Jewelry
Concepts
and
Technology

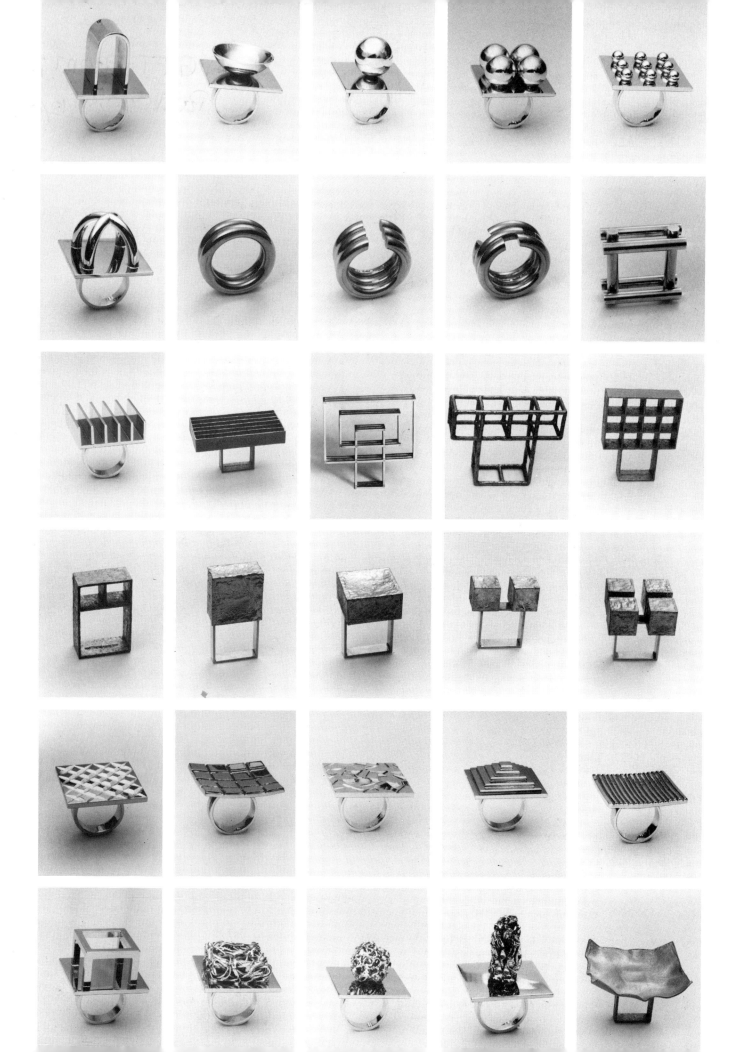

Jewelry
Concepts
and
Technology

OPPI UNTRACHT

DOUBLEDAY
NEW YORK   LONDON   TORONTO   SYDNEY   AUCKLAND

To the memory of two mothers:

Bessie Untracht (1888–1969)
Lempi Hopea (1892–1974)

By the same author:

ENAMELING ON METAL
METAL TECHNIQUES FOR CRAFTSMEN

STAMPED FRONT COVER DESIGN: Basic Forms of Metal: wire, sheet, tubing, and solid.

TITLE PAGE PHOTOS: Numbers refer to photos reading from left to right across pages.

YASUKI HIRAMATSU, Japan. Rings incorporating a great many *basic concepts* employed in *jewelry design* and *fabrication.* Reading from left to right: 1–11: 925 silver, rhodium plated; 12–14: 18K gold; 15–16: 925 silver, rhodium plated; 17: 18K gold; 18: 9K white gold; 19–21: 18K gold; 22–25: 24K and 18K gold; 26–33: 925 silver, rhodium plated; 34: Fine and 925 silver, rhodium plated; 35: 24K and 18K gold; 36–39: 23K gold and silver alloy, 18K gold; 40: 22K gold and silver alloy. Photos: Yasuki Hiramatsu

Published by Doubleday, a division of Bantam Doubleday Dell Publishing Group, Inc., 1540 Broadway, New York, New York 10036

Doubleday and the portrayal of an anchor with a dolphin are trademarks of Doubleday, a division of Bantam Doubleday Dell Publishing Group, Inc.

Library of Congress Cataloging in Publication Data

Untracht, Oppi.
  Jewelry concepts and technology.

  Bibliography: p. 791
  Includes index.
  1. Jewelry making. I. Title.
TS725.U57   739.27
ISBN: 0-385-04185-3
Library of Congress Catalog Card Number 80-2637

PRINTED IN THE UNITED STATES OF AMERICA

8 10 11 9

ACKNOWLEDGMENTS

Flowers in the Garden

Sincere thanks to:

Saara Hopea-Untracht who did the line drawings, typed manuscript, and pampered the writer's psyche. Without her help, this book would not exist.

Bengt Mattsson who inked the drawings with loving care.

Mickey Norman who typed manuscript for years.

Thomas O'Conor Sloane III who initiated this project.

Karen Van Westering, editor par excellence.

Elfriede Hueber for the layout.

Diana Klemin for the book jacket realization.

Deborah Posner for copy editing the manuscript.

Janell Walden for her patience in eradicating vexing oversights.

Eleanor Funk for assistance in innumerable ways.

JEWELERS who generously responded with always-to-be-remembered kindness to requests for photos of their work. Their names, arranged alphabetically by country, follow:

AUSTRALIA
Stokes, John

AUSTRIA
Boltenstern, Sven
Coudenhove, Anita
Skubic, Peter
Symon, Josef

BELGIUM
François, Bernard
Souply, Emile
Wesel, Claude

CZECHOSLOVAKIA
Cepka, Anton
Nováková, Alena

DENMARK
Bisgaard, Palle
Bülow-Hübe, Torun
Exner, Helga and Bent
Flora Danica Jewellery A/S
Fog, Astrid
Gabrielsen P., Bent
Havgaard, Poul
Jensen, Georg
Knudsen, Anni and Bent
Koppel, Henning
Musse, Peder
Nielsen, Kurt
Randers Sølvvarefabrik
Selzer, Thor

FEDERAL REPUBLIC OF GERMANY
Bartsch, Günther
Becker, Friedrich
Bette, Franz J.
Bünck, Werner
Bury, Claus
Dechow, Eberhard
Gasch, Barbara
Huber, Patriz

Immich, Ilse
Jünger, Herman
Lühtje, Christa S.
Munsteiner, Bernd
Nele, E. R.
Reiling, Reinhold
Rothman, Gerhard
Seegebrecht, Bernd
Seibert, Georg
Treskow, Elisabeth
von Mayrhofer, A.
Wagner, Fred

FINLAND
Aarikka, Kaija
Gardberg, Bertel
Häiväoja, Paula
Hopea-Untracht, Saara
Ilvessalo, Kirsti
Juvonen, Helky
Kauppi, Elis
Lehtinen, Martta
Lehtonen, Liisa
Lindholm, Berndt
Linnovaara, Juhani
Lukala, Esa
Minkkinen, Eila
Paaer, Germund
Palonen, Taisto
Rajalin, Börje
Rehnström, Helmer
Rislakki, Eero
Saastamoinen, Reino
Salminen, Mirjam
Sarpaneva, Pentti
Still-McKinney, Nanny
Suuronen, Toivo J.
Tamminen, Seppo
Veriö, Lauri
Vitali, Liisa
Weckström, Björn
Wirkkala, Tapio

FRANCE
Baldaccini, César

Broussailles, Delphin
Champagnat, Jean Claude
Gargat, Henri
Jourdain, Fernand
Lalanne, Claude
Meyerie, Marc
Momiron, Claude
Morobito, Pascal
Penalba, Alicia
Schmid, Michèle
Sylvain, L. B.
Templier, Raymond
Vendome, Jean

HONG KONG
Har, Sui Lai
Huber, Marcus Franz
Piu, Lai Yun
Sang, Chan Ming

HUNGARY
Dobos, Gyöngyvér

INDIA
Nanubhai Jewelers

ISRAEL
Bechar-Paneth, Hanna
Cohavi, Malka
Kaminski, Vered
Shraiber, Rachel

ITALY
Babetto, Giampaolo
Bulgari
Martinazzi, Bruno
Pavan, Francesco
Pomodoro, Gio
Soto, Jesus Raphael
Spalla, Paolo
Villa, Adelio

JAPAN
Hiramatsu, Yasuki
Hishida, Yasuhiko

Mitsuyasu, Takao
Nakayama, Aya
Takabatake, Kotaku
Also see page 772

LITHUANIA
Pakutinskiene, Irena
Pakutinskas, Felkas

MEXICO
Hagsater, Edmée
Poulat, Matilde Eugenia
Soberón, Manuel Rivero
Tane, S. A.
Vargas Ramírez, Fausto

NETHERLANDS
Bakker, Gijs
Herbst, Marion
Niehorster, Karel
van Leersum, Emmy

NORWAY
Bjorg, Toril
Blom, Erik
Juhls, Regine and Frank
Skalstad, Ebba
Vigeland, Pål
Vigeland, Tone

POLAND
Nieniewski, Marek and Lucyna

REPUBLIC OF CHINA
Liu, Wann-Hong

SPAIN
Capdevila, Joaquín
Doria, Puig

SWEDEN
Atelje "3 Städ"
Giertta, Claës E.
Högberg, Anders
Janusch, Bernd
Johansson, Owe

Persson, Sigurd
Taikon, Rosa

SWITZERLAND

Brynner, Irena
Flory, Kurt
Fröhlich, Max
Hintermeister, Margrit
Issler, Katharina
Lang, Eugen
Lindenmaier, Gottlieb
Müller, Friedrich B.
Müller, Rolf
Röthlisberger, Elsbeth
Zschaler, Othmar

UNION OF SOUTH AFRICA

Dill, Dieter

UNITED KINGDOM

Azaro, Rodolfo
Broadhead, Caroline
Burton, Jocllyn
Cartlidge, Barbara
Degen, Joël
de Large, Edward A.
de Syllas, Charlotte
Donald, John
Driver, Michael
Flockinger, Gerda
Gilbert, Wally
Glassar, Brian
Greer, Rita
Hawksley, Anthony
Hensel, David
Heron, Susanna
Jackson, Mike
Jahn, A. C.
Jenkins, Cynthia
Johnston, Geli
Mina, Jacqueline
Myers, Adrian
Osman, Louis

Pinder, Michael
Ramshaw, Wendy
Ross, Jeremy
Shillito, Ann Marie
Spiller, Eric
Tipple, Barbara
Thomas, David
Treen, Gunilla
Ward, James B.
Watkins, David
Whitman, Julia C.

UNITED STATES OF AMERICA

Adell, Carrie
Arentzen, Glenda
Ayers, Ann Sciortino
Baker, Joby
Beetler, Vada C.
Beizer, Samuel
Berg, Janet
Berman, Mona R.
Brown, Judith
Calder, Alexander
Ceasar, Julius
Church, Sharon
Clark, William
Conty, Angela
Copley, Noma
Croft, Michael
Daunis-Dunning, Patricia J.
Davidson, Jaclyn
Davidson, Marilyn Brayman
de la Cueva, Domingo
Ebendorf, Robert
Eikerman, Alma
Engle, Barbara
Evans, Chuck
Fechter, Anita S.
Fisch, Arline M.
Freyaldenhoven, Jem
Gabriel, Hannelore
Gentille, Thomas
Getty, Nilda C. F.

Graham, Anne Krohn
Griffin, Gary S.
Helzer, Richard
Hu, Mary Lee
Husted Andersen, Adda
Jefferson, Bob
Jerry, Michael John
Kacz, Frank
Keens, David W.
Kington, L. Brent
Kran, Barbara Y.
Kuehnl, Claudia
Kulicke, Robert
Lacktman, Michael
Lambert, Rachelle Thiewes
LaPlantz, David
Laws, Margaret
Lechtzin, Stanley
Lent, Anthony
Leupp, Leslie
Lewis, Marcia
Loloma, Charles
Loyd, Jan Brooks
Lumpmouth, Homer
Macrorie, Joyce T.
Mafong, Richard
Markusen, Thomas R.
Marshall, John
Mawdsley, Richard
Metcalf, Bruce
Miller, Frederick A.
Miller, John Paul
Monogye, Preston
Morris, Robert Lee
Moty, Eleanor
Müller-Stach, Dieter
Noffke, Gary
O'Connor, Harold
Paley, Albert
Pardon, Earl
Peck, Lee Barnes
Peck, Naomi Greenburg
Phillips, Ccarol

Pijanowski, Gene
Pijanowski, Hiroko Sato
Porter, Faith
Postgate, George
Pujol, Elliot
Radakovich, Ruth
Radakovich, Svetozar
Renk, Merry
Riis, Jon Eric
Roach, Rodney
Roach, Ruth Schirmer
Roan, Jerry
Roethel, Cornelia
Satterfield, John E.
Saunders, Gayle
Sawyer, George N.
Schaller, Chris
Scherr, Mary Ann
Scherr, Sydney
Schmidt, Robert
Senungetuk, Ronald W.
Shannon, Alice
Shirk, Helen
Skoogfors, Olaf
Soellner, Mitsuko Kambe
Soellner, Walter
Sohier, Emily Bolster
Solberg, Ramona
Stephen, Francis
Szawlowski, Peter
Taylor, Florence Nach
Tsabetsaye, Roger
Tuscon, Myra
Untracht, Oppi
van Duinwyk, George Paul
van Hamel, Nanette
Wallace, Lincoln
Warner, Raymond
Watson-Abbott, Lynda
Wehrman, Sally
Woell, J. Fred
Zelmanoff, Marci
Zilker, Sandra Parmer

JEWELERS

who agreed to undertake the task of producing or allowing work sequence photos or drawings showing their manner of work utilizing a particular technical process. Their names, arranged alphabetically, follow:

Azaro, Rodolfo R.: Casting plastics
Evans, Chuck: Loop-in-loop chain
Gentille, Thomas: Wax-in-wax inlay
Getty, Nilda C. Fernandez: Riveting
Greer, Rita: Hot modeling fused metal
Griffin, Gary S.: Lathe-machined jewelry
Hu, Mary Lee: Wire techniques
Immich, Ilse: Engraving
Keens, David: The use of plastics
LaPlantz, David: Chain mail
Laws, Margaret: Repoussage
Lechtzin, Stanley: Electroforming
Lewis, Marcia: Tapered tubing
Mawdsley, Richard: Tubing uses
Miller, John Paul: Granulation
Paley, Albert: Forging
Pijanowski, Gene: Chip carving; reticulation
Pijanowski, Hiroko Sato: Metal inlay
Scherr, Mary Ann: Etching
Shannon, Alice L.: Cuttlebone casting

Soellner, Mitsuko Kambe: Mercury amalgam gilding
Soellner, Walter: Mercury amalgam gilding
van Duinwyk, George Paul: Stamping
Vargas Ramírez, Fausto: Filigree
Watson-Abbott, Lynda: Investment casting
Weckström, Björn: Injection rubber mold casting

For special assistance and permissions

Individuals:

Joyce Macrorie: For making possible the inclusion of the traditional Mexican filigree work of Fausto Vargas Ramirez
Richard Mafong: For color photos of jewelry
Madan Mahatta: For the use of photos
Eleanor Moty: For the use of drawings
Harold O'Connor: For the use of photos
J. Fred Woell: For the use of drawings
Solange Wohlhuter: For contact with the jewelry world of France
David Zeiger: For a spectacular recovery of lost photos

ORGANIZATIONS AND INDIVIDUALS   associated with them:

Aarikka-Koru, Helsinki (Kaija Aarikka, Director)
Aaron Faber Gallery, New York (Edward Faber, Director)
American Crafts Council, Research and Education Dept., New York (Lois Moran and her staff)
Artwear Gallery, New York (Robert Lee Morris, Director)
Craft Horizons (Now *American Craft*), New York (Pat Dandignac)
Crafts Advisory Committee, London (Ralph Turner)
Den Permanente, Copenhagen (Marianne Bech)
Helen Drutt Gallery, Philadelphia (Helen Drutt, Director)
Electrum Gallery, London (Barbara Cartlidge, Director)
Fine Arts Gallery, California State University, Los Angeles
Finnish Society of Crafts and Design, Helsinki (Mary Wrede)
Galerie Sven, Paris (Sven Boltenstern, Director)
Georg Jensen Sølvsmedie A/S, Copenhagen (Steffen Andersen)
Homestake Mining Co., Lead, South Dakota (Daniel P. Howe)
Indian Arts and Crafts Board, U. S. Department of the Interior, Washington, D.C. (Miles Libhart, Director of Museums, Exhibitions and Publications)
Japan Jewelry Designer Association, Tokyo (Yasuhiko Hishida, former President; and Yasuki Hiramatsu, current President)
Kalevala Koru, Helsinki (Sylvia Sarparanta, Director; Börje Rajalin, Designer)
Fred Manshaw Ltd., London (D. M. Pearlman)
K. Mikimoto & Co., Tokyo (Ryo Yamaguchi, Director of the Ginza Showroom)
Rijksmuseum voor Volkerkunde, Leiden (Dr. A. H. N. Verwey, Curator, Asian Collection)
Schmuckmuseum, Pforzheim (Dr. Fritz Falk, Director)
Society of North American Goldsmiths (SNAG), U.S.A.
Sotheby-Parke Bernet & Co., New York, and *Sotheby's,* London
The L. S. Starrett Co., Athol, Massachusetts (F. H. Clarkson, Jr.)
Swest Inc., Dallas (Earl R. Weaver, President; Joe Mancuso)
Touchstone Gallery, New York (Barbara Hirschl, Director)

The Traphagen School of Fashion, New York (Wanda Wdowka, Director)
The U.S. and Finnish Post Departments (Only *one* loss among the hundreds of letters and packages that found their way over lands and seas to Finland where this book was written)
Johan Philipp Wild, Idar Oberstein, West Germany (Konrad Wild, Director)
The Worshipful Company of Goldsmiths, London (Graham Hughes, Art Director; Susan Hare, Librarian)

Companies for their special cooperation

Aarikka Koru Oy, Finland: Photos of jewelry
Amita Jewelry Corp., Japan: Damascene inlay demonstration
Bühler and Co., West Germany: Rolling mill photos
De Beers Consolidated Mines, Ltd., London: Photographs
Friedr. Dick GmbH, West Germany: File photos and montage material
Dixon Tool Co., U.S.A.: Brush diagram and line drawings
Karl Fischer, West Germany: Montage material
Paul H. Gessewein & Co., U.S.A.: Montage material
Handy and Harman, U.S.A.: Photos and tables
Highland Park Manufacturing, U.S.A.: Photo of lapidary equipment
Alfred Joliot, France: Montage material
Kalevala Koru Oy, Finland: Photos of jewelry
Kultakeskus Oy, Finland: Photos of jewelry
Kultasepänliike Ossian Hopea, Finland: Photos of jewelry
Kultateollisuus Oy, Finland: Photos of jewelry
Kupittaan Kulta Oy, Finland: Photos of jewelry
Lapponia Jewelry Oy, Finland: Photos of jewelry
Metaux Precieux S.A., Switzerland: Photos
K. Mikimoto & Co., Ltd., Japan: Photos of pearl piercing
I. Schor Co. Inc., U.S.A.: Montage material
Myron Toback Inc., U.S.A.: Photo of forms of solder
The L. S. Starrett Co., U.S.A.: Photos of tools
Swest Inc., U.S.A.: Photos of tools, montage material

MUSEUMS   from whose collections objects are shown:

(Credited with the photo captions)

Amsterdam: *Koninklijk Instituut voor de Tropen*
              Rijksmuseum
Ann Arbor: *Museum of Anthropology*
Athens: *National Museum of Greece*
Berlin: *Museum für Völkerkunde*
Bern: *Bernisches Historisches Museum*
Budapest: *Ferenc Hopp Museum of Eastern Asiatic Arts*
Cleveland: *Cleveland Museum of Art*
Copenhagen: *Danish National Museum*
Delft: *Indonesisch Etnografisch Museum*
Dortmund: *Museum für Kunst und Kulturgeschichte*
Helsinki: *Finnish National Museum*
Hyderabad: *Salar Jung Museum*
Jerusalem: *The Israel Museum*
Leningrad: *Hermitage Museum*
              The Russian Museum
Leiden: *Rijksmuseum voor Volkerkunde*

London: *The British Museum*
              Victoria and Albert Museum
              The Wallace Collection
New York: *American Museum of Natural History*
              Cooper-Hewitt Museum
              Metropolitan Museum of Art
              Museum of the American Indian, Heye Foundation
Oxford: *Ashmolean Museum*
              Pitt Rivers Museum
Paris: *Musée de l'Homme*
              Musée des Arts Décoratifs
Pforzheim: *Schmuckmuseum Pforzheim im Reuchlinhaus*
Rotterdam: *Museum Boymans-van Beuningen*
Stockholm: *Hallwylska Museet*
Stuttgart: *Linden-Museum*
Tokyo: *Seibu Museum*
Vienna: *Kunsthistorisches Museum*
Thessalonika: *Folklore and Ethnology Museum of Macedonia*
Zürich: *Museum Bellerive*
              Schweizerisches Landesmuseum

CONTENTS

⑨

⑩

11

12

13

14

15

16

INTRODUCTION

Jewelry plays a greater role in today's world than it ever did in the past. No more is its use only the privilege of the wealthy, for the broadening of the social structure of contemporary society and the burgeoning concepts of what a jewel is or can be has made its use universal. The basic appeal of jewelry lies in the satisfaction of primitive needs. Its use becomes a means of releasing us to fantasize about ourselves, our lives, and our world. Because the motivations for wearing jewelry involve elemental and eternal human concerns, and because jewelry is a portable, intimate art that can be worn and constantly enjoyed, it is safe to assume that the use of jewelry will persist, in one form or another for as long as the human race survives.

The jewelry with which this book is concerned is creative work made mainly by hand technology, but the creative use of machine technology is also discussed. Many of the pieces illustrated have been produced by independent professional jewelers, but a great number are made by non-professional jewelers whose amazing growth in numbers is certainly a phenomenon of our age. To realize how the field of handmade jewelry has expanded, one has only to think of the large number of places where the techniques of jewelry making can be learned today, as compared with the few that existed only 25 years ago. An interesting aspect of this situation is the extraordinary increase in the involvement of women in jewelry making, illustrated by the fact that nearly half the objects shown in this book are designed or made by women. Since most of the jewelry produced today is for use by women, their work is of special interest as presumably it represents a tangible expression of the kind of jewelry that contemporary women would like to wear themselves.

There are several reasons for the growth of interest in jewelry making. Probably foremost among them is that many people have discovered the pleasure and sense of achievement that accompanies the activity of inventing and creating an object. It matters little whether the motive for this activity is to pass leisure time pleasantly; to preserve mental health through absorption in meaningful work; to enjoy the vanity of decorating the body; to engage in a remunerative occupation that pays the rent and fills the stomach; or to attempt to achieve approval, recognition, and fame. Regardless of motivation, craftsmanship is the key that opens the door to the creative experience by which each of us, on any level of capability, can realize the psychological and physical satisfactions which our minds and bodies require. Through creative work, our lives are also enriched in a special way—we are drawn into an involvement with a community of our choice, and this creates the opportunity to form associations with similarly oriented individuals. By sharing common experiences with them, any sense of isolation is eliminated; we can grow in our own capacities while we appreciate the varied accomplishments of others, without, however, abandoning individuality or our right to evaluate and criticize.

Jewelry making can be self-taught, but most beginners

I–1 GEORG JENSEN, Denmark, designer; manufacturer Georg Jensen Sölvsmedie A/S, Copenhagen, 1899. Adam and Eve are depicted in their unornamented innocence in the Garden of Eden beneath an apple tree surrounded by the serpent who created the circumstances that led them to invent the first ornament-cum-clothing: the fig leaf. *Photo: Courtesy Georg Jensen Sølvsmedie A/S*

I–2 MARRAKECH, MOROCCO. The gold bazaar is a feast for the eyes. In some Muslim countries custom declares that women appearing in public must be completely covered, but their love of ornament remains as active as ever, even though their jewelry will only be seen by family, relatives, and close friends. *Photo: Oppi*

learn the necessary metal working processes from instructors of jewelry making courses offered in universities, schools, community centers, and even in classes established by industry for employees. The equipment in such workshops and the quality of instruction range from barely adequate to ideal. Even with a minimum of instruction—given a reasonable amount of patience—a degree of experience and skill can be acquired sufficient to manipulate simple hand tools with increasing certainty. Once the disciplines of materials and techniques are understood and accepted, one can progress to greater challenges. Thereafter, when working independently, as many people do, jewelry can be created in a relatively limited home workshop using long-lasting hand tools that can be purchased with a comparatively small investment. The money and efforts expended are more than rewarded by the results which warm and excite the maker's inner being. Whether they are simple or highly evolved objects, they can be worn with pleasure, given away with pride, or sold.

When instruction and advice are not available from knowledgeable persons, books may have to act as substitutes. To serve this purpose either for the beginner or a committed professional craft jeweler, a field of literature—the instructional craft book—has proliferated in the U.S.A., Europe, and Japan during the last quarter century. In the writer's opinion, an instructional book should be conceived of as both a possible source of inspiration and as a storehouse of information. Though silent on a shelf, a book is always ready as a reference to suggest an insight, to supply an answer that might help to solve a problem, to encourage an awareness of alternatives, or to stimulate the impetus to develop increasingly more challenging skills. These are the concepts that have guided the planning and organization of this book. As far as possible, the information contained herein has been presented objectively, and any expression of personal prejudice in relation to work processes has been avoided in the belief that *all* techniques can engender work of validity and integrity.

The practice of jewelry making has been simplified today by the numerous jewelers' supply houses that exist where tools and materials manufactured by many specialists can be purchased. Established suppliers, formerly only interested in ministering to the needs of professionals, have broadened their range of stock and services to include the requirements of the jeweler for whom the activity is an avocation. Because of the ever growing sophistication in the use of techniques among non-professional jewelers, some larger and more expensive tools and equipment previously used only by professionals or in the jewelry making industry have been modified and manufactured in smaller, less costly models; these include hand power machines, equipment used for vacuum and centrifugal casting, electroforming, lathe work, and metal finishing. Almost all supply houses publish attractive, well-illustrated, annotated catalogs. With these in hand, the problem of a lack of direct access to tools and supplies because of distance is eliminated as all requirements can be filled through mail orders. Even more convenient, materials can be purchased in amounts suited to individual needs, and some materials are semiprocessed to help save time and effort. These developments would be looked upon with astonishment by those in the jewelry field living in less favored areas of the world; we who benefit by them should consider ourselves extremely fortunate.

By far the greater part of the jewelry produced today is created by technical means practiced for centuries, often eons. The form and action of hand tools have developed from the essential nature of the materials upon which they were designed to be used, in conjunction with the simple facts of human anatomy and average strength. As might be expected, their shape and function have changed relatively little. The means of realizing the objects invented by fantasy spring first of all from the materials used, then from the functions of the tools at one's disposal in conjunction with the energy imparted to them. Those who understand the functions of their tools have a far greater chance of success in any work they undertake than those who have no such grasp.

When the material used poses a problem of manipulation, usually the simplest and most direct solution is best. The answer may lie in the selection of the proper tool or tool aid. However, an involvement with tools *per se* can easily lead to seduction by the world of gadgetry. Experience should help one to decide what is a real or imagined tool need, and new tools should be acquired only when an actual necessity for them arises. Because tools act as extensions of the hand, it is only proper that you care for them as you would your own hands. The way in which you use and respect tools expresses not only an understanding of their function, but is an indication of your attitude toward your work.

JEWELRY CONCEPTS AND TECHNOLOGY: The conceptual approach to jewelry making

Should anyone doubt the significance and importance of jewelry, such doubts are immediately dispelled when we reflect on the multitude of concepts that the human mind for centuries has poured into the creation of personal ornament. Though initially intangible to the senses, conceptual thought becomes concrete when creating a unique jewel—first by the evolution of an *idea* that can be communicated in visual terms, then by its *realization* in planar or spacial form through the employment of systems of fabrication.

The means of realization—techniques and work systems commonly used by jewelers—are described and illustrated, by procedure and result, in this book. As an aid in the development of conceptual thinking, they have been organized by concept. Starting with the very basic technological concepts we proceed to those more complex. Individual techniques are grouped in chapters under broader concepts that they share. Finishing processes find their logical place at the end of this book, after all fabrication processes have been covered.

Within particular work areas, concepts, techniques, or objects have been classified into groups to give them coherence, to emphasize relationships or point out differences, or to place them in meaningful sequences. Classification has been used as a method of creating relative order in what otherwise would be an indigestible mass of apparently unrelated information.

To answer the question "why" that comes to mind when certain facts or conditions are mentioned in connection with physical phenomena, an attempt has been made to explain the theory and concepts that lie behind them. It is hoped that the insight and understanding gained will help to alleviate the monotony of routines whose significance may have been unknown or ignored. Any process, even the simplest, has its fascinations once the implications and ramifications of its underlying concepts are realized.

Conceptually organized information can act to stimulate

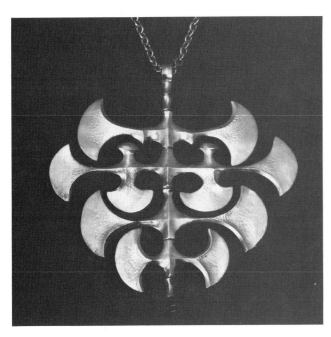

I–3 TAPIO WIRKKALA, Finland, designer; manufacturer Kultakeskus Oy, Hämeenlinna. Gold pendant utilizing the forging concept that metal rod can be hammer spread in characteristic forms. The forging technique leaves a hammer-created surface texture. Each horizontal unit rotates on the central rod spine. *Photo: Courtesy Kultakeskus Oy*

thinking about design because technology is an eternal source of design inspiration. Any single technical concept, for instance simple bending, can be utilized as the basis for the development of a total design. Examples can be seen in the diagrams and work shown in the illustrations for each section. All techniques can be executed on a level simple or complex enough to challenge any degree of skill. It is fortunate that experience is cumulative; this circumstance tends to stimulate our desire for greater challenges and the attainment of ever higher levels of accomplishment. Achieving a new competency within any particular process is often sufficiently satisfying to encourage further exploration.

In the act of creating a piece of jewelry, several interrelated and interacting concepts and techniques are operating simultaneously. To those of us who can interpret the language of the work experience, these concepts and processes, evident in the work, are visually communicated. A jeweler's knowledge increases not only by experience, but by observation. The ability to recognize and understand concepts and processes makes possible a profound "conversation" between the jeweler and any finished work. Though mute, every creation—historic, traditional, or contemporary—speaks volumes in this dialogue.

HISTORIC AND TRADITIONAL JEWELRY: Future perspective through the past

The illustrations in this book cut through the entire history of jewelry making throughout the world, up to the present with its intimations of the future. This time-perspective view includes only a relatively minute fraction of the harvest from the past—a mere selection of traditional jewelry used by culturally distinct ethnic groups—and a sampling of contemporary jewelry. The prime purpose in making this selection so broad is to combat any

unconscious presupposition of cultural dominance which tends to cloud the minds of some Westerners. Valid concepts are not confined to any time or culture.

The terms *traditional* and *ethnic* used to identify that work are more fully understood when we investigate the significance that jewelry made in this context had (and still has where it continues to be made) or the function it served (and still serves) in the society of its origin.

The general decline of traditional usage, and fluctuations in economic conditions have caused most of this work—when made of precious metals—to vanish into the melting pot simply to recover its value as bullion, totally ignoring the worth of the work or its esthetic value. The same fate overcame most historic European work, its demise hastened by relatively rapid changes in fashion. What remains of old, traditional ethnic jewelry and some of the new work is enough to tell us that its character and spirit come surprisingly close to that of handmade, Western-oriented jewelry.

Part of the explanation may be that traditional, ethnic jewelry is usually made to withstand daily usage, and therefore is generally fabricated from heavier materials that give it a certain robustness and vitality. The basic forms of metal used by all jewelers—wire, sheet metal, and tubing—in this jewelry are made by hand and used without much change from their original condition. Their surfaces are commonly left without any attempt to disguise the evidence of process. Usually they are semimatte; the finish is produced manually rather than by unavailable mechanical means which would result in a high polish. Time works to improve the appearance of jewelry worn in a single life-span. The abrasion of touch and use impart a certain softness to edges and surfaces, giving them a tactile patina. To the modern Western eye, these qualities are decidedly attractive.

Traditional jewelry by custom is usually worn in a common ensemble of clothing and ornament used by all the men and women of a community, or of a particular group within it. This explains why designs are often repeated in quantity, though never without variations. The need for repetition accounts for the widely used, timesaving employment of the *unit system of construction,* also used in modern jewelry manufacture. Further economy of time is achieved through the practice of division of labor. Specialists perform various processes on the same object, working

I–4 AJMER, RAJASTHAN, INDIA. Contemporary silver ankle bracelet. This mass-produced traditional ornament employs the unit system of construction. Hundreds of parts are stamped, solder joined, and wire linked, to achieve the tapered cone structure. Hundreds of balls (*gungrus*) are attached by jump rings. The sound created by the balls warns others of a woman's approach. *Photo: Victoria and Albert Museum, London, Crown Copyright*

toward its final unity. Specialization is also common in the contemporary commercial jewelry industry, and some jewelers take advantage of this circumstance by having wax models cast professionally and by having precious stones set by experts.

Technical problems encountered for the first time by a novice jeweler may appear to be new, but chances are that every practical problem that occurs in jewelry making has already been faced and solved myriad times by countless jewelers. Examination of historic and traditional ethnic jewelry reveals an inexhaustible number of concepts locked into the works of every culture, in all periods of time. The wealth of ideas they contain still has relevance for any contemporary jeweler who takes the trouble to ponder the construction of particular works. By mentally reconstructing the sequence of execution, insight can be gained into the entire problem-solving process, and through this, insight into systems we use in our own work. There is no reason why we should deny ourselves the legacy embodied in this vast and rich body of work.

Illustrations of ancient and ethnic jewels have been deliberately juxtaposed in the book with contemporary, Western-oriented work, where specific techniques dominate. Contraposed this way, the works of highly diverse cultures exhibit a decided kinship—because of the forms of the materials used, the concepts involved in their manipulation, and the technology brought to bear upon them. These conditions go beyond style or subject matter, and compress time, distance, and cultural diversity, emphasizing the axiom that *technology is a bond that unites all jewelers*. However, when Western and ethnic or traditional philosophic and social outlook are compared, a profound dichotomy of thinking is revealed. The use of traditional jewelry, still worn in vast areas of the world, involves attitudes that have prevailed in the work of historic periods in various cultures. First of all, the esthetic, creative activity it incorporates is the result of the thinking of many generations of *anonymous jewelers* who have served, and still act as instruments in slowly building up that accretion of community consciousness we call culture. The importance of the *individual* in traditional societies is that of a fragment in a mass which coheres by mutual wish and understanding. In such cultures, esthetic concepts are formed like an amalgam in which individual units of thought are absorbed into one homogeneous compound. Through group acquiescence, jewelry serves the entire society, or at very least, a well-defined group within that society, in specific religious, social, and other ways laid down and accepted by all the members of the group.

In contemporary Western thought, to the contrary, the very existence of the artist-jeweler implies the concept that *individuality* or *ego* and *subjective self-expression* are of prime importance. The creator insists on, even demands recognition and attention, if not from society at large, at least from a well-defined group of peers. Every jewel created becomes a manifestation and affirmation of individuality. The prevailing design idiom, far from being uniform or stable, evolves from current, rapidly changing esthetic concepts—a result of the interstimulation of the ideas of fellow creators, each creator vying with another to produce a more "original" object.

Ideally, to the Western-oriented jeweler, the work experience becomes an exhilarating, almost intoxicating effort of constant self-challenge to concretize a fleeting image. Such an experience is unknown to traditional jewelers who, aside from whatever pleasure they receive from their work, look upon their trade simply as a means of livelihood. Their role is that of an instrument through which the mass fantasy projected by their society is realized. Perhaps the closest approach to the mentality of the traditional jeweler in Western culture is the commercial jeweler who supplies a "conventional" clientele. This work is also anonymous, or at best stamped with the hallmark of the merchant enterprise that employs him or her. The jewelry

I–5 *Left:* PATAN, NEPAL. One of many Samyedyo larger than life-size deity images, a form of the Dipankara Buddha, erected from separate units of head, hands, and ornaments, all mounted on a wickerwork structure. Their display occurs here once every five years during the Panchadana festival. The deity is decorated with traditional ornaments, some similar to those worn by various groups in Nepal, and include a crown (*matu*), with projecting leaves (*kikimpa*), earrings (*dhungri*), necklace (*kanthi*), silver chain (*wohasikha*), and silver coin necklace (*mohama*). *Photo: Oppi*

I–6 *Right:* PATAN, NAPAL. The *Gai Jatra* festival or sacred cow procession, takes place the day after the August full moon. A man representing the god Ram participates, wearing a silver repoussé-worked *matu* ornamented with flowers and silver ornaments traditionally used to decorate images of deities. *Photo: Oppi*

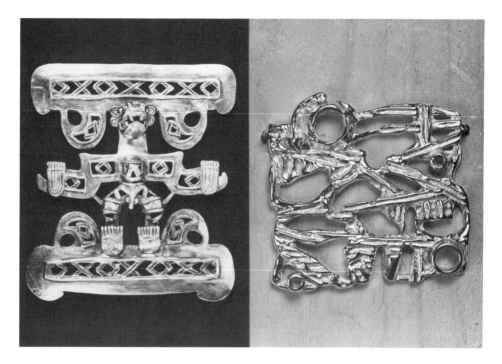

I–7 *Left:* CHIBCHA INDIAN, COSTA RICA. Lost wax-cast gold pectoral ornament made by ancestors of the present Chibcha Indians of Central and South America, who occupied the territory from southeastern Nicaragua to Colombia. This physically balanced, symmetrical image represents a god in human form with a crocodile head. The form of the wax sheet and wire used for the model is retained in the casting. *Photo: The American Museum of Natural History, New York*

I–8 *Right:* EBBA SKALSTAD, Norway, designer; manufacturer Ragnar Skalstad, Oslo. Brooch in cast sterling silver, its surface covered with 24K gold. An asymmetrical, essentially flat work in low relief, pierced with visually balanced openings of negative shapes important in the design. *Photo: Courtesy R. A. Skalstad*

embodies and expresses the artificially created but relatively homogeneous mass fantasy of the moment called fashion.

In historic and ethnic jewelry we encounter cultures that have shown or show a preferential interest in, and in some cases a decided tendency to specialize in a particular technique. Specialization, in such instances, gives rise to the development of new conceptual possibilities that become apparent through exploration within that specialty. Examples of this circumstance have occurred, for instance, in the gold granulation-decorated jewels of the Etruscans, and in the cast ornaments of Central and South America. New ideas were undoubtedly suggested by those already established in the craft, with skills and knowledge built on the experience of yet others who preceded them. The same pattern of developmental growth and accompanying revelation occurs in a single lifetime in the output of a contemporary, individual jeweler who chooses to pursue a special technique or to utilize a specific material or form of material. Such jewelers know that one concept naturally is suggested by and leads to another, and therefore show no hesitation in repeating an idea with minor variations. The result is an entire body of related work whose unity, maturity, and obvious in-depth exploration make it an authoritative, attention-commanding statement.

DESIGN: The marriage of thought to process

Design in reference to jewelry can be described as an intellectual or intuitive concept (both possibly acting simultaneously), in which purposeful planning or mental imagery governs the manner in which materials are used and arranged into a relationship of shapes, forms, and surface treatments to create an integrated object. Because we believe that most individuals possess an innate potential for creativity, and have natural aptitudes that can be developed, design is not discussed as a ready-made formula or an independent subject in this book, though it is every-

where implied or evident in the illustrations. The rapidity with which design concepts arrive and depart today, reflecting rapid social change, would in any case make concrete "suggestions" instantly obsolete.

Current design formulas can be learned and used mechanically, but instead of following such a course we return to and review the craftsperson's eternal sources of design inspiration. When working with metals, jewelry's principal but not exclusive material, the prime source of design is the *metal's initial form,* and *its inherent character;* these in turn relate to the *processes imposed upon it* by the use of tools and techniques. These take precedence over any formal design considerations that may follow and enter into the designing sequence. The form of material itself suggests process because each form of metal embodies a natural range of possible treatments that inspire design. A few examples in metalwork can illustrate this idea. From *wire* comes linear pattern, and the techniques of forging and filigree; from undeformed *sheet metal* comes bending, sawing, and piercing, and when deformed, the processes of repoussage and stamping; from *tubing* comes hollow forms; from *metal ions,* electroforms; *granules,* granulation; and *bulk metal,* any type of casting, as well as negative techniques involving metal removal such as chip carving and file forming.

Superimposed upon the basic concept that a material's initial form and character are related to process, are those considerations of composition and organization termed *formal design elements,* possibly better called *design components* since by their use, an object is composed. No matter how limited they may be in use, or isolated for purposes of discussion, when creating a design, these elements and the above-mentioned considerations are dynamically interrelated in a highly flexible manner; in reality, one aspect can hardly be mentioned without involving another.

The following are the most active general design components for metalwork. *Contrast:* of line with line, and of line with or on shape or form; of outer, positive shape with inner, negative shape (if any); of two- or three-dimensional form with different three-dimensional volumes; of one material with another; of surface textures and finish types; of the colors of metals, or metals and other materials. *Relative scale:* the proportion in size relationship of components to each other; of the piece to the human body. *Balance:* either symmetrical or asymmetrical. *Visual climax* (focal emphasis) is possibly one other design component that can be included, though it is not always present. (See Visual Glossary: Geometric and Morphic Shapes, Forms, and Concepts for an elaboration of concepts that can become design components).

By altering the *position, volume,* or *scale* of any one of these components, the total composition changes through the change of relationships. The possibilities are infinite. In such an exploration, an aspect of relationships previously not apparent may be revealed, thus opening a new road to fields of discovery.

Designing and creating a jewel is a reciprocal procedure of synthesizing the intangible into reality. This is accomplished essentially through a sequence of judgments, decision making, and problem solving, all of which occur when fabricating materials into forms. Initially an inward-delving act of thought in which the mind is searched for a concept that is suitable for development, designing involves the person's ability to select, focus upon, and capture any such nonsensory mental images. Using intuition, a heightened sense of awareness, and a reasoning process modified by an acquired degree of technological experience that dictates what is and what is not possible, these images are then integrated to make a unit. Its components are interrelated in what is felt to be an esthetically satisfying manner; the decisions made are influenced by contemporary design criteria. Finally, the composition—at this point usually a drawing on paper—is physically translated into actual materials. Unless the design concept is the kind that can be conceived with mathematical precision in a drawing and followed, without alteration, as graphically depicted, the designing process may not end here.

For the self-employed artist-jeweler, the externalized process of realization that follows is a solitary act performed as a series of work disciplines that frequently take far longer than the mental formulation of the initial design concept. Often the work process brings to attention unanticipated functional problems or esthetic considerations that must be dealt with. Discoveries and accidental surprises of a positive kind can also occur and be seized upon. Such occurrences establish the necessity of *keeping an open mind* to permit the modification of a design.

Also involved in design development is the maker's ability to visualize the finished work in its ultimate stage—adorning the wearer. Because of possible changes which can occur at any time during work, both designing and creating often continue well into advanced stages of development, in some cases not stopping until all work processing ends and the maker declares the work finished.

The maker is rarely completely satisfied with the result. Between the initial mental conception and the physical realization of the work, some of the spontaneity of the original idea is almost always lost. The effort to minimize or close this gap is what at times provides the force that catapults the maker into the next project, which natural optimism insists will surely be more perfectly realized than the last.

It might be expected that when designing jewelry, practical considerations of size, weight, construction, and the manner of placement on the body would be of prime importance, but the concept of comfort in use is far from universal, nor is there any agreement on just what "jewel comfort" means. Among historic, ethnic, and contemporary jewels are numerous examples which seem to ignore that consideration, and many jewels exist that seem menacing, or decidedly uncomfortable to wear. For example, we have the Indian nose ring, which a Westerner might think is an unquestionably inconvenient ornament. But to an Indian woman—in whose community the ring is *de rigueur*—the question of its convenience or comfort is irrelevant. To her the nose ring is not only an object of beauty, but it serves the function of proclaiming to all that she has attained the matrimonial state and is therefore deserving of deferential treatment.

Western jewelry also includes many examples, historic and contemporary, of irrational factors intruding in the area of design. Tight chokers and belts, oversized rings, heavy earrings, jewels with potentially disfiguring projections and flourishes, forms of body jewelry that either inhibit movement or force the wearer to remain standing during the time they are worn, have been and are in use without any recorded complaints or apparent thoughts of masochism on the part of the wearer, or sadism on the part of the jeweler. Even today, when rationality is considered to be an enlightened and admirable mental state, some of the "best" jewelers produce visually stimulating and inadvertently uncomfortable ornaments, and without doubt these contribute to the excitement generated by contemporary jewelry. While most jewelers would probably insist that jewelry should be designed to be "wearable" (reasonably comfortable and convenient), much media attention is garnered by *outré* work. Possibly, the wearer's motivation is, in some measure, to be the object of that same attention, and this more than compensates for any discomfort or inconvenience experienced in wearing such works.

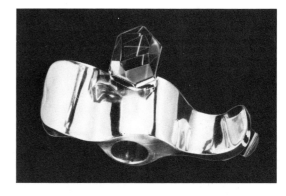

I-9 NANETTE VAN HAMEL, U.S.A. Silver hand jewel with rock crystal. The hollow, lightweight structure spans the width of four fingers. *Photo: Günter Meyer, courtesy Schmuckmuseum, Pforzheim*

TODAY'S JEWELRY:
Conceptual and technological eclecticism

Western-oriented jewelry of what might be termed today's craft movement is more eclectic in terms of creative ideas and technology than ever before. Several powerful but antagonistic concepts are in simultaneous operation, not only in the field of jewelry, but in the creative arts in general. Each of these concepts has adherents, and few are totally unreasonable despite contradictions or even negative thought. It is a tribute to jewelry that such a diversity of expression can be encompassed in these relatively small-scale objects. Given this diversity, and the permissiveness of today's Western-oriented society, it would be unrealistic to expect that any concept *could* bring unity to more than a limited group. Therefore, instead of any attempt by jewelers to modify ideas toward the creation of a synthesis of style for the sake of consistency (as has happened in the past and as recently as the Art Deco period of the 1920s and '30s), all concepts exist simultaneously and all must be tolerated. It remains for the individual jeweler to select and to pursue a direction that is personally, temperamentally, and intellectually satisfying—including the development of new styles.

The field of jewelry has become even more complex because of a widespread and conscious effort to legitimize the acceptance of jewelry making as a valid medium for creative expression on a par with other visual art activities. This viewpoint declares that the jewel is an art form capable of achieving the status of what is termed "a work of art." For those whose definition of a work of art includes the implication that the object created must have no practical function, the ability of jewelry to make this transition is simplified because jewels are, in essence, nonfunctional objects.

Jewelry has always involved technology, formal values, and symbolism, but the scope of its concerns has been broadened by jewelers of today's avant-garde who have introduced the use of philosophical, social, political, psychological, humorous, and erotic themes to a degree never before applied to this field. These themes are active in the world of painting and sculpture—the so-called "major" or "fine" arts—and can equally well come into play and be assimilated by the area commonly designated as the "decorative," "applied," or "minor" arts. The terms "major and minor arts," and "fine and applied arts," in any case have lost their meaning since it is broadly recognized that an object of any material can embody the highest creative achievement. The division of contemporary arts into such classes has certainly outgrown its usefulness and no longer reflects contemporary circumstances. The continuing expansion of themes and the use of subject matter concerned with contemporary attitudes is to be expected, and it is appropriate that creative works should reflect, consciously and unconsciously, the concerns and concepts prevailing in the period of their creation. However, the artist is obliged to aim for a communication of ideas, without which his/her work is understood only for its formal values.

A survey of the work of today's artist-jeweler might bring forth the conclusions that change is the single constant, and that the underlying thrust is *design through conceptual and technological eclecticism.* Given the present diversity of style in contemporary, Western-oriented, creative jewelry, much work does not fit neatly into a single specific category but certain predominating general tendencies, either conceptual or technological, do become apparent.

Jewels concerned with composition, form, or *pure design* remain a distinct body of work. Its main influence originates in contemporary intellectual concepts prevailing in the two- and three-dimensional fields of painting and sculpture. This work is often characterized by precision of construction and execution. In some three-dimensional work, the concepts used to create holloware are adapted to jewelry on a scale suited to this application.

Jewels with dominating surface ornamentation constitute

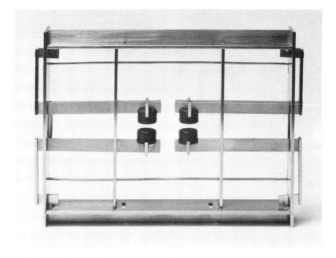

I–10 PETER SKUBIC, Austria. Brooch in chrome-nickel steel with two pairs of red painted magnets. The solderless structure of flat strips is pierced with rectangular holes, the units holding together by the four outer split rectangles that act as clamps, and the force of the magnet pairs. Size 4¹⁄₁₆ × 5¾ in (10.4 × 14.7 cm). *Photo: Courtesy Schmuck International 1900–1980, Künstlerhaus, Vienna*

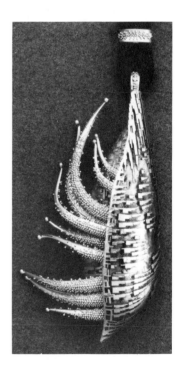

I–11 JOHN PAUL MILLER, U.S.A. Pendant, "Cephalopod," in 18K and pure gold. The tentacles' surfaces are ornamented with round granules, and the body with geometrically shaped gold chips, whose small scale produces a textural effect. The body ground is enameled. *Photo: John Paul Miller*

another important area of interest in which traditional and/or innovative surface-enriching techniques are used. Both ornament and form may range stylistically from abstract pattern or structure, to representational naturalism.

Jewels with an association to nature use subject matter from nature, or employ forms and surfaces that strongly suggest the botanical and mineral world. These are either developed by natural forces and techniques, or are artfully contrived by the use of tools and techniques. The wide use of textured surfaces is a significant development in the jewelry of the last quarter century, representing a widespread interest in the surface treatments possible for the various materials used. An outgrowth of this area of interest is the employment of nonmetallic, organic mate-

I-12 GERDA FLOCKINGER, England. Pair of gold earrings with pearls and diamonds. The organic-looking surface texture is fusion created by natural forces. Length 10.4 cm. *Photo: Günter Meyer, courtesy Schmuckmuseum, Pforzheim*

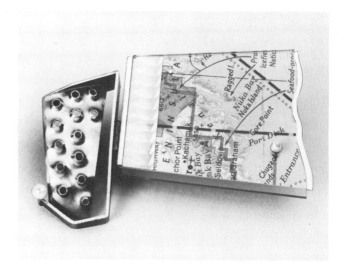

I-13 BOB EBENDORF, U.S.A. Pin in sterling silver with pearls, including a map section covered by a riveted sheet of green Plexiglas. Size 1½ × 3 in. *Photo: Bob Ebendorf*

rials such as fibers, feathers, shell, leather, etc., both in combination with metals, and alone.

Jewels commenting on aspects of contemporary life often incorporate representational images or subjects meant to amuse, provoke, confront, annoy, or shock. Such jewels express a message, overt or cryptic, that ranges from delight in to anger with or sarcastic ridicule of the subject. Collage techniques, and the use of found objects and a variety of nontraditional materials commonly appear in this area because these sources evoke associative or nostalgic ideas and connotations. Often the subject matter has symbolic meaning that calls forth reactions, invites involvement, or in other ways contributes to the message.

Jewels using techniques of the industrial world occupy a distinctive place in the field. In this work, technical processes not traditional to jewelry making have been expropriated and put to use to create jewelry whose character is undisguisedly the result of such processes and no other. In utilizing these techniques, the jeweler erases the boundaries between artistic and industrial technology by applying the creative principle to the industrial process. Inversely, the particular technology has its direct influence on the character of the creation. This area presents another important development of this century; some examples are electroformed, lathe-turned, and stamped jewelry, and jewels that utilize photographic processes.

Jewels that use new or nontraditional materials comprise another area of contemporary interest. This usage generally does not constitute the introduction of new technological concepts because these materials are generally employed in ways that reiterate traditional processing techniques. Plastics, for instance, are formed by means that their nature allows, such as fabrication, carving, or casting—processes that in essence are no different from the processes by which metal or other traditional materials are worked. The novelty of this material lies in its *appearance,* and its *newness.* (This is also the case with the metal titanium, whose use is also new to jewelry.) However, many experimental jewelers return to the use of gold and silver, which remain metals of unlimited potential.

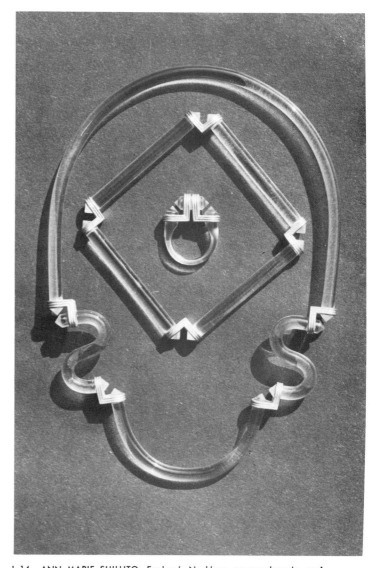

I-14 ANN MARIE SHILLITO, England. Necklace, square bangle, and ring in clear acrylic, with cast silver corner units that make right-angle joins. Basic rod forms with point-tapered ends, and metal angle units are used in all objects. The design is intended for multiple fabrication. *Photo: Ann Marie Shillito*

I-15 BERNARD FRANÇOIS, Belgium. Ring in stainless steel sheets that sandwich plastic inserts, dissimilar materials held together with screws. This exposed, mechanical cold joining device is integrated into the design. *Photo: Günter Meyer, courtesy Schmuckmuseum, Pforzheim*

Jewels using synthetic adhesives are new in jewelry fabrication. Synthetic adhesives allow the efficient cold joining of similar or dissimilar materials in a nonconventional manner. Adhesives have been used in the past for jewelry making, but none had the unique holding power of contemporary adhesives such as epoxy or cyanoacrylate, which are as reliable as solder fusion for withstanding the normal stresses to which jewelry is subject. In the area of *traditional cold joining systems,* the exposure of formerly hidden screws and rivets has become respectable: there is an "honesty" or validity in revealing fabrication methods. Because such elements can now be seen, they too enter the design context.

From the variety of the foregoing, it should be evident that the freedom to experiment with an infinity of options, including a reinterpretation of historic styles, is today's byword, and each of us is welcome to the excitement of the pursuit of discoveries. At some point, however, the "experiment" must lead to a *conclusion,* for which the artist unflinchingly accepts total responsibility.

THE ULTIMATE EXPERIENCE:
Understanding the environment, and self-realization

At the core of the handcraft experience is the development of a fundamental understanding of our physical environment through a personal exploration of the forces and resources present in and on our planet. Guided by imagination and acquired skills, we try to realize our visions using established methods and systems, and by inventing others to exploit the nature of whatever we use.

Through this work we come to realize our greatest human asset, the *creative potential* within us. At the least, the work leads to personal development; for the committed, to a lifetime of fulfillment. Whatever the extent of the involvement, the main reward of the creative experience is its affirmation of the self. Creativity also relates us to other human beings and to our cultural heritage, forming a bridge of continuity between the past, the present, and the future. Using the creative impulse as a tool, we work in our own small way to shape the world in a positive direction, and in the process, participate in its destiny.

Oppi Untracht
Porvoo,
Finland

I-16 GARY GRIFFIN, U.S.A. "Brooch in 12–24 L/R." Fabricated in aluminum, brass, and stainless steel mainly by the creative use of lathe techniques, with monofilament line. Size 2 × 4 in. *Photo: Gary Griffin*

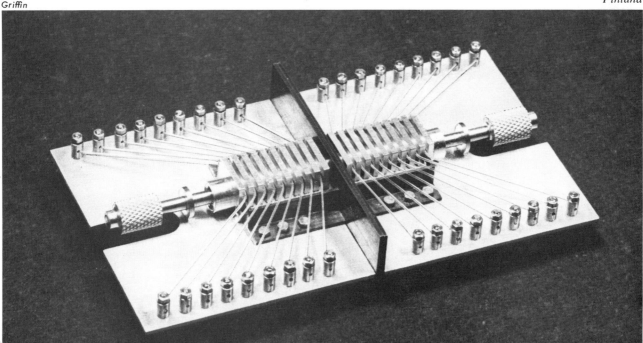

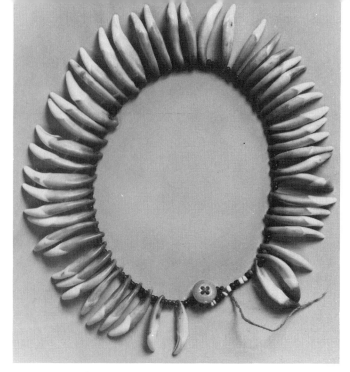

1–1 VIETNAM. Necklace of animal's teeth, glass beads, with button clasp. The use of wild animal's parts for ornament is a totemic emblem by which primitive man attempts to acquire the superior power of the conquered animal's strength, and its courage. Teeth, one of the animal's aggressive weapons, are physical proof of this transfer. *Photo: Musée de l'Homme, Paris*

1–2 CHRIS SCHALLER, U.S.A. Pendant of scrimshawed mammoth ivory slab framed in sterling silver inlaid with ebony, and brown and white mammoth ivory. The fossilized tooth of an extinct Pleistocene herbiverous animal is transformed into a contemporary ornament. Its surface depicts a surviving fierce species of carnivorous animal, *Felis leo*, who by the use of the illustrated bared teeth preys largely on herbivorous animals. The lion is the "king of beasts," and symbolically relates to the sun, and to gold, the "lion of metals." *Photo: Courtesy Aaron Faber Gallery, New York*

1–3 NEW GUINEA. Dressed for a ceremonial sing-sing or traditional dance and country fair, his ornaments include boar's tusks, monkey fur, snake vertebrae, feathers, cowrie shells, cane, and glass beads, representing mastery over animals, birds, reptiles, the sea, and the earth. *Photo: Lehtikuva Oy*

1

THE MESSAGES OF JEWELRY
Why We Wear Ornaments

THE ORIGINS OF JEWELRY

Satisfying psychic and physical needs

Humankind's love of personal decoration must have its roots in the awakened concept of the self-image which developed in the unrecorded past. The first concrete evidence of body ornamentation is seen in cave dwellers' wall drawings believed to be at least 20,000 years old. Since it is fairly safe to assume that the realization that parts of the body could support ornaments predated the idea that humans could represent themselves graphically, the use of ornaments must be even older.

NATURAL SUBSTANCES: Products of the hunt

Anthropologists tell us that our first ornaments were of animal origin, by-products of the hunt, in which animals were killed for food, their skins, or because they were a threat to human existence. Flesh was eaten and blood drunk, and those inedible parts—teeth, claws, horns, tusks, and vertebrae—that were not used to make tools and weapons were strung or pierced and worn as ornaments. It seems probable that this early use of animal parts for ornament was motivated by the metempsychic belief that through physical body contact with the animal's aggressive weapons of attack, its courage, fierceness, and superior power would pass on to the wearer. Besides being concrete displays of trophy evidence only obtainable by the death of the creatures, such ornaments also were a declaration of man's superiority to the vanquished animals, who were far stronger or fleeter.

Other early materials used for ornaments came from vegetative, bird, and insect sources in the immediate environment. Attractive, brilliantly colored but perishable flowers, leaves, fibers, vines, and seeds, as well as the iridescent elytra (wing covers) of beetles, and bird feathers were no doubt used for personal adornment eons ago, as they still are today by some African, Oceanic, and South American peoples during group and private ritual observances.

In assembling these objects into ornaments, esthetic awareness was present, as we see in those ornaments worn today by remote tribal peoples. Parts are often arranged in matched or graded sizes, the most ornamental or highly colored feathers are selected for use, and combinations of materials are chosen for contrasts in texture, form, or color. Assemblies are constructed with care and ingenuity

using methods borrowed from systems employed in the fabrication of shelters, clothing, and implements.

In addition to ornaments, an individual's external physical appearance and the human spirit within could be temporarily transformed by a change of skin color, accomplished with colored earths. With daubs and smears of these same materials, the face could be turned into a patterned mask that symbolically permitted a metamorphosis of persona. Transformations could be made permanent on face and body by tattooing, still in wide use by many peoples.

1–4 ANGOLA, District Huila, Prefecture Sa Da Bandiera. Her headdress is of beads. The divided hair is strung with bone sections and the ends are included in rolled clay lumps. *Photo: Musée de l'Homme, Paris*

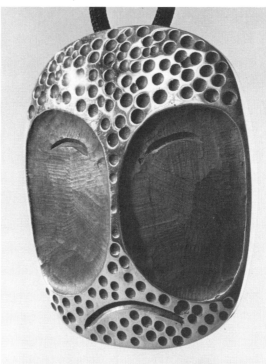

THE BEAD: Transforming durable natural substances into artifacts

Durable natural materials suitable for use as ornaments were also found locally. Uniquely colored, tumble-polished river or beach pebbles attracted attention. In Neolithic times during the late Stone Age, about 15,000 B.C., the technique of *boring through stone* is believed to have been mastered. Such pebbles could then be perforated and a cord passed through the hole, transforming it into a bead that could be tied to the body. Boring was done with palm-rotated *hand drills* with stone bits of *flint* and *chert* (essentially a dark cryptocrystalline quartz or fibrous chalcedony), and later with *bow drills* worked with the help of abrasive powders of crushed stones harder than the pebbles. Bead holes made by such tools are generally conical in shape, since they approach each other from opposite sides toward the center, where they meet.

Surface stone polishing was a technological development that occurred about the same time and made possible the permanent revelation of a stone's true color, previously seen only temporarily when a naturally abraded surface was wet. With these advances, conditions existed to allow the creation of jewelry from durable substances that man could modify or transform in form and surface. The *stone bead,* it can therefore be said, was the first man-created, mineral ornament made by drastically altering the form of the raw material.

By empirical experience the discovery followed that some stones are more highly colored or harder than others, and therefore are capable of a longer lasting, more highly polished surface. This knowledge brought about the concept of the *lapidary art,* which has sent people on an endless search through the mineral world for materials that could serve as beads at first, and much later, as polished stones mounted in metal.

THE USES OF, AND VALUES PLACED ON JEWELRY

THE AMULET: *Protection against the unknown*

In the development of human culture, the idea evolved that the magic act of transformation itself imbued a condition of magic to the changed and perfected object. This belief was projected upon *all* early jewelry, whose prime purpose was for use as an *amulet,* a charm to protect the wearer against real or imagined calamities and threats to life. Belief in their effectiveness furnished humans with a psychological means of combating the hostility of both the real and the spirit-filled world in which they lived.

Jewels such as talismanic beads and objects of metal and other materials were believed to serve prophylactic or curative functions as well. Of extremely ancient usage, such objects held by a string or chain and worn against the skin any place on the body are commonly worn today in many parts of the world. Specific amulet forms developed because their shape and the ideas associated with it, or the material of which they were made were believed to be empowered with the ability to have an influence upon the prime concerns of humans—longevity, good health, wealth, sexual concerns, and luck or the favor of fate. Amulets exist that are believed to have the power to repel the attack of an evil spirit—the evil eye being a common malevolent threat—or a marauding animal. Some offer protection against natural disasters, endemic or epidemic diseases, poisoned bites, or witchcraft, as well as security against myriad other threats to a healthy and happy existence. Still others are used as instruments in magic ceremonies, or as sympathetic magic.

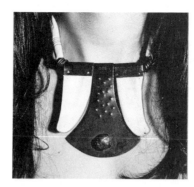

1–9 BEIRUT, LEBANON. Amulet of five alum pieces held together by iron wire. Each part ends in a white metal lunar crescent, and the lowest in the hand of Fatima, both Muslim symbols of good luck, worn as protection against the evil eye. Max. length 6 cm; width 3 cm. *Photo: Musée de l'Homme, Paris*

1–7 BANARAS (VARANASI), UTTAR PRADESH, INDIA. Boy wearing silver neck and arm amulets (*ta'wiz*). When hollow, these contain written paper prayers or incantations. Worn by children all over India in belief that they protect them from various evils that may befall them before adulthood. Some potent charm pendant types are made of tiger's claws (*viaghranakha*). *Photo: Oppi*

1–10 NEPAL. Amulet garland (*raksha ma*) commonly worn by children. Each silver bezel-held object is believed to possess separate protective power. Various seeds, nuts, stones, teeth, animal's hoof, coin, snail shell, etc., are used. *Photo: Oppi*

1–11 BOB EBENDORF, U.S.A. Necklace of silver, copper, and brass, with bone, amber, and animal's teeth, primitive amuletic objects. *Photo: Bob Ebendorf*

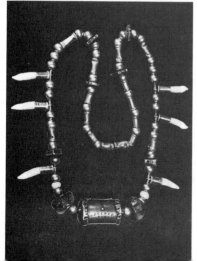

1–12 KAMENG FRONTIER DIVISION, N.E.F.A., INDIA. Hazarikhowa or Kutsun clan woman and child, Village Jamri. Six silver amulet boxes (*melu*) containing magic articles are worn for protection. On her head is a traditional silver fillet (*lenchhi*), and silver earplugs (*rombin*) penetrate large holes in each earlobe. Her face is dot tattooed at the age of ten. *Photo: Courtesy N.E.F.A. Photo Section, Shillong*

1–13 BAHIA, BRAZIL. Silver amulet chatelaine worn suspended from the waist belt. The objects hanging from a two-tiered, ornamented loop include pomegranates, fish, keys, a ladle, coins, grapes, rooster, horse, pigeon, vase, and closed containers, all symbolic magical objects. *Photo: Pitt Rivers Museum, Oxford*

1–14 BIHAR, INDIA. Sunyasi or Sadhu lying on a thorn bed, wearing fillet and bracelet of *rudraksha* beads which are also pinned to his body, along with limes. This act of penance was performed at a country fair to collect money offerings for a sect. *Photo: Oppi*

THE SYMBOL: *Communication with the conscious and the subconscious*

Symbols in the visual arts are shapes, forms, or other representations that suggest either intangible, abstract ideas, or real conditions and objects; an association or resemblance in the mind of the viewer creates a connection between the form and what it symbolizes. A symbol may take the form of an abstract shape or sign, or may appear as a representation of a real, concrete object. Because a symbol has significance beyond what is outwardly seen, the use of visual symbolism exists in our daily lives far more than we consciously realize, the symbol emitting a message that often is only subconsciously perceived. The study of the use of signs or symbols in languages, images, and artifacts as a visual means of expressing thought is called semiology.

Representational symbolic objects were used in jewelry singly or in composite forms whose power, it was believed, helped the wearer to acquire a means of control over the basic concerns of life. Common is the desire for fertility and progeny, often symbolically represented in the ornaments of many cultures by a sun figure (the sun being the source of energy), or a seed (from which life springs). Because fish breed prolifically, they too are fertility symbols. The quest for material wealth is embodied in the use of real or simulated coins in the traditional ornaments worn by many peoples. The desire for love has made common the use of the heart shape. The realization of love is symbolized by the wedding band whose endless circular form in turn symbolizes the promise of eternal devotion.

In the spiritual sphere, forms connected with all religions are frequently adopted for use in jewelry. The flower and leaf, common jewelry motifs, are symbols of identification with life, nature, and the idea of belonging to Greater Creation. Votive offerings in the form of jewels are still given to a supranatural Power.

Even in this rational age, when a scientific explanation exists for all phenomena, we find irrational symbols in use.

1–15 INDIA. Contemporary natural seed (*rudraksha*) necklace. This hard, tubercled nut of the Indian utrasum bead tree (*Elaeocarpus ganitrus*) is endowed with magic properties. Cleaned, stained, and sometimes polished, it is used in rosaries and bracelets worn by Brahmins and Sunyasis, and sold in places of holy pilgrimage. *Photo: Oppi*

1–16 THAILAND, 19th century. Necklace with gilt brass seed pod ornaments, and silver-gilt pendant coins. Seeds symbolize fertility as they possess regenerative forces with fulfillment potential. Coins represent prosperity. *Photo: Victoria and Albert Museum, London, Crown Copyright* ▼

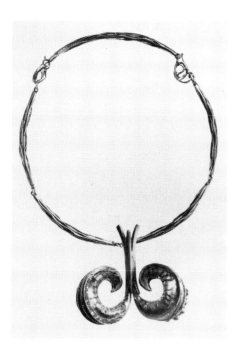

1–17 HANNA BECHAR-PANETH, Israel. "Beans." Silver necklace with cast pendant in the form of seed pods. *Photo: Yacov Paneth*

1–18 TRIPURA, INDIA. Woman wearing a six-strand old silver coin necklace, a symbol of wealth. The silver bracelet-cuff, earrings, and studs are traditional local forms. *Photo: Madan Mahatta*

1–19 KAZAN PROVINCE, U.S.S.R. Udmurt women, a Finno-Ugrian people from parish Mamadeskog, photographed in 1878 wearing traditional status symbol coin decorated headdresses (aison), worn only by married women; short necklace (tśyrtketś); long necklace (tśyrtyveś) and shoulder band (kamali). *Photo: National Museum of Finland, Helsinki*

1–20 KIRSTI ILVESSALO, Finland, designer; manufacturer Kalevala Koru, Helsinki. Gold and silver handmade wedding rings, designs based on old Finnish ornaments. The closed circle is a symbol of wholeness, oneness, and endless continuity, making the wedding ring a widely used symbol of the marriage bond and endless love. *Photo: Otso Pietinen, courtesy Kalevala Koru*

1-21A JERUSALEM, ISRAEL, late 19th century. Jewish silver wedding ring, a type used from the 16th to the early 20th century in the wedding ceremony. Worn by the bride for a week afterward, it was then returned to the synagogue as it was owned by the congregation. The surmounting structure is a synagogue, and unlocks by a hinge and clasp just above the Tablets of the Law. Inside on paper are the Ten Commandments given to Moses on Mount Sinai. *Photo: Frank J. Darmstaedter, Jewish Museum, New York*

1-21B JANET BERG, U.S.A. A contemporary interpretation of the traditional Jewish ceremonial wedding ring, in sterling silver. The roof and side window open and move on hinges. Under the roof, inside the house, is the word *mazel* (luck), and the Hebrew band inscription reads: "I will betroth thee unto me." Height 1¾ in (4.4 cm). *Photo: Janet Berg*

1-22, 1-23, 1-24 TIZNIT and TAFILALELT, MOROCCO. Silver amulets worn by Muslims. *Five*, symbolizing the fingers and toes of man's extremities, is a commonly used amuletic number based on the *quinary* or five-element concept. This amulet *khamsa*, literally meaning "five" or "hand," is commonly worn alone by Muslims on a neck cord or chain, or as an element in larger ornaments. The *khamsa* represents Ali in Iran, and the hand of Fatima, Mohammed's favorite daughter by his first wife Khadija, in other Islamic countries. It also symbolizes the family of Mohammed: the thumb represents the Prophet himself; the first finger Fatima; the second Ali her husband; the third and fourth fingers their sons Hasan and Husain. It protects the wearer against malignant influences of the evil eye, whose power can be nullified by five repetitions of the phrase: *Khamsa fi ainek*, literally, "Five in your eye." The engraved designs on other amulets have additional symbolic meaning. Sun and stars symbolize day and night. A prayer niche (*mirhab*) on a mosque wall indicates the direction toward Mecca, faced by worshipers during prayers. A crescent moon symbolizes Mohammedanism as a religious or political force. Palms, vines, and tendrils symbolize the life force. A lizard moving in the semidesert also is a life symbol. The amulet, above right, has a miniature *khamsa* suspended above the tree-of-life symbol contained within a shape symbolic of female sexuality, flanked by a pair of guardian swords. *Photos: Oppi, courtesy Kabbaj Med. B. Salem, Marrakech Bazaar, Morocco*

1-25 IRAN, late 18th century. Silver necklace with pendant amulets and bells. At top, center, is an agate stone engraved with verses from the Koran; below it hangs a crescent moon (*chand*), symbol of the Muslim faith; below that, a triangular shape, or female symbol enclosing a flower, a symbol of life. These are flanked by two *khamsas*, followed by two crescent moons with pendant stars, the combination of the two a Muslim symbol for the spirit in Paradise. *Photo: Francis Hopp Museum of Eastern Asiatic Arts, Budapest*

1-27 *Left:* HUNGARY, early 17th century. Gold pendant with enamel, set with a diamond and garnets, and hung with pearls; worn suspended by a chain. The subject is the paschal lamb, or *Agnus Dei*, Latin, "Lamb of God," a term applied by John the Baptist to Christ. The lamb, a symbol of Christ and sacrifice, is pouring its life's blood from its chest into a chalice representative of the one used during Communion. By the right leg the lamb holds a cross mounted on a rod. Suspended from the cross is a banner charged with a Maltese cross. The three stones mounted on the lamb's body represent the Holy Trinity: the Father, the Son, and the Holy Ghost in a single Godhead, so that in substance all three are one. An almost identical pendant is in the collection of the Baltimore Museum of Art. *Photo: From the collection of Countess Harley-Teleki, Victoria and Albert Museum, London, Crown Copyright*

1-28 *Right:* ITALY, approximately 1600 A.D. Gold pendant with enamel, precious stones, and pearls, representing a winged Cupid, son of Venus, goddess of love, aiming an arrow in his bow, which upon reaching its victim inflicts the wound of love. *Photo: Rijksmuseum, Amsterdam*

1-26 RAJASTHAN, INDIA. Bhil tribal man wearing a silver amulet pendant stamped with an image of the Bhil goddess Bheru, whose vehicle is a dog. This amulet symbolizes his devotion to the goddess, who in turn offers him protection. *Photo: Oppi*

1-29 NORTHERN INDIA. Hindu, stamped silver pendants worn as protective amulets. Each bears a representation of a Hindu god or goddess. *Top left and second from top*, Ramdeoji on horse; *bottom left*, eight mother goddesses; *center top*, Durga on lion; *top right*, Hanuman the monkey god; three circular sun symbols of Surya, the sun god; *lower leaf shape*, Surya symbol and the horse, his vehicle; above this to the left, Kali; *bottom right*, Ganesh and Lakshmi. *Photo: Oppi*

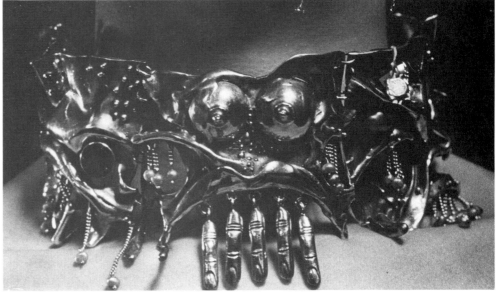

1–30 TIRAP, MON VILLAGE, N.E.F.A., INDIA. Nokte tribal headman, wearing a canework hat ornamented with wild boar tusks, and ivory arm bangles. His coral and millifiore glass bead necklace supports three brass heads, modern effigies symbolizing shrunken human head trophies formerly taken from victims of war. *Photo: Courtesy N.E.F.A. Photo Section, Shillong*

1–31 BARBARA GASCH, West Germany. Silver necklace using magic cult symbols of personal significance. The pendant fingers are reminiscent of trophy jewelry. *Photo: Dölf Preisig*

1–32 ETHIOPIA, 19th century. Silver and white metal pierced work traditional crosses. Since early Christian times, in Ethiopia the cross has been regarded as a powerful amulet and talisman. *Photo: Oppi*

Within the system of astrology, the ancient pseudoscience dealing with the influence of the sun, stars, and planets on human destiny, zodiacal symbols are widely used, and stones are credited with supernatural powers. Particular stones symbolize the planet with which they are associated, and wearing such a stone is believed to influence the fate of any individual born under the planet associated with it.

Many contemporary jewelers speak of their works as being symbolic amulets, another indication that the primitive concept of the jewel being capable of possessing magic powers is far from dead. However, the growing complexity of contemporary society has resulted in a loss of meaning for many traditional symbols originally widely understood. In creative works these are frequently replaced by per-

sonal, private, or even hidden symbols whose intention or meaning may be inscrutable, and that spring from a private fantasy world. In such cases, the limit imposed on communication may be deliberate, since a jewel invested with apparent (but unknown) symbolic meaning becomes a provocation, and either a challenge or an invitation to the viewer to become involved with the "provocateur" in an attempt to understand its significance.

THE JEWEL AND THE JEWELER

THE JEWEL MANDALA: Mapping the jewel-motivation cosmos

An amazingly broad range of motives govern an individual's desire to possess and use jewelry. These ideas are often the result of a person's exposure to the opinions of family, friends, and peers, or to the social and cultural milieu with which one feels identified. Motivations are compounded in complexity by the psychological forces that shape attitudes at all levels of contemporary society, by the circumstances of economics and politics, and by group opinions in general. Today, in addition to this mélange, we are subjected to mass media communication, which pours out constant visual and verbal messages of what an individual should like and possess.

A diagrammatic *jewel mandala* is presented here with the hopes of enabling the reader to better understand the interrelationships of the various forces that contribute to the creation of our desires for jewels. The image of a mandala (the circular, radial "psychocosmogram" originating in India and used in meditation and the invocation of deities) is a particularly useful organizing principle.

At the base of the mandala is the jewel from which radiate those persons who by choice are involved with jewelry through their use of, or interest in it. The three main groups to which these persons belong are the *wearer* who of course is central, the *collector,* and the *investor.* Connected with each of these are types of jewelry that interest them, and the reasons for their interest.

THE JEWEL MANDALA

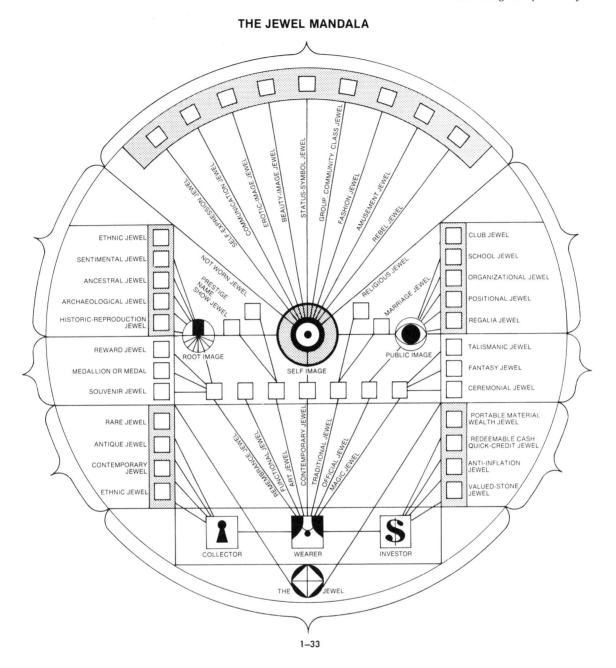

1–33

Most of the mandala deals with the functions that jewelry serves for the wearer. Starting with the more basic types, which are later subdivided, jewelry can be classified into the following groups: jewels whose main function is *remembrance;* jewels that serve an actual *functional* purpose such as holding clothing parts together; jewels with *artistic* purpose, made to express an esthetic; jewels concerned exclusively with *contemporary* concepts; jewels that are dominated by *traditional* concepts; jewels for *official use* that express the hierarchical, structured nature of society; and jewels with *magical powers,* concerned with the irrational and with an individual's inner fantasy life.

All of these uses relate to areas that concern basic aspects of the human being: the *self-image,* the *root image,* and the *public image.*

By *self-image* is meant the inner concept or sense of identity each individual has of his or her being, in which

the whole of the conscious and subconscious personality is integrated; this is the image which he or she desires to project to others. Because of its primal importance, and because it is the origin of self-identification, it is placed at the central axis of the mandala. The motives that govern a person's use of jewelry to express the self cover a broad spectrum of personality needs that together act as an individualizing force. Any single one of these motives may be in operation at a given time, or several can be co-active, even when only one jewel is in question.

Radiating from the self-image are the universal motivations that a jewel's possession can incorporate and satisfy. Primary is the desire for *self-expression,* the affirmation of the ego and the psyche as expressed by an individual's intellectual, emotional, and impulsive activities and predispositions. This basic motivation is shared—the maker experiences it in creating the jewel, the wearer, through the choice he or she makes in acquiring it. That choice may be determined by a wish to *communicate* a general impression to others, or even to supply specific information about the wearer, such as, "I am conventional," or, "I am an extrovert." Of great importance is the desire to enhance one's natural endowments and project an impression of *beauty,* often transformed into an erotic image that may send a provocative sexual message. The desire for *social status* acts as a means of bolstering the feeling of self-importance, and is a powerful and common motive in choosing jewelry. Status may or may not be directly connected with the intrinsic value of a jewel, but it is certainly based on whatever is considered important by the individual and the group or society to which that individual belongs. Connected with status satisfaction is the desire to be *identified with a particular group, community, or class.* An active or passive desire to belong to a *cultural milieu* (which may cut across all social classes) is the automatic result of the acceptance of *fashion-dictated jewelry.* Jewels that satisfy an impulse to *amuse oneself* suggest an attempt to charm others as well. Jewelry can also contain a message *declaring rebellion* against established esthetic attitudes, or even social or political conditions. This declaration can be the result of sincere conviction, or simply be a desire to shock others and attract attention.

Tradition may govern an individual's choice of jewelry, as in the use of *religious* or *rite-of-passage jewelry,* such as *marriage* jewels. These jewels publically declare specific facts about the wearer that he or she wishes to make known. At the other extreme are the jewels that have intensely *magical or private significance,* such as *talismans,* jewels that indulge a secret fantasy, or those used for *ceremonial* purposes. *Sentimental* jewels of *remembrance* may be as personal as a gift from a loved one to commemorate a pleasant experience, an occasion, or an event; or, on a less personal level, they can be a *reward* for services rendered, or an earned achievement in the form of a medal or a medallion. In a special class are *art* jewels purchased because they are created by jewelers of repute; and the prestige of ownership provides the wearer with a feeling of self-importance. In this category are *jewels with double lives*—in one life the jewel is worn, as any jewel; in the other, it is an independent, decorative object placed on a stand or wall—and the *never-worn jewel* meant only for display as an object.

In the mandala, flanking the self-image are the root image and the public image. The *root image* involves an individual's attitudes about his or her origin, and one's jewelry can express a desire to identify with or remember it. These feelings may incline a person to choose to wear *ethnic* jewelry used or produced by one's community of origin. Sentiment or reverence felt for an ancestor can motivate the use of *inherited or ancestral* jewelry. Similar feelings may spark the purchase of jewels manufactured by jewelers of traditional cultures or countries of origin to which one feels connected. *Reproduction* jewels (which are copies of historic or archeological jewels usually found today in museum shops) may induce a feeling of historic connection with the originals. Conversely, a person may opt to forget or obscure his or her origins by adopting the use of the ornaments worn by other groups or strata of society.

The *public image* mainly concerns the use of jewels that have some official or organizational significance. Wearing *club* jewelry involves a desire to belong to a specific and perhaps exclusive group of persons having some common interest or other reason for being a group, and such jewels

1–34 KAMPUCHEA. An *apsara* or Hindu dancing girl in Swerga, Indra's heaven, given in reward to fallen heroes. This example is one of hundreds carved on the stone walls of the Angkor Wat temple monastery, a masterpiece of Khmer art built in the first half of the 12th century A.D. Dressed in a variety of ceremonial jewels that are fantasies of invention by Khmer sculptors, these women of pleasure depend heavily on ornament to enhance their attraction. *Photo: Oppi*

1–35 SAARA HOPEA-UNTRACHT, Finland, designer; Karl-Göran Ahlberg, executor; manufacturer Kultasepänliike Ossian Hopea, Porvoo. Silver ceremonial necklace incorporating the town symbol, worn by the Porvoo city director on ceremonial occasions. Length approx. 40 cm. *Photo: Salmi*

become a means of identifying a fellow member. Similar factors are at work in the wearer of *school* jewelry, which may also involve feelings of sentiment or elitism. *Positional* jewelry is the kind to which the wearer is entitled because of holding an office or a particular position in a society or a community. *Regalia* jewels are those worn by persons to whom certain rights and privileges are due. If such a person is of royal birth, these will include crowns, scepters, ensigns, necklaces of state, and the like. In the case of an office holder in a fraternal organization, such as the Freemasons, a collar of state or other regalia might be worn on ceremonial occasions.

An *investor* may also wear jewelry, but the dominating motive for purchase is the thought that it is a convenient means of concentrating *wealth* in an easily *portable* form. Surplus cash converted into jewelry puts it in a form that can be easily redeemed. If necessary, it is usable as a basis of credit, and the investment becomes a means of keeping up with inflational depreciation in the value of currency. Precious jewelry increases in market value at a rate commensurate with inflation. *Valuable* jewels that stay in a bank vault and are rarely if ever worn belong in this category.

A *collector* almost invariably is a jewel lover, unlike an investor who may or may not actually like the jewelry purchased. A collector's motivations may also be diverse and might include the purpose of investment, but this generally is a consideration of secondary importance. The choices made are highly selective and may follow a decidedly restricted area of interest. *Rarity, antiquity, ethnicity,* or *"avant-garde-ness"* are the most frequent bases for collections, although, of course, not the only ones.

A POLARIZED CONVOCATION OF JEWELERS

We cannot speak of the world of jewelry today without giving due recognition to the *artist-jeweler* upon whom all developments center. He/she is both procreator/genetrix, begetter/conceiver of all the concepts endlessly poured into the jewel object. The term artist-jeweler can be interpreted narrowly to include only influential jewelers, but it can also have an all-inclusive meaning to incorporate both greater and lesser members of this ideologically and physically far-flung family as long as their work contains an element of originality.

To identify each member in the jeweler family, it has been called here to a convocation whose seating plan is polarized horizontally and vertically to indicate diagrammatically how the directions of interest of the various members relate to each other. It must be made clear from the start that the arrangement of this seating plan is *not* to create a hierarchy, nor to give undue prominence to any particular member, nor to divide the family into opposing camps (even though conceptual opposition does occur). The plan's purpose is only to identify and to locate members in a manner that shows their interrelationships. Some members may belong in more than one location. If by some oversight *you* have not been given a place, please understand that the omission was not deliberate, and that you too are invited.

What emerges from this plan is the fact that a remarkable diversity of interests exists within the family. In the light of such diversity, the only means of creating harmony within the family is through mutual tolerance. We all must joyfully accept the many levels and directions that the gift of creativity, a human being's greatest asset, can take.

Therefore, at this meeting, no member is permitted to take an aggressive stance, nor to force another into a defensive position in order to give importance to or gain support for his or her point of view. Neither is there any place for ridicule, or dispute about the greater significance of one direction of interest as opposed to any other. We suggest that any such attack in reality is a disguise for insecurity, and we firmly believe that each member of the family can be strong in his or her own right.

A few points should be made in explanation of the plan. The all-encompassing artist-jeweler is given a position of prominence at the exact center. He or she has forebears in the historic jeweler, who is not present but whose presence is felt. At one end of the hall is the assembly of commercial jewelers, a part of the family in very good standing, but whose contact with other members of the family is unfortunately limited: unfortunate because there is much that can be learned from this branch of the family, as those artist-jewelers who have on occasion crossed over into their territory well know. Commercial jewelers generally supply a mass market by employing mass-production methods, but art production jewelers also exist who create limited-series jewels, often by hand technology. The production team upon whom the commercial jeweler depends to execute the designer's approved ideas is also present. The team consists of highly skilled artisans who are specialists in their particular areas of work.

In the center of the next horizontal pole, at the side of the artist-jeweler, is the independent hand jeweler. To his or her right is the teacher-jeweler and those to whom he or she relates, such as the student jeweler, the hobbyist-jeweler, and the therapy jeweler. The teacher-jeweler also has connections with and may also be an artist-jeweler. At the left on this pole is a virtually unknown member of the family, the anonymous ethnic jeweler who actually has no wish to be anonymous, but remoteness and lack of contact with other, nonlocal jewelers forces this anonymity. This member, also an artist-jeweler, sends regrets, and the message that the only way to meet him or her directly is by travel; indirectly, by studying publications or seeing his or her work in museum collections. Connected with this branch are the members who follow a true folk tradition or an urban tradition which nevertheless bears a distinct cultural identity. Also related, but living physically removed from the source of inspiration, is the jeweler who sympathizes with this branch, and whose work is strongly influenced by ethnic jewelry, the pseudo-folk jeweler.

In the next horizontal pole, at the right is what might be termed the conservative element of the family, though their ideas are constantly being influenced by those of the artist-jeweler. Those jewelers who follow traditional jewelry concepts often pursue the stylistically changing direction of the beautiful jewel, a concept that many contemporary artist-jewelers have abandoned. Unique jewelry whose purpose is simply to be beautiful often makes use of expensive stones, and is produced in the world-famous, long-established workshops found in the major cities of the world.

To the left of the artist-jeweler is the rebel jeweler, the radical of the avant-garde, a pioneer in reform who challenges established concepts of design, subject suitability, materials, etc. At the extreme left are the nihilist jewelers,

A POLARIZED CONVOCATION OF JEWELERS

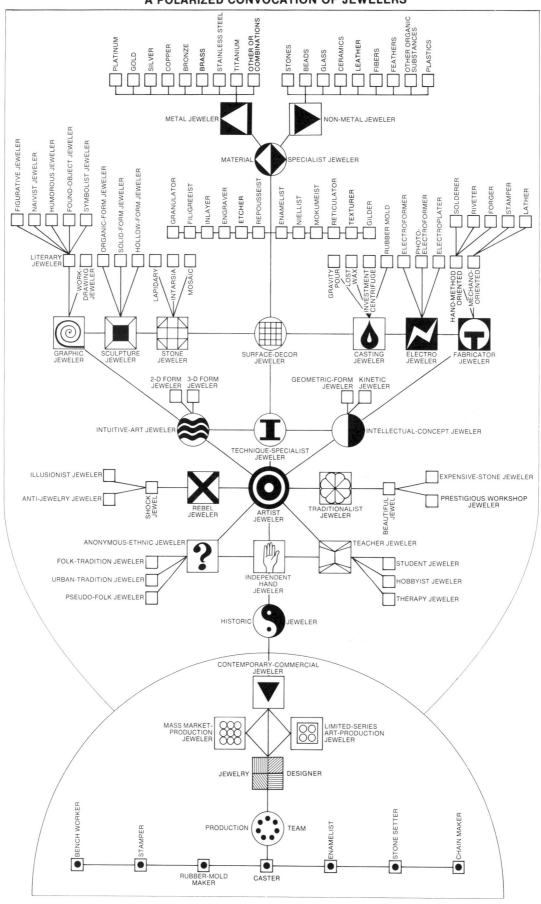

some of whom think that all jewelry is decadent and superfluous, and should be abolished, and that all we need is the illusion of jewelry. Antijewelry jewelers are also necessary because in a culturally free society, following the eternal cycle of creation, flowering, destruction, and re-creation, negation ultimately brings forth an affirmative response.

The following horizontal pole divides from the technique specialist jeweler and branches to the left to the intuitive artist-jeweler, and to the right toward his or her opposite, the intellectual concept jeweler. Continuing in the intuitive direction are the branches to the two- and three-dimensional jewelers who are influenced by graphic and sculptural idioms. Several branches continue from these to follow related paths. Returning to the intellectual concept jeweler, that direction includes the geometric form, and the kinetic or moving-form jeweler, and these are con-

nected with the fabricator-jeweler in the horizontal pole above.

The next horizontal pole includes the major directions of interest among creative jewelers today. At the center is the surface decoration jeweler, flanked on the left by the stone-oriented jeweler and the afore-mentioned graphic and sculpture jewelers. On the right are the casting jeweler, the electro-oriented jeweler, and the fabricator-jeweler. Each of these has attached specialist branches, the largest number emanating from the surface decoration jeweler. A relatively new member of the family is the mechano-jeweler.

At the top of the vertical pole is the material specialist jeweler whose area divides basically into the metal and nonmetal groups. From these follow the many branches that indicate particular areas of specialization.

The meeting will now come to order.

JEWELRY FORMS IN RELATION TO THE BODY

Design and construction conditioned by anatomy

Jewelry design *per se* is not discussed in this book. Ideas concerning design concepts in our times are continually challenged, and alter with such rapidity that advancing any design theory, if such can exist, is like setting up bowling pins to be knocked over. What may be in favor at the moment will soon be regarded with disapproval, humor, or even contempt. We can, however, concern ourselves with certain basic, practical considerations that enter into and influence the creation of a design for any jewel. Regardless of design style, certain factors should always be kept in mind.

Jewelry is for men and women (and occasionally for animals), which means that it must relate to human anatomy: its scale or proportions must be concerned with human dimensions. Almost every part of the human body and almost every item of apparel, has, at one time or another, in one culture or another, been used as a location for wearing a jewel. (See Glossary: Forms of Jewelry.) The form a jewel takes is determined first of all by the place on the body or clothing where it will be worn, modified by thoughts connected with how it will be attached there, and whether it can be worn with relative comfort (though the latter is sometimes sacrificed for other considerations). Such concerns may dictate whether the design is basically conceived of as being *frontal, cylindrical,* or *three-dimensional.*

BASIC FORMS

FRONTAL FORMS

In frontally conceived forms, the jewel is intended to be best displayed from its front side, which by implication means it has a back side. The latter is ordinarily flat, or its points of contact with the body are in a flat plane in a direction parallel to the body. The front side or the portion

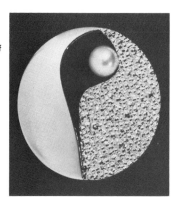

1–37 FINLAND, manufacturer Kultakeskus Oy, Hämeenlinna. A frontal brooch in 14K yellow gold, using contrasting areas of texture and plain surface, with a pearl focal point. *Photo: Courtesy Kultakeskus Oy*

seen may take any dimension from flat to projections at right angles to the body plane. Included in this category are brooches, buttons, clips, pendants, medals, etc.

CYLINDRICAL FORMS

The total form of these concepts is cylindrical, conical, or curved, and they relate to similarly shaped parts of the anatomy on which they are placed. The work may not be seen as a total in actual use on the body, but initially the design is conceived as a total unit encompassing this basic form. Such forms may include frontal or even back elements. Ornaments in this class may be worn on the head, neck, arm, wrist, fingers, waist, leg, ankle, and toes. Head ornaments include crowns, tiaras, chaplets, fillets, and forehead ornaments; neck ornaments include necklaces, chokers, chains, pendants on chains, etc.; arm ornaments include bracelets, bangles, watchbands, and upper arm bracelets; fingers hold rings; waist ornaments include belts and girdles; ankles support anklets; and toes hold toe rings.

1—38 ADRIAN MYERS, England. Silver-gilt cylindrical necklace using similar elements in a reduced-scale, multirepeat format. Partially textured surfaces are fused filings. Units are loop linked for articulation, and pearls are peg mounted. *Photo: Courtesy The Worshipful Company of Goldsmiths, London*

1—40 TIBET. Set of ornaments of human bone (*rus-rgyan*) carved with figures of deities and symbols, worn by Buddhist priests during certain ritual ceremonies. The set includes a crown, ear ornaments, necklace with attached ornaments, upper arm bracelets, chest ornament, sash, and apron. All parts are pierced and strung together. *Photo: National Museum of Denmark, Copenhagen*

THREE-DIMENSIONAL FORMS

Three-dimensional jewels are conceived of in the round, and are worn on parts of the body or in ways that allow the form to be seen from all, or at least several, sides. Such jewels may include hanging earrings, hair ornaments, some brooches, pendants suspended from chains, any other suspended, moving, or spring-mounted ornament, one that projects from a base or is swivel mounted and therefore turns completely around.

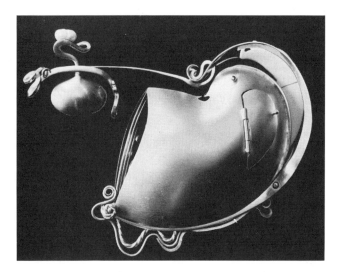

1—39 MARILYN DAVIDSON, U.S.A. Sterling silver and gold pin with ivory, baroque pearls, ruby, and opal. A three-dimensional form, it is held to the garment by a satellite unit clasp (*left*) using a threaded gold tube with a hole through which the pinstem passes, followed by screwing the lower part tight. The side-hinged panel opens to partially reveal a revolving interior construction. *Photo: Michael John Jerry*

FUNCTIONAL CONSIDERATIONS IN JEWELRY CONCEPTS

The size, weight, and shape of a jewel, as well as its position on the body or costume, may determine the system used to hold it to the body or to attach it to clothing and secure it from loss. These general considerations also have to be kept in mind when creating the jewel design. Jewelers' *findings*, the metal parts used to attach jewel parts to each other and to the body or clothing, are of course related to this subject area. (See Glossary: Jewelry Findings.) The term "finding," incidentally, as used by jewelers, is derived from its now obsolete meaning, "support," or what is provided for maintenance.

JEWELRY WEIGHT

The weight that different people can tolerate in any single piece of jewelry varies considerably. Some persons will submit to wearing very heavy jewels and will not mind any possible discomfort, while others will insist on extreme lightness. While weight tolerance may be an individual question involving personality differences, when using precious metals it is also decidedly a question of economics. The greater the weight, the higher the costs and the final price of the jewel.

The control of weight lies first of all in the particular choice of materials, and the thickness of parts. Also of importance is the system of construction: solid, cast forms weigh considerably more than jewels fabricated from hollow forms. It is unwise, however, to reduce thickness to the point where the work becomes flimsy and subject to deformation in ordinary usage. Slimming a ring shank to a dimension where it becomes deformed in use means it will have to be frequently repaired.

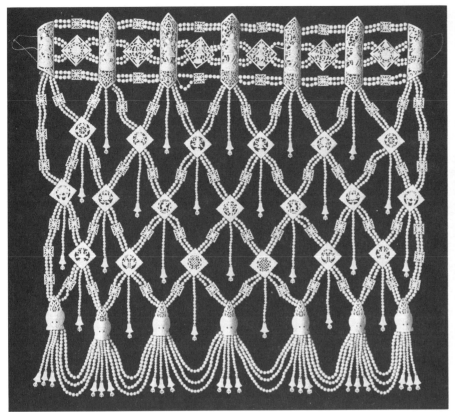

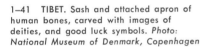

1-41   TIBET. Sash and attached apron of
human bones, carved with images of
deities, and good luck symbols. *Photo:
National Museum of Denmark, Copenhagen*

1-42   FAITH PORTER, U.S.A. "Person in a
Glass House." Body ornament, front view.
This construction was conceived as a
free-standing sculpture, and when not in
use is placed on a mannequin. 120
Plexiglas pieces; 400 crystal glass teardrops;
sixty 72 in Lucite tubing lengths; and 250
crystal and Lucite buttons are held by 3,500
inches of white satin cord inside the tubing.
Photo: Jay Ahrend

JEWELRY BULK

Bulk refers to the *total volume* of a piece of jewelry. The size of a jewel a person may choose to wear bears a direct relationship to the motives that person may have for wearing the jewel. In cases where large bulk is desired, weight can be reduced and bulk increased by fabricating hollow forms. Again, when precious metals are used, the cost of the material may play an inhibiting role on the jewel size. For this reason, precious metal jewelry in general tends to be smaller in bulk and its details finer than when other metals are used. The impression of bulk can be given by the use of wire forms which encompass airy volumes (one reason for the popularity of filigree jewelry). In the Orient, where thin-gauge metal forms are used for bulky shapes, the hollow is filled through an available opening with lightweight shellac which supports the metal and prevents denting.

In any case, jewelry weight and bulk must relate in *scale* and *proportion* with the selected part of the human body on which it is worn.

JEWELRY BALANCE

The problem of jewelry weight can be controlled to some extent by the manner of its distribution or balance. Top-heavy rings require a tight fit or the use of an upper and lower guard ring or plain band to stay in place. Rings can also be counterbalanced by thickening the shanks. Ring shank sides can be made somewhat concave to fit be-

1-43   SWEDEN, Viking period, 9th century. Bronze brooch inlaid with
gold and garnets, front and back view. The vertical pinstem with
hinge and clasp indicates the antiquity of this holding system. Length
15 cm, width 7 cm. *Photo: Antikvarisk-Topografiska Arkivet, Stockholm*

1–44 CHARLES LOLOMA, U.S.A. Cast gold rigid bracelet with gap for placement and removal. The rough surface texture contrasts with the highly polished edge, emphasizing the metal thickness, and visually implying weight. Max. Ø 2½ in. Photo: Courtesy U. S. Department of the Interior, Indian Arts and Crafts Board

1–45 ENGLAND, ca. 1840. Silver pendant brooch set with paste stones. The articulated hanging forms swing freely with movement, causing the stones to scintillate. Photo: Victoria and Albert Museum, London, Crown Copyright

1–46 KURT NIELSEN, Denmark, designer; manufacturer Hans Hansen Sølvsmedie, Copenhagen. Sterling silver articulated bracelet made flexible by concealed jump rings that hold the hollow units together. The total form is conical, allowing a comfortable fit on the wrist. Photo: Courtesy Hans Hansen Sølvsmedie

1–47 ANNI and BENT KNUDSEN, Denmark. Silver bracelet whose design concept is based on repetitions of the ball and socket joint, allowing total articulation. Length 22.6 cm. Photo: Museum für Kunst und Kulturgeschichte der Stadt Dortmund

tween the fingers, and spread out on the underside of the finger. Heavy necklaces can be counterpoised with a back ornament whose weight will help balance the front portion.

A special case is a top-heavy brooch that for some reason must have the position of its pinstem at or somewhat below the horizontal center rather than in the normal position for this finding, which is *above the horizontal center* to prevent the brooch's upper portion from falling forward. This problem can be solved by placing the pinstem at the *vertical center*. If this is not possible, a *double horizontal pinstem* in the form of a U can be used. If a double catch system to accommodate the two pinstem points is not practical in the design, the *upper horizontal pinstem* can be shortened to half the total length of the lower one. In this case, only the lower pinstem engages the clasp, and the upper half-pinstem, called a *sprag*, parallel with the lower one, also engages the cloth. Together, they keep the brooch in place.

SIZED JEWELRY

Size in this sense refers to a *set of specified measurements* used as a legally fixed standard. The best example is ring sizes. The diameter of a ring's shank is divided into numbered or lettered stages that have specific, agreed upon, mathematically stated dimensions that correspond to a normal range of finger thicknesses. Different standards are used in the U.S.A., Great Britain, and continental Europe, and these established standards are also used elsewhere. (See Standard Weights, Measures: "Ring Sizes, Approximate Comparison Table," p. 734.) Of all jewel forms, the size of rings is the only one standardized. The reason is that a ring's size is critical and must be exact or the ring will slip off the fingers and be lost; or it will slip around on the finger, to the wearer's annoyance.

In other pieces of jewelry, size is confined to a certain given range, or is flexible within certain limits. Bracelets based on an oval interior form are sized for women's wrists within a diameter range from 58–66 mm. Necklace sizes depend on neck diameter measurements and cover a wide range of sizes, from a tight collar that requires a clasp, to lengths long enough to simply pass over the head without any need for a closing device.

FLEXIBILITY AND RIGIDITY

Jewels that are generally flat are also often rigid. They may, however, be designed with a degree of flexibility to allow them simply to utilize the element of motion, to permit their placement on the body, or to let them take on the basic shape of the body part on which they are worn. In the latter connection, wide necklaces must be tapered conically toward the neck to lie flat.

In designing and fabricating a jewel, considerations concerning its degree of flexibility or the lack of it must be taken into account. A *permanently rigid* article, such as a bangle, must either be of a suitable size, or it must be provided with an opening to allow its placement on body parts. Another example is a rigid, torque-type necklace. *Semirigidity* is a condition in which the material used remains whole, but in itself has a certain degree of flexibility. An example is a spring-hardened, stiff sheet metal bracelet which can be deformed temporarily to allow it to be placed on the wrist, but once on, springs back to its original shape. *Partial flexibility* can be obtained by introducing a mechanical device, such as a hinge, that permits

be completely concealed from the visible surface by the use of overlapping units held together by movable rivets, sliding rivets, hooks, an internally threaded, flexible metal chain, or even heavy nylon fishing line. Examples of these systems are seen in several of the illustrations in the book.

COMMON JEWEL-SUPPORTING SYSTEMS

HANGING AND TYING SYSTEMS

Among the simplest means of supporting a jewel on the body is to hang it by a flexible chain or semirigid wire, or to tie it by a cord or ribbon onto the body part. Jewels using this system are necklaces, pendants, bracelets, and belts. Hanging systems can also incorporate the use of hooks, loops, swivels, or other systems that allow free movement.

PRESSURE SYSTEMS

Some ornaments hold on to body parts by pressure devices. The pressure may be supplied by the structure of the piece itself, or because it incorporates a spring-energy pressure system, such as the clip used on a brooch or earring. Another common pressure device is the system of an advancing screw, such as the screw wire used to hold earrings. The pressure exerted can be greater when a jewel is attached to an inanimate substance such as cloth, but body parts—the earlobe, for instance—will tolerate

1–48 KABYLE, ATLAS MOUNTAINS, ALGERIA. Pair of silver fibulae cloak pins, employing traditional ornament of blue, green, and yellow cloisonné enamel. The connecting chain and pendant charm box unit utilizes four swivel joints to prevent parts from twisting, as would happen if they were simply linked together. Findings are rivet mounted at the top and bottom of the already enameled main units to eliminate the heat that would be produced by soldering. Col.: Traphagen School of Fashion, New York. *Photo: Oppi*

1–49 PUIG DORIA, Spain. Silver bracelet, semirigid spring construction using an oversized hook with collared rivet clasp to close the gap. The closing device becomes the main decorative design feature. *Photo: Günter Meyer, courtesy Schmuckmuseum, Pforzheim*

1–50 BERTEL GARDBERG, Finland. Necklace of an 18K gold forged wire, using a pressure system to engage an edge-grooved stone. The stone can be changed to any of those shown. *Photo: Oppi*

opening and closing. *Extreme flexibility* can be achieved through *articulation,* in which the total unit is divided into distinct segments that are united by systems that interrelate and reintegrate the whole. There are various means of articulation. They can be visible and obvious, as for example, jump rings. Others are visible but unobvious, since they are integrated with the forms of the parts, as in the case of swivels, and ball and socket joints. Or they can

1–51   IRENA PAKUTINSKIENE, Lithuania. Amber and twisted bronze wire necklace. The outer edge-grooved stones are held in position by pressure from the two-element twisted wire fitted into the groove. The wire units also form the spiral-shaped parts between each two-stone unit. Photo: Bibliothèque Forney, Paris

1–52   FRIEDRICH BECKER, West Germany. Ring in 18K gold with smoky topaz. The stone's pyramid-shaped ends protrude into matching square, tapered-edge holes in the spring-hardened ring shank; the stone is held in place by pressure. Photo: Friedrich Becker

1–53   HENNING KOPPEL, Denmark, designer; manufacturer Georg Jensen Sølvsmedie A/S, Copenhagen. Cast sterling silver bracelet No. 88A. The units incorporate linkage forms, and a hook and eye closing. These normally separate findings are totally integrated with the bracelet forms. Photo: Courtesy Georg Jensen Sølvsmedie A/S

PIERCING AND STUD SYSTEMS

Piercing is a means of holding an ornament that has no permanent position to cloth or other substances by means of a relatively long prong, pinstem, or stick pin. *Studs* are short projecting rods, knobs, or pins, permanently attached to the back of an ornament, which pass through a permanent opening in a part of the human anatomy, or a hole in a garment, such as a buttonhole or eyelet. Ears are pierced to form a permanent opening in the lobe to allow the placement of an ear stud. Studs are often fixed in place by forcing a removable spring clamp onto the tapered stud end after it has passed through the pierced opening. These are used on ear studs and tie tacks. To remove the stud, the clamp must be made to release its grip, after which it is simply pulled off. Studs can also be externally threaded, in which case the clamp has a matching internal thread and is wound on the stud end like a nut on a screw shank. If a stud pin end is plain, pointed, and sharp, it can act as a piercing device and be forced through cloth at any location, and then be held in place by the clamp. Permanent studs can be used to fix an ornament permanently in place on metal or nonmetallic materials.

only a certain amount of pressure without registering pain. Jewelry must therefore be adjustable in pressure to accommodate individual differences. Other pressure systems in which a form can be reduced (tightened) and expanded (loosened) while still holding by pressure are belt buckles, prong and hole systems, slide or ferrule systems, clamps, and snaps. Pressure systems are also used as a means of securing stones in the jewel.

CLASP SYSTEMS

Both flexible and semirigid ornaments can be made to hold on to the body part by the use of a clasp which in general consists of two or more complementary parts that fit together to make a *unit clasp*. Clasps are made in many forms, but all systems must have a method of releasing the hold of the clasp to allow for opening and closing. Release systems may rely on the action of a spring catch, or a hook and spring, while others work on the system of a hinge with a removable pin.

SEWING SYSTEMS

Ornaments can be fixed to nonmetallic supporting substances such as cloth or leather by being sewn to them with needle and thread or with wire that passes through attached loops or through holes in the ornament. The attaching wire or thread can always be severed to release the ornament for cleaning or repair, or for the renewal of the supporting material, and then resewn.

◄
1–54 TINEVELLEY, MADRAS, INDIA. Traditional gold ear and nose ornaments utilizing stud holding systems, worn by a Nadar, a woman of an agricultural caste. Each ornament requires its own pierced hole. In the nose is another stud (*murugu*). The stretched earlobe holds a *pampadam* combining a cluster of balls (*kundu*) and squares (*thattu*), all filled with lac to prevent their becoming dented. Their weight over the years causes the earlobe to stretch. *Photo: Oppi*

►
1–55 FAITH PORTER, U.S.A. "Shell Mail." Body ornament of matching front and back, pale gray blue hand-dyed suede, ornamented with 850 sewn-on natural shell buttons ranging in color from white to gray blue. *Photo: Jay Ahrend*

2
THE MEANS TO CREATION
Working Environment, Facilities, and Implements

THE WORKSHOP

Organizing the working areas

The workshop of a jeweler can be any place in which the activity of jewelry making can effectively be carried out. According to law, a workshop is also defined as a place of manual labor where no machinery worked by mechanical power is employed (which would classify it as a factory). By this definition, many independent jewelers using mechanical equipment are working in one-employee factories, which might better be termed "manufactories."

That a workshop need not even be in one specific loca-

tion is attested to by the existence until early in this century of nomadic jewelers, such as those in Mongolia, who traveled from place to place and set up their "workshops" on open ground or in a tent near a settlement. Until their tools were laid out, their workshops were contained in the traveling bags in which the tools were kept. The fact that such workshops were mobile, that the number of tools used were limited, that there was a total lack of any mechanical equipment and complete reliance on human muscle power, did not prevent these jewelers from creating marvelously complex traditional jewelry, masterpieces of skill and design concepts. Fortunately, a comprehensive collection of the products of these nomadic Mongolian jewelers has been preserved at the outstanding Ethnographical Section of the National Museum in Copenhagen. Actually, the nomadic tradition is still alive today in almost every major Western city where it is common to see young jewelers on sidewalks making jewelry from wire with pliers, their finished work displayed for sale on a cloth spread out before them.

In the West, one-person jewelry workshops are common, as jewelry making is generally a solitary craft in which the same individual is expected to be able to carry out all the processes in the creation of a work. This is not true in the East, or even in large workshops in the West where specialization is more common. But due to the nature and scale of the work, and because the hand tools used are relatively small, it is possible for one individual to occupy very limited space—if necessary, almost within the boundaries of a single worktable. Portable fuel tanks for use in

2–1 RITA GREER, England. Almost all of her minimal workshop is visible in the photograph. Photo: Alan Greer

2–5 SØLVSMIE REGINE & FRANK JUHLS. Exterior of the workshop. Photo: Börje Rönnberg

2–2 BUDAPEST, HUNGARY. The three-person workshop of the jeweler Bartha Lajos. Traditional straight-type goldsmith's workbenches are used. *Photo: Oppi*

2–3 TOKYO, JAPAN. The jewelry workshop of K. Mikimoto & Co., Ltd., of pearl fame. Maximum use is made of the workshop space. *Photo: Kotaku Takabatake*

2–4 KAUTOKEINO, NORWAY. Interior of the workshop of Sølvsmie Regine & Frank Juhls. This spacious, light workshop above the Arctic Circle comes close to being an ideal working environment. Production consists of traditional jewelry worn by the Lappish community of northernmost Scandinavia, and contemporary designs by Regine Juhls. *Photo: Börje Rönnberg*

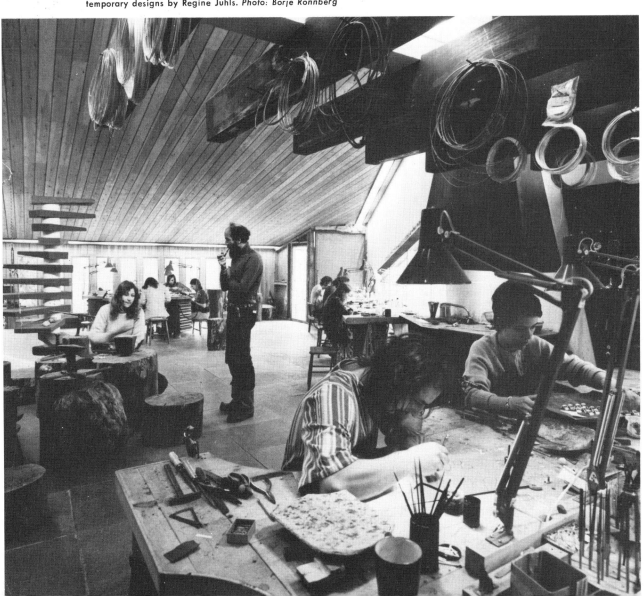

soldering are a great convenience because they allow this activity to take place anywhere in the work space, which can then be used with greater flexibility, further reducing space requirements. Such a workshop can be operated with a minimal expenditure once the basic tools and equipment have been purchased.

At the other extreme, organized workshops exist all over the world where equipment must be duplicated for many workers, each using a separate workbench and hand tools, but sharing the larger workshop tools. (These same conditions also prevail in schools where jewelry making is taught.) In such establishments, it becomes necessary to make an outlay of large amounts of money for equipment, and continuous production to derive the greatest benefit from this investment is the goal.

There is not much use in diagraming an "ideal" workshop—there is no such place, unless you plan and build one from scratch to satisfy your particular needs. More commonly, all real workshop situations, especially small ones, almost always necessitate a compromise between ideal conditions and the actual usable space. One should attempt to make the best use of the space available, guided by considerations like the placement of walls, windows and doors, existing ventilation, and the availability of light, power, and water sources.

THE BASIC WORK AREAS

In any case, for someone starting a workshop, the jewelry making activity *can* be broken down into the need for a few basic areas, though some of the procedures that take place in each can overlap. These basic work areas are: the *fabrication* or construction area; the *heating* or soldering and annealing area; the *acid operation* or pickling area; and the *finishing* or polishing and buffing area. All of these activities are described below. Each employs its own tools and needs certain conditions for proper execution. Other working areas where different activities can take place are also possible.

THE FABRICATION AREA

Fabrication calls for *hand tools,* a *workbench, seat,* and a *bench vise.* The latter two, being important, are placed in a central, convenient position in the workshop. Though a great many tools are available to the jeweler, a starting jeweler can do with a few tools, especially if he or she concentrates at first on a limited number of techniques. A tool becomes indispensable when it is felt that work cannot continue without it. When this happens, buy a high-quality tool that will repay the possibly higher initial expenditure by additional years of usefulness.

THE TRADITIONAL JEWELER'S OR GOLDSMITH'S WORK-BENCH Still in use in European workshops and available from European supply houses, is the traditional curved-top workbench type with a table thickness of at least 2 in (approximately 5 cm), shown in the illustrations. Because it was and is usual for several jewelers to be employed in small workshops, these workbenches are designed to provide space for from three to five or more persons. The curved top half surrounds the worker, providing a convenient working surface. It allows a resting place for tools and elbows, and can support the sheepskin leather apron, called a *basle,* used to catch sawings and filings (*lemel* or *limail*) by hooking it at the undersides. The *bench pin* or *bench peg* is installed in a slot at the inner curve center in

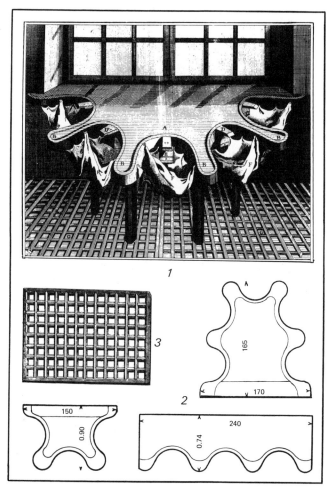

2–6 *TRADITIONAL WORKBENCH AND CLAIES*
1. *Jeweler's traditional workbench (établi chêne "workbench of oak") for five persons, illustrated in Diderot's 18th-century Encyclopédie. Leather aprons attached to the underside of the workbench top are spread on the jeweler's lap to catch lemel or filings.*
2. *Workbenches in this traditional style are available today from Alfred Joliot, Montreuil, France. Dimensions given in the plan views are in centimeters.*
3. *The floor in the illustration is covered with claies or wooden grill units whose purpose is to catch the metal dust and remove it from shoe soles. They are still used today, as for instance in the workshops of the famed Chaumet on Place Vendome in Paris, where they are lifted once a year to collect the dust and reclaim the metal. At Chaumet, a surprising amount of gold is reclaimed annually from this source. Claies are available from the supplier mentioned above, ready-made in units of 1 meter by 35, 50, and 65 cm, which respectively weigh 3, 4, and 5 kilos.*

the table's edge. It is placed with the flat or the sloping surface up, according to individual preference or work requirements. While work is held upon it, the fact that it projects forward from the workbench allows the hands to move freely below it during work.

THE MODERN WORKBENCH The jeweler's workbench used today for one or more persons is more or less standardized. Lemel is collected in a drawer-tray mounted on runners, allowing it to be pulled out when needed, and returned under the bench top when not in use. The normal height for a workbench is 35.5 in (approximately 90 cm), considerably higher than a dining table. The *stool* or *back-*

2–7 *INDIVIDUAL JEWELER'S WORKBENCH,* height 40¾ in, length 39 in, depth 20 in. It is equipped with a retractable bench pan to catch lemel, filing pin holder, mandrel holders, arm rest, three drawers, and has a three-ply laminated top. Total weight: 100 lb. *Photo: Courtesy Swest Inc.*

supporting chair used has a seat 15.75–21.25 in high (approximately 40–54 cm). They have four or three legs, the latter providing stability on uneven floor surfaces. The seat height used depends on the length of your torso, and should bring the eye level somewhat above the workpiece when it is placed on the bench pin, but low enough to eliminate any need to stoop over work when seated. Some workbenches have built-in, exposed racks in which small, constantly needed hand tools can be held. Usually there are small drawers on one or both sides for the storage of tools, boxes, and small items. The table must be sturdy, and not shake when work is done on it. Steadiness can be ensured by fixing the legs to the floor. Benches should be constructed solidly enough to allow a *bench vise* to be fixed at one end of the bench, over a leg which will support and absorb the impact shock when hammering work tools such as small anvils and mandrels held in its jaws.

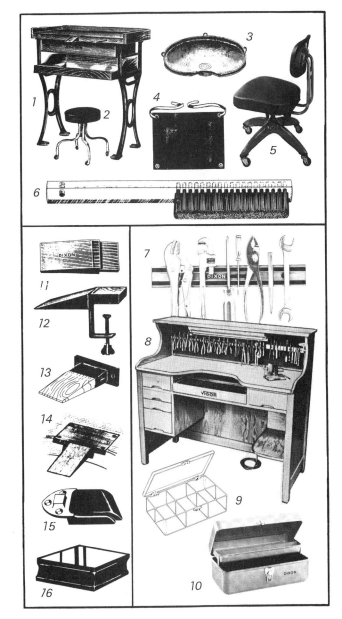

2–8 *WORKBENCHES AND BENCH TOOLS AND EQUIPMENT*
1. *Jeweler's workbench,* single, maple hardwood top and cast iron legs that can be screwed to the floor. *Specifications:* 33 × 17 in; 34 in from floor; equipped with bench pin, arm rest, tool drawer, and lower pan that can be pulled out to catch lemel; weight 65 lb. Also available as a double workbench for two persons working side by side; 65 in long, 17 in deep.
2. *Workbench stool,* padded vinyl seat which is adjustable, on full-sized casters; weight 18 lb.
3. *Filings tray of sheet metal,* for attachment to workbench with curved front by side hooks; with central drilled hole drain beneath which is a container to hold filings swept through the holes.
4. *Split cowhide leather apron,* 24 × 30 in, with corner brass grommets, two of which can hold the waist strings. Can be worn in either direction, the other two corner grommets passed through hooks under the workbench table to allow it to act as a filings apron with smooth surface up.
5. *Workbench swivel chair* with 360° swing, padded seat with adjustable height 17–20 in, and backrest mounted on spring action supports; 2 in ball bearing, rubber-covered casters; weighs 22 lb.
6. *Bench brush,* for sweeping away filings and dust; available with Lucite, seasoned hardwood, or bone handles; stiff nylon or natural bristle in 2⅛–3 in length, 3 or 4 rows; ½–⅝ in width, ½–¹¹⁄₁₆ in trim; overall length 6¾–8¼ in. (*Dixon*)
7. *Magnetic tool holder,* with 1 in wide gripping track; available in 12 or 24 in length. (*Dixon*)
8. *Jeweler's workbench,* specifications: Dimensions 48 in long, 19¾ in deep, 30 in from floor to work surface, 42 in total height; formica-covered worktable top; glued dovetail and pegged joints; five drawers, center drawer lined with filing tray in metal; equipment shelf below right; pegboard back to hang tools; tool racks; strip socket for multiple electric outlets; fluorescent light under hood. (*Vigor*)
9. *Materials box,* plastic, available with 6, 12, or 18 compartments, in 4⅜ × 2⅝ × 1 in; 8¼ × 4¼ × 1¼ in; 10¾ × 6⅖ × 1¾ in. (*Dixon*)
10. *Tool storage chest,* metal with baked enamel finish; 14½ in long, 7½ in deep, 6 in high; with interior-hinged divided tray; padlock closure. (*Dixon*)
11. *Bench pin,* maple hardwood; available 3¾ × 2¼ in; 4¾ × 2⅝ in; 5 × 2⅞ in; tenon slides into matching mortise slot hole in the workbench edge; normally used with the sloping side up for improved work visibility, but also with straight side up.
12. *Bench pin with bench clamp holder;* upper metal surface can be used as an anvil for small work.
13. *Bench pin with cast iron holder,* screwed to bench edge without mortise slot hole; pin held in holder by tightening side thumbscrew; working surface 3⅝ × 2³⁄₁₆ in.
14. *Bench pin with metal holder,* screwed to bench top.
15. *Bench filing block,* iron frame with small square anvil; rubber insert extends 3¼ in from bench edge; used to absorb vibration, keep work from slipping and becoming scarred.
16. *Steel bench plate or block* with mirror-polished surface; 2½ in square, 1¼ in thick; used on a workbench surface.

THE HEATING AREA

Soldering, a heat-producing activity, can take place, if necessary, on this same workbench top if the surface is protected with a *flat refractory board* such as an asbestos composition pressed millboard. If the space is draft-free, soldering can be done in the open without too much heat loss, otherwise a *three-panel screen* made of the same refractory board and joined with angle irons can be temporarily or permanently placed on the bench top to surround the soldering area. The *fuel tank* and *torch* can be drawn within reach, or be left always at the right side. If space allows, it is of course preferable to have a separate soldering table, but even in professional jewelry workshops, the same table is used for fabrication and soldering when work is small. If you have a separate soldering table, it should be located *away* from natural light so that the color of heated metal can be easily observed during soldering.

Annealing is another common heating process that can be carried out in this same area; if the work is large, it may require the use of an *annealing pan*. (See Annealing Steel, p. 237; and Soldering Turntables, p. 399.)

THE ACID OPERATION AREA

Since heat-generating processes such as soldering and annealing necessitate pickling metal objects to clean them, the area in which this process is carried out should be near both the soldering table and a water supply. Because the acid solutions used in pickling produce noxious fumes when heated, adequate ventilation is necessary. Usually small work is pickled in a container on the fabrication workbench, although ideally it should be done at an acid table under a *hood* equipped with an *exhaust fan*. Lacking this, it should at least be near an open window. Some jewelers solve the problem of dealing with acid fumes by using acid substitutes. The acid table surface and the floor in the immediate area should be acid-proof. This same area can be used for etching and all other processes involving the use of acids.

THE FINISHING AREA

Finishing is a final and separate activity. When done by hand, it can be accomplished anywhere on a workbench top, or in one's lap. When a *mechanical polishing lathe* is used, a special area is called for, and it must be near an electric outlet. The polishing lathe must work without vibration (which would quickly wear out a motor). This means it must be fixed on a sturdy, well-supported table, again preferably with the legs fixed to the floor to prevent "creep."

Because lathe-mounted polishing and buffing wheels coated with abrasive materials throw dust into the air when in use, this unit too should include an exhaust, possibly one shared with the system used for the acid table. If an independent *dust-collecting apparatus* is used in conjunction with the polishing lathe, its placement becomes more flexible.

ADDITIONAL WORK AREAS

While most other kinds of work can be undertaken in the areas already described, the techniques discussed below require additional space because of the size of the

equipment they employ, or because the nature of that work, for various reasons, demands it.

Casting, besides using hand tools, requires a surface suitable for the safe melting of metal; lost wax investment casting uses a *burnout kiln;* centrifugal casting, a *centrifuge;* wax injection rubber mold reproduction, a *wax injector* and a *vulcanizer.* All these special pieces of equipment require additional space.

Electroplating and *electroforming* require equipment and a setup that should be separate from other areas because of the use of cyanide-containing chemicals in these techniques. This work area should be enclosed in a well-ventilated space as distant as possible from areas where acid is used, since *acid contamination* of solutions containing cyanide *will generate lethal fumes.*

An area to hold a *bench lathe* and a *drill press* might be provided.

Lapidary equipment such as a *tumbler,* and *sawing, trimming, grinding, sanding,* and *polishing units,* require fixed positions and adequate space, if a jeweler undertakes such work.

Enameling requires a separate area for the *kiln,* an *open surface* upon which hot objects can be safely placed, and *adequate storage* space for materials to keep them dust-free. Enameling is not discussed in this book because, although related to jewelry making, it is a separate activity that deserves lengthy discussion. The interested reader is referred to books on enameling techniques mentioned in the Bibliographies.

GENERAL WORKSHOP REQUIREMENTS

Stationary tools such as a *large anvil, rolling mill, bench cutter, jigsaw, drill press,* or *belt sander* must be fixed in locations that allow free access to them and provide sufficient surrounding work space.

Working light adequate to all these activities is important. Good, natural north light is always desirable because it is shadowless and even. A diffused, overall, artificial incandescent light, and additional, separate, concentrated lights in each work area are needed. Working lights mounted on flexible supports that allow a change in angle of beam are best. For right-handed persons, the light should come from the left.

A *water lamp* can be used if an occasion occurs in which work must be done in a place without electricity, or should this source temporarily fail. This is a device for controlling any light on work, and was used by jewelers, watchmakers, and icon painters before the invention of the electric bulb. It consists of any clear glass globe about 8 in (20.3 cm) in diameter, capable of being filled with water. It may be hung by a cord from a stand, have its own base, or be placed on a base. A little copper sulphate is added to the water to give it a pale blue color and reduce glare. Natural sunlight, or light from a candle, or from an oil or kerosene lamp is allowed to pass through the globe from behind, at a distance and angle that causes the intensified light to project on the work. The light so generated can be so intense as to require the use of a green glass shade or viscope on the globe to protect the eyes from glare. A water lamp can also be used to intensify an inadequate electric light source. A similar device can be improvised.

The *electric supply* calls for several convenient outlets of 110 volts and 220 volts, and the lines should be capable of withstanding the required amperage. When in doubt about the suitability of existing power lines for use with

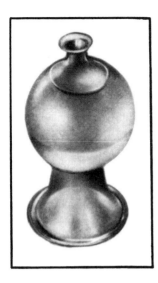

2-9 A GLASS WATER LAMP or *globe* with base. It is placed between the worker and the light source, its position adjusted to make it throw a concentrated bright beam of light on the bench pin or the work, making an illumination covering an area of about 4 in. A substitute is a *bull's-eye condenser* (not shown) which is a large-diameter round lens mounted on an adjustable stand, used in the same way backed with a 100 watt electric bulb.

particular equipment, it is best to consult an electrician and avoid the chance of fire from overloaded lines.

A *gas supply* might be used in cases where portable fuel is not used. In this case, each outlet can be provided with multiple gas cocks to allow the attachment of several rubber gas pipes. A *hand fire extinguisher* should be available in every workshop, no matter what its size.

A *water supply,* with hot and cold water from a *sink with drain board* and *acid-proof drainage pipes* is essential. The water source should be near the acid table as it is used for rinsing after pickling, and near enough to the finishing area for cleaning the work after polishing and buffing. A *metal grille* should be placed over the drain to catch any small part or a stone that accidentally may be dropped during washing.

Storage closets are needed, one to contain tools or work, and another, which can be locked for safety, to hold potentially dangerous and poisonous chemicals, and liquids such as acids. Open shelves are also useful to hold objects that can be left exposed.

A *first-aid box* should be available and well stocked with the necessary items for emergency treatment. Standard items are: an *alkaline acid neutralizer* such as bicarbonate of soda, used with water after thorough rinsing of acid burns; an *acidic alkali neutralizer* such as weak vinegar, used—after thorough rinsing—on alkaline burns; a *heat burn treatment salve;* an *eye cup and boric acid,* used in dilution with water to rinse from an eye a small particle that has entered it; *sterile bandages* and *absorbent cotton,* and a *liquid disinfectant* for cuts; *tweezers, scissors,* and *stick applicators.* In all serious cases, immediately get the aid of a physician. Do not eat food in a workshop as it can become contaminated.

2-10 BENCHWORK LAMPS
1. *Bench lamp* with long, baked enamel shade whose inner white surface reflects light from the two fitted 15 watt standard cool light fluorescent tube lights. Arm is counterbalanced for use in any position, and has a full 24 in swing, and both arm and base are equipped with die-cast swivel joints for ease in positional adjustment. A double-bolt clamp secures the lamp to the bench edge. *Acrylic light diffuser* can be fitted on the shade to help provide a shadow- and glare-free, diffused light over the work area. Weight 11 lb.
2. *Spring-balanced bench lamp* with a 33 in reach, employs a 60 watt incandescent bulb.
3. *Dual-light bench lamp* with telescoping arm adjustable from 25-39 in; two vertical swivels; base rotatable through 360°; utilizes both a 75 watt incandescent bulb, and a 22 watt Circline tube fluorescent light. Either can be turned on separately, or together.
4. *Dual-light bench lamp* with fully rotating swing arm equipped with nickel steel tension springs for balance in any position; with double-bolt bench clamp; uses both a 75 watt incandescent bulb and a 22 watt Circline fluorescent tube light for uniform illumination; either can be used alone. Has an additional outlet in the base for connection of power tools. Weight 12 lb.

OCCUPATIONAL SAFETY AND HEALTH FOR JEWELERS

Jewelers are increasingly aware of work safety requirements and possible health hazards existing in their craft. Wisely, hazards are avoided by reducing risks and taking preventive measures. Warnings against possible mechanical and material hazards are mentioned throughout this book. Many *government* and *private sources* publish information on safety and preventive measures against potential material and equipment hazards employed in the metal crafts. (See *Dealing with Safety and Health,* p. 29; *Safety and Health,* p. 798; and *Safety Equipment,* p. 805.)

Consult also *Safety Equipment Suppliers* in the *classified telephone directory* books (so-called yellow pages) of most large cities. Manufacturers publish *catalogs* describing their products and the hazards against which they offer protection, and they will usually respond to individual inquiries concerning problem solutions.

Safety and Health Equipment: Sensory perception protection

Smell: Respiratory protection Masks and respirators against dusts, mists, airborne particles and fumes; ventilation systems; exhaust fans; filtered polishing systems; industrial vacuum cleaners (wet or dry, or wet/dry); dust accumulators; fume hoods.

Sight: Visual protection Against particles: goggles; safety glasses; impact-resisting glasses; face shields; eye washes; a water source. Against infrared radiation: dark glasses; welding goggles; welder's head shield, or hand screen.

Taste: Oral and internal organ protection Antidotes against accidental ingestion of toxic chemical substances.

Sound: Hearing protection Sound-deadening ear shields; plastic or rubber ear plugs.

Touch: Dermatological protection Barrier creams; disposable gloves for particular substances and processes; detergents and other cleaning material; work clothes (washed often).

Substance protection involving several senses

Heat protection Heat-resisting gloves and gauntlets; face shields; goggles; welder's apron; flame-retarding apparel; flame-control equipment such as a Class D fire extinguisher for use with combustible metals; smoke detectors.

Chemical protection Chemical-resistant disposable gloves; exhaust fans; fume hoods; protective clothing; liquid-impermeable aprons; safety shoes; safety containers for chemicals and acids; chemical storage facilities; chemical-proof drains; settling traps; chemical neutralizers; inactive absorbent material (sand; vermiculite).

Electrical protection Rubber or shock-proof gloves; rubber- or plastic-protected electrical equipment; insulated surfaces for electrical equipment; insulated shoes; grounded electrical equipment; easily reached emergency cutoff switches.

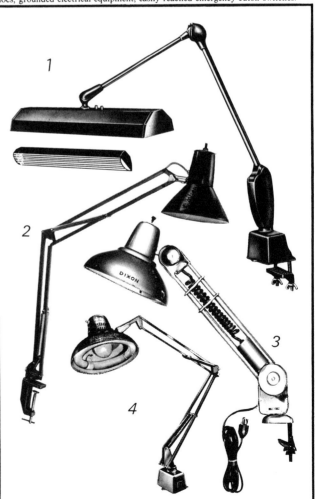

TOOLS

Instruments of technique

THE HAND: Provider of guidance and power

The greatest of tools, and one that is always available to us is that apparatus we call the *hand,* a structure of bones, sinews, and muscles at the terminal part of the arm. This intricate complex includes the fingers and thumb, the hand proper, and the wrist. Altogether, it is a mechanism that by the construction, interrelationship, and interaction of its parts, possesses fantastic mobility. This quality makes possible a great variety of motions, especially due to the capability of the thumb to oppose any of the fingers in a way not given to any other mammal.

By analysis, these hand motions include the basic acts of *reaching,* whose purpose is to move the hand to another location; *grasping* in order to gain control over an object or tool; *disengaging* or grasping to disengage an object; *moving* or *transporting* an object to another location; *positioning* or handling an object to orient, align, or engage it with another; and *turning* or *rotation,* in which the hand, wrist, and forearm move in a radius around the ulna, one of the forearm bones. All of these acts occur time after time in everyday activities as well as in jewelry making. We pay little attention to them except when, because of an accident to the hand, we become deprived of any of these motions.

TOOLS: Extensions of the hand

When we speak of the handcrafts, we mean the production of objects by the skills of the hands in conjunction with the use of tools. It is not accidental that most of our tools have been designed to embody concepts already present in the various hand motions described. For example, the use of hammers and tongs necessitates the act of grasping. In the case of the hammer, the hand alone acts to grasp the handle, and in the tongs the handle-grasping act also occurs, but its hinged design (which allows the opposition of its jaws) permits objects to be grasped by the tool. In rotation, as another example, the bone structure and muscles of the forearm make twisting motions and partial rotation possible; these motions provide the operational concepts of boring tools—such as reamers and awls—and torsion tools—such as the screwdriver.

To increase the efficiency of some tools in performing specialized functions, their form may also incorporate a basic principle of mechanics such as the lever, or the transmission and modification of force or motion. Using these concepts, it becomes possible to design a tool capable of increasing the initial power imparted to it by the hand in order to achieve a *mechanical advantage* or ratio gain of that initial force. For example, the exertion of a normal 40 lb hand pressure on the arms of a 12 in pair of tongs transmits approximately 240 lb of pressure to its jaws and the object held there. This ratio gain is due to the double lever action of its design.

The tool in this way becomes an extension of the hand, making possible acts which the hand alone cannot perform, thereby immeasurably increasing its strength, effectiveness, and usefulness.

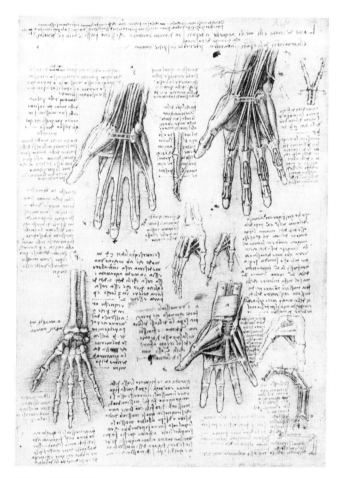

2–11 LEONARDO DA VINCI (1452–1519), Italy. Five pen and ink with chalk studies of dissections of the right hand, depicting bones, tendons, and muscles, and six smaller drawings of digits, including notes. This is page 19,009 Recto in the Windsor volume which is part of the *Codex Atlanticus.* After 1508, in his anatomical drawings, Leonardo was deeply concerned with a study of the anatomy and motor functions of the tendons and muscles of the hand. The notes were written on the completed drawings with his left hand, from right to left (Leonardo was a mirror writer and wrote backward). *Photo: The Royal Library, Windsor Castle. Reproduced by the gracious permission of Her Majesty, Queen Elizabeth II. Copyright reserved.*

SKILL: The mastery over tools and techniques

By acquiring control over, and effectiveness in using a tool, we are developing skill. A skilled craftsperson can be described as someone who has mastered the coordination of the motions of his or her hands with the efficient operation of tools. In the practice of the arts, however, we recognize that it is not dextrous manipulative skills alone that produce masterpieces that move our spirit; only by the joint alchemy of mind, imagination, and skill do materials become transmuted into significant works. Without adequate skill, the realization of fantasy is not possible.

Through mastery of the operation of tools, and of the techniques their use allows, the craftsperson "speaks" to materials, and through his or her creation, communicates to others.

TOOL CATEGORIES ACCORDING TO CONCEPTUAL WORK PRINCIPLES

By placing tools under categorized headings according to the generic work principles by which they function, their conceptual relationship becomes apparent. The tools included under these headings may be used in any techniques where these work concepts are utilized. Their specific manner of use will be found in the processes described in the text.

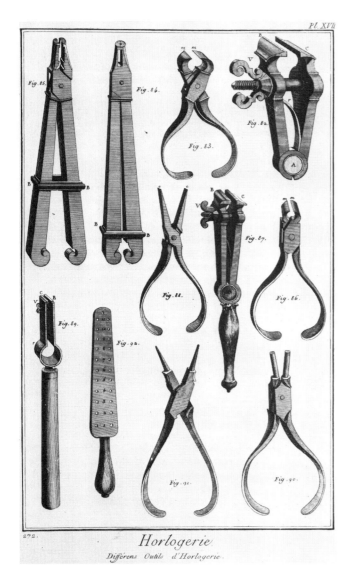

2–12 DENIS DIDEROT (1713–1784), France, compiled *L'Encyclopédie ou dictionnaire raisonné des sciences, des arts et des métiers* which recorded contemporary French crafts and industries. The text is in 17 volumes and is accompanied by 11 volumes of engravings. This literary monument of the 18th century took 21 years to complete (1751–1772), and was the largest encyclopedia of that time. Shown here is a typical full-page engraved illustration of holding tools or pliers used in clock and watchmaking, and also used by jewelers.

HOLDING TOOLS These allow one or both hands to be freed from the work-holding function, permitting the hand or hands to perform other tasks such as guiding the work, or to be used for simultaneously applying another tool upon the work. The form of the tools, and the manner of their use is often conditioned by the need to stand or sit when working. Included in the category of holding tools that allow freedom to both hands are clamps, bench vises, the die sinker's ball, and the lathe. Tools that allow freedom to one hand are the hand vise, ring clamp, pin vise, shellac stick, joint tool, flexible shaft, pliers, tweezers, and tongs.

STRIKING OR PERCUSSION IMPACT TOOLS The oldest tools invented by humanity all act to *move* the metal when it is struck. The most ancient are *direct striking tools* which come into contact with the work, of which the foremost example is the hammer. The oldest hammers were hand-held working heads. The development of the shaft hole or opening in the working head—in stone hammers made possible by boring and in metal hammers, by casting—made possible the insertion of a handle, greatly increasing the leverage and percussive force of this tool. Among the direct striking tools are forging hammers, silversmithing hammers, riveting hammers, automatic hammers, drop hammers, and mallets made of many different materials.

INDIRECT STRIKING PERCUSSION TOOLS These include those struck by a direct striking tool to impart to the former the force necessary to do the work. Judgment is needed to develop a sense of the correct amount of force of impact that is needed. Experience develops control. Among indirect percussion striking tools, all struck by hammers, are chisels, and punches used for repoussage and chasing, stamping, dapping, and rivet setting.

COMPRESSION TOOLS There are two types: those that passively act to resist the pressure brought on the work from one side; and those that actively apply pressure to the work from one or both sides. One-sided passive compression tools include those that are used as a resisting surface against which the work is placed while the work receives the impact force of a percussion tool. In this category are surface blocks, design or swage blocks, dapping blocks or dies, one-piece dies or molds, anvils, stakes, and mandrels. Active compression tools include burnishers, bezel setters, milligrain tools, prong pushers, and beading tools—all used in stone setting. A two-sided active compression tool is the rolling mill.

CUTTING TOOLS Such tools are nearly as old as striking tools. Unlike the blunt-faced striking tools, their points, teeth, or edges must be sharp enough to perform the act of *cutting*. Some are initially sharp but wear out and must be discarded. Others can be resharpened to restore cutting edges. Cutting ability is renewed by different methods, depending on the size and shape of the tool.

The *cutting act* is accomplished by different means with different tools. Among the systems used are lever action shearing, reciprocal action severing, rotational severing, and impact shearing.

In *lever action shearing*, as in hand shears, two opposing, sharp-edged blades that are meant to come together and pass each other along the cutting plane are joined at a fulcrum by a screw, bolt, or rivet. In use the blades are drawn apart by the tool's handles to allow the insertion of the material to be cut. The work is placed as far into the angled opening toward the fulcrum as possible

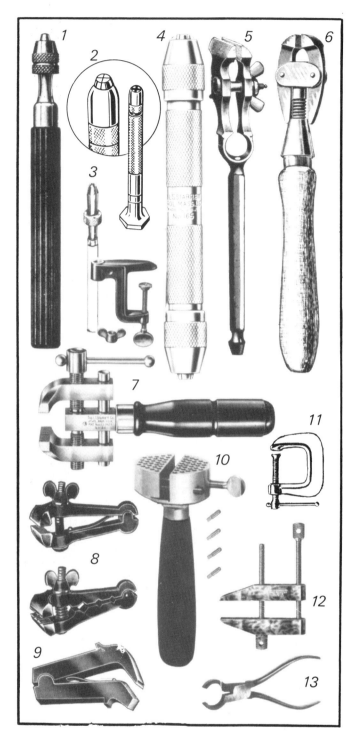

1. *Pin vise* with knurled chuck and grooved wooden handle, used to hold small drills, taps, screws, wire, rod, etc., during work.
2. *Midget pin vise*, steel, with hollow knurled handle, and solid-locking chuck nose that accepts sizes 0.0135–0.031 in (drill sizes 80–68).
3. *Pin vise*, steel, with sliding ring knurled clamp that force pressure closes the chuck jaws, which simplifies one-handed operation; capacity 0–0.051 in, overall length 4⅛ in.
4. *Double pin vise* with reversible collets, 0–0.125 in. Has two size capacities at each end, knurled handle for a firm grip, and a hole that runs through its entire length. One chuck end holds work or tools with diameters 0–0.031 in/0.093–0.125 in; the other 0.031–0.062 in/0.062–0.093 in. (L. S. Starrett Co.)
5. *Hand vise*, steel, with wide spring jaws, tightened by a wing nut, hollow handle.
6. *Lowell pattern hand vise* whose serrated ½ in wide jaws are opened by turning the handle; capacity opening width 5⁄16 in, overall length 5¼ in.
7. *Combination hand vise* which can also be mounted as a *bench vise* by the use of a clamp (illustrated above) by removing the handle and substituting the clamp which can be placed on work table edges from ½–2⅛ in. The ball-ended lever allows considerable leverage over the usual wing nut. Jaw width capacity 1½ in, length about 7 in. (L. S. Starrett Co.)
8. *Hand vises*, two models, both with wing nut jaw closing systems. Top has serrated jaws and spring that keep the jaws open; bottom has grooved jaws and grooved handles with square openings in three sizes.
9. *Hand clamp* with spring jaw opener, held closed by hand pressure. (Karl Fischer)
10. *Universal work holder* with removable handle to allow insertion in a bench vise. Used with pins illustrated, or other engraving block accessories which fit into the holes drilled in its face. These allow work of any contour to be held for sawing, filing, engraving, carving, etc.
11. *C-clamp*, common type, with ball-ended lever.
12. *Parallel clamps*, case-hardened steel, with rounded jaw ends to permit clamping in recesses and under shoulders. A retaining ring holds the loose jaw in alignment while the clamp is opened or closed. Used to hold work while drilling, tapping, and on various machine setups. Available in jaw lengths of 1⅝, 2, 2½, 3, 4, 5 in, with respective corresponding capacities of ¾, 1¼, 1¾, 2¼, 2¾, 3½ in. (L. S. Starrett Co.)
13. *Ring-holding clamp-pliers* with grooved jaws, holds rings up to size 15; 5½ in long.

In *reciprocal action severing,* as in a hand saw, a sharpened, toothed blade is drawn up and back over the material cut, forming a groove or kerf in which small portions are ripped away until the groove deepens sufficiently to sever the material. Included in this group are jeweler's saws, hacksaws, and jigsaws.

In *rotational severing,* the cutting action is continuous in one direction, rather than forward and backward, but the action of the tool on the work is the same. Tools in this group include cut-off discs, ring cutters, and belt saws.

In *impact shearing,* as in the action of a circle or disc punch, the sharpened perimeter of the tool, which may be solid or internally hollow, is forced through the material to sever a blank or make a hole, with or without the use of a matrix. Hollow-patterned dies also operate on this principle.

METAL REMOVAL TOOLS These utilize concepts of boring, linear shaving, rotational shaving, reciprocal abrasion, rotational abrasion, and dispersed abrasion.

In *boring,* as with a twist drill and drill bit, rotational spiral boring penetration occurs, producing a perforation due to the pressure-impelled advance of the drill bit, which shaves chips of the material from the mass. Hand drills, bow drills, strap drills, pump drills, the drill press, reamers, and broaches all work on this principle.

so that maximum leverage action can be brought to bear upon the metal to be cut. The blades are moved toward each other and upon the metal by the simultaneous application of pressure to both handles or levers. The opposing force impinging on the sheet by the blade's cutting edges causes the metal to part along the cutting-line plane in a shearing action. This force can be increased greatly by fixing one lever or handle in a bench vise. Though this makes the lever action single instead of double, it allows greater pressure to be exerted by the movable lever against the sheet metal. This is also true for bench shears. Other lever action shearing tools are nippers, scissors, and snips.

In *linear shaving,* as with all chisels, chips are shaved from the mass while the tool advances in a linear direction, either away from, or toward the worker. Engravers, liners, and scorers all operate by this system.

In *rotational shaving,* as on lathe-mounted work, the cutting tool removes chips and curls from the outer portion of the mass while the work rotates on a fixed axis. Screw plate dies and taps also operate on this principle.

In *reciprocal abrasion,* removal occurs due to the forward and backward action of the tool. Files utilize this movement. Abrasion does not necessarily take place within a single groove, but can occur anywhere on the surface of the material worked. Scrapers can also work by reciprocal abrasive action.

In *rotational abrasion,* as when polishing or grinding is performed by a device mounted on a rotating motor spindle, the abrasive action occurs on the material in one continuous direction. Small portions exposed to the abrasive are removed by gradual wearing away. Rotational burs, and stone seating burs also work this way.

In *dispersed abrasion,* any desired area of the work surface is exposed to the continual, general action of the abrasive, as in the use of a sandblasting machine.

TORSION TOOLS Primarily related to the use of the screw thread, they are of relatively recent development. Torsion involves the act of twisting or turning by the exertion of a lateral force that turns one part around a longitudinal axis, while the other is turned in the opposite direction or is held fast. Screwdrivers, nut drivers, and wrenches with fixed or adjustable jaws are all torsion tools.

MECHANIZED ROTARY-MOTION POWER TOOLS These are an even more recent development of great importance to craftspersons, and a distinct contribution of technology to our age. Partial rotary-motion tools have been in use for thousands of years. In true rotary motion, the tool revolves freely and indefinitely in the *same direction* for as long as power is provided. Rotary-motion tools operated by hand have been used in the past, but in modern times, the invention of the small electric motor has made possible the development of several continuous rotary-motion tools worked by machine energy, provided by electricity. Available today are electric-powered portable and bench drills, power shears, rotary slitting shears to cut circles, circular saws, band saws, jigsaws, lathes, sanding machines, polishing motors, and the widely used, multipurpose flexible shaft, whose accessories perform a variety of types of work. All these tools considerably reduce the time and energy formerly expended upon the tasks performed by the hand-powered earlier models.

The existence of such tools has brought about a change in the craftsperson's attitudes toward tools and work, and this change is still in evolution. Not too long ago, some craftspersons on principle would not allow the use of any tools but those operated by human muscle power to be used on their work. The prevailing thought was that if extrahuman power were used, the result could not in good conscience be claimed to be handmade. The first breakdown of this concept occurred with the acceptance of the polishing lathe to replace hand polishing. Since then the flex-shaft and other power tools have come into common use, and the controversy among craftspersons about using hand tools alone has faded. Nowadays, only their relatively high cost prevents the more general use of power tools by craftspersons.

2–14 *INDIRECT STRIKING PERCUSSION CHASING AND DAMASCENING TOOLS:* The tools of the damascene worker and chaser (*ciseleur*), from Diderot's *Encyclopédie.*

ORGANIZATIONS DEALING WITH SAFETY AND HEALTH

Art Hazards Information Center. Center for Occupational Hazards, Inc., 5 Beekman Street, New York, N.Y. 10038 (212-227-6220). Publish: *Art Hazards News* (Monthly).

Institute of Environmental Health. 110 Vet Science Building, Colorado State University, Fort Collins, Colorado 80523.

Mine Safety and Health Administration. Office of Information, Room 1237A, 4015 Wilson Boulevard, Arlington, Virginia 22203 (703-235-1452).

National Association for Health and Safety in the Arts and Crafts. School of the Art Institute of Chicago, 280 Columbus Drive, Chicago, Illinois 60603.

National Institute for Occupational Safety and Health (NIOSH). 4676 Columbia Parkway, Cincinnati, Ohio 45226. Publish: *Current Intelligence Bulletins.* Local state offices are listed under Health Education and Welfare. Tested products bear *NIOSH* approval.

National Safety Council. 444 North Michigan Avenue, Chicago, Illinois 60611. Publish: *Safety Publications; Safety Data Sheets* for materials.

Occupational Safety and Health Administration (OSHA). Office of Information, U.S. Department of Labor, Washington, D.C. 20210. Publish: *Material Safety Data Sheets* (Form 20). Local state offices are listed under U.S. Department of Labor.

Society for Occupational and Environmental Health (SOEH). 2914 M Street N.W., Washington, D.C. 20007.

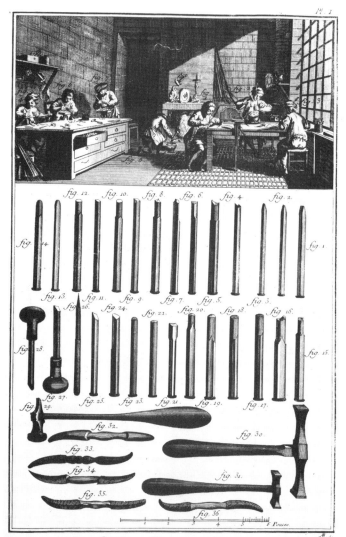

Ciseleur Damasquineur.

3

METAL, THE JEWEL'S RAW MATERIAL
Its Origin, Quality Control, and Variety

METAL

Characteristics and classifications

The word *metal* is akin to the Greek word *metallan,* "to search after" from the Greek *metallon,* and Latin *metallum,* both meaning "a mine or metal." Jewelry has been, and still is made of many other materials, but jewelry making remains essentially an art and technology employing metals. Of the more than 70 pure metals that exist, about 40 have commercial importance, and approximately half that number are used in jewelry itself, or to assist in jewelry making and lapidary work.

METAL CHARACTERISTICS IN GENERAL

Metals are natural elemental chemical or mineral substances, each possessing a distinctive crystalline atomic structure. As compared to nonmetallic elements, metals are heavy, and they are (except for mercury) opaque and solid at ordinary temperatures. When they are mined or extracted from natural deposits in the earth, they sometimes are found in a *native* or pure state. More commonly, they occur as *ores,* which are crude, natural compound minerals containing several components, including one or more metals; the rest is nonmetallic mineral waste matter. It is possible to separate these components because at high heat the atomic structure of metals allows their linkage and fusion to a liquid state, necessary to *smelting,* the thermal process by which metals are liquefied through reduction from ores. The results are refined by various means to convert them to a nearly pure state, the method used depending on the particular metal. They are then cast into *ingots* in preparation for processing them into basic, usable forms. Pure metals possess *specific physical constants* which make their behavior under certain conditions predictable. These properties include their *atomic weight, specific gravity,* and *melting point.*

Most elemental metals are *plastic* (meaning they can be worked without rupture), *malleable* (they permit plastic deformation by compression hammering, rolling, and extrusion), and *ductile* (they permit plastic elongation without fracturing, as in wire drawing), but the degree of these qualities differs with each metal. When proper attention is given to *annealing* (heating, holding the heat, and cooling the metal to cause thermal recrystallization in order to relieve stresses built up in metals due to their subjection to work-hardening processes), fracture can be avoided and the metals permanently deformed into objects of any desired shape or form. The many forming methods used each take into consideration the particular metal's characteristic hardness, rigidity, strength, and degree of resistance to being worked. Metals are generally good heat conductors, which allows them to be joined by thermal methods such as soldering, fusion, and welding; and several are also good conductors of electricity. When polished, metals are lustrous and highly light reflective, which partly accounts for their esthetic appeal. Those that are resistant to *corrosion* (the tendency of metals to revert to their natural state by combining chemically with other elements) retain their luster for long periods of time. Others more quickly react with atmospheric impurities such as sulphur, which in the presence of moisture causes the formation of an adhering, dulling or darkening film of *surface oxidation.* Termed a *patina* in the metal arts, this is often considered a desirable effect.

METAL GROUPS

NONFERROUS METALS

Metals are generally divided into two main groups: *nonferrous* and *ferrous.* The former group includes the noble or precious metals, and base metals. Those in the latter category contain iron.

NOBLE OR PRECIOUS METALS The nonferrous metals can be subdivided into several groups. Foremost among them in terms of use in jewelry, are the *noble* or *precious metals,* a designation that distinguishes them from the base metals also in the nonferrous group. Noble metals include gold, silver, and the so-called platinum six-metal group (platinum, palladium, rhodium, iridium, osmium, and ruthenium). These are "noble" because, rarity aside, they are highly stable chemically, and resist oxidation and corrosion from acids, qualities especially attractive when they are made into jewelry and other objects. Gold and silver are also very plastic, and their general qualities are present in alloys made with them as base constituents. Noble or precious metals are often found as components in base metal ores from which they are separated by refining processes.

BASE METALS Base metals are so called because they are abundant and therefore not precious. Included in this group are aluminum, copper, lead, mercury, nickel, tin, zinc, and many others not ordinarily used by jewelers.

The *light metal group* includes metals with low densities: aluminum, magnesium, titanium, and alloys in which these metals are basic. Another division is the *refractory metal group,* metals with high melting points (above that of iron): titanium, niobium, tantalum, platinum, palladium, rhodium, and their alloys.

FERROUS METALS

Ferrous metals are iron and ferroalloys (alloys containing iron), such as steel, essentially an alloy of iron and carbon plus small amounts of other metals.

ALLOYS

Two or more elemental metals can be combined to make a compound or *alloy.* This is done to change visual properties such as color, or working properties such as increasing hardness, denseness, corrosion resistance, or to lower the melting point of the base metal in the alloy. Heat and fusion are used to mix and unite the components. An alloy of two metals is a *binary alloy,* and a three-metal alloy is a *ternary alloy.* Alloys may contain more than three metals, and hundreds of alloys exist. Base metals are alloyed with each other, and also with precious and ferrous metals. Precious metal alloys are still considered "precious" as long as certain recognized standard proportions are maintained in which the precious metal normally dominates.

GOLD MINING

Disgorging one of Earth's treasures

Gold has always been, and will probably always remain the metal *par excellence* used by jewelers. Gold and jewelry, in fact, are almost synonymous in people's minds because of its ancient use for this purpose, a period of time that covers more than 6,000 years. Its unique position of importance is not simply due to its rarity, but also its appearance, and the very character of the metal itself. In a pure form, its color is a unique bright yellow, which, combined with its ability to take and retain a long-lasting luster, has given gold an ancient symbolic connection with the sun. Because it is chemically inactive when pure, it is almost incorruptible and will not even oxidize in air. This quality gave gold a mystic significance, and a symbolic association with the idea of immortality.

Jewelers and metalworkers since antiquity have appreciated the ease with which gold can be worked by any means and in all decorative processes. Due to its physical characteristics, gold is extremely malleable, which means that by compression it can be squeezed by hammering to incredible thinness. Its ductility and great tensile strength make it possible to draw it, without breaking, into wire of extremely fine section or gauge, and in very long, continuous lengths. Although gold in its pure state is too soft for practical use, it is easily alloyed with other metals; such combinations, while giving it durability, allow it to retain its desirable qualities to a great extent. Alloying also causes gold to take on different colors, depending on the constituents of the alloy and their proportion to the gold. Gold is capable of withstanding great *torsion* (twist or torque), as is dramatically seen by its very early use for gold and bronze *torques,* twisted bar or wire neck ornaments worn by ancient peoples (see Illustration 6–257, p. 252). To all these qualities, we add another of great importance to the contemporary jeweler, the manner in which gold can be used through electrolytic means to plate an inferior metal and give it the appearance of gold, a process far easier than the older mechanical or chemical means of gilding.

Gold was known at least as early as Neolithic times, and possibly earlier. This happened because it was possible to find alluvial gold on the earth's surface with little or no digging, and it was easily identified by its color and bright appearance. Also its relatively heavy weight was noticed. This is due to its high relative density (specific gravity 19.32), surpassed in the precious metals used for jewelry today only by platinum (specific gravity, 21.45), discovered about 1538, and iridium (specific gravity, 22.4), discovered in 1804, and one of the heaviest substances known.

Density in substances is termed their *specific gravity,* expressed as the ratio of the mass or weight of a substance to the weight of an equal volume of water, both at the same temperature. Thus the specific gravity of gold taken at a temperature of $68°$ F ($20°$ C) is 19.32. This expresses the fact that, taken bulk for bulk, gold is $19\frac{32}{100}$ times as heavy as water. For comparison's sake, the specific gravity of silver is 10.49 at the same temperature. A piece of gold jewelry having the same bulk as one in silver is almost twice as heavy, and in the high-karat gold alloys, it is even heavier. Such facts might have an effect on design considerations.

Some sources say that gold was noticed and used even before the knowledge of the existence of copper, the first metal that took the place of stone for implements. It is also claimed that it was through the working of gold for making ornaments that man learned the technology necessary to work other metals. Certainly the jeweler's art is among the most ancient and distinguished of the arts developed for the use of metals, and gold played an important role in this process.

PLACER GOLD: Surface sand and gravel mining

United States law recognizes two classes of valuable mineral deposits, *placers* and *lodes.* Gold is found in all five continents of the world in both forms. The first gold to be discovered in history was, no doubt, the free metallic form called *stream placer gold* (from the Spanish *placer,* and the French *placel* meaning "sand bank" or "alluvial deposit"). Placer gold is obtained in the alluvial or glacial deposits of sand and gravel, often occurring in and near

3–1 *PLACER GOLD MINING*
In 1958 a gold rush started in British Columbia, Canada, in the Cariboo area of the Fraser River. Thousands of prospectors attracted by the chance of finding placer gold flooded the area, and in effect opened the interior of that country to settlement. Placer gold is still mined there today in the traditional way, by pan washing alluvial dirt and gravel. *Photo: National Film Board, Canada/British Columbia*

▶

3–2 *PANNING FOR GOLD*
with a portable plastic sluice box manufactured by the Home Safety Equipment Co., New Albany, Indiana. *Photo: George Brooke*

rivers and streams. Such deposits are the result of erosion through the effect of weather and the abrasive action of water over millennia, on exposed rock outcroppings having gold-bearing quartz matrix veins and lodes. In riverine alluvial deposits gold particles are found exposed or relatively near the surface in sizes that range from fine dust to flakes, spangles, or nuggets, the latter sometimes of great size and weight. Areas near streams and rivers may also contain placer gold; such places are worked by bringing water to them in ditches and then dredging. Placer mining today accounts for about 25% of the gold mined in the U.S.

REEF GOLD: Hard rock mining

The terms reef, lode, ledge, vein, and lead are practically synonymous. Early gold mining in America was for placer gold but this was replaced by reef gold mining in 1873 when the great lodes were discovered in the West.

Reef gold is gold solidly embedded as irregular dendritic masses in white or gray veins or lodes contained in a solid matrix of many kinds of hard rock. Stringers are narrow veins or irregular, reticulated filaments that also go through rock of different material. Gold is also found filling a fissure in the country rock within boundaries that are actually separate from the adjoining rock. The gold in such deposits may or may not be easily visible. Lode-bearing rock can extend for much more than a mile into the earth's surface, which makes it necessary to excavate very deep subterranean passageways when following the lodes. Other metals are usually found combined with gold, both in lodes and solid rock, especially silver, copper, lead, nickel, platinum, uranium, and zinc. Depending on the condition, the gold or the other metal may be the by-product. About one third of all gold mined today in the U.S. is by-product gold. As all these other metals have value, they are separated from each other by refining processes.

PROSPECTING FOR ALLUVIAL PLACER GOLD

In 1968 the officially supported rate of $35 per ounce for pure gold was given up by the world's banks to allow gold to find its real value in the free market. In 1971 the U.S. abandoned the concept that the dollar was converti-

ble to gold, and since then, a floating rate system of the relationships of value between different national currencies has been adopted. The world's central bankers agreed that gold would never again be used as the unit against which the values of all currencies are measured, and that gold would become a commodity like any other. In the U.S., starting December 31, 1974, citizens were permitted to purchase and possess any amount of gold without the permission of the Federal Reserve Bank, formerly needed. This plus the fear of inflation has caused the price of gold to soar.

These conditions have also caused a revival of interest in amateur prospecting for gold. The easiest way to find gold is by searching in alluvial river and stream deposits known to contain it, and the method described here is believed to have been in use since at least 4000 B.C. Prospecting in rivers and streams can be undertaken with the simplest of equipment—a shallow, circular metal pan about 12 in (20.5 cm) or more in diameter, with sloping sides. In this process, called *panning* for gold, the pan is dipped into the water to scoop up about a two-thirds-full complement of river soil or gravel, called *pay dirt, shoot,* or *streak* by the gold prospectors of the U.S.A. during the last century. Larger particles are removed by hand, and the pan is then filled with water and rotated with a circular motion to suspend its soluble and small-particle contents. In this swirling water movement, the lighter particles are carried out of the pan, and, with luck, because of their heavier weight or specific gravity, a residue of gold particles and/or gold ore remain in the pan.

Amateur gold prospectors are at work in at least twenty-one states in the U.S. In response to this interest, one manufacturer has introduced a portable, strong, light-weight, collapsible, black (for gold visibility) plastic sluice box, which is an inclined trough paved with riffles or series of grooves and interstices that catch and retain the gold. This piece of equipment resembles the wooden rock troughs used by the Forty-niners. In ancient times, such troughs were lined with sheepskins, wool side up. Because of the natural grease in the wool, the gold particles clung to it and were later washed off and collected. This system gave birth to the idea of the golden fleece in Greek mythology.

It is claimed that with this new plastic sluice box up to 1.8 tons of pay dirt can be treated by one person in one day, twenty times the amount a single person with a pan

3–3 A PORTABLE, GASOLINE-OPERATED, MOTORIZED DREDGE-CUM-SLUICE BOX in use in the Etowah River in Georgia, in search for placer gold. Photo: United Press International

can process in this time. So, with a modest expenditure, riches are available to the diligent. Wear rubber boots unless you like wet feet.

Taking this idea one step further, another manufacturer offers a portable dredge operated by a gasoline-powered motor and pump, a simplified version of hydraulic mining techniques that are carried out on a large scale. After enough river silt is scooped up to fill the sluice, it is washed by pumped water, the motor is turned off, and the riffles inspected for gold flakes and nuggets which can be further separated by panning.

Perhaps the use of such means is one answer to the problem of the high cost of gold to the jeweler. Jewelers should not deprive themselves of the experience of working with gold.

Two grades of gold are produced at the refinery. The one produced by the *chlorine refining* process tests 0.997+ fine and is called *fine gold*. By further *electrolytic refining* processes, a premium grade, 0.9995+ fine, called *proof gold*, is produced for use in standardizing purposes. The Homestake Mining Company produces an average of 407,400 ounces of gold annually, while 1,000,000 ounces are produced annually from *all* combined sources in the U.S.A. In the Republic of South Africa, which produces 75% of the world's gold (not including Eastern bloc countries), 31,000,000 ounces are produced annually. An estimated 6,500,000 ounces are produced annually in the U.S.S.R.

Less than half of this total is used for jewelry; some is used for dentistry, and the rest for industrial purposes with the electronic industry consuming the greatest amount. (For a further discussion of gold and other precious metals, see Index.)

SECONDARY SOURCES FOR THE RECOVERY OF PRECIOUS METALS

In the United States, secondary source gold and silver is about equal to domestic prime production from mining. Industrial scrap is collected in the form of clippings, stampings, filings, polishings, plated material, contaminated solutions, chemical ware, plated wire, and electronic waste materials. Old jewelry yields about 20% of the total collected. Old fillings and other dental scrap also provide a lesser amount of gold. (See Precipitation and Recovery of Silver from Spent Acid Solutions in this chapter.)

SUBSURFACE GOLD REEF MINING

(As carried out at the Homestake Mining Company)

3–4 1. THE GOLD MINING COMPLEX
This photo shows the sprawling surface complex plants of the Homestake Mining Company in Lead (pronounced "leed"), South Dakota, U.S.A., the largest single gold producer in the western hemisphere. These buildings house the auxiliary services essential to the underground program. In the upper left is the hoisting plant necessary for lifting heavy ores from great depths, which makes modern mining possible. The shaft is 7,212 ft (over one-and-one-third miles) below the surface. At that depth, the rock and air temperature is about 125° F (51.6° C), and cool, dehumidified air must be constantly pumped to the tunnels to allow work to be carried on. About 1,400,000 tons of gold-bearing ore are raised from the mine and processed annually. In the left center is the mill where the ore is ground, and directly above it is the ore stockpile with a conveyer leading to and from the mill. The conveyer brings ore to the mill and tailings (ground stone that has no value) out of the mill. In the lower left and right are the flat-roofed cyanide plants where sand and slime-crushed ore is treated. The refinery is above and to the left of the right-hand cyanide plant, and in it the precipitates are refined to produce chemically pure gold as the end product.

3-5 2. THE GOLD MINE AND MINING
On each level, the ore is located by horizontal tunnels called *drifts* and *crosscuts*. The ores are worked upward in a series of rooms called *stopes* in which the ore is broken down and withdrawn. First 12 ft holes are drilled with properly positioned, jumbo-sized, semi-automatic, self-feed drills fitted with diamond or tungsten carbide-mounted points, and worked with the aid of air compressors. The holes are drilled into the working face of the extremely hard abrasive rock whose gold content is rarely visible, then filled with ammonium nitrate explosives, and a new cut of ore is blasted in a slice 10 ft thick.

3-6 3. GOLD ORE REMOVAL AND BACKFILLING
After blasting, when the dust has settled, the rock fragments are scraped with power shovels, or slushed to a *chimney* or ore pass in the stope floor, and sent by a connecting chute to a level below. After a slice of ore has been removed, most of the space is filled with sand from the mill tailings mixed with cement, called *backfilling*. This provides a support and a floor on which the next slice is broken.

3-7 4. GOLD ORE TRANSPORTATION
On the lower level, the ore is drawn and loaded into an ore car which along with others is hauled to the shaft by an intricate, underground 18 inch gauge railway system with 100 miles of track, covering all mine tunnels. Here it is loaded into a cartridge that measures 10.5 tons at a time, then discharged into a large bucket or *skip*, and finally hoisted to the surface where it is mechanically dry crushed in three stages to ½ in screen size.

3-8 5. REMOVING GOLD FROM ORE: THE MILLING PROCESS
The science of *metallurgy* or the extraction of metal from ores, refining and preparing them for use, now begins, using mechanical and chemical processes. The ore is received by huge 12 × 12 × 6 ft fully automatic *spinning rod mills* in which it is reduced to a sandy ⅛ in particle size which prepares it for the chemical processes of ore extraction. Computers now make all routine adjustments. The crushed ore and water then flows to *ball mills*, similar to rod mills, but 11 ft long by 9 ft in diameter. Each is loaded with about 80,000 lb of steel balls and rotates about 17 times per minute. Here *all* the ore is ground and reduced to a 200-mesh screen to break the gold grains from the rock to a fineness suitable to gold recovery. From here the ground ore flows to *classifiers* which are inclined troughlike machines with slow-moving internal rakes, equivalent to the old rock troughs used by prospectors. In this, particles fine enough are washed away to the next receptacle, and coarser grains are collected and returned to the ball mill for further reduction.

3–9 6. THE CYANIDATION GOLD RECOVERY PROCESS

Gold can be recovered from crushed ore by amalgamation, flotation, gravity concentration, cyanidation, smelting, and combinations of these processes. Amalgamation, formerly widely used, is no longer practiced at this mine because mercury used in this process contaminated the water quality at the plant discharge. Instead, cyanidation and smelting are employed. In the cyanidation process, the fine sandy ore is passed to *sand vats* where it is chemically treated by precipitation. Each vat when filled contains approximately 725 tons of sand when all water has been drained off the top. A cyanide solution is introduced through the vat top, and by gravity percolates and leaches through the sand dissolving 95% of the gold contained in it to form a filtered gravity concentrate, gold-cyanide solution. Extremely finely powdered zinc is added to this solution which is then pumped through filter presses to extract the resulting dark brownish solid matter called *precipitate*. This is the substance subsequently treated in the refinery to produce pure gold.

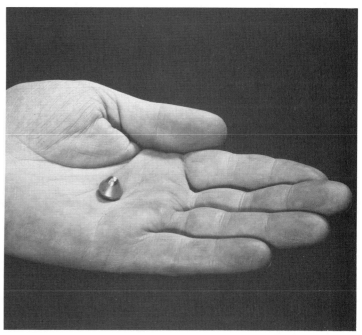

3–10 7. REFINING GOLD BY SMELTING

Native gold is usually found in combination with other metals, as mentioned. In antiquity, the main means of refining gold or separating it from these other metals was by cupellation, a method described at p. 48. Some natural alloys were used more or less as found, such as *electrum*—a name given by the Greeks to an alloy that consisted of approximately 80% gold and 20% silver, and was pale yellow in color. In today's smelting process, the precipitate is mixed with flux and melted, during which time impurities are removed as *slag* or *dross*, a waste product containing mostly silicates. Because this has a lower specific gravity than the metal being smelted, it rises to the surface and can be skimmed off. The result is a crude gold bullion which must be further refined, done by the process of *cupellation*. Today's industrial, large-scale cupellation process is as follows. The crude bullion is remelted and poured into small clay cupellation pots which are placed in small furnaces. In the next process, called *chlorination*, chlorine gas is blown through long clay tubes into the molten gold. Some impurities it contains pass off as fumes. Silver, which is often found combined with gold in the ore, forms a liquid, silver chloride, which because it is lighter than gold, floats to the surface where it is removed by skimming. When silver chloride no longer forms, the gold is poured into what the industry calls *small ingot bars* weighing 35 lb, each bar representing at least 3,500,000 lb of processed ore!

The button of gold seen here in the man's hand weighs 0.227 of one troy ounce, and represents the current yield of gold from *one ton* of rock ore at this mine!

QUALITY CONTROL OF PRECIOUS METALS

Insurance against fraud

MAKING AN INGOT OF PRECIOUS METAL

Metal jewelry making can be said to begin with the *ingot,* a mass of cast metal, usually rectangular or rodlike in form. Besides allowing for ease in bulk metal storage, the ingot is molded metal in a form that is convenient to process into all the basic raw metal forms used by jewelers and metalworkers, including sheet, bar, and wire. An ingot can also be used for casting when it is remelted.

Making an ingot of precious (or nonferrous) metal alloys is well within the means of any jeweler who has a suitable *ingot mold,* and a source of heat sufficient to melt the metal. The ingot can be processed further, even when lacking a *rolling mill* which is the usual tool used to reduce an ingot to sheet, rod, and heavy wire. Because the ingot size used by jewelers is relatively small, the ingot can be *hand hammered* into sheet on an *anvil,* or *drawn down* by forging it with *hammers* to a round rod whose sectional thickness is sufficiently small to allow it to then be drawn through a *hand drawplate* with *drawtongs.* All these methods are commonly used by jewelers, and are described below.

3–12 *GOLD BARS 995.0 FINE QUALITY*, each stamped with a serial number and the mark of the manufacturer who guarantees stated purity. *Photo: Courtesy Metaux Precieux S.A., Neuchatel, Switzerland*

3–11 *ROME, late 4th century A.D. Gold ingot found at Kronstadt in Transylvania in 1887. It was produced, presumably at the Sirmium mint and is stamped with the name of the procurator FLAVIANVS, and of the assayer LVCIANVS. Its weight is 476.2 g; its dimensions 16.5 × 2.2 × 1.1 cm; its purity almost 97% fine. The bar is marked OBRI which means pure gold. The 4th-century solidum (Roman gold coin) was as naturally fine as was then possible. Photo: Reproduced by Courtesy of the Trustees of The British Museum, London*

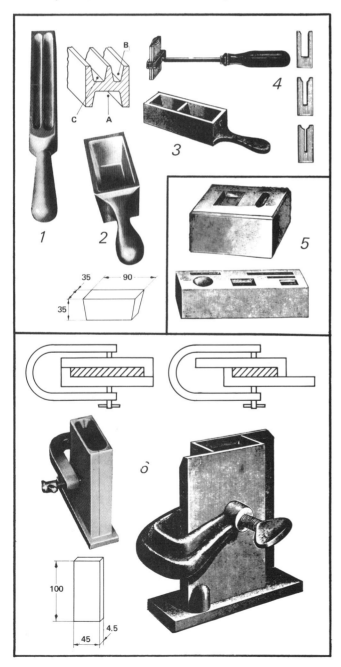

THE METAL USED FOR MAKING AN INGOT

Making an ingot of precious metals is a way of reclaiming *clean, uncontaminated, known and uniform quality waste metal* that has been deliberately and carefully accumulated from filing, cutting, stamping, and other work processes. To be *sound*, (free of foreign matter and internal porosity or blowholes) and homogeneous in composition, precious metal ingots should *not* be made completely of scrap metal, but should include about a 50% charge of new metal. New metal for casting precious metal is sold in the form of *grain* or so-called "bean" *shot*. When precious metal *scrap metal* is used, it must first be prepared in the manner described below. (See Recovery and Refinement of Precious Metal, p. 49.)

When casting a precious metal alloy (or other nonferrous metal alloy), its constituents must be known exactly, and amounts carefully calculated to control exact proportions and achieve a result of known and desired qualities and characteristics. Ingot making enables the jeweler to make precious (or other nonferrous) metal alloys that may not be readily available on the commercial market without a bulk order, to make his or her own solder, and to create a bulk form of metal that might otherwise only be obtainable on special order.

In general, when preparing an alloy, the metals with higher melting points are melted first, followed by lower melting metals.

INGOT MOLD TYPES

The ingot mold evolved from prehistoric times, when a simple depression made in a stone was used for this purpose. This kind of ingot mold can still be used today, and steatite or soapstone is probably the easiest one to use to make a mold. However, nowadays ingot molds are commonly made of cast iron. The design of the mold is important in achieving a sound ingot. Molds with squared shapes produce better ingots than round ones. The ingot molds used by jewelers are of several types. The simplest

3–13 *INGOT MOLDS*
1. *Wire ingot mold, open type. C grcove 9 × 9 × 170 mm; B groove 7 × 8 × 170 mm; A groove 19 × 8 × 170 mm can be used for casting a narrow plate ingot.*
2. *Open ingot mold, capacity 50 oz t.*
3. *Open divided ingot mold.*
4. *Small hand mold for casting small ingots of different thicknesses.*
5. *Platinum ingot brick molds with various shaped depressions, capable of withstanding very high temperatures.*
6. *Adjustable vertical ingot molds that allow various width plate ingots to be made with the same mold. Diagram indicates how the horizontal sliding adjustment is made for casting smaller widths. Dimensions indicate the maximum ingot size capacity of 200 dwt that can be cast with this model. Other sizes are available in all ingot mold types.*

and oldest metal ingot mold is the cast iron *horizontal, open ingot mold.* For producing an ingot bar of a shape suited to rod and wire making in a wire rolling mill, a mold that has a long, narrow, shallow depression varying in length from 9¼–9⅝ in (23.5–24.5 cm), and in width from ⁷⁄₃₂–¼ in (0.56–0.63 cm) is used. Such ingots can also be shear cut into small sections for use in casting. To cast a bar or plate suited to rolling into sheet, a mold with a broad, shallow depression with a capacity of from 50–200 troy ounces of metal is used. Another type is the cast iron *vertical, adjustable, clamp ingot mold.* This type has movable sides that slide horizontally so that the width or volume of metal can be varied according to need, from narrow bars to wide plates.

The better the surface condition of a mold, the smoother the surface of the resulting ingot, and the less work to further process it.

PREPARING THE INGOT MOLD FOR CASTING

The mold cavity must be absolutely clean and free of solid foreign particles which would become embedded in the ingot walls or cause indentations that will result in imperfections in the rolled sheet or wire.

In order to achieve a good surface on metal ingots cast in a metal mold, the mold cavity surface must be *dressed* with a suitable substance. The dressing also has the function of creating a reducing atmosphere in which oxygen is excluded from the mold during the pour, helping to assure a sound surface on the ingot. Also, when the molten metal contacts it, the dressing produces gases whose relative violence causes agitation on the poured metal surface which tends to blow dirt and dross away, thereby preventing their inclusion in the ingot surface. If the dressing is too light, or the pour too slow, the surface will be poor. If it is too thick or heavy, some of the gas evolved may become trapped in the ingot and cause external blisters, or worse, internal blowholes, or the ejection of the molten metal from the mold.

Precious metal dressings in use are a special *mold oil, carbon* in the form of soot applied to the mold cavity by smoking it lightly while holding it over a candle flame, or *powdered graphite* dusted on a very lightly oiled surface. Other substances used for dressings are lard oil, grease, mineral oil, tallow, or combinations of these.

MELTING THE METAL

All casting should be done under conditions of good ventilation, and with suitable protection: *asbestos gloves* for the hands, and *goggles* for the eyes. The amount of metal used should be enough to completely fill the chosen mold cavity in one pour. It is placed in a crucible large enough to hold this amount. If more than one ingot is being made at the same time, the necessary amount should be carefully calculated. Some metals require the use of melting crucibles having particular compositions in order to avoid the absorption of contaminants when the metal is in a molten state. (See Crucibles, p. 513.) Gold and silver and their alloys can be melted in conventional *clay graphite crucibles,* or others made of different compositions. Every metal requires a crucible reserved for that metal alone, or the result will be adversely affected.

Heat the metal in the crucible, completely covering it with a *reducing flame* from a *melting torch* with a tip large enough to create a flame of sufficient size to achieve the necessary temperature. The metal should be melted *as*

rapidly as possible to avoid the inclusion of oxygen or the dissipation through fumes of metals with low melting points in the alloy. Oxygen is excluded because its introduction to the melt adversely affects the metal structure by creating porosity. (See Porosity, Chapter 11.)

To keep the possible introduction of oxygen low, it is advisable to cover the metal with crushed charcoal, which also helps in creating a reduced atmosphere. Before covering with charcoal, sprinkle a pinch of *flux* in the form of boric acid powder over the metal. Flux aids in achieving a homogeneous metal composition, and also helps to prevent the introduction of oxygen into the melt. Now the crushed charcoal can be placed on top. Continue to heat the metal until it is fluid. Gold and silver alloys should be heated to about 338° F (170° C) *above the liquidus* or the temperature at which the metal will flow. This temperature is as low as will allow the whole charge in the crucible to be poured without freezing if one acts with normal speed. Overheating the metal is to be avoided as it will affect the working qualities of the result by creating an oversized crystal structure, and by dissipating the lower melting metals in the alloy through their volatilization as fumes.

POURING THE METAL INTO AN INGOT MOLD:
Teeming

Before pouring the metal, preheat the mold with a torch by passing it over the mold a few times until the dressing starts to smoke. *Never* pour molten metal into a cold ingot mold or it may spatter or be ejected. If the mold is still hot from a previous pour, preheating is not necessary. As soon as the metal reaches the necessary temperature above the liquidus, give it a final stir with a *carbon or graphite stirring rod* to assure its uniformity.

Just before pouring, skim away the charcoal along with any remains of the flux from the surface of the molten metal with a carbon or graphite stirring rod which can be hand held when small amounts of metal are being melted, or held with *tongs* when casting a large ingot. Place a fresh pinch of flux on the melt to aid the flow and to prevent surface oxidation.

In pouring, hold the crucible containing the molten metal with bent crucible tongs and bring it to the heated ingot mold (which must be near the melting area so that the metal does not cool excessively during the transfer). Hold the crucible in position over the mold opening with the right hand, and with the left hand, play a reducing flame (see p. 413) from the torch over the mold at the

3–14 *REFINED GOLD BARS* being poured at the Degussa Precious Metals and Chemicals factory at Frankfurt/Main, Federal Republic of Germany. *Photo: Courtesy Degussa*

Making Gold and Silver Alloys

Gold Alloys	Fine Gold	Fine Silver	Copper	Other Metals	Total Gram Weight
22k (917 gold)					
Light yellow	1.000	0.068	0.023		1.091
Yellow	1.000	0.045	0.046		1.091
18k (750 gold)					
Light yellow	1.000	0.285	0.048		1.333
Yellow	1.000	0.213	0.120		1.333
Deep yellow	1.000	0.167	0.166		1.333
Rose	1.000	0.110	0.223		1.333
Red	1.000	0.050	0.283		1.333
Orange-red	1.000	0.048	0.285		1.333
Deep red	1.000		0.333		1.333
Green yellow	1.000	0.222	0.111		1.333
Green	1.000	0.333			1.333
White	1.000		0.047	0.210 Ni 0.076 Zn	1.333
14k (585 gold)					
Green	1.000	0.532	0.058	0.120 Ni	1.710
Green yellow	1.000	0.474	0.236		1.710
Pale yellow	1.000	0.427	0.283		1.710
Dark yellow	1.000	0.284	0.426		1.710
Red yellow	1.000	0.178	0.532		1.710
Red-orange	1.000	0.103	0.607		1.710
White	1.000		0.342	0.248 Ni 0.120 Zn	1.710
Purple	1.000			0.265 Al	1.265
Silver Alloys					
Britannia (958.4)		1.000	0.0416		1.0416
Sterling (925)		1.000	0.081		1.081
Coin (900)		1.000	0.125		1.125
Coin (800)		1.000	0.250		1.250

The standards used here are British or European in which the requirement is that the result be 1/2k higher than stamped. Any desired amount of alloy in multiples of the total gram weight given here can be made by multiplying each constituent figure in a particular alloy by the desired amount.

point where the metal enters it. Pour the metal slowly but steadily, *without stopping,* into the mold. If the mold is deep, it can be set initially at a slight angle so that the metal does not pour straight into the bottom, which might cause it to splash, or might create unnecessary turbulence. Once the metal nears the top of the mold, the pour is finished, and the mold can be straightened so that the ingot end will be squared to the rest.

During pouring, because of the molten metal's heat, the lubricant burns and creates a gaseous cushion between the metal and the mold walls. The first metal to freeze is that which contacts the mold walls. During freezing, the metal crystallizes and solidifies. As it freezes it also shrinks somewhat so that the metal pulls slightly away from the walls leaving a small air gap, which allows the ingot to be easily removed from the mold. During solidification, shrinkage is slow and is immediately filled in by contacting interior metal still in a molten state. Freezing continues in layers parallel to the mold walls, and the still molten internal pool continues to feed metal to the shrinking, solidifying ingot. Because of the pull of gravity, and the fact that the initially poured metal has already solidified, shrinkage causes a dent to appear at the end of a solidified vertical ingot, or along the exposed side of a horizontal, open-mold poured ingot, even when the mold has been poured full. In

extreme cases, this depressed end of the ingot may have to be cut away, or the side *scalped* by *drawfiling* the surface (see p. 371) to make the ingot dimensions uniform in order to avoid irregularities in the rolled result.

An ingot that is removed from a mold before it solidifies completely, such that some of the liquid core runs out, is called a *bleeding ingot.* When the ingot is *set* or completely *frozen,* it can be removed from the mold. All visible redness should disappear, and sufficient time be allowed for internal solidification to occur. The thicker the ingot, the longer the time needed for total solidification. Because the ingot is still hot, wear *asbestos gloves* when *stripping* or removing the ingot from the mold. Shake it out of an open mold, or open the clamp of a closed mold and do the same. To prevent the formation of surface cracks from cooling too rapidly, pick up the ingot with *tongs,* and bury it in a refractory material such as *pea pumice* to allow it to cool slowly. It is then ready for further processing by methods described below.

3–15   UNION OF SOUTH AFRICA. Refined and polished gold ingot bars, usually 9,960 parts per 10,000, being stamped with individually recorded serial numbers. Each bar weighs 12.5 kg. In this form they are purchased by jewelry manufacturers, industrial consumers, and investors in the free markets of Zürich and London. *Photo: Courtesy Chamber of Mines of South Africa, Johannesburg*

LOWERING OR RAISING GOLD AND SILVER QUALITY

It is possible to lower or raise the quality and amount of gold and silver of a known quality to a desired quality and amount. The tables given here are those used to achieve 18K and 14K gold, and for sterling and coin silver, the precious metal qualities most commonly in use by goldsmiths and silversmiths.

In weighing these metals and the alloy constituents the particular alloy may require, a sensitive scale capable of indicating the required degree of accuracy must be used. To be sure the metal result is actually of the stated, stamped quality, it is common practice for a quality *slightly higher* than the stamped quality to be made. The metal constituents are placed in a crucible, melted, stirred, and poured into a prepared ingot mold, as already described. The resulting ingot can then be processed into sheet, wire, or tubing.

Lowering Gold Quality to 18k Gold (750)

Gold	Add Alloy g	Gold	Add Alloy g	Gold	Add Alloy g	Gold	Add Alloy g	Gold	Add Alloy g	Gold	Add Alloy g	Gold	Add Alloy g
999	0.33200	959	0.27866	919	0.22533	879	0.17200	839	0.11866	799	0.06533	759	0.01200
998	0.33066	958	0.27733	918	0.22400	878	0.17066	838	0.11733	798	0.06400	758	0.01066
997	0.32933	957	0.27600	917	0.22266	877	0.16933	837	0.11600	797	0.06266	757	0.00933
996	0.32800	956	0.27466	916	0.22133	876	0.16800	836	0.11466	796	0.06133	756	0.00800
995	0.32666	955	0.27333	915	0.22000	875	0.16666	835	0.11333	795	0.06000	755	0.00666
994	0.32533	954	0.27200	914	0.21866	874	0.16533	834	0.11200	794	0.05866	754	0.00533
993	0.32400	953	0.27066	913	0.21733	873	0.16400	833	0.11066	793	0.05733	753	0.00400
992	0.32266	952	0.26933	912	0.21600	872	0.16266	832	0.10933	792	0.05600	752	0.00266
991	0.32133	951	0.26800	911	0.21466	871	0.16133	831	0.10800	791	0.05466	751	0.00133
990	0.32000	950	0.26666	910	0.21333	870	0.16000	830	0.10666	790	0.05333		
989	0.31866	949	0.26533	909	0.21200	869	0.15866	829	0.10533	789	0.05200		
988	0.31733	948	0.26400	908	0.21066	868	0.15733	828	0.10400	788	0.05066		
987	0.31600	947	0.26266	907	0.20933	867	0.15600	827	0.10266	787	0.04933		
986	0.31466	946	0.26133	906	0.20800	866	0.15466	826	0.10133	786	0.04800		
985	0.31333	945	0.26000	905	0.20666	865	0.15333	825	0.10000	785	0.04666		
984	0.31200	944	0.25866	904	0.20533	864	0.15200	824	0.09866	784	0.04533		
983	0.31066	943	0.25733	903	0.20400	863	0.15066	823	0.09733	783	0.04400		
982	0.30933	942	0.25600	902	0.20266	862	0.14933	822	0.09600	782	0.04266		
981	0.30800	941	0.25466	901	0.20133	861	0.14800	821	0.09466	781	0.04133		
980	0.30666	940	0.25333	900	0.20000	860	0.14666	820	0.09333	780	0.40000		
979	0.30533	939	0.25200	899	0.19866	859	0.14533	819	0.09200	779	0.03866		
978	0.30400	938	0.25066	898	0.19733	858	0.14400	818	0.09066	778	0.03733		
977	0.30266	937	0.24933	897	0.19600	857	0.14266	817	0.08933	777	0.03600		
976	0.30133	936	0.24800	896	0.19466	856	0.14133	816	0.08800	776	0.03466		
975	0.30000	935	0.24666	895	0.19333	855	0.14000	815	0.08666	775	0.03333		
974	0.29866	934	0.24533	894	0.19200	854	0.13866	814	0.08533	774	0.03200		
973	0.29733	933	0.24400	893	0.19066	853	0.13733	813	0.08400	773	0.03066		
972	0.29600	932	0.24266	892	0.18933	852	0.13600	812	0.08266	772	0.02933		
971	0.29466	931	0.24133	891	0.18800	851	0.13466	811	0.08133	771	0.02800		
970	0.29333	930	0.24000	890	0.18666	850	0.13333	810	0.80000	770	0.02666		
969	0.29200	929	0.23866	889	0.18533	849	0.13200	809	0.07866	769	0.02533		
968	0.29066	928	0.23733	888	0.18400	848	0.13066	808	0.07733	768	0.02400		
967	0.28933	927	0.23600	887	0.18266	847	0.12933	807	0.07600	767	0.02266		
966	0.28800	926	0.23466	886	0.18133	846	0.12800	806	0.07466	766	0.02133		
965	0.28666	925	0.23333	885	0.18000	845	0.12666	805	0.07333	765	0.02000		
964	0.28533	924	0.23200	884	0.17866	844	0.12533	804	0.07200	764	0.01866		
963	0.28400	923	0.23066	883	0.17733	843	0.12400	803	0.07066	763	0.01733		
962	0.28266	922	0.22933	882	0.17600	842	0.12266	802	0.06933	762	0.01600		
961	0.28133	921	0.22800	881	0.17486	841	0.12133	801	0.06800	761	0.01466		
960	0.28000	920	0.22666	880	0.17333	840	0.12000	800	0.06666	760	0.01333		

To **lower** gold of any quality between 24k (999) and just above 18k (751) in order to make 18k gold (750), to one gram of the gold quality given in the left column, add the **total amount** of the **alloying metals** required for the particular gold alloy given in parts in the adjacent right column.

Lowering 18k (750) Yellow Gold to 14k (585) Yellow Gold

Grams	Fine Silver Add	Copper Add	Total Grams =
1	0.16	0.122	1.282
2	0.32	0.244	2.564
3	0.48	0.366	3.846
4	0.64	0.488	5.128
5	0.80	0.610	6.410
6	0.96	0.732	7.692
7	1.12	0.854	8.974
8	1.28	0.976	10.256
9	1.44	1.098	11.538
10	1.60	1.220	12.820

Raising 14k (585) Yellow Gold to 18k (750) Yellow Gold

Grams	Fine Gold Add	Fine Silver Add	Total Grams =
1	0.790	0.043	1.833
2	1.580	0.086	3.666
3	2.370	0.129	5.499
4	3.160	0.172	7.332
5	3.950	0.215	9.165
6	4.740	0.258	10.998
7	5.530	0.301	12.831
8	6.320	0.344	14.664
9	7.110	0.387	16.497
10	7.900	0.430	18.333

Raising Gold Quality to 18k Gold (750)

Gold	Add Gold (999)	Gold	Add Gold (999)	Gold	Add Gold (999)	Gold	Add Gold (999)	Gold	Add Gold (999)	Gold	Add Gold (999)
749	0.00401	719	0.12449	689	0.24498	659	0.36546	629	0.48594	599	0.60643
748	0.00803	718	0.12851	688	0.24899	658	0.36948	628	0.48996	598	0.61044
747	0.01204	717	0.13253	687	0.25301	657	0.37349	627	0.49398	597	0.61446
746	0.01606	716	0.13654	686	0.25703	656	0.37751	626	0.49799	596	0.61847
745	0.02008	715	0.14056	685	0.26104	655	0.38152	625	0.50201	595	0.62249
744	0.02409	714	0.14457	684	0.26506	654	0.38554	624	0.50602	594	0.62651
743	0.02811	713	0.14859	683	0.26907	653	0.38956	623	0.51004	593	0.63052
742	0.03212	712	0.15261	682	0.27309	652	0.39357	622	0.51406	592	0.63454
741	0.03614	711	0.15662	681	0.27711	651	0.39759	621	0.51807	591	0.63855
740	0.04016	710	0.16064	680	0.28112	650	0.40161	620	0.52209	590	0.64257
739	0.04417	709	0.16466	679	0.28514	649	0.40562	619	0.52610	589	0.64659
738	0.04819	708	0.16867	678	0.28915	648	0.40964	618	0.53012	588	0.65060
737	0.05220	707	0.17269	677	0.29317	647	0.41365	617	0.53414	587	0.65462
736	0.05622	706	0.17670	676	0.29719	646	0.41767	616	0.53815	586	0.65864
735	0.06024	705	0.18972	675	0.30120	645	0.42169	615	0.54217	585	0.66265
734	0.06425	704	0.18474	674	0.30522	644	0.42570	614	0.54618		
733	0.06827	703	0.18875	673	0.30923	643	0.42972	613	0.55020		
732	0.07228	702	0.19277	672	0.31325	642	0.43373	612	0.55422		
731	0.07630	701	0.19678	671	0.31727	641	0.43775	611	0.55823		
730	0.08032	700	0.20080	670	0.32128	640	0.44177	610	0.56225		
729	0.08433	699	0.20482	669	0.32530	639	0.44578	609	0.56627		
728	0.08835	698	0.20883	668	0.32932	638	0.44980	608	0.57028		
727	0.09237	697	0.21285	667	0.33333	637	0.45381	607	0.57430		
726	0.09638	696	0.21686	666	0.33735	636	0.45783	606	0.57831		
725	0.10040	695	0.22088	665	0.34136	635	0.46185	605	0.58233		
724	0.10441	694	0.22490	664	0.34538	634	0.46586	604	0.58635		
723	0.10843	693	0.22891	663	0.34940	633	0.46988	603	0.59036		
722	0.11245	692	0.23293	662	0.35341	632	0.47389	602	0.59438		
721	0.11646	691	0.23694	661	0.35743	631	0.47791	601	0.59839		
720	0.12048	690	0.24096	660	0.36144	630	0.48193	600	0.60241		

To **raise** gold quality of any quality between just less than 18k (749) up to 14k (585) in order to make 18k gold (750), to one gram of the gold quality given in the left column, add the **total amount** of **pure gold** (999) in grams indicated in the adjacent right column.

Raising Silver Quality to Sterling Silver (925)

Silver	Add Fine Silver g	Silver	Add Fine Silver g	Silver	Add Fine Silver g	Silver	Add Fine Silver g	Silver	Add Fine Silver g
		909	0.21621	889	0.48648	869	0.75675	849	1.02702
		908	0.22972	888	0.49999	868	0.77027	848	1.04054
		907	0.24324	887	0.51351	867	0.78378	847	1.05405
		906	0.25675	886	0.52702	866	0.79729	846	1.06756
		905	0.27027	885	0.54054	865	0.81081	845	1.08108
924	0.01351	904	0.28378	884	0.55405	864	0.82432	844	1.09459
923	0.02702	903	0.29729	883	0.56756	863	0.83783	843	1.10810
922	0.04054	902	0.31081	882	0.58108	862	0.85135	842	1.12162
921	0.05405	901	0.32432	881	0.59459	861	0.86486	841	1.13513
920	0.06756	900	0.33783	880	0.60810	860	0.87837	840	1.14864
919	0.08108	899	0.35135	879	0.62162	859	0.89189	839	1.16216
918	0.09459	898	0.36486	878	0.63513	858	0.90540	838	1.17567
917	0.10810	897	0.37837	877	0.64864	857	0.91891	837	1.18918
916	0.12162	896	0.39189	876	0.66216	856	0.93243	836	1.20270
915	0.13513	895	0.40540	875	0.67567	855	0.94594	835	1.21621
914	0.14864	894	0.41891	874	0.68918	854	0.95945	834	1.22972
913	0.16216	893	0.43243	873	0.70270	853	0.97297	833	1.24324
912	0.17567	892	0.44594	872	0.71621	852	0.98648	832	1.25675
911	0.18918	891	0.45945	871	0.72972	851	0.99999	831	1.27026
910	0.20270	890	0.47297	870	0.74324	850	1.01351	830	1.28378

To **raise** silver of any quality between just less than sterling (924) to coin silver (830), to one gram of the silver quality given in the left column, add the amount of fine silver (999) indicated in the adjacent right column.

Raising Coin Silver (800) to Sterling Silver (925)

Grams	Add: Fine Silver	Total
1	0.865	1.865
2	1.730	3.730
3	2.595	5.595
4	3.460	7.460
5	4.325	9.325
6	5.190	11.190
7	6.055	13.055
8	6.920	14.920
9	7.785	16.785
10	8.650	18.650

Lowering Gold Quality to 14k Gold (585)

Gold	Add Alloy g	Gold	Add Alloy g	Gold	Add Alloy g	Gold	Add Alloy g	Gold	Add Alloy g	Gold	Add Alloy g	Gold	Add Alloy g
999	0.70769	939	0.60512	879	0.50256	819	0.39999	759	0.29743	699	0.19487	639	0.09230
998	0.70598	938	0.60341	878	0.50085	818	0.39829	758	0.29571	698	0.19316	638	0.09059
997	0.70427	937	0.60170	877	0.49914	817	0.39658	757	0.29401	697	0.19145	637	0.08888
996	0.70256	936	0.59999	876	0.49743	816	0.39487	756	0.29230	696	0.18974	636	0.08719
995	0.70085	935	0.59829	875	0.49572	815	0.39316	755	0.29059	695	0.18803	635	0.08547
994	0.69914	934	0.59658	874	0.49401	814	0.39145	754	0.28888	694	0.18632	634	0.08376
993	0.69743	933	0.59487	873	0.49230	813	0.38974	753	0.28717	693	0.18461	633	0.08205
992	0.69572	932	0.59316	872	0.49059	812	0.38803	752	0.28546	692	0.18290	632	0.08034
991	0.69401	931	0.59145	871	0.48888	811	0.38632	751	0.28376	691	0.18119	631	0.07863
990	0.69230	930	0.58974	870	0.48717	810	0.38461	750	0.28205	690	0.17948	630	0.07692
989	0.69059	929	0.58803	869	0.48546	809	0.38290	749	0.28034	689	0.17777	629	0.07521
988	0.68888	928	0.58632	868	0.48376	808	0.38119	748	0.27863	688	0.17606	628	0.07350
987	0.68717	927	0.58461	867	0.48205	807	0.37948	747	0.27692	687	0.17435	627	0.07179
986	0.68546	926	0.58290	866	0.48034	806	0.37777	746	0.27521	686	0.17264	626	0.07008
985	0.68376	925	0.58119	865	0.47863	805	0.37606	745	0.27350	685	0.17094	625	0.06837
984	0.68205	924	0.57948	864	0.47692	804	0.37435	744	0.27179	684	0.16923	624	0.06666
983	0.68034	923	0.57777	863	0.47521	803	0.37264	743	0.27008	683	0.16752	623	0.06495
982	0.67863	922	0.57606	862	0.47350	802	0.37093	742	0.26837	682	0.16581	622	0.06324
981	0.67692	921	0.57435	861	0.47179	801	0.36923	741	0.26666	681	0.16410	621	0.06153
980	0.67521	920	0.57264	860	0.47008	800	0.36752	740	0.26495	680	0.16239	620	0.05982
979	0.67350	919	0.57093	859	0.46837	799	0.36581	739	0.26324	679	0.16068	619	0.05811
978	0.67179	918	0.56923	858	0.46666	798	0.36410	738	0.26153	678	0.15897	618	0.05641
977	0.67008	917	0.56752	857	0.46495	797	0.36239	737	0.25982	677	0.15726	617	0.05470
976	0.66837	916	0.56581	856	0.46324	796	0.36068	736	0.25811	676	0.15555	616	0.05299
975	0.66666	915	0.56410	855	0.46153	795	0.35897	735	0.25641	675	0.15384	615	0.05128
974	0.66495	914	0.56239	854	0.45982	794	0.35726	734	0.25470	674	0.15213	614	0.04957
973	0.66324	913	0.56068	853	0.45811	793	0.35555	733	0.25299	673	0.15042	613	0.04786
972	0.66153	912	0.55897	852	0.45640	792	0.35384	732	0.25128	672	0.14871	612	0.04615
971	0.65982	911	0.55726	851	0.45470	791	0.35213	731	0.24957	671	0.14700	611	0.04444
970	0.65811	910	0.55555	850	0.45299	790	0.35042	730	0.24786	670	0.14529	610	0.04273
969	0.65640	909	0.55384	849	0.45128	789	0.34871	729	0.24615	669	0.14358	609	0.04102
968	0.65470	908	0.55213	848	0.44957	788	0.34700	728	0.24444	668	0.14188	608	0.03931
967	0.65299	907	0.55042	847	0.44786	787	0.34529	727	0.24273	667	0.14017	607	0.03760
966	0.65128	906	0.54871	846	0.44615	786	0.34358	726	0.24102	666	0.13846	606	0.03589
965	0.64957	905	0.54700	845	0.44444	785	0.34188	725	0.23931	665	0.13675	605	0.03418
964	0.64786	904	0.54529	844	0.44273	784	0.34017	724	0.23760	664	0.13504	604	0.03247
963	0.64615	903	0.54358	843	0.44102	783	0.33846	723	0.23589	663	0.13333	603	0.03076
962	0.64444	902	0.54187	842	0.43931	782	0.33675	722	0.23418	662	0.13162	602	0.02905
961	0.64273	901	0.54017	841	0.43760	781	0.33504	721	0.23247	661	0.12991	601	0.02735
960	0.64102	900	0.53846	840	0.43589	780	0.33333	720	0.23076	660	0.12820	600	0.02564
959	0.63931	899	0.53675	839	0.43418	779	0.33162	719	0.22905	659	0.12649	599	0.02393
958	0.63760	898	0.53504	838	0.43247	778	0.32991	718	0.22735	658	0.12478	598	0.02222
957	0.63589	897	0.53333	837	0.43076	777	0.32820	717	0.22564	657	0.12307	597	0.02051
956	0.63418	896	0.53162	836	0.42905	776	0.32649	716	0.22393	656	0.12136	596	0.01880
955	0.63247	895	0.52991	835	0.42735	775	0.32478	715	0.22222	655	0.11965	595	0.01709
954	0.63076	894	0.52820	834	0.42564	774	0.32307	714	0.22051	654	0.11794	594	0.01538
953	0.62905	893	0.52649	833	0.42393	773	0.32136	713	0.21880	653	0.11623	593	0.01367
952	0.62734	892	0.52478	832	0.42222	772	0.31965	712	0.21709	652	0.11452	592	0.01196
951	0.62564	891	0.52307	831	0.42051	771	0.31794	711	0.21538	651	0.11282	591	0.01025
950	0.62393	890	0.52136	830	0.41880	770	0.31623	710	0.21367	650	0.11111	590	0.00854
949	0.62222	889	0.51965	829	0.41709	769	0.31452	709	0.21196	649	0.10940	589	0.00683
948	0.62051	888	0.51794	828	0.41538	768	0.31282	708	0.21025	648	0.10769	588	0.00512
947	0.61880	887	0.51623	827	0.41367	767	0.31111	707	0.20854	647	0.10598	587	0.00341
946	0.61709	886	0.51452	826	0.41196	766	0.30940	706	0.20683	646	0.10427	586	0.00170
945	0.61538	885	0.51282	825	0.41025	765	0.30769	705	0.20512	645	0.10256		
944	0.61367	884	0.51111	824	0.40854	764	0.30598	704	0.20341	644	0.01185		
943	0.61196	883	0.50940	823	0.40683	763	0.30427	703	0.20170	643	0.09914		
942	0.61025	882	0.50769	822	0.40512	762	0.30256	702	0.19999	642	0.09743		
941	0.60854	881	0.50598	821	0.40341	761	0.30085	701	0.19829	641	0.09572		
940	0.60683	880	0.50427	820	0.40170	760	0.29914	700	0.19658	640	0.09401		

To **lower** gold of any quality between 24k (999) and just above 14k (586) in order to make 14k gold (585), to one gram of the gold quality given in the left column, add the **total amount** of the **alloying metals** required for the particular gold alloy given in parts in the adjacent right column.

Raising Gold Quality to 14k Gold (585)

Gold	Add Gold (999)	Gold	Add Gold (999)	Gold	Add Gold (999)	Gold	Add Gold (999)	Gold	Add Gold (999)	Gold	Add Gold (999)	Gold	Add Gold (999)
		549	0.08695	509	0.18357	469	0.28019	429	0.37681	389	0.47342	349	0.57004
		548	0.08937	508	0.18598	468	0.28260	428	0.37922	388	0.47584	348	0.57246
		547	0.09178	507	0.18840	467	0.28502	427	0.38164	387	0.47825	347	0.57487
		546	0.09420	506	0.19082	466	0.28743	426	0.38405	386	0.48067	346	0.57729
		545	0.09661	505	0.19323	465	0.28985	425	0.38647	385	0.48309	345	0.57970
584	0.00241	544	0.09903	504	0.19565	464	0.29226	424	0.38888	384	0.48550	344	0.58212
583	0.00483	543	0.10144	503	0.19806	463	0.29468	423	0.39130	383	0.48792	343	0.58453
582	0.00724	542	0.10386	502	0.20048	462	0.29710	422	0.39371	382	0.49033	342	0.58695
581	0.00966	541	0.10627	501	0.20289	461	0.29951	421	0.39613	381	0.49275	341	0.58936
580	0.01207	540	0.10869	500	0.20531	460	0.30193	420	0.39854	380	0.49516	340	0.59178
579	0.01449	539	0.11111	499	0.20772	459	0.30434	419	0.40096	379	0.49758	339	0.59420
578	0.01690	530	0.11352	498	0.21014	458	0.30676	418	0.40338	378	0.49999	338	0.59661
577	0.01932	537	0.11594	497	0.21255	457	0.30917	417	0.40579	377	0.50241	337	0.59903
576	0.02173	536	0.11835	496	0.21497	456	0.31159	416	0.40821	376	0.50482	336	0.60144
575	0.02415	535	0.12077	495	0.21739	455	0.31400	415	0.41062	375	0.50724	335	0.60386
574	0.02656	534	0.12318	494	0.21980	454	0.31642	414	0.41304	374	0.50965	334	0.60627
573	0.02898	533	0.12560	493	0.22222	453	0.31883	413	0.41545	373	0.51207	333	0.60869
572	0.03140	532	0.12801	492	0.22463	452	0.32125	412	0.41787	372	0.51449	332	0.61110
571	0.03381	531	0.13043	491	0.22705	451	0.32367	411	0.44028	371	0.51690	331	0.61352
570	0.03623	530	0.13284	490	0.22946	450	0.32608	410	0.42270	370	0.51932	330	0.61594
569	0.03864	529	0.13526	489	0.23188	449	0.32850	409	0.42511	369	0.52173		
568	0.04106	528	0.13768	488	0.23429	448	0.33091	408	0.42753	368	0.52415		
567	0.04347	527	0.14009	487	0.23671	447	0.33333	407	0.42995	367	0.52656		
566	0.04589	526	0.14251	486	0.23912	446	0.33574	406	0.43236	366	0.52898		
565	0.04830	525	0.14492	485	0.24154	445	0.33816	405	0.43478	365	0.53139		
564	0.05072	524	0.14734	484	0.24396	444	0.34057	404	0.43719	364	0.53381		
563	0.05313	523	0.14975	483	0.24637	443	0.34299	403	0.43961	363	0.53622		
562	0.05555	522	0.15217	482	0.24879	442	0.34540	402	0.44202	362	0.53864		
561	0.05797	521	0.15458	481	0.25120	441	0.34782	401	0.44444	361	0.54106		
560	0.06038	520	0.15700	480	0.25362	440	0.35024	400	0.44685	360	0.54347		
559	0.06280	519	0.15941	479	0.25603	439	0.35265	399	0.44927	359	0.54589		
558	0.06521	518	0.16183	478	0.25845	438	0.35507	398	0.45168	358	0.54830		
557	0.06763	517	0.16425	477	0.26086	437	0.35748	397	0.45410	357	0.55072		
556	0.07004	516	0.16666	476	0.26328	436	0.35990	396	0.45652	356	0.55313		
555	0.07246	515	0.16908	475	0.26569	435	0.36231	395	0.45893	355	0.55555		
554	0.07487	514	0.17149	474	0.26811	434	0.36473	394	0.46135	354	0.55796		
553	0.07729	513	0.17391	473	0.27053	433	0.36714	393	0.46376	353	0.56038		
552	0.07970	512	0.17632	472	0.27294	432	0.36956	392	0.46618	352	0.56279		
551	0.08212	511	0.17874	471	0.27536	431	0.37197	391	0.46859	351	0.56521		
550	0.08454	510	0.18115	470	0.27777	430	0.37439	390	0.47101	350	0.56763		

To **raise** gold of any quality between just less than 14k gold (584) and a little less than 8k (330) in order to make 14k gold (585), to one gram of the gold quality given in the left column, add the **total amount** of pure gold (999) in grams indicated in the adjacent right column.

Lowering Silver Quality to Sterling Silver (925)

Silver	Add Copper g	Silver	Add Copper g	Silver	Add Copper g	Silver	Add Copper g	Silver	Add Copper g	Silver	Add Copper g	Silver	Add Copper g
999	0.08000	989	0.06918	979	0.05837	969	0.04756	959	0.03675	949	0.02594	939	0.01513
998	0.07891	988	0.06810	978	0.05729	968	0.04648	958	0.03567	948	0.02486	938	0.01405
997	0.07783	987	0.06702	977	0.05621	967	0.04540	057	0.03459	947	0.02378	937	0.01297
996	0.07675	986	0.06594	976	0.05513	966	0.04432	956	0.03351	946	0.02270	936	0.01189
995	0.07567	985	0.06486	975	0.05405	965	0.04324	955	0.03243	945	0.02162	935	0.01081
994	0.07459	984	0.06378	074	0.05297	964	0.04216	954	0.03135	944	0.02054	934	0.00972
993	0.07351	983	0.06270	973	0.05189	963	0.04108	953	0.03027	943	0.01945	933	0.00864
992	0.07243	982	0.06162	972	0.05081	962	0.03999	952	0.02918	942	0.01837	932	0.00756
991	0.07135	981	0.06054	971	0.04972	961	0.03891	951	0.02810	941	0.01729	931	0.00648
990	0.07027	980	0.05945	970	0.04864	960	0.03783	950	0.02702	940	0.01621	930	0.00540
												929	0.00432
												928	0.00324
												927	0.00216
												926	0.00108

To **lower** silver of any quality between fine silver (999) and just above sterling silver (926), to one gram of the silver quality given in the left column, add the amount of pure copper indicated in the adjacent right column.

	Standard of fineness: Parts per 1000	Maker's mark	British made standard mark	Assay office mark: London	Date letter: 1975
9 K gold	375		375		A
14 K gold	585		585		A
18 K gold	750		750		A
22 K gold	916.6		916		A
Sterling silver	925				A
Britannia silver	958.4				A
Platinum	950				A

Other assay offices: Birmingham ⚓ Edinburgh 🏰 Sheffield 🌹

3–16 OWE JOHANSSON, Sweden, designer; manufacturer Kultakeskus Oy, Hämeenlinna. Silver ring bearing the five hallmarks required by Finnish stamping law on every silver object weighing more than 5 g. Photo: Kultakeskus Oy

3–17 BRITISH HALLMARKS IN CURRENT USE Courtesy Fred Manshaw Limited, London, and the International Gold Corporation Limited, London

THE HALLMARK:
British quality control of precious metals

A hallmark is an official mark on a *special punch* bearing a figure or numbers, imparted by a single blow onto an object made of precious metal that is offered for sale, in order to show that its quality conforms with legal standards. The hallmark is applied to such objects as a means of safeguarding the purchaser against fraudulent practices. Hallmarks are also used on articles made of non-precious metals for purposes of maker's identification, to indicate place and date of manufacture, and to apply other identifying marks.

Official marks to designate and guarantee the purity of precious metal ingots were in use as far back as 2000 B.C. in Egypt when the method was developed of removing impurities (in the form of other metals including silver) from gold, leaving it at least 95% pure. The Romans and other ancient civilizations also made a practice of stamping ingots with an official stamp, usually the name of the ruler or a high official connected with a mint.

Hallmarking as an official governmental function in modern times began in 13th-century France with the use of townmarks, such as at Montpellier. By royal decree in England in 1300 A.D., all articles made of precious metals had to be brought to Goldsmith's Hall in London, the guild hall of the goldsmiths who were entrusted with the testing of all such articles for purity and compliance with set standards. If the article met those standards, it could be stamped officially with the mark of the Goldsmith's Hall, now generally referred to as the *hallmark*, and it could be sold. Such rigid control served to guarantee the purchaser that any object so marked was without question made of the quality of metal the hallmark declared it to be. No other country can surpass this record of vigilance and consumer protection in the field of precious metal manufacture.

Originally the quality test was made by the use of a *touchstone*, for which reason the mark is sometimes referred to as the *touch mark*, and this method is still in use in many countries. It is not as accurate, however, as the ancient method of assaying by *cupellation* used for gold, and *titration* used for silver today. These methods are described below.

BRITISH HALLMARKS

At first, only the mark of the assay office in London, a leopard's head framed in a shield, was used in England, and it is still one of the several used today. In time other marks were added, so that today, an article in *gold* bears five marks, all within different shield shapes. These, in order of their usual appearance, are: the *maker's mark,* which was made compulsory in the 14th century, and since 1720 consists of the first letters of the maker's first and last names; the *British-made standard mark,* which for gold is a crown; *numbers in a shield indicating the karat quality;* the London (or other) leopard's head *assay office mark,* which indicates the place of assaying (today this can also be the anchor of Birmingham, the castle of Edinburgh, or the rose of Sheffield, all also present-day official assay offices); and finally, the *date letter system* which began in the 15th century when alphabetical letter series in a specific style were assigned for use annually by the London assay office. Date letter punches are officially destroyed at the year's end to avoid possible forgery.

Silver articles bear four marks: the maker's mark; the lion passant, first used in 1544, representing sterling silver quality; the assay office mark; and the date letter. The mark for Britannia silver standard is a seated figure of Britannia, which became compulsory in 1697 and replaces the lion passant, plus the others. *Platinum* uses an orb in a pentagonal shield, plus the others.

In Britain, since 1932, the legally enforced standards for gold are 9, 14, 18, and 22 karat (the term *carat* is used in

Great Britain although in the U.S., carat refers to gemstones only). In 1854 9K gold was introduced and legalized so that jewelers could produce gold-containing jewelry in quantity to satisfy the increasing demand of the growing middle class. It contains $^{375}/_{1000}$ parts gold, or 37.5%, a very low amount, not allowed in most other countries. The majority of mass-made British gold jewelry is of this quality. Sterling silver must contain $^{925}/_{1000}$ parts silver; and Britannia, $^{958.4}/_{1000}$ parts silver, the rest usually being copper.

Since January 1, 1975, platinum has also been hallmarked in Great Britain. An orb with a cross within a pentagonal shape is used.

The responsibility for having items hallmarked by the proper authorities is the manufacturers', and dealers are not permitted to sell work not bearing hallmarks. All such articles in a completed but unpolished condition are brought to the assay office nearest to the place of manufacture where they undergo the necessary testing. Actually, a hallmark does not have to be applied when the article is made, but it must be on the article *before it is offered for sale*. Manufacturers find it convenient to have them stamped before the final polishing so that they are then ready, after polishing, for sale without further handling. Articles weighing less than 10 dwt (pennyweights) of gold, or 5 dwt of silver, are exempt from stamping.

If a British-made silver or gold article fails to meet the standard, it is crushed and returned to the maker, whose reputation is then forever suspect. Imported articles failing to meet the standard must be returned to the maker abroad.

HALLMARKING IN OTHER COUNTRIES

Hallmarking is used in all European countries, though it is not compulsory in all. From Europe it spread to Latin America in colonial times. Many countries follow patterns of control that are similar to, if not based on the British system, but differences do occur.

INTERNATIONAL CONTROL AND MARKING OF PRECIOUS METAL ARTICLES

The latest international conference concerning the control and marking of articles made of precious metals occurred in Vienna on November 15, 1972. The contracting states agreed to the appointment of assay offices in their country which would control and maintain the standards of quality and marking formulated at the conference. The signatory countries agreed to accept each other's quality control stamps. Among other regulations, the convention defines technical requirements and standards of fineness for precious metals. It regulates the use of base metal parts, nonmetallic substances, the use of more than one precious metal in one object, and suggests a design for Common Control Marks for precious metals to be used internationally.

PRECIOUS METAL QUALITY CONTROL IN THE U.S.A.

In the U.S.A. hallmarking started in Baltimore in 1814. Today, regulations concerning the stamping of articles of precious metals are controlled by the 1906 Federal Stamping Law (U.S.C., Title 15, Chapter 8, Sections 294–300). Manufacturers are personally responsible to follow these regulations. Violations are punishable by a fine of $500, imprisonment up to three months, or both at the court's discretion. The regulations concerning the marking of arti-

cles made of gold, silver, and other precious metals are available in booklets called *Commercial Standards* (CS), published by the U. S. Department of Commerce in conjunction with the National Bureau of Standards. These booklets are available on payment of a nominal fee from the Superintendent of Documents, U. S. Government Printing Office, Washington, D.C. 20225.

CS66-38   Marking of Articles Made Wholly or in Part of Platinum
            (Effective: June 20, 1938)
CS67-38   Marking of Articles Made of Karat Gold
            (Effective: November 25, 1938)
CS118-44   Marking of Jewelry and Novelties of Silver
            (Effective: August 15, 1944)
CS51-35   Marking of Articles Made of Silver in Combination with Gold
            (Effective: July 1, 1935)
CS47-34   Marking of Gold Filled and Rolled Gold Plate Articles
            (Effective: January 1, 1934)

The standards of laws are constantly revised, and all responsible jewelers should keep themselves informed by writing to the Government Printing Office at the above address for copies of the latest regulations. Effective 1962, stamped gold and silver articles must also bear the name or trademark of the maker. A new amendment to the Stamping Law was passed on November 1, 1970, strengthening the enforcement of the law. In 1976, a new gold labeling act was passed amending the Federal Stamping Law of 1906. It reduces permissible deviations from stamped karat qualities to less than .003 parts when assayed; and when solder is used on the article, to not more than .007 parts.

APPLYING THE HALLMARK TO JEWELRY

In the U.S.A. the hallmark is applied by the maker to objects of precious metals. In the case of gold, the maker is stating that, when assayed (along with the solder used) the hallmarked articles are no lower in gold content (within the allowed legal amount) than the stamped quality. By standard practice, a *stamping punch* made of case-hardened steel (whose surface is much harder than the core) and a *hammer* are used. Individual maker's mark stamps, which can be a name, initials, logo, or insignia, must be registered, and quality marks can be ordered from stamp manufacturers.

GOLD AND PLATINUM   The size of the figures on the stamp are chosen according to the scale of the work. The conventional figures available range from $^1/_{20}$ in, $^1/_{24}$ in, $^1/_{32}$ in, to $^1/_{45}$ in in height. Special sizes can also be ordered to be made. In the U.S.A., gold is stamped 22K, 18K, 14K, and 10K. In Europe, decimal part numbers indicating parts per thousand are used instead, such as 916 (22K), 750 (18K), 585 (14K), and 375 (9K). Platinum in the U.S.A. is stamped "Plat.," and in Great Britain the special platinum stamp, an orb in a pentagonal shield, is used.

SILVER   In the U.S.A. silver is stamped "sterling" when it is 92.5% silver, and "coin" when it is 90% silver, or by the numerical figure. In Great Britain sterling quality is indicated by the stamp of the lion rampant, and the finer quality of Britannia silver ($^{958.4}/_{1000}$) is indicated by a stamp showing the seated figure of Britannia. In other European countries, lower quality silver stamps are allowed, such as $^{830}/_{1000}$.

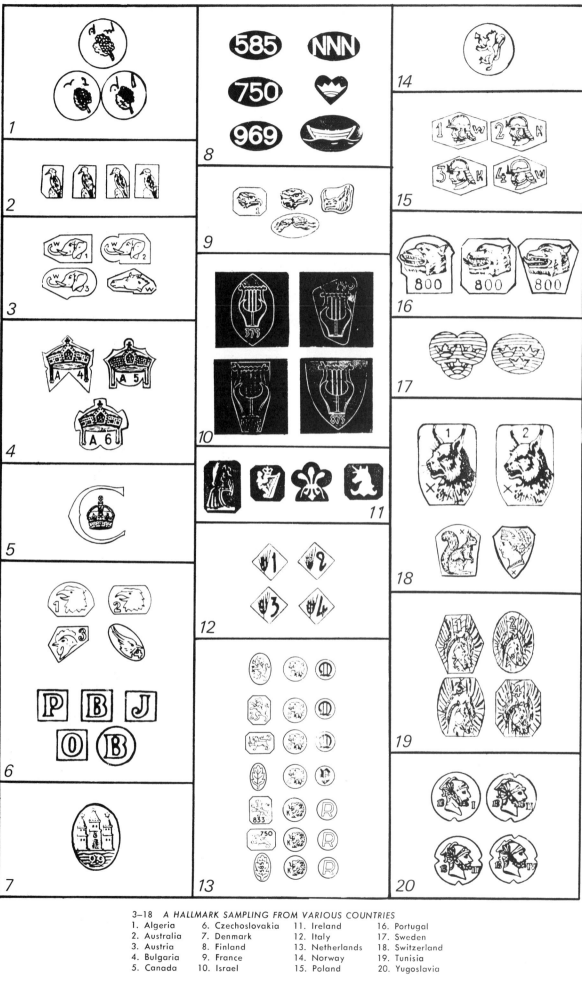

3-18 A HALLMARK SAMPLING FROM VARIOUS COUNTRIES

1. Algeria	6. Czechoslovakia	11. Ireland	16. Portugal
2. Australia	7. Denmark	12. Italy	17. Sweden
3. Austria	8. Finland	13. Netherlands	18. Switzerland
4. Bulgaria	9. France	14. Norway	19. Tunisia
5. Canada	10. Israel	15. Poland	20. Yugoslavia

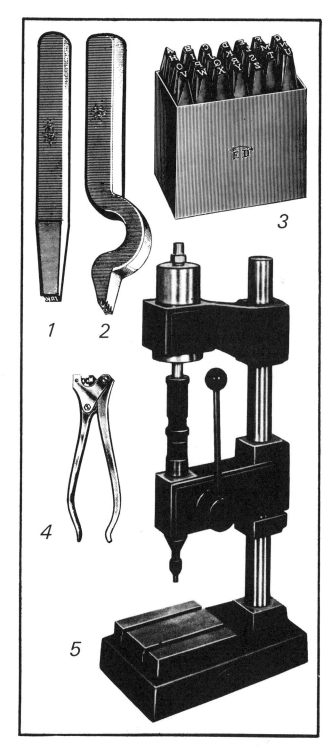

3–19 *QUALITY AND IDENTIFICATION STAMPING TOOLS*
1. *Straight steel, hammer-struck stamp for flat work.* Standard characters are: 10K, 14K, 18K, Sterling, Plat Pall, 10% Irid, 10% Irid Plat. Characters are available in heights of ¹⁄₁₆, ¹⁄₂₀, ¹⁄₂₄, ¹⁄₃₂, and ¹⁄₄₅ in.
2. *Bent ring stamp for stamping the inside of a ring,* whose characters are cut at a radius suitable for the curvature of most ring sizes.
3. *Box of 26 letter stamps* in a hardwood case with cover, available in heights of 0.5, 0.75, 1, 1.5, 2, 3, 4, and 5 mm.
4. *Ring stamp pliers* with three changeable European quality stamp marks: 333, 585, 750. (Karl Fischer)
5. *Hand-operated stamping machine for quality marking.* Stamps make an intaglio or *sunken figure impression,* or a *relief figure impression* in which the figures appear in a sunken rectangle.

OBJECTS OF MORE THAN ONE PRECIOUS METAL   When an object is made of more than one precious metal, if each metal part is *mechanically* joined to the other, for example by rivets, claws, or a bezel, *each part* could be separately stamped with the quality hallmark.

THE STAMPING TECHNIQUE   Stamps can be applied to half-finished work in cases where those places will be difficult to reach after fabrication is completed, or to finished work. Specially bent stamping punches are available for stamping the inside of already formed ring shanks. Stamping should be done on work before any stones are set as the sudden stresses that may be caused by the blow of a hammer on the punch may damage, loosen, or misshape a setting, or the stone may crack. When a work is very delicate in construction, the stamp may be first made on a small plaque of the same quality as the work, which is then soldered to the work. Pieces that are enameled are the most fragile and stamping must be done on them *before* any enameling is done. A hallmark should never be placed straddling a soldered joint.

To stamp a mark, place the object on a flat, smooth, *polished steel plate* or *anvil.* The reverse surface should contact this surface squarely so the object is supported soundly when stamped so that the stamp will not be distorted. Position the *stamping punch* carefully on the work, holding it as vertical as possible, and strike it with *one* sharp blow of a *hammer.* If it is struck twice, there is always the danger that the stamping punch may move slightly causing a blurred shadow image or indistinct marks. Make the mark sufficiently deep so that it will not wear away over time. Different qualities and alloys of metal are of different hardnesses, and the force of the hammer blow must increase with hardness. Gold requires greater force than silver, and platinum even greater force than gold. The beginner is advised to practice making the stamp on a scrap of metal of the same quality as that to be stamped in order to acquire a "feel" for the force needed. The hammer blow on the punch may leave a blemish on the *reverse* side of the place stamped. This is easily removed by rubbing that spot with worn emery cloth.

Other types of stamping tools are also used for quality marking and maker's identification. Among these is a *ring stamp* with two plier-type handles, whose jaws contain interchangeable stamps. The ring is placed in position between the jaws and the handles are squeezed to leave an impression. In the jewelry industry, a hand-operated *bench machine stamp* is used to stamp jewelry.

THE TOUCHSTONE: Approximating quality

The black *touchstone,* also called a *test stone,* is so called because it is used to test the quality of the given precious metals. Assaying by cupellation is a far more accurate method, but the use of the touchstone is much older, and provides a fairly good alternative to the more complex quality-testing methods. Traditionally the touchstone is *basanite* (from the Greek *basanos,* "a test"), also called *Lydian stone.* Basanite is a black, hard, fine-grained, siliceous, extrusive igneous rock. In some places a black flint slate, black basalt, or black ammonites are used.

The touchstone is used in conjunction with a *test needle,* or *test needle sets* available from jewelers' supply houses, each needle quality number stamped and tipped with a piece of a known-quality platinum, gold, or silver alloy,

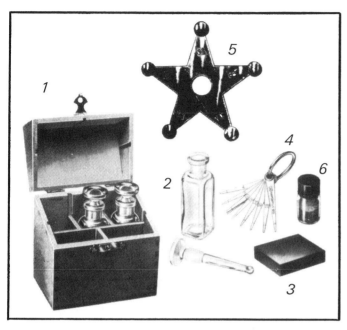

3–20 *PRECIOUS METAL QUALITY TESTING SET*
1. *Wood case containing three ground glass-stoppered acid bottles.*
2. *Glass acid bottle with cover that has attached applicator.*
3. *Black test stone or touchstone.*
4. *Set of gold-testing needles.*
5. *Silver-testing star for testing 400, 500, 700, 800, 900, and 1000 quality silver.*
6. *Schwerter salts for preparing a testing fluid.*

and *acid* stored in a bottle with a ground glass stopper and an attached glass rod that hangs into the acid.

The article being tested is filed in an inconspicuous place in order to expose the true base metal (the object may only be plated). This exposed area is rubbed on the stone with about six forward and backward strokes to form a deposit visible in one place, seen as a one-inch-long streak. Next to this, the test needle, whose tip is of a chosen, known quality of precious metal believed to be close to the quality of the object being tested, is rubbed in the same way, but some space is allowed between this and the first streak. Experts can detect sensation differences—smoothness or roughness, greasiness or dryness—between the standard and the sample during rubbing. They can also judge similarities or differences in the composition by the comparison of the colors of the streaks.

ACIDS USED FOR TESTING PRECIOUS METALS

The following acids can be used to test metal sample streaks made on a touchstone.

GOLD ABOVE 18K
Aqua regia, which in Latin means "royal water" is so called because this *combination* of corrosive acids will dissolve gold and platinum by action of the liberated chlorine, which no acid *alone* will do. This mixture should half-fill a glass bottle with a ground glass stopper having an attached spreader rod used for its application to the test stone (or directly to the sample metal being tested). Once mixed, it will last about three weeks. The usual formula for *aqua regia* is:

Hydrochloric acid:	3 parts	by volume
Nitric acid:	3 parts	by volume

GOLD 18–14K

Nitric acid	49 parts	by volume
Hydrochloric acid	1 part	by volume
Distilled water	12.5 parts	by volume

GOLD 14K AND BELOW
Nitric acid alone

SILVER

Nitric acid	3 parts	by volume
Hydrochloric acid	1 part	by volume

Good silver produces a cheesy-looking foam precipitate consisting of silver chloride. If much copper is present, the acid will turn greenish.

PLATINUM

Hydrochloric acid	9 parts	by volume
Nitric acid	2 parts	by volume

TESTING PROCEDURE

There are many other chemical reaction tests for all metals, but these described are the simplest.

With the glass stopper rod or spreader, or a medicine dropper, place one large drop of the test acid *simultaneously* on both streaks on the touchstone, so that its action can be observed on both. The glass rod should not touch the metal or some of it might be returned to the acid container and thereafter hinder its accuracy. The stopper should not be forced into the bottle too tightly but some air should be allowed to enter to accommodate changes that occur in the acid with time and temperature changes. This is why the container should be only half full of acid.

The acid drop, on touching the surface, comes off the rod and spreads itself—if there is no grease present on the stone—without any assistance. The reaction of the two streaks must now be watched. Low-quality alloys will disappear more quickly when in contact with the acid than high-quality ones. If the article streak is attacked more quickly than the test needle streak, it is of a quality lower than that of the needle. The process is therefore repeated with a lower-karat gold, for instance, until the same reaction is observed in the two streaks.

The metals are not absorbed by the stone. After each use, the touchstone should be immediately cleaned of all streaks to avoid future confusion, by applying *aqua regia,* followed by washing under running water. Acids should not be allowed to dry on the stone as their residue will interfere with the accuracy of future tests. The stone, needles, and glass rod should be grease- and dust-free, and for this reason are stored in a clean, closed box, usually of wood, in which they are sold.

STANNOUS CHLORIDE SOLUTION: Visual testing by color reaction

It is also possible to test the quality of the metal of an object to determine whether it is made of precious metals, by a visual estimate judging of its chemical reaction to acids. In preparation for such a test, file or scrape away a small area on the object, or make a groove in it.

Hydrochloric acid	½ oz
Distilled water	1½ oz
Stannous chloride	½ oz

Dissolve the stannous chloride in the hydrochloric acid and water, then add ½ oz of pure tin, which will slowly dissolve; what remains undissolved will act as a source of tin replenishment. Once the tin is completely dissolved, a new mixture must be made. In any case, this mixture will not last longer than a few days.

Place a large drop of the stannous chloride solution on the scraped or grooved place, and allow it to act. If the result appears as a rich yellow color, platinum or iridium are present. If dark purple, gold is present. Nitric acid is applied first when testing 14K gold, followed by a drop of the stannous chloride solution. If the gold is of 14K quality, it will produce an amber yellow color. When testing for silver, use the silver touchstone test solution first, followed by a drop of stannous chloride. If silver of high quality is present it will result in a thick, creamy white color. If there is copper present, the color will appear greenish, the green deepening as the percentage of copper increases.

CUPELLATION: A method of purifying and assaying precious metals

The process of cupellation is the result of the earliest production of lead and silver, often found together in native ores from which they had to be separated. The process is believed to have been invented about 2500 B.C. in eastern Asia Minor and spread to the rest of the civilized world. Cupellation is still used for this purpose, but it is also one of several methods used today to assay the precise proportion of gold, silver, platinum, and palladium in a given alloy. This is done by following a strict routine, in which the precious metals are separated from any impurities they may contain in the form of base metals, and the weight loss is then calculated. The metal assayed can be in the form of a virgin or scrap metal ingot; or it can be an article made of precious metals whose quality must be tested to see if it contains the required degree of purity to make it eligible for legal hallmark stamping, or to ascertain if the quality of an imported article is suitable for stamping.

The exact total weight of an object is first taken and recorded. A sample of the metal is then scraped from the mass—in the case of an ingot from 12–15.4 grains (1 gram); and in the case of a fabricated article, a smaller amount, taken from a suitably concealed recess so that the article is not visibly defaced. If jewelry being tested is made of several moving parts, samples are taken from each of them as well as of the solder used, since all of these together must pass the quality standard. The total amount of such scrapings is weighed and recorded. If this is an appreciable amount, as when testing mass-produced jewelry, an equivalent will later be returned to the manufacturer.

These scrapings or fragments of gold or silver alloy are then wrapped in a specific quantity of pure lead foil, the ratio between its weight and that of the precious metals being important in order to achieve the desired result. If the alloy is estimated to contain less silver than approximately two and a half times the gold weight, an appropriate amount of silver is added to make up this proportion, a procedure called *inquartation*. This proportion must be established because richer gold alloys when later placed in nitric acid will not otherwise part properly, and the resulting gold will not be pure.

All these are placed in a *cupel,* a small, shallow cup, in ancient times made of a porous, refractory clay, and today

made of bone ash (lime phosphate), or other material such as the burned cores of ox horns. The ash is combined with sufficient water to form a paste which is forced into a circular mold made of cast steel where it is allowed to solidify and partially dry. The cupel is freed by striking the mold, and it then dries completely in air. The result is a highly refractory and porous cupel, whence the term *cupellation.*

The cupel with its metal contents is placed in a *muffle furnace* which is then heated to 1000° C (1832° F). In this heat it is subjected to an air blast that causes the lead to rapidly oxidize to a litharge (lead oxide), melt, and flow around the bottom of the cupel and become absorbed into it. Lead is used because it has the property that when heated and melted in contact with base metals such as copper and tin—the two main non-precious metals usual in such alloys—it causes them quickly to become oxidized, melt, spread, and penetrate the cupel along with the lead oxide. If the amount of lead is correct, its oxide forms a glassy coat on the cupel bottom that allows these other base metals to pass through, but resists the penetration of the gold, silver, or other precious metals. Because precious metals in a pure form have a lower affinity for oxygen than base metals, they resist oxidation and remain on the cupel surface. None of the gold is lost by evaporation under the right temperature, and very little of the silver.

When cupellating silver, it is wrapped with a twist of paper which burns and releases hydrogen which acts as a reducing agent for the lead oxide, and allows the precious metals remaining in the alloy to combine.

When molten, the liquefied remaining precious metal takes on a hemispherical button shape which upon cooling and solidifying retains a shining surface, and is easily separated from the cupel, exposing a rough bottom. If the shape is flat and the surface dull in appearance, this indicates that too much heat was used, and some of the precious metals were lost. If the temperature is too low, the pellet surface and color will be uneven, and some of the lead will remain and be seen as yellow lead oxide scales at the cupel bottom, which cause the button to adhere to the cupel.

The precious metal button is then weighed, flattened, rolled thin, and placed in a solution of boiling nitric acid which dissolves its silver content, and leaves only the pure gold behind as a black powder which is collected by filtration, and weighed. The result is compared with the weight of the original sample taken from the ingot or object, which enables the calculation of an accurate ratio of the amount of gold to the alloying metal it originally contained. In the case of an object, if this result indicates conformity with the standard, it can then be stamped with the appropriate hallmark. An ingot that has an acceptable result can then be processed further into sheet, wire, and tubing of specific quality.

The silver can be recovered from the nitric acid as described below. (See Precipitation and Recovery of Silver from Spent Acid Solutions.)

TITRATION FOR SILVER CONTENT

Titration is a process of determining the concentration of a substance in a solution (its strength) by testing its reaction with another, known substance introduced in a specific amount to the solution. In the case of silver, the sample taken from the article is dissolved in nitric acid and as an indicator, iron nitrate is added. A specific, controlled volume of ammonium thiocynate is titrated with this sample and forms an end point result: a silver salt (silver thiocynate) that sinks to the bottom of the container. Because a known quantity of ammonium thiocynate will combine with a specific quantity of silver, the results can be compared with a standard sample which will indicate the presence of the amount of silver for the amount of ammonium thiocynate added. The exact silver percentage can then be calculated.

RECOVERY AND REFINEMENT OF PRECIOUS METAL

All professional jewelers realize that in work with precious metals, a certain amount of metal is wasted or lost during fabrication and finishing processes. Waste precious metals in all forms have appreciable value, and a careful jeweler can recover them to a great extent as *secondary metal,* or collect them and send them to a *secondary metal refiner.* In any case, strict collection methods should be followed as a regular work habit.

HIGH GRADE SCRAP

Visible, *solid waste metal,* called *fabrication scrap,* results from fabrication processes such as sawing, stamping, and casting, and is considered *high grade scrap* from which a high percentage is recoverable. To reduce the problems involved in small-scale reclaiming such as might be carried out in a jeweler's workshop, certain practices should be followed. Fabrication scrap should be completely cleaned of all foreign matter *before* being stored in clearly labeled, clean, closed boxes or closed glass jars. Metal type of known qualities such as 14K or 18K gold, or sterling silver, must be kept separately. Also includable in this category is *known quality* unwanted or broken jewelry that only has scrap value; unwanted or broken precious metal objects; and dental scrap if of one metal. All these, sorted as to quality, can be combined with fabrication scrap and melted down to form an ingot.

Lemel, limail, or *limaille* from the French *limer,* "to file," is metal dust that results from the friction in filing and sawing. It can easily be collected if the workbench is fitted with a *sheepskin leather apron,* called a *basle,* used smooth side up. This is fixed at the forward edge beneath the workbench top, below the bench pin where filing and sawing take place. If the workbench has a concave, curved front, the free apron side toward the jeweler can be hooked at the nearest curved bench sides, forming a shallow, flexible catchall. Alternately, the apron can simply be drawn over the lap of the worker when in use, or it can be fixed to the waist by attached cords that pass through grommets in the apron corners. When not in use, the apron can be brought forward and hooked to the bench, forming a hanging sack, without removing any lemel that accumulates until the end of the working period.

If the workbench is the rectangular type, it should have a retractable dust-gathering *metal tray* or *shallow drawer* below the bench pin. This is pulled out to catch falling lemel, when sawing or filing start at the bench, and returned to place when work stops. Metal dust of a single metal and quality allowed to fall into this tray can be brushed or tapped together and collected at intervals, as

its accumulation warrants. A *worktable brush* is used to sweep lemel on workbench tops and bench pins directly into the apron or tray. Some European jewelers use a real *rabbit's foot* (available from a butcher) as a brush because metal dust will not cling to the hair or jump around when brushed with it.

Aprons or trays should be used *only* when working with platinum, gold, silver, or other precious metals, and the dust of each metal must be collected separately. *Non-ferrous* and *ferrous metals* should not be allowed to enter and contaminate the collection. For this reason, it is good practice to use separate *files* for each metal. In actual practice, however, even though care may be taken to avoid contamination, a certain amount of iron or steel does in fact enter the collection. Visible broken sawblade parts; steel wool fragments; particles in sizes too fine to be seen, such as rust and natural-wear particles from files, hammers, anvils, burs, and other tools; all of these may possibly become contaminants. *Organic matter* such as asbestos, asphaltum, cement, flux, glue, grease, gum, investment plaster, lacquer, paint, plastic, pumice, sand, shellac, and wax are other possible contaminants.

Hand dust, another source of precious metal filings, consists of small metal particles that cling to the jeweler's hands after sawing or filing. To gather this, in European workshops one often finds a wall-attached *hand rinser* which is a small, manually refillable water tank with a bottom plunger. By simply pushing the plunger upward with the hand, one breaks the seal maintained by water pressure, and sufficient water is released from the tank bottom to fall on the hands held below. Water and solid matter drain into a *settling tank* or *barrel* placed just below the hand rinser. An accumulation of sludge forms at the tank bottom, and periodically the upper supranascent water is siphoned off. When sufficient sludge has accumulated, it is spread out in a *shallow tray* to dry after the liquid has been drained. The metal can then be reclaimed.

Refiners normally accept a minimum of twenty-five ounces of high grade scrap for refining. It does not pay for them to process smaller amounts. The result is assayed and payment made according to established rates, or a credit is recorded to an account against future precious metal purchases. When lesser amounts are involved, the jeweler can refine the collection as described below. Considering the high cost of precious metals, this is a worthwhile procedure.

LOW GRADE SCRAP

Although this consists of sources normally containing 2–5% in volume of precious metal, it is nevertheless worth collecting.

Sweeps are collections taken mainly from the floors of a workshop, or from other surfaces where metal particles can collect. Over a period of time, a surprising amount of lemel can be collected from such sources. Since medieval times, it has been common practice in France for goldsmith and silversmith workshop floors to be covered with an openwork lattice or grille, called *claies,* made in sections of approximately 1 m × 50 cm (40 in × 20 in). (For an illustration of claies, see *The Workshop.*) Ready-made claies are available from French suppliers. The grille openings allow fallen filings to pass through and gather on the floor below. At the same time, the soles of jewelers' shoes are automatically scraped when they walk around the bench area. In large workshops, the claies are lifted once or twice a year (a longer period in small workshops), and the accumulation on the floor is swept and gathered. After several years of use, the claies themselves are burned to recover embedded precious metal.

Mechanical sweeps are dust particles collected in a workshop by a *vacuum exhaust dust collector* with a filter, connected to grinding and polishing equipment. Also in this category are dust, chips, and particles collected with a *manual vacuum machine* from floors, as well as on and around mechanical equipment such as drill presses, grinders, lathes, milling machines, and mechanical engravers used by jewelers.

Polishing cloths, polishing wheels, and *brushes,* are other sources for recoverable precious metals, and should not be thrown away when no longer usable.

Secondary refiners process low grade scrap if the amount is relatively large. It is slowly burned in a closed furnace. The ashes are combined with flux and melted. The result is poured into an ingot mold where the precious metal settles while the slag rises above it and can be separated from the metal.

Metals in solution, such as in plating solutions or acid baths, can be recovered by methods described below involving precipitation or electrolysis. Refiners also use other sources for recoverable precious metal such as film, electronic equipment, and precious metal plated or rolled non-precious metals, but these do not come within the jeweler's scope.

3–21 KULTASEPÄNLIIKE OSSIAN HOPEA, Porvoo, Finland. Traditional brass water container with a lower stopper rod, used to recover precious metal filings clinging to the goldsmith's hands. The rod is pressed upward, water is released and falls, along with any filings, into the barrel below. The collection is emptied every few years, and a surprising amount of precious metal is recovered. *Photo: Nousiainen*

RECOVERY PROCEDURES FROM LEMEL AND SWEEPS

When jewelers themselves do their own recovery, to remove impurities from lemel and sweeps, a certain procedure should be followed to improve the purity of the result.

Iron and *steel* are removed by spreading the collection on a large piece of smooth-surfaced paper, removing and separating large pieces of precious metal scrap, and passing over the rest in a systematic manner with a powerful *hand magnet* to which steel and iron matter will cling.

These are removed from the magnet by lightly tapping its lower part. Repeat the process a few times to be sure all these metals are removed.

Soluble organic matter is removed by boiling the remainder and the large scrap for 2–5 minutes in a container holding 2 pints of water and 2 ounces of sodium hydroxide (NaOH)—caustic soda—a strong alkali, followed by a rinse under running warm water. The results are then spread out on paper to dry. During subsequent melting, solid organic matter that has not been burned away will rise to the surface and can be skimmed off with a graphite *rod* at that time.

Inflammable material is removed by spreading the dried collection out in a clean, plain iron pan or an iron ladle and heating it with a torch flame until any smoking or fuming stops, without melting the metal.

Base metals are eliminated by placing the collection in a flat Pyrex dish containing enough hydrochloric acid to cover the metal, and allowing this to stand overnight to digest all non-precious metals. The container should be placed under an exhaust hood or in the open air. The next day add a solution of half hydrochloric acid and half water and periodically stir with a glass rod during one hour. Silver is insoluble in hydrochloric acid and forms a sludge. It is gathered into a beaker, allowed to settle, and warm water is slowly run into the beaker for a few minutes and allowed to overflow to eliminate the acid and along with it, the base metals in solution. The remaining water is poured off, and the contents dried.

If the collection consists of only silver or only gold the remainder can be melted and poured into an ingot mold, or if wished, further refined by cupellation which will leave behind a button of pure precious metal.

If the result contains both gold and silver these can be separated by methods described under cupellation and titration, or by the following procedure. Measure an amount of soda ash (calcium carbonate in white powder or lumps) equal to one fifth of the total weight of the mass, for use as a flux. Add this to the cooled metal in a clay crucible. Apply a torch flame and melt the contents. The metal sinks to the bottom and the flux appears as a fluid at the top. While stirring, pour off the metal into *cold* water so that it forms small grains. Place these in a mixture of half nitric acid and half water with a volume of about four times that of the metal. Nitric acid digests the silver content into solution, but does not act on any gold present, which remains in granules and is recovered by filtering the decanted liquid. Because the solution still contains the silver, it is saved for processing for silver recovery. After the gold particles are well rinsed, place them in a crucible along with some borax flux and melt them with a torch flame to form a pure gold pellet. The silver is recovered from the acid solution by first diluting it with water to about six times its bulk, and then following the procedure described below.

PRECIPITATION AND RECOVERY OF SILVER FROM SPENT ACID SOLUTIONS

The process of *precipitation* is used to purify certain chemicals, and to recover or extract metals from a *saturated, spent* solution—one in which the liquid cannot take up any more of a substance. An example of such a condition is a spent or saturated pickling solution that has been used to quench silver, to remove firescale, to bright-dip, or to etch. With the price of precious metals today reaching unprecedented heights, the small trouble of processing such acids for the recovery of the precious metals they contain is worthwhile.

First filter the solution to remove insoluble impurities. To reclaim the silver from a saturated nitric acid or sulphuric acid pickle, or one containing both, a chemical change must take place. The acid (nitric in this example, but the same can be done with a sulphuric acid solution), contains ions of silver as $AgNO_3$ and, if alloys containing copper have been placed in it, presumably copper ions in the form of $Cu(NO_3)_2$. To cause the silver to precipitate from the solution, slowly sprinkle finely ground table salt (NaCl) over the surface of the acid solution. (An alternate method is to add a boiling, concentrated solution of salt and water.) Continue to add salt until all cloudiness disappears from the solution. Stir the solution occasionally and allow it to cool if hot.

When the salt is added, the chloride it contains combines with the silver as the silver ions come into contact with the chloride ions. The result is the formation of a compound called artificial silver chloride (AgCl) which will appear as a white, curdlike substance precipitated in the bottom of the container. The silver chloride is stable and will not return to the solution or dissolve in water. The copper ions, however, remain in the solution. Pour off the liquid and flush it away with running water, leaving behind only the sedimentary silver chloride. Rinse this twice with warm water to remove any traces of acid. Dry the result by simple evaporation or with the help of a heat lamp. (Silver chloride is light sensitive and if exposed to light for too long it first turns violet, then brown, but this will not affect the result.) Scrape up the now dry, powdery, white silver chloride and place it in a crucible. Add some metallic silver scrap, and borax flux, and melt the contents with a torch flame. The heat reduces the silver chloride to a pellet of pure, solid silver.

PURCHASING PRECIOUS METALS

In the *U.S.A.*, any individual can purchase the precious metals platinum, gold, and silver from established refiners, who usually set a minimum amount for any single item sold; or through jewelers' supply houses, which normally will sell any amount without imposing a minimum purchase. In *Great Britain,* gold can be purchased from refiners by individuals who possess a license issued by the Bank of England. Application forms are supplied by the refiner, in which the individual states his/her qualifications. It must then be signed by the individual's bank, and sent for approval to the Bank of England. The current price of precious metals is usually published daily in the financial section of most large newspapers, or a bank can be consulted.

Refiners manufacture these metals in a variety of forms and conditions. To avoid confusion and delay, and get exactly what one wishes, when purchasing through the mails, *all specifications* must be stated.

Sheet: State desired alloy, dimensions including length and width, thickness (B.&S. gauge), and working condition (annealed, cold rolled, hardened).

Wire: State desired alloy, dimensions including thickness (B.&S. gauge), shape of cross section, condition (annealed, hard drawn), and if necessary, total weight instead of length.

Tube: State desired alloy, dimensions including outside diameter and wall thickness, inside diameter if this is important, and length or weight.

See the relevant tables in Standard Weights, Measures, and Tables, Chapter 18, for information on the sizes that are available and for data helpful in making calculations. Other forms in which the precious metals, as well as other metals, can be purchased are: ingots, grain, foil, powder, and special drawn and extruded forms. Consult suppliers' catalogs.

NONFERROUS METALS USED IN JEWELRY MAKING

COPPER

Symbol and atomic number: Cu 29
Atomic weight: 63.54
Specific gravity: 8.94
Melting point: 1981.4° F (1083° C)
Boiling point: 4703° F (2595° C)
Hardness, Mohs' scale: 3.0

Copper is believed to have been the first metal used by man, as long ago as 13,000 B.C. By 6000 B.C. the Egyptians were making copper weapons by smelting, casting, and cold working copper. The word *copper* is derived from the Roman source of copper which was the island of Cyprus, in Greek, *Kypros,* in Latin, *Cyprium,* corrupted to the metal name *cuprum,* from which comes the symbol *Cu.*

Today copper is the most widely used of all the nonfer-

rous metals in industry, and it is used extensively in the arts, both in a pure and alloyed state. When pure, copper is a warm, pinkish red color. It is ductile and malleable, as well as being the best metal conductor of heat and electricity. It is easily worked in all working processes, becomes work hardened, but can be easily restored to softness by annealing. Joining fabrication can be done by hard and soft solders, provided the surfaces to be joined are clean and fluxed.

COPPER ALLOYS

Copper and its alloys are the only metals (except for gold) that are not white or gray. A wide color range is possible with copper, from the pink red of pure copper, the gold shades of gilding metal (95% copper), commercial bronze (90%), red brass (85%), and other brasses (80%) which become increasingly more yellow until the yellow brass color characteristic of 70% brasses is reached. At about 60%, the color reverses and becomes more reddish yellow, as in Muntz metal and others, such that their color more closely resembles 85% brass. When alloyed with nickel the color ranges from light pink to blue white. Patinas in great variety are possible on copper alloys. (See Metal Coloring, Chapter 17.)

A great many alloys exist in which copper is the main component. When classified according to working qualities, copper alloys can be divided into two main groups: *wrought alloys* and *casting alloys*. Each of these can be used for the other purpose, but are best for the function for which they are designed.

Another major copper alloy classification is into *bronze* and *brass*. Though in some cases these names are used loosely, *bronze* alloys contain *tin* (Sn), and *brass* alloys contain *zinc* (Zn).

BRONZE

True bronze alloys contain from 5–15% tin. Any alloy having less than 3% tin is considered to be an accidental and not a purposeful bronze, though it is believed that such alloys preceded and spurred the development of true bronzes. Bronze alloys are much harder than pure copper and have twice its tensile strength, but like copper they become work hardened. Some bronze alloys are also sonorous, therefore are used for casting bells, and are called bell metal (bell metal, standard alloy: 78–80 Cu - 22–20 Sn). The ease with which bronze can be cast in closed molds to a great extent accounts for the development of the art of casting. Bronze itself can be used as a mold for stamping and for the casting of metals with lower melting temperatures. In such cases, the thickness of the mold should be greater than the object cast in it as this allows the heat of the molten metal to be readily conducted away from its inner surface so that the casting does not adhere to it.

3-22 PENTTI SARPANEVA, Finland, designer; manufacturer Turun Hopea, Turku. "Puzzle." Bronze rubber mold wax injection cast bracelet in 13 interkeyed parts. Length 18 cm. Photo: Jorma Laine

WROUGHT BRONZE ALLOYS

Commercial bronze: 90 Cu - 10 Zn
  Liquidus temperature: 1910° F (1045° C)
  Solidus temperature: 1870° F (1020° C)
  Hot working temperature: 1400–1600° F (750–875° C)
  Annealing temperature: 800–1450° F (425–800° C)
  Melting and casting temperature: 2237–2282° F
    (1225–1250° C)

This alloy is used for costume jewelry, vitreous enameling, etching, screen cloth, etc. It is suited to all fabrication processes, and can be joined by all grades of hard and soft solder.

Aluminum bronze: 96 Cu - 5 Al
  Liquidus temperature: 1940° F (1060° C)
  Solidus temperature: 1920° F (1050° C)
  Hot working temperature: 1500–1600° F (815–870° C)
  Annealing temperature: 800–1400° F (425–750° C)

This yellow alloy is suited to both hot and cold working, but especially to cold working. It is not suited to severe drawing or stamping, and is difficult to machine. When fabrication methods are employed, silver solders are used with a special flux. Soft soldering is not applicable to aluminum bronzes. All types of flames are used. In powder form it is used as a gold pigment.

Jewelry bronze: 87.5 Cu - 12.5 Zn
  Melting point: 1895° F (1035° C)
  Annealing temperature: 800–1400° F (425–750° C)

Used for jewelry, emblems, as a base for gold plate, and for etched articles. It can be formed by bending, forging, drawing, stamping, spinning, and etching, and has good forming qualities.

CASTING BRONZE ALLOYS

80 Cu - 10 Sn - 10 Pb
Color: Bronze

High-leaded tin bronze. Cast in an oxidizing atmosphere.

78 Cu - 7 Sn - 15 Pb
Color: Gray bronze

High-leaded tin bronze. Pour at the lowest possible temperature in an oxidizing atmosphere.

70 Cu - 5 Sn - 25 Pb
Color: Dull bronze

High-leaded tin bronze. Prepare with the same precautions as above.

85 Cu - 5 Sn - 5 Pb - 5 Zn
Color: Reddish bronze

Has good machining properties.

59 Cu - 0.75 Pb - 37 Zn - 1.25 Fe - 0.75 Al - 0.5 Mn
Color: Yellow

Leaded manganese bronze, free machining.

BRASS

Brasses, as mentioned, are essentially alloys of copper and zinc. If the zinc content is up to 36%, the result is called an *alpha* brass which has good cold working properties. Brasses containing between 36–54% zinc are known as *alpha beta* brasses; and those richer than 45% are called *beta* brasses. The latter two have good hot working qualities. Brass is harder and stronger than copper, is generally malleable and ductile, though the degree varies with particular alloys.

WROUGHT BRASS ALLOYS SUITED TO JEWELRY MAKING

Gilding metal: 95 Cu - 5 Zn
  Liquidus temperature: 1950° F (1065° C)
  Solidus temperature: 1920° F (1050° C)
  Hot working temperature: 1400–1600° F (750–875° C)
  Annealing temperature: 800–1450° F (425–800° C)
  Casting temperature range: 2327–2372° F (1275–1300° C)

Used as a base for jewelry then gold plated, medals, tokens, emblems, plaques, coinage, vitreous enamels and etched articles. This alloy can also be cast. When preparing the alloy, the zinc is added just before pouring, and the melt is under charcoal. The right pouring temperature is indicated by *zinc shine* on the melt. Higher temperatures are avoided as they will cause *zinc boiling*. The melt should be poured into an oil-dressed mold. This alloy can be worked by forming, bending, drawing, punching, piercing, shearing, spinning, stamping, blanking, and coining. It has excellent cold working and good hot working properties. It can be joined in fabrication with all grades of silver and soft solder when flux is employed, and soldering can be done with all kinds of flames.

Red brass: 85 Cu - 15 Zn
    Liquidus temperature: 1880° F (1026° C)
    Solidus temperature: 1810° F (987° C)
    Hot working temperature: 1450–1650° F (787–898° C)
    Melting and casting range: 2192–2237° F (1200–1225° C)
    Annealing temperature: 880–1350° F (426–732° C)

Used for costume jewelry, badges, etching, and tubing. Zinc is added to the melt just before casting, with the same precautions as above. Suited to all methods of working. Has excellent cold working properties and good hot working properties.

Yellow brass: 65 Cu - 35 Zn
    Liquidus temperature: 1710° F (932° C)
    Solidus temperature: 1660° F (904° C)
    Annealing temperature range: 1300–1500° F (704–815° C)

Can be worked by all methods, especially drawing, stamping, and spinning. Can be reduced 90% between anneals.

Forging brass: 60 Cu - 38 Zn - 2 Pb
    Liquidus temperature: 1640° F (893° C)
    Solidus temperature: 1620° F (882° C)
    Hot working temperature: 1200–1500° F (648–815° C)
    Annealing temperature: 800–1100° F (426–593° C)

A special golden-hued alloy designed for all forms of forging and pressing. It can be purchased extruded in rods, and in other forms.

Free cutting brass: 61.5 Cu - 35.5 Zn - 3 Pb
    Liquidus temperature: 1650° F (898° C)
    Solidus temperature: 1630° F (887° C)

Also called free turning brass because it is easily cut on a lathe. (See The Lathe and Machined Jewelry, Chapter 10.) Joining with hard solder is good, and with soft solder, excellent.

Muntz metal: 60 Cu - 40 Zn
    Liquidus temperature: 1660° F (904° C)
    Solidus temperature: 1650° F (898° C)
    Hot working range: 1150–1450° F (426–593° C)

This is the strongest brass alloy with excellent hot forging properties, but with poor cold drawing and forming properties as it is subject to cracking when worked unevenly.

OTHER COPPER ALLOYS USED IN JEWELRY MAKING

Alpaca: 65 Cu - 19 Zn - 14 Ni - 2 Ag
    Used for jewelry, flatware, and holloware, usually heavily plated with silver.
Dutch metal: 80 Cu - 20 Zn
    Yellow and very ductile.
Jeweler's metal: 86 Cu - 12 Zn - 2 Sn
    A type of red brass.
Mosaic gold: 65.5 Cu - 34.5 Zn
    A name derived from alchemy. Used to imitate a gold alloy. The alloy is also used to make ornaments called ormolu that are mercury gilded and used to decorate furniture.
Niello: (See Chapter 9.)
Pinchbeck: 88–83 Cu - 12–17 Zn
    An alloy invented by Christopher Pinchbeck (1670–1732), a London watchmaker, and widely used in Victorian jewelry to imitate the color of gold in cheap jewelry.
Shakudo: (See Chapter 15.)
Speculum: 90 Cu - 9 Sb - 1 Zn; or 66 Cu - 33 Sb - 1 Zn
    Used to make a metal mirror. Highly reflective and corrosion resistant when polished.
Tombac: 75 Cu - 23 Zn - 2 Sn
    A brass alloy used as a base for gilding.

NICKEL

    Symbol and atomic number: Ni 28
    Atomic weight: 58.71
    Specific gravity: 8.9
    Melting point: 2647° F (1453° C)
    Boiling point: 4950° F (2730° C)
    Hardness, Mohs' scale: 3.5

Nickel was first discovered when man seeking flints found heavy metallic meteors that contained from 5–15% nickel. Cronstedt, the Swedish minerologist (1722–1765) recognized and isolated it as a distinct elemental metal in 1751. Long before the Christian era, the Chinese were smelting and reducing nickel ores from the province of Yunan, which they called *paktong*, "white copper." Paktong was actually an alloy of nickel: 30 Ni - 45 Cu - 24 Zn - 1 Fe, and resembles German silver. They used this alloy for household utensils and coinage.

Nickel is a hard, malleable, ductile, nearly silver white metal, capable of high polish, highly resistant to oxidation, and attracted to magnets. Nickel combines readily with other metals, and finds greatest use in alloys in percentages from 80% to as little as 0.5%. It is also used as a plating on other metals. The old "nickel" five-cent coin in the U.S.A. was 75 Cu - 25 Ni.

3-23 RICHARD MAFONG, U.S.A. Pin of silver, gold, nickel, bronze, and brass, with moonstone. Multimetal repoussé work and inlay fabricated in a unit. Height 5 in; width 3¼ in; depth ½ in. Photo: Foster Thompson

NICKEL ALLOYS

Nickel silver: 65 Cu - 18 Ni - 17 Zn
  Liquidus temperature: 2030° F (1110° C)
  Solidus temperature: 1960° F (1071° C)
  Annealing temperature: 1100–1500° F (593–815° C)

This is one of several alloys called nickel silver, and is termed Alloy A. It has a pleasant silvery blue white color, and is the most popular of the wrought nickel silver alloys. It is used for costume jewelry and as a base for silver plate. Available in sheet, strip, rod, and wire. It is suited to all forming and working methods, has excellent cold working properties, and can be joined with hard silver solder, and soft solder, or by welding.

German silver: 65 Cu - 23 Zn - 12 Ni
  Liquidus temperature: 1900° F (1037° C)
  Solidus temperature: 1830° F (998° C)
  Annealing temperature: 1100–1500° F (593–815° C)

This yellow white alloy is used in jewelry, for decorative purposes, and for optical frames. It is highly corrosion resistant to organic products, water, and atmosphere. It has excellent cold working properties, can be fabricated by all processes, joined by hard and soft solders, but is difficult to machine.

OTHER NICKEL ALLOYS

Magnet alloy: 63 Fe - 20 Ni - 12 Al - 5 Co
Monel: 67 Ni - 28 Cu - 5 Fe
Nichrome: 80 Ni - 20 Cr

Used for electric elements in kilns and furnaces as it is high in electrical resistance.

TIN

  Symbol and atomic number: Sn 50
  Atomic weight: 118.70
  Specific gravity: 7.29
  Melting point: 449.4° F (231.9° C)
  Boiling point: 4120° F (2270° C)
  Hardness, Mohs' scale: 1.8

The main source of tin is cassiterite, which when pure contains 78.6% tin. Pure tin has the faintly bluish white color and luster of silver. When pure it retains its natural brightness because of its high corrosion resistance, even in contact with moisture. For this reason it was and is still used in foil form to back translucent stones to increase their brilliance. It is malleable at ordinary temperatures, but brittle when heated. It has excellent casting qualities when included in both high- and low-melting alloys. Tin up to 20% is the main alloying constituent in bronze, pewter (see below) and soft solder (see Soft Soldering, Chapter 10).

For centuries tin has commonly been used as a coating on copper and bronze utensils when these metals have been used as food containers. Old tinned vessels show a partial exposure of the base metal where the tin has worn away, which makes a pleasant color contrast, aside from any practical considerations. There is no reason why this kind of partial tin coating could not be used on jewelry made of brass, bronze, or copper. *Hot tinning* is a simple matter. Cover the clean article with a flux such as zinc chloride, or an oil such as palm oil. Then heat the object to over 450° F (232° C), and while wearing gloves, rub a block

of tin onto the article. Rub the tin that adheres with a cloth folded into several layers to distribute it where wanted.

TIN ALLOYS

WHITE METAL: 92 Sn - 8 Sb

  Casting temperature: 600–625° F (315–329° C)

White metal is a tin alloy similar to pewter. It is commonly used for casting costume jewelry manufactured by the trade either by gravity casting in metal molds, or, more commonly, by centrifugal casting in vulcanized rubber molds (which can be used for from 500–2,000 castings before renewal).

HOLLOW SLUSH CASTINGS White metal or pewter can be used to make *hollow castings* by the method called *slush casting*. In this technique, the mold, of metal, plaster of paris, or investment plaster, is heated to the metal's melting temperature. The molten alloy is then poured in through the pouring gate opening and allowed to stand for a few seconds while the outer shell solidifies. Then the remaining, still-liquid core metal is poured out, leaving the casting hollow.

PEWTER

Pewter is a tin alloy containing small percentages of other metals. There are many compositions that are called pewter, since different countries have established different alloys. In general they can be divided into *leadless* and *leaded alloys*. This consideration is important when the alloy is used to make a container for food because lead can render the food toxic. Modern pewter, generally called Britannia metal, is lead-free, which also makes it less subject to tarnishing and capable of taking a better polish.

LEADLESS PEWTER ALLOYS

  95 Sn - 1 Cu - 4 Sb: Britannia metal
  91 Sn - 2 Cu - 7 Sb: Britannia metal
  81 Sn - 10 Cu - 9 Sb: Another Britannia alloy, also
                called Dutch white metal
  87 Sn - 5 Cu - 8 Sb: Hanover Britannia
  80 Sn - 2 Cu - 6 Sb - 2 Bi: This alloy takes a good polish

LEADED PEWTER ALLOYS

  85 Sn - 4 Cu - 7 Sb - 4 Pb: British pewter
  83 Sn - 2 Cu - 7 Sb - 5 Zn - 3 Pb: Queen's metal
  82 Sn - 18 Pb: French pewter
  80 Sn - 20 Pb: English pewter

Some jewelers work in pewter as it gravity casts well in bronze or iron molds when a large casting series is wanted, or in plaster of paris or investment plaster molds when a limited series is the aim. Compared to the precious metals, pewter is relatively inexpensive. It can be mill rolled into sheet, spun, and is easily worked without annealing. Though far lower in strength than any of the other nonferrous metal alloys used for jewelry, it can be soldered with low-melting tin-lead-bismuth soft solders. A liquid flux for pewter is made of 1 part hydrochloric acid to 18 parts glycerine.

In another use, pewter can be employed to create a *jewel model* from which a rubber mold can be made to be used for wax injection casting, or for use in sand casting.

ZINC

Symbol and atomic number: Zn 30
Atomic weight: 65.38
Specific gravity: 7.131
Melting point: 786.9° F (419.4° C)
Boiling point: 1664.6° F (907° C)
Hardness, Mohs' scale: 2.5

Zinc when pure is a bluish white metal, brittle when cold, malleable at 230–410° F (110–210° C). Zinc does not occur as a native metal, but is roasted and reduced from calamine and other ores.

ZINC ALLOYS

Zinc was produced in India where it was long used for the alloy called *bidri* (93 Zn - 4 Cu - 4 Pb - 6 Sn) long before it was manufactured in Europe where it was first brought by Portuguese traders in the 17th century. Zinc is the main alloying constituent in the copper alloy brass, which was first manufactured about 1200 A.D., but only became common in Europe after 1617. Zinc is used mainly as an alloying metal.

LEAD

Symbol and atomic number: Pb 82
Atomic weight: 207.21
Specific gravity: 11.36
Melting point: 618° F (325.6° C)

Lead has been known at least since 3000 B.C., and probably earlier. It has had ancient decorative as well as practical uses in statuary, architectural ornaments, cisterns, roofing, and plumbing. The main source of lead is galena, a lead sulphide frequently found in association with zinc and other metals, from which it is separated by the flotation process.

In the Parkes flotation process used in the U.S.A., impure lead ore is first melted and cooled below the freezing point of copper, which if present becomes crystallized on the surface and is removed by skimming. The lead then goes to a softening or reverberatory furnace where the temperature is raised, and an air blast over the melt oxidizes any antimony and arsenic present, which forming a skin is then removed.

Placed next in kettles, a small amount of zinc is added to the lead, causing any gold and silver present to immediately leave the lead and combine with the zinc (with which it has a greater affinity). The resulting zinc and precious metal compound is lighter than the lead and rises to the surface. It is skimmed off as a solidified skin, then treated to remove the precious metals. The remainder is almost pure lead.

Lead is used for one or more of its characteristics: heavy weight, high density, softness, malleability, flexibility, low melting point, the ease with which it can be alloyed with other metals, or its high resistance to corrosion. It is, however, low in tensile strength and elasticity.

In connection with jewelry, lead is used either alone or as a constituent in alloys. Alone, lead is used in blocks as a resilient surface upon which metal can be shaped. (See Repoussage and Chasing, Chapter 5.) Lead sheets are used in sheet metal stamping as a *shim* to force the metal being stamped to fill the mold depressions. Lead is used as a liner in containers of other materials such as glass or wood for holding sulphuric acid, to which it is highly resistant (but not for nitric acid), for use with solutions of sulphuric acid having concentrations as high as 96%, at temperatures as high as 425° F (220° C). Lead is also used as a core material in bending and shaping large-diameter tubes.

LEAD ALLOYS

The most important lead alloy to the jeweler is soft solder. (See Soft Soldering, Chapter 10.) Lead is also an ingredient in many nonferrous alloys, placed there to improve their properties of machinability or malleability. Extremely low-melting alloys of lead with bismuth, tin, and other metals are used for cores in hollow objects while they are shaped, then these cores are easily melted out of the shell (see Tapered Tubing, Chapter 7).

WARNING:
Lead, if it enters the human body, is cumulative, and in sufficient quantities is toxic. The most common way this occurs is by breathing in lead fumes. Therefore, when working under high heat with materials containing lead, provision should always be made for good ventilation.

Aluminum alloys are discussed under The Lathe and Machined Jewelry, Chapter 10.

Mercury is discussed under Mercury Amalgam Gilding, Chapter 15.

REFRACTORY METALS USED IN JEWELRY

Refractory metals are metals that have an extremely high melting point, above the range of iron and nickel. A *refractory alloy* contains these metals as minor constituents to provide them with qualities of durability at elevated temperatures, and increased life length. The refractory metals include: titanium, tantalum, niobium (columbium), chromium, hafnium, molybdenum, tungsten, vanadium, and zirconium. These are all used in industrial products that must withstand high thermal stress under extremely high temperatures ranging from 2000–4000° F (1093–2204° C) while maintaining strength.

From this group, only the metals titanium, tantalum, and niobium (columbium) are discussed here because they have recently found use in jewelry. Their fabrication by methods requiring high heat presents problems that are beyond the scope of the jeweler as these processes necessitate the use of equipment and techniques not employed by craftspersons. They can all, however, be cold worked to a degree, and parts can be assembled by *cold joining fabrication systems*.

Their main attraction for the jeweler lies in the fact that they all have the capacity of exhibiting the phenomenon of *optical interference surface colors* (see Titanium Coloring, Chapter 17), where attractive, durable, bright-colored surface oxide films develop due to their reaction with oxygen under the controlled application of heat, or by anodic electrolytic oxidation. (Both methods are described under Titanium Coloring.) These colors are predictable, easily reproducible, and develop from the metal itself without dyes or pigments. Used without coloring, they are highly resistant to tarnishing, which by itself is an advantage in white metals. Tantalum and niobium are rather high priced due to their relative scarcity and the difficulty of their extraction from ores. Titanium is the least expensive, and also the most readily available, and at current rates is one tenth the price of tantalum and niobium. They are all available in sheet, wire, and tubing.

TITANIUM

Symbol and atomic number: Ti 22
Atomic weight: 47.90
Specific gravity: 4.5
Annealing temperature: 1100–1350° F (593–732° C)
Liquidus temperature: 3135° F (1723° C)
Melting point: 3272° F (1800° C)
Boiling point: 5900° F (3260° C)

Titanium, from the Greek *Titanes*, "sons of Earth," was discovered in 1791 by William Gregor (1761–1817), an English clergyman, chemist, and mineralogist, who extracted titanium oxide from a black, magnetic sand found near Falmouth, England. It is believed to be the ninth most abundant metal in the earth's crust, where it is widely distributed, mainly in the prime commercial minerals, ilmenite sands and rutile. The largest deposits are in the U.S.A., Canada, and Australia.

The term *C.P. unalloyed titanium* is used in the metal industry to designate titanium of 99.2–90.0% commercial purity (C.P.). Titanium is extracted from ores at high temperatures and low gas pressure by thermal treatment in a vacuum furnace. Pure titanium is white, lustrous, has a silvery appearance, and can be polished to a high luster. It is light in weight, being a little more than one fifth the weight of pure gold, less than one half the weight of sterling silver, and about one half the weight of steel alloys. Its light weight and its strength permit the fabrication of relatively large jewelry from thin gauges of metal. It has a tensile strength equal to mild steel, and is four times harder and less oxidizable at low temperatures than stainless steel. Titanium is also nonmagnetic, and possesses amazing corrosion resistance. Like other refractory metals, it has an extremely high melting point, and for this reason and because of its great strength, more than 80% of the annual titanium supply in the U.S.A. is used for high-temperature aeronautical purposes (rocket motors, heat shields, and aircraft parts), racing cars, and sports equipment. Because of its inertness and nonirritability to body tissues and bones, it is also used for surgical implants and for suture wire, and could be used for prosthetic jewelry.

Titanium was first produced in commercial quantities during the 1950s, but it is only during the last ten years or so that jewelers have recognized its potential, due to its light weight, corrosion resistance, and its ability to be colored. Avid experimentation in the use of titanium in

jewelry has been in progress in Great Britain, especially among young art jewelers, and is now spreading to the U.S.A. In Great Britain this pursuit has been encouraged by research information made available to the jewelry trade and to craft schools by the metal's manufacturers, and by the research reports published by the Technical Advisory Committee of The Worshipful Company of Goldsmiths in London. Several jewelers show growing expertise in the control of figural designs using the oxide film surface interference colors that are the main attraction of this metal.

TITANIUM FABRICATION

All the basic fabrication methods mentioned here are discussed separately in the text below. Titanium is initially hard, further work hardens, and rapidly becomes embrittled. It may be harder than unhardened, conventional forming tools, and thus damaging to them. It can generally therefore only be worked by craftspersons in ways that do not involve permanent plastic deformation. Though the metal is wearing on drills and saw blades, with patience these processes can be carried out at a slow rate.

TITANIUM SAWING When hand sawing precolored or untreated, plain titanium, use a jeweler's saw blade capable of cutting steel. Oxidized titanium surfaces make the metal even harder. To facilitate sawing, surface oxide should be removed, and oxidizing for color is done only after sawing the workpiece to its final shape. Oxide is removed by pickling, grinding, or sandblasting. (See Titanium Coloring, Chapter 17.) When sawing, always use a lubricant-coolant such as sulphurized or chlorinated oil. The speed of cutting is one-fourth to one-half less than that used to cut hard steel. Guard against too high a cutting speed as the intense local heat that would occur could cause surface cracking.

TITANIUM DRILLING When drilling titanium, a higher temperature develops in the local cutting area than occurs in drilling other metals because titanium is a poor thermal conductor and an inefficient heat diffuser. Drill points may become quickly overheated and lose their temper if certain precautions are not taken. Titanium sheet being drilled should be backed up with an aluminum or soft steel sheet to act as a *heat sink*, and also to minimize the occurrence of burr formation on the side where the drill emerges. Drill titanium with short, high-speed drills, or with carbide tips having a 140° point for holes below ¼ in (6.5 mm), and a 90° or double-angle point for larger holes. Work with a slow speed and heavy feed, and frequently flood the hole with a heavily chlorinated cutting oil lubricant-coolant to reduce friction and heat buildup. Stop the drill at intervals to allow for cooling, and retract it to clear the hole of *swarf* (fine particles) removed by the cutting action.

TITANIUM COLD FORGING Practically speaking, forging is beyond the scope of hand forging methods due to titanium's initial hardness and rapid work hardening. Titanium can be *bent* after heating to 482–572° F (250–300° C).

TITANIUM MACHINING AND TURNING Titanium and its alloys can be machined and turned on a lathe with no more difficulty than steel, using slow cutting speeds, heavy cuts, and sufficient lubricant-coolant. For intermittent cuts, use conventional high-speed tools. For continuous cuts, use tungsten carbide tools with a large nose radius and in-

3-24 GUNILLA TREEN, England. Titanium, silver, and Plexiglas brooch. Flat contour-sawed sheets repeating curved cloud shapes are riveted together, after the titanium was heat colored. Clouds symbolize metamorphosis as they constantly change. *Photo: Günter Meyer, courtesy Schmuckmuseum, Pforzheim*

creased top and side rakes for swarf clearance. Make sure the cutting edges are ground to a good surface finish to avoid galling or seizing the workpiece. Feeds should be as coarse as possible. Titanium has a lower elastic modulus than steel and the workpiece must be absolutely rigid. Excessive pressure must be avoided. Depending on whether pure titanium or a titanium alloy is used, the cutting speed varies from 6–300 feet per minute. Oil-paraffin lubricants are used liberally to overcome the metal's poor heat conductivity, which can cause a fire to occur in accumulated chips and swarf which therefore should be frequently cleared away. Should a fire occur, douse it with dry sand.

TITANIUM STAMPING AND BLANKING The jewelry and watchmaking industries use flat, stamped-out titanium shapes called *blanks* for mass-production items. Blanks are cut with hardened steel dies and punches on hand stamping presses with a load of not more than two tons. This machine is capable of blanking sheet up to 0.080 in (12 gauge B.&S.). Blanking load is directly proportional to the sheet thickness and peripheral area of the blank. If, as in all blanking, the blank is thick in relation to its diameter, it tends to emerge slightly convex on the die side. The lubricant used is chlorinated oil. When a punch press is used, its cutting speed is slowed down to from one-third to one-half normal speed.

TITANIUM ROLLING Rolling must be performed on industrial rolling mills. Those used by jewelers are not heavy enough to use without damage.

TITANIUM GRINDING AND POLISHING (See Titanium Surface Preparation Before Coloring, Chapter 17.)

3-25 METAUX PRECIEUX S.A., Switzerland. Experimental silver jewelry employing Ticolor titanium sheet. *Photo: Courtesy Metaux Precieux S.A.*

TITANIUM HOT JOINING SYSTEMS

Controlling the problems of casting or fabricating titanium objects by methods that require high heat are beyond the scope of craftspersons, but are briefly mentioned here. The main problem for the craftsperson in utilizing heat-requiring processes for fabricating titanium is that it is *pyrophoric,* meaning it can ignite spontaneously when heated in air to temperatures above 2192° F (1200° C). Even more important, because it has an affinity toward atmospheric gases, at elevated temperatures it has a tendency to absorb oxygen, hydrogen, and nitrogen with the accompanying detrimental results of surface hardness and embrittlement.

ANNEALING TITANIUM Heating to proper annealing temperature must take place in a very high vacuum to avoid contamination, and is therefore an industrial process not possible for craftspersons.

BRAZE JOINING TITANIUM This requires a high temperature, and the process cannot take place without an inert gas atmosphere shielding the object. The operation must take place in a vacuum as well, in order to prevent the above-mentioned gas absorption and the formation of refractory oxide films that hinder joining. The same is true of *arc welding* or *resistance welding* titanium. These are not methods commonly used by jewelers.

TITANIUM CASTING Casting titanium is an industrial process done under carefully controlled, oxygen-free atmospheric conditions, using special equipment. Because of the extremely high heat needed to melt this metal, it causes crucibles and conventional mold materials to dissolve. Casting titanium therefore is impractical for the craftsperson.

Titanium inclusions in castings of other metals are, however, possible. Its much higher melting point in this circumstance makes it possible to include a titanium unit in a wax model being prepared for use in casting a metal with a lower melting point. For example, because titanium melts at 3272° F (1800° C), it could be cast with sterling silver which melts at 1640° F (893° C), or karat golds that melt below its melting point. The assembled wax model with the titanium inclusion must be prepared in such a way that the titanium unit is locked with the molten metal form so it is mechanically held in position. The titanium must be enclosed with the wax model in a conventional investment plaster mold to allow the second metal to be lost wax cast centrifugally. After acid cleaning or sandblasting the resulting casting to remove surface oxidation, the titanium part can then be thermally or electrochemically colored. This technique has been used by Ann Marie Shillito. In preparation for immersion anodizing coloring, the other metal(s) must be precoated with a resist or material that protects the surface it covers.

TITANIUM COLD JOINING SYSTEMS

In light of the hot joining difficulties mentioned, the craftsperson is confined to using cold joining fabrication methods on titanium sheet metal (which is available in the normal gauge sizes) and on rod, tube, wire, mesh, and expanded sheet.

Flat titanium components can be joined to each other, or to a supporting unit made of another metal or to some other material, by any of the cold joining methods used for metals and other materials. When the parts are in *one flat plane,* components can be butt edged against each other, in the manner of a mosaic, their edges straight or contoured in matching curves. Multiplaned structures can be created by mounting flat parts in a supporting base constructed to hold them in positions that will create a three-dimensional form. A flat or shaped titanium part can be made with an opening or openings, and can be superimposed upon, or held away from another flat part to create spatial dimension. When these parts are differently colored, the colors of the lower part are seen through the openings of the uppermost part.

Mechanical joining systems such as all types of rivets

and screws that pass through predrilled or tapped holes in the titanium metal can also be used to assemble components. When these are made of a different metal, they can provide color accents.

Retention systems can also be used to hold a titanium unit. Prongs that are a part of a separately fabricated supporting unit of a different metal, or a bezel that holds a titanium unit in the same way as it functions to hold a stone, are possible devices.

TANTALUM AND NIOBIUM (columbium): Their new use in jewelry

Mr. Peter Gainsbury, Director of Research of the Technical Department of The Worshipful Company of Goldsmiths in London, has pioneered in the introduction of information concerning the use of tantalum and niobium (columbium) by craftspersons in jewelry, through the issuance of technical reports. Both these metals can be colored in the same manner as titanium. (See Titanium Coloring, Chapter 17.) The color range is even wider and more brilliant than that of titanium, and colors are not the same for each metal at any given anodizing voltage. These metals, unlike titanium, can be cold worked with normal hand tools and equipment. Rolling, drawing, raising, chasing and repoussage, and stone setting are possible. Their specific gravities give these metals a more substantial feel as compared to the lightness of titanium. Tantalum is closer in working qualities to gold; niobium (columbium), to silver. Their ability to be fabricated by cold forming methods as well as by mechanical joining systems decidedly increases the range of their possibilities. Problems of oxygen embrittlement and the high melting points of these metals, however, do not permit their being annealed, soldered, or cast with ordinary jeweler's equipment. If purchased in an already annealed state, they have a malleability that permits relatively prolonged working before annealing is needed, and they can be stress relieved by heating to a low temperature.

TANTALUM

Symbol and atomic number: Ta 73
Atomic weight: 180.95
Specific gravity: 16.6
Annealing temperature: 2192–3272° F (1200–1800° C)
Melting point: 5425° F (2996° C)
Boiling point: 9800° F (5426° C)

Tantalum is a decidedly bluish metal, highly resistant to corrosion by chemicals. It was discovered in 1802 by Anders G. Ekeberg, a Swedish chemist. Tantalum is named after Tantalus, a wealthy, mythological Greek king —the father of Niobe—who (because he cooked his son Pelops as an offering to the gods) was condemned to eternal torment: placed in water he could not drink, near fruit he could not eat, under a rock suspended above his head threatening to crush him. It is so called because of the tantalizing difficulties Ekeberg experienced in isolating this metal from others, such as niobium (columbium) with which it is commonly found in the minerals colombite, tantalite, and pyrochlore. Tantalum is highly corrosion resistant, and therefore is included in alloys to which it imparts this quality. It is also used to construct acid-resisting chemical equipment.

TANTALUM FABRICATION

Tantalum is very ductile and can be worked by all conventional work processes such as forging, raising, and wire drawing, allowing a 95% maximum work reduction before annealing becomes necessary. Often, depending on the forms created, no annealing is necessary. The metal should, however, be purchased in an annealed state. All cold working processes should be followed by stress relieving to leave the object in a stress-free condition.

TANTALUM HEAT TREATMENTS Tantalum below 302° F (150° C) is one of the most inert of metals, but at higher temperatures it becomes chemically active. It oxidizes in air above 570° F (298.8° C) and a series of bright oxide interference colors (in predictable sequence) starts to develop. At still higher temperatures, tantalum is susceptible to surface contamination during heat treatments that take place in air. Except for deliberate heat coloring, tantalum, niobium, and titanium should not be heated in air unless a protective atmosphere in the form of an inert gas envelops them, or unless heating takes place in a high vacuum. Under temperatures above 1200° F (649° C) they absorb oxygen, nitrogen, and hydrogen and form hard, ultimately severely embrittled surface layers that will interfere with further successful working operations such as drilling, forming, or machining. Observable effects of this contamination are negligible, but become evident when the metal is worked. If stress relieving or annealing must take place in air, the contaminated surface layer must be removed by an acid etch or by abrasion before further work can continue.

TANTALUM STRESS RELIEVING Tantalum is stress relieved to improve ductility and to reduce residual stress resulting from cold working methods. Stress relieving is accomplished by heating the metal to a temperature of 1925° F (1051° C), which is about 100° F (37.7° C) below the metal's recrystallization temperature.

TANTALUM ANNEALING Annealing temperatures of refractory metals in general depend on the amount of cold work performed on them, and the sequence of interim process anneals. Annealing temperatures are therefore not standardized, but those given are typical. *Full annealing* must take place before any severe cold forming operations such as forging and spinning can begin. In full annealing, which occurs in tantalum at approximately 2400° F (1315° C), carried out under a high vacuum, a complete *recrystallization* develops in the metal's structure, and it attains maximum softness as well as improved ductility, but its strength is lowered. The time needed increases in proportion to thickness.

JOINING TANTALUM *Hot joining* can be accomplished using a special copper alloy and flux, but only with special equipment such as a torch-fuel system in which air is excluded and with an inert gas such as argon providing a shielding atmosphere. The inert gas does not enter the joining action, but flows over and around the metal, protecting it on both sides against contamination by atmospheric oxygen and nitrogen. *Welding* can also be performed by special techniques while the object is immersed in water or carbon tetrachloride, which exclude air. These processes can also take place in a *leakproof vacuum furnace* which should have a low *dew point* (water vapor content in its atmosphere at a specific pressure) of −70 or lower.

ACID SOLUTIONS USED IN PROCESSING TANTALUM Tantalum is highly resistant to a variety of acids and chemicals, including nitric acid, hydrochloric acid, acetone, photographic solutions, alcohols, and dyestuffs, especially at normal temperatures. The kinds of acid solutions, and processes in which tantalum is subjected to acids, are similar to those used with titanium. Tantalum is severely attacked by hydrofluoric acid alone, as well as when that acid is combined with nitric acid in etching solutions. It is also slowly attacked by hot concentrations of phosphoric acid and sulphuric acid combinations.

TANTALUM MACHINABILITY It is about equal to that of rolled steel. A light oil cutting lubricant is used with a tool having a rake angle of 28–30°. Though relatively low in hardness, tantalum tends to dull cutting tools and files.

SURFACE TEXTURING To texture a tantalum surface use a high-speed metal or tungsten carbide bur at high rotation speeds.

POLISHING TANTALUM This can be done mechanically with emery to 000, or with levigated alumina. Of the three metals discussed here, tantalum is lowest in reflectivity. It can be brightened by immersion in chemical brightening solutions.

NIOBIUM (columbium)

Symbol and atomic number: Ni 41 (Cb 41)
Atomic weight: 92.91
Specific gravity: 8.57
Melting point: 4474° F (2467° C)
Boiling point: 8901° F (4927° C)

In 1801 Charles Hatchett, an English chemist, discovered an elemental metal in American columbite that he named *columbium*. In 1844 it was rediscovered by Heinrich Rose, a German chemist, who distinguished it from tantalum (with which it is often associated in nature) and called it *niobium*. Its association with tantalum suggested its name: niobium is named after Niobe, a daughter of Tantalus of Greek mythology. She was also a tragic figure: her excessive pride in her numerous children resulted in their death and in her punishment by Zeus, who turned her into a stone in her own form. In 1949 the International Union of Chemistry decided officially to call this metal *niobium*, but *columbium*, its other name, persists and is preferred in some metal literature in the U.S.A.

Niobium is a hard, steely, grayish white metal. Its specific gravity is closer to sterling silver and gold alloys than titanium. It is available in sheet form in gauges down to 0.040 in (18 gauge B.&S.).

NIOBIUM FABRICATION

Generally speaking, pure niobium is the most workable of the three refractory metals discussed here. It is malleable, and can be worked by all conventional cold working processes including forging, rolling, wire drawing, spinning, and repoussage. It has good low-temperature ductility, and hardens at a slow rate. When niobium requires extended fabrication, in order to reduce the danger of cracking and lamination, it is heat treated to a full anneal, which causes recrystallization and greatly improved ductility. However, annealing must be carried out under the conditions described for tantalum. The toughness gained by cold working can be retained by only stress relieving below its recrystallization temperature.

Niobium oxidizes above a temperature of 750° F (399° C), forming a series of surface oxide interference colors that are brighter and in wider variety than for titanium. Like all refractory metals, above this temperature it becomes contaminated with oxygen-containing atmospheres, and even by those considered to be neutral or reducing—causing surface embrittlement and a tendency to crack. From about 500–1750° F (260–954° C) it absorbs hydrogen, resulting in a loss of ductility. As with titanium and tantalum, all heat treatments must be carried out under strictly controlled conditions in a high vacuum.

Niobium is moderately to highly resistant to corrosion in most liquid mediums normally considered to be corrosive, including dilute mineral acids and organic acids. It is etched in a dilute hydrofluoric acid solution which attacks it rapidly. Another reliable etchant contains 30 parts lactic acid, 10 parts nitric acid, and 5 parts hydrofluoric acid. An electrolytic etching fluid that produces a highly uniform grain-boundary definition for surface texture is 90 parts sulphuric acid to 10 parts hydrofluoric acid, used at 2 volts.

NIOBIUM WELDING It is possible to weld niobium under highly controlled conditions using processes in which atmospheric contaminants are excluded, as with tantalum.

NIOBIUM POLISHING Niobium can be polished to a brilliant luster. Initially, a coarse diamond abrasive with a kerosene lubricant is used, and final polishing is done with alumina, using standard procedures.

FERROUS METALS USED IN JEWELRY

IRON

Symbol and atomic number: Fe 26
Atomic weight: 55.85
Specific gravity: 7.87
Melting point: 2797° F (1536° C)
Boiling point: 5430° F (3000° C)

Iron is a hard, malleable, ductile metal commonly found as mineral deposits, usually near the earth's surface. The main iron ores are hematite (70% iron), magnetite (60–70%), limonite (30–50%), and siderite (20–35%).

Meteoric iron was known and used at least 5,000 years ago, but terrestrial iron reduced from ores has been in use only about 2,500 years.

The two basic forms of iron used in the arts are *wrought iron* and *cast iron*.

WROUGHT IRON

Wrought iron is low in carbon, containing less than 0.3%. It incorporates nonmetallic slag in fine streaks, which gives it a directional structure. It is relatively soft

3–26 NIGER-TUAREG (BOUREM), NIGERIA. Heavy-gauge iron pierced work shawl pin in the prevailing geometric tradition, ornamented with copper and brass. It is tied to the shawl end as a weight. The form developed from chest lock decorations and key shapes used in the area. Length 28 cm. Photo: Linden Museum, Stuttgart

but tough, and can be worked by forging methods while cold or hot. (See Forging, Chapter 6.) Wrought iron is used for decorative architectural work and other purposes. Some modern jewelers have experimented with the use of wrought iron for jewelry, sometimes in combination with stones such as rock crystal.

PROTECTIVE COATINGS ON IRON

The main disadvantage of *ordinary* iron is that it is not corrosion resistant and readily rusts or oxidizes when water and oxygen are present. *Wrought* iron, however, resists corrosion because of its slag content; when exposed to such conditions, it becomes coated with a surface oxide film, which protects it from further oxidation.

Artificial protective coatings for iron include specially prepared *paints* which cover it with a protective film; and *chemical coatings* which make possible a pleasing black patina produced by converting the surface to black iron oxide (Fe_3O_4). For this conversion, clean iron is immersed in a commercially available, highly concentrated salt solution for 15 minutes at a temperature of 290–300° F (143–148° C) and then rubbed with a thin film of *sweet oil*.

CAST IRON

Cast iron is iron that is a fusible and fluid metal when poured into a mold to produce a specific form. After solidification it is hard but brittle, due to the multidirectional structure of the crystals. Thin sections consequently cannot be worked without fracturing. Cast iron has been

used in Europe for jewelry in the past—see the finely cast Berlin jewelry of the early 19th century, which was oxidized black to prevent rusting—and in Japan, for *tsubas* (sword guards).

Iron finds many uses in jewelry making, such as in binding wire used to hold parts together during soldering, in soldering nests, and iron mesh heating trivets. More important, iron is the basic constituent of high-alloy tool steel used to make all the tools used by jewelers.

STAINLESS STEEL

Stainless steel is one of the many standardized iron-based steel alloys: one of the most common contains about 12% chromium; another, 18% chromium and 8% nickel. It has come into use for jewelry fairly recently, because though tough to work (a factor that influences design), it is highly resistant to corrosion (because of its constituent alloying metals such as chromium, nickel, silicon, and others) and it takes a high, long-lasting polish. The working properties of stainless steels depend on their composition, but most of them can be worked hot or cold, can be annealed to restore softness when work hardened, and can be welded. Because of the many alloys available, only general information is given here.

SOLDERING STAINLESS STEEL

All stainless steel can be hard and soft soldered. In preparation for both, the surface to be soldered must be absolutely clean. It is advisable to roughen the contacting surfaces with emery paper or cloth.

In *soft soldering,* a special, highly corrosive flux is needed to attack and remove a tenacious film that forms on the surface, in order to allow the solder to "wet" the metal. Solder must be applied immediately, before the surface film re-forms. For good results, the tin content of the solder should be high—from 50–70%. After soldering, the metal must be rinsed and neutralized with an alkaline substance to remove any remaining corrosive flux.

Hard soldering is possible with all stainless steels. The metal should be annealed before hard soldering to relieve stresses from working. The solder must have a high melting temperature and the soldering flux must be suitable for use at high temperatures. The soldering time should be as short as possible. (See Soldering, Chapter 10.) When the solder flows, bonding occurs as a small amount of the base metal dissolves in the molten filler metal, before the base metal fuses.

FINISHING STAINLESS STEEL

Surfaces can be finished matte by scratch brushing, or by the application of abrasives worked in one or several directions, or it can be polished with polishing wheels to a brilliant luster. (See Table, "Wheel Speeds Recommended for Finishing Metals, Plastics, and Wood," p. 655.)

3–27 HENRI GARGAT, France. Stainless steel ring made of an assemblage of sheet strips within a cylindrical section, mounted on a pierced square, solid ring shank. Photo: Günter Meyer, courtesy Schmuckmuseum, Pforzheim

BASIC TECHNIQUES
Processing Sheet Metal Without Deformation

THE ROLLING MILL

Changing metal dimensions by tangential compression

The rolling mill is an important and useful machine, one that should be in every workshop. It is basically used to reduce the thickness of metal in plate or sheet form, while increasing it in both length and width; or to reduce the dimension of round or square wire. Cast ingots can be broken down or reduced to sheets, rods, or wire, if necessary. This is done by passing the metal through the controlled space between the two *rolls* of the machine. If the metal is manually fed to the machine and it is powered by hand force, it is called a *hand rolling mill*. If the rolls are powered by an electric motor, but the metal is still hand fed, it is a *powered hand rolling mill*. If both feed and power are mechanical, it is an *automatic powered rolling mill,* the kind used in industry. The rolling mills used by jewelers and craftspersons are specially designed for small-scale work, which suits their normal needs in this area.

The rolling mill is termed a *two-high rolling mill* when it consists of two rolls mounted vertically, one above the other in an *absolutely parallel* horizontal direction. This is the common type used by craftspersons but there are others used in industry. The size of the mill is stated in terms of the *diameter* of the roll barrel, and the roll's *length,* in that order. Mills used by craftspersons range in

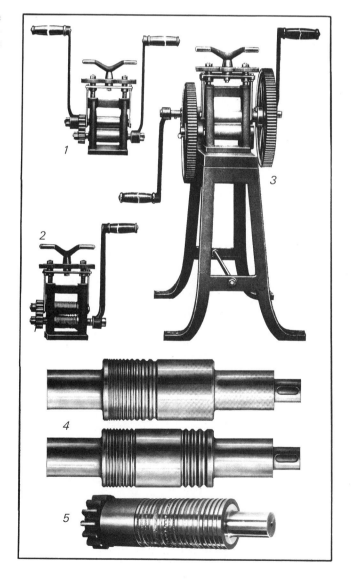

4–1 THE ROLLING MILL
1. *Hand-drive sheet rolling mill,* without bench, and with two handles. The central pressure motion rolls are deeply hardened special quality steel, ground to exactness and highly polished. The frame allows the rolls to be changed. Roll length 60, 80, 100, 120 mm; roll Ø 38, 45, 52, 60 mm; smallest case height 100 × 140 × 250 mm; largest 250 × 420 × 560 mm.
2. *Hand-drive wire rolling mill,* without bench, rolls changeable, same basic dimensions as above. Available groove graduation 2.5–0.6 mm; 4–1 mm; 5–1 mm; 6–1 mm; 7–1 mm.
3. *Hand-drive sheet rolling mill* mounted on a cast iron bench. The two-handled double multiplying power gears allow a large roll gap which makes it suited to breaking down thick ingots as well as for normal use.
4. *Top roll:* half for wire, half for sheet; *bottom roll:* middle part for sheet, right and left for wire.
5. *Pattern roll,* can be inserted in rolling mills that allow roll changing. This roll contains 18 different wire groove designs. (Bühler & Co. Maschinenfabrik, Pforzheim, West Germany)

4-2 *HAND-DRIVE ONE-HANDLED ROLLING MILL* Left: Used to roll sheet and wire, column mounted. When rolling wire and arriving at smaller grooves, the handle is fixed in the journal support on the bearing of the bottom roll. This allows the multiplying power wheel to run the roll at a much higher speed. Rolls are changeable.

HAND-DRIVE DOUBLE-PURPOSE ROLLING MILL WITH FOUR ROLLS Right: Two rolls are used for sheet, and two for wire, column mounted. Equipped with central screwdown for the sheet mill, and single screw for regulating the wire mill. Has multiplying power gears, and two handles on the driving shaft. Max. sheet thickness admission is 4 mm. The frames allow rolls to be easily changed. *Photos: Foto Notton, courtesy Bühler & Co.*

4-3 *BELT POWERED HAND ROLLING MILL* The belt passes to a motor. With power on, the rolls revolve at a continuous, steady rate. The operator is passing small sheets through the rolls with one hand, and receiving them as they emerge from the rolls with the other hand. Kultasepänliike Ossian Hopea. Porvoo, Finland. *Photo: Oppi*

4-4 *THE MANUFACTURE OF SHEET METAL AND STRIP* The sheet passes through at least three stages. Primary and intermediate rolling mills produce a semifinished sheet, then finishing rolling mills produce the final sheet. Sheet thickness is accurately controlled by an automatic gauge control placed close to the exit side of the rolls. When necessary, corrections are automatically fed to the screws or hydraulic cylinders that maintain the gap between the rolls. Here at the Handy and Harman plant, edge-trimmed sterling silver sheet is being fed through the rolls, then cut into strips of various widths. *Photo: Nick Lazarnick, courtesy Handy and Harman*

roll diameter and length from 1¾ in: 3¹⁄₁₆ in, to 4¾ in: 9½ in. Maximum *roll gap* or space between the rolls may also be stated, and this distance determines the maximum *starting thickness* that can be rolled through a parallel rolling mill.

The rolls are made of high-alloy steel, ground and hardened. Those used to roll sheet are flat and highly polished. The rolls work in conjunction with and in opposition to each other against the metal. Rolls may be *cambered* (having a slight convex curve) so that they increase in diameter slightly from the ends toward the middle in order to compensate for their bending slightly under the pressure of a load. The smaller the diameter of the rolls, the more subject they are to wear because they present a smaller total working surface area to the metal at each pass of the metal between them.

The cast iron steel rolling mill frame is called the *housing* which may be *bench-* or *pedestal-mounted* at a convenient working height. The housing contains two *chocks* (blocks), one at each end of the roll. These carry the roll bearings and the sliding which allows the vertical adjustment of the upper roll. The rolls each have a *neck* or cylindrical, parallel projection at each end which fits into the roll bearing. If the housing completely encloses the chocks, there is a window or space at the sides which makes them visible.

In a rolling mill with a single central control handle, parallel adjustment of the roll settings is made by turning the *housing screw* mounted at the top of the housing. This engages two adjustable gears that bear on the top of the roll chocks. In some models the adjusting gears have marked gauges that allow the operator to adjust exactly the *bite* of each successive roll. By turning the control handle or lever, or by using a *spanner,* the top roll moves up or down. In some cases, the housing screw has a *check nut* which can be set to prevent the screw from moving down too far. Some mills have *two* pressure control handles, one at each end, and *both* must be turned the same distance to keep the rolls parallel.

On a hand-operated rolling mill, the drive is provided by the *handle* or *side crank* that causes the turning of two or three reduction gears made of hardened and ground chrome nickel steel. The gears have a ratio of 1:4, which makes roll turning relatively easy. Powered models are made to turn by a belt from a motor shaft to a gear pulley. When the rolls are power driven they are said to be *live rolls.* Models suited for use in small workshops are powered by a 1 hp (horsepower) or 3 hp, 220 volt, single-phase or three-phase motor enclosed within the housing. Hand-driven rolling mills and some of the power-driven ones can usually be made to rotate in a forward or reversed direction, according to need.

ROLLING SHEET METAL

The metal being rolled should be in an annealed condition, always dry, and clean. It should also be scale-free or the scale will become embedded in the surface, and when later removed by pickling, will leave the surface pitted. The rolls must be *absolutely parallel* and preset a certain distance apart, according to requirement. The space between them is called the *gap,* and it can be made smaller or larger.

Each trip through the roll gap is called a *pass.* The metal goes through a series of passes, each time with the gap smaller than the last. The first pass is called the

roughing pass, and the last, the *finishing* pass. It is usual to test the first gap distance by a *dead pass* or one in which no reduction takes place. The roll gap is then decreased to make a *live pass,* one in which metal thickness is actually reduced.

To make the gap distance smaller, turn the gears a quarter turn by moving the spanner at the top of the rolling mill housing. The amount of the turn can be accurately controlled when the gears at the top have a marked distance gauge.

In action, the parallel rolls revolve on their longitudinal axis in opposite directions *toward each other.* Their vertical axis is at a straight angle, perpendicular to the direction of the sheet being rolled. When rolling metal, it should be fed *squarely* to the roll gap. It can be passed through hot, but is more frequently rolled cold. Cold-rolled sheet has a more uniform, smoother surface than hot rolled, and is also harder. Because the rolls are in a fixed position with a gap distance smaller than the thickness of the metal, the rolls exert a squeezing roll force or *bite* upon the metal. This bite is accomplished tangentially by those parts of the rolls that actually contact the metal. The tangent angle between the vertical line joining roll centers and the point of contact with the metal must be *less than 30°.* If it is more, the metal will balk and not enter the rolls.

4–5 THE ROTATIONAL ACTION OF THE ROLLS ON A ROLLING MILL DURING ROLLING.

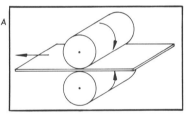

The force exerted upon the metal by the rolls reduces its thickness, and also causes a *roll-separating force* that results from the roll's resistance against the metal. The total turning force applied to the rolls to overcome the resistance of the metal is called *roll torque,* and *roll spring* is the total deformation of the rolls, screws, and housing caused by the roll-separating force. The thinner the desired gauge of sheet metal, the more rigid the mill must be, and the greater the power and torque to be applied.

Always pass sheet metal through the *center* of the rolls. In rolling, the metal is stretched in length (its major directional increase) and in width (*spread*). The amount it is reduced in thickness (shape section, in the case of wire) is termed its *reduction. Pass reduction* is the amount of reduction that results from a single pass. *Total reduction* is the amount that occurs in the entire rolling sequence, from original to final thickness. Do not attempt too great a reduction in any single pass or the mill will be subject to excessive strain. With each pass, *reverse* the sheet end previously fed through the rolls to maintain equal sheet thickness. When rolling sheet to a specific gauge, measure its thickness as it approaches the desired size with a *sheet metal gauge, micrometer,* or *vernier calipers,* and adjust the roll gap appropriately.

When rolling metal, after three or four passes, depending on the metal, it becomes work hardened because its crystal structure is compressed and elongated in the rolling direction, a condition called *grain flow.* In this type of fibrous structure, rolled metal strength is always greatest along the grain flow direction, and weakest at right angles to it. When sheet (or wire) work hardens from rolling it must be annealed to restore it to a softened condition suited to continued rolling—otherwise it may split. Sterling silver normally requires annealing after a 2 mm reduction; alloyed gold after a 1 mm reduction or slightly more. Do *not* anneal sheet metal prior to its final rolling pass but *cold roll* it to achieve maximum surface smoothness and hardness.

EDGES

In hand rolling there is no control over the edge of the sheet which emerges as rolled, a condition called *mill edge*. In industrial rolling, the edge of the final rolled sheet or strip product is controlled by *vertical edging rolls* that give it its mill edge; a *sheared edge* is made by cutting after rolling; a *slit edge* is produced by a slitting machine.

ROLLING WIRE

For wire rolling, both rolls are provided with matching half-round and/or V-shaped grooves, used together to reduce the cross section of round or square wire respectively. Mills exist with *combination rolls* that are partly flat and partly grooved for rolling sheet and wire. Wire grooves are separated by a *collar* or flat, roll-high section. When the rolls come together, the collars completely enclose the groove shape, called a *closed pass*; when they do not close, it is an *open pass*. Grooves are always arranged in order of diminishing sizes. A typical hand-operated wire roll has grooves graduated from 6–1 mm.

When rolling *round wire*, it is entered in the first groove it will fit into so that it is completely enclosed by the matching pair of grooves in both upper and lower rolls, which prevents twisting. The gap should be very small or nonexistent. Small-gauge wire can be gripped at the loose end with a *parallel-jawed pliers* and pulled to place it under tension while it is rolled to keep the length straight. Roll the wire *twice* through the same groove to be sure it has

been reduced to true dimension. Then pass it through the next smaller groove and repeat the same action. When wire must be smaller in section than the smallest rolling mill groove allows, then draw it through a *drawplate*. When rolling *square wire*, avoid the occurrence of corner burrs by reducing its section slowly, and by turning the wire when it enters the rolls to engage alternating corners with each pass.

OVERFILL ROLLING

If a wire is fed to a groove too small for it, the rolls cannot close and collars do not meet, a condition called *overfill*. Feeding wire too small to fill the groove (*underfill*) results in wire that is not dimensionally true.

L. Brent Kington has developed a means of deliberately using the overfill condition in the conventional groove of a wire rolling mill to create bars or wire with side flanges. By deliberately leaving a gap between the rolls and feeding a rod or wire of oversized dimensions to a particular groove, the rolls bear down on the metal and force the surplus to spread in the only direction possible—to the sides. After a few such passes, each time keeping the bar or wire in the same position in relation to the grooves, a flange develops on either side. Such wire can be used in many ways.

WAVY WIRE

If a wire appears wavy after rolling, it has been rolled with insufficient tension. Return it to the rolls, and hold the end taut while rolling it through again.

ROLLING HALF-ROUND AND TRIANGULAR WIRE

To roll half-round wire in a round-groove rolling mill, pass two round wires simultaneously through the same groove. Another method, if the rolls are detachable, is to remove the upper wire roll and replace it with a plain, flat roll. Pass the wire through the rolls, and the flat side of

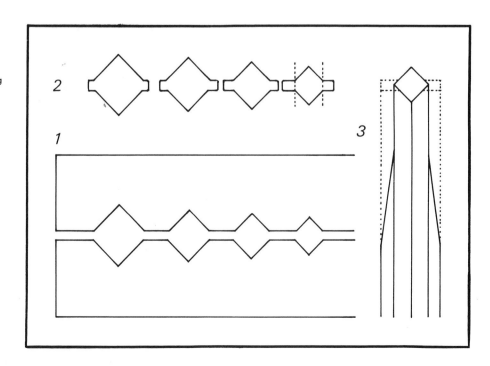

4–6 PREPARING A BAR WITH SIDE FLANGES
1. The square bar is rolled through square wire rolls with a gap.
2. Sections of the bar showing how the side flanges increase as the wire size decreases.
3. The bar with flanges removed to a taper, ready for forge twisting in the manner employed by L. Brent Kington.

the half-round wire will be formed by the flat roll while the groove forms the half-round side. The same can be done to make triangular-section wire from a flat and a square wire roll.

FLATTENING COMPOUND WIRE

Braided wire, twisted wire, wire wrapped around a core, fancy compound twist wires can all be passed through the *flat* rolls to produce a flattened strip with special effects. To achieve round effects, they can be rolled through the appropriate round groove.

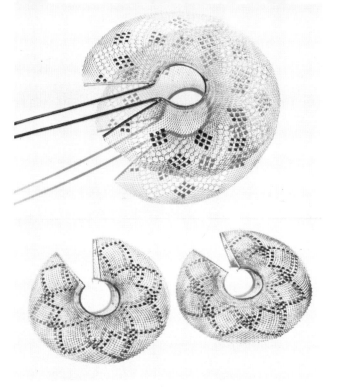

4–7 WALLY GILBERT, England. Hair ornament and earrings using a system of woven fine silver wire heated to the point of fusion to bond their positions at crossings. The maker at times rolls the result through a rolling mill to flatten it. In this case, round 18K gold shot was placed on the resulting mesh in patterned positions and hammered flat to clinch them in place. Openwork circles in the hairpiece were made by inserting a round-shafted pick through the mesh to force the wires apart. The uppermost surfaces were brightened with a hand burnisher. *Photos: Barbara Cartlidge, courtesy Electrum Gallery, London*

4–8 *WIRE AND STRIP OF DIFFERENT PROFILES AND SURFACE PATTERNS* can be produced in continuous lengths with wire rolls engraved with patterns, standard or specially ordered. Typical standard patterns and their numbers are shown here; *left:* with flat profile and surface pattern; *center:* with stepped profile; *right:* with curved profile. Such patterned wire is used for rings, bracelets, borders, and for other purposes. *Courtesy Bühler & Co.*

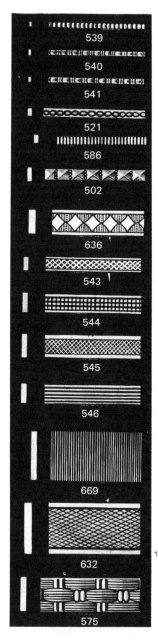

539
540
541
521
586
502
636
543
544
545
546
669
632
575

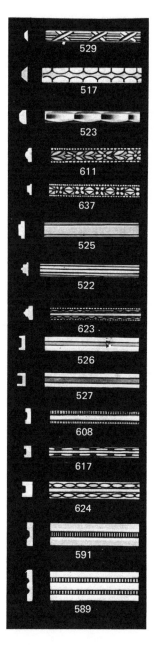

529
517
523
611
637
525
522
623
526
527
608
617
624
591
589

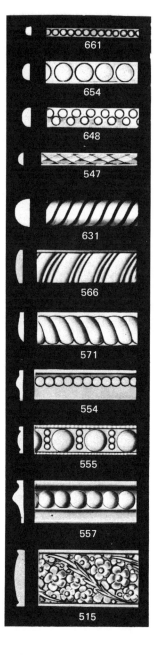

661
654
648
547
631
566
571
554
555
557
515

4–11 BÖRJE RAJALIN, Finland, designer; manufacturer Kalevala Koru, Helsinki. Silver bangle bracelets made of patterned wire whose designs, adapted from old Finnish ornaments, were engraved on wire rolling mill rolls. *Photo: Pietinen, courtesy the Finnish Society of Crafts and Design*

4–9 4–10 SOUFLI, THRACE, GREECE, 19th century. Traditional cast unit woman's belt worn with traditional dress. The buckle with its flanking elements is called *bakirenia* ("made of copper"). *Originally, the central ornament and flanking parts were fabricated of profiled patterned wire* made either in a patterned wire rolling mill or with wire pattern dies. This wire was used as borders around the central units and soldered to the sheet metal base. A mold was then made from the original fabricated piece and a single-piece casting in copper produced from it. The absence of soldered parts simplified the technical problems of applying the blue, green, and pink opaque enamels used to decorate it champlevé style. Bezels holding colored stones were also a part of the casting. The high rosettes of silver wire and shot were formed separately and riveted to the base, the whole then gold plated. The two kissing birds symbolize love, appropriate for the belt's use. Given to a girl by her family, her fiancé, or his family as a betrothal gift, it was worn with the wedding costume, and thereafter until the birth of the third child, then stored as an heirloom. *Photos: Folklore and Ethnology Museum of Macedonia, Thessalonika*

PATTERNED WIRE ROLLS

Patterned rolls for use on wire and strip of any contour section can be ordered from rolling mill manufacturers. Any desired pattern can be engraved on the rolls. A choice can be made from a great variety of patterns offered in manufacturers' catalogs. Such patterned strip is used in making wedding rings, for borders, and for many other purposes.

SOME ROLLING TECHNIQUES

In addition to the normal functions of the rolling mill, some special results can be obtained.

BROADSIDE OR CROSS ROLLING

Turning a piece of metal being rolled through 90° so that the next pass is made along the side edges is called making an *edging pass*. In rolling sheet metal, when the aim is to increase the width as well as the length, if the sheet's dimensions and the roll's length allow, the first few edging passes are made through the rolls in the width of the metal (the direction transverse to the normal longitudinal direction). This causes the metal to spread first to the required width, which it will then retain. When this is reached, the metal is turned through 90° and rolled lengthwise until the required length or thickness is reached.

FLATTENING A BOWED SHEET

Because sheet is flat to begin with does not mean that it will always exit from the rolls in a flat state. If a sheet has emerged correct in dimensional shape but is flexed or curved, it has *bow*, which can be removed by turning the sheet upside down and passing it through the rolls so that a counterdirection is imparted to it and it becomes flat again. Another method is to place the bowed sheet between two clean sheets of flat brass and roll them all. In this case, the brass sheets may become deformed, but the sheet between them will probably emerge flat.

SKIN ROLLING

Skin rolling is rolling a thin-gauge, annealed sheet cold with an absolute minimum of dimensional decrease to give the surface a smoother, brighter, harder skin; a minimum of variation in thickness; and a greater metal temper.

OVALING

If a piece of metal is first rounded at the corners and then rolled, it can be made to assume an oval form. Circular forms will also emerge as ovals. Ovals in turn can be changed to rounds by changing the direction of feed 90° in subsequent passes. Round shot fed broadside to the rolling mill exits as a flattened oval.

PACK OR PLY ROLLING

It is possible to roll sheets in packs or layers simultaneously, known as pack or ply rolling. A very thin sheet can be evenly reduced by rolling it between two thicker, hard metal sheets, and this technique allows it to be handled more easily. The pack is then opened and the sheets separated. *Opening* or *swording* is the term used to

separate pack or stack rolled sheets should they stick together after rolling. A corner is freed, then a blunt knife called an *opener* or *sword* is inserted to cleave apart the sheets.

TEXTURE AND PATTERN TRANSFER BY ROLLING

TEXTURING SHEET METAL

An impression can be made on sheet metal from any material such as metal screening, wire of all weights, clippings, washers, etc., placed between two clean sheets of annealed metal, then passing them through the rolls. The pressure of the rolls forces these materials into the metal so that they make a clear, negative impression on both sheets. The texturing material can then be rearranged on the sheet and a second, overlapping impression can be made on the first. The ingenuity of the reader will suggest other variations. Such sheets can be used in fabricated jewelry, and can also be shaped with nonmarking hammers.

In industry rolls are sometimes shotblasted to texture their surface so that the metal rolled through them also has this texture. Roll pressure is such that any textural variation on the rolls is imparted to the metal rolled through them.

4–12 MARY ANN SCHERR, U.S.A. Gold, silver, and bronze necklace with star sapphire. The engraved silver collar surfaces are ornamented with pierced and solid units made oval in a rolling mill. Pieces of round gold shot of ¼ in Ø were ovalized by running them through a mill, then used for the oval-shaped fringe units. Size 6 × 8½ in. *Photo: The Cleveland Museum of Art, Cleveland*

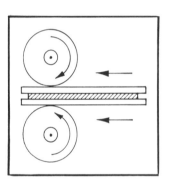

4–13 *TEXTURE TRANSFER* on two sheets rolled simultaneously from an inclusion between them.

4–14 HAROLD O'CONNOR, U.S.A. The rolling mill can be used to make an intaglio or negative impression on the facing surfaces of two annealed sheets by inserting crumpled wire or other suitable substances between them. *Photo: Ron Burton*

ETCHING TRANSFER

Harold O'Connor has used the rolling mill as a means of transferring a design etched on one sheet of metal to a plain-surfaced, annealed contacting sheet. If the etched metal sheet is soft and is not subjected to too much pressure, it can be used to make up to three impressions. Etched steel would allow a greater number of impressions to be made on softer metals.

CORRUGATED SHEET

A corrugated (alternating ridged and grooved) effect is possible on sheet metal by rolling thick sheet through the grooved section of a wire rolling mill. A checkered effect is possible if the sheet is then turned 90° at the next pass.

4–15 HAROLD O'CONNOR, U.S.A. With the rolling mill it is possible to transfer a design or texture etched on a metal sheet to another annealed sheet 22–26 B.&S. gauge, by rolling them simultaneously under average pressure. Photo: Ron Burton

4–16 HAROLD O'CONNOR, U.S.A. "Marrow and Tissue." Brooch in 24 gauge B.&S. sterling silver. The surface pattern was transferred in relief from an intaglio etched zinc plate. Ornamented with a cross-sectional slice of cow bone embedded in cast clear polyester resin. Flat results can be made three-dimensional by annealing them, placing them between two pieces of leather to preserve the surface, and back hammering the metal into a mold depression. Ø 2 in. Photo: Ron Burton

PATTERNED SHEET ROLLS

In industry, entire rolls are engraved with intaglio patterns to order. The negative intaglio designs are imparted to the sheet rolled through such rolls; the pattern appears in relief.

ROLLING DEFECTS

SLIP

Slip occurs when the rolls fail to bite the metal, which then does not move. When this happens, increase the distance between the rolls, or check to see if there is oil on the rolls that is causing the metal to slip.

BANANAING

When rolls are not parallel at the start of rolling, a rolled strip of metal emerges curved, thinner on the convex side and thicker on the concave side. When strip is not fed straight to the rolls it exits in a crescent-shaped condition. Both effects are called "bananaing." A similar effect takes place when sheet has been annealed unevenly, and is therefore harder and softer in parts, so that it exits with an elongation on the soft side while the hard side is shorter. This condition is known as *rockered* or *swept sheet*. The difference in elongation in such a case can be as much as 20%.

4–17 MARY ANN SCHERR, U.S.A. Stainless steel neckpiece with metal strips deliberately bananaed in the same direction. Some units are drill pierced, then mounted in series. Width 3 in; Ø 10 in. Photo: Samuel Scherr

OVERDRAFT AND UNDERDRAFT

If the rolls are of slightly different sizes, or one rotates at a slightly slower peripheral speed, on exit the sheet will tend to curve toward the faster moving roll, a condition called *overdraft* if the upper roll is faster, and *underdraft* if the lower one is faster. This can be done deliberately.

COBBLING

If the metal becomes twisted and does not issue properly from the rolls, it is said to cobble, and the piece itself is called a cobble.

CROWNING

An increase in sheet thickness at the center of the sheet is called crowning. It occurs because the rolls bend when they are too close together for the pass, or because they are worn out toward the center.

BUCKLES AND KINKS

Faulty adjustment of the rolls or in the structure of the rolling mill can result in buckle or waves, an irregular, corrugated, up-and-down wrinkle in the rolled sheet; or kink, a side wrinkle.

ROLL MARK

Should a roll become damaged or scarred, the metal rolled through it may have a roll mark on the surface which cannot be removed. A similar result occurs when the metal being rolled picks up foreign matter that is then rolled with it.

ROLLED-IN SCALE

As mentioned previously, if scale or surface oxides are left on the metal and rolled with the sheet, it becomes embedded in the surface, a condition called rolled-in scale. After pickling, the oxide is removed and the surface is left with an etched pattern, showing depressions where the scale existed. Oddly, this may be a way of achieving surface texture on a sheet.

CRACKS AND FLAKES

If an ingot being rolled is of irregular thickness or is passed through the rolls too many times without being annealed, cracks may form on its surface or edges. Cracking may also occur because of the composition of the metal or because of the way it was cast. Ingots may crack if they contain cold shuts (places where the metal froze due to discontinuous pouring); if the metal was too cold when poured; if the ingot contains too great a percentage of scrap metal; or if the alloy was insufficiently stirred to combine its constituents before pouring. Particles may flake off if the ingot contains foreign matter. If edge cracks are minor, they may be removed, the metal annealed, and the rolling continued. If surface cracks appear, or the edge cracks are major, it does not pay to continue the rolling, as the result will be defective. In such a case, remelt the metal, and pour a new ingot, adding new metal if necessary.

THE CARE OF ROLLING MILLS

When the rolling mill is not in use, the rolls should be moved out of contact with each other. Rolls should be lightly oiled regularly with a good grade of oil about No. 40 viscosity, and a thin film should be allowed to coat the rolls to prevent the formation of rust. Before rolling begins again, remove this protective oil film with a soft cloth or paper, otherwise it will cause slippage. Dust and foreign matter are simultaneously removed.

MEASURING AND MARKING

Tools used to achieve dimensional accuracy

To fabricate any object from the basic forms of metal—sheet, wire, or tube—once the design concept is established, the metal must be cut to necessary dimensions. To avoid waste, the metal is measured and marked before cutting.

MEASURING TOOLS

MARKED MEASURING TOOLS

These are instruments that follow standardized measuring systems, usually divided into subunits or fractions of units. The basic units of linear measurement in measuring metals are the *Decimal* or *Metric System,* and the *British and U.S.A. Measuring System* of inches and feet. (For a discussion of these systems, see British and American Measuring Systems, p. 731.) The marked measuring tools mentioned below are available in either measuring system.

Steel rules are strips of hardened steel marked with stamped measurements on one or both edges, and one or both sides. Stainless steel is preferred as it will not rust. They are used to measure straight, linear distances, for setting measurements on other tools such as dividers or calipers, for guiding a marking tool to make a straight line, for checking the straightness of an edge or surface, and as a guide when scoring a line.

Straight edges are lengths of steel similar to rulers in form but unmarked. Because their edges are "true," they are used to mark straight lines and test the trueness of a surface or edge. (See Tools for Scoring, Chapter 8.)

Squares are right angles used to check 90° corners. Some are unmarked and others have standard measurement marks. Some are rigid, and others have an adjustable handle that allows other angle measurements.

Protractors are instruments for measuring and laying down angles. Several different types exist, but the basic one has a semicircular form, a center mark on the straight edge, and the curve marked with angles from 0–180°.

Spring dividers are tools for dividing and transferring measurements from a rule measure to metal (or vice versa), to inscribe arcs and circles, and to divide line lengths into an equal number of parts. They consist of two tapering metal legs 6 in long, with sharp, hardened points that converge to a spring at the top. From the legs project a side screw holding a knurled round nut that when advanced on the screw, presses the legs together; the top spring controls the tension. When measuring, press together the points and place them against the rule the desired distance apart, then wind the nut down to that distance to hold them in this position. When the leg pressure is withdrawn, the nut is released and slides freely on the screw.

When making a circle or arc, hold the knurled top, place one point on the center mark, and swing the other leg in an arc, allowing it to mark the metal as it moves.

When the dividers are not in use, protect their points by pressing them into a cork.

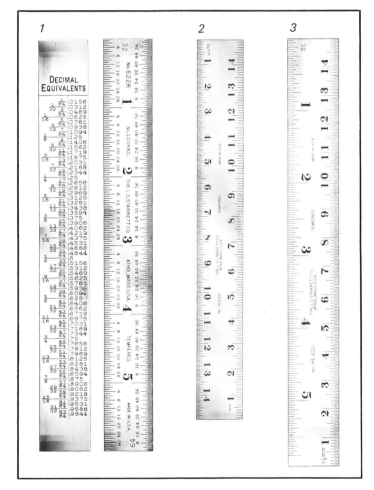

4–18 *STEEL RULES*
1. *Spring-tempered steel rule 6 in long, 3/4 in wide, 3/64 in thick. One side has accurate, machine-divided inch graduations in 32nds and 64ths, the other side has a table of fractions and their decimal equivalents.*
2. *Steel rule, metric measure, 15 cm long, graduated in millimeters and half-millimeters.*
3. *Spring-tempered steel rule, 6 in long, with graduations in both metric and British measure. Front side graduated in half-millimeters and 32nds of an inch, other side in millimeters and 64ths of an inch. Photo: Courtesy L. S. Starrett Co.*

CALIPERS

Calipers are tools similar to dividers but their legs are not straight and pointed. There are two basic forms: the *inside caliper,* whose legs are curved outward and are used for taking inside measurements; and the *outside caliper,* whose legs are bowed toward each other and are used for taking outside measurements. The *hermaphrodite caliper* has one inward-bending caliper leg, and one straight divider leg with an adjustable point. It is used for laying off distances from an edge, or for testing centered work.

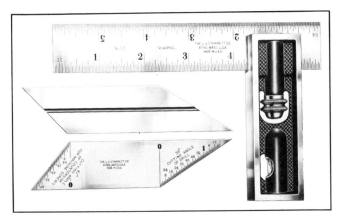

4–19 *DOUBLE SQUARE WITH SLIDING, HARDENED BLADES* 4–6 in long, including a level in the handle. The beveled blade, which can be inserted in the handle to replace the rule, has an octagon angle at one end, and a hexagon angle at the other end. The lower is a drill-grinding blade beveled to 59° at one end with the graduation located to measure perpendicularly to the drill axis. By reading the graduation, the drill center point can be easily and accurately located. The other end is a 41° angle for measuring the cutting angle of countersinks and machine screws. *Photo: Courtesy L. S. Starrett Co.*

After taking a measurement, the caliper can be placed against a steel rule to take a reading.

THE VERNIER CALIPER   This inch-marked type of caliper is used to make highly accurate measurements in thousandths of an inch or finer. Reading a 50 division vernier caliper is done as follows: The bar of the tool (center) is graduated in twentieths of an inch (0.05 in). Every second division represents one-tenth of an inch (0.10 in) and is numbered. On the vernier plate for inside measurement (top) and outside measurement (bottom) the space is divided into 50 parts. These 50 divisions occupy the same space as 49 divisions on the bar. The difference between the width of one of the 50 spaces on the vernier and one of the 49 spaces on the bar is therefore $\frac{1}{50}$ of $\frac{1}{20}$ ($\frac{1}{1000}$) of an inch. If the tool is set so that the 0 line on the vernier coincides with the 0 line on the bar, the line to the right of the 0 on the vernier will differ from the line to the right of the 0 on the bar by $\frac{1}{1000}$ of an inch; the second line by $\frac{2}{1000}$, etc. The difference will continue to increase $\frac{1}{1000}$ of an inch for each division until the line 50 on the vernier coincides with the line 49 on the bar.

To read a vernier caliper, note how many inches, tenths (0.10) and twentieths (0.05) the 0 mark on the vernier is from the 0 mark on the bar. Then note the number of divisions on the vernier from 0 to a line which exactly coincides with a line on the bar.

As an example, in the illustration an object has been inserted and the jaws closed on it causing the vernier to be moved to the right one and four-tenths and one-twentieth inches (1.45 in) as shown on the bar and the 14th line on the vernier coincides with a line, as indicated by the stars, on the bar. Fourteen thousandths of an inch are therefore to be added to the reading on the bar and the total reading is one and four-hundred-and-sixty-four-thousandths inches (1.464 in). (Courtesy L. S. Starrett Co.)

THE MICROMETER   The micrometer is a highly accurate measuring tool whose principle consists of the use of a

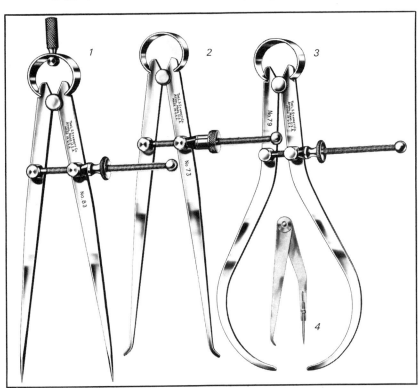

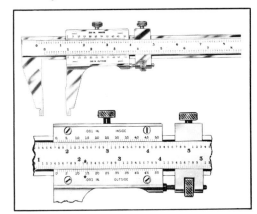

4–20 *DIVIDERS AND CALIPERS*
1. *Spring-type, 6 in dividers* of high-grade steel with two hardened and ground legs, and quick-adjusting, automatic-closing spring nut.
2. *Inside caliper, 6 in,* for taking inside measurements.
3. *Outside caliper, 6 in,* for taking outside measurements.
4. *Firm-joint hermaphrodite caliper* with one caliper and one straight divider leg holding an adjustable point, 4–6 in long, used for laying off distances from an edge, or for testing centered work.

4–21 *THE VERNIER CALIPERS*
Enlarged view of graduations.

ground screw or spindle which is rotated in a fixed nut, thus opening and closing the distance between the two measuring faces on the ends of the anvil and spindle. To measure a piece of work, place the object between the anvil and the spindle faces and rotate the spindle by

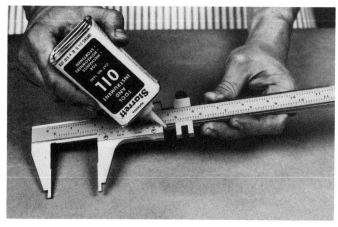

4-22   *LUBRICATING THE SLIDE ON A VERNIER CALIPER*
A special *tool and instrument oil* lubricant is used on hand measuring tools as well as on light machinery. It provides a long-lasting oil film on areas that must be protected against rust formation. *Photo: Courtesy L. S. Starrett Co.*

4-23   *OUTSIDE MICROMETER CALIPERS*
1. These micrometers are available in either British or Metric System measurements. This one is British System in 32nds of an inch with decimal equivalents. Its ample throat depth simplifies making measurements in narrow slots and tight places. The satin chrome finish makes reading easier, and the mirror-finished spindle and anvil ends allow close accuracy. The friction thimble ensures uniform pressure and direct feel.
2. The nomenclature of an outside micrometer caliper. *Photos: Courtesy L. S. Starrett Co.*

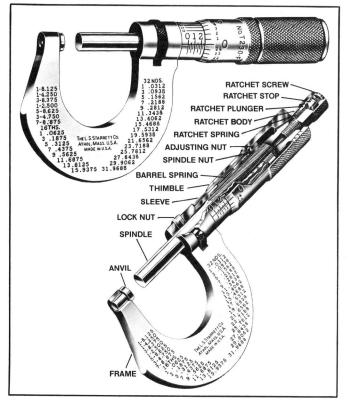

means of the thimble until both anvil and spindle contact the work. The dimension is found from the micrometer reading indicated by the graduations on the sleeve and thimble, as described below.

The pitch of the spindle screw thread is $\frac{1}{40}$ in (40 threads per inch) in micrometers graduated to measure in inches. One complete thimble revolution advances the spindle face toward or away from the anvil face by precisely $\frac{1}{40}$ in (0.025 in).

The longitudinal line on the sleeve is divided into 40 equal parts by vertical lines that correspond to the number of threads on the spindle. Each vertical line therefore designates $\frac{1}{40}$ in (0.025 in) and every fourth line, which is longer than the others, designates hundreds of thousandths. For example: the line marked "1" represents 0.100 in, the line marked "2" represents 0.200 in, and the line marked "3" represents 0.300 in.

The beveled edge of the thimble is divided into 25 equal parts with each line representing 0.001 in and every line is numbered consecutively. Rotating the thimble from one of these lines to the next moves the spindle longitudinally $\frac{1}{25}$ of 0.025 in, or 0.001 in; rotating it two divisions represents 0.002 in. Twenty-five divisions indicate a complete revolution—$\frac{1}{40}$ in (0.025 in).

To read a micrometer graduated in thousandths of an inch, multiply the number of vertical divisions visible on the sleeve by 0.025, and to this add the number of thousandths indicated by the line on the thimble which coincides with the longitudinal line on the sleeve.

Example: Reading to 0.178 in
Refer to the illustration.

The "1" line on the sleeve is visible, representing	0.100 in
There are three additional lines visible, each representing 0.025 in, therefore 3×0.025 in =	0.075 in
Line "3" on the thimble coincides with the longitudinal line on the sleeve, each line representing 0.001 in, therefore 3×0.001 in =	0.003 in
	0.178 in

An easy way to remember is to think of the various units as if you were making change from a ten-dollar bill with the figures on the sleeve representing dollars, the vertical lines on the sleeve as quarters, and the divisions on the thimble as cents. Add up the change and put a decimal point instead of a dollar sign in front of the figures.

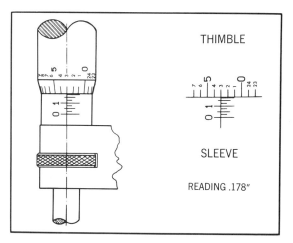

4-24   *EXAMPLE OF HOW TO READ A MICROMETER CALIPER.*

OTHER MEASURING TOOLS

METAL AND WIRE GAUGE MEASURING TOOLS These tools are used to measure the thickness of sheet and wire. The usual form of these gauges is a round circle that has slits along the outer edges in graduated sizes marked on one side with a gauge number, and on the opposite side with its decimal equivalents in inches or millimeters. (See Standard Weights, Measures, and Tables for equivalents of inches and millimeters). To measure a sheet of metal, insert it into the slit that it fits without being forced. Different gauges are made for different standard gauge measures, such as the American Standard Wire Gauge (Brown and Sharpe or B.&S.), the U. S. Standard Gauge for Iron and Steel sheet, the W.&M. (Washburn and Moen) Standard Wire Gauge, and the British (Imperial) Standard Wire Gauge, all also used for sheet metal. (See Wire Gauges: Wire Measurement, Chapter 6; and Standard Weights, Measures, and Tables, Chapter 18.)

WIRE AND TWIST DRILL GAUGES These gauges are in the form of a perforated sheet of high-alloy steel, and are used to measure numbered and lettered twist drill diameters. The reading is taken from the side of the hole into which the drill fits. It can also be used to measure wire. (See Piercing, Chapter 4.)

RING SIZE MEASURING DEVICES These are used to check the size of the inside diameter of a ring shank. This measurement corresponds with the finger size on which a ring is worn for proper fit.

Ring sticks resemble tapered mandrels, but are normally only used to take ring measurements. As no other work is done on them, they may be made of a lightweight metal such as aluminum, or of plastic. They are marked in graduated one-fourth or one-half standard ring sizes in a particular scale such as the U.S.A., British, and European standards. (See "Ring Sizes," page 734.) Some are provided with grooves into which the back of a set stone may go without impeding the accuracy of size measurements taken.

Ring sizers are standardized sets of graduated metal wire circles, all held on a large metal hoop. Each ring of the set is marked with a size number which is accurate within 0.003 in (0.076 mm) as recommended by the U. S. Bureau of Standards, and the sizes correspond with the ring size scale in local use. Sets are made for taking measurements of rings with normal width shanks, and others for rings with wide width shanks.

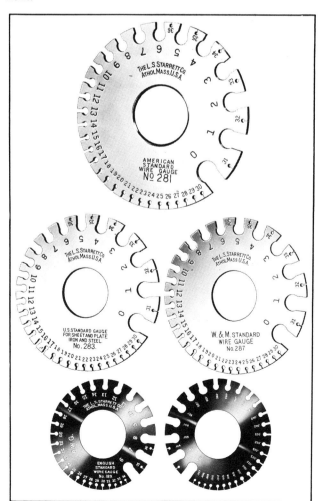

4–25 *SHEET AND WIRE GAUGES*
Top: American Standard Wire Gauge, Brown and Sharpe (B.&S.), for measuring the thickness of nonferrous metal sheet and wire in sizes ranging from 0–36.
Left: U. S. Standard Gauge for measuring 0–36 gauge sheet and plate iron and steel. It is based on weights in ounces per square foot.
Right: Steel Wire Gauge, also known as the American Steel and Wire Company's Gauge, Washburn and Moen Standard, or the United States Steel Wire Gauge. It is used for measuring steel wire and drill rod.
Below: British (Imperial) *Standard Wire Gauge,* also called the Birmingham or Stubbs Iron Wire Gauge. Used for iron wire, and hot and cold rolled steel.
All gauges can also be used to measure nonferrous and precious metal sheet and wire. All have decimal equivalents in inches on the reverse side. Gauges are also available with metric system measurements.

4–26 *SHEET GAUGE MEASUREMENT*
Inserting a piece of sheet metal in a gauge to take a measurement.
Photo: Courtesy William Dixon Co.

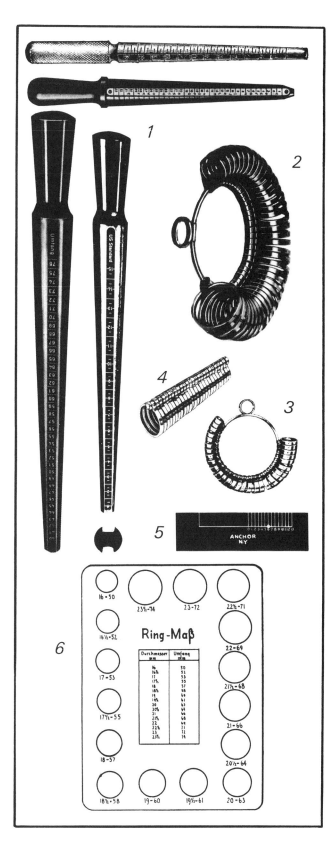

4–27 *RING SIZE MEASURING DEVICES*
1. *Ring sticks, top:* hardened steel with marked quarter size graduations up to 13, can also be used as a regular ring mandrel; *below:* ring stick of aluminum, with four different scales of standard ring size measurement systems; *left:* aluminum ring stick in European ring sizes; *right:* plastic ring stick graduated in quarter sizes from 1–15, with recessed groove to allow for stone culets that protrude below ring shank circumferences, ring tags, or strings attached to rings.
2. *Ring sizer* for normal width ring shanks, marked in half sizes from 1–15, accurate within 0.003 in as recommended by the U. S. Bureau of Standards.
3. *Ring sizer for wide width ring shanks,* graduated in half sizes from 1–15.
4. *Pocket ring sizer,* for normal width ring shanks, graduated in half sizes from 1–13.
5. *Ring gauge,* flat, used to measure metal lengths needed for ring shanks.
6. *Ring map,* cardboard or plastic, flat, European ring sizer pierced with accurate hole measurements, for keeping in a pocket, or sending through the mail to ascertain ring sizes of distant clients.

MARKING TOOLS

CENTER PUNCH (PRICK PUNCH) This tool has a knurled cast steel rod shank with a flat end that is hammered to make the opposite, pointed end ground to a 90° angle put a mark on the metal when struck. This point is used as a measuring reference, and also as a means of steadying a twist drill at the point where it must penetrate the metal.

AUTOMATIC CENTER PUNCH This tool will make a mark without being hammered because it is constructed with a built-in spring mechanism. When the point is placed in position, the shaft is pressed downward, causing the point to automatically rebound and mark the metal.

Both manual and automatic center punches can be used to make dot marks on metal for purely decorative effect, both in linear arrangements and at random, to create textured surfaces.

SCRIBER This tool consists of a steel rod with straight (or one straight and one bent), tapering, hardened point, and a knurled body. It is used to mark a line along a steel rule or straight edge, or a curved instrument, on metal, plastic, ceramic, etc. Some have a carbide point embedded in the tip, and others have interchangeable threaded tips. For an accurate mark, slant the point slightly away from the guide rule so it contacts its true base. (See Tools for Scoring, Chapter 8.)

DESIGN TRANSFER TO METAL

Materials and methods

Some jewelers begin a work by first making a *full-scale rendering* or drawing on paper that realistically represents the object, to be able to visualize its final appearance. From this, a *full-scale working drawing* of the object may then be made showing it in plan view from the front, side, and back, as well as detail drawings that solve construction problems. Working drawings can be used as the basis from which measurements can be taken at different stages of fabrication. Other jewelers work *directly* with the materials used: sheet metal, tubing, or wire.

A design on paper must be transferred directly to flat or formed metal (or other material) to permit a part to be sawed out, or in preparation for etch piercing, saw piercing, engraving, or repoussage. Different materials and methods of transfer of the design can be used, the choice depending on the material and the process to be executed.

Pencil lines drawn directly on polished metal are not satisfactory as the lines, as well as being temporary, are difficult to see. Graphite will not "take" well on a polished surface which must first be given a "tooth" with a fine abrasive paper or pumice powder and water paste.

India ink or *tusche* can be used to draw lines on clean, greaseless metal surfaces, and must be allowed to dry thoroughly.

Felt marking pens with fine points can be used to draw lines on clean metal surfaces, and the lines dry instantly.

Chinese white is a water-soluble, densely pigmented zinc white that is available in tube, stick, or solid block form. It is dissolved and thinned with a *brush* and water, and is painted evenly on clean, greaseless metal surfaces to create a ground on which lines are easily visible. After drying, which can be hastened by gentle heating to prevent flaking, this ground can be drawn on with *pencil, marking pen,* or a *pointed wooden stick.* In usual practice, the lines are then gone over with a *scriber* whose point passes through the paint and leaves a mark on the metal. Scribing is done lightly to avoid deep lines which may be difficult to remove. The paint is then easily washed away with water.

In some cases, especially for small areas, it is sufficient to simply moisten a finger, apply it to the paint, and dab the area with the finger, spreading it on evenly. Other water-soluble paints such as tempera and casein white or yellow can also be used in this way.

Liquid white paints commercially prepared for this purpose are also available.

Yellow ochre powder mixed with a little water (or if necessary for longer lasting coverage, with some water-soluble glue as well) can be used in the same way as white paint. It too can be easily washed away.

Whiting powder which is chalk or calcium carbonate can be mixed with gasoline to a paintlike consistency and applied with a brush. The liquid evaporates in a few minutes, leaving a white residue upon which one can draw or inscribe.

Layout dye is a commercial preparation available in 4 oz and 1 qt cans. It is painted onto a clean, grease-free metal surface, where it dries instantly to an opaque blue or other dark color. Lines inscribed through this coating are highly visible. The dye will not flake off or rub off on hands and clothing. It is not affected by cutting lubricants, nor by the heat generated by machining operations and so can be used in lathe operations. It is easily removed with a cloth moistened with denatured alcohol.

Carbon transfer is possible by rubbing the back of a design paper with a soft lead pencil held with the exposed lead flat against the paper. The paper is attached to the metal with masking tape so it does not move out of register. All the lines of the design are gone over from the front of the paper with a sharp *pencil* or a *stylus* (a tool with a smooth, dull point). Because these lines on metal

4-28 NILDA C. F. GETTY, U.S.A. preparing a metal surface for design transfer by painting it with a quick-drying, commercial, white transfer paint. On this the design is transferred by placing a carbon paper below the positioned drawing, and tracing the lines with a pencil or stylus. *Photo: Les Brown*

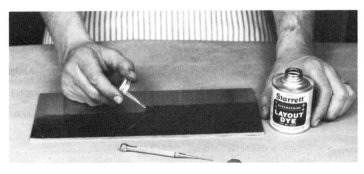

4-29 *APPLYING A BLUE, QUICK-DRYING LAYOUT DYE* manufactured by L. S. Starrett Co. The design is then drawn with a scriber through the dye coat, and exposes the metal. *Photo: Courtesy L. S. Starrett Co.*

alone are easily rubbed off by finger contact, it is advisable to lightly inscribe them before working on the metal, or to first coat the metal with a water-soluble paint and then make the tracing.

Tracing paper on which the design is drawn can also be blackened at the back in the same way as above. It has the advantage of allowing the metal to be visible through the paper.

Cementing a paper drawing to metal is possible if the cement used will not affect the dimensions of the drawing by causing the paper to swell. This means that water-soluble cements or glues are not usable for this purpose. If in doubt about the suitability of a cement, try painting some on the paper in question and watch its reaction. The cement used should hold the paper in place and not allow it to creep on the metal once cutting action starts, or the result will be inaccurate. This system is often used in pierced work.

Rubber cement is a liquefied rubber adhesive most generally used to cement paper as it does not affect it dimensionally nor cause curling. It can be used for temporary or permanent bonds. For a permanent, nonslipping bond, apply the cement with the brush applicator (usually sold with the container) to both the metal and the paper back surfaces, and allow them to become tacky before placing the paper in position on the metal and pressing it flat. To distribute the cement evenly between the two substances and assure complete contact between them, place a straight edge on the paper and draw it over the surface with pressure, which will also remove surplus cement. Allow the cement to dry thoroughly before starting to cut

the metal. Rubber cement is inflammable and highly volatile and its fumes are toxic. It should therefore be used in good ventilating conditions, and not near a flame or other heat source. Since it evaporates quickly, its container should be closed tightly immediately after use. If it thickens excessively it can be thinned with a *cement thinner*. The same thinner is a rubber cement solvent and can be used to remove the paper from the surface of the metal.

Transfer wax, also called *engraver's wax,* is applied to a polished metal surface to dull it by leaving a film on which the design can then be marked with a *pointed stick* or pencil. *Beeswax* or *Plasticine clay* can be used in the same way. In traditional practice after preparing a surface for engraving, it is dusted with powdered chalk or whiting contained in a *pounce bag* made of two thicknesses of a closely woven, circular-cut cotton cloth in the center of which the powder is placed, and the edges drawn together and tied tightly with a string. This is pounced on the wax and leaves a white deposit which increases the visibility of the design when drawn.

The design is marked with the stick which will not scratch the metal surface. Lines are then lightly scratched over with a *scriber,* after which the wax is rubbed off with a cloth, leaving the design ready for engraving.

Transfer wax can be used in another way. A design already drawn on paper is waxed on the back with transfer wax and placed in position on the metal. The paper design is then gone over with a *scriber* which transfers a fine wax line on the metal. This is traced with a scriber and the wax is removed.

CUTTING SHEET METAL

Dividing metal from mass by shearing action

Cutting is the act of dividing metal by penetrating it edgewise with a hand cutting tool that has a cutting edge or edges—to make an incision or divide it into parts; or with a manually operated power cutting tool to sever a portion. In another sense, cutting can also include the acts of drilling, sawing, carving, chiseling, and grinding, in all of which metal is penetrated or removed from the surface. These cutting acts are described separately. Cutting metal is the most basic operation in metalwork.

SHEARING

One of the most basic sheet metal hand cutting tools is the *shears,* which has been in use since the Iron Age. The mechanical principle of shears is that of a *double lever* that pivots around a fulcrum, the central bolt that also serves to hold them together. Each lever has a handle at one end, and the other end is a sharpened, beveled-edge cutting blade, the two blades opposing each other. When hand cutting sheet metal, the sheet is inserted between the jaws of the blades. By pressing the handles together, the cutting edges create a plane of shear stress that allows them to penetrate the metal which initially resists them, but when the force is sufficient, gives way. By a tangential,

perpendicular shearing action, the blades penetrate the metal, shear it, and slide by each other, completing the cut.

SHEARING TOOLS

Several tools perform the action of shearing metal. The larger the tool size, the heavier the metal it will cut.

Scissors are used to cut metal leaf, foil, lightweight sheet metal, and small or soft wire. The blades have plain or serrated edges, and are straight or curved.

Snips are used to cut solder, wire, and thin-gauge metals. They may have bowed or looped handles, and are made with straight blades to make straight cuts, or curved blades to make curved cuts.

Hand shears include a wide range of sizes and forms. The heaviest can cut up to 18 gauge B.&S. metal or more. *Tinner's shears* have wide, looped handles, and cut lightweight metals. Larger hand shears are available in lengths of 7 in, 10 in, 12¾ in. Each of these is available with straight, curved, or "universal" hollow-ground cutting blades that respectively will make straight, curved, or both straight and curved cuts. To increase the leverage on metal when cutting heavy sheet, place one handle in the jaws of a *bench vise* to immobilize it, insert the metal in the

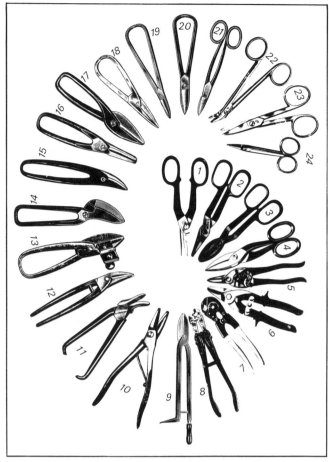

4-32 TAPIO WIRKKALA, Finland, designer; manufacturer Kultakeskus Oy, Hämeenlinna. "Silver Moon." Pendants and earrings of flat, circular sheet forms in concentric and parallel repeats of the same shape in diminishing sizes. All are cut by a circle shear cutting machine. The articulated parts are held by the vertical member. *Photo: Courtesy Kultakeskus Oy*

4-31 HAND-OPERATED METAL-CUTTING MACHINES

1. *Heavy-duty bench shears* with separate, removable handle, for cutting sheet, rod, and flat bars. Replaceable tool steel blades are kept in the opened position by a strong spring to prevent accidental closing. The three models shown respectively have blade lengths of $4\frac{3}{4}$, $6\frac{3}{32}$, and 8 in; cut sheet up to $\frac{1}{8}$, $\frac{5}{32}$, and $\frac{3}{16}$ in; and round bars up to $\frac{3}{8}$, $\frac{7}{16}$, and $\frac{1}{2}$ in. (Swest)
2. *Circular shearing machine* with adjustable ball bearing nut to align the upper blade with the lower one, thus facilitating the cutting action. Cuts from 0–225 mm circles. (Karl Fischer)
3. *Multiple strip shearing machine*, will divide sheet into strips of from less than 1 mm to 65 mm wide. (Karl Fischer)

4-30 SHEARS AND SCISSORS

1. *Ring-handled universal shears*, makes straight or curved cuts in light sheet metal, 7 in long.
2. *Ring-handled duck-bill circular pattern shears* for straight or curved cuts, 10 in long.
3. *Ring-handled straight pattern metal cutting shears*, $12\frac{3}{4}$ in long.
4. *Ring-handled tinner's shears*, straight blade, 8 in long.
5. *Straight-cut, aviation-type, compound-leverage power snips*, cuts up to 18 gauge B.&S., 10 in long.
6. *Compound-leverage power cut type shears*, 11 in long.
7. *Compound lever action sprue handclip cutter*, cuts up to 8 gauge B.&S., 18 in long.
8. *Heavy-duty, vise-mounting sprue cutter*, 14 in long.
9. *Vise-anchored bench shears* for sheet metal, 20 in long.
10. *Right or left side figured cutting open-handled shears* with spring, 215 mm long.
11. *Universal, right or left all figure cutting sheet metal shears*, 260–280 mm long.
12. *Figure cutting shears*, 225–330 mm long.
13. *Bow-handled shears* with attached adjustable millimeter scale, used for straight cutting sheet in widths from 1–100 mm wide. This attachment can be applied to any straight-bladed tin snips.
14. *Bow-handled, curve-bladed shears* that allow ease in access to the cutting groove, 275 mm long.
15. *Bow-handled, curve-bladed hole and sheet cutting shears*, 225–350 mm long.
16. *Bow-handled, universal blade shears*, 225 mm long.
17. *Silversmith's shears* for sheet metal, right hand or left hand, 200–300 mm long.
18. *Bow-handled, pointed, narrow, chain shears*, 150 mm long.
19. *Bow-handled, small-pointed, narrow chain shears*, 176 mm long.
20. *Bow-handled goldsmith's snips* for cutting lightweight metal and solder, straight or curve bladed, 180 mm long.
21. *Ring-handled goldsmith's shears* with straight blades, 180 mm long.
22. *Ring-handled angle-bladed scissors* for cutting wire and lightweight metal, $4\frac{3}{4}$ in long.
23. *Ring-handled, wide-bladed scissors* for cutting soft wire, $3\frac{3}{8}$ in long.
24. *Ring-handled foil cutting scissors*, $3\frac{1}{4}$ in long.

4–33 TANE S.A., Mexico City, manufacturer. Silver bangles of circle and square parts cut from sheet, given dimension by hollow construction. *Photo: Courtesy Tane S.A.*

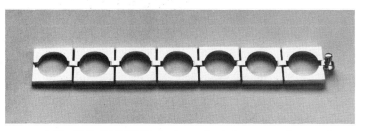

4–34 BENT GABRIELSEN P., Denmark, designer; manufacturer Georg Jensen Sølvsmedie A/S, Copenhagen. The circular openings within each square are made dimensional by box construction. Unit repeats are joined by links to articulate the whole. *Photo: Erik Junior, courtesy Georg Jensen Sølvsmedie A/S*

4–35 MARY ANN SCHERR, U.S.A. "Fringe Necklace." Gold, using the concept of single unit shape repetition. The tapered strip units are mounted by jump rings on a wire frame, and move freely with the wearer's movement. *Photo: Richard Monasterio*

4–36 PETER SKUBIC, Austria. White gold and steel ring using rectangular strip shapes stabilized by joining them to a common ground. The shapes are repeated in graduated sizes. *Photo: Günter Meyer, courtesy Schmuckmuseum, Pforzheim*

shears' jaws, then bring the second handle down on the metal.

Compound-action hand shears have double-levered handles which greatly increase the ability of the blades to cut without requiring more than normal force. They are sometimes called *aviation-type shears.*

Bench shears are manually operated power tools used for cutting heavier sheet metal and rods. This tool, sometimes called *bench alligator shears,* must be bolted to the workbench to make it rigid. It includes a lower, immobile cutting blade, and a moving upper blade that is controlled by a long handle that raises and lowers it on the metal. A spring holds the blade in an open position to prevent accidental closing. The upper blade has a hole into which wire or rod 3/8–1/2 in in diameter can be inserted and cut by bringing the top blade down to meet the lower one. Bench shears are available in several sizes. The larger the model, the heavier the sheet and rod that can be cut with it.

Guillotine shears are hand- or foot-operated power shears similar in principle to the above-mentioned bench shears. The upper blade, which cants slightly to the left, is lowered on the metal which rests on a cutting table. Control over the amount of metal cut is achieved by pushing the metal forward to project—the desired amount to be cut—over the lower, stationary cutting blade. Small models are available, and large models are used in industry to cut heavy sheet metal. (See Illustration 1 in Demonstration 16, Chapter 9.)

CUTTING PRACTICE

When cutting sheet metal, the sheet must always be at a right angle to the cutting blade because a perpendicular plane of shear is the most efficient way to cut metal as the force is brought directly on the metal at its true thickness. Push the sheet as far back as possible into a hand shears' jaws to get the greatest leverage, and cut directly on the marked cutting line. Make each cut as long as the blade length will allow, from one-half to three-quarters of their total length. If the cut is longer than this, open the blades slowly and push them forward in the cut to continue on the same line so that no irregular spurs are created. In cutting, the sheet will probably bend. If this condition becomes bothersome, as when cutting long, narrow strips, immobilize one shear handle in a *bench vise,* and grasp the end of the strip with a pair of *pliers* held in the left hand while the right hand operates the shear handle.

If in cutting, the metal is not at a right angle to the blades, it may become clinched between them. Should this occur too frequently, especially with lightweight shears, the blades may be forced out of alignment, and the shears will become useless due to the looseness of the blades.

SAWING

Severing or contour shaping metal by gradual groove removal

THE JEWELER'S SAW FRAME

The *jeweler's saw frame* with saw blade is probably the most important of all metal-cutting tools used by jewelers in sawing, one of the basic operations in metalwork. Because the saw is used so often, when purchasing a new frame, select one of good quality; the same is true of the purchase of *saw blades*. It is false economy to purchase inferior blades that will break quickly.

The stone saw was developed in Neolithic times and bronze saws came into existence in Egypt about 3500 B.C. Thereafter, saws went through many adaptations of form

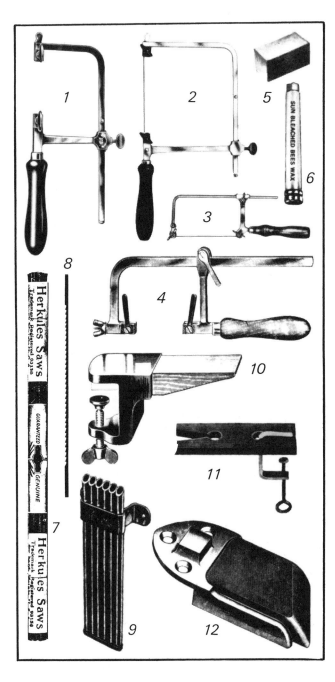

and size in response to the need for specialized uses on different materials. The idea of the saw blade being placed in a frame under tension, the forerunner of today's jeweler's saw frame, originated in ancient Rome.

The adjustable jeweler's saw frame allows the use of blades of different lengths, or portions of broken blades. It consists of two major parts made of flat, tempered, hardened steel, held together by a thumbscrew. The terminals of these parts are mounted with two internally serrated clamps that grasp the saw blade ends. They are tightened upon the blades manually by the thumbscrews or wing nuts provided. Unless discretion is used, they should not be tightened with pliers or their threads will ultimately be stripped. The tool is manipulated by a hardwood handle into which the tang of the lower frame (leg) enters. To adjust the distance between the blade clamps to accommodate a saw blade, loosen the thumbscrew holding the back bar. This allows the inverted L-shaped back bar (spine) with its extension to slide through the box-shaped support at the juncture of the two parts. When the desired distance is reached, the frame is made rigid by tightening the rear thumbscrew. The saw frame in effect then becomes *a spring whose function is to hold the saw blade under tension.*

This spring-shaped saw frame is manufactured with an adjustable depth of throat (from saw blade to back bar) of 2¼ in, 3 in, 5 in (the sizes most used in jewelry making) and in inch intervals from 4–12 in depths, allowing the blade to penetrate the metal up to those depths. The deeper the frame throat, the more difficult it is to balance the saw frame during work, and the handle must be gripped more firmly to keep the blade and the handle perpendicular, the position in which the saw is held in use.

Nonadjustable saw frames are available, but because their blade-holding clamps are a fixed distance apart, only full-sized saw blades can be used with them. Saw frames also exist whose adjustment for tension on the blade is controlled by a tensioning, round, knurled screw, which is a frame-adjusting device that allows greater tension to be brought to bear on the blade once it is clamped in place. Other frames have movable levers for the same purpose. Some are made with saw blade–holding clamps that *permit* rotation so that a change in blade position can point the cutting edge in any direction. This is useful when the position of the back bar inhibits further movement, as the frame can then be swung out of the way.

4–37 SAWING TOOLS AND MATERIALS
1. *Adjustable jeweler's saw frame, 2½ in deep.*
2. *Adjustable jeweler's saw frame, 4 in deep.*
3. *Oval adjustable jeweler's saw frame, 2½ in deep.*
4. *Adjustable jeweler's saw frame with attached tightening levers.*
5. *Block of saw blade lubricating wax.*
6. *Tube of saw blade lubricating wax, sun-bleached beeswax.*
7. *One gross (144) of jeweler's saw blades.*
8. *Single blade in the correct, tooth-down position.*
9. *Saw blade dispenser for attachment to workbench.*
10. *Maple wood bench pin 4 × 2½ in, mounted in 3¼ in top anvil, with screw clamp for attachment on table top up to 1½ in thick.*
11. *Wooden V bench pin held with C-clamp.*
12. *Bench-attached rubber filing block, 5 × 2¼ in, in steel frame, for resting work while filing. Rubber prevents work slippage and scratching.*

THE JEWELER'S SAW BLADE

Jeweler's saw blades, generally termed *piercing saws,* are made of thin, flat strips of a special steel alloy, precisely tempered and hardened. They are used mainly for the cutting of precious, but also nonferrous, and ferrous metals, as well as for cutting softer materials such as bone, ivory, shell, and wood. Their cross section is usually *rectangular,* and some are made with rounded backs to permit their following curves and turning corners more easily. The usual length is 5¼ in (13.3 cm) and except for a distance of about one inch at either end which is straight and toothless (the parts inserted into the saw frame's holding clamps) they bear a continuous series of equal-sized, uniformly spaced teeth on the sawing edge, a saw blade type termed *mill teeth.*

The teeth of the jeweler's saw blade have a *pitch* or *rake* that inclines the *face* (front cutting edge) of the tooth downward at an angle. The curving space from tooth point to throat to the next point is called the *gullet.* In the jeweler's saw blade, the gullet is a concave curve and *not* an angle as in the case of other types of blades. The number of teeth per inch determines its *points,* and the distance from point to point of two contiguous teeth is its *space.* The thickness of the blade is its *gauge,* and its dimension corresponds to and can be measured by a wire gauge. The correct choice of gauge is critical in certain circumstances. The narrower the blade gauge, the less *lemel* or waste metal is produced during sawing.

In manufacture, the teeth are given a *set* (an alternating lateral inclination) so they protrude to the right and left beyond the blade thickness. Because of the set, when sawing, the teeth produce a *kerf* (slit or groove in the metal) that is just a tiny bit larger than the gauge, which allows the blade sufficient clearance during its cutting action to prevent it from becoming overheated and breaking due to

4–38 *THE ALTERNATING SET OF THE TEETH OF A JEWELER'S SAW BLADE, generally used on nonferrous metals, tubing, and softer materials to prevent the blade from jamming or becoming bound or pinched in the kerf. Photo: Courtesy L. S. Starrett Co.*

▼

BLADES
Saws Finer than 4/0 not Illustrated

————————————	4/0
————————————	3/0
————————————	2/0
————————————	1/0
————————————	1
————————————	1½
————————————	2
————————————	3
————————————	4
————————————	5
————————————	6
————————————	8
————————————	10
————————————	12
————————————	14

4–39 *SAW BLADES, ACTUAL SIZE* ▲
Blades smaller than 4/0 not illustrated.

the consequent loss of temper, or being pinched by the kerf sides and jamming or binding to immobility. The idea of set teeth in a saw blade is credited to the Romans. Band saw blades are made with their teeth arranged in a series of waves for the same reasons.

When the blade is mounted in the saw frame, the teeth must point *away* from the throat of the saw frame and toward the metal, as well as *downward* toward the handle. If the teeth point upward, they will lift the metal in the upward stroke, causing chattering in the sawing process and therefore inaccurate sawing results. When they point downward they work to hold the metal in place in the downward or cutting stroke.

The fineness of the saw blade is specified by the number of tooth points in one inch, and a relationship exists between this and the weight and size of the cross-sectional shape of the blade. Jeweler's saw blade sizes are codified, 8/0 being the finest, and 14 the coarsest.

Thin blades are used for fine piercing work as they cut a narrow kerf and have less tendency to bind, but they will buckle if pushed too hard. Coarse blades cut faster and are less likely to break, but form a wider kerf with greater loss of metal. Thin metals require fine blades, and heavier metals generally need heavier blades. The most usual sizes in use for jewelry making, from fine to coarse, range from 3/0, 2/0, 1/0, and 0. Finer sizes are widely used on gold and platinum, while coarser sizes are used on silver. Saw blades are usually sold in a minimum of 12 in one size, or the *gross* which is 12 dozens in one packet. Each dozen is held together with a spirally wrapped hair-fine soft iron wire. This can be easily unwound to release one blade from the dozen. To keep the unused blades together, simply twist the wire around them by twirling the blades with the fingers, while holding the wire taut.

Besides the usual saw blades described, also available for use with the jeweler's saw frame are *spiral saw blades,* whose teeth are arranged spirally around the core. These cut metal in any direction, and are also used for cutting wax, rubber, plaster, plastics, and other soft substances. They are available in sizes 2, 3, and 4 with diameters equal in width to those of piercing saws of the same sizes. *Flat saws* that look like miniature hacksaw blades are also available in sizes 1–12, and are used for heavy-duty, straight cutting.

BLADE STORAGE Saw blades are subject to rusting and corrosion if they are exposed to high humidity, heat, or acid fumes. The best way to store them is to place them in a stoppered tube of glass, plastic, or aluminum, each tube marked with the blade size and number and its decimal equivalent.

STRINGING

To insert a saw blade in the saw frame (*stringing*), first loosen the upper and lower thumbscrews to open the jaws they control. Insert the upper end of the saw blade the full distance into the upper frame clamp jaws, making sure the teeth are pointing straight *down* toward the handle and outward, *away* from the back of the saw frame, and then tighten that thumbscrew. Adjust the distance between the upper and lower saw blade jaws by loosening the back frame thumbscrew, then slide the frame so that the lower blade end just enters the lower saw blade clamp jaws, and tighten the back frame thumbscrew. As the fineness of the teeth makes them hard to see, check to be certain that they point *away* from the throat of the frame and *down-*

Jeweler's Saw Blades

(Thickness and width in decimal inches; with equivalent drill sizes)

Saw Blade Size	Piercing Saw Blades		Drill Size	Flat Saw Blades	
	Thickness	Width		Thickness	Width
8/0	.0063″	.0126″	80	–	–
7/0	.0067″	.0130″	80	–	–
6/0	.0070″	.0140″	79	–	–
5/0	.0080″	.0157″	78	–	–
4/0	.0086″	.0175″	77	–	–
3/0	.0095″	.0190″	76	–	–
2/0	.013″	.0204″	75	–	–
1/0	.0110″	.0220″	75	–	–
0	.0110″	.0230″	73	–	–
1	.0120″	.0240″	74	.0070″	.0290″
1½	.0125″	.0250″	71	–	–
2	.0134″	.0276″	70	.0080″	.0340″
3	.0140″	.0290″	70	.0080″	.0370″
4	.0150″	.0307″	68	.0080″	.0430″
5	.0158″	.0331″	65	.0080″	.0510″
6	.0173″	.0370″	58	.0080″	.0590″
7	.0189″	.0400″	56	.0080″	.0670″
8	.0197″	.0440″	55	.0086″	.0750″
9	–	–	–	.0086″	.0830″
10	.0215″	.0510″	51	.0086″	.0950″
11	–	–	–	.0086″	.1060″
12	.0236″	.0650″	51	.0095″	.1180″
14	.0236″	.0690″	50	–	–

ward by lightly running a finger upward against them. It should catch. Do not use too much pressure or the blade will cut through the skin.

Then, while seated, hold the handle toward you while the rest of the frame points downward, and press the top end of the frame against the edge of the workbench while pressing the handle against the chest. This pressure forces the jaws of the sprung frame toward each other from ¼–½ in depending on the degree of pressure used. The pressure should be just enough to allow the lower end of the saw blade to be guided by the hands, which are both free, into the lower clamp jaws. While maintaining tension on the frame, tighten the lower thumbscrew to close the clamp on the saw blade. Release the pressure on the frame *slowly* to transfer the tension *gradually* to the saw blade; otherwise it may break.

To test the suitability of the blade tension, pluck it with a fingernail—it should emit a high vibrating note. If a saw blade is slack or clamped too loosely in the clamp jaws, it

tends to bend and break. If it is under too much tension in the saw frame, it will tend to twist and work away from the cutting line, and if you try to force it to return to place, it may break.

When a saw blade breaks, it is possible to use the larger section by reducing the distance between the blade-holding clamps. This is one of the advantages of the adjustable saw frame; rigid frames do not allow such usage. Such saw blade fragments do not, however, last long. Before fixing the blade section in place, be sure to open both blade-holding clamps and tap them to remove any saw blade fragments that may have been left behind. Should these remain, clamps cannot be properly tightened on the blade, which may result in breakage or in a tendency to slip from the jaw when sawing. (Parts of old broken blades can be sawed for use in lining up the knuckles of a hinge, through which they are inserted prior to soldering.)

SAWING PRACTICE

There are two main types of sawing actions. One is *severing,* in which an object is cut off and separated into two parts, usually by cutting straight through it. This is often done when cutting through a rod or a tube, but other forms of metal can also be severed. The other is *contour sawing* in which the outline of a shape is sawed out. This usually takes place with sheet metal, but again other forms of metal can be contoured. Combinations of these two sawing acts are also possible.

SUPPORTING THE METAL IN SAWING, AND SAWING POSTURE

To support the metal when sawing, a hardwood *bench pin* is used. It fits into a groove made to hold at the edge of the workbench top, or it can be held by a *C-clamp* to the top of the workbench with the clamp at the left (for right-handed people) to allow work space clearance. The bench pin should be fixed at a height convenient for use when working in a seated position to prevent fatigue and allow looking directly down on the cutting line for accurate sawing. Most jeweler's benches are about 36 in high,

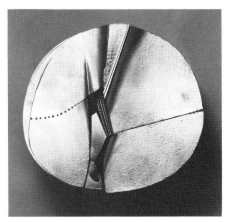

4–40   OTHMAR ZSCHALER, Switzerland. Brooch in 750 gold. Sawing is employed here not only to cut the contours of montage-assembled parts, but to create graphic lines in the composition. Size 8 × 7 cm. *Photo: Günter Meyer*

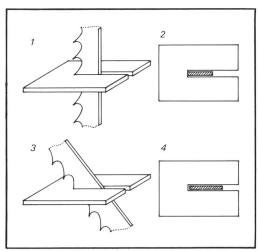

4–41   SAWING
1. The correct, vertical position of the saw blade in relation to the metal being cut, with teeth pointing down.
2. In this position, the blade's sectional contact with the metal is minimal.
3. An incorrect, slanting position of the sawblade.
4. In this position, the contacting surface between the blade and the metal is increased which creates difficulties and makes blade breakage more frequent.

4–42 IRAN, TEKKE TURKOMAN, 19th century. Silver sheet metal necklace (*bukav*) with carnelians. The contour-sawed pierced work base is ornamented with patterned wire and stamped pendants attached to loop-in-loop chains. Max. length 17 in; width 6⅛ in. Photo: Oppi

and the chin is about 3 in above the bench level. This distance is closer to the eye level than when seated in an ordinary chair at a dining table. Such a lowered position allows free arm movement, and may require adjustment in the seat used. The top of the saw frame when at its highest position should be about level with the height of the shoulder. This position in relation to the work minimizes fatigue.

The *bench pin* can be a straight or a slope-tapered wedge, with or without a V-shaped groove, and with or without a small circular opening at the inner apex of its legs. This circular opening allows unobstructed sawing in a restricted area on small work.

Some jewelers prefer to use a bench pin with a sloping upper surface which allows an easier view of the work; they find it more natural to hold the saw frame in a back-canted position, which is still, however, in a perpendicular relationship to the metal.

By keeping the relationship of blade to metal perpendicular, the contact between them remains *minimal,* as shown in the diagram, a condition that is desirable because less metal to blade contact reduces breakage. Holding the blade at an angle to the metal is equivalent to sawing metal of much thicker gauge. A vertically held saw blade also automatically assures a perpendicular edge on the metal cut. If the contour of the edge is to be altered, such changes as chamfering and rounding are done *after* cutting, with files or by other means.

When sawing or filing precious metals, use a *leather lap apron* or *filing tray* placed just beneath the bench pin to catch the lemel or filings as they fall. These should be collected and saved for recovery. Keep filings of gold and silver separate, and if possible, those of different alloys of these metals. To collect filings from the workbench and

bench pin, brush them into the filing tray. Traditionally, a rabbit's foot was used by goldsmiths for this purpose because precious metal dust will not cling to the hair, but any soft-haired bench brush reserved for this use is suitable.

THE SAW AND BLADE IN ACTION

The teeth of a saw blade are *raked* downward. The term *rake* means the angle between the cutting surface of a tool and the plane that is perpendicular to the work surface, and the direction of the tool's motion with respect to the work. This means that the jeweler's saw blade teeth that are sharp only at their bottom edge, cut on the *downward stroke*. With each successive downward stroke, the teeth act to successively tear out minute portions of the metal as they contact and are thrust upon the metal. The fineness of the *bite* depends on the number and size of the teeth in contact with the metal during one full stroke; therefore, aside from size, saw blades that have more teeth per inch will cut finer grooves.

Described below is the manner of sawing a line in sheet metal that can be approached from the metal's *outer edge*. (To saw out *inner areas* that have no access to an edge, the method used is described under Piercing by Sawing, Chapter 4.)

To begin a kerf, place the saw blade against the edge of

4–43 SEPPO TAMMINEN, Finland. "Bird's Song." Necklace made of flat brass sheets stamped with patterns, and applied with brass pellets, the units joined by jump rings. Length 28 cm. Photo: Tauno Tamminen

4–44 ANNI and BENT KNUDSEN, Denmark. Necklace in sterling silver using two similar isosceles trapezoid shapes in alternating directions. The upper is wire brushed matte to further distinguish it from the lower which is polished bright. Photo: Jonals Co.

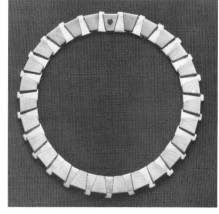

the metal and draw it *upward* lightly a few times, in the same spot. This will create a groove of sufficient depth to keep the blade from wandering when the downward stroke begins.

SAWING LUBRICANT

In good sawing practice, the blade is kept moving smoothly up and down in the kerf. Binding stoppages and breakage can be avoided to a great extent by the use of a *lubricant* which reduces abrasion and erosion while keeping the blade temperature lower, thus prolonging its life. Therefore, initially, and occasionally thereafter, lubricate the saw blade by running it once through a solid cake of *beeswax.* Do not overlubricate as beeswax is sticky and tends to cling to and clog the teeth, reducing their cutting efficiency. If the wax that clings to the blade is found to be excessive, brush it away with a *stiff bristle brush.*

Hold the metal with the part to be cut over the open V of the bench pin. During the sawing, splay the fingers of the left hand firmly over the metal sheet to hold it flat on the horizontal surface of the bench pin, with the thumb beneath it in opposition like a clamp. With the right hand, hold the saw frame handle in a relaxed grip keeping the blade perpendicular to the plane of the metal. Finger pressure on the metal should be sufficient during sawing to keep the metal in contact with the bench pin and to prevent any vertical, chattering motion of the metal which should be avoided as it causes blade breakage. Under ordinary circumstances it is not advisable to use a clamp to hold the metal to the bench pin because then the position of the saw frame when following a curve must be constantly changed instead of the normal practice of turning the metal during sawing to meet the blade. Clamps are useful, however, when sawing a straight line.

Experience has taught that the most efficient cutting action takes place when just enough pressure is exerted on the blade to make its teeth bite freely. Too little pressure allows them to simply scrape the metal which is ineffective in cutting, and too much pressure may strip the saw blade teeth or cause the blade to break. *Dragging* (pressure on the return, upward stroke) can cause the blade to become misshapen and therefore to cut inaccurately, and should be avoided.

To prevent a blade from kinking or buckling, the cutting strokes should be uniform and unhurried. When cutting straight or curved lines, work with full length, regular strokes, exposing as many of the blade's teeth to the metal as possible in one stroke. Short strokes confine the cutting to only a small section of the blade, and this is inefficient as it concentrates too much friction and wear on that small area.

4–45   KAREL NIEHORSTER, Netherlands. Pendant in sterling silver and acrylic sheet. The flat metal sheet acquires illusional depth by the use of perspective. The horse is cast. Size 95 × 95 × 25 mm. *Photo: Hans Hoogland*

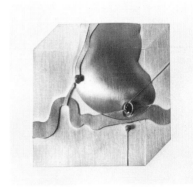

4–46   HERMAN JÜNGER, West Germany. Brooch in gold and silver sheet metal. A tension occurs between the use of perspective in the cube form with its implication of depth, and the ornamentation which is flat because actually the object is two-dimensional. Size 4.5 cm square. *Photo: Ingrid Amslinger*

4–47   BARBARA CARTLIDGE, England. "The Open Road." Silver and gold brooch whose flat forms are given dimension by the use of perspective. The gold steering wheel turns. Modern man's vision follows paved paths that lead to the unknown, using instruments that provide an illusory sense of control. Size 2 × 2.5 in. *Photo: Barbara Cartlidge*

Saw away from the body as much as possible, feeding the metal slowly to the saw blade with the fingers. When following a sawing line, keep the blade somewhat to the *outside* of that line so that the line remains visible after the blade has passed by. This additional, small amount of surplus metal on the shape being sawed is later removed by filing or by other means. When following a curve, move the metal gradually so that the saw frame remains in a more or less constant vertical position while the curve is fed to it.

When sawing is finished, before storing the saw frame with blade, release the lower end of the blade by loosening that clamp to free it and the frame from tension which otherwise places unnecessary stress on both.

SAWING PROBLEMS AND SOLUTIONS

BLADE BREAKAGE

Saw blades usually tend to break long before their teeth wear out, a wasteful situation that can be avoided or minimized. Some of the causes of breakage and the means to avoid them have already been mentioned and others are discussed below.

Not holding the metal tight enough on the bench pin is a major cause of blade breakage. By allowing the metal to vibrate, blade stress occurs, and at worst, the movement of the metal actually interferes with the sawing process.

Exerting too much pressure forward or downward on the blade or forcing it during sawing is another major cause of breakage. Learn to work with only the amount of pressure needed for the work to be accomplished efficiently.

Sharp change in sawing direction is another common cause for breakage. When this is called for, eliminate all forward pressure, draw the blade back slightly, and while

4–48 SAMUEL BEIZER, U.S.A. "Walls of Jerusalem." Silver belt, contour sawed from sheet metal. *Photo: Samuel Beizer*

continuing the up-and-down motion of the saw frame in one position (but with quicker, shorter strokes), gradually turn the metal with the fingers. This action will form a circular hole at that point on the outside of the cutting line. Once the teeth of the blade face the desired direction, sawing can then proceed.

A saw blade too loosely clamped in the saw frame jaws will tend to bend and the blade will break as there is insufficient tension on the blade.

Sawing sideways at the end of a cutting stroke may cause blade breakage. Learn to control and maintain the vertical position of the saw frame and blade.

Excessive speed in sawing causes the blade to heat up due to increased friction and may cause breakage. Use slower, more rhythmic strokes and be sure the blade is lubricated. On the other hand, a too slow speed is also undesirable.

BLADE FREEZE

If a blade freezes in position (or for some other reason must be removed from the metal), do not force it forward or it may break. Remove the blade by loosening the thumbscrew at the top of the saw frame to free it at the end, and draw it gently downward, keeping it perpendicular to the metal plane until it is freed. Start sawing again from another direction. It is usually not advisable to try to saw in the same kerf.

CUT DEPTH EXCEEDS SAW FRAME THROAT DEPTH

When penetrating the metal with a cut, if its depth exceeds the limit of the throat of the saw frame, the back bar of the frame will contact the edge of the metal being sawed and sawing cannot proceed further. Normally, it then becomes necessary to withdraw the blade from the metal, as described above. Backtracking the blade in the kerf to remove it is not recommended as there is considerable risk of breakage. Remove the blade, and after retightening it, approach the cutting line from another, more accessible direction.

TWISTING BLADE DIRECTION TO CLEAR FRAME

If a rigid-clamp saw frame is being used and the circumstances described above occur, professional jewelers sometimes resort to a special solution. While the blade remains in the kerf, it is released from the lower clamp. With *flat-nosed pliers,* the upper section of the blade is twisted 90° just below the clamp while that end is still clamped in

the frame. Replace the lower end in the clamp and release the upper end. Twist the lower end with the pliers in the same way, making sure this is done in the same direction as the upper end. Return the upper end to the clamp and tighten the blade. Skilled jewelers can do this without removing the blade from the clamps. This change in tooth direction brings the frame to one side, out of the way, and sawing can proceed with the frame canted to one side. Blade ends can also be twisted this way before inserting them into the frame when such a difficulty in making a long cut is anticipated.

SAWING THIN-GAUGE METAL

When sawing thin-gauge metal, use fine saw blades since a blade that is too coarse will catch the metal edge and cause it to chatter and buckle.

STACK SAWING

This method can be used with either hand or machine saws. There are times when very thin, flat sheets of metal must be cut. The difficulties involved can be solved by *stack cutting,* in which the thin sheet is sandwiched between two heavier ones clamped together so there is no movement between them. Do not remove the clamp until all the cutting is completed.

Stack cutting is also used when several duplicates of a shape are needed. Take care to keep the position of the saw blade absolutely vertical so that the resulting shapes are the same.

Long strips of thin metal can be cut in this way as they might otherwise twist and become deformed.

INTERCHANGE SAWING

This is a special type of contour sawing in which two different metal sheets, placed one on the other, are cut by close tolerance to the sawing line. Because no change in the contour is necessary, the ground and the figure can be interchanged to create duplicate designs in which the metals are reversed.

USING THE SAW BLADE AS A FILE

Fine saw blades mounted in the saw frame can be used to remove small amounts of metal in the manner of a file from areas that may otherwise be difficult to reach. The blade is used in a rubbing motion in which its *side* is pressed against the metal so that the teeth scrape its surface.

SAWING SPECIAL METALS

The efficiency of a blade's sawing action depends not only on the particular metal being sawed, but on its condition. Thermal or mechanical treatments render metals soft or hard. In some cases, metal that is partly work hardened is easier to saw than annealed or stress-relieved metal.

Stainless steel is sawed using a lubricant of a thin oil and kerosene. Sawing speed is reduced, and enough forward pressure must be maintained to keep all teeth working. Drag (backward pressure on the backstroke) must be avoided.

Aluminum requires a comparatively coarse saw blade with teeth having a little rake and curved gullets or the blade will enter the work too rapidly. Proper clearance of the teeth at the sides is necessary to prevent drag and overheating the blade. Use a mineral base lubricating oil thinned with kerosene, or occasionally apply paraffin wax. Wavy-set hand hacksaw blades work especially well with aluminum.

Copper and *brass* require thinner saw blades as these create less frictional heat.

Nickel and its alloys are very tough and must be sawed more slowly than other metals.

THE HACKSAW

There are occasions when the jeweler must sever heavy bars, rods, and tubing. For these purposes, a *hacksaw*, a metal-cutting handsaw, can be used. The typical hacksaw frame is a long C shape meant to provide blade spring, and the model shown has a pistol grip, rubber-covered handle. Its length can be adjusted to use a 10 in or 12 in (25.4 cm or 30.5 cm) blade length. The blades are made of selected high-speed steel, specially treated for high-speed sawing on hard-to-cut metals such as high-alloy stainless steel, tool steel, chrome steel, Monel metal, and phosphor bronze, as well as softer, nonferrous metals. Each blade has a hole at either end. To mount the blade in the frame, one hole is made to engage the forward peg, and the other a peg near the handle, while the teeth point downward. To place tension on the blade in the frame, first remove all slack by tightening the wing nut, then give it two more turns. The blade tapers in thickness away from the teeth edge toward the back in order to prevent binding. One pitch of teeth cuts a wide range of metals.

GENERAL RULES GOVERNING HACKSAW BLADE SELECTION AND USE

Blades are available with 14, 18, 24, and 32 teeth per inch. For mild materials in large sections, use a coarse-toothed blade of 14 teeth per inch to allow for chip clearance and fast cutting. For general work use an 18-teeth-per-inch blade, and for work ⅛–¼ in thick use a 24-teeth-per-inch blade. For harder materials in large sections, use a blade with 18 or more teeth per inch to distribute the cutting load over more teeth while maintaining good chip clearance action. For unusual work shapes the blade should have two or more teeth always in contact with its

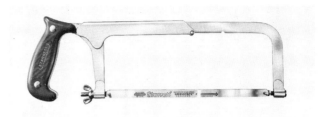

4–49 *HACKSAW FRAME*
It is equipped with a rubber-covered pistol-grip handle; adjustable for use with 10 or 12 in blades. The easy-turning wing nut makes tensioning simple, and the frame is buckle resistant. *Photo: Courtesy L. S. Starrett Co.*

4–50 *HACKSAW BLADES*
Fine- and coarse-toothed high-speed hacksaw blades. *Photo: Courtesy L. S. Starrett Co.*

4–51 *THE RELATIONSHIP OF TOOTH SIZE TO WORK SECTION THICKNESS*. Two or more teeth should always be in contact with the section being cut. *Photo: Courtesy L. S. Starrett Co.*

narrowest section, because if a coarse-toothed blade is used on such objects, it straddles the work, and the teeth may be stripped out. For sawing pipes and tubing use a fine blade with 32 teeth per inch, again to be sure that two or more teeth are in contact with the tube wall. To avoid blade breakage, never use too much pressure on the blade, do not twist the blade, and never tension it too loosely or too tightly.

COLD BENDING SHEET METAL

Changing direction without springback

Cold bending is the act of applying pressure and straining sheet metal to make it move out of a flat plane and to force it to yield and take another shape without the use of heat. The new shape can have curved or angular bends, or combinations of these. The inside of the bend section is called the *bend radius*, which is small in sharp bends, and relatively large in curved bends. Different metals and alloys have different degrees of yield and offer greater or lesser opposition to bending; the thicker the metal is, the greater is its resistance to bending. In the discussion that

follows, we are concerned with the bending of sheet metal and strip. The bending of wire and tubing is discussed separately under those headings.

In bending, the metal is forced beyond its *elastic* or *springback limit* so that it does not return to its original shape, and retains its new form. Change of shape is possible because bending takes place within the plastic range of metal flow. In all bending, *tension stresses* occur, where the outside of the metal at the bend is stretched, and the inside of the bend is compressed. This phenomenon is

4–52 EMILE SOUPLY, Belgium. "Pendant/724." 18K yellow gold with two agates. A single flat sheet is crumple bent to create a three-dimensional form, the folds dictated by the nature of sheet metal. Size 3.5 × 3.75 in. Photo: Emile Souply

4–53 GIJS BAKKER, Netherlands. "Bracelet No. 95." A prefabricated aluminum tube was first cut into edgewise, then cut, parallel to the edge, more than half its length. The cut portion was then pressed down under the rest. Tube Ø 74 mm; width 45 mm; thickness 5 mm. Photo: Rien Basen Adam

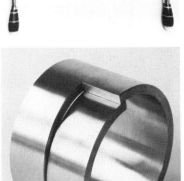

4–54 KURT FLORY, Switzerland, designer; manufacturer Gübelin Fabrication, AG, Geneva. Silver bracelet whose volumetric spiral form is created by bending flat sheet. Photo: Günter Meyer, courtesy Schmuckmuseum, Pforzheim

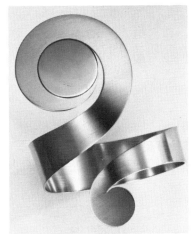

4–55 BOB EBENDORF, U.S.A. Pin of silver, Favrile glass, and a pearl, using a triangular sheet metal strip given a spiral form. The bezel on the glass is made of one sheet divided into small sections, then folded over. Size 3.25 × 1.25 in. Photo: Bob Hanson

common to all forms of metal and to all methods of bending. In angular and curved bending the metal tends to become work hardened along the bend line or over its entire surface because of this development of internal stresses. When bending is excessive, or when the metal is reversed along the same bend line, the stresses build up and cause a structural change. If stresses are not relieved by annealing, the stress limit will be passed, and the metal will fracture.

The opposite of bending is *straightening*, which can be thought of as a reverse bending of a nonflat form to return it to a flat condition. This is done by first annealing the metal to soften it, then placing it on a flat surface such as a *steel bench block*, and hammering it flat with a *mallet*.

METHODS OF BENDING

BENDING WITHOUT DEFORMATION

Bending takes place by either of two methods: with or without deformation. In bending without deformation, the shape of sheet metal is changed by the action of bending forces without a great deal of stretching, contracting, or tearing the sheet. Examples of this kind of bending are angle bending, curling, spiraling, twisting, wrapping, score bending, and tool-assisted bending with *clamps, pliers, mallets, mandrels,* and *bending brakes.*

4–56 FRANCESCO PAVAN, Italy. Necklace of 180 gold and silver units, some oxidized black. Each unit is originally a flat oval, slit through the center, then bent sideways in opposing directions, and joined in overlapping series with ball-ended wires. Photo: Courtesy Schmuck International 1900–1980, Künstlerhaus, Vienna

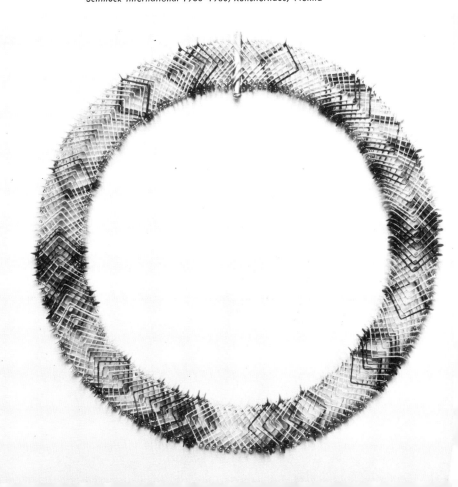

4–57 SIGURD PERSSON, Sweden. Rings made of one flat sheet of silver horizontally laminated with gold. To form the ring shank, holes were drilled, the shank was cut from the form edges, then bent backward. The surface is embellished by stamped intaglio pyramid shapes. *Photo: Sune Sundahl*

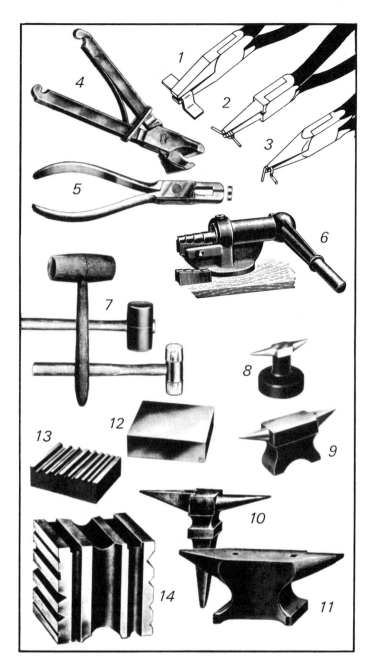

4–58 *METAL-BENDING TOOLS*
1. *Smooth-jawed flat-* or *square-nosed pliers* are used to make angular bends on sheet, strip, and wire.
2. Smoothly tapered *round-nosed pliers* perform bending operations on wire, strip, or sheet.
3. Smooth-jawed *chain-nosed pliers* allow angular bends on wire and strip in short distances.
4. Special *broad-nosed pliers* are used to make a long bend in sheet.
5. *Hollow-chop wire-bending pliers* grip the wire without marring it while it is bent.
6. *Hand-operated ring-bending machine* that can be permanently mounted, or held in a bench vise. It has three interchangeable dies, and is used to bend ring shanks in various sizes.
7. *Mallets* of wood, rubber, and plastic faces replaceable with cast iron, are used to bend metal without marring it.
8. *Small bench anvil* for bending and flattening, with round and flat horns, and a hole for use in riveting; 3⅞ in long, 2⅝ in high.
9. *Bench anvil* 4½ in long, 1⅝ in high.
10. *Anvil with tang* for insertion into a hole in the workbench, or in a tree stump, 8½ in long.
11. *Workshop anvil* for general use, with two horns and two holes, cast steel with tempered face. Available in several sizes, from 65 mm wide, 350 mm long, 14 kg; to 120 mm wide, 650 mm long, 82 kg.
12. *Steel bench block*, ground flat and highly polished, 2¼ in square, ¾ in thick, weighs 1 lb 6 oz. Available in many other sizes.
13. *Steel flat bending* or *design block* with eight variously shaped grooves, 4 in square.
14. *Steel bending block* 2½ in square, with grooves on five faces, including seven V grooves, four flat grooves, and eight half-round grooves.

BENDING WITH DEFORMATION

Bending with deformation means the metal is bent by exerting sufficient force on it to cause it to change its shape due to *stretching* and/or *contracting*. Blocking, bulging, chasing, dapping, doming, forging, forming, modeling, pressing, raising, reducing, repoussage, rolling, sinking, spinning, stamping, swaging, and tapering are all processes in which deformation bending occurs. (See Index for separate discussions of these subjects.)

MANUAL BENDING

Metals can be bent manually, or by the use of tools. In manual bending without deformation, the metal is shaped only by the use of hands, and the bending is done either in air, or against a resisting surface, but still with the fingers. Manual metal bending is possible when the metal is light enough in weight, and in a soft or annealed condition. There is a limit to the thickness and the size of metal that can be bent simply by the use of hand pressure, as well as a limit to the kinds of bends and forms that can be made in this way.

TOOL BENDING

In tool bending, the metal is shaped with the aid of tools. The kind of tool used depends on the type of bend

to be made. The particular tools used are mentioned in the discussion of bend types below.

BEND TYPES

The basic bend types are *angular* or *curved*, and combinations of these.

SINGLE-POINT ANGULAR BENDS

Single-point bends are made at an angle at one place along a straight line. Bends of this type are made with the aid of various tools such as *anvils, blocks, brakes, C-clamps* (called *G-cramps* in Great Britain), *hammers, mallets, pliers, scorers, stakes, rules, straight edges, V-blocks,* and *vises.*

Angular bends on a metal strip can be made with *square-nosed pliers.* To make a right-angle bend, while holding the metal strip in the left hand and the tool in the right hand, insert the strip into the plier jaws, and rotate

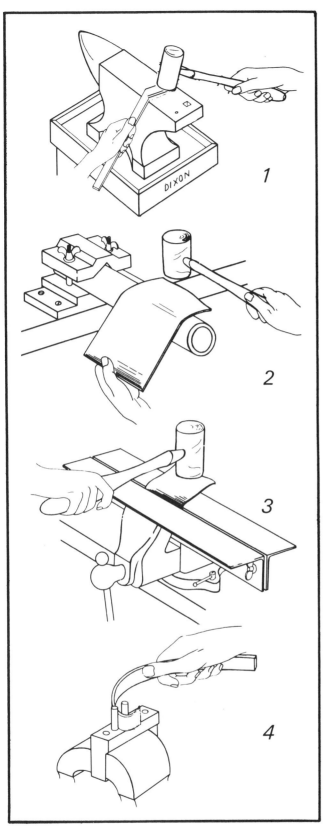

the pliers to the right as far as possible. To perfect the angle, change the pliers to the other side of the bend angle, and repeat the process. Another way to bend strip or sheet easily is to use a *clamp* to hold it to a metal object with a square edge, such as a *steel surfaceblock* or a *flat anvil*. Allow the part to be bent to project out slightly over its edge at the line of bend, and then force it down with a *wood* or *other mallet* to keep marking minimal. A wood block can also be placed against the protruding metal, and the mallet applied to it.

Scoring a straight line on the *inside* of the bend line *before* bending makes a bend of small radius easier to accomplish. Scoring is done with a *scorer*. (See Functional Scoring, Chapter 8.) To facilitate bending a heavy-gauge relatively large sheet, the metal can be fixed upright between *two wooden pads* that line the jaws of a *bench vise*, allowing it to project just beyond them at the marked bending line. Place a wood block alongside the metal and hammer the block with a *mallet* to force the metal to bend along the line. Long bends are difficult to make with accuracy and sharpness, so to give the bend a small radius and sharp right angle, place the block on *top* of the metal, and hammer it down to force the metal against the wooden pads.

4–59 METHODS OF BENDING AND THEIR TOOLS
1. A *single-point angular bend* is being done with an *anvil* and *mallet*.
2. A *continuous, curved surface bend* being done on a *bracelet mandrel*.
3. A *single-point angular bend* done with a *sheet metal bender* or *folding bar* 15 in long, 4 in wide. Smaller versions can be improvised. To secure the metal, it is inserted into the space at the bending line, the wing nuts are tightened to prevent slippage while bending, and it is either bent over with the fingers, or malleted over.
4. A strip being *continuous-curve* bent without marring using a *scroll bender* 3 in long held in a vise. Two steel bending pins used to align the bend are inserted in holes. The distance between them can be adjusted for bending thicknesses of $\frac{1}{16}$, $\frac{3}{32}$, $\frac{1}{8}$, and $\frac{3}{16}$ in. *Courtesy William Dixon Co.*

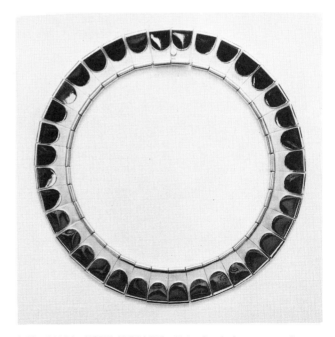

CONTINUOUS-SURFACE CURVED BENDS

In this type of bend, a two-dimensional piece of metal is made to take on a curve or curves that make it a three-dimensional, curved form. Curves are made with the aid of tools or surfaces having the desired contour shape against which the bend is formed. Tools used for this purpose are *round ring mandrels, round* or *oval bracelet mandrels, horned stakes,* and the beak of an *anvil.* Such tools act as the resisting surface against the force of bending carried out with mallets and hammers on the metal.

Curved bends can also be made with hand tools alone, or started with hand tools and finished with bench tools. For example, to bend a ¼ in (6.4 mm) wide, 16 gauge B.&S. metal strip into a circle to form a band ring, the curve can be started with *half-round pliers.* Place the half-round chap on the inside of the curve to avoid making a nick on the strip. Grasp one end and bend it first against the pliers' curved jaw, and then bend the other end. Continue the bend on the remaining parts of the strip to form a circle.

The circle bend can also be achieved by using a *hammer* or *mallet* to force the strip's ends into a curved shape while holding each end in turn over a *ring mandrel* fixed between *wooden pads* placed inside the jaws of a *bench vise.* Continue the bending as far as possible, then close the gap by malleting the circle together while the ring is

4-62   ANN MARIE SHILLITO, England, designer. Stainless steel necklace designed for limited edition production. Flat sheet metal is bent into a three-dimensional form, with the closing device, the front circle, an essential part of the design. Production methods influenced the design concept. *Photo: Günter Meyer, courtesy Schmuckmuseum, Pforzheim*

4-53   JOSEF SYMON, Austria. Brooch, silver, gold, and lapis lazuli, using sheet metal and a concept of repetitions of curving units of similar contour in diminishing sizes, the metals alternating. Ø 80 mm. *Photo: Josef Symon*

4-64   JOSEF SYMON, Austria. Ring, silver and gold, using sheet metal treated with the same concept. *Photo: Josef Symon*

placed upright on a flat surface. The round form can be perfected by placing the ring on the ring mandrel again, and hammering it with the mallet first in one position, then after removing the ring and replacing it on the mandrel in the opposite direction, hammering it again to compensate for the taper in the mandrel. The two ends should butt each other perfectly, closing the gap completely.

BENDING A METAL STRIP EDGEWISE INTO A CURVE OR CIRCLE   Heavy wire or rod of round or square sectional shape can be *bent into open curves, or into a circle* with relative ease by the aid of the kind of *wood bending block* described below. In these cases there is little resistance to the bending operation as not much deformation takes place because these sectional shapes allow easy bending. When a strip of rectangular section is bent into a curve or circle in the direction of its narrowest dimension, greater resistance is encountered because greater stretching takes place on the outer side of the curve and greater contraction occurs on the inside of the curve.

A simple bending device that will not mar the metal can be made from a block of hardwood in which a curved groove is made. With wood chisels and a mallet, cut a groove into one end of the hardwood block in the direction of the grain. The width of the groove should equal the thickness of the strip, and its depth should be greater than the strip width. The back of the groove is made straight, and the front is shaped into a curve of the desired radius. The central point of the curve must remain equal in dimension to the thickness of the metal strip for a tight fit. In other words, the smallest distance between the walls of this curved groove occurs at the groove center.

Clamp the wood block in a *bench vise* with the groove-bearing end facing up. When the aim is to form a circle, use a strip length that is *longer* than the circumference of the final circle, because it is difficult to bend the ends of the strip to the exact curve wanted. The extra length allows the strip ends to overlap so that the rest is closer to a circle; later the surplus is cut away.

Anneal the metal to soften it. (See Annealing Steel, p. 237.) Insert end of the strip, widthwise, into the center of the groove at its smallest point. Draw the rest of the strip sideways in a horizontal plane, forcing it against the groove curve until it comes into contact with it. Shift the strip further into the groove and repeat the process until the curve is completed *halfway* in its length. Repeat the process starting from the other end of the strip, working toward the center again. By the time the center is reached, the circle should be formed and the two ends should overlap. It may be necessary to anneal the strip at intervals during the bending, and to mallet it flat on a true, flat *surface block.* With a *jeweler's saw,* cut through the two strip ends at the center of the point where they overlap. Refine and true the circle by placing the ring on a *mandrel* of suitable diameter, and hammer it where necessary to round the curve. Flatten the circle horizontally with a *mallet* to eliminate any warp. Use a *file* to make the butting ends true, and solder them together.

THE MÖBIUS STRIP   A special form of curved bend is a twisted strip metal form called the *Möbius strip* after the German mathematician August F. Möbius (1790–1868). This bend is a means of giving a two-dimensional form of strip metal a three-dimensional shape without any deformation taking place. It is done by twisting the strip 180°, then joining the ends. The resulting figure has only *one surface* although it is now a three-dimensional form.

4-65 TORUN BÜLOW-HÜBE, Denmark, designer; manufacturer Georg Jensen Sølvsmedie A/S, Copenhagen. Silver brooch No. 374, made of a flat strip warped into a three-dimensional form having one continuous surface. This illustrates the concept of the *Möbius strip*, named after August Ferdinand Möbius, a German mathematician (1790–1868) who first recognized its principle. *Photo: Erik Junior, courtesy Georg Jensen Sølvsmedie A/S*

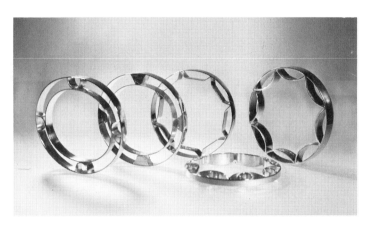

4-66 SAARA HOPEA-UNTRACHT, Finland, designer; manufacturer Kultasepänliike Ossian Hopea, Porvoo. Sterling silver bracelets of bent strips, the units solder joined. The concept of a simple outer form developed internally, is explored. ID approx. 5.8 × 6.2 cm (oval); OD approx. 7.8 × 8.2 cm. *Photo: Oppi*

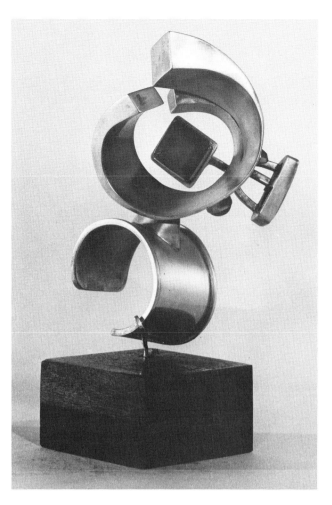

4-67 NANETTE VAN HAMEL, U.S.A. Sterling silver bracelet with jade and amethyst, made with hollow forms. The bracelet is conceived as a dimensional sculpture in miniature, and is provided with a base upon which it stands when not in use. 5 in high. *Photo: Maurice Praga*

COMPOUND SURFACE BENDS

Such bends might consist of curves alone, or curves in combination with straight bends. These are too individual to describe, but examples are seen in the illustrations in this book. They are accomplished with any tools that will produce the desired forms using undeformed and deformed bending techniques.

COMPOUND FORMS MADE OF BENT PARTS

Compound open and closed forms can be made by combining several bent parts by soldering or by other joining methods. These parts can consist of any combination of undeformed, deformed, single-point, continuous-surface, and compound-surface bends.

PIERCING

Penetrating metal laterally or perpendicularly

Piercing is the act of perforating metal (or other materials) so that the tool passes through it to make a hole or opening. The concept of making holes or openings in metal had its origin in prehistoric times when boring tools of bone or stone were used to make holes in softer materials. The Romans used piercing for decorative purposes and called this work *opus interrasile* (Latin *opus,* "work"; *interrasile,* "openings"), and art historians today often use this term to describe pierced work.

There are two concepts implied by the term piercing: one involving *perpendicular* penetration, and the other, *lateral* penetration. Perpendicular piercing indicates that the opening is in an interior position enclosed by an unbroken area of the material pierced; lateral piercing indicates that the material is penetrated from a side, or an edge.

The appeal of the piercing concept lies in the *contrast* between the shapes or lines thus made, and the remaining metal. The interaction between the *negative shapes and lines* in those areas where the material is removed, with the *positive areas* of the remaining material, becomes an important visual aspect of the design.

4–68 SVEN BOLTENSTERN, Austria. Pendant in 18K gold. The egg-shaped repoussé-worked form is pierced internally with an opening in which a star ruby is mounted on silver wires. Height 3½ in, width 2¼ in. Photo: Inge Kitlitschka-Strempel

4–69 DAVID THOMAS, England. Pendant/brooch in 18K gold sheet, set with large central emerald and radiating series of brilliants. The pierced work openings start at the edge and penetrate the sheet, and some contain soldered-in, curved wires. Photo: Angus Forbes

Different tools have been developed to perform the piercing operation. They work according to principles that can be classified under the following categories: *sawing, percussion cutting,* and *boring.* Combinations of these processes are possible on a single work.

PIERCING BY SAWING: Enclosed negative shapes

The invention of the jeweler's saw blade opened pierced work to greater refinement of design, speed, and variety of effect. As a general rule, the blade used in piercing should have a tooth pitch less than the thickness of the metal being pierced. Blades with *rounded backs* facilitate turning and changing the cutting direction in small areas. Saw blades of 4/0 and 5/0 are suited to piercing thin metals up to 22 gauge; 3/0 up to 16 gauge; 2/0 up to 14 gauge; and 1 up to 10 gauge B.&S.

We assume that the design has already been transferred to the metal. Generally speaking, it is good practice to pierce areas before waste metal is removed from the outer shape. To allow the blade to enter an internal area to be pierced or cut out, an initial small hole must be made in the area to be removed, just *inside* the enclosing line of

the shape, at a convenient position. If the metal is thin enough, this hole can be made with a *sharp-pointed punch* or *awl* while resting the metal on a piece of *hardwood* or a *lead block.* The punch may distort the metal where it is perforated, but its flatness can be restored by reversing the metal, placing it on a flat *surface block,* and hammering it down lightly. A small *drill bit* and *hand drill* can also be used to make a small hole for this purpose, or a drill placed in a *flex-shaft.* (See The Twist Drill, p. 94.)

Free the top end of the saw blade from the saw frame, and feed it through the innermost opening to be made. The design side of the metal should face upward. Always start with openings in inner areas and proceed successively to those furthest from the center. Place the metal on the lower clamp of the saw frame. Spring press the frame, insert the upper saw blade end into the upper clamp, and tighten its jaws with the thumbscrew. The blade is now ready for use.

Rest the metal on the *bench pin,* and turn it so that the hole shape is toward the *left,* which leaves the cutting line always visible between the eye and the saw blade. Lubricate the blade with *wax.* Grip the saw handle lightly, raise it to the highest position, and draw it *vertically within* the line, leaving a small remainder to be removed later by filing. Blow away the *lemel* (metal particles) so that the cutting line remains visible. Accuracy in cutting is important, since the more accurate the cut, the less finishing with files will be necessary later. As you cut, shift the metal slightly to follow the curve, which is always cut

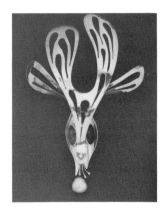

4–71 ARLINE M. FISCH, U.S.A. Ring in silver and 14K gold with citrines and pendant pearl, saw pierced and lightly planish hammered for surface texture. The upper unit is riveted to the base. 4 in long, 3 in wide. Photo: Strüwing

4–72 DOMINGO DE LA CUEVA, U.S.A. "Insight." Bandolier made of flat, contour-sawed sterling silver sheet pierced to create open negative shapes, and words that declare a message. Parts are linked with jump rings. Photo: Frank J. Thompson, courtesy the Fine Arts Gallery, California State University, Los Angeles

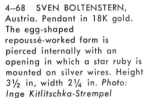

4–70 BARBARA ENGLE, Hawaii, U.S.A. Necklace pendant of sterling silver with Mexican jade beads. After piercing, the surface was ball peen hammered to create a texture and soften hard edges. Photo: Francis Haar

tangentially. The position of the saw frame must remain *vertical,* because if it is slanted, the angle of cutting will result in a distortion of the shape. This is especially important when the thickness of the metal is visible. The reciprocating action of the saw blade should be continuous and steady.

Sharp corners can be cut easily by first drilling a small hole within the angle *before* starting to saw, cutting toward that hole, and once it is reached, turning the metal so that the saw blade faces the next direction. (Another way of turning sharp corners has been described under Sawing Problems and Solutions, Chapter 4.)

Shape piercing is usually followed by the use of *needle files* of appropriate cross-sectional shapes to true the pierced opening. Normally filing is done at a *right angle* to the visible plane of the metal. However, there are occasions when it may be desirable to file an edge at an *acute angle* to the visible surface to make a *chamfer* or bevel that gives the edge, and therefore the metal, the illusion of being thicker than it actually is.

SAWLINE PIERCING: Kerf graphics

In *sawline piercing,* the sawline (*kerf*) itself is used for purely decorative effect much as a line is used in graphics.

4–73 REGINE JUHLS, Norway, designer; manufacturer Sølvsmie Regine & Frank Juhls, Kautokeino. "Lappish Brooch No. 38." Silver, redesigned from old, traditional models. All the line pierced work patterns are made with a jeweler's saw blade starting from a drilled hole into which the saw blade was inserted. Each mobile pendant is chain suspended from a half-dome. *Photo: Börje Rönnberg, courtesy Sølvsmie Regine & Frank Juhls*

4–74 DAVID LAPLANTZ, U.S.A. "Fibula." Fabricated brass and copper, using double saw-pierced kerf lines that radiate from a drilled hole, making decorative, linear pattern. Edge-pierced units are alternately folded over. Length 3½ in. *Photo: David LaPlantz*

In flat metal sawline piercing, paste the paper pattern to the metal, and allow the adhesive to dry to prevent paper movement when work starts. Lines can also be lightly marked with a *scriber,* especially when the surface is curved dimensionally.

Sawline piercing must be carried out with great accuracy because *the finished line cannot be altered.* If the line starts at an edge, sawing begins in the usual way. If the line starts internally, a small hole must first be drilled at the start or the end of the line, or both. Into this hole the saw blade is inserted, and sawing begins. The starting hole can be large enough to itself become a decorative pierced element in the design. If the hole must be unobtrusive, use the smallest possible drill size that will admit the saw blade used. The resulting line can be left bright as it appears after sawing, or it can be oxidized black to increase its visibility.

PIERCING BY PERCUSSION PENETRATION

In piercing by percussion penetration, the piercing tool is placed in position and is worked through the metal by striking it forcibly with a *hammer action tool* in a series of blows. Any tools made of hard, tempered steel and having sharp cutting edges or points that are capable of cutting metal upon impact can be used. Among them are *hand stamping dies* such as *circle cutters,* and *punches, center punches, awls,* and *cold chisels.*

Hand stamping dies of hardened steel are made to remove complete metal blanks from sheet metal and leave an opening. Both the *positive* and the *negative* shapes that result can be used in jewelry making.

One-part circular punches or *dies* are used to cut out circular blanks by placing them on the metal, and hammering the punch through. (See diagram below.)

Circle-cutting dies of the *two-part type* are also used to cut circular blanks from sheet metal, or to pierce a hole of a desired diameter. (See 5–3, number 2.)

Center punches of the one-piece, rigid type whose striking and pointed end are hardened, and with a small point size, are primarily used to locate and mark hole centers prior to drilling a hole in metal with a twist drill. In this case, they are positioned and struck lightly while being

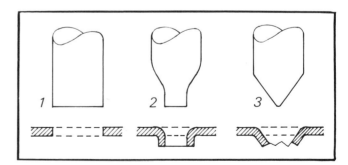

4–75 HOLE TYPES MADE BY PUNCHING, EXTRUSION, AND PIERCING
1. A one-part circular punch or die with sharp edges and a flat face, when hammered through sheet metal makes a clean, round hole and *blank,* both with perpendicular, smooth edges.
2. A tapered punch of small diameter and flat face cleanly punches an extruded hole that follows through to form a clean-edged flange around the sides of the opening.
3. A *sharp-pointed punch* pierces a hole by tearing the metal, forming a ragged-edged flange around the hole sides.

4–76 *CENTER PUNCHES*

1. *Center punches* made of specially selected steel, hardened and tempered their full length. Their square shank prevents rolling when laid down, and knurling provides a firm gripping area.

Length	Body thickness	Point diameter
5 in	$^{15}/_{32}$ in	$^{1}/_{4}$ in
4$^{5}/_{8}$ in	$^{27}/_{64}$ in	$^{3}/_{16}$ in
4$^{1}/_{4}$ in	$^{23}/_{64}$ in	$^{5}/_{32}$ in
4 in	$^{5}/_{16}$ in	$^{1}/_{8}$ in
3$^{11}/_{16}$ in	$^{17}/_{64}$ in	$^{3}/_{32}$ in
3$^{3}/_{8}$ in	$^{15}/_{64}$ in	$^{5}/_{64}$ in
2$^{7}/_{8}$ in	$^{3}/_{16}$ in	$^{1}/_{16}$ in

2. *Automatic center punch* with adjustable stroke, length 5 in, Ø $^{5}/_{8}$ in. The punch handle held upright is pressed down, and the built-in mechanism strikes a perfect *center mark* without a hammer. The blow force, adjustable to suit metal hardness, is regulated by turning the knurled cap. For a deeper indentation, the cap is screwed down; for lighter blows, it is screwed upward. At any single setting, the punch depth remains the same. The point may be removed for reshaping or replacement. *Courtesy: L. S. Starrett Co.*

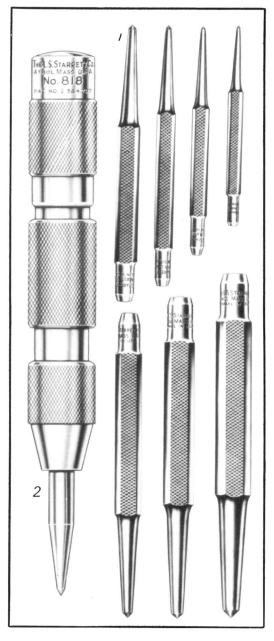

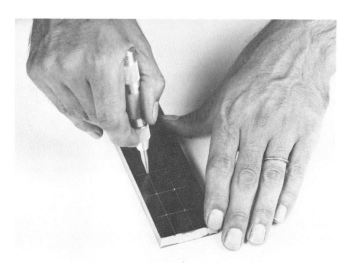

4–77 *THE AUTOMATIC CENTER PUNCH IN USE.* Metals, plastics, wood, or other machinable materials can be center punched with one hand. *Photo: Courtesy L. S. Starrett Co.*

4–78 *INDIA, 19th century.* Matching pair of hollow silver ankle bracelets. The finished form was first engraved, the entire object was then asphaltum filled, and the ground spaces between elements were removed with small, sharp cold chisels. Worked thus from the outside, all sharp edges were bent inward into the form hollow. After piercing, the asphaltum was heated and drained from the form, leaving it hollow. Pierced work lightens the total weight while retaining the form in bulk. To remove and replace the ankle bracelet, the front unit is detached by unscrewing the ornamented screwhead. Traditionally the pattern of a vase filled with flowers and vines symbolizes fertility. Col.: Traphagen School of Fashion, New York. *Photo: Oppi*

held vertically to make a dent in the metal. The same tool can also be used to make a small hole in thin-gauge sheet metal. In raising, a center punch is used to mark a *central reference point* made for making measurements. In India, such a point is called a *bij* or *bija*, which literally means a seed or kernel.

Prick punches are similar in basic shape to center punches, but have sharper, more tapered points. They also can be used to make small holes in metal.

Awls are pointed steel instruments with wooden handles, used primarily to pierce small holes in wood or leather, but they can also be used to make small holes in thin metal.

Cold chisels are so called because these tempered steel tools are meant to be used on cold metal, as opposed to *blacksmith's chisels* which are often used on hot work. They are also generally smaller. (Chisels are discussed under Metal Inlay, Chapter 8.) Small cold chisels can be used to pierce metal.

For ease in piercing, the metal should be *firmly anchored* in place. Use a *clamp* to hold it on a board placed on a workbench, or mount it on *pitch* spread on a board. Once the metal is secure, lubricate the chisel's cutting edge. Hold the chisel *vertically* and strike it with a *hammer;* it will pierce the metal cleanly. When chipping or grooving metal, the chisel is held *at an angle* to the metal. Any distortions that occur from chisel piercing can be corrected by placing the metal on a flat *surface block,* and hammering it flat with a *mallet.* Chisel piercing around a figure on repoussé-worked metal has an advantage over saw piercing in that the edge is turned slightly backward when piercing takes place from the *front.* If the inner side is not exposed or touched when the object is in use, this slight inward bend gives the work a look of added dimensionality.

PIERCING BY BORING

The concept of piercing by the boring motion of a rotary tool extends back to the prehistoric past when reciprocal rotary-motion tools were used. In true rotary-motion piercing, the revolving part of the tool must be free to turn either in *alternating directions by partial turns;* or, as in later developed boring tools, in the same direction by *continuous revolutions.* The tool cuts gradually as it turns, removing or chipping away metal by degrees as pressure is exerted against the point of the tool, which in time penetrates and pierces the metal. The metal can be of any thickness, from a thin sheet to a solid block. Boring can also be used to enlarge the inner diameter of a tube, or to make an existing hole larger. Boring tools automatically leave the metal with a finished, round shape that can be left in that condition for decorative effect. Bored holes are also used to make an opening in the metal to allow work by saws or files.

The *hand push broach* is a partial-turn rotary-motion tool, worked by a series of twisting motions of the hand and wrist. It can be used on any metal, or on other materials such as bone, ivory, shell, or plastics. Though it is a slower method of piercing than a drill, in some cases, as when working on delicate materials, it may be preferred to

mechanically operated drills because the frictional heat is far less and work is safer.

Broaches are used for cutting a new hole, enlarging a hole made by a drill, working on other holes that already exist in a work, and for smoothing round openings in metal or other substances. They are made of a bar of high-quality, uniformly tempered steel, in lengths from 1¾ in to over 7 in (4.45–17.8 cm). On the broach surface is a series of cutting edges, flutes, or teeth that increase in size from the entering end, and run parallel to each other for the length of the taper, less the tang. All broaches are tapered since in concept they work by a *transitional movement* along the axis to enlarge or smooth an opening by gradually forcing the increasing diameter, or feeding the increasingly higher cutting edge into the metal so that each succeeding tooth removes additional metal. The broach has a maximum diameter that is gauged according to the *Stub's Scale,* numbered to correspond with that part of the diameter that is *slightly below* the largest cutting position of the cutting edge. A popular type is pentagonal in cross section, and therefore has five cutting edges or flutes. The lengthwise placement of the flutes on the tool allow metal chips that form during feeding to be ejected so they do not block tool progress.

Smoothing broaches are round, but their action is different from round files as they are meant to be worked with a *rotary motion,* while files work best with a *reciprocating* or *forward motion.*

Broaches can be used as hand tools, or they can be mounted on a *drill press* with the tang end clamped into the chuck jaws. It is also possible to use a broach mounted in a rotary *flex shaft* as an outside shaping tool on soft materials such as plastics, to refine forms, or reach places where length limitation does not permit rotary burs to penetrate.

Reamers are related to broaches, but are generally larger tools worked by hand (or mechanically) and meant for more accurate work. They are used to increase the diameter of holes, to size them, or to burnish them. Their flutes may be straight or tapered. Some are *end cutting;* others are *edge cutting* or *stepped,* a type used to first rough out an opening before it is finished by another tapered reamer.

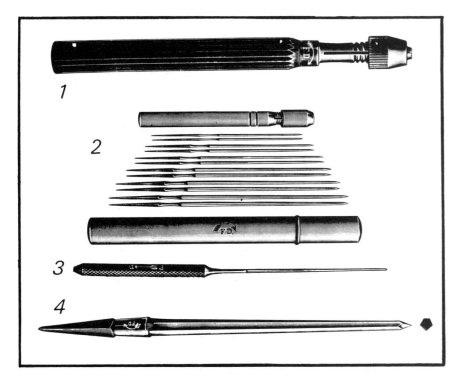

4–79 BROACHES AND REAMERS
1. *Broach holder.*
2. *Set of small broaches with metal container.*
3. *Hand broach with knurled handle which eliminates the need for a broach holder. Sizes 28, 34, 44, 50, 54, 60, and 70 are most commonly used.*
4. *Five-sided ground edge reamer. Each reamer is tapered to a range of five numbers on the twist drill gauge. Available in every fifth number up to 80.*

Flat reamers are used for reaming tapered holes in brass.

Rotary burs and *files* are mechanical rotary-motion tools used mounted on a *flexible shaft.* (See Files and Filing in this chapter.)

Tapping tools fall into the class of rotary hole-making tools, but as they are used to form *internal threads,* and not for pierced work, they are discussed under Screws, Chapter 10.

THE DRILL: Types

The drill is a tool used to make a hole by the concept of reciprocating circular motion, or a continuous-revolution motion. The oldest drills work by the former method, and the relatively recent ones work by the latter. These are used to bore holes of circular shape, or to enlarge a pre-existing hole either in hard substances such as stone or metal, or in soft materials such as wood, plastics, ivory, bone, shell, and others.

THE STRAP DRILL   This was the earliest drill and consisted of a wooden spindle mounted with a *point* or *bit* at one end. To this spindle was attached a leather strap or sinew, turned one or more times around the shaft. To rotate the drill, the strap was pulled back and forth so that the bit turned with an alternating or reciprocal motion. This drill and the bow drill described below required a separate handle made of horn or stone, with a round depression at one end into which the spindle was placed and could rotate freely. This drill type is still in use in some remote places in the world.

THE BOW DRILL   This was in use by the end of the third millennium B.C., and was an improvement on the strap drill. The ancient Egyptian bow drill illustrated on p. 95 is an example. The bow was a separate device, with a string that was wound once around the spindle. To make the spindle rotate, the bow was held in the right hand and moved horizontally back and forth. The left hand meanwhile held the free socket handle in which the spindle rotated. While moving the bow, the socket was pressed down on the spindle to force the drill bit into and through the work.

THE PUMP DRILL   This drill came into use in Roman times. Its advantage is that only one hand is required to hold it once it is in motion, leaving the other hand free to hold the work. The "pump" is a crosspiece that in some types hangs alongside the spindle; in other types it is pierced with a central hole through which the spindle passes, thus allowing it to stand upright. This makes possible better control over the spindle. At the crosspiece ends are holes through which pass a length of cord, which at the halfway point also passes through a hole in the upper end of the spindle. At the lower end of the spindle is a flywheel or weight whose purpose is to impart momentum to the spindle from the force provided by the movement of the hand. Spindle movement starts by slightly twisting the spindle with the fingers, while the crosspiece is held with the right hand. This causes the cord to twist itself around the upper part of the spindle and draw the crosspiece upward. By pressing the crosspiece downward, the cord spiral unwinds and imparts a rotational movement to the spindle. When the crosspiece is at its lowest position, pressure is released and the momentum of the flywheel causes the cord to make a reverse twist on the spindle which then rotates in the opposite direction, creating a reciprocal rotational action. By repeating this action, the drill is kept in constant motion until the work is com-

pleted. If drills that cut in both directions are used, cutting action is also continuous.

This was the type of drill used to bore holes in stone beads. The immobilized bead was first entered from one side, penetrated halfway, then reversed and penetrated from the opposite side until the holes met. Because the drill bit was tapered, the hole shapes were biconical. The same ancient drill and method is used today in Cambay, India. Stone artisans there supplied the whole ancient civilized world with semiprecious stone beads, and still do so today.

THE HAND DRILL   Along with the *twist drill* (*drill point* or *bit*) it holds, this drill operates with a *continuous-revolution rotary motion,* and is the newest of all unmechanized drilling tools. It is a compound tool and consists of a separate hand drill or holding device, in which the drill point or cutting instrument is mounted. The tool is designed so that the point is made to rotate continuously around its longitudinal axis, and at the same time, move axially to pierce through the material being bored. A hole is made by the combination of the driving end of the hand drill (which transmits the *torque* or *rotational force*) and the *pressure force* on the point that does the actual boring into the material.

The normal hand drill (called an *American drill* in some European countries), often termed an "egg-beater drill," consists of a wooden handle holding a solid steel frame or spindle. Its other end bears a screwed-on *three-jawed chuck* which can be opened by turning the knurled casing counterclockwise—opening the jaws—and closed by turning it clockwise—closing all three jaws simultaneously on the inserted drill shank. Most chucks on hand drills are fitted to accept twist drill shanks in sizes ranging from 0–¼ in (0–0.64 cm).

THE TWIST DRILL

The *twist drill* (drill bit) placed in the holding device today is a standard type that gets its name from the manner in which the helical *channels* and *flutes* are spirally formed around its body. The most common angle of flutes to shank is 30°. The *shank* is the plain end that is inserted into the holding device. Actual cutting is accomplished by the conical *point* of the drill, not the flutes. Cutting edges occur at the intersection of each body flute and its termination at the point; the usual, two-flute drill has a point with *two cutting edges* or *lips* on an angle of 59° to the drill axis. Because the drill revolves in a clockwise direction, the lip edges are ground at a 120° angle from the lips so that they cut away small chips of metal with each turn of the drill. The flutes have the function of bringing chips or cuttings up from the hole being drilled to the metal's surface to carry them away, and by their presence, a lubricant can be introduced to the cutting edges. After some time, the cutting edges may become dulled. They can be resharpened, but this is a job requiring skill and care since the correct cutting angle of 59° and the lip clearance angle of 120° must be maintained or the drill will not work efficiently.

Cheap drills are made of rigid carbon steel, and are quickly worn out. They can, however, be used to drill relatively thin sheets of silver and nonferrous metals. It is advisable to purchase the best drill made of a high-alloy steel called *speed steel,* because they last longer and cut best at higher speeds, especially when they are used on mechanical flex-shafts and drill presses.

THE DIAMOND DRILL   An extremely useful drill to the jeweler, it is used in cutting hard metals and piercing stones. It has embedded in its point particles of hard abrasives such as industrial diamonds, silicon carbide, tungsten carbide, or boron nitride. These must be used with a lubricant, such as oil or running water, especially when boring holes in stones, to prevent them from becoming overheated by friction and cracking or chipping as a result.

4–80   ANCIENT DRILL TYPES
1. The *ancient Egyptian bow drill*, with copper bit and separate, hollow handle.
2. The *pump drill* with weighted flywheel.

4–81   DRILLS
1. *Archimedean-type hand drill* used with small drills. The central hand piece is pushed up and down to rotate the drill. Length 4 in.
2. *Automatic drill* pressed down by the handle to operate. Chuck instantly releases or holds drill points by slight thumb pressure. Handle contains compartment for 12 drill points.
3. *Hand drill* with gear and three-jawed chuck that holds 0–¼ in round-shanked twist drills. Length 11 in.
4. *Breast hand drill*, held horizontally with breast pressed against support and one hand on rotating handle and other on stable handle. Length 350 mm. Holds drills up to 8 mm shank diameter.
5. *Fluted twist drill*, high-speed steel, straight shank, available in sizes 30–80.
6. *Spiral pivot drill*, high-speed steel, right hand, fast helix type with positive rake angle, used for drilling steel.
7. *Flat pivot drill*, high-speed steel, with 0° rake angle, used for drilling mild steel, brass, aluminum, etc.
8. *Twist drill assortment set* in graduated sizes in container with hinged cover.
9. *Twist drill gauge index*, used to determine the size of a twist drill.

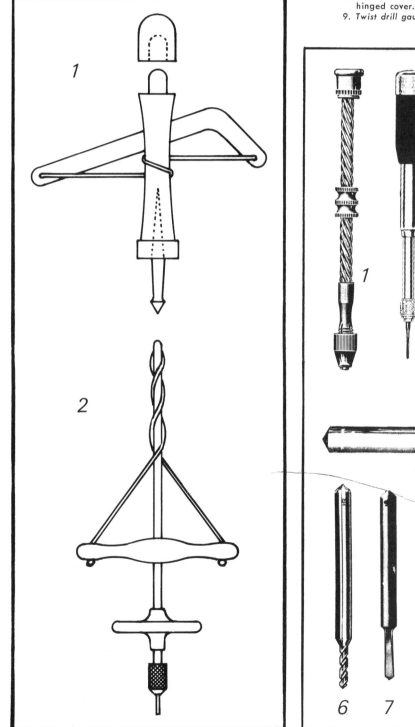

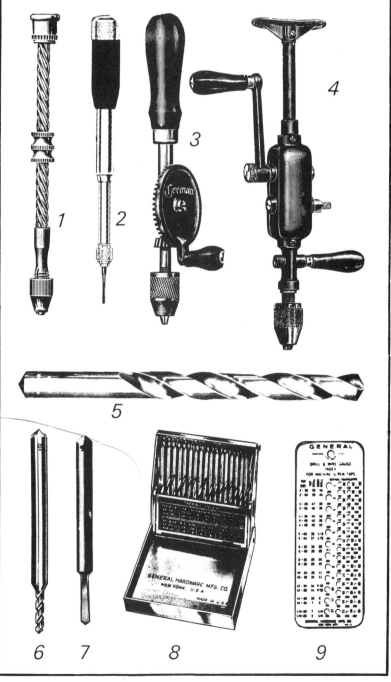

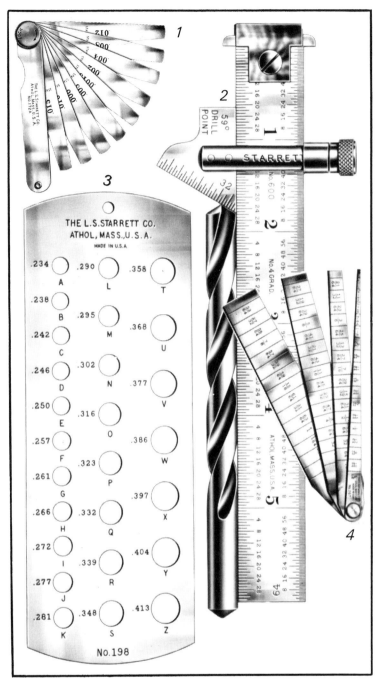

4-82 GAUGES

1. *Thickness* or *feeler gauge* with tempered steel leaves and locking device to fix leaves in any desired position. Used for checking clearances from 0.0015–0.012 in.
2. *Drill point gauge, 59°.* Designed specifically for use in drill grinding to check the correct drill point angle of 59°, and the correct drill lips for clean-cut drilling at maximum speeds and feeds. Has a 6 in removable hook rule combined with a sliding head adjustable to any position along the rule, and locked by a thumb nut. The head is beveled to 59° and is graduated in 32nds along that face for measuring the drill lips which should be equal in length. Can also be used as a plain rule or with a tri-square, slide caliper, or depth gauge.
3. *Standard letter-size drill gauge,* range A–Z, made of hardened, ground and polished steel. Letter-sized drills can be quickly and conveniently checked for size accuracy by inserting the drill in the hole that it fits tightly. Each hole is letter marked, and has a decimal equivalent in inches, in diameters of 0.234–0.413 in. Length 6¼ in, width 2⁵⁄₁₆ in, thickness ⁵⁄₆₄ in.
4. *Taper gauge* of spring-tempered steel, specially designed for rapid measurement of tube IDs, holes, and slots. The tapered leaves measure diameters or widths from ¹⁄₁₆ to 1¹⁄₁₆ in, in 64ths of an inch. Approx. 1 in wide by 5¼ in long. *Photo: Courtesy L. S. Starrett Co.*

USING THE DRILL

To insert and fix a twist drill into a hand drill, hold the chuck end pointing upright with the left hand. With the right hand, wind the drill handle counterclockwise which will cause the chuck jaws to open, but only open them wide enough to admit the shank which should be *fully* inserted in the jaws so it is rigid and accurately centered. While still holding the chuck, tighten the jaws by turning the drill handle clockwise. Make sure the axial direction of the twist drill is *straight* and *true* or it will wobble in use.

A *drill start mark* is made before drilling a hole. Place the metal on a *surface block* to mark the exact center of the hole. Place a *center punch* point on that spot, and hammer it lightly once. The small depression that results is used to place the drill point, and keeps it from wandering from that spot when the drill motion is started. For large

4-83 4-84 NILDA C. F. GETTY, U.S.A. Headpiece in sterling silver and 860 silver with opals, front and back view. Fabricated of pierced parts, linked with forged units, and ornamented with reticulated parts. Back view shows a small container, opened. *Photo: Les Brown*

DRILL SIZE SYSTEMS

Drills are available *singly,* or in *sets,* in standardized, graduated sizes. Five different size series are in use: (1) *Decimal sizes* in flat drills, from 0.002 in to 0.080 in in half-thousandth steps. (2) By *numbers* from 80, the smallest (0.0135 in) to 1, the largest (0.228 in) diameters. (3) By *letters* from A–Z (0.234–0.413 in diameters). (4) By *fractions* from ¹⁄₆₄ in to 3½ in (in steps of ¹⁄₆₄ in from ⅛ in to 1¾ in diameters; steps of ¹⁄₃₂ in from 1²⁵⁄₃₂ in to 2¼ in diameters; and steps of ¹⁄₁₆ in from 2⁵⁄₁₆ in to 3½ in diameters). (5) By *millimeters* (available in steps of 1 mm from 0.10 mm to 10 mm; and half-tenths from 0.10 mm to 2.80 mm). (See Table, "High-Speed Steel Twist Drills," p. 740, for the relationship of inch to millimeter sizes to each other.) Usually, each twist drill has its size number stamped on the shank.

drills, the drill start mark can be made with a pointed *bur* held in a *flex-shaft.* When such a place is being marked for making a hole in an area to be pierced, place the center punch just *inside* the line that outlines that area. An *automatic spring punch* can also be used to form a center mark. Position its point, and press the handle downward. This action releases a spring that makes the point rebound on the metal, where it leaves a dent. In some cases when using large twist drills, it may be necessary to deepen the marked spot with an *awl* by rotating it in that spot.

The metal must be immobilized, or the clockwise motion of the drill will cause it to revolve, in which case the point cannot get a grip on the metal and no cutting action is possible. Anchor the metal to a *wooden board,* immobilizing both with a *C-clamp.* By another method, hammer *small nails* into the board at positions touching the metal where the clockwise turning of the drill force will be *opposed.* This placement depends on the shape of the metal being drilled. Drills mounted in a flexible shaft handpiece are usually of small diameter, and work with such speed that resistance is diminished. In this case, it may be sufficient to hold down the metal manually. *Masking tape* can also be used to hold down small metal pieces on a scrap wood board.

Position the point of the twist drill in the dent which will hold it in place once it starts to rotate. The hand drill chuck revolves by putting clockwise pressure on the handle. This action turns a large, circular gear or *rack* of cast iron that has machine-cut teeth which mesh with the spindle-mounted, tapered, small *pinion gear* which has matching teeth. The drive is thus transferred from the handle to the twist drill by the use of *rack-and-pinion gears,* a mechanical principle used to drive other geared tools. The difference in the ratio of the gear sizes accounts for the fast action of the twist drill.

Hold the drill handle upright with the left hand while pressing downward on the point, and turn the gear handle clockwise with the right. Start and finish drilling with *slow revolutions*—at the beginning in order to establish the opening, and at the end to prevent drill breakage as the drill emerges through the metal. Once the hole is established, place a little *light machine oil* on the twist drill, or on the metal, to facilitate the drilling action and reduce the buildup of frictional heat. Use little pressure when using twist drills smaller than number 60 or they will bend or break. When using small drill points, the weight of the hand drill itself is usually sufficient to do the work. After the hole is made, *reverse* the motion of the hand drill to remove the point from the metal without breakage.

THE VERTICAL DRILL PRESS

Holes can also be made with a *vertical drill press,* an electrically driven machine that is named after the means of feeding the drill to the metal: the drill is forced downward by means of a controlling lever or drill press handle until the drill passes through the metal. The smaller models that satisfy the needs of the jeweler are driven by a ¼–½ hp motor, usually equipped with *two-, three-, or four-step pulleys* which allow a fairly wide range of speeds by shifting the belt position from smaller to larger diameter steps to increase the speed. By this means, spindle speeds with a range of from 7,500–30,000 rpm are possible. Some motor heads can be tilted to make possible quicker belt position changes. Others have a foot-controlled *rheostat* that allows speeds to be gradually increased or decreased simply by foot pressure.

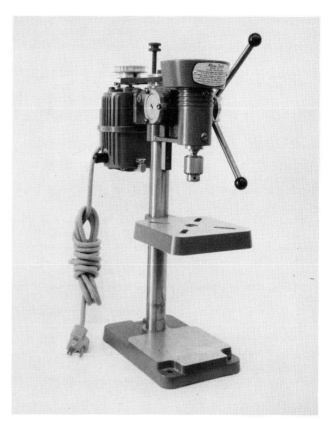

4–85 *THE CAMERON MICRO DRILL PRESS* has dead-true spindle parallelism with the column. Maximum table with spindle squareness is 0.001 in 5 in. The quickly adjustable table, 4 × 4 in, with ⅝ in center hole, locks in precise squareness. Six spindle speeds from 7,000–30,000 rpm provide a wide range of cutting speeds. It has a smooth-acting rack-and-pinion feed, and return spring, and maximum spindle feed travel is ¼ in. Holes from 0–⁵⁄₃₂ in to the center of a 5 in circle can be drilled. Maximum chuck to base distance is 7 in. It is powered with a ⅛ hp, continuous, heavy-duty, two-speed motor. Overall height is 17 in. Photo: Courtesy Swest Inc.

The size of the drill press is given in terms of the largest piece of work through whose center it is possible to drill. Thus a size with a 5 in circle, suitable for use in jewelry workshops, means that the distance from the *center of the spindle* to the front of the *vertical supporting column* is 2½ in (6.35 cm). It is therefore not possible to make a hole in an object that is deeper than 2½ in from any point on the object.

A typical *drill press* used in a jewelry workshop is a small-model precision machine, about 17 in (43.2 cm) high. It is used for drilling holes of relatively small diameter in much the same manner as the much larger drill presses used in industry to drill large holes. The drill press consists of four main parts: the *base* supporting the entire mechanism; the *column* to which the base, table, and the mechanism are attached; the *table* (on which the work is placed) which can be raised or lowered and is clamped in position on the column a maximum distance of 5¾ in (14.6 cm) from chuck to table, is slotted to hold clamps, and has a central hole for the drill to pass through; and the *head* or *mechanism* which consists of a balanced, vertically revolving spindle that operates smoothly and rigidly without chatter, on ball bearings inside the movable sleeve known as the *quill.* The spindle axis and the column axis must be *dead true* so that the drill runs true without wobbling.

The spindle with quill move downward a maximum distance of about 1¼ in (3.18 cm) by means of a simple *rack-and-pinion feed mechanism* moved by a *feed lever*. In most machines, the feed lever is spring loaded, so that when released, the quill and spindle return to their normal upper position. A *locking device* exists that makes it possible to lock the spindle in any intermediate position. The maximum distance possible between the chuck and the table on such a model is 5¾ in.

The spindle is fitted with a *geared, three-jawed chuck*, either screwed on, or held by a *Morse taper* (in which system tapers vary from 0.600–0.630 in/ft depending on the number of the taper). The usual chuck capacity will hold drills that make holes up to ⁵⁄₃₂ in (0.397 cm). Its jaws are opened and closed with a *chuck key*.

To use a drill press, open the chuck jaws with the chuck key, insert the drill shank to its depth capacity and tighten the chuck jaws with the key to close them on the drill shank. Raise the table with the work clamped on it so that the work is near the drill point when the spindle is in its normal raised position. Set the drill press at the desired speed by shifting the belt to the proper pulley (the choice of speed will depend on the material being drilled, and the kind of twist drill used). (See Table, "Suggested Drill Cutting Speeds and Feeds," p. 756.) Choose a speed as near as possible to those suggested for the work at hand. Lubricate the drill with a drop of oil to avoid overheating. Lubrication may have to be repeated if drilling is extended, as when drilling a deep hole into thick metal.

While standing or sitting before the drill press, with the right hand lower the drill by bringing the feed lever toward you until the drill point touches the premarked drill start position on the metal. Do not apply continual heavy pressure when drilling, but instead, press lightly down with *interrupted thrusts*, and lift the drill repeatedly. By decreasing pressure intermittently in this way, the buildup of frictional heat is minimized. In the case of deep holes, drill removal allows the chips to be cleared from the hole. If the feed is too heavy, the drill will run the risk of breaking. Should the drill squeak, this indicates it is blunt. When the drill will not operate except by unusual pressure, this indicates that it is dull. It should be resharpened or replaced. If the drill turns blue, it has been overheated by prolonged frictional heat, and its temper has been drawn. Such a drill cannot be used any longer without retempering it to straw-yellow color. (See Tempering Steel for Tool Durability, p. 239.)

Only *high-speed drills* should be used when cutting metal with a drill press. For cutting soft materials, *carbon steel drills* can be used, but the suggested drill speeds should then be *cut in half*. In general, the larger the drill size, or the harder the metal or object being drilled, the slower the speed must be.

In drilling, do not try to hold a small article on the drill press table simply by hand pressure. *This is a dangerous mistake.* Instead, use a *clamp* to hold it to the table. An experienced operator can hold a piece of metal in a *hand vise* while it is drilled.

It is generally easier to drill holes in flat metal or in concave shapes. When drilling a hole in a concave shape, avoid exerting too much pressure or the work may become deformed. Flat metal sheets can be shaped *after* they have been drilled with holes for decorative effect, provided they are sufficiently annealed.

An object can be mounted on a softwood board which the drill enters. If not, when the drill passes through the metal, its point enters the hole at the center of the drill

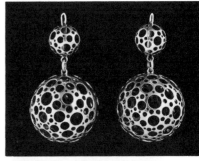

4–86   LIISA VITALI, Finland, designer; manufacturer Kultakeskus Oy, Hämeenlinna. "Leppäkerttu" (Ladybug). Silver hanging earrings with pierced work holes made with different sized twist drills ornament the hollow ball form, reduce the total weight, and create an ever changing pattern through the light-admitting openings. Photo: Courtesy Kultakeskus Oy

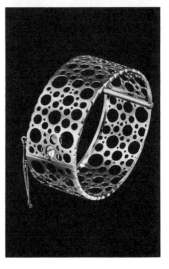

4–87   LIISA VITALI, Finland, designer; manufacturer Kultakeskus Oy, Hämeenlinna. Silver bracelet with drilled pierced work holes. The square wire soldered to the inside edge of the long strip gives the form strength and visual edge thickness. Photo: Courtesy Kultakeskus Oy

press table and therefore is not damaged. When drilling is finished, raise and return the spindle head to its highest normal position, and stop the motor. The work can then be released from the clamp. If the drill is sharp, and excessive pressure has not been applied, the hole should be clean and without burrs. If there are burrs, however, remove them with *fine emery paper*.

For precision work, as when for instance drilling a blind hole in preparation for making an internal screw thread, the drill press can be mounted with a *dial indicator* that registers the depth of a hole while it is being drilled.

With proper *adaptors*, the drill press can also be used for tapping, milling, planing, sanding, grinding, and buffing. Drilling can also be done on a *lathe*. (See The Lathe and Machined Jewelry, Chapter 10.)

Twist drills can also be mounted, as mentioned, in *flexible shafts* for use in drilling small holes because the capacity of the chuck on a flex-shaft is suited only for small twist drills. This capacity can be increased somewhat by the use of an *adaptor collet*. Flex-shafts must use high-speed drills because their normal speed of operation is faster than that of most drill presses. Speeds are controlled by a foot rheostat.

PIERCED WORK POSSIBILITIES

PATTERNED PIERCED WORK

The surface of a pierced work object can be *decorated* by any of several techniques, such as engraving, stamping, punchwork, carving, repoussage and chasing, planishing, texturing, or other decorative surface embellishment processes.

DIMENSIONAL POSTPIERCING FORMS

Flat pierced work can be planned by first making paper models so that after piercing, parts of the metal are bent up, down, or outward, to create a more three-dimensional form. The *illusion* of dimension can be created in several ways. Engraved lines can be placed in a way that implies the passage of positive parts over other parts. In another way, pierced holes can be surrounded by soldered-on wires to give them an appearance of depth.

PIERCED WORK BACKING: Cagework

It is common for ornamental pierced work to be left as is—open at the back so that light can pass through the openings. Alternately, the object can be *backed up* with a solid base of the same or contrasting material, called *cagework*. An entire back can be made of a semiprecious stone slab, wood, leather, cloth, etc. When metal is used, the backing can be *permanently oxidized black* to make a contrast to the polished pierced work mounted above it. The backing can also be polished *mirror-bright* so that with movement, light flashes through the openings. Such a backing can be mounted by screws to make it possible to remove the backing when repolishing is necessary; or the mounting can be permanent, using rivets, a bezel type of construction, by soldering, or by other techniques. The pierced work and backing can be flush against each other, or the backing can be concave in relation to a flat or convex upper pierced work part, in which case light can enter the space between.

4-88 FINLAND, early 20th century. Silver pierced work and engraved Art Nouveau (Jugend) identification monograms clipped or sewn to the inside of coats, on purses, wallets, cigarette boxes, etc. All are of flat sheet, but dimensional effect is achieved by engraved lines that imply the overlapping or intertwining of forms, and surfaces are texturally differentiated. Largest height 3½ in. Col.: Kultasepänliike Ossian Hopea, Porvoo. *Photo: Oppi*

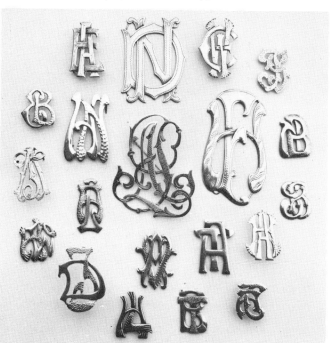

4-89 MANUEL RIVERO SOBERÓN, Mexico, designer; manufacturer Tane, S.A., Mexico City. Sterling silver pendant achieving a pierced work effect by superimposing and soldering separate pierced units upon each other. A variety of differently sized and shaped openings result, all relating to the basic unit shape. Size 12 × 12 cm. *Photo: Courtesy Pedro Leites, Tane, S.A.*

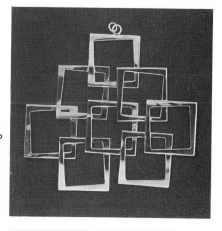

4-90 FRIEDRICH MÜLLER, Switzerland. Cuff links, 18K rose gold, the top saw-pierced sheet backed by a solid sheet, and the pierced area colored. Ø approx. 20 mm. *Photo: Mario Tschabold*

4-91 BHUTAN. Contemporary gilded silver pierced work matching pair of cloak clasps with connecting chain. Worn at the shoulders to secure the traditional woman's costume. The main pattern used on both clasps and links is the endless knot, a Buddhist symbol of longevity. Piercing is done with small, sharp chisels. *Photo: Victoria and Albert Museum, London, Crown Copyright*

PIERCED INLAY: Filling pierced work openings

Wires formed into filigreelike shapes can be soldered into pierced openings in solid sheet metal. If the pierced work is soldered to a backing, such openings can be filled with a viscous or fusible material such as a resin or liquid plastic, a solid material like crushed stone mixed with epoxy, a mosaic of stones, niello, or enamel. Such mate-

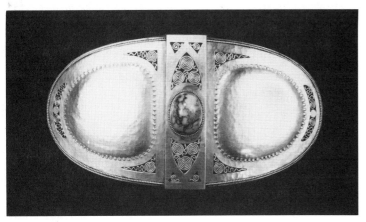

4–92 A. VON MAYRHOFER, Munich, Germany, 1912. Silver belt buckle with turquoise. The repoussé-worked sheet has pierced openings that are filled with wire spirals. *Photo: Günter Meyer, courtesy Schmuckmuseum, Pforzheim*

rials can partially or completely fill the pierced opening, in which case the finished surface can be treated as one continuous piece and leveled with abrasives or files, followed by a uniform polishing.

The pierced cavity can also be filled with a *different metal,* one whose color contrasts with the rest, or that is capable of being treated with chemicals to achieve a different patina. Such inlays must be cut to the exact shape of the opening to fill it completely. This is done by placing the finished opening on the inlay metal and tracing its shape with a *fine-pointed tracing stylus.* Once the inlay is cut out and its edges finished, it is soldered into place.

FILING PIERCED WORK OPENINGS

Files are used as an adjunct to piercing to refine shapes that have been opened first by other tools.

OTHER SAWING TOOLS USED FOR PIERCED WORK

Compass saw: A narrow-bladed saw for cutting curves.
Keyhole saw: A saw used to pierce openings such as keyholes. It is similar to a compass saw, but has a narrower blade.
Jigsaw: A sawing machine with a narrow, vertically reciprocating saw blade that is removable. It is used to cut curved and irregular lines, and for ornamental openwork.
Scroll saw: A saw with a thin blade stretched in a frame, foot or motor powered, used for sawing curves.

ETCH PIERCING

Etch piercing is the piercing of metal by the use of an etchant. (See Photomechanical One- or Two-Surface Etch Piercing, Chapter 8.)

HEAT PIERCING

Openings can be pierced in metal by melting away parts with a *micro-torch* having a hot, concentrated flame.

FILES AND FILING

Removing metal by attrition

A *file* is a hardened steel tool whose surface or surfaces are covered with parallel rows or furrows of sharp teeth or cutting ridges. Files are used for cutting, abrading, shaping, and smoothing metals (and a variety of other substances) by the gradual removal of material when the teeth, under pressure, pass over, engage, and cut into it, removing small amounts. A great many different kinds of files exist, each used for particular purposes, classified on p. 101. Filing is a basic technique used by jewelers, and the file is one of the most important shaping and finishing tools.

Before the use of metal tools, stones of various degrees of hardness and surface roughness were used to abrade different materials. The bronze file came into use during the Bronze Age. It contained 18–30% tin, and was suited for use on soft materials only. True files as we know them today developed with the use of iron late in the Bronze Age, when both flat and round forms were developed. Mild steel files were used by the Romans, but these were limited in size. The earliest account of the hand manufacture of files occurs in the 12th-century treatise of Theophilus, *On Diverse Arts,* and the process remained essentially unchanged until the middle of the 18th century. Mechanical manufacture of files began in France in 1750, and several machines were developed, mostly by French-

men, between 1756 and 1862. An important improvement was the development of various techniques of carburizing the file teeth to render them hard enough to abrade hard metals. From then on, machine manufacture made possible the development and standardization of special files for use by many trades. New files for special uses are still being invented today.

FILE MANUFACTURE

Blank file steel stock is prepared in various widths, thicknesses, and cross sections; the most basic shapes are rectangular, square, triangular, round, and half-round. Many other shapes also exist. The blank is rough shaped by heating and forging with trip-hammers and rolls to form the tang and point. The *tang* is the narrow, tapered part of the file that engages the handle. The blank is annealed and slowly cooled to soften the steel, to make its internal structure uniform, and to prepare it for tooth cutting. It is next brought to its final shape by grinding and milling. The surface is drawfiled to make it truly flat or curved.

The teeth are formed by a reciprocating hard steel chisel that strikes rapid successive blows on the soft blank as it moves past the chisel, cutting into and displacing the steel without removing it, into the desired tooth structure.

The most important step in file manufacture is hardening. To harden the teeth, by one method, the file is heated in a molten lead bath at a controlled temperature, then immersed in a quenching solution which brings the very top of the cutting edges to maximum hardness.

By another method for hardening, the file is treated to prevent its oxidation which would affect its sharpness. It is first submerged in a solution containing about three pounds of salt dissolved in one gallon of water, or to saturation, then stiffened to a creamy consistency with flour. Into this the file is dipped. The purpose of the flour is to help get a maximum of salt on the file surface. It is immediately heated to a uniform cherry red by holding the tang end with tongs and introducing it to a forge fire or special heating ovens. The salt immediately forms a firm coating that fuses on the file as the water evaporates. The file is then quickly quenched in fresh water as cold as possible to prevent warpage. The way it is quenched is important. Except for the half-round file, all files are immersed perpendicularly into the water as quickly as possible to cool them uniformly. The half-round is held perpendicularly to the water level but moved horizontally somewhat toward its round side to prevent its warping backward. They are then brushed with powdered coke and water to clean them, and rinsed two or three times to take away any remaining salt which otherwise could cause rusting. After a dip in lime water and drying, they are coated with an oil and turpentine mixture while still warm.

In some cases, before oiling the teeth are further sharpened by sandblasting. The tang is then tempered for hardness, and the file is oiled.

GENERAL CLASSIFICATION OF FILE TYPES

The *length* of the file is almost always given exclusive of the *tang*. The measured distance lies between the *heel* where the tang begins, and the *point* or opposite end. (Needle files are an exception; their *total length* inclusive of handle is given.) Generally the length has no fixed proportion to width or thickness.

In classifying files, we refer to their *profile, type of section, cut,* and *fineness* or *grading.*

PROFILE

The *profile* is based on its general outline. It may be a *taper* (*pointed* file) in which the point is reduced in width or thickness, or both. The tapering occurs for one half to one third its length from the point toward which it converges. *Slim files* are files that are very narrow in proportion to their length and are graded as *slim, extra slim,* and *double extra slim tapers. Blunt files* have parallel edges and their sides are uniform in sectional shape and size from tang to point; or they may taper somewhat, but the point is blunt.

TYPE OF SECTION

The file type name refers to its cross-sectional shape or style. A *section* or *cross section* is what the end view of a file would look like if it were cut squarely across its greatest width and thickness from the tang end. The three most general cross-sectional shapes are *quadrangular, tri-*

4–93 *THE WORLD OF FILES.*
Photo: *Courtesy Friedr. Dick GmbH, file manufacturers, Esslingen am Neckar, West Germany*

angular, and *round,* and from these are derived other irregular forms, classed as *miscellaneous.* Generally, as a file increases in length, its cross-sectional size also increases.

CUT

Each type of file is made in a range of *tooth character* and *coarseness* or *cuts,* as well as in different sizes. The tooth character can be *single, double, rasp, curved,* or *special. Single-cut* files have a single series of teeth cut at an angle of about 25° normal with a center line of the surface or at a right angle to its length. These are used with light pressure to produce a smooth surface finish, or to keenly sharpen the edge of a cutting tool. *Float* files are coarser grades of single-cut files used on very soft metals like lead or aluminum, or on wood and other soft materials. *Double-cut files* have two series of diagonal teeth: the first called the *overcut* or *crosscut* is at an angle of 25°; and the second, called the *upcut,* crosses over the first at an angle of 45–50°, and is finer than the first. Double-cut files are used with heavier pressure than single-cut for fast metal removal, but tend to produce a rougher finish. They are suited for use on harder metals, such as iron and steel, but are not well suited to soft metals which tend to fill and clog the teeth. *Rasp-cut* files have individually formed, disconnected teeth made by a sharp, narrow, punchlike cutting chisel. They are very roughly cut and are mainly used for quick removal of soft materials such as lead and aluminum, and also on plastic, wood, or leather. In *curved-tooth* files, the teeth are formed in arcs across the width of the file. They are used on soft or hard metals. Special cuts are made for other specialized uses.

FINENESS (GRADING)

The tooth coarseness or cut can be *coarse* or rough, *bastard, second, smooth,* or *dead smooth.* The *coarse* cut is the coarsest of all and is used for heavy work and rough metal removal. *Bastard* cut is a file coarseness between coarse and second cut and is used for relatively rough metal removal. *Second* cut is a file coarseness between bastard and smooth and is used for finishing. *Smooth* cut is a file cut of less coarseness than second cut, and produces a smooth, almost unmarked surface, especially after drawfiling. *Dead smooth* is the finest of the standard cuts, used for finishing.

File Cuts:	Teeth	per in
Coarse:	14–22	per in
Bastard:	22–32	per in
Second:	30–42	per in
Smooth:	50–68	per in
Dead smooth:	70–120	per in

Superfine files such as needle files and Swiss files are graded by *numbers* ranging from 00, the coarsest, to 6, the finest. The most commonly used are from 00–4, and for average work, numbers 1 or 2 are used. The tooth count for these files is given separately in a chart below.

FILE FAMILY GROUPS (Arranged alphabetically)

BRASS FILES   Used for brass and soft metals, are cut at an angle that prevents clogging, with a short upcut angle almost squarely across the file, and a fine-cut long angle overcut of about 60°. This angle cut prevents grooving and clogging by breaking the filings. It bites deeply with less pressure, and produces a smoothing effect.

CURVED-TOOTH FILES   Made with milled, curved-line-cut teeth instead of straight-line-cut teeth, usually having a radius of about 1½ in. Because their teeth are curved, they are self-clearing of chips. They are made rigid in a conventional, tanged form. In a flexible form, the file has a hole at each end by which it is fixed to a special holder that flexes the file into a bowed curve. Used in industry on both soft and hard metals, and on flat or curved surfaces. Made in standard, fine, and smooth cuts, in parallel, flat, square, pillar, pillar-harrow, and half-round types.

DOUBLE-ENDED FILES   Coarse cut from the points toward the middle which usually has a blank area for holding, these files are used at either end. They are mainly meant for filing hard waxes, plastics, and other soft materials, and weigh about two ounces.

ESCAPEMENT FILES   These have the same fineness as needle files. They were created originally for use in clock- and watchmaking when forming the *escapement,* a part of a watch that controls the motion of the wheelwork and other parts. Besides the usual shapes, there are *balance wheel* (one side, right angle; other side, half-round), *rounding off* (half-round with face safe), *notch* (for very narrow notches), and others. The length of the cut area varies according to the shape, from ¾ in to 2½ in (1.9–6.4 cm); total length 5½ in (14 cm); and cuts, available in size numbers 00, 0, 2, 3, 4, 6.

FLOAT FILES   Also called *lead float files,* these coarse, short-angle, single-cut files are used on extra soft metals such as lead, babbit metal, and others to rapidly shear away the metal under ordinary pressure. Light pressure results in smoothing the surface.

MACHINISTS' FILES   These are mostly double-cut files of various shapes, used in industry where metal must be removed rapidly, and where smoothness of finish is not important. Length ranges from 4–16 in (10.16–40.64 cm), and are available in most sectional shapes.

MILL FILES   These files are so named because they are widely used for sharpening circular mill saws, though they also have other uses such as drawfiling, general smooth-finish filing, lathe work, and on brass and bronze. In effect, they are general-purpose files, 12 in, 14 in, or 16 in long, single-cut, slightly tapered in width for about a third of their length, and in thickness also. They are usually made with two square edges that also cut as well as the sides, but some have one or two round edges designed to be used for sharpening saw blades. They are available in all the standard sectional shapes and degrees of coarseness.

NEEDLE FILES   These narrow, fine-cut files are made in many sectional shapes, and are widely used by jewelers, watch and clock makers, and tool- and diemakers for precision work, sometimes done under magnification. They have rounded, knurled tangs up to 2¾ in long, used as a handle to provide a comfortable grip. They are available from some manufacturers with plastic-coated handles that are *color coded* for cut identification. Measures include their *total length* which can be 4 in, 5½ in, 6¼ in, and 7¾ in, the cut portion ranging from 2½–4⅛ in. They weigh approximately one ounce each, and are often sold in *sets* of assorted, commonly used sectional shapes, described below. Cuts range from the coarsest, 00, to the finest, which is 8.

PLASTIC FILES These are files of various types, used to finish and shape plastic objects. When used on hard plastic, the file removes the material as a light powder, and on soft plastic the material is removed as shreds. A special curved-tooth *super-shear file* is available for soft plastics. It has single-cut coarse teeth with a 45° angle that reduces clogging.

RASP FILES These have disconnected, individually formed, coarse teeth, made for use on soft materials. They are available in flat, half-round, and round shapes. *Cabinet rasps* are smaller and finer and are used for finer shaping work.

RIFFLER FILES The name is derived from the French *rifler,* "to file." They come in a variety of shapes, with curved, fine points at both ends, and a plain center section used as a handle while either end is used. They are designated by shape and cut, and are used by jewelers and

diemakers (for which reason they are also called *die-sinker's files*) to work in depressions and otherwise inaccessible places, which is possible because of their curved ends. They are available with various degrees of cut fineness.

STAINLESS STEEL FILES Because of the chromium and nickel content in stainless steel, this alloy is extremely hard. As general-purpose files are quickly worn out when used on it, files are made specifically for use on stainless steel that have a special steel composition which provides them with good wearing qualities. They are available in a variety of shapes and sizes. They must be used with light pressure, in slow, steady strokes to allow rapid metal removal and good finish.

SWISS PATTERN FILES This group comprises a large series of fine-cut files whose shape and manufacture originated in Switzerland. They are made of a chrome steel alloy for hardness and durability, in various shapes, and a range of special cuts. The points are small, and their

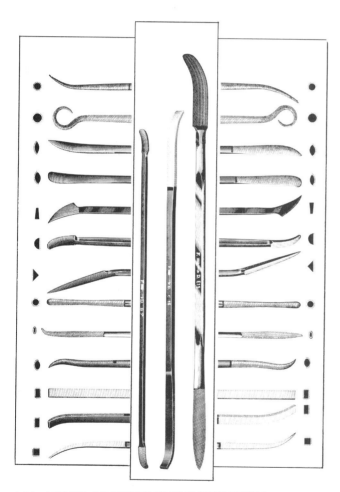

4–94 ASSORTED DIE-SINKER'S OR ENGRAVER'S RIFFLERS
In three lengths 6, 6¼, and 7 in. Courtesy: Friedr. Dick GmbH, West Germany

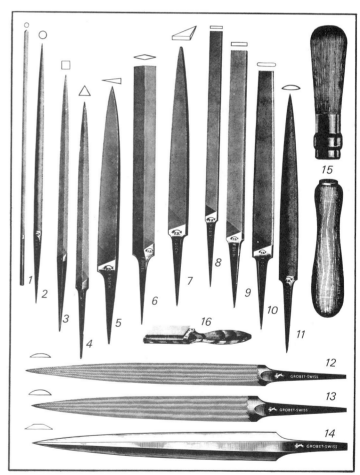

4–95 SWISS PATTERN FILES, 6–8 in long.
1. Round, parallel
2. Round, tapered
3. Square
4. Threesquare
5. Knife edge
6. Diamond or slitting
7. Warding
8. Pillar
9. Hand
10. Crochet
11. Crossing
12. Half-round, ring
13. Half-round
14. Barrette
15. Two wooden file handles
16. File card or brush

tapered files have longer tapers than conventional American pattern files. They are designed for precision work in jewelry making, silversmithing, diemaking, clock- and watchmaking. Flat files should be used with a slow, smooth, lateral forward stroke. To assure a deeper cut and smoother finish when working with half-round, round, and oval files, rotate them clockwise on the forward stroke. They are available in cuts from coarse to fine (00–6), 6–8 in (15.2–20.3 cm) long, tang length 2 in (5.1 cm), weight between one and two ounces.

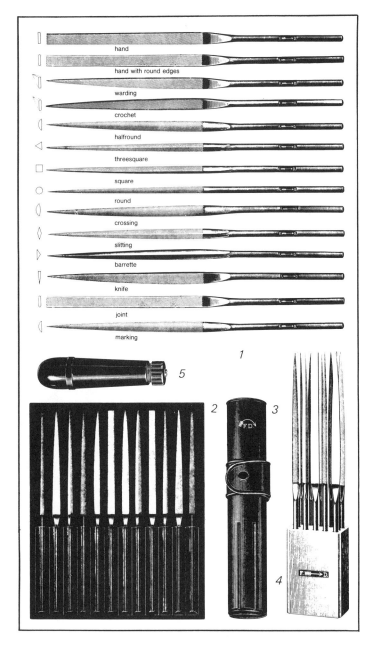

4–96   NEEDLE FILES WITH ROUND HANDLES
1. A selection of various *cross section* needle file types, total length 5½–7¾ in (140–200 mm).
2. An *assortment* of needle files in a plastic case.
3. The closed case.
4. An *assortment* of needle files in a container with a wooden stand.
5. Screwhead Bakelite file handle, adjustable, 80 mm.
   Courtesy: Friedr. Dick GmbH, file manufacturers, West Germany

Teeth Count by Size Number on Files Used by Jewelers

00 = coarsest; 6 = finest

	Size No.	Teeth per inch upcut
Files 10" and over:	00	30
	0	38
	1	51
	2	64
	3	79
	4	97
	6	142
Files 4 – 8"	00	38
	0	51
	1	64
	2	79
	3	97
	4	117
	6	173
Needle and Escapement Files 4 – 7¾"	00	51
	0	64
	1	79
	2	97
	3	117
	4	142
	6	213
Rifflers	0	64
	2	97
	3	117
	4	142
	6	213

SWISS PATTERN, ESCAPEMENT, AND NEEDLE FILE SECTIONAL SHAPES

The files most widely and usually used by jewelers, die sinkers and watchmakers are types known as hand files (6 in [15.2 cm] long), Swiss pattern files (6–8 in [15.2–20.3 cm] long), and needle files (4–7¾ in [10.2–19.7 cm] long). These files are manufactured in over a hundred shapes, further multiplied by a range of sizes, cuts, and tapered and blunt forms. Not all shapes and cuts are available in each category or size. Certain shapes such as flat, square, triangular, barrette, half-round, and round are most commonly used, but special circumstances may call for any of the other shapes available. When one or more edges or sides are left *uncut* so as not to cut adjacent surfaces, it is called a *safe edge* or *safe side*. Both small and large files may be used without, but preferably with separately purchased handles which fit over the tang by pressing them on, or by holding the file point upward, inserting the tang into the handle, and then gently tapping the handle end on a hard surface. It is not advisable in work to ever hold a file on its cutting portion as perspiration causes corrosion, and oil imparted to the file may cause it to skip.

The common shapes are:

FLAT   Rectangular section, slightly tapered in width and thickness, blunt, double-cut on edges and sides, sometimes with one small safe edge.

HAND   Rectangular in section, parallel in width, but bellied or tapered in thickness from the middle, both ways. Double-cut, one safe edge, bites deeply for fast metal removal. Suited to accurate work and finishing flat surfaces. It should be used with a handle.

PILLAR Narrow, rectangular in section, parallel in width, with one or both edges safe, tapered in thickness from the middle both ways, usually double-cut. Narrower and thicker than a hand file, suited to narrow work like filing slots. Also made in extra narrow section.

WARDING (ENTERING) Rectangular section, tapered to a narrow point. Narrow thickness suited to filing narrow spaces and notches.

EQUALING Narrow rectangle, cut on four sides, blunt.

ROUND-EDGE JOINT Rectangular section, but narrow edges that are curved and cut, with long, flat safe sides, blunt.

MILL Rectangular in section, slightly tapered in thickness and width from the middle to the point, sometimes has one round edge. Ordinarily single-cut but when blunt is usually double-cut. In fineness usually bastard- or second-cut.

SQUARE (FOURSQUARE) Square in section with four equal filing sides, double-cut on all sides, tapered or blunt. Used for general surface filing, for slots, and in the heavier weights sometimes preferred over flat or narrow pillar because of its heavier cross section.

TRIANGULAR An equilateral triangle (three equal sides) in section, tapered or blunt if used for sawtooth filing; double-cut with edges left sharp; and single-cut. Used for filing internal angles. Available in needle files with end bent into a curve, top flat, safe edge.

BARRETTE Truncated triangle in section, long flat side cuts, two smaller sides and safe edges. Allows filing close to an angle without removing adjacent metal.

CANT Isosceles triangle in section, edges parallel, obtuse angle between the sides, blunt.

KNIFE Triangular in section with very acute vertex angle of about 10°, double-cut on sides, single-cut on the edges, wider safe edge, tapers to a point in both width and thickness. Used for working with acute angles.

CROCHET Narrow rectangle in section, short ends rounded, tapered to a point.

GREAT AMERICAN Triangular in section, but base is curved, blunt.

LOZENGE (ONGLETTE) Lozenge- or diamond-shaped rhombus, tapered.

SLITTING Narrow lozenge section, blunt. Used for making narrow, V-shaped grooves.

FIVE CANTED Shaped like a pentagon, 108° angles, blunt.

SIX CANTED Shaped like a hexagon, 120° angles, blunt.

ROUND Circular section, conically tapered or cylindrically blunt, double-cut. Used to file circular openings or concave curved surfaces, and to enlarge holes.

RATTAIL A small-diameter, round-section file, tapered, ¼ in (0.64 cm) or less in section. Used to enlarge small, round holes and to work concave contours.

HALF-ROUND Flat on one side, curved on the other side, but not equal to a semicircular cross section, tapered toward the point in width and thickness. Flat side is always double-cut, curved side is usually double-cut except for smooth, second cut which is single-cut.

HALF-ROUND SLIM (RING FILE) A tapered half-round shape of narrower width than ordinary half-round, its size suited to filing the inside of ring shanks.

MARKING Half-round section, curved side cuts, flat safe side, tapered.

CROSSING (DOUBLE HALF-ROUND) Curved and cut on both sides, tapered or blunt.

OVAL Approximately elliptical in section, tapered.

SCREWHEAD Narrow-edged oval, used for filing small slots in screwheads, blunt, sometimes without tang.

PIPPIN Similar to Great American but smaller, shaped like a tear or an apple seed in section, tapered.

AURIFORM Curved on both sides and very small.

THE USES OF FILES

Files are used to remove surface defects and edge burrs (also called a fraze), to trim and true edges to their final dimension, to round or bevel edges, to true grooves and notches, to enlarge holes, to make slots, to shape corners and forms from solid stock, to refine forms and planes, to shape pierced openings, to remove unwanted solder, for finishing and smoothing, to sharpen cutting tools, as well as for many other purposes. The choice of the right file for the particular use on particular metals or other materials assures more efficient, faster, and better results. The factor of size, shape, and cut of file are basic considerations when selecting a file.

Typically, different files are used on an edge after sawing to trim and smooth it (such as flat, pillar, or hand); on flat or convex surfaces (flat-faced files); on curved or concave surfaces (half-round, round, oval, riffler files); on a notch or slot (warding, equaling, round-edge joint); on a round hole (round, rattail); and on a square hole (square file). Other considerations may be the degree of smoothness or accuracy wanted (coarser or finer; double- or single-cut files); the location to be filed; and the kind, hardness, or amount of metal to be removed.

To avoid work contamination, separate files should be reserved for exclusive use with the precious metals, the nonferrous metals, ferrous metals, and very soft metals. If, for instance, particles of lead are left on precious metals, when heated the lead will eat into the metal and create pits.

The file should not be used to do work that is more easily, efficiently, and quickly done by other tools—such as the removal of large amounts of metal, better done by saws, chisels, or scrapers.

FILING TECHNIQUES

All files are designed so that their *teeth cut on the forward stroke.* Use just enough pressure on the forward stroke to keep the file cutting at all times, and no more than that. A file rapidly becomes dull if it is allowed to slide, especially over hard metals, and too much pressure causes the teeth to chip or become clogged which reduces file efficiency. Push the file forward with a smooth, steady, even stroke. It is always advisable to use the *full length* of the file with each stroke so that one area does not become worn out while the rest is hardly used. On the *backward stroke,* lift the file from contact with the metal, or turn it

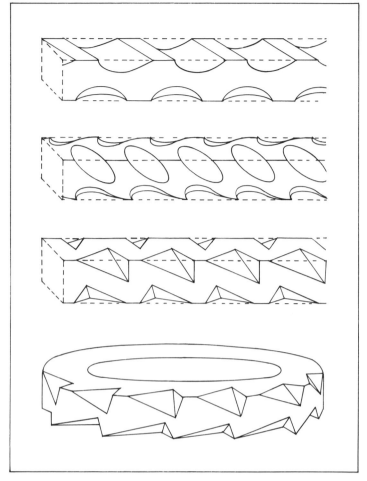

4-97 *FILE PATTERN SHAPING ON SOLID STOCK BY METAL RE-MOVAL FROM MASS*
Three solid bars and a solid ring are shown here to illustrate the creation of regularly repeated patterns made on them with the use of files to remove metal for decorative effect. In the first and second figures, only *curve-shaped files* are used. The third, and the ring below use *flat-surfaced files.* When shaping solid stock to irregular forms, the file shape is chosen according to the desired curvature or straight shape to be created.

slightly so that its pressure against the metal is not more than its own weight. Avoid dragging pressure which will wear out the teeth.

In hand filing with small files, the worker is usually seated, and the work should be placed at eye level or about six inches below it. The work can be hand held firmly while a part is braced against the workbench edge, a *file block,* or a *bench pin* fixed in the edge of the workbench. Holding tools as a *hand vise, ring clamp,* or *pin clamp* (depending on the work shape), can be used to firmly hold the work when filing, especially when it is small, with the tool braced for rigidity against the bench pin or within its apex. Unless the clamp has leather-lined jaws, it may be necessary to protect the work from becoming marked by the clamp by placing a strip of leather above and below the place of clamp contact. This is especially needed when large *C-clamps, bench clamps,* or *bench vises* are used to hold large work. In some cases, a strip of cardboard, sheet metal such as copper or brass, or two blocks of wood placed on either side of the metal within the vise jaws can be used as protecting materials.

When using large files on large work held in a bench vise, the worker stands with the work clamped in the vise

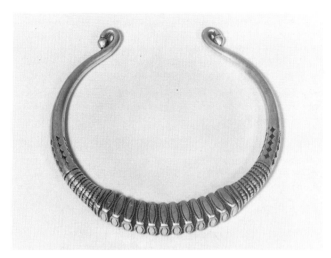

4-98 NORTH INDIA. Traditional torque, solid silver forged neckpiece (*hansuli*), ornamented with postforging patterns created by first filing away regularly repeated portions of the form, then embellishing them with engraved and stamped patterns. Col.: Dietlind Bock-Meinardus. Photo: Salmi

at elbow level. The grip and stroke of the file is different from that used with small files. *Both hands are used,* the right grasping the handle with its end up against the fleshy part of the palm below the joint of the little finger, and the point end grasped with the thumb and first two fingers. For light pressure, the thumb and fingers holding the point lie at nearly right angle to the file. When holding a large file with one hand, hold it in the same way as a small file, with the index finger extended.

Straight flat filing consists of holding the file firmly with the right hand with the index finger extended on top of the file in the direction of its length. Push the file straight ahead, or at a slight diagonal angle to the metal and pass its entire length over the work. In general, when removing surplus metal, pass the file over a distance on the part filed and not just in one place, in order to avoid forming grooves (unless of course you are deliberately making a groove or slot). If a file leaves marks or decided grooves on an edge or surface, and to assure surface flatness, change the angle of work slightly, or reverse the direction of filing to smooth them away with the strokes that follow. Small parts can be filed for metal removal or where flat surfaces are wanted by holding the part with the fingers, and rubbing it against an *immobilized,* clamped-down file. For filing slots and angles, use files with appropriate *safe edges* where needed to prevent metal removal from adjacent areas.

Curve filing consists of filing convex or concave surfaces or edges with the file held as described above. Carry the stroke across the work in the direction of the curve with a smooth, even rocking or rolling motion, or a curved directional stroke by rotating the wrist. Do not keep the file in one place unless deliberately cutting a curved groove. For shaping *convex* surfaces or edges, flat files are usually used; for *concave* surfaces or edges, round or oval files or rifflers are used. Move the file across as well as along the curve.

Shape filing or filing solid stock to a form begins with larger files, proceeds to finer ones as the form nears completion, and finishing is done with a series of gradually finer abrasive papers.

Drawfiling is a method of filing used to make a surface,

an edge, or (simultaneously) several edge pieces perfectly smooth, flat, and level. When a considerable amount of metal is to be removed, a *double-cut hand file* works fast but tends to leave small ridges on the work. Where a smooth surface is wanted, use a *single-cut mill bastard-cut file,* which can also be used to finish work done with a double-cut file. A short-angle-cut file should not be used for drawfiling because it is likely to scar the metal instead of shaving or shearing it.

In drawfiling, the worker stands, and the work is fixed in a bench vise, projecting above the vise's jaw level. In some cases, especially when the work is of irregular shape, a sheet can be held to a block of wood by headless wire brads driven into the block at intervals around its perimeter. Be sure the nail top is *below* the metal's surface, or it will catch on the file. Place the block holding the metal in the bench vise. Grasp the file firmly with two hands, one at each end, and alternately push and pull it *sideways* across the work with the length *transverse* to the direction of its motion.

For *lathe filing,* see The Lathe and Machined Jewelry, Chapter 10.

FILE CLEANING

Clogging (also called *pinning*), or allowing the file teeth to become filled with or collect metal chips, greatly reduces file efficiency, and the trapped metal may scratch a work surface. To prevent clogging the end of the file should be tapped lightly on the bench after several strokes to loosen chips. The file can also be rubbed with chalk *before* use as this does not reduce its ability to cut but will impede clogging.

Files should in any case be cleaned occasionally. This is done with a *file card,* or a *file brush* that includes a card on one side and a brush on the other. The card is stiffer than the brush and is generally used on coarse files, and the brush is used on finer files. Hold the file by the tang end with the point resting on the bench, and rub the card or brush over it in a diagonal position. If the pinning is not removed this way, use a scorer, or the edge of a piece of soft brass or soft iron to remove it. Grease or oil is removed from a file by the application of chalk, which absorbs it. The chalk is then removed by the file card or brush. Grease on a file will cause it to skip.

FILE STORAGE

There are several acceptable methods of storing files when not in use. They can be placed vertically, tang end in a series of holes drilled in a wooden slab, to prevent contact of their working surfaces. Special file cases are available. Small files are often kept in a plastic sheet holder that has pockets in which each file is held separately. Files should never hit against each other in storage. They should not be thrown into a drawer or kept together in one box. They should be stored in a dry place to prevent rusting which corrodes the teeth.

Old files never lose their usefulness, even when they are broken. It is common practice to use old, worn files on soft metals. They can be ground down to make other tools that get rough usage, such as a *solder probe* or *pick.* Old files can be formed into knives or used for trimming buffing wheels.

ROTARY FILES, BURS, AND ABRASIVE POINTS

The development of portable power tools for jewelry making has brought about a greatly increased use of *rotating files, burs, abrasive points,* and a variety of other accessories. The versatility of power-driven tools such as the *flexible shaft* and its attachments (all scaled to sizes needed in jewelry making) makes them the most important innovation in this field. With them, the time needed to perform the operations of grinding, shaping, texturing, finishing, and polishing are considerably reduced.

The flexible shaft (flex-shaft) through which rotary power is transmitted to the attached tool is usually purchased with its own motor, but *adaptor shafts* which allow them to be worked by attachment to the rotary spindle of different motors (such as buffing motors, bench model drill presses, and lathes) are also available. The shaft is mounted with a *straight* or *angled handpiece* containing an adjustable, key-controlled chuck to hold the shank of files, burs, points, mandrels, arbors, adaptor chucks, and other accessories below a specific shank size diameter. The shanks of these items range from ⅛ in, ³⁄₃₂ in, ¼ in, up to ⁵⁄₃₂ in. When purchasing a handpiece, the choice of chuck capacity must be considered carefully, as this limits the maximum size of shaft usable without recourse to an *adaptor* that allows the use of larger shanks.

Rotary files and burs are generally made of high-speed steel, and have spirally formed, fluted cutting edges. Burs are also made of carbide, which has up to one hundred times the cutting life of high-speed steel, though they are brittle and must be used with care. Worn carbide burs are reground and refluted by the manufacturer for a nominal charge. The teeth of *hand-cut rotary files* are made by an expert with a hammer and chisel. They are discontinuous and not in flutes, making them suited for use on dense metals as tough as die steel because the teeth dissipate frictional heat. Ground burs are cut by a machine-driven grinding wheel from blank stock and have continuous flutes that extend from base to nose. Intermediate flutes lead into the main flutes on round and oval shapes. Ground burs in general are more efficient than hand-cut rotary files as their fluted teeth free themselves of chips.

Shape	Section	Size Width x Thickness approx. inch
Rectangular		.208 x .047
Half-Round		.208 x .071
Triangular		.138 (side)
Square		.100
Round		118 (dia.)

4–99 *DIAMOND FILES* in sizes and shapes resembling needle files. They have diamond particles bonded to their all-metal shanks. Available in the basic sectional shapes in coarse (100–120) grit, and fine (230–270) grit for use on nonferrous metals, ferrous metals (stainless or hardened steel), for lapidary use in shaping stones, and use on glass and ceramics. *Courtesy Highland Park Manufacturing*

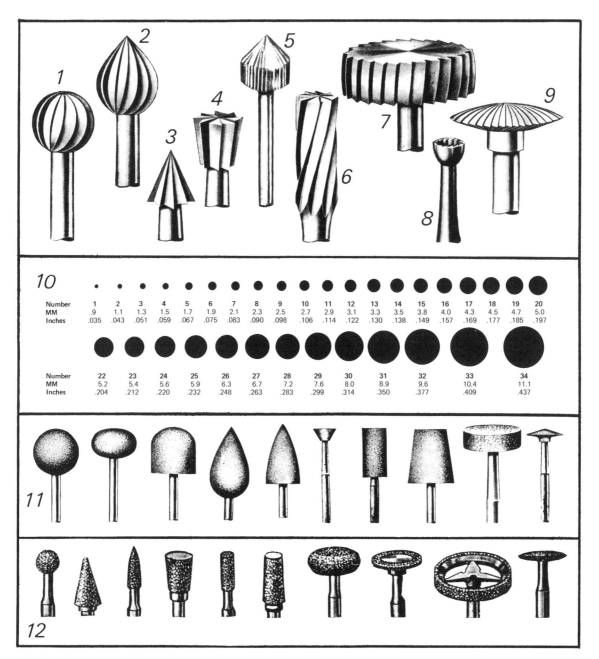

4–100 *ROTARY CUTTING INSTRUMENTS*
Rotary Files, Basic Shapes
1. *Round;* 2. *Bud;* 3. *Cone;* 4. *Inverted cone;* 5. *Stone-setting cone, 45° bearing;* 6. *Cylinder;* 7. *Wheel;* 8. *Concave;* 9. *Knife-edge wheel;* 10. *High-speed bur size chart (there is no size 21);* 11. *Silicon carbide bur shapes;* 12. *Diamond-embedded rotary cutting instrument shapes.*

BASIC SHAPES OF STEEL AND CARBIDE ROTARY CUTTING BURS

It is important when using rotary cutting burs to select the shape that best suits the purpose. These are available in high-speed carbon, tungsten, or vanadium steel and carbide. The diameters of heads range from No. 1 (0.035 in, 0.9 mm) in 34 sizes to No. 34 (0.437 in, 11.1 mm), (see Illustration 4–100). Shank sizes are ⅛ in, ³⁄₃₂ in, or ¼ in, in diameter.

ROUND AND ROUNDED Ball-shaped, pear-shaped, barrel, oval.

BUD Pointed ball shape; *flame:* longer pointed shape than bud; *tree:* straighter sided, blunter end than flame.

CONE Tapered sides, pointed end; *short cone:* shallow cone; *cone reamer, slim reamer:* fewer and straighter flutes, longer taper, available in straight- or cross-cut edges.

INVERTED CONE Flat sides taper away from the flat or round end toward the shank.

STONE SETTING CONE Flat-sided cylinder with cone-shaped end, used to drill holes for stone setting; bearing 45° or 90°: cone-pointed end, sides converge toward the shank.

CYLINDER Cylinder shape, straight sides, regular with all sides toothed, safe end, safe sides with cutting end, round end.

WHEEL Disc-shaped with square cutting edge, safe inside, safe outside, round edge, knife edge, thin edge.

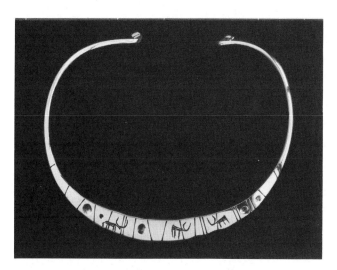

4–101 RONALD W. SENUNGETUK, Alaska, U.S.A. Torque of sterling silver forged wire. The reindeer motif is engraved in the metal by the use of a small rotary file mounted on a flexible shaft, then the intaglio portions were colored. Size 5 × 5 in. Photo: Howard Ringley

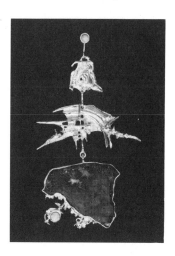

4–102 REGINE JUHLS, Norway. Silver pendant with lapis lazuli and two small turquoises. This fabricated piece was worked over in parts with circular files mounted on a rotary shaft. Photo: Börje Rönnberg, courtesy Sølvsmie Regine & Frank Juhls

CONCAVE Cup-shaped, concave, hollow end with interior teeth, used to round wire ends, tips, prongs, and exposed ends.

MISCELLANEOUS Any that fall outside these categories.

THE USE OF HIGH-SPEED STEEL ROTARY FILES AND BURS

When using high-speed steel rotary files and burs, to achieve best results certain procedures should be followed. The pressure should be even to avoid bumps. The head diameter determines the speed at which they can be used (see accompanying table: Suggested Speeds for Medium-Cut Rotary Files and Burs). They should be sharp. It is very important to insert the shank *fully* and bring the chuck holding the shank as *close to the bur head as possible* to assure safe control and to avoid wobbling. Coarse-cut files and burs are used for greater metal removal, medium-cut are used for most situations, and fine-cut for achieving an extra smooth finish. Burs can also be used for final surface texturing, in the process called *milling*.

Approximate Speeds Suggested for Medium-Cut Rotary Files and Burs (in rpm)

Head Diameter	Mild Steel	Cast Iron	Bronze Copper	Aluminum
1/8″	4600	7000	15000	20000
1/4″	3450	5250	11250	15000
3/8″	2750	4200	9000	12000
1/2″	2300	3500	7500	10000
5/8″	2000	3100	6650	8900
3/4″	1900	2900	6200	8300
7/8″	1700	2600	5600	7500
1″	1600	2400	5150	6850
1 1/8″	1500	2300	4850	6500
1 1/4″	1400	2100	4500	6000

For fine cut, speeds should be decreased about one third.

PROBLEMS AND SOLUTIONS IN THE USE OF STEEL BURS

If the bur *does not cut,* but slips, or if its shaft moves within the collet, the collet-retaining nut may be loose and should be tightened; the bur shaft may be too small for the collet used, and either the bur shaft size, or the collet should be changed. If the bur *cuts slowly,* its teeth may be dull, and it must be replaced; or its diameter may be too large for the job, and a smaller bur should be used. If the bur *cuts unevenly,* the cutting speed may be too slow and should be increased; or the bur may be too small in diameter for the job, and a larger one should be used. If the bur *cuts too quickly,* it may be too large or too coarse for the job, and a finer toothed or smaller bur should be used. If the bur *overheats and its cutting edges become dull quickly,* it may have been used for too prolonged a time without lifting it away to allow it to cool off. Overheating should be avoided as it causes a bur to lose its temper. Overheating may also occur if the bur is used with an insufficient amount of lubricant, such as *wintergreen oil;* or it may be used at too high a speed or with too much pressure, in which case reduce both. Should the *shaft bend,* or the *bur break off the shaft,* entirely too much pressure has been used, or the bur shaft was not sufficiently deep in the collet. Reduce pressure, and be sure the shaft is as deep within the collet as possible. If burs are *dull,* their cutting edges can be sharpened by etching the bur in a cold nitric acid solution, prepared with 6 parts distilled water to 1 part nitric acid. Let the bur soak in this solution for 15–30 seconds, then rinse and dry it.

CARBIDE BURS

Carbide burs last up to a hundred times longer than high-speed steel burs, which makes their higher cost a worthwhile investment. Their flutings, rake, and coarseness are somewhat different from those made of high-speed steel. They can be used on either hard or soft materials. Their shapes are similar to those of steel, and the shanks are 1/8 in or 1/4 in (3.18 or 6.35 mm).

CARE OF CARBIDE BURS Carbide burs are hard but relatively brittle and must therefore be treated more carefully than high-speed steel rotary files and burs. Never throw them on a workbench or place them in contact with other tools. Store them upright with their shafts in a container with separate holes or in an improvised wooden holder, preferably covered.

Recommended Speeds for Carbide Burs of Medium Cut

Head Diameter	rpm	Head Diameter	rpm
1/8″	45000	5/8″	18000
1/4″	30000	3/4″	16000
3/8″	24000	7/8″	14500
1/2″	20000	1″	13000

DIAMOND DENTAL ROTARY CUTTING INSTRUMENTS: Shank dimensions

Diamond rotary cutting instruments have industrial diamonds set in their cutting surfaces. They are used in jewelry making to create surface textures on metal by *milling*

the surface. Different textural effects are made by changing the directional pattern of the milling action. To create an all-over texture, consistent application in the same direction is followed. This direction can be crossed over by another to create a different texture. The degree of fineness of the diamond results in different textural effects.

Use these cutting instruments with turpentine as a coolant.

The diameter of the shank or latch end of the rotary cutting instrument has specific, standardized dimensions.

Class	Diameter in inches	Shank length in inches
1	0.0919 – 0.0929	0.420
2	0.0919 – 0.0929	1.100
3	0.9117 – 0.0929	0.2095
4	0.0624 – 0.0631	0.400
5	0.145 – 0.150	0.370
6	0.1485 – 0.1488	0.534
7	0.0920 – 0.924	0.519

MILLING

Rotary grinding metal for peripheral or face removal

Milling is a metalwork process in which metal is removed from a workpiece by a form of grinding that employs a rotating, high-speed, multiple-toothed *steel cutter* with side and/or end cutting edges; a cutting tool made of a *very hard substance* such as tungsten carbide; or a *diamond-embedded* tool. The process is also known as *frazing* when it involves the mechanical reaming or enlarging of a hole, or the shaping and dressing of a surface using fluted revolving cutters or burs, also called *frazers*. With every rotation of the cutting tool, each tooth, or the cutting surface, takes a small amount of metal away from the workpiece in the form of very small chips. By powered rotary motion, the tool is used to *shape* metal (or other

substances), *dress* metal surfaces, *rout out* surplus metal from the mass, or to *create surface textures.*

Milling can take place on flat or dimensional workpieces mounted on a *milling machine,* designed specifically for milling functions. It can also be done on almost any machine that allows the mill cutting tool to be rigidly held and rotated while the workpiece is fed into the cutter, or where the workpiece is made rigid and the tool is moved into or across it. *Lathes* mounted with a *milling table* and a *milling vise* can be used for milling, and in this case, the cutter shaft is held *horizontally.* A *drill press* in which the cutter shaft is held *vertically* can also be used for milling. Work can be hand held on a sandbag or a rubber sheet and milled freely by the use of a mill cutting tool such as a *rotary file* or a tungsten carbide or diamond *bur* or *frazer* mounted in a *flexible shaft,* in which case the mill cutter shaft can be oriented in any direction in relation to the work, and can reach any part of it.

The best results in milling are attained when the tool and the workpiece are held *rigid.* Lack of rigidity causes tool chatter which results in excessive tool wear, possible bending of the tool shaft, breakage of tools, unsatisfactory surface finish, and inaccuracy.

Because in all milling actions the teeth of the mill cutter remove small chips of metal from the mass, when working with precious metals, the chips should be gathered and saved for reclaiming.

The *feed* or *cutting speed* used depends on the metal (or other material) being milled. In general, harder metals require faster milling speeds and softer metals, slower speeds. Avoid too high a speed when using metal rotary files as they may overheat, reducing their cutting life. If frictional heat is carried to an extreme, the cutter will lose its temper and be rendered useless.

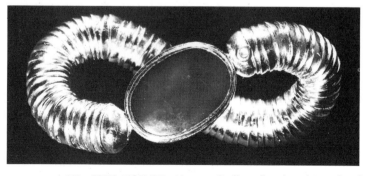

4–103 TONE VIGELAND, Norway. Sterling silver bracelet made of nesting half-domes strung on a chain, with a central agate. The dome surfaces are peripherally freehand milled to create a surface texture by using a *rotary file* mounted on a flex-shaft. The U-shaped pin clasp is next to the stone. *Photo: Abel*

MAIN TYPES OF MILLING ACTIONS

The basic types of milling actions refer to the type of cutter used, and the relationship of its shaft to the surface milled. In *peripheral milling* the cutting action is performed by peripheral teeth on the cutter whose shaft works in a direction *parallel* to the cutter teeth. In *face milling* cutting is done by the cutter face, and its shaft is in a direction *perpendicular* to the surface of the metal. In *end milling* the cutter has cutting edges on the face and the periphery, and can be used on either or both sides, on flat or irregular workpiece surfaces.

PERIPHERAL MILLING

Peripheral milling utilizes a milling cutter form of any of a wide variety of cylindrical shapes, depending on the work. Narrow- or large-diameter, long cutting face, drum-shaped *plain cutters* such as cylindrical rotary files (see Rotary Files, Burs, and Abrasive Points in this chapter) whose toothed sides are arranged in spiraling grooves, when mounted in a *lathe* can be used for slotting, or when in a *flex-shaft* can be used to shape perimeters, and also to dress and texture large flat or convex surfaces.

Contour milling or cutting the curved edge profile of a sheet metal shape with a mill cutter is done with a peripheral cutter at a right angle to the edge.

Profiling in stacks, or processing the periphery of a *series* of the same shapes in metal, plastic, or other material, is possible. The sheets are arranged in layers, clamped or glued together temporarily or permanently, and a small-diameter, long cutting edge peripheral cutter is used. This can be fixed vertically in position in a *drill press,* and the work moved against it, or placed in a *flex-shaft,* and the tool moved freely against the workpiece which can be hand held or clamped to a working surface.

FACE MILLING

Face milling primarily employs *end mills,* cutting tools that have end cutting teeth and possibly also side cutting teeth. They can be used to make round holes, or holes of irregular shapes. End cutting tools with *safe sides* (no side cutting teeth) can be used to create single or multiple circular patterns on a flat metal surface by just coming into contact with them; to make circular or curved shapes, or grooved depressions; and to trepan (perforate) metal. If the cutter also has side cutting teeth, it can be used to enlarge holes.

Mill grooving or *channeling* is done on the face of the metal with *wheel cutters, side cutters, circular saws,* or *wheel files,* of any diameter. The cutter's tooth width used depends on the groove width wanted. Cutters with narrow cutting edges can also be used to sever metals.

Mill carving can be done on the face of a sheet or block of metal, using a drum, ball, tear, tree, or other convex cutter fixed in the handpiece of a flex-shaft. The particular shape used depends on the area to be removed, and the desired form. These special shapes can also be used to texture an existing surface.

DIAMOND MILLING

Diamond milling is a milling process carried out on sheet metal or solid stock jewelry mass-produced by an *automatic-copy diamond milling machine.* It is capable of performing all types of milling operations by the use of mounted diamond or carbide cutting tools, and produces bright-cut or matte-textured surfaces. A variety of machines exists. Many separate *index* head attachments, rotatable through 360°, and accessory devices with adjustable speeds are available. These can be attached by bolts to different machines to adapt them to a variety of uses.

Milling can be carried out with the cutter spindle in vertical, horizontal, or controllable intermediate positions. The machine has an expandable clamp mounted in a threaded nose, suited to hold work of various sizes within a maximum limit. With the work held horizontally, milling can take place in three main directions: *vertically, longitudinally,* and by *lateral transverse* (a direction opposite to longitudinal). Attachments are available to allow automatic rotation, and to-and-fro movement. A typical workpiece size limitation of a machine designed for use in jewelry manufacture is: vertical movement 90 mm (3.6 in); longitudinal movement 80 mm (3.2 in); lateral transverse movement 100 mm (4 in). The work area can be divided into any number of divisions.

In some machines, the tool head holds a single diamond-mounted milling tool that performs all functions; in others, two or four tool holders are used, each tool performing a separate function. When a single tool is used, it can rotate at 6000 rpm; when two or four tools are used, a slower 3000-rpm rate is employed. When the total area worked is small, the speed can be faster than when it is large.

A *master model* clamp-fixed in the machine can be used as a *face milling guide* or cam for the cutting action. *Cams* in general are rotating or sliding devices that can be mounted singly or in series on a machine. They are precision-shaped units designed to rotate or slide at a set rate, and impart a particular, exactly timed movement to the cutting tool. Cams are used when profiling a shape in peripheral carving, or for perpendicular carving, grooving, or channel milling actions. When a master model is used, normally a one-to-one ratio between the model and the work exists, which means an exact reproduction is made.

Various machine actions are employed. In one machine, the workpiece is fixed in a quick chucking device, and rotates horizontally in a path around and against a very rapidly rotating cutting tool mounted on a fixed center. On another model, the work spindle moves around a workpiece that is itself moved by one or more cams, according to the shape and surface design requirements.

The work can be flat, concave, convex, cylindrical, symmetrical, or asymmetrical. An endless variety of highly precise and faultless surface patterns and textures can be produced by surface milling on flatwork, concave, or convex units such as earrings, pendants, buttons, and medallions. The same can be done on flat chains or flexible, linked bands of the broad, machine-made type used as necklaces, bracelets, or watchbands, and on cylindrical rings, bangles, or bracelets. Entire three-dimensional forms can be milled from solid metal stock to make rings, pendants, or watchcases by first contour milling, then milling interior shapes to hollow them out (as in a watchcase); or entire volumes such as the inner portion of a ring shank can be removed and the surfaces can then be diamond mill decorated.

It is common for silver diamond-milled jewelry to be rhodium plated to preserve the surface and the characteristic effect of diamond milling. Properly plated rhodium is almost completely tarnish-proof, and its hardness helps

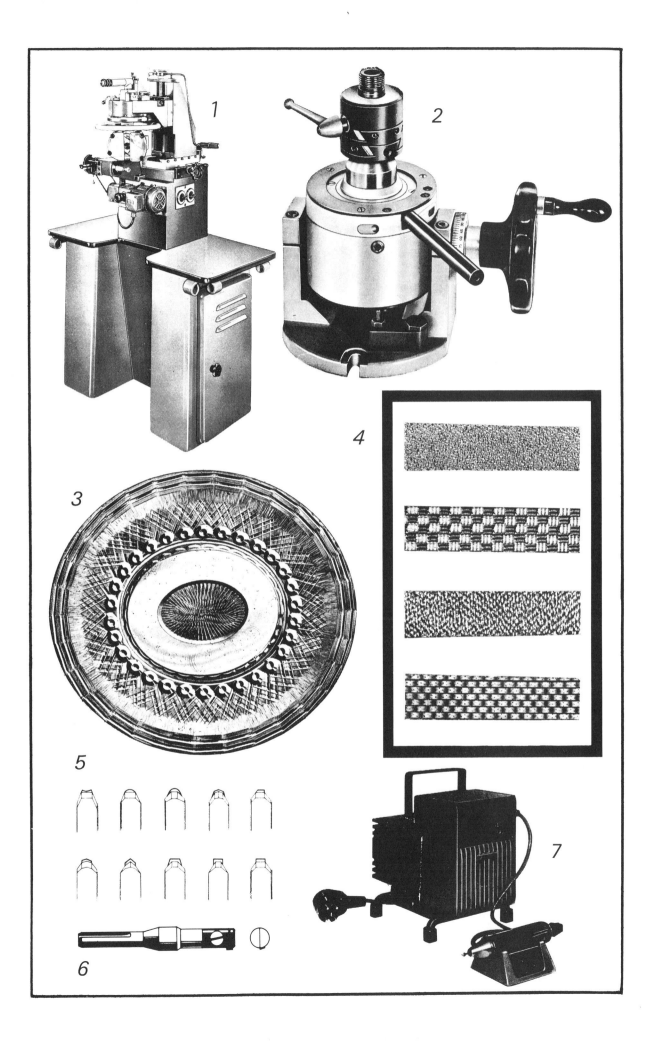

to preserve the flat, sharply faceted angles created by diamond milling. It also has the ability to take a high polish which gives these facets the glittering, brilliant appearance that is unique to this technique. Automatic matte- or satin-finished surfaces and textures are also possible.

As in the case of all automatic machines and the processes possible with them, it takes a certain investigative mentality and a willingness to experiment to utilize them creatively. Unfortunately, the expense of these machines places them beyond the sphere of use by individual jewelers, unless a used one should become available, or a fortunate opportunity should arise to allow a creative jeweler to use one for experimental purposes. The scope for the utilization of the diamond milling machine and its products in creative contemporary jewelry is decidedly great and totally untapped. Possibilities exist for the use of already diamond mill-cut, unmounted units or parts of units in precious or even nonferrous metals to be imaginatively incorporated into work designs. Such products hopefully could be made available by companies possessing these machines.

HANDPIECE-MOUNTED DIAMOND MILLING TOOLS

Precise *freehand bright cutting* can be accomplished by using *individual diamond milling tools* without the danger of the tool overheating, as previously mentioned. Each tool has a different surface area and cutting edge profile, as illustrated, and they are designed for use on small work. The tool is mounted in an adaptor chuck that can be fitted into an ordinary flexible shaft handpiece that operates at the normal speed of from 10,000–18,000 rpm. These tools, have, however, been designed for high-speed use as milling can be achieved at high speeds with far less pressure, and with greater efficiency. To achieve such high speeds, special, *fast-frequency drive motors* capable of 18,000–48,000 rpm are built into special handpieces that are used with a *portable transformer* as a power source. In some arrangements, the cutter is counterbalanced for better control and ease in movement of the tool.

With these tools, a great variety of ornamental milled surface textures and other milling uses are achievable. Each tool profile produces a different effect. A great advantage of their use is that they can be employed not only on the usual flat, convex, or concave surfaces, but also on surfaces with completely irregular contours. Compared to the cost of an automatic-copy diamond milling machine, this equipment is inexpensive, and well within the reach of the hand craftsperson.

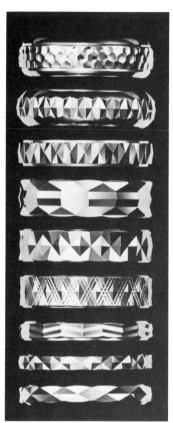

4–105 KULTAKESKUS OY, Hämeenlinna, Finland, manufacturer. Wedding rings in 14K gold, surfaces decorated with diamond mill-machined patterns. Any geometric pattern can be created by following a *master model* clamped onto the machine's copying head. The resulting surface is typically bright cut. *Photo: Courtesy Kultakeskus Oy*

4–104 *MILLING EQUIPMENT AND RESULTS* (opposite page)
1. Automatic-copy diamond milling machine designed for the decoration of jewelry, available from Tousdiamants, Meyrat-Luisoni S.A., Moudon, Switzerland. It is shown here with a special *GT-4 horizontal cutter headstock* rotatable through 360°. With a 150 mm diamond cutter head, it operates at 3000 rpm; with a 25 mm diamond cutter head at 6000 rpm. The base casing contains electric and hydraulic equipment. Height from floor to top approx. 160 cm.
2. *Indexing head attachment*, also available from Tousdiamants S.A., can replace the GT-4 unit above, and is attached by two bolts to the machine. It is used for machining and decorating oval shapes with 0–12 mm difference in axis. The unit is inclinable to the horizontal, and is fitted with a degree scale for intermediate positions.
3. *Diamond-milled bright-cut oval unit*, a sample of the work possible with the above attachment.
4. *Flat, flexible, linked unit bands* with examples of bright-cut surface textures made by to-and-fro and rotational movements of diamond milling tools.
5. *Bright-cutting diamond milling tools* used freehand while mounted in a flexible shaft handpiece. An endless variety of bright-cut surface textures are possible using the various profile shapes.
6. The *adaptor chuck* used to hold the above diamond milling tools in the handpiece.
7. *Special handpiece* with small interior motor, and *portable transformer* that allows milling tool rotation speeds of up to 48,000 rpm. (Karl Fischer)

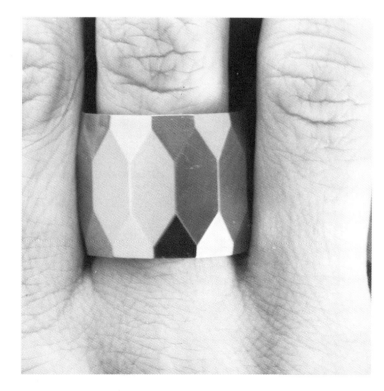

4–106 *Right:* MARY ANN SCHERR, U.S.A. Collaboration with FRANK KACZ, U.S.A. Band ring, stainless steel, mill-machined surface pattern. *Photo: Richard Davis*

5

SHEET METAL
Forming by Deformation Techniques

SHEET METAL STRUCTURAL DISTORTION

Three-dimensional form through deformation

Metals are constructed of atoms in a crystalline arrangement. When these atoms are subjected to stress, as when working a metal sheet with a hammer or other impact tool, the lattice or space between the atoms becomes distorted. If the applied stress is less than the force holding these atoms together, they return to their original positions and no distortion occurs. If the stress force is greater, the *elastic limit* is exceeded; the atoms become displaced along cleavage planes, and a change in their relationship or dimension occurs due to *plastic flow*. In other words, *permanent deformation* takes place. This happens when a hammer makes a dent in metal.

This act embodies one of the most important properties of metals and their alloys: under the force of impact stress, *deformation* (a re-forming movement due to the plastic flow of the metal's atom bonds and its crystal structure) is possible *without rupturing the metal*. Lacking this property, metals could not be shaped by mechanical work methods such as doming, embossing, repoussage, stamping, forging, drawing, spinning, riveting, etc.

A limit exists, however, in the amount of plastic flow or stress any given metal will allow at a given temperature. Once this is exceeded, its condition changes and it becomes what is termed *work hardened,* and its malleability, ductility, and tensile strength decrease. Should work continue beyond that point, fracture will occur in those places most stressed. This is especially rapid when metal is cold worked. Fortunately, one can sense, by the behavior of the metal, when these limits are being approached. At that time, conditions of stress can be relieved, and the metal rendered workable again by heating (annealing) it, which causes a re-formation of the crystal lattice that renders the metal soft and again capable of plastic flow without cracking.

DOMING

Stretch punching a hemisphere

A *dome* in its fullest and most perfect form is a hollow, metal hemisphere of any diameter size. It can be an independent unit, in which case it is made from a disc blank cut out with a *disc cutter* (see Blanking, p. 135), or a part of the sheet on which it is formed.

DOME-MAKING TOOLS

The tools used for forming a dome are a *dapping* or *doming punch,* and a *dapping* or *doming block* or *die*. The *dapping punch* is a cylindrical tool steel shaft, flat at the end on which it is hammered, and round, almost ball-shaped at the opposite end. Dapping punches can be purchased individually, but they are also sold in sets of 31 sizes, the ball end in diameters of 2–32 mm. The ball ends fit matching semicircular depressions in the doming block

5–1 NORWAY. Lappish bridal couple. The bride wears as many ornaments as she owns, and borrows others for the occasion. The groom's brooch is simpler. *Photo: Lehtikuva Oy*

5–2 REGINE JUHLS, Norway, designer; manufacturer Sølvsmie Regine & Frank Juhls, Kautokeino. Silver Lappish brooch partly gilded, a modern design based on traditional Lappish motifs. Three concentric rows of gilded half-domes hang forward from wire rings, fluttering and flashing with the wearer's movement. Ø 14 cm. *Photo: Börje Rönnberg, courtesy Sølvsmie Regine & Frank Juhls*

5–3 DISC-CUTTING AND DOMING TOOLS

1. *Set of 18 circle-cutting punches, 3–14 mm in diameter.*
2. *Matching hole plate with 18 holes containing a 2 mm (5⁄64 in) slot for inserting sheet metal up to 1.829 mm (13 B.&S. gauge; 0.072 in).*
3. *Dapping punches in tool steel, available in 31 graduated sizes.*
4. *Metal-covered box for holding dapping punches, repoussé work or chasing tools.*
5. *Combination small jeweler's anvil and design block with dapping die depressions and straight grooves of various shapes.*
6. *Design swage block in steel with dapping depressions and grooves of various shapes.*
7. *Hardwood dapping block, 2¼ in cube, and matching wooden punches.*
8. *Dapping block in steel 29 mm thick, with 24 semicircular depressions, smallest 2 mm, largest 32 mm.*
9. *Conventional steel dapping die, 2½ in cube, with six working surfaces, and many sized depressions.*

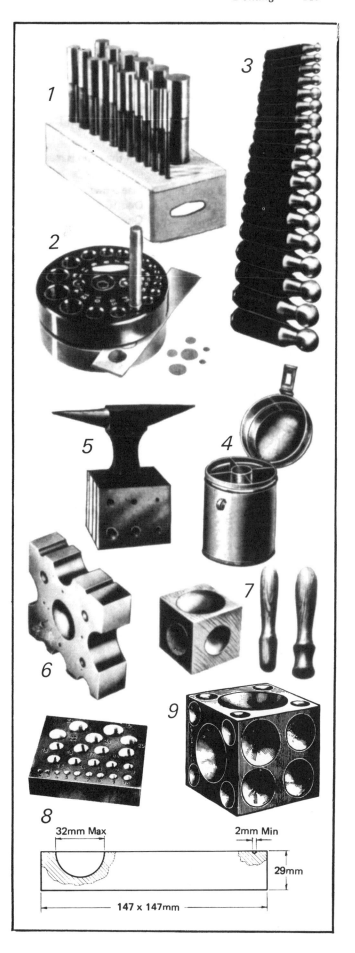

or die, which is the matrix, and can be of brass or steel. The traditional block used by jewelers is a 63 mm (2½ in) cube (smaller ones are also available), whose six sides are each faced with from one up to five polished, semicircular concave depressions or cups in graduated sizes from 2–50 mm in diameter, whose depths vary with the diameter. A *rectangular* dapping block with all the depressions arranged in rows on one surface is also available, one model having 27 depressions ranging in diameters of 3–26 mm. Also available is a *hardwood dapping block* and matching *wood punches,* with shallow cups for forming shallow domes.

MAKING A DOME

When lacking a dapping die block, a *lead block* can be substituted as a surface on which to shape the dome. In this case, first a hollow is formed in the lead block with a *dapping punch.* The disc blank is placed over it, and the punch, placed in the exact center of the disc, is hammered down to force the disc into the depression. (Place a piece of paper between the lead and the metal disc to avoid contamination from the lead. If lead is present on the dome, it will eat into the metal when it is heated.)

When making a dome, select a disc with a diameter larger than the dome you intend to make as it loses about one third of its diameter when made into a hemisphere. Place the annealed disc in the first cup in the dapping block that it fits into levelly, just below the surface. Place the corresponding dapping punch vertically over the center of the disc and

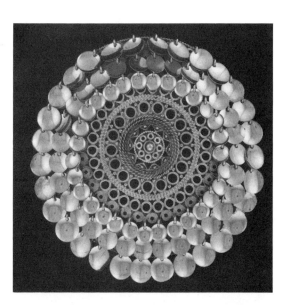

5–4 ELIS KAUPPI, Finland, designer; manufacturer Kupittaan Kulta Oy, Turku. Gold ring with concave domes and diamond. Photo: Courtesy Kupittaan Kulta Oy

5–5 SAARA HOPEA-UNTRACHT, Finland, designer; manufacturer Kultasepänliike Ossian Hopea, Porvoo. Silver ring with convex gold domes mounted on a silver base, designed for use on the middle finger. Photo: Oppi

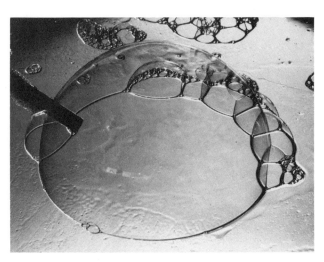

5–6 SOAP BUBBLES. These most ephemeral of convex domes are the source of inspiration used by SIGURD PERSSON, Sweden, as the basis of a design concept for jewelry. Photo: Sune Sundahl

5–7 SIGURD PERSSON, Sweden. Silver, open-ended bracelet ornamented with soap bubble-structured half-domes. Photo: Sune Sundahl

hammer the punch end until the tool forces the disc to touch the bottom of the cup depression. To deepen a dome, place it in the next smaller cup, and with the corresponding punch, hammer it again to the bottom of the cup. This can be repeated, each time moving the dome to the next smaller depression without skipping any, until a dome of the desired depth and/or diameter is achieved. If the dome's edges become irregular, replace it in a depression that brings its edges level with the upper die surface, and *file* them level. Outside contours on the flat blank to be domed can, however, be deliberately shaped by sawing and filing to any regular or irregular shape, then domed.

USING DOMES

Domes have been used in jewelry since antiquity. Half-domes can be soldered convex side up to a sheet metal surface. In this case, make a small hole in the base sheet at the center of its position to allow the escape of trapped air and gases which expand when heated. If this is not done, complete soldering of the dome's edges to the base will not be possible, and worse, the dome may explode. Two domes of the same diameter can be soldered together to make a round ball or bead. At least one hole must be drilled into one dome, for the same reason. If the result is to be a bead, drill a hole in *each* dome before soldering; the holes can be used for stringing. Drill the hole or holes from the inner or concave side of the dome while holding it on a wood board. This will prevent its becoming deformed under pressure. It is possible to pierce a flat disc blank with a pattern of openings *before* doming. Keep in mind that after doming a certain distortion of the pierced openings will occur, a fact that may or may not be important. Domes can also be made of a sheet composed of a mosaic of married metals; rigid wire mesh or screening; or expanded metal sheet.

When making a dome as an *integral part of a sheet,*

place the sheet with the position for the dome directly over the depression in the dapping block, place the dapping punch exactly over the center of the depression, and hammer the punch to force the metal downward into the cup.

Domes with *irregular shapes* such as tear, pear, or oval can be made by using a punch with such a shape, or a combination of punch shapes, and a *lead block* in which a depression of the desired shape has been formed. Domes with flat faces such as triangular- or square-based pyramids are also possible. A *bezel block* can be used to shape a dome with a pointed head, but the *bezel punch* that matches the block depression is too sharply pointed and will penetrate the metal. In that case, if an unpenetrated dome is wanted, start the depression form with a *blunt-pointed punch.* Anneal the metal in stages, and use gradually more pointed punches to stretch the metal slowly. It will not be possible to bring the point to reach the bottom of the bezel cup, but the point can be achieved with the blunt-pointed punch, or a shaped punch made for this purpose from hardwood.

5–8 SAARA HOPEA-UNTRACHT, Finland, designer; manufacturer Kultasepänliike Ossian Hopea, Porvoo. Silver brooch and ring using round and pyramid-shaped domes, shot, and flat spiral wire. Photo: Oppi

5–9 DAVID WATKINS, England. Necklace in silver and yellow gold utilizing seven quarter-domes, fabricated with sheet metal to form closed shapes. Tubular units and hollow beads are strung on a chain, fastened by a screw-apart bead. Ornamented with red, white, and blue enamel. Photo: Bob Cramp

5–10 WERNER BÜNCK, West Germany. Bracelet in gold and silver using half-domes and tubing. Photo: Günter Meyer, courtesy Schmuckmuseum, Pforzheim

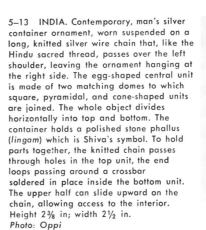

5–11 RAYMOND WARNER, (Navajo), U.S.A. Silver necklace with turquoises and pendant. Squash blossom pendants are made of joined half-domes with sheet metal attachments. Length 22 in. Photo: Courtesy U. S. Department of the Interior, Indian Arts and Crafts Board

5–12 THOR SELZER, Denmark. Man's tie ornament made of silver beads joined by round wire links. Photo: Sven Aage Andersen

5–13 INDIA. Contemporary, man's silver container ornament, worn suspended on a long, knitted silver wire chain that, like the Hindu sacred thread, passes over the left shoulder, leaving the ornament hanging at the right side. The egg-shaped central unit is made of two matching domes to which square, pyramidal, and cone-shaped units are joined. The whole object divides horizontally into top and bottom. The container holds a polished stone phallus (lingam) which is Shiva's symbol. To hold parts together, the knitted chain passes through holes in the top unit, the end loops passing around a crossbar soldered in place inside the bottom unit. The upper half can slide upward on the chain, allowing access to the interior. Height 2⅜ in; width 2½ in. Photo: Oppi

5–14 BÖRJE RAJALIN, Finland, designer; manufacturer Kalevala Koru, Helsinki. Silver and gold necklace using spherical beads and balls with sheet metal tube attachments alternating with spectrolite stones set in tube sections. Photo: Pietinen, courtesy Kalevala Koru

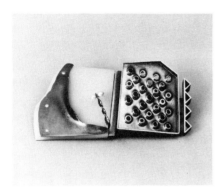

5–15 BOB EBENDORF, U.S.A. Sterling
silver and 14K gold pin with pearls and
amber acrylic. Holes drilled in flat sheet
were hammered with a round punch over a
dapping block to form small raised domes.
Size 3¼ × 1½ in. Photo: Bob Ebendorf

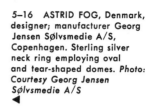

5–16 ASTRID FOG, Denmark,
designer; manufacturer Georg
Jensen Sølvsmedie A/S,
Copenhagen. Sterling silver
neck ring employing oval
and tear-shaped domes. Photo:
Courtesy Georg Jensen
Sølvsmedie A/S
◄

5–17 KAIJA AARIKKA,
Finland, designer; manufacturer
Aarikka Koru, Helsinki. Silver
rings using the pierced bead
form whose repeated openings
create a decorative pattern.
Photo: Studio Wendt, courtesy
Aarikka Koru
▼

5–18 DAVID LAPLANTZ,
U.S.A. Fibula with a dome of
copper, silver, and brass made
from flat sheet strips formed
into a dome, set in a bezel
that is saw cut into small
sections pushed over onto the
dome. The beads are of bone,
threaded brass tube, and brass
edge-hammered for texture.
Photo: David LaPlantz
◄

REPOUSSAGE AND CHASING

Free punching relief and intaglio forms

Repoussage is a method of using the quality of plasticity in metal to shape sheet metal with punches and a hammer by degrees to form a relief. In the process, there is no loss of metal as it is stretched locally and the surface remains continuous, though it may be cut through later. The English word used for this process is derived from the French verb *repousser*, literally "to push again"; colloquially "to thrust back," and its adjectival form, *repoussé*, a word that has come to be widely (though incorrectly) used as a

5–19 PANAMA,
Pre-Columbian. Gold
alloy repoussé-worked
mask. Photo: Victoria
and Albert Museum,
London, Crown Copyright

noun to designate this work. The proper noun is *repoussage*, and the adjectival form should be used as a descriptive term as in *repoussé work*.

The noun *chase* refers to a prolonged hollow, groove, furrow, channel, or indentation, and from it comes *chasing*, the process of refining, detailing, and ornamenting sheet or cast metal forms by the use of chasing tools. The adjectival form is *chased work*.

The use of the repoussage technique dates back to the Bronze Age, and in different eras, the craftsmen of Assyria, Mesopotamia, Greece, Rome, Scythia, Nepal, India, and rococo Europe produced masterpieces. Repoussage and chasing, its companion process, are relatively slow techniques, but with them the jeweler can achieve a maximum of form with one continuous surface of sheet metal of essentially the same thickness. This basic process, one that every jeweler should master, allows full consideration to be given to the development of form and its decoration. The results are personal, and the play of light and shadow on the work shows any degree of subtlety in modeling the form. Direct contact of the tool is usually visible in the result, a condition not always so apparent in other techniques of work where all evidence of the working method is eliminated.

5–20 ELSBETH RÖTHLISBERGER, Switzerland. Bracelet of thin gauge silver sheet ornamented with low relief repoussage, and mounted on an inner clear Plexiglas support, the strip fixed at the ends by the hinge and clasp mountings. *Photo: Courtesy Schmuck International 1900–1980, Künstlerhaus, Vienna*

5–21 AKEN/ASHANTI, GHANA. Gold repoussé-worked soul washer's badge, worn by a priest who guards the purity of the soul of the *asantehene* or ruler, since it is believed that its condition influences the well-being of the kingdom. *Photo: Reproduced by Courtesy of the Trustees of The British Museum, London*

5–22 TIBET. Silver charm box pendant (*gau kerima*) worn in Kham in eastern Tibet. The central repoussé-worked gilded plaque with a turquoise stone is mounted by rivets in a depression in the silver case, the latter consisting of two repoussé-worked units, one with a flange that fits into the other. Length approx. 2½ in. *Photo: Oppi*

5–23 BODNATH, NEPAL. Bhotia woman wearing a *gau kerima* supported by a separate string which makes the longer strand of beads of turquoise, red coral, and ceramic (the magic *zhi* bead) take on a wide curve. *Photo: Oppi*

The techniques of repoussage and chasing cooperate to develop the form to completion. By strict definition, in repoussé work, the sheet metal is given form mainly by stretching, incidentally thinning the metal outward from the reverse side. In chasing, forms are outlined, modeled, refined, undercut, and textured mainly by pushing the sheet (or cast metal) back from the obverse or front side. Generally speaking, therefore, repoussage tools create *relief* effects, and chasing tools create *intaglio* effects. The two processes normally alternate on the same piece. In a conventional work sequence, the outline is chased on the front of the blank sheet metal; repoussé work on the back of the sheet follows to establish basic forms; chasing from the front then refines and models forms, and creates details and textures. This sequence is repeated until the desired form and detail are achieved. The final result takes full advantage of the effect of light reflection and shadow in the form or forms.

Procedures may, however, vary. It is possible, for instance, in *flat work chasing* to work the metal in linear patterns from the front only, a process in which no metal is removed, as in engraving. Low relief can be made by first pushing the ground back from the front with repoussage tools, then continuing to work the piece from the front with chasing tools. The work can also start on the back without outlines, directly with repoussage tools; or follow a design drawn or traced on the back in line, or lightly enscribed on the metal.

REPOUSSAGE AND CHASING WORK SURFACES

In general, the metal being worked should be supported wherever the tool strikes it, particularly when creating larger forms, or its effect will be uncontrolled. It is therefore placed on a surface that has the necessary degree of resiliency, depending on the work. When the tool is struck, the jeweler should have the sensation that the metal has not been struck "in air," but has contacted the supporting material which has answered the blow. This is indicated by the sound of the blow—supported blows on metal emit a higher sound than unsupported blows (which sound hollow and dull).

LEATHER AND WOOD

The choice of supporting material depends on the work. When chasing line patterns on flat metal or making a low relief, one needs no resiliency or, at most, only a little. In this case the work can be done on a *dampened piece of leather* taped to a flat, solid surface. Work can also be nailed to a close-grained, *hardwood slab,* the headless nails placed about ⅛ in (0.32 cm) from the edge of the metal to allow for expansion, then driven over onto surplus metal sections of the blank so they do not scar the actual work.

LEAD BLOCKS: A semiresilient working surface

Lead blocks of any size and at least 1 in (2.5 cm) thick are used as a semiresilient working surface upon which the metal can be shaped. The softness of lead offers limited resistance to impact from the much harder steel repoussage or chasing tool. Because lead melts at a low temperature, there is a danger of lead contaminating the metal worked upon it. Small lead particles that cling to the work's sur-

5–24 REPOUSSAGE AND CHASING MATERIALS AND AIDS

Repoussage or chaser's pitch constituents

1. *Pitch,* sold in bulk by the pound.
2. *Powdered pumice,* used as a pitch filler.
3. *Venetian turpentine,* used as an emollient to keep pitch soft.

Other work-supporting or filling materials

4. *Chaser's or engraver's cement sticks* used spread on a surface to hold work, or heated to liquefy it and poured into the cavity of hollow repoussage objects to act as a cavity filler to help them retain their shape against use and impact. Each stick is 7¼ × 1⅛ × 1 in, and weighs ½ lb.
5. *Shellac sticks,* transparent, used spread on a surface to hold work in progress, or as a permanent cavity filler in a completed object, especially those made of thin-gauge metals. Each stick is 7 × ⅝ × ¼ in.
6. *Sealing wax stick,* used to fill the concave depressions at the reverse side of a finished flat or curved, but open-backed repoussage unit to help retain its shape, and applied before mounting such a unit.

Pitch containers and their supports

7. *Shallow metal tray* filled with pitch, used for repoussage on relatively large, flat work objects. A tray 8 × 10 × 1 in has a capacity for approximately 4 lb of prepared pitch.
8. *Deep cast iron chaser's bowl,* with round bottom to permit the work surface to be tilted in any direction by shifting it on the supporting pad or stand. Bowl alone weighs 5 lb; with pitch and stand, approx. 8 lb 8 oz; Ø 5 in.
9. *Shallow cast iron chaser's bowl,* with supporting felt pad, total weight 5 lb; Ø 6½ in.
10. *Leather ring pitch pad* or *engraver's block pad* or *cushion,* one-sided, stuffed; Ø 6 in. Rubber or wood rings are also used for pitch bowl pads.
11. *Leather ring pitch bowl* or *engraver's block pad* or *cushion,* two-sided, stuffed; weight 1 lb 4 oz; Ø 6 in.
12. *Cylindrical leather belting pitch bowl stand.*
13. *Pressed felt pitch bowl* or *engraver's block stand* with concave depression to accommodate bowl bottom; Ø 5 in; weight 8 oz.
14. *Circular braided fiber mat,* in container, used as a support for a pitch bowl; large work; or solid *surface blocks* during work to absorb percussion impact. Available in 40 mm or 50 mm diameters. (Jolliot)

Other work surfaces

15. *Leather cushion,* sand filled, used as a pitch bowl support, or as a repoussage or engraving working surface to hold the object, weight 1 lb 12 oz.
16. *Canvas sandbag,* 2 in thick, 7½ in wide, 12 in long, weight 8 lb.
17. *Solid hardwood block* upon which viscous pitch is spread to hold work during repoussage, chasing, or engraving, etc.
18. *Small lead block,* 3½ in square, 1 in thick, weight 6½ lb.
19. *Lead block in iron base* which allows the work-scarred lead to be smoothed and leveled by direct heat when necessary, size 5 × 3 in.

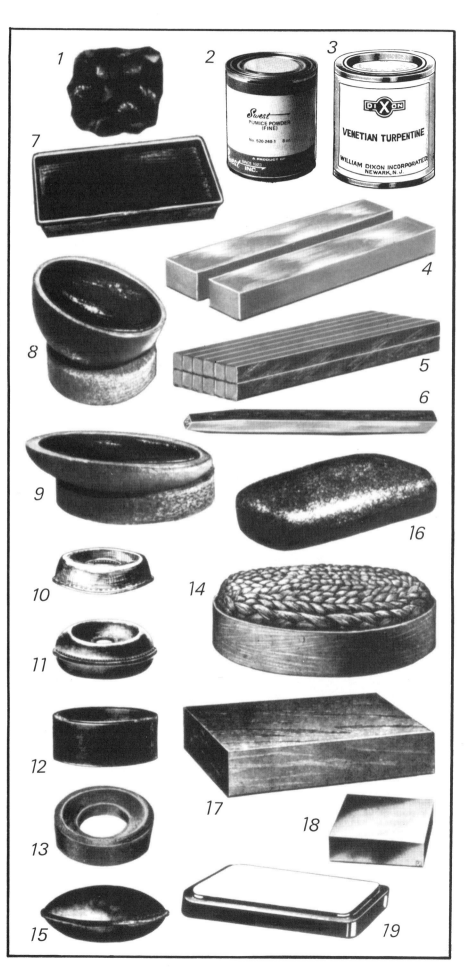

face, or to the hammer face and from there imparted to the metal, will eat into the work when heated above the melting point of lead and form a spongy-looking alloy with gold, silver, or copper alloys. The only way to remove such a defect is to cut or file it away. Protection from lead particles is offered by placing a piece of heavy paper on the lead block. Always be sure all traces of lead are removed from the work either mechanically or chemically before it is heated.

Lead blocks are easily cast or restored to a level surface when they become distorted after working. A sand mold, or even a temporary wood mold can be used to shape the block. Melt the lead with a torch in an open *iron casting ladle* or *cast iron, lead-melting pot*. Because lead oxidizes quickly when exposed to air, apply rosin or linseed oil to the surface to reduce oxidation during heating. Just before pouring the lead into the mold, skim off the surface dross. The lead will then look bright. Pour it immediately into the mold cavity, allow it to solidify, and then break it out of the mold.

THE PITCH BOWL

Despite the additional housekeeping problems, the most usual and versatile material for repoussé work and chasing is a composition termed *chaser's pitch*. This combination of materials has the property of adhering to and holding the metal (even when it is being constantly hammered) that is unmatched by other materials or systems. At room temperature, it offers just the support and resistance necessary to the metal under work, no matter what its shape. Because this composition is viscous when heated, it can be poured to completely fill the hollows at the back of any form of sheet metal in relief, and it will completely fill a three-dimensional, hollow object, which allows working externally on the object.

The pitch composition can be placed upon any hard surface, or into any receptacle used to hold the work. For work of sizes commonly made by jewelers, the usual pitch container is a hemispherical, heavy, *cast iron chaser's bowl*, available in diameters of 5–9 in. Its dimension limits the size of work done upon it. When filled with pitch and possibly other supporting material below the pitch layer, such bowls weigh 8–20 lb and are consequently very stable. A bowl of 6 in diameter and depth requires approximately 3 lb of pitch to fill it, and one with an 8 in diameter requires 5 lb. Because of its semicircular bottom, the bowl can rest on a *circular leather* or *felt pad* with an open center, a *wood block* with a hollow that matches the form of the bottom of the bowl, a depression in a *sandbag*, or on a *triangle* made of three strips of wood nailed together. In repoussé work and chasing, the angle of work must be frequently changed. All these devices allow the bowl to be easily seated, turned, and tilted, while it remains in a balanced position at any working angle. The angle between the tool's axis and the working surface is easily controlled, and can be changed as necessary, which allows the force delivered by the hammer to be efficiently transmitted to the metal.

When the work size exceeds the size limitation of the conventional pitch bowl, the pitch composition can be placed into any other container having sufficient weight, such as a *rectangular pan* made of heavy metal. It can also be spread on a *hardwood board* or tray of any size, in a thickness of at least one inch. To keep these containers immobile under the hammer blows, they can be held by a *clamp* to the worktable. A pitch-spread board of suitable size can be clamped in a *die-sinker's ball vise*. For economy's sake, any deep container can be half filled at the bottom with small pebbles or broken brick and the molten pitch composition poured on top of it. These filler materials also add weight to the container which helps to keep it steady.

PITCH COMPOSITION

The traditional repoussage working surface is *chaser's pitch* which is usually a composition combining three substances: *pure pitch*, a *filler* (or stiffener), and an *emollient* (softening medium). The ratio of these constituents to each other determines whether the result is hard, medium, or soft. Hard chaser's pitch is used as a surface upon which inlay work is done as this work requires greater support, and medium and soft compositions are used for repoussage, the softer for work that must be done in greater depth.

Pitch, a form of asphalt, ranges in consistency from hard and brittle, to soft. It melts when heated, burns with much smoke eventually to an ash, is insoluble in water but soluble in petroleum products such as gasoline (petrol) and the oleoresin product turpentine or oil of turpentine. Refined pitch is available in bulk. By itself this is generally too soft for use in repoussage, and must be combined with fillers to give it the desirable degree of resilience-resistance. Chaser's pitch, Burgundy pitch, and Swedish pitch are interchangeable and all are available. Bdellium, a gum resin obtained from various trees of the genus *Commiphora*, similar to myrrh, is sometimes used in India. Other resins (natural substances of vegetable origin produced mainly as an exudate from evergreen trees) are used as a constituent in some repoussage compositions, usually in combination with pitch, in various proportions.

Fillers are *additive substances* used to control the "body" or degree of stiffness of the composition. These can be brick dust pulverized from old brick, powdered pumice, or plaster of paris.

Emollients are used to soften the consistency of the pitch composition. These may be linseed oil, vegetable oil, tallow, petroleum jelly, or the superior Venice turpentine (a yellowish resin exuded from incisions in the bark of the European larch (*Larix decidua*).

Pitch solvents are used whenever it becomes necessary to remove pitch from metal. Pitch can always be burned off until it is completely consumed and forms an ash, but, if burning is not possible or advisable, a solvent such as kerosene, turpentine, or hot paraffin can be used.

PREPARING THE COMPOSITION

Melt the pure pitch under low heat in a thick *cast iron pot* that distributes heat evenly, until it becomes viscous.

Typical Pitch Repoussage Compositions

Type	Pitch	Filler	Emollient
Hard	3 parts	3 parts	0.1 parts
	7 "	7 "	0.5 "
Medium	5 "	10 "	3 "
	7 "	10 "	1 "
	6 "	8 "	2 "
Soft	5 "	3 "	1 "

Do not allow it to bubble or boil, an indication that it is too hot. Add the filler material a little at a time, stirring it in constantly with a *stick,* but not too vigorously or unwanted air bubbles will become included. When all the filler is uniformly mixed with the pitch, slowly add the emollient or softening substance and stir it in well. The percentage of emollient may have to be seasonally adjusted, more in winter and less in hot seasons. Additional filler can be added to the composition in warm seasons to stiffen it. The individual recipes given can also be adjusted. Pour the composition into the pitch bowl, or onto the tray or board. Level the surface with a *spatula,* mound it somewhat at the center, and smooth the surface by passing a flame over it. Do not overheat the composition as it may ignite. Burnt pitch is useless as it loses its resiliency, becomes cinderous, and must be removed. Allow the pitch to cool and solidify. It is important to remember that no matter what container is used, the pitch must be in complete contact with the underside of the metal worked in order to fully support it, and no air pockets should be allowed.

PUNCHES IN GENERAL

The general term *punch* covers a wide variety of tools used in many different techniques. All are one-piece tools (though they may be used in conjunction with a second tool). They have a *striking end, a shank,* and a *working end.* What classifies a tool as a punch is its manner of use: the striking end is struck to force the working end to move the metal. The tool that strikes it is usually a *hammer,* but alternately can also be a *metal bar* or a flat-surfaced *hardwood stick.*

Generally the stock from which the tool is made is a straight piece of tool steel, or brass or bronze rod; it can be round, square, or rectangular in cross section. Sometimes it is tapered toward the working end and/or toward the striking end.

Punches are specifically known by the operations they are designed to perform. Among these are punches used for beading, bending, bezel forming, blanking, center marking, chasing, coining, curling, cutting, dapping, die stamping, doming, embossing, figure and letter punching, matting, outlining, patterning, perforating, piercing, planishing, prong pushing, quality marking, repoussage, rivet head forming, stamping, signature punching, stone setting, and texturing.

The working end is shaped according to the function it must perform, and is generally hardened and tempered. *Dull*-ended punches, depending on whether they are used on the obverse or reverse side of the metal, form depressions, bosses, relief or intaglio shapes, or level the metal. *Sharp*-ended punches make grooves, cut into or pierce metal. *Dull* hollow-ended punches form indented circles or mounds (or other shapes), and *sharp* hollow-ended ones can cut into or remove metal and make holes or blanks. *Pattern*-ended punches impart their patterns to the metal.

REPOUSSÉ WORK AND CHASING PUNCHES

The punch-type tools used in repoussage and chasing are similar in form and function, and to some degree are interchangeable, depending on the scale of the work. Catalogs list them *all* as chasing tools. In general, however, repoussé work tools are heavier and blunter than chasing tools to facilitate stretching the metal, their main task. Chasing tools are generally used for smaller, more exact and refined detail work, and are therefore smaller, finer, and exist in more varied working end shapes. The lengths and section sizes of these punches are given below.

To provide a better grip on the tool, square or rectangular stock is used, sometimes forged thicker toward the center for this purpose. The shank edges are rounded somewhat so their corners do not press uncomfortably into the fingers when under pressure during use. These shapes allow the working end of the tool to be kept in the same position relative to the work, because they do not tend to turn as will round-shanked tools. This is especially important when the working end has a form that is oriented in one direction (as is often the case) and the tool must follow that direction of work. It is not important when the working end is round, as in the case of round punches and dapping tools.

MAKING REPOUSSAGE AND CHASING TOOLS

A variety of forms of repoussage and chasing tools are available, ready-made, from jewelers' supply houses. Many jewelers prefer, however, to make their own tools, and create unavailable shapes. They purchase a *blank* or *brindle* which is an unshaped, straight length of tool steel rod of square, rectangular, or round stock, in a dimension that suits the working end shape to be made. For chasing tools, the length should be about 4–5 in (10–12.7 cm) and the cross section $\frac{5}{32}$ in, $\frac{3}{16}$ in, $\frac{7}{32}$ in, ¼ in (3.9 mm, 4.7 mm, 5.5 mm, 6.3 mm) square. Some repoussé tools may be of heavier stock, again depending on the shape of the working end. Chasing tools of brass are occasionally used, however, because this alloy is relatively soft, they wear easily and do not keep their shape as well as steel.

To form the taper, the stock is annealed to dull red and forged down to its basic shape with *forging hammers,* on an anvil. The shape is refined by *drawfiling,* followed by *finer files.* Shank edges are rounded with files. The working end is shaped into the particular form and dimension desired. Hollow faces are drilled out or rotary burs are used to shape them. The working end is then smoothed with progressively finer grades of *abrasive cloth.* Only the working end is given a high polish. If the shank were polished, it would slip in the fingers during work. Finally, the working end of the tool is hardened and tempered to dark yellow. (See the Index for Hardening and Tempering.)

COMMON REPOUSSAGE AND CHASING TOOL SHAPES

A set of approximately 20 shapes is considered standard for the general needs of this work, but specialists in these techniques may use up to a hundred or more punches, often making special shapes to satisfy particular needs.

Repoussé work and chashing punches are used to do linear work, embossing, modeling, outlining, detailing, patterning, and leveling. The degree of relief or intaglio varies. Their working ends are hardened, tempered, and highly polished (except for pattern punches, which are not polished), to allow them to move easily on the clean metal surface *without any lubrication.* To assure most efficient functioning, they should be repolished with rouge on a buffing wheel from time to time. Their edges and points

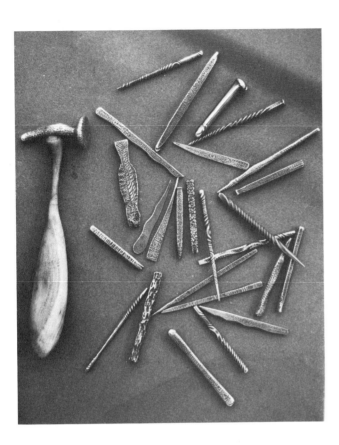

5–25 GARY NOFFKE, U.S.A. Set of hand-forged tool steel chasing tools. Square-sectioned tools, and tools with patterned, ridged surfaces will not turn in the fingers when gripped during use. Tools: 2½–4 in long; hammer: 8 in long. *Photo: Barbara Daniels*

5–26 REPOUSSAGE AND CHASING TOOLS
1. *Tracer and liner punches of various profiles.*
2. *Embossing and cushioning punches.*
3. *Modeling punches.*
4. *Ground leveling and planishing punches.*
5. *Matting and grounding or graining punches.*
6. *Hollow-faced circle punches.*
7. *Chasing hammer head, 4–7 oz, available with face of* $^{15}/_{16}$, $1\frac{1}{8}$, *and* $1\frac{1}{4}$ *in Ø.*
8. *Chasing hammer with straight, oval handle.*
9. *Pistol-grip handle, weight 1 oz.*

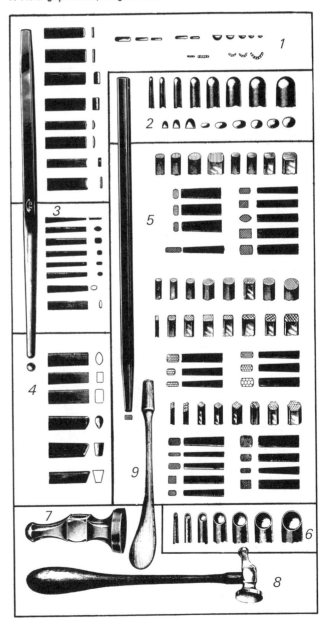

are generally rounded so that they do not unintentionally puncture the metal.

Among the several classes of repoussage and chasing punches, each made in variations of shape and in several graduated sizes, are the following:

TRACER PUNCH   The tracer punch, also called a *liner,* is probably the most important chasing tool. It is blunt-ended, round-cornered, and shaped like a chisel. Its narrow-edged face, usually rounded in sectional contour, may be of various widths. It may also be either *bevel* edged or *hollowed* longitudinally in the face length. The face width may vary from $\frac{1}{64}$–$\frac{1}{8}$ in (0.39–3.17 mm). *Uses:* Tracers are used from the *front* surface to delineate an outline in the form of a narrow groove, called a *trace.* Traces are also visible at the *back* of the metal and can therefore be followed when later bulging forms with repoussage tools. They are also used to refine and undercut forms, and for *flat chasing* in which the design is worked flat from the front only, in a linear pattern. *Curved tracers* have a curved working end of uniform thickness, and are used to follow a small curve in chasing and inlay work, or to impart a curved form to the metal with one blow.

EMBOSSING AND CUSHION PUNCH   These punches, also called *embossers,* have flat, smooth, highly polished working faces whose edges are smooth so they do not cut the metal or form angular marks as a squared tool would. They are made in various sizes. The face can also be a small, blunt, decorative figure imparted by one blow to the metal from the back, and seen as a raised *boss* at the front. *Uses:* In repoussage these punches are used to strike

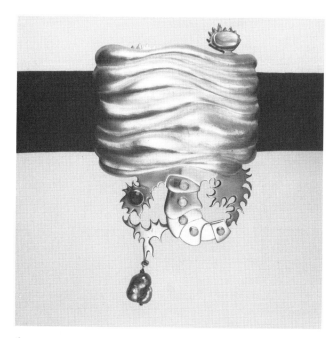

5–27 BARBARA Y. KRAN, U.S.A. Belt buckle combining a repoussé-worked fine silver unit with fabricated units in gold, sterling, and copper; edges turned back for rigidity; with moonstone, amethyst, opal, and hanging blue baroque pearl. Photo: Ian Rogers

5–28 JERRY ROAN, (Navajo), U.S.A. Silver wrist guard (ketoh) with turquoise, mounted on a leather strap. Length 7⅜ in. Photo: Courtesy the U. S. Department of the Interior, Indian Arts and Crafts Board ▼

the metal from the reverse side and block out or raise forms or bosses into relief at the front side. As raising the form to a desired height may not be possible in one operation, work may be continued after annealing the metal.

MODELING PUNCH This is the largest group of punches, generally termed "chasing tools." They have a variety of half-round, round, oval, oblong, triangular, curved, and other profile shapes, and flat or convex working ends. They are made in many sizes. *Uses:* These punches are used to shape and refine relief forms from the *front* of the metal; to give definition, detail, and crispness to a form; and to heighten the contrast of light and shadow by making undercuts.

GROUNDING OR LEVELING PUNCH This is a round, oval, or square punch with a flat face and rounded edges used after the initial stages of repoussage done from the back. (When forms are pushed out from the back, the sheet metal tends to warp its initial flat or curved plane.) *Uses:* Especially in the early stages of repoussage, this tool is used to restore or *set down* the metal, or to form a ground around a figure from the front of the work. A *hardwood stick* with an appropriately shaped end could also be used for this purpose.

PLANISHING PUNCH This is a punch with an oval or round, relatively large, flat face. *Uses:* Once forms are raised to their final shape, planishing punches are used to level, smooth, condense, toughen, texture, or polish surfaces. They are also used in inlay work to force the inlay metal into the groove in the parent metal, to close the burrs over on it, and make it level with the ground.

MATTING OR GRAINING PUNCH These punches have a broad, flat working face that is engraved with various textures, or small patterns in endless variations. Some are striated and create linear effects; others make small dotted or mounded effects, parallel squares, etc. *Uses:* The impressions made from the front with these punches are placed side by side or in overlapping arrangements, repeated without limit to fill an area, often to make a background to a figural design. Characteristically, they create a dulled, lusterless surface—the reason they are called matting tools—chosen to provide a contrast with a polished, raised area or figure. In some circumstances, while creating this texture, they simultaneously depress the ground around the figure. When a ground around a well-defined figure is being matted, start the work at the outline and work *away* from it so that the ground close to the figure is flattened. Hold the tool perpendicularly to the metal surface, and above the surface. Shift its position after each hammer blow. Pattern impressions can be made side by side, or they can overlap.

DOTTING PUNCH This is a pointed punch. *Uses:* To make single dot impressions, groups of dots, to texture an area with closely placed dots, or to make lines of a series of dots.

HOLLOW-FACED PUNCHES These well-tempered punches have a hollowed-out face so that their relatively sharp edges will create a well-defined figure. An example is a *ring punch* which imparts a small circular shape to the metal. This is available with figures in several dimensions. *Uses:* To make a small circular imprint, and also to raise a small dome-shaped dot on the metal, as in the Japanese technique called *nanako*. If the circular figure is repeated in overlapping series, it can create a textured

5-30 SARMATIAN, 1st century A.D. Gold collar whose three central tube rings open at the back by a hinge. The friezes above and below consist of eight repoussé-worked and chased eagle- or lion-headed fantastic animals in procession, grouped into four pairs composed of an attacker and a victim. Turquoise, coral, and glass set with lac into depressions emphasize the animals' eyes, shoulders, and hindquarters. The ground between figures was completely removed by chisel piercing. This very important historic work is one of the best extant examples of Sarmatian animal-style ornaments. The Sarmatians, an ancient people believed to be the Slav's ancestors, lived in the region north of the Black Sea, and were kin to the Scythians. This ornament was discovered accidentally in 1864 in the Khokhlach Barrow or grave mound near the Novotscherkaszk area in the Rostov region. Ø 17.8 cm; height 6.3 cm. *Photo: Hermitage Museum, Leningrad*

5-29 GYÖNGYVÉR DOBOS, Hungary. Copper repoussé-worked and chased rigid bracelet, first made flat, then shaped. The leveling-punched ground sharply defining the flat ground plane from the dimensional figure was textured with matting tools for contrast with the smooth-surfaced figure. *Photo: Oppi*

5-31 EILA MINKKINEN, Finland. Silver bracelet with open-backed repoussé-worked forms. The ground is textured with a planishing punch for visual contrast with the figure. *Photo: Eeva Rista*

area. Large-sized circular hollow punches are used as dies to cut a circular blank from sheet metal.

DOMING PUNCHES   Also called *bossers, domers, dapping,* or *ball punches,* these have a round, ball-shaped end, and are made in many graduated sizes. *Uses:* Primarily intended for use in conjunction with the matching shaped and sized hemispherical depressions in a *dapping block* which is a matrix for making domes or half-spheres from circular blanks. (See Doming, Chapter 5.) They can, however, also be used as punches to form depressions or raised parts from either side of the metal.

5–32 LAURI VERIÖ, Finland. Silver pendant with turquoise. Flat sheet, pierced and modeled, and surface textured with a variety of chasing tools. Surface texture was an interest characteristic of the North European Art Nouveau movement. Liners, matting tools, circle and dot punches were used. The file-beveled edges impart an illusory depth to the relatively flat form. Length 3 in. *Photo: Vatanen*

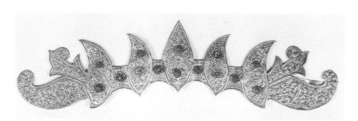

5–33 PALEMBANG, SUMATRA, INDONESIA. Gilded tin, repoussé-worked head ornament with low-quality diamonds (*inten-inten*), worn by young, single men during special festive dances. Length 17 cm. *Photo: Courtesy the Indonesisch Ethnografisch Museum, Delft*

THE CHASING AND REPOUSSÉ WORK HAMMER

The force imparted to the punch to make it do its work comes from the blow of a *chasing hammer*. When striking chasing and repoussage tools, it is very important to be able to pay full attention, without distractions, to the effect the punch is having on the metal. All judgments concerning form or pattern development in these processes revolve around this consideration. It must be possible to strike the punch end without having to watch the fall of the hammer on the punch.

This need to focus on the effect rather than the process brought about the development of the special shape of the chasing hammer head. Typically it has an unusually large, circular, flat, polished face at one end in diameters of $^{15}/_{16}$ in, 1⅛ in, 1¼ in (2.4 cm, 2.9 cm, 3.2 cm). The face is hardened and tempered, therefore will not become dented or marked when striking the punch. With such a broad striking surface, the task of making contact with the small punch head becomes simple and can be done automatically and mindlessly. At the other end of the head is a small ball peen that can be used for forming rivet heads and other work. The hammer is designed to balance well due to the shape of the approximately 1-oz, 10-in-long hardwood handle which emerges from the head as a round, slender rod and has resiliency and spring in action; this reduces the jarring vibration to the hand. Its diameter gradually swells toward the other end and flows into an oval, round, or pistol-grip shape which is comfortable to hold. The hammer head should be fixed firmly on the wooden handle so it will not come loose during work.

Hammer and handle in total weights of 5, 6, or 8 ounces are available. The weight chosen must relate to the punch size and the work to be done. When working, a balance must be sensed between the strike force, the tool size, and the metal thickness. Adjustments to these factors make a difference in the result. Too much force makes the punch move too fast, become displaced, or even pierce the metal, while too little force or too light a hammer can make the blow totally ineffective. Too heavy a hammer used on a lightweight punch will make it jerk, jump, or skip on the metal. As mentioned, some craftspersons substitute a broad, flat piece of hardwood or a flat metal bar for the chasing hammer.

METALS USED FOR REPOUSSAGE

Almost any metal and its alloys used by craftspersons can be formed by repoussage techniques. Some metals are more suitable to the process because they are more malleable, while others are too stiff to respond easily to the amount of pressure normally exerted on the metal by hand power and tools. The metals most likely to be used by a jeweler for repoussage are gold of any karat and suitable sheet thickness, usually 22–26 gauge B.&S.; silver, pure, sterling, or coin, 20–22 gauge B.&S.; and copper, 18–22 gauge B.&S. Stiff metals such as nickel and brass are more difficult to work, but, like all the above metals, can be annealed when they become work hardened to restore their working qualities.

METAL REPAIR

Metal fracture can happen if the metal is too thin to begin with; if the metal is forced into form too vigorously and rapidly and becomes stretched too thin or unevenly; or if the work time is too extended instead of stopping to anneal the metal and restore its malleability. In such a case, repairs should be undertaken immediately to prevent further damage. From the *back*, flood the area with hard solder of a color matching the metal, or if necessary, solder a patch to the back of the area, and file down its edges to blend them smoothly into the rest.

THE REPOUSSAGE AND CHASING PROCESS

DEMONSTRATION 1

MARGARET LAWS makes a silver vest of relief-modeled forms

Photos: Jane Lougee Bryant

PREPARING THE METAL

1 The metal to be worked in repoussage or chasing can first be cut to its contour, or a blank larger than the final dimension can be used, from which the work is cut out when finished. This system is especially suited to making several small pieces on the same sheet, rather than separately handling small, possibly complex shapes. To be better able to anchor the metal in the pitch, the surplus ends of a cleaned and annealed piece of 22 gauge B.&S. sterling silver are bent to a right angle. First the bending line is marked and the part hammered over the straight edge of an *anvil* with a *rawhide mallet*. By another method, the bend can be made by inserting the part to be bent between the legs of a steel *folding bar* clamped in the jaws of a bench vise.

2 Cut small tabs along the sides with *snips*, and bend them down 90°. Once these tabs are inserted in the pitch, the sides of the metal cannot be displaced by hammering during the work. The cutting is done here with powerful *aviation-type snips* designed with a compound leverage arrangement for greater cutting power. It will easily cut metals up to 18 gauge B.&S.

BEDDING THE METAL TO THE PITCH COMPOSITION

3 Lightly grease the back of the metal to facilitate its removal later, then warm it with a torch. With a gentle, moving flame, heat the pitch in depth but do not allow it to overheat and become too soft. When the pitch has cooled off but is still plastic, mound it somewhat toward the center with wet fingers. Press the metal into the pitch with a tool or stick deeply enough so it is properly bedded and all air below it is pressed out. Do not press the metal so deeply that it becomes difficult to remove it later. When

bedding small pieces, with greased fingers press a small amount of pitch over the edges to anchor the metal in place. Avoid getting pitch on the surface to be worked, and wipe it off should this occur. Allow the metal to cool and the pitch to solidify, but do not let it get too cold during work or when the metal is struck, it may become disengaged from the pitch surface. If the pitch shows signs of excessive hardening during work, pass a flame over it lightly.

TRANSFERRING THE DESIGN TO THE METAL

4 Transfer the design—with one-sided *carbon paper* and a pencil or round-pointed stylus—to the front of the metal, before or after it is placed on the pitch. Any of several other methods of design transfer can also be used. If a form is to be made without an outline, the repoussé work can start directly from the *back*. In this case, the design would have to be transferred *in reverse* to the metal surface, that side then becoming the back. If working on the back, the outline can be lightly marked on the metal with a *steel scriber*. If a scriber is used on the front, remember to make the marks very light as they are otherwise difficult to remove.

LINING-IN THE OUTLINE

5 Here the design outline is done from the front with a *tracer punch* in conjunction with a *chasing hammer*. When using all repoussage and chasing tools, hold the punch in the left hand between the thumb and the next two or three fingers placed toward the top, middle, and bottom of the tool. Allow the fifth or small finger to rest on the metal to give leverage, keep the tool steady, and help guide it. Hold the hammer in the right hand and with wrist action apply light, rhythmic, rapid blows to the punch. Watch the working end of the punch and the line that it follows on the metal. *Do not watch the tool's striking end or the hammer!* If the punch is held in the correct position, the broad face of the chasing hammer will hit it easily, and the tool will move along the line. Gauge the force of the blow by watching the result.

The liner punch should lean slightly away from you, and move forward toward you on its heel, its upper end slightly raised, and by a series of oblique indentations, form a continuous line. If the angle is too high, the tool will dig into the metal, and if it is too low, it will slip and not follow the groove being made. The correct angle for each tool must be tested—they are not the same. Strike the tool with the hammer at an angle perpendicular to its length. With each hammer blow, the punch digs into the metal and moves forward, gradually cutting a *channel* or *chase* into the metal. Its progress should be slow and smooth, and it should not move in jerks and jumps which would create a line with distinct, disjointed sections. In this way, the lines are *chased-in* or *lined-in*. The sharper

1

2

3

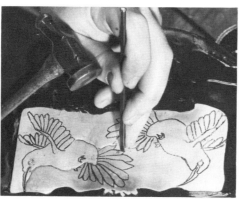

4   5   6

the curve of the line, the shorter the tool face should be. Special small curves can be made with *curve-faced tracers*.

REVERSING THE METAL

6 Once the chased outline is completed from the front, the repoussé work process can commence from the back, guided by the chased outline which is easily visible there as a raised ridge. Remove the metal from the pitch by heating it with a soft flame, and lifting it off with *tweezers* or *pincers*. (For work without flanges embedded in the pitch, a sharp blow administered to a cold pitch bowl bottom will usually jar it loose.)

7 Pitch adhering to the metal can be removed by a *solvent* or by *heat*. First place the metal on a refractory surface, pitch face up, and heat the metal until the pitch is in a liquid state, then wipe off as much as possible with a plain cloth. Remove the rest by rubbing the cooled metal with a turpentine-saturated cloth. Alternately, as shown here, burn off the pitch to reduce it to an ash, and rinse it off. The metal becomes somewhat annealed in this process,

but a full anneal may be needed. In any case, whenever inserting the metal into the pickle to clean away firescale, be sure it is entirely free of all traces of pitch or oil. The acid will not remove these substances which will act as a resist and will cause the acid to eat into the metal surface unevenly and create undesirable surface irregularities.

8 After pickling, rinsing, and drying the metal, flatten the bent edges and tabs, and reverse their direction. Reheat the pitch surface, and replace the metal on the pitch, with the back now facing up.

REPOUSSAGE

9 Push back the metal from this side with *embossing* and *cushion punches* to block out, establish, and stretch main forms toward the front surface. Most of the time, repoussage tools are held firmly, but not too tightly, almost perpendicularly to the metal, or leaning slightly back away from the direction of tool movement. When necessary, as here, a heavier chasing hammer is used to exert additional force to stretch and raise the form.

7   8   9

10   11   12

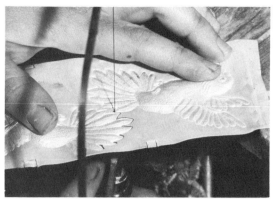

13   14   15

It is possible to test the degree of relief to see if it is satisfactory or if more work is needed, by pressing an oil-mixed clay such as Plasticine, or soft wax into the depression, and then lift it off. The pattern can then be seen in relief as it appears from the front.

10 When the main forms are blocked out and the desired degree of relief is achieved from the back, remove the metal from the pitch to work the details of the design by *chasing* from the front surface. Anneal the metal to overcome work hardening which can be sensed when the tool no longer has any effect on moving the metal and has become stiff. Clean the metal by immersing it in the pickling bath, and rinse and dry it.

GROUNDING

11 When the repousséd forms are deep, the forward pressure from tools often causes the ground plane to become warped. Flatten it to one plane by placing the metal, face up, on a flat surface and pushing it down with a flat-faced *grounding punch,* a *small mallet,* or a piece of *hardwood with a shaped end.* If the metal is thin enough, this can be done simply by pressing the tool down manually.

12 Before returning the metal to the pitch surface, reverse the holding tabs to their original position. Place solid lumps of pitch into the depressions in the metal and melt the pitch to fill them completely to make the back surface level. The pitch will now support these relief areas when worked. Allow the pitch to cool and solidify. It is simpler to melt pieces of pitch into indentations this way than it is to press the metal deeply into the pitch and force

it to fill the depressions or to pour molten pitch into the indentations, as must be done in the case of hollow objects. Cover any remaining exposed portions of the metal on the back with a thin layer of pitch to facilitate its adherence to the pitch surface. Place the metal on the pitch and heat it, pressing it down until it adheres, but take care not to overheat it.

CHASING

13 With variously shaped and textured *chasing punches,* model and chase-in final details and textures. The chasing tool assortment is seen on the right.

FINISHING

14 Remove the work from the pitch and clean it. Saw out the finished repousséd and chased forms from the sheet. Save the scrap metal for other uses or for reclaiming. File and buff the edges and rub the surfaces of the form with fine pumice or tripoli on a cloth or with the fingers to smooth them and bring them to the desired degree of brightness or matteness. Highly polished surfaces are generally too light reflective and tend to confuse rather than reveal repoussage forms. An intermediate degree of brightness can be achieved by scratch brushing. Areas can be brightened by burnishing.

15 The parts are being assembled to plan for the position of the jump rings to which chains will be attached to hold the units together.

16, 17 The finished vest, front, and a detail of the back section.

16   17

5-34 CHRISTOPH BECK I, Basel, Switzerland, 1682. Crown of the Silver Guild. Repoussé-worked and chased flowers and leaves, made separately, were mounted on a wire framework. Height 14 cm; Ø 18 cm. *Photo: Rijksmuseum, Amsterdam*

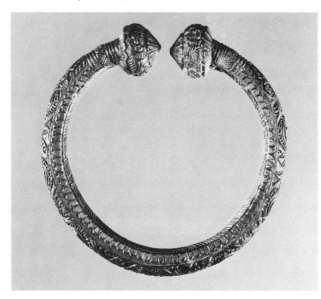

5-35 RAJASTHAN, INDIA. Traditional silver ankle bracelet (*kara*). The hollow, seamed tube form was pitch filled, and the design worked with chasing tools from the outside. When finished, the pitch was drained by heat. Ø 5 in. Gift of Mr. and Mrs. J. H. Wade. *Photo: The Cleveland Museum of Art, Cleveland*

HOLLOW-FORM REPOUSSAGE

Repoussé work can be made in relief seen *frontally* or it can be applied to a *three-dimensional* form. Completely three-dimensional forms occur in jewelry, made of sheet metal or tubes, and can be repoussé worked entirely from the *outside* after the basic form is completed. (See Bulging and Reducing Tubing, p. 267, for a method of working repoussage on empty forms or tubes from the *inside*.) In hollow-form repoussage the form is filled with heated liquid pitch. If there is more than one opening, the others must be temporarily closed to contain the pitch until it solidifies. This can be done by binding lightly greased pieces of metal over the openings, and later knocking them off when the pitch has hardened. In some cases it may be useful to push a *round* or *square wood stick* through the opening in the object into the still plastic pitch and leave it until the pitch hardens. The free end can be clamped in a vise to hold the article in any position to accommodate different working angles. When the repoussage is finished, the pitch with stick is melted out.

POSTREPOUSSAGE TECHNIQUES

Once the repoussage and final surface finishing are completed, in a design consisting of a figure and ground, the ground can be *colored* to make a visual contrast with the raised form (which is left uncolored) and to increase the effect of dimension through the illusion of greater depth. Finished repoussage units can be worked further with any of several other techniques. Some of these possible supplementary processes are: enameling part or all of the visible surface (basse taille enameling); engraving; etching; granulation; inlaying; and stone setting. Repoussage done on very thin-gauge precious metal, used to reduce costs, can be reinforced for strength by enameling the unseen inside surface, or by coating it with several applications of a liquid resin such as an epoxy.

5-37 CHINA, 19th century. Repoussé-worked brooch with pierced work ground and engraved details. The entire surface is covered with transparent blue enamels in the basse taille technique. Col.: Mickey Norman. *Photo: Oppi*

5-36 ELLIOT PUJOL, U.S.A. Fibula of copper and brass, with green patina. The central tubular units were repoussé-worked into concave forms from the outside. The lunate forms of self-edged copper sheet were surface textured with matting punches. Ø 5 in. *Photo: Ron Sittz*

5-38 GEORG JENSEN, Denmark. Silver repoussé-worked pin. Contrast between the figure and ground is achieved by coloring the ground. Wings on fabulous animals indicate the sublimation of those qualities ascribed to that animal. *Photo: Erik Junior, courtesy Georg Jensen Sølvsmedie A/S*

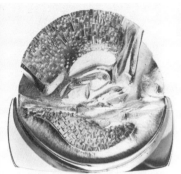

5–39 GEORG SEIBERT, West Germany. Gold and silver pendant. Low-relief dimension is visually increased by coloring the depressions. *Photo: Günter Meyer, courtesy Schmuckmuseum, Pforzheim*

5–40 JOHN MARSHALL, U.S.A. Gold and silver repoussé-worked and chased brooch. The subtly modeled surface is texturally enriched by gold-granulated chips. *Photo: University of Washington Audio-Visual Production Services*

FABRICATION WITH REPOUSSAGE UNITS

There are many possibilities for the fabrication of jewelry made entirely or in part of repoussage units. The whole repoussé-worked object can be treated as a single unit, or a series of units can be assembled in various ways. One such unit can be mounted in a bezel in the same manner as a stone is mounted. It could be mounted on a contrasting metal, or inlaid with a different metal. It can be combined with or mounted on a nonmetallic material such as ivory, bone, tortoiseshell, plastic, wood, or glass. Repoussage units can be joined to a ground, or to other units, using pegs, permanent or movable rivets, screws, or hinges. Work can be sewn to a soft material such as cloth or leather by drilling small holes near its edge and stitching it to the other material with tough, durable thread or wire, or by passing small split-shank rivets through the hole and spreading the shank ends at the reverse side. Units can be joined to each other with loose or soldered-on jump rings through which other rings, chains, flexible foxtail chain, or a nylon filament can pass to hold them together. A repoussage unit can be soldered to a flat ground that projects beyond the limits of its contour, or to a backing that exactly follows the contour to make a closed form that gives the appearance of weight while actually—because the result is hollow—remaining light. A form without a backing can have a wire soldered to either the upper, visible edge to form a frame, or to the under edge to give the object the illusion of visual weight by making it seem to be made of a heavier metal—at the same time giving the unit structural strength. Several separately made repoussage units can be soldered together, or joined by any other means to make a three-dimensional, sculptural unit. The possibilities are endless.

5–41 BOB EBENDORF, U.S.A. Three repoussé-worked and chased copper and silver belt buckles with engraved, stamped, and saw-pierced details. *Photo: Bob Ebendorf*

5–42 KABYLE, ATLAS MOUNTAINS, ALGERIA. Silver upper arm bracelet. The springy, repoussé-worked cylindrical form opens and closes by lifting the central cloisonné-enameled and coral-decorated strip to release the hooks. Col. of the Traphagen School of Fashion, New York. *Photo: Oppi*

5–43 ARLINE M. FISCH, U.S.A. Sterling silver pendant/perfume flask, repoussé-worked, chased, and fabricated to hold a glass perfume bottle. The head is hinged to expose the stopper when tilted. Height 4 in; width 1¼ in. *Photo: Arline M. Fisch*

▶

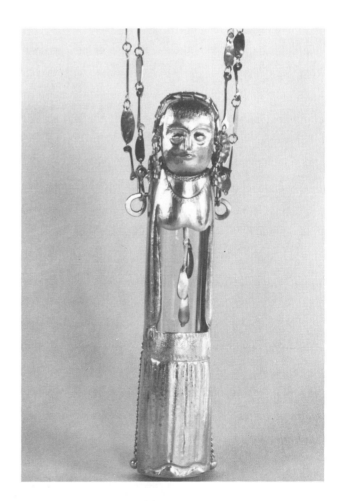

5-44 SVEN BOLTENSTERN, Austria. Necklace of 18K gold and silver with smoky quartz crystals in wire mounts. Backed, hollow, repoussé-worked linked forms allow visual bulk with minimal weight. *Photo: Inge Kitlitschka-Strempel*

5-46 BARBARA GASCH, West Germany. Calla lily brooch; the leaf in repoussé-worked 14K yellow gold, and the lily in white gold. The spring-mounted, trembling lily stamen unit ends in a large pearl surrounded by small pearls. The worm at the bottom is ornamented with green chrysoprase stones and projecting stiff bristles. Flowers symbolize life's transitory nature, and in the West, the calla lily is associated with funerals. The worm, symbolic of death, is already at work on the leaf and bloom at the peak of their maturity. *Photo: Astrid Mucs*

5-47 HELEN SHIRK, U.S.A. Sterling silver bracelet with moonstones. Large sculptural forms are in 18 gauge B.&S. sheet, shaped on a sandbag. The open-backed forms visually thickened and strengthened by edge wire, become closed forms when the bracelet is worn. Size 3½ × 2½ in. *Photo: Helen Shirk*

5-48 BRUNO MARTINAZZI, Italy. "Metamorfosi." White gold and 20K yellow gold bracelet. The repoussé-worked parts are backed by sheets to close the form. The surface is scratch brushed, except for the fingernail which is highly polished for contrast. *Photo: Courtesy Martinazzi*

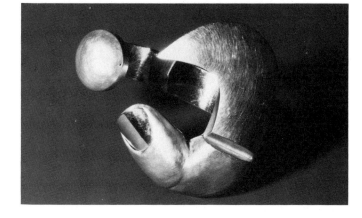

5-45 GEORG JENSEN, Denmark, 1924. Silver armband No. 30. Individual repoussé-worked and chased units are hollow and backed by sheet cut to the unit silhouette. Every enclosed space is pierced with two small holes to allow the escape of expanding gases during soldering. The interflanged units are held together by hinge pins. *Photo: Erik Junior, courtesy Georg Jensen Sølvsmedie A/S*

STAMPING

Impressing, blanking, or embossing by impact pressure

The concept of stamping evolved in ancient times. The process that produces shaped units is believed to have developed from the earlier technique of repoussage, which is far more time-consuming, as a means of avoiding the tediousness of having to make multiple, identical units. Innumerable ancient necklaces, bracelets, and other forms of jewelry utilized stamped patterns and parts. At an early age the stamping process was also used to manufacture coinage. The use of real coins as well as stamped imita-

tions has been common in jewelry, as a wealth symbol, almost since the beginning of the use of stamped coinage.

With the introduction of the stamping technique came the concept of tools used for mass production. Stamping is also largely responsible for the concept of *componential jewelry*, a very important system used in jewelry design, in which many repeats of a single or a few different units are combined to form the jewel. This system was used in ancient jewelry, and is still used today because it considerably reduces the time needed to make such jewelry, with an accompanying reduction in labor costs. Mechanically stamped jewelry reached a peak of importance with the growth of industrial techniques in the 19th century. The then greatly expanded jewelry industry aimed to satisfy the demands of the masses by mass manufacture, a concept still active.

There is no reason for the individual jeweler of today to look down upon stamping because it is mechanical. Making jewelry of stamped forms can be creative: it is the artist who controls the tool shapes and die forms used, and who chooses the manner in which the results are assembled.

5–51   JULIUS CEASAR, (Pawnee), U.S.A. Nickel silver neckerchief slide using stamping punch ornaments for pattern. *Photo: Courtesy U. S. Department of the Interior, Indian Arts and Crafts Board*

STAMPING CONCEPTS

Stamping is a process in which a tool or die is forcibly struck into sheet metal for one of three purposes; impressing, blanking, or embossing.

5–52   NAVAJO INDIAN, U.S.A. Contemporary silver belt buckles with stamped patterns. *Photo: Oppi*

5–49   EASTERN NEPAL. Contemporary silver necklace (*gopoma*) worn by brides. All the stamped units are closed by sheet at the back, then lac filled through an opening, and chased. Several spaced threads that pass through side holes hold them together. *Photo: Oppi*

5–50   ISFAHAN, IRAN. Traditional silver necklace worn by Christian Armenian women until the beginning of this century. Stamped units of birds, fish, and flower buds, closed at the back, are joined and held by links. The end hooks at the back are fixed into the clothing. *Photo: Oppi*

IMPRESSING

Impressing is the act of making a mark by pressure. In *impression stamping*, a pattern is made on flat sheet metal with a *stamping punch* that bears a linear figure at its working end in comparatively sharp, projecting outline that leaves an impression on the surface of the metal when struck with a hammer. Improvised punches can be used for the same effect.

BLANKING

Blanking is the act of stamping out a flat shape of special contour, or a three-dimensional form, called a *blank*, by the use of a sharp-edged *blanking punch*, alone or in conjunction with a *blanking die*. The larger or more dimensional the blank is, the more likely it is that greater mechanical force must be applied to produce the blank.

EMBOSSING

Embossing is the act of stamping to force out a shape in cameo or intaglio. This process is done with the aid of a *stamping punch* or *die*. When the resulting form is positive, or in relief, it is termed *in cameo* (from the Italian *cammeo*, "a gem carved in relief"). When the form is negative or concave, it is termed *in intaglio* (from the Italian *intagliare*, "to engrave, cut, or carve a design into a substance below its original surface"). In the case of sheet metal, these forms can be used with the positive or negative side uppermost. The shape formed can be relatively small—as when it is made with a small, hand *embossing punch*—and the resulting *boss* is usually one of several such elements placed in an arrangement on the still intact sheet. When it is large—as when made with a *one- or two-part die*—the embossed stamping or shaped sheet may itself be a unit or the entire object.

PUNCH AND DIE STAMPING BY HAND METHODS

IMPRESSING: *Direct punch pattern stamping*

Direct punch stamping consists of using a one-piece, ready-made punch or an improvised, self-made *pattern-bearing steel punch* shaped by carving, filing, or engraving, to impress a pattern on sheet metal. The pattern is imparted directly to the metal surface by striking the punch with a hand-held hammer while the metal rests on a supporting surface.

The impression punch is called a *single-blow punch* because the pattern is normally made by striking the punch with a single blow of the hammer, which is the unifying concept behind this diversified group. Pattern punches can be subdivided into two groups: those used for *decorative purposes* such as an impression punch that imprints a decorative figure, and those that impress a normally *nondecorative* figure on metal such as a trademark, quality mark, letter, number, or a stamp with some other figure used for identification or other purpose.

5–55 TIZNIT, SOUTHERN MOROCCO. Contemporary silver fibula (tezrzag) worn by women with the traditional costume in pairs at the shoulders. Ornamented with stamped and engraved patterns and enameled bosses, and set with glass stones. A variety of traditional ornaments are manufactured by the many jewelry establishments in Tiznit. *Photo: Musée de l'Homme, Paris*

5–53 GERMANY, 5th–6th centuries A.D. Solid gold torque collar found in Trolleborg, Flackarp Parish, Skåne, Sweden. Made from melted-down Roman gold *solidi* coins, equal in weight to about 284 solidi. Decorated with patterned stamped punch impressions in the relatively soft metal. Ø 21.5 cm. *Photo: Antikvarisk-Topografiska Arkivet, Stockholm; Museum of National Antiquities, Stockholm*

5–54 *DETAILS OF STAMPED PATTERNS* on other solid gold rod torques, also in the Museum of National Antiquities, Stockholm. *Photo: Sören Hallgren, ATA, Stockholm*

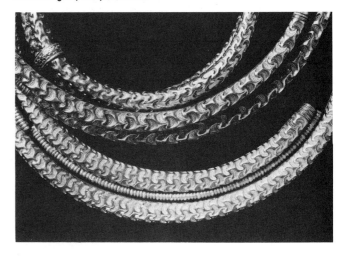

5-56 TIZNIT, SOUTHERN MOROCCO. The complete ornament consists of two *tezrzags*, and connecting pendants which hang between them on the breast. *Photo: Oppi*

5-57 KALEVALA KORU, Helsinki. Stamping dies used in a stamping press for production jewelry. *Photo: Oppi*

5-58 KALEVALA KORU, Helsinki, manufacturer. Silver stamped unit cuff links made of a single, small, machine-stamped unit. Designs are based on motifs taken from Finnish Viking Period ornaments. *Photo: Otso Pietinen, courtesy Kalevala Koru*

Resisting surfaces are used for impression stamping when the metal is flat and a single-blow punch is used to make an impression on its visible surface. This can be a *flat steel block* or *anvil*. By using a resisting support, the punch makes a clear, deep impression in the metal, and there is only a ghost image of the pattern at the back of the metal.

Place the punch and strike it with the hammer in one judicious blow (a second blow may result in a double or unclear image). Practice on scraps of the same metal as that being worked to get a feel for the amount of pressure needed to get a good stamped imprint. An individual stamped unit can be made or, by repeating a unit in masses or overlapping impressions, a textural area can be created. After stamping on flat sheet metal forms, they can be shaped into dimensional forms by using mallets of soft, nonmarking materials, and/or wood or metal shaping blocks and molds.

BLANKING: *Shearing a form of special contour*

USING A ONE-PART STAMPING DIE TO SHEAR A CIRCULAR BLANK

A *stamping die* is a device used to cut out or shear a shape or blank of a certain contour, and/or to impart a relief pattern to sheet metal. This is done by striking the die with a hammer, as in hand stamping, or by mechanical pressure.

The principle of die stamping or shearing a blank from sheet metal by hand can be illustrated by the stamping of a flat, circular blank with a *one-part, hollow, steel shearing die.* This consists of a steel rod or punch that ends in a hollow, sharp-edged circle form whose cutting edge is hardened and tempered. The metal to be blanked is placed on a sheet of soft brass. The die is placed exactly upright on the metal, held by its shank. Its end is struck a few times, making the die shear through any metal softer than the die

5–59 SUMATRA, INDONESIA. Gold pectoral, basically a flat sheet edged with a twisted wire, decorated with small, individual embossing punch patterns applied from the back in sequences that parallel the contour shape. The front lunette-shaped unit with repoussé-worked flower and vine design, is held by thin wire stitched at intervals through holes pierced in both sheets. *Photo: Courtesy the Rijksmuseum voor Volkerkunde, Leiden*

5–60 SWEDEN, 6th-century A.D. Gold bracelet found in Lojsta Parish, Fride, Gotland. These thin, circular medallions struck with individual stamping punches from both front (intaglio parts) and back (relief parts) were widely used by Germanic and Scandinavian people after the fall of the Roman Empire. Nordic medallions imitated late Roman gold coins with imperial portraits, but usually show a profiled head over a horned animal. Believed to have been talismans, they were worn as a woman's necklace pendant, strung through the top loop. *Photo: Antikvarisk-Topografiska Arkivet, Stockholm, Museum of National Antiquities, Stockholm*

itself. If the blank is not loosened, without shifting the die position, rock it gently in all directions while hammering. The result is a blank, flat, circular disc.

USING A TWO-PART DISC-SHEARING DIE

A more complicated die is a *two-part die* consisting of a *matrix* that is used in conjunction with a shearing punch to shear away a blank from sheet metal. An example is a *two-part circular disc shearer.* The matrix consists of two solid steel blocks mounted one above the other with a space between them. Both are pierced with vertical perforations or holes of various diameters from ¼–⅞ in (6.34–22.22 mm). The metal being sheared is placed in the slot between the two parts of the matrix below the selected hole size. Place a thin sheet of brass below the sheet metal being sheared to support it and to help to achieve a flat result in the blank. Each matrix hole is matched in size by a punch.

To facilitate the action of *shearing* (in which metal is cut by a moving edge working against a fixed edge, or two moving edges working against each other as in *hand shears*), the edge of *one* of the cutting members, the punch or the matrix die, is angled or *sheared* so that something less than the full perimeter is cut. When the *punch face* is sheared or beveled and the die wall remains vertical, the result is a flat sheet and a slightly curved stamping or blank. When a flat blank is wanted, the *die* is beveled or sheared and the punch remains straight. The thinner the sheet metal, the less die clearance is needed. Softer metals have a tendency to flow into the die just

prior to fracture, which is why stamped blanks of soft metal have curved edges.

The clearance between the punch and the die hole is small so that the punch just fits into it. The punch is placed into the hole, and its exposed end is hammered with one good blow. This forces it to move at a plane of shear perpendicular to the plane of the metal, and it pierces a blank from the sheet at the die rim. The cutting action is tangential so that little or no edge crushing occurs. The sheet is then removed from the slot, the resulting blank drops out, and the sheet can be moved to its next position for shearing the next blank. Metal up to 14 gauge B.&S. (0.641 in, 1.629 mm) can be sheared with such a device.

When many blanks of similar shape are sheared from one strip or sheet, they are cut as close to each other as possible to minimize the amount of metal waste that remains. If the silhouette of the shape allows, they are *nested* within each other. In some cases, the pierced sheet itself can be used creatively.

EMBOSSING: *Raising a surface relief with shaping hand punches*

Embossing or shaping a pattern in relief in sheet metal can be done manually with a small hand punch, an open, one-part die, or a closed, two-part die; or by mechanical pressure on dies. When using small hand punches, shape stamping can be done in intaglio from the back surface of the metal, and the result is later seen in cameo from the front. The metal is placed on a *yielding surface,* the choice depending on the depth of the embossed pattern. A piece of leather on a wood block, a softwood board, a lead block, or chaser's pitch can all be used. Place the metal sheet, back surface up, on the supporting material. Position the shaping punch on the metal and hammer it down to the desired depth. When using a larger punch to create a higher relief, it is helpful to first make a shaped impression in the supporting material with the punch alone. If this is a lead block, first hammer the punch into the block, then place the annealed sheet metal on top of this, replace the stamping punch in position directly above the depression and hammer the metal into it.

5–61 INDIA. Contemporary pendant made from a single large hand stamping from a bronze die. Originally it was one of a matching series on a giant necklace worn by processional elephants on festive occasions. Set with small turquoise stones. Height 5 in; width 4½ in. *Photo: Oppi*

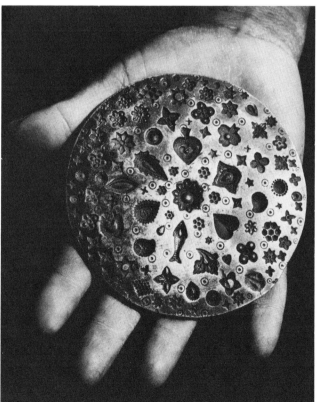

5–62 NORTH INDIA. Contemporary bronze *intaglio jeweler's die* (variously called *thasa, thappa* or *chhancha*), in wide use by Indian and Nepalese gold and silversmiths for making small pattern stampings used in jewelry. The die depressions are spaced sufficiently for any to be selected for a stamping. The shallow patterns stamped between them simply decorate the die and delight the jeweler. The stamped units are cut from the sheet and soldered on silver and gold jewelry, often to conceal joints. *Photo: Oppi*

5–63 NURISTAN, AFGHANISTAN. Contemporary, rigid, silver torque (*tawq*) necklace, worn by Pashtu women. Small, decorative, stamped units are borders, space fillers, and support bezels holding lapis lazuli stones at the center and coral in side rosettes. Ø 20.5 cm. *Photo: Oppi*

▼

DIE SINKING: Preparing a one-part, open, intaglio die

Die sinking is the art of forming or shaping a depressed, intaglio relief pattern in a die block. The pattern is meant to be reproduced in cameo relief on the sheet metal placed on the die. By hand stamping or machine stamping it becomes deformed and conforms to the die's cavity shape. If the deforming is excessive the metal may develop cracks unless annealed. Smaller dies meant for reproduction by hand stamping can be made from a block of brass or bronze ½ in (1.27 cm) thick. Larger, heavier dies for use on mechanical hammering or stamping machines are made of a block of special die steel alloy, forged to give it the correct grain flow for maximum strength. Special, very strong zinc alloys are used for dies in mechanical stamping (see p. 141). The stronger the metal used for the die, the greater the number of impressions or stamped blanks that can be made with it.

In the field of artistic and industrial metalwork, the die sinker who prepares the die is a highly qualified and valued specialist, especially as he or she must work to very exacting specifications. Experimental die sinking is well within the means and ability of any craftsperson familiar with even a few of the die-sinking techniques mentioned below.

Open dies made of a thick block of cast bronze are among the earliest dies used to stamp out a form from sheet metal, and they are still in use in jewelry making. These dies make possible shaped stampings that are larger than stampings that can be produced by hand punches because the surface area of an open die is bigger. The pattern is made in the smoothed, flat, uppermost face of the squared and trued die block, and a flat, blank border is allowed around the pattern to form the *flange* or *flashing* of waste metal that is later cut away. The pattern is traced and drawn on the block with a steel scriber. The intaglio portions can be sunk by any hand or by a mechanical tool capable of excavating the metal. The techniques of drilling, using rotary burs and files, milling, chipping, carving, engraving, and chasing with their appropriate tools can all be used. *Riffler files* (often called *die-sinker's files*) are commonly used in die sinking because their curvatures suit them for use on intaglio surfaces.

During the sinking of the die, the appearance of the work can be checked at intervals by pressing a wad of stiff but plastic wax into the depression, then withdrawing it. The pattern appears on the wax in relief as it would appear on the metal at that point. Alterations can then be made where necessary. The intaglio surface can be left as the tools have made it, or it can be smoothened with fine abrasive papers, then polished with tripoli, and buffed with rouge on a polishing wheel.

RELIEF STAMPING WITH A ONE-PART, OPEN, INTAGLIO DIE

The important concept in the use of all open dies is that the metal is not restricted at its outer shape, but is permitted to flow in the direction of least resistance and freely enter the die cavity. To make a stamping of more than shallow depth from such a die, place the die on an anvil and put the annealed sheet metal over the die intaglio. Be sure the entire cavity is covered, and the sheet size allows for surplus metal to form the flange. To assist in making the image on the stamping clear and sharp, and to force the metal to completely fill out the die depression, place a ¼ in (0.63 cm) sheet or several thin sheets of *lead* on top of the metal sheet to act as a shim. In industry, lead shims are used for the same purpose when drop hammering sheet metal into dies.

Hammer the lead with a heavy, somewhat convex-faced hammer, but not one that is too heavy or the die may fracture under impact. If the intaglio pattern is shallow and small enough to be covered by the size of the hammer face, a single blow from the hammer on the lead sheet may be sufficient. When stamping with a drop hammer, no lead sheet would be used with a shallow die as long as its dimension is less than the size of the hammer face. For reproducing deeper intaglio patterns, several blows will be needed to force the sheet metal into the deepest parts of the depression. The hammer blows work against metal *springback* (the tendency of the metal to want to retain its original shape) and force the metal to take on the shape of the die cavity.

Take care not to allow the metal sheet to move while it is hammered, or the impression may be multiple, therefore blurred and unsatisfactory. When the lead is removed, the sheet is easily withdrawn from the die because it has no undercuts. Its surface is usually satisfactory, it accurately reproduces the image in the die, and needs no finishing other than polishing. It is generally not good practice to return the stamping to the die a second time because of possible inaccuracy in its register. If restamping is necessary, the flange is helpful in making sure it is replaced in

5-64 NEPAL. Silver pendant with turquoises. The entire work is an assembly of prestamped and prefabricated units, including stamped gallery wire, stamped pendants and small decorative units placed on wire work or sheet metal grounds. Col.: Traphagen School of Fashion, New York. Photo: Oppi

5-65 NEPAL. Tamang woman wearing a silver neck ornament with stamped decoration. Photo: Oppi

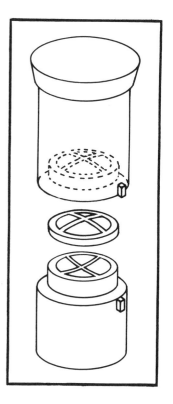

5–66 KURASAN, IRAN. Turkoman woman's silver breast ornament with flat gold stamped unit decorations soldered to every larger unit; with carnelian stones. Length 55 cm. Photo: Musée de l'Homme, Paris

the exact same position. This can be tested by seeing that there is no lateral movement between the stamping and the die. Finally, the superfluous flange is removed by sawing it away with a jeweler's saw.

COINING: Relief stamping by hand with a two-part, closed die

The two-part, closed stamping die has been used since antiquity to make a stamped pattern in relief on sheet

metal or thicker blanks of circular form. It was widely used since the 2nd century B.C. by the Greeks who employed a two-part, closed, bronze stamping die and punch to make coins and medallions. Closed stamping dies have cavities that prevent the metal from spreading as it is compressed. The lower part is called the *anvil* or *lower pile die* and contains the design in intaglio. The upper or second, hand-held part is called a *trussel,* and contains either the obverse pattern in intaglio, or if a thin sheet of metal is being stamped, the same pattern in cameo to match that of the other half. These two parts are each marked or keyed on the outside in some way to make sure that the two faces of the dies are in correct relation to each other. The annealed metal blank to be stamped is placed on the anvil die. The trussel die is placed in position over it. By the impact of a hammer blow on the shaft extending from the upper die, the die parts are brought to bear upon the metal inside, and if the dies are in the proper relationship to each other, the force is exerted equally over its entire surface. The higher the relief, the more force needed to make a complete stamping. Because the metal is completely enclosed in the die cavity, it flows into the depressions. If there happens to be a surplus of metal, this is forced out between the two die parts at the parting line (the line between the die parts) and forms a *fin* or thin projection that is later removed.

MECHANICAL COIN STRIKING In modern coin minting practice, and in the manufacture of gold-filled jewelry, closed, two-part dies are mounted on a mechanical drop hammer. The metal blank of the exact size and weight necessary to fill the die cavity must be absolutely clean, free of grease and moisture. Any small foreign particle on the blank will make its mark on the result, and can cause the die to split. The blank is therefore degreased, pickled, wire brushed, and dried before being placed in the die cavity (which must also be absolutely dry because metal will not flow into cavities containing moisture). The punch (or upper die part) is allowed to fall upon the anvil die, striking a single blow. By instantaneous pressure, the blank is shaped to a very accurate relief reproduction of the intaglio die. If no heat treatments have been used, the stamping comes from the die with a bright, smooth, burnished surface.

FINISHING SHEET METAL STAMPINGS

High-relief stamped units of thin sheet metal can be made stronger by flooding the depressions on the reverse side with easy flow solder. To strengthen it further, a wire can be soldered around the outer perimeter at the underside edge to form a frame. It is filed even with the edge and creates the illusion that the stamping is made of a much thicker sheet of metal. Or, a decorative wire frame can be soldered to the upper side at the perimeter for strength.

A stamping can also be backed with a soldered-on flat sheet of metal. If this completely closes the form, an air space exists between the stamping and the backing, and a hole must be provided for (in the backing sheet or elsewhere) to allow for the escape of expanding air during soldering.

If the stamping is of thin metal, it is common practice to fill the hollow space at the back (or inside when two stampings are joined) with a supporting substance such as *sealing wax, shellac,* or a *liquid synthetic resin* such as epoxy. This is done to strengthen the upper surface and to prevent its denting easily. The above-mentioned traditional materials are heated to a viscous state and poured into the hollow at the back, or through an opening in the object. Should the filler solidify before the space is completely filled, gently heat the object to allow the filler to settle inside, then complete the pour. (One way to avoid a necessary opening from being visible in the result is to plan for it at a place in the design where later it can be concealed, such as below a bezel where a stone or other mounted ornament will later be placed.)

STAMPING WITH POWER MACHINES

Craftspersons and jewelers today are making inroads on the domain of industry, and are finding a challenge in the use of industrial power machines normally not within their sphere. Almost all of these machines are originally developed from concepts that originated in hand tools. Examples are the drop hammer, stamping press, power lathe, metal spinning lathe, and the press brake.

Industrial power machines perform specific functions and processes to achieve precise results. The craftsperson's interests are explorative and innovative, and he or she seeks to use them in creative ways which may at times be contrary to industrial goals. Such results may be totally the product of the machine, used creatively, or a combination of machine-made parts and others made by hand processes.

Power tools may be present in a school metal workshop, or a factory to which a craftsperson may have access. Factories periodically replace old equipment and the scrapped models that are still serviceable can be purchased for a nominal fee.

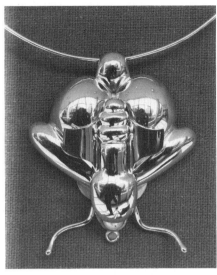

5–68 GEORGE PAUL VAN DUINWYK, U.S.A. "Bee." Sterling silver pendant with cultured pearl, aluminum die stamped as one unit on a drop hammer. Photo: van Duinwyk

If you are fortunate enough to have access to a drop hammer or power stamping machine, it can enter your assembly of useful tools. Once the dies are completed, the machine can quickly produce uniform results by a power that no individual could manually exert on the metal. For jewelers interested in producing and selling *work in series,* this is one tool that increases production and lowers costs.

Obviously, cautions of safety are necessary. *Extreme care* and *constant alertness* are needed to avoid accidents. Fingers should always be well away from the machine's moving parts when in action. As with any tool, an *understanding* of the principles of operation, and the development of *proper work habits* is the best accident insurance.

DROP FORGING AND STAMPING WITH A DROP HAMMER

The *drop hammer* is a power machine that can be used for drop forging and stamping. In *drop forging,* solid metal bars and stock are worked by a mechanical hammering action to change both their *form* and *section.* In *drop stamping,* sheet metal is changed in *form* but not in section by hammer impact or by a kneading or squeezing action, depending on the kind of machine used. Dies are used for both forging and stamping.

Drop hammer machines are used for mass production of small parts in industry, and can also be used for making stampings for jewelry. Their sizes range from small to very large, extremely heavy machines that require installation of special foundations firm enough to support their weight and the force of their impact in use. Small bench model stamping machines are widely used in the mass production of jewelry, and in some jewelry factories, large floor models are also used for this purpose.

DROP HAMMER TYPES

The drop hammer's energy develops when the hammer is raised by manual or mechanical means and then falls freely through a given distance onto the work placed on the anvil of the machine below. The weight of the hammer and the distance it falls determine the force of the blow. Two basic kinds of drop hammers exist: a *gravity drop hammer* and a *direct power drop hammer.*

Manual lift drop hammers are the simplest of gravity drop hammers, in which the *head* (also called *hammer, tup,* or *ram*) is lifted by manual force by pulling down on a strap or rope that works in conjunction with a pulley action system.

The hammer's position can be controlled by a hand clutch, latch, or foot treadle which when released, allows the ram to fall (by simple gravity) between *guides* or *column ways* onto the die placed on the anvil or bed below. This type is used by van Duinwyk in the photo demonstration series on p. 142. A drop hammer that falls by gravity acts more quickly than the slower stamping press. Its capacity is indicated by the weight of the head without an attached punch, and its maximum blow energy. The one seen in the photo series has a 1 ton blow, but machines with far greater capacities exist. The larger the weight of the head, the larger the size of the bed of the machine. A typical 500 lb head has the dimensions of 18 in × 30 in (45.7 cm × 76.2 cm), and one with a 10,000 lb head has bed dimensions of 88 in × 84 in (223.5 cm × 213.4 cm).

Direct-power pneumatic drop hammers have a system whereby the weight is raised by steam or air pressure. The hammer still falls freely, but it is given increased downstroke energy by pressure on a piston above, which produces a controlled, low-pressure blow, or a fast, high-pressure wallop (better for work on large parts). In the *steam drop hammer,* the ram is set in motion by a steam valve which controls the lifting of the ram and also exerts a force on its fall which has an impact force of 500–50,000 lb. *Air drop hammers* are constructed basically in the same way as steam drop hammers, but derive their power from compressed air.

Board gravity drop hammers have a ram that is lifted by one or more boards at the top of the machine that pass tightly between two rollers whose action on the boards causes them to rise. When they have rolled upward to the desired height (a full stroke is not invariably used), they are released mechanically and the ram drops by its own weight and strikes the die with impact force. Power comes from a lineshaft and pulleys, or a direct motor drive. These have a falling head weight capacity of 400–10,000 lb. In industry they are generally used to produce stampings from *engraved steel molds,* to stamp out smaller and lighter parts, and to perform basic shaping functions on *blanks* of metal that may later be shaped further and hand finished.

STAMPING PRESSES

The stamping press is used mainly to shape sheet metal with dies. It consists of a frame similar in construction to that of a drop hammer. The upper ram instead of being suspended is mounted on a *double- or triple-threaded screw* which is turned by the action of a large flywheel by two friction discs that rotate on opposite sides of the wheel. Manipulated by a crank, the screw rotates rapidly in the direction that brings the ram downward on the die placed on the anvil, and hits it with a sudden *bump* rather than with the impact blow of a free-falling ram. To raise the ram, the discs reverse the screw, causing the ram to move upward. The ram speed on a screw press is slower than that of a drop hammer, and can be controlled by a hand lever. This type of press was used by the author for open forging a wire necklace without a die (see p. 145).

In industry, other types of presses exist, such as the *hydraulic press* driven by water or steam pumps. These can be used for very large forgings.

5–69 KULTAKESKUS OY, Hämeenlinna. A screw-type stamping press used to stamp jewelry parts and flatware. Photo: Oppi

ZINC ALLOYS USED FOR DIMENSIONAL DIE CASTINGS

A major industrial use of zinc is as a metal alloy for casting pressure dies used in stamping. The preparation of such a die is described here briefly for those who may be interested in further pursuing this method. The zinc used in this alloy should be as pure as possible to make die castings that are stable in dimensions. Typical zinc alloys are the following:

	Zinc Alloy AG 40A		ASTM Zinc Alloy XXI	
Zn	95.774	parts	92.00	parts
Al	4.0	parts	4.5	parts
Cu	0.10	parts	3.5	parts

In addition, small amounts of other metals (Mg 0.04; Pb 0.005; Cd 0.004; Sn 0.002; and Fe 0.075) are added to the first alloy.

These alloys have a melting point of about 720° F (382.2° C). The lower the melting point of the alloy, the greater is the die life and the more accurate are the dimensions of the result. Alloys with lower melting points enable one to stamp metal of thinner gauge than alloys having higher melting points. These alloys have excellent casting characteristics, are cast at low temperatures, and are low in cost. Dies can be made quickly by sand casting, and they have greater strength and better impact resistance than all other die casting metals except copper alloys.

With the drop hammer, these zinc stamping dies can be used to make 50–500 stampings, depending on the complexity of the die shape. The die gradually wears, so that the definition of the stamping may not be as sharp toward the end of the die's usefulness. When it must be discarded, it can be remelted and recast.

CASTING THE ZINC ALLOY DIE

When using the drop hammer for making dimensional stampings from sheet metal, an upper punch and a matching lower die are used. One is positive and the other negative. To make the *die*, a plaster pattern is first made in the exact shape of the form, without undercuts so that the stamping can be easily removed. If dimensional exactness is the aim, the model should be made slightly oversized, by ⅛ in per foot, because on cooling, the cast die metal shrinks that much.

The plaster pattern is placed in an open sand casting frame or flask and surrounded by packed foundry sand. When the pattern is removed, a cavity remains into which the molten zinc alloy is poured. An allowance is left around the edges of the form for a flashing on the sheet metal, and projecting studs about ¼ in (0.6 cm) thick can be allowed on the model for use as a means of attaching the die on the drop hammer, so that it can mate accurately with the punch. A die block without studs can be placed in a *die holder* which is a plate having holes or slots for fastening it to the *bolster* or bed of the drop hammer or press.

After the casting cools, the die's working surface is usually very smooth, and the skin of the casting is its strongest part. Usually it does not require any further finishing, but the working surface can be sanded, buffed, and polished if desired.

MAKING A PUNCH FOR USE WITH THE DIE

Punches to match the die are usually made of lead alloys containing 6–8% antimony. Because these alloys can be poured at a temperature about 70° F (26.6° C) lower than the melting point of the zinc alloy used for the die, the punch can be poured directly against the die's working surface while the die is at room temperature. There is no need to make a separate pattern for the punch. To assure accurate matching of the working surfaces, after casting place a piece of sheet metal of the gauge to be used between the punch and the die, put both on the drop hammer anvil and strike them with a hammer.

The die is clamped down to the hammer bed. The hammer is lowered, and when the punch is in position on the die, it is attached to the hammer head by soft steel bolts which are best for this purpose as they withstand great impact. The bolts pass through holes drilled in the projecting studs, and the punch is held by nuts on the upper side of the head.

FORMING A CONTOURED BLANK WITH A DROP HAMMER

The shaped or contoured blank can be made with one blow if the metal is annealed and of thin enough gauge. If thicker metal is used, several blows are applied, especially if the sheet requires severe deformation to make the matching contours of punch and die meet. In this case, it is necessary to remove the sheet and anneal the blank periodically to relieve work hardening caused by the compression and stretching that occurs in the stamping process. With an open die (one that does not confine the edges of the sheet), an oversized piece of metal is used so that a flashing of surplus metal is formed. At the moment of impact, the metal fills out the depression of the die. The flashing allows the stamping to be replaced accurately in the die after removal and annealing. It is trimmed away from the finished stamping by sawing along the flash line.

DIE STAMPING WITH A DROP HAMMER DEMONSTRATION 2

GEORGE PAUL VAN DUINWYK makes a stamped pendant-necklace

Photos: van Duinwyk

MAKING THE FLAT SHEET METAL DIE

1 In industry, making a die to exact specifications is an expensive process. By preparing one's own die, the jeweler reduces these costs to a minimum. Minor variations in the die are not objectionable, and may even be welcome. The full-scale design, traced from an exact drawing, is glued flat with water-soluble Elmer's White Glue to a sheet of annealed tool steel, 5½ in × 5½ in, and 8 gauge B.&S. in thickness, from which the die will be cut. With a drill, a hole is made in each enclosed area in the design that is to be cut out. These holes allow saw blade access. A No. 1 saw blade is inserted through an opening, then tightened in a *jeweler's saw frame*. While keeping the saw blade as vertical as possible, each of these shapes is carefully and accurately sawed out. Saw blades may break, and new ones are inserted in the same kerf and the cutting continued. Lines that appear as ridges on the finished piece are made with a single-kerf cut. After piercing, the inner walls of the negative openings are smoothed with a *file* to be sure they are perpendicular to the sheet.

2 Because the stamped sheet metal will reproduce the slightest surface texture of the die at any point of contact, the die surface is deliberately milled or textured with a *tear-shaped carbide rotary bur* mounted on a *flex-shaft*. The bored holes in the design are reamed, which will produce a round, stepped form, using a standard *machinist's reamer*, or a *drill* of suitable size. Other die surface treatments to impart texture are also possible, such as using a grinding wheel, chip chiseling, or pattern stamping with a punch.

HARDENING AND TEMPERING THE DIE

3 *Pattern* and *silhouette* stamping dies cut from the same steel, after sawing and finishing must be hardened and tempered. The paper pattern is no longer needed on the pattern die and has been removed under running hot water. The dies are placed in a cold *furnace*, and the galvanometer device that controls its temperature is set to 1500° F (815.5° C), following manufacturer's specifications for hardening the particular steel used. It is kept at this temperature for at least an hour and a half for a good soaking heat.

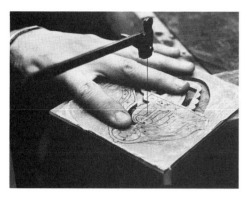

1 2 3

4 The die is removed from the furnace with *tongs,* is placed without delay in an expanded metal *quenching basket,* and quickly submerged and agitated in commercial quenching oil. Delay and lack of agitation may result in uneven cooling, which will cause the die to be irregularly hardened and possibly to break when used. The die is scrubbed with a *wire brush* to remove surface scale, and is replaced in the furnace—this time set at 1000° F (537.7° C)—for tempering. After two hours, it is removed and quickly quenched again. This leaves the die with a spring temper that allows great flexibility and resistance to shock during the stamping process.

5 A test is done using a sheet of 22 or 24 gauge B.&S. copper to see the result before using expensive precious metal. Copper, brass, or other metal could also be used for the final result. Copper responds well to the drop hammer impact, flows into the die for a considerable depth, and shows good surface detail. Sterling silver tends to be more difficult (stiff and brittle) and therefore needs more frequent annealing.

ASSEMBLING THE FOLLOW-DIE
LAMINATE

A *follow-die* is a progressive die consisting of two or more parts in a single holder. In preparation for stamping, a laminate is assembled, consisting of the *pattern die;* the *sterling silver sheet* of 22 gauge B.&S.; a *copper sheet* of 24 gauge B.&S. which serves as a shim to level the metal, prevents shearing by helping to absorb the hammer impact, helps the metal fill the die and pick up detail, and prevents contact between the silver and the lead sheet below; *two lead sheets* of 2 gauge B.&S. used to provide a push to the silver when it is expanded into the mold's negative cavities; and finally, *two plates of mild steel, ¼ in (1.27 cm) thick,* one placed over and the other under this assembly, to impart an even impression to the sheet metal when struck.

Through *all* these, two ¼ in holes were bored, into which the bolts that hold the laminate together are inserted to key them all together. This is especially important during the first few drop hammer blows. By holding the sheets together, the bolts prevent mismatching or *offset,* a fault in drop hammer stamping sheet metal that occurs when the top and bottom dies get out of line. No nuts or washers are used as they tend to be cumbersome. The bolts may not be needed after the first few strikes because the sheets themselves have already partially bulged where they have been forced into the die openings, the bulging keying them all together. The other drilled depressions seen in the lower left corner of the die were simply made to test the die's hardness. If several lead shim sheets are used behind the copper and silver blanks, the bolts are kept in the holes throughout the entire stamping sequence to prevent the sheets from shifting which would spoil the silver sheet by causing *offset* or an unclearly struck image. On smaller dies, more force is used on the first strike and keying bolts are not used.

USING THE DROP HAMMER

6 The drop hammer is raised to the safety position. The assembled die and blanks with bolts in place is positioned below the hammer head on the drop hammer anvil bed. The bed must be absolutely flat and in a plane parallel to the ram in order for the impact of the hammer to be evenly distributed on the metal.

7 The drop hammer weighs 5 tons and is mounted on a spring impact absorption assembly. This machine incorporates an electrically assisted gravity drop hammer weighting 275 lb that can be elevated (has a "daylight" distance of) 4 ft. The hammer is raised between the frame's two side guides up to the head piece by a system of pulleys. A safety releasing lever is provided that holds the ram in position while the die assembly is placed on the bed, whose maximum die size allowance is 12 in × 12 in

4 5 6

BLOCKING OUT THE FORM

The first strike must be done carefully to *block out* or establish an initial shape on the metal. In this arrangement of dies, the relief forms of the metal expand *upward* through the die openings as the die pushes the ground downward. Under this pressure, the silver and copper become toughened, their physical properties of tensile and compressive strength are increased, and the result is a work-hardened sheet. If the strikes must be repeated, it becomes necessary to anneal both silver and copper sheets to render them workable again. The follow-die laminate is removed and disassembled, and the metal is annealed, pickled, and dried thoroughly. Annealing also prevents the development of internal folds or wrinkles, and fracturing at the edges.

There is no difficulty in returning the metal to its proper position in the die as its bulged areas fit it in place. The assembly is struck once in one direction, then turned to the opposite direction, with the same side up, and struck again. This is done to assure the even expansion of the metal in the die, a safety precaution taken because the drop hammer is about 50 years old and its anvil may not be absolutely level. (Turning is not necessary on a new machine.) This sequence is repeated as many times as necessary. The limit of the depth of a stamping in this case is just short of the thickness of the die sheet.

The silhouetted second die is used as a means of outlining the form of the first. In this case, this die is placed over the already struck laminate and hammered three or more times to deepen the whole form. The previously struck section rises within this outline shape. In this case, after the second or third strike, the pattern die is placed over the silhouette die to allow space for expansion; otherwise the bulged metal might reach the drop hammer face and the highest forms would be flattened by that contact.

After the silver form is raised to the desired level by the lead sheets, the lead and the copper sheets are removed. A sheet of 12 gauge B.&S. pewter is placed behind the silver.

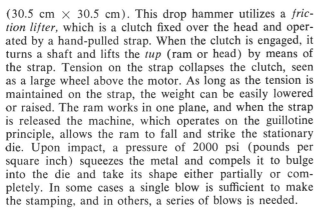

(30.5 cm × 30.5 cm). This drop hammer utilizes a *friction lifter,* which is a clutch fixed over the head and operated by a hand-pulled strap. When the clutch is engaged, it turns a shaft and lifts the *tup* (ram or head) by means of the strap. Tension on the strap collapses the clutch, seen as a large wheel above the motor. As long as the tension is maintained on the strap, the weight can be easily lowered or raised. The ram works in one plane, and when the strap is released the machine, which operates on the guillotine principle, allows the ram to fall and strike the stationary die. Upon impact, a pressure of 2000 psi (pounds per square inch) squeezes the metal and compels it to bulge into the die and take its shape either partially or completely. In some cases a single blow is sufficient to make the stamping, and in others, a series of blows is needed.

The laminate is reassembled and struck once or twice to ensure accurate reproduction of surface detail.

CUTOFF: REMOVING THE FLANGE

8 The flange of the sterling silver sheet is removed by sawing it off, and the edge of the stamping is filed.

FINISHING THE NECKLACE

9 A strip of silver, ½ in wide, was soldered at an angle of 45° around the perimeter of the stamping. To this strip, a square wire was soldered to give the edge thickness. Parts of the form were struck from the reverse side with *doming punches* to push them forward.

Here we see the finished necklace with stamped unit pendant. Areas where the metal contacted the die reproduce its surface texture. The bulged areas which did not touch the die surface appear smooth. The neck elements holding the stamped plaque are of 18 gauge B.&S. sheet, fabricated over stakes, and planished. The lower sections were forged from 2 gauge B.&S. square silver wire and were soldered to the rest. Square edging wire was also added to the sheet metal parts of the neckpiece to give it visual thickness and strength while keeping the weight down. The findings at the back of the neckpiece were fabricated from drawn tubing, sheet, and wire. The catch is essentially a nut and bolt concept.

10 and **11** Front and back view of the stamped plaque pendant. Behind the plaque at the base of the forged lower part of the neck element is a three-part hinge. The pin for the hinge is attached to a horseshoe-shaped fitting, which in turn is held by a rotating pin to a holed disc soldered to the plaque, an arrangement that allows movement in all directions. Once the rear catch is unscrewed, the two side parts open in opposite directions which the rotating hinge allows. The pin holding the pendant is threaded and held by a small silver nut, threaded internally. This arrangement makes it possible to disassemble the two main parts for repairs.

5–70 OPPI UNTRACHT, U.S.A. Necklace of copper, brass, and sterling silver wire formed entirely on the stamping press. Fine silver shot was used to form stamped "rivets" that clinch parts together without the need for solder. *Photo: Oppi*

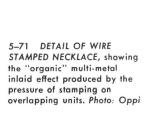

5–71 *DETAIL OF WIRE STAMPED NECKLACE,* showing the "organic" multi-metal inlaid effect produced by the pressure of stamping on overlapping units. *Photo: Oppi*

OPEN FORGING: Free use of the drop hammer

The drop hammer can be put to use without dies to create jewelry that has its own distinctive appearance. These are some observations based on experience. Dies are always used with the drop hammer. It is possible, however, to think of the drop hammer simply as a power hammer whose instantaneous pressure can form metal, as in forging. With this idea in mind, a drop hammer was used by the author to explore some of the possibilities of such an application.

In this case, both the ram head and the surface of the drop hammer bed are plain and flat, equivalent to the face of a hammer and an anvil. To allow for the control of the blow, and to limit it to a local area of the work, *blank steel blocks,* true and with smooth surfaces, in any shape —round, oval, square, oblong—and in any size, were placed on the anvil bed and the work placed on top of them. Only that particular area of the work on top of the block was exposed to being struck in any single blow. At the time of impact, there is no constraint on the metal which flows freely as it is compressed.

DROP HAMMER FORGING A WIRE OBJECT

Wire of any metal and any gauge can be used, freely combined by the techniques of weaving, braiding, twisting, lashing, knotting, plaiting, crumpling, or by other means. After shaping the wire into the form it must have it is placed on top of the selected small steel block, and the ram is dropped on it. The impact flattens the wire into a rigid structure that holds together without solder. If a unit is made that is smaller than the ram head, only one blow is necessary. If the unit is larger, as in this case, the object must be shifted, and each adjacent area flattened in turn. The wires that cross each other interpenetrate.

All such flattened wire forms have an organic look. Even a single wire appears to be varied in width because of its position and the degree of pressure it has undergone.

OTHER POSSIBLE USES OF THE DROP HAMMER

Partial flattening of the unit is possible while the rest remains as it is. For instance, a unit can be placed on a round steel block *smaller* than the unit size so that only the round area within its diameter is stamped flat.

Instant riveting is possible by placing a pellet of soft metal such as fine silver or soft brass over a crossing of wires. Under the pressure of the drop forge, such pellets are flattened and the wires they cover are pressed into them, and thus held in place. A conventional rivet with one head already formed can be placed in a hole drilled through two or more sheets, the preformed head underneath, and the end is then flattened by a blow from the drop hammer to form the other head by instant impact.

Instant inlay of wire into sheet is also possible, though

not completely reliable or predictable. A hard wire such as hardened bronze or steel can be placed on an annealed sheet of metal of a contrasting color such as silver, copper, brass, or aluminum, and stamped into it by a drop hammer. Experiments with small units may suggest combinations that can then be made in larger units. Small units can be used as pendants or earrings.

Textured surfaces can be made on sheet metal by placing any suitable material such as wire mesh, small scraps, cut lengths of wire, washers, or crumpled wire on an annealed sheet of metal. The ram is then allowed to fall on these and force an impression from them to the sheet. After the texturing material is removed, the surface can be enriched by placing more of the same on it and hammering it again.

A *duplicate* of a textured surface can be made by placing a blank sheet over the textured one, then drop hammering them together. This leaves an identical impression in reverse on the second sheet, which can then be used for objects that require duplicate surfaces, such as a pair of earrings or cuff links.

Object impressions in intaglio can be made by placing any object with a unique silhouette on a sheet of metal. Manufactured articles such as a key, hairpin, fork, comb, watch parts, springs, razor blades, or any other flat metal object can be used. A complete image (or part of one) could be incorporated in a piece of jewelry. The drop hammer is also capable of impressing an image on a sheet metal of things far more fragile, such as feathers, seeds, leaves, small branches, and other objects from nature. The effect resembles a fossil image in stone.

Ready-made, existing stamping dies can be used. Metalsmiths who use drop hammers usually possess a stock of out-of-date, abandoned dies carved with patterns no longer

in use. A search through these might uncover medallions, heraldic emblems, or organizational insignia from which stampings can be made. The results can be used in a free manner for purely decorative, possibly amusing collage effects.

Many other possibilities will suggest themselves to anyone who has the opportunity of drop hammer play.

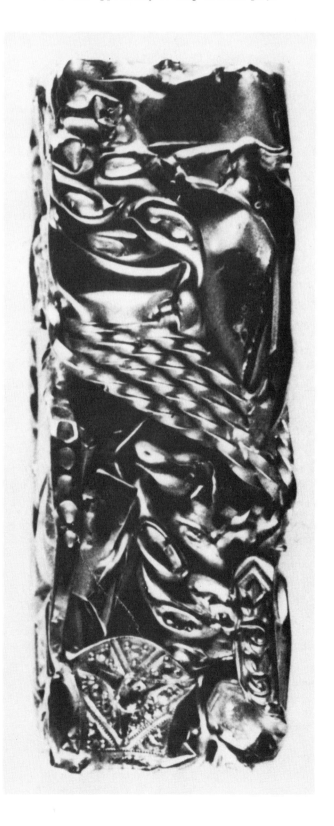

5-72 CÉSAR BALDACCINI, France. Two "compression" pendants made of discarded pieces of precious metal jewelry turned in for melting and refining. They have been crush stamped into rectangles on a drop hammer press that compresses them into an interlocked solid mass in which individual parts are still recognizable. Height 6 cm. *Photo: Courtesy Galerie Sven, Paris*

6

WIRE

The Uses of Drawn or Extruded Flexible Filaments

WIRE

Manipulating line into shape and dimension

One of the basic forms of metal available to the jeweler is wire, a form that has a great many possible applications. *Wire* can be defined as any metal uniform in cross section, in sizes that range from a fine thread to a slender rod. In industry the limits are from 0.001–1.00 in (0.025–25.4 mm) in cross section diameter. For the craftsperson, the range is more restricted, 0.005–0.324 in (36–0 gauge B.&S.; 0.13–8.23 mm), and the most commonly used gauges are 12–24 B.&S.

The ability of metal to be drawn into wire is due to its inherent *ductility*, (not to be confused with the property of *malleability*—its ability to be hammered laterally into sheet). In descending order of ductility are: gold, silver, platinum, iron, copper, aluminum, nickel, zinc, tin, and lead. In descending order of malleability are: gold, silver, aluminum, copper, tin, platinum, lead, zinc, and iron. Gold and silver are very well suited to extreme reductions and elongations because of their high ductility. One ounce of pure gold is capable of being drawn into a hair-fine filament 35 miles long.

The use of wire is believed to have begun with the application of gold wire to jewelry making and not, surprisingly, with wire of other metals for other purposes. Its earliest use is traceable to Egypt at approximately 3000 B.C., and to the Assyrians and Babylonians about 1700 B.C. Because examination shows irregularities in this wire, and no drawplates of metal or any other material have been found as yet, it is believed that the method used to make the earliest wire consisted of cutting thin, straight or spiral strips from a sheet of metal with a flint chisel, annealing and straightening them, and then exploiting the malleability of metal by edge forging or swaging the strip, followed by rolling it between two flat surfaces of stone or metal to round the wire. Wire was also made by twisting thin strips into a tight spiral or *spill*.

THE DRAWPLATE AND DRAWTONGS

Wire is now handmade by the use of a *drawplate* and *drawtongs;* semimechanically by means of a *drawbench;* or mechanically where the wire is drawn through dies auto-

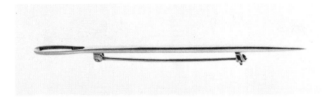

6–1 NOMA COPLEY, U.S.A. "Needle." Gold straight wire brooch. Photo: Tracy Boyd

6–2 GEORG JENSEN, Denmark, designer, 1929; manufacturer Georg Jensen Sølvsmedie A/S, Copenhagen. Square wire, round bangle bracelet, possibly the simplest wrist ornament ever made. Photo: Erik Junior, courtesy Georg Jensen Sølvsmedie A/S

6–3 ANNI and BENT KNUDSEN, Denmark. Silver wire bracelet made of one continuous wire bent into alternating loops to make a closed form. Photo: Oppi

matically. The invention of the drawplate is of utmost importance as it allowed the manufacture of almost unlimited lengths of wire from any ductile metal. Also, by altering the shape of the drawplate opening, wire having sections of different shapes could be made. It is uncertain when this tool in metal form first came into existence. Hardwood drawplates *may* have preceded those of metal but as wood is perishable, if they existed, they have disappeared. Archeologists tell us that metal drawplates were

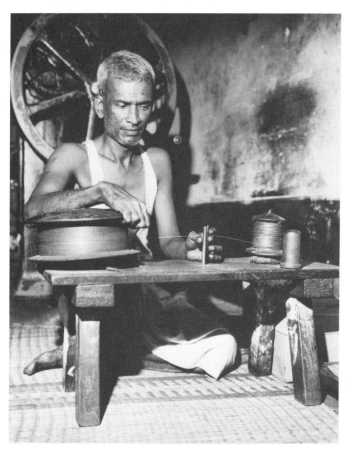

6–4 VARANASI (BANARES), INDIA. Wire drawer reducing the section of silver wire. The drawing reel has a removable and replaceable brass bushing or sleeve to resist wear and reduce friction, and is mounted on a steel axle fixed in the bench top. He turns the reel by its flanged top edge. The wire is wound on an idling reel and passes through a vertically held drawplate die made of high-carbon steel, onto the drawing reel. When a drawplate hole wears out or becomes enlarged, the drawplate is hammered on an anvil to close the hole which is then reamed to the desired size. After the entire wire length passes through, it is rewound, and reduced in the same way, each time passing through a smaller hole in the drawplate die. This ancient method of reducing the section of long lengths of wire is accomplished in the small area of a workbench. Photo: Oppi

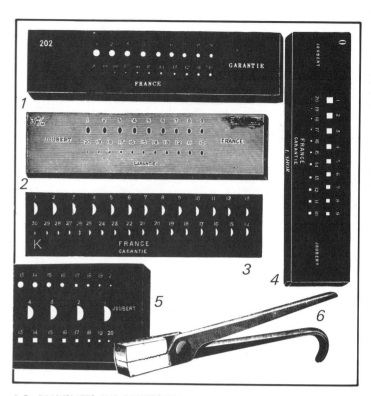

6–5 DRAWPLATES AND DRAWTONGS
Each drawplate is available in several sizes, each with a different range of hole sizes. 1. Round hole drawplate; 2. Oval hole drawplate; 3. Half-round hole drawplate; 4. Square hole drawplate; 5. Combination hole shape drawplate; 6. Hand drawtongs.

used by the Persians in the 6th century B.C., that they were used in Roman times, and first came into use in Europe in the 10th century A.D. The European drawplate is first mentioned in writing in the fascinating mid-12th century account by Theophilus (*On Divers Arts,* The University of Chicago Press, 1963, Chapter 8, p. 87). Its widespread use occurred with the development of chain mail armor in medieval times, though some of this wire was hammered out. This form of body protection demanded great amounts of iron wire, and wire drawing on a commercial scale occurred in Europe as early as the end of the 13th century.

Today wire is generally bought by many jewelers from refiners and suppliers in the form and dimension and condition (annealed or spring hardened) they wish to use. The most common cross section used in jewelry is round, but manufacturers make other shapes such as square, rectangular, triangular, oval, hexagonal, octagonal, half-round, half-oval, and flat.

6–6 UGANDA. Young Suk woman, wearing wire collar rings and earrings of brass, worn with glass bead necklaces. Photo: Musée de l'Homme, Paris

Because of expense, it is not possible for most jewelers to invest in a wire stock of all sizes and shapes, and also, some suppliers will only honor orders of relatively large amounts of any single size or shape. It is still common, therefore, for craftspersons to buy the heavier gauges of wire, 6–10 gauge B.&S., and from them make their own thinner wire by use of the drawplate. Round wire can be altered longitudinally to take on other sectional forms as for example square, triangular, and half-round by the use of drawplates having appropriately shaped openings. Drawplate manufacturers will make up drawplates with a great variety of different openings.

It is also possible to impart other shapes to wire laterally by the use of *swage dies,* as when making beaded wire, or to stamp wire with patterns. These processes are described beginning on p. 168.

Craftspersons have a habit of saving all waste or *scrap metal* by placing it in dust-free, covered boxes or containers to guard against contamination and carefully labeled to control uniformity of quality. When a sufficient amount has accumulated, this scrap can be used to make wire by melting it and pouring it into as long and thin an ingot as possible. Following the ancients, this ingot can then be forged down in a grooved *swage block* or on a *flat surface plate,* turning it constantly while it is hammered. When the now extended rod reaches an appropriate size, it can be annealed and fed through the forming grooves of a *wire rolling mill.* The smallest diameter obtainable with the rolling mill is about 0.80 in (2.03 cm). When it reaches a reduction of section suited to the openings of a *drawplate,* human strength can then pull it through to reduce it still further to finer dimensions and shapes.

wide use are listed below, and their tables can be found in Chapter 18, Standard Weights, Measures, and Tables. The lower the numerical value, the thicker the wire or metal will be, and conversely, as the number value increases, the size becomes smaller.

BROWN & SHARPE GAUGE (B.&S.); AMERICAN WIRE GAUGE (A.W.G.) This variously named system is the general wire gauge used in the U.S.A. for the measurement of wire and sheet metal in nonferrous alloys.

BRITISH (IMPERIAL) STANDARD WIRE GAUGE (S.W.G.) This is the legal standard gauge for all ferrous and nonferrous wire and sheet metal used in Great Britain and Canada. Often the word "Imperial" is omitted.

STUBBS IRON WIRE GAUGE (STUBBS) an American gauge and BIRMINGHAM WIRE GAUGE (B.W.G.) a British gauge. These two scales have the same values. In Great Britain this scale is used for measuring iron, copper, brass, and drawn steel wire, and drill rods. In the U.S.A. it is used for drill rods only.

WASHBURN AND MOEN GAUGE (W.&M.) and AMERICAN WIRE AND STEEL CO. wire gauge. Used for measuring steel and iron.

BIRMINGHAM METAL GAUGE (B.M.G.) Used in Great Britain by goldsmiths for gold, formerly for silver, also for copper, brass, and nonferrous metals. Gold and silver are now measured by the British (Imperial) Standard Wire Gauge.

WIRE GAUGES: Wire measurement

Several standardized numbering systems exist for the accurate measurement of wire diameter, and the same systems are also used to determine the thickness of sheet metal. The *wire gauge* is a device meant for taking such measurements. In its usual forms (see Measuring and Marking, Chapter 4; Illustration 4–25), it is a thick steel plate, usually round, but sometimes rectangular in shape. Along its edges are notches in graduated sizes. Each notch is stamped on one side with the appropriate common gauge number that indicates the diameter or thickness values of wire and sheet, respectively, in that particular standard measurement. On the other side it is marked with its corresponding decimal equivalent in inches or millimeters, or both. By placing the wire (or sheet) into the groove into which it fits tightly without being forced, a quite accurate measure can be taken. Greater accuracy in measurement is possible in cases where close tolerances are wanted by the use of other measuring devices, such as *micrometers* or *vernier calipers.* (See Tables, "Wire Gauge Standards, U.S.A.," p. 738; "British Standard Wire Gauge," p. 739; "Birmingham Metal Gauge," p. 739.)

Several different standardized numbering systems exist in different countries, and often more than one is in use. The specific wire gauge system used must therefore be mentioned or it will be almost impossible to understand the measurement. Some systems are designed for use when measuring particular metals. The most important ones in

6–7   L. B. SYLVAIN, France. "La Bicyclette." Gold wire brooch whose wheels revolve and handlebars turn the front wheels. This piece exemplifies the suitability of the material to the subject and the use of many lengths of wires of different gauges reassembled by soldering to create essentially flat shapes. Length 5 cm. *Photo: Richard Charpagne*

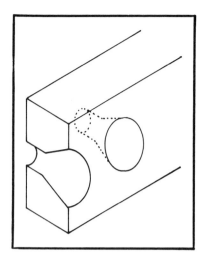

6-8 *DRAWPLATE HOLE SECTION* showing the taper.

WIRE MANUFACTURE BY HAND

WIRE DRAWING WITH THE DRAWPLATE

The *drawplate* is a single-action die usually made of a 3⁄16 in (0.47 cm) thick sheet of any of several alloyed steels or chilled iron, hardened to make the openings resistant to frictional wear. Every drawplate has a series of spaced openings or perforations normally graded in size with the largest opening on the left. On a single drawplate, these holes may be of the same shape or more than one shape may be present. Common openings are: round, square, half-round, and triangular, and a great many specially shaped openings can be provided on special order from drawplate manufacturers.

Each hole is smoothly and accurately made. Its shape must be perfect, since any irregularity in an opening is imparted to the wire drawn through it. For instance, a nick in an opening will appear on the whole wire length as a streak or ridge. It is important to maintain the drawplate by keeping it well oiled when not in use to prevent the formation of rust that might corrode and thereby distort the opening shape.

The holes taper from the back toward the front, larger at the back and smaller at the front. For a short distance between these holes, it is straight. If the taper were too great the hole edge angle would be too sharp and the metal passed through it would be stripped instead of compressed. The taper is used to facilitate the entrance and reduction of the wire which must always enter the opening through the larger end of the taper at the *back* of the drawplate. Each opening at the front face is number stamped and is visible to the drawer for reference. These are *not* gauge numbers, but simply designate hole size sequence.

The drawplate is the working member used to form, modify the shape of, and elongate wire. These changes occur while the wire is pulled through the hole, the resistance of the stationary drawplate exerting a constricting force against the wire as it passes through the hole. In the process, wire diameter or sectional area and shape decrease, and simultaneously, wire length increases. As the wire is passed through successive openings, reduction is progressive since each opening is smaller than the last.

In wire drawing, the force of compression causes the crystal orientation or metal structure to run in the direction parallel to the longitudinal axis of the wire. In contrast, when wire is forged, the compression is irregular, occurring unequally in the direction of the hammering or rolling; as a result, this kind of wire is not as structurally strong as drawn wire whose structure is uniform. Drawing compression also automatically increases the *temper* of wire, making it tougher and springier. There are circumstances in which hardened, springy wire is more desirable than annealed, soft wire, and vice versa.

LUBRICANTS FOR WIRE DRAWING: Drawing compounds

All wire should be lubricated before drawing as the lubricant, by reducing friction, considerably facilitates its passage through the drawplate. The lubricants used for wire drawing are: beeswax, paraffin, oils, fats, tallows, pulverized soap, soap and water solution, greaseless soaps, and specially prepared drawing compounds and greases.

When selecting the lubricant for wire drawing (or for other formation processes requiring a lubricant), consider what the subsequent operation will be. Ease of lubricant removal might enter the question of choice. If, for instance, soldering operations follow, soap that can be removed by brushing in a hot water rinse is preferred. Oils and greases can be removed by emulsifiers or ammonia, soap and water applied with a stiff brush, but they are harder in general to eliminate completely. Heat is used to volatilize a lubricant, but should be avoided unless the wire must in any case be annealed, because some lubricants become caked on under a high temperature and their removal then may be stubbornly resisted. (In such a situation, heat it in an acid pickle bath.) The choice of lubricant also may depend on the needs of the particular metal, or the number of drafts (passage through a drawplate) a wire will be drawn. Heavier lubricants are used for multiple drafts, light ones for limited drafts.

Be sure that the wire comes into complete contact with the lubricant *before* passing through the drawplate hole. For liquid lubricants dipping and allowing the lubricant to drain off is sufficient since adequate lubricant clings to the surface of the wire. Semisoft solids are spread over the surface with the fingers; solids are rubbed evenly over the wire surface. It is inadvisable to apply lubricants to the drawplate hole because its distribution on longer lengths of wire is uneven.

SUGGESTED LUBRICANTS FOR DIFFERENT METALS

Gold and *silver, pure:* no lubricant needed.
Gold alloys: paraffin oil plus a small amount of vaseline.
Silver alloys: liquid soap, beeswax.
Copper and *brass:* an aqueous solution, 3–5% by weight, of a good grade of soap powder or chips, kept slightly warm to prevent jelling.
Brass: A cheap lubricant and a traditional one is fermented bran liquor made of 1 lb of bran to 5 gal of water, allowed to ferment for one week, then filtered. This has a strong odor that may be objectionable to some. Brass is sometimes drawn dry with powdered soap.
Steel: a light petroleum oil; powdered soap plus lime; grease. By one method, the wire is covered with lime before drawing, then baked, and drawn with a dry soap lubricant. Fine steel wire is drawn with a soap solution.
Stainless steel and *Monel metal:* petroleum oil. If a water-based lubricant has been used, be sure to dry the drawplate thoroughly and oil it lightly before putting it away.

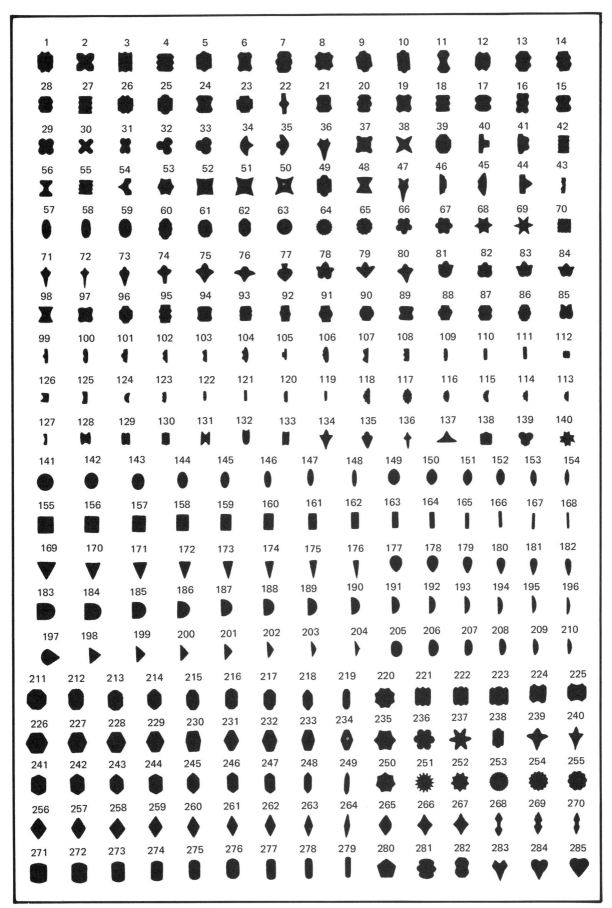

6–9 *PROFILE SHAPES OF DRAWPLATE OPENINGS* Available on special order from Karl Fischer, Pforzheim. The number is over the shape. *Courtesy Karl Fischer*

THE WIRE DRAWING PROCESS: *Manual drawing*

Before drawing, anneal the wire to put it in the maximal state of ductility. To avoid damage to the drawplate openings, the wire should be absolutely clean and free of residual firescale which can result in imperfectly drawn, scratched wire, and can reduce the life of the drawplate opening. Mount the drawplate with its *longitudinal* direction clamped *horizontally* but upright in a strong, well-anchored bench vise whose jaws or chaps are smooth faced or lined with brass sheet. This position provides the maximum support to the drawplate which is under considerable stress when drawing pressure is applied. *Never* mount a drawplate in a vise with its long axis in a *vertical* position as the pulling force may cause it to fracture. Be sure the small openings on the face side point toward you.

TAGGING A DRAWING DOG FOR GRIPPING

Tagging, the first step in drawing wire or tubing, is the forming of a tapered shape at one end by clipping, hammering, swaging, filing, or grinding that end to a gently tapered (but not *sharp*) point. This point is called a *dog,* any device used to facilitate gripping, clutching, or holding something. In this case, the *draw dog* makes it easier to draw the wire or tube through the hole in the drawplate. Pass it through the first hole that allows entry but just resists the passage of the true wire diameter. The draw dog must protrude at least ¼ in (0.63 cm) at the drawplate face, as otherwise it cannot be grasped without breaking off.

DRAWING A ROUND WIRE

Grasp the draw dog with *drawplate tongs* (also called *drawtongs* or *drawing pliers*), a tool made for the purpose of pulling wire through a drawplate. It has a blunt, squared-off nose that allows a maximum amount of wire to be gripped as close as possible to the drawplate face, and the jaws are serrated to allow them to hold the wire without slippage during the drawing pull. It has one straight and one curved handle, which permits it to be held firmly during drawing or to be attached to a drawing chain in a drawbench (see p. 155). When tension is placed on the drawtongs the jaws clamp on the wire end automatically. When starting hand drawing, draw the end through the first openings at half strength, but once the wire's true diameter is neared, exert full strength. It is desirable to avoid a jerky pull and in particular it is important to make the last draw as continuous as possible. The wire must pass *perpendicularly* through the vertical plane of the drawplate to keep it straight and round. If the wire is pulled at an angle to the drawplate, damage may occur to the wire. Repeated abuse causes the openings to wear, reducing their accuracy, and can change circles into ovals. For this reason too, the drawplate must be mounted at hand pulling level.

If the wire is heavy and a drawbench is not available, a simple system can be used to increase pulling power. Pass a rope around your hips and attach its ends to the curved drawtong handle, then pull with full body weight while holding the tong jaws closed on the wire end.

To obtain the desired size, repeat the drawing process, each time passing the wire through successively smaller openings, never skipping any, so that the size is reached by a *gradual* reduction.

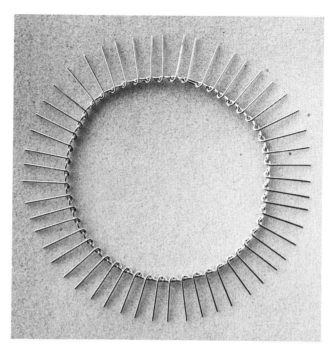

6–10 ANNI and BENT KNUDSEN, Denmark. Silver, straight wire, open-ended necklace made of individual units, each ending in a loop that engages its neighbor. *Photo: Oppi*

6–11 JESUS RAPHAEL SOTO, Italy, designer; manufacturer Gem Montebello, Milano. Red and white gold earrings of mobile straight wire held by a common bar. *Photo: Ugo Mulas*

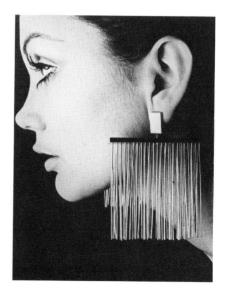

DRAWING WIRE IN SHAPES OTHER THAN ROUND

Basically the same procedure is followed when drawing oval, triangular, or square wire with a drawplate having openings so shaped. To keep the result from becoming twisted, take care to maintain the perpendicular position of the wire in relation to the drawplate. As an aid to keeping square wire straight, place two hardwood boards at the *back* of the drawplate, held in place by *C-clamps,* as close together as possible so that the opening between them just allows the wire to pass through.

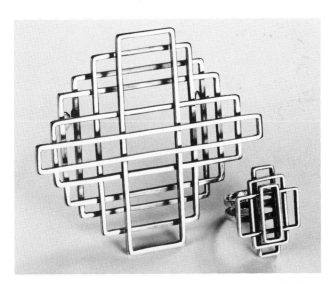

6-12 KAIJA AARIKKA, Finland, designer; manufacturer Aarikka Koru, Helsinki. Silver square wire brooch and ring made of closed form, rectangular-shaped units in graduated sizes, piled one upon the other and solder joined. *Photo: Studio Wendt, courtesy Aarikka Koru*

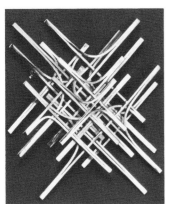

6-13 DAVID THOMAS, England. Yellow 18K gold square wire brooch combining straight and curved wire units. *Photo: Courtesy The Worshipful Company of Goldsmiths, London*

6-14 JOHN STOKES, Australia. Silver necklace made of straight sections of square wire. *Photo: Doug Munson, courtesy the Touchstone Gallery, Inc., New York*

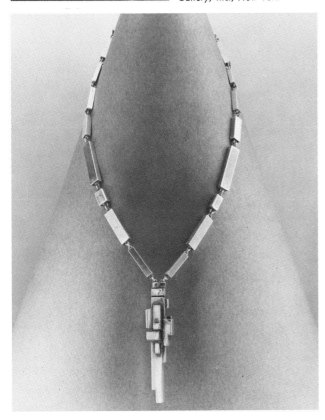

When lacking a drawplate having half-round openings, and wire of this shape is wanted, one with round openings can serve as a substitute. For this, bend the wire length in half, tag-hammer the two *free* ends, and pass them simultaneously through the drawplate opening. Once the two ends are through the drawplate, C-clamp a thin-bladed knife in place at the back and as closely as possible to the drawplate. Pass its point between the two parts of the wire. This system helps to maintain the upright direction of the division between them and the wire will emerge this way when drawn. Repeat the drafts in progressively smaller holes, shifting the knife each time, until each wire forms the half-round shape in the desired dimension. In the same way, two wires having triangular cross sections can be formed in a drawplate with square holes, though this is more difficult.

ANNEALING WIRE

When pulling wire through a drawplate die, its plastic deformation causes frictional and internal heat, and by compression the metal becomes work hardened. Some metals such as pure gold and fine silver do not work harden appreciably, and can be drawn until they reach the desired dimension. Lubrication in this case is not needed but it does make the job easier. *All alloys,* however, tend to be harder than pure metals, and become work hardened and, *in extremis,* become brittle and break. Before this happens, *anneal* the wire after a few drafts whenever it seems to be very stiff in order to restore its ductility.

To anneal wire, first shape it into as small and compact a coil as possible, tucking in the loose ends but allowing them to be visible. The coil form is used as it guards against local melting since it distributes the heat more evenly. To compact the coil, wrap it either with the end of

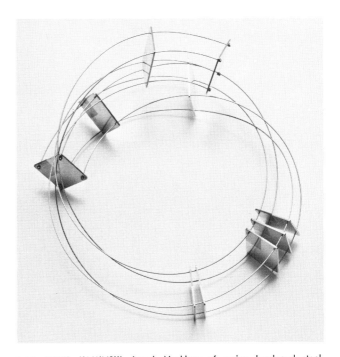

6-15 VERED KAMINSKI, Israel. Necklace of spring hardened steel wires that are spaced by passing through the four corners of silver squares with a quartered brass insert. A conventional closing device is unnecessary since the steel keeps its springlike curvature. *Photo: Courtesy Schmuck International 1900-1980, Künstlerhaus, Vienna*

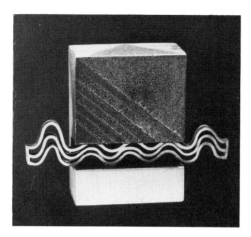

6-16 JOAQUÍN CAPDEVILA, Spain. Square silver wire brooch with wood and plastic, the wires bent into undulating curves. *Photo: Günter Meyer, courtesy Schmuckmuseum, Pforzheim*

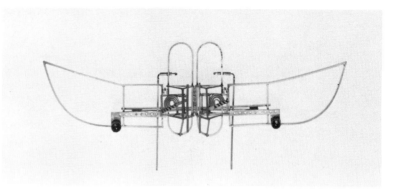

6-17 ANTON CEPKA, Czechoslovakia. Brooch with wings, made mainly of square silver wire, with two blue stones. *Photo: Courtesy Schmuck International 1900–1980, Künstlerhaus, Vienna*

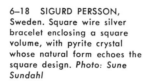

6-18 SIGURD PERSSON, Sweden. Square wire silver bracelet enclosing a square volume, with pyrite crystal whose natural form echoes the square design. *Photo: Sune Sundahl*

the same coil or with wire *of the same metal* as that being annealed. This is done so that in subsequent pickling there is no need to first remove the restraining wire (as would be necessary if iron wire, for instance, were used to bind the coil).

Most metals achieve a satisfactory anneal at a temperature well below the transformation range, and a full anneal is not necessary for drawing. Of greater importance is *uniformity of degree of anneal* which leaves all the wire in the coil in the same degree of softness. Wire that is unevenly annealed and has harder and softer sections may break when drawing due to the uneven pull such wire needs. Attainment of annealing temperature is indicated by the fusion of a flux coating into which the whole coil is dipped prior to annealing. Place the coil on an *iron wire mesh* to allow the heat to envelop it completely. Pass a large, soft, reducing flame over it evenly. Watch the wire ends. They show redness before the surface does and this is another way of judging anneal completion. Wire coils can also be annealed in a furnace or kiln which has the advantage of equalized heat. Interior temperature can be controlled by observing the thermocouple dial.

Quench the wire in water or pickle to remove fused flux and firescale if any, rinse, and dry. Remove the restraining wire, and continue to draw until the wire again starts to work harden. The more drastic the wire diameter reduction, the more frequently annealing is necessary. The need for annealing must be judged by the wire condition. Ordinarily, alloys can be drafted through at least four holes before annealing becomes necessary.

STRAIGHTENING WIRE AFTER DRAWING

Even with proper precautions such as a straight pull, finished hand-drawn wire tends to curve. To straighten a long length, anneal it if necessary, place one end in a *bench vise*, hold the other end with the *drawtongs* or *heavy pliers*, and gently pull the wire taut several times. To straighten it further, pass the wire over the edge of a bench pin in the direction opposite to the curve.

6-19 PAULA HÄIVÄOJA, Finland, designer; manufacturer Kalevala Koru, Helsinki. Gold ring of round wire and strip, all parts butt joined. The single outer cube form is internally divided. *Photo: Studio Wendt, courtesy Kalevala Koru*

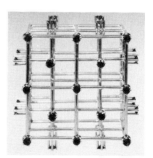

6-20 WERNER BÜNCK, West Germany. Round wire white gold brooch with rubies, basically a cube divided internally into square unit modules, the wires lap and butt soldered. Size 32 × 32 × 32 mm. *Photo: Werner Bünck*

6–21 HELGA and BENT EXNER, Denmark. White 18K gold ring with hematite stone squares. At crossings, the wires are flattened and pierced to give the round wire sufficient surface to pass through. The wire ends act as pegs that fit the stones' holes, and the stones are cemented on them. *Photo: Svend Thomson*

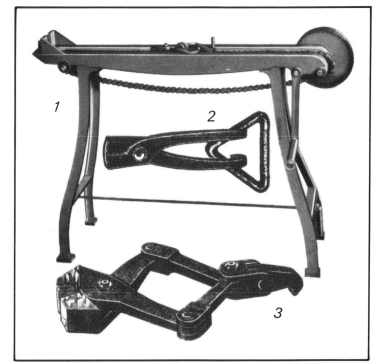

6–23 DRAWBENCH AND DRAWTONGS
1. *Drawbench with hand drive, continuous chain system, fitted with an interior geared wheel that allows two speeds for light and heavy draws. The handle is moved to another pivot for direct drive.*
2. *Drawbench tongs with two curved handles, fitted with a hook to engage the chain.*
3. *Drawbench tongs 30 cm long, with articulated handles that cause the jaws to automatically close on the wire when drawing commences. (Joliot)*

6–22 KULTAKESKUS OY, Hämeenlinna, Finland. Drawplate clamped on a drawbench while the wire is being guided through it by hand. It can also be fed from the reel if the quantity is sufficient to warrant its spooling. *Photo: Oppi*

THE WIRE DRAWBENCH: A semimechanical method

When wire is drawn manually, usually relatively short lengths are processed. The longer or thicker the wire is, the less convenient or more difficult it is to draw manually.

For such occasions, some shops are equipped with a powerful *manual wire drawbench* by which *great and continuous* force can be brought to bear on the wire. It is also possible to use the drawbench to draw wires of irregular cross section, such as contoured moldings, by passing the wire through a *drawswage* of the desired contour instead of a drawplate. (See ahead.)

Drawbenches vary in design, but a typical one might be about 5 ft (1.5 m) long and would consist of a rectangular, rigid frame, usually of wood, mounted on legs that are firmly fastened to the floor. At one end is a fixed cleat arrangement against which the drawplate (or swage block) presses while under the pressure of the pull, or there may be a clamp that holds the drawplate perpendicular to the direction of drawing. At the other end there is a winch with a long, strong, metal handle(s). In arrangements that use an endless-chain table, which allows drawing unlimited lengths by moving the clamp forward on the wire once it has reached drawbench length, the

winch has a toothed gear that engages the openings of the cable that passes over it. The wire clamping device is attached to the cable and its jaws are tightened on the wire by a butterfly nut. In some cases one uses *drawtongs* having two curved handles that are formed into a hook which engages a heavy ring or stirrup attached to the cable. Once the wire is passed through the drawplate (or swage block) and its end placed in the clamp or drawtongs, the winch crank handles are turned, placing tension on the cable and wire which is then steadily drawn, and wound around an uptake reel. The wire is released to pass it through the next smaller opening, then again engaged in the clamp or drawtongs, and the same procedure follows until the desired dimension is reached. Heavy wires require the exertion of considerable force on the handles.

DRAWING GOLD-PLATED SILVER WIRE

Silver wire can be gold plated and drawn to very fine dimensions, a process long practiced in India. This is possible because the two metals, gold and silver, have a compatible degree of ductility. No matter how finely the wire is drawn, it remains coated with the gold. In India this process was used for making gold-plated silver wire the thickness of a thread, which was used in weaving brocaded textiles and in embroidery. Today electroplated gold on silver wire is used. The coating of gold on the silver in the hand process is thicker and more permanent than electroplated gold. There are many uses for such wire as for instance in interworked wire processes where the wire is not subjected to heat.

The silver bar or heavy wire must be *absolutely clean.*

Roughen its surface by filing it with a coarse file to raise a surface burr. Use gold leaf of sufficient thinness to be flexible, *not* rigid gold foil. Cut the *pure gold leaf* so that its width is equal to the circumference of the silver bar. Wet the gold leaf with a thin flux to cause the gold leaf to cling to it, but do not flood it. Roll the bar over the gold leaf on a flat surface. Do not cover the bar ends but allow the silver to be exposed. The gold leaf should make a single layer on the silver bar and weigh 2–3% of the silver bar weight. With a polished *planishing hammer,* beat the whole bar surface to make the adhesion of the two metals complete.

Heat the bar to redness in a furnace or kiln (or with the reducing flame of a torch). Remove the bar with *tongs,* allow it to cool, then place it in cold water to cool it completely. Rub the whole surface with a *burnisher* to smooth down the gold and eliminate air pockets. Inspect the bar for bare places. If these exist, they must be repaired by adding more gold leaf in the same way. Return the bar to the kiln, heat it again, and reburnish it. The gold should now cover the surface with a uniform thickness and appear smooth. If you wish a thicker gold plating, apply a second layer of gold leaf in the same way.

Lubricate the bar with beeswax and roll it through the wire rolling mill. When its dimension is sufficiently reduced, form a draw dog on the plain silver end and draw it through the drawplate. Once the drawing is established, clip off the plain silver end and form a new draw dog. Continue drawing until the desired dimension is reached. In the entire drawing process, the gold remains on the surface of the silver core, forming a durable plating.

INDUSTRIAL WIRE DRAWING

In industry, wire is made by *continuous drawing* in very long lengths on a mass scale of manufacture. To form the wire section shape, diamond, corundum, or other very hard stone (or tungsten carbide) is drilled to the required shape and mounted in the *die block* which has a round disc shape. Diamond dies are preferred for making very fine wire, and chromium steel or tungsten carbide is used for drawing dies having special shapes.

Cold drawing is done on a *wire drawing frame* consisting of a bench mounted with several *drawing blocks,* cylinders or drums which rotate and pull the wire through the drawplate while winding it upon itself in a coiling motion. Before passing through the die, the wire goes through a trough containing a lubricant. Wire drawing machines develop a drawing force of from 1 kilonewton to 2.5 meganewtons (100 kilograms-force to 250 tons-force).

PROFILED WIRE MADE WITH A DRAWSWAGE

Narrow, flat strip wire or moldings of any desired length, but without undercuts, can be drawn by hand through a *drawswage.* This is a specially constructed *profile die,* generally not available ready-made, but which can be made by hand. The working die parts resemble a pair of swage blocks, but are used like a drawplate, hence the name of this tool. By using different pairs of die shapes—which are removable—profiled, contoured moldings of various cross sections can be achieved.

The *profiled wire drawswage* is an assembly of several parts, as seen in the diagram. It consists of an outer frame

which is rigid and strong, made from a solid, rectangular block of tool steel. The dies fit into the opening and are held in place during drawing, in this design by the taper of the sides of the opening which the dies match. (In another drawswage design, the inner frame opening is squared and contains side channels into which projecting flanges on the die sides fit, the top of the frame being removable). Normally, *two-part dies* are used, one above the other, with the open profile space between them. To bring pressure on these dies from above, one or two large (but not too long) screws with perforated heads—through which a steel rod is placed to facilitate turning by increasing leverage—are wound downward to press the dies tightly together, by stages, as necessary.

The opening between the two die parts forms the profile shape of the strip. This opening can be shaped to any profile by the maker, using files, chisels, and gravers. The die's working surface must be highly polished to aid in drawing. In one possible arrangement (see in the drawing), only the upper die is shaped, and the lower die is left flat. Strip drawn through such an arrangement emerges with a profiled upper surface and a flat back. In a second type, also illustrated, both obverse and reverse are shaped, either with matching, parallel profiles a specific distance apart according to the desired resulting thickness, or with different upper and lower profiles. The upper die forms the obverse, and the lower the reverse of the result. When preparing such dies, the appearance of the section as a positive form can be tested by hand pressing the pair of dies over a strip of wax which then takes on the form of the die opening. Alterations can be made accordingly.

Unlike in an ordinary drawplate, where the opening tapers toward the front only, these dies must be left to their *exact dimensions at the center,* and taper toward both front and back. The opening must be free of any sharp edges which would scar the metal passing through them. When the dies are finished, they are hardened and tempered in the same way as is done with tools.

THE PROFILE WIRE DRAWING PROCESS

Insert the die parts in the drawswage frame, with one end of the annealed, dried, and lubricated metal strip be-

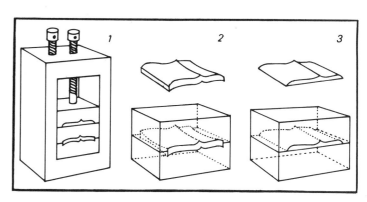

6-24 PROFILED WIRE DRAWSWAGE BLOCK AND DIES
1. The *drawswage die block holder* containing three die shapes, shown enlarged at the right. The block is threaded at the top to hold two tightening screws whose heads are pierced with holes for the insertion of a separate tightening rod.
2. A *pair of drawswage dies,* shaped with an upper and lower form to profile both surfaces of the wire drawn through them. The resulting shape is seen above.
3. A *pair of drawswage dies,* with the upper one shaped and the lower one flat, used to make profiled wire with only one surface shaped. The resulting shape is seen above.

6–25 BARBARA CARTLIDGE, England. Silver and 18K gold pendant on chain. The door, which opens on hinges, is a feminine symbol, implying an entrance, accessible by a golden knob. It opens to reveal an interior. The doorframe resembles profiled wire, but is made by combining wires of various cross sections. *Photo: Cyril Wilson, courtesy Electrum Gallery, London*

6–26 BARBARA CARTLIDGE, England. "The Bedroom." Silver and gold pendant, with furnishings made of sheet metal and wire. The room with its commonplace accoutrements and the occupant's possessions symbolize comfort. Size 3.25 × 2 in. *Photo: Günter Meyer, courtesy Schmuckmuseum, Pforzheim*

tween them, projecting about a half an inch to allow it to be grasped by *drawtongs*. Secure the whole assembly upright in a *bench vise*. Because the strip is not yet shaped, there will be a space between the two die parts. This space will gradually be made smaller between drafts until the dies come together and the strip achieves its true dimension.

Clamp the drawtongs on the strip end, and with a continuous pull, draw the strip through the dies just short of the end. Loosen the frame screws, remove the strip, and replace it with the original end projecting as before. Take care to replace it *exactly* in position or the drawing will be inaccurate. Tighten the screws gently to take up any slack between subsequent drafts. Continue drawing until the strip takes on the true section of the die openings. If the strip becomes work hardened after the first few drafts, it must be annealed, pickled, dried, lubricated, and replaced in the drawswage.

CUTTING WIRE

Cold chisels are used to cut through thin-gauge wire of regular cross section by placing the wire on a soft brass sheet and pressing or hammering the chisel downward. Since the brass is softer than the chisel the cutting edge will not be dulled. The end of the resulting cut may not be perfectly square—if it must be perfect, allow a little extra brass and trim it with a *flat file*.

Nippers are a form of pliers. The word *nip* comes from the Danish *nippe*, "to pinch," which is what they do when severing wire. Nippers are made having *side, end,* or *diagonal,* sharp, beveled cutting jaws. Because they are strong, nippers can be used to cut wire of considerable thickness.

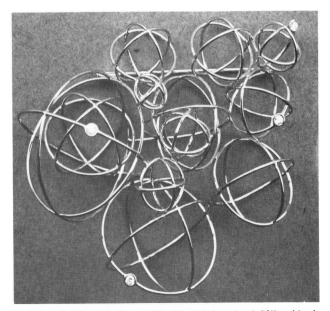

6–27 L. B. SYLVAIN, France. "Continent." Brooch of 18K gold wire and brilliant-cut diamonds. Curved round wires are used to define a cluster of 11 airy, almost weightless volumes asymmetrically arranged. *Photo: Oppi*

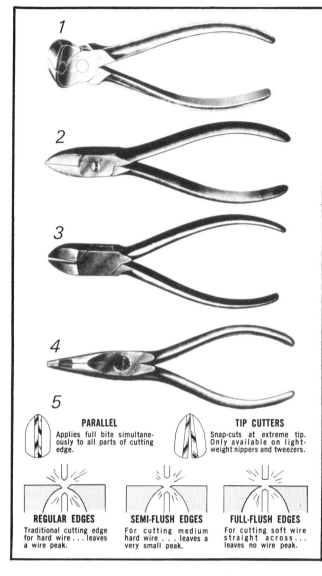

5

PARALLEL
Applies full bite simultaneously to all parts of cutting edge.

TIP CUTTERS
Snap-cuts at extreme tip. Only available on light-weight nippers and tweezers.

REGULAR EDGES
Traditional cutting edge for hard wire . . . leaves a wire peak.

SEMI-FLUSH EDGES
For cutting medium hard wire . . . leaves a very small peak.

FULL-FLUSH EDGES
For cutting soft wire straight across . . . leaves no wire peak.

Hand shears can be used to cut wire of larger diameter. *Heavy-duty hand shears* can have their lower grip clamped in a bench vise while cutting to allow increased leverage. *Heavy-duty bench shears* have a rigid lower blade, and a movable upper blade which contains a hole of from ⅜–½ in diameter. Rods up to these diameters are placed within the hole, and the upper blade is then brought down toward the lower blade to sever the rod.

Sprue cutters are a form of heavy-duty shears that are capable of cutting round sprues up to 8 gauge B.&S. in diameter.

The *jeweler's saw frame and blade* can be used to sever wire when an accurate cut must be made. Use a fine saw blade that puts more than two teeth in contact with the metal at all times. Hold the wire down on a bench pin, draw the blade gently downward to form a starting groove, then cut through slowly, keeping the blade perpendicular to the wire's length to make a clean cut.

USING WIRE WITHOUT CHANGING ITS SECTIONAL SHAPE: Shaping and bending

Wire can be shaped and bent with the fingers if the shape is not too complex nor the radius of the curve too small, and if the wire is not too heavy. Otherwise, tools must be used to bend wire without changing its sectional shape.

PLIERS

Probably the most common tool used to shape wire, ribbon, and strip is the pliers. The word relates to Old French *plier*, "to fold." The earliest ancestor of pliers is the pincers or tongs used by blacksmiths. Pliers are a developed form of pincers. Today they are made of cast or

6–28 NIPPERS
These tools are generally made with box joints or lap joints.
1. *End-cutting nippers*, for cutting wire not reachable by other shaped nipper blades.
2. *Side-cutting nippers*, for easy access to restricted places.
3. *Diagonal-cutting nippers*, the traditional wire cutter for all normal wire-cutting operations, used close to the tip.
4. *Snipe-nosed pliers* with a side cutter.
5. The *regular, semi-flush*, or *full-flush shape* of the cutting edges of nippers determines the appearance of the cut wire ends. Different wire hardness requires different types of nipper cutting edges. Hard wires are best cut with regular-edged nippers.

6–29 BOB JEFFERSON, U.S.A. Copper, sterling silver, gold, and ivory belt buckle. Square wire is shaped to outline solid flat sheet metal forms planished for surface pattern. Size 3 × 8 in. Photo: Frank J. Thomas, courtesy Fine Arts Gallery, California State University, Los Angeles

6–30 SIGURD PERSSON, Sweden. Round gold wire necklace. The shaped wire of the clustered unit encloses volumes inspired by transparent bubble formations. *Photo: Sune Sundahl*

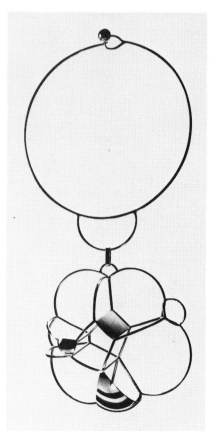

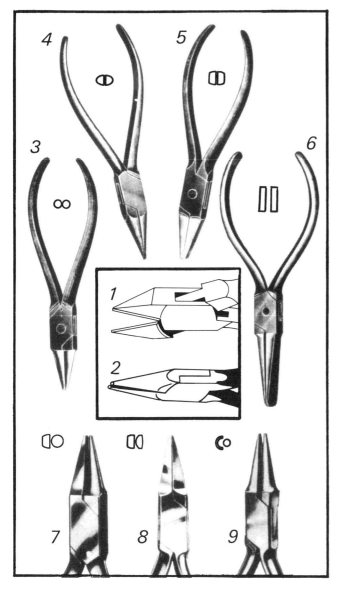

6–31 *PLIER CONSTRUCTION TYPES AND SHAPES*
1. *Box joint* constructed pliers retain their alignment and do not develop looseness.
2. *Lap joint* construction with a rivet is generally used in larger pliers and nippers to bring the fulcrum nearer to the jaws for greater leverage.
3. *Round-nosed pliers.*
4. *Snipe- or chain-nosed pliers.*
5. *Flat-nosed pliers.*
6. *Duckbill-nosed pliers.*
7. *Flat- and round-nosed pliers.*
8. *Flat- and half-round-nosed pliers.*
9. *Round and hollow chop pliers.*

drop forged steel, hardened and tempered, and available plain and polished, or nickel plated. Pliers and pincers are used for any task requiring the act of pinching, which involves squeezing, compressing, seizing, or gripping actions. (The word *pinch* comes from the French *pincer,* "to pinch," and from it we get the related word *pincers,* an instrument with two handles that, like pliers, work on a pivot, and have jaws or chops shaped for performing the actions mentioned.)

The *principle of the lever* lies behind the operation of pincers, pliers, and nippers as well as other tools such as tweezers, snips, hand shears, bench shears, tongs, forceps, and sprue cutters. In its simplest form, a lever is any rigid object such as a stick or bar of metal that can be turned around one point called the *axis* or *fulcrum.* By applying force to one end, the other exerts a force in the opposite direction against the resisting fulcrum. A simple example of the lever principle at work is a stick (the lever) placed over one rock (the fulcrum) to move a second rock (the object of resisting force) by placing the stick end under the second rock. The force brought to bear on the lever end by pressure against the fulcrum gains great *mechanical* advantage in transmittal, thus multiplying *human* strength.

Pliers (and the tools mentioned above) may be described as double-levered instruments, whose two handles or levers are joined and rotate around a common fulcrum —the hinge joint, which allows both levers to pivot in opposing directions. By bringing the handles toward each other, both lever ends (now called *jaws* or *chops*) simultaneously close on whatever is placed between them—the object or resisting force. The force transmitted to the object held is considerable.

Plier handles are generally curved to have a certain springiness which helps them to exert maximal force. Some pliers have a built-in *return* spring that keeps the jaws apart when the pliers are not in use. Handles are sometimes provided with plastic-covered grips which aid in holding them securely. Plastic grips can also be bought separately, placed in boiling water until soft, then forced over the plier handle and allowed to cool and harden. Such handle castings allow the pliers to be fitted with *double-leaf springs* which can be inserted, but are not attached to the handles and are therefore removable.

PLIER JOINT CONSTRUCTION

Three basic kinds of construction are used at the fulcrum hinge. They are the *lap joint,* the *box joint,* and *parallel-action jaws.*

Lap joints (also called cross lap joints), are used when the fulcrum should be near the jaw to provide greater leverage. They are held together by rivets and are the least expensive type. *Box joints* are stronger, retain their alignment relationship even under great strain, the jaws open and close smoothly, and they never develop looseness even after considerable use. They only open a predetermined distance, however, while lap joints allow a greater opening. Both lap and box joint plier jaws form a *tapered* jaw opening when in use. *Parallel-action jaws* are designed with a compound lever system that when open allows the jaw throat and jaws to stay in a *parallel* relationship to each other for their entire length. This condition is useful when the pressure must be exerted with exactly opposing force to hold an object without slippage, as when holding a flat object, or when pulling on an object. Plumbers sometimes use pliers having a *slip rivet joint* that allows the jaws to be opened wider than normally. These are sometimes used in jewelry making.

JAW CONDITION, SIZE, AND SHAPE

The condition, size, and outer and inner shape of plier jaws are designed according to the type of work that will be demanded of them. Regardless of size and shape, the jaws may be *smoothly polished* or *serrated* (also called rough) so that they have a milled, filelike surface that, though it provides a good grip, can also mar the surface of articles grasped. The choice of whether to use smooth or serrated pliers is often faced in jewelry making. If you cannot afford two sets of pliers in the most common shapes, get the serrated ones. If necessary, serrated jaws can be temporarily covered with glued-on strips of leather so that they will not mar the work, but under no circumstances should the inner surfaces be altered by filing, since removing metal inside the jaws will diminish the accuracy of their position in relation to each other.

The size or length of plier jaws is usually in proportion to the total length of the tool. If the jaw length is longer than normal, it is termed *long nosed,* and they provide extra reach. *Bent-nosed* pliers are those whose jaws take a change of direction at an angle to the normal axis.

A great variety of jaw shapes are available, some designed for basic uses in situations that occur commonly in jewelry making. Others have very specific, specialized uses. Several special-use pliers used by dentists have been adopted for use by jewelers. Almost all basic, and many special-function pliers have *tapered* jaw noses.

BASIC PLIER JAW SHAPES

Round nose: Both jaws are completely round; used for making curved bends on wire and strip, and for making loops and coils.

Chain nose or *snipe nose:* Inside jaws are flat, outside shape of both jaws form a circle or oval when closed, and are tapered to a point; used for forming loops (by grasping the wire end within the jaws, then wrapping the wire around the *outer* nose shape) and to make small-radius curves.

Half-round nose: One jaw is half-round, the other, flat; used to make curved bends.

Flat nose: Both jaws are flat; used to make angular bends, and for pulling motions.

Flat-round nose: One jaw is flat, the other is round; used in appropriate situations.

Duckbill nose: Both jaws are broad and flat; used for gripping ribbon, strip, wire, and sheet.

Hollow chop: The term *chop* or *chap* means a hollow, movable jaw, and chops are two jaws with a space between them. In *hollow-chops* or *hollow-chaps* pliers, one jaw is concave and the other is convex, or both are concave; used for grasping wire or rod endwise without marring the metal.

Round and hollow chop: One jaw is round, the other concave; used to grasp objects having a narrow-curved sectional shape.

Pliers made for specific, specialized functions have functional rather than shape names. A great variety of these exist. Some of the more common ones are as follows:

Rivet-setting: Used for setting wire rivets on findings.

Ring-holding: Have large, circular, hollow jaws; used to hold round ring shanks and other round forms when filing and polishing.

Prong-setting or *stone-setting:* Used to force prongs against a stone being set in a prong setting.

Bow-opening: Have outer ridges in both nose parts; used to open rings and links, and to form closed links.

Loop-closing: Have hollowed jaws; used for grasping and closing small loops, jump rings, and links without marring or twisting them.

Combination: Pliers designed to serve more than one distinct function, such as one with a conventional nose shape, also having a side cutter or nipper.

JAW AND PLIER LENGTHS

The common pliers are available with jaws in different lengths, and with jaws that are smooth or serrated. A variety of overall lengths is also available. Some typical dimensions are *jaws:* ¾ in, 1 in, 1¼ in, 2 in, 2½ in; overall lengths: 4 in, 4½ in, 5 in, 5¼ in, 6 in.

Consult suppliers' catalogs.

BENDING BLOCKS

When finger pressure is insufficient, wire can be bent with the help of a *bending block.* This is an improvised hardwood block containing a straight or curved groove. The wire is placed within the groove and pressure is exerted simultaneously on both sides of the wire to form the bend. If the radius of the curve is small, a narrow block is used, and if the radius is great, a wider block is used. The groove can be made to curve somewhat. After the first bend, the wire can be shifted in the groove to continue the curve.

MANDRELS

Metal *mandrels* are manufactured for the purpose of bending. Usually these are tapered, and in section may be round or oval. Any *cylindrical bar, heavy tube,* or *pipe* can be used as a form upon which wire is bent. Bending can be manual or the wire can be tapped around the mandrel with a wooden mallet. It is also possible to place the wire across a groove in a wood block, swage block, or design block, put the mandrel on top of it, and hammer the mandrel to force the wire into the groove shape. This can also be done with wire strip. Some blocks have a hole into which wire can be inserted endwise, then bent manually or with a mallet to form an angle bend.

Wrapping wire around a mandrel to make links is described under Chain Mail, Chapter 6. To make a *single loop* from heavy wire, wrap the wire once around a mandrel whose diameter corresponds with the inside diameter of the desired loop. Allow the ends to pass each other side by side. Remove the loop, place it flat on a bench pin, and with a jeweler's saw and blade, cut straight through both wires. To close the ends, before soldering, use *two pliers* in the manner described under Chain Mail, Chapter 6.

6–32 *PLIERS NOSE SHAPES*
1. *Round nose;* 2. *Chain nose;* 3. *Flat nose;* 4. *Half-round nose;* 5. *Half-round and concave half-round nose;* 6. *Round and flat nose;* 7. *Round and concave half-round nose;* 8. *Round and hollow-chop nose;* 9. *Half-round and hollow-chop nose.*

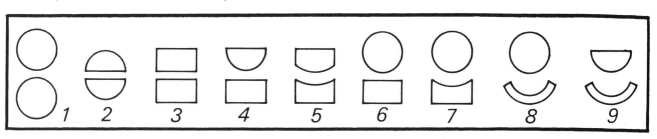

SPIRAL MAKING

Spirals and coils (a form of spiral), both widely used in jewelry, are basic forms that can be made with wire. Wherever a form has a radical force and outward growth, or continuous movement combined with a movement of rotation, the result is a *spiral*. The spiral form is found in an infinity of objects in nature, from microscopic marine shells to celestial galaxies. Spirals are seen in the way seeds form on plants, in tendrils, flower petals, pine cones, the pattern of leaf growth, hair, some feathers, and spider webs. The representation of these natural forces has always been attributed with mystic significance, and has fascinated creators in the arts. Some of the earliest metal jewelry was made of wire shaped into spiral forms.

Symbolically, the spiral represents the concept of growth, expansion, and cosmic forces in nature. It is also used to symbolize the relation between a circle and its center; to emphasize the potential center, the curve either emanating from or returning to that center which in some cultures is thought of as a hole through which man escapes the material world to the world beyond. Spirals also symbolize all cyclic phenomena.

rapidly; they can also be formed eccentrically, as in spiral ovals. The simplest spiral, discussed by Archimedes in his 3rd-century B.C. book *On Spirals,* is called *spiral of Archimedes.* It is also called the *arithmetic spiral* because with each revolution, the distance from the point of origin increases arithmetically. This type is known to the jeweler in the form of a wire that moves outward from the center in a *tightly closed development,* each turn continuing to touch the previous one, with no space between them. It can also be made with an *equal space* between each spiral revolution.

The spiral called *equiangular* has an *open development* that in its most regular form follows a regular geometric progression. Such a spiral is seen in the cross section of the chambered nautilus shell where the curve cuts the radius vector at an angle of 85°. All its radii are cut at the same angle, for which reason it is called an *equiangular spiral.* The larger the angle, the tighter the spiral; conversely, the smaller the angle, the more open it becomes, expanding rapidly with each rotation of the figure.

A *double flat spiral* is one that has changed direction from its progression outward to an inward or reversed direction, forming a *duplicate* of itself while returning to a second central point.

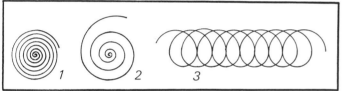

6–33 *SPIRAL TYPES*
1. The *flat plane,* closed-development Spiral of Archimedes.
2. *Equiangular,* open-development spiral.
3. *Cylindrical* helix spiral.

6–34 LIISA VITALI, Finland, designer; manufacturer Kultakeskus Oy, Hämeenlinna. The design utilizes basic spiral types, with a helix spiral used for the ring shank, and flat spirals for ornaments. *Photo: Courtesy Kultakeskus Oy*

6–35 MAX FRÖHLICH, Switzerland. Pendant in flat spiral form, and bracelet in helix spiral form made of red and green plastic-coated electrical wire. The plastic is welded together at the back by using an electrically heated soft soldering iron. *Photo: Walter Kern, courtesy Museum Bellerive, Zürich*

TYPES OF SPIRALS

FLAT PLANE SPIRAL

A spiral developed to the right or left in a flat plane can be described as a two-dimensional figure that is produced by a rotating, infinitely expanding movement (or the opposite way, by a contracting movement to a central point). It winds in a continuously growing curve around a central point, moving with each axial turn further away from that center (or toward it). Spirals can be *tight* or *open,* changing slightly in radius vector, or changing

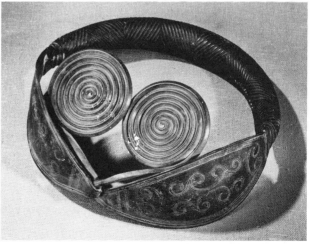

6–36 SWEDEN. Bronze Age. Sheet metal necklace ornamented with two square wire flat spirals that form the closing. Found in Halland, Sweden. *Photo: Antikvarisk-Topografiska Arkivet, Stockholm; National Museum of Antiquities, Stockholm*

6–37 LIISA VITALI, Finland, designer; manufacturer Kultakeskus Oy, Hämeenlinna. Silver flat wire flat spiral ring. Photo: Courtesy Kultakeskus Oy

CONE SPIRAL

Other spirals develop on more than one plane, and are therefore three-dimensional. If any of the flat plane spirals grow *in depth* from the central point outward, the result is a *cone,* which when seen directly from above looks exactly like the spiral developed on a flat plane.

HELIX SPIRAL

The spiral called a *helix* moves endlessly in uniform curves of *constant diameters* throughout its length in one direction. Such is the case of wire made to form a *cylindrical coil.* The same helical motion occurs when a screw thread is being cut by hand by means of a screw plate, taps and dies, or on a lathe by simultaneous rotary and endwise motion, at a constant rate. If this spiral proceeds in a circle, and rejoins itself, it is called a *spherical spiral* or *coil.*

6–38 NORTH CENTRAL SUMATRA, INDONESIA. Karo woman, Batak tribe, northwest uplands north of Lake Toba, wearing two *padoeng-padoeng,* traditional heavy earrings made of solid silver flat spirals. The left is worn pointing forward, and the right backward. Because of their weight, they are supported by the head shawl. The wire is made by drawing it through a drawplate. In some cases, a small, grooved part is removable to make an opening, and can be returned to lock the earring in place, but most such earrings are permanently placed, and the woman must lie near the anvil while the second spiral is formed. Photo: Archives of the Koninklijk Instituut voor de Tropen, Amsterdam

6–39 IRAN, TURKOMAN. Pair of silver earrings, using flat spirals, wrapped and twisted wire, and stamped forms. Photo: Oppi

6–40 RATANAKIRI, KAMPUCHEA. Woman wearing a helix spiral form, tapered cylinder wrist bracelet of copper wire. Photo: J. Matras, Musée de l'Homme, Paris

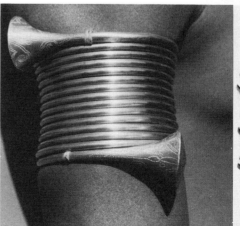

6–41 NORTH EAST FRONTIER AGENCY, INDIA. Traditional Naga man's ornament. Brass wire helix spiral form upper arm bracelet ornamented with terminating finials. Photo: P. N. Mago

6–42 GERMUND PAAER, Finland, designer; manufacturer Kalevala Koru, Helsinki. Brass helix spiral form upper arm sheet metal bracelet ornamented with twisted wire flat spirals, based on an old Finnish snake motif. Photo: Otso Pietinen

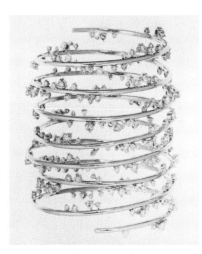

6–43 CHAN MING SANG, Hong Kong, designer; manufacturer New Universal Jewellery Co., Hong Kong. White gold wire helix spiral bracelet mounted edgewise with 285 diamonds of different sizes. *Photo: Courtesy Diamond Importers Association of Hong Kong*

6–44 ANNI and BENT KNUDSEN, Denmark. Silver triangular-shaped spherical helix spiral armband, reinforced and rigidized by an inside soldered wire which also renders its spacing permanent. *Photo: Jesper Høm*

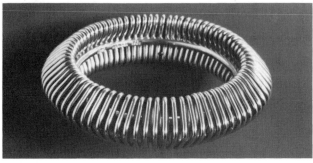

SPIRAL MAKING PROCESSES

FORMING FLAT PLANE SPIRALS FROM WIRE

To form thin-gauge wire into a spiral, anneal the wire to make it flexible and better able to retain a curved shape. In some cases the very end of the wire is tapered with a file to a point to start the spiral very small. Grasp the very end of the wire with the jaws of *round-nosed pliers* and wind the first turn around one of the jaw noses, forming a small-radius circle. If the circle is not small enough, use *flat-nosed pliers* to reduce the diameter by bringing pressure on its outer shape. If it is not absolutely round (which it must be to form a round spiral), gently shape it with pointed *snipe-nosed pliers*.

Insert this first completely circular turn in the smooth jaws of *flat-* or *square-nosed pliers* held in the left hand with the spiral pointing to the right in a clockwise direction. Continue to form the spiral by half turns with the right hand, each time winding it tightly against the preceding circle. Shift the position of the growing spiral 90–180° with each turn, and continue wrapping until the desired spiral diameter is reached. As the spiral size increases, insert it more deeply in the plier jaws. Do not exert excessive grasping pressure as this will mark the surface. *Parallel-jawed pliers* are good for this function.

To coil medium-gauge wire, which is more difficult to shape into small-diameter circles, the start must be fixed in place. With *flat pliers*, bend the first quarter inch at a right angle to the rest of the wire, and hammer the bend flat. Place the bent and flattened end *alongside* a small-diameter, stiff metal rod clamped in an upright position in the jaws of a *bench vise* so that the wire and the rod are both fixed in place. Wind the wire once tightly around the rod to form the first, innermost spiral coil, and if you

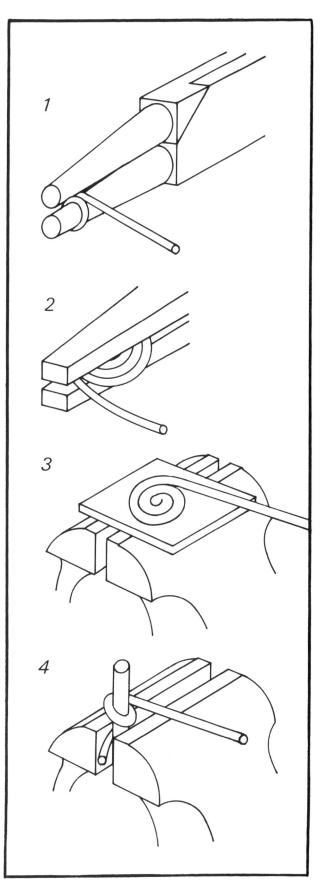

6–45 SHAPING SPIRALS FROM WIRE
1. With *round-nosed pliers.*
2. With *flat-nosed pliers.*
3. With a *flat plate* having a central hole, and the wire through it, anchored in a vise.
4. Forming a helix spiral around an *upright mandrel* anchored in a vise.

wish, make a second coil. Remove the wire and mandrel from the vise and cut off the perpendicular start. Place the spiral in the smooth jaws of larger *flat-nosed pliers* and continue building the spiral as described above.

To form a spiral with heavy-gauge wire, begin as above but do not remove the bent start end. Instead, pass it through a hole drilled through a flat sheet of metal resting on the chops of a bench vise, and clamp the wire start end in the vise so that the first coil rests level on the sheet, with the turn in a clockwise direction. With your fingers, bend the coil slowly. The beginning, smaller coils are the most resistant to bending, but the difficulty decreases as the spiral's size grows. While winding the coils, press them down with the fingers to keep them flat. Continue until a spiral of the desired diameter is reached.

FORMING A HELIX SPIRAL FROM WIRE

A *helix spiral*, commonly called a coil, is one that is formed with wire to have the shape of a right circular cylinder. This is done by wrapping the wire around a hardwood or metal *mandrel* in the manner described under Chain Mail, Chapter 6 to form rings or jump rings of identical size used in chain making and in assembling jewelry parts. Remember that the mandrel forms the *inside diameter* dimension of the coil, and the total outside diameter of the coil is this distance plus the thickness of two wires.

There are several possible uses for helix-shaped spirals. They can be left as finished; curved to form a continuous, spherical spiral helix loop; stretched to form an open helix; or hammered flat with a mallet on a surface block. The use to which such forms can be put is related to *scale* whose variants are the *size of wire* used, and the *diameter of the spiral*. Fine helix spirals of thin-gauge wire can form an ornament around the bezel of a stone; when flattened it can form a border. Larger spirals can form the basis of the concept for an entire piece of jewelry such as an earring, bracelet, or necklace.

SHAPING SPIRALS DIMENSIONALLY

It is possible to shape a flat spiral into a dome or cone shape. To dome a spiral, hold it over the appropriate groove of a *wood shaping block* or a *metal dapping block*. Hammer the wire gently into the depression with a round-ended *dapping punch*, or if the spiral is large, with the round end of a *soft fiber mallet*. Two spirals formed on the same wire with a plain length between them and shaped to domes can be combined and made to hold a ball or bead, with the plain center section twisted into a loop for suspension.

To form an *open, cone-shaped spiral*, first form the spiral flat, then push or pull the center outward with a tool.

To form a *closed, tapered spiral cone*, the wire must be wrapped around a *tapered mandrel*. The wire start must be flattened and fixed alongside the mandrel which is placed taper upward in a bench vise. The spiral form starts with the largest dimension and progresses toward the smallest. One may need the aid of pliers to form the smallest diameters. Tapered spiral cones come right off the mandrel. Such forms can be used in a variety of ways, again depending on scale.

TWISTED WIRE

Wires are twisted upon themselves, or together in endless combinations to make *compound twisted wire*. The most successful results pay attention to variations in *scale* for contrast, that is, using wire of different gauges, and to the combination of differing sectional shapes. Wires of the same or different metals can be combined, the latter for color as well as pattern contrast.

All wire must be annealed before twisting so that it will twist easily. In twisting, wire becomes work hardened, so the result should be annealed *after* twisting if it is to be formed further. If twisted wire is bent in a hardened state, it may crack or break at its weak points.

When joining the ends of twisted wire of the same pattern, do not cut them *across* the twist but rather, *diagonally* at the angle of the twist so that the join will be invisible. Twist direction is usually to the *right*, but wire can also be given a *left* twist.

6–46 ALEXANDER CALDER, U.S.A. Brass wire necklace with flat spirals shaped into cone spirals. Photo: Victoria and Albert Museum, London, Crown Copyright

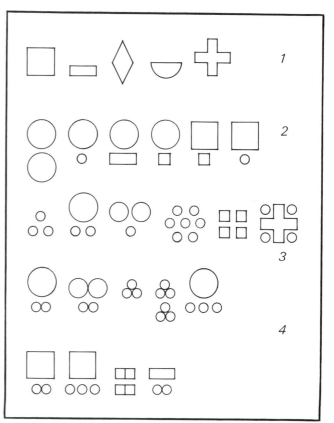

6–47 ELEMENTS AND COMBINATIONS SUITED TO TWISTING
1. Mono-elements that will give a self-twist.
2. Bi-elements.
3. Multi-elements.
4. Compound elements, round; square; oblong and round.

TWIST TYPES

MONO-ELEMENT TWISTS

A single element or strand of wire having any section shape *except* round can be twisted either to the *right* or *left,* as can all other wire combinations. Clamp one end of the annealed wire in a *bench vise* and fix the other in the jaws of a *hand drill.* If the wire is heavy, use a strong metal *hand vise* or *clamp* instead of a hand drill. Hold the wire taut horizontally and wind the handle of the drill forward for a right-hand twist or backward for a left-hand twist. If the turning is *fast* the twist quickly becomes dense; and if *slow,* it is more open. The twisting operation can, however, be stopped at any point when the wire achieves the desired degree of twist. When the twist of one length of wire must be duplicated, count and record the full turns given to the first wire and repeat this number in making the second. Mono-twist can be used alone, or as an element in bi- or multi-twists.

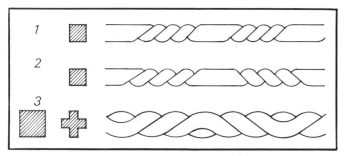

6–48 *TWISTS ON MONO-ELEMENTS*
1. Wire with partial, *unidirectional twists.*
2. Wire with *alternate direction twists.*
3. Wire with *alternate direction twists.*

6–49 GIJS BAKKER, Netherlands. Square aluminum wire armband. The wire is shaped by giving it a quarter turn twist. The ends are soldered together to make a Möbius-type form. Size 70 × 70 × 120 mm. Photo: Rien Bazen

BI-ELEMENT TWISTS

Bi-twists consist of *two single elements.* Both elements can be plain, untwisted wire, or one or both can be mono-element twists. Variations and contrast in appearance are obtained by changing the *size* of one element in relation to the other.

If both elements are the same, the entire length can be bent in half, the loose ends clamped in a bench vise, and the looped end engaged by a *steel hook* clamped in the

6–50 RANDERS SØLVVAREFABRIK, Denmark, manufacturer. Silver bangle made of two strands of twisted wire, drawn through a shaped drawplate. Photo: Lisco

6–51 FELKAS PAKUTINSKAS, Lithuania. White metal twisted wire and amber pendant. The stones are edge grooved to hold the wires. Photo: Courtesy Bibliothèque Forney, Paris

6–52 MARCI ZELMANOFF, U.S.A. Silver, 14K gold, and copper 22–28 gauge B.&S. twisted wire neckpiece, with shaped sheet bosses. Size 9 × 9 × 5 in. Photo: Bob Hanson

6–53 THAILAND. Contemporary, traditional silver bracelet, worn by Meo hill tribe women. The twisted wire ends are solder flooded and forged into a solid mass, the wires are twisted to form a volume, and the opposite end is treated similarly. This heavy bracelet must fit the wrist snugly to support its weight. *Photo: Oppi*

chuck jaws of the hand drill. To facilitate making the twist with different wire, the elements at one end can be soldered together and that end placed in the hand drill chuck jaws before twisting.

MULTI-ELEMENT TWISTS

Three or more strands *without any previous twisting,* or with any of them being mono-twists, are twisted together simultaneously to make a unit.

COMPOUND-ELEMENT TWISTS

One or more elements that have already been made into bi- or multi-element twists *before* they are combined, are twisted with other elements to make a *compound-element twist.* First twist the smaller elements, then the larger, then combine them into one compound twist. Because of the irregular section shape, solder their ends together to hold them in place.

OPPOSING DIRECTION TWISTS COMBINED

Two bi- or multi-elements, each twisted in the *opposite* direction, are then combined by twisting them together to

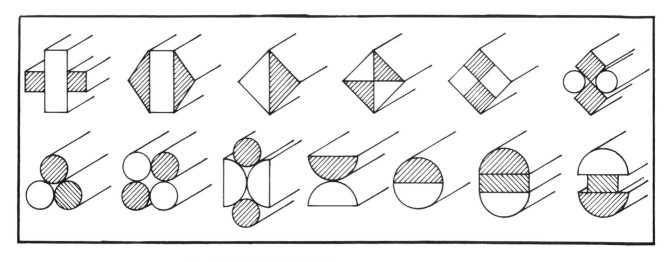

6–54 COMPOUNDS FOR TWISTING
Compounds of longitudinally soldered wires of various sections, weights, and different metals, in preparation for twisting.

6–55 GEORG JENSEN Sølvsmedie A/S, Copenhagen, manufacturer. Silver bangles of compound twisted wire, the last cut into sections and alternating with plain square wire. *Photo: Jonals, courtesy Georg Jensen Sølvsmedie A/S*

6–56 RANDERS SØLVVAREFABRIK, Denmark, manufacturer. Silver bangle made of two double strands twisted, each in the opposite direction, drawn through a drawplate, then soldered together to make a chevron pattern. *Photo: Lisco, courtesy Randers Sølvvarefabrik*

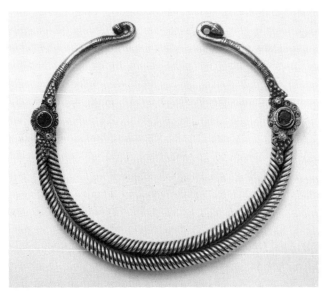

6–57 JELLALABAD, NURISTAN, AFGHANISTAN. Silver torque (tawq) made of two wires twisted in opposing directions, attached to forged wire ends engraved with patterns. The side rosettes of stamped sheet metal and carnelians cover the join. Ø 22 cm. Photo: *Bernisches Historisches Museum, Bern*

6–58 RANDERS SØLVVAREFABRIK, Denmark, manufacturer. Silver bangle made of two strands twisted together, then both pulled through a drawplate, and one strand unwound. Photo: *Lisco, courtesy Randers Sølvvarefabrik*

the right or the left. When twisting a combination of right- and left-twisted elements to the right, the left-twisted element has a tendency to become partially untwisted, and vice versa.

PARTIAL ONE-DIRECTIONAL TWISTS

A single wire is given an intermittent twist by immobilizing one part in a bench or hand vise, and applying the twist to the desired area with a second hand vise placed at the point of the twist limit. The twists are separated by sections of untwisted wire, and all the twists go in the *same direction.* It is possible to facilitate twisting by annealing the wire *locally* in the area to be twisted, while the rest remains harder and therefore resists twisting as readily.

ALTERNATE TWISTS

A single element is given partial twists in *opposing directions* in the same way as shown in Illustration 6–47. These twists can be spaced by plain, untwisted sections, or can alternate continuously. This type of twist was commonly used for square and cross-shaped wire or bar to make torques during the Viking period in Scandinavia and in other locations in Europe as well.

POST-TWIST TREATMENTS

Wires can be treated in several ways *after* they are twisted, for special effects.

UNWOUND TWIST

After twisting two or more elements together, one (or more) of them is *untwisted* from the rest by releasing it at one end and unwinding it slowly, without distortion, against the direction of the twist. The released mono-element result has the form of ripples or waves. It can be

used as is, or after manual or mechanical flattening. A variation of this process is to twist the wire, then roll it in a rolling mill, and finally unwind the element from the rest. Such wire is both wavy and alternately flat and depressed where parts have crossed.

HAND WINDING ON TWISTED WIRE

A mono-element, usually a small-gauge one, is wound *by hand* on top of a bi- or multi-element twisted wire. The added element can be a mono- or multi-element that replaces one that has been removed or unwound, and can be different in scale and appearance. In winding, the added element follows the path of the one removed. If an additional element is added to a multi-element in this way, it must follow the grooves of the twist direction so that it becomes integrated with the structure of the rest.

WRAPPING WIRE WITH ADDITIONAL ELEMENTS

Additional mono-, bi-, or multi-elements can be hand wrapped around any supporting core. The core can be a straight or twisted mono-element, a twisted bi-element, multi-element, or compound element. The effect is most pronounced when the core is sufficiently large to show a variation in the result. Multi-element twisted steel, silver, copper, and bronze wires were often wrapped around the grips of smallswords made from the 16th through 19th centuries, their purpose to provide a better grip on the sword. Sometimes the wrapping is done over shaped cores. The combinations and effects are very beautiful, and museum collections should be studied.

RESHAPING TWISTED WIRE

Finished wire already twisted can be reshaped by applying longitudinal or lateral compressive pressure.

DRAWING TWISTED WIRE

To stretch or partially smooth the shape of twisted wire, solder one end together and hammer or file it to a taper. Pass the tapered end through a drawplate. After a few passes, all the surfaces touching the outer circumference of the wire become flattened, while the rest is compressed and stretched in length. The resulting shapes of some multi-element twisted wires can be interesting. Such wires can also be unwound and used as mono-elements.

FLATTENING TWISTED WIRE

The simpler combinations of twisted wire can be effectively flattened to stretch them *widthwise* by pounding them with a *polished planishing hammer* on a *surface plate,* or by running the wire either widthwise or lengthwise through the rolling mill. If the twist was loose when flattened, the wires will show openings between each twist, but tight twists may not show such spaces. If the same wire is rolled very flat, the holes may close because of the spread of the wire.

FILING TWISTED WIRE

A less drastic method of flattening the uppermost surfaces of a flat strip of twisted wire is done by filing. Use a large, flat, bastard-cut file to remove the metal, followed by a smooth-cut file.

USES OF TWISTED WIRE

Twisted wire can be put to many decorative and structural uses. Combined elements make patterns of light and dark that can be a very satisfying detail in a design.

By itself, a length of twisted wire can be made into a *rigid bangle bracelet.* Rigid bangles have been one of the most enduring and popular simple forms of ornament for both women and men throughout history. In India, the bangle (from the Hindi word *bangri*) is a symbol of the state of matrimony for women. Therefore, when a Hindu woman becomes a widow, she breaks the glass ones and discards any other bangles and never wears them again. Bangles can be made of alternating sections of twisted wire and plain wire, in which case their sections are cut square at a plain part to make a butt joint when soldered together. Otherwise the joint is made by cutting across the twist in the same direction as the twist angle to make a neat, invisible joint. *Compound bangles* are also possible by soldering together several bangles to make a *band* bangle of any width, usually with the ends disguised by an added part.

Twisted wire can be applied to jewelry and metalwork as an ornamental border or used to frame a unit. It can be used structurally to form the shank of a ring, to decorate a bezel, to form a frame or filler unit in filigree, when braiding wires for ornamental purposes, to make links for chains, and in chain mail, to mention a few uses. It can also be wrapped around other elements for textural effect.

TWISTED WIRE FABRICS

Twisted compound wires made of different weights and of different colored metals can be soldered together alongside each other to make a flat compound fabric that can be used in various ways. By careful arrangement a pattern

can be made by using varicolored wires that have been given a right and/or a left twist. They can be combined with plain wire and soldered together in various arrangements and combinations. After soldering they can be hammered manually or run through the rolling mill to produce a flat, patterned, openwork sheet that can then be used in any way as an element in a design. Such sheet could even be shaped dimensionally. (See Twist Lamination, p. 369.)

TWISTED WIRE INLAY

Compound wires of *different colored metals* can be drawn through the drawplate until they acquire a completely round form, striped spirally like an old-fashioned barber pole. This variegated wire can be inlaid in metal of yet another color by the normal wire inlay process.

ALTERING THE SHAPE OR SURFACE OF WIRE

SWAGE SHAPING BEADED WIRE

Beaded wire is round wire that has been given the appearance of a string of matched round beads. Its use in metalwork and jewelry is ancient.

THE BEADING TOOL Beaded wire is made by the use of a bronze or steel *beading tool,* which consists of a matching pair of swage blocks, in effect a two-part die. This can be relatively easily made if a ready-made tool is not available, from steel blocks into which the depressions are formed by *round carbide burs.* Both halves bear a matching straight series of identical, concave, hemispherical depressions, so that when placed together, they form connected sphere-shaped cavities. The blocks engage each other by means of two keys in order to make sure they are aligned. Each single "bead" in the series on each mold half is slightly less than a full hemisphere at the sides where it contacts the next bead. The space between beads forms a depression but at that point, upper and lower dies do not meet so that the wire formed in the mold is not cut through. The small fillet that results joins each bead to the next in the wire length.

MAKING BEADED WIRE To make beaded wire, place the start of the annealed wire over the beaded groove, allowing the wire to project a little beyond the far end so that the position of the wire can be seen. Place the upper die half over the lower and engage the keying flange in the groove of the lower half. By resting on the wire, the upper die half holds it in place initially; once the bead shape is started the bead itself keeps the wire in position. With a mallet, hammer the upper half until the two die halves meet, an indication that the beaded wire is formed and has taken the shape of the mold cavity. To be sure the beads are full spheres and the fillet between them depressed equally all around, turn the wire a quarter turn at intervals during hammering, until at least one full revolution is made.

To continue the beading on the same wire, release the upper mold half and shift the wire to a position where the last full bead rests over the first depression in the lower die. Replace the upper die half and repeat the process until the desired length of beaded wire is formed. Before shaping beaded wire, anneal it so that it can be smoothly curved.

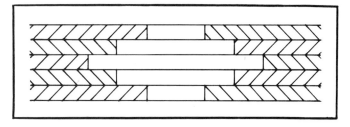

6–59 *SOLDER JOINED WIRE COMPOUNDS*
A flat fabric made of *alternately* twisted and plain wire segments arranged in a pattern and butt soldered together.

1–1

1–2

Plate 1–1   GERHARD ROTHMAN, West Germany. Brooch fabricated from stainless steel and gilded copper sheet metal. *Photo: Günther Meyer, courtesy the Schmuckmuseum, Pforzheim*

Plate 1–2   HELEN SHIRK, U.S.A. Neckpiece fabricated from copper and silver forms raised from sheet. *Photo: Richard Mafong*

Plate 1–3   SAARA HOPEA-UNTRACHT, Finland. Rings with domes fabricated from silver sheet, and shot. *Photo: Oppi*

1–3

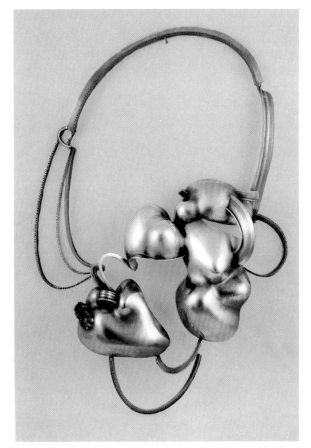

Plate 2–1 ANNI and BENT KNUDSEN, Denmark. Bracelet fabricated from die-stamped silver sheet and wire. *Photo: Courtesy Anni and Bent Knudsen*

Plate 2–2 ROBERT SCHMIDT, U.S.A. Brooch of silver with 14k gold appliqué, drop hammered on a bronze die, and surface acid etched. *Photo: Ira Garber*

2–1

2–2

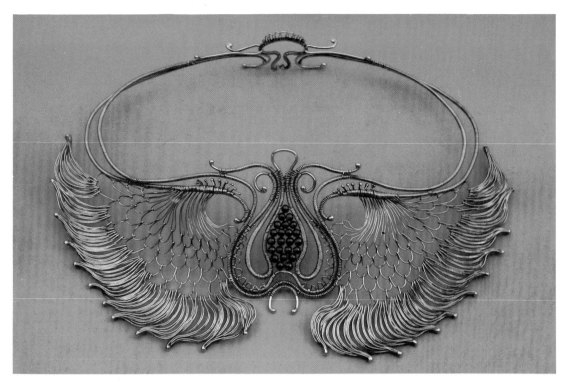

3–1

3–2

Plate 3–1 MARY LEE HU, U.S.A. Necklace
made of fine and sterling wire, with garnets.
Photo: Mary Lee Hu

Plate 3–2 MARCI ZELMANOFF, U.S.A.
Neckpiece of single element and twisted
bi-element fine silver wire, with inserts of
gold, silver, and copper repoussage sheet
forms. *Photo: Richard Mafong*

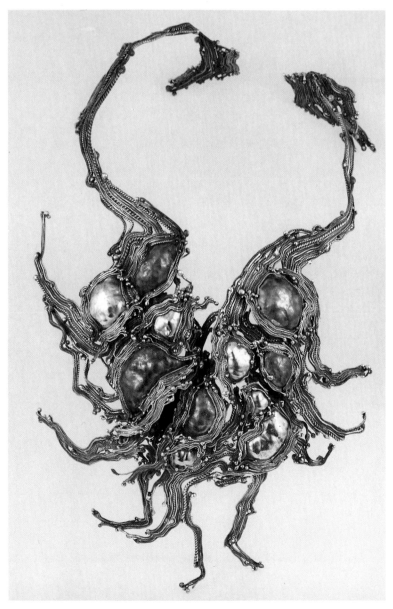

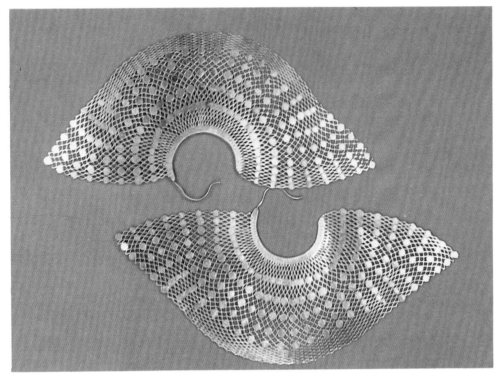

4–1

4–2

Plate 4–1 WALLY GILBERT, England. Earrings woven of sterling silver fused wire, inlay clinched with 18k gold shot. *Photo: Peter Parkinson*

Plate 4–2 OPPI UNTRACHT, U.S.A. Necklace of interworked power-stamped silver, copper, and brass wire, clinched with flattened fine silver bean shot. *Photo: Oppi*

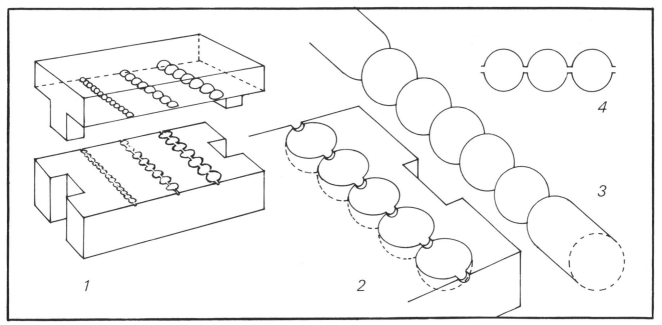

6–60 SWAGE SHAPING BEADED WIRE WITH BEADING WIRE DIES
1. The *two-part beading wire die*.
2. An enlargement showing the *die depressions*.
3. The resulting, partially formed *beaded wire* made from round wire.
4. Sectional view showing the connecting *fillet* between the beads.

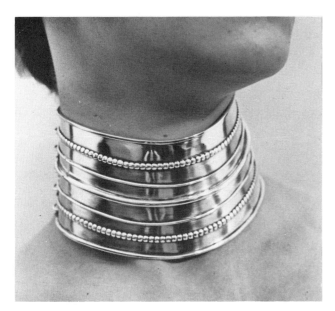

6–61 MARY ANN SCHERR, U.S.A. "Afro." Sterling silver collar. The form is decorated with round and beaded wire. Width 3 in; Ø 7 in. *Photo: Richard Margolis*

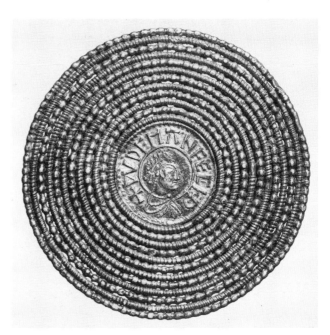

6–63 ENGLAND, late 10th century A.D. The Canterbury Brooch, found in Canterbury, Kent, now in the Ashmolean Museum, Oxford. The design consists of 12 separate concentric circles of alternating beaded wire and twisted wire, with central stamped portrait, and an Anglo-Saxon letter inscription. Ø 7.9 cm. *Photo: Ashmolean Museum, Oxford*

6–62 TIBET. Silver bangle (*dugpa ngulgi dudong*) with central red coral flanked by turquoises, and four turquoises at the back. Tibetan jewelers make frequent use of beaded wire to define and strengthen the edges of forms, and as accents around bezels. *Photo: Oppi*

▲

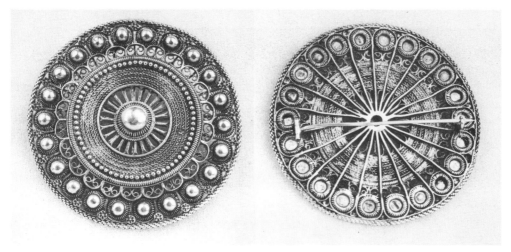

6–64 SCHVANHOVEN, NETHERLANDS, 18th century. Cloak clasp, silver, front and back view. One of a pair converted to a brooch. Jewelers in Schvanhoven are making similar ornaments today. Made entirely of wire in a variety of forms including straight, twisted, compound twisted, beaded, and spiraled, and ornamented with large pieces of silver shot. The back view shows the use of radiating flat wires to which the front wires are soldered for structural support. Ø 3⅛ in. *Photo: Oppi*

6–65 YASUHIKO HISHIDA, Japan. "Weeping Willow." Brooch of gold with rubies. Made of round wire that has been textured by pointed tools. *Photo: Courtesy Japan Jewelry Designers' Association, Tokyo*

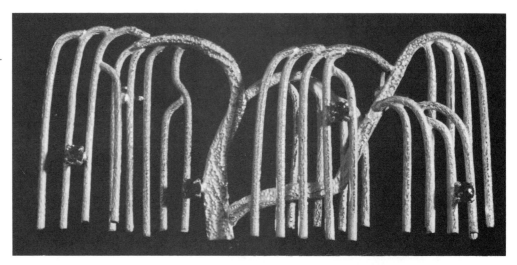

STAMPING WIRE WITH PATTERNS OR TEXTURES

Wire of any regular shape can be manually stamped with a regularly repeated pattern or texture created by the use of *design punches, matting punches, hollow punches, hammers,* or other tools.

Fix the wire in the groove of a *design* or *swage block* whose contour it matches. Place the punch over the wire and hammer it once with a sharp blow to impart the pattern. Shift the punch to the next position and do the same until the desired length of patterned wire is completed. The pattern appears on the upper surface. Such wire can be used in straight or bent forms. When bending, use pliers whose jaws are lined with leather so they will not mar the pattern.

ROLLING WIRE

The use of the *rolling mill* to perform various functions on wire has already been mentioned. Some additional points can be made in this connection.

MAKING STRIP FROM WIRE *Strip* can be made from wire. To form the strip as straight as possible, align the rolls in an absolutely parallel relationship to each other. This can be controlled by first closing them until they touch, then turning the two adjustable gears the *same distance* so that the roll gap is uniform and parallel. If the gears are marked with a gauge, adjustment is easier. When the rolls are not parallel, the wire will tend to curve when rolled toward the side with the wider gap.

6–66 MATILDE EUGENIA POULAT, Mexico. Silver necklace using flat, punch-textured wire spirals that form the chain links. In the pendant, undulating wires form loops as decoration, and to suspend free-hanging ornaments set with small turquoises, used throughout. *Photo: Oppi*

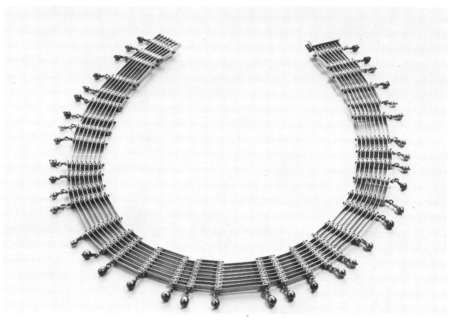

6–67 GOTTLIEB LINDENMAIER, Switzerland. Yellow 18K gold neck-lace wtih 38 natural pearls, made of straight, flat strip wire whose ends only are curved to allow interlocking. Parts are held by a pin from which pearls hang. Photo: Hans Baumann

To help achieve a straight result, get an assistant to grasp the emerging end of the strip with *parallel-jawed pliers* and to pull on it as it emerges from the rolls. Strip can be straightened if necessary by annealing, then hammering it edgewise with a mallet on a flat surface block in the direction against the curve. It is easier, however, to take preliminary precautions.

ROLLING PATTERNED WIRE Rolls are available with *intaglio* patterns already engraved in the wire rolling grooves, and special patterns can be ordered from roll-making specialists. By rolling wire through such rolls, the pattern is automatically imparted to the wire *in relief*. Wire of this type is used for wedding rings, borders, and bangles. (See Illustration 4–11.)

ROLLING WIRE TO CHANGE SECTION SHAPE Because ordinary wire rolling mills usually have grooves for forming both *round* and *square* wire, the rolling mill can be used to change the shape of a single round wire to a square one. (See The Rolling Mill, Chapter 4.)

FORGING WIRE

Forging wire, a basic method of shaping wire, is discussed under Forging, Chapter 6.

DROP FORGING WIRE A *drop hammer* or *stamping press* can be used to create an intertwined, flat wire structure that requires no other means to support or hold its parts. (Suggested methods are discussed under Open Forging, p. 145.)

GALLERY WIRE

Gallery wire, also called *gallery strip,* is stamped, patterned wire or strip manufactured by refiners. The name is derived from the fact that their patterns resemble architectural colonnaded galleries. The *open type* is designed with a pattern of upstanding parts on one side that allows those parts to be bent over, as when this form is used in a coronet setting to mount a stone. The *closed type* usually has a perforated pattern of regularly spaced openings, and is used in borders and in other ways. Though this wire is conventional in nature, it can also be used in a contemporary design idiom.

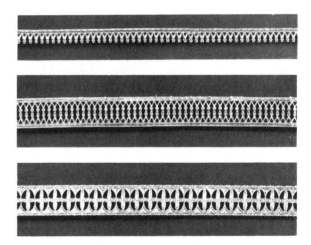

6–68 GALLERY WIRE
Above: Gallery wire, machine stamped, open and closed type, perforated. (Myron Toback, Inc., New York)
Below: Gallery wire, closed and open type. (Comptoir Lyon-Alemand Louyot, Paris)

6–69 AFGHANISTAN, KUDGI TRIBE. Woman's silver torque. The elaborate ornament is constructed of mass-produced units, mainly of flat and half-round wire, and ornamented with red and blue glass stones. The suspended parts are spread over the breast by two side hooks that pierce the clothing. Torque Ø 6 in; length of pendants 8 in; width of pendant ornaments as shown 18 in. Col.: Armi Ratia. *Photo: Matti Pietinen*

FILIGREE

A traditional wire technique of captured air

Filigree is an ancient form of delicate, open or backed wirework, normally of gold or silver, but also other metals. The English term is from the Italian *filigrana,* a compound derived from the Latin *filum,* "a thread of wire," and *granum,* "a grain or bead." The use of these terms to describe the process alludes to the early practice of ornamenting this wirework with small balls of metal (granules or shot), a technique still used today, though filigree work may consist entirely of wire.

In ancient times, the filigree technique was used in Mesopotamia, Egypt, Etruria, Greece, and Byzantium. In ancient Greece and much later in Hungary and Russia, filigree was often combined with enamel, as it still is in the backed filigree work of Ioánnina, Greece, and in the U.S.S.R. Today filigree work is still actively produced in traditional regional styles in Algeria, Bulgaria, China,

Egypt, Greece, Hungary, Iceland, India, Israel, Italy, Jordan, Latvia, Lebanon, Malta, Mexico, Morocco, Norway, Poland, Portugal, Spain, Sumatra, Tunisia, U.S.S.R., Yemen, Yugoslavia, and elsewhere.

The extremely wide distribution of the filigree process in jewelry making is an indication of its continued popularity. People admire and purchase it. There is much in the traditional filigree process that is compelling and admirable, if one takes the time to examine good pieces carefully. We can appreciate the fine filigree masterpieces of the past without feeling intimidated or competitive about them. Several outstanding contemporary craftspersons have made attempts to reinterpret the process in a nontraditional, contemporary design idiom, exploiting its structural possibilities.

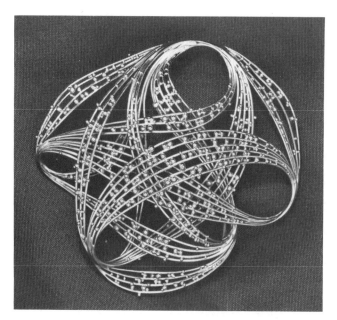

6–70 DAVID THOMAS, England. Asymmetrically designed filigree brooch in 18K gold. The traditional combination of wire and granules are used in a contemporary design idiom. Granules and wires are joined as in granulation with copper as an eutectic weld. The granules join the wires, and give the structure strength. *Photo: The Worshipful Company of Goldsmiths, London*

FILIGREE STRUCTURAL TYPES

There are four basic types of filigree, and many variations of these. The first type, the one most commonly thought of as being typical of filigree work, is *openwork filigree*. In this, the wirework is without any backing, and generally consists of heavier wire frames within which lighter weight wire units are held, the unit joined by solder at points of contact. In the second type, *ground-supported filigree*, all the wire is soldered to a ground of sheet metal or woven wire mesh. The use of a supporting surface greatly simplifies construction and soldering. Only when the wire dominates the design can this type of work be classified as filigree work. When the wire is sparse and open, it is simply called wirework. The third type is a *combination* of these two: completed units of openwork filigree are attached to sheet metal or other grounds by *non-soldering methods* such as split rivets, rivets, bezels, claws, or by other means. A fourth type is filigree to which *another material is added,* such as enamel (*à jour,* or backed), niello, or a plastic resin that fills the spaces between the wires which have first been soldered together.

There are some great advantages in openwork filigree. There is no other jewelry making technique that uses such a minimum of metal material to achieve such a maximum of extraordinarily light form. The wire may be less than half of the actual surface of a form; the rest is air. The

6–71 JANET BERG, U.S.A. Five 960/1000 silver wire filigree rings; *left* with amber; *center* with amber; *right* with garnets and green onyx. Twisted and untwisted wire forms are used in a variety of systems in conjunction with round and flattened shot. *Photo: Janet Berg*

6–72 IOÁNNINA, GREECE. Silver filigree bracelet of wire backed by sheet, with enameled petal and berry forms, and stamped wire borders. *Photo: Oppi*

low expenditure on metal makes favorable pricing possible, and the labor often costs more than the materials. The technique demands patience, small-scale manipulatory skills, and good vision. The problem of visibility can be solved by working in a good light under a *floating magnifying glass,* or by wearing *binocular magnifiers,* even when your vision is good. It is also possible to make the *scale* of the work *large* by using heavy-gauge wires to give it a new, simplified look.

FILIGREE CONSTRUCTIONAL CONCEPTS

To design in filigree, one must bear in mind the concepts that are basic to its character, and design accordingly. First of all, designs are essentially *linear* because the main element is wire in many forms. An important concept of openwork filigree is the idea of *unit construction.* Commonly, the design is made of framed units that contain smaller elements. In general practice, smaller units are combined by soldering them together to make larger units, but they can also be joined by loops and jump rings so that movement is allowed between them.

Another concept in *traditional* filigree construction is that the *wires never overlap*—they *abut* or touch each other by round or flat edges. This makes it possible for all the units to hold together within the frame by lateral tension *in one plane,* which greatly simplifies joining them. It also makes possible the formation of a flat plane at the *reverse* side, which is useful in subsequent shaping, if this is done.

With these concepts in mind, a drawing for a design made on paper to exact size can serve as a guide to construction, and be used as a means of making measure-

6–73 TURKEY. Silver filigree money purse worn suspended from c belt. The symmetrically organized heavy frame wires are densely filled with intricate filler wire forms. *Photo: Oppi*

6–74 SAN'A, YEMEN. A Jewish bride photographed in the 1930s, wearing traditional flowers and ornaments, including the filigree-worked traditional necklace *lebbe,* suspended around her chin. *Photo: The Israel Museum, Jerusalem*

6–75 SAN'A, YEMEN. "Lebbe." Traditional necklace of gilded silver filigree and granulation work with small blue stones. The design consists of many separate geometric filigree units, joined by jump rings. *Photo: David Harris, The Israel Museum, Jerusalem*

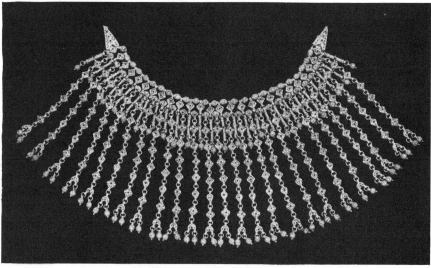

ments. During the forming of the units, parts can be placed upon the drawing to check their size and shape.

FILIGREE WIRE PROCESSING

Many of today's craftspersons are fortunate to have available from suppliers wire already drawn to almost every dimension and section. The majority of craftspeople who work in places where traditional filigree work is being done today do not have that option. They must prepare their own wire by drawing. (See Wire Drawing with the Drawplate, p. 150.)

After drawing, most filigree wire passes through four processes before it is ready to be used to form shapes: annealing, straightening, twisting, and flattening. *Annealing* is done prior to shaping to soften the wire so that it can be easily bent. *Straightening* is next: one end of the wire is fixed in a bench vise, the other end held in the serrated jaws of pliers or hand vise, and the wire is pulled sharply (which also stretches it slightly). Straightening can also be done by holding and pulling the wire over a large, round mandrel. *Twisting* two wires together is done with the aid of a hand drill. (See Bi-Element Twists, p. 165 for a description of this process.) *Flattening* of round wire for use as frame units, or flattening twisted filler wire, or textured wire is the last preparatory step. The simplest way to flatten wire is to place the wire on a flat, polished metal surface such as an anvil or surface block, and hammer it with a flat-faced planishing hammer by applying regular blows while moving the wire length at a steady rate so that the flattening is uniform. Wire can also be made flat by pulling it through *fixed rolls* (see Demonstration 3, p. 181), or by passing it through the flat rolls of a rolling mill. Flat wire has the advantage of being easily shaped into curved or spiral forms because the flat side always runs perpendicular to the curve of the shape.

FORMS AND SIZES OF WIRE USED IN FILIGREE

Wire of several forms can be used for filigree, including: round, flat, square, textured, twisted, spiral, beaded, wrapped, and braided wire. If desired, almost all of these forms can be hammer flattened or passed through a rolling mill.

The gauge of wire used depends on the scale of coarseness or fineness of the filigree being done. In most common traditional filigree jewelry, a relationship exists between the size of the frame wire and that of the filler wire. The range of frame wire size is 20–26 gauge B.&S.; for filler wire, 22–30 gauge B.&S. *In general,* frame wire is from two to four gauges larger than filler wire. This scale and size relationship can of course be deliberately changed to a nontraditional wire gauge range. However, it is good to remember that the contrast of wire sizes and the play of light on a filigree surface of different wire weights creates surface variation and is therefore an important part of the appeal of filigree work.

6–77 HELMER REHNSTRÖM, Finland, designer; manufacturer Kalevala Koru, Helsinki. Contemporary Finnish filigree bridal crown of a type traditionally worn in Scandinavian countries. The square wire frame is filled with flattened, twisted silver wire units. The crown is held to the hair by two pins. Bridal crowns first came into use in Scandinavia during the mid-15th century, their inspiration being the chaplet worn by unmarried noblewomen. Peasants made crowns of less valuable tinsel, silvered and gilded glass beads, and ribbons, supported on wire structures. *Photo: Otso Pietinen, courtesy Kalevala Koru*

6–76 MANINDJAN, WEST SUMATRA, INDONESIA. Bride wearing a traditional wire and filigree bridal crown, plus many other ornaments. *Photo: Koninklijk Instituut voor de Tropen, Amsterdam*

BASIC FILIGREE WIRE USES

FRAME WIRE   Frame wire forms the shape that contains and supports the filler wires. A single piece of filigree jewelry may contain several subframe units, joined with larger, heavier wire frames which give the unit strength. The frames emphasize the *main theme* or *structure* of the design, revealed by their movement, while the filler wires supply a counterpoint of detailed, patterned richness. Frames are always used in openwork filigree, and can also be used in ground-supported filigree, though their function there is more decorative than structural.

Frames are ordinarily of flattened round, square, or rectangular wire, but can also be made of twisted wire. After shaping, the frame is hard soldered closed before the filler wire units are placed within it so that the internal pressure of the filler wires will not force it open during soldering.

FILLER OR PATTERN WIRE   Finer wire is used to form the small filler units that fill the frame. In traditional filigree, these small units are generally made of two fine wires twisted together, then flattened. The height of the flattened wire can be equal to the height of the frame wire, but never more. Its flatness makes it possible to keep the filler units pressed against each other within the frame. In ground-supported filigree the filler units need not be as compact as those in openwork filigree where their pressure against each other holds them in place.

6–79 *BASIC FORMS OF FILLER UNITS* Common filler unit forms used in filigree construction.

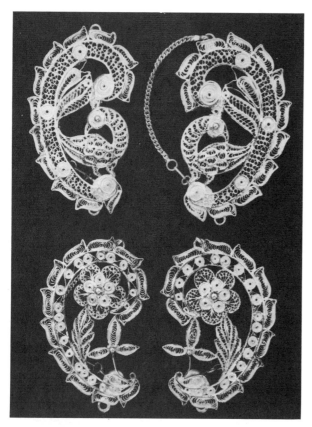

6–78 CUTTACK, ORISSA, INDIA. Contemporary silver filigree earrings (*kana*) designed to cover the entire ear. They are held in place by chains slipped over the ears, clips at the ear tops, and a pierced earlobe finding. The upper peacock design, and the lower flower design use many basic filler wire unit shapes. Cuttack is an important filigree manufacturing center where many workshops flourish, employing hundreds of people. *Photo: Oppi*

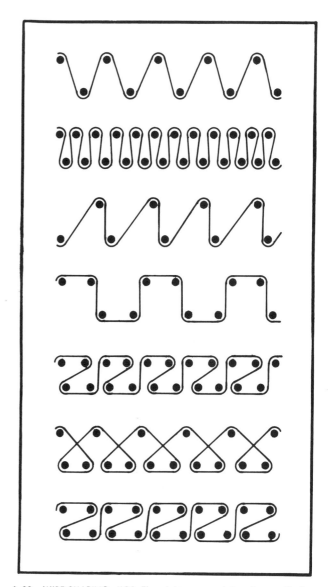

6–80 *WIRE-SHAPING JIGS* The dots represent headless nails hammered into a wooden board.

FILLER WIRE UNIT SHAPES

Filler wire shapes generally consist of some form of spiral, loop, or other curling, curved shape, and combinations of these. Traditional filigree workers all over the world give specific names to the basic filler wire forms they use repeatedly. Some of the basic shapes and their variations are shown in the accompanying illustration. These, in all sizes, can be combined in infinite combination. Further variations are achieved by using contrasting wire weights, and twisted or plain wire. Shapes and their leaders can be elongated. Changes in the forms can be made during shaping by squeezing them together with the fingers or by pressing their sides with a tool, for instance, to force a circular form into an oval shape. A very useful tool for shaping is a *pointed steel probe* which can be used to stretch out or compress spiral forms, to separate curves within a form, or bring them to touch at a single point. It can also be used to adjust the positions of whole filler units in relation to each other once they have all been placed within the frame. *Tweezers* are also commonly used.

WIRE-SHAPING JIGS These can be made by hammering small straight pins or *headless* nails into a wood ground. The pins can be placed in many configurations to achieve different patterns for making separate filler units, or continuous patterns that can be used for borders and outlining. Their positions must be drawn on the wood with accuracy to assure the regularity of the result. Some schematic possibilities are shown in the diagram. If the pins are headless, and placed perpendicularly, the wire can be lifted away by gently forcing it upward with a tool.

FILIGREE SHAPING TOOLS

Before use, filigree wire should be in an annealed state to facilitate shaping. The shaping of units is simple and does not require complicated tools. Fingers are as important as other tools for shaping, and for guiding the wire to the shaping tool. The main tool for shaping lightweight wire is *tweezers,* and for heavier wire, *pliers,* the pointed, round-nosed form being most useful. To cut wires at terminating points, *nippers* or *cold chisels* are used. When using a cold chisel, the wire is placed on a piece of soft brass to avoid dulling the chisel's cutting edge, and the cut is made square by simple pressure (for heavier wire, the cut is made with a hammer blow on the chisel).

Holding tools such as a *ring clamp* with leather-lined jaws, *old pliers* with leather strips pasted inside their jaws, broad flat-nosed pliers, or a hand vise are useful in retaining and stabilizing certain shapes while forming.

6–82 TIZNIT, SOUTH MOROCCO. Young artisans in one of the many existing workshops, fabricating flat filigree units used for traditional ladies' belts worn in that area. *Photo: Oppi* ▶

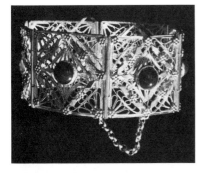

6–83 TEL AVIV, ISRAEL. Contemporary geometric design filigree bracelet, mounted with corals. Made by Yemenite jewelers at the Maskit workshop. *Photo: Courtesy Maskit*

6–81 SAARA HOPEA-UNTRACHT, Finland. Silver filigree pendant whose outer, heavy frame of square wire contains the inner elements made of flat wire, scroll- and spiral-shaped forms, sections of square tubing, and shot. By enlarging the scale of normal filigree units, a more robust appearance is achieved. *Photo: Oppi*

FILIGREE CONSTRUCTION

In openwork filigree, all units are made *flat* which simplifies their construction and soldering. Completed parts or total unit forms can be shaped three dimensionally *after soldering*.

Place the shaped and joint-soldered unit frame on a clean, flat surface such as a flat sheet of metal or plate glass. Professional filigree workers do not pin down their frames before filling them in preparation for soldering, but there may be cases, as when making a large form, when this can be helpful. Pick up a filler unit with tweezers and insert it in the frame. Place other units alongside. Since the wire of the fillers is flat, the units contact each other; when the frame is filled, the tension is distributed laterally in one plane, which is the reason that it is important when shaping filler units to keep their sides vertical. At intervals press down the fillers with a flat tool to force all units to contact the base plane on which they rest, which makes the entire undersurface uniformly flat. As mentioned, the position of filler units can be adjusted in relation to each other by teasing them with a steel probe (an old dental tool serves nicely for this purpose). No large areas are left open without fillers as this would result in a weakened structure. Tension from the pressure of unit against unit and the confining frame should be enough so that when the frame is lifted, the filler parts do not fall out. If they do, there are not enough filler units inside the frame, or they are placed in a way that is not mutually supporting. On the other hand, too many units should not be squeezed in a frame to the point where the tensions between them become so great that they may spring out of the frame.

The situation is different when, as is sometimes the case, filler units are placed on the *outer edge* of a frame, and must be soldered to it at their point of contact. Here it is useful to hold the parts together by adding some gum, such as gum tragacanth, to the flux, and to construct the piece on a *sheet of mica*. Unnecessary movement is avoided by placing the mica on the soldering surface at the start.

STONE SETTINGS

Constructions in filigree can also include settings for stones. These can be mounted in conventional bezels placed in strategic positions on top of the filigree wire once the unit has been soldered. Designs are often planned so that the position of the stone setting occurs at the juncture of wire ends to conceal them. Granules are often used for the same purpose. High box settings can be used to raise the stone well above the wirework level, and the box is then covered with wirework to integrate it visually. Bezels can also be raised and supported on arcades of wirework.

SOLDERING OPENWORK FILIGREE: Wire to wire

Openwork filigree is a wire-to-wire soldering situation. Preparing the unit on a *mica sheet* has some advantages. If the piece employs wires of different weights, which is usual, they can be pressed down so they all contact the sheet, making the thicker wires project upward while the wires of *all* thicknesses are level at the back.

Another way to prepare a framed filigree unit for sol-

dering is to place it on a block of charcoal whose surface has been made flat by rubbing it on a flat sheet of abrasive paper held on a truly flat surface. Lift the unit with tweezers to the charcoal, or push it off sideways from its resting surface onto the charcoal. Cover it with a flat sheet of metal or a flat tool, and gently press it into the charcoal to a depth of about half its frame wire thickness. This is done because soldering heat tends to expand the wire, and embedding it holds the unit in place. Because of its highly refractory nature charcoal retains the heat and helps the solder to quickly reach its melting temperature.

Greasy substances, including oil from the fingers must be avoided at all times in filigree work as the grease will act to inhibit the successful flow of solder.

Prepare a mixture of borax, water, finely powdered solder, and some gum to make a thin paste. (The gum helps to hold the parts together.) Paint this on the clean wire at the junctions of forms and their contact places. Alternately, paint all joints to be soldered with a thin gum and flux mixture, dip small snippets of solder into this mixture, then place them at the junctions to be soldered. Do not use too much solder as a surplus will flood the wire, coarsen its appearance, and be almost impossible to remove.

When heating filigree work, there is a risk of applying too much heat and melting the wire. It is therefore good practice to diffuse the heat by applying the flame from below. If for some reason this cannot be done, *move the flame constantly* when bringing the metal up to soldering temperature. Heating the work from below is simplified when the work is mounted on a piece of mica sheet placed in turn upon an *iron mesh* that is elevated on a *ring stand*. In this arrangement, the flame can easily be applied from below. The mica, a natural insulator, helps to deflect and distribute the heat evenly to the wires. A freely flowing solder should be used. Watch the solder closely, and *the instant it flows,* withdraw the flame.

Try to solder an entire unit in *one* soldering operation. When joining several units together, or when adding loops needed to join sections to other sections by jump rings, or when soldering findings, always use a lower melting solder than that used for the other joints. Pickle the piece after each soldering. Upon removal from the pickle, never handle the work with the fingers—use clean tweezers instead.

It is common in traditional filigree work for the important wire junctions and sometimes selected focal points in a design, such as the centers of spirals, to be covered with a decorative element such as round or flattened shot; convex or concave half-domes; stamped, small, flat, geometric units; or other forms. Besides concealing such places, they give strength to the filigree structure. They also provide dimension and highlights. In another, ancient variation, granules are soldered *between* the wires rather than on top of them, another way of giving the structure strength.

SOLDERING GROUND-SUPPORTED FILIGREE:
Wire to sheet

Soldering ground-supported filigree is simplified by the fact that all the pattern wires lie in contact with the base, which may be flat or shaped dimensionally. The soldering techniques used in these circumstances are those of soldering wire to sheet. It is not necessary for the whole wire length to be soldered to the ground: interval soldering is acceptable. Wire ends should always be soldered. It is possible to give such a piece lightness, after the wires are soldered in place, by piercing parts of the ground with a jeweler's saw to create open areas.

SHAPING FILIGREE UNITS DIMENSIONALLY

If the finished unit is to be kept flat and needs flattening after soldering, place it on a flat surface, put a piece of leather on top of it, and tap it carefully with a horn or wood mallet. If the unit must have an angular bend, use a pair of pliers, but take care not to scar the wire by lining the plier jaws with leather. Units can be adjusted to curved forms, but not shaped drastically without misshaping the wires or causing the unit to fracture. To give a unit a gentle curve, place it in the depression of a *dapping block,* or if an irregularly curved shape is wanted, one can be made in a lead block and the unit placed into this, then hammered *lightly* from the back with a suitably shaped *punch.*

FINISHING FILIGREE

After soldering, brush the work with a *brass wire brush* (machine polishing filigree is dangerous and should be avoided), then pickle it. Silver filigree emerges from the pickle in a dead white condition, and gold filigree appears matte. Traditionally, it is left this way except for the upper surfaces of the frame wires, and possibly also those of the

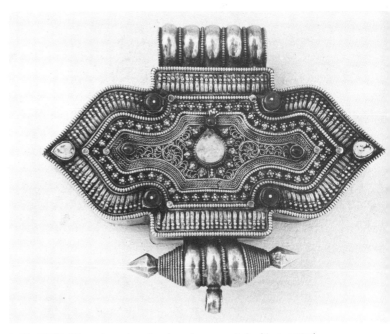

6–85 TIBET. Silver charm box (*ngul gau*) ornamented with a central area of filigree work, surrounded by beaded wirework and a series of small, stamped unit borders. Turquoise and coral stones accent central and terminal points. Width from point to point 6¼ in; height 5¼ in. *Photo: Oppi*

6–86 LAHUL SPITI, HIMALAYA, PUNJAB, INDIA. Woman wearing traditional silver ornaments including several large *gaus,* as an adjunct to festive dress. *Photo: Oppi*

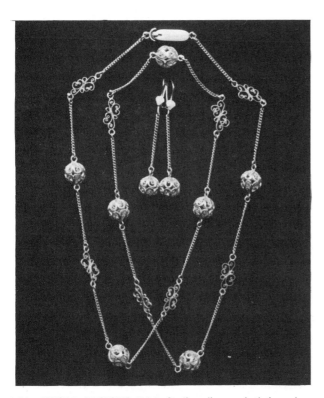

6–84 JOYCE T. MACRORIE, U.S.A. Sterling silver neck chain and earrings with filigree beads. To make filigree beads, two separate petal-shaped parts are made flat, their diameter depending on the size of the planned bead. The center of each is a small wire circle which will be used later to thread the bead. After flat soldering these parts, each "flower" is placed in turn over the depression of a *dapping block,* and lightly tapped with a *dapping punch.* The unit is moved progressively from the large starting depression to increasingly smaller ones until the two units are shaped into identical half-domes. Their upper or contacting edges are filed across to assure proper meeting of the two halves. The halves, held together with *iron binding wire,* are soldered, forming the bead. *Photo: Joyce T. Macrorie*

filler wires which are burnished with a *burnisher* and soapy water lubricant. These shining surfaces create a pleasant contrast with the matte dullness of the rest. Copper filigree is gold or silver plated. Silver filigree can be gold plated, and then edge burnished.

It is also possible to oxidize silver filigree by submerging the whole piece into a liver of sulphur solution, rinsing and drying it, then rubbing it with the fingers dipped into whiting or fine pumice to remove surface oxidation, while the rest is left dark.

If there are any stones to be mounted, this is done *after* all the above processes are complete.

FILIGREE COMBINED WITH OTHER TECHNIQUES

It is not necessary for an entire work to be made in the filigree technique alone. Separately made filigree units can

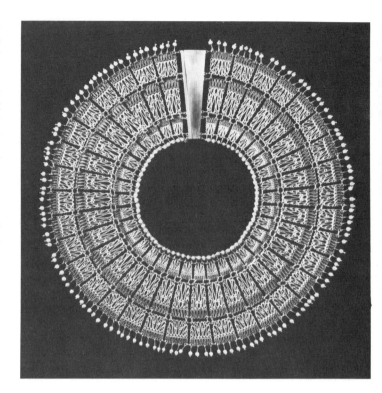

6–87 KALEVALA KORU, Helsinki, manufacturer. Reproduction of an old Finnish silver filigree brooch with central rose quartz and spectrolite stones. An injection rubber mold is used to make a wax model for casting from the original. With great fidelity, it reproduces the technique of ground-supported filigree in a single casting. *Photo: Courtesy Kalevala Koru*

be combined with other techniques. These units can be joined to other parts by soldering, or by the use of cold joining systems, such as pegs, rivets, split rivets, or screws.

FILIGREE REPRODUCTION WITH A RUBBER MOLD

Open or backed filigree-type construction models can be used as a *pattern* to make a *rubber mold* for the purpose of reproducing them in quantity. The only limitation is the dimension capacity of the mold, though this can be overcome by soldering smaller units together to make larger units after casting. With proper care in processing, the rubber mold is capable of producing wax models with great fidelity to the original. (See Rubber Mold Wax Injection, Chapter 11.)

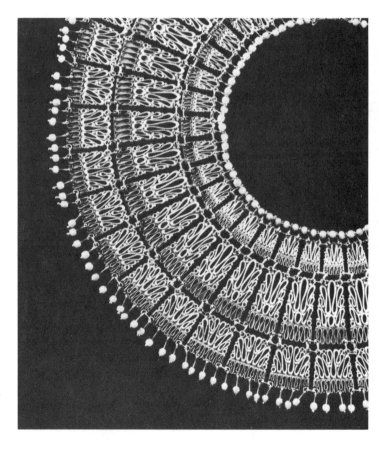

6–88 MICHAEL CROFT, U.S.A. "Tutankhamen Defiled." Filigree necklace (and detail) whose three basic sterling silver openwork filigree units are made by casting from rubber molds. They are then enameled in several hues of red and blue, and gilded with 24K gold vermeil. The units are joined by jump rings to make a flexible fabric. Red glass beads ornament the inner and outer borders. *Photo: David Ring*

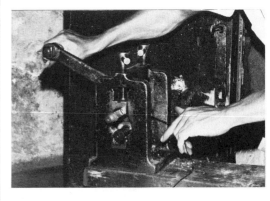

1

2

3

GOLD FILIGREE: The Oaxaca, Mexico, method

DEMONSTRATION 3

FAUSTO VARGAS RAMÍREZ makes a filigree earring.

Photographer and informant: Joyce T. Macrorie

In Mexico, traditional gold filigree jewelry is still done at locations including Iguala, Mérida, Tehuantepec, Juchitán, Tuxtla Gutiérrez, and Oaxaca, to mention a few, their products all stylistically different from each other. The filigree jewelry of Oaxaca, discussed here, follows jewelry styles prevalent in 17–18th-century France and Spain, and the necklaces, bracelets, pendants, earrings, and rings with their usual accompaniment of pearls have a unique old world charm.

Before gold prices first skyrocketed in the 1970s, this jewelry was made in 14K or 18K gold, but today 12K is generally used unless a higher karat quality is specified. The favored bright yellowish orange appearance of pure gold is, however, maintained by a final electroplating process.

The technique of making Oaxacan filigree is essentially the same as elsewhere, though some unique practices are followed. The procedures described here are those practiced by one of its outstanding makers today, Fausto Vargas Ramírez. They illustrate how an economy of means, improvisation, and an utter simplicity of tools can be used to create works of great delicacy. In spite of its delicate appearance, however, well-made filigree jewelry is surprisingly strong.

The earring (*arete, arracada*) is a major jewel in Oaxacan filigree and certain *traditional designs* have been per-petuated over the years, each with its special name. Among those designs well known among the local people are: *el gusano* ("the worm," after a worm that is found in the maguey plant and eaten french-fried with tequila), *el jardín* ("the garden," a floral pattern), *el eme* ("the M," after the configuration of seed pearls), *el ramo* (the "branch" or "bouquet"), and *calzoncito* ("little pants," shaped like a bow-legged child). Besides earrings, necklaces, bracelets, chains, pendants, rings, and matching sets are also made.

PREPARING THE INGOT FOR WIRE MAKING

1 The metal is alloyed by weighing the ingredients and melting them in a crucible with a torch, then poured into an ingot mold. The ingot is washed in acid and rinsed in water containing soda, an alkaline solution that neutralizes any remaining traces of acid; then it is rinsed again.

2 The ingot is forged to a square shape on an anvil to fit the grooves of a wire rolling mill.

3 It is then reduced in the rolling mill to a size suitable for drawing.

DRAWING THE WIRE

4 The drawplate is mounted in a bench vise, and the wire, lubricated with beeswax, is pulled through with drawtongs. At intervals the wire is annealed to relieve work hardening and render it soft.

The wire is drawn to two basic sizes. One is for the frame wire (*cuadrado*) which is either rectangular or square in section. A thinner wire for filler shapes (*cartones*) is also made. To make square or rectangular wire, round wire 20–22 gauge B.&S. is run through the flat section of a rolling mill. Filler wire is made by drawing the wire through from two to five drawplate holes smaller than those used for the frame wire, and it emerges about

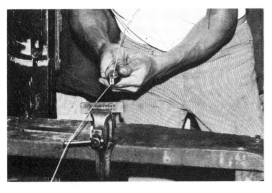
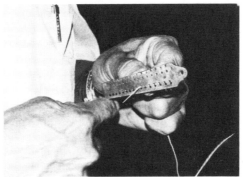
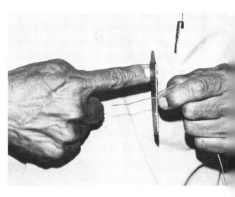

4

5

6

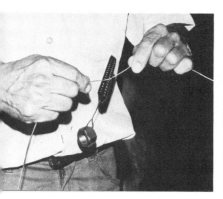

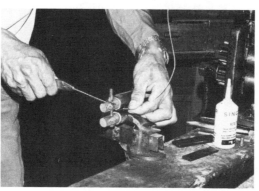

7

8

9

22–24 gauge B.&S. Still finer gauges are used for more delicate work. (Generally finer wire is used in the beautiful gold filigree work done in Tuxtla Gutiérrez, Chiapas, and Mérida, Yucatán.) First the outer frames are formed with pliers and their juncture soldered.

TEXTURING WIRE WITH THE SCREW PLATE

5 By a process that seems to have been invented by Oaxacan goldsmiths, the round filler wire is given a spirally ridged texture in a unique way. One wire is threaded into the hole of a screw plate.

6 The screw plate is flipped over with the fingers and with each turn moves further down its entire length.

7 The technique can be accelerated by attaching a weight to the far end of the screw plate (here a large nut was attached with a wire). The wire is held tightly, and the screw plate is whirled around it. As it moves along the wire, it makes a thread in the same way as if a screw thread were being made. The weight of the nut and the centrifugal force keeps the screw plate moving along by momentum.

FLATTENING THE WIRE

8 This spirally textured wire is then flattened by drawing it *manually* in an improvised *flattening mill* consisting of two ¾ in (1.9 cm) diameter steel tubes mounted with wing bolts at either end so they can be brought together and tightened to gradually decrease the space between them. The effect is similar to that achieved on a rolling mill, but the action is gentler. In this case the hands pull the wire instead of it passing through the rolls under pressure. Both wire and rolls are lubricated. The

flattening process consists of about 20 pulls through the flattening mill, and care must be taken to avoid breaking the fragile wire. In this process, besides becoming flattened and widened somewhat, the wire is also stretched in length. Though the sides are flattened, the edges retain the serrations given to the wire by the screw plate, now somewhat farther apart than they appeared originally. The appearance of this patterned edge when seen in the finished work resembles that of a flattened, twisted wire, which was probably originally used for fillers and may be the reason that this procedure was adopted.

PLACING THE FILLERS

9 The filler wires are formed with fingers and pliers. Some of their forms are a single spiral (*medio-cartones*); a double inverted spiral (*calavera*); a double, tendril-shaped spiral (*pavo*); and ovals (*ojillos*). These are placed along the outer edge of a frame wire or within a frame with tweezers, allowing no large gaps between them.

10 As the filling of the frame proceeds, the units are pressed down with the fingers and the handle of the tweezers. Upon completion, the fillers compactly fill the frame, so that the unit can be picked up without their falling out.

SOLDERING

11 The solder is made by the jewelers themselves. Hard solder for gold is made of 24K gold, to which one part fine silver is added, plus a small amount of copper and brass. Silver hard solder consists of two parts fine silver and one part brass. The same solder hardness is used throughout on a given object. The solder strip is cleaned to be oxide-free. Only enough solder paillons are cut with snips for immediate use. The flux is prepared several times

10

11

12

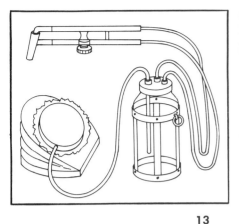

13

14

15

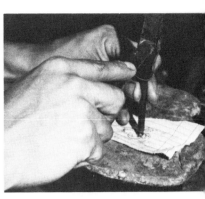

16

each working day, and is a lump-form borax, rubbed with some water in a clean metal jar lid.

12 The work is placed on a charcoal block, and the joints are painted with flux with a fine brush (sometimes made of dove's feathers). Each piece of solder is coated with flux as it is placed at important junctures on the work.

13 A *mouth torch* is used for small work with the flame from a glass jar containing gasoline from which a wick projects. For most soldering, a *homemade torch* is used with ordinary gasoline as fuel, mixed with air that comes from a *foot-operated bellows*. This torch is capable of producing a tiny, pointed flame which is used to melt the filigree solder; it can also be adjusted to make a flame of a size sufficient to melt one ounce of gold for casting.

The standard postsoldering treatment consists of immersing the work in a hot sulphuric acid pickling solution, followed by a rinse in cold water, and always followed by a dip into a solution of one tablespoon of baking soda to two cups of water. After this the work is massaged with the fingers, then finally rinsed in water. Between solderings, the piece is also cleaned with a brass wire hand brush to remove adhering flux.

ASSEMBLING

14 If a design has multiple units, they are assembled and soldered together. If they are to be joined in a flexible way to each other with jump rings, loops are now soldered on.

17

18

15 Mountings for stones are also soldered on at this point. Large pearls are often set in a metal cup which is drilled through with a pump drill to make a hole in preparation for mounting. The finished piece is sanded on both sides *while flat* because in that form sharp projections are more easily eliminated. Careful work requires little smoothing at the front.

SHAPING

16 Parts are occasionally shaped dimensionally by placing them over a depression in a *dapping block* or a *lead block*. When using the latter, a piece of paper is placed between the block and the work to avoid lead contamination.

FINISHING FILIGREE

In preparation for electroplating with 24K gold, the piece is pickled, rinsed, boiled in a soda solution, boiled in a detergent solution, then rinsed thoroughly in water. An enameled pan holds the gold plating solution that contains potassium cyanide, hence the precaution of *removing all acid traces* from the work as the combination of cyanide and acid would create lethal fumes. The electrical current is provided by flashlight batteries, attached to the work by wires. Gold plating with 24K gold gives the work a bright yellow color characteristic of pure gold, much admired by Mexicans, but not understood by most Americans and Europeans who are conditioned to think that the lower alloy gold colors represent the real color of gold.

After hand brushing the result, finishing is done entirely by hand burnishing. The upper surfaces of the wires are burnished bright with a *burnisher* lubricated with soapy water. The burnisher is held with the handle inserted between the index and the middle finger while the tip is manipulated with these fingers plus the thumb. This manner of holding the burnisher allows the greatest degree of control over the tool.

STONE MOUNTING

17 Pearls are traditionally used in Oaxacan filigree jewelry, though red coral and other stones, real or synthetic, are occasionally used. Old Oaxacan filigree jewelry work used pearls from China and India, imported via Acapulco, and these are still highly valued. Today's pearls come from Japan and are cultured, baroque, or regular, white or colored, large or small.

Several different pearl-mounting techniques are followed. Single large pearls are rigidly mounted by melting one end of a suitable length of fine gold wire to a ball. The plain end is passed through the pearl, then from the front through the drilled hole of the pearl cup mount. The ball appears at the front on top of the pearl as a decorative knob and also conceals the drilled opening. The unseen back end of the wire is twisted to a knot. Moving-mount dangling pearls, single or in series, are strung on the same kind of wire with an end-melted ball. The plain end is passed through the frame or an opening in the filigree wire, shaped into a loop, and its ends twisted around itself. Seed pearls are also strung in single or multiple series, each on a plain wire. These are mounted rigidly at the front of the piece, and sometimes in channels provided for them in the construction. The beginnings and ends of the wire are passed through to the back of the piece where they are twisted to a knot, or wrapped two or three times around a heavier frame wire. If the series of seed pearls is long, at the halfway point the stringing wire may pass through a loop soldered to the main body to anchor the series in place. To form a circlet, series of pearls are strung on a wire whose ends are simply twisted together. They hold to the piece by loops in the manner already mentioned. Grapelike pearl clusters are made by threading each pearl separately through a ball-ended wire, then the wire "stems" are twisted together to form one unit which is suspended from a loop. Cut stones are set in conventional claw settings or in bezels.

18 After stone setting, a final burnishing finishes the piece, a gold wire pendant earring with pearls, approximately 3 in (7.62 cm) long.

CHAINS

Integrating interlinked, interlooped, flexible systems

The chain in precious metals, by itself has a long history of use as a jewel. Chains alone are used decoratively as necklaces, bracelets, belts, hair ornaments, or fillets, to mention only a few examples. Functionally, they can support other ornaments, such as pendants, earrings, watches, medals, keys, and eyeglasses, and in endless ways can be used as a device for connecting parts of an ornament.

Symbolically, the chain alone evokes an image of bondage (which may mean willing bondage to a loved one). In some societies it is a symbol of marriage, a symbol of a link with ancestors and the past, or in abstract form, a symbol of eternity.

In its basic form, a *chain* consists of a series of similarly shaped units that intercept or pass through one or more preceding units. Each unit is normally able to move freely within the last so that the total chain length is *flexible*. *Repetition* of units, *flexibility,* and *endlessness* are ideas inherent in the concept of a chain. Therefore, any construction having these qualities may rightfully be designated as a form of chain.

THE LINK: The chain unit

The *link,* also called a *loop,* is the basic chain unit. Ordinarily it is made of wire and is round or oval in form, but it can also be of special shapes as long as these function as links. The wire used for links can be round, square, half-round, flat strip, twisted wire, or patterned wire. The units of one chain may all be the same, or they may vary in a regular or an irregularly repeated sequence. Units can also be made of other forms of metal such as sheet or tubing, or they can be forged. The manner of their linkage may be obvious and exposed or completely concealed. As long as they are linked in some way as units and they are not strung on a continuous supporting strand (in which case they would be termed beads), they are termed links, and the total is a chain.

GENERAL CHAIN TYPES

Chains may be grouped according to some major factor in their construction or appearance. The most basic division is between *linked* and *interworked* chains as these are different concepts of construction. The former uses short lengths of wire, and the latter uses a wire of continuous length. Within the linked chain category, chains can be divided into those whose links are *undeformed* and those which are *deformed*. Within each category, variations are possible by changing wire *size,* sectional *form,* and the *scale* of the link.

UNSOLDERED OR SOLDERED LINKS Either *unsoldered* or *soldered* links can be used in chains. Single unsoldered links are obviously not as strong as soldered ones, and cannot be depended upon to hold any weight that might cause them to stretch and open. When heavier wire is used, however, the links are more rigid and the chance of their opening is reduced. Unsoldered spiral links increase in strength with the number of loops in the spiral. In general practice, however, most chain links are soldered.

SIMPLE LINK CHAINS These are common chains whose unit is undeformed and constant throughout, interlinked in series in which one link intercepts the other. The wire of which it is made can be of any gauge, depending on the desired weight and/or strength of the result.

ROUND OR FLAT CHAINS Round chains are constructed three dimensionally and have no front or back, while flat chains are worn with one side flat on the body.

GRADUATED CHAINS Chains whose unit size gradually increases from small at the back to largest at the front are called graduated.

ROPE OR CORD CHAINS These chains are made of round or oval links left in an *undeformed* shape, each passing through two or three of the previous links so that their

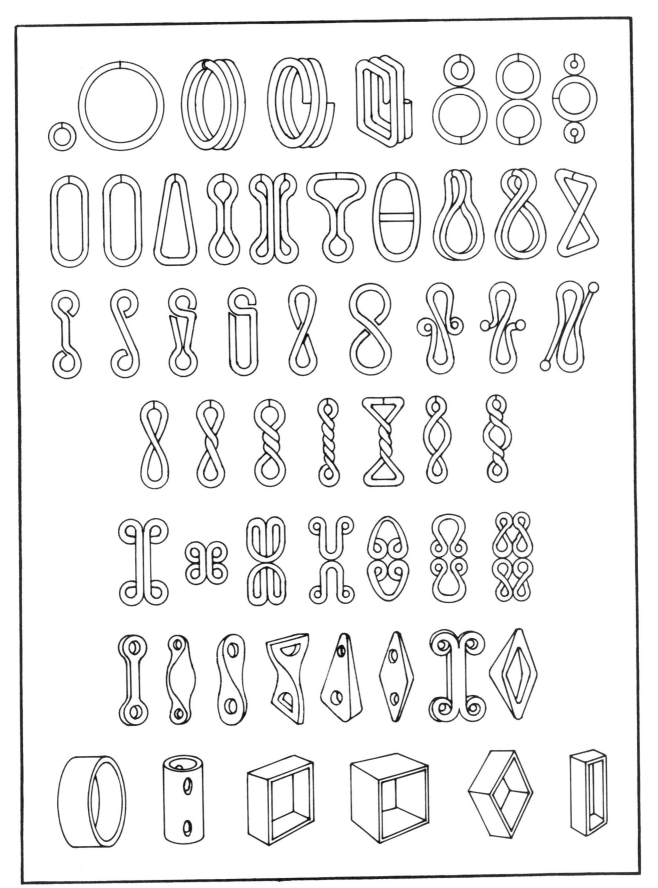

6-89 *CHAIN LINK TYPES*
Wire, forged units, and sections of ready-made tubing used for chain
links.

6–90 LAOS and NORTHERN THAILAND. Contemporary Meo man's silver chain necklace with unsoldered links made of wire spirals, with padlock style forged and engraved pendant. This is an amulet believed to protect them from evil spirits. The chain ends are often attached to a torque-like neckpiece with the pendant hanging below. *Photo: Oppi*

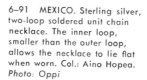

6–91 MEXICO. Sterling silver, two-loop soldered unit chain necklace. The inner loop, smaller than the outer loop, allows the necklace to lie flat when worn. Col.: Aino Hopea. *Photo: Oppi*

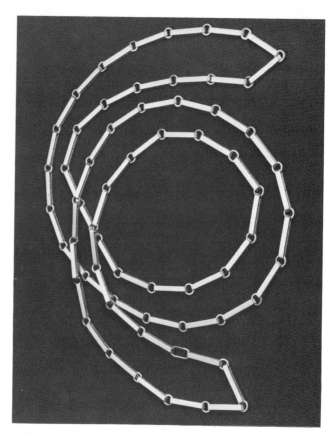

6–92 MICHAEL DRIVER, England. Silver chain of flat strip links and round wire loops. By changing the scale of parts, totally different-looking chains can be made with the same elements. *Photo: Courtesy The Worshipful Company of Goldsmiths, London*

6–93 KULTAKESKUS OY, Hämeenlinna, Finland, manufacturer. Soldering a link in a gold rope chain necklace of graduated link sizes, each of which engages the two previous links. A small gold solder snippet is placed on the join, and the link held in air with tweezers, the rest hanging below. The link is placed within the stationary flame of the torch which simply lies on the workbench. *Photo: Oppi*

6–94 KULTAKESKUS OY, Hämeenlinna, Finland, manufacturer. Oversized rope-type chain, each uniform link made of sheet strip formed into half-round, hollow links. *Photo: Oppi*

6–95 BERTIL GARDBERG, Finland, designer; manufacturer Kalevala Koru, Helsinki. Silver anchor-type chain of cast units linked by flat strip loops. *Photo: Studio Wendt, courtesy Kalevala Koru*

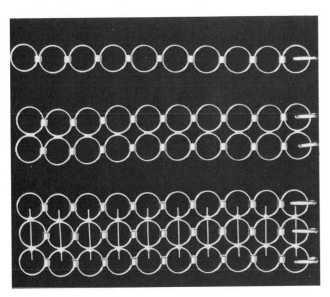

6-96 KAIJA AARIKKA, Finland, designer; manufacturer Aarikka Koru, Helsinki. "Peilikuvana" (Reflection). Silver round wire bracelets. The same-sized loops and linking system are used for the top single unit, and the soldered loop pairs and triplets, the latter pierced with a straight wire. Length 19.5 cm. *Photo: Studio Wendt, courtesy Aarikka Koru*

6-98 KAIJA AARIKKA, Finland, designer; manufacturer Aarikka Koru, Helsinki. Silver brooch using a series of interlooped chains. *Photo: Pentti Pietinen, courtesy Aarikka Koru*

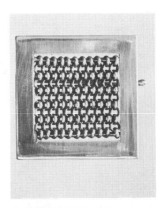

6-99 ADELIO VILLA, Italy, designer; manufacturer Giuseppe Villa, Milano. Necklace of 18K gold with handmade, soldered link, flattened curb chain, each alternating chain twisted in the opposite direction, forming a chevron pattern effect. The result is very flexible. *Photo: Franco Berra* ▼

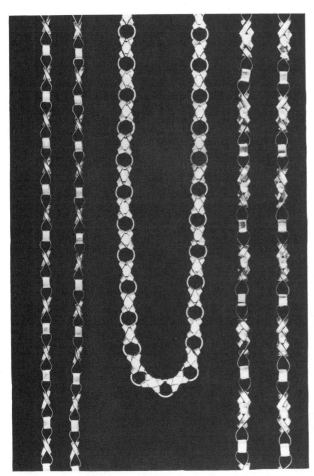

6-97 SAARA HOPEA-UNTRACHT, Finland, designer; manufacturer Kultasepänliike Ossian Hopea, Porvoo. Three silver chains, each rigid link made of flat sheet metal bent into dimensional forms. *Left* chain has one soldered joint; center, no soldered joints; *right*, two end-soldered joints. The last is in the collection of Margaret O'Conor Sloane. *Photo: Salmi*

6-100 *Left*: SAARA HOPEA-UNTRACHT, Finland, designer; manufacturer Kultasepänliike Ossian Hopea, Porvoo. Silver pendant with spectrolite. The surface of the ground sheet is decorated with alternating rows of commercial Venetian (or box) and curb chains, soldered flat in concentric series to form a textural area. *Photo: Oppi*

6-101 *Right*: Close-up of the pendant. *Photo: Oppi*

6–102 BARBARA GASCH, West Germany. Silver loop-in-loop chain belt with links that diminish in size toward the tail end. The snake head cast from a snake's skull has emerald eyes and gold fangs. To close the belt, the head's spring jaws bite the body. Length 90 cm. Photo: Astrid Mucs

combination produces an effect of twist that resembles a rope, though in fact no twisting occurs.

TWISTED AND UNTWISTED CHAINS Twisted chains generally have links of the same size and weight. They are assembled first in an untwisted form and then are given a twist so that all the links become equally and regularly deformed, nest within each other, and the chain becomes shorter in length. In the process of twisting, the wire also becomes hardened. Individual loops can be twisted and combined with plain, untwisted loops. Untwisted chains are generally more open in character than twisted chains.

RIGID-UNIT LINK CHAINS This category comprises chains in which the main unit is made of rigid metal in forms that may be of sheet, tube, wire, or cast units. These are joined to each other by visible links, concealed links, or any other system of interlinkage that allows flexibility in their total length.

MULTIPLE OR COMPOUND CHAINS These are chains that are constructed separately, and then joined to each other *edgewise, side by side* for their *entire length,* or at regular *intervals.* The result is a flexible or rigid band. The joining can be done by interlinking, by sewing, or by soldering.

LOOP-IN-LOOP CHAINS These chains are constructed of soldered *loops* by a system shown in the demonstration photo sequence ahead. The resulting chain, depending on the system used, appears openly or closely woven, but in fact is not woven but interlooped.

KNITTED WIRE CHAINS These are chains in which a thin-gauge wire of *continuous length* is knitted into a tube by any of several systems to form interlocking loops. There are no separate links. The texture is compact and highly flexible. The round, hollow tube that results can be flattened to make a band or tape, and units can be combined side by side to make wide bands. (The system is shown under Making a Knitted Wire Tube, p. 232.)

FANCY CHAINS Chains in which the wire links are not just simple rings or ovals, but of some special form comprise another category.

6–103 *Left:* NEPAL, MORANGIA DISTRICT. "Seven Star" (*sat sari har*) silver necklace used by Tharu women, worn with the five loop-in-loop chains at the front and the ornamented portion at the back. *Photo: Oppi*

6–104 *Right:* Tharu woman wearing the necklace. *Photo: Oppi*

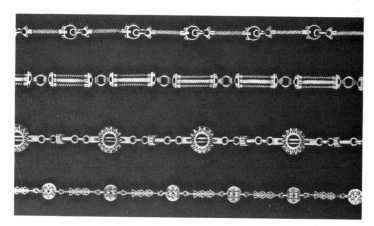

6–105 RICHARD MAWDSLEY, U.S.A. Fabricated sterling silver chains using small-dimension tube sections of various shapes, twisted and round wire, etc., in symmetrical arrangements. *Photo: Illinois State University Photograph Service*

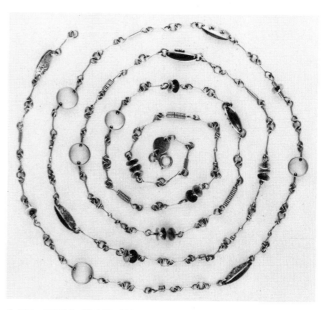

6–106 RUTH S. ROACH, U.S.A. Chain of 14K gold made of a variety of link shapes using tubes, discs, wire spirals, fused and granulated units, etc., interspaced at intervals with round swivel units to prevent the chain from tangling. Length 50 in. *Photo: Bob Carvill*

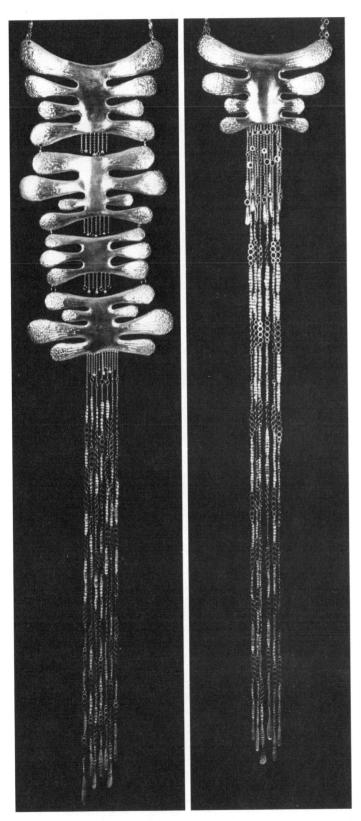

6-107 ARLINE M. FISCH, U.S.A. Sterling silver body necklace, front and back view. Some chain links consist of 24 gauge B.&S. sheet silver hammered into form on a lead block with a dapping punch, then sawed into shapes; others are a series of butt-soldered rings hammered flat; tumble polished. Width 10 in; length 52 in. *Photo: Bradford Palm*

MAKING PLAIN LINK CHAIN

The factors that influence the choice of wire size used are *total chain weight* and *chain density*. In general, thin, lightweight chain is made of 24–20 gauge B.&S. wire, medium-weight chain is made of 18–16 gauge wire, and heavy links are made of 9 gauge wire or hollow tubing which lightens the actual weight of large links. Very dense chains which would also therefore be very heavy can be made with thinner wires. The most commonly used wire shape is round in cross section, but half-round, or twisted wire are also used.

ANNEALING THE WIRE

Regardless of the material used, certain practices apply to all chain making. The wire should always be annealed to render it maximally flexible and to remove all springiness which would interfere with link making. (The method of annealing wire is discussed under Annealing Wire, p. 153.)

FORMING LINKS

The wire is then coiled on a *round mandrel* or *spit* of the desired section size to form the links, the coil is removed from the mandrel, the links are cut, and then butted. (These methods are all described under Chain Mail, Demonstration 5, p. 200.)

SOLDERING LINKS

Dip each link in liquid flux and place them spaced apart but in series on a *charcoal block* or other flat *soldering surface* so that they can be soldered one at a time. The seams should be pointing away from the flame source. Place one small snippet of easy-flow hard solder on top of each joint so that the solder straddles the joint and touches both sides. If the chain will be twisted later, use a harder solder. Use a *small torch tip* to pass the flame around each link first to dry the flux, then apply it briefly to the link and the solder. The flame must not linger on the link or it will melt. Withdraw the flame as soon as the solder flows, and proceed to the next link, repeating this procedure for each. Normally only half the needed number of links are soldered separately this way; the rest, in the course of assembling the chain.

To form a chain, intercept two soldered links with an unsoldered one. Grasping each end of the open link with *one pair of pliers* in each hand, close the open link as de-

6-108 KAIJA AARIKKA, Finland, designer; manufacturer Aarikka Koru, Helsinki. Silver rings using alternating bands of square wire and chain that is immobilized between them by soldering the links to the contacting bands. *Photo: Studio Wendt, courtesy Aarikka Koru*

scribed on page 202, in Illustration 12. Hold the unsoldered link in air, joint up, clamped in *self-locking tweezers,* with the two soldered links hanging below as far from the joint as possible. Apply some flux to the joint with a *flux brush,* and place one small solder snippet on top of the joint. No more than a small amount of solder is needed, because a surplus will form a bulge at the joint. With the same small torch tip, pass a flame around the link to dry the flux, then concentrate the flame tip on the solder with brief touches, avoiding overheating, until the solder flows. *Immediately* withdraw the flame. After making as many of these three-link groups as are needed, they can be joined to each other by an unsoldered link in a similar manner.

JOINING LINKS BY FUSION WITHOUT SOLDER

In a method developed by Jean Stark and Robert Kulicke, the link seam can be fused without solder. The method is fusion welding used for granulation. Plate the butted links with copper or dip them into a copper salt solution. Place them three or four at a time on a charcoal block, or in a small kiln with a glass cover. Depending on the size of the wire used, heat them for 10–30 seconds. Apply a No. 1 torch tip flame either in front of the joint, on the joint, or encompassing the whole link, again depending on the wire size. Heat to a temperature near fusion, at which point the joint will close in a fusion weld, and form a link without the bulge that may occur if solder is used.

FORMING A TWISTED CHAIN

Twisted chains (called *curb chains* in machine manufacture) can be easily made by hand from chains of regular, round, or oval, medium hard soldered links. Remember that the length of a twisted chain is less than that of the same chain before twisting, and compensate for this by making it long enough to begin with. The amount of the loss depends on the degree of the twist. The whole chain length must be twisted at the same time as it is very difficult to exactly match the degree of twist in separately twisted sections.

Anneal the chain to soften the metal if necessary. Clamp one end of the chain in a *bench vise,* and grasp the other end with a *hand vise.* Keeping the chain taut, turn the hand vise slowly while maintaining mild tension on the chain. Under this torsion, the links become twisted and automatically line up, one nesting within the other. Suspend the chain after twisting to see if all the links lie in one direction, and if they do not, continue the twisting till they do.

FLATTENING A CHAIN

Flattened chains are used in cases where it is undesirable for a chain to turn in use. A flattened chain normally stays flat once placed on the body. Not all chains are suited to flattening. Only those with soldered links can be flattened, as unsoldered links will open in the process.

To flatten a chain, hammer a headed nail through the first link into a flat hardwood board. Turn the board so that the chain hangs loose and all the links are *in the same relation to each other,* then stretch it tight and hammer a nail through the last link into the board. The soldered ends should be positioned so they will be covered by adjoining links. Hammer the chain lightly with a *wooden*

mallet to the desired degree of flatness. Once the flatness is established, the chain can be placed on a flat steel surface and flattened further. The effect of flatness can be increased without sacrificing strength by stretching and anchoring the chain as before and filing the highest surfaces. Flatness can be made more uniform if the chain is run through the rolls of a rolling mill. Be sure the rolls have been set at a distance apart that will not compress the links to the point of weakening or even destroying them. It is also possible to flatten twisted chain in the same way. The chain will appear even flatter if its upper surface is leveled with a *file.*

COMMERCIAL CHAIN

Commercial chain is any chain manufactured by *chain-making machines.* Great ingenuity has been shown in their invention, which is based on a rationalization of the hand chain-making process. Chains are manufactured in the precious metals in all the usual standard alloys of gold and silver, as well as rolled gold, bronze, brass, copper, nickel, stainless steel, etc.

Because the patterns produced are so numerous, it is almost impossible to classify them, but some broad divi-

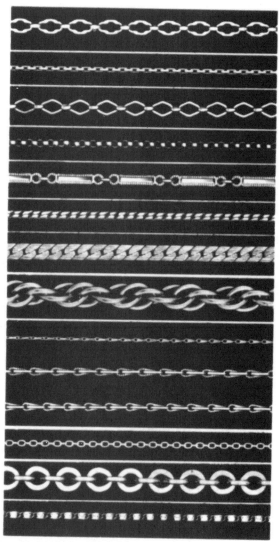

6-109 COMMON MACHINE-MADE CHAINS
An assortment of machine-made chains, available in gold, gold filled, and silver. *Courtesy Myron Toback, Inc.*

6–110 MARY ANN SCHERR, U.S.A. Stainless steel necklace with natural crystal. The design uses a graduated-length series of machine-made trace chains that fall in a chainette or catenary curve, a shape naturally assumed by a chain with fixed ends hanging free in equilibrium under gravity forces. *Photo: Richard Monasterio*

6–111 TAPIO WIRKKALA, Finland, designer; manufacturer Kultakeskus Oy, Hämeenlinna. Commercial gold trace chain hangs as an ornamental fringe from the animal's ears. *Photo: Courtesy Kultakeskus Oy*

sions can be mentioned. It must be remembered that each type is available in many variations.

Trace chain probably takes its name from the obsolete usage of the word in the sense of meaning a line, series, or succession. The word is still used to designate a pair of chains on a harness extending from a collar to a whiffletree attached to a drawn vehicle. They are made of equal-sized round or oval links placed in alternating horizontal and vertical planes to each other so that the chain does not lie flat.

Guard chain is a type of trace chain, but made with convex, half-round, hollow broad wire instead of plain round wire. It sometimes is called *belcher chain.*

Curb chain takes its name from the meaning of the word curb, "crooked" or "bent." It also has a meaning in horse parlance, referring to the chain attached to the upper part of the branches of a bit, used to restrain the horse by drawing against its lower jaw. This chain is first made as a trace chain, then twisted so that the links become bent and therefore lie flat. *Filed curb chain* is filed flat after being twisted.

Rope chain is a compound trace chain in which each new link engages and passes through the two or more previous links so that the links advance spirally and the result resembles a twisted cable or rope.

Venetian chain, also called *box chain,* is a form of trace chain in which all the links are square, and the opening small so that the result looks like a square chain.

Fancy chains are chains with specially designed links. Some are developments of those mentioned, and others are novelty inventions.

6–113 SVETOZAR RADAKOVICH, U.S.A. Silver bracelet using free-hanging series of commercial rope chain. *Photo: Svetozar Radakovich* ▶

6–112 AURES, DOUAR MENAA, NARA, ALGERIA. Silver pectoral with two 5 cm Ø fabricated fibulae connected by five smaller units from which hang 67 commercial, 10 cm long, guard chains ending in engraved sheet pendants. Worn with the fibulae fixed at the shoulders to hold a garment in place. *Photo: Musée de l'Homme, Paris*

6–114 ILSE IMMICH, West Germany. Silver medallion pendant with various stones, suspended by eight commercial Venetian chains interspersed with pearls and smoky quartz beads. *Photo: "Simone" Luino*

192

MECHANICAL CHAIN MAKING

In mechanical chain making, one continuous length of wire is used. While passing through the machine, it is processed by four separate actions, all performed automatically: the link is formed; the link is cut; the link is interlooped with the last link in the already completed chain; and the link is closed. These machines are capable of making many types of chains in all wire gauges. The fastest can produce 6,000 links in an hour.

Soldering the links closed is also done automatically. Normally, the chain is dipped into powdered solder after it comes off the machine, the surplus solder is removed, and to keep the links from being soldered together, powdered chalk is dusted on the chain. By another method, wire with a solder core is used, eliminating the above process. The chain is fed through a conveyer-type furnace that has a controlled, reducing atmosphere so that oxidation of the metal does not occur, and when it emerges, is soldered. Finishing may consist of polishing, hammering, diamond milling, or grinding. The chain is then cut into lengths suited to its use.

HANDMADE VS. MACHINE-MADE CHAINS

Most jewelers who make individual pieces that require the use of chain prefer to use one that is handmade as these are generally more compatible with the character of handmade jewelry. This feeling seems to be diminishing, however, and commercial chain is seen in ever greater use combined with parts that are hand fabricated. The suitability of machine-made chain depends very much on the kind of chain it is and on its finish. When oxidized or given a surface treatment similar to the main part, certain machine-made chains combine well with hand-fabricated parts. Most important is the choice of a chain that is visually related in weight and appearance to that of the work it holds. Chains can be constructed partially of machine-made and partially of handmade units.

Machine-made chain can be thought of as a form of *raw material* that can be used to ornament jewelry in decorative ways. In this way, a chain can surround a bezel, be soldered in side-by-side lengths to cover a surface and create a textural effect, or be hung in groups as a tassel or fringe, to mention just a few possible such uses.

SINGLE LOOP-IN-LOOP CHAIN MAKING

A serviceable chain can be made from a single loop-in-loop system. The process is simple and the result can be varied by changes in the gauge of the wire, and the form of the individual link.

Make circular loops by wrapping wire of the chosen gauge around a wooden dowel or metal mandrel in the usual way. Cut through the loops, solder the links, and shape them into ovals, either allowing some inner space or completely flat with sides touching. (See methods discussed on p. 194.) Form the loop into a circle by bending it with *pliers* over a wood dowel or metal mandrel whose diameter is the size of the inner diameter of the loop. Allow a portion of both ends of the loop to project upward by pinching them with the pliers. Open this upper projecting section by inserting and rotating a *round pick* or similar tool so that the opening is large enough for the two-wire thickness of the next loop to be passed through it. Pass one end of the next loop, already similarly shaped, sideways through this opening and turn it to its proper position. Continue this process with all remaining loops until the desired length has been reached.

6–115 *AUTOMATIC CHAIN-MAKING MACHINE* The wire is fed from a spool to the machine, and finished chain emerges at the front, bottom. Photo: Oppi

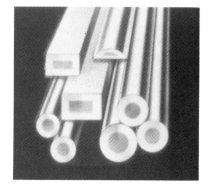

6–116 FRED WAGNER, Pforzheim, West Germany. Round and profiled wire with interior core of hard solder, available with exterior of 925, or 835 silver; karat gold alloys; rolled gold; and other metal alloys. This wire is used mainly in the chain-making industry to automatically solder closed formed and butted links that **pass through a tunnel kiln.** Soldering can also be done with a torch.

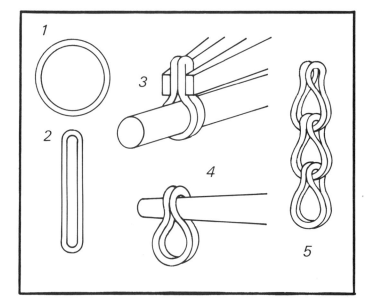

6–117 *MAKING A SINGLE LOOP-IN-LOOP CHAIN*
1. Circular loop.
2. Loop shaped to an oval.
3. Oval loop formed with pliers over a wooden dowel, ends pinched vertically.
4. Vertical end opened by the insertion of a pick.
5. Loop passed through loop in sequence.

6–118 ALESSANDRO CASTELLANI, England (son of *Fortunato Pio Castellani* [1793–1865], Italy). Pair of temporal pendants from a diadem, and a necklace, made in 1865, faithfully reproducing the 4th-century B.C. Hellenistic Greek originals found 1864 in a tumulus near Vyeshesteblevshaya village on the Taman peninsula, in ancient Phanagoria, Southern Russia. The originals are now in the Hermitage Museum in Leningrad. This illustrious jeweler family was famed for their stylistic and technically accurate reproduction of ancient jewelry. These reproductions were purchased for £88 by the Victoria and Albert Museum in 1884 from the Castellani Collection, which also contained important antique jewelry that served them as models.

Both these jewels employ a typical ancient Greek construction system involving an assemblage of hundreds of parts by the use of supporting and unifying *chains* whose end links pass through loops on the parts they hold. The *temporal pendants* depict Achilles' mother Thetis who lived in the sea, riding a sea horse and carrying the breastplate (*left*) and the greaves (*right*) of the impenetrable armor she ordered Vulcan, the celestial metalsmith, to make for her son for use during the Trojan War. The lower half of the rims alternate with rosettes and studs, from which hang 12 single loop-in-loop chains in vertical and diagonal directions, forming a flexible and stable network. At their junctions, which are emphasized by small rosettes, in five rows (6-5-4-5-6 in each row) hang four different-sized hollow pendentive units in the form of *amphorae*, Greek jars used to contain oil and wine, presented to winners at games and victories, mostly granulation decorated.

The *necklace* employs a main supporting strap chain made of a **six-wale wide loop-in-loop fabric that terminates in repoussage** finials in the form of lions' heads whose jaws grasp rings that serve as a fastening. To the lower strap edge is attached a row of 43 alternating rosettes and studs. Attached to 20 rosettes are groups of three single loop-in-loop chains from which hang three rows of different-sized amphorae (21 small, 22 medium, 21 large in each row). The first and last rosettes hold only two chains. A total of 64 single loop-in-loop chain lengths are used in the design. The central chain of the triple groups hangs straight and holds the medium-sized amphorae; the other two fall in diagonal directions and join in pairs to hold a large amphora which because of this triangulation stays in place. The smallest amphorae are attached to the studs. Total necklace length 15 in. Photo: Victoria and Albert Museum, London, Crown Copyright

MULTIPLE LOOP-IN-LOOP CHAIN MAKING

DEMONSTRATION 4

CHUCK EVANS shows the technique of interlocking deformed links

Photos: Chuck Evans

CHOICE OF SYSTEMS

The loop-in-loop chain-making system is one of the basic and most ancient concepts in chain making. In this system, a chain can be constructed by using from 1 up to 12 loops within each other. In a two-loop chain, an oval-shaped loop is passed through a similar loop bent into a U shape. The result is a chain that is square in cross section, and one that is more open in texture density and less flexible than a three- (or more) loop chain. The latter are more complicated to make and necessitate more material, but are denser, round in section, and flexible.

CHOICE OF MATERIALS

The choice of round *wire gauge size,* and the *diameter* of the basic loop are the variables. Any change in these factors will make a difference in the dimensions of chain diameter and length, and in the character of the finished chain. In the demonstration, a 3 loop-in-loop chain using 22 gauge B.&S. round silver wire is shown. The *hardwood dowel* used as a loop-making mandrel has a ½ in di-

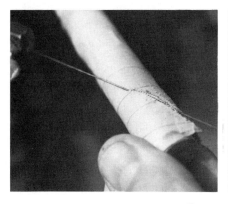

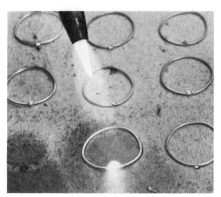

1   2   3

ameter. The final, finished chain has a diameter of ³⁄₁₆ in. It requires about 30 rings per inch. A 20 in chain of this type uses about 600 loops made from approximately 77 ft of wire. The finished chain weighs about 2½ ounces.

MAKING THE LOOPS

1 The wire is annealed sterling silver. Secure a 1 ft (30.5 cm) section of a hardwood dowel firmly in a *bench vise.* Carefully and uniformly wrap the wire around the end of the dowel. Each single turn in the wire coil is called a *wap.* Three inches of wrapped wire of these dimensions will make about 115 loops or jump rings. Tightly wrap two layers of *masking tape* around the coiled wire to hold the loops in place so that when they are cut, they will not spring off the dowel. With a *No. 1 jeweler's saw blade,* cut along the axis of the dowel in a spiral direction through both tape and wire.

2 By spiral cutting, each loop is left with a diagonal scarf joint cut for soldering, a type that because of its greater surface contact adds strength to each ring, and therefore to the total chain. Remove the loops and peel off the tape. There is no residue from the tape to interfere with soldering.

SOLDERING THE LOOPS

3 With the fingers or with *pliers,* shape the loop joint so the overlapping parts touch. If the sawing has been done carefully, the joint is well fitting. Lay the loops on a flat *asbestos pad.* Flux each joint and place a snippet of hard solder on top of each. With a *small tip torch,* solder each loop. The result should not require any filing. Pickle the loops, wash and dry them.

CONVERTING ROUND LOOPS TO OVALS

4 The round loop must be converted to an *oval,* the basic shape used in loop-in-loop chain making. The object is to change the shape but *not the total dimension,* and to

avoid stretching the loop. For this purpose, *round-nosed pliers* have been file grooved on the outside of each nose part, the same distance from the nose end. This groove holds a single loop for shaping. Pliers exist that are made especially for this purpose, have several grooves at intervals, and are called *bow-opening pliers.* Place the round loop on the pliers with its sides within each of these grooves. Be sure the *soldered joint* is in the *center* of the loop. This is important because in this way, the joint will be concealed *inside* the chain construction. Spread the plier jaws apart only enough to convert the round loop to an oval shape, easily done as the wire is in an annealed state from the heat of soldering.

STARTING THE CHAIN

5 A two-, three-, (or more) loop system could be followed. In each case the loops must be initially arranged to cross each other in a regular, evenly spaced arrangement. In the system illustrated here, three loops cross each other in the manner shown, with their ends 60° apart.

6 These are soldered to the end of an upright copper or brass rod of about ⅛ in (3.2 mm) diameter. It is important that each loop be soldered squarely to the rod since this is the point of stress when the interlooping starts.

7 Clamp the rod with the loops on top into a bench vise.

8 Bend the loop ends upward with the fingers to make them almost vertical, a position that best allows them to receive the loops that follow.

LOOP-IN-LOOP PLACEMENT

9 To line up and open the loop ends to facilitate the passage of other loops through them, an old, *modified dental tool* is used, but any tapered metal pick of suitable diameter would work. The looping can start at any point,

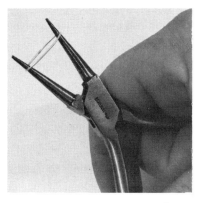

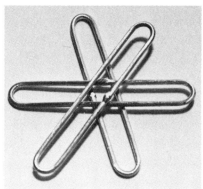

4   5   6   7

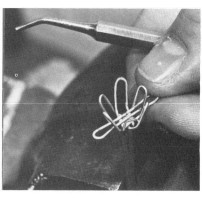
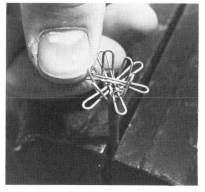

8   9   10   11

and continue in either a clockwise, or counterclockwise direction, but whichever direction is chosen must be continued until the chain is finished. Here the first loop is placed in position.

10 The second and third loops are in place, each one all the way through the two opposite loops, and on top of the loop placed before it. At this point, two rounds of "sets" (six loops) are in place, the first which was soldered to the rod, and the second which has just been added.

11 With the fingers, bend the ends of the loops upward to a vertical position.

THE TWO-LOOP INTERPASS SYSTEM FOR A DENSER CHAIN

12 In the three-loop system described and illustrated here, *chain density* is increased by passing each subsequent loop through the *two previous ones* from here on rather than through only the last one. The pass that starts here is important as it establishes the basic two-loop interpass system. Before passing the loop through, line up the opposite loops by inserting the dental tool.

13 Insert each of the next three loops under *two loops* of the previous two sets.

14 From this point onward, repeat the procedure already described: first line up the opposite openings with a dental tool, then insert a loop through the two previously placed loops, in the established direction. After each set of three loops is in place, bend the set upward with the fingers.

If you wish a chain that has a more open appearance, and one that uses less material and is therefore lighter in weight, it is of course possible to follow a system of inserting the loops only through the *last* loop, and not two loops. Openness can be decreased by using loops of shorter length.

15 After approximately 2 in (5.1 cm) of chain length have been made, remove the rod from the vise, place the chain completed so far on an *anvil,* and while rotating it, gently hammer it with a *rawhide mallet* to round the form and make the texture more compact. Return the rod to the vise and continue the loop-in-loop process.

FINISHING THE CHAIN

When the chain looping is finished, its surface can be made more uniform by carefully drawing it through at least two openings in a *drawplate* made of hardwood or steel. At the same time, the chain is lengthened somewhat. Pass the starting rod through the drawplate hole and grasp it with *drawtongs.* Pull the chain through the drawplate in this direction so that the pressure is not contrary to the direction of the bend of the loops.

After drawing, saw off the starting rod. If the chain is in two parts, each of them should run in the same direction when worn, so the chain must be cut in half. The ends of the chain are unfinished, and the usual practice is to cover them with chain-ending devices such as a sleeve or casing made of a section of tubing slightly larger than the chain diameter, to which a loop or hook is soldered. They should be prepared beforehand. They are placed at the chain ends and the chain is soldered into them. The chain can now be finished. It can be gold plated, polished bright, or colored by oxidation chemicals.

CHAIN PATTERN VARIATIONS

Color variations can be introduced by using loops made of different colored metals, such as copper, gold, brass, or shakudo. These can alternate in any combination or sequence in a regular or in an irregular manner. *Tapered chain* can be made by decreasing the loop size combined with a gradual decrease in wire gauge size used for the loops. *Twisted wire* can be used for links to produce a

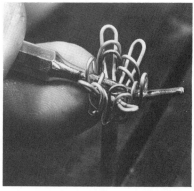
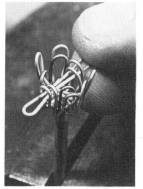

12   13   14   15

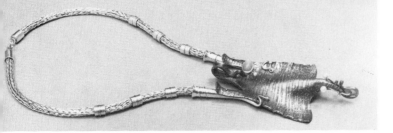

chain with a textured surface. The chain can be *twisted* after it is finished, but this results in some loss of flexibility. It is possible to *flatten* a loop-in-loop chain by hammering it gradually with a *rawhide mallet,* annealing the chain between courses to render the wire softer.

16 Pendant and loop-in-loop sterling chain, by Chuck Evans, U.S.A., with pearls and moonstone. The pendant is of forged and textured 16 gauge B.&S. bronze with sterling elements; the chain is threaded with sections of gold tube.

Photo: Photo Service, Bowling Green State University

CHAIN COUPLINGS

Chain couplings are findings and other means of uniting the ends of a length of chain, or of connecting the chain to an object such as a pendant, watch, earring, bracelet, or other form of jewelry in which chain might be used. Chains long enough to go over the head need no couplings, but those too short to be put on this way do. A coupling also allows a long chain to be wrapped many times around the neck or the wrist, then closed.

Couplings may be placed at the back where they are not meant to be seen but simply be functional. The coupling can also be highly ornamental, and in this case it can be worn at the back *or* at the front. Among the couplings used for chains are catches, hooks, jump rings, loops, swivels, toggles, capped and looped ferrules, as well as others. (See Glossary: Jewelry Findings.)

CHAIN MAIL

A unit system of intertextured construction

The importance of chain mail and armor to the jeweler lies in the wealth of functional and design concepts that they incorporate. Many of the systems of construction they employ are based on the repetition of units, and their decorative forms can be utilized by the jeweler. Museum collections of chain mail and armor are well worth studying as a source of inspiration.

Chain mail is a flexible fabric made of interlocking metal rings or links made of wire, or wire links in combination with metal plates. The term *mail* can be used to mean a single link or an entire garment made of mail, such as those articles used for defensive armor in Europe and throughout the East, starting as early as the 2nd century B.C. and continuing well into the 17th century.

The earliest types of body armor were made of leather or skins to which metal rings or small plates were sewn or riveted, inside or outside the armor, or were held between layers of leather or cloth. The use of whole garments made of chain mail consisting entirely of interlaced metal links, as chain mail is generally thought to be, came into very wide use in Europe from the 10th through the 13th centuries, a time often called the "Age of Mail." The most common protective articles made of chain mail were the *hauberk* (a tunic), *chausses* (leg coverings), *camail* (a chain cape or neck guard attached to a helmet); even *gauntlets* (gloves) were made of mail. It was usual to wear a quilted garment beneath the mail such as the *acton* or *gambeson* worn beneath the hauberk.

CHAIN MAIL CONSTRUCTION

Before the 13th century, mail was made from iron wire produced by forging. The fine *cast iron drawplate* which then came into use greatly facilitated and expedited the wire making process. (It is probably due to the large demand for wire for use in chain mail construction that the drawplate was introduced.) In the 14th century water

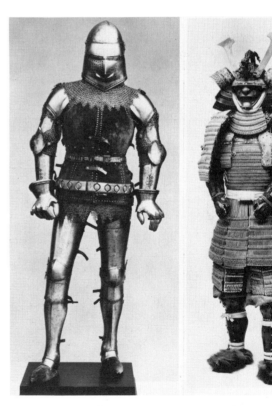

6–119 *Left:* ITALY. Armor from about 1400 A.D., showing the use of a chain mail hauberk beneath a leather cuirass, and a chain mail collar. Metropolitan Museum of Art, Bashford Dean Memorial Col., gift of Helen Fahnenstock Hubbard, 1929. *Photo: Metropolitan Museum of Art, New York*
Right: JAPAN. Suit of armor made by Yoshihisa Matahachiro, ca. 1550 A.D., Muromachi period. Made of over 4,500 black-oxidized, gold-lacquered steel plates, numerous gilded bronze mail links, 265 yards of orange silk braid, 1,000 rivets, and leather. Col.: Metropolitan Museum of Art, Rogers Fund, 1904. *Photo: Metropolitan Museum of Art, New York*

6–120 HUNGARY. Fine silver chain mail hauberk, a tunic form coat of mail worn exposed or below sheet armor, made for György Rákóczi II, a heroic, 17th-century reigning prince of Transylvania. Decorated with gilded silver stamped bosses in star and rosette shapes containing a stone, attached to the mail by means of prongs folded over at the back, inside the garment. Some are arranged to simulate a choker and necklace. Length 85 cm; width 50 cm. Photo: J. Karáth, National Museum of Hungary (Magyar Nemzeti Múseum), Budapest

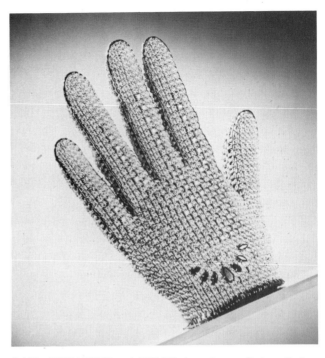

6–122 MARC MEYERIE and GRIVAUD, Lyon, France. Chain mail glove made of 18K yellow gold wire interlinked loops that required more than 10,000 solderings, and the work of 12 persons who completed it in 1,600 working hours. Mounted with 200 diamonds, each $^{10}/_{100}$ pt, and a total of four carats of emeralds. Weight 620 g (1.36 lb). Photo: René Basset

6–123 NETHERLANDS. Sterling silver chain mail evening purse, a type popular during the 1920s. Made of alternating rows of heavy, flat wire loops and thin round wire loops. The frame is decorated with repoussé work and wire. Photo: Museum Boymans-van Beuningen, Rotterdam

6–121 KAIJA AARIKKA, Finland, designer; manufacturer Aarikka Koru, Helsinki. Brass chain mail garment made of die-stamped units joined by wire jump rings. Photo: Courtesy Aarikka Koru

power was utilized to facilitate wire drawing in a system where a water wheel turned a crank having an attached rope that ended in a wire-grasping tong held by a stirrup. More easily drawn wire, such as that made of gold, silver, and copper, continued to be drawn by hand through drawplates. Mail was not often made of precious metals, but mail exists where elaborate geometric patterns were assembled in one fabric from links of iron, brass, and copper. Precious metals were, however, widely used to ornament chain mail armor.

Most mail is made of round links, but the Japanese made frequent use of a network of round links from which oval links radiated. The central, round links engaged four or six ovals respectively, making a square or hexagonal arrangement. The wire used in European mail is usually of the same dimension throughout the garment, but in Oriental mail, wire sizes varied and was heaviest where maximum protection was needed. The links were made by wrapping the wire around a mandrel, then cutting the resulting coil to form individual rings. Mail made of links that were left open was the least valued, and the better grades had welded or riveted links joined by one, two, or even three rivets. To avoid the tedious job of closing the thousands of links used in one garment, mail was sometimes made of double or triple spirals, cut from one continuous coil. Where heat was employed, as in welding a join, the iron mail had to be tempered to restore its hardness, essential for protection.

In ordinary mail, the common system has each link passing through four others (see Illustration 6–124) in a regular, consistent, interlocking arrangement. Even when using this basic system, depending on the wire gauge chosen, its appearance can vary from an open network to one

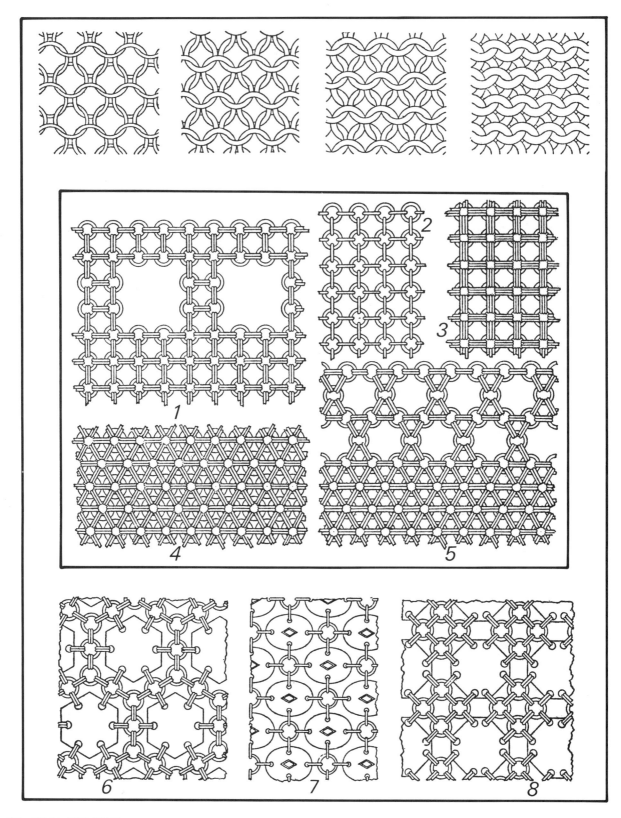

6-124 *CHAIN MAIL TYPES*

Top: By increasing the wire gauge in a transition from ordinary wire mail (left) to double mail (right), while the OD of the links remains the same, the ID decreases progressively, until finally, the openings become closed.

Center: Japanese link mail types. 1. Square, *vertically and horizontally linked* pattern. 2. Square pattern, single links. 3. Square pattern, three-turn links. 4. Hexagonal pattern, *diagonally linked*, with heavygauge wire central link. 5. Hexagonal pattern, small-gauge wire cen-

tral links. Both linking systems shown allow the creation of open spaces.

Below: Plate and link mail. 6. Hexagonal plates, connected *vertically, horizontally,* and *diagonally* by wire link mail. 7. Elliptical plates connected *vertically and horizontally* by link mail. 8. Octagonal plates connected *diagonally* by link mail. *Line drawings from* A Glossary of the Construction, Decoration and Use of Arms and Armor, *by George Cameron Stone, with permission of Jack Russel, publisher.*

so dense the openings are hardly visible. The choice of wire gauge is therefore important. If the wire is a thin gauge and the link size relatively large, the result is an open net. If the mail diameter remains the same and the gauge is increased, the openings are reduced. As the internal diameter of the link decreases, the opening between the links grows smaller. When the link wire gauge is more than half the inside diameter measurement of the link, the resulting mail has no visible opening. Its appearance can be varied by using round wire, flattened round links, or twisted wire. Whatever the wire gauge or form, the construction must lie flat and possess the considerable degree of flexibility that is its basic advantage.

MAIL AND PLATES

Some Japanese mail was made of a mixture of mail links and flat or shaped plates of sheet metal linked by mail. These small plates were usually geometric in shape, the most common forms being the square, rectangle, circle, oval, hexagon, and octagon. The plates could be treated with a variety of decorative techniques such as piercing, repoussé, inlay, etching, engraving, stamping, gilding, riveting, etc.

Depending on the shape of the basic plate unit, the structure was either vertical and horizontal, or diagonal. These systems can be adapted for jewelry making. Diagonal systems are especially suited to forms such as necklaces that must have a fabric that will lie flat over shaped surfaces, i.e., the shoulders. In vertical and horizontal arrangements, shaping can be achieved in a necklace, for instance, by starting with a small unit near the neck and

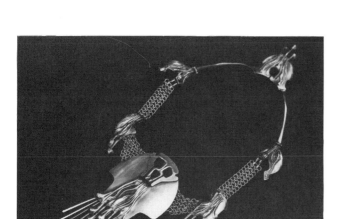

6-125 NILDA C. F. GETTY, U.S.A. "Mask." Sterling silver neckpiece with repoussé-worked sheet metal units joined by chain mail sections. It opens by a double hook attached on the right to the top of the chain mail section. *Photo: Les Brown*

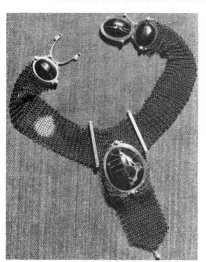

6-126 CHARLOTTE DE SYLLAS, England. Chain mail choker made of mild steel given a blue patina in a kiln. Mounted with carved mosaic stones, the front one containing an emerald. *Photo: Courtesy The Worshipful Company of Goldsmiths, London*

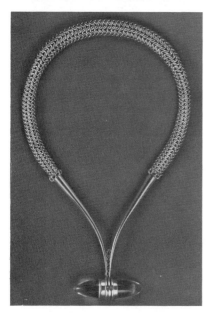

6-127 MICHAEL PINDER, England. Neckpiece in sterling silver with a tubular-shaped neck band made on a flexible chain mail module, the link sizes decreasing toward the extremities. Other parts are fabricated from sheet and wire. Two self-cut, high cabochon rock crystals are set end to end with the fastening mechanism between them. Size 225 × 145 mm. *Photo: Peter Parkinson*

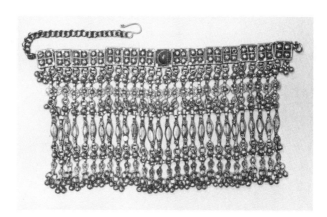

6-128 EGYPT. Bedouin silver ornament (*Kirdan*) worn suspended across the face. The construction consists of vertically and horizontally linked, stamped, and wire-made units which maintain their position, as in chain mail. *Photo: Oppi*

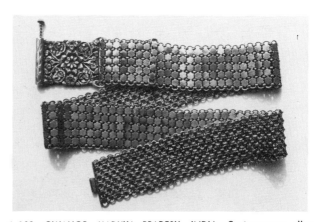

6-129 GWALIOR, MADHYA PRADESH, INDIA. Contemporary silver chain mail belt, employing a very flexible system of links soldered together in vertical series, and covered with six-petaled, stamped flower units soldered to the links. Vertical units are then interlinked horizontally with loose jump rings. The closing screw (*above left*) is a straight wire length wrapped spirally with a thinner wire. This engages a split tube (*below left*) in which a similar spiral or wire is soldered, that intermeshes with the screw. *Photo: Oppi*

6-130 MARY ANN SCHERR, U.S.A. Collar of 14K gold with 50 diamonds *en tremblant*. The structure consists of vertical, rigid elements interlocked by the prongs projecting from alternating units which engage the loops of their neighbors. Photo: Richard Monasterio

6-131 ENGLAND. Victorian silver necklace with pendant, 1885, that opens up and originally contained two daguerreotypes. The necklace uses a link and plate system, each flower-shaped plate stamped with a star, a motif repeated on the pendant. Flexibility between links and plates permits the necklace to lie flat on the wearer. Col.: Dietlind Bock-Meinardus. Photo: Oppi

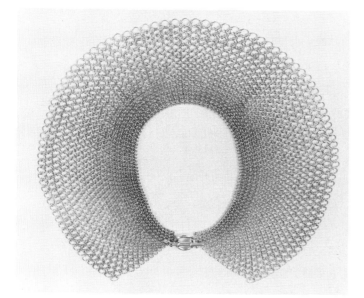

6-132 PEDER MUSSE, Denmark. Sterling silver chain mail collar. Made in graduating link sizes, the smallest toward the neck to allow for the expanding circle diameter, and to make the necklace flat on the body when worn. Photo: Little Bobby Hanson

then gradually increasing the unit size as it moves away from the neck.

Articles of mail were sometimes decorated with studs, flat or in relief, applied on top of a mail ground by rivets, bent prongs, or in other ways. This idea can also be adapted to use in decorating chain mail jewelry.

6-133 MARY ANN SCHERR, U.S.A. "Circles and Lines." Stainless steel necklace, the units assembled with straight, hook-ended stainless steel wires whose rigidity permits shape retention. Photo: Richard Monasterio

6-134 U.S.A. Head ornament made from the pull-open mechanism (pop tops) of soft drink cans, linked in a chain mail system. Worn at the traditional Easter Parade on Fifth Avenue in New York. Photo: Lehtikuva Oy

MAKING CHAIN MAIL LINKS AND PLATES

DEMONSTRATION 5

DAVID LAPLANTZ makes a chain mail necklace

Photos: Shereen LaPlantz

MAKING THE LINKS

1 The method of making links described here is the same as that for making jump rings used in chain making. The wire in 10–15 ft (3.0–4.5 m) lengths is drawn through three or four drawplate holes to stiffen it and bring it to the desired dimension. Gauge is chosen according to need. The simplest way to make the chain mail links is to wrap the wire around a *metal mandrel* in the form of a straight round bar, as tightly as possible, holding one end with the

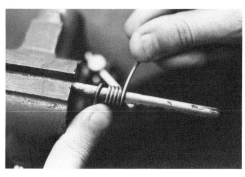

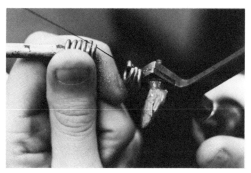

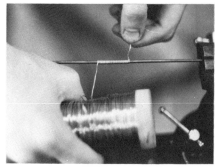

1

2

3

left hand while the right hand wraps the wire. There should be no space between the turns or the links will not be of identical size. (A hole can be drilled in the mandrel into which the wire end can be inserted to hold it in place while the rest is wrapped. Other wire-wrapping systems are also possible.)

Round spirals can generally be easily forced off the mandrel, but oval or other shaped links may resist removal. To facilitate spiral removal, before wrapping the wire, wrap the mandrel spirally with a piece of tissue paper and secure it at both ends with masking tape. When the wrapping is finished, burn the paper away with a torch flame. The added thickness of the paper, now eliminated, is enough to allow the coil to be easily pushed off the mandrel. Here the mandrel end has been sawed with a groove so that when the links are cut from the coil, the saw blade is unobstructed, which keeps breakage of blades to a minimum.

2 At each turn of the spiral, cut the wire straight through with a jeweler's saw. Feed the coil to the blade at an angle so that only the upper turn is cut. The cutting line should be kept straight to make the links the same size. When cut through, some of the links gather on the saw blade, and others fall off, but are caught in a tray kept below the sawing place for this purpose, and also to collect metal filings, especially if precious metal is used.

3 In preparation for making a spiral link used in the design, the link itself a spiral shape (see photo of the finished piece), a heavy-gauge wire is stretched between two *fixed vises,* then wrapped with a smaller gauge wire. When the wrapping is finished, the coil is compressed horizontally simultaneously from both sides to tighten it and give it uniformity. Later, the wrapped wire is itself wrapped around a larger mandrel to form spiral links, cut into separate links in the same way as above.

MAKING THE HEXAGONAL PLATES

4 The plan for the basic construction system for the necklace shows how the plates will be held by the mail links.

5 To make the hexagonal plates, a cardboard *template* or pattern is cut out, then used to make a metal template with which the remaining hexagons were created. To assure angle accuracy, a *protractor* is used.

6 To save the work of having to saw two sides of the hexagon, since the design calls for 29 plates, a strip of metal the exact width of the hexagon is cut out first. The template is traced at one end of the strip with a *scriber.*

7 Measurements are made with a *ruler* and *dividers* to mark the exact location of the holes to be drilled through the plates, through which the mail links will pass. Drilling is done in the intact blank since it is easier to handle a strip of this size than small, individual, cut-out hex-

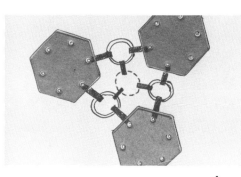

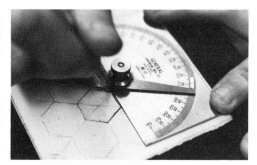

4

5

6

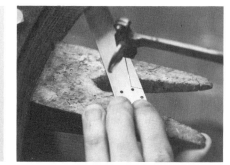

7

8

9

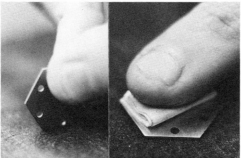

10   **11**   **12**

agons. The drill locations are marked with a *center punch* and *hammer* to keep the drill from wandering.

8 Whenever drilling with a *mechanical drill press,* wear a *full face shield* for protection against flying metal fragments. The metal is placed and held tightly on a wooden block on the drill press table, and the chuck is lowered by the hand lever until the drill touches a hole location. The lubricated drill is made to pierce all the holes in the hexagon, taking care to avoid drill breakage by not feeding the drill to the metal with too much pressure.

9 The metal hexagon is cut from the strip with a *jeweler's saw.* The cutting line follows the outer side of the marked line to allow for trimming to true size.

10 The sawed sides are trued by holding the hexagonal plate on a bench pin and filing the sides vertically so that the resulting edges are square.

11 The final truing of the edges and smoothing of the surface of the hexagon is done on a 400-grit Wet-O-Dry *sandpaper.* To simplify holding the small hexagon while finishing the flat surfaces, a section of about 2 in (5 cm) of *masking tape* is rolled up, sticky side out, and placed on the metal. It grips the part and the finger so the hexagon is easily moved up and back. All the plates are given the same surface sanding treatment, in one direction.

JOINING THE LINKS

12 Joining the chain mail links and plates is done with the help of two *flat-nosed pliers.* The link is used in exactly the condition in which it comes on sawing it from the coil. To close an open link, grip one end with flat-nosed pliers, and the other end on the side opposite the first with a second pair of pliers. Bend the link ends first laterally, away from each other to make the link become stiffer, and then toward each other until its ends are perfectly aligned and opposite each other, end to end, as closely as possible. The links are not soldered closed as they do not bear much weight.

13 The finished neckpiece after assembly of the chain mail links and plates. Some of the hexagons have been given various additional surface treatments: straight line and circular scoring done with a *scriber* and a pair of *sharp-pointed dividers* respectively, and piercing with additional holes. The links made of circlets of spiral wire are below. The wire on which the assembly of chain mail and plates is mounted is wrapped with silver wire and bent to a hook at the ends. This supporting wire passes through the chain mail links in a way that keeps them in position. The hexagon plates and the copper links are gold plated, and decorative chains of links below are silver plated. The entire neckpiece has been made totally without soldering.

Photo: David LaPlantz

14 A detail of the necklace.

13

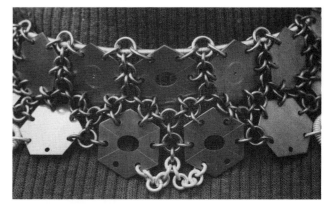

14

6–135 Right: CHAIN MAIL CONSTRUCTIONS
David LaPlantz illustrates possible linking systems. *Photos: David LaPlantz;* read left to right (ver. = vertical; hor. = horizontal)

Photo A: VERTICAL CHAINS

1. Single-single
2. Double-single
3. Triple-single
4. Double-double
5. Triple-double
6. Single-single, staggered link
7. Double-double, staggered link
8. Double-single/ single-double
9. Triple-triple, overlap link
10. Double-double/ double-triple, overlap link
11. Triple-triple, overlap link with loose pickup link

Photo B: DOUBLE AND TRIPLE VERTICAL CHAINS

1. Double-single ver. joined to double-single ver. with hor. single link through ver. single links
2. Single-single ver. joined to single-single ver. with hor. single link through alternating ver. single links
3. Double-single ver. joined to double-single ver. with hor. single links through ver. doubles and singles
4. Double-single ver. joined to double-single ver. with hor. single links through ver. single links, and through inside double links

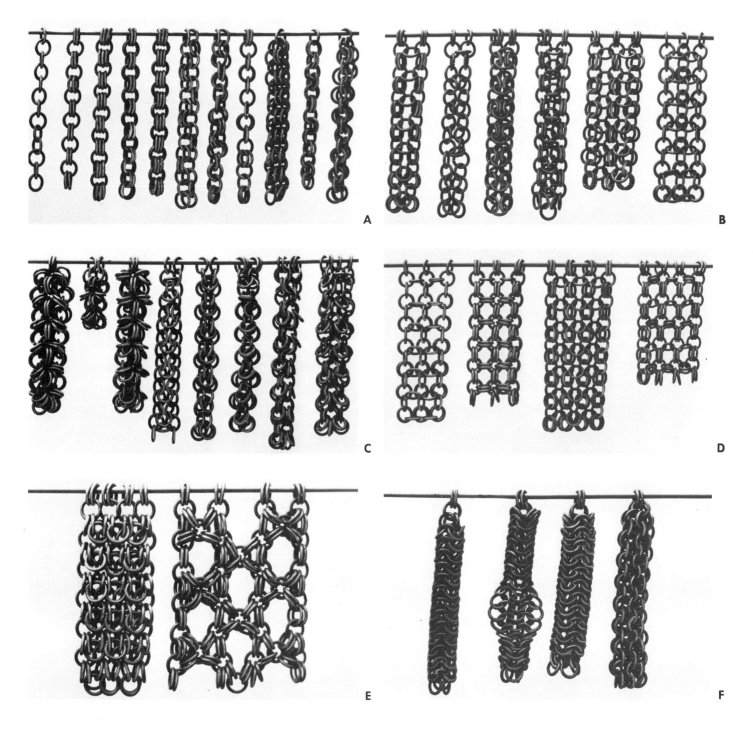

A

B

C

D

E

F

5. Three double-single ver. joined by hor. single links through ver. single links

6. Three double-single ver. joined with hor. single links through ver. double links

Photo C: VERTICAL CHAIN VARIATIONS

1. Tube of four double-single ver. chains joined by hor. double links held with ver. single links

2. Tube of three rows of single-double ver. chains joined by hor. double links connected with ver. single links

3. Same as C-2, with larger diameter links

4. Variation of B-2. Single-single ver. chain joined to single-single ver. chain with hor. single links through pairs of ver. single links

5. Two single-single ver. chains joined with single links through both chain sides on alternating links

6. Two double-single ver. chains joined with hor. single links on both chain sides, which tightly pulls single links, and makes double links come together

7. Three single-single ver. chains joined with hor. single links (variation of C-2)

8. Four single-single ver. chains joined with hor. single links (variation of C-1)

Photo D: JAPANESE MAIL MESH VARIATIONS

1. Three double-single ver. joined with hor. single links through ver. double links

2. Three double-double ver. joined with hor. double links through ver. double links

3. Four double-single ver. joined with hor. single links through ver. single links

4. Four double-single ver. joined with hor. alternating double and single links through ver. single links

Photo E: JAPANESE MAIL MESH VARIATIONS

1. Four double-single ver. joined with hor. single links through ver. inside double links; both front and back

2. Hexagonal structure: Four double-single ver. joined with double diagonal links through ver. single links; these diagonal pairs joined with ver. single links

Photo F: COMPOUND CIRCULAR STRUCTURES

1. Hor. link chain, six links across

2. Hor. link chain, opened up (variation of F-1)

3. Hor. link chain, larger diameter links, eight across

4. Ver. chain system, double-singles joined with single-singles

WIRE AND STRIP IN INTERWORKED PROCESSES

Using concepts employed with fibrous materials

In the history of the development of technology, archeologists and anthropologists tell us that fiber technology preceded textile weaving, which in turn preceded metal technology by thousands of years. It is not surprising therefore that some of the technical knowledge gained in the use of fibrous materials was ultimately transferred to metalwork. Some of these transitional processes and their concepts are discussed here. Besides their most important use in the creation of fabrics of fiber, they all have been and still are in use by various world cultures in making and decorating objects in metal, including jewelry.

Returning to man's earliest skills, some contemporary jewelers are focusing their attention on a restudy and exploration of the fibercrafts to reinterpret the wealth of technical concepts to be found in this area and reconsider their possible application to and utilization in new directions for metal jewelry making.

Of all the fibercraft processes, those used in basketry relate most closely to the kind of results achievable when metal is substituted for fibrous materials, because as structures, at least some of the elements used in baskets require an inherent rigidity, a condition natural to metal. The basic components or elemental shapes of fibers interworked in basketry and mat making, which are the very earliest fiber-made artifacts, are the *round form* (as in reeds and rushes; cane, vines, twigs, and osiers; yarns, cords, and ropes) and the *flat strip* (as in plant leaf strips, mid ribs, split stalks, stem sections, and flattened cereal stalks; bamboo or wood strips). These substances and forms possess a broad range of flexibility or rigidity, and can be of any diameter or thickness, width and length. When these forms are translated into metal, the same variables are encountered. Although the scale may be considerably reduced in the sizes suitable for use in jewelry making, *round wire* or *tubing* takes the place of round forms, and *metal strip* replaces fiber strip. Such a substitution is easily made because of the obvious physical similarity between the forms of these materials.

Round wire offers no directional resistance (because of its uniform section and round form) and can be bent into any curves or angles. This condition makes round wire a more versatile shape than metal strip, and also allows a high degree of control and uniformity in the results. *Strip metal* can be bent to any angle or curve in the direction of its flat surfaces, but only to a very limited degree in a sideways direction. It can also be wrapped flat spirally around a core, or given a limited self-twist. These basic ways of shaping wire and strip are the foundation for their use in construction and decoration.

Other parallels can be drawn from similarities in the field of woven textiles. Most textile fabrics are made of spun and twisted threads. Although wire is drawn rather than spun, two or more wire elements can be twisted together to make a multiple-ply element that in structure resembles twisted-ply yarn. Twisted wire elements can take the place of any single strand wire or strip element used in many of these systems of construction. (See Twisted Wire, Chapter 6.)

6–136 ORISSA, INDIA. Tribal woman wearing a headdress of fiber strips with woolen tassels held to the head by twisted cords. *Photo: Madan Mahatta*

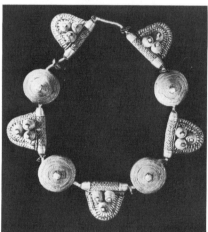

6–137 MALI. Straw diadem worn by the Songhai, who live below Timbuktu in the bend of the Niger River. Mostly Muslim, these people mixed with Moors and the Fulah, and formed a powerful empire from the 10th to the 16th centuries. The diadem is made of flattened straw stalk dyed yellow with saffron, sewn and threaded with cord, and set with wax. It employs spirals, double-strand twists, square braid, and wrapping techniques. *Photo: Musée de l'Homme, Paris*

Metal, on the other hand, has certain unique advantages when worked in fibercraft processes that fibers do not possess. Besides being easily bent, after twisting, metal elements can be untwisted and each element retains its twisted form. It can be riveted or soldered as a means of permanently joining parts, adding new material when a continuous length has run out, or to finish the edges of textures. Instead of being bent back into the texture, the usual way of finishing ends in fiber products, wire and strip ends can be spread by forging to prevent their slipping out of a texture, and wire ends can be melted to form a ball which gives a finished appearance to loose ends.

Even though by its nature metal lacks the elasticity possessed by most fibers and yarns, there are almost no technical difficulties that cannot be solved when applying metal wire and strip to the interworked processes discussed below. Certain considerations should, however, be kept in mind when using fibercraft techniques to create metal jewelry. When necessary, as for bracelets, necklaces, and belts, fabrics must be created that by their system of construction give the metal and their resulting form a needed degree of flexibility without causing fracture in use from bending. The size and shape of forms must be such as can be comfortably worn as ornament on the human body. Special attention must be paid to the avoidance of sharp points and projecting parts on which things can catch; this generally concerns the finishing of the *edges* of structures.

WIRE SUITABILITY TO PROCESS

The wire used for interworked processes is best purchased in *spool form,* especially because in the small-scale gauge range in which it will be used, it will probably be needed in relatively large quantities. Having it on a spool makes wire easier to handle, keeps the wire smooth, and reduces the occurrence of snarls and tangles. Its availability in long lengths eliminates the need to make the frequent joins necessary when short lengths are used.

The wire chosen must be suited to the technique being employed. It must be physically possible to manipulate it with the fingers or the hand tool used. The choice of *gauge* is directly related to the frequency with which, or the distance in which the wire must make a *change of direction,* and the *degree of radius curve* it must form. Techniques such as weaving in which the wire can travel relatively long, straight distances before returning, present no gauge size problem, while at the other extreme, as in knitting and crocheting where the radius curve of the wire element changes drastically in short distances, and in addition must be manipulated with a tool, gauge becomes critical.

Technical considerations therefore may automatically narrow down the range of wire size that can be used. If a scale of difficulty could be set up for the various techniques discussed here in terms of the relative difficulty in manipulating wire in increasing weights, from easy to difficult, it might read thus: weaving, twining, plaiting, braiding, interlinking, wrapping, lashing, knotting, stitching, crocheting, and knitting.

Wire flexibility to a certain extent can compensate for dimensional adjustment. Flexibility depends first of all on the particular metal; for example, 24K gold, fine silver, and pewter alloy are more flexible than other metals and alloys. Another factor in flexibility is whether the wire after drawing has been left in a work-hardened state, or if it has been annealed. Wire that tends to become work hardened can always be annealed again to restore flexibility, and if its surface becomes oxidized in the process, it must be pickled after annealing. When purchasing wire, it is possible to specify that you want it in an annealed condition.

Wire surface condition is important in processes where hand tools are used to manipulate the wire, as in crocheting and knitting. Given any single wire size, if its surface is smooth, lacquered, or plastic coated, there will be less friction between it and a tool so it can be worked more easily than if it were not smooth.

Wire reduction in long lengths is possible when a wire of a certain gauge must be made smaller. Obviously, the size of a normal workshop is too small when many feet of wire are drawn in one straight line, an impractical procedure. If a drawbench is not available, a smaller bench top arrangement such as has been used since ancient times can be improvised. (See Photo 6–4, p. 148.)

METAL QUALITIES IN RELATION TO INTERWORKED PROCESSES

Gold in 24K maintains its softness and flexibility in all work processes and need never be annealed. It is, however, expensive and very soft so that fabrics and structures made of it alone tend to become easily misshapen or crushed. For this reason, it is better to use 18K or 14K yellow gold, which is flexible. Gold alloys generally retain their flexibility in decreasing order of the gold content of the alloy. Some colored gold alloys are designed to be initially hard, and others easily become work hardened, but most can be annealed to restore flexibility when necessary. For knitting and crocheting, gold wire 0.255 mm (30 gauge B.&S., 0.010 in) is suitable. *Gold-filled brass,* which is brass covered with a layer of hard gold of appreciable thickness, is less expensive than all gold wire, but should not be subjected to many annealings as each pickling or repolishing will reduce the thickness of outer layer of gold.

Silver in a *fine* or pure state is suitable for all interworked techniques as it retains its softness and flexibility after all work processes. Sterling silver and silver of lower qualities tend to become work hardened and may require periodic annealing.

Copper when in an annealed state retains its softness for a relatively long time, and is suited to all interworked processes. It is available from electrical suppliers, in spooled wire form as it is used for current-carrying coils in motors and electromagnets. A very wide range of sizes and surface finishes such as lacquer and plastic coatings are manufactured. Such finishes are retained during work unless the metal is subjected to chemicals, heat, or rolling, in which case the finish is destroyed. For crocheting and knitting, a size larger than 0.32 mm (28 gauge B.&S., 0.0126 in) is difficult, but any gauge smaller than that is usable.

Brass and bronze are copper alloys which in some compositions—there are many—tend to be stiff, brittle, and easily work hardened. They can, however, be purchased in a specified annealed state, and can be annealed when they harden in work.

Nickel wire alloys such as *nichrome* and the so-called *German silver* tend to be relatively stiff, but they can be annealed. They are used in the electrical industries.

Aluminum wire is lightweight and suited to all processes. It has a lower melting temperature than all the metals mentioned and when soldered requires special fluxes.

Stainless steel is a ferrous metal that in wire form tends to be very springy after being drawn. Annealing it is tricky as correct temperature control is necessary to keep its composition intact. It is not recommended for knitting and crocheting, but can be used in small sizes in all other techniques.

CLASSIFICATION OF FIBERCRAFT TECHNIQUES

While the majority of interworked fibercraft techniques require the use of fingers alone, some require the help of very simple hand tools, and others a mechanism for the construction of a fabric. These conditions hold true when substituting metal for fiber. For the sake of conceptual grouping, we have classified these processes according to the lack of tools needed, or the hand tool or mechanism needed to execute them.

Finger-worked processes include wrapping and coiling; braiding; plaiting; interlacing; twining; lashing; sewing; embroidering and tapestry embroidering; and knotting.

Hand-with-hand-tool-worked processes include crocheting; knitting; and other techniques requiring some form of rod, hook, or other simple hand-held tool, instrument, or device.

Hand- or mechanism-worked weaving processes include finger weaving, loom weaving, and any mechanical process used in industry to manufacture machine-created intertwined, braided, or woven fabrics that can be used as raw materials in making jewelry.

Within any single system of construction, a great variety of effects are possible, because many variables or alternatives exist. Wire or strip can each be used alone, or in combination in one work. A *change of scale* of either element can result in a completely new look. Wire and strip can be used in techniques that require one or more *continuous-element filaments,* in those that utilize *short lengths,* and in *combinations* of these. *Color variations* can be introduced by a change of metal, or the use of plastic-coated, lacquered, or anodized and dyed metals. A finished product of nonferrous metals can be electroplated with silver or gold to prevent oxidation, or the result can be deliberately oxidized. In some cases, metal wire and strip can be *combined with fibrous materials* for the sake of greater flexibility, or for support, or simply for visual appeal.

FINGER-WORKED PROCESSES

WRAPPING AND COILING WIRE AND STRIP

Archeologists inform us that wrapping and coiling are the most ancient and simplest of the techniques used in basket making, where the concepts of wrapping and coiling used in metal work probably originated. These techniques are different from all other fiber-using methods that resemble weaving in that they do not follow the two-element, opposing warp and weft concept basic to woven structures. In the wrapping concept, a supporting foundation element or *core* is implied, around which the second or *wrapping element*—a very pliable wire or strip—is spirally wound or wrapped. Because the wrapping element follows a spiral, it always slants slightly in relation to the core direction. When the wrapped result is itself bent into a curved spiral, it becomes a *coil.* In the *coiling* system, by continuing the wrapping, extending the coil and adding it to the periphery of the spiral construction, binding it to the previous coil by linked loops, flat or dimensional, self-supporting, rigid forms can be developed in any direction.

THE CORE   The core can be *permanent.* In metal, it may consist of a single solid wire of any gauge or shape such as round, square, triangular, or irregularly shaped wire; a compound element such as a group of twisted wires which simulates the kind of core made of multi-strand fibers used in coiled basketry; or a plastic or metal tube which considerably lightens the total weight of the work. The core can be *uniform* in dimension in its entire length, or gradually *tapered* in its length. When using cores of uniform length to make spiral forms, the final ending is tapered by filing or drawing down to bring it smoothly into the main circular structure. The core can be left partly exposed or completely concealed by the wrapped element. In the case of metal, the latter can be an advantage as when wire of a precious metal is wrapped around a nonferrous metal or plastic core which is concealed, but the core gives the element the desired diameter dimension. Flexible plastic cores impart their flexibility to such a wrapped unit. If the core is rigid enough it can simply be hand held while it is wrapped with the fingers, but a core made of a flexible,

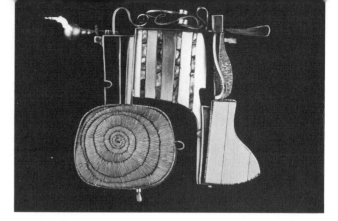

6–138 RICHARD MAFONG and JON ERIC RIIS, U.S.A. Pin of forged silver wire and fabricated parts ornamented with abalone shell mosaic, ivory inlay, and a pearl. The metallic thread unit is wrapped around a core of unequal thickness to form a flat spiral coil, inserted in an edge-textured strip wire frame. *Photo: Richard Mafong*

6–139 MITSUKO KAMBE SOELLNER, U.S.A. Necklace using spiral wire elements to form the neckpiece and ornament the upper front portion. Lower part is shakudo inlaid with silver wire. *Photo: Walter Soellner*

6–140 *DETAIL WITH ALTERNATING SPIRALS* of shakudo and silver wire soldered to each other at intervals, and to a small, square plaque that passes over them. *Photo: Walter Soellner*

6–141 THOMAS GENTILLE, U.S.A. Neckpiece of gold-, bronze-, and silver-wrapped wire, with epoxy inlay. *Photo: Robert Lee Morris, courtesy Artwear, New York*

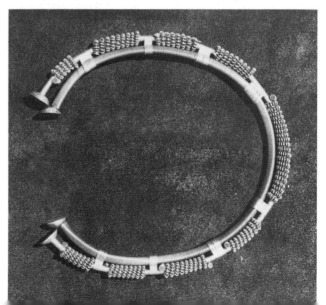

6–142 EUGEN LANG, Switzerland. Necklace in 18K gold, with five baroque pearls. An irregularly twisted pair of wires with open intervals is wrapped with a third wire. *Photo: R. Humbert*

small-gauge wire or plastic may have to be stretched between two clamps while being wrapped.

The core can be *temporary*. Because of the relative rigidity of metal wire, even-diameter spirally wrapped, or regularly tapered spirally wrapped coils can be made on a temporary core such as a straight wooden dowel, a bendable fiber or plastic material, or a metal mandrel. When wrapping is completed, the resulting coil is removed, or destroyed by heat, leaving an independent coil or helix spiral of equal-sized loops, or a regularly tapered cone with a central opening. (The method of making such coils and their uses are discussed under Spiral Making, Chapter 6.)

LINKING WRAPPED UNITS A single wrapped unit can be used alone, in which case the beginning and the end of the wrapping wire must be secured. This can be done by soldering the ends to the core or to the coil itself, or by drilling a hole in the core where the wire begins and ends and passing these ends into the hole, where they can also be soldered to hold them. A series of wrapped units can be linked or joined to each other in adjacent layers to form a structure such as a flat or dimensional spiral, a sinuous up-and-back form, or a cylindrical form, and of course combinations of these. The join can be made in ways that are invisible, regularly visible, or dominant to the extent of completely obscuring the presence of the core or coil, such that only the joining element is seen.

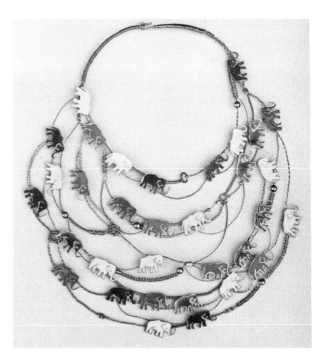

6–143 LYNDA WATSON-ABBOTT, U.S.A. Silver wire necklace ornamented with elephants enameled in opaque white, yellow, orange, and blue. The lengths of twisted and wrapped wire sections are linked and articulated by jump rings and beads at intersections. *Photo: Lynda Watson-Abbott*

Invisible joining utilizes a thin wire, threaded on a needle if necessary, to sew the wrapped units together at their point of contact. *Regularly visible* joining is done by *tie-bands* during the wrapping of the core. After completing a certain specified number of turns of the wrapping element around the core, a tie-band is made by passing the element either *completely around,* or *through* the texture of the adjacent unit, and the wrapping (wire) then continues until the next joining tie-band is made. To help pass the wrapping wire end through tightly wrapped textures, the point of a straight, round-shafted tool, such as an *awl* whose thickness equals that of the wrapped wire gauge, is forced through, and the end is passed through that opening. It is possible to make a space between adjacent coils and to create an openwork effect by deliberately separating and holding the coils apart. This is done by first passing the joining wire through or around the adjacent coil as usual, but then wrapping the wire once *around itself* between the coils to form a loop that makes the separation, then continuing the wrapping. *Cores completely covered*

6–144 MARY LEE HU, U.S.A. "Neckpiece No. 11." Constructed with a warp of 28 gauge lacquered nickel alloy electrical wire, and a weft of double 26 gauge fine silver wire, with old Venetian glass beads made for trading in Africa. The wrapping system is basically coil construction, in a herringbone pattern resembling a satin weave system. Spacing the supporting warp wires further apart broadens the form; bringing them closer together converges the form. *Photo: Mary Lee Hu*

6–145 DARBHANGA DISTRICT, BIHAR, INDIA. The same system is used in this flattened *sikki* grass stalk, nearly 2 ft high elephant and rider basket. The upper portion is a cover. Made by women, it is used at marriage ceremonies. *Photo: Oppi*

by the linking element are also possible. Instead of wrapping individual core units, the wrapping element is passed over two or more adjacent cores in a regular, herringbone, or other pattern, making each pass close to the next so the core eventually becomes invisible and the linking element in fact becomes the surface. This system is often used in basketry.

6–147   RAJASTHAN, INDIA. Bhil tribal woman wearing traditional silver ornaments. The torque (hansli, vadla) is widely used by several groups in the area. This one is made of hollow, tapered tubing, completely wrapped with fine plain or twisted wire, and has attached pendants. Photo: Press Division, Photo Section, Government of Rajasthan

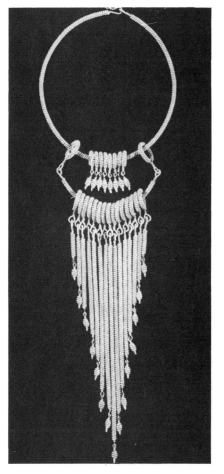

◀ 6–146   WANN-HONG LIU, Republic of China. In this brass wire necklace, the wire is first wrapped helically around a core, then this unit is wrapped around a second core whose ends are used to form loops by which parts are joined. Photo: J-Jen Lin

6–148   GUJARAT, INDIA. Silver vadla worn by Rabari tribal women. The tapered tube core is soldered to a solid wire exposed at the back. It is wrapped with plain wire, in turn wrapped at intervals with helix spiral secondary wires, and ornamented with bi-element twisted wire. The hooked opening is worn at the front. Photo: Oppi ▶

6–149   RAJASTHAN, INDIA. Below: Traditional, contemporary necklace whose main wrapped wire ornament is made of one single, continuous wire. The rosette flat spiral coils of three, four, five, and six turns, were later flooded with solder to maintain their position. Wires between them are helically wrapped with fine wire as the shaping and wrapping progressed. Wrapped wire jump rings support the suspended pendant ornaments. Photo: Oppi

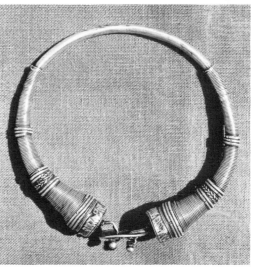

6–150   REVERSE SIDE OF THE NECKLACE showing the wrapping construction system. The main core wire has been forged flat at the front to support the spiral rosettes. The necklace opens by a hinge on one side, and is held by an ornamentally headed screw at the other side. Photo: Oppi

A great variety of effects are possible by changing the size of the core or the gauge of the wrapping wire, by using strip instead of wire as the wrapping element, by using different colored metals, and by other variables.

WRAPPING A HELIX SPIRAL COIL AROUND A CORE   It is possible, when wrapping a single core, to add a helix spiral coil to the wrapping element for decorative effect. In this case the helix spiral can be wrapped *directly* around the wrapping wire while wrapping is in progress, or, if a larger diameter coil is wanted, it can be *made separately* first around a removable core which is later eliminated, leaving the coil empty. The wrapping wire is then wrapped around the core until the point of introducing the coil is reached. The coil is then threaded on this wire, and the wrapping continues around the core, taking the coil spirally with it. Any surplus coil can be cut at the necessary point and removed from the wrapping wire which then continues to be wrapped on the core.

Separate units of a helix-coiled wire wound spirally can be made in a similar way. A length of the helix coil is made and the core removed. The supporting wrapping wire is inserted, and is wrapped with the coil around a temporary small-diameter core, then removed. The wrapping wire inside the coil projects from either end of the wrapped spiral. It can be formed into loops at either end, or at one end and the other end introduced into the spiral texture and closed. Such units can be used as a pendant, a bead in a series, or as a link in a chain.

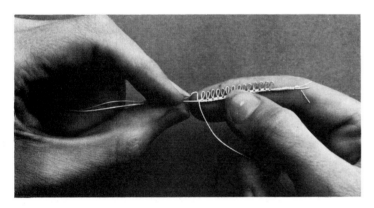

6–151   MARY LEE HU demonstrates using three wires and fingers to make a series of single loops of 26 gauge B.&S. silver wire along one side of a stiffer 22 gauge B.&S. sterling silver core wire. The wire used to make the loops is carried along the top of the core wire, and the loop is formed by lifting it up with the thumb, then pushing it back with the nail of the index finger, as shown. The third or wrapping wire is brought across and around the core wire three times from the back, between each loop. Photo: Mary Lee Hu

6–152   *Top: A FINISHED, WRAPPED, SINGLE LOOP LENGTH* is formed into a helix spiral with overlapping loops. *Below:* A three-size, graduated loop construction. The result can be shaped in any way desired. Color variations are possible by using different metals, or lacquer-colored wire. The ends are loose to show the system. Photo: Mary Lee Hu

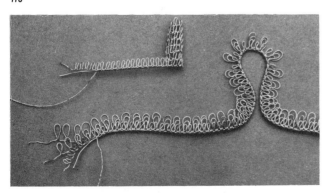

6–153   DRAA VALLEY, SOUTHERN MOROCCO. Silver earring with carnelian worn suspended from the temples before the ears by Haratin women in the Bani and Tata region. The wire-wrapping technique is used to hold the two loop units together, and the diagonal pass of the wrapping wire between the loops keeps them from stretching apart. Photo: Didoni, Linden-Museum, Stuttgart

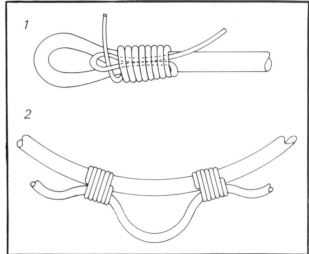

6–154   SEIZING
1. Seizing a loop;   2. Seizing a pair of elements in series.

SEIZING

Seizing is a method of wrapping wire around the end of a loop made at the end of a core to make it secure. The procedure, which works best with small-gauge wire, is as follows: Shape the core wire element to the desired loop size, tapering the end by filing it so it flows smoothly into the form of the core. Bend a thin, flexible wire wrapping or whipping element into an open loop, making sure the free end is longer than the intended length of the wrapped or whipped area. Place the whipping element loop flat on the core loop, and start to wrap or whip the wire tightly around the core and over the wrapping wire loop, in a close spiral, working toward the core loop until the desired distance is wrapped. Pass the working end of the wrapping element through its own still exposed loop, and while holding that end tightly to keep tension on the spiral, pull on the *starting* end of the wrapping wire. This brings the remains of the wrapping wire under and through the spiral. Continue to pull until a loop of the wrapping wire appears, then grasp its free end and pull the remainder through the spiral. The two wrapping wire ends are now together. Cut them off flush with the spiral.

6–155 FRIEDRICH BECKER, West Germany. Brooch of 18K gold wire with 108 varicolored oriental pearls. Nine wires terminate at twelve juncture points where they are soldered together. Each wire extends from the juncture and is used as a peg to mount a pearl. The pattern resembles a wrapping technique with the support removed. *Photo: Walter Fischer*

BRAIDING: *Combining wire and strip by oblique interlacing*

Braiding, from the Anglo-Saxon *bregdan,* "to move to and fro," is a process of interworking one set of no less than three, but possibly more, odd or even number of strands to form a close or open weavelike structure or braid, also sometimes called a plait. In British usage braiding is called plaiting, but there are differences that make a separation of these terms useful. The basic difference is that the braiding process usually (but not always) results in a relatively narrow band or fabric, while a plaited fabric can be of any width, such as a mat. Also, all the elements in braiding tend to go in one more or less oblique direction, while in plaiting (discussed separately on p. 212), the elements are usually at opposing right angles to each other.

In its simplest form, three-strand braiding, the outer right and left strands are alternately passed over the inner strand. When all the strands are of equal size and shape, in the resulting braid each strand takes an equally balanced, diagonal, sinuous course through the resulting ribbonlike structure. Many variations in braid making are possible. Instead of using a single strand as a unit, two, three or more strands can be treated together as one unit; they are *always,* however, kept in the same flat and parallel relation to each other throughout the braid length. Braids can be made of any number of strand units.

In braiding with metal, because ordinarily each strand takes a winding course through the texture, round wire in single or multiple units is easier to braid than strip. Because of metal strip's nature, it resists side-to-side movement and will form kinks at the point of the change in direction of the curve if it is of too small a radius. Theoretically such kinks can be hammered to stretch the metal at that point to make the strip flat again, and braiding can continue. When using strip in multi-strand braiding, the more common way to keep the strip flat before it returns is to fold it over on itself at the edge of the braid at an angle that points its length in the direction it is to take in its next course through the braid.

The general term for the decorative use of interworked flat metal strips is *strapwork.*

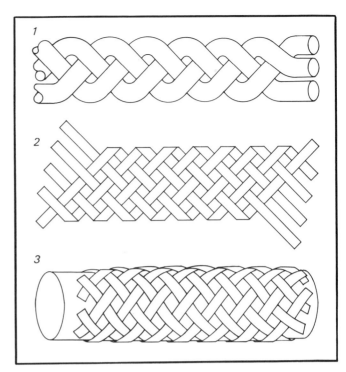

6–156 BRAIDING
1. Standard three-strand braiding; 2. Flat strip, five-strand braiding; 3. Flat strip, tubular braiding.

6–157 ISRAEL. Contemporary Yemenite-type silver brooch with turquoises and coral beads, manufactured by Maskit, Tel Aviv. The framing braid is made of four-strand units, the outer plain, and the inner of two twisted wires, one pair to the right, and one pair to the left. *Photo: Maskit*

6–158 SILESIA, ca. first half of the 19th century. Steel wire bracelet. The basic flat braided band is made of wire prewrapped with fine steel wire. The frontal knotted ornament is held by a smaller braid that continues around the bracelet. Edge lashing holds the flower-shaped, polished, stamped steel paillettes. Ø 6.2 cm. *Photo: Reproduced by Courtesy of the Trustees of the British Museum, London*

TYPES OF BRAIDS

There are several basic types of braids, named after their structure, appearance, or use. Only a few of them can be mentioned here.

Flat braids are the most common. They are made of

round wire or strip to produce a narrow, flat, equal-width texture. Flat braids are very easily bent edgewise into curves after they are completed.

Divided braids are possible in multi-strand braiding. At the start, the strands are braided into a single unit. At any point, the number of strands can be divided equally or unequally and each unit formed into an independent braid of narrower width. These divided units can be reunited at any point and the result is an openwork structure.

Shaped braids of multi-strand units are created when working in metal by controlling the tension of the braiding elements, or by bending the braid form as it proceeds. The braid is worked from one edge only, passing those outer strands diagonally through the others, which remain straight and parallel to each other. By increasing the tension on the diagonal strand after each pass through the other strands, a flat braid can be made to curve in its width. Shaped braided forms are useful in giving dimension to braided textures used for jewelry forms.

Circular and hole braids can be made by the use of a core of wire, rod, or tubing. The number of strands used increases with the core diameter, and the core size determines the diameter of the finished braid. The strands are placed around the core and held in place by passing a heavy-gauge iron binding wire twice around them, then

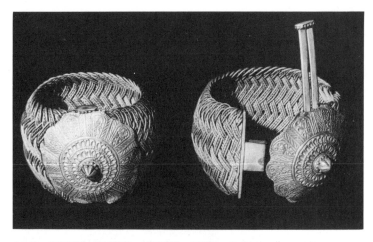

6–161 INDORE, MADHYA PRADESH, INDIA. Braided silver wire upper arm bracelets (*bazuband*). The shaped braid is made of a three-element wire unit: two round wires flanking a twisted wire. The closing finding is in the form of a U-shaped flat wire that engages a box-shaped opening mounted behind the central stamp-decorated ornament into which it is forced. *Photo: Oppi*

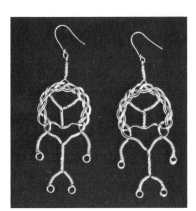

6–159 WANN-HONG LIU, Republic of China. Silver earrings whose three-element wire braid divides, intertwists, and ends in loops. *Photo: Wann-Hong Liu*

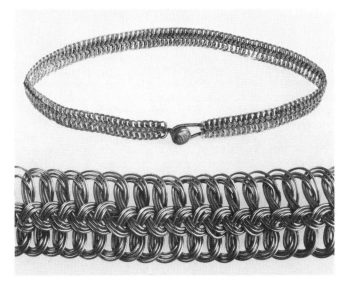

6–160 THAILAND, 19th century. Flat braided belt made of three-unit brass wires, the start, wrapped with a wire, formed into a loop; the finish, attached to a brass button to make the closing device. *Photo: Gisela Croon, Museum für Völkerkunde, Staatliche Museen Preussischer Kulturbesitz, Berlin*

6–162 AYA NAKAYAMA, Japan. Two necklaces, one with a fabricated pendant in 950 silver, the other with a fabricated neckband in 950 silver, both using silk threads and fine silver wire. Both employ the same concept, with the placement of materials reversed: a sheet metal fabricated unit is integrated with a silk yarn braided unit by intermediary wires. The traditional Japanese silk braiding technique *kumihimo*, used in the past for the ornamentation of armor, helmets, and swords, is used today for making braids that go around a Japanese woman's kimono sash (*obi*). These two materials, metal and yarn, have in common their fine filament form, and can be braided together, each blending with the other. In terms of bulk, each must match the other. As their dimensions are known, a *calculator* is used to determine the necessary number of filaments in each material. The fine silver wire soldered to the fabricated unit is initially braided in the manner to match the particular braiding structure used for the silk. The other end lengths are left irregular so that when braided into the silk, the two materials seem to dissolve into each other. *Photos: Left: Nobu Watanabe; right: Seibu Museum, Tokyo*

twisting its ends together tightly. Round wire or flat strip can be used, round wire resulting in an open texture, and strip in a flatter and tighter texture. The sum total of the width of the strips used should be somewhat less than but *never more than* the total circumference of the core. An even number of strands are used. The braiding continues in a spiral direction around the core, and must always be sufficiently tight so that the texture lies flat on the core surface. Tightly woven circular braids are very strong and retain their circular shape. The core can be left within the braid to support its shape, or it can be removed. To remove a circular braid from a core, grasp the braid at both ends and push the hands toward each other. This pressure will flex and slightly expand the diameter of a diagonally structured circular braid, allowing the core to be pulled or pushed out.

Tapering, conical, circular braids can be made on a cone-shaped core. At the starting point at the cone apex, all the strands are tied together, and during braiding, they gradually expand to form an openwork on the cone shape. It is possible to remove the core when the maximal expansion has been reached, and continue to braid the strands in an ever smaller diameter until all the elements return to a point, forming a bicone.

Circular braids can be used in their original uniform size. When they are core-free, they can be stretched or squeezed at one point to cause that point to contract in diameter. When they contain a core, the opposite can be done, that is, they can be expanded at a point by pushing a section from both sides toward that point, which makes the braid swell there and expand in diameter. To hold such an expanded (or contracted) shape, the adjacent constricted sections can be tied by wrapping them tightly with a wire that also holds them in place.

Commercial cable sheathing made of copper, brass, or nickel wire, or of flat strip is machine-made circular braid. Its main use is as a casing for a core of electrical wire and its insulators. Cable sheathing can be purchased in many diameters and densities and used as a raw material to create dimensional jewelry forms in the ways already described. (Mechanically woven flat braid in various widths are also available in copper and brass.)

6-164 LAHUL-SPITI, UTTAR PRADESH, INDIA. Tapered tube and half-dome ball necklace from the Himalayas, ornamented with wrapped and braided wire, supported by knitted wire chains. Side flowerets contain enamel, and corals edge the large flanking beads. *Photo: Oppi*

THE USES OF BRAID IN JEWELRY

Braid can be used in jewelry in many ways. A flat braided band can be used alone, or several similar (or different) braided units can be joined edgewise to each other by sewing them together with a thin wire, or by soldering. Such a straight flexible fabric can be used for a belt or bracelet. Narrow or wide flat braids can be wrapped around cylindrical or tapering cores, in a circle or spirally, for decorative effect. Braids can be made to form a flat circle or can be used edgewise at the perimeter of the circle. Braided rings can be used for earrings or in other constructions. Flat braid can be used as a border or frame for a unit. Round braid can be used as a chain in the many ways that chains are used.

PLAITING

Plaiting is a method of forming a fabric with fingers by diagonally interweaving or interlinking any number of elements, usually strip of the same width and material, or multiple strands of wire. With plaiting, a variety of fabric types and structures can be made including ropelike forms; narrow, flat, ribbonlike forms; fabrics of any width or length such as mats; open fabrics such as nets; and three-dimensional, cylindrical forms such as baskets.

Flat plaiting with strips resembles *weaving* when the structure is made of two opposing elements that meet at right angles, and *braiding* in that the weaving is accomplished in diagonal progression. Flat strip plaiting can also be done with three crossing elements, each exposed overpass forming a parallelogram instead of a square or rectangle. Interlinked plaiting done with wire employs one set of parallel elements interlinked with adjacent elements. (Because of the wire form, this kind of plaiting resembles twining and is discussed below separately under Open Twining Interlinking One Set of Flexible Elements, p. 217.)

In flat strip plaiting, the result is also flat, and when using wire for systems that meet at right angles, the texture has a more dimensional appearance. When the work starts at the upper right-hand corner (or the upper left-hand corner) which is usual as when making a flat mat, it must thereafter consistently follow the chosen direction. In the most common plaiting, a single element passes over one and under one element, repeated regularly throughout. At the lower left-hand corner where the fabric ends, the element is brought into the texture by being bent inward at the edge, returning to the right.

The result in its simplest form, when using strip and the

6-163 ANITA S. FECHTER, U.S.A. Neckpiece using industrial, circular, braided copper wire cable sheathing. Its form and structure allow stretching, compressing, and flattening, as well as sewing units together. The result was electroplated to bond crossings and rigidize the structure. Size 4 × 8 × 7 in. *Photo: American Crafts Council, New York*

one-over-one-under system, is a diagonally woven *checker-board pattern* of squares. Different weaves are possible, however, such as the so-called *basket weave* in which two parallel elements pass over two units instead of one to create squares containing four elements; and the *twill weave* in which a single element passes over two elements, and the next single element does the same, but is staggered by one element so that a stepped effect is established. Many variations on these basic systems are possible, and the introduction of color differences in the opposing or alternating elements introduces further variation.

Normally when using flat strip, each element can be brought close to the last so that no open spaces appear in the texture, but deliberate openwork plaiting is also possible, and occurs automatically when using wire instead of strip. Other variations are possible by using both strip and wire in the same fabric. With both strip and wire, various surface textures are possible by twisting the strip or wire upon itself on the upper, visible surface *before* passing it under the next element. In the case of strip, this creates a pointed, projecting triangle, and with wire, a loop is formed. If this is repeated consistently an all-over texture results, or the twisted pattern can be confined only to certain areas.

6–167 MARY LEE HU demonstrates openwork plaiting with a three-element unit of 22 gauge B.&S. fine silver wire. The structure starts from a six-pointed star base begun on a board to which the wires were nailed to hold them in position until sufficient plaiting is completed to stabilize the texture. To lock each element in place, alternating elements must be pulled up or pushed down, the element introduced is then positioned, and the opposite, alternating elements are raised or lowered. This also acts to prepare the texture for the introduction of the next element. *Photo: Mary Lee Hu*

6–168 NEPAL. Three-strand open plaiting of a split bamboo basket for keeping chickens. The same structure is possible by translating bamboo splits into metal strip or wire. *Photo: Oppi*

6–169 MARY LEE HU, U.S.A. "Neckpiece No. 15." The basic warp, 26 gauge B.&S. fine silver wire is used throughout in groups of three elements. The front portion is formed into three-strand open plaiting and continues on both sides, wrapped with lacquered copper electrical wire in groups of six. These are held equidistantly apart by lashing wires. The remaining warp is seized in crossing groups of six. Size 8½ × 14 in. *Photo: Mary Lee Hu*

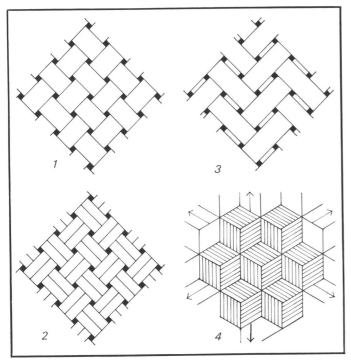

6–165 PLAITING
1. Checkerboard; 2. Basket weave; 3. Twill; 4. Three-strand plaiting.

6–166 MALKA COHAVI, Israel. Upper arm bracelet made of diagonal checkerboard-plaited copper strips, the texture 6 cm wide by 18 cm long. The comblike closing device of black wood is 4.4 cm wide and 14 cm long. *Photo: Ada Savidosky*

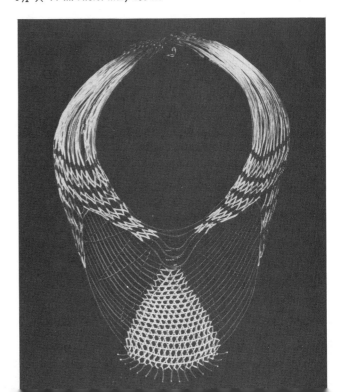

INTERLACING

Interlacing consists of making a structure using a *vertical warp* and a *horizontal weft*. Basically, a single weft element passes over one and under the next warp element without any twisting between them which would make the system Twining. (See p. 217.) Interlacing most closely resembles textile weaving when making flat forms in that the warp element passes through the length of the fabric and the weft element passes up and back. When interlacing dimensional, hollow forms, the weft continues in an endless spiral around the entire form until it is finished. The material used can be strip whose flat surface is always parallel with the wall of the form, or wire. A variety of weaves are possible, each resulting in different visual effects.

Basketry is the best example of the use of interlacing systems. The word *basket* is believed to be derived from the Celtic *basc*—bracelet—from a method of making bracelets by coiling or interlacing strands of natural substances. It is often done with wickers which are small-diameter, circular twigs or osiers. For this reason, objects made with these materials are sometimes referred to as "wickerwork," but this describes the material used and not the interlacing technique. Round wires of any diameter can substitute for wickers when transposing the interlacing technique to metal, and being nondirectional, they can be bent to any angle or curve.

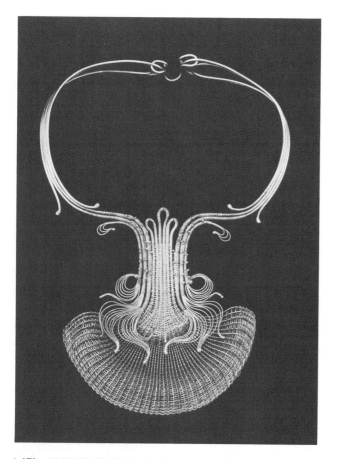

6–170 MARY LEE HU, U.S.A. Necklace of silver and lacquered copper wire of various gauges B.&S. (14–26), utilizing interlacing systems as well as wrapping. The small balls are projecting wire ends, melted singly or in groups. *Photo: Rauno Träskelin*

INTERLACING FLAT AND DIMENSIONAL FORMS

Interlacing (and Twining, discussed on p. 217) is commonly used as a system of making *flat* and *dimensional* forms in mat making and basketry. A common type of basket construction is the *stake frame basket* which utilizes more or less rigid, round or flat *stakes* in single, double, or multiple units. The stakes are supporting elements equivalent to a warp, and are spaced apart equidistantly to form a frame through which the *rand* (the flexible filling element equivalent to the weft) is interlaced or twined, usually at right angles to the stakes, in a process called *randing*. In all basket construction of this type the development starts at the *center* of the base, proceeds to the *development of the form,* and is last concerned with *finishing the edge.*

FLAT, CIRCULAR STRUCTURES

In making flat, circular or oval structures by traditional spiral interlacing, construction begins at the center. The supporting stakes can be arranged in several different ways to form the center, depending on whether round or flat stakes are used. The main center systems can be seen in Illustration 6–171. When working with fibrous substances, the stakes are often temporarily tied at the center, but metal stakes have the advantage that they can be soldered together at their central point of contact. Also, the start of the weft rand can be soldered to them, or can be twisted around one stake to anchor it before interlacing or twining begins.

(It should be mentioned here that flat forms can be developed by an entirely different approach. For instance, a wire frame can be made first in any shape. The space can then be crossed with a warp by wrapping wire around the frame to anchor the elements, in a radial manner or in a vertical and horizontal arrangement. Upon this foundation, randing can be done by interlacing, twining, or other technique, and the result is a framed, flat unit.)

THE START: Construction centers suited to metal

Star center: Round stakes are bent so they touch at the center, usually with one group going in one direction and the other group overlapping it going in the opposite direction. In metal, their point of contact is soldered together, and the individual stakes are then bent to radiate outward equidistant from each other. When a simple *over-and-under alternation* of the weft is used, there must be an *odd number* of stakes, and when a *double-strand twining* system is followed, the number of stakes can be *even* or *odd*.

Four-cross center: Multiple units of round stakes are arranged in a foursquare, interlocked crossing. After a few turns of the randing around this central unit, the individual parts of the multiple can be spread apart equidistantly, in pairs or individually, and treated thereafter as separate stake units.

Fan center: Flat strip stakes cross over each other in sequence at a common, central point and appear like the ribs of an opened folding fan. In most cases these units are spaced equally apart. In metal, the central point at which they cross can be drilled with a hole and all of the units riveted together to hold them in place.

Solid pierced center: A solid material in disc form (wood for fibers, sheet metal for metal) is pierced at its periphery with holes into which round stakes are placed

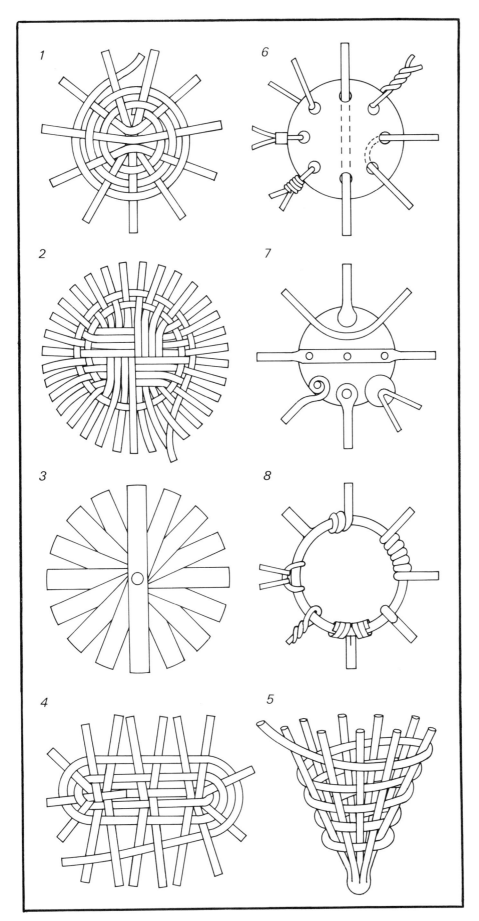

6–171 BASKETWORK STARTS IN METAL
1. Star.
2. Four-cross.
3. Fan.
4. Oval.
5. Pointed.
6. Solid, pierced.
7. Spoke, soldered, riveted.
8. Ring, wrapped.

and fixed. When using an even number of stakes, a single unit can pass through one hole and be brought out through the opposite hole at the opposite edge of the disc. The disc holds the stakes in position, ready for randing.

Soldered or riveted spoke center: In metal, the wire stakes left round or flattened at one end by forging can be soldered to the edge or surface of a metal disc which acts as the center. The stakes radiate like spokes of a wheel from the disc. They can also be held to the disc by rivets.

Ring center: With metal, the center can be made of a wire ring of any size, soldered at its joint. The wire stakes can be attached to this ring by wrapping their ends around it, by looping them to it, or by soldering them endwise to the ring.

Oval center: To create an oval form, round stakes are tied in pairs (or larger multiples of two) and placed in parallel series a certain distance apart. The number of pairs used depends on the length of the oval. Randing starts at the first pair, continues at right angles along one side of the stakes, then returns on the other side, turns, and thereafter continues in an oval spiral around the stakes.

Pointed center: All stakes converge to a point where they are held together and from which they radiate outward to form a conical shape. Wire stakes can be joined to a point by soldering, or they can be fused at the point of contact, where they form a ball.

DEVELOPING DIMENSIONAL FORMS FROM FLAT BEGINNINGS

Flat, circular, interlaced or twined forms made using any of the above-mentioned centers can be developed into dimensional forms, the flat part becoming the base. To make a *cylinder,* the stakes must take a sudden bend at a right angle; for a *cone* shape, they bend obliquely; and for a *curved* form, they bend gradually to the contour curve of the form. Metal stakes have the advantage over those of fibrous materials because they can be bent at more drastic angles without breaking, and round wire stakes can be bent to any direction or contour.

After a form has grown vertically or outwardly, the stakes can be made to converge gradually or suddenly to constrict the form; if desired, it can be brought to a point, a round closing, or even turn inward.

As a conical form expands, it often becomes necessary to add additional stakes at regular intervals within the structure in order to keep the distances between the stakes from becoming too great, because the randing in that case would then be required to jump longer distances and the structure would become too loose. These extra stakes are forced into the already randed sections alongside existing stakes, and if they are metal they can be soldered in place. Another way of increasing their number in metal work would be to divide a strip stake at the point where additional stakes are needed and then rejoin them by soldering if it becomes necessary for their number to be decreased, as when the form becomes restricted.

Because the forms used in adapting these techniques for use in jewelry making are decorative and not functional, the aim is not necessarily to create a container, and the form can be without a base. A bead form, for instance, could be made from a section of a metal tube of suitable diameter, leaving the top and bottom edge intact, then dividing the rest into vertical sections that are expanded outward to form the shape and act as stakes, through which the randing can be interlaced or twined.

6–172 KASHMIR, INDIA. Unstripped willow osier, diagonally interlaced randing chicken-holding basket. The conical form has been developed from a flat beginning. *Photo: Oppi*

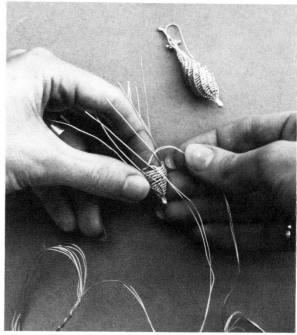

6–173 MARY LEE HU demonstrates diagonal interlacing using 22 gauge B.&S. round silver wire stakes whose start has been fused to a ball. The densely textured randing is 28 gauge B.&S. fine silver wire, double-twine interlaced so either an even or odd number of stakes can be used. By spreading the stakes outward, the form increases in diameter, and by pressing them together the form is constricted. Instead of being held perpendicular to the randing, the stakes are worked at an angle so they develop a diagonal, spiral movement in the texture. The system is used here to make a hanging earring. *Photo: Mary Lee Hu*

Interlacing and twining the randing around the stakes of dimensional forms can be done in any of the ways described for flat constructions or dimensional baskets. The randing can be done with one unit, or two or more acting as a single unit, the multi-unit stake making a denser, more rigid texture. Instead of keeping the stakes straight and at right angles to the randing, they can be bent obliquely so they form a spiral around the dimensional form as it develops. Endless numbers of variations in visual effect are possible by combining round and flat randing, using the techniques of interlacing and twining.

THE FINISH: Completing the edge

If a form is developed in the basic manner of a stake frame basket, which covers a wide range of possible struc-

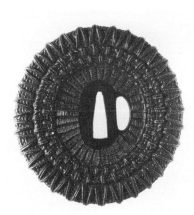

6–174 JAPAN. Sword guard (*tsuba*), 18th century. Iron tsuba (*shingen*) faced on both sides with brass wire woven through pierced holes. The edge was finished with three different systems using couching and lashing techniques. *Photo: Cooper-Hewitt Museum, New York*

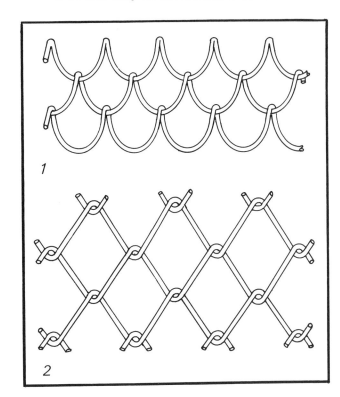

6–175 *TWINING*
1. Single-element, open twining to one side.
2. Single-element, open twining to both sides.

tures, or by other methods, the edge must be finished. When fibrous substances are used, reinforcing the edge gives it strength, but edge strength is not important in metal where finishing is done for visual rather than functional reasons. There are many ways of finishing edges, and edge finishing is actually simplified when using metal because of the possibility of using solder to hold all elements together.

Nonsoldered finishing systems are the same as those used with fibrous materials. By a common system for baskets that utilize the warp and weft concept, with round stakes as warp, their ends (round wire in metal) can be bent and returned to the texture, forced in a curve into the space occupied by the following stake. Repeated regularly, the edge becomes a series of twined loops, each passing over the other. Wire stake ends can also be formed into a loop or spiral which is left projecting, or bent over the edge.

A separately made framing edge element can be added to the form. A strip, thick wire, compound of twisted wires, braided wires, or a spiral coil can be held to the edge by wrapping, whipping, or lashing it with a thin wire that penetrates the main structure at regular intervals and holds the edging element in place.

Solder-finished edges can also be used. The last elements of warp and weft can be soldered together and the edge smoothed with files. Any of the above-mentioned framing elements can be soldered to the edge. Projecting stake ends can be trimmed to equal lengths and then fused to form a ball at each end.

TWINING

OPEN TWINING INTERLINKING ONE SET OF FLEXIBLE ELEMENTS

Open twining uses any number of one set of parallel elements (wires) to form a network. In interlinking these elements, each one intercepts the element on one side, or alternately a right- and a left-hand element. The earliest and best example of this system was its use in fishing nets; the same concept was utilized in carrying nets and bags, and today is used in salad-rinsing racks and wire fences. When these articles are made of plied fibers that are elastic, the structure tends to be drawn together when not in use, and it must be stretched out and distended to be able to see the interlinking system. When the system is transposed to metal wire, the elements can be made to stay spaced apart

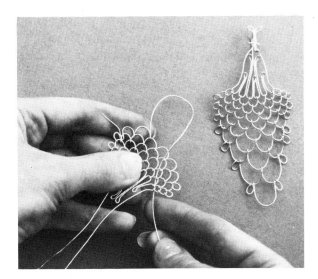

6–176 MARY LEE HU demonstrates single-element, open one-side twining to create an earring. Each row of 22 gauge B.&S. fine silver wire starts with a separate length whose end is brought forward, placed in the loop of the previous row, and pulled until the loop that forms is the desired size and shape. *Round-nosed pliers* may be used instead of fingers. The effectiveness of this system depends on precision in loop size and shape. *Photo: Mary Lee Hu*

because of the rigidity of wire, or to collapse into each other, but in either case, the structure still retains its degree of flexibility.

With this same system, spirally formed constructions are also possible. Networks of this type can also be knotted together at their points of crossing.

6-177 MARY LEE HU, U.S.A. "Neckpiece No. 18." Made of fine and sterling silver, fine gold, and gold-filled brass wire. The lower winglike portion is made of 22 gauge B.&S. gold-filled brass wire using single-element open twining to one side. Photo: Mary Lee Hu

6-178 FRANCE. Wire salad-washing basket, circular construction, open twining to two sides; seen from above. Photo: Oppi

TYPES OF TWINING

Close twining consists of twining a single element tightly around each repeated vertical element (and sometimes around a rigid, horizontal supporting element as well), then passing on to the next. Each time the twining element is pulled tightly so there is no space between the intercepted elements other than the thickness of the twining element.

Spaced parallel twining can be done with *one* flexible twining element of wire around a rigid element or wire or strip. The twining wire passes once around the rigid element, and a space is allowed before it does the same with the next rigid element. To make a more rigid structure, the twining wire can pass once around itself before going on to the next point.

When using *two* flexible twining elements, the system is called *paired twining*. In this case, each member of the unit passes around the rigid element from the opposite direction, then they meet, and twine around each other a specific number of times before continuing to the next rigid element. In this case the number of times the flexible elements twine around each other between the rigid elements determines the distance the latter are kept apart.

Spaced radial twining is done in the same way as above, but in each subsequent row of twinings a regularly increasing number of twists are made between the rigid elements. For instance, the first course may be done with only one twist, the second with two, the third with three, etc. This arrangement makes the rigid elements radiate away from each other in matching radial directions. For additional rigidity, a curved wire support can be incorporated in the twining elements. Radial structures are suitable for forming necklaces, bracelets, and other conical forms.

Free twining consists of a single, or multiple elements that are intertwined in symmetrical or asymmetrical arrangements.

LASHING OR LATTICE TWINING

Lashing is a form of twining, and consists of binding together two or more sets of rigid elements placed vertically and horizontally, or diagonally, or both, by the use of one or more flexible transverse elements. When the aim is to create an openwork, the process is called *lattice twining*. Latticework is characterized as an openwork structure of parallel, intersecting elements, placed flat within a frame, or shaped into dimensional forms.

TWINING USING TWO SETS OF OPPOSING ELEMENTS

Two-set twining is the process of turning one set of elements to mesh with successive elements of the opposite set that run in a direction perpendicular to the first. The twining element is flexible, and usually the opposing element is rigid but it too can be flexible. Depending on which element does the twining, it is termed *warp twining* (lengthwise twining), or *weft twining* (widthwise twining). In the result there is a suggestion of the diagonal in the twining element in its relation to the element twined, because in passing around it is deflected and slants to one side. In close twining these regularly repeated elements take on a decided diagonal appearance.

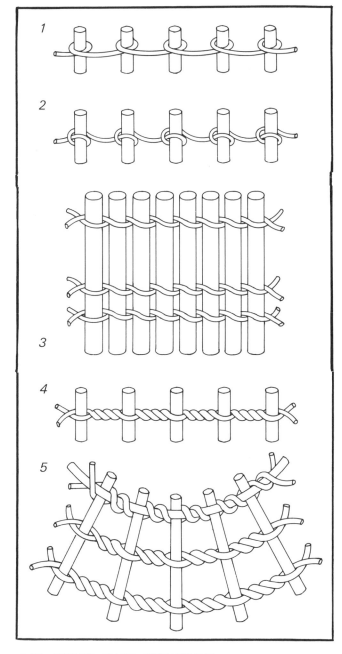

6-179 *TWO-SET, SPACED, WEFT TWINING*
1. Two single, opposing elements, parallel twining.
2. Two single, opposing elements, self-locked, parallel twining.
3. *Top:* Paired element, close twining, double row.
   Bottom: Paired element, close twining, double row.
4. Double-element, paired, parallel twining.
5. Double-element, paired, spaced radial twining.

6-180 MARY LEE HU demonstrates a single twisted, spaced, radially twined form in progress. The stakes are 19 gauge B.&S. lacquered copper wire, and the randing is paired 26 gauge B.&S. fine silver wire. *Photo: Mary Lee Hu*

6-181 HONG KONG. A two-element, intertwined rattan palm stem carpet beater, made in one continuous length, seized to the handle by a split and coiled rattan. The same twining system can be used with wire. *Photo: Oppi*

6-182 ANGLO-SAXON, late 8th–early 9th century A.D. The Windsor pommel ornament on a sword hilt, silver on separate, detachable gold panel held in flanged sides. Decorated with one intertwined heavy-gauge round wire representing two symmetrically interlaced snakes, each consuming the other's tail. This is interwoven with one long, and several short two-element twisted wires, ending in granule clusters soldered to hold the wires to the base. Some wires are soldered at crossings and in a few places to the border, but otherwise are free of the base panel, which is 2 cm high and 1.75 cm wide. *Photo: Ashmolean Museum, Oxford*

Lashing is accomplished by making the continuous flexible elements pass over and twine around the rigid elements at their crossing point in such a way as to snare or bind them to each other, or to a third rigid element, which prevents them from slipping or moving because they are held under tension. Lashing differs from knotting because knots are made by passing an end through a loop, which is not done in lashing. (Knots can of course be used to hold elements and make structures rigid, as described below.) The lashing element is *flexible* and *continuous*, passes over and around the unit juncture, then passes on from that lashing point to the next. Its continuity makes the tension on the flexible element possible so that the structure holds together. Because of the regularly repeated manner in which most lashing is done, the results create a rhythmic visual pattern.

In all lashing systems *multiple* as well as *single series* can be made, either next to each other, or spaced apart (another way of introducing pattern). Most systems that can be used with parallel rigid elements are also applicable to radially placed elements.

Cross-tie lashing uses one or two lashing elements, and the path of the flexible element differs accordingly. When using a single lashing element, the cross is done in the same way in which a cross-stitch is done in embroidery. When two lashing elements are used, they both are used

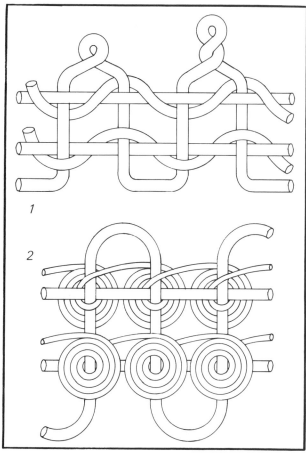

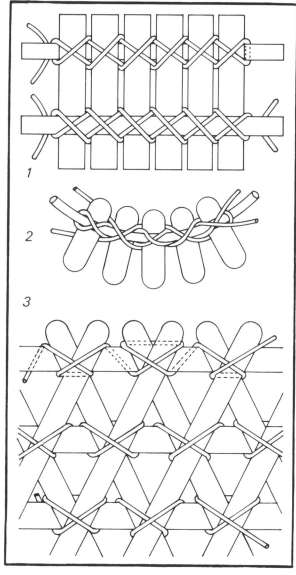

6–183 *LASHING*
1. Sinuous lashing, *upper:* front view; *lower:* back view.
2. Spiral lashing, *upper:* back view; *lower:* front view.

6–184 *CROSS-TIE LASHING*
1. *Top:* One-element, return, cross-tie lashing.
   Bottom: Two-element, cross-tie lashing.
2. Two-element, radial, cross-tie lashing.
3. One-element, diagonal, lattice lashing.

6–185 BATAK TRIBE, SUMATRA, INDONESIA.
Wooden comb with handle wrapped with brass wire. The teeth are lashed together radially with brass wire mainly in rows of buttonhole stitches. *Photo: Oppi*

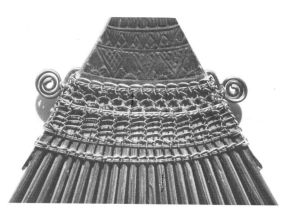

6–186 *DETAIL OF THE COMB* showing the buttonhole stitch lashing system.

6–187 KENYA. Masai woman wearing five traditional collar-necklaces of colored glass beads strung on concentric, parallel rows of completely covered steel wires held rigidly together in flat sequence by radiating wires lashed around each row at intervals between the beads. *Photo: Jorma Poutanen*

6–188 ANGLO-SAXON, 9th century A.D. Gold ring found in 1877 at Dorchester, Dorset. The main, heavy, continuous wire forms the heads and bodies of two symmetrically intertwined snakes. These are lashed with a second, smaller gauge, continuous wire that starts at one side of the ring shank and continues through to the other side, thus rigidly holding the main forms. Ø 2.4 cm Photo: Ashmolean Museum, Oxford

6–189 REAR VIEW OF THE RING showing the lashing wire construction.

simultaneously. The first one crosses the rigid elements in one oblique direction, and the second in the opposite oblique direction, forming a cross on top of each rigid element. By cross-tie lashing, rigid elements can be held closely together or be spaced apart. In *radial cross-tie lashing* the rigid elements are lashed to a wire that has been preformed to a curve, but the lashing system is the same as with elements that are parallel.

Cross-tie lashing can also be used to hold small units in series to a substructure of two or more rigid supporting elements. The two lashing elements pass in a cross over the small unit, then twine around the supporting member, and make a cross over the next small element. As a variation, supporting elements can be lashed together and hold the small unit between them.

STITCHING: Joining and decorating metal by sewing and embroidery processes

Stitching is probably man's oldest means of joining and of decorating units of nonwoven or woven fabrics made of fibrous substances. During Paleolithic times, skins were the material sewn together to make clothing, and later felt and woven cloth parts were assembled by stitching them together. The basic concept of all stitching and embroidery is that the foundation material is penetrated with holes

221

made with a piercing tool to allow the passage of a flexible element (thong, thread, wire) which is then pulled sufficiently tight to place the flexible element under enough tension to hold that element to the foundation and keep the parts together. This concept can be utilized with any flat or dimensionally shaped rigid materials including metal, wood, plastic, or others.

Many of the great variety of stitching and embroidery stitch systems can be used in metalwork by substituting wire of suitable gauge and flexibility for thread as the joining element, and sheet metal or wire mesh for cloth. Once the pattern is laid out, holes are pierced through the metal at the proper positions with a *small high-speed drill*. Even though it is flexible, the stitching wire ordinarily is sufficiently rigid so that a needle is not necessary (though it can be used), and the wire passes easily from the point of entry to an exit hole. To minimize the movement between the parts of such structures, make the hole as nearly equal in size as possible to the wire gauge diameter employed. This helps to eliminate looseness and compensates for the lack of elasticity of the wire. Starts and ends can be twisted onto the work so that entire works can be constructed without soldering, but they can be soldered to the supporting metal at their beginning and end as well.

BASIC STITCH GROUPS

The two basic stitch groups that categorize almost all stitches are straight stitches and curved stitches. *Straight stitches* are straight from one point to another, and include running, solid line, and crossed stitches, to mention a few. *Curved stitches* are those that follow a curved path by being brought out of the straight line direction by one or more additional stitches, and include buttonhole stitches, chain stitches, and others. Only some of the most basic stitches suited to use with metal can be shown here in diagrams. Books on stitchery will provide a profusion of other stitches that can be used. Almost all basic stitches can be used either for functional or purely decorative purposes. They can be applied to join overlapping or abutting sheet metal forms or to decorate a surface with a linear pattern in wire; some are suited to decorating the edges of metal forms.

6–190 HIROKO SATO PIJANOWSKI, U.S.A. Pin with a central repoussé-worked part held to the three-row coil-wrapped fiber frame by stitching it at intervals with the same metallic wrapping thread, passed through drilled holes. Photo: Bill Burchell

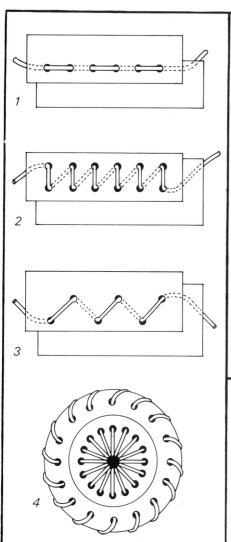

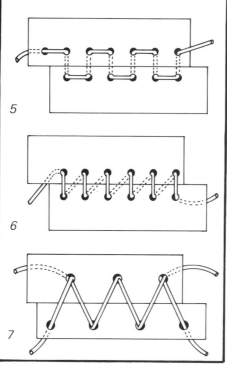

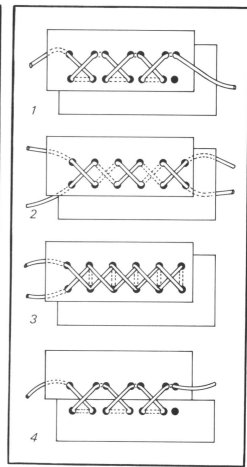

6-191 STRAIGHT LINE
STITCHES
Lapped
1. Horizontal running stitch.
2. Vertical running stitch.
3. Diagonal running stitch.
4. Radial running stitch.
Butted
5. Horizontal.
6. Vertical.
7. Diagonal.

6-192 CROSSED STITCHES
1. Each cross is made before the next; lap join.
2. Crosses are made as a series of parallel, slanting half-stitches, followed by a second journey of crossing stitches; lap join.
3. A crossing system in which the back has vertical stitches; lap join.
4. Same system as the first; butt join.

6-193 *Left:* CURVED
LINE STITCHES
1. Buttonhole stitch: *top, front,* lap join; *bottom, reverse side.*
2. Chain stitch: *top, front,* lap join; *bottom, reverse side.*
3. Buttonhole stitch: *edge.*

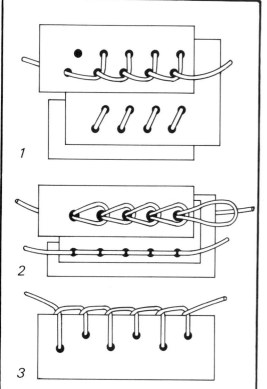

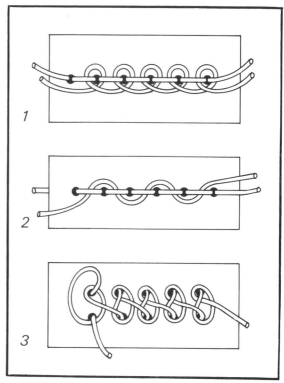

6-194 COMPOSITE STITCHES
1. Whipped backstitch; 2. Threaded backstitch; 3. Braid stitch.

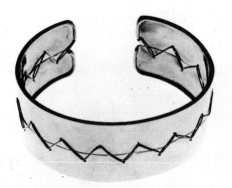

6-195 NOMA COPLEY, U.S.A. Bracelet in 18K gold of two butted sheet metal forms joined with diagonal, two-element running stitches in wire. *Photo: Tracy Boyd*

6-196 SOUTH INDIA. Collar of steel spikes, used to train dancing girls. The units are regularly drilled with pairs of holes, and stitched together through them by cords which form a pattern in the design. *Photo: Victoria and Albert Museum, London, Crown Copyright*

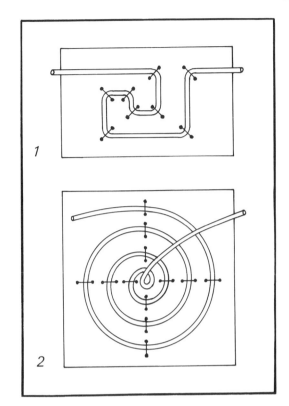

6-197 COUCHING
1. Straight couched stitches; 2. Curved couched stitches.

COUCHING

Couching is a type of embroidery in which thread (in this case, relatively heavy-gauge wire, too heavy for use as stitches) can be shaped into any pattern and held to the surface by short stitches with a fine thread (wire) that passes over it at intervals, holding it down. Plain, round, patterned or twisted wires could be used as the laid or couched element.

TAPESTRY EMBROIDERY

Tapestry embroidery can also be transposed to metalwork.

In *tapestry embroidery,* a foundation of a meshwork such as canvas is used to support the decorative thread (wire). All or only a part of the foundation mesh is covered by stitches. Instead of using canvas, woven wire mesh of silver, copper, brass, or nickel in any coarseness can be used for the foundation. Wire of the same or a contrasting colored metal can replace thread. If a nonwoven, molded plastic mesh is used as a foundation, it is possible, when using interlocking or overlapping stitches, to burn away the plastic foundation and leave only the wirework embroidery which can then be used mounted on a ground, or flattened by running it through a rolling mill.

Using accessory articles with metal wire is yet another possibility. These can be bones, feathers, horn sections, quills, seeds, shells, semiprecious stones or other objects from nature. Fabricated objects such as beads, bells, coins, glass, mirror, metal plaques, and sequins of all shapes could be used. According to their nature, if they can be pierced or have holes, they can be strung on wire individually or in a sequence such as a strand, then stitched to the surface with an auxiliary wire. They can also be knotted to the structure with wire. Objects with holes can be made

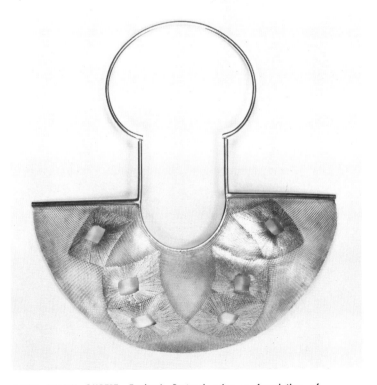

6-198 WALLY GILBERT, England. Pectoral using a foundation of woven sterling silver wire, 28 gauge B.&S., made on a frame, then embellished with extra wire embroidery. The rectangular patterns with open centers are done in buttonhole stitch which creates a finished opening edge. The result is hammered flat. The wire crossings are fusion welded in place to give the structure rigidity, and soldered to an end- and side-supporting sterling silver tube structure. Wire surfaces are polished and burnished. *Photo: Peter Parkinson*

a part of the wirework structure while the construction process is underway, and become incorporated into the result.

KNOTTING

Conceptually, a *knot* is formed when the ends of a length of a flexible unit of a cord, wire, or plastic are interlaced by making a loop and passing the end through it in a prescribed over-and-under sequence. When the unit loop and/or ends are pulled tightly, the knot becomes structurally "tied" or immobilized at a point on its own length, or upon another supporting element. Characteristically, at that point, a lump or knob is formed of the intertwined element, called a knot. One can also use more than one flexible unit at a time.

A rope or other element used to make a knot consists of two main parts relative to the knot: the *working end* (or ends) which is manipulated to create the knot; and the *standing part* which is not manipulated. When the ends of the element are inaccessible, some knots are formed by making a loop in the element, called a *bight*, between the working and standing parts. In knot terminology, a *hitch* is used to fasten an element to an object, or to its own standing part; and a *bend* is used to fasten two elements together.

All knots depend on *friction* where the parts cross over each other to prevent movement. When friction is decreased, as when using smooth, sliding materials such as plastic and metal, the ability of the knot to hold when weight is placed upon it is decreased, but when knots are applied to jewelry, this is not normally a problem as the scale is small and the weights involved are relatively light. Normally, when two elements are joined they are of the same weight, but some knots can be made with elements of different weights. This condition assumes importance when relatively great weights are placed on the knot as smaller elements tend to be pulled out of larger elements.

Knotting is a means of forming a raised knob on an element; a way of attaching an element to a supporting element; a means of attaching elements to each other to

6–200 RANDERS SØLVVAREFABRIK, Denmark, manufacturer. Cuff links made of square silver wire tied in the form of a knot. *Photo: Lisco, courtesy Randers Sølvvarefabrik*

make them a single unit; or a way of creating netlike, openwork structures by knotting together many elements at fixed positions where they meet or cross. Knots by themselves can be used either *functionally* or *decoratively*, and they can simultaneously serve both purposes. The knotting concept is at the basis of several decorative processes that employ yarns, among them lace making, tatting, and macramé, all of which are techniques where round metal wire of the proper gauge and flexibility can substitute for yarn.

A few applications of knots and knotted structures to jewelry can be mentioned. Single knots are commonly used to space beads to prevent friction; as a separate, decorative wire unit, they can be a link in a chain, or a means of joining fabricated or cast forms; knotted or knotlike structures can be made of plain and/or twisted wire and mounted as decoration on a sheet metal ground; an entire piece of jewelry such as a ring, bracelet, or necklace can be in the form of a nonfunctional or functioning knot; knotted structures in netlike forms, such as can be created by net making, macramé, or lace making can be made in metal wire as jewelry. For detailed instructions on the latter techniques, readers are referred to specialized texts on these subjects.

The patterns made by knots, and knotlike structures or configurations have been simulated in jewelry since antiquity in nonflexible forms. These have been used for their decorative value, or for reasons of symbolism connected with specific knot forms.

KNOT STRUCTURES

Knots can be started either from the left or the right, passing under or over the first loop. Some knots appear different on their reverse face, others are identical on both sides, and they can be structurally symmetrical or asymmetrical. Consult the accompanying diagrams for the construction of the various knots described below. In metal, ends or contact points can be soldered together to make the form permanent. Free ends can be fused to a ball shape, and knot forms can be joined by links to make a series of units into a flexible chain.

Because of the great number of knots and their variations, only some of the more basic types and a few variants can be given here. Some of their names originate with sailor's knotting.

Movable knots are those made with one active element that engages a second, passive element that is not a part of the knot, such as a straight wire along which the knot can be moved, a jump ring, a hook, a hole in sheet metal, or a finding.

Simple overhand knot: The simplest of all knots, it is identical on both sides, and will not pull apart. It is used at times at the end of an element to prevent it from slipping out of a hole.

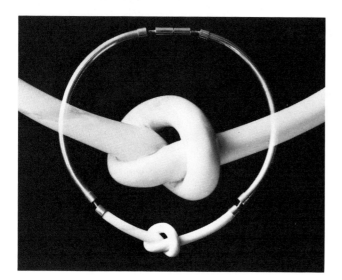

6–199 CAROLINE BROADHEAD, England. Necklace of silver tubing and ivory carved into a simulated one-element overhand knot. *Photo: Ray Carpenter, courtesy Electrum Gallery, London*

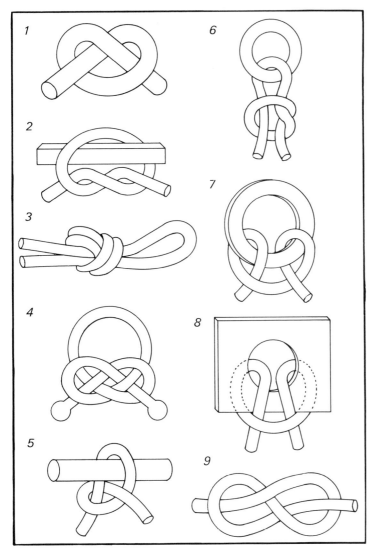

6–201 *KNOT STRUCTURES*
1. Overhand knot, one element.
2. Simple knot, two elements.
3. Loop knot.
4. Prolonge knot.
5. Half hitch knot, two elements.
6. Slip knot, two elements.
7. Clove hitch knot, two elements.
8. Cow hitch knot, two elements.
9. Figure eight knot, one element.

6–202
10. Cat's paw knot, two elements.
11. Square knot, two elements.
12. Granny knot, two elements.
13. Mesh knot, two elements.
14. Fishnet knot, two elements.
15. Carrick bend knot, two elements, ends seized.
16. Surgeon's knot, two elements.

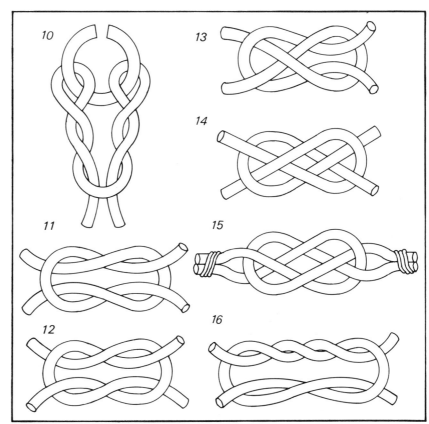

Half hitch: An over-one-under-one interlacing system, it is asymmetrical, with dissimilar faces. It is used by sailors in knotting rope, and in pillow lace making.

Slip knot: This is a movable, sliding knot with two dissimilar faces, so called, because when used alone without engaging a passive element, it -can be unreeved (pulled apart) simply by pulling on one end. It is actually an overhand knot with a loop rather than an end pushed through the loop.

Clove hitch: This knot is made with two identical, contiguous loops of two half hitches that pass over the second element. When tightened it is asymmetrical, but has two identical faces. It is an especially good knot to attach wire to a cylindrical form.

Cow hitch: This is composed of two contiguous, simple half hitch loops over the second element, each facing in an opposite direction, making it symmetrical, but with dissimilar faces. It is commonly used to anchor an element to a loop, hole, or buckle, as when starting knotted constructions such as macramé.

Cat's paw knot: This knot is related to the cow hitch, but several extra twists are made in the bights before slipping them over the open ends of a loop or a hook.

Immovable knots are those in which both the elements used to make the knot are active, and when tightened, they lock upon each other and do not move.

Square knot: An easily tied and very popular fixed knot, it is also called a *reef knot*, or *Hercules knot* because it is so strong. It is one of the oldest knots in use, and in ancient Greece was believed to have healing properties. It is made of two interlocking loops in which the terminal and standing parts are together and parallel to each other. It is symmetrical, and both faces are identical.

Surgeon's knot: This knot is related to the square knot, but has an extra overpass or twist in the first overhand knot which holds it in place while the second overhand turn is tied.

Granny knot: This is similar to the square knot, but is greatly disliked and avoided by sailors because it tends to slip and jam when subjected to excessive weight. The

6-204 6-205 KALEVALA KORU, Finland, manufacturer. Bronze cast pendants adapted from finds of Viking age Finnish brooches. Various forms of the so-called "endless knot" were used as a protective symbol of long life, eternity, and infinity by many world cultures. *Photo: Otso Pietinen, courtesy Kalevala Koru*

6-206 MELONG, KIBOR, SPITI, INDIA. Brass pendant (*srubtsi*) inlaid with silver. Its central pattern, a Tibetan form of the endless knot (*dpal-be*) is one of the widely used Buddhist Eight Glorious Emblems, or good luck symbols. *Photo: Museum of Anthropology, University of Michigan*

6-203 GREECE, 4th–3rd century B.C. Center ornament from a gold diadem with garnets using the knot of Hercules motif, a form of a square knot widely used in ancient Greek jewelry, symbolizing strength. Purchase, Joseph Pulitzer Bequest Fund, 1958. *Photo: Metropolitan Museum of Art, New York*

two elements pass over each other in an asymmetrical sequence, though the faces are identical.

Mesh knot: Also called the *weaver's knot* or *sheet bend knot,* it is made with two interlocking loops, is asymmetrical, and has two dissimilar faces. It is frequently used to join two elements of different sizes.

Fishnet knot: Used to join the free ends of two elements, it is made of two loops that cross within each other. It is asymmetrical, and has two dissimilar faces.

Carrick bend: This is a very secure, decoratively patterned knot used originally to join large ropes. Its ends are lashed or whipped to secure the loops formed, in the process called *seizing.*

MIZUHIKI-SAIKU: A Japanese form of ornamental knot work

In Japan, a decorative form of knotting and tying called *mizuhiki* (the term for both the material used and the result; *saiku,* "work") is a highly developed art. By the techniques of knotting, interlacing, intertwining, looping, bending, and spiraling, simple or complex formations of knots and loops are made into attractive ornaments that are tied around gift packages. By transposing the paper material used into *two-ply, twisted wire,* these knotting systems can easily be used to make jewelry.

The technique is believed to have originated in ancient India where it was practiced in the early days of Buddhism for making religious decorations. From there it traveled to China, and then to Japan, the path of so many of the arts of ancient Japan. At first, the custom of using these knot works for decorating and tying ceremonial gift packages was limited to use by royalty and the nobility. The original material used was linen thread made stiff by glue. In time, many different knot patterns were developed, and their usage filtered down to the lower classes who substituted the paper cord still in use today. This cord is made of thin strips of paper spread on one side with paste, then spirally twisted and allowed to dry stiff while retaining flexibility. The old traditional colors are red, white, silver, gold, and black, but today about 30 different colors are used. Gold- and silver-colored strands are made with an aluminum-coated paper. Colored plastic core wire is also in use now, completely wrapped with matching colored synthetic yarns that give the cord the appearance of silk.

Ready-made mizuhiki cord is prepared in units of five, seven, and nine strands (odd numbers are considered auspicious). Two groups of five are sometimes combined and used for tying marriage gifts as their total, the number ten

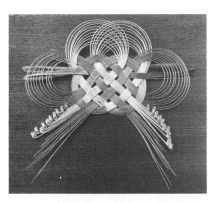

6–207 JAPAN. *Musubi* knot work decoration *(mizuhiki)* for a gift parcel, made of gold and silver paper cord. Size 8¼ × 7¾ in. Photo: Oppi

6–208 ARLINE M. FISCH, U.S.A. Necklace of twisted fine silver and brass wire strands, in the form of a traditional Japanese *mizuhiki-saiku* knot. Photo: Arline M. Fisch

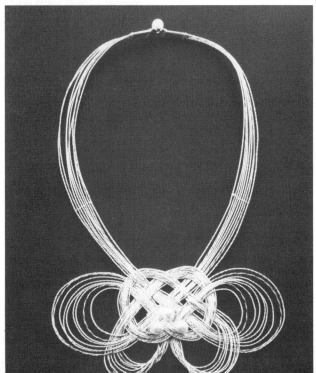

is considered lucky. All of these units are joined at the center with a glued paper strip of the same or contrasting color to hold them flat together when forming the knots and loops which normally lie flat, though they can also be made three dimensional. Mizuhiki are available in lengths of 60 cm (23⅝ in), 75 cm (29½ in), or 90 cm (35⅝ in) because these lengths are convenient to handle. Each single strand is about 1 mm (0.04 in; 18 gauge B.&S.) in thickness.

In the traditional mizuhiki, certain colors and combinations have an association with different types of events, and various forms of knots *(musubi)* are used to make particular configurations that are traditionally considered to be appropriate for certain occasions.

The basic knots used to join *two different* mizuhiki strands to therefore make *four-ended configurations* are the square knot, the fishnet knot, and the bow knot or double slip knot. Others are used when only *one* mizuhiki strand, therefore *two ends* are used. These knot patterns, each different, are given names such as baby turtle knot, pine tree knot, bamboo knot, peach knot, and plum blossom knot. Braiding *(kumihimo)* is also used in the form of three-strand braiding *(mitsuami)*, four-strand braiding *(yotsuami)*, etc.

From all of these basic configurations of knots, more elaborate patterns can be created by repeating them either widthwise or lengthwise in series using long mizuhiki strands. Individual knots can be elaborated by adding and intertwining additional loops to the initial knots. Units can also be made separately initially, then interworked to create more complex units.

Not only symmetrical, flat, patterned structures are made with these knots, but also three-dimensional knotted structures depicting subjects from nature. The chosen subjects are highly symbolic, and their meanings are widely known in Japan, so that subjects are chosen for their suitability to the particular occasion. On wedding gifts, for instance, any of the following could be used: the crane or turtle (both suggesting long life), the pine (steadfastness), the plum blossom (bravery), or the cherry blossom (purity), to list a few.

The knot work is done almost entirely with the fingers, holding the mizuhiki strands flat to preserve their proper sequence. Only a very few simple tools are needed. To form helix spirals *(rafen)* at strand ends, a metal rod with a slotted end is used. A single strand end is fixed in the slot to hold it while the spiral is formed by rotating the rod. Such spirals are only used on decorations for happy occasions, otherwise the strand ends are left straight *(massuguna)*. Another tool resembles a pointed scriber and is used to enlarge a knot part to allow the passage of ends through it. Scissors and nippers are used for cutting, and pliers for sharp bending. To hold unfinished parts and loops together while others are worked, contact tape can be placed at the back where needed, and later removed. The separate wires of a loop made from one unit are often spread apart to vary the spaces between them, and they are also bent to give them changes of direction. In some constructions, certain juncture points are held together with a thin wire twisted below to make it invisible. In the case of metal wire, junction points can be soldered if necessary.

Knotted wire units made in this way can be used for brooches and earrings, and when long wire lengths are used, the ends can form a neckpiece around the neck to hold a frontal knot construction; in a similar manner, a bracelet can be made.

HAND-WITH-HAND-TOOL-WORKED PROCESSES

SINGLE ELEMENT INTERLOOPED STRUCTURES

Crocheting and *knitting* are two important interlooping techniques that utilize a single, continuous element and a hand tool or tools to form a structure by drawing loops through previously made loops. When the interlooped fabrics are made of yarn or thin-gauge wire, only that part of the element near the tool's working end need be drawn through the previous loop to form a new loop. The length of the looping element can therefore be "endless" or unlimited, and the wire used can be held on a spool.

In some applications of these systems, however, the *whole length* of the wire is passed through the loop, making it necessary to use relatively short lengths and to solder new ones to the end of the old when it is consumed in the structure. Drawing the length through loops many times tends to stiffen or work harden the wire (particularly disadvantageous when making small loops); however, at intervals the working wire can always be formed into a coil and annealed to restore its flexibility.

CROCHETING: Vertical and lateral interlooping

The word *crochet* is derived from the Old French *croc,* "a (single) hook," the hand tool used in this interlooping or chaining process by which openwork or dense fabrics of yarn or soft, annealed wire are created. Crocheting is normally done with a single, hooked, hand tool, and knitting is normally done with a minimum of two straight needles. (Exceptions exist: *hairpin crochet* uses a two-pronged, hairpin-shaped tool; tubular forms can be knitted on a single curved needle; and in knitting tubular chain, described on p. 232, only one straight tool is used.) The crochet hook is designed to make it convenient to shape and draw a loop through an existing loop, a process basic to the crocheting technique. The use of a hook, however, is not confined to crocheting. A hook is also sometimes used in knitting, especially when knitting with wire, because it helps to make wire manipulation easier.

Crocheting makes use of both vertically and laterally interworked loops of *chain stitches* and stitches based on the chain stitch, each one securing the previous one through which it is drawn. By the nature of the continuous, interlooped structure of the chain stitch, each stitch locks the previous one, but the loops can be unraveled by pulling on the still unused element. Therefore, to finish and lock the last stitch at any point where this may be necessary, the element is cut off and its end is drawn through the last loop and pulled tight, the last loop acting as a knot.

The *loop size* made depends on the *hook size* in relation to the size of the element. Fine steel hooks are used to make small loops from fine elements, and for larger loops and heavier weight yarn or wire, larger diameter bone, aluminum, plastic, or boxwood hooks are used. Different hook size numbering systems are used in the U.S.A., the U.K., and continental Europe, and separate ones are used for hooks made of steel, aluminum or plastic, and wood. An *international numbering system* exists based on the diameter (in millimeters) of the hooks. Loop size or *stitch gauge* as it is called in crochet terminology, is also con-

6–209 LIISA LEHTONEN, Finland. Lacquered copper (0.85 mm; 20 gauge B.&S.) electrical wire crocheted necklace, with handmade black and red Indian glass beads. Photo: *Oppi*

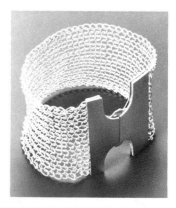

6–210 KATHARINA ISSLER, Switzerland. Sterling silver wire, open-loop knitted bracelet. The strip was knitted flat, then curved into a cylindrical form. Its ends are sandwiched between the two sheet metal parts of the clasp. Photo: *Thomas Von Wartburg*

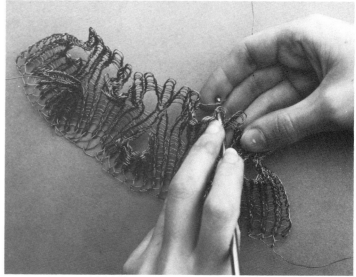

6–211 MARY LEE HU demonstrates the use of a crocheting needle to create a flat structure from 24 gauge B.&S., dark bronze, anodized aluminum wire, but the system is knitting despite the tool used. This is possible because wire, unlike yarn, maintains its rigidity, and the unworked loops need not be held on a second knitting needle. Stitches can be dropped or added without the need of spare needles. Here three, four, or five stitches have been dropped and simply bent forward while the knitting continues past them. Returned to later, they are worked with a new wire into a tube form, as seen on the left. The structure starts with a series of simple twisted loops, seen at bottom, later removed. Photo: *Mary Lee Hu*

trolled by *tension* or the pull exerted with the fingers on the wire when each loop is formed. There is a limit to the size of wire gauge that can be manipulated with a crochet hook, and much depends on the flexibility of the wire.

Fabrics of almost *any form* can be made by crocheting. A flat fabric is made by working the loops in equal rows forward and backward to form squares and rectangles. The structure can also grow radially from a point by gradually *increasing* the number of stitches, or diagonally to a point by *decreasing* the stitches, to make triangular segments. A flat strip can be made and then developed radially. Flat, spirally created circular or oval forms are possible. Forms can develop to create a hollow, cylindrical, or tubular structure by working the loops continuously in a spiral. A great variety of netlike structures are possible. Most important in the use of crocheting for making wire jewelry is that *the structure can be added to at any point.* This makes it possible to develop a work in any direction once a basic foundation or form has been established.

For *basic crocheting techniques,* and the use of elaborate stitches that are compounds of loops made before releasing them from the hook in order to make openwork fabrics, interested readers are referred to specialized texts on crocheting.

KNITTING: Vertical interlooping

Knitting is the technique of interlooping a single, continuous element by making a series of connected loops that have been placed on a blunt-pointed rod or *knitting needle* pass singly in sequence from a left to a right needle while engaging a new series of loops, thus forming a continuous, vertically interlooped fabric. The earliest knitting is believed to have been done on the four fingers of the left hand, or on a series of pegs arranged in a row or a circle. From these beginnings, two basic systems evolved. One uses a minimum of a pair of *knitting needles* or *pins,* as mentioned above, and the other uses a series of *pegs* placed in a single or double row, or in a circular ring.

The technique of knitting with wire is exactly the same as for yarns, except that the stiffness and lack of elasticity of wire imposes certain limitations. There are many excellent texts available on the subject of knitting to which those who are interested can refer. Therefore, conventional needle knitting is not discussed here.

It might be mentioned, however, that because of the stiffness of wire, once a foundation has been established, a knitted fabric can be created with a *crochet hook* since the loops will not unravel. In spite of the use of this tool, the system is still considered knitting as it is the *structure of the resulting fabric* that determines the classification, not the tool used.

CROSSED KNITTING This is said to be the oldest form of knitting. It differs from ordinary knitting in that instead of the loops being left open, they are taken from the needle with a half turn which causes a cross to form at the base of each loop. The right may be crossed over the left, or vice versa. The result in wire is a denser-looking texture.

FINISHING KNITTED STRUCTURES IN METAL When knitting with metal wire, the edge loops can be finished off on a knitted structure in ways that differ from those used to finish yarn knitting. A heavy wire can be passed through the loops of the last row and then bent to form a circle that acts as a suspending device to hold the worked part around the neck. Two knitted units can be joined by passing a stiff wire through alternate loops at their edges to

lock them together. Wire ends can be bent, balled, spiraled, forge spread, etc., to prevent the texture from raveling or coming apart. Wire loops can be individually twisted upon themselves with pliers. A thin wire can be passed through each loop in succession and whipped once around each before passing on to all the others to keep them in place.

It is also possible to finish an edge of a knitted fabric by crochet work. A knitted unit can be sewed to a wire frame pierced regularly with holes, onto hole pierced sheet metal, or onto a leather or cloth ground.

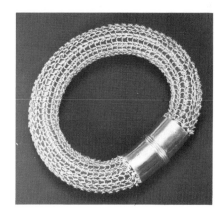

6–212 KATHARINA ISSLER, Switzerland. Sterling silver wire, open-loop knitted tube bracelet, containing a clear, flexible plastic tube to keep its form. The knitted tube end loops engage matching spaced tabs projecting from the sheet metal central tube ornament. Photo: Thomas Von Wartburg

PEGGED RING-KNIT WIRE TUBES

Knitting a tubular form spirally from a continuous wire by the use of a round, hollow-centered ring that bears a circle of an equally spaced series of upright or outward-slanting pegs, is one of the most ancient methods of knitting with yarns or wire. The concept using wire was practiced in ancient Greece, and many other cultures, and is still practiced today for making knitted tubular "chain" used to support ornaments. In Cuttack, India, for instance, manufactories exist that employ a hundred women who hand knit silver wire tube of this type all day long, and the process is also widely used in Nepal.

Circular peg-knit tubes often make use of the system of crossed knitting because a cross-knitted tube is much denser in texture and therefore more substantial-looking than tubes of the same construction and amount of material knitted with open loops. Because of the spiral structure, knitted tubes always have a *central opening* which makes it possible to insert a wire or even a tube within their length. Such knitted tubes should not be confused with loop-in-loop chains which they sometimes externally resemble when the texture is tight because *wales* with

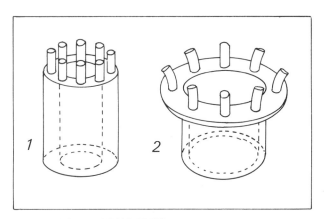

6–213 *PEGGED KNITTING RINGS*
1. Wooden tube with metal or nylon pegs.
2. Molded plastic pegged ring.

diagonally slanting wires are formed in both techniques. In these cases, the only way to know the method of construction used is to take apart one end of the tube which instantly reveals the use of oval links (used in loop-in-loop chains), or a continuous wire (used in knitted tubes).

Depending on the tube diameter and its density, a knitted tube can be put to the same uses as chains. In short lengths they can link other forms. In a long, flattened form they can be used singly or in multiples as belts. Usage is multiplied by the fact that knitted tube, round or flat, is *highly flexible* and easily takes on any curved form.

The *pegged knitting ring* device can be improvised from a wooden or plastic spool or tube into which wooden or nylon pegs are sunk and cemented, or headless nails are hammered. It is advisable when making such a device to predrill each peg or nail position with a hole slightly smaller than the peg or nail thickness to avoid splitting the material. Ready-made knitting spools of this type, and molded plastic pegged rings are available and can be purchased in hobby or toy shops.

The initial *diameter of the tube* depends on the diameter across the ring from peg to opposite peg position, and is always somewhat less than the diameter of the central hole as the tube tends to draw together under work. Tubes of fine wire can be knitted from ⅛ in diameter upward. The initial tube size that can be made with each such ring is more or less fixed, and rings of different diameters are needed to knit different sizes of tubing. The diameter of a finished tube can be reduced by drawing it through a drawplate. The *density of the tube texture* depends mainly on the relative closeness of the pegs. A four-peg knitting ring produces a *square-sectioned tube,* but any number greater than four will produce a round tube.

The *loop-lifting tool* used to pass the wire over the peg during knitting can be a plastic, nylon, or metal, dull-pointed, polished knitting needle or crochet hook, or a tool can be improvised (see the tool used in the demonstration Making a knitted wire tube, on p. 232).

The pegged ring knitting method used depends on the desired result. The simplest technique is *cross knitting.* To start, slip knot the wire end and pass the loop over any peg. Progressing in a clockwise direction, pass the wire across the *inside* of the peg, then once counterclockwise around that peg and on to the next peg. This forms a crossed loop on the peg with the cross on the *inner* side facing the tube hole. Do the same with all the pegs in the circle. In the second round (and all subsequent rounds), pass the wire in the same crossed way around one peg at a time, but always *above* the wrapped wire already there. While holding the loose wire end and the ring with the left hand and allowing some "give," with the right hand and the *loop-lifting tool,* lift the lower loop over the second or top, most recent loop and on over the top of the peg, toward the hole; then release it. Repeat the process with each of the pegs in turn, never skipping any. The tube develops in a spiral of interlooping loops, moving downward within the central hole of the ring. When after a few rounds enough of a tube develops, grasp its end below the ring hole and tug it downward. The tug stretches the loops in a vertical direction, and the amount of tug applied is another way of regulating the tube diameter. This tugging motion should become automatic after each loop is passed over a peg, and it should be uniform to keep the diameter of the tube uniform.

When tube knitting with wire, do not be disappointed by the irregular appearance of the initial tube, because as the work progresses, it becomes more even. The irregular half inch or so of the starting section can later be cut away. For this reason, plan for an extra allowance of wire material.

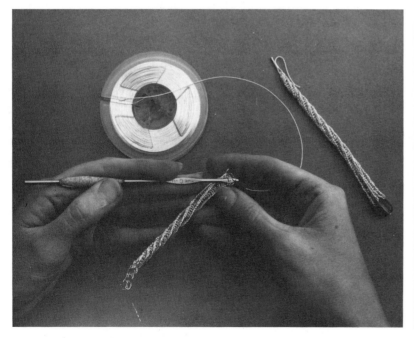

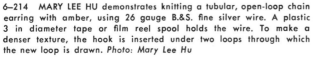

6–214 MARY LEE HU demonstrates knitting a tubular, open-loop chain earring with amber, using 26 gauge B.&S. fine silver wire. A plastic 3 in diameter tape or film reel spool holds the wire. To make a denser texture, the hook is inserted under two loops through which the new loop is drawn. *Photo: Mary Lee Hu*

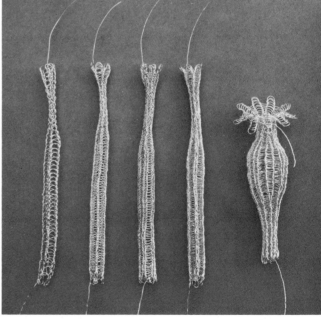

6–215 MARY LEE HU demonstrates open knitted tubes made with the same size crochet hook. From *left to right* are four five-loop circumference tubes. In the first, each loop is drawn through a single loop of the previous row; in the second through two previous loops; in the third through three loops; and the fourth through four loops. With each increase in loop numbers drawn through, the texture becomes denser. In the fifth example, a nine-loop circumference tube is shaped by gradually increasing the loop size and pulling the structure outward, and constricted by decreasing the loop size and pressing them inward with the fingers. *Photo: Mary Lee Hu*

6–216 NEPAL. Tamang woman wearing a traditional necklace (*sang-la*). The central repoussé-worked charm box (*jantar*) contains a written charm (*mantra*), and is suspended by five knitted wire tubes (*bhayeko sikri*). Photo: Oppi

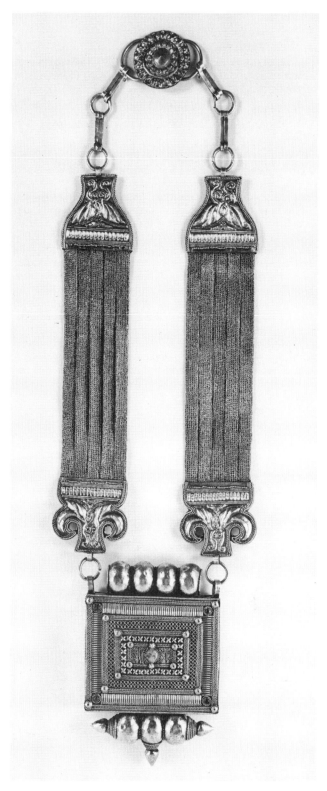

The ring knitting method allows the use of a long length of wire wound on a spool as only the immediate section near the peg is formed into a loop. If, however, a long length of wire is not available and relatively short lengths must be used, solder a new length of wire to the old one as needed.

To *finish* the ends of the knitting after reaching the desired tube length, carefully remove the loops from the pegged ring with the loop-lifting tool. As a safety precaution, draw a separate wire through the loops to prevent the last line of loops from raveling, and twist its ends together.

Variation is possible in the appearance of the result. By using a thin or a thick peg, the size and shape of the loop is different. *Vertical density* of the wales that develop depends on the distance between the pegs, close pegs making close wales; spaced pegs, spaced wales. *Horizontal density* can be increased by cross wrapping more than the normal two rounds of loops on the peg at the same time. For example, in *triple-loop knitting*, a *third* loop is cross wrapped above the normal two. The *lowest loop* is lifted over the two above, so that each loop encloses *two loops* instead of one. Three or more loops can be leapfrogged in this way and with each increase in number, the horizontal density of the result increases.

A round tube can be flattened with a *mallet* which doubles its thickness. A metal strip can be placed within a partially flattened tube, the tube flattened further upon it, and the strip then withdrawn. This flat core serves to bring all the wires to a more level plane. It is also possible to pass the flattened tube (with or without the strip core inside) through a *rolling mill*. Rolling cannot be repeated—with each roll the wires cut more deeply into each other at their crossing points, become weakened, and may break.

Round tube can be decreased in outside diameter by passing it through two or three holes in a metal or wooden

6–217 EASTERN NEPAL. Silver necklace of the *sang-la* type. The very fine wire knitted tubes have been flattened into a double strip, sewn to other units with twisted wire. The flower-shaped back ornament (*hup*) is typical of these necklaces. Photo: Ferdinand Boesch

drawplate. Drawing also tends to make the tube appear more regular, and at the same time, increases its length. To make the texture more dense and the shape more round, place a *round wire core* of a gauge that matches the inside opening within the tube before drawing it. The inside diameter will be maintained and the wires forced to its curvature and surface. The core wire can be removed after drawing, or it can be left inside. If it is of a different color than the wire used for the tube, you may wish to leave it in for contrast.

MAKING A KNITTED WIRE TUBE: Self-supported knitting

Because of the relative rigidity of wire, the pegged ring used to make a hollow knitted wire tube can be dispensed with. In the system described here, the circle of starting loops made of twisted wire in the manner shown in the diagrams can stand alone: it substitutes for the pegged ring. Each individually made loop is crossed at its base, so this method is also *cross knitting,* but there are differences between this procedure and pegged ring knitting. First, the texture grows upward from this base rather than downward into the ring hole. There is no wrapping of the wire around a peg or drawing loops through loops. Instead the loops are formed by passing the whole wire length through two adjoining loops and around a pick which shapes them. Other differences will be seen in the description.

In the system described here, a knitted tube or "cord chain" is made with a continuous length of 25 gauge B.&S. wire. The *pointed pick* used to form the loops can be

made from a 16 gauge B.&S., straight, rigid steel wire mounted in a hole drilled in a wood dowel that serves as a handle. The loops are formed around the wire which therefore must be uniform in section to keep the size of the loops uniform. Before use, sterling wire should be annealed but not wire of fine silver. Three-foot wire lengths are the most convenient to handle. When this length is consumed, a second length can be soldered to the end of the first. After soldering, smooth down the solder and remove oxidation by rubbing the joint area with a piece of abrasive cloth.

1 To start the construction, twist a series of loops together from one wire length passing from one to the other in the manner illustrated in the first diagram. For a round tube, five or more loops can be used. The greater the number of loops, the larger the tube diameter. In this example, eight loops are used. These are all twisted in the same direction from one length of wire, and the loops are arranged in a circle. On this base the tube will be knitted.

2 Push the pick through the first two loops so they are bent at right angles to each other. This makes it possible to pull the wire through the loops in a straight line without any resistance from the loops. Also, it then becomes easier to keep the loops uniform in size as they are made.

3 Remove the pick from the loops and place it in a vertical position against the first loop (A). Bring the wire through the back of the first loop, pass it around the tool, then cross it over on itself, out through the same first loop, and then through the next one (B). This makes a large loop of the wire which is then pulled down against the pick until the loop is tight around it, as illustrated.

4 While holding on to the wire to keep it tight against the pick and toward the pick tip to avoid crushing the loops opposite, raise the pick upward in an arc to a horizontal position, bringing the loop to a vertical position above the loop to which it is attached. These steps constitute the basic procedure. From here on, the first three steps are repeated.

5 Push the pick through the next two loops to align them as in diagram 2.

6 Next follow the same procedure as in diagram 3 using the second loop (B). The previously formed loop is visible.

The next step is a repeat of the procedure in diagram 4. Continue these steps around the circle of loops until the end of the wire is reached and a new length is soldered on. Continue working until the desired tube length is reached. The tube grows with relative rapidity, this eight-loop tube increasing about an inch and a half in an hour.

To make the finished tube appear more uniform, first anneal the tube. Then insert a brass, copper, or steel core wire of a gauge equal to its inside diameter into the central hole in the entire tube length. Leave an exposed portion to be grasped later when removing it. This core wire supports the tube and keeps it round while it is drawn. Draw the tube through at least two holes in a metal or wood *drawplate* slightly smaller than its diameter. If the tube wales have become spirally twisted in fabrication, straightening it is possible to a limited extent by having an assistant exert a countertwist on it during drawing. Conversely, the twist can be increased by deliberately turning the tube in its direction of twist as it passes through the drawplate. After drawing, grasp the core wire end with *square-nosed pliers* and withdraw it. The result is a flexible, lightweight, knitted tube.

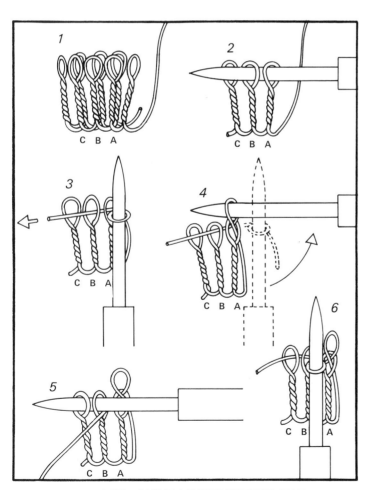

6-218 *MAKING A KNITTED WIRE TUBE CHAIN*

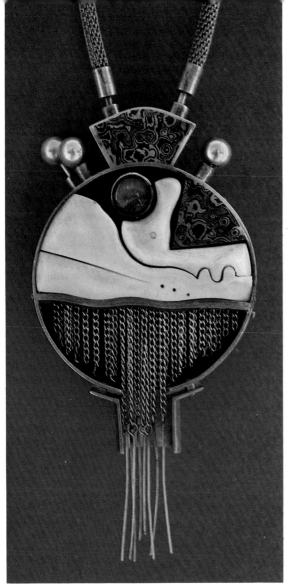

5-1

5-2

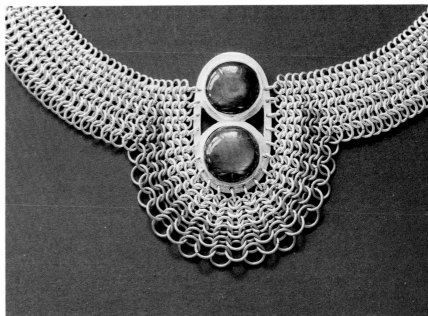

5-3

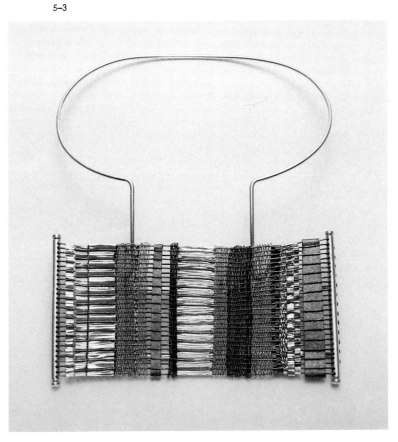

Plate 5-1 FRANCIS STEPHEN, U.S.A.
Pendant fabricated in silver and brass
married metals, using free-hanging
silver chain. *Photo: Francis Stephen*

Plate 5-2 MICHAEL PINDER, England. Necklace of chain mail with
silver and colored titanium links, and
two Finnish spectrolites. *Photo:
Michael Pinder*

Plate 5-3 MARGRIT HINTERMEISTER,
Switzerland. Necklace woven of
silver, gold, aluminum, colored titanium, and iron wire. *Photo: Thomas Von
Wartburg*

6–1

6–2

Plate 6–1   YASUKI HIRAMATSU, Japan. Bracelet and ring forged from gold strip. *Photo: Yasuki Hiramatsu*

Plate 6–2   BRENT KINGTON, U.S.A. Bracelet forged from a sterling silver bar, colored. *Photo: Brent Kington*

Plate 6–3   ALBERT PALEY, U.S.A. Brooch forged from heavy silver and gold wire. *Photo: Bruce Miller*

6–3

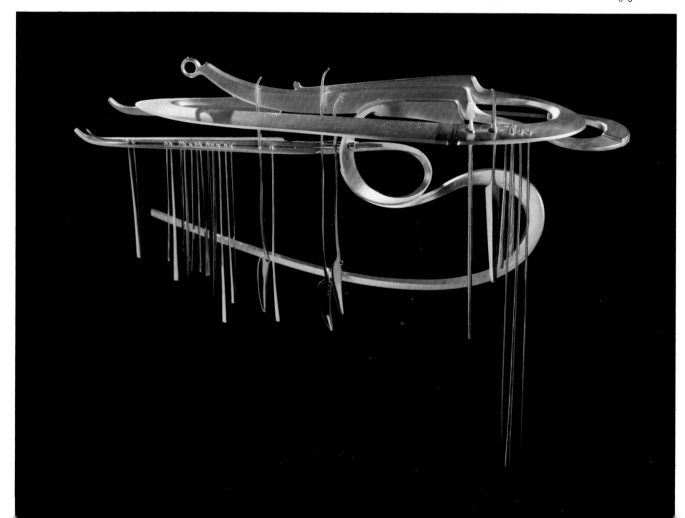

7–1

Plate 7–1 MITSUKO KAMBE SOELLNER, U.S.A. Silver belt buckle, Kyoto-style damascene inlay in gold and silver with black lacquer ground. *Photo: Walter Soellner*

Plate 7–2 CYNTHIA JENKINS, England. Ring of gold tubes into which diamonds are set. *Photo: Courtesy Crafts Council, London*

Plate 7–3 ELLIOT PUJOL, U.S.A. Ring of externally repoussé worked brass tubes. *Photo: Elliot Pujol*

7–2

7–3

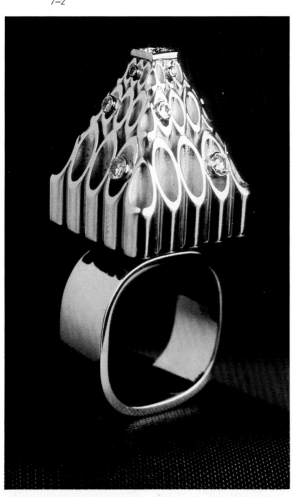

8-1

Plate 8-1   GUNTHER BARTSCH, West Germany. Brooch
fabricated with front in a mosaic of sterling silver, copper,
and brass married metals, backed in silver sheet. *Photo:
Thomas Goldschmidt*

Plate 8-2   PATRICIA DAUNIS-DUNNING, U.S.A. Cuff in
married metal inlay of interchanged silver and copper, the
holes cut with a circle disc cutter, then the discs are fused
in place. *Photo: Patrician Daunis-Dunning*

Plate 8-3   DAVID HENSEL, England. Bracelet of several
carved hardwoods, inlaid with silver wire, awabi and
abalone shell. *Photo: Barbara Cartlidge, courtesy Electrum
Gallery, London*

8-3

8-2

6–219 *DRAWING THE FINISHED KNITTED WIRE TUBE* with its brass wire core through a drawplate clamped in a bench vise. The assistant is twisting the tube as it is drawn to align the loop wales. *Photo: Oppi*

HAND- OR MECHANISM-WORKED WEAVING PROCESSES

WEAVING WITH METAL WIRE AND STRIP

Weaving is the most important of the hand- or mechanism-worked processes that can be used to interwork wire and strip elements. In all weaving, the basic concept involves the insertion and interlacing of a set of *horizontal* (width) elements called the *weft* through a set of *vertical* (length) elements called the *warp*.

Metal in wire and strip form can be woven on a loom without difficulty, but it is unnecessary here to discuss the operation of a conventional loom to weave metal elements, because within the probable scale and size range of metal fabrics woven for use in jewelry, and given the stiffness of metal, almost the same results can be attained *without the use of a loom*. Should the reader be interested in using a loom for weaving metal elements, a vast literature on simple hand weaving exists which can be consulted, and the relevant information applied to metal weaving. What follows, therefore, relates to *finger weaving*, done without a loom.

Finger weaving systems relate to systems used in basketry and plaiting, discussed earlier in this chapter. Basic weaves are discussed only briefly here.

THE BASIC WEAVES

To create what are called the basic weaves, the weft elements pass over and under the warp elements in specific, predetermined sequences. There are four main basic weave systems: plain weave, twill weave, satin weave, and open weave. From them come many derivative weaves.

Plain weave, also called *tabby weave,* consists of an interlacing order in one *pick* or weft row, of *over one, under one* warp element. In the following pick, the sequence alternates, the warp formerly passed over is passed under,

6–220 SAARA HOPEA-UNTRACHT, Finland, designer and chain knitter; K-G. AHLBERG, assembler; at Kultasepänliike Ossian Hopea, Porvoo. Silver necklace using three cross-knitted wire tubes, with fabricated parts and pendant using right circular cones. *Photo: Oppi*

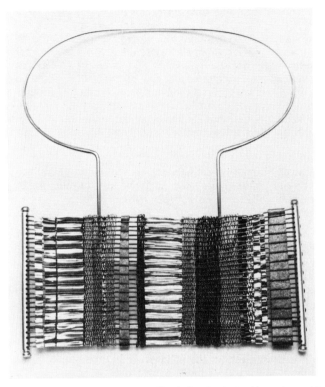

6–221 MARGRIT HINTERMEISTER, Switzerland. Necklace in multimetals. From a silver wire neckband, a plain-weave woven unit is suspended. The continuous iron wire warp passes through equally spaced holes drilled in the two silver end bars. The weft includes wire and strip in gold (999, 917, 750 yellow, 750 rose); fine and sterling silver; copper; anodized aluminum (pink, blue, yellow, white); colored titanium (brown, purple); and zinc-coated iron. Woven unit size 5⅞ × 2¾ in; total weight 94.4 g. Photo: Thomas Von Wartburg

and vice versa. Each pick is forced against the last to lock the previous weft in place by pressure to reduce or completely close the space between them.

Rib weave is one of the derivatives of plain weave and consists of passing the first weft pick *over two adjacent* warp elements, then *under two*. In the next pick, the weft passes over *single alternating* weft elements. In the resulting texture there is a tendency for the weft elements to become compressed so they partially or completely cover the warp elements. The horizontal *weft* element thus dominates, a texture called a *weft-faced rib*. If the same system is followed in a vertical direction, the *warp* element tends to dominate the texture and the weft becomes concealed to make a *warp-faced rib*.

Basket weave, another derivative of plain weave, consists of *two adjacent* weft elements passing over *two adjacent* warp elements, and the order is *alternated every second* pick. The appearance of the result is somewhat different when using wire or strip, but in each case the same structural pattern of squares develops, resembling the patterns achieved in basket making, hence the term basket weave.

Twill weave is done by making each successive interlacing of warp and weft occur with the intersection taking place *one warp end to the right* (or left) so that a *diagonal movement* occurs in the resulting pattern which is typical of all twill derivative weaves. The usual twill systems are *over two, under two; over three, under one;* or *over one, under three,* all in diagonal progression. There are

many weaves derived from the twill, among them the well-known *herringbone weave.*

Satin weave, some authorities claim, is a derivative of twill weave. In this system, the single warps or wefts interlace or are bound in a dispersed sequence, in which adjacent wefts are never bound by the same warp. The sequence is *regularly repeated,* however, and produces a smooth-faced fabric often without any apparent diagonal movement, with either the weft or warp making long floats on the fabric surface. Its application to uses in metal is limited because of the long floats unless the scale of elements is small, as they would make a loose structure. The appearance resembles long-float, wrapped coil work where the wrapping element predominates, though of course the techniques are entirely different. Wide belts are made this way in Egypt.

Open weaves produce openwork fabrics, often by utilizing the techniques of *twining* and *wrapping* to create stability in the position of the warp and weft elements in the open areas. Typical open weaves are *leno* and *gauze weaves,* and their derivatives. In these weaves, two or more elements lock on each other while they are held in place by a third element. This can be accomplished by crossing the warp ends in pairs or groups or twisting them, then passing the weft through or wrapping it around them. By alternating these open areas between tight, plain-woven bands, the open spaces are secured. Open weaves are particularly suited to metal wire in any scale.

THE FINGER WEAVING PROCESS

Most weaving processes require a means of holding the warp element by one or both ends, or at the center, in a way that allows the weft element to be introduced. When weaving with yarns, this is normally accomplished by means of a *loom mechanism* which is designed to hold the warp at both ends, under tension. On most looms, alternating sets of warp ends can be lifted or depressed at will, and the weft pick is easily introduced in the space or shed. Controlling texture density is also simplified by the use of a weft-beating mechanism on the loom. Metal wire and strip, however, characteristically possess an inherent stiffness, and though inelastic, have sufficient flexibility to allow the acts of weft introduction and beating to be accomplished *manually,* without a loom, when weaving rectangular, flat pieces. Since for jewelry the amounts of woven metal fabric needed and the scale of the work are both relatively small, any of the weaves described above can be created on a small scale by that most ancient preloom method of weaving, *with the fingers alone,* securing the warp at one end only.

The warp element can be of wire, strip, or a combination of both. Wire warp can be easily held in place during the introduction of the weft by hammering a series of equidistant headless finishing nails at a slight angle away from the weaving direction into a *softwood board.* The warp ends can then be individually twisted around the nails, or a wire length can be bent in half, its center twisted into a loop which is passed over the nail so two warp strands hang from the same nail, while the rest hang loose. If strip is used (alone or in combination with wire) for warp, a hole can be drilled in each strip end and a nail hammered through it into the board. To prevent sideways movement of the warp elements, a length of *draftsman's tape* can be passed temporarily across the warp near the nails.

The weft element can be made of a *continuous length* of

wire wound on a spool that passes back and forth after completing each pick so that each return secures the warp in the width direction of the fabric. *Cut lengths* of wire and/or strip can also be used for weft—in which case the fabric is open at the sides and the weft strips must be *longer* than the width of the texture, projecting somewhat beyond its edges to keep the warp ends from coming loose.

Weaving the weft through the warp is done from the top downward, with the warp lying flat on the board, by lifting every other *warp end* only with the fingers, passing the weft below them, then allowing them to return to a flat position, or by pressing them down with the fingers. In the next return pick, the alternate warp ends are lifted and the weft is inserted. To compact the density of the texture, after the second pick is introduced, and after each pick thereafter, when working with a wire warp a *metal comb* can be used to push the wefts together toward the nails. With a warp made of strip or of wire and strip combinations, a *straight stick* or *metal rule* is used for this purpose while the warp ends are raised, before pressing them down.

Certain common weaving faults should be avoided. If a continuous weft is used, and a straight-sided fabric is the aim, *pull-in,* or the tendency of the edges of a fabric to draw toward each other, can be eliminated by allowing a sufficient weft length. Pull-in is more easily controlled with metal than with elastic yarns since, once it is established, the exact width can be measured and maintained in the nonelastic wire. Pull-in can however be done deliberately to make a fabric with concave sides. To prevent the formation of a *downward bulge* at the center when using cut-length wefts, hammer small nails in a straight line through the texture against the wefts. As the work progresses and new nails secure every third or fourth new weft, old nails can be removed.

FINISHING THE WARP ENDS When the necessary amount of woven fabric is completed, the warp ends must be secured first to keep the weft from raveling. While this is being done, the last wefts are held temporarily in place by nails or a strip of draftsman's tape placed across the end of the woven texture. *Without heat,* the warp ends can be finished by twisting them together in pairs or groups; by passing them through a sheet metal shape or a finding in which holes have been drilled the distance apart that matches the distance between warp elements, then twisting these together at the back; by braiding or knotting them together and allowing the remaining ends to form a straight or spiral fringe, or to be formed into loops from which beads or other hanging ornaments can be suspended. *With heat,* the ends can be soldered to each other, to a part of the work, or to another unit; be fused to each other to form a unit; or be fused into balls.

FINISHING THE WEFT SELVAGE The *selvage* is the lengthwise edge of the fabric at its two sides. If a *continuous-weft* wire type is used, a smooth, warp-containing selvage is automatically produced during weaving. If a *discontinuous weft* made of separate units for each pick is employed, some means of finishing the selvage must be decided upon. The means chosen depends first of all upon whether the edge will be visible in the finished work. If not, extending weft picks can simply be bent back to the unseen surface, or they can be soldered to the outermost parts and the rest clipped away. If they will be seen, a decorative selvage treatment is called for, and some of the edge-finishing techniques used in basketry can be used.

6–222 KATHARINA ISSLER, Switzerland. Tabby-woven bracelet in matched width sterling silver strips. The same bracelet is shown flat, and closed as when worn. Each unit has a wire frame which acts as a decorative thickened edge, and structurally holds the strips. In one direction, the strips pass around the edge wire and their ends return within the woven structure. In the other direction, the strips act as hinge lugs or knuckles that hold all the units together by alternately passing around the wire frame between units, from both sides. Each strip in the first and last row of a single unit has been pierced and riveted to hold together the lug loop and the intervening layers, and the rivet heads form decorative raised disc rows. The sheet metal unit clasp has a bent edge that engages a free wire end in the last unit. Photo: R. Christensen

Weft units can be twined with each other to make a thickened edge along the fabric with the tips facing the back; the ends can be passed over each other and be forced to re-enter the texture at regular intervals, which conceals them while forming a series of interworked loops. If weft ends are long, they can be knotted or braided together. Wire ends can be made to enter a hole drilled in side strips or a frame, and then be upset hammered to form an expanded rivet head which holds the fabric within the frame or to the side strip; and they can be forge hammered flat to spread them, which keeps them in place.

Once the warp ends and the weft selvage have been secured, the woven fabric can be handled without coming apart. It can be left as woven, flattened with a mallet, or even run through a *rolling mill* to flatten it and spread the dimension of the elements.

USING WOVEN FABRICS IN JEWELRY

Entire pieces of jewelry such as rings, pendants, necklaces, bracelets, hair bands, belts, and bags can be made from rectangular units of woven fabrics. For some of these uses, the fabric can be left flat, and for others it can be easily shaped to a curved form around a *mandrel* with a *mallet* in the warp direction or length. It can also be shaped to any regular or irregular three-dimensional form. Curved units such as a cylinder or a spiral can be used independently, or they can be mounted on and supported by or under a curved foundation of sheet metal or plastic.

When a woven fabric is shaped to a cylinder for independent use, the matching warp ends can be soldered together, and if this is done carefully, unit end to unit end, the join will be invisible and the structure continuous. Straight woven pieces do not lend themselves to being tapered into cone shapes. If this is the aim, the fabric should be woven initially in one or two parts as a radially curved form, progressing from a narrow to a wide width, or vice versa, the single unit then shaped to a cone, or the two units joined. Radial forms in metal wire and strip are much more easily made by shaping the elements through finger weaving by the board and nail system than with a loom.

Parts of a piece of jewelry can be made of a woven fabric while other parts are fabricated or cast. The woven parts can be mounted or joined to the rest by any suitable cold or hot joining method. A flat woven fabric can be cut to any outer contour, but before this is done, *all* the ends at the perimeter of that shape must be soldered to each other where they are in contact or to a supporting frame placed either on top or behind the fabric while it is intact. Then it can be cut without disintegrating. Such a piece can then be shaped dimensionally in a shallow *die* or *mold* with a *mallet* and used with either surface uppermost.

MACHINE-CREATED FABRICS

Machine-created fabrics are mechanically made, interlooped, interlaced, intertwined, braided, woven, or welded wire products that have a great many applications in various fields. For example, braided wire products of copper and aluminum are widely used as electrical cable sheathing and for the conduction of electrical current in automobiles. Mechanically made wire screening is used for sieves, filters, insect excluders, fences, traps, and nets.

These fabrics can be utilized by jewelers as a raw material with which jewelry design concepts can be developed. They are available in many different metals, in almost any dimension and practically unlimited length, and can be thought of as a raw material like any other metal material used by the jeweler.

Round, braided, straight strip can be easily bent to any curve, and flat braid will still stay flat after bending it into a flat plane curve. Both round and flat braid can be compressed to expand the woven texture, or condensed to constrict it, and either can be tied into dimensional or flat knots.

Wire screen can be angularly bent, curved, hammered into dimensional forms, hammered or pressed into one- or two-part dies, cut out to any contour, and pierced with regular or irregular openings. Individual strands can be removed from the total, and what remains drawn together with an interworked wire as in *drawn work,* and wire screen can be used as a foundation for other decorative processes. (See Filigree, Chapter 6.)

Woven fabrics can be used as a *ground* upon which additional ornamentation can be applied. New metal elements can be introduced *diagonally* into the fabric by interlacing them between the old. The fabric can be embroidered with wire of a contrasting metal. Repoussé work relief units, stones in premade settings, or other metal forms can be mounted upon the fabric by soldering, with screws, or with split-leg or ordinary rivets. Units can also be sewn in place with wire passed through holes drilled in them, around an element in the fabric, then twisted together at the back.

Woven fabrics can be *combined with other materials* such as cloth, leather, fur, and feathers. These can be used as a ground upon which the metal fabric is mounted, the materials can be introduced to the texture during weaving, or they can be added to the finished fabric as decoration.

FORGING

Fabrication by percussion to move metal mass

Forging is the act of plastically deforming metal into desired shapes by hot or cold fabrication methods, utilizing the ductility and malleability of metal by exerting compressive force upon it, mainly through the *intermittent blows of a hammer.* Forging is also done mechanically. The term *fabricate* is related to the Latin *fabri-,* "blacksmiths"; fabrication originally was the work of blacksmiths. Today fabrication means the manufacture of an object to form a whole by uniting parts.

Hot forging is essentially a blacksmith's technique by which metal objects mainly of iron and steel are formed while in a red- to white-hot state. Traditional hot forging techniques are used today by the jeweler in making hand tools of the simpler types, such as repoussage and chasing punches, chisels, and gravers. Though the jeweler may occasionally work hot metal, more generally it has been annealed and cooled to room temperature, and then is worked by *cold forging* which still remains a basic technique used in jewelry making.

The discussion that follows deals first with hot forging

in reference to *steel tool making* to provide an understanding of what happens in tool manufacture, whether undertaken by the jeweler or the professional tool maker, then covers cold forging as used in jewelry making.

FORGING AND HEAT TREATING TOOL STEELS

Tool steels consist of high-carbon steel, high-alloy steels, and high-speed steels. These are used to make tools that perform the mechanical operations of forging, stamping, bending, sawing, cutting, and other basic working operations. Depending on the particular function, tool steel must possess many or all of the following qualities which are imparted to it by the composition and manufacture of the steel, as well as by tool design. These qualities include hardness, the ability to withstand wear, toughness, freedom from distortion caused by the heat generated by cutting edges or the action of tool against work, resistance to

6–223 BENT GABRIELSEN P., Denmark. Forged gold bracelet with moonstones. The wire is transformed from its original round section to external concavity. Forging rigidizes and spring hardens the metal. *Photo: Bent Gabrielsen P.*

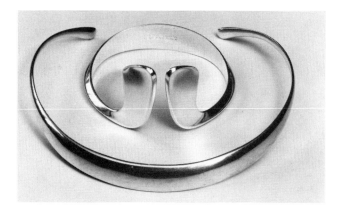

6–224 ERIK BLOM, Norway, designer; manufacturer David Andersen, Oslo. Taper-forged sterling silver neckband and bracelet, with edges beveled for dimensional emphasis. *Photo: Teigens Fotoatelier, courtesy David Andersen*

chipping and breakage, and resistance to distortion and cracking caused by impact or sudden changes in temperature during use.

The capacity of a tool to hold its cutting edge increases with its carbon content, and tool steels contain the relatively high amount of between 0.5–1.05% carbon, and 0.60–1.15% manganese. Alloying elements of vanadium, tungsten, molybdenum, chromium, and cobalt are used in varying percentages in a great many different high-alloy steels to toughen them or impart other characteristics. *High-speed steels* are alloy steels used for tools that must operate at high speeds where friction creates high heat. Without the addition of these hardening elements, and the manner of heat treating the tool after manufacture, such tools would quickly become soft, lose their temper, and stop functioning. When properly treated, high-speed steel's cutting performance is 3–50 times greater than unalloyed high-carbon steel of the same hardness.

The normal sequence of steel tool making involves forging, annealing, quenching, hardening, and tempering.

FORGING THE TOOL

The purpose of forging tool steel while it is either red or white hot is not only to physically create a tool of a certain shape or size, but at the same time to improve the physical properties of the inner structure of the metal. At the start, after heating, the beginning hammer blows on the metal are light, then increase in strength as the metal flows. The metal is worked sufficiently over its entire surface to ensure correct and uniform internal grain development. Too little force in hammer blows works the outer layers more than the inside. The decision of when to increase the hammer impact is learned by experience. Sufficient force is applied to work the metal through until the final shape and dimension is reached. When the tool during forging becomes *work hardened,* and the hammer blows no longer make an impression on its surface, it must be heated to anneal or soften it for further shaping.

ANNEALING STEEL

When working metals to make tools and objects the metal, because of *compression,* becomes hard, retains stresses that make it brittle, and resists further shaping which, if forced, may cause it to crack. It was discovered early that this hardness and brittleness could be eliminated, and the metal restored to its original workable condition by heating it to a temperature that varies with different metals (see Table, p. 238).

The process of heating any metal to restore its workability is called *annealing* (from the Anglo-Saxon, *neal*

meaning "to kindle, burn, or bake"). The annealing process can be *repeated* again and again which makes it possible to work a metal object in several stages until it reaches its final shape.

During annealing the distorted, compressed grain structure of the worked metal is transformed and replaced by a new, larger, strain-free grain structure, a condition that occurs naturally when the temperature of work-hardened metal rises above the specific minimum annealing temperature. The lowest temperature at which this occurs is called its *recrystallization temperature,* and is a function of the purity of the metal, the length of time the annealing temperature has been maintained, and the degree of prior deformation of the metal from work.

Ordinarily, if in annealing tool steel a neutral or reducing flame is used in which all oxygen is consumed by the flame, tool surface protection is not necessary to avoid *scaling,* nor to prevent *decarburization,* in which the surface carbon, necessary to a steel alloy with good working properties, is lost as a result of oxidizing conditions. Oxidation occurs when the flame has more oxygen than it consumes. Carbon loss can, however, occur from prolonged overheating which should be avoided in any case as it causes excessive grain growth which weakens the metal's structure. The presence of scale will also cause decarburization.

Annealing is done by placing the object in an *annealing pan* filled with *lump* or *pea pumice.* The torch flame is generally large and bushy, to cover the object as evenly as possible. It is played on the object for just long enough for the heat to uniformly and completely penetrate the metal. The time needed for this to occur increases with the bulk of the object or tool. Tools should be turned with *tongs* during annealing to as much as possible heat all parts equally and at the same rate. Long, slender tools should be heated while held vertically with tongs. High-alloy steels such as high-carbon, high-speed, and high-chromium steels require twice as much heating as low-carbon steels. Avoid too rapid heating which causes uneven metal expansion that can result in the formation of internal cracks, especially in the case of high-carbon steels.

POST-ANNEALING PROCEDURE

Annealing is followed by *air cooling,* or *quenching.* In tool making, the annealed tool is usually quenched in

The Annealing Temperatures of Some Metals

Metal	°F	°C	Melting Point °F	Melting Point °C
Aluminum	640-670	337-354	1220.4	660.2
Britannia metal	No annealing required		563	295
Copper	700-1200	371-648	1981.4	1083
Yellow brass	800-1300	426-732	1660	904.4
Muntz metal	800-1100	426-593	1650	898.8
Forging brass	800-1100	426-593	1650	898.8
Bronze	800-1250	426-676	1550-1900	843.3-1037.7
Nickel	1500-1700	815-926	2651	1455
Nickel silver	1100-1500	593-815	1960	1071
Monel Metal	1500-1700	815-926	1325	718.3
Gold, pure	No annealing required		1945.4	1063
Gold, alloys	1200-1300	648-710	1615-1825	879.4-996
Silver, pure	572	300	1760.9	960.5
Silver, sterling	1200	648.8	1640	893.3
Steel (depending on carbon content and alloy)	1375-1650	746-898.8	2802-3000	1538.8-1648.8

water or another quenchant. When working with nonferrous and precious metals, the quenchant may be water or a dilute pickling solution so that surface scale is simultaneously removed. Though quenching occurs after annealing, it is most important after hardening, and is discussed there.

HARDENING TOOL STEEL BY HEAT TREATMENTS

After the tool has been shaped (or reshaped) by forging, grinding, and polishing to its final form, it must go through the process of *hardening*. The ability of steel to be hardened by fairly simple operations is probably the single most important fact of metallurgy, since to this quality we owe the availability of the hard, sharp tools so essential to all metalwork. Hardening is accomplished in industry most often by the use of a kiln or furnace in which all parts of the tool are uniformly heated. The tool is turned and exposed to the heat on all surfaces to assure uniformity of crystal structure change.

Craftspersons perform the hardening process by the direct use of a torch flame, called *flame hardening,* also used in industry at times. The correct flame atmosphere depends on the steel. Generally speaking, most tool steels require a reducing or neutral flame to keep scale formation minimal. Alloys containing manganese require a slightly oxidizing flame. Unlike kiln or furnace hardening in which the tool is uniformly heated, flame hardening makes possible *selective hardening* of *parts* of the tool, such as the point, edge, blade, or face, because the flame can be easily directed to that particular part. As craftspersons often use the hardening process to *reharden* a tool, flame hardening is common. In most tools, those parts other than the working parts mentioned are left in a less hard state to leave them resilient.

To flame harden a tool, heat it *rapidly* to a medium cherry red heat, about 1450° F (787.7° C) with a high-temperature flame that should cover the area to be hardened, and then quench it. (Quenching methods are described below.) In flame hardening the *surface layer* of the tool is heated *above the transformation range,* in which internal *austenite,* a certain desirable crystal structure, forms. During quenching this crystal structure disappears and is transformed or decomposed to *martensite,*

the hardest constituent in steel. As a result of hardening, the tool develops a hard outer layer—actually a relatively thin skin if the duration of the flame exposure is short, and thicker if a longer soaking heat is used—whose depth can vary from 3/32–1/8 in (0.24–0.32 cm).

CASE HARDENING OR CARBURIZING

Case hardening or *carburizing* is another method of hardening finished tools. The purpose of carburizing tools is to *introduce or increase the carbon content* in the *surface layer,* thus making the outer surface of the tool rich in carbon content, in amounts substantially greater than in the metal below. The result is a hardened surface that greatly increases tool toughness. This is done by heating the tool while it is in contact with a carbonaceous material —gas, liquid, or solid—to a temperature above the transformation range, and keeping it at that temperature for some time. Quenching follows, and a case is produced with a surface layer harder than the interior. The tool then possesses internal strength and toughness, while its outer, harder surface allows it to withstand great stress during work. Case-hardened steel takes a better and longer lasting polish than steel not case hardened.

QUENCHING HEATED METALS

Quenching, from Middle English *quenchen,* "to decrease, extinguish, disappear," is the process of suddenly cooling heated metal to extinguish its heat. In quenching a tool after flame hardening, hold it with tongs and immerse it quickly into a tank containing a liquid *quenchant* or *quenching medium.* Rapid quenching results in maximal metal hardness. Quenching also imparts a fine grain structure to the metal which increases its qualities of hardness, toughness, and the ability to retain its shape after use.

QUENCHING MEDIUMS

WATER Water between 60–80° F (15.5–26.6° C) is the most common quenching medium. Previously used or boiled and then cooled water is preferred. Once the tool is immersed in the water, agitate it to cool it as quickly as possible through the transformation range, and remove it *before* it is completely cold—at a temperature just below

200° F (93.3° C), or when the water surface contacting the metal stops boiling. As the boiling point of water is 212° F (100° C), this temperature can easily be judged. Water cools plain carbon steel on the surface at the rate of 1800° F (982.2° C) per second. The rate of cooling also depends on the mass and shape of the tool, as well as its movement in the quenching medium.

OIL Oil is best used as a quenchant when heated to 100–150° F (37.7–65.5° C), and *cold oil must be avoided.* Any presence of water in the oil is undesirable, yet oils are sometimes used that are water soluble. Avoid oil quenching near heating equipment that uses oxygen, as a fire may result. Oil cools the metal on the surface at approximately 135° F (57.2° C) per second. As a quenchant it is therefore considerably slower than water. The tool is removed from the oil when the surface of the tool ceases to flash-fire upon removal from the oil.

BRINE Brine is water with a saturated salt content of 10% by weight. It is used at a temperature of between 60–80° F (15.5–26.6° C). Brine has the advantage of causing steel to shed its surface scale more readily, thus producing a cleaner tool surface, as well as one having more uniform hardness.

AIR Air cooling is done with certain types of steel which by this process attain a shock-resistant outer case. The source can be still air, fan-produced air, or an air blast from a high-pressure line. The tool is held or supported so that the air can flow all around the metal and thus provide uniform cooling.

The choice of quenchant depends on the content of the tool steel alloy, and the cooling speed needed to harden it. Hammers after casting are locally hardened, and the striking face is quenched in water or brine; pliers are oil quenched; gravers and chisels are usually water quenched; and tools with cutting edges like shears are water quenched.

The quenching tank should be large enough to contain the whole tool, and enough of a volume of the quenchant should be placed in it to completely envelop the tool, or if the tool is large, that part being hardened. By using a sufficient volume of quenchant it is also easier to keep the liquid at a proper temperature and assure a *uniform* result.

When the tong-held heated tool is submerged in the quenchant, agitate it vigorously to be sure that the medium contacts all parts at a more or less uniform temperature. In quenching, heat is released from the solid object only by the transfer of heat from the inner mass to the surface where it is dissipated. Agitation acts to expose new volumes of the quenchant to the surface and therefore allows it to be cooled more quickly. It also avoids air pockets and minimizes warpage. If a tool is held still and partially submerged in a quenchant, it may ultimately break along the quenching line as stresses have probably developed there.

The tool is removed from the quenchant when it is below 200° F (93.3° C). Never allow the tool to remain in the quenchant until it becomes completely cooled.

Warpage should be avoided. It occurs most frequently as a result of nonuniform quenching, therefore agitation in the quenchant is important. When warpage does occur, its degree depends on the size and the shape of the tool, the steel of which it is made, the manner in which it was heated (partially or uniformly), and the suddenness of the quench. Generally speaking, tools that are water quenched

tend to warp more than those which are oil quenched, and air-quenched tools warp least. Short tools warp less than long or thin ones. Thin tools should be quenched while held vertically. Another cause of warpage is tempering too rapidly. If the tool becomes warped in quenching, straighten it while it is still hot.

After flame hardening and quenching, the chemical composition of the steel is not changed. However, it is in a state of *brittleness,* which is the reason it is followed by tempering, a process that reduces brittleness.

TEMPERING STEEL FOR TOOL DURABILITY

Tempering or "letting down" follows hardening and consists of gently reheating the metal to a predetermined temperature *below* the transformation range (to the degree of temper that is necessary for its use), and then cooling it. Tempering acts to reduce the hardened tool's brittleness, makes it more durable, increases its resistance to abrasion, provides strength and ductility, and puts it in a condition of maximum toughness in relation to its hardness which enables the tool to best resist fracture by shock, bending, or twisting. High-carbon steels can attain high surface hardness; some plain carbon steels can be hardened throughout. The alloying elements in alloy steels reduce the tool's tendency to soften upon tempering.

When the tool is removed from the quenching bath, it is in a strained condition during which the danger of cracking is greatest. The tool should not be allowed to go cold before tempering begins, but should be cool enough to be hand held. Heat for tempering *slowly,* since too rapid heating causes a rapid release of stresses that may result in warpage, and there is less control of the temperature. Slow heating also assures the deepest possible penetration of the desired temperature.

Tempering can be done in mechanically controlled conditions, as in a kiln, a procedure used by tool manufacturers, but individual craftspersons usually apply the heat by a torch flame or a Bunsen burner. It is also possible to place small tools in contact with a red-hot piece of steel, about 1 in (2.5 cm) from the point, or edge, or directly upon the surface being tempered, and allow a heat transfer to take place. In usual practice, only that part of the tool that does the work, such as the point, blade, or face is tempered.

TEMPERING STEEL BY COLOR JUDGMENT

Proper temper temperature can be judged by observing the color change that takes place on the *polished* tool part being tempered. Here, under heat, the metal assumes a specific sequence of optical interference colors caused by the formation of a thin film of oxide and the way light reflects from the surface. Each color indicates an approximate degree of heat of the surface at that time, and these colors are used as a guide to judging the metal's temperature. As the tempering temperature increases, the metal's ductility increases and its hardness decreases. Once the desired temperature is reached, the tool is immediately quenched in water or oil. It is now in an intermediate state of toughness, roughly between that achieved by annealing and quench hardening.

If the metal is overheated during tempering, the whole process of annealing, quenching, and tempering must be repeated.

Tempering Temperatures: Judgment by Heat-Produced Colors on Polished Steel

Color	Temperature		Temper	Tools, etc.
	°F	°C		
Light straw	400	204.4	Very high	Engraving tools, files
Straw yellow	428	220	High	Finishing tools, lathe tools, scrapers, twist drills, razors
Golden yellow	469	242.7		Cold chisels, hammer faces
Dark brown-bronze	500	260	Medium	Drills
Purple or peacock blue	531	277.2		Chasing punches, dies, other punches, gouges, shear blades, springs
Full dark blue	550	287.7	Low	Hot chisels, knives
Pale blue	610	321.1		Hacksaws, other saw blades, needles, screwdrivers
Gray-black	630	332.2	Soft to dead soft	Too soft for steel tools

TOOLS USED IN THE FORGING PROCESS

THE ANVIL: The impact-receiving surface

The *anvil* is the iron block on whose working surface hot or cold metals are formed by forging with hammers. Originally it was a flat, leveled stone. Small bronze anvils were developed in the Bronze Age for use in making the smaller, finer metal objects made then. These often had an attached lower spike or *tang* that could be driven into the ground or into a groove in a wood support to secure them to position.

Today's anvil is made of a forged or cast iron core to which steel parts are welded. The main parts are the following: the flat, rectangular top or *face* which is cantilevered over the base, made of ½–1½ in thick steel welded to the body and drawn to a hard temper. When struck, a good anvil will emit a ringing note (for which reason it is called a "ringing anvil"). The *beak* or *horn* is the horizontal, flat or conical projection from the face, and is used for shaping curved forms. Opposite the horn is the *heel* or *squared tail* which is punched with a ½–1 in square *har-*

die hole to receive the shank of a chisel when cutting through metal, and into which most forging tools and some smaller anvil tangs will fit, and a round, ½ in diameter *pritchell hole* into which round stock is placed for bending. Between the face and the horn is a drop and a smaller rectangular extension called the *table*. The rest of the body narrows to a *waist,* then into a spreading *base* and *feet*. In manufacture the working surfaces are welded to the core, then hammer shaped. The whole is heated to cherry redness then plunged into cold water to harden the working surfaces which are grindstone leveled and smoothed and polished with emery and crocus.

The craftsperson finds an anvil weighing about 25 lb sufficient for his or her needs, but for heavier work as in silversmithing and blacksmithing, anvils weighing up to 300 lb are made. To mount such a heavy tool so that it does not move when struck, traditionally it is placed on a section of a hardwood tree trunk whose height places the anvil face level with the knuckles of the worker when his arms hang loosely at his sides. Well below eye level, this height allows the full hammer weight to strike the work without strain or excessive bending, and takes advantage of the added force of gravity. The anvil base is held to the tree trunk support by large nails. Special heavy steel stands are also used for anvil mounts.

OTHER WORK SURFACES FOR FORGING

Miniature horn anvils with round and flat horns and a hole for shaping rivets are used by the jeweler for small forging. Typical working surfaces are 3⅞ in × 2⅝ in (9.84 cm × 6.67 cm); or 5¾ in × 2¼ in (7.30 cm × 5.72 cm).

Train rail sections about 12 in (30.5 cm) can be used as an anvil. One end can be ground to a beak shape, and the whole working surface should be polished.

Surface blocks or *bench blocks* are cast iron or steel plates whose five upper or all six surfaces are true,

6–225 GOULIMENE, SOUTHERN MOROCCO. Jeweler forge hammering a small silver ingot on an anvil anchored in the earthen floor in preparation for use in forming a forged wire ornament. *Photo: Oppi*

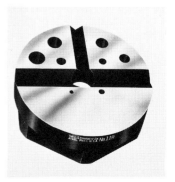

6–226 *ROUND BENCH BLOCK* Made of alloy steel, hardened and ground top and bottom. Weighs 5 lb, has a working surface of approx. 4⅞ in Ø; 1½ in high; has nine holes varying from ⅛–³⁷⁄₆₄ in Ø; and two V-grooves at right angles. Base is hexagonal to allow it to be held rigid horizontally in vise jaws. *Photo: Courtesy L. S. Starrett Co.*

smoothly ground, case hardened, and polished to a mirror finish. They are therefore accurate for use in bending right angles, for flattening work, and shaping small forms. Their sizes and thickness vary.

Swage or *design blocks* are steel blocks 4–18 in (10–46 cm) square, and between 2½–3 in (6.4–7.6 cm) in thickness. In a typical model, two of the sides are serrated with half-cylinder grooves whose widths vary from ⅛–2 in (0.32–5.1 cm). The other two sides may have V-shaped grooves in a range of sizes, or other shapes. The block is used placed on an anvil or held in a bench vise. Rod and wire are placed in one of its grooves and hammered to change their sectional shape, or to reduce their size. The flat sides may contain depressions of various shapes, or holes that pass completely through the block. Into these, metal pieces or lengths can be placed and shaped or bent by hammering.

Bench vises are made with an *anvil* surface on the immobilized part attached to the workbench. These can be used for occasional anvil work. A *leg vise* is a heavy vise that has a leg or extension between it and the floor. The leg supports the vise when it is used to hold a heavy anvil that must take heavy blows.

6–227 *BENCH VISE WITH ANVIL* Has full 360° swivel base whose position is controlled by a swivel wrench lock. Jaw width is 3 in, max. jaw opening 3 in, and has pipe-sized jaws to allow it to hold round tools such as mandrels. Weight 19 lb. *Photo: Courtesy L. S. Starrett Co.*

Combination bench pin and anvil units that clamp onto a worktable are available and provide a small hammering surface.

Hardwood tree stumps called *steadies,* cut perpendicularly to the floor with a height of from 30–40 in (76–102 cm), and of diameter of approximately 18 in (46 cm), have hollows of different diameters and depths used for shaping scooped out of their upper surfaces, and a hole to hold an anvil tang. They are old, traditional, and very useful forming surfaces or places to hold an anvil.

STAKES

Stakes are large and small anvils used mainly by silversmiths to make holloware or flatware, but also by any jeweler when the occasion arises to shape and form metals. They are made in a great variety of shapes designed for general or specific functions. Almost all have a single *tang* which projects below the working surface and enters a hole in the workbench containing a *metal bench tool socket* to hold the anvil firmly in place. Tangs can also be placed into a hole in an *extension arm*, also called a *horse extension*, clamped in a bench vise, placed in the hardie hole of a large anvil, or in a hole in a tree stump. The few anvils without tangs must be clamped in a vise's jaws to hold them. Because of the variety of forms, only an arbitrary division can be made among them based on their number of working part projections (not including the tang).

TWO-PROJECTION STAKES These are generally called *T-stakes* or *tee-stakes* because of their general conformation

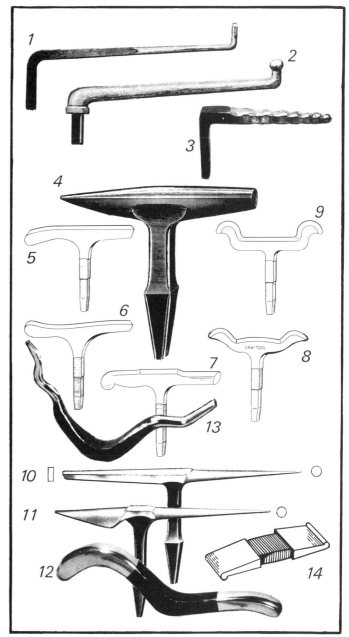

6–228 *SILVERSMITH'S ONE-PROJECTION STAKES*
1. *Snarling iron,* end Ø ¼ in, length 16½ in, weight 2 lb.
2. *Snarling iron,* end Ø ¾ in, length 16½ in, weight 2 lb.
3. *Spout and handle iron,* 6½ in long.

SILVERSMITH'S TWO-PROJECTION STAKES: T-STAKES
4. *Standard bick iron* (also called bickern, beakiron, beakhorn) T-stake with one tapered horn-shaped arm, and one cone-shaped arm, length 11 in, width 1½ in, height 7½ in.
5. *Common T-stake* with downward bending arm and square arm, length 11 in, width 1½ in, height 7½ in.
6. *Common T-stake* with round-ended upward-bending arm, and sloping square arm, length 12 in, width 1½ in, height 7½ in.
7. *Raising T-stake* with ball end, central anvil surface, and elliptical end with 70° undercut, length 12 in, height 7½ in.
8. *Spout T-stake,* length 10¼ in, width 1½ in, height 7½ in.
9. *Cow's tongue T-stake,* length 10½ in, width 1½ in, height 7½ in.
10. *Blowhorn T-stake* with tapered mandrel and square-tapered arm, total length approx. 20 in.
11. *Beakhorn T-stake* with tapered mandrel, and tapered elliptical horn arm, total length approx. 18 in.

SILVERSMITH'S TWO-PROJECTION STAKES WITHOUT TANG: CRANK STAKES
12. *Crank stake* (crank means bent or crooked) held in a vise, length 15 in, width 1⅜ in, weight 6 lb.
13. *Handle and spout crank stake,* held in a vise, each arm 9 in long, weight 3½ lb.
14. *Anvil bar,* held in a vise for straight edge work, width 3 in, thickness ⅞ in, length 10 in.

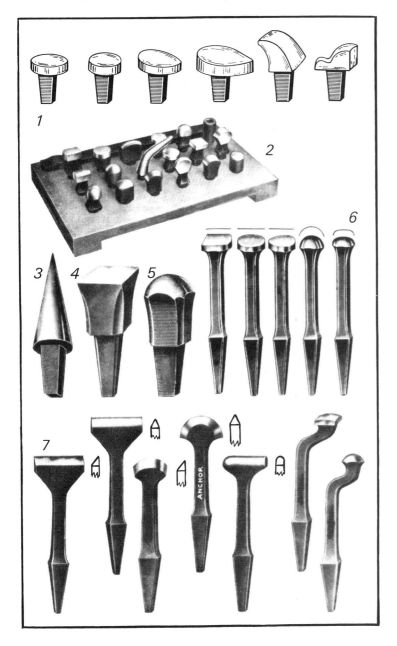

to the shape of the letter T. They have two ends that project horizontally or obliquely beyond the tang. These vary according to their functions. Not all of them have specific names, but some are named after their function and others after their resemblance to some other form. Among them are raising stakes, crimping or valley stakes, cow's tongues, blowhorns, and common T-stakes.

ONE-PROJECTION STAKES   These have only one oblique or horizontal projection from the tang. Among these are spout stakes, flaring stakes, and snarling irons.

NONPROJECTION UPRIGHT STAKES   These have forms that are centered directly above the tang. Among these are round head, mushroom, ball, dome, half-dome, bottoming, planishing, oval, spoon, dish, pan, corner, concave, hollow, cone, straight, taper, horn, creasing, fluting, square teest (*teest* is a general name for a small anvil), half-moon, hatchet, and others.

All working surfaces must be kept highly polished and greased when not in use for protection against rust. If a

6–230   STAKE AND ANVIL HOLDING DEVICES

1. *Standard stake and anvil holder* that accommodates most T-stakes, screwed to the bench, height 4 in, width 5 in.
2. *Offset extension arm,* vise held, used for stakes and anvil heads.
3. *Vertical extension arm,* height 7 in, width 1¼ in.
4. *Right-angle extension arm,* held in vise or stake holder.
5. *Double extension arm* for stakes, anvil heads, and anvils, with central flat anvil, length 16½ in, width 1¾ in, height 9 in.
6. *Multi-stake holder,* holds all standard stakes and anvils vertically, and also has a horizontal 1 in diameter hole with clamp handle permitting the use of the special horizontal anvils *below.* (Craftool)
7. *Horizontal anvils* used with the multi-stake holder *above; upper right to lower left:* ball with flat side; concave bowl with round, flat reverse surface; concave bowl within a square, with square, flat reverse surface; heart anvil with variously shaped work surfaces.

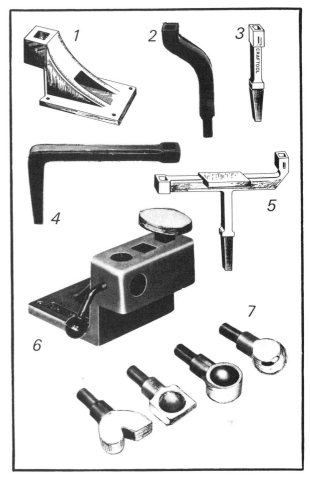

6–229   SILVERSMITH'S NONPROJECTION UPRIGHT STAKES

1. *Anvil heads,* left to right: flat head or bottom stakes, Ø 1¾ in; dome head, slightly rounded, Ø 1⅝ in, height 1⅝ in; teaspoon head, length 2 in, width 1¼ in; tablespoon head, length 3 in, width 1¾ in; slope head, length 1¾ in, width 1¼ in; valley head, length 1¾ in, width 1⅛ in.
2. Assortment of *anvil heads* in a *rack.*
3. *Cone anvil stake* (taper iron), cone length 5 in, largest Ø 1⅞ in, height 7 in, weight 2¼ lb.
4. *Flat, square anvil stake,* top 4 in square, height 10 in, weight 17½ lb.
5. *Mushroom stake,* Ø 3½ in, height 9¼ in.
6. *Mushroom stakes,* height 10½ in, *left to right:* flat, three square, one round edge, 2½ in square; flat, round, Ø 2 in; egg-shaped, domed, 2 in wide, 2½ in long; high dome, round, Ø 2 in; shallow dome, round, Ø 2 in.
7. *Hatchet- and fist-type forming and planishing stakes,* all 1¾ lb, except as noted. *Left to right:* straight, single-bevel face, width 2⅜ in, height 9½ in; straight, double-bevel face, width 2⅜ in, height 9½ in; rounded, half-moon, single-bevel face, width 2⅜ in, height 9½ in; rounded, half-moon, double-bevel face, width ¼ × ¾ in, height 1¼ in; rounded face, width 2⅜ in, height 9½ in; bent, square, shallow dome, Ø 1⅝ in, height 11¼ in, weight 3½ lb; bent, round, full dome, Ø 1¾ in, height 11¼ in, weight 3½ lb.

working surface becomes nicked, this defect will be imparted to any metal placed over that position and struck with a hammer. The work surface in this case must be refinished by grinding, if necessary, and repolished.

Metalsmiths now carve stakes from *devcon* or *nylon blocks* which are both hard and resilient.

MANDRELS

In metal forming techniques, a *mandrel* is a straight or tapered metal bar of circular, oval, or other section used as a core around which metal may be forged, bent, or shaped. On occasion, wood mandrels are used, but metal ones allow greater accuracy. A *straight mandrel* of solid metal rod is used as a core when wrapping wire around it to form links. Long, *tapered steel mandrels* called *triblets* are circular, oval, oblong, square, or octagonal in section, and are used for shaping and enlarging rings and conical forms. Special tapered mandrels are made for shaping conical bezels. Hollow mandrels of large tapering circular or oval forms are used to shape rigid bracelets and large cylinders.

6–231 BEZEL, RING, AND BRACELET MANDRELS (triblets)

1. *Round steel bezel mandrel*, small Ø 10 mm, large Ø 22 mm, 7½ in long.
2. *Oval steel bezel mandrel*, small Ø 5 × 6 mm, large Ø 16 × 18 mm, 7½ in long.
3. *Square steel bezel mandrel*, small Ø 4 mm, large Ø 20 mm, 6 in long.
4. *Hexagonal steel bezel mandrel*, small Ø 3 mm, large Ø 14 mm, 11¾ in long.
5. *Octagonal steel bezel mandrel*, small Ø 2.5 mm, large Ø 10 mm, 8 in long.
6. *Oval bracelet mandrel*, small end 1⅜ × 1⅞ in, large end 3 × 3½ in, 6 in long plus 3 in tang. These gray iron-hardened, cast, polished mandrels are used for forming bracelets and oval forms. Similar mandrels are available with round section.
7. *Bezel and ring mandrel vise* (upper right) with small and large openings to hold small- and large-diameter mandrels. It is kept in place by the bench pin vise (*below it*) which overlaps and clamps it down. The mandrels are tightened in position with thumbscrews. The oval bracelet mandrel (*far left*) has a rectangular tang of the same dimension as the wooden bench pin (*below it*) that fits into the slot of the bench vise.
8. *Ring mandrels* of hardened tool steel, with engraved, marked graduations. *Left to right*: size range 7–19; size range 1–13; size range 1–13, with longitudinal groove for holding a ring set with a stone. Used for shaping, straightening, sizing or gauging, and enlarging rings, and when setting stones in rings.
9. *Ring stretcher* that will enlarge a ring shank in platinum, yellow gold, and silver up to three sizes, white gold to one size. The ring is placed in size position on a mandrel, one with a groove used if stones are present. The plain back of the shank is rolled with any of the five rollers set in the holder whose shapes will accommodate a variety of ring shank sections. Any standard steel mandrel is grasped in the roller holder, and the upper handle is raised and lowered which makes the roller pass over the shank and stretch it.

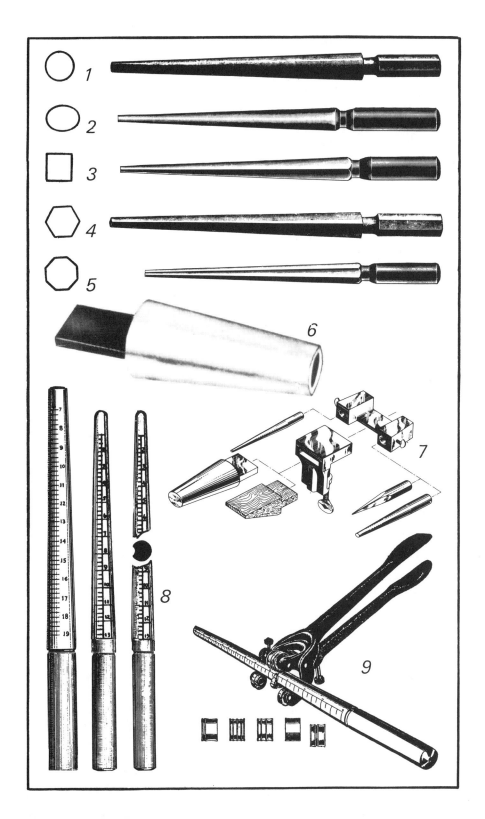

SHAPING SHEET METAL WITH A MANDREL

Sheet metal and strip as for a ring shaft can be curved or shaped into a completely cylindrical form by placing the sheet over the depression in a design block or a groove in a wood block, putting a straight mandrel on top of it, and hammering the mandrel down with a wood mallet until it forces the metal to the bottom of the depression. If a cylinder is wanted, the edges of the sheet can be hammered down on the mandrel until they meet and form a seam, thus completing the cylinder. Lubricate the mandrel to facilitate its removal after the form is finished.

FORGING A CIRCLE OR CYLINDRICAL FORM ON A MANDREL

A ring or cylinder *without seams* can be mandrel forged, starting with a metal disc. First drill or punch a hole in the center of the disc large enough for the mandrel to pass through. Using flat-faced hammers, forge the metal by upsetting its edges, turning the disc gradually, and exposing all edges equally to hammer blows. Anneal the metal at intervals, and work it until a circle of the desired thickness or width forms around the mandrel.

THE HAMMER: A percussion impact tool

Hammers are the main tools of the group used for *striking,* the basic act employed in shaping metals by forging. A hammer consists of two basic parts: a *lever* which is the *handle, shaft,* or *haft,* usually made of a springy hardwood such as ash or hickory (or today also from fiberglass), upon which in crosswise position is fixed the *metal hammer head.* The head contains a *hole* or *eye* into which the shaft is forced and is held on the handle by a malleable iron wedge driven into a split in the handle's end.

HAMMER HEADS   Hammers are our oldest tools, the first extension of the hand. Prehistoric hammers were made of stone and had no handle but acquired one at the end of the Paleolithic Age. This tool-holding device greatly increased the leverage that could be imparted to the tool. Today a variety of hammers are designed to execute special functions in metalwork, their form derived from that function. The various *shapes, sizes,* and *weights* of hammer heads are made of drop-forged tool steel, and their working faces have been hardened, tempered, and polished.

On either side of the head's shaft hole are flat areas called *cheeks.* The *working ends* can bear two similar, but differently sized *striking faces* that may vary in degree and type of curvature (flat, convex or crowned, dome, or ball). The *face edges* can range from square to completely rounded and merging with the head. The length of the *head extension* from center hole to face can vary from very short to long to give it reach. The hammer can also have one regular face opposed by a different shape at the other end, or both ends can have irregular shapes.

A common, *all-purpose hammer* used in forging is the *ball peen hammer,* often called a *machinist's* or *engineer's* hammer, and we take this as a basic example for further description. At one end it has a face that is flat or slightly convex that can be used for striking and planishing or smoothing metal. At the opposite end is the *peen (pein* or *pane)* which is round or ball shaped, thus giving the hammer its name. Other hammers can have a *straight peen* running in the same direction as the shaft, or a *cross peen*

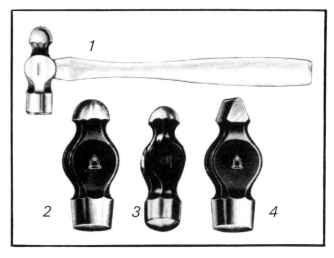

6-232   *THE BALL PEEN HAMMER*
1. *Hammer with hickory hardwood handle.*
2. *Hammer head with one flat and one ball peen face.*
3. *Hammer head with one convex and one ball peen face.*
4. *Hammer head with one flat and one cross peen face.*

running in the direction perpendicular to the shaft. The peen end is used for many functions such as drawing down, stretching, or bending, by striking the metal. Indentations or grooves are formed by the impact that causes the metal to move plastically by deformation without rupture.

HAMMER WEIGHT   Hammers of a single form are often made in various *weights* or *sizes.* The heavier the weight, the greater the impact of each blow. The hammer weight is chosen according to the work to be done. In jewelry work, the hammers used may range in weight from a few ounces to five pounds (a heavier hammer cannot be comfortably lifted with one hand).

HAMMER SHAPING AND MAINTENANCE   It is sometimes necessary after purchase or accidental damage to a hammer to modify, "dress," reshape, or polish the face, or to round its edges. Reshaping can be done by forging, but this is hard work, and grinding can substitute for it, but should not be drastic. Cool the grinding wheel and the hammer by allowing cold water to drop on both while grinding so that the friction of grinding will not create heat high enough for the hammer to lose its temper. If the grinder is not near water, it should be piped to it by a rubber or plastic hose, or use a pail with a small hole at the bottom into which a length of tubing is forced to serve as a spout that drips water on the work. Drip rate can be controlled by a clamp-type clothespin.

Follow shape grinding or surface grinding with polishing the surface or face with fine-grit paper abrasives, then with tripoli on a polishing wheel, and rouge on a buffing wheel to achieve a mirror finish. Hammer faces should always be kept highly polished and free of scratches and dents which otherwise will be imparted to the metal with each blow.

If a hammer becomes softened by overheating, it must be retempered. After all shaping and surfacing, remove the handle, heat it to cherry redness, and quench it in brine. Polish a portion of the face to be able to see the change of color; temper it to a golden yellow, then quench it in water.

HAMMER STORAGE AND SURFACE PROTECTION   When not in use, hammers should be placed in a dry location in racks or stands that hold each one separately to keep their

6–233 *PORTABLE HAMMER AND ANVIL RACK*
The lower shelf has a wooden grill into which the anvil tangs fit. Designed by BERTIL GARDBERG, Finland, for use in his workshop. Photo: Oppi

faces from hitting each other. If the tool will not be used for a long time, cover the metal with a thin coat of petroleum jelly or oil it lightly to prevent rusting and preserve its high polish. Wipe off the protecting lubricant before use. Should rust appear on a hammer (or other tool), soak the metal for 24 hours in a half-and-half solution of kerosene and gasoline in a covered container, then wire brush and repolish the surface.

HAMMER CATEGORIES

Categorizing hammers is difficult because many hammers are used for *more than one purpose,* or a hammer may have *two working faces* designed for completely different functions. Certain basic divisions can, however, be made.

HAMMERS USED FOR INDIRECT STRIKING

In one group are hammers that are always or occasionally used to strike an *intermediary tool* that contacts the metal, such as *punches* of any kind, *stamps, dies,* and *puncturing tools.* A hammer always used for striking is the broad, flat face of the chasing hammer used to strike chasing and repoussé punches. The flat face of an *all-purpose* hammer such as that of a ball peen hammer, can be used to strike cold chisels, center punches, design and hallmark stamps, one-part circle-cutting dies used to make a blank, or a sharp-pointed tool to penetrate sheet metal. Flat-faced planishing hammers whose flawless, polished faces must be preserved, should *not* be used for any of these purposes as their faces may become marked.

HAMMERS USED FOR DIRECT STRIKING

The category of hammers used to work metal directly is much larger and includes all those used for shaping, raising, and finishing forms. Though intended mainly for creating holloware, these hammers also are used in jewelry making.

Forging hammers used for forging thick metal forms weigh considerably more than those used for light forging. A sledgehammer used by one person may weigh up to 6 lb. To make it easier to lift repeatedly, it is made with a shorter thicker handle than others. Their faces may be rounded or cross peen, used respectively to spread or to thin and taper metal.

Silversmithing hammers are used in the starting stages of raising, and for forging, have well-rounded or oval faces in a variety of contours, and range in weight from 3 oz to 2¾ lb. Heavier hammers are used in initial forming stages, and lighter ones at later form refining stages.

Embossing hammers, sometimes called *doming hammers,* are silversmithing hammers that have smaller, rounded faces. They are used to emboss or raise forms on sheet metal, and for sinking forms, usually from the inside while the work rests on a resilient surface. They weigh between 6 oz and 2 lb.

Raising hammers have rectangular, blunt or wedge-shaped cross peen faces of different widths and degrees of edge sharpness. Edges are usually rounded to minimize cutting the metal. They are used to strike the outside of forms to raise them by stages from flat sheet to dimensional forms. In some, the face is set at a slight angle, pointing inward to the handle, to help drive the metal to the anvil or stake and simultaneously compress it. They weigh from 11 oz to 3½ lb. *Collet hammers* are related in shape to raising hammers but are generally lighter in weight. They are used to shape concave forms and for edge thickening.

Planishing hammers, including *bottoming hammers,* have round or square faces available in large to small diameters. The face may be flat, or slightly convex (called *crowned* or *full*). They are used to smooth, level, or planish metal surfaces, usually after they have been worked by other hammers such as peen hammers that have made dents and ridges in the work. Because planishing hammers are flat or only slightly convex they must be struck true center to avoid marking the metal with the face edges. *Spotting hammers* are a form of planishing hammer and have a slightly convex face that leaves a spot on the metal upon impact, hence the name. Planishing hammers weigh 4–12 oz.

Special function hammers for direct striking include the *riveting hammer* which has a slightly concave, round or square face, and is available in weights from 2½–9 oz; and a *blocking hammer* which has a large hook shape head extension that allows it to reach inside deep forms, and weighs 8 oz.

THE USE OF THE HAMMER

Some general comments can be made about practices related to the use of hammers in forging and other hammering operations.

The *stance* of the worker in relation to the work and the distance from it are important for efficiency and comfort. First establish the *striking level* in relation to whether you work in a standing or sitting position. The anvil face in either case should be even with the forearm when in the horizontal position at the completion of a stroke. Adjust the striking level of the anvil accordingly.

When executing a hammer stroke, keep the upper arm against the side. Hold the hammer handle with a firm grip toward the end (*not* near the head, as this imbalanced position limits efficient hammering), the index finger extended for control alongside the handle. In *light hammering,* the striking movement is made mainly with the wrist, which moves the hammer in short arcs while the rest of the arm moves minimally. In *heavy hammering,* greater

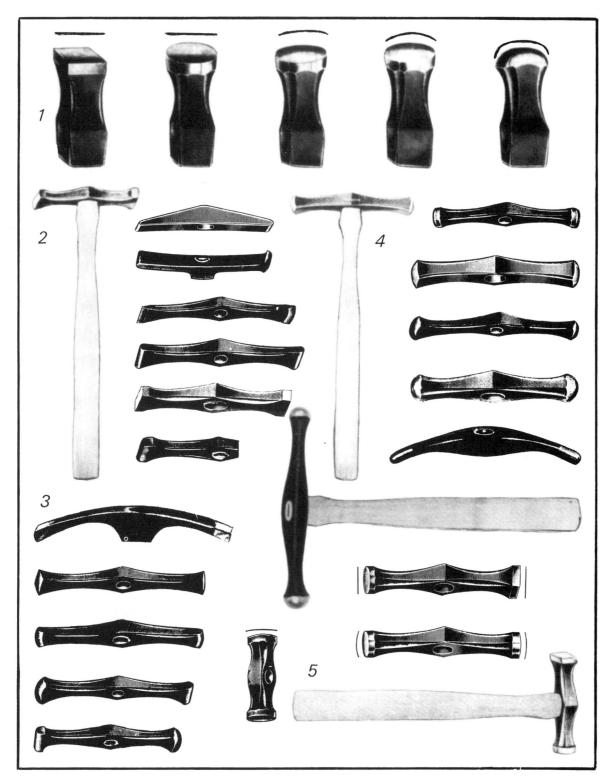

6-234 *SILVERSMITHING HAMMERS*

1. *Basic hammer face shapes:* square, flat; round, flat; round, slightly convex; round, convex; oval, ball.

2. *Raising hammer shapes:* both ends cross peen, straight; one end cross peen, other end rounded cross peen; both ends wedge shaped, one straight, the other curved; collet type, both cross peens straight and rounded, different sizes; both cross peens square, different sizes; one-faced hammer, rounded cross peen.

3. A selection of other *raising hammers* with various face shapes.

4. *Embossing, doming, or forming hammer shapes:* round, convex; square, convex; domed; large ball; small ball.

5. *Planishing hammer shapes:* long head, one face round, the other square, both flat; both ends oval, one slightly convex or crowned, the other more convex; short head, both faces round, one flat face, the other slightly convex for spotting.

impact must be brought to bear on the work. The whole forearm may move as much as a radial arc of up to 90°, and the hammer head which extends beyond the hand moves in an even greater arc. By a law of physics, *mass multiplied by acceleration equals force,* therefore, the hammer weight and the speed of fall determine the impact force. By choosing a hammer of a proper weight and controlling the rate of the blows and their arc distance, the force of impact can be controlled. These decisions are based upon experience.

Normally in jewelry making the blows struck are relatively light. The degree of impact force needed is regulated by the weight of the metal being worked, and the particular metal, which can be yielding and soft or tough and rigid. For example, in repoussé work where relatively thin-gauge metal is shaped, the blows are short-arced, rapid, and light on the punch; while in forging thick metal, the blows are less frequent, fall in greater arcs, and are considerably heavier in impact. *Scale of work* also determines the size and weight of hammer and degree of impact. In work that requires a prolonged series of blows, as when raising, planishing, or texturing metal, a hammering rhythm is established that helps to coordinate the movement of the arm and the tool.

THE EFFECTS OF HAMMER IMPACT ON METAL

Springback is the ability all metals have to be subjected to deformation *up to a certain limit,* and then return to their original size and shape. If the force of compression exerted upon the metal exceeds its elastic or springback limit, it becomes changed in shape and size. This is what happens when metal is forged by hammer blows in bending, shrinking, stretching and elongating techniques that give it a new and permanent form.

In *direct metal hammering,* the aim is to make the hammer work on the metal through a percussive impact applied to a specific place. Generally the face falls squarely on the metal, and oblique strokes are avoided as they can irregularly scar the metal rather than move it. In *indirect metal hammering,* as when striking a tool with a hammer, the aim is to transfer the impact from the struck tool to the point where the tool contacts the metal. In both cases, the force of the blow makes the metal move in some way by *displacement* or *deformation.*

MULTIDIRECTIONAL MOVEMENT: Flat impact spread forging

The basic concepts of forging relate to the *shape of the hammer face* and the *angle of its impact* on the metal. By the proper choice of hammer shape and by control of the striking angle, the metal can be deformed in any desired direction. When striking metal squarely with a flat- or convex-faced hammer, and the metal is supported, it spreads *in all directions* from the point of impact and in the direction of least resistance. The flatter the face, the broader the extent of the area struck; the more convex it is, as in a dome or ball face, the smaller the area struck. These actions occur in spotting, smoothing, planishing, and bottoming.

SELECTED DIRECTIONAL MOVEMENT: Angular impact reduction or stretch forging

A rectangular, regularly curved face, as the cross peen of a raising hammer, when struck squarely on the metal forces it to move at a *right angle* to the point of impact. This occurs in the act of forming longitudinal grooves, as when crimping or fluting, or when rounding. If the same hammer strikes at an *acute angle* to the metal, or if a hammer is used that has a face whose curve angles slightly downward in the direction of the handle (as in the case of some raising hammers), the metal moves *in the direction of the angle* or obliquely. This occurs in raising and forging when stretching, shrinking, and tapering the metal. When these acts are performed toward or at the *edge* of the metal, the result is thinning.

PERPENDICULAR DIRECTIONAL MOVEMENT: Upset forging

By striking a flat-faced hammer at a *right angle* to the *end* of a bar or wire, as when making a rivet head, or striking a cross peen hammer at a *right angle* to the *edge* of sheet metal, called respectively upsetting and edge thickening, the metal spreads in a direction *perpendicular to the axis* of the form.

6–236 CLAËS E. GIERTTA, Sweden. Forged silver ring with hammered surface texture. Photo: Sven Petersen

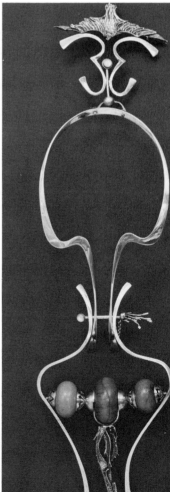

6–237 NILDA C. F. GETTY, U.S.A. "Tribal Flight." Sterling silver forged neck/body ornament, with African amber and moonstones. It unscrews at the point where the lower unit is attached to place it on the neck. Photo: Les F. Brown

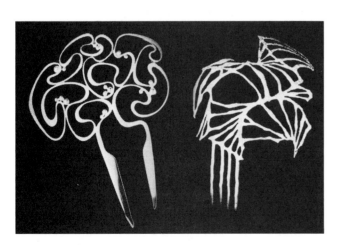

6–235 PÅL VIGELAND, Norway. Forged hair ornaments, the left made of a single forged wire, calligraphically thick and thin due to forging. The right is pierced work, with forged surface texture. Photo: Pål Vigeland

248

MALLETS AND RESILIENT HAMMERS

Mallets and hammers made of various materials that are softer than metal are used in forging and otherwise to bend, flatten, and shape metal without marking its surface. *Wood-headed mallets* use hardwood such as boxwood or other close-grained wood and are formed with their end grain perpendicular to the face for added strength. They are available in flat, domed, or cross peen faces, in various sizes. *Rawhide mallets* are made of spirally wrapped, tough, rawhide (untanned) leather in different head diameters and lengths. The protective coating of shellac painted on the face of a new rawhide mallet must be sandpapered off before it is first used. *Leather-faced wooden mallets* exist. *Horn mallets* are available in conical shapes that are the natural horn form. *Rubber mallets* have the disadvantage of rebounding after they strike the metal. Less liable to rebound are mallets made with *detachable, threaded-on brass or nylon faces,* the latter available in eight degrees of hardness, from super soft to extra hard. Their advantage is they can be replaced when worn.

COLD PUNCHES AND COLD CHISELS

These chisels are so called because they are used on cold work. They are smaller in size than hot work chisels and punches, but like them are also used in forging to cut metal and make grooves and holes. (See Repoussage and Chasing, Chapter 5 and Metal Inlay, Chapter 8.)

BASIC FORGING OPERATIONS

USING HAMMER AND ANVIL

Whether the metal is worked hot or cold, the forging techniques which comprise most of the basic ways (apart from casting) of shaping metal are the same. Forging can be done on solid bar, wire, sheet, or cast metal.

ROUNDING UP

In rounding up, sometimes called *roughing,* a flat-faced hammer is used on square bar or wire stock to take it through stages in which its corners are hammered. When done methodically, as when shaping a square bar into a round one, the square's edges are hammered, while the bar rests flat on the anvil, to form a hexagonal shape in section. The edges of this shape are then smoothed with the hammer to make a totally round form. Rounding up also works to rearrange the crystal structure of the metal, consolidating and therefore strengthening it internally.

SWAGING

Swaging can be a form of rounding up, but is also used to otherwise change the cross section of a bar by hammer blows. This can be done while holding the metal on a flat anvil surface, but is more frequently accomplished by placing it in the groove of a *swage block* whose shape and size is selected according to need, and like a die, controls the form that results. Depending on circumstances, the metal is either turned constantly as it is hammered and shaped, or kept stationary as for instance when a half-round or triangular form is swaged. Swaging is also a

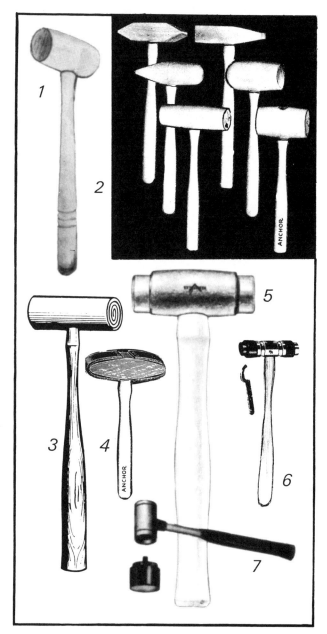

6-238 MALLETS AND RESILIENT HAMMERS
1. *Boxwood-headed mallet* with wooden handle, head 2⅜ in long, face Ø 1⅜ in, length with handle 10½ in.
2. *Wood-headed forming mallets:* wedge shape, wedge and dome, narrow flat face, wedge and oblong face, flat and dome face, broad flat face, heads 3–5½ in long. *(Anchor)*
3. *Rawhide mallet* with wooden handle, head lengths available from 2⅛–3¼ in, Ø 1–2 in in one-eighth-inch progressions.
4. *Wood wedge-shaped mallet* with strip leather face.
5. *Cast iron base hammer* with rawhide faces, wooden handle.
6. *Metal hammer* with detachable, threaded-in faces available in fiber, nylon, or brass; with wrench to remove and tighten faces. *(Abbey)*
7. *Nupla hammer holder* available in various weights from 6 oz to 3 lb, with removable plastic faces graded and color coded in eight degrees from extra hard to soft; separate tip with attached thread, available Ø 2, 1½, and 1 in. *(Abbey)*

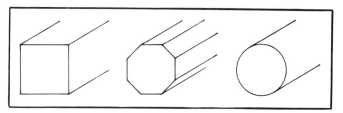

6-239 ROUNDING UP

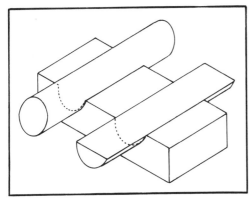

6-240 *SWAGING*

means of reducing the section of a tube by repeated, opposing blows to gradually make a decrease in diameter, or when tapering a tube end to a smaller opening.

DRAWING DOWN OR FORGING DOWN

Drawing down is the act of reducing the cross section of a metal bar to increase its length without much increase, if any, in its width. This is accomplished by hammering it with a cross peen hammer to a taper. There are three basic tapers. A *round taper* is one in which the bar is drawn down equally on all sides so that it eventually forms a conical point if the process is continued. A *flat taper* is one in which a square or rectangular bar is drawn down on two opposite sides, first with a cross peen hammer on one or both opposing sides, then with a planishing hammer on the other two surfaces or edges, to contain and continue the line of the taper. If the taper is allowed to spread or expand toward the thin end, it is called a *fishtail taper*, a type used when forming the cutting ends of some chisels. *Piping* is a form of taper that consists of forming a hollow in a bar that tapers in its longitudinal direction. Piping can also occur unintentionally when the top and bottom surfaces of a bar stretch while the metal between those surfaces does not, thus forming side grooves or *pipes*. Where these are undesirable, they are eliminated by hammering the sides on which they appear at an early stage. Drawing down is usually followed by planishing.

COUNTERDIRECTIONAL DRAWING DOWN

Counterdirectional drawing down is an application of plain drawing down and not actually a separate process, but as it is used so much in forming forged jewelry, it is mentioned here. In counterdirectional drawing down, two opposing tapering planes are formed on the same bar so that their opposition resembles a *tetragonal sphenoid* or wedge-shaped form whose wedges taper to a point in opposite directions when the piece is short. When these opposing planes are formed on a long bar or wire, and that bar is curved instead of straight, the opposing planes merge gradually into each other to present the sculptural appearance, due to subtle changes in planes, evident in most forged jewelry.

SETTING DOWN

Setting down is a means of reducing the cross section of a part of a forging. Only that area is worked while the rest remains as is.

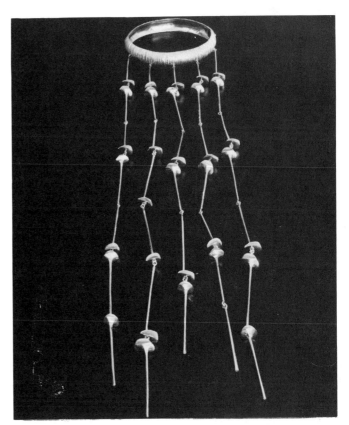

6–241 DIETER MÜLLER-STACH, U.S.A. "Body Chimes." Silver neckpiece, 800/1,000. The 34 hanging units were made by lost wax casting, their stems forged after casting. Length 28.5 in. *Photo: Dieter Müller-Stach*

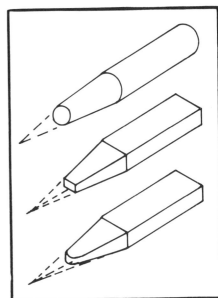

6–242 *DRAWING OR FORGING DOWN*

6–243 TORUN BÜLOW-HÜBE, Denmark, designer; manufacturer Georg Jensen Sølvsmedie A/S, Copenhagen. Forged sterling silver wristwatch armband with smoky quartz watch glass. *Photo: Courtesy Georg Jensen Sølvsmedie A/S*

6–244 *THE TETRAGONAL SPHENOID* (wedge)

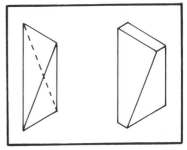

6–245 CLAUDE MOMIRON, France. Forged gold ring with malachite, with smoothly modulated transitions from thick to thin on different planes.
Photo: Claude Momiron

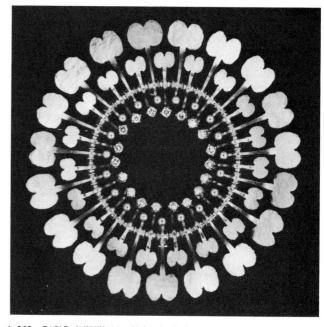

6–250 TAPIO WIRKKALA, Finland, designer; manufacturer Kultakeskus Oy, Hämeenlinna. Forged 14K gold brooch with diamonds, showing the typical surface texture of forged hammer marks, left intact, on the two sets of 19 repeated units strung on a chain. *Photo: Courtesy Suomen Taideteollisuusyhdistys, Helsinki*

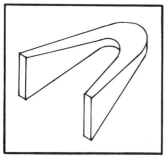

6–246 ONE-DIRECTIONAL DRAWING DOWN ON A CURVE

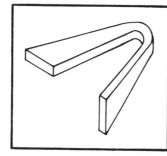

6–247 OPPOSITE, TWO-DIRECTIONAL DRAWING DOWN

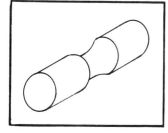

6–248 SETTING DOWN

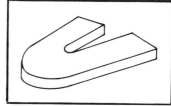

6–249 SPREADING

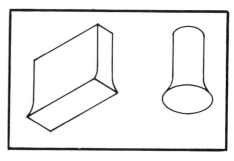

6–251 UPSETTING A BAR OR A SHEET EDGE

SPREADING

In spreading, the metal is thinned or widened or both by hammering it with a *cross peen hammer* with blows angled to the direction toward which the desired spread should take place. The metal is then flattened and smoothed to remove hammer marks by a *planishing hammer* while the work rests upon and is supported by an anvil or stake of appropriate form.

UPSETTING

Upsetting is the reverse of drawing down. Its purpose is to *thicken* the metal by hammering it in the direction contrary to its longitudinal axis, as at the *end of a bar,* causing it to bulge out; or in its developmental direction, as at the *edge of a sheet,* causing it to become edge thickened. Corners of sharp bends of bars and wire are upset to spread them and make the bend rigid.

In upsetting, the metal is held upright or horizontally with the hands, tongs, or in a vise while it is worked by a hammer at its end or edge. Thick bars can be upset by pounding the bar itself on the face of an anvil, a process called *jumping up.*

FORGING BY HAMMER, ANVIL, AND OTHER TOOLS

CUTTING

Cutting metal can be done while the metal is hot or cold. A relatively thick bar such as an ingot can be cut by hammering a *cold chisel* at the severance point first on one side, then on the other. The metal can then be easily broken off at the point of the groove by striking it off with a hammer. If there is any danger of dulling the chisel or scarring an anvil face, place the ingot on a piece of soft brass before cutting. Thick sheet metal can be cut by placing it vertically in a *bench vise,* then hammering the projection with a sharp cold chisel to sever it. This method can be used as a means of reducing or trimming thick stock.

SLITTING OR SLICING

In slitting, *sharp chisels* are driven through sheet metal or bars to make a cut in order to divide the metal into parts that can then be spread apart at the cut line. A broad shape can be slit into several smaller ones that can then be shaped by forging or other means into subsidiary forms that remain a continuous part of the larger mass.

6–252 *SLITTING*

6–253 SIGURD PERSSON, Sweden. Forged silver bracelet whose hollow terminal forms are inspired by seed shapes. *Photo: Sune Sundahl*

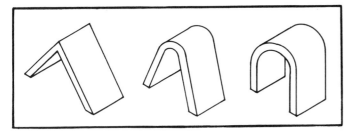

6–254 *BENDING*

6–255 TORIL BJORG, Norway, designer; manufacturer David Andersen, Oslo. Each repeat unit of this forged sterling silver bracelet is made with one wire, forged and bent to link with the previous one. *Photo: Teigens Fotoatelier, courtesy David Andersen*

BENDING

Bending in forging is an important process, and is discussed in Chapter 4. To those remarks we add here only what specifically relates to bending metal in forging.

Forge bending in most cases consists of hammering bar, rod, or wire with *forging hammers* while holding the work on an *anvil* or *stake*. Both nondeforming and deforming angular and curved bends are used in forging. Most characteristic of forging, however, are bends that warp the

metal out of its normal, flat plane by torsion. In this case, the metal is twisted by the exertion of a lateral force from hammer blows that causes it to gradually turn about its longitudinal axis at the place worked while the rest remains the same as before, or is then hammered to twist it in an opposite direction. Torsion is a way of creating a smooth flow of one surface plane into another that so often indicates that a piece of jewelry has been made by the forging process.

In torsional bending or planar deformation, the initial bending of the rod or wire can be done with *pliers* if the metal is small in scale; when heavier it is hammered into the depression of a *swage block, metal mold,* the hollow in a *tree stump,* or over a *mandrel.* The work is then transferred to and held against a metal-resisting surface such as an *anvil, stake* of suitable shape, or a *surface block,* and forcefully hammered with *forging hammers* along the plane of torsion. Greater force is needed to permanently stretch and shrink a plane than is needed for simple bending. The plane warp can be left as it is after hammering, or it can be filed smooth.

TWISTING

Twisting is a method commonly used in forging to create a form or to decorate it. It too depends on the force of torsion. It is most commonly done on solid wire or bar stock that has lengthwise edges so that the pattern of the twist can be seen. Twisting can be done while the metal is hot or cold. If a continuous twist is the aim, the entire piece of metal must be annealed. If the metal is to be twisted in one place or in a relatively small area, it can be annealed *locally* with a torch flame, while the rest is left in a harder state. The softened area is more easily twisted and the rest remains intact.

A single, right-angle twist can change the plane of rectangular stock to the opposite direction by a rotation of 90°, and the form can then be forge shaped and developed further as described above. A square bar or other ridged shapes can be self-twisted in as many turns as desired along its entire length. Thinner gauge square wire can be twisted with a hand drill. (See Twisted Wire, Chapter 6.) Depending on thickness, short lengths of wire can be twisted by placing one end horizontally in a stationary *vise,* while the other end is grasped by a pair of *pliers, hand clamp, spanner wrench,* or *tap wrench.*

Wires and bars formed of a composite of several units having different cross-sectional shapes, or made of different metals can be twisted together. These can first be joined in their length by soldering, or only at their ends to facilitate their being twisted; the twist itself then serves to hold the units together. Lengths of twisted wire can be shaped further by bending, forging, or rolling.

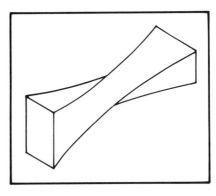

6–256 *TWISTING*

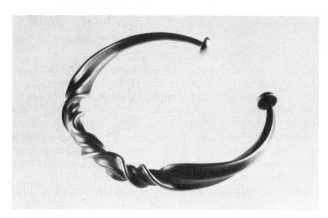

6–258 L. BRENT KINGTON, U.S.A. Oxidized sterling silver forged bracelet, with gold domes at the ends. The cross-sectional shape and pattern of reverse twists was inspired by the Vendel torque. Instead of welding the flanges together, the stock was extruded by an open roll pass through the rolling mill wire rolls, in the manner shown in the diagram. The ridged end areas contrast with the convolutions of the central area. *Photo: Myers Walker*

6–259 L. BRENT KINGTON, U.S.A. Forged sterling silver bracelet with gold wire and shot end ornaments. The form is typical of twisted wire stock forged work. Ø 3 in. *Photo: Myers Walker*

6–260 L. BRENT KINGTON, U.S.A. Oxidized sterling silver forged bracelet with end balls in gold. The twist pattern results from twisting square stock. Ø 3 in. *Photo: Myers Walker*

6–257 DENMARK, Late Bronze Age, Period VI, approximately 6th century B.C. Bronze forged Vendel torque found at Rigerup, Holbak County. Such torques are believed to have been imported to Denmark from North and East Germany. Four flanges were welded to a bar in a cross-form section, narrowing toward the ends which terminate in a hook-clasp. The entire length, first straight, was twisted while hot, at intervals, in opposite directions. Seventeen have been found in Denmark, frequently in pairs, indicating, as contemporary bronze statuettes show, that they were so worn. *Photo: Danish National Museum, Copenhagen*

FULLERING TO PARALLEL DRAW DOWN

Fullering is making grooves or hollows in forged metal with a *cross peen hammer,* or making necks and shoulders in a bar by the use of grooves in a *swage block.* A rod can be drawn down parallel by placing it over the edge of a flat-edged *stake* or a *fuller,* and hammered on the opposite side by a *cross peen hammer,* followed by a *flat-faced hammer.*

ROUTING TO REMOVE MASS

Cold chisels can be used to rout out depressions in thick metal, to scoop out a furrow, to completely remove an area, or to make a depression. (See Metal Inlay, Chisels in General, Chapter 8.)

PUNCHING TO PIERCE METAL

In punching, a cold, sharp-pointed, hand-held *punch,* a *chisel,* or a *tapered drift* (a tool similar to a punch, used to enlarge a pre-existing hole) is forced through the metal to create a hole or opening, or to enlarge one, while the metal rests on an anvil or other surface. The punching tool should emerge through the metal into the hardie hole or pritchell hole in the anvil face, or into a softer metal or wood surface on which the metal has been placed. When punching this stock, the punch is brought almost through, the piece is turned over, and the action is repeated from the opposite side. The difference between punching and drilling a hole is that in punching, no metal is removed, while in drilling, chips of the metal are continuously removed until a hole is formed. A punched hole has its special appearance because the metal volume is the same as at the start, only spread and bulged at either side of the opening. A mandrel can then be inserted into the hole, and the part worked by forging to spread the metal around the mandrel in a direction opposite to the rest.

METHODS OF JOINING FORGED PARTS

COLD, RIGID JOINS

RIVETING   Riveting is used for joining work-hardened forged parts that must remain in that condition, and therefore cannot withstand any hot joining processes. A hole is pierced through the parts and a rivet is passed through it, then hammered down to form a head at either end. The join can be rigid or movable. (See Rivets and Riveting, Chapter 10.)

SCREWING   In joining parts with screws, a hole is drilled and tapped through the parts and the screw threaded in it. The screw can then be made permanent by forming a second head at the end opposite the head, as with a rivet. (See Screws, Chapter 10.)

BOLT AND NUT   A bolt is a threaded pin or rod that has a head (of any shape) at one end and a screw thread on the straight, nontapering shaft. The shaft is passed through a hole in the coupled parts and is secured by threading the shank with a matching threaded nut. (See Bolts and Nuts, Chapter 10.)

COLLARING   A collar is a band or encircling ring hammered to surround two (or more) parts being held together to restrain their motion partially or completely. The collar is open where its ends meet. It is sometimes used to cover an opening or an end to prevent endwise motion. In cross section it can be flat, round, or half-round, or combinations of these.

WRAPPING   Wire or strip metal can be wrapped several times around parts to be held together. The methods of doing this are greatly varied. (See Wrapping and Coiling

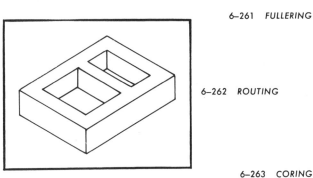

6-261   *FULLERING*

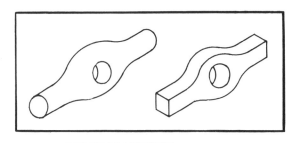

6-262   *ROUTING*

6-263   *CORING*

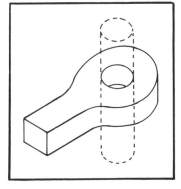

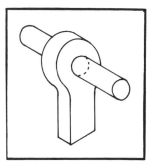

6-264   PUNCHING

6-265   HOLLOW FORGING ON A MANDREL

CORING

In coring, a sharp, *hollow punch* is used to cut a circular piece out of the metal.

HOLLOW FORGING MANDRELS

A mandrel can be inserted into a hole formed in the metal, and the part worked by forging to spread the metal around the mandrel in a direction opposite to the rest to form a ring or cylinder. Transitions from round to square can be made this way.

6-266   *Left:* MICHAEL JOHN JERRY, U.S.A. Forged wire and fabricated sterling silver neckpiece with agate slab, moonstone, and pearls. Size 11 × 6 in. Photo: Michael John Jerry

6-267   *Right:* Detail of the forged neckpiece showing the agate slab placement. To put on the neckpiece, the two small spirals are pinched together and pulled down and back, releasing the collar. A white gold hinge behind the agate frame swings the stone out of the way to allow the collar to come down and unhook. Photo: Michael John Jerry

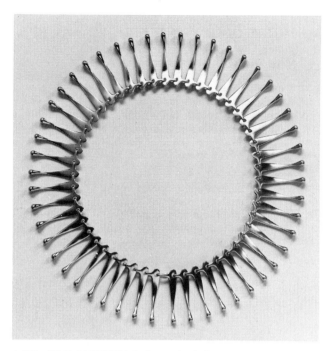

6-268 BENT GABRIELSEN P., Denmark, designer; manufacturer Georg Jensen Sølvsmedie A/S, Copenhagen. Forged silver necklace using 50 repeats of the same unit, each hooking into the next by a forge-spread and bent end. *Photo: Erik Junior, courtesy Georg Jensen Sølvsmedie A/S*

Wire and Strip, p. 206.) If the wire is stiff, its ends will stay in place; if not, certain techniques must be employed to prevent the wrapping from raveling.

COLD, MOVABLE JOINS

COLD PUNCHING HOLES   A hole can be punched through with a *cold punch* and other parts, links, bolts, and hinge pins can then be passed through this hole to make a movable connection.

LINKS AND HOOKS   Separate links of wire can be used to hold parts that have holes in them for this purpose. Hooks that are an integral part or extension of the main body can pass through a hole or loop in an adjoining body.

BALL AND SOCKET   A ball and socket joint is a *universal joint* or coupling that permits swiveling and turning at any angle (free movement of the parts joined). Essentially it consists of a rod extending from one part passed through a hole or fitting into a cup of another part. To keep it in place, the rod end is forged or upset to make it larger than the diameter of the opening. Depending on the design of the parts, such a joint can swivel completely or stay in a chosen position. In any case, the members are freely movable.

HINGING   If a hinge is forge formed as an integral part of two adjacent members, the parts can be held together and operate as a hinge by inserting a hinge pin. (See Glossary: Jewelry Findings.)

HOT JOINING METHODS

Methods of hot joining forged parts can be used, but normally this softens the forged parts as the heat anneals them. Parts *can* be planished after heat joining to work harden them, depending on the design situation.

Welding is a method used to join not only ferrous, but nonferrous metals as well. Ferrous metal welding is a large subject, and the reader is referred to special texts dealing with this area of metalwork. For nonferrous welding, see subjects dealing with metal fusion techniques.

Spot welding, is a form of welding in which two parts are welded at isolated points rather than in a continuous seam by the use of an *electrical spot welding machine.* This is largely used in the field of commercial jewelry, for making eyeglasses, and in making repairs where a more widely diffused heat would endanger the piece. It is rather surprising that the small, hand-held spot welding apparatus available has not been more widely adopted by individual craftspersons for use in fabricating jewelry.

Soldering forged parts is also possible. (See Soldering, Chapter 10.)

FINISHING A FORGED METAL SURFACE

Planishing metal after final forge shaping is the smoothing of the surface to remove minor irregularities and any undesirable visible signs of other work processes. This is done by the use of an 8–13 oz flat- or slightly convex-faced, highly polished *planishing hammer* when the surface to be planished is convex, and a somewhat more convex-faced hammer when the surface is concave. In this traditional finishing method, the work is placed over a supporting, highly polished, smooth-surfaced stake whose contour closely corresponds to that of the object to be planished. The purpose of planishing is *not to shape* the metal, but to give the *surface a final texture.* Therefore, to prevent work distortion due to stretching, the work must *make contact* with the stake's surface which will then support it against the hammer blows, and its shape will be retained. The supporting surface area must be larger than that of the contact area of the hammer face when it strikes the work.

Planishing is done by placing a series of relatively rapidly delivered, light but equally weighted, regularly spaced, overlapping blows on the object's surface. Their sequence depends on the shape of the object, and may follow a concentric, spiraling, or radiating path. Each blow overlaps the last, and the object is always kept in contact with the stake surface by shifting it according to the area worked. Because of the local compression that occurs on the work at the point of each percussive hammer blow, the visible surface develops a series of bright, facetlike marks at those hammer contact points as planishing progresses. When properly supported, the undersurface of the work becomes smooth and bright. To best be able to see the progress and development of the facet marks while planishing is in progress, first pickle the work to a matte, dead white. Each blow of the hammer will then appear as a shining spot. Edges may become misshapen during planishing, but they can be filed smooth once planishing is completed.

Filing a surface after forging is another finishing technique. Whether to leave a surface with its obviously hand-forged hammer marks, or to reduce the form to its basic shape by removing all evidence of the forging process and refine the work surface to a specular, mirrorlike, reflecting smoothness, is a matter of personal choice. Both hammered and smoothed surfaces are legitimate, and combinations of the two can coexist in a single work. *Files* of all cuts and cross sections may be used to level risings, to smooth and refine surface contours, to eliminate work marks, and to give a surface uniform flow. Coarse files are used first to take the surface down to the deepest groove level, followed by finer files to eliminate the coarse file marks.

Texturing, in which surface character is created by the use of tools such as *engraving liners,* or *rotary milling burs* such that light is reflected in various ways, is another finishing technique.

Stamping the surface partially or totally with *small-patterned stamps* can be done to give a surface textural richness and a special character.

Hand polishing the surface after forging gives it a soft, semibright finish. This can be done with *steel wool,* leaving the surface with a matte, parallel-scratched appearance.

Mechanical polishing can create an effect ranging from semimatte, achieved with a *scratch brush,* to a high mirror finish, achieved by the use of abrasives and buffing and polishing wheels.

FORGING IN ACTION

DEMONSTRATION 6

ALBERT PALEY makes a forged brooch

Photos: David Darby

The process of making a piece of jewelry by the technique of forging imposes the same structural problems, considerations, and skills as are involved when making a large construction in forged wrought iron, though differences in metal and scale impose differences in design. In making jewelry by forging, the metal is generally worked by *cold forging,* shaped primarily by hammer blows aided at times by the use of other tools. An exception occurs when using platinum, palladium, and their alloys which are often hot forged at temperatures ranging from 1472–2372° F (800–1300° C).

In the development of the form of a piece of jewelry such as this forged brooch, Paley does not begin by making a fully developed drawing of the design concept. Instead, based on his knowledge of the possibilities of tools, materials, and techniques, he relies on an intuitive approach to the design. A design idea is often triggered by an aspect of the forging process itself, and modified by a structural or mechanical necessity. The form develops during the work, taking on changes of shape and plane suggested by the special technology unique to the forging process. Every forming process—be it forging, casting, or fabricating—contains its own esthetic concepts, unique to that particular process, which the craftsperson must investigate and exploit to create a design having integrity.

Additional practical considerations enter into design development. Size, weight, stability, and the mechanical means of placing the piece on the body or attaching it to clothing are factors that each exert their influence.

In creating this brooch, Paley wished to make the design a statement in metal alone, using the forging technique as the means of determining the form, therefore no stones or other materials were used.

ANNEALING

1 Unless the metal is already in an annealed condition, ready to be forged when purchased, anneal it so that it has an optimal hot or cold working character. The ¼ in (6.35 mm) square sterling silver bar used to create the main form is placed in an *annealing pan* containing *pea pumice* and is heated uniformly with a soft, reducing flame that is kept moving at an even rate over its entire surface. When annealing, it is important to bring the metal to the proper annealing temperature for that particular metal. Overheating should be avoided as it causes the metal to form unnecessarily large crystals that result in its structural weakness, and under work, may cause it to crack. To assure the accuracy of the desired annealing temperature, which in the case of silver is particularly critical, apply a *flux* that matures at a known temperature to the entire surface by brushing, dipping, or spraying. Because flux matures to a glassy state at about 1000° F (590° C), this indicates the desired annealing temperature is near. Sterling silver is annealed at 1200° F (648° C). By another method of judging annealing temperature, small, round, pill-like *Thermo Pensils* are placed next to the metal. This proprietary product is made of a material that matures at a specific temperature, and the pill is watched so that when this occurs, the flame is removed.

After every anneal, pickle the metal to remove the flux and any surface oxides. Scratch brush the surface to relieve it of any adhering oxide particles which otherwise would be forged into it and become the cause of undesirable surface irregularities.

FORGING

2 The most effective initial forging tool is a narrow-faced, rounded, *cross peen hammer.* Forging hammers are made in several weights and one is chosen according to the need. Each hammer blow on the bar makes a ridged dent in the metal which causes displacement, increases temperature, and spreads the metal widthwise, especially at the edges. Edge spread called *shouldering* is sometimes undesirable and must be watched, because it may lead to

1

2

3

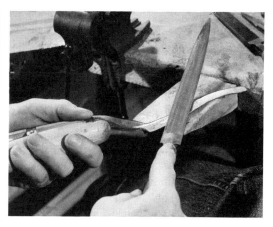

4   5   6

cracking; if necessary eliminate it by forging the edge in the opposite direction.

At the start, a basic, transitional forged form—a tapered wedge shape is *drawn down* from the square silver bar by hammering it with a 2 lb *cross peen hammer* in blows that fall perpendicular to the work while it is held on the flat, polished face of an *anvil*. Other basic sectional forms can also be made from a bar as seen in this chapter. One with exciting possibilities, often seen in forged jewelry, and used here, is the *tetragonal sphenoid*. This is formed by working the wedge shape from opposite sides, increasing the taper and spread in a direction away from its origin. Two opposing planes then develop at right angles to each other. If the form is straight, these planes remain intact and are clearly seen. In the case of this piece, the form will be extended to a long, curved, ellipsoidal shape, so that the warp of its planes ultimately brings the same planes together where the form closes.

To achieve a maximal directional change and visible separation of the planes, only one pair of sides is worked at a time, and the metal is annealed before changing the direction of the work. By limiting the direction of the hammer blows this way, internal stress occurring in the metal because of compression forces is reduced, which eliminates the chance of edge cracking.

After initial drawing down with the cross peen hammer, the surface is worked with a slightly convex-faced *planishing hammer* to level the hammer-raised ridges; if not, the highest ones might become folded over and would ultimately develop into surface cracks. The round planishing hammer also acts to distribute the metal in all directions while it levels.

3 By working and thinning the metal through blows of the cross peen hammer in the side *opposite* to a desired direction of bend, a slight curve, bend, or warp of plane is achieved. Through repeated blows, the direction of shaping and widening the metal is controlled. If, however, the curve is sharp, the stock must be initially bent by hand, by a tool such as pliers, or by hammering it to the desired shape *before* forging starts.

PLANISHING

4 Planishing or smoothing a surface to a plane is accomplished by hammering the metal with a smooth-faced, slightly convex *planishing hammer* while the work is placed on a resisting or supporting surface such as an *anvil*. The anvil face must be absolutely clean, smooth, and dent-free or the metal will pick up these irregularities. Planishing is used as a means of achieving a refinement of transitional warp-curved planes and forms.

5 The surface on which planishing is done may be the curved beak of a forging anvil or an *anvil stake* chosen for its appropriate size and shape, whose extension is placed in the anvil's hardie hole, or the work may be placed directly on the flat face of the anvil. When metal is planished or otherwise cold worked, it is condensed and toughened because of changes in the grain shape of its crystal structure due to compression, a condition called *work hardening*. As a result, each forged element of the several of which this brooch is made is placed in a state of rigidity, a condition Paley uses to advantage. As his jewels are generally large, their total weight becomes a major consideration. In order to preserve the work-hardened strength of the forged parts, they are intentionally assembled by *cold working* processes such as riveting, swaging, and wrapping. Where

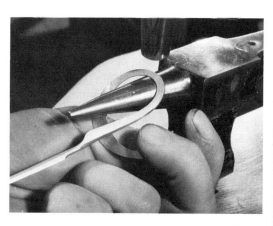

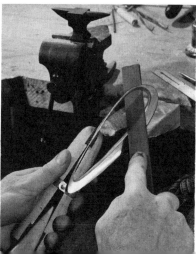

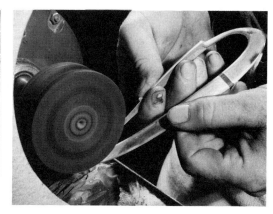

7   8   9

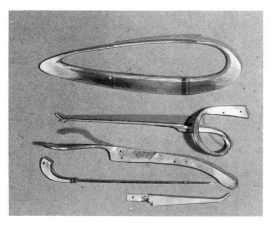

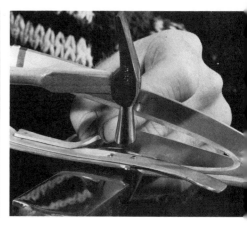

10   11   12

soldering is the method of joining, the parts being joined automatically become annealed during soldering and thereby softened. Jewels that are made with extensive soldering generally depend for their strength on mass or the mutual support of structural parts of the piece. By employing cold worked assembly methods, the work-hardened strength of large, relatively thin, light parts is preserved and can be utilized for structural rigidity.

REFINING FORM AND FINISHING

6 Forged surfaces can be left showing the subtle texture of hammer blows, or they can be leveled, smoothed, and refined by filing and finishing. Here the shape of the forged form is refined initially by a *coarse-cut file,* followed by *fine-cut files.* The file shape chosen for use depends on the contour of the plane being filed. (See Files and Filing, Chapter 4.)

7 Even after filing, a form can be subtly altered, or work hardened if necessary, by using a planishing hammer. Any marks that result can again be removed by files.

8 Edges are refined by the use of a fine-cut file. *Beveling* or file faceting the edges at an angle to the main planes draws attention to the *mass* more effectively than does a flat surface with straight edges, and it also emphasizes the line movements that develop when edges curve. Further finishing consists of using *emery paper* in successively finer grits, starting with 350, proceeding to 450, and ending with 600 grit. The surface is next rubbed with *fine pumice,* and then scratch brushed.

9 Here we see that the ellipsoidal form made from the silver bar was soldered at the union where, because it seemed "natural and logical," a section of a copper, silver, and gold laminate was placed to serve as a visual focal

point on the frontal plane of that form. After soldering, the form was again hardened by working it with a *mallet.*

Most of the surfaces on Paley's jewelry are scratch brushed to a satin finish and not highly polished, because he feels that the linear character of forged forms is confused and interrupted by multiple, bright reflections. In this case, however, to achieve highlights on the beveled edge only of the ellipsoidal form, it is polished with a *felt lap* which, because of its hardness, preserves the edge and the relative flatness of the plane. Small recessed areas inaccessible to buffs and laps can be reached with a *hand burnisher.*

10 The major elements of the piece are seen here before assembly. Each piece has been drilled at positions appropriate to receive the joining rivets. In the development of the design, it was initially decided that the vertical back plane of the ellipsoidal shape (seen here in a thin, upended position at the top) was the logical place for the placement of the pin-holding device, and was also a suitable surface where other parts could be riveted. The joining system of *overlapping riveted plates* as a means of creating multiple, flowing forms, developed from this practical, structural necessity. These three elements (plus the pinstem), their placement, and interrelationship established the *basic* structure of the brooch. A fourth element was needed and was made to project the ellipsoidal form to a position perpendicular to the body and to support it in that position.

11 In placing the pinstem so as not to interfere with a major element, a secondary element was introduced to hold it and its hinging device. A pin guard or closing device was forged out of heavy sheet and placed at the back of the ellipsoidal shape at the end opposite the pinstem hinge. The end of the pinstem is threaded and held by screwing it into an internal thread made with a *bottoming tap and die.* Here the hinged section is fitted and joined, to be held in place by a rivet.

12 The work-hardened elements are here being joined together by the use of rivets made of sections of silver wire. A riveting hammer is used to form the rivet heads and then hammer them flush with the surface plane of the part on which they appear. After filing, emerying, and scratch brushing, the rivet head becomes invisible and does not interrupt the visual flow of the planes.

13 It was decided to utilize the space created by the forward projection of the ellipsoidal shape by incorporating elements that hang from its forward part as well as from another part of the brooch structure. These would be

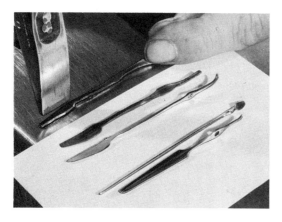

13

mobile as they hang in air away from the body. Because they are mounted loosely in drilled holes, they are set in motion by movement of the wearer.

Shown here is the development of some of these small, gold, hanging elements, starting with rough forging, through intermediate stages, to a refined, polished form. The use of a high polish of these parts was a deliberate choice as a means of catching and reflecting light and to establish a reference to body movement, thereby accenting such movement. The contrast these bright parts make with the satin finish of the rest creates visual variety.

The addition of these vertical parts meant added weight, thereby creating a need for the fourth supporting element mentioned above. This element thus serves a dual function —that of holding the ellipsoidal shape in its forward projecting position, and of providing an area from which the free-hanging elements can be suspended.

14 The finished piece, Brooch No. 75-1, is 9 in wide and 6 in high (22.9 cm × 15.2 cm); weight 5½ oz t.

Photo: Bruce Miller

The hanging elements in 14K yellow gold employ internal hinging in the outer ring, and an axial form in the lower left. The smaller gold elements use a ball and socket joint that allows radial movement, and because they are loose and move, these elements contrast with the structural rigidity of the forged forms. Another contrast occurs between their verticality and thinness, and the horizontality of the heavier forged forms.

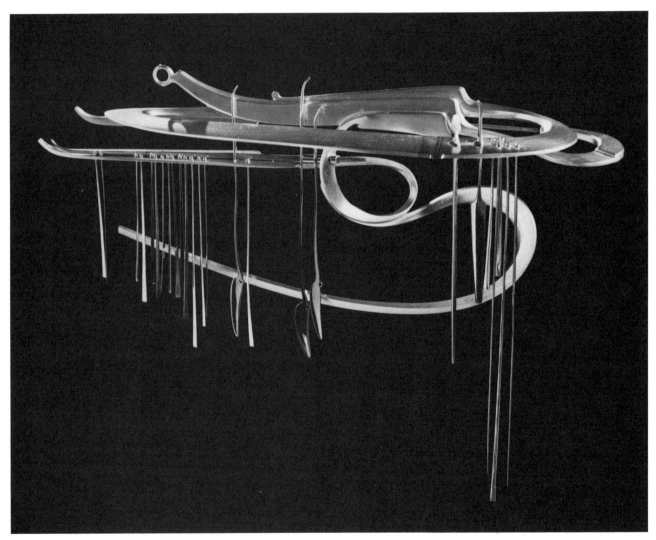

14

7

TUBING
The Uses of Fistular Forms

THE TUBE

Hollow, uniform, seamless, or seamed

Tubing is a basic metal form that is hollow, pipelike in shape, and ordinarily uniform in wall thickness and diameter throughout its limitless length. *Seamless tubing,* also called *chenier* in the jewelry trade (from French *charniere,* "hinge"), is manufactured in precious metals in different shapes (the common ones being round, half-round, oval, square, hexagonal, and rectangular), and in various wall thicknesses, and diameters. These are available through dealers in precious metals. Seamless tubing of nonferrous metals is also available from suppliers dealing in these metals.

As a raw material, the tube is extremely useful to the jeweler, who employs it in functional and decorative ways. It is not always possible, however, to stock tubing in all the dimensions or shapes desired. In such cases, *seamed tubing* can be made with relative ease from sheet metal and will suit most purposes equally well. Round seamless tubing can be *reshaped* to many other forms by the use of drawplates having openings of the desired shape. Tube can also be *tapered* by hand methods. Making, reshaping, and tapering tubing methods are described below.

SEAMLESS TUBE MANUFACTURE BY EXTRUSION

Seamless tubes of the regular sectioned forms used by jewelers are manufactured by the process called extrusion, which in principle is the opposite of drawing. *Extrusion* is the mechanical manufacture of metals into a continuous hollow (or solid) form. Extruded tubing is uniform in cross section, and of any length. The earliest machine for extrusion was invented in 1797 and was used for making

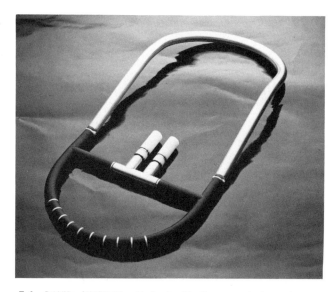

7-1 DAVID WATKINS, England. Necklace employing aluminum tubing and acrylic plastic rod, with gold inlay. Hinges connect the upper tubing with the lower unit. Width 12.8 cm. *Photo: Mike Hallsen*

lead plumbing pipes. Several different types of machines are used today. A basic principle is the use of a vertical hydraulic press incorporating a cylinder that holds the near molten metal, a ram that forces or pushes the metal out through the restricted orifice of a die fixed on the lower ram face, and a core mounted in the center of the cylinder that makes the hollow, and determines the tube's

Round Gold and Silver Seamless Tubing

Common sizes available. OD = outside diameter; ID = inside diameter.

Heavy Wall (24 B.&S. = 0.020")			Medium Wall (26 B.&S. = 0.015")				Thin Wall (30 B.&S. = 0.010")		
OD B.&S.	OD Inches	ID Inches	OD B.&S.	OD mm	OD Inches	ID Inches	OD B.&S.	OD Inches	ID Inches
8	0.128	0.088	2.75	6	0.236	0.206	8	0.128	0.108
10	0.101	0.061	4.5	5	0.196	0.166	10	0.101	0.081
12	0.080	0.040	6.5	4	0.157	0.127	12	0.080	0.060
							14	0.064	0.044
							16	0.050	0.030
							18	0.040	0.020

7-2 SEAMLESS TUBING
Extruded mechanically, this tubing is available in various sectional shapes, in all precious metals and their alloys. *Manufactured by Ferd. Wagner, Pforzheim, West Germany*

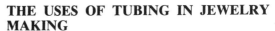

THE USES OF TUBING IN JEWELRY MAKING

FUNCTIONAL USES

Tubing has a variety of functional uses. An important use is in hinge or joint making to form *hinge lugs,* also called *knuckles.* Its use for hinge joints is why tubing is sometimes referred to as *joint wire.* (For the use of tubing in hinge making, see Glossary: Jewelry Findings.) Tubing is used to make handmade *findings* such as round clasps, pinstem clasps, and safety catches. A section of tubing can form a loop finding, such as is used at the top or back of a pendant, through which the supporting chain or cord passes. Tubes can also be an element in a constructed *chain.* Tube sections are used as a pinstem instead of a solid wire or rivet. Tube *ferrules* (a metal ring or bushing placed around two wires) hold straight or tapered wires together to strengthen them, or make a tight joint by forcing the ferrule onto the wires. Sections of tube can be used as *spacers* between parts. Tubes can be used as *sleeves* to cover a wire or another tube.

DECORATIVE USES IN STRAIGHT FORMS

A great advantage of tubing for decorative use is its relatively light weight. Probably its simplest decorative use is in sections to make *beads* that are strung together endwise, concealing the cord or chain of a necklace or bracelet. Besides being strung lengthwise, by drilling a hole through their diameter, they can be strung widthwise. Holes can be drilled in them simply for decorative effect, which also lightens their weight. Tube sections can be soldered together in their length to make a form of masses of tubes of different sizes and lengths. They can be soldered in *perpendicular butt joints* by first filing the abutting tube with a curved file to make it fit the shape of the abutting tube, then soldering them together. *Short cross*

inner diameter when one is called for. The metal solidifies on exit. Different sized and shaped products are produced by changing the dies and cores. Gold is available in 14K yellow and white, and 10K yellow, but may be ordered in other compositions and qualities. Silver is sterling. Gold is available in minimum 2 in, maximum 12 in lengths; silver in minimum 12 in lengths. Measurements may also be given in fractions of an inch:

Round, OD: 1 in, ¾ in, ⅝ in, ½ in, ⅜ in, ¼ in, 5⁄32 in, ⅛ in, 3⁄32 in, 1⁄16 in.
Square, OD: ½ in, ⅜ in, 5⁄16 in, ¼ in, 3⁄16 in, ⅛ in.

Other shapes may be available on special orders from refiners.

In the field of jewelry, examples of *solid-form extruded shapes are:* stepped bezel wire; half-round, triangular, and square wire of large dimensions; and decoratively shaped wire moldings. Soft solder is also extruded in both solid and hollow core forms, the latter filled with rosin core flux.

7-3 KAIJA AARIKKA, Finland, designer; manufactured by Aarikka Koru, Helsinki. Sterling silver bracelet using seamless tubing for a standard three-knuckle hinge. *Photo: Seppo Vikman, courtesy Aarikka Koru*

7-4 GIAMPAOLO BABETTO, Italy. Necklace of gold tubing sections strung on a round leather thong and riveted in position. *Photo: Hubert Urban, courtesy Schmuck International 1900–1980, Künstlerhaus, Vienna*

7-5 TONE VIGELAND, Norway. Sterling silver necklace and bracelet made of tube sections with surfaces textured by milling with rotary file mounted on a flex-shaft; threaded on chains. The oval ornament of the necklace was first soldered with gold applications, passed through a rolling mill, and reticulated. The headed pin closing is inserted into a three-knuckle hinge. The bracelet closes with an engraved box clasp. *Photo: Abel*

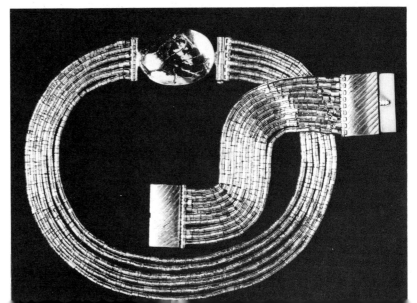

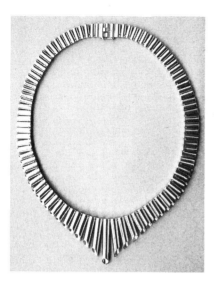

7–6 FERNAND JOURDAIN, France. Necklace of 18K internally linked gold tube sections. The diagonally shaped openings of the front tubes were filed to matching angles by fixing them upright in sequence in pitch. The series was then filed simultaneously. Col.: Solange Wohlhuter, Paris. *Photo: Oppi*

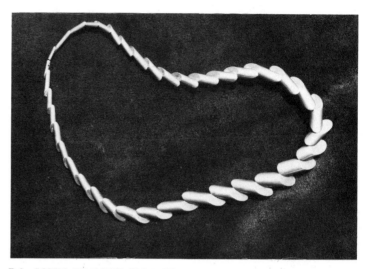

7–9 ROBERT LEE MORRIS, U.S.A. "Zeta." Necklace in sterling silver tube sections with closed ends pierced with a hole through which a steel cable passes. *Photo: Robert Lee Morris, courtesy Artwear, New York City*

sections of tubes can be soldered together *edgewise* to create an openwork pattern of ringlike shapes, which can also be soldered onto sheet and filled with enamel or other substance. Such sections can also be soldered together *in layers* to create openwork patterns.

DECORATIVE USES IN ALTERED FORMS

The concept of curved tubing introduces a whole range of decorative possibilities. Tubing surfaces can be enriched by decorative processes such as etching and milling. Elements can be added to tube, such as soldered shot. Wire can be wrapped around tubing. In this case, a simple way to hold the wire end is to drill a hole in the tube at the wire starting point, place the wire in the hole and solder it there, then wrap the tube with the wire, and do the same with the finishing end. Tubing shapes can be altered by repoussage, bulging, and tapering.

7–10 THOMAS R. MARKUSEN, U.S.A. "Pendant 1978E." Fabricated from brass tubing sections telescoped within each other, bronze rod, sterling silver discs, and baroque pearls. *Photo: Thomas R. Markusen*

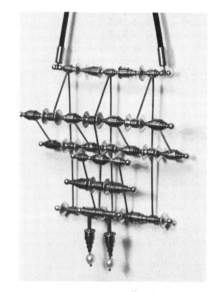

7–11 BOB EBENDORF, U.S.A. Pin fabricated of gold, silver, brass, and blue acrylic, with pearls. The design incorporates gold tubes of different diameters longitudinally soldered to each other, and silver tubes mounted endwise in the acrylic. *Photo: Don Hanson*

7–7 KASHMIR, INDIA. Contemporary traditional bracelet using tubing sections in flower groups of seven, soldered to a sheet base which is raised from the main bracelet body by another tube section. *Photo: Oppi*

7–8 TAPIO WIRKKALA, Finland, designer; manufacturer Kultakeskus Oy, Hämeenlinna. Gold ring with massed tubes soldered together longitudinally, each topped with a concave dome and a central shot ball. *Photo: Courtesy Kultakeskus Oy*

DRAWING SEAMED TUBING

Drawing is the shaping and stretching of tubing and wire by pulling them through a series of diminishing sized holes in a drawplate to reduce sectional area, increase length, change shape, and incidentally harden the metal.

Straight tubes with a lengthwise seam are made with a drawplate from a strip of sheet metal cut from the rest with shears. The final *outside diameter* (OD) of a drawn tube is controlled by the size of the last hole in the drawplate through which it passes. Without the use of an interior core, the *inside diameter* (ID) cannot be controlled but is predictable to a degree by doubling the wall thickness and subtracting this figure from the OD. Tube wall thickness depends on the gauge of the sheet metal used. Choice of sheet metal gauge depends on the ultimate purpose of the tube. Take a tube made for a hinge as an example. As a general rule, hinge tubing has an ID equal to half the tube's OD. The sheet suitable for most jewelry hinges ranges from 20–30 gauge B.&S. The smaller the tube's diameter, the thinner the gauge size used. The walls of hinges using short knuckles are thicker than those made with long knuckles.

The *width* of the sheet strip used to make a tube of a specific diameter is slightly more than three times the diameter of the drawplate opening aimed at for the tube's final size. This amount is based on the mathematical fact that the ratio of the circumference of a circle to its diameter is expressed by the Greek letter π (pi), a symbol having the numerical value of $3.14159265+$, or approximately $3\frac{1}{7}$. As when drawing wire, the tube formed is lengthened as it is drawn through the progressively smaller holes of the drawplate. Even so, the strip *length* should be longer than the length of wire needed because allowance must be made for waste at the starting end.

Be sure the strip is cut accurately, is uniform in width, and has parallel edges throughout its length that are finished true (that is, perpendicular to the sheet) or they will not meet evenly along the seam length when curved. To assure a good *butt joint*, drawfile the strip's long edges square. Remove any kerf that results from filing by running a *scraper* lightly down both sides of the edge length.

With *hand shears* or *bench shears*, cut one end of the strip to a flat-pointed taper for a distance of about one inch. Be sure the flat point of the taper occurs in the cen-

ter, or the tube will not shape evenly or pull correctly. When the tapered end is shaped to a cone it is called a *drawing dog*, and is passed through the drawplate first.

A certain amount of preshaping of the strip length is necessary, and different shaping methods are possible. One way is to place the strip into a half-round, longitudinal depression in a *swage block,* or a similarly shaped semicircular, long groove in a *hardwood shaping block.* With any suitably shaped *cross peen hammer,* while the strip rests edgewise in the groove, beat it at a right angle to one edge along its whole length, at the same time forcing it into the groove so that it is converted lengthwise by upsetting into a U shape.

Another method shapes the curve by the use of a smooth-surfaced *straight steel mandrel* or round rod whose diameter matches that of the groove of a *swage block* on which the strip is placed. Put the mandrel on top of the center of the strip and hammer it down to force the metal into the groove so that it forms a U shape. Further shape the tapered drawing dog end as small, round, and closed as possible with a *flat-faced hammer* by placing it on a *surface block* and rotating it while hammering.

Before drawing, anneal the entire strip, pickle, rinse, and dry it thoroughly. For simple tube drawing, lubricate the outer surface of the strip with a soft, water-soluble soap (avoid grease as it is more difficult to remove), that can simply be washed away.

A *round-holed drawplate* is used for tube drawing. The maximum size of the tube diameter that can be made with a particular drawplate is several openings smaller than its largest one, as the tube must pass through several openings before it becomes round. The minimum size depends on whatever is practical with this technique and the gauge of metal used.

Feed the tapered tube end or drawing dog through the first hole that barely resists its passage. The first draw is for *preliminary shaping,* and the fit need not be one that sharply reduces the tube diameter. Grasp the draw dog with the *drawtongs.* This will cause the tapered cone to collapse, but this does not matter and has no effect on the drawing action. Draw the tube through the drawplate in as few pulls as possible, with slow, steady pressure, and not with sudden jerks which may break the draw dog and necessitate making a new one. (If a new drawing dog must be made, saw through the tube on a diagonal.) Place the tube in the next smaller drawplate opening and pull it

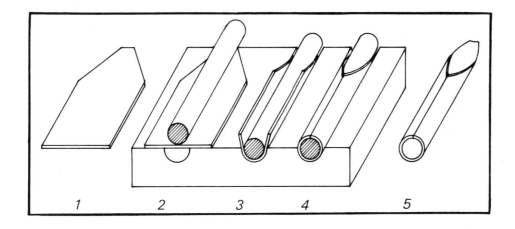

7–12 FORMING A TUBE FROM SHEET METAL

1. Cut the strip to a width that is equal to the circumference of the mandrel that represents the ID of the resulting tube. If the tube is to be drawn through the drawplate, cut one end to a taper to form a draw dog.
2. Place the strip over a grooved depression in a design block whose depth is sufficient to accommodate the mandrel, and put the lubricated, straight mandrel on top of the strip.
3. Hammer the mandrel down on the strip to force it into the groove.
4. Hammer the upright strip edges over the mandrel to close them and form the tube.
5. Remove the mandrel from the tube with a hammer.

through. The edges rapidly curve inward, approach each other and finally meet squarely, thus forming the tube. Continue drawing through progressively smaller holes until the desired tube diameter is reached. Draw with the seam facing upward so that it is visible during drawing. To keep the seam straight and prevent twisting, clamp a *knife blade* at the back of the drawplate with its thin edge toward the drawplate and the point inserted in the seam. The knife point serves to guide the seam so that it feeds straight into the drawplate opening. Remove the knife blade before the last draft when the seam is closed.

There are circumstances when a tube with a diameter exceeding the drawplate's capacity must be shaped. In this case, a *smooth, straight metal mandrel* is used, lubricated to facilitate its removal. The beginning procedure is the same as described for making a lengthwise U shape. At this point, force the edges down on the mandrel with a wooden mallet so that they close toward each other. If the edges do not meet, withdraw the mandrel by placing it in a hole drilled in a wood block equal to the diameter of the mandrel. Pass the mandrel through, and while pulling it out, the block will stop the tube and prevent it from being drawn through, thus releasing the mandrel. Place a lubricated, *smaller diameter mandrel* in the tube and hammer it down. To round the tube at the seam, place the seam downward in the groove of a swage block and hammer it down. Remove the mandrel as described above.

SOLDERING A TUBE SEAM CLOSED

The seam of a tube can be left unsoldered, or can be closed by soldering, depending on circumstances. Before soldering a seam, saw off the tapered draw dog end with a *jeweler's saw.* Do not remove it with shears as this will misshape the tube end. Make sure there is no grease inside the tube; if there is, heat it with a torch until all grease is consumed, then pickle, and rinse it in running water. Pass a *file* or a *scraper* along the seam to help the solder flow. In cases where the seam is to be hidden in the construction, mark it at regular intervals by taking small nicks out of it so that its location is visible later—a useful reference in its orientation and placement. Before soldering, flux the seam and wrap the tube tightly with a spiral of soft iron binding wire, anchored tightly at both ends to prevent the soldering heat from opening the seam.

If the seam is a tight butt, as it should be, small amounts of solder will run long distances when led by the torch flame. Therefore, place a small amount of solder at one end of the seam. After bringing up the temperature of the metal, concentrate the flame at the end with the solder, and when it starts to melt, use the flame to draw it as far as it will go. When it stops, touch a stick of solder to that place and continue to draw it on with the flame until the whole seam length is soldered. Avoid flooding the seam with solder as this might reduce the ID, and in the case of small-diameter tubes, use of too much solder may even close the opening.

SEAMED AND SEAMLESS TUBE FORMING WITH CORE WIRE AND MANDRELS

DRAWING TUBES TO EXACT INSIDE DIAMETERS

When drawing seamed tubing to a *specific* ID, use a core of steel wire that measures to the exact gauge

desired. If a seamless tube is used, force the lubricated wire into the tube. Its length should be several inches longer than that of the tube so that the wire is exposed at one end. When the wire reaches the draw dog end of the tube, the taper can be hammered flat to clinch it there. The drawing proceeds as usual, and the tube closes down around the core wire which because it is steel and harder than the precious or nonferrous metal being drawn, resists reduction while the other metal is compressed. When the metal lies flat upon the steel wire core, the correct dimension has been reached, and the drawing is stopped.

To remove the steel core wire, first cut off the drawing dog end where the core wire is clinched, to free it. Place the wire that protrudes from the opposite end of the tube into the *front side* of the first drawplate hole through which it will easily pass without any reduction. With *drawtongs,* pull out the core wire from the *back* of the drawplate. The tube will be stopped when it contacts the drawplate.

REMOVING A WIRE OR TUBE CORE FROM CURVED SEAMED TUBING

The core used in shaping tubing can be a wire, as described, or another tube. When bending seamless tubing to a curve with the wire core inside, if the curve is not too severe, the formerly lubricated core wire or tube can be pulled out with a drawtongs and drawplate as described above.

With seamed tubing, after curving, some precautions can be taken. Heat the tube and quench it in sweet oil where it should remain for 15 minutes. With *pliers* (if the core wire is not already protruding), bend back the tube at the end to expose the core wire or tube. Wrap the outside of the shaped tube at the point directly behind the bent-back part with *binding wire.* This will hold the seam together at that point and not allow it to open under the pressure of removing the core. Then continue as above.

REMOVING A COPPER OR ALUMINUM CORE FROM GOLD TUBE BY ACID

To remove the core after bending gold tubing with a copper tube core, immerse the tube in a nitric acid solution which will attack the copper but not the gold. This method takes longer than the extraction of a core by pulling it out, but is used when tubes have been given drastic curves that make core removal by other means impossible. Acid entry is easy when a copper tube has been used as a core, and is used for large-diameter tube bending.

With this technique, any lubricating grease present must be removed by heat since its presence would inhibit the action of the acid. To help the acid enter the tube, drill a few small holes at intervals along the gold tube. Holes can be soldered closed later. At intervals lift the tube with *copper tongs* to drain the acid inside and allow fresh acid to enter the tube. Rinse the tongs after use.

Aluminum tubing or wire can be used as a core with gold and silver tubing, as when making hollow gold tube links for a chain. To dissolve the aluminum, place the tube in a solution of sodium hydroxide ($NaOH$), a strong caustic alkali commonly called caustic soda or lye. This dissolves the aluminum, and its action is faster if the solution is heated. Wear *rubber gloves,* and work in *good ventilation.* Rinse the result thoroughly.

1   2   3   4

RESHAPING THE SECTIONAL FORM OF SEAMLESS TUBING

DEMONSTRATION 7

RICHARD MAWDSLEY draws round tubing to a
hexagonal section

Photos: Jerry Liebenstein

1 Seamless, round tubing of precious and nonferrous
metals can be reshaped to assume a variety of different
cross-sectional forms by the use of a *drawplate* that has
openings of the desired shape, clamped in a *bench vise*.
The diameter size limit of the tube depends on the size of
the drawplate openings. Larger diameter tube drawing
requires the aid of a *drawbench* since greater power is
needed than is possible with hand drawing. The round tubing that can be hand drawn ranges from 6–16 gauge B.&S.

The *wall thicknesses* of most tubing in the size range
that is used by jewelers is 0.020 in, 0.015 in, or 0.010 in
(0.51 mm, 0.38 mm, 0.25 mm), the vast majority being
the latter. Tubes with a wall thickness of 0.010 in and 14,
16, or 18 gauge B.&S. diameter can be reshaped *without a
core wire* because, with care, their walls will not collapse
and a well-defined shape is possible. Larger sizes require a
core wire support.

Here we see a variety of round and square, extruded,
seamless sterling silver tubing as manufactured by refiners
in various sizes.

2 The *length* of a tube that can be reshaped by hand
drawing with a drawplate varies. Length is limited by the
difficulty of removing the supporting core wire from the

reshaped tube. Relatively large diameters such as the one
illustrated, which is 6 gauge B.&S., can be reshaped in
lengths up to 6 in (15 cm) or longer if a drawbench is
used. In large-diameter tubes the core wire is heavier and
therefore stronger, so that more pulling force can be exerted upon it at the time of removal. When tubing of small
diameter is used, only short lengths can be made since the
finer-gauge core wire cannot withstand a great deal of
stress. Experience and experiment are the only way to determine the possibilities and limitations when using tube of
a particular size and wall thickness with differently shaped
drawplate openings.

The length of round tubing here is sawed at an angle so
that the severed end produces a tapered shape. When sawing tubing, use little pressure before arriving at the mid-
point.

Since in reshaping such short lengths of tubing the reduction of the form is not drastic, the tube should *not* be
annealed before or during the drawing process. The tube
becomes work hardened and as a result springs away
slightly from the core wire while it is drawn down upon it;
this is a help in extracting the core wire.

3 Crush the tapered end with *drawtongs* to create a
drawing dog that extends sufficiently through the drawplate to provide enough metal to be firmly grasped with
the drawtongs.

4 Lubricate the outside of the tube, always in the
same position, and pull it through a series of diminishing
sized drawplate holes so that it starts to take on the
shape of the opening. Here a drawplate with hexagonal
holes is used. When pulling tubing through a drawplate,
start the pulling action with a gradual buildup of force
instead of applying a sudden jerk which may cause the
draw dog to break.

5 When the shape is established, squeeze or force a

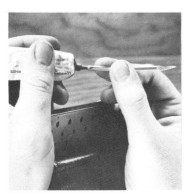

5   6   7   8

9   10

liberal amount of *lubricating grease* of the type used for gun or fishing reel maintenance into the tube from the end opposite the taper.

6 Draw a core wire to the same shape and ID size that the *completed,* reshaped tube will have. This wire is used to select the starting tube size—whose opening should be slightly larger than the largest cross-sectional dimension of the shaped core wire. With the core wire, work the grease into the tube, forcing it in fully. Allow at least an inch or more of the core wire to protrude at the end opposite the draw dog. This end will later be grasped to remove the core.

7 With the core wire in place, draw the tube through the first drawplate hole that just resists its passage, then pass it through successively smaller holes in regular order, not skipping any holes. The tube will take on the shape of the drawplate opening, its angles becoming sharp and well defined. When approaching the smallest hole through which the tube will be drawn, it may be necessary to make a slight sacrifice of shape sharpness (or shorten the tube length) in order to be sure that the core wire can be pulled out. If the tube is drawn through too small a drawplate hole, it will become so firmly compressed on the core wire that its removal will be impossible.

8 After the last draw, the core wire must be extracted. To do this, insert the core wire *backward,* that is, from the *front* of the drawplate hole as shown here. Select a hole that allows the core wire to pass through tightly but without resistance, and is too small for the *tube* to pass through. The draw dog end is now farthest away from the drawplate opening.

9 With the *back* of the drawplate opening toward you, grasp the protruding end of the core wire with the drawtongs and withdraw it. This process is made easier by the lubricating presence of the grease. In this reversed po-

sition, the drawplate acts to prevent the passage of the reshaped tube which presses against it, while the pulling force exerted on the core wire effects its removal.

10 Burn the grease out of the inside of the tube by annealing, followed by pickling and rinsing.

11 Here we see a cross section of the original round stock tube used at the start, and the resulting hexagonal cross section of the reshaped tube.

12 These are other shapes and sizes of reshaped tubing that Mawdsley has made and uses in his work.

TUBE SHAPING

STRAIGHTENING TUBING

Short lengths of tubing can be straightened if necessary by rolling the tube, with little pressure, between two flat, true surfaces until the deformation has been eliminated. Do not press too hard or round tubing may become oval in section. To straighten a longer length of tubing, counterpressure must be applied against the direction of the curve, and this is done with a *grooved hardwood shaping block,* described on p. 266.

BENDING TUBING

When bending tubing, the metal form is changed beyond its elastic springback limit. The metal weight is redistributed: the inner curve wall becomes thicker because of compression and reduction in length, and the outside curve wall becomes thinner because it stretches. These changes cause the difficulties experienced in bending tubing. When a tube is not supported during bending, it tends to buckle on the inside curve, and the outside curve wall tends to move toward the *neutral axis,* which is normally in the center of the tube opening when it is straight but which shifts toward the thicker, inside curve wall when the tube is bent. There is little stretch at the beginning and the end of the bend, and the inside shape of the tube at the bend becomes oval.

To counteract this tendency, the use of a *core material*

7-13 WERNER BÜNCK, West Germany. Gold and silver bent tube bracelet with domes and balls covering open ends. Ø 80 mm; width 35 mm. *Photo: Flemm*

7-14 NETHERLANDS. Victorian gold, bent tube bracelet with diamonds. The fluting was done by drawing the tube through a drawplate with an appropriately shaped opening. The helix spiral wire section acts as a spring and gives the bracelet flexibility when placing or removing it. *Photo: Rijksmuseum, Amsterdam*

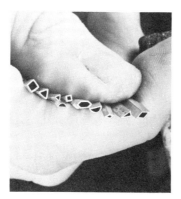

11   12

makes tube bending with little or no shape change possible, and it is helpful if the tube metal is in an annealed condition. The core material acts to support the tube wall and prevent it from kinking or collapsing during the bending process. Various materials can be used for a core: the choice depends on tube wall thickness, the diameter of the tube, the *bend radius* or degree of bend in the curve, and convenience in use under the particular circumstances. For bending a tube into simple curves, a *solid core* such as wire, or a tube of a smaller diameter which fits into the tube to be bent can be used. The core material is lubricated with a light oil so it can be inserted and removed easily. After bending, the core material is pulled out with pliers. Fast or compound curves make the withdrawal of solid cores difficult or impossible, unless the core is of a metal that can be etched out by an acid that does not affect the original tube. For instance, aluminum can be used as a core in gold, and etched out with an etchant that only works for aluminum, as mentioned.

Soluble cores can be used. One such material is *hypo crystals* (sodium hyposulphite, $Na_2S_2O_4$), which is also used as a fixing medium in photography. This substance is available as a dry, crystalline salt which is heated to 104° F (40° C), poured into the tube which has been closed by *masking tape* at one end, then allowed to cool and solidify. It will support the tube during bending, and because it is water soluble, can easily be dissolved out of the tube with hot water when its work is completed.

Cores that can be melted out by heat are also possible, and these include wax, thick grease, pitch, and low-fusible metal alloys. (See Tapered Tubing, Chapter 7.) Before using them, lubricate the inside of the tube with oil to facilitate core removal later.

Dry cores such as fine sand can be used, first closing one end of the tube with masking tape, filling the tube, then closing the other end with the same material. After bending, the tape is removed and the sand poured out.

When bending tubing it is important to avoid denting the tube wall because such blemishes cannot be removed easily, and they cannot be filed away. One way to prevent the tube surface from becoming scarred is to wrap it spirally with *soft binding wire* which keeps the surface from coming into direct contact with the bending device. Another possibility is to lubricate the outside of the tube and insert it into a tight-fitting *flexible plastic tube*. The plastic protects the tube surface and to a degree acts as a support when bending. It is easily removed by pulling it off, or, if the curves are compound and this is not possible, it can be burned off (in which case *allow for proper ventilation*).

TUBE-BENDING DEVICES

MANUAL FORCE   Bending the tube *in air with the hands* is the simplest way to bend tube, and is possible for tubing

7–15 JOSEF SYMON, Austria. Silver brooch with hand-bent tubes. Photo: Josef Symon

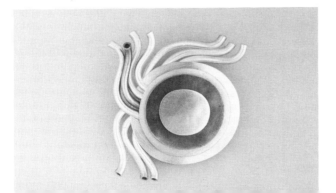

without a core if the tube is of small diameter, but is safer with a core. Proceed slowly, exert pressure first on the tube ends, if possible. It is difficult to bend the very ends of a tube into a curve, and provision should be made for this in cases where it matters by starting with a piece of tubing longer than the final needed length. Selected curved portions of the tube can later be sawed away from the rest.

A large-diameter round or tapered tube can be bent manually by first hammering it with a *mallet* into an oval shape, then bending it against the direction of the oval. If the bend is not completed before the tube returns to a round shape—and it will—hammer the round to an oval again and continue the bending.

MANDRELS   Any suitably shaped round or curved tool such as a *triblet* or an *anvil*, depending on the desired curve radius, can be used as a shaping device. By manual pressure, press the tube slowly against the mandrel with the fingers, shifting the point of pressure often until the tube acquires the desired curve.

HAND PLIERS   These can be used to bend small-diameter tubing. Use half-round or round-nosed pliers, and guard against scarring the tube by wrapping a piece of leather around it. Proceed slowly, shift the point of bend, and exert a counterpressure with the fingers to help form the curve.

A SCROLL BENDER   This can be used to bend tubing in the same way as it is used for scrolling solid wire and flat strip, if the tube has a core.

GROOVED WOOD BLOCK   This is discussed below. (See Demonstration 9 for bending a tapered tube with *bending pins*, and see Using Wire Without Changing Its Sectional Shape, Chapter 6 for additional suggestions.)

A TUBE-BENDING BLOCK   This steel block has round depressions of various sizes drilled in its face. A tube end can be bent by inserting the tube into the tightest opening possible, then bringing pressure to bear slowly on its end.

BENDING LARGE TUBING WITH GROOVED BLOCKS

The tube must have a core of fine sand, wax, sealing wax, pitch, or lead when bending it with a *grooved hardwood shaping block*. These blocks are easily made, and can contain several grooves in progressively sharper curves. The very ends of the grooves are rounded to avoid damaging the tube where it contacts that point.

The fundamental principle involved is one of *distributed counterpressure* which prevents tube collapse, most likely to occur when using pressure at only one point. Insert the tube in the selected block groove and form the *center* of the curve first. By slowly applying bending pressure at one tube end, the other end becomes wedged in the groove, and the wood block supplies counterpressure. The pressure brought to bear on the tube must be sufficient to exceed its elastic limit and set up just enough strain so that when released, the tube maintains the curve. Sensitivity must be acquired to detect the limits of this strain. Proceed slowly and by stages. To shape the tube curve further, shift its position in the groove, or change it to a more sharply curved groove. The ends of the tube are shaped last. When the desired curve is reached, melt out or remove the core material. The same method, *in reverse*, can be used to *straighten* curved tubing, using progressively straighter grooves in the shaping block. Where a sharp curve must be made, the tube can be *locally annealed* at the point

7-16 ELLIOT PUJOL, U.S.A. Externally worked brass tube ring formed with hammers and chasing punches, while the interior was pitch filled or held on a mandrel. *Photo: Ron Sittz*

7-17 ELLIOT PUJOL, U.S.A. Gold-plated brass tube torque with concave depressions created by working the tubes externally with chasing tools while the tubes were pitch filled. Length 12 in. *Photo: Ron Sittz*

where that curve is to occur. Apply pressure to the stiff parts, and the softer, annealed part will bend more easily.

BULGING AND REDUCING TUBING

Cylindrical tubing of larger diameters can be made to assume other shapes by forcing the tube *inward* or *outward* locally to dimensions larger and smaller than its original diameter. *Bulging* is a process in which the metal is made to swell outward or expand from its original surface level to form a protuberance. In effect, the process is a form of repoussé work in which pressure is applied from *within* the tube. Inversely, tubing can also be *reduced* locally in section from *without,* or shaped locally into concave forms by hammering or chasing.

To achieve outward local pressure from within, a *miniature snarling iron* or *recingle* is used. This tool is used by the silversmith in far greater size to reach within and work hollow forms from inside. In miniature, it has been used for centuries in Nepal to help form bulged areas in small, closed-form repoussé work, as when making religious images of their deities by the repoussé process (at which they were masters), and when making traditional forms of shaped tube jewelry such as the ornament worn in Nepal

7-18 *Left:* NEPAL. Goldsmith (*sakyabikshu*) using a miniature snarling iron to outwardly bulge a hollow gold ornament worn by Nepalese married women. He works in the traditional position, squatting on the floor, with knees drawn up to his chin. *Photo: Oppi*

7-19 *Right:* NEPAL. Woman wearing the gold tube ornament (*tilari*), suspended from strings of glass beads. *Photo: Oppi*

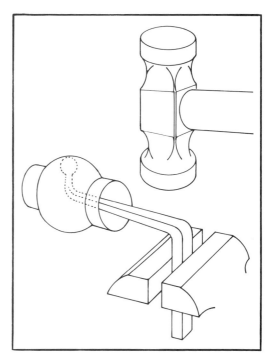

7-20 *A MINIATURE SNARLING IRON*
This self-made tool is used to bulge small hollow forms, such as tubing, outward from within.

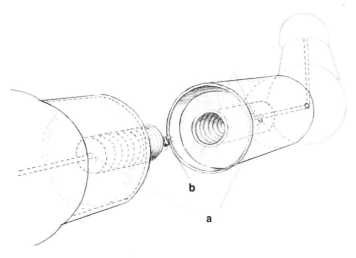

7-21 *THE SCREW-TUBE CATCH SYSTEM*
Diagram shows the manner of threading the parts on a nylon string. The screw catch consists of two tube sections. Inside one tube a smaller tube with an internal thread is mounted, and in the other is a tube with an external matching thread. The nylon string passes through a hole (a) in the closed end of the externally threaded screw tube, then through a small-diameter tube whose ends (b) are pinched upon it to hold it in place. The same is done in the second part. *Drawing: Suzanne Ross*

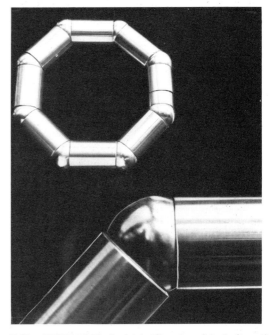

7-22 JEREMY ROSS, England. Silver bracelet of alternating 17.5 mm diameter tube sections and standard silver balls. The screw-tube closing system and the manner of joining the parts are illustrated in the diagram. *Photo: Ray Carpenter, courtesy Electrum Gallery, London*

by married women, called the *tilari* (see illustrations). This useful miniature tool cannot be found in any supply catalog, but can be easily made by forging a square rod of tool steel, bent to basic shape; a small ball is formed as a head at one end, and the tool then hardened and tempered to a light straw yellow color. It can be made in several sizes to fit into tubes of different diameters.

The miniature snarling iron is used in exactly the same manner as its larger counterpart in silversmithing. First anneal the tube. Fix the leg or tang end of the tool in a bench vise. Insert the ball end inside the tube which is held in the right hand, with the ball positioned where the bulge is wanted. Tap the shaft just above the clamped tang end with a small hammer held in the left hand. With each blow of the hammer, the end inserted in the tube vibrates, the ball kicks upward, each time making a bump appear on the tube wall. By watching the position where the bumps appear, and moving the tube accordingly, the bulging can be controlled. The effect of this tool's action is exactly as if a repoussé punch had been used on the open work.

Once the bulged shapes reach the desired size, the tube shape can be refined by working it from the outside. Fill the tube with pitch and insert a square rod into the pitch before it solidifies. With this rod the tube can be held in the jaws of a vise while it is worked. The tube could also be anchored on a pitch bowl or pitch block, but the first method leaves its outer surface clean and it can be easily turned as needed. The form is then worked with chasing tools.

This method can be used to make a series of shaped beads on one tube, and when they are finished, they can be cut apart with a saw blade.

THREADING TUBING

Tubes of regular, round section can be threaded on the outside *or* the inside in the same way as solid wire or bar is threaded externally, or a nut is threaded internally. In this form, tubes can be used to cold join parts.

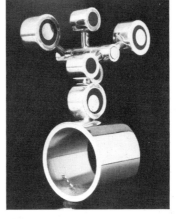

7-23 BRIAN GLASSAR, England. Silver ring with kinetic upper portion. The ring uses tubes turned from rod, and tubes fabricated from sheet metal with soldered seams. Portions are filled with red polyester resin. *Photo: Angela Turner, courtesy Electrum Gallery, London*

7-24 MARION HERBST, Netherlands. Bracelet of four ready-made copper plumbing angle tubes connected by spiral cable tube sections, chromium plated. Inner circumference 18 cm; tube Ø 3 cm. *Photo: Hans Hoogland*

7-25 GIJS BAKKER, Netherlands. Chromium-plated copper tube bracelet, the tube cut at an angle of 45° to insert a soldered section cut with matching angle ends. Size 95 × 95 × 15 mm. *Photo: Rien Bazen*

7-26 JOHN DONALD, England. Gilded silver brooch with central crystal idocrase (vesuvianite). Made of radially mounted tubes of various diameters, their ends cut at angles to create oval-shaped openings. Max. Ø 2.2 in. *Photo: Courtesy The Worshipful Company of Goldsmiths, London*

7-29 *JOINT TOOLS* They are so called because they are designed to hold tubing while it is squarely cut, and tubes are commonly used **for hinges or joints. Various types are shown, hand or vise** held, some with guides to allow the cutting of any number of the same lengths. American, French, and German manufacture. ▼

7-27 HANNA BECHAR-PANETH, Israel. Necklace of cast silver etched tube shapes, mounted on differently colored rolled leather. *Photo: Yacov Paneth*

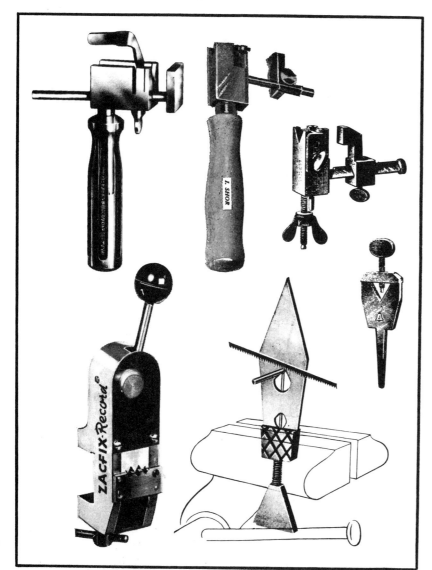

7-28 *WOODEN JIGS FOR TUBE CUTTING*
1. A wooden *V-jig* in which the tube is cradled while its end is sawed with a jeweler's saw.
2. A *two-part clamp jig* held together with a C-clamp while the tube is cradled in a groove between the jig parts and is cut.

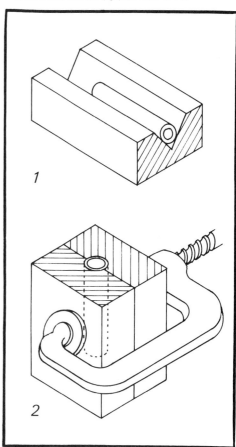

1   2   3   4

ORNAMENTAL TUBE USE IN JEWELRY

DEMONSTRATION 8

RICHARD MAWDSLEY constructs a brooch mainly with tubing

Photos: Jerry Liebenstein

SAWING, SHAPING, AND HANDLING TUBING

1 An efficient and simple way to saw a tube from a length of stock is to hold it with the fingers over a small notch made in a wooden *bench pin*. A tube *holding jig* or so-called *joint tool* can be used but has a limited range of sizes of tube, and some jigs tend to mar the tubing.

2 It is easier to hold a long length of tubing than a small length, therefore, *before* the needed tubing length is cut from stock, its end should be refined to the required condition. In cutting tubing, a *burr* or thin ridge of roughness is left by the cutting saw, and this also occurs when filing. Here a tube is being *deburred* by the use of a *cup-shaped bur* held in a *pin vise*, and rotated on the tube end with the fingers. Precise fittings of small parts are more easily made when burrs are removed.

3 To straighten round tubing and short (less than 1 in) wire lengths, roll them back and forth on a flat *steel surface block* by applying light pressure with another flat steel surface. Here a *tube-bending block* is used.

4 When filing small pieces of tubing or wire, hold them with a pair of *parallel-jawed pliers*. This type of pliers will securely hold tubing being worked without exerting the pressure that comes from tapered-jaw pliers that might crush the tube.

5 Lengths of specially shaped tubing can be held firmly when filing by placing them in grooves made in the jaws of *old pliers*. The groove shape corresponds with that of the tube held. Again, avoid squeezing the pliers too tightly or the tube shape may become distorted or crushed.

BENDING TUBING WITH A WIRE CORE

This method works effectively only on tubing whose diameter is between 16–12 B.&S. gauge (0.5082–0.08080 in; 1.290–2.052 cm). Success also depends on the tube wall thickness. Tubing of small diameter and heavy wall thickness can be bent without a core wire.

6 Do not cut the needed tube section from the stock until *after* it is bent. Anneal the tube and force a liberal amount of light grease inside.

7 Use a core wire whose diameter is just enough smaller than the inside of the tube so that it can slide easily in and out. Insert and move the core wire back and forth several times within the tube to distribute the grease for a distance of about ¼ in (0.6 cm) more than the

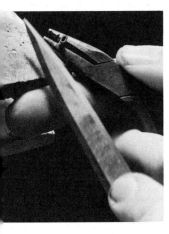

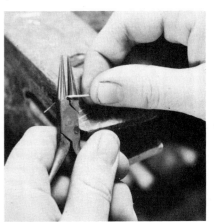

5   6   7   8

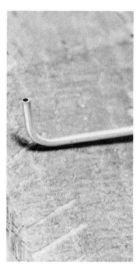

9   10   11   12

length of the tube that will be affected by the bend. Leave the core wire inside the tube.

8 Here the tube is bent with *round-nose pliers*. Use the fingers only to gradually apply bending pressure on the tube, and do not hammer it with a mallet which might distort or mar the tube.

9 To remove the core wire, clamp the entire bent area in a leather-lined *ring clamp,* and pull the wire out with *pliers,* a job made easier by the grease inserted previously. Annealed core wire is easier to remove than hard wire and it is less likely to distort the bent shape as it emerges.

10 The bent tube is ready to be cut off from the stock to the desired length.

SOLDERING TUBING

11 The soldering area is beside the workbench, but separate. The *torch* is an oxygen-natural gas type, and rests on an *automatic fuel cut-off system.* For most soldering operations, the *coiled asbestos soldering block,* lower right, is used.

12 Rub clean a 12 in piece of 26 gauge B.&S., ¼ in wide hard solder strip with *steel wool* then with *snips* cut the end into an evenly spaced fringe, and form snippets or *paillons* by then cutting straight across the fringe. Prepare only as much solder as you estimate will be needed for the *immediate* soldering operation so that it is sure to be clean each time. Store these snippets in a separate, marked box for each type of solder. On a single work, Mawdsley uses about 40% hard silver solder, 55% medium solder, and 5% easy solder in its fabrication.

13 A large-section tubing part with a small tube already soldered to its side is being soldered here onto a circular sheet base. Solder is placed with tweezers *inside* the large tube so that it leans upon the inner tube wall, but also touches the sheet circle.

14 The unit is lifted with *tweezers* to apply the heat evenly from below with the torch flame. On melting, the solder flows into the seam.

15 After pickling, this piece is mounted on a small standard *watchmaker's lathe* which is very versatile in holding small forms, and is held in a chuck by the large tube section while the supporting sheet circle is turned true to the desired size. At the same time, the middle of the sheet is also removed with a sharp cutting tool. Though this lathe is not powerful, it is a valuable tool for jewelers, as the scale of work is generally small.

16 Other small pieces of tubing and wire are to be soldered in place to this now open-ended unit. The parts are held in *self-locking soldering tweezers* mounted on a stand with a universal joint. The *flux* being applied is a creamy mixture composed of *powdered boric acid* and *methanol alcohol* (CH_3OH, a light, volatile, inflammable liquid obtained by the distillation of wood or by synthetic manufacture, used as a fuel or solvent). This is painted with a *brush* on *all* surfaces *except* the seam where the parts are to be soldered, to protect the metal surface against the formation of surface oxide. The torch flame ignites the inflammable methanol which burns off, leaving an even deposit of boric acid which forms a glassy protective oxygen barrier coating when heated.

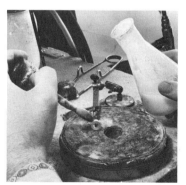

13   14   15   16

17   18   19   20

17 A hexagonal tube part with one end cut at an angle (and slightly longer than needed) is dipped into the liquid flux and placed in position with tweezers.

18 *Liquid Oxide Dissolving Flux* (a proprietary product) is applied with an *eyedropper* to the area where these small parts will be soldered in place.

19 A solder paillon is placed in position, resting on the hexagonal tube area that extends over the end of the already assembled section, but also touching the assembled section. It is placed there so that if the solder leaves a *skull* (residual solder mark), it can be removed when the surplus diamond-shaped tube is later sawed away.

20 Heat is applied and the solder flows along the seam. A steel *soldering pick* or *probe* is held in readiness to poke back into place any of these elements that the heat might cause to move out of position.

21 Individual sections are assembled and soldered together. Here a small wire was soldered inside a tube on the upper part to form a peg that fits into a hole prepared in the flange below, thus assuring the desired relationship between the sections.

22 As the work progressed, four such sections were soldered together, a side was cut off, and a flat sheet was added along with additional embellishments. This assembly is ready to be soldered to another section, a larger one made of many different reshaped and round tubes. One with a spirally grooved surface is drawn in a special drawplate having notched holes, and the drawtongs twisted while drawing to create the spiral. The left section is propped in position on a scrap of copper tubing.

23 Both sections are fluxed, and a paillon of solder is placed on the forward end where the two sections meet. The solder rests on the slightly longer surplus metal. The heat is applied and when the solder's melting temperature is reached, it is used to draw the solder to flow and fill the ½ in (1.26 cm) long joint.

24 The piece is pickled, using Sparex No. 2 placed in a Pyrex beaker, then put into an *ultrasonic cleaner*. The pickling action is fast and since it does not get very hot, it does not send out fumes excessively. This pickle must be changed often because after some use the cavitation (formation of a vacuum in the pickle) is inhibited and efficiency is lessened. Stainless steel containers can be used in the cleaner with heated Sparex. When the solder flowed, it left a residual skull mark on the surplus part where it rested. Here it is cut away.

25 The cut is smoothed with a fine-cut *barette file.*

MAKING CONE SHAPES FROM TUBING

26 Here a cone shape is being made from a ½ in length of round tubing. Place the tube section into the depression of a *round-shaped bezel block*, which is a hardened steel slab having graduated, tapering cone-shaped depressions meant for forming standardly tapered bezels used in stone mounting. In this demonstration, the bezel block acts in a function similar to that of a *dapping die*. Because tubing is used, these cones will be open at the apex end. The bezel block uses the tapered *bezel punch* meant to be used with this block, its working end a positive of the negative hole shape. By hammering the punch, the tube is gradually forced into the depression, expanding

21   22   23

24   25   26

at the upper end and contracting at the lower end. The form can be more sharply defined by then moving it to a larger depression. As it is worked, it must be periodically annealed to relieve the great stresses that occur. In this case, three anneals were needed to shape the cone.

27 Through hammering, the cone usually becomes lodged in the bezel block depression, but it can be removed by punching it out from the reverse side through the hole provided for this purpose that opens to each forming depression at the back of the block. A converted *old dental tool* is used here for this operation.

28 Now the round cone is annealed and converted into a square pyramid by using a *square-shaped bezel block,* along with the accompanying *square-shaped punch,* in the same manner as described above.

29 To make the base of the square pyramid perpendicular with its central axis, *while it is still in the depression,* it is filed down with a *flat file* until its edges are level with the bezel block surface.

30 A small round tube, 18 gauge B.&S. diameter, is being soldered onto one pyramid surface for embellishment. As before, the small tubes were cut slightly longer than needed. The solder paillon is placed against the tube in a position that will be covered by another tube that is to be soldered next to the first. While soldering takes place, the pyramid is held in air by a pair of self-locking tweezers.

31 Five such small tubes are soldered onto the surface in this way. Their ends are then made even with a side plane of the pyramid with a *file*. During filing, the assembly is held with the aid of the *square-tapered bezel punch*

that was used to form the square pyramid, while pressing the pyramid against the end of the bench pin to hold it rigidly in place. After filing, the ends are finished with *emery paper,* and the assembly is cleaned for the next soldering operation.

32 The pyramid will now be soldered to a base of flux-covered sheet metal. In soldering operations of this nature, a larger piece of sheet metal is used than is needed. After soldering, the base will be sawed to size. In this way, problems of critical placement or movement during soldering are avoided. One rather large paillon of solder is leaned against the pyramid in a position that eventually will be at the back. Heat is applied first to the side opposite the solder, then the flame is moved to the solder. The surplus sheet helps draw the heat to the whole joint. As the solder starts to melt, it is drawn around the joint with the flame.

33 After pickling, the assembled form is cut from the sheet with a *jeweler's saw.*

34 Once the assembled form is filed and refined with emery paper, it is fitted, cleaned, and is ready to be soldered to the main unit. A small piece of solder is positioned at the back with a *brush*. This will only serve to tack the part in place as the fitting and angular placement in this case is tricky, especially since the form being joined rests on a curved surface. The rest of the piece is entirely coated with surface-protecting flux. When just a small area is tack soldered in this way, if the part moves during soldering, the solder can be more easily remelted and the angle corrected by prodding the part with an ever-ready steel soldering pick.

35 Once the tack soldering operation is completed, and

27   28   29   30

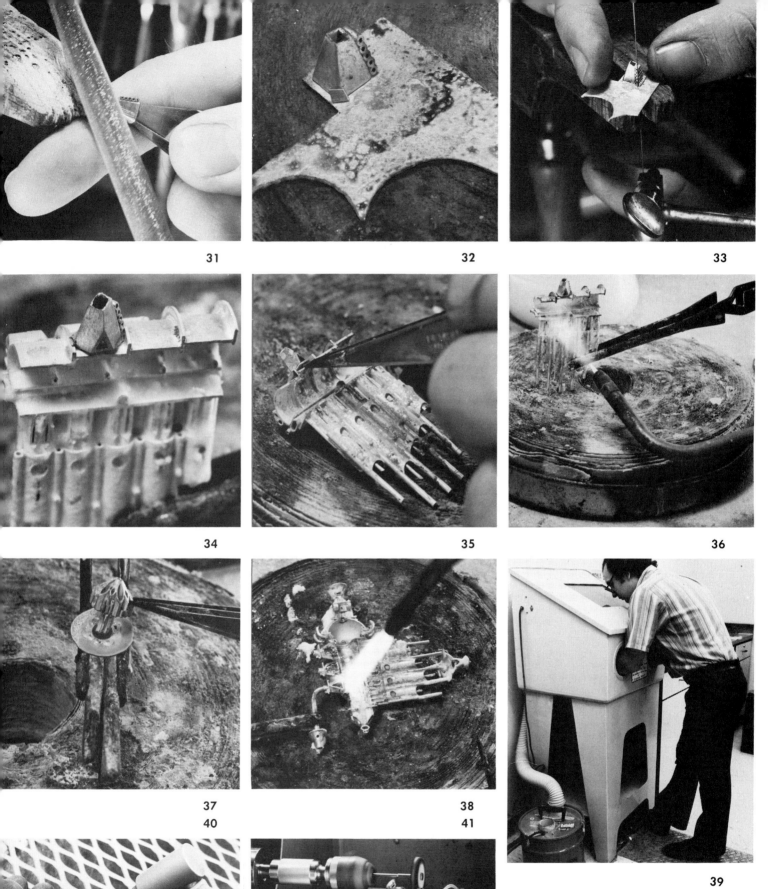

31

32

33

34

35

36

37

38

40

41

39

42   43   44

the angle checked, a larger solder paillon is placed at the joint; when this flows, it completely fills the joint.

36 The entire piece is held upright in *self-locking tweezers,* and the flame is applied from below at an angle that simultaneously heats both parts until they reach the temperature needed to melt the solder.

37 A base is being soldered onto a circular form made of variously shaped tubing and wire. In this case, the technique of *sweat soldering* is used. The solder has been *premelted* in pools onto the base at what will be the points of contact, and the circular form is laid on top. The core of this assembly projects through the opening of the base and was deliberately left longer than needed so that after soldering, the assembly can be easily grasped for further treatment. The circular base is resting on the jaws of self-locking tweezers held apart the necessary distance by two small pieces of *transite* inserted between the jaws. The heat is applied and when the premelted solder remelts, the circular form sinks into it and is held in place.

38 The circular part is seen here joined at the bottom center. The first of the three armlike forms made of tubing with spirally shaped surface grooves is soldered in place. These are among the last parts to be soldered, and the final appearance of the brooch now begins to be apparent.

FINISHING OPERATIONS

39 Once all the soldering operations are completed, the brooch is ready for finishing. After first soaking it in pickle for an extended period to achieve a thorough pickling and remove all foreign matter, the entire piece is sandblasted with a dry, fine, silica sand grit. The entire *sandblasting machine* is shown here. All work takes place within the enclosed box which has two openings and attached rubber gloves to protect the hands. The air pressure is activated by a foot pedal depressed by the right foot. The sand ejected from the gun inside falls through a grate and collects outside in a bucket placed alongside the machine, and can be used repeatedly.

40 Here we see the rubber gloves, and the *gun* that ejects the sand. It is held about 2 in (5 cm) away from the piece. Below is the grate through which the sand falls. Areas of the piece that will have a polished finish are protected by masking tape. Sandblasting produces a "frosty" finish, and the process can also be used for deburring, but its action must be watched on delicate work as it will rapidly wear away metal if the blasting is prolonged.

41 The piece is being polished in areas where this is practical by means of a *chuck-type spindle* used on the buffing motor to hold a mandrel mounted with a ⅛ in wide, ¾ in diameter *felt buff* whose working surface has been shaped to fit the surface polished. *Bobbing compound* is used for the first stage in polishing. As with all felt buffs, it is very important that the buff be kept in *continuous motion* over the surface or an excess of metal will be removed locally. The stones are mounted on pegs.

42 Areas difficult to reach are polished by the use of a *thrumming cord* on which either tripoli or rouge is applied. Mawdsley here holds the soft cord anchored at one end, then inserted in the piece, and held tightly. The piece is then pulled up and back on the taut thrum.

43 The final cleaning is done in an ultrasonic cleaner which removes all traces of polishing compounds.

44 The cleaned piece is oxidized with liver of sulphur which makes it uniformly black. Oxidation is removed from selected parts of the surfaces and embellishment by use of an *end-bristle brush* mounted in a *flexible shaft,* using wet pumice as an abrasive. The final finish is done with a *scratch brush* and soapy water.

45 The finished brooch in sterling silver and green jade balls, half-drilled, and placed on a peg made of a piece of twisted wire, and held there by an epoxy cement. The balls rest on a concave domed disc that acts as a seat. The brooch dimensions are 3⅜ in wide, 3¼ in deep (8.6 cm × 8.3 cm), and its weight is 1 ounce troy.

Photo: Brian Braye

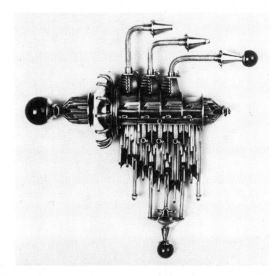

7–30 RICHARD MAWDSLEY, U.S.A. "Feast Bracelet." Sterling silver with jade and pearls. Tubing is used extensively, both structurally and as ornament, and also for the vessels which were turned from tube on a miniature lathe. Top length 4½ in. *Photo: Jerry Liebenstein, Illinois State University Photo Service*

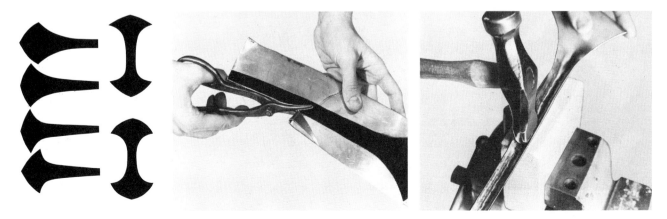

1   2   3

TAPERED TUBING

Transmuting flat sheet into coniforms

Silversmithing processes can be applied to jewelry making. Forming a tapered tube from sheet metal, and using a masonite die in which sheet metal forms are sunk are examples illustrated in the demonstration below.

TAPERED TUBE FABRICATION

DEMONSTRATION 9

MARCIA LEWIS makes a neckpiece using tapered tubing

Photos: Rolland Schlieve

MAKING THE TAPERED TUBE

1   These are typical template patterns for tapered tube blanks, either with a single attenuated taper, or with both ends large and tapering toward the center. Such forms are similar to those used to make tapered spouts on holloware pouring pots.

2   A cut-out paper template pattern is rubber cemented in place to the 22 or 24 gauge B.&S. sheet metal, and cut out with *hand shears*.

3   The metal is annealed (the paper burns away), and a *cross peen hammer* is used to sink the lower, narrow area into a groove made in a soft *pinewood block* clamped in a *bench vise*. The groove was made by striking the wood along a line with the cross peen hammer. It could also be made with a *wood rasp*.

4   As a result of forcing the metal into the groove, its sides rise upward in a transverse curve. The planishing end of the hammer is then used to strike the edges from the outer side until both sides meet in a coniform butt joint. The smallest end is closed first, and the hammer is worked upward toward the increasing diameter of the conical tube.

5   The seam, which now meets about halfway along the tube length, is painted with flux, hard solder snippets are placed along it at intervals, and the lower section is soldered. A *soldering pick* is held in readiness to manipulate the solder if necessary.

6   The larger end of the tapered tube can now be closed. Using a *cross peen hammer,* starting from the narrower end and working gradually toward the wider end, the metal is formed in a wood block groove as before, and the edges are gradually brought toward each other. Annealing this end may be necessary when the metal becomes work hardened.

7   The wide end can be closed with the help of an *anvil* used by silversmiths for shaping conical forms, such as the beak of a *bick iron, funnel stake, spout stake,* or a *tapered bench stake,* shown here, while the tang end is anchored in a bench top hole or one in a wood stump, or clamped in a bench vise. A *cross peen hammer* is used to force the seam edges toward each other.

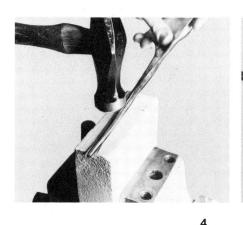

4

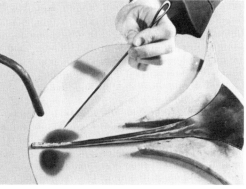

5

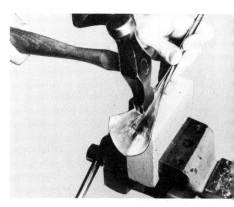

6

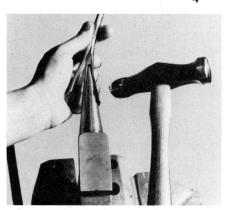

7

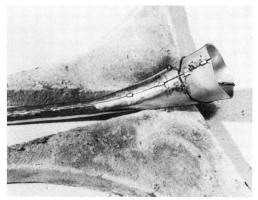

8

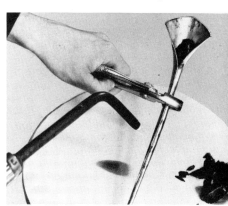

9

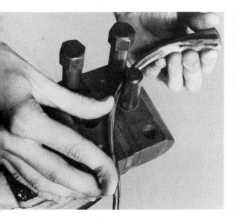

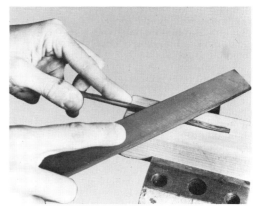

10   11   12

8 To secure the *binding wire* on the tapered form without it slipping from position, a length of heavy-gauge iron wire is folded in half and twisted at the center with *pliers* to form a loop. The two loose ends are separated, passed around the tube, their ends twisted together and bent over to form a hook that passes over the edge of the tube into its hollow. To further tighten the wire so that the seam is held closed during soldering, the loop is twisted more tightly. The entire seam can be soldered closed, as shown here, or left partially open.

9 The design calls for a partially open-ended tube, as seen here. In the finished piece, two tubes form the neck-piece. The V-shaped tube opening is therefore later closed by soldering a flat plate of metal cut to that shape so that the flat part fits against the back of the neck for comfort in wearing. (See Photo 18.)

The tube must now be bent to the required curve. Before bending, pour some light oil into the tube to coat the inner surface. This facilitates the later removal of the *chaser's pitch* now to be placed inside the tube to provide support to the walls and prevent them from kinking or collapsing when the tube is bent to a curve under pressure. Small pieces of pitch are placed into the opening at the large end. While holding the tube upright, large opening up, with ordinary *household pliers*, the lower tube area is heated and tapped gently on the workbench to make the pitch descend and fill the narrower portion of the cavity. More pitch is added as needed until it runs out the small end, an indication that the tube is filled and without air pockets. The small end is placed into cold water to make the pitch solidify there. Still more pitch is added and the upper portion only is heated until the whole tube is filled.

10 To hasten the cooling and solidification of the pitch,

the tube can be immersed in cold water. When the pitch is firm, bending the tube can commence. The same method of bending can also be used to bend heavy, *solid rod or wire.*

BENDING LARGE-DIAMETER TUBING

Bending can be done between any two *firm, vertical, cylindrical, stationary posts* of metal or wood. These mandrels work on the *principle of the lever,* such that when the lever is in equilibrium, the power and the weight are to each other inversely as their respective arms. In this case, the tube is the lever. It is wedged between the two posts to acquire the mechanical advantage of this system of acquiring leverage. The *weight* (the first post) presses against the first lever arm (the tube from the end to the fulcrum). The second post is the *fulcrum* or support against which the second arm of the lever (the rest of the tube) also presses when the force or *power* is applied manually by finger pressure on the far end of the tube. Because the posts are rigid, under pressure it is a *lever* that gives way, unlike the usual case in which the *weight* gives way. The trick is not to allow the lever or tube to give way at one point only or buckle. By slowly shifting the position of the tube and gradually pressing it against the fulcrum at a series of places all up and down the length of the curve, it will by degrees assume whatever curve you wish. Do not try to rush the process.

Any final shaping or texturing of the surface is done while the tube still contains the supporting pitch. It is then melted out by holding the tube with *pliers,* larger end down, over a *pan* placed there to catch the molten pitch as it emerges. With a gentle torch flame, *gradually* heat the tube from the lower end, moving upward slowly as the pitch melts, runs, and falls into the pan. *Do not try to rush the process* by moving the flame upward too quickly

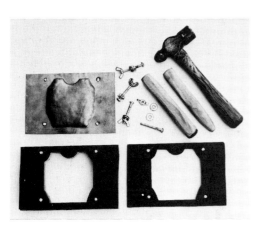
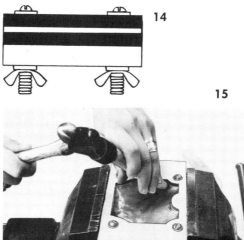

14

15

13   16

or by overheating the pitch—it may expand to the point where it will explode the form and do you injury. *Do not take this warning lightly.*

The oil put earlier into the tube should help in clearing it of all pitch. If any still adheres, the tube can be heated in its whole length to burn remaining pitch to an ash which can then be rinsed out, followed by pickling and rinsing to clean the tube.

FORMING TAPERED SOLID ROD WITH THE WIRE ROLLING MILL

11 The design calls for the use of tapered *solid* metal rod to be added to and form extensions from the main form, to be used as hooks from the tapered tube neckpiece that holds the pendant purse. Solid rod can of course be drawn down by basic forging methods with a hammer on an anvil, but an alternate and quicker method is to use the *round wire rollers* of a *rolling mill*. The rod is inserted into the appropriate groove in the wire rolls, rolled forward a certain distance, and then rolled back. It is then inserted into the next smaller diameter groove, rolled forward but not as far as before, and back again. This process is repeated, each time feeding the rod to a progressively smaller groove until the desired degree of taper is reached.

12 The resulting taper is not smooth. To remove the ridges that form on the rod where the mill pass has stopped, and shape it to a smooth taper, it is placed into a groove made with a *rasp* in a *pinewood block*. While holding the rod firmly and rotating it slowly, it is filed round and tapered smooth with a *large, flat double-cut hand file*. After finishing, the rod is cut to the desired length and the parts soldered to the main form, as can be seen below. The joint between the tube and rod can be filed to make them appear to be continuous. The rod can be shaped further with *half-round pliers*.

USING A MASONITE DRAWING DIE TO SINK-STRETCH SHEET METAL

13 A *drawing die* is one used to shape sheet metal into concave shapes by pushing it into the die cavity with a *drawing punch*. The metal is prevented from wrinkling by the use of a metal blank holder which grasps the outer edge firmly. A drawing die differs from an ordinary form-ing die because the latter has no blank holder. By the silversmith's method of sink stretching sheet metal used in making holloware, the main form of the purse-neckpiece is blocked out. The die drawing components and the tools used are shown here. Below: two identical *die sections* cut from *Masonite* (a hard composition board) drilled in four places to allow the passage of the four bolts. The pressure from the bolt head and the butterfly nut used at the bottom is distributed over a large area by the use of washers, one placed beneath the bolt head, and the other above the butterfly nut, so that they will not be forced into the masonite and plywood when they are tightened. Upper right: a *ball peen hammer* and two self-made *hardwood drawing punches,* a blunt-ended one to push down the main form, and the other pointed but curve-ended, to shape the edges. Upper left: the unfinished resulting die-shaped form of 22 gauge B.&S. sheet brass.

14 The diagram shows the placement of the assembled die parts. In sequence from top to bottom: the top black band is one of the Masonite dies; the white band is the metal; the black band is the second Masonite die form; and the white at the bottom is a solid piece of flat plywood cut to the same OD as the Masonite, and used to form the bottom, thus limiting the expansion of the metal to the thickness of the lower Masonite die form. If a deeper result is wanted, a thicker, hollowed out lower part can be used. The plywood is also drilled with holes in the same positions as those in the Masonite dies. Bolts, washers, and butterfly nuts are in position holding the die parts together.

15 The planishing end of the *ball peen hammer* is used to drive the *hardwood punch* into the annealed metal to force it down into the die depression until it contacts the plywood below. In the process, the metal flange (rim) external to the form is held rigidly between the die forms by the bolts, while the form is bulged to a curve.

16 When the form has been shaped, the die is disassembled and the metal removed. Its concave part is then filled with pitch, melted level, and the piece is fixed, convex side up, in a *pitch bowl*. Here the form will be refined and detailed with *chasing punches* driven by a *chasing hammer*. The flange is left intact until detailing is com-

17

18

19

pleted since it can be hammered to return the outer edge of the shape to one flat plane if the form becomes warped in the process. The lines sketched on the form are guides in the chasing operation. When the work is finished, and the pitch removed, the flange is cut off with a *jeweler's saw*.

17 Here we see the front and back of the purse hinged together and opened flat. The tapered wires are shown here soldered in place. Those on the upper right side of the front of the purse are yet to be bent into final shape, while those on the upper left are formed into finished curves. Additional sheet metal forms have been fabricated and soldered to the main form at the sides and the bottom corners.

18 At the top is the tapered tube torque used as a device to hang the purse around the neck. It has been chased with ridges at the wide end. The ends of the tube forms have each been closed by an 18 gauge B.&S. end plate. On one of them is an opening, and on the other a projecting part that enters the opening. The two parts are pivoted and lock together. Below is the closed, finished, but unpolished purse, without the python skin which, after the purse is polished, will be glued to the central area, to a corresponding area on the back, and around the lower portion of the neck tubes.

19 The finished "Python Purse."

Photo: Dennis Dooley

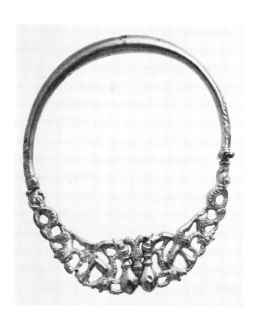

7–31 NORTH INDIA. Contemporary neckpiece (hansuli) made of hollow tapered silver tubing, except for the two curved forged silver end pieces which are solid. In fabrication, the pre-shaped and soldered, tapered plain tube was pitch filled. The forms were then created externally with chasing tools. Additional ornamentation in the form of engraved lines (including the name of the owner in Urdu) and small round punch marks were added. The pitch was melted out, the tube cleaned, and the solid ends soldered on. *Photo: Oppi*

7–32 CELTIC, 4th century B.C. Gold necklace found in 1962 concealed at the base of a massive boulder at Erstfeld, Uri Canton, Switzerland. Consists of a separately made tapered tube support, repoussé decorated at the sides, and held to the rest by a pin. In front is a repoussé-worked hollow unit depicting fabulous creatures with human and animal heads and parts. Max. Ø 16.6 cm. *Photo: Schweiz. Landesmuseum, Zürich*

7–33 MARGARET LAWS, U.S.A. Sterling silver necklace with repoussage and chased work central and rear dragons set with synthetic sapphires, the front one flanked by two dragons ornamented with cloisonné enamels. The hollow side pieces are double-tapered tubes formed from sheet. To fill the tubes with pitch for working them externally, pitch was first dribbled onto an oiled surface and allowed to solidify. The tubes were placed upright in a sandbox, one end plugged. The pitch "strings" were fed into the small tube end opening while the tubes were heated with a torch, and feeding continued until the hollow was filled. Chased line patterns on the outer surface were made while the tubes were straight and fixed on a pitch surface. Tubes were then hand bent to a curve, and the pitch was melted out. Length 10 in. *Photo: Margaret Laws*

7–34 MANIPUR, INDIA. Kabui Naga tribal woman wearing a necklace of three strands of silver tapered tubes supported on lengths of loop-in-loop chain, interspersed with large brown seeds and coral beads. *Photo: Press Information Bureau, Government of India, New Delhi*

CORES FOR SHAPING LARGE-DIAMETER TUBES

LOW-MELTING ALLOYS USED FOR CORES

Certain low-melting, easily fusible alloys have unusual mechanical and physical properties that allow them to be utilized for cores when bending tubes, as well as for other processes in jewelry making. These alloys are mainly combinations of bismuth, lead, tin, cadmium, indium, and sometimes other metals. Their main characteristic is that they melt at temperatures *lower* than that of any single metal of their components. Many of them *become liquid at temperatures below the boiling point of water* (212° F, 100° C) so they can be easily melted out of a tube or a matrix. The melting points of their *component metals* are:

Metal	Symbol	Melting Temperature	
		°F	°C
Lead	Pb	621	327
Cadmium	Cd	610	321
Bismuth	Bi	520	271
Tin	Sn	449	232
Indium	In	313.5	156.4

The low-melting alloys are used in the metal industry where they have been given a variety of different names after their inventors. Some of the better-known alloys are given below. Their compositions are not standardized, and they may vary according to different sources where several different compositions are attributed to each. Some are called "Anatomical Metal."

The low-fusible alloys given below are *eutectic*, which means their components are in such proportion that the melting point in this combination is as low as is possible with these particular metals. Usually this means they melt suddenly at a particular temperature. Noneutectic low-fusible alloys have a wider melting range according to circumstances, and there are hundreds of them, only a few of which are given here.

Bismuth is a metal that expands upon cooling and solidifying. Its percentage in the alloy therefore influences the alloy's behavior. Alloys containing more than 48–55% bismuth expand during the first 12–24 hours after solidification; those containing about this amount do not change in volume; and those with less, shrink—as do most metals—upon cooling, and pull away from molds. Therefore, alloys containing a higher amount of bismuth are very well suited to reproduction processes, since with expansion, the metal presses into the fine detail in the mold or matrix.

ADDITIONAL USES OF LOW-FUSIBLE ALLOYS

The use of low-fusing alloys as a core when bending, shaping, or tapering tube has already been mentioned. There are several other uses in jewelry making, all of which take advantage of their ability to be melted at low temperatures. They can be used for making a matrix for electroforming; as dies for lost wax patterns; in reproduction from plaster patterns; in metal spinning to fill a form that must be shaped to a narrow neck; in anchoring tubes and rods inside constructions; in chucking gemstones when they are ground and polished; and for making sheets to be used to hold down clamp pads.

Eutectic Low-Fusible Alloys: Compositions and Melting Temperatures

Bismuth	Lead	Tin	Cadmium	Indium	Melting Temperature	
					°F	°C
44.70	22.60	8.30	5.30	19.10	117	46.8
49.00	18.00	12.00		21.00	136	58.0
51.60	40.20		8.20		197	91.5
52.50	32.00	15.50			203	95.0
55.50	44.50				255	124.0
58.00		42.00			281	138.5

FILLING TUBES WITH LEAD OR LOW-MELTING ALLOY CORES

Lead alone can be used as a core for bending and shaping tubes of diameters greater than ½ in (1.27 cm). The low-melting alloys previously discussed have one disadvantage—their tendency to be brittle because of their bismuth content, though this does not apply to all of them. Lead is more malleable and has tenacity, suiting it to forms that must take drastic bends, though it requires a higher temperature to melt it out of the tube.

In pouring both lead and low-melting alloys, precautions must be taken to protect yourself against accidents. Always wear *asbestos gloves* and a *face shield* in case of splashing, and work in a *well-ventilated* place.

To facilitate the later removal of low-melting metal from tubes, it is advisable to put a coating of a *dressing material* inside the tube before the metal is poured. This can be a light oil, poured into the tube, then decanted and allowed to drain, or a mixture of whiting and gum made into a thick, viscous paste, which after decanting must be allowed to *dry thoroughly*. *Never* pour molten metal into a tube that contains water: the water will become steam whose pressure may possibly cause tube fracture and acci-

Low Melting Alloys Developed by Metallurgists

Alloy Name	Composition Percent				Melting Temperature	
	Bi	Pb	Sn	Cd	°F	°C
D'Arcet's alloy	50	25	25		200.7	93.7
Lichtenberg's "	50	30	20		196.9	91.6
Lipowitz's "	50	27	13	10	140.0	60.0
Newton's "	50	31	19		202.1	94.5
Rose's "	50	28	22		212.0	100.0
Wood's "	50	25	12.5	12.5	159.8	71.0

Non-Eutectic Low-Fusible Alloys

Bismuth	Lead	Tin	Cadmium	Temperature	
				°F	°C
50.50	27.8	12.40	9.30	158-163	70-72
50.00	34.5	9.30	6.20	158-174	70-78
50.72	30.9	14.97	3.40	158-183	70-83
42.50	37.70	11.30	8.50	158-194	70-90
35.10	36.40	19.06	9.44	158-210	70-98

dents. Place a *wooden stopper* or *cork* into one end of the tube, and place that end into a box containing *dry sand*. Place the whole assembly near where the metal will be melted so it does not have to be carried long distances to be poured. The tube should stand upright. Before pouring, heat the tube with a *torch* as molten metal should not be poured into a cold tube since the temperature shock can cause it to be ejected.

Melt the metal in a *ladle* or in a *melting pot* with a pouring lip, and pour it into the tube at a slow, steady rate without stopping until the tube is filled. Allow it to stand and the metal to solidify, and then remove the cork or stopper. The tube can now be shaped.

REMOVING THE CORE After shaping, to remove the low-melting alloy, if it is one that melts below the boiling point of water, submerge it in a container of water, and bring the temperature up to the boiling point. Lift the tube with tongs and if a stopper has been used, turn it so the metal can drain out into the water. Repeat submersion and draining until the tube is emptied. If lead is used, hold the tube with *tongs* with the widest opening down over an iron container to catch the molten lead. With a torch flame, heat the part *nearest the bottom opening*. As the metal there starts to flow out, gradually move the torch upward, melting out the rest of the lead until the tube is emptied. *Never* start this heating at the *center* of a tube filled with lead or it may explode.

7–35 WILLIAM CLARK, U.S.A. Brass tapered tube, spiral necklace made from seamed tubing while it contained a lead core to support it during bending. *Photo: Peter Wolfgang Behn*

8

SURFACE ORNAMENT WITHOUT HEAT
Metal Removal Techniques

ENGRAVING

Forward-pressure linear metal removal

In general, engraving can be described as the art of carving or cutting incisions into any material less hard than the tool used to make them. Characteristically, in the process of forming the groove, some of the material is removed from the parent object. As a decorative technique, engraving on metal was preceded by earlier graphic embellishments on a variety of nonmetallic materials such as shell, bone, ivory, gourds, coconut shell, bamboo, wood, and stone. Our earliest engraving tools were made of beveled, pointed flint, found in the Upper Paleolithic culture in Western Europe. Shortly after we entered the Age of Metals, stone tools were replaced by sharp, pointed tools of copper or bronze, and eventually iron. With the iron

8–2 JELLALABAD, AFGHANISTAN. Conically tapered silver bracelet (*kara*) with glass stones, worn by Pashtu women. The engraved central area is flanked by bands of beaded and stamped wire. The hinged closing opens by the withdrawal of the pin. Height 8 cm; Ø 6.5 cm. *Photo: Bernisches Historisches Museum, Bern*

8–1 THAILAND. Contemporary silver necklace worn by Yao Yin, Meo and Karen tribal women in the northern hill area, and in Burma. Three increasing sized units are each forged from a separate round wire to a frontal thickness of 2 mm. Two rings hold them in a slightly overlapping position. Their flat surfaces are completely *flat chased* in curved lines with floral, butterfly, bird, and fish motifs. Borders are stamped. The difference between chasing liner tool and graver engraving (besides the difference in tools) is that in the former, no metal is removed from the furrow, but instead it is depressed and a ghost pattern of the lines appears as a ridge on the reverse side; while in the latter, metal is removed and no trace of the line appears on the back. Col.: Dietlind Bock-Meinardus. *Photo: Oppi*

8–3 TOIVO J. SUURONEN, Finland. Brooch with ivory relief carved entirely with engraver's tools. Finished by rubbing with levigated pumice, then mounted in a silver frame. Size 2 × 2½ in. *Photo: Ragnar Damström*

tools, in about the 11th century B.C., the art of engraving as we know it now can be said to have really begun. The knowledge of hardening and tempering helped reduce the chance of a tool chipping and splintering, and engraved embellishment became more controlled and refined.

The ancestor of our current engraving tools is the chisel, which works on the principle of the *wedge*. Cutting action occurs in these tools because by applying forward pressure on the tool, held at an angle to the surface worked, the sharpened wedge-shaped working end can easily be made to gain entry and penetrate the metal. Specialized chiseling tools such as gravers were developed to satisfy the need to cut smaller scale incisions into small objects and jewelry for decorative effect.

Engraving is used today mainly as a means of decorating metal, but gravers can still be applied to the same materials engraved by primitive man, as well as to new materials such as plastic. It is a skilled technique that includes special branches such as lettering, and craftspersons exist who practice only this. Any person who has patience for and enjoys highly controlled techniques, with practice can become, in time, a skilled engraver.

THE USES OF ENGRAVING ON JEWELRY

Engraving owes its basic appeal to the brilliant play of light and dark, the contrasts between the parent metal's surface and the incised grooves on it. The most beautiful is *bright cut engraving* which takes advantage of the variety of relatively shallow groove width cuts possible with engraving tools; the use of slanting cuts at different angles; and subtly changing contours that reflect light with every change of direction.

Any design composed of lines and points, or that can be done by small-scale carving is possible by engraving. Such designs can be scriptatory, representational, totally abstract or textural patterns, reliefs or intaglios.

A conventional, ever popular form of engraving is the monogram and inscriptions on objects and jewelry, often

8–5 LINCOLN WALLACE (Tlingit), Alaska, U.S.A. The Tlingit Indians of Alaska use woven blankets or ceremonial robes (*chilkat*) on which appear animal forms, heads, and abstract shapes that have symbolic meanings and form family crests. The designs engraved here are based on such subjects. Ø 2½ in. *Photo: Courtesy the U. S. Department of the Interior, Indian Arts and Crafts Board*

8–6 TOIVO J. SUURONEN, Finland. Silver belt buckle in the form of a monogram. Pierced sheet metal is given the appearance of relief by means of engraving tools. Size 4½ × 4¼ in. *Photo: Courtesy Suuronen*

8–7 TUAREG, SOUTH MOROCCO and MAURETANIA. Contemporary man's ring, silver, engraved, with enamel inlay. *Photo: Matti Pietinen*

8–4 GELI JOHNSTON, England. "H is for Hoop." Silver, gold, and ivory pendant. The reverse side is engraved "This is for you," and stamped with hallmarks. This pendant in the form of a child's school slate is a sandwich of two ivory frames riveted together to hold the 0.66 mm thick silver sheet. Width 39 mm; length 59 mm. *Photo: Ray Carpenter, courtesy Electrum Gallery, London*

for sentimental or for commemorative purposes. Gravers are used in the traditional manner of setting faceted stones, a highly specialized use of the technique. A purely practical use of engraving tools is the removal of surplus solder on jewelry. Gravers are used for engraving details such as a line pattern or figure on inlaid metals or other inlaid materials. Inlays can also be modeled or carved with gravers. Gravers are used to carve details in intaglio in dies, another specialized skill called die-sinking. Engraving can be the initial step utilized with other techniques. Engraved lines can, for instance, be filled with niello, and this, indeed, is one of the earliest decorative uses of engraving. By the technique of *basse taille* (French, "low-cut") enameling, a metal surface is engraved with a design in relief which is then completely covered with a single, transparent enamel whose color varies with the depth of the engraving. Transparent liquid resins can be substituted for enamel and after hardening, if the design calls for such treatment, can be leveled with the metal and polished. Gravers are used to raise a stitch or small spike on metal, against which a wire or sheet edge can be positioned and held during soldering. These are but a few of the uses of the engraving tools.

The technique of *flat chasing* employing a *thin edged tracer punch* to make lines resembles engraving, but the difference lies in the fact that in engraving, metal is removed, but in chasing, no metal is removed, and the line therefore has a different character. (See Photo 8–1, p. 283.)

ENGRAVING TOOLS AND ACCESSORIES

LIGHT SOURCE AND MAGNIFICATION DEVICES

Engraving in jewelry work proceeds slowly, and is generally small in scale. It is therefore essential to work by a good, shadowless, natural north light or diffused electric light that for right-handed people falls on the work from the upper left and can be adjusted to need.

Even persons having naturally good vision find that doing small work is simplified by using a suitable magnifying device which facilitates watching the progress of the tool, and allows close inspection of the results. The use of a magnifier also reduces eye strain of which the worker may be unaware. When selecting a lens, the normal distance between the eye and the work in the working situation must be taken into account, as well as the degree of magnification desired.

The *laws of optics* follow these principles: As the power of magnification of a lens *increases,* the working distance, field of view, depth of the field of focus, and the diameter of the lens *decrease.* This can be illustrated by a sample table on p. 286.

To leave the hands free, the *magnifier* used must be a type that does not have to be hand held during work. The usual types are worn attached before the eyes by an eyeglass-holding device; stand on the workbench surface between the eye and the work; or are suspended above the work. They are all adjustable to easily permit convenient positioning. A useful standing type is a *bench magnifier* with a 3X lens having a diameter of 2.5 in (6.35 cm), mounted on a heavy base that holds the lens 3.5 in (8.89 cm) above the work.

In wide use are *binocular loupes* fitted into a frame held on the head by a padded, adjustable headband. If necessary, this type can fit over eyeglasses. The lenses allow magnification viewing with both eyes, and are available in powers of 1.5–3.3X, giving a range of in-focus depth from 4–8 in (10.2–20.3 cm). Also used are lightweight, *clip-on telesights* that are attached to eyeglasses, and are hinged so they can be flipped upward when not in use. For those who do not wear glasses there is a type attached to lensless eyeglass frames because of the convenience in supporting them in this way. All magnifying devices can also

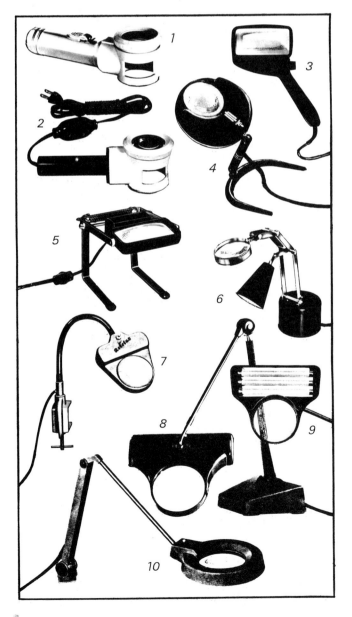

8–8 *ILLUMINATED WORK MAGNIFIERS*

1. *Hand magnifier*, battery powered, provides shadowless illumination on the 2 in field viewing area; fixed focus 1⅛ in distance nonachromatic lens; 5X magnification.
2. *Hand magnifier*, electric line powered, same lens as above.
3. *Bausch and Lomb hand magnifier* with 4 × 2 in rectangular lens having a 9 in focus; equipped with miniature 110 volt bulb and heat sensor that turns power off if overheating occurs; lens ground and polished ophthalmic glass.
4. *Standing magnifier*, round lens. All standing magnifiers have adjustable-position lenses, and leave both hands free for work.
5. *Standing magnifier*, rectangular 4 × 2 in lens, adjustable from 1–6 in above the work, and tiltable to any angle; 7 watt 115 volt bulb; aluminum stand folds for storage.
6. *Magnalite illuminated lamp* with separately mounted and adjustable magnifying lens and light; arm extends to a 12 in max.; stands anywhere on the worktable.
7. *Circular illuminated magnifier* with fluorescent cold-light tube lights; lens mounted on flexible gooseneck; fixed to bench by a single clamp.
8. *Circular large-field lens illuminated magnifier* available with a 3½, 4½, or 8X dioptic lens, 120 mm Ø, mounted in a universal swivel joint; carrying arm 350 mm; available with bench clamp or bench stand foot. (*Fischer*)
9. *Reverse view of the former lamp* showing the placement of the three fluorescent tube lights.
10. *Circular illuminated magnifying lamp*, using 22 watt circular fluorescent tube light that surrounds the lens; feed pipe extended length 10.5 mm; supplied with workbench clamp. (*Fischer*)

Lens Power, Focus Depth, and Working Distance

Power of Lens	Depth of Focus		Working Distance	
	Inches	Centimeters	Inches	Centimeters
1.5X	6.0	15.24	20	50.8
1.75X	5.5	13.97	14	35.5
2X	5.0	12.7	11	27.9
2.5X	4.0	10.16	10.0	25.4
3X	3.5	8.89	5.0	12.7
3.3X	3.0	7.62	4.0	10.1
4X	2.5	6.35	2.5	6.3
5X	2.0	5.08	2.0	5.08
7X	1.5	3.81	1.5	3.8
8X	1.25	3.17	1.2	3.0
10X	1.0	2.54	1.0	2.5

be used for other close work: correcting faults; inspecting condition of the work in progress; or working with stones and their settings.

An *eye loupe* is a single lens (monocle) mounted in a cylindrical, black plastic frame. Because its lenses fall in the area of large magnification, they are generally not used for work in progress, but are used more often for inspection. Monocular eye loupes for persons with normal vision can be hand held before one eye, screwed into the eye like a monocle, or held in place by a headspring that passes around the forehead and acts as a clip. *Spectacle loupes,* used by persons who must wear eyeglasses, can be clamped to the eyeglass frame, and swing up and out of the way when not needed. Other forms of magnifiers used for inspection are available, some with built-in illumination. To prevent eyeglasses and lenses from fogging because of perspiration, mix equal parts of water, denatured alcohol, and glycerine and apply this with a cloth to the lens.

WORK SURFACES AND HOLDING DEVICES

Engraving is possible with the work kept completely immobilized, but generally it is desirable to be able to move and control its direction when a change of work angle is necessary. The need for mobility depends on the work's size, shape, material, and the direction and type of lines being engraved.

SIMPLE HOLDING SYSTEMS

In the simplest engraving situation, the work is braced on a flat surface simply by hand pressure. That surface should be one that will not let the object slip, and that allows it a degree of maneuverability when necessary. *Dampened leather* with the nap side up is sometimes used. Large, dimensional, shaped work can be held on a *leather sandbag,* the bag first covered by a soft chamois to prevent scratching when the work is turned. A ring can be held on a paper-wrapped *ring mandrel* onto which it is tightly jammed to prevent its slipping during work, or it can be held by the leather-lined jaws of a *ring clamp.* Flat or slightly dimensional work, depending on its shape, can be secured in a *clamp,* or *cemented to shellac or pitch* spread on a board and melted with a torch. A *pitch bowl* can also be used.

A device suited to holding jewelry and small objects is a *shellac stick* consisting of a horizontal wooden disc whose surface is spread with a ⅛–¼ in (0.32–0.64 cm) layer of shellac, to which is attached a handle that can be hand held or braced against a bench pin. The shellac is heated to soften it, and the warmed work is pressed into it. The shellac is allowed to cool and harden, which can be hastened by plunging it into cold water. To remove the object, warm the shellac and pry the work off, or while the shellac is cold tap the disc with a *mallet,* and the blow will usually release the work. The solvent for adhering shellac particles is denatured alcohol.

Small work can also be secured in various types of *clamps.* One made for engraving or for holding other kinds of work in progress is a split-faced, vise-type *peg clamp* which has an attached wood handle that can be braced in the V-cut of a bench pin. In its face are many drilled holes into which loose metal pegs can be inserted in positions that conform to the size or shape of the work. The two faces are then brought together to make the pegs grip the work, and their position secured by a thumbscrew. Similar separate *peg-holed faceplates* can be mounted on two rectangular pieces of wood through which pass two threaded rods. Thumbscrews tighten the wood pieces so that the mounted pegs hold the work.

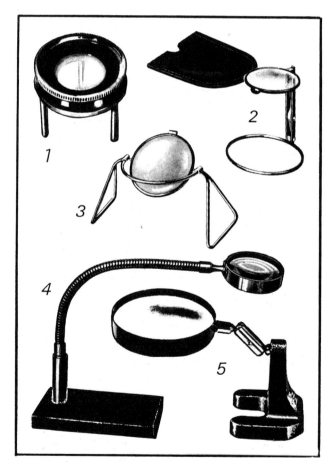

8-9 WORK MAGNIFIER LENSES, PORTABLE AND BENCH MODELS
1. *Three-footed standing loupe, 6X magnification, Ø 28 mm. (Fischer)*
2. *Pocket lens, mounted on a collapsible stand; with leather case.*
3. *Tiltable pocket lens on wire stand that collapses flat; available in Ø 40, 45, and 50 mm. (Fischer)*
4. *Work magnifier lens mounted on a gooseneck flexible arm, with heavy base.*
5. *Peer bench work magnifier lens, with 3X magnification, 2½ in Ø lens having a working distance of 3½ in; attached to a ball joint arm which allows lens movement in any direction; on a heavy horseshoe base; total height 3½ in.*

8–10 OPTICAL DEVICES

1. *Bi-convex, Plexiglas-mounted single, pocket lens,* 2½X power.
2. *Doublet bi-convex lens,* highly corrected, distortion-free magnifier in metal mount, power 12X.
3. *Single-lens eye loupe,* available with lenses having 4–10X power, with working distances of 2½–1 in respectively.
4. *Triple-lens loupe* used for critical close-up inspection, with working distance of 1 in, power 10X.
5. *Spring metal head clip* attachable to eye loupe for use when two-hand operations must be performed.
6. *Binocular loupes* with ground and polished lenses, providing three-dimensional magnified viewing for both eyes, with adaptable headband. Will fit over eyeglasses. Available in focus ranges of 4–20 in, 3½–1½X powers respectively. Auxiliary lenses can be added for additional magnification.
7. *Clip-on telesights* attachable to eyeglasses, with prismatic lenses, in lightweight frames, flip forward when not in use, weight 2 oz. Available with 3–1¾X power, having working distances with a range of 5–13½ in respectively.
8. *Single-lens spectacle loupes* that can be clamped to eyeglass frames. The lenses swing upward when not in use. Available in 10–1.7X powers, with a working distance range of 1¼–6 in respectively.
9. *Extension tube miniature pocket telescope* with three powers, 40, 50, and 60X, used for close-up examination of distant objects such as those in cases in museums.

8–11 ENGRAVER'S WORK-HOLDING DEVICES AND ACCESSORIES

1. *Half-sphere engraver's bowl* of cast iron, meant to hold pitch to which work is anchored, Ø 140–270 mm; weight 2–8 kg. Used for engraving large objects that cannot be accommodated by an engraver's block.
2. *Engraver's and die-sinker's ball* with single screw-on clamp, weight 1.7 kg.
3. *Four-clamp engraver's and die-sinker's ball;* Ø 85 or 115 mm; weight 4 or 8 kg.
4. *Leather cushions* or engraver's ball pads, used to provide a rest for engraver's bowls and blocks; round 12–18 cm, full 8–22 cm, cylinder 12–18 cm diameters.
5. The *Victor engraving block* with adaptor plates, one fixed, one pivoting, with 3½ in wide work-holding capacity and deep-throated jaws, sphere Ø 5 in, and weight 15 lb. The turntable revolves on radial and thrust bearings which eliminate all side shake, and allow response to the slightest touch. Sold with attachment accessories described in 7.
6. *Universal work holder* for holding small, irregularly shaped work to be engraved, filed, etc., and usable with most engraving block accessories. The handle can be removed and the holder inserted in a bench vise.
7. *Engraving block accessory set,* including, clockwise from upper left: small, bent, rubber-covered pin; large, bent, rubber-covered pin; locket holder; button holder; large, straight, rubber-covered pin; concave pin; triangular pin; watch holder; small, straight, rubber-covered pin.
8. *Extra accessories,* clockwise from upper left: Victor 4-in-1 pins; ring holder for engraving inside rings; button holder; male pin.

THE DIE-SINKER'S BALL

Similar to the above in mechanical principle is the professional, weighted *diemaker's ball* used by *die sinkers,* professional craftspeople who engrave steel dies in intaglio. In all of these, the round lower portion rests in a *sandbag, felt ring,* or on a *piece of wood* with a matching depression, and the weight of the ball keeps it from moving too freely. At the top of the diemaker's ball is a vertical, deep, wide groove into which the die block or work mounted on a board spread with shellac, sealing wax, or pitch, is placed and held by one or two thumbscrews that seize the board edgewise and grip it.

THE ENGRAVER'S BLOCK OR BALL

The most versatile holding device used by engravers is the professional *engraver's block* or *ball,* which is a form of vise, and a precision-made tool. It consists of two main parts. At the top is a crown holding a vertically split chuck that when closed has a diameter of 3–5 in (7.62–12.7 cm) or more. Its jaws open into two equal, semicircular halves that form a deep, vertical throat. The distance the jaws can be moved apart is controlled by turning a screw, on which the jaws are mounted, with a *hand key* that is used to tighten and release the jaws. Under normal circumstances, the circumference of the tightened jaws is small enough to permit them to be gripped and partially encircled with the fingers of the left hand and thus control the movement of the whole block.

Rotation of the position of the upper portion with the jaws locked on the work is made possible by the fact that the crown at its horizontal division is mounted on bearings in the ball below, so that the crown can be rotated by slight hand pressure around a horizontal axis like a turntable while the lower half of the block is immobile. The bearing mount is rigid enough to keep the crown free of unwanted movement or looseness. Work position can be easily and gradually changed *in one plane,* which allows the forward stroke of an engraving cut to be easily fol-

8–12 MARTTA LEHTINEN *using an engraver's ball placed on a circular leather cushion, in the workshop of Kultasepänliike Ossian Hopea, Porvoo, Finland. Photo: Oppi*

lowed through, essential for engraving. The lower part of the ball remains in one position, but because its surface is polished, when necessary it can be easily moved on its supporting cushion to change the angle of the work plane. At its largest diameter, the engraver's ball is 5–7 in (12.7–17.8 cm) and its total weight of 18–28 lb makes it stable on its cushion support.

The crown face has many drilled holes, and in some models, an *adaptor plate* with a greater number of holes than in the basic face can be fitted into it by pegs. In this case, one of the adaptors has two lower engaging pegs and is therefore stationary, while the other, with one peg, can be pivoted. This feature simplifies their adjustment to each other when inserting irregularly shaped work. Into these holes can be inserted variously shaped attachments and accessories designed to grip work having a variety of contours and sizes by its edges.

ENGRAVING BLOCK ACCESSORIES All *accessories* used with the engraver's block are held to the crown face by attached pins whose diameters fit snugly into those of the drilled face holes. These small work-holding accessories are made in shapes that experience has shown are most useful. They are generally used in opposing sets of two or more, depending on the need. Among them are vertical cylinders with grooves or side notches all around the cylinder, triangular pins, cone-shaped pins, shaped holding jigs with rubber sleeves to keep work from being scarred, ring holding clamps, and others.

In cases where the work is smaller than the distance between pegged accessories, it can be temporarily cemented to a larger sheet of copper spread with shellac.

Besides their use in engraving, such holding devices can also be used to hold work on the block when doing chip work or carving, and in special circumstances when setting stones, filing, sawing, and polishing.

THE BURIN: THE ENGRAVER'S BASIC TOOL

The general name for an engraving tool is a *burin* (from the Old English *borian,* "to bore"), and it is also known as a *graver* (from the Anglo-Saxon *grafan,* "to dig or excavate"). Gravers are also called *scorpers,* especially when used for purposes other than engraving line patterns.

The graver consists of two parts: the metal rod or *shaft* bearing the cutting end, and the *handle* into which the other shaft end or tang is inserted.

Since the power to make an engraving tool perform comes from the forward pressure on the tool from the cupped palm of the hand (and not from the impact force of a hammer stroke, as with chisels and punches), the tool must be comfortable to hold and push. This is why the burin's wooden handle is rounded. Handle shapes in mushroom, pear, or round forms can be chosen according to preference. The choice of handle size depends on the hand size of the engraver—small hands require short handles, and large hands, longer ones. Completely round handles are used on burins that are bent or *heeled.* When the burin shaft is straight or only slightly heeled, a handle with the lower third of the handle's hemispherical shape cut off is used, held with its flat lower surface parallel to the work. This shape allows the burin's cutting edge to make a more shallow angle with the metal, permitting smoother cutting action. It also eliminates the chance of the handle's edge catching on the metal. If this portion of the handle is removed by the craftsperson, trimming should take place *after* the metal burin has been inserted to assure its correct relationship with the cutting edge.

Gravers are normally too long for use when purchased. Shortening can take place at the tang end, the cutting end, or both. The *tang* is the tapered extension of the burin shaft opposite the cutting end, and is inserted into the handle. To shorten the tang, place the tool upright in a bench vise with the amount to be removed protruding above its jaws. While wearing an *eye shield,* strike off the surplus with a hammer, in a direction away from you. It should break off evenly. Restore the taper of the tang by grinding and then by filing. In some cases, regrinding the tang taper is all that is needed to size the tool.

To prepare the handle to receive the tang, place it in a vise with its narrow end upright. This end is encompassed by a metal ferrule to strengthen it and prevent its splitting when the tang is forced in. Drill a hole straight into the center of the handle end, its diameter slightly *smaller* than that of the tang at its widest point. Remove the handle and grip the graver shaft vertically in the vise, tang end up. Position the handle above it, guide the tang taper partially into the hole, and hammer the handle straight down until the whole tang is within the handle. Burins can also be purchased already mounted in handles.

BURIN OR GRAVER SHAPES

The burin's *shaft* is made of a rod of a good grade of tool steel which when hardened and tempered is capable of engraving all metals normally used by the jeweler. In cross section (relative to the work position of the cutting end) it can be rectangular, square, diamond-shaped, triangular, oval, or round. Each of these forms gives a differently shaped cutting tip, which in turn results in cuts having different characteristics. All graver shapes are available in several sizes or widths of cutting end.

Flat: This graver is rectangular in cross section, with a flat cutting edge that makes flat-bottomed cuts. *Scorpers,* also rectangular, are used for purposes of metal removal

8–13 ENGRAVER TOOL HANDLES
These hardwood handles have steel ferrules to prevent splitting and add strength. Shapes are chosen for comfort, hand size, tool length or angle to the work. *Courtesy Karl Fischer, Pforzheim.*

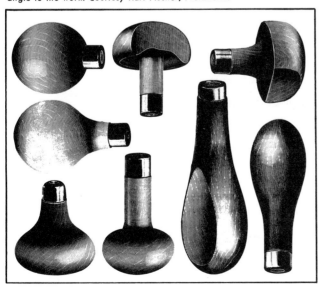

Graver Shapes, Cutting Angles and Faces

Graver Type	Normal Cutting Face Angle	Number of Set-off Faces	Angle of Set-off Face
Flat	30-45°	0	0
Square	30-45°	2	5-10°
Lozenge	30-45°	2	5-10°
Onglette or point	30°	2	0
Knife	30-45°	2	5-10°
Spitsticker	60-65°	0	0
Dotter	30-45°	0	0
Round	60-65°	0	0
Oval	60-65°	0	0
Liner	30-45°	0	0

other than engraving. They make flat cuts, and are used to remove larger amounts of metal.

Square: An equilateral square in shape, it is held in a position such that its lower corner cuts the metal.

Lozenge: This equilateral rhombus, diamond-shaped with two acute and two obtuse angles, makes a V-shaped cut with an acute angle.

Onglette or point: Pointed in shape, its width forms an outward-swelling curve, unlike the *knife* whose sides are straight, and it makes V-shaped cuts.

Knife: The very acutely angled triangular-shaped point makes deep, narrow, V-shaped cuts.

Spitsticker: (*Spitz* is German for "point.") The point of this drop-shaped graver is used especially to outline designs. (The term is also used for a small, pointed chisel used for making very small, sloping cuts between the stones of a setting.)

Dotter: The rectangular shaft is flat at the top and rounded at the bottom and is used for making dots or round-bottomed cuts.

Round: The shaft is flat at the top and rounded at the bottom where it cuts rounded grooves. It may also have a completely round shaft.

Oval: The shaft is completely oval, and makes U-shaped cuts.

Liners: Liners were originally made for the photoengraving industry where they are still used. In jewelry engraving, they are used to create a variety of linear and textural effects, such as the Florentine finish. (See p. 296.) Their cutting edge is flat and regularly grooved with lines that run lengthwise on the surface below the cutting edge so that the grooves remain after any shaping and polishing. The lines are made in varying numbers, degrees of fineness, and width.

Beaders or perloirs: In setting a faceted stone, first a knife-edge graver is used to raise a spur toward the stone, which is then rounded to a ball shape and pressed with a beader or perloir down onto the stone's girdle to hold the stone in place. This is a round punch with a half-dome hollow end, mounted with a graver's handle.

GRAVER SIZES

Each graver shape is manufactured in a series of width sizes, from narrow to wide, and each size has a number. For example, *flat gravers* are available in size numbers 36–49; *round gravers* in numbers 50–63, etc. The lower the number, the narrower is the graver. Certain sizes and widths are favored for particular work, such as stone setting.

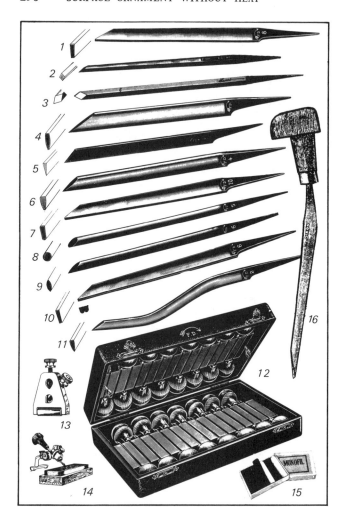

8–14 GRAVER SHAPES
1. *Flat.*
2. *Square.*
3. *Lozenge.*
4. *Onglette or point.*
5. *Knife.*
6. *Spitsticker.*
7. *Dotter.*
8. *Round.*
9. *Oval.*
10. *Double round.*
11. *Spitsticker, double bent.*
12. *Set of 30 gravers of the basic shapes in several different sizes, with handles, contained in a box.*
13. *Graver sharpener having two angle openings and roller that passes over the oilstone.*
14. *Graver sharpener, Crocker pattern with rest, can be set at any angle by turning the index.*
15. *Monofil, a wax crayon composition that is used to fill engraved lines with any of several colors, then polished smooth with the metal surface.*
16. *Graver with handle.*
Courtesy Karl Fischer, Pforzheim.

8–16 *Right:* KULTAKESKUS OY, Hämeenlinna, Finland, manufacturer. Cuff links of 18K gold engraved in perpendicular directions with lining gravers. *Photo: Courtesy Kultakeskus Oy*

8–15 *Left:* BÖRJE RAJALIN, Finland, designer; manufacturer Kalevala Koru, Helsinki. Silver cuff links engraved in parallel, straight lines. *Photo: Pietinen*

PREPARING A GRAVER FOR USE

TRIMMING A GRAVER

In use, the graver is held in the right hand, grasped by the thumb opposing the index and middle fingers, with the other fingers resting on or near the work. The point projects beyond the end of the thumb for ½–¾ in (1.3–3.4 cm). When purchased, the standard graver is usually too long. As hand sizes vary and the amount of this distance is important for control, the length of the graver usually requires shortening to make the total tool length, including

the handle, about 3½–4 in (9–10 cm). As mentioned, if the amount to be removed is small, it can be taken from the tang end. The graver is highly tempered and brittle, and can be easily reduced in length from the cutting end by breaking it off, following the same procedure as described above for shortening the tang. The cutting end must then be reground to restore the point.

Initial reshaping of the cutting face is done while holding the tool at the correct angle, first to a *rotating grinding wheel* that is coarse rather than fine because these build up less frictional heat. Prolonged grinding causes metal to overheat and may result in a loss of tool temper and point

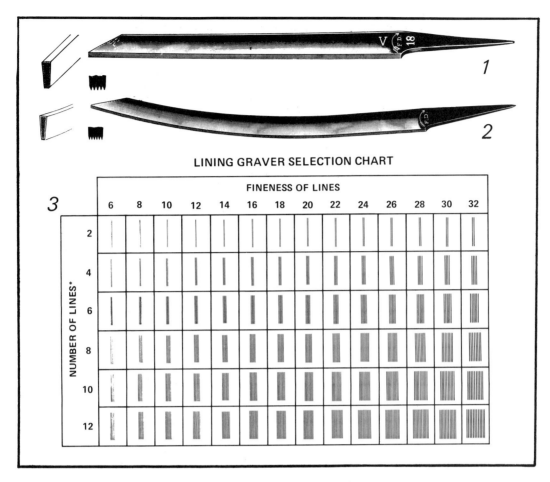

LINING GRAVER SELECTION CHART

8–17 *LINING GRAVERS FOR CREATING A FLORENTINE FINISH*
1. *Straight.*
2. *Bent.*
3. *Lining graver selection chart.* The number of lines shown represents those in most common use.

strength, and should be avoided. Cool the tool at frequent intervals by dipping it in cold water. Final shaping is done with a fine-grained grinding wheel.

MAKING THE SET-OFF FACES

The first step in preparing the graver's cutting point is usually to grind away a small angular portion of the *upper* part of the graver shaft which does no cutting. This is done with a *soft emery wheel* for a distance of up to 1 in (2.54 cm). The purpose of this removal is to present less metal to the whetstone to be ground when sharpening and reshaping, thus reducing the time needed for these processes. It also allows better visibility of the tool point during cutting.

For certain gravers (see Table, p. 289, "Graver Shapes, Cutting Angles and Faces") it is then usual to cut away a flat portion from each sloping plane of the undersurface of the graver's point to make what is called a *set-off angle*. Its purpose is to prevent the point from digging into the metal too deeply when the graver is held in a normal position on flat work. Because the tool can then be held more steeply, grasping it with the fingers is easier when working on concave surfaces. The set-off also prevents handle contact with the work and reduces the possibility of point breakage.

It is usual to form the set-off faces before making the angle of the cutting face. As the Table shows, only gravers having flat-planed cutting surfaces are given a set-off. Set-off faces on curved cutting points would destroy those cutting shapes. To compensate for the lack of set-off on such tools, they are *bellied* (see below). On most gravers, the set-off is short, and its angle can vary approximately 5–10° from the horizontal, depending on the particular graver, whether a flat or concave metal surface is being engraved, and other variables. Greater set-off angles, up to 45°, are sometimes used on concave surfaces. Generally speaking, however, the larger the set-off angle, the more difficulty there is in being able to observe the cutting edge during work. It is of particular importance that the cut-off planes be highly polished since these planes make contact with the metal during cutting, and any roughness impedes the graver's progress and may cause the raising of a burr which then must be removed. When grinding a pair of set-off faces on a graver, take care that the resulting central ridge at the point where the two planes meet is lined up with and is a continuation of the original lower shaft ridge. Normally, the two set-off faces are equal, but there are exceptions, as when *heeling* a graver (see p. 293).

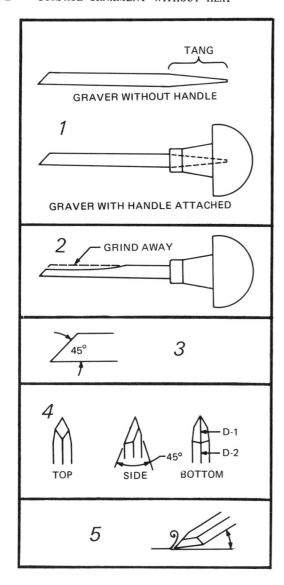

SHARPENING THE CUTTING FACE

Gravers can, of course, be hand held when their cutting face is sharpened and polished. (See Table p. 289 for suggested angles for each basic shape.) Accuracy in maintaining the correct angle and a flat plane on the cutting face, both essential, is difficult and requires long experience. Where this is lacking, the best procedure is to use a *graver sharpener* device, of which several types are available. These devices hold the graver rigidly at a chosen, preset, constant angle to the whetstone.

WHETSTONES, OILSTONES

The graver sharpener is used in conjunction with a *whetstone* or *oilstone*. Whetstones in general use attritional rubbing to sharpen or *keen* and polish any metal tool that

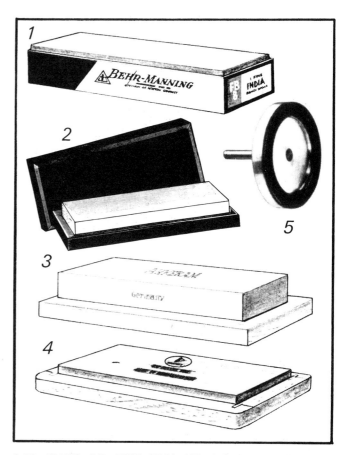

8-18 TRIMMING A GRAVER

1. To prepare a graver for use, select a handle shape that is comfortable for your hand. Small hands generally use short handles, large hands long handles. Drill a hole into the handle somewhat smaller than the tang section, straight into the vise-held handle. If the graver, which is brittle, must be trimmed to a required length, one way of doing this is to place it in a vise with the surplus projecting above the vise jaw level, then strike it off with a hammer. Place the graver in a vise, tang end up, press the handle over the tang and hand force it into the hole, then hammer the handle down until the entire tang is inside it. Handles with cut-off lower portions must be oriented in relation to the shape of the graver so that portion is at the bottom.

2. To reduce the area that must be polished on the cutting face of the point, first grind away the upper portion of the graver at the point end, for a distance of about one inch, unless the graver is a type that will have set-off faces.

3. Grind the graver *cutting face* on grindstones to the appropriate angle according to the requirements of the various graver types, as given in the table.

4. For gravers that require *set-off angle faces*, these must be ground off *before* grinding off the top. The cuts of the set-off angle (D-1) must be true with the existing center line at the graver bottom (D-2).

5. Gravers with set-off angle faces allow their use at a greater angle to the work, thus reducing the chance of making excessively deep cuts.

Courtesy Swest Inc.

8-19 GRAVER AND OTHER TOOL GRINDING AND SHARPENING STONES

1. *India bench oilstone,* has a coarse grit on one side, fine grit on the other side, 6 × 2 × 1 in., packaged.
2. *Arkansas bench stone,* permanently mounted in a hardwood box, 6 × 2 × ¾ in.
3. *Arkeram bench stone,* made of a combination of powdered Arkansas stone and a ceramic composition, fired for solidification. Has a cutting ability somewhat more than the natural Arkansas stone. Boxed, 6 × 2 × 1 in.
4. *Ruby bench stone,* a very hard artificial abrasive stone. Can be dressed and resurfaced by rubbing two such stones together with some boron carbide powder sprinkled between them. Boxed, 8 × 2 × ½ in.
5. *Diamond-charged graver sharpening lap wheel,* for use on tungsten carbide gravers, but not for soft metals; 2 in Ø, 3/16 in arbor mount.

requires a sharp edge or point. They may be artificial or natural. Some are used dry and others are lubricated with water or oil.

An *Indian oilstone* is an artificial whetstone made of an aluminum oxide abrasive. It is sold already impregnated with oil and therefore requires only a small additional amount of oil to keep the minute metal particles afloat and to prevent *glazing*—the impregnation of the stone's pores with fine particles of metal removed from the tool when it is shaped or keened. Glazing is a cause of inefficient metal removal because the metal slips on the stone's surface. Oilstones are available in coarse and medium grit for cutting, and in fine for polishing. After some use, accumulated old oil should be washed off with a hot soap and water solution, and the stone should be allowed to dry before new oil is added. One drop of oil smoothed and spread with a finger is sufficient. Oil prevents edge burn when high friction occurs.

In good graver sharpening and polishing practice, an Indian oilstone is used first for sharpening, followed by a fine-grained *Arkansas stone* for polishing. This is a superior variety of novaculite, a very hard, fine-grained siliceous rock thought to be of sedimentary origin, found in the Ouachita Mountains in the state of Arkansas. Another suitable natural whetstone is the *Water of Ayr* or *Ayr stone* that comes from Ayr, Scotland, and is also called a *Scotch stone*. This is a fine-grained slate, used with water for the same purpose as an Arkansas stone. The slime released by attritional rubbing is wiped away with a damp sponge. If a graver is used directly after being prepared only by a rough stone, its point may quickly break.

To assure angle accuracy and flatness of the cutting face, both the whetstone and the graver must be on the *same level plane*. The best surface for this purpose is a sheet of *plate glass* on which both the whetstone and the graver held in the graver *sharpener* are placed, fixed at the necessary angle. The graver contacts the Indian oilstone over which surface it is moved up and back or in a figure eight until the cutting plane is flattened to the proper angle. It is then polished in the same way on the Arkansas stone.

Once the cutting face is polished, the set-off faces are polished and burrs removed with an extra fine emery cloth, or 4/0 emery paper placed flat on the plate glass sheet. Always move the graver on the abrasive in strokes *away* from the cutting edge, and at all costs avoid rounding the cutting angles which would make the tool unusable. Burrs can also be removed by forcing the graver point to penetrate a piece of hardwood. All the graver's cutting surfaces should now be bright and smooth. To achieve the brightest possible cut, after stoning, strop the tool on a *piece of leather* on which some *diamantine* (an artificial corundum) has been placed. Traditionally, graver sharpness and readiness is tested by touching the cutting edge to your thumbnail, on which it should catch. If instead it slips or skids off, its cutting edges are not sufficiently sharp. To resharpen a graver after it becomes dulled from use, replace it in the graver sharpener device and resharpen the cutting faces to the same angle as before. If the graver has set-off faces, these are sharpened first, then the top, and finally the cutting face, followed by burr removal.

Professional engravers have several sizes of each basic shape of graver, some straight, some heeled, some with shallow-angle cut-off faces, others with greater angles. Drastic graver shape alteration should not be necessary except for special circumstances.

HEELING A GRAVER

When it is necessary to cut a curve to the right or left, a graver will more easily cut in these directions if it is *heeled* or *beveled* toward the desired direction. A *bevel* is the slanting angle that one plane makes with another when it is not at a right angle. To bevel or heel a graver to favor the right or left when cutting, the set-off faces are made so that the shorter one faces the side of preference, and the longer one is on the other side. The cutting point is thus slightly canted in the direction of the desired side toward which it will naturally tend to gravitate when cutting the curve. A directionally heeled graver has the advantage that it produces a metal chip at the inside of the curve rather than at the front of the graver point, which allows the line being engraved to be seen more easily.

If in its forward movement a graver leaves a scratch before the cut, it is insufficiently heeled or bellied for the shape of the work.

BELLYING A GRAVER

The greater the angle of the set-off, the more difficult it is to see the cutting edge of the graver during work. Many engravers therefore find it advisable, especially when working on flat or concave surfaces, to *belly* or bend the forward end of the graver shaft near the point to a curve, instead of increasing the angle of the set-off. Bellying allows the position of the graver handle to be somewhat raised during flat work and therefore easier to grasp. Also, the cutting point can be lowered closer to concave work, and the set-off angle diminished, which makes for easier, smoother engraving.

To belly a graver, first remove it from the handle and rub the whole surface with soap to prevent the development of firescale which would otherwise form as the forward portion is heated to redness with a torch to anneal the metal. Avoid overheating which may destroy the metal's working qualities. Place the hot shaft, point down, into a ½ in (1.27 cm) deep hole drilled in a vise-held wood block. Grasp the tang end with pliers at the point where the shaft is complete in section, and bend it into the desired curve. The shaft will bend at the point where it emerges from the hole as this is where resistance ends. Be sure to insert the graver in the hole in the correct position in relation to the bend so that the point is properly aligned after bending. Alternately, the graver can be placed over a mandrel and struck with a wooden mallet. It can also be bent by holding it with two pliers, one on either side of the point of the bend, and applying pressure. Once a graver is bellied, it should be left that way. Bellied gravers are difficult to straighten.

In the process of annealing the graver to soften it for bending, it has lost its *temper*. To retemper it, polish the cutting end surfaces, smear them with a little oil (which makes it easier to see the color change), and heat the graver to a light straw color in the usual way before quenching it in water. Then reinsert the burin into the handle.

PREPARING THE WORKPIECE FOR ENGRAVING

SURFACES AND METALS ENGRAVED

Normally the metal surface to be engraved is smooth and flat, however, engraving can be done on surfaces with any curvature or texture. Ordinarily, before engraving, the object is finished and has its *final surface condition,* ranging from a bright mirror polish to a textured surface. Rough textured surfaces contrast visually with sharply engraved linear patterns.

Various degrees of resistance to the engraver's forward movement are encountered depending on metal hardness and the direction of crystalline structure. Gold, silver, copper, nickel, zinc, and their alloys are relatively soft and easily engraved. Titanium and steel, though hard, can also be engraved. Plastics such as Plexiglas can be engraved as well, although the burin leaves a slight burr on the line.

Japanese metalworkers engrave bonded laminates made of as many as 15 alternating layers of copper and shakudo alloy, or other combinations of metals. V-shaped or round-sectioned gravers are used to make angular or round-bottomed cuts into the laminate, the cuts varying in angle, width, and depth. Within each cut the varicolored, striated structure of the laminate is revealed, and the technique is used to create patterns. Postengraving coloring brings out the color differences of the metals in the laminate. The Japanese generic term for engraving or carving with gravers or chisels is *bori.* Gravers are also used to create relief or three-dimensional results. *Usu-niki-bori* = low relief; *chiu-niki-bori* = half relief; *atsu-niki-bori* = high relief; and *maru-bori* = carving with burins in the round.

TRANSFERRING A DESIGN TO METAL

To avoid scratching the undersurface of flat work held on a sandbag, place a clean *chamois* over the sandbag, or when other holding systems are used, glue a soft paper to the back of the workpiece with a water-soluble glue that can be removed later with warm water. Depending on whether the surface to be engraved is flat or curved, smooth or textured, several materials and methods can be used to directly draw, trace, or transfer a design directly to metal. (See Design Transfer to Metal, Chapter 4.)

Because it is difficult to see and follow a design line on a brightly polished metal surface, it is common practice before transferring a design to dull the metal's reflectivity by

finger-daubing the surface with a substance such as a paste made of yellow ochre and water (whiting or casein white paint could also be used). Once dry, lines can be drawn directly or traced onto this surface, and the substance is easily later washed away with water.

HOLDING AND USING A GRAVER

For those interested in engraving, which in its best form is the work of specialists, what follows can only be basic hints of manners of work. Much can also be learned about the uses and techniques of engraving from the examination under magnification of good samples of old or new engraved work, regardless of whether you find the subject or treatment suits contemporary taste.

The success of engraving depends on the *complete control* of the graver, achieved by the coordination of the hands and the wrist. To achieve such coordination, nothing replaces practice and experience. Take care! Loss of tool control can be the cause of nasty wounds to the left hand. Therefore, the manner of holding and using the graver is important. The beginning engraver is advised to practice holding the tool and making the basic cuts described below on a piece of scrap metal (usually copper). It is best, however, to use the same metal as that of the workpiece planned, since different metals vary in hardness, offer different degrees of resistance to cutting, and require varying degrees of pressure; the control learned on one may not translate immediately to another.

Hold the graver firmly, but not tightly, with the handle snug against the palm heel. About ½–¾ in (1.27–1.91 cm) of the cutting end should project beyond the thumb of the right hand which presses against the graver in opposition to the first two fingers, while the last two fingers rest on and slide over the metal surface. The right thumb rests on or near the metal. The wrist controls the upward, downward, and sideward movement of the graver as well as its angle of inclination, and its action is very important. Assuming that the work is mounted on an engraver's block, the left thumb may press against the right thumb as

8-20 KALEVALA KORU, Helsinki, manufacturer. Silver fibula with patterns engraved in the rockered line technique, modeled after a fibula found at Kekomäki, Finland. *Photo: Otso Pietinen, courtesy Kalevala Koru*

8-21 GELI JOHNSTON, England. Silver brooch with ivory. The half-timbered house, the ivory roof, and the garden wall are all engraved. *Photo: Geli Johnston*
▼

8-22 ENGLAND, ca. 1870. Victorian ornamental silver comb engraved with a great variety of line types and techniques. *Photo: Oppi*

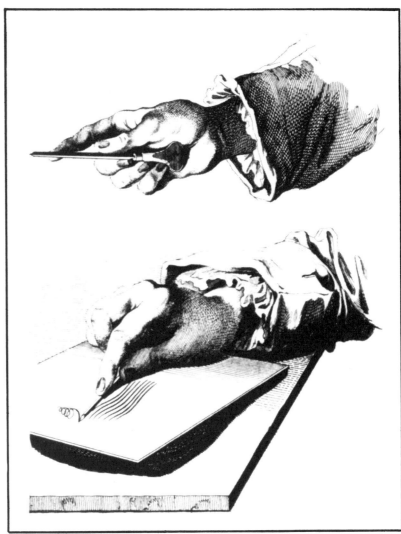

8-23 *THE CORRECT MANNER OF HOLDING AND USING AN ENGRAVING TOOL,* as illustrated in Diderot's *Encyclopédie.*

a means of helping to control the pressure exerted on the tool by the right hand. The other fingers of the left hand grip the ball crown, preferably below the working plane, to get them out of the way so they do not encounter the graver point should it slip.

Keep the tool lubricated during work to prolong its sharpness, to increase its cutting efficiency, and to increase the brightness of the cut. Touch it at intervals to a wad of absorbent cotton saturated with genuine or synthetic *wintergreen oil* or *mineral oil.*

STARTING AND ENDING A CUT

Place the graver on the metal at the point where the cut line begins and hold it at the angle that corresponds with the set-off angle. Move it forward, away from you, cutting into the metal by pressure. The start will always taper slightly where the tool enters the metal surface. As the tool cuts through the metal, it incises a groove and removes a thin strip or metal curl. The depth of the cut depends on the angle at which the graver's cutting point is held in relation to the metal plane. If the angle is too steep, the graver will dig into the metal and probably stop cutting; if too shallow, it will tend to skip. Sharp gravers incise a line nearly free of *burr,* the raised edge or ridge which can occur at either or both sides of the channel cut

in metal when using a sharp tool. According to the degree of sharpness and the shape of the graver's cutting end, the cut from each tool takes on a unique appearance. When a line of even width starts weakly, it can be made sharp by repassing the graver over that part of the line from the *reverse* direction, then bringing the graver up sharply at the starting point.

LENGTH OF CUT

The length of a cut is as long as can be efficiently accomplished in *one continuous movement*—usually about ½ in (1.27 cm) for the beginner. An experienced engraver can carry a cut forward for a longer distance. If a line must be made in segments of several strokes, as is often the case, it should proceed in the same cut, at the same depth, while the tool is held at the same angle to the metal as before. In this way, one cut merges imperceptibly into the last.

WIDTH OF CUT

To widen a line, rotate the graver on its axis to a greater angle than used the first time, then pass over it for a second time. Lines can also be made wider by cutting them more deeply into the metal, or by using a wider tool in the same cut. Or, several cuts can be made alongside each other. A flat graver can be run in a narrow line to widen it. Areas can be removed to a certain width by making two separate, parallel cuts, and then using a *scorper* to remove the metal between them. The same can be done when the aim is to remove the metal ground around a figure. First cut an outline, then remove the ground with a flat graver or scorper. The ground can be left plain or can be textured.

SHAPE AND DEPTH OF CUT

The shape of a cut depends first of all on the tool used. The degree of depth and the angle, upright or canted to one side, at which the tool is held act as variables for any given tool. Generally speaking, flat-pointed gravers produce flat-bottomed cuts; round-ended gravers, round-bottomed cuts; and knife, lozenge, diamond or square gravers make V-shaped grooves with different degrees of slope. When the depth of a cut is uniform, the sides are parallel.

ROCKERING AND ROLLING

Rockered lines, also called *wriggled lines* or *tremolo engraving,* are relatively simple to make by alternately and rapidly rotating a graver from side to side—causing it to bite alternately left and right—from one corner to another as it progresses forward. This action which can be done with flat or round gravers, creates a zigzag linear effect, as regular as the hand motion has been regular, and as wide as the tool width. The degree of fineness of the effect depends on the amount of forward pressure and the angle at which the graver is held. Rockered lines are sometimes used to fill a figure with a texture.

Rolling a cut, also called *shading,* is done to make a groove that starts at a point, widens gradually to its greatest width, and then returns gradually to a point. This is done with a vertically held graver that makes a V-shaped groove. Start with a shallow cut that gradually deepens and widens by rolling the hand to one side, then gradually straighten it until it reaches the vertical position again at the terminating point.

CURVED CUTS

Curved cuts are more easily made than straight cuts. They are best made with bellied or heeled gravers. The curve is produced by coordinating the forward cutting action with the simultaneous turning action of the block. At the start of the line, push the graver forward while leaning on the right thumb which acts as a pivoting point for all curved cuts since the graver moves around it. With the left hand, gradually turn the metal toward the right as the graver moves left following the line. It is generally easier to turn the work to accommodate the direction of the line than to make a drastic change in the position of the graver, which would be necessary if the work were fixed. Moving the work with the left hand while graving with the right also allows the possibility of making longer cuts in one movement. Practice teaches coordination of these two movements.

HATCHING AND STIPPLING

By massing and repeating lines to cover an area, various textural effects are possible. Single lines can be made in parallel series, their distance apart varying from large to

small, and their depth, from shallow to deep. *Crosshatching* consists of two series of parallel lines, one traversing the other. The angle at which this occurs can range from right to oblique, the latter called *diagonal hatching. Stippling* effects are done by using pointed gravers and placing small dots or short lines closely together.

8–24 TUAREG, SOUTH MOROCCO. Silver ankle bracelet (qelqal) worn in pairs by nomadic Tuaregs who travel between Mauretania, Algeria, and Morocco. The engraved geometric patterns are typical of the traditional nonfigurative designs used in this area by Muslims whose religion precludes the representation of human and animal forms. *Photo: Oppi*

FLORENTINE FINISH

The *Florentine finish* is made with a *liner.* Its effect is that of a network of lines that cover an area or a whole surface with a texture. By keeping the direction of the cuts parallel, by crosshatching, or making curved strokes, a great variety of different effects can be obtained. For a regular result it is better to make the graver strokes short and overlapping. Experiment will reveal many possibilities. Florentine finishes are usually left as cut, but here again experiment is the byword.

CORRECTING ERRORS

To correct shallow errors in the form of grooves caused by slips of the graver, go over the mark with a *burnisher,* using soapy water as a lubricant, and *always rub in the direction of the cut,* not across it. To correct deeper errors, depending on their depth and the thickness of the metal, first make the surface level with a *scraper* which shaves off the necessary amount, then smooth the surface with a burnisher. To completely erase a shallow engraving on a flat area, file it with a *second-cut file,* then go over the area with a fine *pumice stone.* Also available is a chuck-mounted *hard stone* (Arkansas stone) *point,* which can be rubbed over the area.

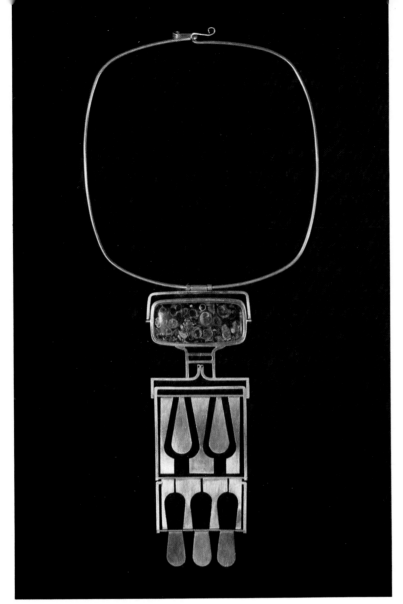

9-1

Plate 9-1 JOHN E. SATTERFIELD, U.S.A.
Necklace of sterling silver, with photoetch-
pierced units. *Photo: John E. Satterfield*

Plate 9-2 ELEANOR MOTY, U.S.A. "Reflections." Pin with image photoetched on silver,
with leather and abalone. *Photo: Eleanor
Moty*

9-2

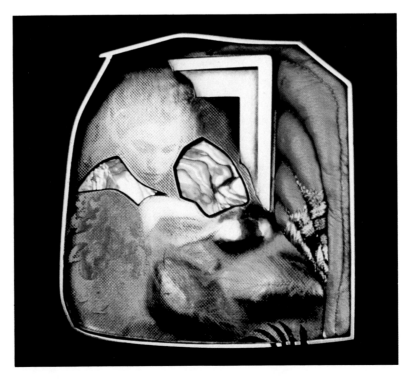

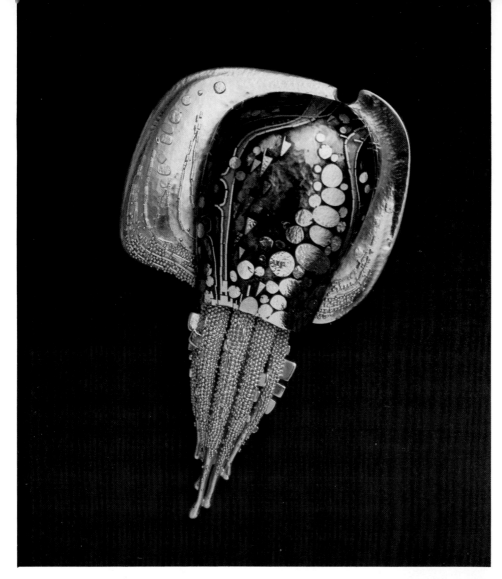

10—1

10—2

Plate 10—1   JOHN PAUL MILLER, U.S.A. ''Cephalopod.''
Pendant/brooch fabricated in 18k gold, with granulation
and enamel. *Photo: John Paul Miller*

Pate 10—2   JOHN PAUL MILLER, U.S.A. ''Talisman.''
Pendant/brooch fabricated in 18k gold with 22k gold chip
granulation. *Photo: John Paul Miller*

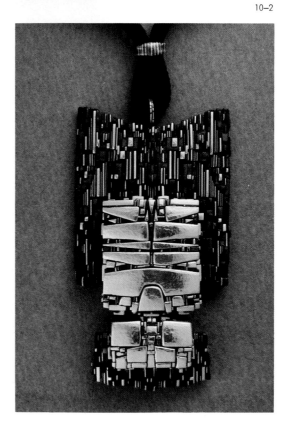

Plate 11-1   ANNE KROHN GRAHAM, U.S.A. Chain fabricated with surface fusion ornamented units, employing swivel links, with opal, moonstone, garnet, amethyst, and carnelian. *Photo: Anne Krohn Graham*

Plate 11-2   HIROKO SATO PIJANOWSKI, U.S.A. Brooch with stand, in twist-laminated sterling silver and copper. *Photo: Gene Pijanowski*

11-1

11-2

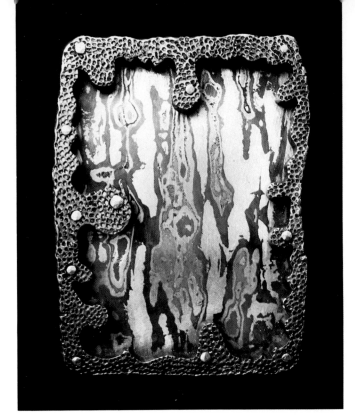

12-1

Plate 12-1 PETER SZAWLOWSKI, U.S.A. "Belt Buckle No. 10." Fabricated of mokumé sheet of fine silver, copper, bronze, and brass, riveted between a textured sterling silver unit frame and stainless steel. *Photo: Courtesy American Crafts Council*

Plate 12-2 MAREK and LUCYNA NIENIEWSKI, Poland. Bracelet fabricated of silver strip and ebony, articulated with two-headed screws, one internally threaded to receive the other. *Photo: Marek Nieniewski*

Plate 12-3 HANNELORE GABRIEL, U.S.A. Ring fabricated of sterling silver and 18k gold, with moonstone. *Photo: Hannelore Gabriel*

12-2

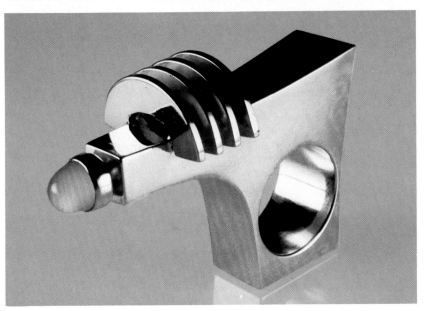

12-3

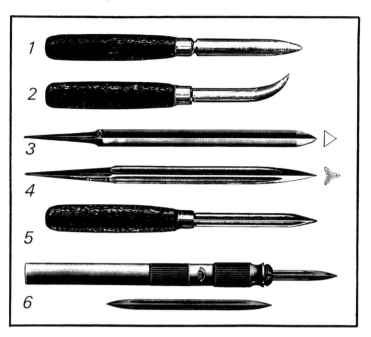

8-25 BURNISHERS AND SCRAPERS
1. *Straight,* wooden-handled burnisher.
2. *Curved,* wooden-handled scraper.
3. *Triangular* scraper with tang.
4. *Hollow-ground triangular scraper,* with tang.
5. *Hollow-ground triangular scraper,* with wooden handle.
6. *Hollow-ground triangular, double-pointed scraper* that can be inserted into a metal chuck-type handle.

POLISHING

As mentioned, the work being engraved should be in its final state of finish before engraving is done on it. If, however, the surface around an engraved area must be polished for some reason, use a high-speed spindle rate, a fine cotton buff, and move the work constantly. Avoid overpolishing as this will cause the edges of the engraved lines to become rounded and the effect of their crisp brilliance will be diminished. Hand polishing is probably preferable to machine polishing in such a case. Remove rouge from the engraved cuts by using a soap-laden *brush* dipped into water containing ammonia, then rub in a circular motion. Rinse in water and dry. Engraved lines can be deliberately oxidized to make them appear dark on a polished ground. High surface polish must be carefully restored without removing the oxidation.

THE STORAGE OF GRAVERS

Before storing, dry and lightly oil your gravers to prevent rust formation. Protect the cutting point by placing it into a hole made in a cork, or by placing the cutting end into a hole drilled in a wood block so it stands upright along with others. On no account should gravers be put away loose, where their cutting edges can hit other tools or each other and become damaged. For the sake of efficiency, gravers should be maintained in a sharp, polished state so they are always ready for use.

8-26 PATNA, BIHAR, INDIA.
Contemporary silver repoussé-worked pendant *(panwa).* The pan leaf shape and facing peacocks are popular Indian folk art motifs. The entire relief area was engraved after repoussage.
Col.: Saara Hopea-Untracht.
Photo: Oppi

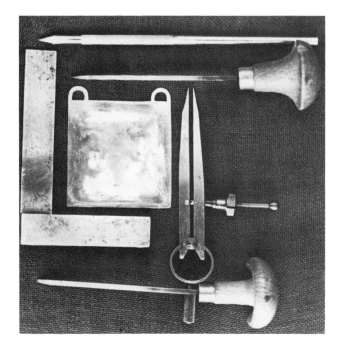

1

2

ENGRAVING PRACTICE

DEMONSTRATION 10

ILSE IMMICH engraves a silver pendant

Photos: Günter Grabher

In this sequence, flat gravers are used almost entirely in the rockered line technique.

1 The metal was cut and its edges finished with an abrasive paper. The surface was then scratch brushed. The tools used to prepare and execute the design are shown.

2 To lay out the main guide lines of the design, a *scriber* and *right angle* are used. The center is marked, and vertical, horizontal, and diagonal divisions are established with lightly enscribed lines. Using a *compass*, other equal divisions are marked off.

3 Using three flat gravers of different widths, the engraving is started from the center and worked around each side of the square, then the work proceeds gradually toward the edges. The rockered lines are formed by moving the graver alternately to the right and the left by "rocking" the hand as the line moves forward. If corrections are necessary, they are made at the end when the work is completed.

4 The finished silver pendant engraved with rockered lines. Size 2¾ in. (7 cm) square.

Photo: Oppi

4

3

8–27 KEL-AIR TUAREG, MAURETANIA. Engraved, double amulet silver pendants, mounted on leather thongs. The form and its decoration are derived from shapes and patterns used on leather bags in the Sahara region. Height 6.2 cm; width 7 cm. Photo: *Linden Museum, Stuttgart*

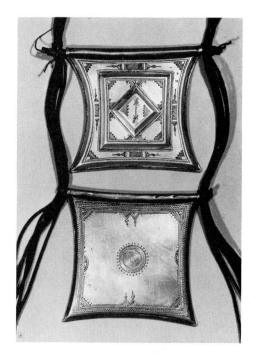

SCORING

Backward-pressure linear metal removal

Scoring is related to engraving in that a groove or furrow of metal of varying depth is removed from flat metal or other materials. Scored lines are made more simply than engraved lines, and because of their uniformity, the lines appear to be produced mechanically. An important difference lies in the manner of handling the tool. In engraving, the grooved line is created by a *forward* motion of the tool *away* from the worker, while scoring is accomplished by a *backward* movement of the tool *toward* the worker. Actually, scoring can be described as a controlled form of scratching, scribing, or scraping, terms that relate to the degree of groove depth in the result.

DECORATIVE AND FUNCTIONAL PURPOSES OF SCORED LINES

Scoring can be used for decorative or functional purposes. In decorative scoring the resulting lines are visible as a part of the design; in functional scoring they are no longer seen in the result.

Decorative scoring includes the use of straight or curved lines; segmented or dash lines; parallel series of lines; and crossed lines in which two or more series of parallel lines pass over each other in perpendicular, oblique, or curved directions. With these elements, a wide range of variations and effects are possible.

Functional scoring includes the use of a scored guide line made for use in the operations of making measurements, sawing, or cutting; and scored lines are used when bending sheet metal, as described below.

TOOLS FOR SCORING

A *scorer* can be any metal tool that is capable of making a clean, smooth groove in the surface of the chosen material, and the part that contacts the material scored must be very sharp to be effective. Scorers can be divided into *straight, conically tapered point*, and *bent, beveled-point* types. Lines of quite different character are made with each, and they are held in different ways during scoring.

Straight, conically tapered point types include *scribers* made entirely of tool steel; those with steel handles and a carbide tip; and scribers that have an industrial diamond, ruby, or sapphire mounted in the tip. Though a bent, tapered-point scriber also exists, the bent-ended scorer differs in that its bent end is beveled and relatively broadly angled to a point.

Bent, beveled-point scorers are available made of a flat strip of tool steel whose tang end may be mounted in a wooden handle, and the portion bearing the point is bent to a 90° angle from the rest. Bent-ended scoring tools can easily be improvised from any suitable piece of tool steel. An old chisel, or a worn out flat file could be used as the raw metal. In this case, heat one end to redness, and forge-bend the last ½ in (13 mm) of the tool to a 90° angle. If the scorer is to be used to prepare the sheet metal for a *perpendicular bend, grind* the bent portion to a point that has an angle of 90°, allowing angles of 45° from the horizontal on either side. To create the sharp cutting edge and point, grind a bevel in the outer edge of the bend, and

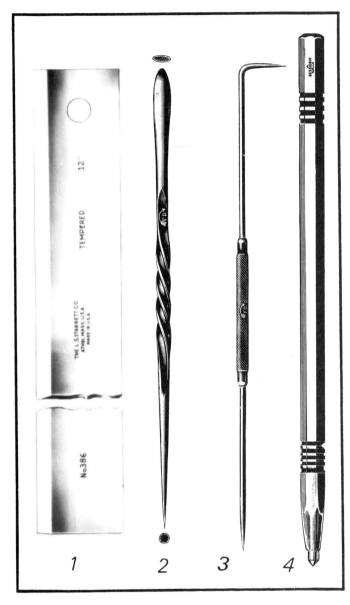

8-28 SCORING TOOLS
1. Steel straight edge, beveled on one side, tempered, available in lengths of 12, 24, 36, 48 in. Has a hole at one end for hanging it up.
2. Steel scriber, straight.
3. Steel scriber, straight and bent end.
4. Diamond-pointed scriber.

then smooth and sharpen the bevel and point on a *whetstone.* Harden the scorer's point end by tempering it to straw yellow. Scorers can also be ground to steeper or broader cutting angle ends, the angle slope of the resulting scored line varying accordingly. In all cases, the resulting line in the metal has two decidedly *visible angles,* sloping downward to a V shape in the groove. The use of such a scorer for grooving a bend line is described below.

DECORATIVE SCORING OF FLAT SURFACES

STRAIGHT LINE SCORING WITH A CONICALLY TAPERED POINT SCRIBER

Place the metal on a *wood block* to which it is fixed at its edges with *screws* or *nails.* C-clamp the wood block to a *flat-topped workbench.* Alternately, the metal alone can be secured directly to the workbench by placing a wood block or a flat, smooth piece of steel over a part of the metal, leaving the area to be scored exposed, then C-clamping the wood block or steel plate to the bench. As a precaution against accidental marking from a slipped scoring tool, the unworked area of the metal can be covered with strips of *masking tape.*

A *straight edge* is used as a guide when scoring straight lines with a *scriber.* This is an unmarked tool steel bar that has an accurate, straight, beveled edge which has been hardened. The straight edge is also often used as an aid in drawing straight lines on metal when laying out a work, and to test the flatness of a surface. All straight, tapered-tip scorers make a mark on the metal with the point tip, and are only sharp there, therefore they glide easily and do not scrape against the straight edge. On the other hand, bent and beveled scorers cannot be used with a straight edge because their sharp, beveled edge would come into contact with the straight edge and damage edge accuracy by taking small shavings from it.

To make a scored line with a tapered-tip scriber, place the straight edge in position, and either hold it firmly in place with finger pressure, or *clamp* it down. Place the scriber's point alongside the straight edge, and keeping them always in contact, draw the scriber *toward you* over the metal. The sharp point will gouge a fine line on the metal surface, the depth of the line varying with the amount of pressure placed on the tool. By definition, a scored line is much heavier than a guide line because the former is meant to be *permanent,* while the latter is *temporary* and therefore is lightly marked to make its removal possible. As a means of better control when scoring a line, it is advisable to first establish a light guide line, then deepen or score it by passing over the line as many times as is judged necessary. If hand held, the straight edge must remain in the same position, and the point must enter the same groove each time. Light slipped lines may be removable with a *Scotch stone* or *paper abrasive,* but deep slipped lines are difficult or impossible to remove, and may have to be flooded with solder to eliminate them. As with all scored lines, the *shape of the groove* depends on the angle and shape of the point of the scriber or scorer.

CROSSED LINE SCORING

When scoring crossed lines, care must be taken at the *crossing points* to prevent the scriber or scorer from leaving the line past that point, or from cutting a deeper or wider groove than is wanted in that place.

CURVED LINE SCORING

Curved lines, or a complete curved figure such as **a** circle or an ellipse, can be scored for decorative purposes. To guide the tool, use a *metal guide* such as a *French curve;* a *metal template* with openings of the same figure in several sizes; or a *piece of metal* cut to the desired curve. Follow the same procedure as described for straight line scoring, but try to make the curve in one continuous stroke. Circles can also be scored by mounting and centering the metal on a powered rotating tool such as a *lathe,* and then using a *pointed, diamond-shaped lathe cutting tool* as a scorer. Concentric circles can be scored by shifting the cutting tool point the desired distance away from the last scored circle, and repeating the process.

8–29 REINHOLD REILING, West Germany. Silver brooch using diagonal and cross-scored lines. Photo: Reinhold Reiling

8–32 PAULA HÄIVÄOJA, Finland, designer; manufacturer Kalevala Koru, Helsinki. Gold ring whose form was first cut flat, the lines then scored, after which it was shaped into a warped plane to form a ring shank whose ends were soldered together. Photo: Studio Wendt, courtesy Kalevala Koru

8–30 FRIEDRICH B. MÜLLER, Switzerland. Brooch whose steel base is scratch brushed in one direction. Upon it is mounted a small gold square bearing the numbers, and a screwed-on sheet of transparent red acrylic, the latter scored in circular and straight lines with a divider point. Ø approx. 65 mm. Photo: Mario Tschabold Steffisburg

FINISHING A DECORATIVE SCORED LINE

Decorative scored lines do not have to be treated in any way after they are made but can be left bright or can be colored black. It is also possible to fill them with enamel, niello, resins, or liquid plastics. These materials can be leveled flush with the metal's surface leaving the added material only in the scored line which is then sharply defined.

DIMENSIONALLY SHAPING A FLAT SHEET BEARING SCORED LINES

It is possible to shape a scored flat metal object into a three-dimensional form. This can be done simply by bending the object into a curve or curves. Small forms, or parts of forms can be shaped with a *punch* on a *doming block*, the scored lines on them becoming curves over the surface of the form that results. Larger sheets can be shaped with a *mallet* or a *nonmarking hammer* into a *shallow wooden mold* or over a *stake* of suitable contour.

8–31 SOUTHERN MOROCCO. Used in the Ait Baamrane-Lakhsas-Ifrane, Sahel Atlantique area, and the region of Ouad Massa. Contemporary silver necklace with coral beads, made in the Bazar Berbere, Tiznit, Morocco. Traditionally it consists of eight circular pendants scored with parallel or spiral lines, the shape and decoration symbolizing the sun and fertility. The lines are sometimes niello filled. Photo: Oppi

FUNCTIONAL SCORING

SCORING A STRAIGHT LINE FOR BENDING WITH A BENT-ENDED BEVELED SCORER

Scored lines made with a bent-ended beveled scorer can be used for decorative purposes as well as the functional purpose described here. To make a *perpendicular bend* along a scored line, use a bent-ended scorer having a 90°-angle point. The scored line made with this scorer allows the sheet to be bent accurately and with a small bend radius along that line. This bending technique is especially useful when the metal object being bent is small, as when making a box clasp. Scoring and bending can also be used when making larger rectangular or other geometric boxlike fabrications, or simply any straight, bent-angle form that may be used in a jewelry design and holloware.

Accurately measure and mark the line of bend on the metal with a *pencil*, then using a *straight edge*, go over the penciled line with a *tapered-point scriber* to initially establish the straight line. This will then be deepened and shaped by the *bent-ended scorer*. Anchor the metal securely to the workbench to be certain it will not move. Grip the scorer with the right hand, thumb on top. Guide the scorer with the first two fingers of the left hand placed near the cutting point in front of the fingers of the right hand. Place the point of the tool at the far end of the guide line and slowly but steadily draw the scorer toward you to remove metal from the groove in as smooth, continuous, and even a manner as possible to maintain an even groove depth. (If the groove depth is greater at the ends, which tends to happen, after bending there will be a space there.) This first scoring ordinarily is not to the final depth, but is followed by several other smoothly executed passes of the scorer in the same groove. If you must use a straight edge to assist in making a straight groove, use one to which possible edge damage will not matter.

When a *sharply angled outside corner* of small radius is wanted on the bend, repeat the scoring until a V-shaped groove is formed approximately halfway through the thickness of the sheet. In this case, groove readiness for bending can be judged by observing the *back* of the metal. Scoring stops when the scored line appears there as a scarcely visible ridge, an indication that there is very little metal left in the groove. If a *rounded outside corner* is wanted on the bend, less metal is removed and a shallower incision is made in the groove.

BENDING SCORED METAL

Bending metal along the scored line can be done by several means, depending on the size of the work. Small work might be bent with the fingers alone, with *pliers* on one side of the work, or with *two pliers* placed on either side of the bend. For larger work, clamp the metal, back side up, on a flat surface such as a *steel surface block* with the shorter work part projecting beyond its edge, and with the scored groove lined up with a corner of the block. Using simple finger pressure all along the line, or using a *block of wood,* press the projecting metal downward along its entire length. The two sides of the chamfered score line inside the bend will meet. The sheet will automatically form

a right angle because the scored line was created with a 45° angle on each groove side. Bending can also be done in a similar way by placing the work against a *straight steel* strip fixed in the jaws of a *vise.*

Because the actual amount of metal holding the parts together is thin, never try to *rebend* metal along a scored line unless you deliberately wish to break it off, which is what will happen. Since the corner is actually weak, it is advisable to strengthen it. Flux the line inside the bend, and place a piece of solder at one end. Heat the metal and draw the solder along the line with a torch. If needed, add an additional piece of solder to the groove with a *soldering pick,* or from a fluxed solder stick, placing it at the point where the solder stops flowing. Continue to draw the solder through the remainder of the groove.

CHIP CARVING

Metal volume removal from mass with chisels

HISTORIC CHIP CARVING: Kerbschnitt

Chip carving metal with *metal-cutting chisels* as a technique dates at least from Roman times. Early Germanic metalwork, and that of the North Sea Scandinavian area were also often so decorated, and as a result of Anglo-Saxon migrations, the technique spread to England, Scotland, and Ireland. This metal technique was called *kerbschnitt,* literally "chip carving." It is believed to have had its origins in the carving of softer materials such as wood and bone, and was also carried out directly on bronze with metal chisels. The same name was also applied to work in which wax models were created to resemble chip-carved effects. Sometimes impressions were taken from chip-carved designs made in bone, then cast in gold or other metals to make relief ornaments. Such castings in nonferrous metals were then frequently gilded with mercury amalgam to make them resemble gold, and applied or fixed to another object by means of rivets.

Chip carving was responsible for the character of the very popular *cut steel jewelry* made during the end of the 18th and the start of the 19th centuries in Woodstock near Oxford, England, and Tula, in Russia, was also famed for its chip-carved steel as well as its niello work. In this jewelry, the heads of rivetlike steel studs, round, oval, or other shape, were chip faceted by cutting them in planes to form rose-cut patterns by the use of flat, sharp chisels. These were then mounted on a supporting pierced work silver or brass ground into which holes had been drilled, in densely packed arrangements, and the minute rivet shaft that projected from behind each decorated head was hammered and fixed in place. The rivet heads of the upper surface almost completely covered the ground so that it appeared to be paved with faceted stones. Three-dimensional beads were also chisel faceted in this manner, pierced and strung, and used in combinations with constructions of the above-mentioned types. Cut steel studs such as these decorated a whole range of personal jewelry items including shoe buckles, buttons, brooches, bracelets, combs, chatelaines, necklaces, and tiaras.

8–33 SWEDEN, 7th century A.D. Bridle mount found at Vendel, Uppland. The mount was first cast, then chip carved. Photo: S. Hallgren, Antikvarisk-Topografiska Arkivet, Stockholm

8–34 MYCENAE, GREECE, 15–14th century B.C. Upper surface of a gold ring, found at Tirinto, carved in intaglio with an offering scene depicting fabulous animals bringing gifts to a king. Possibly used as a seal. Largest Ø 5.6 cm. Photo: National Museum, Athens

CONTEMPORARY CHIP CARVING

Today, returning to the original concept, chip carving is a technique that employs *sharp chisels* of all sizes and shapes (see Chisels in General, p. 306), and a *hammer* which is used to force the chisel obliquely into relatively thick sheet or cast metal, in order to remove portions from the metal by the impact of hammer blows. The contemporary approach to chip carving adopts a freedom that has greatly enlarged the possibilities of this technique as a means of creating a surface pattern on metal. Instead of trying to imitate faceted stones, the reflective quality of the chip facet can be used as a means of ornamenting the entire surface of a metal object. The technique can be used alone, or in combination with other decorative processes on the same object.

Chips can be made in various ways. The chip planes can all be cut at the same angle, or combinations of intersecting angles can oppose each other in any arrangement. The shape of the cut can be varied from the usual flat one to concave or V-shaped cuts made with chisels having appropriate sections. Cuts can be spaced or repeated in close series. Chisels of different widths of the same cut can be used in one work. By varying the depth of cut the appearance of the result will change. Leaving the raised *burr intact,* provided it is not sharp, introduces yet another pattern. Combinations of these means can be used on the same surface, or confined to different parts of the same work.

Polishing the result is avoided as this would soften edges, modify the crisp-cut look, and reduce the ability of the cuts to reflect light.

CHIP CARVING WITH CHISELS

DEMONSTRATION 11

GENE PIJANOWSKI investigates chisel-cut textures

Photos: Gene Pijanowski

1 Chisels for chip carving in the basic V, round, and flat cutting edge shapes, also used for inlay work.

2 The work is fixed to pitch spread on a wood block. The chisel is hammered into the metal, removing metal chips. Various textural effects or patterns can be made by changing the direction of the cut; by repeating the cut in the same direction; or by varying the depth of the cut. Linear effects are also possible.

3 Belt buckle with chip-carved textures. Top: Cuts made with a curved chisel in diminishing depths. Center: Faceted planes cut with a flat-bladed chisel. Around the center: V-shaped chisel cuts.

 **1**

 **2**

3

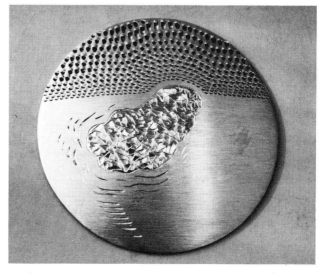

8–35 CLAËS E. GIERTTA, Sweden. Silver cross whose surfaces are carved with chisels. The chain is forged. Height ca. 8 cm. *Photo: Sven Petersen*

METAL INLAY

Excavation succeeded by insertion techniques

The concept of the process of *metal inlay* involves the permanent insertion of wire or sheet metal forms of one metal into an excavation created in the surface of an *already finished* metal object made of a contrasting colored metal. There are several methods by which this can be done, and they are described below. In traditional inlay work the inlaid metal does *not* appear at the reverse surface of the work, nor does the inlay make use of heat as a means of joining the metals, though the results of these methods can *appear* to be inlay. The retention of the inlay depends instead upon the *mechanical holding action* of a *burr* raised at the edge of the excavation made to receive the inlay, and an *undercut* to hold it in place after the inlay has been forced into the recess. Most frequently, the inlaid metal is then made level with the surface of the parent metal, but several variations are possible in which the inlaid metal is in *relief*. (See Flush Dot Inlay, p. 312.)

JAPANESE INLAY WORK (HON ZOGAN)

The process of inlaying metals is one that has been perfected and in wide use for centuries by specialists in Japan. Since jewelry worn by women in the Western sense was almost nonexistent in Japan in the past, the use of metal decorative techniques such as inlay was concentrated on objects used mostly by men. Foremost among these were the highly valued sets of sword furniture (collectively called *sorimono, kanagu* or *kodogu* for different sword types) used to decorate the swords worn by every samurai. These were often made to order by specialist artisans and their hereditary descendants who created schools in particular decorative techniques. The swords were decorated with subjects of significance to the owner and his family, such as the adopted crest (*mon*) of a clan to which he belonged, subjects from mythology, and symbolic themes. All the inlay techniques in practice, and there were many, were used to ornament the sword guard (*tsuba*). It had three holes, one for the sword blade, and the other two for the skewer (*kogai*) and a throwing knife (*kozuka*) to pass through and be held alongside the blade. The handles of the skewer and the throwing knife were also ornamented, and along with the pair of hilt ornaments (*menuki*) constituted a set (*mitokoro mono*) that were often done by the same family of craftsmen. The pommel cap (*kashira*) and the ferrule at the opposite end of the hilt next to the guard (*fuchi*) also made a set. The scabbard ornaments such as the end of the chape (*kojiri*) that covered the point, the ring for attaching it to a belt, and the ornaments at the open end of the scabbard (*koiguchi*) were all decorated. A study of these sword and scabbard parts reveals an astounding range of other decorative metal processes besides inlay. The scale of the decoration is so very small that a magnifying glass must often be used. Clearly both the makers and the users of these objects appreciated this exquisite attention to detail, careful workmanship, and great artistry.

In addition, inlay was also done on ritual objects, and

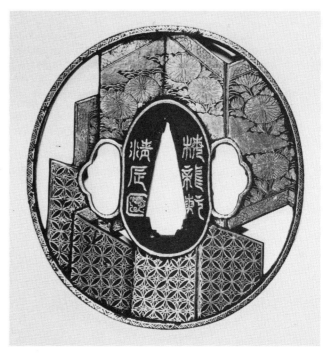

8–36 JAPAN. Iron *kenjo style tsuba* by Bairiuken Kiyotoki, early 19th century. This type, given as a present to a superior, was always inlaid in geometric diaper or floral patterns with gold wire (*nunome zogan*). This style originated with Jiuchiya in Kyoto. This design represents a pair of ornamented folding screens. The signature seal of the maker (*kakihan*) is also inlaid in gold wire. Bequest of George Cameron Stone. *Photo: Cooper-Hewitt Museum, New York*

objects made for secular use such as vases, decorative plates, boxes, and finger grips on the movable panels that are used in Japan to divide rooms.

The processes described below are those that were practiced by traditional Japanese craftsmen of the past, and are still in use today. We are particularly indebted to Gene Pijanowski and Hiroko Sato Pijanowski, who have made a study of the Japanese inlay processes, and have so graciously shared their knowledge.

JAPANESE INLAY WORK TYPES

The general term for inlay work in Japanese is *hon zogan*, or *zogan*, which is equivalent to the Western term *damascene work*. Several specialized techniques of inlay work are recognized, and each has its established name, a circumstance unique to Japanese artisans.

Hon zogan (*hon,* "flush") is the general term for flush inlay made by first cutting grooves in metal, then undercutting them, and hammering in wire or sheet metal flat with the base metal plane.
Sen zogan is the flat inlay of round wire, flush with the ground, or in relief.

Hira zogan is the inlay of sheet metal flush with the base metal.

Takaniku zogan or *taka zogan,* literally "mound" inlay, is the inlay of raised or high relief forms made of solid sheet metal, repoussé-worked sheet, or cast metal forms. These forms can also be carved, engraved, or themselves inlaid.

Hira shizuku zogan is the inlay of dots made flush with the surface.

Shizuku zogan is raised dot or domed dot inlay, also called "raindrop," and "toad skin" inlay.

These processes are all described below in the demonstration process photos. In addition, there are other forms of inlay work.

Nawame zogan is the inlay of compound, multi-metal twisted wire, inlaid as in *sen zogan.*

Uttori zogan is a form of *taka zogan* where large, thick pieces of cast metal are set in a surrounding flange. The projecting inlaid metal is then carved or inlaid with other metals, or it can have been carved or inlaid in advance.

Nunome zogan, literally "cloth inlay," consists of first engraving a flat surface with crosshatched lines with a serrated liner to raise a series of burrs on the entire surface and give it a texture that resembles woven cloth. On this prepared surface wire or gold leaf is then inlaid. The process is described below.

Kinkeshi zogan, ginkeshi zogan are respectively gold amalgam inlay and silver amalgam inlay (*kin,* "gold," *gin,* "silver," and *keshi,* "amalgam"). This process consists of inlaying a mercury amalgam of precious metals into grooves made in the metal, then volatilizing the mercury and leaving the precious metal behind. The process is described under Amalgam Inlay, p. 674. Very small dots representing mist, and signatures were made in sword ornaments in this way.

Other processes that are not strictly inlay according to Western concepts of the process, but a form of mosaic, are classified by the Japanese as a form of inlay. *Kirihame zogan* or "sawing inlay" is a *pierced work inlay* in which parts of the ground are pierced through completely and replaced with parts having exactly the same shape, but of another metal, then soldered in place. The inserted inlay can be flat or in repoussé work relief. A variation is one in which a prepared mosaic of different colored metals is then inlaid in a pierced parent metal, and soldered in place. One type is a mosaic of alternating squares of contrasting colored metals, others are laminates of different metals.

METALS USED FOR INLAY

At the basis of the appeal of the inlay process is the contrast between the color of the metal inlaid and the ground metal. The greater the "palette" of metal colors used, the more varied the work can appear. For jewelry making, any combination can be used. In relief or sheet metal inlay, the metal inlaid can be of any contrasting color. In wire inlay, it is usual for the wire to be of either gold or silver or both, and the ground can be of any color that will contrast with these metals.

Fine gold, karat gold, fine silver, sterling silver, copper, brass, bronze, iron, steel, or the Japanese alloys *shakudo* and *shibuichi* all can be used in any combination.

THE GROUND METAL (jigane)

The minimum thickness of the ground metal should be 14 or 16 gauge B.&S., gauges thick enough to allow excavations to a depth suitable to receive the inlaid metal. Thicker metal can of course also be inlaid, as can cast metal pieces.

THE INLAID METAL (mongane)

The inlaid metal should always be *well annealed* to allow for maximum malleability so that it is easily spread into the undercut when struck, and takes on the form of the recess into which it is pressed or hammered. Fine gold and fine silver are well suited to use as inlay metals because they are naturally soft and do not become excessively work hardened when hammered. Round wire in gauges of 18 to 22 B.&S. are commonly used. Much finer wire is used in the inlay process called *nonume,* where it can be placed anywhere on the surface, which is completely grooved. Sheet metal inlay in thicknesses of 22–24 gauge B.&S. are recommended. Sheet metal thinner than 24 gauge B.&S. may become too thin after leveling, and the inlay runs the risk of falling out of the recess.

PITCH: The traditional ground metal holding surface

The working surface most favored for inlay work has always been pitch (*yani*). This material firmly holds and supports the ground metal which is cemented to it, and offers just the right amount of resistance to the impact blows of the tools used. Pitch is used for the same purpose in repoussage, and the reader is referred to that section in Chapter 5 (see p. 121) for a discussion of pitch and pitch compositions. In the Table, "Typical Pitch Repoussage Compositions" (see p. 121), "Hard pitches" are listed that are suited to inlay work. The pitch composition used for inlay must be harder than for pitch used for repoussage, because in inlay work the ground is not altered in shape and the pitch serves only to hold the metal firmly in place during the inlay process; while in repoussage it must give to the shaping of the metal. If the pitch is too hard, however, the work may spring from the ground when the metal is struck. It may be necessary, as in repoussage, to alter its composition somewhat to render it suitable to seasonal temperature changes.

Inlay work can be done with the metal placed on the pitch in a pitch bowl that rests on a circular cushion. (See Illustration 5–24, p. 120.) This allows the work to be angled to whatever position may be necessary, and makes it easier to do inlay work on convex surfaces. Traditional Japanese inlay workers, however, use a special maple or other hardwood board (*yani dai*) approximately 5 in × 8 in × 2 in (12.7 cm × 20.6 cm × 5.1 cm). To give the board weight, a rectangular hole is made in the center of the board, and chipped stones or pebbles are placed in it, or lead about 1¼ in (5.7 cm) thick is cast in the hole. The cooled but still viscous pitch is poured over the hole and spread over the rest of the board with a stick to a thickness of about 1 in (2.54 cm), this being the limit of the depth of the metal shape placed upon it. Objects of greater depth can be accommodated by mounding the pitch at the center. The concave part at the back of the work must be completely supported or the ground metal will move when struck. Avoid pouring the pitch while it is still too hot, or it will run off the board.

To secure the ground metal to the pitch, heat the pitch surface with a soft flame just enough to soften it. Place the ground metal on the pitch and press it in at its center with a hammer handle until the entire undersurface is in total contact with the pitch. Avoid sinking the metal into the pitch. Allow the pitch composition to cool and solidify. It is then ready for the inlay work to start.

When the time comes to remove the work from the pitch, heat the work only enough to allow it to be pried loose from the pitch (do not burn the pitch), then lift it away with *tweezers*. To remove pitch from the inlaid metal when the work is completed, *never use heat* as this might cause the metal to warp and destroy the inlay. Instead, with a wooden stick, scrape off as much of the pitch as possible while it is softened. The rest is dissolved by using a pitch solvent such as lacquer thinner in which the article can soak, or by rubbing it with a wad of cotton soaked with turpentine.

THE INLAY TOOLS

Three basic tools are used in the inlay process: the metal-cutting *chisel* (*tagane*), the *hammer* (*kanazuchi*), and blunt, noncutting *repoussage* or *chasing punches* (also called *tagane* with modifying adjective). Chisels are made of high-carbon cast tool steel, and are used to make the incisions in the parent or ground metal into which the inlaid metal will go. The hammer is used to propel the chisel, and to strike punches for various functions.

CHISELS IN GENERAL

A *cold chisel* is a sharp-ended steel tool forged from a bar of tool steel containing 3.5% nickel or chrome in the alloy. It has three parts: the *striking end*, the *shaft*, and the *cutting edge* or *blade*. Chisels are used to bevel, carve, cut, chip, dress, engrave, gouge, pare, pierce, remove, rout, and shape metal, and in a special form, to turn solid metal or other material on a lathe.

THE STRIKING END A metalworker's chisel, unlike a woodworker's chisel, does not have a tang that fits into a wooden handle. Its working end, which is where it is struck, is blunt and flat, and usually is the *same* in section as the stock; *smaller* in section in the case of chisels with tapered stocks; or *larger* than the stock, tapering outward. If an outer taper develops at this end during the course of long hammering and use, it is termed a *mushroom head* because of its shape. This sharpened form is undesirable as it may weaken the tool and be the cause of accidents to the hands, and is removed by grinding it off. In some cases, such a head may be formed deliberately to provide a chisel with a larger striking surface. To make the chisel penetrate the metal, it is struck with a *hammer, stick,* or *metal bar*. The striking end is left soft to better take the impact since it might break if it were hard and brittle. When cutting metal with a chisel, watch the cutting end, not the striking end.

THE SHAFT, STOCK, OR TAPER This is the tool's handle. The *blank* or unshaped or unfinished bar of tool steel from which a chisel is made can be square, rectangular, hexagonal, octagonal, or round in section. It can be straight its entire length, or it can be given a taper toward the working end, the striking end, or both, by drawing it down when forging the tool. Tapering can also be accomplished by grinding or drawfiling when shaping the tool. The shaft corners are smoothed down to make the tool more comfortable to grip.

THE WORKING END This is the part of the tool that cuts into the metal when the chisel is used. To make the cutting end better able to penetrate the metal, the last 1½ in (3.8 cm) of the cutting end is tempered and hardened, then repolished before final sharpening and honing.

The concept of the chisel shape is based on the principle of the *wedge,* a shape that, when held at a suitable angle, allows it to enter the metal by its sharpened edge, the smallest part of the wedge shape. This is called the *nose* or *blade* of the tool and has been bevel sharpened to shapes and dimensions suited to the usual cutting tasks demanded of chisels. Its function and shape determine the angle of the bevels. They are created by working the tool on a water- or oil-lubricated whetstone while holding it at the desired angle, then honing it on a *leather sharpening strop* coated with a suitable fine abrasive such as diamantine. A sharp, properly hardened and tempered chisel can enter into and completely penetrate metal of relatively great thickness and of any hardness less than that of the tool itself, which is to say all metals ordinarily used by jewelers.

COLD CHISEL TYPES

Most cold chisels (so called because they are used on cold work), are named after their shape or use, and almost all chisels are made in several sizes of each shape, used according to the dimensions needed. Some of the more common forms are the following:

Flat or chipping chisel: A flat chisel used for general purposes, for chipping, cutting thick sheet, and for excavating straight-sided, flat grooves. Its corners are slightly curved so that it does not dig in excessively. It should be held firmly about ½ in (1.3 cm) from the striking end, and its edge should be slightly lubricated. The metal removed comes off in curls or chips.

Crosscut or cape chisel: A straight-edged, narrow blade used for cutting grooves and slots. When removing a large area, its edges can be cut first with a crosscut chisel, and the waste metal between excavated with a flat chisel.

Diamond: A diamond-pointed, square-sectioned chisel, used for cutting square corners.

V-shaped chisel: A chisel that cuts V-shaped grooves, often as an initial groove. It is followed by chisels having edges of other shapes to alter the shape of the groove.

Round-nosed chisel: A chisel with a hollowed, rounded cutting edge, used for making round-bottomed incisions.

Half-round chisel: A chisel with a solid section and round-bottomed cutting edge, used to cut curved grooves, and to cut out holes by chipping.

SEN ZOGAN — LINE INLAY

F: FRONT   B: BACK   S: SIDE VIEW   ga: GAUGE B.&S.

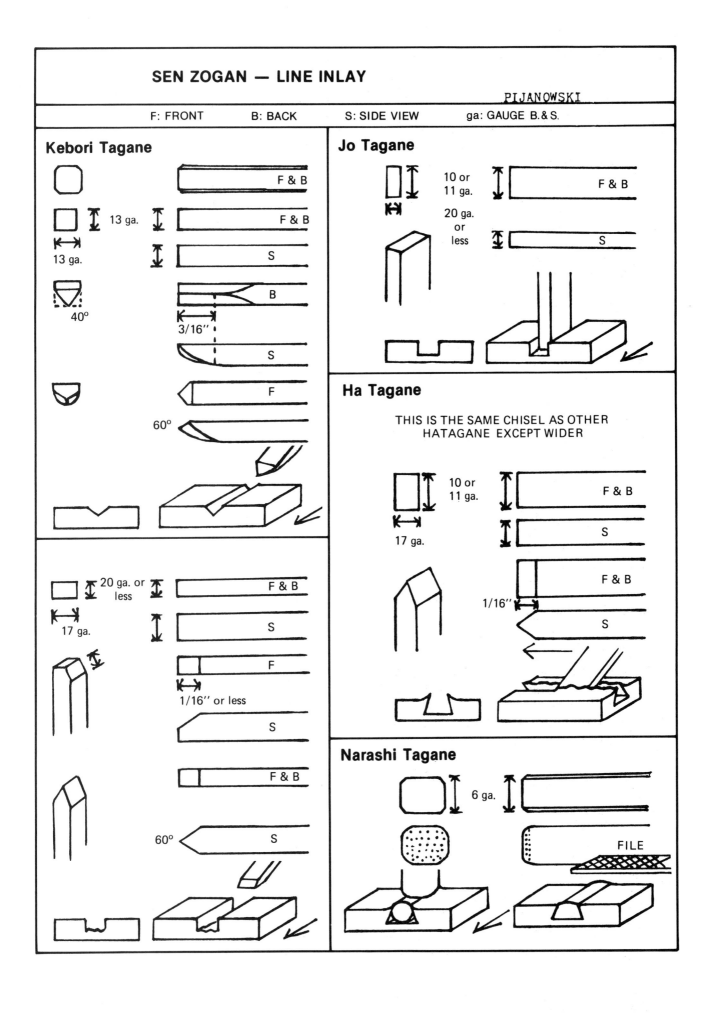

Kebori Tagane

F & B

13 ga.   F & B

13 ga.   S

40°

B

3/16''

S

F

60°

20 ga. or less

17 ga.

F & B

S

F

1/16'' or less

S

F & B

60°   S

Jo Tagane

10 or 11 ga.

20 ga. or less

F & B

S

Ha Tagane

THIS IS THE SAME CHISEL AS OTHER HATAGANE EXCEPT WIDER

10 or 11 ga.

17 ga.

F & B

S

F & B

1/16''   S

Narashi Tagane

6 ga.

FILE

THE JAPANESE INLAY PROCESS

DEMONSTRATION 12

HIROKO SATO PIJANOWSKI inlays a pendant

Photos: Gene Pijanowski
Japanese terminology supplied by Hiroko Sato Pijanowski

THE BASIC JAPANESE CHISELS USED (tagane)

The Japanese inlay chisels are made in five graduated sizes, Nos. 1–5.

Kebori tagane: A bellied, V-shaped grooving chisel with straight sides used to cut into the metal to make the initial inlay groove, then followed as a guide by the next chisel used. When a wire is to be inlaid, the chisel's width must be equal to that of the gauge of the wire. When a shape is being excavated, the outlines are first made with this chisel, and the metal between them is then excavated.

The faces of the point must be formed symmetrically and true or it will not cut a straight groove, but will favor one or the other side. If the front triangular bevel is not at a sufficiently steep angle, it will bury itself in the metal and possibly break. If it is too shallow an angle, it will slip on the metal and not cut. See the diagram on p. 307 for correct face angles.

Ha tagane: A straight chisel, square in front view and triangular in side view, with faces beveled to a knife edge. This chisel follows the *kebori* chisel. In its narrowest size, it is used to deepen the perpendicular-sided groove in the metal. Its width must equal the gauge of the wire to be inlaid. In a wider width, it is also used to excavate surplus metal when preparing a recess for a sheet metal shape to be inlaid. It is also used to undercut a groove and raise a burr.

PUNCHES USED FOR INLAY

Punches are tools that plastically deform metal without cutting or removing any metal. In Japan punches and chisels are both called *tagane*. Each chisel and punch has its special function and a word that describes its use is added to the generic term *tagane,* as for example: *narashi tagane,* "leveling punch." All these Japanese tools have their Western equivalents in chasing (*ukibori*) and repoussé work (*uchidashi*).

PLANISHING PUNCH (SOBAYOSE TAGANE) A bent-ended punch used in wire inlay to straighten the burr raised in a groove to align it or make it more vertical. This is done by inserting the end into the groove under the undercut and tapping it along. It is made with a flat end for use in straight lines, and a curved end for use on curved lines.

EMBOSSING, CUSHION, OR MATTING PUNCH (NARASHI TAGANE) A blunt, flat-ended, round-edged leveling punch, used while held in a vertical position at the juncture of the burr and the inlay to tap down or level a burr over the edge of the inlay. It is also used to push down an inlay into its groove. The working end must be wider than the wire gauge being set down, and it is sometimes roughened before tempering by striking it with a coarse file to prevent its slipping off round wire when hammered.

TRACER PUNCH (JO TAGANE) A rectangular-sectioned, flat-ended punch (*hira jo tagane*) whose width is narrower

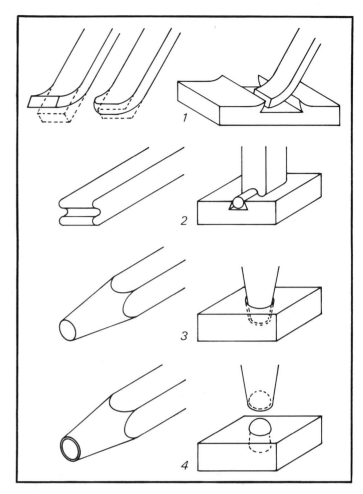

8–38 *INLAY PUNCHES WITH SPECIAL FUNCTIONS*
1. *Planishing punch (sobayose).*
2. *Hollow-ground tracer (tunnel narashi tagane).*
3. *Round punch (maru jo tagane).*
4. *Round hollow punch (nanako).*

than its depth, used to set down and flatten the bottom of the groove made in the ground to better accommodate the inlay, as in wire inlay. Its width must correspond to the gauge of the wire being inlaid. In another form it is a curve-ended, crescent-shaped punch used for deepening curved grooves (*magari jo tagane*).

HOLLOW-GROOVED TRACER (TUNNEL NARASHI TAGANE) A tracer with a longitudinal groove in its end, used to set down a wire inlay yet leave it raised from the surface of the ground.

ROUND PUNCH (MARU JO TAGANE) A solid, round section, flat-ended, tapering punch, used to make round depressions for the inlay of round wire.

ROUND, HOLLOW OR CUPPED PUNCH (NANAKO TAGANE) A round-sectioned punch with a hollow end, used to shape a small dome on inlaid wire as in *shizuku zogan,* or to imprint series of small circles called *nanako,* "fish roe," as when texturing a ground. Nanako circles of minute, sometimes almost microscopic size were spaced at equal intervals in linear, geometric, or random patterns.

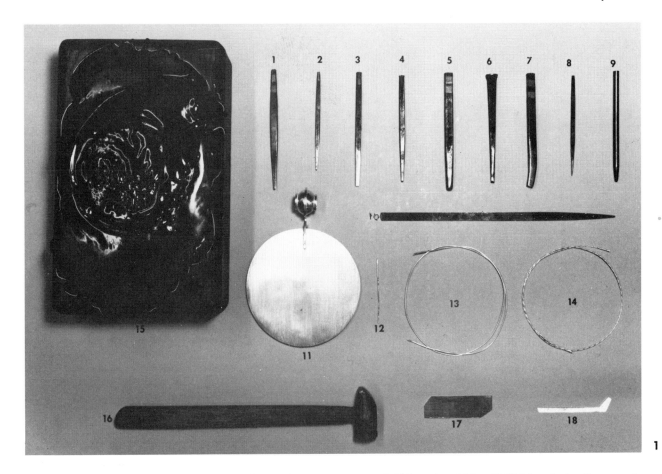

1

1 Tools and materials used for the inlay demonstration.

    1. *kebori tagane*. 2. No. 1 *ha tagane*. 3. *jo tagane*. 4. No. 2 *ha tagane*. 5. *narashi tagane*. 6. No. 3 *ha tagane*. 7. *sobayose tagane*. 8. *maru jo tagane*. 9. *nanako tagane*. 10. file (*yasuri*). 11. ground metal (*jigane*). 12. 18 gauge B.&S. round fine gold wire (*kin sen*). 13. 20 gauge B.&S. round fine silver wire (*gin sen*). 14. 20 gauge B.&S. round twisted copper and fine silver wire (*nawame sen*). 15. pitch spread on a board (*yani dai*). 16. Japanese hammer (*kanazuchi*), *otafuko* No. 6. 17. inlay metal (*mongane*). 18. 22 gauge B.&S. shakudo inlay shape (*mongane*).

2 This diagram illustrates the different types of inlay work that will be done on the demonstration piece.

    1 Line or "wire" inlay (*sen zogan*)
    2 "Flat" or flush sheet inlay (*hira zogan*)

    3 "Mound or high relief" inlay (*takaniku zogan*)
    4 "Flat dot" inlay (*hira shizuku zogan*)
    5 "Raised or domed dot" inlay (*shizuki zogan*)

3 The finished 16 gauge B.&S. copper disc ground metal (*jigane*) is fixed in the pitch. Because no heat process can be used on the object after inlay, it must be finished in every way, except for final polishing and coloring. The base metal should be at least two gauges thicker than the wire to be inlaid in it.

FLUSH WIRE INLAY (sen zogan)

CUTTING THE INCISION

4 Draw the design on the metal with a *steel scriber* (*kegaki*). Carve a V-shaped channel in the metal ground following the line which goes in a direction straight toward the worker with a *V-shaped chisel* (*kebori tagane*). Slant the chisel's striking end *away* from you. Move the chisel at

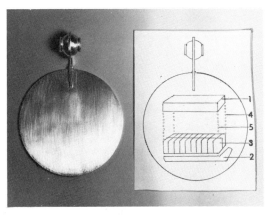

2

3

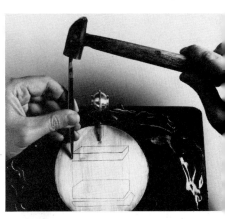

4

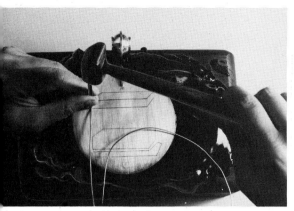

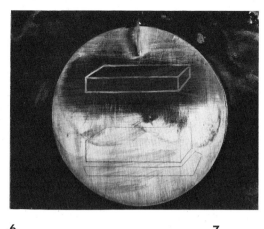

5   6   7

an angle of 30–40° along the line toward you by hammering it with light taps on its striking end with the hammer that hits at an angle of 90°. This forces it forward while it removes a curl of metal from the sheet.

DEEPENING AND BROADENING THE INCISION

After the V-shaped groove is made, to deepen the groove, hammer a square-ended excavating chisel (width No. 1 *ha tagane*) whose cutting edge width is equal to that of the wire gauge being inlaid into the groove. Work in the same direction as before. The bottom of this groove may now be rough. Smooth and beat it down to a depth equivalent to two-thirds of the wire's thickness with a *square-ended tracer punch (jo tagane)* held perpendicular to the metal and moved along the line toward the worker. Its size must also just fit the groove so that no alteration of groove width occurs.

UNDERCUTTING THE INCISION

Shift the work 90° so that it crosses in a direction in front of the worker. The undercut of the incision is done with a *flat cutter chisel* with a sharply beveled knife edge (width No. 2 *ha tagane*) by setting it inside one side of the groove at an angle of 30–40° from the groove bottom, then driving it down the line. While making the undercut, it also raises a burr along one side of the line. Turn the work 180° and do the same with the same tool along the other side of the line so that both sides are now undercut and with raised burrs. Straighten the burr and make it point in a more upward direction by using a *bent-ended planishing punch (sobayose tagane)*, a straight one for straight lines, and a curved one for curved lines.

INLAYING THE 20 GAUGE B.&S. FINE SILVER WIRE

5   Turn the work so the line points straight toward the worker. File flat the end of the fine silver wire to be inlaid, and insert it in the groove at the start of a line by tapping it in lightly with a flat-ended *embossing* or *cushion punch* (*narashi tagane*) whose end is wider than the wire. Hold the punch above the wire in a vertical position. Move the punch along its length, and with each blow, force the annealed and softened wire into the groove to make it take its shape, and fill in the undercuts so that it cannot come out—the basic system for holding all inlays. A *hardwood punch* with the proper end shape could also be used for this function. At the same time that the punch is pushing the wire into the groove, it is also flattening the burrs on the wire edges, helping to hold the wire in place. At the end of a line, use a sharp-edged cutting chisel (*ha tagane*) to cut off the wire.

LEVELING THE WIRE INLAY AND SETTING DOWN THE BURR

6   Level the wire inlay to the plane of the ground, by first filing, then sanding it with a *400* or *600 grit sandpaper*. If the purpose is to shape the wire longitudinally to raise it in relief, this can be done with a polished *hollow-grooved liner punch*. First smooth the edges along the wire with fine emery cloth. Then place the punch so that its groove is over the wire and its edges straddle the wire. Then hammer the punch along the line forcing the wire into the groove and at the same time pushing down the burr on its edges. Once the wire is flat, remove marks left on the outer edges by the tool with a smooth-faced level-

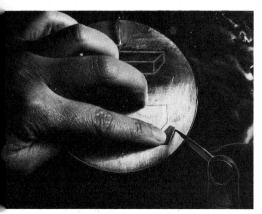
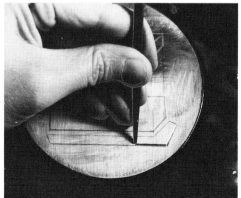
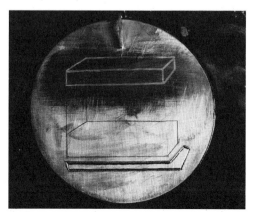

8   9   10

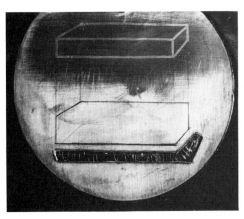  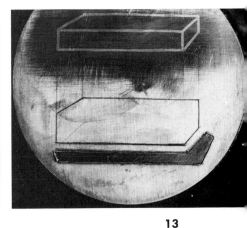

11   12   13

ing punch (*narashi tagane*). Hold it perpendicular to the ground and close to the wire, and with light taps work it along the length of the inlay. Avoid heavy blows as they will cause marks that are difficult to remove.

FINISHING THE SURFACE

7 Here we see the finished surface after sanding with the positions of the shapes of the sheet to be next inlaid marked on the ground with a *scriber*.

FLUSH SHEET METAL INLAY (hira zogan)

8 The metal of this shadow form to be inlaid is 20 gauge B.&S. shakudo. The inlay is to be flush with the ground, therefore this gauge is adequate. The blank is sawed out with its edges at a 90° angle to the horizontal plane. Its upper edges are then beveled with a *file* to an angle of 20–30° from the vertical. Anneal the blank.

Align the blank to *one line* in its enscribed position, and deepen that line with a scriber held at an angle so that its point touches the point of contact between the blank and the base. Place the work, now mounted on the pitch board, so it is perpendicular in front of you. Hold a cutting chisel (width No. 2 *ha tagane*) between the thumb and first two fingers with its striking end slanting *away* from you and its cutting edge on the line, and drive it toward you along the line. The incision should be neither too deep nor too shallow. The cut raises a burr along the marked line.

9 When one line is done, return the blank to its posi-

tion against the newly raised burr, and draw a second line along its next side, as before. Turn the work so this next line points toward you and make an incision as before. Continue in this way until all the lines enclosing the blank are incised.

The purpose of this procedure is to be sure that the shape within the incisions exactly fits that of the blank so that it will not be loose. If the excavated space is too wide, which tends to happen if the entire outline is made in *one* tracing, the blank will be too small and cannot be inlaid.

10 Here we see the work with all four incisions made. Place the blank in position to test its fit within the raised burrs. Make any necessary adjustments carefully.

11 Excavate the metal between the burrs with *cutter chisel* (width No. 3 *ha tagane*) to form the recess. The depth of metal removed should equal that of the thickness of the inlay blank so that it will be flush with the ground when finished.

12 Smooth and straighten the burrs with a *planishing punch* (*sobayose tagane*) by placing its working edge against the *inside wall* of the recess and tapping it lightly. Take care not to increase the dimensions of the incision.

13 Again place the shakudo blank in the recess in the ground to see if it fits properly, and make any necessary adjustments.

14 With light taps, hammer down the burr on the blank with a *cushion punch* (*narashi tagane*) held vertically with its face over the burr along the edge of the inlay blank, moving it along until the entire burr is set down. Level the surface with a file followed by fine abrasive papers, or by a *horizontal belt sander* if this is available.

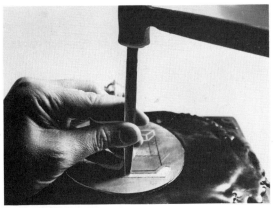  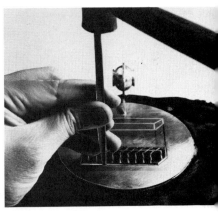

14   15   16

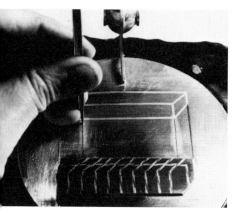

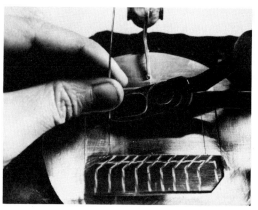

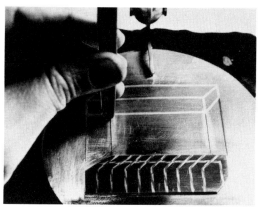

17   18   19

RELIEF OR MOUND INLAY (takaniku zogan)

15 Relief or "mound" inlay is almost the same in method as flat sheet inlay, with the difference that the finished inlay is in relief above the surface of the ground. The recess does not have to be excavated as deeply as in flat inlay.

A shakudo blank is prepared in this case from 18 gauge B.&S. in the same manner as described for the last. A heavy gauge is used as this inlay will project in relief *above* the surface of the base.

MULTI-METAL WIRE INLAY (nawame zogan)

The shakudo blank is seen here with an inlay of a patterned wire made of round twisted copper and fine silver already in place. Both wires were originally 20 gauge B.&S. After being tightly twisted together, they were drawn through a *drawplate* until they were 20 gauge B.&S. The place between the two metals is then flooded with easy-flow hard solder to unify and strengthen the wire which can then be treated as a single wire, and inlaid by the wire inlay method (*sen zogan*). The use of such patterned wire in inlay is called *nawame zogan*, (*nawame* = rope).

16 Chisel a groove and excavate the surplus ground metal, then raise and straighten the burr in the manner described on p. 311 for Photo 12. File the edges of the blank to a bevel, and place the blank in the excavation. Here the burr is being pushed down alongside the inserted blank with a vertically held *tracer punch* (*jo tagane*), not an embossing punch.

In some cases, the form of the inlay may be made *con-*

vex by hammering it from the back before placement to dome the shape somewhat. After it is placed, it is hammered down to force it into the undercut, then the burr is set down. It is also possible for the inlay to be a casting in relief, repoussé-worked sheet metal, or layers of sheet metal soldered to each other. In all cases, their edges are beveled to an angle, and the form is then inlaid in the manner described for sheet inlay.

FLUSH DOT INLAY (hira shizuku zogan)

In this process, wire is inlaid *endwise* into the ground, so that when the inlay is completed, as round wire is used, it is a flush round dot. The ground should be at least 16 gauge B.&S. and the wire used here is round, 20 gauge B.&S. pure gold. Finer wire can also be used but requires smaller tools and greater care.

17 Punch a hole straight down in the ground metal to half the depth of its thickness with a *flat round punch* (*maru jo tagane*) whose diameter is one gauge smaller than the round wire being inlaid. After punching, rotate the tool clockwise while tapping it lightly so that an undercut is formed. At the same time, the size of the hole is increased to 20 gauge B.&S. which is the size of the inlay wire used. *File* off one end of the annealed wire flat, and place it in the hole.

18 Cut the wire off with *side nippers* a little above the level of the ground, and file the cut end flat. It is also possible to precut a length of wire, file both ends flat, and place it with *tweezers* perpendicularly into the hole.

19 Place a *blunt-ended embossing punch* with a face large enough to cover the wire and tap the punch to force the wire to fill the circular recess. *File* the surplus metal

20   21   22

off to level the dot inlay flush with the ground, then sand the surface smooth.

RAISED DOT INLAY (shizuku zogan)

20 This inlay process is started in the same manner as flush dot inlay. First hammer the round punch straight down, then rotate it clockwise while tapping it with a hammer to make an undercut and enlarge the hole slightly to the desired diameter.

21 The wire used for these raised dots is pure gold, 20 gauge B.&S. Place the wire upright in the hole and cut it off a little *above* the level of the ground. To create the domed, rounded end, a *round hollow-ended punch (nanako tagane)* is used. Hold this vertically over the wire end and tap it straight down. In the hammering, the wire end fills the hemispherical depression in the punch and forms a dome. After the first few taps, rotate the punch while tapping it to round the raised dot evenly.

The same round, hollow-ended *nanako punch* is commonly used in Japanese metalwork to create a ground pattern, surface decoration, or texture by striking series of small circles in straight or diagonal lines one next to the other, the effect called "fish roe surface." The diameter of the dot varies between 0.04–0.08 in (1–2 mm), the small size making it necessary to place them entirely by touch. In some cases, a flat inlay of different colored metals is gone over with a continuous *nanako* pattern that passes over from inlay to ground without interruption.

22 Remove the piece from the pitch and place it in a lacquer thinner (acetone) to remove the pitch. Do not use heat in cleaning the work as it might cause the inlay ground to warp and the inlaid metal to fall out.

POSTINLAY PATINATION

When the inlay work is finished, polished, and cleaned, it is then patinated. The natural color range of the metals and alloys used can be increased considerably by the use of chemical coloring agents. This is one of the reasons that in Japan, metals that accept chemical patination well are favored for inlay work. Foremost among these are *shakudo* and *shibuichi,* both discussed under Mercury Amalgam Gilding. (See Chapter 15.) When these are treated with the favored coloring chemical *rokusho* (also Chapter 15), shakudo takes on a rich purplish black color, and shibuichi a grayish silver color. The same chemical, rokusho, reacts differently in the same bath with copper, giving it a reddish brown patina, while it does not affect the pure gold and pure silver. Another coloring solution used is a combination of 50% ammonia and 50% liquid soap which gives shakudo a brown color, improved by rubbing. The Japanese call metal inlays of several alloys on one object *iroye* ("colored picture") because besides natural color differences, each metal develops its own color under patination.

23 The finished pendant, ground metal disc, copper, 16 gauge B.&S., diameter 3 in (7.4 cm).

Technique	Part	Metal (B.&S. gauge)
Wire inlay (*sen zogan*)	upper box	fine silver, 20 gauge
Flush sheet inlay (*hira zogan*)	lowest shadow form	shakudo, 20 gauge
Relief inlay (*takamiku zogan*)	lower box form	shakudo, 18 gauge
Rope wire inlay (*nawame zogan*)	compound wire on lower box form	fine silver and copper, 20 gauge each, drawn to 20 gauge
Flush dot inlay (*hira shizuku zogan*)	flush dots	pure gold, 20 gauge
Raised dot inlay (*shizuku zogan*)	raised dots	pure gold, 20 gauge

23

VARIATIONS OF INLAY

INLAY IN A CROSSHATCHED GROUND (nunome zogan)

In this inlay process, instead of cutting grooves and recesses for the inlaid wire and sheet, the entire ground surface or selected areas on it become the field for a freely placed, normally precious metal inlay, though soft brass or copper can be used. The surface or areas are *crosshatched* to make a rough texture capable of holding an inlay that can completely or partially cover the ground into which it is hammered. This system is called *koftgari* in Trivandrum, India; *tela-kubi* in Qasvin, Iran, where it is used to inlay gold wire on three-dimensional steel animals carried in Moharram processions; *taraceado* in Toledo, Spain, where steel jewelry and ornamental objects are produced; and *nunome zogan* in Kyoto, Japan, where it is used for the decoration of jewelry and objects. Old armor from East and West was commonly ornamented by this technique, and examples are preserved in many museums. Surprisingly, this alternative to the more time-consuming inlay technique already described is referred to in some sources as "false damascene," a derogatory term. Both techniques are valid, and each is capable of its own perfection. The crosshatched ground inlay method described here is prac-

8-39 TORAHIKO MINAI, damascene inlay artisan working at the Amita Jewelry Corp., Kyoto, Japan. Because steel is the base metal of the damascene work produced here, to hold work in progress, a *permanent magnet chuck* is used, manufactured by the Kanetsu Kogyo Co. Ltd., Osaka, Japan (Model KMT-1018 shown). The steel ground form is placed on the flat upper slab, and magnetic action is activated by a lever. Reversing the lever position deactivates the magnet, allowing the release of the steel. *Photo: Oppi*

(Surface preparation is also done mechanically today on large sheets which are then cut into shapes.) The surface now has a texture resembling a finely woven cloth. The result is lightly etched in a nitric acid solution, and overetching is avoided to retain burr sharpness. The metal is washed and dried.

INLAYING WIRE OR SHEET IN THE PREPARED GROUND The ground is anchored in a *pitch bowl* or on a *board* spread with pitch, or is *clamped* to a *steel block*. The design is drawn on the toothed ground in pencil or waterproof ink. Inlays of fine precious metal wire or sheet need no annealing. Lower quality metals should be preannealed to increase malleability. Three basic inlay tools are used: a *small-peen hammer* to hammer in wire, a *pointed tool* to help guide wire directionally, and a *sharp chisel* to sever a wire end. Thin sheet is cut out or stamped to shape before inlay.

The wire line start is anchored in place simply by tapping it with the hammer peen. Thereafter, while leading the wire along the design line with fingers and pointed tool, hammering follows, tapping it permanently into place. Wire line width can be increased by placing wires alongside one another, or a whole area can be filled this

ticed by the highly skilled craftspersons of the Amita Jewelry Corporation in Kyoto, Japan.

PREPARING THE GROUND METAL The ground metal used in Kyoto is a flat *mild steel,* approximately 16 gauge B.&S. Other hard metals or alloys capable of being "toothed," such as bronze or a nickel alloy, could be used. Domed or dimensionally formed grounds can also be inlaid in this method, but flat grounds are not made dimensional *after* inlay because of the risk of loosening the inlay. To prepare the ground, a very *finely serrated liner chisel* (a *liner graver* could also be used) is hammered in one direction over the entire ground or a part of it, raising straight, very fine, parallel serrations with continuous burrs intact. A second series of lines is made at an oblique angle *over* the first, creating a surface like a double-cut file.

8-41 MITSUKO KAMBE SOELLNER, U.S.A. Hair clip and hairpin of mild steel, inlaid in the Japanese damascene (*zogan*) manner with 24K and 18K gold and fine silver. The ground is covered with black or brown lacquer. *Photo: Walter Soellner*

8-40 AMITA JEWELRY CORP., Kyoto, Japan. Their inlay process in four simplified steps, from left to right: 1. Lines are chiseled by hand with liner chisels on the steel ground in two opposing directions. 2. The design in 24K or lesser karat golds and fine silver wire is hammered into the crosshatched surface. 3. The surface is acid etched, cleaned, rusted, and passivated, then coated with four layers of black lacquer. 4. The lacquer is rubbed with powdered charcoal as an abrasive until the precious metal design is exposed. Enough remains to leave the ground a matte black, the lacquer protecting the steel from rusting. *Photo: Salmi*

way. Cut-out sheet metal shapes are inlaid by hammering them in position. Only finished inlaid areas are *burnished* to further force the inlay into the toothed ground whose serrations and burrs hold the inlay in place. Finished flat work is held on a *surface block* and completely planished with a *planishing hammer* to eliminate any remaining *nunome* ground texture.

Steel grounds left untreated and exposed might eventually develop rust. Japanese craftspersons cover grounds with a protective organic lacquer coating. To first clean and prepare the surface, it is painted with an alkaline solution of 18 grams of powdered ammonia dissolved in 180 cc of water. After two hours, a second coat is applied. The rinsed, cleaned object is then left submerged in water for 48 hours to brown it or build up an even layer of rust or hydrated red ferric oxide on its surface. To seal it from further rusting or corrosion, and to arrest, fix, and passivate the oxide rust formation, it is placed in a solution of 15 grams of tannic acid to 5 liters of water. (In an older method, a strong solution of green tea, which contains tannic acid, was used.) This is brought to a boil, and after 15 minutes the rust is converted to black iron oxide, and the object is removed, rinsed, and dried.

APPLYING THE LACQUER (URUSHI) Immediately afterward, to avoid contamination and assure good adhesion, the *entire surface* is coated with a natural organic resin lacquer (*urushi*) made from the milky sap tapped from the Japanese varnish tree *urushi-no-ki* (*Rhus verniciflua*), then boiled, skimmed, and filtered. Its chief component is *urushiol* ($C_{21}H_{32}O_2$), a water-soluble phenol that is poisonous in liquid form. As contact can cause skin inflammation, hands must be protected with *rubber gloves*. To color the naturally brownish lacquer, dry dye pigment, usually black, is added, though other colors can be used. A little water as a solvent extender liquefies it to an oily, flowing consistency, and the lacquer is then brushed over the entire surface. Normally it is dried in a humid atmosphere, but it can also be heated to about 320° F (160° C) and dried without harm. (Remove it from the heat when vapors cease rising.) Once dry, the result is hard, and resistant to acid, alkali, and humidity. Lacquer is applied in four layers. Each application is dried with heat, then rubbed with powdered charcoal and water as an abrasive to prepare the surface for the next coat. The final coat is rubbed down to the metal inlay level which is higher than the ground, therefore exposed first, leaving the ground covered with lacquer. The inlay is *burnished* where desired for selective matte and polished effects. Sometimes bright line details are engraved into the inlay. The surface is finished with rubbed-on paste wax, or sprayed with a clear lacquer. Units meant for jewelry are mounted in gold-plated bezel settings or frames.

TOLEDO CROSSHATCHED GROUND INLAY

The crosshatched ground inlay done in Toledo, Spain, follows the same basic inlay procedure, but the steel ground is heat oxidized black instead of being lacquer covered. Some special techniques are used here. Different weight wires and different colored golds are combined in the same work. Silver wire often outlines patterns. After inlay, lines are sometimes patterned with a *round hollow-ended punch* struck once, then moved to the next position. A series of tiny half-dome shapes are raised on the inlay. The effect is like an inlay of beaded wire. In the opposite manner, a small, *round-ended punch* is used to stamp

8–42 TOLEDO, SPAIN. Contemporary steel brooch inlaid with silver and gold wire in two colors, typical of the geometric style of much Toledo work. The ground is given a black patina by heat. Ø 2⅜ in. Photo: Oppi

semicircular depressions in unburnished (therefore matte) wire inlays. The depressions appear as a series of bright, concave spots in a matte ground. These effects greatly enrich the surface appearance of the work. The backs of the steel ground metal are highly polished and lacquered.

ENCRUSTATION OR OVERLAY

A distinction must be made between the concept of *inlay* and *encrustation* or *overlay*. Very often both words are applied indiscriminately to the process of inlay. Inlay and encrustation are related in that a second material is physically joined to the surface of the first. In metalwork, an inlay is introduced *into* the ground and held *mechanically*, that is, by an incision and undercut. An encrustation can be held to the ground *chemically*, that is, by the addition of a third substance, most usually with the join made by *soldering*—as when joining metal to metal—but it can also be done by *adhesives* or *cements*—as when joining nonmetallic substances to metal, or metal to nonmetallic substances such as shell, tortoiseshell, ivory, etc. It can also be held *mechanically* by rivets. But by strict definition, in all cases it rests *on the surface* of the ground.

METAL MOSAIC

A distinction must also be made between *metal inlay* and *metal mosaic,* which can appear the same from the front. In metal inlay, a supporting ground runs beneath all the inlaid metal. In a metal mosaic, different metals are *butt joined edgewise* to each other by soldering to form one continuous surface (which may be partially raised), but there is no underlying, supporting metal sheet, and the joins can usually be seen at the back. When the work is done carefully, a mosaic can be reversible.

METAL MOSAIC (KIRIHAME ZOGAN) In this process, a ground metal sheet is saw pierced, and into that opening, a second metal of the same shape and size is inserted and

8–43   JAPAN. Shakudo *tsuba* inlaid with multicolored sheet metals in the *iroye* or "colored picture" style. The leaves and blossoms are engraved after inlay. Signed: "Saiya" (Shonai School), 17th century. *Photo: Victoria and Albert Museum, London, Crown Copyright*

8–44   PETER SKUBIC, Austria. White gold brooch with a butt-soldered mosaic sheet of striped white and yellow gold. Size 38 × 38 mm. *Photo: Narbutt-Lieven & Co.*

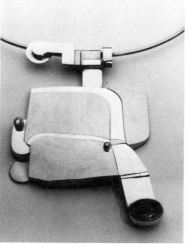

8–46   BERNARD FRANCOIS, Belgium. Pendant with diamonds and one moonstone, using a mosaic of yellow and white gold, sweat soldered to a base sheet. Size 6 × 6 cm. *Photo: Bernard François*

8–47   ALBERT PALEY, U.S.A. "Pendant No. 136." Fabricated from a butt-soldered mosaic of sterling silver, 14K gold, and copper, dimensionally formed; with a cameo, four pearls, and Delrin forms. Size 12 × 4 in. *Photo: Roger B. Smith*

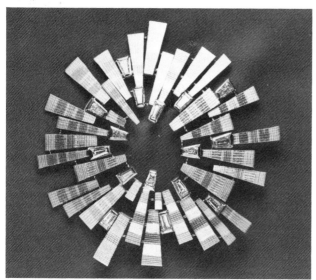

8–45   JOHN DONALD, England. Sunburst brooch with baguette diamonds. Each radial part is butt soldered in a mosaic of different colored golds, the surface matte textured. *Photo: Courtesy The Worshipful Company of Goldsmiths, London*

soldered. In Japan this is referred to as a form of inlay, but it is termed a *mosaic* in the West. A related Mexican technique is called "married metals" (*metales casados*). The same pattern appears on both sides, a fact that can be used to advantage in a piece of jewelry where both sides are seen when it is worn.

The area to be pierced is enscribed and sawed out of the ground metal. The edges of the pierced area are filed true and perpendicular, then placed in position on the ground. A line is enscribed within the pierced shape exactly at the base of the sheet where it contacts the second metal. The shape is then cut along the *outside* of the enscribed line to allow for some metal to be trimmed away until the shape matches the opening in the ground. Or, the shape to be inlaid can be made first, then traced on the ground which is then pierced. In this case, the opening is cut on the *inside* of the enscribed line to allow for trimming. In either procedure, the shape is then placed in the opening and soldered in. The surface is leveled by an abrasive. The inserted metal can be flat or a dimensional shape made by any means necessary.

MOSAIC SHEET   Mosaics can be assembled of pieces of different colored metals in any pattern, then soldered together edgewise in butt joints. The resulting sheet can be handled like any other sheet and shaped dimensionally by any cold working method.

INLAY OF NONMETALLIC SUBSTANCES IN A METAL GROUND

Nonmetallic substances such as wood, wood powder mixed with epoxy, mother of pearl, coral, bone, ivory,

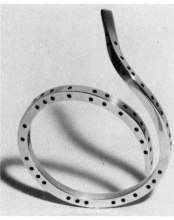

8-48 THOMAS GENTILLE, U.S.A. "Fall." Forged brass armlet, pierced with drilled holes inlaid with an ebony and epoxy mixture. *Photo: Hans Christian Graber*

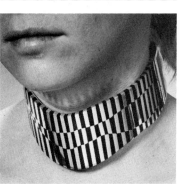

8-49 SYDNEY SCHERR, U.S.A. Sterling silver collar inlaid with alternating ebony strips. *Photo: Doug Moore*

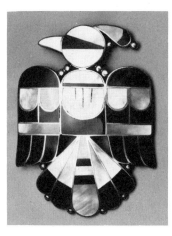

8-50 MYRA TUSCON, (Zuni) Pueblo, U.S.A. "Thunderbird." Silver pin with inlays of mother of pearl, tortoiseshell, and jet fixed in upstanding cloisons. Height 3 in. *Photo: Courtesy U. S. Department of the Interior, Indian Arts and Crafts Board*

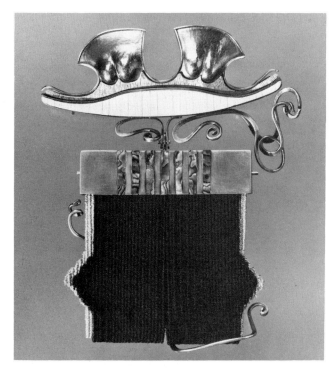

8-51 RICHARD MAFONG and JON ERIC RIIS, U.S.A. Sterling silver and gold pin inlaid with ivory and abalone shell, with a section in woven tapestry. Size 5 × 4 in. *Photo: Andrew N. Foster*

plastic, stones, or glass can be inlaid in a metal ground. This is done either by first making an excavation or depression in the base metal to receive the inlay, or by fabricating upstanding parts having spaces for the insertion of the inlay between or into them. Wire enclosures, for instance, can be soldered to a ground sheet, and the spaces between them inlaid with any of these materials. Some substances such as wood mixed with epoxy will adhere to a clean metal surface, and other materials call for the use of a suitable cement to hold the particular material to the ground. Generally an epoxy will work with most of those mentioned. If in doubt about the holding efficiency of a particular cement, make a trial join before using it on the final work.

LIQUID METAL INLAY

Powdered metals mixed in suspension in epoxy or other adhesives are available on the market, sold in tubes. These cold "liquid metals" can also be used as inlays in depressions of a ground metal of a contrasting color. The preparation of the ground metal usually includes roughening the areas to receive the liquid metal in order to provide a "tooth" which aids in its adhesion. Read and follow instructions provided with the particular product. Once this material has hardened, the surface can be sanded level with the base, then polished either by hand or on a polishing lathe. The result appears as a metal inlay.

INLAY OF METAL INTO NONMETALLIC GROUNDS: Piqué work

Metal wire or sheet cut or stamped into small shapes can be inlaid into nonmetallic grounds. A traditional technique of this type is *piqué work* (from the French *piquer,* "to prick, puncture, insert, or eat into a surface"), in which gold or silver wire and small stamped shapes are inlaid into tortoiseshell. This work first became popular in France during the 17th century, after which it was introduced to England by Huguenot refugees. It retained its popularity during the 18th century and most of the 19th century when mechanical mass production took over and caused a decline in its acceptance.

In traditional piqué work, when wire or small shapes were forced *endwise* into tortoiseshell, the technique was termed *piqué point* (French *point,* "hole or dot," therefore "dotted piqué"), and when lengths of straight or twisted wire were *laid flat* into the base, it was called *piqué posé* (French *posé,* "to lay down on the side").

In either case, the process consists of cutting lengths of wire, heating them, and while holding them with *pliers,* forcing them—endwise or flat—into the tortoiseshell, horn, or plastic base. (When wood is used as a base, holes must be drilled first to receive the inlay.) The heated metal melts the ground material locally. It can be left to cool, or dipped into cold water to solidify the ground. Normally, any surplus metal protruding above the surface is filed flush with the ground surface, but it can also be left in relief. Small rivet heads and dimensionally stamped shapes were used in this way. Small-diameter tubing is also used today, their inlay forming small round or other forms. Larger sheet metal forms can be secured by the use of wire rivets or pegs soldered to their backs. These can be allowed to pass completely through the ground material, and then be bent over on the reverse side to clinch them.

These techniques are used in Mexico today where silver

wire and mother of pearl are inlaid into cut-out shapes of tortoiseshell which are then mounted in fabricated silver settings: In India, brass and white metal wire in various sectional shapes are inlaid endwise and lengthwise into horn and plastic to make intricate patterns on combs and bangles.

ELECTRODEPOSITED INLAY

It is possible to first etch (or otherwise make an intaglio design in a ground metal), then stop out the ground and back of the object with a resist leaving only the intaglio areas exposed, then use electrochemical deposition methods to inlay a different metal of a contrasting color into the depressions. (The basic method is described under Photoelectroforming, as Bi-metal electrodeposited inlay, p. 713.) Some results of this technique might be termed "electrodamascene."

8–52 8–53 DAVID HENSEL, England. Three carved wood acrobatic figural bracelets employing several hardwoods whose density and fine, compact grain allow detailed carving, and take a high polish. Specific density (or gravity) refers to this condition in seasoned wood with a standard average of 15% water content. Wood with a density greater than 1.0 will sink in water. Some of the woods used are described here, arranged alphabetically:

African blackwood: Dalbergia melanoxylon
Specific density: 1.2
Heartwood dark purplish brown with predominating black streaks. Exceptionally hard and heavy, fine even texture, is slightly oily and therefore takes an excellent finish, can be tapped for screw threads almost like metal.

Brier (or briar): Erica arborea
Specific density: 0.8–0.9
Root of the white or heath tree of Southern Europe, used for making smoking pipes. *Brierroot* is the common name used to designate the burl or flattened hemispherical excrescence that grows on the trunks of many trees such as *Kalmia, Mountain Laurel, Rhododendron,* and *Smilax,* used for the same purpose.

Common barberry: Berberis vulgaris
Specific density: 0.8–0.9
Bright yellow wood when freshly cut, darkening after exposure. There are 200 species in this genus, some of which are bushes, others small trees. The wood is hard and has an even grain with very small pores.

Ebony: Diospyros
Specific density: 0.8–1.2
Black heartwood sometimes streaked with dark brown. There are several species in this genus, all extremely hard and heavy.

English boxwood: Buxus sempervirens
Specific density: 0.83–1.14
White or light yellow wood approaching ivory in texture and color. Heavy, tough, very close grained, even texture, smooth, and capable of acquiring a bright surface.

Flowering dogwood: Cornus florida
Specific density: 0.9
Equivalent in the U.S.A. to the English boxwood above.

Indian rosewood: Dalbergia latifolia
Specific density: 0.85
Heartwood dark purple with black longitudinal streaks, extremely hard, close grained, with moderate-sized pores; also called Bombay blackwood.

Yew wood: Taxus baccata
Specific density: 0.67–0.82
Bright orange brown, or warm light brown, heavy, tough, resilient and fine grained. Though considered a softwood, it has many hardwood qualities.

The bracelet figures are hinged at the waist to allow opening and closing, and have wire loop and ball closing findings. Garments are inlays of square silver wire, abalone, awabi, and white mother of pearl. Eyes are inlaid with abalone irises and ebony pupils. Inlays are held in grooves by a *cyanoacrylate adhesive* (commercial product *Cyanolit*). This is a powerful, clear, nontoxic, instant contact adhesive developed for bonding small items of similar or dissimilar materials.

8–54 FRANCE, first half of the 19th century. Magnifying glass mounted in a tortoiseshell, piqué-decorated case, inlaid with gold wire *piqué point* work, and flat sheet metal forms in *piqué posé* work. *Photo: Österreichisches Museum für Angewandte Kunst, Vienna*

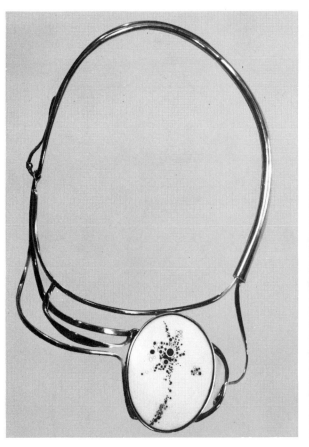

8–55 JOHN E. SATTERFIELD, U.S.A. Silver necklace with ivory plaque into which *piqué point* silver wire and tubing has been inserted through holes made completely through the ground (when one-sided patterns are created) or partly through (when two-sided patterns are the aim). Tubes are flared slightly to fix them in place. In addition, epoxy resin mixed with a catalyst and color in powdered form is forced into some holes with a flexible knife. After setting, the entire surface is sanded with 400 or 600 grit wet/dry sandpaper. The process is repeated for another color. The colors used here are red and black. Plastic, nylon, Teflon, Delrin, or wood could also be used as a ground for piqué work. *Photo: Oppi*

8–56 MARY ANN SCHERR, U.S.A. Sterling silver neckpiece whose design was created by photoetching. After the design was etched, the resist was left intact and the object returned to a gold plating bath for the electrodeposition of gold in the still exposed areas. Once the resist is removed, the depressed areas, now gold plated, appear as a gold inlay in a silver ground. The process may be termed "electrodamascene." *Photo: Rauno Träskelin*

8–57 *Above right:* IRAN. Muslim black coral rosary inlaid with *piqué* white metal wire. *Photo: Oppi*

8–58 PARTABGARH, INDIA. *Thewa* work brooch, a traditional technique done for at least the last 200 years exclusively by members of certain related families. The very small-scale design is pierced from a thin 22K gold sheet with small chisels. This is laid on a flat sheet of low-melting blue, green, or red glass cut to the desired silhouette, backed by fine silver foil, placed on a mica sheet, and heated in a charcoal-fired kiln whose heat is high enough to fuse the gold to the glass. After careful cooling, the gold is embellished with engraved details, and the result is fixed in fabricated mountings. In the last century, these craftsmen made a quantity of European-style jewelry to satisfy foreign demand, as well as objects like boxes and trays, ornamented with such units. The latter are still made today from gold-plated silver. Size 2 × 2 in. *Photo: Victoria and Albert Museum, London, Crown Copyright*

8–59 DAVID HENSEL, England. Ring in hardwoods and silver. The six-petaled parts open on hinges to reveal carved, crowned heads in various woods. The reverse side of the petals and the ring shank contain inlays of round wire and tubing in the *piqué point* style. Some tubes are inlaid with ivory, and *piqué posé* sheet metal flower-shaped units are also inlaid. *Photos: David Hensel* ▼

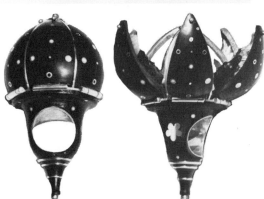

THE ACID ETCHING OF METAL

Selective metal removal by chemical action

The word *etch* is derived from Dutch and German words meaning "to eat or corrode." In this process, metal objects are etched by being immersed in an acid solution. To protect all unetched parts against acid attack, their entire surfaces—front, edges, and back—are coated with an acid-repelling substance called a *resist,* while *selected portions* on one or more surfaces in a pattern or design are left exposed to the acid's action. Gradually, the acid dissolves and corrodes these exposed places down to a desired level below the original surface, while the protected metal remains intact. Any of several separate biting and digesting menstrua or chemical agents that dissolve metal, or a combination of them can be used for this purpose depending on the metal being etched. These etching solutions are composed of inorganic mineral acids, organic acid solutions, or mixtures of these two. Some acids work best with particular metals, and some that have little or no effect on particular metals, will in combinations dissolve them into solution.

Success in the etching technique lies in the careful control of the etching acid solution strength, the application of the acid-resisting substance to the metal, the manner and skill with which the design is exposed through the resist, and in timing and judging the acid's action so that the etched figure appears in the metal in the desired depth and degree of regularity.

The distinction between acid etching, pickling, and acid cleaning is a matter of degree. Because acids are used for all these, there is often an overlapping of the terms and the techniques used. In general, acid pickling is of much shorter duration than etching. The solution has a greater percentage of acid, and its action is more severe, while acid cleaning uses a weaker solution mainly as a final or near final preparation of the metal for other processes.

THE USES OF ETCHING ACIDS AND PROCESSES

Etching is used in jewelry making to create a figural design, pattern, or texture on a metal surface. The etched areas are either important or minor parts of the design. The main figure can be left at the original metal level *in positive relief,* or it can be an etched out area *in negative intaglio.* From these conditions come the terms *relief etching* and *intaglio etching.*

Etching can be used for the following purposes:

To prepare a recess in metal for the inlay of another material such as a contrasting metal, niello, enamel, resins, wood and epoxy-resin mixtures, shell, or other substances.

An all-over texture can be etched on a metal sheet which can then be cut and shaped dimensionally into any form and used as a part of a fabricated work. Parts of the surface of an already fabricated work can be textured.

Breakthrough etching employs acids that etch completely through a metal sheet to create planned openings and achieve a pierced design without the use of a jeweler's

8–60 LYNDA WATSON-ABBOTT, U.S.A. "Matthews Inspired Neckpiece." Constructed in three parts, with hinged joints. The main figure is etched in relief, the outline in intaglio, using soft and hard grounds. *Photo: Lynda Watson-Abbott*

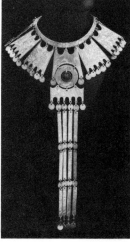 

8–61 *Left:* MARY ANN SCHERR, U.S.A. Sterling silver torso necklace with lapis lazuli. Many sheet metal units, etched in line patterns are joined by jump rings. Size 13 × 20 in. *Photo: Richard Monasterio*

8–62 *Right: DETAIL* of the torso necklace.

saw or chisels; to make slots; or to create an object with a special contour.

Double- or multi-sided etching is a means of etching a sheet of metal by allowing the etchant to work on both sides of the metal simultaneously. The time needed for breakthrough is halved. In this case, the workpiece must be suspended in the etchant by a resist-coated wire.

Etched results can be combined with other decorative surface techniques. For instance, lines can be engraved to introduce a sharp, controlled, bright line to contrast with the softer quality of an etched line or textural area. Repoussage or three-dimensional surfaces can be etched for any of the above purposes.

MATERIALS USED IN THE METAL ETCHING PROCESS

FOR THE PRE-ETCH METAL PREPARATION Cleaning: Pumice powder, chalk, whiting, or other suitable powdered abrasive; a water source.

FOR THE TRANSFER OF THE DESIGN TO THE METAL Tracing paper bearing the design; masking tape; pencils, hard and soft; metal scribe.

FOR THE ACID RESIST AND ITS APPLICATION Commercially prepared asphaltum, or a composition made to a recipe; (alternatives to asphaltum: beeswax, resin, lacquer, or stop-out varnish); soft applicator brushes, ½–1 in (1.3–2.5 cm) width sizes; paper towels.

FOR THE CREATION OF DESIGN DETAILS Metal scribe; wood stick, mounted steel needles.

FOR THE ETCHING BATH PROCESS Acid; glass measuring graduate or beaker; glass or plastic stirring rod; glass acid bath container large enough to hold the workpiece being etched; distilled or boiled water; feathers to agitate the acid solution and remove sludge; scribe to test the depth of etch; a water source.

FOR POSTETCH METAL CLEANING Turpentine, paint thinner, or other suitable resist solvent; rags; paper towels.

ACID FIRST AID MATERIALS (See Acids: Handling Precautions, p. 326. Barrier cream can be spread thinly on the hands to prevent harmful effects of acid contact, should this occur.

THE ETCHING PROCESS

DEMONSTRATION 13

MARY ANN SCHERR relief etches a pendant

Photos: Douglas Moore

CREATING THE DESIGN

1 The design is accurately drawn on the tracing paper or any smooth, translucent paper. Part of this design was created with the help of a plastic template or stencil of circles. After placing the selected shape on the paper, a sharp pencil is used to trace the inside outline of the shape, guiding it around the edges of the opening. French curves can also be used to create smooth, flowing, curved lines, and straight edges for straight lines.

CLEANING THE METAL

2 Scrub with fingers or a brush all surfaces, front, back, and edges of the metal with a finely powdered abrasive such as pumice, chalk, or whiting, to remove grease and any other contaminating foreign matter. The resist will not adhere properly to anything but a chemically clean surface. The surface is clean enough when water poured over it will cover it and cling to it by surface tension in a thin film for at least 30 seconds without any water break. Such a break indicates the existence of grease, and the cleaning process must be repeated in areas where this happens. Dry the metal carefully with a clean paper towel. Never touch a cleaned surface directly with the fingers as skin oil and fingerprints will be immediately imparted to the metal, and this will affect the ability of the resist to adhere in such places. Leave the metal covered with a clean, dry paper towel to prevent the development of surface oxidation. For the same reason, some etchers place the prepared metal in a container with distilled water, not tap water which may contain contaminants that encourage oxidation.

COVERING AGENTS: THE ACID RESIST AND ITS APPLICATION

3 The conventional material used to resist acid action on the metal is an asphaltum (sometimes termed "asphal-

Typical Hard Ground Resist Compositions

Constituent	Recipes (in parts)					
	1	2	3	4	5	6
Asphaltum	4	3	2	2	2	
Beeswax			2			8
Burgundy pitch	2		1	0.5		
Mastic gum		6				
Pitch				0.5		
Rosin					2	10
Tallow						2
Turpentine					12	10
Wax, white	1	10		2	2	

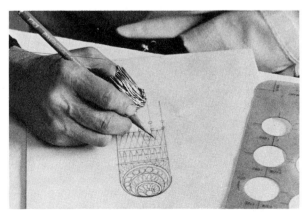

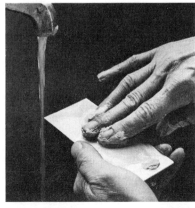

1   2   3

tum varnish"), a preparation containing asphaltum, pitch, and wax, commonly known to graphic etchers as a *hard ground*. This preparation can be purchased ready-made, but a craftsperson can also make his or her own mixture and in this way meet any special conditions, such as seasonal atmosphere and temperature changes. To compensate, it may be necessary to alter a mixture, therefore its constituents should be known. Additional wax makes the result softer; additional pitch makes it harder and more brittle.

Asphaltum is a blackish brown natural bituminous deposit found in various countries, or obtained as a residue from certain evaporated petroleums, coal tar, or lignite, or as a by-product of petroleum derived from distillation. It can be hard and brittle, or in a plastic state. It melts on heating and if the temperature is high enough burns with a smoky flame. It is soluble in turpentine and unaffected by acids. Upon exposure to air it loses its essential oils and becomes hard. Besides its use in resists, it is used for road paving, roofing, paints, and varnishes.

Burgundy pitch or *fused colophony* is an opaque, yellowish brown, hard, brittle resin exuded from the Norway spruce, the balsam fir, the balsam poplar, and certain pines. It is a residue of the process of distilling turpentine from this exudate.

Mastic gum is a clear to light yellow gum-resin exuded from the mastic or pistachia tree of the Mediterranean area. The gum-resin is gathered from incisions made in the tree bark and dissolved in turpentine to remove impurities. It is soft at 90° F (32° C), melts at 105–120° F (40–48° C), and is soluble in oil of turpentine and hot alcohol. It is used in lacquers and resin-oil varnishes, and widely used as a picture varnish.

Pitch is an artificial asphalt, a fusible, pyrogenous residue obtained by the destructive distillation of wood, coal, and bones. It varies in consistency from a viscous liquid to a brittle solid, and is near black in color.

Rosin, or more properly *colophony* is a translucent, light yellow to reddish brown, brittle, easily fusible, solid residue remaining after the distillation of turpentine from pine wood. It is soluble in oil of turpentine, alcohol, and acetone. It is used on violin bow strings for traction.

Tallow is extracted by melting it from the membranous and fibrous matter of the ox and the sheep. When pure it is white and almost tasteless. Its solid consistency is due to the large proportions of glycerol esters of stearic and palmitic acids. It is used as an additive to casting waxes, and as a lubricant in spinning. Its presence in acid resists makes the resist less brittle.

Turpentine, from which a colorless essential oil called *oil of turpentine* is obtained by distillation, comes from the oleoresin derived from various species of pine, balsam, fir,

and larch trees. In the distillation process, several by-products are obtained, one of which is rosin. Turpentine is a solvent for all the materials mentioned here and is widely used as an oil painting medium.

Wax is obtained from animal, insect, mineral, petroleum, and vegetable sources. The most important insect source is beeswax, widely used in the arts as a lubricant, as an additive to resists and pitch compositions, as a filler, etc. The best quality is prepared from one-year-old honeycombs from which the bee larvae have not yet emerged, and is a bright yellow (darker yellow when older), though it can be bleached white. It is compatible with all the natural materials used in acid resists. Its melting temperature range is 142–149° F (61–65° C), it dissolves in oil of turpentine, and is very resistant to acids. Plant, mineral, and petroleum waxes all are soluble in oil of turpentine.

When preparing an asphaltum-based resist, first melt the wax and pitch together, then add the asphaltum and other ingredients. Mix them thoroughly, stirring them continuously over a low heat, allowing the mixture to simmer. *Do not boil or overheat* which would cause it to burn. The result is a black, opaque, viscous substance which can be made thinner if necessary with its solvent, turpentine. To keep it viscous, store it in a well-closed container so that its volatile oil constituent does not evaporate, which would cause the resist to harden.

When applying a resist that is basically wax, avoid an excessively thick layer by heating the metal and dipping it with *tongs* into the molten wax in a container, then hold it vertically by the edges and allow the surplus wax to drain off. To make lines enscribed in wax more visible, smoke the surface by moving it constantly over a candle flame to deposit a film of carbon on it. After etching, remove the wax by immersing the metal in boiling water. Remove any remaining wax film with an emulsifying detergent.

OTHER ACID RESISTS

Stop-out varnish is a quick-drying varnish used to make quick repairs in places where the asphaltum has lifted away from the metal, or where it has been nicked in handling. Such places are discovered upon inspection during etching. It can also be used if the etching is to be done in two depths, a method described on p. 324.

Resist pens developed for the electronics industry for use in preparing printed circuits are available. They dispense a resist which can be drawn as a fine line on the clean metal surface. The result must be baked before etching.

APPLYING THE ASPHALTUM COMPOUND RESIST

As soon after cleaning as possible, paint the dry metal with a thin, even coat of the prepared asphaltum com-

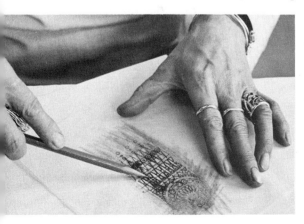

4   5   6

pound only on the side of the metal that will be etched. Allow the resist to dry to the point of tackiness, when it still can be touched without pulling away from the metal. With fresh asphaltum this takes about half an hour. Working the resist in this flexible condition eliminates the problem of asphaltum chipping that might occur if you enscribe the metal when the asphaltum is completely dry and hard. At the same time, prepare a small sample of the metal being etched to use later as a test piece when judging the bite strength of the acid solution.

The metal used here is a 2 in × 4½ in (5.1 cm × 11.4 cm) piece of sterling silver. It is wise to use a sheet of metal that allows a *margin of surplus* all around the shape. This surplus will later be cut away to the true contour of the piece with a *jeweler's saw*. Its purpose is to avoid the risk of the acid attacking the edges of the object.

TRANSFERRING THE DESIGN FROM PAPER TO METAL

4 To transfer the paper design to the metal, blacken the reverse side of the paper with a soft lead pencil. A piece of carbon paper could be used instead.

5 Place the metal with the asphaltum-covered surface to be etched up on the table, and anchor it with straight pins to prevent its movement. With *masking tape,* fix the tracing paper, *design face up in exact position,* to the metal plate. Lightly trace the main outlines with a *pencil* or *stylus* to impart graphite to the asphaltum surface. The finer details can be added directly to the metal later with greater accuracy. Lift the tracing paper often during the process of tracing to avoid its sticking. Avoid excessive pressure which can cause thin places in the asphaltum resist where acid can attack the metal.

6 Remove the tracing paper and develop the design directly on the metal with a metal-tipped *rounded-point scriber* sharp enough to part the semisoft resist without cutting into the metal surface. Normal pressure on the tool produces the desired result. Lightly brush away any small particles of resist removed in the process.

7 Once the design is completed, stand the metal up and paint the asphaltum resist on the back and the edges and any other areas where acid contact is to be avoided, and allow it to dry.

Never try to thin an already prepared resist, or to revive very old, dried asphaltum, because the proportions are then no longer in balance and its reliability is questionable. It must be discarded. Avoid rapid drying out of the asphaltum by keeping it in an airtight container.

SUGGESTED ALTERNATIVES IN ETCHED DESIGN DEVELOPMENT

This demonstration workpiece is an example of *relief etching,* in which the line pattern is etched to define the forms left in relief at the original metal level. The reverse, *intaglio etching,* is also possible; that is, a pattern is created in which the etched-out areas become the main design forms and the ground is left in relief.

Areas can be blocked out by cutting shapes in draftsman's tape to make a *frisket* (adhesive-backed stencil), which is fixed to the metal before painting the surface with asphaltum. When the asphaltum is dry, the frisket is removed. *Coated frisket paper* in several degrees of stickiness is available at art material suppliers—use one with a *light* sticking power.

Rubber or metal stamps can be pressed into asphaltum spread on glass and quickly stamped on the metal. Textured surfaces can be dipped into asphaltum and then pressed on the metal to impart the texture.

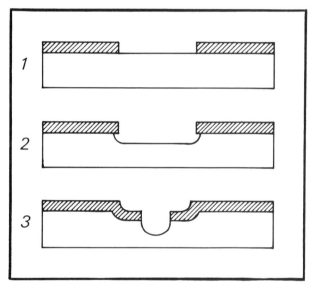

8-63 THE ETCHING PROCESS
1. The *metal with the resist* (shaded area) applied, leaving direct access of the etchant to selected areas of the metal surface.
2. The *etched area of the metal* after a *first etch* showing how the etchant undercuts the resist slightly, due to the etch factor, thus broadening the etched area on the surface of the metal.
3. After a *second resist* has been applied to partly cover the first etched surface, the *second etch* progresses to a new level.

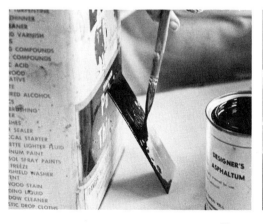

7

8

9

Figures can be painted on the metal with a brush dipped into asphaltum, and the areas between them etched away. Asphaltum can be spattered on the metal with a stiff brush, or stippled onto the surface with a sponge to achieve a texture. Lines can be enscribed through asphaltum-textured surfaces.

The etching process can be carried out in two (or more) stages. In the first, the pattern is etched to a certain depth. When reaching this level, remove the metal from the bath, rinse, and dry it. Carefully paint over the areas etched to the first depth with quick-drying *stop-out varnish*. When this dries, return the metal to the bath to etch out the second level. To allow this treatment, metal of at least 16 gauge B.&S. minimum thickness should be used, otherwise there is a risk of making the second depth parts too thin or even eating through the metal.

ACIDS: Handling precautions

Before proceeding to the use of acid etchants, mention must be made of precautions necessary to handle acids. Any acid is potentially dangerous if it is not handled correctly and with care.

Any work involving acids should be done near a ready supply of *running water*. Upon *skin contact* with acetic, hydrochloric, nitric, or sulphuric acids, immediately flush the area with lots of warm running water. If the area is burned, freely apply baking soda (sodium bicarbonate, $NaHCO_3$) dissolved with enough water to make a paste. This is an alkaline substance that neutralizes acids. A solution of ordinary ammonia water is also effective for this purpose. *Household ammonia water* is a dilute solution of about 28% ammonia gas (NH_3) in water. Keep the sodium bicarbonate and a prepared bottle of ammonia water at hand when using acids. In *eye contact,* in case of splashing, promptly flush the eye with plenty of water for at least five minutes. As soon as possible, consult a physician. Work in a *well-ventilated area* that has an efficiently operating exhaust fan to remove the harmful acid fumes. When it is necessary to bend over a container holding acid do not do so for an extended period of time. Sulphuric acid is corrosive to the mucous membranes of the nose and mouth. It is a wise precaution to use *goggles* and a *face mask* for protection against splashes. Coat the hands with a *barrier cream* and wear *rubber gloves* when the hand must be immersed in the acid. A protective *rubber apron* or a jacket will protect your clothing. Above all, work with considered action. *Never work in a rush.* Never put a cut finger into an acid solution. Never eat food or drink in a workshop, especially when acids are in use; and never smoke in the presence of acids.

PREPARING THE MORDANT OR ACID ETCHING SOLUTION

8 When making up acid solutions, remember the rule: *Always pour undiluted acid into water,* and *not* the reverse which causes a dangerous, violent spattering and fuming, especially in the case of sulphuric acid. Stir the acid into the water with a *glass* or *acid-resistant plastic rod* to help it combine more quickly with water. In mixing these liquids, heat stresses occur in the solution, and they can cause a glass container to crack, with disastrous results. Slowly blending the acid and the water lessens the chances of such an occurrence.

The common *acid container* used in etching by jewelers is one made of heatproof glass, in a shape, size, and depth suited to the article to be etched. Shaped pieces require deeper containers than flat pieces.

It is safer to use *distilled* or *boiled water* warmed to about 120° F (48° C), and not hot or cold water when making up acid solutions. Measure the acid in a *marked beaker* or *graduate* and while stirring, add it slowly to the water, according to the proportion used. In this case, approximately one-third acid to two-thirds water is recommended. Other proportions are given below. If spillage occurs, clean it up quickly with a sponge while wearing rubber gloves, then rinse the sponge under warm running water, because in the future, even when dried, its contact with other chemicals can cause an undesirable reaction.

When storing acid after use, put it in a *clearly marked, well-closed glass container,* placed at eye level out of the way, in a well-ventilated place where it is not subjected to heat. The container should not be filled to the top. Some air space should be left to allow for expansion in changed atmospheric conditions.

It is good practice to perform a *test* of the action of the solution on the previously prepared test piece. After observation of the acid action on the metal, if necessary, measures can be taken to change the proportions of the solution. Such a test should be made each time an etching bath is used to avoid the risk of destroying all the work done on the metal to this point.

Observe the action of the acid on the immersed test piece. If the solution is too strong, bubbles of gas will form on exposed metal parts *immediately* after immersion, and if very strong, gas may rise visibly. Solutions that are too strong tend to lift the resist off the metal. To correct this, add small amounts of *water* slowly to the solution, an act no longer dangerous because the solution is already much diluted. A total lack of visible action means the solution is too weak (if it is one that has been exhausted, it is said to be "spent"), and more *acid* must be slowly added to the solution and stirred in. An acceptable solution strength is one in which the exposed areas of metal *first* appear to become opaque, and *shortly afterward* form active gas bubbles.

9 Once the proper solution strength has been achieved the workpiece itself can then be safely immersed in the etching bath. Do *not* just drop it in as this might cause a disastrous splash. Use *copper acid tongs* for this purpose, and release it *gently,* then rinse off the tongs under running water. Another way is to rest one end in the solution and slowly lower the other end by means of a *cotton* (not wool which will dissolve) *cord* that has been looped around the metal. If the cord is left in place it can also be used to lift the piece out of the acid for inspection. *Bamboo photographer's tongs* can also be used to handle the metal. Be careful not to mar the resist in handling the work. Always rinse hands under running water if they have contacted the acid.

COMMON ACIDS USED FOR ETCHING

Hydrochloric acid (HCl), specific gravity (sp gr) 1.20, 40%, is also called *muriatic acid.* It is a colorless, aqueous solution of hydrogen chloride gas in water, made by the action of sulphuric acid on common salt. It fumes strongly in moist air. Most commercial preparations contain 37% acid dissolved in water.

Nitric acid (HNO_3), sp gr 1.42, 91%, commonly called *aquafortis,* is an inorganic, colorless, corrosive, and caustic liquid. A water solution containing more than 86% nitric acid is called *fuming nitric acid.* Dilute solutions of nitric acid are usually used for etching.

Sulphuric acid (H$_2$SO$_4$), sp gr 1.83, 87%, commonly called *oil of vitriol,* is an inorganic, colorless, corrosive, oily liquid widely employed. Miscible in all proportions with water, it destroys wood and other organic substances.

Aqua regia (Latin, "royal water"), is a very corrosive, fuming, yellow liquid made by mixing three volumes of hydrochloric, and one volume of nitric acid. It is so called because this combination of acids will corrode and etch gold and platinum, the "royal" metals, by the action of liberated chlorine. Both these metals are *insoluble* in either acid alone. When preparing aqua regia, stir the acids constantly, and work under a *fume hood.*

MORDANT SOLUTIONS FOR VARIOUS METALS

All metals can be etched if the proper *mordant* or etching menstrum is used and a suitable resist (one that can withstand the action of the particular mordant) is applied. Some etches can be used for several metals, but other metals react best to etching with special mixtures of various acids. Because all acids are water soluble, any etching solution can be weakened by adding water. Most solutions are used at room temperature, but their action can be hastened by heating. Generally speaking, slower etches are preferred to fast etches which may cause the resist to be lifted away from the metal, or etch an undercut in the wall of the groove.

If *soldered joints* exist on the work, no matter what acid is used for the etching solution, the joint should be protected with an acid resist or the acid will attack and weaken it. When handling metals being etched, use only *copper, bamboo,* or *plastic tongs,* and not iron or steel which will contaminate the etchant solution.

Acids are described as *chemically pure* (cp) if they contain less than one part per million of *any single impurity,* and a total of less than one part per ten thousand. Concentrated (conc.) acid is *undiluted* from the concentration in which it is usually offered for sale. *Specific gravity* (sp gr) is the ratio of the weight of any volume of a substance whose standard is *water* for solids and liquids, and *air* or *hydrogen* for gases, taken at the same temperature. When it is said that sulphuric acid has a specific gravity of 1.83 when pure, this means that bulk for bulk, at a given temperature, it is 1.83 times as heavy as the same volume of water. As all acids have a greater specific gravity than water, they will tend to settle at the bottom of the container holding the water if they are not mixed. Once mixed, however, they will not separate. If the water of an etching solution is allowed to evaporate, the remaining chemicals and the dissolved metals they contain crystallize. Silver can be recovered from spent acids. (See Precipitation and Recovery of Silver from Spent Acid Solutions, Chapter 3.)

Gold
Dilute Aqua Regia
Nitric acid	1 part
Hydrochloric acid	3 parts
Water	40–50 parts

Silver, strong
Nitric acid	2–3 parts
Water	1 part

Silver, weak
Nitric acid	1 part
Water	3–5 parts

Copper and *Brass,* fast etch
Sulphuric acid	1 part
Water	2 parts

Copper and *Brass,* slow etch
Hydrochloric acid	1 part
Potassium chloride	0.2 parts
Water	9 parts

Nickel Silver (German silver)
Use a concentrated solution of nitric acid, clear, clean. and white (free of impurities)
Nitric acid	1 part
Hydrochloric acid	3 parts
Water	according to strength desired

Steel and *Iron*
Hydrochloric acid	1 part
Water	1 part

Steel and *Iron,* deep etch
Nitric acid	1 part
Water	1 part

Steel and *Iron,* light etch
Nitric acid	1 part
Water	4–8 parts

Pewter
Nitric acid	1 part
Water	4 parts

STRENGTH-TIME-TEMPERATURE FACTORS

The action of the acid on the metal is a function of *strength-time-temperature* factors. The *strength* of the acid depends on its proportion to the water and other chemicals in the solution. Weak solutions take a longer time to act on metal and strong ones are quicker. Weak solutions tend to eat down into the metal at a more or less straight angle, while strong ones tend to eat it at an ever broadening angle. The result may be the thickening of a line, or an undercut. When using etching as a means of preparing the metal for an inlay of another substance, an undercut may, however, serve a good purpose. If a shallow surface design is the aim, a slower, weaker solution is generally preferred, to minimize the chance of distorting the design.

Time is a factor that can be utilized to compensate for the normal rate of the acid's action. Long, slow bites in weak solutions can achieve results roughly equivalent to short bites in stronger solutions. Under normal conditions, the time for an etch takes from 10 minutes to half an hour, but may take longer, depending on other variables.

Temperature control can compensate for lack of strength and shorten time. Warm or hot solutions are more active than cold ones. A weaker solution can be made to act more quickly by heating it, and a stronger solution can work more slowly by cooling it.

AGITATION OF THE ETCHANT

Agitation or movement of the mordant solution is a means of increasing the speed of the etching and reduces severe *undercutting* (lateral or sideways etch). *Etch factor* is the etch depth divided by the amount of sideways etch at an edge where resist meets metal. An etch factor of 2 means the etch depth is twice as large as the undercut. Agitation also helps to achieve a smoother surface on the etched metal areas. Use a *feather* to brush away the reaction and residual products such as bubbles and sludge. Feathers are not affected by dilute acids—they are dyed in acid solutions. By agitation, new surfaces are continually presented to the etchant. Conversely, for a textured surface, only agitate the etchant occasionally. The unmoved gas bubbles and sludge tend to block the even action of

10

11

12

the ctchant, causing the metal to reveal its crystalline structure. The stronger the etch, the rougher the surface.

INSPECTION OF THE ETCH

As the exact time needed for the action of the acid is not known in advance, it is necessary to pay close attention to the progress of the process by inspecting the article every 5–10 minutes. To test the depth of the etch, lightly draw a *scribe* across a groove, taking care not to dig into the resist. If a noticeable drop is felt, a satisfactory etch is taking place. At intervals it is advisable to lift the metal from the etching bath to inspect it. At this time, if necessary, repairs can be made to the resist. Rinse and dry the metal, apply quick-drying *stop-out varnish* or *lacquer,* and when this dries, return it to the mordant. When etching is finished, remove and rinse the work under running water, and dry it.

RESIST REMOVAL WITH SOLVENT

10   After etching, asphaltum-based resist can be removed by pouring its solvent, *turpentine,* over the metal and rubbing with an old, *stiff brush* or a *soft cloth.* A fine-grade *steel wool* can be used in case of difficulty, and *paint thinner* will also work. Allow good ventilation to avoid inhaling fumes.

11   Here we see the finished etched plate after resist removal, and before it is cut with a *jeweler's saw* to its final contour.

12   The finished, etched pendant contoured to its final shape and size, now 1¾ in × 4½ in. The sterling silver necklace includes a cabochon amber stone, beads of tubing sections and amber strung on a chain, and tassels made of fine commercial chain.

The etched lines can be left bright or oxidized with a potassium sulphide solution (liver of sulphur) to turn them black. The raised surface is freed of oxide by relieving or hand rubbing it *in one direction only* with 0000-grade fine steel wool.

Photo: Richard Monasterio

ELECTROCHEMICAL ANODIC ETCHING

(For information on electrical equipment and its employment, see Electroplating and Electroforming Equipment and Conditions, Chapter 16.) An electrochemical etching process is possible by first soldering a copper wire to the workpiece, then coating the object's surface with one of the usual acid resists. The piece is made *anodic* by attaching the wire to the current source or batteries, then immersing it in an electrolytic solution. A plate of metal the same as that of the work, lead or steel, is made the cathode. Etching is accomplished by the electrochemical dissolution of the metal. This process has the advantage that it is much quicker than simple etching in still solutions. The electrolyte does not eat out undercuts as

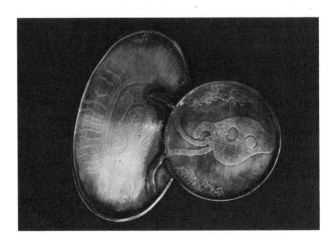

8–64   HAROLD O'CONNOR, U.S.A. "Ziggy-Zygote." Brooch in 14K gold and silver. The pattern was transferred from etched plates to a blank sheet by co-rolling them through a rolling mill. Width 2 in. Photo: Ron Burton

readily, and the etched lines are sharply defined. The electrolyte used for copper can be a dilute solution, 1 part sulphuric acid to 20 parts water; and for silver, a silver nitrate solution; both electrolytic solutions are used at a temperature of 68–140° F (20–60° C), at a current density of 5–10 A/dm².

A recommended resist for this process consists of:

Asphaltum	4 parts by volume
Pitch	1 part
Wax	4 parts

Its application and use is exactly the same as for ordinary etching. To be certain the metal is protected, this can be applied in a second layer after the first has dried.

STENCIL ETCHING METAL SHEET USING LIGHT-SENSITIZED GELATIN

Coat a clean, flat metal sheet or plate with *spirit varnish,* and allow this to dry hard. Prepare the following light-sensitizing solution under subdued light, preferably in a darkroom.

Gelatin or gum arabic	5 parts
Red potassium dichromate ($K_2Cr_2O_7$)	1 part
(store in a lightproof bottle)	
Distilled water	100 parts
Black pigment, water soluble, wet or dry	

Solution good for 1–2 days.

SOLUTION PREPARATION AND APPLICATION   Mix the gelatin and the red potassium dichromate *separately* in a portion of the heated distilled water until each is thoroughly dissolved. Combine them and the remaining water. The result is a saturated solution. Add and completely stir in enough pigment to color the solution for better visibility of the resist. The potassium dichromate is the light sensitizer, and when exposed to light, renders the gelatin (or gum) hard and insoluble.

Because the prepared surface is not light sensitive until it is nearly dry, the following can be carried out in subdued artificial light. Pour the solution over the tilted metal plate held in a *shallow tray* until the entire surface is evenly covered. Remove the plate from the tray, wipe off any solution from the back with a *sponge,* and stand it at an angle in the warm, darkened darkroom to dry, or hang it up by a corner clip. Alternately, the sensitized solution can be applied with a soft, clean *brush* in overlapping strokes, first in one direction, then in the other. The coating must be smooth. After 10 minutes, the gelatin should set. Drying time can be shortened by the use of an ordinary *fan* that circulates air, but do not direct air at the plate.

EXPOSURE   To expose the stencil and plate, *under darkroom safety light* conditions, place the full-sized, high-contrast stencil in contact with the gelatin-sensitized or emulsion surface of the plate, placing both together in a *photocontact printing frame,* or in a *vacuum frame.* Use a negative stencil for a positive image, and a positive stencil for a negative image—emulsion or dull side down if the image is on film. If the light box or vacuum frame are not available, in the following order, from bottom to top, make a sandwich of an inch thick *foam rubber pad,* then the prepared plate, sensitized gelatin up, then the stencil, and last, a clean *sheet of plate glass* sufficient in size to completely cover the plate. The latter is used to press the stencil flat to the plate, because dimensional accuracy

8–65   REINHOLD REILING, West Germany. Brooch with photoetching on silver, gilded, and framed in silver. Photo: E. Augenstein

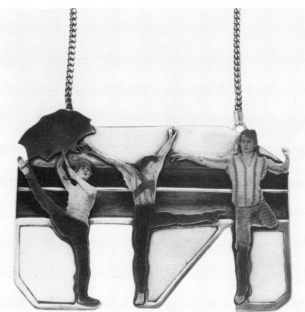

8–66   ANN SCIORTINO AYERS, U.S.A. "Baryshnikov/Jazz/Dance." Pendant in 14K gold, sterling silver, and ivory. The photoetched images were done with a fine screen, and sawed completely from the plate in silhouette. Photo: Courtesy the Aaron Faber Gallery, New York

depends on total contact of the stencil and the sensitized surface.

Expose these with a *quartz* or *arc lamp,* or an *infrared lamp.* If these are not available, depending on the plate size, use between one and four *500 watt photoflood bulbs,* each mounted in a *reflector.* Bright daylight can also be used as a light source, but requires a longer exposure. Place the light(s) about 18–24 in away from the plate; the larger the plate, the greater the distance needed to light it evenly. *Exposure time* varies with the distance of the light from the plate and the type of light used. A sun lamp might require from 3–15 minutes, and a photoflood light from 20–45 minutes or more for the hardening reaction of the potassium dichromate to take place in reaction to the ultraviolet light. To determine proper exposure time, it is advisable to make a test beforehand on a similarly prepared *trial plate,* using the same photo stencil resist. Using a *timer,* expose portions of the plate across its surface at 7–15 minute intervals, as when making a test strip for a photo enlargement.

When an extended exposure time is used, play a *fan* on the glass to draw off accumulated heat which otherwise might cause the film stencil to buckle. Turn off the exposure light, turn on the *yellow safety light,* and remove the stencil and plate.

DEVELOPMENT   Wherever the sensitized gelatin has been exposed to light it becomes hard and insoluble after development. To develop the plate, place it, gelatin side up, in a *tray* of distilled water heated to 100° F (37.7° C). Agitate the solution until those parts of the gelatin that were shielded from the light by the stencil, and therefore are still soluble, are dissolved down to the varnish, and the image appears. This may take at least 15 minutes, depending on gelatin thickness. When the varnished surface appears in unexposed areas, rinse the plate in cold water to chill the gelatin and stop further dissolving action. The general light can then be turned on. Do not touch the gelatin surface while it is wet. Handle the plate by its edges. Lay it flat and allow the result to dry in air, or with the help of a fan, until the gelatin is hard. Remove the spirit varnish from the exposed areas with a *cotton swab* containing *spirit alcohol* which will not affect the hardened gelatin. Cover the edges and back of the plate with an acid resist.

ETCHING   Immerse the plate, stencil side up, in the mordant for the particular metal, in a shallow, heat-resistant glass tray. Etch the metal to the desired depth by gently rocking the tray to agitate the mordant. When this is achieved, after rinsing, strip the gelatin from the plate with very hot water, and eliminate the remaining varnish with spirit alcohol.

Images can be superimposed upon each other on the same etched plate by repeating the entire process, using the same or different stencils. By the use of a *screen,* this system can also be used to reproduce a halftone image. (See Halftone Photoetching on Metal, on p. 334.)

ETCHING PURE GOLD-PLATED COPPER USING THE GOLD AS A RESIST

Pure gold plate in thickness of at least 0.5 mil (⁵⁄₁₀₀₀ in; 0.127 mm) is used in the electronic instrument industry as a stop-off resist in etching printed circuits on other metals. Because the gold is highly resistant to sulphuric acid, this suggests possible applications for the use of gold as a resist, for instance, on copper. Decorative effects would be possible by applying gold (by flooding, electroplating, or soldering) to copper in a pattern, and then etching the exposed copper areas in sulphuric acid, possibly with contrasting textural effects. The gold portions, if

of sufficient thickness, will then stand up in relief, while the copper will be in intaglio. The copper ground could then be given a dark patina to contrast with the gold.

The possibilities of varied effects in the technique of etching are endless, offering a challenge to the ingenuity of the etcher.

For the etching of ivory, see Organic Materials Used in Jewelry, Chapter 12.

DISPOSAL OF SPENT ACID SOLUTIONS

For the disposal of acid solutions, see Pickle Disposal, p. 420.

PHOTOMECHANICAL ONE- OR TWO-SURFACE ETCH PIERCING

Photomechanical etch piercing, sometimes called breakthrough etching or chemical milling, is a process that includes the blanking out of a unit of any shape from a flat sheet of metal, and simultaneously precision piercing the unit with openings in any degree of complexity called for in a design. The process involves the preparation of an artwork master stencil which is used to make a resist stencil on the metal for use in etching. The *artwork master stencil* or mask can be created by cameraless, nonphotographic techniques, or by the use of a camera and photographic techniques, and both methods are described below. Artwork preparation employing either method is similar to methods employed in the preparation of a *mechanical* (the final artwork made by commercial artists for reproduction). The transfer of the image on the artwork stencil to the metal to form a *metal resist stencil* is always accomplished by photodevelopment processes. The metal resist material is a proprietary product that is light sensitive and works positively or negatively, and its composition is designed for use with particular metals and their etchants.

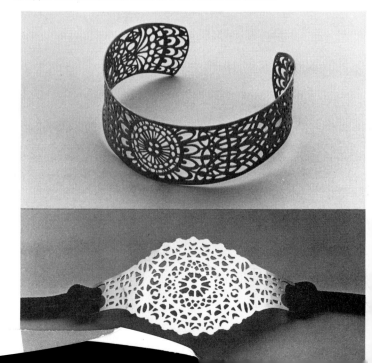

8–68 MARY ANN SCHERR, U.S.A. *Top:* "Neck-lace." Lace-inspired neckpiece in 20 gauge B.&S. brass-plated black chrome, created by photomechanical two-surface etch piercing. Size 1½ in wide; 10½ in long; Ø 7 in. *Bottom:* Gold-plated 20 gauge B.&S. brass photomechanical two-surface etch-pierced belt ornament, also usable as an upper arm ornament. Size 5¾ × 3 in. *Photos: Bob Hanson*

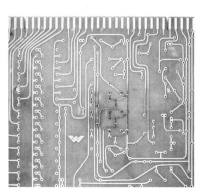

8–67   *PURE GOLD ELECTRIC CIRCUITS*
Etched in relief on copper, they are used in electronic instruments. *Photo: Courtesy Degussa, Precious Metals and Chemicals, Frankfurt/Main*

In etch piercing, the one time etching process may be used for *single* or *double surface etching,* depending on metal thickness. In effect, the acid etchant takes the place of the main cutting tool used by jewelers in traditional hand piercing, the jeweler's saw. The techniques employed in the photoetch process were developed for use in the electrical and electronic industries, in the former case for etching printed circuits from sheet metal, and in the latter case for making high precision, flat sheet metal components from relatively thin sheet metal. Only recently have these methods been adapted for use in jewelry making.

ADVANTAGES OF THE PHOTOETCH PIERCING PROCESS

In jewelry making, there are several advantages in the use of the etch piercing process involving photographic techniques. First, *very thin* metal sheets can be pierced that formerly could only be achieved in hand saw piercing by sandwiching such a sheet between two thicker sheets. Photoetch piercing is accomplished with far more *ease, speed,* and *accuracy* than by hand sawing, and with *less chance of error.* Because of the mechanical nature of the process, *highly accurate reproduction* is realized by using suitably prepared artwork. Any flat black and white or solid area design can be photoetched, with the use of a stencil whether it has a simple or highly complex contour or silhouette, and with any number, size, or shape of openings. As a natural outcome of this technical process, *multiple production* can be carried out. There is no limit on the number of units that can be reproduced from the original artwork master stencil which can be used indefinitely to re-create the resist stencil on metal. Limited series production is possible and ultimate cost is reduced. Situations may occur, as in the case of a highly complex pierced work unit, in which it is feasible to make just one object. Because the surface of the sheet metal is protected by the resist during etching, prepolished metal can be used, and after the resist is removed, little finishing is needed on the object. Etched contours are free of burrs that accompany hand-sawed pierced work. After the etching process, the metal is left physically unaltered from its original condition as etching does not subject it to any work stresses. Therefore, if a preannealed sheet is used, the result can be shaped three dimensionally to a certain extent, as described below. Any number of postetching secondary processes can be carried out on or with etch-pierced results.

ARTWORK PREPARATION OF A NONPHOTOGRAPHICALLY PRODUCED MASTER STENCIL

Photomechanical methods can be used to create an infinite variety of textures and pattern effects on the surface of a metal sheet. The discussion here, however, centers on the preparation of artwork for a solid line or area design, not a halftone which is discussed separately ahead. The materials and methods described here are suited to creating a *master design* stencil in which *pierced openings* are dominant in the result. Piercing can be in *line, area,* or both, but in any case, the pierced work concept presupposes the creation of a design whose remaining parts will physically hold together as an entity by a *common, connected ground.*

Whether nonphotographic or photographic means are employed to create the master stencil, because the design is reproduced on flat metal, a *flat image artwork* or *stencil* is called for as it must ultimately be placed in intimate contact with the photoresist-covered metal to avoid any unwanted distortion of the image—as would happen, for instance, if it were used on a curved surface. (Theoretically it is possible to apply a stencil image made on a flexible, transparent base to a curved surface by forcing them into contact in a *vacuum printing frame.* However, the equipment needed, and the problems of exposing all surfaces equally to light, plus the realizing of an even thickness of photoresist material on a curved surface to render it equally protected from etchant attack, together make successful achievement quite difficult.)

USABLE ARTWORK MATERIALS   Only those materials that can be easily photographed, or that have sufficient density when backlighted to be suited for use in the preparation of an *artwork master stencil* for use in etch piercing are mentioned here. Additional materials are also available when the aim is to surface etch a design on metal. The manner of the use of these materials resembles the techniques used in the production of an art mechanical or paste-up prepared by a commercial artist for reproduction by a platemaker for use in printing.

Cellulose acetate plastic film sheet, 0.003 in or 0.005 in in thickness, of the clear type used in graphic artwork preparation is the basic material used in this process in which the artwork is carried out in *exact size.* This material is *dimensionally stable* under changes in environmental temperature and humidity, and will not shrink or become distorted when worked upon, factors especially important when an identical design is to be reproduced on two sheets which must be in *exact register,* as when they are employed in two-surface etch piercing. *Vinyl* and *polyester drafting film* are superior to acetate when dimensional stability is critical, and are similarly employed, but they are more expensive.

Ink or *paint* of a suitable composition can be used directly on clean acetate, vinyl, or polyester sheets to create a freehand design transparency. When only opaque, adhesive-backed tapes are used to make the design, plain, glossy films can be used. To allow ink, paint, and adhesive tapes to hold on this nonabsorbent surface, the working side of the sheet is given, or is already prepared with, a "tooth" which is a matte or frosted coating that does not interfere to any appreciable extent with the transparency of the sheet when it is backlighted for photographing. The frosted surface also allows changes to be easily made in the design as it does not show the effects of errors that are scraped away with a *frisket knife* or *razor blade.* Opaque inks or paints can be applied with brushes, pens of various kinds, or other dispensers to achieve various widths of lines, or to fill in areas in ways possible with the particular instrument of application. Ordinary water-based opaque inks and paints will not adhere to a plastic surface but will bead, and when dry, will crack or peel away. *Proprietary acetate liquid mediums* can be added to these inks and paints according to supplied instructions to overcome these difficulties and render them flexible and less brittle when dry. The exact amount used must be estimated and tried on a test piece of the same material. The amount must not be excessive or the ink or paint will become translucent, and it is essential that *all substances applied to artwork sheets be opaque.* Opaque acetate inks with the necessary amount of acetate medium are manufactured for use on plastic sheets, and can be applied with a *brush* or pen. Should the ink thicken due to evaporation, *thinners* are available. *Acrylic paints* generally work well on plastic films and have the advantage of being waterproof when dry. Clear plastic sheets are also available already printed with a blue grid, used in lining up elements or repeats. The grid is eliminated by a filter when artwork is photographed.

Adhesive-backed sheets are manufactured, and others have an *opaque coating* on one side which can be scratched or scraped away with any *sharp-edged blade, frisket,* or *stencil knife* such as an X-Acto, leaving the transparent base intact. Another type which can be back-lighted is a *plastic cut-and-peel sheet,* which is covered with a nonactinic, photographically opaque, colored film layer laminated to a clear or translucent base. The colored layer alone can be cut through by using a very thin, sharp blade and gentle pressure. No knife marks should be made on the clear base as it may crack or tear in such places. The colored film can then be stripped off the base leaving clear design areas. *Swivel knives* are friskets with the blade mounted in a revolving handle that allows curved lines to be made without changing the hand position.

Dye markers consisting of a tube containing non-water-based dyes dispensed by capillary action through a felt or nylon tip can be used. Particular brands must be tested to see if the dye will adhere evenly on the plastic sheet employed.

Printing on plastic sheet is also possible using a suitable opaque ink, applied directly with a line cut, linoleum block, or rubber stamp.

Rub-off transfer-type letters, symbols, patterns, lines, textures, etc., are available from various manufacturers and can be incorporated in a master stencil. They are printed in opaque ink on the *back* of a clear plastic supporting sheet, backed with a transparent, waxy adhesive. After positioning the symbol exactly where it is to appear on the paper or plastic artwork sheet, it is transferred by pressure rubbing the element from the *front* of the supporting sheet, using a *burnisher* or other smooth instrument. When the supporting sheet is then lifted away, the item is left behind, bonded to the plastic artwork sheet. To avoid a waxy halo around a letter or element on the artwork sheet, try to rub only the element and as little as possible of the surrounding area.

Drafting tape is opaque when backlighted and has gentle adhesion and a crinkled surface which permits its easy removal. It is available in a wide range of widths, and can be cut into any shape.

Photographic tape is a drafting tape whose matte black surface and adhesive are light-proof, and is also available in various widths. Because of its opacity, it can be used to produce stencils or masks in all photographic processes, and it can be cut into any desired shape and applied to artwork.

Chart tape is an adhesive-backed plastic tape, available in many widths, designed for use in producing lines on maps. It is applied directly to artwork with a little pressure, and trimmed with a razor blade or knife. This tape has the advantage of having a degree of flexibility which allows it to be bent into curves, provided they are not too sharp. All of these tapes are usable in creating openwork patterns suitable for etch piercing.

Photostats, either duplicates or reversals, can be made from the original artwork or master stencil on light-sensitive, glossy, high-contrast paper, in duplicate size, reduced, or enlarged, and in any number. This is specialized work done to order by photostat service houses. Photostats can be used in cases where several repeats of a single design must be lined up and combined in preparation for photo-graphing them onto one film which will be used as a master stencil when several units are simultaneously etch pierced from one metal sheet.

Cameras are used to reproduce original artwork onto stencils on film, positively or negatively. The camera used must allow a suitable negative size capacity. The resulting negative or positive film can be used as a master artwork stencil. In industry, special cameras are used for artwork reproduction.

Light boxes or *tracing boxes* are used as a background when photographing artwork prepared on a transparent plastic sheet. A light box can be improvised by placing a clear glass covered with a translucent paper, or a frosted glass on top of a box containing fluorescent lights or tungsten bulbs. Lighted up, the glass is used for tracing, photographing artwork, transferring typographic elements or artwork from one sheet to another. Guide lines drawn or printed on a separate translucent sheet can be placed below the artwork to assure accuracy when lining up and mounting several units on one sheet. Lacking a light box, an ordinary window pane can be used as a substitute during daylight hours, the work temporarily taped to the glass.

With all these varied materials, the possibilities for design are enormous. The preparation of a nonphotographically produced master stencil might also be the least expensive way of using the photoetch piercing process. A final advantage is that original artwork and master design stencils can be *easily stored* in dustproof boxes for future use, and require little storage space.

PREPARING A PHOTOFABRICATED TRANSPARENCY FOR USE AS A MASTER STENCIL

A prepared artwork design can be reproduced photographically to transfer it to film for use as a master stencil or *transparency* in processing a photoresist on metal for etching. The term "transparency," as used here, means either a positive or negative working image on film. The photofabrication methods involved are exactly the same as those discussed under Photoelectroforming (see Chapter 16), but the effect is exactly the reverse. In photoelectroforming, exposed areas on the metal are *built up* by additional metal; in surface photoetching, exposed areas are *partially etched away;* and in photoetch piercing they are *totally removed.*

Generally the design is first drawn on paper in nonreflecting, matte black ink or paint with pen and brush, though other opaque matte materials can be photographed on film for reproduction. When designing on paper, in order to reduce minor irregularities and assure dimensional accuracy, one usually makes it at least five times larger than the final size on the film, but occasionally up to ten or more times larger. The artwork must be highly accurate, should have good definition, and solid areas must be uniformly blacked in as it is reproduced *exactly* as it appears.

As the design will ultimately be reduced in size, the various elements must be of *sufficient width* to make them viable and not overly fragile after reduction. Lines, for instance, must be of a thickness that will withstand not only mechanical photoreduction, but also the physical, lateral reduction that occurs during etching due to the *etch factor* (the ratio of depth etch to sideways etch or undercutting of the resist) that normally takes place during the etching process. If dimensions are critical, the etch factor can be compensated for by thickening or oversizing outside dimensions in the artwork, and undersizing the inside perforation shapes.

Making corrections on a design drawn in black paint or india ink can be accomplished by scraping with a *razor blade,* or by the use of an *opaque white paint* that is capable of covering those materials without their bleeding through. This can be applied with a pen, brush, or airbrush, depending on the nature of the correction. Opaque white paint is also used for silhouetting or outlining an area around the contour of the design shape in order to achieve a high-contrast image on film, or to eliminate a background.

To reduce the time and work necessary for an etchant to pierce through the metal, when large areas are to be pierced within the blank, they can be etched through *in outline only* instead of dissolving their entire surface and volume. This action can be provided for in the artwork by leaving an outline around the shape, but solidly filling in the rest of the shape instead of leaving it blank. The resist covering such an area will protect it from etchant attack. To prevent the entire blank or an internal perforated part from dropping into the etchant once its outline is pierced, a small rectangular connecting section or tab can be drawn from it to the outer remaining sheet of metal or to an adjoining part, to hold it in place. When thick metal is to be two-surface etch pierced, this connection can be drawn on *only one* of the two matching stencil films used; the connection is thus etched from one side only, to half its thickness. The connection is removed after etching by severing it with a cutting tool.

A very high-contrast working orthochromatic reproduction contact film such as Kodaline Reproduction Film 2566 (Estar Base), or 4566 (Estar Thick Base), or similar products, can be used to make a master stencil for contact printing. This film has a stabilized gelatin emulsion that assures outstanding dimensional stability. The camera must have a lens capable of very sharp focus, and must accommodate a negative large enough to include the whole design *in final, exact size,* and allow some blank marginal space around it. When focusing, use the working lens aperture where possible. The image can be accurately measured on the ground viewing glass of a large camera, and the camera must be fixed to a rigid tripod. *Exact* sizes are necessary because the film negative result will be placed *in contact* with the photoresist-prepared metal.

To avoid shadows and provide the best contrast between opaque and clear areas, the artwork is taped for photographing to the frosted glass top of a *light box,* or to the translucent paper covering a clear glass. To avoid distortion, the mounting surface must be *parallel* with the film plane, and *perpendicular* to the lens axis. Front light is directed at the artwork at an angle of 45° to prevent light-scatter surface reflections from bouncing back from the artwork into the lens. Light must be even and sufficient for the normal range of light sensitivity of the film used, and this can be determined by the use of an accurate *light meter.* Film time exposure and development instructions provided with the film must be followed strictly according to recommendations made by the film manufacturer.

After the master stencil film is developed, fixed, and dried, it is placed, emulsion side down, on a light box and inspected with a *magnifying glass.* Pinholes and thin places that otherwise would be etched into the metal surface are eliminated by retouching such places on the film with *opaque, black film retouch paint,* applied with a *fine hair brush.*

PREPARING THE RESIST ON METAL AND ETCHING THE MASTER STENCIL

Metal surfaces are photosensitized by the use of light-sensitive resists which act as a stop-off stencil material. The remarks here apply to the use of the material for surface etching and etch piercing. The metal used should be oxide-free, clean, defect-free, and *flat,* the latter to assure an even deposit of the resist which will then provide equalized surface protection from the etchant. Some metals require a *conversion coating treatment* of their surface which acts to increase photoresist adhesion, and to minimize the etch factor (see Table on p. 332). The edges and back of the metal sheet must also be protected against etchant attack by covering them with either the same resist, which must then also be light exposed to make it insoluble, or another material such as *plater's contact tape* or *etcher's stop-out lacquer.* The positive or negative image is established on the metal by placing the stencil in contact with the surface and exposing it to light. (For a discussion of the application and the development of the resist and other details, see Photoelectroforming, Chapter 16.) After exposure to ultraviolet radiation, in a positive image those portions of the resist exposed to light are rendered insoluble because the molecules subsequently cross-link when in contact with the alkaline solvent developer, and this action plus its adherence to the metal is what allows the resist material to become a stencil on the metal. The unexposed areas, protected from light by the opaque areas of the stencil, are dissolved away, leaving them open to the attacking action of the etchant. Postbaking the resist to toughen it is necessary to prevent its failure when strong etchants are used, and the time of immersion is extended, as when etch piercing.

The etch piercing method permits very thin metal sheets, 24 gauge B.&S. (0.0201 in or 0.5 mm) or less, to be etch pierced. When thin metal is etch pierced, only one master stencil can be used, and in this case, the resist image is formed only on *one side* of the metal. The back and edges of the metal are covered with resist. The etchant composition and strength differs for each metal to be etched as each has a different degree of corrosion resistance.

The etchant is allowed to eat completely through the metal and penetrate it from one side. Edges are usually very well defined. To reduce the tendency for all metals to be undercut due to the etch factor, agitate the solution continuously during etching. This can be done by moving the solution or the object; by allowing air to bubble through the etchant; or by the use of a *magnetic stirrer.* Generally speaking, the thicker the metal, the greater the discrepancy between the original width of the object and the result. To achieve a straightwall edge, the metal can be overetched to reduce the etch factor bevel.

PREPARING DUPLICATE MASTER STENCILS FOR DOUBLE-SURFACE ETCH PIERCING

Metal up to 18 gauge B.&S. (0.0403 in, 1.024 mm) can be *double-surface etched* to pierce it with dimensional accuracy, but if critical accuracy and strict tolerances are not essential in the dimensions of the jewelry part being etch pierced, thicker metal could also be two-surface etched. The thicker the metal, the longer the etch time that is necessary, and the greater is the need for the resist to remain intact. Resists which fail in places during etch-

Resists and Etchants Used on Metals in Photofabrication

Metal	Kodak Resist	Etchant
Aluminum	KMER (Kodak Metal Etch Resist) constituted for deep etching and piercing. Postbake at 250°F (121°C) for 10 minutes. KTFR (Kodak Thin Film Resist) formulated to meet more exacting requirements. Postbake as KMER.	Use proprietary conversion coating bath, then etchant: Photoengraver's grade ferric chloride (42-degree Baumé)—one gallon; hydrochloric acid, conc. 38%—12 ounces. This solution generates heat and must be cooled below 110°F (43°C) in use.
Copper and copper alloys	KPR (Kodak Photo Resist). KPR2, KPR4 (the higher the number the greater the coating thickness due to increasing viscosity). KOR (Kodak Ortho Resist) sensitive to tungsten light.	Solutions of ferrichloride (42 degree Baumé). Electrolytic etch: Solutions of ammonium chloride saturated with sodium chloride.
Gold	KTFR, KMER	Aqua regia: Hydrochloric acid 1 part Nitric acid 3 parts Mix with constant stirring under a hood, use cold. Electrolytic etch: Alkaline 10% sodium cyanide solutions, steel cathode, 6 volts.
Nickel and nickel alloys	KMER, KTFR	Conversion coating: Phosphoric acid, 1 volume; water, 3 volumes, immerse for 3 minutes at 170°F (76°C), then etchant: Nitric acid, conc. 1 volume Hydrochloric acid 1 volume Water 3 volumes
Platinum	KMER, KTFR	Degreasing dip: Hydrofluoric acid 48% solution, 30 second immersion, rinse under running water, dry, etch in aqua regia at room temperature
Silver	KTFR, KMER	Sulfuric acid (Sp. gr. 1.84) 20 ml Chromium trioxide 40 grams Water 2000 ml Electrolytic etch: Nitric acid 15% by volume and water; stainless steel cathode 2 volts
Stainless steel	KTFR, KMER	Conversion coating: Nitric acid 20% by volume and water, at 150-160°F (65-70°C), immerse for 15-20 minutes, then etchant: Hydrochloric acid (37%) 1 volume Nitric acid (70%) 1 volume Water 3 volumes Electrolytic etch: Hydrochloric acid, conc. 37%, 1 volume; water, 3 volumes; stainless steel cathode; 6 volts
Titanium	KMER, KTFR	Hydrofluoric acid, conc. 48% 1 part Water 9 parts Combine at 1/2ml per minute at 85-90°F (30-32°C); or use: Hydrofluoric acid, conc. 10% Nitric acid 20% Water 70%

ing can be patched after the metal is rinsed and dried by applying stop-off varnish where needed.

Registration, or exact correspondence of the position of the two film copies of the same image used to make the resist image on the metal, is absolutely essential. One of these films is placed on the *front side* of the metal, and the other on the *reverse side.* Unless these two are in exact register, the two-sided etch will not meet at precisely the same position, and as a result, the pierced openings will become enlarged while the metal between them is reduced in width, and narrow elements may be completely destroyed. The standard register mark used in commercial artwork, sometimes called a *target mark,* is a small circle containing a centrally placed cross that extends beyond the circle. This may be hand drawn on artwork to register overlay guide line sheets or identical copies. Register marks are also available printed on adhesive-backed tape. Units can be cut from the tape roll and placed in exact corresponding positions on each overlay sheet to assure their being perfectly lined up.

When *thin metal* is double-surface etched using two identical stencils, one system that can be used to maintain their registration before exposure is to tape them together at one edge, emulsion sides out. The metal, coated with resist on *both* surfaces, is placed between the two stencils and taped in place to prevent its movement, then exposed.

When *heavy-gauge metal* is to be double-surface etched, the above system is not accurate as the metal's thickness may prevent the stencil from lying flat. In this case, it is preferable to *punch* the tape-joined stencils with at least three holes spaced apart at one edge, and to drill identical holes through the metal at corresponding positions *before* it is coated with the resist. Then line up these holes by placing them over *pegs* whose diameter matches the hole size, the pegs fixed the same distance apart in a flat wooden stick. Both stencils and metal will then automatically be in register.

To expose such a sandwich of stencils and metal, in industry the assembly is placed in a vacuum printing machine, and both sides are simultaneously exposed to ultraviolet light. Lacking such a machine, a *contact printing box,* or an improvised one such as is illustrated in Photoelectroforming (see Chapter 16) can be used. In the latter case, first one side is exposed, then the other, taking care that the metal and stencils do not move when the metal is turned. After development, the resist image on the metal is ready for etching.

TWO-SURFACE ETCH PIERCING

Spray etching techniques are used in industry for two-surface etching. The prepared metal sheet is suspended above a solution-collecting container while its surfaces are forcefully played upon by a jet-propelled etchant spray that simultaneously dissolves metal and washes away chemical products and residues, thus constantly exposing new layers of metal to the etchant's action.

Electrochemical etching is also possible provided the design has *connecting tabs* between all parts to allow the current to pass to them. The object is made the cathode and immersed in a highly conductive acid electrolytic solution suited to the particular metal being etch pierced. This process is quick, and acid consumption is minimized.

Tank etching by conventional immersion in a tank containing the etchant is the simplest, though the slowest method. When two-surface etching takes place under these conditions, two alternatives are possible. The object can be vertically suspended in a deep, vertical tank by an attached wire that passes through one of the register holes while the other end is attached to a crossbar which can be raised and lowered for agitation. Alternately, it can be placed in a shallow tank, but in this case, to allow the etchant to make easy contact with both metal surfaces, a means must be devised to raise it horizontally from the tank bottom. The tank is agitated by rocking it gently, or by other means. Residues can be removed from the surface of the metal during etching by occasionally swabbing it with a feather.

After the etching process, if edges appear to be too mechanical-looking, this effect can be altered after the resist is removed with its solvent, by the use of an overall etch, by abrasives, or by sandblasting.

SECONDARY PROCESSING USING ETCH-PIERCED RESULTS

Surface texture both surfaces of a single, unmounted etch-pierced unit to make it reversible. Surface texture *before* etch piercing by manual or mechanical means: the pierced unit; the base on which it is mounted; or both, differently, for contrast before joining them.

Sweat solder laminate a thin etch-pierced unit to a thicker base of a contrasting color which is seen through the openings.

Patina color depressions of the above differently from the pierced upper sheet for the sake of stronger color contrast.

Fill openings in the above with enamel or synthetic resins in the *champlevé* style. The openings of a single unmounted unit can be filled with enamel in the *plique à jour* or backless enamel style.

Inlay metals or nonmetallic materials such as shell, ivory, stone, wood, or plastic into the pierced openings. Solder metal inlays in place, and bond nonmetals with appropriate cements.

Photograph the pierced work result to make an exact, new stencil, then surface etch its negative shape or intaglio into a second, differently colored metal to be used as a base, to a depth that allows the pierced unit to fit into the depression either flush with the ground, or slightly raised above it. Solder these parts together to make it appear an inlay.

Etch pierce a design in sheet metal, but not its silhouette. Cut the outer contour into different shapes; die stamp a blank containing the pierced work by manual or mechanical means.

Superimpose two similarly etch-pierced units, but shift their position to create an overlapping pattern; or superimpose two units having completely different pierced work designs. When these are flat, solder together contacting places. By leaving a space between them (one or both must be made convex), an optically shifting pattern occurs with changes in the viewing angle where the two designs overlap and are seen through each other. A convex unit can be soldered edgewise to a flat pierced ground, or two convex pierced units can be joined edgewise.

Mount pierced work units in a metal frame or one of another material.

Heat reticulate the etch-pierced unit for use by itself; reticulate a pierced work unit and join it to a smooth-surfaced, or other contrasting textured base.

Electroform the finished etch-pierced unit to create a textural surface and soften its edges and outer shape.

Bend the etch-pierced shape along straight lines, making the bend sharp by first scoring a line *inside* the bend angle, or by etching a bend line into the metal. *Three-dimensional forms* can be created by preplanning the form and bends.

Curve or shape the result dimensionally, which—depending on the metal, and on the character and extent of the etch-pierced openings—is possible to some degree provided the curvature is modest. Because the structure and condition of the metal are not physically altered in any way in the etching process, the metal is left stress-free. Preannealed metal can be etch pierced to simplify postetch shaping. When shaping, to prevent damage to a surface condition or image, cover the metal surface to be worked with a protective layer of an adhesive-backed contact sheet, or with overlapping strips of masking tape. Shape the metal with resilient *softwood-, rubber-,* or *nylon-faced mallets* while holding the object over a suitably shaped *stake* or *mandrel.* Use the same mallets to shape the unit into a wooden or masonite sinking mold. Shape an etch-pierced object without kinking by placing it between matching positive and negative forms, dies, or molds, then subject these to manual or mechanical pressure.

Use the waste metal negative shapes remaining after the photoetched blank is removed from the sheet metal to fabricate other objects.

HALFTONE PHOTOETCHING ON METAL:
Graduated tone photoreproduction

Any image that consists of *continuous tones* of varying degrees of light and dark, graduated from white through grays to black, or from highlights to shadows, can be photographically reproduced on any flat metal sheet (copper, silver, gold, etc.) by preparing a *halftone etched plate*. The halftone process was invented by the British photographer Henry Fox Talbot around 1852, and used thereafter for commercial printing. A *halftone* is a tone-graded image etched on a flat metal plate on which the tones are reproduced by a graduated series or pattern of dots and checked spots, normally invisible to the naked eye. They are all on the same original metal plane, *in relief*, not intaglio. When a halftone plate is prepared for letterpress printing, it is called a *cut* or *block* and is used as a means of achieving a printed reproduction of a tone-graded image on paper or other materials. Here, however, the aim is to produce a *metal plate* etched with a halftone photoimage which is then used as a design element mounted in a piece of jewelry. The technique will only be briefly described here to suggest the contemporary possibilities open to the jeweler in using such an image. For greater detail, the reader is referred to data booklets available from the Eastman Kodak Co., Rochester, New York 14650; Dynachem Corp., Santa Fe Springs, California 90670; to other companies elsewhere who manufacture the photographic materials used; or to texts on halftone platemaking.

CREATING A HALFTONE IMAGE ON METAL

To create a halftone image on a flat sheet of any gauge of metal, first clean the plate to make it grease-free by rubbing it with a dilute ammonia and whiting mixture, with fine pumice powder, or by using a solution of one part glacial acetic acid to three parts water. While holding the plate by its edges to avoid touching the surface, rinse it under cold running water, and observe it for water break. Should water break occur, this is an indication that grease is present which would prevent proper adhesion of the photoresist, and the plate must be recleaned until an even water film covers the surface without break. Give the surface a "tooth" by then etching the plate in a weak nitric acid solution. Rinse and dry the plate with a *clean paper towel*, or with a cold or hot *air blower*. Any resist material should now adhere to the plate.

Without delay, in a darkroom with a yellow or red *safety light* on, coat the plate evenly with a light-sensitized resist. (See Stencil Etching Metal Sheet Using Light Sensitized Gelatin, Chapter 8.) Besides the gelatin and potassium dichromate mixture mentioned there, proprietary photosensitive resist compounds such as Dynachem or Kodak KMER, KTFR, and KPR photoresist products can be used. These products must be thinned to the proper consistency according to provided instructions, and they come with their own developer and stripper. Some photoresists are rendered insoluble and therefore acid resistant only if exposed to *ultraviolet light;* others require *tungsten light.* Some photoresists are *negative working,* others *positive working.* For example, to reproduce an image positively with a positive working photoresist requires a transparency of reverse values. Allow the resist-covered plate to dry in the dark. (See Photoelectroforming, Chapter 16.)

HALFTONE SCREENS

To transfer a continuous toned image to a photoresist-coated plate to make a halftone, a *screen* must be used. Line screens used professionally in halftone platemaking consist of two optical glass or plastic sheets engraved or etched with parallel lines a specific, uniform distance apart. The lines are filled with an opaque substance, and the sheets joined, face to face with transparent cement. The lines are placed at right angles to each other, making a screen of transparent squares with the lines running in a diagonal direction, 45° to the outer, normally rectangular screen shape. *Screen size* is measured by the number of lines in one linear inch. From coarse to fine, this number may be: 50, 55, 60, 85, 120, 133, 150 to 200 or more.

Flexible acetate film contact screens are also available, manufactured with printed lines in any desired screen size. They are less expensive than professional glass screens and are easily stored, but they must be handled carefully to avoid scratches.

Kodalith autoscreen film has a 133 or coarser halftone screen incorporated in the film during manufacture. The negative-value photographic image exposed on this transparency, when developed and used produces a *positive halftone image.* To convert this to a positive-value image transparency for use in making a negative-value halftone image on the plate, it is contact printed on a regular Kodalith film, which is then developed and used.

When an etched halftone plate is inked and printed, the optical effect achieved *on paper* is an impression of smoothly graduated tones. The finer the screen size, the greater the detail visible in the printed result. The normal printed dot-visibility limitation is a 55 line screen, used in newspaper photographs. In a 120 line screen or more, used in photolithography, the printed dots are no longer visible to the naked eye. When the aim is to produce a metal sheet with an easily visible image, a coarse 60–85 line screen is recommended because in this higher contrast result, the image is more easily seen.

A *deliberately coarsened screen* is sometimes used for decorative graphic effect. This can be done by enlarging a halftone transparency, projecting all or a part of it onto the photosensitized plate. In such an enlargement, the regimented nature of the halftone dot structure is easily visible. In a positive image, dark area dots run into each other leaving small, clear, isolated pinholes; in light areas, small dark points of widely spaced dots are isolated. On a positive-image halftone plate, in dark areas more of the original surface metal is retained after etching, and in light areas more of it is eaten away.

Besides the usual diagonal screen of squares, *special halftone screens* are available, each creating a unique effect in the result. These are used in coarse grades or their effect will not be visible. In a *vertical screen,* the lines of the squares run vertically and horizontally, instead of diagonally as in the commonly used screen, and its effect is different. A *straight-line one-way screen* has lines in one direction only, the lines swelling and contracting to form highlights and shadows. A *curved-line one-way screen* has concentric lines around a central point or in a series of arcs. A *wavy-line screen* creates an image with uniformly wavy lines crossing it, and a *linen screen* creates a clothlike texture on the image. Other screen types are also available.

EXPOSURE

Glass screens used by professional halftone makers are held in special cameras between the lens and the film, a few millimeters in front of the image plane. When using a flexible acetate film contact screen, it is placed on top of the image transparency which is in *direct contact* with the sensitized metal sheet in a light box (or as described in Stencil Etching Metal Sheet Using Light-Sensitized Gelatin, Chapter 8), covered with a sheet of plate glass to assure total contact, then exposed to a battery of lights from above. The light must cover the image *evenly* with the same intensity. During exposure, the screen splits up the image tones onto the sensitized photoresist-plated surface. The opaque screen lines prevent the passage of light, and the transparent squares allow varying amounts of light to pass through, depending on the values in the image. The time of exposure, and the kind of light used depend on the photoresist used and the distance of the light from the photosensitized plate. Experimenting with a text plate is necessary.

DEVELOPMENT

The method of development and fixing, and the proper chemicals to use for these processes must be those particular to the photoresist used. Instructions are usually packed with the product, and data sheets can be consulted.

ETCHING

Once the image is exposed and developed and the photoresist is dry and hard, the image is made permanent on the metal plate by *etching.* With the edges and the back of the plate protected with a suitable acid resist, the plate is now etched with the etchant appropriate for the particular metal and the resist used. (See Table, Resists and Etchants Used on Metal in Photofabrication in this chapter.)

Agitate the acid solution to avoid the accumulation of sludge in the etched-out areas. It is common practice in industry to increase the contrast in the image by applying a stop-out varnish to the dark-toned areas once they are sufficiently etched, then after further etching, the medium-toned values are stopped out. The final etch is for etching out the highlights to reduce their dot size and therefore lighten them. This procedure requires intermittent inspection with a magnifying glass to observe its condition. The entire process may take 20 minutes. Care must be taken to *avoid overetching* as the halftone image, which is very shallow, is easily eaten away.

To make the finished halftone image more visible, in a negative manner, the ground in the finished etched plate can be colored with an appropriate coloring chemical. (See Metal Coloring, Chapter 17.) The surface dots can then be rubbed with an impalpable abrasive, or lightly buffed to make them bright. This leaves coloring in the depressions, and the dots are polished, thus creating a negative-image effect. In another way that gives a positive result that looks more like a photograph, the plate is first cleaned by a solution (not with abrasives) down to the base metal. After drying, the *surface dots only* are thinly inked with a film of an appropriately pigmented ink applied with a *brayer* (printer's hand inking roller) to spread the ink evenly over the raised dots without forcing it into the etched-out depressions, as happens in relief printing. Once the ink has been allowed to dry, the surface is then sprayed with a compatible protective lacquer. The halftone plate must then be mounted by cold fabrication methods.

Silhouetted image halftone plates are made by engraving a line around the image, then cutting the image out with a *jeweler's saw* to separate it from the ground. If sawing is done carefully, the engraved guide line may not be necessary.

To increase halftone image visibility, or to change the surface metal from, say, copper to silver or gold, the halftone metal plate may be electroplated. A lead wire must be attached to the plate to immerse and suspend it in the electrolyte. (See Electroplating, Chapter 16.) Small plates require from ¾–1½ volts, and 20–40 amps per square foot of surface. Higher voltages must be avoided or the image will be destroyed or "powdered." It is not advisable to electroplate halftones with very fine screens as the electrodeposited metal tends to fill the depressions between dots and destroy the image. Electroplated halftone results can also be colored, as above.

POSTHALFTONE TREATMENTS

A halftone image is not sacred, and may be further manipulated by other decorative methods. For instance, line patterns may be engraved or scored upon the image plate. Parts of the surface can be removed with chisels or by milling, for example, to create a textured ground around a figure. A stone or stones may be set upon the image by making a separate stone mount such as a bezel, then drilling a hole in the plate, passing a screw attached to the base of the mount through the hole, and then fixing the mount in place with a nut. Separate repoussé-worked units can be mounted on the plate in relationship to the halftone image configuration to produce a contrast between an illusory three-dimensional image with actual three-dimensional forms.

9

SURFACE ORNAMENT WITH HEAT
Metal Fusion Techniques

RETICULATION

Samorodok, or the self-born technique of fusion texturing

The term *reticulation* is from the Latin *reticulum,* diminutive of *rete,* "a net." In general it means to divide or mark a surface with intercrossed lines that resemble or form a network or web. The term is used in reference to several materials and processes. In glass manufacture it describes glass with two sets of lines that intersect; in photography it indicates a network of textural configurations that are accidentally or deliberately produced on a negative by a rapid expansion and shrinkage of the swollen gelatin of the film being processed, roughly parallel to what happens in the case of metal reticulation. These conditions suggest the formation of a surface having a textured or patterned appearance, which also applies to reticulated metal.

The use of the term reticulation in reference to metalwork is recent. The earliest use of reticulated surfaces created on sheet metal occurred during late Victorian times in Czarist Russia, and in Scandinavia. The Russian term for this process is *samorodok* which literally means "born by itself," referring to the fact that the texture is self-created in a natural way, except for the provision of heat. The technique was used by Fabergé and other Russian goldsmiths of that era. From Russia it spread to Finland where it is called *hehkutus,* literally "glowing," or *rypytetty* meaning "wrinkled." In Swedish it is called *krympad,* also meaning "wrinkled." Objects such as cigarette boxes, card cases, eyeglass cases, and liquor flasks were made of reticulated sheet metal, still used for these

items in Scandinavia. Its international use in jewelry, however, did not occur until the recent development of widespread interest in surface texture in jewelry.

The reticulation of sheet metal probably owes its origin to observations made when accidentally overheating a sheet of metal being annealed. In the reticulation process, at an intermediate stage between the normal annealing temperature and metal's melting temperature, a surface can be produced on sheet metal that has a texture formed of ridges and depressions in a marked relief pattern that resembles aged skin. If heating is continued still further, the metal collapses and melts.

Normally these events would be termed a disaster, and an inept waste of good metal. Today, however, the technique has become one of the standard tricks in the bag of the modern jeweler. What is especially appealing is the organic appearance of the texture, due to natural causes. With experience and a certain control gained by trial and error, it is possible to control the technique, at least partially, and to predict the general configurations and patterns that can be produced.

There are two basic uses to which the process of reticulation can be put. One is to reticulate sheet metal *prior* to its use, and then employ the result as a raw material for a component in jewelry. The other is to reticulate an *already formed* or *fabricated unit,* or an entirely completed piece of jewelry. Examples of these uses are illustrated.

9–1 A. K. (unknown), St. Petersburg, Russia, after 1896. Cigarette box, 84 zolotnik to 96 zolotnik (875/1000) silver alloy; 56 zolotnik to 96 zolotnik (583/1000) gold alloy thumbpiece mounted with a cabochon sapphire; the interior silver gilt. This box is a typical example of the Russian *samorodok* or reticulated surface made popular in Czarist Russia by Fabergé and his contemporaries. Height ⅝ in; length 3¹⁵⁄₁₆ in; width 2¹³⁄₁₆ in. The India Early Minshall Collection, The Cleveland Museum of Art. *Photo: Cleveland Museum of Art, Cleveland*

9–2 GENE PIJANOWSKI, U.S.A. Silver brooch of a single reticulated sheet, framed in square wire. *Photo: Pijanowski*

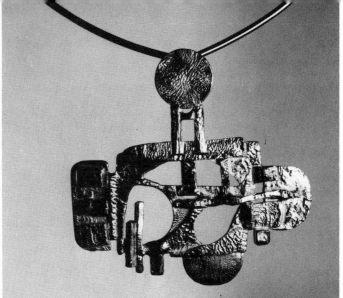

9–3 HAROLD O'CONNOR, U.S.A. Brooch of parts of silver and gold reticulated sheets organized within a unifying form, and soldered to a base sheet which curves upward to form a framing edge. Only the silver parts are colored. *Photo: Ron Burton*

9–4 ATELJE "3 STÄD," Helsingborg, Sweden. The pendant is made of reticulated parts, the entire piece again reticulated after assembly. *Photo: Sune Sundahl*

METALS USED FOR RETICULATION

Different metals and alloys can be subjected to reticulation. Pure silver can be reticulated, but more usually, silver copper alloys ranging from 92.5–80% silver are used. Pure and alloyed gold was commonly reticulated by Fabergé, and plain copper and its alloys can also be reticulated.

When using silver of 820/1000 quality, a common European alloy, thicknesses down to 0.511 mm (24 gauge B.&S., 0.0201 in) can be reticulated with care. Heavier gauge sheets also can be reticulated, but sheets thinner than this tend to melt away or form holes if overheated. The thicker the sheet, the stronger and longer the heat that is required. For an all-over, even-textured reticulation, the metal should be flat, evenly worked, and free of deep scratches. Bent sheet metal can be reticulated and will form patterns that relate to the bend configuration.

THE THEORY OF RETICULATION

Reticulation is in effect a by-product of annealing whose main function is to relieve residual work stresses in the metal by the application of heat. But whereas in annealing any visible change in the surface appearance of the metal, or unusual change in its structural constitution is considered undesirable, when reticulating the surface of sheet metal, these changes are pushed to the limit.

The physical change that takes place in reticulated sheet metal is the result of several *variables*. Most important is *temperature* which is above the normal limit used for annealing, but below actual melting temperature. For example, sterling silver is normally annealed at 1200° F (648.8° C), and its melting point is 1640° F (893° C), allowing a range of 440° F (226° C) within which its reticulation takes place. The *time-temperature heating cycle* which includes heating, holding, and cooling, is important. The relationship of these factors is drastically changed from that used for annealing. When reticulating, the heating period is rapid, the holding period short, and the cooling is sudden.

In normal annealing, the heat is distributed more or less uniformly on the metal to achieve a homogeneous crystalline metal grain growth, but in reticulation the heat is deliberately *concentrated locally* on an area to cause a drastic difference between its condition and that of the adjacent metal, until reticulation takes place, and the torch is then moved on.

The *time duration of the heat concentration* and the *temperature of the flame* are both important because they influence the creation of thermal stresses and grain growth distortion in the metal, both of which have an effect on the reticulated pattern. Maximum grain growth distortion occurs at the time of maximum temperature, and is also affected by the *heating rate*. The use of a rapidly heating, strongly oxidizing flame results in greater metal surface and substratum surface oxidation, in manners that depend on the method used, described below. Old hands at reticulation claim that the *pressure of the air* in the gas flame makes the surface move, more or less according to *its force* and the *rate of movement of the flame*. It is by varying these variables that differences in the appearance of the reticulated surface becomes possible. These then are the conditions that act to change the structure and nature of the metal, and cause the development of a variety of reticulated textural patterns. The three different methods of reticulation described below each cause a different structural effect.

RETICULATING SILVER ALLOY

METHOD 1

PRERETICULATION SURFACE COPPER DEPLETION

The cleaned surface of the silver copper alloy discussed here is first prepared to deplete it of its copper content and form a pure silver surface layer on the metal. This is done by heating the sheet to a full annealing temperature of about 1200° F (648.8° C). During this heating, which lasts for 5–10 minutes, a copper oxide surface scale develops and is removed by quenching the metal in a sulphuric acid pickle containing up to 33% acid. The sheet is left with an almost copper-depleted surface film of pure silver, and is then scratch brushed. To totally deplete the copper and further thicken the silver-enriched surface, the same annealing and acid quench treatment is repeated four or more times. The final surface on the sheet is a thickened coat of dead white, pure silver. Any surface oxidation that occurs during subsequent heat treatments is far less than it would be if the copper content had been allowed to remain intact.

RETICULATION HEAT TREATMENT

The metal so prepared is then heated with an *air-gas torch* to a point below melting. Experienced reticulators claim that better results are achieved if the *surface* on which the object is placed for reticulation to be carried out is preheated. During heating, a change in the metal structure occurs. From the elongated, compressed, more or less parallel-to-surface-oriented crystal structure that is characteristic of rolled sheet metal, a complete recrystallization occurs, the crystals enlarging, becoming less stratified, and more dendritic in nature.

Other changes also occur during heating. The outer surface remains silver enriched, but immediately below it, and between it and the interior original silver copper alloy, an intervening copper-enriched subsurface stratum forms due to internal subsurface oxidation. While the interior metal is in a molten state, copper is fed there to both sides of this substratum from adjacent areas of the silver copper alloy. In alloys with a high silver content the substratum is black cupric oxide (CuO), and in those with high copper content, it is brick red cuprous oxide or copper suboxide (Cu_2O). The presence of this copper-bearing substratum plays a role in this method of reticulation as it allows the pure silver surface layer to remain intact.

With proper heat control, the pure silver surface does not melt, while the interior original silver copper alloy does. At the time of maximum temperature the core expands as it melts. When the flame moves on to new surface areas, the core freezes and contracts due to the sudden change in temperature as it air cools. This causes the unmelted silver surface layer to take on the characteristic reticulated, wrinkled appearance as it conforms to the change in the subsurface structure, accommodating itself to the shrinkage that takes place. The *critical point of readiness* of the metal to develop a reticulated surface must be judged by its *color and appearance under the flame*. Care must be taken to move the flame to new areas immediately before the surface shows signs of melting, which can be judged by a slight glistening look. By coordinating the *amount of heat applied,* the *duration* of its application, and the *rate of movement* of the torch flame, a more or less homogeneous textural effect can be produced.

METHOD 2

RETICULATION WITHOUT INTERNAL COPPER OXIDE SUBSTRATUM

By a second process, using a similarly prepared copper-depleted surface silver copper alloy, the metal is heated only to a redness that is sufficient to cause reticulation as the torch flame is moved slowly along. In this result, the surface remains silver enriched, and an outer oxide layer forms, but is thin. This technique acts to *prevent* the formation of the internal copper oxide substratum mentioned above.

POSTRETICULATION SURFACE TREATMENT

In the above two methods, the surface oxide that forms on the sheet during reticulation is afterward removed by pickling the metal in a 10% sulphuric acid solution brought near the boiling point. This dissolves the copper and silver oxide surface scale and restores the surface to the same silver-enriched, dead white state it formerly had after surface copper depletion. The sheet is then ready to be processed further.

METHOD 3

DIRECT RETICULATION

By a third process, the simplest of all, no prereticulation depletion of the copper in the surface is carried out. Instead, the reticulation is simply done directly on the unmodified alloy, allowing a normal development of copper silver surface oxidation to take place. The same substratum of copper-enriched oxide also occurs. The outer oxide scale is removed *after* reticulation by boiling the metal in a normal 10% sulphuric acid pickle which restores the surface to the original silver copper alloy. The results are the same as the first two methods, but this method does not create a silver-enriched surface. If, however, a pure silver surface is wanted, the reticulated sheet can *then* be copper depleted, as on p. 337, as a postreticulation process, and finally scratch brushed.

RETICULATING SHEET METAL
DEMONSTRATION 14

GENE PIJANOWSKI explores reticulation possibilities

Photos: Pijanowski

METAL PREPARATION FOR RETICULATION

1 To reticulate sheet silver, clean the metal and anneal it on both sides. The surface becomes oxidized as a result, and this must be removed with an acid bath of 8–30% sulphuric acid, until the sheet turns dead white. (For gold and its alloys use a nitric acid pickle bath.) Brush the sheet with a feather during pickling to agitate the acid, hasten its action, and remove the sludge that accumulates on the surface of the metal. Remove the sheet and rinse it.

Scratch brush both surfaces with a *soft brass crimped wire brush wheel* and a lubricant (detergent in solution; or, as in Scandinavia, stale beer). Scratch brushing does not remove any metal but cleans the surface. Repeat the annealing and pickling process from four to six times, scratch brushing perhaps half that many times between, but not after the final annealing and pickling. When annealing, the flame should have a fraction more air than usual so that by rapid oxidation, firescale develops on both metal surfaces. The purpose of the alternating annealing and pickling process is to build up an outer coating of pure silver on the surface, removing surface copper content by oxidation and depletion.

THE RETICULATION WORKTABLE SURFACE

2 The *refractory surface* upon which the reticulation is done must be *flat* when flat sheet is reticulated, and it

1   **2**   **3**

must be clean and moisture-free. An *asbestos* (or other refractory) *sheet,* preferably mounted on a *turntable base,* is recommended, but *firebrick,* or a flat, new *charcoal block* can also be used. If necessary, clean a used asbestos sheet by scraping off any remains of accumulated flux or other foreign matter, and run a flame over it to be sure it is dry. Here we see several sheets laid out at one time to be reticulated in turn.

THE RETICULATION FLAME

3 The kind of flame used, its *size, length,* its *angle* to the metal, and the *path* of its movement are all important factors that each has its influence on the result which will vary with differences in these conditions. Strength of the air force introduces the element of *pressure* from the air blast which causes the melted metal surface to move.

Hold the torch with a steady hand and pass the oxidizing, forceful flame slowly over the metal to bring it to annealing temperature. From then on, a single torch can be used, but it is helpful to use *two torches,* one with a softer flame to maintain total metal temperature, and the second torch to create the reticulated pattern. Starting at one end of the sheet, concentrate the reticulating torch flame on the area. Once the reticulation pattern commences, and the surface seems to crawl and wrinkle, move the flame forward slowly. Watch the formation of the reticulated pattern, and advance the flame accordingly.

FLAME PATH PATTERN AND DURATION

4 By moving the flame over the sheet in a specific, parallel *flame path pattern,* different patterns will develop. Variations in the *degree of relief* depend on *flame duration.* When the flame lingers longer in one place, reticulation increases in scale and dimension. Therefore, when a pattern with less dimension is wanted, the flame should be moved immediately once reticulation starts. Even with such controls, it is not possible to predict in advance *exactly* how the result will appear. To learn maximum control, note the conditions that prevailed when achieving a particular effect, and repeat them. The main precaution is to avoid overheating the metal.

Here we see reticulation results on three sheets and on a metal tube. At the upper right is a reticulated pattern resulting from a spiral flame path; below it is a sheet with a flame path parallel to the sheet's length. In the lower left is a sheet partially reticulated with a few melted holes; resting on it is a reticulated tube.

5 A finished brooch by Gene Pijanovski, made of a reticulated sterling silver sheet, with rutilated quartz and zircon.

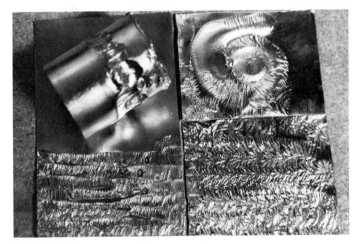

4

5

VARIATIONS IN RETICULATED EFFECTS

Reticulation variations are possible. A sheet can be only partially reticulated, or one spot can be reticulated to make a textural accent while the rest is left intact. Instead of an all-over reticulation, plain areas can alternate with reticulated areas. It is possible to create a sharper definition between a reticulated area and a plain area by coating the area where reticulation is *not* wanted with a thick paste of a refractory material such as clay, asbestos, or sodium silicate to act as a heat sink and reticulation inhibitor, leaving areas to be reticulated exposed. A sheet of steel can be laid across the metal to act as a heat sink and protect what is underneath in the same way that the refractory material insulates the area it covers and prevents the full effect of the heat on the metal in those places.

9–5 DAVID W. KEENS, U.S.A. Neckpiece of sterling silver, 14K gold, agate, and cast polyester. Included in the composition is a partially reticulated silver sheet inlaid with gold. *Photo: David W. Keens*
◀

9–6 *Above:* OLAF SKOOGFORS, U.S.A. Gold-plated sterling silver pin with two baroque pearls. The elements are separately forged cast units, reticulated, and fusion constructed. Size 2 × 2¼ in. *Photo: Jack Simon, courtesy Helen Drutt Gallery, Philadelphia*

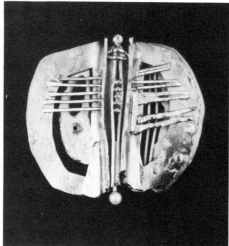

9–7 BERND JANUSCH, Sweden. "Vattenblomman" (Water Flower). Silver pendant of concave circular forms reticulated after shaping, causing the reticulation lines to run inward perpendicular to the edge. Ø 10 cm. Col.: Eva Dickson. *Photo: Bernd Janusch*

RETICULATING PREFORMED SHAPES

A relatively recent innovation is the reticulation of an entire finished piece of jewelry, or completed, fabricated unit parts of jewelry made of sheet metal or thin castings. Such preformed parts are reticulated, then joined to the rest of the work. In such cases, great care in heating is necessary as overheating can cause partial or complete collapse, especially when the parts are dimensional and unsupported. The condition of the metal surface must be closely watched, and when reticulation has started, the flame must be withdrawn immediately. An interesting result occurs with dimensional forms when they are heated at the edges first—the reticulated pattern develops from the edge toward the interior of the form, resulting in a pattern that seems to grow organically from the form and relate to it. Such patterns also will develop around large open places such as a hole preformed in the sheet toward which the pattern becomes oriented.

Because the surface of a sheet of metal newly reticulated is in an oxidized condition, to restore it to its natural base metal, necessary in order to solder it to another part, it must be pickled, rinsed, and scratch brushed. These steps may have to be repeated several times if the oxidation is particularly heavy.

USING RETICULATED SHEET

The reticulated sheet can be used as an entity, or parts can be selected and cut from a sheet and used in combination with other fabricated parts and forms. The sheet can be used exactly as it appears after reticulation, or the degree of relief can be reduced by partially flattening it with a *wooden mallet*. It is also possible to run the sheet through a *rolling mill* once to flatten it; do not bring the

9–8 REGINE JUHLS, Norway. Silver earrings. The form was sawed from sheet silver, then fused to round its ends and create a reticulated surface texture. *Photo: Börje Rönnberg, courtesy Sølvsmie Regine & Frank Juhls*

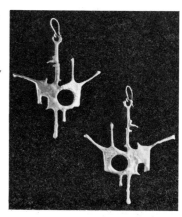

rolls too close or the pattern may be removed by the pressure.

Flat reticulated sheets can be shaped dimensionally to a certain extent by the use of forming dies, mandrels, or punches while the sheet is fixed on pitch. There is a limit to the amount of shaping and bending the sheet will take before it cracks, though cracks can be repaired by flooding them with solder. The edges of a reticulated sheet can be bent or curved back, and then backed with a plain, flat sheet to which it is soldered. To hold the reticulated sheet to the backing sheet, use a backing larger in dimension than the reticulated sheet, bind them together with binding wire, then solder them together. Be sure to make a small hole or spiracle at the back to allow for the air expansion that takes place when soldering closed forms. After soldering, cut or saw away the surplus flange, and file the edges to finish them. Pieces of reticulated sheet can be set in a bezel constructed to receive them, in the same way as when setting a stone.

COLORING RETICULATED SURFACES

The surface of a completely pickle-cleaned reticulated sheet can be reoxidized with a liquid oxidizer applied with a brush (see Coloring Metals, Chapter 17). The texture can then be emphasized by dipping a wet finger into a finely powdered whiting or other mild abrasive, and rubbing to relieve the highest ridges. The highlights that appear on these raised portions and the shadows left in the depressions emphasize the dimensionality of the relieflike surface.

It is also possible to leave the last surface coating intact, then partially relieve it, in the same manner as above. This can be done if the metal will not undergo any further heat treatments, as when placing a reticulated component in a mechanical mount.

FUSING METAL

Using heat to plastically form metal

To fuse metal is to render it partially liquid or fluid on its surface, and in some cases to melt it completely by heat. Fusing, apart from its application to soldering, is normally done to partially melt the metal to create a fused form, or to join parts by bringing their contacting surfaces to a molten state so that they join each other by an interpenetration of their atoms without the use of an intermediary metal such as solder. At this point the heat is immediately withdrawn as further fusion may result in the total collapse of the form. Because the natural forces of gravity, molecular attraction, and capillarity have been at work in the fusion process, the appearance of fused forms has an affinity to organic shapes.

SHOT MAKING: Forming a metal ball by total fusion

A separate ball of metal called a *shot* because its size range resembles that of gun shot, can be made by fusion. First make a semicircular depression in a *charcoal block* with the round end of a *dapping punch* the size of the ball being made, by rotating and grinding it into the charcoal block. Blow away the loose dust. Cut a length of wire or use a piece of scrap metal, dip it in flux, and place it over the depression. Heat the metal until it fuses into a ball shape. Gradually reduce the air to make the flame a reduction flame, and then *gradually* withdraw the flame. Because it is bathed in a reduced atmosphere, the ball should have a shining surface. If it does not, allow the ball to cool before pickling it.

If several balls of the same size are wanted, the amount of metal in each must be the same. This can be determined by weighing them on a *goldsmith's scale,* or, if the exact size is not critical, wires of approximately the same lengths can be cut. Several extras can be made and a final selection of those of closest size used. Beyond a certain size, balls made this way tend to become flattened in shape

when the force of gravity acting on its greater volume is greater than its surface tension. A ball can be deliberately made with a flattened side by placing the metal on a flat charcoal surface instead of in a rounded depression.

THE USES OF SHOT IN JEWELRY

Solid spheroid forms or shot have been used as a decorative element in jewelry since the discovery was made centuries ago how the laws of nature work to easily allow small solid metal balls to be made. (See Gold Granulation: Practice, Spheroidizing, p. 359.) If the quantity of metal is very small, such as filings, solid spheres can be made that are so tiny that when they are used to cover a surface, as in ancient Etruscan jewelry, they are not recognizable as balls to the naked eye. They also found use in sizes large enough to approach that of a medium-sized pearl, beyond which their weight becomes objectionable and hollow sphere construction takes over.

In any size between this range of extremes, their employment can take several forms. Single spheres of shot are used as accent points because smooth-surfaced spheroid forms always act as natural light reflectors—any part of their surface bounces existing light back from any angle to an observer. Shot clusters multiply the highlight pinpoints which can contrast with flat or slowly curved adjacent areas upon which light reflection is diffused or sporadic. Shot also contrasts with any other form of surface ornament or treatment. Arranged in linear series of the same or graduated sizes, shot is used to delineate flat areas, to outline dimensional forms, to emphasize a transition from one plane to another, or as a border. Shot of the same size can be arranged geometrically in series or groups to form units placed on and soldered to a ground that supports them. They can be used to fill a shape completely and thus become a textural area such as one defined by an outline wire, an etched depression, or a pierced area. Shot of any size can be used alone struc-

9–9 ROSA TAIKON, Sweden. "Baro Ilho" (Great Heart, in Romany). Silver necklace of flat sheet forms ornamented with twisted wire borders and surface decoration, and shot balls in graduated sizes. Length 190 mm; width 90 mm. Col.: National Museum, Stockholm. Photo: Sven Nilsson

9–10 SHOT BALLS IN GRADUATED SIZES being placed in series to ornament a unit of a silver belt, prior to soldering them in place. Photo: Björn Langhammer

9–11 ROSA TAIKON, Sweden. Silver belt made of units ornamented with wire and shot. Photo: Björn Langhammer

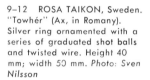
9–12 ROSA TAIKON, Sweden. "Towhér" (Ax, in Romany). Silver ring ornamented with a series of graduated shot balls and twisted wire. Height 40 mm; width 50 mm. Photo: Sven Nilsson

9–13 KABYLE, ATLAS MOUNTAINS, ALGERIA. Traditional silver necklace with shot ornament, yellow, green, and blue enamel, and set with coral stones. This richly elaborate necklace has 50 individual, linked parts. Photo: Oppi

9–14 SWAT, PAKISTAN. Traditional silver bracelet, a hollow form ending in stylized lion heads with open mouths, ornamented with repoussé work, engraving, and dot punch work. Mounted with large solid balls made by fusion, and squares. Photo: Salmi

9-16 MIXTEC INDIAN, OAXACA, MEXICO. Cast gold ornament of a man's head. Different sized shot is used to outline forms. These were made of small wax balls in the wax model before it was cast by the lost wax method. Height 1⅞ in. Photo: *Museum of the American Indian, Heye Foundation, New York*

9-15 BATAK TRIBE, SUMATRA, INDONESIA. Gold bracelet whose basic structure is four tubes with interfitting flanges. Stamp-patterned wire, and twisted wire in spirals and borders outline shot-filled shapes that create textural areas. Round and flattened shot discs are used to conceal wire terminals. The large end balls are two half-domes soldered together. Photo: *Rijksmuseum voor Volkerkunde, Leiden*

9-17 BERNDT LINDHOLM, Finland, maker; ANDERS HÖGBERG, Sweden, designer. A silver pierced work unit is soldered to a ground sheet, and the openings filled with gold shot. The outer rim and central concave dome are gold. Photo: *Jan Olsson*

9-18 SOUTHERN MOROCCO. "Cross of Agades," or "Southern Cross." Silver pendant with stamped wire decoration and shot used singly and in groups by Tuaregs in the region of Goulimene, Tan-Tan, and Tarfaya. Col.: Ruth Christensen, Copenhagen. Photo: *Oppi*

9-19 SAN'A, YEMEN, end of 19th century. Traditional silver necklace (*ma'nage*), still made today, alternating with 366 shot-constructed beads, and 366 faceted solid beads, making a total of 732. Each shot-constructed bead is made of 36 small shot units, therefore at least 13,176 shot pieces were used for the shot beads. Straight length 42 cm; weight ca. 500 g. Photo: *David Harris, Israel Museum, Jerusalem*

turally; several units can be soldered together to form independent, compound units; or such preconstructed units can be joined to existing forms to make projections. These and other uses make shot a valuable raw material for the jeweler.

FUSION FORMING A BALL AT A WIRE END

Any length of wire can be made to form a terminal ball under the heat of fusion. The size of the ball depends on the thickness of the wire used as this determines the amount of molten metal the wire will hold. To form such a ball or bead on wire, hold the wire vertically *in air* with *self-locking tweezers*. Dip the lower end in flux, and apply a short, hot flame until it melts and forms a small round ball. The molten metal increases in size if the heat is prolonged until its weight causes it to drop off. The flame should be removed before this occurs. The opposite end of the same wire length can also be treated to form a ball by reversing its direction and pointing it downward. Such units can be soldered to jewelry as decorative ornaments, or they can be used in other ways, such as forming them into an S-shaped clasp. Straight wire projecting from already fabricated forms can be balled in the same way by holding the piece in air with the wire pointing downward, then heating it as described.

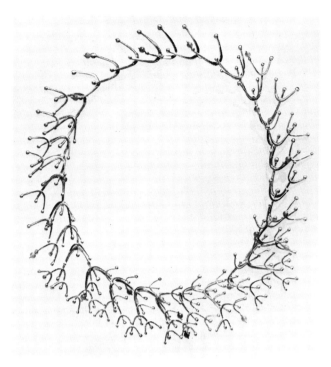

9-20 MERRY RENK, U.S.A. Yellow 14K gold wire necklace with jade beads. The linked units have ball-fused ends. Col.: B. Gibson, San Francisco. Photo: Robert Boni

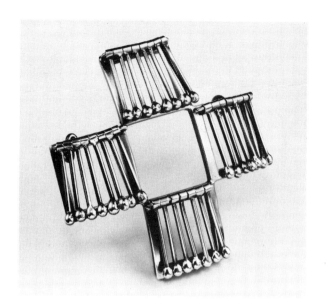

9-21 KAIJA AARIKKA, Finland, designer; manufacturer Aarikka Koru, Helsinki. "Sielun Messu" (Requiem). Silver pin in cross-shaped square wire frame ornamented with hanging wire lengths whose free ends have been fused to ball forms. The other end is soldered to a tube section, and strung on a wire held by the frame. Photo: Studio Wendt, courtesy Aarikka Koru

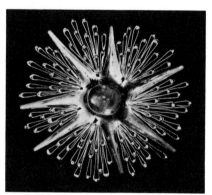

9-22 DAVID THOMAS, England. Brooch of 18K yellow gold, using doubled wires whose closed ends were fused to form a ball. The central repoussé-worked unit is set with a cabochon emerald. Photo: The Worshipful Company of Goldsmiths, London

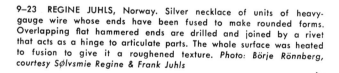

9-23 REGINE JUHLS, Norway. Silver necklace of units of heavy-gauge wire whose ends have been fused to make rounded forms. Overlapping flat hammered ends are drilled and joined by a rivet that acts as a hinge to articulate parts. The whole surface was heated to fusion to give it a roughened texture. Photo: Börje Rönnberg, courtesy Sølvsmie Regine & Frank Juhls

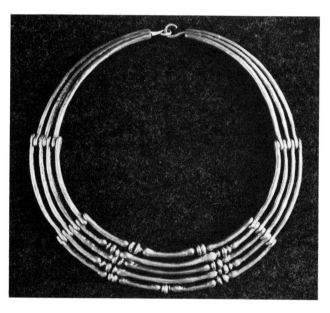

FUSING WIRE, SHEET, AND WASTE METAL FORMS

Exploration of the unpredictable offers an intriguing and fascinating direction to follow. For those interested in such a path, surprises are found in the results obtained from fusing larger metal forms to each other. Because of the lesser degree of control in the process, a fused mass of collected scrap metal, though possibly appealing, by itself cannot rightfully be called a creative work, unless one wishes to take credit for the laws of nature. There are, however, legitimate ways in which such forms can be used, for instance, by combining them with other forms created by controlled techniques so that a relationship is established between the accidental and the planned.

Wire and other forms of most metals can be fused to like types (wire to wire, sheet to sheet), or in mixed combinations. All pieces must be chemically clean, and free of firescale. Dip them in flux, then place them with tweezers on a flat soldering surface, such that at some points they are in physical contact. Arrangements that include some open spaces are usually more successful. Apply a rather large, reduced covering flame to bring all surfaces simultaneously to the same degree of surface melt. When the surface glows and the forms sink into each other, they

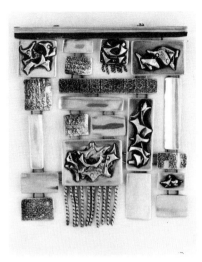

9-24   CLAËS E. GIERTTA, Sweden. Silver bracelet made of a flat sheet of contoured metal whose surface was reticulated, then shaped. The forged wire forms were then fused to it in an overlapping and crossing pattern. *Photo: Sven Petersen*

9-25   SHARON CHURCH, U.S.A. Cuff bracelet with a silver ground that was divided into many parts. While flat, these units were fused together with 14K yellow gold, fed into the joint from the edge and drawn along by heat. The form was hammer shaped on a bracelet mandrel, the silver then etched with nitric acid leaving the unaffected gold in relief. *Photo: Don Manza, courtesy Aaron Faber Gallery, New York*

9-26   RUTH S. ROACH, U.S.A. Man's pocket ornament. The surface of some parts were textured by sprinkling on sterling silver filings, then patterned with a dental tool prior to fusion. Some are layered small scrap silver pieces fused to rectilinear grounds. All parts are articulated with jump rings. Width 3¼ in; height 3¾ in. *Photo: Bob Carvill*

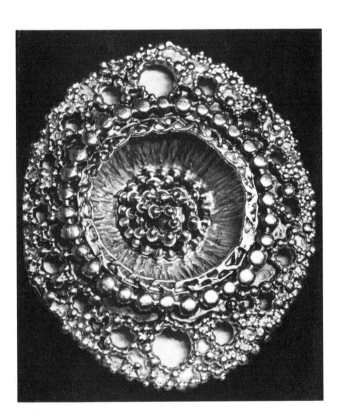

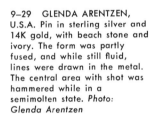

9-29   GLENDA ARENTZEN, U.S.A. Pin in sterling silver and 14K gold, with beach stone and ivory. The form was partly fused, and while still fluid, lines were drawn in the metal. The central area with shot was hammered while in a semimolten state. *Photo: Glenda Arentzen*

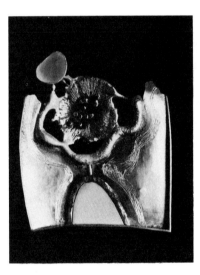

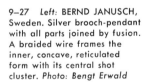

9-27   *Left:* BERND JANUSCH, Sweden. Silver brooch-pendant with all parts joined by fusion. A braided wire frames the inner, concave, reticulated form with its central shot cluster. *Photo: Bengt Erwald*

are fused. Remove the flame before they collapse. Overheating causes progressive melting of the forms so that they withdraw into themselves because of increasing surface tension. Their shapes become more and more rounded until eventually a molten puddle is formed.

During the fusing process, while the torch is held in the left hand, a *steel soldering pick* can be held in the right hand to prod parts into position. As an experiment, different colored metals can be fused together. At the point of fusion, a form can be struck with a steel hammer or block that covers it completely or partially, thus flattening and spreading it in an unpredictable and hopefully interesting pattern. The entire result can be hand hammered, drop hammered, or rolled in a rolling mill. Undesirable parts can be eliminated by sawing them off, and if necessary, weak sections can be supported or spaces between forms bridged with additional pieces of metal by soldering.

9-28   ALMA EIKERMAN, U.S.A. Sterling silver bracelet fabricated with textured sections with fused surfaces. A steel point was used to draw and push the surface while fluid. Col.: Rita Grunwald. *Photo: Ross Simmons*

9–30 CLAËS E. GIERTTA, Sweden. Silver ring made of forged forms that were subjected to fusing temperature in order to round edges and reticulate surfaces. *Photo: Sven Petersen*

9–31 GEORGE PAUL VAN DUINWYK, U.S.A. Pendant in sterling silver with moonstone, tourmaline, and citrine. After preliminary fabrication, the surface of the textured part was covered with silver filings which were then fused to the base. The frame was then fabricated from square wire, and the result gilded. *Photo: George Paul van Duinwyk*

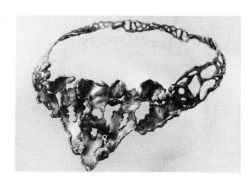

9–31A IRENA BRYNNER, Switzerland. Necklace, 18K gold, cast and parts micro-welded together. *Photo: Max P. Linck*

FUSED TEXTURES

The high temperature necessary for fusion to occur causes the surface of the metal to take on a characteristic wrinkled-looking appearance because it expands upon being overheated, then contracts upon cooling. This texture can be left intact, or parts can be removed by filing, then polishing the form smooth and bright at those places.

Textural surfaces can be deliberately created on metal by fusion. One such process involving sheet metal alone or dimensional forms is *reticulation* (described in this chapter), in which the surface develops a texture due to overheating.

Another fused metal textured surface can be created by first covering the base metal with flux, adding small elements such as metal filings, small scraps of wire, shavings, or paillons to it by sprinkling or sifting, and then fusing them to that surface by heat. The added elements can be of the same metal as the base, or of a different, contrasting colored metal. They can be fused just to the point where they become a part of that surface but still stay in relief upon it, or to the point where they begin to level and melt into the surface. The surface can be left as it is, or when a contrasting metal is used, it can be hammered flat for a multicolored pseudo-inlay effect.

MICRO-WELDING

Fusion welding is a technique of joining, cutting, piercing, surface or edge texturing sheet or cast metals using *welding equipment* that requires high heat. The welding process is common in industry, and is also used by metal sculptors. In recent times, *miniature welding equipment* has been developed for very small-scale welding jobs, the process called *micro-welding*. The small size of this equipment and the *micro-flame torch* used with it, makes the process of fusion welding suitable for use by jewelers. It can be used by jewelers who work with platinum, but also on all other metals used by jewelers. Those interested in this process are referred to books dealing with the subject of fusion welding.

HOT MODELING: Tool shaping fused metal

DEMONSTRATION 15

RITA GREER hot models an owl brooch

Photos: Alan Greer

Hot modeling is a method of shaping metal with a tool while it is being fused. Parts prepared this way can then be joined to each other by fusion. This method of directly sculpting metal with simple tools while it is in a surface-molten or completely molten state has been adopted by some jewelers as a means of creating parts of jewels or entire pieces. Surfaces can be textured in this process in a manner that is unique to it.

1 The working surface used here is a refractory *platinum melting block* which provides a noncrumbling slab on which to work. A small, intensely hot flame is played closely on the metal *throughout each stage*. The modeling must be done quickly before the work melts or collapses.

Here the repoussé-worked silver body of the owl with the face sawed out is being textured on the breast by fusing on gold filings. These are stroked with the end of an old *file* to shape downward, featherlike furrows while the torch flame plays on the area and keeps it in a surface-molten state.

2 A V-shaped piece of silver is being fused to the

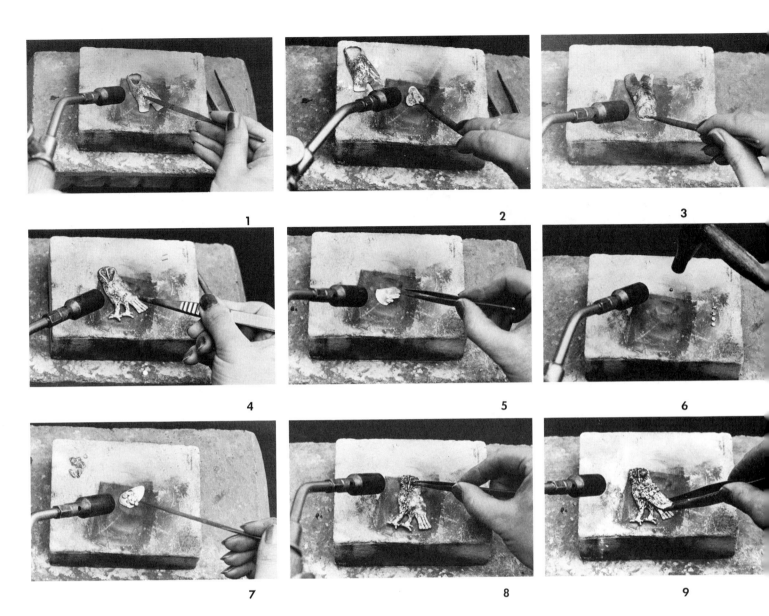

1	2	3
4	5	6
7	8	9

repoussé-shaped and chased face of the owl to form the upper part of the beak. It is modeled to the rest with the file under the flame.

3 Before each stage of joining one major part to another, their contacting surfaces are filed and fluxed, but the rest is left oxidized as it is. This helps to prevent already finished areas from melting. (Surfaces to be worked are also prefiled or scraped and fluxed.) Here the face is fused to the body as it rests in the cut-out opening made to receive it.

4 The tail and legs shaped under fusion from wire are already fused to the body. Small lengths of silver wire are being fused on to texture the juncture of the legs to the body.

5 Wing feathers cut from thin sheet silver are being modeled into shape before fusing the unit to a repoussé-formed wing shape.

6 Small wing feathers are made by heating a silver granule to the melting point, then flattening it with a hammer. Already flattened discs are seen on the right.

7 Small feathers are being fused to a repoussé-shaped sheet metal wing while the file manipulates their position.

8 A gold granule is being fused to the face to form an eye. The other eye and beak have already been fused in place. The eye, held by tweezers, is quickly dropped on the surface as soon as it starts to melt.

9 The finished wing, made separately, is being fused to the body. After this, the work was heated and boiled in pickle to remove all firescale. A cut-out flat sheet matching the owl's silhouette, pierced with a spiracle hole to let gases escape, was then soldered to make a back, and finally the brooch findings were soldered in place.

10 Polishing, buffing, and coloring complete the process. Here we see the finished owl brooch.

10

9–32 RITA GREER, England. "Night Travelers." Silver and 18K gold pendant, fused and hot modeled. The girl's head symbolizes sleep, during which the owl and the fish are both active, darkness keeping their movements secret from humans. Height 3.75 cm; width 5 cm. Photo: Alan Greer, courtesy Electrum Gallery, London

HOT PRESSURE MOLDING SMALL FORMS

Small forms can be *pressure molded* to take on any intaglio depression shape made with a *shaped punch* or carved directly into the flat surface of a refractory material such as a *charcoal block,* a block of *investment plas-*ter, or other suitable material. An approximation of the amount of metal needed to fill the cavity is cleaned and fluxed, then placed over or into the depression and melted with a reducing torch flame. When the metal becomes fluid, to force it to fill the mold completely, a thick, *flat steel block* is placed directly on the molten metal which does that and also flattens the back of the casting at the same time. Surplus metal will be forced out to form a fin or flange on the casting which can be removed by sawing or filing, if desired.

Three-dimensional objects can be formed in this way from two parts made in matching dimensions, then soldered together, back to back. Larger pieces so made tend to become heavy; to lighten them, surplus metal can be removed from their backs by *milling* it out with a *rotary bur.* Because in this case there is a hollow between the two parts, a hole must be drilled in one part before joining, to allow for an equalization of air pressure during soldering. Such hot pressure molded parts can be combined with sheet metal forms in fabricating jewelry.

FUSION INLAY

Fusion inlay involves making a recess in a sheet metal or cast metal object by engraving, chiseling, drilling, or saw piercing, then filling the recess by flooding it through fusion with a different colored metal. For example, the cleaned and fluxed recesses on a gold, copper, bronze, or shakudo alloy object can be fusion flooded with a silver alloy hard solder, which is white in color and therefore a contrast with all these metals. The surface is then leveled uniformly by filing so that the white solder-filled recesses become sharply defined. The surface is then polished and buffed.

GRANULATION

Fusion weld bonding ornamental units

Granulation (from Latin, *granulum,* diminutive of *granum,* "grain") is a metalwork process that takes its name from the manner of joining small, usually round balls or granules to a base. Normally the base is sheet metal, but the same process can be used to join granule to granule, granule to wire, wire to wire, chip to sheet, wire to sheet, sheet to sheet, and any other combinations of these, at their point or surface of contact. The means by which this is accomplished is by a *fusion welding bond,* therefore the term *granulation* when used here must be understood to mean *fusion welding.* The process works best with gold, but can also be used with silver.

THE FUSION WELD BOND: Theory

The ability of metals to be welded is influenced by their metallurgical, chemical, physical, and thermal characteristics. *Fusion welding* is fundamentally a process in which the objects or metals to be joined are brought to a molten state at their abutting or contacting surfaces. The term *welding* implies that the surfaces are joined in a mol-ten state, and *fusion* implies that an interpenetration of atoms occurs.

The *weld* is a localized union between the parts, formed in a relatively short time. During this period, the metal objects' surfaces are heated from room temperature to plasticity which occurs at a high temperature. In this state, the metals' surface atoms become mobile and because of thermal action are agitated and shuffled so that they exhibit a random or disordered distribution. The atomic structure of the molten metals in contact breaks down, opens up, and interacts. For this reason, copper—the joining alloying metal ordinarily used in this process—can penetrate the base metal, either gold or silver, in both directions and become diffused into both the base and the granule at their boundaries, which in the case of a ball is a very small interface of contact between it and the base. At even such small intersurfaces, when the temperature is sufficiently high and other conditions are present, a *contact alloying* takes place due to the action of atomic forces. This localized alloying is characterized by *intermolecular penetration.* Because of laws concerning the melting points of alloys, this fusion takes place at a temperature *lower* than

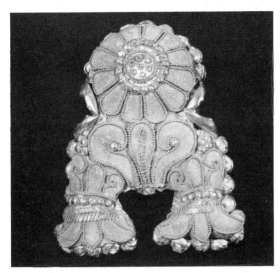

9–33 INDIA, Shunga Period (185–72 B.C.). *Triratna* (Sanskrit, "three jewels"). The trident shape used is symbolic of the three precious jewels of Buddhism: the Buddha; the Law (*dharma*); and the Order (*sangha*). The same trident shape, called *trisula* (Sanskrit, *tri,* "three"; *sula,* "sharp instrument"), is the emblem of Shiva, the Hindu god, and denotes his functions as Creator, Preserver, and Destroyer. When these symbols are worn as an ornament, they are believed to protect the wearer. The pendant, shown *full size* (2¼ in high), is one of two identical pieces, between which goes a barrel-shaped bead 2¼ in long, all three originally suspended by chains as one necklace. Their base forms, made of sheet metal by repoussage, are completely covered with gold granules. Purchase: John L. Severance Fund. *Photo: The Cleveland Museum of Art, Cleveland*

9–34 *DETAIL OF THE TRIRATNA PENDANT*
This shows the use of three sizes of granules in its decoration: large, medium, and small. The large granules emphasize points in the design by catching light; the medium-sized granules outline the shapes in the design; and the extremely small granules are used as fillers between the outlines to completely cover the ground surface where they are used. The fact that the diameter of the flower is approximately 1⅛ in makes this a *tour de force,* and indicates that an ancient tradition existed in India for the art of granulation. *Photo: The Cleveland Museum of Art, Cleveland*

9–35 DHARAN CANTONEMENT, NEPAL. Nepalese jeweler preparing a nose ring (*nakh phuli*) in 22K gold for granulation fusion welding. The nose ring ground was hammered out of a gold coin, and its surplus outside the pattern will be removed after granulation. The granules are being selected and placed with tweezers on the gummed surface. Small granule groups in three-ball arrangements, stamped pyramid shapes, and the central bezel are all fused to the base at the same time. *Photo: Oppi*

9–36 *THE WORK PLACED ON A MICA SHEET*
Both are put on a charcoal block which is hand held in air to allow its position to be moved as necessary to receive the flame heat. The heat source is a mouth blowpipe and a small kerosene lamp. An old beer can holds the quenchant. *Photo: Oppi*

9–37 NEPAL. Tamang woman wearing a gold-granulated nose ring, and a gold ear ornament (*chyaptesun*) with wirework decoration and flattened shot fused to its surface. *Photo: Oppi*

9–38 REVALSAR, HIMACHAL PRADESH, INDIA. The gold-granulated, septum-anchored nose ring (*bulak* or *kundu*) and gold nose stud (*luang*) are symbols of marriage. *Photo: Oppi*

9–39 NAGAR VILLAGE, KULU, HIMACHAL PRADESH, INDIA. Gold nose ring (*balu*), 22K, with granulation used extensively in the borders, and in the structures that enclose beads. This elaborate ornament strung with seed pearls and rubies is supported by a double, gold, loop-in-loop chain anchored by a hook to the hair. Ornaments like this are worn by married women at festivals such as the famed Dusserah at Kulu, and are discarded if the woman becomes widowed. A *kundu*, also bordered with granulation, and a *luang* are also worn, necessitating three holes in the nose. *Photo: Pran Nath Mago*

the separate melting points of the individual component metals being joined. The presence of carbon also acts to reduce the melting point. Metals possess the characteristic of being soluble into each other when molten, the degree of intersolubility depending on the combination. Those normally used in granulation techniques work well together.

Once surface fusion occurs, the heat is withdrawn from the metal. The bond then solidifies by *recrystallization* as on cooling the atoms assume definite positions in a crystal lattice. Under microscopic inspection an examination of the join shows that the transitions of the copper and the gold atoms are *gradual* and not abrupt, occurring in intermediate stages. In other words, there is no line of demarcation between the structure of the metals joined, their surfaces having diffused irregularly into each other. The finished weld is therefore *homogeneous,* and there is no evidence of the juncture. Because of the minute area of the join, the depth of the fusion is not great, but it is sufficient to hold the parts firmly together.

JOINING GRANULE TO BASE: Chemical and thermal action on copper and binder

To fully understand the concept central to the technique of granulation, the basic theory outlined above—the method of making the granules hold and become joined to the ground and each other with a *minimal join*—must

be discussed in greater detail. Unless otherwise specified, the following discussion refers to round granules joined to a sheet metal base.

To effect such a join, the use of solder in any form for purposes of joining is eliminated, because no matter how finely divided solder is, it will occupy too much space between and/or below the granules. This would rob them of their appearance of simply sitting miraculously on the base surface, which is the charm of the granulation technique. By examining any granule-decorated object with a *loupe,* one can determine whether it is true granulation or if the granules are held by conventional soldering techniques. The presence of fillets of solder which start at the base, curve upward, then outward and upward to the granule base is immediately apparent. In true granulation, the granule retains its complete, spherical form, and only a *minimally visible* joining fillet exists. Some visible fillet *must* exist in order for the bond to be strong enough to function. The higher the karat of the gold, the smaller the necessary fillet. There is also a relationship between the size of the granule and the size of the fillet needed to hold the granule firmly to the base. Large granules attract and develop proportionally larger fillets than small granules.

Several techniques can be used to join a granule to a base. All of them have in common the exploitation of physical and chemical laws by which an interaction takes place between the metal and the other substances used when they are heated to certain temperatures.

COPPER: The welding material for gold and silver alloys

To make the join, the granule (chip or wire) or the base, or both, are coated with a combination of *copper* in a chemical or solid form, plus an *organic binder*. The interaction of the copper and the carbonized binder when heated cause the surface of the grain and the base metal to melt at a temperature *lower* than that of the core alloy of the granule and base which therefore remain solid and do not collapse unless they are overheated.

By the most practiced methods, the forms of copper used are a *copper salt* or a *copper solid*. Among the *copper salt substances* that have been used successfully (mixed with an organic binder or glue and sometimes borax glass flux) are: copper hydroxide, $Cu(OH)_2$; copper chloride, $CuCl$ or Cu_2Cl_2; copper sulphate, $CuSO_4$; or copper acetate, $Cu(C_2H_3O_2)_2$. The *solid copper forms* used are: finely divided black copper oxide, CuO; red copper oxide, Cu_2O; copper oxide or firescale, which is a combination of black copper oxide on the outer surface and red copper oxide on the inner surface, both formed *directly* on the granule and/or the base surface by applied heat; copper deposited on the granule or the base, or both, by immersion in a spent nitric acid solution that has been used as a pickle for alloys containing copper, and therefore, when a piece of iron is introduced to this solution a copper flashing is produced on the surface of immersed objects by galvanic action; or a deposit of copper applied on the granules by the use of a copper plating solution. (For fine silver granulation, 3 parts antimony trioxide, Sb_2O_3 or Sb_4O_6, and 1 part borax glass flux is a recommended intermediary welding material.)

THE ORGANIC BINDER: A colloidal substance

The organic binder used to hold the granule to the base is a *colloidal substance,* for which reason the process is sometimes referred to as "colloidal hard soldering," but this term is misleading as no solder (which implies a form of a conventional lower melting fusible metal alloy) is used. *Colloidal fusion welding* might be a more correct term. A *colloid* is a viscous, gelatinous substance in fine subdivision and dispersion, dissolved and suspended without settling in water. Examples of colloids are gelatin, starch, and albumen. Colloids have the property of not becoming coagulated by salts, and have no effect on the vapor pressure of the solvent (water), for which reasons they do not bubble up as does unfused flux, and possibly cause the granules to move when their water content is heated to evaporation.

Colloidal organic binders used in the granulation process function in two ways: *mechanical* and *chemical*. Mechanically, the binder makes the granule initially adhere physically to the contacting surface and to other granules when they are arranged in a design pattern, before the heat is applied due to its adhesive quality and simple surface tension. The colloid is always an organic substance for chemical reasons to be made clear.

Animal or fish organic glues, or *vegetable gums* are the colloidal substances used for this purpose. Organic glue is a hard, brittle, usually impure gelatin obtained from boiling the skin, hoofs, and bones of animals, the result called *hide glue. Fish glue,* also organic, is made by boiling the sounds (air bladders) and skins of fish, which produces hard-drying fish glue types called *Seccotine* or *isinglass.* These gelatins, which are brittle when dry, are dissolved into and mixed with water to prepare them for use. All water used in the granulation process should be *distilled water* to avoid the possible interference of impurities. Because the glues and gums become tenacious and viscid when mixed with water, they can be applied with a brush. The amount of water used to create the necessary binder consistency must be judged, and depends on granule size. Thicker mixtures are needed as the size of the granule increases.

Organic vegetable gums are exuded or extracted from plants, shrubs, and some trees. They are glutinous when moist, but harden on drying, and then are usually pulverized and sold in powdered form. Basically they consist of complex organic acids, called gum acids, or their salts, which upon *hydrolysis* (the chemical process of decomposition involving the addition of water, induced by the presence of a dilute acid, an enzyme, or other agent) yield *starches* or *sugars* which *carbonize under heat.* The fact that carbon is produced when gums are heated is very important in the granulation process.

The most common vegetable gums used are *gum acacia* or *gum arabic* (these are essentially the same, or come from the same or similar sources), *Acacia senegal* or *Acacia arabica; gum tragacanth,* which is an exudate from a shrub *Astralagus gummifer;* and *agar-agar* from certain seaweeds, especially *Red Algae Rhodophyceae.* In some places in the East, orchid root gum is used. Some granulists add a little *borax glass* (fused borax or sodium tetraborate, $Na_2B_4O_7$) to the copper binder, but it does not seem to be essential to successful granulation.

When *joining granules to a metal base,* several different systems are used for coating and preparing both granules and base for heating. Some granulists apply the copper and binder to granules and base *separately.* It is more usual, however, for copper and binder to be *combined* with distilled water to form a paste. This is then applied to the base to which the granules will be joined, but only in the area that the granules will cover. Each granule is held by *tweezers,* dipped into the copper-binder preparation, then placed on the workpiece. Alternately, a *brush* that has been dipped into this preparation first is used to lift up and place each granule, automatically coating it with the preparation in the process. Only the minimum of binder needed to hold the granule is used. Once all the granules are placed, any surplus copper-binder preparation must be removed from exposed areas with a dampened brush. If it were allowed to remain on the workpiece, the copper content in the preparation would become fused to that area when heat was applied and would be seen as a discoloration, or would possibly cause pits in the surface.

When *joining granules to granules* to make an object completely of granules alone, or granules to wire, as for instance was done in China and is still done in India in making granule beads, caps to hold beads, or hairpins of unbacked wire and granules, another procedure can be practiced. When *flat* arrangements of granule groups are wanted, they are coated with a brush with the copper-binder preparation, and placed on a *sheet of mica* to which they will not adhere when heated. Using this concept, it is possible to make such a unit of granules alone, and after fusion joining to place it on a sheet metal unit to

join it there. When a *shaped* unit such as a hemispherical bead cap is to be made, a depression of the desired size is made in a *charcoal block*. The granules coated with the copper-binder preparation are lifted with a brush and placed in position within the depression which acts to support them, starting at the bottom and working upward. The same system could be used to create forms made entirely of granules, or granules and chips, on a larger scale.

All copper-binder preparations must be allowed to *dry thoroughly* before being heated. Excessive moisture remaining when the workpiece is heated, can boil and cause granule displacement.

BASIC GRANULE ARRANGEMENT AND GROWTH PATTERN SYSTEMS

Certain basic systems exist in which granules can be arranged, and from which unit growth pattern systems can be developed. These systems can be classified as follows: *linear or serial systems; geometric massed systems; random systems; varied sized or shaped granule systems;* and *three-dimensional systems.* In a jewelry work, granules arranged in such systems can be used as subordinate or dominant elements in its design.

LINEAR OR SERIAL SYSTEMS

For the purpose of this discussion, we assume the traditional concept that all granules are *round,* and of the same size in a single figure, also that all granules (except for three-dimensional arrangements), are in *contact with a base* to which they are fused (they can just as well be fused only to each other, without a base).

A single granule is the simplest element in all systems, and can be used alone in a figure as an accent. All systems begin with *one* and proceed on the basis of the positional relationship of *one to others.*

9–40   CHINA, 7–8th century A.D., T'ang Dynasty. Total length 28 cm; width 1.75 cm. Pair of silver-gilt hairpins, the ornamented section framed by a U-shaped wire that also forms the pins. Gold tubes with the seam on the inside are ornamented with alternations of scrolled wires and serial granulations. The openwork central section (8 cm long × 1.1 cm wide) consists of round wire tendril scroll and floral petal shapes, wires butting so all are in one plane. Along the inner edge of the scroll wires, granules are arranged in series, and also completely fill the flower petal units whose spaces are randomly packed with granules. Granules were placed over junctures to strengthen joins of wires to wires, and the entire inner wire construction is joined by granules at points of contact to the outer tube frame. Some such joins are intact, and others have broken away, but granules are in place on adjacent wires and tubes.

Backless granulation is a term that could be used for this granule and wire fabrication system. For its achievement, parts must have been supported during fusion weld heating using a suitable flat refractory material such as charcoal or sheet mica. The sheet metal lower section is also granule decorated on both sides. The joins include wire to wire; granules to wire; and wire and granules to sheet and tube. If, in addition, one considers the *scale* of the work, this is a truly extraordinary achievement. *Photo: Reproduced by Courtesy of the Trustees of The British Museum, London*

Linear or serial systems are established by adding other granules to the first. When these are all placed in a single line, we have a *linear series growth pattern.* When that line follows a curve, we have an *open curve linear series,* and when a curved line's ends meet and a figure is formed that encloses a space, we have a *closed curve linear series.* Linear systems can also be used to delineate geometric forms, free forms, or to create representational figural subjects. In all the above-mentioned one-to-one linear growth pattern systems, the *space between granules* has the same configuration, made by two abutting concave hemispheres, as illustrated in the drawing on p. 354.

GEOMETRIC MASSED SYSTEMS

In geometric massed systems, *groups* of granules are arranged in certain relationships to each other that come about because of the round granule form. Since these arrangements are geometric, a geometric rhythm is created

9–41 *Left:* TARQUINIA, ETRURIA, 7th century B.C. Gold-granulated bracelet whose entire linear design of geometric patterns, warriors and horsemen, is made of minute granules fused on a flat sheet metal ground. *Photo: Reproduced by Courtesy of the Trustees of The British Museum, London*

9–42 *Above: DETAIL OF THE SAME BRACELET,* one of a pair, showing the linear granule design. The bracelet width is 1⁷⁄₁₆ in (3.75 cm), and the length shown here is 1¹¹⁄₁₆ in (4.25 cm), which gives an idea of the fineness of the work scale. The best Etruscan granulation was produced during the 7th and 6th centuries B.C. *Photo: Reproduced by Courtesy of the Trustees of The British Museum, London*

9–43 *Right:* CAERE, ETRURIA, 7th century B.C. Gold granulation-decorated bracelet, one of a pair, whose figures formed in the sheet by repoussage are completely outlined with minute granules placed mainly in grooves. At the bottom is a fastening tongue. Granulation was the most important Etruscan decorative process used in jewelry, and the technique developed there to far greater refinement than in Greece. *Photo: Reproduced by Courtesy of the Trustees of The British Museum, London*

9–44 *Left: DETAIL OF THE SAME BRACELET;* width 2³⁄₁₆ in (5.5 cm); length 2⁹⁄₁₆ in (6.5 cm). Fine gold wires twisted to right and left are used as borders, and were fused to the ground along with the granules. *Photo: Reproduced by Courtesy of the Trustees of The British Museum, London*

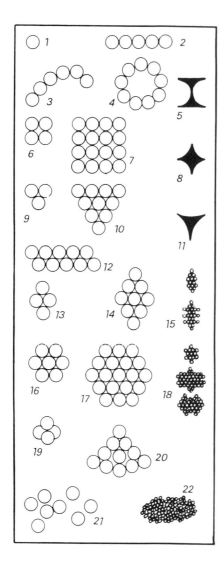

two side by side, one above in the space between them, and one below in the lower space. From this growth patterns generate variations of the lozenge—which can be thought of as a *double equilateral triangle*, base to base.

Hexagonal systems utilize a minimal unit of seven granules, forming the basic six-sided hexagonal figure from which growth patterns generate. Because this is also a three-axis figure, the spaces between granules are *concave triangles*.

From each of these basic geometric systems an infinite number of variations in arrangements can be made, each developing from the basic generic growth pattern figure. *Units* of any of these can be placed in repeats near other similar or differently formed units with a space between them. Entire surfaces can be covered with geometrically arranged granules so that no base metal is seen. Geometric systems can be combined with linear or serial systems.

THREE-DIMENSIONAL SYSTEMS

It is also possible to place granules three dimensionally, that is, to place *granules on top of granules*. When this is done, either the lowest tier is fused first, and the subsequent tiers are fused in sequence, or two or more tiers are fused simultaneously, depending on the complexity of the pattern and the possibility of physically placing one above another. Regular constructions can be made with spheres, and freely arranged constructions are possible with round or other shaped granule forms.

Pyramids are an example of a regular three-dimensional construction made with granules of the same size, on either a triangular or a square base. The one illustrated here has a triangular base. In the granule pyramid development, each diminishing level of granules rests in the spaces that occur between the granules of the level below.

Free three-dimensional constructions can be made using granules of different sizes; by layering chips; with combinations of chips, granules, and wires.

RANDOM SYSTEMS

In random systems, granule placement is deliberately irregular and haphazard, depending on chance or accidental arrangements. The spaces between granules are therefore *irregular*.

within the figure because they are all oriented in relation to the axes that pass between their centers. This rhythm expands in all directions as the figure follows any growth pattern. Arrangements in which a single granule contacts more than one other are stronger, the strength increasing with the number of contact points.

Squared systems have a minimal unit of four granules, with the two axes between all granule centers at right angles to each other. The massed granules are arranged in ranks. Each individual granule touches *four granules* when completely surrounded by others, and the growth pattern is always at right angles. The space shape between granules in this case has *four points* and might be termed a *concave square*.

Oblique systems contain three axes in the granule arrangement, one horizontal, one oblique to the left, and one oblique to the right, the three together forming triangulations. The minimal unit in this system is a *triangle* formed by three granules, one placed in a position halfway between and above or below two others. In all oblique systems, the *space* between the granules is the smallest that is possible when massing round granules. This space shape has *three points*, and might be termed a *concave triangle*. One simple arrangement that develops from this beginning is the *double linear series* often used in borders. By adding to this a *third series*, on one side only, skipping a placement between each granule, a *triangular repeat series border* is made.

Lozenge system minimal units consist of four granules,

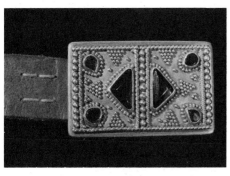

9–46 *Left:* ROBERT KULICKE, U.S.A. Silver belt buckle ornamented with fine silver granulation and garnets. The twisted wire borders and the bezels were fused to the ground in one granulation-fusion operation. Length 3.9 cm; width 2.3 cm. *Photo: Hank Simon*

9–47 *Right: THE BELT WITH BUCKLE, TONGUE OR MORDANT* with emerald, and ornamental black plaque, all granulation decorated. *Photo: Hank Simon*

9–48 CORNELIA ROETHEL, U.S.A. Gold linear-patterned granulation-decorated bead, the two half-dome parts separated by a lapis lazuli disc; threaded on a cord. *Photo: Cornelia Roethel*

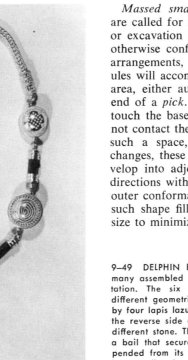

Massed small-sized granules in random arrangements are called for in some designs, placed within a depression or excavation in the base, within a wire cloison, or in an otherwise confined or delineated space. In such crowded arrangements, because of their spherical shape, the granules will accommodate themselves to the smallest possible area, either automatically, or by being prodded with the end of a *pick*. Because of gravity, all granules will try to touch the base within the space. Surplus granules that do not contact the base, or that extend beyond the contour of such a space, can be removed. As the space contour changes, these self-made geometric arrangements may develop into adjoining geometric arrangements that change directions with each change in axis direction. Because the outer conformation of the figure usually remains irregular, such shape filling is usually done with granules of small size to minimize irregularity.

9–49 DELPHIN BROUSSAILLES, France. Gold necklace fabricated of many assembled parts, including 13 units with granulation ornamentation. The six round dome units are each ornamented with a different geometrically arranged granulation pattern, and are spaced by four lapis lazuli cylinder beads capped with ornamented tubes. On the reverse side of each round unit is set a Sassanian intaglio of a different stone. The central, large, bell-shaped, granulated pendant is a bail that secures a Mesopotamian stone-engraved stamp seal. Suspended from its sides are two quadruple loop-in-loop chains ending in centrally pierced emerald terminals held by ball pins. The same chain construction is used at the front and back where the closing consists of a quadruple loop and hook. Ball and socket, and rivet hinge joints are used to hold various units to each other. The maker uses granules in sizes of 0.010, 0.013, 0.014, 0.018, and 0.025 in. *Photo: Courtesy of Ares Gallery, New York*

9–50 BALI, INDONESIA. Contemporary silver bracelet ornamented with minute fine silver granulation. Represented on each hinged panel is the mask of the Barong, the two-man dragon who appears in traditional Balinese dances. *Photo: Oppi*

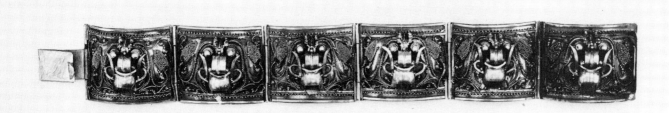

Pulviscolo, which in Italian literally means "fine dust," is a term used by contemporary Italian granulators to designate one such random arrangement, also used by the Etruscans, especially at Vetulonia, near Lake Prile. Here the size of the granules is so small that when they are distributed within a space, the surface appears to the naked eye as a *texture* rather than an agglomeration of grains, and only by the use of a magnifying lens can one confirm with certainty that the individual units are in fact granules.

VARIED SIZE GRANULE SYSTEMS

As initially mentioned, in the foregoing discussion, the assumption has been made that all the granules in the systems described are of the same size in a single figure, the traditional granulation concept, but of course they need not be. Any design can be created using several different granule sizes with either the same sized granules used for different portions of the pattern, or by using a combination of graduated granules within the same figure. When *different sized granules* are used in the same design, the figure, area, or surface can be arranged geometrically, nongeometrically, symmetrically, asymmetrically, or in random arrangements.

DIMENSIONAL SURFACES

In the previous discussion, it has also been assumed that the surface on which granules are placed is flat. Granules can be placed on any *dimensional* surface as well, and held in position by an organic adhesive. That surface can be a single convex or concave plane as in a hemisphere. It can also be a complex repoussage on which the granules are used to outline a representational or abstract figure, or to partly or completely cover a form.

MISCELLANEOUS FORMS USED IN FUSION WELDING

Besides round granules, *flattened granules* which then become small discs, *chips* of any polygonal shape, or *wire* in round, square, rectangular, and multi-element twists in a round or flattened state; as well as butt-edged and lapped sheet can all be "granulated," a term that in these cases seems inappropriate because the forms of these units are no longer granules. However, the process that holds them together or to a base is still *fusion welding*. Any of these forms can be combined and used on the same object.

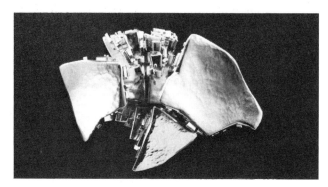

9–51 JOHN PAUL MILLER, U.S.A. "Fragment No. 3." Pendant/brooch in 18K gold. The compound structure with several forged and planished units are ornamented with rectangular chip granules. *Photo: John Paul Miller*

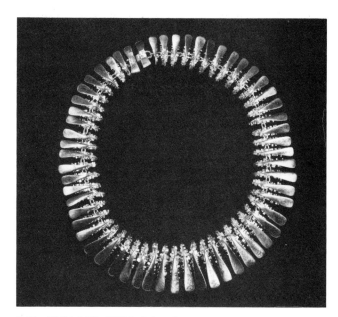

9–52 JOHN PAUL MILLER, U.S.A. "Sunburst." Necklace of 18K gold. Each of the 59 forged units is ornamented with rectangular chip granules, and linked by oval loops. *Photo: John Paul Miller*

A special use of fusion welding can be carried out in preparation for cloisonné enameling in which wires of square or rectangular section are used to form the cloisons. By fusion welding these cloisons, bent to any shape, to the base (in this case both are precious metals), the problem of the interference of solder (which would otherwise be used) with the enamel, is eliminated.

THE EFFECT OF THE REDUCING ATMOSPHERE HEAT

Once the granule is held to the metal base with gum or glue, and some form of copper covers or is applied to it, and it is dry, the next step is to apply the heat to this assembly. Heat may be applied by a torch (*torch fusion*) or a kiln or furnace (*kiln* or *furnace fusion*), and in some practices, *both* are used.

Granulation must take place in a *reduced atmosphere*, meaning one in which *oxygen is excluded* as much as possible, because of the *chemical changes* that occur during the process, as explained below. (The means of creating such an atmosphere with a torch are explained under Soldering, Chapter 10.) When the temperature is sufficiently high, and a reducing atmosphere exists, and the granule-holding substance is suited to the process, the two metal parts can be joined at their contacting surfaces *without conventional solder.*

Under heat, in the reduction atmosphere, the compound of copper plus adhesive undergoes a *chemical change* in which *the nonmetallic elements are removed*. In this process, at an *intermediate heating stage*, the following takes place:

At 212° F (100° C) the colloidal gelatin or starch becomes carbon and separates from the copper oxide; by 1112° F (600° C) the binder becomes completely carbonized or converted to a residue of carbon; at 1562° F (850° C) this carbon residue combines with the remaining oxygen in the metallic salt or solid, and passes off as a carbon dioxide gas, thus carrying away those elements no longer necessary to the chemical success of the process after having served their chemical and mechanical functions. This leaves behind a thin film of *pure copper* on the granule and/or base metal. The copper is formed because when metallic oxides are heated in the presence of carbon in a reduced atmosphere, they are reduced to a pure metallic state.

This can be expressed by chemical formulas as follows:

Copper hydroxide:

$$2Cu(OH)_2 + C \rightarrow 2Cu + CO_2 \uparrow + 2H_2O \uparrow$$

That is: Copper hydroxide plus carbon under reduction heat yields copper, and carbon dioxide and water which pass off into the air as a gas and vapor respectively.

Copper chloride:

$$CuCl_2 \rightarrow Cu + Cl_2 \uparrow$$

That is: Copper chloride under reduction heat yields copper and chlorine which passes off as a gas.

Black copper oxide (cupric oxide, CuO):

$$2CuO + C \rightarrow 2Cu + CO_2$$

That is: Cupric oxide plus carbon under reduction heat yields copper and carbon dioxide which evaporates leaving pure copper.

Red copper oxide (cuprous oxide, Cu_2O):

$$2Cu_2O + C \rightarrow 4Cu + CO_2 \uparrow$$

That is: Cuprous oxide plus carbon under reduction heat yields copper and carbon dioxide which passes off as a gas.

In starting with granules copper plated either from a spent acid solution or a regular copper plating solution, the copper is already present in a metallic state. The gum acts as a binder and when turned to carbon under heat has another function:

The organic carbon in the presence of copper also has the effect of *lowering the melting point* of the surface metal alloy somewhat. This fact plays a part in allowing the fusion of the molten copper and the metal surface to take place *before* the core metals have attained their melting point. The surface melt occurs at a temperature below the fusing point of the separate constituents in a state of pure metals.

It is known that pure copper melts at 1981.4° F (1083° C), and pure gold at 1945.4° F (1063° C); 18K gold melts at a range of 1700–1810° F (926.6–987.7° C) depending on the alloy, and 14K gold, 1540–1767° F (837–963.8° C). All these are below the melting point of pure copper and pure gold. When copper exists in an alloy of gold, it acts to lower the melting point to a minimum of 1623.2° F (884° C), the liquidus of binary alloys of copper and gold. The fusion of an 18K red gold alloy (75% gold, 25% copper) occurs at 1634° F (890° C). These figures point out the reason that the *choice of alloy* used in the granulation process is of extreme importance.

TIME-TEMPERATURE RELATIONSHIP

The time during the heating period in which the joining takes place bears a relationship to the necessary temperature. The heating period must be long enough and the temperature high enough for both *liquation* and *capillarity* to occur. At the heart of the successful conclusion of the granulation process is the individual's ability to judge the moment and the duration of when these conditions obtain, usually covering a period of only three or four seconds. For this short time interval, the temperature remains in the plastic range of one or both of the surfaces of the metals joined, and does not reach the liquidus temperature

of the core metal before the fusion weld bond has been completed and the heat is withdrawn.

SURFACE TENSION AND CAPILLARITY

The copper left on the granule surface is very thin. It is also low in *surface tension* (also called *interfacial tension,* the *interface* being the outermost layer of the surface), a property of the surface film of anything in a liquid state. In surface tension, particles lying below the interfacial film are acted upon equally from all sides, and normally are attracted inward in a state of cohesive equilibrium.

When a higher temperature is reached, the copper film and the precious metal below it melt and become fluid. In melting, the interface metal expands and becomes extended, making it necessary for the molecules in the interior to move to the liquid on the surface, thereby working against the cohesive forces of the liquid copper which has a higher energy than the liquid below it. It behaves like a thin elastic membrane, breaks, contracts to the minimum area at the point of contact, and acts according to the laws of *capillarity* (which is the direct result of the action of surface tension).

Capillarity is a physical characteristic of a liquid (the molten metal surface) in contact with a solid (the unmol-

9–53 JOHN PAUL MILLER, U.S.A. Gold necklace with beetle whose elytra and other parts are ornamented with spheroid granules. Col.: The Cleveland Museum of Art, Silver Jubilee Treasure Fund, 1953. *Photo: The Cleveland Museum of Art, Cleveland*

  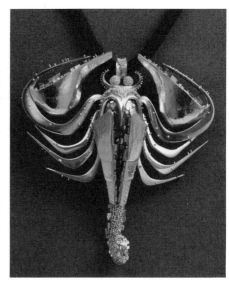

9–54 JOHN PAUL MILLER, U.S.A.
"Gunard." Pendant/brooch in 18K and fine
gold, with enamel, ornamented with
spheroid and flattened sphere granules.
Photo: John Paul Miller

9–55 JOHN PAUL MILLER, U.S.A.
"Octopus." Pendant/brooch in 18K and fine
gold, with enamel. Photo: John Paul Miller

9–56 JOHN PAUL MILLER, U.S.A.
"Scorpion." Pendant/brooch in 18K and
fine gold. Photo: John Paul Miller

Granulation Procedures

Gold Used	Welding Substance	Glue or Gum for Granule Placement	Heat Source
Rosenberg-Treskow 900/1000 gold 50/1000 silver 50/1000 copper	The granule is coated with gold carbide as a result of being formed in charcoal, the carbide having a melting point 160°C below that of the gold used	Spittle, which contains ptyalin, the amylase of saliva, an enzyme that accelerates the hydrolysis of starch, a complex carbohydrate. Spittle itself is weakly alkaline.	Reducing torch flame or kiln with reducing atmosphere
Littledale 750/100 red gold (250/1000 parts copper, or 125/1000 parts copper and 125/1000 parts silver)	1 part copper hydroxide (a copper salt. Salts are any of a class of compounds derived from acids by the replacement of part or all of the acid hydrogen by a metal. Salts are formed by the reaction of acids with metals and oxides, and other ways). Cupric hydroxide $Cu(OH)_2$ finely divided, or other copper salts.	1 part organic glue, as siccotine + water, or gum tragacanth + water, or gum acacia + water. Mix with copper hydroxide fo form a paste, apply with a brush to granule during granule placement.	Reducing torch flame, heat to 1634°F (890°C)
Wilm-Roethel 750/1000 red gold 585/1000 red gold containing copper	At the start, copper chloride, then halfway: copper oxide, flux, water, one third each	Flux and water. Borax flux the ground and place granules.	Reducing torch flame
750/1000 red gold 585/1000 red gold both containing copper	Pre-heat granules and base metal separately to achieve copper oxided surface with an oxidizing torch	Borax flux the ground and granules	Reducing torch flame
Miller 750/1000 yellow gold	Preheat granules only for surface oxide. Place them on depletion-gilded nearly 24k gold surface base metal	Gum tragacanth on brush when placing granules	Reducing torch flame, object placed over charcoal bed
750/1000 red gold	Coat base with finely divided copper oxide powder mixed with gum	Gum tragacanth mixed with borax used on brush to place granules	Reducing torch flame
Kulicke-Stark 22k gold (22 dwt 24k gold, 1.5 dwt fine silver, .5 dwt copper or fine silver)	Depletion gild the base. Plate or paint the base metal of electrum (gold silver alloy) with copper by immersing it in copper-saturated nitric acid, in which some iron such as a piece of iron binding wire is present and in contact with the granules to cause the plating action, or by applying it with a brush. Coat granules with same for gold, but not silver unless they are large.	Hide glue and water, proportioned 1-10 respectively for flat surfaces. Add 1 part hard soldering flux to the above for curved surfaces.	Heat in small kiln with glass cover till red, then apply reducing torch flame.

ten metal base and the granule or contacting granules). The molecules of the liquid have a force of attraction for each other and for the contacting solid if it is compatible (as the metals are in the case of granulation). The molecules of the molten copper and gold attract each other. When the copper migrates to the points of contact between granule and granule, and granule and base (the latter by now also in a state of surface fluidity), its molecules on the touching surfaces form a minute fillet or junction, invisible due to the circular grain shape. The copper and gold then intermix and both the join and the immediately contacting surfaces become an interalloy. *At this crucial point, the heat is removed.* Immediately the liquid metals crystallize and form an intermediary alloy at the point of contact, thus effecting a weld bond join of relatively good bonding strength, achieved with a minimal amount of fillet metal.

The types of surface finish in the result after pickling depend on certain variables. Under reduced heating conditions, these variables include: the content of the alloys of gold or silver used; the specific copper-containing welding chemical used with a particular alloy; the strength of the organic binder (which ultimately means its carbon content); and the degree of heat this combination requires to form a satisfactory weld-bonded fillet. After pickling, the surface appearance of the result can range from brightly shining, smooth-surfaced granules, or frosted granules, on a bright or frosted ground; to undesirably reticulated or pitted surfaces on granules and/or ground. Experimentation is necessary to determine which chemicals work best with which alloys, and the strength of organic binder needed for particular alloys. Some directions are indicated in the table that follows. Resulting surfaces can of course be altered by manual or mechanical polishing and buffing, or by chemical means such as the use of bright dip acid solutions.

GOLD GRANULATION: Practice

DEMONSTRATION 16

JOHN PAUL MILLER illustrates one granulation method while making a pendant/brooch

Photos: John Paul Miller

Shown in the following sequence is only *one* of the several gold granulation techniques used by the artist. Here an 18K gold granulation ornamented pendant/brooch in the form of a cephalopod is fabricated.

SPHEROIDIZING: PREPARING THE GRANULES

1 Long, thin strips are cut from a sheet of 34 gauge B.&S. 18K yellow gold (75% gold and 25% copper and silver). Hand- or foot-operated *guillotine shears* are used for this purpose. The strips are fed endwise to the shear blades, and shear cropped into small, more or less uniform pieces. Alternately, fine wire arranged in a bundle can be cut by *hand* or *bench alligator shears*. Very small granules of the *pulviscolo* type can be made from coarse filings of precious metals.

2 The resulting minute square and rectangular gold chips can be granulated to the base in that form, a practice often followed by Miller. Frequently they are formed into small, round balls or granules, the traditional form used for granulation. The process of making these small, round balls is called *spheroidizing,* which is the heating, fusing, and cooling of metal that results in a rounded or globular form. The term can also be used to describe the making of larger balls called *shot,* normally too large for use in granulation. *Shotting,* a process by which the refiner prepares metal in rounded pellets for use in casting, is also a form of spheroidizing.

By a metallurgical principle, when small amounts of metal are melted to the *liquidus point,* a cohering surface tension force causes them to contract, or become reduced to a form having the smallest possible surface area consistent with the material and the force of gravity in a shape that can contain the liquid result. In this case, the shape is a *sphere* which when small enough becomes a granule when allowed to cool and solidify in this form. The sphere shape has the minimum surface-to-volume ratio.

To accomplish spheroidizing by one method used by Miller, the gold chips are sifted on a leveled layer of *powdered charcoal* placed in a *stainless steel container.* These chips are distributed so that as much as possible they do not touch each other, because if they do, they will join under heat and form larger balls when the larger mass of metal fuses. A second layer of charcoal is sifted over the chips to a depth sufficient to prevent the next distribution of chips deposited upon it from sinking through the first. For this reason, the charcoal should not be too finely powdered. Only three or four layers are so made in the container, their total depth being about 1¼ in (5.7 cm). If you make too many layers at once you risk the interior not reaching the necessary temperature. More granules than you expect to use are made because of the relatively wide variation in sizes that results as a function of the inequality of chip sizes.

3 The container with charcoal and gold chips is placed in an *electric kiln* preheated to about 2000° F

1   2   3

4   5   6

(1093.3° C). A container 4 in × 2.5 in (10.2 cm × 5.7 cm) requires about 20 minutes in the kiln for the chips to contract to their smallest surface and form spheres, each separated from the other by the powdered charcoal. The loose physical condition of the powdered charcoal does not resist the spheroidizing process or cause any surface flatness, as would occur if solid, flat charcoal or other refractory material is used, unless a depression is made for each granule, obviously impossible when they are very small, but possible when making shot.

4   The container is removed from the kiln and its contents are poured directly into another *container of water* and some detergent, and the charcoal is washed away, leaving behind the gold granules, which because of their weight, gather at the bottom of the container. The presence of the charcoal surrounding each granule during formation creates a reducing atmosphere around each sphere so that their surfaces remain bright and oxide-free. Even slight variations in chip sizes result in spheres of many slightly differing diameters.

5   Because ornamental granules are generally grouped by size, they are now sorted into eight different diameters by sifting them through a *series of sieves,* starting with the one having the smallest mesh openings, and continuing to those progressively larger. No. 8 is the smallest granule of uniform size and has an 0.008 in (0.205 mm) diameter; No. 2 is the largest uniform size and is 0.030 in (0.762 mm) in diameter; and No. 1 is large, ungraded sizes.

6   The granules selected for use are placed in a container of pure or 18K gold, put into a *small electric kiln* having a *heatproof glass cover* so they can be observed, and are heated to 1200° F (648.8° C) and kept at that temperature for several minutes. During this time, their surfaces, which contain copper, become oxidized and uniformly covered with black cupric oxide, CuO, also

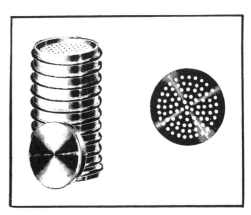

9–57   *TEN-TIERED SIEVE.* This is used for sorting the sizes of spheroid-shaped granules to obtain uniformity of size. Sieves are available and can be made to specifications by Karl Fischer, Pforzheim.

called copper monoxide, or black oxide of copper; in jeweler's parlance it is called firescale. Below the outer layer of black copper oxide is red oxide of copper, Cu_2O, also called copper suboxide, cuprous oxide, and copper hemioxide. The difference in its composition from black copper oxide is due to the fact that it has been created under reduced atmospheric conditions. The outer layers become black copper oxide because they are exposed to a greater amount of atmospheric oxygen. The granules emerge from the kiln looking like black poppy seeds, making them highly visible during their placement in a pattern.

7   8   9

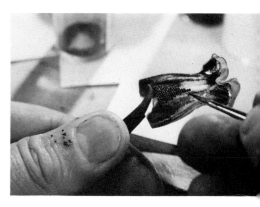

10   11   12

DEPLETION GILDING: PREPARING THE SURFACE

7 The next aim is to develop a surface of nearly pure gold on the repoussé-worked and chased form on which the granules will be applied. This is done by a process called *depletion gilding,* an ancient technique for creating a final surface of nearly pure gold on any object made of even low gold content alloys. In the process, by chemical means, all metals in the alloy except the gold that exist in the outer surface are removed. In the present context, the need to create the pure gold surface on the 18K gold base is that it will act more favorably in this particular granulation technique. Some oxide may form on a depletion-gilded surface when it is heated, but very much less than if the surface had not been gold enriched.

Depletion gilding involves three steps. The first is to heat the object in the electric kiln to 1200° F (648.8° C) which causes the copper molecules in the outermost layers of the alloy to combine with oxygen, oxidize, and form a firescale on its surface.

8 The next step is to immerse the object in a hot, dilute solution of nitric acid which dissolves the surface scale (cupric oxide), leaches out surface copper, and leaves a greater number of gold molecules exposed than formerly. The nitric acid attacks only the copper (and the silver, if any is present in the alloy), not the gold. The object is rinsed well in running water to remove acid traces.

9 The surface is next scratch brushed which has the effect of burnishing it without removing any metal, and compressing it at the same time. For this, a *nickel silver, fine crimped wire brush* fed a constant thin stream of soapy water as lubricant, is used.

These last three steps are repeated in sequence a maxi-

mum of three times as a surface more gold enriched than this seems to result in a weaker joint of the granule. The surface thereafter acts almost as one of pure gold.

GRANULE PLACEMENT: USING GUM AND BRUSH TO MANIPULATE GRANULE POSITION

10 A thin coat of a special soldering investment plaster slurry, used for holding parts together while soldering, and a great help in other difficult soldering operations (see Soldering, Chapter 10), is here applied to the edges of the work to prevent them from becoming overheated during the soldering process that follows. Edges are always attacked by heat first and therefore tend to melt before the rest of the metal has reached a high enough temperature; the plaster by its insulating refractory property prevents this from happening.

11 A solution of *gum tragacanth* is prepared. One-tenth of a gram of gum powder is combined with half an ounce of water, which makes a relatively thin solution. A *brush* moistened with this gum solution picks up the granules and deposits them on the upper thumb where they are checked for uniformity of size and shape.

12 Granules are transferred to their position on the metal base which is hand held with *self-locking tweezers.* In the process of transfer, each granule becomes completely coated with a gum amount sufficient to hold the granule in place. To assist the gum in its job of holding the granules in place, the work is turned so that the area of granule placement is facing upward.

13 The granules positioned in one area are allowed to dry before turning a three-dimensional form in another direction to place granules on another part. As the amount of moisture in the gum is small the gum dries in air, and ordinarily it is not necessary to heat the work to hasten

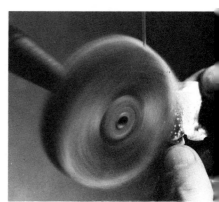

13   14   15

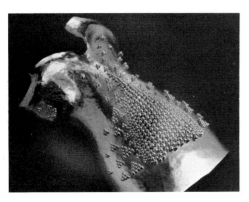

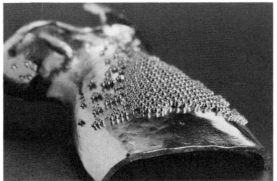

16   17   18

drying. The gum, however, must be *thoroughly dry* so that excess moisture will not boil up under subsequent heating and cause possible granule displacement.

GRANULATION: GRANULE FUSION WELD BONDING

14 The piece is held in air above a premade bed of glowing charcoal in a *brazier* by clamping two stainless steel *self-locking tweezers* at either end. To free the hands, they are then laid flat on and anchored to a *heating frame* placed on either side of the brazier level with its top. Sometimes a piece is placed on a *fine iron wire screen.* Discretion must be used, as holding tools can act to absorb too much heat. The glowing charcoal under the piece works to establish a uniform temperature over the entire piece, a condition essential to the success of the process. The edges of a large surface heat faster than the center and the heat from the charcoal tends to balance the heat supply.

The flame of a *torch* set to a reducing condition is applied to the work from above (out of view). Its size is sufficiently large so that the outer flame envelope shields and further protects the metal by excluding and preventing atmospheric oxygen attack. Heating is fast to avoid the dissipation of carbon formed from the binder. For large areas, Miller uses a *fluxing unit* set to introduce a small amount of gas/flux into the flame and increase its reducing condition. Creating a reducing flame, and its control by playing it over the metal without overheating it, are critical for successful granulation. Contrary to normal heating practice, a bright light is used during the heating in order to better observe the changes that occur to the surfaces of the base metal and the granules as the temperature of the metal rises.

Under the heat of the reducing flame, in the reduced atmosphere, it is the chemical change that occurs that allows the joining of a granule to the base. The black cupric oxide, CuO, on the granule surface turns to cuprous oxide, Cu_2O. The gum carbonizes, and the oxygen in the cuprous oxide combines with the carbon and passes off as carbon dioxide gas, leaving behind a very thin film of pure molten copper that completely covers the granule surface. The copper in a high-alloy gold acts to lower the melting temperature to a minimum of 1623.2° F (884° C), the liquidus temperature of the copper and gold alloy used which also contains some silver.

As the workpiece nears red heat, the granules look dark, and the surrounding carbonized glue becomes bright red. As the heating continues and the liquidus of the alloy is approached, the surface tension of the copper film breaks

down and, because of capillarity, the copper flushes and migrates to the point of contact between granule and base, in the manner of solder when it becomes liquid in a joint. Usually the enriched, almost pure gold surface becomes bright, but the granules shimmer, as does the area immediately near them where some of the copper flows over it.

At this point—the "moment of truth" in granulation—in a few seconds a welding and bonding action takes place. The touching metal surfaces are in the plastic range of both the copper and the gold, but under controlled conditions the rest of the metal does not reach the liquidus temperature before the completion of the bond or the metal would collapse. The bond occurs when the molecules of the molten copper flow to the contacting surfaces by capillary attraction, and in this action, the contacting atoms of both metals interpenetrate. Thus the granules join where they touch each other and the base simultaneously. The success of the whole process, even after careful preparation and meeting all other necessary conditions, depends upon the judgment of that point at which the above action has taken place in the final, critical few seconds. The flame is then immediately withdrawn. At this point, the metal turns black upon cooling.

The point of contact is a small fillet of a copper gold alloy. As mentioned, there must be a sufficient fillet to make the joint firm, and it can be seen under magnification, but to the naked eye it seems not to exist. Overheating is to be avoided since this may cause a large fillet,

19   20

which will also occur if there is too much copper in the welding medium.

It is sometimes necessary to make two or more applications of granules, and the second and subsequent firing process becomes even more critical.

FINISHING: SURFACE PROCESSING AND ASSEMBLY

15 The piece is pickled to remove the surface firescale. All cleaning action must be *gentle* and done with great care in this delicate work. The surface is burnished with the same *nickel wire brush* as before, using soapy water as a lubricant. The spindle is operated at the slow speed of 1800 rpm.

16 Here we see the completed granulated unit which is only a part of the total pendant/brooch.

17 These close-ups show by the reflection of the inverted image of the granule in the mirror-bright surface of the base metal, that the point of its contact to the base is absolutely *minimal*. This is the main characteristic of successful granulation.

18 The base metal is 18 gauge B.&S. (0.040 in or 1.024 mm), and the smallest granules here are eight thousandths of an inch (0.008 in or 0.205 mm).

19 The assembled basic units of the incomplete pendant/brooch. The central section ornamented with granulation is $1\frac{7}{16}$ in $\times$ ¾ in (3.6 cm $\times$ 1.9 cm).

20 The completed pendant/brooch. Enamel has been fired in the spaces between the granules and chips in the upper section. The tentacles are also granulated with chips and flattened pellets, as well as round granules.

METAL LAMINATION FABRICATION

Bonding and patterning multi-metal composites

Lamination fabrication, a basic metal use concept, can be described as the making of a stratified or multilayered ferrous or nonferrous metal composite consisting of two or more individual *laminae* (singular, *lamina*) of different metals, originally in the form of sheet, strip, wire, or rod, fused or bonded together to make one structural unit. The *laminate* that results is then manipulated in various ways to create a surface pattern that utilizes all the component metals in the composite.

Lamination compositions are increasingly in use in creative jewelry. The visual appeal of their surface patterns is more important in this area than the functional character of the result (as when a laminate is made for use in the blade of a cutting instrument).

DAMASK STEEL: Pattern in cast crucible steel or fabricated laminates

The origin of all lamination fabrication processes is in the manufacture of patterned blades made of what in the West is commonly called *damask* or *Damascus steel* (discussed in this chapter). There are, in fact, two basic means of creating patterned ferrous blades because there are two distinctly different kinds of damask steel, each with a patterned structure brought out by different means. One is *cast crucible steel,* and the other a *fabricated laminate of wrought iron and steel.* Though the jeweler's interest centers on fabricated patterned laminates, crucible steel will be discussed first to differentiate between the two types, and to provide a historic background for modern developments.

WOOTZ: An old Indian carburized cast crucible steel damask

Old Persian and Arabic texts indicate that the manufacture of cast damask steel and patterned blades made from it originated in India from where it spread westward to the Middle East, and eastward to China, Japan, and Indonesia. Since pre-Christian times, skilled steelmakers in the Hyderabad-Deccan area of India produced a superior steel widely recognized for its outstanding qualities, and exported throughout the "civilized" world of that time. Production continued until the 19th century when the common use of military and ceremonial swords virtually ended, and its manufacture which was relatively expensive, was wiped out by cheap imported European iron and steel whose use rapidly spread in India with the growth of the Indian railways.

This steel is called *wootz* in Western literature, but according to Yule (*Hobson-Jobson,* page 972) this is not a term in any Indian vernacular language, but is a corruption of the South Indian Kanarese word *ukku* (pronounced *wukku*), meaning "hardenable steel." Today the Hindi and Urdu word for hardenable carbon steel is *fulad,* taken from the Persian.

Wootz was *cast crucible carbon steel* made from a magnetic ore called magnetite (Fe_3O_4), which in a native state contains up to 72% iron. It was a superior cast carbon steel that with proper control maintained the quality of *malleability* not normally found in cast iron (which is usually brittle). In India it was prepared by placing in a *crucible* two parts of chipped pieces of mild steel, one part finely broken cast iron, and flux. (Wrought iron can be substituted for cast iron.) Mixed with this and covering it to the crucible top was crushed charcoal, and sometimes other organic matter which was carbonized by the reduced atmosphere heat. The crucible was closed with a cover to exclude oxygen and retain the gases that formed within, and placed with several similarly charged crucibles into a *furnace* for simultaneous melting. The charge in each crucible was small, about 5½ lb (2.4 kg) of metal which was brought to a boiling melt under high heat. In some cases, after the initial melt occurred, about 5.29 oz (150 g) of silver was then added to the charge. The load was recovered with fresh charcoal, and the crucible was then closed and reheated. The charcoal was subjected to sufficient air blast from a hand-operated *bellows* to raise the temperature above 2800° F (1538° C), necessary for melting iron.

Carburization of the metal took place during melting

due to the presence of charcoal inside the crucible. *Carburizing* is a process in which the metalloid carbon becomes alloyed with the iron by contact and diffusion during high heat. This process is of the greatest importance as without it the manufacture of hardenable steel used for blades and hand tools would not be possible as the tools would not be hard enough to function effectively. The degree of carbon penetration is a time-temperature dependent process, therefore the melt was kept at a uniform high temperature for a period of about six hours. In this time, the carbon (in the form of carbon monoxide gas, CO) mixed with the charge and penetrated it, combining with the iron to the extent of becoming up to 1.7% of the total composition. When the alloy in addition contained 3% nickel, even greater toughness and impact or shock resistance as well as hardness resulted, conditions important for swords. Charcoal was also used as fuel for the fire, and acted as a deoxidizer to exclude and absorb atmospheric oxygen.

When the heat was stopped, the melt was allowed to *slowly cool and solidify* in the crucible at a pace with the cooling of the furnace, which took about three hours. By cooling the metal in the crucible, its temperature was kept uniform throughout the cooling process, and metal's structure was even, unlike metal that is quenched or air cooled. The *slow rate of cooling down* through the solidification range was important because the change that took place in the metal structure during this intentionally long cooling period is what produced cast damask steel with large grain and structural pattern. During cooling, an allotropic change took place. The excess, hard, brittle cementite (Fe_3C) or iron carbide contained in the metal composition by stages called phase changes became segregated into a laminated type of structure. This consisted of high- and low-carbon areas of hard cementite and softer ferrite that developed in the crystalline structure along extremely extended straight dendritic axes. In this phenomenon, coarse laminated plates of ferrite and cementite were included in the same structure, causing a *natural,* self-created macrostructure whose pattern was visible even without magnification. It has been called *crystalline damask* to differentiate it from fabricated welded laminate patterned damask.

The cast crucible steel broken out of the crucibles had the form of round cakes 5 in (12.7 cm) in diameter and ½ in (1.27 cm) thick. Because it was malleable, it could be used for fabricating laminated welded damask blades, but it was also widely used *alone* forged into patterned blades, with or without a plain steel cutting edge welded to it. After cleaning the ingot it was forged into shape, and during this time, the straight pattern structure gradually became wavy due to the breaking up and distortion of the large crystals in the direction of working. This pattern of orientation closely resembled small patterned structures found in multilayered fold-fabrication lamination damask steel.

After hot forging, the blade was annealed to redness, then hardened by quenching. An important heat treatment because of its effect on the metal's structure, *quenching* involves the rate at which the quenching medium extracts heat from the surface, and the rate at which the heat by thermal conductivity diffuses from the center of the metal object to its surface. In the case of swords where the metal is not thick, the first was more important. The rate of heat loss is proportional to the difference in temperature between the metal and the quenching medium. Each medium varies greatly in its ability to extract heat from a hot

steel object. Experience proved which quenchant, whether water, oil, brine, or air, worked best, and at what temperatures for particular steels. Swordmakers considered this information so important that they often kept it secret, even from their apprentices who had to learn from observation.

In proper quenching, internal stresses produced by hot and cold working were relieved without causing warpage or cracking. This involved the manner in which the blade was introduced into the quenchant. Usually the blade was held horizontally in a vertical plane over the quenchant, then was brought straight downward, its cutting edge entering the quenchant first. Indian blade makers used agitated boiling oil as a quenchant when making damask blades to retain large crystal structure. A cold quench reduces crystal size and increases the possibility of the development of external local cracks that begin at deep tool marks and sharp corners, and internal cracks that form along the main axis of the object.

Tempering the finished blade followed final quenching and polishing. Tempering relieved any remaining internal stresses that might cause brittleness, warpage, or cracking; improved the toughness of the blade by causing a transformation of some of its components to ferrite and cementite; and provided the blade with the desired degree of hardness.

DAMASK STEEL FABRICATION: Welding and patterning a ferrous laminate

Lamination fabrication became possible with the technological development of permanently bonding physically separate pieces of metal by fusion welding. This process is *ferrous metal forge welding* or *fire welding* which occurred about 1000 B.C. in the Middle East (probably in Persia), whence it spread—to Europe about 800 B.C., to China during the 3rd century A.D., and to Japan before the 8th century A.D. Lamination was used in the manufacture of dagger and sword blades, and much later, for gun barrel making. In this technique, two or more sheets, strips, or bars of iron, or of iron and steel, are heated to the high temperature necessary for welding, and while hot, are placed into contact and hammer forged to fuse them together, making a *laminate* or composite bonded metal unit.

In all ferrous metal welded blades, the laminate combines alternating layers of a malleable, soft, nonhardenable but easily weldable *wrought iron* (the term *wrought* indicates any metal shaped by forging, rolling, or drawing) and hardenable and temperable *steel* with a high carbon content up to 1.7%, possibly containing a nickel content up to 3% as well. In this laminate composition, after a series of treatments in which they are worked together, the steel content serves the function of strengthening the blade, rendering it hard, and giving it "edge," and the wrought iron content provides it with characteristic elasticity. Lamination techniques in time became more controlled and refined as *esthetic* awareness of the appearance of the blade's patterned structure, as seen on its surface after polishing and etching, was more appreciated and valued. Several techniques developed for manipulating the laminate in various ways during manufacture to deliberately develop specific types of surface patterns that resulted from the particular method used, and these were given names. Because such patterns were also structural, they enhanced the blade's functional qualities.

Welded and patterned iron and steel broadswords were made in the West by the Merovingian Franks and the Vikings as early as the 7th century A.D., but those produced in the Middle and Far East—in Persia, India, and Japan —were functionally superior because in those countries the knowledge of metals and their forging had developed into a very high art. In tribute to this skill, the general Western term *damask* or *Damascus steel* is used today for a laminated blade having a variegated structural composition and visible surface pattern. This designation was adopted at the time of the seven principal Crusades during the 11th to 13th centuries when Europeans came into direct contact with the East. Crusaders believed that the superior military blades they found in use were made in Damascus, but in fact the blades made there were inferior. Damascus, however, was a crossroads of trade between East and West, and blades manufactured elsewhere were a local trade staple. Nevertheless, the term *damask steel* (not to be confused with *damascene work,* the mechanical *inlay* of one metal into another) persists in English and most other European languages, as for example in French, *acier damassé;* Italian, *acciaio damaschine;* Spanish, *acero damasquino;* and German, *Damast-Stahl.*

The superior quality of Indian wootz was recognized by the blacksmiths of Persia in Khorassan, Kerman, Isfahan, Qasvin, and Shiraz, famed centers of pattern welded swords from the 16th to 18th centuries. The best of these employed wootz steel, in old Persian called *faqirun,* in middle Persian *hundwani* or *hindi* (lit. = made of Indian steel), and in modern Persian *ruhina,* which was welded to soft wrought iron. It was a Persian concept that soft wrought iron was female, and hardenable carbon steel was male; therefore in laminated damask steel where they were combined, a synthesis or balance of the sexes was achieved by lamination (*waraqa*) through forge welding.

The advantage of all carburized steels is that blades using them can be made very hard by quenching alone, or by quenching and color tempering. As mentioned, not only the method of manufacturing the laminate, but also the manner of quenching, the temperature of the quenching medium, and the particular quenchant used were important in achieving high-quality final hardness. Persian pattern welded and etched sword blades (*jouhar* = etching acid; *jouhar-dar* = etched damask steel) in a highly organized trade were exported to countries of the Middle East and South Asia, including India, thus completing the cyclic journey of wootz. They were greatly prized and emulated in India where 17th-century swordsmiths eventually equaled their Persian colleagues in skill.

Elsewhere, elaborately fabricated laminated and forge pattern welded daggers (*kris*) were made of damask steel (*pamor*) by the Pandai-Vesi or blacksmith caste of Indonesia. Japanese swords were also made of laminates of wrought iron (*yawarake*) and steel (*hagane*). They probably surpassed all others in refinement of lamination and pattern fabrication techniques, as shown by the rich vocabulary that developed to describe the great attention given to detail during manufacture, and to differentiate between the patterns achieved (of which over 100 were given individual names). Japanese swords did not, however, enter the world market. In Japanese one term for a welded and patterned laminate is *mokumé,* which is discussed in Mokumé Gane in this chapter.

WATERED STEEL: Structural pattern made visible by macroetching

Watered steel is a general term used to describe a finished, laminated or cast crucible steel blade whose pattern due to lamination fabrication or internal structure is made visible after manufacture. This term is based on the technology employed in a final treatment where the blade's surface is subjected to a mild acid macroetch that visibly brings out the pattern and metal structure on the surface. (This technique is described on p. 371.)

BASIC LAMINATION FABRICATION SYSTEMS: Structural concepts used for pattern development

Essential to the lamination fabrication concept is the combining of metals and alloys of *different compositions* and/or *colors.* This condition, exploited by postlamination processing, makes possible the development of surface pattern. The laminate can therefore be *decorative* as well as *structurally functional.* In decorative patterning treatments, ultimately all the metals and alloys used in the laminate, by various methods, are made to appear on the face or upper visible surface of the composite. They can be either *flush* with the surface, or in microscopic to palpable *relief,* thereby physically as well as visually defining their boundaries within the laminate structure, and emphasizing differences between the constituents.

In all the lamination fabrication systems used to create a decorative color, or color plus dimension surface pattern, the sequence of metals is chosen for *color contrast,* which is more varied in the case of nonferrous laminates. The patterns developed are controllable to a degree, depending on the system of lamination used, the precision followed in creating the laminate, and the manner of processing the laminate once it is formed.

There are three basic lamination fabrication systems: *horizontal lamination; vertical lamination;* and *twisted lamination.* With each of these, characteristic surface patterns can be developed by subsequent treatments of the laminate face. The same systems used to fabricate ferrous laminates for blades are used on a smaller scale when making objects or jewelry of nonferrous laminates.

HORIZONTAL LAMINATION: *Cut and stack pattern development*

In horizontal lamination fabrication, the layers of the composite are piled *horizontally in parallel series* of a desired number of initial total thicknesses. In this parallel relationship, the uppermost layer, which is a single metal, is the *face.* The thickness of a horizontal laminate can be that of a sheet, plate, or slab, depending on the initial thickness of the layers and later, the extent to which the laminate is reduced dimensionally. A *sheet* is generally

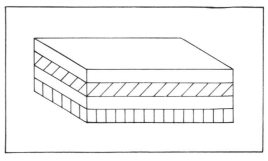

9-58 *HORIZONTAL LAMINATION, FOUR ELEMENTS.*

considered to be ⅛ in (3 mm) or less in thickness; a *plate* is from ⅛–1½ in (3–38 mm) in thickness; and a *slab* is over 1½ in (3.8 cm) thick, and its width is more than double its thickness.

Though a laminate can be used as initially formed, at this stage it is usually a semifinished product meant to be forged or rolled to reduce its thickness to slab, plate, or sheet size, incidentally reducing the thickness of its layers at the same time. The result is then cut into parts, stacked, and bonded to increase total thickness and the number of layers.

PREPARING THE LAMINATE CONSTITUENTS

To make a horizontal laminate, a set of sheets or strips of the same length and width, and of the same or varying thicknesses are first prepared. The size of the starting unit depends on the ultimate use intended for the laminate, and how far the total thickness will be reduced. When ferrous metals are used, a certain percentage of metal is lost at each heating due to scaling (the amount depending on the heating atmosphere and temperature), and this must be compensated for when deciding on the initial unit size.

All burrs must be removed after cutting the unit to size, and the unit must be completely *flat* to assure good layer contact which is essential to successful fusion. Otherwise air holes can develop between layers and become inclusions that will cause difficulties during subsequent processing. The *sequence* of touching metals should be different, and when the intention is to double the layers, the top and bottom layers must be of different metals. (For the choice of metals usable for a *nonferrous laminate,* see The Metals Used for a Nonferrous Mokumé Laminate in this chapter.) All contacting surfaces must be *chemically clean,* and the layers must be placed in *exact alignment* with each other. In the case of ferrous laminates which must be handled when placing them into or removing them from the fire, alignment is preserved by temporarily binding them together at both ends with a *heavy-gauge iron binding wire,* removed after initial welding is achieved. The total number of layers used depends on the number of metals in the laminate composition, and the degree of coarseness or fineness aimed for in the finished face pattern. Laminate layers are rapidly increased by dividing and stacking when a larger number of initial layers, between four and six, for example, are used.

FORGE PERCUSSION WELDING A FERROUS LAMINATE

Wrought iron is easily weldable to other wrought iron without the use of flux, but flux aids the welding of iron to steel. Flux is used because while these metals are heated and exposed to air, they rapidly oxidize, and the oxide is visible as the development of surface scale. This form of oxidation inhibits welding or fusion between layers, and must be minimized or eliminated. To assure good layer fusion and to make whatever oxide does form fusible enough to be squeezed out from between layers during forge welding, *borax flux* is sprinkled between the layers when preparing the stack. The flux fused by the heat acts as a deoxidizing compound, prevents further oxidation, and lowers the oxide fusion point.

The laminate, held at one end by *tongs,* is buried edgewise into the forge fire, and covered by a sulphur-free fuel (sulphur interferes with fusion), such as *charcoal* or *coke* to exclude air and keep oxidation and scaling down. The

air blast introduced to the fire from below through the tuyere or nozzle by which air enters the forge, should be *slow and steady* as this rate of inflow contains sufficient oxygen to heat the metal *uniformly* and *in depth.* A high-velocity air blast would rapidly bring the metal to welding temperature, but it only increases the oxygen forced into the fire, and the surplus causes a thicker scale to form on the metal. Too rapid heating is avoided also because it makes the metal expand unevenly which may result in internal cracking. With controlled air volume input, only as much oxygen is introduced to the fire as is consumed by the fuel during combustion, therefore the surface oxidation on the metal is minimal.

The metal is made red hot, approximately 1400° F (760° C), removed from the fire with tongs, and the surface is sprinkled with flux. It is then returned to the fire and brought to an oily yellow to near white heat, approximately 2500° F (1371° C), at which temperature the metal starts to emit a few sparks. This high heat, necessary for welding to take place, is just below the upper limit of the metal's plastic range, and the surface becomes molten and appears fluid. Metal "burning" or overheating occurs at incandescent white heat when many sparks are emitted, and is avoided since it renders the metal unworkable—it becomes brittle, and internal voids and oxide inclusions may develop.

When the laminate reaches welding heat, it is removed from the fire by *tongs.* Because heat loss is rapid, forge welding the laminate layers together must be carried out during the relatively short time that the metal retains its welding heat range, and before the oxide solidifies. This is as long as it glows visibly white to yellow, as judged in the semidarkness of forge workshop conditions. The time of heat retention depends on metal volume—it is longer when the metal is heavier.

The laminate is tapped on the *anvil* to remove loose ash, etc., and placed flat on the anvil face, which immediately starts to draw heat away from it, with the layers parallel to the surface. It is rapidly hammered with a 1½ lb *flat-faced hammer* which provides enough force to affect the entire cross section of a laminate ⅝ in (1.59 cm) thick. Heavier hammers are used as the thickness increases. The starting blows immediately make the weld and force out trapped liquid oxide, fuel ash, and flux. The first blow is made at the center, followed by others outward from the center alternately to the right and left of a strip laminate for its entire length. By another method, the first blows can be made at one end, then continued in the opposite direction. With controlled force and light blows, the interface layers become diffused into each other along their planes of contact and are welded together. By the time the laminate has been evenly worked over its entire face, bottom, and edge surfaces, air pockets will be eliminated.

When the metal ceases to glow bright yellow, it has cooled down too much for welding to be possible. Now that the weld is at least partially completed, the end binding wires are no longer needed and are removed. If any slippage has occurred between layers, protruding parts must be ground off to smooth the sides. The laminate is returned to the fire for a second heat, and the same forge welding operation is repeated, continuing from where the first was stopped, to complete the weld. Depending on the laminate size, two or more welding heats may be necessary.

Forging down follows welding and can be carried out at bright yellow to bright red heat. The top and bottom surfaces are hammered to draw out or uniformly reduce the laminate thickness and stretch it in length in preparation for division and stacking. The manner of forging, meaning the *angle of blows* to the work and the *direction* in which hammering is done, has a distinct effect on the damask pattern created in a solid metal or in a laminate because pattern development depends on metal structure as well as laminate composition. If the work is forged lengthwise, due to grain flow, the metal crystal structure becomes elongated and the pattern appears in long lines. If it is forged equally in all directions, the pattern is crystalline and amorphous. If it is forged in alternating directions, the pattern is undulating and wavy. Pattern distortion takes place by hammering the edges at alternating positions along the sides.

When the sides of a laminate are forged, they must be left in an even state if doubling is still to follow. During edge forging, care is taken to avoid folding over any metal as this will cause a *cold shut* or unjoined flange on the surface. Once the desired number of layers is achieved in the laminate, it can be deliberately forged unevenly. For example, it can then be tapered in thickness toward one side, as when making a blade, which will distort the pattern in that direction and cause it to stretch toward the thinned area.

Nonferrous laminates can also be fused by heat alone. The process requires the use of a *furnace* or *forge* where temperature can be controlled. The specific temperature required for the fusion or localized melting to take place at the interface between the laminate layers changes with each laminate composition. Finding the proper temperature and the time necessary for a prolonged soaking heat to allow partial melting to take place requires experimentation. Fusion bonding by the use of solder is simpler. These processes are described under Mokumé Gane in this chapter.

CUTTING AND STACKING THE LAMINATE

To increase the number of layers in the laminate, in this system it is divided across its width into parts with a *saw, chisel,* or by other means suited to severing the particular laminate thickness. After removing burrs, the parts are stacked as were the individual units, aligned exactly one above the other, then fused. In ferrous laminate patterned blade making, washes of impurities such as *metallic oxides* are sometimes introduced between the layers before stacking or folding because their presence affects the final patterning of the blade by distinctly demarking the layers on the surface of the finished composite.

The following table gives the arithmetic progression of the number of layers achieved when a laminate of two, three, four, five, or six layers is cut into two, three, or four parts which are then stacked and welded or soldered together, and when the process is repeated from one to seven times. The smaller the number of layers in a given thickness, the coarser and bolder the pattern. Doubling and thickness reduction increase the number of layers in a given thickness, and consequently the pattern becomes finer. Ultimately the metal structure becomes practically homogeneous in composition, and the possibility of pattern development in effect is lost.

CREATING THE FACE PATTERN IN THE HORIZONTAL LAMINATE

If no other treatment is given to a horizontal laminate, the result is simply a parallel, stratified, *cladded* or sandwiched, layered composite metal unit with a single metal without pattern appearing on the face surface. This is the nature of *gold-filled sheet* in which a gold sheet is sweat soldered to either side of a silver or base metal sheet and then rolled down together to the desired thickness. Another example is fusion welded Sheffield silver plate (1–10 ratio of silver to copper). The purpose of lamination here, however, is to create a decorative surface face pattern—which can be accomplished in various ways—once the total number of layers and the appropriate thickness of the laminate is reached. Methods by which this can be done to a horizontal laminate are discussed under Mokumé Gane in this chapter.

FOLD LAMINATION: Doubling and bending for pattern development

Fold lamination employing sheet or strip is a means of increasing the laminate layers when making *horizontal* or

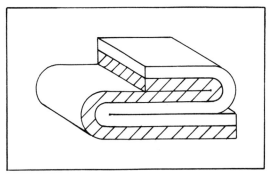

9–59 FOLD LAMINATION, TWO ELEMENTS.

Horizontal Cut and Stack Lamination: Layer Progressions

Number of Welds	Starting Layers					Starting Layers					Starting Layers				
	2	3	4	5	6	2	3	4	5	6	2	3	4	5	6
	Cut into 2 Parts and Stacked					Cut into 3 Parts and Stacked					Cut into 4 Parts and Stacked				
1	4	6	8	10	12	6	9	12	15	18	8	12	16	20	24
2	8	12	16	20	24	18	27	36	45	54	32	48	64	80	96
3	16	24	32	40	48	54	81	108	135	162	128	192	256	320	384
4	32	48	64	80	96	162	243	324	405	486	512	768	1024	1280	1536
5	64	96	128	160	192	486	729	972	1215	1458	2048	3072	4096	5120	6144
6	128	192	256	320	384	1458	2187	2916	3645	4374	8192	12288	16384	20480	24576
7	256	384	512	640	768	4374	6561	8748	10935	13122	32768	49152	65336	81920	98304

vertical laminates. In *horizontal fold lamination,* the laminate is folded in half lengthwise upon itself, which doubles the total layer number. The fold is hammered down to bring the inner faces together. The contacting two parts of the original face layer are the same metal. Because they now meet, after they are hot forge fused, a thicker layer of that metal appears at the center of the laminate at that time. In effect, one layer is lost which does not occur in planned cut and stack lamination where the top and bottom layers that come into contact are of different metals.

Nonferrous interfaces can be solder fused after folding. When joined, a thin line of solder will appear between them, unless the metal contacting the solder is the same color as the solder. Nonferrous laminates can then be forged or rolled to decrease thickness and increase length. Folding, forging, or rolling is repeated until the desired number of layers and the total laminate thickness are reached.

MOSAIC LAMINATION: Pieced pattern development

Mosaic lamination is a method of further processing a horizontal or a vertical laminate. Once the laminate has its final number of layers and thickness, the result, usually in the form of a bar, is cut in vertical, diagonal, or horizontal cross sections of equal width or thickness. The direction of cutting depends on which of the above-mentioned systems are being processed. These sections are laid out flat, face up, on a *refractory soldering surface,* arranged in a regularly repeated or random pattern, with the units butted next to each other. They are then fused or soldered together to make a single fabric with a patterned face surface. The units can also be placed on a backing sheet of metal to which they are fused or soldered. The result can be forged flat, or run through the *rolling mill* if the thickness must be reduced. The surface can then be scalped by filing or grinding to clearly expose the pattern. (See Mokumé Parquetry: Mosaic lamination in this chapter.)

VERTICAL LAMINATION:
Perpendicular pattern development

In *vertical lamination,* from the start all the strip constituents used are placed *perpendicular* to an imaginary base, *side by side.* Using strip, the face of the laminate develops from the arrangement of the narrow or edge dimension of the layers, the rest positioned perpendicular to the face. When rod or wire are used, the units, normally but not necessarily of equal width, are placed and fused *next to* each other. In all cases, from the very beginning *all* components are visible on the surface. The ultimate

thickness of a vertical laminate made of an aggregate of sheet metal edges is greater than that of a horizontal laminate in the form of a sheet whose face is on the flat plane side.

STRAIGHT-PATTERN VERTICAL LAMINATION

Bar, ribbon, or wire vertical laminates can be treated in a variety of ways to create straight face patterns if the laminate form is kept straight and if the units are *cut,* not folded. As in horizontal lamination, to double layers the laminate is divided, stacked *edges upward* in a vertical position, and fused or soldered. Forging or rolling will reduce thickness and increase length and width. The result, which usually is thick, can then be divided in a direction *parallel* to the face. The sections can be made in thicknesses equivalent to or greater than sheet used by jewelers, and then arranged in any pattern with the face upward, and joined, mosaic fashion.

CURVED-PATTERN VERTICAL LAMINATION

If in vertical lamination *folding* techniques are used, the face pattern will form in *curves.* The manner of creating curved face patterns with vertical laminates is infinite, and only a few basic suggestions will be explored.

When *ferrous* laminates are worked they must be heated to redness before bending or the metal will crack at the bend where greatest stresses take place. The parts are hot forged and welded together.

When *nonferrous* laminates are bent, low-temperature annealing is necessary when the metal becomes work hardened to restore softness and workability. The folds are soldered together. After heat treatments, nonferrous laminates are pickled to remove the surface oxidation that forms. They must then be *neutralized* by washing them in a soda and water solution. This is done because any remaining acid traces may inhibit the solder flow at such places and cause a discontinuity in the solder between layers. Should they occur, unjoined pockets in the laminate might split apart later during working. When cracks, splits, or separations occur at any time during the lamination process, nonferrous metal laminates *must be repaired before work continues* by soldering them together or flooding them with solder.

Soldering a curved-pattern vertical lamination can be done in one operation once the laminate is formed. By another method, each fold is soldered together as it is made before continuing to make the next fold. This means that as many solderings will have to be undertaken as there are folds.

The laminate strip can be folded in regular serpentine or

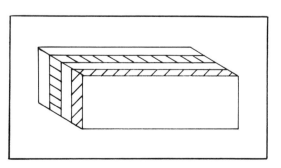

9–60   *VERTICAL LAMINATION, FOUR ELEMENTS.*

9–61   GEORGE N. SAWYER, U.S.A. Two wedding rings made with an outer surface of a vertical laminate of 14K yellow and red gold, sterling silver, and copper, backed by 14K red and yellow gold liners. The laminate relief surface is created by a 50% concentrated nitric acid etchant solution which attacked the copper and sterling silver, but not the gold. The surface was rubbed with a fine-grit abrasive paper to restore the color to the red gold whose copper content was leached out by the etchant, and then polished. Vertical lamination makes these rings suited to extended wear. Wide ring 10 mm; narrow ring 7 mm. Photo: Vern Hammerlund

accordion fashion. The spaces between the folds are closed by placing the unit *edgewise* on an *anvil* and then applying a *hammer*. The interfaces are fused or solder joined, depending on whether ferrous or nonferrous metals are being worked. (See Cold Bending Sheet Metal, Chapter 4, for various methods by which bends can be accomplished.) The result can also be forged to a bar shape, its length divided, and the parts joined *side by side* with their faces up, to make a composite pattern. The forging process will compress, stretch, or deform the pattern in different ways, depending also on the direction of work.

Another method is to fold the laminate strip back and forth in *free curves* of irregular length, in the same or in different directions. In this case, the curves appear not only at the fold ends, but anywhere within the unit, and the outer contour of the work becomes *irregular*. The contour can be left irregular, or the unit hammered edgewise to compress its parts into a regular geometric shape such as an oval, circle, square, rectangle, or triangle. It is also conceivable that a curve-folded laminate could be made with open spaces between solid areas.

The laminate thickness need not be uniform, as after rolling. It can be forged to a taper toward the edges, or in the reverse way, forged with an internal depression, and thickened toward the edges.

Thick, nonferrous vertical-fold laminates can be divided in a direction parallel to the face to achieve several repeats of the same pattern. The number of sectional divisions possible depends on the total laminate thickness and the thickness of each section into which it is divided. When such a division is the aim, the total laminate thickness is planned in advance. Sectional units can be used separately, or in series, for example in a necklace, or butt edge joined mosaic fashion. If *alternating faces* of the sections, that is, the two faces in contact in the same cut, are placed face upward, *mirror image patterns* become available for use. Finally, in all systems, the surface can be scalped or etched (see below) to expose the pattern or give it relief dimension.

An important advantage of the vertical lamination system is that the metals that appear in the pattern face continue *in depth* through the entire laminate. Therefore in postlamination treatments such as etching, the visible pattern is essentially unaltered, nor will the result be affected by abrasion in use. The disadvantage of this system is that thin sections are not easily shaped dimensionally to an appreciable extent without the danger of some joins coming apart. Joint fracture is minimized by low-heat annealing the section before shaping, or by soldering the section(s) to a *backing sheet* which because it lends support, makes dimensional shaping easier to accomplish.

SPIRAL LAMINATION: Coiling laminates from a center in one plane

Spiral lamination in general is the forming of any suitable laminate into a spiral configuration that starts from a center and coils spirally outward in a flat plane. This is not a basic lamination system, but another means of pattern development using vertical lamination systems with strip or twisted wire constituents, or a combination of these. The result is heated to fusion, or flooded with solder to fill the spaces. The entire unit can be fused or soldered to a backing sheet which helps to retain flooded solder. The face can be left in relief, or be scalped flush to better expose the pattern made by the various metals in the laminate.

9–62 *SPIRAL LAMINATION, STRIP, TWO ELEMENTS.*

9–63 HIROKO SATO PIJANOWSKI, U.S.A. Pendant made of a fabric of right- and left-hand–twisted bi-element wires joined to make a faggoted twist laminate. After twisting, the wires were drawn through a round-holed drawplate to give them a uniform cylindrical section. The central spiral laminate consists of alternating silver with copper, and copper with shakudo wire bi-elements. The vertical laminate portion surrounding the spiral consists of alternating right- and left-twisted silver with copper wire bi-elements. Wires were butt soldered, and sweat soldered to a silver backing sheet. The result was hammer forged flat to close gaps and form a solid surface which was file scalped flat and smooth to reveal the pattern. The sheet was shaped to a gently undulating curve and soldered top and bottom to another flat backplate with a top space allowed between sheets for the passage of the supporting brown silk cord. Size 2 × 2½ in. *Photo: Oppi*

TWIST LAMINATION: *Torque-created pattern development*

In twist lamination, the constituents are usually round or square wire, rods, or bars of uniform section, in different metals. Though no widely accepted dividing line exists, generally speaking, a *rod* is ³⁄₁₆–½ in (4.7–12.7 mm) in diameter; and a *bar* ⅝–3½ in (15.8–88.9 mm) in diameter. A basic unit suited to twist lamination pattern development has a minimum of two parts but more can be used. These are fusion or solder joined to make a com-

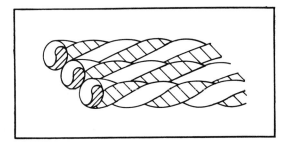

9–64   *TWIST LAMINATION, TWO ELEMENTS.*

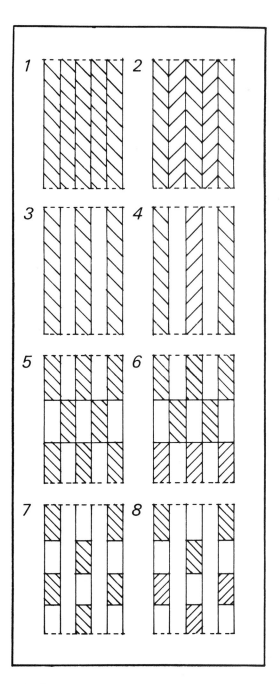

9–65 *SCHEMATIC REPRESENTATIONS OF COMBINATIONS OF VARI-
OUS TYPES OF FAGGOTED OR TWISTED UNITS*
Some are combined with plain units, as arranged in groups prior
to welding to make a patterned laminate by forging or rolling.
1. All units twisted in the same direction.
2. Alternating units twisted in opposite directions create a chevron
pattern.
3. Units twisted in one direction alternating with plain units.
4. Units twisted in opposite directions alternating with plain units.
5. Units partially twisted in one direction separated by untwisted
parts, placed in a staggered arrangement.
6. Units partially twisted in opposite directions separated by
untwisted parts, placed in a staggered arrangement.
7. Units partially twisted in the same direction alternating with plain
units.
8. Units partially twisted in opposite directions alternating with plain
units.

pound wire or rod, the join carried out either before or
after twist formation. Applying *torque,* or twisting them
together around a central axis causes the different metals
to form a helix spiral around each other, and this basic
fact predetermines the characteristic pattern types that can
later be achieved.

Methods of twisting wire of dimensions suited to use in
jewelry are described under Twisted Wire, Chapter 6.

Twist tightness can be expressed on the basis of the
number of twists per inch, or per centimeter. This number
depends partly on the dimension of the constituents, and
the number or turns given to them when twisting takes
place. The pattern achieved later depends on the *degree of
twist tightness,* and the *number of metals and alloys* used
in the unit. Because twisting can be done in a clockwise or
a counterclockwise direction, *direction of twist* is another
means of creating twist lamination patterns, as described
below. As a result of twisting, the *initial length* of the unit
decreases: as the twist becomes tighter, the unit length becomes shorter. This dimensional loss should be kept in
mind and allowance made for it.

Before a twisted unit is used, if it has sharp edges they
should be removed as they may cause splits or cracks in
the laminate during its formation.

It is also possible to draw twisted wire units through a
drawplate to make the unit section round in order to facilitate butt joining and reduce the possibility of openings occurring between units when they are joined in groups. If
the elements of the twist have not been soldered together
before twisting, they should be soldered together after
twisting *before using a drawplate.* The reason is that during drawing, the elements tend to slip on each other or become untwisted to a degree which reduces the sectional
size of the unit by the end of drawing.

FAGGOTING: Uniting twisted components
to create pattern

Straight or twisted units can be combined in groups,
termed *faggoting.* When twisted units are faggoted into a
composite, after forging and/or rolling they produce a
patterned fabric that possesses a type of face pattern that
can only result from using twisted units. Units can be
placed side by side in various combinations and sequences,
then joined and flattened to achieve a variety of face patterns. Some of the possible combinations are shown in the
diagram. For example, in the simplest one, *all* the units
are twisted in the *same* direction. Units twisted in *opposite*
directions can *alternate* to achieve a chevron effect.
Twisted units can alternate with *untwisted,* plain units of
the same or different sectional size or metal. Still other
patterns will result if *partially* twisted units, or *alternate
reverse twist* units are combined, etc.

9-66 GAYLE SAUNDERS, U.S.A. Pendant made of a twist lamination using wires of sterling silver, 18K yellow gold, and 14K green and pink golds combined into one fabric by soldering, then rolled in a rolling mill to make a flat sheet. The sides contain mother of pearl inlays in an amber-colored epoxy cement. Size 3½ × 2½ × ⅜ in. Photo: Gayle Saunders

When using nonferrous metals, the *metal colors* have an important effect on the appearance and degree of contrast in the pattern, which can be bold or subtle. Silver and copper, or silver and shakudo will make a strongly contrasting pattern. Silver and gold, gold of different colors, gold and copper, brass and copper, brass and silver, or other metal and alloy combinations will each appear different.

Once the unit sequence is decided upon, and they are placed in contact with each other along their entire length, they are joined by fusion or solder. Forging or rolling follows to make a flat sheet or ribbon, depending on the section size and number of units placed side by side. Any open spaces that might remain between units or that develop as a result of forging or rolling can be flooded with solder of the appropriate color. Silver solder can be deliberately flooded between units made from nonwhite-colored metals to introduce a third color element to the laminate. If the laminate thickness allows, the result can be divided horizontally in line with its axis to make two

identically patterned units, each of which could be divided widthwise into as many parts as wanted. The entire laminate can be *sweat soldered* to a base strip or sheet of metal that completely backs it.

POSTLAMINATION TREATMENTS

SCALPING THE LAMINATE TO EXPOSE FACE PATTERNS

In the finished twist laminate, the pattern made by the various metals is to a great extent concealed within the unit, and after forging or rolling may not appear as clear as it can be. Scalping is a way of bringing the true structural inner pattern to the surface.

Scalping consists of removing the upper layers or a certain amount of metal from the surface which is leveled in the process. Scalping can be done *manually* with a *hand drawfile* worked across the surface while the laminate is immobilized in a *holding device.* (See Drawfiling, p. 106.) A *coarse-cut file* is used first to remove the metal quickly, followed by a *fine-cut file* to remove file marks. Thick laminates can be scalped *mechanically* on a *grinding wheel,* but because grinding action is fast, it must be carefully controlled to avoid too much metal removal. The surface is then filed with a *smooth-cut file,* and finally, all scalped surfaces are finished with *paper* or *cloth-backed abrasives.*

CARVING THE LAMINATE FOR PATTERNED RELIEF FORMATIONS

Any laminate of sufficient thickness, and especially vertical laminates, whose depth allows greater scope for forming, can be directly carved to relieve the flat look. Face reliefs can be carved with rotary burs of different forms. The depressions and directions of change caused by carving will create different configurations in the face pattern with each change of curve or plane angle, as when carving a strongly grained piece of wood. Laminates formed into a bar or rod can be mounted on a lathe and *turned* into any shape. Here again, the pattern of the laminate layers will change with the contour of the form, creating a flowing pattern over its surface.

MACROETCHING OR "WATERING" THE LAMINATE FOR RELIEF DIFFERENTIATION

An effective traditional method of revealing the crystal structure or the component metals in any laminate, whether ferrous or nonferrous, is to macroetch the result. Etching accentuates the gross structural details in the laminate so they become more visible to the unaided eye. Any suitable etchant can be used, depending on the metals in the laminate composition. (See The Acid Etching of Metal, Chapter 8.) First the surface must be *polished,* and the object made *absolutely clean* to permit the maximum and even action of the etchant on the metal. Strong solutions will act faster than weak ones, but in the case of some metals may cause pitting and surface roughness. In general, therefore, weaker etchants are used. Because any single etchant will attack each metal or alloy in a ferrous or nonferrous laminate at a different rate, and in some cases not at all, the result becomes a *relief* in which some metals remain prominent, and others are depressed in various degrees below the original face level.

Ferric laminates such as sword blades of soft iron and hard steel are "watered" by first polishing the surface, then heating it slightly, and traditionally, applying a ferric sulphate solution $(Fe_2SO_4)_3$ to it with a cloth. *Ferric sulphate* is a compound made from ferrous sulphate by oxidation with nitric acid. This is allowed to remain on the metal for a short while, then it is rinsed off. Though the etch is shallow, it is enough to reveal and increase the definition of the crystallization that occurs in the structure of the composite metals, especially between the layers of the laminate, and in this way the pattern is brought out. The etchant readily attacks soft ferrite, but hard areas of cementite and those with nickel are hardly etched at all. Some etchants will visually intensify the metal differences in the laminate by *coloring* as well as etching them. Blade portions with high carbon content become dark, iron is colored from gray to black, and nickel steel remains bright, as do flecks of nickel or silver wherever they appear in the composition. The etched result is rubbed slightly to remove the superficial colorant, and then with an alkaline solution such as soda and water to stop acid action and neutralize any remaining acid traces.

FINISHING: Coloring and polishing

Finishing treatments on patterned nonferrous laminates are discussed under Mokumé Gane, in this chapter, and also under Types of Finish on Metals, Chapter 14. Ferric laminates can be waxed or oiled, then heated to a black heat and cooled, to prevent undesirable rust formation. *Rust* is a hydrated oxide of iron $(2Fe_2O_3 \cdot 3H_2O)$ which forms on iron when it is exposed to air and moisture, and corrodes it. Some types of rust are desirable as a final surface as at a certain point rust becomes stabilized and rusting halts.

MOKUMÉ GANE

A Japanese fusion-layered patterned laminate

The analogy between the appearance of the natural structure of wood and metal face-patterned laminations was apparent to Japanese metalworkers who called one of their generic lamination systems *mokumé*, which in Japanese means "wood grain or wood burl." Gane means "metal," therefore *mokumé gane* translates as "wood grain metal." This basic designation was modified by various additional descriptive terms to indicate different conditions and the appearances of various face patterns as well as processes.

The analogy is based on the fact that in most woods, annual growth rings (because of seasonal variation in their growth rate) appear in striated color bands that give cut and smoothed lumber its characteristic surface grain pattern. *Horizontal* lamination patterns can be compared with those that appear on a board when a log is quartersawed by cuts made lengthwise in the trunk. *Vertical and spiral* lamination correspond to patterns that occur when a log is cut sectionally, across the trunk, revealing its end grain. *Twist lamination* can resemble a section through a burl or the growth that forms on the trunks of many trees, the pattern taking a random, twistlike form with flowing, wavy, or knotted contortions.

Though the term *mokumé* was used in Japan to include ferrous as well as nonferrous laminates, as used hereafter in this text it must be taken to mean a nonferrous laminate that might also include precious metals.

The nonferrous horizontal mokumé lamination process described below first was used about 300 years ago by the celebrated Takahashi family in Japan to create sword mountings and sword guards (*tsuba*). Mokumé in sheet form is still used today by specialist craftsmen in Japan for making small or large holloware objects. The foremost living craftsman who works in mokumé is Tetsuji Shindo (aged 83 in 1975), and he lives in Akita City where he raises large forms from horizontal lamination mokumé sheets. We are concerned here with the use of mokumé in jewelry.

9–67 CLAUS BURY, West Germany. Two single plane objects using gold, silver, copper and their alloys and plane linear perspective orthographic projection to create illusional three-dimensional forms. The main figures are married metal mosaics, the parts soldered with silver and gold solders, visible to create linear color elements in the design. The ground into which the figures are inserted consists of strips of multi-metal mokumé type laminates, joined in more or less parallel series. The resulting unit has been somewhat convexedly shaped. Photo: Hubert Urban, courtesy Schmuck International 1900–1980, Künstlerhaus, Vienna

THE METALS USED FOR A NONFERROUS MOKUMÉ LAMINATE

When preparing a nonferrous mokumé laminate, any combination of nonferrous metals can be used provided that their melting points fall within a fairly close temperature range, all higher than the solder used to join them, and if their degree of malleability and ductility are compatible. Copper is always one of the metals used because its malleability tends to impart this characteristic to the whole laminate. Bronze alloys are not used in heat fusion laminates as their component lower temperature metals create difficulties. It is important that the sequence of colors in the laminate layers be as contrasting as possible to make the resulting pattern maximally visible. The choice of color sequence might be influenced by the fact that lower melting metals preferably should alternate with higher melting metals which support them during heat treatments. Laminates can also be made completely of noble metals though their cost is obviously higher than nonferrous metals. Yellow gold can be used as a *face metal* in an otherwise nonferrous laminate. In this case, it will predominate in the face color, and its loss in patterning development is least. Metals that *accept chemical coloring* well, such as copper, and the Japanese alloys shakudo, shibuichi, and kuromi-do (copper 99%, arsenic 1%), contribute richness to the mokumé pattern after patination. Of these three, the first two alloys can be made by a craftsperson. Kuromi-do cannot—due to its poisonous arsenic content. It can, however, be used safely, if available.

Metals and Alloys Suited to Mokumé Laminates

(in decreasing order of their melting points)

Metal	Melting Point °F	°C	Composition (in parts)
Copper	1981	1083	99.9 Cu
Shakudo	1952	1066	75 Cu- 4-25 Au- 5-20 Sb
Gilding metal	1950	1065	95 Cu- 5 Zn
Gold, fine	1945	1063	99.9 Au
Silver, fine	1761	960	99.9 Ag
Shibuichi	1720	937	75 Cu- 25 Ag
Yellow brass	1710	930	65 Cu- 35 Zn
Sterling silver	1640	893	92.5 Ag- 7.5 Cu
Coin silver	1615	879	90 Ag- 10 Cu
Gold, 14k yellow	1615	879	58.5 Au- 41.5 Cu

Compare temperatures here with those shown in the table of **Silver Solder Compositions** under **Soldering**.

CREATING A NONFERROUS MOKUMÉ GANE: Horizontal lamination

The process of making a horizontal nonferrous mokumé metal sheet involves three basic procedures: first creating the laminate composite, then the pattern on the laminate face, and finally reducing the laminate to a usable thickness.

PREPARING A NONFERROUS MOKUMÉ LAMINATE: Wet bonding by solder fusion

In solder fusion lamination, fusion, called wet bonding, depends on the melting point of the solder. The relative strength of the bond is determined by the solder alloy used.

To make a nonferrous horizontal mokumé laminate sheet suited to convenient use in jewelry, either strips or sheets of metal can be used. The surface should be *flat*, and as free as possible from any defects such as pits or scratches which might interfere with interface fusion by causing solder discontinuity. The *size* decided upon should be the same in all units used in the laminate, and depends

on the ultimate purpose of the result. The *thickness* of the layers preferably should be equal, but a thicker sheet of copper can be used as the final bottom layer, added (when the laminate is stacked and doubled) last when the laminate is completed to support the other layers and to provide sufficient dimension for the manipulation of the upper layers during pattern development. Any *number of layers* can be used, depending on whether the intention is to start with all the layers needed for the laminate and not double them but only decrease their total thickness, or to increase the number of layers by cut and stack lamination. The greater the number of layers in any given thickness, the thinner is each constituent, and the finer the resulting face pattern.

A typical starting sheet size for use in jewelry might be 2½ in (6.35 cm) square, each sheet in 18 gauge B.&S. (0.040 in, 1.024 mm). A typical composite might include copper, bronze or brass, and sterling or fine silver, which without coloring would provide a pink, yellow, and white combination. However, any of the other metals mentioned in the table could be used, possibly with copper placed in alternating layers. When rolled to reduce the laminate thickness, the metals tend to keep their initial ratio of relative thickness, as in the case of clad metals that are rolled. Because the color of the final face metal tends to predominate in the appearance of a horizontal laminate, it should be chosen with this in mind. If gold is used as the face metal, a 28 gauge B.&S. sheet (0.012 in, 0.305 mm) can be used, soldered *last* to a finished cut and stack laminate before face pattern development starts.

Suppose that *five layers* are used in the initial laminate. If the metals are not purchased in an already annealed and absolutely flat condition, anneal and carefully flatten each of them on a smooth, *flat surface block* using a *rawhide* or *softwood mallet* which will not leave scars. The flat state is very important as each sheet must *completely contact* the next to aid in capillarity by which the solder flows evenly at the interfaces between layers and joins them into one laminate. After heating, it is essential that all surfaces be carefully *pickled* to remove any traces of firescale. The metal should be handled only by clean *tongs*, or if by fingers, at the edges only to avoid imparting fingerprint grease to the metal. The presence of any traces of acid, grease, scale or other foreign matter could become the cause of air pockets at interfaces, and result in an unsound laminate. After pickling and rinsing, boil the sheets in an alkaline solution of two tablespoons of washing soda to one quart of water which will neutralize any remaining acid, then rinse them under running water, and dry them with a clean *paper towel*. Rub the sheets at contacting surfaces with a medium grade of *emery cloth*, and brush away any dust with a *clean brush*, rinse, and dry. Spread borax flux evenly on the entire upper surface of each of the pieces with a *brush*. If the flux crawls, that place is contaminated and the surface must be cleaned again. Set aside the piece that will be the top or face of the laminate. Place the remaining *four* units spaced widely apart on a clean, flat, solid *refractory soldering surface*.

The solder used in bonding the laminate layers should be low in zinc content, and free of cadmium because the low boiling points of these metals may result in their distillation, which, trapped between layers, might cause internal blisters. The solder should have a sufficiently high melting point to permit rolling the laminate without its becoming brittle, and to allow the finished laminate to be annealed and solder joined during fabrication without affecting the original soldered bond. It is suggested therefore, that *medium hard silver solder* be used. Avoid easy-flow solder for lamination bonding because, under repeated heating, by the end of bonding, its greater percentage of lower melting elements may volatilize, causing the solder and thereafter the laminate to become brittle or short. Reserve easy-flow solder for fabrication purposes with the finished mokumé sheet.

Hold a cleaned, flux-covered medium hard solder stick in the left hand, and heat the metal with a *torch* having a large, soft, neutral flame. When the proper melting temperature is reached, indicated by the maturing of the flux, touch the solder stick to the sheet surface, and while moving it along, flood each surface completely and as evenly as possible. Spread the solder on the surface with an *iron* or *steel soldering pick* to which it will not adhere. Do not allow the solder to remain in uneven puddles or mounds as these will prevent good surface contact between the stacked sheets, and when the solder melts, they will cause a sudden slump that may displace the sheets from their alignment. Use only enough solder to cover the surface.

Pickle the four pieces and make sure any oxide on the *reverse side* is removed, rinse them well, neutralize as described, and rinse again. Scrub the solder-covered surface with *pumice powder,* or with a scratch brush while holding the metal with a clean *paper towel,* then rinse, dry, and reflux the soldered surface evenly. Avoid a surplus of flux as trapped flux pockets can form that might interfere with total bonding. Allow the flux to dry, then stack the four layers with the solder side up in the desired order, making sure that the edges are aligned. Place the fifth or top layer—with both sides fluxed—on top of the stack. Some makers then bind the stack with heavy-gauge *iron binding wire,* kinked to allow for metal expansion during heating (see Soldering Jigs, Chapter 10).

By another method, *sheet solder* can be used instead of puddling solder on the metal. Sheet solder can be purchased in thin gauges. If the solder sheet you have is not thin enough, pass it through a *rolling mill* to thin it to about 32 gauge B.&S. (0.007 in, 0.178 mm). Cut the sheet to the dimension of the laminate units. Clean and flux it on both sides, allow the flux to dry, and place one solder sheet between each of the laminate layers. Bind them together with iron binding wire.

SWEAT SOLDERING THE LAMINATE TO JOIN LAYERS

The units are *sweat soldered* together, a process in which metal parts previously covered with solder are joined. Heat the laminate evenly with a large, soft, neutral or slightly reduced torch flame. Move the flame constantly over the surface and bring the metal's temperature up quickly so that the solder melts before the flux is spent. *Avoid overheating* as blistering may occur leaving voids between the layers. Heat just until the solder reaches a molten state—it will appear as a bright line between the layers at the edge. Should any layers shift during soldering and become displaced, correct the position while fusion is occurring by prodding it into place with a *soldering pick* held in readiness for such an eventuality. As soon as fusion occurs, carefully place the flat of an *old file,* or a *soldering pick* across the center of the top piece, and apply moderate pressure to force the sheets together. This pressure will spread the molten solder into an even layer, and force out surplus solder, flux, and any trapped air. Alternately, just after the solder fuses, place a clean,

9–68 VADA C. BEETLER, U.S.A. Ring fabricated in sterling silver, and a shaped horizontal mokumé laminate section employing fine and sterling silver, 14K and 18K gold, copper, and brass, with sterling silver in the uppermost layer. Mounted in the ring is a casting in bronze of the lichen *Cladonia verticillata.* Size 28 × 20 mm. Photo: Vada C. Beetler

smooth, *flat steel block* on the laminate, and wearing an *asbestos glove,* press down gently to apply hand pressure. Maintain this pressure until the solder solidifies. Do not quench the laminate, but allow it to air cool. With a five-layer, 18 gauge B.&S. sheet laminate, the result is a composite close to 4 gauge B.&S. (0.204 in, 5.189 mm). If in the result one of the metals in the laminate expands and projects beyond the rest, trim off the protruding portion by filing or grinding it away. It is important that the layers be of equal dimensions before doubling.

Do not yet pickle the laminate after soldering. Clean it with hot water and a brush, and inspect its edges. If solder gaps are discovered between the layers, scrape and reflux the laminate, apply solder snippets there and reheat the metal to fuse the solder. Alternately, a solder stick could be applied to that place when the metal reaches sufficient heat. Now, after cooling, pickle the laminate thoroughly, wash, neutralize, rinse, and dry it well with a paper towel so that moisture does not get on the rolls in the next process.

ROLLING THE LAMINATE TO REDUCE THICKNESS

It is possible to *forge* the laminate to reduce its thickness, in which case the entire surface should be worked evenly. Forging takes more time and effort and rolling is probably preferable as it reduces the thickness evenly and leaves the surface evenly worked. Rolling a many-layered laminate presents certain problems. Theoretically, if all the sheets have been bonded together at interfaces with solder, it should be possible to *reverse* the direction of rolling with each pass in order to keep the laminate flat, without causing layer separation. In fact, because the different metals in the laminate vary in degree of ductility, and variations in solder contact and thickness may be present, stresses between the layers occur during rolling. When the direction of rolling is reversed, two-directional stress takes place and where greatest, may result in local laminate separation due to solder failure and cause a rupture between layers. If this should happen, rather than discard the sheet, before proceeding further, paint the whole surface with flux to minimize the formation of surface scale, reheat the laminate, and when the existing solder flows again, place the laminate immediately under pressure in the same way as before to close the rupture. To be on the safe side, therefore, continue rolling the laminate in the *same direction,* each pass entering the rolling mill gap at the same end, and keep the same surface upward. If after the final pass the sheet is bowed, anneal it, place it on a flat surface, bowed side up, cover it with a rigid, flat *steel block,* and hammer it flat.

As a result of rolling the sheet will increase somewhat in width, but its greatest increase will be in its length. After a few passes, the sheet will become work hardened, and will require a between-pass anneal, followed by pickling, rinsing, and drying. This procedure is probably necessary approximately once with each decrease in gauge number. In rolling, edge deformation may occur. If the sheet will be divided for stacking and doubling, trim and true the edges with a *file* after flattening.

To increase the number of laminate layers, cut the trued sheet in half widthwise with a *jeweler's saw* to avoid its distortion from the flat plane which might occur with other means of cutting. Remove any edge burrs with a backed abrasive sheet. Be sure the contacting surfaces are chemically clean. Flood the upper surface of *one* of the halves with solder, and follow the same procedure as before. Place the sheet without a soldered surface on top of the solder-flooded sheet, make sure their edges are aligned, and sweat solder the two five-layered units together. Pickle, rinse, neutralize, and rinse again. If any more doubling takes place, the procedure is repeated in the same way.

The original laminate had five layers, and now there are ten. Roll the laminate to about 14–16 gauge B.&S. (0.064–0.050 in, 1.629–1.270 mm), which can be checked with a *wire gauge, micrometer,* or *vernier calipers.* In the next doubling, there will be 20, then 40, and finally after five such doublings, 80 layers. This is the *maximum* desirable in this gauge range because after this, the patterns made on the face become so fine they lose their effectiveness. The lamination process can, of course, stop short of 80 layers, in which case the face pattern will be bolder and coarser. In the *final* rolling, leave the sheet at about 14–16 gauge B.&S., as this thickness is most advantageous in the face pattern development process.

PREPARING A NONFERROUS MOKUMÉ LAMINATE: Diffusion weld bonding method

Diffusion weld bonding is a method of preparing a nonferrous and/or precious metal mokumé laminate whose layers coalesce and permanently fuse in a continuous bond at each contacting interface, forming a solid fabric. Lamination is accomplished without the use of an intermediary, liquefied, lower-fusing filler metal between layers, such as silver hard solder, but by the use of *heat* elevated to a suitable temperature, in conjunction with pressure. The laminates described here are ultimately meant to form sheets, blocks, or bars, but the same methods could be used, for instance, to make a multi-metal cylinder using tubes of different metals and alloys that telescope into each other, ending with a central solid rod. Regardless of its form, the result is a type of multi-metal fusion cladding, which is then processed further by mechanical and chemical treatments for surface pattern, the latter char-

acterized by the exposure of laminate layers in the face surface.

Laminate bonding methods: At this point, it is well to review the methods used by craftspersons in bonding gold, silver, copper, and their alloys. None of these basic techniques can be considered an "imitation" of another, as some metalsmiths would suggest. Each is a legitimate technique that is used, as circumstances require, exploiting its particular possibilities and limitations.

Metal lamination bonding methods can be categorized into those employing a filler metal, such as solder, between the laminate layers, and those that do not; and those requiring pressure, and those that do not. Combinations of these conditions are possible.

Puddle bonding: One metal is completely melted onto the surface of another having a higher melting point, without pressure.

Moist bonding: Solder with a wide plastic range is used between laminate layers. Before reaching its melting point, it is allowed to liquefy under heat, while other phases in the solder remain solid. Pressure is or is not used.

Wet bonding: Free-flowing hard solder alloy with a melting point below that of the metals being bonded is used between layers. It becomes completely fluid at the time of bonding, and wets the surface by capillary attraction. Pressure is or is not used.

Weld bonding: The layers are joined without solder using pressure and heat within the plastic range of the metals joined. Their core does not reach liquidus temperature, but the bond is formed by a local liquid state of the metals at their contacting surfaces, a condition known as diffusion, sometimes called "sweating."

Regardless of whether solder and pressure are used or not, all these methods require certain conditions for successful lamination bonding. First, the composite metals must be in complete surface contact. All metal surfaces must be chemically clean, that is, initially free of any foreign matter, especially oxides. Any oxides present are soluble in molten metal. Should this occur, the oxide hinders fusion. Oxygen introduced to the metal also causes embrittlement, and reduces its mechanical properties such as ductility and formability. During heating, most metals readily oxidize; therefore, a shield is needed to keep the metal surfaces free of oxide formation, and to exclude oxygen from the surrounding air. This can be accomplished either by the use of flux between the laminate layers and over the whole stack; or by creating and maintaining a reduction atmosphere around the laminate, meaning one relatively free of oxygen; or both. Finally, the method used to introduce and apply heat should be capable of creating an even distribution of a temperature high enough throughout the entire composite to effect the bond.

Except for puddle bonding, it is usually advisable to apply pressure to the laminate, either during the heating period, at its end, or at both times. When pressure is applied, it must be maintained sufficiently long to assure total contact between the component metals for a good, permanent bond to occur over all contacting surfaces. The amount of pressure needed depends on the bonding method used, the metals in the laminate, the size of the contacting surfaces, the thickness of the metals and the base metal, the temperature used by the particular method to make the bond, and the degree of malleability of the component metals at bonding temperature. The relative amount of pressure needed for the above-mentioned methods, in increasing order, are: puddle bonding (none); wet bonding; moist bonding; and weld bonding. During laminate bonding employing solder, pressure is placed on the layers when the solder flows. In solderless bonding, to create pressure, the laminate is prepared by tying it with heavy binding wire; by clamping it together; or, in conjunction with wire binding, by placing it between steel pressure plates, or within a steel sheet-metal box. Depending on the method used, the heat for bonding can come from a large flame torch, a forge fire, or an open box or closed box furnace using gas or electricity for heat.

Diffusion, to a lesser or greater degree, is a phenomenon common to all fusion bonding techniques employing heat alone. In diffusion bonding, the laminate is made by welding the constituents without the presence of a total liquid phase. Actually, a highly localized melting and alloying takes place at the interfaces or planes of contact. Upon arriving at the correct temperature for interface melting to occur, the heat is held at that temperature to allow a movement and interpenetration of metal ions between adjacent contacting laminate metal planes, due to both heat and pressure. The metal's crystal lattice structure, in effect, opens up at the interfaces, the atoms move and interpenetrate, forming local alloys, at a temperature below the melting points of the constituent metals and alloys. This heat-produced effect between metals in contact is described as "sweating" because the metal there generally appears bright and liquid.

Diffusion weld bonding a laminate: The lamination technique described here now is one followed by Hiroko and Gene Pijanowski, acknowledged masters of the process, with additional elements, developed as a result of experience in blacksmithing techniques, by a research team of teachers and students at Southern Illinois University at Carbondale.

Select equal-sized metal sheets for the mokumé laminate. Traditionally they are also of the same thickness. When a sheet is being prepared for use in jewelry, 14 gauge B.&S. would be suitable, except for the bottom sheet, normally copper, which is thicker. Equal thickness, however, is not technically necessary. The lowest sheet is thickest because later this permits maximum pattern exploitation of all the metal layers above it. Prepare the sheets for bonding by annealing and flattening them with a *mallet* on a truly flat surface such as a *steel surface block.* Eliminate obvious surface defects on both sides by rubbing them with a 320 grit silicon carbide *abrasive paper.* Because clean oxide- and grease-free metal is essential to successful lamination, pickle, rinse, and if necessary, degrease the sheets with denatured alcohol, or by rubbing them with a pumice paste till they show no waterbreak.

Assemble the sheets, aligning them in a stack in the desired metal and color sequence. The sheet size, thickness, and layer number used depends on the purpose of the laminate. For jewelry making sheets, from 8–20 layers could be used, making a total of from 3¾ to 14 inches in thickness. Place metals or alloys with lower melting points between sheets of a higher melting metal, usually copper. If brass is used, it should not contact silver alloys, as their proximity causes difficulties. Most metals and alloys tend to maintain their relative thickness ratio during subsequent reduction by forging or rolling.

Possible means of creating pressure have been mentioned. For use in this method employing a laminate of copper and its alloys, prepare two ¼ inch (6 mm) thick *steel plates,* the same size as the stacked sheets, to act as pressure clamps. Coat the deburred and cleaned plates on one surface with a *yellow ochre paste.* When this parting substance contacts the top and bottom of the stack, it will prevent the fusion of the plates to the laminate. Place one plate on top and one below the stack, and using heavy 12 gauge B.&S. *iron binding wire,* tightly bind the assembly twice in both directions. The immobilized layers cannot move laterally during heating, but they do expand. Nonferrous metals and alloys have a relatively higher coefficient of expansion than steel. When heated, the wire-bound, expanded strata press against each other, which aids in surface contact while also expelling any intra-layer gas pockets.

In laminates containing pure silver or silver alloys, because their melting point is lower than copper, fusion occurs at a lower temperature than with a copper and copper alloy laminate. In this case, even heat and its control become more critical. To help in maintaining an even heat, and to prevent slippage between earlier melting silver layers and other metal layers at the time of fusion, place the stack in an open-topped, 18 gauge B.&S. *mild steel box* which can be easily made of one flat sheet with bent-up sides. Make its wall height equal to the stack height plus the thickness of one steel pressure plate. To accommodate the stack, make the interior bottom size slightly larger than the laminate sheet size. Cut away an inch wide opening at the center of the side that will be visible during heating to be able to watch the stack condition. Coat the box interior with yellow ochre for the same reason as above, and let it dry completely. Put a steel pressure plate below and on top of the stack, place these inside the box, and, as before, bind the whole assembly, including the box, with heavy binding wire.

A *forge* is the heat source. Because initially all forge fuels produce smoke and noxious fumes, these must be drawn away by an exhaust hood above the forge fire. Good ventilation is absolutely essential to avoid health hazards. To retain and equalize the fire heat around the laminate, build an improvised, three-sided heat chamber with walls two firebricks high, and a roof of a ¼ inch thick steel plate. The interior space should be somewhat larger than the laminate stack to permit it to be manipulated. Pack the outside seams with wet sand to make the chamber airtight in order to keep maximum heat within the chamber. Place a ¼ inch thick perforated steel sheet or a heavy steel grille grate on the floor, its openings allowing air entry while it supports the burning fuel. The grate should cover the duck's nest opening but be raised slightly above it by side supporting firebricks to permit air entry to the fire.

Start the fire in the usual blacksmith's manner with crumpled paper and wood chips. Add 8–10 handfuls of broken charcoal. Ignite the charcoal with a torch or charcoal lighter fluid. When it begins to burn with a blue flame, start a gentle air flow from a hand-cranked or a power-operated blower with a regulatable rheostat control, the air entering the fire from below through the tuyere, or air pipe. Add 2–3 handfuls of sulphur-low blacksmith's coal, or coke, broken into small pieces. As the coke ignites, add 8 more handfuls of coke, and increase the air input to raise the temperature within the chamber. An established fire is smokeless and burns evenly with a blue flame. To maintain the fire and raise the temperature, add green or dampened coke around the fire, and continue the high air input rate. Do not allow the coke to become more than half consumed, by adding more over it while it burns. If the coke becomes red hot, the fire will first be too hot, and will then hollow out or die down internally. When blue flames fill the chamber, this indicates that atmospheric oxygen there is being completely consumed, that a reduction environment, conducive to successful lamination, exists in the chamber, and even heat is radiating throughout. The time has come to insert the laminate.

Wearing *asbestos gloves,* with *tongs,* place the laminate into the center of the chamber. Reduce the air input, but continue it sufficiently to keep the chamber filled with flames. Heat the laminate for 10–20 minutes, its bulk determining the time needed to bring it to red-orange heat. Keep adding additional green coke to contain the fire and maintain the heat at the desirable level.

During the heating period, to avoid overheating the stack at the back and bottom, turn the stack twice with tongs at time spaced intervals, bringing front to back, and top to bottom. While turning, do not withdraw it from the chamber or the metal will oxidize.

Observe the laminate to make a visual judgment of its state of readiness in terms of its color and condition. Toward the end of the heating period, it will appear uniformly red-orange. In a copper and copper alloy laminate, diffusion may take place at a temperature between 1400–1900° F (760–1038° C). Maintain the laminate at this red-orange state for a few minutes to permit interface molten metal fusion to occur. To test its readiness, scrape a *steel pick* lightly across the exposed laminate edges. If the resulting mark appears uniformly bright, the layers have fused.

Remove the laminate from the chamber, place it on an *anvil,* and quickly, working from the center outward, tap the stack top lightly with a *wooden mallet.* Tapping pressure aids welding by further compressing the surface molten layers into total contact, and simultaneously driving out any intralayer trapped gas pockets. Return the still red laminate to the chamber, raise it again to red-orange heat, remove it to the anvil, and tap it again with a mallet. Quickly clip off the binding wires with *nippers,* and remove the steel plates with edgewise hammer blows. While it is still red hot, and till it cools down to blackness and becomes work hardened, hammer forge the laminate billet down to at least half its original thickness. The degree of thickness reduction also depends on its initial size, its purpose, and the treatments for pattern that will follow.

When the laminate contains silver or silver alloys, watch the silver during heating. It will be first to turn bright red-orange, and will form a eutectic alloy weld with copper at between 1100–1400° F (593–760° C), a temperature range considerably lower than in the case of an all-copper laminate. At the point where the silver sweats, the weld has been accomplished. Remove the laminate and treat it as above. Before forging, clip off the binding wires, remove the upper steel plate, turn the box bottom up over the anvil to extract the laminate, then remove the lower steel plate. Do not forge laminates containing silver till after the redness in the silver dies down. Do not quench the laminate, as this sudden cooling may cause uneven cooling stress between the various metal components, and

possible delamination or rupture between layers due to unequal rates of contraction. Allow it to air cool.

When the result is cool, with a *hacksaw,* trim away any uneven projections from the laminate sides, and smooth them with a *coarse cut file.* Laminates meant to be used as one metal sheet can be further reduced in thickness by forging or cold rolling them down to ¼ inch to prepare them for sheet metal pattern development. During dimensional reduction, anneal the laminate when it work hardens.

Estimated starting and resulting sheet size (Pijanowski)

Sheet size (14 gauge B.&S.)	Laminate layers	Result (14 gauge B.&S.)
2 in sq. (5.1 cm sq.)	10	4½ in sq. (11.2 cm sq.)
3 in sq. (7.6 cm sq.)	13	8 in sq. (20.3 cm sq.)
4 in sq. (10.2 cm sq.)	19	14 in sq. (35.6 cm sq.)

Thicker laminates can be cut into bars or strips, then processed in these forms for pattern using normal forging techniques. The more the laminate is deformed, the greater is the importance of a good bond between layers that will not separate during work. Pattern development involves mechanical techniques such as surface and form distortion manipulations, metal removal, forging or rolling, and chemical treatments, all described farther on.

CREATING A MOKUMÉ FACE PATTERN: Horizontal lamination

POSITIVE CURVED FIGURE PATTERN DEVELOPMENT: By convex forms

The pattern developed on the face of a horizontal mokumé laminate can be developed by various methods. By this system, place the laminate face down on a yielding surface such as *pitch,* a thick piece of *wet leather,* or a *lead block.* In the latter case, first put a piece of heavy, strong *wrapping paper* over the lead block to avoid possible lead contamination by contact because any remaining lead particles will eat into the heated surface and cause pits. Using the same or different sizes of *dapping punches* and a *hammer,* from the *back* raise low domes or protruding bosses that appear in *convex relief* on the face of the laminate, but are intaglio from the back where they are made. The arrangement of the bosses can be *regular* or *random,* each resulting in a different kind of face pattern. Their height should not be more than two-thirds the laminate thickness. Reverse the sheet, immobilize it *face up* with a *clamp,* and slowly file away the highest places with a *flat bastard-cut file.* Watch the progress of the metal as it is removed, and expose the layers of different colored metals by tangential filing action. If the number of layers in the laminate is not great and you know the total, you

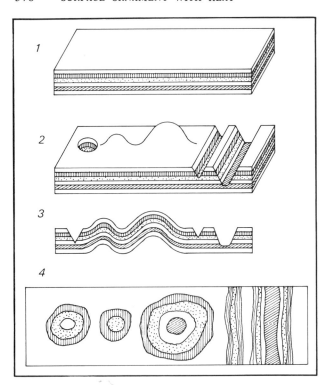

can count those you expose and stop short of making a hole. Should a hole occur, it can be repaired by flooding it with solder from the back, or a patch of the same or a contrasting metal can be soldered to the back to fill it.

Roll and level the laminate until the sheet surface is flat, or when it reaches a thickness of about 16–18 gauge B.&S. (0.050–0.040 in, 1.290–1.024 mm). Where the different metals have been exposed on the face, a mokumé wood grain pattern appears, while the rest remains the original face metal. In this development, because the metal was removed from circular domes and bosses, the resulting pattern appears in more or less concentric circles and curves, as in burl wood grain. The bossing, filing, and rolling process can be repeated more than once on the same face to develop the pattern, but each time the sheet is rolled it becomes thinner.

Pattern variations can be created. Instead of round bosses, oval, long, or irregular shapes can be raised from the back of the sheet with *repoussage tools*. When using a *file* the metal is removed from these shapes, the resulting exposed layers each follow their contour in the same way as seen on a topographical map where the elevation lines pass around hills. Combinations of round and oval forms are also possible.

9–69 MOKUMÉ PATTERN FROM A HORIZONTAL LAMINATE: Positive and negative patterns
1. The sweat-soldered horizontal mokumé laminate.
2. Treating the mokumé laminate with convex, positive forms, and concave, negative forms: a drilled hole; a small and large dome; a shallow and deeply filed groove.
3. Side view of the above showing the raised and excavated forms.
4. The mokumé laminate face pattern resulting from the above treatments after rolling the sheet through the rolling mill to a uniform thickness.

9–70 CHUCK EVANS, U.S.A.
Pendant with moonstones, fabricated parts in sterling silver and 820 silver, supporting a hinged horizontal mokumé laminate form made of sterling silver, nickel silver, brass, bronze, and copper, in 80 layerings. *Photo: Photography Service, Bowling Green State University*

NEGATIVE PATTERN DEVELOPMENT:
By intaglio or metal subtractive methods

Different patterns result when the metal is removed in *intaglio* from the *face* of the flat laminate while it is fixed on a *pitch*-spread surface, in an *engraver's ball*, or otherwise immobilized. Long straight grooves can be made partially or completely across the laminate's width or length, in parallel, converging, or crisscrossing arrangements, with a *triangular-* or *curve-sectioned file* to expose the lower layers. A basic principle of layer exposure within a groove or negative shape is that the *steeper* the groove angle, the *closer* the layers of the laminate will appear on the face after rolling, and the *shallower* the groove angle, the *further apart* each layer will appear. Straight grooves will be seen after rolling as parallel long stripes, diamond shapes, etc. By using *gravers* or *chisels*, any kind of straight or curved figures in regular or irregular patterns, or even representational figures can be excavated. All the above treatments are followed either by hand forge flattening on an anvil with a hammer, or rolling in a rolling mill to bring the depressions made by the tools to the same plane as the face. The metal subtractive method can be repeated more than once in the same laminate face, possibly in a direction opposing the first.

Surface reliefs can be created by metal subtractive methods provided the sheet is sufficiently thick. Carving can be accomplished with *carborundum-mounted abrasive points, diamond-mounted burs,* shallow-angle *high-speed steel burs, rotary files*—all mounted on a *flexible shaft handpiece.* These miniature grinding tools can make any desired depressions in the mokumé sheet face. In another type of relief development, the laminate can first be pierced through with *drilled* holes, and the hole *sides* then filed or carved at an angle to reveal the laminate strata around them. These two methods can be combined in the same relief. Such a treatment would *not* be followed by forging or rolling which would destroy the relief.

Etching can be used as a method of creating a linear pattern in the laminate by dissolving the metal locally down to any depth, the design controlled by the help of a resist. (See The Acid Etching of Metals, Chapter 8.) Etching can be used on vertical laminates to etch the metals in the face, as already described under *Macroetching* or *"watering"* above. As a result of etching a multimetal laminate, the surface may take on an all-over copper or silver color due to electrolytic action. This flashing can be removed by cleaning the surface with a *scratch brush,* or a cut-and-color abrasive can be used until the laminate metal color variations are restored.

PRESSURE NEGATIVE PATTERN DEVELOPMENT Another technique for creating pattern involves no initial metal removal, but employs *local compression.* For a line pattern, any *small-diameter cylindrical mandrel* can be laid flat on the laminate surface and hammered to make a groove in it. This pressure depresses the laminate layers immediately below, and after the surface is scalped, the laminate layers appear in lines parallel to the groove. Any small, flat metal object with a distinctive contour, such as a key, could be used in the same way to create a distinctive impression pattern.

By another method, small pressure patterns can be made with *blunt hand stamping punches.* These can be of any shape or pattern as long as their configurations are large and bold enough to be easily seen. Even *letter punches* can be used to spell out words or phrases. Punched impressions can be single or in groups or series, placed regularly or irregularly on the face surface while the laminate rests on a hard resisting surface such as a *surface block.* The pressure causes a local depression of the upper layers. Later when scalping the surface down to the desired level, the laminate layers form concentric lines eddying around the stamped figures. This type of pattern cannot be forged as this would destroy the pattern, but it could be rolled.

MOKUMÉ PARQUETRY: Mosaic lamination

Make a bar of 1 in (2.5 cm) wide strips (smaller or larger dimensions can be used) of different colored metals, aligned and sweat soldered together. The thickness, or the number of layers used, and the bar length depends on the size and quantity of repeats needed. Do not run the bar through the rolling mill to reduce its thickness but retain the initial thickness. With a *jeweler's saw* squarely cut *equal* cross sections off the bar end to make many duplicate units of equal thickness. Rub the face and bottom surfaces of each unit on a flat sheet of backed abrasive placed on a hard, flat surface to smooth them. Arrange these units in an opposing direction pattern on a flat soldering surface, in contact, side by side, in the manner of a wooden parquet floor. Paint the entire surface with flux, place medium or easy solder at the joints of the units, and solder them together to form a sheet or strip as large as desired.

If the soldering surface is flat, the result should be level at the bottom. To level the face side as well, drawfile it with a *flat file* having a large surface, which simultaneously will remove any surplus surface solder. If the result is rolled, it will become thinner, but it will also stretch and distort the pattern. However, softening its rigid geometry may not be objectionable. Such a flat patterned sheet can be used as is, can be soldered to a sheet metal backing, cut into any shape, or formed dimensionally to a limited extent.

SPIRAL MOKUMÉ: Vertical strip lamination

Spiral mokumé is a variation of vertical lamination in which the *edges* of the constituents become the laminate face. Cut flat strips of various metals about ⅜–½ in (0.95–1.27 cm) wide and 12–18 in (30.5–45.7 cm) long. Anneal the strips, flatten, pickle, and neutralize them. Lay them out flat, side by side, and flood hard solder on all but the last one, on one side only, covering a distance of from ¼–½ in (0.64–1.27 cm) from one end. Scratch brush the solder-flooded ends on both sides, flux them on both sides, and arrange them in contact, flat side to flat side, with the strip ends staggered to create a tapered beginning that makes starting the spiral center easier. Add the last piece without solder but fluxed, to the group, and bind them with wire together at a point slightly beyond where they are solder flooded. Stand the group on edge and fan the strips apart to keep the solder from advancing beyond their point of contact. Apply heat and solder that end together. Pickle the result, rinse and neutralize it, and rinse it again.

With *pliers* or other tools form the strips into a tight, touching spiral coil. Bind the outside of the spiral together with wire, and place it, edges up, on a flat refractory surface. Apply flux to the spaces between the strips, or dip the whole unit into flux, and flood the spaces with medium

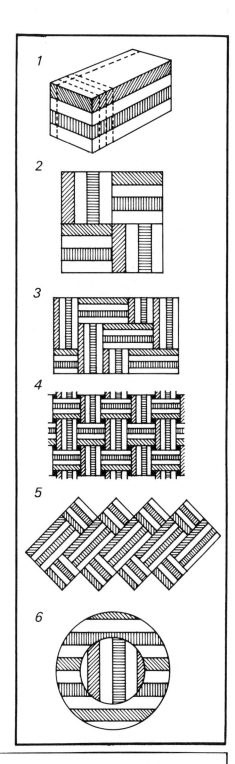

9–71 MOKUMÉ PARQUETRY MOSAIC FABRICATED FROM A HORI-
ZONTAL LAMINATE

1. The horizontal mokumé laminate from which cross sections or longitudinal cuts can be made.
2. A mokumé parquet mosaic of square sections.
3. A parquet mosaic of oblong sections.
4. An openwork parquet mosaic from oblong sections, leaving small
holes; or made of continuous, woven strips.
5. A diagonally patterned parquet mosaic of square and oblong sections.
6. A round mokumé form cut from mokumé sheet.

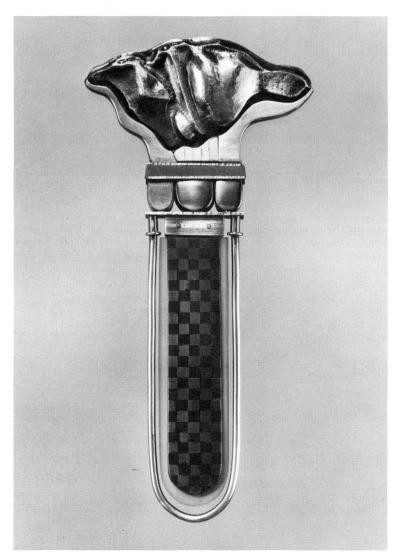

9–72 RICHARD MAFONG,
U.S.A. Brooch in silver, nickel
silver, ivory, and acrylic,
employing repoussage, chasing,
fabrication, and riveting
techniques. A unit in bi-metal
mokumé parquetry in a
checkerboard pattern is used
for the lower portion, backed
by an acrylic sheet form and a
bent tube form. Size 3 × 6
in. Photo: Andrew N. Foster

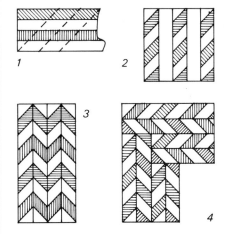

9–73 MOKUMÉ DIAGONAL-PATTERNED MOSAIC SHEET: Made from
diagonal cuts through a horizontal laminate or a vertical laminate

1. The horizontal laminate through which diagonal cuts are made.
2. Alternating diagonal-patterned laminate strips with solid metal
strips.
3. Herringbone or chevron pattern of diagonal strips used in alternating directions.
4. Parquet mosaic of vertical and horizontal chevron pairs.

hard solder. *File* the face to remove surplus surface solder and level the surface.

A strip spiral laminate can be divided by sawing it parallel with the face to make thinner sections. These can be passed through the rolling mill to distort the circular spiral to an oval form, or they can be forged to soften the regularity of the pattern. Both processes can be followed by scalping. If parts open up, flood those places with medium hard solder before proceeding further. A relatively small coil of this dimension when forged or rolled down to 16–18 gauge B.&S. makes a sheet of considerable size.

MOKUMÉ WIRE LAMINATES:
Straight and twist lamination

Patterned nonferrous laminates made of straight wire or of units of twisted wire in various metals are another possibility. *Straight wire laminates* can be composed of square or round wire of the same or different gauges, but with not too great a gauge difference. Select wires of different metals and cut them into the same or different lengths. Arrange the wires in the desired sequence of colors, *side by side* in a parallel arrangement to form a unit or strip of multicolored metal. The same wire can run the entire length of the strip, or a single continuous unit can be made of wires of different metals of matching gauge size and section. The wires are hard soldered together, and the result can be forged or rolled flat. The multicolored, striped sheet or strip that results can be bent into a spiral, formed in other ways, or cut into flat units and reassembled in the manner of a mosaic laminate.

Twisted wire lamination using compound wire elements of different metals in one unit has already been discussed under Twist Lamination, p. 369.

MISCELLANEOUS PROCESSING OF FINISHED MOKUMÉ LAMINATES

USING SHEET LAMINATES

Once the face pattern on the nonferrous laminate is finished, it can be worked by any method used to work sheet metal. Units of any shape can be sawed from a sheet and used to create whole objects, or portions of objects. The entire surface or part of it can be treated in any of the cold working decorative processes such as piercing, engraving, texturing, etching, or punch stamping. The laminate can be used as a ground for the inlay of precious metal or nonferrous metal wire, placed in directions or forms counter to those of the face pattern, a technique used by Japanese metalworkers in the past.

SHAPING MOKUMÉ SHEET

Generally speaking, finished, annealed, face-patterned, *solder bonded mokumé laminates* can be worked as any other sheet, provided that the distortion of the laminate is not too drastic. It can be gently shaped into three-dimensional forms in *wooden* or *Masonite molds,* or over a *stake* or *mandrel* using a *wood* or *plastic mallet;* dome shaped with *dapping dies* in a *dapping block;* or worked with *repoussage* and *chasing punches* while mounted on pitch. The greater the deformation or stretching, the more chance there is of splitting or cracking the laminate. To reduce this possibility, the laminate must be annealed at

9–74 RACHEL SHRAIBER, Israel. Silver bent tube bracelet with a section in a horizontal laminate of silver, copper, and brass mokumé sheet formed into a seamed tube. Photo: Ilana Volish

stages during forming, and work should proceed slowly. If a crack or split should appear between parts, flood it with solder, file off the excess, and continue working. *Duffusion weld bonded laminates* allow far greater three-dimensional deformation.

JOINING A MOKUMÉ LAMINATE IN FABRICATION

Soldering a solder bonded mokumé unit to other fabricated parts is possible if *easy solder* is used, and the temperature is kept as low as possible to avoid the separation of the laminate layers already joined with medium solder. A *solder inhibitor* painted over the laminate joins will help to protect them during soldering. Hard solder can be used with diffusion weld bonded laminates.

Cold joining methods can be used without difficulty to join mokumé parts to a fabricated work. Riveting, screwing, the use of bezel or prongs to mount the mokumé unit can all be used, depending on the design.

FINISHING THE MOKUMÉ SURFACE

POLISHING MOKUMÉ Mokumé parts in jewelry are not usually given a high mirror polish because greater light reflection minimizes the differences in the metal colors, making them less visible. Instead, a semimatte finish is preferred. This can be achieved manually by the use of *steel wool,* a *fine abrasive sheet,* or pumice; or mechanically by wire brushing, or by the use of a coarse-particle abrasive compound. For contrast, the parts in which a mokumé unit is mounted could be polished mirror-bright.

COLORING MOKUMÉ Coloring a patterned mokumé laminate is a way of heightening the color contrast between the metals and alloys in its composition. Normal coloring solutions can be used, though they may not work equally well on all the metals and alloys in the laminate, each accepting or rejecting the color in varied degrees.

A weak solution of potassium sulphide is traditional for use in coloring nonferrous metals, followed by a water rinse and a light rub with a cloth. This can be repeated to deepen the color. Exposing the surface to the fumes of ammonia is another possibility. (See Metal Coloring, Chapter 17 for other suggestions.)

When the laminate contains the Japanese alloy shakudo, using the coloring solution *rokusho* is traditional (see Mercury Amalgam Gilding, Chapter 15). Ordinary exposure to air in time will cause natural surface oxidation due to the sulphur content in the atmosphere. Coloring can also be done by heating methods.

Once a work is satisfactorily colored, to preserve the patina, oil or hot wax can be applied to the surface, then rubbed with a cloth. For those not purist-minded when it comes to patinas, the surface can be *lacquered* with a clear lacquer painted or sprayed on a clean surface. Make sure no grease is present or the lacquer will not hold.

QUALITY STAMPING OF LAMINATES

When nonferrous base metals are combined with precious metals in a laminate, the result cannot be quality stamped with a precious metal hallmark since it can only be placed on articles made *entirely* of the metal and quality so stamped. An exception in laminates would be one made of any combination of different colored golds, *all of the same karat.* For example, a work can be made of 14K red, green, yellow, and white golds, using the gold solder appropriate to this quality gold. This could be stamped "14K" as the total gold content in each constituent is of the same quality. When a laminate is mounted by a mechanical holding system, that is, without being joined to it by solder, the precious metal portion of the holding device can be stamped with the appropriate quality stamp.

NIELLO

A fusion-inlaid contrast alloy

In the search for and sensual enjoyment of metal alloys having different colors and degrees of fusibility, by empirical experiment, at an early time alloys that melted at low temperatures were developed. One such alloy is *niello* which is black in color. As long as 3,000 years ago in Dynastic Egypt, methods were developed for inlaying this easily fusible sulphurized alloy into gold and silver parent metal objects. Once the surface was polished, the dark pattern created by the niello inlay and the bright color of the parent metal offered endless possibilities of pleasing contrast. That this opposition of colors was much appreciated is evident from the fact that the use of niello was so widespread geographically, and that its use covers such a long period of time. The Persians, Migration Period peoples, Greeks, Romans, Celts, Anglo-Saxons, Germanic tribes, and Byzantines, among others, all used niello in their metalwork and jewelry. Renaissance Italian artisans brought the process to a peak of perfection. Their pre-eminence accounts for the fact that almost all European languages use the Italian term *niello,* from the Latin *nigellus,* diminutive of *niger,* "black," to indicate this technique.

Until relatively recently, niello work was also done in Turkestan in Central Asia, the Caucasus region in Russia, and in Turkey. In Russia, niello which is called *chern,* "black," has been employed since Byzantine times. Nielloed objects are still made at Tula, near Moscow, a place that since the 16th century has had an outstanding reputation for metalwork. Another Russian center active since the beginning of the 18th century is the town of Veliky Ustiug in the Vologda Region, where a contemporary factory called Northern Niello continues the production of niello ornamented silver jewelry, cigarette cases, and other objects. Further afield, niello is still used on jewelry in a few centers in Southern Morocco; and it is flawlessly executed in the workshops of Bangkok in Thailand where niello, there called *krueng tome,* is used to decorate mass-produced silver jewelry and small *objets de poche.*

THE NIELLO COMPOSITION

Prepared niello consists of a *ternary* or *three-metal alloy* of silver, copper, and lead (some formulas also include small amounts of other metals). These are combined in

9–75 RUSSIA, 12–13th century, from Terehovo, Orlov District, U.S.S.R. Cylindrical silver bracelet in two hinged sections. The engraved figures were mercury gilded, and the ground is in niello. These bracelets were ritual ornaments believed to have magic, protective powers connected with fertility. Worn in pairs, they held up both yard long sleeves of the festive gowns worn by women during the pagan Rusalia ritual celebrating the summer solstice. Most are divided horizontally into two zones, the upper—with arches representing sky—enclose humans, animals, or birds, and the lower zones contain other subjects. The two lower left panels here contain the *simargl,* a pagan winged dog, the guardian of vegetation, and the birds are symbolic messengers between heaven and earth. Length 15.9 cm; width 7.1 cm. Photo: Courtesy The Russian Museum, Leningrad

specific proportions in a melt to which sulphur, a nonmetallic element, is added to make the result a *metallic sulphide compound.* Niello, like most alloys, has characteristics of color, hardness, density, and fusibility that are quite different from those of its separate component metals, though the fused niello alloy is homogeneous and compatible with the base or parent metal of the object. Niello melts at a temperature lower than two of its main metals—silver and copper—and possesses far more tenacity and hardness than its third—lead.

The application of niello in its final form, bonded to the parent metal, is accomplished by *heat* which causes the niello compound to fuse, become viscous, flood the depressions, and become permanently cemented to the parent metal base. For these reasons it can be called a *fusion-inlaid alloy* process.

When after fusion the surface is reduced to the parent

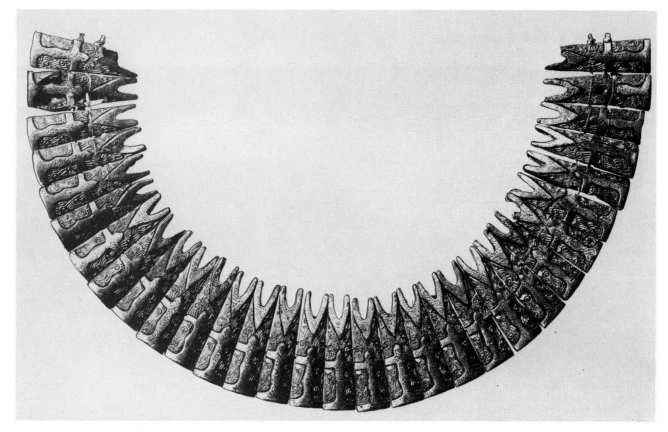

9–76 SWEDEN, about 1000 A.D., from Grötlinge Parish, Gotland. Bronze necklace, each unit mounted with silver parts whose engraved, knotted rope patterns are nielloed. Col.: Museum of National Antiquities, Stockholm. Photo: Nils Lagergren, Antikvarisk-Topografiska Arkivet, Stockholm

metal plane and then polished, the solid niello metallic composition has a reflective, permanent, uniform color that ranges from dark gray to a deep black according to the composition of the alloy. The proportion of its constituent metals also affects the relative toughness of the result. An increase in the amount of lead makes niello brittle, but it also helps to reduce the heat needed for fusibility, and allows the alloy to flow easily and fill even delicately engraved lines. The amount of copper in the alloy to a great extent determines its hardness. The silver helps to lower the melting point of the copper. The amount of sulphur added to the alloy during the melt affects the depth of the black color. A smaller amount of sulphur results in a niello with a decidedly grayish tone, while an ex-

cessive amount, which most recipes call for, deepens it to a rich black.

Commercially prepared niello is sold by the kilogram from several European companies, such as Karl Fischer of Pforzheim, West Germany.

PREPARING THE PARENT METAL FOR NIELLO

In a design, the niello inlay can form the negative space or ground surrounding a figure in the parent metal, or it can be the positive element, the figure itself surrounded by the parent metal as a ground. Traditionally in jewelry the niello base metal has been gold or silver, but other metals whose melting point is considerably higher than that of the niello alloy, such as copper, brass, bronze, nickel alloys, or

Niello Formulas

(in parts, arranged from minimum to maximum silver content)

Niello Origin	Silver (fine)	Copper	Lead	Other	Sulphur
Augsberg	1	1	2		In excess
Cellini	1	2	3		In excess
Persian	1	5	7	Ammonium chloride 5	24.5
Thailand	1	5	3		In excess
Russian (Tula)	1.5	2.5	3.5		12
Theophilus	2	1	0.5		In excess
Bolas	2	4	1	Antimony 1	In excess
Wilson	6	2	1		10
Fike	6	2	2	Borax 1-2	10 or more

The term **parts** can be translated to read pennyweights, grams, grains, or ounces, depending on estimated need. (See **Tables of Weights and Measures**, and **Conversion Tables**.) The melting range of prepared niello depends on the proportions of the constituents, and may be anywhere from 824°F (440°C) to 1040°F (560°C).

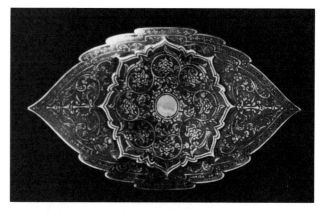

9–77 PADANG HIGHLANDS, SUMATRA. Silver intaglio repoussé-worked belt buckle with niello-filled ground and figure in the parent metal. Length 17 cm. Photo: Courtesy the Indonesich Ethnografisch Museum, Delft

9–78   MOROCCO. Complete head ornament (*right*), silver, with four pendants engraved with line-patterned figures filled with niello. Courtesy a private collector in New York. Detail, a pendant from Taghmout, Ida Oundif, Central Sous Region, Anti-Atlas. Niello work is also done in Ait Seghrouchen, Ait Youssi, Marmoucha, and Ida ou Kensous in Southern Morocco. Ø 2½ in; length 5¼ in. *Photos: Oppi (left); Alan Fairley (right)*

steel could also be used. Both sheet metal and castings are suitable as a base.

Any tool can be used to make the depressions to receive the niello in the parent metal. Engraving, chiseling, chasing, stamping, repoussage or etching can all be employed. The pattern can be linear and consist of very fine lines, of larger areas, or a combination of both. It is preferable that the ground metal should be of *one piece* and not made of soldered parts, because the solder may melt, contact the niello and create difficulties. Try for a more or less uniform depth in making the incisions or depressions of the pattern, no more than 1/64–1/32 in (0.4–0.8 mm). If an incision is deeper than 1/32 in (0.8 mm), the niello needed to fill it may harbor trapped air bubbles. *Keying* the depressions by roughening their surfaces is desirable as a way of helping to secure the niello to the parent metal, but there is no need to undercut the depressions as the niello bond to the base metal after fusion is complete.

PREPARING THE NIELLO ALLOY:
The first melt of the compound

Weigh the clean metals of the alloy on a scale. Divide them into small pieces with *shears* or other means as they are more easily melted in this form. Use a new, clean, *carbon-containing crucible* to limit the inclusion of oxygen in the melt.

When melting metals in any multi-metal alloy, the components may vary greatly in fusibility. In the sequence of melt, it is good practice to first melt those having the highest melting point because they are least fusible, and follow this by those having increasingly lower melting points, which are more fusible and thus more likely to be

volatilized at the elevated temperatures used for the higher melting metals. Therefore, when preparing the niello alloy, first fuse the copper (melting point 1981.4° F, 1083° C) with the silver (melting point 1760.9° F, 960.5° C), with a pinch of borax flux to promote liquefaction and to control the intake of atmospheric oxygen. When these reach a melt, stir them with a *charcoal stick* or *graphite rod*. Moderate the heat and add the lead (melting point 621.3° F, 327.3° C) which has been mixed with a portion of the sulphur. If any antimony (melting point 1166.9° F, 945.7° C) is used, this is also added now. Stir when molten, then add the remaining crushed or powdered sulphur.

The sulphur used should be in as pure a state as it is possible to obtain. *Flowers of sulphur,* mentioned in some niello recipes, is a pure sulphur powder resulting from the condensed vapors that occur during the distillation process used when purifying sulphur. The expression "in excess" refers to the fact that some of the sulphur is lost in fumes, and more than is called for in the recipe is therefore used to retain the required amount in the alloy. When sulphur is placed in the crucible and heated, it ignites in air and burns with a blue flame. At the same time, it emits the highly malodorous and suffocating gas and fumes of sulphur dioxide, not poisonous but highly objectionable. Avoid inhaling it when preparing niello indoors by carrying out the melt under a fume hood equipped with a well-functioning exhaust. If done out of doors, position yourself upwind on a breezy day so the fumes are carried away from you.

Play a reducing flame on the crucible bottom and sides until it becomes a dull red and the contents are fully fused. The melt should take place at the lowest temperature at which the union of the ingredients can occur. When it happens, stir the mixture vigorously to assure its homogeneity. Undissolved particles can become the cause of difficulties as they may later form gas holes in the fused niello. Place a ½ in (1.3 cm) thick cover of ground charcoal on top of the molten metals to induce a reduction atmosphere and to prevent the introduction of free oxygen into the melt. Continue to play the reducing flame on the crucible but do not overheat. Once fusion is complete, grasp the crucible with *tongs.* With the left hand, cover the top with a piece of *transite* to hold back the charcoal, but allow just enough of an opening to pour the contents onto a clean *stone* or *steel slab,* where it will form a round, solid "cookie." Before this has a chance to cool, with a hammer, beat the alloy thinner. When it cools, to continue the thinning, reheat it with a torch but not to redness or it will melt and run. The beating work hardens and embrittles the alloy which makes it easier to break up. Once cold, the niello compound is friable and can be easily crumbled and reduced to a powder. Break the niello into small pieces. Place them into a container and wash them with water. If there are any particles of charcoal still present, they will rise to the surface and can then be poured off. (By another method, pour the niello into a clean, heated, slightly oiled, narrow *ingot mold* to form a niello "stick" which can be fed into a depression while a torch flame plays on the end in contact with the parent metal.)

GRINDING NIELLO TO A POWDER WITH MORTAR AND PESTLE

A *mortar* (the container) and a *pestle* (the grinding tool) are used by the jeweler to grind relatively small amounts of substances like niello, enamel, or dry, solid gums into a pulverized form. Those made of porcelain, agate, or another hard stone are recommended for grinding niello. Iron or brass mortars are not suitable as these may contaminate the mixture. Grind only the amount of niello you anticipate using immediately and keep the rest stored in lump form in an airtight container as it deteriorates less rapidly in that form and under those conditions. Place a small amount in the mortar, cover it with water and apply pestle pressure in a circular motion. Grind the niello to the desired fineness. For most applications an adequate grind is 80 mesh, which means that there are 80 openings per square inch in the *screen* used to sift the ground powder. Powdered niello can be separated from coarser grains into specific degrees of fineness by dry sifting it through a wire screen of the desired fineness. Any coarser matter is returned to the mortar to reduce it to a finer state. The degree of grind fineness used depends on whether the niello is meant to fill large areas, in which case a coarser grind is suitable, or fine lines, for which finer powder is used.

To get rid of foreign matter such as abraded mortar material that may enter the powder during grinding, rinse the niello powder by placing it in a clean glass jar, cover it with water, stir it, allow the particles to settle, then pour off the water. Repeat the process until the water poured off is clear.

STORING NIELLO Niello in a powdered state cannot be stored for long periods since the compound tends to deteriorate by combining with atmospheric oxygen and moisture and by sulphur evaporation. In this condition, niello will not fuse smoothly, nor is its color as uniform. Such changes occur to a lesser degree when lump niello is stored absolutely dry in airtight containers.

APPLYING THE NIELLO POWDER

The technique of applying niello resembles the application of enamel in the champlevé technique of enameling. The base metal object to which niello is applied must be *completed* as no work can be done on it after nielloing.

The surface must be absolutely clean, oxide- and grease-free. To assure a good flow of niello when melted, add some liquid flux to the niello to make a paste. This flux consists of a dilute solution of *sal ammoniac* (ammonium chloride, NH_4Cl). (Alternately, *borax* can be used as a flux.) Also apply the flux to the metal surface to receive the niello. With a *small spatula,* place the niello paste over the lines and into the depressions where it is wanted, loading it a little higher than the base metal level because it will shrink considerably when fused. Take off any surplus liquid by touching a clean cloth or absorbent blotting paper to the edge of the niello. It is easier to load niello on a flat or somewhat convex surface than on a completely three-dimensional one (in which case, add a small amount of diluted gum tragacanth to the niello to help hold it in place). Confine the placement of niello to the desired area because any scattered grains on the surface will also be heat fused and will have to be removed later. To cover fine lines, place the niello over the entire area of the lines. Allow the niello to dry in air before firing, or hasten the drying by placing the object on a *hot plate* at low temperature, or by heating it gently from below with a *torch flame* until all vapor ceases to rise.

NIELLO FUSION:
The second melt of the compound

The object nielloed can range in size from a small plaque to a large piece. Pieces with niello on one side are easier to fire than three-dimensional pieces, and this is why the shape of the majority of nielloed pieces is relatively flat or gently convex. The work placed on an *open mesh heating frame* is easily heated from below with a torch having a reducing flame. The compound of sulphides that comprise niello tend to alter undesirably under heat if they absorb oxygen. Therefore, a reducing flame atmosphere is advisable. In Thailand, charcoal is used as a base upon which niello is fired as it helps to establish a reduced atmosphere around the work. Larger pieces can be placed within a *heat shield* constructed of charcoal blocks or refractory brick. The work must be in a raised position on props of these or other materials to support it on the heating frame and to allow room to play the flame on the work from below. It is also possible to fire the niello by placing the work on a heating frame into a *kiln* preheated to 1000° F (537.7° C) in the same manner as in enameling. Heating in an open heat has the advantage of allowing the niello surface to be accessible so that during fusion, if necessary, it can be poked and guided with a *steel pick* into places where it may be needed. Three-dimensional objects being nielloed must be supported on *improvised racks* suited to the particular shape. These should hold the piece in places where the support will not contact the niello.

It is most desirable to create as even a heat as possible *simultaneously on the whole work* so that all of the niello matures at the same time. Otherwise part might run before the rest has fused. During firing, watch the niello. At fusing temperature, which varies with the particular alloy, the

9–79 MICHAEL LACKTMAN, U.S.A. Ring of 14K gold with niello. Short gold wire lengths have been fused with the niello, and the entire surface polished smooth. Photo: Walter Sheffer

9–80 AIT SEGHROUCHEN, CENTRAL ANTI-ATLAS, MOROCCO. Contemporary silver breast ornament (*choka*), also used as a diadem. Made of engraved units filled with niello, joined by links and chains, and supported by two fibulae. The niello technique has attained a high degree of perfection in this area, and is applied to a wide range of traditional jewelry forms. *Photo: Oppi, courtesy Aux Arts Islamiques, Marrakech*

grains will melt, become viscous, sink down, flood the depressions, and become cemented to the parent metal. Withdraw the flame *at once* when the surface becomes smooth and shining, as the *niello will run if overheated.* (One old source calls for heating the niello just until it fuses, then allow it to cool, rub it with borax, and heat it again to a final fusion.) Overheating the niello can cause it to eat into the base metal because of its lead content. Allow the niello to cool in air, and *never quench it.* Once fused, niello is very stable, and is tougher than enamel. Ideally, niello should be given only one firing, and this should be the aim.

INCLUSIONS IN NIELLO

It is possible when the niello is in place initially as a paste before fusion, to introduce inclusions to areas containing niello, in the form of metal wires, small granules, or shot of precious metals. When fused, the niello acts to hold these in a kind of *fusion inlay*. Intricate patterns can be developed by this technique, which was practiced in ancient Egypt.

FINISHING THE NIELLOED SURFACE

Traditionally, the fused nielloed surface is *finished level* with the plane of the parent metal, regardless of whether this surface is flat or curved. This is done by slowly and carefully scraping it away with a *sharp steel knife,* or by grinding away the surplus with a *fine-grade stick abrasive* such as 400 or 600 grit carborundum and water, or a *water of Ayr stone* used with pumice paste. Take care to

make frequent observations after washing off the ground sludge and *do not rush the process.* Fine shallow line details can be quickly worn through if too much niello is removed. When you can just see the contour delineation of the nielloed areas exposed, stop the stone abrasion and continue the leveling with *dry crocus cloth* which is finer. Then hand buff the surface carefully with tripoli until the design becomes clearly delineated, and follow this with a final machine polish with rouge. At this point, the niello has taken on a surface gloss equal to that of the metal, and its true depth of color is revealed. (In old niello work, the final polish was achieved by burnishing.)

ENGRAVING PARENT METAL AND NIELLO

It is possible after niello fusion and leveling to engrave linear details in the parent metal sections of the finished piece, or the niello itself if it is a hard composition. Experiments on a piece of nielloed scrap metal of the same metal base and niello composition as that contemplated for engraving will indicate whether the alloy you use is suitable. When engraving, it is advisable to mount the work on an *engraver's block* or other firm holding device. A holding system that requires heat, such as mounting it on pitch, should be avoided.

9–81 AIT HADIDU, MOROCCO. Bride wearing the silver with niello *choka* as a diadem, attached to a cloth headdress; and amber beads. *Photo: René Bertrand, Marrakech*

REPAIRING NIELLOED WORK:
The third melt of the compound

In the process of leveling the niello, air bubbles trapped below the original surface level may be exposed, and these, now forming pits on the surface, must be filled. Repeated firings may be the cause of internal air bubbles, and old powdered niello has a tendency to pit, as will niello that is not homogeneous in composition. In cases where it is discovered that the niello was insufficient to fill recesses, these places can also be added to and brought to the same level as the rest by a *third firing*. If such faults are discovered in the process of leveling, do not take the niello through further processing.

To repair a surface, it must be absolutely clean and grease-free. If necessary, break open the hole with a *pointed tool* or *scraper* to expose its full extent. Apply the sal ammoniac or borax flux, and load the depression with enough niello to assure its being filled after firing. Do the same to insufficiently filled depressions. Refire the work, and when cool, process the surface as before.

Third firings have a tendency to dull the blackness of the niello alloy, probably because a portion of its sulphur content is vaporized in the process. This is all the more reason to work carefully and try to avoid more than a single firing of the applied niello.

MOUNTING NIELLOED ELEMENTS

A unit with niello decoration can be mounted on a larger work by setting it in a bezel, like a stone, or holding it by claws or rivets. A nielloed part can be screwed to the rest if a hole is drilled through it; the screw, attached to the other part, passes through this opening and is secured at the back by a nut. The nielloed part can be fabricated at the start to include bent projections or flanges which after nielloing can be passed through waiting holes and be bent back to hold the part in place.

10
FABRICATION
Building Fragments into Units

SOLDERING

Joining fabricated parts by intermediary metal alloy fusion

Hard soldering, from Latin *solidare,* "to make solid," is also called *brazing* in industry because brazing implies that there is no melting of the metals being joined, and only the solder is melted. *Soldering* is the joining of similar or dissimilar metals by the use of solder and the application of heat to the object. *Solder* is an intermediary nonferrous alloy whose composition in a molten state becomes extremely fluid, and has an affinity for the metals joined. The proportions of the metal components in solder alloys are constituted to give them the thermal property of melting and running at a flow point temperature *lower* than the melting point of the parent metals being joined. The solder flows freely in the space between the parts to bond them, or in the joint space where it acts as a permanent filler. In the bond that results, a diffusion of the filler metal into the base metal by local penetration along grain boundaries occurs *without fusion* of the base metal.

Hard solder is so called because of the high temperature needed to melt it. It is used in joining metals with melting points higher than 800° F (426° C). Hard solders used in jewelry making melt at red metal heat, and have a melting point that ranges from 1150–1600° F (620–871° C). Hard solder is also called silver solder, or silver brazing alloy because its main constituent is silver. Normally its color and composition are similar to the parent metals being joined, but this is not always the case. Because hard solder alloys are malleable and ductile, they are fabricated in sheet and wire forms.

Soft solder is made of low-melting metals, and has a composition that melts below 800° F (426° C). Most of these alloys melt below 700° F (371° C), a temperature below red heat. The technique of soft soldering is discussed separately on p. 422.

This subject starts with a discussion of the nature of the precious metals most used in jewelry: platinum, palladium, gold, silver, and their alloys, and the solders used with them.

SOLDERS FOR PRECIOUS METALS AND THEIR ALLOYS

PLATINUM AND PALLADIUM

Platinum–Atomic symbol and number: Pt 78
  Atomic weight: 195.09
  Specific gravity: 21.45
  Melting point: 3217° F (1769° C)
  Boiling point: 8185° F (4530° C)

Palladium–Atomic symbol and number: Pd 46
  Atomic weight: 106.7
  Specific gravity: 12.02
  Melting point: 2826° F (1552° C)
  Boiling point: 7200° F (3980° C)

Platinum was known in South America in the 16th century but did not come to Europe until 1741. In the next 100 years, all the other related noble metals of the platinum group were also discovered. They arrange themselves in a triad of pairs: platinum-palladium; iridium-rhodium; osmium-ruthenium. The first of each pair has almost twice the atomic weight and density, and a higher melting point than the other. Platinum and palladium are the most important and abundant, and their main source today is from copper-nickel ores mined in Canada.

Of the metals in this group, platinum and palladium and their alloys are the most widely used in jewelry, for several reasons. They and their alloys are highly resistant to oxidation, suphidization, and corrosion in air. When polished they retain a high degree of reflectivity. Their relatively great strength assures their reliability in holding precious stones in settings. Palladium is less expensive than platinum. Palladium that has been hardened with ruthenium is now commonly used by the jewelry industry for diamond settings in white gold rings, because of its strength and because its whiteness enhances the appearance of the diamond. Palladium is less dense than platinum or gold, therefore larger jewelry can be made with less weight. Palladium is added to gold and silver alloys to improve tarnish resistance. Rhodium is the whitest, the most reflective, and tarnish resistant of the platinum metals and is used for plating silver and other metals. Iridium and ruthenium are used mainly as alloying metals.

The main problem in the use of the platinum metals is their high melting point which requires a hotter flame than is needed with other jewelry metals. About 1856 the invention of the oxyhydrogen torch made possible the attainment of the high temperatures needed to solder, melt, and cast them. Today soldering and melting are accomplished with a torch using oxygen plus one of the fuel gases (oxyacetylene is favored). Hollowed-out, solid *lime blocks* or *zircon refractory crucibles* are used for melting and casting platinum and palladium. Crucibles containing silicon are avoided as they contaminate these metals and cause them to be hot-short or brittle when heated. Just before casting, the metal is deoxidized with 0.05% calcium boride. Synthetic graphite or pure copper ingot molds are used.

Platinum and palladium when pure are moderately hard, and the addition of up to 5% of alloying metals iridium, rhodium, ruthenium, gold, silver, or copper makes them even harder. Pure or alloyed, these metals are highly ductile and malleable, and can be beaten in the same way as gold into leaf ⅟₂₀₀,₀₀₀ in (0.000127 mm) thick. They can be worked in all cold working techniques including rolling, forging, spinning, and drawing, the latter using dry soap powder as a lubricant. They work harden more quickly than gold or silver and must be given intermediate anneals when this happens. If steel hammers have been used on them, or if they have come into contact with other steel tools, before annealing they must be *pickled* in hot hydrochloric acid to remove surface iron traces which otherwise will diffuse into the metals during heating and contaminate them, and the iron is not removable. Platinum and its alloys are annealed in an oxidizing atmosphere, but palladium is annealed with nitrogen or hydrogen fuels because oxygen dissolves into it. Platinum is

annealed to a white heat; palladium to redness. (Palladium develops a bluish surface oxide when red hot, but this disappears as the metal is heated further, as in soldering.) After annealing temperature is reached, both are quenched immediately in water. When palladium is quenched, the blue surface oxide is removed. Recommended annealing temperatures for these metals range from 1650°–2010° F (898°–1098° C), depending on whether the metal is pure or alloyed.

PLATINUM AND PALLADIUM SOLDERS

Refiners manufacture a wide range of solders for use with platinum, palladium, and their alloys. Solders are binary or ternary alloys. Some contain 60–70% gold and the remainder is platinum, palladium, related metals, or silver. The composition is designed to be white in color, and have a melting point high enough for use with these high-melting metals. From highest to lowest melting point, the common solders available in the U.S.A. are the following:

Platinum and Palladium Solder Types with Melting Temperatures

	°F	°C
Iridio Welding	3092	1700
Welding	2912	1600
Extra hard	2732	1500
Hard	2552	1400
Medium hard	2372	1300
Medium	2192	1200
Soft	2012	1100
Extra soft	1832	1000

Of these, the solders that melt at high temperatures have a platinum base. Others are normally palladium based, but other alloying metals such as gold, silver, or copper are used, each giving the result some special property. The solders most commonly used in jewelry making are in the melting range of 2372–2732° F (1300–1500° C). The first soldering starts with solder having the highest melting point, and those that follow melt at about 212° F (100° C) lower than the last used. Soft and extra soft solders with the lowest melting points are used for repairs. Fine gold can be used as solder if the color difference is unimportant. Platinum and palladium heated with an oxyhydrogen flame can be hammer welded at red heat temperatures, about 2282° F (1250° C).

SOLDERING PLATINUM, PALLADIUM, AND THEIR ALLOYS

Cleanliness is very important, as is a well-fitting joint. Lightly file the joint parts to prepare them for soldering. Place very small pieces of solder at the joint. Use *proprietary fluxes* for the platinum metals, or use self-pickling gold flux.

Unlike gold or silver, platinum and its alloys (but not palladium in a pure state) are highly resistant to oxidation in air at high temperatures. *Oxidizing conditions* are maintained throughout heat processes to avoid contamination. Hot reducing flames are *avoided* with platinum alloys because they make the surface brittle, and almost always result in contamination. Oxidizing flames leave the surface smooth and in a condition that is easily polished. Because the high-temperature white heat used in soldering and melting platinum is harmful to the eyes, protect them by

10–1 *TYPICAL 1-DWT PACKETS OF PRECIOUS METAL SOLDERS.*

wearing *dark* or *blue glass goggles* when these processes are carried out.

Do *not* use a compressed air and gas flame as it is not hot enough. Instead, use natural gas-oxygen, or oxy-acetylene (which produces the best surface), and an *oxidizing flame*. Heat the joint slowly with a small, hot, localized flame, and *avoid overheating*. Since platinum and its alloys do not oxidize after being heated, postsoldering pickling is not necessary until the *last* heat operation is completed. The object is then pickled in hot hydrochloric acid to dissolve any adhering flux. The platinum metals are highly resistant to normal 10% solutions of nitric and sulphuric acid used with gold and silver, but are attacked by and soluble in *aqua regia* (a mixture of nitric and hydrochloric acid). Palladium is attacked by and soluble in strong nitric acid solutions.

STAMPING PLATINUM AND ITS ALLOYS FOR QUALITY AND CONTENT

In the U.S.A., approximately 14% of the platinum and 10% of the palladium available are used for jewelry. The rest is used for a great many industrial and electrical purposes. The regulations concerning the stamping of jewelry made of platinum are based on platinum that uses iridium as a hardener in the alloy. Regulations are not provided for other platinum and palladium alloys which are widely used in Europe. Soldered platinum articles must contain a minimum of 95% platinum metals and those without solder (cast), a minimum of 98.5%. If the alloying metal is more than 5%, the word for the dominating alloying metal is placed before the word platinum in the stamp, as for example "Iridium-platinum," and the alloy must have a content of at least 75% platinum. For an object to be stamped palladium it must contain 98.5% if unsoldered (cast) and 95% if soldered.

GOLD

Gold–Atomic symbol and number: Au 79
  Atomic weight: 197.2
  Specific gravity: 19.32
  Melting point (fine):   1945.4° F (1063.0° C)
  Boiling point: 5380° F (2970° C)
  Casting temperature: 2000–2370° F (1100–1300° C)

The purest gold is .9995+ fine, is called "proof gold," and is used for standardizing purposes. For use in jewelry, gold is refined to 0.997+, and is called "fine gold."

GOLD AND THE KARAT

Pure gold is too soft to be used for jewelry as it is subject to rapid abrasion. It is therefore alloyed with other metals to make it harder, to produce a cheaper alloy of a specific quality, or one having a distinct color. For purposes of identification and quality control, the percentage of gold in all gold alloys is standardized, though the amount of the other metals the alloy contains is not. This fractional gold percentage or *proportion* is termed its *karat content*, which is abbreviated as "K" in the U.S.A., preceded by a number that indicates a specific quality, as in "18K."

A confusion exists between the word *karat* as a term that indicates the *proportion of gold content* to that of alloying metals in a particular alloy, and *carat* which is a *unit of weight measurement* for precious stones, such as diamonds, pearls, and others. The term *carat* and its ab-

breviation "C" (or sometimes "ct") is given in some dictionaries to indicate *both* uses, probably because the word *carat* has *both* meanings in British usage. To avoid confusion, as their meanings are not synonymous, there should be an international agreement to use the word *karat* and *carat* and their abbreviations "K" and "C" for these separate and distinct meanings.

The term *carat*, incidentally, is derived from the name of the bean of the carob tree (*Ceratonia siliqua*) of the Mediterranean region, which grows in the form of a long pod containing small seeds. The pod and its contents are called *carob*, or commonly "St. John's bread." Because of their uniformity of weight, these seeds were long ago adopted as a standard of weight for precious substances. Today *one carat* equals 3.086 g tr, or 200 mg in the International Metric Carat measuring system used for stone weight measurements. accepted in 1913 in the U.S.A. but widely used prior to that in Europe. The carat is divided into four grains, each 50 mg, sometimes called *carat grains*.

THE PROPORTIONATE FINENESS OF GOLD ALLOYS IN TERMS OF KARAT Pure gold is expressed as *24 karat:* 24K is 100% gold or fine gold. Qualities below this are divided into 24 parts to express their *proportionate degree of fineness*. The standardized proportions universally used in alloys of gold are shown in the table below. One karat is a 24th portion of the total weight of the alloy. The remainder is the alloying metal or metals.

GOLD ALLOYS

The gold alloys used in jewelry are described by *karat* and *color*. Gold can be alloyed with most metals, and in any proportion. The proportion and metal(s) used determines the color of the alloy, its working qualities, and its suitability for use in fabrication, casting, or enameling.

Gold and Alloy Percentage in Standard Karat Gold Alloys

Gold Karat		Alloy	
Parts	Percent	Parts	Percent
24	100.00	1	4.17
23	95.83	2	8.33
22	91.67	3	12.50
21	87.50	4	16.67
20	83.33	5	20.83
19	79.17	6	25.00
18	75.00	7	29.17
17	70.83	8	33.33
16	66.67	9	37.50
15	62.50	10	41.67
14	58.33	11	45.83
13	54.17	12	50.00
12	50.00	13	54.17
11	45.83	14	58.33
10	41.67	15	62.50
9	37.50	16	66.67
8	33.33	17	70.83
7	29.17	18	75.00
6	25.00	19	79.17
5	20.83	20	83.33
4	16.67	21	87.50
3	12.50	22	91.67
2	8.33	23	95.83
1	4.17	24	100.00

The colors of gold alloys generally fall into the color groups red, yellow, green, and white. Other colored alloys exist, but are rarely used. Most colored alloys used in jewelry are *ternary alloys,* meaning the alloy contains three metals. The most common combination is gold, silver, and copper. Small amounts of other metals are added to create special colors, or to alter the working qualities of the alloy in some way. For example, zinc is added as a deoxidizer, to lower the melting temperature, to reduce hardening upon cooling in air, and to lighten the alloy color (it makes reddish alloys yellower). Although all alloys of a *given karat* have the same gold content, the alloying metals may be in different proportions and change the mechanical qualities of the alloy.

In the U.S.A. 14K yellow gold is the color and quality most favored and used, and white gold is second. In Europe, 18K yellow gold is most favored. In India only 22K gold is used. The widest color range is available in 14K and 10K gold alloys, controlled by the ratio of silver to copper. Yellow golds are the easiest to work. High-karat white golds which were first offered as a substitute for platinum are the most difficult to work with as they are brittle and subject to fire cracking. White gold is often rhodium plated by electrodeposition to provide a bright, nontarnishing finish.

Gold of 18K is very resistant to tarnishing, but 14K and lesser karat golds tarnish slowly in air. The lower the karat the more rapid the tarnishing rate, though this may not be obvious in their appearances because of their color. Tarnish on gold jewelry is greatest on people who perspire and it shows as a dark smudge on their skin. This happens because perspiration contains sodium chloride and other salts and these interact with the high silver and copper content in low-alloy golds to form a dark salt deposit that due to friction appears on the contacting skin. Such persons should avoid using jewelry with low-karat gold alloys.

Because of the many different alloys and the wide range of karat purity, only a *sampling* can be given here of the components of some gold alloys. These alloys are expressed in terms of parts per 100 or the percentage of any alloying portion.

GOLD ALLOY COMPOSITIONS

Yellow gold, 22K
 Au 91.67–Ag 5–Cu 2–Zn 1.33

Red gold, 18K
 Red: Au 75–Cu 25
 Rose: Au 75–Cu 22.25–Ag 2.75
 Pink: Au 75–Cu 20–Ag 5

Yellow gold, 14K
 For enameling: Au 58.33–Cu 29.7–Ag 10.0–Zn 1.97
 All-purpose: Au 58.33–Cu 29.2–Ag 8.3–Zn 4.17
 Standard: Au 58.33–Cu 31.2–Ag 4.0–Zn 6.47
 Casting: Au 58.33–Cu 30.0–Ag 5.0–Zn 6.67

Green gold, 18K
 Green, soft: Au 75–Ag 25
 Light green: Au 75–Cu 23–Cd 2
 Green: Au 75–Ag 20–Cu 5
 Deep green: Au 75–Cu 6–Ag 15–Cd 4
 Blue: Au 75–Fe 25
 Purple: Au 80–Al 20

Gold, 12K
 Red: Au 50–Cu 50
 Yellow: Au 50–Cu 34–Ag 16
 Yellow: Au 50–Cu 40–Ag 10
 Green, soft: Au 50–Cu 6–Ag 44
 Dark green: Au 50–Cu 10–Ag 40

White gold, 18K
 White: Au 75–Pt or Pd 25
 White: Au 75–Pd 10–Ni 10–Zn 5
 Gray white: Au 75–Cu 8–Fe 17
 Blue white: Au 75–Fe 25

White gold, 14K
 Casting: Au 58.33–Cu 22.1–Ni 10.8–Zn 8.77
 All-purpose: Au 58.33–Cu 23.5–Ni 12.2–Zn 5.97

White gold, 10K
 All-purpose: Au 41.67–Cu 32.8–Ni 17.1–Zn 8.4

GOLD SOLDERS

Gold solders are alloys of gold, copper, and silver, and some also contain small amounts of the lower melting metals cadmium, bismuth, zinc, or tin. The percentage of the metals in their composition is designed to make the solder match the color of the karat gold on which they are used so that soldered joins are not visible. The lower melting metals such as electrolytic pure zinc also reduce the melting point of the solder alloy, but beyond a certain percentage solder brittleness increases. Each solder alloy designated for use with a particular karat gold will flow at a lower melting point than that designated alloy gold. The best choice of solder has a temperature differential approximately 212° F (100° C) below the fusion temperature of the alloy being soldered. Compositions are made suited to use with almost any type of gold color and alloy which makes the maintenance of quality standard and acceptable joint strength an easy matter. Most gold solders assay at 0.50–0.75 karat *below* their designated karat number. When a gold article is stamped, the allowance for the content of the solder is only *one percent.*

When gold solder is prepared, the copper and silver are melted first under a cover of carbon boride flux, the lower melting metals are melted separately under a zinc chloride flux, then all are combined with the molten gold under a carbon boride flux, covered to exclude atmospheric oxygen, and poured into an *ingot mold.* When cool, the ingot taken from the mold is rolled to sheet or wire of the desired thickness. When the metals copper and silver are added to gold, even though separately the melting points of these metals are high, their combined melting point in the solder is lower. As the gold content in the solder alloy decreases, the melting point also decreases.

Typical Gold Solder Compositions

Type	Composition			Melting Point Range	
	Gold	Silver	Copper	°F	°C
Low karat	45	30-35	15-20	1146-1500	619-816
General purpose	60	12-22	12-22	1335-1535	724-835
High karat	80	3-8	8-12	1374-1617	746-871

All these contain from 2-3% Sn and from 2-4% Zn.

Some craftspersons use a gold alloy two or more karats lower than the gold to be soldered instead of using an available or self-prepared solder. Thus an object of 18K gold is soldered with 16 or 15K gold; 14K with 12 or 10K. The lower karat gold melts at a lower temperature, and its color can be chosen to match that of the gold being soldered.

White gold solders contain the same metals as the white gold alloy they are used with, but their proportions differ. Because white golds have comparatively high melting points, soldering them must be carried out with care. White gold solders are purchased ready-made from the same refining company from whom the white gold alloy is bought because their compositions must match, and each refiner makes its own solder. Instructions for their use are available from the manufacturer.

Extra easy: For repairs and final soldering.
Easy: For repairs and secondary soldering.
Hard: For general purpose, color matching, and sizing.
Very hard: For enameling and casework.
Welding: For use in spot welding.

FORMS OF GOLD SOLDER When ordering gold solder, state the *color* and the *karat* of the gold to be soldered. Gold solders are available in conventional one-pennyweight (dwt) pieces which is a sheet ¼ in × ¼ in × ¹⁄₁₀₀ in (0.6 cm × 0.6 cm × 0.0254 cm), 30 gauge B. & S., a standard thickness. Sheets are stamped with the color and karat with which they are used. Gold solder is also available in 10 dwt amounts of preclipped wire packed in bottles; in strip, wire, machine-cut pieces, and powder. Always store each quality and color gold solder in a separate, clearly labeled container.

GOLD SOLDERING When soldering gold alloys, first coat the object by dipping it into or painting it with an *antiox-idizing medium* such as boric acid in alcohol in the form of a thin paste to prevent its surface from becoming oxidized due to heat. Use the highest karat gold solder possible with the gold being soldered, and a color that matches the object. To select the solder most suitable, you should know the karat of the gold you use and its melting point, as well as that of the solder used with it.

The same principles and practices used when soldering silver with silver hard solders and when pickling, apply to gold and gold solders. Joints should be well fitting, surfaces clean, well fluxed, and a reducing flame should be used. Do not flood the joint with solder, but use the smallest amount of solder that will do the job. Paste fluxes that fuse at high temperatures are made for use with gold, but ordinary borax mixed with alcohol to a thick paste can also be used. A most suitable flux for use with gold hard solders that melt above 1400° F (760° C) is made from *borax glass*. This is borax fritted or presmelted by placing it in a crucible and heating it to fusion, when it becomes a transparent glass, to drive off all mechanically and chemically combined water. It is then ground to a powder and mixed with alcohol. Gum tragacanth can be added to help hold the solder to difficult places. As in the case of all soldering operations, but especially when fluxes containing alcohol are used, *good ventilation* is essential to draw away fumes which may be toxic to sensitive persons.

If several solderings are necessary on the same work, start with the hardest solder and proceed to the softest. Use a solder thinner than the object being joined. Solder in a darkened area and watch the *solder* for an indication of heat readiness. *Do not watch the color of the metal* because gold does not show redness until shortly before its melting and collapsing point is reached. When soldering an article made of a combination of gold and silver, use silver hard solder or gold easy solder to avoid overheating and melting the silver.

Karat Gold Solders and the Gold Qualities Used with Them

	Yellow Gold			F°		C°	
Type	Karat	Color	Use with	Melt	Flow	Melt	Flow
Extra easy	6k	Light	Any k	1215	1285	657	696
	8k	”	10 & 14k	1165	1275	629	690
	10k	”	10 & 14k	1190	1295	643	701
Easy	8k	”	10 & 14k	1065	1315	573	712
	10k	Pale	10 & 14k	1335	1380	723	748
	14k	”	14 & 18k	1330	1390	721	754
Hard	8k	Light	10 & 14k	1360	1485	737	807
	10k	Yellow	10 & 14k	1225	1475	662	801
	10k	”	14k	1425	1485	773	807
	12k	”	18k	1465	1520	796	826
Very hard	6k	Pale	10 & 14k	1340	1405	726	726
	8k	”	10 & 14k	1370	1435	743	779
	10k	”	14k	1395	1450	757	886
	14k	”	18k	1460	1525	793	829
Welding	10k	”	14k	1430	1470	776	798
	12k	”	14k	1465	1510	796	821
	White Gold						
Easy	6k	White	Any k	1280	1395	693	757
	10k	”	10 & 14k	1295	1350	718	732
	14k	”	14 & 18k	1300	1375	704	746
Hard	8k	”	10k	1330	1450	721	787
	12k	”	10 & 14k	1335	1440	723	782
	16k	”	14 & 18k	1325	1490	718	810
	19k	”	18k	1440	1640	782	893

Handy and Harman

GOLD QUENCHING After annealing to a dull red, yellow, red, and green, gold 14K and above can be air cooled or quenched hot. White gold should be allowed to cool before quenching to avoid its cracking. Red gold is quenched hot to avoid hardening.

SILVER

Silver–Atomic symbol and number: Ag 47
    Atomic weight: 107.8
    Specific gravity: 10.49
    Melting point: 1760.9° F (960.5° C)

Fine: Ag 99.9 + trace metals

Britannia silver: Ag 95.84–Cu 4.16
    Melting point: 1688° F (920° C)

Sterling: Ag 92.5–Cu 7.5
    Melting point: 1640° F (893° C)

Coin silver: Ag 90–Cu 10
    Melting point: 1607° F (875° C)

European silver: Ag 83–Cu 17
    Melting point: 1525.8° F (829.8° C)

European silver: Ag 80–Cu 20
    Melting point: 1507° F (819.4° C)

High fine silver is 0.9995+ pure or higher. It is used for laboratory purposes.

Fine silver contains at least 0.9990 parts silver, the remainder being very small amounts of copper, iron, lead, and traces of other metals. It is available in bars, as bean grain, flake, powder, sheet, strip, foil, wire, rod, and tubing, as is sterling silver.

Britannia silver is an alloy of high silver content introduced in Great Britain for use in holloware for which it is still occasionally used. It is too soft for general jewelry usage.

Sterling silver, called *standard silver* in Great Britain, is the most common silver alloy used for jewelry, holloware, and flatware in the U.S.A. and Great Britain, as well as in other countries. Because fine silver is too soft for most uses, this alloy was developed by adding 7.5 parts copper to 92.5 parts silver which results in an alloy of suitable hardness and with good working qualities. The name "sterling" comes from the fact that the silver coinage of Great Britain before 1920 was of this standard. Because of the increase in the value of silver, it is no longer used as coinage there, or in other countries. The U.S. Stamping Law requires that for an object to qualify being stamped "Sterling" it must assay at least 0.921, and with soldered parts, the entire article must assay at least 0.915.

Coin silver as this term is used in the U.S.A. is a 90% silver alloy which was the standard for the silver content in U.S. coinage in the past, but is no longer used for this purpose. The term remains, however, and this alloy is occasionally used in jewelry.

Continental European silver of 83% and 80% alloy standards are today commonly accepted and used by many European countries for jewelry, holloware, and flatware. These standards have been agreed upon by the signatory nations of the 1972 Vienna Convention on the control and marking of articles made of precious metals. Articles made of these qualities are so stamped.

All these silver alloys can be soldered without difficulty, provided that the proper preparations, procedure, and type of solder are employed.

SILVER SOLDER, HARD SOLDER, OR SILVER BRAZING ALLOYS

Silver solders or hard solders, also called silver brazing alloys, are termed *silver solders* because their main component is *silver,* and they are designed mainly for use on silver. They are also free-flowing solders as opposed to braze welding alloys which are bead forming. Silver solders can be *binary alloys* of silver and copper (the best contains silver 72% and copper 28% and melts at 1433° F [778° C]). More generally they are *ternary alloys* containing silver, copper, and zinc, each as pure as possible. The proportions of these metals vary to make solders that have different melting points. As the silver content decreases, they become increasingly yellowish. As the zinc content rises, the alloy becomes more brittle. All silver solders are intended for use with, and to approximate the color of sterling silver. Some contain additional small amounts of other metals which are introduced to make an alloy with special characteristics, or to affect color, strength, or fusibility. These alloys are calculated to provide the jeweler with a melting range that falls between their melting point and their flow point, from 35–150° F (1.6–65° C) in the examples given below. This gives the jeweler some leeway in the control of solder flow.

The *melting point* or *solidus* of a metal is the temperature at which melting begins during heating, or at which the metal finishes freezing upon cooling; the *flow point* or *liquidus* is the temperature at which melting is complete during heating, or at which freezing starts during cooling.

STEP SOLDERING The classification of solders according to their melting point is helpful because they are commonly used to perform *sequential* or *step soldering operations.* In this technique, when a series of soldering operations are anticipated on a single object, they are performed employing first the hardest, and last the softest solder, in sequence, in order to avoid melting previously made joints. In general, however, when only one solder is used, it is good practice to use the solder that melts at the lowest melting point possible in order to reduce the chance of overheating the metal. When special strength is needed, medium or hard solder is used. Hard solders are used on silver, but can also be used on gold alloys in circumstances where the solder is not seen and color matching is not a consideration. They are also used on nearly all nonferrous metals and their alloys with which they have an affinity. Because of their zinc content, they can also be used on iron and steel, and on nickel alloys as well, though they do not work as well on these metals as on the precious and nonferrous metals.

THE BASIC HARD SOLDER TYPES:
IT: This is the solder with the highest melting point. It is used for casework, and on an object that will be enameled after soldering. Enameled metal requires a solder that melts at a temperature higher than that needed to fuse enamels, as otherwise the solder will flow and interfere with the enamel, possibly creating tensions that will cause the enamel to crack. Care must be exercised in the use of this high-melting solder as its flow point is close to the melting point of sterling silver.

Hard: This solder is used for a first solder in step soldering, when a work has many joints and must pass through more than two separate solderings. In such cases, for each soldering, a solder with a lower melting temperature is used than was used in the previous solder-

Silver Solder Compositions (Silver Brazing Alloys)

Solder	Component Percentage				°F		°C		Color
	Ag	Cu	Zn	Other	Melting	Flow	Melting	Flow	
IT	80	16	4		1330	1490	721	810	White
Hard	75	22	3		1365	1450	740.5	787	White
(Braze 750)									
Medium	70	20	10		1275	1360	690.5	737.7	White
(Braze 700)									
Easy	65	20	15		1240	1325	671	718.3	Gray-white
(Braze 650)									
Ready flow	56	22	17	5Sn	1165	1200	629	665	Gray-white
Easy flow	50	15.5	15.5	16Cd 3Ni	1170	1270	615	687	Yellowish

Handy and Harman

10–2 PLATINUM, GOLD, AND SILVER SOLDERS
Solder is available in sheet, rod, wire, strip, clipped, powder, paste, and 1 dwt sheet forms. Photo: Courtesy Myron Toback, Inc.

ing. Hard solder would be followed by medium, and then easy.

Medium: This is a general-purpose solder, frequently used before easy solder as its melting point is sufficiently above that of easy solder to keep it from melting when the latter flows.

Easy: This is used when there are only a few joins that are *spaced relatively wide apart.* It is also used as a last sol-der in step soldering. It flows easily, and is deeply penetrating.

Ready-flow and *easy-flow:* These solders have the lowest melting point of hard solders, and are generally used for repair work. Because their silver content is so low, they are yellowish and approach the color of brasses.

FORMS OF SILVER SOLDER These malleable and ductile solders are available in *sheet* 2 in × 6 in (5.1 cm × 15.2

cm), 26 gauge B.&S., weighing approximately 1 ounce; in *strip* ¼, 26 gauge B.&S., weighing ¼ ounce per foot; in *stick* ⅛ in × 20 in (0.32 cm × 50.8 cm), 20 gauge B.&S., and ⅙ in × 20 in (0.4 cm × 50.8 cm), 20 gauge B.&S.; and in *wire, clipped,* and *powder* forms. When ordering, specify the type of solder wanted, its gauge and dimensions. A new form of solder is combined with a binder and flux in a paste, housed in a plastic, hypodermic-type dispenser from which it is ejected directly onto the work. (See Solder Paste, p. 404.)

JUDGING APPROXIMATE TEMPERATURE OF HEATED SILVER BY COLOR A way of judging the approximate temperature of silver when heated during soldering is by its color. Color appears first at the edges of sheet metal and the ends of wire, and is best seen if soldering takes place in a darkened area. The first visible red color occurs at 900° F (482° C). At 1200° F (648° C) silver is a dull red, and at 1400° F (760° C) it is cherry red. At this temperature ordinary borax becomes fluid. At 1500° F (815° C) silver is orange red. Do not unintentionally heat silver above this point as it starts to break down structurally as grain size increases, and sterling will collapse and melt at 1640° F (893° C).

SPELTER SOLDERS

Spelter solders are alloys of copper and zinc in about equal proportions and are yellow in color. They are used to join objects of copper, bronze, and brass. Also used for their free-flowing properties are alloys called *phos-copper,* an alloy of phosphorus and copper that melts at 1380° F (748° C), and *sil-phos* an alloy of silver, copper, and phosphorus that melts at 1300° F (704° C). These are all used with the same fluxes as for silver hard solders, and the methods are the same. Higher melting spelters are also available that are melted with acetylene welding torches, but these are unsuited to jewelry making.

For those situations when copper, bronze, or brass objects must be joined by soldering, silver hard solders can of course be used. Seams can be almost invisible if the joint is tight fitting. Spelter solders are often used with these metals because the color more closely approximates them. If necessary, seams can be concealed by copper plating copper objects, and in finishing, color-oxidation chemicals can be used.

PREPARING YOUR OWN SOLDER

In the West, and in highly industrialized countries, all solders are available ready-made from manufacturers and refiners or through jewelers' supply houses. This happy state of affairs is *not universal* in other places in the world where jewelers commonly prepare their own solders and do not think they are suffering a hardship. There are occasions when any jeweler may wish to make his or her own soldering alloy: to be certain of a solder's contents, when the supply of solder runs out and cannot be immediately replenished, or for the simple satisfaction of the experience.

The preparation of a solder alloy is no more difficult or mysterious than the preparation of any other alloy. Once you know the composition and formulas of the alloys, which are all available, the basic procedure is to melt them, one at a time, in a crucible, *in order of their melting point*—highest first, followed by the next lower, and the lowest. Take care not to overheat or prolong the melting unnecessarily, especially when the lower melting metals are added or they will volatize and change the nature of

the alloy. While playing a reduced flame on the crucible's contents, sprinkle a pinch of flux on the molten metal surface, stir with a *graphite stirring rod,* and when they are well mixed, pour the crucible's contents into a *small, heated ingot mold* with the reduced flame playing on the alloy. *Do not pour molten metal into a cold mold* or it will spatter. Allow the ingot to cool and completely solidify, quench it, dry it, and run it through the *rolling mill* to form a sheet of the required thickness, usually about 24 gauge B.&S. Because solder alloys are malleable and ductile, they can be rolled into rod, stick, or wire form by using the wire rolls of the rolling mill; they can also be rolled into sheet; and strip can be made by passing a wire through the flat rolls to flatten it.

MARKING, CUTTING, AND STORING SOLDER SNIPPETS

MARKING The most common solder form used in jewelry making is as snippets cut from strip or sheet solder. The jeweler usually uses at least three grades of silver solder hardness: hard, medium, and easy-flow, and a harder IT grade for work that must be enameled.

Before cutting solder into small pieces, some *hardness identification system* for marking the solder sheet or strip should be decided upon, and *thereafter followed consistently*. Any marking system can be used. Sheet or strip can be *letter stamped* with a code letter, such as IT, H, M, E (IT, hard, medium, and easy-flow). A system of *dots,* stamped on the solder can be used if no letter stamps are available. Four dots for IT, three for hard, two for medium, and one for easy-flow.

CUTTING Before cutting, solder sheet or strip is cleaned by rubbing the surface with *steel wool* or a *paper abrasive.* Thereafter it should be handled with paper to avoid imparting finger grease to its surface. To cut snippets or *paillons* (from French *paille,* "spangle") use *solder snips.* The blades should open and close easily, but the handles should not be so loose as to fall together by their own weight because the cutting edges will not come together properly. If snips are not available, use *straight-bladed hand shears.* First cut a fringe about ¼ in (0.6 cm) into the sheet or strip end, making a series of parallel cuts from 1/32–1/16 in apart (1–2 mm). Hold the solder in the left hand with the index finger extended alongside the snips' or shears' blade along the top of the fringe to prevent snippets from flying, and hold the snips or shears in the right hand. A perpendicular cut across the fringe makes small rectangles. This shape of snippet is preferred as it can be placed lengthwise flat along seams, and will leave less *skull* or solder remnant after the solder flows. Allow the snippets to fall into a shallow cardboard box over which the cutting takes place. From there they are transferred into the appropriately labeled solder container. Cut only the approximate amount of snippets you anticipate using. Solder snippets that lie unused for extended time periods can become oxidized, causing soldering difficulties. Oxidation can be minimized by using an airtight container.

STORING Accidental substitutions of solder hardness can be disastrous. Therefore, always store solder snippets in the same place, and the container must be *clearly marked. Boxes* compartmented to hold different solder grades are available. Commonly solder is stored in small, clean, covered metal or plastic boxes, a separate one for each solder grade.

BASIC TYPES OF JOINTS

A *joint* is a place where two or more parts are united or made to fit together. The union can be permanent as when soldering, riveting, or welding, or movable as in other joining methods such as certain kinds of riveting, screwing, flanging, folding, and bending.

BUTT JOINTS In a butt joint, two ends come together squarely at their extremity without scarfing or chamfering.

LAP JOINTS In a lap joint, one part or layer overlaps another. A special type is a *sleeve joint* in which one tube fits inside another.

SCARF JOINTS In a scarf joint, the join is made by chamfering, beveling, notching, halving, or otherwise cutting the two parts so that they correspond with each other where they overlap. Such joints can also be made by the use of a *plate* that overlaps the joint and is secured by rivets.

All the joints shown here are made with the basic forms of metal used by the jeweler: sheet, wire, and tubing. Many of the situations illustrated can also be used when joining or assembling cast sections, or when combining cast and fabricated parts. In some cases, solder would not be needed, though it could be used. We do not include all conceivable combinations, as this is obviously impossible.

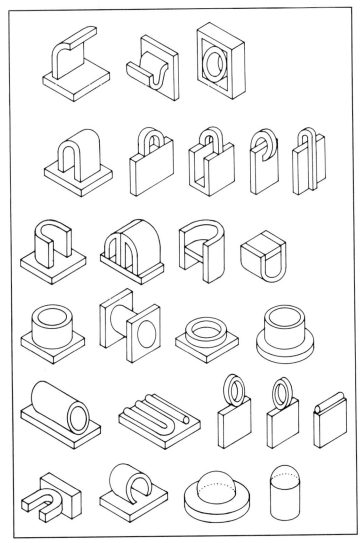

10–4 *BUTT JOINTS, CURVE TO FLAT.*

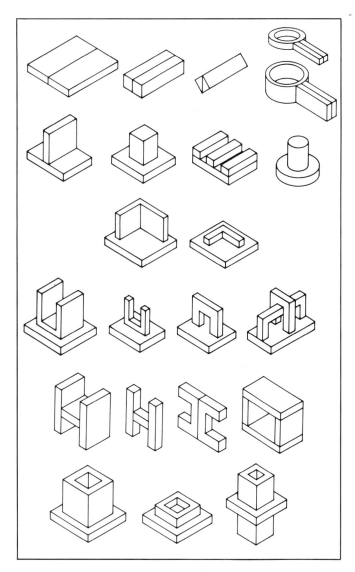

10–3 *BUTT JOINTS, FLAT TO FLAT.*

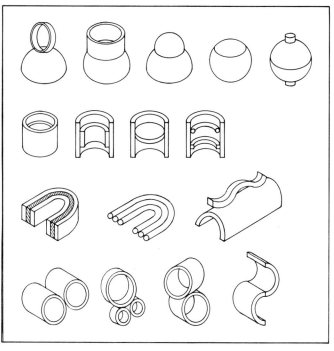

10–5 *BUTT JOINTS, CURVE TO CURVE.*

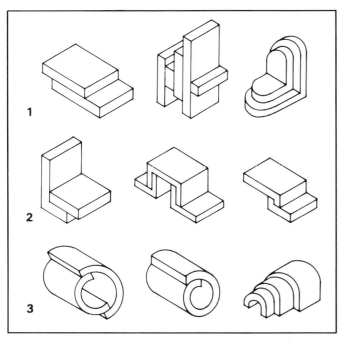

10–6　LAP JOINTS: 1. Flat to flat; 2. Corner lap; 3. Curve to curve.

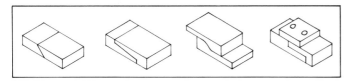

10–7　SCARF JOINTS.

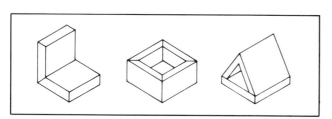

10–8　CHAMFERED OR BEVELED JOINTS.

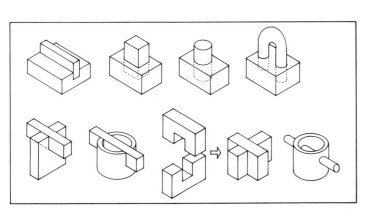

10–9　SLOT AND PENETRATION JOINTS.

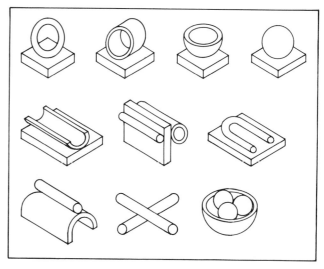

10–10　POINT- OR LINE-OF-CONTACT JOINTS.

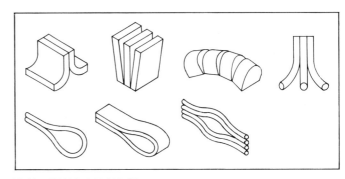

10–11　SPREAD GAP JOINTS
This consists of the joining of two forms only by their contacting edges or surfaces, their physical shape making larger surface contact impossible.

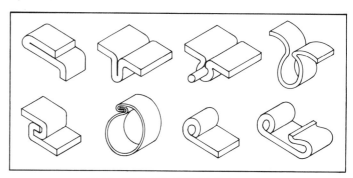

10–12　BEND AND FOLD JOINTS.

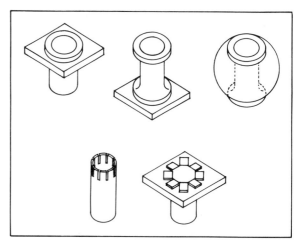

10–13　FLANGED JOINTS.

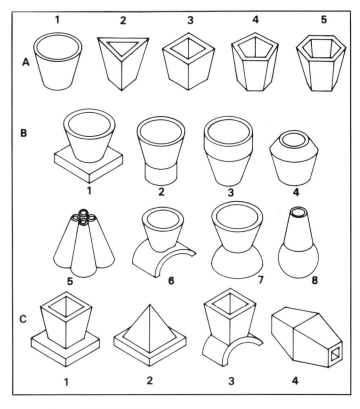

10-14 *FRUSTUM FORMS*
A. *Frustums of Common Geometric Figures*
1. Circle (cone); 2. Triangle (pyramid); 3. Square; 4. Pentagon;
5. Hexagon.
B. *Hollow-Cone Frustum Joints*
1. Cone to flat; 2. Cone to cylinder; 3. Cylinder to cone; 4. Cone
to cone; 5. Cone to cones; 6. Cone to curve; 7. Cone to dome;
8. Cone to ball.
C. *Hollow-Pyramid Frustum Joints*
1. Inverted pyramid frustum to flat; 2. Pointed pyramid to flat; 3.
Inverted pyramid frustum to curve; 4. Pyramid to pyramid.

The joint situations represent *basic concepts* that have
been used repeatedly in both historic and contemporary
metalwork and jewelry. In context, the forms need not be
simply geometric or abstract, but can be shapes or forms
using these principles. It is quite possible to create a
design for an entire piece of jewelry based on any single
joining concept shown here. A simple *change of scale* can
produce a completely different result, as can the repetition
of the same concept. Combinations of several joint types
and object forms can of course be used in the same work.

SOLDERING JIGS

A *soldering jig* is any device used in soldering to apply
pressure upon, fasten, support, or enclose a workpiece to
make it stationary, or to hold in position the parts being
soldered in cases where simple gravity alone cannot be
depended upon to do the job. This definition covers a wide
range of devices and systems, some made specifically for
this use, others improvised to suit circumstances. Jig
choice depends on the situation's requirements, and its
successful use may depend on the jeweler's experience and
ingenuity. As a general suggestion, the best jig to use is the
simplest one that will work.

Jig materials and techniques for their use vary widely.

Typical jig types and situations in which they are used are
discussed here. Sometimes tools or materials intended
primarily for other purposes can also be used as jigs.

BINDING WIRE

Soft iron binding wire is probably the most common soldering jig. It is available in spools or coils in 18–32 gauge
B.&S.; heavy-duty 18–22 gauge; medium-duty 24–26
gauge; light-duty 28–32 gauge. When lacking heavy-gauge
wire, several strands of a lighter gauge wire can be twisted
together.

When using iron wire as a jig, pass it around the parts
to be held or forced together, and twist the two ends together with pliers. To avoid causing dents in the object
from twist pressure, it is customary to also twist the wire
at a position opposite to the ends into a loop. When the
work is heated, this loop will give somewhat, allowing object and wire expansion. Another method used to allow for
expansion is to make a *kink* with pliers in the wire portion
passing around the object. (See Illustration 10–19). Place
the wire so it will not slip off the workpiece during soldering. Its position can sometimes be fixed by passing a second wire around the object crossing the first.

Whenever possible, wire jigs should not be placed where
they will be subject to a direct flame because they can
melt under high heat. Flame contact can be avoided by
choosing a flame direction that does not intercept binding
wires, or by placing the wire at a distance from the joint
being soldered. If a direct flame cannot be avoided, make
its duration on the wire as brief as possible by moving the
flame on the work.

Binding wire jigs help to make a close-fitting joint, but
must not be depended upon to excessively force together a
bad fit. Joints should *fit well from the start.* Wire jig pressure is meant to prevent parts from moving due to expansion during heating.

Remove all binding wire from the workpiece *before*
placing it in the pickle. Otherwise an electrolytic plating
action occurs in which silver is coated with a copper
flashing that is difficult and time-consuming to remove.
Also, the acid solution is rendered useless as it becomes
contaminated and must be discarded.

HEAVY WIRE

Heavy steel, nichrome, Monel metal, or other nickel
steel wire compositions are used to make rigid, temporary
supporting jigs. Nickel alloy wire is especially suitable as it
takes high heat without distortion or loss of strength. A
length can be used straight, or bent into a right angle, a
clip, or other shape with pliers. Such forms can be used to
hang work from the wire during soldering to permit heat
access below the workpiece, or to hold work supported
upright. Bent into a loop or U shape with ends cut
diagonally with *nippers* to make sharp end points, staple-
shaped wire jigs can be driven into a charcoal block or an
asbestos coil or board to hold down work.

PINS

Straight steel pins without or with small or large heads
can be used to hold work in place by forcing them into the
supporting refractory soldering surface, against the work
to immobilize it. *Cotter pins,* ready-made or made from a
heavy wire bent in half, can be used as a clip to hold parts
together, one leg passing above and the other below the
parts. Their ability to exert pressure is retained if a high

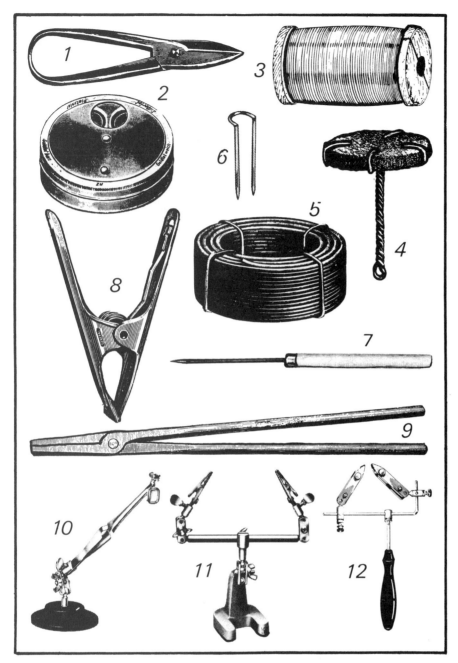

10–15 SOLDERING JIGS
1. *Solder-cutting snips,* 7 in long.
2. *Solder storage box* with revolving cover whose circular opening allows access to only one compartment at a time. (*Joliot*)
3. *Spool of soft iron binding wire* available in 16–30 gauge B.&S., in ¼ lb spools.
4. *Soldering mop,* nest, or wig, made of coiled iron binding wire, supported by a heavy-gauge wire handle and frame.
5. *Coil of heavy-gauge iron wire* used to hold work to a soldering surface when made into pins and supports.
6. *Wire pin* made of heavy-gauge iron wire, used to hold work to a soldering surface when soldered.
7. *Soldering pick* with wooden handle, made of a special, nonbreaking, hard alloy that permits shaping, used when soldering all precious metals with high melting points, without contamination. (*Swest*)
8. *Soldering clamp* with spring 4, 6, or 9 in long with 1, 2, or 3 in openings respectively. Can also be used to clamp other materials. (*Abbey*)
9. *Soldering pincers* or tongs, 6–8 in long.
10. *"Third-hand" soldering stand* on heavy base with self-locking or slide-locking tweezers mounted on a swivel joint that allows any work-holding position.
11. *Double alligator clamps* soldering stand with heavy base supporting a universal ball joint that permits any work-holding position.
12. Hand-held *Parker slide locking soldering clamp* with ball joint, that holds small parts at any angle while soldering.

melting point metal such as nichrome wire is used. (Cotter pins of other metals are used as a metalwork joining device, their legs inserted through a cotterway hole or slot, then bent in opposite directions at the back.)

SOLDERING NEST

A *soldering nest, soldering mop, soldering boss,* or *soldering wig* is a heavy steel supporting wire frame bent into a horizontal circle, then twisted below to form a handle. Over the circular part, a binding wire is wound or wrapped in all directions and hammered to form an intersecting, open wire mass resembling a bird's nest, mop, or wig. Work being soldered is either embedded in the wires of the nest, or bound to them with additional wire lengths. Its advantages are that the torch flame can be directed at the work from all directions; it can be hand held and turned during soldering; or propped upright.

RING STAND AND HEATING FRAME

A *three-legged ring stand* or *tripod* over which a *heating frame* is placed can also serve as a soldering jig. Work can be supported by laying it on the heating frame or iron, stainless steel, or nichrome wire mesh; or held to the mesh by binding wire. This device allows the torch flame to be directed toward the work from below, a form of induction heating used when direct heat is inadvisable.

SOLDERING TURNTABLES

A *soldering turntable* has a base and a shallow tray 6 in, 12 in, or 18 in (15.2 cm, 30.5 cm, or 45.7 cm) in diameter, mounted on bearings that permit the tray to revolve. The tray is filled with *small-lump refractory pumice* on which the work is placed during soldering or annealing, for which reason it is also sometimes called an *annealing pan.* By turning the tray, the flame can play uniformly over all workpiece parts. When it is used for annealing, the pumice holds the heat and the annealing temperature is quickly reached. A substitute can be improvised from a pumice-filled Chinese *wok* or hemispherical cooking pan placed on a ring and turned by its handles.

SOLDERING PICKS

A *soldering pick,* also called a *pointer, pike* or *spike,* is a straight, rodlike, pointed steel instrument, with or without an insulating handle. It can have one straight and one curved end, or only curved ends. This useful tool, easily improvised from an *old dental tool,* should be at hand ready for use in every soldering operation. Because steel melts at a much higher temperature than silver and gold solder, the pick does not run the danger of becoming molten or misshapen at the temperatures used to melt solders.

Soldering picks serve several uses. They can aid in solder flow by drawing the molten solder along a seam or into a cavity; replace a dislodged solder snippet that must be pushed back without stopping the heat flow; place pressure upon parts being soldered; and in other ways. By dipping the pick point in flux, it can be used to pick up and place a small premelted solder ball of suitable size just before soldering temperature is reached in cases where only a small amount of solder is needed, or where additional solder must quickly be added to a joint in a heated work.

MECHANICAL SOLDERING JIGS

Mechanical soldering jigs are any tools, devices or contrivances designed specifically for, or easily adaptable to the purpose of soldering.

TWEEZERS

Tweezers are pincerlike instruments used for acts of grasping, squeezing, twisting, extracting, or handling an object. Any kind of tweezer can be used as a soldering jig, but those with locking points are preferred to those without. *Plain steel soldering tweezers* available with flat-edged shanks; with points that are sharp, blunt, curved, spatulate, outward curved, or in other shapes can be used according to circumstances. When small work is soldered, it can be hand held with tweezers *in air* during soldering—a method used extensively by professional jewelers. If work must be held longer, tweezers are available with heat-resistant fiber grips, or gloves can be worn.

Self-locking or *cross-locking tweezers* have a spring lock. When pressure is applied on the gripping section, the points open; when released they close and lock on the work placed between them. Work can be held without paying attention to the act of constantly exerting pressure on it. Once locked on the work, they can be laid on the soldering surface, or placed in suspension above a heat source. They are available with different shaped points suited to various work situations. They are particularly useful when soldering chain links as one link can be isolated and held in air, while paying attention to the torch flame.

Slide-locking tweezers have an almain-type rivet permanently fitted into a groove at the center of both curved tweezer legs. By sliding the rivet toward the joined end, the points open; sliding it toward the points closes the legs

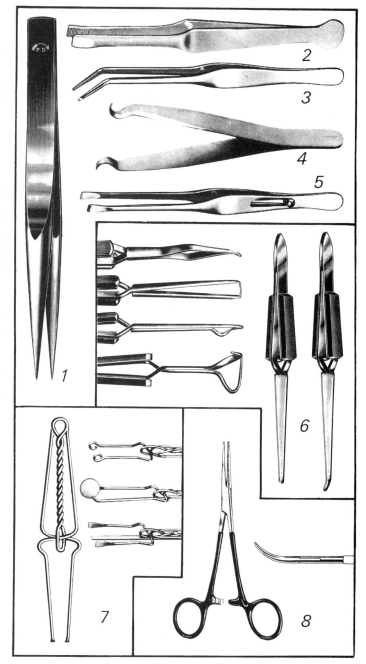

10–16 *TWEEZERS FOR SOLDERING AND OTHER USES*
1. *Pointed, heavyweight, 7 in long.*
2. *Square point, serrated, 5 in long.*
3. *Angle end, pointed, 6¾ in long.*
4. *Ring-holding, 5 in long.*
5. *Slide-locking, 6⅝ in long.*
6. *Self-locking, straight point, and angle point, fiber-insulated handles; various other point shapes, all approx. 6½ in long.*
7. *Self-locking, wire, flat point ³⁄₁₆ in wide; loop point Ø ¼ in; flat disc Ø ⅝ in opposed by right-angled point; flat point ³⁄₁₆ in with table rest leg; all approx. 5½ in long.*
8. *Straight, long-nosed, serrated-jaw clamp, locks in two positions; also available with curved end.*

on work inserted between them. The tweezer is then used as a handle on the work.

The so-called *"third-hand"* soldering stand consists of a heavy, cast iron base on which a swivel is mounted that holds one or two self-locking or slide-locking tweezers. The swivel allows work to be held in any position, freeing the jeweler's hands.

CLAMPS

A *clamp* is a device that holds parts together as a unit in a compression coupling by pressure brought to bear on the parts through a screw movement, a spring, or a wedge.

Special pairs of clamps are designed for use in soldering. The simpler one has two slide-lock clamp tweezers mounted on a bar by a swivel ball universal joint screwed to a bent bar, supported by a hand-held wooden handle. Another device follows the same basic construction principle, but the clamps are mounted on a stand or base that allows both hands freedom. This has spring-closing alligator jaws that open under pressure and close on the work when released, like a clamping clothespin. They are made of lightweight metal so do not conduct much heat away from the work they are holding.

SOLDERING MANDRELS

Refractory material mandrels are used as soldering jigs. One is a replaceable, tapered mandrel made of *carbon* or *graphite,* clamp mounted above an asbestos board. It holds forced-on rings in any position. Another is made of a tapered length of *asbestos,* about 8 in (20.3 cm) long, and is used in the same way.

PLIERS, PINCERS, TONGS, AND FORCEPS

Old pliers, otherwise useless, can be used to hold parts together during soldering. *Never* allow a good pair of pliers to be subjected to heat as they will lose their temper.

Pincers and tongs of small size can be used to hold work being soldered. As they do not have automatic holding systems, continuous pressure must be maintained.

Forceps used by surgeons, dentists, and watchmakers can be used for holding or exerting traction upon work. Clamp types with ratchet stops hold work securely while soldering takes place.

Heavy-gauge round iron wire or strip in 3–5 in lengths, bent with *pliers* to an angle to keep them stationary, can be used as props to raise a workpiece above the soldering surface and create a space below it that allows heat to flow there.

REFRACTORY MATERIALS USED FOR JIGS AND SOLDERING SURFACES

Refractory materials are nonmetallic substances that are resistant to the oxidation action of heat, are therefore poor conductors of heat, are not affected by reduction, and fuse with difficulty. This makes them suitable for use under conditions where high temperatures, as when soldering, must be withstood. Refractories are classified as *acid* (silica, fire clay); *basic* (magnesite, dolomite); or *neutral* (graphite, chromite), to correspond with the character of the contacting metal with which they are charged so that no chemical interaction occurs.

Refractory materials are available in powder form which can be converted into a paste or slurry that hardens, as grains that are loose or embedded in another material, or as a solid such as a sheet, block, or other form.

ASBESTOS

Asbestos is essentially a calcium-magnesium silicate that has the unique property of being incombustible and indestructible at red heat because of its poor conduction of

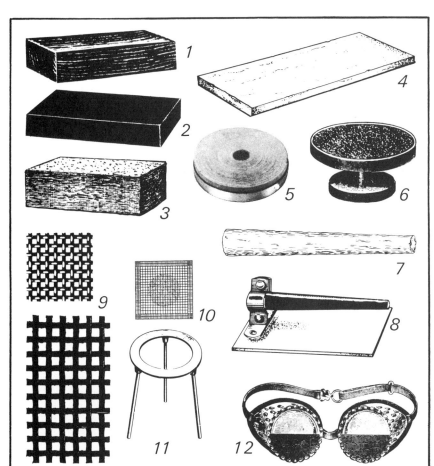

10–17 SOLDERING SURFACES
1. Charcoal soldering block.
2. Pressed charcoal block, longer lasting.
3. Magnesium soldering block, soft and porous to allow work being soldered to be pinned down upon or pressed into the surface, 6 × 3 × 12 in.
4. Hard asbestos board, ½ in thick, available 6 × 6 in, 12 × 12 in, and 12 × 24 in.
5. Spirally coiled asbestos strip in steel tray; Ø 5½ in; depth 1 in; allows work to be forced between coils or pinned down.
6. Rotary soldering and annealing pan on ball bearings, filled with lump pumice, Ø 12–18 in.
7. Asbestos ring mandrel on which rings are placed for soldering, leaving the hands free, length 8 in.
8. Carbon tapered mandrel ring-soldering stand, asbestos board base, with screwed clamps to allow replacement of the mandrel. It can accommodate rings from size 4 up, and can be used with an electric soldering machine. Length 6 in.
9. Investment spider or heating frame of steel wire, 18 and 10 gauge B.&S., 6 × 6 in, 12 × 12 in.
10. Wire heating frame with asbestos borders and center to spread the flame placed beneath it when it is on a ring stand. It can also be used flat on a charcoal or asbestos surface to allow heat flow beneath the work.
11. Tripod ring stand used with wire mesh heating frame when work must be heated from below. Can also be used with an alcohol lamp or Bunsen burner.
12. Goggles that can be worn during soldering to reduce glare and make solder flow more visible. Lower two thirds is dark glass, upper third clear.

heat. It is found in nature as a fibrous stone in the form of a hardened mass, long fibrous masses, or long silky fibers. These fibers are finely divided or powdered for manufacture into composition materials such as Portland cement, a nonconducting plaster. Another binding material, *transite board,* commonly used as a surface upon which heating can be done, is a proprietary composition and an example of such a combination. Asbestos fibers can also be spun into a yarn that is woven into cloth that is fireproof, such as the cloth used to make *asbestos gloves* which are worn when handling hot objects and when moving metals in crucibles after melting and casting. Asbestos boards can be cut to size and held together with angle irons, bolts and nuts to make a three-walled low partition or booth placed on a table to eliminate drafts from the soldering area. Asbestos in ½ in (1.27 cm) thick sheet or millboard is commonly used as a refractory surface for soldering. It is valued by jewelers because it is long lasting, does not expand or contract, and in small pieces can be hand held while soldering takes place upon it (a great convenience in certain circumstances). As already mentioned, it is also available in the form of a tapered mandrel upon which rings are placed for soldering. In the form of thin, flexible strip about 1 in (2.5 cm) wide, it is wound into a coil and placed in a shallow, round, metal receptacle to make an *asbestos coil soldering block.* Because of its construction, this has the advantage of allowing pins to be easily forced into it to hold work in place during soldering, or the work itself can sometimes be wedged between the coil layers to hold it stationary and upright. *Small pieces of asbestos* can be used to support or prop up work while it is being soldered. *Asbestos mulch,* made by adding water to a loose-fibered asbestos strip, can be packed around a stone to keep it cool while making a repair or working on another part of the object.

In recent years, research has indicated that there is a possibility that asbestos fiber dust inhaled into the lungs, where it remains and accumulates, in combination with irritants introduced into the system by smoking, creates a condition favorable to the development of cancer. High temperatures dissipate moisture in the form of steam, and may cause asbestos particles to enter the air and be inhaled. Therefore, keep an asbestos soldering surface dry, and avoid having wet substances such as flux permeate it. The chance of a nonsmoker, or a non-production jeweler being affected is small, but anyone who is constantly exposed to the presence of asbestos should use a substitute composition board in a hard form and should give up smoking.

Soldering boards to replace asbestos millboard are now available, made of a new material that involves no health hazard. A high-purity china clay is blown into an aluminosilicate ceramic fiber, and formed into hardened boards 0.4 in (10 mm) thick, or into blocks. This substance is very low in thermal conductivity, highly resistant to thermal shock, extremely stable at high temperatures up to 2300° F (1260° C), is completely noncombustible, and is unaffected by water, steam, or oil. One such product, called *Cerfi-Board* is available at Charles Cooper (Hatton Garden) Ltd., London.

CHARCOAL

Charcoal is a black, porous form of carbon prepared from animal or vegetable substances. The charcoal used by jewelers is made from dry wood with the bark removed since charcoal made from internal wood will not crackle

or cause flying sparks when subjected to heat. Charcoal is made today in a kiln from which air is excluded, in a reduced atmosphere. The resulting charcoal constitutes between 16–27% of the original weight of the wood used. It burns without smoke, but in impure forms it can also yield dangerous carbon monoxide gas which in sufficient amount can cause headaches and in large quantities can be lethal. *Always use charcoal in a well-ventilated room.* Unused charcoal is not subject to decay and can be saved for a long time. It burns slowly, but heat can be increased by fanning it or blowing air on it through a tube or bellows. Eventually it is completely consumed, leaving a gray ash residue. Most hardwoods produce good charcoal. There is a relationship between the structural quality of the wood grain and the resulting charcoal.

CHARCOAL CHARACTER FROM COMMON WOODS
Ash: shining black, spongy, firm
Beech: dull black, spongy, firm
Birch: velvety black, bulky, firm
Chestnut: glossy black, compact, firm
Elm: fine black, moderately firm
Holly: dull black, loose, bulky
Laburnum: dull black, compact, very hard
Mahogany: black tinged with brown, spongy, porous
Norway pine: shining black, bulky, very soft
Oak: Shining black, close, very firm
Sycamore: fine black, bulky, moderately firm
Walnut: dull black, close, firm

THE USES OF CHARCOAL
Charcoal has the longest history of use by jewelers as a refractory material. A bed of charcoal was and still is used as a heat source for smelting, making alloys, casting, cupellation, forging, and for almost any other metalworking or jewelry making process that requires heat. It was used as a surface upon which soldering, granulation, enameling, and nielloing were and still are done.

Work can be surrounded by charcoal blocks to confine and conserve the heat from a torch flame to a small area, prevent its dissipation, and therefore hasten the work's buildup of heat to soldering temperature. A charcoal block is soft enough and porous enough to allow work to be pinned to its surface in preparation for soldering. Before using a charcoal block, heat it with a torch to evaporate any moisture it has absorbed from the air—a practice that will prevent it from cracking in use. Because charcoal is a poor conductor of heat, professional jewelers often pick up and hold a block on which work has been placed while soldering. Blocks can be smoothed level with a *coarse file,* then carved, and a depression can serve as a unique, one-time mold into which molten metal is poured to make a casting. The charcoal obtained from some woods contains silica, and in a crushed form, is sometimes used as an abrasive to polish metals. In Japan it is used as a final polishing agent on cloisonné enamels.

FIREBRICK

Firebrick is hard or soft, made of highly refractory fireclay which is any natural clay having a fusion point greater than 2912° F (1600° C) so that it is capable of withstanding high temperatures. Soldering tables are sometimes made of hard firebrick for this reason. A typical composition is $Al_2O_3 \cdot 2SiO_2 \cdot 2H_2O$ (alumina, silica, and water). Single bricks or pieces of brick can be used to prop up work being soldered. Bricks can be used to make an enclosure that keeps drafts away from the soldering area. Covered crucibles made of firebrick are available for use in melting gold, which melts quickly in this container.

PEBBLE PUMICE

Pumice is a type of hardened volcanic glass froth full of minute air cavities which make it very light in weight. Pebble pumice (also called pea pumice or lump pumice), is a good refractory material used in soldering or annealing turntables. Work can be made to stand up wedged between the pebbles. Pumice in powder form is used as an abrasive and is available in various grades of coarseness for this purpose.

CARBORUNDUM GRAINS

Carborundum is a trade name for a synthetic silicon carbide (SiC) manufactured in very hard, black, iridescent crystals by heating carbon and sand together in an electric resistance furnace. In a crushed form in various grit sizes it is used as an abrasive for grinding purposes, bonded to cloth or paper backing or in grinding wheels. In its loose form the coarser grit such as No. 6 can be used as a refractory, placed in a container such as a chaser's bowl, an annealing tray, or a baking tray for use as a soldering surface. Because of its granular form, it has the advantage of allowing objects otherwise difficult to position for soldering to be embedded in the grain with only the part to be soldered protruding. It has a minor disadvantage in that it tends to draw some heat away from the work, and is therefore best used for small work such as rings.

REFRACTORY INVESTMENT PLASTER

The normal use of refractory investment plaster is in making molds used in lost wax casting techniques. Increasing use has been made of this material as a soldering aid. Its excellent refractory qualities allow it, once solidified and *dry,* to withstand high temperatures without crumbling, and this is essentially the reason for its use to hold metal parts to be soldered together in positions that otherwise would be very difficult to manage.

The parts are first held in position by sticky wax on a glass slab. The prepared investment plaster is brushed or dribbled around the parts to hold them in place, with the portions to be soldered left exposed. It may be necessary to construct a temporary retaining wall of lightweight cardboard around the object to hold the plaster slurry in place until it sets, at which time the cardboard is removed, and the assembly is removed from the glass slab.

The wax is removed manually if possible or scraped away. Any remaining wax melts when the plaster is then dried slowly with a mild torch flame. The plaster is dry enough when steam has ceased to rise. The exposed parts can then be cleaned by scraping off any plaster in the way of the seam and any wax residue. Soldering then takes place. After soldering, the plaster is washed away, leaving the joined metal parts. As such joints are generally made with otherwise unsupported parts, they are vulnerable to coming apart during future soldering unless supported.

FLUXES USED FOR SILVER OR HARD SOLDERING

In silver soldering the use of a *flux* is essential. The word *flux* comes from the Latin *fluxus,* "flow," and the function of flux is to aid solder to flow. *Flux* is any substance, or combination of substances capable of promoting the fusion of metals joined by the use of heat and a solder or metal filler.

Flux is used in soldering mainly because the temperature necessary for solder to melt and flow causes unpro-

10–18 *HARD SOLDERING FLUXES AND MATERIALS*
1. *Slate borax grinding dish,* 5 in square.
2. *Slate borax grinding dish,* round, Ø 5 in.
3. *Borax cake or junk,* approx. 2 oz; borax cone, approx. 4 oz.
4. *Flux paste* for nonferrous and ferrous metals and alloys.
5. *Sable brushes* for applying flux to joints to be soldered.
6. *Brass scratch brush* bound in metal holder, used to clean joints prior to soldering.
7. *Silver solder* combined with flux and organic binders in a viscous paste form, contained in plastic, disposable hypodermic-type syringe that allows the compound to be quickly dispensed to a precleaned joint with minimal waste. Contains ½ oz of solder plus flux and binder. Available in hard, medium, and easy-flow solder types.
8. *Battern's Self-Pickling Liquid Flux* for use with platinum, gold, and silver.
9. *Abgasflux,* a proprietary compound of borax flux in an alcohol base, used with a gas tank so that flux is deposited through the gas line onto the work, making fluxing the work unnecessary.
10. *Yellow ochre,* used as a solder inhibitor or antiflux, ½ lb can.
11. *Kool Jool,* a proprietary heat-sink compound paste used on work to protect soldered joints and stones from heat damage during soldering and in repair operations.
12. *Glass fiber scratch brush* used for cleaning metal prior to soldering, 50–100 g.

tected metal surfaces to oxidize readily. If such oxides are allowed to be present during soldering, they will inhibit the flow of solder. By its presence, flux prevents the formation of oxides and dissolves or "fluxes" any oxides that may form. Some fluxes are called "self-pickling" because they contain additives that make them capable of dissolving oxides already present. Fluxes also have the function of reducing the surface tension of solders when they are in a molten state, thus permitting them to flow more easily.

Fluxes can be purchased in solid, powder, paste, and liquid form. Special proprietary mixtures with secret formulas are available in paste and liquid forms. In general, the proprietary fluxes are made with a mixture of borax and boric acid with fluorides and potassium salts added. These become fluid at temperatures higher than 1100° F (593.3° C), and therefore are suited for use with solders that melt above that temperature. For solders that melt at temperatures higher than 1400° F (760° C), it is best to use the common mixtures of powdered borax and boric acid made into a paste by adding hot water, because this flux remains active at higher temperatures.

BORAX SOLID FLUXES

The common fluxes used for jewelry making and metalwork generally contain some form of borax. They are used as an aid in soldering nonferrous metals—such as gold, silver, copper, nickel, tin, zinc, and their alloys—with hard solder. *Borax* is sodium tetraborate ($Na_2B_4O_7$), a colorless, crystalline salt, white when pure. At 1400° F (760° C) it becomes a thin fluid that under heat is capable of dissolving the metallic oxides that form on the surfaces of most metals used by jewelers. Borax is available from jewelry and chemical suppliers as solid, compressed cones or cylinders called a *borax junk* ("junk" refers to a thick piece or lump) weighing between 2–4 ounces. With this economic form, the flux is freshly prepared for each soldering occasion. This is done by grinding or rotating the cone under hand pressure in a *borax dish* or plate made of slate or another material, into which a little hot water has been placed. The resulting milky white paste is applied to the joint with a *brush*.

BORAX POWDER

Common *borax powder* can be purchased inexpensively in some grocery stores and pharmacies. It can be used instead of the cone form, but when mixed with water, it has a tendency to crystallize and solidify. Borax contains approximately 47% water of crystallization in the dry state, and this is driven off when it is heated. It is the mechanically combined water in the paste that causes the flux to swell and bubble, and this action can cause the displacement of solder snippets. Even when the borax flux has been allowed to dry, not all the moisture is evaporated, especially when humidity in the air is high. *Fused borax* or *borax glass* will not froth as much as common borax and therefore is preferred, but it should be mixed with *alcohol* to make a paste, and not water which causes it to return chemically to its state as common crystalline borax. Whenever a flux contains alcohol, work under good ventilation to avoid inhaling harmful fumes.

Borax powder is prepared as a paste for soldering, or used as a liquid painted on the metal surface for scale prevention. It is also used dry when melting and casting metals, a small amount sprinkled on the surface of the molten metal acts to increased fluidity and absorb impurities.

BORAX PASTES

With the addition of a small amount of liquid, borax is made into a paste which allows a greater concentration of borax where it is applied. Several proprietary pastes are available. A typical one becomes fluid and dissolves oxides at 800° F (426.6° C), and is active between 1100–1600° F (593.3–871.1° C). Some have special compositions that make them suited to special purposes, and jewelers' supply catalogs should be consulted. Some are suited to normal soldering and others to shorter duration soldering and are chosen accordingly.

Boric acid made into a paste is sometimes used alone as a flux because it melts and spreads over the metal at a low temperature and thereafter protects it from oxidizing during heating. This is why it is often mixed with plain borax (75% borax powder to 25% boric acid powder), especially when using solders that melt above 1500° F (815° C) to provide extended protection. When preparing this combination, dissolve them to excess in boiling water until the solution becomes tacky. One ounce of monoammonium phosphate ($NH_4H_2PO_4$) is added to one quart of the *cooled* result.

SOLDERING FLUIDS

In general, most soldering fluids are not suited to prolonged soldering situations, for which paste fluxes are preferred. Several proprietary mixtures are available, such as *Battern's Self-Pickling Liquid Flux*. When using liquid fluxes, it is advisable to decant a small amount into a separate small container in order to not contaminate the rest. All such containers should be provided with an airtight stopper to prevent evaporation.

A liquid flux is made by preparing a supersaturated solution of boric acid powder and denatured alcohol. Work dipped into this is then heated in a well-ventilated place to burn off the alcohol, leaving the object coated with a boracic layer that during the heat of soldering forms a borax glass that prevents the surface from becoming covered with oxide, and consequently subsurface firestain is also avoided.

A longer lasting liquid flux for firescale prevention can be made of 3 parts boric acid powder, 2 parts borax powder, and 2 parts disodium phosphate (Na_2HPO_4), a crystalline salt that occurs in blood and urine, but is made synthetically. Mix these with some water to form a paste, then slowly add water (1 quart to 210 grams of solid) and boil until clear.

A special form of liquid flux, usually methyl borate, is manufactured with an alcohol base and sold in quart or gallon containers. These can be attached with a coupler to gas tanks and used mixed with the soldering fuel. The flux is ejected through the gas line to the torch along with the gas and onto the work, giving the flame a greenish color. The surface hit by the flame is sprayed with a constant stream of flux which eliminates the need to apply flux directly to the work before soldering, though this can be done for added protection. This arrangement can be an advantage in prolonged soldering, and in mass production.

SOLDER PASTE

Solder pastes, increasing in use in recent years, are blended mixtures formulated from specific color and karat gold alloy uniform sized *powders* of specific fusion point, plus an *organic binder* that holds the metal powder in suspension and that when heated evaporates leaving minimal or no residue, and a flux that is compatible with the binder. This is available in a *plastic syringe* from which it passes through a tube needle. Dispensing can be done manually, or by using an attached electropneumatic device, some of which supply compressed air. Though this paste is now used mainly in the jewelry industry as a time-saver and for its ease and precision in placement, its use by individual jewelers also has these advantages plus economy through the exact control of amounts used. Solder and flux are applied in one operation, and because of the dispensing system, can be placed in areas otherwise difficult to reach, or where solder paillon placement is impractical. Its stability allows storage and use for more than one year, and its cost is slightly higher than conventional solders.

PRESOLDERING OPERATIONS:
General recommendations

METAL AND HANDLING TOOL CLEANLINESS

Cleaning the metal before soldering is *very important* to a successful soldering operation. Impurities such as dirt, foreign matter, grease, oxide, graphite, or carbon, if present can hinder solder flow. *All* parts of the workpiece must be clean, but in particular, the joint and its immediate area must be *absolutely chemically clean* before soldering can take place. Anyone not taking the necessary cleaning steps does not understand what takes place in the soldering process, and is creating unnecessary difficulties.

METHODS OF CLEANING METAL FOR SOLDERING

(For additional information on types of soil on metals, general methods of cleaning metal, degreasing, cleaning mediums, and related information, see Metal Finishing, Chapter 14.) Any of the following methods are used by jewelers to prepare metal for soldering.

DEGREASING AND CHEMICAL CLEANING Degreasing is the first step in the total cleaning of a workpiece. If grease in any form is present, it must be eliminated. Pickling in an acid solution for chemical cleaning follows. (Pickling and bright dipping are discussed on p. 417.)

MANUAL CLEANING Manual or mechanical means can be used to clean a workpiece, depending on circumstances and the availability of equipment. Manually, the metal can be rubbed with *abrasive papers* such as a fine grade of crocus cloth, carborundum, or with fine, clean *steel wool*. Joints can be scraped with a *steel scraper*, triangular in section, edges sharp, solid or hollow sided, with an average blade length of 2½ in (6.35 cm). (Scrapers are also used to scrape away excess solder; smooth or level metal surfaces; slightly increase the inside size of a bezel, etc.) Filing the joint with a *fine-cut file* also prepares it for soldering.

MECHANICAL CLEANING Metal can be cleaned by a crimped wire *scratch brush* mounted on a polishing motor, or with a *tampico bristle brush* and paste pumice. (See Metal Finishing, Chapter 14 for other methods.)

THE ULTRASONIC CLEANER Ultrasonic cleaners are now available in convenient smaller sizes and are finding favor with increasing numbers of jewelers. Cleaning work with one is faster than any conventional cleaning method, very efficient, and effortless. Units have a stainless steel tank that holds the special cleaning solutions recommended by manufacturers for use with their machines and particular metals. Instructions should be followed. The unit contains an ultrasonic generator, and a transducer to convert electrical energy into mechanical energy.

To clean large objects, the tank is filled with the cleaner solution. For cleaning small objects such as jewelry, smaller stainless steel, heat-resistant glass or plastic beakers are used, held in place inside the tank by a *beaker-positioning cover* as otherwise the vibrations would move them. Work is held suspended in the solution on a stainless steel wire hook and should not rest on the bottom; or it is placed on a rack with large openings to allow the penetration of sound waves. Solution temperature influences a cleaner's effectiveness. When the current is turned on, the solution will heat up, but this takes time, and built-in heaters are available, as are built-in timers. The most effective temperature is well below boiling.

Ultrasonic cleaning action depends on *cavitation*, a phenomenon in which the high-frequency, high-intensity, ultrasonic sound waves are introduced to the solution. As they pass into the solution in every direction, these shock waves cause the rapid formation and violent collapse by implosion of countless, minute bubbles or cavities. Their implosion at the instant of collapse occurs as a series of pressure points against the work surface so that they effectively scrub it.

When the current is turned on, ultrasonic energy penetrates into all cavities and crevices of the work that are in contact with the liquid cleaner, therefore its cleaning action reaches parts that are difficult or impossible to reach by ordinary mechanical cleaning methods. The chemical action of the cleaner is accelerated, and the time necessary for the dissolving of soils is shortened.

Ultrasonic cleaning solutions are used to clean work before soldering to remove all organic soils, and after soldering and casting to remove firescale, investment plaster, and other foreign matter. Jewelry having transparent stones where dirt has caked up in inaccessible places is also easily cleaned. After a few seconds in the cleaning solution, the cleaned work is removed by *stainless steel* or *bamboo tongs*—it should not be handled with the fingers—then rinsed and dried.

LIVE STEAM JET CLEANER Professional jewelers use live steam jet cleaners to clean jewelry of contaminants, especially prior to electroplating. Small tank units are now available for use by individual jewelers. The live steam is produced by an electrically heated or gas-heated tank containing water. By controlling a valve or a foot pedal, steam under 20–65 pounds of pressure emerges from a pipe onto the work which is held in tweezers just below the jet. The work is turned in all directions to allow the steam jet access to all parts. Contaminants are blasted out of recesses in seconds, leaving the work clean, and there are no chemicals to be removed.

WORK FIT

As a result of soldering, the space between the two parts being joined is filled with solder, then called a *solder fillet*. Distance between parts joined should be *minimal* to create a condition favorable to capillary or solder flow. If spaces are too wide, capillary attraction is weakened because the power of gravity acts against solder flow. Close-fitting joints give the best results, and the maximum joint clearance should not be more than a few thousandths of an inch. To assure a close-fitting joint, parts must be well finished and free of burrs which prevent proper contact. Large solder fillets are weaker than small ones, and it is a mistake to count on solder filling a poorly fitting joint. The solder fillet should be practically invisible.

SOLDER AMOUNT

The amount of solder used must be controlled. *Use only the minimal amount needed* to fill the gap. Beginners tend to use too much solder and flood the joint. This is unnecessary once it is realized how far a small amount of solder will flow in a well-fitting joint.

SOLDER SIZE

The thickness of solder snippets should not be greater than that of the parts being joined. Less heat is then needed to melt them, and there is less risk of overheating the metal. Small snippets also melt more quickly.

APPLYING FLUX AND PLACING SOLDER

Paint the joint and its adjacent area with flux, applying it with a *soft hair flux brush* dipped into the solder paste or liquid. Areas to be protected against the development of firescale or firestain can also be painted with flux, or the whole workpiece can be dipped into a flux solution, drained, and allowed to dry or heated gently to dry it. In some cases the work will already have been jigged to close the joint, and in others, parts are then assembled. Set the work in a position favorable to the flow of solder, with the seam as nearly horizontal as possible in order to use gravity as an aid.

Solder used in the form of snippets must also be flux coated. Lift them with *tweezers* and dip them into flux, then position them on the work. A *solder flux brush* can be used to place snippets. First dip the brush into the flux. When lifting the snippet with the brush, it automatically becomes flux coated.

Every soldering situation is *unique* and demands its own solution as to solder placement. Some *general suggestions* as to practice can, however, be made.

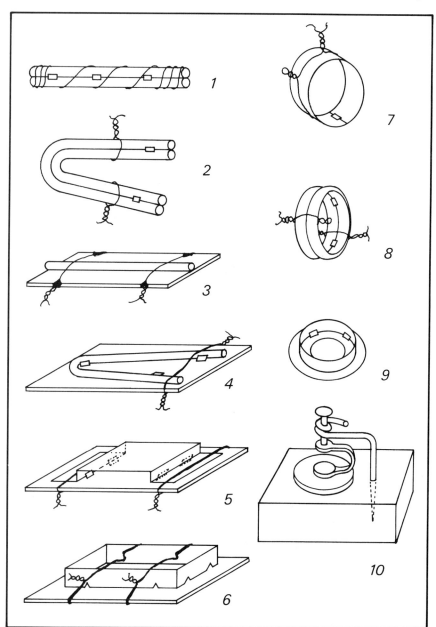

10–19 *TYPICAL SOLDERING SITUATION JIGS AND SOLDER PLACEMENT*
1. Iron binding wire wrapped the full length of a wire-to-wire joint.
2. Binding wire used in separate ties at intervals.
3. Binding wire used in conjunction with nicks made in the edges.
4. Binding wire to hold down wire ends.
5. Binding wire to hold down sheet, solder placed internally.
6. Edge soldering with graver-raised "stitches" to hold a part in position. The wire is bent or kinked to allow for expansion of the metal during soldering heat.
7. Binding wire given a twist to allow for expansion when soldering a cylindrical form.
8. Soldering two wires together with binding wire tied at opposite sides, solder placed within.
9. Soldering a bezel edgewise, with solder placed inside.
10. Soldering an ear wire finding supported by a heavy-gauge, bent iron binding wire pin forced into the soldering surface.

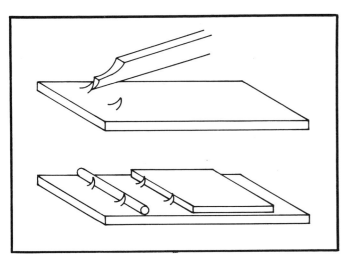

10–20 RAISING A STITCH WITH A GRAVER
Stitches are used to hold a wire or sheet pressed against it in place during soldering.

Sheet joint soldering: Space solder snippets fairly wide apart on long joints. Only use one or two small snippets for short joints. Try to make the solder contact *both parts* being joined. For example, place it *in* the joint. If possible, put solder snippets in positions where there is less likelihood of creating a *solder skull* (a remnant of solder or "solder ghost" visible at its former position after the solder flows). This will eliminate the need to clean away that spot later with a file or abrasive. Examples of such locations are the insides of ring shanks and bezels, or on surplus metal that later will be removed. If this is not possible, place the snippet right on top of the joint, or in the angle of contact between the parts being joined.

Wire soldering: Place the snippets on top of the wire, or leaning against the wire and its supporting base part. Heat the metal *from below,* and when the solder melts, draw it along with the torch. When soldering wire to wire, place the solder at both ends of their length, apply the heat from below to a point between them, and the solder will run toward the heat. Other examples are shown in the jig illustration.

VISUAL JUDGMENT OF TEMPERATURE BY METAL COLOR

In the soldering operation, during heating metals slowly take on visible color changes that roughly indicate the temperature they have reached. Visual temperature judgment by heat color is a means of knowing the approximate condition of the metal at that stage in the soldering sequence. The *light source* in the soldering area should be shielded or turned off during soldering to best note color changes in the metal, more easily seen in a dull light. Sterling silver color changes are as follows:

First visible redness:	900° F	482.2° C
Dull red:	1200° F	648.8° C
Cherry red:	1400° F	760° C

Sterling silver should not be heated much beyond the latter point as it starts to break down, and the object might collapse. (For a point of reference, IT hard solder flows at 1460° F or 793.4° C.)

SOLDER INHIBITORS

When soldering parts together, it sometimes becomes necessary to apply a *solder inhibitor* or substance that will *prevent* the flow of solder. With its use, solder flow can be confined to or restricted from a part. An outstanding example is when making a hinge. (See Glossary: Jewelry Findings.) When solder is overheated it tends to spread over a surface as a film. Solder inhibitors prevent this from happening, and are often used on visible surfaces for this reason. Liquid proprietary solder inhibitors are available. Other common substances used as solder inhibitors include the following:

Powdered rouge: a fine red powder of ferric oxide, made by calcining ferrous sulphate.
Whiting: chalk or calcium carbonate ground to an impalpable powder.
Yellow ochre: an impure iron ore, also called *limonite* or *loam.*
Yellow ochre casein paint: already in a pastelike form, this adheres easily to a clean metal surface, does not disengage from the metal when heated, and is easily removed afterward.
An 18th-century account suggests an inhibitor made of three parts clay and one part horse dung.

Mix these inhibitors with only enough water to make a paste, and to aid in their better adherence, add some organic gum such as gum tragacanth. Paint the paste in the desired area with a soft-haired paintbrush. Take care not to allow it to enter a place where solder flow *is* wanted.

Solder inhibitors can also be used for the purpose of protecting a joint that has already been soldered when it must be subjected to the heat of another soldering. They can also be used to protect fine work such as small-gauge wires that might otherwise run the risk of melting during a soldering operation.

Solder inhibitors should be removed from the work *before* it is placed in a pickle as otherwise the bath becomes contaminated and weakened. This is especially true of inhibitors that contain any form of iron. After soldering the inhibitor may become caked on the work. If it resists removal by brushing with warm water and a *stiff hand brush* or *metal scratch brush,* it may then be necessary to boil the piece in an alkaline solution, brush it again until it is clean, and then place the work in pickle.

BURNING FUELS:
The energy source of heat

COMBUSTION

Combustion is the combination of an oxidizer with a fuel that results in light and heat. *Heat* is the name for *energy* as it passes from one body to another by thermal flow processes. The most common oxidizer is *oxygen*. Once ignited, an ordinary flame burns simply by using the oxygen in the atmosphere surrounding it. The chief combustible element in all fuels is *carbon,* usually in combination with free hydrogen, or with hydrogen in combined forms (as hydrocarbons).

The simplest and most ancient mechanical system of introducing air to the fuel is the *mouth blowpipe* (described on p. 410) by which the human lungs act as a bellows and force oxygen through any ordinary flame as a means of increasing its heat output. An increase in the velocity of the flow of oxygen to the flame results in raising its temperature. The earliest mechanical substitute for the human lungs was the *bellows*, which increased the air velocity to a flame at a steady rate. It was operated manually or mechanically by foot pressure. The value and efficiency of such systems is proved by the fact that they are still in use today by jewelers and metalworkers in various parts of the world.

Human ingenuity and modern technology have given us far simpler ways—though in themselves the mechanisms are far more complex—for the forced introduction of air to a flame: the use of oxygen stored under pressure in tanks, or by the use of a compressor. In combination with these compact and reliable sources of oxygen, any of several fuels available become capable of burning with a heat in a temperature range of approximately 3500–6000° F (1926.6–3315° C), more than sufficient for carrying out *all* functions requiring high heat that are used by craftspersons in metalwork.

We are fortunate to have several excellent fuels to provide energy/heat needed for metalwork. We must only choose *which* of them we prefer to use. When making a choice, the following factors must be considered.

FUEL PORTABILITY

Portability is of prime importance as this allows functions requiring heat, such as soldering, annealing, and casting to be carried out in any area of a workshop. All fuels available from commercial suppliers in pressurized steel, cylindrical tanks (described on p. 409) meet this requirement. Convenient carrying units facilitate the portability of tanks and accompanying accessories.

Small hand-held torches with expendable, pressurized containers holding propane or butane gas are also portable. Their use, however, is severely limited because their small size generates only enough heat for small work. The frequent need to replace the fuel container makes them relatively costly.

Natural gas, commonly used in some jewelry making torches, is available in most large cities, but is a relatively nonportable fuel. Piped into the workshop at *fixed* locations, it is controlled by a gas cock or outlet valve that regulates its flow. To overcome this limitation on mobility more than one outlet can be installed at different workshop locations, and rubber extension tubes can be used. They should not be too long as they can become snarled and possibly cause accidents.

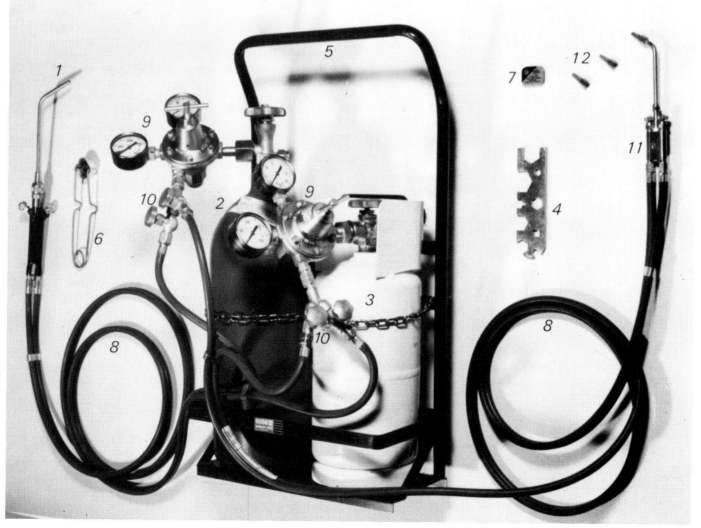

10–21 *PORTABLE PROPANE/OXYGEN COMBINATION UNIT*
This unit has two permanently fixed torches, one for soldering, the other for melting; 1. Soldering torch; 2. Oxygen tank; 3. Propane tank; 4. Wrench; 5. Carrier; 6. Spark lighter; 7. Flint refills; 8. 16 ft hose; 9. Regulator units; 10. Y-connectors; 11. Melting torch; 12. Torch tips. *Photo: Courtesy Swest Inc.*

OXYGEN

Oxygen (chemical symbol, O), essential for combustion whether the fuel is a gas, liquid, or solid, is a colorless, odorless, tasteless gas that constitutes about 23% by weight, and about 21% by volume of this planet's natural atmosphere. Oxygen produced artificially in a tank is 99.5% pure. By itself, oxygen is nonpoisonous, is not dangerous, cannot explode, and will not burn unless combined with a fuel and ignited. The result is *combustion,* a chemical process which is an intense form of oxidation.

The manner of compressing and storing oxygen into a tank was invented in 1877 by Raoul Pictet, a Swiss physicist. By condensing oxygen gas at a temperature below its critical temperature, −284° F (−140° C), it becomes a pale blue liquid that can safely be placed into a strong, compact, pressurized cylindrical steel tank capable of withstanding 500 atmospheres pressure. Today tanks are available in several sizes. A convenient size used by jewelers has a 19 ft³ (cubic feet) capacity, though tanks with larger capacities can also be used. Similar tanks are used for compressed liquid fuel gas storage, discussed below.

Oxygen and fuel gases are released from the tank by a *controlling valve* placed at the opening to which a *pressure regulator* is attached containing valves capable of reducing the high storage pressures to a pressure suitable for ignition. This makes possible any flame temperature or particular flame type desired. A certain air volume is needed to burn one gas volume, the amount varying with particular gases, hence the need to control the volumetric relationship between gas and air.

Pressure regulators have one or two gauges. When there are two, the larger one indicates tank pressure; the smaller one, the reduced line pressure, generally set at 6 psi (pounds per square inch) for soldering purposes. The regulator works on a diaphragm system in the valve. Before attaching a regulator to a *new* oxygen tank, "crack" the tank—that is, open the tank valve for a second, then close it. The short oxygen escape blast expels any dust or foreign matter in the outlet. Dust blown into a regulator when opening a tank valve can cause clogging and malfunction. Screw the regulator onto the tank valve without forcing the connection or threads may be damaged. Never use grease or oil on oxygen tank or regulator connections when making attachments as it may clog valves. Once a regulator is attached, keep the adjustment handle or regulator screw in the "open" position to prevent the diaphragm damage possible if the tank valve is suddenly opened and pressure suddenly exerted upon it.

If pressure correction is necessary at this point, reset the gauge. Hereafter, to close the oxygen, only use the valve on the tank, or the torch valve. A change in pressure is not normally necessary, and frequent changes should be avoided as valve parts may wear out.

COMPRESSED AIR

Compressed air is air under greater pressure than air in the atmosphere. The *air compressor machine* is a form of pump, available in small models for use with a single torch. It is operated by a motor whose horsepower (hp) size depends on the need (available: ¼ hp, ⅓ hp, ½ hp, 1 hp, 2 hp, or 5 hp). Portable units have motors operating at 1725 rpm. They supply *direct, continuous* air pressure, and do not require separate air storage tanks. A typical, general-purpose, portable compressor should be capable of developing 35 psi, at 1.70 cfm (cubic feet per minute)

displacement or more. More powerful stationary models piping air to two or more torches 10–12 ft from the compressor require a separate air storage tank. Not all torches are usable with compressed air. When in doubt, consult your supplier.

Compressed air is a possible oxygen source for soldering torches. It can also be used for sandblasting, air blast cleaning, air gun spraying, the operation of grinders, power presses, and wax injection machines. When used for heating purposes, the resulting maximum flame temperature is about 1000° F (537.7° C) cooler than oxygen. It is therefore somewhat less effective for melting and casting large amounts of metal. Compressed air systems also tend to accumulate water which can cause flame sputtering and blowout.

Temperatures Attainable with Gas and Compressed Air

Fuel	Maximum Temperature	
	°F	°C
Natural gas	3565	1962
Propane	3497	1925
Acetylene	3848	2120

LIQUEFIED PETROLEUM GAS FUELS

Most of the energy that the jeweler consumes today is produced by the combustion of *organically derived fuels* combined with air. These fuels are different liquefied petroleum gases compressed under pressure in tanks. They are easily converted to a gas fuel by low-pressure vaporization, their escape and pressure change controlled by the tank valve regulator. Common gas fuels used by jewelers are natural gas, propane, butane, acetylene, hydrogen, and manufactured gas, the last two least used. They are mixed either with oxygen or compressed air. In some cases they are used with torches that allow mouth-blown air, or air from a foot-operated bellows.

NATURAL GAS AND OXYGEN Maximum temperature: 5120° F (2826.6° C) Natural gas comes from wells bored in the earth at widespread locations where natural reservoirs trapped the gases that developed as a product of organic matter decomposition through the action of heat from the earth's core. Its *composition varies* from one location to another, but invariably its chief constituent is *methane* (CH_4), a gaseous hydrocarbon compound that is lightweight and odorless. A typical composition of sweet natural gas (free of hydrogen sulphide) as found is 82 parts methane, 4 parts ethane, 3 parts propane, 3 parts butane, 2 parts hexane, and 5 parts heptane. Butane (C_4H_{10}) and propane ($CH_3CH_2CH_3$) belong to the large *methane series,* and are usually removed and sold separately as liquefied petroleum gas fuels. A typical natural gas composition supplied to users contains 93 parts methane, 5 parts ethane, and 2 parts propane. Other heavier, saturated hydrocarbons in the methane series are gasoline, kerosene, and the solid paraffin. Acetylene is also made from natural gas.

Liquefied natural gas (which liquefies at −258° F or −161° C), compressed in tanks, is recommended as the most practical fuel for jewelry making. It is portable, economical as it is the least expensive of fuel gases, and burns slowly unlike hydrogen which is consumed quickly. Natural gas is also available piped into a workshop through street main conduits in pipes of ¾ in (1.8 cm) diameter, at pressures that start at 25–36 psi in the large mains, reduced to about 8 psi by regulating devices. Its availability by direct piping eliminates the purchase of one tank (and subsequent replacements) and one regulator gauge, necessary with other fuels in tanks. When purified, natural gas is odorless, but it is usually given a *mercaptan* (oils of unpleasant smell) odor so that if it escapes it can be detected before it reaches an explosive amount. Since natural gas varies at different locations, consult your local supplier as to which torch to use for the local gas mixture.

PROPANE GAS AND OXYGEN Maximum temperature: 5252° F (2900° C) *Propane* is a heavy, gaseous hydrocarbon that also occurs naturally dissolved in crude petroleum. It consists of propyl and methane, and is therefore also of the methane series, belonging to the *paraffin series.*

Propane gas mixed with oxygen burns with a clean, carbon-free flame at a temperature somewhat hotter than natural gas. It is inexpensive, and tank refills are widely available, as it is a fuel commonly used for cooking in rural areas, by campers, and in trailers. A heating unit consisting of one propane and one oxygen tank can each be fitted with a Y-shaped connection adaptor that allows two (or more) torches to be used with the same two tanks. One of these connections can be mounted with a torch and tip large enough to use for annealing and melting, and the other with a torch and tip suited to normal soldering.

ACETYLENE AND OXYGEN Maximum temperature: 5850° F (3232.2° C) Acetylene (HC:CH) is a colorless, gaseous hydrocarbon formed by the direct union of carbon and hydrogen in the electric arc, by the incomplete combustion of other hydrocarbons, and by other means. It has an unpleasant odor similar to ether, due to the presence of impurities. It is the main fuel used for welding, and in the proper torch, produces the hottest, brilliant white flame. It does not burn clean (clean burning means that *all* the carbon in the fuel is consumed and *no* carbon deposited on the work) unless a small amount of oxygen is applied when igniting it. Because the flame heat is so high, it is used for platinum, a metal that requires the highest heat of all the precious metals for soldering, casting, and fusion; it is also used for certain bronze alloys that require high melting temperatures. Of all the gases mentioned, it is least desirable for the jeweler unless he works with platinum. If it is used, the torch must be kept in constant motion to avoid overheating and melting the work.

MANUFACTURED GAS *Manufactured* or *artificial gas* is made from coal, coke, or petroleum. The most common are *coke-oven gas, oil gas, producer gas, hydrogen gas, nitrogen gas,* and *water gas,* all named after the manner by which they are manufactured. They are not recommended as gas fuels for the jeweler as they contain carbon monoxide which is lethal, even in rather small amounts.

TORCHES AND ACCESSORIES:
Equipment for utilizing heat

THE TORCH

A torch is any portable, hand-controlled mechanism utilizing fuel and air combined in a flame that is used to perform metalwork heating functions. Torches vary from very simple mechanisms to complex constructions. The term *blowpipe* implies that air is introduced to the flame by mouth blowing, and *torch* implies mechanical air introduction, but in some metalwork literature these terms are used interchangeably. Because usage of the term "blowpipe" might be misconstrued, the word "torch" is used in this text.

THE MOUTH BLOWPIPE

The 8–10 in (20.3–25.4 cm) long *metal mouth blowpipe,* also sometimes called a "French torch," is a torch form whose ancestor was the first and simplest of all torch devices: a natural hollow reed. This instrument was first used in small metalwork such as jewelry making to increase a flame's heat by forcefully introducing oxygen to it from man's bellows—the lungs—blown through the mouth. By this simplest of means, rapid flame oxidation elevates its temperature enough to melt relatively small amounts of metal, alloys, and solder. Blowpipes can be used with any nonpressurized flame, such as from an oil lamp, alcohol lamp, or a Bunsen burner.

A typical metal mouth blowpipe is a conically tapered brass tube, straight, or bent at the narrow end to direct the flame sideways on the work to make it visible to the worker. The small end has a very small, pinhole-sized orifice that increases the pressure of the air jet forced through the tube by gentle and continuous mouth blowing via the larger ¼ in (0.63 cm) diameter opening which can be fitted with a *wood mouthpiece.* Some mouth blowpipes have a ball-shaped reservoir which evenly regulates the natural variations in oxygen content and air flow pressure from the lungs. Mouth blowpipes are also available in the fixed bench-type torch, constructed of two tubes, one that introduces gas fed to it from the gas source through an attached rubber tube, the volume controlled by a valve, while through the other air is supplied simultaneously from the mouth. Some have a larger opening at the small end for producing a larger flame.

To use an ordinary mouth blowpipe, or a bench-type mouth blowpipe, inflate the cheeks with air, and blow it gently through the pipe. Train yourself to take fresh air into the lungs *through the nose* so that blowing pressure is not interrupted to take a breath and is even and continuous. Irregular blowing is to be avoided as it causes the metal and solder to alternately heat up and cool off, not a good practice.

To produce a medium-sized, soft, blue reducing flame for preheating the whole object, turn the blowpipe with its curved end pointing downward and toward the left at a 45° angle. Harder blowing produces a larger, hotter flame due to increased air pressure. To make a smaller, more pointed, hot flame used locally to cause the solder to flow once the work is preheated, angle the blowpipe sideways until the flame becomes sharp, blue outside with a light blue cone half as long as the flame length inside. Its hottest point (approximately 2012° F, or 1100° C—or higher) is just before the inner cone and this part should contact the solder and the area surrounding the joint, causing quick solder flow. If less heat is wanted, simply increase the distance between the flame and the work.

Because a mouth blowpipe (but not a fixed bench-type blowpipe) is limited to a relatively small-sized flame, mouth blowpipes are used for small work, but most jewelry *is small,* or made in small sections. Its universal use until recent times, and continued worldwide use today

10-22 SOLDERING TORCHES

1. *Brass mouth blowpipe, available lengths 8, 10 in. (C. R. Hill)*
2. *Wooden mouthpiece for blowpipe. (C. R. Hill)*
3. *Mouth blowpipe with ball, removable to eliminate collected saliva, length 10 in. (C. R. Hill)*
4. *Combination mouth blowpipe, used with mouthpiece with tubing, or with compressed air tube, length 10 in. (C. R. Hill)*
5. *Torch used with city gas. (Karl Fischer)*
6. *Torch for acetylene with changeable tips: fine, medium, large. (Karl Fischer)*
7. *Torch for propane with changeable tips: fine, medium. (Karl Fischer)*
8. *Torch used with natural, artificial, mixed, propane, butane, acetylene gas with air or oxygen by changing to a suitable tip, length 10¼ in. (Swest)*
9. *Midget torch, length 6¾ in, used with medium- or low-pressure natural gas, oxyacetylene, or liquid petroleum gas. (Swest)*
10. *Torch for natural gas with three extra tips. The same torch is available adapted for use with acetylene, butane, hydrogen or artificial gas with oxygen or compressed air. (Swest)*
11. *Torch for use with all bottled gases, or city-supplied gas. (Karl Fischer)*
12. *Large melting torch for use with all gases. (Karl Fischer)*
13. *Large torch for acetylene and oxygen, with two tips, used for annealing and casting. (Swest)*
14. *Flint spark lighter.*
15. *Rubber tubing, ¼ in ID, ⅜ in OD.*
16. *Torch holder, screws on bench side, and torch supporter hook, length 10½ in, screws into bench.*

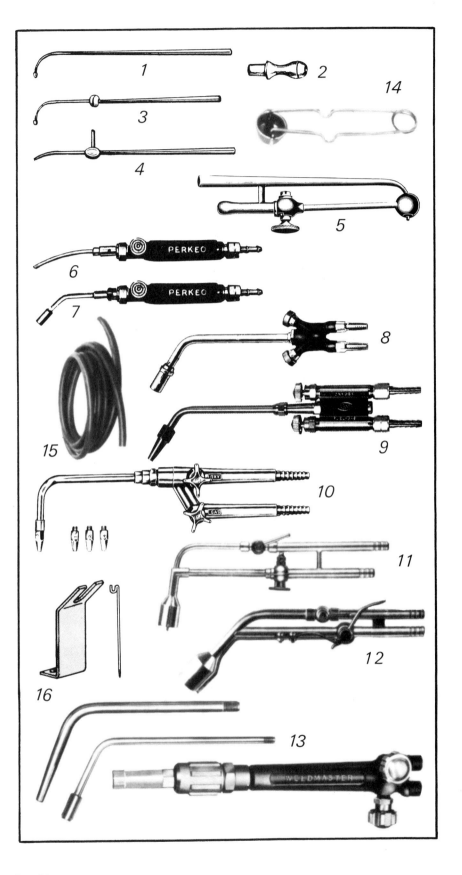

testifies to its effectiveness, and no other means of making a hot flame is more economical.

To help increase a blowpipe's efficiency, shield the work to insulate it against rapid heat loss from cross drafts by surrounding it with a refractory material such as charcoal blocks, and place the work itself on refractory material.

THE FOOT BELLOWS AND TORCH

In another ancient system, compressed air is fed through a tube to a torch from a *foot bellows*. Different systems are used. Gas torches are designed to use air from a foot bellows, or air mechanically blown from a compressed air system. In either case, the air volume is controlled by a torch valve for uniform flow. In another system, liquid fuel is fed under bellows-created pressure to a second tube, and the fuel and air are premixed before emerging from the torch nozzle. This is a Mexican system. (See Filigree, Chapter 6.) Bellows are still used today because they most economically achieve oxygen velocity increase. With a little practice, the necessary foot pumping action becomes automatic. Foot bellows are available with an air-holding reservoir requiring slower, less frequent pumping.

MODERN TORCHES

Modern torches with interchangeable tips are designed for a variety of circumstances demanded in jewelry making. Some torches are used with *one specific gas fuel,* such as natural gas, town gas, or tanked gas. Others can be used with different fuels simply by changing the tip to one suited to the gas used. All employ a combination of oxygen or compressed air and fuel. When purchasing a torch, consult your tool supplier for advice about which model is suited to the particular gas and air combination you will use.

Internally, the construction of the torch varies according to the fuel used, but externally almost all have two open-ended tubes for the attachment of two rubber hoses, often color coded, that conduct air to one and fuel to the other. The on-off control, volume, and regulation of flow for each is controlled by a hose cock valve with a lever handle, or a knurled knob. The extension tubes take the flame far enough away from the torch to allow it to be hand held without discomfort. Various metals are used in torch construction. A standard type such as the *Hoke torch* is made of solid brass machined stock and seamless tubing, and the entire unit is nickel plated. A general-purpose jeweler's bench torch averages 9 in (22.85 cm) long and weighs 8½ ounces, so it can be hand held for normal time lengths without hand fatigue. Smaller and larger torches are also available for specialized work. The *Prestolite* (acetylene) torch is used with a single fuel tank, and the torch has a single valve and control, and a pistol grip; the tank a capacity of 40 ft³.

TORCH TIPS Torch tips, also called *jets, nozzles,* or *heads,* are designed for use with particular fuels, in combination with mouth-blown air, compressed air, or oxygen. In most modern torches, the tip alone can be screwed off the extension tube end, or the extension tube and tip are one unit and come off together when changing sizes or changing fuels. With any fuel-air combination, the work a single torch can do is considerably increased by changing its tip type or size. At least *three different torch tips* for any one torch are advisable, and even more are often available.

Torch tips are changed to achieve different flame sizes needed for different scale work, or to increase or reduce flame size to perform a particular function. A relationship exists between the area or volume of metal to be heated and the amount of heat needed for the work. Small tips are used for pinpoint flames on small work; a medium tip is used for a medium-sized flame and general soldering; and a large tip produces a brush flame used for annealing, melting, and casting. On standard torches, large tips have a capability of melting up to 5 ounces of precious metal.

Melting torches are large torches whose main function is to melt large charges of metal placed in crucibles or in open forging hearths. The angle of the flame to the metal is important. The flame should deflect off the work be-

cause if it bounces back toward the torch, it may lift off the torch and become extinguished.

THE BUNSEN BURNER The Bunsen burner is a gas torch that produces a premixed flame. Credit for its invention in 1855 goes to Robert Wilhelm Bunsen of Heidelburg. This first economical, hot, blue gas flame started the use of gas in cooking. Typically, a Bunsen burner has a 4–5 in (10–12.7 cm) long upright tube (though horizontal tube Bunsen burners also exist) that admits air through small holes at the bottom. Their openings are adjustable to increase or reduce flame size. Gas admitted through a tube attached to the bottom mixes with the air and burns at the tube top with an intensely hot, smokeless, blue flame of low luminosity. The flame has two zones: the *oxidizing section* just above the inner, nonluminous, blue cone, and the *reducing section* inside the inner, bright blue cone. Flame temperature can be greatly increased by placing a *nickel wire* or *stainless steel screen cap* over the upper tube end.

The Bunsen burner has many uses in jewelry making, but is not used for soldering. Its main limitation is a relative lack of flame mobility as it is used standing on a table, often in conjunction with a *tripod* covered with a *wire mesh* on which work is placed. It can be used for any work placeable on top of a flame.

Fixed gas fuel burners, and *gas furnaces* are also available. Though not used for soldering, they are used to heat pickle, for annealing and enameling, and in gas kilns for mold burnout in casting.

HEATING ACCESSORIES *Regulators* for the oxygen and fuel tanks must be bought. This precision unit fits all standard tanks. Regulators reduce the high tank pressure of 250 psi under which oxygen and fuel are stored to a normal 15 psi delivered to the torch assembly for normal soldering and melting, or 25 psi used for forging and case hardening steel. Regulators are equipped with single or dual stages, the former used with one torch, and the latter, when two torches are used simultaneously. The desired pressure is uniformly maintained once it has been set on the *regulator dial pressure gauge.* When a tank is not used for long periods, regulator valves should be relieved of pressure with the dial gauge reading "0" to take the pressure off the 3 in (7.6 cm) stainless steel diaphragm. At the same time, turn off the *tank valves,* making sure they are properly closed to avoid fuel leakage, then open and close *torch valves* to relieve them of pressure. Some fuel tank regulators have an indicator showing remaining contents, marked at quarter-tank intervals. Replacement can be anticipated.

Rubber hosing is used to connect bellows, Bunsen burners, and torches to the air and fuel source. With some fuel tank arrangements, only 6 ft (1.8 m) of hose is needed, and others have up to 16 ft (4.8 m). Separate hoses used for air and fuel are color coded to avoid confusion in hookups. Also available are *dual hoses* made with two passages welded together, each with its own connectors to the torch. Two types of connection are possible, depending on torch design. Some torches have stepped, tapering tube ends over which a hose end is simply forced until it is securely engaged. Others have an attached threaded metal coupling made leakproof by a hex nut tightened on the threaded tube end with a *wrench.* The most common inside diameter (ID) is ¼ in (0.64 cm), but ³⁄₁₆ in, ⁵⁄₁₆ in, and ⅜ in (0.48 cm, 0.79 cm, and 0.95 cm) are also available.

Spanner wrenches in sizes matching the needs of particular tank and torch assemblies are usually provided with the tank. They are used to attach and remove regulators to tanks, and hoses to torches and tanks.

Y-connectors are optional, and are used to attach two hoses to dual-stage regulators on fuel and oxygen tanks.

Tank carriers are optional, but convenient. They hold one or two tanks (one oxygen, one fuel) secured by chains, and have hose racks and a handle to allow lifting and carrying the whole assembly to another part of the workshop.

Spark lighters with removable, replaceable, striking spark flints are the safest and easiest to operate when igniting a flame. Unlike for a match, you need only one hand to strike a spark and light the torch when using a spark lighter.

THE ANATOMY OF A FLAME

A *flame* is a body of self-propagating, burning gas or vapor, caused by combustion or oxidation reactions of gases combined with atmospheric or mechanically introduced oxygen. The two basic flame types are *diffusion flames,* and *premixed flames.*

DIFFUSION FLAMES A diffusion flame (a candle flame is a typical example) results from the combustion of solid fuels (wax) or liquid fuels (oil) and atmospheric oxygen. The fuel and the oxidizer are initially separate, but mix when they burn, fuel and oxidizer *diffusing* into the flame zone while combustion products and heat are diffused out. This flame structure has an outer luminous envelope because carbon particles freed from the fuel hydrocarbons are present, though almost complete combustion takes place there. Generally speaking, the *less luminous* the flame, the *hotter* it is: more efficient combustion of the fuel is taking place. This luminous envelope is followed by an invisible gas layer (called a *streamer* in a premixed flame) caused by incomplete combustion of burning gases. The innermost zone contains unburned vapor. The flame's hottest point is just inside the streamer tip, and the inner cone-shaped zone has little heat. Such a flame can have a maximum temperature of 3632° F (2000° C). By forcefully introducing an oxidizer, as when blowing air through a flame with a blowpipe, a diffusion flame can be converted to a premixed flame, and in the process, becomes much hotter.

SMOKE AND THE FLAME Smoke is gas in the air that is visible due to the presence of fine solid particles of carbon. Smoke indicates *incomplete combustion,* as all fuel carbon is not consumed. A smoky flame, besides being wasteful, is unsuitable to jewelry making. For jewelers, the old motto

should be amended to read: Where there is smoke, there is not enough fire.

PREMIXED FLAMES In a premixed flame blown oxygen, pressurized oxygen, or compressed air is combined with gas before combustion. In a torch, this occurs at the fuel-air exit point where combustion begins. Premixed flames are more complicated in coloration and structure, and their appearance varies with the fuel source and the amount of oxygen introduced. *Size* and *color zone structure* are the chief means of knowing a flame's composition.

A smoky flame, as explained above, contains unconsumed carbon and indicates that insufficient oxidation is taking place. If more air is mixed with the fuel gas in this flame, smoke disappears. The flame, formerly yellowish, becomes bluer, hotter, and partially loses its luminosity because of more complete carbon combustion. Since the flame contains more oxygen, the metal surface to which it is applied oxidizes. If used in casting such a flame will introduce free oxygen by dissolution into the melt, especially in the case of silver which is highly receptive to free oxygen; this is the main cause of porosity in a casting. For these reasons, and others, an excess of oxygen in a flame is generally undesirable in jewelry making.

Premixed flames may be *laminar* or smooth flowing when a balance of air and fuel flow exists, or *turbulent* when the air or gas flow enters the flame at an excessively high speed.

FLAME TYPES IN PREMIXED SYSTEMS

Most torches allow flame adjustment by control of the volume and velocity of introduced oxygen and fuel. This makes possible changes in the proportion of gas to air. There are three recognized premixed flame conditions: oxidizing, reducing, and neutral. It is important for the jeweler to learn to distinguish between their appearances. In some torches only one flame type is produced. In such cases, use that part of the flame with the desired atmosphere, generally identifiable by *position* and *color.*

THE OXIDIZING FLAME An oxidizing flame has a surplus of free oxygen introduced from an air source (oxygen tank or compressed air). Generally it is a clear blue, and when the air is excessive, the blue darkens, the flame shortens, and it hisses and roars. If such a flame must be used, place the metal *just beyond* the flame tip. An excessively oxidizing flame is, however, generally not recommended in jewelry making (soldering platinum is an exception) because oxygen present in large amounts causes the metal surface to form a heavy oxide coat called *firescale.* Also, because of its intense heat, it can easily burn or melt the metal. In general, an oxidizing flame is smaller in length than a reducing flame from the same torch and fuel source.

THE REDUCING FLAME To *reduce* is to *deoxidize.* A reducing flame is low in oxygen, luminous, yellowish, and contains elements that will unite with oxygen contained in substances placed within it. Its action on an oxygen-free metal surface is to raise its temperature. Because it is low in oxygen, it causes little or no surface oxidation on metal. To obtain a reducing torch flame, once the flame size is established, introduce just enough oxygen to cause the disappearance of the yellowish tinge. When used, place the metal in the area *just within* the tip of the innermost light blue cone. In heat treating processes such as soldering and annealing, a reducing or neutral flame is desirable. In

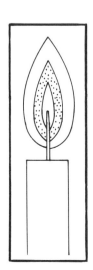

10–23 *THE ANATOMY OF A DIFFUSION FLAME*
A candle flame consists of an outer luminous envelope of burning gases, followed by a streamer of invisible gases, and an inner cone of unburned vapor.

cases where mechanical control is not possible, as a means of oxidation control, apply an oxygen-inhibiting substance, such as flux, on the metal surface.

THE NEUTRAL FLAME   The neutral flame is balanced between an oxidizing and a reducing flame. Only enough air for combustion is present, and neither oxidation nor reduction takes place. It is probably the flame type most widely used among jewelers for soldering and heat treatments. In general, to achieve a neutral flame, once the flame size is established, introduce just enough air to make it appear *slightly* yellowish blue.

FLAME APPEARANCE

In an *oxygen-gas* (natural, propane, butane)-*fed torch*, the oxidizing flame has a small, deep blue inner cone, and a bright, luminous blue outer envelope. The reducing flame has a greenish blue inner cone surrounded with a yellowish portion, enveloped by a blue outer layer ending in a reddish blue tip.

In a *natural gas-compressed air-fed torch*, the oxidizing flame has a deep blue inner cone surrounded by a luminous lighter blue, and a very pale blue tip. The reducing flame has a longer, deep blue inner cone ending in greenish blue, surrounded by a luminous envelope followed by a blue outer layer ending in a pale blue tip.

In an *acetylene* (Prestolite)-*fed torch*, the oxidizing flame has a large greenish blue inner cone surrounded by a thin, bluer envelope ending in a pale, sky blue tip. The reducing flame also has an inner but much smaller greenish blue cone surrounded by a dirty yellowish gray, enveloped by an outer darker blue ending in a sky blue tip, but the flame in general has a faintly yellowish tinge.

THE FLAME IN USE

IGNITION TEMPERATURE AND DELAY TIME   Before a gas fuel can burn, its temperature must be raised to the point where *ignition* occurs. This point depends on the rate at which chemical reactions take place, on the ignition method employed, and on the fuel form. *Ignition delay time* is the interval between the application of the igniting flame and the moment when observable combustion begins, and with the kinds of fuels jewelers use, is a fraction of a second.

IGNITING AND EXTINGUISHING A FLAME   To ignite a gas-air torch flame, hold the torch in the left hand with the tip opening pointing *away* from you. First turn the fuel gas on *low,* then in the shortest possible interval, with the right hand bring a *lighted match,* a *spark lighter,* or *pilot light* to the fuel outlet to ignite it. Some torches have a built-in pilot light. When a torch will be used repeatedly during a short time period, leave a small pilot light burning on an *alcohol lamp* or a *Bunsen burner.* A torch flame should not burn unnecessarily as this can lead to accidents.

Once the fuel is lighted, *slowly increase the gas volume.* Without air, the flame becomes a large, bushy, possibly smoky yellow flame. Then *gradually introduce the air or oxygen,* slowly increasing its velocity until the flame reaches the condition of neutrality or reduction described above. Too much oxygen or air can blow out the flame altogether. When this happens, do *not* try to reignite the flame immediately—this can be dangerous as gas in the surrounding air can ignite and explode. Instead, turn off both the gas and the air valves, air the workshop to allow the gas in the air to dissipate, and start again.

Always use a torch tip of the size appropriate to the work. A tip too large or too small can be a hindrance to successful soldering.

To *turn off* a flame, first gradually diminish the air flow and close the air valve, then *slowly* close the fuel valve. This procedure will avoid *backflash,* in which the gas burns inside the internal gas jet instead of the external jet of mixed air and gas.

THE SOLDERING OPERATION

In soldering there is no direct fusion of metal to metal as in welding, but fusion occurs in the intermediary alloy —the solder. Through the use of relatively high heat, when the solder alloy melts, its surface tension is reduced, a condition aided by the presence of flux, and it becomes extremely fluid. The solder then flows and *wets* the clean, fluxed surface of the metals being joined.

Solder flow is aided by *capillarity,* a physical condition in which the surface of a liquid has a molecular attraction for a solid with which it has contact. This is why solder flows between contacting surfaces, or follows the narrow space in a joint, and aided by heat, fills it for the distance in which capillary attraction has force. Once the heat is withdrawn, the solder solidifies and makes a solid joint with the parent metal.

Another condition aids in the unifying function of solder in a joint. During the heating period prior to solder flow, the crystals of the metal in the parent object expand and grow, and minute spaces open between them which the solder fills when it flows. Therefore, a *limited diffusion* occurs between the solder and the parent metal at the contacting surfaces, forming a localized alloy which strengthens the bond. The degree of fusion varies with different metals and alloys, and with the solder composition.

Fusion of the solder can take place without the collapse of the heated object because a *temperature differential* exists between the melting points of the solder and the metal being joined. In some cases, this differential may be as little as 50° F (10° C), which makes temperature control during soldering critical, but it can be as much as 200° F (93° C), which allows greater leeway.

The *length of time of heat exposure* has a bearing on the soundness of the result. Heat must not be unnecessarily prolonged once the solder flows as this can affect the composition of the solder and its strength.

THE THREE STAGES OF A SOLDERING CYCLE

It is generally good soldering practice to make the soldering cycle as brief as possible. This decreases the chance of spending the flux, overheating the parts, or volatilizing the lower melting constituents in the solder, and the problems that ensue.

The soldering cycle can be divided into three main stages: the preheat; localized heat; and heat withdrawal.

1   THE PREHEAT: Heating the whole work

By one of the basic laws of thermodynamics, in a free interchange of radiant energy heat flows from a hot body (the flame) to a cold body (the work) in contact with it, and by conduction, the hotter body loses energy while the colder body gains the energy given off, until at a certain point, the two bodies reach the same temperature.

This law applies to the soldering situation. No solder will flow until the parent metal being joined, as well as the solder, have both reached solder flow temperature. It is therefore bad practice in soldering to simply place the flame directly on the solder when heating starts and wait until the solder flows. More than likely, the flux will be spent, the metal will oxidize, and the solder will melt and form a ball. Instead, first generally *preheat the parent metal* in the area *around* the joint. Move the torch in a circular motion at a uniform speed, slowly in ever smaller circles or figure eights around the joint. Finally, when the temperature is sufficiently high, which can be judged by the appearance of the flux and the metal, concentrate the heat on the joint and directly on the solder.

FLUX APPEARANCE DURING SOLDERING Changes that occur in the appearance of the flux must be watched as an indication of the approach of solder flow temperature. At first, steam rises as the water chemically combined and mechanically included in the flux evaporates. The flux swells up, and becomes a white, porous-looking mass. Withdraw the flame for a fraction of a second at a time to allow it to subside. If an excessive amount of moisture is present in the flux, this swelling may cause a displacement of the solder snippets which may then have to be pushed back in place with a *soldering pick*. It is therefore good practice to draw off the moisture carefully with the flame. The flux then settles down smoothly, loses its opacity, becomes viscous and is converted into a translucent borax glass·which is shiny and reflects light. In this state it protects the metal surface from oxidation by forming a barrier that excludes air contact with the metal surface, and dissolves any oxides that may form. This occurs *before* the solder reaches the melting point, and indicates that the melting point of the solder is approaching. The heating can now be accelerated by bringing the flame locally onto the joint. If the time lapse between the formation of borax glass and solder flow is relatively great, the flux coating will become *spent* or exhausted, in which case it is no longer chemically active and protecting the metal against the formation of oxides. Should this occur, more flux may have to be added to complete the soldering cycle.

2 LOCALIZED HEAT

In the localized heat that follows, confine and concentrate the flame on the joint and the solder, but still move it somewhat. As soon as the solder visibly flows, lead it along the seam with the flame.

CONDITIONS INFLUENCING SOLDER FLOW *Capillarity* or the relative attraction of the molecules of a liquid for those of a solid it contacts, and the reduction of surface tension on the molten solder due to heat have been mentioned as reasons for solder flow. Solder will tend to flow in a joint, or even over a surface, toward the direction of that part of the metal having the highest temperature. This fact (known since ancient times) can be utilized once the solder has started to flow to deliberately tease or draw it along a joint. By slowly moving the torch flame the solder will move with the heat. If, however, the gap distance between the parts is too great, heat and capillary action will not work, which emphasizes the need for well-fitting joints.

It is surprising how far a small amount of solder will

flow in a well-fitting joint. By watching the solder flow you can judge the rate at which to move the torch. The solder, in the case of silver solders, flows along like a bright silver streak. When this stops, remove the torch from the work because the solder has become extended as far as the capillary action will take it. Ordinarily, enough solder to complete the seam should be in place before soldering starts. If there has not been enough, at this point, additional solder must be added. A small solder ball melted beforehand and waiting in readiness for such an event can be picked up with the heated and fluxed soldering pick and placed without interruption of the process. Heating can then continue until the seam is filled.

FLAME CONDITIONS DURING SOLDERING
Flame type: Use a soft, neutral or reducing flame. Avoid a short, sharp, intense oxidizing flame that will cause rapid oxidation of the metal and solder, and quickly consume the flux.
Flame size: Do not use a flame larger than is necessary for the work. For localized or spot soldering, once the work is preheated, reduce the flame to a medium size. When work size increases, flame size becomes correspondingly larger. For annealing use a large, bushy, soft flame.
Flame motion: Oscillate the flame constantly in the area of the joint or part being soldered. Avoid a stationary flame because a hot spot might develop and cause local melting, or the work might collapse.
Flame height: For efficient heat use, hold the flame at the height at which it contacts the metal in the correct flame area, and its hottest part.
Flame angle: Flame angle should be as nearly vertical as possible, but the flame should not deflect back to the torch because it may be suddenly extinguished.

3 HEAT WITHDRAWAL

It is important to learn to recognize the proper moment for flame withdrawal. Judgment comes with experience. At times, as in granulation, judgment of the correct withdrawal moment may be critical to success. In general, do not allow the flame to linger on the soldered area any longer than necessary. When the solder fills the joint, allow the flame to remain just a fraction of a second longer, then immediately withdraw it. Slowly turn off the air first, then the fuel, to extinguish the flame.

ALTERNATIVE SOLDERING SYSTEMS

STICK FEED SOLDERING

Stick feed soldering can be used when snippets cannot be conveniently placed. A straight, cleaned, flux-coated solder stick, or a strip cut from sheet solder is held in readiness in either hand if the stick is long enough, or with *tweezers*. The fluxed work is heated until flux condition indicates soldering temperature is approaching. Briefly touch the solder stick to the joint, allow some to become molten under the flame and run in the joint, remove the stick, and draw the solder along the joint with the flame. If more solder is needed, repeat the process.

CONDUCTION SOLDERING

Conduction means transmitting heat to an object through an intermediary conductor material. In *conduc-

tion soldering, torch flame heat is not applied directly to the object, but is generally applied *from below* while the object rests on a *sheet of mica,* an *iron sheet,* or an open mesh iron or nichrome wire *soldering screen* or *heating frame.* These can be placed on a *tripod* or *ring stand* to lift the work and allow heat to be directed at it from below. Heat so applied is transferred by even diffusion from the supporting object to the work, bringing up its temperature gradually and evenly. This soldering method is used when joining delicate parts which might collapse and melt under direct heat, as in filigree work, and when joining wire to sheet.

SWEAT SOLDERING

In *sweat soldering* two clean, fluxed, lap joint parts with solder between them are heated until the solder flows and joins them. In some situations, the upper part is pressed with a soldering pick to force the solder to spread between the parts while it is molten. Alternately, one or both contacting surfaces can be preflooded with molten solder, then placed together, and the parts heated until the solder melts and joins them.

COMMON SOLDERING PROBLEMS AND SUGGESTED SOLUTIONS

Underheating causes solder to ball on the surface. This can happen when the parent metal is insufficiently heated before heat is played on the solder. Balling can also result from dirt or oxide present on the metal surface or joint. When it happens, stop the work, reclean it, reflux it, add new solder, and follow normal soldering procedure.

Overheating can cause pinhole development in exposed solder joints because the zinc or other low-melting metal in the solder alloy has volatilized. It can also make solder flow over areas adjacent to the joint where it is not wanted, and in some cases, it can even flow *away* from the joint. This can happen when too much solder is used. Wire and the corners of forms heat up quickly, often faster than the parent body and run the risk of melting. In such cases, use a soft flame, move it constantly, and use a long-lasting flux. Remove the flame as soon as the solder flows and do not prolong heating. Overheating metal also causes melting and collapse.

Preheating by lining up work, as in series soldering, is generally not advisable. If this system is used, arrange the work so that flame splash from the unit being soldered does not pass over the next. Should this happen, the flux on the next piece will become spent and the work oxidized before soldering is completed on the previous unit.

Joining different thicknesses of metal may be a problem. The thicker member tends to conduct heat away from the thinner one. The solution is to direct the preheat flame to the heavier part until it is near solder flow temperature, then let the flame cover both parts at the joint.

Joining different metals may cause difficulties as one may become overheated before the other reaches soldering temperature. The solution is to preheat the metal having the highest conductivity, or use a solder with a lower melting point.

Joining large surfaces may require a longer heating cycle because more heat is absorbed by the parts. First preheat the parts well away from the joint with a large flame to bring the heat of the unit up as quickly as possible and to minimize heat loss due to radiation and conduction. Then concentrate the flame on the joint and solder.

FIRESCALE: A surface, inorganic metal soil

Soil is any foreign substance on a metal surface that will hinder any process to be performed. *Firescale* is an inorganic metal soil that develops on a metal surface after heat treatments. Its extent and thickness depends on the degree of heat, the length of time of heat application, and the amount of oxygen imparted to the metal from the air and/or from the flame.

Light scale occurs on work annealed in a reducing atmosphere and is easily removed in an acid pickle solution, a process called *descaling.* Extended oxygen contact from an oxidizing flame creates a heavier scale. The difficulty of scale removal increases with its thickness.

Copper alloys heated to high temperatures in oxidizing conditions form a *double* oxide scale film. The *black outer layer* is cupric oxide (CuO), also called black copper oxide or copper monoxide. The *red inner layer* is cuprous oxide (Cu_2O), also called red copper oxide or copper suboxide. This inner layer is less rich in oxygen because it has had less oxygen exposure. Cuprous oxide is tenacious and more difficult to remove than cupric oxide. Excessive cuprous oxide will form if there is oil on the metal during heating.

When metal is immersed in a pickling or acid solution, these oxides are converted into a readily soluble metallic salt. In dense developments of oxide scale, however, pickle penetration is relatively slow. Therefore a *scale-loosening dilute acid solution,* is often used first, followed by *scale-removal solution* containing an oxidizing agent such as sodium dichromate. When the scale loosener is heated, it penetrates the outer oxide layer and converts the inner, lower oxides to higher oxides that are more readily dissolved. Simultaneously the subsurface oxides swell and disrupt the outer layer, which disintegrates. Depending on the metal, and on the thickness and nature of the firescale, descaling in pickle can take from a few seconds to as much as 20 minutes.

FIRESTAIN: A subsurface scale

Silver alloys containing copper repeatedly subjected to high heat treatments without being properly protected with scale-inhibiting flux or other inhibitors will develop a subsurface scale, commonly called *firestain* or *fire* by silversmiths and jewelers. This appears as a shadowlike, dark gray patch or patches below the surface. Firestain is more likely to occur as the alloying copper content increases. Eventually, this suboxide penetrates the grain structure, which becomes harder than the original silver alloy. Where it exists near a soldered joint, the joint is weakened since it hinders solder flow. Ordinary pickling may temporarily obscure its presence by leaving the surface thinly coated with pure silver from which the copper has been leached, but firestain appears again when the surface is polished. When allowed to remain, firestain may spoil the work's appearance, and its presence hastens further oxidation or tarnishing.

PREVENTING FIRESTAIN FORMATION To avoid firestain formation, take advance *preventive* measures. The simplest measure is to *precoat the entire article:* with a paste mixture of flux applied by a brush; by dipping the heated object into a flux solution then draining and allowing it to dry; or by spraying it with flux. A fixative sprayer, insecticide hand pump, or other sprayer can be used. Preheat the article beforehand somewhat so that the spray will dry on contact. Reheat the work and spray it with a second coat of flux. During soldering, at an elevated temperature the flux fuses and forms a glassy coating on the metal that seals the surface against oxygen contact so firescale and firestain do not form. After soldering, fused flux is removed with pickle or an ultrasonic cleaner.

CURING TREATMENTS TO REMOVE OR TREAT FIRESTAIN

Acid: Paint joints front and back with protective molten wax. Immerse the work for short intervals in a strong 50% solution of cold nitric acid, remove, and rinse. Observe the result by scratch brushing. Repeat this procedure until the subsurface firestain level is dissolved.

Abrasives: If metal thickness allows, remove firestain with abrasives. Polishing with tripoli usually is not enough unless firestain is shallow, but it can be tried first. Otherwise, use a *wet* waterproof abrasive paper, *dry* emery paper, or pumice paste and a felt buff. Alternately, rub the surface with a fine Arkansas stone, or a file.

Electrostripping: Electrolytically strip the silver by deplating with the article as anode. Remove the work at intervals to observe its condition as excessive stripping roughens the surface.

Electroplating: After polishing and thoroughly cleaning, electroplate the entire article using a pure silver or rhodium anode to completely cover the firestain.

Creating a uniform firestain: Make the entire surface appear a uniform bluish gray firestain color by annealing the work until it just shows redness. Allow it to cool somewhat, then pickle it. Repeat the process about six times, then polish with rouge.

POSTSOLDERING OPERATIONS

PICKLING OR ACID DIPPING

The word *pickle* describes any salt or vinegar and water solution used for preserving foods, and in general refers to solutions for steeping or soaking substances. *Metal pickling* is acid dipping, or the act of immersing and soaking metal in a dilute acid solution primarily to chemically remove or dissolve surface oxide or subsurface firestain formed on metal during heat treatments such as annealing, soldering, casting, and fusing. Pickling is also a means of removing other acid-soluble soils such as fused flux, investment plaster, and carbonaceous deposits.

SAFETY PRECAUTIONS

For *safety precautions* followed in handling and using acids, see Acids: Handling precautions, p. 324.

ACIDS USED FOR PICKLING, BRIGHT AND MATTE DIPPING

ORGANIC ACIDS This group of acids was commonly used on metals centuries before the discovery of mineral acids. Organic acids used in metalwork are: *citric acid* ($HOOC$-$CH_2C(OH)COOHCH_2COOH$), contained naturally in citrus fruits; and *acetic acid* (CH_3COOH), contained in vinegar, from 4–12%. Either of these acids mixed with common salt ($NaCl$) can be used to clean copper and its alloys, or to remove light scale on gold and silver.

MINERAL ACIDS Acids in this group commonly used by jewelers include: *nitric acid* (HNO_3), discovered in the 12th century A.D.; *sulphuric acid* (H_2SO_4), discovered in the mid-16th century A.D.; and *hydrochloric acid* (HCl), discovered in the 17th century A.D. (Also see Common Acids Used for Etching, p. 324.)

THE ACTION OF ACIDS IN PICKLE BATHS

A wide variety of pickle baths are used to achieve different results. Their action depends on their *composition, concentration, temperature,* and *immersion time.* These interrelated factors vary with the metal pickled, its condition, and the desired result.

CONCENTRATION Because all acids are *water soluble,* solutions of different strengths are easily achieved. A pickle solution's strength should not disturb the metal surface more than desired, but should be enough to do the work. Pickling solutions are generally weaker than etching solutions, which are meant to corrode the metal and act faster. For normal pickling operations, acid concentrations range between 5–10%, with some exceptions.

TEMPERATURE Some pickle solutions work best at room temperature, and others at elevated temperatures. Heat hastens the action of any acid solution. It is *not considered good practice today,* however, to bring pickling solutions to a boiling temperature because unhealthy, noxious fumes are released into the air, and pickling is just as efficiently accomplished *below* boiling temperatures. In jewelry making, it is common practice for jewelers to immerse work in pickle directly after soldering, while it is still hot. Work should *not* be red hot on immersion because besides possibly cracking the metal, acid spatter occurs, and excessive fumes evaporate into the atmosphere. Wait instead until the metal air cools somewhat before immersion, and cover the acid container immediately after immersion.

A solution containing a low concentration of acid works best when heated to 150–180° F (65–82° C). If, however, a cold solution is used, the acid can be increased to 10% to compensate for the decrease in thermal activity. When heating a glass container holding pickle, diffuse the heat over a large bottom area and do not concentrate it in one place or the container may break.

TIME OF IMMERSION The time needed for the pickle to remove the firescale or firestain depends on soil thickness in relation to acid concentration and temperature. If stronger solutions are used, the immersion time is shorter, and weak solutions require longer immersions. In normal immersion time periods, the parent metal below the soil is not seriously attacked because immersion is relatively brief and the object is removed from the pickle before this can happen. Remove work from the pickle as soon as the firescale or other soluble soil dissolves. The longer metal remains in acid solutions, the more surface corrosion occurs. Prolonged acid activity may result in *overpickling,* which creates a pitted surface, especially in cases where firescale was unevenly distributed.

THE USE OF OXIDIZING AGENTS When metal is immersed in acid, water-soluble metallic salts are formed by the chemical action of the acid on the metal and the oxides present. When oxides resist solubility, chemical oxidizing agents can be added to the acid solution. For instance, when dissolving red cuprous oxide, which is highly resistant to oxidation in acid solutions, *sodium dichromate* ($Na_2Cr_2O_7$), a red, crystalline salt oxidizing agent, is added to convert it to lower oxides that are readily dissolved. Another is anhydrous ferric sulphate ($Fe_2(SO_4)_3 \cdot 9H_2O$), added to sulphuric acid as an oxidizing agent to remove oxides from copper and its alloys, nickel, and stainless steel. (See formulas on p. 421.)

GREASE REMOVAL Acids will not attack metals coated with organic fatty substances such as wax, oil, grease, some lubricants, soap, and greasy binders in polishing compounds. These acid-resisting substances may be invisible, but to make a simple test to determine their presence, run cold water on the object. If rapid surface water break results, grease in some form is present. A clean surface allows a water break–free film to persist for at least 30 seconds after drainage. Greasy substances remaining on work immersed in pickle will foul the pickle and make it perform unevenly, and therefore must be removed.

Grease removal from objects can be done by heat. An object just soldered is grease-free. When grease is known to be present, remove it by boiling the work in a hot alkaline solution such as washing soda and water, or in a detergent; or place the work in an ultrasonic cleaner containing a cleaning solution. A mechanical means of removing grease from simple shapes is to scrub the surface with powdered pumice and a brush, then rinse with water.

Grease removal from the pickle solution is sometimes necessary when greasy objects have been immersed in it. When grease comes off the object, it floats on the surface because it is not acid soluble. When work is immersed in the pickle, it becomes grease coated. To remove floating grease, place a clean paper towel flat on the pickle surface, allow it to absorb the grease, then with tongs quickly remove and dispose of the towel. Repeat this procedure if necessary. The surface of a pickling solution should be occasionally inspected for the presence of an oil slick.

PICKLE CONTAINERS FOR USE AND STORAGE

Pickle solution containers or *tanks* for use or storage must be acid resistant. Containers for the use of solutions must have large openings; those used for storage, small openings that can be tightly closed with a cover. Large openings with tight covers can serve both purposes which does away with the need to transfer solutions from one container to another.

The choice of container material depends on the type of acid, in some cases its strength, its use, and simple convenience. A pickle container widely used by jewelers for cleaning work is a *copper pickle pot* with a handle to move it easily to and from the heat source, and a pouring lip to transfer the pickle into a storage container. Copper containers cannot be used for acid storage because copper is rapidly dissolved into the pickle from the pot itself and the acid is quickly spent. Pyrex or other heat- and acid-resistant glass does not have this limitation, but cannot be used for hydrofluoric acid which corrodes glass, and glass is fragile. (Hydrofluoric acid is not recommended for use by any but the most experienced craftspersons, and under the best conditions because its fumes are highly corrosive, even to eyeglasses.) *Polyethylene plastic* containers are used for storage because this substance is inert and does not react with acids, but it cannot be heated. Stainless steel, ceramic vitrified stoneware, and lead- and rubber-lined containers are used with various acids. The container

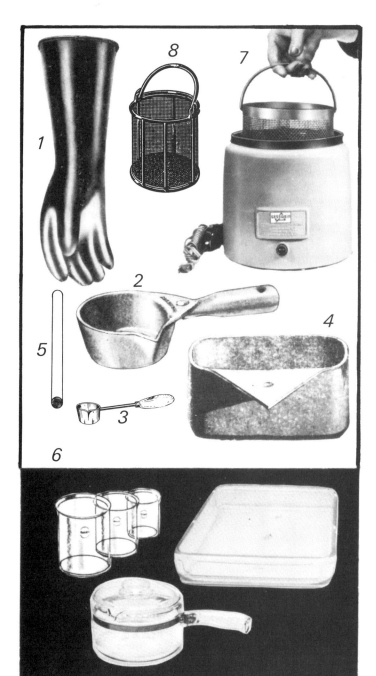

10–24 *PICKLING EQUIPMENT*
1. *Rubber gloves*, heavy-duty, 14 in long, used when working with acids or steam.
2. *Copper pickle pan*, of a heavy gauge, with riveted, hollow copper handle into which a wood rod extension can be hammered; 4½–6 in Ø, used for heating nitric acid or acid substitute solutions.
3. *Lightweight copper pickle pan* or boiling-out cup, 4 in Ø, with wooden handle, used for small work and weak acid solutions.
4. *Oblong, heavy-gauge copper pickle pan*, available in sizes from 80–260 mm. (Joliot)
5. *Glass or polyethylene stirring rod*, used when preparing acid solutions, or when agitating acid baths.
6. *Pyrex glass containers* used for pickle solutions; upper left: Pyrex beakers 1500 ml, 1000 ml, 600 ml, can also be used for plating solutions; right: Pyrex tray, 9 × 14 in; bottom: two-quart pot with handle, pouring spout, and cover.
7. *Electric pickler*, contains 1½ qt, 7 × 7¾ in, AC, 115 volts, 125 watts. Work is placed in a stainless steel or polyethylene basket and immersed in the pickle solution which is automatically maintained at an even temperature as long as it is connected.
8. *Stainless steel or polyethylene immersion basket* for use with electric picklers, or for normal pickle solutions, the latter if not heated above 180° F.

for use should be large enough to hold the object, and deep enough to allow the solution to completely cover it.

Clearly label all acid and pickle storage containers. Place them in a safe, cool, dry, easily reached location, preferably not above eye level, and not near tools or supplies that can be attacked or corroded by any escaping fumes. The storage time limit of a pickle solution depends on how much it has been used. Unused acids can be stored indefinitely *provided the cover is tight.*

PREPARING AND USING THE PICKLE

For the preparation of acid solutions, see The Acid Etching of Metals, Chapter 8.

Some additional points can be mentioned. To introduce any dry materials to a pickle solution, first dissolve them in water. Stir the solution with a *glass* or *plastic stirring rod* when pouring *any* liquid into pickle. If in time small amounts of acid must be added to the pickle to keep it active, or if the solution is transferred to a container with a small opening, use a *plastic funnel*. In all cases, *always pour slowly.* Avoid splashing by pouring it close to the container or funnel, not from a height. When adding acid to water in a container, always stir the solution so that heat stresses do not develop in the solution as they can cause glass containers to crack. *Always keep acid antidotes handy* and ready for use, work with acids near a *ready supply of running water,* and under good ventilation conditions.

Before placing any object into the pickle, first allow it to cool below red-hotness, then remove any *iron binding wire.* Never allow an iron tool to enter the pickle. Because iron is anodic to copper, an object in a solution containing any copper will become coated with copper. Place and remove objects into and from the pickle with copper, plastic, wood, or bamboo *tongs.* When porous tongs are used, reserve them for use with a particular acid or pickle solution. When immersing large objects, use a stainless steel, nichrome, or Monel metal *basket.*

AGITATION OF THE PICKLE Upon immersion, the acid attacks and softens the firescale, and the surface soon appears uniformly gray. Pickle action is considerably accelerated either by agitating the *object* with tongs, or by agitating the *pickle solution* with a stirrer. If the object lies stagnant, gas pockets may form that prevent pickle contact with the surface, thus stopping the acid's action there. Agitation makes the acid concentration more uniform so that the pickling rate is even on all surfaces. It is sometimes helpful, especially when pickling seamless tubes, to lift the work from the pickle with tongs, drain the acid, then replace it. This exposes the metal surfaces to fresh acid solution.

RINSING After pickling, all objects must be rendered acid-free. This is done by rinsing the object held by *tongs,* under cold or warm running water. Some jewelers dip the workpiece before or after rinsing in a soda solution (4 ounces to 1 pint of water) to neutralize the acid. This is

10–25 PICKLING EQUIPMENT
1. *Copper pickle tongs* used to immerse and remove articles from pickle solutions, 9 in long.
2. *Copper pickle tongs* with double jaws, 9 in long.
3. *Copper forceps,* 10 in long.
4. **Bamboo tongs,** 8 in. (20.3 cm) long, used with one acid only.
5. *Stoneware ceramic crock* with cover, used for pickle solutions and storage. (Allcraft)
6. *Lead container* with cover, used for acid solutions. (Joliot)
7. *Inert polyethylene containers* with friction-fit, vapor-tight covers, heavy walls, capable of withstanding temperatures up to 180° F (82° C), used for acid solutions and plating solutions. Available in 1–5 gal sizes, heights 9½–16¼ in; widths 6½–10¼ in.
8. *Sulphuric acid substitute,* Sparex No. 2, a granular, dry, proprietary compound that is prepared by mixing it with water according to given instructions.
9. *Swestex,* a pickle compound used for the removal of firescale from precious and nonferrous metals when mixed with water according to instructions. Available in 10 oz and 2½ lb cans.

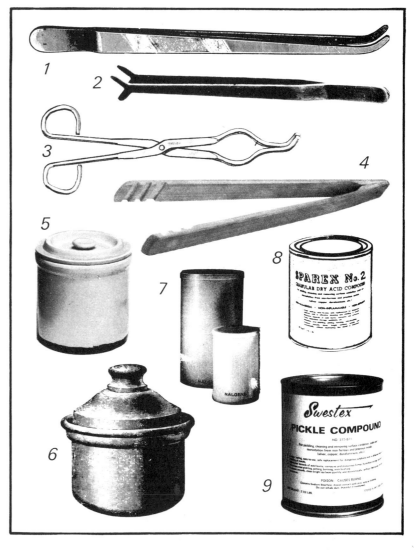

done especially with hollow objects where traces of acid may be trapped and cause corrosion later. If the object is neutralized after rinsing, a second rinsing must follow.

DRYING Dry the work with a clean *paper towel*, a clean *soft cloth, heated sawdust, heated crushed corncob,* in a *hot air* blast, or under a *heat lamp. Avoid touching the surface* if the work is to be followed by surface operations such as plating, electroforming, or lacquering.

PICKLE DISPOSAL Pickles used with alloys containing copper turn green as dissolved copper salts accumulate. Deep green solutions contain a saturated copper salt content in solution, are no longer active, and must be discarded. (See Precipitation and Recovery of Silver from Spent Acid Solutions, Chapter 3.)

To dispose of a *small* amount of pickle, do not simply dump it undiluted into a drain as this will corrode and damage the drain. Turn on a large volume of water, and pour the pickle slowly into this flow to dilute it. *Large* amounts of pickle must first be *neutralized* by introducing an *alkaline substance* such as powdered lime, or bicarbonate of soda. A rough proportion is 100 grams of neutralizer to 4 liters of solution. Allow the acid solution with neutralizer to stand for a while, and then flush it away with a large amount of running water.

ACID SUBSTITUTES

Acid substitutes or "safety pickles" are available for those who do not want to handle acids. They are manufactured in a dry powder form whose ease in handling and safety in storage are their main advantages. The powder is mixed with water in recommended proportions given with the product. Proprietary preparations of this type are Sparex No. 2, manufactured in the U.S.A. and available in 1 pound containers or larger amounts, and English products such as Shor Safe T Pickle, and Hoben Davis Safety Pickle.

A typical composition consists essentially of *sodium hydrogen sulphate* (NaHSO$_4$), or sodium bisulphate, which is a by-product in the manufacture of nitric acid, in a caked mass called *niter cake,* and in solution called *sulphamic acid.* This powder is mixed at a recommended concentration of 2.2 pounds to 1.2 gallons of water (1 kg to 4.55 liters of water) to produce a solution of pH 0.65–0.8. (In a smaller proportion: one teaspoon to one pint of water.) When this is brought to the boiling point, the result is sodium pyrosulphate (Na$_2$S$_2$O$_7$), and if the heating continues, sulphur trioxide forms and, in combination with water, acts as a dilute solution of sulphuric acid of about 6%. This removes metal oxides with less efficiency than a normal 10% sulphuric acid solution used for pickling.

PICKLING SOLUTIONS FOR VARIOUS METALS

PLATINUM PICKLE

Hydrochloric acid   10–20% by volume
Water   remainder
Use hot in a heat-resistant glass container. Before annealing platinum, pickle it to remove traces of iron or other base metals imparted to it during tool working. If not removed, they will diffuse into the platinum during annealing and cause uncorrectable irregularities.

GOLD AND GOLD ALLOYS

AQUA REGIA
Nitric acid   1 part by volume
Sulphuric acid
    (or hydrochloric acid)   3 parts by volume
"Royal water" solution is so called because it dissolves gold and platinum. When preparing this solution, add one acid to the other *very slowly,* since heat is chemically generated in the process of combination.

GOLD PICKLE
Sulphuric or nitric acid   1 part by volume
Water   5–10 parts by volume
Use at 125–175° F (51–79° C) in a stoneware or heat-resistant glass container. In cases where hollow parts might trap acid, pickling should be followed by boiling in an alkaline solution such as washing soda and water to neutralize acid traces. If not neutralized, trapped acid will continue to corrode the metal. Should moisture contact dried acid, it will become reactivated. Follow neutralizing with a warm running water rinse, and dry the object.

WHITE GOLD PICKLE
Sulphuric acid   10% by volume
Potassium dichromate 1% by volume
Water   remainder
Gold bright dip and matte dip are the same as those given for copper.

SILVER AND ITS ALLOYS

SILVER PICKLES
Nitric acid   2 parts by volume
Water   1 part by volume
Use at room (or elevated) temperature in a copper or heat-resistant glass container.

Sulphuric acid   5–10% by volume
Water   remainder
Use hot in a heat-resistant glass container.

FIRESCALE REMOVER FOR SILVER, WITH OXIDIZING AGENT
Sulphuric acid   1 pt
Sodium dichromate 2–4 oz
Water   1 gal
Use at 80–120° F (26–48° C) in heat-resistant glass or stoneware container. Immersion time must be judged by visual inspection, but should not be too long or etching will occur. Rinse thoroughly in hot then cold water, and neutralize. Dry well. Solutions with oxidizing agents can be used 3–5 days, then must be discarded.

SUBSURFACE FIRESTAIN REMOVER AND BRIGHT DIP
Sulphuric acid   2 parts by volume
Nitric acid   1 part by volume
Water   1.5 parts by volume
Hydrochloric acid
    or sodium chloride small amount
Slowly add one acid to the other, with *great caution,* as heat is generated. Use in a heat-resistant glass container. Hydrochloric acid increases luster, but in excess will cause spottiness. Rinse in cold running water, then wash with a hot soap and water solution.

COPPER AND ITS ALLOYS

COPPER PICKLE
Sulphuric acid   1 part by volume
Water   9 parts by volume
Use at room temperature or from 125–150° F (51.6–65.5° C) in a heat-resistant glass, stoneware, or copper container.

OXIDIZING AGENT
Add 4–8 ounces of sodium dichromate per gallon of above pickle when removing red cuprous oxide.

FIRESCALE REMOVER FOR COPPER (FAST)
Sulphuric acid   2 parts by volume
Nitric acid   1 part by volume
Water   5 parts by volume
Use at room temperature. Allow a short immersion, then rinse. Use this solution before bright dipping, in a copper, stoneware, or heat-resistant glass container.

BRIGHT DIP FOR COPPER AND ALLOYS
Nitric acid   25% by volume
Sulphuric acid   60% by volume
Hydrochloric acid 0.2% by volume
Water   remainder
The hydrochloric acid produces a bright, lustrous surface. Sodium chloride (NaCl) or common salt may be substituted for the hydrochloric acid in the same amount. Because this solution engenders heat, immerse the first acid container halfway into a second container of cold water. Sometimes some wood soot is added, stirred in, then skimmed off, as it helps to assure a uniformly bright surface and counteracts the tendency of hydrochloric acid to result in spottiness. Use at room temperature, immerse and rinse immediately in cold running water, then neutralize in a detergent solution to avoid acid stains.

MATTE DIP FOR COPPER AND ALLOYS
Sulphuric acid   35% by volume
Nitric acid   65% by volume
Zinc oxide or zinc sulphate
  ($ZnSO_4$)   1 lb/gal of solution
No water is used. Agitate the solution occasionally. Use at 180° F (82.2° C) in a heat-resistant glass container. The resulting matte surface can be made coarser by increasing the nitric acid, and finer by increasing the sulphuric acid. Dip, rinse, and dry. Parts can be left bright if they are protected by a lacquer resist that is allowed to dry thoroughly before use, and later is removed by a solvent such as acetone.

NICKEL AND ITS ALLOYS

NICKEL SILVER
Because the oxide scale on nickel alloys and stainless steel is difficult to remove, a *scale-loosening solution* is used first, followed by a *scale-removal solution*. If the scale is not heavy, the first may be eliminated.

SCALE LOOSENING
Potassium permanganate, $KMnO_4$
  (oxidizer)   3–12 oz/gal
Soda ash   3–12 oz/gal
Water   1 gal
Use at 170–212° F (91.6–100° C) in a heat-resistant glass container, for 10–30 minutes, with agitation, then rinse and use:

SCALE REMOVER AND PICKLE FOR NICKEL AND MONEL
Sulphuric acid   13 oz/gal
Ferric sulphate, anhydrous (oxidizer)   13 oz/gal
Water   1 gal
Use at 140° F (90° C) in a heat-resistant glass container.

NICKEL SILVER PICKLE
Sulphuric acid   1 pt
Sodium dichromate   ½ lb
Water   5 gal
Use at room temperature or at 150° F (65.5° C) in a heat-resistant glass container.

STAINLESS STEEL
In pickling stainless steel, copper or bronze should not be present or copper will be electrolytically deposited on the steel. Use steel tongs to handle the object.

SCALE LOOSENING
Sulphuric acid   12 oz/gal
Water   1 gal
Use at 180° F (82.2° C) in a stainless steel or heat-resistant glass container.

SCALE REMOVAL
Hydrochloric acid   5 parts by volume
Nitric acid   1 part by volume
Water   14 parts by volume
Use at 125–160° F (51.6–71° C) in a heat-resistant glass container.

BRIGHT DIP
Nitric acid   4 parts by volume
Phosphoric acid   1 part by volume
Acetic acid   5 parts by volume
Hydrochloric acid   1 part by volume
Use at 160° F (71.1° C) in a heat-resistant glass or stoneware container. Before bright dipping stainless steel, passivate it by immersion in a hot 5% sulphuric acid solution. Passivating is a treatment that removes contaminating iron particles in the stainless steel surface placed there by tools, dies, etc., during processing. If allowed to remain, these particles will later rust and cause discolorations. Follow bright dipping by washing and drying. If the article will be polished, passivating can be eliminated as the iron particles will be removed by abrasion during polishing.

UNSOLDERING
There are occasions when parts that have already been soldered together must be separated. In this case, paint flux on the joint to be separated. Paint joints that must remain intact with a solder-inhibiting paste. Protect exposed surfaces against firescale formation by coating them with flux. Pin the lowest part to a charcoal block or asbestos coil block, and leave the part to be removed exposed. Fix *self-locking tweezers* to the part to be removed, and heat the joint to be separated with a small flame. Watch the solder in the seam. At the moment when it turns bright, pull or lift away the part. A *soldering pick* or an *old pair of pliers* can also be used to help hold down or push away a part if necessary. Do not prolong the heating unnecessarily or other joints may become overheated and come apart.

422

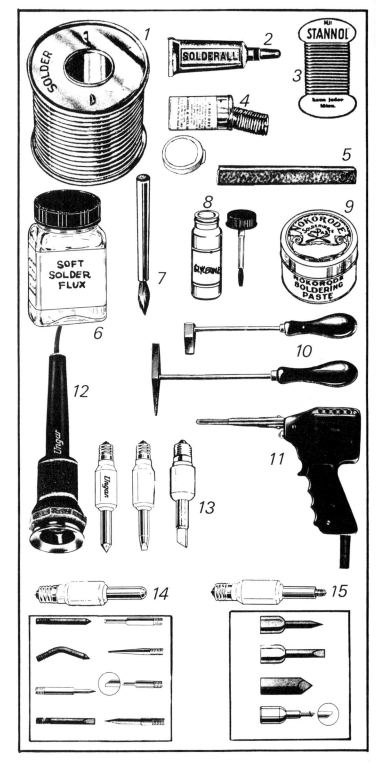

10–26 SOFT SOLDERING MATERIALS AND TOOLS

1. *Spool of solid wire soft solder.*
2. *Solderall,* a soft solder in paste form combined with a flux in a 1½ oz tube.
3. *Hollow-core soft solder containing resin flux.*
4. *Stay Bright,* a soft solder alloy for use with silver, brass, and copper, flows at 400° F (204° C), remains bright, and will take gold plating. (Container cover below.)
5. *Bar of bismuth soft solder, used on pewter, 1 oz.*
6. *Soft solder liquid flux,* mildly corrosive, for use on brass and white metal.
7. *Soft solder liquid flux brush applicator* with aluminum handle, length ¹¹⁄₁₆ in.
8. *Glycerin with brush applicator,* used with hydrochloric acid as a flux for fast soldering action.
9. *Nokorode,* a noncorrosive soft soldering flux paste for use on all metals but aluminum, 2 oz metal container.
10. *Hammer form and double-ended externally heated soldering irons* with copper tips mounted on steel rods held in a wooden handle.
11. *Mentor electric soldering pistol,* 55 watts, 110 or 220 volts, with changeable tips.
12. *Ungar electric pencil-type soldering iron,* 47.5 watts, 110 or 220 volts, with many interchangeable tips for soldering miniature, subminiature, and microminiature work, with standard insulated handle.
13. *Interchangeable screw-in tips* for the above in pyramid, chisel, and knife form.
14. *Screw-in tip* used with ⅛ in thread-in tiplets in box below. *Left column:* pencil, offset pencil, stepped pencil, chisel. *Right column:* stepped chisel, tapered needle, microspade, ultra fine.
15. *Screw-in tip* used with ¼ in thread-on tiplets in box below. Pencil, chisel, pyramid, stepped microspade.

SOFT SOLDERING

Soft solder is an easily fusible alloy of tin and lead, and in some compositions also includes antimony and bismuth. These metals melt at a temperature below 700° F (371° C), which defines them as "soft" solders. Its use in jewelry making is generally limited, the main use being to join earring wires, cuff link backs, and other findings to jewelry when the parts to which they are attached cannot take the higher heat of hard solder without becoming damaged, or to keep the spring hardness of the findings being soldered. It is also sometimes used for repairs, again when the work cannot be subjected to higher temperatures. Most jewelers try to avoid its use by using findings that can be attached to presoldered finding parts by cold joining methods such as riveting. Some countries will not allow articles made of precious metals that make use of soft solder to be hallmarked. A special use of soft solder alloys is its use as a seal disc that is stamped with an official customs or personal cipher, then attached by a string to articles or parcels placed in bond.

The proportions of various soft solder alloys and their flow points are given in the chart on p. 423. Of all these, the most popular general-purpose solder used is *half-and-half* (50% tin; 50% lead), and *fine* (60% tin; 40% lead). In repair work, however, soft solders having an even lower flow point temperature may have to be used on occasion. In the soft solder composition, tin serves as the major metal-wetting ingredient. The melting point of these alloys is lower than that of tin or lead alone. These solders will wet all common metals except aluminum.

SOFT SOLDER FORMS

Soft solder is available as *extruded wire* and in other forms. One is a *tube* whose hollow core is filled with flux. Another is a *paste* called *fusion solder* and in one composition it combines pulverized soft solder alloys, flux, and a cleaning agent.

SOFT SOLDER FLUXES

Soft solder fluxes are classified as *corrosive* or *noncorrosive,* and are available in *liquid* or *paste* form. As in the case of hard solders, the flux acts to prevent surface oxide formation during soldering; to promote the mutual contact between the atoms of the metal being joined and the solder atoms; and to lower molten solder surface tension so that when heated it will flow freely into the joint, and by gravity and capillarity, will wet the metals being joined.

Corrosive soft solder fluxes are more efficient in preventing oxidation than noncorrosive ones. A typical liquid cor-

Soft Solder Compositions

Metal Percentage				Flow Point Temperature	
Tin	Lead	Antimony	Bismuth	°F	°C
10-20	90-80			567-531	279-277
15-35	85-65			543-523	283-242
38-40	62-60			462-460	238-237
45	55			437	225
50	50			421	216
60	40			376	191
63	36.5	0.5		359	181
50	49.5	0.5		358	181
45	54.5	0.5		359	181
40	59.75	0.25		360	182
39	48		13	343	172
40	10		50	240	115
24	26		50	200	93

10–27 HOMER LUMPMOUTH (Arapaho), Oklahoma, U.S.A. An electric soldering torch in use. Photo: Courtesy U. S. Department of the Interior, Indian Arts and Crafts Board

rosive flux is made by dissolving 6 ounces of zinc chloride (ZnCl$_2$), a white, caustic salt, in a pint of alcohol or water. Another is made by dissolving small pieces of pure zinc in hydrochloric acid until all bubbling ceases and the acid is "killed." Some ammonium chloride (NH$_4$Cl) (also called *sal ammoniac*) is added to make the flux more efficient. The ideal corrosive soft solder flux contains 71% ZnCl$_2$, 29% NH$_4$Cl, and melts at 354° F (178° C), or very near the melting point of soft solders, thus offering extended protection. Store liquid fluxes in well-stoppered bottles. A popular corrosive flux contains 75% petroleum jelly, 20% ZnCl$_4$, 5% NH$_4$Cl, and a little water as an emulsifying agent.

Noncorrosive soft solder flux pastes are mild fluxes made by dissolving rosin in alcohol or kerosene. They are not as effective as corrosive fluxes in preventing or removing oxidation. Commercial proprietary preparations such as Nokorode soldering paste, are available.

THE SOFT SOLDERING PROCESS

Compared with hard solder, soft solder is relatively low in strength. Joint strength depends on solder adhesion to the metals joined. Wetting power and solder penetration, and conditions that permit these are therefore important. The contacting parts must be well fitting, clean, and free of all foreign matter. Clean the metal by abrasion with steel wool, an abrasive paper, a file, or a scraper, or by chemical solutions. Lap joints are the strongest as their large contacting surfaces add strength to the joint.

Apply liquid flux with a brush, and paste flux with a wooden stick. Use only a minimum amount on the surfaces to be joined. Solder can be placed on the metal with a soldering iron, described below, or small solder snippets can be placed in contact with the parts being joined, if necessary hammering them flat to place them between parts in order to minimize movement at the time of solder flow.

SOLDERING IRON SOFT SOLDERING *Soldering irons,* also called *soldering coppers* are of two types: one heated *externally,* the other heated *internally.* All have copper tips as copper is a good conductor of heat and electricity. A tip without electrical attachment is heated externally by

applying or holding it over a flame. A tip heated internally has an electric wire that conducts current to the tip. Both types have wooden handles to allow them to be hand held.

To use a soldering iron, first clean the tip well with steel wool or a paper abrasive. Then heat and rub it over a cake of *solid sal ammoniac flux,* or dip it into another flux. Load it with solder by rubbing the tip against the solder, melting it on the tip's last half inch. Place the tip near the joint to allow a heat transfer to take place, then draw it along the fluxed seam to let the solder flow from the tip into the seam. Add more solder and repeat the process if necessary. Soldering irons are not frequently used by jewelers, who usually prefer to use a torch flame to melt soft solder.

SOFT SOLDERING WITH A TORCH Soft soldering can also be done using a torch flame as the heat source to melt the solder. The work is prepared by cleaning the joint, applying flux, and placing solder snippets along it. The soldering time should be as short as possible. The parts to be soldered together must be heated to solder-melting temperature before the solder will flow. Use a small, soft torch flame and gently heat the area adjacent to the joint until the solder shows signs of melting by becoming *bright.* Then concentrate the flame on the solder, which will flow when its melting point is reached. Remove the flame *immediately* and do not overheat the solder. Allow the work to stand until the solder solidifies; it will appear *dull* at that point. Parts can be pressed together with a *soldering pick* until this happens. The work can then be lifted with *tongs* and cooled under running water. Remove all surplus flux. Removal must be complete, especially when corrosive fluxes are used. Boil the work in a detergent to emulsify greasy flux.

SOFT SOLDER REMOVAL

Soft solder can be removed from a cleaned gold or silver jewel by placing it in a hot solution of hydrochloric acid in a heat-resistant glass container, and keeping it there until all the solder has been digested by the acid. Be-

fore immersion, scrape off as much of the exposed solder as possible. Remove and rinse the work.

It is also possible to heat the work to the point when the soft solder liquefies, and pull the parts to be separated apart with *tweezers.* While the solder is still in a molten state, it can be wiped away with steel wool from exposed surfaces. Any remainder can be removed with abrasive paper or a file, or if that would endanger the surface, it can be digested by acid, as above.

SCREWS, BOLTS AND NUTS, AND SCREW JOINTS

Mechanical cold fabrication by torsion-pressure holding systems

SCREWS

A *screw* is a mechanical fastening device that applies pressure on the parts being joined, the pressure acting to hold them together. The basic concept of *any mechanical device* is that it serves to transmit and modify motion and/or force to produce a desired effect or work. The screw, in several forms, does exactly that.

The mechanical system of joining jewelry parts by means of screws alone, or screws and/or bolts with nuts can be resorted to not only when joining metal to metal, but when joining *dissimilar materials,* such as metal to plastic, metal to wood, metal to ivory, etc. Screws are also useful in cases where heat cannot be applied, for example as when joining a separately made enamel-ornamented unit to a larger work, or a stone set independently in a separate metal bezel to a ground of metal or another material by means of a screw previously soldered to its back. Screws are sometimes used to take the place of a rivet when the work is too delicate to withstand hammering. Screws have the unique advantage of being able to be removed to disassemble work for purposes of repair, or to repolish otherwise inaccessible areas, such as a reflective backplate. Screwheads are often concealed in jewelry, but today they are at times deliberately exposed as a decorative joining device.

THE PARTS OF A SCREW

In its common form, a screw consists of a *slotted head* which can have any of several shapes, and a cylindrical *shank* or *spindle* that is grooved in its total or partial length with a helical spiral consisting of one or more *threads,* also called *worms* or *ribs* in some cases. The thread utilizes the concept of the *inclined plane,* which classifies the screw as a *simple machine.* (The six simple machines are the screw, the lever with fulcrum, the wheel and axle, the pulley, the inclined plane, and the wedge.)

The same mechanical principle of the inclined plane in the form of a screw is utilized in a holding device such as a clamp or vise, in the transmitting of motion as in a micrometer, and as a provider of power as in the operation of a tool such as a lathe. In the screw, the inclined plane winds in a helical spiral around the solid metal or hollow cylinder shank, and becomes the threads or ridged ribs which are uniform in section, but possibly different in shape, depending on the work they are to perform. It is

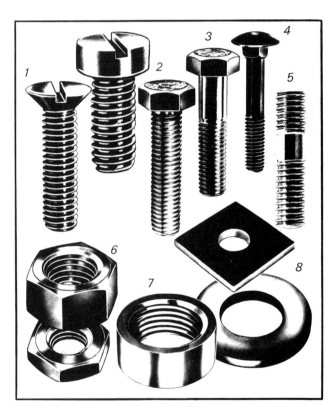

10–28 *SCREWS, BOLTS, NUTS, AND WASHERS*
1. *Metal screws with slotted or grooved heads, the first with a cone or flat head, the second with a cap head.*
2. *Hexagonal-headed screw-bolt with full thread.*
3. *Hexagonal-headed bolt with half threaded and half plain shank.*
4. *Oval-headed bolt with square base for setting into a square hole to immobilize the head, with half threaded shank.*
5. *Headless or grub screw with plain center to allow tube threading from both ends.*
6. *Hexagonal screw or bolt nuts, wide and narrow.*
7. *Sleeve nut or screw coupling.*
8. *Square washer; round washer.*

the thread's inclined plane that converts the screw's rotation into *straight-line motion,* and the holding power of screws, and bolts and nuts depends upon the threads.

Right-hand threads, when seen from the head, turn in a clockwise direction, while *left-hand threads* (commonly

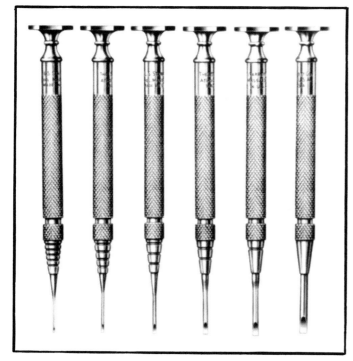

10-29 *JEWELER'S, WATCHMAKER'S, AND OPTICIAN'S SCREWDRIVERS* These are adapted to fine, delicate work on small screws. The knurled steel tubing bodies and concave swivel knobs provide for good grasping. The tempered steel blades are held in chucks whose number of grooves designate blade sizes. They vary in width from 0.025–0.100 in. For convenience in carrying, the blade can be reversed into the body. *Photo: Courtesy L. S. Starrett Co.*

point may cause the threads to wear out or become stripped, which renders the screw useless. Therefore, you must learn to sense the correct moment when to stop exerting pressure, when maximum torque tension exists.

SCREWHEAD TYPES

Most screws have a *slotted* or *grooved head* into which the screwdriver is inserted to wind and tighten the screw, or to loosen and remove it. The head can be of several shapes, depending on how the screw is to function. Some of these are the following:

Cap: A straight-sided, cylindrical form.

Flat (cone): A cone shape tapering toward the shank, commonly used with a countersunk surface to make the head flush with the plane of the work surface.

Round: A semicircular head that projects above the surface.

Oval: A curved, low-profile shape that projects upward less than a round head.

Headless: Without a head, the solid or tube shank itself being slotted, driven home either flush, or below the surface (also called a grub screw). In the latter case, the remaining circular depression may be filled with a tight-fitting round *plug* of the same or contrasting metal to make the screw presence invisible. So-called *headless screw rivets* are short, threaded cylinders whose shank length is a fraction more than the thickness of the parts joined. Once threaded in place, both ends are hammered to form shallow or flush heads that are then permanent.

Decorative: Any ornamental head shape attached to a screw or bolt shank.

Thumb: An oval, flat or concave, knurled or smooth-surfaced projection joined perpendicularly to a screw or bolt shank that permits tightening it with the thumb and forefinger. It is often found on tools such as the jeweler's saw frame, and clamps or holding devices of various types that are tightened manually.

THE PARTS OF A SCREW THREAD

Crest: The top point where adjacent sides of the inclined plane of a thread meet.

Root: The bottom surface where adjoining adjacent sides of the thread form a groove.

Pitch: The distance from any crest to the adjacent one, measured parallel to the shank axis.

Lead: The amount of axial movement of any point on the screw thread during one complete revolution.

Single thread: A screw having a single helix crest around the shank, from beginning to end.

Multiple thread: A screw with more than one helix around the shank, such as a *double thread* which has *two* in which the lead between each distinct thread is twice as long as the pitch.

Threads are divided into two basic types: those used for *fastening,* and those used to transmit *power* and *motion,* as in lathe lead screws, vises, and clamps.

used in jewelry in the East) turn counterclockwise. When the threads are *external* they are called *male threads,* and when they are *internal, female threads.* Any round hole of a proper size in solid metal can be threaded internally to match an externally threaded screw, but the most common form of internal threading occurs in a *nut.* This is a square- or hexagonal-sectioned metal part, perforated with a hole that contains the female thread, its size coordinated with the screw or bolt with which it is meant to mate. (Bolts and nuts are discussed on p. 427.) Screws and bolts used for metal are cylindrical and have blunt ends, but screws used for wood are tapered and have pointed ends. Wood screws form their own internal threads in the material as they enter.

Screws are inserted in the threaded hole made to receive them, and are rotated by the aid of a *screwdriver.* A screwdriver is used to drive or force the screw spirally in place, called "screwing it home," by inserting its wedge-shaped end into the slotted groove of the screwhead, each turn causing it to advance. Jewelers and watchmakers use very small screws which require specially made miniature screwdrivers to tighten them. One such screwdriver consists of a single knurled handle with a chuck into which blades of various sizes can be inserted to allow the interchange of blades.

SCREW THREAD FIT As both parts being joined are threaded with mating threads, they mesh as the screw advances until, when fully wound home, the screwhead comes down tightly on the parts joined, or in the case of a bolt and nut, until both come tightly together bringing two-sided, clamping pressure upon the parts being joined. A *close screw thread fit* is one in which there is a minimum of shake or play, and the interference of the metal is zero. Continuing the screwing torque pressure beyond this

10-30 NOMA COPLEY, U.S.A. "Screw Head." Cast 18K gold cuff links in the form of cone- or flat-headed screws; with wire links. *Photo: Tracy Boyd*

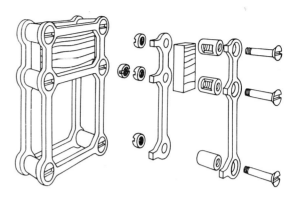

10–31A Exploded drawing showing the parts used in the assembly of the ring at *left*.

10–31   JOËL DEGEN, England. Four rings using the cold fabrication system of screws and threaded parts to hold units together.

Top left: Ring of titanium and stainless steel with striped agate sandwiched between them.

Top right: Ring with two blue anodized titanium sheet units separated by silver tube spacers, joined by gold flush-headed screws with stainless steel shanks. The green-dyed moss agate stone is held by four tubes notched to accommodate it. Exploded drawing showing the parts used in the assembly of the ring at *left.*

Bottom left: Ring with 1½ct emerald-cut diamond, set in a white gold cup on a yellow gold shank. The channel-grooved outer titanium discs and the cup edges hold the stone. Stainless steel flush-headed screws are threaded into holes tapped in the gold shank.

Bottom right: "Worry" ring. Constructed with an upper cylinder that revolves by a shielded ball bearing placed inside. Above this, a tubular structure holds the upper round diamond. Around the cylinder are 12 baguette diamonds held in place by holes in two titanium discs. Below is a disc with 12 tapped holes which hold the 12 screws circling the central diamond, and bind the entire structure. The gold shank is faced on both sides with titanium discs fastened by flush-headed stainless steel screws. *Photos: Joël Degen*

10–32   JOËL DEGEN, England. Bangle bracelet of three metal layers: stainless steel, silver, and blued titanium. Pierced hole diameters are slightly smaller than those of the lenticular-shaped red carnelians. Once parts are screwed together, the stones hold in place. Screws pass from the steel side to engage the titanium sheet in which meshing holes are threaded. *Photo: Courtesy Crafts Advisory Committee, London*

Thread types

Thread name	Angles between sides of thread	Description
Fastening threads		
American National Standard		
Coarse (ANC)	60°	squared-off crest, rounded root
Fine (ANF)	60°	squared-off crest, rounded root
British Association Thread (BA) metric	47.5°	rounded crest and root
V-thread, American	60°	sharp crest and root
Whitworth (BS), British	55°	rounded crest and root
European, metric		
French (NF)	60°	rounded crest and root
German (DIN)	60°	rounded crest and root
Swiss (VSM)	60°	rounded crest and root
Unified National System U.S.A., U.K., Canada, 1948		
Coarse (UNC)	60°	rounded crest and root
Fine (UNF)	60°	rounded crest and root
International Standards Organization (ISO), metric, 1963		
Coarse (ISOC)	60°	flat crest and rounded root
Fine (ISOF)	60°	flat crest and rounded root
Power and motion threads		
Acme	29°	squared-off crest and root
Buttress, one face vertical, other angular	45°	squared-off crest and root
Square	90°	squared-off crest and root

Commercial metal and wood screws, and bolts and nuts are available in many sizes and head shapes, made of iron, steel, copper, brass, bronze, aluminum, and nylon. Small sizes suited for use in jewelry are available from watchmakers' suppliers. Screws in precious metals are also available. All screws and bolt and nut types can of course be made by the jeweler from any metal according to need, by methods described below.

BOLTS

Metal screws pass through parts and are seated in the drilled and tapped mating threads that have been prepared to receive them. Tapered wood screw threads form their own threads as they penetrate the material. Bolts are different from screws in that normally they pass *completely through* an unthreaded hole in the parts joined without being screwed into them, and hold the parts together by the help of a nut wound onto the end of the shank. When tight, friction between the thread and the nut, as well as the helical pressure on the nut wound on the bolt, prevents its becoming loosened, unless excessive movement or vibration occurs. Bolts have special threads, but may also be threaded with normal screw threads, in which case they are sometimes called *screw bolts*.

Bolt heads commonly are square or hexagonal to allow them to be gripped with a wrench, or they may be of several other shapes similar to those used on rivet heads. (See Rivet Head Shapes, Chapter 10.) They may also have a head of any decorative shape when visible and used in jewelry.

Washers may be used with screws, bolts, and rivets. They are plain or decorative rings of metal, leather, nylon or another material, and are placed between the screw, bolt, or rivet head and the upper work surface. Their purpose is to form a seat for the head, to protect the work surface against which they are drawn by increasing the area of pressure (useful when using thin metal), to prevent a tightened head from being pulled through the opening, and to prevent loosening from vibration by locking the screw or bolt in place through an increase in the area of friction.

10–33 PETER SKUBIC, Austria. Stainless steel rings based on the bolt and nut concept. Height 42 mm. *Photo: Peter Skubic*

NUTS

Nuts are square or hexagonal blocks of metal, perforated and internally threaded, and are used at the end of a screw or bolt to draw and hold parts together. The *sleeve nut* is an internally threaded cylinder made of tubing, also called a *screw coupling* or *screw socket*. The threading can be all in the same direction, or half right and half left. Such a coupling can be used to join two threaded wire ends, rods, or tubes, one from each side.

CONSTRUCTION

MAKING A PSEUDOSCREW

Screws are believed to have been invented by about the 4th century B.C. It is possible that the idea was inspired by nature in the form of shells whose eroded, exposed inner spiral structures were thrown up on beaches. In Roman times, screws were made by winding a triangular wire around a cylindrical rod, with one flat side against the rod. This wire was also used as a guide to file, chisel, or gouge the spiral groove into the shank cylinder.

10–34 *Left: DETAIL OF THE CLOSING DEVICE* contained within the back bead that divides in half. The psuedoscrew is made of a wire wrapped spirally around a wire shank, which fits a spirally wrapped screw cylinder formed in the screw's grooves, then mounted within the second bead half. *Photo: Jan Olsson*

10–35 *Right:* BERNDT LINDHOLM, Finland, maker; ANDERS HÖGBERG, Sweden, designer. Necklace of square-wire silver openwork spheres in graduated sizes, decorated with small, concave gold discs, separated by small gold beads. *Photo: Jan Olsson*

A similar, simple device that functions in concept like a screw and sleeve nut is often used today in India on jewelry as a closing device for belts and bracelets. No *screw plates* or *taps,* the tools normally used today for forming a thread on screws and in nuts, are needed. First cut a suitable length of round wire for the shank core, and solder on a head, often a round, solid ball. Starting at this head, tightly wrap a round wire in a close clockwise spiral around this shank to its end. Solder the start and the end of the spiral to the core wire to keep it from moving on the shank core. The wrapped wire is now equivalent to the *external* or *male screw.* It must mate with an *internal* or *female screw,* normally contained in a nut. Carefully wind the same gauge round wire spirally clockwise onto the groove depressions of the spiral on the male screw, and cut off the end. This outer spiral is equivalent to the nut screw or a sleeve nut. It is easily removed from the male screw by unwinding it counterclockwise with the fingers, like a nut. The resulting nut-spiral can then be mounted in the work, often inside a tube of suitable size. This pseudoscrew and nut set must mesh as they have been formed upon each other.

MAKING A SCREW OR BOLT

Round wire or rod is used as the raw material for the screw or bolt shank. In some bolts, the part of the shank just under the head is made *square,* a form that fits into a matching square hole in the metal being joined, thus preventing it from twisting when the nut is turned hard on it in tightening. This idea can be used as a way of fixing a screw or bolt with an ornamental head which must be placed in one particular, immobilized position.

A head can be formed on the shank by immobilizing it in a vise using a strip of leather on both sides to prevent its becoming flattened from the pressure. The head is then formed with a *rivet hammer,* upsetting it with the square peen, then rounding it with the flat peen. It can be shaped further in a half-round depression in a *dapping block* or *rivet block,* and smoothed if necessary with an abrasive paper. The head must be large enough and heavy enough

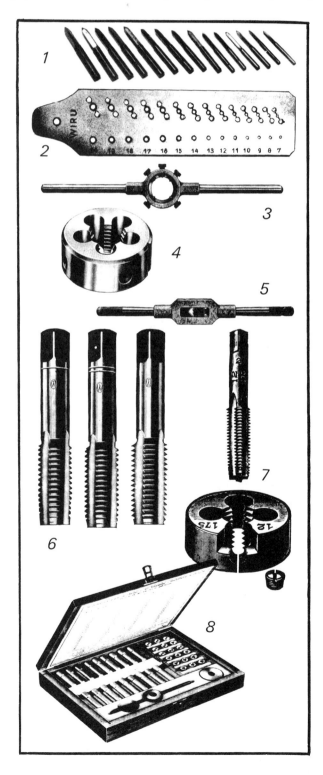

to offer proper resistance to the pressure of its tightened condition to prevent the head from being pulled through the hole. The slot in the head can then be formed by starting the groove with a triangular file to establish its proper position, then changing to a square file to complete it to the required depth.

DIE THREADING AN EXTERNAL THREAD WITH A SCREW PLATE The *screw plate* is a threading die for hand forming external threads on screws and bolts. It consists of a highly tempered tool steel plate pierced with one or more threaded holes, progressively increasing in size, that are circular or double notched for the clearance of metal chips. Screw plates are usually sold with a matching set of *taps,* the tool used to form an internal thread, described below.

When making an external thread, select the screw plate hole whose inner thread diameter is less than the diameter of the shank so that it will cut into the shank and form threads. Clamp the screwhead in a vise with the shank pointing perpendicularly upward. Place the selected screw plate hole flat on the trued shank end, and press the screw plate down hard over the shank to fix it in a starting position. Turn the screw plate handle clockwise and the screw plate grooves will automatically start to cut into the shank as the screw plate advances. Continue to wind the screw plate until the desired depth of thread is formed on the shank, then reverse the direction and unwind the screw plate until it is removed. If the diameter of the shank is too large for the chosen hole, the screw plate may break, or it will stop advancing and if the turning continues the threads already formed will be stripped or worn off. Before this happens, unwind the screw plate and move the shank to the next larger opening in the screw plate, and proceed as before.

DIE THREADING AN EXTERNAL THREAD WITH A CIRCULAR DIE A solid or a two-part circular cutting die can also be used to form the external threads on a screw or bolt. This die is placed in the depression of a two-handled *stock* made to hold dies with the same outer diameter, but with different sized cutting capacities. The stock depression is provided with a shoulder to keep the die from being forced out in use. The stock is also equipped with external set screws that are tightened, and pass through its frame into matching holes in the die perimeter to secure it.

The screw shank with its end filed square and its edge slightly chamfered to ease the start is placed in a vise

10–36 *DIE THREADING AND TAPPING TOOLS*
1. *Taps* of hard steel in a set of 15 in decreasing sizes from ³⁄₃₂–³⁄₁₆ in, to correspond with the hole sizes of the screw plate.
2. *Screw plate* with 14 double-notched holes and 14 single holes, for making small right- and left-hand V-threads.
3. *Circular stock* or round die holder with handles, used for making external threads. In use it rests against the inside shoulder and is screwed tightly in place by five externally mounted set screws surrounding the stock.
4. A *circular, button* or *spring die* used for making external threads on screws up to Ø ½ in. The thread-forming chaser ridges and the metal clearance holes which also provide cutting edges to the die are seen, as well as the outer rim with holes into which the retaining set screws fit.
5. *Tap wrench* with an adjustable lever handle used to hold the square end of taps.
6. *Hand taps,* set of three used when making internal threads of large diameter, and when making blind holes. The first is a starting or *taper tap,* the second an intermediate or *plug tap,* and the third a finishing or *bottoming tap.*
7. A *numbered set of taps and circular dies* for making a matching internal and external thread on a nut and screw respectively. A set screw to hold the die in the stock is at the side.
8. *Goldsmith's taps and circular dies,* a set in 18 sizes with handled stock for each. (Karl Fischer)

pointing perpendicularly upward, and the die whose diameter matches or is slightly larger than the core diameter of the shank is pressed down on its trued end. The shank is then lubricated and turned by half turns and partial reverse turns, advancing until the initial threads are properly established by the die's cutting threads. By hand feeding the die progressively on the shank, threads are formed by degrees until the desired thread depth is reached. The stock is then rewound in reverse to remove the die.

FORMING INTERNAL THREADS ON A NUT WITH A HAND TAP To thread a nut for use with a screw or bolt, cut a rectangular piece of sheet metal thick enough to engage a distance of at least three thread crests, otherwise it will not hold on the screw efficiently. Mark its center with a *center punch*. Using a *tap drill* whose number corresponds with the tap size used, drill a hole straight through the center. The drill's diameter should be slightly smaller than or equal to the core diameter of the thread, called tapping size. (Alternately, a hole can be made in the uncut metal, then threaded, and the nut cut out later in any form; an internal thread can also be made at any location on any irregular metal form to hold any part.)

To cut an internal thread, a *hand tap* is used. This is a square-headed, cylindrical or conical hard steel tool having peripheral cutting threads. It is fluted lengthwise to allow for chip clearance and the access of lubricant to the cutting area. Taps are numbered to match the die used to make an external thread. The tap moves forward into the metal with a combined rotary and axial motion, allowing the threads to form in a spiral. The tap is hardened but brittle and easily subject to breakage if unnecessarily forced, therefore it must be handled with care. The tap is held in a solid or an adjustable *tap wrench* which has a central, square opening sized to match the square end of the tap, and is turned by grasping its two handles. Small taps such as those often used by watchmakers and jewelers in combination with a screw plate may be held and turned by inserting their end in a square hole near the handle of a screw plate which then becomes the tap handle.

To make an internal thread in a nut, place the nut flat, clamped in a vise with the tapping hole upright, and place a drop of water-soluble oil in the hole as a lubricant (none needed for brass) to facilitate cutting action. Place the tap, with its handled wrench dead center, upright in the hole. While exerting even pressure on both handles, turn the wrench handle clockwise a quarter turn to work the tap into the hole, then reverse it an eighth turn to break the chips that form which otherwise will resist the tap's advance. Repeat this procedure, gradually advancing through the metal until the tap passes through with its full diameter. When true diameter is reached and the tap turns smoothly and without resistance through the nut, reverse

10–37 TAP AND DRILL GAUGE
This shows the correct size tap drill for any common size machine screw tap in National Fine (NF) or National Coarse (NC) Thread Series. The gauge also shows the correct body size drill to use. The 60 holes are marked with the number size and decimal equivalent of the drill that fits each hole. For example: a size 2-56 tap (No. 2 tap with 56 pitch) uses a No. 50 tap drill and a No. 44 body drill. *Photo: Courtesy L. S. Starrett Co.*

Equivalent Tap Drill, Tap, and Screw Wire Sizes

Tap Drill Size			Tap Sizes			Screw Wire Size	
Number	Decimal Equivalent		Size No.	Outer Diameter Inches	Root Diameter Inches	Closest Decimal Equivalent Inches	B.&S. Gauge
	Inches	mm					
53	0.0595	1.512	1-64	0.0730	0.0527	.0808	12
50	0.0700	1.778	2-56	0.0860	0.0628	.0907	11
47	0.0785	1.994	3-48	0.0990	0.0719	.1019	10
43	0.0890	2.235	4-40	0.1120	0.0795	.1144	9
38	0.1015	2.578	5-40	0.1250	0.0925	.1285	8
36	0.1065	2.705	6-32	0.1380	0.0974	.1443	7
29	0.1360	3.454	8-32	0.1640	0.1234	.1819	5
25	0.1495	3.802	10-24	0.1900	0.1359	.2043	4
16	0.1770	4.498	12-24	0.2160	0.1619	.2294	3

the turning direction to remove the tap. It may be necessary to use a second tap with sharper threads to finish the thread.

TAPPING A BLIND HOLE   A *blind hole* is one that does not penetrate the metal. If such a hole is needed, the usual practice is to use three taps, the first a starting or *taper tap*, the second an intermediate or *plug tap*, and the third a finishing or *bottoming tap*, the three comprising a set. (In England they are respectively called taper, second, and plug taps.) The thread-making chaser ridges on each of these are progressively sharper, the first two start with a taper to allow easier entrance, and the last has full threads in its whole length. The distance the tap must penetrate can be controlled and measured with a *depth gauge*, but lacking this, the tap can be marked or a washer can be screwed on the bottoming tap at the correct depth to act as a stop and so avoid breaking through the hole bottom. The procedure is the same as for an ordinary thread, each tap used in its turn.

10–38   PETER SKUBIC, Austria. Finger jewel worn *between the* fingers, made of stainless steel, silver, and red and blue glass balls. The lathe-turned parts can be moved to adjust size by winding a screw contained within the central tube stem. Height 53 mm. *Photo: Peter Skubic*

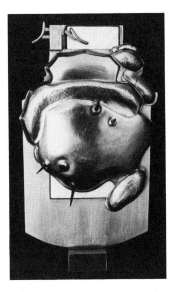

10–39   JEM FREYALDENHOVEN, U.S.A. Pin with flat nickel backplate to which the central chased silver unit is held by hidden screws fixed from the back. Flexible nylon spikes protrude from holes. Silver upper left and bottom box shapes are inlaid with diagonal nickel stripes. Black acrylic blocks are filed to make wide black edges around the inlaid and laminated ivory. Height 5 in. *Photo: Jem Freyaldenhoven*

10–40   FRIEDRICH B. MÜLLER, Switzerland. Brooch with red gold cast face, black acrylic back on which a stainless steel plate is screw mounted. On this is a screw-mounted black acrylic panel with light-emitting diodes (LED optical actives) activated by an electronic device powered by three back-mounted batteries. Diodes emit flashes in a sequence of 265 different combinations, the "picture-to-picture" interval approximately half a second. The device is made by André Claude Godet, Thun, Switzerland. *Photo: Mario Tschabold*

10–41   EBERHARD DECHOW, West Germany. Gold brooch with aquamarine. Exposed gold screws are used to hold the central circular unit to the frame and the stone mounting. Width 6.2 cm. *Photo: Günter Meyer, courtesy the Schmuckmuseum, Pforzheim*

10–42   RACHELLE THIEWES LAMBERT, U.S.A. "Pincushion." Steel bracelet with an inner 1/8 in square steel framework soldered to the outer plates to allow parts to be screwed together with cap-headed, unslotted screws. The blue steel patina is obtained with a commercial "gun bluing" solution. The interior is stuffed with fabric and embroidery floss. Size 4½ × 4 × 1½ in. *Photo: Bill Synk*

10–43   POUL HAVGAARD, Denmark, designer; manufacturer Lapponia Jewelry Ltd., Helsinki. "Adam and Eva." Silver ring with a hidden screw below the cast top that permits the interchange of upper spare parts on the ring shaft. *Photo: Winifred Zakowski, courtesy Lapponia Jewelry Ltd.*

RIVETS AND RIVETING

A cold percussion closed pressure joining system

Jewelry can be constructed by joining parts with rivets, joining devices that do not require heat, but are cold closed. The basic, conventional *rivet* is a malleable metal pin, usually cylindrical in shape, used to hold two or more metal parts together. A rivet consists of a *head* at one end, a *shank* which passes through the holes made in the parts being joined, and a *tail* or the end opposite the head, formed into a second head.

RIVET CONDITIONS USED IN JEWELRY

Rivets can be used in jewelry in different conditions. A *fixed rivet* is one that permanently immobilizes the parts joined by tight pressure exerted on the parts between the top and bottom heads. A *pivotal rivet* does not have a tight fit, but permits the movement of the enclosed parts with the rivet shank acting as a pivot that allows the parts to move in a fixed radius on the shank, the rivet acting as a spindle. This can be accomplished by inserting a thick piece of paper under the rivet heads, and when the riveting is completed, burning the paper away. A *sliding rivet,* also called an *almain rivet* which originated in use with armor, is one whose shank moves or slides within a groove. It is used when sliding movement is required. Although it slides, its installation can be permanent, or it can be removable along with an attached part, as when it is used as a fastening device for necklaces and bracelets. A *fixed almain rivet* can have a round or square shank whose diameter must equal that of the slot, the head diameter being larger than the slot so it does not pass through. By sliding up and back, the attached parts can move a total distance equal to the slot length, thus providing flexibility. *Removable almain rivets* require the presence at the slot end of a shape in the slot equal to that of the rivet head, allowing the rivet to be removed since the head passes through the opening.

The *brad* or *integral rivet* takes its name from the headless nail called a *brad.* This term was adopted in forging to indicate a rivet type made by shaping the end of a

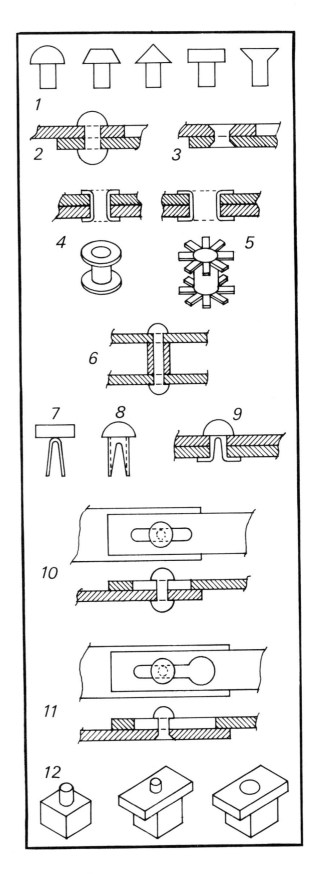

10–44 *RIVET TYPES*

1. *Rivet head shapes,* left to right: Buttonhead or snap; flathead or pan; steeple or conical; square; countersunk or flush.
2. *Buttonhead rivet* with both ends set down holding two sheets of metal.
3. *Countersunk* or *flush rivet* set down holding two sheets of metal.
4. *Tube rivet* with flanged top and bottom, set down holding two sheets of metal.
5. *Tube rivet* with saw-divided flanges.
6. *Rivet* used with *tube sleeve spacer* to hold apart the two units joined and allow flexibility.
7. *Split rivet* with square head and bent wire shank.
8. *Split rivet* with buttonhead and tapered, solid, split shank.
9. *Buttonhead split rivet* set down with legs spread.
10. *Permanent, fixed sliding* or *almain rivet,* the slot smaller than the rivet head; plan and elevation view.
11. *Removable sliding* or *almain rivet,* with slot that develops an opening equal to the head shape so it can pass through; plan and elevation view.
12. *Brad, tenon,* or *integral rivet, left:* the brad formed on the stock; *center:* the brad entered in a hole in the second part; *right:* the brad rivet head set down flush.

10–45 EMMY VAN LEERSUM, Netherlands. Bracelet in aluminum, bent and riveted. *Photo: Courtesy Museum Bellerive, Zürich*

10–46 BÖRJE RAJALIN, Finland, designer; manufacturer Kalevala Koru, Helsinki. Silver bracelet made without soldering. The two front balls are screwed together, and the almain sliding rivet closing locks because of the spring hardness of the bands. *Photo: Otso Pietinen, courtesy Kalevala Koru*

10–47 RUTH S. ROACH, U.S.A. "Weeds." Sterling silver bracelet with 14K gold shot soldered to 16 gauge B.&S. wires joined to the front, spring-hardened frame unit. The mirror-finished, plain inner band reflects the image of the weed units, creating a sense of depth. Four almain or sliding rivets at the back (seen in the rear view) fit the keyhole slots of the textured and oxidized front frame unit, allowing removal of the inner band for polishing. *Photo: Bob Carvill* ▶

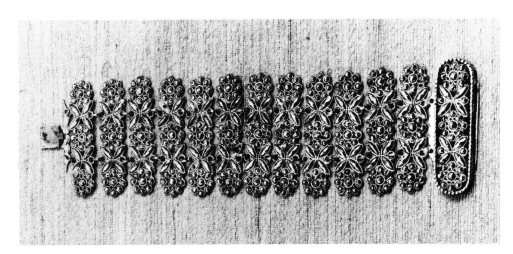

10–48 WOODSTOCK, ENGLAND, late 18th or early 19th century. One of a pair of bracelets, surface ornamented with densely placed steel rivet studs each with an integral rivet that passes through a solid or pierced work baseplate and is riveted at the back. The visible heads are rose cut and highly polished. Here the baseplates are linked together, but complex structures of several interlocking baseplates joined at the back by riveted crossing bars were also made. This cottage industry was centered mainly at Woodstock, north of Oxford. Similar work was done in France and at Tula near Moscow. *Photo: Victoria and Albert Museum, London, Crown Copyright*

10–49 *Left:* BERBER, SOUTH MOROCCO. Silver bracelet with each upstanding square-shanked, pattern-stamped unit, equivalent to an extended and ornamented rivet head, joined to the band as a brad or integral rivet, its shank passing through to the inside of the cylindrical bracelet surface, and the tail hammer spread. Ø 11.7 cm. *Photo: Linden Museum, Stuttgart*

10–50 *Right:* DAVID LAPLANTZ, U.S.A. Pin fabricated of mild steel, copper, and brass, using headed rivets and tube rivets for function and decoration. Length 2½ in. *Photo: David LaPlantz*

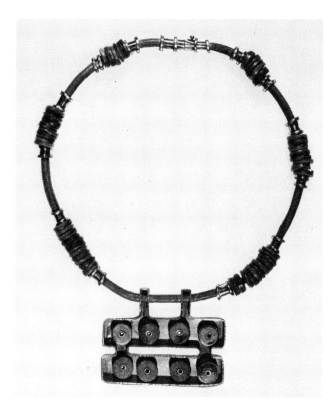

10–51 RAMONA SOLBERG, U.S.A. Necklace with fabricated silver pendant to which disc-shaped Tibetan rosary beads made of human skull bones (thod-'phreng) are held by flanged tube rivets. The neckpiece uses the same beads in groups spaced by silver tube beads and sections of round leather thong. Photo: University of Washington, Audio-Visual Production Services

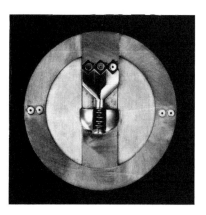

10–52 REINHOLD REILING, West Germany. Yellow and white gold brooch ornamented with rivets with centrally drilled holes. Photo: Günter Meyer, courtesy Schmuckmuseum, Pforzheim

head can be kept from turning by making the legs from square or flat wire and making a square hole to match. This type of rivet is widely used in Tibetan jewelry and metalwork. Split rivets with decorated heads can also be used as *studs* in materials other than metal, such as wood, plastic, tortoiseshell, leather, or cloth.

RIVET HEAD SHAPES

There are several different types of preformed rivet heads, each named according to its shape. The more common ones are: *buttonhead* or *snap* which is half-round; *flathead* or *pan* which tapers upward away from the shaft

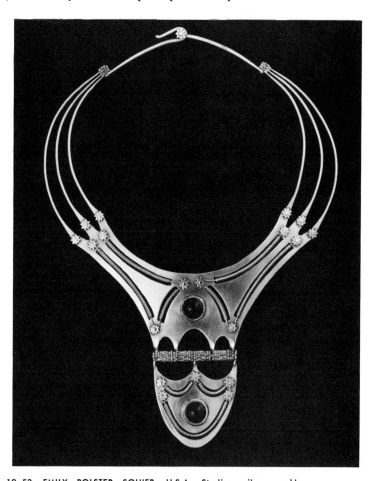

10–53 EMILY BOLSTER SOHIER, U.S.A. Sterling silver necklace, mainly rivet constructed. The star shapes sawed from sheet are decorative rivet washers used to form a seat for the rivet heads, and were drilled and countersunk before sawing. After assembly, including the looped wire ends of the wrapped wire units, both rivet ends were hammered to form a raised head at the front that fills the countersunk area. The free-floating crystal spheres are set in a sawed-out, domed disc soldered at the back. The ball was placed from the back and the straight bezel closed over it, just as for any cabochon stone. Length 8½ in; width 6¼ in. Photo: Sohier and Olaf Skoogfors

10–54 ANNI and BENT KNUDSEN, Denmark. Silver bracelet in two rigid units made of square wire, held together by a rivet hinge joint, the parts between square wires sleeved by nine tube sections that allow the relative movement of the inner rivet shaft. Photo: Knudsen

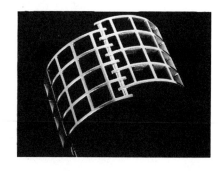

square or round stock bar to the form of a headless rivet, joined structurally to the part from which it projects. The projecting rivet, which is an integral part of the main body, is passed through a hole in the next part and a rivet head is formed at its only end to hold them together; this process is called *bradding*. There are many situations in jewelry construction in which this system or a variant of it could be used.

Split rivets have a conventional head, but their shank is bifurcated or longitudinally divided into two (or more) parts that might better be called legs. The legs can be made from a rod sawed just short of dividing it in two, or a metal strip or wire bent to a U shape, then soldered to a head. When such rivets are used, the head is often a decorative one, possible because this rivet is not subjected to hammering. The legs pass through the holes in the metal sheets, and the parts that protrude beyond them are bent backward, like a paper clip, to fix the head in place. The

and has a flat top; *steeple* or *conical* which tapers to a point; *square* whose sides are straight and top flat; and *countersunk* or *flush* which is tapered toward the shank to fit a similar taper made in the metal with a rotating bur, and has a flat top. Except for the countersunk rivet, the heads of all these project above the metal surface.

It may not be possible to purchase ready-made rivets in desired sizes in the precious metals, but they can easily be made from round wire. Entire pieces of jewelry can be assembled with rivets alone; the rivet heads can be visible, or rivets can be used in unobtrusive ways to hold parts together.

RIVET SETTING

DEMONSTRATION 17

NILDA C. FERNANDEZ GETTY utilizes rivets on a pendant

Photos: Les F. Brown

SETTING OR COLD CLOSING A FIXED, FLUSH-HEADED RIVET

1 Measure the diameter of the wire used for the rivet shaft with *calipers* or *micrometer*. Select a *twist drill* of exactly the same size, and mount it in a drill or in the chuck of a flexible shaft.

2 Place the point of a *center punch* or, used here, an *automatic center punch* over the marked exact center of the hole. An ordinary center punch is then hammered, but this automatic type is pushed down on the body to release the striking mechanism, which is adjustable for light or heavy strokes.

3 Place the work on a wooden surface and drill the hole simultaneously through *both sheets* being riveted. Hold them tightly together, or tape them together with *masking tape* so they do not move and the hole stays properly aligned. A *high-speed drill* is used here. The resulting hole size should allow the rivet shaft to enter in a tight push-in fit.

4 The simplest rivet is made from a straight length of wire, here silver. It should be a little longer than the combined thickness of the two sheets to allow the formation of the heads from the surplus. This head will be flush and the rivet is a fixed rivet so the parts are permanently held together without movement. The rivet head formed must have a wider diameter than the hole so it does not slip out. Before forming the head, file the end of the shank wire flat and perpendicular to the shank so that when it is ham-

mered to form the head, the same amount of metal is available to spread in all directions.

5 To set down a flush rivet, place the work on a *flat surface block*. Be sure the rivet shank end lies flat on its surface and is perpendicular to it.

(If you are using a rivet with one preformed head, such as a common buttonhead, place the shank in the holes and force the rivet down until its shoulder rests flat, squarely against the metal. Then place the head into a *rivet block* or *dapping block* depression that matches the rivet head size.)

To head the rivet, first use the cross peen of a lightweight *riveting hammer*. While the work contacts the block, strike light blows on the edge of the shank, and turn the work with the left hand until a full circle has been made. Reverse the rivet and work and repeat this from the other side of the rivet. Continue to upset the rivet end until the rivet holds the sheets tightly together. Then hammer the rivet head to spread it.

If the rivet shank is too long, or if the head on one side has been favored more than the other in the setting down, the shank may bend. Straightening it is very difficult or impossible. Remove the rivet by sawing off one head; then extract it and make a new rivet.

If construction indicates that the rivet pin may become twisted in use, or will allow unwanted movement, provide against this eventuality by using a square-shanked rivet and a matching square hole.

6 To hammer the head flush with the rest of the metal, flatten it with blows from the round planishing face of the rivet hammer, which will spread and level the head.

INVISIBLE, COUNTERSUNK RIVETS

A *countersunk bur* could also be used first to form a tapering depression in the metal before the rivet head is set down. In this case, the flush rivet can be almost invisible if it is of the same metal as the metal being joined.

SETTING DOWN A HEADED RIVET

Headed rivets can be set down with a *rivet set* (also called a *riser*) and a *rivet snap*. The set is a punch with a depression at its end that matches the rivet shank. The snap is another punch that at its end has a cup-shaped depression used to form the second rivet head (assuming the rivet already has one head), or for shaping both heads. A *combination rivet set and snap* tool exists, housed in an oval-shaped punch that has both depressions at the same end.

Assuming a rivet with one existing head, the total length of the rivet shank should be 1½ times the thickness of the sheets being joined, the extra allowance used for forming the second head. Proper shaft length is important to avoid

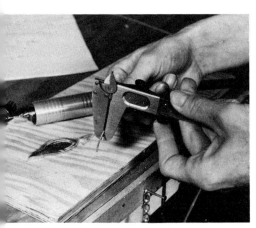
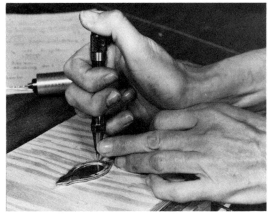
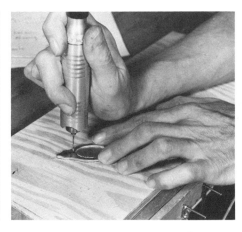

1   2   3

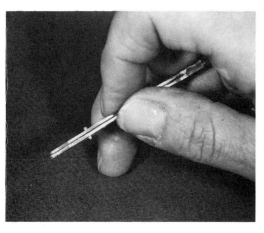

4   5   6

shank bending. Also avoid a hole that is too large or the shank will not be supported vertically and will bend under head forming. Place the rivet snap upright in a bench vise and set the existing rivet head in its depression with the shank pointing upward. Place the rivet set over the shank end and hammer it until the metal touches the rivet shoulder. Remove the set and hammer the shank end with a *cross peen hammer*, first hitting it squarely on end, then slowly placing the blows in rotation around the shank edge to make it form a roughly rounded head. When movement of the sheets held between the heads ceases, remove the snap from the vise and place the original head in the depression of a *dapping block* that fits it. Place the snap over the newly formed head and hammer it sharply two or three times which should be sufficient to form a well-rounded head.

If a *series of rivets* are made in the same piece of metal, the distance from center to center of each rivet position is termed the pitch. In this case, drill the positions for all the holes through the *top sheet,* and only *one* of the holes through both sheets. Set the first rivet in this hole to hold the sheets together, then drill the holes in the second sheet through the hole in the upper sheet at each pitch location. The reason for this procedure is that it is very difficult to accurately drill several holes in two sheets of metal and be sure there was no movement between them. The remaining rivets are then set down.

HOLLOW TUBE RIVETS

7 A hollow tube rivet is an annealed section of open-ended tubing placed through a hole drilled in metal sheets

equal in diameter to the outer tube diameter. Its length must be at least twice the total thickness of the sheets being joined. To make the upper and lower ends flange outward and so hold the sheets together as a rivet, place a *round-ended punch* of a size larger than the inner tube diameter upright in a vise. Place the lower end of the tube rivet over the punch end, and, at the same time, place a similar punch over the top end. An assistant holds the work while this is done. Hammer the top punch, which will cause both ends to deform in an outward-curving flange.

8 Repeat this on both sides of the tube with a broader, round-ended punch to spread the flange. Once the metal between is held firmly, place the tube rivet end on a flat surface block, put the same punch on top of the opening, and hammer the flange flat. Do the same from the other side.

In a variation, a tube rivet can be prepared by first cutting across the tube walls with a jeweler's saw blade so that it is divided into sections that can be easily bent back to form petallike parts following the same procedure.

USING A RIVET SLEEVE AS A SPACER

9 In this case, a rivet is being headed to hold two parts together, but between them, the rivet wire has been covered with a *length of tubing* or a *sleeve*, which by definition is any tubular part meant to fit over another part. Besides working to keep the two sheets a set distance apart, the sleeve can act as a hollow axle or quill to allow relative movement for the rivet shaft inside.

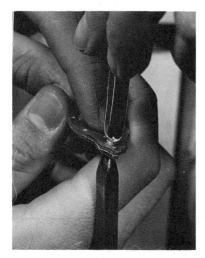

7   8   9

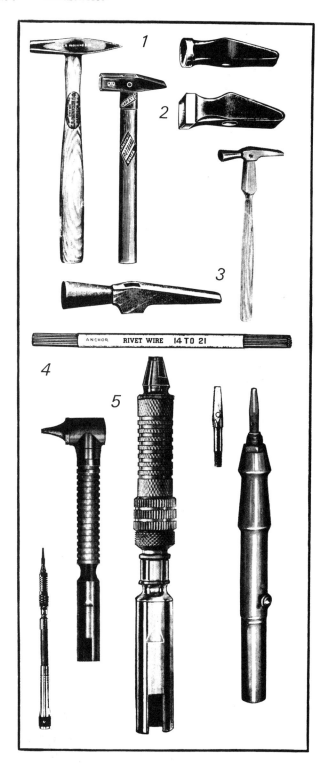

10–55 RIVETING TOOLS AND MATERIALS

1. *Round-faced riveting hammer* of drop-forged steel, available in light (2 oz), medium (4 oz), heavy (6 oz), and extra heavy (8 oz) sizes.
2. *Square-faced riveting hammer*, available in six sizes, head length 3–4½ in, face Ø ⅜–⅝ in; weight 2½–9 oz. The cross peen is used to upset form the rivet head, and the flat face to planish or flatten the head.
3. *Small, Swiss-style watchmaker's hammer*, available in head lengths from 2–3 in; can be used in setting down small rivet heads.
4. *Nickel silver and brass rivet wire* sold in assorted gauge sizes in 1 oz bundles. For use in riveting pinstems to joint findings, and cuff link findings.
5. *Automatic reciprocal cam-action handpiece hammers* for use attached to a flexible shaft and quickly detachable. A typical model operates with a ³⁄₃₂ in stroke at speeds up to 5000 rpm. The strength of the stroke power impact is adjustable by turning a knurled wheel, and some models are available with an extra heavy spring for heavier work. Used with a flat anvil for setting down rivets, and for setting bezels and stone prongs in stone setting. Equipped with a carbide-tipped pointed stylus it can be used for marking, texturing, scribing, and engraving. *Left to right:* handpiece with flexible duplex spring; rigid handpiece with hammer head collet mounted at a right angle to the shaft; separate anvil hammer head, detachable and available in several sizes and weights; rigid handpiece with attached anvil hammer head.

10 The work is reversed and the rivet head is smoothed on the other side. A hinge with rivet has also been used in this design. (See Glossary: Jewelry Findings for the method of making a hinge pin.)

11 Front and back view of the finished brooch entitled "In Faith . . . Deceived, I," from a series called Proud American Medals. The brooch employs sterling silver, enameled fine silver, 14K gold, and copper, with moonstone, corals, golden sapphire, and an insert of an old photograph. Parts are joined by the use of flush-headed fixed rivets, and articulated parts by hinges containing riveted permanent hinge pins made of rivet wire, as seen in the back view. Size 10 in × 4 in × 3¾ in. (25.4 cm × 10.2 cm × 9.5 cm)

Photos: Claire Braude

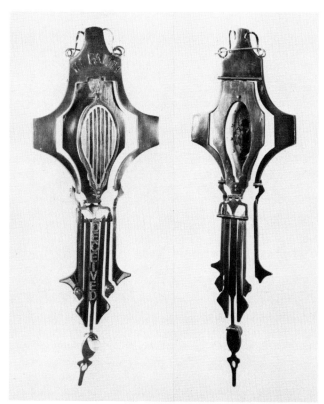

10   11

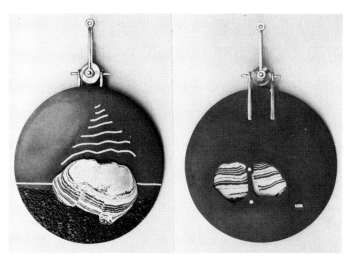

10–56 GENE PIJANOWSKI, U.S.A. Shakudo pendant inlaid with silver wire. A separate, central mokumé overlay form is held to the disc by two rivets, as seen in the reverse side photo. The lower textured portion is chip carved in facets. *Photo: Gene Pijanowski*

MOUNTING AN OVERLAY BY SOLDERED RIVET PIN SHANKS

A metal overlay can be rivet mounted on a sheet metal backing by soldering lengths of round wire perpendicularly to its back to act as rivet shanks. Their length should be sufficient to project through the back and allow a head to be formed. To mark the exact position where they must pass through the ground metal, first cover the area with a thin layer of wax. Place the overlay in position and press the pin ends into the wax. Drill a hole at each marked position with a diameter matching the rivet shank wire. Remove the wax and clean the piece. Place the pins over the holes, and press them through. With *nippers* cut off any surplus rivet shank at the back, but allow enough to remain for forming the rivet head. File the end of each pin flat. Place the work, pin ends up, on a rigid surface, or, if the front surface must be protected, on a piece of wet leather. Gently hammer the rivet pin ends to form a head, using a lightweight *riveting hammer.*

The same procedure can be used to mount a metal overlay on nonmetallic materials, or in reverse, to mount nonmetallic materials on a metal ground.

THE LATHE AND MACHINED JEWELRY

Rotational fabrication systems

The *lathe* is a manually or mechanically operated machine tool that holds and rotates a nonmetallic or metallic raw stock workpiece on a horizontal axis. By the process of *turning,* which is the progressive, subtractive rotational removal of bulk from the work, achieved by means of engaging the work with a sharp-edged cutting tool, it is formed by degrees into a preconceived shape and size. When *external* surfaces are so generated on the work, the process is called *turning;* when *internal* surfaces are created by the same action, the process is termed *boring.* Both processes may be performed on the same workpiece mounted on the same lathe. Because of the rotational movement of the work, the forms generated are *cylindrical,* variants of the *cone,* or *compound shapes.*

Evidence has been discovered in the Near East of the use of the lathe for turning nonmetallic objects by the 8th century B.C., and possibly even earlier in the Indus Valley civilization around 2000 B.C., in what is now a part of Pakistan.

The concept of the lathe is believed to have derived from that of the *bow drill.* Both the bow drill and the primitive lathe share the use of a string to impart rotary motion to the cutting tool, but there are also differences between them. On the lathe, the spindle does not bear the cutting (turning) tool, but instead holds the rotating object while it is worked, and its axis of rotation is horizontal rather than the normal vertical position of a drill, which depends partially upon gravity to produce a force upon the work. The horizontal workpiece position necessitates a second bearing at the other end of the lathe to hold and secure the object as when *turning between centers,* probably the oldest of the work-holding methods. Another difference is that the drill action translates circular motion to a linear boring motion that is an extension along its vertical axis of rotation, while the most common cutting action of a lathe tool is a lateral, horizontal, external shaving cut parallel to the rotary motion of the work, with the cutting tool position normally perpendicular to the axis of rotation of the work. Also, the lathe's cutting tool is a separate, independent, nonrotating, stationary or slowly moving instrument that requires a support or holding device to allow it to be fed against the work, while on the drill the tool is held by the rotating shaft and rotates with its movement.

Although the lathe is among our most ancient tools, *machining* (as the act of using the lathe and other power machines and their techniques is termed today) to make entire pieces of jewelry may be among its newest applications. Until recent years, this important mechanism has been thought of as belonging to the realm of the metal industries, and the use of mechanical power machines by the hand jeweler was believed to be a threat to the mystique of jewelry making. The conflict between the "organic" and the "mechanical" look in jewelry is no longer relevant as any approach to jewelry design is now acceptable. The distance between the bench-worked jewel made exclusively by hand tools and processes, and the power machine-made jewel is being bridged by the creative, imaginative use of the machine which brings with it an entirely new esthetic in jewelry design. Today an international group of jewelers inspired by this new esthetic have turned to using the lathe, reappraising and revitalizing the formal evolution of its main product, the *externally turned object.* Others have exploited the *internal* lathe cutting operations of drilling, reaming, boring, screw cutting, threading and tapping—all typically utilized when lathe turning machine parts—to create machinelike but nonfunctioning assemblages in the form of rings, bracelets, necklaces, etc. The validity of using this versatile tool, not just for occasional use, but consistently as a basic means of making entire pieces of jewelry is incontestable.

Perhaps the initial expense of a lathe and the commitment demanded by its ownership and use as a major tool system in a jeweler's creative work has limited its wider use until now. However, the cost of a small workbench model such as would be suitable to the scale of jewelry objects is not much more than that of an automatic drill press or a centrifugal machine. The existence of such lathes as the *Unimat,* or the *Edelstaal Machinex 5* with their possibilities for use in other work processes, makes such tools very useful in the workshop.

Because the techniques of the modern lathe are numerous, and the literature on its use is extensive, only basic information will be given here to illustrate its application to modern jewelry making.

THE PRIMITIVE MANUALLY POWERED LATHE

The most ancient prototype of the modern lathe, probably in continuous use for more than 3,000 years, is still widely used in India to turn nonmetallic and metallic materials. This is the *kharad* or lathe shown in the photo; its operation is described in the caption.

With this primitive lathe, the Indian *kharadi* or lathe worker can turn small or large objects of great refinement from wood, ivory, horn, plastic, and vegetable ivory. (The latter is the nutlike seed of two palms—*Phytelephas macrocarpa* and *Coelococcus amicarum*—which has a very hard endosperm about as large as a hen's egg, and is used in India in turning and carving small objects.) The list of products made on such lathes is lengthy, and includes items of jewelry such as beads and other round and cylindrical forms, as well as many containers and *objets de poche*. Though these items are made of waste pieces of

ivory left over from the manufacture of larger objects, they invariably are finely contoured, and lovingly detailed.

Decoration and finishing processes are carried out on the object while it rotates on the lathe. Often grooves are cut into the surface of the rotating object with a sharp, pointed tool, and these are then filled with colored lacquer in dry, stick form. Because this lacquer is applied to the object while it rotates, frictional heat melts it and causes it to fill the grooves. The lacquer surface is then leveled

10–58   JAIPUR, RAJASTHAN, INDIA. Ivory pomanders or scent holders (*gonda*) also used for snuff by men and women. These 2 in long holders have handles that are turned on the same primitive hand lathe described. The carved, hollow head is internally threaded on this lathe to engage the external threads at the handle end. Perfume-drenched cotton is stuffed into the head. Drilled holes allow perfume scent to emerge when the carrier brings the scent holder to the nose to help disguise encountered unpleasant odors. *Photo: Salmi*

10–57 *AN INDIAN LATHE WORKER* (*kharadi*). Squatting before his manually powered lathe (*kharad*), he uses a free-hand and foot-held tool to make a wooden rolling pin (*belen*) (a finished one rests on the floor). The lathe headpiece on the worker's right is a square wooden post fixed in the floor bearing a stationary, finely tapering, horizontally mounted steel spindle or center upon which a workpiece is fixed. The tailpiece on the worker's left is a movable wooden block that has a fixed, tapered steel spindle or center to hold the other workpiece end. Distance between headpiece and tailpiece centers is adjusted to hold any length of work simply by bringing the movable tailstock end toward the fixed headstock end, then anchoring the tailstock in place with a large stone, seen at the worker's left. The worker's feet are used as much as the hands to control tools and work, and rest on the tool rest, a square length of wood placed loosely on the floor before the lathe.

The workpiece-rotating implement is a curved wooden bow with a loose cord attached to both ends, the cord looped one or more times around a workpiece part. To rotate the workpiece (the number of revolutions depending on the workpiece diameter and bow length) first the bow is pushed forward *away* from the operator, causing it to rotate clockwise. When the bow is pulled back *toward* the operator the workpiece rotates in a *counterclockwise* direction. Rotation occurs by the friction of the cord on the workpiece (as in the case of the cord around a *bow drill* shaft). By repetition the workpiece rotates with an *intermittent* or *reciprocal forward and backward motion*.

At the *return bow stroke* when the workpiece rotates *toward* the operator, the cutting tool, held in the left hand and supported by the wood bar tool rest, is brought against the workpiece which turns upon the tool's cutting edge, and chips are removed. As the tool is guided by the operator's toes, he literally hand-and-foot feeds the tool against the workpiece. When the forward bow stroke reverses the workpiece rotation direction, the cutting tool is withdrawn from the work, to be reapplied when the direction is again counterclockwise. *Photo: Oppi*

smooth with the object's surface by *scrapers,* and the entire object is polished with fine sandpapers and abrasive powders.

BASIC CONTEMPORARY LATHE CATEGORIES

The *contemporary lathe,* in contrast to the manually powered lathe, is electrically powered, and the spindle rotation is *continuous* in the direction toward the operator who stands before the machine. The electric motor provides the necessary power to rotate the work continuously, and a manually or mechanically held cutting tool is fed to the work which turns at a selected rate, making possible the maintenance of a desired rate for the removal of matter from the raw stock. Lathes are classified by the manner of their control in use.

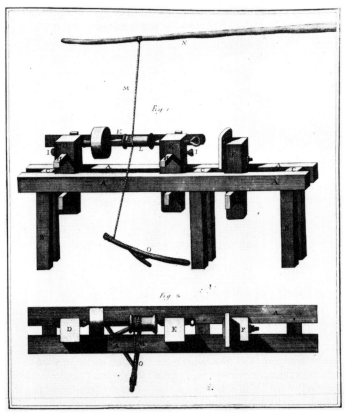

10–59 A POLE LATHE, Diderot's *Encyclopédie,* 18th century. This concept, at least 2,500 years old, was used in Europe since Classical Greek times. It consists of a bed frame raised on legs (Fig. 1, A, B, C), holding uprights (D, E) equivalent to headstock and tailstock, between which the work (L) is revolved. The pole (N) of resilient wood forms a spring that projects over the bed, and a cord (M) is attached to its end, then wrapped around the work (K) mounted between the lathe spindles, finally passing downward for attachment to a foot treadle (O). (Fig. 2 shows a plan view of the lathe.) Upon depressing the treadle, the pole is pulled downward, and the cord spins the work a number of times in a forward direction toward the worker. Upon releasing foot pressure, the bent pole springs back to reverse the motion in the return, drawing both cord and treadle upward. While turning the workpiece in the counterdirection, it winds the cord back to its original position, preparing it for the next treadle impulse. By delegating reciprocating, discontinuous rotary lathe motion to a foot function, both hands are freed to hold the tool which rests against a board (not shown) placed on the two projecting members (H). The tool cuts work only on the treadle downstroke when work rotates in a forward direction. The workpiece is cleared of shavings on the upstroke.

Manual lathes are without automatic controls, and the operator regulates all operations. They are used generally for making unique workpieces or small numbers of parts. In industry they are used to make prototypes that will be reproduced on automatic-production lathes.

The main systems for holding work on a lathe are the same for manual or mechanical lathes. These include holding the workpiece firmly *between centers* in the headstock and tailstock; in a *chuck;* clamped on a lathe *faceplate;* or on a *straight or tapered mandrel* fitted to the headstock spindle. These systems are described in detail ahead.

The cutting tool is not held rigidly by the machine, but is hand held, supported on a tool rest. This system, called *freehand turning,* allows the tool to be freely worked from any angle around contour curves in the workpiece. (See Manual Tooling and Manual Lathe Tools, p. 444.)

Semiautomatic lathes vary in the degree of automation and the attention needed in working them.

Automatic lathes were introduced for economy of production. They need no operator attention once the work is loaded and the mechanism programed. Machining takes place automatically in a predetermined sequence, and the lathe stops when the work is finished. The operator usually removes the finished work from the lathe and loads it with new work, but in industrial practice, this is also sometimes done automatically

In each category several lathe versions exist, and the various lathe manufacturers make available a vast number of modifications. For instance, more complex lathes are equipped with automatic lengthwise and crosswise travel, screw-cutting drive, quick-change gear boxes that permit rapid changes to different speeds, and some have multitool holders and attachments that allow a series of operations to be carried out on the same object, either simultaneously or in sequence.

LATHE TYPES

The lathe chosen depends on the needs in producing the particular object. For the purpose of making lathe-turned jewelry, the jeweler will probably use the type capable of making small parts that require average to close tolerances. Considerations of choice aimed at quantity production, important in the metal industry, are generally not important to the jeweler who normally uses a lathe to make a unique piece, or a relatively small production series. Because jewelry parts are in a small-scale range, smaller lathe types meet these requirements. Larger lathes can, however, be used to turn small work since the principles of turning are the same regardless of lathe size.

THE MINIATURE LATHE In this group are small bench lathes used for turning small work. The *Unimat lathe* is a precision bench lathe with an overall size of 14½ in × 4 in × 5 in (36.8 cm × 10.2 cm × 12.7 cm), a 3 in (7.6 cm) swing, a distance between centers of 7 in (17.8 cm), a chuck capacity of 2¼ in (5.7 cm), and is capable of a tolerance accuracy of 0.002·in (0.051 mm). This lathe is shown in use under Plastics in Jewelry, Chapter 10. It can be converted to perform the multipurpose operations of grinding, drilling, milling, and polishing by altering the relationship of its parts and by adding the necessary components. A similar, versatile miniature lathe is the *Machinex 5,* manufactured by American Edelstaal, Inc. (See illustration 10–60.) *Watchmaker's lathes* constitute a group of small bench-type precision engine lathes made especially for turning objects of small diameter and

10–60 *THE MACHINEX 5 MULTI-PURPOSE MINIATURE LATHE,* manufactured by American Edelstaal, Inc.
This small-scale metalworking lathe capable of machining to small tolerances, has a capacity that relates to small-scale jewelry objects. Bed: 20 in; 10 in capacity between centers; 5 in swing over the bed; cross slide swing: 3⅛ in. Carriage travel: 9¼ in; cross slide travel: 3 in. Headstock bore: ⁹⁄₁₆ in; spindle collet capacity: ½ in. Tailstock spindle designed for a No. 1 Morse taper; spindle travel: 1³⁄₁₆ in. Permanent magnet, ¼ hp, 115 volt motor with six-speed nonslip V-belt drive, providing slow spindle speeds of 250 rpm for use with large objects, and 500, 1500, 2000, 3000, and 4000 rpm for turning small objects. The entire headstock assembly can be unclamped and attached to the 16 in vertical, steel, rotatable column, and a drill press handle can be attached to convert the lathe into a *vertical drill press* with an 8 in vertical capacity, and ¼ in drill chuck capacity. With attachments it can also be used in this position as a milling machine, precision grinder, and polisher. *Photo: Courtesy American Edelstaal, Inc.*

length with great dimensional accuracy. In the smallest, which is designed to make parts for watches, workpiece capacities range from ⁵⁄₃₂–½ in (0.397–1.270 cm), with chuck capacities up to ½ in (1.27 cm) maximum. A common arrangement has five cutting tools arranged in the form of a fan, all adjustable by means of micrometer screws.

TOOLROOM LATHE   A small engine lathe designed for accurate cutting when work must be held to close tolerances.

ENGINE LATHE   A general, all-purpose lathe with a back-geared, cone-driven headstock, and a screw-cutting capacity. It can be used for straight turning, facing, cutting tapers, and a wide variety of work. This is the lathe type used in the demonstration photos on p. 450ff.

GAP-BED OR GAP-FRAME LATHE   A lathe with a bedway that does not reach the headstock, or with a deep notch in the bed to allow the turning of short objects with large diameters. It allows the workpiece to be face worked while held near the headstock, or workpieces with attached protrusions to be turned. Such work otherwise must be turned on a larger lathe.

TURRET LATHE OR CAPSTAN LATHE   A lathe that developed from the engine lathe, but has no tailstock. This hand-operated or semiautomatic lathe is versatile, and can be used for small work. The tool-holding device or *turret* holds a number of cutting tools fixed in a capstan tool holder. This rotates, allowing each tool to be brought into action in sequence on the workpiece for successive actions that can include turning, forming, and cutting off. It is used in industry for repetition work and for long production runs, often with the shapes controlled by the use of templates.

AUTOMATIC SCREW-CUTTING LATHE   A highly accurate slide-rest lathe that has a lead screw and pitch suited to cutting threads. It is used particularly by watchmakers on bar stock for making long, slender parts.

SPINNING LATHE OR MANDREL LATHE   This heavy spindle lathe is used for a branch of lathe work *totally separate* from the above-mentioned turning lathes: *lathe spinning.* It is used to make *hollow sheet metal forms* or *shells* from flat sheet metal blank discs. The blank is held between the block and a live center in the headstock. Once it is centered and revolves, it is dimensionally shaped with any of several simple, round-ended hand tools which force the blank against a solid or segmented wood or metal block or form called a *chuck.* No metal is removed, but edges may be trimmed.

LUBRICATION OF THE LATHE

Lubrication of the lathe with a machine oil lubricant is necessary for efficient lathe operation, and to minimize wear on the machine. The *lathe parts oiled before use* include all the gears and bearings, the oil holes in the tailstock, the cross slide, and the bedways. When work is turned between centers, the tail centers must be oiled to reduce heat buildup at the point of contact.

LUBRICATION OF THE TOOL AND THE WORK

Some free-cutting metals are cut "dry," that is, without the use of any lubricant. Sometimes only a blast of cool air is used to cool the work during cutting. With the majority of metals, however, a *cutting fluid* or *liquid coolant* is used. The use of a cutting fluid bears a direct relationship to the power required for cutting the workpiece, and allows increased speeds by minimizing friction between the tool and the workpiece. Lubrication also enhances accuracy, improves surface finish, and lengthens the tool's cutting life. Besides acting to cool both the work and the cutting tool, it flushes away *swarf* or the resulting metal chips removed from the workpiece. This function is especially important when drilling deep holes. Another function of lubrication is to act to prevent the buildup of a welding deposit on the tool's cutting edge (see p. 440).

The coolant can be applied directly to the work with a *brush,* or it can be allowed to drip from a *drip can* fixed directly above the cutting edge, thus constantly applying additional fluid to the cutting tool edge and the work surface.

CUTTING FLUIDS   Cutting fluids are either prepared proprietary products meant for specific uses, or simple lubricating substances, the choice depending on the metal being turned.

Soluble oil mixed with water in various concentrations is a fluid lubricant widely used in cutting. The usual mixture

Lubricants for Cutting Tools

Material	Turning	Chuckling	Drilling Milling	Reaming	Tapping
Tool steel	Dry or oil	Oil or soda water	Oil	Lard oil	Oil
Soft steel	Dry or soda water	Soda water	Oil or soda water	Lard oil	Oil
Wrought iron	Dry or soda water	Soda water	Oil or soda water	Lard oil	Oil
Cast iron	Dry	Dry	Dry	Dry	Oil
Brass	Dry	Dry	Dry	Dry	Oil
Copper	Dry	Oil	Oil	Mixture	Oil
Babbit	Dry	Dry	Dry	Dry	Oil

is 1 part oil to 20 parts water. This oil is nonflammable, and nontoxic, and can be used with almost all metals.

Straight mineral oil, sulphurized mineral oil containing 4% active sulphur, and *proprietary compound blends* of cutting oils containing lard, rapeseed, or petroleum oils are also used to improve cutting action, and to eliminate vibration-caused chatter.

Nonoil cutting fluids are proprietary mixtures that are also available.

Plain water, water with an alkali, turpentine, paraffin, wax, or a soft soap and water mixture are also used on occasion.

WORKPIECE MATERIALS

Workpiece raw stock can be any material that can be cut with lathe cutting tools. This includes almost any metal, but preferably those rated high for their ease in machining or turnability, and *nonmetallic materials* such as wood, ivory, bone, horn, or plastic. These materials can be *entirely solid,* as in the form of a bar or rod; *hollow* as in the case of a seamless tube (which can be used to reduce the total weight of the finished work); or a *solid or hollow cast object* which is turned to true its shape, to improve its surface finish, or to ornament it externally.

Regular sectional shapes in the form of a metal bar or other material having a round, square, or any polygonal shape whose maximum radius variation lies within the capacity of the particular lathe, can be used. Parts of this original raw stock shape can be retained in the result, while only sections of it are turned. Solid stock blanks are generally cut *longer* than their final dimension to allow for the removal of waste at the ends where the centers, or the jaws of a holding chuck might mar it. The *maximum length* of a workpiece is limited to the distance of the lathe carriage travel. Several workpieces in either repeats of the same form, or in different forms can be produced on the same stock length to save the time of setting each one up separately, then parted-off, or sawed apart manually once finished.

Laminations of different colored metals can be made by soldering layers or rods together, or a lamination can be made employing metal, hardwood, ivory, horn, and plastic, joined in any order with a suitable cement. When such a composite substance is turned on the lathe, it is preferably run with the lamination layers in the direction perpendicular to the rotating axis which eases the tool's cutting action as the same material is presented to the tool's edge in one complete revolution, but with care and slow speed

10–61 MIKE JACKSON, England. Acrylic neckband with silver and acrylic pendant. The eight identical acrylic parts are fixed-tool lathe turned, and the ½ in diameter silver rings at the center are fabricated. The acrylic parts are cemented to the silver. *Photo: Mike Jackson*

and feed the lamination can also be turned with its layers parallel to the direction of the spindle axis. The resulting forms with their striated variations in color, and/or dissimilar materials, in vertical, horizontal, or even diagonal directions, can be quite decorative in jewelry.

METAL MACHINABILITY

Machinability of a metal is the term used to describe the *force* or *power needed* to shape the metal by the various lathe cutting operations; its *cuttability* as indicated by the rate at which a drill can penetrate the metal in a given time; the *time* it takes to cut off a given cross-sectional area; the *quality of the surface* after being tool cut; and the *life of the cutting tool.* The lathe-working jeweler will find it easier to use any metal or alloy that is *free machining,* meaning it is suited by its composition and state of hardness to be easily cut with lathe tools. The *standard of machinability* is *free-cutting brass,* described on p. 442. Alloys that have a high machinability rating are specifically designed to include constituents that make them maximally machinable, least wearing on tools (thereby assuring maximum tool life), and that result in a good surface finish on the workpiece.

Due to the great heat generated in cutting some metals, a tendency exists for a *welded deposit* or *edge buildup* to occur on the tool's cutting edge which acts to reduce its cutting efficiency and also is a major cause of surface roughness in the result. To a great extent this condition can be minimized by the use of the proper cutting fluid, and by removing all grinding marks and scratches from the tool's cutting surfaces. When burrs build up at the workpiece's cut edges, they can be removed with a conventional triangular *scraper* while the work revolves on the lathe.

Factors that affect machinability are the composition and structure of the metal being cut; the size and shape of the workpiece; the size and shape of the cut; the cutting speed; the material, shape, and condition of the cutting tool; the rigidity of the tool and the work-holding device; the particular cutting process employed; and the cutting fluid used.

CHIPS AND MACHINABILITY   The *appearance of the chips* produced when cutting metal on a lathe is an indication of, and is used as a standard of its machinability. The surface of a machinable metal can be sheared away cleanly and rapidly in small, brittle chips—the most desirable type —or by short, brittle curls. The workpiece surface should be left smooth, well finished, and be free of cutting tool marks. Indicating the degree of machinability *in decreasing order* are: small, brittle chips; small, brittle curls; fairly open coils or closely wound helixes that are easily breakable and free themselves easily from the tool and the lathe; and long, continuous, tight, strong, tough curls that do not break easily, and run the risk of tangling with the tool and the lathe.

Swarf is the term used to describe fine metallic particles such as chips removed by a cutting tool during the operation of the lathe. When using precious metal, swarf and chips should be collected for reclaiming. They must be uncontaminated by other metals.

Surface finish is influenced by the rigidity of the lathe and the tool; the relationship of workpiece metal to type of cutting fluid; the feed rate per revolution; and the nose radius of the tool. A tool with a large nose radius can operate at a faster feed rate than one with a small nose radius, whose feed rate must be reduced and compensated for to achieve a good finish.

METALS USED FOR LATHE TOOLING

Gold and silver alloys that are hard and brittle are generally best in machinability, but all alloys of precious metals can be machined with proper care. Because of the value of these metals and their relatively heavy weight, when solid stock is used, turned parts employed in jewelry will probably be small. A way of overcoming size limitations is to use hollow tube forms or hollow cast shapes. In machining these metals, carbide-tipped tools are used for facing cuts at a speed of 350 fpm (feet per minute); grooving is done at 115 fpm with a high-speed tool. Carbon steel drills are used for drilling at 5000 fpm (for a typical drill 0.040 in [1 mm] in diameter). When machining *gold-filled metal parts,* ordinarily cutting takes place at the facing ends in the core metal, therefore the choice of cutter depends on whatever that *base metal* may be. For nickel silver cores, carbide tools are used, and for pure nickel cores, high-speed steel is used. It is also possible to make cuts on the object in a direction parallel with the axis of rotation to create striped effects by removing the overlying gold to expose the core metal. Castor oil is the preferred lubricant for precious metals, and because sulphurized lubricants cause complications, they are to be

10–62   WENDY RAMSHAW, England. Silver necklace with gold parts. The grooves in the face-turned circles, the turned tubular beads, and the solid pendant parts, are filled champlevé style with turquoise, blue, and gray enamels. The three contour-turned pendants are supported on a hinge which provides articulation. Length 20 cm. *Photo: Bob Cramp*

avoided. As mentioned previously, precious metal chips and swarf should be collected for reclaiming.

Copper and copper alloys are divided into three groups in respect to machinability: free-cutting, moderately machinable, and difficult to machine. Wrought copper and copper alloys in bar form are recommended over cast copper. The metal alloy that is rated ideal in machinability and is used as the *standard of machinability* upon which the *Machinability Index* is based is *Alloy 360 free-cutting brass* which contains 61.5% copper, 35.5% zinc, and 3.0% lead. This alloy is given a rating of 100, and the rating applied to other metals and alloys as to machinability is in relation to this figure. *Lead* in the alloy, and its use in other alloys improves machinability because it increases the brittleness of the alloy which causes the chips to break off readily in short curls rather than in long stringers. It also acts as a lubricant for the cutting tool, reduces tool wear, and requires less tool pressure. Free-cutting brass is available in sheet, bar, and tube form.

Other copper alloys recommended for their machinability are:

Alloy 544 Free-cutting phosphor bronze
(88 Cu–4 Zn–4 Pb–4 Sn) Machinability Index 80

Alloy 798 Leaded nickel silver
(46.5 Cu–10 Ni–41.5 Zn–2 Pb) Machinability Index 60

Alloy 385 Architectural bronze
(57 Cu–40 Zn–3 Pb) Machinability Index 90

Alloy 377 Forging brass
(59 Cu–39 Zn–2 Pb) Machinability Index 80

Some copper alloys are machined dry, but a cutting fluid is recommended to increase the possible speed and feed levels, improve surface finish, increase tool life, and enhance accuracy. Water-soluble oils are used as an anti-weld agent for the tool. The fluid consists of 1 part oil to 20 parts water. To improve the surface, a light mineral oil, or mineral oil with 5–20% lard oil is used especially in the case of alloys that make tough, stringy chips, and also when cutting fine threads. Sulphurized oils have a tendency to stain copper and its alloys and are therefore avoided.

Nickel and nickel-base alloys are machined with carbide single-point tools as are *iron-base alloys*. They need tough tools as they have a tendency to work harden rapidly during machining. This condition can be minimized if the metal is work hardened before machining, a condition that exists naturally in cold drawn rod; therefore *do not anneal such alloys*. To produce the smoothest finish, use sharp tools which cut instead of push the metal, and do not allow the tool to dwell too long in a cut.

Nickel alloys recommended for their machinability are:

Nickel 200 (99.5 Ni - 0.06 C - 0.25 Mn - 0.15 Fe - 0.005 S - 0.05 Si - 0.05 Cu)

Monel 400 (66.0 Ni - 0.12 C - 0.90 Mm - 1.35 Fe - 0.005 S - 0.15 Si - 31.5 Cu)

These are examples of high- and low-nickel alloys suited to machining.

Nickel alloys can be cut without any cutting fluid, but it is also possible to use almost any cutting fluid. Ordinary sulphurized mineral oil is recommended, but the workpiece should be cleaned *immediately after machining* to prevent staining.

Aluminum alloys designed for their machinability are free-cutting and high in strength. They are superior to pure aluminum in machinability because of their metallurgical structure. They offer maximum machining speed depending of course on the complexity of the design. As aluminum has approximately one-third the density of brass or steel, the result is lighter in weight than other alloys. This permits the use of larger forms which in other metals might be excessively heavy. These alloys are generally noncorrosive, and capable of retaining a good finish. Some of the many recommended machinable aluminum alloys in order of desirable small chip size and the quality of their surface finish are: A 140 Temper F, A 750 Temper T5, A 2001 Temper T3. The recommended cutting fluid is a soluble oil emulsion, a mineral oil, or an aqueous chemical solution, all of which should not contain sulphur because aluminum alloys will stain.

Stainless steel is more difficult to machine than carbon steel because in an annealed state it has greater tensile strength, it work hardens more rapidly, and because of its carbide content it causes greater tool wear. "Gumminess"

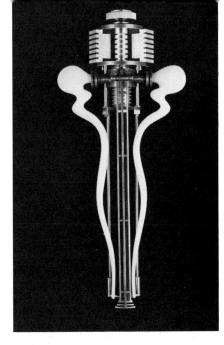

10–63 GARY S. GRIFFIN, U.S.A. "Departure in ⅜–16." Brooch in aluminum, copper-plated brass, and carved Delrin. All the basic fixed-tool lathe working processes have been employed in its creation. *Photo: Gary S. Griffin*

10–64 TAKAO MITSUYASU, Japan. Brooch in lathe turned aluminum, the central unit suspended under tension by steel wires. *Photo: Hubert Urban, courtesy Schmuck International 1900–1980, Künstlerhaus, Vienna*

in machining causes a buildup on tool edges and excessive tool heat, thereby shortening tool life, and results in a poor finish. To achieve a good finish, use cemented carbide-tipped tools, heavier feeds, and slower speeds to reduce work hardening and tool buildup. Greater machine power is needed as the steel is generally purchased in an annealed, quenched, and tempered condition.

Low-carbon martensite grades of steel are free-machining and produce the best results. Among these are the free-machining types 410, 416, 405, 303, and 439F, all of which are good because their structure is somewhat brittle which results in good chip breakage. These steels contain as additives *sulphur,* which minimizes tool edge buildup and allows greater speed with reduced power, as well as prolonged tool life; *selenium,* which improves the surface finish; and *lead,* which improves machinability. These may be contained in the alloy singly, or in combinations.

As a cutting fluid, water-soluble oils in the proportion of 1 part oil to 12–20 parts water are widely used for stainless steel and other types of steel. These cutting fluids can be applied to the cutting area in copious amounts to flush away chips, lower heat conductivity, and induce coolness.

DESIGN AND ORNAMENTATION OF WORKPIECE FORMS

Regular shaped workpieces constitute one category of machined forms, and are the type that the jeweler is most likely to use. Regular shapes have turned faces that are created mainly by using the tool in a *perpendicular* or *angular direction* to the central axis of the object. The results are all *variants of the cylinder*, made with any combination of *flat surfaces, curves, angles*, and *tapers*.

The basic external cuts can be used creatively whether lathe tools are used *freehand*, or *fixed* on the lathe. Within the limitation of mainly cylindrical forms, an infinite number of variant contours and compound forms can be invented. The only technical design limitation on the externally lathe-turned object is that all details must allow the entry of a *single-point tool* into the cut. When the object is not made for a mechanical function, but for a creative purpose, tools can be used with exploratory freedom, using any of the following concepts.

WORKING A WORKPIECE EXTERNALLY
- Using workpiece stock with an initial sectional shape such as round, square, pentagonal, hexagonal, or octagonal, whose original form is partially retained in the result
- Varying the tool: using tools with differently angled cutting edges; using tools with compound contour-shaped cutting edges
- Varying the cut depth; varying the cut angle
- Repeating the same width cut at regularly spaced intervals and depths; or spacing the same or varied width cuts at irregularly spaced intervals and different depths
- Using external, helical spiral thread cuts for decorative effect
- Using surface linear or textural cuts, such as knurling, regularly or irregularly repeated
- Alternating contour cuts with linear and/or textural cuts

WORKING A WORKPIECE INTERNALLY, OR BY FACING CUTS
Internal or facing cuts allow another area of design possibilities. The workpiece ends can be penetrated endwise to make internal holes; and a disc, or the ends of a workpiece, can be face worked in any of the above-mentioned ways.

Irregular shaped workpieces constitute a second category of lathe turnings. These are common in industry, and generally require adjustments to accommodate them, or special lathe facilities. In many such cases, the chuck, the workpiece, or the spindle must be counterbalanced to equalize the distribution of the unequal weight of the object.

POSTLATHE SURFACE DECORATION   After turning, the object's surfaces can be ornamented by *hand methods*, employing any of the decorative processes. Materials such as niello, opaque or transparent enamel, lacquer, or liquid resins can be added to grooves, and into textured depressions, or over textured surfaces on the workpiece to create color contrast.

DIAMETER ACCURACY OR TOLERANCE

Tolerance is a term that indicates a specific maximum allowance for error in dimensions from an accepted standard which specifies a required degree of accuracy. Such a high degree of accuracy is attainable on lathe-turned workpieces because the lathe has automatic or manual systems of measurement that permit the close control of cutting operations. This condition is absolutely necessary when a piece must be made to *close dimensional tolerances*, or when making *identical repeats* of a particular shape. It is also important when *mating* two parts that must fit each other accurately to effect a join, and when *making screw threads*.

Turning diameters is the term given to turning a workpiece to specific tolerances. Diameter accuracy is controlled by the dial setting on the *cross slide positioning dial* which on precision lathes is graduated in 0.001 in (0.025 mm) increments. This ensures the fitting, mating, and functioning of parts.

Accuracy of dimensions are checked on the work with the *lathe at rest*, by the use of *calipers, vernier calipers*, or a *micrometer*, depending on the degree of accuracy wanted.

When work is done freely and is without mating parts, turning diameters is of lesser importance, and esthetic considerations become dominant.

MANUAL TOOLING AND MANUAL LATHE TOOLS

Manual tooling consists of moving an *unattached, unmounted* cutting tool made of tool steel or tungsten carbide freely over the workpiece surface from any angle to make a unique compound shape with free contours that cannot easily be achieved when tools are rigidly fixed in the tool holder of a mechanical lathe. The cutting tool is supported in an *adjustable tool rest*, and the work turns toward the operator over the tool's cutting edge. The tool rest acts to steady the tool by providing a counterpressure against the direction of revolution of the workpiece. Because the tool can be moved freely across the tool rest and into the work, the workpiece form can be developed and altered at will during the cutting operation. Hand turning metal is not difficult once practice teaches tool control.

Manual or *hand turning tools*, also called *lathe chisels*, can be used for turning nonmetal or metal materials. All

10–65 WENDY RAMSHAW, England. Set of seven silver, hand-held tool, freehand lathe-turned rings. The projecting approximately 1¾ in high units have regularly shaped contours turned from solid metal bar stock. Forms are groove banded on the lathe, and grooves are inlaid with turquoise, blue, and gray enamels. When worn, ring order in the set is interchangeable. When not in use, rings are returned to a screw-apart Perspex stand, also lathe turned, where they can be enjoyed as a freestanding miniature sculpture. *Photo: Bob Cramp*

lathe tools, manual or mechanical, are designed to achieve the basic lathe turning operations of *planing, surfacing, contouring, tapering, slotting, grooving,* and *screw cutting.*

Lathe hand turning chisels in the majority are those with a *single point.* The most common face cutting shapes are *spear point, round nose, skew right, skew left,* and *parting.* Cutting tools are available ready-made, or their cutting edge shapes can be ground from a solid bar of tool steel. After shaping by grinding, the tool's cutting edge can be hardened and tempered in the usual way. The tang end is inserted in a hardwood handle. In use a tool may become dulled and need resharpening. When resharpening a tool, its original shape and cutting edge angle should be retained as far as possible.

Round-nosed tools, as the name implies, have a rounded point or nose radius; *flat-edged tools* have straight edges. *Round-nosed roughing tools* are used for initial roughing cuts, and *round-nosed finishing tools* for final shaping and finishing. *Right-* or *left-side-skewed tools* have side cutting edges and are used for cutting shapes that must be side trimmed, for entering corners, and in facing operations. *Parting* or *cut-off tools* are used for cutting off finished work from the stock. Other shapes may be needed according to circumstances, and are relatively easily made.

Profiling tools are broad-edged tools whose cutting ends are shaped into irregular contours. They are often made from old files, and are used when several small identical shapes or parts of shapes must be cut from the same form in identical sizes. A *beading tool* has a depression that leaves a raised ridge or bead on the work, and is an example of a profiling tool.

Hand screw-threading tools are used to make external threads, and *inside screw-threading tools* are used to make internal threads. *Outside* and *inside thread chaser tools* are used to round off sharp threads after they have been cut either manually or automatically. Making a thread manually on a lathe requires experience as the tool must be moved along the blank at the correct rate of speed to create the necessary number of threads per inch.

HAND TOOL FEEDING METHOD

When using manual lathe tools, they must be *rigidly* hand held, and are applied to the workpiece with the handle held in the right hand while the left hand grasps the tool shank. The thumb presses the tool down on the tool rest placed before the work in a tool rest holder attached to the lathe.

An upright *fulcrum bar* is placed in one of a series of holes in the tool rest to help steady the tool while it is pushed against the workpiece. Work is held between centers, or in the jaws of a chuck in the headstock. Normally the tools move from *right to left* to make cuts parallel to the axis of the work, so the object must be reversed when working the left end. It is worked from *front to back* when facing or end turning a surface.

FEED AND SPEED

Feed is the manual or automatic rate of advance or carrying forward of the cutting tool to produce progressive tool operations upon the workpiece by moving the cutting tool *along* or *into* the work to a desired depth. *Manual feed* is controlled by hand pressure when the tool is hand held, and is performed on a lathe with a mounted tool by turning the feed handle. On automatic lathes the tool's feed rate is set on the lead control and is therefore automatic.

The *feed rate* used depends on the strength and degree of rigidity of the workpiece, and also that of the lathe; the degree of workpiece hardness; and the amount of metal to be removed in each operation. Also important are the width and depth of the cut, and the desired surface finish.

Roughing cuts use heavier or coarse feed rates at slow speeds, and every subsequent cut must overlap the last. *Finishing cuts* use a fine, light feed at higher speeds that leave little or no tool marks. Feed rate is therefore related to the speed of rotation of the spindle, and this basically depends on the kind of metal being cut. The highest possible speed is selected for a particular metal or purpose.

When machining metals rated high in machinability, and when using *high-speed tools,* the *surface feet per minute* speed can range from 40 sfpm (medium-carbon steel), 150 sfpm (stainless steel), 300 sfpm (brass), 400 sfpm (aluminum). With *carbide-tipped cutting tools* speeds can be doubled. These speeds are considerably lower than those used for turning relatively soft materials such as plastics and wood.

Chatter is the undesirable vibration that occurs during lathe operations and is evident by the noise, the blurred appearance of the workpiece while rotating, and an uneven finish on the work. It occurs either because the work is revolving off-center, or the tool is not sufficiently rigidly mounted in the tool holder. Both conditions must be checked and immediately corrected.

MECHANICAL TOOLING AND MECHANICAL LATHE TOOLS

Mechanical tooling utilizes a *fixed cutting tool* whose cutting edge or edges can generate only *one surface at a time* before another surface can be generated. Therefore, in any design to be executed by mechanical tooling, its details must be reachable with the sharp cutting point or edge of the tool. To make compound shapes, the tool, or the workpiece position, or both, must be changed.

Mechanical lathe turning tools are mostly of the *single-point* lathe tool type: small, square- or rectangular-section cutter bars made of tool steel. A typical dimension is about ⅜ in (9.5 mm) square. Some are available tipped with tungsten carbide which can withstand high-speed cutting. Other tips are removable and disposable after they wear out. The tool is held in variously shaped *tool holders* mounted on the lathe, and tooling work generally proceeds *from right to left,* though tooling action can also be reversed. As in manual tool cutting operations, in mechanical turning the form is first roughed out with *roughing tools,* then worked with *finishing* or *facing tools.*

Roughing tools are always used to first preform the object. They make the heaviest cuts, 0.01–0.03 in (0.25–0.76 mm). The individual tool shape used depends on the contours of the workpiece. Some of the basic shapes of single-point roughing (and finishing) tools are: *square* (end cutting); *straight; slanted* or *skewed* (to one side at a standard angle, called *offset*); *angled* (lead angle); *curved* (round nose); and *pointed* (slotting and cutting-off tools).

Finishing tools, also called *forming* or *profile tools,* are used for light cuts of 0.002–0.01 in (0.005–0.025 mm), and a typical tool has a nose end curvature with a radius of 1/32–1/16 in (0.793–1.587 mm). As the name implies, it is used to finish contour profiles and bring the metal down to its final form. During this work, when turning to *exact*

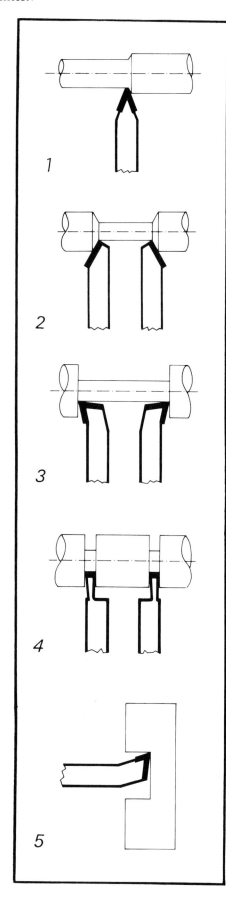

10–66 *COMMON LATHE TOOL SHAPES*
(and their position in relation to the work)
External cutting tools:

1. *Single-point tool,* round nose, used for general external cut work to reduce the workpiece size. Its tip is ground to a small radius.
2. *Straight-nosed roughing tool,* right- and left-hand types. The right, used to cut toward the headstock, is more commonly used.
3. *Corner tools,* left and right, used to make sharp, right-angled corners.
4. *Parting-off tools,* canted left and right. They have narrow cutting edges designed to cut a narrow slot and expose a minimum amount of metal to the cutting edge. They are tapered backward to avoid binding the tool sides in the groove.

Internal cutting tool:
5. *Square-nosed boring tool,* used to make internal cuts. Boring tools have cutting edges on the portion of the tool that is bent or set off at an angle from the rest. This form is designed to allow access to the boring position on the workpiece. *Drawings courtesy American Edelstaal, Inc.*

diameters, dimensions must be tested frequently with calipers.

Facing tools or *side tools* are used to face or finish the ends and shoulders of a workpiece. They are raked to the *right* or *left side* to make cuts in those directions. Care must be taken to avoid catching a lathe center when turning between centers.

Parting-off or *cut-off tools* have a front angle clearance of 5–15° with the work to minimize the size of the *teat* or small projection at the center of the piece where it breaks off from the stock. The aim is always to meet the workpiece exactly at the center line.

Thread-cutting tools and their use are described below, and in the text accompanying the photo sequence.

Diamond lathe cutting tools are made of correctly shaped diamonds that have been embedded in the end of a steel shank, oriented there to present a hard edge (not a cleavage direction) to the object on which it is used. This tool can perform turning, boring, drilling, threading, and tapping operations. Though its initial cost is high, with proper use it retains its edge sharpness and cutting ability for a long period of time. Even with intensive use it outlasts the hardest lathe cutting tool by at least 25 times. Diamond will cut even the hardest metal alloys, and is also usable on soft materials like plastics. In the watch industry this tool is used to turn watch parts, and in the jewelry industry it is used to achieve fine contour detail on objects such as wedding rings, and produces a very fine surface finish on gold and silver lathe-turned objects.

NOMENCLATURE OF TURNING TOOL ANGLES

Rake is the term used to describe the angular relationship between a turning tool's cutting face or a tangent to the tool face at a given point, and a given reference plane or line. In a single-point lathe tool, the reference plane is one of the surfaces of the original, basic shape of the tool blank which is a square or rectangle in section. The rake angle is designed to give the tool a slicing action on the workpiece in a particular direction in order to turn the resulting chips or curls away from the work as otherwise they might scar it, or prevent its proper functioning later. The rake angle made on a tool varies with the particular metal being turned. Steel generally requires a 10–15° rake, copper and brass a 10° rake, and aluminum a 10° rake.

Back rake angle is the angle on a single-point tool made between the *end plane* of the cutting face and the reference plane at that point perpendicular to the tool base. When

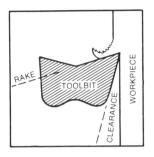

10–67 *TOOL RAKE AND CLEARANCE IN RELATION TO THE WORKPIECE.*

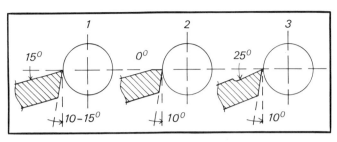

10–69 *CUTTING ANGLES USED ON THE LATHE*
1. Steel   2. Copper and brass   3. Aluminum

the angle slopes downward from the cutting point toward the shank, the angle is termed *positive;* when it slopes upward from the cutting face toward the upper shank plane, it is termed *negative.*

Side rake angle is the angle on a single-point tool between the cutting face and the reference plane which is the *side plane* of the tool perpendicular to the tool's base. If the angle slopes downward away from the cutting edge toward the *opposite shank side,* it is termed *positive;* if it slopes upward it is *negative.*

Relief is the removal of tool mass or material *behind* or *adjacent* to the tool's cutting edge. Its purpose is to provide *clearance* and prevent the tool from rubbing on the work, called *heel drag.*

End relief angle, also called *front clearance,* is the angle between the tool's end face and a perpendicular line drawn from the cutting edge to the shank base, measured at a right angle to that cutting edge. It prevents the face cutting edges from rubbing in the cut on finished surfaces and therefore marring the resulting finish.

Side relief angle is the angle between a tool's side flank on a side cutting edge and a perpendicular line from that edge to the tool's base, measured at a right angle to that cutting edge.

End cutting-edge angle is the angle between a tool's end cutting edge and a line drawn perpendicular to the tool's side plane.

Side cutting-edge angle, also known as the *lead angle,* is the angle between a side cutting edge and the same side plane of the tool shank.

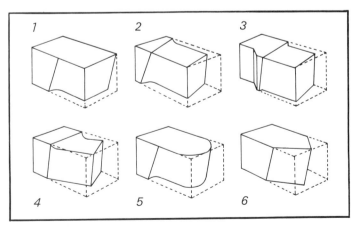

10–68 *COMMON SINGLE-POINT LATHE TOOL SHAPES*
The original solid, square, tool steel bar is indicated by a dash line in relation to the tool shape achieved by grinding the metal away from the solid bar.

1. End cutting
2. Straight
3. Offset
4. Lead angle
5. Round nose
6. Threading

Nose radius is the contour or radius of the rounded, curved part between the tool's end cutting edge and a side cutting edge, or the convergence of two sides of the cutting edge of the tool. That portion of the tool is ground into a curve to remove what may otherwise have been a fragile corner that might break. When the radius is large it is strong and is therefore used on rough cutting tools, and small-radius curves are used on tools used for light feeds.

Clearance angle is the angle or gap between a plane that contains the flank of the tool and a plane that passes through the cutting edge in the direction of relative motion between that edge and the workpiece being turned. This angle varies with the metal undergoing turning. For steel it is 15°; for copper and brass the tool is set exactly on the work center at 0°, and the same is done when cutting a thread; and for aluminum it is 25°. If the tool is set *too low,* the point vibrates or chatters, digs in, wears away, and may push the work off-center. If the tool is set *too high,* little or no cutting is accomplished; the work rubs behind the point as it does not come into contact with the tool. This condition causes the tool to become heated, and if it continues, the tool will ultimately lose its temper.

When the cutting tool engages the work as it rotates, a tangential force is created which when multiplied by the speed at which the workpiece surface moves gives the *net horsepower* needed to remove the metal from the workpiece. The necessary power increases with the toughness of the alloy being cut. The power needed to move the tool longitudinally is negligible.

SAFETY PRECAUTIONS

CLOTHING AND HEALTH SAFETY

1 Cover or tie back any loose hair when working on a lathe. Belt ends, ties, loose clothing, gloves, or any other such items of apparel that might become caught in a lathe part should be removed or secured. Jewelry on fingers, neck, and head should also be removed.

2 Wear a *protective body apron, goggles* to protect the eyes against flying chips, a *dust mask* if the work produces dust in the air, and *nonslip shoes.*

OPERATIONAL SAFETY

3 Keep the work area *clean* and free of unnecessary objects. Remove wrenches and adjusting keys from the lathe part on which they are used, and place them away from the lathe, *not on it,* as vibration might cause them to fall into the lathe when in operation and cause it damage.

4 The lathe should be *grounded* to protect the operator from electrical shock when it is *ON*. All machines are supplied with a *three-prong* grounding plug that fits the correct receptacle in the outlet. Only three-wire extension cords should be used. Lathe, lathe accessories, and the area and floor around the lathe should be *dry*.

5 Clean the lathe of swarf, broken or curled chips *before* starting work, always while the machine is *OFF*. These waste substances might interfere with the proper functioning of the lathe. Never try to clean them away while the lathe is in motion, as this can be very dangerous.

6 Before mounting chucks, or inserting a center, wipe out the spindle hole to eliminate the possible presence of foreign matter which would prevent the true centering of the chuck or the center's position.

7 Tighten all necessary bolts and screws on work-holding devices and tools so they cannot come loose during operation and cause damage to the machine, or become a safety hazard to the operator.

8 Be sure the lathe switch is on the *OFF* position before plugging in a lathe outlet cord, to avoid its starting unintentionally.

9 Spin the headstock *manually before* turning the power switch to *ON* for mechanical operation, to be sure the lathe is functioning properly, and that the workpiece clears stationary lathe parts.

10 Do not remove belt guards or other accessory guards when the machine is in motion.

11 Make the necessary adjustments on a lathe, or turn on the reverse lever, *only when the lathe is stopped, never while it is in motion*. First turn off the power, then wait until all motion ceases and the lathe comes to a *full stop*, then make the adjustment.

12 Do not reach across the lathe while it is in motion.

TOOL SAFETY

13 Never force the lathe in any way beyond its normal capacity or the motor may stall and become damaged. Never force a tool beyond suggested rates of speed, or make tools do work they were not designed to do.

14 Always feed work into a cutting tool with the work rotating *against* the tool's edge.

15 Tools must not be allowed to work unattended.

16 Keep tools sharp and clean for optimal performance. Check their condition before use to see that they are not damaged and will operate properly.

17 Use lubricants or coolants on the lathe, the tool, and workpiece when necessary.

18 When the lathe is turned off, it should not be left unattended until it comes to a dead stop.

PRIMARY LATHE OPERATIONS: External cuts or feeds

Longitudinal feed is the movement of the tool in a direction *parallel to the central axis* of the workpiece in order to remove mass from the piece longitudinally. Face flatness depends on the perpendicular alignment of the cross slide to the axis of rotation. The cutting tool makes a *first pass,* which is a single cutting trip parallel to the rotation axis across the work, in the direction from right to left toward the headstock so that the bearing will receive the cutting thrust. This is followed by a *second or shaving cut* in the same direction to increase the accuracy of the first cut and to smooth the surface. Thereafter as many cuts are performed as are needed to finish the form.

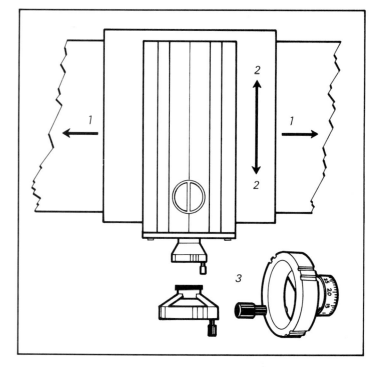

10–70 *THE TWO BASIC FEED DIRECTIONS OF A LATHE TOOL CARRIAGE*
1. *Lengthwise:* Along the lathe bed, parallel with the workpiece center line or axis, termed the *longitudinal carriage feed.*
2. *Crosswise:* On a cross slide, at a right angle to the axis, termed the *carriage cross-feed.*
3. Both movements are controlled by *feed screws* through the manipulation of *graduated handwheels.* The carriage slides along the bed and the tool moves to the left or right of the operator by turning the *lead screw handwheel.* For crosswise movement, the *cross-feed handwheel* is turned. All handwheels are provided with calibrated, resettable dials, here graduated in one-thousandths of an inch. By first positioning the dial at zero, the tool can be advanced by stages until the desired depth of cut is reached on the workpiece. *Drawing courtesy American Edelstaal, Inc.*

Cross-feed is the straight *forward* or *transverse* movement of the tool *perpendicular* to the central axis and drive of the workpiece. When the tool is fixed or held in one position, the result is a straight incision or *slot* on the work whose width matches that of the tool width. Slots can be widened by subsequent parallel perpendicular cuts, and a series of slots can be made on a work by spacing them.

Compound feed is the *diagonal* or *angular* movement of the cutting tool in relation to the central axis of the workpiece, resulting in an angular cut. Angles are made by changing the alignment of the cross slide, or when working manually, by moving the tool at an angle toward the workpiece center *at a steady rate.*

Taper-cut feeds are automatically controlled, and consist of a gradual, smooth *reduction in diameter* along the workpiece. The angle of the cut depends on the rate of exchange between the axis of rotation and the angle at which the cutting tool on the carriage proceeds in relation to it. Cutting angles are set by fixing a graduated compound mounted on the carriage worktable to controllable angle gradations, on some lathes every 15°.

Contouring or curved-cut feeds to produce *convex* or *concave* forms can be done manually or mechanically, normally on work mounted between centers, and using curve-ended tools. Mechanical tools are fixed in position on the lathe and are hand fed to the work, the approach angle of the tool shifted for each part of the curve. In manual curve or contour cutting the tool is hand held, and its position can be changed gradually and smoothly in relation to the work to create the desired curve or contour simply by supporting the tool against the tool rest. This free type of contour feed creates the curved surfaces characteristic of hand-shaped cylindrical workpieces. The result in all cases can be finally smoothed with appropriately shaped tools, or with *files* held against the work as it rotates. Lastly, the surface can be smoothed with a fine grade of *emery cloth* held against the revolving workpiece.

Superimposed feeds involve the use of any combinations of the above feed types or the use of different tools to create superimposed effects, as in knurling, threading, and other operations that create textured surface effects.

SECONDARY LATHE OPERATIONS

EXTERNAL CUTS

Knurling is the external milling of two opposing direction, raised, diagonal ridges to form a regular lozenge-shaped pattern on a cylindrical form while it rotates. It is often done on the cylindrical handle of a metal tool to give it an easy-grip, nonslipping surface when the tool is hand held during use. A knurled surface texture has decorative as well as functional value, and can be used to ornament a workpiece.

Knurling a workpiece mounted on a lathe can be done either with a *hand-held knurling tool,* or mechanically with a hard steel *knurling roll tool or die* clamped in the tool post. These are pressed (manually or mechanically) against the workpiece and moved at a definite rate, first feeding the tool to the left for the desired distance in the usual way. With sufficient pressure the tool produces the desired depth of diagonal groove pattern on the rotating article. The lathe spindle motion is then reversed, and the same, or a different pattern is made in opposition to or crossing the first by feeding the tool back to the starting position. In the result, a lozenge-shaped pattern is formed on the workpiece surface.

Knurling of another type is used in architecture, and in turned work in general. In this case, it consists of a series of close, parallel (not crossing) ridged forms made on the cylindrical shape. One such common design is the bead and reel, but much more elaborate forms can be invented. The result can be centrally divided longitudinally into two matching halves which can be used mounted flat side down side by side or one above the other.

Facing is turning work done on a workpiece by using a cutting tool in a transverse direction on those surface planes which are at a *right angle* or *radial* to the longitudinal axis.

Parting-off is an action done with a narrow-bladed tool whose function is to cut a workpiece into two parts; to separate the finished part made on a single workpiece stock length from which other parts are to be made; or to remove waste from the facing ends of a finished workpiece.

Threading a workpiece by mechanical means on a lathe is the process of forming *external threads* on a cylindrical part. When making jewelry, such a thread may be made for a functional or a decorative purpose.

INTERNAL CUTS

The secondary lathe operations of *drilling, reaming, boring,* and *tapping* are normally carried out on a workpiece that has been initially externally turned to a half-finished, or a finished condition. These operations are only defined here, and are described in Demonstration 18 below.

Drilling is the making of a penetrating, round opening longitudinally along the axis of a workpiece, either *partly into* the solid to make a *blind* hole, or *completely through* the solid at its axial center to make a *through* hole. The tool used is a *drill* which is a rotating, end cutting tool with one or more cutting lips, and one or more helical or straight flutes whose purpose is to allow chips to emerge and cutting fluid to enter the hole made. The hole is actually a negative cylinder in form.

Reaming is the process of finishing or sizing a drilled hole which by common practice has been made at least ⅟₆₄ in (0.397 mm) undersized. The tool used is a *reamer* which is helically fluted with cutting edges, and is fixed in the tailstock. With the reamer, the hole is made more accurate in dimension than is possible with a drill.

Boring is turning applied to true the internal wall or side surfaces of an existing hole. In the process of boring, the hole is enlarged to obtain a maximum in precision sizing, surface finish, accuracy, and location. *Boring tools* exist in straight, right-angle, and oblique forms. They are held in the tool post normally, and the work, held in a chuck or faceplate, revolves against the tool's cutting edge or point.

Tapping is the internal threading of a negative, cylindrical form produced in a solid, in order to make internal threads of all types and pitches. It is accomplished with *taps* which are internal thread-cutting tools.

MACHINING JEWELRY

DEMONSTRATION 18

GARY S. GRIFFIN shows the use of fixed tool lathe techniques

Photos: Gary S. Griffin and American Edelstaal, Inc.

The illustrations shown here are not meant to demonstrate the fabrication of a particular work, but to show typical lathe work tools and techniques by which machined jewelry can be made.

TYPICAL MATERIALS AND TOOLS (Clockwise from left to right)

1 (1) *Rods of free-machining brass.* Other brasses more difficult to machine make necessary frequent regrinding of conventional tools. (2) *Square bar of aluminum alloy* 6061 Temper T6, machines well, is free cutting, produces very small broken chips. It is corrosion resistant, strong, relatively lightweight, and capable of acquiring an excellent finish. (3) *Square bar of Dupont Delrin* white plastic, which carves easily and is resilient. Because it adheres to itself and to other materials with difficulty, mechanical fastening systems are used in its assembly with metal parts to hold it together. (4) *Beryllium copper wire* is used for pinstems. After shaping, it is temper hardened in a kiln to give the metal additional strength and a characteristic springiness that suits this alloy for this purpose. Because beryllium is toxic, pinstems are copper plated to

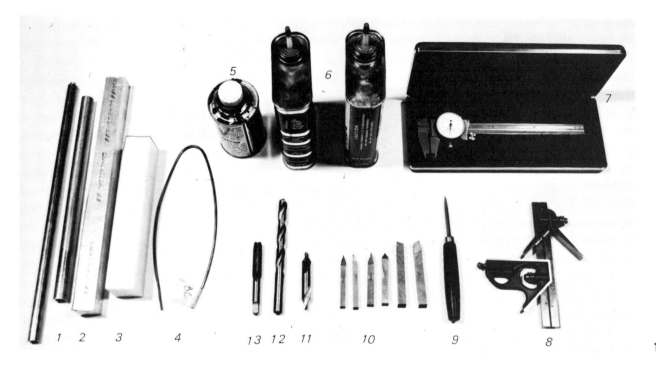

prevent possible reactions. (5) *Layout dye* is painted on cleaned metal surfaces prior to their being worked. When dry, the working and dimension lines inscribed through the dye are readily visible. (6) *Cutting fluids* (two oval cans) are used to improve machinability and surface finish. This fluid is a proprietary, low-viscosity compound especially suited to deep drilling and tapping operations. (7) *Dial calipers* are used for taking accurate precision measurements of both outside and inside diameters. Griffin tries to keep his work to a tolerance of ± 0.002 in (0.051 mm). (8) A *combination square* used for layout work, and for locating centers on cylindrical stock. (9) A *scraper* of standard triangular section, used for deburring. (10) *Six lathe tool bits* of standard high-speed steel containing 5% cobalt. (11) *Center drill,* makes a small hole that prevents the standard twist drill used next from wandering. (12) A *standard twist drill* used to drill holes. (13) A ½–13 *standard taper tap* used for threading internal holes.

THE LATHE AND ITS COMPONENTS

2 The *Rockwell engine lathe* shown here is a standard metal workshop lathe. This one is used in the School for American Craftsmen at the Rochester Institute of Technology. It has all the standard lathe features and components, and is designed to perform all standard lathe functions, including screw cutting. This lathe has its own stand, but smaller models can be placed on a bench at a convenient working height, which is with the top slide at elbow level when standing before the lathe. All lathes should be fixed *level,* and made rigid by bolts that pass through the bench top; if on a stand, the stand should be bolted to the floor.

The *capacity* of a lathe is stated in terms of its *swing* which is the largest work diameter possible to be passed over the bedways; the *maximum work length* it will accommodate when the work is mounted "between centers" in the headstock and tailstock; and the *carriage travel distance.* All of these measurements set the maximum limit

on the width and length of the workpiece. On this lathe, the work diameter or swing capacity is 14 in (35.56 cm), and the length capacity is 54 in (1.37 m). For the sake of comparison, the corresponding dimensions for the small *Machinex 5 lathe* (see caption, Illustration 10–60), also shown in some of the photos that follow in order to demonstrate alternative work procedures, can be referred to.

Lathe parts can be divided into four groups, each with a general function: *the structural parts; the power unit; workpiece-holding systems;* and *tool-holding systems.* These are discussed now in this order.

LATHE STRUCTURAL PARTS

Numbers included in parentheses after lathe parts mentioned in the text below refer to numbers in Photo 2.

The *bed* or *bedways* (1) is the main milled casting of the lathe, and is the foundation upon which the other parts are mounted, to which they are attached, or by which they are supported. Its *rigidity* is essential, and this requirement is common to all lathes. On larger lathes the bed generally has two longitudinal tracks or guides upon which the tailstock can be moved forward toward, or backward away from the rigid, fixed headstock. On small lathes, the bedways may be two parallel rods. The carriage assembly mounted with the tool holder also moves along the bed.

Running the length of the lathe bed and parallel to it are two shafts. The upper one is the *lead screw* (2) which provides the drive for the carriage, and because it is ground with an accurately machined square or Acme thread, controls carriage movement at a regular rate, especially important when the lathe is used for cutting threads. The *lead screw-reversing lever* (3) in the headstock is used to control the direction of carriage movement. The lower shaft is the *feed rod* (4) which is plain on one side and has a keyway machined into its entire length on the other side. It regulates the feed motion, which is controlled by the *feed-reversing handwheel* (5) in the carriage apron.

The *headstock* (6) at the left end is a separate casting bolted to the bed. It is the part of the lathe that provides

the driving end as its housing contains the gear drive. It also holds the ball bearings in which the mounted main *spindle nose* (7) rotates. The spindle or mandrel is a shaft that has a morse taper hollow, which is one of five standard tapers that allow small tool shanks to fit into and be held in the spindle. The size of the taper depends on the size of the lathe. The tapers vary from 0.600 to 0.630 in per ft, depending on taper number. The hollow is threaded to permit attachments to be mounted, such as a chuck that holds a workpiece. Some headstock spindles are hollow all the way through to the left which makes it possible for work of considerable length to be passed through them and extend beyond the headstock while held in a chuck and worked. The *tailstock* (8) is a casting on the right end, and carries centers or tools, as well as acting to support the work at the end opposite the headstock. It is mounted keyed on the bedways so its center and that of the headstock are easily aligned. It can be moved along the bedways to any position toward or away from the headpiece and the work. It is locked in place by the *tailstock clamp handle* (9) or a *tailstock clamping screw*. The tailstock also has a hollow spindle or barrel with a morse taper to allow the placement of centers, tools, or other fittings and accessories.

LATHE POWER UNIT

The *electric motor* (10), the source of power, is usually mounted at the rear left, and is not visible here as it is contained within the *headstock casing* (11). The motors on small lathes may employ as little as 1/10 hp, and in the metal industry, motors of 75 hp and higher are used in giant lathes. In a *single-cone lathe* such as this, the *stepped-cone driving pulley* mounted on the motor shaft communicates and transmits motion energy or *drive* from the motor spindle to the spindle on the lathe, and indirectly to the workpiece, by means of a *V-belt* that goes the short distance from the motor pulley to the stepped-cone pulley on the headstock spindle. Continuous length V-belts and the matching shaped pulley grooves transmit power without slipping, and belt tension is adjustable. These parts are concealed here by the guarding headstock housing or casing, but are sometimes visible in small lathes.

Variation in *spindle speed* can be chosen according to the needs of the operation performed (such as roughing or finishing), the tools used, the metal worked, the depth of cut, and the diameter of the workpiece. At any given spindle speed, an increase in diameter also means an increase in surface speed on the object. Different spindle speeds are achieved by shifting the position of the belt from the *constant speed countershaft* on the motor to the different *stepped cones* by a handle. The smaller the diameter of the cone pulley on the headstock shaft, the faster the spindle speed, and vice versa. A *quick change gear adjusting lever* (12) in the *quick change gear box* (13) makes the change automatically. Its handle causes the drive pin to engage the pulley and transmit a direct drive to the spindle. The pulley can also be made to idle on the spindle with the back gears disengaged. Large lathes also have a *back gearing system* in the headstock, engaged or disengaged by a handle. These gears permit extra slow speeds, as slow as 50 rpm, which is slower than permitted by the cone pulley. Maximum speeds are about 1500 rpm on most metalshop lathes, but on industrial lathes the maximum can be as high as 7200 rpm. When changing any gears to control speeds, the motor must be *off* and the lathe *at rest*.

WORKPIECE-HOLDING SYSTEMS

The three most important methods of holding rotating work are *between centers, in a collet or a spindle chuck,* or *on a faceplate.* The work done with the aid of these holding devices is respectively called turning between centers, chuck work, and faceplate work. Often surplus material is left on the workpiece to allow for the various methods of holding the work on the lathe, and this surplus is removed once the lathe work is completed.

CENTERS

As mentioned, the tailstock contains a *morse taper-holed sleeve* or *dead spindle* (14) that by friction can hold a *dead center* (so called because it does not rotate), or a *live center* (so called because it contains a bearing that allows the point to rotate with the spindle or mandrel nose, and the work). *Half-centers* have only half a point (divided lengthwise), and are used in the tailstock because, when making facing cuts, the side of the point that is removed faces the worker and permits a tool to *nearly* approach the workpiece center (the actual center must be avoided). The *tailstock handwheel* (15) is worked by hand to advance and retract the sleeve, and to make fine longitudinal adjustments of the center's position. *Before* starting to turn work between centers, the point of the center in the headstock must accurately meet the point of the center in the tailstock. This is tested by bringing the tailstock center point to the left to touch the headstock

center point. If necessary, lateral adjustments can be made by loosening the *tailstock clamp* and/or the *stop pin* at the base of the tailstock, and shifting the tailstock to align the center points of tailstock and headstock *exactly.* The tailstock is then reclamped in place. With the live and dead centers perfectly aligned, work held between them can be turned its full length with concentric precision. It is also possible to remove work from its mounting between centers and later replace it for further work, still maintaining the accuracy of its position.

Centers consist of two parts: a *tapered rod* that fits into the self-holding conical recess in the spindle shaft or the tailstock barrel, and a cone-shaped tapered point. The dead center's point is always made of hardened steel as the

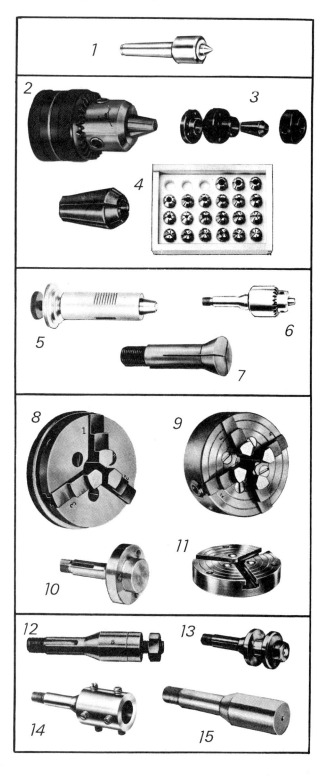

10-71 *TYPICAL WORKPIECE-HOLDING DEVICES*
(These are meant for use on a Unimat lathe)
1. *Precision live center with two ball bearing races.*
2. *Jacobs-type drill chuck,* ¼ in capacity. The chuck screws onto the lathe headstock or tailstock spindles, and is opened or closed by a key. It holds drill shanks from No. 70-¼ in, and is accurate to 0.003 in.
3. *Collet chuck,* capacity 5⁄16 in, designed for precision drilling and milling. The chuck body has a precision-ground, tapered bore to hold the collet sizes mentioned below. The collet-closing nosepiece grips or releases the collet when tightened or loosened. A separate threaded chuck plate is provided.
4. *Single collet, and collet set,* double tapered, precision ground to fit the above chuck. Because they are *alternately split,* they are more flexible and even clamping pressure is possible which results in greater accuracy. Cased sets are available in 21 different inch sizes 1⁄64–5⁄16 in; and 16 millimeter sizes 0.5–8.0 mm in 0.5 mm steps.
5. *"WW"-type watchmaker's precision lathe spindle* which can be interchanged with the regular spindle for use with standard "WW"-type jeweler's collets and accessories. Has precision roller bearings in front, and a matched pair of radial thrust ball bearings in the rear that assure accuracy within 0.0004 in.
6. *Precision drill chuck, type "WW,"* for use with watchmaker's spindle above, has a capacity of 0–4 mm.
7. *Precision "WW"-type collet* for watchmaker's spindle. Available in sets in inch sizes 1⁄32–¼ in; and millimeter sizes 0.1–7.0 mm.
8. *Three-jawed universal chuck,* 2¼ in max. capacity, self-centering, reversible steel jaws. Scroll, guideways, and jaw teeth are all hardened steel and precision ground for an accuracy within 0.003 in. The chuck can be mounted on a lathe headstock, or a tailstock spindle, and also on the cross slide.
9. *Four-jawed independent chuck,* 2¼ in max. capacity, with cast iron body and reversible jaws, each of which can be adjusted individually to grip square, rectangular, hexagonal, or irregularly shaped workpieces. Round parts can be chucked off-center to turn eccentric parts and cams. The chuck can be mounted on a lathe headstock or tailstock spindle, and on the cross slide.
10. *Chuck mounting arbor* used to adapt the three-jawed universal chuck, or the four-jawed independent chuck for use with the watchmaker's spindle.
11. *T-slotted faceplate,* 2⅝ in Ø, with three T-slots and three threaded holes for fixture screws. Can be used on the lathe spindle or the cross slide in conjunction with a mounting plate.
12. ½ in *slitting saw arbor.*
13. ⅜ in *grinding wheel arbor.*
14. *16 mm capacity set screw chuck.*
15. *Blank arbor.*

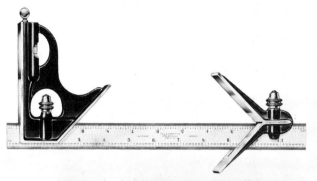

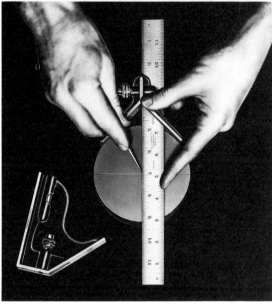

10–72 Top: *COMBINATION SQUARE WITH SQUARE HEAD AND CENTER HEAD, AND 12 IN TEMPERED STEEL RULE* accurately machine divided, with *spirit level* in the square head. This tool is used to locate centers. When mounted, the square or center head can slide on a central groove (on reverse) along the rule blade, and lock bolts hold them at any position on the blade. They and the rule can also be separated and used. The accurately ground equal-length faces of the center head permit the finding of centers on small- or large-diameter discs, cylinder ends, and other round work.

10–73 Bottom: *THE CENTER HEAD AND RULE* (with the *square head* removed) is used here to accurately locate a disc center (on any round work). With the center head faces pressed against the disc, and the rule blade flat on the workpiece, one diameter was drawn with a *scriber*. The disc was shifted approximately 90°, and a second line is being enscribed. The point where they intersect is the disc center. *Photo: Courtesy the L. S. Starrett Co.*

work must rotate upon it, but the live center is often left soft. The points are ground to a 60° angle which corresponds with a similarly angled depression made in the center of the ends of the workpiece with a *60° countersink.* These angles *must correspond* to allow the work to be properly gripped, supported, and revolved between centers by a surface larger than its extreme points.

To make this depression, first the center must be located. This is easily done with a *square* that has an attached *center head* which is a right angle bisected by the edge of a blade, the latter sometimes permanently fixed, sometimes removable. When the center head is pressed against any circular object, such as the end of a cylinder, the blade edge bisects the circle or cylinder head with a di-

ameter. This line is enscribed, and the center head is shifted to bring the blade edge to nearly a right angle to the first line, then a second line is enscribed across the first. The point where these two lines intersect is the bisector of a chord, and the center of the circle. Therefore in finding this center by these means, no actual measurements are necessary.

This point is marked with a *center punch.* The center is then drilled with a shallow hole, *slightly deeper* than is needed in order to leave a *small space* that acts as a reservoir for lubricant which prevents excessive center point wear. In this hole the correct angle is formed by a *countersink* with a 60° point, but not so deeply as to leave a ridge around the countersunk hole as the center point must contact the hole sides. The fit of the center rod into the spindle nose recess must always be tight; therefore, before its insertion, the recess must be inspected to be sure it is free of foreign matter such as metal chips, as otherwise the work will not run true.

In mounting a workpiece between center points for turning, the tailstock is advanced toward the headstock enough to hold the work in place between the centers without forcing. The tailstock is then locked in place. A dead center point must always be well lubricated as the work turns upon it while the center itself remains stationary. Depending on circumstances, live centers, sometimes referred to as *running centers,* can also be used in the tailstock, especially when turning work at high speeds. To remove a dead center, the sleeve is retracted, which brings the end of the tailstock screw against the rear of the center and forces it out. If the headstock and tailstock barrels are hollow, live or dead centers can be knocked out by inserting a rod from the rear through the hole, then pushing them out.

COLLETS AND CHUCKS

3 Various kinds of collets and chucks, *all jawed devices,* are used to hold small- and large-diameter work in the threaded spindle nose of the headstock or the tailstock from which the center has been removed. A *collet* is a small chuck attachment that fits into the lathe spindle. Its tapered, split jaws, and accurate hole in round, square, or hexagonal shape, holds small work of those sectional shapes, or tool shanks such as on drills or milling cutters, in accurate positions, and without damaging their surface. They are made in sets with jaw holes that vary by a few thousandths of an inch or millimeter. The workpiece or tool must be inserted far enough into the jaws to allow them to be firmly and accurately gripped. Some collet jaws are the type that are controlled by a *removable key* that is placed in a pinion and turned. Whenever a key is used to tighten or loosen an accessory, it should not be laid to rest on the lathe as it can fall and cause damage to a working lathe. On some collets the jaws are simultaneously closed

by manually tightening a knurled closing collar, as in this photo. When screwed back into the spindle's nose threads, the spindle's core taper causes the collet's jaws to be squeezed, become compressed, and so grip the workpiece or the tool shank placed in them. For high-precision work, a *draw-in spring collet* is used in which the outer surface, when drawn against the taper inside the chuck, is forced against the workpiece or tool shank and held there. It is released by pushing the other way which causes the jaws to open by spring action. After use, carefully wipe any collet with an oily rag to keep it clean and maintain its accuracy.

A *drill holding chuck* (16) can be mounted in the tailstock spindle which allows it to be fed into and out of the work which is fixed in a headstock-held chuck or collet. The simplest type is opened and closed by turning the knurled case, and others are worked with a *key* (seen in Photo 2 lying on the bench top at the right). They are mounted on an arbor with a taper that fits into the spindle nose or tailstock barrel.

Small-step chucks are also available, concave with concentric steps for the external gripping of a disc to be faced, or convex for internal gripping of a central hole in a disc.

A *universal chuck* (17) is already mounted in Photo 2 on a *backplate* that screws into the headstock spindle nose, or it is first screwed and bolted onto a backplate. It is so called because its *three jaws,* each numbered to correspond with the slot number it occupies, are geared to allow them to *close simultaneously* on a round or regular polygon-sectioned workpiece, or a tool shaft with a round section. *One* screw, operated by a *hand chuck key* (seen in Photo 2 lying on the headstock housing above the name Rockwell), moves *all* the three case-hardened, one-piece, machined, stepped jaws in or out, to open or close them upon the workpiece. Of great convenience is the fact that the workpiece is automatically self-centered. This makes it easier to operate than an *independent chuck* (see Photos 13 and 15), also mounted on a backplate, and provided with *four hardened, serrated step jaws,* each of which is controlled *independently* by a *hand tightening key.* These jaws are *reversible* (as are also those of the universal chuck) to allow a workpiece to be held inside or outside. Depending on the need, they can be inserted into their slideways in whichever direction is best suited to hold the particular workpiece. The presence of four independently movable jaws allows this chuck to accommodate any work of an irregular shape which can be placed off-center; and it also permits accurate centering. Because the work is not automatically centered in this chuck, it is first centered in the jaws by eye, then its position is adjusted.

FACEPLATES AND FACING CUTS

4   A *faceplate* is a large-rim, machined, cast iron disc provided with holes, slots, or T-slots through which a bolt head can pass. A workpiece can also be attached to a faceplate by other arrangements, such as clamps that are used to hold irregularly shaped workpieces. The faceplate holds work on which *facing cuts* are made, and these are cuts made perpendicular to the axis of rotation at the *end* of a workpiece, or on a flat workpiece held in this position. The faceplate is held on the spindle nose thread.

In some cases, work being face cut can be held and turned by a *lathe dog,* an angled device that is clamped to the spindle end of the work, and held by its tail which is engaged in a slot in the faceplate. When the faceplate revolves, the attached dog causes the work to turn with it

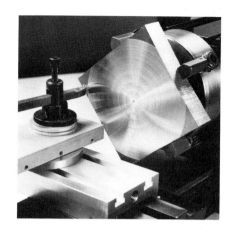

4

by communicating motion to it from the revolving faceplate.

Depending on its shape, work can also be held in a three-jawed universal chuck, or a four-jawed independent chuck, as in this photo of the *Machinex 5 lathe.*

When making a facing cut, *right-* or *left-hand side offset* or *corner tools* can be used, depending on the workpiece shape and how the tool is mounted. Tools are normally set at a 45° angle to the work plane (although perpendicular cuts can also be made) and they are fed across the work with the cross-feed handwheel. Several light cuts are made, usually from the center outward when a large surface is being face cut, in order to avoid strain on the motor. Slow speeds are used for large-diameter work, and the speed can be increased as the diameter diminishes, as on small work. The cross slide should be capable of traveling the full distance needed to accomplish the cut in one action. In cases where the center cannot be reached, or where a stub is allowed to remain that connects the main workpiece body to a smaller waste piece, the waste can be cut off once the work is removed from the lathe, using a *hacksaw,* or a *jeweler's saw,* depending on its thickness.

TOOL-HOLDING SYSTEMS

The *carriage assembly* (18) or *compound slide* is power activated. It bears and conveys the *cutting tool mounting,* manually or automatically, along the bed to the workpiece by moving along the threaded lead screw at a rate according to selected gear ratios. When moving it manually along the bed to make cuts parallel to the central axis, the large *apron handwheel* or *carriage handle* (19) is turned. The carriage holds an accurately machined saddle (20) that spans and rests on the bed, and contains a dovetail bearing along which the *cross slide* (21) it carries moves. The tool-holding device is held and clamped to an auxiliary slide mounted on the main cross slide. The cross slide can move at right angles to the spindle axis, its position controlled by the *micrometer-dialed cross-feed handle* (22) at the center-top of the carriage apron. This moves a cross slide screw which turns in a nut fixed in the carriage. A *swiveling compound rest* (23) that allows angular cuts and turning tapers, here carries a *turret-style tool post* (24) on the cross slide (other tool-holding devices, mentioned below may also be mounted on it), and is controlled by the *tool slide handle* (25) or cross-feed handle for lateral or longitudinal feeds.

Tool-holding systems of different types are available for

use on lathes. If the tool is a *small cutter bit,* it can be held in a tool holder whose shape fits into the lathe's tool post (see Photo 14). Some small lathes use a *centrally screwed pillar* with a tightening screw that puts pressure on a pressure plate under which the tool is placed and held. The *tool post* or *tool stock* is a centrally slotted post or pillar through which the tool shank passes, and is held down by a single tightening screw (see Photos 4 and 6). Another type is a *side-slotted* or *block tool post* which is a casting held on a pillar (see Photo 7). The tool is clamped or locked in the slot by screws, usually with the slot facing the left as most work is performed toward the direction of the headstock. This unit is mounted in a T-slot or dovetail in the *cross slide worktable* (26). By advancing the cross slide, the tool can travel perpendicularly *across* the lathe bed to make facing cuts or slots on the work. In the *four-way turret-style tool post* (see Photo 8), up to four tools can be held at once, and it can be rotated to present each tool in turn to the work. In this device the tools are held by a *turret-style lock,* but they can also be held in a horizontal position by *holding bolts* that are tightened down evenly upon the tool shank by a *hand wrench.*

All tool points should *minimally overhang the tool post* to keep the tool *maximally rigid.* The cutting edge is placed on the center, or slightly below the center, but *never above center.* Any tool's position can be adjusted when necessary by inserting *packing strips* of *shim sheet metal* beneath it to align the tool point to the correct position in relation to the center.

A *steady rest* is a lathe accessory used for steadying and supporting slender, long, small-diameter workpieces or tubing during turning, or a headpiece-held workpiece that must be end drilled or faced. It can be attached to the carriage in which case it travels or moves along with it and is termed a *traveling steady,* or clamped to immobilize it in any position on the lathe bed, in which case it is termed a *fixed steady.* Steadies can be used instead of the tailstock to support a workpiece that is longer than the lathe's length capacity, the surplus passing through the headpiece barrel.

The *apron* (27) is the front, vertical part of the lathe carriage, and is a casing bolted to the underside to protect the handwheel mechanism by which the carriage is moved. It incorporates the apron controls including the *feed-engaging lever* or *feed-reversing handle* which acts to feed the work transversely to the longitudinal axis of the bed or to retract it from the work. It also can carry a *split nut lever* which engages the apron and the lead screw to allow the carriage to travel automatically along the bed, as when threading.

LATHE TECHNIQUES

TURNING

5 *Turning* is the general term used to describe the manual or mechanical operation of metal removal from a workpiece which is held in one position on the lathe and rotates against the edge of a cutting tool brought to bear upon it. Generally the tool is moved along the workpiece axis, normally from right to left; at an angle to the work; or perpendicular to that axis. Due to the pressure of the hard tool on the workpiece, its outer layer is compressed and removed by the action of the cutting edge. In automatic turning, the *tool cut depth* is set by adjusting the cross slide position, as is here being done by Griffin, by turning the micrometer-dialed cross-feed handle; or by adjusting the position of the compound rest. When turning large-diameter work, to compensate for the increase in surface speed, the work is made to revolve at a slower speed than for small-diameter work.

ROUGHING

6 *Roughing cuts* are the initial cuts that reduce the workpiece radius by tool penetration into the workpiece. They are made at *slow speed* which is easier to control. Here on a Machinex 5 lathe, the tool is accomplishing a transition turning operation that is common, turning square stock into a cylindrical form. This stage has been reached by a series of roughing cuts made by feeding the cutting tool along the work with the lead screw handwheel. Roughing cuts are generally relatively deep, the depth depending on the degree of metal hardness, the desired degree of finish, and what the lathe construction will allow without strain. Roughing is generally done without too much regard for finish as the work will be processed further. The total of roughing cuts performed reduces the work to a diameter somewhat greater than its finished dimension, leaving an allowance of about 0.010 in (0.254 mm) remaining for the finishing operation. The longitudinal feed of the carriage toward the left is started by the operator who first turns the carriage handwheel to bring the cutting tool to the right of the workpiece, then turns the lathe manually to test the depth of cut. When this appears satisfactory, turning can proceed either manually by hand feeding the work to the tool, or with the carriage power feed engaged, automatically, at a slow spindle speed, proceeding along the work up to a set point when the rotation is stopped. The work is lubricated at intervals if required with a *brush* that has been dipped in the lubricant. The tool is made to pass over the work the necessary number of times to achieve the desired dimension. Diame-

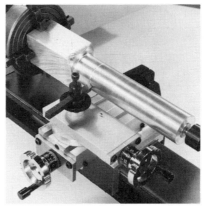

5   6   7

ter size is checked at intervals with a micrometer or another measuring device.

Roughing leaves the work with a relatively rough, somewhat ridged surface. In cases where work is turned between centers, and parts of the far left are not yet fully turned, the workpiece is removed from the lathe by withdrawing the dead center and the tailpiece, its position reversed, and it is returned between centers. The carriage is moved manually to the starting position, and the remainder is then turned with the same tool, moving past the first stop point on the work so that no ridge remains.

TAPERING

Tapering, in which short tapers or angular cuts, or chamfering is done, is most easily accomplished by setting the tool-holding compound rest at the necessary angle, clamping the carriage in place, adjusting and setting the tool by using the cross slide, then cutting the taper by hand by feeding the compound rest to the work. Long tapers are made by offsetting the tailstock center, making it out of line with the headstock center, the lateral distance between centers being half the total taper on the length of the workpiece.

FINISHING CUTS

7 *Finishing cuts* are usually made with a sharp, round-nosed tool in the same way as roughing cuts, but at higher spindle speeds. Because the cuts are *very light,* only about 0.005 in (0.127 mm) in depth, a fine, threadlike chip, as seen here, is removed in this operation. The high speed results in a very smooth, mirror surface, and with it the work is brought to its final diameter. If the work is being *turned to tolerances,* measurements are frequently taken during finishing to check diameters. This is done with *outside calipers, vernier calipers,* or a *micrometer,* depending on the degree of accuracy wanted.

SLOTTING

8 *Slotting* is the process of forming an equal width groove in a workpiece by bringing a *narrow parting-off tool* only partially into the workpiece. In this case, a 1 in (2.54 cm) square aluminum bar stock held in a four-jawed independent chuck is being slotted for decorative purposes. The turret-style tool rest in which two tools are clamped is visible here.

9 A close-up of the slotting above, looking down on the minimally projecting cutting tool held by the tool post. The short distance it overhangs or projects from the tool holder ensures maximum tool rigidity. These slots are being made at measured intervals into the stock. The tool is hollow ground behind the cutting edge, and tapers back slightly from the cutting edge to allow clearance from the work, to prevent it from becoming jammed in the slot or rubbing the slot sides.

FILES USED FOR WORKPIECE SHAPING

Files can be used to *shape* the small forms that are used in jewelry, or to *finish* and *refine* the forms begun with other lathe tools, while the workpiece is mounted and revolving on the lathe. When employing a file for this purpose, a high spindle speed is recommended. Ordinarily *single-cut mill files* are used, but to eliminate possible drag or tear, overcome "chatter," and reduce file clogging, a self-clearing, fast-cutting, special *long-angle file* whose teeth are cut at a much greater angle than those of a standard mill file, is recommended. Because of its rapid cutting action, care must be taken against allowing it to cut too deeply too quickly. With this file, the surface can be brought to a silky smoothness. *No. 4* or *No. 6 Swiss pattern files* of different sectional shapes can also be used, the sectional shape selected to fit the specific contours of the work.

Unless making a groove, files should not be held stationary and rigid, but should be constantly stroked against the workpiece as it revolves, using a gliding, lateral motion that helps to prevent scoring and the formation of ridges, as well as allowing the file to clear itself of chips. The file is held in *both hands* in the same manner as described under Drawfiling, p. 106. Only as much pressure as is necessary to do the work is exerted on the file, as excessive pressure may cause small-section files to break. When lathe filing, never allow the hand to touch the workpiece as the oil and moisture thus imparted to it will cause difficulty in permitting the file to get a "hold" on the metal.

DRILLING

10 *Drilling* a hole into the workpiece is a common lathe operation. *Drills* may have *parallel* or *cylindrical shanks* that are used in a three-jawed drill chuck inserted and held in the center socket of the tailstock, or *morse-tapered shanks* that can be fitted directly into the tailstock barrel without a chuck. When small drill sizes are used, they can be accommodated by the use of *taper adaptors* that fit into the chuck. The type of drill used, whether of high-speed or carbon steel, depends on the degree of hardness of the workpiece; the degree of rigidity in the setup; the hole size; whether the drill is being used to start or to enlarge an existing hole; and the degree of tolerance required. Drills can be reground freehand when dull, or with the aid of a *drill-grinding jig* to achieve the correct cutting angle on the drill point. Different metals require different drill point angles and clearances. A backing-off angle of 12° is usual.

Especially when making a larger hole, the workpiece is usually center punched first, then—with the punch mark accurately aligned with the spindle axis—drilled with a

8   9   10

small-diameter drill guide hole. This hole gives the correct position for the *larger diameter twist drill,* keeps it centered on the cone of the first hole, and helps prevent it from wobbling or wandering once drilling starts. The work to be drilled is here held in a revolving independent chuck on the headstock and *rotates,* and the drill held in a tailstock drill chuck is rigid and *stationary.* The drill is advanced and fed manually into the securely fixed workpiece by turning the tailstock screw handle. The feed rate must be judged by feel. Excessive pressure is avoided as the drill can overheat, lose its temper, and its cutting edges can be chipped. Slow spindle speeds are used for large drills, and faster speeds for small-diameter drills. The drill is alternately fed to the workpiece and withdrawn as judged necessary, to free the hole and the drill flutes of chips. Brass and aluminum can be drilled dry, but other metals require lubrication. When lubrication is necessary, the hole and the tool are liberally supplied with a cutting fluid such as a light machine oil. Because the stock being drilled here is square, it appears as a blurred form during rotation.

11 Here a large, flat workpiece is to be drilled on a Machinex 5 lathe converted to a vertical drill press (see Photo 20). Any workpiece to be drilled must be securely fixed so it does not move during drilling. The workpiece here is held on the cross carriage by *clamps.* T-bolt heads are passed into T-slots in the cross slide which is used as a worktable, and pass through strap clamps that grip the work by tightening nuts and washers upon the bolts. When through holes are drilled, the workpiece must be fixed in a way that allows the drill to clear the worktable, holding tool, or lathe part that may be beneath it. A plywood board could be placed below the work for this purpose.

12 With the Machinex 5 lathe converted to a vertical drill press, a cylindrical workpiece is here held in a *machine vise* mounted on the cross slide worktable. The *high-speed metal drill* used is a short set drill type that has a short shank and flutes. It is held in a drill chuck mounted on the spindle nose. The workpiece is being lubricated while drilling progresses with pressure applied by lowering the drill press hand lever, also used to retract the drill. (For recommended drill speeds, see Table, "Suggested Drill Cutting Speeds and Feeds," p. 756.)

REAMING

Reaming is a rotary operation that uses a *reamer* with one or more straight or twisted flute cutting elements called *teeth,* to enlarge, true, or finish an existing hole to size or contour. Because in drilling the drill makes a hole slightly larger than the drill diameter, when drilling a hole to exact tolerance, first a hole 0.005–0.006 in (0.127–0.152 mm) *undersized* is made. It is then enlarged to size with a reamer of the proper dimension.

A *tapered-shank reamer* is held in the tailstock in the same way as a drill, but during work, it is also supported by the walls of the metal around the hole. It is fed *manually,* slowly and evenly, forward into the hole, and made to revolve by hand turning the feed wheel. The work must be well lubricated. Reaming can also be done mechanically, but that is best left to experts. When hand reaming is carried out, less initial stock difference is left between the drilled hole and the reamed hole size because otherwise the pressure needed to manually force the reamer through the metal is too great. Reaming does not improve the position or alignment of drilled or bored holes.

BORING

13 *Boring* is an operation involving turning an internal surface on a rigidly held workpiece, either with the tool rotating and the workpiece held stationary, clamped to the cross slide; or with the workpiece rotating and the tool held rigidly in the tool post in true relation to the spindle's axis. The boring tool can be a single-point, straight, L-shaped, or inclined-point cutter. *Straight* and *L-shaped cutters* are used when boring *through holes* (in which case clearance must be allowed past the workpiece to permit the tool to emerge without damaging equipment beyond the hole); and the *inclined cutter* is used when boring *blind holes.*

When boring is done with a rotating workpiece and a stationary cutter (as seen here on a Machinex 5 lathe), the cutting tool is the *small-bit type* inserted into a clamp at the end of a rigid *boring bar,* as shown upper left. For rigidity, the bar is here held in a *spring box clamp* fixed on the carriage, and centered parallel with the bedways. The cutting tool's edge can overhang or project beyond *one* or *both* sides of the diameter of the bar. Clearance is allowed to prevent the tool heel's underedge (or edges) from contacting and rubbing against the hole wall, and to allow the chips to emerge, as otherwise they might jam the tool in the hole.

Boring is a fairly simple way of accurately cutting, sizing, and finishing relatively large-diameter holes from ¼ in (6.3499 mm) upward, holes larger than those normally drilled by jewelers. The liberally lubricated workpiece is here clamped in a headpiece chuck but can also be held on a faceplate, and revolves as the tool is hand fed or fed automatically into the hole. Boring tools are used with light, continuous cuts. Forcing must be avoided, especially when the tool is mounted in a boring bar, and when L-shaped borers are used because their length inclines them to be somewhat springy. Because this springiness might affect accuracy, several cuts are made without changing the tool setting, in both directions, that is, inward and out-

11   12   13

ward, until no cutting action takes place. This procedure compensates for possible bar or tool shaft bend which might result in a tapered rather than a straight hole. After boring is completed, the exterior and facing ends of the work are turned and trued.

THREADS AND THREADING

14 Threads used on screws, bolts, and workpieces exist in a large number of forms and standard pitches. (For a description of these, and the *terminology* of screws, refer to Screws, Bolts and Nuts, and Screw Joints, Chapter 10, and the chart "Thread Types" on p. 426.)

Threading is the cutting or forming of *external* screw threads which are projecting helical ribs on a cylindrical object. When the object is mounted on a lathe, the work is most simply done by the use of a *round thread-cutting die.* To facilitate the start of the die on the workpiece, its edge is chamfered 45° by holding a *flat file* against it as it rotates. A solid, nonadjustable, one-piece die can be used, fixed in the tailstock in which a *die holder* is placed to receive, center, and hold it. It is important that the die be brought *squarely* to the workpiece as otherwise it will only form half a thread on the object. The chuck is rotated *manually* while pressing the die on the lubricated object end, by turning the tailstock handwheel. As soon as the die grips the workpiece and starts to cut, the tailstock does not need adjustment since the die pulls the holder along the workpiece while the chuck is turned manually. After two rotations, the die is reversed half a turn to break the swarf curls that form.

MECHANICAL EXTERNAL THREADING

Mechanical external threading on a lathe-mounted workpiece can be executed on any lathe equipped with screw-cutting equipment. (A lathe without this capability is called a *plain lathe.*) External threading can be carried out on solid cylindrical stock, on tubing, or on a projecting part of a workpiece. All these forms are used in jewelry fabrication.

Mechanical screw threading is described here only briefly, and in its simplest form: *single-point tool thread making.* Other mechanical thread-making devices are also used on lathes, including multiple-point thread cutter tools; adjustable threading dies; thread rollers; and special lathes that exist only for the purpose of thread making.

Functional external threads are meant to mate with internal threads on another object, produced by *taps.* Therefore, the same American, British, or Metric thread must be formed on *both* parts to allow mating.

In screw cutting, the carriage must move along the bed and the lead screw at a predetermined rate to make the tool cut a regular thread of the correct lead. To do this, the tool must be coupled to the headstock mandrel through gearing, and different threads require different

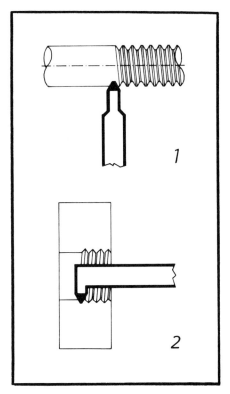

10–74 SCREW-CUTTING TOOLS
(and their position in relation to the work)
1. *External threading tool,* its position perpendicular to the workpiece when cutting a full thread.
2. *Internal threading tool,* its position inside the hole also perpendicular to the workpiece.
Drawing courtesy American Edelstaal, Inc.

gearing. Simple lathes have a supply of *change wheels* or gear wheels used to make up the various *gear trains,* which are a series of meshed gear wheels arranged to transfer rotational motion or drive from one shaft to another at a particular speed in relation to that of the other shaft. This drive transmits power from the headstock spindle to the lead screw, causing the cutting tool mounted on the carriage to move at a regular rate of turns per inch (tpi) along the lead screw. Change wheels are stamped with the number of teeth they have, are selected according to the thread to be cut, and are mounted by hand on the lathe. Instructions are provided with each lathe indicating which train of gears should be used to achieve the desired thread. In expensive lathes, a *quick change gear box* is incorporated in the headstock. By this arrangement, gearing is changed through the manipulation of levers.

Because lead screws are made with various pitches, the movement of the workpiece is a definite distance for each spindle revolution. For example, a lead screw having 8 threads per inch will cut an 8-pitch screw thread. If a 16-pitch thread is wanted, the stud gear with half as many teeth as the screw gear is used to make the workpiece advance at the proper speed ratio of mandrel speed to lead screw speed.

Here threading is being carried out on a brass rod by the use of a single-point tool. The workpiece is first fixed between centers on the lathe, or it can be fixed in the jaws of a chuck in the headpiece, provided that its length is not more than five times its diameter, in which case it would not maintain sufficient rigidity for this operation. In this

14

photo, the turret tool holder has been replaced by a conventional *slotted tool post* mounted on the cross slide. The tool bit is held by a nut in the tool holder whose shaft passes through the slot in the tool post. To put pressure on and hold the tool holder rigidly in position, a *hand wrench,* seen mounted on the top tightening nut, is used.

The single-point thread-cutting tool used must have the *correct angle form* for the desired screw thread. If it is not purchased already with this form, its point must be ground to the necessary angle. In the grinding operation, point angle accuracy can be tested by holding the result against a *screw-cutting and tool-setting gauge,* in effect a *template* having border notches in various standard pitch angles. The same guide is also used when mounting the tool in the correct position in the tool post. To be sure that the tool is set square to the work, which must be the case when cutting both faces of the thread at once, and to give the thread the correct angle and form, the tool point must be exactly at the center of the cut. A proprietary non-oil cut-

10–75 29° *ACME STANDARD SCREW PITCH AND TOOL-SETTING GAUGE* with ground and hardened angles and edges. Used for testing the tool angles ground to the desired angle, and for setting tools on the lathe at the correct angle when cutting Acme threads which have a side inclination of 14.5° (29° included angle). Their depth is the same as square threads which they are replacing in machine construction because of their strength and greater ease in cutting. One side is a depth-of-thread scale, and the other is a threads-per-inch scale. *Photo: Courtesy the L. S. Starrett Co.*

ting fluid is used to lubricate the cutting tool and the work.

In *manual feed thread making,* first the diameter of the screw blank or workpiece is reduced 0.005 in (0.127 mm) to prevent the crests of the finished thread from being stripped or torn in use. The half nuts are engaged, and a trial run is made with the single-point tool making a very light cut. By just allowing it to touch the workpiece, a helical spiral is scratched on the work, the cutter moving across the workpiece surface from right to left at a regular rate of advance so the marks are separated. The tool is withdrawn, the half nuts are disengaged, and the carriage is returned by hand to the right, at the starting position. The scratch is checked for accuracy with a *screw pitch gauge,* and if correct, the cross-feed dial indicator is then set to zero, and the cutter is set to make a 0.003 in (0.075 mm) deeper cut. By engaging the half nuts, the workpiece is positioned to present the tool to the same place on the work as previously so it cuts in the same groove. The tool is fed to the workpiece with the manual feed handle.

When the first shallow cut is finished, the cutting tool is withdrawn from the work by turning the cross slide handle one complete turn. The lead screw is disengaged simultaneously, and the cutter is again returned to the starting point. After resetting the cross-feed dial again at zero, a second, 0.003 in (0.075 mm) deeper cut is made further into the spiral. The form and pitch of the thread can be checked with a *thread profile guide template.* As many cuts are made as necessary, the last cuts removing only 0.001 in (0.025 mm), until ultimately the necessary amount of metal is removed. This depends on the thread size, pitch, and percentage of full cut depth. To test the result, a *matching standard-threaded hexagon nut* can be threaded onto the screw thread, on which it should move *smoothly.*

Internal threading of a larger sized hole can be done with an *internal screw-cutting tool* mounted in the tool post, or with *taps,* the latter described below. Internal screw-cutting tools are used in the same way as boring tools. Because of their length, they tend to spring, therefore a *series of cuts* are made without increasing the cut depth until the tool stops cutting, after which it can then be advanced to cut more deeply into the workpiece.

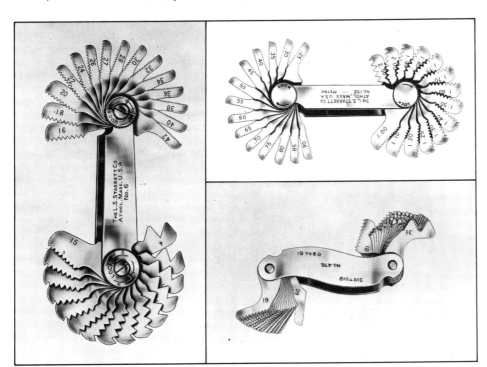

10–76 *SCREW PITCH GAUGES* allow quick determination of various thread pitches. A steel case contains a number of size-marked folding leaves at both ends, which can be brought out singly, and held in place by a locking device. Each leaf has teeth corresponding to a *particular pitch* which can be matched with the workpiece thread, so that the correct pitch can be read from the leaf marking. Different screw pitch gauges are made for the various screw thread measurement systems in use. Shown here are, **left:** *American National and U. S. Standard 60° Screw Pitch Thread Gauge,* with 30 pitch leaves, and a range of 4–42 threads per inch; **lower right:** *Whitworth Standard 55° Screw Pitch Thread Gauge,* with 30 pitch leaves, and 3½–60 threads per inch; **upper right:** *Metric French Standard and International Standard 60° Screw Pitch Gauge,* with 28 pitch leaves, and a range of 0.25–2.50 mm. *Photo: Courtesy the L. S. Starrett Co.*

THREAD CHASING

Though not always necessary, the final sizing and finishing cuts can be done with a manual or mechanical *thread chaser tool*. These tools have a serrated edge that matches that of the grooves in the thread. By manually or mechanically pressing the chaser's serrated end against the finished threads and into the grooves, the thread crests and roots are rounded and rendered less sharp. *External* and *internal thread-chasing tools* exist, the former with the teeth perpendicular to the tool shaft, and the latter with the teeth running parallel with the shaft, which is bent to permit the teeth to contact its sides when inserted into the hole. Manual chasers are hand held, supported on a tool rest fixed parallel to the workpiece. They are advanced to contact and register with the thread, the chaser held at the center line. With the lathe revolving the workpiece, the thread is allowed to move the chaser along the lubricated workpiece to the end of the thread, then it is withdrawn. Mechanical external thread chaser tools are fixed square to the workpiece in a special *spring chaser carrier*. While the workpiece revolves, the chaser moves mechanically along the thread length at the same speed used in thread making. In either case, a *separate* chaser tool is used for *each thread pitch*.

TAPPING

15 *Tapping* is the forming of an *internal screw thread* in a predrilled hole whose diameter equals that of the *thread core,* the additional metal left for the formation of the threads. The workpiece shown here is held in a four-jawed independent chuck in the headstock because this chuck best holds the square shape, and its rigidity assures true centering. When tapping by *manual power,* first the undersized hole is drilled into the workpiece. A *Jacob's-type drill chuck* is used in the tailpiece to hold the tap in an absolutely perpendicular position to the work. With the work remaining motionless, a *hand tap wrench* is placed over the square end of the tap shaft, and with it the tap is turned by hand in a clockwise direction to establish a grip on the workpiece. The first two internal helical grooves that form are then sufficient to hold the tap in the correct position. The tap is then released from the tailstock which is moved to the right, out of the way. The tap wrench is replaced on the tap shank and turned manually until the tap reaches the required depth within the hole. After each two revolutions, the tap is reversed a half turn to break swarf curls that form within the tap flutes. To remove the tap, it is turned counterclockwise out of the workpiece.

16 In this photo, a tap is being started in a previously drilled hole as described above. The workpiece is clamped on a Machinex 5 lathe that has been converted to a drill press which can also be used for tapping. Here the tap is started in a countersunk hole, its shank held in the drill chuck to establish its correct vertical position in relation to the workpiece. The chuck is then turned by hand while applying moderate pressure from the feed handle. The tap is *not* operated under power on this machine or it will break.

Power tapping is done with the tap also held by a tap wrench whose handle is long enough to make contact with the bedway side and so prevents the tap from rotating since in this case, it is the work that rotates. The lathe is operated at slow speed, and the tap is fed into the workpiece by gently turning the handwheel on the tailstock.

PARTING-OFF

17 *Parting-off,* also called *cutting off,* is the severing or dividing of a workpiece with a *parting-off tool.* The work is firmly held in a headstock chuck, and the part to be removed is not supported in the trailstock. Here the workpiece is a cylindrical brass unit held in a three-jawed universal chuck. With the lathe operating at slow speed, the lubricated parting-off tool is advanced perpendicularly into the workpiece toward its center at a rate that allows the tool to cut continuously. When the center point or axis is reached, the workpiece is severed. A small teat or raised central point may remain, and if so, is removed by filing or an abrasive paper.

SURFACE FINISHING

18 *Surface finishing* involves bringing the workpiece surface to a desired final condition. Each part can be separately finished while revolving on the lathe, before assembly. Sharp edges and burrs must be removed. This can be done by a *file,* used in the manner discussed above when using a file for shaping. Following filing, a *cloth-backed abrasive* of the desired grit can be used to remove any surface marks. As illustrated here, a strip of this material can be held by both hands at its ends, passing around the workpiece and held stationary, or moved along its length as necessary. To get into crevices and angles in the contour, a piece of the same cloth can be folded into a small pad, and the doubled edge pressed into the position while the workpiece revolves. The finer the grit, the brighter and smoother the finish. To give the work a mirror finish, this can be followed by a cloth that has been rubbed over a bar of one of the usual finishing abrasives, such as rouge, and pressing the cloth against the revolving work. To avoid accident, only expose a small area of the cloth to the work, and be sure to hold back any loose cloth.

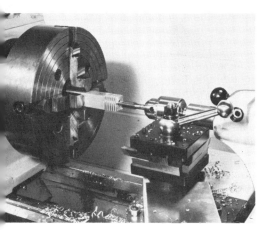

15   16   17

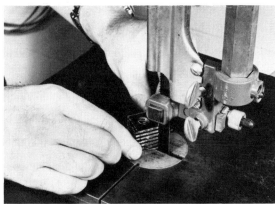

18 **19** **20**

POSTLATHE OPERATIONS

Postlathe operations are those performed on the workpiece after all lathe operations have been completed, or they can be independent operations. They are performed with hand tools, or various power tools designed for the purpose. Some miniature lathes, as mentioned, can be converted to accomplish those operations that can be carried out by rotary motion.

CUTTING

19 Here the workpiece is being sawed into two parts on a *band saw*. The purpose in this case is to expose non-functional, internal threads for their decorative value. Three basic cutting directions are possible: longitudinal, perpendicular, and angular. *Longitudinal section cutting* divides the work into two parts. When it occurs at the medial point, the parts are equal, but it can also be done at more than one parallel position producing unequal parts. *Perpendicular, transverse* or *cross section* cutting divides the work in a direction perpendicular to the longitudinal axis, ordinarily achieving circular sectional shapes if the workpiece is cylindrical in form. Any number of cross sections can be made on the workpiece. *Angular or oblique section cutting* is done at any angle, and when the form is cylindrical, the sections are oval.

MILLING

20 *Milling* as a mechanical process is normally carried out on a *milling machine*. Here a Machinex 5 lathe has been set up vertically to convert it for use in milling operations, and also for use as a vertical-spindle drill press. To do this, the headstock assembly is unclamped from the bed's dovetail guideway, removed, and remounted on the sliding head mount of the 16 in long vertical column. The two clamping screws are tightened with a *torque wrench* to approximately 100–125 *inch-pounds* to ensure a square position, and the same is done when returning it to the lathe bed. (The measurement "inch-pounds" is used in mechanics, as are "foot-pounds," an inch-pound being equal to one-twelfth of a foot-pound. The latter is a unit of energy equal to the work done in raising one pound avoirdupois against the force of gravity to the height of one foot.)

The movable handle is inserted in the mount's socket, and the lock screws are tightened. The handle is operated as on a drill press to lower or raise the entire head. With the handle lifted to the upright position, the feed mechanism is disengaged from the column rack, and the head can be hand lifted or lowered to any position on the column.

21 The workpiece is securely mounted in a *clamp* that holds it rigidly as otherwise it might rotate. (See Milling, Chapter 4 for a general discussion of the process.) Various types of *mill cutting tools* can be used, depending on the function they are to perform. Here a circular cutter is milling a keyway in cylindrical stock. Longitudinal feed is used wherever possible, with the work fed to the cutter. The work is oriented for "up" milling, the cutter's teeth always moving forward along the cut line opposing the feed direction. The cutter's teeth should not turn downward and back because this direction causes the teeth to pull the workpiece under the cutter, and will make the cutter climb

21 **22** **23**

and break. Milling with small cutters should be carried out with moderate spindle speed, and with large cutters at slow spindle speed. *The work must be lubricated.*

22   Here a *ball-ended mill* cutter is being used to mill a cavity. This shape allows a wall that joins the base with a filleted recess, and it can be used to make rounded grooves.

GRINDING

23   *Grinding* is another rotary motion operation that can be carried out on a lathe. Here the headpiece of a Machinex 5 lathe has been set vertically on a post, and a grinding wheel has been mounted in the spindle. The cutting edge of a tool is being ground, the tool mounted in a clamp fixed to the carriage at the proper angle. Workpiece surfaces can also be ground. Grinding wheels should operate at the high speed of 5000 sfpm (surface feet per minute). During grinding, eyes must be protected against flying particles by wearing *goggles.* Each pass of the wheel is light, and removes only a few thousandths of an inch of metal. The larger the surface area that is ground, the lighter the cut. If the surface appears mottled, the wheel has become glazed by the presence of embedded metal particles in its surface. The surface layer must be removed by lightly dressing the wheel with a *grinding wheel dresser* (see Illustration 14–1; 13) to expose fresh abrasive.

ASSEMBLY FABRICATION SYSTEMS FOR LATHE-CREATED PARTS

MALE AND FEMALE UNITS   In assembling finished lathe-made parts, various systems can be used. The concept of male and female units is basic. *Male units* have a projecting part that fits into a corresponding hollow female unit (negative). *Female units* have hollow parts into which a corresponding projecting male part (positive) is inserted. The surface of the fitting parts can be smooth or threaded.

PRESS FIT   Units with smooth surfaces made to exact tolerances are so close fitting that they can be joined simply by *pressure,* a method also called a *driving fit,* or an *interference fit.* The projecting part on one is forced or mated into a recess on the other.

SHRINK FIT   In shrink fitting, two close-fitting or mating parts are held together by expanding the outer part with heat, and while it is still hot, a cold mating part is forced into it. Both parts are then cooled and the outer heated part *contracts* over the inner part to form an inseparable joint.

CONVENTIONAL METAL SCREWS   Separate from the workpiece, these can also be used to join lathe-made parts. *Rods* of any length can be threaded and substituted for conventional screws, and units screwed on the rod ends will hold together. *Tubes* can be internally and/or externally threaded to act as screws. Units can be connected *in series* by the use of short connecting threaded parts.

CONVENTIONAL FABRICATION TECHNIQUES   Conventional techniques that are *not* the result of lathe processes can also be used to hold lathe-made parts together. Hot fabrication soldering, or cold fabrication systems such as riveting can be used. *High-bond adhesives* can be used to hold parts, especially when joining different materials such as metal to plastic, ivory, or wood.

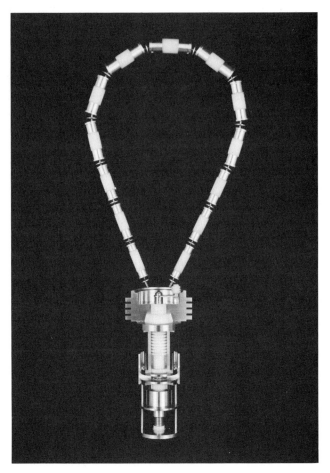

10–77   *Above:* GARY S. GRIFFIN, U.S.A. "Pendant in ⅜–24." Lathe-fabricated necklace in aluminum, brass, Delrin, and Teflon. *Photo: Gary S. Griffin*

10–78   *Below: THREE-QUARTER VIEW OF THE PENDANT,* illustrating the variety of systems used in the assembly of its parts. *Photo: Gary S. Griffin.*

PLASTICS IN JEWELRY

Fabrication using synthetic solids and liquids

The first synthetic plastic was a cellulose nitrate called *celluloid,* invented by John Wesley Hyatt of Albany, New York, in 1868. The next important invention occurred in 1909 when Leo Hendrik Baekeland invented Bakelite, a synthetic resin named after him, which resembled and was used in ways similar to hard rubber. Since then, with the phenomenal development of the plastic industry after World War II, more than 50 new plastic compounds have been developed and have found commercial use.

BASIC PLASTIC TYPES: Thermoplastics and thermosetting plastics

Two main groups of plastic exist, each of which behaves in a different manner. Within each group are products sold under different trade names.

Thermoplastics are plastics that are capable of being softened by heating, and hardened by cooling a number of times without chemical change occurring.

Thermosetting plastics are plastics that can undergo a single, nonreversible heating and cooling cycle that changes them to a hard, infusible solid. This process is achieved by the use of heat and/or curing agents.

THERMOPLASTIC GROUPS

Acrylic: Good in temperature resistance, acrylics are produced in different types, each designed to have specific properties to meet the demands of special purposes such as resistance to heat or crazing. Plexiglas and Perspex are acrylics, and are used in costume jewelry.

Acetate resin: High in strength and toughness and in chemical resistance to acids.

ABS plastic (Acrylonitrile butadiene styrenes): Good in chemical resistance to acids.

Cellulosic: These are among the toughest plastics available. They withstand moderate heat, and are produced in a wide range of colors. They are used in eyeglass frames, telephones, pens, etc.

Fluorocarbon: They are tough, will not absorb moisture, and are used to form laminations.

Polyamide: A group that includes *nylon* which is a family name within this group. Nylon is tough, high in tensile, impact, and flexural strength. Used in filament and solid form in many applications, and in textiles.

Phenolic: Among the oldest and cheapest of the cold-molded plastics, resistant to heat and most corrosive agents, these plastics are outstanding in dimensional stability and resistance to cold flow. Used in laminating, adhesives, and protective coatings.

Polyethylene: The largest in volume production of all plastics, it is produced in low, medium, and high density. Nonbreakable, flexible, easily processed, low in cost, highly resistant to chemicals, it can take low temperatures and is also heat resistant, but should not be worked near a flame or heating device.

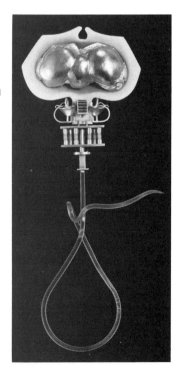

10-79 JEM FREYALDENHOVEN, U.S.A. Brooch in fabricated gilded silver with thermoplastic forms in acrylic, polycarbonate (a fluorocarbon) and nylon (a polyamide). The top white acrylic part was vacuum formed in a cupped shape to accommodate the repoussé-worked silver unit. The short columns are silver tubes containing force-fitted nylon rods, and the polycarbonate rod tail is thermoformed. Height 12 in. Photo: Case Crenshaw

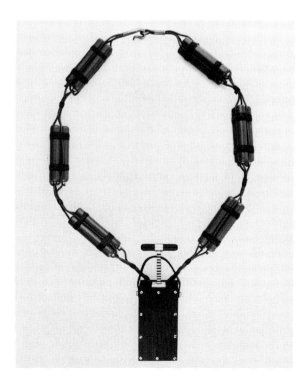

10-80 WILLIAM CLARK, U.S.A. "Dynamite Necklace." Fabricated silver, wood, and flexible electric wire coated with colored polypropylene. Photo: William Clark

Polypropylene: Resistant to solvents, greases, and oils, it is used in dishes, wire coating, and packaging.

Polystyrene: Produced in several different types, it is resistant to chemicals, and to most household acids and heat. Because it is odorless, it is used for kitchen items and food containers.

Silicone: Used as a releasing agent in molds and dies.

Urethane: Especially used for foamed plastics in forms used for mattresses, sponges, pads, and insulating cloth. They are good in resistance to chemicals, and outstanding as an adhesive for synthetic fibers.

Vinyl: Made in several different types, all resistant to water, heat, cold, oils, foods. Used for hoses, phonograph records, shower curtains, etc.

THERMOSETTING PLASTIC GROUPS

Alkyd: Resistant to high temperatures but affected by temperature changes, it is widely used for buttons and buckles.

Casein: Takes a high polish but is affected by a wide range of temperature variations. Available in many colors in all forms, widely used for beads and buttons.

Epoxy resin: Hard and durable, epoxy resins are often blended with phenolic and urea resins because these are heat convertible. Available in liquid solutions for use as adhesives, it is also made in flexible film and foamed blocks.

Melamine: Used for adhesives, decorative laminates, and dinnerware.

Polyester: Easy to handle, it is long lasting and can be formed at room temperature at low pressure to achieve a superior hard surface. While liquid, it can be colored as desired.

Phenol formaldehyde: One of the oldest plastics, this group includes Bakelite.

Aniline formaldehyde, pheno furfural, and the *aminos* also belong to the thermosetting group.

MANUFACTURE OF PLASTICS

FORMS IN WHICH PLASTICS ARE AVAILABLE

The main forms in which plastics are available as a raw material and for molding are powder, granules, flakes, pellets, and as liquid resins. The semifinished forms in which they are available for fabrication are film, sheet, foamed block, filament, rod, and tube. These forms can be transparent, translucent, opaque, one-colored, multicolored, or as laminates.

PLASTIC MANUFACTURING PROCESSES

The main plastic forming processes are: *film and sheet making,* including cast and extruded sheet and calendered sheet; *extruding,* by which film, sheet, filament, rods, tubes, and pipes are made and wire is coated; *laminating plastics,* which is done by low or high pressure and heat or by the use of cements; *reinforced laminating,* in which glass fiber, paper, fabrics, or other reinforcing materials are laminated by the use of liquid resin solutions; *molding* or making a half-finished or finished product by the use of a mold; *coating* textiles, papers, etc. by *dipping* them into liquid resins, then calendering them through heated rollers. Film and sheet making, extrusion, and coating of standard items are commercial processes that employ spe-

10–81 GUNILLA TREEN, England. Three Perspex rings of flat sheet plastic pierced with cloud-shaped openings filled with liquid resins. *Left:* Blue with clear and ivory; *Center:* Clear with blue and green; *Right:* Transparent yellow with clear. Size 1½ in square. *Photo:* Horst Kolo

10–82 BERND SEEGEBRECHT, West Germany. Ring in fabricated silver with bent tube Plexiglas cemented into tube-shaped metal parts. *Photo:* Günter Meyer, courtesy Schmuckmuseum, Pforzheim

10–83 HAROLD O'CONNOR, U.S.A. Ring in opaque white Plexiglas with inner 18K gold band, edges flanged to grip the Plexiglas form. The flat ring rectangle was sawed from ½ in thick sheet, placed in an oven heated to 250° F (121° C) for several minutes to soften it, then bent and held with two pliers until cold and rigid. The finger hole was cut out and the form filed to shape and finished. The 24K gold 30 gauge B.&S. inlay relief was formed by forcing the sheet into a carved Plexiglas intaglio mold with a blunt tool. Cut out, it was mounted in an excavated depression with plastic cement. *Photo:* Ron Burton

cial machinery but that can be duplicated on a small scale by hand methods. Simple forms of lamination and molding are well within the means of the craftsperson for use in jewelry making. Some of these processes are described below.

PLASTIC WORKING PROCESSES

In addition, ready-made plastic forms such as sheet, rod, and tube can be worked by any *manual fabrication method* such as sawing, drilling, lathe turning, filing, and carving. By the use of heat and adhesives to join units, the range of possible treatments for plastics is considerably enlarged. The results can be manually or mechanically finished by sanding, buffing, and polishing. All these processes are discussed below in relation to their application to plastics.

SAFETY PRECAUTIONS WHEN USING AND STORING PLASTICS

When working with plastics in a *solid state,* or in a *liquid state* that necessitates the handling of catalysts and

0.0

activators, possible hazards exist that must be avoided. These are hazards to the skin, the eyes, and the respiratory system from fire and explosion. As elementary precautions, always wear adequate protective clothing, work in a well-ventilated atmosphere near a water supply, and have the necessary protective and counteracting materials handy.

Solid or liquid plastics each present different hazards. When using liquid polyester resins (which are commonly used by craftspersons), because they as well as the activators and catalysts used with them are inflammable, proper *storage* and *protection against fire and explosion* is necessary. Manufacturers recommend using liquid resins within three months of purchase, but unused resins remain usable as long as they remain liquid, which is possible for six months to one year if they are properly stored. The temperature of the storage place must be kept at 68° F (20° C) or below, and the place must be dry and dark. This is why they are stored in glass or polythene (a contraction of "polyethylene") plastic containers, two-thirds full so the resin does not contact covers or caps. The same is done with activators and catalysts but these require additional precautionary treatment. Activators are put in a tin can, and catalysts in a polythene plastic container, but each of these must be placed into *separate covered metal storage drums,* which also serve the purpose of creating a dark environment. Each drum should be put in a different storage place such as separate metal cabinets, because if their fumes are allowed to mingle, fire or explosion is possible. Liquid resins are placed in containers not exposed to light or higher than normal temperatures because otherwise they will gel in a few days and no longer be usable.

Any cloth, paper, or other disposable material that has been in contact with a resin, activator, or catalyst should be disposed of immediately after work by burning, because they are potentially combustible. *Do not store.* Never smoke while working with plastics, or work near a bare flame, a heated oven, or any other heat source.

Skin protection is recommended when working with polyester resins because they contain grease solvents that cause them to stick to the skin and may cause irritation. *Polythene plastic gloves* protect hands, but if they interfere with the work, hands can be protected with a *barrier cream* spread on them before work starts. Should resin contact the skin, remove it with a proprietary *resin removing* or *cleansing cream,* or *acetone* before the resin hardens and removal is more difficult, followed by immediate washing with warm water and soap. Catalyst or activator contact should be quickly washed off with warm water as they can cause burns. Because acetone is a plastic solvent, it is used to clean plastics from tools and brushes.

Eye protection against solid particles propelled in the air during manual or mechanical fabrication and finishing processes, and protection against splashes when handling liquid resins and chemicals is achieved by wearing *goggles* or a *face shield.* Should any of these materials contact the eye, wash it with copious quantities of water, then with a *2% aqueous solution of sodium bicarbonate, which should always be kept in readiness nearby.* See an eye doctor as soon as possible after contact and first aid, because effects are sometimes delayed.

Respiratory protection is necessary against plastic dust or fumes that come from burning plastics out of a mold as when casting, and from chemical fumes. This is achieved mainly by always working in a well-ventilated place, preferably near an efficient exhaust fan. Fumes and toxic gases may become concentrated in a closed place and be the cause of eye and respiratory irritation. If your eyes water in the workplace, the fume concentration is at an unacceptable level. When machining, trimming, filing, or abrading plastics, always wear a respiratory mask and goggles as protection against irritation to the membranes of the mouth and nose from the dust and particles that are by-products of those operations.

PLASTICS IN SOLID FORM USED IN JEWELRY

DEMONSTRATION 19

DAVID W. KEENS fabricates a brooch using plastics shaped by various methods

Photos: David W. Keens and William Wadley

FABRICATING THE METAL STRUCTURE

1 Using a small *Unimat-SL lathe,* a fabricated part is machined down to turn it true to its center axis.
2 Machined forms are soldered to fabricated forms with the help of two "third-hand" *self-locking soldering tweezers* mounted on universal ball joints. Where necessary, the solder is guided in its flow by a steel-pointed *solder teaser.*
3 After the pinstem and catches are soldered on, surfaces are finished and scratches removed with an *abrasive stick* where necessary.
4 *Silicon carbide paper* in fine 400 grit is used for smoothing and finishing.
5 The surface is polished with a *bristle brush wheel* and powdered pumice.
6 A *drill press* is used to drill a hole through the body of the silver form. This hole will contain silver tube rivets by which two Delrin forms will be joined to the metal.

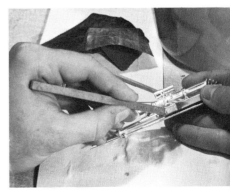

1   2   3

4   5   6

MEASURING AND MARKING SHEET PLASTIC

7 Delrin plastic is available in sheet, block, and rod forms, in various thicknesses and diameters. To protect their surfaces from becoming scratched, sheet plastics are usually purchased with both sides covered with *masking paper* that has an adhesive on the contacting side. If the surface of the plastic must be retained, the paper is left intact. Design contours can be easily drawn directly on it or transferred to it from a master drawing with carbon paper.

When drawing an outline for a shape, allow a minimum of waste by placing the outline as near to the edge as possible. Allow about 1⁄16 in (0.16 cm) margin for the sawing kerf and for finishing the edges by sanding or other methods. If a *compass* is used to make a circle or a curve, use very slight pressure to keep the pointed leg from passing through the masking paper and marking the plastic. If the paper has already been removed and a circle must be drawn, temporarily place a piece of masking tape at the center point to receive the pointed compass leg.

An unmasked plastic sheet can be marked directly with a nonscratching, greasy *glass-marking pencil,* as seen here. If a line must be enscribed in the plastic, this is done with a sharp-pointed tool such as a *scratch awl.* If the line must be straight, the awl is used in conjunction with a *steel rule* or *straight edge.* The forms outlined here on the Delrin will be attached to the outer upper part of the silver form in the position shown.

FABRICATING PLASTICS BY MANUAL AND MECHANICAL MEANS

SAWING PLASTICS WITH POWER TOOLS

8 *Power saws* are used for cutting outside and inside contour shapes. Always wear *goggles* to protect the eyes against flying chips. Have a source of light that is directed on the work so it is not in shadow. The working table of these saws should be at a convenient height, somewhat below elbow level when standing before the machine, the usual working position.

THE BAND SAW: OUTSIDE SHAPE POWER SAWING *Outside shape power sawing* is done first to free the shape from the surplus plastic. It is usually done with a *band saw,* as in this case, as this saw is primarily used for shape cutting, though it can also make straight cuts. Leaving the masking paper intact helps to control the chips. The *band saw blade* used is a fine-toothed metal cutting blade, 1⁄8 in (0.31 cm) wide, with 7–10 points per inch, which is capable of cutting a radius of 1⁄2 in (1.27 cm). As with most blades, the teeth have a *set* wider than the kerf, so under normal sawing circumstances, the blade should not bind. The blade on a band saw is a *continuous pulley type* and runs around a lower power supplying wheel, and an upper guide wheel in a downward direction against the material being cut. An average saw blade is 10 in (25.4 cm) or 12 in (30.5 cm) in diameter. The narrower the blade, the easier it is to cut small-radius curves. Adjust the *blade guide* to the proper height according to the thickness of the plastic to give the blade maximum support.

When cutting sheet plastic, allow the blade to enter the material at a tangential angle near the cutting line so the saw blade kerf flows smoothly alongside the line and the blade does not have to make a drastic, sudden change of direction, which is difficult as the blade is flat in section. If it is anticipated that such a change will be necessary, instead of backing out of the kerf (the usual method when sawing manually), to allow the blade to turn, drill a hole *in advance* at the turning point large enough so that it can change direction. Make any sharp turn slowly to prevent blade binding or breakage. If a curve is too small in radius for the blade used, make the cut in several tangential passes. On *outside cuts* always follow *outside* the line to

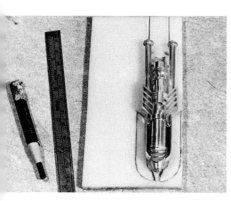

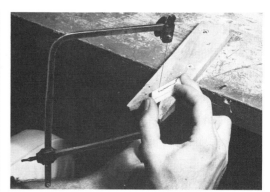

7   8   9

leave material for later removal down to true dimensions. To avoid an accident when sawing a long, narrow strip with the help of a T-guide, use a *wooden pusher stick* to finish the cut.

When cutting stock less than ½ in (1.27 cm) thick, a fast speed of 3000 sfpm can be used; for thicker stock use a slow speed of 1500 sfpm or less. Always feed the work slowly to the saw blade and allow it to dictate the feed rate rather than forcing the speed. Feed the work to the blade with both hands, but apply feed pressure only to the right side of the plastic while the left hand acts as a guide, or the blade might bind. Avoid force feeding as it causes blade and plastic overheating and possible blade breakage or loss of temper. Dull blades can also be the cause of overheating, and they break easily, so they should be resharpened or replaced.

Plastic sheet less than 1 in (2.5 cm) thick does not need a *coolant fluid,* but to prevent overheating, melting, or fusing thicker material, slow the blade speed rate and apply a coolant fluid of 10% soluble oil and water to the blade with a brush. If the material seems to be overheating, indicated when a melted ridge accumulates on the plastic while sawing, slow the feed, apply some lubricant, and if necessary, back the blade out of the cut slightly before continuing.

THE JIGSAW: INSIDE SHAPE POWER SAWING *Inside shape power sawing* of small-radius curves and intricate shapes is usually done on a *jigsaw* which, unlike the band saw, can also be used for pierced work because the blade is easily removable. First drill a hole in the waste part of the inner shape to be removed, making it large enough for the blade to pass through. Use a 5–6 in (12.7–15.2 cm) long, coarse-toothed, medium-temper blade designed for use with plastics. The blade is easily detachable from the jigsaw, and can be released from either the top or the bottom blade-holding chucks. Brush the table clear of any chips to be sure the plastic sheet is level during cutting so the cut edge will be perpendicular to the level plane of the sheet plastic. Place the clean plastic on the saw table, insert the blade through the hole made in it—checking to be sure its teeth are pointing *downward and outward* toward the operator. Refasten each blade end in the top and bottom chuck. The adjustable guide post behind the blade supports it when cutting. The attached holding feet are sprung to keep the work down and they press against it when lowered. The maximum thickness of plastic that can be cut on a jigsaw is about 2 in (5.08 cm).

In a jigsaw the blade moves up and down in a *vertical reciprocating motion.* Before turning on the power to start the saw, turn the saw *one revolution manually* to see if the blade is fixed correctly. Should it bend, the adjustment is incorrect, and one chuck should be moved toward the other.

If the blade locks, they are too close and one must be moved further away from the other.

Plastics are easily cut on a jigsaw at a speed of 1000–1200 rpm. For accuracy while cutting, press down on the plastic with both hands to keep it flat on the saw table. On *inside cuts,* always follow *inside* the line to allow waste for removal later. Control the direction of cutting by slowly pressing the material toward the blade. Avoid fast feeding or the blade may come loose from the chuck or break. Make turns slowly to prevent the blade from binding or breaking. Never try to pick up small waste pieces as they come free (or small workpieces being cut) while the blade is still in motion. Remove all waste *after the saw blade stops.*

9 A *jeweler's saw* is being used to cut a concave curve. The blade cuts on the outside of the line. Keens is left-handed, and positions would be reversed for a right-handed person. The procedures for hand sawing plastic are the same as for sawing metals by the same process. Coarser grade jeweler's saw blades can be used for thick stock and finer blade for thin stock. The jeweler's saw has the advantage of allowing small-radius curves and intricate shapes to be cut.

10 After file trimming the inside contacting surfaces of the plastic shapes, they are tested to assure a close fit against the metal form. The outer portions are then also shaped and brought to their final dimensions with *files.* The whole surface is hand rubbed with dry abrasive papers in 220 and 320 grit, then a wet abrasive in 400 grit to smooth the Delrin and give it a visually soft finish.

DRILLING PLASTICS WITH A VERTICAL DRILL PRESS

11 Plastics can of course be drilled with *hand drills,* but a *drill press* offers great control and accuracy. One of the finished Delrin shapes is held in position to the metal form with *masking tape.* The previously drilled holes are used as a guide from the reverse side to drill a hole in the plastic through which the tube rivet will pass. The same procedure is followed for the matching second Delrin part.

When a *drill press* is used for drilling holes perpendicularly into plastic, the center of the hole must be accurately marked by manually rotating a *sharp-pointed tool* at that place. If the *twist drill* used is ¼ in (6.35 mm) in diameter or larger, its point should be ground to a short lead angle of 26° which prevents the drill from grabbing the plastic as it passes through. Select the desired drill size with this lead angle number marked on its shank. Open the three-jawed drill press chuck with a *chuck key,* insert the drill bit shank fully, then close the chuck with the same key. If the hole is to be drilled *completely through* the plastic sheet, place a flat piece of wood on the drill table and put the plastic on top of it to prevent its lower

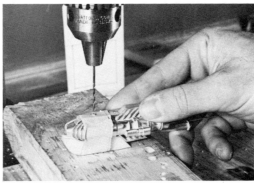

10   11   12

edge from chipping as the drill emerges through the plastic. Raise the table with the wood and plastic on it until the drill point almost touches it, then lock the table in place. Set the gauge at the height at which the drill just passes the plastic's thickness. Test this depth by moving the plastic and wood to one side, and manually lower the drill with the drill press handle until it just passes the top surface of the wood. For a *partially penetrating hole,* set the drill press gauge similarly to the desired depth in the plastic, then set the stop on the drill press at that point.

When drilling plastics with a 1/16 in or 1/8 in diameter drill it can run at maximum speed; run a 1/4 in drill at 3000 rpm; a 3/8 in drill at 2000 rpm; a 1/2 in drill at 1500 rpm; and a 3/4 in drill at 1000 rpm. During drilling, do not place too much pressure on the drill as excessive pressure may cause the plastic to crack or break. When making a hole completely through thick plastic do not try to accomplish this in one operation as the motor may stall. First make a partial penetration, then bring the drill upward to clear the hole of shavings which otherwise may melt and stick to the drill, then return the drill in several stages if necessary and complete the hole. Overheating plastic by drill-produced friction can result in a clogged or uneven hole.

When drilling a *large hole* through a small plastic part, hold the plastic with *hand pliers* or clamp it to the table with a *small clamp* or *vise* as otherwise the drill may grab the plastic and carry it around, which can be dangerous. While holding the tool with the left hand, turn on the power, and with the right hand slowly move the drill downward by the drill press handle until it contacts the plastic, then drill slowly through it in stages, as described.

If making a large-diameter hole of a depth greater than 1 in (2.54 cm), first drill a 1/8 in diameter *pilot hole* at the exact center of the hole position to a depth just short of passing through. Then fill the hole with wax or heavy oil as a drill coolant and to assure a smooth-sided hole. Drill the hole as above with the large-diameter drill.

When drilling a hole at an *angle* to the plastic surface, first fix the drill press table to the angle desired, and fix the plastic in position on the table with a *clamp* to keep it in place. It is easier to make an angular hole if you first drill a small, shallow hole at the position while the plastic is held in a horizontal position; there may be difficulty in making the drill grip the smooth surface of plastic otherwise.

A small *sanding drum* can be mounted in the drill chuck of the drill press and used to sand small inside curves at a slow speed, using light pressure.

12 The alignment of the drilled rivet holes in the Delrin parts is tested to be sure they coincide with these in the metal form by temporarily passing the tube used for the rivets through the holes. The rivets are set later when assembling all parts.

FORMING PLASTICS ON A LATHE

13 The same operations used to turn metal parts on a lathe can be used on plastics, but some differences are worth noting. Here a small, stepped Delrin part is being lathe turned from a round rod shape while clamped in a universal three-jawed chuck. As it is held only by the chuck, this arrangement is called *faceplate turning.* When a longer length is turned between centers, it is termed *cylinder turning.* The part in this case will be cut longer than its final length to allow for end trimming, especially if a *live center with claws,* often used for wood turning, is used to hold it. When a clawed live center is used, the end is marked for the center and a 1/8 in (3.18 mm) drill is drilled 1/4 in (6.3 mm) deep. A kerf 1/8 in deep is next sawed across the end through the center for the claws to penetrate and hold the plastic. For the dead center end, only the hole is made, but this center is lubricated to avoid its overheating as the dead center is stationary, and overheated plastic will discolor.

Most plastics are turned dry, but the use of a 12% soluble oil solution will help to keep it cool. If a nonround shape is being turned round, it is safest to first remove its corners because when turning a square shape to a round form, the plastic can chip, crack, or break as the tool forcefully contacts it irregularly. Sharpen the lathe tool in the same way as for soft metals, but allow plenty of clearance and a negative rake to allow for a *scraping cut* and not a chipping cut.

When lathe cutting plastics with *hand tools,* bring the tool guide or rest up to the work and fasten it with the handle clamp. Turn the lathe manually for one full revolution to be sure the work clears the tool guide. Plastic is turned at a speed of 1400–1725 rpm. Hold the tool against the tool rest for better control. Apply the tool cutting edge or point gradually to the plastic while holding the handle down with the hand on one side, with the other hand holding the tool to the top of the guide, its forefinger moving in the guide groove. Remove small portions of the plastic in cuts that may be irregular at first, until the form becomes round. When the shavings come off in long ribbons, the form has become round. At intervals during turning, if necessary (as when working from a full-size master drawing), check dimensions with *calipers* or other cylinder-measuring tool. To refine a form and create details, apply the round-nosed, pointed, skewed, marking or parting tool selected with light pressure so the surface is smooth.

14 Plastics can be shaped while they rotate on the lathe by using *solid stick abrasives.* They can also be

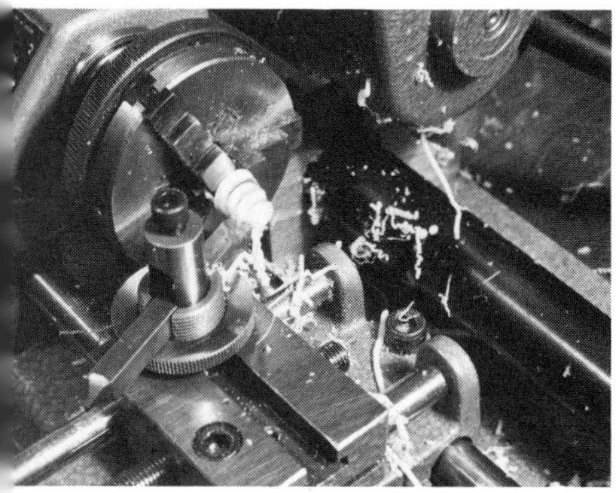

13

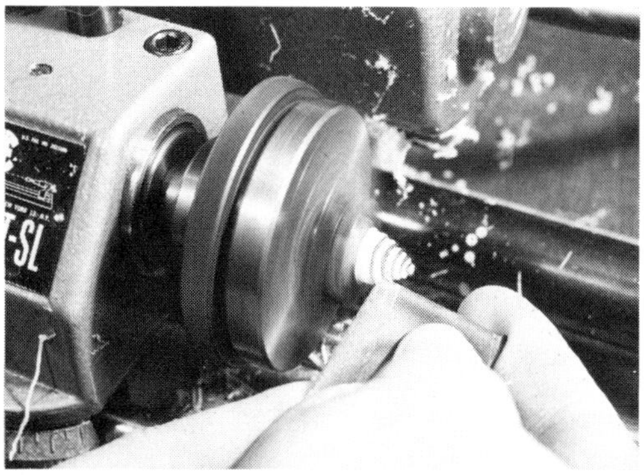

14

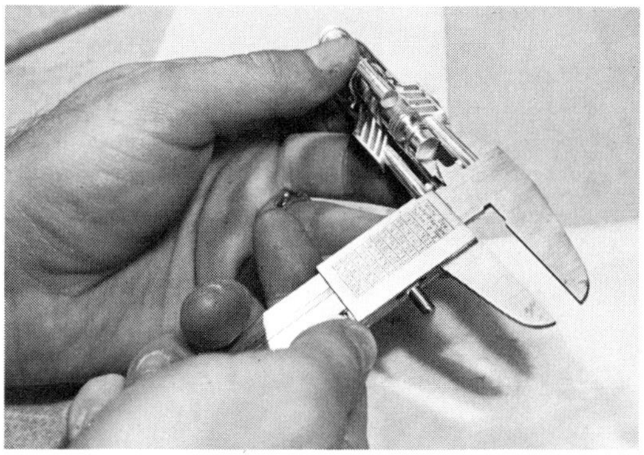

15

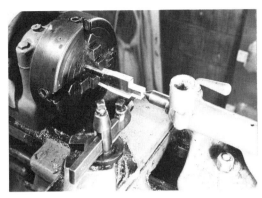

16   17   18

shaped with a *mechanical sanding belt,* or a *disc grinder* and corundum wheels.

Finishing a form or a surface can be done, as shown here, while the form rotates on the lathe and a folded piece of abrasive paper of fine grit is pressed against it.

TURNING AN ACRYLIC PART TO EXACT TOLERANCES

15 *Vernier slide calipers'* inside jaws are used here to obtain an *internal measurement* of the inner diameter (ID) of a tubular part. Into this a *tenon* or projecting part left on the plastic form when the rest is cut away will be inserted, the tube acting as a mortise to hold it. The acrylic tenon must be precisely machined to exact tolerances to fit this dimension as it will be a press-fitted joint.

16 A *band saw* is used to cut out the marked-out dimension for the blank shape of a form made for the brooch from a thick sheet of transparent acrylic.

17 The irregularly shaped acrylic part is mounted in the four jaws of an independent chuck on a larger lathe, its axis lined up with the still square end to be tenon shaped which is held by a center in the tailpiece.

18 The tenon has been machined to a round form and its diameter is being checked for *external dimension* (OD) with the *external measuring jaws* of *vernier calipers.* The tenon is cut to an exact tolerance measurement that fits the internal dimension of the tube into which it will be force fitted.

19 The rest of the acrylic shape is oval and irregular, so it will be shaped by mechanical and manual tools. After the tenon is finished, surplus acrylic material is trimmed off with a band saw to bring the shape closer to its final form.

FILING PLASTICS

20 Plastics can be filed to remove waste, to produce a flat surface, or to smooth inside and outside curves with any coarse-toothed *hand file* whose teeth do not become quickly clogged. For rough shaping, a coarse, nonclogging *vulcanite* (hard rubber) file can be used, or as shown here, a nonclogging plastic metal *float file* can be used. A 00-cut file is suitable but as it becomes clogged with plastic it must be frequently cleaned with a *file brush*. To reach concave sections, coarse *riffler files* are used.

Holes made in plastic with a drill press and twist drill can be smoothed by inserting a *circular file* mounted on a mandrel in the drill press chuck. A 3 in (7.6 cm) section of a broken *rattail file* can be used in the same way, so do not throw away broken round files. Round files used in a drill press should rotate at 1725 rpm. Besides making round holes, oval and slot shapes can also be made with rotating round files.

CARVING PLASTICS

After all initial shaping is finished, the quickest and most convenient way to make details in plastic forms is by *subtracting* material from the mass or *carving* it with any suitable cutting tool. In the small-scale work with which the jeweler is involved, hand tools can of course be used, but far quicker is the use of any suitable form of *bur, router, saw, disc, abrasive point,* or *high-speed twist drill* placed in a rotary *flex-shaft* operated at 4000–5000 rpm. When selecting an accessory for this purpose keep in mind the *maximum arbor diameter* acceptable by the chuck of the flex-shaft.

Carving plastic can be *external* or *internal*. External carving is done to establish an outer shape, and internal carving creates internal voids that in clear plastic can be seen externally. Into such voids colored liquid plastic resins or dyes can be injected. When carving clear plastic internally, *watch the progress of the carving from both top and sides* because refraction makes distance judgments difficult. Internal carving is done with high-speed twist

19   20   21

drills whose points are sharpened to a 60–75° angle. When regrinding such a drill point, use the grinding wheel at a slow speed to avoid overheating the drill which otherwise will lose its temper. Also, at intervals during grinding, dip the drill into a container of cold water to cool it. Place a new cutting edge on the lip of a reshaped drill point by grinding a lip clearance back into the drill flute end with an emery disc.

SANDING PLASTICS MANUALLY

21 Once the object has reached its final form, *sanding plastics manually* is done with *abrasive papers* or *cloths* of various grits. Use coarse 120 grit abrasives when much material must be removed during rough shaping, and increase the fineness in stages up to 400 grit or finer. If a surface must be leveled, use a medium, not a fine grit, and rub the plastic on an abrasive paper placed on an absolutely true, flat surface. Thermosetting plastics are sanded dry near a good exhaust fan, and thermoplastics are sanded wet, which keeps them cooler—which is important as they are subject to heat distortion. Wet sanding produces a finer surface as water acts as a lubricant, and at the same time dust in the air is reduced.

As plastics are a relatively soft material as compared with metal, matter is easily and fairly quickly removed manually as the cutting action of the abrasive is fast. This means that *light pressure* is always called for.

When sanding a form to *round* or *shape* it, first mark the area to be removed with a *felt-tipped marking pen* or a *glass-marking pencil* by drawing a circle around the area, then drawing parallel hatched lines through this shape. These lines are removed during sanding, and act as a guide to indicate where additional removal must take place. When rounding a shape, always remove the corners first, then repeatedly rotate the workpiece to achieve the desired curve.

Final finishes can cover a wide range—from the translucent, frosted finish being made here on the acrylic part with a wet 400 grit paper, to a highly glossy surface. A worked surface can be restored by manual polishing to a high gloss which returns it to its original transparent state, but this takes longer and is more quickly and efficiently done mechanically.

When using either hand or machine methods to sand plastics, work near an efficient *exhaust system* or wear a good *face mask* to avoid the inhalation of harmful dusts or vapors. An exhaust has the secondary purpose of cooling the worked plastic, especially when mechanical sanding takes place. Should dust get in your eyes, immediately wash them with water, then with a dilute solution of boric acid.

SANDING FLAT PLASTIC SURFACES MECHANICALLY

Mechanical belt, disc, and *vibrating sanders* can be used when sanding flat plastic surfaces. Belt sanders are constructed with a rigid flat table and rotating end rollers, over which an *endless abrasive-coated cloth-backed belt* is placed, and revolves with the motion of the rollers. This shape makes it possible to sand flat surfaces on the flat table portion, and convex and some slow-curved edge surfaces on the curved roller portion, provided the curve is suited to that of the roller. Belt and disc sanders operate at the relatively slow speed of 1100–1750 rpm. To keep the abrasive on the belt from wearing out unevenly and to get maximum use from it, move the plastic from side to side while sanding: *do not hold it in one position.*

When mechanically sanding a surface *level*, keep the worked surface in light contact with the abrasive, and when a pass is finished, withdraw it straight upward or away from the abrasive. Keep pressure light because when excessive pressure is applied, the plastic seems to bounce off, and the fast rotating speed tends to burn it, indicated by its surface turning opaque white.

SANDING SHAPED PLASTIC FORMS MECHANICALLY

When using mechanical means to sand plastics, removal of the material takes place at a much faster rate than when doing the same work by hand, and this must be kept in mind. Symmetrical or cylindrical plastic objects can be sanded while they are mounted in a *lathe;* if small, they can be mounted in the chuck of a *drill press* or a *flex-shaft.* Because in these cases only *one end* of the object is supported as the form revolves, apply very light pressure or the plastic may overheat as the rate of rotation is rapid in such devices; at worst, the object may snap off.

Flex-shaft-mounted *miniature sanding discs, brushes* and *buffs* can be used to reach places otherwise inaccessible, and are particularly useful for creating a final surface on irregularly shaped forms.

Disc sanders can be of the miniature sanding disc type mounted on a mandrel whose arbor is placed in a flex-shaft, or the larger discs used with a portable drill; or a fixed-position motor with a revolving metal disc attached to the shaft or mounted in the jaws of a chuck can be used. On this a disc of abrasive paper is placed. Instead of a metal disc, a wood disc with an attached arbor can be faced with a sheet of abrasive paper glued to its surface. To glue the paper down, apply the adhesive evenly to its back surface and allow it to dry for at least 24 hours or it will loosen in use. Paper discs of various degrees of coarseness can be prepared in advance for use when needed. With large discs, always work in the lower front quarter segment of the disc as it revolves toward you; this is the safe sanding area and the dust is thrown downward.

FINISHING PLASTICS

FINISHING ON THE POLISHING LATHE

When plastic parts are carved or turned or otherwise worked with tools from sheet, rod, or bulk forms, they must be finished. The connotations of the terms used in finishing plastics are not the same as the same terms used when polishing metals. *Buffing* plastics, also called *ashing*, is the removal of tool, process, or sanding marks from the surface. Buffing may replace sanding in some situations and leave the work with a matte surface produced by semiashing, cut-down buffing, or intermediate buffing, or the surface can be brought to a dull luster, called luster buffing. Any one or more of these methods might be employed on a workpiece, or might be the aim of the final finish. *Polishing*, when finishing plastics, *follows buffing*— the reverse of when finishing metals—and means the production of a high luster and the brilliant, reflective surface finish of which most plastics are capable.

Plastic parts hand shaped or machine shaped usually require buffing and polishing to remove tool marks, sanding streaks, or buffing passes with coarser abrasives. Do not attempt to polish plastic to a high luster before all tool marks have been removed by sanding and buffing as the surface will not be satisfactory. Buffing and polishing can of course be done manually, but mechanical means are much quicker and more uniform.

The most important consideration when buffing and

polishing plastics is to *avoid excessive pressure of the workpiece against the wheel* because by creating excessive frictional heat the surface will creep, become burned, develop a cloudy appearance, or become nonuniform in texture, and overheating may cause cracks to appear in the work months later. To avoid overheating, always use a proper lubricant, and do not allow the work to remain in stationary contact with the wheel, but *move it constantly* during buffing and polishing operations. When finishing plastics mechanically, the recommended buffing and polishing speed of the motor shaft is 1725 rpm, and 4000 sfpm (surface feet per minute) is the most effective speed on the wheel perimeter, though speeds of 2000–5000 sfpm are also acceptable.

BUFFING: SMOOTHING AND SEMIGLOSS

THERMOSETTING PLASTICS

Buffing plastics to smooth out irregularities takes a longer time than polishing. For thermosetting plastics, use greaseless compounds on compressed muslin buffs for rough work, or flexible, full-disc, unstitched muslin buffs of at least 8 in (20.3 cm) in diameter for normal work, at a 1725 rpm spindle speed. This will remove surface defects from sanding and machine operational marks, and contours will smooth at 5000 sfpm.

Buffing for a smooth, semigloss final finish is done with a fast cut-down buffing compound of the low-grease type containing fast-cutting abrasives that do not leave much residual dirt. Loose pocketed or sewn muslin buffs are used, depending on the work to be accomplished, and for flat work use wide-faced buffing wheels with the same compound at 4000–6000 sfpm.

THERMOPLASTICS

Wet ashing is used on thermoplastics to smooth irregular surfaces because they are more subject to overheating. To make a matte surface, use 00-grade or 1-grade wet pumice and water on a full polishing disc loose muslin buff at a speed of 4000 sfpm. Apply both abrasive and water frequently to the wheel.

Because these plastics are easily distorted by excessive heat, a special compound has been developed for buffing that is different from those used in metal finishing. It provides enough lubrication to minimize the heat generated, and contains fine white silica and tripoli in a grease binder. Pocketed and ventilated buffs with metal centers are recommended for preliminary work at a 3000–4000 sfpm peripheral speed.

POLISHING: LUSTER BUFFING FOR HIGH GLOSS

THERMOSETTING PLASTICS

Polishing plastics requires much less pressure on the work than buffing. Also, the work must be moved around much more rapidly. For luster polishing to a smooth finish without dulled areas or streaks, use a very low-grease compound that has unfused aluminum oxide powder, on a loose muslin disc buff at 4000–5000 sfpm. According to some practice, the compound is applied to the *work* and not the wheel, then removed from it with the wheel.

THERMOPLASTICS

For a high gloss, the article must first be thoroughly washed and dried to remove any traces of previously used abrasives. Use a soft-packed muslin buff and a fine buffing compound, at 3000–4000 sfpm.

SOLVENT POLISHING

Solvent polishing consists of using a liquid chemical to melt the surface of plastic to give it the appearance of having been mechanically polished. This is resorted to when small interior surfaces cannot be polished, even with miniature wheels. Carefully apply ethylene dichloride ($C_2H_4Cl_2$), also called Dutch oil, a heavy, colorless liquid with a chloroformlike odor, with a brush directly to the part, but avoid contact with already polished surfaces which will become marred. Work in a well-ventilated place. Allow the chemical to evaporate, and the surface to harden.

SHAPING PLASTIC BY MANUAL THERMOFORMING

22 *Thermoforming* is a process in which the plastic in solid or laminated sheet form is heated, then shaped manually by pressure in air or in a mold to force it to take on a shape. Plastic forms can be shaped by thermoforming either before or after surface finishing. As acrylic is a thermoplastic, it can if necessary go through several heating operations to soften, shape, and reharden it. Thermosetting plastics can only be heated once, then they set hard. The form here is being heated over an ordinary *electric hot plate,* while wearing *thick gloves* to insulate the hands from the heat needed to soften the plastic enough to allow it to be shaped, about 350° F (176.6° C). Above this heat, blisters will form in the plastic. The form is rotated constantly until it shows evidence of pliability. The whole form, or only a heated area can then be shaped.

23 Thermoforming the heated and pliant thick acrylic form by simple pressure with the fingers. When it has the desired shape, it is hand held until it cools and becomes hard and set in position.

Thermoforming thermoplastics is also possible when using a sheet or laminate of plastic. The plastic can be heated in an oven at 350° F (176.6° C), and when soft, it is removed and pressed into the contours of a mold while wearing thick gloves. Hold the plastic in place under pressure, or place a negative mold on top of it to apply pressure until the plastic sets and hardens. In *drape forming* sheet plastic, the object is placed over a positive mold and heated until it slumps or drapes into the mold depression, then it is forced into the mold as above. The result is relatively uniform in thickness.

24 Before mounting the plastic parts, the metal part is brought to its final finish. It is oxidized with liver of sulphur, and highlights are made with ruby powder. In this exploded view, all the plastic parts are seen in their position relative to their placement in the work.

25 The Delrin forms are riveted in place by flaring the ends of the tube rivets. The central parts are spaced with tube sections shouldered to fit them into their position. They are held together as a unit by a rod that has a head at one end and passes through a hole in all the other units, ending in a hole drilled in the shoulder-stepped plastic end

22   **23**

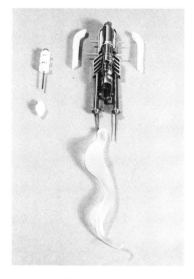

24

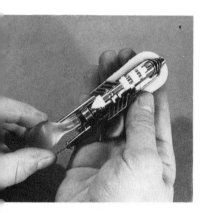

25

26

piece to which it is held by a force fit. The tenon of the acrylic form is press fitted into the tube that holds it. As insurance against accidental removal, a small amount of epoxy cement is applied to the groove that will receive the tenon before forcing it in.

26 The finished brooch, No. 2–3, in sterling silver, copper, and brass, with Delrin and acrylic. Length 7 in (17.8 cm), width 1¼ in (3.18 cm), depth 1 in (2.54 cm).

Photo: David W. Keens

LAMINATING SHEET PLASTICS

LAMINATION BY PRESSURE:
Thermal method

Any transparent, opaque, or colored sheet thermoplastic such as acrylic (which includes Lucite, Plexiglas, and

Perspex) can be *laminated* or joined in layers after heating. In industry, lamination is done in forming presses, but on a small scale it can be done manually or with the help of improvised hand presses, under relatively low pressure. Always wear *thick gloves* when handling heated plastics, and work in a well-ventilated area. Lamination can be done in the open over a heating surface such as a *hot plate* or an *electric stove,* or in an *oven* capable of being heated to at least 400° F (204° C). When heating over a hot plate, the plastic can be heated only locally, which allows local lamination if this is the aim, while heating in an oven brings the temperature of the entire object to a uniform degree while the object rests on a clean metal tray placed on a rack. If shaping follows lamination, the entire object must be heated uniformly as portions cooler than the rest will break when bent.

To laminate sheet plastic manually, place the clean, grease-free layers of the laminate together, and heat the object. The temperature range for softening plastics is 250–350° F (121–176.6° C). When in a matter of minutes the plastic softens, remove it from the heat source and place it on a clean, *flat metal sheet,* or if making a dimensional lamination, in a *die* or *mold* of wood or sheet or cast metal. When flat, press the laminate plastic layers together manually while wearing gloves, or by placing a weight over it that covers it evenly and completely. Two thick, unbending flat sheets of metal can be placed below and on top of the sheets being laminated and the two clamped together. If a mold is used to shape the plastic while it is laminated, it can be pressed manually into the mold, a shaped wooden pressing form can be used, or a positive of the mold can be pressed over the plastic to force it to take the negative mold shape.

Hold the plastic under pressure until it cools and sets hard. Plastic ⅛ in (3.18 mm) thick set hardens in approximately 90 seconds; ½ in (1.27 cm), in 120 seconds; and 1 in (2.54 cm), in 130 seconds—therefore laminating and mold shaping must be done quickly after removal from the heat source. Overheated plastic will develop internal bubbles and external blisters that cannot be removed. It is possible to reheat thermoplastic if it has not fully taken on the desired mold shape in the first attempt, but after three reheatings, the material becomes more difficult to shape. In most cases, laminates are best made flat first, then shaped. If a strip laminate is bent to a particular shape, a jig made in advance can be used. The reheated plastic is placed and held in the jig until it hardens. When shaping a one-piece bracelet from a laminate, for instance, after the second heating it is placed around a *metal bracelet mandrel* and shaped.

POSTLAMINATION TREATMENTS FOR PLASTIC LAMINATES Laminates made of different colored layers of plastic can be carved to expose striated strata, or turned as a solid on a lathe, the layers running horizontally, vertically, or diagonally with the form.

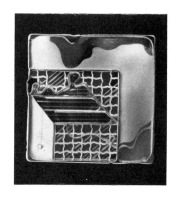

10–84 DIETER DILL, Union of South Africa. Gold brooch with diamond and Plexiglas. A striped, colored laminated plastic sheet is used as a backplate, the pattern seen through a square wire mesh. A partially frosted Plexiglas overlay is held in the remaining framed area. *Photo: Günter Meyer, courtesy Schmuckmuseum, Pforzheim*

INCLUSIONS BETWEEN HEAT- AND PRESSURE-FORMED LAMINATIONS

Inclusions of different materials between laminated sheets is possible. The choice of materials included depends on the temperature necessary to make the lamination and how this heat affects the particular inclusion material. If the inclusion is affected by heat, lamination can be done by nonheat methods, as with cement, described below.

Any metal in any form such as wire, sheet, screening, powder, or particles can be used for heat-made inclusions in laminates. Other materials such as glass fiber in yarn or woven form and other textiles can be used. Liquid metallic dyes or powdered colored plastic dissolved with ethyl dichlorate can be injected between laminated sheets with a *hypodermic needle.* The laminate can be deliberately overheated to cause it to form internal bubbled textures, or the contact of the sheets can be so uniform that the bond is invisible. Where the inclusions are thick there may be a tendency for the sheets of the laminate to stay apart partially and air bubbles may in this case become trapped. As with plain lamination, it is possible to make the inclusions in the *flat* laminate first, then reheat the laminate to bend it into a form such as a bracelet or collar.

The laminated plastic with inclusions can be bonded manually by hand pressure, especially when the object is small. Alternately, it can be placed in a *press* which is then tightened upon it. A simple press can be improvised from two ⅜ in (9.5 mm) thick, smooth-surfaced metal sheets, bolted together or held by *C-clamps.* It is also possible to make the lamination by placing the whole assembly in such a press cold, and then putting the unit into an oven heated to 400° F (204° C) for about 15 minutes, after which it is removed, retightened, and heated again another 15 minutes at the same temperature. It is then removed, cooled, and released from the press.

LAMINATING PLASTICS:
Liquid cement method

Two or more level layers of sheet plastic can be laminated, and well-fitting, clean plastic parts can be joined by the use of *plastic cements,* also called *plastic glues* or *adhesive solvents.* Clear plastic can be joined to clear, clear to colored, colored in layers, or plastic can be bonded to metal, wood, ceramic, glass, or stone. Prepare all materials and gather all tools needed in advance, since in most cases cementing work must be done quickly. Work on a metal, glass, or marble surface in a well-ventilated place.

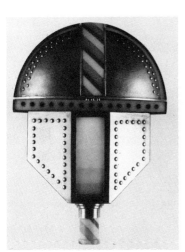

10–85 RICHARD HELZER, U.S.A. "Brooch EL7708." In sterling silver, bronze, and diagonal and horizontal laminations of acrylic plastic, the bottom one lathe turned. Photo: Richard Helzer

10–86 SANDRA PARMER ZILKER, U.S.A. "Striped Snake Tail with Halo Connective." Pin fabricated from sterling silver and 14K gold, with amethyst, moonstone, and garnet. The laminated, manually thermoformed acrylic section, and the bent plastic tubing are fixed to the metal units with rivets and cement. Size 3½ × 4½ in. Photo: Sandra Parmer Zilker

For cementing acrylic plastic to the same material, the common adhesive solvent is ethylene dichloride. Another cement is a 60% methylene chloride and 40% methyl methacrylate monomer mixed in a paper cup. When a monomer is used, if the surplus is to be stored for future use, add one drop per ounce of an oxidizing catalyst to prevent polymerization or solidification of the cement. It is best to try to *mix only the amount needed* and discard leftovers, mixing fresh cements for each use.

To cement one polished surface to another by *hand pressure,* soak both surfaces in ethylene dichloride for 10 minutes, drain the surplus, hold both parts separated in air for 30 seconds, then bring them together and hold them together for 2 minutes until the cement starts to set. *Clamps* can be used to hold parts together, but take care not to allow surplus cement on the surface where it is not wanted as it can cause crazing. Allow the parts to stay clamped together for about 4 hours. When gluing a round rod into a drilled hole, place the cement there with a glass medicine stopper, and spread it with a wooden dowel to coat all surfaces. Also immerse the contacting part of the rod into the cement for 10 minutes, drain the excess, press the parts together, and allow the same 4-hour curing time while under pressure.

When cementing plastic to plastic, metal, wood, stone, ceramic, or glass, a *clear* or *opaque epoxy cement* can also be used. It is usually supplied with the preactivated resin in one tube and the catalyst in another. Follow the instructions given for their use. To cement two surfaces, apply the carefully prepared mixture to both surfaces and allow them to set for 30 seconds, then press but do not clamp the surfaces together. Allow a 24-hour drying period. If the join must be made in a vertical position, use masking tape to hold the parts together.

BUTT JOINT CEMENTING Sheet or rod plastics of different colors or patterns can be cemented together with plastic cements in butt joints. If the parts are of the same thickness, the result is a level sheet mosaic whose surface can be smoothed to a true level. The prefinished parts can also be made of different thicknesses, that project forward at different levels, but are flat on the back, to make a dimensional relief.

Apply only the necessary amount of adhesive to the contacting edges because when the parts are pressed together, any surplus will rise to the surface and, because most cements act as a solvent, surface defects may result at points of overflow. Remove any surplus immediately with absorbent cotton, or scrape it off with a knife. Once the cement has set, the assemblage can be surfaced again by polishing if necessary.

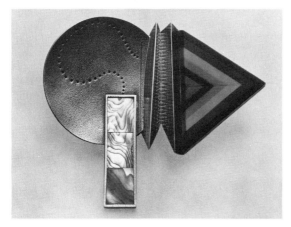

10–87 LESLIE LEUPP, U.S.A. Brooch in bronze with butt joint— cemented, laminated colored plastic, and abalone shell inlay. Size 5½ in, largest dimension. *Photo: Rauno Träskelin*

PLASTICS IN LIQUID RESIN FORM

The development of plastics in a liquid resin form has made possible a whole new range of techniques in jewelry making. The plastic can be used as a "paint," *applied in thin layers* on a wide range of materials with which it will make a strong bond, and it can be used in any *casting* technique to make solids of plastic alone or of plastics containing inclusions.

THE NATURE OF LIQUID PLASTIC POLYESTER

The most useful plastic in liquid resin form to the craftsperson is *polyester,* a thermosetting plastic derived from coal tar and petroleum. In use it goes through three stages: in the first, it is a liquid; in the second, it sets and becomes a solid; and in the third, it becomes an infusible solid that cannot be reshaped by reheating. Unlike other thermosetting plastics, it does not evolve volatile by-products in the setting process, and it sets simply by contact pressure. In the relatively small amounts that are used in jewelry, this plastic is sufficiently hard to resist normal wear.

It is not necessary to have a knowledge of chemistry to use or cast plastics. As long as manufacturer's instructions are followed, a satisfactory result can be achieved fairly simply. Particular compositions are designed to suit particular fabrication techniques and the final properties of a cured polyester is determined by its ingredients and their proportions. Without going into the chemical compositions of polyester plastics, it is sufficient to know whether a particular composition is suitable for the intended use, and this information can be obtained from the supplier or is already available on the product container. Therefore, no specific polyester is mentioned here and only general considerations are discussed.

TRANSLUCENT AND OPAQUE PLASTICS:
Pigments and fillers

Pigment pastes dispersed in a plasticizer are used to uniformly color any liquid polyester resin. They are available translucent or opaque in a fairly wide range of colors that can be used singly or mixed together to make intermediary colors. The pigment available from suppliers will

not affect the resin cure, are color-fast upon exposure to sunlight, and do not cause the resin to discolor. To color the resin, about 2.5% pigment paste by resin weight ratio must be added, and this percentage can be increased to deepen the color. Acetone is used to dissolve powdered plastic pigments when these are used, before mixing them with the resin.

Fillers can be added to the resin, up to 30% by volume, to make it textured or opaque. Pigments are usually added at the same time as are fillers. When coloring filled plastics, the pigment percentage used is relative to the resin content alone, and not the total content. All fillers increase viscosity, reduce shrinkage, and increase strength; some increase hardness; and most act to retard the gel time and cure time. They also increase bulk and reduce costs, the main reason they are used in the plastic industry.

The main *inert fillers* are precipitated calcium carbonate and silica powder, but other stone dusts such as marble and slate are also used. Iron or other metal filings, sintered metal powders, and dry sawdust are also used as fillers. Each substance produces a different surface texture or appearance, especially where color contrast exists between filler and resin.

Well-mixed fillers are kept in suspension by the resin. They should be stirred in with care to avoid air entrapment. A mixture of filler to resin can be used in ratios from 30/70 to 50/50 but not more or the resin may not be sufficiently viscous to fill the mold cavity and enter undercuts, avoid bubbles, and ensure the escape of air from the resin when it is poured into the mold.

Sintered metal powders (*brass* for a gold effect, *aluminum* for a silver effect, as well as *copper* and *bronze*) can be added as a filler and cast into a block that can be carved or turned on a lathe. This combination when polished on a wheel with suitable abrasives acquires a glossy appearance that makes the object appear metallic. Use one part sintered metal powder by weight to three parts resin. Store sintered metal powders in sealed polythene bags to prevent oxidation from air contact, which darkens them.

COLD POURING POLYESTER RESIN

Polyester resins by themselves are unstable and at normal or higher room temperatures in time they will set and slowly cure or harden. To hasten this curing action and cause it to occur within a reasonable time period, *curing agents* are added to the liquid resin. The choice of curing agents and the quantity used determines the rate of curing and the final properties of the cured resin.

CATALYSTS The curing agent added to all liquid resins is termed a *catalyst* or *hardener.* Those used for polyester resins are almost always organic peroxides that decompose in the presence of heat or through the chemical reaction of *activators* (described below). Catalysts are sold as a liquid or paste because in the pure state they can explode upon decomposing. They help reduce the speed of hardening, reduce heat buildup, and prevent cracking. Normally about 2% liquid catalyst or 4% paste catalyst of resin weight is used in cold curing, but less is used for small amounts of resin, though never less than 1%. (See Table on page 475.) In such small amounts, the catalyst is measured with a *glass eyedropper,* or through the dropper spout provided with the catalyst containers.

ACTIVATORS Activators, also called *accelerators,* are added to the resin to control the setting time of cold curing resins by hastening the decomposition of catalysts. Usually they are cobalt soaps or amines, available combined with a solvent in solution. About 1–2% by weight is added to the resin to slow down the hardening process. If insufficient activator is used the resin may stay undercured. Activator is also measured with an eyedropper in small amounts.

PREACTIVATED RESINS   Some resins are sold *already containing* the normal amount of 2–4% by weight of activator, which is an amount sufficient to make them cure fairly fast at normal room temperature once the catalyst is added. When adding a catalyst to a *preactivated resin,* no problems exist.

PREPARING THE RESIN FOR CURING

To prepare a resin for curing use a graduated paper cup. When *both* activator and catalyst must be added, certain careful procedures are necessary. *The activator and the catalyst must always be kept separated from each other as they can react violently or explode when combined.* Work with each one separately. First add the catalyst, mix it well with the resin, and then put it away. Work at a normal room temperature of 68° F (20° C), and do not attempt to cure a resin below 60° F (15° C) or it will be undercured. Once the catalyst has been added, the resin has a pot life of 3–30 hours at room temperature before hardening.

A short time before use, add the activator to the already catalyzed resin, in amounts as suggested in the Table below. To control the gel time, vary the amount of activator, but not the amount of the catalyst. A larger amount of activator decreases the gel time, and a smaller amount increases it. If the resin must be used in a higher than normal atmospheric temperature, reduce the amount of activator.

EXOTHERMIC HEAT   During the curing of a resin, after the catalyst and the activator have been added, *polymerization* occurs in which the resin molecules are organized into another compound which is higher in molecular weight, causing a change in the physical properties of the resin—from a liquid to a solid. In this process, at the time of setting, a considerable amount of heat is generated, called *exothermic heat,* which can be as high as 320° F (160° C). This heat speeds the resin cure. The generation of heat becomes an important consideration when casting resins in a rubber mold, or when embedding substances whose appearance or condition may be affected by such temperatures. Generally speaking, the shorter the gel time, the higher the heat, but if the gel time is too rapid, internal stresses develop in the resin that cause cracking. In curing small castings in molds, the heat problem is lessened as most of the heat is dissipated into the mold.

SETTING TIME   Various factors influence the setting time of polyester resin, and also its final condition. If the *catalyst content* and/or the *activator* is decreased, the gel time is increased. Catalyzed resin that has been stored will set in a shorter time than uncatalyzed stored resin. *Low atmospheric temperature* increases the gel time. *Large-*

bulk resins cure in shorter time than a thin laminate of the same material and composition. *Fillers* generally increase setting time, and the greater the filler content, the longer the set time. The *presence of moisture* in a filler or in an object embedded will retard the cure time. Some *pigments* increase setting time, others reduce it.

POSTCURING CONTROL CONDITIONS   Polymerization continues slowly for some time after the resin initially sets. Curing conditions after setting should therefore continue to be controlled for satisfactory long-term results. For at least two weeks the object should be kept at room temperature, after which time the resin reaches a condition of stability. It is possible to accelerate maturing by increasing the *heat gradually* after the resin has set to 140° F (60° C); or at least 24 hours after setting, heating the result to 176° F (80° C) for three hours. The longer the period between setting and postcuring treatment, the easier full cure becomes.

SURFACE TACKINESS   The top of a cured, open-mold casting is often *tacky,* and this provides a surface that grips subsequent layers that may be added. If, however, this surface is the final one, such tackiness must be removed. This can be done by cleaning it with acetone and a brush, or by abrading it with dry or wet 120, 320, or 500 grit abrasive papers. If the final surface is to be clear and have a high gloss, it is then buffed and polished with a suitable polishing compound on a polishing wheel.

THE USES OF LIQUID POLYESTER RESINS

COLD POLYESTER RESIN "ENAMELING" ON METAL

Applying polyester resins in a way that resembles enameling on metal is possible *without the use of heat,* and with far less difficulty and expense. The metal surface to receive the resin should be grease-free, chemically clean, and "toothed" to hold the resin. This latter operation is done by rubbing it with an abrasive, by roughening it with a file, by engraving, by milling the surface with a rotary bur, or by etching a design upon it. Toothed surfaces act to key the resin and prevent its delamination after curing. Any type of polyester resin can be used as long as a suitable amount of catalyst is added just before placement to assure proper hardening. Prepare small amounts of as many colored resins in the desired hues, tints, and shades as you will need for the work. Use proven, permanent, translucent or opaque dyes or pigment colors. Small amounts can be mixed on a glass slab that has first been waxed and polished with a non-siliconized wax so that the glass releases the resin remnants when they set and the palette can be cleaned. Larger amounts can be mixed in small glass containers with covers so the resin, without catalyst, can be stored for future use.

When applying the colored resin to the metal, when a preactivated resin is used, place a small amount on the glass palette and add a few drops of liquid catalyst. The correct amount is 2%, but in such small quantities, this

Catalyst or Activator Amounts Added to Resin Weight (approximate)

Resin Weight		1 oz 28 gms	2 oz 50 gms	4 oz 100 gms	9 oz 250 gms	1 lb 450 gms
2% Liquid catalyst or activator	Ounces	18 drops	36 drops	72 drops	1/6	1/3
	Milliliters	0.6	1	2	5	9

ing, or otherwise. Into these depressions translucent or opaque resins are placed until the amount is level with the metal. The field (French, *champ*) or ground is raised (French, *levé*) to the same height as the metal surface so that each color is surrounded by a metal wall and thereby compartmentalized. Each color fills the depression only and is separated from the others by an area of metal. Once the resin sets and hardens, in both cloisonné and champlevé types the surface can be leveled to one plane by an abrasive (as is done traditionally with these techniques in true enameling), then polished to smoothness and gloss with a polishing wheel.

BASSE TAILLE RESIN Sunken (French, *basse*) cut (French *taille*) resin, like its enamel counterpart, consists of a design cut to various depths on the surface of a metal sheet, using any technique by which metal can be removed from a mass. The *entire surface* is then covered with a layer of transparent resin. Where the depressions cut from the metal are deepest, the color appears darkest because it is thickest, and it is lightest at its highest or thinnest parts. Often the technique is enriched by working the metal first in repoussage, or by other metal-shaping techniques. The light reflects through the colored resins from the variously treated metal surfaces and cuts.

PLIQUE-À-JOUR RESIN This method in true enameling is technically difficult to achieve, but in resin enameling, it is relatively simple. The work is characterized by pierced openings in a sheet or metal, or openings between a filigree arrangement of wires, filled with *translucent resin* which when hardened, allows the passage of light because the *openings are backless*. To support the resin in place until it sets and hardens, each opening is backed with a

10–88 LYNDA WATSON-ABBOTT, U.S.A. "Butterflies." Silver necklace of cast and fabricated units ornamented with colored liquid polyester resin in the champlevé and basse taille styles. The butterflies and dragonflies have orange, yellow, and brown resin, and the leaves, greens and blues. Size 9½ × 6 in. *Photo: Lynda Watson-Abbott*

must be approximated. Mix the catalyst thoroughly with the resin by stirring them together with a wooden stick. If the resin does *not* contain a preactivator, the activator must be added first, 3% or 27 drops per ounce of resin, or 1 drop per gram, mixed thoroughly with the resin; the catalyst is *then* added.

Apply the resin to the metal with a brush or stick just as you would apply paint. Colors can be mixed by combining different colored resins beforehand on the palette, or they can be blended on the work itself. Some resins can be built up dimensionally by adding several layers, after each layer cures.

Various traditional enameling techniques can be *simulated*.

CLOISONNÉ RESIN In cloisonné resin work, an outline design is made with bent wires that are soldered on edge in place. The partitions (*cloisons*) are then partly or completely filled with resin, level with their height. Shrinkage is about 7% and can be compensated for by mounding the resin somewhat.

CHAMPLEVÉ RESIN This technique is the opposite of cloisonné in that a single metal surface is used into which design spaces are excavated by engraving, gouging, etch-

10–89 RACHELLE THIEWES LAMBERT, U.S.A. Hollow silver beads ornamented with bone and liquid polyester resin colored with earth-toned transparent liquid dyes. The resin was inlaid with a toothpick into depressions made by soldering the pierced parts onto sheet metal grounds, the result appearing like champlevé-style enameling. After curing, plastic surfaces were smoothed level with the metal ground using abrasive papers, then polished flush. Length laid straight 17 in; central bead 1⅝ × 1¼ in. *Photo: Rachelle Thiewes Lambert*

10–90 JOYCE T. MACRORIE, U.S.A. Silver filgree chain with openwork wires in each unit filled with transparent, colored, liquid epoxy resin, then filed, sanded, and polished flat down to the wire surface, in the *plique-à-jour* style. *Photo: Joyce T. Macrorie*

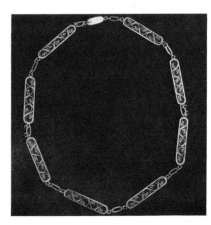

piece of *masking tape*. Once the resin is hard, the tape is stripped off. Additional resin can then be added in subsequent layers to increase the amount or deepen the color, either at the front, the back, or on both sides. It is advisable, where possible, to apply a *clear counter-resin* to the whole back of the object as it will further hold and secure all the individual resin parts within the openings.

CASTING LIQUID PLASTICS:
Cold contact molding

Plastics in a liquid state can be cast by various techniques and for different purposes. Casting a plain block, casting a shaped form, and embedding objects in a cast form are basic methods that can employ liquid resins. Many technical variants are possible.

CASTING A BLOCK OF RESIN FOR MACHINING

Liquid thermosetting resins such as polyester can be cast into a solid block to be machined on a lathe, or used in other ways that require a block form. This simple process is useful when a premade block of suitable size is not available but a stock of liquid resin is at hand.

For casting a block of resin, use a polythene or similar plastic container, such as one used to hold cosmetic or detergent products, because this type of plastic will not adhere to the cast block of thermosetting plastic resin which is therefore easily released, especially as it shrinks in setting. Be sure the container is clean and dry. The container (its bottom cut off), and the base (a clean glass slab) are waxed to a high gloss with any non-siliconized wax. Stand the container squarely on the glass slab and seal the seam by applying Plasticine to the outside edge at the point of contact with the base.

Use a resin that cures with low exothermic heat because in this case the chance of the block forming internal cracks is lessened. For making small blocks with a resin that already contains a preactivator, add the usual 2% liquid catalyst, and for larger blocks reduce this amount to 1% or 1.5%. Stir the catalyst carefully with the liquid resin to avoid the introduction of air. Pour the resin in a slow stream into the mold and allow it to stand until hard. Resins containing low catalyst amounts will take longer to cure, the time varying from 1–4 hours. Allow the resin to remain in the mold for 12 hours during which time it will shrink about 7% so it can be easily removed from the mold. Some resins leave a tacky, air-inhibited top surface which can be mechanically removed by filing or with abrasives. Allow the block to stand in air for several days at a constant temperature to harden it further. It can then be machined on a lathe or worked in other ways. After 4–6 weeks the resin will harden even more, making machining difficult; therefore it should be machined before this time period has passed.

CASTING POLYESTER RESIN

DEMONSTRATION 20

RODOLFO R. AZARO uses a silicone rubber mold
Drawings: Rodolfo R. Azaro

Cold cure silicone rubber molds of small size can be used for series castings in polyester resin. Silicone rubber molds are strong, accurate in detail reproduction, and are flexible so that castings with deep undercuts are possible as the mold can be bent to release them. Also, when polyester resin is cast in this material, the resin surface that contacts the mold hardens without tackiness and does not stick to it.

The silicone rubber is cured by mixing it with a certain amount of a curing agent, catalyst, or hardener sold with the rubber. Use the proportions provided in the instructions given with the particular material purchased. Silicone rubber is low in shrinkage and will not deteriorate quickly, therefore its relative expense is compensated for by its long use. It cannot, however, be remelted to make a new mold as with some other mold products.

1 The *master pattern* or model can be made of any material that has a surface firm enough to allow it to be painted with silicone rubber, or over which the silicone rubber can be poured. Metal, wood, plastic, plaster of paris, or Plasticine clay, as in this case, can be used as a model material. Porous materials must first be sealed by painting them with shellac. All details in the master pattern are accurately reproduced, therefore the final surface must be finished exactly as wanted. The model is mounted on a *flat glass slab* which will not warp.

A *one-part open mold* is all that is necessary if the model is a flat relief or has a flat back, as in this case. The flat side of the model should be well anchored in place so it does not float out of position when the mold material is poured.

2 Build a temporary wall of strips of heavy cardboard, glass, or wood around the model high enough to retain the

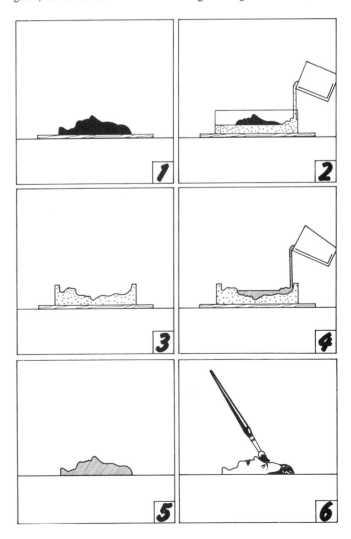

silicone rubber when poured to a depth of about ½ in (1.27 cm), at a distance of ½ in (1.27 cm) from the model at any point to the wall. Seal the wall seams either with Plasticine clay or strips of draftsman's tape so the mold material will not leak out when poured.

A *two-part closed mold* is needed if the model is three dimensional in the round. In this case, sink the model halfway into a prepared block of Plasticine and place a retaining wall around its squared-off edges. Key the clay block, which represents one half of the mold, by making at least three depressions in it on the portion outside the model that will contact the second, matching part.

Prepare the silicone rubber in a disposable paper cup, or a metal, ceramic, or glass container. Add the curing agent or catalyst in the recommended proportion, and stir the two together with a flat stick. Avoid including any air in the mix, and if a *vacuum table* is available, use it to extract any air.

Paint a thin coat of the silicone rubber mixture all over the surface of the model to be sure no air bubbles come in contact with it. To avoid the introduction of air, pour the mix into the mold in a thin stream until the model is covered at least ½ in (1.27 cm) above its highest point. Allow the rubber to cure or harden at room temperature, or in a temperature of 149°F (65°C) for from a few hours up to 24 hours, depending on the nature of the material and manufacturer's recommendations.

3   In the case of a one-part mold, remove the mold walls. Extract the Plasticine model from the mold by flexing it, leaving a negative mold of the model. Clean the mold to remove any Plasticine traces with detergent and warm water, dry it, and place it on the table, cavity upward. If the second part of a two-part mold must be made, reverse the first part, remove the clay half but allow the model to remain in place. Replace the mold walls making sure they are high enough to hold the second mold part. Apply a thin layer of liquid mold release or parting agent, or petroleum jelly to the cured mold half. Pour the same mixture of rubber and curing agent into the mold as before and allow the second half to cure. Remove the walls, separate the two mold halves, extract the master model and clean the mold. Burn or cut a pouring gate and attached sprue opening into one end of the mold up to the inner mold cavity.

When polyester resins are cured the exothermic heat buildup may be as high as 320°F (160°C), so the rubber mold should be postcured to a temperature at least 10 Fahrenheit degrees (6 Celsius degrees) higher than the curing temperature of the resin used by heating it at this temperature in an oven for several hours.

As a mold release substance, wipe the mold cavity surface with a very thin coating of petroleum jelly.

4   The size and type of casting will decide which of the several different polyester resin types should be used. For jewelry, because of the need to keep the weight of the object low, the sizes of the castings will probably be small and therefore lightweight. This eliminates some of the problems encountered when making large castings. Small quantities of resin can be mixed in disposable waxed paper cups, but not in cups made of polystyrene, which will soften and become unusable. Here a preactivated polyester resin with added catalyst is poured slowly in a thin stream to fill the mold level with its height.

5   When the resin has set and hardened, lift it out of the mold which can be flexed for its release if undercuts exist. The mold can then be used to make repeats of the model.

6   In this case, the plastic casting will be painted. Before any resin casting is painted, all traces of any mold release agent must be removed or the paint will not adhere. Use a detergent mixed with warm water and a soft brush to eliminate all traces of greasy mold release substances. In some cases it may be necessary to abrade the surface with a finely powdered abrasive made into a paste to "tooth" the surface sufficiently to accept the paint. Rinse the abrasive away. Before painting any plastic surface, it must be absolutely dry. A wide variety of plastic-based paints are compatible with polyester resins. First a ground color is painted on, and when this is dry, details can be added. In a piece such as a brooch, a metal finding is cemented to the back.

10-91 10-92 RODOLFO R. AZARO, England. "First Men on the Moon." Cast polyester resin necklace on nylon thread. The casting is painted with plastic enamel. Ø 5⅛ in. The same techniques were used for the brooch "King Kong." Size 3¾ × 3⅜ in. *Photos: Ray Carpenter*

EMBEDDING OBJECTS IN LIQUID TRANSPARENT POLYESTER RESIN

The idea of embedding natural specimens in translucent synthetic resin has its prototype in the insects found trapped in amber, a natural fossil resin of great age. Since ancient times when trade along the Amber Road extended from the Baltic Sea countries—the source of amber—to Greece and Rome, and branched out to the Middle East and the Far East including Tibet and China, pieces of amber containing complete insects have been especially valued. Today, by the use of synthetic resins in a liquid state, it is possible for any craftsperson to emulate this natural process.

THE EMBEDDED OBJECT   To minimize the problems of embedding, use dry specimens that need little or no pretreatment. These might include dried insect specimens, dry natural plant parts, metal objects in any form, small machine parts, natural or synthetic threads or cloth, sticks, shells, stones including pebbles, semiprecious tumbled or cabochon-shaped stones, synthetic or real faceted stones, pieces of colored glass or plastic, etc. Letters printed on transparent polyester film can be embedded by cementing them in place. Dried objects can be stained to color them with spirit-soluble stains or penetrating dyes such as those used in biology microscopy laboratories to penetrate the pores of the substance, such as the basic dye *haematoxylin*, or the acid dye *eosin*. For further information on stains, refer to biology textbooks.

10–93   PASCAL MOROBITO, France. Gold pendant in the form of a telephone dial, with the owner's telephone number in diamonds embedded in clear acrylic that fills the enclosed space; suspended by a gold chain. *Photo: Courtesy Morobito*

10–94   JAN BROOKS LOYD, U.S.A. "Entomology Necklace No. 1." Silver, brass, amber, ebony, and insect specimens. The latter must be cast in liquid polyester resin before they are completely dry as otherwise they become extremely brittle and require great care in handling. Air within the insect body tends to be forced out by the exothermic heat occurring during the polymerization of the curing resin, causing unwanted trapped air bubbles, but this can be overcome by injecting liquid resin into the partially dried body cavity through a hypodermic syringe before casting. Length 12 in. *Photo: Jan Brooks Loyd*

If an object has delicate parts, before embedment its entire surface can be sprayed with several applications of a lacquer to strengthen it, which also helps to preserve its natural color. Broken parts such as insect legs or plant parts can be refixed in place with a colorless plastic adhesive such as epoxy used in the smallest possible amount. It is also possible to embed plant specimens such as flowers whose color must be preserved by preliminary chemical treatment, and wet specimens which must first be dehydrated, but these processes properly done require considerably complex preparations, and are not discussed here.

THE EMBEDDING PROCESS   The embedding process utilizes a water-clear polyester resin that can be poured in depth and cured without cracking. It can be tinted to any light color by the addition of any transparent coloring pigment which allows the embedded object to remain visible. The resin should be of *low viscosity* to allow it to penetrate into and make contact with all of the surfaces of the object. With low-viscosity resins the chance of intervening air bubbles between the object and the viewer is reduced. As such bubbles obscure the view, the avoidance of trapped air is the main problem encountered in embedding objects.

Depending on whether the casting is to be seen from all angles or whether the result is frontal (meaning it has an upper and lower surface), will determine the manner in which the objects are placed. If the casting is seen frontally, it is possible to back it with an opaque, colored resin to increase visibility; the choice of color depends on its general tonality.

THE RESIN MOLD   When casting the object in a block of resin, the mold base can be a glass slab, and strips of glass can be used for the walls, their position adjustable in a swastikalike arrangement to accommodate a casting of any size. Aluminum strips bent at right angles can also serve as walls. Both glass and metal must be *wax coated* and *polished* to resist the adhesion of the resin and allow its easy release after solidification. The seams at wall corners and the base must be sealed against leakage in the manner already described. Ready-made polythene and polypropylene plastic forms such as ice cube containers can also be used as small molds since the polyester resin will not adhere to them. Do not use polystyrene plastic containers as polyester resin will dissolve them. If in doubt about the nature of the plastic, make a preliminary test by placing a small amount of the prepared polyester with catalyst added in the container and observe the reaction. Small boxes of aluminum foil and silicone rubber molds of any shape can also be used.

OBJECT POSITION   When the upper surface of a casting will be the one in contact with the mold, the object is placed *upside down* so it will be seen in its proper direction through the top surface after the casting is removed from the mold. If all the surfaces of the casting will be processed after casting, the position of the object can be in any direction, unless as in the case of multilayered castings, they must be in a specific relationship to each other.

RESIN PREPARATION   Prepare the resin in measured amounts in a disposable, wax-lined mixing cup. Do not scrape its sides or particles of wax may become included in the mix. If the resin already contains a preactivator, only the catalyst or hardener, a powerful oxidizing agent, must be added. The oxidizing agent will reduce exothermic heat in setting (which might affect some objects), make shrinkage minimal, and extend the curing time to about 2½ hours which is desirable in order to prevent cracking that may occur if the resin hardens too rapidly. The usual resins require 2% catalyst for 4 oz of resin (1 ml for 2 oz); 1½% for 4–10 oz castings; 1% for 10–16 oz castings. When mixing in the catalyst, stir it gently to avoid the introduction of air bubbles. As a guide, 4 oz of resin will make a ⅜ in (9.5 mm) thick slab, approximately 12 in (30.5 cm) square.

Pour the resin in the level mold to a shallow depth of about ¼ in (6.35 mm). This will form the surface upon which the specimen or object will rest. If this is the *back* of the casting, the resin used can be opaque or colored differently from the rest, or the same clear resin can be used throughout. Break any air bubbles that rise to the surface, or remove them with a clean stick, and set the mold aside for the resin to cure at a normal room temperature at 68° F (20° C). *Cover* it with a paper sheet to keep dust from settling on and sticking to the surface.

After two or three hours the resin hardens at the bottom, but a thin upper layer remains liquid. This liquid layer will anchor in place an object laid on it, especially if the object is light in weight. Do not wait longer because if the resin hardens too much, the following layer may not adhere properly to the first, or a division may be seen between them instead of the block appearing as a solid. After another quarter or half hour, the liquid portion will harden sufficiently to hold the object firmly in place and the second pouring can be made.

As the exothermic heat released from the first layer during setting will hasten the curing of the following layer, the amount of catalyst added to the next batch is reduced slightly. Objects of heavier weight that will not be displaced in the second pouring can be positioned now after a small amount is poured, and the remainder of the second batch is poured over them. If they move, they can be prodded back in place with a stick.

If only a single object is being embedded, the resin is poured to the desired depth to completely cover it. When several objects are placed at different levels, each level requires a separate pour. Remove any trapped air bubbles by stroking them out with a needle, then breaking them at the surface where they rise. Set the mold aside to cure at normal room temperature. If the object is embedded upside down, a final thin layer of an opaque or colored resin can be poured to act as a backing when the previous covering layer has set, if desired.

MOLD RELEASE   Once the block has cured, it can be released from the mold. Ordinarily removal is not a problem if the right mold materials have been used, and because the resin shrinks up to 7% on curing. If, however, the casting resists removal, tap the mold lightly, and if this does not work, immerse the whole assembly in very hot water for 10 minutes, remove and reverse its position, and immerse it for the same time period in cold water. Repeat the process if necessary.

Upon normal removal, the upper air-inhibited surface may be tacky. (Tackiness can be removed in ways described in *Surface Tackiness,* p. 475.)

In some cases, especially where the specimen is hard, it may become separated from the resin and coated with a layer of air. This is called *silvering* because it appears to be covered with a layer of silver. To remove this trapped

10–96   SUSANNA HERON, England. Silver necklace in three units with transparent black, translucent off-white, and bright opaque green polyester resin poured as a liquid inlay into the spaces in the fabricated metal unit made to receive them. Metal and resin are flat in the manner of plique-à-jour enamel. Units are held together by jump rings. *Photo: Courtesy the Crafts Advisory Committee, London*

air, heat the block to 150° F (70° C) in water of that temperature, then clamp it in a press and keep it under pressure until it cools.

FINISHING   One or two hours after mold release the block can be processed by cutting, sawing, or filing it to shape as it is still easily worked at this point; also less dust is generated at this time than after full curing. After a few days it becomes progressively harder and can be turned on a lathe with a general-purpose tool, top raked to approximately 25°, at a slow feed, with a speed of 300 rpm. The resin must be fully cured before final finishing which can be done on the lathe with suitable abrasives starting with 320 grit and ending with 600 grit, then with polishing compounds on a polishing lathe wheel.

MOUNTING   The result can be mounted in metal in any of the ways by which a stone can be mounted, it can be cemented to other parts, a hole can be drilled through it and a jump ring inserted, it can be riveted in place, etc.

PLASTICS GLOSSARY

Accelerator, activator, or promotor: These are substances added to liquid resin plastics to cure them. They are active oxidizing materials such as manganese, cobalt soaps, or amines, used in conjunction with a catalyst to hasten the polymerization process at room temperature, and to speed the set of the resin.

Acetone: An organic, carbonyl liquid, CH_3COCH_3, used as a solvent for many organic compounds. It is mixed with plastic pigment powder to make a liquid plastic dye, and also to remove surface tackiness that occurs after the liquid resin has set.

Adhesive: Any liquid or paste form of plastics used to bond plastics and other materials.

Annealing: Heating plastic near its melting point to prepare it for welding.

Air bubbles: Pockets of air that form between laminations of plastic sheet, or in liquid resins. In sheet they are

10–95   BJÖRN WECKSTRÖM, Finland, designer; manufacturer Lapponia Jewelry Ltd., Helsinki. "Big Drop." Silver pendant with acrylic cast in a two-part steel mold, with deliberately included random-patterned trapped air bubbles, either left clear, or injected with liquid colored dyes through a small drilled hole, then cemented closed. The casting is trimmed, polished, and fitted to the metal mount by a keying peg, or flanges in the metal part designed to receive them, and cemented in place under pressure. *Photo: Winfrid Zakowski, courtesy Lapponia Jewelry Ltd.*

pressed out before the plastic cures, and in liquid resins they are teased out with a needle. They also may be deliberately injected into plastic resins while in a liquid state for decorative effect.

Air inhibition: The surface of some, but not all polyester resins remains tacky if cured in open air, the effect due to air inhibition.

Blisters: Surface defects that form on overheated plastics.

Catalyst, hardener, or initiator: To cure plastic resin more rapidly by initiating polymerization, a chemical compound (generally an organic peroxide) or catalyst is added.

Contact molding: Molding plastics without the application of heat.

Crazing: Cracks that appear in set plastic due to improper heating, overheating when buffing, the improper use of thinners and glues, and from other causes.

Curing: The transformation of a liquid thermosetting resin to a solid plastic by chemical reaction, accomplished by adding a catalyst or curing agent to the resin which produces specific chemical reactions that generate heat; or by subjecting the resin to heat. Cold curing resins are cured in air, and hot curing resins are cured in a stove, after an accelerator has been added.

Curing time: The time it takes for a resin to become completely polymerized.

Cushion: Softening the surface of plastic by soaking it in a solvent while preparing it for gluing or cementing.

Decorative sheet: Combinations of colored plastic sheets.

Dry coloring: Coloring plastic by tumbling it in a drum containing dyes and pigments.

Exothermic heat: The heat generated by resins during the polymerization reaction.

Expanded plastics: Plastics expanded to multicellular structures characterized by low density. Example: Styrofoam.

Extrusion: Forming a continuous shape by heating, and then forcing the plastic through a mold into a cooling station.

Fabrication: Working plastic by machining or other forming processes to create a finished piece.

Filler: A substance added to resin to increase bulk or to give it special properties.

Film: Plastic in thin sheet form, 0.010 in (0.025 cm) or thinner.

Gel: Polyester resin in a jellylike consistency between a liquid and a solid, or when partly cured.

Gel time: The time it takes or a resin to set in a nonfluid, gelled state.

Hot stamping: Pressing heated metal dies or stamps on plastic to form a contour or to make an impression. A heated die can also be used to impart a pattern if it is coated with dyes or pigments.

Jig: Any tool or means of holding heated plastic parts in a particular form or configuration while they are cooled to a certain shape.

Lamination: Bonding several layers of plastic sheet together by heat and pressure; or cold bonding with transparent plastic cements.

Low-pressure resin: A resin used to make laminates in molds at low pressure.

Maturing time: The time needed for a cast resin to become completely cured or stable.

Mold: A form used to shape plastics by injecting or pouring the plastic in a liquid state, or by pressing it

into a heated solid form so that it solidifies under pressure into the shape of the mold cavity. A mold with a convex working surface is a *male mold;* a mold with a concave working surface is a *female mold;* a *matched mold* is one having two close-fitting parts between which the plastic is pressed.

Mold release: A substance used to coat molds to facilitate the release of the casting and prevent it from sticking to the mold, also called a *parting agent* or *releasing agent.*

Molding powder: Plastic in granules; filler or coloring pigments ready for use in the operation of molding.

Opaque plastic: Plastic that does not allow the passage of light.

Optically clear plastic: Plastic that is transparent.

Pellets: Plastic in beadlike shapes used when heat forming plastics in molds.

Pill: Plastic in a compressed tablet having a specific weight, used when accuracy in measurement is necessary in molding plastics.

Polymerization: A chemical reaction that occurs when a liquid resin sets to become a solid in curing; the molecules link together, thus changing the liquid to a solid.

Postcuring: Applying external heat to cause a resin to cure to a stable state in a shorter time than occurs when curing takes place in air at normal room temperature.

Pot life: The time period during which a liquid resin to which a catalyst and activator have been added remains unstable and therefore capable of being worked, at the end of which period it gels.

Preheating: Heating a plastic before it is molded in order to decrease the time for the molding cycle.

Premixing: Preparing plastic by mixing resin, filler, and other materials with it before use.

Resin: Plastic in a liquid or semiliquid state, used with the addition of a catalyst and activator and heated to form an object.

Sandwich: Two or more layers of plastic material stacked to form a laminate, used in making composite colored sheets, or when bonding inclusions.

Shelf life: The period of time during which a resin can be stored and still remain unstable.

Solvent: A liquid substance such as acetone that will dissolve dyes, and powdered and solid plastics.

Tacking: Spot fastening two items together by heat, a solvent, or glue to temporarily hold them together prior to welding or lamination.

Tackiness: A condition of semisolidity in which the air-inhibited surface of cast and set plastics remains sticky to the touch.

Thermoplastic: A plastic that can be repeatedly softened by heating and hardened by cooling without involving chemical change.

Thermosetting plastic: A plastic that can undergo a single nonreversible heating and cooling cycle that changes it to a hard, infusible solid, achieved by the use of heat or curing agents.

Thinner: A liquid substance such as acetone that acts to thin or soften plastic.

Translucent plastic: Plastic that is colored so that a certain amount of light passes through, but it cannot be seen through.

Viscosity: The resistance of a liquid to flow. A highly viscous liquid is thick, and a liquid low in viscosity is thin.

11

CASTING

Methods of Giving Form to Molten Metal

GRAVITY POUR CASTING

Exploiting Earth's centripetal force

THE DEVELOPMENT OF CASTING TECHNOLOGY

Vast new possibilities of working metal beyond the scope of Stone Age techniques using stone tools to cut, split, chip, and bend opened up with the realization that metal ores could be *smelted* and the resulting purified metals could be *cast*. Because metal becomes fluid and plastic when heated to a high enough temperature, entirely new forms in *unlimited variety* could be made, provided the metal in its molten state could be *contained until it cooled and solidified*. This became possible with the development of the *mold* by whose use the whole process of *casting* developed.

The casting process developed late in the 4th millenium B.C., and with it began the art and science of *metallurgy*, or the extraction of metals from ores, which is believed to have started with copper. About a thousand years later, the metallurgy of gold, silver, antimony, and lead, and the alloying of bronze were also established. Spurred on by an ever developing technology, casting techniques proceeded from the simple one-piece open mold to the two-part closed mold. Eventually the process of casting a *replica* of an object first created in an expendable material such as wax by the use of an expendable mold also evolved to overcome the problem of undercuts, and with this the process of lost wax casting, also of great antiquity, was established.

All of these processes are still in use by jewelers today, and are described in this chapter. Some are still practiced in the same primitive manner of their inventors. Others have developed into greatly refined techniques using specially prepared materials to satisfy the increasing demand for accuracy in reproduction.

GRAVITY POURING METAL

It is good to remember that for many centuries before the recent and widespread adoption by craftspersons of the practice of vacuum or investment casting, the most common casting method for jewelry (as well as for large objects) was *static casting* or *gravity pouring*, by which the metal fills the mold cavity simply through the force of gravity. This relatively easy, quick, ancient system is still widely used today. Craftspersons who do not possess cen-

trifugal casting equipment, or do not have the space to accommodate it, need not abandon the idea of casting. The only real physical requirements are a *well-ventilated area*, a worktable and floor surface that are fire resistant in the case of spills (a sheet of *transite* or another heat-resistant material in solid form can be laid on the worktable and floor), a *crucible, crucible tongs,* and a *means of heating* the metal to render it molten, which can be accomplished by using any of the usual fuels employed with a *torch tip.* Normally, all of this is already available to the jeweler.

MOLD TYPES

Molds can be either of two types: *reusable* to make several castings, or *expendable* for one-time use only. Reusable molds can be the *one-face type* with the pattern in one mold half, and the other half flat and used for placing pressure on the molten metal to force it into the mold cavity; or a *two-part, two-faced mold,* with both parts bearing patterns, and the parts keyed to each other for proper alignment, producing *two-sided* or *three-dimensional* castings. Expendable molds are more usually used by the craftsperson and may be any of the above. These also allow the use of a pattern with *undercuts* or parts that might cause mold damage in their removal. Expendable molds are made of an amorphous material such as clay or plaster because these materials allow the casting of objects whose form is too complex to cast in a reusable mold.

ALTERNATIVE MOLD MATERIALS

The basic processes of gravity pour casting (described on p. 484 in Cuttlebone Casting) can be carried out using a mold made of any of several materials. Molds can be made of any substance that can be easily *impressed, shaped by pressure, carved,* or *poured* and then allowed to solidify. The important requirement is that these substances must be able to retain their form without disintegrating when they are subjected to the high heat of the molten metal used.

Clay is the most primitive of these mold materials and is used in different grades of fineness for making *terra cotta molds. Refractory clay* is best as it can withstand high temperatures without physical change. In the lost wax casting process, the first and finest clay is used to cover the model which is usually made of a temporary material such

11–1 MALI. One-piece gravity-poured lost wax cast bronze bracelet used by the Bambara tribe near Bamako. The wirelike surface appearance results from the method of creating the model. A wax compound is first drawn into long strands. These were shaped by twisting in pairs, like wires, or by weaving them together in a basket-woven texture. They were laid down on a clay core (removed after casting), and the mold was built up over the model with clay. Ø 4½ in. Photo: Musée de l'Homme, Paris

as wax or resin, in order to achieve optimal definition. This is followed by coarser grades of clay that have been mixed with a refractory material such as brick dust, sand, or pulverized refractory brick. The purpose of these additives is to make the clay mold wall *more porous* and *allow the escape of gases* formed during the heat of the pour. Molds of refractory clay can be dried and used green, or they can be fired (with the opening to the mold cavity pointing downward so that the expendable model can drain out as in lost wax casting); or in the case of two-part molds, the model can be removed and the mold biscuit fired to make it solid. If the mold has no undercuts, it can be used many times to make a casting. It is also possible to deliberately remove parts of the mold to allow the metal access to the undercuts, and after the casting is removed, this additional metal on the result can be eliminated by filing, chasing, carving, chiseling, or other means.

Soft stone has been used as a mold for casting metal for thousands of years, ever since pre-historic man cast the first copper ax. Some pre-Hispanic gold pectorals made by the Indians of Central and South America were cast in stone molds. Suitable, easily carvable stones used in ancient times for molds include chlorite, gabbro, limestone, pumice (a lightweight, hardened volcanic lava glass froth with a characteristic texture of minute bubbles), tufa stone (a porous rock composed of the finer kinds of volcanic detritus), slate, and the most common, soapstone or steatite (a soft, dense, easily carved talc that hardens after heat and needs no parting agent). Today, preformed and dried cast blocks of the same investment plaster that is used for centrifugal casting can be easily carved to make an open mold for casting a one-faced relief, or a two-part mold for casting three-dimensional objects. Some of these materials have their distinctive texture, while others are

completely smooth thus allowing castings with smooth surfaces. When casting an open-faced relief, inclusions of a contrasting metal can be allowed to set in the plaster to partially embed them, then the molten metal can be poured into the cavity. When the investment plaster is removed, such inclusions are keyed to the casting and project from its face.

Wood can be used to make an open mold for the casting

11–2 BERLIN, PRUSSIA, late 18th through mid-19th centuries. Cast iron jewelry cast in metal chill molds, produced in Prussia and also France during this period. Phosphoric cast iron containing not more than about 0.7% phosphorus was used because the addition of this element renders the iron more fluid than when normally molten, permitting intricate, thin-sectioned castings. Though this type of cast iron is rather hard and brittle, when used for jewelry brittleness was not an objection. The peak of its production occurred during the War Of Liberation against Napoleon in 1813–1815 when the Prussian government asked the wealthy to contribute their jewels to support the national cause, in exchange for which they were issued this jewelry. A great variety of forms were made. The skill with which the casting was accomplished gave Berlin founders a high reputation. This example combines formalized popular "Gothic" and naturalistic units. Here a central floweret is backed with a polished steel disc (paillette or sequin). The result was lacquered black to prevent rusting. Photo: Österreichisches Museum für Angewandte Kunst, Vienna

11–3 BERLIN, PRUSSIA. Cast iron bracelet ca. 1820, signed Berlin Geiss. Six identical units are linked by loops. A box clasp is concealed behind one, covered with a flower unit. Photo: Victoria and Albert Museum, London, Crown Copyright

of low-melting metals. First soak it in water before use, as is done when using wood for glass-making molds. *Hard charcoal* makes a carvable, open mold. *Metal molds* are of course used for casting, and can be made from bronze by carving out the cavity with chisels, gravers, and die-sinker's tools. They should be dressed with a coating of a parting material before casting to ease the removal of the casting. *Sand molds* are also sometimes used to gravity pour cast jewelry. This is not a method ordinarily used by jewelers since surface texture is not as accurately reproduced as in lost wax casting.

CUTTLEBONE CASTING:
Creating the mold cavity by pressure

Cuttlebone has long been in use for casting pieces of jewelry having forms without undercuts. Such forms are suited to the limitations of the cuttlebone as a casting material, and exploit its possibilities. Cuttlebone casting is economical and relatively fast.

Cuttlebone is a white, firm, calcareous internal shell or bone of a ten-armed marine mollusc called a cuttlefish, of which there are many species varying in size from small to enormous. Cuttlefish inhabit all ocean waters, but the chief source of the cuttlebone used by jewelers in the West is the European cuttlefish *Sepia officinalis*. The bone supports the soft parts of the cuttlefish—which differs from its relative the squid in that it possesses this internal sepium shell or bone, while the squid does not. Once the creature has died, the bone is found thrown up on the shore where it is abundant, which probably accounts for the reason that in French it is called *biscuit de mer* or "sea biscuit." These are collected, but the main source of sepium is from the cuttlefish captured for food in nets by fishermen, from which the bone is extracted.

11-4 EDMÉE HAGSATER, designer; manufacturer Tane S.A., Mexico. Sterling silver necklace, sand cast in sections, the design inspired by cactus forms. Ø 42.5 cm. *Photo: Courtesy Tane S.A.*

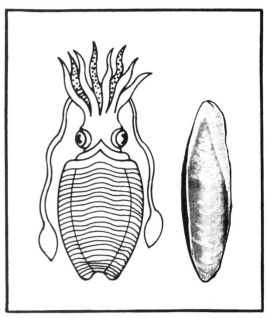

11-5 *THE TEN-ARMED SEPIA OFFICINALIS* and the internal calcareous shell or bone extracted from it, called the *cuttlebone*.

The bone obtained from suppliers is white, clean, and dry. It should be of good quality, firm in structure and not too coarsely grained. An average size is 6 in (15.2 cm) long by about 3 in (7.6 cm) wide, and about 1½ in (3.8 cm) thick. Smaller and larger ones are also available—Chinese cuttlefish produce cuttlebone up to 14 in (35.6 cm) and those extracted from tropical cuttlefish can be even larger.

Cuttlebones are often hung in the cages of captive birds who eat portions of them as a source of lime and salts, so they can often be purchased from pet shops.

The *size* and *thickness* of the cuttlebone naturally limit the size of the casting that can be made with it, especially when a single bone is used to make one object. Therefore, purchase as large a bone as you can find. The work can be made larger and deeper by using two cuttlebones for the same mold, or by planning a design that is made of several separately cast parts that are then joined by fabrication methods.

Cuttlebone is lightweight and relatively fragile. It should be handled carefully and not subjected to *excessive* pressures that will cause it to crumble. Its hard outer surface is easily cut through with a thin-bladed saw and the softer interior is carved with simple cutting tools. Its substance can withstand the high temperatures of molten metal without disintegration, only becoming charred.

Because it is easily crushed under pressure, cuttlebone can be used to produce a casting having either relatively smooth surface as when a smooth-surfaced model is pressed into it; or, when carving directly into it, a surface that reproduces the natural pattern and textured structure of alternating hard and soft ridges or striations. These ridges can be seen in the demonstration piece on p. 488-89, and in some of the other illustrations.

PREPARING THE CUTTLEBONE

The bone is whole when purchased. Its texture is not

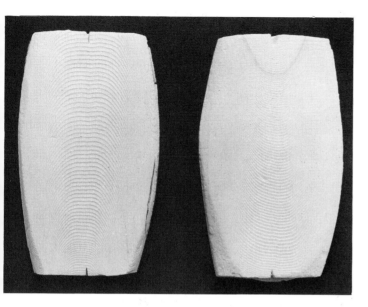

11–6 *TWO CUTTLEBONE SHELLS* about the same size, used for one mold in the demonstration ahead. The ends have been cut off with a jeweler's saw and a fine blade. The working surfaces were rubbed flat on sandpaper, then against each other for a close fit. The ends are center marked for future alignment. The typical striated surface texture due to structure is visible. *Photo: Michael Brechner*

uniform—internal ridges are harder than the spaces between them. It has thin, projecting edges that tend to be fragile and crumbly and are therefore removed. To cut away parts and divide the bone, use a small, thin-bladed, fine-toothed saw to minimize loss. Because of the normally shallow thickness of the bone, there is a limit to the depth possible for the mold cavity. The choice of bone size depends on the size of the model. This natural limit can, however, be overcome by various ways.

USING A TWO-PART CLOSED MOLD

We will assume that the model to be cast is a heavy, relatively simple man's ring, a type that is often cast with the cuttlebone. Such a basic form can be developed and embellished further by other techniques after casting. For this object, one large bone is sufficient. Cut it in half at the center where it is thickest. Flatten the two facing surfaces true by rubbing them on a piece of *fine sandpaper* placed on an absolutely flat surface such as a *plate glass slab*, rubbing each in turn with a circular motion to avoid rounded edges until they are level. The touching, inner surfaces of the mold must be completely flat. If they do not fit together tightly, they will not contain the molten metal and the result will be an incomplete, unsuccessful casting. It is *not* good practice to rub the two surfaces *upon each other* as the result is not always satisfactory and too much material can be lost. Brush or blow away any dust loose on the surfaces.

THE MODEL OR PATTERN

The model, free of undercuts, can be of any material strong enough to withstand the necessary pressure without becoming misshapen. The conventional materials used are lead (which is easily formed) or brass (when the model will be used repeatedly). Other possible materials include plastic, wood, or sealing wax. Any suitably shaped and sized, rigid "found object" such as a lead casting, wire mesh, or fused metal forms, can be reproduced by the use of the cuttlebone.

PLACING THE MODEL

The ring model can be made with an open, split shank so that the size can be adjusted according to the needs of the particular casting. If the surface of the model is smooth, coat it lightly with *castor oil* which will facilitate its release from the cuttlebone. Hold one half of the cuttlebone mold with the thickest part *up* in the left hand and place the model ½–1½ in (12.7–38.1 mm) from the top with the ring shank up and the heaviest part down. With the right hand, slowly and firmly press the model into the cuttlebone which will give way under this pressure, until it is well seated about one-third to one-half its depth. Brush or blow dust with air from your torch.

KEYING THE MOLD PARTS

In this process, it is important that the two mold parts after separation be replaceable in exactly the same relation to each other after the model has been removed. This is necessary to avoid a *shift casting,* which is a faulty casting caused by the misalignment of the two mold parts. To assure a perfect match, insert *mold pins* in the two mold parts so that they lock together as an insurance against mismatching mold parts.

Three pins made of short lengths (depending on the bone thickness) of 16 or 18 gauge B.&S. copper wire are pressed halfway into the mold, two at the upper, thickest part of the bone, far enough away from the model and the pouring gate that will be formed later so they do not interfere with them. The third is placed toward the bottom of the bone, not too close to its edge.

Now put the second half of the mold in position exactly opposite the other half. While you are in a seated position, hold the two parts between your hands which are between your knees so that knee pressure can also be exerted upon the mold. With hand and knee pressure, press the two parts together slowly but firmly until they meet. If a small model is being made, a gentle, slightly rocking pressure (without sidewise motion) exerted by the hands alone is sufficient.

With the model still enclosed, shape the outer parts of the cuttlebone. Rub the upper, thickest part on a flat *sandpaper* or with a *flat, coarse file* to even that end. Cut away and square the thin sides, cut off the bottom and smooth all surfaces flat with sandpaper.

On these now flat outer surfaces, another system of keying the parts can be used. With a *smooth file* or *small saw,* carve or cut one or more lines or grooves into the bone *across the parting line of the mold parts* in the manner shown in Illustration 11–17. Later, when the mold parts are separated and must be reassembled, these lines act as a guide in their alignment.

With gentle pressure, separate the two mold parts, but leave the model in place. This is done to avoid possible damage to or breakage of the mold cavity in the next step. It will now be seen that the pressure on the mold parts has forced the metal key pins mentioned above into the opposite mold half. Make sure they are in place in the *same half* of the mold. Blow or brush away dust but do not use high air pressure as this might cause mold damage.

MAKING THE POURING GATE AND VENTS

The mold requires a *pouring gate* for the admission of the molten metal, and some *vents* leading outward from the mold cavity to allow for the release of gases that form during casting. If gas is not allowed to escape, it will be trapped and cause a counterpressure against the molten metal, which will not then completely fill the mold cavity. Such gases can also cause damage to the mold.

The pouring gate is simply a flat, conical depression—flat because the relatively shallow depth of the bone will not allow a round-shaped cone. Its width should be about two-thirds of the ring's diameter, not larger or it will require an unnecessary amount of the molten metal to fill it. In one half of the mold, with a *sharp knife* first carve this cone shape, large diameter up, diminishing downward until its apex reaches the enclosed model, the mold cavity. Its depth should be minimal, perhaps no more than 1 in (2.54 cm) at maximum and if possible less, but sufficient to contain a reserve of molten metal during the pour to act as a feeder when the metal cools, solidifies, and draws upon it.

A few vents spaced at intervals are made with the point of a *knife*. These can be made in only one half of the mold. Start at the mold cavity (the model is still in place), and move *outward* and *upward,* gradually decreasing in size as they radiate outward. They should *not* reach the outer edge of the mold, but go only halfway, because if they extend to the outer edge a gas back-pressure is created that prevents the metal from flowing into them too easily.

Now with fingers or *tweezers* gently lift the model from its embedded position in one half of the mold, and remove it. There should be a sharp, negative impression of the model left in the cavity. The greater its accuracy, the less work there will be later when finishing the casting. If the model has any sharp projections, it may be advisable at this point to use a *sharp, pointed knife* and carve into the mold *at those places* to make the points a bit deeper or larger, to make sure the metal will fill those places. Any excess can later be removed, which is much easier than adding metal to the final casting. Blow away dust with some air from the *torch,* but do not use a strong blast.

PREPARING THE MOLD SURFACE FOR CASTING

If the impression from the model has been made carefully, it should not be necessary to do anything more to the mold cavity surface before casting. However, once the model is removed, it is the practice of some jewelers, in order to achieve an impression with optimal definition, to dust the impression with *finely powdered graphite* (or to coat the surface with carbon from a candle flame). Replace the model in the mold cavity, press the mold parts together again, and carefully separate the mold sections and remove the model. In this case, no further treatment of the mold surface is possible.

Another technique to produce a maximum of surface accuracy in the casting—or if the mold is to be used for more than one casting—is to strengthen the mold surface by painting it with a prepared dressing consisting of the following:

Borax	¼ teaspoon
Sodium silicate	1 teaspoon
Hot water	½ pint

The *sodium silicate* ($Na_2O \cdot 2SiO_2$), commonly called *water glass,* is a powder that dissolves in water to make a syrupy liquid. It is extensively used as a fireproofing agent and protective coating, and acts to harden the surface to which it is applied, because, once it dries, it forms a hard, transparent film. This dressing allows the mold to better withstand the heat of the molten metal without excessive deterioration. Do not use more than one teaspoon of this mixture for each half of the bone. Allow it to sink into the cuttlebone, then dry the cuttlebone by placing it in a *low-heat oven,* or under a *heat lamp* until all moisture evaporation ceases. It is necessary to dry the cuttlebone to avoid the detrimental action of steam at the time of the pour.

Reassemble the mold parts and check to see that the exterior guide lines match up and that the three key pins lock together accurately. Bind the parts together at two locations, toward the top and the bottom, with a *soft iron binding wire.* Twist their ends together with *pliers.* Be sure when doing this that the wire is no tighter than necessary as wire too tightly twisted will cut into the bone and cause it to crumble.

USING A THREE-PART MOLD

In some cases there are advantages in using a *three-part mold.* The process described here again uses a man's ring as the model. Three-piece molds are particularly suited to ring designs that have straight projecting claw settings or a dimensional front portion, again, *always without undercuts.*

Refer to the diagram. The cuttlebone must be cut into three parts. The two end pieces contain the mold part for the ring shank, and the third or central part contains the front part of the ring. The width of the central part (3) should be a bit more than the total width of the thickest parts of the two other parts (1 and 2) when held together in a vertical position. After cutting, rub parts 1 and 2 on sandpaper so that their touching surfaces meet perfectly. The parting line of these two vertical parts must meet the horizontal part (3) perpendicularly.

Place the ring with the front part toward the thick end of bone 1, with its shank projecting about ¼ in (6.35 mm) past the end. Place bone 2 over it and press these together until they meet. Saw off the excess on both sides to make the sides flat. Saw off the thin top. Enscribe saw-drawn guide lines across the parting lines to act as a guide when reassembling the mold parts. Carefully separate parts 1 and 2 and remove the model. Reassemble these parts and tie them together, making sure that the guide lines match. On the end that will eventually contact part 3, rub the surface so that it is at a right angle to part 3. Continue rubbing parts 1 and 2 together until you reduce that end to the point where you reach the mold cavity of the inner surface of the ring shank. Separate parts 1 and 2, replace the model, and press them back together again. The front face of the ring now projects out beyond them. While holding parts 1 and 2 together, carefully press the ring face into part 3. Tie all parts together, then file away any excess parts of part 3, making its sides continuous with 1 and 2. Guide mark the parting lines between parts 1 and 2 and 3. Carefully take the mold apart by first removing part 3, then separating parts 1 and 2, and remove the model. Carve a conical pouring gate into parts 1 and 2 up to the model cavity, and make vents that point upward toward the pouring gate. If the model has projecting parts, such as claws, deepen them in part 3 with

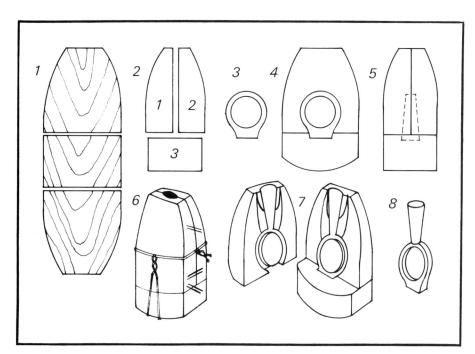

1. The *cuttlebone cut into three parts.*
2. The *three parts assembled* (1, 2, 3).
3. The *ring model.*
4. *Front view* of the ring model in place between the three parts.
5. *Side view* showing the position of the ring model in the mold.
6. The *mold assembled* and tied with soft iron binding wire, ready for casting. The diagonal lines on the sides are scratch lines over the parting line between mold parts, put there to simplify their correct alignment.
7. *Part 1 of the mold removed after casting,* with the other two parts and the casting still in place.
8. The *casting with attached sprue,* removed from the mold.

a well-tapered knife point, for reasons discussed above. Blow out any loose dust particles. Reassemble the mold, making sure that all guide lines match at the parting lines. Bind together the three parts with soft iron binding wire, as shown in the diagram. The mold is now ready for pouring.

DIRECT CARVING OF A CUTTLEBONE MOLD CAVITY

DEMONSTRATION 21

ALICE SHANNON cuttlebone casts a pendant

Photos: Michael Brechner

By the use of a directly carved mold cavity, it is possible to make a casting with undercuts with a cuttlebone. In this case, of course, the undercuts will destroy those parts of the mold that lock in the undercuts after a single casting. The mold cavity can be carved into only *one half* of a two-part mold in which case the result is a relief, backed up with a flat second half that forms a flat back on the

casting. To be able to visualize the result *before* casting, an impression can be taken of the carved area with a soft material such as a *soft wax* or softened *Plasticine clay.* Take care not to exert too much pressure when taking such an impression. After examining such a result, the mold cavity can be altered by additional carving.

It is also possible to carve directly into *both halves* of the mold. If the halves must correspond, mark a center point at the top and bottom of the two parts and use these marks to line up a similarly marked drawing on tracing paper whose outline can then be traced onto the cuttlebone. Another method is to carve both mold halves in such a way that *parts overlap* in places to be sure they become one unit in the casting. In this case, both sides of the resulting casting are different, and some flat parts will be seen from either side to contrast with those that are in relief.

CUTTING TOOLS FOR MOLD MAKING
1 Here we see some of the simple tools used in the process: a *brush* to remove carved particles and dust; a *pencil* to draw the design; *binding wire* to hold the mold parts together; and various *cutting tools* to do the carving. The shape of the tool influences the shape of the cut made

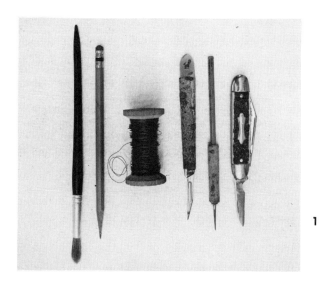

1

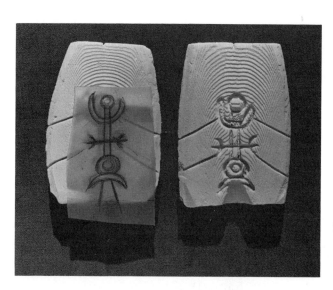

2

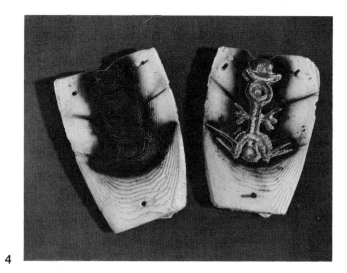

3   **4**

with it. Other improvised tools might be used; for instance, a round-ended dapping punch could be utilized to make a semicircular depression that will become a dome on the casting. Remove all loose particles after carving by brushing or blowing them away by air from your torch.

2   The design was first carved into one half of the mold, then transferred *in reverse* to the second half by the use of a tracing, then carved there. Vents have been scratched from the mold cavity upward, and a pouring gate has been cut out at the top for the entry of the metal.

THE GRAVITY POUR CASTING

3   During the pour, in all cuttlebone casting the only pressure on the metal to fill the mold is the force of gravity. The mold has been tied with binding wire, positioned with the pouring gate *up,* and pressed into the dampened sand that fills a container improvised from aluminum foil. (It could also have been held in place by two refractory bricks.) As an additional precaution to deal with possible escape of molten metal, the lower half of the mold has been wrapped with a thin sheet of asbestos, made wet to make it flexible. After wrapping, the asbestos has been al-

lowed to dry somewhat before casting. The surface on which the casting is done should be of a fire-resistant material such as an asbestos coil, slab, or refractory brick. To facilitate the escape of air and gases from the cavity during the pour, incline the mold somewhat to one side, toward the worker.

Alloyed gold or silver is commonly used in cuttlebone casting. For an average man's ring, 15–20 grams of alloyed gold would be used, and about 8–11 grams of sterling silver. Other metals can also be used such as casting bronze, brass, or pewter. The amount of metal needed to fill a casting made in a carved mold must be estimated, and it is better to err on the generous side than to have too little metal to fill the mold.

THE CRUCIBLE

Low-melting metals can be melted with a blowtorch in an *iron pouring ladle*. High-melting metals are placed in a *crucible* to be melted. This can be one commercially manufactured, or one can be improvised from a carved out depression in a block of charcoal. Charcoal has the added advantage of creating a reduced atmosphere around the molten metal, thus preventing the metal from excessive oxygen absorption.

THE POUR

Weigh and place the dry metal in the crucible and heat it with a reducing flame until it contracts to a ball. If new metal must be added, preheat it with a torch and place it carefully with *tongs* into the molten mass; do not drop it in. Preheat one end of a *graphite rod* with a torch and stir the molten metal to mix the contents. Sprinkle a pinch of borax on the metal to facilitate its combination and to exclude the absorption of atmospheric oxygen or oxygen from the flame. Heat the mold by playing the torch on it just prior to pouring. Grasp the crucible with *crucible tongs,* and allow the metal to cool just to the point when the surface appears wrinkled. If the metal is too hot when poured, excessive gases will be created in the cuttlebone that will add undesirable porosity to the casting. While keeping the reducing flame playing on the metal, pour it slowly and without interruption of flow into the mold pouring gate.

The rate of pour should be continuous, neither too fast, as this creates turbulence and possible porosity, nor too slow, or the metal will cool off too much and not fill the mold cavity.

5   **6**

Stop the pour when the mold cavity is completely filled to the top of the pouring gate. If the amount of metal has been correctly calculated, there should be no surplus. (A *poured short mold* is one into which insufficient metal has been poured to fill the mold cavity, resulting in an incomplete casting.) If, however, there *is* a surplus, the crucible must be emptied after each pour. In this case, pour off any remaining metal into an ingot mold that has been warmed and is ready nearby for this purpose. Molten metal should not be allowed to solidify in a crucible bottom because its removal is difficult, and parts of the crucible are likely to chip off and become undesirable inclusions. Immediately after pouring, place the emptied crucible in a box containing dry sand, prepared beforehand and waiting, to allow it to cool off slowly, which will prolong its life. Store the cold crucible in a warm, dry place so it does not pick up moisture.

4 Allow the mold to stand for a few minutes while the metal solidifies. Cut off the binding wires with *snips* or *nippers*. While wearing *asbestos gloves*, gently pry open the mold parts with a thin *knife blade*. Remove the casting with a pair of *small tongs*. If there are no undercuts, it should come out easily. Quench it in a pan of cold water or under running water.

FINISHING THE CASTING

To finish the casting, with a *jeweler's saw*, cut off any fins or flash projections at the parting line, attached vent projections, and the pouring gate. Metal removal can also be done with *sprue-cutting clips, hand files*, or *rotary files* mounted on a *flexible shaft*, depending on the position and the amount of metal to be removed. Pickle the casting, rinse, and dry it.

If a *high finish* is the aim, the casting as taken from the mold is not as smooth in surface as that which can be achieved by lost wax, centrifugal casting. It is necessary to first prepare the surface with files and abrasive papers, then polish and buff it with polishing wheels.

5 and **6** The finished necklace with the sterling silver pendant, 2¾ in (7 cm) long, weight 2½ oz. Its form follows the astrological symbol for Mercury, the ruler of craftspersons and those who work with their hands. The necklace is strung with silver tube beads, ivory, Persian turquoise, carnelian, and wild boar tusks. Its total length is 31 in (78.7 cm).

REUSING A CUTTLEBONE MOLD

In casting, due to the rapid but uniform washing action caused by the molten metal on the cuttlebone, the cavity surface deteriorates, details become eroded, and the textural surface is coarsened. However, it is possible that a texture-loving jeweler might not consider such deteriorated surfaces objectionable, and even an advantage. Making a second casting does not take much additional time—it can be tried. If it is unsuccessful, the metal can be remelted in the next casting and there is no loss.

It helps to restore some toughness to the mold by recoating it with the borax and water glass mold wash solution. If a model has been used, some definition can be restored by recoating the mold cavity surfaces with carbon, replacing the model, and closing and pressing the mold parts together. Remove the model and cast as before.

The waste parts removed from the cuttlebone can be ground to a powder and used as a coarse polishing agent for silver and other metals. Old, no longer usable cuttlebone molds can also be pulverized and so used.

11–8 HANNA BECHAR-PANETH, Israel. "Two Olive Trees." Silver pendant, cuttlebone cast, with fabricated chain. Pendant 2 in square. Photo: Yacov Paneth

11–9 NILDA C. F. GETTY, U.S.A. "Ryujin" (Japanese dragon king of the sea). Silver brooch in which cuttlebone-cast parts are used in combination with repoussage units, with lapis lazuli and carnelian. Photo: Les F. Brown

LOST WAX CASTING

Replacing a mold-voided temporary model with metal

In lost wax casting, an *expendable, one-part mold* is formed around a model also made of a material that is expendable, the main substance used being *wax* or a composition in which wax is a major ingredient. This can be removed from the mold with low heat without damaging the mold. In its place is left a void or mold cavity that is then filled with molten metal which replaces the wax and takes on its former form.

The technique is widely known as *cire perdue,* from the French *cire,* "wax," *perdue,* "lost," hence in English, *lost wax.*

The main attraction of lost wax casting for the jeweler is the fact that the *plasticity* of the modeling wax is unrivaled by any other material used in jewelry making. Because it is a substance that can be used in either a solid or a liquid state, wax is capable of developing form in any manner possible with these conditions. This means its treatment in the invention of form and surface texture is quite literally unlimited. Making a casting from a wax model therefore takes the place of all the time-consuming techniques used by the fabricator-jeweler who achieves results by the methods of sawing, forming, soldering, and additional decorative processes. If the wax model is well finished—always the aim, since the casting will exactly reproduce the wax pattern—postcasting finishing processes are also minimal. Another important point is that wax is easily voided from a mold at a low temperature.

The creative experience in the casting process takes place in making the wax model, and in the ability of the maker to create form, invent texture, and preconceive how that form and its surface will appear after casting in

metal. The actual casting of the metal is a routine technical process, not without its own skills, of course. The jeweler who works exclusively in casting must be satisfied by the fact that actual contact with the metal is indirect, except for its manipulation in the molten state and in the finishing and decorating operations that may be necessary afterward.

11-11   RUSSIA, 10th century A.D. Animal subject fibula, cast silver, partly gilded; found near Jalca. Length 8.8 cm. Photo: Courtesy The Hermitage Museum, Leningrad

LOST WAX INVESTMENT CASTING

The adoption of the method of producing dental castings by the lost wax process was first introduced by William Taggart in 1907. Because investment casting assures great accuracy, the process revolutionized dentistry which previous to this depended mainly on amalgams and the malleting or welding of pure gold foil into a tooth cavity to fill it. In dentistry no allowance for shrinkage can be made. This requirement set off a search for a casting mold material that would make possible the greatest accuracy in reproducing the wax model. The material developed is the *investment plaster composition* used today. Gold contracts about 1.25% when cast, and by 1932 investment plasters were formulated that when preheated before casting provided an expansion of about 1.4% which almost exactly compensated for the shrinkage of the gold alloy in casting.

The literal meaning of the word *invest* is to surround, envelop, or embed. This is exactly what happens in *investment casting,* in which the plaster mold material, called the *investment,* completely surrounds the model as one continuous substance. The viscous nature of the investment when it is first prepared as a slurry is what makes possible the casting of a model of *any conceivable shape.* In all casting methods that employ an invested wax model, such as *centrifugal casting, pressure casting,* and *vacuum casting* (all described in detail below), the result cannot be extracted from the mold without destroying it com-

11-10   LYNDA WATSON-ABBOTT, U.S.A. "Sheep Bracelet." Cast silver. The model was carved from very hard wax, then decorated with elements added in a softer wax. The inner edge was hollowed out to reduce weight, then enameled opaque white after casting. Photo: Lynda Watson-Abbott

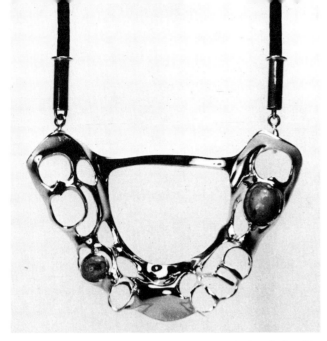

11–12 EMILE SOUPLY, Belgium. "The Second Smile of the Gioconda," Pendant 727. Cast 18K yellow gold, with two opals. *Photo: Emile Souply*

pletely. In these casting methods, the mold can be used *only once.*

ADVANTAGES OF THE INVESTMENT CASTING TECHNIQUE

Accurate reproduction is the greatest appeal of the lost wax investment casting technique to the jeweler. Any form and detail that can be invented with wax and translated into metal can be reproduced. For this reason it has been widely adopted in the last 30 years by many independent jewelers as well as by jewelry manufacturers.

Dimensional accuracy within 1.5% in casting is important in dentistry where centrifugal casting is widely used, but close dimensional tolerances are generally not significant in cast jewelry. There are cases when size or fit are important as in the size of a ring. Compensation for shrinkage can be made by forming the ring shank of the wax model slightly smaller than needed and somewhat thicker. Surpluses are trimmed away when finishing the piece.

Other advantages of investment casting are savings in time and labor. The amount of waste or scrap metal is considerably reduced, almost unlimited production repeats are possible by reproducing any model through wax injection in rubber molds, then casting the replicas in multiples by lost wax investment casting. A casting achieved with the centrifugal investment casting method is more dense, has a closer grain structure, and less porosity than the casting that results from any gravity pour casting.

LIMITATIONS

The main limitation of the centrifugal investment casting process is the limitation of the maximum size of the casting that can be made in a flask. This can be overcome, however, by planning a design so that parts can be joined by soldering, or assembled in other ways to make larger units.

11–13 LYNDA WATSON-ABBOTT, U.S.A. "Aerial View Neckpiece." Cast sterling silver, oxidized. A clay mold was first made in reverse (intaglio), dried, and painted with molten wax to a thickness of about 14 gauge B.&S. to produce a positive model. This was separated from the clay by dissolving the latter in water. After adding details, the entire model was divided into sections suitably sized for centrifugal casting. The cast units were assembled with U-shaped pins whose rectangular heads were formed to appear as houses. Size 11 × 8 in. *Photo: Frank J. Thomas, courtesy Fine Arts Gallery, California State University, Los Angeles*

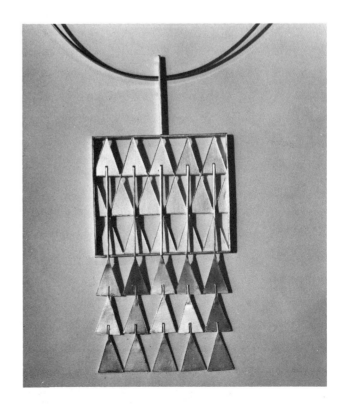

11–14 MAX FRÖHLICH, Switzerland. Sterling silver pendant cast from forms cut with a knife and straight edge from sheet wax 0.7 mm thick. The raised ridge edges on each piece result from cutting. The parts were assembled after casting and cleaning without further finishing operations. Size 165 × 75 mm. *Photo: Max Fröhlich*

Castings in general do not exhibit any *directional structural properties*, as, for instance, do forgings. Castings therefore tend to be brittle when bent. They are also less ductile than forged or extruded metal because they lack the longitudinal crystal structural direction which exists in metals formed by other methods.

WAX COMPOSITION FOR INVESTMENT CASTING

The exact composition of commercial dental waxes used to make a model for investment casting is a proprietary secret, but their basic constituents are known. All these constituents must burn away and leave a solid residue of less than 0.1%. Unconsumed residue becomes an inclusion in the casting, causing porosity and surface pitting.

Natural and chemical waxes are used, including beeswax, candelilla wax, carnauba wax, ceresin wax, and paraffin wax. The specific gravities of all basic waxes and prepared wax compositions vary from 0.815 to 0.996, or slightly below 1.00 at 77° F (25° C). If a wax floats, its specific gravity is less than 1.00, which is that of water. (See page 512.) These are all solids that become viscous at a temperature range of 113–220° F (45–104° C). Each of them has different characteristics such as soft or hard, brittle or flexible, tough or elastic, dry or sticky, slippery or tacky. They are combined in certain compositions and proportions to produce a wax that has specific qualities. For example, beeswax and carnauba wax have little or no effect on the melting point of paraffin, but the composition is tougher. Certain combinations produce a wax with a glossy surface.

Composition waxes that melt at temperatures between approximately 136–250° F (57.7–121° C) are manufactured for use in dentistry and jewelry making to achieve the desirable casting qualities of low thermal expansion, ease in flow, and absence of residue after burnout, all of which are important in achieving a satisfactory casting. The ability of wax to flow at a certain temperature limits its thermal expansion, which relates to accuracy of reproduction, important in sized jewelry.

Oils and *fats* are added as a lubricant to aid in the movement of the solids in the heated wax composition when it becomes plastic and viscous. Animal fats are not

11-15   J. FRED WOELL, U.S.A. "First Class Fare." Pendant in cast silver, opened end. Made in several parts joined after casting to create three-dimensional and articulated forms. Height 2¾ in; width 3 in; depth 1 in. *Photo: J. Fred Woell*

11-16   SIANG FRONTIER DIVISION, N.E.F.A., INDIA. Traditional ornament, lost wax cast brass discs (*benyop*). Worn by young girls and women of the Gallong tribe, in various numbers on a cane string around the loins, the largest covering the pubic region, with the smaller, graduated sizes toward the thighs. After first child bearing, it is discarded, and given to a daughter or a female relative. Among the Khemsing tribe of N.E.F.A., women wear it as a necklace (*kamlolak*). The model is made from strands of a resin-wax compound, wound into spirals and ornamented with twisted pairs. After investment in a clay mold and wax elimination, it is cast by gravity pouring. *Photo: Victoria and Albert Museum, London, Crown Copyright*

11-17   SIANG FRONTIER DIVISION, N.E.F.A., INDIA. Young girl of the Gallong tribe, Village Siduk, wearing the *benyop*. *Photo: North East Frontier Agency, Photo Section, Shillong, Assam*

used in these waxes as when heated they tend to separate from the solids.

Resins provide luster and smoothness to the surface and prevent flaking and cracking. When molten wax cools and solidifies, it crystallizes and becomes rigid, and this condition is aided by the resins it contains. Natural resins added to wax compositions are copal, rosin, damar, and balsam, all derived from the sap of trees, and the insect-exuded resin: shellac.

Fillers are added for bulk. The fillers used are barite (a mineral), chalk, polyethylene plastic, pumice, soapstone (steatite), starch, and talc.

Additives such as solid aerosols are included in small amounts in rubber mold injection waxes to provide ease in removal from rubber and plastic molds.

TYPES OF WAX

Hard carving wax is used in subtractive methods of constructing a model. It is hard enough to be cut or carved with all cutting, carving, and scraping tools, wax files, drills, etc., and it can be turned on a lathe. It is not brittle, resists flaking and chipping, and does not adhere to cutting tool surfaces. It can be blended with a softer wax to make a wax having intermediate hardness, or flushed over a softer wax to make it possible to carve details into it.

Building or sculpture wax is a medium hard wax that is usually applied by additive methods such as melting it on a spatula and depositing it on the model in a liquid state, but can also be added in a solid state by welding on parts, to build up the model by successive additions of layers or sections. It remains plastic, can be bent, pinched, or carved, and keeps details well.

Soft wax is capable of being easily bent with or without warming, but is too soft for carving. It is used by itself to make a model, it can be added in a molten state to build a model, and it can be blended with a hard wax to give it more body. It is also used to seal joints.

Tacky wax sticks to an object without being heated when pressed against it, or will stick to itself. It is used to hold mounted metal parts in position while pouring an investment slurry around them to hold them together when preparing to solder them in cases where such a soldering position is otherwise difficult. When the investment sets, the tacky wax is removed, the parts are soldered, and then the investment plaster is removed.

Sticky wax is a hard, fast-setting wax that, when heated and pressed against an object and then allowed to cool, will stick to the object. It is used to lift a stone from a wax model setting, or from a metal bezel when testing it for size. It is also used for welding different kinds of waxes together, repairing wax models, and for joining sprues to a model.

Water-soluble wax is soluble in warm water. It is primarily used to make a core over which nonsoluble wax is placed; when the model is completed, the water-soluble wax is melted out, leaving a hollow. It can be hard enough to carve.

Injection wax is a plasticized wax containing polyethylene plastic and is the hardest of all waxes. It is used when making wax-injected patterns in rubber or metal molds. Its strength reduces the chance of model breakage, it allows easy removal from the mold, and it shrinks minimally.

In addition, manufacturers describe their wax by the function they are generally designed to perform, such as:

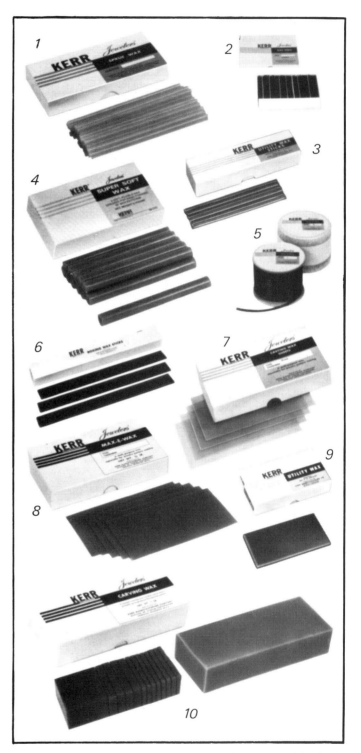

11–18 *MISCELLANEOUS FORMS AND TYPES OF KERR JEWELER'S PATTERN WAXES*

1. *Sprue wax,* for spruing and mounting the wax pattern.
2. *Wax wires,* boxed in assorted sizes.
3. *Utility wax sticks,* for buildup, filling small imperfections by rubbing on a surface, and for filling sprue bases.
4. *Super soft wax,* adheres to itself, has sufficient rigidity to resist bending or distortion, also used for spruing.
5. *Wax wire* in ¼ lb spool form.
6. *Boxing wax sticks,* slightly tacky, adheres readily to itself and other waxes without heat.
7. *Casting wax sheets,* flexible and transparent for tracing designs from paper.
8. *Max-e-wax sheets,* in regular or hard, pliable, multipurpose, boxed in assorted thicknesses.
9. *Utility wax sheets,* adhesive, for model buildup and other uses.
10. *Carving wax,* smooth, carvable and toolable, can be sawed, drilled, filed, and lathe turned, in 1 lb block bulk form, 3 × 7 × 1½ in, or sliced in various thicknesses.

1

Gauge	Actual Size										
	Round	Half-Round	Square	Rectangle	Ribbon	Bezel	Uncut Bezel	Triangle	3-prong	4-prong	6-prong
2											
4											
6											
8											
10											
12											
14											
16											
18											
20											

2

Gauge	Actual Size	
	Round	Half-Round
6		
8		
10		
12		
14		
16		
18		
20		

3

Gauge	Actual Thickness
22	
24	
26	
28	

4

Gauge	Actual Size
6	
8	
10	
12	
14	

5

Millimeter	Gauge	Actual Thickness
½ mm	23 gauge	
1 mm	18 gauge	
1½ mm	14 gauge	
2 mm	12 gauge	
3 mm	8 gauge	

11–19 CROSS-SECTIONAL SHAPES AND THICKNESSES OF VARIOUS WAX FORMS
1. Jeweler's wax wires in available cross-sectional shapes, 4 in lengths.
2. Jeweler's wax wire available in ¼ lb spools.
3. Jeweler's casting sheet wax, sheet 3 × 5½ in.
4. Jeweler's sprue wire wax, 4-in lengths.
5. Jeweler's sheet Max-e-wax, for maximum use, sheet 3 × 5½ in.

general purpose, build-up, modeling, sculpting, patching, welding, spruing, and casting.

FORMS OF WAX

Special forms of wax are made by several manufacturers for use in the dental and the jewelry industries. Generally all waxes made for these purposes are compatible. In the U.S.A. their gauges correspond with the Brown and Sharpe metal gauge system, and this should be understood wherever gauge is mentioned. In other countries it is available in millimeter thicknesses. The basic forms in which wax is available are wire, bars, sticks, sheet, blocks, bulk, and extruded shapes.

WAX WIRE   Wax wire is available in round, half-round, square, rectangular, and ribbon forms.
Round wire is available in 20, 18, 16, 14, 12, 10, 8, and 6 gauge diameters.
Half-round is available in 14, 12, 10, 8, and 6 gauge diameters.
Square wire is available in 14, 12, and 10 gauge diameters.
Rectangular wire is available in 12, 10, 8, 6, 4, and 2 gauge widths.
Ribbon or strip is available in 14, 12, 10, 8, 6, 4, and 2 gauge widths. It is thinner than rectangular wire.
Sprue wire, a round wire used for sprues, is available in round 10, 8, and 6 gauge diameters.
These are all available in 4 in (10.62 cm) lengths,

boxed. Round and half-round wire are also available in quarter-pound spools of continuous length.

WAX STICKS AND BARS   Wax sticks and bars are bulkier forms of wax sold in longer lengths and larger boxes.

WAX SHEET   Different waxes are available in boxed sheet, in 32, 30, 28, 26, 24, 22, 18, 14, 12, and 8 gauges. Not all types are available in this wide gauge range. A typical sheet size is 3 in × 5½ in (7.6 cm × 14 cm), and larger sheets are available in thicker gauges. Some sheet wax is thin and transparent enough to be placed over a design drawn on paper, and the silhouette then cut out with a sharp-bladed knife.

BLOCKS AND BULK   Wax sold in blocks is generally meant for carving. Bulk wax is meant for melting, casting, blending, and for pattern injection in rubber molds. It is available in blocks of 1 pound, and in cartons containing up to 50 pounds.

EXTRUDED WAX FORMS OF IRREGULAR SHAPE   The smallest irregularly shaped extruded wax form is stepped bezel wire. This is available in 10, 8, 6, 4, and 2 gauge B.&S. Another extruded form is round, 6 in (15.2 cm) long *ring tubes,* either solid or hollow, with an inside ring diameter of ⅝ in (1.59 cm). The hole can be in a centered position, or off-center, and one side of the tube can be left flat. Outer diameters of ⅞–1⅜ in (2.2–3.5 cm) are available. The wax that such ring tubes are made of is hard, which allows it to be cut with a saw into sections and used as a base upon which a ring model can be developed by carving or by building up with other waxes.

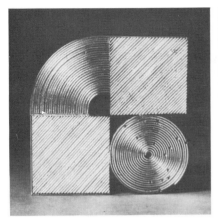

11–20 THOMAS GENTILLE, U.S.A. Pin of 18K cast gold. The model was made entirely of wax wires in flat, straight, curved, and spiral arrangements. The back has a different design. Size 3½ in square. Col.: Brenda Meredith. Photo: Otto Nelson

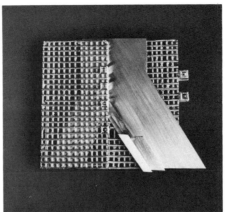

11–21 REINHOLD REILING, West Germany. Brooch in 785/1000 cast gold, with diamonds. The wire mesh was made of fine wax wires laid in opposing directions. Photo: E. Augenstein

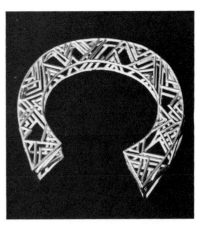

11–22 THOMAS GENTILLE, U.S.A. Bracelet in 14K cast gold, the cagework model constructed entirely of wax wires used dimensionally. Ø 9 cm; ends 3 cm; center 1 cm. Photo: Hans Christian Graber

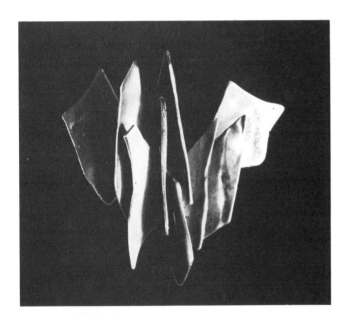

11–23 ALICIA PENALBA, France. Cast silver clip made of sheet wax used essentially in its original form, cut and shaped, then wax weld joined. Photo: Michel Chilo

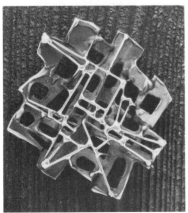

11–24 RONALD W. SENUNGETUK, Alaska, U.S.A. Pin cast in sterling silver. The wax model was made of a flat sheet backing pierced with holes, over which a wax wire structure was built, thickened at joints by the heat of a wax-welding tool. The ground is oxidized to contrast dimensionally with the polished wires. Photo: Howard Ringley

11–25 BAR AND TUBE RING STICK WAX
Wax suitable for carving, in 6 in lengths.
1. Round, solid bar.
2. Round, center hole tube.
3. Round, off-center hole tube.
4. Flat side tube.
5. Ring developments possible from these forms.
6. Outside diameter dimensions available are given. All tubes have ⅝ in IDs.

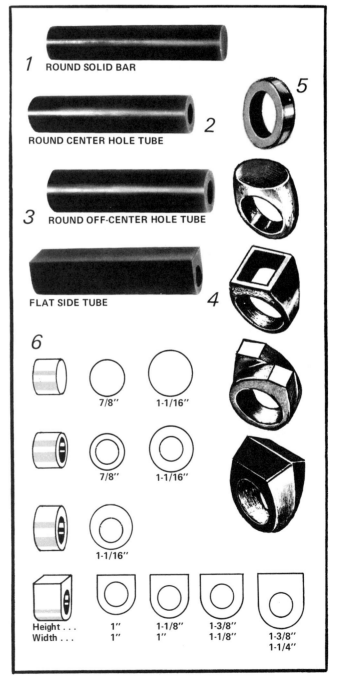

1 ROUND SOLID BAR

2 ROUND CENTER HOLE TUBE

3 ROUND OFF-CENTER HOLE TUBE

4 FLAT SIDE TUBE

5

6

7/8"   1-1/16"

7/8"   1-1/16"

1-1/16"

| Height . . . | 1" | 1-1/8" | 1-3/8" | |
| Width . . . | 1" | 1" | 1-1/8" | 1-3/8" 1-1/4" |

Colors are added to commercial waxes simply to identify a particular manufacturer's types. Color is a way of remembering which wax has been used to make which parts of a model. Unfortunately there is no standardization of colors among manufacturers to mean a particular type of wax. This kind of standardization would certainly be very helpful. Waxes are available in yellow, pink, orange, red, purple, blue, brown, green, black, and white.

NON-WAX MODEL MATERIALS

In a search for new effects and subjects, today's jewelers have used expendable materials other than wax to make a model. The prime requirement for any model material is that it *must burn out completely* in the mold and *leave no residue.* Theoretically, a casting can be made from objects found in nature made of suitable organic or inorganic materials. This may lead to the temptation to cast insects, leaves, plant buds, and the like. Their use for jewelry is a question of taste. Other artificial, expendable materials such as plastics and Styrofoam can also be used. In this case, precautions must be taken against breathing their fumes *which may be toxic.* Use a strong exhaust fan in a well-ventilated area.

WAX-MANIPULATING TOOLS AND MATERIALS

WAX-SHAPING TOOLS AND SURFACES

Heat is a basic tool for shaping, forming, and finishing wax. Starting with the heat from the fingers and hands, maximum 98.6° F (37° C), the next hotter heat source is warm to hot water, maximum 212° F (100° C). Beyond that, the heat from a flame is used. Flame heat is of course far greater than is needed to melt wax, therefore when shaping a model with a flame, pass it through the flame quickly, unless the wax is deliberately to be melted.

The alcohol lamp produces the best flame: one that burns clean with a minimum of free carbon, because if carbon is deposited on the wax model, its presence may cause the casting to be porous. Therefore, a candle flame is *not* recommended for use in model making because it causes carbon buildup on the model and contaminates it.

The best clean heat source is supplied by the flame of an *alcohol lamp* that uses *methanol* or *methyl alcohol* (CH$_3$OH) as a fuel. Alcohol is a light, volatile, inflammable liquid that boils at 148° F (64.5° C). It is made for industrial use by distillation from wood, for which reason it is commonly called wood alcohol or wood spirit. It is also made by synthesis from carbon monoxide and hydrogen under high pressure in the presence of catalysts. It is also called denatured alcohol because a poisonous substance is added to it to make it impalatable, otherwise it is like ordinary ethyl alcohol in most properties. *Ethyl* or *ethanol alcohol* (C$_2$H$_5$OH) is obtained from fruits, grains, and vegetables that have undergone fermentation, and is commonly called proof spirit or common alcohol. It can also be used as a fuel, but is more expensive than methanol alcohol.

Bunsen burners can also be used as a heat source by adjusting the flame to a carbon-free blue. When using any flame, place it against a dark background to make it more visible and to reduce eye strain.

11-26 SPIRIT LAMPS AND BUNSEN BURNERS
1. *Glass dental lamp with screw-adjustable wick and cap that prevents fuel evaporation; bowl Ø 2½ in; capacity 1½–3½ oz.*
2. *Glass lamp with flat sides, allowing any angle position; Ø 3⁵⁄₁₆ in; wick, ³⁄₁₆ in.*
3. *Spherical glass lamp resting in nontipping nickel-plated metal base, adjustable to any angle; Ø 3 in; capacity 5 oz.*
4. *Tin lamp with hinged flame extinguisher.*
5. *Portable brass lamp with screw-on cover.*
6. *Oval brass lamp.*
7. *High heat Bunsen burner with needle valve gas control, and air control; for either artificial or natural gas, height 4½ in, used with ¼ in tubing.*
8. *Horizontal Bunsen burner for use with city gas or propane gas.*

Wax presses or extrusion syringes fitted with a die shape at the wax exit end are used to extrude wax wires and rods in long lengths. These can be purchased or improvised. An electrically heated wax extrusion device called a *Matt Gun* is available. A hard but flexible wax in the form of a pellet is inserted into the gun. To assure wax wire results of even diameter, hold the gun 3 inches above a flat wooden table surface, and press the feed rod. Move the gun at a regular rate in a straight line across the surface. The wires emerge from the nozzle, whose size can be changed. Long lengths of wax wire can be used in any manipulation method, but are especially suited to interworked processes such as braiding, knotting, weaving, or crocheting.

Mandrels are used to form *curved models* such as rings or bracelets. To facilitate the removal of the wax model

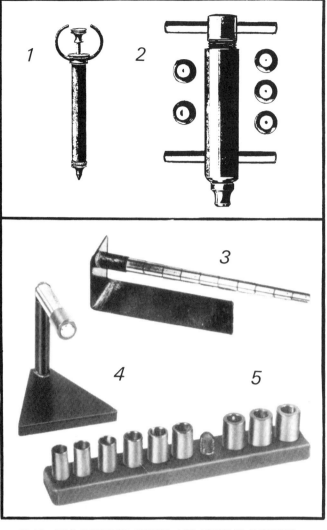

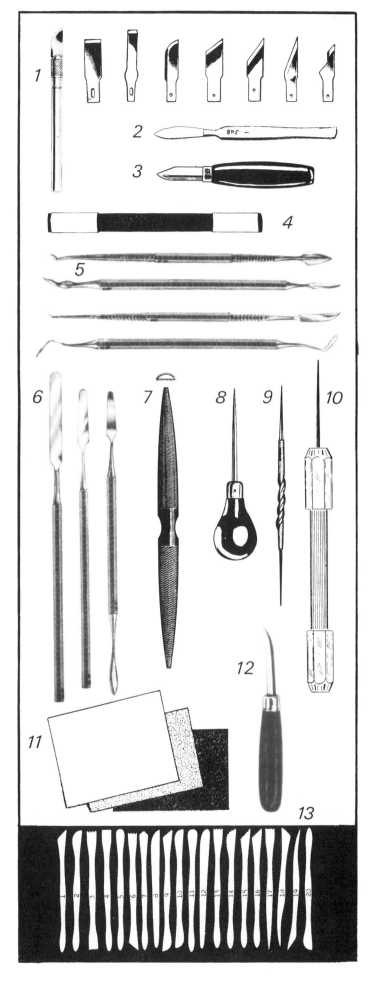

11–27 WAX EXTRUSION PRESSES AND FORMING MANDRELS

1. *Syringe* for extruding liquid wax into wire.
2. *Wax press* for extruding wax wires, with interchangeable dies in various sizes and shaped openings.
3. *Stepped ring mandrel* for table use, rotatable while in stand, or detachable for hand use when working on wax models of rings to assure size accuracy; also used in setting stones.
4. *Kerr ring mandrel* consisting of an aluminum die-cast stand that holds short, sized, marked, machined, hardened, anodized aluminum *ring sleeves* that can be smoothly rotated fully on the stand arbor, or hand held. Wax models are easily released from the mandrels.
5. Set of *full-sized ring sleeves*, sizes 4–13 (15–22 mm) with storage stand, for use on the Kerr mandrel; half sizes are also available. The heat from molten wax is quickly absorbed, which allows faster wax buildup.

11–28 WAX-MANIPULATING TOOLS AND MATERIALS

1. *X-Acto knife* with metal handle, blade chuck, and interchangeable blades of various shapes, 1–2 in long, ¼–½ in wide.
2. *Stainless steel scalpel*, 6 in long, 1⅝ in handle.
3. *Bench knife* with wood handle, total length 5 in, steel blade length 1¾ in.
4. *Spiral-toothed saw blades*, 5 in long, can be used for cutting wax, plastic, and rubber in any direction without changing saw handle direction.
5. *Wax carvers* of stainless steel with serrated handles, in several shapes for carving, shaping, and patching wax models, used with heat, approximately 7 in long.
6. *Spatulas* of stainless steel, approx. 7 in long, blade 1⅛–2 in long.
7. *Wax file*, double ended, for shaping wax models, does not easily clog, and is cleanable, length 8 in.
8. *Awl*, 5 in long, blade length 2¾ in, used cold.
9. *Scriber*, 7 in long, used cold.
10. *Pin vise*, 3¼ in long, with double-ended chucks, jaw capacity 0–3 mm.
11. *Abrasive papers* for shaping and finishing hard wax models.
12. *Burnisher* with curved blade, available in lengths 1½–3 in.
13. *Boxwood clay modeling tools*, can also be used to model soft wax and for carving, 6 in long.

from these mandrels without distortion, first lubricate the mandrel with a thin film of glycerin or a light oil, or wrap it with a thin plastic film. Rings are commonly built up to the desired shank diameter on a *sized ring mandrel* for size accuracy. Construct a ring model one size smaller than needed to allow for postcasting finishing operations in which the inner ring shank is enlarged. Bracelets are formed on *bracelet mandrels*. Smooth metal or plastic rods of any size can also be used as mandrels as long as they are prelubricated. Do not use a porous material without wrapping a plastic film around it first or the wax will adhere to it.

Plate glass slabs are used to construct *flat models*. When working directly on glass first coat it with a thin film of lubricant to facilitate wax model removal. When forming dimensional models on a flat surface, a core of water-soluble wax of the proper shape can be laid down first and the model built up on it with regular waxes. Later, the water-soluble wax is melted away leaving the rest in the desired form. A piece of white paper placed under a plate glass working surface will help in making visible unwanted foreign matter.

WAX-CUTTING, -CARVING, AND -SCRAPING TOOLS

Knives and *scalpels* in any shape are used to cut wax, depending on the need. *Razors* can be used to cut or scrape wax, as can old *dental carving tools*. These tools can be used cold or hot. Hard wax mounted on a *lathe* can be cut with any *pointed metal tool* while the lathe rotates. A *jeweler's saw* and *blade* can be used to sever wax. *Files* made especially for removing wax or soft materials can be used. Do not use regular metal-cutting files which are ruined by the presence of grease. If such a file is used, it must thereafter be reserved for use with wax. Hard wax can be carved with *chisels,* or even *engraved* to create details or linear patterns. A *flex-shaft bur* can be used to remove wax. All waste wax can be saved and used for building-up processes using heat.

WAX-PIERCING TOOLS

Any *pointed metal tool* of suitable size can be used to pierce wax, either while cold or when heated. *Needles* mounted in a wooden dowel handle are used to make small holes in wax and also to transfer small amounts of wax to a model under construction. Larger holes can be made with a *heated round wire*. An *awl* can be used. *Hand drills, power drills, rotary files,* and metal *burs* can be used for hole making and to remove wax, and are not spoiled by contact with wax.

WAX-MODELING TOOLS

Metal spatulas can be used cold or heated to model wax by pressure. *Wood spatulas* and *clay modeling tools* of any shape can also be used. *Burnishers* can be used to press down the wax surface or shape it.

WAX-WELDING TOOLS

Wax-welding tools are a very important group of tools greatly depended upon to work up or build up a wax model. They are always *heated* to shape the wax in its most plastic state. The most common wax-welding tool is an *all-metal spatula* with cup-shaped tip, single or double ended, 5½–6½ in (14–16.5 cm) long. To transfer wax to

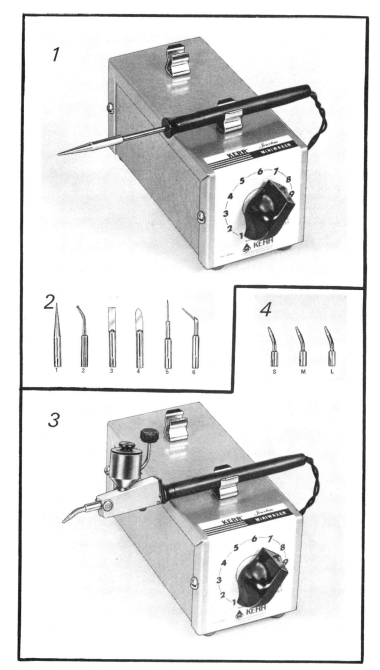

11–29 ELECTRIC WAX WELDER AND PEN
1. *Kerr miniwax* welder with electrically heated tips for carving, adding, texturing, smoothing, and finishing wax models. The heat control allows a wide range of heat levels. Available with 115 or 230 volts.
2. *Individual tips,* interchangeable, used with the welder in tapered-point, ball-point, flat-spatula, spoon-spatula, straight-needle, and bent-needle shapes.
3. *Kerr miniwax pen* used in wax buildup on a model, detail development, and texturing. Wax is placed in the reservoir bowl, the desired heat level is selected on the control, and by pressing the release knob, a continuous flow of wax is deposited through the tip. Available with 115 or 230 volts.
4. *Small, medium, and large tips* used with the miniwax pen.

a model, apply the heat to the tool shank—*not to its tip end*—by passing it through the flame or holding it there for a short while. Then touch it to the wax, which melts onto the horizontally held spatula end, where it stays. Heat the shank again briefly and deposit the wax on the model. To remove wax from the tool, heat it and wipe it off on a clean cloth. The same heated tool alone can be used to smooth the surface of a wax model, to shape it, and also to remove wax from the model.

Electric wax-welding tools can be set by thermostatic controls at any desired temperature needed by a particular wax to carve, weld, sprue, texture, smooth, or otherwise work and finish the wax model. They are available with interchangeable, differently shaped tips. *Electric waxing pens* are mounted with a small reservoir filled with liquid wax that is dispensed by pressing a release knob to deposit controlled amounts of wax on the model. In effect, they are electrified versions of the *tjanting tool* used in Java to dispense hot wax in batik work.

Paintbrushes dipped in molten wax can be used to apply wax to a model, but this must be done quickly before the wax solidifies. Liquid wax can also be dispensed from a heated *glass eyedropper* or a heated *glass* or *metal syringe*. Wax can be kept in a molten state ready for use by placing it in a metal container over a small alcohol flame, or by using an *electric wax-melting pot* with automatic temperature control. Molten wax can be poured into molds.

WAX-FINISHING MATERIALS

Various materials are used for finishing the wax model. depending on the type of wax used. Soft waxes are smoothed by passing the model quickly through a flame. Hard waxes can be smoothed with *sandpaper, abrasive papers,* or by rubbing with a moist *chamois leather,* or with care, on a *polishing lathe* using a soft cotton buff or brush reserved for this purpose only, and a short dwell time.

PREPARING THE WAX MODEL

The wax model is of prime importance as its degree of perfection determines the quality of the resulting casting in metal. When making a wax model, the maker must form the mental habit of visualizing its appearance translated into metal—which makes concrete all the plastic properties of wax. To learn what these properties are and take full advantage of them, the beginner must experiment with all kinds of wax in all the ways described below, then select those directions that are most appealing and challenging.

Besides esthetic considerations, the model maker must also keep in mind practical considerations such as ultimate metal weight and size in relation to flask size. Unnecessary thickness in the model should be avoided, but on the other hand, the wax should not be so thin that the model cannot be cast without the risk of the metal being unable to fill the mold cavity. If stones are to be used, ways must be solved in advance for their placement and retention. (See Preparing a Wax Model for a Stone Setting in this chapter.) If the casting is to be combined with fabricated parts, the means of joining them must also be planned in advance. In other words, the maker must develop a habit of thinking the work process through from the beginning to the end and try to anticipate and solve problems that may arise.

BASIC WAX CONSTRUCTION CONCEPTS

Because of the many possible approaches to the use of wax in model making, only some general points will be mentioned here about construction. Wax can be used by

11–30 IRENA BRYNNER, Switzerland. Cast gold wedding ring with diamonds and gray baroque pearls. The fluid character of the surface results from flaming the finished wax model. Photo: Tommy Yee

only *slightly modifying the original form* in which it is purchased as sheet, wire, and rod so that these forms are still recognizable as such in the results. Models can be *built up* by utilizing the structural possibilities of the wax and adding wax to wax so that ultimately the original wax form is lost. A model can be constructed by *subtractive means,* that is, by starting with a larger mass and removing wax from it with tools as is done in stone sculpture. And wax can be *melted to a liquid* to fill a mold and create a form that has no relation whatever to the raw forms of wax. Combinations of these concepts are of course also possible. Examples of these various approaches to the wax as a raw material are seen in the illustrations. Specific techniques in wax manipulation are described below.

The choice of approach to the wax determines the kind of wax used. A particular design concept may suggest the kind of wax needed for its realization. In general, structural forms are best begun with an *armature* or framework of a hard wax such as sprue wax because it can withstand handling and higher temperatures, and will maintain the rigidity of the form built up upon it. Medium hard and softer waxes can then be used to build up wax veneers to develop the shape and contours, and details and textures can be made in hard wax.

The aim in model buildup is to make the model *as complete as possible* to reduce to an absolute minimum the work of finishing the metal casting. The final model must be complete in size, surface, and details such as texture and stone-holding devices. After *flaming* or passing the model briefly through the flame as a possible final smoothing process, its surface should be left smooth and glossy, and the model is then ready to be sprued.

BASIC TECHNIQUES OF WAX MANIPULATION IN MODEL BUILDING

The techniques that follow are used to form a wax model for casting. They can be divided into several major classifications of methods used to manipulate the wax: *manual manipulation,* in which the wax is shaped by hands and fingers alone without any removal or addition; *pressure,* in which a tool or surface is used to force the wax to achieve a form; *mechanical manipulation,* in which the wax is altered by the use of a tool that divides, removes, or otherwise shapes it.

Heat plays an essential part in shaping wax. The degree to which the wax is subjected to the heat source determines whether it is simply softened, surface melted, or liquefied. Of the heating manipulation methods, the most important is *welding,* in which heat is used, with or without a tool, to join otherwise cold parts at localized positions. *Fusing* is the joining of parts to create a form by subjecting the wax to heat that causes it to slump and change shape, or by sufficiently softening its surface so that it adheres to other surfaces. *Melting* includes any method in which the wax is first turned into a liquid state.

MANUAL MANIPULATIONS

When handling any wax, *cleanliness* is very important. Dust or small particles adhering to the surface of the model will be reproduced in the casting, and therefore must be avoided.

Bending and shaping: Wax in sheet, wire, or rod form can be bent while it is immersed in water warm enough to render it plastic, approximately 140° F (77.7° C).

Twisting: Sheet or wire can be twisted under water warm enough to allow it to be so manipulated without breaking or melting.

Stretching: While in a softened, plastic state, wax can be stretched to a limited extent, depending on the particu-

11–31 BJÖRN WECKSTRÖM, Finland, designer; manufacturer Lapponia Jewelry Ltd., Helsinki. "Kneeling Woman." Brooch in cast sterling silver with spectrolite. The model was made of wax forms softened, cut, bent, and twisted while warm and plastic. Photo: Winfrid Zakowski, courtesy Lapponia Jewelry Ltd.

11–32 EMILE SOUPLY, Belgium. "La rosée est une longue patience." Cast sterling silver pendant with carved ivory rose, and blue pearl. The panel made of wax wires in an interwoven net was pressed flat, then cast, and mounted in a fabricated frame. Symbolically, the white rose represents virginity and perfection, but roses in general have erotic connotations, one in full bloom corresponding to the beauty of the loved one. This rose is enhanced by a fresh pearly dewdrop (rosée), the moisture of sustenance. Nets symbolize entanglement, the power to capture and bind. Height 17 mm; width 10.5 mm. Photo: Morian

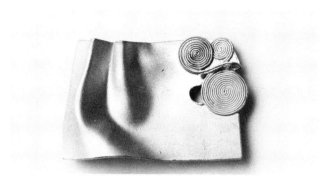

11–33 MAX FRÖHLICH, Switzerland. Brooch cast in 18K yellow gold, using the elemental wax forms. On a dimensionalized sheet of 22 gauge B.&S. sheet wax, wax spirals are pressed only enough to make contact to prevent form distortion. Size 50 × 75 mm. Photo: N. Monkewitz

lar wax. If only a *part* of the wax is *heated locally,* that part alone can be made to stretch. A dome can be formed in a sheet by heating only that area and pressing it upward with the thumb. A wire can be diminished locally in cross section by stretching.

Braiding, weaving: Wax wire, when made plastic by warmth can be braided or woven to form a texture, employing wire of the same or varying dimensions. The result can be left as it is and incorporated into a design, or flattened, and otherwise shaped.

Spiraling: Wire can be shaped into spiral forms, flat, or dimensionally around a mandrel such as a wooden dowel.

PRESSURE MANIPULATIONS BY TOOLS OR SURFACES

Extrusion: Waxes can be forced into rod or wire forms of any cross-sectional shape by pressing molten wax through a *wax press,* or *syringe* mounted with an opening die of any contour. Extrusions can be laid straight in any length, or can be guided to form curved configurations by trailing them onto a cold, flat glass slab, lightly lubricated to facilitate removal once the wax has solidified. The result can be used in this form, totally, partially, or with modifications.

Rolling: A preformed shape of wax in sheet, rod, wire, or any combination of these can be passed over with a smooth roller or pressed flat with a wood block to flatten it.

Positive relief textures or forms: A roller with a textured surface, or carved with *intaglio* forms will impart the pattern *in relief* to the wax surface over which it is rolled.

Negative intaglio impression textures and forms: A negative surface texture can be formed on a sheet of wax by pressing a softened wax sheet directly onto *fabricated material* such as a textile or a wire screen (or the object can be pressed onto the wax), then passing a roller over it. Any *natural object* such as a leaf, a stone, or a crystal having a textured surface, can be used in this way.

Press molding: Solid but plastic wax made warm by kneading it in the fingers, by warming it over heat to a point short of melting, or by submerging it in warm water, can then be pressed into a *permanent* or *temporary* mold made of metal, clay, paper, charcoal, cuttlebone, etc., to take its image or surface. The result can be cast separately and applied to flat or curved metal

11–34 MAX FRÖHLICH, Switzerland. Pendant in cast 18K yellow gold. The basic forms of each unit were first modeled in plaster, and the wax sheet was pressed upon this, then the wax wires were applied. *Photo: Max Fröhlich*

11–36 EMILE SOUPLY, Belgium. "Le Marabout." Brooch/pendant in 18K cast yellow gold with crab claw and two white pearls. The wax sheet has been impressed on a textured surface, then shaped. *Photo: Morian*

surfaces, used as a unit in an assemblage, or joined to another wax form, then cast. The mold may have to be treated first with a suitable parting substance such as talc, oil, liquid soap, or glycerin, depending on what it is made of.

Using mandrels and forming surfaces: Mandrels are any forms of metal, wood, cardboard, or other material formed into a basic shape, and then used to give shape to a wax model under construction. The wax can be pressed around a *bracelet mandrel,* for instance, to

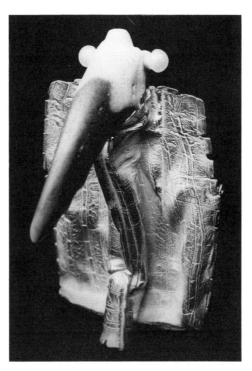

11–35 HAROLD O'CONNOR, U.S.A. Cast sterling silver cuff links. Their surface texture is a reproduction taken from a piece of iron-stone-clay, accomplished by using an elastometric impression material with a polysulphide or silicone base. Kerr Permlastic impression compound was used here, but Kerr Elasticon or other similar preparations can also be used. These compounds are used by dentists in restorative dentistry, as when making crown or inlay impressions. It is sold in two tubes, one containing the *base* (in the case of polysulphide containing 80% polysulphide polymer and 20% inorganic filler such as zinc oxide, calcium sulphate or silica); the other the *catalyst* or *accelerator* (containing 78% lead peroxide, 3% sulphur, and 19% inert oil). The base is usually white and the accelerator brown to assure uniform mixing, indicated when both colors are completely blended. The compound is available in light, regular, or heavy body forms, used according to preference. Both ingredients are mixed in equal parts (or according to manufacturer's instructions), then thickly spread on the dry, clean surface to be duplicated. After a 10–15 minute curing time, the compound sets and can be peeled away, as it is elastic, tough, and springs over even severe undercuts without tearing or breaking. The mold is accurate, minutely detailed, dimensionally stable, and compatible with gypsum or electroforming baths. In this case, a positive was made from the mold by applying liquid wax with a brush to the mold cavity, building it up to the desired thickness. Upon hardening, the wax was removed by stretching the mold. Any textured surface or form can be reproduced, and the mold is reusable. *Photo: Ron Burton*

11–37 LYNDA WATSON-ABBOTT, U.S.A. Neckpiece in cast 900 coin silver. The model was made by pressing wax sheets into a mold made of cut-out cardboard parts. Other parts were fabricated. *Photo: Lynda Watson-Abbott*

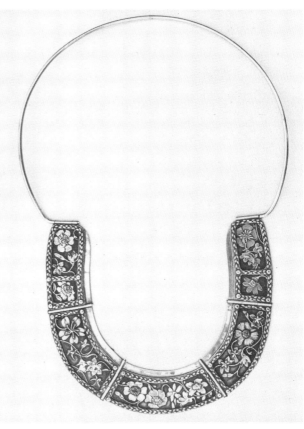

create its initial shape or a *ring mandrel* can be used to make a ring model of an accurate, specific size. This basic wax form can then be developed by additive methods used in wax forming.

Adding a casting to an existing surface: In some cases, wax models are made into castings that must fit an irregularly shaped surface of an object that already exists in metal. The process is called casting-on. The wax can be pressed onto that shape in the desired position and be made to conform exactly to it. When cast, it fits closely and can be successfully soldered in place without alteration. This is what a dentist does when he makes an inlay.

Spreading soft wax upon hard: Soft wax can be spread over the surface of a hard wax sheet to create a rough-textured surface by pressing it with an unheated *spatula*.

Burnishing: Wax surfaces can be cold smoothed with a metal or hard stone *burnisher* lubricated with liquid soap into which the tool is dipped at intervals as required (the tool will otherwise skip and not work smoothly). The surface becomes compressed and shiny, lightly streaked with the tool strokes. A piece of soft *chamois leather* can also be used to burnish wax.

MECHANICAL MANIPULATIONS

CUTTING

Cold: Wax that has been warmed slightly so that cut edges do not splinter can be cut with any *sharp-bladed tool* such as a *scalpel* or *single-edge razor blade*. Thick, hard wax can be cut with a *jeweler's saw frame* and a No. 4 blade.

Hot: All wax can be cut with a *heated metal scalpel*. Metal dental tools made of stainless steel have thin blades that are quickly heated while the handle stays cool to the touch. They are also used for trailing and carving wax.

PIERCING

Cold: All wax can be pierced to make regular or irregular openings. A *drill, awl, broach, needle,* or any other piercing tool is suitable.

Hot: Piercing is facilitated by first heating any of the above tools. However in this case, a residual ridge of molten wax will form around the shape of the opening, but it can be scraped away if undesirable. Cold piercing does not result in such a ridge.

CARVING, TRIMMING, OR SCRAPING

A subtractive method of forming, carving can be done with any cold cutting tool. To remove large amounts of wax quickly from bulkier models, use a heated tool.

FILING

Wax can be removed by the use of special *nonclogging wax files,* or by single-cut, rasp- or curved-tooth files of a coarseness suited to the material. Avoid clogging fine files with wax.

SANDING

Wax can be removed and surfaces smoothed by the use of various grades of *sandpapers* and other types of *abrasive papers*. Do not allow any particles of abrasive material to become embedded in the wax as these can cause imperfect castings.

11–38 DIETER MÜLLER-STACH, U.S.A. "Neptune's Admiration." Neckpiece cast in sterling silver. The seaweedlike model forms were cut from wax sheets, the parts cast separately, then joined by hinges and ball and socket joints. Rainbow-colored oxidation. Length 13 in; width 6½ in. *Photo: Dieter Müller-Stach*

11–39 EMILE SOUPLY, Belgium. "Pendant 7424." Cast sterling silver. The model was formed of scraped wax surfaces. *Photo: Yves Auquier*

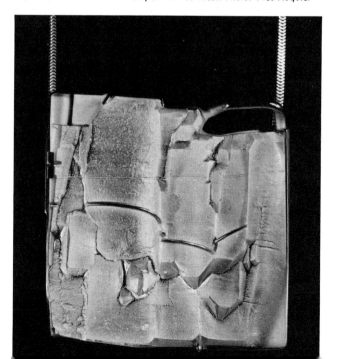

11–40 *BAR OF HARD CARVING WAX BEING TURNED ON A UNIMAT LATHE WITH CARVING TOOLS* The result can be invested and cast as a unit, then used as such, or divided into parts. *Photo: Ron Burton, courtesy Harold O'Connor*

11–41 FLORENCE TAYLOR, U.S.A. Cast sterling silver brooch with peg-mounted pearl. The model was made of 24 gauge B.&S. sheet wax held over a flame to soften it, then crushed to shape. The small balls were made by dropping molten wax from a heated spatula onto the surface. Ø 2½ in. *Photo: Florence Taylor*

11–42 JUHANI LINNOVAARA, Finland, designer; manufacturer Lapponia Jewelry Ltd., Helsinki. The upper white gold unit is stamped sheet metal, fixed by rivets to the lower, cast yellow gold unit. The highly polished, flowingly contoured top unit contrasts with, and threatens to envelop the roughly textured, rigidly rectangular lower unit. *Photo: Winfrid Zakowski, courtesy Lapponia Jewelry Ltd.*

11–43 JACLYN DAVIDSON, U.S.A. "The Rumor." Cast sterling silver ring. The model surface was tool scraped to create texture. *Photo: J. David Long*

TEXTURING

Cold: Any wax surface can be textured by using a cold tool to score, scratch, or otherwise mark it. The effects depend on the nature of the tool.

Hot: A heated tool will produce yet another range of textural surfaces. Experiment on scrap wax to discover effects that can be achieved.

LATHE TURNING

Solid rods or bars of wax of suitable hardness—usually those types containing plastic additives—can be mounted on a *lathe* and turned to any shape. Such shapes can then be cast. Turned parts can be reproduced in quantity by means of a *rubber mold*. The resulting casting can be mounted on the lathe, trued to a desired accuracy, or further refined in shape or detail.

HEAT MANIPULATIONS

WELDING

Welding in connection with wax forming is the joining of wax elements to each other by the use of heat applied directly to the wax at the join of parts. This can be done by heat applied with a flame, or by the use of a heated tool, which offers the model maker more control. Sheet wax can be joined in butt or lap joints. Be sure that every join is complete or structural weakness will result in the model. Wire and rod can be joined to like forms or to other wax forms by drawing a heated tool along their point of juncture.

FUSING

Wax in any form or combination of forms can be laid in a pattern on top of each other and the whole subjected to sufficient heat from above with a flame to fuse them into one unit. All or parts of such fused forms can be used in creating a model. The fusing can take place on shaped surfaces to give the result a particular basic configuration or form, a method that can be called *slump molding,* or *slump fusing.*

MELTING

In this category are all forms of wax manipulation in which the desired form is achieved by first bringing the wax to a molten state.

Dripping round dots or lumps: Round dots or lumps of similar or different shape and size can be formed on any wax surface by heating small amounts of wax on a *spatula* to a molten state, and allowing the wax to drip from the tool onto the desired place in the wax model. If the wax is dripped while too hot, the ball will tend to be

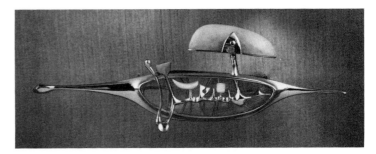

11–44 SVETOZAR RADAKOVICH, U.S.A. Cast pin in 18K yellow gold, with white jade and ivory. The highly refined forms were made of a model whose parts were carefully welded together to reduce finishing processes to a minimum. Length 3 in. *Photo: Svetozar Radakovich*

flattened, but if the wax is allowed to cool somewhat before dripping, it will be more rounded. Small, fine spheres are made from wax on a heated *needle mounted in a wooden dowel,* and a spatula is used for making larger spheres. *Automatic wax-heating tools* are now available that keep wax at a desired temperature. Ball making is simplified with such a tool.

Trailing: Wax in liquid form can be trailed from a heated tool or a suitable heated container holding molten wax such as a *glass medicine dropper* or a *syringe* onto edges or surfaces of wax models. Mechanically heated waxing tools are also good for this purpose.

Modeling or building up: Wax can be built up and quickly added to the model by the use of a *brush* dipped into molten wax, while it remains in a molten state.

Spreading: Immediately after application while wax is still soft enough, it can be spread with a *metal or wood spatula* over the surface before it sets.

Blowing: Excess *molten* wax can be blown away, as when increasing a hole size freshly made in sheet wax with a heated tool.

Flame smoothing: The wax surface of a model can be made smooth by quickly passing it through or near an *alcohol flame* (low in carbon), or by passing a flame over a stationary model. This is often done as a final stage in wax shaping to eliminate undesirable tool marks. Wax should not be overheated more than slightly above its melting point as this causes brittleness and excessive shrinkage on cooling. Too much flame heating can reduce sharp detail and make the model look too soft.

Flame shaping: Forms can be deliberately created by simply subjecting the wax to the flame and allowing it to melt away parts, edges, or make holes. A small, round ball can be formed at the end of an upright projecting wax rod to be used as a prong in setting stones in a jewel.

Free pouring: Molten wax can be dripped or poured freely onto a surface or into water without any restraining container to give it form as it solidifies. The resulting forms are completely accidental, formed by the nature of the material and its interaction with the contacting surface. Its appearance may be determined in part by the particular material upon which the wax is poured or trailed. A flat, cold glass slab will produce one effect; a metal surface, a container of cold water, a surface of crushed ice, or snow, others. It is possible to cast these results as they occur, further manipulate them by heat, or to use selected parts in a design assembly combined with other techniques of wax model making, or other methods of fabrication.

Controlled pouring: Casting wax: Molten wax can be poured into any mold from which the resulting casting can be easily removed without major distortion. Suitable mold material can be clay, paper, cardboard, lead, charcoal, a cuttlebone, built-up Masonite, Styrofoam, etc. Each material has its own character that can be exploited to advantage. To ease removal of the model, it may be necessary to first prime the mold surface with a parting material such as oil, talc dust, powdered graphite, liquid soap, or whatever is most suited to the particular material.

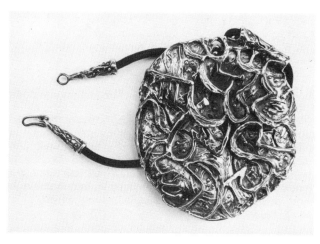

11–45 ALICE SHANNON, U.S.A. Pendant in cast 14K gold. Surface pattern and texture were developed by trailing molten wax on a sheet wax ground, and by tool modeling. *Photo: Ron James*

11–46 BARBARA ENGLE, Hawaii, U.S.A. Pendant in cast sterling silver with ivory beads. The model was made by pouring molten wax from a height into cold water where it solidified in a chance pattern. *Photo: Francis Haar*

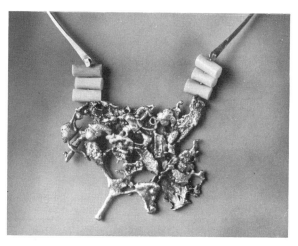

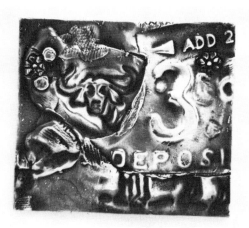

11–47 J. FRED WOELL, U.S.A. "3¢ Buffalo." Cast silver pin. The model was made by first making plaster molds from a number of relief surfaces. After plaster set and removal from the surface, the mold was soaked to saturation in water; hot wax was poured into the cavity and allowed to solidify to the desired thickness, the surplus then poured out. The wet plaster released the wax casting easily. A collage was made using several castings, cutting and welding them to make a unit. The result was then cast. Height 1¾ in; width 2⅛ in; depth ⁵⁄₁₆ in. *Photo: J. Fred Woell*

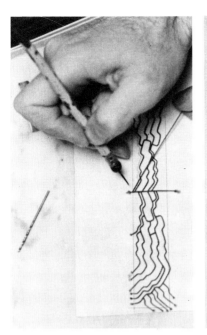
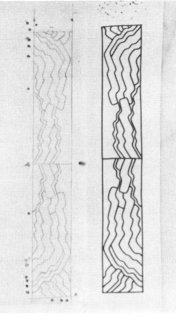

1   2   3   4

WAX-IN-WAX INLAY

DEMONSTRATION 22

THOMAS GENTILLE forms a rigid bracelet
exploiting wax characteristics

Photos: Hans Christian Graber

1 The design is constructed in 20 gauge, green, round wax wire, which is hard and can withstand the pressure to which it will later be subjected without deforming. All gauges mentioned here are B.&S. gauge. The pencil line drawing on the paper beneath is followed precisely. To avoid differences in depth, all the wire is of the same gauge. One end is anchored to the paper by touching it with a heated tool, while the other is manipulated and finally also anchored at its terminating end, both times *outside* the design margin. The excess is later trimmed away. The paper therefore supports the wire construction. To help bend the wire into curves, any stiff, round rod, such as the *drill* seen here, can be used as a *mandrel*. The improvised forming tool used here is a favorite with the demonstrator, made of the pointed end of a needle, the eye end cut off and forced into rubber eraser mounted on a pencil.

2 The line design is seen here in the original line drawing, and in reverse in the wax, now removed from the paper after the surplus ends were trimmed. It has been framed with the same gauge wax wire to prevent its becoming distorted in this transfer. If desired, such a frame could be removed after inlay. At the top right are small wax slivers used with a *heated tool* to fill each juncture, first at the front before removal, and then at the back after removal. Welding the junctures on both sides is necessary to prevent the wire from coming apart during the pressure of inlaying.

3 For the ground, a special wax is prepared consisting of equal amounts of beeswax (bleached or unbleached) and microcrystalline wax, a combination that is

softer than the hard wire wax later inlaid into it. It is dark brown in color. These ingredients are *measured in volume while liquid,* stirred well to combine them, and poured into a level, improvised container made of a sheet of aluminum foil with edges bent up. Here the wax solidifies into a slab approximately 5/16 in (7.9 mm) thick but any thickness is possible. A portion of the result was cut off and is being heated over an *alcohol lamp* to soften it.

4 The wax is kneaded into a long, flat shape of uniform thickness, somewhat larger in dimension than needed to cover the wire inlay pattern. In this process, it is necessary to reheat the wax several times to keep it plastic. The total finished length is approximately 6¾ in × 1¾ in (17.1 cm × 4.4 cm).

5 The wax wire pattern is placed on a paper having a slight texture, and the base wax, while still warm and pliable, is laid over it. Starting at one end, it is pressed down with the fingers, working toward the other end. The

5   6

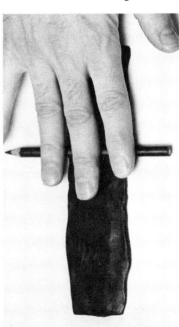

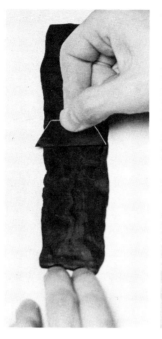
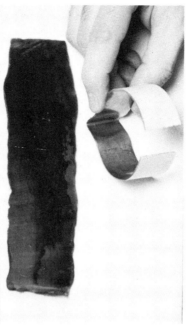
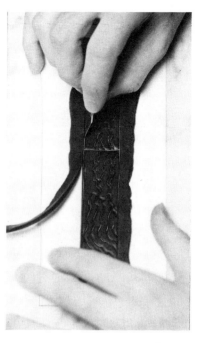

| 7 | 8 | 9 | 10 |

texture of the paper (or other supporting substance) is important as this registers on the wax surface and becomes a part of the final cast surface. The supporting material must allow easy release of the wax when it is removed, and its suitability for this can be tested with a scrap of the same wax before use. With the fingers, the base wax is pressed over its total surface to be sure the pattern wax is inlaid equally into the base wax. To see if the inlay is sufficient and uniform, lift the wax from the paper for inspection.

6 To further embed the inlay, a *round pencil* or *dowel* is rolled over the base wax with firm but gentle pressure, an action that also serves to level the back. After every few passes of the roller, the front side is checked to see if any area needs additional pressure.

7 Here the paper is pulled away, showing the wire wax inlaid into the base wax.

8 The wax is returned face down to the same surface

and scraped with a straight steel edge such as the *mat blade* used here, to level the back and reduce it to the desired uniform thickness. In this process, the blade may unintentionally gouge into the wax at either end of the stroke, or nick an edge, for which reason the surplus has been left. Since the surplus will be removed, such an event is not as disastrous as it might otherwise be, and does not require time-consuming repairs. The blade is heated over the alcohol flame because, when warm, it will easily slide the entire length without leaving unwanted terminal stroke deposits or freezing in mid-stroke. After a few passes, any wax that accumulates on the blade can be removed with the fingers, and when the blade is heated, any remaining wax can be removed with a *paper towel*.

9 The base wax is shown here scraped level on the reverse side. On the right is an 18 gauge B.&S. rigid sheet of copper formed into a *mandrel* for shaping the wax to the bracelet form. A smooth paper has been rubber cemented to the outer surface which will contact the wax, to assure its easy removal.

10 The model is placed face side up and the surplus wax trimmed away with a slightly warmed, *sharp blade*. At this point, the inlay wire frame could have been cut away if desired, but it is retained here as a part of the design.

11 Here is the resulting wax model whose final thickness is approximately 9 gauge B.&S. A portion of surplus wax has been left outside the frame at either end to provide detail-free pressure points when shaping the wax over the mandrel, and to serve as easy positions for the attachment of the sprues for casting.

12 To facilitate the removal of the wax from the mandrel after the model is bent to shape, a coat of household oil is first spread over the paper glued to the mandrel and on the back of the model.

13 The wax strip is heated carefully and then slowly and gently bent over the mandrel by exerting even pressure with the fingers. Accidental contact with the fingernails is avoided because a nick occurring in the wax at this point would be difficult to repair. Care is taken not to allow the wax to slip from the mandrel.

| 11 | 12 |

13   14   15

14 Once removed from the mandrel, the wax model is placed on smooth cardboard to prevent its becoming marred. At this point, the central section of the model behind the point was filled with wax to form a shape continuous with the inner form of the bracelet, and to strengthen the form which is subject to stress when placed on and removed from the wrist.

The wax model was then placed to harden in the freezing section of a refrigerator. Next it was sprued at the surplus edge and inside, so that later sprue removal would not destroy the pattern or textured surfaces.

The process of lost wax casting by the use of a *centrifuge,* employed to cast this bracelet, is described on p. 510 under Centrifugal Casting.

Once cast, the inner surface was filed to final smoothness, a process more easily performed in metal than on the wax. The outer surface with the wax inlay pattern was hand polished, and the inner surface was polished by a *felt ring buff* mounted on a *polishing motor* arbor. The front surface was then oxidized and the highlights restored to increase the effect of relief.

15 The finished bracelet in sterling silver. Dimensions: side-to-side diameter: 2½ in; from point to leg: 2¾ in; gap between legs: 1³⁄₁₆ in; width of bracelet: 1 in.

PREPARING A WAX MODEL FOR A STONE SETTING

Stone setting literally means "stone seating." When you set a stone in a piece of jewelry, you are placing it in its *seat* and fixing it there in a way that holds it securely. The use of a stone in a jewel is not to be considered as an afterthought. It must be planned as a part of the initial concept of the design, not only for esthetic but for technical reasons. We deal here with technique only, and leave esthetic considerations to the creator. In the following discussion, stone setting in relation to wax model making and casting are considered. (For a separate discussion of stones see Stones and Their Setting, Chapter 13.)

A variety of methods can be used to set a stone in a wax model. Almost all the basic methods used in setting stones in fabricated work can be utilized in cast pieces. In addition, the caster can make use of certain unconventional ways of setting stones in a casting so they seem to grow organically from the setting, especially when using natural crystals, and this perhaps is unique to casting.

A stone setting can be made of wax wire, sheet wax, or both, depending on the requirements of the stone and the model design. The character of the wax is important in making a stone setting. It should be a hard wax capable of bending without brittleness, and of being carved or sanded if necessary. The wax should be firm enough to take a sharp impression from the stone when it is trial placed in the wax model to be sure it sits well, and it should resist distortion when a low heat is applied, as is sometimes necessary, when removing a stone from a wax model after a trial fitting. *The stone should fit the setting when the wax is cold.* If wax is worked in a warm atmosphere and allowed to stand for some time before casting, because of internal stresses it may become distorted and the setting may no longer be accurate in shape or size. If a delay in casting under such circumstances cannot be avoided, place the finished wax model in a refrigerator, or in cold water until it is ready to be invested.

STONE SETTING TYPES:
Flange, claw, prong, or peg

The type of setting chosen for use with a stone depends on the stone form: whether it is a natural crystal, cut in cabochon, faceted, or ball shaped like a bead or pearl. In all cases except the latter, for the stone to fit properly in its seat a space must be allowed between the seat of the stone and the base of the holding device so it does not impinge upon the stone when forced over it. Pressure against a stone's edge will cause it to fracture at the pressure point, even in the case of a very hard stone. The space must be only large enough to avoid impingement. If too much space is allowed, the stone may be loose in its setting, and normally, no stone should be allowed to move once set. Stones are not set until all work is completed on the object.

FLANGE SETTINGS

In terms of stone setting, a *flange* is a rigid part of the model that projects partially over a stone, or an upstanding portion that partially or completely surrounds a stone, and is bent over it to hold it in place. A bezel is a flange. In cases where a part of the stone is slipped under a rigid flange, it must be opposed by a device such as a prong or claw that can be bent over the stone to hold it in position. In this system, the prong is left upright in the wax model as it must be possible for the stone to be inserted for a trial size and placement in the wax, and then removed. If this cannot be done in the wax model, it is also not possible in the casting. The rigid flange can be heavier than any part that must be bent. In the wax, the parts to be bent should be made somewhat thicker than they ultimately will be. After casting they are reduced in dimension by a *hand file* or a *rotary file*.

A precaution about bending a casting is necessary. Cast metal tends to be brittle because its crystal structure is not all oriented in one direction as it is in metal that is rolled or extruded and is therefore much more easily bent. Bending a cast projection like a prong or a claw has its hazards as it is subject to fracture. To avoid this, file the prong or claw as thin as is structurally sound, anneal it before bending and quench it properly to render it maximally soft. Immobilize the object, place the stone in its seat and *gradually* bend the flange, prong, or claw in place with light hammer taps on a *bezel bender*, a *hollow-ended punch*, a *burnisher* or other tool suited to the circumstances. Never plan on reopening a cast part once it has been bent as this will almost invariably result in fracture.

CONVENTIONAL BEZEL   A conventional bezel or collet is an upstanding flange that surrounds the stone. Inside the bezel is a level supporting ledge or *shoulder* upon which the stone rests. Bezel wax wire is extruded with this shoulder as a part of the bezel wire. Because in setting the bezel is folded over on the stone, cast bezels must be filed thin enough so this can be done. In a variation, parts of the bezel can be removed in the wax leaving only sections of

11–48 LEE BARNES PECK, U.S.A. Cast sterling silver ring with 24K gold plate. The mounted handmade glass and hematite stone parts are cemented into upright flanges prepared in the model to receive them. Length 3 in; height 3 in; width 1¾ in. *Photo: Neil Anderson*

it, called *cramps*, to be folded over the stone to confine or restrain it by contraction. This bezel type is called a *cramp setting*.

GYPSY SETTING   A cabochon or faceted stone can be mounted flush with the outer surface of a smooth flange already shaped in a folded over position as a part of the form of the wax model. In this case, the stone is inserted *from below*, and is held in place by another flange or by prongs that fold over *from below* and are not seen from above.

CLAW SETTINGS

Claws and *prongs* are similar in concept as they are projections pushed over a stone to hold it in place. Usually claws are used in groups of three or more rising from a common base to encompass a single stone, and a prong can be used singly or in groups. A *claw* is a tapering projection, so called because it resembles the sharp nail of an animal. Claw settings are usually reserved for use with transparent and faceted stones because their open structure allows the admission of light to the stone, therefore giving it more brilliance by light refraction. Claws can be of many different shapes, they can be single or bifurcated, but they all grip faceted stones just above the girdle. The claw should not touch the edge of the stone when it is bent over the stone in the final setting. Too little space allowance around the stone's edge might cause the stone to chip when the claw is bent over it.

Wax wires of 16, 18, and 20 gauge B.&S. are used to make a claw setting. When the wax claw setting is ready the claws project upward or outward. Warm the stone and press it straight down into the claws to make the stone girdle fit snugly into them. Allow the wax to cool and cut any surplus wax away. It should then be possible to release the stone by pushing it upward out of the setting from the back. If the stone resists displacement, heat a tool, put it in contact with the stone, allow the heat to spread in the stone, and then release it. By another method of stone release, warm a wad of sticky wax and place it in contact with the stone. Allow the wax to cool, and then lift it straight upward. If the stone is not too firmly embedded in the wax, it will rise with the sticky wax. This method can be used to release any stone.

CLAW AND BALL SETTINGS   This type consists of a claw ending at its extremity in a round ball. This type is favored in cast metal stone setting and its form evolved from the possibilities of wax. In making such a setting, the

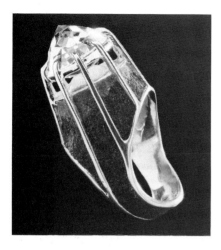

11–50 GEORGE POSTGATE, U.S.A. "Temple of Light." Cast 14K gold ring with citrine mounted in a claw setting over an opal to magnify and intensify its opalescence. Between side claw extensions, channels approximately 0.5 mm in depth were prepared in the wax model. These surfaces, cleaned and grease-free on the casting, received an inlay of crushed lapis lazuli and turquoise mixed with epoxy, the color of one fading into the other. Once set, this mixture is permanent and very durable. It can be left as is; stoned down to a level, matte surface; or polished. *Photo: Peter Pfensick*

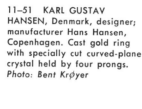

11–51 KARL GUSTAV HANSEN, Denmark, designer; manufacturer Hans Hansen, Copenhagen. Cast gold ring with specially cut curved-plane crystal held by four prongs. *Photo: Bent Krøyer*

11–52 ALICE SHANNON, U.S.A. Cast 14K green gold ring with square-cut opals and peridots mounted with ball-ended claws. *Photo: Jack Biterman*

PRONGS

A *prong* is a tapering, pointed, projecting spur that rises from a setting. It is usually heavier than a claw, and can be independent or used in groups. Prongs are often used to hold irregularly shaped stones. Their position is made in the wax setting while the stone is in place by judiciously choosing those locations that will hold it. In some cases, a prong can be cut from the same sheet wax used for the rest of the setting, and bent upward. After casting, they are bent over the stone.

PEGS

Pegs are cylindrical lengths of wax wire, uniform in section and joined in an upright position to hold any mounted stone that has a hole of a matching diameter drilled halfway in it. The usual stones set on pegs are ball-shaped stones and pearls. If a thin peg is needed, to be sure it is

11–53 REINO SAASTAMOINEN, Finland. Silver pendant with natural geode of stalagmitic chalcedony, commonly called "chalcedony rose." The model sheet wax was shaped to conform with the contour of the individual stone, held in place by prongs that are a part of the original model wax sheet. *Photo: Erkki Talvila*

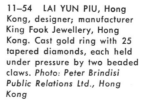

11–54 LAI YUN PIU, Hong Kong, designer; manufacturer King Fook Jewellery, Hong Kong. Cast gold ring with 25 tapered diamonds, each held under pressure by two beaded claws. *Photo: Peter Brindisi Public Relations Ltd., Hong Kong*

claw is made first, then a small ball of melted wax is placed at its end. A mimimum of three such "balled" claws surround the stone, and the ball with its claw is pressed down upon the stone.

COMMERCIAL CLAW SETTINGS Settings of this group, called *crowns*, are available ready-made in a highly plasticized wax in standard sizes for use with stones of standard sizes and shapes. These can be incorporated by welding onto an existing wax model, and they can be modified according to wish. (See Prong and Claw Setting, p. 622, for more details on claw setting.)

not too thin to cast, it can initially be made of a heavier wax wire, and after casting it can be carefully filed to the thinner diameter necessary. Formerly, pegs were made bent to help hold the mounted stone, but today with the use of epoxy cements as a binder, this is not necessary and straight pegs are used. It is also possible to drill a hole in the casting, insert a peg made of a length of wire and solder it in place. It is far less trouble, however, to make the peg in wax wire and weld it *in situ* in the wax model.

PRESSURE SETTING

A stone can be mounted without claws, bezels, prongs, or pegs by holding it in place by pressure from parts of the main body of the form that, once the stone is in place, are forced toward each other. This kind of bending of a casting is risky, though it can be done with care.

PRECAST SETTINGS

Settings can be made separately in wax and cast independently of the rest of the work, then mounted on it by soldering. The practice is called *piece casting.* Piece-cast settings can also be mounted on a casting with screws or rivets attached to them.

FABRICATED SETTINGS AND CASTINGS

Jewelry can be made partially by casting and partially by fabrication. For instance, the shank and main parts of a ring can be cast, and the stone setting entirely fabricated and soldered to the casting. The problem is to integrate the design of the setting with the cast portion, a not impossible task.

CENTRIFUGAL CASTING

Flinging molten metal from a rotating center outward into a single-use investment plaster mold

In the lost wax casting process here described, the casting is created by the use of a *centrifuge,* a machine used for centrifugal casting. This technique is also used in industry, dentistry, and for making commercial as well as art jewelry. To have an initial basic understanding of the centrifugal casting process, it is first briefly summarized.

Once the model has been invested in a flask mold in which it is embedded in investment plaster, and the wax has been eliminated from the mold by heat, the flask mold is mounted on the centrifuge next to a crucible in which metal in an amount sufficient to fill the mold cavity is placed. The metal is made molten, and the arm of the centrifuge holding the flask mold and the crucible is released so that they revolve rapidly. At the instant of release, due to the rapid rotation, the molten metal is flung outward from the center of the machine into the adjacent mold cavity. Provided that sufficient metal has been supplied, the mold cavity is filled and the metal is trapped and held by rotational pressure or *centrifugal force* for the amount of time it takes to solidify. The casting is then released from the single-use mold, so called because it is destroyed in the process.

The sequence of the centrifugal casting processes to be

11–55 ROLF MÜLLER, Switzerland. Symmetrical necklace in sterling silver, with 19 tourmalines. The cast units, made in separate parts, were solder joined after casting by round wire sections, making the necklace rigid. *Photo: Thomas Von Wartburg*

11–56 ALICIA PENALBA, France. "Dryade." Cast gold collar made in units joined after casting by a flexible system. Visual volume was created with minimal weight by hollow construction sheet wax forms. When the open backs rest against the body, they are not seen. *Photo: F. Gennari*

described is: spruing; mounting the model in a flask; investing the model; burning out the wax model to create a mold; mounting the flask mold on the centrifuge; melting the metal; releasing the centrifuge; freeing the casting from the investment; removing the sprues; and cleaning and finishing the casting.

SPRUING THE WAX MODEL

The finished wax model is prepared for casting by adding the necessary *sprues* which are wax wires or rods that are attached to the model between it and the pouring gate former (also called the *sprue base,* see p. 512), or to a wax button. When the model is invested in the casting plaster mold, and the wax is melted out, the space left by the wax sprue (or sprues) makes a channel (or channels) through which the flowing molten metal feeds to the mold cavity. In centrifugal casting, no gates or risers, which are used in casting larger metal objects, are made to carry off the gases—which instead escape through the porosity of the investment plaster of which the mold is made.

The *wax sprue B.&S. gauge size* needed for a particular model varies with the model size and shape and the metal in which it is cast. Heavier models require wax wire sprues of relatively larger diameters, but generally not larger than the average thickness of the wax used in the model. Delicate models use sprues of smaller diameters. A sprue of suitable size allows the metal to flow rapidly into the mold and reduces the chance of turbulence in the flow of molten metal into the mold cavity, thus reducing the chance of porosity in the casting which is highly undesirable and to be avoided. If the sprue is too narrow, the metal may freeze or solidify before the cavity is filled, and this can result in an incomplete casting with a porous surface. Gold can be cast with the smallest sprue because it retains heat well; silver requires heavier sprues than gold because it tends to solidify more rapidly; bronze needs larger, short sprues, and more of them than the above-mentioned metals. If there is any doubt about the sprue size to use, it is better to err on the larger than on the smaller side. Gold needs 12, 14, or 16 gauge B.&S. sprues; silver, 10, 12, or 14 gauge B.&S. sprues; and bronze, the same as silver or larger. The *length of the sprue* should be no more than is necessary.

Sprue placement varies with the particular model design. In general sprues are joined to the model at places where they will cause the least damage to its appearance when finally cut away after casting. They can be straight or curved, but never bent at a sharp angle. Never place a sprue in a position where it will be difficult to remove after casting. Usually this means that sprues are attached to the *back* or the *edge* of a model, the latter especially if the model is large. They should lead to its heaviest parts, those parts to which the greatest amount of metal must flow during casting.

To *weld join a sprue to the model,* hold it in contact and place a *heated spatula blade* to that point. As soon as the wax melts, withdraw the spatula and hold the sprue in place until the weld solidifies. Be sure the weld is secure so that it will not loosen during the investment of the plaster. The point of attachment to the model should be neat, and as large as the full sectional diameter of the sprue; otherwise a "pinch" will be created that will constrict the metal flow into the mold cavity. Where the sprue leads to a thick model part, this contact point can be enlarged by adding a small fillet around the sprue at that point to double the

sprue thickness there and form a *feed ball* of molten metal which is drawn toward the mass as it solidifies. Do not lead a sprue at a right angle to the model's flat surface as this will cause turbulence of metal flow and porosity in the casting. Instead, angle it toward the point of metal entrance *at an angle of less than 45°,* preferably 20–30°. Holding the model upright, no point on the model should be *lower* than the main point of metal entry into the mold cavity as this might cause a pocket of trapped air and that part of the mold cavity would not be filled. If, however, this cannot be avoided, and also when making heavy castings, attach an *extra sprue* of 18 gauge B.&S. wax wire to this lowest or thickest point, and lead it to a point away from the central pouring gate (which during casting will be filled with molten metal) at the top of the mold. This projection allows the wax of the lower part of the model to drain, and during casting becomes a pressure release vent that permits air there to emerge during casting so that it does not offer resistance to the flow of molten metal to that mold part. The *number of sprues used* depends on the size and complexity of the model. Simple, bulky models such as a man's ring, may need only one large sprue, while delicate, thin-sectioned wire models such as filigree may need several sprues. When multiple sprues are used, as is usually the case, they must all *converge to one point,* not more than ½ in (1.27 cm) below the model. At the converging point, to provide additional metal, some casters add a short, ¼ in (0.64 cm) piece of straight, thick wax and attach this to the sprue former or the wax button, if one is used.

Multiple model casting consists of mounting several small models and casting them in the same flask which contains the mold. In this case each model has its own sprue that leads to a single common wax button. Position the models so that they do not touch, and in such a way that the distance between each of them and to the *side* and *top* of the flask is not less than ¼ in (0.63 cm). Center the models in the flask space as much as possible. Their

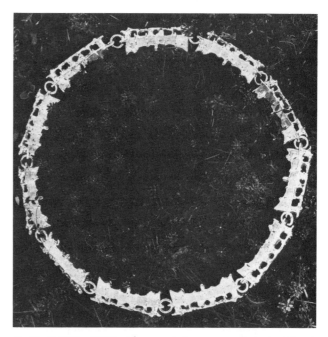

11–57 REGINE JUHLS, Norway, designer; manufacturer Sølvsmie Regine & Frank Juhls, Kautokeino. Cast silver necklace. The units are repeats of rubber mold wax-injected models. Length, stretched out 43 cm. Photo: Börje Rönnberg

position can be tested by placing the empty flask over the model, and adjustment can be made if necessary.

Tree mounting is a system of mounting several smaller models by attaching them to a *single* central heavy sprue. (See Multiple "Pincushion" Spruing and Tree Spruing, p. 543.) Make sure the main sprue is thick enough in cross section to allow the metal to fill the attached patterns and to feed metal as needed to them during their solidification when the sprue metal acts as a metal reservoir. The total amount of metal that can be used in this kind of casting is determined by the total metal capacity of the centrifugal casting machine, and the crucible used with it. The models must not be less than ⅛ in (3.2 mm) from each other.

"Pincushion" mounting is a system in which several small models are mounted on a common sprue former, each model with *its own sprue* to the former.

DETERMINING THE AMOUNT OF METAL NEEDED FOR A CASTING

Once the sprues are joined to the model, and before attaching them to the *pouring gate former,* the whole wax assembly with attached sprues must be *weighed* to determine the amount of metal needed for that particular casting. There are two ways of approximating this amount. One is by *bulk displacement* and the other is by a *wax weight–to–metal weight ratio.*

BULK DISPLACEMENT MEASURE

Fill a *marked, glass graduate* large enough to contain the model with water. Attach the model to a *stiff, thin wire* and submerge it in the water. Because wax is less dense than water, it will float. Therefore, be sure it *all* goes below the water level by pushing it downward with the wire. Then with a *glass-marking pencil,* mark the level to which the water rises (or note it down), and remove the model. Place pieces of the chosen metal for casting in the same measure until the water level reaches the height just marked. The *metal bulk* now matches the *displaced water bulk.* Add an extra from 1–4 ounces of metal for the sprues and the button, the lesser amount for a small and greater for a large object, or when multiple sprues are used. This extra amount of *reserve metal,* besides compensating for shrinkage during metal solidification, also provides the "push" that forces the metal to fill the mold cavity as densely as possible, thereby reducing the chance of porosity.

WAX-WEIGHT–TO–METAL-WEIGHT RATIO

The second method of arriving at the amount of metal needed for a casting is by using a *wax-weight–to–metal-weight ratio.* In this case, a different *number factor* is used for each metal because each of them has a different *specific gravity* which the factor number approximates. First weigh the model on an accurate *precision scale* with all wax sprues and the button attached. Then *multiply the weight by the factor number given above right.* The result is the weight of the metal needed for the casting. If you first record the weight of the separate model, then attach the sprues to it and weigh their total, the weight of the model can be subtracted from the total to give the separate weight of the sprue assembly. Once the weight of the wax model is known, it can be translated into metal weight and metal cost. The result might become the cause of model alterations to reduce metal weight.

Metal Weight to Wax Weight Factor

Metal	Factor
Platinum	22
Palladium	13
Gold 22k	18
Gold 14k	14
Gold 12k, 10k	12
Pure silver	10.5
Sterling silver	10
Bronze	9
Brass	8.5
Dried organic model, cast in sterling	18

MOUNTING THE MODEL ON THE POURING GATE FORMER

To prepare the model for casting, it must be mounted upright on a metal or rubber *pouring gate former* (usually called a *sprue base,* an ambiguous term). This part does form a base for the *flask* or metal cylinder that holds the poured mold plaster, by a flange around its perimeter into which the flask edge fits or snaps tightly to make a leakproof seal. In terms of the resulting mold it also has another function. At its center rises a mound or cone shape about ½–1 in (1.27–2.54 cm) high. This shape acts to automatically form the depression in the plaster mold that becomes the *pouring gate,* a widened cup-shaped depression into which the released molten metal flows and by which it is directed as rapidly as possible because of its shape to the sprue opening in the mold. The molten metal forms a button in this mold depression. The name "pouring gate former," more clearly indicates its prime function.

The pouring gate former can be of several kinds, depending on the method of casting used, or on individual preference. Sometimes, but not always, this form has a central hole. When it does, as is usual with cone shapes, the *outer concave shape* under the base is filled with heated tacky wax then allowed to solidify. At the cone apex opening where some of this wax is exposed, the converging ends of the sprues of the wax model are securely attached by welding with a *heated spatula* to prevent the wax model from breaking loose during investment procedures. For additional security, a heated *steel sprue pin* can be inserted through this external wax to pass through the hole in the former into the main sprue or the model itself. This pin provides strength to the mounting when it is vibrated later to remove air bubbles from the plaster slurry of the mold. *Be sure to remove the pin with pliers* just *before* placing the mold in the burnout or wax-eliminating kiln or it will prevent the wax from draining. If the pouring gate former has no hole, as is usually the case with mound shapes, its *inside convex shape* is primed with a molten layer of wax to which the sprue is attached. Some rubber pouring gate formers have a central cup that is filled with wax to form a sprue button. This can be converted by a separately fitting, conically holed insert to make the former a base for use in *tree spruing,* discussed under Rubber Mold Wax Injection, p. 536, where multiple model "pincushion" spruing is also discussed.

A flat flask base with no rising mound or cone can also be used. In this case, place a smoothly rounded, semicircular button of tacky wax in the center of the base, its amount roughly equivalent to the contents of a cone-shaped former, and weld the model's sprue ends neatly to it. When the wax is melted out, this button forms the pouring gate. In all cases, the pouring gate former must be free of all traces of old investment plaster, and be clean to prevent contamination of the mold. Before use (except in the case when the above-mentioned tacky wax button is added, and it is done *after* the wax button is mounted), coat the pouring gate former with a light film of oil which will help to separate it from the plaster after setting when the pouring gate former must be removed.

When space saving is critical, it is also possible to mount a model on a shallow wax button attached to a clean, flat glass slab. Once the button is in place, oil the rest of the glass for the reasons stated above. Place the flask with the model-mounted button at its center, then close the seam of contact on the outside of the flask with Plasticine clay or putty to make it airtight. After the plaster has been poured into the flask and it has set, remove the seal and the flask can be removed.

THE CENTRIFUGAL CASTING FLASK

The *flask* or investment-containing cylinder that is used in centrifugal casting to hold the mold can be made of seamless heavy 16 gauge B.&S. mild steel. Repeated use of this metal causes it to oxidize and deteriorate, and for this reason, the more expensive but longer lasting flask of stainless steel which is capable of withstanding higher temperatures without disintegration is preferred. (Flasks used for vacuum casting have walls perforated with numerous holes to allow air to be drawn out.)

HEIGHT AND DIAMETER Flask height and diameter limit the size and to some extent the shape of the casting that can be made with it. Some typical dimensions used by jewelers and available from supply houses are the following:

HEIGHT		DIAMETER	
IN	CM	IN	CM
2¼	5.71	1¾	4.44
2⅝	6.67	2⅜	6.03
2½	6.35	3	7.62
2¾	6.98	3½	8.89
4	10.16	3⅜	8.57
5¾	14.60	4	10.16

For each diameter, a matching pouring gate former must be used. When choosing a flask size to use, remember that a minimum allowance of approximately ¼ in (6.35 mm) must be made between the outermost-reaching parts of the wax model and the flask walls. About a ½ in (12.7 mm) minimum is allowable at the top between the model and where the plaster ends, but not more because a larger amount will hinder the escape of gases through the plaster when the molten metal enters the mold cavity. A used flask should be cleaned with a *wire brush* to free it of old investment plaster or rust which might contaminate the investment.

USING A TIN CAN AS A FLASK When a model with its sprues has a shape that cannot be accommodated in a cylindrical flask, or if one of sufficient size is not available, it is possible in such a situation to use a one-time substitute seamless tin can for casting. The thin-gauge steel of which it is made can easily be bent to an oval, squarish, or other shape. Place an asbestos liner within the can, and for reinforcement, bind the outside with a few turns of heavy-gauge iron wire at top, center, and bottom. Cut a large can down to required height, and remember that in

the case of a sling-arm centrifuge, both the flask-can and the crucible must fit on the arm. When placing the flask-can in the flask cradle after burnout, be sure the sprue gate opening is *centered* on the crucible baffle opening so the molten metal flows unimpeded into the mold.

CRUCIBLES

The term *crucible* comes from the Medieval Latin word *crucibulum,* which refers to the hanging lamp or eternal light that burns before the cross of Christ. Crucibles are vessels or pots used to contain metals to be melted, to prepare an alloy, or to calcine or fuse other materials. All these processes require the use of high temperatures, therefore crucibles are made of a highly refractory substance that can withstand such heat. The common refractories used for crucibles are the following:

Acid refractories: silica, clay, fireclay;
Basic refractories: magnesite, dolomite, alumina, zirconia;
Neutral refractories: chromite, graphite, silicon carbide.

In some crucibles, these materials are combined to make a crucible with characteristics suitable for use with a particular metal. The substance of the crucible should not act upon the material it holds when heated. Crucibles range in size from very small (an inch or less as used in assaying), to very large (capable of holding several hundred pounds of metal as in smelting). Because these substances do not crack under high heat, crucibles are thin in relation to their size.

CRUCIBLE SHAPES Though varied in shapes, most crucibles are simple conical containers, some with a pouring lip. Those used on centrifugal casting machines have special shapes designed to suit their being mounted on this machine. They have flat bottoms that fit the crucible carriage on the centrifuge arm and a flat pouring end pierced with a hole or nozzle that is placed up against the crucible carriage baffle plate also pierced with a correspondingly placed hole. The flask is placed in the adjacent flask rest in a horizontal position with the mold gate and sprue opening pointing toward the crucible hole so that the molten metal can pass directly into the mold when the machine is activated.

CRUCIBLE SIZES The sizes of crucibles used for centrifugal casting are graduated and designed to contain a certain maximum amount of metal. The size to use will depend on the needs of the casting. A typical small crucible has a capacity of 1 oz of gold; a medium size, 2½ oz of gold; and large, 7½ oz of gold. They are numbered according to capacity.

CRUCIBLE-TO-FLASK SIZE RELATIONSHIP This relationship is important. For efficiency, use the *smallest* size of both needed for the work. In some cases, only crucibles and flasks of a particular size can be used with a particular size of casting machine, and in other cases, one machine allows a range of crucible and flask sizes to be used. The larger the machine, the bigger these can be. A machine having a 4–6 in (10.2–15.2 cm) arm length is capable of larger capacities. Manufacturers' recommendations for particular machines should be followed.

USING A NEW CRUCIBLE To prolong the life of a new, unused crucible, coat the inside with an equal part mixture of borax and boric acid before its first use, then heat

11–58 *CRUCIBLES, METAL-MELTING TOOLS AND MATERIALS*

1. *Clay crucible, dish type,* for melting gold and silver, from 1¾ in ID × ⅝ in deep for 20 dwt; to 4 in ID × 1⅜ in deep for 175 dwt.
2. *Melting dish* for all metals, capacity up to 6 oz.
3. *Wesgo high-backed metal-melting dish* for all metals, the shape retains the flame. Small, capacity up to 10 oz; large, capacity up to 20 oz.
4. *Wesgo high-temperature platinum-melting crucible,* capacity from 3–6 oz.
5. *Crucible with wooden handle,* capacity 6 oz gold.
6. Four *Kerr clay crucibles* for use with a carriage (*see right*) on Kerr Centrifico casting machines. *From left to right,* capacities are: 1 oz gold; 2½ oz gold; 7 oz gold; 12 oz gold.
7. Two *crucible carriages* with baffle plates; *left:* for standard and 4 in Kerr centrifugal machines, holds 1 oz and 2½ oz crucibles; *right:* for 4 and 6 in machines, holds 7 oz and 12 oz crucibles.
8. *Burno refractory firebrick crucible* with cover for quick melting of gold with a blowpipe, sizes 2⅜ × 1½ × 2 in, capacity 25 dwt; to 3⅛ × 2½ × 3 in, capacity 100 dwt. This crucible with cover is held by wire, spring-jointed tongs, 17 in long.
9. *Dee graphite and carborundum crucible* for melting gold, silver, and bronze, used with the Dee, Kerr, and Ecco casting machines.
10. *Carbon crucible* for the Thermotrol casting machine.
11. *Round sand crucible* for melting large amounts of metal, and for the preparation of alloys.
12. *Dixon round assay sand crucible* with pouring lip. Height 2⅝–6½ in; top Ø 1⅝–1½ in.
13. *Triangular sand crucibles,* a shape easy to pour, available in several sizes.
14. A single triangular *sand crucible,* any of its three corners can be used as a pouring lip.
15. *Crucible of natural flake graphite and silicon carbide* bonded with plastic fireclay, available in a wide range of sizes, heights of 3–9½ in; top Ø 2⅞–7 in. Used for pit, tilt, or induction furnaces.
16. *Sand crucible with cover,* available in a wide range of sizes: 3–14 in high; top Ø 1⅞–9¾ in; capacity 0.13–17.5 lb of water (1 lb water = .96 pt or 27.7 cubic inches).
17. *Smelter's glasses* of dark blue glass, worn to reduce glare in melting and soldering operations.
18. *Crucible tongs* with one bent leg, spring type, for holding crucible with cover, 17 in long.
19. *Scissor-type tongs* for holding *graphite stirring rod,* length 21 in, available with jaws that will hold graphite rods of ½, ¾, or 1 in Ø.
20. *Bent-nose steel crucible tongs,* 36 in long, for holding and pouring small crucibles.
21. *Bent-nose steel crucible tongs,* 36 in long, for holding and pouring medium- and large-sized crucibles.
22. *Kerr Super Flux,* 8 oz can, and *Fluxite* in jar, for application on metal being melted.

it slowly with a torch flame to anneal it, and allow it to cool slowly. Thereafter, never start a melt by placing flux in the crucible bottom. Not all crucibles require annealing, but it is never good practice to direct a high, roaring flame on a new, unused crucible; always heat it slowly.

Maximal Temperatures for Crucible Use

Crucible Material	°F	°C	Uses
Sand	2600	1426.6	Gold and silver casting, bronze, and brass
Silica quartz	2800	1537.7	Gold and silver casting, bronze, and brass
Alumina	2980	1637.7	White gold, nickel-containing alloys
Clay-graphite	3000	1648.8	Gold and silver casting, bronze, and brass
Magnesia	3580	1971.1	White gold, nickel and nickel alloys
Zircon	3600	1982.2	Platinum, palladium, ruthenium
Zirconium	3990	2198.8	Gold and platinum refining
Graphite	5430	2998.8	Melting palladium, platinum, ruthenium

CRUCIBLE AND FLASK TONGS *Crucible tongs* used to handle a hot crucible usually have bent-nosed jaws, and two *reins* or handles, and must be handled with two hands. If the handles are enclosed by a *coupler* or ring that is slipped over the reins and pushed down toward the ends tightly, the jaws will close and clamp on the crucible, and the tongs can be handled with one hand. *Flask tongs* used to hold a flask when removing it from a furnace after wax elimination and burnout, are usually made of a single, bent piece of spring-hardened steel. This form permits the tongs to be held with one hand, thus allowing furnace doors to be opened and closed with the other hand. Their two ends are curved to a semicircular form that allows the flask to be grasped when the legs are pressed together, and released when the pressure is taken off the legs. These forcepslike tongs were inspired by the oldest crucible holder, a single green twig bent into a U shape. Heavy flasks are also held by two-armed tongs.

PAINTING THE MODEL WITH A WETTING AGENT

To break the surface tension on the wax model, done to allow the plaster to cover and contact its surface evenly, it is painted with a brush with a *wetting agent* commonly called a *debubblizer*. This can be a commercial preparation, a mixture of glycerin and alcohol, or a solution of liquid green soap. Alternately, the entire model can be dipped into the wetting agent, and the surplus allowed to drain, be shaken off, or blown away. If the flask will be debubblized by the use of a vacuum pump, a special commercial solution called Vacufilm can be used. Allow all such liquids to dry on the wax model surface from 20 minutes to one hour. Models must be dry to prevent local dilution of the investment which causes roughened surfaces in the casting. Bubbles that remain on the model cause a space in the investment mold that will appear as a positive nodule on the casting.

THE INVESTMENT PLASTER COMPOSITION

The investment plaster composition consists of a binder, a refractory, and modifiers. The *binder* which keeps the silica in suspension, as it otherwise would settle, is calcined gypsum, which is a mineral, widely distributed in nature, in one form a dihydrate of calcium sulphate ($CaSO_4\cdot2H_2O$). This is turned into dental stone, a hemihydrate of calcium sulphate ($CaSO_4\cdot\frac{1}{2}H_2O$) which is harder and stronger because of its crystal structure, by calcining the former under steam pressure in an autoclave, the result now sold under the trade name Hydrocal. It is the prime ingredient in dental casting investments, used because when calcined, 75% of its water content is eliminated, therefore it requires less water, and its elongated crystals are dense which makes it about two and a half times stronger than ordinary gypsum. The *refractory* is quartz and crystobalite, crystalline forms of silica. Crystobalite (SiO_4) is prepared commercially by calcining selected quartz to 2732° F (1500° C). Its ability to expand and contract when heated allows the extreme heating and cooling of the investment without its cracking. The mold can therefore expand during wax burnout, which compensates for cast metal shrinkage upon solidification. The *modifiers* are added to reduce plaster expansion, adjust the setting time, increase strength, and prevent gypsum shrinkage when it is heated much above 573° F (300° C). Modifiers include boric acid (H_3BO_3), potassium sulphate (K_2SO_4), common salt ($NaCl$), and sodium potassium tartrate ($NaKC_4H_4O_6\cdot4H_2O$). Wetting agents are added to increase slurry flow capacity, and defoaming agents to aid in air removal from the slurry during vibrating or vacuuming.

To produce a consistently reliable product, the Kerr Company, a foremost supplier, tests the raw materials in the investment casting composition to assure high-quality casting results. Tests are made for *uniformity of particle size* to assure smoothly cast surfaces; *characteristic slurry flow* when first mixed; *work time* or the period during which the investment slurry can be handled, from the start of mixing to set time; *setting expansion* degree whose maximum is reached 2–4 hours after hard setting, depending on volume; *vacuum rise* or the rise and fall of the slurry under a bell jar when on a vacuum table, which indicates the speed at which and degree to which the air is removed from the mix; *thermal expansion* or the extent to which metal when heated will expand, which should be equivalent to the extent that cast metal will contract upon its becoming solid; and *crushing strength* at casting temperature to determine mold strength.

11–59 INVESTMENT CASTING TOOLS AND SUPPLIES
1. *Kerr Satin Cast investment plaster:* 25 lb carton; 10 lb container; Cristobalite inlay investment, 3½ lb container.
2. *Stainless steel spatula* for mixing investment plaster, 3⅝ in long, ⅞ in wide.
3. *Rubber plaster-mixing bowls,* flexible black rubber to allow quick cleanup, 1 pt and 3 pt capacities.
4. *Investment mixer,* fits on rubber bowl, hand turned.
5. *Triple-beam balance,* 2610 g capacity, 0.1 g sensitivity, for weighing dry investment plaster prior to mixing. Beam calibrations: front 10 × 0.1 g; rear 100 × 10 g; center 500 × 100 g. Separate weights in grams.
6. *Interval timer* for timing investment mix, can be set for 1–60 minutes.
7. *Graduates,* plastic, for measuring liquids, or for use in the displacement method of measuring casting metal, capacity 16 oz or 500 cc; 240 cc; 500 cc.
8. *Sable hair brush* for painting models with surface tension reducing agents, or for applying investment.
9. *Vibrator* with three-speed switch for low, medium, or high vibration levels to eliminate air bubbles in investment.
10. *Kerr Vacufilm,* a surface tension reducing agent painted on the wax model before investment is applied, to eliminate the formation of surface bubbles, and allow close adaptation of the investment to all surfaces, in 3–8 oz bottles.

Investment plaster must be kept dry before and after use to prevent it from absorbing moisture from the air, otherwise its working characteristics will be altered, causing surface roughness on castings, or mold cracking that results in fins forming on the casting, or totally unsuccessful castings. The investment plaster contained in a closed plastic bag should be kept in a drum with an airtight cover.

PREPARING THE INVESTMENT SLURRY

The *work time* of the investment you use must be known to you, since investment must be completed before the plaster sets. In a characteristic work time covering a period of *10 minutes,* the time might be divided as follows: 3–4 minutes to mix the investment; 2–3 minutes to debubble the slurry; 30 seconds to pour the slurry into the flask; 1½ minutes to debubble the flask; half a minute to cap the flask to bring the slurry to its top; 1½ minutes for the plaster to set. In the next 2 minutes, the surface of the investment will "frost" over, i.e., the gloss of water on the investment surface will disappear since it is absorbed into the set plaster.

The *water-to-powder ratio* used in mixing the investment slurry is most important as it determines the physical properties and setting time of the resulting set plaster. Do not guess at these proportions, but *carefully follow manufacturer's instructions* as given, for instance, in the chart below (courtesy of Kerr). Use an *accurate scale* for dry measures, and a *container marked in cubic centimeters* when measuring liquids. Any deviations from the suggested proportions will result in a change in the degree of expansion, therefore a change in the dimension of the casting, and possibly a weakened plaster that might crack. Surplus water causes a reduction in strength of the set gypsum, or may cause water marks to appear on the model. Too thick a slurry due to an excess of investment may fail to contact the model completely, or not fill the flask properly. The need for accurate measurements is self-evident. In setting, a certain amount of surplus water evaporates in the process and leaves 10–15% pore space in the set investment through which gases can later escape.

The table given below provides a reference to determine the correct amounts of investment and water required for flasks of different dimensions. It was developed specifically for use with Kerr Satin Cast investment, and Kerr Bril-

Cast investment. Both these investments have a powder-to-water ratio of 40/100, and a working time of 9½ minutes, plus or minus 30 seconds. The top figure represents *investment,* and the lower figure *water.* Platinite investment is a composition developed for casting platinum and other high-melting temperature metals used in jewelry.

Draw the necessary water from the tap and allow it to stand for one hour before use to bring it to room temperature, between 70–80° F (21–26° C), and to allow embodied air to escape. Water and powder temperature 74° F (23.3° C) is ideal. Colder water slows work and setting time, and hot water speeds it up. Measure the water in a sufficiently large *measuring graduate* marked in cubic centimeters (cc), and pour it into the *rubber mixing bowl.* Rubber mixing bowls are used because they are easier to clean after residual plaster sets and hardens as they can be flexed to crack it off. Before measuring the investment plaster, agitate the contents in its container to assure a uniform distribution of its ingredients which have a tendency to separate according to particle size if they have been subject to vibration during storage. Measure the necessary amount by weighing it on an accurate *triple-beam scale* calibrated in grams or ounces (ounce measurements can be converted to grams if necessary). The amounts used should be somewhat more than the total that you estimate will be necessary to fill the flask since this must be done from *one* prepared batch.

Always add the investment to the water, and not the reverse, to assure even, quick wetting of the investment and a smooth slurry consistency. Sift the investment plaster through your fingers into the water *slowly* to prevent air entrapment into the mix. Combine *all* of the measured ingredients to maintain their ratio accuracy. Avoid air bubbles in the mix because, as mentioned, they tend to become attached to the surface of the wax model and become hollows in the mold, and are cast as bumps on the casting. When correct procedure is followed, the investment will combine smoothly with the water and not form lumps. The bowl contents can be mixed with a broad *hand spatula,* or a *mechanical hand spatula* which fits on the top of the bowl with a flange and is rotated by an attached handle. Electric mixers should operate at 120 rpm, and are turned on before adding investment to the water already in the mixing bowl. To bring the contents to a smooth, creamy slurry may take 30–120 seconds, depending on the amount.

Investment and Water Requirements for Various-Sized Flasks

Flask Diameter	Flask Height							
	2″	2½″	3″	3½″	4″	5″	6″	7″
2″	5 oz 57cc	6 oz 68cc	7.5 oz 85cc	9 oz 102cc	10 oz 114cc			
2½″	8 oz 91cc	10 oz 114cc	12 oz 136cc	14 oz 160cc	16 oz 182cc	20 oz 228cc		
3″	12 oz 136cc	15 oz 170cc	18 oz 205cc	21 oz 240cc	1½ lb 274cc	30 oz 340cc	32 oz 410cc	2¾ lb 500cc
3½″	1 lb 182cc	1¼ lb 228cc	1½ lb 274cc	1¾ lb 320cc	2 lb 364cc	2½ lb 456cc	3 lb 548cc	3½ lb 640cc
4″	18 oz 205cc	23 oz 262cc	27 oz 308cc	2 lb 364cc	2¼ lb 410cc	3 lb 546cc	3½ lb 637cc	4 lb 728cc
5″					3¾ lb 682cc	4¾ lb 864cc	5½ lb 1000cc	6½ lb 1182cc

VIBRATING THE INVESTMENT TO REMOVE AIR

Hand spatulating results in some air being trapped in the mix. If no vibrator is available to remove bubbles, place the mixing bowl on a raised stand, and tap the container. The bubbles will rise to the surface and can be broken with the spatula. A more efficient manner of removing bubbles is to use a *vibrator,* a platform mounted over a motor, equipped with a three-speed switch for low, medium, and high vibration levels. Place the mixing bowl with its contents on the platform, hold it in place with a hand, turn the vibrator up to *high,* and when air bubbles rise, break them with a spatula. Air can also be eliminated with a *vacuum unit,* the most efficient system, discussed below.

PAINTING THE MODEL WITH INVESTMENT

A means of being fairly certain that air bubbles will not be present on the model's surface is to paint the model (which is already mounted on the gate former) with a good *hair brush* dipped into the prepared investment slurry, making sure that all surfaces, including those of the sprues, are completely covered. Before this dries, place the flask (asbestos lined or not—see below) over the model to engage the flange in the gate former. The outer seam between the gate former and the flask can be sealed (luted) with sticky wax to be sure it does not leak when filled with investment.

THE ASBESTOS LINER FOR FLASKS

Some casters do not use a ⅟₁₆ in (1.6 mm) thick asbestos strip to line the inside of the flask, and others find it useful. Its function is to provide a cushion for the expansion of the investment plaster during the burnout. It has been found that a dry asbestos liner reduces hygroscopic expansion, but nevertheless, a wet liner is commonly used. It should be cut so it makes one complete turn inside the flask without any overlapping. To find the needed length, place a string around the flask. Use this measure to cut the asbestos strip, test its length, then trim it if necessary. Its height should be ½ in (12.7 mm) less than the flask height, so that when it is centered, there is a distance of ¼ in (6.4 mm) left at the top and bottom. Dip the asbestos sheet quickly in water which softens it enough to make it easy to press it tightly against the inside wall of the flask.

FILLING THE FLASK BY HAND

When a metal pouring gate former is used, it must be luted to the flask with modeling clay or soft wax to form a seal. The flask can be filled with investment by hand, without a vibrator or vacuum table. In this case, to reduce the chance of trapped air as the investment rises, when pouring the slurry into the flask tilt the flask to one side. When the flask is nearly filled, straighten it to a vertical position and complete the fill. Lightly tap the top edge of the flask with a metal tool to cause any bubbles in the slurry to rise, and break them. We assume that the correct flask size has been chosen for the particular model. If it cannot be avoided that the top of the model is considerably more than ½ in (1.27 cm) below the flask top, it is only necessary to fill the flask to that distance above the model since an additional thickness restricts the penetration of gases through the investment pores during casting.

USING A VIBRATOR FOR AIR REMOVAL

When filling the flask and using a *vibrator* to remove air, wrap a *paper collar* around the flask that projects about 1½ in (3.8 cm) above its upper edge and secure it with a rubber band or a piece of draftsman's tape. This is to contain possible investment overflow and spatter. The model must be securely fixed with wax to the gate former so it will not break loose in the process of vibrating. A means of securing it is to heat and insert a *metal sprue pin* through the external wax button and the hole in the sprue gate former into the main sprue. Be sure to *remove this pin before burnout.* Place the flask ensemble on the vibrator table. While holding the flask down with the fingers, slowly start to pour the prepared investment into the flask. As it is poured, start the vibrator at a slow speed, and when it is filled nearly to the top, turn it on full speed. Vibrate the flask until no more bubbles appear on the investment surface which should take no longer than 30 seconds. Remove the flask from the vibrator. If on settling, the plaster does not completely fill the flask, and the model is no more than ½ in (1.27 cm) below its top, add more to bring it level with the flask top before it sets. Allow the paper collar to remain until the plaster sets, then remove it.

USING A VACUUM TABLE FOR AIR REMOVAL

By another system, after the investment is mixed, it can be debubblized by the use of a *vacuum table* which is more efficient than a vibrator in air removal. This is a machine that has a spring-mounted table covered by a rubber pad with a central hole. Over this a glass or plastic *bell jar* which takes its name from its shape, is placed. A standard jar has a 9 in (22.9 cm) diameter and is 8 in (20.3 cm) high, limiting the size of flask that can be placed under it. The air is evacuated by a *vacuum pump* connected by a tube to the central hole in the table and the pad, and makes a partial vacuum in the bell jar by suction. The machine has a gauge that indicates the degree of vacuum which is lower in density than sea level atmospheric pressure.

Mix the prepared investment to a slurry for two minutes, then place the mixing bowl on the vacuum table under the bell jar. Turn on the vacuum pump, and close the relief valve. The needle on the vacuum gauge almost immediately indicates 20–25 psi. The investment will rise and boil, then fall. As it rises in the bowl, with your fist, strike the table sharply at one corner to cause the table to vibrate, which it will do since it is mounted on springs. This vibration helps eliminate air bubbles. Allow about 10 seconds of boiling, then open the valve, turn off the pump motor and release the bell jar. This action takes about 1½ minutes. From here on the investment preset time is approximately 8 minutes.

It is generally not necessary when using a vacuum table to prepaint the model with plaster slurry though this can be done as an added precaution. Again, wrap the flask with a paper collar to contain the spattering of the investment when it expands and boils. Pour the investment to a level that covers the model but does not quite reach the top of the flask. Scrape the rest out with a spatula into the flask. Place the flask on the same vacuum table, cover it with the bell jar, and subject it to the vacuum in the same way as before. Once it starts to boil, allow 10 seconds, then open the valve and turn off the pump. This action should take about 1½ minutes. Remove the bell jar. The return of normal atmospheric pressure forces the investment densely against the model. If the flask is not "capped" or filled to the top, pour in additional investment, enough to complete the unfilled portion. Set the flask aside on a *level surface* and allow the plaster to set.

INVESTMENT PLASTER SET

When the investment plaster in powdered form comes into contact with water, it begins to return to its original, natural, solid form. A chemical change occurs that turns the hemihydrate to the dihydrate form of calcium sulphate which causes it to expand slightly and set, a process accompanied by the release of heat. At a temperature of 73° F (23° C), the setting time varies from 5–25 minutes. It is advisable to use up the entire work time available to avoid the occurrence of free water rising to the mold surface. In rising, free water causes water marks on the wax model. Do not disturb the investment-filled flask until the investment sets.

All techniques using plaster involve some thermal and hygroscopic expansion. The amount of thermal expansion depends on the investment composition, temperature, water-to-powder ratio, and the rate and duration of the heat of burnout. Thermal expansion in air varies from 0.6–1.5% at 932–1292° F (500–700° C). Using a dry asbestos liner in the flask reduces hygroscopic expansion, and a wet asbestos liner increases hygroscopic expansion. The investment plaster will set in one to six hours, depending on flask size. When the surface water starts to disappear around the flask edges, the investment has reached "gloss-off" or water-loss time, and has set.

SCREEING THE PLASTER LEVEL

Once the plaster is set, its top surface which may mound above the flask is screed off level with the flask top with any *straight-edged steel strip* longer than the flask diameter. This assures its fitting well against the backplate of the centrifuge. If several molds are made at one time, the leveled area can be marked with any identification number or a notation of the amount of metal needed, and the metal used for that mold by scratching it in with a *pointed tool.* Such markings remain visible through the burnout.

REMOVING THE GATE FORMER

After the investment is set, the rubber or metal gate former can be removed. First remove any metal sprue pins or plastic pins with *pliers.* A rubber gate former is carefully twisted to break the seal, then is simply pulled off. If a metal gate former resists removal, gently pry it loose with a tool, or heat it where it contacts the sprue wax at the gate former where resistance to its removal is greatest, by holding that part briefly over an *alcohol lamp flame.* With a *knife,* scrape the outside of the flask free of any investment that has accumulated there, and *sponge* away loose particles. Loose particles should not be allowed to be present in the sprue cavity where they would form an obstruction to molten metal entry.

THE BURNOUT:
Losing or eliminating the wax

Two to four hours air drying setting time should be allowed for small flasks, and four to six hours for larger

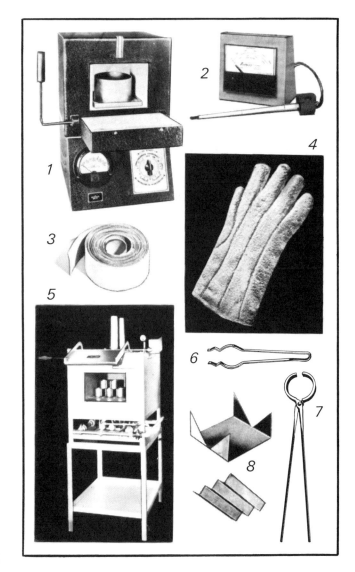

11–60 BURNOUT EQUIPMENT AND TOOLS
1. *Electric burnout furnace,* muffle 4 in high, 4¾ in wide, 5 in deep, with embedded elements, top vented, with built-in pyrometer and preselected heat-holding controls for any temperature up to 1800° F (982° C), AC 110 v, 110 w, will accommodate one flask. (Gesswein)
2. *Swest pyrometer* for wall mounting and use with furnaces and kilns without pyrometers. Measures temperatures from 70°–2300° F (21°–1260° C) with accuracy, has 5 in extension lead and 8 gauge B.&S. thermocouple.
3. *Strip asbestos* for flask liners, in 12, 34, or 100 ft rolls.
4. *Asbestos glove* used to protect the hands against high heat.
5. *Baker gas burnout furnace* with ribbed hearth for easy wax drainage, of long-lasting Carbofrax refractory, cased in a welded steel construction, vented. Will accommodate several flasks, the number depending on size, used in production casting. Must be installed with a *vent hood* above the furnace and *exhaust fan* to eliminate fumes. No. 24 has a heating chamber 13¼ in wide, 21 in long, 8 in high, and uses 150 ft³/h (cubic feet per hour) of 525 Btu gas.
6. *Flask tongs,* one-piece spring construction, one-hand style, 20 in long, for flasks up to 5 in Ø.
7. *Flask tongs,* two-piece, two-hand manipulation style, heavy-duty, 36 in long, for large-sized flasks.
8. *Stainless steel trivets:* four points, 4 × 4 × 2½ in high; reversible, corrugated, 4 in wide, three grooves; 6 in wide, three grooves; used to elevate flasks to allow wax elimination during burnout.

flasks to ensure the development of maximum investment strength. The remaining moisture and wax (or other model material) can then be burned out of the mold and eliminated completely, leaving a carbon-free cavity to receive the molten metal. This is done by using a *burnout furnace* or *kiln*.

THE BURNOUT FURNACE OR KILN

The *burnout furnace* or *kiln* used by self-employed jewelers is usually heated electrically, and the larger models used by production jewelers are usually heated by gas. They are provided with a vent to allow fumes generated in this process to emerge, and must be placed under a *hood* near a *fan exhaust* that draws the fumes out of the room. Proper ventilation is extremely important as the *fumes can be a health hazard.*

The furnace must have a *muffle chamber* large enough to accommodate the *maximum size of flask* or *flasks* that can be used on your centrifuge. It should have a *built-in pyrometer* which accurately indicates the chamber temperature, and a *power switch control* that makes possible the control of the temperature at any point within the maximum heat of 2000° F (1093° C). If there is any reason to doubt the accuracy of the pyrometer reading, or should you wish to test its accuracy, use a commercially prepared pellet such as *Tempil* whose composition is designed to melt at a specific stated temperature. Place one of these on a piece of *asbestos* on the top of the flask in the furnace. When it melts, which can be observed through the furnace peephole, note down the temperature indicated on the pyrometer gauge and see if it corresponds with the known melting temperature of the pellet. If these do not match, you must find the cause and correct it. This may require the help of an electrician. A kiln used for enameling can also be used for wax elimination provided the manufacturer recommends such usage.

With *flask tongs,* place the flask toward the back in the center of the muffle chamber where it will be hottest. Heat the furnace to 300° F (148° C). Be sure the flask is placed *with the sprue opening pointing downward.* To gather any molten wax and moisture that may initially emerge from the flask, and to protect the furnace floor, place a *wax collection metal or refractory tray* with raised edges in the furnace. On it place *three triangular-sectioned refractory sticks* such as are used in ceramic making, in a position radiating equidistantly outward from a center. The flask placed on these will then be raised above the tray which allows wax drainage space and air access. *Ceramic pottery stilts, expanded steel sheet* cut to size, or *steel trivets* can also be used for this purpose.

THE BURNOUT CYCLE: Curing the mold

Curing in this sense consists of heating the plaster compound to render it insoluble to molten metal. To accomplish this, a *burnout cycle* is employed, divided into from three to five temperature levels. Heat buildup must be controlled to prevent the mold from cracking, and to be sure to eliminate all moisture and combustible material in the mold to achieve a good casting result. A too rapid burnout may cause *spalling* or the collapse of a part of the inner mold wall into the cavity, so that it becomes an inclusion in the casting. The cycles recommended here can be applied using a furnace that has either a manual or an automatic temperature control device. A *timer* is recommended to remind one when the next cycle is due to start,

otherwise keep a written record of the cycle as it proceeds. As can be seen from the chart on p. 520, the duration and speed of the burnout cycle depend on the flask size. During the cycle, avoid opening the door of the furnace as this causes the inside temperature to drop 200 Fahrenheit degrees (93 Celsius degrees) or more, depending on how long the door is left open. This temperature shock might cause the investment to crack.

First stage: The furnace is heated to 300° F (148° C), higher than the melting temperature of *all* waxes, so the wax is drained from the flask, and all the free moisture in the investment is eliminated as steam. This initial temperature level must be brought up slowly because the greatest expansion of both investment and wax occurs between the temperatures of 200–300° F (93–148° C). If this stage is speeded up, the excessive steam pressure and pressure from the expanding wax will cause the investment to crack. A cracked mold cannot be cast successfully as the metal runs into the cracks and will be insufficient to fill the mold cavity. In this case, all the work of making the wax model and investing it is lost, so take the proper precautions. On the other hand, the temperature must not be .allowed to drop below 450° F (232° C) during burnout or the mold may crack due to flask metal contraction.

The wax must be removed before the temperature rises above 360° F (148° C), and below *wax flash point* when wax burns. It should not be allowed to burn as smoke damages the kiln elements. The wax will drain into the wax collection tray in about 1–1½ hours. The flask is lifted with tongs, the tray is removed with another pair of tongs, and the flask replaced on a support. A carbon residue remains in the mold. Its presence is indicated by the surface color of the investment which up to 1000° F (537° C) appears black. After this, it turns gradually gray, and at the end of the cycle, the sprue gate appears red, and the exposed investment should appear pure white in color. If any discolorations are still present, this is an indication that all the carbon has not been eliminated. Incomplete burnout can be the cause of a lack of sharpness in the casting, and at worst, the unconsumed products can become inclusions in the casting, or the cause of surface roughness or porosity. Its presence can also cause *back pressure* in the mold cavity so it cannot be completely filled. To aid in completely burning out residual wax or other model material, the furnace atmosphere should be kept an oxidizing one.

Second stage: The burnout cycle continues slowly up to 700° F (371° C). After this, stresses decrease and the temperature increase is rapid. Generally investments expand until they reach a temperature of 1112° F (600° C), after which there is no appreciable change.

Third stage: The temperature is quickly brought to the normal maximum of 1350° F (732° C) when all carbon and chemically combined moisture are eliminated. Larger flasks require a division of five stages to reach this maximum temperature (see Table on page 520). Never heat the investment beyond this maximum or its characteristics will change and cause a rough-surfaced, brittle casting, or one with dark, discolored surface stain that may not be removable, even by acid pickling.

Fourth stage: The burnout is complete, but the temperature must be allowed to drop to adjust the mold to the temperature proper for casting a metal or alloy and assure its being able to enter the mold cavity without undue resistance from gases. Generally speaking, for heavier pieces, proper casting temperature is 700–900° F (371–482° C);

Suggested Wax Elimination Burnout Cycle

5-hour cycle			8-hour cycle			12-hour cycle		
Flasks up to 2½″ × 2½″			Flasks up to 3½″ × 4″			Flasks up to 4″ × 8″		
Time Period	°F	°C	Time Period	°F	°C	Time Period	°F	°C
1 hour	300	148	2 hours	300	148	2 hours	300	148
1 hour	700	371	2 hours	700	371	2 hours	600	315
2 hours	1350	732	3 hours	1350	732	2 hours	900	482
						4 hours	1350	732
1 hour adjusted temp.			1 hour adjusted temp.			2 hours adjusted temp.		

for delicate patterns 900–1000° F (482–537° C). (The casting temperatures recommended for specific metals and alloys are given in Table, "Recommended Casting Temperature for Metals," on p. 524.) The flask can be held at this final casting temperature for some time if a delay in casting is necessary.

Remember that after the flask is taken with tongs from the furnace and placed in the centrifuge cradle, a time interval occurs in which the metal must be melted in the adjacent crucible. The heat of the torch playing on the crucible can help to maintain the flask temperature, but some loss of heat does occur. If it is a large melt, allow an appropriate initial temperature in the flask. Smaller flasks cool off more quickly than larger ones.

THE BURNOUT OF NON-WAX MODELS

Casting models to make replicas of experimental organic or inorganic materials other than wax, such as insects, plants, paper, plastics, cloth woven of organic or synthetic fibers, is possible if the material of which they are made can be completely consumed and leave no ash residue. Because this is difficult to ascertain in advance, there is always some degree of risk involved. These objects or substances may require strengthening or an increase in dimension before being invested. Thickening can be done by painting them with or dipping them quickly into molten

11–61 HAROLD O'CONNOR, U.S.A. The model was made from a flexible sheet of 1.5 mm thick foamed polyethylene, a common packing material. Cut into a shape, it was heated with a small torch, the heat causing the piece to contract, curl, and shrink, and its edges to melt and become rounded. The result is an organic-looking, lightweight form with a rough surface texture. To increase its thickness, the undersurface was painted with molten wax—not too hot, to prevent the form from melting locally. It was then sprued with more sprues than normal for a similar sized wax model to assure a successful casting. The model, painted with a surface tension breaking solution or wetting agent, was invested, and the flask was subjected to vibration or vacuum pressure to assure complete air evacuation. In the burnout (well vented to dispel noxious fumes) the polyester was completely consumed, leaving no residue, and the mold was cast. Photo: Ron Burton

wax, and stiffening by spraying them with a liquid plastic or lacquer. Using short sprues may help obtain a satisfactory casting. To be sure of as complete a burnout as possible, at the third stage of the burnout cycle, bring the maximum temperature to 1500° F (815° C), maintain it at that point for some time for a soaking heat, then reduce it to casting temperature.

WARNING

Potentially *toxic fumes* may occur during the burnout of most plastics. The area where the burnout furnace is placed should be well ventilated with a proper exhaust system since inhaling such fumes can cause health problems. The kiln or furnace should be well vented.

THE CENTRIFUGAL CASTING HAND SLING

The earliest use of *centrifugal force* to place relatively small amounts of precious metal under sufficient pressure to fill a small mold such as is used for jewelry making, was accomplished by the use of a *hand sling device*, still used by some jewelers today for centrifugal casting. When a *centrifugal casting machine* is not available, or an inexpensive system must be used, this method employing the hand sling can still be used. If it is not available, it can be easily constructed.

The *hand sling* consists of a smoothly rounded wooden handle large enough to be gripped well, with a steel ferrule attached at one end to which a heavy steel or iron wire loop is welded. Through the loop there may be a swivel loop to prevent kinking. (In another construction, a rod ending with a rivetlike restraining head is inserted into the handle, and the first link in the chain passes around and rotates around the rod.) The flexible arm consists of a "chain" of straight wire links looped at each end, followed by three or more others to form a chainlike series whose total length is approximately 18 in (46 cm). Attached to the far end of this chain is a circular, basketlike, flat-bottomed platform or flask cradle unit made of a disc approximately 3½ in (9 cm) in diameter, surrounded by an upstanding flange about 1 in (2.5 cm) high. Attached to the platform is an upward-curving wire loop joined to the last arm link. The total height of the platform and supporting loop is approximately 5 in (12.7 cm), but can relate to the height of the flask used.

The *platform* is designed to hold the mold-containing flask when it is removed with *tongs* from the *burnout furnace*, and to support and suspend it while it rotates. The mold must be prepared with a depression at the top deep enough to hold the amount of metal necessary for the particular casting. The metal is placed in this depression and heated with a *melting torch*. Once it reaches a temperature

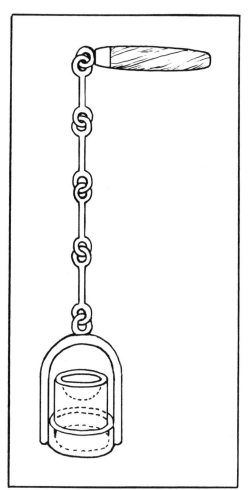

11–62 *A TYPICAL CENTRIFUGAL CASTING HAND SLING.*

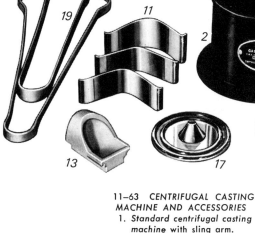

11–63 CENTRIFUGAL CASTING MACHINE AND ACCESSORIES

1. *Standard centrifugal casting machine* with sling arm.
2. *Base* containing heavy steel spring.
3. *Central shaft pin*, cocked, and retaining nut.
4. *Counterweight arm.*
5. *Two counterweights* in place on arm.
6. *Additional counterweights.*
7. *Crucible and flask sling arm.*
8. *Crucible carriage.*
9. *Vertical baffle plate.*
10. *Flask cradle pins.*
11. *Flask cradles* for flasks of different sizes.
12. *Centrifugal casting flasks* of various sizes. This machine will accommodate flasks with up to 3½ in Ø, and 2⅝ in high.
13. *Crucible* with 2½ oz gold-melting capacity.
14. *Crucible* in place on the crucible carriage.
15. *Stop rod pin* in up, cocked position holding the sling arm in place.
16. *Small-sized pouring or sprue gate former.*
17. *Large-sized pouring or sprue gate former.*
18. *Flask tongs*, 15 in long, used with all flasks.
19. *Crucible tongs*, 11 in long.
Photo: Courtesy Kerr Dental Mfg. Co.

above the liquidus of the metal being cast, while firmly gripping the sling handle, the standing slinger swings the flask *clockwise* in a vertically rotating path in a room space sufficiently high to allow clearance. About five to ten revolutions are performed during which the centrifugal force of the rotation flings the molten metal away from the center and, forcing out all air, makes it completely fill the mold cavity. The flask remains in place on the platform due to the same centrifugal force. The first rotations are the fastest in order to quickly create maximal centrifugal force, and the last rotations are slowed down to bring the mold to a halt, when it is set aside to cool.

Anyone who is new at using this simple but effective device is well advised to first make several practice "dry runs" to acquire the knack of performing a smooth clockwise or counterclockwise rotating operation, whichever is most comfortable for the particular individual.

THE CENTRIFUGAL MACHINE

The type of *centrifuge* or *centrifugal machine* normally used by individual jewelers works in a *horizontally* revolving plane. Others exist, however, in which the rotation is at an *angle* to the vertical, or in a *vertical* position. For safety's sake, the centrifuge should be surrounded by a *sheet metal shield* which will stop any accidental splashing of molten metal that might occur during an unsuccessful

casting operation or *metal runout* due to mold rupture. A typical model consists of a *base* bolted solidly to the *work-table* so there is *no vibration* in its action. Vibration must not exist if metal spattering is to be avoided. The centrifuge is placed with the manufacturer's nameplate, which indicates the front, facing the operator's position, and with the stop rod to the left of that position.

The base contains a central shaft and an oversized, powerful steel spring that provides the energy for the rotation of the machine's two arms. These are mounted at the top of the spring housing, on the central shaft pin around which they revolve while held there by a retaining nut. One arm holds the *counterweight,* and the other arm holds the *crucible* and the *flask.* Oil the central shaft *before* and *after* each use of the centrifuge to assure smooth operation.

THE COUNTERWEIGHT

The *counterweight* is mounted by a central hole that either fits on a straight rod on the arm, or is screwed on a threaded rod and held in place by a threaded tube that acts as a nut. The counterweight must balance the combined weight of the crucible, the molten metal, and the flask containing the mold. This second arm can be stiff, or articulated on a pivot, the latter called a *sling arm,* because when the centrifuge is set in motion, it slings or whips the molten metal into the mold cavity as it straightens in motion. Some models allow the size of the sling arm to be changed to accommodate flasks of different sizes.

CRUCIBLE AND FLASK POSITIONS

The *crucible* is held on the second arm by a *carrier* or *carriage* that snaps into position. Its shape is designed to conform with the bottom shape of the crucible used. The crucible rests up against a *vertical baffle plate* or *shield* against which it exerts pressure when the centrifuge revolves. The baffle plate is pierced with a *central hole* that lines up with the *nozzle* or opening at the adjacent end of the crucible. Through this hole the molten metal passes in a direct line into the sprue gate of the mold in the flask placed opposite it, and then into the mold cavity.

The *flask* is held immediately after the baffle plate in a *flask rest* or *cradle* whose size and shape must match that of the flask used. Sometimes flasks and their cradles are numbered for corresponding identification. The purpose of the cradle is to automatically position the flask so its central sprue gate is lined up with the nozzle of the crucible without any need for further adjustment. On large jewelry casting machines, the flask is bolted in place.

There is a relationship between the size of the machine, its arm length, the maximum crucible capacity size, and the flask size that can be used with it. A sample of these relationships is given in the following chart.

Capacity of Typical Centrifuge Machines

Crucible-Flask Arm Size	Crucible Capacity (maximum)	Flask Size (maximum)
4"	2 1/2 oz gold	3 1/2" dia., 2 5/8" high
4"	7 oz gold	3 1/2" dia., 4" high
6"	12 oz gold	4" dia., 6" high

BALANCING THE CENTRIFUGE

The balance between the counterweight and crucible-flask weight is done *before* burnout. Time cannot be taken for balancing *after* burnout because a rapid loss of heat from the mold would occur. Each flask must be individually balanced as its weight varies, even when the flask size is the same as one used previously.

To balance the arms, loosen the arm-retaining nut on the central shaft pin to allow free up-and-down movement, necessary for balancing. If the centrifuge has a sling arm, line it up straight with the counterweight arm. Place a cradle of the correct size on the arm, then place the flask containing the invested mold in the cradle, with the pouring gate pointing toward the crucible carrier shield. When using the largest flask capacity on some machine, a flask cradle is not needed as the flask in this case rests on the side guides of the backplate. Slide the crucible carrier against the flask and cradle tightly by pushing the far end of the crucible against it with *tongs.* Tongs are not actually needed now as the flask is cold, but must be used when placing the hot flask after burnout, and their use now is practice for that time.

The heavier weight of the crucible-flask arm end will now angle that arm downward. To balance its weight, on simple machines place the counterweight bearing a stamped number that corresponds with the flask number on the counterweight arm by sliding it onto the rod as far as it goes. More advanced machines allow more refined adjustments. The counterweight is screwed on a threaded rod, and its position adjusted until a balance is achieved between both arms, then a nut before and after the counterweight locks it in place. For a casting of 60 grams or less, one weight is sufficient, and for more than 100 grams, two weights are used. The retaining nut on the central shaft pin of the centrifuge is then tightened enough so that the arms do not vibrate in rotation. The machine is now properly counterweighted. Remove the flask for the burnout.

PREPARING THE CENTRIFUGE FOR CASTING

During the last hour of the burnout cycle, the centrifuge is prepared for casting. The arms have already been counterweighted and balanced. The crucible is in place on the crucible carriage. Dampen a strip of asbestos that has been cut to fit the floor of the crucible, and press it down to fit the inner shape. This *asbestos liner* acts as an insulator that shortens the time needed to bring the metal to a melt, and it protects the metal placed in the crucible from absorbing impurities or loose particles from the crucible. To make sure that the crucible nozzle opening is not covered by the asbestos liner, press a pointed tool through the hole to clear the opening. Use a fresh asbestos liner with each casting, and discard old liners. If you wish, an *asbestos pad* can be cut out and placed upright against the crucible carriage backplate, but again, be sure you make a central opening in it to correspond with the opening already there. Also, be sure the crucible fits tightly against this asbestos pad.

WINDING THE CENTRIFUGE SPRING

The *centrifuge spring* must now be tightened. With one hand, turn the arm in a *clockwise* direction. The number of turns necessary to wind the spring varies with the machine—manufacturer's instructions should be followed. A heavy-duty spring may require only one complete revolution. Other centrifuges require two complete turns for a small flask, three for a medium flask, and four for a large flask. Be warned that there is a *danger in overwinding the spring* because if too much pressure is exerted upon the metal when the spring is released, its weight is increased to the point where the extra force can cause the metal to break right through the mold, take out the back of the investment, and destroy the mold. On the other hand, if the spring is insufficiently wound, there may not be enough pressure upon its release to force the metal to fill the mold.

To hold the centrifuge arm in place, after winding, raise the *stop rod* from its slot in the base housing, and bring the arm past it, then back against it so its counterclockwise pressure holds it up. This it will continue to do until it is released later. The flask position should be away from the operator with the inner chamber of the crucible in a position facing toward the operator, at the other side of the central shaft pin, so its chamber is accessible for directing the torch flame into it to melt the metal.

11-64 CASTING MATERIALS, TOOLS AND EQUIP-MENT

1. *Metal casting grain pellets, top to bottom:* gold, silver, brass alloy, silicon bronze alloy, pewter clippings.
2. *Jelrus Handy Melt,* a portable, electric, rapid-melting furnace with pyrometer, 110 V AC or DC, 1250 W, also available 220 V.
3. *Refractory brick* or *soldering block* upon which hot flasks can be placed when removed from the centrifuge, and for use in soldering; standard size 3¾ × 2⅛ × 3¼ in.
4. *Transite asbestos composition board* for the same purposes as above.
5. *Stirring rods* for mixing molten metal: graphite, slate pencil, carbon, the latter of ½ in Ø, 12 in long.
6. *Sprue cutter* with compound lever, angled jaws, and plastic-covered handles, 9 in long.
7. *Sprue cutter* with pointed jaws, compound-lever construction; one handle can be held in a vise for one-hand operation, 9 in long.
8. *Heavy-duty bench model sprue cutter,* with long lever arm and cam-type action for minimum effort, maximum cutting power; blades are replaceable.
9. *Stiff bristle hand brush* for cleaning casting after shakeout: *brass wire hand brush* for the same purpose, 10 in long.
10. *Handy Sandy,* a bench-top model *sandblasting machine,* left side with attached glove, right side with hinged door access to chamber, enclosed light socket, magnifying front viewing glass lens, chamber 8½ × 10½ × 13 in deep.

11-65 SAARA HOPEA-UNTRACHT, Finland, designer; manufacturer Kultasepänliike Ossian Hopea, Porvoo. Fine silver "bean" shot or grain, the form in which it is purchased for casting purposes. Used with soldered links to make a necklace. Photo: Oppi

PREPARING THE CASTING METAL

The means of determining the amount of metal needed to cast a particular model has already been discussed in this chapter. Before the flask is taken from the burnout kiln, place the accurately weighed metal in the crucible. All new metal can be used, the best type being casting metal in pellet or grain form, or used metal from formerly cast pieces, such as clipped off buttons and sprues can be included, but only up to half of the total metal being cast or porosity will result. The latter must be *absolutely clean,* free of any particles of flux, investment, surface oxide, grease, solder, or other foreign matter. (If allowed to remain, such substances will become inclusions in the casting, affect its accuracy, surface, and become a cause of porosity.) Some casters premelt the metal *before* removing the flask from the burnout kiln, then remelt it after the flask is in place. Others find there is enough time to place the flask in the cradle, and then melt the metal. Some casters start the melt with only a portion of the total amount of metal in the crucible, melt that, then add the rest and melt it. Others prepare the crucible by fusing borax in it as a liner, then heat the crucible to a red heat, place the metal in the crucible, and bring it to casting temperature. The flask is placed in position and the centrifuge released.

TORCHES AND FUEL USED FOR MELTING CASTING METAL

The *torch* used for casting must be capable of producing and maintaining a flame of sufficient size and strength to melt the casting metal in the shortest possible time. Delays in the melt at this stage may cause an undue time lapse during which the flask may cool too much, in which case cold shuts may result in the casting.

A *reducing flame* is used to keep the introduction of oxygen to the casting metal at a minimum and prevent the formation of oxide which would reduce metal fluidity. Some types of torch fuel are less adaptable to realizing a hot, reducing flame than others. The most suitable fuel is an oxygen-propane combination whose flame tends to be more compact, which makes it possible to limit it more closely to the area of the crucible and the melt. Oxyacetylene fuel with a torch tip that allows a maximum of gas flow can also be used. Relatively small amounts of metal such as up to 5 ounces of silver can be melted with a gas-air torch.

PORTABLE METAL-MELTING FURNACES

Another possibility is a *portable electric melting furnace* which is also used to prepare alloys. A typical model is about 10 in (25.4 cm) high and 8 in (20.3 cm) wide, and weighs about 6¾ lb. Models are available equipped with a pyrometer, and can quickly reach the melting temperature of 1800° F (982.2° C), sufficient to melt 25 oz of gold or silver in 12 minutes; 15 oz in 10 minutes; and 5 oz in 6 minutes. As they are equipped with *graphite crucibles* 4½ in (11.4 cm) high by 1⅜ in (3.5 cm) diameter, no flux is needed and the atmosphere within the container remains reducing. Other metals can be melted in the same furnace, but a separate crucible must be used for each metal.

PLACING THE FLASK ON THE CENTRIFUGE

Flask placement and melting the metal can be carried out by one person, or with the help of an assistant. If you have an assistant, he or she transfers the flask from the burnout furnace, wearing *asbestos gloves,* and the molten metal is prepared by the other person. The flask is lifted with *flask tongs* and placed horizontally on the centrifuge arm with its back up against the backplate, making sure that the sprue gate opening points toward the crucible. The crucible and its carrier are pushed with tongs so the baffle plate is tightly up against the flask. If only one person must do the work of placement and metal melting, flask placement is first, followed by metal melting and pouring. If the flask has been heated to the necessary casting temperature for the metal (at right), its transfer from the burnout furnace to the centrifugal machine should be carried out without delay for minimum heat loss, but *great speed* is not necessary, and *may be dangerous.* The true temperature inside a flask drops an average of between 41–50 Fahrenheit degrees (5–10 Celsius degrees) every 4 minutes because heated investment is a poor heat conductor. This allows the operator sufficient time to make the transfer and then heat the metal, without rushing.

MELTING THE METAL IN THE CRUCIBLE

Light the torch and adjust the flame to a tri-cone reducing condition. Direct it at the metal in the crucible so its reducing zone plays on the metal with the center cone about ¼ in (6.35 mm) from the metal. If another part of the flame plays on the metal, its surface will appear dull as surface oxides will form. When the correct flame zone is in contact with the metal, the metal appears bright and shining. Adjust the flame distance until this occurs. Cover the metal with the reducing flame at all times during the melt up to the time of its release into the mold. This is done to eliminate the inclusion of free oxygen in the melt as its presence is the main cause of porosity in the casting and incomplete mold filling. The flame should enter the crucible somewhat from one side so it fills it in a spiral direction and does not bounce back into the torch. At the same time the adjacent flask mouth is being heated which helps in metal flow and maintaining investment temperature.

When the metal becomes hot, apply a pinch of casting flux from a supply placed nearby. Once the metal has contracted to a rounded form, add another pinch of flux. The flux coats the metal and also acts to prevent oxygen from coming in contact with it, and prevents the formation of oxides and the inclusion of free oxygen in the melt. If the metal appears dull, again add a pinch of flux or a small pinch of saltpeter (potassium nitrate, KNO_3, a strong oxidizer). Avoid using too much flux as an excess might be washed into the mold with the melt, and if so, will form surface pits on the casting. One way of reducing the oxygen in a melt is to stir it with a *carbon rod.* If any foreign particles appear on the metal surface, pick them off with a *slate pencil, carbon stirring rod,* or a *graphite rod.*

All metals should be melted in the shortest possible time. Carry the temperature somewhat *above* the melting point so it will flow readily, but never heat it until it boils, or prolong the heating excessively as the lower melting metals in the alloy will vaporize, changing the constitution

Recommended Casting Temperature for Metals

Metal or Alloy	Metal Casting Temp.		Flask Casting Temp.	
	°F	°C	°F	°C
Platinum	3000	1648.8	1400	776.6
Gold, 14k white	1925	1051.6	950	510
Gold, 14k yellow	1825	996.1	900	482.2
Gold, 10k white	2025	1107.2	1000	537.7
Gold, 10k yellow	1850	1010	950	510
Silver, sterling	1775	968.3	800	426.6
Bronze	1950	1065.5	900	482.2
Copper	1900	1037.7	800	426.6

Metal casting temperature varies slightly with the metal or alloy used. Generally, the metal is heated from 100-150° F (37.7-65.5°C) above its liquidus temperature. The flask temperature also varies with its size. The amounts given here are a close approximation of what is required.

of the alloy and altering its characteristics. Also, if metal is overheated and poured at an unnecessarily high temperature, it will shrink more as it solidifies than would the same metal poured at a lower temperature. Overheated sterling silver and alloyed gold castings often appear black when released from the mold. This occurs because the copper content in the alloy rises to the surface during solidification. It can be removed by pickling in an acid bath, or by electrostripping.

CASTING METAL ON THE CENTRIFUGE

When the metal reaches proper casting temperature, judged by its bright, rippling surface, prepare to release the centrifuge arms. Hold the torch in the left hand with the flame playing on the metal. Extend the right arm, put your fingertips on the counterweights (or grasp the handle behind them if there is one), and pull the crucible arm back clockwise against the spring *gently* to avoid spilling metal from the crucible. This causes the stop pin to be released and fall back into its slot in the centrifuge base. Just before lifting your fingers away to allow the centrifuge arms to start their revolution, the casting arm should be unmoving and *steady;* if not, arm vibration, metal spattering, and wear on the bearings will result. Be sure the torch tip is high enough to clear the flask and crucible after arm release. Straighten your fingers, and together lift your arm and the torch simultaneously *straight upward* above the machine. The centrifuge immediately starts to revolve. Turn off the torch flame.

THE CENTRIFUGAL ACTION

The casting spins on its own axis as rapidly as the spring allows for approximately 2–5 minutes. Upon the first rotation of the arm, and in the first few seconds of the arm's rotation, the molten metal in the crucible is flung through the crucible hole into the sprue gate and into the mold cavity. The rate at which it exits from the crucible is controlled by the diameter of the crucible nozzle opening, the inside diameter of the sprue in the mold, and the weight of the metal used in the casting; a greater weight exerts a greater force. Because the heat of the mold is sufficiently high, the metal remains liquid long enough to pass into all parts of the mold. While the centrifugal force impels the metal outward from the center of rotation, it is mechanically restrained because the mold cavity walls are fixed. This force of the continuing rotations is great enough to hold the metal densely against the mold walls without backpouring through the sprue opening or pooling in the lower portions of the mold for the time necessary for it to solidify.

The speed of rotation varies from 500–1200 rpm. The force of this rotational speed is expressed as the term "g," the symbol for the gravitational acceleration of a mass toward a center by centrifugal force in pounds per pound. In centrifugal casting, the range is from 50–100 g's, meaning from 50–100 times the force of gravity. The pouring speed is therefore many times faster and the pressure far greater than that produced by gravity alone, as in a static gravity pour.

Metal freezing starts from the outermost position of the casting inward toward the central sprue. The hotter metal accumulates nearer the axis of rotation, stays hot longest, and acts as a feeding reservoir to the rest of the casting. The denser parts are the outermost metal and the heavier parts of the casting because of their greater volume of metal. Density helps the metal to eliminate gases during casting, and also to eliminate porosity in those parts.

Never try to stop the rotation of the arms of a centrifuge. Allow the spring to expend its force, the arms coming to a rest at their own rate. This will take a few minutes. The exception is when using a vertically spinning centrifuge. When its spin slows and is nearly stopped, halt it so the arm holds the crucible and flask at the bottom of the arc with the sprue end pointing upward so that any metal still in a molten state cannot escape.

Put on *asbestos gloves* and hold the *tongs* in readiness for when the arm stops revolving. Lift the flask from its cradle and place it, sprue upright, on a waiting *asbestos pad*. Allow it to cool and the metal to solidify for 3–5 minutes for a small flask and for up to 10 minutes for a large flask.

THE SHAKEOUT: Freeing the casting from the investment

Allowing the investment to cool too long makes its removal from the casting difficult. On the other hand, immersing the flask in water too soon may cause the metal casting to crack or brittleness in the casting. The best way of judging shakeout readiness is to start when all the redness has disappeared from the sprue gate opening in the mold, and the button of metal there has turned black. Lift the flask with tongs and submerge it in enough water in a *pail* to cover it so it will not spatter. Use a pail because the disintegrated investment can be caught in it and later disposed of. If you place the flask under running water, the investment will run down the drain and possibly clog it. By subjecting the investment suddenly to water and shaking the flask in the process, the investment quickly disintegrates and normally the casting will fall out of the flask. If it does not, tap the flask with a *mallet* to

11–66 L. BRENT KINGTON, U.S.A. "Bird Ring." Cast 18K gold. The skull, a reminder of the mortality of living creatures, is also a receptacle of transmuted thought. Winged creatures are universally a symbol of spiritualization, or the soul that upon death flies from the body. *Photo: Myers Walker.*

11–67 JEAN CLAUDE CHAMPAGNAT, France. "Scorpion." Cast silver ring. The scorpion is the eighth zodiacal sign. The body becomes the ring shank. *Photo: Oppi*

help crack it up. In the cast jewelry industry, after subjecting the flask to water, the casting is shaken out by the use of a *pneumatic vibrating ram or hammer* held against the flask. Remove the asbestos liner from the flask and clean away any adhering investment.

CLEANING THE CASTING: Fettling

Fettling is the cleaning, trimming, and finishing of a casting once it has been removed from the mold. On inspection, the casting may not be free of all traces of investment. If stubborn traces still remain after scrubbing it with a *stiff bristle brush* under running water, other methods may have to be used. It may be possible to pry them loose with a *wooden tool* or *hand pick,* taking care not to scratch the surface. Investment can also be removed by *compressed air, steam jet blasting,* or by submerging the object in a cleaning solution in an *ultrasonic cleaner.* Pickling by acid may be necessary to remove investment and surface oxides to clean and brighten the casting.

CLEANING A CASTING BY AN ACID BATH

The high casting temperature causes the casting to emerge from the process with a black, oxidized outer layer. This must be completely removed from the casting as well as from the sprues and buttons, especially if the latter are to be saved for use in future castings. For this reason, do not sever sprues and buttons from the casting until the oxide is removed.

The pickling bath used for silver is 1 part sulphuric acid to 8 parts water. For gold use 1 part hydrochloric acid to 10 parts water. A Sparex No. 2 pickling solution can be made from 2 tablespoons of Sparex added to 16 ounces of water. Prepare enough pickle to completely cover all parts of the casting, and place it in a deep enough *Pyrex glass container.* As mentioned, the pickle should also remove remaining investment plaster, but may not succeed in removing all of it without several repetitions of the process.

Either heat the casting until it is a dull red color, and submerge it in the pickle with *copper tongs* without splashing, or put it cold into the solution and heat the pickle to a point below boiling. Agitate the casting in the solution, and after approximately 10 minutes, remove it with tongs to inspect the progress of investment plaster and oxide removal. If either still exists, brush the casting under running water and return it to the pickle. Finally, rinse the casting in water, neutralize any remaining acid traces by submerging it in an alkaline solution of sodium bicarbonate and water, then rinse and dry it.

A nontoxic, safe, and inexpensive solution that acts as a solvent for the residual inert silica in investment plaster that remains on a casting, and that also partially removes surface oxide from gold, silver, and their alloys, recommended by the Technical Advisory Committee of The Worshipful Company of Goldsmiths, contains the following:

Ammonium sulphate	150 g/liter
Glycerol (A water-soluble tertiary alcohol)	25 ml/liter
Water	1 liter

Boil the object in this solution using separate containers for white or yellow gold. Follow by pickling to remove remaining oxide. This solution can also be used as an ultrasonic cleaner bath which accelerates the process.

11–68 BARBARA GASCH, West Germany. "Lizard." Cast 14K gold ring worn on two fingers, the body on the index finger, and the tail curving around the middle finger. The lizard is a symbol of regeneration because when it loses its tail, a new one grows to replace it. *Photo: Astrid Mucs*

11–69 NAOMI GREENBURG PECK, U.S.A. "Clasped Hands." Cast 14K gold ring. Two clasped hands traditionally symbolize a mystic marriage. Height 1½ in; width ¾ in. *Photo: Neil Anderson*

11–70 JACLYN DAVIDSON, U.S.A. "Wheeel" Cast sterling silver ring hollowed internally to lighten weight. *Photo: J. David Long*

FINISHING THE CASTING

Remove buttons and sprues of small cross section with *nippers*, or by sawing through them with a *jeweler's saw and blade*. If *sprue cutter shears* are available, use them for the removal of heavy sprues. Do not use them on delicate work as the clipping action might distort the casting, but use a saw blade instead. Cut the sprue off as near as possible to the actual casting without removing any of the metal that is a part of the casting itself. Trapped air bubbles that have been cast on the object can be ground off with *rotary files*. Buttons and sprues removed from a casting are called "returns" as they can be reused, if uncontaminated with foreign matter, in another casting.

Hand finishing to remove sprue contact points and surplus metal is done with *hand files, chisels, gravers,* or *chasing tools,* whichever may be appropriate to the situation. After filing, remove any surface marks left with a *fine-grit abrasive paper* or *cloth*. The last smoothing is done with *crocus cloth*. The removal of sprue ends from castings by grinding is called "snagging."

Findings such as ear wires, tie tacks, posts, pins, and safety catches are hard soldered to the object before the last stages of finishing. After this, the object will not be subjected to any process requiring high temperatures. After soldering, remove surface oxide by immersing the work in an acid pickle. In some cases, the surface oxide might just be rubbed or polished to relieve the color only where a bright finish is wanted.

Machine finishing utilizes any suitable mechanical device. The *flex-shaft* mounted with *small rotary files* or *abrasives* is convenient for reaching parts of a piece that are otherwise difficult to reach, such as undercuts, details, and the inside of ring shanks. For selective polishing, use a small polishing mop or wheel mounted on the flex-shaft. For overall polishing and form smoothing, use a regular *polishing motor, buffing wheels,* and suitable *abrasives*. (See Metal Finishing, Chapter 14, for details.)

Coloring comes after final polishing and is the last step in the finishing process. (See Coloring Metals, Chapter 17.)

Stone setting follows coloring and is the last process in completing the work as stones cannot be subjected to any process that requires heat. Preparing a wax model for a stone setting has already been discussed and should be referred to again. The process of setting a stone in a casting is essentially the same as setting a stone in a fabricated setting. Remember, however, that cast metal is brittle as compared to fabricated metal, and therefore take greater care in bending cast bezels, claws, and prongs when setting the stone. To thin a claw in preparation for bending it over a stone, grind away a portion of its *inner* side so its outside appearance remains unchanged.

The problem of size accuracy enters into the stone-setting process. If a small percentage of shrinkage in the casting affects the accuracy of the setting for a particular stone, it may be necessary to grind away a part of the setting to allow the stone to fit.

POROSITY: A major casting fault and its causes

Porosity is unsoundness in cast metals caused by the presence of small pores, holes, or voids in the metal. Porosity in a casting is a major fault. The problem of porosity has been mentioned, and is summarized here. *Blowholes* are related to porosity but are larger in scale. A blowhole is a hole produced in a casting when gas is trapped in the mold when it is filled, or by gases that evolve during the solidification of the metal. Because it cannot escape, it creates a small pocket within the metal.

SYMPTOMS INDICATING THE EXISTENCE OF POROSITY

Surface porosity is indicated by a rough area on the casting surface that will not take oxidation, will not be wet by solder, and may resist the smoothing process. It is sometimes possible to remove it by filing.

Internal porosity consists of a porous, uneven internal structure that is the cause of brittleness and weakness in the metal. An internally porous part may crumble when bent, as when turning down a claw, or a part may collapse if subjected to pressure. Internal porous areas may show up when finishing the casting. When filing in finishing, such an area of roughness defies smooth finishing. In some cases it may become necessary to rout out the area and replace it with clean metal, or flood it with solder.

CAUSES OF POROSITY IN AN INVESTMENT CASTING (In procedural sequence)

Faulty spruing that causes an inhibited flow of metal into the mold—resulting in turbulence—creates porosity as a consequence. Sprues that are too small in section do not allow the metal to completely fill the mold, so it expands with less pressure and becomes porous.

Incomplete burnout, indicated by a grayish color or streaks of black in the investment, is evidence of the *presence of carbon* in the investment and/or the mold cavity. When the mold is filled, the carbon permeating the investment prevents the escape of gases which become trapped in the metal. When carbon exists on the inner mold surface, surface porosity results in the casting. Unconsumed residue of the model due to incomplete burnout may leave particles of carbon behind that can become a cause of surface or internal porosity.

Too hard air pressure from the torch flame, or the use of an oxidizing instead of a reducing flame during the melting of the metal may be the cause of the introduction of oxygen to the melt. The presence of oxygen in the melt is the main cause of porosity.

A *lack of flux,* or an *insufficient amount of flux* applied during the melt results in oxides that form being swept into the casting, causing porosity. If old metal that has not been cleaned properly but is still flux coated is used in the

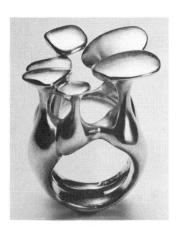

11–71 PEDER MUSSE, Denmark. "Svampevaegst" (Mushrooms). Solid cast sterling silver ring. *Photo: Tue Lütken*

melt, a *surplus of flux* is dissolved into the melt and brings air along with it.

Old metal in excess of the maximum allowable in a single casting, may already contain porosity, which is then introduced into the melt.

Protracted heating or overheating the metal causes a structural or compositional change in the metal because the low-melting metals in the alloy are vaporized. The resulting space left by these metals in the alloy structure allows the absorption of oxygen into the melt.

Excessive speed and pressure from the centrifuge when wound too tightly will cause the metal to flow into the mold cavity too quickly, resulting in inner *turbulence,* a cause of porosity.

An insufficient amount of metal for the casting due to faulty calculation results in a small or nonexistent button which means insufficient back pressure on the rest of the metal in the mold, causing it to expand and become porous.

Trapped gas pits in the metal during shrinkage, called *pinhole porosity,* consists of a sprinkling of small holes in a casting. As vents are normally not made in a mold in investment casting, the only way gases (which always develop during casting) can escape is through the pores of the investment. Any condition that prevents this escape causes the gases to remain trapped within the mold and to enter the casting. One cause is the choice of a flask that is too large for the particular model. This results in too thick a surrounding layer of investment which makes it more difficult for evolved gases to emerge through the investment pores. Another cause, incomplete burnout of the mold, has been mentioned.

Unequal cooling of the casting causes uneven shrinkage which can result in porosity.

CENTRIFUGAL CASTING: Practice

DEMONSTRATION 23

LYNDA WATSON-ABBOTT uses an intaglio clay mold to form a wax reiief model for casting

Photos by Lynda Watson-Abbott and Richard Miller

1 The design is drawn on paper. This is not always done, but was needed in this case to plan the divisions of the Masonite pressing stamps subsequently used.

2 A traced copy of the design is ready to be glued with rubber cement on a ⅛ in (3.2 mm) thick piece of Masonite composition board, a thickness that allows design parts to be accurately cut out.

3 The design contains five parallel façade levels. Following this plan, the Masonite is cut into five horizontal pieces, each one forming a silhouette for each level. Holes are drilled through each Masonite part to allow wooden matchsticks to be inserted into them for use as handles with which pressure can be brought on the patterns to force them into the clay.

4 The five Masonite silhouettes with matchsticks inserted into the holes, and their edges smoothed, are ready for use as press stamps.

5 Into the ¾ in (19 mm) thick clay slab each stamp section is pressed to a varying depth. The part forming the foreground is pressed most deeply so it will project foremost, and each successive level is pressed less deeply to produce an illusion of distance. The total depth used is ⅜ in (9.5 mm).

6 To these basic intaglio forms, further details are added or cut away, keeping in mind that all forms will ultimately appear in reverse as a relief. Pieces of wood and metal are shaped for use as stamps to form the desired detail shapes. Parts of the relief requiring greater detail are made of porcelain clay which lends itself to more sharply defined forms. In some cases, thinly rolled clay is cut into forms and applied.

7 The clay mold form in a flat, shallow pie tin is placed in an ordinary, cold baking oven which is then slowly heated to 250° F (121° C) to evaporate moisture and harden the clay. In this case, drying takes about 20 minutes, but the time will vary with the moisture content of the clay. The clay is allowed to cool until it can be comfortably handled.

8 Wax is melted and carefully brushed over the clay (which is still warm) to fill the details in the intaglio mold.

9 Successive layers of wax are brushed on and the thickness is built up until all depressions are filled and a relatively uniform thickness of about 10 gauge B.&S. is reached. The surface seen here is the back which is smoothed with a gas flame issuing from a rubber tube into which the tube of a glass eyedropper filled with cotton has been inserted. This arrangement produces a soft flame that can be used in smoothing wax models in final stages.

10 The clay mold with the applied wax is soaked in

1

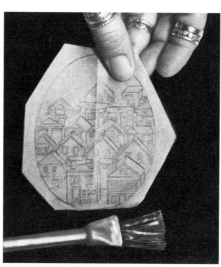

2

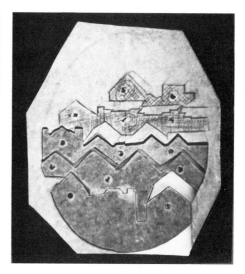

3

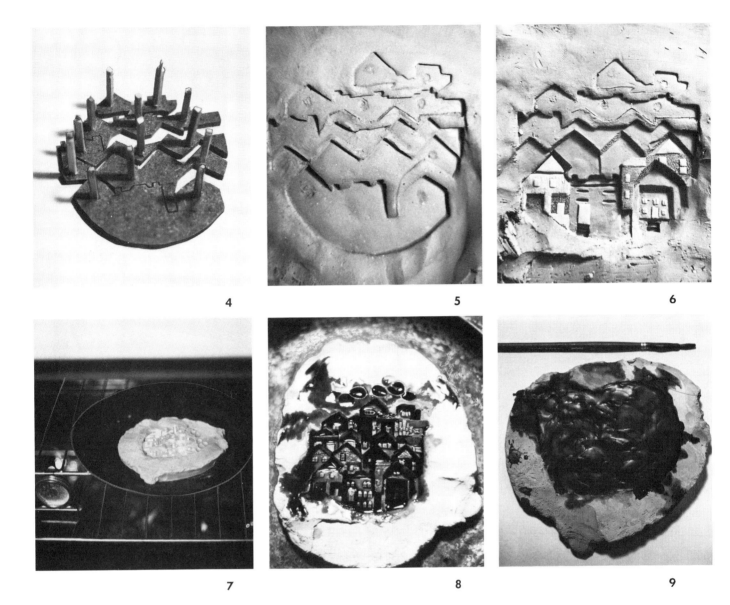

4

5

6

7

8

9

cool water, and the dissolving clay is removed with a soft bristle brush.

11 The wax relief model with almost all of the clay removed is shown here.

12 Many fine details not achieved with the clay are then added directly to the wax model with an *electric wax welder* having a fine needle point. The model is trimmed

with a knife to an oval shape, and a half-round wax wire is added to frame the work.

13 Heavy, 10 gauge B.&S. wax sprues are attached to the back of the model, the sprues converging toward a point where a wax button will be attached later. The model is positioned at an inclined plane to facilitate the filling of the cavity of the mold later during casting. Here

10

11

12

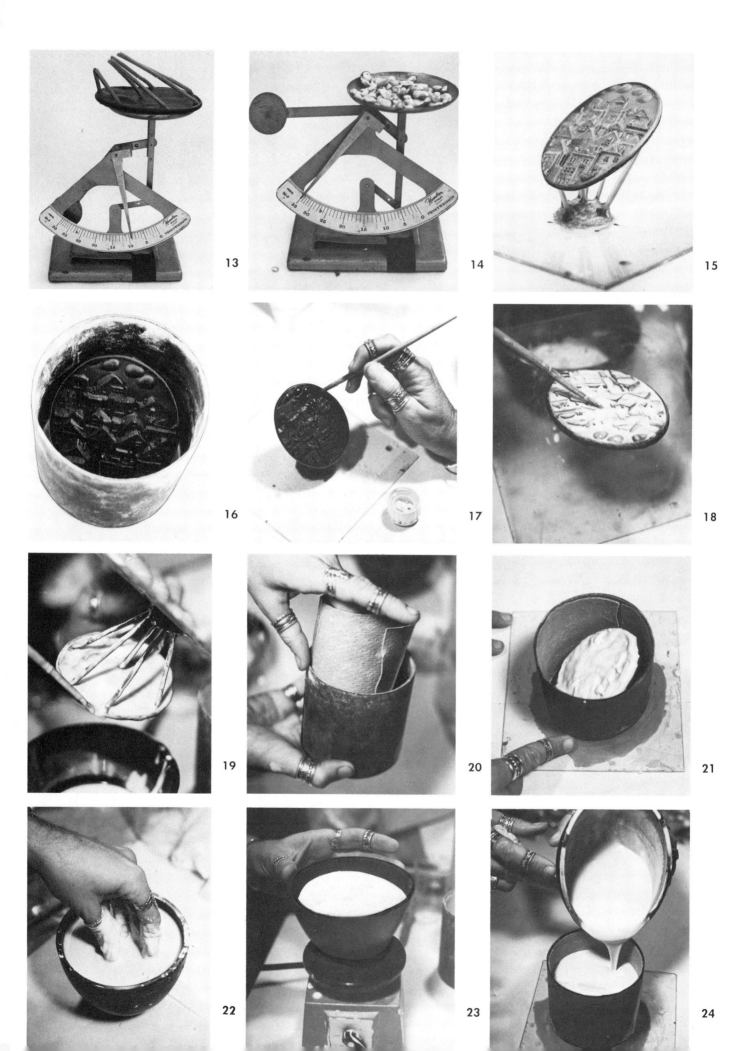

13

14

15

16

17

18

19

20

21

22

23

24

25   26   27

the model is being weighed with sprues attached to determine the amount of metal needed for this casting. The wax model weighs 9.5 dwt (pennyweight troy).

14 Sterling silver casting shot is weighed. The amount needed is calculated by multiplying the total wax weight by a factor of 10, then adding a quarter of this amount for the button. A total of 120 dwt is used. Because of the maximum weight limitation of the scale, this amount is weighed in four batches to make up the total.

15 The model sprues are attached to a wax button prepared on a sheet of Plexiglas. Its position is determined beforehand by placing the flask over the model to make certain a clearance of about 5⁄8 in (1.59 cm) exists between the model and the flask walls.

16 The flask is placed again over the mounted model to check its position and clearance.

17 The flask is removed and Kerr Vacufilm debubblizing solution is painted on the wax model.

18 A small batch of investment plaster is mixed in a rubber mixing bowl and applied to coat the model face. This mixture is the same as the investment plaster prepared later to fill the flask.

19 The reverse side of the model is also covered with investment slurry.

20 A moistened strip of measured asbestos is placed within the flask as a liner. It is moistened to relax the asbestos so it will take on the flask shape.

21 The flask is positioned over the model. An oil-mixed clay is pressed all around the point of contact between the flask and the Plexiglas sheet to make an airtight seam to prevent the escape of investment slurry.

22 A new batch of investment plaster is prepared to fill the flask. Lumps are squeezed with the fingers to make a smooth mix.

23 The rubber investment container is placed on a vibrator and vibrated to eliminate air bubbles from the mix.

24 The flask is filled to the top with investment and allowed to stand while the plaster sets.

25 After the plaster sets, the flask is separated from the Plexiglas sheet, and the wax button is removed, revealing the sprue ends which are seen here as dark spots. If the button was made smoothly, shaping the pouring gate is not necessary, but if not, it can be scraped smooth at this point with a round-edged tool.

26 This is a *homemade front-loading burnout kiln* of firebrick, with a *pyrometer*. The flask is placed inside with the pouring gate opening down, and a 6–8 hour burnout cycle commences to eliminate all wax from the mold as well as all carbon. At 500° F (260° C) the flask is turned so that the pouring gate points upward.

27 The *sling-arm centrifugal casting machine,* counterweighted, and with the weighed grain metal already in the crucible which is in place on the crucible carrier is shown here. The machine arms have been wound clockwise three turns, and the arm-retaining pin has been raised to hold the arm in place under tension, ready to receive the flask after burnout.

28 While wearing asbestos gloves, the flask is removed from the kiln with flask tongs after the burnout.

29 The flask is placed in position in the flask cradle on the centrifugal machine with the sprue pouring gate facing the crucible, and the crucible is pushed with tongs against the baffle plate and the flask so they are tight against each other and lined up.

30 The metal in the crucible is melted with a reducing flame from an oxyacetylene torch. The retaining pin is released and drops into the base in preparation for the release of the arm which is held manually at the counter-

28   29   30

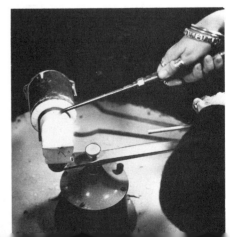

31   32   33

weights while the torch flame plays on the metal until it is in a molten state and ready for casting.

31 The centrifugal machine casting arm has been released by simultaneously lifting the hand and the torch upward. The arms revolve and the metal flows by centrifugal force into the mold cavity. The flask is removed from the casting machine with tongs after all motion has stopped. The button appears well filled, which is an indication that the casting is probably successful. The flask is set aside and allowed to cool for about 5 minutes until the button metal appears black. It is then immersed with tongs in cold water, removed, and reimmersed, the process repeated until all hissing stops, which indicates its temperature is below that of the boiling point of water. It is then left in the water.

32 The flask can then be removed and the casting shaken out. This is the casting with sprues and button still attached, and some investment plaster still adhering.

33 Remaining investment is removed from the casting with a stiff brush, and after pickling to remove surface oxides, the sprues are cut off.

34 The finished, sterling silver coat button, 3½ in × 4¾ in (8.9 cm × 12.1 cm), weighing 4.7 ounces.

34

CASTING METAL ON METAL: Ganga-Jumna

A second metal can be *cast on* an existing casting, or on a one-piece construction of metal sheet or heavy wire that has no soldered joints. The combination of metals is chosen for color contrast, and is possible because of the difference in their melting points. This technique has been used in India for hundreds of years in the manufacture of cast copper or bronze images of deities which are then decorated with elaborate ornaments in brass made in a second lost wax casting on the first. It is called *Ganga-Jumna* decoration, named after the blending of the muddy (gold) waters of the Ganges River at its confluence with the blue (silver) waters of the Jumna River at Prayag, a place of great sacredness to Hindus. The term was broadened to include any object in which one metal decorates another by casting or inlay. Today, this method might be termed bi-metal casting.

First the base form is made of a metal having a higher melting temperature than the metal to be cast upon it. Thus, for instance, sterling silver can be cast on copper, bronze, titanium, or gold; brass or gold on nickel; and gold on steel. The base form is brought to a finished state, and the wax for the second metal is built up in position directly on top of it. To be sure the casting will hold on the base form—since they will not fuse at points of contact—some form of undercut, interlocking, interpenetration or envelopment of the casting and the base is necessary in the construction. An undercut groove can be made in the base form at the position where the two forms overlap, or grooves can be made at the edges and the wax can be forced into them. The wax can penetrate the base form at some points where holes are made so that an interlocking cast peg or even a rivet form with a head on the reverse side is created, or the wax can partly or completely envelop the base form. When the wax overcasting is complete, run sprues to it, invest the object in a flask, burn out the wax, and cast as usual. Careful temperature control is necessary to avoid melting the metal of the base form.

PRESSURE CASTING

In the basic concept of *pressure casting,* a dense casting is created by the impact of suddenly created pressure on the molten metal which acts to force it into the mold cavity. In the concept of pressure, an *applied force* acts against an *opposing force* distributed over a surface.

Open-mold casting illustrates this principle. In this simple type of casting, still in wide use by jewelers in many places in the world, small castings with flat backs are created. First a negative mold depression is carved into a one-part open mold made of a piece of charcoal, steatite (soapstone), or a block of set and dried investment plaster. Metal sufficient to fill the cavity is placed into this depression, and heated with a torch flame until it melts. A flat metal surface such as a steel block (the applied force) is brought down on the molten metal which is forced to fill the mold cavity against the back pressure resistance of gases that occur in the mold cavity (the opposing force), the metal displacing the air and other gases that form and escape through the investment. The applied force is maintained by the weight and mass of the block for the short time needed for such a small metal casting to solidify into a positive form taken from the negative form of the mold cavity.

Steam pressure casting is a more advanced type of pressure casting, one that utilizes the force of steam. *Steam* is water converted to a vapor state and expanded by heat which brings it to the boiling point, 220° F (100° C), or beyond. When expanding steam is trapped or placed under pressure, it generates a force which can be utilized as energy or the driving power to execute mechanical processes, such as in this case forcing the molten metal through the sprue hole into the mold cavity. The limitation of the process as applied here in an improvised setup is that only relatively small castings can be made by its use.

Sprue the model within the mold with a short, small-diameter sprue no more than 14 gauge B.&S. (0.0641 in, 1.629 mm). This diameter is small enough to prevent the molten metal from flowing of its own accord by gravity through the sprue until forced to do so. Invest the model with investment plaster within a cylindrical casting flask. When the plaster is set, make a cup-shaped, rounded

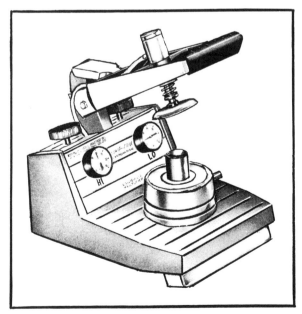

11–72 *TRI CASTER FOR PRESSURE CASTING*
It accommodates flasks 1½ × 2–3½ × 4 in. (C. R. Hill Co.)

depression in the investment at the sprue gate end. This depression will hold the necessary metal for the casting, and air. Heat the flask and mold by the usual burnout process to 1200° F (648.8° C) for silver casting.

To apply the pressure and create the steam, a simple improvised *pressure flask cover* is made. For this purpose, a metal jar cover which in essence is a flanged disc, can be used. Attach a wooden dowel to it with a screw, to serve as a handle. Line the cover with a few layers of *asbestos sheet* which is made wet for each use in casting. Allow enough of the flange on the cover to be free so it will overlap the flask. The inside diameter of the cover must be sufficiently greater than the outside diameter of the flask to permit its quick placement over the flask. (Ready-made pressure covers that work on the same principle of manual impact are commercially available.)

While wearing *asbestos gloves,* remove the flask from the *burnout kiln* with *flask tongs,* and place it on a heatproof *refractory surface* such as a *kiln shelf* or an *asbestos block.* Place the necessary amount of metal into the sprue depression, sprinkle it with casting flux, and quickly heat the metal with a *torch* to a molten state. Bring the pressure cover with its wet asbestos lining down directly upon the flask, and hold it there firmly. This causes an instant generation and expansion of trapped steam from the moisture contained in the asbestos. The steam forces the metal through the small sprue opening into the mold cavity. Hold the pressure cover in place for at least 30 seconds to keep the metal under pressure until it solidifies in the mold.

PRESSURE AND VACUUM CASTING

Jewelry supply manufacturers have used the positive, applied pressure principle in combination with negative vacuum pressure to devise a more complex mechanism, such as the Tri Caster, that allows a predetermined casting pressure to be uniformly applied to the mold to eliminate the possibility of excessive pressure which might cause mold fracture. The casting metal is placed over the sprue opening in the heated, burned-out flask, and melted. Because the metal is melted directly over the sprue opening in the burned-out flask and not in a separate crucible, when manual pressure is then applied by a lever that brings down a cover on the flask, turbulence in the metal (which occurs during its delivery from a crucible to the mold cavity) is eliminated. This mechanism utilizes a graduated pressure system, starting at low pressure, then building up to higher pressure, both levels preadjusted on gauges on the mechanism. The result is a slower entrance of the metal into the mold, which, combined with a coupled vacuum pump, eases the passage of gases through the investment pores. Peak pressure is maintained until the metal has solidified.

VACUUM ASSIST CASTING

In vacuum assist casting, the force of gravity is assisted by the *negative pressure* of a partial vacuum created in the mold to force the metal against the resistance of gases to fill the cavity. Any metal can be cast by this method, but it is particularly suited to casting alloys that include oxidizable metals or that are subject to gas absorption. The advantage of vacuum assist casting is that it makes possible the use of larger casting flasks than those used in

11–73 VACUUM CASTING EQUIPMENT
1. *Vacuum assist casting table with vacuum pump, 115 v, 60 cycle, AC, 23 in wide, 13½ in deep, weight 65 lb.*
2. *Casting table or baseplate with intake hole, and silicone rubber pad.*
3. *Investment table.*
4. *Rubber pad, 10 in square.*
5. *Plastic bell jar, Ø 9 in; height 8 in.*
6. *Spring mount to allow vibration.*
7. *Vacuum gauge.*
8. *Control knob.*
9. *Pouring crucible with attached wooden handle, 6 oz gold capacity.*
Photo: Courtesy Swest Inc.

centrifugal casting, and the casting of a greater amount of metal than is possible with the centrifugal casting machines used by most craftspersons. Also, the cost of vacuum assist casting equipment is less than centrifugal casting apparatus, the process is relatively simpler, and the results comparable.

When preparing the model for vacuum assist casting avoid making parts less than 22 gauge B.&S. in thickness as they may fail to fill completely. To avoid the premature cooling of the molten metal when poured, use larger sprues, or more of them than would be used with the same model if cast centrifugally. The sprues should be short and in as nearly a vertical position to the plane of the flask end as possible to make it easier for the metal to fill the cavity. In this position, there is also less chance of cracks developing in the mold. After mounting the model on the sprue former, paint it with a wetting agent such as green soap and water, or Vacufilm (a commercial preparation) to break surface tension.

THE VACUUM ASSIST CASTING TABLE

Jeweler's suppliers have devised a table top *vacuum assist casting table* suited to use by individual craftspersons. It contains a vacuum pump capable of creating a partial vacuum for either of the two purposes for which this table is designed: air bubble removal from investment, or vacuum assist casting of molten metal.

One unit has a 10 in (25.4 cm) square, single, aluminum table or baseplate that can be used for both purposes. Another, made by Swest, has *two* tables, side by side, each

for its own purpose. On one side is the *investment table* with a central opening over which a *rubber investment pad* 10 in square with a matching central opening is placed. Over it goes a glass or reinforced plastic *bell jar* whose size limits the size of the mixing container or flask that can be placed beneath it. An average bell jar size has an 8 in (20.3 cm) diameter and is 7 in (17.8 cm) high, but larger sizes are used on vacuum tables equipped with greater motor pump power. The air within the bell jar is evacuated by the motor pump through a tube attached from the hole to the motor. The container with the premixed investment is placed under the bell jar, and the air is partially evacuated by the pump. A flask containing the invested model can be placed there for the same purpose, with a stiff paper collar taped to its upper portion to contain rising investment. This platform is mounted on jiggle springs to allow it to vibrate when it is struck at an edge with the hand or a tool. The vibrations assist in air removal from the investment.

On the other side is a rigid aluminum *casting table,* also with a central intake hole, on which a *silicone rubber pad* or a dampened *asbestos pad,* either one having a matching central hole, is centered over the hole in the baseplate. On this the hot flask is placed after burnout when ready for casting. The unit is fitted with a *filter trap* between the pump and the table to prevent moisture or investment particles from being drawn into the pump. The machine normally draws 27–29 inches of mercury at one level. A *vacuum gauge* indicates the vacuum in inches of mercury as the latter reacts to the pressure pumped by the motor. A control knob activates the vacuum action in either the investment table or the casting table.

To check the functioning of the system, place a half-filled glass of water whose temperature must be 72–80° F (22–26° C) under the 8 in diameter plastic bell jar placed on the investment table, and turn on the vacuum pump. Within 40 seconds, the water should begin to bubble violently. If it does not, the bell jar is not making complete sealed contact with the rubber pad. This can be achieved by moistening the rubber pad with a sponge soaked with water or a liquid green soap and water mixture before positioning the bell jar, which when placed on such a wet surface, will better grip the pad and form a tighter air seal.

THE VACUUM ASSIST CASTING PROCESS

In the vacuum assist casting process, it is important that chances of investment fracture be avoided, because in the case of cracks, air and molten metal are drawn through the investment by the vacuum pump and the casting is destroyed. Mixing the investment correctly in the manner already described under centrifugal casting is therefore critical. Heating the investment *slowly* through the critical heat range of 350–600° F (176–315° C) when cracking is most likely to occur, is also important. After mixing for 2 minutes, place the investment-filled mixing container on the vacuum table under the bell jar, turn on the vacuum pump, and allow the mixture to boil for 1 minute while the air is evacuated. Turn off the vacuum, remove the bell jar and the container, then place the flask containing the mounted model in its place. The seam between the sprue gate former and the flask must be luted (sealed) with sticky wax or Plasticine clay which contains oil to make that seam airtight, or the investment will be drawn out by the vacuum. Place a 1 in (2.5 cm) strip of *draftsman's tape* or stiff paper around the upper edge of the flask to temporarily extend the flask height and contain the investment spatters that arise. At first, pour in the investment while the flask is canted to one side to eliminate the chance of air entrapment under model parts, and as it is filled, but before it reaches the top, gradually straighten the flask to a vertical position when the model is covered. Replace the bell jar over the flask. Close the valve and turn on the vacuum pump for 1½ minutes, which should be enough to remove all air bubbles from the investment. Remove the flask, fill it to the top with investment plaster, and place it aside for about 30 minutes for the plaster to set.

To be sure the flask makes a good sealed contact and has a firm seat on the rubber pad, it must have a smooth, even edge. After plaster set, remove the draftsman's tape, the sprue pin and gate former, and scree the closed side opposite the sprue gate opening level with a *straight edge,* or, if the model size allows, shape it to a cup-shaped hollow with a *curved steel rib* or template such as is used in ceramics. In the latter case, be sure there is at least ¼–½ in (6.4–12.7 mm) thickness of investment from the furthest extremity of the model end to the end of the investment. *Excessive* investment thickness here may prevent the effective operation of the vacuum in drawing out gases, and during the pour it may hamper drawing the metal into the mold.

While the burnout is in progress, prepare an *open crucible* by lining it with a ¹⁄₁₆ in (1.5 mm) thick moistened sheet of asbestos, or by coating it with a borax and alcohol paste, then while the crucible is on a refractory brick, fire it with a torch to fuse the flux to the crucible bottom. When weighing the metal, it may be necessary to use up to 25% more metal than would be used for a comparable model cast centrifugally, in order to fill the extra large or additional sprues. Place the weighed metal in the crucible. In preparation for casting, place a *protective screen* over the central intake orifice on the casting table, then center the *silicone rubber pad* on the table.

An inexperienced caster using the vacuum assist method may need the help of an assistant. One person prepares the melt, and when the burnout and the melt are ready, the other removes the flask from the burnout furnace, places it on the rubber pad, activates the motor and closes the pump valve. The metal is then poured into the flask. These steps must be coordinated.

After the burnout, place the flask on the silicone rubber pad (or a moistened asbestos pad) with *crucible tongs.* This silicone rubber composition can withstand a temperature up to 1000° F (537.7° C). The transfer from the burnout furnace to the casting table must be quick to retain as much heat as possible in the investment, therefore the furnace and the vacuum assist table should be near each other. Position the flask directly over the intake hole with the sprue gate opening *upward.* After flask placement, test the seal by turning on the pump and watch the vacuum gauge indicator; it should quickly indicate 20–25 pounds of vacuum, expressed in inches of mercury. If it does not, there is a leak somewhere between the flask and the pad. In that case, quickly lay the tongs across the flask top, and press down on the flask to force it to become seated in the rubber pad. If there is still no seal, there may be some foreign matter such as investment plaster at the flask edge

which prevents contact, or far more seriously, a crack exists in the investment through which air is drawn. In the latter case, the mold cannot be cast by the use of a vacuum assist and it is useless to pour the metal.

The *melt* of the metal starts when the burnout cycle is completed. When heating the metal do not bring the torch tip too close to the metal or the flame will blow out, and when the torch is withdrawn, it will reignite with an explosive effect that may cause the metal to be blown out of the crucible, or later, when the heat is prolonged with the torch after the pour, it may be blown out of the mold. For vacuum assist casting, the metal in the crucible is heated higher above its liquidus (more than 50–100 Fahrenheit degrees [10–37 Celsius degrees]) than for centrifugal casting. When its surface seems to play under the flame, turn on the vacuum pump motor and close the valve. As soon as the gauge indicates the correct degree of vacuum pressure, lift the crucible with tongs that fit it well, and quickly but steadily pour the metal into the sprue gate of the flask. A crucible with an attached metal handle that controls a bottom opening in the crucible, called a *drop metal crucible,* is available. When the metal is molten, it is held over the sprue gate and triggered with a finger to open the bottom trap and drop the metal directly into the sprue gate.

After pouring, play the torch flame on the sprue button for a few seconds. Because the atmospheric pressure on the closed end of the mold is reduced by the vacuum, the lowered pressure causes a quicker escape of air and other gases that might otherwise resist the passage of the metal through the pores of the investment. Gravity, aided by the vacuum, immediately draws the molten metal into the mold cavity. If the walls of the investment are too thin and the weight of the metal great, the pressure of the metal may cause a rupture in the investment, and in such a case, the metal will run out of the mold and the casting will be destroyed.

Remove the torch flame, open the vacuum valve to release the vacuum, and turn off the pump motor. Allow the flask to cool for 2–10 minutes depending on the size of the casting, until the button surface freezes and becomes dark, then remove the flask from the casting table. The casting can be shaken out by immersing the flask in room temperature water, as usual. Avoid hammering or in any way misshaping the flask as this will affect its ability to form a good seal in future use. The usual procedures of removing the sprues, cleaning, and finishing follow.

VACUUM PUMP AND MOTOR MAINTENANCE

The oil in the pump acts as a filter against contaminating substances. From time to time, the oil level should be checked to see that it is properly maintained, or the oil should be changed after every 50 castings. To add oil, place the spout of a container with lightweight machine oil into one of the holes of the exhaust cap, and pour in the oil until the indicator shows it has reached a marked level. Surplus oil can be released, or a complete oil change made by opening the drain cock and catching the oil released in a container. The rear bearings of the vacuum pump motor must be oiled with a few drops of oil once a year.

RUBBER MOLD WAX INJECTION

Duplicating a master model with a reusable flexible mold

The concept at the basis of this system of duplicating a master model is the use of *thermoplastic compounds, rubber* and *wax,* that when heated take on any form, and when cooled will set and retain that form. This method of mass producing wax models from a master rubber mold for use in investment casting is widely used in the jewelry manufacturing industry today. It is also finding favor with growing numbers of independent jewelers who wish to support themselves by their craft. They use it as a means of producing exact reproductions of a jewel, *in series,* which reduces costs and time, and makes it possible to sell their work at favorable prices.

11–74 FINLAND, Viking Age reproductions manufacturer Kalevala Koru, Helsinki. Cast bronze belt buckles inspired by old finds reproduced in series by rubber molds. *Photo: Otso Pietinen, courtesy Kalevala Koru*

MAKING THE MASTER MODEL

The *master model* of a jewel to be cast can be made of any material that can withstand approximately 300° F (148.8° C) required to vulcanize rubber, without becoming misshapen. Remember that the wax-injected replica *exactly reproduces all details* of the master model, including surface texture, therefore take great care in finishing. Models can be made of silver, brass, bronze, or gilding metal. If they are mirror buffed, their removal from the mold is easier. Sometimes models are made of tin, chromium or rhodium plated, as these materials will not stick to the rubber mold after vulcanization. If a *sized object* such as a ring is being made, allow for 10% shrinkage when making the model; the shrinkage occurs when the replica is cast in wax, and to some degree, during investment casting as well. When the model is finished, dust it with *fine talc* loaded on a *stiff bristle brush* before placing it on the rubber. This lubricant will help later in allowing the model to be parted from the vulcanized rubber mold.

THE SPRUE FORMER

It is common practice to hard solder a *sprue former rod with an attached nozzle-button former* to the model at a point where it will not interfere with the design, and in a position that allows the model to lie as flat as possible in the mold. Hard solder is used because soft solder is weaker and subject to disintegration by exposure to heat during vulcanization. A typical brass rod sprue former is ⅛ in (3.17 mm) in diameter and is about ¾–1½ in (1.9–3.8 cm) long, the length depending on the requirements of the model. Generally speaking, sprues should be as short as possible. They should join the pattern without any decrease in dimension at the point of contact because this would restrict the flow of molten metal to the mold cavity. If the model happens to be made of a nonmetallic material, the sprue former can be attached to it with any suitable adhesive cement. When the wax is injected into the mold, the sprue and attached nozzle-button automatically become a part of the resulting wax model, and later, the metal casting. If a heavy model is being cast, a larger sprue may be needed, and if very delicate work such as a filigree model is being cast, it may be necessary to use two sprues. Ready-made sprue formers with attached nozzle-button formers are available from casting material suppliers. Separate nozzle-button formers are available pierced with a central hole into which the sprue rod is passed.

THE MOLD FRAME

The vulcanizing process calls for the use of a *metal mold frame* to contain the rubber mold material in which the model is embedded. The frame is usually of heat-conducting aluminum or steel. It can be a *one-piece frame,*

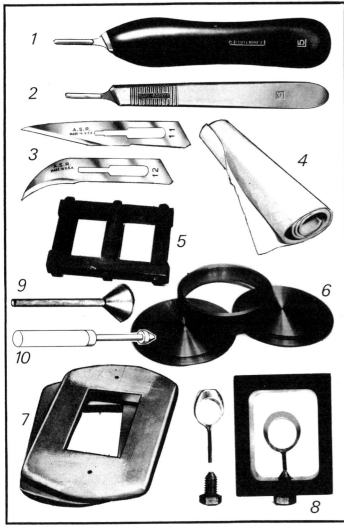

11-75 TOOLS AND MATERIALS FOR PREPARING RUBBER MOLDS
1. Bard-Parker *rubber mold–cutting knife* with plastic handle.
2. Bard-Parker *rubber mold–cutting knife* with steel handle.
3. Changeable *straight and curved or hooked blades* for these handles.
4. *Mold rubber,* ⅛ in thick sheet, 16 in wide, cloth-backed, available in regular hard, or super soft qualities.
5. Welded steel *rubber vulcanizing frame,* with two-mold capacity. Frames with three- or four-mold capacities are also available.
6. Steel *round rubber mold frame and plates,* Ø 9 or 12 in.
7. Two-part, cast aluminum *rubber vulcanizing frame.* The lower half has two projecting pegs that key it to the matching holes in the upper half.
8. One-part cast aluminum *rubber vulcanizing frame* with rounded inside corners. A *removable sprue former* (disassembled at left) holds the model with attached sprue rod in position during packing and vulcanizing. Available in a wide range of sizes and thicknesses.
9. Brass *sprue rod* and attached *sprue gate former* that assures correct fit of the wax injection nozzle, and acts as a locating pin when dividing the mold.
10. *Sprue burning mandrel* with insulated wooden handle, used to form a sprue gate when no sprue former is employed, by heating it with a torch or Bunsen burner, and pressing it into the sprue end of the rubber mold where it burns a matching depression in the mold.

sometimes with demountable sprue attachment, or a *two-piece frame,* one part fitting above the other. All faces are ground true and absolutely flat to assure close fit and accurately matching parallel surfaces with those of the platen in the vulcanizing press. Large welded steel frames are available for use on large vulcanizers. These can accommodate from two to four molds which are vulcanized simultaneously.

537

MAKING A TWO-PART MOLD WITH A SEPARATOR

The purpose of using a *separator* when forming a rubber mold is to facilitate the division of the two-part rubber mold after it has been vulcanized. For the less experienced craftsperson, a two-piece mold frame and the use of a separator is the easiest method of rubber mold making, therefore this method is described here first.

PLACING THE MODEL IN THE MOLD FRAME

The process of placing and centering the model in the mold frame can be facilitated if a two-piece mold frame is used that has a groove or cradle on the inner surface at one of the small ends with half of a cylindrical-shaped opening in one mold frame half, and half in the other. Together, when the frame is assembled, they form a full cylinder. In this case, solder a tube of a diameter matching the opening to the end of the sprue nozzle-button. When this along with the attached model is placed in position between the closed mold frame, the model is automatically clamped rigidly in the proper position. By another method, the sprue forming rod is sawed in half lengthwise to within ⅛ in (3.17 mm) of its attachment to the model proper. Later the separator material is forced into this groove and helps to hold the model in place. There should be a minimum ¼ in (6.35 mm) clearance around the model and the sides of the mold frame. Position the model in a way that will allow it to be easily divided at a center line to simplify the removal of the wax replica later.

THE SEPARATOR MATERIAL

The *separator material* can be any thin-gauge metal such as aluminum foil, or the cloth which adheres to and protects the cleanliness of the mold sheet rubber when it is purchased. Cut out the separator sheet of 38 gauge B.&S. aluminum, copper, or brass foil, and make its size a little larger than the outer dimension of the two-part mold frame. One half of the frame has *projecting pins* which act to accurately register the position of the assembled mold halves. Place the foil or cloth separator on a flat surface, put the mold half with the pins over it, and tap the frame lightly to make an impression of the pin's position on the separator material. Remove the frame, and at those marked places, cut holes into the separator exactly the size of the pins, as indicated by the impression.

11-76 PENTTI SARPANEVA, Finland, designer; manufacturer Turun Hopea, Turku. Bracelet cast in silver or bronze in seven sections, hinge joined. The design is based on traditional Carelian lace motifs. The rubber mold allows high-fidelity reproduction of very intricate patterns. Length 7½ in. Photo: Jorma Laine

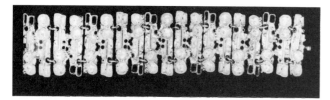

11–77 REGINE JUHLS, Norway, designer; manufacturer Sølvsmie Regine & Frank Juhls, Kautokeino. Silver cast bracelet in ten parts, linked with jump rings. The original handmade model was reproduced by rubber molds. Length 19 cm. Photo: Börje Rönnberg

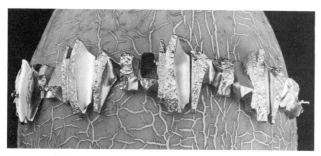

11–78 BJÖRN WECKSTRÖM, Finland, designer; manufacturer Lapponia Jewelry Ltd., Helsinki. "The Bear." Gold bracelet cast in parts by rubber molds, assembled by hinges. The design uses an alternation of rough-textured and smooth planes. Photo: Winfrid Zakowski, courtesy Lapponia Jewelry Ltd.

Next assemble the two parts of the mold frame with the separator between them. While they are so held together, trim away all excess parts of the separator material that projects beyond the frame with *shears*. While the parts are still assembled, mark the separator material at the *inner dimension* of the mold frame with a *scratch awl* or pencil. Separate the two parts of the mold, and remove the separator.

Place the separator on a flat surface. Set the model at its center, and with a pencil, draw an outline of its outer shape completely around it, allowing an additional ⅛ in (3.17 mm). With a *sharp knife* or *shears*, cut out this outline shape. Mark the position of the sprue forming rod and attached sprue holder, and also cut away the separator in this area unless a split sprue rod is used.

In such a two-part mold, provisions must be made for the *four mold keys*, one at each corner. At the four corners of the separator in the visible space within the frame of the mold, and approximately ⅛ in from the inner mold wall, cut out four square holes, about ⅜ in (9.52 mm) each. These open places in the separator will allow the rubber of both halves of the mold, when vulcanized, to join and become *one* at these spots. Later, the four mold keys can be formed at these places, where they will act to automatically and accurately position the two parts of the mold. To help assure easy separation, dust microfine powdered graphite over the surfaces to be separated after vulcanization. The fineness of this powder assures a very smooth surface.

THE UNCURED RUBBER

Uncured rubber is available in rolls, sheets, and strips of smooth-surfaced rubber of ⅛ in (3 mm) thickness or thicker. Besides ordinary production rubber, special flexible types are available for use when *severe* undercuts make more than usual bending around the model neces-

sary, for use in cases where low shrinkage is essential, when easy flow around intricate designs is needed, and for use with flat models. Soft mold rubber is used for thick molds, and firm rubber for thin molds. Rubber sheets are covered on one surface with an adhering cloth or plastic material in order to keep that surface absolutely clean, free from dust, grease, and foreign particles. In practice, after the rubber is cut out to the desired dimension, the adhering protective cloth is stripped off just prior to placing the rubber in the mold. This same protective cloth is used to form a *mold separator*.

The rubber manufactured for use in molds vulcanizes or cures at 300° F (148.8° C) in 30–45 minutes. It is low in shrinkage, high in flexibility, provides accurate detail, can be easily marked and cut, and is long lasting. After curing, it forms a rubber that can be easily bent, which is necessary when releasing the wax-injected pattern, and it quickly returns to its original form. Also available in sheets is already vulcanized rubber, impressed with a small three-dimensional pattern of diamond shapes. This type is sometimes used as a separator in a two-part mold. It is also used to form *mold keys* or *guide patches*. In the latter case, small squares are cut out and applied to one half of the mold which it sticks to easily, with the embossed pattern up. During vulcanization, a negative, matching pattern is automatically formed in the opposite mold half, the two patterns effectively acting to key the mold. Fresh rubber as purchased with its protective cloth is automatically clean. When it is stripped and handled, the fingers must be absolutely grease-free. If it is necessary to clean rubber sheets (or a mold about to be used that has become grease infected), submerge it into a container holding *acetone*, allow it to drain in the container, and then lay it out to dry; or rub it with a clean cloth impregnated with *acetone, benzene, naphtha, carbon tetrachloride*, or a substitute. The rubber used for vulcanizing must be absolutely clean or the mold will develop air pockets where the grease has prevented its welding during vulcanization.

PACKING THE MOLD FRAME WITH RUBBER

Mark the rubber sheet into divisions equal to the dimension of the inner mold frame. To determine the number of rubber thicknesses needed of the standard ⅛ in (3.17 mm) thick rubber, measure the thickness of the mold frame. As an example, a frame 1 in (25.4 mm) thick requires eight layers, four on one side of the pattern, and four on the other side. Cut the rubber with *scissors* or a *sharp knife*. Place one half of the two-part mold frame, inner part up, on a flat table surface. Strip off the protecting cloth from the cut rubber sheets and place half their number into the mold frame. (If a one-piece mold is used, fill it halfway.) Every model has its special requirements. If the model is deep, it may be necessary to cut out its silhouette in the inner sheets to allow space for it. It also may be necessary to force small pieces of rubber into recesses of the model where it is thought that the rubber will not be sufficient to fill the space, as for instance inside a ring shank. These pieces should be packed in tightly to be sure that the details in the model are filled. It is usual to pack in somewhat more rubber than may seem necessary, to be sure to fill the mold.

Place the separator over the filled mold half. If a split sprue is used, first force the separator into the split before placement. If you are using a mold frame with a reamed sprue holding cradle at one end, or with a sprue holder that is screwed into the mold frame, place the sprue with attached model in position next. If embossed rubber keys or guide patches are used, place these now. Smear some talc over only the embossed key patches to keep them separate from the rest during vulcanizing as an aid in finding their exact location when later cutting the mold apart.

Now place the second half of the mold frame to engage the first. Stuff pieces of rubber over and around the model as needed, then place the remaining sheets of rubber on top of these. The procedure is the same as before, but in reverse. Dust the final top and bottom exposed sheets with talc to prevent their adherence to the vulcanizer's platens. The prepared mold unit is now ready for vulcanization.

VULCANIZING THE UNCURED RUBBER MOLD

Hot vulcanization was discovered by Charles Goodyear in 1839. The process of vulcanization improves the physical properties of crude rubber. It is hardened, strengthened, and its qualities of flexibility and elasticity are improved. In other rubber-manufacturing processes such as tire making, vulcanization is done by the use of sulphur compounds. The rubber used for wax model mold making is designed to be cured by heat alone.

OVEN VULCANIZING   The simplest way to vulcanize rubber in the mold is to make an assembly of the mold, covered top and bottom with a *pressure plate* made of a ¼ in (6.35 mm) thick aluminum sheet, predusted with talc, all clamped together securely with *C-clamps*. This whole assembly as a unit can then be placed into any *preheated oven* that is large enough to hold it, and can be heated to the necessary 300° F (148.8° C). The process takes 30–45 minutes, depending on the requirement of the rubber and its bulk. Overheated rubber can char and become brittle around the model. Underheated rubber will not cure fully,

and will have a texture like putty when cooled. It can be reheated to the correct temperature. *Caution:* When handling any heated mold, wear *asbestos gloves,* and allow for good ventilation. After the first 10 minutes at full temperature, tighten the clamps; and after 25 minutes repeat the tightening to prevent possible leakage and to put maximum pressure on the rubber to take the form of the model. During vulcanizing the rubber solidifies into one mass, and tends to shrink. If it is not tightened, the result may be a faulty mold.

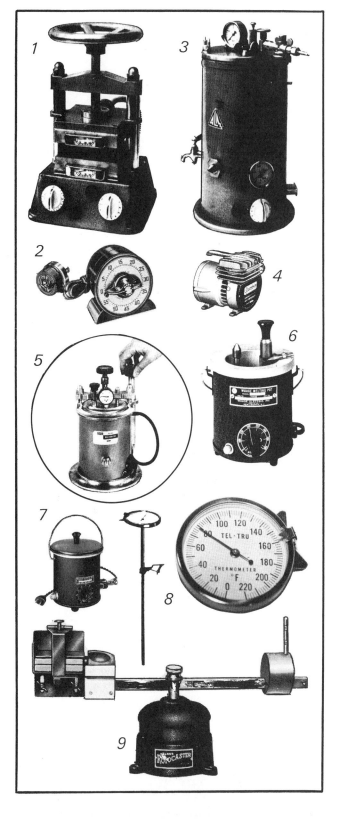

11–79   *RUBBER VULCANIZING AND WAX INJECTION EQUIPMENT*
1. *Screw press–type electric rubber vulcanizer,* with regulated temperature on both upper and lower platens, each with its own temperature gauge. Platens are 140 × 170 mm, max. platen gap height is 75 mm.
2. *Electric timer* into which the vulcanizer is plugged, and which will turn it off at any predetermined time up to 60 minutes.
3. *Wax injector,* a closed pressure pot, used with a separate air compressor, has pressure regulator and gauge 1–30 psi (between 7–10 psi are normally used for casting jewelry wax), thermostatic temperature controls, drainage cock, automatic safety pressure release valve, one discharge nozzle; wax capacity 4 liters (approx. 8 lb); height approx. 18 in; Ø 10 in.
4. *Air compressor,* small, suitable for use with a wax injector, providing pressures up to 35 psi, with ¹⁄₁₂ hp motor, 115 v, length 8½ in, width 6 in, height 7 in, weight 12 lb.
5. *Kerr wax injector* containing its own manually adjustable air compressor system, pressure gauge, with a range up to 30 psi, wax capacity 1 qt (approx. 2 lb), Ø 6½ in, height 10 in, 115 v or 230 v, AC.
6. *Waage hand hydraulic wax injector* with thermostatic controls, wax capacity approx. 2 pt (1 qt), and upright wax injection nozzle.
7. *Waage electric wax-melting pot* with cover, thermostatic controls to keep the wax at a constant, set temperature, available in capacities from 1 pt to 20 gal, 110 v, AC.
8. *Dial thermometer,* hermetically sealed stainless steel, accurate to within ½° F, in stem lengths of 6, 8, or 12 in, with a dial range temperature of 0–220° F for use with wax pots, injectors, and plating solutions; or 50–400° F for use with vulcanizers; and others up to 1000° F.
9. *Centrifugal wax-casting machine,* 16 in arm length, with adjustable rubber mold clamp, sliding crucible carriage, and counterweight. To make a wax casting in a rubber mold, the mold must be lubricated with a mixture of tincture of green soap and alcohol. The mold is clamped on the holder with the crucible nozzle inserted into its sprue gate, the spring is wound three or more turns, and the heated, liquid wax is ladled from an open casting wax pot into the warmed aluminum crucible. The centrifuge is then released to cast the wax in the mold.

THE VULCANIZER AND VULCANIZING Vulcanization is normally done by the use of a *vulcanizer*. This machine combines heating units with a press that holds the assembled mold while its rubber contents are subjected to heat. Various models are designed for use by individual jewelers and factories. Smaller bench or table models are available. A typical small model has two absolutely level *platens* approximately 5 in × 7.5 in (12.7 cm × 19.1 cm), and has a maximum opening between them of 3.5 in (8.9 cm). The larger the platen, the larger the mold that can be accommodated. The lower platen is fixed in the base, and the upper platen can be moved up and down like the jaws of a vise by a wheel-handle lever mounted on a heavy central pressure screw, 1 in (2.54 cm) or more in diameter. Models variously have two, three, or four machine guides that hold the upper platen rigidly enough so that when moving and fixing the platens they remain in a position parallel to each other. This makes it possible for equal pressure to be brought on the whole mold. Both platens are heated electrically (115 volts, AC, 300 watt, and 200 volts, AC, 300 watt models are available) by an automatically controlled, liquid-type thermostat set in the base. They can attain a constant set temperature up to 450° F (232.2° C) by adjusting the marked knobs and controls. They usually have an external thermometer indicator, and pilot lights to indicate when they are working. Separate *automatic timers* are available into which the vulcanizer's outlet is plugged so that after a preset time, the current will automatically shut off.

Lift the talc-dusted mold with a *broad spatula*, and place it in the *center* of the preheated lower platen so that pressure on it will be uniform. In the jewelry industry, the mold is placed between *two pressure plates* made of rigid, ¼ in (6.35 mm) thick sheets of aluminum whose size corresponds with the outer dimension of the mold. These are used to prevent the heated rubber from contacting and possibly sticking to the vulcanizer's platens. The contacting surfaces of the pressure plates (or the vulcanizer's platens when no pressure plates are used) can be sprayed with an *aerosol silicone coating* which acts to allow easy release of the rubber mold after vulcanization. Screw down the vulcanizer's top platen onto the mold assembly. After an interval of 10 minutes, screw the platens together more tightly to increase the pressure on the rubber and take up any slackness. Tightening can be repeated after 20 minutes. After 30 minutes to as much as 1 hour, depending on its bulk, the rubber is vulcanized to a solid mass or block that completely surrounds the enclosed model.

Remove the mold assembly while wearing *asbestos gloves*, set aside the pressure plates, and place the mold on a heatproof surface to cool, or submerge it in water at room temperature. Cooling takes 20–40 minutes. If no separator has been used, remove the rubber mold from the mold frame simply by forcing it out. If a two-part mold was used and it does not budge, rubber fins may have formed at the parting line. Insert and draw a *flat-bladed knife* along the inner mold frame to cut the fins and release the mold. If a sprue forming device or mold separator has been used, the mold parts must be separated before the mold can be removed. Both mold halves can be marked with a number or name for identification with a heated, blunt-pointed metal tool.

DIVIDING THE RUBBER MOLD

The rubber mold is now ready to be divided in half up to the enclosed model which must of course be removed.

The *mold-cutting knives* can be of several types. All have a short, sharp cutting blade similar in size and shape to surgeons' *scalpels*. In some the blade is permanently attached to a metal handle, and others have a plastic handgrip-shaped handle that has provision for the removal and replacement of blades of different shapes. Two basic blade shapes are the most useful: a *straight*, pointed blade, and a *curved* one.

A rubber mold with a separator can be divided with relative ease. The procedure for dividing a solid rubber mold is more difficult and requires practice and skill. The basic idea in dividing a mold is to do so in a way that facilitates the later extraction of the injected wax pattern.

We consider the mold made with a separator. The parts at the four corners meant to form the keys must be dealt with first. Into a *bench vise*, place one corner where a separator divides the mold. With the fingers, stretch the corresponding other half away from it to allow the knife blade access to one of the corner keys. With the blade make four cuts of uniform depth perpendicular into the opposite mold half following the boundaries of the separator as a guide. This forms a *rectangular key*, but it is still attached at its fifth side to the other mold half. Stretch the mold further away, make a fifth incision parallel to the separator, freeing the key. Follow the same procedure for the remaining three corner keys.

Next, hold one half of the mold in a vise and with the fingers stretch it away from the other half but toward you. This will expose the remaining ⅛ in (3.17 mm) around the model which is then cut up to the mold cavity and the still enclosed model. Use long knife strokes, if possible directed away from the model to avoid doing it damage. At intervals in the cutting, dust the just cut mold parts with talc to keep them from sticking. In this way the mold is divided into two parts and the model is freed and removed. Remove the separator material. The two mold parts should fit together perfectly.

Inspect the inner surface of the mold cavity for possible small flaws as these can be corrected at this point. To make corrections, heat a *metal modeling tool* in an *alcohol burner* flame or over a *Bunsen burner* flame, and very carefully smooth the flaw away. An *electric wax welder* can also be used. If necessary, small bits of vulcanized mold rubber can be added, as for instance in the case of a small hole that needs to be filled.

MAKING A ONE-PIECE RUBBER MOLD WITHOUT A SEPARATOR

Rubber mold makers in the jewelry industry ordinarily do not use a separator, but favor a one-part mold frame and one-piece mold. Often even the sprue former is eliminated. In this case, after the solid mold is vulcanized, a sprue opening is *burned* into the mold from one edge up to the model with a heated metal rod of ⅛ in (3.17 mm) diameter. The nozzle shape is made next with a *nozzle burning mandrel* whose shape matches that of the nozzle of the wax injector machine to be sure of a tight fit. Its point is heated with a torch and pressed into the mold at the sprue hole to the proper depth.

DIVIDING THE ONE-PIECE RUBBER MOLD

Dividing a one-piece mold is an art that requires experience and is learned with practice. The mold must be cut in half, but in some cases, the upper half can be thinner than the lower. There is no separator to serve as a guide in dividing the halves. With a *mold knife* make a ⅛ in (3.17 mm) cut all around the center of the mold edges. Grip one corner of the lower half in a vise to hold it firmly. Stretch the upper part away. If no rubber key studs have been placed at the corners (they can be used even in the case of solid molds) form a key by making four cuts, described on p. 540, into one half of the mold only. If the four key patches have been used, expose their position by cuts in the mold edges. Make the corner keys by five cuts described on p. 540.

Assume that a sprue and nozzle-button have been used. Spread the mold halves apart and start the cuts at the left side of the sprue button. Holding the blade parallel with the large mold surface, cut along the sprue until you penetrate the mold up to the model. Thereafter, always make the cuts long and sweeping, starting at the model and ending at the mold edge. Continue to cut along the parting line of the model toward the mold edge, progressing gradually in a clockwise direction around the model until you reach the other side of the sprue and the mold is divided into two parts. The irregularity of the cuts in the rubber surface also acts to key the two mold parts together. In some cases, one of the short edges of the mold is *left uncut,* and acts as a hinge to hold the mold parts together. This eliminates the need for keying the mold.

RELEASING UNDERCUTS

A model with *shallow* undercuts can be easily released when the mold is bent open. A model with *severe* undercuts may not be easy to release, even when the rubber mold is bent backward after wax injection. Provision must now be made for such cases to allow the easy release of wax-injected models. Each model with undercuts has its own particular problems. One of the skills of the rubber mold maker lies in finding the best way to release it. If release of the model from the mold is not easy, the whole purpose of the rubber mold is defeated.

Study the position of the undercut. Try to imagine the best direction in which a cut can be made that would release it. Make a judicious cut perpendicular to the mold at that point up to the model and out to the mold edge. Do not make more such cuts than are really necessary as too many will weaken the mold and possibly affect its accuracy. To test whether the model can now be released without force, hold the mold half and bend it back with the fingers. The model should come out easily. If it does not, decide where it is still being held back and make another cut at that point.

11–80 CLAUDE WESEL, Belgium. Yellow gold fabricated ring reproduced in limited series by rubber molds. Severe undercuts are no problem in rubber mold reproduction. *Photo: Bernard François*

Rubber molds, when handled with care, can last a long time, depending on how much they are used. In the jewelry industry a mold in production can last for two years or longer.

INJECTION WAXES

The waxes used in injection wax model making have the same range of characteristics as the dental waxes used to hand form a model for one-time reproduction by lost wax casting with investment plaster. The wax should possess both hardness and flexibility. It should run easily at a moderate temperature somewhat above its melting point (which varies with different waxes), so its properties are not impaired by overheating. It should not adhere to the mold, should be flexible when warm so it is easily released from the mold, should be strong enough to bend without breaking, and should burn out completely after being invested. Seasonal atmospheric and temperature differences may necessitate a change in the type of wax used to one that is harder in summer and softer in winter. Some injection waxes are plasticized to harden them and minimize pattern breakage. These are especially suited to making intricate, delicate patterns. The wax is bought in bulk, or in flake form which makes it easier to be melted in the *wax injector tank.* Approximately 2 pounds of wax make 1 quart of molten wax. Place an appropriate amount in the injector tank according to its capacity. (A new injection wax available from Kerr called Accu Injection Wax has a built-in releasing agent that eliminates the need for talc or other releasing powders or rubber molds.)

11–81 JUDITH BROWN, U.S.A. "Celery Necklace." Cast in silver or bronze. Impressions were taken from real celery stalks with a dental elastometric impression material, then reproduced in wax. Pieces with greater total dimension than 6 in in any direction were divided, and later reassembled. The cast metal result was then worked over for detail. From this metal master model, a rubber mold was made for wax injection to produce an edition of 25 necklaces. *Photo: Peter Stettenheim*

THE WAX INJECTOR MACHINE

The *wax injector machine* can be either of two basic types. One works by a manually operated injection pump whose handle is pushed down while the mold is held against the nozzle. By *manual hydraulic ram action,* molten wax is forced to fill the mold cavity. The other works by *air pressure,* either contained within the tank or produced by a separate *air compressor.* A typical model of either type has an insulated tank with a capacity of one quart of molten wax, a thermostatic control, a built-in thermometer that indicates temperatures up to 220° F (104.5° C), and a drain cock to allow the wax to be "bled" or completely evacuated when it becomes necessary to change the type of wax used. Some machines have a small tank opening into which the premelted wax must be poured, and others have an opening large enough to admit the wax in chunk form, eliminating the need to premelt it. Large models used in production have a larger wax capacity of up to 4 quarts. They may have *two* nozzles instead of the usual *one,* allowing two workers to use the same injector. After pouring wax into a tank, or when placing it in bulk, wait until its temperature rises to working heat before use.

Wax injection machines that operate by air pressure have an air gauge that indicates pressure up to 15 pounds, an air pressure regulator, and an air pressure release or safety valve. The normal air pressure used ranges from 5–15 psi (pounds per square inch). Avoid using too high a pressure as it will cause the wax to swell and blister. Five psi is sufficient in most cases.

Injection nozzles are placed low at the front or, in cases where the tank is mounted on a stand, at the bottom. The nozzle shape must *exactly match* the shape of the sprue opening in the rubber mold. A tight fit ensures a maximum of pressure on the wax while it is being injected. The nozzle is mounted on a spring and when the mold is pressed against it, a valve opens up and allows the hot wax to be injected into the mold by manual hydraulic pressure, or by air pressure. When the mold is removed, pressure on the spring in the valve is released and cuts off wax flow. At the proper wax-melting temperature, the nozzle should not leak, nor should the wax freeze, but should readily fill the mold cavity. A normal working temperature range for wax is 140–160° F (60–71° C). Wax much hotter than this may develop air bubbles that will fix themselves to the mold surface and the result will be useless.

MAKING A WAX-INJECTED REPLICA

To prepare the vulcanized rubber mold for wax injection, lay the two parts open on a table, or hold each separately in the hand. Dip a *stiff bristle brush* into the container of *talc,* and work it over the entire inner mold surface. A *small cloth bag* containing talc powder can also be used, but a brush is more efficient. Blow away any excess deposit of talc as any loose remainder can affect mold accuracy. Excessive talc between mold parts can be the cause of fins on the model because it does not allow the two parts of the mold to make perfect contact. The talc lubricates the mold surface and prevents the wax model from sticking to it. Molds that have been lying idle before use must be cleaned with benzene or carbon tetrachloride which should be allowed to evaporate before the mold is dusted with talc. Make a new application of talc after every three or four injections of wax.

Assemble the mold and place a *flat Masonite pressure board* about ¼ in (6.35 mm) thick and a little larger than the mold dimensions on each side of the mold. Hold these pressed together with the sprue opening forward. Press the mold's sprue opening firmly against the nozzle of the wax injector so that they couple tightly. The wax will automatically be injected into the mold cavity and fill it. The time

this takes is a few seconds. Different models may require more or less time, and a few practice runs will soon tell you how long filling time should be. Catch any wax that drips in a small container placed below the nozzle. This wax can be reclaimed and used again, and so can the wax from imperfectly cast models that must be discarded. Hold the mold, sprue end upright, for about a minute, keeping pressure on the pressure boards while the wax solidifies, then lay it down.

RELEASING THE WAX REPLICA

Allow the mold to cool 1–5 minutes, depending on the bulk of the model, on its side. If models are made in rapid succession, the mold retains heat and may have to be allowed to rest longer.

When removing the wax model from the mold, avoid excessive bending of the mold as this can cause the model to become misshapen or break. It also will cause unnecessary wear and tear on the mold and shorten its life. When releasing sized pieces, such as rings, even more care is needed to avoid distortion. With the mold lying flat on a table surface, start at the sprue end and carefully remove the upper half of the mold. Normally, with the upper half of the mold off, the model is exposed in the lower half. If any wax fins are seen, cut them away with a knife while the replica is still in the lower mold half. Fins should not develop if the mold parts fit tightly together and sufficient pressure has been applied on them when the mold is held between pressure boards during wax injection. Should fins persist, this indicates the mold is wearing out from repeated bending, and it may have to be replaced.

Lift the second mold half and while holding it between the thumb and fingers of the left hand, gently bend it backward. This should allow the release of the replica with the right hand. Avoid distortion of the replica. In cases where a mold undercut exists, pressure may have to be increased at that part to release the model. In some cases, only a part of the mold may have to be bent back to release the undercut. Should model distortion occur, correct it immediately while the wax is still warm. Injection waxes have a "memory," and if severely distorted, the replica will warp once it cools and sets.

Inspect the wax model for surface faults. If a fault cannot be easily repaired, reject the model. It does not pay to use a defective wax model as both time and material will be needlessly lost. Use only perfect models. To determine the even thickness of a model, hold it up against the light. Color differences will be seen if there are variations in the thickness of the wax. Models with excessively thin parts should not be cast as the casting will probably be incomplete at its thinnest sections. Minor surface defects can often be corrected with a heated *spatula* or an *electric wax welder.* Small pits due to small bubbles can be filled with an additional amount of wax placed with a heated tool. Where a parting line appears on the model at the juncture of the two mold parts, it must be scraped off with a *knife.* It is far easier to remove this in the wax model than in a metal casting.

At this point, the model will ordinarily have a sprue button attached to the sprue runner. The button can be cut off with a heated *spatula,* but the sprue is left attached. It is preferable for wax models to be used as soon as possible because if they lie waiting, they may become subject to heat and thereby distorted. If, however, it is necessary to store them, make sure they are placed in a cool spot.

0

11–82 TURUN HOPEA, Turku, Finland, manufacturer. Tree-spruing production series of wax-injected models. The central wax rod trunk sprue is mounted on a central cone of a rubber sprue gate former. Using an electric welding spatula, the wax patterns are welded to the sprue at close intervals in an upward-pointing radial angle, forming a treelike arrangement, from which comes the method's name. The total number attached depends on the model size and the metal-holding capacity of the crucible and the centrifugal casting machine. *Photo: Jorma Laine, courtesy Turun Hopea*

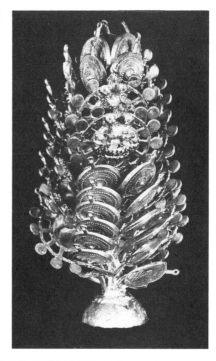

11–83 *A BRONZE CASTING OF TREE-SPRUED MODELS* after the removal of all investment plaster. Height 7¹⁄₁₆ in. Photo: Jorma Laine, courtesy Turun Hopea

MULTIPLE "PINCUSHION" SPRUING AND TREE SPRUING

In repeat production it is economical to use as large a flask as possible and cast as many replicas as can be accommodated in the same flask at one casting. Two systems of mounting several models simultaneously are used.

Multiple "pincushion" spruing is a system in which all models stand upright and their sprues come to a common, large, main *rubber sprue former.* At its center is a convex mound that is primed with a layer of wax with a heated *mandrel.* When mounting the wax model, first form a hole in the base wax and insert the model's sprue end, holding it upright till the wax solidifies. Models are spaced as equally as possible. In the invested mold, the mound will become the concave cavity into which the molten metal will run to the several sprue ends there. After investment, when the sprue former is removed, each separate sprue end can be seen. Each end is enlarged somewhat in the plaster with a *knife.*

Tree spruing is a system used when many smaller sized models are cast in one flask. These are arranged around one thick, *central, vertically positioned wax sprue* mounted in hard wax placed in the center pouring gate former hole. To this, the sprue end of each model runs obliquely and is joined, starting from the bottom, then proceeding upward. Finally the surplus of the central sprue is removed at the point where the last model is joined. Because the mounted models resemble a tree trunk with spreading branches, this system gets the name of *tree spruing.* Enough space must be allowed *between each model* to prevent the plaster between them from breaking down under pressure from centrifugal casting force. A space of ³⁄₁₆ in is the thinnest distance allowable between waxes, but ¼ in is safer. Make sure the sprue cross section of each model fully contacts the central sprue so that the opening through which the molten metal flows is maximal. Position the sprue at an angle to the trunk sprue to minimize the turbulence of the molten metal as it enters the cavity. Excessive turbulence is one of the causes of porosity. Mount the models with a *heated spatula* or an *electric wax welder* by touching it to the point of contact of both model and trunk sprues, then

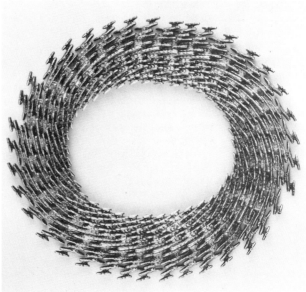

11–84 ANTHONY HAWKSLEY, England. Silver-gilt collar of 37 identical, surface-textured units made with wax models from a rubber injection mold, tree cast. Photo: Victoria and Albert Museum, London, Crown Copyright

hold the model for a few seconds while the wax solidifies and hardens.

When mounting a tree-sprued assembly for pouring the investment plaster, push a pair of heated stiff wires at right angles through the heavy bottom end of the trunk sprue, then hang the tree upside down in the flask by resting the two wires on the flask edges. The distance between the treetop and the flask base should be no less than ¾ in (1.9 cm). Once the flask is filled with investment plaster and has set, remove the two supporting wires. (From here on, casting by *centrifugal machine* follows the same procedure already described under Investment Casting in this chapter.)

COLD RUBBER MOLD MAKING

A *cold rubber mold compound* made to set by the addition of a *catalyst* has been developed. It is capable of producing models with great accuracy and with only about 1% shrinkage between the pattern and the mold. It allows the manufacture of a mold without the use of a vulcanizer, and the reproduction of models made of materials that would otherwise be damaged or destroyed by the heat of vulcanizing. This composition consists of two compounds: a black polysulphide rubber, and a separately packed curing agent or catalyst. Following manufacturers' instructions on quantity, pour the catalyst into the rubber compound to activate its curing, and when it is well mixed by stirring, pour it around a model mounted in a mold frame. This mixture will cure at room temperature, 75–80° F (23.8–26.6° C) in 24 hours. The time can be shortened to 3 hours by heating the mold in an oven at 150° F (65.5° C). Thereafter, cutting the mold apart to release the model is the same as described for vulcanized rubber molds.

USING TRANSPARENT PLASTIC MOLD MAKING COMPOUNDS

Also available today are flexible plastic mold compounds that can be used to form transparent solid molds. Because this is a liquid composition, packing the mold is not necessary, unlike the case of rubber, and no mixing is required because it is a single mixture.

To prepare the model, attach it to a sprue and fix it to stand upright at the base of a U-shaped metal mold frame with one plate of heat-resistant glass *C-clamped* or *spring clamped* on both sides. The prepared mold compound is opaque when poured into the open end of the mold to fill it completely. Stand the whole assembly upright in an oven heated to 350° F (176.6° C) for approximately 30 minutes. At this point, it solidifies and becomes transparent. Shrinkage is minimal. Remove the clamps, the glass slabs, and the mold frame. Treat the mold as an ordinary rubber mold. The process of cutting it into two parts is facilitated by the fact that the compound is transparent.

In use, if kept clean, talc or another model-releasing material is not needed as the compound is self-lubricating. Because of its transparency, the injected wax is also visible, which helps ascertain that the mold cavity is completely filled.

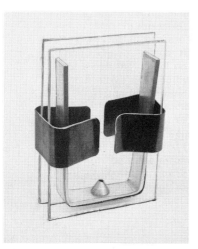

11–85 *TRANSPARENT PLASTIC MOLD FRAME* with Pyrex side plates, U-shaped metal three-sided frame with attached sprue gate former, and two C-clamps, size 2 × 3½ in, the frame available in several widths from ½–1¼ in. Used for cold casting models that cannot withstand heat without becoming deformed. Photo: Courtesy Swest Inc.

MAKING A RUBBER MOLD FOR USE IN WAX INJECTION

DEMONSTRATION 24

BJÖRN WECKSTRÖM designed production brooch

Photos: Oppi Untracht, taken at Lapponia Jewelry Ltd., Helsinki

1 A sheet of vulcanizing rubber is cut into strips in the width of the inner mold frame with a *straight edge* and a sharp *cutting tool.*

2 The strip is divided with *scissors* into lengths that match the mold frame.

3 The rubber sheet is cleaned, if necessary, with benzene and a clean cloth.

4 The bronze model of the brooch is positioned on the rubber sheets.

5 Its outline is drawn and the rubber is cut through with a *scalpel* to accommodate the model.

6 The hole in the rubber has been cut and the model placed within.

7 The vulcanized, patterned rubber keying tabs are placed at each corner.

8 The *one-part mold frame* is filled with rubber with the model packed inside.

9 The mold with an *aluminum plate* on top and bottom is in position in the *vulcanizer* whose upper platen is screwed down on it.

10 With vulcanization completed, the mold assembly is removed while holding it with *asbestos gloves,* and is placed in water to cool.

11 The rubber mold is removed from the frame and one corner is lifted to start the separation of the two parts of the mold. One corner key tab is visible.

12 This mold has been made with a separator. Here it is cut with a *scalpel* to allow the release of the wax model from an undercut. A *surgeon's clamp* is used to hold it open while the cut is made.

13 The mold is shown spread apart to expose the cuts at the top and bottom that release the undercut.

14 The inner mold surface is being repaired with an *electrically heated wax welder.*

15 The nozzle opening is being formed in the mold with an *electrical nozzle-forming mandrel.*

16 The original silver brooch, the bronze model, and the two-part, opened, vulcanized rubber mold.

17 One mold half is dusted with *talc* with a *stiff bristle brush* before assembly.

18 The *two-part mold,* assembled and ready for wax injection with the nozzle opening up, and a *Masonite board* on top and bottom to apply pressure on the mold to keep it closed.

19 The mold assembly is pressed against the nozzle of the *wax injector,* and the released pressure forces the wax into the mold cavity. A small puff of talc may be emitted indicating the cavity has been filled.

20 The rubber mold assembly right after wax injection. The nozzle hole is wax filled.

21 The rubber mold assembly resting to allow the wax to chill in the cavity and solidify.

22 One corner of the rubber mold is lifted with the thumb to start the separation of the mold halves and release the wax replica.

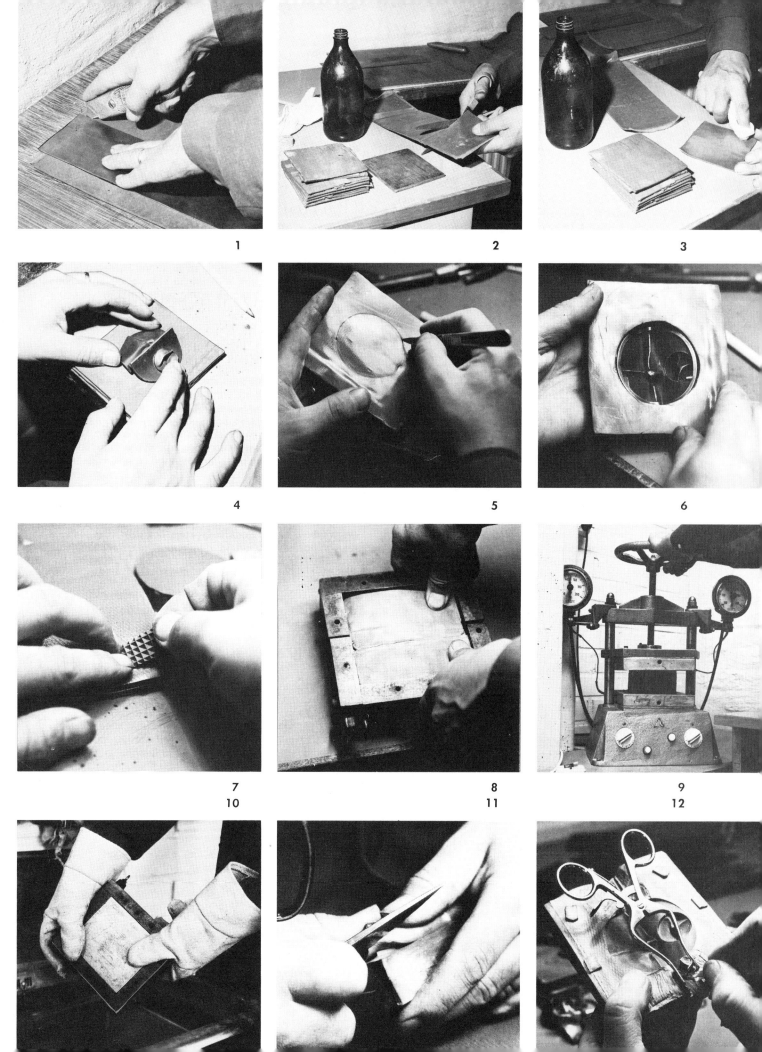

1

2

3

4

5

6

7

8

9

10

11

12

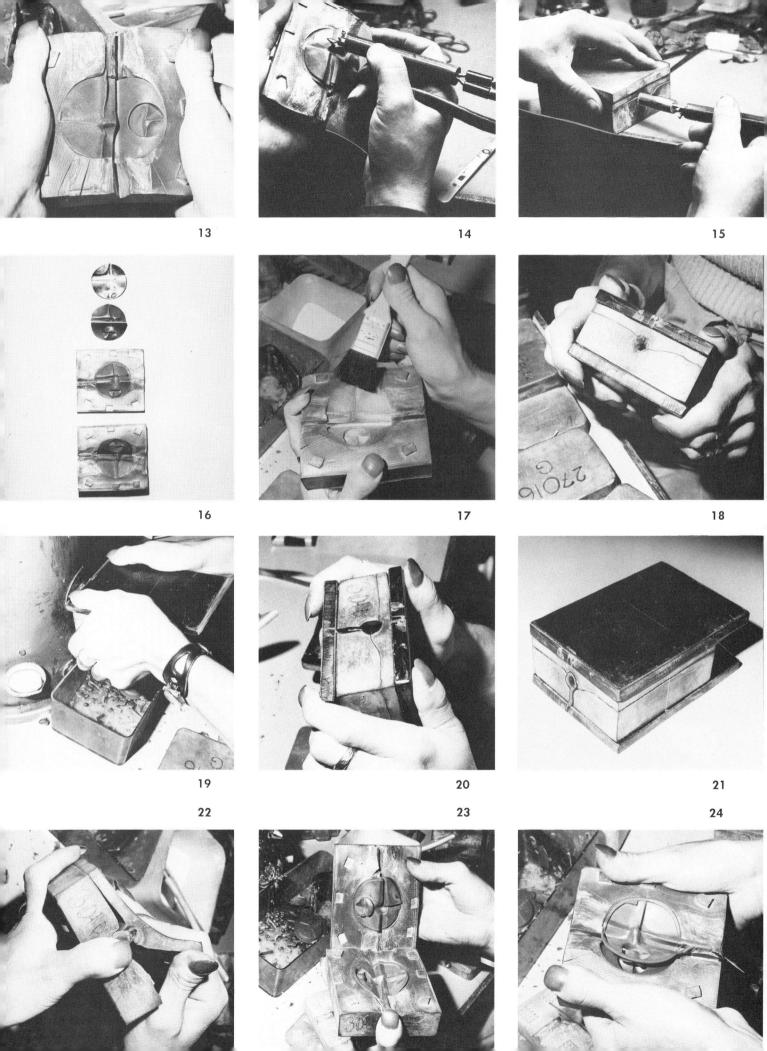

13

14

15

16

17

18

19

20

21

22

23

24

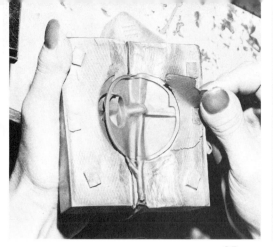

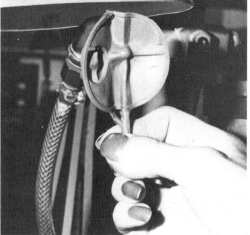

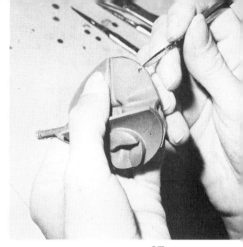

25

26

27

23 The opened mold, with the wax replica in place in the thicker lower half.

24 The lower mold half is bent to release the wax model from undercuts.

25 A wax fin is broken off from another model before releasing the replica.

26 The replica is examined against a light to see if it is uniform in thickness. Pressing the halves together too hard during wax injection can cause areas that cannot be cast successfully because they are too thin.

27 A *scalpel* is used to remove a fin at the parting line by scraping.

28 In the so-called *pincushion* method or arrangement, the rubber sprue former is primed with wax with a heated *iron mandrel* to receive the models.

29 This is weighed on a *scale* to determine the amount of metal needed for this casting. The wax replicas below are ready for mounting.

30 Sprue lengths are shortened in preparation for mounting.

31 Four replicas have been mounted upright on the sprue base, like pins in a pincushion, by welding them to the primed wax on the *sprue former* with an *electric spatula*. (A *heated knife* or ordinary *spatula* can be used as well.) Models are placed at least ¼–⅜ in (6.35–9.52 mm) from the flask walls, and can be as close as ⅛ in (3.17 mm) to each other, but must not touch. The flask height chosen should allow at least ½–¾ in (12.7–19.1 mm) space at the top to prevent metal breakthrough.

32 The final assembly of five mounted wax replicas

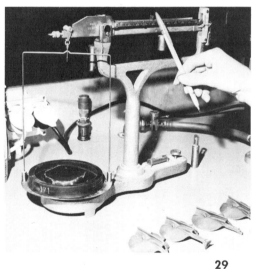

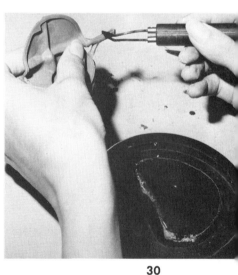

28

29

30

31

32

33

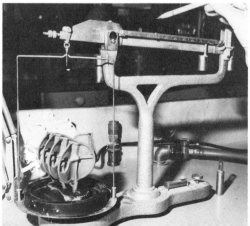

34

35

36

37

38

39

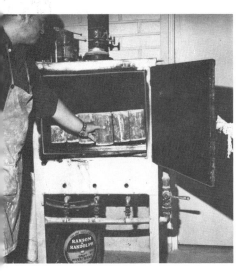

40

41

42

43

44

45

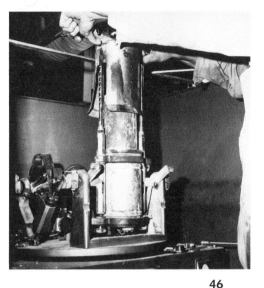

46 47 48

49 50 51

and sprue former is weighed to determine the amount of metal needed for their casting.

33 A *stainless steel flask* is being placed over the mounted replicas.

34 Several flasks containing different wax replicas are placed inside a *vacuum air evacuator machine.*

35 The flasks have been filled with investment slurry.

36 The vacuum machine is clamped in place over the flask container chamber and the air is sucked out, eliminating all air within the flasks.

37 After removal from the vacuum machine, the surplus plaster on each flask is screed off with a straight *steel scraper.*

38 Once the investment plaster is set, the rubber sprue former is removed. The ends of the sprues of each of the five models in the flask can be seen.

39 The investment plaster is marked with a recorded casting identification number before wax burnout.

40 The flasks are placed, sprue opening down, in a *wax-eliminating oven* to evacuate the wax model from the mold and leave a cavity for casting.

41 The flasks are placed on shelves in a *burnout kiln* to completely eliminate the wax before casting.

42 *Casting silver* in pellet form is seen in the container with the spoon at the left. The amount needed for the casting in this specific flask has already been calculated. Normally about 60% of the total goes to the models and

40% to the sprues and buttons. It is weighed out on a scale, the amount is recorded, then placed in a loading funnel at the right.

43 The silver is funnel fed to the *crucible* mounted in the *centrifuge.* The crucible is heated electrically to melt the metal and bring it to the correct casting temperature.

44 The flask, ready after burnout, is being removed with *tongs* from the burnout kiln.

45 The flask is brought to the *centrifugal machine* and is mounted above the crucible with its sprue openings down toward the crucible.

46 A *flask sleeve* is placed over the flask to hold it in place directly above the crucible.

47 The flask sleeve is locked tightly on the side guides. This machine can accommodate two flasks for simultaneous casting. When only one is cast, as in this case, a *counterweight* (the bar) is placed on the mounting where the other flask would ordinarily go on the opposite side of the machine.

48 The centrifugal machine is released, spins around, and the molten metal fills the mold cavities.

49 After casting, the flask held by *tongs* is submerged in cold water to start the disintegration of the investment plaster.

50 While the flask is held with tongs, a pneumatically operated *vibrating ram* is used to further disintegrate the investment plaster and shake out or release the

casting from the flask. A different casting in a treed arrangement is emerging from the flask.

51 The casting is cleaned in a *sandblasting machine* to free it of any remaining investment plaster. The worker holds the casting inside by putting his hands through the outside openings in *mounted rubber gloves,* and watches the progress of the work through the glass shield.

52 The sprues are cut off with a powerful *mechanical sprue cutter.* All sprue metal is collected in the box at the left, as this is reclaimed. The sign on the lamp says "save electricity."

53 Björn Weckström, Finland, designer; Lapponia Jewelry Ltd., Helsinki, manufacturer. "Vela," Space-Silver brooch created from the rubber mold wax-injected model in the process described above; cast in sterling silver. Ø 2³⁄₁₆ in (5.6 cm).

Photo: Max Petrelius

52

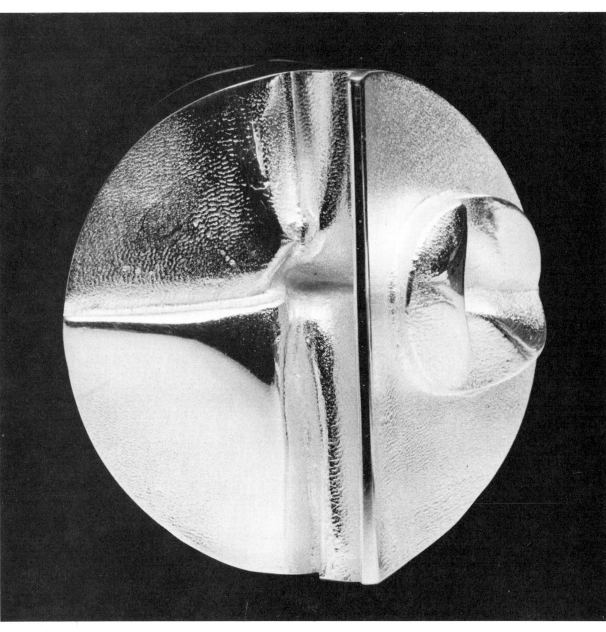

53

12

NATURAL MATERIALS IN JEWELRY
Using Nature's Valued Nonmetals

ORGANIC MATERIALS USED IN JEWELRY

Employing products of formerly living organisms

Organic substances that are the by-products of once living animals, birds, plants, and water life have been used since antiquity for ornamental purposes. Among the earliest of such materials were those from animals and birds primarily hunted for food and skins. In the leisure following satisfaction of hunger, people had time to experiment with decorative uses for the remains (bone, teeth, horn, tusk, and feathers). Other dead organic matter was discovered contained within the land or in riverbeds (fossils), thrown up by the sea (amber and shells), or within the depths of seas and lakes (pearls, coral, tortoiseshell).

Today all these materials are available with no more effort expended than is needed to make a trip to a supplier, or to write a mail order. Most of them (except for pearls, amber, and coral) are relatively inexpensive as compared, for instance, with the cost of inorganic, semiprecious and precious stones. Their use in jewelry offers a wide range of choice in color and visual effects that contrast and harmonize well with metals and other substances from which jewelry is created.

IVORY

Specific gravity: 1.70–1.93
Hardness, Mohs' scale: 2–3
Refractive index: 1.54

Ivory is calcareous matter in the form of teeth from certain mammals. The main source for use in the arts is *elephant tusk,* actually the elephant's two incisor teeth that are fixed in its upper jaw. (It is also obtained from the teeth of other animals, mentioned below.) Its substance consists of *dentine* which is like bone, but denser and harder. This material develops in the form of a matrix containing closely placed, minute, parallel tubules or canals that start from the inner pulp cavity, and radiate in all directions from it forming a fibrous mass with a longitudinal grain. The tubules contain a gelatinous substance which in part is responsible for the high gloss attainable when polishing ivory. The dentine forms in more or less concentric layers or rings, as can be seen in a cross section. Each ring is about 1 cm (0.3937 in) in thickness, and represents 6–8 years' growth.

In *structure,* an elephant's tusk is a round, tapering, curved cone. The tusk is open ended, a type of tooth that

builds up and continues to grow during the entire life of the animal, and is never worn down, as are, for instance, the closed-root teeth of the hippopotamus or humans. Young elephant tusk, except for the tip, is completely hollow, the conical basal cavity space containing the nerve tissue or pulp of the tooth having been removed once the tusk was taken from the elephant. The surface of this inner cavity is often brown. As the elephant matures, the pulp cavity becomes shorter because the dentine fills its anterior end and pushes the solid portion forward. The tusk then remains hollow for only about half its length or less, starting at the jaw where the hollow diameter is largest, and tapering as it progresses forward toward the tip. The outer surface of a tusk, called its "bark," is grayish white, and this portion is generally shaved away before the ivory is used to expose the inner, whiter portion. In commerce, the ivory considered superior is as white as possible, dense, fine grained, and elastic.

Ivory can easily be distinguished from bone by the appearance of a transversely cut and polished section which, because of the manner of its growth, displays a unique

12–1 GUNILLA TREEN, England. Two brooches of ivory cross sections covered with clear acrylic, joined with silver rivets. The pulp cavity of the upper one contains mobile pearls and opals, and the lower one, mobile opals. Each growth ring seen in the section is approximately 1 cm (0.3937 in) wide, and indicates 6–8 years of the elephant's life. These show four rings, therefore this tusk came from an elephant about 32 years old. Also clearly seen is the characteristic secondary dentine which in ivory always has a crisscross pattern in concentric layers. Size 60 × 40 mm. *Photo: Horst Kolo*

structure. This is seen as a rhombohedral-patterned network of intersecting arcs, called the lines of Retzius (after A. A. Retzius, 1796–1860, a Swedish anatomist). This formation, though somewhat less visible in young ivory, is not found at all in a similarly cut section of bone, which instead shows specks or stripes. Bone also has a "drier" look than ivory, which appears as if it is soaked in oil because of its gelatinous content.

The appeal of ivory is based on its pleasant appearance, tactile quality, relative durability, and especially on its workability. It can be sawed, filed, scraped, drilled, turned, etched, engraved, carved, dyed, and polished, but not welded like horn. Considering the fact that ivory is a relatively porous organic material, it is surprisingly durable, as attested to by the existence of very ancient ivory objects. Aside from its physical qualities, part of the reason for the preservation of ancient ivory artifacts may be attributed to the fact that ivory has no secondary uses, unlike metal, for instance, which can always be melted down and reused.

TYPES OF IVORY

Green ivory is a tusk cut from a living elephant (which can be done without its discomfort or death provided the nerve tissue is left intact); ivory from a killed elephant; and ivory from one just recently dead.

Dead ivory is found on an elephant that has died a natural death, and whose tusks have been exposed to the elements for some time afterward; or ivory that has been kept in storage under unfavorable conditions for too long a time so that it has completely dried out. (To prevent the occurrence of drying out and accompanying *checking* or cracking, the exposed ends of a newly cut cross section are normally coated with a layer of *wax*, and the tusk is stored in a cool, dry, dark place.)

Cured ivory is ivory that has been kept in a favorable, cool atmosphere such as above for at least 20 years.

Fossil ivory is ivory from prehistoric, extinct mammoths and mastodons who lived until the Ice Age. Their remains have been discovered in northern permafrost lands. Actually it is not a fossil material since it is only frozen, and not replaced by minerals as in fossilized matter. Its use was important during the 19th century when it was found in quantity buried in large riverbanks in northern Siberia in Russia, and in Alaska and the Yukon. It is brittle, often checked, and yellows quickly upon exposure. This source has been used up, mostly for the manufacture of piano keys, and since the mid 1950s, synthetic plastics have replaced ivory on the keyboard.

Old ivory in the form of *sheet* may be recovered from a derelict piano, and *bulk ivory* in a highly usable form can be found as old billiard balls which occasionally turn up in antique or junk shops. The patina color and network of surface checking acquired by old ivory is visually very appealing, and can be retained when such a piece is used in jewelry fabrication.

African ivory comes from both male and female African elephants, and until the recent ban on the import of ivory to the U.S. was the main ivory source, and provided the greater portion of the quantity available. Though its quality may vary regionally, it is still considered to be a superior material because it is generally denser in texture, and finer grained than Indian ivory. When initially worked, it is not as white as Indian ivory, but it is less liable to yellow, and in fact lightens with age and becomes more opaque. Like all ivory, it hardens upon exposure to air. African elephant tusks can reach a maximum of 10 ft (3 m) in length, and a pair can weigh up to 220 lb. Hong Kong is a major African ivory-carving center.

Indian ivory is found only on the male elephant. It is more grainy and easier to carve than African, but does not take as fine a polish as the latter, and it has a tendency to check with age. Indian elephant tusks can reach a maximum of over 7 ft (2.1 m) in length, and a pair can weigh up to 170 lb. Indian elephants are fewer in number than African, and in India the elephant is domesticated and used as a work animal.

ALTERNATE SOURCES OF IVORY

Hippopotamus incisor and canine teeth (specific gravity 1.80–1.95) can weigh up to 30 lb, but are normally about 6 lb. Their hard, thick outer enamel resists working with normal tools and must therefore be removed by acid or large, strong cutting and scraping tools to expose the inner, pure white, hard, tough, easily carvable ivory inside. This is closer grained than elephant ivory, but without grain pattern. It is subject to cracking and splitting with age.

Walrus tusk or canine teeth (specific gravity 1.90–2.00) can grow up to 3 ft (0.9 m) long in curved lengths, are oval in section, and weigh 7–15 lb. This ivory is nearly as white as elephant ivory, but is denser, and has a darker, marbleized interior pattern. Walrus tusk ivory is used by Eskimos, but due to the mass slaughter of large Arctic walrus herds, it is now scarce. *Fossilized walrus tusk,* called *beach ivory* by Alaskan Eskimos, is sometimes found thrown up on Arctic beaches. It is mottled brown and violet in color.

Narwhal ivory is produced by a 16 ft (4.8 m) long porpoise (*Monodon monoceros*) that belongs to the family Delphinidae, and inhabits the Arctic Ocean. The male of this species develops a spirally grooved, straight tusk up to 8 ft (2.4 m) long which grows forward from the left side of its upper jaw, and is sometimes accompanied by a corresponding or shorter tusk from the right side. This tusk, which rarely comes to market, was thought in medieval Europe to be the horn of a unicorn, and to have magical properties. It is close grained, and similar in texture to elephant ivory.

Sperm whale teeth are relatively short, stubby, hard, heavy, and well marked with fine concentric lines. The grainy, furrowed outer surface of a raw tooth is rough and is removed with a *wood rasp* or *metal file* to level the surface. Sanding follows with 120–220 grit *silicon carbide abrasive papers* to smooth the surface, and finally with *steel wool* for a satin finish. Mechanical polishing tends to overheat the ivory rendering it hard and brittle and resistant to carving and engraving tools.

Wild boar tushes or tusks are curved, sometimes almost forming a circle. They are relatively small in thickness, and 3–12 in (7.6–30.5 cm) in curved length. They are generally used intact to be identifiable. In primitive cultures, their use in jewelry was a symbol of bravery (the boar is very fierce when fighting for its life, and therefore a worthy adversary).

Hornbill ivory is the dense, carvable substance found in the solid casque attached to the upper bill of the helmeted hornbill bird that inhabits Southern Asia, Indonesia, and Africa. Its interior is cream colored, and it is grainless and softer than elephant ivory.

13-1

Plate 13-1 WENDY RAMSHAW, England. Necklace in lathe turned sterling silver and gold, and fabricated parts, with enamel. *Photo: Bob Cramp*

Plate 13-2 CLAUS BURY, West Germany. Brooch fabricated in various alloys of gold. *Photo: Günther Meyer, courtesy the Schmuckmuseum, Pforzheim*

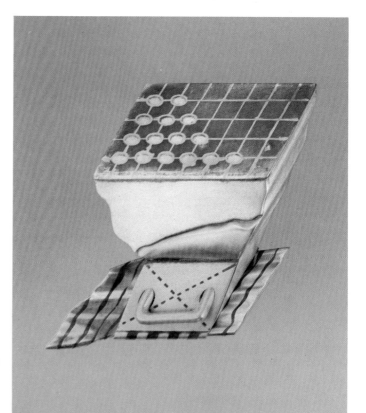

13-2

14-1

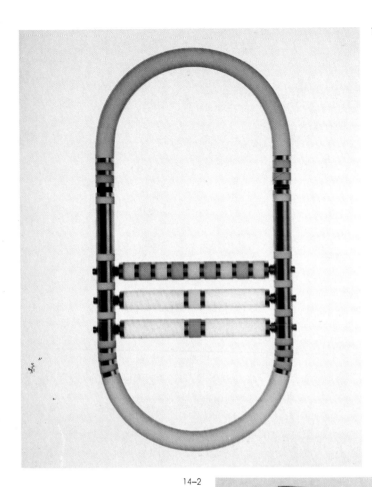

Plate 14-1 DAVID WATKINS, England. Hinged loop necklace fabricated of sterling silver and dyed acrylic rod. *Photo: Bob Cramp*

Plate 14-2 LYNDA WATSON ABBOTT, U.S.A. Brooch fabricated of brass and colored silver, with agates, polyester and acrylic sheet. *Photo: Lynda Watson Abbott*

Plate 14-3 BRUCE METCALF, U.S.A. "Ziz-Zag Pin." Fabricated of silver, copper, brass, wood, and Delrin. Colored with enamel paint intended for plastic military models, applied over a zinc chromate primer, and coated with clear urethane automotive paint. *Photo: Bruce Metcalf*

14-2

14-3

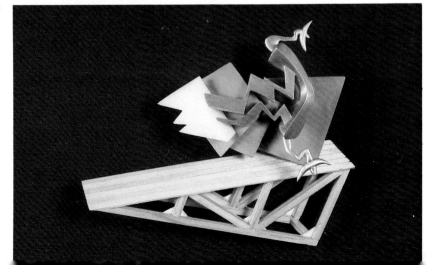

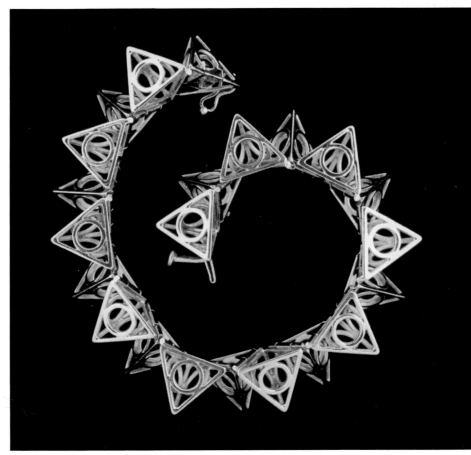

Plate 15–1   CARRIE ADELL, U.S.A. "Tetrahedron."
Bracelet in cast and fabricated gold, the units
hinged together. *Photo: Murray Warren Photographics*

Plate 15–2   J. FRED WOELL, U.S.A. "One More for
the Road." Pendant in cast brass. *Photo: J. Fred
Woell*

Plate 15–3   ANTHONY LENT, U.S.A. Pendant in
platinum and 18k cast gold, graver carved and
chased, with rubies and Mississippi River freshwater
baroque pearls. *Photo: Don Manza, courtesy Aaron
Faber Gallery, New York*

15–2

15–3

Plate 16-1 MARY ANN SCHERR, U.S.A. Necklace in sterling silver, gold, and brass, with walrus tusk sections, black coral, jade, and fire opals. *Photo: Sam Scherr*

Plate 16-2 BARBARA TIPPLE, England. Choker necklace of ivory inlaid with 18k yellow gold, with nine carats of diamonds. *Photo: Courtesy De Beers Consolidated Mines Ltd.*

16-1

16-2

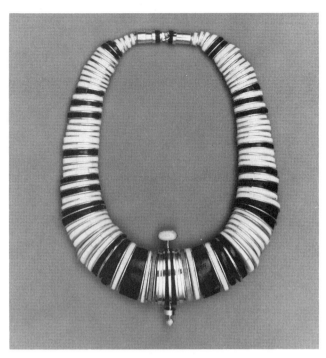

12-3 MARY ANN SCHERR, U.S.A. Sterling silver, gold, and brass necklace utilizing the natural ellipsoid sections of walrus tusk in graduated sizes. Black coral, jade, and three fire opals are also used. Photo: Richard Monasterio

12-4 TUENSANG DIVISION, N.E.F.A., INDIA. Naga man wearing a necklace of two wild boar tushes, the enlarged canine teeth of the upper and lower jaws of the boar with which it digs for food and viciously defends itself. The use of teeth trophies for personal decoration is considered a sign of bravery. The headdress is of massed, clipped feathers. Photo: Courtesy Photo Division, Ministry of Information and Broadcasting, Government of India.

12-5 JAMUDA VILLAGE, GUJARAT, INDIA. Ivory bangles (hathi dant chura) lathe turned, and worn in graded sizes on the upper arm. In Gujarat and Rajasthan, as many as 17 upper arm and 9 lower arm bangles can be worn at once, making a total of 52 bangles on both arms. Photo: Oppi

12-2 WALRUS TUSKS
Two tusks hang perpendicularly downward from the upper jaw of the sea cow living in Arctic regions. Oval in section and open ended, they can be over 2 ft long. The outer white layer gradually turns yellow upon exposure, and the core is darker than the exterior, and is composed of small, round crystals. Without the intersecting line pattern found in elephant ivory cross sections, it has an easily recognized, handsome marbled effect once the interior is exposed. Col.: Bertel Gardberg. Photo: Oppi

USES OF IVORY IN JEWELRY AND SMALL OBJECTS

Because of the internal hollow in an elephant tusk and its circular sectional shape, a series of cross sections cut from that part of a single tusk will automatically form cylindrical rings in graduated diameter sizes. The fact that the diameter of an elephant's tusk pulp or nerve corresponds to the dimensions of the average human wrist and arm makes elephant ivory a natural traditional source for bangles, and these have been used since time immemorial as ornaments in many cultures. Sections with the smallest diameters have long been worn by Tibetans for magic thumb rings, and as hair ornaments. Solid ivory has been used to make hairpins, hair ornaments, combs, earrings, rings, seals, dice, chessmen, dagger handles (and handles in general), spoons, and containers. Ivory can be used for the ornamentation of many other substances. It is an economical material because it receives maximal use and there is hardly any waste. Even very small scraps can be employed as an inlay material or in a mosaic, and therefore have value.

PROCESSING IVORY

Fresh ivory is easier to cut from bulk because it still contains its full gelatin and moisture content. Old ivory is harder and more difficult to cut because it has dried. To cut off a section, fix the piece in a *vise,* wrapping the part that contacts the vise jaws with cloth or leather to prevent damage to its grasped surface. Any *fine-toothed saw* can be used, the blade as thin as is practical to reduce the percentage of waste from sawing. At intervals, pour water into the cut to reduce the buildup of frictional heat, and to act as a lubricant. Though objects of some thickness, such as bangles, are made from cross sections, when ivory is cut into pieces for carving purposes, it is generally cut into slabs whose grain runs lengthwise. Because the fibrous structure runs in the direction of the longest dimension the mass is stronger. Thin objects made of cross sections have far less structural strength, and tend to be brittle.

CARVING IVORY With patience, ivory can be carved into any form, and there is almost no limit to the amount of small-scale detail possible because of its density, uniformity of texture, close grain, and elasticity. Ivory should be carved as soon as possible after a part is cut from a larger stock as the freshly cut surface is then in a maximally carvable condition. Upon exposure, this surface will dry and harden in air. Because ivory is hygroscopic, carvability and flexibility can be restored by covering the object with a damp cloth and allowing it to stand for some time to absorb the moisture. It can also be wiped with a dampened sponge at intervals during work, or when set aside,

12–8 EARL PARDON, U.S.A. Pin/pendant fabricated in 14K gold, ivory, and ebony, with emerald. Ivory and ebony strips are laminated into one unit and held together by gold rivets, as are the other ivory parts. Photo: Courtesy Aaron Faber Gallery, New York

12–6 GELI JOHNSTON, England. Gold earring (one of a pair), with carved ivory teddy bear on a swing. Photo: Geli Johnston

it can be wrapped with sponges dampened with clean water.

Use *small, sharp chisels* and a *mallet* to rough out the initial shape, but avoid excessive force in the blows to prevent cracking and chipping. If an object in subsequent carving is small or difficult to hold in the hands during work, it can be mounted on a base such as a *shellac stick* to free both hands for work. Use *scalpels* for scraping a surface to remove fine shavings when developing a form, and *sharp knives* for detailing. Finish forms and surface condition with *hand rasps, files,* and *rifflers* of appropriate shape and fineness of cut, or by the use of *mechanical miniature rotary tools* worked with a *flex-shaft,* frequently lubricating the surface with water to prevent overheating. Final surface smoothness is achieved with *abrasive cloths* and *papers,* or *steel wool.*

Ivory can also be *pierced* using *drills* and a *jeweler's saw* in the same way as when piercing metal. Ivory can be *turned* on a *lathe,* a technique still widely used in the Orient, and one that reached a high degree of development during the 17th and 18th centuries in Germany and Flanders.

JOINING IVORY The limitation imposed on an object's dimension by the size of a single piece of ivory can be over-

come by fabricating an ivory object from several pieces and then joining them as a unit. This technique has been important throughout the history of the use of ivory. Joining can be accomplished by the use of mechanical joints such as mortise and tenon, scarf, etc., and by the use of rivets that pass through the parts to be joined. To insert a rivet, a hole equal in diameter to that of the rivet must first be *drilled* through the parts. To be sure these parts are properly lined up, they must all be assembled and drilled *simultaneously.* In some instances, this may mean that parts have to be held together temporarily by *adhesive tape,* or a *water-soluble glue,* later removed. For hole position accuracy, and to avoid the occurrence of splinters on the visible surface at the drill entry point, cover that area with a pressed-on piece of *draftsman's tape,* mark the hole position on the tape, then slowly drill a hole through in one continuous operation. Tape can also be applied to the back at the point of drill exit to prevent chipping there. The rivet can be a close-fitting, rodlike section of ivory which will then be almost invisible, or made of deliberately visible gold or silver wire, the rivet head appearing as an inlay. Do not use other metals as they will ultimately discolor the area around them.

Ivory parts can also be joined to each other, or to a surface or holding device of another material, by using nonstaining *polyvinyl acetate emulsion* adhesive that will not discolor ivory. If necessary, this adhesive can also be removed by its solvent, acetone. Ivory units can also be held to a metal base by mechanical means such as claws, bezels, screws, wire loops, and crossing metal bands.

SURFACE SMOOTHING AND POLISHING IVORY These processes can be done *manually* using a soft, clean *flannel cloth* impregnated with a *colorless* cut-and-color compound, followed by white rouge; or *mechanically* with the same substances placed on *clean flannel buffing wheels* mounted on a *polishing lathe,* but take care not to overheat and embrittle the ivory. The final surface can be manually brought to a bright luster by rubbing it with a small amount of *sweet oil* such as almond oil applied to a soft cloth, or by use of *white wax,* similarly applied. Neither of these substances should be left on the surface in any appreciable amount. Their use acts to limit the amount of moisture released or absorbed, and therefore helps to maintain the stability of the ivory and prevent checking.

BLEACHING IVORY To bleach ivory to a whiter appearance, first rub the surface with a thick *pumice* or *whiting and water paste,* then rinse and dry it. Under conditions of good ventilation, and while wearing *rubber gloves,* immerse the object in a bleaching solution of *20% by volume hydrogen peroxide.* Remove and inspect the object at

12–7 BENIN, NIGERIA, 16th century A.D. Carved and pierced ivory armlets of tusk sections. Made by craftsmen of the Benin sculptors' guild (Igbesamwan). Carved ivory objects were made only by royal permission, and were used only by the king as royal regalia. Left: two tiers of figures alternating head to foot, carrying and interspersed with snakes. Right: the oba or chief of Benin, wearing a decorated tunic, hat, and jewels, seated on a throne with hands upraised, alternating with a decorative motif. Heights approx. 4¾ in; Ø approx. 3⅛ in. Photo: Reproduced by Courtesy of the Trustees of The British Museum, London

intervals, and repeat the immersions as necessary to achieve the wanted degree of whiteness. Finally rinse and dry the object.

CLEANING OLD IVORY To clean old ivory without changing its color, prepare a solution made by adding 1 teaspoon of ammonia to 1 cup of acetone. Into this dip a *cotton swab* mounted on a wooden stick, and upon its removal, press out the surplus solution. While wearing *rubber gloves* to avoid skin contact, and working under good ventilation to avoid the inhalation of fumes, rub the object with the swab, changing the swab as it becomes soiled.

IVORY RESTORATION Because ivory is hygroscopic, it reacts to environmental humidity, absorbing or losing moisture from the air. This characteristic may cause it to shrink or swell, conditions that may result in warpage or the development of cracks. Thinner sections of ivory are more subject to these effects than thick ones. Ivory also tends to shrink with age as its moisture and gelatinous content gradually evaporate. Therefore, when accuracy of dimension is a factor, or when joining two parts of ivory by the mechanical means of an internal and external thread, seasoned or aged ivory is preferred as its dimensions have become relatively more stabilized. Very old, dried, and shrunken ivory can be *restored at least partially,* and cracks reduced or closed by immersing the object in a cool gelatin and water solution, then slowly heating the solution to near boiling, followed by a slow cooling. This treatment brings back a degree of firmness and solidity to the object.

ETCHING IVORY To etch ivory, first polish the surface to its final state, then clean it with a *stiff brush* and a detergent solution to remove all grease, and dry it. A simple *acid resist* or *stop-out* is a semihard wax dissolved to a liquid state with alcohol, then painted on the ivory with a *brush.* Another is rosin varnish, melted and applied with a brush, and allowed to dry thoroughly after application. An effective resist can be made from 1 ounce of pure white wax, 1 ounce of solid mastic, and ½ ounce of asphaltum. Reduce the mastic and the asphaltum separately into a powder, melt the wax in a vessel, sprinkle in the mastic, stir them together, then add the asphaltum and stir until the mixture is homogeneous. Heat the combination to a liquid state, and paint it only in the areas to be protected, leaving exposed those parts to be etched. Alternately, depending on the system of design development used, the entire surface can be covered with resist and then engraved, exposing the engraved parts to the action of the acid. To store this resist for future use, pour any remains into lukewarm water, knead it with the fingers until cool, then roll it into balls about one inch in diameter, and wrap these in a lintless cloth or a plastic sheet. Store them in a glass jar with a tightly closed cover. Before starting to create the design through the resist or with it, all other parts of the ivory object that must be protected against attack by the etchant must be covered with resist.

When using the system in which resist is applied only to selected areas of the design, first trace or draw the design directly on the ivory surface, and apply the resist where that surface is to be retained leaving the rest exposed to the action of the etchant. When using the system in which the entire surface is covered, the design is drawn through the dry resist using a *pointed wood or metal tool* to create linear details as well as larger areas.

IVORY ETCHANT

Hydrochloric acid	1 part by volume
Acetic acid	1 part by volume
OR	
Sulphuric acid	1 part by volume
Water	5–6 parts by volume

This acts quickly.

Immerse the ivory into the mordant, etch the design to the desired depth, remove and rinse it in cold water, and dry it. To eliminate the resist, apply alcohol or turpentine to a soft cloth and rub it off.

GILDING GROOVES ETCHED INTO IVORY To gild the negative grooves of the etched pattern, first carefully paint only those places with an adhesive size. (See Cold Gilding with Metal Leaf, Chapter 15.) While the gold leaf is sandwiched between two sheets of tracing paper or the paper of the book in which it is sold, cut it into pieces or strips of the shapes needed. Carefully remove the top layer of paper, pick up the leaf with a *dry brush,* and place it over the groove or area. Press it down with the brush, and allow the size to dry. Once this happens, remove surplus gold leaf by rubbing the object with *absorbent cotton.*

ENGRAVING IVORY Ivory in flat sheet or three-dimensional form is more easily engraved in the direction of the grain, which runs lengthwise in the direction of the tusk, than across the grain, which might cause chipping unless the tool is sharp. To make ivory less brittle before engraving, cover it with a damp cloth for a few hours. As an aid to visibility of design, thinly daub a paste of a yellow or black, *water-soluble paint* on the surface to create a color contrast between engraved lines and the ground, and also to eliminate surface reflections. Draw the design on this surface with a *2H* or *3H pencil* in the same way as on metals.

Use very sharp *flat-planed gravers.* Grind the cutting face to an angle of 15–20°, and make set-off angles to allow the tool to be held at approximately 15° from the horizontal. These angles are shallower than are generally used on metal and are suggested to prevent the graver from digging into the ivory which will result in chipping and an unevenly cut line. Because of the shallow cutting angle, however, *guard against graver skid.* One way to reduce the chance of chipping is to first make a shallow line then deepen it, passing over the cut again. Another way to avoid chipping is to reverse the engraving direction when chipping seems imminent. Fine lines can be scratched in with a *needle* fixed in a *pin vise,* or the point of a sharp *scalpel* can be used. Work with a good strong light, and use *magnifying loupes* or *glasses* to make lines more visible. Mistakes can be shaved away with a *knife blade* or filed locally with a *riffle file.*

COLORING ENGRAVED AND ETCHED LINES IN IVORY: SCRIMSHAW WORK Lines engraved in ivory can be permanently colored for visibility and decorative effect, as in scrimshaw work. *Scrimshaw* is a general nautical term used by old-time sailors to designate any neat piece of mechanical work. Today it is used to designate carved and engraved ivory objects made by 18th- and 19th-century windjammer sailors as a pastime during long voyages. Bracelets, rings, fans, cane handles, and boxes were made from whale's teeth, walrus tusk, or bone, and engraved with a variety of figural patterns and subjects. The surface was filed, scraped, then sanded smooth or rubbed with steel wool. The incised lines were colored, usually black, by rubbing an oil based pigment made of charcoal or

12–9 JOBY BAKER, U.S.A. Talisman in engraved ivory into whose lines black ink has been rubbed to make them more visible. The ivory slab is an old piano key, and is held by claws in an engraved silver mount, pierced at the back with "windows" that reveal engraved line images on the slab's back. The pendant is suspended on black waxed cotton fishing line interspersed with silver beads, and terminates in a hook and eye closing. *Photo: Leonard Nimoy*

lampblack, or other colored pigment, into them. Today black india ink or printer's inks can be used. Some sailors possessed special small boxes filled with tools used for scrimshaw work, and those who did this work were called *scrimshanders.*

Etched lines can be colored black before the resist is removed by immersing the work into a silver nitrate solution. Upon removal and exposure to light, the lines will become a permanent deep black or purple. The resist is then removed with an abrasive.

When flat sheet ivory is engraved or etched, and *printer's ink* is used as a pigment, after the ink is rubbed into the incisions and the rest is wiped from the surface, it is possible to make a *print* of the design on paper before the ink dries in exactly the same way as when hand printing a metal engraving or etching. This method can be used as a means of making and keeping a record of designs used.

In a process common in India, lines grooved into ivory are filled with an inlay of any *colored lac* in stick form, its consistency much like sealing wax which is available in any color, including silver and gold. This is heated and rubbed into the grooves of the warmed object, and is allowed to harden. The surface is then rubbed smooth and level with an abrasive paper, leaving the inlay color only in the grooves, and the final surface is repolished. This effect can also be accomplished by painting sufficient applications of *liquid, colored lacquers* into the grooves to fill them, then once the lacquer has dried, removing the surplus as above. *Liquid, colored plastic resins* can also be applied with a brush in the same way. Thick lines or relatively wide intaglio areas should first be given a "tooth" with a *graver* to help hold the plastic or other filler in

place. By a reverse process, an ivory surface can be completely dyed, then the lines scratched or scored in it, leaving a pattern of white lines on a colored ground.

STAINING AND DYEING IVORY Left in its natural state, when ivory ages it develops a yellowish to brownish patina, depending on the extent of organic substances and chemicals with which it comes into contact. Such a surface patina can be *simulated* on a newly carved and polished work by immersing the clean object for a few minutes in a concentrated solution of *tea* whose *tannic acid content* acts as a stain to produce a yellowish to brownish surface color, depending on its strength. This works best on carved or textured surfaces. The stain can be rubbed off high surfaces and left in depressions. This technique is openly (and secretly) used by merchants to instantly "age" an ivory object.

Because ivory is porous in structure, it is easily stained or dyed. Staining can be unintentional, as when ivory comes into contact with salts developing on copper, brass, or iron mounts which have become corroded (ivory readily absorbs metallic and other salts); or coloring can be deliberate, as when staining or dyeing ivory. A *stain* is a chemical coloring substance that has an affinity for ivory and can penetrate and be absorbed into its pores. It is thinner in consistency than paint or pigment, and is usually applied with a *brush locally* in a particular area of the work. *Dyeing* involves the use of *mordants* and coloring substances called *dyestuffs* or *dyes,* and the process generally implies the *total immersion* of the object in a *dyebath* so that all parts exposed to the dye are colored simultaneously, permanently, and uniformly.

Dyeing ivory is generally more successful if done *before the surface is polished* as the dye can then more easily penetrate the pores. The mordants and dyes used for dyeing can be almost any natural or synthetic substances used to color fibrous materials, though some dyes are more successful than others. Colors form a permanent bond with the ivory and are long lasting provided that the colored surface is not subject to constant abrasion. Deliberate gradation of color can however be achieved on an already dyed object by rubbing the surface to thin and lighten the color in those areas wanted.

As to which dyes to use, considering the enormous variety of dyes available, experiment is the only answer. Follow the instructions given with a particular dye, and try the color first on a scrap of the same ivory to see the result. Intermediate colors are possible by overdyeing, first with one color, then with a second color. Upon the removal of the ivory from a total immersion dyebath, it should be immediately plunged into cold water to reduce the chance of fissures that may occur from the heat of the dyebath. If after dyeing the result appears dull, the surface can be polished as already described. Polishing will cause a deepening of the color.

Pigments have also been used to color portions of ivory objects, but because pigment forms an appreciable layer on the surface, it tends to flake off due to the expansion and contraction of the ivory. Pigments are therefore generally less permanent or desirable than stains and dyes which actually penetrate the ivory pores.

CHRYSELEPHANTINE WORK

The term *chryselephantine* (from Greek *chrysos,* "gold"; and *elephas,* "ivory") describes objects made of a combination of gold and ivory. Work done in chryselephantine in Minoan and Classical Greek times was thought to be extremely luxurious as both materials were very precious. The term can be applied to the overlay or the inlay of gold into ivory, or the inlay of ivory into gold. This latter combination was commonly used in art nouveau jewelry.

INLAYING SHEET METAL AND OTHER MATERIALS INTO IVORY

Inlaying metal, mother of pearl, stones, etc., into ivory can be done by two methods. In the first method, form the depression in the ivory to receive the inlay, and make sure that its edges are *perpendicular to the surface* and not sloping inward as this would diminish the actual dimension of the depression. Place a tracing paper over the depression, and rub the paper with a *soft lead pencil* to get an exact image of its contour. Transfer this outline to the metal (or other material) and cut it out accurately with edges *square*. Adjust the shape with a *file* of the proper cross-sectional shape where necessary. Cement the inlay in place.

By the second method, first shape the metal (or other material) inlay, place it on the ivory surface, and with a *fine-pointed needle,* score the outline *at its contact point with the ivory.* First engrave the inlay outline, then excavate the ivory within its limit with *gravers* to a uniform depth that, if a flush inlay is the aim, corresponds with the thickness of the inlay material. Take care that the ivory edges and those of the inlay material butt as uniformly as possible so that there are no gaps which otherwise would have to be filled in. The inlay can also protrude above the surface, or even be in the form of a relief, an effect commonly used in jewelry.

When placing the inlay, do not force it into the depression as this might cause the ivory to chip or even fracture. If the inlay does not easily fit the excavation, inspect it with a *magnifying glass* to locate the point of resistance, and either file away the interfering inlay material, or remove the necessary base material.

Inlays of metal or other materials can be held to the ivory by adhesives or cements. A traditional method and a safe one when inlaying larger sheet metal or cast metal forms, is to solder wire pegs to the back of the metal inlay, drill holes in the ivory at corresponding positions to receive them, insert a small amount of adhesive into the holes and under the inlay, then press the inlay pegs in place.

INLAYING METAL WIRE AND TUBE IN IVORY Metal wire and tubes can be inlaid *endwise* into ivory as a form of *piqué* work. Drill a hole into the ivory to a desired depth, using a drill dimension that matches the gauge of the inlay wire so its fit is tight. Press the wire into the hole, then nip off any protrusion with *side or end nippers,* and smooth the end. If tubing is inserted, use a *saw* to remove the surplus just short of the surface, then *file* the tube end level with the ivory, and polish the surface. Wire can also be inlaid *lengthwise* by first engraving a line equal to the wire gauge, applying epoxy or another adhesive in the groove, then pressing the wire in.

INLAYING IVORY INTO ANOTHER MATERIAL Ivory can be inlaid into another material such as metal or wood that acts as a ground. Make an excavation in the ground with *gravers* or small *chisels,* cut the ivory to its shape, then cement it in place. Metal wire cloisons can be soldered to a base metal sheet and the ivory, cut to individual cloison shapes, can be cemented in place. In both cases, after inlay the surface can be smoothed flush with a cloth abrasive, then polished with pumice followed by smoothing with a cut-and-color composition, and finally, with white rouge.

STONE MOUNTING ON IVORY

Gems mounted in premade, individual metal bezel settings that have an attached rivet peg or screw at the back can be set on an ivory surface. Drill a hole in the ivory large enough to pass the peg or screw into it. Place some epoxy into the hole to act as added insurance to anchor the setting in place. A screw can be backed with a nut to hold the setting securely. Instead of a peg, a length of tubing can be soldered to the back of the setting. Its length should be slightly more than the thickness of the ivory. To hold the setting in place permanently, this surplus can be burnished to shape it into an outward-spreading flange which clinches the tube.

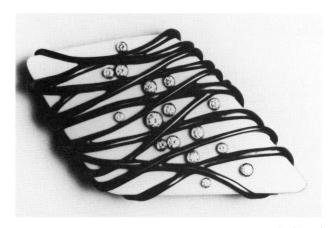

12-10 KOTAKU TAKABATAKE, Japan. Pin in ivory wrapped with red copper wire oxidized black, with 14K white gold inlay-mounted diamonds. Photo: Yasuhiro Izuka

BONE

Specific gravity: 2.0
Hardness, Mohs' scale: 2.50

Bone is the hard tissue which composes the adult skeleton of most higher vertebrates. It consists chiefly of calcium phosphate, $Ca_3(PO_4)_2$, a mineral arranged in concentric lamellae, and organic matter. Bone is dense, hard, and rigid, though internally porous, and many bones have a central cavity containing bone marrow.

Bone has its own character that makes it sympathetic as a material for use in jewelry. Because bone from various animals is inexpensive, dense bone is sometimes used as a substitute for ivory. The chief way to distinguish bone from ivory is by its structure and appearance. When cut across the grain, it looks more fibrous and lacks ivory's striated pattern. It is somewhat heavier than ivory, but usually less hard. After it has been processed for use, it lacks the abundance of natural gelatin contained in ivory, and this also accounts for its "dry" appearance.

To prepare raw bone for use, first scrub it with soap and water using a stiff brush. Then boil it in a dilute hydrochloric or sulphuric acid solution to remove the organic gelatinous matter. The resulting liquid, once the acid is recovered, contains the soluble tissue gelatin that is used to prepare animal glues. The clean bone is then bleached white with an aqueous solution of chlorine, a powerful bleaching agent, and dried.

Bone is soft enough to be worked with all tools. Though it tends to be brittle, it can be carved and pierced to an appreciable degree. It can also be stained, dyed, and polished, but does not retain as high a luster as ivory. In Bali, large bones are shaved spirally to form flat sheets of equal thickness, in the same way as continuous wood veneers are made. These are then elaborately carved and pierced into stiff fans and other objects.

Bone ash is the white, porous residue from bones that have been calcined *in air*. Crushed into a powder, it is used for cleaning jewelry, and for making *cupels* used in cupellation for the refinement of gold or silver.

Bone black is a black, carbonaceous substance made by the gradual application of heat to calcine bones contained in a *closed vessel*. In the process, the organic matter is destroyed, leaving carbon in a finely divided state. The result, after treatment and grinding is a deep black pigment known as *bone black* or *ivory black,* which is usable in all techniques requiring a black pigment.

TEETH

The teeth of carnivorous animals known for their fierceness are among the earliest objects used for personal ornaments. Primitive man is thought to have had the animistic belief that by placing such teeth in contact with his body, the courage and strength of the original possessor was transferred to himself. Often certain specialized teeth such as canines, fangs, and small tusks were preferred as these are the teeth that do the most damage.

The fact that teeth roots are not permanently ankylosed with the jawbone makes possible their removal intact. The enamel-coated crowns are highly polished and hard, making them durable. The dentine or softer part of a tooth embedded below the gum is easily pierced, allowing it to be strung into necklaces, belts, etc., or to be sewn to garments.

The popularity of toothlike forms for pendants today, and the relative scarcity of large ones, has resulted in the imitation of these shapes in a variety of other materials such as shell, coral, ivory, jade, and bone.

TORTOISESHELL AND HORN

Specific gravity: 1.26–1.35

Tortoiseshell is obtained from the hawksbill turtle (*Eret-*

mochelys imbricata) who lives in all tropical and subtropical seas. The shell most highly prized by jewelers comes from the east coast of New Guinea, Celebes, and Brazil. Its carapace or shell which is rarely more than 2 ft (0.6 m) long is covered with 13 central, thick, horny, overlapping plates called the *heart* (known in the trade as *blades*). The 5 central blades and the 4 blades on each side are used, but there are also 24 small marginal plates which are considered inferior. The largest single blade reaches approximately 14 in × 8 in (35.6 cm × 20.3 cm) and weighs about 9 ounces. They are separated from the skeleton by heat. In color they are mottled, opaque, rich browns marbled with translucent yellow. The shell is harder and more brittle than horn, and is less fibrous, but is worked in the same way as horn. Small pieces can be welded together to make larger pieces, as with horn, and it takes a high polish. Tortoiseshell is now widely imitated in plastic. Real tortoiseshell fuses to a black mass when heated and smells like burning hair; plastic chars and smells like burned milk.

Horn is a tough, fibrous epidermal substance that consists chiefly of keratin, an albuminoid found in hoofs, nails, tortoiseshell, feathers, and hair. Horn substances have been widely used in jewelry in the past, and interest in their use is having a revival in contemporary jewelry. The horn of antelope, bison, buffalo, caribou, cow, deer, elk, goat, ibex, moose, ox, reindeer, sheep, and rhinoceros can all be used. The curved and pointed horns of cattle, sheep, goats, and true antelope are unbranched and permanent. Branched horns are usually shed annually, and are more like bone.

The horns of cows, bulls, water buffalo, and sheep are solid from the pointed tip for a certain distance, then they are hollow. They can be cut in cross section to make discs where solid, or circles with a central opening where hollow. Often the coloration follows the horn's structural shape as the horn develops in layers with age, much like the development of a small tree trunk. The largest, seamless, circular forms can be used as bangles and can be decorated with metal.

Horn is relatively light in weight, and attractively warm to the touch and on the skin. It varies in hardness with the animal, and is tough and fibrous, but can be easily worked with metal tools. Horn can be carved, shaved, scraped, sawed, pierced, drilled, die punched, and solid sections can be turned on a lathe. Both horn and tortoiseshell are used to make brooches, buckles, earrings, bracelets, combs, and diadems.

12-11 MARQUISE, SOLOMON and TONGA ISLANDS, POLYNESIA. Forehead ornament (kap-kap) worn by chiefs. Made of nacreous tridacna clamshell at center and sides, overlaid with pierced work tortoiseshell ornaments, mounted on braided fiber ground. *Photo: Musée de l'Homme, Paris*

12-12 *MARQUISE ISLANDS CHIEF.* 19th-century drawing. He is wearing a kap-kap ornament with feathered headdress. *Photo: Musée de l'Homme, Paris*

12–13 GEORG JENSEN, Denmark, 1905. Back comb of tortoiseshell, ornamented with sterling silver and corals. *Photo: Courtesy Georg Jensen Sølvsmedie A/S*

12–14 MARIA TRIBE, BASTAR, MADHYA PRADESH, INDIA. Marriage ceremony dancer wearing bison horn headdress with suspended cowrie-shell tassels, and jungle cock and peacock feather plumes. *Photo: Photo Division, Ministry of Information and Broadcasting, Government of India*

POLISHING TORTOISESHELL AND HORN Tortoiseshell and horn can be polished to a high gloss and when polished, are often partially translucent. After polishing, the colors deepen in a pleasant range of natural blacks, browns, beiges, grays, and whites. Polishing is done with buffing wheels on a polishing machine with the usual but *colorless* polishing compounds. Tripoli or pumice can be used first, followed by white rouge, or a cut-and-color composition without grit can be used to achieve a high gloss. Polishing can also be done manually with a nonscratching polishing compound, but takes longer. The material acquires and retains a long-lasting high luster.

WELDING TORTOISESHELL AND HORN TO MAKE SHEETS Most tortoiseshell and horn already cut into sheet form can be welded together permanently to make larger sheets due to the nature of these materials. They are not water

soluble, but can be softened by soaking them overnight in water. First rub the surfaces and wash them to remove any external foreign matter which must not be allowed to remain. Any grease on the horn or tortoiseshell hinders welding. For this reason, do not touch sheets that are to be welded together, but handle them with *wooden or bamboo tongs.*

File the edges of the two pieces to be welded *to a taper* so they are flat and smooth at the point of overlap contact. Place them into boiling water for half an hour to soften them. While the parts are still hot, overlap the tapered edges and quickly place the pieces between two smooth, polished *metal sheets* that are sufficiently thick not to bend, and *clamp* them together. Plunge the whole assembly into boiling water until the horn softens again. Tighten the clamps during this time. After half an hour, remove the assembly and plunge it into cold water. Keep it there until the horn cools and hardens, then remove the clamps. The joint is permanent, and in most cases, is invisible after polishing. The result is a flat sheet of horn, uniform in thickness, which can be worked further.

MOLDING TORTOISESHELL AND HORN SHEET To mold these materials, first cut them to the required size, then soak them overnight in water. Boil the sheets for half an hour to soften them, then place them between the positive and negative parts of a *two-part, open, heated metal mold,* which is then clamped together. The mold should not be too hot or the horn will become scorched or will burn. Boil the assembly in water for 15 minutes. Then plunge the assembly into cold water and allow it to cool and harden in its new form. Do not remove the horn too soon or the shape may warp. Trim away excess flanges with a *saw.*

DYEING HORN The natural color of horn ranges anywhere from black through grays, browns, and beiges. If desired, horn can be dyed with synthetic dyes. Experimentation is necessary to find the dyes that will color horn. Dyeing should be carried out on the finished article, after it has been polished to its final luster. It may be necessary to repolish the article after dyeing. It is preferable to use a dye that does not require a high-temperature solution to avoid the possibility of warping the article.

If the tortoiseshell or horn is partially translucent, its color can be altered by placing a nontarnishing, *pure tin sheet* underneath it to reflect light through the horn. *Colored foils* can also be used to back these materials and alter their natural color. This technique was widely practiced in France during the 17th century by the famous furniture maker, André-Charles Boulle. He also, inciden-

12–15 ORISSA, INDIA. Contemporary water buffalo horn section bangles, inlaid with piqué work in brass, white metal, and ivory. *Photo: Oppi*

tally, used inlays of bone, ivory, and mother of pearl in his furniture.

INLAY INTO TORTOISESHELL AND HORN Horn can be inlaid with metal wire and/or sheet, a form of work called *piqué*. (This is described under Metal Inlay: Inlay of metal into nonmetallic grounds, p. 317.)

CLAWS

The long, sharp, curved claws on the toes of animals, especially those of vicious animals that have great strength and who use them as a weapon to seize, dig into, and hold their prey, have long been used for ornaments, especially in Eastern countries. Anthropocentric man believed them

to impart the strength and courage of the original possessor to himself. In India, tigers' claws especially have always been considered valuable talismans, worn singly or in outward-curving pairs in a metal mount. The use of tigers' claws in jewelry in Victorian India was especially favored by foreign women living there. They were mounted in silver or even gold settings in various arrangements in brooches, belt buckles, bracelets, and necklaces.

SHELL CAMEOS

Cameos are carvings of a figure in relief on shell or stone. (For stone, see Gemstone Carving and Engraving: The glyptic art, in Chapter 13.) The opposite of a *cameo* is an *intaglio* or negative carving, rarely found in shell, but common in stone, such as in engraved stone seals. For at least two or more centuries, the center for shell cameo carving has been the town of Torre del Greco at the foot of Mount Vesuvius near Naples, Italy. Here hundreds of traditional carvers are at work, descendants of cameo-carving families, in this still highly active craft industry.

Though shell cameos were originally meant to substitute for gemstone cameos, shell cameo carving today is a separate and important art in the jewelry world. Carving a

12–17   F. R. NITOT, France. "Coronne de Sacre." Gold-plated silver crown made for Napoleon's coronation in 1804, and also used for his wedding to Marie-Louise. Now in the Galerie Apollon, the crown jewels collection, Louvre, Paris. Napoleon wished to use the 10th-century crown of Charlemagne, but it was hidden in Austria, and this was made and worn instead. From a circlet of eight laurel leaves rise four crossing arches, surmounted by an orb and cross finial. Many antique Roman stone cameos and intaglios are mounted on the crown, reflecting contemporary interest in Classical antiquity. *Photo: Service de Documentation Photographique, Paris*

12–16   CHINA, ca. 1860. Necklace employing gold-mounted tiger's claws, in China believed to be a powerful talisman against sudden fright, and able to imbue the wearer with the animal's courage. Between the claws and joined by chains are filigree units ornamented with felicitous subjects having symbolic meanings. Included are *phoenixes*, symbolically associated with the sun, fire, good luck, and prosperity; the *butterfly*, a symbol of joy and conjugal felicity; the *carp*, symbol of abundance, freedom, and harmony in connubial bliss; and the *lotus flower*, a symbol of purity and perfection. *Photo: Victoria and Albert Museum, London, Crown Copyright*

12–18   CLAUDIA KUEHNL, U.S.A. "Last Time." Silver brooch fabricated with outer oxidized silver base, followed by a gold-plated upper arch, and an ivory arch beneath which are three back-mounted carnelian stones, followed by a layer of tortoiseshell. Spires of baroque pearls, a peridot at the arch point, and the central shell cameo relate to the architectonic forms. *Photo: Evon Streetman*

cameo from shell, which is relatively soft, is far easier than carving one from hard stone. Though the prices of shell cameos are therefore comparatively lower than those of similar quality carved from gemstones, the best shell cameos command high prices.

The shells commonly used for cameos are mainly the large, heavy, tropical marine univalve shells of the genus *Cassis* (from the Latin for "helmet") of the family *Cassisidae*. The main shells employed are *Cassis cameo, Cassis rufa, Cassis madagascariensis,* and related species, whose common names are shield shell, bull's mouth, black helmet, horned helmet, and queen conch. *Strombus gigas* or the fountain shell which has an expanded outer lip is also used. These shells are imported to Italy from the West Indies, mainly from the Bahamas, from Madagascar, and from the Maldive Islands. In these shells, the uppermost, porcelaneous surface is a white to cream-colored layer with a thickness of from one to two millimeters, and from it the figure is carved in relief in varying thicknesses that appear opaque to translucent in contrast with the ground. The ground color that lies beneath the outer layer can be pale orange, pink, rose, deep terra-cotta, red brown, or nearly black.

In making a cameo, the selected shell area is first cut away from the rest with a *rotating circular mechanical saw*. The outer shape is then ground on a *mechanical grinding wheel*. The figure is carved with sharp *steel gravers* having different cutting edge shapes, similar to those used in engraving metal. Today some carvers also use *power-driven miniature carbide abrasive* or *diamond wheels,* mounted in the handpiece of a rotary *flex-shaft*. Details are carved while wearing magnifying glasses. The finished cameos are polished on *polishing lathes* with *soft wheels* and suitable abrasives.

The cameos vary in size from very small ones suited to be mounted in rings or earrings, to those several inches in diameter used for brooches, pendants, bracelets, and necklaces. Large cameos are relatively rare because they require very high-quality work in order to get high prices. All sorts of figural and allegorical subjects were and are still used, but the female head in profile remains the most popular subject. Most contemporary jewelers consider cameos old-fashioned and conventional. Their use in creative modern jewelry is, however, on the increase. Some jewelers appreciate the skill with which they are done, and others even find them amusing. At times they are used with the effect of a collage, to provide a striking stylistic contrast to their contemporary environment.

A *lavoro di commesso* cameo is a shell cameo with elaborate ornamental inlays of metal, enameled metal, or stones. This type of polychromed cameo was inspired by Renaissance hard stone cameos. When the inlays delineate details of clothing or ornament on the figure represented, the cameo is called a *cameo habillé*. Cameos are also carved in coral, ivory, jet, and lavastone, but these are of one color.

CORAL

Specific gravity: 2.60–2.70
Hardness, Mohs' scale: about 3.5

Coral is not a mineral, but is the axial, opaque, calcareous or hornlike skeleton made of calcium carbonate and organic matter, produced by various soft, jellylike anthrozoans and a few hydrozoans or polyps. The living creature is also called coral, and exists in warm seas,

12-19 GIO POMODORO, Italy. Gold collar with natural branch and cabochon coral, and rubies, all parts articulated. Photo: Sala Dino

requiring a temperature of 55–60° F (13–15.5° C), normally at a depth of 15–20 feet, but is also found in much deeper waters, though size decreases with depth. These compound animals live in immense colonies that together secrete separate cells joined by their proximity in branchlike forms in which they live. Their hard, dense skeletons solidify into a stony mass that stands on a thicker "foot" attached to a submarine rock, and this foot makes it hard to remove. The stem is seldom more than one inch in diameter, and the branches are even smaller.

The red coral of the Mediterranean and Japanese waters, *Coralium nobile* and *Coralium rubrum* are widely used in jewelry as a semiprecious stone. Red coral develops nearer the water surface, and flesh-toned and white corals, at greater depths. Until the first quarter of this century, coral was found in quantity in the coastal waters around Naples, Calabria, Sicily, Corsica, Sardinia, Spain, Provence, Algeria, and Tunisia. These areas have diminished or ceased to exist as coral producers due to water pollution and overfishing. The main source of coral today are Japanese waters and those of the Sumatra coast, but some comes from the Red Sea and from the Persian and Arabian Gulfs. The most valuable is the deep red coral called *moro*, but pale rose pink called *angelskin*, and a lighter pink called *demiangelskin* are also desirable. White and white touched with pink are less popular.

The most important coral cutting and carving center in Europe is at Torre del Greco near Naples. Its proximity to former coral sources accounts for its establishment at this place, but today most of the raw coral used by the coral-working craftsmen, who also carve shell cameos, comes

12-20 ALICE SHANNON, U.S.A. Pin in 14K gold with black branch coral and Biwa pearls. Photo: Jack Bitermann

from Japan. Hong Kong is the most important Eastern coral carving center where skilled craftsmen work in an Oriental style. Besides carving selected material into small objects, often floral or figural, coral is made into beads and cabochons. Because of size limitations, large beads are rare. All coral is sold by gram weight and priced according to quality, color, and size.

Coral is easily shaped and cut by files, rotary cutters, and abrasives, and takes a high polish. To test the genuineness of coral, place a drop of acid on it: its main constituent, calcium carbonate, will visibly effervesce. Upon excessive heating, it loses its color and decrepitates.

Coral has long been believed to have talismanic virtues, and has been used for this purpose since antiquity. It is especially prized in the Far East where it is frequently cut *en cabochon*. In Nepal it is carved into the shape of the deity Ganesh, the Hindu god of wisdom and remover of obstacles, then mounted in jewelry. In India, where the power of stones on the human condition is an ancient belief, coral is said to emit powerful yellow cosmic rays that dry up ailing human lymph nodes and cure rheumatism and other diseases. In Italy it is believed to avert the malignant influences of the evil eye. *Black coral* is less known and used. It is found in Japanese waters, the Indian Ocean, the Caribbean Sea off the coast of Cozumel in Mexico, and in the Maldive Islands. East Indians call it *akabar*, and the Italians call it *giojetto*. It is horny in structure, is carved much like horn, and can take a high polish. It was popular in Persia until recent times for making large bead rosaries that were often inlaid with wire or tubing in the manner of piqué work. (See Metal Inlay, Chapter 8, Illustration 8-55.)

AMBER

Specific gravity: 1.08–1.10
Hardness, Mohs' scale: 2.50–3.00
Refractive index: 1.54

Amber is the yellow, fossilized, transparent to translucent to semiopaque, resinous gum exuded by the ancient, coniferous fossil tree *Pinites succinifer* that grew in forests during the Oligocene. In the course of time, the trees became buried, and because of heat and pressure the resin they exuded became fossilized. Amber is an organic substance and is not a mineral. Like other resins, it is light in weight, warm to the touch, and can be easily burned (the reason for its Dutch and German names, respectively *barnsteen*, and *bernstein*). During the life of the tree, it was exuded in viscous form, and because of this, insects that existed in the climate in which the tree grew and who often sit on trees or live in bark fissures, were frequently imprisoned in the amber in which they were caught and by which they were covered. Pieces containing insects such as ants, bees, beetles, flies, gadflies, gnats, and wasps are highly valued. Air bubbles, and vegetable and organic matter can also be inclusions.

The word *amber* is derived from the Arabic *anbar*, "ambergris," with which it was confused. Amber has been used for ornament, mostly as beads, since the Bronze Age. Upon being rubbed, amber generates a negative electric charge which makes it magnetic and capable of picking up light objects such as paper. Because of this, the Greek called it *elektron*. This is also the reason that it has been thought of as a mystic stone possessing magical properties, therefore long used as an amulet, especially in the Near and Far East. Its property of becoming electrically charged is a problem to polishers because during polishing, if not carefully cooled, its electrical charge can cause it to fly into splinters. Professional amber polishers are often seized by wrist and arm tremors because of the electricity amber generates. Its magnetic quality is sometimes used to distinguish the real from imitation amber, but this is not a reliable test as some plastics possess the same qualities. A better way to judge genuineness is by its specific gravity, or by its sweet aromatic smell after burning a particle.

The amber found in undersea deposits is called *sea amber,* and when mined from pits is called *pit amber.* Constitutionally they are the same. The main sources of amber today are the countries along the Baltic Sea, including East Prussia in East Germany, Poland, Estonia, Latvia, and Lithuania. It is also found in smaller amounts in Siberia, Greenland, eastern England, the Netherlands, Burma (a hard red variety: Burmite), and in valleys of the Himalaya foothills. In the Baltic region it is commonly thrown up by the sea on the sandy shores after rough weather loosens submerged particles. Inland it occurs in

12-21 MARY ANN SCHERR, U.S.A. Sterling silver wire necklace covered with multi-metal wrapped wire, holding amber bead sections separated by silver domes, and discs of silver, brass, and blued steel. Photo: Doug Moore

bluish clay and alluvial soils with beds of lignite. It is now systematically mined in areas where amber-bearing trees are known to have existed by breaking up earth deposits with strong blasts from water hoses, followed by sieving. It is also collected from the beds of small streams and from sea cliffs.

In color amber ranges from whitish yellow to bright yellow to brown red. The best pieces used for gems in jewelry are bright, transparent yellow, but are rarely completely clear and often contain inclusions, opaque areas, and fissures. Amber is soft enough to be easily cut and carved with ordinary steel blades or abrasives, and shaping is done on a whetstone or with successively finer grades of abrasive papers. Polishing to a bright, glassy surface can be done on a polishing machine with felt or flannel polishing wheels loaded with chalk and water, or tin oxide, followed by a rubbing with vegetable oil. The final gloss is created by rubbing with a flannel cloth.

PRESSED AMBER: Ambroid

Pressed amber, called *ambroid,* is made of powdered waste amber, chips, and inferior amber pieces. These are heated to approximately 185° F (85° C) to make the material pliant and form a mass. The reconstituted mass is placed in a mold and heated to approximately 450° F (200° C), then pressed to form a block, or extruded under pressure. The results can be cut and shaped into beads or formed into large objects such as cane handles and cigarette holders, or carved. Ambroid is considered inferior to natural amber. It can be detected by its misty look, flowing structural lines, and may contain trapped, elongated air bubbles. Ambroid is stronger than natural amber.

Pieces of amber can be joined by smearing their contacting surfaces with linseed oil, and while holding them tightly together with a tool, heating them until they become welded. If opaque amber is baked at a low temperature for several hours, it becomes more transparent. Only about one-fifth of all amber found is suitable for use in jewelry, hence these attempts to use inferior material and reconstitute pieces. Many imitations of amber exist, made from natural resins which resemble amber, and from synthetic resins.

MOTHER OF PEARL: Nacre

Specific gravity: 2.65–2.78
Hardness, Mohs' scale: 3.5
Double refraction: 1.57

Mother of pearl is a general term meaning a hard, silvery or iridescent, brilliant internal layer that occurs in *several* kinds of shells of oysters, abalone, mussels, snails, and other Mollusca. The nacre substance is manufactured by secretion from the mantle of the shellfish while its shell grows to protect itself. Not all these molluscs produce pearls, but some do, and pearls are made of the same substance.

The color of nacre varies with the species producing it, from dead white to yellow, green, or variegated purple, pink, and blue. Nacre consists of layers in series, lapped over each other in an imbricated manner so that their edges show a series of lines with waved margins. Sometimes it appears chatoyant when its structure, which contains a multitude of microscopic wrinkles or furrows, runs across the surface in a parallel direction. When it is iridescent, the structure of any slice of the shell is such that it

12-22 RANGOON, BURMA. Contemporary mother of pearl heart pendants, pierced and engraved. *Photo: Oppi*

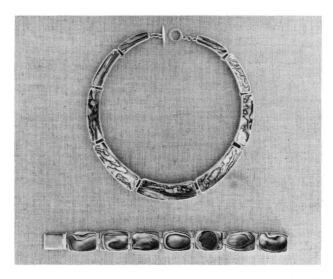

12-23 PALLE BISGAARD, Denmark. Silver necklace and bracelet inlaid with abalone shell (*Haliotis gigas*). *Photo: Jens Buhl*

causes interference to light in a way that produces a chromatic effect. The brilliancy of the iridescence depends on the thinness of the laminae or nacre layers.

Some of the Mollusca producing nacre are the genus *Pentadenae* around Cape Comorin in India; *Aviculata margaritafera* in Ceylonese waters; *Haliotis gigas, Haliotis iris,* and *Haliotis splendens,* whose common name is abalone, in California waters; *Turbo petholatus* from South Pacific islands; and others come from the Persian Gulf, the Red Sea, the Straits of Malacca, the Indonesian Archipelago, the Philippines, and South Africa. In commerce they are known on the market by the name of the place of their origin, and some of the popular colloquial names are flat shells, ear shells, green snail shells, and buffalo shells.

In some shells such as some of the species of the genera *Trochus* and *Phasianella* the nacre is of sufficient thickness to allow sections to be carved to a considerable depth with abrasive tools and drills, or to be made into round beads up to 20 mm (0.8 in) in diameter, while in others like abalone, the thickness ranges from 1 mm up to about 4

12-24 SAARA HOPEA-UNTRACHT, Finland, designer; manufacturer Kultasepänliike Ossian Hopea, Porvoo. Necklace of 18K gold with abalone shell and eight Finnish spectrolites. *Photo: Oppi*

PEARLS

Specific gravity:	Oriental pearls:	2.68–2.74
	Japanese cultured:	2.72–2.78
	Australian cultured:	2.70–2.79
	Freshwater pearls:	2.68 average

Hardness, Mohs' scale: 3–4
Double refraction: 1.57

NATURAL PEARLS

Natural pearls, generally termed *Oriental pearls* because they come mainly from Oriental waters, are a dense, shell-like, lustrous concretion formed in pearl oysters, clams, abalone, mussels, giant conch, and giant clams living in salt waters. Because pearls are organic in origin, they are not mineral gems. Pearls have been in wide use for personal ornament since prehistoric times. The great shell mounds found at prehistoric sites indicate that the use of pearls must have occurred at an early date. The major reason for their immediate adoption for ornamental purposes is the fact that they can be used *as found*, they require no cutting or polishing because of their natural luster (though polishing may be carried out), and need only piercing which, because of their relative softness as compared with mineral stones, is easily accomplished.

The true pearl oyster is a nacreous-shelled, scallop-shaped, bivalve mollusc of the genus *Pinctada*, of which there are several species. *Pinctada margaritifera*, or *Pinctada vulgaris*, is widely distributed in the Persian Gulf where the world's best natural pearls are found in beds off Bahrein, and also in the Red Sea and the Indian Ocean.

mm (0.04–0.16 in) which allows low cabochons or flat pieces for inlays to be used.

Mother of pearl is of little intrinsic value, but its natural beauty makes it an attractive material. Its structure resists cracking and splitting, and it is relatively hard. It is easily cut into blank shapes with a *jeweler's saw* or a *lapidary's trim saw*, formed into flat pieces with *files, rotary abrasive wheels*, or on a *grinding machine* or *lapping wheel*. Mounted on a dop stick, it can be polished like a cabochon cut stone with tripoli followed by rouge, with a cut-and-color compound followed by tin oxide, or by tumbling. It can be drilled, fret sawed, carved, or acid etched to make contrasting polished and dull areas. Depressions or lines engraved on the surface show up best on light or colorless nacre, and these can be filled with lac or resin in a contrasting color.

Polished nacre can be set like any stone in a bezel or prong setting. In inlay work where it is probably most often used, whether in metal, wood, or stone, it is often set flush with the surface in contact on a common base, or in cloisons, and is held in place by a suitable cement such as epoxy. The whole upper surface is leveled flat at the same time with an *abrasive stick*, or by using a *220 grit silicon carbide lapping wheel* mounted on a *polishing motor*. It is polished for luster with tin oxide and retains its luster for relatively long periods of time if the surface does not suffer from abrasion in which case it becomes dull, but the polish can easily be restored. Mosaics of nacre should not be allowed to come into prolonged contact with water which attacks the cement and ultimately loosens the shell.

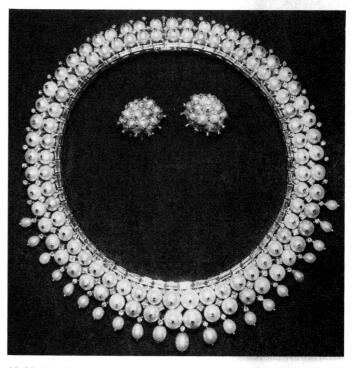

12-25 NANUBHAI JEWELERS, Bombay, India, manufacturer. Platinum necklace with 104 round pearls, 21 pendant oval pearls, 156 diamonds between the pearls, 57 emerald-cut diamonds, and 125 small rubies covering the holes in each pearl; with matching earrings. *Photo: Oppi*

Related species are found in Japanese waters, the South Pacific Island waters, off the northern coasts of Australia, in the Gulf of California, and in the Caribbean Sea off the coasts of Venezuela and Panama. The quality and amounts of natural pearls produced in these places differ widely, and since the advent of cultured pearl production, fishing for natural pearls has diminished.

NATURAL PEARL DEVELOPMENT Pearls develop in the mollusc as an abnormal growth around a minute foreign body. Sometimes this is a grain of sand that accidentally becomes lodged between the mantle and the shell of the mollusc, but more often it is a parasite, or the egg of the flat tapeworm deposited by that parasite who eats a hole through the shell into the oyster's mantle. If this object cannot be released or ejected (which the mollusc tries to do by repeatedly snapping its shells shut), as it is a source of irritation to the mantle tissue, the mollusc is stimulated by stress to isolate the substance by manufacturing a secretion from the entire external mantle surface. This consists of a crystalline calcium carbonate ($CaCO_3$) called *nacre* which is deposited around the irritant, and is the same smooth substance called *mother of pearl* used to develop shell growth and inner shell lining. Pearls that develop in the mantle are called *cyst pearls* or *mantle pearls* though they may ultimately work their way out of the mantle and lie loose between it and the shell, but they also develop in other parts of the mollusc. Those that remain free and unconnected to the shell do so because the mantle makes slight contractions that cause them to roll about. Usually they are also trapped in a mantle sac that develops around them. These conditions account for the round or rounded shapes of pearls. Other pearls become connected to the shell, or to each other as more than one pearl can develop in a single oyster. (See Glossary of Natural and Cultured Pearl Types on p. 568.)

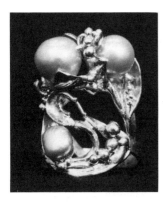

12–26 ILSE IMMICH, West Germany. Ring in yellow gold with beige and white pearls. Photo: Simone Luino

In the shell, the nacre layers lie parallel to the shell's surface. In a round pearl, in time the nacre is deposited around and completely envelops the irritant or nucleus object in extremely thin, interstratified, concentric layers or laminae. Also included in the substance is some organic matter called conchiolin. Like the inner surface of the mollusc's shell, the overlapping layers on the pearl consist of 82–86% nacre which is a form of aragonite, and 10–14% organic conchiolin ($C_{30}H_{48}N_2O_{11}$). The irregular, ridged, exposed edges of the nacre structure cause light interference which accounts for the highly iridescent appearance of the best pearls, and this same iridescence also appears in the shell when it is cut and polished.

FRESHWATER PEARLS

Freshwater pearls are found in freshwater mussels (Unionidae) which live in streams, lakes, and rivers of all continents. The most common freshwater pearls available on the market today are *biwa pearls* which are cultivated in Lake Biwa in Japan, and *China pearls* which are cultivated in China. These pearls are generally not round, but occur in a variety of irregular shapes. Their color is more often than not a creamy white and relatively low in luster, but pearls of good luster are also found. The color range of freshwater pearls is more varied than that of natural or cultured saltwater pearls. When natural freshwater pearls are collected, hand rakes, tongs, or drags, or hand picking methods are used. It has been discovered that pearls are found mostly in shells that are imperfect or distorted, and this is also the case with natural pearls found in saltwater oysters. Freshwater pearls are also cultured in cages suspended from rafts in the same general manner as saltwater cultured pearls. In the past, freshwater pearls have been lower in value than saltwater pearls, but because of demand, this situation is changing and good quality freshwater pearls can command high prices as well. Their nacreous shells have been used for pearl button manufacture, but this industry has declined with the introduction of plastic buttons made to resemble shell.

CULTURED PEARLS

Cultured pearls are created artificially, mainly by the mechanical introduction of a perfectly round mother of pearl bead or *nucleus* to the interior of the mantle of a live oyster. The core causes the oyster irritation and stress, so that in order to isolate the nucleus, it deposits the pearlescent substance upon it in exactly the same way that it produces nacre for shell construction and in making natural pearls. The difference between a natural pearl and a cultured pearl is that in nature the introduction of the nucleus is accidental and it is very small, while in the case of cultured pearls, it is introduced artificially and the nucleus is large in order to reduce the time necessary for a fair sized pearl to develop. In a cultured pearl the total thickness of the nacreous layer is thin compared to that of a natural pearl in which the nacreous layer develops from the small nucleus and therefore comprises almost the entire pearl.

The idea of inducing an oyster or mussel to manufacture nacre around an artificially introduced nucleus is believed to have started in China during the 12th century. Round pearls, however, were not the aim. Instead, as was also done during the 19th century, small mother of pearl or metal images of the Buddha, and other forms, were inserted and cemented in rows against the inner shell of the river mollusc *Dipsus plicatus*. In time, this mussel deposited a coating of pearlescent nacre upon such a figural nucleus. The image was cut from the shell, backed, and sold as a good luck charm for a good price in Buddhist countries.

A method of artificial round pearl culture was developed by Carolus Linnaeus, a Swedish botanist (1707–1778) who also used freshwater mussels into whose shell he bored a hole and introduced a limestone nucleus, but this method, sold to the Swedish government, was never commercialized.

Credit for successful pearl culture goes to the Japanese. In 1896 Kokichi Mikimoto established a business in the cultivation of *half pearls,* accomplished by cementing a mother of pearl half bead to the inner oyster wall. He also produced button pearls which developed with a flat side. At the same time he was attempting to create round pearls with controlled regularity and not by occasional accident as happened. Other persons in Japan at this time were also investigating means of solving the problems of cultured round pearl manufacture. Credit for first developing the intermantle, nucleus-inserted method along with a tissue graft to create completely spherical cultured pearls, according to postwar investigation, is now given to Tokichi Nishikawa, a marine biologist of the Japanese Bureau of Fisheries who accomplished this in laboratory conditions by 1905 but never received a patent for his system which is now used by the entire industry, and is described below in greater detail.

Mikimoto also produced round pearls, but by another method patented in 1908. In 1916 Mikimoto was granted a patent as inventor of round pearl production. He then purchased the rights to the use of the Nishikawa method and this method was then adopted by his organization. There is no doubt that Mikimoto was the first to produce cultured round pearls in quantity, and to make a commercial success of marketing them, for which reason the press gave him the title "The Pearl King." Today other companies also produce cultured pearls, such as Yamakatsu, Takashima, and Yakota, but the K. Mikimoto & Co. Ltd. of Tokyo is without competition in the now highly organized cultured pearl industry.

CULTURED PEARL PRODUCTION METHOD To help nature to create round cultured pearls, first round beads from 2–9 mm (0.08–0.36 in) in diameter are manufactured from mother of pearl shell using the shell of the freshwater pig-toed clam found in the Mississippi River Valley. This material has been found to be best for this purpose, and is imported to Japan from the U.S.A. This nucleus constitutes 75–90% of the total diameter of the cultured pearl, depending on how long the oyster is permitted to produce nacre.

The three-year-old, mature *Pinctada martensii* oyster is the main host for cultured pearl production. It is brought from the waters where it is cultivated, cleaned, and placed in running water to make it open its shells, whereupon a bamboo wedge is inserted between them to hold them open. In a 30-second operation, a skilled worker places the oyster in a clamp that keeps it open. By means of a hollow grafting needle, the worker penetrates and makes an incision in the outer skin layer (epithelium) of the mantle, fractures the secondary skin (parenchyma), and introduces up to 20 very small nuclei, two 6 mm (0.16 in) nuclei, or one large nucleus into the incision. Along with these goes a small square section of graft mantle tissue taken from another oyster and placed there to stimulate nacre production, and some epithelial cells which help the oyster to form a pocket in the mantle that eventually embraces the nucleus. Though there are some losses, most healthy oysters survive this operation, accept the implant, and live to produce nacre upon it for at least three or more years. It takes approximately three years for 1 mm (0.04 in) of nacre to develop around a nucleus.

About 50 oysters are then returned to one wire cage which is then submerged in 7–10 ft (2–3 m) of saltwater, suspended from floating rafts in sheltered waters, such as the pearl farms at Ago Bay where 65% of Mikimoto production takes place, and Toba Bay. Each

raft holds about 60 cages or about 3,000 oysters. Periodically they are hauled up for cleaning, then returned to the water. Here they remain for three to seven years. They are harvested in winter months because the nacre produced at this time is considered best.

The pearls are graded for size, quality, luster, and color by trained workers. They are drilled and strung into graduated or matched strands that are sold by *momme.* (A momme is a Japanese unit of weight equivalent to 3.75 grams.) Pearls of 6–7 mm (0.24–0.28 in) diameter are considered average in size; 8 mm (0.32 in) are large; and 9–11 mm (3.36–0.44 in), very large, and the limit in maximum size possible with the akoya oyster. The price jumps considerably with each increase in diameter.

Since 1957, the export of any but quality pearls from Japan was prohibited by law. All export pearls are inspected, and if found acceptable, are given a seal of approval. In this way, quality production for export is upheld.

THE BASIS OF PEARL QUALITY JUDGMENT

Size, shape, luster, surface condition, and color are the bases for judging both natural and cultured pearl quality, and are important in this order.

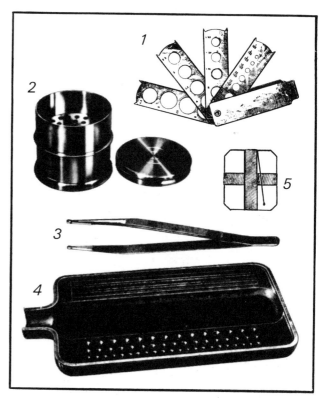

12-27 *PEARL SORTING AND STRINGING TOOLS AND MATE-RIALS*
1. *Pearl and round stone diameter gauge, with four leaves having openings from ¹⁄₁₀₀–6 mm carats, seven leaves from 0.2–40 grains.*
2. *Pearl sieve with interchangeable, accurately calibrated, holed plates of brass, 51 or 77 mm Ø, each with different sized openings for sorting pearls. Lacquered brass or nickel plated.*
3. *Pearl tweezers with round, concave, ivory-tipped points, 160 mm long.*
4. *Pearl and stone sorting tray, black, used to arrange them in graduated series, 150 × 350 mm, or 3¾ × 7 in.*
5. *Pearl and bead stringing thread of multiple-ply natural silk or nylon, 2 meters long, with one or two attached needles, wound on cardboard.*

SIZE   Certain oysters are capable of producing pearls of small size only, and other species can produce larger pearls. All other factors being equal, pearl size is of paramount importance. Natural pearls are weighed in *carats,* which measurement is converted into *pearl grains* (the weight in universal use for natural pearls) by multiplying carat weight by four. Thus there are 4 grains in 1 carat, and 1 grain equals 50 milligrams. Today the *weight* of pearls is only used in connection with natural pearls, and natural pearl fishing has diminished considerably due to the development of the cultured pearl industry. Because cultured pearls have artificial, solid centers, they are measured instead by *caliber,* measured in millimeters. A natural pearl of 5 grains approximately equals a cultured pearl of 5.5 mm (0.22 in).

In 1893 George Frederick Kunz (1856–1932), a gem expert after whom kunzite is named, stabilized the use of the grain as 4 grains per carat, and he is also responsible for setting the present use of the millimeter as a size standard for round pearls. The *Kunz gauge* which he devised is available as a cardboard sheet pierced with graduated holes into which a pearl can be placed to determine its millimeter diameter and weight. This gauge came into wide use at the start of the 20th century. Pearls are also measured by the use of any millimeter gauge.

SHAPE   The regular pearl shapes most sought after are *completely round,* which are further graded into perfect spheres; *slightly off-round* (detectable only by instrument measurement); and *off-round* (detectable by visual inspection). Other popular shapes are *drop,* which has one end that tapers nearly to a point while the other end is rounded, like a drop of water; *pear,* which resembles a typical pear shape; *egg,* which resembles a typical egg shape; *button,* which is domed at the top and has a shallow, flat curve at the other side; and *double button,* whose upper and lower surfaces are flat-curved. Still other irregular shapes are described in the Glossary of Natural and Cultured Pearl Types on p. 568. Pearls that have regular parts but are otherwise defective in form are sometimes cut into parts that can be used separately.

LUSTER   The characteristic luster or sheen of a pearl is termed its "orient." This results from the interference and the diffraction or modification that light undergoes in passing by the edges of the microscopic ridges or fine striations that constitute the pearl's surface structure. These ridges break up the light and cause the surface to produce the effect of iridescence. The term luster is based on a relative judgment; therefore when purchasing a pearl, its luster is best judged by comparing it with that of other pearls. Experts can detect subtle differences, and often use poetic terms to describe luster. The pearl appears as a "silver-veiled moon," "polished silver," or a "mirror." In cultured pearls, five grades of luster are recognized: very bright, bright, medium, slightly dull, and dull.

SURFACE CONDITION   The surface of a pearl ranges from smooth to grainy or rough, and this condition depends mainly on the species of the oyster that created it. Although pearls develop in concentric layers, surface defects may occur. The type of defect and its extent cause a proportionate decrease in the value of a pearl. Four grades of *flawlessness* used by the pearl trade are: flawless to the naked eye (the use of a lens will reveal defects in even the most "perfect" pearl), slightly spotted, spotted, and heavily spotted. Other defects include depressed point dots, raised dots, color spots, raised ridge, raised band, irregular projection, bump or growth, surface split, and subsurface split. In use, a split can occur in a pearl if it is suddenly subjected to a drastic change in temperature.

Some defects can be corrected by peeling off the outermost layers of a pearl, called *skinning.* This is a job done only by experts who are specialists in this technique, and even then with risk. Bumps ordinarily cannot be removed as they leave even more visible spots. Acids affect calcium carbonate, therefore will attack the pearl's surface, as will highly acidic perspiration.

COLOR   Evenness of color in a pearl is very important, and the color range is very wide. Specialists classify pearl colors as rosé rosé, rosé, white rosé, cream, white, blue white, yellowish white, brown rosé, yellow rosé, brown, gray, yellow, and hard yellow. Other colors also occur in freshwater pearls. The most favored conventional color is a silvery white, but women in one part of the world favor rosé tones, and in other areas creamy tones are favored.

Color and luster judgment of pearls is always done in diffused natural daylight, never by artificial light, by placing the pearls against a neutral, medium-value gray ground. Several pearls (or strands) should be placed near each other when examining pearls, as comparison brings out differences. Actually, accurate judgments of this kind as well as judgments of value take years of experience to develop. Therefore, reliance upon the judgment of a reputable dealer is important.

Fantasy or fancy colors are the deeper ones found in natural pearls which can be deep gold, green, purple, and black. When gray black, brown black, blue black, or green black natural pearls also possess perfect shape and good luster, they are very desirable. Coal black is the least desirable of the black pearls on the pearl market.

Dyed pearls are generally cultured pearls that have been dyed to give a string of pearls the color unity it otherwise would not have. Dyed pearls are also available singly. They are considered to have less value than pearls with natural color, but can be attractive in their own way. Yellowish pearls, the least desirable of the light colors, are sometimes dyed black by soaking them in silver nitrate, exposing them to light which turns the silver nitrate black, then polishing them. Pearls are sometimes stained to increase pinkness, and it is common to bleach cultured pearls in a warm, dilute solution of hydrogen peroxide for one week. To see if a pearl is artificially colored, observe the hole where it is drilled, as dyeing is done before drilling. If the internal color is vastly different from the exterior, the pearl is probably dyed.

COMMERCIAL CATEGORIES OF CULTURED PEARLS TODAY

The round cultured pearl is still the ideal pearl shape, and dominates the pearl market today. Conditions of pollution in the original Japanese waters used for pearl oyster culture has limited production and caused the development of pearl farms in other suitable waters in Japan and elsewhere. As a result, the price of round cultured pearls of good quality, and of pearls in general has increased considerably over the recent past years. Consumer interest consequently is growing in the less expensive, nonround pearl types which traditionally are considered inferior. When the prejudice in favor of round pearls is overlooked, the organic, asymmetrical, irregular pearl forms become attractive in their own right. Physically they are made of the same substance, and they may possess color and iridescent luster equal to the best round pearl. To the jeweler and jewelry designer, their forms, especially those of freshwater pearls which can develop in quite extraordinary shapes, may suggest many possible uses in contemporary jewelry. They are either strung in strands in combination with stone or metal beads, or used individually or in groups with metal jewelry. Irregularly shaped pearls are increasingly accepted by the public, and their production is growing. Present tendencies indicate that they will become ever more important in fulfilling the demands of the pearl market.

Cultured pearls today are produced in various locations, the main ones being Japanese and Australian coastal waters. To indicate pearl type, the *pearl shape,* or its *place of origin* are used as designations in the commercial pearl market. The following are the main pearl groups available today:

Akoya: The classic, round cultured pearl, named after the *Pinctada martensii* oyster (called *akoya-gai* in Japanese) that produces it in Japanese coastal saltwaters. Its size is 2–11 mm (0.08–0.44 in) maximum. It is available in white, white rosé, white green, cream, gold, and blue gray tones. Pearls in this category that are dark green, dark blue gray, or black, are always dyed.

Keshi: Irregular or baroque-shaped akoya pearls that develop after the oyster has ejected the nucleus. They are available in the same color range as akoya pearls.

Biwa: Freshwater mussel pearls cultivated in Lake Biwa in Japan. They are generally without a solid nucleus as the oyster normally will not accept one. The pearls are usually ovoid and baroque in form, but other, often bizarre forms also develop. A variety of colors are produced from the typical lustrous creamy white color, to white rosé, salmon orange, gray blue, brown violet, and brown.

Burma: Large-diameter, saltwater-cultured oyster pearls with a creamy luster, produced in small quantities.

China: Freshwater mussel pearls cultivated in China. They resemble the biwa pearl, but are made with nuclei, and develop in various forms including forked types that are even more irregular than biwa pearls. Rose tones predominate, but other colors such as white, green white, green rosé, salmon orange, dark wine red, and violet are also available.

South Sea: Pearls cultivated only by the *Pinctada maxima* oyster in the warm saltwaters of the Indian and Pacific oceans, especially off the coast of Australia, but also in the Bay of Bengal off Burma, and in Philippine and Indonesian waters. They are the largest of all cultured pearls, ranging from 10–20 mm (0.4–0.8 in). Their colors resemble those of the akoya pearl, and range from white to white rosé, green white to green, various golds, and blue gray.

Tahiti: Large saltwater pearls cultivated in Tahitian waters, and often black in color.

GLOSSARY OF NATURAL AND CULTURED PEARL TYPES

Akoya is the Japanese name for both the classic cultured pearl of round shape, and the *Pinctada martensii* oyster which produces it.

Baroque pearls are natural or cultured pearls having nonround, nonsymmetrical, curved or contorted, irregular shapes that frequently are variations on the round form. They are found in both saltwater and freshwater pearls, and constitute the greater part of the pearl harvest. Large

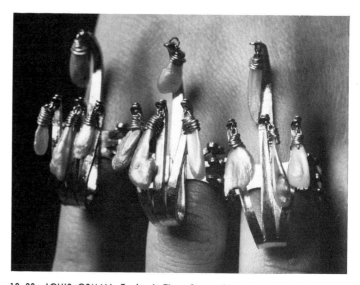

12-28 LOUIS OSMAN, England. Three-finger ring in 18K gold. The wing, petal, dog-tooth, and baroque pearls are pierced at one end, then mounted by a wire passed through to form a loop seized with a spiral wrapping. The loop is connected to a swivel that penetrates the rigid ring part, thus allowing the pearls to turn. Photo: Courtesy The Worshipful Company of Goldsmiths, London

baroque pearls were popular for use in jewels during the Renaissance when their shapes suggested their employment in figurative motif jewels for use as bodies of human, animal, and bird forms. *Oriental baroque* is a trade term for a baroque saltwater pearl to distinguish it from a baroque freshwater pearl. *Semibaroque* is a pearl that is visibly not round, but is less irregular than a baroque pearl. *Pearl coq* is a large, hollow baroque, therefore light in weight. A *hinge pearl* is a baroque whose ends are pointed or pinched because they developed near the mollusc's hinge.

Biwa pearls are cultured freshwater pearls produced by the up to 9 in (22.86 cm) long mussel *Hyriopsis schlegeli* which lives in Lake Biwa, near Kyoto, Japan. Culture starts when the oyster has a circumference of 1 cm (0.4 in). It is kept in cages for three to five years until it acquires a circumference of 15–17 cm (6.0–6.8 in). At this point, as many as 20 small squares of epithelial tissue from another mussel are inserted in the interior of the edge of the mussel's mantle. Solid nuclei are not used as the nature of the mussel's structure does not allow their acceptance. The irritation caused by the transplants causes the mussel to deposit nacre around these particles, and ultimately the pearls develop. Pearls 4–6 mm (0.16–0.26 in) in diameter require three years to develop; 6–8 mm (0.26–0.32 in) take from four to five years; and those 9 mm (0.36 in) or larger, a longer time.

Blister pearls, also called *chicots* (from the French, "stump"), are *natural* half pearls that start their development inside the shell of an oyster when small boring worms or parasites pierce the shell and penetrate to the body of the oyster. To protect itself against this intrusion and close the shell opening, the oyster manufactures a quantity of nacre over it. Ultimately this builds up and becomes a protrusion or knob integrally attached to the inner shell surface. When these are found with good hemispherical shape and luster, they are cut from the shell, backed with mother of pearl, and sold. Some are too thin for use unless they are filled with a supporting material, while others are nearly solid. The pearl market differentiates between blisters as hollow, half full, or three-quarters full. Jewelers mount them in a bezel, like a cabochon stone so that the flat underside and the edge are not visible. Blister pearls are not considered to be of great value, but often are attractive when of good color and luster. A high-domed blister pearl is called a *turtleback*.

Button pearls are natural or cultured pearls that have a flat side.

Cultured pearls are pearls that are started artificially in a suitable species of mature oyster, usually at least three years old. Living epithelial mantle tissue cells from another, sacrificed oyster, plus a round nucleus of mother of pearl are graft inserted into the oyster's mantle. The stress which the oyster experiences upon the intrusion of this foreign substance causes its mantle tissue to secrete nacre around the nucleus to cover it and render it smooth and less annoying. After a period of from three to five years during which the thickness of the nacre layer increases, the pearls are harvested.

Cyst pearls are those that develop either naturally or by cultivation in a cyst or sac within the oyster's mantle.

Dog-toothed pearls are elongated, narrow, and come to a point. They are a type of baroque pearl of low value.

Double or twin pearls are two (possibly more) pearls united or bridged by a common nacreous coating, but still retain their individual shapes.

Drop pearls have the shape of a drop of water—rounded at the bottom, and tapering in the other direction to a point, or to a smaller, rounded end.

Dust pearls are very small seed pearls that are pierced, strung, and sold.

Freshwater pearls are any pearls produced in mussels in freshwater, naturally; by nucleation; or by the introduction of epithelial mantle tissue.

Half pearls are those that have been sawed from a pearl that may have a defect in the other part which makes it unusable. Some pearls have an elongated shape from which two half pearls can be sawed. Half pearls are set in a manner similar to that of a cabochon stone.

Mabe pearls (pronounced "mah-bee"), also sometimes called *mobe* (pronounced "moh-bee") pearls, are *cultured* half-sphere pearls. The best quality are produced by the giant South Sea oyster (*Pinctada maxima*) in Australian coastal waters. They are created by inserting a half-sphere mother of pearl nucleus and attaching it against the inner shell surface in contact with the flat part. There it is allowed to remain for two years. This oyster produces nacre upon this nucleus about twice as fast as does the Japanese oyster *Pinctada martensii* used for cultured pearls. The result is sawed from the shell. Often the nucleus in the undersurface separates from the rest, or it is removed. Into this depression a second, convex-bottomed piece of mother of pearl, shaped to fit, is keyed into the recess with a projection, and is cemented in place. Mabe pearls can be as large as 25.4 mm (1 in) across, and are mounted like a cabochon stone.

Mommes (pronounced "mommies") are small cultured pearls usually less than 1 mm (0.04 in), but not larger than 6 mm (0.24 in) in diameter. They are sold in Japan in lots by the *momme*, a Japanese weight equal to 3.75 grams, into which these pearls are grouped.

Natural pearls are those that form under natural conditions in an oyster, mussel, other bivalve, or gastropod mollusc, without any interference by man, and are found by chance when pearl fishing. The best come from the Persian Gulf near the island of Bahrein, and in the trade are called *Indian pearls* because they are sent to Bombay, India, for piercing, classification, and stringing.

Oriental pearl is the name that was given to natural salt-water pearls before the development of the cultured pearl, because they were fished mainly from Oriental waters. The term is now used loosely in reference to any natural pearl, regardless of its geographic origin.

Paragon pearl is what a superior, perfectly spherical pearl of larger than average size, and good color and luster is sometimes called. It is also called a *master pearl*.

Seed pearls are small, round, sometimes irregularly shaped natural pearls weighing less than a quarter of a grain.

Wing and petal pearls are colored pearls of irregular shapes resembling the forms after which they are named, and are found in freshwater pearls. They are considered to be of low value.

DRILLING AND MOUNTING PEARLS

DRILLING PEARLS

Round pearls can be purchased *half drilled* for mounting on a peg, or *drilled through* for stringing or mounting them in other ways. Baroque pearls with a long and short axis can also be purchased drilled in these ways, and sometimes drilled through at one end to allow them to be mounted as a pendant.

Pearl-drilling jigs are devices used to hold and immobilize a round pearl to prevent it from slipping or twisting when a hole must be drilled into or through it. Several pearl jig types are available from jewelers' suppliers, but it is also possible to improvise one. The simplest jig, used especially when irregularly shaped pearls are drilled, is a *dop stick* of the type used to mount a stone when it is being ground to a shape or polished. This consists of a wooden dowel with squared ends, loaded with sealing wax at one end. The wax is softened by heat, the pearl pressed into it, and the wax is allowed to cool and harden, holding the pearl in place. The stick is then secured vertically in a bench vise, and the hole drilled. A *shellac stick* can also be used for this purpose. A simple pearl-drilling jig for round pearls can be made from a flat strip of mild steel or brass. At each end of the strip, at measured distances apart, a hole is drilled of sufficient size to allow a drill bit to pass through with some clearance. Using these holes as a center guide, matching pairs of depressions or domes are formed with a *dapping punch*, in corresponding pairs one at each end of the strip, in graduated sizes that will accommodate from 2–8 mm (0.08–0.32 in) diameter pearls. The strip is then folded over in half and hammered flat until each pair of depressions coincide to make a full dome. Just before inserting a pearl into one of these positions, line the lower depression with a small piece of *two-sided draftsman's tape* to hold the pearl in one position and prevent slippage. Attach the jig to the workbench top with a *C-clamp* to hold it steady while drilling takes place, and allow it to project beyond the table edge to allow for the passage of the drill through the pearl.

Pearls are relatively soft and are usually drilled with a *hand pump drill* and special *pearl borers* whose cutting end shape is designed to clear the hole of drilled material as drilling progresses. If ordinary drill bits are used to *half drill* a pearl, place a piece of tape on the bit at the position that indicates where the drilling should stop. Drill slowly so as not to pass this mark. When selecting a drill

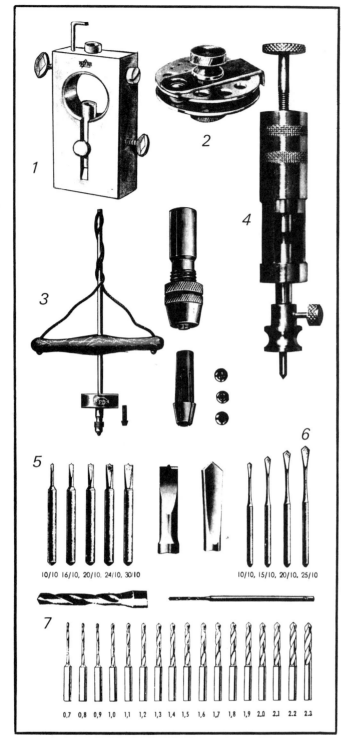

bit size, remember that strung pearls require smaller holes than peg-mounted pearls. Drilling may also be done with very sharp, small drills mounted in the collet of a flex-shaft handpiece.

Before drilling a pearl, examine it to see if there is any point of defect which can be used as the position at which the hole can be made, thereby concealing the defect. Carefully roughen that place by rubbing the pearl lightly on a piece of *fine paper abrasive* to allow the drill point to grip the pearl surface and not wander during the start of drilling.

When a hole must be *drilled through,* this can be done by carefully and slowly drilling in *one pass,* provided the drill is sharp. At intervals the pearl is made wet to prevent its overheating, which might cause it to crack. Some drillers place pearls under water while drilling to keep them cool. If a worn or dull drill is used to drill through the pearl, it may cause chipping of the pearl hole where the drill exits. To avoid this, drilling is often done in *two passes* from opposite sides so the hole meets at the center. This requires accurate marking at opposite ends, and maintaining an absolutely vertical drill position. To assure alignment, a pearl drilled halfway can be placed with its hole over a vertical peg which holds it upright while the other half of the hole is drilled.

DRILLING AND MOUNTING PEARLS

DEMONSTRATION 25

Methods used by K. Mikimoto & Co. Ltd., Tokyo, Japan

Photos: Courtesy K. Mikimoto & Co. Ltd.

1 By one method, the pearl is simply hand held and drilled with a stationary *electric drill.*

2 When many pearls are to be drilled at once, the pearl is mounted in a *two-jawed clamp* or jig which holds it firmly in place while the automatic drill moves on it in a horizontal axis to the desired depth, or completely through.

3 Drilled pearls are set on a straight peg which our Mikimoto informant says is sufficient to hold them because of the strength of the epoxy cement used. Here cement is being applied to each peg before the pearl is pressed onto it.

4 The pearl is forced on the peg while held by *tweezers.*

5 The finished hair ornament (*kanzashi*) in gold-plated sterling silver, with plum blossom pearl buds and

12–29 PEARL-HOLDING JIGS AND DRILLING EQUIPMENT

1. *Pearl-holding jig.* Pearl is inserted in brass cup mounted in central opening, pushed upward and secured in place with a thumbscrew. Drill is inserted through the upper bushing to assure dead center drilling. Adjustable drill stop (*upper left*) prevents drill from passing beyond set point when drilling halfway through a pearl. Entire jig can be placed under water during drilling.
2. *Pearl-drilling clamp,* another type of drilling jig with 13 graduated sizes, of nickel-plated steel. (*Karl Fischer*)
3. *Hand bow drill* with adjustable drill chuck and changeable collets to accommodate different drill shank sizes up to 8 mm. Used when drilling, and also when engraving stones as it allows great control; also used for drilling metal.
4. *Pearl-boring tool* used for through and half-through drilling. Can be regulated to stop the drill at half-through position. Uses a drill with up to 2 mm thickness, thicker capacity can be ordered. (*Karl Fischer*)
5. *Pearl drills,* different sizes, all with same $\frac{3}{32}$ in shanks. The correct chisel edge assures concentricity with proper clearance angles, sizes 0.9–2.3 mm.
6. *Spear drills,* different sizes, used for drilling soft substances.
7. *Twist drills,* high speed, small sizes, all on same $\frac{3}{32}$ in shanks, sizes 0.7–2.3 mm.

1

2

3

4

5

6

flower centers, and carved ivory buds. These are traditional Japanese bridal ornaments, still used because many Japanese brides are married wearing traditional dress.

6 *Kanzashi* hair ornaments worn by apprentice geisha girls (*maiko*).

Photo: Japanese Tourist Bureau, Tokyo

PEARL-HOLDING AND -SETTING SYSTEMS

There are several ways in which pearls can be fixed and held to a jewel, depending on whether they are fully drilled, half drilled, or undrilled.

FULLY DRILLED PEARL-HOLDING SYSTEMS *Stringing pearls* is commonly done on strands of *multiple-ply silk* or nylon that is made for this purpose. This is sold with an attached "needle" made of fine twisted brass wire at one or both ends of the thread. The wire is of small enough gauge to pass through average pearl holes. The thread is knotted between each pearl to prevent one from rubbing against the other and wearing out at points of contact. Knots also limit loss should the strand break, the knot acting to hold the others in place. Wire is also used to string and hold pearls in jewelry. In historic and traditional jewelry small seed pearls, and also large pearls are often strung on precious metal wire which at intervals is made to pass through small, upstanding metal loops soldered on the main jewel body to hold the strand in position. Such strands can form circles, or straight or curved lines. The wire ends are twisted together with *pliers* at the back, or at some other place on the jewel where it will not be seen.

Pendentive pearls are hung from a jewel to allow them

movement, the method used again depending on whether they are fully drilled or half drilled. The simplest way to suspend a fully drilled pearl with its hole vertical is to make an *eye pin* out of a suitable wire length with *round-nosed pliers* forming a small loop at one end. The other end is passed through the pearl and is formed into another loop which engages a loop on the main jewel body. Another system is to form a wire length into a *head pin* by fusing one end into a ball with a torch. Because the ball is larger than the hole, it supports the pearl from below, and a loop is formed at the other end as before. In India, small seed pearls are commonly mounted in bunches as pendants by using lengths of fine gold wire. Each clean wire held by *pliers* is made wet by dipping it into a gum solution, then one end is dipped vertically into dry, powdered enamel. The enamel is fused with a *torch* while holding the wire vertically in air, the lower, enameled end forming a small colored ball or head on the wire which supports the pearl from below. The enamel colors favored for this purpose are transparent red so the ball looks like a small ruby, or transparent green so it resembles an emerald, but transparent or opaque enamel of any color can be used. The wire pin is passed through the pearl, through a loop in the jewel, and then returned and twisted with the fingers or pliers around the remaining exposed pinstem. Another system uses one of the above methods plus a small metal cup or cap with a central hole, one placed below and the other above the pearl. These systems can also be used to hold a fully drilled pearl *rigidly* to a jewel, the stem projecting outward, perpendicular to the jewel. In this case, the wire end, and any existing end ornament are seen from the front, and can be more decoratively treated.

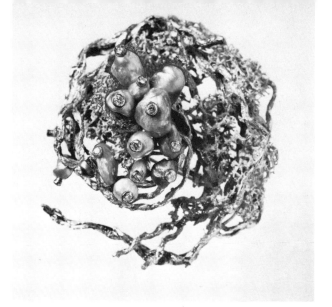

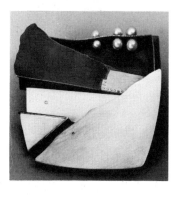

12-30 JEAN CLAUDE CHAMPAGNAT, France. Brooch cast in yellow gold from a seaweed model, with pink baroque freshwater pearls, each held by a screw with a diamond head. *Photo: Gerard Merlino*

12-31 BOB EBENDORF, U.S.A. Pin in sterling silver and 14K gold, with white acrylic, and three pairs of pearls, the pair sharing the same peg. *Photo: Bob Ebendorf* ▶

The other end of the wire must be formed into a knot or otherwise held at the back of the jewel.

Screw wires can also be used to hold a pearl in place by penetrating the pearl and the mounting, then held by a nut placed on the threaded stem at the back. A decorative screwhead can be soldered on the stem end, or it can even be made to hold a small stone.

Pearl bails consist of a half loop or ring, or any semicircular decorative device used to hold a pearl or another stone by passing from one side, over an end, to the opposite side. The ends are often fabricated with perpendicularly projecting pegs placed there to penetrate a horizontal, fully drilled hole in a pearl. Some epoxy cement applied to the peg ends secures the bail in place.

Split-shank pegs are made of two separate wires drawn through a *drawplate* until together they form a compound round wire shape of the necessary gauge. To use these to mount a fully drilled pearl, by one method, one of the pair ends can be soldered to the main jewel body, the pearl passed over the upstanding other ends, and its projecting ends are then bent with pliers to form two small outward-curving decorative scrolls at the pearl front. By another, reverse method, one pair of stem ends are fused together at one end to form a common ball, the rest is passed through the pearl from the front which leaves the ball visible, and the other ends are spread apart at the back of the jewel, flat against it, like a split rivet.

HALF-DRILLED PEARL HOLDING SYSTEMS *Rigid pearl pegs* soldered or cast in place are commonly used to hold half-drilled pearls to any position in a jewel. When a pearl is set flush against the surface, for security, the minimum peg length should be equal to half the pearl diameter; and to assure a tight fit, the gauge of wire used for the peg should be very close to the size of the hole drilled in the pearl. Because *epoxy pearl cements* are so reliable, pegs need not be bent to make a tight fit within the hole, but can be used straight. The pearl cement is applied either to the peg, or to the pearl hole, and the pearl is simply pressed down upon the peg, surplus cement is wiped away, and the piece laid aside to allow the cement to harden.

Cups and caps are used to suspend half-drilled pearls as pendants from above, and the pearl appears with its surface whole. *Button caps* have a loop soldered to their convex side; *pegged button caps* have a peg soldered to the concave side as well. The pearl is cemented to the concave cup, or to the projecting peg, and suspended from the top loop. Caps can have any decorative shape, or be split into sections so its parts can be pressed down on a pearl, as is done with a pearl of irregular shape.

12-32 FRIEDRICH BECKER, West Germany. Brooch in 18K white gold, with 241 peg-mounted pearls, 12 tube-mounted diamonds, and central rhodolite. Ø 50 mm. *Photo: Gerd Knobloch*

Pearl claws can be fabricated, but are also available ready-made as cast findings. They are used to hold a half-drilled pearl in a ring, earring, or other jewel form. A peg is included in the center of the claw base when the claw lengths are less than the diameter of the pearl and simply serve a decorative, not a functional purpose. Claws longer than the pearl's largest diameter are pressed over to hold it in place, as when setting a stone.

UNDRILLED PEARL HOLDING SYSTEMS *Pearl cages* are wire constructions in which undrilled pearls are enclosed. *Pearl cups* are concave metal mounts into which a pearl may be placed. *Bezels* of any type can be used to hold half, blister, or mabe pearls.

Undrilled pearls can simply be cemented in place, but this is an "unprofessional" method ordinarily used for costume jewelry. If this method is chosen, before gluing the pearl, examine its surface for defects, and apply the cement to the least desirable spot, which will then not be seen. To help provide traction for the cement, roughen the place of cement contact first by lightly rubbing that area on a sheet of fine abrasive.

PEARL CEMENTS

The professional use of pearl cement is to hold a drilled pearl on a metal peg in a setting. Several commercial pearl cements are available. One is a very strong *epoxy-type cement* sold in two tubes, one containing a resin, and the other a catalyst. The two are mixed together in equal

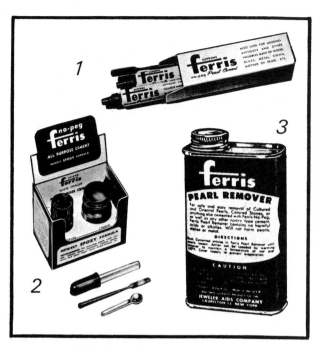

12-33 PEARL CEMENTS
1. *Ferris epoxy cement* in two tubes with spatula to mix equal amounts of the resin and catalyst, 2 oz tube.
2. *Ferris No-Peg*, all-purpose epoxy cement set, with paste hardener, supplied with spatula, measuring spoon, and dropper, available in pearl color or transparent, 4 oz, hardener 2 oz.
3. *Ferris pearl remover*, a solvent for epoxy cements containing no harmful acids or alkalis, will not harm pearls or stones. The article is soaked in the solvent until the cement loosens. Can be heated to 150° F (65° C) to speed action, but must be covered to prevent evaporation.

ual appetites. Other birds, common or rare, whose feathers are especially colorful, uniquely marked or shaped, have always been hunted for their plumage alone.

As accessories to dress, feathers have long been an article of trade in the world of fashion, and demand has fluctuated with the dictates of style. The extent to which fashion's edicts have been accepted in the past, and a former total lack of governmental control over the fate of birds with the desired plumage at times resulted in their mass slaughter, sometimes almost to the point of extinction. Today most countries have passed laws, or are being pressured by growing world public opinion into passing laws that regulate or completely prohibit the killing of certain birds, especially those considered to be endangered species. Countries that were formerly a common source of ornamental feathers from indigenous species, or from seasonally migrating birds that regularly passed through their territory, now usually have laws forbidding the *export* of the plumage of wild birds. Countries sympathetic to the moral concept calling for the preservation of endangered species have cooperated by prohibiting the *import* of certain feathers, while allowing others. In the U.S.A. almost all of the wild birds are forbidden species, and their feathers cannot be imported. However, the feathers of permissible domestic birds, and some common wild birds can be imported. Among the latter are feathers of prolific wild birds such as ducks and some pheasants. These birds are legally hunted, though hunting is seasonally regulated, and their

amounts, only in the quantity needed for immediate use, just prior to cementing. Another is an *alpha cyanoacrylic cement* that sets in about one minute. This is a very strong cement, but it must be applied with a stick, taking care to avoid skin contact since the fingers can become glued together.

If it should be necessary to remove a pearl from a jewel after it has been cemented in place, as when making a repair, commercially prepared solvents are available for particular cements, called *pearl cement remover*. These loosen the cement without harming the pearl surface, the stone (if any), or the metal.

FEATHERS IN JEWELRY

Feathers, which constitute the ensemble of plumage of a bird, in recent years have seen a revival in jewelry. The concept of employing feathers for personal adornment, however, is as ancient as primitive man's interest in self-decoration. As well as for the obvious appeal of their form, texture, and color, interest in the use of feathers is due to their evocation of fantasy, the feather implying an image of sensuousness, airiness, and otherworldliness. Birds appear as a symbol of flight in art, literature, and mythology, and their unique airborne mobility among living creatures has long been the object of envy. Because birds have always been an important source of food, their plumage, a by-product of this usage, was readily available to nourish as well the flights of fantasy that satisfy spirit-

12-34 SOLOMON ISLANDS CHIEF. His costume of state consists of ornaments made of local feathers, shells, and fibers, and also includes imported trade beads strung in geometrically arranged armbands, a belt, and a crossing body necklace. *Photo: Musée de l'Homme, Paris*

feathers come to market mainly through poultry suppliers. Societies such as the National Audubon Society in the U.S.A. (950 Third Avenue, New York, N.Y. 10022) monitor conditions in the bird world, and alert proper government agencies and the public in general to circumstances threatening to the existence of birds.

Ornamental feathers and plumes are more commonly found on the male bird who ordinarily is more brightly colored than the female (she frequently is protectively colored to blend with her environment for protection of the eggs during nesting). The male's ornamental plumage serves to attract the female during the process of courtship when it is often displayed before mating. An outstanding example of this practice is the peacock who rustles his fantastic spread of tail and covert feathers for these purposes. The peacock is native to South East Asia and to India where it is considered sacred. In Indian mythology, the peacock is the vehicle (*vahana*) of Saraswati, a river goddess who is the goddess of speech, wisdom, learning, invention, imagination, the creative arts and sciences, and the tutelary deity of writers, poets, and artists; the peacock also carries Karttikeya, the god of war. Because of its sacred nature, the peacock is never killed in India, or only surreptitiously and at great risk to personal safety should this act become known to others. Peacock feathers are nevertheless widely used in Indian arts. Fortunately, nature has kindly provided birds with a seasonal ability to molt. Based upon this fact, large peacock ranches have been established in India near Calcutta, Jaipur, and Madras.

All birds *molt,* a process in which they periodically shed or drop their mature feathers to make room for new ones. Most birds molt once annually, but others more frequently, the number of molts varying with the group and species. Normally molting takes place directly after the breeding or incubating season. During this period, the males of many species develop an especially attractive or bright, seasonal, nuptial plumage which some species display in a courtship dance that is a prelude to mating. Thereafter these feathers are dropped. Molting normally occurs in a specific sequence on various parts of the bird's body, and in a certain sequence of feathers in those places.

The peacock molts his tail feathers around September, and these are collected when found in nature, and at this time also become available at the peacock ranches. In the same way, the molted feathers of house pets such as canaries and various parrots can be a feather source. Keepers of pet shops, or local zoos having aviaries might be induced to cooperate and collect molted feathers dropped by the exotic specimens in their care. In addition to these sources, supply houses exist to cater to the theatrical costume and millinery trades, and they can be located in the classified pages of telephone directories of most large cities.

Most feathers sold in the feather trade are taken from slaughtered domestic fowl. Feathers *can* be plucked from living birds as once a feather is fully grown, it contains no living cells. When a feather is plucked, the end of the papilla is torn away, but this quickly heals and the bird regenerates a new feather in its place. The feathers used as writing and drawing quills, still occasionally used, are plucked from the wings of geese, crows, and swans. Feathers taken from live birds, or birds only recently dead are more brilliant and retain their color and liveliness, and are also more durable than those taken some time after death.

BIRDS WHOSE PLUMAGE IS COMMONLY USED FOR ORNAMENT

Of the world's 20 orders of birds, the plumage of the 9 mentioned here have commonly been used for ornamentation, though practically *all* bird feathers have probably been used in various locations by different people at one time or another.

Anseriformes: Waterfowl, domestic or wild; raised for food, or shot for sport; includes ducks, geese, and swans.

Ciconiiformes: Long-legged wading birds; includes egrets, flamingos, herons, ibises, roseate spoonbills, and storks.

Columbiformes: Doves, wild and domestic pigeons, and sand grouse.

Coraciiformes: Mainly tropical, usually brightly colored birds consisting of the rollers and their allies, include bee-eaters, hornbills, and kingfishers.

Galliformes: Fowllike birds; when domesticated, termed *poultry,* includes domestic chickens and turkeys. Among the wild birds of this order are pheasants, grouse, guinea fowl, partridge, peafowl, and quail.

Passeriformes: Perching birds; the order includes about 5,000 of the approximate total of 8,600 species of birds in the world. In this order, to mention a few, are the bird of paradise, bluebird, cardinal, cedar waxwing, crow, finch, fly-catcher, green jay, green shrike-vireo, lark, oriole, raven, scarlet tanager, swallow, thrush, titmouse, wren, etc.

Piciformes: Woodpeckers and their allies, including toucans.

Psittaciformes: Parrots; comprising more than 300 species, including the cockatoo, lovebird, macaw, parakeet, etc.

Trochiliformes: Hummingbirds; an order which exists only in the New World.

THE PLACEMENT AND STRUCTURE OF FEATHERS

Feathers can be described as the epidermal (skin) outgrowth constituting the external covering or plumage of birds. They are composed of a hornlike protein called *keratin* of which epidermal tissue such as nails, hair, horns, and hoofs are also made, and they are shaped in a light, strong, and flexible structure. Feathers are found only on birds, and their presence therefore characterizes this group, avifauna. It is due to the existence and manipulation of feathers, and a light, bony frame, that birds possess their unique power of flight.

FEATHER TRACTS *Feather tracts* or *pterylae* are those sharply defined areas on the skin of a bird's body where feathers grow, the places between tracts being either bare, or covered with down. All birds have the same basic feathers which grow in specific body areas. The feathers growing on any single bird are of several different forms and colors. However, in birds of different species, the feathers in the corresponding parts of the body may be developed differently or be differently colored. Some of these feathers are more desirable for decorative uses than others.

FEATHER STRUCTURE The structure of a typical feather consists of a *barrel, calamus,* or *quill* which is a cylindrical central stem or supporting shaft whose proximal part or that part nearest to the point of attachment to the bird's body is hollow and grows from a follicle of the skin, at

12–35 A. C. JAHN, England, ca. 1901. Brooch of a carved bone angel's head enveloped by wings, repoussé-worked in silver and parcel gilt, with pearls and an opal. In art forms, the head symbolizes the receptacle of the spirit, and wings also symbolize spirituality and otherworldliness. Humeral and alar tract feathers are meticulously and faithfully delineated. Photo: Victoria and Albert Museum, London, Crown Copyright

whose base is a *papilla*. Internally the calamus is filled with a lightweight, pithy substance which can be easily removed. The *rachis* or distal part of the quill furthest away from the body attachment is solid, furrowed on the reverse side for structural strength, and bears the feather end or *vane*, which is divided into two *webs*. Each web consists of a series of numerous slender, somewhat obliquely directed, parallel processes called *barbs*. Each barb has smaller, flatter branches called *barbules*, and from them develop *barbicels*. In most feathers the barbicels pointing toward the feather tip have *hamuli* or microscopically small, hooked ends underneath, which serve to hook together the barbules of adjacent barbs; in this way they unite the whole series of processes into the vane or web. Should the barbs become separated, the presence of the hamuli make it possible to re-engage the barbules and to rejoin and smooth the feather, an act the bird accomplishes when preening with its beak. It can also be done with the fingers, one above and one below, by running them down the feather length from quill to rachis. Feathers in a badly disjointed condition can be restored by holding them before a kettle spout issuing steam, then running the fingers down the feather's length. When the hamuli do not exist in a feather, as for example in down and some ostrich tail and wing feathers, it is soft and fluffy, and is termed "decomposed."

FEATHER TYPES ON A SINGLE BIRD The feathers existing on a single bird are of the following types, any of which can be used in jewelry.

Contour feathers: These grow in tracts and comprise almost all of the exposed feathers that give the bird its particular form. They have a hollow-based central shaft from which the barbs and barbules grow on the rachis that continues from it. Most are used for locomotion, and also to preserve body temperature.

Semiplumes: Loosely webbed, downlike feathers with little or no vane, these feathers lack hamuli on the barbicels.

Down feathers: These loose, soft, fluffy feathers have long barbs, a short rachis, or none, and no hamuli to hold the barbs together. They are used for insulation.

Powder down feathers: These feathers have no commercial value. They consist of feathers whose tip disintegrates and produces a talclike powder on the bird that provides water resistance, as well as being a plumage conditioner.

Filoplumes: These have long, hairlike centers, and generally divide at the end into a tiny vane.

Ornamental auxiliary plumes: Some species grow specialized feathers that are purely ornamental, and develop only before the courtship period of the mating season and last until the end of the incubation period, after which they are dropped. They take on a variety of forms and are often quite showy.

THE FEATHER TRADE

In the feather trade, feathers are first of all generally divided into two groups: common and ornamental. *Common* feathers are used for stuffing and similar practical purposes, and *ornamental* feathers have decorative uses. Common feathers generally come from domestic fowl, and are a by-product of the poultry industry. The greater percentage of ornamental feathers used today comes from certain domestic fowl, but some are from permissible, plentiful wild birds with attractive plumage, or wild birds that are domesticated and raised for their feathers.

As mentioned, feathers are collected after molting, but more commonly, they are pulled or plucked by hand from the slaughtered bird. The mechanical removal of feathers employs very hot water which causes all feathers to be simultaneously removed from the skin, but this destroys the feathers which turn mushy and quickly start to rot.

CLASSIFICATIONS IN WHICH FEATHERS ARE COMMERCIALLY AVAILABLE

In the feather trade, besides the common and ornamental categories, feathers are further classified according to the *particular bird* from which they come, such as chicken, duck, goose, ostrich, peacock, pheasant, or pigeon, these being the most common feathers used. Feathers are processed and come to market in various forms. Most of the ornamental feathers available today are sorted and prepared by about 3,000 female *plumassières* or feather-working artisans living in Hong Kong, Taiwan, and Macao. The classifications are as follows:

1 *Loose:* Sold by the pound
  a) *Mixed:* Smaller and softer feathers, in several sizes.
  b) *Sized:* Sorted according to type, and in sizes: small, medium, large; or by the inch: 3 in, 3¼ in, 4 in, and 5 in (7.6 cm, 8.2 cm, 10.1 cm, 12.7 cm).

2 *Bundled:* Sold by the piece in bundles of 100
These feathers are larger than 5 in (12.7 cm) including the quill, and tend to be of the stiff type.

3 *Strung:* Sold by the yard, or the pound
These feathers are sorted by type and quality so that all are the same. They are graded in half-inch sizes, and strung on strings.

4 *Glued or stitched to a base:* Sold by weight, amount, or unit
These selected feathers are available glued or stitched to

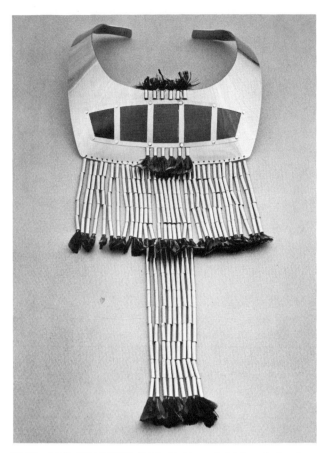

12–36 MARY ANN SCHERR, U.S.A. Necklace of stainless steel contour-sawed sheet metal and severed tube sections. Ornamental peacock feather clusters are mounted by inserting and gluing their combined rachises into the tube ends. The upper section contains rhomboid-shaped liquid crystal panels that monitor body temperature and air pollution, their color changing upon exposure to alterations in the atmosphere. This ornament serves a functional as well as a decorative purpose. In collaboration with James Ferguson, Thomas Davidson, and International Crystals Co. Size 8 × 16 in. *Photo: Richard Monasterio*

cloth bands 2–6 in (5.1–15.2 cm) wide by 24 in (61 cm) long; or on pads approximately 4 in × 4½ in (10.1 cm × 11.4 cm), depending on the type of feather. Bands to which feathers are sewn can be cut into smaller parts, and feathers attached to pads with glue can be individually lifted off with tweezers after steaming.

5 Skins: Sold by the skin
This is the smallest classification in terms of volume of sales. It is however commonly used by jewelers because the purchase of a whole skin makes available a wide assortment of feather types, sizes, and colors. The feathers are rarely used still mounted on the skin, but are generally removed from it. Skin *parts* such as wings and necks with their attached feathers are also used, the most popular being the neck skins of pheasants and roosters.

BLEACHING AND DYEING FEATHERS

Most decorative feathers are used in their natural state because of the beauty of their coloration and form. Less interesting types can be bleached and/or dyed almost any color.

In preparing them for these processes, the feathers are first tied with thread around the quills to form small bundles. This makes handling them in the subsequent proc-

esses much easier. As a first process, they are washed to remove their natural oil coating and any adhering dirt, both of which would impede their acceptance of dyes. Washing is done in a water and detergent solution mixed with some washing soda, hot but no hotter than the hand can bear. The feather bundles are immersed in this solution and drawn through the hands from quill to vane, an action that is repeated for 5 or 6 minutes to squeeze out the foreign matter. Soaking follows in a new, warm, soapy solution for about half an hour, after which they are rinsed in three cool water baths in succession. If the feathers are to be used undyed in their natural condition, they are then dried. First they are struck against the hand to remove surplus water, then hung upside down, quill end upward, in a well-ventilated, naturally warm or artificially heated place, but *not in direct sunshine*. During the drying period, from time to time the bunches are shaken to open the feather's barbs and fluff them up.

When dyeing, to achieve bright colors, unless the feathers are naturally white or a relatively light color, they must first be bleached. Any natural color remaining will affect the appearance of the final dyed color. There is, however, a limit to which natural color can be bleached from a feather, and very dark feathers cannot be bleached pure white. Bleaching may not be necessary if dulled colors are the aim, or if the feathers are to be dyed dark colors.

One *bleaching solution* is a 30% dilution of hydrogen peroxide (H_2O_2) which is an oxidizing agent that readily decomposes into oxygen and water. To this enough ammonia is added to make the solution neutral (pH7). Weaker or stronger solutions can be used to remove a relatively smaller or greater degree of color. The feathers are immersed completely, and the container is covered with a piece of flat plate glass, then placed in a dark place. The feathers are allowed to steep in this solution for from 10–12 hours, depending on the amount of color to be removed and the degree of whiteness desired.

Another bleaching solution contains a dilute solution of potassium dichromate ($K_2Cr_2O_7$) which is also an oxidizing agent, to which a small amount of nitric acid is added. The feathers are allowed to soak in the same way as above for 3–4 hours, after which they are soaked in a dilute sulphuric acid solution to remove a greenish cast they may have developed in the former solution, then thoroughly rinsed.

Once bleached, a feather will not return to its former color, but if left white, yellowing may occur with age. After rinsing, the feathers to be dyed are *not* dried; they are dyed while wet, a condition that helps the dye to penetrate all parts more quickly and uniformly.

The *dye solution* is prepared in a pan large enough to contain the whole feather without the need to bend it. The dyes can be any single *natural dye* used with its proper mordant; mixed natural dyes; or *synthetic dyes*. After a first dyeing, entire feathers can be overdyed with a second color to achieve a compound color, or they can be partially dyed a second color by simply dipping the desired portion into the dyebath. When synthetic dyes are used, the instructions given with the particular dye must be followed. If possible, use *less than boiling* temperatures since feathers cannot take prolonged immersion in temperatures over the boiling point of water (212° F, 100° C) without becoming damaged. After dyeing, the feathers are hung upside down, as when drying, and are smoothed with the fingers. At intervals they are shaken to restore their form and fluffiness.

Feathers that are dyed will not be attacked by moths or cockroaches, but natural colored feathers must be kept in napthalene as a protection against insect attack.

FEATHER MOUNTING IN JEWELRY

Feathers are used in earrings, pendants, necklaces, bracelets, upper arm bands, crowns, diadems, headbands, barrettes, ponytail ornaments, chignon rings, on combs, in hair ornaments, waistbands, etc. Their texture, color, lightness, and mobility make a pleasant contrast when combined with solid materials.

The flexibility and structure of a feather allows it to be used in many ways and simplifies its mounting. Individual quills can be mounted in a bezel, ring, or a cross section of tubing, with the addition of a suitable cement. Quills can be pierced very simply by heating a *needle* or *wire* of appropriate thickness for the desired hole size, then pressing it through. They can then be mounted by stringing them with a *thread, nylon fishing cord,* or a *wire* that passes through the holes. Mounting in this manner can be flat in series, or several feathers can be tied into groups to make dimensional bunches. Groups can also be *glued* together, and their combined shafts then wrapped with silk cords, the thread end secured by passing it through the quills with a needle, or by gluing it in place.

CHINESE KINGFISHER FEATHER INLAY JEWELRY

In China, gold and silver filigree jewelry whose units were inlaid with parts of feathers of the kingfisher (*fei-ts'ui*) were made as early as the T'ang Dynasty (618–906 A.D.) for court use. Those that survive today were made mainly in Beijing (Peiking) and Guangzhon (Canton) in the 18th and 19th centuries. The feathers used were mainly from the water kingfisher (*Alcedinidae*) and the wood kingfisher (*Halcyonidae*), especially *Halcyon smyrnensis* which was the most common of the kingfisher species in China. Due to the popularity of this jewelry, it was, unfortunately, hunted almost to extinction. Similarly colored feathers from the Indian kingfisher and Indian roller or bluejay were exported in quantity from India to China during the 19th century to supply the demand. These feathers were used for comb decorations, earrings, brooches, and other forms of jewelry faithfully depicted in ancestral portraits. Particularly spectacular were the elaborate feather-decorated filigree crowns worn by performers of Chinese opera. A large industry in the export of feather decorated jewelry existed in China until the 1930s.

The unique aspect of these ornaments is that the feathers had to be patiently cut to a specific shape, and glued in place using a thin layer of adhesive so as not to destroy the feather's iridescence. To cut a vane into shapes, it must first be stripped from the rachis, but a *part* of the rachis must be allowed to remain to hold the barbs together or the feather will simply disintegrate.

For those interested in feather inlay today, the following method could be employed. To have better control in cutting a feather to shape, first paste it to a lightweight cardboard with a temporary, water-soluble glue. Cut it to shape with very sharp *scissors*, then soak it off the cardboard with water, and place it on an absorbent paper towel to dry. It can then be glued in place upon a cement-spread surface, using a permanent cement that will not penetrate the feather and cause discoloration.

12–37 MERRY RENK, U.S.A. Neckpiece in gold and silver with abalone shell (*Haliotis splendens*) inserted in the settings from the back and held by prongs. The form suggests a bird, its head surrounded by a feather ruff, and wings outspread. This and other nacreous shells, as well as many feathers, produce the same *iridescent interference color effect* created by optical interference. In this phenomenon, white light, which is a composite of all the spectral colors, upon striking a surface of a certain structural nature is refracted, broken up into its constituent colors, and dispersed in a shifting rainbow effect. The use of iridescent shell produces a result comparable to an inlay of iridescent feathers, in this case achieved by a more durable material. *Photo: Laurence Cuneo*

12–38 THOMAS GENTILLE, U.S.A. Pin cast and fabricated in 18K yellow gold, with recessed areas inlaid with green iridescent feathers cemented in place. Size approx. 2¼ in square. *Photo: Otto Nelson*

13

STONES AND THEIR SETTING
Inorganic Minerals Employed in Jewelry

STONES

Selected fragments of terrestrial bounty

Soon after discovering the existence of buried mineral treasures in the form of stones and crystals in the Earth's crust, we began placing a value on those that were rare, colorful, and hard. Magical or prophylactic properties attributed to them increased their value, and such ideas persist in some cultures even today. In India, for instance, certain stones are still worn primarily as amulets because they are believed to avert diseases, misfortunes, and malefic influences, and to prolong life. Attractive stones have been used as an adjunct to metal jewelry almost since the start of the use of metals for jewelry making, to bring color to the metals they did not possess.

PRECIOUS, SEMIPRECIOUS, AND SYNTHETIC STONES

In modern times, gemstones used in jewelry are given values based on their weight, size, luster, brilliance, transparency, degree of perfection, durability, portability, and availability. Stones owe some of these qualities to their specific chemical composition and their physical characteristics which make possible their identification. When in doubt, stones can be referred to gemologists who have studied these characteristics and have scientific means of determining their presence. The relative rarity of stones possessing some or all of these qualities has resulted in the classification of gemstones into *precious* and *semiprecious* groups. Today science has devised ways of manufacturing many gemstones by artificially reproducing their crystal structure, and the results are termed *synthetic stones.*

PRECIOUS STONES Traditionally these are diamond, ruby, emerald, and sapphire. Good specimens are certainly among the most costly of stones used in jewelry, but the term "precious" is relative. Outstanding examples of "semiprecious" stones may actually exceed the value of inferior "precious" stones. The more perfect a transparent precious stone—that is, the freer it is of inclusions, blemishes, flaws, or cracks when examined with a magnifying glass of 10X magnification power—the greater its value.

SEMIPRECIOUS STONES All other stones believed to be sufficiently attractive when cut and polished to be usable in jewelry are considered semiprecious. These are found in nature in quantities large enough to take them out of the rare or precious stone category. Their degree of hardness

remains of prime importance and must be within a range that renders them durable and allows ordinary wear without undue surface impairment.

Transparency, translucency, and opacity constitute yet another basis of classification within the semiprecious group. These states ordinarily influence the manner in which the stone is cut. Transparent stones usually are cut with facets to allow maximal dispersion of light within the stone. Opaque stones are generally cut *en cabochon.* (See p. 598.) Translucent stones may be cut either way. This is not to say that transparent or opaque stones ought not be prepared, or are not prepared in other than normal cuts.

13–1 PUEBLO INDIAN, U.S.A. This woman is wearing traditional Zuñi-style silver jewelry ornamented with cabochon-cut turquoises, first used in American Indian jewelry around 1890. *Photo: Western Ways*

SYNTHETIC STONES This group includes artificial reproductions of almost all the major precious and some semiprecious stones. In most cases, the synthetic stone has the same general physical properties of specific gravity and refractive index as the corresponding natural stone. Though synthetic stones have far less value than the natural stone they imitate, they are not inexpensive.

By a method originated by Auguste Verneuil in France in 1891, many synthetic stones are formed today from components of alumina and a powdered oxide whose choice depends on the color desired. These are passed through a vertical blowtorch in a furnace whose flame is made extremely hot by feeding it oxygen and hydrogen. The fused results fall as droplets onto a rotating ceramic pedestal called a *candle,* and gradually form an upward-growing stalagmite or tapered cylinder called a *boule* which is allowed to cool. Its size, which can be up to 200 carats for a ruby, or even larger for other stones, is big enough to be cut and used as a gemstone once it is removed from the pedestal and split horizontally. Detection of a synthetic stone is possible by microscopic internal examination which generally, but not always, reveals a curved structural formation. This, however, depends on the stone. Synthetic stones have a more homogeneous formation than natural stones which frequently display inclusions and other irregularities.

Synthetic *stars* are also produced in stones by adding a small amount of titanium oxide to the powder before fusion. The material is heated to a temperature high enough to cause the titanium to precipitate as needles of rutile which orient themselves to the crystal's axes, thus forming the star.

Synthetic spinel was manufactured commercially by the 1930s, and when colorless, is brilliant, and therefore used as a diamond substitute. Other synthetic stones were developed to simulate the diamond. A synthetic material without any natural equivalent is strontium titanate, commercially called Fabulite or Starilian, first synthesized in 1955 and intended to simulate the diamond. Yttrium aluminum garnet, commercially called YAG, when colorless, is another. These two have a dispersion of respectively six and four times that of diamond, therefore greater brilliance. Rutile was used to synthesize a stone in 1948, commercially called Titania, which when almost without color, has a fire six times that of diamond. All these synthetic stones have a hardness far less than diamond, usually about 6, Mohs' scale. In 1955, General Electric (U.S.A.) succeeded in truly synthesizing the diamond, and now produces them in quantity, but these are of an industrial grade and not of gem quality.

Chatham emeralds were synthesized by Caroll F. Chatham (U.S.A.) in 1935, by Linde Air Products of America in 1967, and Pierre Gilson (France) in 1969, among others.

THE ANCIENT MINING OF STONES

According to archeologists, precious and semiprecious stones were first mined during the following periods:
Upper Paleolithic (300,000–12,000 B.C.): Amber, calcite, chalcedony, jasper, obsidian, quartz, rock crystal, serpentine, steatite
Mesolithic–Neolithic (12,000–2500 B.C.): Agate, amethyst, fluorspar, jade, jet, lapis lazuli, nephrite, turquoise
Pre-Dynastic Egypt (3500–3000 B.C.): Alabaster, beryl, carnelian, chrysocolla, feldspar, hematite, malachite

Metal Age I (3000–2200 B.C.): Azurite, onyx, sardonyx
Metal Age II (2200–1200 B.C.): Bloodstone, chrysoprase, emerald, magnesite, topaz
Early Iron Age (1200–500 B.C.): Blue chalcedony, sapphire, spinel, rose quartz
Late Iron Age (500–50 B.C.): Aquamarine, diamond, moss-agate, opal, ruby, zircon

THE STRUCTURE OF GEMSTONES

Most gemstones are minerals that have developed under certain favorable conditions that cause the mineral to solidify in the form of *crystals,* symmetrically arranged, their forms being the external expression of their inner molecular structure. These crystals can be small or very large, and have the property of growing externally over long periods of time. Often they develop faces that make them appear faceted. The angles remaining between these faces and any other additional malformations stay constant with each particular mineral, and internal structural angles are a means of identifying the crystal.

The laws of symmetry that follow form the basis of the classification of crystals into six (or seven) main systems. Each system is recognized by the unique arrangement of axes it possesses which identifies it as a family.

Plane of symmetry is an imaginary plane passing through the crystal that divides it into two halves that mirror each other. Several such planes can exist in a single crystal.

Axis of symmetry is the number of times a crystal being rotated 360° or one complete revolution on an imaginary axis assumes a position in space that makes it appear *identical* to the way it looked at the start of this rotation. This can occur two (digonal axis), three (trigonal axis), four (tetragonal axis), or six times (hexagonal axis) in one complete revolution.

Center of symmetry can be described as a line drawn through a center point that intersects opposite crystal faces at distances identical from the center point; or in another way, center of symmetry can be said to be similar faces and edges having corresponding positions on the sides of a crystal opposite a central point.

THE SIX CRYSTAL SYSTEMS OF GEMSTONES

In the formation of gemstones there are six (some crystallographers say seven) recognized groups of crystallization systems, the classifications based on the relative lengths and inclinations of the axes to which they refer. These are *cubic, tetragonal, hexagonal, orthorhombic, monoclinic,* and *triclinic.* These are basic, ideal shapes, as shown in the diagrams, which in fact seldom occur as perfect, separate entities in nature. More commonly, specimens are jumbled or massed, and smaller crystals form on the sides of larger crystals.

CUBIC SYSTEM (isometric, regular) Has three axes, all of equal length and at right angles to each other; nine planes of symmetry, three axes of symmetry, and a center of symmetry.

Stones in this system: diamond, fluorite, fluorspar, garnet, pyrite, lapis lazuli, sodalite, spinel.

TETRAGONAL SYSTEM Has three axes all at right angles to each other, with two horizontal lateral axes of equal length, and the vertical axis either longer or shorter than

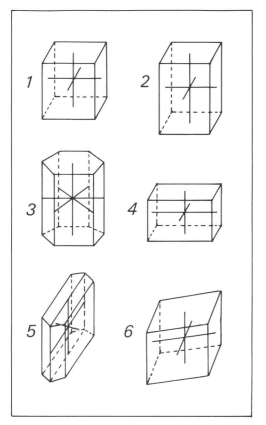

13-2   *THE SIX MAIN CRYSTAL SYSTEMS OF STONES*
1. Cubic or Isometric   4. Orthorhombic
2. Tetragonal   5. Monoclinic
3. Hexagonal   6. Triclinic

13-3   *A ROUGH GEM DIAMOND CRYSTAL* as found in a mine embedded in kimberlite or "blue ground." Its isometric or cubic crystal form is an octahedron, its characteristic or *habit* shape, is clearly observable. *Photo: De Beers Consolidated Mines Ltd.*

the lateral axes; five planes of symmetry, five axes of symmetry, and a center of symmetry.

Stones in this system: cassiterite, idocrase, rutile, scapolite, zircon.

HEXAGONAL SYSTEM   Has four axes: three lateral axes of equal length that intersect at 60° to each other, and the fourth axis vertical, either longer or shorter than the lat-

eral, axes, and at a right angle to the plane in which the others lie. It has seven planes of symmetry, seven axes of symmetry, and a center of symmetry.

Many crystallographers incorporate the *rhombohedral* or *trigonal system* as a division of the hexagonal system because their axes are similar. The main axis has threefold symmetry instead of the sixfold symmetry present in the hexagonal system. It has four axes of symmetry and three planes of symmetry.

Stones in the hexagonal system: aquamarine, apatite, beryl, calcite, emerald. Stones in the trigonal system: corundum, ruby, sapphire, tourmaline, transparent quartz.

ORTHORHOMBIC SYSTEM   Has three axes which are at right angles to each other, all of different lengths. The main vertical axis is either longer or shorter than the lateral axes; it has three planes of symmetry, three diagonal axes, and a center of symmetry.

Stones in this system: andalusite, barite, chrysoberyl, olivine, peridot, topaz.

MONOCLINIC SYSTEM   An oblique system with three axes of different lengths, two at right angles to each other, the third inclined at an angle to the plane containing the other two. It has one plane of symmetry, one diagonal axis, and a center of symmetry.

Stones in this system: azurite, diopside, epidote, feldspar, gypsum, jadite, kunzite, malachite, moonstone, nephrite, orthoclase, serpentine, sphene, spodumene.

TRICLINIC SYSTEM   Has three axes, all different lengths, none at 90°, but all inclined to each other. It has a center of symmetry but no axes or planes of symmetry.

Stones in this system: labradorite, plagioclase feldspar, rhodonite, spectrolite, turquoise.

Cryptocrystalline stones have such fine crystals massed in structural, granular form that they can be seen only with a microscope. In this group are agate, jasper, chalcedony, and flint. *Amorphous stones* have no crystalline forms, and include opals, obsidian, and amber.

OPTICAL AND OTHER PROPERTIES OF GEMSTONES

Color is one means of identifying a stone, but this method is not always reliable, especially in the case of transparent stones, as several which are popularly thought of as being one uniform color actually exist in several colors. This is why other properties including *refraction, dispersion, hardness,* and *specific gravity* are also important.

Color in a stone is due to an impurity, usually present in a small quantity in the form of unpaired electrons or transition metal ions. The specific color depends on the environment's symmetry, and the strength of the bonding around the ions. In transparent stones, uniformity of color is important, but there are exceptions, such as the watermelon tourmaline which when sectioned reveals several colors. In semiprecious opaque stones, color variation is frequently desirable, and colors can occur in patches, zones, stripes, concentric arrangements, in blended areas, or in other formations.

Luster is the surface quality of a polished stone, or the way in which it reacts to light by refraction and dispersion (as in the case of transparent stones), and by reflection (as in the case of opaque stones). Some stone lusters can be variously described as adamantine (as diamonds), vitreous (as quartz), metallic (as hematite), waxy (as topaz), silky (as cat's and tiger's eye), resinous (as amber), or pearly (as moonstone).

Refraction is the ability of a polished, transparent mineral to bend or deflect a beam of light from the entering direction to a new direction when it strikes a second or subsequent surface. The *index of refraction* is the amount a beam of light will bend, and depends on the mineral's structure. This amount can be measured on a *refrac-*

tometer which is used by expert gemologists to identify a gemstone; *each* mineral has a *specific* index of refraction (see Table below).

Dispersion is the amount of refraction that occurs when a light beam strikes a polished gemstone; this depends on the inner structure of the gemstone and the wavelength of the light, which in turn depends on its color. A white diamond has a strongly chromatic dispersive ability because white is composed of all wavelengths which are widely

Characteristics of Some Common Gemstones

T = transparent; Tr = translucent; others are of varying degrees of translucency to opacity, or combinations of these. + = see below.

Species	Hardness (Mohs)	Specific Gravity	Refractive Index	Dispersion	Durability
Diamond (T)	10	3.52	2.42	high	high
Corundum	9				
Ruby (T)	9	4.00	1.77	low	high
Sapphire (T)	9	4.00	1.77	low	high
Chrysoberyl (T)	8.5	3.71	1.75	low	high
Alexandrite (T)	8	3.68-3.78	1.75	low	high
Cat's eye (Tr)	8	3.68-3.78	1.54-1.75		high
Spinel (T)	8	3.60	1.72	low	high
Topaz (T)	8	3.54	1.63	low	med.
Beryl (T)	7.75	2.70	1.58	low	high
Emerald (T)	7.75	2.66-2.77	1.56	low	high
Aquamarine (T)	7.75	2.68-2.70	1.57-1.575	low	high
Garnet (Tr)	7.5	3.70-4.16	1.74-1.89	med.-high	high
Zircon (T)	7	4.02	1.81	high	high
Tourmaline (T-Tr)	7	3.06	1.63	low	high
Quartz (T-Tr)+	7	2.65	1.55	low	high
Chalcedony (Tr)*+	7	2.65	1.55	low	high
Spodumene (T)	7	3.18	1.66	low	low
Kunzite (T)	7	3.13-3.31	1.66-1.68	med.	low
Jade					
Jadite (Tr)	7	3.33	1.66	none	high
Nephrite (Tr)	6.5	2.96	1.62	none	high
Peridot (T)	6.5	3.34	1.68	low	med.
Opal (Tr)	6	1.97-2.20	1.45	none	low
Feldspar	6				
Moonstone (Tr)	6	2.50-2.55	1.52-1.54		high
Labradorite (Tr)	6	2.70-2.72	1.52		med.
Spectrolite (Tr)	6	2.70-2.72	1.52		med.
Obsidian (T)	6	2.33-2.60	1.48-1.51		med.
Olivine (T)	6	3.30-3.50	1.65		high
Peridot (T)	6	3.30-3.50	1.66		high
Epidote (T)	6	3.25-3.49	1.73-1.76		high
Hematite	5.5-6.5	4.95-5.30	2.94-3.22		high
Apatite	5	3.16-3.22	1.64-1.65		med.
Lapis lazuli	5	2.76-2.94	1.50		med.
Sphene	5	3.45-3.56	1.95-2.05		med.
Sodalite	5	2.13-2.29	1.483		med.
Rodonite	5	3.53	1.73-1.74		med.
Turquoise	5	2.60-2.80	1.61-1.65		med.
Jet	3.5	1.10-1.40	1.64-1.68		low
Azurite	3.5	3.80	1.48-1.65		low
Serpentine	3.5	2.50-2.70	1.57		low
Marble	3	2.71	1.48-1.65		low
Malachite	3-4	3.70-4.00	1.87-1.98		low
Amber (T-Tr)	2.5	1.03-1.10	1.54		low
Steatite	1-1.5	2.7-2.8			low
Alabaster	1-1.5	2.20-2.40	1.52		low
Gypsum	1-1.5	2.30			low

+Quartz: Includes amethyst, citrine, milky quartz, rock crystal, rose quartz, rutilated quartz, smoky quartz, and tourmalinated quartz.

*+Chalcedony: Includes agate, aventurine, bloodstone, carnelian, chrysoprase, jasper, onyx, sard, sardonyx, and petrified wood.

separated when white light strikes it, therefore causing it to sparkle and flash in prismatic colors. Dispersion is best seen in a faceted stone that has been cut to a form whose angles take advantage of its dispersion ability by trapping and reflecting the light back to the observer.

Pleochroism occurs in colored gemstones that because of their structure possess *double refraction*. This causes them to appear to possess different colors in the same stone when seen from different directions. Stones that possess pleochroism are green tourmaline which has a marked two-color effect and therefore shows *dichroism,* and alexandrite which has three colors and therefore exhibits *trichroism.*

Chatoyancy (from French *oeil-de-chat,* "cat's eye") is a property of stones in which one or more parallel, undulating, or wavy lines of light appear on a polished surface, a condition best seen when the stone is cabochon cut. In tiger's and cat's eye stones, chatoyancy is the result of the inclusion of needlelike shapes or tubes of foreign bodies oriented in parallel bundles that catch entering light and cause it to move with a change of direction. Tourmaline, beryl, and chrysoberyl when cabochon cut also show chatoyancy.

Asterism is the effect of a "star" in a stone due to the existence *of several sets* of such needlelike inclusions, and can appear in a ruby, sapphire, aquamarine, garnet, or other stone provided it is properly oriented when cut. Because of the shape of the crystal structure in rubies and sapphires, the star is arranged in three crossing directions, 120° apart, thus forming a six-pointed star. In garnets, because their crystal structure is isometric, only two such crossings occur and that "star" is really a four-pointed cross.

Cleavage lines are yielding surfaces always parallel to the actual or possible crystal faces along which a crystal can be split, which is done when a transparent crystal is large enough to be divided. The parts are then cut into faceted stones that best display their color and dispersion. Fragments of massed crystals (called a *druse*) too small to be otherwise utilized recently have become popular for use in their natural state.

SPECIFIC GRAVITY OF GEMSTONES

Specific gravity or degree of density is the ratio of the weight of a volume of a substance with an equal volume of another substance taken as a standard. For solids the standard substance is water. At 4° C (39.2° F) one cubic centimeter of water weighs one gram, therefore its specific gravity is 1. When the identification of a stone is in doubt, the measurement of its specific gravity is an important means to ascertain it. For example, diamond has a specific gravity of 3.52, meaning it is three and a half times heavier than an equal volume of water. The specific gravity of a colorless zircon (which to a non-professional resembles a diamond) is 4.02, which means that bulk for bulk it is heavier than diamond.

To determine the specific gravity of a stone, by one method, it is first weighed in air and this weight recorded. Then it is suspended by a string from a counterpoise beam scale and fully immersed in water at 4° C. The weight that registers on the scale is taken as its specific gravity.

STONE HARDNESS: Mohs' scale

A scale meant to indicate the approximate *relative hardness* of stones was devised by Friedrich Mohs, a Ger-

man mineralogist (1773–1839). It is based on the ability of one stone to be scratched by another, or to itself be scratched. In order of hardness, from hardest to softest, he rated the more usual stones employed by jewelers as in the chart on p. 581. That this rating is relative is shown by the fact that diamond is proportionately much harder than corundum, one degree lower on the scale, than such an equally stepped numbering system would indicate. *Stone hardness testing pencils* are available for testing stone hardness. A stone's degree of resistance to abrasion is often a factor in deciding how it is mounted in jewelry.

Gemstone Names in Various Languages

English	French	Spanish	Italian	German
Agate	Agate	Agat	Agata	Achat
Amazonite	Amazonite	Amazonito	Pietra della amazonè	Amazonenstein
Amber	Ambre	Ambar	Ambra	Bernstein
Amethyst	Améthyste	Amatista	Ametista	Amethyst
Aquamarine	Aquamarine	Agua marina	Acqua- marina	Aquamarin
Aventurine	Aventurine	Avenchiurin	Auven- turina	Aventurin
Beryl	Béryl	Berilo	Berillo	Beryll
Bloodstone	Jaspe sanguin	Piedra de sangre	Ematite	Blut jaspis
Carnelian	Cornaline	Cornalina	Carniola	Karneol
Cat's eye	Oeil-de-chat	Ojo de gata	Occhio di gatto	Katzenauge
Chalcedony	Calcédoine	Calcedonia	Calcedinio	Chalcedon
Chrysoberyl	Chrysobéril	Crisoberilo	Crisoberillo	Chrysoberyll
Chrysoprase	Chrysoprase	Crisopraso	Crisopraso	Chrysopras
Citrine	Citrine	Topacio falso	Citrino	Citrin
Coral	Corail	Coral	Corallo	Koralle
Crystal	Cristal	Cristal	Cristallo	Kristall
Diamond	Diamant	Diamante	Diamante	Diamant
Emerald	Émeraude	Esmeralda	Smeraldo	Smaragd
Fire opal	Opale feu	Opalo de fuego	Opalo di fuocco	Feueropal
Garnet	Grenat	Granate	Granato	Granat
Hematite	Hématite	Hematita	Ematite	Blutstein
Ivory	Ivoire	Marfil	Avorio	Elfenbein
Jade	Jade	Jade	Giado	Jade
Jasper	Jaspe	Jaspe	Diaspro	Jaspis
Jet	Jais	Azabache	Giavazzo	Gagat
Labradorite	Labradorite	Labradorita	Feldspato opalino	Labradorit
Lapis lazuli	Lapis lazuli	Lapis lazuli	Lapislazzuli	Lapis lazuli
Malachite	Malachite	Malaquita	Malachite	Malachit
Marble	Marbre	Marmol	Marmo	Marmor
Marcasite	Marcasite	Marquesita	Marcassita	Markasit
Moonstone	Pierre de lune	Piedra de luna	Pietra lunare	Mondstein
Moss agate	Agate mousseuse	Agata musgosa	Agata muschiosa	Moosachat
Obsidian	Obsidiane	Obsidiana	Obsidiana	Obsidian
Olivine	Olivine	Olivina	Loivina	Olivin
Onyx	Onyx	Onix	Onice	Onyx
Opal	Opale	Opalo	Opalo	Opal
Pearl	Perle	Perla	Perla	Perle
Peridot	Péridot	Peridoto	Peridoto	Peridot
Quartz	Quartz	Cuarzo	Quarzo	Quarz
Rose quartz	Quartz rose	Cuarzo rosada	Quarzo roas	Rosenquarz
Ruby	Rubis	Rubino	Rubino	Rubin
Sapphire	Saphir	Zafir	Zaffiro	Saphir
Sard	Sardoine	Sardonica	Sardonio	Sard
Sardonyx	Sardoine	Serpentina	Serpentina	Sardonix
Smoky quartz	Quartz enfumée	Cuarzo quemado	Quarzo fumoso	Rauchquarz
Sphene	Sphène	Esfenio	Sfenio	Sphen
Spinel	Spinelle	Espinela	Spinello	Spinell
Spodumene	Triphane	Spodumeno	Spodumeno	Spodumen
Sunstone	Aventurine orientale	Aventurina oriental	Venturina	Sonnenstein
Topaz	Topaze	Topacio	Topazio	Topas
Tourmaline	Tourmaline	Turmalina	Tormalina	Turmalin
Turquoise	Turquoise	Turquesa	Turchese	Türkis
Zircon	Zircon	Circon	Zircone	Zirkon

STONES AND ASSOCIATIONS

Months and Birthstones

January	Garnet
February	Amethyst
March	Aquamarine or bloodstone
April	Diamond
May	Emerald
June	Moonstone or opal
July	Ruby
August	Peridot or sardonyx
September	Sapphire
October	Opal or tourmaline
November	Topaz or citrine
December	Turquoise or lapis lazuli

Astrological Stones

Capricorn the Goat	December 22 to January 20	Ruby, moonstone
Aquarius the Water Bearer	January 21 to February 19	Garnet, sapphire
Pisces the Fish	February 20 to March 20	Amethyst, chrysolite
Aries the Ram	March 21 to April 20	Bloodstone, diamond
Taurus the Bull	April 21 to May 21	Sapphire, moss agate
Gemini the Twins	May 22 to June 21	Agate, beryl
Cancer the Crab	June 22 to July 22	Emerald
Leo the Lion	July 23 to August 23	Onyx, ruby, diamond
Virgo the Virgin	August 24 to September 23	Carnelian, jasper
Libra the Scales	September 24 to October 23	Chrysolite, opal
Scorpio the Scorpion	October 24 to November 22	Aquamarine, topaz
Sagittarius the Archer	November 23 to December 21	Turquoise, carbuncle

The Twelve Tribes of Israel

Levi	Garnet
Zebulon	Diamond
Gad	Amethyst
Benjamin	Jasper
Simeon	Chrysolite
Issachar	Sapphire
Naphtali	Agate
Joseph	Onyx
Reuben	Sard
Judah	Emerald
Dan	Topaz
Asher	Beryl

The Twelve Apostles

Peter	Jasper
Andrew	Sapphire
James	Chalcedony
John	Emerald
Philip	Sardonyx
Bartholomew	Sard
Matthew	Chrysolite
Thomas	Beryl
James the Less	Topaz
Jude	Chrysoprase
Simon	Hyacinth
Judas	Amethyst

STONE WEIGHT: The metric carat

The *carat* (ct) is a unit of weight generally used for faceted precious stones (especially diamonds), and transparent semiprecious stones. The International Metric Carat (M.C.) of 200 milligrams (3.086 grains troy) was made standard in the United States in 1913—it was already established in many European countries—and has been since generally recognized internationally. A single carat is divided into four grains (sometimes called *carat grains*) used in weighing natural pearls.

1 carat = $3\frac{1}{16}$ (3.086) grains troy
1 carat = 0.007 ounce avoirdupois
1 carat = $\frac{1}{5}$ gram = 200 milligrams
1 carat = 100 points
$\frac{1}{2}$ carat = $\frac{50}{100}$ points = 0.50 points
$\frac{1}{4}$ carat = $\frac{25}{100}$ points = 0.25 points
$\frac{1}{8}$ carat = $\frac{12.5}{100}$ points = 0.125 points

NATURAL STONE FORMS USED IN JEWELRY

All forms in which stones are found naturally, as well as those to which they can be cut and polished have been and are used in jewelry. When using a natural form, it may only be necessary to polish its surface, trim its size or shape down to a suitable outer contour with a stone-cutting saw, drill a full or partial hole into it, or grind the back flat to facilitate mounting.

Pebbles are small, rounded stones worn to shape by the action of water, sand, and natural tumbling or grinding against each other or harder stone. They are found in streams and riverbeds, on beaches, and in outcroppings where they are embedded in matrices of softer substances such as clay. Depending on the actual composition of the mineral, pebbles can be transparent, translucent, or opaque. Sometimes they already have beautiful shapes that are sufficiently polished by natural abrasion to reveal their true color and need not be altered in any way. The surfaces of others can be hand polished to bring out their color in the same way that any stone is polished; they can be mechanically tumbled which rounds the form while polishing it; or deliberately altered by grinding, sanding, and polishing to a conventional form, as is done by a lapidary.

Crystal fragments, or massed crystal clusters can be used in their natural form provided that their scale is sufficiently small and that their weight falls into an acceptable range. Total weight can be lessened by grinding off the back of a crystal cluster. Crystals can be set in appro-

13-4 PAOLO SPALLA, Italy, designer; manufacturer Ferraris & Co., Valenza. Brooch with natural stone pierced with a hole into which a gold insert is placed, surmounted by fabricated and cast units. *Photo: Günter Meyer, courtesy the Schmuckmuseum, Pforzheim*

13-5 JOHN STOKES, Australia. Silver ring fabricated of sheet metal, holding a natural columnar rock crystal druse by claws projecting from the structure. *Photo: Doug Munson*

priate mountings, often in claw-type settings. Gemstone crystals used in jewelry are pyrites, Chatham emeralds, amethysts, rock crystals, tourmalines, and others.

Geodes are hollow balls of mineralized earth resulting from the filtration of silica-containing groundwater inside which beautiful crystal formations occur as complete linings. When these hollow balls are broken open, the inner surface contains sparkling crystal surfaces, fragments of which, called a *druse,* can be mounted in jewelry. *Nodules* are solid geodes and are cut into slab sections which often reveal elaborately patterned formations in colors that differ with mineral content. Parts of these slabs can then be cut and shaped to cabochons, or they can be used flat. *Thunder eggs* are solid agate-centered nodules found in riverbeds, and can be slabbed and used in the same way.

Rough is any gemstone specimen in bulk. It can be collected by an individual in the field, or purchased from a lapidary supplier. When intended for use in jewelry and not as a specimen, stones "in the rough" are occasionally used as found, but often they are either tumbled or cut into slabs which are then subdivided and polished as cabochons, or faceted by a lapidary.

Fossils are impressions or traces of a formerly living animal, shell, or plant, or footprints or tracks from past geological ages, preserved or petrified in stone which is

13-6 ELEANOR MOTY, U.S.A. Choker neckpiece in fabricated, photoetched, and electroformed silver, with Plexiglas inserts. The central natural columnar quartz prismatic crystal nodule is held by claws, enlarged by electroformed nodules. Size 7 × 7 × 2 in. *Photo: Courtesy the American Crafts Council, New York*

13-7 ALICE SHANNON, U.S.A. Silver necklace of centrifugally cast sections, with central geode of stalagmitic chalcedony. This is a cryptocrystalline translucent variety of quartz, commonly pale blue or gray in color, popularly known as "chalcedony rose." It is found in the Mojave Desert in southern California, and in Brazil. The mineral, 7 in hardness, is deposited from solution in geode linings, and forms a layer of relatively uniform, small size crystals called a druse. Here it is held in place by bent-over claws, and mounted with a gray baroque pearl. *Photo: Jack Bitermann*

13-9 E. R. NELE, West Germany. Necklace in gold in the form of a mermaid, embodying two complete ammonites, suspended by double strands of shell disc beads. Width 8.9 cm. *Photo: Günter Meyer, courtesy the Schmuckmuseum, Pforzheim.*

13-8 JEAN CLAUDE CHAMPAGNAT, France. "Blackbird." Sterling silver pin with natural black slate slabs mounted in rough-textured bezels. At the top is a cluster of white and colored diamonds, and red corals. On the reverse side are springs used to place tension on wires that stretch across front portions. The pin is supported by the use of a *sprag-type* finding with one long prong and one short sprag. Length 6 in. *Photos: Oppi*

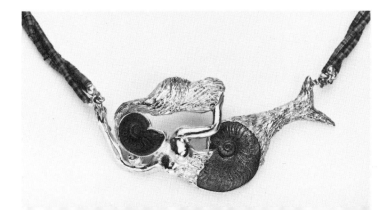

often of the sedimentary type, or in nodular masses. Sometimes the fossil is in layers of strata and is inseparable from the rock formation. It is found when dividing the strata by breaking them apart. Fossils such as shells and crustaceans are also found in stones such as marble when it is slabbed and polished flat. At other times, the fossil is made of a different mineral and is called a *pseudomorph*, a substance formed by a process of substitution, infiltration, incrustation, or alteration. A fossil of this type is the *ammonite* which is any of numerous extinct fossil shells of cephalopods of the group *Ammonoidae*, all having the shape of a flat spiral. In India, the ammonite is called a *salagramma* and is worshipped by followers of Vishnu; it is valued according to the number of its spirals and perforations. They can be found embedded in the retaining material, or free in riverbeds, released by the action of running water or because the softer holding material has disintegrated. Ammonites were abundant during the Mesozoic (the Age of Dinosaurs), and are between 200 million and 70 million years old. They have been used in contemporary jewelry in their entirety, or sectioned and polished flat.

Petrified wood is another pseudomorph, found, among other places, in the Petrified Forest in northern Arizona. There, the original organic matter, the tree trunk, was converted millions of years ago into stone by the infiltration of water containing dissolved mineral matter such as calcium carbonate, or silica, plus traces of iron and manganese impurities which give petrified wood its rich color. In time, the organic substance was replaced particle by particle, and the original structure was retained. Petrified wood can be slabbed, shaped, and polished to take a high luster.

THE LAPIDARY ART:
Stone shaping and polishing

A *lapidary* (from Latin *lapidarius*, "pertaining to stone" or *lapis*, "stone") is a person who cuts, polishes, or engraves precious and semiprecious stones. By the art of lapidary, those qualities in stones that we find attractive, such as their true color, luster, and brilliance, are revealed.

The subject of lapidary work is a vast one, and the interested reader is referred to a book specializing on this subject. A jeweler may never have to prepare a stone for a piece of jewelry since cut stones are so readily available from suppliers. Even so, you should become familiar with the labor and skill involved in producing even a simply shaped and polished stone, to fully appreciate the result, and to be able to pass this appreciation on to a client. Some phases of lapidary processes useful to the average jeweler are referred to briefly in this section.

TUMBLING: Mechanical shaping and polishing stones

The simplest way to polish and prepare stone material for use in jewelry is by *tumbling*. A purely mechanical process, tumbling duplicates the abrasive action that occurs in nature when rocks fall upon each other in rivers and oceans, and with sand as an abrasive, in time become rounded or pebble forms. By the use of a *mechanical tumbler*, what takes natural forces eons to accomplish can be made to happen in a few hours or weeks, and the result will have a high degree of surface finish rare in nature.

13–10 *TUMBLER, MODEL 12TM*, manufactured by Highland Park Manufacturing. Steel drum with 12 lb capacity; removable heavy rubber liner for quieter operation; self-aligning nylon bearings; double-pulley plastic-covered drives; slip-free carriage rollers; motorized. Overall dimensions 12¼ in wide × 12 in deep × 14 in high. *Photo: Courtesy Highland Park Manufacturing*

For a description of the tumbling process, see any good textbook on stone preparation.

METHODS OF MOUNTING TUMBLED OR BAROQUE STONES

The result of tumbling is polished stones possessing rounded, organic, or so-called *baroque* shapes that are irregular. These can be mounted in jewelry in various ways.

BAIL AND CAP MOUNTING Pendant baroques can be mounted by a *bail* which in a basic form is a metal loop from which two arms project and grasp the stone. *Caps* are bell-shaped forms with arms whose positions can be shaped to fit the stone's surface contour. At the point of contact between the arm and the stone, it is usually advisable to roughen the stone's surface with a *pointed silicon carbide stick* to provide a better gripping area for the cement used. A small amount of a cement such as epoxy is mixed according to instructions and applied to the inner bail or cap arm surfaces, and also to the corresponding contact area on the stone. The bail is then pressed upon the stone. If the fit is proper, its arms should hold in place without springing away, but if necessary, it can be temporarily placed into a clamp to hold it down. Any surplus cement that emerges is removed with a clean stick such as a toothpick, and the stone is placed with the bail upright in sand until the cement hardens. The pendant can be hung from a jump ring anyplace in a jewel, from a chain, etc.

PEGGED BAILS Some bails are made with *inner projecting pegs* or short wires of 22 or 24 gauge B.&S. at the *end* of each of two arms. These are intended to fit into holes drilled into the stone at corresponding positions, and act as a means of securing the grip of the bail on the stone. Before pressing the pegs into the stone holes, some cement is placed in the hole to secure it.

RIVETED BAILS A bail whose arms have *drilled holes* can be used to mount a stone with a drilled-through hole, such as a bead or pearl. A head can be formed at one end of the rivet or joint wire, then passed through the bail and stone, and a second head carefully formed at the opposite end with a small *watchmaker's riveting hammer* while the preformed head rests in a depression of matching size in a *dapping block* to support the rivet while hammering. A split rivet could also be used in this case and its projecting shank legs simply bent back.

PEGGED CAPS A pegged cap is a small dome with a loop soldered to the convex side and a peg soldered to the concave side. It is used with a stone that is drilled at a right angle to its surface to a depth sufficient to receive the peg. Before inserting the peg, place a small amount of epoxy cement into the hole and also in the concave side of the cap. Press the peg into the hole until the cap is seated

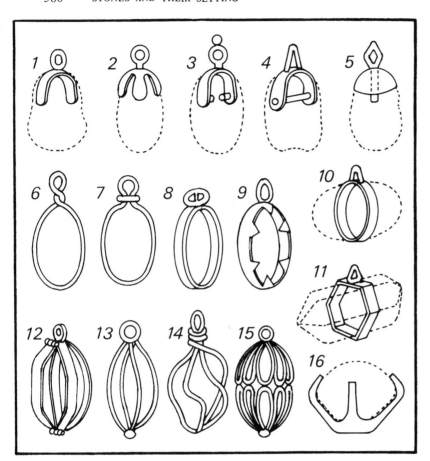

13–11 *MOUNTINGS FOR BAROQUE STONES AND CRYSTALS*
 1. Bail, plain, two arms
 2. Bail, four arms
 3. Pegged bail with two arms
 4. Rivet bail
 5. Pegged cap
 6. Single wire surround, twisted self-loop
 7. Single wire surround, soldered ends, clinch ring
 8. Strip surround, vertical
 9. Strip surround with claws
10. Strip surround, horizontal
11. Strip surround, formed to fit crystal shape
12. Cage mount, strip, with one hinged side, rivet closed
13. Cage mount, wire with ball end, separate loop
14. Cage mount, bent wire, self-loop
15. Cage mount, wire, symmetrical
16. Prong and claw mount

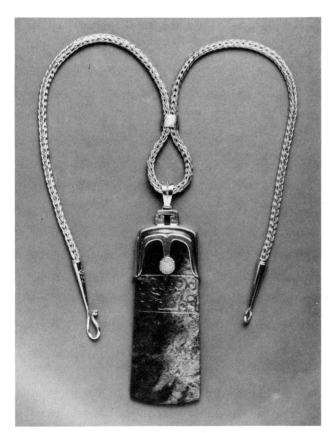

13–12 FREDERICK A. MILLER, U.S.A. Pendant with bail-type mount; 18K gold, with granulation detail, holding an archaic-style 16th-century Chinese carved jade. The mount leaves the jade intact, obviating drilling or tapping. Loop-in-loop 14K gold chain. *Photo: John Paul Miller*

against its surface, then set it aside upright in sand until the cement hardens.

WIRE SURROUNDS   A baroque stone can be held by a circle of wire with a self-loop that fits into a groove made in the circumference of a stone. To determine the amount of wire needed, bend a length of iron binding wire into the groove, and allow some extra for the formation of the self-loop, then straighten the wire and measure its length. Solder the ends of the wire finally used to this length to make one large loop that includes the future self-loop material. Place the wire into the stone groove, press it in with the fingers, and allow the surplus to project at the point where the self-loop is to be formed. Work this end together with *flat-nosed pliers.* Grasp the loop that results and gently twist the wire around until the self-loop is formed with enough twists at its base next to the stone for the surrounding wire to hold. Avoid overtwisting the loop or the wire will become overstressed and break.

STRIP SURROUNDS   Plain, flat strip surrounds, minimally 1/8 in (3.18 mm) wide or wider, of fine silver or other easily compressed metal can be used to mount a baroque stone, a regularly shaped stone, a flat slab-cut stone, or a crystal specimen in either a vertical or horizontal position. First the strip length needed to fit around the stone must be calculated. This can be done in the same way as when using a length of binding wire to determine the length needed for a plain bezel. (See Settings Used for Cabochon-cut Stones in this chapter.) Solder the ends of the strip together and solder an upright loop to the outer strip surface for stone suspension. Press the surround with the fingers around the stone which it should fit closely but without excessive forcing. Should the fit prove to be tight, rub the inner surface with an *abrasive paper* to enlarge it slightly. With a *burnisher,* first fold over the opposite ends a little at a time, working both edges of the strip to make it grasp the stone. Continue to the point halfway between at the sides and do the same, then slowly fold over the rest. Finally, smooth the whole surround down with the burnisher. In this mount, both sides of the stone are visible.

PRONG AND BEZEL MOUNTING Baroque and freeform stones can be mounted in claw settings with preplanned positioning of the claws to suit the particular stone. At least three claws are normally needed to secure the stone. Conventional settings in bezels are also possible, and these systems are discussed ahead. To set a baroque stone in a bezel, one of its sides must be ground flat up to the point where the slope of its surface starts to be less than 90°. This is to make it possible for the bezel to grasp the stone which otherwise it cannot do. Before grinding, select the best surface to remain face up. Baroque stones were com-

monly used in medieval jewelry before the art of stone faceting became so highly developed.

CAGE MOUNTING Baroque stones can be held in a wire cagelike construction of three or more wires that converge at top and bottom points, and have an attached upper suspension loop. Such cages, simple or elaborate, can be fabricated first, and the wires spread apart to allow an entry point for the stone. After the stone is in position within the cage, the wires are forced back in place. Cages can also be made in sizes larger than the stone dimensions, and after the stone is inserted, the wires can be kinked with *pliers* at an angle flat against the stone surface to shorten their length and hold the stone in place. Cages can be made deliberately oversized so the stone moves within them. They can be used as pendants, or joined in series like beads.

DRILLING A HOLE IN A STONE

A hole can be drilled partially or completely through a gemstone with proper tools and patience. Generally speaking, the smaller and deeper the hole, and the harder the substance drilled, the greater the difficulty. However, holes were drilled in gems in ancient jewelry with extremely simple means by methods similar in concept to those used today, using drills and abrasives far inferior to those available now. The ancient hole driller, still in use, was the hand-held *bow drill;* a *hollow copper tube* was the drill bit; the abrasive was *sand* or *powdered emery;* and the lubricant, *water.*

13–13   LYE PARISH, GOTLAND, SWEDEN, Viking Age. Necklace using silver surrounds with double-sided spaced claws holding each rock crystal ball. To set the stone, it was placed into the surround whose claws on one side were already bent to hold it. The claws on the opposite side were then bent over. *Photo: Antikvarisk-Topografiska Arkivet, Stockholm*

13–15   KAREL NIEHORSTER, Netherlands. Sterling silver pendant with gilded blinds, and cast resin hand holding balloons made of unpierced glass spheres, epoxy cemented to wire "strings" with a projecting end flange. Size 95 × 95 × 25 mm. *Photo: Hans Hoogland, courtesy Electrum Gallery, London*

DRILL TYPES

Today, *flat, high-speed steel drills* (see Drilling Pearls, p. 569) held in a *hand drill,* a *flex-shaft,* or a *bench drill* are used to make holes in soft substances up to Mohs' scale 3, such as shell, amber, malachite, marble, and aragonite. For drilling harder substances (Mohs' scale 5–7) the bur/drill used is made of *solid tungsten carbide,* made of solid metal whose tip or surface is *diamond grit embedded,* or made of *diamond grit sintered with metal.* Also used for larger holes are *thin-walled tube core drills* made of steel, copper, or brass and embedded with diamond; or plain metal used in conjunction with loose silicon carbide grit or a prepared diamond compound.

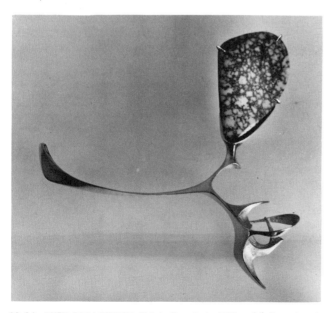

13–14   RUTH RADAKOVICH, U.S.A. Brooch in 18K gold, forged and fabricated, with freeform Nevada spiderweb turquoise held by three claws. *Photo: Svetozar Radakovich*

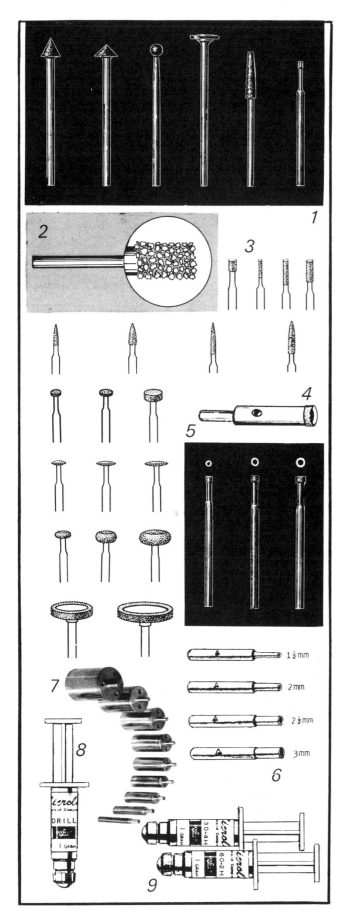

The difference between using solid and hollow drills is that in the first, *all* of the material in the hole is ground away, and in the second, a *core* is cut away from the stone. When making a hole of ¼ in (6.35 mm) or larger, it takes far less time to use a hollow drill than a solid one as far less stone material must be ground away. At intervals, cores must be removed from the drill or they will block further drill progress through the hole. Drills that cut cores usually have a ⅛ in (3.17 mm) or larger side opening into which a rod or wire can be forced to eject the core.

In *mounting a drill,* those with small-diameter shanks such as ³⁄₃₂ in (2.38 mm) can be placed in a *flex-shaft chuck.* Such drills have solid tips of from 1.5–2 mm (0.06–0.08 in) and must be used with care and minimal pressure as they are breakable. It is difficult or impossible to remove a broken drill end from within a hole. Drills with larger shank diameters normally are mounted in a *precision drill press,* held firmly in the chuck, absolutely centered with dead true spindle parallelism, and should operate without any trace of wobble.

LUBRICANTS *Lubricants* are not necessary when drilling soft materials with a hardness up to Mohs' scale 3 if care is taken to lift the drill away from the substance every few seconds to allow it to cool, but to be sure, water can be used as a coolant, dripped continuously from a suitable plastic container on the stone drilling point. Harder materials drilled with diamond-containing drills require a lubricant which can be water, a light oil, a water-soluble oil, or if a diamond compound is used, a suitable extender. These are added repeatedly near the hole with a *small brush,* or dripped in place from a container. It is also possible to submerge the entire stone (or if a large stone is being drilled, its drilled area alone) in a coolant in a manner described on p. 589. Besides acting as a coolant, lubricants also wash away stone flour and abrasive particles and allow new abrasive to come into contact with the stone.

DRILLING AND CARVING ABRASIVE GRITS Loose *silicon carbide grit* used for drilling with metal tube drills and for carving stones may range from grit grades 80–300 or finer. For carving, the choice of which to use depends on

13–16 *STONE HOLE DRILLING AND CARVING TOOLS*
1. *Diamond-plated burs* used for stone carving, *left to right:* countersink 60°; countersink 90°; ball 3 mm; wheel 6 × 1 mm; reamer tapering from 3 to 1 mm; drill 1½ mm.
2. *Diamond-plated bur,* enlarged, with solid metal core and positive kerf clearance to eliminate jamming, operated at 5000–7000 rpm.
3. *Diamond-sintered wheels* in which the diamond grit is combined with sintered metal, in various shapes, *top to bottom:* straight cylinder, flat head; reamers with flame heads; flat-edged wheels; knife-edged wheels; round-edged wheels; heavy-duty wheels. All in various sizes.
4. Core *drill* with diamond-embedded point, ¼ in Ø with side opening for core clearance; also available, Ø ⁵⁄₁₆, ⅜, ⁷⁄₁₆, and ½ in.
5. Core *drills* with diamond-embedded points, no side opening, small sizes.
6. *Metal tube core drills* 1½, 2, 2½, and 3 mm, used with separate abrasive grit.
7. *Metal tube core drills,* set, with end notches to catch the grit, in sizes up to 1⁹⁄₁₆ in, used with separate abrasive grit at approx. 1500–1800 rpm, mounted in drill press chuck.
8. *Diamond drilling compound* with natural or synthetic diamond grit, used when drilling holes with a metal tube drill. It is available in various *micron sizes.* Used with a *compound extender fluid* when necessary.
9. *Diamond lapping and polishing compound,* used with a compound extender on flat, shaped, or carved stone surfaces for polishing. Available in various grits.

the hardness of the stone material and the degree of surface smoothness wanted. For hole drilling, the finer grades are used on the hardest stones. *Diamond compound* used for drilling, carving, and polishing stone is today applied from a color-coded particle-size plastic syringe containing 1, 2, or 5 grams. Diamond compound ranges in particle size from 45 microns to ¼ micron. A *micron* is a unit of length equal to one thousandth of a millimeter or about 0.000039 in. The coarser grades are used for carving and drilling, and the finest for polishing stone. Squeeze about ¼ in (6.35 mm) from the syringe onto the stone. Apply the drill gently without pressure at a slow speed, and lift it away from the stone frequently. This compound is used in conjunction with a *compound extender fluid* available in a dripper bottle holding 1–4 ounces.

Diamond compound micron size and its mesh equivalent

Micron size	Mesh equivalent
¼	100,000
½	50,000
1	14,000
3	8,000
6	3,000
9	1,800
15	1,200
30	600
45	325

MAKING YOUR OWN TUBE DRILL You can make your own larger sized tube drills by force fitting a tube section of the desired diameter onto a round steel arbor of a size that will fit into a drill chuck. While it is so inserted, to true the cutting edge of the tube, bring it down and run it against a flat piece of abrasive paper placed level on the drill table. Then spread the tube end *slightly* to flare it outward in order to provide drill clearance and prevent jamming. To spread the tube end, insert a round rod and rotate it slowly, then place a knife blade against the tube end and lightly hammer it to make notches in the tube end every ¹⁄₁₆ in (1.6 mm). These will catch the abrasive and oil mixture and help the tube drill to function more efficiently.

HOLE-DRILLING PROCEDURE Drilling a hole in very hard stone requires the use of a diamond-plated drill or sintered diamond and metal drill, or a metal tube drill with separate abrasive. Mount the stone with *dopping wax* on a waste slab of a softer stone. Clamp the slab in place on the drill table so it does not move with the hole position directly below the drill. For ease of penetration, the drill must enter the stone's surface at a *right angle* or as nearly this as possible. Depending on the stone's shape, this may mean that the stone has to be positioned on a mound of wax to make such an entry possible. For large stones being drilled, build a wall of Plasticine around the hole area to a height that will allow dripped lubricant to be caught and retained. Where necessary, this wall can allow the whole stone to be submerged under the lubricant-coolant poured into this depression.

To start a hole, use either a *diamond-point scriber* or an oil-lubricated *small ball-shaped bur* to break the surface at the exact center of the desired hole and make a small concave depression there that will allow the entering drill to grip the stone to prevent its slipping and scratching the stone's surface. Should a scratch occur, it may be possible to remove it with some diamond compound applied with a small felt wheel, depending on its seriousness.

When drilling a hole in stone, in all cases work must *proceed slowly*, drill speeds must be moderate, and the pressure upon the stone light. Work the drill by just touching the stone, raising it frequently from the hole to clear it. Lubricate the hole with water or other coolant applied with a brush or dripped to reduce any buildup of frictional heat which, if allowed to develop, will cause the stone to crack. Allow fresh abrasive to enter the hole with the lubricant which will at the same time remove *swarf*, the slimy combination of grinding abrasive, fine stone flour, and metal drill particles mixed with lubricant. If these procedures are not followed, chances are increased for cracking the stone and losing all the time spent thus far in shaping it.

A *critical point* occurs during hole drilling: when nearing the last millimeter before the drill passes through the stone to complete the hole. If this is not done at a *greatly reduced speed and pressure,* the chance is great of the drill causing the outer hole edges to chip.

When metal tube drills are not in use, immerse them in oil or kerosene to prevent corrosion or rusting.

THE USES OF DRILLED STONES IN JEWELRY *Half-drilled stones* can be mounted rigidly on a peg to which they are cemented with epoxy. They can also be used in a mobile form as a pendant by cementing a swivel or looped peg mount into the hole, and passing a second loop through it to suspend the stone, secure it, and allow its movement. A second stone can be seated in a partially-drilled-through opening made in a base stone and cemented in place without any metal mount as an inlay, either flat or in relief.

Fully drilled stones find their greatest use as *beads*, believed to be the earliest jewels. Beads are generally globular, but they can be of any form, and for that matter, of any natural or synthetic material. What makes a bead a bead is that it is *fully perforated* to allow a supporting cord, chain, or wire to be passed through it. An undrilled or half-drilled ball is a sphere which can of course be used as a bead if it is provided with a mount that permits stringing or attachment. Piercing variations for beads exist, such as the common Chinese system of piercing a bead with a transverse hole which is met by a second hole that penetrates the bead in a direction perpendicular to the first hole and meets it in an inverted T. This system allows a bead to be immobilized and not only strung horizontally, but vertically as well to meet others. Beads such as this with holes at angular intersections can be strung with a fine, flexible, twisted wire "needle" to which the cord is attached. Another common system involves parallel holes through which the string supporting separately strung bead rows can penetrate, the multi-holed bead serving to keep the strands separate. Oval or long baroque beads can be drilled through at one end in a direction perpendicular to their long axis to allow them to be used as a pendant. These are only some of the various

13–17 NOMA COPLEY, U.S.A. Pin in 18K gold with fully drilled ruby, sapphire, and pearl, each mounted on a headed rivet whose extended bright-polished shank passes through the matte-surfaced, bent sheet metal base. *Photo: Tracy Boyd*

ways in which beads can be pierced. The ways in which they are combined and strung are infinite.

Stones can be drilled through perpendicularly to their faces to allow the mounting of a metal ornament on their surface, the base stone acting as a ground. This is done sometimes to mount a stone of a contrasting color, and to combine an opaque with a transparent stone. To mechanically join the upper stone to the base, a screw or tube can be soldered to the back of the metal mount or the setting holding a stone, and then passed through the hole to the back of the base stone. There a nut can be placed on a screw end, and a tube can be flared like a tube rivet to secure the ornament. Unset fully drilled stones can be mounted directly to a metal base with a screw or rivet in this same way.

13–19 GWALIOR, MADHYA PRADESH, INDIA. Woman making *lamp beads* or wire-wound glass beads by hand. On her left are glass rods in various colors. Resting on the sand-filled bowl are the mandrels: prepared lengths of nichrome steel wire coated by dipping into liquid white clay. Before her is a battery of five torches (the "lamp") whose merging gas flames make one hot flame. A clay-coated rod is held in the right hand, while the left manipulates a glass rod in the flame that melts it onto the rotating wire. The glass forms a round bead whose size depends on how much glass material is used. Additional colors are added from thinner glass rods to the bead surface, as seen here. While the beads are in a molten state, they can be rolled in crushed colored glass, then while the bead rotates in the flame, the addition can be smoothed and rounded with a curved steel tool. Cylinders can be made by rolling the mass on a flat metal surface while still plastic. Rods holding finished, spaced beads are implanted upright in the sand-filled bowl to cool. Cold beads are removed from the rod simply by forcing them off, or by placing one rod end in a vise jaws and grasping the other with heavy pliers, then pulling on the rod to stretch it and reduce its sectional size. In either case, the protective clay disintegrates, leaving a bead with hole ready for stringing. Wires can be recoated with clay and reused. *Photo: Oppi*

GEMSTONE CARVING AND ENGRAVING: The glyptic art

The art of carving and engraving gemstones is called the glyptic art, a *glyph* being a channel or groove (from the Greek *glyphe,* "carving"). In this process, figural designs are either incised into the stone, called *intaglio,* or appear in relief, called *cameo.*

Gem engraving is an ancient art that seems to have first appeared about 4000 B.C. in the form of the cylinder seal of Mesopotamia. The decorative art of carving jade, a gemstone of first importance in China, started there more than 3,000 years ago and reached a high degree of skill as early as the Shang Dynasty (1766–1122 B.C.). Gem engraving was also practiced in Egypt where the cylinder seal first used was replaced by the scarab, a gemstone carved and engraved to the shape of the sacred beetle (*kheprer*) that was the symbol of the god Khopri, the generator of new life, virility, and resurrection. The carved scarab was also used by officials as a seal for documents, its flat, lower surface carved with the name of the king or

13–18 KHWAREZM, UZBEK S.S.R. Silver, parcel gilt pectoral with central filigree ornament hung with 10 chains bearing 157 fully drilled coral beads, and turquoise-studded pendants, subdivided into smaller strands holding spiral wire-strung coral beads. Pectoral length, not including neckband 13 in. *Photo: Oppi*

13-20 FRANZ J. BETTE, West Germany. *Left:* ring in sterling silver with carved nephrite stone. *Right:* ring in 18K white gold with carved dumortierite, a bright blue or greenish blue basic aluminum silicate named after Eugène Dumortier, a French paleontologist. The stones are carved to the maker's design in Pforzheim, West Germany. *Photos: Sibylle Küsters-Hassenpflug*

13-21 INDIA, Mogul period, 17th century. Archer's rings respectively of carved carnelian, rock crystal, and jade, inlaid with gold, diamonds, and rubies set into carved depressions, held by the Indian *kundan* style of gem setting. Though decorative, this ring form was primarily functional. It was worn on the thumb with the ring lip pointing up and on the underside, to improve the archer's use of his bow and arrow. The bow string was hitched behind the lip, and only the outstretched thumb and forefinger were used to draw the string. Upon release, by separating these fingers, the ring lip was drawn forward by the string which then slipped off. The arrow's flight range was greater and steadier than in the Western three-finger pull and release. *Photo: Salar Jung Museum, Hyderabad, Hyderabad-Deccan, India*

13-22 PAOLO SPALLA, Italy, designer; manufacturer Ferraris & Co., Valenza. Natural egg-shaped rock ring with a gold tube set into the hole to form a ring shank. The top is capped with a yellow and white gold repoussage appliqué of an embryo bird with a cabochon ruby eye set in a closed bezel, surrounded by pavé-set diamonds. Size 55 × 40 mm. *Photo: Gallone Moreno, courtesy Ferraris & Co.*

official in hieroglyphics surrounded by a cartouche. When pressed into clay it left a relief signature. Scarabs were carried on a string by a pierced hole, or commonly were mounted in a ring by passing both ends of a wire through the same hole, then wrapping these ends around the shank. In later times they were widely used as amulets.

The Minoans, Greeks, Etruscans, and Romans all appreciated engraved gems. The Greeks wore carved gemstones as rings made in a manner similar to the scarab setting described above, as bracelet ornaments, and as pendants suspended from a belt tied to the waist. Romans wore them set immobilized in gold mounts, and as pendants. Gemstone engraving was revived again during the Renaissance when interest in the Classical period was renewed. Old engraved gemstones were discovered in excavations, and their style was emulated. These were worn in medallions, pendants, rings, and in hat brooches. After this period, interest again declined, but was renewed in Europe during the late 18th and early 19th centuries at the time of the neoclassic revival. During this time, shell cameos made in Italy became important as a relatively inexpensive substitute for gemstone cameos which were then also reproduced in quantity. Today gemstone carving is still practiced in India, China, Hong Kong, West Germany, and Italy, and by a few scattered individuals elsewhere.

INTAGLIO AND CAMEO

The earliest gemstone carving was in *intaglio* in which the design is carved in the *negative* below the flattened or somewhat domed gemstone surface. This condition allowed the carved stone to be pressed into a soft substance such as clay or sealing wax where it left a mirror image of the design in relief. *Cameo* carving in which the design is created by cutting away the ground and leaving the figure *in relief* did not begin until the late Hellenistic Greek period when gemstone carving came to be appreciated for its artistic, ornamental value rather than for the functional aspect an intaglio seal served. Greek cameos were often

13-23 ROME, end of the 1st century, A.D. "Gemma Augustea." Banded onyx cameo, believed to be the most skillfully executed cameo extant from Roman antiquity. The upper tier shows the Emperor Augustus Tiberius seated beside Rome, being crowned in victory by a personified *Oikoumene*. The lower tier depicts conquered peoples. *Photo: Meyer, Kunsthistorisches Museum, Vienna*

13-24 HELLENISTIC GREECE, 3rd century, B.C. Onyx cameo of a Ptolemaic royal couple, carved in several layers to exploit the natural color banding of the stone. Photo: Kunsthistorisches Museum, Vienna

13-25 NEPAL, early 19th century. Silver-gilt clasp-buckle, the entire surface covered with carved and engraved precious and semiprecious stones in the local style called jadau work. Col.: Metropolitan Museum of Art, Kennedy Fund, 1915. Photo: The Metropolitan Museum of Art, New York

13-26 BERND MUNSTEINER, West Germany. Brooch in 750/1000 yellow gold, with flat zard onyx stone in naturally colored layers, with cabochon rubies. By a method that is a contemporary extension of the cameo-carving technique, the onyx is corundum sandblasted to form relief patterns that expose underlayer color strata, and also create matte areas that contrast with those polished. A series of stencils are used to shield and protect untreated stone parts, to establish edges, and create steplike contoured depressions. Photo: Baumann

made of banded agate or sardonyx carved with the color layers running horizontal to the visible upper plane, so that as many as four levels of carving, each in a different color in the stone, could be achieved. It was usual for a white figure to appear on a dark ground. When a translucent white layered, black based onyx stone is used, and the cutting is done in the white layer to create various tonalities by varying the depth, the result today is termed a *nicolo* cameo.

In addition to the above-mentioned stones, practically all other known gemstones were also used for engraving. The range of available stones increased considerably in Greece after the conquests of Alexander the Great when a rich variety of colored stones began to be imported from India and Sri Lanka. Most of these stones have a hardness of about 7 Mohs' scale, but some are even harder. In Mogul India and in Persia even the diamond, the hardest of all stones, was engraved with the signatures of its possessors by the use of diamond powder as an abrasive.

GEM ENGRAVING: Tools and Techniques

The tools used for gemstone engraving today are essentially the same as those used in 4000 B.C. The stone must be mounted in a substance that prevents its movement, but when it is large, it may also be hand held. In ancient times, a hand-operated *bow* or *pump drill* using drills of many sizes and shapes was used in conjunction with powdered quartz sand, corundum, or emery as abrasives. Carving was accomplished by changing the direction of the cutting tool in relation to the stone, adding abrasive powder as needed to the area carved. Stationary wheels with a belt drive were also used, and in this case, the stone must be hand held at the desired angle and brought to the wheel dressed with abrasive. Vasari in his book *On Technique* (1568) describes the Renaissance Italian process. As the carving proceeded, the carver tested the appearance of the intaglio by taking test impressions of it in wax. This

allowed examination of the work, and additional stone material was then removed where necessary. Cameo carving did not require such testing as the work is positive. In an interesting late Roman technique, when making an intaglio in a transparent stone, once the work was polished after carving a gold sheet was pressed into the depressions and the reverse side was polished. This allowed the image to be seen through the stone in relief, the gold reflecting through the stone.

Today, *silicon carbide* and *diamond-sintered drills and burs* in a great variety of shapes and sizes are available for use in conjunction with a *flex-shaft handpiece,* and these can be used on stones or shells. Diamond polishing compounds are also manufactured for use on miniature buffing wheels. Stone carving can also be achieved by what might also be called *dry etching,* through the use of *corundum sandblasting.* Portions of the stone to be protected can be covered with a stencil material strong enough to resist the sandblast, such as *adhesive tapes.* By directing the hard corundum sand against the exposed areas of the stone, those places will gradually be worn away, creating depressions in the surface. With these advanced and efficient means available, it is surprising that more persons are not interested in gemstone carving as an art.

STONE MOSAICS IN JEWELRY

In the concept of a *mosaic,* a surface decoration is fabricated by assembling and permanently abutting small, differently colored shapes of a material such as colored stones, glass, or a synthetic substance to create a unit having a surface pattern. The individual parts are shaped to fit beside each other in the pattern so that normally, a minimum or none of the substance that binds them together is visible.

Stone and glass mosaics for architectural ornament have been made since classical antiquity, but their use in miniature scale that could be termed *micromosaic* for decoration in jewelry first occurred in Italy during the mid-19th century. Two distinct systems were used: the first was known as *Roman mosaic* and employed glass; and the second was called *Florentine mosaic* and utilized semiprecious stones. The concepts in these old techniques are full of possibilities for further developments in a contemporary idiom.

ROMAN MICROMOSAIC:
The assembly of miniature tesserae

The system used in Roman mosaic is based on the pictorial wall, floor, and ceiling decoration made in Classical Rome and Byzantium. Interest in this technique was revived during the 19th century as a result of the impact of earlier and current discoveries made in the excavations of Pompeii and Herculaneum. The miniature mosaic method was first adopted for use by Fortunato Pio Castellani whose fine glass micromosaic miniatures were set in granulated gold frames. This process was copied and coarsened by countless others whose descendants are still active in

Italy today fabricating such pieces mainly for the tourist industry.

In this micromosaic technique, each small individual part, called a *tessera,* is a uniformly colored glass rod, and most *tesserae* (plural) used in a single mosaic are generally of the same sectional size. In some, cross-sectional shapes are suited to the form of the subject, such as flower petal, or border shapes. Many lengths of such tesserae are cemented together in parallel positions side by side, their ends at the upper surface aligned in one flat plane perpendicular to the rods, or in a curved plane. By placing different colors next to each other, floral or architectural subjects are created. Greater or lesser realism is achieved, depending on the section size of the individual tessera rod which can range from incredibly fine to coarse. Once the entire pattern is assembled and the cement hard, it becomes possible to cut across all the tesserae sectionally with a *trim saw* to achieve two or more identical cross sections whose face surfaces can then be polished level. The finished unit is sometimes set into an excavation in a frame made of a stone slab, or more usually in a metal mount, traditionally of filigree, to make brooches, earrings, bracelets, or necklaces. It is possible to imagine this process translated into fine plastic rods instead of glass, with geometric figure designs.

FLORENTINE MOSAIC: *Pietra dura, stone inlay*

Florentine mosaic is a form of stone work known as *pietra dura* (Latin, "hard stone"), a process in which sepa-

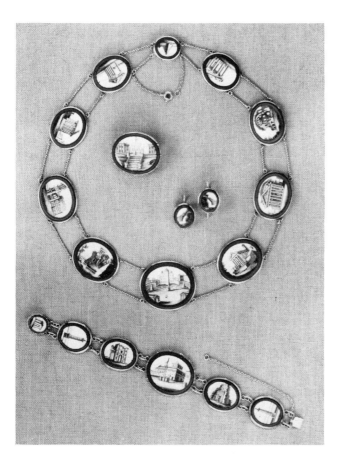

13–27 ITALY, early 19th century. Parure including a brooch, bracelet, earrings, and necklace, all containing Roman glass micromosaics set in gold. Necklace: 42 cm long; bracelet: 17 cm long; brooch: 3.2 cm Ø; earrings: 2 cm long. Col.: Schmuckmuseum, Pforzheim. Photo: Günter Meyer, courtesy Schmuckmuseum, Pforzheim

13–28 BROOCH FROM THE SAME PARURE. Photo: Günter Meyer, courtesy Schmuckmuseum, Pforzheim

13–29 ROGER TSABETSAYE, (Zuñi Pueblo), U.S.A. Silver bracelet with mosaic of turquoises, coral, mother of pearl, and jet cemented to the base. Width 2½ in. Photo: Courtesy U. S. Department of the Interior, Indian Arts and Crafts Board

13–30 T. BIANCHINI, Italy, ca. 1870. Bracelet of five linked oval gold frames, each holding a Florentine *pietra dura* mosaic with a visible black marble ground inlaid with multicolored semiprecious stones in flower patterns. Col.: Hallwylska Museet, Stockholm. *Photo: Courtesy Hallwylska Museet, Stockholm*

13–31 PRESTON MONOGYE, (Hopi), U.S.A. Cast silver bracelet whose divided, textured surface incorporates a multi-stone mosaic inlay of rectangular sections of ironwood, turquoise, coral, and jet, set in a visible metal ground. Width 1⅜ in. *Photo: Courtesy U. S. Department of the Interior, Indian Arts and Crafts Board*

rate units of various hard stones are cut to fit together in a pattern and inlaid into a *common stone ground*. *Intarsia* from the Italian *intarsio* means "inlay" in general, but more specifically refers to the inlay of wood veneers, ivory, or metal into a wood ground. The term *Florentine intarsia* sometimes used to describe this work in stone is therefore inappropriate.

Florentine pietra dura mosaic is still being done today in Florence, Italy, and the best work is as skillful today as in the past. There are actually two basic systems of working. A *visible-ground mosaic* is one in which shapes are cut out and inserted into a depression in a common stone ground made to receive them. The ground is seen surrounding the unit, is a part of the final surface, and often acts as a frame. In an *invisible-ground mosaic*, the parts fit together in the manner of a jigsaw puzzle and the ground is invisible, but one still exists and backs the parts which are cemented to it. (In yet a third type, but one not used in Florentine mosaics, the parts are cemented to each other and form a unit without any supporting backing.)

In either case, work starts with a *cartoon* or exact size master drawing of the design on paper in which the subject is divided into sections, each to be substituted by a different piece of stone cut to that shape. In planning the design, avoid sharp-angled internal corners which are difficult to cut in stone, by dividing the form at such points. To aid in keeping track of the work, as it is possible that many pieces may be of the same material or close to each other in size or shape, give each part a number, preferably with those within a single subject or in proximity numbered in sequence. Make two or three accurate tracing paper copies of the original design with a *fine-pointed hard lead pencil*, to keep the lines as thin as possible. Avoid varying the thickness of lines in this outline drawing because this may result in inaccuracy when later fitting the cut-out parts together.

MOSAIC WITH VISIBLE GROUND

The method described here for making a visible-ground mosaic inlay was used to elaborately decorate the Taj Mahal in Agra, India, built during the 17th century. The mosaics there are said to have been supervised by a Florentine mosaicist. Descendants of the original pietra dura craftsmen who executed the work are still at work in Agra outside walls of the Taj Mahal where they make pietra dura plates, boxes, and table tops.

The stones used in pietra dura work are generally opaque, uniformly thick, 1 mm (0.04 in) slabs of agate, aragonite, carnelian, coral, jasper, lapis lazuli, malachite, marble, onyx, opal, and turquoise. Ideally, the more uni-

form the slab thickness, the flatter the surface will be and the less grinding needed when later lapping the surface flat. When a realistic design is being executed, the area of the stone used for a particular piece may be carefully selected for *gradations of color and tone,* dictated by their position in the design. Otherwise, *pattern silhouette* and *color combination and contrast* is more important. When the pattern consists of geometric forms, the work resembles wood parquetry; when representational, scenic, figural, or floral subjects are made, the result resembles wood marquetry.

Mosaics executed in this style start by tracing the outline of a single numbered shape, following the line exactly from a copy of the master cartoon. Place the same number on both sides of the stone with a *stone-marking stylus*. Cut the part out of the paper following the line accurately, and paste it on the selected portion of the stone slab with a non-water-soluble cement that will not curl paper or cause it to change its dimension. Allow this to dry.

Cut the stone shape out on a *trim saw,* close to but not touching the outline. To cut sharp inside curves, first remove as much stone as possible with straight cuts. Then make several short cuts perpendicularly into the stone's edge toward the marked outline but ending short of it. Trim off the surplus by using *pliers* held in a gloved hand and breaking it off by nibbles. The remainder can be removed with a *grinder,* or, if the parts are small, with a mechanized *miniature abrasive wheel* on a *flex-shaft,* using water as a coolant-lubricant until the final shape is achieved. Try to keep the sides of the part vertical, or only slightly inclined toward the back, but be sure the shape of the face side is kept intact.

Place the cut-out part in position face up on the ground stone and trace its outline, making sure the *tracer* makes a mark *absolutely vertical* to the part edge to avoid a loose fit that will leave spaces that will have to be cement filled, and therefore would be visible. Several units can first be joined to make one by cementing them together edgewise, and the result treated as one shape, if this simplifies the work.

With a *small sharp chisel* of appropriate shape, and using a lightweight *chasing hammer* to strike its end, excavate the ground within the shape outline on the base stone to a depth equal to that of the unit thickness. To make this work easier, traditionally a soft stone such as marble is used as a base. The depression could also be ground into the base with an abrasive *silicon carbide rotary bur* or a *diamond-impregnated metal bur,* using water as a coolant. Test the part at intervals for fit, removing the ground wherever necessary. Stone outline shape and ground depression shape must match exactly or the cement will be visible in the gap. Cement the part in place and continue with the rest of the design in the same manner. When all parts are in place and the cement has hardened, lap the surface flat and polish it.

MOSAIC WITH INVISIBLE GROUND

When making a mosaic with an invisible ground, a mirror image or reverse tracing of the design will be needed. The simplest way to make one is to place a sheet of *carbon paper,* face up, below the paper onto which the design has been traced, then go over the lines again, and use the side with the carbon line as the mirror image. Its use is described ahead. Number the parts to correspond with those on the master cartoon.

Cut out one part as before using a positive of the shape glued to the stone, and when it is finished, place the part and glue it face down temporarily on the intact mirror image tracing with a *water-soluble cement.* The paper serves the purpose of aligning the face surfaces of all finished parts. When all are completed and glued to the paper, a stiff paper frame is improvised around the outer contour of the mosaic and held to the paper which must be supported by a hard, flat surface, with Plasticine placed around it outside the frame. The cement is poured into this walled area to hold the parts together.

CEMENTING THE MOSAIC The cements used can be any fine-grained cement that will set hard, such as a dental or casein cement. Synthetic epoxy such as clear or opaque

Araldit can be used following manufacturer's instructions. For mosaics with a visible ground, place the cement into the ground depression, press the mosaic part into it, and wipe away any rising surplus. In the invisible-ground mosaic, prepare a sufficient amount of cement and pour it into the retaining frame, working it into the spaces if necessary with a *stiff brush.* Cover the back with the backing material which can be a single thin slab cut to the contour

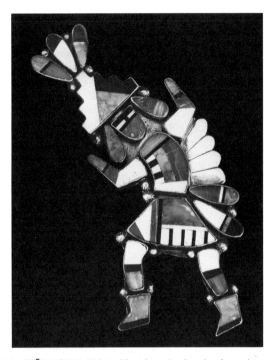

13–34 ZUÑI INDIAN, U.S.A. Silver brooch of a dancing rain god, set with a mosaic of turquoise, coral, jet, and mother of pearl. Most units are compound mosaics of these stones, cemented together and set as one stone in fine-toothed edge bezels, the teeth rubbed over the stones to hold them. *Photo: Courtesy U. S. Department of the Interior, Indian Arts and Crafts Board.*

13–32 SAQQARA, EGYPT. Trapezoidal shrine-shaped gold pectoral of Rameses II, XIXth Dynasty. The frame is topped by hollow tubes for the suspending chain, and contains a divine vulture with outstretched wings, and a cobra, surmounted by a smaller winged deity topped by a cartouche of Rameses II. The entire surface is inlaid with a glass mosaic, each part separated from another by fusion-joined upstanding cloison wires. Some mosaic parts are missing, and their places show traces of cement. Col.: Louvre. *Photo: Archives Photographiques, Caisse Nationale des Monuments Historiques, Paris*

13–33 KOTAKU TAKABATAKE, Japan. White gold, 14K pin with flat-lapped, angular-cut nephrite, onyx, and bloodstones set in cloisonné mosaic style with areas of pavé-set diamonds. *Photo: Yasuhiro Izuka*

13–35 TIBET. Silver ornaments worn suspended by cords tied to hair before the ears. The surface is covered with a turquoise mosaic set in lac by heating the lac and the stone, and pressing them together. *Photo: Ferdinand Boesch*

of the entire mosaic, and press it down. Allow the cement to harden. (If the mosaic is backless, it becomes even more important that the sides of the individual parts be cut to abut each other *exactly* since the parts hold together by cemented sides.) Allow the cement to harden, then soak the whole mosaic in warm water to soften and remove the paper from the mosaic face and edges. When the parts have been made flat to begin with, the result should be flat. The face surface can be given a final leveling polish.

In Victorian Florentine mosaics, the result was treated as a single stone, and was set in a bezel mount in brooches, earrings, bracelets, and necklaces. *Parures* or matching sets of these items were often made and worn together as an ensemble during the 18th and 19th centuries.

CONTEMPORARY USES OF MOSAICS IN JEWELRY

In contemporary interpretations of the mosaic concept, modifications in traditional methods have already been employed. By one method, the metal to receive the mosaic is fabricated first and provided with a depressed area to receive a stone or glass mosaic. When this has been assembled, the face is then ground flat with *hand abrasive sticks,* or on a *mechanical lap wheel.* Sections of a mosaic can be separated from each other by the use of soldered

13-37 OPPI UNTRACHT, U.S.A. Three 18K gold-framed brooches holding mosaics of semiprecious stones, all units cut to order in the same length, but different in width and sectional shapes. Clockwise: overlay of yellow topaz; mosaic: tiger's eye, yellow jasper, hawk's eye, iron pyrite, and red jasper. Mosaic of rhodonite, white agate with green lace, tiger's eye, iron pyrite; oval moonstone at top, and rounded square smoky quartz at bottom. Mosaic of malachite, hawk's eye, green-dyed onyx, chrysoprase; with round moonstone. *Photo:* Oppi

cloisons in the manner of ancient Egyptian, Anglo-Saxon, and Celtic jewels, as well as in modern American Indian channel work, and Mexican stone and shell inlay jewelry.

By varying any of the basic elements that characterize a mosaic, a completely new appearance can be given to the result. The scale of its parts can be increased, or large and small elements can be deliberately combined. Instead of aiming for a uniformly flat final surface, each of the tesserae can be of a different height. Parts of the mosaic can be polished flat and a depression can be left into which a relief-carved element can be fitted and cemented. Mosaics can be made of a combination of stone and metal, or of synthetic materials alone. The use of modern cements simplifies the permanent joining of dissimilar materials.

METAL MOSAICS

Metal mosaics can be made following the same system as for Roman mosaics, substituting metal wires and rods of differently colored metals and cross-sectional shapes. Tubing can be incorporated with wires, and wires inserted into the tube. These compound elements can be soldered together in groups, then cut into sections which can then be joined together to make a mosaic sheet. Spaces remaining can be filled with colored lacquers, epoxy, enamel, or flooded with solder and then filed flat to expose the pattern on the surface.

CABOCHON-CUT STONES

The noun *cabochon* used to describe a stone form commonly used in jewelry is derived from the French *caboche,* "head" or "pate," and indicates a smoothly polished, unfaceted stone whose visible form is curved like a bald pate or the crown of a head. The earliest stones used in metal jewelry were set *en cabochon,* that is, with their polished, convex surfaces upward. Today, the cabochon cut remains

13-36 CHARLES LOLOMA, U.S.A. "Lizard." Silver brooch inlaid with a turquoise and ironwood mosaic. *Photo: Courtesy the American Crafts Council, New York*

Comparison of Gem Sizes (round)

Stone Size (ss)	Pearl Size (ps)	Milli-meter (mm)	Inch ('')	Carat (ct., ideal cut)
1	4-5	1.00	3/64	.005
2	6-7	1.125		.01
3	8-9	1.25		
4	10	1.50	1/16	.02
5	11-12	1.75		
6	13-14	2.00		.03
7	15-16	2.125	5/64	
8	17-18	2.25	2/32	.046
9	19-20	2.50		.06
10	21	2.75	7/64	.078
11	22-23	3.00	1/8	.10
12	24-25	3.125		.113
13	26	3.25		.127
14	27	3.375	9/64	.142
15	28-29	3.50		.161
16	30	3.75		.197
17	31-32	4.00	5/32	.235
18	33	4.125		.26
19	34	4.25		.27
20	35	4.375	11/64	.308
21	36-37	4.50		.32
22	38-39	4.75		.394
23	40	5.00	3/16	.475
24	41-42	5.25		.535
25	43-44	5.375	13/64	.575
26	45-46	5.50		.62
27		5.75		.70
28-29		6.00	15/64	.80
30		6.25		.90
31		6.50	1/4	1.02
32		6.75		1.14
33-34		7.00	9/32	1.27
35-36		7.50		1.57
38		8.00		1.90
39		8.25		2.08
40		8.50		2.28
41		8.75		2.48
42		9.00		2.70
43		9.50		3.18
44		10.00		3.70
45		10.25		3.97
46		10.50		4.27
47		11.00		4.93
48		11.50		5.63
49		11.75		6.00
50		12.00		6.40

popular mainly for use on translucent and opaque semi-precious stones, but it is also used sometimes for transparent and precious stones, especially those that show chatoyancy or asterism. The curved form of a cabochon-cut stone has a quality of its own, capturing and reflecting moving light in a liquid, flowing way quite unlike the flashing manner in which light is refracted in faceted stones.

A simple engineering concept lies behind the mounting of a cabochon-cut stone in a metal setting. From the outer perimeter or *girdle* of the stone which is its largest dimension, its form *slopes inward* to a greater or lesser extent. The slope does not have to be very great—only *a few degrees less* than the perpendicular or 90° is sufficient. The stone is held in a metal mount by various means that take advantage of this angle. These can range from three inward-bent points, to a continuous inward-sloping wall or *bezel* that is forced to lie flat against the stone's surface. Cabochon stone setting is discussed on p. 599.

CABOCHON STONE CUTTING

Cabochon-cut stones are probably in wider use in contemporary art jewelry than other stone cut types. They can be purchased ready-cut in a great variety of different stones, shapes, and standard dimensions. However, even if a jeweler never cuts a cabochon, the knowledge of what is involved is important. For cabochon stone cutting, the reader is referred to the bibliography for books on stone preparation.

STONE SHAPES AND CUTS

In describing a stone, a distinction must be made between its shape and its cut. The *shape* of a stone refers to its outside configuration when looked at in *plan view*. This

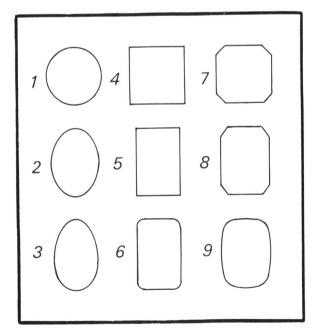

13-39 *CABOCHON STONE SHAPES*
1. Round
2. Oval
3. Pear
4. Square
5. Rectangle (cushion)
6. Oblong
7. Octagon-square
8. Octagon-rectangle or long octagon
9. Cushion Antique

13–38 BÖRJE RAJALIN, Finland, designer; manufacturer Kalevala Koru, Helsinki. Gold bracelet using cabochon Finnish rose quartz, smoky quartz, and Lapland garnets. The entire concept consists of open-backed shoulder bezels interspersed with a few gold domes. Two hinges make the opening and closing device. *Photo: Otso Pietinen*

is its true periphery or contour, called the *girdle*. The *cut* of a stone refers to the form given to the visible surface alone in the case of most opaque stones; or to both the upper, visible surface and the lower surface in the case of transparent stones, particularly when faceted. *Heights* in all stone cuts are made in a wide range from shallow to very high, and shapes can be of *any dimension*.

Common shapes for cabochon stones are round, oval, square, cushion (rectangular), oblong, cushion antique, octagon-rectangle (rectangle with corners removed), octagon-square (square with corners removed), and pear. Most of these shapes are also used in faceted stones, and some special shapes and cuts exist for faceting alone that are not used for cabochons. (See Faceted Stones in this chapter.) Numerous other special shapes are used for cabochon-type and flat-cut stones. Included among these are transparent stones which are combinations of cabochon and facet, such as edge-faceted and pavilion-faceted cabochons.

Cabochon cuts are variations on the convex curve. Starting from a straight, flat stone, any convex form that rises from it becomes a cabochon curve. Normally the stone bottom is flat and unpolished in the case of opaque stones because it is not seen, but translucent and transparent cabochons are also polished below. The upper form may rise directly from the flat back, or the under edge at the

13–41 SIGURD PERSSON, Sweden. Gold ring with very high cone-shaped cabochon of rutilated quartz, set in a closed bezel. *Photo: Sune Sundahl*

13–42 PATNA, BIHAR, INDIA. Five-strand (*panch lara*) silver necklace. Each of the 285 tear-shaped pendants is set with a hand-cut low cabochon glass unit backed by a piece of pure tin foil to give the glass reflective brilliance, and is set into the bezel with lac. As much care is given to the shaping of these glass "stones," common in Indian jewelry, as to genuine stones. *Photo: Oppi*

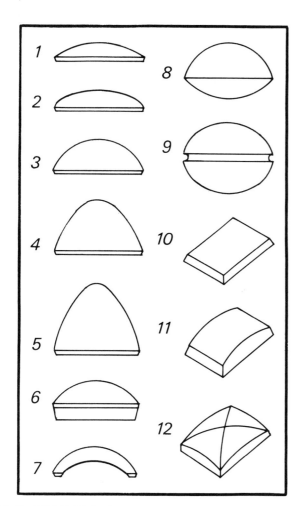

13–40 CABOCHON CUTS

1. Low
2. Medium, regular, or standard
3. High
4. Cone
5. Tallow dip
6. Doublet
7. Hollow
8. Double-bombé
9. Double-bombé, grooved
10. Flat cushion
11. Buff top
12. Bent top, cross faceted

perimeter or girdle can be *chamfered* to a 45° angle made during cutting to give the edge strength and help prevent possible chipping during setting when under pressure. Chamfering also sometimes helps to seat a stone on a bezel shoulder (see p. 600) where a fillet of solder forms between it and the outer bezel at their place of contact. Chamfering is not technically necessary to setting provided the shoulder of the bezel is free of all obstructions, such as surplus solder, or a mismated bezel joint.

Cabochon cuts in common use in order of increasing slope of curve are called *low, medium* or *regular, high, cone,* and *tallow tip*. A less common cut is *hollow* in which the undersurface is hollowed to a concave form and then polished. Hollowing is done to thin dark-colored transparent or translucent stones to reduce color density and make the stone appear lighter in color when light passes through it. The opposite of this is the *double cabochon* in which the lower surface is a convex cabochon, usually, but not always with a profile lower than that of the upper surface. This cut is used on light-colored transparent or translucent stones to increase color density by increasing stone thickness, and both sides are polished.

A variation of the above cut has a grooved edge or girdle made as a means of mounting the stone in a manner that allows it to be seen from both sides. This is used for both transparent and opaque stones, and normally both sides have the same form. A *cushion* or rectangularly shaped stone can be cut with one barrel vault curve, or with cross vault curves that intersect and form a diagonal cross making four triangular shapes that mount to a peak at the crown. Other variations on regular forms are also occasionally made, and cabochons with irregularly shaped cuts are made to avoid the loss of stone material. Special shapes can be ordered from most professional lapidaries.

SETTINGS USED FOR CABOCHON-CUT STONES

A *stone setting* is any system used in jewelry making that securely holds a stone permanently in place, and displays it to best advantage. Stones are used in metal jewelry because their color combines well with the color range of metals, and their ability to reflect light combines well with metal color and luster. They often are used to create a focal point or climax of interest in a design, and in most cases, the stones used have a hardness that makes them extremely durable in normal use.

Many systems of fabricating a setting for a cabochon-cut stone are used. Basic types are discussed here. The diagramed examples utilize a round shape, but the same systems can be used for any stone with a regularly curved shape, or one whose contour is irregular. Stones with sharply angled corners are also set in continuous bezels (see below), but in this case, while the bezel is still flat, its corners are filed to a V shape to permit the bending and meeting of the sides to a sharp angle at corners, avoiding the formation of bumps of surplus metal there. Interrupted mountings, or those which are not continuous, such as picket, prong, and divided bezels can also be used for straight-sided shapes.

THE BEZEL AND BEZEL TYPES

REGULAR OR PLAIN CURVED VERTICAL BEZELS *Bezel* is derived from the French *biseau,* "chamfered, sloping, or beveled edge." In its basic, regular, plain, and most common curved form, a bezel (or *collet,* as it is also called) is simply (at the start) a vertically upstanding strip of metal normally the same as the base to which it is joined, completely surrounding the stone at the girdle. Its height and the thickness of the metal used depend on the stone size, depth, and proportion to the rest of the design. Its lower edge is joined by soldering to the base, and is parallel to the stone base, if the metal base is *flat*. If the metal base is *domed,* the inner bottom bezel edge must be chamfered to match the dome slope angle to make a smooth joint. If the base is *curved* or *cylindrical,* as in a ring, the lower bezel edge must follow that curvature. In all cases, the *upper edge* remains *straight*. When a bezel is placed on a flat surface, the stone can rest or be *seated* directly on the flat base. In cases where the base is domed or curved, an *inner shoulder* must be soldered within the bezel to provide a seat for the stone, as described on p. 600.

Into this upstanding wall with its butt-joined seam, the stone, which must *exactly fit* the enclosed space, is placed and seated with its flat base perpendicular to the bezel wall. The top bezel edge is often filed thinner than the rest to facilitate its then being pressed over the *stone slope* with a tool to hold the stone in place, as described on p. 600. Final pressing is done with a *burnisher* in a rubbing motion—the reason that plain bezels are also called *rubover settings*. When the base is solid, no light passes through the setting from the base or below, in which case it is called a *closed setting*.

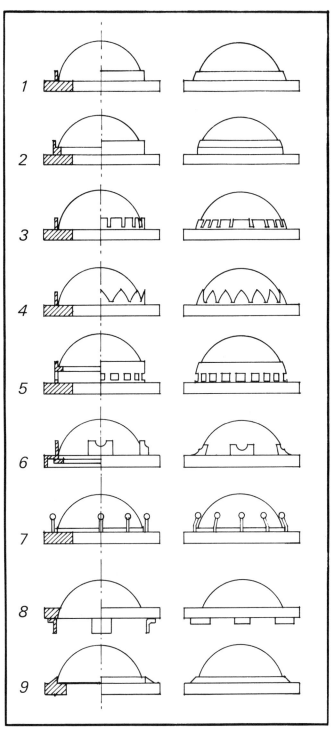

13–43 *SCHEMATIC REPRESENTATIONS OF MOUNTED CABOCHON-CUT STONES*

1. Regular or plain bezel
2. Shoulder or bearing bezel
3. Picket or segmented bezel
4. Prong bezel
5. Bezel mounted on gallery wire
6. Divided bezel
7. Wire and ball prong
8. Reverse flange mounting
9. Gypsy or paved mounting

13-44 RODNEY ROACH, U.S.A. "Timeless." Silver bracelet with low cabochon, rutilated quartz set on a shoulder bezel. The watch, as all circular forms, can be thought of as a *mandala*. A watch minus its face and mechanism may symbolically comment on the futility of an excessively time-patterned life. *Photo: Bob Carvill*

13-45 SAARA HOPEA-UNTRACHT, Finland, designer; manufacturer Kultasepänliike Ossian Hopea, Porvoo. Necklace of 18K gold with carnelian, smoky quartz, and eight matched banded agates which are cut from the same slab rough in parallel series. The stones are set on backward-tapered shoulder bezels. *Photo: Oppi*

13-46 *DETAIL OF THE NECKLACE BACK* showing the tapered shoulder bezels that minimize the metal seen around the stone at the front. *Photo: Oppi*

RIGHT ANGLE BEZELS   For stones that require *right angle bezels,* such as squares and rectangles, strip bezel wire up to 18 gauge B.&S. may be used. The simplest solution in the construction of a right angle bezel is to make it of two L-shaped parts, the short leg exactly the length of one side of the stone, and the long leg longer than its corresponding side. To bend each part squarely at a right angle, with a corner of a *square file,* file a V-shaped groove halfway into the metal at the exact angle position. With *pliers,* bend the strip to a 90° angle. Solder these parts at the bent corner to strengthen them. Place the two parts against the stone. The two long legs will extend in opposite directions beyond the square or rectangular stone shape. Mark the point where the surplus extension starts on the outside, remove the parts, and use these marks to reposition the bezel on a soldering surface, then solder the parts together. Saw away the surplus leg extensions. Test the bezel around the stone, and if it is slightly small, file away some metal from its inner surface. Solder the bezel in place on the work. When setting the stone, if its slope is steep, it may be necessary to thin the top bezel edge from the outside, or to file away some metal from each corner to permit the bezel to be forced down flush on the stone without forming corner bulges.

SHOULDER BEZEL   A *shoulder bezel* contains an inner, close-fitting additional *collet* or *bearing,* upon which the stone base rests. When the bearing is made of flat strip, its height is less than that of the outer bezel, and it is lap joined to it with solder. A shoulder can also be made of round wire soldered in place at the correct height. *Extruded shoulder bezel wire* is manufactured with a step profile and is also used for this purpose, thereby eliminating the need to make and solder in a separate shoulder collet. When fabricating bearing bezels from flat strip, after the two touching parts are assembled and soldered, the inner edge forming the shoulder must be free of all obstructions such as corner fillets that may rise above the shoulder edge or plane, because this would prevent the stone's base from resting, as it must, *squarely upon the shoulder.* The stone must enter the bezel *without friction.* If more than a necessary amount of solder is used when joining a collet in place, a solder fillet may form at the upper edge on the join between the outer bezel wall and the shoulder due to capillary attraction. This fillet reduces the actual bezel diameter and the stone will no longer fit in the bezel. Unless the stone has been chamfered at its base, any such fillet must be removed with a *graver* or a *pointed abrasive bur.* Once the stone is seated squarely on the shoulder, the thinned upper bezel edge is pressed over the stone slope in the normal way, as described below.

Reasons for using a shoulder bezel on domed or curved bases have been mentioned. Another function of a shoulder used with a flat-based bezel is to raise the stone higher from the base than when the stone rests directly on the base metal plane. Shoulder bezels are also used where only an *open space* exists below the stone, thus providing a place for the stone to rest.

PICKET OR SEGMENTED BEZEL   A *picket bezel* is so called because it resembles a fence made of a series of slats placed next to each other to form an enclosure. A series of equally spaced straight cuts are made perpendicularly into the upper edge of the bezel metal with a *fine-toothed saw blade,* to at least half the bezel width, remaining joined at a common base. A small hole can be drilled beforehand at the lowest point of each cut, and the cut made to meet it. The stone is placed in this enclosure, and the pickets are pressed over it with a flat-faced tool such as a *bezel setter*. When the picket bezel has a shoulder, the picket segments are cut just to that point.

PRONG BEZEL The word *prong* is derived from Middle English *pranglen,* "to press or pinch," which is what occurs when prongs hold a cabochon or faceted stone. A *prong bezel* can be made of one metal strip cut into a series of triangular, flat, joined prong forms, normally equidistantly apart. Prongs can also be cut from the base metal itself and raised up to form the stone opening, the stone resting on a separate inner shoulder. In a variation of the latter type that eliminates the need for a shoulder, each vertical prong alternates with one left horizontal to support the stone from below. Prongs made of round, half-round, triangular, or rectangular wire can be soldered to the *outside* of a vertical or conical sheet metal bezel which then acts as a shoulder below the stone and is not seen from above in the finished setting. (The manner of holding the prongs in an upright position for soldering, and the manner of setting a stone in prongs is described under Prong and Claw Setting, p. 622.)

GALLERY BEZEL WIRE *Open gallery wire,* commercially available or hand pierced, is used in setting cabochon or faceted stones to permit the admission of light from the setting sides when the stone is transparent or translucent to increase its brilliance. The stone can be mounted with a cylindrical or conical base. The pattern of the open portions of the wire provides ornamentation and gives the form dimension. Some gallery wire is made with upper, separated, pronglike projections in series which are used to hold the stone. In any case, the gallery wire itself must be provided with an inner bearing for the stone, fabricated and soldered inside the already joined form to support the stone, unless one is already a part of the wire when purchased. It is also possible to mount a bezel on the top edge of gallery wire which supports it while prongs attached outside hold it.

DIVIDED BEZEL In a *divided bezel,* a series of relatively widely spaced projections are either formed from an opening in the base and bent upward, or separate units are fabricated and soldered to project from the base. The stone rests in this case on a flat ring soldered beneath the base, and the projections are bent down over it.

13–47 FRIEDRICH BECKER, West Germany. Gold ring, 18K, with flat-topped, barrel-shaped tourmaline set in a divided bezel. *Photo: Friedrich Becker*

BALL AND WIRE PRONG WITH BEZEL Wire with fused end balls used as claws can be soldered to the outside of a low, plain bezel and are made to stand upright by first vertically drilling holes that match the wire gauge used, in-

serting the wire prongs into each hole with the ball upright, then soldering them in place. After placing the stone in position, the ball prongs are pushed over it.

REVERSE BEZEL FLUSH MOUNTING To mount a flat-based cabochon-cut stone, or a flat-topped stone with a flat base *flush with the metal surface* or rising directly from it without the transition of a bezel, the bezel can instead be soldered to the *reverse* or *undersurface* of the base. Instead of a full bezel, tabs could be used, spaced at the primary and intermediate cardinal points. In this case, the upper surface opening must be made sufficiently *smaller* than the stone girdle to prevent its passing through; it acts as a shoulder in reverse. Usually its inner edge is filed with an *inward-sloping chamfer* at an angle that matches the slope of the cabochon face. The stone is placed face upward from the reverse side into the bezel, and the bezel (or tab) is forced down over its base and burnished flat to the stone base.

GYPSY MOUNTING The gypsy mounting, used for both cabochon and faceted stones of round, oval, square, or rectangular shape, resembles the reverse flush mounting, but is accomplished in the opposite way. A hole whose diameter is smaller than the stone girdle is drilled into the thickened upper portion of the base which usually is a casting, but thickening can be also accomplished by fabrication. To create a seat for the stone, a shoulder is carved from the upper surface into this opening leaving a raised burr, bent outward all around it. The stone is seated on the shoulder, and the burr is forced over its girdle with bezel-setting tools. In the result, the base metal smoothly meets the stone which projects above the setting. Faceted stones when used with the gypsy setting are sunk into the setting with their table almost flush with the metal surface. A minimum of the girdle is covered by the burr flange so as not to appreciably reduce stone diameter visible size.

13–48 PETER SKUBIC, Austria. Ring in 14K white gold with an octagonal rectangle emerald of 3.90ct set in a bezel, and eleven brilliants totaling 12ct set in gypsy type settings. *Photo: Peter Skubic*

MAKING A PLAIN VERTICAL CURVED BEZEL AND SETTING A CABOCHON IN IT

Bezel wire in the form of a flat strip of fine silver—which takes a higher temperature than sterling, and whose softness allows it to be more easily compressed over the stone—is available in several widths, and in plain or ornamented forms. Lacking this, a straight, even strip of 24–28 gauge B.&S. metal can be cut from sheet for silver, or 26–30 gauge B.&S. for gold.

The bezel *width* depends on the stone size and slope

angle. Proportionately wider bezels are used on larger stones, or those whose slope is more vertical in order to extend the gripping surface on the stone. Aside from practical considerations such as these, the selection of bezel width is also a matter of personal preference, judgment of proportion of bezel width to stone size and shape, and appropriateness in design, as well as visual weight. Generally speaking, however, use a width no wider than seems necessary, and do not conceal too much of the stone with the folded-over portion of the bezel.

The *length* of a bezel strip for a circular stone, for example, can be calculated by the use of a formula for determining the circumference of a circle, which is: diameter times π ($\pi = 3.1415$). This amount can be marked on a straight bezel strip, plus a little extra for filing the ends true. The bezel strip is cut through with a jeweler's saw if the strip is heavy gauge, or with *straight-bladed shears* or *snips* if thin.

A simple way to determine bezel length for all regular shapes *without calculations* is to hold the stone, face upward, on a flat surface (assuming the back is flat), and wrapping the bezel strip around the stone *at the girdle* making sure the bottom bezel edge contacts the surface squarely. Fine silver bezel wire is soft which makes bending into such a small radius (and later contraction) easier. If sterling silver or other silver alloy is used, or a low-karat gold which tends to be stiff, these will probably have to be annealed first to decrease their spring resistance to bending. While holding the strip tightly around the stone girdle, with a *scriber*, mark the point where the strip overlaps its starting end. Straighten the strip, allow a little extra for squaring the ends true to make a well-fitting joint, then cut the strip. File both ends squarely up to the mark, or *slightly less than the mark*, for reasons described below.

Another method of determining bezel length is to surround the stone girdle with a length of a soft, 24 gauge B.&S. *iron binding wire,* and twist the ends until the loop that forms fits tightly up against the girdle. Then cut the loop, allowing the twisted portion to remain intact, spread it into one straight line, measure that distance, transfer this to the bezel strip, and cut it.

Soldering a bezel closed begins by bending the bezel strip into a circular shape, either with the fingers alone, or by forcing it around the stone or a *ring mandrel* or *bezel mandrel,* or by using *round-nosed pliers.* Adjust the shape until the ends meet squarely and completely—which should be the case if they have been filed square. At this point, if measurements have been accurately taken, the bezel shape for regular curve-shaped stones need not be exactly the same as the stone for which it is being prepared. Final shaping can take place *after* soldering the joint. Straight-sided and irregularly shaped bezels must, however, be made and maintained in their correct shape during the entire bezel-making and end-joining processes.

Press the ends slightly past each other to give the bezel "spring," then return them to a butting position which normally they will hold due to metal spring tension. Binding wire can be used for this purpose if necessary, but in this case, avoid overtightening the wire by overtwisting its ends together as this may cause the bezel to collapse. Flux the clean joint and place it, joint down, on the soldering surface. With a borax-loaded *soldering brush,* place a snippet of hard solder *inside* the joint, and solder it closed with a *small torch tip* taking care to withdraw the flame as soon as the solder flows and not to overheat and melt the

bezel. Pickle the bezel, but if you have used iron binding wire, be sure to remove it *before* pickling.

To shape the bezel to the correct form and *to size* it, place it over the stone and press it down to the girdle. If the bezel is being prepared for an oval stone, the seam should be at one side, not at the small end. Do not be alarmed if the bezel now seems to be slightly too small for the stone.

To enlarge a round bezel, place it on a *round bezel mandrel* (oval, square, and hexagonal bezel mandrels are also made for those shapes), and while turning it, lightly tap it while turning it only a few times on the outside using a *small flat-faced planishing hammer.* Do not attempt to increase its size too much in one operation; after only a few taps, return the bezel to the stone to test its size. Repeat the process until the size is *snug but not tight.* Slight differences in size can be adjusted simply by filing the inside bezel surface with a *half-round fine-cut needle file* or *rattail file.* It is far easier to slightly *increase* the size of a bezel than to decrease it, which is the reason, mentioned before, for making the bezel length slightly undersized. If the bezel is too large, there is no recourse but to saw it apart at the soldered joint, scrape away the solder, take away the surplus from that position, then resolder it —which is probably more time-consuming than simply starting from the beginning and making a new bezel.

To square the upper and lower bezel edges and make them parallel, alternately rub them on an *absolutely flat* piece of *abrasive paper* of about 300 grit. If the bezel is of a size and thickness that can take handling at this point without losing its shape, file the outer side of the upper edge with a *fine-cut flat needle file* to thin it, in order to simplify its compression later on to the stone slope. Do not thin the edge to razor fineness as this will only make a weak bezel with low holding power. If the bezel is too fragile at this point, thinning can take place after it is soldered to the base. At that same time file marks can be smoothed away with a fine *cloth* or *paper abrasive* or *crocus paper.*

To solder the bezel to the base, after a final test for fit with the stone, place it in position with or without a soldering jig to hold it in place, depending on circumstances, and flux the joint. Place only enough small hard solder snippets of the same or next lower melting hardness, at intervals *inside* the bezel area at its point of contact with the base. Heat the piece *from below,* and do not direct a flame onto the bezel, which may melt because of its thinness. This soldering operation can take place at the same time as others that must be done with the same solder hardness so that all solder flows at the same time. Surplus solder inside the bezel base, if any, must be removed, and this can be done with a *hollow scraper,* or an *abrasive bur* mounted on a *flex-shaft.*

Setting a cabochon stone in a bezel in a piece of jewelry is a final process, executed *after* fabrication, finishing, and coloring have been completed. The success of setting a cabochon stone depends first of all on the accuracy of the bezel size and shape, then on a methodical and careful carrying out of the remaining techniques.

When preparing a bezel to receive a stone, it may be necessary when testing its seat to place and remove the stone in the bezel several times. To make placement and removal easier, a wad of *sticky wax* designed for this function can be used, alone or at the end of a stick. By pressing the wax to the upper stone surface, it can be lifted away, provided the bezel is not overly tight. In that case, access to a stone stuck in a bezel should be attainable from below by means of at least a small hole made at the center of the base inside the bezel area. Through this, a *pointed tool end* or a *wire end* can penetrate to prod the stone and unseat it. It is common practice to make a setting with a hole at the base, especially when transparent or translucent stones are used, in order to admit light. Another reason is that completely closed settings in silver tend to darken in time due to oxidation, and this affects the appearance of such stones. For this reason, in old jewelry, to avoid such darkening below a closed-set transparent stone, and to give the stone brilliance, a piece of pure tin, silver, or gold foil, either of these possibly also colored to influence stone color, was placed beneath the stone. In closed settings these metals resist oxidation even after long periods of time. (See Foiled Stones in Closed Settings, p. 614.)

BEZEL SETTING TOOLS

Bezel setting tools that can be used to set cabochon stones include: a *setting tool;* a *bezel pusher;* a *bezel rocker;* an *automatic hammer;* and a *burnisher.* A *setting tool* has no handle and resembles a straight steel punch, rectangular in section, tapered to a flat, rectangular working face ⅛ in × ³⁄₁₆ in (3.17 mm × 4.76 mm); or smaller. A *bezel pusher* is a square steel or brass shaft 3⅓ in (8.9 cm) long, with a highly polished working face ⅛ in (3.17 mm) or ³⁄₁₆ in (4.76 mm) square; the opposite or tang end anchored in a round wooden handle similar to an engraver's handle, designed for comfort in gripping. A *bezel rocker* is made of steel or brass, and also has a tang set in a round wooden handle, and its working end flares out to a semicircular form about ½ in (12.7 mm) wide, with a curved face ³⁄₁₆ in (4.76 mm) wide. *Automatic hammers* are described under Rivets and Riveting (see Illustration 10–55). *Burnishers* are described under Metal Finishing (see Illustration 14–4), and under Engraving (see Illustration 8–25). The use of these tools for stone setting is described below.

When an object such as a ring is being set with a stone, its shank is gripped in the upper, leather-lined jaws of a *ring clamp* with the portion including the stone setting protruding upward. These jaws are held closed by forcing a *wedge* between the lower jaws of the clamp which is then held in the left hand braced against a worktable edge, or in the V-slot of a *V-board.* A *shellac stick, engraver's block,* or a *ring mandrel* can also be used to hold the work, depending on its form. Other work can be placed on a piece of wet leather on which it will not slip. It is especially important that the stone be resting squarely on the base or the shoulder that supports it because the pressure that will be exerted on the bezel and then transmitted to the stone is equalized and distributed evenly around the stone perimeter. The chance of the stone cracking during the contraction of the bezel over its slope is then considerably diminished.

BEZEL SETTING A CABOCHON STONE

USING A SETTING TOOL This tool is especially suited to use on bezels thicker than 20 gauge B.&S. On thick bezels, the upper edge is usually filed thinner than the rest from the outside to make it easier to force down. Force the bezel onto the cabochon stone's slope by holding

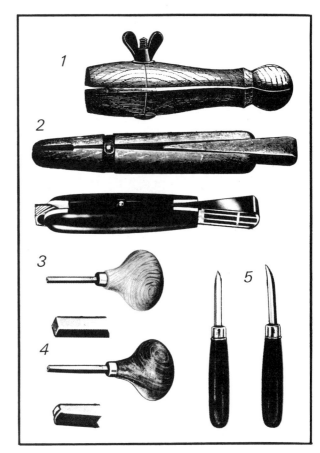

13–49 *CABOCHON STONE-SETTING TOOLS*
1. *Ring clamp* in two parts with leather-lined jaws which are tightened on the ring shank by a butterfly nut.
2. *Ring clamps,* used to hold a ring during work and stone setting. Leather-lined jaws firmly grip the ring shank once the wedge is forced between the two parts at the opposite end. *Top:* wood model; *bottom:* Dupont nylon plastic model with leather-lined jaws, and nylon wedge.
3. *Bezel pusher,* square-ended steel shank, used to force a bezel over a stone slope, mounted in wooden handle, total 3½ in long.
4. *Prong pusher,* groove-ended steel shank, used to force prongs or crown points over a stone girdle, total 3½ in long.
5. *Burnishers,* steel, oval section, highly polished blades, used to smooth bezels over stone slopes after the bezel pusher has forced it down. Also used in surface finishing to compress and brighten metal. *Left:* straight blade; *right:* curved blade; available in blade lengths 1½, 2, 2½, and 3 in long.

it at an angle against the bezel base. With a *chasing hammer, lightly* strike the tool's end, and gradually force the bezel down. Work the tool by raising its angle to the bezel till it almost reaches the bezel edge. Work *slowly,* and avoid too great an impact on the tool, or the stone may crack. To fix the stone on its seat so that it no longer moves, repeat the same at the opposite side, and at cardinal points, then work the rest down between these positions.

USING A BEZEL PUSHER Because the force when using this tool comes from hand power, it works best on bezels thinner than 20 gauge B.&S. Hold it in the right hand with the handle cradled in the palm, the thumb and forefinger holding the shaft. Bring the tool to the bezel base with its vertical face toward the bezel. In an upward-turning motion, roll the bezel over onto the stone slope. Repeat this at the position opposite then, as described above. Do not rush the process or allow the pusher to slip as it can fatally scratch the stone face.

USING A BEZEL ROCKER   This tool works best on thinner-gauge bezels. Hold the tool in the same way as the bezel pusher. Place one edge against the bezel base, and rock the tool back and forth in a sideways motion against the bezel. Gradually raise its position till the bezel is forced against the stone. Repeat as above from cardinal points, then the rest.

USING AN AUTOMATIC HAMMER   This miniature power hammer is a handpiece attached to a *flex-shaft*. Because the anvil heads are detachable and changeable to several sizes and weights, this tool can be used on bezels of all weights. The stroke on a typical model is ³⁄₃₂ in (2.38 mm), and its length is adjustable by turning a knurled wheel. Speeds can be regulated up to 5000 rpm. Hold the hammer at an angle against the bezel, and force it down on the stone as above.

USING A BURNISHER   In the next step, dip a *burnisher* in soapy water, and systematically rub it over the entire bezel to smooth the surface and compress it fully to the stone slope. Normally this action will remove any irregularities in the bezel surface and leave it bright.

Should the bezel edge become uneven, it can be trimmed by careful use of a *pointed engraver*. Now give the bezel its final polish by rubbing it with a *cloth* to which some *rouge* has been applied. Wash the stone and its setting with detergent and warm water, using a *brush* if necessary.

FACETED STONES

Stones with *facets* (French, "little faces") have surfaces that are cut into a systematic arrangement of intersecting, flat planes, normally made in relation to the crystal structure of the particular stone. Generally speaking, it is usual for transparent stones with a high refractive index to be cut into facets, but opaque stones at times are also faceted on their upper surfaces to catch and reflect the light. The prime function of facets on a stone is to exploit its optical properties in order to increase its appearance of brilliance, dispersion or fire, and to heighten any existing color. This occurs when entering interior light is multiplied as it is refracted and reflected from inside cut plane to plane, and then is dispersed outward toward the viewer.

13–50 PAULA HÄIVÄOJA, Finland, designer; manufacturer Kalevala Koru, Helsinki. Gold brooch with brilliant-cut smoky quartz stones set in tube settings with inner bearings. *Photo: Studio Wendt, courtesy Kalevala Koru*

FACETED STONE SHAPES

The *shape* of a faceted stone refers to the configuration of the *girdle*, the stone's largest perimeter or section which outlines the plane that divides the front of the stone from the back, or the top from the bottom. It is seen in its true configuration from the plan view of the stone.

The *cut* of a faceted stone is the specific, systematic arrangement of flat planes ground into the stone's surface. Specific ideal relationships of facet angles have been found empirically and scientifically to achieve the greatest refractive dispersion.

PRINCIPAL GIRDLE SHAPES

The principal girdle shapes are round, oval, square, antique, rectangle (pillow), and hexagon. The term *long*, as in *long hexagon*, means the shape is extended on opposite sides. Other shapes are included below.

Principal and special girdle shapes can be grouped according to basic configurations: *curved shapes; three- and four-sided shapes; six- and eight-sided shapes;* and *miscellaneous* or *fancy shapes.*

CURVED SHAPES
Round and oval: These are the principal curved shapes.
Antique square: A curve-sided square shape with rounded corners, also called a cushion or pillow shape.
Antique rectangle: A curve-sided rectangle with rounded corners, also called a cushion or pillow shape.
Pear; pendaloque; pippin: A *pear*-shaped stone has a symmetrically curved shape larger at the bottom and narrowing toward the top, reminiscent of a pear. The shape is also called *pendaloque* (French, "pendant"), indicating one of its common uses. *Pippin* means "seed," which the shape resembles.
Navette; marquise: These synonymous terms refer to a symmetrically curve-sided, elliptical boat shape with equally shaped points at both ends. *Navette* in French means "incense box," and *marquise*, is a title of nobility. Normally it is brilliant cut with 58 facets.

THREE- AND FOUR-SIDED SHAPES
Triangle: A figure that has three touching lines with three points or interior angles. *Equilateral triangles* contain three equal angles; an *isosceles triangle* has two equal sides; a *right-angled triangle* has one right angle; an *obtuse triangle* has one obtuse and two acute angles; a *curvilinear triangle* has curved sides; a *scalene triangle* has no equal sides. Stones in these shapes are generally small, cut in step or French cuts, and in traditional settings are often used as accessories to larger stones.
Square: A shape with four equal sides, and interior right angles. They are cut in French, cross, step, and other cuts.
Rectangle (cushion or pillow):   A four-sided figure with two short and two long parallel sides and interior right angles. They are cut in almost any style.
Baguette: French for "rod, wand, or stick," which describes these narrow, rectangular, small stones, usually made from cleavage fragments of a larger stone. In traditional settings they are step cut, used as accessories to larger stones, and often are set in channel settings.
Trapeze: A trapezoidal, four-sided figure with two short, opposite, parallel sides, and two long, opposite sides that taper equally toward each other; sometimes called a *keystone* shape.

13–51 STONE GIRDLE SHAPES
Curved shapes:
1. Round
2. Oval
3. Antique square (cushion or pillow)
4. Antique rectangle (cushion or pillow)
5. Pear
6. Navette or marquise.
Three- and four-sided shapes:
7. Triangle
8. Square
9. Rectangle
10. Baguette
11. Trapeze
12. Spear
Six- and eight-sided shapes:
13. Hexagon
14. Long hexagon
15. Octagon
16. Long octagon
Miscellaneous:
17. Barrel

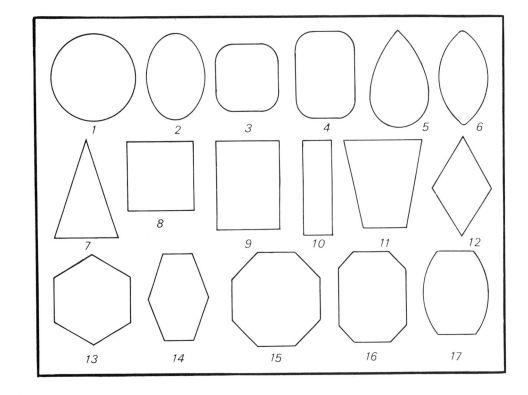

Spear: A rhombus or lozenge-shaped four-sided figure having four equal, straight sides bounding two matching acute and obtuse angles. It is commonly called a *diamond* shape in playing cards.

SIX- AND EIGHT-SIDED SHAPES

Hexagon: A six-angled polygon with six sides, all of which are equal in a *regular hexagon*. In stones, this shape is called a *hexagon round* when its outline fits into a circle, and a *hexagon oval* when its shape fits an oval shape.

Long hexagon: A hexagon with two opposite long sides, or four long, and two short sides.

Octagon: A polygon with eight equal sides and angles. A *long octagon* or an *octagon-rectangle* (a rectangle with corners removed) has two parallel long sides and is associated with the emerald cut.

MISCELLANEOUS OR FANCY GIRDLE SHAPES

These are shapes that do not fit into any of the above categories, and are used with less frequency. Among them are the *barrel* which has two short, straight sides, and two long, curved sides; the *heart* which can be either a faceted heart shape or a cabochon heart shape; the *kite* which is a four-, five-, or six-sided polygon; the *prism* which is a form whose faces form parallelograms that are parallel to the vertical axis and whose base can be triangular, quadrangular, rhombic, etc.; *irregular polyhedron,* or a figure formed of many unequal sides, usually more than six; *shield* which has a flat top and two curving, intersecting sides; *half-round* or a half-circle; and others.

FACETED STONE TERMINOLOGY

Because among the gemstones used in jewelry the diamond is very high in refractive dispersion, the basic facet

Stone Girdle Shape Names in Various Languages

Shapes English	Formes French	Formas Spanish	Formas Italian	Formen German
Round	Rond	Redondo	Rotondo	Rund
Oval	Ovale	Ovalado	Ovale	Oval
Antique-square	Antique-carré	Antiguo-cuadrado	Antico-quadrato	Antik-quadratisch
Antique-rectangle	Antique-rectangulaire	Antiguo-rectangular	Antico-rettangolare	Antik-rechteck
Pear	Piriforme	Pera	Pera	Birnenform
Navette	Navette or Marquise	Naveta	Navetta	Navette
Triangle	Triangle	Triángulo	Triagolo	Dreieckig
Square	Carré	Cuadrado	Quadrato	Quadrat
Rectangle-cushion	Rectangulaire-coussin	Rectangular-cojin	Rettangolare-cuscino	Rechteck-kissen
Baguette	Baguette	Varita	Bacchetta	Baguette
Trapeze	Trapèze	Trapeza	Trapezio	Trapez-förmig
Spear	Lancéolé	Lanza	Lancia	Lanzen-förmig
Hexagon	Hexagone	Hexágono	Esagono	Sechseckig
Long hexagon	Hexagone-long	Hexágono-largo	Esagono-lungo	Gelängtes-sechseck
Octagon	Octagone	Octagona	Ottagono	Achteckig
Long octagon	Octagone-long	Octagona-largo	Ottagono-lungo	Gelängtes-achteck
Barrel	Tonneau	Barril	Barile	Tonne

cuts used on stones in general have developed mainly for application to this paragon of gems. The same cuts or modifications of them and the terms used to describe them are also employed in reference to other precious and semi-precious stones. A *brilliant-cut diamond* is used here as an example.

The parts of a *round brilliant* can first of all be divided into two main sections, each separated from the other by the *girdle* which in plan view is the perimeter or contour

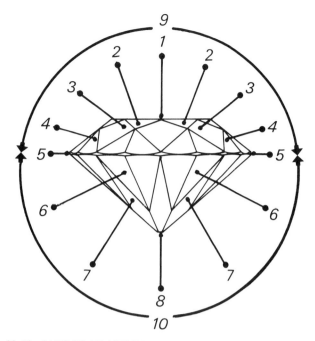

13–52 PARTS OF AN AMERICAN BRILLIANT-CUT DIAMOND

Crown:
1. Table
2. Star facet
3. Bezel facet, crown main facet
4. Crown girdle facet
5. Girdle

Pavilion:
6. Pavilion girdle facet
7. Pavilion main facet
8. Culet

Entire form:
9. Crown
10. Pavilion

that constitutes its round shape. The part above the girdle which is the front or top of the stone is called the *crown*. The part which slopes downward away from the girdle, or the back or bottom of the stone is the *pavilion*.

The *crown* starts at the uppermost plane with the octagonal-shaped *table* which is parallel with the girdle. Sloping away from the table are 8 triangular *star facets* whose bases rest against the table and whose apexes point away from it. The remaining 8 larger quadrilateral facets that touch both the table and the girdle edge are the *crown main facets* or *bezel facets*. The other 16 triangular facets whose bases rest on the girdle are called the *upper girdle, cross,* or *skill facets*. Altogether, in a brilliant-cut diamond, these crown facets total 33 in number, including the table.

In the *pavilion*, the facets slope beneath the girdle to a bottom point or *culet* (from French *cul*, "bottom"), cut off in a small plane parallel with the girdle on large stones to prevent splintering when polishing and when the gem is worn. Because the setting often offers sufficient protection, culets are not used in some large stones, and they are not used in most small stones. In a rectangular stone, the culet is a thin, flat ridge. The culet is seen in plan view of a round stone exactly at the center of the table, or in a rectangular stone as a line at the longitudinal center of the table. From the culet, the 8 four-sided, long or *main pavilion facets* slope upward to the girdle, touching both girdle and the culet. Between them at the girdle are 16 *lower girdle facets* that correspond with the 16 *upper girdle facets*. These extend to midway between the girdle and the culet in the traditional brilliant, but more recently, to two-thirds the distance. The total facets in the pavilion number 25, including the flattened culet. On a brilliant-cut diamond, there are therefore a grand total of 58 *facets* whose corners meet at points.

To achieve maximum brilliance, by one set of propor-

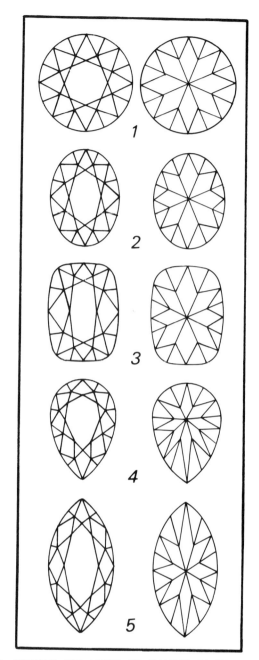

13–53 BRILLIANT CUT APPLIED TO VARIOUS FORMS, crown and pavilion view, all 33/25
1. Round; 2. Oval; 3. Pillow or antique; 4. Pear; 5. Navette or marquise.

tions, the ideal crown angle between the bezel facets and the girdle plane is about 35°, and that between the pavilion facets and the girdle plane are about 41°. The height of the crown mass constitutes 14.6% of the total, the depth of the pavilion 43.1%, and the table diameter is 57.5% of the diameter of the girdle. Other proportions also exist which vary slightly in amounts.

THE PRINCIPAL CUTS OF FACETED STONES

Faceted stone cuts can be grouped into two main categories: those used predominantly on straight-sided *preforms* (the basic stone shape before faceting) whose girdle shapes can be a square, rectangle, octagon, or triangle;

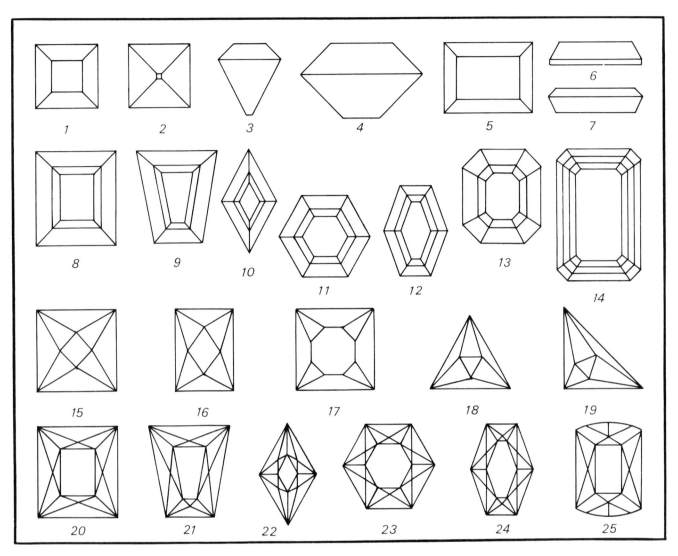

13–54 *STONE CUTS*
Table cuts:
1. Table cut, crown, octahedron diamond crystal, 5/5
2. Table cut, pavilion, with culet
3. Table cut, side view
4. Table cut, side view, another proportion
5. Table cut, rectangle, 5/1
6. Table cut, rectangle, crown bevel
7. Table cut, rectangle, crown and pavilion bevel, 5/5

Step cuts:
Four-sided girdles
8. Step cut, rectangle, 9/9
9. Step cut, trapeze
10. Step cut, spear or lozenge
Six-sided girdles
11. Step cut, hexagon, round
12. Step cut, long hexagon, oval

Eight-sided girdles
13. Step cut, octagon, emerald cut, two crown steps, 17/33
14. Step cut, long emerald cut, three crown steps, 25/25

French cuts:
15. French cut, square with square table
16. French cut, rectangle with lozenge table
17. French cut, square, with octagonal table
18. French cut, equilateral triangle, with equilateral triangle table
19. French cut, right angle, with isosceles triangle table

Crosscuts:
20. Crosscut, rectangle
21. Crosscut, trapeze
22. Crosscut, lozenge
23. Crosscut, hexagon
24. Crosscut, long hexagon
25. Crosscut, pillow

and those used on conical preforms whose girdles have round or curved shapes.

CUTS USED ON STRAIGHT-SIDED PREFORMS

TABLE CUT; FLAT-TOP CUT The *table cut* is one of the oldest stone cuts and originated in the old practice of grinding or cutting off the top and bottom tips of the natural octahedron crystal form in which the diamond is found. From this developed all other faceted cuts used on transparent stones. In its simplest form, called *single bevel*, the upper surface or crown has a flat table surrounded by a single beveled edge, and the back is lapped flat. In another form called the *double bevel*, the crown and the pavilion are both beveled. Additional bevels may be placed on the pavilion. In today's table-cut stones, used especially for small, square, transparent stones, but also on larger stones, the pavilion may be cut to a point, and when rectangular, to a ridge, both of which may be cut off to form a culet plane parallel with the girdle. Table cut is also widely used on translucent and opaque stones, and for stones intended for use as intaglios because the large, flat surface provides a suitable area for engraving.

STEP CUT   The *step cut* is among the oldest cuts and is still very popular today. Because of its relative simplicity it has a modern appearance. It developed from the table cut by increasing the number of front and back facets. It is used mainly on square, rectangular, and other straight-sided stones, and sometimes also on the pavilion of stones whose crown may be cut differently. In the step cut, a series of rectangular facets on the crown proceed in rows or steps on the outward-curving preform from the large table which has the same shape as the stone's girdle, to the girdle, and also from the girdle on the pavilion to the culet. In long shapes, the culet is a ridge that resembles an inverted tent ridge. In its developed form, the step cut has at least 50 facets or more. It is commonly used on diamonds and light-colored stones.

Baguette-shaped diamonds are usually step cut. *Caliber stones* are step-cut diamonds or other precious stones in various geometric shapes, smaller than 6 mm (0.24 in), and calibrated in 1 mm (0.04 in) sizes so they can be matched.

Emerald cut is a form of step cut on a long octagon shape with both sides stepped. It is so called because it is commonly used for emeralds, though it is also used on other transparent stones, and sometimes on the crown of opaque stones.

FRENCH CUT   The *French cut* is used on small stones with square, rectangular, and triangular girdles. From a table with a small square or triangular shape, two sets of triangular-shaped facets are made. One series has a common base with one side of the table and their apexes extend to a corner of the girdle, and the other set has a base at the girdle and an apex meeting a corner of the table. The pavilion is step faceted in two or three rows. In conventional settings, these are often used as accessories to a larger stone, or used in massed arrangements.

CROSS CUT; STAR CUT   This popular modification of the step cut is used on rectangular, long octagon, and other shaped stones. Using the rectangle shape as an example, this cut has a large, four-sided table parallel to the girdle shape (in other shapes the table repeats the girdle shape to which it is parallel), and the steps are divided into triangular cuts that radiate from the table, crossing each other at oblique angles, meeting at corners. There may be two, three, or more rows or series of facets on the crown between the girdle and the table. This cut is commonly used on colored stones.

CUTS USED ON ROUND AND CURVED PREFORMS

ROSE CUT   The *rose cut* developed during the 16th century for use with round diamonds. The back is lapped flat, and the crown preform, which follows a dome shape, has a height usually equal to half the girdle diameter, and is cut into three series of triangular facets. Two of these are placed around the girdle, and a third at the center consists of 6 facets that form a shallow, hexagonal, pointed apex, so there is no table. Altogether there are 24 crown facets, though on small stones modified rose cuts have 18 or less. The rose cut is now used rarely, mainly for small diamonds that are made of flat cleavage fragments from larger stones. It is still used for garnets, and for pyrites which when cut to this form are called *marcasites*. Some-

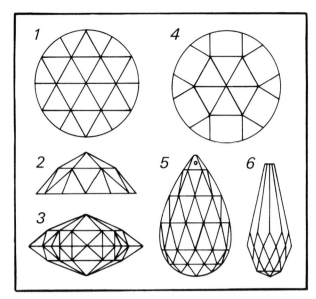

13–55 ROSE CUTS
1. Rose cut, crown view, 24 facets
2. Rose cut, side view, flat bottom
3. Rose cut, double, 24/24
4. Modified rose cut, 18 facets
5. Briolette
6. Drop

times two rose-cut stones of the same diameter are placed back to back. A single stone cut to a rose form on both sides is called a *double rose,* and its crown and pavilion have the same symmetrical shape. This shape is used as a pendant. Other cuts such as the briolette and drop, described on p. 609, are related to the rose cut.

THE SINGLE CUT   Round and curved preforms are cut with the brilliant cut, cuts from which it derived, or cuts that developed from it. The origin of the brilliant cut is the circular form *single cut,* now only used on small diamonds that weigh less than 0.03ct. It has a crown with a central octagonal table from which a single series of facets radiate to the girdle, making a total of 8 facets. The pavilion has a single series of 8 triangular-shaped facets that correspond with those at the crown girdle, and taper to a pointed culet. Though called an 8/8 cut, the total facet number is 17, including the table.

THE STAR CUT; OLD ENGLISH DOUBLE CUT   The *star cut* has a pentagonal, hexagonal, or octagonal table, each of whose sides are the base of a triangular-shaped facet whose apex extends to the girdle, together forming a five-, six-, or eight-pointed star. Between each of these are triangular-shaped facets whose bases form the girdle. The crown of a star with a pentagonal table has 11 facets, a hexagon 13 facets, and an octagon 17 facets. The pavilion has two rows of facets: those touching the girdle are broad triangles, and those meeting at the culet are rhombus shaped. The pavilion of a star with a pentagonal table has 10 facets, that with a hexagonal table 12 facets, and that with an octagonal table 16 facets—so these stones have a total of 21, 25, and 33 facets respectively. This cut is used on round, elliptical, and cushion-shaped stones.

The *double cut* is a modification of the single cut and has an additional 16 triangular-shaped facets around the crown and pavilion sides of the girdle, thus increasing the stone's dispersion.

IDEAL BRILLIANT CUT; FULL CUT   The *ideal brilliant cut* exhibits the fire of diamonds to great advantage, and is a

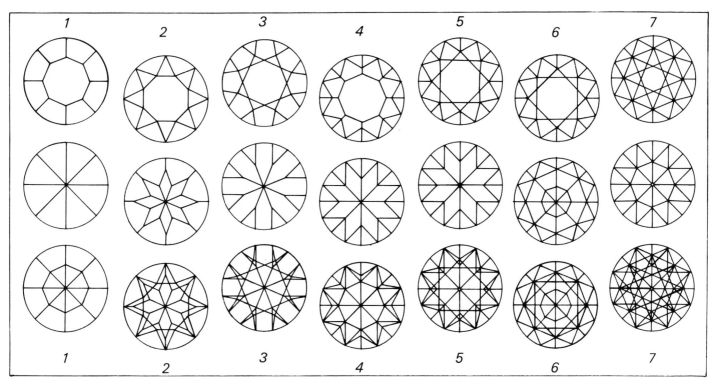

13–56 DIAMOND CUTS
Top row: crown cuts; center row: pavilion cuts; bottom row: combination of crown and pavilion cuts on the same stone.
From top to bottom:
1. Single cut 8/8; 2. Old English double or star cut, 16/16; 3. Three-quarter brilliant cut, 24/16; 4. Double cut 24/24; 5. Brilliant cut 33/25; 6. Brilliant-cut crown; step-cut pavilion 32/40. 7. American brilliant cut 48/32.

system that developed at the end of the 17th century when laws of refraction were discovered by physicists, and analytical geometry developed as a mathematical science. It is used primarily for round diamonds, but several modified brilliant cuts are also used on transparent stones with curved or elliptical girdles, and oval sections, such as the pear and navette shapes. Because the ideal round brilliant has a minimum total of 58 facets—32 on the crown plus the table, and 24 on the pavilion plus the culet—it is called a 33/25 stone. The *single* or *half brilliant* has 28 or 32 facets, 16 on the crown, and 12 or 16 on the pavilion.

In a *double brilliant* cut, also called a *split* or *trap brilliant*, used on large stones to reduce the loss of weight in grinding, the main facets are divided into two triangles, making a total of 72 facets, 40 in the crown and 32 in the pavilion. The *American double brilliant cut* has an extra row of facets around the smaller sized table, making a total of 66 facets, and in a modified form in which the main facets are double cut, has a total of 82 facets. The *twentieth-century cut,* a modified and more complex brilliant developed in recent times, has 40 triangular and

rhomboid-shaped crown facets, and 40 four-, five-, and six-sided facets arranged in the pavilion, making a total of 80 facets. Its table is replaced by a series of low rhomboid-shaped facets sloping to a central point.

BRIOLETTE This form may be described as a double rose cut with an elongated cone-shaped upper crown and a rounded pavilion shape. The entire surface is covered with triangular or rectangular facets. Its apex is either pierced horizontally with a small hole for suspension purposes, or drilled vertically for the insertion of a peg from the mount, making it possible to use it either suspended or upright. It is cut from natural crystals having this shape to avoid loss. In another form of briolette, the top forms an extended cone shape, and the bottom a cone whose height is about one third that of the part above the girdle, each part angled sharply from the girdle.

DROP; PAMPILLE This is an elongated cone-shaped form rounded at the bottom where it is cut in lozenge-shaped facets meeting at an apex at the bottom, as in a rose cut, and with long lozenge-shaped facets tapering toward the top. It is usually mounted by suspension.

SPECIAL FANCY CUTS

Besides the regular cuts on regular stone crystal shapes, special cuts have been devised to retain the maximum bulk of both regular and irregular shapes. Some irregular (meaning "unconventional") cuts are applied to *cleavage splits* from larger diamond crystals, to *chips* (stone parti-

13–57 AMERICAN BRILLIANT-CUT DIAMOND PROPORTIONS
1. Crown view, 33 facets including the table.
2. Pavilion view, 25 facets including the culet, total 58 facets, or a 33/25 stone.
3. The table area comprises 57.5% of the total girdle diameter dimension: the crown is 14.6% of the total mass; and the pavilion 43.1% of the mass.

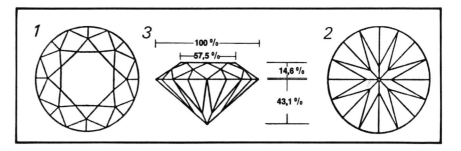

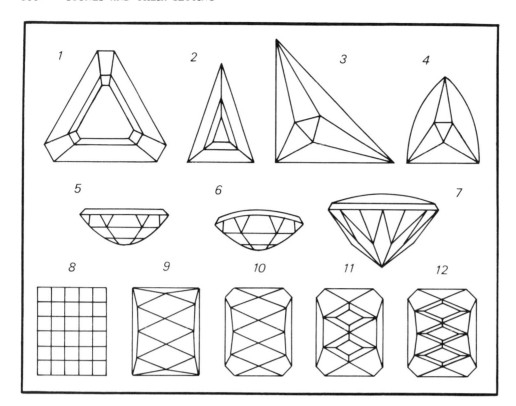

13-58 *SPECIAL FANCY CUTS*
1. Equilateral triangle, step cut.
2. Isosceles triangle, step cut.
3. Right triangle, French cut.
4. Curve-sided triangle, French cut.
5. Flat top with step-cut pavilion.
6. Buff top with step-cut pavilion.
7. Buff top with brilliant-cut pavilion.
8. Chess cut.
9. Bent-top rectangle, triangle cut.
10. Bent-top octagon, triangle cut.
11. Bent-top octagon, step triangle cut.
12. Bent-top octagon, step triangle cut.

cles less than one carat), and to *flats* or thin, flat pieces. Several of these cuts are used on diamonds, but also on semiprecious, transparent stones.

Chess cut: The *bombé* (outwardly curved) preform surface is entirely covered with small, square facets.

Triangle cut: The bombé surface is entirely covered with small triangular facets.

Prism cut: The rectangular stone is cut with rectangular shapes that resemble prisms.

Buff top: The round, oval, rectangular, or elliptical stone has a crown curved like a low-domed cabochon, either with or without a beveled edge, and the bottom or pavilion is faceted.

Bent top: A rectangular stone whose crown follows a bombé curve or arch which is cut into a series of triangular facets.

ASYMMETRICAL CUTS

Any stone whose facets are not arranged in a symmetrical pattern is asymmetrically cut. Some jewelers cut their own stones in this manner, or have the cooperation of lapidaries willing to cut stones to order in nontraditional, asymmetrical forms. Asymmetrically cut transparent stones possess unusual visual effects due to the unconventional manner in which light is reflected from faceted prismatic shapes, through crossing planes, and angular grooved incisions made in the manner of the ornamentation of cut crystal glassware.

CUTTING AND POLISHING A FACETED STONE

Most jewelers who use faceted stones purchase them ready-made from lapidaries. To really appreciate the great skill involved in faceting stones, the reader is referred to specialized texts on the subject. It is essential that a jeweler understand these processes also to be better able to judge faceted stone quality.

13-59 BERND MUNSTEINER, West Germany. White gold pendant with 76.50ct citrine and six brilliants. The citrine is free cut in an unconventional form with groups of intersecting parallel surface incisions whose angles refract the light with each shift of direction. Cut stones of this type are a specialty of this jeweler's work. *Photo: Baumann*

Stone Cut Names in Various Languages

Cuts English	Taille French	Tallas Spanish	Taglio Italian	Schliff-formen German
Cabochon				
Low cabochon	Cabochon bas	Cabochon bajo	Cabochone basso	Flacher cabochon
High cabochon	Cabochon haut	Cabochon regular	Cabochone alto	Cabochon
Cone cabochon	Cabochon cône	Cabochon cono	Cabochone cono	Kegel cabochon
Faceted	*Facetté*	*Faceteado*	*Sfacettato*	*Facettierter*
Flat top/flat back	Plat et inverse plat	Plano y revers plano	Piano e inverso piano	Flache tafel/flache Rückseite
Flat top/faceted back	Plat et inverse facetté	Plano y revers faceteado	Piano e inverso sfacettato	Flache tafel/facettierter Rücken
Step	Echelonné	Escalera	Scalino	Treppenschliff
Emerald	Émeraude	Esmeralda	Smeraldo	Smaragd
French cut	Taille français	Talla francesa	Taglio francese	Französischschliff
Cross cut	Taille traversé	Talla cruzada	Taglio croce	Kreuzschliff
Rose	Rose	Rosa	Rosa	Rosenschliff
Single cut	Taille singulaire	Talla singular	Taglio singolo	Einzigschliff
Star cut	Taille étoile	Talla estrella	Taglio stella	Sternschliff
Brilliant	Brilliant	Brillante	Brillanti	Brillantschliff
Bombed top/single bevel	Bombé et une face	Bombe y una faceta	Bomba e una facetta	Gemugelt/eine facette
Bombed top/double bevel	Bombé et deux faces	Bombe dos facetas	Bomba inverso due facette	Gemugelt/zwei facetten
Bombed top/faceted back	Bombé et reverse facetté	Bombe y reves faceteado	Bomba e inverso sfacettato	Gemugelt/facettierter Rücken
Checkerboard	Damier	Talla damero	Damiere	Schachbrettschliff

COMPOSITE STONES

Composite stones are made by assembling and cementing or fusing layers of natural stones in strata parallel to the girdle; or joining stones and glass with colored cements to make them appear as one stone. The upper portion or crown is usually the valuable natural stone, though exceptions exist. These compositions are then faceted, or shaped into cabochons.

A *doublet* is a composite stone consisting of two layers, usually with a natural top layer cemented to a colored glass bottom layer. In some doublets both layers are of natural stone joined together to create a larger stone or to improve color. Because in doublets the crown is usually the natural hard stone, resistance to surface scratching is retained. *Triplets* are less common than doublets, and consist of any composite having three layers.

Doublets and triplets are mounted in settings where their joining edges are concealed, therefore more difficult to detect. When the fact that a stone is a doublet or triplet is not made known to the purchaser, the practice is fraudulent. If, however, this fact is known and accepted, and the price is lower than an entire stone of similar quality and size, the practice is acceptable.

SOME COMMON DOUBLETS AND TRIPLETS

Opal: A thin upper layer of quality opal of good color is cemented to a second layer of an inferior opal, or to a backing of black onyx or black glass in order to increase color visibility and depth. In opal triplets, the top layer is clear quartz, the center opal, and the bottom black glass.

Garnet: An almandine garnet upper layer is fused to colored or clear glass, then faceted.

Emerald: In an emerald doublet, a thin, upper layer of real emerald is cemented to a deeper colored glass base to improve its color. Two clear quartz layers are cemented together with a thin layer of green gelatin or a green-colored liquid matter in a cavity between them, the result called an emerald *soudé* (French, "soldered"). Two synthetic white spinels are cemented together with a green plastic cement.

13-60 *COMPOSITE STONES: Doublets and triplets*

1. *Doublet:* Top layer real stone, bottom layer glass of the same color.
2. *Doublet:* Top layer real stone extending to the girdle, lower quartz or glass.
3. *Doublet:* Top and bottom clear real stone, joined by cement.
4. *Triplet:* Top and bottom layer clear quartz, with a pocket of colored liquid between them.
5. *Triplet:* Top and bottom layer a transparent stone, center layer a deeper colored glass.
6. *Triplet:* Star sapphire made with a top layer of a rose quartz star, center layer of blue glass, bottom layer mirrored glass.
7. *Triplet:* Top clear quartz, center opal, bottom black onyx or black glass.

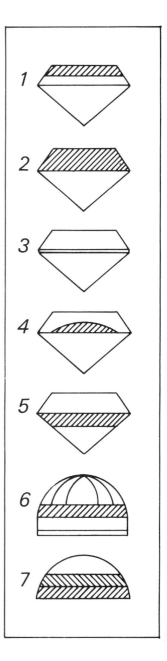

Diamond: A doublet has an upper layer of real diamond, and the bottom is clear quartz, white zircon, or rock crystal.

Ruby: In a doublet, the upper layer is real ruby, the lower red glass.

Star sapphire: A triplet consists of a top layer of a cabochon rose quartz star, a center layer of blue glass, and a backing of mirror glass.

GEMSTONE SUBSTITUTES

Throughout history in the use of gemstones for jewelry, their relative rarity and high cost has resulted in the use of substitutes. Ever since early Egyptian times, the favored substitute has been some form of glass. The Egyptians made common use of colored glass made of quartz coated with colored glazes, or powdered soda-lime silicate glass frits into which metallic oxides were introduced for color, the compound then vitrified by heat. Even in gold jewelry worn by pharaohs such substitutes were widely used to imitate their classic gem counterparts: turquoise, carnelian, and lapis lazuli.

Paste, as any glass composition used to imitate transparent or opaque gemstones is called, was also in wide use during the first two centuries of the Roman Empire. During the Middle Ages paste stones were sometimes combined in the same work with real stones, probably when the natural stone was unavailable. During the Italian Renaissance in the 15th and 16th centuries, colored glass "stones" used in jewelry were backed with foils in closed settings to improve color and luster. With the increased and popular use of diamonds during the late 17th and early 18th centuries, a brilliant, lustrous, and highly refractive transparent glass containing lead oxide as a flux was introduced for use as an imitation. When new it resembled the diamond in its high color dispersion, and its ability to be polished to brilliancy. Because glass is relatively soft, however, it was easily scratched and facet edges chipped, ultimately giving it a worn appearance.

Strass was one such glass composition, supposed to have been invented by an Alsatian, Georges Stras who started work in Paris in 1724. It was an immensely popular, brilliant lead glass consisting of a silicate of potassium and lead with borax, alumina, and white arsenic. Faceted strass paste gems were set in metal mounts that were as carefully fabricated as jewels employing real precious stones.

By the mid-19th century when open settings were generally adopted, paste was relegated to use on obviously imitation diamond jewelry. The use of foils was practically abandoned, and paste gems instead were "silvered" at the back by the same process used to mirror glass. Since then the use of "stones" completely of glass has been confined mainly to inexpensive novelty jewelry.

Today plastics are commonly used to substitute for gems in costume jewelry.

SETTING A FACETED STONE

The term *setting* is a noun used to describe ways by which a faceted stone can be mounted, and a verb that describes the action by which this is accomplished. Inherent in the concept of stone setting is the idea of stone seating, or creating a means by which the stone rests in the work, is fixed in place, and held securely without danger of loss.

A variety of systems exists for setting a faceted stone in a jewel, and those of primary importance are given here. Within this range of possibilities, a single stone may be used as the main focal point in a metal setting that remains visible, groups of stones can be set together to form a cluster or unit, or entire surfaces of the work may be dominated by stones with the metal serving a purely functional role of stone holding, and at times being so unobtrusive as to be almost invisible.

The type of setting selected for use with a particular faceted stone is governed to some degree by traditional usage, adapted today to suit the contemporary design idiom if desired. Of prime importance is the character of the stone, its degree of transparency, its refractive index, and fire. Other influencing factors to be considered are the importance of the individual stone in the design of the work, and the manner by which the stone can best be displayed. At times the entire design of a work evolves around the use of a particular stone or combinations of stones. Some jewelers whose quest is an adventure into untried paths have defied custom and have invented unconventional stone-setting methods, some of which can be seen in the illustrations.

Standard faceted stone-setting systems can be generally classified under the basic concepts of *closed settings, open settings,* and *group settings.* Some systems can be used to create either a closed or an open setting, and in each of these, several variations and modifications are possible. Several of these systems have French names or make use of French terminology, because France led the Western world in jewelry manufacture and design during the 18th century when this terminology was adopted internationally.

HANDLING STONES

Because of the relatively small size of stones used by jewelers, handling them may at times cause difficulties. These are solved by the use of handling materials and tools.

Sticky wax formed into a cylindrical shape can be pressed onto the table of a stone and will attach itself readily to it, then set hard quickly. With this material the stone can be placed in a setting to test its size, and lifted out of a setting without damage from dropping.

Shellac sticks are used to hold work when a stone is being set in it. The shellac is heated to make it plastic, and the work is pressed into it, leaving the stone setting up and exposed. When it cools, the shellac hardens and holds the work. To release the work, the shellac is warmed to make it plastic, and the work is pried loose.

Stone-handling tweezers are finely tapered and have internally serrated jaws to facilitate gripping a stone at its girdle. They are available with straight or curved jaws.

Gem tweezers with retractable jaws are used to grasp a stone, and are especially useful when handling small stones.

Stone shovels are used when making a selection of stones from many laid on a *velvet-covered pad* which prevents them from rolling. The selected stones set aside with tweezers are scooped up with the shovel and placed into a paper folder.

Paper folders for stone storage are traditionally used in the jewelry trade. To make a typical folder using a piece of paper 8½ in × 11 in (20.3 cm × 27.9 cm), the standard American letterhead size, hold the paper vertically and draw lines dividing it vertically into three columns:

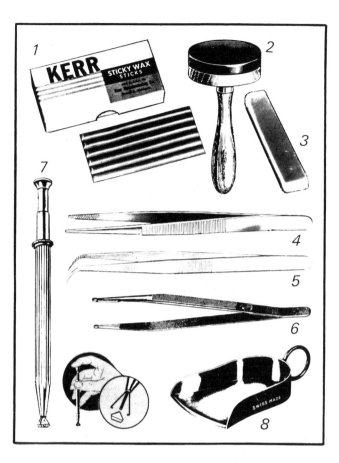

13-61 *STONE-HANDLING TOOLS AND MATERIALS*
1. *Sticky wax sticks,* a hard, fast-setting wax used for attachment to loose stones when test placing or lifting them away from a setting in preparation.
2. *Shellac stick* with wooden handle and disc base, upon which a shellac preparation is spread. This is softened by heat and the jewelry is pressed into the surface to immobilize it while it is worked, having a setting prepared, or stones mounted.
3. *Bar of shellac* applied to a shellac stick. After melting it by heat, it is spread on the surface to the desired depth.
4. *Stone-handling tweezers* with inner serrated jaws, used to lift and handle loose stones without damage; approx. 6 in long.
5. *Stone-handling tweezers* with inner, serrated, curved jaws and very fine points; 5½ in long.
6. *Pearl and round stone tweezers* with ivory-lined jaws ending in concave cups; approx. 6 in long.
7. *Three-prong gem tweezers.* The three prongs are controlled by a spring plunger in the handle, operated as shown. When the plunger is pressed, the prongs move forward and open, allowing the stone to be grasped, and when the plunger is released, the prongs retract into the handle and close around the stone. When not in use, the prongs contract into the handle. Approx. 6 in long.
8. *Stone shovel* for handling small stones, 2½ × 2 in.

13-62 SAARA HOPEA-UNTRACHT, Finland, designer; manufacturer Kultasepänliike Ossian Hopea, Porvoo. Brooch in 18K gold with a combination of cabochon and faceted stones in round, oval, antique cushion, octagon, and drop shapes, set in open-backed shoulder bezels. *Photo: Oppi*

►

2⅛ in, 4¼ in, 2⅛ in (5.4 cm, 10.8 cm, 5.4 cm). Draw lines across the paper width, from the top downward: 1 in, 2½ in, 2½ in, 2½ in, 2½ in (2.5 cm, 6.3 cm, 6.3 cm, 6.3 cm, 6.3 cm). Fold the bottom division of 2½ in across the paper width. Then fold the two 2⅛ in sides vertically so they meet at the center. Continue folding from the bottom upward at the 2½ in divisions three times, ending with a 1 in foldover flap. Flatten the seams by running a *hard edge* over them. The folder, now 4¼ in × 2½ in, has a foldover flap that points downward and the stones are resting inside at the bottom of the first horizontal fold so they will not fall out when the folder is opened to inspect them. On the outside at the folder top, write the name, size, price, date of purchase, amounts of stones, etc. contained within. Folders can be filed standing upright in a container of the same width, in alphabetical order to make them easy to find.

CLOSED SETTINGS

In *closed settings,* the stone is normally only open to light from above the girdle.

BEZEL SETTINGS FOR FACETED STONES

The same kind of collet bezels described earlier in this chapter for cabochon stones can also be used to make a closed setting for a faceted stone. When the stone is transparent, this normally is not done because light from below is excluded, which limits the ability of the stone to display its brilliance. Open-sided or -backed shoulder bezels are, however, commonly used as in this case, light does reach the stone's pavilion from the side or below.

The *cup bezel* is a special type, made by utilizing the concave side of a dome whose depth must be greater than the depth of a faceted stone from girdle to culet. A cup bezel can be used closed for opaque stones, or when transparent or translucent stones are used, an opening can be made either at the cup sides or its base to admit light. Stones have a natural seat in the angle of the dome, but one can be also made with a *graver.* Alternately, an upstanding edge of a fitted collet or wire can be soldered

13–63 BENT GABRIELSEN P., Denmark, designer; manufacturer Georg Jensen Sølvsmedie A/S, Copenhagen. Silver ring with flat-topped stone set in a cup bezel. *Photo: Courtesy Georg Jensen Sølvsmedie A/S*

within the dome below its edge to serve as a bearing or shoulder. The top edge is thinned with a *file* and the stone is set with stone-setting tools. Finally the cup edge is *burnished* over the stone's girdle edge in the same manner as when ordinary collet bezels are finished.

KUNDAN SETTING

The word *kundan* in Hindi means "pure gold," and is applied to a *flush stone closed setting* type commonly practiced in India in the ancient past and still in use today for both cabochon and faceted stones. If the stone has a flat bottom, a flat setting is gouged out of the base metal (or jade) with *gravers*. A stone with a pavilion culet has its bearing seat made in the same way as described below for a gypsy setting. Instead of burnishing down the raised burr, it is at first allowed to remain intact. The stone is placed in its setting. A *foil* of 24K or *pure gold* is folded longitudinally several times to form a narrow strip. One end of this is anchored at a starting point at the stone's edge by pressing it down with a *burnisher* into the space between the stone and the setting flange. The gold strip is then led with the hand and pressed with the burnisher completely around the stone, then the surplus is cut off. The foil is burnished down all around the stone, and, at the same time, the flange burr is leveled with it. Because pure gold is *completely weldable* in a cold state simply by compression, it forms a solid wedge that permanently holds the stone in place. Sometimes the foiled area around the stone is then ornamented by circling it with a *milli-graining tool* (see p. 621) which impresses it with a beaded pattern while at the same time compressing it further. It can also be shaped into a four-cornered depression whose shining surface reflects light to the stone. Because this is a closed setting, the stones are usually foiled below.

FOILED STONES IN CLOSED SETTINGS   Until the end of the 18th century, it was common practice in Europe for all transparent stones set in closed settings to be backed by pure silver, gold, tin, or colored foils from which light would be reflected through the stone's crown to increase its color intensity and brilliance. This practice is still carried out in India for both cabochon and faceted transparent stones, and is also common in *costume jewelry* which is mass-produced jewelry made of non-precious metals and imitation stones. During the 19th century, claw settings that were left open at the back to allow the admission of light to the stone were generally accepted, thus eliminating the need for foils. This change was partially due to the general improvement in the techniques of faceting precious and semiprecious stones.

When foils are used they are highly polished to increase their reflectivity. A piece large enough to fill the space is simply pressed into the bottom of the setting with a clean,

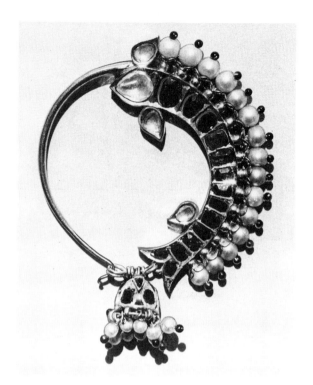

13–64 HYDERABAD, HYDERABAD-DECCAN, INDIA. Nose ring (*nath*), 22K gold, worn by married women. The fish form is a symbol of fertility. It is set here with diamonds and rubies in *kundan* closed settings, with each stone foiled below to increase its color and brilliance. Each of the outer row of pearls is held on a gold wire ending in a fused-on, red, transparent enamel ball that appears to be a round ruby. The other wire end passes through the setting and is knotted at the back. *Photo: Oppi*

dry, blunt-ended *punch*. The foil is usually held in place with a little cement spread on its back. Alternately, foil is sometimes pressed around the bottom surface of the stone which is then set. In a completely closed setting such as this, because the foil is sealed from atmospheric contact, and due to the nonoxidizing nature of the metal foils used, the foil remains bright.

GYPSY OR BEVELED SETTING

The *gypsy setting* is so called because it was favored in the gold jewelry worn by people of that community in Europe. It was generally popular during the 19th century. In this setting, a thin flange which serves as a bezel is formed from a bevel made in the body of the work itself, which accounts for its sometimes being referred to as a *beveled setting*. In the result, the cabochon or faceted stone is sunk into the opening with its girdle flush or continuous with the body form, for which reason it is sometimes also called a *flush setting*. When setting a stone this way in a fabricated setting, the metal of the body at the seat must be thick enough to allow such shaping, but this is normally not a problem when making a gypsy setting in a cast piece where the walls are normally relatively thick.

To set the stone, first *drill* a center hole whose diameter is smaller than that of the stone. Into this hole drill a vertical-sided seat with a *stone-setting bur* whose outer diameter snugly matches that of the stone's girdle. File the flanged area surrounding the stone with a *round hand file* or a small rotating *circular file* or *bur* to thin it so it can be forced over the stone. The holding flange should not be too deep or too much of the stone will be covered, thus unnecessarily reducing its diameter. Seat the stone and force or chase the surrounding metal flange over it by using a *flat-faced smooth* or *matting punch* with a *hand hammer* in the same way as when setting a stone in an ordinary bezel. (A *power hammer* mounted in a *flex-shaft* can also be used for this purpose.) In the result, the flange forms a smooth wall around the stone that merges with the body of the work. Next smooth the flange-bezel with a *burnisher* around the stone. Since part of the area around the stone has been filed away to thin the flange, a slight depression may be apparent. To eliminate this, file the surrounding area smooth, then polish it.

SEAMLESS TUBE SETTING

In a tube setting, the stone is literally placed within the open end of a section of precious metal seamless tubing whose ID (inside diameter) matches the stone girdle diameter. The tube length can be any height. Tubes can be used to create either a closed or an open setting.

A *closed tube setting* is actually an extended straight-sided bezel and is made in the same basic way. The tube length is soldered flush with the base or placed within a drilled hole and soldered. To form an *inner bearing* or *shoulder,* a wire circlet can be soldered inside; or a squared-off shorter tube whose OD (outer diameter) matches the ID of the tube used can be press fitted by forcing it into the first, then soldering it in place there the necessary distance below the upper edge of the outer tube. The outer upper tube end is thinned by filing from the outside, the stone is positioned, and the flange is pressed over its girdle with a burnisher in the same way as for a common bezel.

By another system, a tube is selected whose ID is slightly less than that of the stone's girdle but whose outside diameter is greater than that of the stone. A shoulder is formed within the tube wall with a stone-setting bur whose diameter matches that of the stone's girdle diameter; or one is formed with a graver. The tube edge is thinned, the stone placed on the shoulder, and the flange is burnished over it.

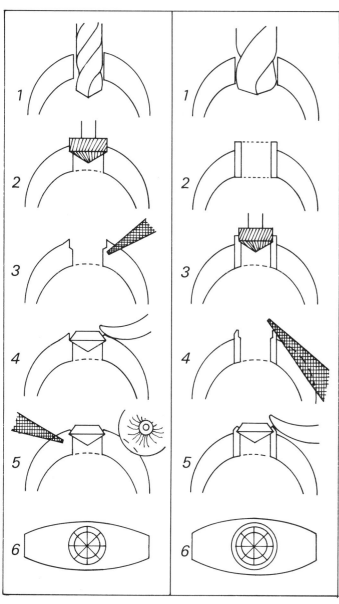

13–65 GYPSY STONE SETTING (left column)
1. *Drill* the stone opening with a *drill* size smaller than the stone's diameter.
2. *Grind* a bearing into the hole using a *stone-setting bur.*
3. *File* away the metal around the bezel edge to reduce the thickness, leaving a raised ridge around the stone.
4. *Seat* the stone and *burnish* the bezel down on it.
5. *File* the metal surface smooth, and polish.
6. The finished gypsy stone setting.

TUBE SETTING A STONE (right column)
1. *Drill* an opening whose size exactly equals the tube's OD.
2. **Insert the tube section, forcing it in if necessary with a mallet for a tight force fit.** Solder the tube in place.
3. *Grind* a bearing for the stone with a *stone-setting bur* into the tube end.
4. *File* the tube outer edge at an angle to thin it.
5. *Seat* the stone and *burnish* the tube end over it.
6. The finished tube stone setting.

13–66 FRIEDRICH BECKER, West Germany. Ring in 18K white gold with a brilliant-cut rhodolite stone mounted in a gypsy or beveled setting. The polished surface below reflects light upward through the stone. Photo: Walter Fischer

13–67 FRIEDRICH BECKER, West Germany. Kinetic 18K white gold brooch with brilliants, rubies, and emeralds, mounted in tube sections. The tube is joined to a wire structure that acts as a moving axle. The stone colors and the construction pattern reflect on the mirror-polished concave surface of the oval form. Ø 47 × 50 mm. Photo: Walter Fischer

13-68 JOCELYN BURTON, England. Gold necklace made entirely of tube sections mounted with diamonds. Tubes are butt joined in groups, and connected with loose wire rivets, leaving the entire structure flexible. *Photo: Courtesy De Beers Consolidated Mines, Ltd., London*

13-69 FRIEDRICH B. MÜLLER, Switzerland. Ring in white and fine gold, with Indian moonstone in a tapered bezel; sapphire, diamond, and coral in tapered tube bezels; and ivory inlaid with gold tube inserts. *Photo: Mario Tschabold*

An *open tube setting* can be created simply by making openings in the tube wall below the shoulder. These can be drilled or sawed and filed to shape. Another system commonly used is to form the upper portion of the tube into prongs. In this case, first an inner shoulder is made by a *bur* or a *graver*. The position of the prongs is marked and their shape drawn on the outer tube wall. They are then formed either by filing the tube wall to the desired depth, or by sawing them out. If the prongs are made just short of the shoulder, the setting remains a closed one. They must extend below the shoulder to make an open tube setting so that when the stone is seated in the remaining portion of the shoulder inside the prongs, the opening extends below the shoulder which allows the entrance of light. The claws are made in the usual way (described below) and forced over the stone's girdle. Several stones can be set

this way by butt soldering the desired number of tubes together side by side, and their tops can all be at the same level or at different levels.

TAPERED TUBE SETTING A tapered tube formed from sheet metal with the seam soldered closed can be used as a setting. A straight-sided tube can be taper stretched outward by hammering it on a *tapered ring mandrel* or other small-sectioned steel object of suitable shape and size, such as a *tapered round punch* end.

FRUSTUM SETTING

A *frustum* is a truncated, right conical, equilateral pyramidal, rhomboidal, or other regularly *tapered* geometric form intersected between two planes parallel with the base. When such a form is constructed from sheet metal, it is hollow. Frustum forms are often used with their larger diameter upward to make a setting for both cabochon and faceted stones. By its use, the stone is raised to a desired height from the base plane. Total depth is generally determined on faceted stones by the distance from pavilion to culet to make certain that the culet does not extend beyond the back and contact the wearer, for instance the finger in a ring, or body in a brooch or pendant. Because the setting tapers to a smaller size below the stone, it is seen only minimally from the front, one of the main reasons for its use. When a frustum form is used for square, rectangular, or octagonal stones, it is sometimes called a *box setting*.

The manner of laying out the frustum of a cone, square pyramid, and rectangular pyramid on a flat sheet of usually 22 gauge B.&S. metal is shown in the accompanying illustration. This figure can be drawn directly on the metal, taking the measurements from the stone itself. The lines are gone over with a *scriber* and the frustum is sawed out with a *jeweler's saw*. It can also be traced on the metal from a paper drawing, and the lines then gone over with a scriber. The greatest possible accuracy is needed to make the form meet perfectly after cutting and bending. The thickness of the metal must be taken into account and added at corners. After sawing out the flat frustum, it is shaped to true dimension with a *file*, then formed. A *cone frustum* can be shaped over a *tapered ring mandrel* with a *wooden* or *plastic mallet* until the seam meets, and is then soldered closed.

To shape *frustum forms for straight-sided stones*, to facilitate bending all the bend lines are scored with a scorer before bending the flat metal pattern. Take care not to penetrate the metal to more than half its thickness or it will become too weak, and when bent, may crack along the bend line. To bend the form along the three scored lines, place the pattern on a flat surface and hold a *straight edge* over the long portion extending from the first line, and along the line. With the fingers, raise the short length of metal upward along the scored line. Do the same for the short length of metal extending outward from the third line. Bend the center line with *long-nosed flat pliers* with which the other angles can also be adjusted until the bent angles and the seam of the joint abut cleanly. Solder the joint and the scored corners to reinforce them.

USING THE FRUSTUM SETTING The frustum setting can be used to hold a stone in a *closed-sided setting* in which the stone rests below the girdle, with the addition of claws to hold it, or in an *open-sided setting* that extends above the girdle and is folded over on the stone to hold it. In both cases, the bottom is usually open to admit light. Closed-sided frustum settings have a bearing soldered inside to support the stone, or one can be formed in the base metal with a graver. When the stone rests *inside* the frustum, the portion above the bearing is filed thinner from the *outside* to allow it to be more easily bent over the stone, as with an ordinary bezel. In the case of all angled frustum forms bent over the stone girdle, the corners above the bearing must be removed to form 30–45° angles (depending on the angle of the stone's crown slope) to allow the sides to be bent over upon the crown without the development of corner bulges that otherwise would occur. These corners should meet squarely so the bezel edge appears to be continuous. It is also possible to remove the sides and only leave the corners projecting to act as claws; or to remove the corners completely and leave only the sides to be folded over the stone.

Open-sided frustum settings are more usual because they allow the entry of light to a transparent stone. In this case, the sides of the one-piece frustum below the bearing can be *pierced* with openings in any pattern that will not weaken the structure. In other variations, the part extending from the bearing upward can be cut or filed to form claws which can be bent over the stone's girdle.

Separately made *claws* of wire tapered below to half the top dimension can be soldered to the outer side of the frustum at corners, sides, or in other placements. The use of claws makes it possible for the frustum's upper edge to act as a bearing ledge or shoulder for the stone. That edge is in this case filed at an angle to match that of the stone below the girdle and to support it. When claws are used, the stone must fit the setting while the claws are straight, and the supporting frustum setting is invisible from the top. The claws are soldered on separately while the setting is held in air with *tweezers*. Surplus metal is filed away,

claw thickness is thinned from the outside, and the claws are bent over the stone girdle to hold it.

LAYING OUT THE FRUSTUM OF A HOLLOW CONE

1 Measure the stone's diameter at the girdle, and the vertical distance from the girdle to the culet. When the stone is to fit *within* the cone (not resting on the upper frustum edge as a shoulder), to these measurements add the additional amount needed to allow for the upper edge of the frustum to be either burnished over the stone's girdle, or formed into claws, and an amount to extend below the culet to prevent contact with the body.

2 Using these dimensions, draw lines forming the side or elevation view of the cone ABCD.

3 Extend lines AB and DC until they intersect at the apex Z.

4 Using the distance DZ as a radius and Z as a center, draw an arc from G to E; using the distance CZ as a radius, draw an arc from H to F.

5 Measure the distance AD and mark this off 3½ times along the arc, the first point forming G; the arc is GE.

6 From the first point G and the last point E, draw a line to the apex Z. Where this line intersects the arc HF, points H and F are established.

7 The shape contained within GHFEG is the flat cone pattern which is laid out on the metal and cut out.

8 After shaping the cone with a mallet on a *tapered round ring mandrel,* points EF and GH meet to form the join which is soldered closed. The hollow cone frustum setting is then ready to be treated in a variety of possible ways.

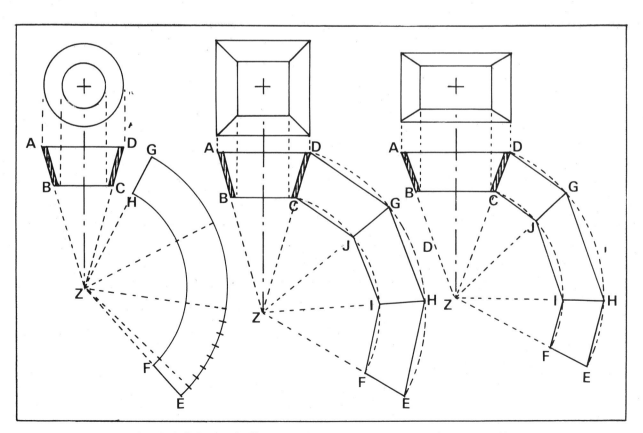

13–70 *LAYING OUT THE FRUSTUM OF A HOLLOW CONE, A HOLLOW SQUARE PYRAMID, AND A HOLLOW RECTANGULAR PYRAMID.*

LAYING OUT THE FRUSTUM OF A HOLLOW SQUARE PYRAMID, OR A RECTANGULAR PYRAMID

1 Draw the profile elevation or side view of the square (or rectangle) with measurements determined from the stone. Depending on whether the stone is held by the frustum or by attached claws, the measurements are respectively larger or smaller than the stone's girdle size.

2 Extend lines AB and DC until they intersect at the apex Z.

3 Using the distance DZ as a radius, draw the arc DE; using the distance CZ as a radius, draw the arc CF.

4 Measure the distance AD with *dividers* and mark it off three times on arc DE.

5 Draw straight lines from G and H toward Z until they intersect arc CF, at which places points J and I are established. Lines DC, GJ, and HI will form the corners of the frustum.

6 Draw a straight line from D to G; G to H; H to E; C to J; J to I; and I to F.

7 The shape contained within ADGHEFIJCBA is the flat pattern for the frustum of the square pyramid; it is laid out on the metal and cut out.

8 *Score* lines DC, GJ, and HI to facilitate bending the metal at these points to form the frustum. After bending, the lines AB and EF meet to form the join which is soldered closed.

Laying out the frustum of a hollow rectangular pyramid is done in the same way as described here for the hollow square pyramid. The difference is that when marking the side lengths on the arc, the distance for the long and the short rectangle sides must alternate, as shown in the diagram.

BEZEL BLOCK AND PUNCH FRUSTUMS   An alternative to laying out and shaping a frustum from flat sheet is to stamp press one from a flat sheet metal blank with the aid of a *bezel block* and *matching collet punch*. This tempered steel block is actually a single-action open die and is available with round, oval, square, rectangular, antique cushion, antique long cushion, long octagon, or navette tapering depressions, each block having a series of one shape in graduated sizes. The metal is forced to conform to these shapes by a corresponding and matching *bezel block collet punch* whose angle slope or taper matches that of all the depressions in the block so that the same punch can be used for all sizes. Normal or deeply tapered bezels can be made, depending on the angle of the depressions in the

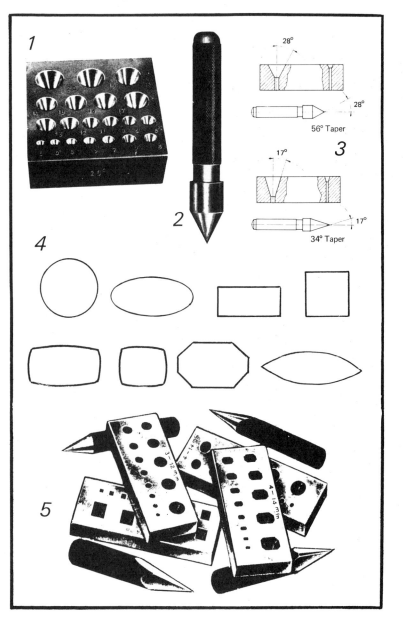

13-71   TAPERED BEZEL BLOCK AND PUNCH

1. *Round-shaped bezel block*, tempered steel, accurately machined, highly polished, with 28° (56° total) taper in 20 graduated size depressions, weight 4 lb 12 oz.

2. *Round bezel block punch* for use with the above block, its angle of taper the same as all size depressions in the same block.

3. Diagrams showing 28° (56°) and 17° (34°) taper of block and punch, the former for normally tapered bezels, the latter for deep-tapered bezels made from punched sheet metal discs.

4. Standard bezel shapes, and the size range in which blocks of these shapes are available. *Top row; left to right*: round, oval, rectangle, square; *bottom row*: antique long cushion, antique cushion, long octagon, navette or marquise.

Shape	13-hole block	8-hole block
Round	3–12 mm	7–18 mm
Oval	4–14 mm	8–20 mm
Rectangle	4–14 mm	7–18 mm
Square	3–10 mm	5–16 mm
Antique long cushion	4–14 mm	8–20 mm
Antique cushion	3–10 mm	5–16 mm
Long octagon	4–14 mm	7–18 mm
Navette	4–14 mm	7–18 mm

5. Assortment of bezel block shapes with their punches.

particular block. The size of the depression used depends on the size of the stone. An advantage of this method is that any number of identically sized frustum collets can be made and sizes can be easily matched.

To make such a frustum-shaped bezel, position the flat or domed and annealed *disc blank* (or other contour-shaped sheet metal blank for long forms), drilled with a center hole, directly over the opening of the desired size. Place the *punch* vertically directly over the blank's center—which should correspond with the center of the die depression—and by degrees, with repeated strokes hammer the punch straight down, forcing the metal into the depression. For maximal flow and stretch, and to avoid tearing the sides of the frustum, the metal may have to be annealed at an intermediate point. Then hammer the punch until block wall, metal, and punch end make total contact, simultaneously sizing the frustum and bringing it to its desired contour.

Without a center hole, the punch pierces the sheet, tears a jagged hole at the center, and the upper frustum edge will also probably be uneven. For this reason, allow a sufficient amount of waste metal in the disc blank for trimming. To make the upper edge level with the top of the block, perpendicular to the taper, leave the frustum within the depression holding it in place, and *file* any protruding parts with a file large enough to cover the opening. Should the edge still be uneven, place the frustum in the next smaller depression and file away the rest of any protruding edge. This can be repeated for trimming later if necessary to reduce the frustum height as all openings have the same internal angle slope. To straighten the frustum's small end, remove it from the depression, poking a stiff wire or tool end through the hole at the bottom of each opening if it resists removal, and place it, trued top down, on a level surface. File away the metal with a *flat file* large enough to cover the whole end at one time while holding it down with the fingers. Any of the same treatments already suggested for the flat sheet, fabricated frustum can be applied to a finished stamped one.

It is also possible to start a stamped frustum by using a section of annealed seamless or seamed tubing (see Tubing, Demonstration 8, Photos 26–29). Place this in an upright position within the selected depression of the bezel block. Place the punch directly over the tube end and hammer it down. In this case there will probably be less trimming to be done than when a flat sheet blank is used. Because the upper edge is stretched it is thinned, and the lower edge is compressed and thickened in the resulting frustum, this variation serves the frustum's use as a bezel.

The finished frustum bezel is then soldered to the work. If the object has a curved surface, as in a ring shank, the bottom edge must first be filed to conform to this contour. This is done by rubbing the base of the frustum on a stationary *half-round file* of similar diameter, or on a piece of *cloth backed abrasive* wrapped around and fixed to a *ring mandrel,* or, in some cases, wrapped around and bound to the object itself.

OPEN SETTINGS

Any setting that allows the entrance of light from below a transparent, faceted stone's girdle through the pavilion facets is termed an *open setting,* or *à jour* (French, "open to daylight").

BEAD SETTING: **Raising a bead with a graver and beader**

Faceted stones, occasional cabochon stones, and full and half pearls, are often held in various types of closed and open settings by what are called beads. A *bead* is a spurlike projection raised with a *graver* from the base metal of the workpiece at positions around the girdle perimeter of the stone, then rounded to a bead or grain form with a *beading* or *graining tool,* and pressed against the stone. Beads are formed at cardinal points around the stone and hold it in place in the setting. When the surface from which the bead is raised is flat, it is called a *flat setting.*

To form a bead, while the workpiece is immobilized, with the stone in place, starting approximately one millimeter from the stone and working toward it, the graver is forced into the metal at an angle of about 30° along a line radiating from the stone's center. As the cut moves forward, while the graver's point is still embedded within the metal, the graver is raised to nearly a right angle. This elevates an approximately $\frac{1}{16}$ in (1.6 mm) long triangular-shaped, curved spur of metal above the surface which projects over the stone's girdle. When the bead on the opposite side of the stone is formed, they act together to hold the stone in position. Four beads are used to hold stones under 15 points, and six or more for larger stones.

The size of the bead increases in proportion with the stone size. Small beads used for stones 10 points or less are formed with a *No. 51 round graver* from single small spurs. Large beads formed by a *No. 52 round graver* from one large spur are used for holding stones up to 20 points. Still larger beads are made by first making two diagonal cuts with a *knife-edged graver* or *spitsticker* in the form of a V with its apex pointing *away* from the stone in order to isolate the amount of metal needed for the spur. Then a *blunt-shaped round graver* is forced into the V at a position halfway from the apex, and while rocking it from side to side, a cut is made into the metal to raise the spur. During this rocking motion, the graver's position is slowly elevated, causing the cutting edge to dig deeper into the metal to thicken the spur at its base, and the spur is automatically pushed toward and over upon the stone's girdle. In making the next spur the work is turned 180° to form one opposite the last, anchoring the stone in place.

To form the spur into a *bead* or *grain* as it is sometimes called, a *beading tool* or *graining tool* is used. This is a straight steel shaft tapering at its end to a round, concave dome shape. Sets of beading tools, each with a bead hollow in its end, are usually available in sets of twelve graduated sizes, and shafts can be interchanged in the chuck of a single separate wooden handle used for all sizes. The size chosen for use depends on the size of the bead to be made. While holding the beading tool shaft with the thumb and second finger, with the index finger resting on top of the tool for control, encompass the spur end within the hollow end of the beading tool, holding it at an angle pointing toward the stone. In the same act of raising the spur and pushing it forward against the stone's girdle, rotate the tool with a rapid side-to-side motion. This action automatically transforms the spur into a bead while pressing it over on the stone, and its base remains attached to the base metal. When the beading tool is lifted away, a raised, polished, round bead is in position. The same is done with the remaining spurs made for that stone, alternating to opposite sides to keep the stone levelly seated.

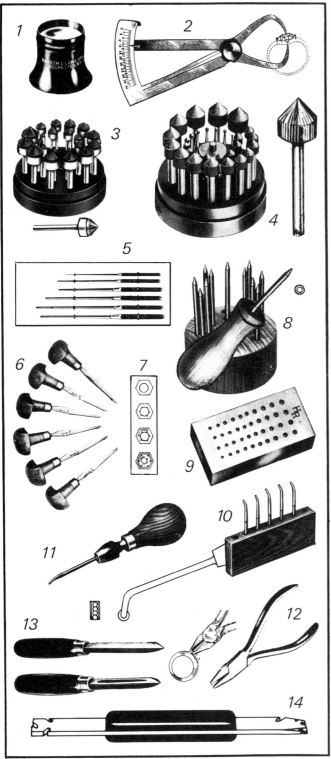

13–72 STONE-SETTING TOOLS

1. *Eye loupe*, single lens, available in 2–10X power enlargement, at working distances of 5–10 in. Used to examine work in progress during stone setting.
2. *Moe degree gauge and diamond weight calculator*, made of polished steel, plain points, with easily read indexes graduated from 0.1 mm to 160 mm capacity; used to measure the girdle diameter and the depth of stones, and settings. From such dimensions, the carat weight of a diamond can be computed while the stone is still in the setting, by comparing the width and depth measurements in an available set of tables.
3. *Stone-seating burs* with ⅛ in shanks, used to drill a seat in a setting; with end cutters and safe sides; set of 22 graduated for stones of ¹⁄₁₆–2cts; Ø from 2.5 mm (size 1) to 9.0 mm (size 22).
4. *Stone-seating burs* with ⅛ in shanks, with both end and side cutters, set of 30, graduated from 1.0 mm (size 1) to 10.0 mm (size 30), in stand with plastic cover.
5. *Set of cutting broaches* with knurled handles, used to enlarge a tapering hole.
6. *Set of gravers* in wooden handles, with differently shaped points, used in raising a bead, and trimming and shaving stone settings.
7. *Model stone-setting plate* illustrating the steps in bead setting a stone in a flat-top setting.
8. *Set of 12 beading tools* mounted in a wooden block, in graduated sizes: 2–0, 1–0, 1–10; used to form a bead to hold a stone in a setting. Wooden handle permits the changing and holding of all sizes; end view of beading tool showing the hollow where the bead is shaped.
9. *Beading tool plate*, brass with a hardened steel bead in each of the 40 depressions in eight standard sizes. The end of a worn or misshapen beading tool is inserted in the hole size selected, and the tool rotated against the bead to reshape it.
10. *Set of milligrain wheels*, mounted in wooden block, available in sizes 2–9; detail shows the position of the wheel at the end of the shaft, and an end view of the wheel showing the round depressions within the side wheel rims that form the milligrains.
11. *Milligrain wheel* mounted in the screw chuck of the wooden handle.
12. *Prong-bending and -lengthening pliers* whose jaws have one concave and one ball end; 5½ in long.
13. *Scrapers, top*: triangular, solid; *bottom*: triangular, hollow, both with curved ends. Used to deburr, remove excess metal and solder from fillets in joints, or to adjust the bearing of a stone in a setting.
14. *Prong lifter*, steel with plastic handle, can be used at various angles to safely pry prongs away from a stone to remove it for remounting or when a worn claw or prong must be repaired.

Skill in the bead-raising technique can be easily acquired by practicing on a scrap of the same kind of metal as that to be used in order to develop a feel for the right amount of pressure needed against the resistance of a particular metal and the stone.

In traditional practice, after raising all the beads of a setting, the surplus metal around each bead is carved away with a *right-* and *left-sided graver* to isolate and elevate the bead, thus clearing it from the surrounding metal. This is the most painstaking part of the bead-making process, and requires practice. The metal is shaved away to the right and left of the bead in several shallow cuts, using the right-sided or left-sided, pointed, polished graver according to the direction being followed. Each cut is made as long as possible, and the cuts must avoid approaching the bead directly as this would involve the risk of also cutting the bead itself away. The final cuts are made with a *highly polished flat graver* to leave the metal surface bright, which makes unnecessary the polishing of this area and subjecting the stone to possible damage during polishing.

When the end of a beading tool becomes worn or misshapen, it can be reshaped by placing its end in the proper number marked, sized depression of a hardened steel *fion block* or *beading tool plate* that corresponds with a particular sized tool. Each depression has a bead attached at its bottom, its size in proportion with the tool size. Under forward pressure, the tool is rotated there until its

In possible variations, a ridge is raised with a graver, divided with a graver, and turned into a series of beads of the same size, as is often done in a pavé setting. (See p. 628.) More than one bead can be formed at a single position by raising adjoining spurs that converge at that point. A stone can be set, for instance, with beads in triangular groups of three, two against the girdle, and one behind and between them. It is possible to use this bead-raising technique not to hold a stone but simply to create a decorative effect by covering a whole surface or area with raised beads, with a result that resembles coarse granulation.

edge and shape are reshaped, restored, sharpened, and polished. A new beading tool can be made by placing an appropriately shaped steel rod into the depression with its end perpendicular over the bead and hammering it down to form the depression at its end. The tool is not tempered and hardened to reduce the chance of damaging a stone.

MILLIGRAINING

Milligraining is the process of producing very small, beadlike forms in series along the edges of bezels, or around a stone setting. This traditional form of stone-setting ornamentation is done to make a small faceted stone appear larger by increasing the points of reflected light in the setting. There is no reason why this technique should not be used on a jewel of contemporary design.

The *milligrainer tool* with which this is done consists of a metal shaft mounted in a wooden handle. The shaft's working end is divided into two legs to mount and hold a very small steel wheel between them by a horizontal rivet. The concave rim of the wheel is engraved with a series of shallow, semicircular depressions with sharp edges. When the wheel is rolled over a raised metal edge, a linear series of small beads or *milligrains* are formed, for which reason the tool is sometimes called a *beading roulette*. The tool is available with wheels in at least ten different sizes, each containing uniform depressions.

There are a few different ways of making the milligrains. A single track can be engraved parallel to the edge of a surface for the wheel to roll upon. Two parallel lines can be engraved anywhere on the work for the wheel's rims to roll upon. The upstanding edge of a plain collet bezel, or any upstanding edge for that matter, can be milligrained without a track as long as the milligrain wheel rim can securely straddle the edge.

To form the milligrains on any malleable metals, the wheel lubricated with a light machine oil is simply pressed against the metal and rolled back and forth over the line, lines, or edge. The wheel is narrow enough to get to most places, but should a corner be inaccessible, the pattern can be supplemented by using a small, *hollow-ended punch* of the same size, which with a *hammer* can make a single bead impression at a time.

In preparation for anticipated milligraining on a strip bezel edge, the edge should not be finally pressed against the stone, but left extending somewhat away from it to make it accessible to the tool. As the milligrainer passes over the edge, the bezel is automatically pressed against the stone while it is patterned.

It is possible to use the milligrainer tool in contemporary ways for which it was not intended. For instance, an area on a jewel can be textured by first scoring a series of parallel lines, then rolling the milligrainer along them. Lines can cross each other. The milligrainer can also be used to texture wax models being prepared for casting, dipping it in water at intervals to prevent its sticking to the wax. The tool should be dried and oiled afterward to prevent it from rusting in storage.

13–73 KULTAKESKUS OY, Hämeenlinna, Finland, manufacturer. Gold wedding band with two rows of four carré-set diamonds each held by four beads, and ornamented with milligrained perimeters. *Photo: Courtesy Kultakeskus Oy*

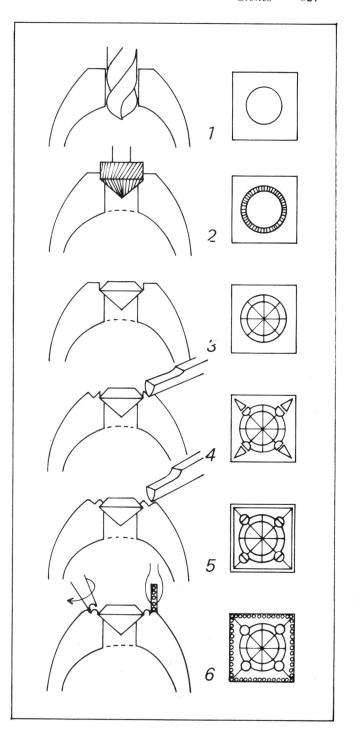

13–74 *MAKING A FLAT-TOP CARRÉ SETTING WITH FOUR BEADS*
Side view and top view of the result
1. *Drill a hole through the metal smaller than the stone's diameter.*
2. *Grind a seat or bearing centered on the hole with a stone-setting bur of the same diameter as that of the stone. This can also be done with a graver.*
3. *Seat the stone which should rest on the bearing with its girdle slightly below the surface of the metal.*
4. *Raise four spurs toward the stone with a graver held at an angle of 45° to the metal surface.*
5. *Trim the metal around the bead and stone by degrees with a chipping action, first at the corners, then from corner to corner until the metal around the stone reaches a level slightly below the stone's girdle. With a knife-edged graver, engrave a line parallel to the edge of the square outer shape of the setting to form a "track" for the milligraining tool. Bright cut the remaining surfaces with a flat graver.*
6. *Form four beads with a beading tool, then press them over the stone's girdle to hold the stone in place. With a milligraining tool, milligrain the edge of the square.*

CARRÉ SETTING

Beading and milligraining are used in several traditional types of stone setting. A typical example is the *carré setting* (from French *carré*, "squared"). This term is used in the jewelry trade to designate a setting in which one round stone is placed in a square, *flat-topped setting* which is one that starts with a flat plane in the case of a ring. The carré setting can also be repeated in a work to make a series of settings to form squares, multiple rows, etc.

First a hole is drilled through the work at the center of the stone's position. This hole should be smaller than the stone's girdle. Then a *stone-setting bur* with a diameter slightly smaller than the stone's girdle is used to make a shoulder to seat the stone. The size of the opening it makes is slightly larger than its diameter due to vibration and will just fit the stone's size. The stone is placed in the seat and corner spurs are lifted with a *graver* to hold it in position. The spurs are then formed into beads, and the surplus metal is trimmed away with gravers. The outer raised ridge around the square is engraved with an inner parallel line and the edge is *milligrained*.

In setting diamonds by this system in a yellow or colored gold jewel, the setting itself is often of white gold or platinum because its color is more compatible with the stone and makes the stone appear larger.

Sometimes, as in a *star setting*, bright-cut lines are engraved radiating from the stone toward the outer edge of the square to provide the illusion of larger size by reflecting light.

13–75 BÖRJE RAJALIN, Finland, designer; manufacturer Kalevala Koru, Helsinki. Brooch in gold and platinum with corderites set in carré settings in groups of four, with four beads holding each stone. The setting perimeter is milligrained, and sides are cut with slotted openings to admit light. The diamonds are set in round, open-shoulder bezels with milligrained edges. *Photo: Otso Pietinen, courtesy Kalevala Koru*

PRONG AND CLAW SETTING

A *prong* is a slender, usually straight but possibly curved, projecting, rigid metal part attached to a bezel or base, used in groups to hold a stone. It can be fabricated from wire or sheet, or can be stamped or cast. In section, the prong can be round, triangular, square, or rectangular, and it can be uniform in section throughout its entire

13–76 FRIEDRICH BECKER, West Germany, designer; manufacturer Fa. Diamass, Dusseldorf. *Brilliant-cut diamond demonstrator*, used with customers to illustrate diamonds cut in sizes from 0.10–2.0ct. Made of wire-brushed stainless steel with synthetic white sapphires held by four prongs and claws bent up in parallel pairs from the flat holder. *Photo: Walter Fischer*

length, or it can taper. Inherent in the concept of a prong is the fact that it ends in a bent-over portion called a *claw* which contacts and holds the stone above the girdle. Claws can be tapered to a pointed shape, rounded, or squared off, and a single prong can terminate in two or more claws. In normal practice, the aim is to make the claw as unobtrusive as possible so that little of the stone is covered, but at times the claw is made bulky to attract attention.

À JOUR OR OPEN SETTING   Because prongs are spaced with openings between them, the *sides* of the setting or mounting of which they are a part can be open, allowing light to enter the stone from below the girdle. This gives a transparent stone brilliance and life. To utilize this effect, transparent and translucent faceted stones normally are set in *prong and claw settings*. A typical six-prong setting for holding a single stone (usually a diamond) raised above a ring shank was introduced by Charles L. Tiffany in 1886 and remains popular today. It is called the Tiffany setting, and is described on p. 624. It is not unusual, however, to find that translucent or opaque cabochon-cut stones with asterism are also set in prong and claw settings. (See channel setting ahead for *à jour cutting* from *below*.)

FABRICATING PRONG AND CLAW SETTINGS   A minimum of three prongs and claws are normally needed to hold a stone in place, though exceptions occur. For conventionally shaped stones, usually four, six, or eight prongs are used. Prong and claw settings can be fabricated by the jeweler. Some examples of the endless possibilities are shown here. The greater the number of parts, the more difficult the fabrication.

A *cup prong setting*, the simplest prong and claw setting for a small faceted stone, can be made from a flat sheet metal disc whose thickness and diameter must relate to the stone size. On this, a four-, six-, or eight-prong arrangement is laid out, marked with a *scriber*, cut out with a *jeweler's saw*, and shaped to contour with a *file*. The flat result is placed over a circular depression earlier hammered into a *lead block* with a *round-ended dapping punch* of appropriate size. The punch is held vertically at

13–77 *FABRICATING PRONG AND CLAW SET-TINGS*
1. *Small cup prong setting*
   A. The flat pattern
   B. Forming the cup prong with a punch
   C. The finished cup prong setting
2. *Bezel with attached prongs*
   A. Made of one piece of metal
   B. Made with separate prongs soldered to a straight-sided bezel
   C. Made with separate prongs soldered to a cone frustum bezel
3. *Box and prong setting*
   A. Bezel with octagonal pyramid frustum, top view
   B. Prongs attached to bezel by solder, claws grooved to form a seat for the stone
   C. The set stone with claws forced over its girdle

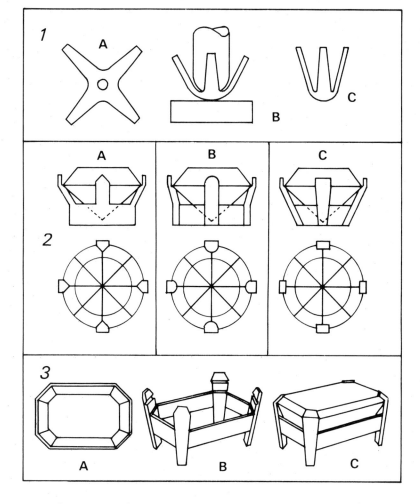

its center and hammered straight down. As the punch descends, the flat pattern is deformed, the prongs move upward, and the bottom becomes cupped. *Flat-jawed pliers* are used to straighten the prongs. If it is decided to also straighten the cup sides which still curve toward the bottom, a hole can be drilled into the center of the bottom, and the setting can be placed in the depression of a *conical* or *square bezel block* and hammered into it with a *bezel block punch.* The setting is then ready to be soldered to a base.

A *bezel with attached prongs* is another relatively simple prong setting, made by first fabricating an ordinary straight-sided bezel from sheet metal, wide enough to cut prongs from it, and smaller in diameter than the stone girdle so the bezel is not seen from above. The prongs are cut from the upper edge and made to slant back from the bezel at the same angle as the pavilion, then to straighten upward. The stone rests on grooves made across the angle bend, and the remaining claw ends are bent over onto the stone.

Separate prongs can be fabricated and soldered to the outer side of an ordinary bezel of any shape, and are treated in the same way. A *tapered-cone bezel* can be made with wire prongs tapering to a point at the bottom soldered to its outer side. In all these examples, only the bent-over claws can be seen from the top view. The bezels shown are solid, and the claws lift the stones to allow light entrance from below the girdle. The same systems can be used with the stone resting on the top edge of the bezel itself which in this case becomes the shoulder, but the bezel

would have to be pierced to allow light to enter the stone from below the girdle.

A *box and prong setting* made for a faceted emerald-cut stone, because of its octagonal shape and the several parts and solderings, is probably the most exacting of all prong settings. This can be made in several ways. In the system shown here, a box or crossbar to which the prongs will be attached is made first, either by fabricating it from flat sheet by the frustum method, or by the use of an *octagonal-shaped bezel block* and *punch.* The box could also be cut from thick metal, then the inner opening and its outer counterpart filed to the angle of the stone's pavilion. Four matching, separate prongs that taper downward or are straight are made from flat sheet. Prongs can also be forged from round or square wire. These are made longer than actually needed to allow for trimming after soldering.

To solder the prongs in position on the box which is placed on a *charcoal* or *magnesium block,* force the prong ends to the same depth marked on the prong into the soldering surface in contact with the box. Then solder them to the box using a high-temperature hard solder. After pickling, surplus prong length at top and bottom is cut, sawed, or filed away. The procedures that follow are the same as for any prong and claw setting, and are described below.

READY-MADE PRONG SETTINGS Ready-made cast or stamped prong settings, called *heads* or *chatons* (French, "settings"), can be purchased for use in rings or any other form of jewelry. They are manufactured in metals of

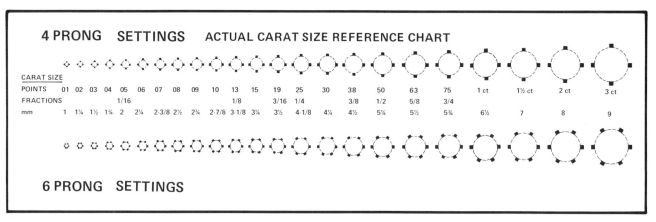

13–78   CARAT SIZE REFERENCE CHART OF FOUR- AND SIX-PRONG
SETTINGS. Courtesy Swest Inc.

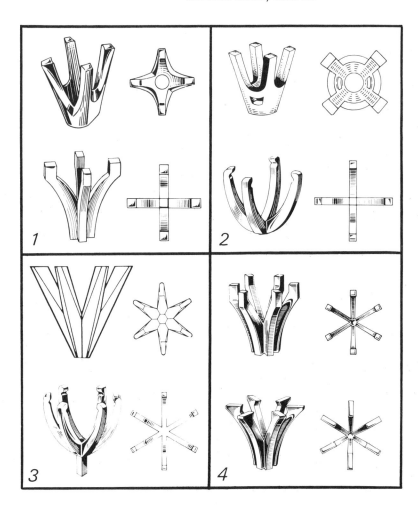

13–79   PRONG SETTINGS, READY-MADE CAST OR
STAMPED
These can be purchased from jewelry suppliers in
four-prong (1 and 2), and six-prong (3 and 4)
types. Most forms are available for stones of carat
sizes 1/8, 3/16, 1/4, 1/2, 5/8, 3/4, 1, 1 1/4, 1 1/2, 1 3/4,
2, 2 1/2, and 3, in 14K white or yellow gold, and in
other alloys. Courtesy Swest Inc.

13–80   KULTAKESKUS OY, Hämeenlinna, Finland,
manufacturer. Ring in 14K yellow gold with faceted
amethyst held in a modified fishtail claw mounting
in which only the very small ends of three triangu-
larly joined claws at each location are bent over the
stone with a pusher, covering very little of it. The
two outer claws are holders, and the center claw is
decorative. Photo: Courtesy Kultakeskus Oy

alloy, color, and quality that match the rest of the work.
They are available in round, oval, square, rectangular,
marquise, or other shapes, in sizes that are calibrated by
carat size, point size, stone diameter, or length and width
dimension, all meant to hold stones of standard shapes and
sizes. Some degree of adjustment is possible by bending
the prongs inward or outward with pliers, but cast prongs
are more brittle than fabricated prongs.

These settings are manufactured in a number of styles.
A round *coronet* or *crown setting* is so called because of
its resemblance to a conventional pinnacled crown worn

on the head. Other types are fishtail, split prong, triple
prong; still other, nameless types have prongs that curve
inward, outward, or have prongs that are narrow or broad
at the top. If the correct size is chosen, these only require
soldering in position to be ready for stone setting.

SETTING A STONE IN A PRONG AND CLAW
SETTING: Tiffany type

Once the prong setting is soldered in position, whether it
is hand fabricated or commercially cast, the manner of

seating the stone is the same. Fix the object in a *ring clamp* or other holding device that holds it rigidly, but allows mobility. For convenience in the test placement and removal of the stone, attach it at the table to an upstanding, cylindrical wad of *sticky wax.* By one method—used for round stones, but more usually for stones having other shapes—when the prongs slant outward at a sufficient angle to allow it, place the stone within the prongs in a level position. The girdle must be below the prongs' upper level and must rest against all of them. In any setting, the stone's culet should not project below the setting's base line. On the inside of each prong, mark the position of the girdle with a *scriber,* then lift away the stone with the wax wad.

Using a *triangular-shaped needle file,* make a notch in each prong at a position just below this mark, then file each position to a depth of at least one-third of the prong's thickness to form the stone's seat. By thinning the prong at this point it becomes easier to bend the prong over the stone later to form the claw at that point. For accurate seating and security, the lower angle so made should match that of the pavilion angle of the stone, and if it does not, file away any surplus to make it match. This angle supports the stone from below and provides a larger bearing surface than just the girdle edge, and is a means of avoiding later possible stone breakage under the pressure of forcing the claws down. Pavilion seat angles vary with different stones, therefore it is necessary to test accuracy by replacing the stone with the wax and checking its angle of contact to the prongs. Seat angles can also be formed with a *flat graver* by slowly shaving away portions of the metal, testing the stone until the correct angle is achieved.

When prongs are steeply inclined or very wide at the top, a different method can be used to seat a round stone within them. Place the stone on the prong ends to see if the girdle covers no more than one-third of the prongs' thickness. Should the stone exceed this amount, and the prong shape permits, bend all the prongs slightly outward an equal distance with *pliers.* Prongs can also be stretched apart equally and simultaneously by placing a *round-ended repoussage tool* whose diameter equals that of the

13–81 SIU LAI HAR, Hong Kong, designer; manufacturer Tai Hang Jewellery Ltd., Hong Kong. White gold ring with 1.96ct emerald-cut diamond set in two prongs and claws, with the culet resting in a groove on the ring shank for a third point of support. *Photo: Courtesy Peter Brindisi Public Relations Ltd., Hong Kong*

13–82 FRIEDRICH BECKER, West Germany. Ring in 18K white gold with two identical step-cut tourmalines mounted culet to culet in four straight prongs. *Photo: Walter Fischer*

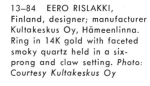

13–83 KULTAKESKUS OY, Hämeenlinna, Finland, manufacturer. Ring in 18K white gold with four heavy prongs that hold the diamond in beveled claws. *Photo: Courtesy Kultakeskus Oy*

13–84 EERO RISLAKKI, Finland, designer; manufacturer Kultakeskus Oy, Hämeenlinna. Ring in 14K gold with faceted smoky quartz held in a six-prong and claw setting. *Photo: Courtesy Kultakeskus Oy*

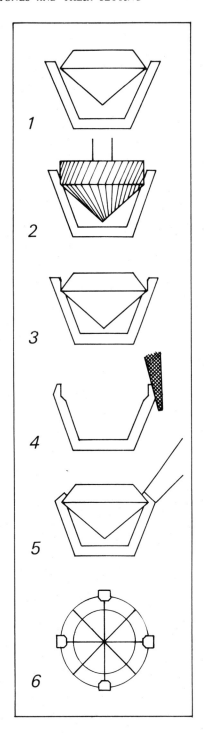

inner diameter distance between prongs, vertically into the opening between them, and lightly hammering it down. If this widening procedure is not possible, a setting of larger diameter must be used.

Measure the stone's girdle diameter with a *degree ligne gauge*, a *micrometer*, or *calipers*. Mount a *stone-setting bur* that matches or is slightly smaller than this dimension in a *flex-shaft* collet. While the object is secured vertically in a *clamp, shellac stick,* or by other means, gradually lower the bur perpendicularly into the center of the prongs' opening and grind them downward up to the point that will become the stone's seating position. Allow the bur to rotate at no more than medium speed to avoid excessive vibration which might cause too great an enlargement of the seat and a loose fit. *File* away any edge burr that may form, or remove it with fine *crocus paper*. Place the stone in the claws to see if the girdle is level; if not, make necessary adjustments.

13–86 PAULA HÄIVÄOJA, Finland, designer; manufacturer Kalevala Koru, Helsinki. Gold ring with specially cut smoky quartz held in a fabricated setting by four small prongs above the girdle, and two small prongs at the culet base. *Photo: Studio Wendt, courtesy Kalevala Koru*

13–85 *STEPS IN SETTING A STONE IN A PRONG AND CLAW SETTING*
1. Place the stone level within the prongs, and mark its girdle position.
2. Remove the stone and either *file* a seat notch in the prongs, or use a *stone-setting bur* to grind a shoulder in the prongs.
3. Place the stone in the seat to test the seat angle.
4. Trim and thin the outer claw surface, and form its shape with a *file.*
5. Replace the stone, force or set down the claws over the stone following a sequence of alternate sides, using a *grooved* or *flat prong setter.*
6. The finished setting from the top view showing four claws holding the stone in place.

13–87 JEAN VENDOME, France. "Nocturne." Fabricated gold and platinum ring with three step-cut aquamarines resting on box bezels and held by claws; and five brilliants mounted in four-prong and claw settings on frustum cones. *Photo: Frédéric Arlotti*

From the seat upward, the remaining portion of the prong now becomes the claw. Claws can be treated in several ways, depending on the design and the initial prong shape. Shaping a prong is done on its *outer surfaces only,* leaving the inner surface intact to avoid a change in stone seat size. A *rotary file* can be used to shape the claw to form a tapered or blunt point, or a squared end; a *cup bur* can be used to round a prong end; or the prong can be divided by sawing it into two equal parts which are then spread apart in divergent directions. In many cases, claw sides and what will become its upper surface thicknesses are diminished with a *hand file,* again on the outer side only. By thinning the metal the need for excessive pressure when bending the claw is eliminated.

In preparation for bending, smooth the claws' outer surfaces with a fine *abrasive paper* and remove any remaining scratches with *rouge* and a *polishing cloth.* Claws can also be mechanically polished with *miniature buffs* on a *flex-shaft* to avoid as much as possible later subjection of the stone to this treatment. If mechanical polishing is done, take care not to misshape the prongs or wear them away with the abrasive.

To set the stone in the prong seat, using *flat-jawed snipe-nosed pliers,* or *parallel-jawed pliers* (both without serrated jaws), slightly bend each claw to a vertical position so the stone can still enter and be seated. In large settings the claws can be bent to slightly less than vertical so the stone can be snapped in place. It is sometimes possible when setting a stone with a flaw to place it in a position where a claw covers the flaw. Assuming that this setting is on a ring (it can be on any piece of jewelry), immobilize the ring to facilitate setting the stone. To do so, place the ring on a *ring mandrel* that has been wrapped with a thin rubber sheet to help the ring to gain traction and prevent its sideways movement, or in the leather-lined jaws of a *ring clamp.*

THE SHELLAC STICK AND ITS USES   A *shellac stick* is traditionally used during stone setting to hold the workpiece in place, and allow it to be manipulated. In a common form, it consists of a horizontal wooden disc or platform with an attached wooden handle. Shellac sticks of various other shapes are used to accommodate the shape of the workpiece. In all cases, their upper surface is covered with a thick coating of a shellac-pitch, or a sealing wax composition. To prevent the shellac from adhering to the work later, first paint the lower surface of the object with a thin slurry of *chalk* and allow it to dry. Heat the shellac with a torch flame, and if necessary, mound or otherwise shape it to conform to the underside contour of the work to completely support it. While it is still soft, press the object into it only to a depth sufficient to hold it. *Do not allow the shellac to rise into and fill any stone-setting holes.* While it remains plastic, some of the composition can be molded with the fingers over the edges of the work at places to help hold it, always leaving the stone-setting areas free. As the shellac cools it hardens, and this can be hastened by dipping it in cold water. In work, hold the shellac stick by the handle with the left hand, with the handle base wedged into a V-board groove, or up against a worktable edge to keep it rigid while the stone is set. After setting the stone, to remove the work, first remove any shellac from overlapped edges, and gently pry the work loose with a *blunt tool,* tapping the tool end with a hammer if necessary. Any shellac adhering to the work can be removed with its solvent, alcohol.

STONE-SETTING TOOLS   When using manual force alone to bend the claws over a stone, a commonly used tool is a *grooved prong setter.* This is a wooden-handled small tool with a straight, short, steel or brass shaft about 3 in (7.6 cm) long. It looks like a bezel pusher, except that its end is centrally grooved to allow the claw to be cradled in the depression while the tool is rocked to push the claw over the stone by gentle hand pressure. This tool end shape helps in avoiding the hazard of scratching the stone should the pusher slip in the setting down process. Another claw-setting tool is a square-sectioned, *two-angled pusher* whose end is two-thirds flat in the direction perpendicular to the tool shaft, while the rest is at an angle of 45°. This allows the accommodation of different angles of work. Another tool used has a flat, square end whose surface has been roughened with a file to provide a grip on the claw and prevent slipping. Still another pusher has a round shaft and a circular, flat end which is often used for final pushing. Special *prong-bending pliers* are also available for this purpose. Where claw shape and setting size allows, a *claw pusher* used for setting small round stones consists of a round shaft with a circular, hollow-domed end large enough to encompass *all* the claws of a single setting at one time. This is held vertically over the claws, and while all are cupped within the hollow, it is hammered gently down, bringing them all down on the stone simultaneously.

Stone breakage resulting from too much pressure exerted on the stone in setting down the claws is the major hazard. The stones used in a claw setting should be of a hardness of at least 6 Mohs' scale. Stone breakage also occurs when bending the claw *short* which pinches the stone girdle and chips it at the place of contact. Should a gap between stone and claw still remain after using hand and tool pressure alone to force a claw on the stone, either of two methods can be tried. First *file* the claw still thinner from the outside (though excessive thinness should be avoided as this makes a weak claw) and try hand pressure with a tool again. Alternately, place a *round, flat-ended punch* called a *closing tool* squarely on the claw, and tap the punch end lightly with a *small hammer* until the gap is closed. In lightweight settings used for small stones, claw thickness may be small enough to only require the use of a *burnisher* to force the claw onto the stone. To keep the stone seated squarely, set the claws down in pairs on opposite sides of the stone.

After the claw is set down, if necessary it can be trimmed to final shape with a *file* having a safe side, edge, or surface on the part that contacts the stone to avoid scratching it. Lacking this, a safe edge can be made on a file by grinding the teeth off on an *Arkansas* or *India oilstone.* The amount of claw metal visible on the stone crown in the finished setting should be minimal to allow as much as possible of the stone to be visible, without, however, being so small as to hazard its loss. Polish the claw to final smoothness with hand polishing tools, or by mechanical polishing with *miniature buffs* mounted on a *flex-shaft,* using abrasives suited to the amount of repair needed. There should be no roughness remaining on the prong or claw which might catch clothing or hair. The setting can be inspected with an *eye loupe* and corrections made if needed.

GROUP SETTINGS

Group settings are those in which several stones are set together to form a *cluster;* to cover a surface, called a *pavé setting;* or in linear series, called a *channel setting.*

CLUSTER SETTING

This is the placement of several stones in an isolated group, usually in a circular relationship. Stones of the same size can be used, or stones of different sizes. They can be held by beads or in a prong and claw setting. Cluster settings in standard precious metal alloys for use with small stones are available commercially in a large variety with the beads already cast in place. They can also be fabricated, as shown in Illustration 13–89.

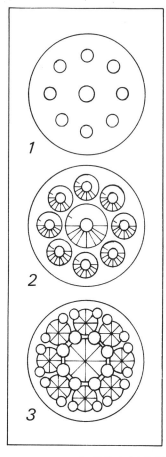

13–88 KULTAKESKUS OY, Hämeenlinna, Finland, manufacturer. Ring in 14K gold. In the nine-stone brilliant cluster or rosette setting, the eight outer stones are mounted by four prongs and claws, and the center larger and higher stone is held by eight prongs. *Photo: Courtesy Kultakeskus Oy*

13–89 *PAVÉ SETTING A NINE-STONE CLUSTER WITH BEADS*

1. Measure the diameter of the stones and mark their positions on the metal so that they barely touch each other, allowing approximately 1 mm extra metal beyond the cluster. *Center punch* each position and drill a small hole through the base metal at each stone's center point. The base can be domed slightly if desired.
2. Using a *stone-setting bur* with an outside diameter matching the stone diameter, grind a bearing seat centered on the small hole in the base metal for each stone, starting with the central one. Do not force the bur through the metal but only partly through, leaving the hole sides slanting downward toward the hole.
3. Starting from the center and working outward, or from one side and working across, raise spurs for beads at the locations that will hold the stones. With the stone in place, use a *beading tool* to form each bead, pressing it over onto the stone to hold it in place. In this setting, the inner row of beads also holds one side of the outer row of stones. Prongs can be used instead of beads to hold the stone. In this case, four to six holes are drilled at each prong position for a single stone, and the prong wires are inserted and soldered in place. The stone is set in the prongs as already described. The cluster mount can be soldered or otherwise held to a base in a way that permits light to reach the pavilions of the **stones.**

PAVÉ SETTING

Pavé (French, "paved") is a term used in the jewelry trade normally to indicate the setting of small, usually round, faceted or cabochon stones or pearls of the same or very nearly the same size, close together so they cover an entire area. The metal supporting them is almost completely concealed by the stones which appear to be girdle to girdle, level with each other. Because a large percentage of the metal is removed in making the setting holes, heavy-gauge metal is used to strengthen the construction. The surface can be flat, convex, concave, or combinations of these. In order to preserve this form visually, the stones are set as nearly as possible with their tables in the same plane, which helps give the paved effect. According to the design, the stones can be placed in concentric circles, rows, diagonal or straight-line series, or irregularly.

To pavé set stones, first mount the object on a *shellac stick.* Mark the position for each stone (they should barely touch each other) with a sharp, *pointed scribe,* or a *pointed graver.* Drill a hole through the center of the metal at each location, its size slightly smaller than the stone's girdle diameter. Either *engrave* a shoulder for each stone, or use a *stone-setting bur* to make one.

The normal method of holding the stones in a pavé setting is by the use of raised beads. Place the stones in position, one at a time, starting from left to right. In the manner already described, with a graver, raise the necessary spurs for them, if possible in a regularly placed arrangement to give an even effect. A minimum of three beads, but more usually four, are made for each stone. It is often possible in tight arrangements for a single bead at one position to hold two adjacent stones. If in the stone arrangement spaces occur between stones, these can be filled with extra beads which are merely decorative. If the space is relatively large, it is also possible to set an extra, small stone at that place. When all the spurs have been raised, shape them into beads with a *beading tool,* making small adjustments to align the beads where necessary.

An effect similar to a pavé setting can be achieved by mounting many small stones in prong and claw settings placed next to each other on a surface. In this case, mark the positions of each of the stones with a circle that matches their girdle size. Drill at least four holes *within each circle* at cardinal points, each to hold a prong. Match the hole size to the gauge of the wire used to form the prongs. Place lengths of this wire longer than that needed for the final prong length in each hole with its end projecting somewhat through the base. Because they fit tightly.

13–90 RAYMOND TEMPLIER, France. Brooch in platinum with onyx, matte crystal, and pavé-set diamonds, each held by four beads. In this art deco jewel, the outer setting frame is milligrained. *Photo: Musée des Arts Décoratifs, Paris*

13–91 ENGLAND, late 19th century. Necklace with diamonds mounted in silver and gold made to be divided so the lower portion can be used as a tiara. Composed of a chain of round diamonds in closely linked carré collets that support an elaborate fringe of pavé-set foliate and scroll motifs, with the outer larger round stones in tapered collets held by eight claws. Photo: Courtesy Sotheby Parke Bernet & Co., London

they will stand upright. When all are in position, solder them in place. Cut or grind off the surplus of the projecting ends flush with the back. Drill a hole at the center of each four-prong arrangement for the admission of light. Set the stones in the prongs by forming claws in the usual way.

CHANNEL SETTING

In a fabricated *channel setting,* a series of quadrilateral, straight-sided, normally transparent and faceted stones, are set next to each other so that no metal appears between

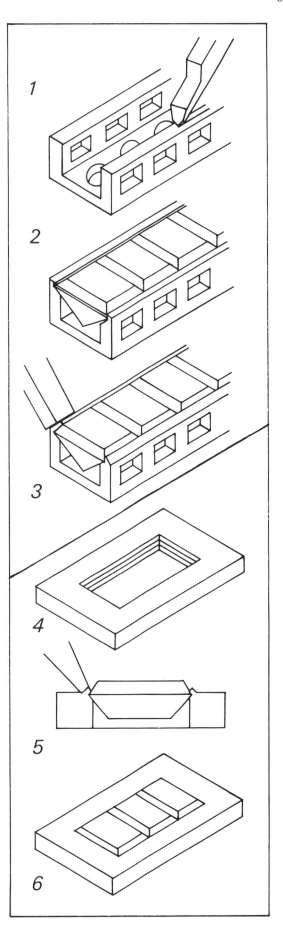

13–92 *FABRICATING A CHANNEL SETTING*

Raised channel setting
1. Cut the channel setting race with a shoulder bearing using an onglette graver held at an angle of 60° to the metal. A hole has been drilled below each stone setting, and an opening made in the channel sides to admit light to the stone.
2. Place the equal sided stones, girdles barely touching, in the channel on the angle's shoulder, with their girdles resting below the channel's upper edge which is still upright.
3. Set the channel edge down on the stone's girdle using a flat-faced stone-setting tool. Go over the channel edge with a highly polished burnisher. The edges can be milligrained.

Flush channel setting
4. Pierce an opening in the thick base metal, less than the total dimension of the stones to be set together, side by side. With an onglette or other graver sharpened to the right or left side, carve a shoulder in the opening to seat the stones.
5. Remove some metal from the setting around the stones, but leave the ridge of the original metal thickness around the setting. Place the stones, and with a flat-faced punch, chase the metal around the stones onto their girdles.
6. The finished flush channel setting.

13–93   JEAN VENDOME, France. " 'S' Ring." White gold with step-cut aquamarine mounted in an open-ended channel setting, held under tension from both sides. This view shows the stone's pavilion and culet ridge. *Photo: Frédéric Arlotti*

13–94   ADDA HUSTED ANDERSEN, U.S.A. Gold ring with table-cut citrine and smoky quartz in open-ended channel settings. *Photo: Paul Parker*

13–95   MARKUS FRANZ HUBER, Hong Kong. White gold ring set with baguette-shaped diamonds in channel settings, with 1, 2, 3, 4, and 6 baguettes on each level, totaling 16. *Photo: Peter Brindisi Public Relations Ltd., Hong Kong*

13–96   MICHÈLE SCHMID, France, designer; manufacturer Jean Desmousseay. Ring in white gold with tapering, curved channel-set diamonds in diminishing sizes. *Photo: Michel Plassard and Uwe Ommer, courtesy Centre d'Information du Diamant, Paris*

13–97   FRANCE, 20th century. Platinum and diamond necklace, the stones completely dominating the almost invisible platinum which serves only to support them. Baguette diamonds are channel set, small round diamonds are pavé set, and large round diamonds are set in open-shoulder frustum cone bezels, those at the sides in four-claw settings, and those at the back counterpoise in six-claw settings. *Photo: Courtesy Sotheby Parke Bernet & Co., London*

the stones on two of their sides which touch each other at the girdle. Step-cut stones cut to calibrated standard sizes for use together are called *calibré* or *calibré-cut*. They are supported in the setting on the other two sides by two upstanding, parallel races, tracks, or *channels*, hence the name. These form parallel, straight ledges when the stones all have right-angled sides, or curved or tapering ledges when they have a quadrilateral keystone shape (two parallel and two converging sides). The base plane on which the channel rests can be flat, convex, concave, or

combinations of these forms. Because the stones are matched as closely as possible in size and color, a single series forms a *line;* by placing channels next to each other, a series of lines becomes an entire *area.*

Channel settings are common in commercial jewelry, especially when small baguette diamonds are employed. Making them is a professionally demanding act requiring care, patience, and experience. The process is briefly described as follows.

When the channel base holding the sides is metal sheet, it is common practice to cut openings below each stone, called *à jour cutting* because they are intended to admit light to the stone. If the setting permits, *à jours* are also made in the sides, below the girdle. These are made with

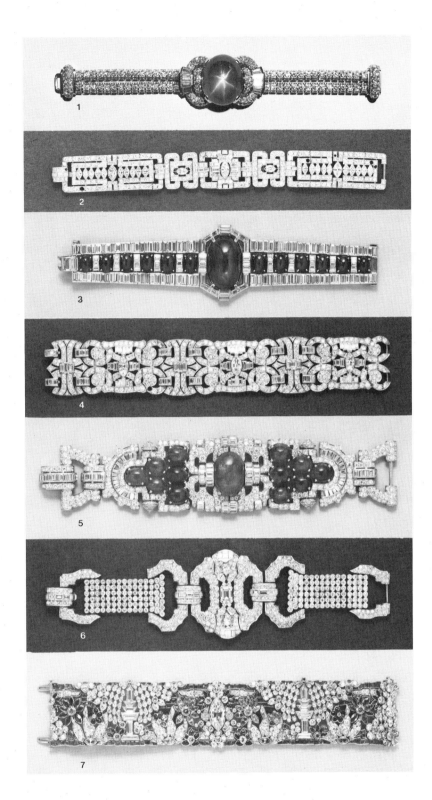

13–98 U.S.A. *BRACELETS OF THE 1920s–1950s.*

From top to bottom:

1. Platinum double strap mount centering on a 100ct star sapphire held by four claws; 334 round diamonds in flat-top beaded settings; 16 baguette diamonds comprising approx. 16ct in channel settings.
2. Platinum openwork geometric mount set with 25 marquise-shaped diamonds totaling approx. 4.95ct, in milligrained box settings with two end beads; 17 baguette diamonds in channel settings, and 305 round diamonds (6 missing) weighing approx. 13.15ct in pavé settings.
3. Platinum mount centering on a cabochon ruby approx. 76ct, held by four claws; flanked by 12 cabochon rubies weighing approx. 42ct, each held by four claws; with 186 baguette diamonds weighing approx. 42.75ct, set in channel settings.
4. Platinum openwork mount set with three marquise-shaped diamonds weighing approx. 2.75ct; 406 round diamonds in pavé settings, and 105 baguette diamonds with a total weight of approx. 20.50ct, in channel settings.

5. Platinum openwork mount centering a cabochon emerald weighing approx. 29ct held by four claws; flanked by 12 cabochon emeralds weighing approx. 60ct, each held by four claws; with 444 round pavé-set and 125 baguette channel-set diamonds weighing approx. 40ct.
6. Platinum mount centering on four square-pronged, corner-held emerald-cut diamonds weighing approx. 2ct; 6 pear-shaped, four-prong-held diamonds, and 16 baguette diamonds weighing approx. 4ct; and 498 round diamonds weighing approx. 20ct (182 set in rows à jour).
7. Platinum openwork mount in the form of two fountains made of 12 fancy-shaped diamonds weighing approx. 7ct; each spouting 30 drop-shaped diamonds; and garden flower motifs centering on a fancy yellow marquise-shaped diamond of approx. 4ct; the flowers formed by 92 fancy colored diamonds weighing approx. 7ct; 400 round diamonds; and numerous emeralds, rubies, and sapphires. Most of the round- and curve-shaped stones are set in rub-over bezels, some in pavé mounts, and the straight-sided stones are in channel settings. *Photos: Courtesy Sotheby Parke Bernet Inc., New York*

a *saw,* held at an angle slanting toward the stone, thus forming an internal chamfer when made at the side, or an external chamfer when made opposite the stone.

Mount the work with the channels soldered in place on a *shellac stick.* Cut a continuous shoulder in each of the upstanding channels with an *onglette graver,* sharpened right or left as needed. Place the stones in this channel groove and test them for size. Make small adjustments in the channel width with a graver as necessary to accommodate small changes in stone size. Place the stones in the channel. Using a *flat-ended punch* and a *small lightweight hammer,* chase the channel sides against each stone in turn to hold it in place. It is also possible to form beads to hold the stones in the channel.

A variation of a channel setting is one that resembles a

gypsy setting in principle, in that the base metal itself is used to form the channel and hold the stone. In this case, make a hole in the base metal whose shape matches that of the stone but is smaller than its girdle. Using a *graver,* form a shoulder along the sides of the hole to seat the stone. The shoulder angle must conform to the angle of the stone's pavilion just below the girdle. If an undercut is made in the channel sides, the stone can be snapped in place. Chase the metal over the stone's girdle edges with an appropriate *punch* and *hammer.*

MÊLÉE CHANNEL   Mêlée (French, "mix or blend") is a name used in the trade to indicate a small diamond cut from a fragment of a larger stone. Its size ranges from one-fourth to one-twelfth of a carat. When such stones are set in a channel, it is termed a mêlée channel.

13–99   JEAN CLAUDE CHAMPAGNAT, France. Gold ring with triangular, cushion, and round brilliants, each held by a single claw perpendicular to the base against which they are supported. *Photo: Del Bocca*

13–100   JEAN CLAUDE CHAMPAGNAT, France. Gold ring with three groups of six diamonds held in cubes by prong and claw settings. *Photo: Del Bocca* ▼

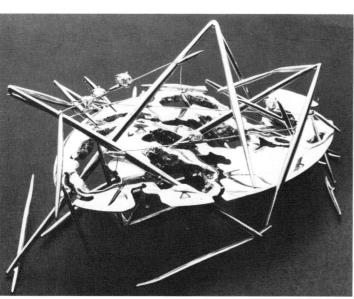

13–101   JEAN CLAUDE CHAMPAGNAT, France. White gold brooch with brilliants mounted in three-prong settings attached to tapered tubes through which a wire is passed. These wires are held under tension by springs mounted at the back. The whole form is constructed with the lowest wire sections parallel to the body plane to support the brooch in air, away from the body. *Photo: Del Bocca*

14

METAL FINISHING
Achieving Desired Surface Appearance

METAL FINISHING TECHNIQUES

Manual and mechanical

Metal finishing is a broad term implying that the surface of a metal object is altered, or brought to a new surface. This is done by several basic means including: *cleaning solution techniques, hand and mechanical techniques, chemical pickling techniques,* and *metallic coating techniques.* Depending on the ultimate objective, one or more of these processes may be used on the same object.

TYPES OF SOIL ON METALS

In metal finishing, a prime objective is the removal of soil on metal. Various types of metal soil are possible, and the choice of cleaning process depends on the kind of soil it is. Soils on metals can be *oil-based liquid compositions* that may or may not be saponifiable; *semisolid compounds* or mixtures of abrasives and liquid binders that are either saponifiable or not; and *solid compounds* that contain some oil but are mainly solids; oxide scale; and miscellaneous surface contaminants. These substances may be organic or inorganic. Knowing the composition of the soil you are trying to remove determines the appropriate cleaning medium.

ORGANIC

Saponifiable: Animal and vegetable oils, fingerprints
Unsaponifiable: Mineral oils, waxes
Miscellaneous: These include soils that are changed chemically due to heat-generated changes of the metal. For example, in polishing or buffing, the excessive frictional heat generated turns the free fatty acids contained in polishing compounds into hard substances and caked metal soaps which are very difficult to remove. Such substances also change chemically due to aging and drying out.

INORGANIC

Scale and smut: Metallic oxides that occur when soldering, and metallic residues that occur in etching.
Polishing compounds: Some substances in abrasives, grinding and polishing residues and grits
Miscellaneous: Fused soldering flux, lacquer, etc.

CLEANING SOLUTION FINISHING TECHNIQUES

By the use of *cleaning solutions,* soil in the form of organic or inorganic dirt on the metal surface is removed before subjecting the work to further finishing processes. The object is dipped, soaked, boiled, or rinsed in the solution, depending on the need, the type of soil, and the cleaning substance used.

THE MECHANISM OF CLEANING ACTION

In *detergency* or cleaning action, one or more of the following phenomena may take place:
Wetting is the first requirement of cleaning soil from metal. In wetting, surface action agents in the cleaning liquid loosen metal soil by displacing air and lowering surface and interface tensions.
Emulsification occurs after wetting, and is the dispersion of two mutually immiscible liquids (oil and water) by agitation, temperature raising, and other factors.
Solubilization is the process by which oil solubility is increased in water by the use of a surface active agent.
Saponification is the reaction between any organic oil containing fatty acids and free alkalis to form soaps which can then be eliminated by washing them away.
Deflocculation is the process by which solid soil is broken down into very fine particles then dispersed in the cleaning media which allows them to be discarded.
Mechanical action is important in almost all metal detergency, as it greatly increases the efficiency and speed of soil removal. Manual scrubbing or brushing, hand or mechanical agitation of a solution, moving the work in the solution, and electrolytic cleaning are mechanical processes frequently used in most cleaning circumstances.
Rinsing is the removal of soils in solution by their dispersal through running water. The water temperatures from a water tap can vary considerably during summer and winter. A warm water rinse at 100–110° F (37.7–43° C) is desirable after an alkaline cleaning operation since cold water may cause some alkali to return to a solid state and adhere to the metal surface.

CLEANING MEDIUMS

The particular cleaning medium used alone or in soil removal solutions depends on the type of soil to be removed. The choice includes emulsions, detergents, acids, solvents, and electrocleaners, all used in cleaning mediums to remove various types of soil.

Emulsions are dilute solutions of organic alkaline solvents, 1 part solvent to 50–100 parts water, combined and used hot, at 130–160° F (54–71° C), to remove semisolid or solid soils from metals, and to dissolve and emulsify mineral oils and other unsaponifiable oils from polished work. A common example used in cleaning jewelry is a soap and ammonia solution made of 1 level teaspoon soap flakes, 1 teaspoon ammonia, and 1 quart of water. The object is boiled in this solution, or can be brushed with it, then is rinsed under warm running water. Agitation with a brush helps to dislodge soils from grooves and corners. Alkaline cleaners effectively remove all kinds of fluids and soils left by polishing and buffing compounds, and are the least expensive to use. If a bath is used, agitate it to prevent oil float which otherwise will be redeposited on the work when it is removed.

Detergents work by wetting, emulsifying, dispersing, and solubilizing soils. They contain buffering salts, sequestering agents, dispersants, inhibitors, wetting agents, and soaps. They are used especially after polishing and buffing processes, the solution heated to a temperature range of 150–220° F (65–104° C), in concentrations of from 4–10% by volume (6–12 oz per gal).

Acids are not used to remove polishing and buffing compounds, but are used to remove metal oxides such as surface firescale and subsurface firestain. Specific acids or combinations of acids are used for specific metals. Organic and inorganic acids remove soils by attacking the surface and dislodging particles by dissolution, etching, or emulsification. This is accomplished by immersion, soaking, agitation, brushing or hand wiping, and rinsing to remove the sludge that forms in the process. (This process is discussed under Pickling or Acid Dipping, p. 417.)

Solvents are any substances that are used to dilute or dissolve another substance. They are capable of decompos-ing, breaking up, loosening, and dissolving all or part of another substance by dissipating or disintegrating it, then dispersing it in a removable form. The solvent used must be appropriate for and active on the particular soil to be removed. Some are fast drying and others slow drying, some are used cold and others hot or cold. Solvents can be applied with a saturated cotton pad or with a brush, and the object is either hand scrubbed with these; soaked in the solvent; or sprayed with it so the solvent runs off with the soil. Solvents are sometimes used as a first step to soften soil substances that are not saponifiable, and the object is then subjected to alkaline cleaning or emulsion cleaning methods to remove the rest.

WARNING:
These generally colorless liquids, each of which has a particular, characteristic odor, are sometimes highly inflammable, or give off strong, toxic vapors that are hazardous to health. Use a solvent only in circumstances of good ventilation, preferably near an exhaust fan. Always use *clean* solvents and provide a shallow container to catch used solvent or drippings. Most soils dissolved by solvents can be wiped off metal with a clean cloth or paper towel which should be *immediately discarded* as they are a fire hazard. Do not store solvent-impregnated materials.

HAND AND MECHANICAL FINISHING TECHNIQUES

The choice of techniques employed in hand or mechanical metal finishing depends on the desired result. Among the many hand and mechanical techniques used are *grinding, abrasive blasting, tumbling, burnishing, polishing, brushing,* and *buffing* which are discussed here in this order.

GRINDING

Grinding consists of the physical removal of metal by the help of a bonded abrasive in paper-backed, cloth-backed, stick, or wheel form. These are worked by hand

The Chemical Composition of Solvents and Substances They Work Upon

Solvents	Chemical Composition	Substances Worked Upon
Ammonia	NH_3	Greases, soaps, oils, buffing compounds
Acetone	CH_3COCH_3	Lacquer, rubber cement, resins, fats, oils, plastics, many organic compounds
Methyl alcohol (methanol)	CH_3OH	Resins, shellac, varnish, oils, fats
Ethyl alcohol (ethanol)	C_2H_5OH	Resins, shellac, varnish, oils, fats
Turpentine	–	Oils, fats, asphaltum, oil-based paint, rubber, dried polishing and buffing compounds
Benzene	C_6H_6	The same substances as turpentine, but is a stronger solvent
Kerosene	–	Lubricants, pigmented paints
Carbon tetrachloride	CCl_4	Pigmented paints, greases; also used as a fire extinguisher
Trichlorethylene	$CHCl:CCl_2$	Lacquer, non-water-based adhesives
Water	H_2O	Water-based substances

Electrolytic cleaners and cleaning devices are discussed under Metallic Buildup, p. 680.

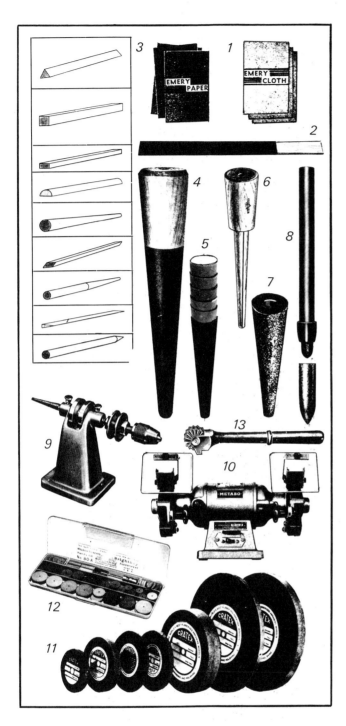

14-1 HAND AND MECHANICAL GRINDING TOOLS AND MATERIALS

1. *Paper- and cloth-backed abrasives in sheet form.*
2. *Hand grinder with layers of emery paper, grits of 4/0, 3/0, 2/0, 0, 1, 2, 3, mounted on a wooden stick. Used layers are stripped off.*
3. *Hand grinding stone sticks or slips in various shapes: triangle 2½ × ⅛-3½ × ⁵⁄₁₆ in; square 2½ × ⅛-3½ × ⁵⁄₁₆ in; flat rectangle 3½ × ½ × ³⁄₁₆ in; half-round 4 × ¼ in; round tapered 4 × ⁵⁄₁₆ × ⅛ in; lozenge or diamond 3½ × ⅜ × ¼ in; conical round 4 × ³⁄₁₆ × ¹⁄₁₆ in; knife edge 4 × 1 × ¹⁄₁₆ in; round 4 × ¼-½ in.*
4. *Cone inside ring shell mounted on a solid wood mandrel drilled for use on a tapered spindle, 4½ in long.*
5. *Assorted grit replacement shells, used for smoothing and finishing the inside of ring shanks.*
6. *Split wood mandrel approx. 4 in long, used with flat cloth-backed abrasive cut to fit into the slit at one end, the remainder wrapped counterclockwise for a right-hand mandrel around the mandrel to the desired thickness, then held by a rubber band.*
7. *Solid corundum lathe cone in medium and fine grades, long lasting.*
8. *Brightboy stick metal mandrel, 5 × ⁵⁄₁₆ in with chuck to hold replacement points 1 × ⁹⁄₃₂ in, for manual use on internal deep cavities and narrow channels.*
9. *Grinding head on which a grinding wheel or other grinding and polishing equipment can be mounted, operated by a motor with a V-belt. Can have a step pulley attachment to allow several speeds by changing the V-belt to a different groove.*
10. *Double grinding motor 220 volt, 185 watt, 150 × 20 mm, ¾ hp, 3000 rpm with plastic eye shields.*
11. *Cratex rubber-bonded grinding wheels, available in a variety of diameters and thicknesses.*
12. *Brightboy small rubber-bonded abrasive wheel assortment in fine and extra fine grades, ½-1 in Ø, with mandrel and chuck for mounting on a flex-shaft.*
13. *Wheel dresser used to restore a flat working face on a grinding wheel that has become cupped by placing it against the wheel while it rests on the tool rest and drawing it horizontally across the wheel.*

coarsest to finest numbered 2, 1, 0, 00, and 000. Coated papers or cloths to which *Turkish emery* (a natural compound of aluminum oxide and iron oxide), *artificial aluminum oxide* or *carborundum* (artificial silicon carbide) is bonded by high-glue (used dry) or synthetic resins (used dry or wet) are available. The edges of Turkish emery wear smooth without fracturing which is desirable for fine grinding operations; artificial aluminum oxide is sharp, hard, fast cutting and long wearing; and silicon carbide fractures when dull to present new, sharp cutting edges to the work. Paper backing is used for hand abrading operations and cloth for either hand or mechanical grinding. They are manufactured in flat sheets or strips used for manual grinding, and belts, wheels, discs, cones, drums, and shells used mounted on portable or stationary belt sanders, grinding or polishing motors, and flex-shafts. They are manufactured in grits from 6–240 mesh, and also in increasing finenesses up to 600-mesh grade.

WARNING:
When using these abrasives with a mechanical power source, always wear *goggles* or a *face shield* to protect the

or placed on a grinding head or other machine to remove excess metal, round a contour, create a shape, smooth a surface, or to reshape or dress the edge of a tool. Of all the metal-finishing processes in which metal is removed, grinding is the roughest and is generally used for preliminary surface conditioning that is followed by smoothing, polishing, and buffing.

HAND AND MACHINE GRINDING WITH BACKED ABRASIVES

Flint sandpaper is sometimes used to grind a metal surface though this abrasive is not as long lasting as the abrasive mentioned below. It is available in grades from

eyes against flying particles. If dust is generated, wear a suitable *dust respirator,* and work near an exhaust.

In *manual grinding* of flat surfaces, the metal is rubbed back and forth without rocking on the abrasive sheet which is placed on a flat, smooth surface; and in contour shaping, the abrasive is rubbed on the metal. With each change of abrasive fineness, rotate the metal 90° to be better able to note progress by seeing the elimination of the direction of the previous, coarser scratches as they are replaced by those made by the finer abrasive in the new direction. The hand grinding process is slower than machine grinding.

In *machine grinding,* each form of the mounted abrasive has its uses and limitations. Strips of abrasive cloth are inserted into the slot of a wooden ring mandrel and wrapped around it. These are mounted on a polishing spindle to grind the inside of rings. When using a flat disc, the face cuts and not the rim, so grinding direction does not have to be changed. In *belt grinding,* the belt is backed up by a hard or soft contact roll that provides opposing pressure to the work. Generally, flat or convex shapes are ground in belt grinding as the belt is not usually flexible. The life of the belt depends on the speed at which it is used, the hardness of the metal being ground, and the degree of pressure of the work against the belt. Always use light pressure, especially important with a new belt as excessive pressure causes glazing, until the belt is broken in and maintains a uniform cutting action. Waterproof backing cloths permit the use of a lubricant in the form of water or a water-soluble oil that drips on the work.

HAND GRINDING STONE STICKS

Grinding stones are used as whetstones to sharpen a tool. (For a discussion of their use in this connection, see Engraving, Chapter 8.) In *stick form,* square, half-round, round, triangular, etc., abrasive stones Water of Ayr or Scotch stone, Arkansas stone, Washita stone, and various coarsenesses of carborundum are also used by hand with water to smooth surfaces, rub away scratches, and to shape edges and contours. The stick can be shaped in contour or section for use on particular surface forms. Grinding is followed by smoothing and polishing.

GRINDING WHEELS

Grinding wheels are solid compounds of abrasives that are bonded in a vitreous baked clay (code letter **V**), rubber bond (**R**), or plastic bond material (**B**). The common abrasives used are aluminum oxide (**A**) or silicon carbide (**S**). Grinding wheels are manufactured in a series of grit sizes from very coarse to very fine grades. They are used on the work in order from coarsest to finest, the finest making scratches so fine as to be indistinguishable from those made by polishing compounds (used on a polishing wheel) and which can be eliminated by polishing. The coarse grit sizes range from 6–36; medium grit from 36–60; and the finest are available from 70–600 grit. The degree of wheel composition hardness is designated by letters. Very soft: C–G; soft: H–K; medium: L–O; hard: P–S; very hard: T–Z. Most grinding wheels are printed with these identifying code letters.

These wheels are pierced with a hole that corresponds in size with the diameter of the standard grinding and polishing motor shaft on which they are mounted and tightly held by flanged retaining discs and threaded nuts so there is no vibration in their use which would be dangerous. The grinding head or motor is provided with an ad-

justable work rest on which a tool being ground or the work rests and is supported while being ground. The wheel normally turns away from the worker, and grinding is done by the wheel rim or face against which the work is pressed and passed slowly up and back. The top, forward quarter of the wheel is used when the wheel turns away from you. It is also possible to work a grinding motor with the wheel running toward you, in which case the lower, forward quarter section is used and grinding proceeds more rapidly. Especially when grinding tools to reshape or resharpen them, the wheel must be lubricated with water which drips on the wheel while it turns, in order to avoid overheating the metal. Overheating a tool will cause it to lose its temper.

Solid grinding wheels are used with motors that rotate at 1750 rpm, with a wheel surface speed of between 5000–6000 sfpm. (See Table, "Polishing and Buffing Wheel Perimeter Surface Speed Calculation," in this chapter.) They should not be used at less than recommended speeds or their cutting capability will not be realized; nor above maximum speeds, or safety will be endangered. Never force a grinding wheel as local high temperatures are generated by friction in the work, and the wheel breaks down excessively. Too little pressure causes the wheel to become rapidly glazed, decreasing its efficiency.

In *progressive grinding,* a series of wheels of decreasing grit size are used. The initial grit removes a major part of the unwanted metal, and the removal is completed by successively finer wheels. With each grit change, the direction of the wheel on the metal is changed 90° to remove previously made grinding scratches. The work should be brushed before each change to remove any remaining abrasive particles. In grinding it is good practice to stop the grinding action enough above the base metal to leave sufficient metal for further finishing. The work should be done under water lubrication; if this is lacking, dip the piece in cool water from time to time.

WHEELS PREPARED WITH ADHESIVES AND GRIT

For grinding and coarser polishing operations, an abrasive grit can be made to hold on a cloth or leather polishing wheel surface with hide glue or, more commonly today, commercially made cement compounds and adhesives.

Hide glues: Use only a good quality of hide glue. Melt only as much as is needed at one time because when prepared hide glue stands unused, it decomposes rapidly by bacterial action. Soak the flakes or ground glue for an hour, then melt them, preferably in a thermostatically controlled glue pot at 145° F (62.5° C). Avoid prolonged melting or overheating because this reduces glue strength. Use sterile brushes to apply the glue, and wash and sterilize the glue pot after use to avoid contamination of the following batch. The proportion of glue to water varies with the size of the abrasive used.

Abrasive grit size	Dry glue percentage by weight to water
200	20
150	25
100	30
80	33
60	35
46	40
36	45
30	50

14-2 TURUN HOPEA, Finland. Silver grindings from sprue ends on castings here being removed are caught in the downdraft of a vacuum pipe and carried away to a central collection tank. The accumulation is periodically removed and sent to the refiners to reclaim the precious metal. *Photo: Turun Kuvaus*

Heat the wheel and the abrasive grit to 120° F (48.5° C). Brush the glue on the wheel face and sides, then roll the wheel in a container holding the grit. Place the wheel in suspension on a nail and allow it to dry for an hour or two. Apply a second coat of glue (or cement) and abrasive in the same way. Dry the wheel in a well-ventilated place for 24 hours. Avoid contamination of glue and grit by keeping each separate. When the wheel is dry, "break" its surface by striking it with a round metal bar at intervals diagonally across the face. When it becomes necessary to reapply abrasive, true the wheel face with a wheel rake and follow the same procedure.

Cements: Commercially manufactured cements and adhesives have the advantage that they can be used at ordinary room temperatures, do not need melting pots, can be dried more rapidly, tolerate higher frictional heat, are flexible, and can be used for coarse and fine grits. Follow manufacturer's recommendations for application.

Recommended speeds for wheels with *glued abrasives,* are between 6000–8000 sfpm. At higher speeds overheating occurs and the glue will break down. At lower speeds the abrasive tends to rip out.

RUBBER WHEELS

Rubber wheels are made of a rubber composition impregnated with abrasive grit. They are used for fast cutting and polishing, shaping, firescale removal, and semigrinding operations. Brightboy wheels are of this composition, and are available in conventional shapes in all sizes, as well as in end wheel cone forms, and as sticks used by hand to eliminate local scratches from a work. These wheels can easily be shaped with a coarse file while rotating to suit special contours and circumstances.

637

ABRASIVE BLAST CLEANING AND TEXTURING

Abrasive dry blast cleaning can be used as a dry method of removing non-oily and non-greasy substances such as firescale, dry soils, paint, lacquer, and investment from objects of all metals of any size or shape, and to remove burrs. More frequently in jewelry making it is used on metal and plastics to create frost-textured matte surface effects with low reflectivity. A common abrasive material in 50–80-mesh grit used is called "sand," a category that includes natural and synthetic materials such as sand, emery, quartz, garnet, pumice, dolomite, novaculite, stone powders, and carborundum. These are forcefully thrown against the metal and, because they are nonmetallic, do not contaminate it. This is accomplished by *sandblasting equipment* which utilizes compressed air to propel the abrasive in a stream through the nozzle of an *air blast gun* connected by tubes to the sand and air sources. The blasting is done in an enclosed chamber or cabinet (see Demonstration 8, Photos 40 and 41 under The Tube, Chapter 7) to confine the flying particles and dust. The cabinet is equipped with fixed, internal, *heavy rubber gloves* for the hands as protection against sandblast contact because the high-velocity particles bounce off the gloves. The blast

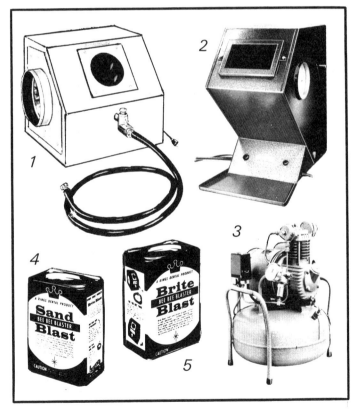

14-3 *SANDBLASTING EQUIPMENT AND MATERIALS*
1. *Handler "Junior"* sandblaster, bench-top model, 9 × 9 × 9 in, with interior illumination, large window, instant-action gun with stainless steel nozzle, air line hose 3½ ft long that operates on an air line with 30–60 lb pressure, self-sealing vinyl sleeve prevents sand leakage, with cleanout plug for cleaning cabinet interior, one hand hole, portable weight 5 lb.
2. *Protempo* sandblaster 330 mm wide, 530 mm deep, 520 mm high, with one or two hand holes. (Karl Fischer)
3. *Compressor F105B,* two cylinder, 220/380 volt, used with sandblaster. (Karl Fischer)
4. *Sand Blast,* a white quartz abrasive used for cleaning, scale removal, coating removal, frosted or satin finish, preparation for plating.
5. *Brite Blast,* cleans and leaves the metal with a bright luster finish in one operation, eliminates the need for stripping before plating.

should be kept moving to avoid excessive local metal removal, unless this is wanted. After contact with the work, the abrasive medium passes through a wire mesh, expanded metal, or perforated plate to remove coarse contaminants, and is returned to a storage container from which it is recirculated.

More than one size particle of a substance is usually used at a time to avoid clogging the feed pipes to the gun. Depending on the abrading particle size, coarse, medium, or fine matte surfaces are possible on the metal. The "sand" should be uniformly mixed in the supply tank as any grit change causes a somewhat different effect. In abrasive blasting, some metal is removed from the object, especially from corners, and the abrading continues as long as the blast persists. The abrasive reaches places in the work that otherwise could not be conveniently filed, or are more difficult to polish.

WARNING:
When using sandblasting equipment, wear *safety goggles* to protect the eyes against stray abrasive particles which can cause an embolism or blood clot. An adequate *sand collector* should be used so the air breathed is dust-free.

PREFERENTIAL BLASTING

Sandblasting an area of a workpiece partially, called *preferential blasting,* can be accomplished by *masking off* areas with a material that can resist the impact of the abrasive. *Masking tape* cut into any shape to cover the areas to be protected is best as it is easy to remove by simply stripping it off when work is finished. Wax or heavy lacquers are sometimes used, but are not as convenient as their removal requires solvents. Some *frosted finishes* are made by fine sandblasting followed by scratch brushing.

GRAVITY SANDBLASTING

For lack of any sandblasting equipment, to achieve an abrasive-blasted matte surface, an old, very simple and reliable method uses the *force of gravity alone.* Sift sand through a fine mesh to remove all very fine particles and dust. Sift it again with a coarser mesh to remove any very coarse particles, and use those that remain of *medium size.* Place this in a container that has a spout from which a steady stream of sand can easily flow.

The help of an assistant is needed unless the sand container is rigged in a way that allows its control by a cord pulled on it. The assistant mounts a stepladder with the container of sand. The greater the distance the sand falls, the more successful and quicker the result. Two or three meters (6½ or 10 ft) if possible is a good height. Work in a draft-free place. The work is held by the second person at floor level over a container such as a large pan with steep sides used to catch the falling sand. The person on the ladder pours the sand in a steady stream and the work is held at the contact point of the fall, *at an angle* to it so that the sand does not pile up on it and the development of the surface can be watched. The pouring continues until the desired degree of matte surface is reached. The results are perfectly satisfactory.

TUMBLING OR BARREL FINISHING

Tumbling or *barrel finishing* consists of tumbling or rolling metal or stone objects in a rotating *barrel, ball mill* or other container along with an abrasive, a combination

of fine abrasives such as tripoli, sand, or tin oxide, soaps, detergents, water, and combinations of these. In tumbling, a *rolling friction* causes slight deformations in the surface which ultimately wear it to uniformity. In the metal industry, tumbling is used as a method of cleaning, descaling, deburring, grinding, and burnishing metal objects. Its main use to the hand jeweler is for tumble grinding and polishing stones used in jewelry. The method is completely automatic.

BURNISHING

Burnishing is a form of hand (or machine) polishing to make a metal surface shining and lustrous by friction and compression with a burnisher tool, so that polishing is accomplished *without the removal of any metal.* In hand burnishing, the working end of the burnisher consists of a hard substance that compresses the metal, thereby toughening it and causing it to remain bright for a long time period. In *total burnishing,* an entire surface is so polished, and in *selective burnishing,* only parts of the object are made bright, as in filigree work, while the rest is left matte by a previously accomplished process such as acid pickling, scratch brushing, or sandblasting. Burnishing is a means of polishing otherwise inaccessible places in a work. In the East, it is the only polishing method used on jewelry as mechanical polishing is a luxury known about, but rarely used. Burnishers are also used to turn down a bezel on a stone, then to polish the bezel.

BURNISHERS

Burnishers have wooden handles into which tips are permanently fixed and secured by a metal ferrule. Tips are variously made of very hard, highly polished, hardened and tempered steel, agate, bloodstone (green chalcedony spotted with red), or hematite (a metallic-looking iron ore). All these hard substances take and retain a high polish, which is necessary or the tool would scratch the metal

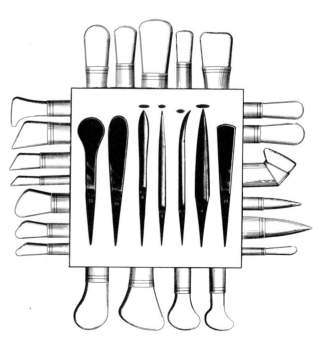

14-4 *BURNISHING TOOLS*
Outside frame: Forms of bloodstone burnishers. (Karl Fischer) Inside frame: Tip forms of unmounted polished steel burnishers. (Friedr. Dick GmbH)

surface instead of smoothing it. Tips are shaped in many forms, each meant to accommodate different work contours which they should match as nearly as possible.

Burnishers must be kept highly polished, which is done by rubbing them in a groove in a *thick leather strip* or *strop* on which some *porcelain rouge* or *diamantine* abrasive has been applied. Red rouge is *not* used, nor is any other polishing compound that contains *iron oxide* because if this substance is imparted to the metal, it will cause subsequent discoloration. After use, steel burnishers should be coated with wax to prevent their rusting and to preserve their smooth surface, and stone tools can also be protected in the same way. Burnishers should be stored in leather or thick cloth bags to keep them from hitting against hard surfaces and thereby becoming marked or chipped.

Lubricants are necessary for burnishing or the tool will drag on the metal. The earliest lubricant used for burnishing metalwork was human spittle, a turbid, viscous substance which is weakly alkaline, slippery, and always available. Soap that is soda-free and dissolved in water, or detergent and water can be used. Dip the burnisher into the lubricant when starting, and again when it starts to stick or skip on the dry metal surface. Both object and lubricant must be absolutely free of any abrasive grit or dust.

HAND BURNISHING

The burnishing process requires a *good light* to be able to observe its progress. Place the work on a nonslipping surface, such as a *felt* or *leather pad*. Dip the burnisher in the lubricant, and rub it systematically back and forth in the *same direction* on the metal when a uniform surface finish is wanted. Each stroke forms a *bright streak* that should overlap the last. The skill of the process lies in blending these strokes uniformly so that streaks are not visible. A deliberate textural streaking can also be accomplished by crossing strokes. To compress the surface even more for a longer lasting finish, burnish the surface at a

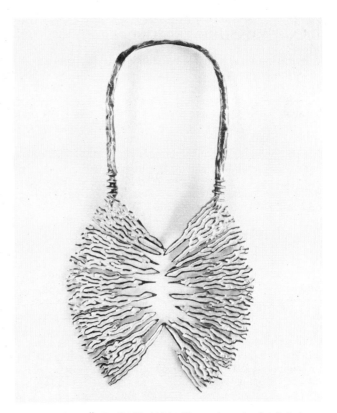

14–6 DIETER MÜLLER-STACH, U.S.A. "Forms from the Sea." Body ornament in 800/1000 silver, created by lost wax casting. The neckband is oxidized, the pendant parts acid-frosted silver, and the upper edges (appearing dark) are burnished bright with hand burnishers. Length 15 in; width 8½ in. Photo: Dieter Müller-Stach

right angle to the first until all opposing marks are obliterated. After burnishing, rub the work with a *soft chamois* and *white rouge,* wash the work in a *soap and ammonia solution* to clean it, then dry it, preferably in *warm sawdust.*

MECHANICAL BURNISHING

Mechanical burnishing is a tumbling process that removes no metal. It is used in the production jewelry industry to polish gold and silver objects to a bright finish, but the hand craftsperson does not burnish mechanically. The process consists of placing many cleaned parts or whole articles in a *burnishing barrel* where they are tumbled by a motor at from 30–60 rpm for 10 minutes to 8 hours, depending on the work to be done. Included with the work are pieces of *tumbling shot* or miniature pieces of highly polished, hard steel units in various shapes such as round balls, slugs, diagonally cut cylinder sections, pins, and diamond shapes, each designed to make contact with another contour. The barrel is half filled with the work and the burnishing shot pieces, and over them is placed a covering amount of a detergent and water mixture. After burnishing, the pieces are removed, rinsed, and dried in sawdust. The shot must also be thoroughly cleaned and dried, then stored in alcohol which is rinsed off before the next use, and which acts to prevent the formation of rust on the shot. Rust is to be avoided as it pits the shot which would then scratch the work being burnished.

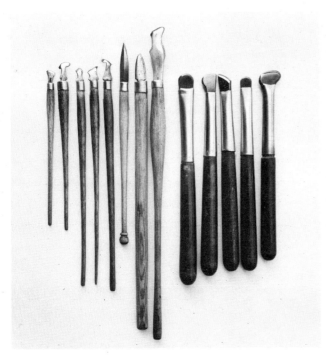

14–5 BURNISHING TOOLS WITH SHAPES MADE TO SUIT VARIOUS WORK CONTOURS. The tools at the *left* are steel; at the *right*, hematite. Photo: Oppi

HAND POLISHING AND BUFFING

When metals are formed by manufacturers, their surface condition is generally very good. In subsequent operations, by the use of tools, shaping abrasives, heat, and chemicals, the surface becomes unacceptable or flawed and must be brought to a satisfactory condition by polishing and buffing. These activities can all be done by hand, by machine, or both.

Hand polishing was the common practice of old, and for lack of any polishing equipment, it is still effective though time-consuming. It is still preferable in many cases, especially when because of the shape, size, or delicate condition and construction of the work, problems would arise if it were polished mechanically.

Hand polishing and machine polishing are rarely one-step procedures. More usually several stages are necessary in achieving the final result. The general sequence in arriving at the desired finish for precious and nonferrous metals may include a combination of the processes of grinding, polishing, burnishing, lapping, hard buffing, color buffing, and mirror buffing, in order of increasing degree of polish. For most of these processes, more than one technique, material, or tool can be used, and because of the multiplicity of available materials and tools used for polishing, confusion as to their use arises. In general, if the jeweler becomes familiar with all of these materials by deliberate exploration and carefully observes the results of each, he or she will be able to select for use those best suited to a general or a particular purpose.

It should be understood that after finishing, a piece of jewelry should be completely clean, free of any abrasive compounds used in its finishing, and if colored, the coloring should not rub off on any garments or the skin of the wearer.

In all metal finishing, according to metalwork parlance, *polishing is followed by buffing.* These terms have specific meanings. *Polishing* is a preliminary step in which some metal is removed from the surface of the work by abrasives. Its purpose is to bring the work surface to a state in which flaws are eliminated to prepare it for a final finish by buffing. In *buffing* very little if any metal is removed during this process which uses much finer abrasives than are used in polishing, and the work surface is brought to the desired degree of brightness. In finishing a surface, the aim may not be to bring the work to a mirror-bright finish, and one can stop at any intermediate stage in the finishing process.

HAND POLISHING MATERIALS

Many of the materials used in hand polishing are the same as those employed in mechanical polishing. Their form, however, is suited to application by hand, and the energy used to apply them is muscle power.

Abrasives backed with paper or cloth are commonly used alone to remove burrs, shape edges, eliminate surface scratches, and prepare the work for finer abrasives and buffing. All the usual abrasives in particle form glued to the backing are available including aluminum oxide, silicon carbide, quartz sand, garnet, and crocus. They are manufactured in a wide range of degrees of coarseness.

Abrasive composition in solid stick forms of various cross-sectional shapes are made to include silicon carbide or aluminum oxide in a range of grit coarsenesses. They are rubbed on the metal to remove scratches, smooth edges, and reach difficult places in the work.

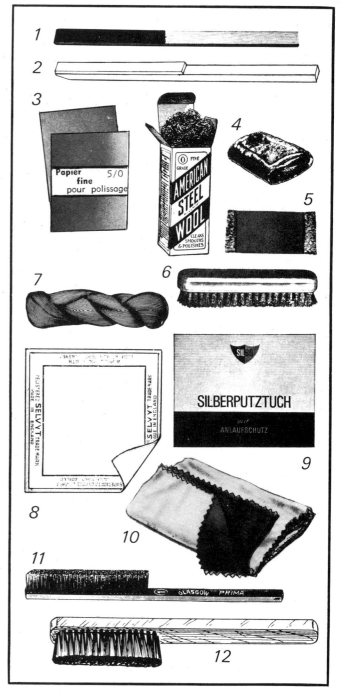

14-7 *HAND POLISHING TOOLS AND MATERIALS*
1. *Chamois leather hand polishing buff,* wood handle, leather ½ in wide, overall length 8 in.
2. *Felt hand polishing buff,* wood handle, felt ⅞ in wide, overall length 11 in, used with rouge for high-luster finish.
3. *Crocus paper for fine polishing,* available in several grades of fineness.
4. *Steel wool,* grades 4/0, 3/0, 2/0, 0, 00, 000, 0000 in order of increasing fineness.
5. *Crimped brass wire hand scratch brush* bound in a metal holder.
6. *Brass wire hand scratch brush,* five rows, 150 mm long, 35 mm wide.
7. *Thrumming thread,* without knots, for use with tripoli or rouge.
8. *Selvyt hand polishing cloth,* England, washable, available in several sizes between 5 × 5 in and 21 × 21 in.
9. *Silbo silver hand polishing cloth,* West Germany, 35 × 30 cm.
10. *Hand polishing cloth,* U.S.A., one side for rouge, the other for final cleaning.
11. *Glasgow hand washout brush* with wooden handle, four-row natural bristle portion 4½ in long, ⅝ in deep, overall length 10¼ in, available in six grades of stiffness.
12. *Lucite-handled washout brush* with four rows of nylon bristles 3 in long, ½ in deep, overall length 7½ in.

Hand polishing sticks or *buffs* are available in flat, round, and half-round shapes. To about half the 8–11 in (20–28 cm) long, ½–1 in (1.3–2.5 cm) wide wooden stick, sheets of abrasive are glued or held to simplify their use on the work, and to provide a firm base that offers resistance to the pressure needed in their use. The plain wood end forms a grip handle. Emery, garnet, flint sandpaper, or artificial abrasives bonded to paper or cloth are held to the stick by glue. In the form of a pad of many layers, the topmost sheet is consumed and discarded to expose the next one. Other polishing sticks in straight or curved forms are covered with leather or felt glued to half their length. Upon these surfaces an abrasive is applied and the stick is rubbed on the metal.

Steel wool made of fine steel shavings is used to clean metal, for polishing, and to create a scratched finish that resembles that done with a mechanical wire brush. The fineness of the scratches depends on the fineness of the steel wool which is graded from coarse to fine as Nos. 2, 1, 0, 00, 000, and 0000. It is usual for the polishing action to be maintained in one direction so that the scratch lines on the metal are parallel.

Metal wire scratch brushes with handles are used with a powdered pumice and water paste for the same purposes as mechanical wire brushes, namely to clean a surface or give it a scratch finish.

Polishing cloths such as Selvyt are manufactured already impregnated with proprietary compositions of polishing chemicals. They bring the surface to a final degree of luster, and some can be used on plastics and glass. After use, wash the work thoroughly with a detergent and water, and dry it.

Impregnated cotton pads such as Duraglit are saturated with a polishing chemical. They are rubbed on the metal to remove soil, the work allowed to dry, and then it is rubbed with a clean, soft cloth to bring it to a high luster. The work must be washed with a detergent and water to remove residual chemicals, then rinsed and dried.

Levigated powdered abrasives are used in both hand and machine polishing. To *levigate* means to reduce a substance to an impalpable powder by grinding it while moist. Any abrasive such as pumice, rouge, alumina, magnesia, or chalk can be levigated, then applied to metal with a cloth. Alumina is probably the cleanest to handle. To prevent dry levigated abrasives from rising as dust in the air, a light oil is mixed with them. In this light but not pasty form, pumice is commonly used to polish jewelry and holloware. A cloth can be dipped in this mixture and rubbed on the work, or it can be kept in an open container near the polishing motor and the work dipped in it before it is touched to the polishing wheel. The use of pumice in this semidry form is easier than applying it as a water-wet paste to a wheel.

Polishing or abrasive pastes can be made of any levigated abrasive by adding water, oil, water and detergent, or a weak ammonia solution. Such pastes can be applied to the work with a soft cloth, or they can be placed on a suitable buffing wheel and used in mechanical polishing.

THRUMMING

Thrum is a weaving term meaning any mass of fibers, thread, or loose, coarse yarn. Thrumming in metalwork is a form of hand polishing parts of a work that are otherwise inaccessible, by the use of a length of coarse, soft threads or thrum charged with an abrasive. Thrumming thread is available in coarse, medium, and fine grades.

14–8 KULTAKESKUS OY, Hämeenlinna, Finland. Polishing and buffing wheel rack. In the trough before the polisher levigated powdered abrasive is heaped, into which the work is occasionally dipped during polishing. *Photo: Oppi*

They can be used in bunches or singly, depending on the need. One end of the thrum is tied to any rigid member, held tight, and charged with a bar of tripoli or rouge by rubbing it along its length. Only *one* type of polishing compound should be used on a particular set of thrums. The free end is then passed through an opening or depression in the work and is then held tautly with the left hand. The work is moved up and back on the thrum with the right hand, changing its angle of contact as necessary to reach the desired places. Additional abrasive is added when needed. Thrums work quickly, and the work must be examined often. The thrum is withdrawn when the work is finished. (See Demonstration 8, Photo 42.)

DEBURRING OR EDGE BLENDING

A *burr* is an irregular ridge raised on metal as a result of the use of a tool. Burrs occur after grinding, along a newly sawed line, an engraved or chiseled line, etc. Deburring is not a single finishing procedure, but any method that produces the desired result which is the removal of burrs and the breaking of sharp edges on the metal to blend them or give them a rounded contour or radius without changing dimensions. Deburring can be accomplished by hand filing, scratch brushing, and hand or mechanical polishing with an abrasive. Normally, it is done as a part of the mechanical finishing operations of polishing with a muslin buff charged with tripoli or a greaseless compound. Deburring is done by passing a wheel or brush *across the edge* and not in line with the edge which would flare the wheel layers or brush ends and wear them out unevenly. It can also be done manually by the use of steel wool or crocus paper.

MECHANICAL FINISHING OF METAL SURFACES

Mechanical finishing involves the achievement of a finish by the aid of mechanical means, as differentiated from its achievement by hand or chemical means. Almost all the materials mentioned are available in normal sizes for use on mechanical bench grinders and polishing lathes, and in miniature sizes for use on flexible shafts.

POLISHING

Polishing is an abrading and smoothing operation done with relatively hard-faced polishing wheels mounted on a polishing motor. Polishing follows grinding and precedes buffing. In polishing, tool marks and scratches from previous processes are eliminated from the work, giving it a uniform surface and preparing it for buffing. A considerable amount of metal is removed from the surface, and the action of the abrasive and the wheel leaves a line pattern on the metal surface, actually fine scratches that go in the direction over which the wheel has passed. *Cross polishing*, or changing the direction of the polish swipe 90° with each contact, is a means of achieving an evenly abraded surface. It also shows if the entire surface has been equally abraded which occurs when all the lines of the former direction are removed.

BUFFING

Buffing always follows polishing in the mechanical buffing of metal, very fine abrasives are used on softer wheels than are used in polishing, and little or no removal of metal occurs, but the metal is *burnished*. The resulting smoothed metal surface ranges from a semibright to a high mirror finish with maximum specular reflectivity in which no lines made by abrasive action are apparent.

POLISHING AND BUFFING MOTORS

Polishing and buffing motors or lathes used for normal polishing and buffing operations in jewelry making range in power capacity in increasing strength from $\frac{1}{10}$–$\frac{3}{4}$ horsepower (hp). The motor must be powerful enough to

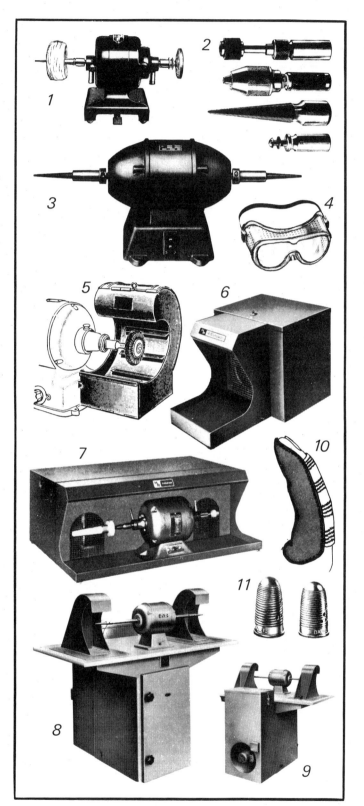

14–9 MECHANICAL POLISHING AND BUFFING EQUIPMENT

1. *Small polishing motor*, used for grinding, polishing, and buffing small work. Height to shaft center 3¾ in, with tapered spindle on left, and guard wheel arbor on right; $\frac{1}{15}$ hp motor, ¼ in shaft, 110–130 volt, AC.
2. *Baldor brass chucks* with standard tapered shaft holes (0.370 at rate of ¼ in per ft). Top to bottom: arbor band; bur; tapered spindle for soft-centered wheels, lead center, or wood lap, spindle length 4½ in; hard wheel chuck. All are marked L or R indicating they are for use on the left- or right-hand motor shaft, with threaded shaft holes, available for ¼, $\frac{5}{16}$, ⅜, ½, or ⅝ in shafts.
3. *Polishing lathe*, long ½ in shaft, heavy-duty, ½ hp, 115 or 220 volt, AC, 60 cycles, single-speed 3450 rpm, height of shaft from table 5½ in.
4. *Protective goggles*, vinyl plastic ventilated frames, worn while using polishing lathe.
5. *Splash pan* with openable back and front, used with water in base to catch dust, wheel lint, and abrasive thrown off by polishing and buffing wheels. Fits over average-sized wheels with sufficient clearance allowance. Size 12 × 6½ × 10½ in.
6. *Portable dust collector* with replaceable fiber glass filter, and built-in suction fan, 110 volt, 60 cycle, AC; size 10 × 10 × 17½ in.
7. *Double-spindle polishing lathe* with double-opening dust collector, bench model with lights under hood on both sides; length 32 in,

depth 21 in, height 10¼ in; accommodates wheels with up to 6 in Ø.

8. *Double-spindle polishing lathe with dust collector* in the table level, *floor model* with cabinet. Blower motor 220/380 volt installed in lower cabinet, also large suction fan, fiber glass filters; table 17¾ × 32¾ in; table height 32¼ in.
9. Rear view of the above showing the placement of the fan.
10. *Finger cot*, leather with elastic, worn on index finger for protection against buff burning or rouge deposit, and clean work contact.
11. *Finger cots*, rubber, perforated and ridged for ease in gripping, in thumb and finger sizes, used to hold work when finishing on buffing wheel without leaving fingerprints.

keep the wheel rotating at the rated speed without slowing down or stalling when pressure is brought to bear against the wheel, even when considerable pressure is used. Light work motors simply rest on the workbench and stay in place by their weight alone, but it is preferable to mount a motor securely to the workbench which itself is anchored to the floor. With these precautions, the motor shaft works with true concentricity and does not vibrate in use which would cause wear and dangerous wheel chatter. It is recommended that the motor be the type constructed with sealed, permanently lubricated ball bearings so that no dust can accumulate to hinder its functioning.

Polishing motors generally have two hardened steel, unbending, straight or tapered shafts, one at either end, so that two different finishing operations can take place, although some models have only one shaft. Standard shaft sizes are ¼ in, ⅜ in, ½ in, or ⅝ in (6.35 mm, 9.52 mm, 12.7 mm, or 15.9 mm), with the ½ in shaft in most common use. A shaft can hold a *tapered spindle,* a *straight arbor,* or a *chuck.* Tapered spindles are used to hold soft-centered wheels and allow quick wheel changes; straight shafts hold arbors used to mount hard-centered grinding, polishing, and buffing wheels; and chucks are used to hold drills, flex-shaft extensions, or other rotating mechanical tools or devices. Some shafts are tapered and others have a flat side to allow the set screws of spindles and arbors to be tightened upon them so they do not slip. The shaft rotates *toward the worker,* therefore spindles and arbors are not interchangeable for either side, but are marked R or L to identify them for use on the right or left shaft. The shaft and attachment should be long enough to allow contact with the surfaces of work of normal size, which means they must project far enough away from the motor casing to allow access to both sides of a wheel. Shaft extensions are available. A normal height of the shaft from the table is 4½ in (11.4 cm) which allows a wheel with a maximum diameter of 6 in (15.24 cm) to be used. It is common practice to place the polishing wheel on the right and the buffing wheel on the left shaft.

POLISHING HEADS Electric motors with one set speed can be used with V-belt-driven *polishing heads,* the belt passing from a pulley mounted on the motor shaft to a pulley on the polishing head. In the V-belt arrangement, the belt is forced into the taper-sided pulley groove, and makes positive contact with its *sides.* It should ride in the groove level with the top, and not above or below it. The tension should be such that there is no slipping, and the shorter the belt, the tighter it must be. The pulleys must be in perfect alignment to avoid excessive wearing of the belt. To find out the correct belt diameter needed for a particular setup, pass a nonstretching string around both pulleys at the groove bottom, and cut it where it overlaps; then add ¾ in (1.9 cm) extra so the belt does not touch the bottom of the pulley groove while in action. Pulleys are designated by their overall inside diameter (ID) and groove width, ½ in (1.27 cm) wide belts being most common. Pulleys are available in series of graduated diameter sizes that can be used on the polishing head and motor shaft to provide a wide range of surface speeds to the wheel mounted on the polishing head shaft. Straight arbors with flanges, tapered spindles, chucks, or arbor-chuck combinations can be mounted on the shaft of the polishing head; when purchasing them, remember to specify if they are for use on the right or left side.

POLISHING AND BUFFING DUST COLLECTION In metal grinding, polishing, and buffing, dusts from wheels, abrasives, and the metal are raised in the air. To avoid inhaling them, which can be harmful, wear a *respirator mask.* The simplest dust-catching device is a *splash pan* or *lathe splasher* which is a sheet metal hood or shield that fits around a wheel and is placed below and behind it, its size allowing some space for maneuvering the work position in relation to the wheel. Inside its base is a removable, shallow pan into which some water is placed before work starts. As the wheel rotates, a good portion of the dust is caught and held in the water. The tray can be emptied at intervals and refilled with fresh water. Some splash pans are lighted internally for better work visibility, and others are provided with plastic, adjustable shields.

Dust collectors are available that are much more efficient in dust gathering as they work by suction fans to draw away dust, lint, abrasives, and metal particles through intake holes behind the arbor shaft. Their efficiency depends on the power of the fan. Some of these are portable, others are housed in units placed on the workbench, or are contained in independent cabinets and have hoods that extend beyond the spindle. The dust is drawn through a flexible, large-diameter hose attached to a dust collector or drum. Some are provided with replaceable filters in front of the blower wheel so the collected matter does not come in contact with the suction fan or motor and clog it or cause malfunctioning. If precious metals are polished, the dust that is collected should be processed periodically to reclaim the metal.

A *polishing booth, box,* or *cabinet* can be constructed with a sloping front tempered glass panel, hinged to allow access. The booth should be large enough to completely enclose the polishing lathe with attached polishing wheels, and allow room enough for manipulating the work. It should be fixed on the polishing lathe table so it does not move with vibration. At the front make two horizontal oval holes for the insertion of the arms. To retain the dust, over these openings, fix stiff but flexible rubber sheets, cut radially toward the center of the opening. An internal light bulb at each end is needed for work visibility. Make an opening at the back to accommodate the shape of the exhaust of the dust collector used, and fix it in place.

POLISHING SPEEDS Polishing motors are made to rotate at a single speed of 3450 *rotations per minute* (rpm); or have two speeds, 3450 rpm and 1725 rpm, the latter, slower speed used for some polishing situations and for grinding. The *polishing speed* or the rate at which a polishing or buffing wheel moves over the surface of the object is expressed in terms of *surface feet per minute* (sfpm), which is the linear velocity of the rotating wheel's perimeter. This speed rate depends on the *wheel size,* and the *rpm of the shaft* of the polishing motor. Given the same shaft rpm, the larger the diameter of the polishing wheel, the greater will be its peripheral speed. As the wheel diameter increases, more wheel perimeter contact occurs with the metal in a given time period, therefore, the rate of the metal cutting is also greater. The recommended sfpm speed depends on the metal being finished, the kind of wheel in use, the particular abrasive used, and the type of finish desired. These considerations involve numerous variables, and only general recommendations can be given.

If a motor has only one speed, by choosing the correct wheel diameter intermediate sfpm rates can be achieved. At any single shaft speed, a smaller diameter wheel has a slower sfpm rate, and a larger diameter wheel a greater sfpm rate. (See Table next page.)

Polishing and Buffing Wheel Perimeter Surface Speed Calculation Chart (in feet per minute)

rpm at Arbor or Spindle	Diameter of Buffing Wheel in Inches										
	4	6	8	10	12	14	16	18	20	22	24
	Surface Speed in Feet Per Minute										
800	837	1256	1675	2094	2513	2932	3351	3770	4189	4608	5026
900	942	1413	1885	2356	2827	3298	3770	4241	4712	5184	5655
1000	1047	1570	2094	2618	3141	3665	4189	4712	5236	5760	6283
1100	1152	1727	2304	2880	3455	4031	4608	5183	5760	6336	6911
1200	1256	1884	2513	3142	3769	4398	5027	5655	6283	6912	7540
1300	1361	2042	2723	3404	4084	4764	5446	6126	6807	7488	8168
1400	1466	2199	2932	3666	4398	5131	5865	6597	7330	8064	8796
1500	1571	2356	3142	3927	4712	5497	6284	7069	7854	8640	9425
1600	1675	2513	3351	4189	5026	5864	6703	7540	8378	9216	10053
1700	1780	2670	3560	4451	5340	6230	7121	8011	8901	9792	10681
1800	1885	2827	3770	4713	5654	6597	7540	8482	9425	10368	11310
1900	1989	2984	3979	4975	5969	6963	7959	8954	9948	10944	11938
2000	2094	3141	4189	5236	6283	7330	8378	9425	10472	11520	12566
2100	2199	3298	4398	5498	6597	7696	8797	9896	10996	12096	13194
2200	2304	3455	4608	5760	6911	8063	9215	10367	11519	12672	13822
2300	2408	3612	4817	6022	7225	8429	9634	10839	12043	13248	14451
2400	2513	3770	5037	6284	7540	8796	10053	11310	12566	13824	15079
2500	2618	3927	5236	6545	7854	9162	10471	11781	13090	14400	15708
2600	2722	4084	5445	6807	8168	9529	10890	12253	13613	14976	16336
2700	2827	4241	5655	7069	8462	9895	11309	12724	14136	15552	16964
2800	2932	4398	5864	7331	8796	10262	11728	13196	14660	16128	17592
2900	3037	4555	6074	7592	9110	10629	12147	13667	15184	16704	18221
3000	3141	4712	6283	7854	9425	10996	12566	14137	15708	17280	18850

POLISHING AND BUFFING WHEELS

The main function of polishing and buffing wheels is to carry the abrasive over the work to achieve a metal removal (cutting), or a coloring action, and to generate enough heat to cause burnishing or plastic metal flow of the metal surface. To do this, polishing and buffing wheels are mounted on polishing motors. The desired result is achieved with the proper wheel type on which the properly selected abrasive compound is applied and made to contact the metal for a long enough time, called the *dwell time,* to perform the job. Many kinds of wheels are available, and any of a great number of abrasive materials are used on them. The proper choice of wheel and abrasive makes the difference between a satisfactory or an unacceptable result. A single wheel should be used with *one* abrasive type, and to avoid confusion, should be *marked* on its walls to indicate which abrasive is used. This will avoid contamination.

The diameters of wheels used most often in polishing and buffing jewelry are 3 in, 4 in, 5 in, and 6 in (7.6 cm, 10.2 cm, 12.7 cm, and 15.2 cm), and wheels of larger diameter up to 24 in (61 cm) are made, graduated at one-inch intervals. Wheels approximately ¼ in (0.64 cm) thick are termed *regular* and have an average of 20 ply; those approximately ⁵⁄₁₆ in (0.8 cm) thick are *heavy;* and those ⅜ in (0.95 cm) or more are *extra heavy.*

WHEEL TERMINOLOGY

Wheels are also known as *buffs, bobs* (hence the term "bobbing," a form of polishing), *mops,* or *dollies.* For the sake of clarity, the general term *wheel* is used here. Wheel parts have specific functions.

Face: The working edge of the wheel or face is the portion that contacts the metal, and holds the abrasive. It can be specially contoured to fit specially shaped surfaces, the contouring done with a *wheel rake* or an *abrasive stone* while the wheel rotates. (See Dressing or Raking in this chapter.)

Sides or walls: The sides or walls of the wheel might occasionally be used and therefore can be loaded with abrasive, but ordinarily they are not used for polishing or buffing as in stitched wheels the stitching will wear out and the wheel will disintegrate. Good buffing practice does not allow the exertion of so much pressure that the wheel walls become deformed.

Center: The center is the reinforced area around the arbor hole or central opening. See separate discussion below.

Arbor hole: The arbor hole is the central opening through which an arbor shaft passes, whose size it must match to prevent looseness. When a wheel is meant for use on a tapered spindle on which it is wound to make a tight fit, it has a smaller hole than one used mounted on an arbor. See the discussion on p. 645.

Stitching: Heavy cotton thread is sewn or stitched through the layers of the material of which the wheel is made to hold them together. The stitching provides the wheel with the desired degree of stiffness, hardness, or softness. The closer the stitching rows, the stiffer or harder the wheel, and the further apart they are, the softer the wheel.

Wheel hardness: Very hard and hard wheels are used to polish flat surfaces, and will not chamfer edges. Medium soft wheels are used in decorated parts which must not be flattened. Soft wheels follow contours, and blend surfaces without disfiguring the work shape or removing metal. Very soft and mushy wheels tend to wrap around contours, do not remove blemishes, but are used for high coloring.

Wheel hardness	Stitch distance
Very hard	⅛″
Hard	¼″
Medium soft	⅜″
Soft	½″
Very soft	¾″
Mushy	unstitched wheels

WHEEL CENTERS AND HOLDING DEVICES

It is very important that the wheel center and the area around it be strong enough to withstand the tremendous forces brought to bear upon a revolving wheel. The two basic wheel types are those used on straight arbor shafts and those used on tapered spindles. These different mounting methods determine the size of the wheel's opening. Wheels on arbors have holes that must match that of the arbor diameter to prevent looseness which causes vibration and ultimate motor damage. Loose wheels will not run true, and are dangerous as they chatter, and the work cannot be held against them. Such wheels must be thrown away.

Arbor-mounted wheels are mounted with *metal flanges* having a central hole that matches the arbor diameter, ¼ in, ⅜ in, ½ in, and ⅝ in (0.64 cm, 0.95 cm, 1.27 cm, and 1.59 cm). One flange is placed on either side of the wheel, flanked by a *retaining nut* that screws onto the threaded arbor. Both nuts are tightened together in directions counter to each other with *wrenches* to lock the wheel firmly in place. This assembly should not be placed too close to the end of the shaft because it is possible that by vibration or faulty tightening the nuts may loosen and fly off. To avoid such an event, test the tightness of the nuts before each use of the wheel.

Tapered spindle wheels have a smaller opening than those used on straight arbors. The central area is hardened to keep it from wearing out so that in repeated use the hole will not become unduly enlarged and the wheel will hold on the spindle. Shellac, leather reinforcing discs stitched to both sides, or lead poured into the central core are used for hardening purposes. The wheel is mounted on the spindle simply by winding it against the spindle's increasing conical diameter while it is in a vertical position. The pressure forms threads on the wheel's center to match those of the spindle. As mentioned, spindles are made for use on the right or left side of the motor. Because the motor shaft rotates *toward* the worker, the thread on the spindle works *against* that direction and the wheel in use automatically becomes tightened on the spindle.

CLOTHS AND FIBROUS MATERIALS USED FOR WHEELS

Many kinds of woven cloths and other fibrous materials are used for wheels, and the main ones are discussed below. Each is used for a particular range of purposes for grinding, cutting, or coloring metals. The choice of the wheel material and the abrasive best suited to the work depends on the desired finish. The strength and flexibility of a cloth in a wheel varies considerably with its texture, weight, and whether it contains any stiffening chemicals or substances. Wheel cloth may be untreated, or treated before or after manufacture with substances meant to increase the cloth strength, give it more body, increase its ability to retain polishing and buffing compounds, reduce or increase its flexibility and its ability to cut—and some additives even act as a lubricant. None of these substances affect the metal worked or leave it streaked.

Whatever the material, the wheel should be reserved for use with either *greasy* or *greaseless* types of abrasives or compounds. Grease penetrates the material, and once used, the wheel can no longer be used with a greaseless compound, which it will not hold properly.

Soft wheels are used in cases where the surface is irregular and fast metal removal is not the aim, while hard, rigid wheels are generally used on flat surfaces and for rapid metal removal. Generally speaking, wheels made of flat discs of cloth are safer than those made of units in other forms as these may come apart in use.

Wool wheels are made of selected, tightly woven woolen cloth, and are used for high-color buffing on precious and soft metals.

Flannel (cotton) wheels with a heavily combed nap on both sides of the cloth (domet flannel) or a nap on one side (canton flannel) are soft, do not scratch, and are used with various rouges for high-color buffing luster on metals and plastics. Flannel is made in 6, 8, 10, and 12 ounce weights.

Muslin is the most popular and commonly used of all cloth wheels. Relatively inexpensive and versatile, muslin wheels are used for cut-and-color operations on precious metals, softer metals, and on plastics. The lower the *weight number* of the cloth, the heavier it is, and the lower the *thread count*, the lighter the cloth. Lightweight, loose-disc muslin wheels are used for coloring and are flexible so that they can reach contoured surfaces. Closely woven, heavier, stitched and stiffened muslin is used on wheels for polishing and cutting operations on brass, copper, nickel silver, and steel. They are made in a wide range of hardness.

Canvas discs are the hardest of the cloth wheels, and those whose layers are cemented together are harder than those stitched. Canvas discs are often cemented to the sides of buffs made of other kinds of cloth in order to keep their walls from breaking down, to prevent the face from becoming mushroomed or spread out, and to protect the stitching on the layers below.

Pressed felt wheels are available in densities from extra soft to rock hard. In cases where the metal surface is flat, the face must be of uniform density, squared and true. Knife-edged types are used to polish crevices, and in cases where edges and corners must be retained. Felt wheels are also available in other shapes. If necessary, felt can be easily contoured. Coarse-grit abrasives can be used with felt, but generally finer abrasives and compounds are used. Because of its relative hardness, the action of a felt wheel is fast, and for this reason, the work should not be held too long in one position as this may result in local excavations. Hard felt wheels are used with tripoli at a spindle speed of 2000–3450 rpm.

Nylon mesh loose-ply wheels, 4 in (10 cm) in diameter, with reinforced centers, are impregnated with abrasives in coarse (150) and medium (180) grits. They are used to achieve a satin finish without the use of abrasive compounds. They follow contours well, and are long lasting.

DRESSING OR RAKING: Reshaping and cleaning wheels

When a cloth wheel is new, its face is usually flat as this is generally the most efficient shape for work. Sometimes new wheels are rough trimmed and must be dressed or shaped to flatten the face surface. In use, wheels wear out, and the face may become irregular or misshapen. To restore a wheel face to flatness, the sharp teeth of a *wheel rake* are used to remove excess cloth and true the face and a *pumice* or *emery wheel dressing stick* gives it the proper nap, both while held horizontally against the face as it rotates. In want of a wheel rake, a coarse-toothed *old hacksaw blade* can be used.

WHEEL GLAZING   When an excessive buildup of abrasive compound occurs on a wheel, because of friction heat it becomes glazed and will not polish the metal. The glaze consists of a mixture of abraded metal, used abrasive compound, and used wheel debris, and must be removed. If a wheel has become contaminated it may be restored to good working condition by removing the outermost layers

with a wheel rake or dressing stick. In this process, much lint and abrasive dust is thrown into the air, therefore, wear a *respiration mask* and work near a good exhaust ventilator.

Occasions occur when a wheel face must be shaped to accommodate a special contour, and this can be done with a wheel rake held against the wheel face at the desired angle, or by rounding the face.

Never wash a cloth wheel to clean it as this may remove its chemical constituents, soften binders, and loosen cloth fibers, thereby decreasing its efficiency, or ruining it totally.

LAPPING WHEELS

Lapping is a form of polishing used on work that has sharp corners, or large, flat areas that must be preserved.

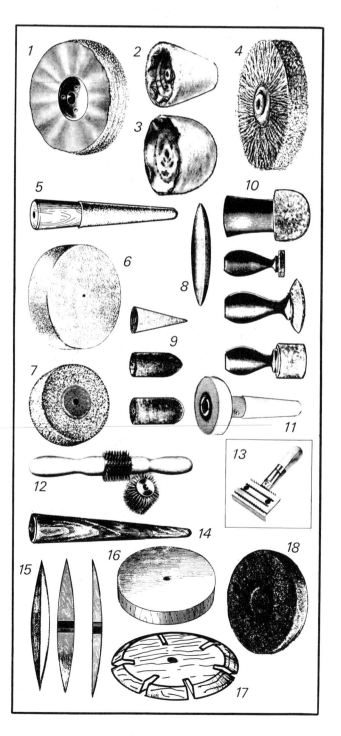

14–10 POLISHING, BUFFING, AND LAPPING WHEELS

1. *Loose muslin wheel* with metal center.
2. *Tapered loose muslin buff*, 2, 2½, 3, 3½ in Ø available.
3. *Goblet loose muslin buff*, 2, 2½, 3, 3½, 4, 5, 6 in Ø available.
4. *Cotton string wheel*, wood hub with metal center, available in 2½, 2¾, 3, 4 in Ø; in two, three, four rows; used for high polish with rouge, or satin finish with greaseless compound; extremely flexible over irregular contours.
5. *Tapered, felt inside ring buff*, on wood mandrel, felt portion in 3, 4, 5, 6 in lengths.
6. *Solid felt wheel*, square edge, with pinhole center, uniform texture, in rock hard, hard, medium, and soft; Ø 4, 5, 6, 7, 8 in; face widths ⅛, ¼, ½, ⅜, 1 in.
7. *Solid felt wheel*, reinforced center.
8. *Solid felt wheel*, knife edge, rock hard; Ø ½, ⅝, ¾, 1, 2, 2½, 3, 4 in.
9. *Felt cones*; top: pointed cone; center: blunt point; bottom: rounded; medium and hard densities; Ø ¼, ⅜, ½, ¾, 1 in; depths ½–2 in.
10. *Various contoured solid felt small end wheels* mounted on wooden mandrels, for use on tapered spindles.
11. *Combination felt wheel buff and inside ring buff* mounted on wood mandrel permitting inside ring and outside ring polishing without changing buff.
12. *Wheel dresser*, used on cloth and felt buffs.
13. *Lea buff rake and evener*, works on face of fiber buffs without tearing it or breaking threads.
14. *Wood inside ring lap*, solid, 4¼, 6, 7 in long; 1¼–⅜ in taper; drilled to fit tapered spindle.
15. *Wood lap*, knife edge, both sides tapered (section view), or one side flat (section view); 4 and 6 in Ø.
16. *Soft wood lap*, flat faced, used with rouge, diamantine, tripoli; 6 in Ø, 1 in thick.
17. *Wood lap*, beveled and split for see-through lapping; with four, six or eight slits; 6 or 8 in Ø, ½ in thick.
18. *Plastic-bonded abrasive wheel*; hard, medium, soft; medium, fine, extra fine grits; 1½–6 in Ø; ¼ or ½ in wide.

For this purpose, the wheels are made of a material that has little or no "give" under pressure. Hard felt, close-grained wood, and leather-faced wood wheels, are used. Metal wheels are also used including brass or lead which hold grit abrasives on their face surfaces, and tin or steel wheels which are used for mirror-bright lapping. In lapping, the work is brought in contact with the wheel face or its sides or walls, depending on the circumstances. As with other wheels, a different lap wheel is used for polishing and for buffing. Lapping wheels are also used for cutting gemstones and glass.

Wood lapping wheels can be dressed or trimmed with a *wood-cutting chisel* while in rotation to shape them to particular contours. They are 2–6 in (5.1–15.2 cm) in diameters, ½ in, or 1 in (1.3 cm or 2.5 cm) thick, and have slightly convex sides. Leather-faced wood wheels are used for flat surfaces in cases where a minimum of flexibility is wanted.

Split lapping is a method of finishing flat surfaces by the use of a hard felt or wood lap with four or more *radial slits* cut from the outer rim edge toward and nearly reaching the central hub. When the lap is lighted from above, and work is held against the opposite or working surface of the revolving lap, the work surface being lapped is visible while the wheel moves. Visibility is increased if the perimeter of the lap edge is painted black. This visual effect is due to a stroboscopic action that takes place. It allows work to be quickly completed to the desired state in one operation without any need to remove and inspect it.

CUT-OFF DISCS

Cut-off discs are very thin wheels made of strongly cemented abrasives. They are used to cut through metal like a circular saw, as when removing sprues or cutting tubing. They are available in large and very small diameters.

POLISHING AND BUFFING WHEEL TYPES

UNSEWN DISCS AND FULL-DISC WHEELS These wheels are made of discs of cloth cut from sheets of muslin of the following counts: 86 × 93; 80 × 92 (the most popular); 64 × 68; and 48 × 48. The higher counts are used for cut-down polishing, and the lower counts are used for coloring. They are assembled 18–20 ply, and sewn with a single row of stitching around the central arbor hole. Double layers of discs are turned with their threads lying in different directions so that the wheel will wear evenly and not become square in shape as it would if they were all in the same direction. Because of its looseness, this type is extremely flexible and will not catch on irregular surfaces. It is recommended for polishing chains and delicate work. *Packed wheels* are made of discs of alternating large and small diameters.

Wheel designations are standardized to specify their description. For example, a wheel 6 in × 3 in, No. 2 pack type, 18 ply, 86 × 93, 2.50 yard, spiral, 1.25 in arbor hole means: the wheel is 6 in (15.2 cm) in diameter on a 3 in (7.6 cm) center, No. 2 pack type, section of 18 ply thickness, warp of 86 threads by 93 weft threads per inch, cloth weight 2.50 ounces per yard, and has a central hole of 1.25 in diameter.

SEWN OR STITCHED WHEELS When the layers of cloth are sewn together in various ways with a strong cotton thread, they become dense and more suited to "cut" the metal surface to remove scratches and surface imperfections, as well as being better suited for use on hard metals. The closer the stitching rows, the denser the wheel. Because of its stiffness, stitched wheels do not conform to the contours of the metal. The types of stitching used are:

Spiral: This is the most common type, used on full-disc wheels and almost exclusively on pieced wheels.

Concentric: The stitching is done in concentric circles around the center hole. The result is a stiff, dense wheel that becomes harder as it wears close to a stitched line, and softer when that line has been worn through, releasing the cloth from that point to the next stitched circle.

Radial: This sun-ray pattern makes a wheel that is more uniform in density and one that forms pockets in which the abrasive compound is held. There are two types: *straight* radial stitching in which all the lines are straight, equidistant, and cross the wheel diameter; and *radial arc* stitching in which each line forms a curved arc, crosses at the center, and is equidistant. A variation has concentric stitching in the central area, and from this the arcs start and radiate.

Square sewn: This is sewn in parallel lines equidistant from each other and crossing over the entire buff in a perpendicular direction, thus forming squares. The result is a stiff wheel with pockets that hold polishing compounds.

Other stitch types: Parallel, curved, tangent, zigzag, ripple, and petal, all of which also hold polishing compound in pockets.

PIECED WHEELS In this type, layers of irregularly shaped pieces of cloth are built up to a thickness of about ⅜ in (0.95 cm) and sewn together in any of the stitching patterns mentioned. They are a cheaper substitute for full-

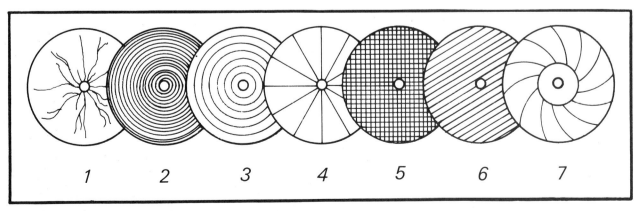

14-11 *POLISHING AND BUFFING WHEEL STITCH TYPES*
1. *Unsewn disc.*
2. *Spirally stitched wheel.*
3. *Concentrically stitched wheel.*
4. *Radially stitched wheel.*
5. *Square-stitched wheel.*
6. *Parallel-stitched wheel.*
7. *Curve-stitched wheel.*

disc wheels, but not as well balanced because not all the cloths are on the bias. They have an outer cover of a full disc for appearance's sake. Because they are made of pieces, they wear out quickly.

PACKED WHEELS   In this type, small spacer discs are inserted between the layers to soften the face. The number of such inserts determines the degree of softness and flexibility. They are used for coloring operations.

FOLDED OR POCKET WHEELS   This type consists of circles of cloth that are folded twice to make a quarter-circle segment and form a pocket open at the wheel periphery, or folded three times to make a superpocket which is more dense and therefore has greater cutting power than the former. In assembling this wheel, each segment overlaps the previous one halfway to form the circle. These are sewn around the arbor hole part of the distance toward the face. The fold pockets hold the compound, and are flexible so they follow contoured work. If the wheel is run with the fold open toward the work, it *cuts;* in the reverse direction it *colors.*

PUCKERED OR SHIRRED WHEELS   The air-cooled, puckered or shirred wheel is a relatively new type. It has a central split metal drum into whose channel continuous lengths of shirred or puckered cloth that has been cut and sewn on the bias at a 45° angle is placed and held. The cloth frays and ravels less than conventionally constructed cloth wheels. The central metal drum has openings that ventilate and cool the wheel in action. These wheels are rated by numbers, the highest has the greatest cloth density and face pucker, and the higher the face density, the greater its cutting power. They are used for fast cut-down operations.

SPOKE AND FLAP WHEELS   Spoke wheels are made with units of cloth placed at right angles to the wheel's direction of rotation so they radiate like spokes from a central holding arbor of metal. In action each flap reinforces the previous one and wipes it, which gives it superior coloring ability. Its advantage is its great flexibility for contour work. It is also hard wearing and runs smoothly and cool. These wheels are made in varying densities and plies.

STRING WHEELS   Wheels, buffs, or mops, also called *string brushes,* are made of strong, soft cotton string fastened to a hub. They are used where great flexibility is wanted as in final coloring operations. Their form and construction allows them to follow irregular contours. With greaseless compounds they produce a finish that ranges from dull satin, to bright butler, to high gloss. *Cord* wheels of similar but denser construction produce coarser results.

LEATHER WHEELS   Leather wheels are generally of a porous leather that will hold the abrasive. They are made of discs—loose, stitched, or cemented together in increasing degrees of hardness. They are resilient, tough, and springy, and are generally used for fine polishing and coloring hard metals. They work faster and last longer than cloth or felt wheels, and are also more expensive. Porous and resilient bull neck leather, buffalo neck leather, and walrus hide which has a fine grain all hold abrasives well. They are used at a lower speed than cloth polishing wheels to quickly produce a mirror finish. When used with very fine activated pumice and peanut oil they produce a fine satin polish on sterling silver. The article must then be degreased in an ammonia and soap solution with a brush.

Chamois leather, stitched wheels are soft and are used with rouge to attain a highly reflective finish on metal.

Sheepskin discs of russet, bark-tanned leather, stitched or cemented together are used for cutting where greater flexibility and less density is needed. White, alum-tanned sheepskin wheels are used for coloring metals, and for buffing metals that contain lead to avoid surface drag.

The hardest and most rigid type is a lapping wheel made of belting leather that covers the face of a wood wheel. It is used on flat surfaces in the same way as other lap wheels.

END MANDRELS AND END WHEELS

Wood mandrels about 4½ in (11.4 cm) long and tapered conically are screwed in a horizontal position onto the end of a tapered spindle. Some are solid wood drilled with a tapered hole and others have a lead core to aid in holding it on the spindle. Over the mandrel goes a cloth-backed, grit-covered shell that matches it in shape. They are used to grind the inside of ring shanks, inner bracelet surfaces, and concave forms. Felt-covered wood core mandrels are used with rouge or other abrasives to polish similar surfaces. Another type is split in half lengthwise and into the split is inserted one end of a piece of cloth-backed abrasive which is then wrapped around it in the direction counter to that in which the spindle turns, and is held in place by a rubber band at the inner end. Mark them R or L (see below).

Solid felt ring mandrels or *pointed, solid felt cones* of similar conical shape are used with rouge to polish and color the inside of rings and on concave surfaces. Once they are threaded right or left, they must be used only on those sides, because if they are reversed, the existing internal thread will be stripped. Mark the right R and the left L.

End wheels, also called *mops* and *bobs* can have a wooden core that screws on the end of a tapered spindle, or they may have a stiffened cloth center. To the core is attached puckered cotton cloth, string, or felt that forms a ball shape. They are unstitched, very flexible, and are used from the side or end on interior surfaces of objects, or on concave surfaces that are inaccessible to an ordinary wheel. Mark them R or L.

Miniaturized polishing and buffing wheels mounted on metal shafts are a kind of end mandrel used on a *flexible shaft* for most of the functions for which mandrels and mops are used.

Wheel storage: When not in use, wheels, unless wet, should be put away in a covered box or in a drawer reserved for them alone, so they are not exposed to airborne abrasive contamination. Wet wheels should be dried before being stored.

BRUSH CLEANING AND FINISHING

Bristle or wire wheel brushes are used to clean or finish metal. Brushing is a process that cannot be classified either as polishing or buffing as it produces its own unique surface results. Brushing is done to remove firescale, as an intermediary step in polishing and buffing practice to remove scratches and polishing marks, to prepare a work for another surface treatment such as electroplating, to deburr metal, to clean an irregularly shaped surface or one having crevices or decoration on some depth, and to create a final, matte or satin finish.

The results achieved depend on the variables of *brush construction* which includes the *type of fill material* (fiber, or straight, crimped, or twisted wire), *trim* or fill material

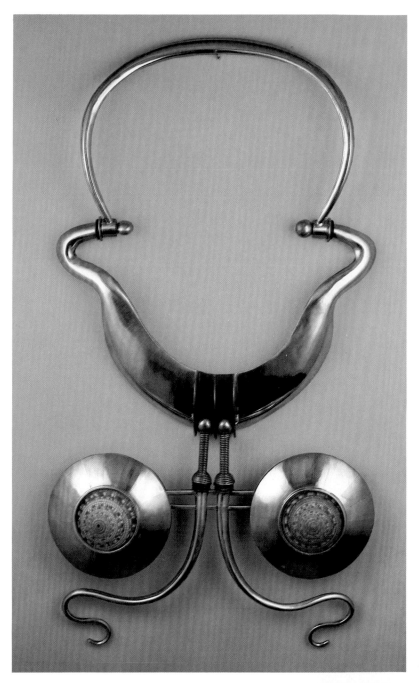

17–1

Plate 17–1   SALLY WEHRMAN, U.S.A. ''Ceremonial
Neckpiece II.'' Fabricated of silver, brass, and
copper, with two shells. *Photo: Richard Mafong*

Plate 17–2   JACQUELINE MINA, England. Ring in
18k gold with nacreous shell and diamonds. *Photo:
Courtesy Crafts Council, London*

17–2

18-1

18-2

Plate 18-1 OPPI UNTRACHT, U.S.A. Brooch
of fabricated 18k gold with modular mosaic
of red jasper, pyrite, hawk's eye (blue
crocidolite), yellow jasper, tiger's eye
(yellow brown crocidolite), and yellow topaz.
Photo: Salmi

Plate 18-2 CHARLES LOLOMA, U.S.A.
Bracelet of silver with three-dimensional
mosaic of turquoise, ivory, coral, lapis lazuli,
and black onyx. *Photo: Courtesy American
Crafts Council*

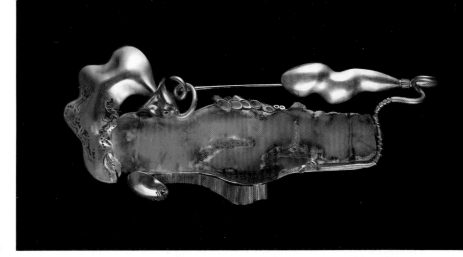

19-1

19-2

Plate 19-1 MARILYN DAVIDSON, U.S.A. "Green Brooch." Fabricated of silver, gold, and brass, with chrysoprase slab. Col.: Metropolitan Museum of Art. *Photo: Michael Jerry*

Plate 19-2 SAARA HOPEA-UNTRACHT, Finland. Necklace fabricated of 18k gold, with serially cut, matching striped agates, and carnelian, amber, and moonstones. *Photo: Oppi*

Plate 19-3 ELISABETH TRESKOW, West Germany, 1928. Ring fabricated in yellow and white gold, with diamonds, moonstones, and pearls. *Photo: Günther Meyer, courtesy the Schmuckmuseum, Pforzheim*

19-3

20–1

20–2

20–3

Plate 20–1   JEAN VENDOME, France. ''Fifth Avenue.'' Ring fabricated in gold and platinum, with diamonds. *Photo: Larousse*

Plate 20–2   KOTAKU TAKABATAKE, Japan. Brooch in fabricated gold, with diamonds, coral, black onyx, and mother of pearl. *Photo: Courtesy K. Mikimoto & Co. Ltd., Tokyo*

Plate 20–3   ANGELA CONTY, U.S.A. Necklace fabricated in 14k multicolored golds, repoussé worked and chased, with amethyst geode, faceted amethysts, and pearls. *Photo: Don Manza, courtesy Aaron Faber Gallery, New York*

length (short, medium, or long), and *density of fill* (light, medium, or heavy). Of great importance in the achievement of a particular result is the speed of rotation at which the brush is used, and the dwell time.

BRISTLE WHEEL BRUSHES

Bristle wheel brushes used in jewelry finishing most commonly employ a natural fiber such as *China hog bristle*, a short, stiff, coarse hair from the back of swine, or *tampico* which is a strawlike bristle not as tough as hog's hair, made of a mixture of plant fibers from various species of the Agave genus, shipped from Tampico, Mexico. Synthetic fibers such as *nylon* are also used in brushes and wear longer than natural fibers, but pick up more dirt.

The bristles are usually about ⅝ in (1.59 cm) long or longer and are mounted on metal-centered hardwood or plastic hubs, or all metal hubs bored to fit the standard diameters of straight arbors or tapered spindles. They are available in various densities in one to four parallel rows, or rows that taper toward each other to narrow the face. The common sizes used on jewelry polishing motors are in diameters of 1¼–3½ in (3.18–8.89 cm). Those used on flex-shafts are made in miniature sizes, with soft or stiff bristles in natural fibers, synthetic fibers, or wire, in one or two rows, with ¾–1½ in (1.9–3.8 cm) diameters, in straight, cup, or end bristle shapes.

Bristle brushes are used at shaft spindle speed of 1750 rpm. At this low speed, they remain flexible. As the speed increases they become more rigid and the face narrows progressively. Higher speeds do not appreciably improve the work capacity, but only speed up the wear on the bristle.

WIRE WHEEL BRUSHES

Wire wheel brushes are made of straight or crimped brass, nickel, Monel, or stainless steel wire. Brass wire 0.0025 in, 0.003 in, 0.004 in, and 0.005 in (0.064 mm, 0.076 mm, 0.102 mm, and 0.127 mm) are used; nickel

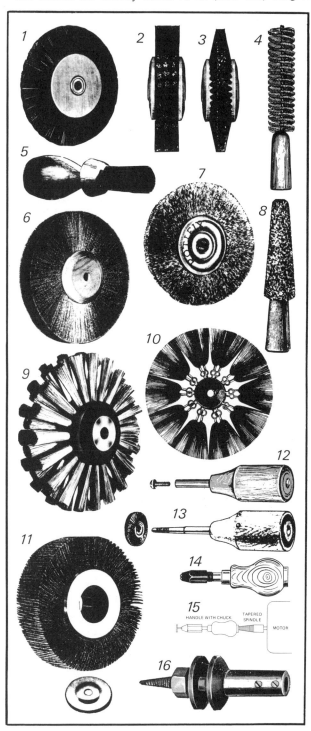

14–12 *BRISTLE AND WIRE BRUSHES*
1. *Bristle brush wheel* with hardwood hub, metal center, available with one, two, three, four rows; Ø 2½, 3, 3½ in; hubs 1¼, 1½, 2 in.
2. *Upright, straight bristle* three-row wheel, 3 in Ø.
3. *Converging, wedge-shaped bristle,* three-row wheel, 3 in Ø.
4. *Straight spiral ring end brush* on wire mount with wood handle for tapered spindle; 4½ in long.
5. *End brush* on wood handle for ⅜ or ⅝ in tapered spindle; available with 1, 3, 5, 7, 9, 10, 12, 19, 23 knots.
6. *Crimped wire scratch wheel brush* with wooden hub and lead center for tapered spindle; continuous set; available in brass, steel, or nickel silver; wire thickness 0.0025, 0.003, 0.0035, 0.004, 0.005 in; Ø 2, 3, 4, 5, 6 in; one, two, three, four rows.
7. *Crimped wire wheel* with metal hub, continuous set.
8. *Brass crimped wire end brush* on wood mount for use on tapered spindle.
9. *Straight wire wheel* on nylon hub with metal center, knot set, three rows.
10. *Straight wire wheel* with knots linked to metal hub, a loose mount for maximum flexibility. (Karl Fischer)
11. *Abrasive flap wheel* mounted on metal hub, for use on straight arbor to which it is held between two metal flanges (one seen below) one on either side; 6 × 1 in, available in all common grits from 40–400.
12. *Mounted screw end mandrel* for use with unmounted wheels with ³⁄₃₂ and ⅛ in center holes; with drilled end for mounting on a tapered spindle. Allows the use of small-diameter unmounted wheels on a normal sized polishing lathe.
13. *Mounted MK spindle* with tapering threaded end on which small metal-hubbed wheels with ⅛ in hole can be wound and held as on a miniature tapered spindle; made for use on either right or left side.
14. *Mounted small chuck* with open capacity of .085–.128 in, allowing ³⁄₃₂ and ⅛ in mandrels, on reinforced wood mandrel for use on a tapered spindle; overall length 3½ in.
15. Manner of mounting the chuck on a tapered spindle held on normal sized polishing motor shafts to allow miniature wheels, etc., to be mounted in chuck jaws. (Swest Inc.)
16. *Arbor-tapered spindle combination* for ⅜, ½, or ⅝ in shaft, with right or left thread.

wire is 0.003 in; and steel wire, 0.003 in. For gold and silver, brass and nickel wire are most commonly used. Wheels are made with a metal center in wood or plastic hubs or all metal center, and have from one to six rows of bristles. Brush diameters for polishing lathes range from 1½–6 in (2.9–15.2 cm). A great variety of miniature wire wheels are available for use on flex-shafts. End bristle brushes are available in various shapes.

USING BRISTLE AND WIRE BRUSHES

The speeds at which wire and bristle brushes work on polishing lathes is considerably slower than that used for cloth or leather wheels. Brushes have the advantage of running cooler than cloth wheels so there is less likelihood of the work becoming overheated. This slower speed gives the brush a desirable softness or cushion that allows it to conform to irregular surface shapes and reach recesses in the object. It also allows the work to be hand held without the danger of the skin on the fingers being torn.

In work, both bristle and wire brushes should be pressed only *lightly* as excessive pressure will cause the bristles to bend and wires to become misshapen and take on a mushroom shape, reducing their efficiency. In wire brushes, it is the pointed wire *ends* that do the work, and when the wires are deformed by excessive pressure, their sides and not the ends whip over the metal surface with little effect. This poor practice will result in wires and bristles wearing out much before they should. From time to time, both bristle and wire brushes should be reversed to keep the bristles and wires straight so they will wear evenly. Newly reversed wire brushes work efficiently.

Wire brushes can be used without or with abrasives, but except for the removal of firescale when they are used dry, they are almost always used with a lubricant. Unless a lubricant is used, a brass wire brush may make a deposit on gold or silver and cause silver to look yellowish. When a brush is run wet, very little or no metal is deposited or removed. After a brush has been used with a lubricant, hang it to dry on a nail hammered into a board, then store it when dry. As in the case of cloth wheels, their use should be confined to greasy or greaseless abrasives.

SCRATCH BRUSHING   Scratch brushing with bristle or wire brushes can be done manually or mechanically as an intermediary step in metal finishing, to remove firescale, to prepare a surface for another process, or as a final finish. All scratch brushing is worked wet with a lubricant. The most common lubricant is soap and water. Quillai bark from the soapbark tree (*Quillaja saponaria*) which is naturally rich in saponin is also used in a pulverized form as a detergent or lubricant. A mixture is prepared in advance by mixing one heaping teaspoonful of quillai powder with one gallon of hot water; stir and allow it to stand for several hours. Either dip the wheel in the lubricant, or apply some periodically to the brush face while the wheel rotates. Beer or ale is also used as a lubricant.

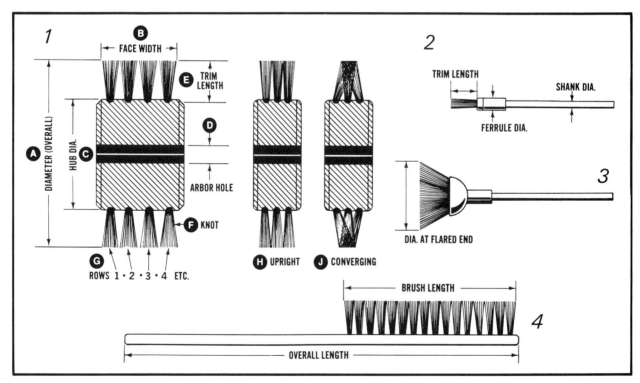

14–13 *BRUSH TYPES AND TERMINOLOGY*
1. *Wood hub bristle wheel brushes*
   A = *Diameter:* The distance across the brush from face to face. For maximum efficiency, use the largest possible brush diameter.
   B = *Face width:* The distance across the brush face which is the working surface.
   C = *Hub diameter:* The diameter of the wood or metal core to which the fill material is anchored.
   D = *Arbor hole:* The central hole in the core used for mounting the brush on a spindle or motor shaft.
   E = *Trim length:* The length of the fill material in a single hub hole.
   F = *Knot:* One tuft of fill material in a single hub hole.
   G = *Rows:* The number of knots placed in the face width.

   H = *Upright tuft:* A wheel whose fill material is set perpendicular to the hub face.
   J = *Converging tuft:* A wheel whose fill material is set in a direction tapering toward the face center, making for a stiff brush.
2. *End brush* for use with a flex-shaft, available in trim lengths: ¼, ½, ⅝ in; shank Ø ³⁄₃₂, ⅛ in.
3. *Cup brush* for use with a flex-shaft, diameters at flared end available in ½, ⁹⁄₁₆ in.
4. *Standard washout brush* for use with cleaning solutions, available in brush lengths of 2⅛, 2⅜, 3, 3⅜ in; in widths of ½, ⅜, ⅝ in; trim lengths of ½, ⅝, ⁹⁄₁₆ in; three or four rows; overall lengths of 6¾, 7¼, 8¼ in.
Drawing courtesy the William Dixon Co.

For *hand scratch brushing* jewelry, brass or steel wire 0.003 in (0.076 mm), or extra heavy spring steel wire brushes with or without hardwood handles are available in several sizes 2–4 rows wide by 10–20 rows in length.

For *mechanical scratch brushing* jewelry of gold, silver, and nonferrous metals, the following wire brushes are recommended: brass, 1½ in diameter, ⅛ in wide, wires ¼ in long; brass, 2½ in diameter, ⅛ in wide, wires 9/16 in long; nickel silver, 2½ in diameter, ⅜ in wide, wires ¾ in long. Use these with warm water, a soapbark solution, or stale beer. Brushes are used at a spindle speed of 1750 rpm, with wheels capable of 2500–6500 sfpm, depending on wheel diameter, with minimal pressure.

SATIN BRUSH FINISHING When making a satin or matte finish with a bristle or fine wire brush wheel, apply abrasive compounds to the wheel while it rotates. In general, abrasives do not adhere as well to bristles and wires as they do to cloth or leather wheels. Lubricants are used to help them adhere, as well as to facilitate finishes. Compounds in use on brushes tend to be transferred back to the metal and are moved along as the brush ends contact them. Therefore apply small amounts frequently instead of overloading the wheel.

A common lubricant and abrasive combination for satin brush finishes is a slurry or paste of pumice with water, which is applied on the work or the wheel. To help a greasy-type red rouge bar abrasive adhere to brushes, first dip the bar into kerosene before applying it to the rotating wheel. Emery is used in a grease-based paste form as is pumice to remove burrs and to round edges. Greaseless compounds adhere more easily than pastes because of the binders they contain. The speeds used with brushes vary from 1200–3450 rpm shaft speed to achieve 4200–6000 sfpm speeds depending on the size and construction of the brush and the desired surface effect. All brush finishes must be followed by thorough cleaning to remove abrasives and grease.

ABRASIVES

Abrasives have the function of abrading metals, plastics, stones, glass, and other materials in order to shape them or to impart a desired finish to their surface. They play an extremely important role in jewelry making and in lapidary work. Several natural or synthetic materials are used as abrasives, singly or in combinations, in various forms:

Solid: Abrasive substances, natural or synthetic, are formed into sticks, bars, or wheels in many sizes and degrees of coarseness.

Grit: The solid abrasive is crushed to a desired particle size.

Powder: The abrasive material is ground and levigated to an impalpable consistency so it can be combined with a liquid to form a paste or slurry, or combined with other substances to make a solid composition bar.

Composition: The abrasive is formed into a bar by combining it with a supporting material, one meant to provide lubrication, or both.

Mounted: Powder or grit abrasives of specific graduated and rated sizes are mounted by adhesives on a backing of paper or cloth.

NATURAL ABRASIVES

These fall mainly into groups of stones or oxides of metals.

Flint: This is a hard, impure variety of quartz, and is gray, brown, or black in color. Reduced to particles, it is mainly used on sandpapers or flint papers. Flint is the oldest of all natural abrasives used by man.

Silica: Silicon dioxide (SiO_2) occurs naturally in crystalline form as quartz or sand which is impure silica, and as an element in other materials. It is the most common of all solid minerals. Ground to a fine, soft, white powder, it is used to color nonferrous metals. It is also produced artificially and combined with carbon as silicon carbide.

Garnet: A brittle, red, brown, or black mineral silicate containing aluminum, magnesium, or calcium. In its coarser almandite or andrite variety it is crushed and used as an abrasive, mounted on paper backing, and called *garnet paper.*

Ruby: Corundum ruby powder is used for very high polishes on gold. (See Corundum below.)

Tripoli: Also called rottenstone, it is probably the most widely used fast-cutting abrasive in finishing jewelry. It is a very friable, soft shistose deposit of amorphous silica and other substances in a homogeneous yellowish gray or white rock form. It is almost entirely composed of the skeletons of the microscopic animal life that formed a siliceous limestone with a silica content of over 80%. Tripoli is named after its original main source, Tripoli, Libya.

Tripoli used for polishing cuts the metal and leaves it with a dull finish. It is usually followed by buffing with rouge. Before buffing, the work should be well cleaned to remove any traces of the coarser tripoli abrasive. Tripoli is available in powdered form, or combined with a greasy binder in a polishing compound bar. The binder consists of stearic acid, grease, or tallow. It is there to provide lubrication and to create drag between the wheel and the work to make it cut faster. A water-soluble tripoli composition bar is also available. Powdered tripoli is also combined with other abrasives in compositions that cut faster than plain tripoli, some acting as cut-and-color compositions. Initially the tripoli cuts sharply, then breaks down in size, making a finer cut that acts to color the metal.

Chalk: A soft, white or gray limestone, mainly of calcium carbonate, chalk is composed of minute marine shells of Foraminifera, and yields lime when burned. It is used in an impalpable powder form as a fine abrasive, or is mixed with binders in polishing compounds. *Whiting* is a form of chalk, used as a powder when *highlighting* or partially removing oxidized coloring from finished work to give those parts a luster that contrasts with the areas left oxidized.

Lime: Pure lime is calcium oxide (CaO), obtained by calcining shells, limestone, or other forms of calcium carbonate. *Venetian lime* is used with flannel to remove fingerprints from mirror-polished surfaces as it will not scratch the metal. *Vienna lime compounds* (also called lime compounds, or nickel-buffing compounds) contain almost pure calcium and magnesium oxides that produce high color on nickel, copper, brass, and aluminum.

Pumice: This is a white, gray, or brownish solid of rapidly cooled and hardened volcanic glass that is filled with minute air holes which make it very light in weight. This is ground to a coarse, medium, or fine powder and is used dry or mixed with oil or water to form a controllable paste or slurry that can be applied to wheels or brushes. It is used as an abrasive in cleaning metals before polishing and buffing operations, and is also mixed with other substances in abrasive compounds.

Corundum: A naturally occurring, extremely hard mineral, aluminum oxide (Al_2O_3), next in hardness to the diamond. Pure and transparent corundum is a gem, according to its color called ruby, or blue, white, or yellow sapphire. Non-gem-quality ruby and sapphire are crushed to a powder and used as a fine abrasive. (See Ruby on p. 651.)

Emery: A natural black substance containing 57–75% aluminum oxide, as well as corundum and iron oxide, used mounted on paper or cloth backings. It is also used in a grease or tallow stick, and as a paste on tampico brush wheels for a bright satin finish. Emery was the standard metal-polishing medium until the heat-treated artificial abrasives entered the market.

Iron oxide: Includes any of the three compounds ferric oxide, ferrous oxide, and ferrosoferric oxide. These can be found naturally or they can be produced artificially. They are used in combination with binders in bar form, as in rouge, or mounted on a cloth backing, as in crocus cloth.

Crocus: A deep yellow, dark red, or purple, coarse iron oxide, also called *colcothar* or *crocus of Mars,* left as a residue when calcining ferrous sulphate to a higher degree of temperature than when making rouge. *Crocus of Venus* is cuprous oxide.

Tin oxide: A fine white powder used to polish semiprecious stones.

Cirium oxide: Used to polish stones that cannot be given a satisfactory surface with tin oxide.

ARTIFICIAL ABRASIVES

Artificial abrasives have been produced synthetically since the end of the 19th century. They are harder, purer, more uniform, and longer lasting than natural abrasives, and are commonly used in all the forms in which abrasives are prepared. They are used to rapidly "cut" the metal by abrasion to remove grinding lines, pits, or tool marks. Compounds containing these abrasives are considerably harder and sharper than tripoli in cut-down polishing.

Aluminum oxide: A very sharp, tough, durable abrasive in grain form, used in all forms of abrasive. The grain shape makes it suitable for mounting with adhesives on cloth or paper backing, and gives it good bonding properties. It is made from the fusion of bauxite and iron filings at high temperature. Fused aluminum oxide is probably the abrasive most in use in metal finishing today.

Silicon carbide: Harder than aluminum oxide, this dark purple, iridescent compound of silicon and carbon (SiC) is made by heating sand and carbon together in an electric resistance furnace. Its trade name is *carborundum.* Crushed into grain form, it is applied to wheels by first covering their face with liquid hide glue which is flexible and used for high-polishing situations, or a silicate-based cement suited to fast-polishing situations. The grit is then applied to the binder and it is allowed to dry. It fractures easily in use when dull, presenting new cutting edges to work. Artificial abrasives are available in screened sizes: 24, 30, 36, 60, 80, 90, 100, 120, 150, 180, 220, and 240 grit; and as *flours:* 280–600 grit.

POLISHING AND BUFFING COMPOSITIONS

FAST-CUTTING COMPOSITIONS: These are used for *polishing* in which the abrasive cuts down or removes some of the metal surface and edges.

COLORING COMPOSITIONS These are used in *buffing* in which little or none of the metal is removed, but it is burnished to a lustrous finish by light touches to the wheel, called *fanning.*

CUT-AND-COLOR COMPOSITIONS These double-duty compounds occupy a position between fast-cutting and coloring compositions. They are used for deburring, and to produce a satin finish. Generally, they are of the same type as fast cut-down compounds, but because of their composition, have less drag on the metal. The degree of cutting and brilliance achieved lies between that possible with cutting and coloring compounds used separately for either operation. The most popular compounds in this group generally contain aluminum oxide, silicon carbide being less in use—although some contain both—in grits from 120–240. Well known in this group are Lea compounds. In some designed for use on nonferrous metals, white silica powders are blended with tripoli and a grease binder. On ferrous metals, coarsely powdered, unfused aluminum oxide, or fused and unfused combinations are used. This is the type used to polish tools such as hammer, stake, and anvil faces, followed by rouge buffing. For an intermediate luster, use 6000–8000 sfpm.

All these compositions should be transferred to the wheel as it rotates, so that frictional heat melts the compound and it dries quickly. Relatively small amounts should be applied at frequent intervals during polishing and buffing rather than in one large application. Excessive amounts are to be avoided because under high pressure and frictional heat the surplus tends to become packed and caked or glazed on the work, and is difficult to remove. All of the compound bar can be used down to the nubbin or bar end, which is too short, but it can be remelted.

In general, polishing or cutting operations require greater sfpm rates than are used in color buffing. Gold and silver are considered softer metals and require a lower sfpm rate, nonferrous metals a medium rate, and ferrous metals such as stainless steel take the highest rates. Higher rates of speed than are necessary only act to wear down the metal rapidly, or to burn the wheel and wear it out more quickly. Follow recommended wheel speeds for particular operations with these compositions. Excessively high speed also wastes the composition which flies off the wheel.

GREASY OR GREASELESS COMPOSITIONS Abrasives used in *bar form* must be held in a binder-carrier medium. This can be of a greasy or greaseless type, making a grease-based or greaseless composition.

Greasy compositions use binders containing a mixture of fats and waxes of vegetable, mineral, or animal origin, among them stearic acid, tallow, petrolatum, and hydrogenated fatty acids, glycerides, or fish oils. The grease in these compositions creates a high degree of "drag" between the wheel and the metal which results in an increase in its cutting action. The grease, however, penetrates the wheel material and reduces its life. Because of grease penetration, these wheels must be reserved for *exclusive use with greasy compounds.*

The grease base is combined with fast-cutting abrasives in finely powdered form. Abrasive to binder proportions vary according to the desired result and the particular combination of ingredients. Greasy cut-down polishing bars for nonferrous metals contain tripoli, and those used on other metals contain fused and unfused aluminum oxide.

To avoid composition back-transfer, after the compound has been applied to the wheel, allow the wheel to rotate for 20–30 seconds to dry, then bring the work to the wheel. For cut-down polishing for preliminary smoothness with a greasy abrasive, use 6000–8000 sfpm. After polishing, a light film of grease remains on the work which must be removed.

Greaseless compositions are entirely free of grease and consist mainly of a gelatin-glue binder base plus fast-cutting abrasives. When they are applied to a rotating wheel, the heat generated by friction causes them to melt and be transferred to the wheel. A great advantage of greaseless compounds is that after polishing there is no grease to be removed, and usually there is no deposit of compound left on the metal unless it has caught in the depressions of the work. Final cleaning is therefore simplified. These compo-

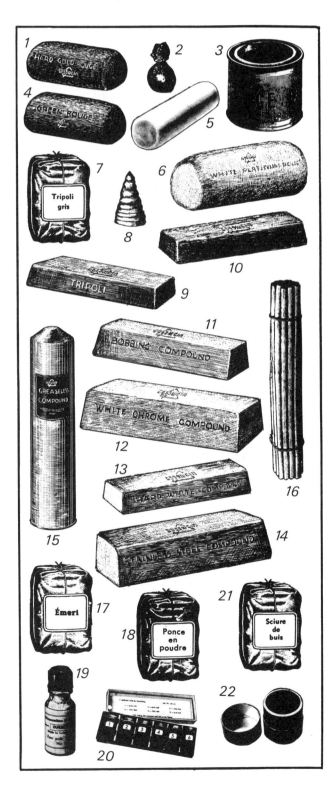

sitions are usually furnished in approximately 2 pound bars enclosed in cylinders of aluminum or plastic to keep them from drying out. Aluminum tubes are cut away only ½ in (1.27 cm) at a time as the bar is used, to expose just the necessary amount of abrasive composition to the wheel. Plastic jackets can be torn away, or after first removing the end, worn away by friction in use. Once the container is opened, cover the open end with a tight-fitting plastic cap, as dried out abrasive is very difficult to apply. They are available in many grades, containing 50–240 grit abrasives. Typical and most popular are those containing silicon carbide and/or aluminum oxide in the 120–240 grit range for coarse, scratched finishes to fine satin finishes respectively. Aluminum oxide in 240 grit is favored for a satin finish on nonferrous metals. American emery and hard silica compositions in fine grades are also used for these metals.

Finishes of varying degrees of dullness from an almost bright luster to an almost totally unreflective surface can be achieved with greaseless compounds, depending on the abrasive it contains, and the kind of wheel used (loose, almost bright; sewn, dull). A butler finish is made on silver

14–14 POLISHING AND BUFFING COMPOSITIONS
1. *Hard red rouge* for gold; ¼, ½, and 1 lb bars; for high polish on precious metals.
2. *Greasy red rouge ball,* for gold and silver, adheres to wheels.
3. *Red rouge powder,* for application to cloths for use in hand polishing.
4. *Green rouge bar,* for final buffing on platinum, rhodium, chrome, and stainless steel; ¼ lb bar.
5. *Yellow rouge* for gold, silver, and base metals.
6. *White rouge* for buffing platinum and other precious metals, also nonferrous metals; ¼, ½ lb bars.
7. *Powdered tripoli* (French, *Tripoli gris*) for use in hand and wheel polishing, the latter in levigated compounds.
8. *Venetian tripoli cone,* a fine-grit abrasive.
9. *Tripoli,* 1 lb bar, for surface scratch removal prior to using rouge.
10. *Platinum tripoli,* fast cutting, 1 lb bar.
11. *Bobbing compound,* for use on gold and silver, 1½ lb bar.
12. *Hard white chrome compound,* grease base with white alumina, for fine cutting, 3 lb bar.
13. *Hard white compound,* dry, for cutting and semifinish on precious metals.
14. *Stainless steel compound* with grease base, containing 240 grit aluminum oxide, 3 lb bar.
15. *Greaseless compound* of which several proprietary preparations are available, left in protective tube to prevent drying out, open end kept in water when not in use; applied on polishing wheels and allowed to harden; used for butler finish; available in 120, 150, 180, and 240 grit abrasives, 2½ lb tube.
16. *Charcoal sticks,* used as a mild abrasive to remove surface scratches.
17. *Emery powder* (French, *émeri*), fast-cutting abrasive.
18. *Powdered pumice* (French, *ponce en poudre*), used for cleaning surfaces and removing surface defects.
19. *Diamantine powder,* a fast-cutting abrasive used on leather wheels, and *leather strops* to polish hard steel tools, and in stone polishing; available in three grades in ¾ oz bottles. (Swest Inc.)
20. *Silicon carbide powders,* set of six grades, used for cutting, polishing, and finishing hard materials; in ¼ oz bottles. (Swest Inc.)
21. *Boxwood sawdust,* sifted, used to dry jewelry after final washing.
22. *Sawdust case,* used to hold objects in sawdust during drying, shaken together. Has central screen and removable end caps; 3 in Ø, 3 in high.

with a compound containing finely divided soft silica and unfused aluminum oxide. Extremely fine greaseless compounds with special lubricating binders are available for bright butler finishes. For satin, butler, and brushed finishes, use 5000–6000 sfpm speeds.

Greaseless compounds lie on the face of the wheel and do not penetrate it. If grease is present on the wheel, they will not adhere, therefore the wheel should be reserved exclusively for their use. After the application of the compound, as in the case of other compounds, allow the wheel to rotate for 30 seconds before use to dry the compound. Repeat this each time new compound is applied. When using coarse (80–120 grit) compounds, to help the compound hold on the wheel better and last longer in use, a quick-drying glue can be applied to the wheel first.

BUFFING ABRASIVE COLORING COMPOSITIONS

These compositions do not cut the metal but remove minor defects by flowing or burnishing it, and they color the metal, bringing it to a smooth, scratch-free, lustrous, reflective, specular surface finish. In these compositions where fast cutting is not required, the finest abrasives are used. For gold and silver, various types of red rouge compositions are used; for brass and aluminum, soft white silica powder in finer grades; for brass, powdered lime; and for nickel alloys and stainless steel, fine, unfused aluminum oxide powders or chromium oxide.

These abrasives are combined with a binder or carrier that acts to lubricate the metal, helps the abrasive hold on the wheel face, and helps prevent the work from overheating due to excessive frictional drag. In *hard buffing* they are used with higher count wheels (86/93), and in *color buffing* where a scratch-free, lustrous surface is the aim, a softer, lower thread count wheel (64/68) is used with milder buffing compounds such as rouge. *Wiping* is a form of buffing in which a dry or only lightly dressed wheel is used to brighten color. Color buffing and wiping for a high-gloss or mirror finish utilizes 6000–8000 sfpm.

Any remains of buffing compound that dries out on the metal becomes a metallic soap that is difficult to remove. Therefore, the work should be cleaned as soon as possible after buffing.

ROUGE   Rouge is the most common composition used to color buff precious metals—which must be *dry* when buffed to prevent rouge smear. Its ingredients have the right qualities to achieve a high luster. *Rouge* is a red, brown, or pink composition that contains fine, almost pure ferric or ferrous iron oxide. In its manufacture, ferrous sulphate or iron salts are gently calcined or heated to redness when the iron as oxide separates from the acid. This is in the form of a white powder which is placed in another crucible and reheated to redness until no vapors rise. The residue is a soft, powdery iron oxide. Fused umber, aluminum oxide, chromium oxide, or diamantine may also be added. Strictly speaking, rouge should contain iron oxide, but the term has been extended to include fine buffing abrasive compositions used for the same purpose that contain no iron oxide, but that instead substitute the above-mentioned abrasives. These can be used on metals on which iron-containing rouge should not be used.

Because most rouges contain iron, unless they are removed completely after buffing, the iron will ultimately cause the metal to discolor. If the rouge cakes or smears on the work, too much rouge has been applied to the wheel, or the sfpm speed is insufficient. It is useless in this case to increase the pressure of the work against the wheel as this will simply burn the rouge and make it form a hard coating on the metal that is difficult to remove. Instead, increase the spindle speed, or if this cannot be done, use a wheel of greater diameter.

The rouge types are:

Red rouge: The red rouges available include *dry:* the standard type used on gold and silver, some of which are water soluble; *medium dry:* fast polishing and coloring, used on silver, copper, and brass; *medium wet:* cuts slightly and produces a high finish on all nonferrous metals; and *greasy:* used on greasy wheels. Tallow or rosin are used as a binder for greasy or dry types respectively.

Pink rouge: A combination of rouge and white diamond compound.

Ochre rouge: Used for gold alloys, contains yellow ochre.

Crocus rouge: Contains crocus powder which is a coarse grade of red iron oxide powder.

Green rouge: A chromium oxide rouge, iron-free, used on the platinum family metals for an extremely bright finish, and also to polish hard ferrous metals such as stainless steel.

Porcelain rouge: Not used on gold and its alloys, but used on hard-to-buff metals such as steel to provide a fast mirror surface. Rouges containing iron are not used on steel as they cause a discoloration.

Black rouge: A hard rouge used for highly reflective finishes.

OTHER POLISHING AND BUFFING COMPOUNDS   These are proprietary compositions whose exact ingredients are not made public.

White rouge-lime compound: Used on platinum and white gold for high color, and also on other nonferrous metals. Wheels used for gold should not be used on platinum or palladium as a transfer of gold occurs on their surface that will give them a yellowish cast. To buff them, first use a tripoli compound, then white rouge applied on a 64/68 weave cotton wheel 4–8 in (10.2–20.3 cm) in diameter, at a spindle speed of 3450 rpm. Follow this by cleaning with a hot water and ammonia and soap solution; then rinse and dry.

White diamond: A dry compound used in bars, sometimes combined with other abrasives such as tripoli; leaves a dull, scratch-free finish on gold, copper, and white metals. It is used to clean metals before plating.

Diamantine: A fast-cutting abrasive used for stone polishing and steel. It is often used on a leather strop to polish steel tool faces. Available in several grades of fineness.

Bobbing compound: A wet and tacky or medium dry, fast-cutting compound used to remove scratches from gold, silver, or plastics; leaves a dull appearance. It is often used on wool wheels, brushes, or lap wheels to which it adheres well.

Emery pastes: Black, fast cutting, 120–180 grit, used on polishing wheels and tampico brushes.

Rubber finger cots, ridged and perforated, fit over the ends of fingers, and are used for holding jewelry when it is being polished. They prevent leaving fingerprints, and protect the fingers against heat and the friction of the abrasive.

TYPES OF FINISH ON METALS

A large range of finishes are possible on metal, from a dull, coarse matte, nonreflecting surface, to a high mirror gloss. The finish selected depends on the maker's wish. The means by which it is accomplished depends upon the kind of equipment available to achieve it, the kind of metal to be finished, its original surface condition, its shape, size, or construction, the wheel type used, and the polishing or buffing compound used. Parts of one work can be finished in different finishes for the sake of contrast or to emphasize construction. It is not always the aim for a piece to be finished with a high gloss, and a finish somewhere between coarse matte and mirror may be a final one.

MATTE FINISH A bright or dull matte, nonreflecting, frosty finish with an even texture can be made by sandblasting, achieved by a mechanical sandblasting gun or by a gravity sand drop. Other matte finishes are achieved by acid dips.

SEMIMATTE A semimatte, scratched-line finish, somewhat reflective, with underlying luster can be produced by a metal wire scratch brush or a bristle brush, manually or mechanically, with or without the use of an abrasive.

SATIN FINISH: DIRECTIONAL Coarse, medium, or fine lines pass in *one* direction across a surface, produced mechanically with a cutting abrasive compound on a cotton wheel, or manually by rubbing with steel wool, or with cloth- or paper-backed crocus or other fine abrasive.

SATIN FINISH: NONDIRECTIONAL Coarse, medium, or fine lines go in *all* directions across a surface and blend with any surface marks or scratches, produced with a cut-and-color composition and a muslin or flannel wheel. Hand-produced, dull satin finishes are done with fine-grit abrasive cloths, or fine abrasives applied on a cloth.

BUTLER FINISH A type of deadened satin finish of fine parallel lines, this is the brightest of the "lined" finishes. It is meant to simulate the finish imparted to metal by prolonged exposure to hand-rubbed polishing, and is so called after the butler, who in wealthy households was in charge of plate and its maintenance. A dull butler, butler, or bright butler finish can be achieved according to the degree of brilliance desired, by hand rubbing with a sharp

cutting compound such as a 240–320 grit emery cloth, or by machine with an unstitched muslin wheel having a 64/68 weave, with a 240 grit greaseless compound, at a spindle speed of 1750 rpm and 4500 sfpm.

BURNISHED FINISH A hand or mechanical bright finish, it is directional when done with a burnisher on a large surface by hand, and is nondirectional when done by machine in a tumbler.

MIRROR FINISH A very bright, highly reflective surface having no evident abrasive pattern and no surface defects, done with rouge and a loose muslin or flannel wheel at 7500 sfpm. Scratches that appear on mirror finishes come from contamination of a coarser abrasive, brought to the metal by dirty hands, grit under fingernails, abrasive left on the metal from previous cutting and polishing operations, or contaminated wheels. The work and the hands should both be washed before final mirror polishing takes place. Mirror finishes are subject to fingerprints as soon as the surface is touched, therefore some polishers wear *cotton gloves* during mirror polishing. Fingerprints can be removed with levigated Vienna lime applied with a soft, clean cloth. After final washing, dry the work in warm sawdust, not with a cloth.

ULTRA MIRROR FINISH For an extremely bright finish, after mirror finishing, use a loose, soft canton flannel wheel with a slurry of lampblack and kerosene as a lubricant.

POLISHING AND BUFFING WHEELS IN ACTION

When a cloth, wire, or bristle brush wheel rotates at the high speeds used on a polishing lathe, tremendous centrifugal force causes its walls to flatten; the wheel becomes stiff, and in ordinary circumstances, the face surface becomes uniform, presenting a flat plane to the contacting metal. This force, as much as the wheel material and the abrasive used, gives the wheel its working qualities and produces the result.

Wheel Speeds Recommended for Finishing Metals, Plastics, and Wood
(speeds in surface feet per minute)

Material	Polishing or Matte Finish	Satin or Semimatte Finish	Buffing or Mirror-Bright Finish
Aluminum	4000-5000	3000-5000	6000-7500
Brass	5000-7000	3500-5500	5000-8000
Bronze	5000-7000	3500-5500	7000-8000
Britannia metal	2000-5000	2000-4000	3000-4000
Copper	5500-6500	4500-6000	5500-7000
Gold	5000-6000	4000-7500	6000-8000
Nickel and alloys	6500-7500	5000-6500	7000-8000
Pewter	2000-4000	2000-3500	3000-4500
Plastics			
Thermosetting	2000-6000	4500-5500	4000-5000
Thermoplastic	3000-5000	3000-4000	3000-4000
Silver (sterling)	5000-6000	5000-7500	6000-8000
Stainless steel	6000-8000	4500-5500	8000-10,000
Wood	sanding 3500	sanding 5500	5000-6000
Zinc	5000-6000	5500-6000	6000-8000

For wheel diameter selection to achieve these speeds, see **Polishing and Buffing Wheel Perimeter Surface Speed Calculation Chart**

When the wheel revolves, it turns *toward* the worker and exerts a *downward* pressure. It is therefore important when using a polishing lathe to bring the metal at a *tangential angle* into sideways-moving contact with the revolving wheel *only in the area of its forward lower quarter segment*. If contact is made with other wheel areas, or in a way that opposes the direction of the turning wheel, the work can be torn from the hands, causing not only damage to the work but possibly an accident to the worker.

WARNING:

When using a mechanical polisher, always make sure loose clothing is confined. Long hair should never hang loose, but should be tied back. Remove from the fingers any rings that have projections as they might be caught. Certain shapes of work may have to be supported by holding them on a flat piece of wood. Chains being polished should be wrapped firmly around a flat stick, and only a short length of the chain at one time is presented vertically parallel to the direction of the wheel, while making sure the rest is gathered in the hands and does not dangle loose. Delicate work (especially of wire) is best polished by hand. Never work with an unbalanced, chattering wheel (which is noticeable when the rotating wheel face instead of being sharply defined appears as a blur, indicating that a true working plane does not exist).

If the workpiece should get caught in a moving wheel, *withdraw the hands immediately*. Do *NOT* try to rescue it. As soon as the situation is assessed, turn off the polisher. Your fingers are worth far more than any object!

THE PROBLEM OF FRICTIONAL HEAT

In all machine polishing and buffing operations, *sliding friction* or the act of rubbing one body against another is

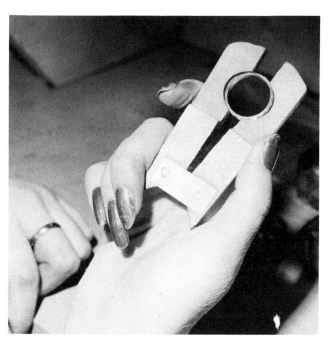

14–15 KULTAKESKUS OY, Hämeenlinna, Finland. *WOOD RING HOLDER.* A device with brass hinge used to grasp rings while filing, or when polishing their inner shank surface with a felt end ring mandrel. *Photo: Oppi*

at work. Because of the resistance created by the still body (the work) against the moving body (the wheel), *heat* is generated in both. The greater the force or pressure exerted by the work on the wheel, the greater is the heat generated and retained, especially if the work is of metal

Polishing problems, causes, and suggested corrections

Problem	Cause	Suggested solution
Wheel chattering	Enlarged central hole; wheel shape not true	Use a softer density wheel; true the wheel with wheel rake; be sure motor vibration is not the cause; if hole is enlarged excessively, discard wheel
Cutting too slowly	Unsuitable abrasive, wheel density, or sfpm speed	Use a coarser abrasive, harder wheel density; increase the wheel sfpm speed
Rounded edges; cutting too fast	Wheel too soft; abrasive too coarse; too much pressure used	Use a flat-faced, more rigid wheel with less pressure, and a finer abrasive
Wheel glazed	Too much abrasive applied to the wheel; too much frictional heat buildup; speed too high	Clean wheel face with wheel rake to remove caked compound; apply less compound; use a harder wheel density; reduce pressure; change to wheel with smaller diameter
Unwanted overlap marks	Wheel too hard; abrasive too coarse	Use wheel of softer density; dress wheel to a rounded contour
Rouge buildup on work	Work is wet; speed too high; frictional heat too high from excessive pressure	Buff with work dry; reduce speed or use a smaller diameter wheel; apply medium pressure; shorten dwell time
Finish too dull or too coarse	Abrasive too coarse; wheel too hard	Change to a finer abrasive; use softer buff, and higher sfpm speed
Burned finish	Speed too high; frictional heat from excessive pressure	Reduce speed or use smaller wheel diameter; change to coarser grit abrasive

which conducts heat well. A certain amount of pressure is needed to cause the metal surface to move, called *starting friction*, but there is a limit to the pressure necessary. The wheel works best with a fair charge of abrasive and firm pressure, but never so much that the wheel in motion becomes distorted in shape. Excessive pressure will cause the work to be worn away too rapidly, and excessive frictional heat may cause the abrasive binder to burn, become hardened and glazed on the wheel, or caked on the work from which it is removed with difficulty.

In machine polishing and buffing, the work must be firmly held with the fingers. Holding small objects such as

jewelry while the heat builds up rapidly can be a problem. Some solutions are possible. One is to wear *rubber finger cots,* or *cotton* or *thin leather gloves,* all of which act as insulators. Heat buildup can be kept to a minimum by making the polishing passes or dwell time short and allowing a short, cooling interval between passes. Work can be held on a piece of wood which is a low heat conductor. With care, small work such as a ring can be held in a *ring clamp* or other holding device or on a *wooden mandrel* while being polished.

REMINDER:
To avoid contamination, use separate polishing and buffing wheels for greasy and greaseless compounds. After each finishing operation is completed with a particular abrasive, clean the work and wash your hands.

14–16 *FLEXIBLE SHAFTS*
Karl Fischer models
1. Hanging type, permanent table installation, motor operates on 220 volt, 180 watt, models capable of 1400, 3000, 6000, 8000, and 12,000 rpm.
2. Hanging bracket, side rotating.
3. Hanging system with wheel.
4. Hanging type with workbench edge clamp.
5. Pedestal type on wheels for mobility, with swinging tray to hold accessories, and foot rheostat.
6. Foot rheostats, press-down and side-swinging types.
7. Goldsmith's handpiece, collet accepts 0–3 mm shafts.

Foredom flexible shaft
8. Handpiece with $\frac{3}{32}$ in collet, four other size collets available, oil-retaining precision bronze bearings.
9. Miniature high-speed bench grinder with removable flexible shaft, 36 in long, attached with a motor coupling for $\frac{1}{4}$, $\frac{3}{8}$, $\frac{5}{16}$, and $\frac{1}{2}$ in shafts; operates at speeds from 1500–14,000 rpm; height to shaft $3\frac{3}{8}$ in; motor 110–130 volt, AC-DC; shaft available with a permanently fixed handpiece, or with a handpiece-detaching system.
10. Bench type, $\frac{1}{10}$ hp universal motor mounted on stand; 36 in flex-shaft; speed range 0–14,000 rpm; 110–130 volt, AC-DC, 220 volt also available.
11. Hanging type, otherwise same as above.
12. Handpieces, interchangeable: end of flex-shaft is simply plugged into the handpiece, and disengaged by a sharp pull.
13. Handpiece, general heavy-duty use, with adjustable key-type chuck for shank sizes up to $\frac{5}{32}$ in, with grease-sealed bearings.
14. Handpiece with speed-increasing mechanism for speeds up to 35,000 rpm; for use with small carbide and diamond tools for high-speed drilling, die grinding, deburring, etc.; with $\frac{1}{8}$ in precision collet, others, available to $\frac{1}{4}$ in.
15. Miniature hammer handpiece with $\frac{3}{32}$ in reciprocating motion stroke and adjustable impact control, used in jewelry making for light riveting, peening, texturing, stone setting, etc.; works at continuous speeds up to 5000 rpm; replaceable flat anvil point.
16. Handpiece with duplex flexible spring connection. Almost all handpieces are also available with this connection.
17. Jacobs-type chuck key used to open and close chucks.
18. Rheostat foot switch, with 12 in long motor connection; usable with two- or three-blade plugs; outlet cord 6 ft long; with three-blade plug and adaptor for use with two- or three-blade receptacles; used with any universal motor of $\frac{1}{10}$ hp or less; 115 or 230 volt, AC-DC.

FLEXIBLE SHAFT EQUIPMENT AND ACCESSORIES

Flexible shafts and the *accessories* used with them probably constitute the single most important advance made in the field of jewelers' tools in this century. By the use of this universal, motorized instrument, almost all of the fabrication processes that can be adapted to execution by rotary motion power can be performed. This is done with suitable accessories which are miniaturized to a scale that relates to the requirements of jewelry making. With them, the techniques of grinding, deburring, sanding, carving, milling, countersinking, drilling, filing, sawing, slotting, brushing, polishing, buffing, and even hammering can all be carried out. The versatility and timesaving aspects of this tool make it practically a necessity in a modern jewelry making workshop.

The basic elements that make up the flexible shaft complex consist of the *motor* which generates power, the *flexible shaft* connected to it through which the power passes to the operating end and which, because of its flexibility, allows movement in any direction, a *handpiece* which is a device designed to hold the great variety of *accessories*, and a *rheostat* which is a resistor for regulating the current input by means of variable resistances to control the number of motor revolutions per minute (rpm), therefore speed.

Motor mounting for convenience is available in models that can be suspended by a bracket; hung from a swinging arm permanently fixed to a workbench, or clamped to its edge; mounted on a base for use as a bench model; or mounted on a wheeled pedestal.

Motors with 110–130 volts, up to 60 cycles, in various models are of ⅟₁₅, ⅟₁₀, ⅛, or ¼ hp, and can operate at *direct drive* to attain speeds up to 14,000 rpm, or in some models by an easily changed *geared drive* which through a three-to-one *reduction gear* makes low-speed operation possible without any loss of power under load. New models have a *feedback circuit* that supplies only the power needed for the torque necessary to do the work so that power waste is reduced.

Flexible shafts (flex-shafts) are generally 31–37 in (79–94 cm) long, and supply even torque and smooth control to the handpiece regardless of the curvature taken in use. They are available with a permanently fixed handpiece, or an end plug that allows the handpiece end to be attached by simple hand pressure into a socket, or quickly detached by pulling them apart. Separate, heavier model flex-shafts are available designed for adaptation and use on other motors, electric drills, drill presses, or other power sources. Some can be attached to these sources directly, or by the use of a ball bearing *motor coupling* that matches the diameter of the motor shaft.

Handpieces, either fixed or detachable, are available in a variety of types, and catalogs should be consulted. Usually they are grease-sealed for self-lubrication, with roller or ball bearings. In most, an accessory is placed in the handpiece collet by sliding a surrounding sheath back to expose the collet into which the accessory is inserted. The sheath is then slid forward to lock the shank of the accessory in place, and provide a stationary gripping device over the rotating collet. If the handpiece is fitted with a chuck of the Jacobs type, it is tightened by a key. Handpiece collets are available in several sizes to accommodate accessory shafts of various diameters, and the chuck will accept shanks of various diameters up to a certain capacity limit beyond which *adaptor chucks* are used; their shafts are locked in the jaws of the existing chuck. The entire handpiece can be rigid, or include a *flexible duplex spring connection* that further increases its flexibility and maneuverability in small work.

Rheostats are installed in the *hand- or foot-operated control switch,* the latter placed on the floor, that serves as the on-off switch and speed regulator. In foot controls, used more commonly than hand controls, the further down the foot presses the pedal lever or single-pole button contact switch, the faster the speed. When the foot is re-

14–17 *ACCESSORIES FOR USE ON FLEXIBLE SHAFTS:* Mountings and unmounted wheels

Mountings

1. *Tapered screw end mandrels for mounting soft-centered wheels, ³⁄₃₂, ⅛ in shanks. For machines with shafts driven counterclockwise use left-hand threads; for machines driven clockwise use right-hand threads.*
2. *Pressure-prong mandrel for use with paper disc abrasive wheels, ⅛ in shank.*
3. *Snap-on split-shank mandrel for use with paper disc abrasive wheels, ⅛ in shank.*
4. *Screw end arbors for mounting stiff abrasive wheels, with reinforced shanks; shown with screw removed and screw in place; ³⁄₃₂, ⅛ in shafts.*
5. *Screw end arbor with extra reinforcing flange; ³⁄₃₂, ⅛ in shafts.*
6. *Adaptor chucks: small capacity 0–0.065 in; medium capacity 0–0.089 in; large capacity 0–0.1250 in; ³⁄₃₂, ⅛ in shanks; used for grasping accessory shafts larger than handpiece allows, and for use with small drills; chuck jaws are shown removed, and with top view.*
7. *Miniature tapered spindle for use on miniature grinder and polishing machine, or straight mandrel ¼ in held by chuck, or ¼ in motor shaft.*

Unmounted wheels

8. *Midget buffs; high-count muslin 16 ply, one row stitched, ½, ⅞ in Ø; chamois stitched with center leather patch for gripping spindle, ¾ in Ø, for use on ³⁄₃₂, ⅛ in mandrels.*
9. *Hard felt wheels; top: crevice ½ in Ø, tapered edge; bottom left: ⅛ in thick; Ø ½, ¾, 1 in; right: tapered cone, blunt end.*
10. *Brushes; top left: conic brush, natural black bristle; black, hard bristle brush, ¾ in Ø; center: white bristle brush, soft, ¾ in Ø; right: nylon, 1 in Ø; bottom: perlon end brush; steel, brass, or nickel silver wire brushes, Ø ¾, ⅞, 1 in.*
11. *Abrasive wheels; top row: Brightboy wheel, ¼ in square edge, available in ⅞, 1½, 2, 3 in Ø; nylon-bonded abrasive wheels in a wide range of diameters and thicknesses; red aluminum oxide porcelain-bonded grinding wheels with squared edge, available in a wide size range; knife-edged silicon carbide grinding wheels available in a wide range of diameters and thicknesses; bottom row: Mizzy heatless grinding wheel, coarse composition, for rough texture finishing, and deburring, available in a wide size range; rubber-bonded pumice points, pointed and blunt, soft and flexible; tapered cone rubber-bonded pumice, ½ in Ø; cup-shaped rubber-bonded pumice, ½ in Ø; rubber pumice wheel, rounded edge, available ⅞ × ⅛ in; ⅝ × ³⁄₃₂ in.*
12. *Adhesive-backed paper abrasive disc holder, flexible, available in ½, ¾, 1, 1½, 2 in Ø; paper discs available in 60–320 grits; cut-off wheel, perforated to allow work being cut to be seen, and to cool the cutting action, 1.25 × 0.025 in; solid abrasive cut-off discs, extra thin, strongly cemented abrasive, will cut through metal at high speed; Ø ⅞, 1½ in.*
13. *Drum sanders, Ø ¼, ⅜, ½, ¾ in; ½ in width, used with special mount having a ⅛ in shank.*
14. *Diamond wheels; top: flat disc with wide area diamond impregnated; Ø ⅝, ¾, ⅞, 1 in; edge only impregnated, same sizes; cone shape, edge impregnated; bottom: barrel diamond wheels available with ⅛, ⅜, ¼ in rims, used for carving, grooving, etc., on hard materials.*
15. *Disc slotting saw, high-speed steel, available in a very large range of diameters, thicknesses, teeth per inch, and center bore sizes. Used for cutting all metals, thin-walled tubing, and other thin materials. Saw is mounted on a supporting arbor, shank 0.150 in.*

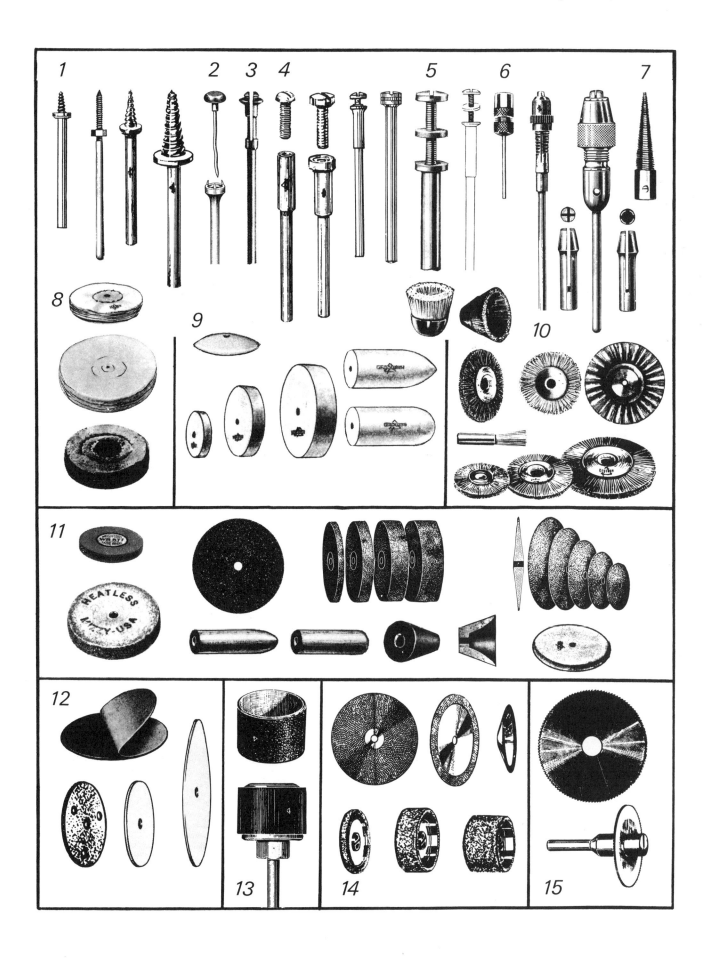

moved from the pedal, the control returns to the "off" position.

Accessories used with the flex-shaft can be generally divided into *unmounted* and *mounted types,* the former requiring a separate mandrel or chuck chosen according to the needs of the particular device to be mounted, and the latter usually already permanently mounted on a mandrel. The same wheels used in normal, large sizes on polishing lathes and grinding motors are all available for use on the flex-shaft, but in *miniature sizes* designed specifically for this machine.

Accessories can be further grouped into the *fibrous* group which includes muslin, leather, felt, and natural bristle wheels; the *metal group* which includes wire brushes, rotary files and burs, cut-off saws, and diamond-embedded wheels; and the *abrasive group* which includes a great variety of paper- and cloth-backed abrasive wheels, rubber- and ceramic-bonded wheels incorporating a homogeneous mixture of different abrasive materials such as pumice, silicon carbide, and aluminum oxide, unmounted or permanently bonded to a steel shaft. As the abrasives wear down, their shapes and dimensions change but they remain useful on different contours until the end. All of these are available in a variety of sizes and shapes that are suited to work on specific contours and in crevices. (See Rotary Files, Burs, and Abrasive Points, Chapter 4.)

For greatest efficiency, any of these accessories should be used at recommended speeds which vary with the accessory material and the substance they are worked upon. Speeds that are too slow can cause a lack of control in some cases, as with circular files. The shaft must be *fully inserted* into the collet or chuck to provide total support and prevent wobbling. Pressure should always be light and never so much that it causes or forces the wheel to slow down or stop. This is an indication that the power of the motor is being exceeded. Overloading can damage the entire mechanism. In some cases the material worked upon may require a coolant-lubricant, as in the case of stone, and in others they can be worked dry, as in the case of metals.

RESPIRATORS: Protection against particle and gas inhalation

Respirators or *face masks* should be worn by the jeweler to cover the nose and mouth whenever protection against the inhalation of dusts and gases is necessary. There are several different types of respirators on the market which offer protection against the following:

Dusts which come from mechanically generated particle matter, usually in the size range of 1–10 microns. *Fibrous dusts* can cause the growth of lung scar tissue, and *toxic dusts* are systemic poisons.

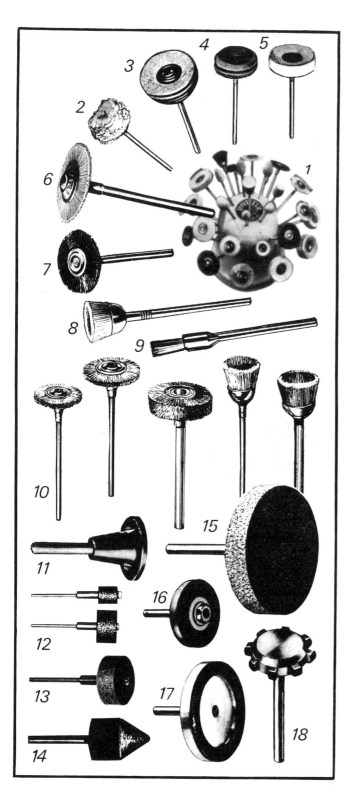

14–18 *PERMANENT MANDREL-MOUNTED WHEELS FOR FLEXIBLE SHAFT*
  1. *Assorted buffs, wheels, and brushes on bench top stand, all with ³⁄₃₂ in shafts.*
  2. *Unstitched muslin buff, ⅞ in Ø.*
  3. *Heavy-weight muslin buff, layered, 1 in Ø.*
  4. *Chamois wheel, ⅞ in Ø.*
  5. *Hard felt wheel, available in a variety of diameters and shapes.*
  6. *Bristle brush, white, available in soft or stiff bristles, one or two rows; Ø ¾, 1⅛, 1½ in.*
  7. *Bristle brush, black, available as above.*
  8. *Cup-shaped natural bristle brush, cup ⅝ in Ø.*
  9. *End brush, natural bristle.*
  10. *Brass, steel, or nickel silver wire brushes, wire 0.005 in, mounted on ³⁄₃₂ and ⅛ in mandrels, in flat, cup, and end shapes, one or two rows.*
  11. *Famco adhesive disc holder, flexible rubber mounted on ⅛ or ¼ in steel shank; head Ø ½, ¾, 1, 1½, 2 in.*
  12. *Sanding drums, ⁷⁄₁₆, ²⁷⁄₃₂ in band size; ³⁄₃₂ or ⅛ in shanks; in coarse, medium, and fine grits.*
  13. *Rubber-bonded abrasives, available in a variety of diameter sizes and thicknesses, in various grades, with ³⁄₃₂ in mandrel shank.*
  14. *Cone-pointed Rotaflex rubber-bonded abrasive, on ³⁄₃₂ or ⅛ in shanks. Other shapes also available.*
  15. *Silicon carbide stone wheel, 2 in Ø, ⅜ in thick, mounted on ³⁄₁₆ in arbor; a wide range of other sizes available.*
  16. *India stone wheel, ½ in Ø, ¼ in thick, on ³⁄₁₆ in arbor, fine grit.*
  17. *Diamond-charged lap, OD bonding material impregnated, 2 in Ø, ³⁄₁₆ in arbor.*
  18. *Sintered hard metal wheel on 2.35 or 3 mm shaft; used for texture decorating surfaces.*

Extremely small and/or toxic particles consist of very finely divided and/or particulate matter, as well as living organisms such as bacteria and certain viruses.

Fumes are chemically generated solid particles of *metallic origin,* usually in the size range of 0.1–1.0 micron.

Smokes are chemically generated solid particles of *organic origin,* usually in the size range of 0.05–0.5 micron.

Mists are liquid particle matter usually of 5–100 microns.

Gases are aeriform fluids without independent shape or volume that emanate from heat or combustion, and from substances such as acids, ammonia, etc.

These substances can be excluded from the respiratory system with at least 99.98% efficiency by the use of filters, screens, and chemical cartridges which are mounted in the respirators. Specific filters have been developed for use against particles, and the cartridges absorb gases. Some respirators allow the interchange of filters and cartridges according to the need. When not in use, the respirator should be placed in a well-closed container to prevent internal contamination.

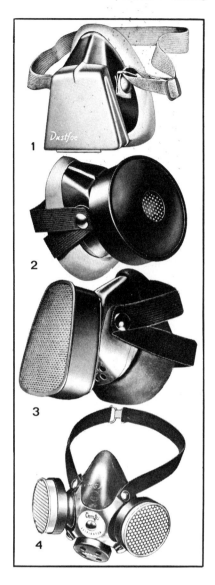

14–19 *RESPIRATORS*

Manufactured by Mine Safety Appliances Company

1. *Dustfoe 66 respirator,* has an aluminum facepiece that allows shaping to individual face contours, edged with neoprene sponge face cushion which creates an airtight seal; filter protects against all dust concentrations, fibrous and toxic dusts, and mists.

2. *Dustfoe Ultra-Filter respirator* weighs 6 oz, has a double strap, contains a filter against toxic radioactive aerosols and dusts, fine-particle smoke, airborne bacteria, and certain viruses and mists.

3. *Gasfoe respirator* has an aluminum facepiece, neoprene cushion, double strap, and four interchangeable and replaceable chemical cartridges which offer protection against light concentrations, up to 0.1%, of organic vapors, acid gases, ammonia, or metallic mercury vapors. Each cartridge is made to specifications that offer protection against the particular hazard. It also has auxiliary screens and static-web filters to prevent clogging during spraying operations.

4. *Custom Comfo respirator* has double filters, rubber facepiece, and chin cup which all conform to face contours. Filters are interchangeable and can be installed against dusts, mists, fumes, toxic aerosols, extremely fine particles, and smoke, according to the need.

15
METALLIC COATING TECHNIQUES
Changing the Base Metal's Surface Appearance

COLD GILDING WITH METAL LEAF

Mechanical application of precious metals

LEAF METAL

Leaf metal is thinner than foil, varying from $\frac{1}{8000}$ to $\frac{1}{10,000}$ mm in thickness. The ability of any metal to be pounded to such thinness is due to its malleability and ductility. As gold, silver, and palladium all possess good malleable and ductile qualities, they are made into leaf under highly controlled conditions by a combination of machine and hand techniques, or by hand alone.

Leaf metal can be used to cover fabricated or cast objects made of other metals, or other materials such as wood, stone, plastic, or plaster. It is the least expensive method of giving an object, or a part of it, the appearance of being made of the metal of the leaf. Gold (and hereafter silver and palladium leaf should be understood to be included) leaf application is a *mechanical cold gilding process,* not a chemical process, and is therefore free of any toxic, poisonous, or dangerous to handle substances. The length of life of the gilding is determined by the thickness of the leaf, or the number of layers of application, and the degree of friction the object receives in use. There are possibilities for the use of cold gilding in jewelry in circumstances where the leaf can be placed on protected surfaces that receive little or no outside contact. It could, for instance, be placed in depressions, or under rock crystal. Considering the price of gold, its use in leaf form deserves further exploration.

SIZES AND PACKAGING OF GOLD LEAF

The standard dimensions of gold leaf in the U.S.A. is 3⅜ in × 3⅜ in (85 mm × 85 mm), and in Europe 3⅛ in × 3⅛ in (80 mm × 80 mm). For protection against tarnish and ease in handling, each sheet is placed loose between chemical-free tissue paper which is formed into the smallest unit, a "book" containing 25 leaves, enclosed in one individual paper envelope. A "pack" is a standard unit that contains 20 books or 500 leaves. Packs are wrapped, sealed, and placed in boxes 4 in × 4 in (10 cm × 10 cm), the total weighing about half a pound. One thousand 22K gold leaves weigh only 10 grams. Allowing for normal *laps* (overlapping at the edges) in covering a surface continuously with leaf, a book of 25 leaves will cover the very large area of approximately 1½ square feet.

TYPES OF GOLD AND OTHER LEAF

23K gold leaf (whose gold content is actually higher) is also known as *loose* or *board gold.* It has the rich yellow color of pure gold. It will not oxidize because of its purity, and need not be protected by any final coating for this reason, but can be protected against abrasion.

23K glass gold leaf is also known as *window gold* because it is used to make signs in gold on shop windows, etc. These are specially selected sheets free from joins.

patches, thin areas, pinholes, lumps, unsound centers, or other blemishes, so that when burnished, a uniformly brilliant finish is possible.

22K deep gold leaf is a European product, and has the color of pure gold.

18K lemon gold leaf, sometimes called *light* or *green gold,* is alloyed with silver to create this color. Because it will tarnish in time, it must be covered with a final, protective, clear lacquer.

16K pale gold leaf, sometimes called *white gold,* is alloyed with silver and is lighter in color than lemon gold leaf. It too must be protected by a final coating to prevent discoloration.

Silver leaf readily tarnishes on exposure to air, therefore requires protection with a final finishing substance.

Palladium leaf is made of unalloyed palladium, a metal of the platinum group. It is white, and has the advantage over silver of not oxidizing in air, after burnishing.

GOLD LEAF PRODUCTION

DEMONSTRATION 26

Traditional techniques as modified today

Photos: Courtesy J. G. Eytzinger GmbH

There are very few craft techniques as old and unchanged as the art of making gold leaf, a process that is datable to 1600 B.C. in Egypt. The technique as described and illustrated here, is as carried out today at the J. G. Eytzinger GmbH in Fürth (Bay.), West Germany, who have been specialists in gold leaf manufacture since 1867.

Gold (or other metal) leaf beating is the art of reducing gold to extremely thin leaves by beating. Originally this was done only with hand hammers, and in some places in the world this is still so, but today, the process time is shortened by the use of a mechanical hammer as well. The finer the gold quality, the easier it is to beat into leaf, and the greater the alloy percentage, the more difficult beating is, though leaf is also made from gold alloys.

PREBEATING PREPARATIONS

1 Pure gold alone, or the metals used in a particular gold alloy including pure silver and copper, usually all in bean shot form, are accurately weighed on a scale. In these illustrations, a 22K gold alloy is used. The metal or metals are placed with some borax as flux in a *clay crucible* and heated in a *gas melting furnace* that liquefies them at 2192° F (1200° C). A *cast iron ingot mold* previously greased and heated is placed near the furnace, the crucible is lifted with *crucible tongs,* and the metal is poured in a continuous stream into the ingot mold until the crucible is emptied. The resulting ⅝ in (1.59 cm) thick ingot is annealed in hot charcoal ashes to soften it and free it from grease. While still hot, it is worked on a *steel block* with a 3 pound *flat-faced forging hammer* to reduce it in thickness in preparation for entering it in a rolling mill. When necessary, the ingot is annealed to soften it.

ROLLING THE INGOT TO RIBBON DIMENSIONS

2 The result is passed through the perfectly flat rolls of a *rolling mill,* annealing it frequently whenever it shows signs of becoming work hardened in order to avoid the formation of cracks, until it is formed into a ribbon about ¼₄₀ mm (0.000285 in) thick. Because the aim is to produce a metal ribbon with a uniform 4 cm (1.6 in) width, the mill is equipped with vertical edging rolls that give it this mill edge width.

GOLD BEATING

3 The gold ribbon is carefully measured and marked with *dividers,* and cut into 1⁹⁄₁₆ in (4 cm) squares with *shears.* The aim is to make each square as nearly equal in weight as possible to avoid excessive surplus. These squares are placed in a *goldbeater's book* which in the commencing beating consists of 480 sheets of *goldbeater's skins* made of calfskin vellum or parchment created from the outer pellicle or membrane of a calf's gut. In the following stages, the goldbeater's book pages may be prepared from the tougher outer membrane of the large intestine of the ox, or from a bull's appendix. Each sheet is 4¾ in (12 cm) square. Today, because the cost of vellum books is very high, books are also made with leaves of PVC plastic leatherette. This produces a slightly more shining leaf, so for duller surfaced leaves, leather books are still used.

The sheets may be loose, or stitched together along one edge like a book, hence the name. When loose sheets are used, approximately 20 extra sheets are placed at the top and the bottom of the pack. Each sheet has been rubbed with calcined, finely powdered plaster of paris, applied with a *rabbit's foot* or a *brush* to prevent the leaf from sticking to the sheet which would cause it to tear. The book or loose sheets are tied together, then slipped into a

3

4

5

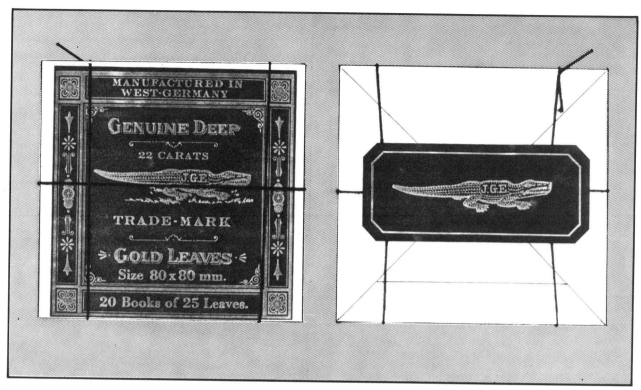

15-1 *FRONT AND BACK VIEW OF TYPICAL PACKAGING OF 20 BOOKS OF 22K GOLD LEAF,* 25 leaves in a book, each 3⅜ × 3⅜ in (80 × 80 mm). Brand name "Krokodil," manufactured by J. G. Eytzinger GmbH, West Germany. Each leaf is interfaced with orange-colored tissue paper. The paper wrapping is tied with a cord and sealed at the back with a sticker bearing the trademark as a guarantee of quality.

strong, encircling *vellum case* that has two open sides, and this is next placed into a second, similar case, but at right angles to the first, so that all sides are closed, and the whole is a compact, square mass. This may be placed within a *retaining wooden frame.*

GOLDBEATER'S HAMMERS

Before the use of mechanically operated hammers which reduce the time and work necessary to produce the leaf, the entire hammering process was done with hand *goldbeater's hammers* whose shape and weights are designed specifically for this process. The first hammer used, called a *flat* or *commencing hammer,* weighs 6–7 lb (2.7–3 kg), has a circular, slightly convex face about 4 in (10 cm) in diameter, and its head tapers conically backward to a height of about 6 in (15 cm) to a short handle which makes it easier to lift. At intermediate stages, a lighter weight *spreading hammer* that weighs 4–5 lb (1.8–2.2 kg) with a more convex face and a head diameter of 2 in (5.1 cm) is used. The last one, called a *finishing hammer,* is the heaviest of all, weighing 12–24 lb (5.4–11 kg) and its face is the most convex.

THE COMMENCING BEATING

In the procedure illustrated here, as shown in the photos, the book is placed in the bed of a *mechanical spring hammer* which rains steady blows upon it. Between blows, the operator moves the book slightly to cause the hammer blow to strike it at a different position to spread the metal evenly.

When the book is *hand hammered,* the working surface is a well-anchored *steel* or *marble block* about 12 in (30.5 cm) square, and about 18 in (45.7 cm) thick. To keep the book from movement, in some establishments it is enclosed in a wooden frame. While holding the commencing hammer in the right hand, the book is forcibly struck in a regular pattern, starting at the center and working spirally outward so the gold is squeezed out laterally. The book is turned over frequently so that both sides receive equal pressure. Occasionally the book, which is flexible, is bent or rolled between the hands to loosen the gold leaves from the pages to allow them to extend freely. This is also done because the friction of beating causes the metal and the book to become hot, and this action ventilates and cools both. Loose books are sometimes taken apart to shift central leaves to outer layers to equalize the impact of the beating action, and assure a uniform stretching of the leaves. Beating continues until the leaves have expanded nearly to the size of the vellum sheet. They are then removed from the book by *wooden tweezers* to which they will not cling, and are piled up in a stack.

QUARTERING AND SPREAD BEATING

In the process called *quartering,* each sheet is cut with a knife into four equal squares of about the size of the original piece of gold. These pieces are placed in a different goldbeater's book of 1,300 pages made of ox gut which is tougher than calf's vellum. A second or *spread beating* follows, in this case with the same mechanical spring hammer, but in the hand process, with a *spreading hammer.* In the latter case, the book is folded occasionally to ventilate it and free the leaves from the pages, as before. Hammering continues until the leaves extend to the book page size when they are about 5½ in (14 cm) square, and about ⅟₆₉₀ mm (0.00004 in) thick.

QUARTERING AND FINISH BEATING

4 Once more the result is quartered as before with a knife so that each part is equal in size and weight. This last time, each part is placed between the pages of a vellum sheet book. This is placed on a marble block, and beaten by hand with a heavy 24 lb (11 kg) broad, convex-faced *finishing hammer*. The final size of the square averages 3–3.75 in (7.6–9.5 cm), and is about ⅟₁₀,₀₀₀ mm in thickness. It is possible to beat the leaves even thinner, but in this case, there is much waste in broken leaves, and greater skill is required. Also, leaves that are too thin are difficult to handle, and are less durable.

TRIMMING THE LEAF

5 In the last step, the finished leaf is trimmed to a regular square. Each leaf is separately lifted from the vellum book with wooden tweezers, placed carefully on a *leather cushion,* and blown to make it lie flat upon it. The leaf can be cut to size with a sharp-edged *length of cane,* by simply pressing its edge into the gold. Today a more usual device is a *square cutting frame* made of two pairs of parallel, sharp-edged knives (shown in this photo), adjustable to a square of any size. The leaf is visually centered within the opening, and the cutting frame is pressed upon it, which simultaneously removes the surplus from all four sides of the square. All waste is collected for reclamation. The leaves are placed by wooden tweezers into small 25 page books made of a soft, smooth-surfaced paper to which the gold will not adhere. Earlier, these pages were prepared by rubbing them with chalk or rouge to prevent leaf adherence. After packing, the leaves are ready for sale and use.

MECHANICAL SURFACE GILDING

Porous materials must be prepared before they can be gilded. A *ground* is made on the surface to receive the leaf by smoothing, filling, and sealing the surface to close the pores and make it nonabsorbent. A typical ground material for porous substances, called *impression* in French, consists of white lead, half its weight of yellow ochre, and a little litharge (lead monoxide). Each of these is ground fine separately, then they are combined and mixed with linseed oil, and thinned with turpentine. The mixture is applied in several very even, thin coats, allowing each application to dry thoroughly before the next is applied. When dry, the surface is smoothed to dullness with powdered pumice applied with a woolen cloth. It is then sealed with shellac, varnish, or lacquer.

Metal surfaces to be gilded should be absolutely clean, and scratch brushed or rubbed with an abrasive paper to give the surface a "tooth." Any grease present will prevent the *size* from adhering.

GOLD SIZE

Gold size is a viscous, adhesive preparation applied to a surface in an even layer to assure even drying, and used to fill the pores of a material to be gilded as well as to provide it with an adhesive surface to receive and hold the leaf. Size is available from gilders' supply houses, and their exact composition is a proprietary secret. *French size* is considered the best and is most widely used. It contains bolus clay which in France is colored red because it contains iron oxide, or Bohemian bole which is yellow in color and resembles yellow ochre. Colored size is used as a ground for gold, but for white metals, a clear size is used. A typical size might contain fat oil, the latter thinned with turpentine, japan varnish, and for use with gold, some chrome yellow pigment. These are all passed through a fine strainer.

Two size types are available, a *slow-drying oil size,* yellow or clear; and a *quick-drying size,* clear. The slow size dries to the correct *tack* (degree of stickiness) in 12–18 hours, and holds its tack at moderate temperatures for at least 6–10 more hours, longer at lower temperatures. Quick-drying size takes 10–30 minutes to dry. Generally speaking, the slow-drying size is preferable for surface gilding because it allows the surface of gold leaf applied to it to be burnished to brilliance, the result is more elastic, and the gilding more durable. Because it holds its tack for a long period, work can proceed more slowly than when using a quick-drying size.

To test tack readiness, touch the surface with your knuckle, which is less likely to contain grease than a fingertip. It should not stick, but when pulled away, you should feel a slight pull and hear a slight "tick." It is important that the size be in the correct state of dryness. If it is not dry enough, it will force its way through the gold, and if it is too dry, the gold will not adhere. All applications of size should be allowed to dry in a dust-free atmosphere. Small objects can be placed in a covered box from which one side has been removed for ventilation, to keep atmospheric dust from settling on them from above. Because silver leaf is heavier than gold or palladium leaf, the size for silver should be one-third to one-half weaker than that used for gold.

APPLYING THE GOLD LEAF

Place a piece of heavyweight cardboard under the gold leaf book to give it supportive stiffness. Fold back the upper sheet of protecting paper and expose the desired amount of leaf, allowing for an overlap of about ⅛ in (0.32 cm). With the fingernail (or a *knife*), cut the foil using the folded paper as a guide.

When gilding, work in a still atmosphere free of drafts since rapid air currents can cause total leaf destruction. Draw a *gilder's tip,* which is a thin, flat, broad, soft brush made of camel's or badger's hair, over your own head hair. This is done to charge the brush with static or frictional electricity, an electricity of stationary charges produced by rubbing together two unlike bodies. Lay the charged brush lightly on the gold leaf. The attractional electric force makes the leaf adhere to the brush. Lift the brush and attached leaf to the tacky surface, and lay it on lightly, without pressure. The leaf will automatically adhere to the size because of its tacky condition. Take care that the brush does not touch the size or the leaf will be torn. In cases where the surface to be covered is irregular, the leaf can be pressed down with clean, dry cotton wool, or by a dry, small brush. Continue applying new leaf parts, placing each addition so it overlaps the last by about ⅛ in so that no seams are seen. Inexperienced gilders can use a *transfer gold silk paper* to remove the gold leaf from the book and apply it with minimal loss.

Allow the size to dry thoroughly for one or two days. Readiness can be judged by appearance. The dry parts will appear bright, and parts still wet will be dull and lusterless. When all is dry, burnish the whole surface by rubbing it briskly but lightly with a high-quality absorbent cotton such as *medicinal cotton* which is free of impurities, or with a piece of clean *plush velvet*. Any gold that did not adhere will come off, including the ⅛ in overlap, leaving a continuous join. Save the burnishing cotton as it contains gold. The brilliance of the burnish depends to a great extent on how accurately you have judged the state of tackiness. If desired, a second layer of gold leaf can be applied directly on the first to create a thicker gold covering. If the gold is 22K or better, the new leaf will adhere by simple contact with the old. If less, it is probably wise to repeat the sizing process before applying new leaf.

PATCHING

A well-done job should not require patching. If, however, areas are imperfectly covered or holes remain, cover the *entire* surface with clear size, but take care not to damage the existing leaf by harsh rubbing. Apply small pieces of leaf to those areas where it is needed. When the size is dry, burnish the surface again.

PROTECTIVE COATINGS

A protective coating of clear varnish or lacquer can be sprayed over the leaf to keep low-karat gold, or silver from tarnishing, and to supply abrasion resistance. Never apply any protective coating substance until the sizing has dried *hard*.

MERCURY AMALGAM GILDING

Depositing precious metal by heat

MERCURY

Symbol and atomic number: Hg 80
Atomic weight: 200.61
Specific gravity: 13.55 (at 68° F [20° C])
Freezing point: −37.97° F (−38.87° C)
Boiling point: 675° F (356.9° C)

Mercury is the metal used for a chemical method of gilding (and silvering) called *mercury amalgam gilding* (or silvering), and sometimes *fire gilding* for reasons described below. Mercury is a heavy, silver white metallic element, and the only metal that is *liquid* at ordinary temperatures. The common name for mercury is *quicksilver* (*quick* meaning "living"), the term derived from its normally fluid state. Its Latin name, *argentum vivum*, has the same meaning. The main sources of mercury are cinnabar, calomel, and a few other minerals from which it is roasted and its vapors condensed. It is also found combined with silver in a natural amalgam. Commercial mercury has a nominal purity of 99.7%, the rest traces of several metals.

AMALGAMS

One of the characteristics of mercury is that it readily forms a union with many metals, and such a union or alloy is called an *amalgam*. The derivation of the word came to us from the Arabic term *al-malgham,* "the assembly," via European alchemists who derived much of their knowledge of chemistry from the Arabs. (Other etymologists believe it is from the Greek *malagma*, "a poultice of soft composition that is spread.")

Amalgams are an alloy of mercury as the base metal with another metal or metals, made in most cases by simply bringing finely divided amounts of the added metal into contact with the mercury at room temperature, sometimes aided by heat, and sometimes by the addition of a dilute acid. Many metals can be made into an amalgam. Mercury unites directly with antimony, bismuth, cadmium, calcium, gold, lead, magnesium, potassium, silver, sodium, tin, and zinc, and less easily with aluminum, copper, and palladium and its related metals. Metals having high fusing points, often called refractory metals, such as iron, nickel, titanium, and platinum, do not readily react with mercury, except by electrolysis of their saline solutions, or by other means.

Mercury readily amalgamates with gold and silver. Because amalgams contain mercury, they can wet almost any metal surface, provided it is clean. Amalgams can be easily decomposed and the mercury dissipated by vaporization in a moderate heat, leaving a residue of the precious metal behind. These qualities made mercury extremely valuable in the metal arts. For the latter reason, this method of gilding is also called *fire gilding*. Articles made of less valuable metals could be gilded to give them the surface appearance of gold, always the most esteemed metal in all cultures. Mercury amalgam gilding was and still is widely practiced in the East, especially on ritual objects and on images of deities, and possibly its use there predated its use in the West. In Europe, mercury amalgam gilding did not occur until the Roman period when the process was used in gilding silver and bronze objects and sculpture. From then on, this method of gilding retained its importance until the mid-19th century when it was superannuated by the invention of electroplating.

Vermeil is a term related to the pigment vermillion, because both have a common connection with mercury. (Vermillion is a compound of 100 parts mercury to 16 parts sulphur.) The French term vermeil has been long used to designate a silver, bronze, or copper object plated with gold, originally by the use of a mercury and gold amalgam and heat, as described here. Today the term vermeil is loosely used in commerce simply as a fancy term for gold plating on silver by any means.

Mercury amalgam gilding has seen something of a revival in the arts because of its advantages, and because of the diverse effects possible in mercury amalgam gilding techniques. The gold in the amalgam makes a firm bond with the surface of the metal gilded, and is extremely long lasting because it is more than just a thin skin, as in the case of ordinary gold electroplating. The gilding is highly resistant to oxidation, and protects the article against corrosion, a fact well proved by the many ancient mercury-gilded articles excavated by archeologists and found in a well-preserved condition because of their surface gilding.

Gilding with mercury-gold or mercury-silver amalgams works best on metals that are slightly fusible, as silver, copper, bronze, brass, and other copper alloys such as shakudo. Iron and steel do not take gilding, but if their surface is partially or totally copper plated first, or inlaid with copper, the copper areas will take gilding. Other intermediate metals can also be used: solder can be flooded on a metal surface (see Gilding Puddle-Bonded Solder on Steel in this chapter); or the surface can be flooded with a brazing alloy using high heat from an acetylene flame or welding torch.

SAFETY PRECAUTIONS AGANST MERCURY POISONING

Theophilus in his 12th-century treatise *On Diverse Arts,* the first Western record of craft technology, warns: "Be very careful that you do not . . . apply (mercury) gilding when you are hungry, because the fumes of mercury are very dangerous to an empty stomach and give rise to various sicknesses against which you must use zedoary (turmeric) and barberry, pepper and garlic and wine."

While the danger in the inhalation of mercuric fumes was recognized, these fanciful homeopathic cures certainly offered no protection to medieval craftsmen who are known to have taken insufficient precautions when working with the widely used mercury gilding method. Today we know that mercury in any form is poisonous to the human system. The potential dangers in its use must be pointed out; with proper precautions, however, they can be avoided.

Mercury is highly toxic and is therefore normally handled in glass containers. It can be absorbed directly through the skin, ingested, or inhaled as a vapor. It accumulates in the system and a certain amount can be lethal. Mercurialism is a chronic, slowly progressing disease, ordinarily acquired from the inhaling of small amounts of mercury vapor over a long period of time. Excessive inhalation results in marked mouth inflammation, profuse saliva flow, tooth loosening, sore throat, listlessness, muscular tremors (called "hatter's shakes"), and abdominal pain. Long exposure may cause corneal opacity, lung and kidney damage, and mental disturbance characterized by excitement followed by depression and irritability. Any of these symptoms can occur singly, or all may be present simultaneously.

Facing this formidable list of possible ailments, no sensible craftsperson will fail to take the necessary precautions when handling mercury. Store it in well-stoppered, clearly marked *glass containers.* Avoid direct physical contact, and wear *rubber gloves* when handling it.

Should direct contact occur, wash thoroughly with soap and water. Never eat food in the workshop, and wash hands thoroughly before eating after using mercury.

The greatest danger from mercury is its inhalation as fumes. To avoid inhalation when volatilizing mercury, wear a *respirator mask* specifically designed to filter out mercuric fumes. In industry, the acceptable concentration of mercuric vapor in the air is less than the level of 0.1 mg per cubic meter of air, a very small amount indeed. Working with mercury out of doors is a way of diminishing contact, but even there, to avoid fume inhalation always work against the wind so that fumes are taken away from you. When working with mercury indoors, it is *essential* to use an efficient system for condensing the mercuric vapors in order to return mercury to a solid state in which it can be reclaimed. A simply fabricated system for condensing mercury is described on p. 670. By taking the appropriate precautions, craftspersons can completely eliminate any chance of mercuric poisoning.

PREPARING A GOLD-MERCURY AMALGAM FOR GILDING

DEMONSTRATION 27

WALTER SOELLNER devises a closed venting system

Photos: Soellner

1 Cut 24K gold foil or thin sheet into very small pieces, or use coarsely powdered gold if this is available. Extremely fine particles do not amalgamate readily. The metal must be clean and oxide-free as oxides retard the mercury amalgamating reaction. Add the gold to the mercury held in a *Pyrex container,* a *porcelain fireproof crucible,* or a *refractory clay crucible* lined with moistened alumina or yellow ochre. The proportion is 1 part gold to 4–6 parts by *weight* of mercury. Place the container (a *beaker* is used here) on a *tripod,* or *three-legged ring stand.*

2 The equipment used in this case is illustrated. Place a *rubber stopper* with a hole in it into the beaker, and into the hole insert a *bent glass tube* whose purpose is to vent the mercury vapors emitted during the process into a *second beaker* placed to one side and somewhat below the first. It is half filled with water, and the tube end should be under water.

Heat the first beaker with an *alcohol lamp* placed below the tripod until the mercury starts to boil, but do not overheat or allow the mercury to come to a full boil which

1

2

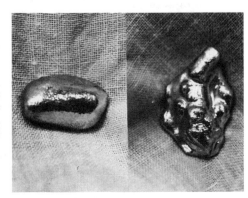

3

will cause excessive vapors to rise. Heat speeds up the amalgamation process, causing the atoms of mercury and the alloying metal to migrate and diffuse into each other at a faster rate than would occur at room temperature. While heating, gently shake the beaker (or the crucible with *crucible tongs*) as agitation hastens the amalgamation process. Allow the amalgam to cool. Examine it to see if traces of gold are still visible, and if so, repeat the heating process until amalgamation is complete.

3 Amalgams are liquid when an excess of mercury exists, and solid and pastelike, but readily fusible, where the alloying element dominates. To reduce the liquid amalgam to a pasty state and to eliminate excess mercury, when the amalgam cools, pour it into a double thickness of clean *cotton* or *linen cloth* stretched over a *dish*. (By a traditional method, it is poured into a *wet chamois leather bag*, or one made of a strong but porous canvas.) While wearing *rubber gloves*, enclose the mercury in the cloth by wrapping and twisting it around, then tighten the twist and squeeze the lump to wring out any excess liquid mercury present. It emerges through the cloth openings (or the chamois pores), and since this still contains a small amount of gold, it is gathered in a *glass container* and saved for future use when preparing a new amalgam. In the photograph, on the left we see the amalgam as it appears when first poured, and on the right as it remains in the cloth after it has been squeezed. At this point it is a pasty, malleable, crystallized metallic compound mass about the consistency of butter, and firm enough to register a fingerprint. Using an *iron spatula,* place the amalgam in a *ground-glass-stoppered container* with just enough *distilled water* to cover it, and be sure to label the contents.

By another method, heat 8 parts of thin gold pieces to redness, and place them immediately into 1 part of mercury heated just short of boiling. The gold will be absorbed quickly into the mercury to form the amalgam. Pour the amalgam onto a cloth submerged in water in a glass container. Collect the mercury by gathering the cloth corners, squeeze out and collect the surplus as above, and store the resulting amalgam under distilled water as above.

SILVER-MERCURY AMALGAM

Sprinkle finely divided silver powder on mercury in an *iron container.* Heat the contents to 482–572° F (250–300° C), and stir the mixture for a few minutes. Allow the amalgam to cool, and treat it as above.

MULTI-METAL AMALGAMS

It is possible to alloy several metals simultaneously with mercury to form multi-metal amalgams. Gold alloys of any karat can also be amalgamated. The result will have the color characteristic of that particular alloy.

MERCURY NITRATE SOLUTION: Quicksilver water

A weak solution of *mercury nitrate*, $Hg(NO_3)_2$, commonly known as *quicksilver water* (*shiyosansuigin eki* in Japanese, and *hwang shing-yoh* in Chinese), has been used in the East for centuries in the process of amalgam gilding and silvering as a means of assisting the amalgam to adhere to the surface of the metal being gilded or silvered. This solution is prepared in advance under a *hood* having a *strong exhaust* as the combination of chemicals disengages fumes that must be drawn off.

The solution consists of 10 parts of mercury to which is added 10 parts by weight of nitric acid, HNO_3 (specific gravity 1.33). Apply a gentle heat to the heat-resistant *glass container* to help the acid digest the mercury. When digestion is complete and the mixture is cool, add 25 times its initial combined weight of distilled water, and store the result in a closed, clearly marked *glass jar*.

By the Kambe Soellner method for making a small amount of mercury nitrate, add one small pea-sized drop of mercury to five tablespoons of pure nitric acid which has been placed beforehand in a *glass container*. Stopper the container, and gently mix these together by shaking the container. Allow the combination to stand for two days until the mercury is digested by the acid. Slowly add one cup of water to the result.

QUICKING

The article to be gilded must be annealed, its surface oxidation removed, and the object must be chemically clean. To do this, plunge it when hot into a dilute solution of sulphuric acid to which a small amount of common salt has been added. When all the oxidation on the surface is removed, scratch brush the object, wash it in water, and dry it, preferably in sawdust. The surface should appear slightly dulled due to the scratch brushing, and the gold in the amalgam will hold to this surface better than it does to a highly polished surface.

By the process commonly called *quicking,* to this prepared surface, the dilute mercury nitrate solution can be applied in several different ways for different purposes or effects. (These are described on p. 674 under Techniques in the Use of Precious Metal Amalgams in this chapter.)

SHAKUDO: A favored Japanese copper alloy

We digress here to discuss *shakudo,* one of the several important copper alloys used in the arts in Japan, and used here in the demonstration object. Each of these alloys has its own character and is subtly different from others, a condition appreciated by the Japanese who have acquired the ability of discerning such differences. Among them, shakudo is probably most highly esteemed because its composition provides it with the ability to acquire various patinas ranging in color from a unique reddish brown to a bluish black or velvety black color when treated with the coloring compound called *rokusho,* discussed on p. 671. Shakudo was widely used for sword mountings, for decorative metalwork, and for casting sacred images, and it is still used in Japan today.

Shakudo compositions vary widely according to different sources, but all have one factor in common, which is that in addition to a 97–75% copper content, the alloy contains a minimum of 3% and a maximum of 25% pure gold. It is believed that the presence of gold is responsible for its being capable of acquiring the above-mentioned patina. Its very fine crystalline texture may also be due to the gold content, and suits the alloy to engraving, repoussage and chasing, and to inlay. It is also favored for inlay because the patina it takes contrasts well with inlays of precious metals. This contrast is also apparent in the mercury-gilded object described here.

Shibuichi is another much favored Japanese alloy, the name meaning "four parts," a designation that refers to the metals in its composition. Basically it is about 60–70% copper, the rest varying from 10–40% silver, plus small amounts of tin, lead, or zinc. When the silver percentage is high it is called *rogin,* literally "misty silver." It is much harder than shakudo, takes a high polish, and can be patinated to a silvery gray color with rokusho. Many other alloys are also used.

PREPARING A SHAKUDO OR SHIBUICHI ALLOY

Weigh and cut the metals used into small pieces to facilitate their mixture when melted, then clean them thoroughly. Heat a *furnace* to 1500° F (851° C), cool it to 1300° F (704° C) to create a nonoxidizing atmosphere, then bring the temperature up to 1800° F (982° C). Put the metals in a *crucible* into the furnace, or if the melting furnace is provided with a permanent crucible, directly into that, and continue heating to 2000° F (1093° C). Stir the metals with an *iron* or *graphite rod*. When the metals are completely molten, the alloy will not adhere to the rod.

An *ingot mold* must be prepared by coating it with a parting agent such as a layer of carbon produced from the flame of a *paraffin candle*, and the mold must be heated before pouring the metal into it. Pour continuously at one end of the mold cavity from which the metal will flow and fill the rest of the groove without cold shuts. When the ingot has cooled, roll it through a *rolling mill* to the desired gauge, annealing it several times during the rolling process to render it soft enough to continue rolling without the danger of its cracking. After each anneal, be sure to pickle the metal to remove firescale before rerolling, and be sure it is dry. There must be no firescale present, or when it is patinated the coloring solution will not take effect in those places.

KINKESHI: A Japanese amalgam gilding method

DEMONSTRATION 28

MITSUKO KAMBE SOELLNER parcel gilds a shakudo pendant

Photos: Walter Soellner

The Japanese term for gold is *kin;* for silver, *gin;* and for an amalgam, *keshi*. Kinkeshi is Japanese for a gold amalgam or gold amalgam gilding; *ginkeshi* is a silver amalgam or silver amalgam silvering.

The basic method of applying the amalgam to a metal surface is shown in the demonstration that follows in which Mitsuko Kambe Soellner works in the traditional Japanese manner to parcel gild a pendant made of the copper-gold alloy *shakudo*.

1 The shakudo metal unit is anchored to pitch on a block, and the crosshatched fan design is worked with *chasing punches* and *chisels*.

2 This detail shows that the depth of the chased and chiseled grooves need not be great, because deep marks require repeated applications of the amalgam to cover the surface, while shallow grooves need only one or two applications.

TOOLS AND MATERIALS FOR KINKESHI

3 The materials used, starting clockwise from the bottom include: a *steel-handled applicator with copper spatula ends* to spread the amalgam, a *large jar* containing the mercury nitrate solution, a *small jar* holding the gold-mercury amalgam, a *paintbrush* for applying the mercury nitrate solution, *two wooden modeling tools*, and a *steel tray* used as a work surface because small amounts of amalgam can be easily picked up from this amalgam-resisting metal. In the center is the work to be parcel gilded.

PREPARING A METAL SURFACE

In mercury amalgam gilding, as in all other gilding processes, the metal surface must always be *grease-free, oxide-free,* and *chemically clean,* or the amalgam will not adhere to it. To prepare the surface, it is first degreased with a detergent, then pickled in a dilute solution of nitric acid, and thoroughly rinsed. If a bright, shining surface is the aim, the result is improved by giving that surface a high polish before beginning the process. Because rouge contains iron oxide as well as grease, both of which will prevent the adhesion of the amalgam, all traces of these must be removed with a detergent and *cleaning brush*.

Dip the brush *used only for this purpose* in the mercury nitrate or quicksilver water, and paint it over the area to receive the gilding. Rinse the work and the brush to wash away the acid.

THE AMALGAM-SPREADING SPATULA

An *amalgam-spreading spatula* can be easily made of an iron bar to which spatulate-shaped copper ends are soldered. One end is straight and the other curved to accommodate differently shaped surfaces. The amalgam will not adhere to the iron, but will hold on the copper during its transfer to the work.

4 Dip the spatula into the mercury nitrate solution, pick up some of the amalgam, and spread it on the area as smoothly as possible in a fairly thin coat. Spread and even the amalgam further with a *wood modeling tool*. Continue until the whole area or surface to be gilded is coated. Rinse the object under running water, or dip it into a container of water, then gently blot the surface dry with a *paper towel*. Place the work on an iron surface such as an *iron mesh heating frame* as this metal resists mercury con-

1

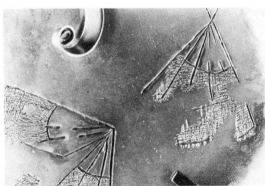

2

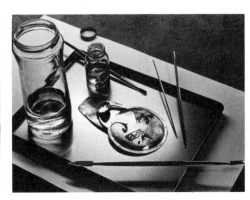

3

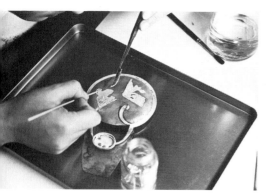

4   5   6

tained in the fumes that result in the volatilization that follows.

A CLOSED CONDENSER SYSTEM FOR MERCURY RETRIEVAL FROM VAPORS

5 The mercury in the amalgam must now be volatilized as a vapor, and the poisonous mercurial fumes must be efficiently eliminated from the atmosphere to prevent their inhalation. Seen here is a *closed condenser system* devised by Walter Soellner which eliminates mercury vapor from the atmosphere, and retrieves the mercury allowing for its reutilization. The parts are made of steel and fiber glass, both materials not receptive to mercury. Metals that *are* mercury receptive must not be used. The arrangement consists of a *cylindrical container* in which the object is held while heated, and a *fan* at the top that sucks the vapors through the attached *flexible steel pipe* that leads to a *steel pan* filled with water where the condensed mercury is trapped. Also seen are a pair of *rubber gloves* and a *respirator mask*.

6 *Type CMH respirator mask* designed specifically for protection against mercury fumes. It is manufactured by the Pullmosan Safety Equipment Corp., Flushing, New York, U.S.A. The inscription reads: "For use in nuisance concentrations of mercury vapors not exceeding 0.1% by volume or not exceeding 10 times latest threshold limit value as set by the National Institute of Safety and Health (N.I.O.S.H.). Do not use in atmospheres containing less than 19.5% oxygen by volume at sea level."

VOLATILIZING THE MERCURY: DRYING OFF

7 The process of volatilizing the mercury is called *drying off*. Wear *rubber gloves* and a *mercury vapor mask*. Hold the amalgam-coated object with *tongs* (or on an *iron mesh* held by tongs) in the side opening of the circu-

lar hood. Hold a gentle torch flame below the work, and move it constantly. The heated mercury now appears like a mirror, and mercury vaporization occurs at a temperature above 675° F (356.9° C), its boiling point. If a much higher temperature is used, the gold in the amalgam will permeate the base metal and produce a spotty surface. Therefore, heat the work slowly in a controlled manner and do not use excessive heat. Fumes are sucked by the fan through the pipe which does not have to rise much above the hood since mercury vapor does not rise very high but starts to decline immediately. While passing through air, the fumes cool, and the mercury condenses and returns to its normal solid state as liquid droplets that accumulate at the pipe end in the water-filled container where they are trapped and gather into a mass. The container has a central depression toward which the mercury gravitates and forms one mass. From there the mercury can be easily collected later by pouring off the water, and picking it up with the copper-spreading spatula, then storing it in a container for reuse. Thick areas of the amalgam at this point can be spread over a surface by brushing over them with a wad of absorbent cotton. The surface will soon appear a dull matte white, then, when no visible white fumes rise, it appears a dull yellow as only the gold remains on the work as a finely grained deposit. Allow the object to cool, then wash it with a brush in water acidulated with some vinegar. If the amalgam layer was unevenly applied, the gilding may appear uneven. Such an effect may be desirable, but if an even layer of gilding is wanted, repeat the process one or more times.

BURNISHING THE GILDING

8 For a bright finish, the gold deposit must now be burnished. The *burnisher* is a wooden-handled tool in which is fixed a hard steel, hematite, or agate head shaped in various forms to fit different contours. Ivory or other

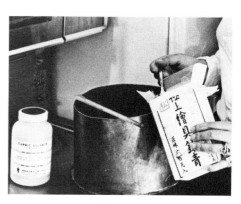

7   8   9

animal teeth were used in medieval Europe to burnish amalgam-gilded objects, and to burnish gold leaf applied to illuminated manuscripts.

In burnishing metal, a lubricant is necessary to achieve the best results. Soapy water, saliva, ale, and beer are all used for this purpose. Water sharpened with vinegar gives the tool a "tooth" that aids in the burnishing action. Dip the tool in the lubricant and rub it back and forth over the area, always *in the same direction,* until the desired degree of brightness is achieved. Because the burnisher is worked in one direction, the deeply lustrous reflection is also directional, varying from a brilliant shine to very dark, depending on the angle of light reflected from the burnished strokes. Burnishing also *compresses* the gold to the base metal *without removing any gold,* which would occur with other methods of polishing. This helps to make the gold more adherent and longer lasting. Rinse the work in cold water to remove lubricant traces, and dry it with a clean *linen cloth* or with *sawdust.*

THE SHAKUDO COLORING PROCESS: USING ROKUSHO

The shakudo base metal is given a dark reddish brown to black patina that contrasts with the gilded areas of the work by using the previously mentioned chemical preparation known in Japan as *rokusho,* which in Japanese simply means "green blue powder." The contents of this special compound as prepared commercially are a proprietary secret, and it is purchased by craftspersons in Japan in ready-made packages. Commercially prepared rokusho is available to members of the Japanese Metalsmiths Association from: Kikuyakenzakuhun Co., 1-28-9 Higasiueno Taito-ku, Tokyo, Japan.

ROKUSHO FORMULAS

Several different formulas are known, however, each claiming to be the *true* rokusho. The results obtained with them may vary somewhat, but can be as successful as the commercial preparation. This indicates that several different chemical compounds will act in a similar manner.

Rokusho No. 1

Copper acetate	$Cu(C_2H_3O_2)_2 \cdot CuO$	6 g
Calcium carbonate	$CaCO_3$	2 g
Sodium hydroxide	$NaOH$	2 g

Dissolve these chemicals in 150 milliliters of distilled water in a heat-resistant *glass container,* and allow the solution to stand unmolested for one week or more. Siphon off the clear liquid result at the top, and add 1 liter of distilled water. Mix these and store the solution for future use. It will last according to how often it is used, and whether it becomes contaminated. When ready for use, add 2 grams of copper sulphate to this amount.

Rokusho No. 2

Copper acetate	$Cu(C_2H_3O_2)_2 \cdot CuO$	4 g
Copper nitrate	$Cu(NO_3)_2$	1 g
Cupric chloride	$CuCl_2$	1 g
Copper sulphate	$CuSO_4 \cdot 5H_2O$	4 g

Dissolve these in 1 liter of distilled water.

Rokusho No. 3

Cupric acetoarsenate	$Cu(C_2H_3O_2) \cdot 3CuAf_2O_9$	55 g
Copper sulphate	$CuSO_4 \cdot 5H_2O$	55 g
Distilled water	H_2O	½ gal

Grind these chemicals together, boil the water, add the chemicals, and stir the solution until they dissolve. Cool the solution before use.

Rokusho No. 4

Copper acetate	$Cu(C_2H_3O_2)_2 \cdot CuO$	60 g
Copper sulphate	$CuSO_4 \cdot 5H_2O$	60 g
Acetic acid	CH_3COOH	½ gal

Use vinegar (acetic acid), diluted 4.5–12% with water.

Rokusho No. 5

Copper sulphate	$CuSO_4 \cdot 5H_2O$	60 g
Salt	$NaCl$	22 grains
Water	H_2O	2½ oz

Boil these together, then cool the solution before use.

PREPARING A PROPRIETARY ROKUSHO CHEMICAL SOLUTION

9 If the commercially prepared rokusho is used, put 5.6 grams of rokusho powder and 5.6 grams of copper sulphate into 2 qt of water, bring them to a boil, and then allow the solution to cool to room temperature.

PREPARING THE METAL FOR PATINATION

In all cases, the metal must be absolutely clean, free of all firescale and grease, and polished the same as before gilding. After the usual cleaning operations, boil the work in water, then rinse it in ordinary pickle followed by a running water rinse, or a rinse in distilled water. Rub the surface with *fine pumice* using a clean *bristle brush,* and rinse it. As the object is now clean, touching it must be avoided as this might deposit greasy fingerprints on which the patina coloring will not take. Instead, handle the work with *paper towels.* It is good practice to attach a copper wire to the work by which it can be handled until the patination process is completed. Place the work in distilled water to keep the surface wet.

In the procedure that follows, use only copper or wooden instruments when handling the work, and *avoid iron* which upon contact with the solution would produce a galvanic action and plate the object with a copper flashing rather than coloring it. Mix all ingredients well, be sure they are totally dissolved, and work at suggested temperatures. The color achieved may not be exactly the same each time it is applied. Worked metal objects can be colored more easily than cast metal objects.

APPLYING THE PATINA

10 Prepare about 1 pound of grated or ground-up *white Oriental radish, Raphanus sativus longipinnatus* (Japanese: *daikon;* Chinese: *loh-bak choi*), a long, tapering white radish larger than a carrot. (Red radish can be used if white radish is not available, and if neither of these is available, try powdered white radish.) Save the juices. Add 5 parts of water to the total amount of grated-radish-plus-juice weight.

11 Throughout the remaining processes, handle the object only by the attached copper wire. Heat the rokusho in a large, deep copper pot to about 100° F (37.7° C), but do not let it boil. Lower the work by its attached wire into the solution, and move it constantly, removing it occasionally to observe the progress of the patina color formation. *Never allow the work to become dry* during this procedure or it will form water marks and irregular color will result.

12 After a period of about 10 minutes, when the color appears dark enough, remove the work and immediately cover the surface with grated radish, rubbing it gently with clean fingers. The radish is rather strongly alkaline which is probably the reason that it helps color retention in the chemical interaction that takes place. Rinse the work with

10   11   12

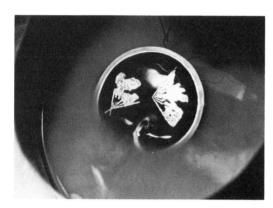

13

14

water, and rub the surface with *baking soda* which also is alkaline, then with pumice, and rinse it again.

13 To deepen the color, return the object to the rokusho solution again. Remove it after a minute or so, immerse it immediately in water, then return it to the rokusho solution again. Repeat this procedure several times. Now bring the rokusho solution to a boil and allow the object to remain suspended by the wire in it until the final color is achieved. Remove, rinse, and dry the work. Coat the surface with a *light oil* to deepen the color, or cover it with a light coat of *hot wax*, and rub off the surplus with a soft cloth.

14 The finished pendant with attached South American pheasant feathers. The contrast between the gilded areas and the rokusho-colored ground is evident.

Pure gold, high-karat gold alloys, and pure silver will resist chemical coloring action if these metals are present in an object being colored. If the object has an inlay of sterling silver, or silver of a lower quality which contains copper in its alloy, these alloys may become yellowish in the rokusho solution. In such a case, stop the process, and repeat the cleaning steps. Dry the metal, and coat the silver parts with *shellac* dissolved in denatured alcohol, CH_3OH (99% IPA methylated spirit). Once this is thoroughly dry, the coloring process can then be continued as described. The shellac acts as a resist, and once the coloring process is completed, it can be removed by dissolving it with alcohol applied to a piece of absorbent cotton, then rubbed over those areas. The work is then finished with oil or wax as above.

GILDING PUDDLE-BONDED SOLDER ON STEEL

DEMONSTRATION 29

WALTER SOELLNER parcel gilds a steel belt buckle

Photos: Soellner

1 The steel buckle is fabricated, polished, cleaned, and its surface coated with flux.

2 Melt hard solder alloy in wire form (content: silver 75%, copper 22%, zinc 3%) by feeding it to the torch flame and guiding the puddles that form in a pattern on the steel. *Puddle bonding* is a method of joining one metal having a lower melting point onto another with a higher melting point.

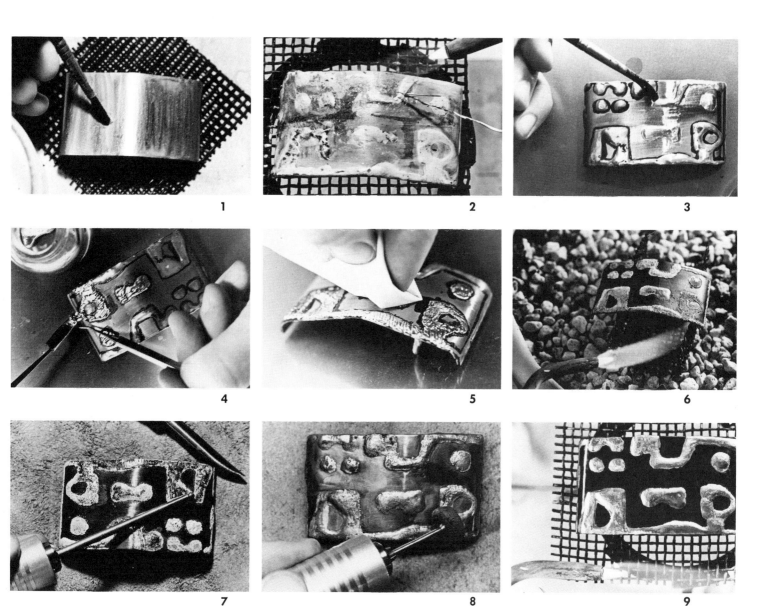

1   2   3

4   5   6

7   8   9

3 Polish the puddle-bonded metal surface and make it chemically clean. Paint mercury nitrate solution over the puddle-bonded areas that are to be gilded to assist in the adhesion of the amalgam.

4 Apply the mercury-gold amalgam to the desired areas in the manner already described.

5 Absorb any surplus mercury nitrate with a paper towel to prevent it from bubbling under the amalgam when the latter is heated.

6 Volatilize the mercury under a hood and exhaust, as previously shown, by heating the object slowly from below while it is placed on an *iron mesh heating frame*. If the heating is too rapid, the amalgam will lift off the surface. When the silver color of the amalgam turns to a light gold color, and mercury vapor fumes no longer rise from the object's surface, the heating is finished. Allow the work to cool off in air before removing it from the hood enclosure.

7 Burnish the gilded areas with a *burnisher* to the desired degree of brightness. Burnishing can also be done *mechanically* by using a *steel dapping punch* that has been mounted in a *flex-shaft*, as shown.

8 Polish the steel areas with a *rotary miniature buff* and abrasives, the buff mounted on a flex-shaft, and make the surface chemically clean.

10

9 Color the steel to a heat-created patina with a soft torch flame applied to the object from below to be able to watch the color development, and when it reaches the desired blue black, quench the object in *oil*. Rub on a final application of wax to protect the black iron patina.

10 The finished belt buckle.

TECHNIQUES IN THE USE OF PRECIOUS METAL AMALGAMS

TOTAL GILDING

When one or several small objects are to be *totally gilded,* clean and place them with *steel tweezers* in an *iron* or *steel pan.* Pour in enough mercury nitrate solution to completely cover the objects. Move the objects in the solution to be sure each surface is entirely coated. Remove them with the tweezers, and rinse them thoroughly with water to remove all traces of acid. Apply the amalgam as already described.

SPOT OR BRUSH GILDING

The surface of an object can be *partially gilded* to contrast that area with the natural color of the base metal. To heighten such a contrast, the exposed base metal parts can be given a coloring patina after gilding is completed. Paint the mercury nitrate solution in those spots on the metal to be gilded. The brush could also be used to apply the solution in a calligraphic manner, leaving the remaining ground exposed. Wash off the acid, and apply the amalgam which will adhere only to those treated areas.

AMALGAM INLAY

Gold and silver amalgam can be *inlaid* in recesses or lines made in the ground by means of tools. The amalgam is applied with a *spatula* to fill the depression, then volatilized as usual. It may be necessary to make several applications of the amalgam to completely fill the depression, if this is the aim. The result can be left rough as it appears, or the amalgam-deposited metal can be smoothed by an *abrasive cloth* to the level of the ground. In the latter case, the result appears similar to a solid metal inlay. *Dental amalgams* that are used to fill tooth cavities can be applied in the same manner. Dental amalgams are de-

15–3 WALTER SOELLNER, U.S.A. Sterling silver neckpiece, die formed in a hardwood mold carved to this shape. The form was pierced with round holes into which shakudo half-domes were set from the back and soldered in position. On them, gold-mercury amalgam (*kinkeshi*) was applied random patterned in droplet form. The amalgam was volatilized, burnished, and the shakudo patinated with *rokusho.* Photo: Walter Soellner

signed to *expand slightly* on hardening, which locks them in place when there is an undercut in the object.

BRIGHT OR DEADENED MATTE FINISH

The gilded surface can be burnished bright, or parts can be made bright and others left matte. The entire surface can be left matte and rough, as it appears after volatilization. If the surface has been made rough *before* gilding, it will appear matte afterward.

ORMOLU GILDING

Ormolu (French *or,* "gold," *molu,* "milled or ground") is a French mercury gilding technique that was carried out in the 18th and 19th centuries, before the invention of electroplate gilding. Bronze alloy objects such as candelabra, clocks, and furniture mounts were gilded and finished

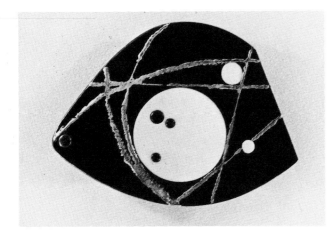

15–2 WALTER SOELLNER, U.S.A. Shakudo brooch into which holes were pierced for the ivory inlays, the holes then backed with sheet bronze. Into this a line pattern was chased, and the lines filled with several applications of gold amalgam by the amalgam inlay technique (*keshi-zogan*). The result was then patinated. The ivory discs were cut to shape to fit the depressions. Holes were drilled and filed into the central disc to hold cabochon garnets. Both ivory and garnets were epoxied in place. Photo: Walter Soellner

with a combination of brightly burnished and matte areas. According to a contemporary account of this process, the mercury gilding and finishing process was done as follows:

The object was first mercury gilded as usual. Before rendering areas matte, the areas to be subsequently burnished must be protected. This is done by preparing a mixture of whiting, gum, and bruised sugar, dissolving these in enough water to make a thick paste. The result is painted over the areas to be protected for burnishing. The work is next placed on an *iron rack* and heated until the protecting paste turns brown by partial carbonization. The areas left exposed are coated with a mixture of equal parts of salt, nitre, and alum dissolved in some water. The work is returned to a charcoal fire and heated until the saline coating becomes homogeneous, nearly transparent, and fused to the surface as a crust. The work is next plunged into cold water which simultaneously removes the saline crust and the bright area's protective paste. It is then washed in a weak solution of nitric acid, rinsed well in water, and dried in air, with a clean cloth, or in a drying stove. In the result the treated gold appears matte. The areas to be bright are then burnished.

15–4 MITSUKO KAMBE SOELLNER, U.S.A. *Meguriwa*-style neckpiece, inspired by old Japanese armor neckpiece forms so named. Fabricated from sheet silver, copper, and shakudo. Shakudo surfaces were silver solder flooded in a free pattern, and those areas were mercury amalgam gilded, then burnished. The unit was given a patina with *rokusho*, leaving the shakudo parts dark, and the copper parts reddish brown. Chains, some pendants, and the neckpiece are silver. *Photo: Walter Soellner*

15–5 *DETAIL OF THE NECKPIECE* showing the texture of gilded areas. *Photo: Walter Soellner*

15–6 15–7 15–8 TEKKE, SALOR, and SARYK TURCOMAN TRIBE, TRANSCASPIAN REGION, 19th century. Three traditional ornaments, a type still made today in modified forms without gilding in Ashkhabad, Turkmen S.S.R. Typically, the construction consists of heavy, flat silver sheets engraved with stylized patterns (*islimi*) whose main figures were then mercury gilded, and the ground left silver. The color contrast between figure and ground gives the impression of a pierced work bi-metal combination. The large main forms usually are outlined with borders of twisted and patterned wire, cut and shaped to necessary lengths and forms. Other characteristic embellishments are contour-stamped pendants attached to main units by jump rings or loop-in-loop chain, and the use of cabochon or flat-topped carnelian stones.

The six-sided pendant (*ansuk* or *ghursakcha*) (width 12 in; height 9 in), is worn by the Mari-Tekke either at the back or on the breast. The pendant of the neckpiece (*kesurga* or *adamlyk*) (length 9½ in; width 4 in) now mounted on a necklace of amber, carnelian, black coral, and silver beads, was originally one of a pair used as head temple ornaments. The waist ornament or half belt (*ghushak*) (length 15 in) is held on heavy clothing by two large, sharp hooks, forming a half circle at the front, with the chain-hung pendants making a swinging fringe. *Photos: pendant, Bern Historical Museum, Bern; neckpiece, Ferdinand Boesch; half belt, Oppi*

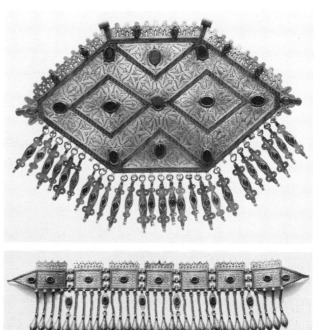

APPLYING GOLD LEAF OR POWDER

A sheet of pure gold leaf, or gold powder can be applied to a base metal that has first been painted with the mercury nitrate solution, rinsed, then plated with *mercury alone* painted on the surface with a brush. The area then can be covered completely or partially with gold. When leaf is applied, it must be placed on the surface with great care because it cannot be moved once it contacts the mercury. The work is then heated to volatilize the mercury, leaving the leaf adhering to the surface, and this is then burnished. The process can be repeated to apply additional layers of gold leaf to make a thicker, more durable coating. Gold and silver leaf can be applied to the same work.

Gold powder can be sifted onto the surface, and the mercury then volatilized, leaving a speckled gold effect. The gold can be left dull or burnished. The ground can be colored for contrast with the gold.

POSTGILDING LINE ENGRAVING

After gilding has been finished, a line design or other pattern can be engraved through the gilded areas into the base metal. These lines can be left bright, or if the base metal allows, they can be oxidized or colored to create a dark line pattern on a gold ground. The oxidizing or coloring chemical will not affect the pure gold of the gilded areas.

15-9 *ALENA NOVÁKOVÁ, Czechoslovakia S.S.R.* Carved wood bracelet ornamented with gold leaf and silver leaf applied by cold gilding, and bright colored acrylic paint. *Photo: Hubert Urban, courtesy Schmuck International 1900–1980, Künstlerhaus, Vienna*

15-10 HELGA and BENT EXNER, Denmark. Sterling silver square wire ring whose surface is rough mercury amalgam gilded by applying the amalgam unevenly and thickly. For contrast, the seven balls are smoothly gilded and finished bright. *Photo: Svend Thomsen* ▶

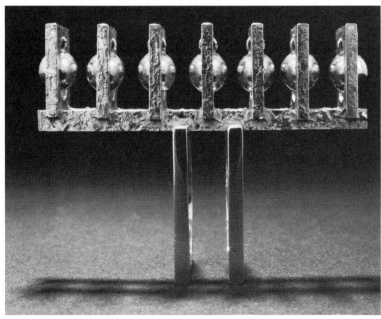

16

METALLIC BUILDUP
Electrolytic Molecular Creation of Surface and Form

ELECTROPLATING

Depositing metals through electrolytic mediums

Electroplating in general is the *deposition by electrolysis* of an adherent coating of one metal or alloy upon an object made of another metal or alloy, or on a nonmetal object made *electroconductive,* while these are in an acid, neutral, or alkaline aqueous solution called an *electrolyte.* To effect the deposition of metal upon the *matrix* or *mandrel* (the object to be plated) it is made the *cathode* or *negative electrode* in the electric circuit, and the ions of metal in the electrolyte pass to it from the *anode* or *positive electrode* also in the solution.

Of the over 30 metals that can be electrodeposited on other metals from aqueous solutions, only some 15 are now used commercially. Those used most commonly in plating jewelry are platinum, palladium, rhodium, gold, and silver, the latter three predominant. They are extensively applied to jewelry made of lower qualities of the precious metal alloys, and to copper and copper alloys such as brass and bronze, nickel alloys, and white metal. Ferrous objects can also be plated with precious metals provided they are properly prepared by first giving the object an undercoat of a nonferrous, conductive metal, usually copper or nickel, as otherwise the plating will not adhere. In the same way, metal deposition is also possible on nonmetallic objects if they are first made electroconductive. (See Electroforming in this chapter.)

REASONS FOR ELECTROPLATING

The high cost of precious metals has altered the view of many art jewelers who formerly were prejudiced against the use of precious metal electroplating in art jewelry. It is recognized here that electroplating is a process requiring both knowledge and skill, and that it may not be possible for techniques as practiced in industry to be duplicated in an individual studio-workshop. However, the knowledge of what is involved in electroplating is of importance to every jeweler, whether the process is used or not. Electroplating (like electroforming, which has already been adopted by art jewelers) is a process that can be undertaken with equipment modified to the needs and circumstances of an individual jeweler. Its application to jewelry (again, like

electroforming) can follow directions and usages that are not limited to industrial aims, thus enlarging its potential for creative use by the individual jeweler.

16–1 FLORA DANICA JEWELLERY, A/S, Denmark. Fresh, natural leaves of various plants are used as a mandrel. Sprayed with an electroconductive, metallized lacquer, they are electroplated in silver, and finally gold plated. The result retains the original leaf mandrel and all its fine detail. From *left to right,* starting at the top row: rosa glauca, rosa canina, rosa rugosa, sagitta, beech, chervil, mahonia, clematis, and parsley. Lengths 4–6 cm. *Photo: Courtesy Flora Danica Jewellery, A/S*

16–2 FLORA DANICA
JEWELLERY, A/S, Denmark.
Electroplated natural parsley
pendant with joined loop,
suspended on a wire
neckpiece. Photo: Courtesy
Flora Danica Jewellery, A/S

Electroplating may be undertaken for a variety of purposes—ornamental, technical, or economic. *Ornamental* reasons, which are primary, are to provide the object's surface with a pleasing appearance different from that of its base metal, to improve its luster, and to increase its surface reflectivity which it will retain for a relatively long period of time. By *selective plating* in which only parts of an object are plated and the rest is left in its original state, decorative effects are possible.

The *basic technical* reason for plating an object with precious metals is the fact that such a plating gives the object a resistance to oxidation and corrosion. As an example, silver alloys oxidize or tarnish in time, and for this reason, when a white metal result is the aim, silver objects are sometimes rhodium plated because rhodium is highly resistant to oxidation and is capable of a high luster. Copper and its compounds also become oxidized when exposed to sulphur compounds in the air, which gold plating prevents. High-karat gold plating is done on low-karat gold alloy jewelry in cases where persons using such jewelry have skins that are allergic to the copper content of low-karat alloy golds, or highly acidic skins which cause copper-alloyed gold jewelry to leave a black deposit on the skin, actually a form of corrosion. Precious metal plating renders the base metal impervious to corrosion of this type, but for complete protection, the plating must be thick enough and hard enough to make it resistant to attack. Soft or thin deposits of gold must be renewed when they become worn and the base metal is exposed.

Other technical reasons include the plating of objects made of gold-filled or gold-rolled metals whose cut ends expose the other metals, necessitating plating to cover them. At times, gold or other metal plating is undertaken to increase the total dimension of an object, or a part which has inadvertently or deliberately been made undersized. Plating is also used in repair or restoration work to replace a worn part by building up metal on it while the rest has been stopped off with a resist. In such cases, the plating coat must be at least as hard as the original metal it matches. Nonmetallic substances such as plastics can be metal plated once they are made electroconductive, either for decorative reasons, or to construct a shell over them which is later removed, a process common in electroforming.

Economic factors for plating revolve around the fact

that the high price of gold has sent many jewelers searching for ways of giving their work the appearance of gold, which plating will accomplish, without the expense of a solid gold object. Objects of an inferior quality gold, or one of a non-precious metal are deliberately disguised by plating to make them appear to be made of a more valuable metal. There is nothing morally wrong about this so long as a purchaser is aware of the facts.

PRINCIPAL PROPERTIES OF PLATED COATINGS

PLATING THICKNESS

Plated coatings are measured in *microns,* a micron being a unit of length equal to the thousandth part of one millimeter, equivalent to 0.00004 of an inch. Plating thicknesses on jewelry vary from less than 1 micron to 40 microns (0.00004–0.0016 in). The thickness given to the plating on an object depends on the function it is to serve, and on the method of plating. Thickness is controlled by the degree of current density used, the duration of immersion, the throwing power of the solution, the shape of the article, and its position in relation to the anode. The thickness of the plating influences such factors as its degree of ductility, resistance to cracking, freedom from pinholes, porosity, resistance to tarnish and oxidation, and resistance to scratching and wear.

Government finishing specifications set standardized requirements for electrodeposited gold platings as follows:

Class 00	0.00002 in thick, minimum
Class 0	0.00003 in thick, minimum
Class 1	0.00005 in thick, minimum
Class 2	0.00010 in thick, minimum
Class 3	0.00020 in thick, minimum
Class 4	0.00030 in thick, minimum
Class 5	0.00050 in thick, minimum
Class 6	0.00150 in thick, minimum

Flash or "color" plating covers the base metal with a very thin deposit less than one microinch (one millionth of an inch) thick. This is done in a coloring bath of the dip or immersion type using proprietary solutions. (See Immersion or "Dip" Plating in this chapter.)

Strike plating according to government specifications is any plated metal 10 microinches or less thick. Gold plating often is preceded by a strike plating of another metal, usually copper, but sometimes nickel or silver, to seal the final gold plating from porosity, and to more readily prepare the surface for the acceptance of gold. The minimum plating thickness in which plating functions as the metal plated is 0.00005 in. When gold is used over silver to prevent tarnishing, from 0.03–0.05 mil thickness is used. Up to 0.3–0.8 mil is applied for greater wear or corrosion resistance.

Heavy decorative plating of gold 10–50 microinches thick is used on jewelry of better commercial types, and is used when the object plated is made of base metals that are subject to wear and abrasion. Metallic coatings heavier than this enter the realm of electroforming in which the deposit becomes heavy enough to become an independent object.

COLOR

Color in gold plating is a dominant consideration. A wide range of gold alloy colors are possible, ranging from pure gold or 24K which has a decidedly bright yellow color that cannot be imitated by any but pure gold anodes, to colors that result from the metal proportions used in particular gold alloys. Because in electroplating, more than one metal can be electrodeposited at one time in the same solution, the plating of color gold alloys are possible. For a *pale yellow gold* deposit the solution can contain potassium gold cyanide, potassium nickel cyanide, and potassium copper cyanide; for a *green gold deposit* potassium gold cyanide, and potassium silver cyanide (increasing the silver percentage or adding cadmium makes the deposit greener); for a *pink gold deposit* potassium gold cyanide, potassium copper cyanide, and potassium nickel cyanide (increasing the copper percentage makes the deposit more pink).

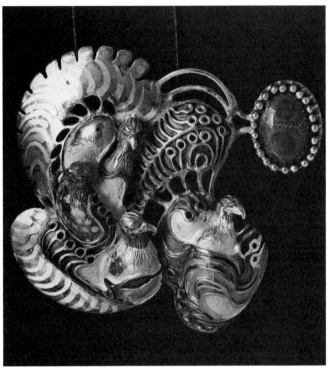

16–3 LEE BARNES PECK, U.S.A. Bird pendant cast in sterling silver, with petoskey stone (fossilized coral whose organic remains have been replaced by agate, calcite, chalcedony, or jasper). The completed wax model was larger than the casting flask capacity, and therefore was divided into parts, each cast separately, then reassembled by soldering. To create a *tri-metal effect* of gold- and copper-plated areas on a silver ground, areas of the cleaned surface were painted with a resist, and exposed parts first plated in 24K gold. A second resist was applied over the gold-plated parts and other areas to be protected, and exposed areas were then plated with copper. The resist was removed with a solvent. The plated result can be lightly buffed, or brightened with a burnisher. Plating is relatively durable on pendants where abrasion is minimal. Plated high areas on rings are subject to wear, but recessed and otherwise protected areas where abrasive contact is low can be plated for color. *Photo: Larry Gregory*

POROSITY

Small pores may exist in the plating if it is not successful. These are important only when they expose the base metal; corrosion can develop at such a point and spread. Protection against corrosion from porosity pinholes is usually accomplished by first plating the base metal with a metal known to be corrosion resistant, such as nickel.

ADHERENCE

Cases of poor adherence are immediately detected if after plating the deposit lifts away from the base metal in part or as blisters. This can happen if the surface was not clean prior to plating; or if, after plating, the object is subjected to bending, twisting, hammering, or stretching. As finished and plated jewelry is not subject to further working, the latter is less likely to occur, unless the article is accidentally subjected to stress.

HARDNESS

It is possible to control the hardness of plated metals by control of the conditions of electrodepositing and the composition of the electrolyte.

LUSTER AND REFLECTING POWER

Bright plating solution compounds are available, and additives called *brighteners* can be included in made up electrolytes to achieve heightened reflectivity. By pre-polishing the object's surface to a mirror finish, the plated result will also be bright. Plated articles can be subjected to polishing, but a loss in the thickness of the plate results from the polishing abrasives. Plated surfaces can be burnished, in which case there is no metal loss.

FACTORS INFLUENCING ELECTROPLATED RESULTS

The achievement of a satisfactory result in electroplating depends on conditions and variable factors in effect both before and during plating. Pre-electroplating variables concern the *metal condition* and its *surface preparation*. During electroplating variables involve the *equipment*, the *anodes, composition of the bath, current density, bath temperature, agitation,* and *filtration*. All of these are discussed below; this section concerns pre-electroplating preparations.

BASE METAL SURFACE CONDITION

All electrodeposited metals are crystalline in structure and orientation. Large crystals result from elevated temperatures and agitation. Small crystals develop from high current densities, the addition of brightening agents, and low metal concentrations in the electrolyte.

The *composition* of the base metal is important as its structure may affect reactions in preplating operations of cleaning and pickling.

The *condition of the surface* to be plated is very important. Its degree of polish, the presence of cracks, scratches, pores, or inclusions have a direct bearing on the way in which the crystal deposit develops, the existence of porosity in the result, and its appearance. To assure good adhesion of the electroplate to the base metal, an intimate linkage of the atoms in both must occur, and this is not possible when impediments exist in the form of grease, scale, or other impurities. They must therefore be removed.

CLEANING METAL SURFACES PRIOR TO ELECTROPLATING AND ELECTROFORMING

The degree of cleanliness required of a metal object before it is ready to accept electroplating and electroforming is greater than that necessary in preparations made for most other working processes. It is of critical importance that the surface be unquestionably *chemically clean,* which means that absolutely no foreign matter can be present, otherwise the plating will not adhere. Since the type of substances that may be contaminants on a metal surface vary considerably, so do the means used to remove them. The cleaning operations used here fall into four (or more) basic groups, the most important being: *mechanical, organic, chemical,* and *electrochemical.* Of these, the method used depends on the condition of the particular metal surface, and the result desired. Therefore, more than one of these processes may be employed on a single object. Of these processes, mechanical cleaning techniques, organic cleaning, and solvent cleaning have been discussed in detail under Metal Finishing in Chapter 14, and chemical cleaning has been discussed under Presoldering Operations in Chapter 10. They are mentioned briefly here insofar as they concern electroplating.

MECHANICAL CLEANING This includes grinding, scratch brushing, sandblasting, steaming, polishing, and buffing. These processes are done to remove scale, burrs, and surface scratches. Most important in relation to plating is that by mechanical polishing a smooth surface is also produced in the plated result which reduces the amount of polishing necessary and minimizes the possible accompanying loss of precious metal in postplating polishing.

16–4 *STEAM JET CLEANING MACHINE*
It ejects a high pressure steam jet from the tube, removing all organic substances present on a metal surface. *Photo: Courtesy Swest Inc.*

ORGANIC CLEANING This is the removal of nonbonded organic matter such as grease, fingerprints, oils, waxes, the remains of buffing compounds, etc., by the use of cleaning mediums such as detergents and hot alkaline solutions. The latter is also used to neutralize acid traces. Nonmetallic surfaces such as wax, plastics, plaster, and wood (the latter two already sealed with a sealant) used in elec-

troforming are cleaned if necessary with a wetting agent and a detergent by dipping in a solution containing these, or by light scrubbing with a soft clean sponge in this solution, followed by a thorough rinse under warm running water, holding the object with a paper towel, and then allowing it to dry. If the object is being prepared for electroforming, after drying it is then sensitized by applying an electrochemical lacquer.

SOLVENT CLEANING This method is used to remove soils that are not saponifiable and must be broken down by the use of a solvent that dissolves them. Lacquer, plastic, resin, paint, shellac, varnish, etc. (substances often used as resists or for decorative purposes), are removed with the solvent proper for the particular substance. Residues are removed by the use of other suitable cleaning mediums.

CHEMICAL CLEANING This involves the use of acid cleaning processes such as pickling to remove fused flux, scale, and to dissolve oxide films formed in previous cleaning operations. Acid solutions are also used to microetch the surface of a metal object, which besides cleaning it, exposes its true crystal structure, thus increasing the bonding ability of the atoms of the base metal and those of the electroplated metal. Such a surface when deeply etched can also be electroplated and left with a crystal pattern for textural effect. The corroded surfaces of long used anode plates often develop beautiful crystallized surface formations and parts of such a sheet of metal could be used in fabricating jewelry with textured areas.

ELECTROCHEMICAL CLEANING PRIOR TO PLATING

Electrochemical cleaning utilizes cleaning solutions plus an electric current to perform the work. Often a final process before plating, it is also used to clean a metal object in preparation for other purposes. *Electrolytic cleaners* are alkaline or acidic solutions placed in a tank into which the object is immersed by an attached copper wire. Either a *reverse* (anodic), *direct* (cathodic), or *periodic reverse* (alternately anodic and cathodic) *current* is run through the solution which causes the gas generated close to the metal surface to produce a high level of agitation or scrubbing action that removes the soil from the object.

The *water break test* can be used to determine the effectiveness of a cleaning operation, and will indicate the presence of contaminants. Water is allowed to flow over the surface. If when the object is withdrawn, a thin water layer clings evenly to the entire surface, it is clean. Should the water film break, this indicates the presence of grease or another foreign substance, and the article must be cleaned again.

In electrocleaning, burning of the work may occur if a too low temperature, too high voltage, too high current density, or an improper cleaning compound are used. The electrodes should be periodically removed and cleaned.

ANODIC CLEANING The work is made anodic (positive) by attaching a copper wire to it, then to the anode contact. It is submerged by the wire into a commercial, hot alkaline electrocleaning solution at 120° F (48° C) in a stainless steel tank which is the cathode. Low 1–6 volt current, and 30–35 amp/ft^2 are run through the solution, higher amperages used if the object is very badly soiled. For most purposes, a cleaning time of ½–2 minutes is sufficient.

A suitable cleaning solution can be made by dissolving an ounce of a household cleaner in a quart of water, then heating it to approximately 180° F (82° C). This solution will remove saponifiable greases and oils, polishing and buffing compounds, etc. However, these substances rapidly contaminate the electrocleaner which must be changed relatively frequently.

Electrostripping is the process of anodically electrolytically removing or stripping especially adherent solids, surface metal from an object, a surface oxide, or an old plating of metal that must be removed before replating takes place. After electrostripping, the entire surface of the object is left chemically clean, bright, and ready for electroplating.

The object is made the *anode* and suspended by a copper wire in a special proprietary electrostripping solution containing cyanide, or a made-up one containing a weak acid solution. The current is turned on before the object is immersed so it completes the circuit upon immersion. A cathode plate of the same base metal as the object (or if precious plating metal is being stripped, of the same precious metal to be recovered) is also immersed in the solution to receive the stripped metal. The stripping container should be placed in a sink or in a tray as rapid stripping action may cause the solution to boil over. A separate container should be reserved for exclusive use with the stripping solution to avoid possible contamination should it be used for other solutions.

The stripping action should be carefully watched as once the surface metal is stripped, the base metal will be attacked and etched, which may not be desirable. To avoid etching, it is necessary to control current density, temperature, and the concentration of the acid or other cleaning agent in the solution. Periodic reversal of the current is sometimes employed to keep the surface smooth.

An old electrodeposited gold plate can be stripped from copper and its alloys by placing the object as an anode in a 5% solution of hydrochloric acid, at 6 volts. The object must be removed as soon as the gold is stripped off.

An electrostripped object can be scratch brushed to improve its luster before being electroplated again with gold. To again render it chemically clean, it must be returned briefly to the cleaning solution, and then thoroughly rinsed. Stripping may leave the surface of some metals electrochemically passive, but the object can be reactivated by pickling and then rinsing. It is then ready for plating, but should there be any reason to delay its being placed in the plating solution, the object is immersed in clean distilled water to prevent the formation of surface oxidation from air contaminants.

As stripping solutions are used, their action slows down, and ultimately they may develop a tendency to pit the surface, at which point they must be discarded.

CATHODIC CLEANING The work is made cathodic (negative) and the same equipment, current densities, and voltage are used as in anodic cleaning. In this case, hydrogen is liberated from the surface of the work at twice the volume as is oxygen in anodic cleaning, which therefore creates the effect of increased gas scrubbing. For this reason cathodic cleaning is sometimes used as a precleaner followed by anodic cleaning.

PERIODIC REVERSAL CLEANING Direct current (DC) is used, as in all plating operations, and the work is made alternately cathodic and anodic by a preset cycle on the periodic reversal unit, at 6–15 volts. This removes smut, oxide, and scale without the danger of etching, and prevents the deposition of metallic film or nonadhering metallic particles.

After electrochemical cleaning, if there is still reason to doubt its cleanliness, the object is dipped into a 5% by volume solution of sulphuric acid for 5 seconds, rinsed in cold water, dipped into a sodium dichromate solution (one ounce per gallon of water) rinsed in cold water, and then electroplated.

IMMERSION OR "DIP" PLATING

This form of plating is also known as *galvanic plating* after Luigi Galvani, the Italian physiologist who discovered dynamical or current electricity about 1780. It works on the principle of which position the metal the object is made of occupies in the electromotive series, in respect to the metal in the form of a dissolved salt in the solution.

The *electromotive (force) series* is an arrangement of metals ordered according to the amount of electromotive force set up between the metal and a solution of the salts of another metal in which it is placed. Each metal is electronegative to any of those that precede it, and electropositive to those that follow it. Therefore, in this order, without the use of an applied electric current, each metal is displaced and plated by the metal in the salt solution of those that precede it, and displaces and plates those that follow. The series (shortened to those common metals likely to be used by a jeweler) is as follows: aluminum, zinc, chromium, iron, nickel, tin, lead, copper, silver, mercury, rhodium, platinum, gold.

The less noble metal is immersed by an attached wire of the same metal, into a proprietary noble metal salt solution, such as Engelhard's Atomex gold, held in a wide-mouthed glass jar. During the deposition, the metal object releases ions into the solution by anodic dissolution and these are replaced by the noble metal ions in the solution which are deposited upon the object. The released base metal ions become a contaminant in the solution, therefore when such a bath is depleted of its noble metal content, the entire solution is *discarded*.

Gold and silver are commonly and easily immersion plated on copper and copper alloy objects. The deposits, however, are thin, ranging from 10–15 millionths of an inch (microinches) of gold maximum. Keeping the object immersed will not increase its thickness as once it is completely covered, the plating action stops. Typical formulas of such solutions follow.

IMMERSION FORMULAS

IMMERSION GOLD PLATE ON COPPER
ALLOY SOLUTION

67% potassium gold cyanide	½ oz/gal
Potassium or sodium cyanide	3½–4 oz/gal
Soda ash or sodium carbonate	4–5 oz/gal
Temperature	140–180° F (60–82° C)

IMMERSION SILVER PLATE ON COPPER
ALLOY SOLUTION

Silver nitrate	1 oz/gal
Ammonia	10 oz/gal
Sodium thiosulphate	14 oz/gal
Use at room temperature	

IMMERSION RHODIUM PLATE ON SILVER
OR COPPER ALLOYS SOLUTION

Rhodium (as chloride)	0.6 oz t/gal
Hydrochloric acid	32 fl oz/gal
Use at room temperature	

BRUSH PLATING

Brush plating of gold, silver, rhodium, copper, or nickel is a simple means of *locally plating* parts of a metal object with a minimum of equipment, and without the need to immerse the object into a plating bath. Its function is to plate small areas on metal objects such as jewelry, and also to repair plated areas that have become worn away.

The equipment needed is minimal. As an electrical power source, a DC *rectifier* can be used, if available. Otherwise any *lead acid battery* that is capable of producing at least 6 volts can be used. Four 1½ volt dry cells can also be used as a power source, connected to each other in series by short wires that pass from the anode of the first to the cathode of the second, etc., leaving one end anode free for the connection to the brush, and one end cathode free for connection to the object. In small models available from suppliers, two flashlight batteries held within the "brush" are sufficient. If a current attachment must be made, the brush is attached to the anode or positive pole by an *alligator clip* with attached *copper wire,* and the object is attached to the cathode or negative pole, preferably with an *ammeter* between them to measure the current and control the plating thickness.

What can be termed a *plating brush, stylus,* or *applicator* can be improvised by using an 8 in (20.3 cm) length of stainless steel rod, or a rod of the metal being applied which in this case also serves to deliver metal anodically to the object. Its end is shaped to a point, cupped, convex, or flat, depending on the shape of the surface being plated, and the ends can be interchangeable. Leaving both ends exposed, the rod is forced into a tight-fitting *plastic* or *rubber tube* which acts as an insulated handle, or the same area can be wrapped with overlapping turns of *rubber electrical tape.* To create an applicator that will conduct current and spread the metal in solution, the working end of the stylus is wrapped with a layer of absorbent cotton covered with surgical gauze, both tightly tied to the stylus-brush with string, or held there by rubber bands. The anode wire is attached to the opposite end.

WARNING:

In *all electroplating operations,* avoid electric shock through direct contact with any activated electrical equipment. For safety's sake, always wear insulating, dry *rubber gloves.*

The surface to be plated must be absolutely clean and the rest of the object as well. Local cleaning on a small scale can be accomplished by rubbing the area with a *fine-grit abrasive paper,* then wiping it with a cloth dipped into naphtha to eliminate sanding dust and possible fingerprints which would hinder plating. A paste of water and *pumice* or *600 grit aluminum oxide* can also be used. This is followed by a thorough water rinse which allows the cleanliness of the surface to be water break tested at the same time. Should water break occur, repeat the cleaning process, and test the surface again.

If less than the total surface of the work is to be plated, a resist is needed to protect the unplated portion. Mask out those parts with *contact plater's tape. Wax* can also be used, painted on the surface while molten, or a *stop-off varnish* can be used and allowed to dry thoroughly.

To activate the surface when cyanide alkaline plating solutions are used, first dip the object into a 3% or weak solution of *sulphuric acid,* then rinse it *thoroughly* under running warm water. The *plating solution* used is one of the prepared types available from any plating supplier, sold in a plastic or glass container. These solutions are about double the concentration of solutions prepared for use in plating tanks. Pour only a small amount of the solution anticipated as sufficient for immediate use into an *open glass container* and place it nearby. Do not use too much at one time as the entire amount decanted must be used up since remaining used solution should not be returned to the stock container as it can cause contamination of the entire contents. Always tightly close the stock container to prevent air contact which can cause deterioration.

Attach the object to the *cathode* with the *ammeter* between it and the power source. Use 5–7 volts for a stainless steel anode to plate small areas, and a larger voltage for larger areas, possibly up to 20 volts for a 3 in² area.

Attach the *plating "brush"* to the *anode,* and immerse its cotton-covered end into the prepared container of plating solution for about 5 seconds. With parallel strokes applied at the rate of about one per second, systematically brush the surface in the lengthwise direction of the area, or use a circular motion, and cover the entire area with overlapping strokes. Work for 25 seconds at a time (use a *timer*), then immerse the brush again into the solution for 5 seconds, and work another 25 seconds. Watch the metal deposit. If it appears dull or becomes black, decrease the voltage or work the brush more rapidly. Repeat the applications until a plate of the desired thickness is in place. Disconnect the work and the "brush" from the electrical source. Rinse the work well under running water, and dry it with a clean, dry cloth. Remove the resist. To brighten the surface, rub it in one direction for a smooth effect, or in different directions for a patterned effect that will pick up light as the object moves. For a semimatte effect, apply a pumice paste, but this will remove about 10% of the plate thickness.

ELECTROPLATING AND ELECTROFORMING EQUIPMENT AND CONDITIONS

Electroplating and electroforming equipment are basically the same since the basic principles involved apply to both. The differences between these techniques lie in the manner of their use, the formulation of the bath to control its metal ion concentration, the time of immersion, and other factors. A plating bath for silver may contain about 4 troy ounces of silver per gallon, and in an electroforming bath about 10 troy ounces of silver per gallon. Therefore the metallic buildup on an electroforming matrix is faster than in electroplating. In electroplating, the goal is to change the color of the object's visible surface whose original condition is generally preserved; while in electroforming, metal deposition is allowed to continue beyond this point to develop sufficient thickness to create an independent object. Also, the surface appearance may be allowed to develop unpredictably, according to the electroforming potential. In electroforming, the surface finally seen is the outer one which develops and changes with the progress of the metallic buildup. The inner surface contacting the matrix is an exact negative reproduction of that surface and normally is not seen in the electroform. Should the inner surface be the one desired, a negative matrix could be used. In general, the aim of electroplating is to permanently coat and color the object with a metal,

16–5 ELECTROPLATING EQUIPMENT

1. *Soluble anodes* of silver, copper, brass, and nickel, and insoluble stainless steel, 1 × 6 in.
2. *Anode of 24K gold*, approx. ¾ × 1 in.
3. *Glass beaker* containing a circular *insoluble platinized titanium anode.*
4. *Paper filters*, cone shaped.
5. *Paper filter*, accordion folded.
6. *Ribbed glass funnel.*
7. *Plastic funnel.*
8. *Copper wire* for current connection leads to the object plated.
9. *Stainless steel storage containers* with covers and handles, used for plating baths, or with electrocleaners and electrostrippers, 1¼, 2¼, 3¼ qt.
10. *Polypropylene plastic beaker* for use with investment remover or other solution that will attack glass, 400 ml.
11. *Pyrex glass beaker* for use with hot liquids, available in 100, 250, 600, 1000 ml.
12. *Stainless steel beaker* without handles, 600 ml.
13. *Stainless steel beaker cover.*
14. *Connector leads* with alligator clamps, each wire covered with a different colored insulator, 31 in long, used to fasten leads to bus bars.
15. *Alligator clamp.*
16. *Plating immersion thermometer*, floating type, with a temperature range of 20–230° F (−6–110° C).
17. *Electric hot plate* with single burner with thermostatically controlled heat from 0–500° F (0–260° C) graduated by 25 degree increments, 6 in Ø, 3⅜ in high.
18. *Single gas burner hot plate*, also available with two burners.
19. *Electric hot plate* with double burners, one with 1100 watt tubular element, and the other with 550 watt tubular element, with infinite heat control knobs. (C. R. Hill Co.)
20. *Galvanofix electroplating outfit* for small work, with voltmeter and attached adjustable clamps, 8 × 5⅞ × 4 in (20 × 15 × 10 cm). (Karl Fischer)
21. *Wilaplat-Junior Electroplating outfit* with rectifier regulatable for 10 amps, 0–10 volts, 33½ in long × 8⅝ in high (85 × 22 cm), with three glass or plastic tanks and connected bus bars. (Karl Fischer)

and in electroforming the aim is to create a self-supporting metal object, and the equipment is designed to produce these results.

A separate area or workbench should be set aside in the workshop for these processes to eliminate the need to dismantle and reassemble the equipment. When not in use, all bath containers must be covered to exclude dust from entering the solutions. The setup must be near a sufficiently powered electrical source, have hot and cold running water nearby, and be supplied with good ventilation.

The degree of sophistication of the equipment used is up to the individual and the means at one's disposal. These processes can be performed with relatively small-scale, simple equipment whose capacity is limited to small objects. Equipment used in some schools and in industry are more elaborate and have large-size object capacity.

RECTIFIER The electrical power source of direct current is the rectifier. All electroplating and electroforming is done using unidirectional or *direct current* (DC). Since it is generally more common for the current provided to be os-

16-6   ELECTROPLATING SILICON RECTIFIER OR PLATING MACHINE
This is a heavy-duty, variable-transformer-type unit, operating on 115 volt, 50/60-cycle electric source, that converts AC, 250 watt, 10 amp input to 0–10 volt infinite continuous DC output. It is equipped with a DC ammeter and voltmeter; marked positive (anode) and negative (cathode) terminal connector clips; easily accessible fuse (uses a 3 amp fuse); pilot light; in 18 gauge B.&S. steel cabinet, size 12 × 7 × 6 in. (Swest Inc.) Photo: Courtesy Swest Inc.

16-7   THE RECTIFIER IN USE
Shown in use here to plate fine gold on a ring. The solution is heated to 140° F (60° C), and not allowed to boil. The 24K gold anode is immersed and its attached wire bent over the beaker edge. The alligator clip on the positive (anode) lead is clamped on the anode wire. The other clamp on the negative (cathode) lead is attached to the wire holding the article. The dial is turned to 6 volts, and the switch is turned on. The article is immersed for no longer than 30 seconds, during which time it is turned so that all surfaces face the anode part of the time. The article is removed, the current is turned off, and it is rinsed in warm water, rubbed with baking soda to brighten the plate finish and neutralize any remaining acid traces, then rinsed and dried. Photo: Courtesy Swest Inc.

cillating or alternate current (AC), a rectifier is used, so called because it rectifies AC to DC by suppressing half of each cycle.

Rectifiers allow the control and variation of the voltage passing through the plating bath. Though direct current may vary in strength, it always flows in the same direction. From the normal entry of 110–220 volts, rectifiers reduce the output to the usual potential of 6–12 volts. Most plating takes place at 6 volts. The voltage used also depends on the surface area of the work and the current density used. The rectifier should not be placed over a plating tank, but to one side.

In periodic reverse current, the current that comes from the rectifier is transmitted to a periodic reverse unit which is preset on a cycle that makes the positive terminal negative, and the negative terminal positive for short periods of time so that an anode briefly becomes a cathode, and a cathode an anode. This reversal allows for plating and deplating, and the control of the development of a smooth plating or surface texture. When the deplating cycle is long, the surface becomes smoother, and a shorter deplating time makes for a rougher or more nodular surface.

Proper current density must be established for smooth and dense deposits in electroplating. Current density is expressed as the amount of current in amperes per square foot of cathode surface (amp/ft²) that passes through the solution in the direction of flow during a unit of time. The term ampere (after French physicist A. M. Ampère), is an internationally used unit of the intensity or quantity flow of the electric current equal to the current produced by one volt acting through a resistance of one ohm, and is equal to one coulomb per second. Amperage means the current consumed in a tank during plating, which starts when the cathode is also immersed. Current density must be within the established limits, lower when the bath is at room temperature, higher when its temperature is raised or when insoluble anodes are used and when the metal content in the electrolyte is increased. Proper current density in electroplating produces uniformity of plating thickness, and controls the quality of the coating. A current density that is too high may be the cause of roughness, porosity, brittleness, burning, or cracking of the electrodeposit. Current density can be regulated by a rheostat, by changing the bath constituents, or by changing the ratio of area of anode to cathode.

To control electrical output, each tank should ideally be provided with an ammeter, a voltmeter, and a rheostat.

AMMETER   An ammeter, or ampere-hour meter, is an instrument that measures in amperes all the electric current flowing in series through an electrical system to which it is attached. It is used as a guide that indicates the need for replenishment of gold or other metals, brighteners, and conducting salts.

VOLTMETER   A voltmeter is an instrument used to measure the volts or units of electrical force or pressure, in voltage which is the difference of potential between different points of an electrical circuit. A voltmeter is always connected in parallel with the circuit whose voltage is to be measured, across the bars in the plating setup. Overvoltage is an excess of plating voltage necessary in all plating baths to deposit the metal satisfactorily on the cathode.

RHEOSTAT   A rheostat is an adjustable resistor constructed to allow resistance to the passing of electric current in a circuit through it to be changed by dissipating and cutting down amperage and voltage without opening the circuit to which it is connected. The regulation of the current density passing through an electrolyte is thereby made easy.

ELECTROLYTE   An electrolyte is the solution containing metallic salts in the tank that acts as a conductor through which the current enters and leaves the circuit.

ANODES   Anodes are usually rectangular metal plates with a hole at one end or an attached hook for hanging. The plate form is most commonly used as it exposes the maximum surface for dissolution in the electrolytic solution in which the anode is hung. In large units, soluble anodes in bar form are also used. Through the anode which is attached to the positive or anodic electrode in the circuit, current enters the bath, which is the conductor. Anodes must be clean, and are fully immersed in the solution.

Soluble anodes are made of metals that slowly dissolve into the solution when the current is activated, and release metal ions, maintaining its more or less constant metal concentration and its pH value. In the soluble metal anode group are pure gold, alloyed golds, pure silver, copper, and nickel. Anode efficiency must match cathode efficiency, which is accomplished by making sure the area of the anode is equal to or larger than that of the cathode. When there is greater ratio of anode to cathode, control of the metal deposit thickness, the character of the surface, and its quality are easier. More than one soluble anode may be used in a single tank, placed at spaced positions around the object being plated in order to increase the metal in the solution and make its deposition on the object more uniform. In small setups, the anode may be bent to form a cylinder that surrounds the object which is suspended by an attached wire in the center space. Soluble anodes used in electroforming are consumed much more rapidly than those used in electroplating.

If a precious metal anode turns black in use, this indicates the bath is too weak; if silver becomes white the current is too strong; in a balanced bath a silver anode is gray while current is on, and turns white when it is off.

Insoluble anodes are permanent, meaning that though they pass current to the electrolyte, they are inert and release no metal into the solution. The bath metal content instead is first established, then replenished as needed by periodically adding concentrated metallic salt preparations to the electrolyte as it becomes depleted by use. These solutions are available from plating suppliers and must be used according to instructions. Because soluble anodes do not always dissolve at the same rate at which metal is deposited at the cathode, both a soluble and an insoluble anode (called a *companion anode*) are sometimes used in the same plating bath to heighten current density, and to maintain a desirable, uniform metal concentration in the bath. The insoluble companion anode prevents the soluble anode from going into the solution too quickly. Stainless steel is used in alkaline baths, but not in acid or chlorine baths or it would dissolve and contaminate the bath. Pure nickel anodes are used in acid baths, or nickel alloys such as Monel or Inconel.

Anode bags of high-count, densely textured fabrics of glass fiber, Orlon, Dynel, polypropylene, nylon, or cotton are used to encase a soluble anode while it is immersed in the electrolyte. Its function is to gather and hold impurities that exist in and are released from all dissolving anodic metals in the form of a sludge. This is prevented from entering the solution which would otherwise become contaminated and hinder success in plating and electroforming. The bag is used for one metal only, and is periodically cleaned by boiling it in water.

CATHODES *Cathodes* are negative electrodes through which a current leaves the conductor. The object being electroplated or mandrel being electroformed is the cathode in the circuit. It is suspended in the electrolyte by an attached copper wire, or a wire of the same metal as is used in the electroplating or electroforming bath. The wire end is attached to the cathodic bus bar or to the cathode terminal on the rectifier or battery. The current cycle is not completed until the cathode is immersed in the electrolyte after the current has been turned on.

BUS BARS OR TANK RODS *Bus bars* or *tank rods* are electric conductors that serve as common anodic or cathodic connectors in a circuit. They are placed across a tank or over a series of tanks. Separate anode and cathode bars are used to conduct current from the rectifier to which they are attached by wires or clips. Anodes are hung from the anode bar, and for short plating intervals, a wire attached to the cathode or object can be held against the cathode bar, or for long immersions, hooked to or suspended from it by wrapping the wire end around the bar. When large tanks are used, bus bars are held above them by insulated supports. Anode and cathode bars must be kept clean so that nothing interferes with their efficiency.

Leads and *alligator clips* are used to bring the current from the rectifier to the anode and cathode, or to the bus bars.

Copper wire, which is a good electrical conductor, is used to conduct the electric current to anode and cathode, and to hold the work suspended in the electrolyte. The object is also handled by the attached wire as *it must not be touched during the entire electroplating process,* for reasons of contamination prevention and avoidance of electric shock. The object is attached to the wire either by simply hooking or twisting the wire around a convenient place, or it may be soft soldered to the object, at a place of contact that will not affect its appearance. Usually only one wire is used, but it is also possible to attach several wires to different parts of a mandrel to give better current distribution. Also, the position of the wire can be changed during plating to make a more uniform deposit on the object. Several small items can be attached to one wire in series, and several wires can be combined into one twisted, cablelike unit, each lower end then spread radially to hold a small item for plating. The object must be attached to the cathode wire *before* immersion as contact with the solution closes the electrical circuit which allows deposition to take place.

ELECTROPLATING AND ELECTROFORMING SOLUTION CONTAINERS

Several different materials are used for the containers and tanks that hold the solutions used in electroplating and electroforming. They can be small or large in capacity, depending on the setup and the relative scale of the equipment. All tanks should be provided with covers to prevent contamination from the air when not in use.

Stainless steel tanks are used for alkaline cleaning baths, and alkaline plating baths containing cyanide.

Glass of the heat-resistant, toughened type such as Pyrex is temperature shock resistant and very resistant to acid corrosive agents, but should not be used for hot caustic solutions. The container size can range from a small beaker as used in brush plating, to a large immersion tank. To avoid breakage, they are sometimes externally covered with wood shields. Because they are transparent, work in progress is easily seen which is an advantage, and glass is easily cleaned.

Ceramic crocks made of vitrified stoneware are chemically acid-proof and are used for small acid plating baths, mostly for gold, silver, and other precious metal plating. Because of their acid resistance, they are also used for bright dips, and for nitric acid pickling solutions. They are subject to damage from thermal shock, therefore hot solutions should not be placed in a cold tank—the tank should be warmed first.

Molded polyethylene or polypropylene plastic containers and tanks are less fragile than glass or ceramic and are suitable for neutral and acid electroplating and pickling solutions, but cannot withstand very high temperatures, or direct contact with a heat source.

Enamel-lined tanks are suitable for small baths, but tend to chip. If the base iron is exposed in such a chip, it may cause solution contamination and have an adverse influence on the plated result. Other types of tanks are also used in industry.

ELECTROLYTIC BATH CONTENTS

WATER   *Water purity* is of prime importance in all plating and electroforming operations. Should tap water contain iron, or a high content of calcium salts, the deposit will develop roughness. If chlorides are present in concentrations of more than 0.05 ounces per gallon they will encourage the growth of nodular deposits. Pitting occurs if organic particles are present. When the objective is a perfectly smooth plating, *distilled* or *deionized water* is used for the bath and for tank replenishment.

COMPOSITION OF THE BATH   Baths used in electroplating are *acidic, neutral,* or *alkaline* in composition, and for the sake of efficiency, this condition must be controlled.

PH: CONTROLLING BATH ALKALINITY, NEUTRALITY OR ACIDITY   The system used for bath control is *pH value.* Control is necessary because in electroplating operations, the relative alkalinity or acidity of the solution has an effect on current efficiency in particular electrolytes, as well as the rate of soluble anode corrosion, and the properties and appearance of the resulting deposit. The term *pH* is a symbol used to indicate the relative alkalinity or acidity of a solution. The pH scale ranges from 0–14 with 7, the mid-number, indicating a neutral condition, that is, neither acid nor alkaline. As the pH value decreases below 7, the solution is increasingly acid; and as the value increases above 7, it is increasingly alkaline or basic. Control of pH is common practice in maintaining acid and neutral gold solutions. Generally speaking, it is necessary to keep the major bath constituents constant within plus or minus 5% of the optimally desired amounts. When proprietary solutions are used, the manufacturer's recommendations as to degree of acidity or alkalinity should be followed.

The simplest and fastest way of determining the pH value of a solution is by the use of *pH papers* and color matching, though other methods exist. These are strips of absorbent paper impregnated with an indicator chemical whose color varies with each value. They are immersed in the electrolyte solution, and upon removal, the resulting color of the dipped portion is compared with a printed color chart, or a color printed on the strip. If necessary, the solution can then be adjusted toward greater acidity or alkalinity. Color comparisons should be made in good daylight or artificial light approximating daylight in color balance.

Typical pH papers are divided into the scale that follows. A single indicator covers only a small range in the pH scale, therefore figures overlap.

pH range	Indicator
1.2– 2.8	Meta cresol purple
3.0– 4.6	Brom phenol blue
3.8– 5.4	Brom cresol green
5.2– 6.8	Brom cresol purple
6.8– 8.4	Phenol red
8.0– 9.6	Thymol blue
9.6–11.2	LaMotte purple
11.0–12.6	Sulpho orange
12.0–13.6	LaMotte violet

THE FUNCTION OF CYANIDE IN AN ELECTROLYTE   Potassium or sodium cyanide acts to dissolve the metal from a soluble anode and forms a complex salt which prepares it to be electrodeposited on the cathode (the object). In proprietary solutions, concentrated cyanide and metallic salts are diluted with distilled water to form the bath. The purpose of free cyanide in a bath added at intervals in the form of sodium or potassium cyanide is that it raises the conductivity and improves the throwing power of the solution. *Throwing power* is the ability of the solution to deposit metal into depressions and onto parts of the object not directly exposed. The throwing power of a bath generally increases as it is used. While a solution stands and is not in use, the free cyanide content gradually diminishes and must therefore be replenished. Cyanide in a solution slowly changes to carbonate, therefore old and used gold solutions have a tendency to plate darker gold tones. Chemically pure calcium sulphate powder, 1–3 ounces per gallon, stirred in well, can be used to precipitate excess carbonate, removed by filtration after it settles to a white sediment.

Coatings from acid bath deposits are easier to buff to a high luster than those from cyanide baths. However, by the use of current interruption or periodic current reversal techniques, the metal luster achievable in high-concentration cyanide baths is improved.

CYANIDE=POISON!   Safe handling practice

ALWAYS WORK UNDER CONDITIONS OF GOOD VENTILATION. The chief danger in using cyanide-containing solutions, widely used in precious metal plating, is that they are a potential source of the most deadly of poisons and possibly fatal *hydrogen cyanide gas* which has a characteristic odor of peach blossoms. This gas is created by the action of acids on cyanide. Contact can come about when an object is inadequately rinsed after pickling in an acid solution or a bright dip solution. A dragover of acid on the object which is then placed in a cyanide plating or cyanide rinse solution will cause hydrogen cyanide gas to develop. To minimize such a possibility, first of all, all solutions containing cyanide must be kept well separated from any solutions containing acid. Any object exposed to an acid- or a cyanide-containing solution must be *THOROUGHLY RINSED,* preferably first under running water, then in deionized water which is free of impurities, *before* being immersed in a solution containing cyanide or acid in order to prevent the formation and release of hydrogen cyanide gas. **ALWAYS WEAR RUBBER OR PLASTIC GLOVES** when handling chemicals containing any form of cyanide, or when working with solutions containing cyanide as it can be *absorbed through the skin.* **WASH HANDS IMMEDIATELY** and thoroughly if they come in contact with cyanide. **NEVER ALLOW FOOD IN AN ELECTROPLATING OR ELECTROFORMING WORKSHOP** where chemicals containing cyanide are used as cyanide can be unwittingly ingested. **PRACTICE UTMOST CARE** and never work absentmindedly in plating rooms. **AVOID SPILLING SOLUTIONS,** but should this occur, while wearing gloves, mop up the spilled matter immediately with paper towels, and dispose of them in a safe way. Clean the spilled area with copious amounts of water. Do not take home the shoes worn in plating rooms as some cyanide can be transferred to floors and carpets and endanger the lives of children and pets. **KEEP CHEMICALS CONTAINING CYANIDE LOCKED IN A STORAGE CABINET** to which only a responsible person has the key.

CYANIDE SOLUTION DISPOSAL Before discarding old solutions containing cyanide, they should be neutralized by adding sodium bicarbonate. Never allow them to come in contact with any solution containing acid as this will generate the deadly hydrogen cyanide gas. For the same reason, never pour any solution containing cyanide down the same drain into which an acid solution has been poured. In such cases, be sure the remains of the acid solution has been neutralized and totally flushed away, and that the drain is also neutralized by pouring an alkaline solution down it, such as one containing sodium bicarbonate or sodium carbonate.

BRIGHTENERS The plated results normally appear matte. The upper parts of such a surface can be polished and the rest left matte. When a semibright or bright finish is wanted on the entire surface, *brighteners* or organic agents are added to the plating bath in small amounts per gallon at frequent intervals rather than in a large amount at one time. Among the substances used for this purpose are alcohol, aldehydes, dextrin, furfural, gelatin, glue, milk, molasses, sugar, and some sulphonic acids. In cyanide baths, these substances form molecular complexes with the electrolyte that have an influence on the growth and orientation of deposited metallic crystals, producing long, fine crystals that make for a bright appearance. Brighteners are available as proprietary preparations, and the amounts recommended and the conditions of their use should be followed, as otherwise dullness, pitting, and blistering can result.

BATH TEMPERATURE Some plating and electroforming baths are used at room temperature, approximately 68–72°F (20–22°C). Others must be heated almost to a boil for greater efficiency. Hot baths give off fumes which should be drawn off under a *hood* to an *exhaust*. Bath temperature must be kept within the prescribed limits because there is a direct relationship between temperature and the rate of and quality of deposition.

HEAT SOURCES *Electric hot plates* or *gas burners* are used in small workshops to maintain bath temperatures. It should be possible to control them by several heat stages. Small glass beakers when heated should not come in direct contact with a flame but a metal screen should be placed under them to deflect the flame and spread the heat.

Immersion heaters of inert stainless steel, or *fused quartz immersion heaters* with automatic controls are available in a wide range of sizes. They are commonly used to maintain recommended bath temperatures by hanging them in the electrolyte at one side of the tank.

Solutions used when electroforming on plastic models or mandrels with plastic inclusions must not be too high in temperature or deformation of the plastic may result. *Thermoplastics* such as cellulose acetate, methyl methacrylate, styrene, and others in this group should not be subjected to temperatures higher than 95°F (35°C), and *thermosetting plastics* such as the phenolics and ureas should be subjected to temperatures not higher than 130°F (54°C).

Plating thermometers of the immersion, floating type, or the dial type capable of registering up to 220°F (104°C) are used to check bath temperatures.

BATH MAINTENANCE The maintenance of the bath is very important. When a bath is in use, it constantly undergoes changes in composition. This means that its constituents are not in constant balance, and if in due time they are not returned to their original balanced condition, good results will not be realized. Chemical balance is important whether you are working with a small- or large-scale operation. The silver and free cyanide content should be checked at regular intervals. Impurities such as sulphides, organic decomposition products, traces of other impurities or other loose floating particles must be filtered out. Solutions should be raised to proper levels by adding water when needed, temperature should be checked to be sure it stays within the proper range, anodes of the soluble type must be watched and replaced when they become inadequate, and large tanks must be cleaned at least once a month if they are in constant use. All containers and tanks must be *covered* when not in use to reduce evaporation and eliminate the entrance of airborne contaminants.

The main contaminants of plating solutions come from the dissolution of the base metal of the object being plated, contaminants that are introduced on the work plated from previous baths, the use of impure salts and anodes, new anode bags and filter cloths, remains of buffing compounds on the article, the water used, and from dust and dirt from the environment.

AGITATION Agitating the solution, or moving the object in the solution (which has the same effect) results in an increase in current density and metal buildup. Agitation may be produced *manually* by moving the solution or the object by its attached wire, by the use of oscillating rods, magnetic agitators, or by rotating the electrodes.

Magnetic stirrers consist of a Teflon-covered magnet coupled to a rheostat-controlled motor by magnetic force. They are small enough not to take up much space, and are placed below the container or tank. When heavy plating or rapid electroforming is in progress, their mechanical stirring action rapidly agitates the solution and causes the constant exposure of new ions of metal to the object or mandrel surface so that rapid metal deposition takes place.

Tank rod agitator motors are used in large installations, attached at one end of the tank and with Bakelite rollers at the other end. They automatically move the tank rod back and forth, and with it the attached cathode which agitates the electrolyte.

FILTRATION *Paper or fiber glass filters* are used to line *plastic* or *ribbed glass funnels* when measuring liquids, when pouring solutions from or returning them to storage containers, and when cleaning an electrolyte at intermediate stages to filter out any impurities and solid particles they may contain.

Tank filtration, either intermittent or continuous, keeps the solution free of suspended matter and prevents the accumulation of impurities that would foul the electrolyte. Pure silver, for instance, although the ideal anode for metal buildup, is never actually absolutely pure. As a silver anode's surface erodes into the solution, small amounts of impurities are dissolved with it in the form of carbon particles and trapped oxides that are released. In addition, sediment that always develops, and dirt particles that enter the solution from the atmosphere must be removed. If these substances are not filtered out, they will be the cause of rough, nodular, nonadhering deposits on the object. Filtration is especially necessary when using agitation as it raises these contaminants into the solution from the tank bottom where they otherwise tend to gather. When very heavy metal deposits are applied, as in electroforming, filtration is essential.

Electric filters containing Dacron and activated carbon filters, can be placed at one side within a tank where they constantly work to filter out impurities and contaminants.

MECHANICAL AIR-CLEANING SYSTEMS   Control of air condition is important during plating and electroforming processes in order to reduce possible health hazards. Corrosive fumes rise from plating solutions which should be eliminated from the atmosphere.

Exhaust hoods and *fans* are used in workshops as an aid in fume removal. Hoods should project above and enclose all or as much of the tank surface area as possible to help the exhaust fan placed at the end of the ventilating system create an effective air flow that removes the fumes which are drawn through the pipe or duct to the point of discharge. When working, your head should be in front of the hood opening, not under the hood. The recommended hood slope to the exhaust pipe is 45°, and the vertical flanges at the lower hood edge should be deep.

A TYPICAL CYANIDE GOLD PLATING PROCESS CYCLE

Not all of these processes need be carried out on the same piece.

- The article is polished to the desired surface finish.
- The article is cleaned of organic polishing contaminants by boiling it in an organic solution.
- Brushed and rinsed under running water.
- Electrolytically cleaned of chemical contaminants in an alkaline electrocleaning solution, first as a cathode, then as an anode.
- Rinsed in running water.
- Cleaned of mineral contaminants by light etching (electrostripping) as an anode in a weak sulphuric acid pickling solution.
- Rinsed thoroughly in running water.
- Scratch brushed, redipped in pickle, and thoroughly rinsed again.
- Always first connected to the cathode before it touches a metal-containing solution. It is given a bright nickel strike plate which is a minimum of 0.05 mil in thickness, usually accomplished in about a 10-minute immersion. This plate provides the object with a sealed barrier and hard underplate that eliminates porosity and prevents future corrosion, thus protecting the decorative properties of the gold plate.
- Rinsed and dried.
- Areas not to receive plating or metal buildup are stopped out with a resist.
- Dried.
- For good gold plate adhesion and to activate the surface, the article is first given a gold strike before its final gold deposit by dipping it into a solution of potassium gold cyanide (0.1 oz t/gal gold and 6 oz/gal potassium cyanide).
- To avoid tarnishing, the article is placed immediately as a cathode into the regular gold electroplating baths. The current is turned on to close the circuit as the work is immersed and allowed to remain 30–45 minutes for a heavy gold plate.
- Hot rinsed in distilled water; the water is saved for use as a solution replenishment for the gold bath as it contains gold and plating chemicals.

- May be scratch brushed to burnish the surface if brighteners are not used. Other finishing processes such as hand burnishing with a soap solution lubricant, or buffing can be done.
- Washed in very hot water and dried in warm sawdust, by hot air, or in a warming oven.
- Heavy gold plate requires no protection, but a thin gold plate may have to be lacquered to prevent tarnishing.

PLATING FORMULAS

GOLD PLATING

Decorative gold plating today is capable of brilliant, thick, ductile, wear-resistant deposits in a variety of gold alloy colors. Generally when making a thin deposit low current densities are used and no agitation. To produce heavy deposits the solutions used contain high gold contents and use high current densities and agitation. Faster plating speeds are obtained at higher temperatures and with increased agitation. When soluble anodes are used, metal content in the bath is maintained by free alkali cyanide. When insoluble anodes of type 304 stainless steel are used, complex gold cyanides must be added to the solution in the form of concentrated proprietary solutions (which are diluted with distilled water) to maintain the bath's gold content. Deposits for decorative purposes should be uniform and heavy, and if a bright surface is wanted, bright enough to eliminate the need to mechanically buff the result with the concomitant loss of gold and reduction of plate thickness.

There are many possible gold plating solution compositions. Those that follow are given as typical examples. All weights referred to in the following formulas are avoirdupois weights.

TYPICAL GOLD CYANIDE FLASH PLATING BATH

Metallic gold	¼ oz t/gal
Cyanide, free (KCN)	2 oz/gal
Phosphate (K$_2$HPO$_4$)	2 oz/gal
pH	11.8
Current density	1–10 amp/ft²
Temperature	130–160° F (54–71° C)
Anode	insoluble stainless steel

Composition of Typical Colored Gold Plating Solutions

Color	Gold	Other Metal	Free Potassium Cyanide	Potassium Carbonate
			in grams per liter	
24 karat yellow gold	1.5		8.0	15
Red gold	1.5	Copper 1.0	8.0	15
Green gold	1.5	Silver 0.1	8.0	15
Yellow gold	1.5	Copper 0.8 Silver 0.15	0.2	15
White gold	1.5	Nickel 5.0 Zinc 0.5	3.0	15

All metals in the form of salts.
pH about 10.5-11.8.
Temperature range from 110°-150° F (43°-65° C).
Current density: 1-10 amp/ft².
Anode: insoluble stainless steel.

Conditions of Plating Solution Usage

Solution	Parts	Water Parts	Temperature °F	Temperature °C	Voltage	Maximum Area Square Inches
Rhodium (isothermal)	1	None	110	43	4V	39
Rhodium 217 or 219	1	None	110	43	4V	39
Gold	1	None	140	60	6V	80
Silver	1	3	70	21	2V	238
Copper	1	3	100	37	6V	39
Nickel	1	None	70	21	2V	48

Use with distilled or de-ionized water.

16–8 *PROPRIETARY PLATING SOLUTIONS*
(*Swest Inc.*)
1. *Isothermic Rhodium Plating Solution, 1 qt.*
2. *Isothermic Rhodium Concentrate (Syrup), 3 g, 30 cc concentrate; 10 g, 100 cc concentrate. Usage: 10 cc syrup (1 g rhodium) to 1 pt distilled or deionized water, plus 10 cc sulphuric acid.*
3. *Fine Gold Plating Solution, 1 qt; also available in 18K yellow, pink, and green gold.*
4. *14K Yellow Gold Plating Solution, 1 qt.*
5. *Concentrated Gold Plating Solution, contains 1 oz t of fine gold; 1 pt makes 2 gal.*
6. *Coloring Solution for use in fine gold plating solutions, used according to suggested proportions per quart for 14K and 18K yellow, 18K pink and green colors.*
7. *Atomex Immersion Gold Solution, Engelhard.*
8. *Silver Plating Solution, 1 qt makes 1 gal.*
9. *Copper Plating Solution, 1 qt makes 1 gal.*
10. *Nickel Plating Solution, 1 qt makes 1 gal.*
11. *Electro Cleaner Solution, 1 qt makes 1 gal.*
12. *Electro Stripping Solution, 1 qt makes 1 gal.*
13. *Oxy-Black Solution, used to electrolytically color a metal object; used with a special anode; 1 qt makes 1 gal.*
14. *Stop-out lacquer, and stop-out thinner-remover.*

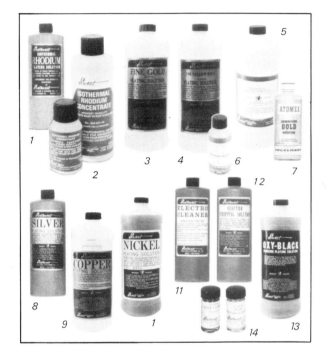

THICK GOLD PLATING BATH

Metallic gold	1 oz t/gal
Cyanide, free (KCN)	2⅔ oz/gal
Phosphate (K_2HPO_4)	2⅔ oz/gal

Other factors same as above

NO FREE CYANIDE BATH

Metallic gold	1 oz t/gal
Potassium phosphate (KH_2PO_4)	4 oz av/gal
pH	6.5–7.5

Other factors same as above

SILVER PLATING

Silver plating is a process widely used to make objects appear to be made of silver, and in creating electroformed jewelry. Electrolytes that contain cyanide are most widely used for silver plating and electroforming (though other bath types are also used and electrolytes not containing cyanide are growing in importance). The cyanide content promotes good adhesion and such baths have good covering and throwing power. Deposits can be made smoother and brighter by the introduction of additives containing small amounts of sulphur compounds such as ammonium thiosulphate and carbon disulphide, and these also suppress the excessive buildup at peaks called *treeing*.

The silver anodes used are not less than 999.5 fine because otherwise traces of impurities can cause the develop-ment of a blackish scum on the anode (then called a "black anode") which limits the anode's corrosion, causing interference with the bath composition. To minimize this possibility, a high free cyanide content and high current density are used to assure good corrosion and silver transfer from the anode into the solution and to the object/mandrel. Anode-to-cathode-area ratio should be two-to-one for good results.

Scratch brush the surfaces as silver resists adhering to mirror-buffed finishes. Any stainless steel, glass, or stoneware tank may be used. The purpose of the first silver bath or *strike solution* is to preplate the surface, which is necessary so that the plate deposit that follows will adhere. This bath is low in concentrated silver but high in cyanide content. When preparing to immerse a mandrel into a silver bath, it is important to make electrical contact with the cathode before immersion. This is especially necessary in silver strike baths where relatively high voltage is used, because the hydrogen generated helps promote better metal coverage on the cathodic mandrel. The silver strike coating is produced in 1–2 minutes. Then follows immersion in the second, regular plating solution which builds up the plating or electroform deposit to the desired thickness. When thick, smooth deposits are wanted, periodic reversal current is used. Brighteners can be added to help form a dense, white-bright silver plate. After plating, scratch brush or hand burnish the plate which can then be given a higher polish if wanted. Soft solder will not accept silver plating. If soft solder is present, the area must first be copper plated before the silver strike bath.

SILVER STRIKE BATH FOR NONFERROUS METALS

Silver cyanide	0.5–0.7 oz av/gal
Free sodium cyanide	8–12 oz/gal
Sodium carbonate (optional)	1.2 oz/gal
Current density	15–25 amp/ft^2
Voltage	4–6
Temperature	70–85° F (21–29° C)
Time of immersion	1–2 minutes
Anodes	silver or stainless steel

TYPICAL SILVER PLATING BATHS

	Regular	High speed
Silver cyanide	2.5–4.4 oz/gal	6.0–7.3 oz av/gal
Free potassium cyanide	4–6 oz/gal	6.0–7.3 oz/gal
Potassium carbonate	3–12 oz/gal	3.0–10.7 oz/gal
Potassium nitrate	–	3.0–12.0 oz/gal
Potassium hydroxide	–	0.4–1.6 oz/gal
Current density	5–15 amp/ft^2	25–100 amp/ft^2
Voltage	about 1	about 1
Temperature	70–90° F (21–32° C)	105–115° F (40–46° C)
Anode	fine silver	fine silver

Brightener: ammonium thiosulphate, 0.003 gram/liter or 0.17 grain/gallon added every four hours.

RHODIUM AND PALLADIUM PLATING

The practice of plating silver objects, particularly silver jewelry, with rhodium to make a thin, hard, white-bright, highly reflective and oxidation-resistant surface began around 1930 and is finding ever wider acceptance today. It is also used on nickel and copper. The proprietary solutions containing rhodium have good throwing power and the operation is simple. Use only *Pyrex glass containers* for the bath. The concentrate is added to the bath *after* the acid content has been mixed with distilled water as otherwise it may not yield good deposits. The normal rhodium deposits sufficient to cover the base metal are from 0.000006 in to 0.00001 in. Heavier platings up to 0.001 in require special sulphate solutions. Rhodium plating is harder and more reflective than palladium plating, but palladium is used when thicker deposits (from 0.0001 in and heavier) are wanted. The plating will appear *as bright as the surface on which it is applied*, therefore if a bright surface is the aim, which is usual, the object must be *polished bright*. If this cannot be done satisfactorily with the metal used, first plate it with nickel which will take a high polish, then plate with rhodium. After cleaning and electroplating, rinse; dip in cyanide, rinse thoroughly; sulphuric acid dip (1–10), rinse; nickel flash plate, rinse; sulphuric acid dip (1–10); rhodium plate, rinse first in cold water, then in very hot water; dry immediately.

RHODIUM DECORATIVE FLASH PLATE BATH

Rhodium (proprietary sulphate solution)	¼ oz/gal
Sulphuric acid (concentrated)	2½ oz/gal
Current density	20 amp/ft^2
Voltage	3–5
Temperature	105–115° F (40–46° C)
Time of immersion	1–2 minutes
Anode	insoluble platinum

Rhodium-plated objects cannot be repaired by methods requiring heat as the plating becomes discolored. When repairs are necessary, all plating must be stripped from the object; the repairs done; the object repolished; and then replated with rhodium.

PALLADIUM BATH

Palladium in the form of a chloride	50 g/liter
Sodium chloride	20 g/liter
Hydrochloric acid	18 g/liter
pH	0.4
Current density	1 amp/ft^2
Voltage	2–4
Temperature	158° F (70° C)
Time	1–3 minutes
Anode	soluble, very pure palladium

PLATINUM PLATING

This platinum solution is orange in color and is boiled until it becomes pale yellow, at which point the platinic chloride has been transformed into a complex of ammonium phosphate. Because this bath is operated with insoluble platinum anodes, each time the platinic chloride is periodically replenished, the boiling procedure must be repeated. Over a period of time chlorides will gradually accumulate in this bath, and eventually good deposits become impossible. Platinum plating wears well and does not tarnish. It can be deposited over the precious metal alloys and nickel.

PLATINUM BATH

Ammonium phosphate	20 g/liter
Sodium phosphate	100 g/liter
Platinum as platinic chloride	4 g/liter
Water	1 liter
Current density	1 amp/ft^2
Voltage	3–4
Temperature	194° F (90° C)
Time of immersion	30 seconds–2 minutes
Anode	insoluble platinum

COPPER PLATING

Copper is commonly used as an underplate deposit in a multi-metal plating process, and as a first plate in electroforming, though an entire electroform can be made completely of copper. It can be deposited from *alkaline* or *acid baths*. The widely used alkaline copper plating baths contain alkaline cyanide and produce a heavy deposit with relatively uniform thickness over the entire surface. Cyanide electrolytes produce a harder deposit than acid bath deposits. Acid copper plating baths are also extensively used to electroform copper but have less throwing power and the metal distribution is not as efficient as the alkaline baths. Copper sulphate baths are the most frequently used of acid copper baths, both for undercoating and for electroforming, as they are simple to prepare and control. Heavy copper deposits of any thickness can be produced, and brighteners can be added for a bright surface finish. *Current interruption* or *periodic reverse plating* are practiced to produce a uniform distribution of copper on complex shapes, and this procedure also acts to reduce plating time and the amount of metal used.

TYPICAL ACID COPPER PLATING BATH

Copper sulphate	26–33 oz/gal
Sulphuric acid	4–10 oz/gal
Current density	20–40 amp/ft^2
Voltage	6
Temperature	70–120° F (21–48° C)
Anode	copper

TYPICAL CYANIDE COPPER PLATING BATH

Copper cyanide	3.5 oz/gal
Sodium cyanide	4.6 oz/gal
Sodium carbonate	4.0 oz/gal
Sodium hydroxide	until solution reaches pH 12
Rochelle salt	6.0 oz/gal
Current density	20–40 amp/ft^2
Voltage	6
Temperature	130–160° F (54–71° C)
Anode	copper

NICKEL PLATING

Nickel is used as an undercoating for some metal plating processes, and also for a final decorative finish. Dull deposits can be buffed to a high luster, or brighteners can be added to the solution for bright nickel plate deposits. Nickel platings are highly resistant to corrosion and are therefore often used on silver objects to seal off porosity before gold plating takes place. Agitation is necessary to ensure even, thin coatings. Distilled water is used in solutions. The anode is of cast nickel, placed in a cotton bag to prevent products of anode disintegration from entering the bath.

NICKEL PLATING BATH ON COPPER, BRASS, STEEL

	Low current density	High current density
Nickel sulphate	16 oz/gal	30–40 oz/gal
Ammonium chloride	2 oz/gal	
Nickel chloride		6 oz/gal
Boric acid	2 oz/gal	4 oz/gal
pH	5.3	high: 5.0–5.2 low: 2.0–2.5
Current density	10–20 amp/ft^2	25–50 amp/ft^2
Voltage	4	4
Temperature	70–90° F (21–32° C)	100–150° F (37–65° C)
Time	4–5 minutes	4–5 minutes

NICKEL, ELECTROFORMING

Nickel sulphate	40–60 oz/gal
Nickel chloride	0–2 oz/gal
Boric acid	4–6 oz/gal
pH	3.5–4.5
Current density	25–200 amp/ft^2
Voltage	4
Temperature	100–140° F (37–60° C)
Time	4–5 minutes

FINAL RINSING AND DRYING

Rinsing is done to remove the solution remaining on the object from the previous tank to be sure that it is not introduced to the following tank as a contaminant. If any plating solution dries on the surface of an object, it will later cause local spotting and tarnishing, especially if the object is lacquered. The best rinse is under running water; cold or warm can be used, but the latter is preferred as it speeds up the removal of films by lowering their viscosity, and it quickly carries soluble impurities away. In large-scale operations, *still rinses* in tanks are also used, especially when precious metal plating solutions are in use, because the *dragout* of precious soluble metal salt that may cling to the object can be gathered in such a tank and reclaimed.

Some rinsing tanks are provided with a rubber hose that brings fresh water to the bottom of the tank and causes it to overflow, thus constantly changing the water and carrying surface films away.

In cases where chemical purity is essential and the available water supply is doubtful, still rinses in water of known quality, such as distilled water or deionized water are used.

The final rinse at the end of a plating sequence is usually *very hot*, at least 180–212° F (82–100° C)—the thinner the metal the higher the temperature—to allow any water adhering to the workpiece after the object is withdrawn from the rinse to evaporate by the heat it contains. Rapid drying after plating is necessary to prevent the formation of water marks and stains from chemical traces remaining, or minerals in the water itself. To hasten drying, rinsing can be followed by immersing the object in *warm sawdust;* placing the object under an *infrared heat lamp;* by blowing hot air against the object with a device such as a *hair dryer;* or by placing the object in a *heated drying oven.*

ELECTROFORMING

Synthesizing form and texture by electrochemistry

Electroforming is the process of synthesizing a metal object by controlling the *electrodeposition* of metal passing through an *electrolytic solution* onto a metal or metallized form. The metal source is either a *metallic anode* placed in the solution and gradually dissolving into it, or is in the form of metal salts contained in the solution, and the immersed object is the *cathode*. The dissolution action occurs when the electric current passing through the electrolyte from anode to cathode liberates positively charged metallic ions from the soluble anode and/or the solution, and renders them mobile, causing them to seek a path to the negatively charged cathode upon which they deposit themselves. The resulting, slowly built-up metallic object is an *electroform*, which ultimately is self-supporting.

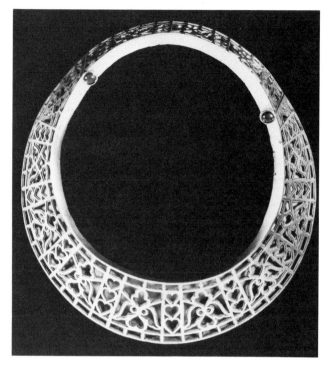

16–9   GREEK WORK FOR GOTHIC TRIBES OF DACIA, 4th century A.D.
An *electroformed reproduction* of the gold gorget with garnets, from the
so-called Treasure of Athanaric, found in 1837 in Pietroasa (Petrossa)
village, Buzau District, Romania. Treasures like this were hidden during the Hun invasions when dangers threatened the owners who never
recovered them. The pierced work, elevated sheet, backed by a solid
sheet, is an outstanding example of *cagework* which gives the form
additional dimension by casting shadows on the ground sheet. Electroformed reproductions of famous works were commonly made for
display in museums during the end of the last century. Original, col.:
National Museum of Antiquities, Bucharest, Romania. *Photo: Victoria
and Albert Museum, London, Crown Copyright*

The word *electroforming* was established by Blum and
Hogaboom in their classic book *Electroplating and Electroforming.* When the process was first invented in the
mid-19th century, its most suitable application was then
thought to be for the multiple reproduction of three-
dimensional art works which could be made available to a
large market at low cost. This use reached a peak at the
turn of the century when the use of electroforming for industrial purposes developed and became more important,
as it still is today. The process is used, for instance, for
making exact reproductions of historic jewelry and objects
in museum collections. Its relatively new use for the creation of *unique* (meaning one of a kind) pieces of jewelry
embodies the concept of utilizing industrial techniques and
processes for creative purposes in ways never intended or
imagined by industry.

The techniques and equipment used for electroforming
and electroplating are basically the same with the
difference that in electroplating, electrodeposition is carried out on a finished, existing object, and in electroforming the object itself is created by electrodeposition. Because the electroform is a self-supporting structure, the
thickness of the deposition during electroforming is considerably heavier and denser than the thin deposit made
on an object during electroplating.

The object upon which the initial and/or final electrodeposition takes place is a three-dimensional *mandrel*,
also called a *matrix, master, mold,* or *model.* This can be
fabricated in advance from any of a variety of possible
materials to full size, shape, and desired surface condition.
The different types of mandrels fall basically into *permanent* and *expendable* types, and are discussed below.

The appeals of the process for use in jewelry making are
several. It allows latitude for the realization of results that
are generic to this process alone and not possible by any
other working method available to the jeweler. Of particular importance are the special textural effects and surfaces
which are progressively developed and can be stopped at
any point by the creator. There is no technical barrier to
realizing forms which can be unprecedentedly complex.
Though the aim is ordinarily to create a single, unique object, it is also possible to *reproduce* an object in any
quantity from a permanent master mandrel. Because the
normal thickness of an electroform is about 22 gauge
B.&S. and electrodeposited metal is dense and the forms
rigid, one can create relatively large objects of light
weight. Any metal used for jewelry can be used to make
electroformed deposits, or can be electroformed upon, including gold, silver, copper, nickel, and their alloys, rhodium, platinum, and palladium, and even iron or steel if it
is pretreated to make it electroconductive. Finally, the
only limit on the *size* of an object that can be electroformed is the capacity of the tanks containing the electroforming solutions. Electroforming equipment can be
relatively minimal or highly sophisticated. In the latter
case, its high cost usually implies a more than casual commitment to this process. Though some potentially dangerous chemicals, such as cyanide, are used, the hazards can
be eliminated by carefully controlled work habits.

CREATING THE MANDREL: Preliminary work prior to electroforming

The fabrication of a mandrel is the starting point of the
electroforming process. There are several different types of
mandrels possible, the choice depending on the concept involved.

MANDREL TYPES

PERMANENT, NONADHESION MANDRELS   These are those
intended to be withdrawn or separated from the electroform and used repeatedly thereafter. Their shape must
be such that allows extraction, removal, or stripping of the
electroform. Usually this means that if the form is three
dimensional, it is tapered and without undercuts, convex
or concave, or is developed on a relatively flat surface.
When used they must be absolutely *chemically clean* to
allow separation. To help in separation, surfaces are commonly brush coated or sprayed with a thin but still conductive separating film of powdered graphite.

PERMANENT, SINGLE-USE ADHESION MANDRELS   These are
made of materials that become incorporated in the final
electroform and are *not eliminated.* They can be completely visible, partially visible, or completely invisible in
the final electroform. Because they are used as a base
upon which electrodeposited metal will permanently adhere, or as an ornamental part of the total result, their
shape is not of technical but of esthetic importance, the
only technical consideration being to devise a system that
allows them to be retained as part of the final electroform.

EXPENDABLE, TEMPORARY, SINGLE-USE MANDRELS   These
are made of a material that is used to initially establish an

16–10 RAMONA SOLBERG, U.S.A. Silver brooch with amber, fabricated from a contour-sawed sheet. Bezel and the central areas of each projecting part were stopped out with lacquer. The object then became a single-use adhesion mandrel upon which metal was built up, and a textured surface developed in the electrodeposited areas. Photo: William Eng

16–12 HANNA BECHAR-PANETH, Israel. "Scales." Necklace with interlocking beads and other forms strung on a wire. Made with expendable, single-use wax mandrels, electroformed in sterling silver. Total length 17¾ in. Photo: Yacov Paneth

16–11 THOMAS GENTILLE, U.S.A. Copper electroformed pendant with tie-dyed cord. The top disc is 14K gold, electroformed into position. The small round and square copper units below and to its left and right are 24K gold foil covered with transparent enamel, and electroformed in place. The large central bronze disc is covered with a copper electroformed pattern whose preparation is described below. The bottom disc is ⅛ in thick copper, and contains a 24K gold foil base covered with a pattern of 24K gold cloison wire and transparent enamel, the unit electroformed in place. In preparation, the areas to be electroformed were covered with *masking tape* cut into shapes with a *razor blade*. Exposed areas were painted with ordinary nail lacquer as a resist. When this dried, the tapes were peeled off. After the copper electroform buildup, exposed metal was colored dark brown by repeated dips in dilute, warm liver of sulphur solution, and rinsed between dips. The surface was rubbed with wax in several applications. Photo: Bernard Vidal

electrodeposited form and is then deliberately eliminated or destroyed at an intermediary or final stage in the electroforming process. This means the mandrel must be made of a material that presents no problems in elimination. The remaining metal electroform is an independent metal object.

INTERNAL AND EXTERNAL SURFACE MANDRELS These are those in which either of these surfaces are of prime importance in the result. This implies the preparation of a mandrel in a way that is suited to these circumstances. Normally the jeweler using the electroforming method is

concerned with reproducing the *external* or *visible* surface of a dimensional mandrel, and therefore makes a positive mandrel which is reproduced by a *positive* electroform. When the *internal* surface is of prime importance, the mandrel is termed a *negative* mandrel. Though internal surfaces are not normally visible in jewelry, there are circumstances in which they require special attention. Examples are constructions that open to reveal the inside, such as a locket or boxlike object, or the inner surface of a bracelet where it contacts the wrist. There are cases in which an inner surface must be made to a certain size or tolerance that matches a fitting, finding, or another part of the work that it engages in a compound-unit construction.

MATERIALS USED FOR MANDRELS

Different materials are used for mandrels. The choice of material may depend on the unique nature of the substance which is important to the final appearance of the electroform. Points to be considered when selecting a mandrel material are: whether the mandrel is to be permanent or temporary; the degree of difficulty in its fabrication and surface preparation; whether it is electroconductive or inert (but can be made to accept metal deposition from the electrolyte); and the ease with which it can be retained in or eliminated from the electroform.

MATERIALS USED FOR PERMANENT, NONADHESION MANDRELS

Usually these are made of stainless steel which has a naturally passive surface that allows poor adhesion, permitting the electroform to be easily removed. In some cases, a thin film of graphite, which does not prevent electrodeposition, can be applied to a permanent mandrel as it acts as a parting agent to prevent permanent adhesion. Steel, copper, or brass mandrels plated with a flashing of nickel or chrome also allow separation of the electroform as the plating acts as a nonadhering surface.

Plastics can also be used to make permanent mandrels as long as surfaces are smooth and shapes are without undercuts. Epoxy resins used for casting, vinyl plastisols, rigid vinyl sheets (which can be heated to soften them, then pressed over flat or shaped textured surfaces to be reproduced), can be used.

MATERIALS USED FOR PERMANENT, SINGLE-USE ADHESION MANDRELS

Metals without a natural oxide film such as gold, silver, copper, and brass, whose surfaces are chemically clean and possibly also mechanically roughened or etched to encourage adhesion, can be used. Electrodeposited metal that builds up on these metals will adhere if proper cleaning preparations and procedures are carried out. If there is a doubt as to the ability of the electrodeposited metal to hold on the mandrel, one technique is to allow the deposited metal to build up in a way that *locks it* upon the base metal by forming an undercut around corners and edges, through holes, or in other ways.

Metal wire, tubing, or *sheet* in gauges that are normal for jewelry fabrication can be used as a mandrel or a part of one, as well as very thin foils, perforated metals, and screening. Cast metal objects can also be used, but surfaces must be mechanically roughened or etched as built-up metal adhesion is not as good as on fabricated metal surfaces. Special metal structures such as mokumé laminates or copper plate photoetchings can be introduced as a *metal inlay* and the buildup allowed to develop around their edges to hold them, but their faces must be protected by a resist to keep them intact.

Nonmetallic materials can be employed as single-use mandrels upon which metal is electrodeposited because high heat is not used in the electroforming process. Their use is one of the advantages of this process. Such substances, when visible in the result, can be permanently "set" or embedded in the electroform that is allowed to build up around their edges, across corners, or partially over surfaces in ways that hold them in place. Such objects have also been termed "grow-ons." Objects such as single stones or groups of stones, stone slabs, natural crystals, flat plastic laminates, three-dimensional cast or carved plastic units, lenses, prisms, glass, etc., can be used as possible inclusions. Soft stones such as pearls, cameos, opals, or turquoises will be affected by electroplating and electroforming solutions and should not be used. In some cases these materials can be completely coated with a resist that is later removed, and room temperature plating solutions can be used. To encourage the buildup of metal around their edges to hold them in the manner of a frame, bezel, or claw setting, these parts can be painted with an electroconductive lacquer. If in addition to these materials, the mandrel also contains wax, these materials must be of a nature that can withstand, without damage, a temperature of 212° F (100° C) needed to eliminate the wax. It is probably wise to bring up the heat gradually and reduce it gradually to avoid thermal shock to some materials such as stones.

Any material that has a desirable surface texture, that can be made to retain its shape, and that can be made electroconductive can be used. If this is a substance of no intrinsic decorative value in itself, or is nondurable, and provided it is light enough in weight, once it is completely covered with a metallic deposit, it can be *left* as an *internal core* inclusion. Leather, textiles, fibrous materials, paper, and cardboard can all be used in this way.

MATERIALS USED FOR EXPENDABLE, SINGLE-USE MANDRELS

These can be divided into *metallic* and *nonmetallic groups.* In either case, they are temporary, and it must be possible to eliminate them with ease. If their surfaces are porous, they must be presealed and made impervious by a sealant.

METALLIC EXPENDABLE SUBSTANCES USED FOR MANDRELS These include a *soluble metal alloy* or an *easily fusible, low-melting metal alloy* that can be melted out of the electroform by hot water or hot oil once a sufficient metallic buildup has been achieved that will allow the object to retain its shape after the alloy has been eliminated. (Such alloys are given under Tapered Tubing: Low-Melting Alloys Used for Cores, p. 281.) Their maximum melting points are about 280° F (137° C). To be more certain that all traces of these alloys are eliminated after melting, the mandrel made of such metals is coated with a thin parting film of graphite before the electroforming buildup starts. This prevents direct contact of buildup metal with mandrel metal, and minimizes the possibility that remaining traces will dissolve in acid electrolytes and attack the metal used for the electroform. These alloys can be reclaimed and reused.

NONMETALLIC EXPENDABLE SUBSTANCES USED FOR TEMPORARY, SINGLE-USE MANDRELS These materials can be fabricated in ways suited to the particular substance. Often they can be cast or machined, opening the possibility of creating mandrels whose forms are the distinct result of these processes. The surface of the result must be completely clean, free of cleaning compounds, sufficiently rinsed, dried, and covered with an electroconductive lacquer.

WAX This is the prime expendable mandrel material because it is supremely manipulatable, melts at low temperatures, is easily eliminated, and can be made electroconductive. The same dental waxes used in investment casting are suitable provided they do not include oil. (The many ways in which wax can be used to fabricate a mandrel have been discussed under Lost Wax Casting, Chapter 11.) Wax has one drawback and that is that some compositions will soften and possibly become misshapen when first submerged in a solution whose temperature is even only somewhat higher than room temperature. Therefore, only waxes that are known to have higher melting points should be used and the temperature of initial electroforming baths should be especially controlled until a sufficient metallic buildup has occured that rigidizes the mandrel and thus eliminates the softening hazard.

PLASTIC This is the second most common expendable mandrel material used, and it is also used as a permanent inclusion. Various synthetic resins in solid form such as acrylic or Perspex, PVC, and polyesters can be fabricated or machined in any suitable way. Liquid plastics such as epoxies can be cast and the casting used as a mandrel. Foamed plastics such as Styrofoam can also be carved to create an electroform with a distinctive surface texture. All of these will accept metallic silver electroconductive lacquer either painted or sprayed on. In cases where they are very light in weight, they may be permanently retained as a core. They can also be separated from the electroform

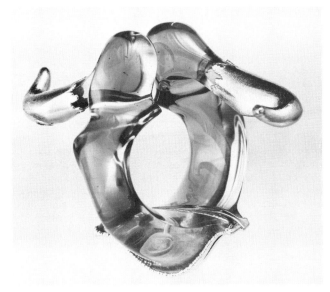

16–13 STANLEY LECHTZIN, U.S.A. Bracelet, electroformed silver gilt. The carved and polished amber polyester was used as a permanent inclusion mandrel. The two electroformed end forms lock over its conical sections. The bracelet opens halfway with a fabricated hinge held to the polyester by a grown-on electroform metal deposit. Photo: Stanley Lechtzin

16–15 CLAUDE LALANE, France. Belt using natural wisteria blossoms, electroformed as a single-use mandrel in copper, then electroplated with 18K gold. Photo: Courtesy Galerie Sven, Paris

mechanically by stripping them off, provided the electroform shape allows this. If they are destroyed by burning them out, take the precaution to do this under a fume hood where good ventilation is assured as *plastic fumes are toxic*. Lightweight or hollow plastic mandrels may be buoyant in the electrolyte, so it may be necessary to weight them with a nonconductive weight such as a piece of stainless steel or plastic-coated lead attached with a wire or a hook to keep them submerged.

CELLULOSIC MATERIALS Wood, paper, textiles like cotton, linen, or rayon can be used if stiffened and sealed with shellac to make them impermeable. Besides the possibility of burning these out, they can also be dissolved in a zinc chloride solution, Schweitzer's reagent (cupric oxide or hydroxide in ammonia), and other solvents.

PLASTER OF PARIS OR INVESTMENT PLASTER Completely dried plaster can also be used, but because its surface is porous, it must be completely sealed with liquid resins or acid-resistant varnishes to prevent it from absorbing fluids which would gradually bleed out over the surface during subsequent processes and affect the result. Plaster must be used in a way that allows it to be removed or dissolved later in dilute sulphuric or nitric acid solution, depending on the metal that is electrodeposited.

NATURAL OBJECT MANDRELS Any plant, leaf, or flower can be used if they will stand up to the process of being sprayed with an aerosal polyurethane lacquer to seal the

surface and to stiffen and strengthen them sufficiently to allow them to hold a second sprayed coating of silver electroconductive paint, or to be covered while wet with a flake silver powder whose surplus is tapped off when the lacquer dries.

FOUND OBJECT MANDRELS Objects of a suitable size and section thickness can be used as a basis for a mandrel. If the object is to be permanently incorporated within the body of the electroform, it must be sufficiently light in weight, and if to be burned out, of a material that will allow this.

COLLAGE MANDRELS Wax impressions taken from textured surfaces, natural, ready-made, or found object mandrels, perforated sheet, screening, or whatever substances will accept the sensitizing paint can be combined to make a collage mandrel.

THE INFLUENCE OF MANDREL CONFIGURATIONS ON METAL BUILDUP

Flat surfaces tend to get greater buildup at the periphery and edges, if the edges are squared.

Convex shapes are easily evenly plated. When edges are squared, buildup occurs at corners and angles; when edges are rounded plating is more even.

High peaks get greater buildup at the peak because projections of any kind are places of high current density, and deep depressions which are places of low current density get less buildup.

Sharply angled forms and edges get greater buildup at peaks and squared edges.

Flanges get greater buildup at end edges than at the inside angle, unless this angle is formed with a rounded radius.

Flat-bottomed grooves get greater buildup at upper peaks than at the groove bottom.

Deep V-shaped grooves get greater buildup at upper peaks than in the groove bottom.

Deep concave shapes get a buildup that decreases toward the deepest parts.

Rings and tubes get a more or less even buildup at their outer surfaces, and more at the edges if they are

16–14 J. FRED WOELL, U.S.A. "My Favorite Chair." Cast silver brooch made from paper relief matrices used by printers to make an electrotype. The paper was moistened slightly, then hot wax was poured on its surface. Upon cooling, but before total solidification, the wax was stripped off. Parts of images so made were assembled by softening them in warm water, then pushing the parts against each other to join them. This wax model was sprued and cast by centrifugal casting, but could also have been realized in metal by electroforming. Photo: J. Fred Woell

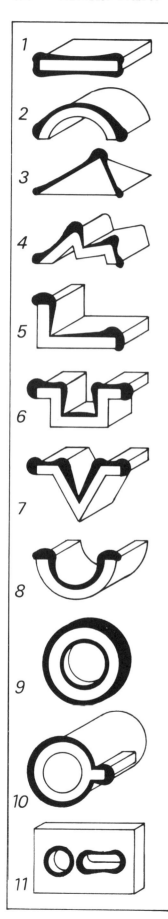

16–16 *HOW MANDREL CONFIGURATIONS INFLUENCE METAL BUILDUP*
 1. Flat surfaces.
 2. Convex shapes.
 3. High peaks.
 4. Sharply angled forms.
 5. Flanges.
 6. Flat-bottomed grooves.
 7. Deep V-shaped grooves.
 8. Deep concave shapes.
 9. Rings.
10. Tube with attached flange.
11. Holes and slots.

squared. Interior tube surfaces build up more slowly than exterior surfaces.

Holes and slots that are small, narrow, or closely spaced get greatest buildup at their squared-off edges, less if these are rounded.

To summarize, in general, complex shapes take longer to plate or electroform than simple shapes. Convex forms plate more easily than concave; round edges are covered more evenly than square edges; sharp inside corners get less buildup than high peaks and projections. These facts can be used in a positive or negative manner. What may be undesirable when the aim is an evenly plated coating may be desirable in free electroforming. In electroforming, for instance, the excessive buildup at peaks, ridges, and squared edges may act to define a form or create a textural effect that provides an element of interest in the appearance of the result.

PREPARING MANDRELS FOR ELECTROFORMING

The preparation of a mandrel's surface, whether it is of a permanent or temporary nature, has a definite effect on the character of the electrodeposited result. Many resulting qualities—degree of surface brightness, porosity, roughness, hardness, solderability, and blistering—are related to surface conditions prior to plating. Prebuffed, highly polished metal mandrels produce bright surface results, though brightness can also be increased in the result by adding brighteners to the solution. Roughness can result from faulty cleaning. Cast surfaces receive less satisfactory electrodeposits than wrought surfaces.

THE USE OF ARMATURES FOR STRUCTURAL SUPPORT

Making a viable mandrel structure in wax or plastic depends on how the substance is used to form the man-

16–17 STANLEY LECHTZIN, U.S.A. Brooch, electroformed silver gilt, embedding an agate slab sectioned through a geode. The electroformed deposit developed as a retaining bezel around the stone's edges and natural central openings where electroconductive lacquer had been painted. The fabricated wire armature serves a partially decorative function where it forms a spring-spiral, and then becomes a pinstem that engages a sculptural catch form. In use, the pinstem is concealed in the clothing. *Photo: Stanley Lechtzin*

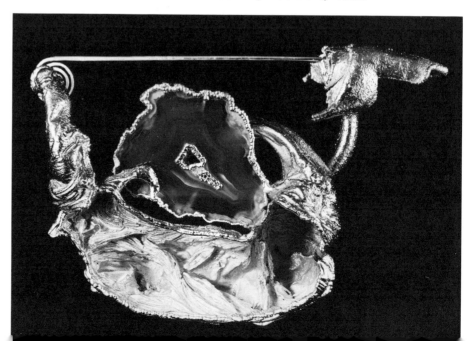

16–18 LEE BARNES PECK, U.S.A. Copper electroformed pendant. The lower section was first cast in silver. Other parts are based on found objects. The circular forms were cut and shaped from plastic drinking straws, wax coated and joined in rows. Wax wires, 18 gauge B.&S., were used to join the cast unit to the circles. The top units were added: a series of ladies' fake pearl hatpins (permanently embedded within the electroform). Units were embellished with perpendicularly joined lengths of 18 gauge B.&S. wax wires. The sterling unit was stopped out with resist lacquer. After the rest was made electroconductive with silver lacquer, the piece was electroformed in copper. The wax mandrels were eliminated, the work was gold plated, and the resist lacquer removed. *Photo: Neil Anderson*

drel. Keep in mind that the thickness of the deposit of metal on the wax or plastic mandrel, or on another mandrel material, should be roughly equal to that used in the fabrication of metal objects. Think ahead and try to imagine the result as it will be in metal and anticipate points of potential structural weakness that might need reinforcement in the mandrel. Though it is possible to fabricate reinforcing parts and solder them to existing multipart electroforms to hold them together, or to join electroformed units to fabricated units by any means used to join metal to metal, one of the advantages of the electroforming process is that the electroform alone can be a complete and finished work.

An *armature* or skeletal framework made of wire, tubing, or sheet metal can be incorporated into the mandrel for support when the shape of a form requires reinforcement, or when several forms made of wax must be joined. The armature can be completely concealed within the wax, or parts can be covered and others exposed and

treated in a decorative way to incorporate them into the design concept. Armatures can be adapted to other functions, as when a wire armature's ends are extended and used to make a pinstem and catch for a brooch. A work-hardened pinstem will retain its spring, and should be completely polished, and covered with a resist. A design can be conceived in which the entire metal portion is actually an armature made to hold a major, nonmetallic unit or units.

THE USE OF FINDINGS IN ELECTROFORMS

When findings are needed, handmade findings better suit the organic nature of the electroformed result. Premade fabricated pinstems, bails, hooks, rings, ear wires, hinge knuckles, clips, etc., can be incorporated into the mandrel material to become a permanent part of it by metallic deposits that build up around or over parts of them to hold them in place. They can also be soldered beforehand to a metal armature. Such an armature with attached findings can be incorporated into a wax mandrel with an *electric waxing tool* or by applying molten wax with a *brush*, with parts left exposed to allow them to be joined to the main body by metal growth. Findings can be attached to grease-free surfaces on plastic mandrels by an appropriate cement, and an electroconductive lacquer is then painted around their point of attachment to permit a metallic buildup continuous with the main metal form so that they will be held. All the *working surfaces* of any finding should be protected with a resist against metal buildup to keep them functional.

If half-drilled pearls are used, wire pegs meant to hold them after the mandrel is electroformed must be incorporated into the mandrel, coated with a resist to prevent metal growth upon them, but with their bases left sufficiently exposed to allow the pegs to be joined by metal deposition.

APPLYING METALLIZED ELECTROCONDUCTIVE SUBSTANCES TO MANDREL SUBSTRATES

The mandrel must be finished in every respect, and completely dirt-, dust-, and grease-free. Parts of any nonconductive mandrel meant to receive a metal deposit during electroforming can be made *electroconductive* by using a *brush* to cover them with a *water-impervious lacquer* or *shellac* containing suspended reduced *silver, copper metallic particles*, or *graphite*. When the entire surface of the object is to be made electroconductive, the metallic lacquer can also be sprayed on. The spray is directed at the mandrel from a distance that allows the application to dry almost instantly as it covers the object.

It is possible to prepare your own electroconductive lacquer by combining dry, grease-free silver or copper powder with a metallic lacquer, shellac, or synthetic resin. Prepare only what will be immediately used as the metal tends to cause the lacquer to jell. *Silver conductive paint*, is available and consists of an epoxy base with 60–80% silver powdered metal pigment, the percentage lower when it is used as a spray. If after its application to the mandrel the surface shines, this indicates that the percentage of lacquer to metal is too high and the lacquer has covered the metallic particles, or that the compound was not mixed well enough to put the metal particles in suspension. In such a case, the paint will not conduct electricity in the solution. One remedy is to depolish the surface by a dry ab-

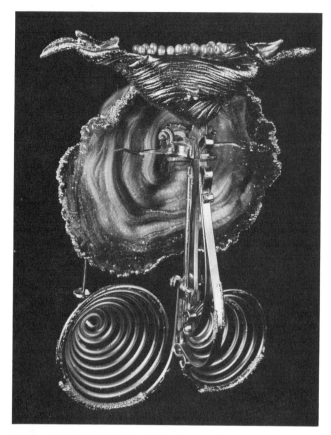

16–19 STANLEY LECHTZIN, U.S.A. Brooch, electroformed silver gilt with chalcedony rose and biwa pearls. The brooch combines fabricated and wax mandrel units. Spiral wire and flat strip units are partially textured by electroformed deposits. The chalcedony rose geode is edged and held by electroformed metal after electroconductive lacquer was painted on its edges. The upper unit was made using a wax mandrel. *Photo: Stanley Lechtzin*

rasive blasting, and another is to apply a new coat of lacquer containing the proper proportion of metal. The lacquer must be thoroughly dry before electroforming can begin.

RESISTS USED FOR SELECTIVE METAL DEPOSITION

Resists are substances applied to the surface of a mandrel to make the area they cover *nonconductive* to *prevent* the adhesion or buildup of metal at that particular place. They can be used to protect a metallic or nonmetallic inclusion in the mandrel, to form a sharp demarcation on visible surfaces between those that are plated or electroform deposited and those which are not, to create an area of contrast in metal color between the existing metal and the electrodeposited metal, and to protect the working surfaces of findings to keep them operative. Before any resist can be applied, the mandrel surface must be absolutely clean and dry or the resist will not adhere properly. Metal deposited on an unclean surface may lift off while the mandrel is in the electrolyte. Resists are often applied to the mandrel before the initial immersion in the electrolyte, but if necessary, they can also be applied at any intermediate stage to stop metallic buildup at some places on the object, and conversely, they can be removed at an intermediate stage to allow metallic buildup to take place.

Wax derived from petroleum is commonly used as a resist. It must not contain oil or other organic material that will dissolve into and contaminate the solution. The wax is heated in a container to a temperature approximately 50° F (10° C) above its melting point to keep it liquid while it is applied, and to allow better adhesion. Warmed metal parts will hold wax best, and it can be applied with a *soft brush,* or by dipping. After metal deposition, wax is removed by boiling the electroform in hot water. *High-temperature stop-off wax* that can be used in plating baths at temperatures up to 275° F (135° C), is available. The *exposed* portions of a wax mandrel will resist a deposit of metal in such places. It is possible, as is done in etching, to coat a metal surface with wax, then draw through the wax with a pointed stylus to expose a linear pattern that will accept metallic buildup at such places.

Stop-off lacquer of a viscous type is used when the bath temperatures will be too high to permit the use of wax. To be made visible, these lacquers are usually given a color, such as white or red, by mixing a dye or pigment into them, and those stopped-off portions can be watched during electroforming to be sure they stay intact. The lacquer used sometimes depends on the substance to which it must be applied. Vinyl lacquers are used on metal or plastic and dry in 10–15 minutes. From two to four coats are applied, each allowed to dry before the next one is applied. Thinners are available that reduce lacquer viscosity, or remove the lacquer later after use by either soaking, or rubbing with a thinner-impregnated cloth. Most lacquers can also be steamed off.

Varnishes such as copal can be used, provided they are of the drying type. Asphaltum varnish is generally *not* used, especially when the mandrel must be submerged in solutions containing cyanide.

Draftsman's or plater's tape, a pressure contact tape, can be used as a resist as it easily adheres to dry surfaces, will withstand immersion in solutions, and can be easily peeled off after use. It can be cut into any shape and placed on flat surfaces to form sharp divisions between plated or electroformed areas and plain areas. Rubber tape is also usable. When covering cylindrical parts, it is wound tightly and stretched, with each turn covering the former turn halfway. Rubber tubing can be used to stop off cylindrical parts which it fits, and the tube ends are sealed with wax.

THE ELECTROFORMING PROCESS

The mandrel must never be touched before the electroforming process is finished to avoid depositing fingerprints and grease on it which would hinder metal deposition at such places. Therefore, throughout the electroforming process, the mandrel is handled by an annealed wire and suspended from it in the electrolyte. The wire should preferably be of the same metal that is being used in the plating solution, or of copper. It is attached to the mandrel in the manner best suited to the material of which the mandrel is made. It can be welded or soldered to a metal mandrel; embedded in a wax mandrel by an *electric* or *manual spatula;* or attached to nonconductive materials in a way that allows contact with surfaces activated by metallic lacquer. For short immersions, the wire's other end is held in contact with the cathode bus bar, and for long immersions it is either hooked to or wrapped around it. When no bus bar arrangement exists,

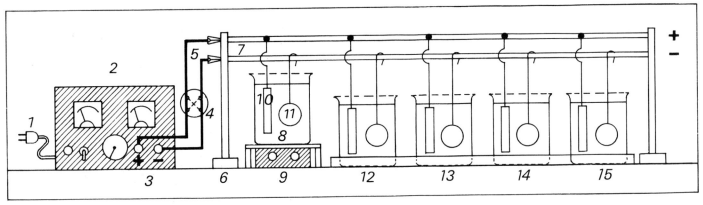

16-20 *SCHEMATIC REPRESENTATION OF A POSSIBLE ELECTROFORMING SETUP AT TABLE LEVEL*

1. The *electric line* with *plug* (AC current).
2. The *rectifier* that converts the AC current to DC current.
3. The *anodic* (positive) and the *cathodic* (negative) *terminals* on the rectifier.
4. The *periodic reversal current unit.*
5. The *lead lines* connected to the bus bars by *alligator clips.*
6. The *bus bar stand.*
7. The *anodic* (upper) and *cathodic* (lower) *bus bars.*
8. *Electrocleaning bath* in a *stainless steel tank.*
9. *Hot plate,* or *magnetic stirrer* and *stand* for solution container.
10. *Stainless steel anode* attached by a *copper wire* to the anodic bus bar.
11. The *object* being electroplated or electroformed attached by a *copper wire* to the cathodic bus bar.
12. *Acid copper strike bath* in a *glass beaker* with *copper anode.*
13. *Silver bath* in a *glass beaker* with *silver anode.*
14. *Bright nickel plating bath* in a *glass beaker* with a *nickel* or *stainless steel anode.*
15. *Gold plating bath* in a *glass beaker* with a *platinum-clad titanium anode.*

the anode wire goes directly to the anode contact and the cathode wire to the cathode contact on the rectifier. Anode and cathode wires must not be allowed to touch or the fuse will blow to interrupt the circuit, necessitating replacement of the renewable fuse.

THE COPPER STRIKE BATH

When a mandrel is to be electroplated in silver, it is first immersed in a copper bath to give it a copper plating. This bath can be acidic and contain copper sulphate and sulphuric acid, or alkaline and contain cuprous cyanide. A copper strike is applied to the mandrel as a first step because if it were placed directly into the silver cyanide bath, the metal in the metallic lacquered surfaces would immediately be attacked and would dissolve more rapidly than the rate at which metal could be deposited on it. The current is turned on before the object is immersed, and the attached copper wire must contact the cathode bar. After 15 minutes in the agitated copper sulphate solution, a thin layer of copper is deposited from the anode upon the mandrel-cathode wherever metal and metallized lacquer parts are exposed. Because copper has a great affinity for silver, the mandrel will readily receive a buildup of pure silver when placed in the silver bath that follows. The mandrel is removed from the electrolyte by its attached copper wire, and is rinsed in clear running water. It is then ready for immersion in the silver electroforming bath.

INTERMEDIARY MANDREL CHANGES Before placing the mandrel into the silver bath, it is possible to make minor changes in it. The layer of copper now present is very thin and can easily be cut through with a knife in order to open up some areas, spread others apart, to allow the entry and electrodeposit of silver in such places.

THE SILVER BATH: First immersion

Either acid or alkaline baths can be used to deposit silver. Alkaline baths contain complex cyanides and are more commonly used than acid baths. They are preferred because cyanide compounds have superior throwing power than acid bath constituents. *The dangers faced in the use of cyanide-containing solutions have already been discussed under* Electroplating on p. 686, *and proper precautions should be rigorously followed.*

Initial electroforming must be carried out at a very low current density of 1 amp/ft² until the deposit is thick enough to increase the current to the recommended level. If full current is applied initially, the metallic coating on the mandrel may be electrically burned up. Recommended bath temperature is about 90° F (32° C), and it is constantly filtered and agitated. If agitation is manual, use a *plastic* or *glass rod, not* a metal rod.

The *throwing power* of the plating solution depends on current density, anode and cathode efficiency, a greater ratio of anode to cathode surface, multiple anode placement, temperature control, and other factors. The prime objective is relative uniformity of thickness, even on irregular surfaces. As mentioned, additional buildup tends to occur on high spots and sharp edges which attract more metal during deposition than low places. Such irregularities can add to the attractive organic quality that is possible in this technique. A means of controlling thickness and avoiding rough textures on an electroform is by *periodic reversal* of the current. The *periodic reversal unit* is attached between the rectifier and the anode and cathode in the circuit. By the use of a switch, the current can be reversed on a preset cycle, alternately making the anode the cathode and vice versa. When the object becomes anodic it is partially deplated and its surface becomes smoother. The shorter the deplating time, the rougher and more nodular the surface texture will be. When a portion of an object reaches a desired condition, it can be removed from the bath, rinsed and dried, and that portion can be stopped off with a resist to prevent further change; then the object can be reimmersed, and the process continued.

ACHIEVING A RAPID PLATING RATE A faster rate of deposition of metal can be achieved by using a salt in the electrolyte, causing a high diffusion rate of ions; by increasing the metal concentration on the electrolyte; by raising the temperature of the electrolyte; and by increasing the agitation.

After the work has been in the electroforming bath for one or two hours, the silver deposit has accumulated to approximately one-third its final thickness. The metal is then rigid enough to withstand handling without the need for the supporting mandrel material, which can now be eliminated. The mandrel is removed from the electrolyte by the handling wire, and first rinsed in a still tank (where reclaimable precious metal can be gathered), then under running water.

EXPENDABLE MANDREL ELIMINATION

If the mandrel is of wax, small holes are drilled in the metal electroform at unobtrusive places to permit wax evacuation. The electroform is immersed in boiling water, and the wax melts out through the holes. Once the wax has been removed, it is possible to judge the approximate thickness of the metal deposit, which cannot be done while the wax is still in place. On the basis of how long it took to achieve the present deposit, an estimate can now be made of the remaining time needed to attain the desired metal thickness. Any wax film remaining on the work must be eliminated by electrocleaning the electroform in an alkaline solution, after which it is rinsed.

Non-wax mandrel substances such as paper, plastic, etc., if not too heavy, can be allowed to remain in the electroform. If they must be eliminated and are completely contained in the metal buildup, they can be burned out by first drilling holes, as before, and then applying a *torch*. The holes are necessary not only for residual ash removal, but because expanding gases develop during burnout, and if no holes exist, this gas could cause a closed, hollow electroform to explode. These materials could also be eliminated by placing the mandrel in a burnout oven heated to the appropriate temperature. Be sure this is done under conditions of good ventilation, especially important when a plastic mandrel is removed. The firescale formed on the metal is eliminated by an acid pickle bath followed by a *very careful and thorough rinsing and neutralizing* in an alkaline solution. There should be no remaining traces of acid on the object when a cyanide solution is used next.

Mandrels holding stones, a decorative plastic, or any other material that would be affected by heat during burnout must be made of wax as this is the only suitable waterproof, low-melting substance available.

THE SILVER BATH: Second immersion

The object is reimmersed by the attached wire in the silver electrolyte and the wire is reattached to the cathode bar. There it remains for from three to four additional hours until the object reaches a desired thickness of approximately 22 gauge B.&S. It is removed and rinsed.

COLLAGE ELECTROFORMS

It is possible to combine electroformed units that are made separately by using normal soldering techniques. Electrodeposited metal is relatively dense, and parts can be shaped to a degree, though this is not advisable as they tend to be brittle due to internal stress. Electroformed parts can be joined to fabricated parts by cold joining methods such as riveting.

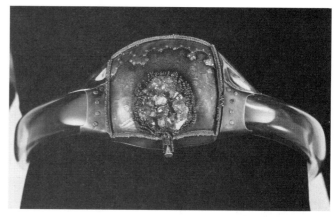

16–21 ELEANOR MOTY, U.S.A. "Dodge City Cowboy Band." Vinyl belt with brass and copper fabricated and electroformed buckle containing a copper photoetched plate riveted to the structure, with a garnet crystal electroformed in place. Behind the crystal the buckle encloses batteries that light up the stone by fiber optics, the on-off switch being the .22-caliber cartridge container at the bottom, center. The outer frame was given an electroformed texture, and the buckle assembly riveted to the vinyl belt. Size 6½ × 4 × 1½ in. *Photo: Frank J. Thomas, courtesy the Fine Arts Gallery, California State University, Los Angeles*

FINISHING THE FINAL SURFACE

When the object emerges from an electroforming bath without brighteners, its surface is normally matte, a dead white in the case of silver. Unless it is left that way, such a surface can be polished to a pleasant semibright finish by scratch brushing it with a *nickel alloy wire brush* using soapy water as a lubricant. This process will burnish accessible surfaces without removing any metal. Because only upper surfaces can be reached, however, the result may have a contrast of bright and matte surfaces between those that are raised and those recessed. When brighteners are used in the electrolyte, the entire surface, including depressions inaccessible to a polishing wheel, is left relatively bright.

ELECTROCHEMICAL POLISHING Electrochemical polishing combines the effects of pickling and bright dipping. It can be done to achieve an intermediate or final finish as when

16–22 JEM FREYALDENHOVEN, U.S.A. Brooch in copper, bronze, and acrylic. The main form created in wax sheet was electroformed in copper with acrylic inserts. The central bronze unit was fabricated and joined to the electroform. Height 8 in. *Photo: Case Crenshaw*

preparing a metal surface for plating; to brighten a plated surface; or to produce a final bright surface on a metal object, especially when mechanical polishing of inaccessible areas is not possible. The final finish is not mirror-bright as when mechanical polishing techniques are employed, but is acceptable as a final finish.

The work is made *anodic* and placed in a proprietary electropolishing solution. Its content promotes the formation of a passive, thin oxide film on the object which attacks peak areas more rapidly than valley areas, thus to some extent evening out microirregularities, and making the surface smoother, therefore brighter. High temperatures and current densities are used, and the instructions provided with the electropolishing solution should be followed.

GOLD PLATING AN ELECTROFORM

The object can of course be left in its original metal with a bright or oxidized finish. It can also be gold plated to prevent tarnishing. The cost of plating an object to have it appear gold is considerably less than if the entire electroforming process had been carried out in gold, which is also possible. Nickel plating normally precedes gold plating of a silver electroform. This is done to provide the gold plate with a hard undercoat, and to seal the base against porosity, future corrosion, and subsurface oxidation. A bright nickel plate is used to create a bright gold-plated result.

The gold plating process has already been described (see A Typical Cyanide Gold Plating Process Cycle in this chapter), and gold plating an electroformed object follows the same procedure as when gold plating any other metal object.

ACRYLIC AUTOCLAVE CASTING AND ELECTROFORMING A BROOCH

DEMONSTRATION 30

STANLEY LECHTZIN creatively uses two industrial processes

Photos: Daniella Kerner

The photo series seen here on the development of an acrylic and silver electroformed brooch can be divided into three main groups. In the first series, Photos 1–3, Stanley Lechtzin uses a photographic process to transfer an image from a copper plate to a rubber mold. In the second series, Photos 4–16, the acrylic autoclave curing cycle is demonstrated. In the third series, Photos 17–45, the electroforming and electroplating processes are shown. The result is a "photo cameo" in acrylic mounted in an electroformed gilded-silver decorative structure that also serves the purpose of an armature.

TRANSFERRING THE PHOTO IMAGE FROM NEGATIVE TO RUBBER MOLD

1   To transfer the coarse screen negative image to the polished, sensitized photoresist-covered copper plate, the *negative* is placed on an ultraviolet light source, the copper plate is placed upon the negative, and exposed to light.

2   The image is developed and fixed on the polished copper plate (whose edges and back are covered with *plater's tape* as a resist) by etching it in an iron chloride solution while the tank is over a *magnetic stirrer*.

3   The image will be transferred from the copper plate to a sheet of silicone rubber, and from there to an acrylic plastic sheet. A retaining mold is formed around the plate from four *L-sectioned aluminum strips* to which the plate is taped at the bottom, and whose outside corners are filled with Plasticine to make them leak-proof. The prepared silicone rubber mix is poured into the mold over the face of the copper plate, and allowed to cure. The cured rubber mold is stripped off the copper plate and placed face up within a second mold frame constructed in the same way as the one above.

THE ACRYLIC AUTOCLAVE CURING CYCLE: Transferring the image to acrylic

4   The acrylic slurry or dough must be prepared from two components: a *polymer* and a *monomer*. The finely granulated *Lucite acrylic resin* 4F-EMB methyl methacrylate polymer is weighed on a *triple-beam scale*. The ratios used can vary from 30 parts polymer/70 parts monomer, to 70 parts polymer/30 parts monomer. Lechtzin uses 68 parts polymer/32 parts monomer.

5   The dye used to color the acrylic mix (the same as is used for polyester) is poured into a *clean beaker* and weighed on an *electronic scale*.

6   The thin, water clear liquid H-112 methyl methacrylate *monomer* which has been filtered through a *hard paper filter,* is poured slowly into the beaker containing

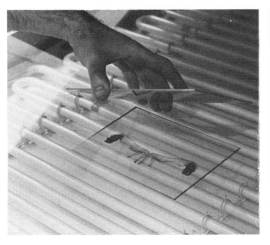

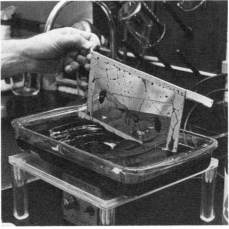

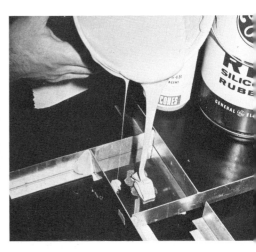

1   2   3

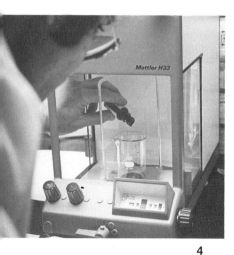

4

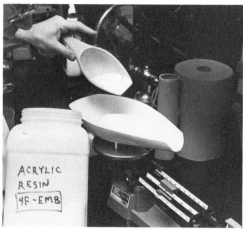

5

6

the dye, placed on a scale to control their recommended proportions. These two substances are mixed together. The *polymer* is then poured slowly into the monomer-plus-dye mix in a thin stream and stirred manually with a metal spatula to avoid lump formation. (Both polymer and monomer are products of E. I. du Pont de Nemours & Co., Wilmington, Delaware.) Mixing continues until the mix will not settle, and it forms a doughlike mass. This proportion of polymer-monomer mix takes about 10 minutes to become gummy and nonpourable, but this time will vary with mix composition, temperature, and degree of polymer fineness. (Mixes with smaller amounts of polymer take longer to prepare.) The mix is then covered and allowed to stand about 15 minutes at room temperature or lower until it becomes a semirigid dough. Any air bubbles within the mix will be forced out by the pressure within the autoclave, which will be used for casting.

7   The slurry mix is poured over the face-up negative silicone rubber photo image in the mold to reproduce it as a positive image in acrylic.

CASTING THE ACRYLIC IN THE
AUTOCLAVE

8   The purpose in using acrylic rather than a commonly used polyester plastic is that the result is harder, therefore more durable and resistant to surface abrasion and deformation, and clearer and more brilliant. The prepared mold is placed in the *autoclave* for acrylic polymerization or curing to take place. The autoclave is

a very strongly constructed, airtight vessel or chamber which can be filled with superheated steam or gas under pressure, and is capable of attaining a temperature above 212° F (100° C). (A *pressure cooker* is a type of autoclave.) To autoclave a material is to subject it to a heat-pressure process whose purpose, in this case, is to use positive pressure to eliminate air bubbles within the polymer/monomer resin mix casting, to hasten its curing time, and to achieve a hard acrylic result. The amount of pressure applied depends on the mix composition, the mold thickness, and the curing temperature used.

9   The autoclave lid is lowered into position, and bolts and holes engaged. Lechtzin is tightening the autoclave lid nuts to an initial torque of 22 foot-pounds, always alternating to opposite sides, then a final torque of 30 foot-pounds. Before bringing the autoclave up to pressure, the air is bled out for 4 minutes. Moderate pressure of 150–175 psi, and moderate temperature is then introduced to the chamber in the form of dry nitrogen gas (carbon dioxide could also be used). These gases are inert and therefore safe to use as they avoid a possibly explosive mixture. The starting temperature within the autoclave is about 70° F (21° C). The thermostat is set at 150° F (65° C), to which the internal temperature then rises. This temperature is maintained for about 12 hours (overnight) until polymerization is nearly completed. The thermostat temperature setting is then raised to 180–220° F (82–104° C) and held there for 8 hours for final cure and maximum hardness, then turned off. The time necessary

7

8

9

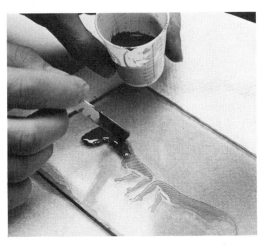

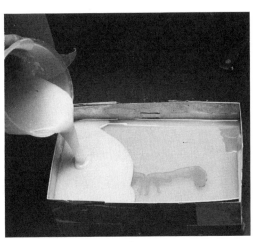

10   **11**   **12**

for full curing depends on the size of the mold and the temperature within the autoclave. (The dough could also be cured under the pressure of a *standard laboratory-sized hydraulic press.*) Doughs with a 2:1 polymer/monomer mix shrink about 7% when undergoing polymerization. The mix is strongly exothermic, giving off about 130 calories/gram. If a bubblefree result is to be achieved, it is necessary to keep the heat of the reaction at a temperature below the monomer's boiling point during polymerization. At the autoclave pressure of 160 psi used here, the monomer will not boil.

After a cure time of approximately 20 hours during which the mold cools down to room temperature once more, it is removed. The silicone rubber is stripped off, leaving a sheet of acrylic bearing a positive image from the rubber mold that matches the image on the original copper plate.

10   The cast acrylic image is then permanently pigmented by preparing a liquid mix of an opaque pigmented polyester, and spreading this over the image areas. Polyester and acrylic are compatible with each other in the subsequent casting. After the polyester has cured, the surplus is sanded down to level the color with the acrylic sheet so the color remains within the confines of the depressed image contour.

EMBEDDING THE IMAGES IN ACRYLIC

11   A new mold wall is constructed around the first sheet bearing the image, made about 2½ in (6.3 cm) high

to accommodate the approximately 2 in (5.1 cm) total thickness of the block to be formed next, which will incorporate the first cast acrylic sheet. A new monomer/polymer slurry is prepared, poured into this mold, and the assembly goes through a second cycle in the autoclave.

12   In this interval, a second image (the two heads) has been prepared in the same way and incorporated into the same block in a third cycle through the autoclave. The final block is approximately 2 in thick $\times$ 8 in $\times$ 10 in (5.1 cm $\times$ 20.3 cm $\times$ 25.4 cm), and contains two layers of embedded photo images after the third autoclave cycle. It is seen here after the removal of the mold walls. The block will then be shaped to form the "photo cameo" unit of the brooch.

13   After drawing the contour of the shape on the cast acrylic block with a *marking pen*, parts of the block were cut away with a *band saw*. The remaining form is being shaped here with a *high-speed air grinder*, and *carbide burs*. A *dust respirator* is worn to avoid dust inhalation.

14   The finished acrylic form is wet sanded with increasingly finer grit pieces of 80, 120, and 360 grit *waterproof abrasive paper* under running water.

15   Selected portions are *sandblasted* to produce a matte surface, while the rest is painted with hot wax for protection.

16   The clear portions are buffed to a final finish on a *polishing lathe* using a *high-count cotton wheel* and Learok 304 abrasive.

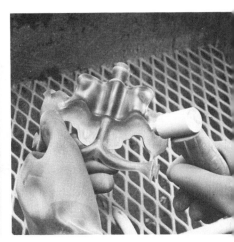

13   **14**   **15**

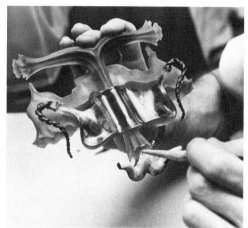
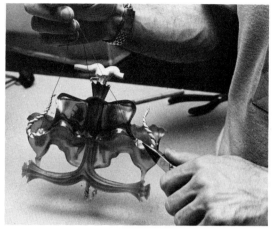

16   17   18

THE ELECTROFORMING CYCLE

ATTACHING WAX MANDREL UNITS IN PREPARATION FOR ELECTROFORMING

17 Wax mandrel units are added to parts of the finished acrylic unit in stages. Upon these the electroforming will take place. Acrylic alone, like all plastics, is nonconductive in the plating bath, therefore does not attract metallic buildup and needs no resist. Here the first four wax additions have been shaped and added: the three spirally twisted units at top and sides, and the lower, bifurcated unit (the form is being held upside down). The latter is being painted with an *electrically conductive silver lacquer*, applied with a *brush*.

18 After the wax parts have been lacquer coated, *copper contact wires* are attached to temporary silver wire hooks which act as contacts and are later cut off. These have been embedded into small holes drilled in the acrylic form. Current will pass through these wires to the parts being electroformed. In this photo, the work is seen from the back, but the placement of the image in relation to the acrylic form parts can be seen, the heads in the clear portion, and the figures below seen through matte-surfaced forms whose frontal surfaces are clear.

APPLYING A COPPER FLASHING TO THE MANDRELS

19 A preliminary copper flash plating is applied to the electroconductive lacquer-coated wax mandrel units. The object, hand held by the attached copper wires, is immersed in the bright acid copper bath, and the wires are placed in contact with the central cathode bus bar. Copper anodes can be seen at the right suspended by hooks from the anodic bus bar, and a similar series hangs from another bus bar (out of view at the lower left) so that the object is surrounded by copper anodes and receives an even coating. The mandrel remains in this bath for 15 minutes.

ATTACHING FINDINGS AND NEW WAX ELEMENTS

20 Two pinstem findings have been fabricated from wire for the brooch, hammered to a work-hardened springiness, their ends filed to points, and finished smooth. They are attached to the copper-flashed mandrel part by a soldered-on perpendicular end disc using a *quick-curing epoxy cement* in a twin dispenser that simultaneously supplies epoxy resin and catalyst.

21 After the epoxy has set, the pinstems are covered with *vinyl plater's tape* which acts as a resist on these parts while they are in the plating baths.

22 Silver electroconductive lacquer is applied to the pinstem joint area left exposed to prepare it for metal buildup.

23 A bright acid copper flash plating is applied to the newly added elements by immersing the work in the copper plating tank. Because the plastic is buoyant in plating solutions, a *plastic-coated lead weight* has been attached to

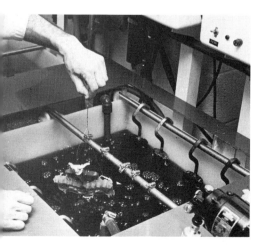
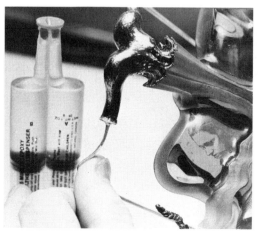
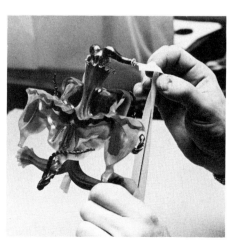

19   20   21

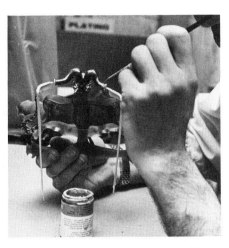

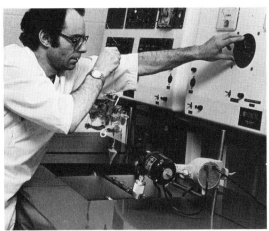

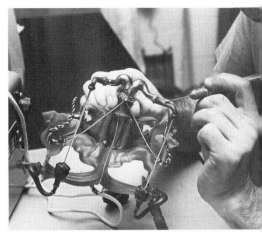

22   23   24

the bottom of the work to keep it submerged in the bath. Lechtzin is adjusting the *amperage* and *voltage* on the *rectifier* to 3 volts, 10 amps. (The motor seen below is a *stirrer* used when making up new baths.)

24 Additional wax forms, extensions from the first, are added to enclose the upper portion of the pair of pinstems. Wax forms that act as pinstem point sheaths have also been added below, attached to the bottom of the acrylic form, and wire hook contacts have been placed in holes drilled in the acrylic. The surface of these wax forms is refined with a *wax float file* and an *X-Acto knife blade*.

25 Silver conductive lacquer is applied to the new wax form additions, and all are copper plated.

26 Two additional tendril forms have been added to pegs projecting from the acrylic form, and then copper plated. Here a wax petal form is added to one of the tendrils. The reason that the tendril stems now are smooth instead of being spirally twisted as they have been up to this point, is that Lechtzin decided he did not like the twisted tendrils and changed them to others with smooth surfaces.

27 A round silver disc stamped with a trademark, the word *Sterling,* and the name Lechtzin, used as a signature plate and quality stamp on each of his works, is joined to the back of the form with quick-drying cement. Its surface is stopped off to prevent metallic buildup using a product called *Micro Peel,* manufactured by the Michigan Chrome and Chemical Co., Detroit, Michigan. The plate's edges

are left exposed to allow metallic buildup there to form what in effect is a bezel that will hold it in place.

28 After all new wax mandrel additions have been painted with an electroconductive silver lacquer called *Electrodag 416,* manufactured by Atcheson Colloids Co., Port Huron, Michigan, the work is given a final bright copper flash, then rinsed in water from which it is here being removed.

THE FIRST SILVER BATH

29 The assembly is immersed in the first silver plating bath containing a silver cyanide solution. It is allowed to remain there for 1 hour, then removed and rinsed in running water.

ELIMINATING THE EXPENDABLE MANDREL

30 Wax escape holes are made with a *drill* mounted in the handpiece of a *flex-shaft* into the partially electroformed elements. Through these holes the wax mandrels still inside will be drained.

31 The wax is boiled out of the electroforms. (Boiling temperature does not affect the acrylic.)

32 The work is initially cleaned with detergent cleaning solution in an *ultrasonic cleaner.*

33 It is then immersed in a 180° F (82° C) electrocleaning bath, here covered with floating plastic balls to prevent evaporation. Upon emergence, it is rinsed with running water. All surfaces are now chemically clean and again ready to receive a silver deposit.

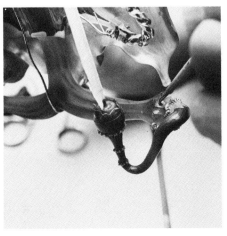

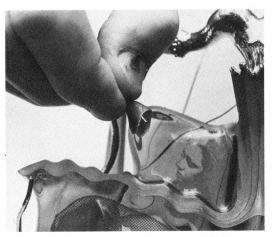

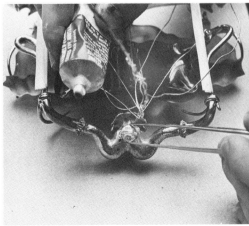

25   26   27

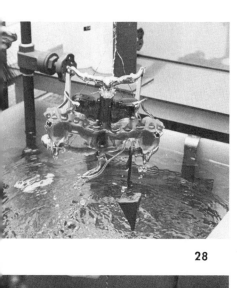

28

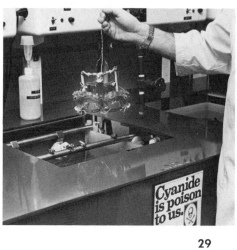

29

30

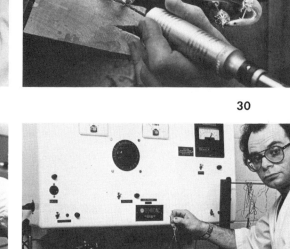

31

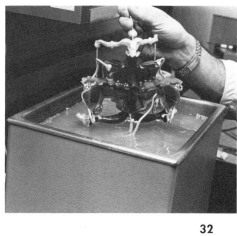

32

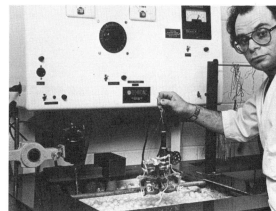

33

34

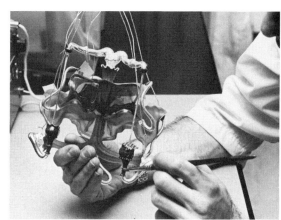

35

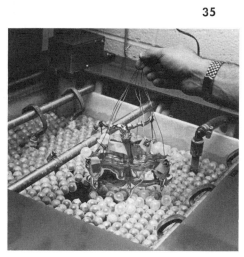

36

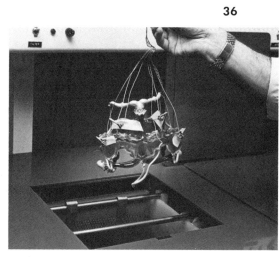

37

38

39

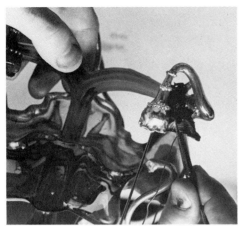

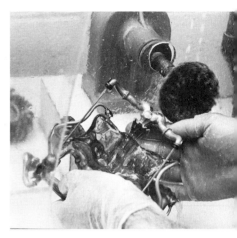

40   41   42

THE SECOND SILVER BATH

34 The amperage and voltage are adjusted on the rectifier to approximately 2 volts, 6 amps, in preparation for the second and final silver electroforming bath.

35 After immersion in the silver bath for approximately 3 hours, the work is removed. The deposit of silver has now reached a thickness of approximately 22 gauge B.&S. (0.0253 in, 0.6426 mm), and a nodular buildup has occurred around some peaks, ridges, and edges. An anode bag can be seen here in the upper left, placed around the soluble silver anode to contain impurities which the anodes release.

36 The Micro Peel resist is applied with a brush to selected areas which are to remain silver. Although Lechtzin is touching the surface with his fingers, this does not matter because the next step will be electrocleaning.

GOLD PLATING

37 The work is electrocleaned, rinsed thoroughly, and dipped into an acid solution to neutralize any alkalinity remaining from the cleaning bath. This also reactivates the surface to make it metal conductive. A typical gassing action is visible, the hydrogen bubbles rising to the surface.

38 After being rinsed again, the assembly is immersed in a bright nickel plating bath. This is done to seal the silver surface to reduce the possibility of future tarnishing due to the diffusion of silver into the gold plate, and to provide the gold plate with a hard base. The work is removed after 10 minutes. The small pieces of tape seen attached to the work are there to protect the acrylic from the stop-off resist.

39 The work is immersed in the agitated gold plating bath for 45 minutes. Upon removal, all exposed metal parts are covered with a dull surface of a heavy electrodeposit of pure gold. The inert platinum-clad titanium expanded metal anode can be seen hanging by hooks from the anode bus bar.

40 The resist is peeled off the petal-shaped pinstem point sheaths to expose their surfaces which are still silver.

41 These silver portions are immersed in a liver of sulphur solution which oxidizes them black. The pinstem point guard on the right has been colored after dipping, and the one on the right is still silver.

42 After rinsing, the brooch is scratch brushed with a nickel wire wheel with soapy water as a lubricant to burnish the gold deposit and create lustrous highlights.

43 A detail of the finished electroformed portion of the brooch holding the trademark-quality-signature disc. The electroformed deposit built up around its edge functions like a bezel to hold it in place.

44 The finished brooch is placed into an *air-circulating oven* heated to 175° F (79° C) where it remains for 10 hours to *thoroughly anneal* the acrylic casting. This is done to avoid the chance of cracking or crazing developing in the acrylic as it ages. At the end of this annealing period, the temperature is reduced to room temperature *slowly* to avoid the introduction of new stresses.

45 The finished "Photo Cameo Brooch No. 56D," with cast brown and green acrylic, and green and red photo-etched images, electroformed silver gilt. Size 6½ in × 6½ in × 3 in, 1975.

Photo: Stanley Lechtzin

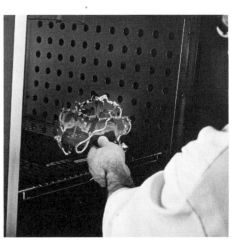

43   44

PHOTOELECTROFORMING

Using light to impart an image to metal and to create form

Photoelectroforming is based on the concept of employing photographic processes for the surface treatment of metals. The technique was developed for industrial usage, but can be creatively exploited in jewelry making and metal decoration. The process can only be described here briefly, and for greater detail, data booklets and pamphlets are available from Department 454, Eastman Kodak Company, Rochester, New York 14650, U.S.A., the company that developed the light-sensitized resists mentioned here.

THE PHOTOELECTROFORMING PROCESS SEQUENCE

The steps in the process can be summarized as follows, and are then described below.

1 An original master design is prepared on paper in *black and white* only as this process is best suited to high-contrast images. Transparencies of any subject can be used provided they are of the high-contrast type. A halftone image can be created to reproduce continuous tone images by the use of a 60-line or coarser screen transparency sheet placed between the image and the photosensitized mandrel. (See Halftone Photoetching on Metal, Chapter 8.)

2 *The high-contrast transparency* of the artwork is made with a *camera* on film or on a photosensitized glass sheet, and in effect acts as a stencil. The transparency must be the *exact size* of the image to be reproduced because it will be used as a *contact transparency*. Other types of *nonphotographic stencils* can also be improvised using any suitable opaque materials that can be placed in *flat contact* with the mandrel plate.

3 The flat sheet metal mandrel surface is coated with a photoresist and dried.

4 The stencil image placed in close contact with the photoresist-coated mandrel surface is then exposed to ultraviolet radiation.

5 The exposed image is chemically processed to fix it on the mandrel and form a *mandrel stencil* which adheres firmly to its flat surface.

6 Plating, electroforming, or etching then follow.

The acids and chemicals used are corrosive and toxic,

therefore wear *rubber* or *disposable plastic gloves,* and work under conditions of good ventilation.

PREPARING THE MANDREL SURFACE TO RECEIVE THE PHOTORESIST

The mandrel can be any flat metal sheet of platinum, gold alloy, silver alloy, copper or copper alloy, nickel or nickel alloy, stainless steel or other metals, or a base metal plated with one of these. Its surface should be smooth and free of haphazard scratches, and it should not be unidirectionally scratched as when finished on a belt sander. The mandrel must be made *chemically clean* to assure the adhesion of the photoresist. Cleaning procedures are done just before the resist is applied to be sure the metal surface does not develop any oxidation film. Any of the cleaning methods already described, or a combination of them can be used, including mechanical cleaning, solvent cleaning, detergent cleaning, dilute acid cleaning, electrosonic cleaning, or electrocleaning. All cleaning procedures are followed by a *thorough rinsing* to free the surface of any traces of cleaning chemicals. The surface is dried and coated with the resist immediately afterward.

Gold: Clean chemically with a detergent. Rinse under running water, heat dry.

Silver: Clean with a fine pumice paste and make certain all pumice residue is removed by using a clean brush on the surface during the rinsing, or dip the mandrel into a weak solution of nitric acid to give the surface a slight etch. Rinse under running water, and dry in room temperature to avoid the development of an oxide film.

Copper and its alloys: Immerse into a weak solution of ferric chloride for 10–15 seconds, then dip it immediately into a 10% by volume solution of hydrochloric acid. Rinse well under running water and dry at room temperature to avoid reoxidizing the surface.

Nickel and nickel alloys: Clean with a fine pumice slurry and rinse under running water. Immerse for 3 minutes in a solution of 1 volume of concentrated phosphoric acid to 3 volumes of water, at 170° F (75° C). Rinse in running water, and heat dry with an air blower.

Stainless steel: Clean with pumice, and rinse in water. Immerse in a 20% nitric acid solution at 150–160° F (66–71° C) for 15–20 minutes. Rinse under running water, and heat dry with an air blower.

THE KODAK PHOTOSENSITIVE RESISTS

The following Kodak resists are recommended for use with particular metals. They are available in quart containers or larger. Other manufacturers also make resists used for these purposes.

Gold: KTFR, KMER
Silver: KTFR, KMER
Copper and copper alloys: KPR, KPR2, KPR3, KPR4, KOR
Nickel and nickel alloys: KMER, KTFR, KPR2, KPR3, KPR4, KOR
Stainless steel: KTFR, KMER

The resist consists of a light-sensitized photopolymer resin in an organic solvent solution. When exposed to ultraviolet radiation, the resin polymerizes and sets, becomes adhesive to the base metal sheet to which it is applied and hardens enough to withstand immersion in the usual etching and electroplating solutions. Resists are capable of reproducing exact detail without any dimensional change.

Resists are available that are either *positive-working* or *negative-working.* When a *negative-*working resist is used, the areas *exposed* to light are polymerized and made insoluble while those areas that receive no light are soluble and are dissolved by a developer that exposes them to its chemical action. When a *positive-*working resist is used, the *unexposed* areas remain on the mandrel surface after development. This concept can be used to create either a positive or a negative image. Different kinds of films are used for positive- or negative-acting resists.

Resists contain no dangerous chemicals, but skin contact can irritate some people. Therefore, wear *rubber* or *plastic gloves* while handling them. Should any resist contact the skin, immediately wash the area in running water. Some resists are inflammable and must not be used near any heat or spark source. Resists must be used under conditions of good ventilation to eliminate toxic vapors of the solvents that are used in conjunction with them.

THINNERS

Particular thinners are manufactured for use with particular resists. Some resists are low in viscosity and form thin coats, others are highly viscous and form heavy coats. Thinners are used to decrease the viscosity of a resist; to thin one from which the solvent has evaporated and made thick; or to prepare a resist to a consistency suitable for spraying. After adding and thoroughly mixing a thinner with a resist, give the air bubbles that form time to rise and break. Thinners should be stored in their original containers which must be kept tightly closed to avoid the evaporation of their solvent content.

METHODS OF PHOTORESIST APPLICATION

Because all resists are light sensitive, they must be handled and applied under darkroom *safelight* conditions in all processes until image development is completed. The recommended safelight is a *red fluorescent tube.* There should be no ultraviolet radiation present from natural light as this can cause fogging of the resist which renders it useless.

Before applying the resist to the prepared and clean metal mandrel surface, allow the mandrel to return to room temperature. Depending on the method of application used, either only the working surface, or all surfaces of the mandrel will be coated with resist. In cases where only one surface is coated, before the mandrel is subjected

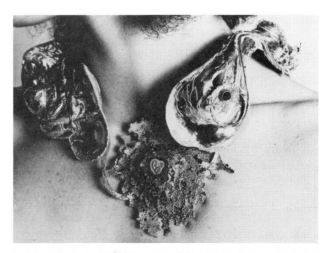

16–23 MONA R. BERMAN, U.S.A. "Cloud." Neckpiece fabricated from sterling silver. The central nonadhesive, stripped-from-mandrel photoelectroform is ornamented with a central stalactite slab. The side repoussé-worked sterling silver units with photoetched surfaces are set with amethysts, and parts are forged. *Photo: Gerald Wenner*

to electroplating, electroforming, or etching, the unprotected parts must also be coated with another resist such as *stop-out lacquer* or *plater's tape.*

The thickness of the resist layer should be only the amount needed for the process that follows. Processes involving short immersions need only thin resists, long immersions thick resists, and deep etching requires a heavy resist coating. In cases where a resist is hung vertically to dry and tends to "wedge" or form a coat that tapers from thin at the top to thick at the bottom, after the first coat dries the mandrel can be given a second coating and hung to dry in a position in reverse of the first to compensate for uneven thickness.

Depending on the method of application, the resist can be poured from its container onto the mandrel placed horizontally in a *glass tray;* or the resist can be contained in a vertical, narrow, *deep stainless steel tank* into which the sheet is dipped.

Dip coating is the simplest method of applying the resist. The mandrel is held at one corner by a *stainless steel clamp* or *self-locking tweezers,* or by a *wire* that is hooked through a hole drilled in the waste portion of the mandrel, immersed in the resist placed in this case in a deep tank, then withdrawn and held above the tank to allow drainage. Inspect the surface to see that it is bubble-free, and hang the mandrel in a dark, dust-free place until it hardens. Drying can be hastened by baking, described below. As both surfaces are coated in this case, the *back* of a negative working resist-coated mandrel should also be exposed to light when the time comes for development.

Flow coating consists of pouring a pool of undiluted or diluted resist on the horizontally placed plate which is then tilted in various directions to allow the resist to spread over its entire surface. The plate is then placed on a *raised support* such as two dowel sticks in a horizontal position; propped up at an angle; or hung vertically and allowed to dry at room temperature.

Whirl coating is done by placing the mandrel in a horizontal position in the center of a *turntable,* pouring the resist in a pool at the center, then revolving the turntable to cause the centrifugal action to force spread the resist evenly over the mandrel surface. An old 78 rpm *phonograph turntable* can be used as a substitute, or a *potter's banding wheel.*

Spray coating is done using a resist diluted to recommended consistencies with appropriate thinners applied with 20 psi *compressed air* and a *spray gun* held 12–14 in (30.5–35.6 cm) from the mandrel surface, in a well-ventilated *spray booth.*

PREBAKING THE PHOTORESIST ON THE MANDREL

The photoresist must be *completely dry* or it will not respond well to the light exposure. To hasten drying, first it is air dried at room temperature for about 10 minutes until the surface is no longer tacky. To assure complete drying and the removal of residual solvents which can be the cause of unsuccessful image development, the resist is then prebaked. Thin coatings may not require prebaking but it is recommended for heavy coatings. Baking takes place in an *oven* equipped with an intake and outlet exhaust for the elimination of solvent vapors. Be sure these vents are open and working when the oven is used. The mandrel is hung by a *hook* in the oven for 10–20 minutes at a temperature of from 176–250° F (80–121° C) following manufacturers recommended times for particular resists. The lowest temperatures are used for copper. A general rule is to bake at the lowest possible temperature for the shortest possible time that assures complete drying, because prolonged heating progressively hardens the resist resin and thus lengthens exposure time. If for any reason the prepared mandrel is to be used the following day, it must be stored in a *lightproof container.*

PREPARING THE STENCIL OR TRANSPARENCY IMAGE

If a photo transparency is used for design transfer, the original design is reproduced with a high-contrast orthochromatic reproduction film such as Kodaline Reproduction Film 2566 (Estar base) or 4566 (Estar thick base). The film transparency (or any prepared stencil) must be *exact size* as that wanted in the reproduction.

A stencil can be made by cutting an image out of a thin, stiff opaque paper or acetate film, or a design could be drawn on acetate film with a felt-tipped marking pen. This is placed on the resist-covered mandrel plate, and a thin, clean sheet of glass put over it to keep it flat. Another possible stencil could be made from a piece of glass covered with an adherent black opaque paint, or by using a sheet of uniformly exposed and developed film which becomes a solid black. These are then scratched through with various tools to create an image.

EXPOSING THE PHOTORESIST TO ULTRAVIOLET RADIATION

As mentioned, photoresists are sensitive to ultraviolet light, or so-called black light, the radiant energy of ultraviolet rays. The rays of this light are outside of the visible

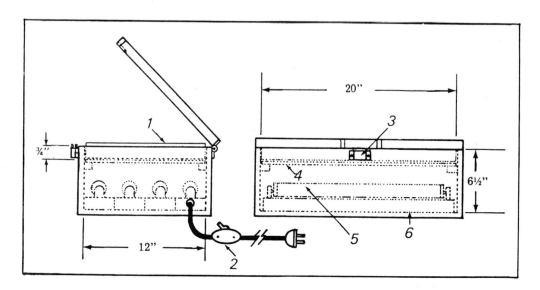

16–24 *LIGHT BOX FOR EXPOSING THE PHOTORESIST*
1. Foam plastic sheet, 1 in thick.
2. Off-on line switch.
3. Magnetic catch to hold box lid closed. A latch or hook could be used instead.
4. Plate glass, ¼ in thick.
5. 18 in, 15 watt F 15T8-BL fluorescent unfiltered black light.
6. One of four fluorescent 18 in light fixtures.
This and the following drawing from Photography in the Crafts edited by J. Fred Woell, courtesy J. Fred Woell and Eleanor Moty

spectrum, but are evident by their photographic action, and are harmful to the eyes. Therefore, ultraviolet radiation exposure of the photoresist takes place in a *light box* under darkroom conditions.

AN IMPROVISED LIGHT BOX   A *light box* can be improvised if one is not available. Eleanor Moty suggests one fabricated from wood. Its interior dimensions would be 20 in long, 12 in wide, 7 in deep (50.8 cm × 30.5 cm × 17.8 cm). The hinged lid lifts from the long side, and is held closed by a contact magnet. At the bottom, installed in parallel series are four 18 in (45.7 cm) long fluorescent bulb light fixtures that each hold a black light, 15 watt, F 15T8-BL unfiltered fluorescent tube. An inner molding ledge 1½–3 in (3.8–7.6 cm) above the light tubes, and ¾ in (1.9 cm) from the upper box edge supports a ¼ in (0.635 cm) thick plate glass the size of the box interior. Near where the electric line emerges outside the box, an on-off switch is placed.

In industry, exposure is made in a *glass-topped vacuum frame* which excludes oxygen from the surface of the resist as some are oxygen sensitive, and assures close contact between the transparency negative and the mandrel resist stencil surface.

Working away from the light source, the image is placed emulsion side up in the center of the plate glass in the light box, and the photoresist-covered mandrel is placed over it with the resist contacting the transparency. A 1 in (2.5 cm) thick piece of foam rubber the size of the interior dimensions is placed over these, and the light box lid is closed, pressing the foam sheet down against them, assuring contact.

The *exposure time* depends on several variables such as the thickness of the resist, its degree of solvent retention, the nature of the original metal mandrel surface (dull surfaces prolong exposure time), the strength of the light source, and the distance of the light source from the resist. With all these variables in operation, the necessary exposure time will have to be determined empirically by making a *test plate* employing the same metal and resist. As is done in ordinary photography, using a *masking cardboard* and a *timer,* make exposures on the test plate every 15 seconds, then develop the plate to see which exposure best suits the particular set of conditions. Once the information has been acquired from such a test it can be used for the same setup in the future.

During exposure, use a *photo timer* which will turn itself off after a preset time interval, or an ordinary timing device turned off manually. At this time, if a negative-working photoresist has been applied to the mandrel by dipping, also expose the back of the mandrel to ultraviolet radiation so the resist will also develop there.

DEVELOPING THE EXPOSED PHOTORESIST COATING ON THE MANDREL

The exposed resist is developed in the *darkroom* under a *safelight,* or in a subdued incandescent light to which the resist is not sensitive. Temperature and washing must be carefully controlled. The developer is poured into a *glass tray* to about a ½ in (1.3 cm) depth, and the mandrel is immersed slowly without splashing. Particular developers are used for specific resists, each formulated with its own solvent. Development takes place in less than 3 minutes, during which time the tray is gently agitated, and the soluble parts of the resist dissolve.

The manufacturer suggests that development be done in *two trays* or *tanks,* each containing the same developer. The total developing time is divided between them, starting in the first and finishing in the second. The reason for this procedure is that the first tray may become exhausted from dissolved resist before development is completed, which may cause the resist to be redeposited on the mandrel. The mandrel is removed and *spray rinsed* with cold water. Used resist is *discarded.*

The developing time should not be longer than needed to remove the soluble resist parts or excessive swelling and puckering may take place in the insoluble parts. Swelling can also be an indication that the original metal surface was not clean, the film may be too thick, the resist was insufficiently prebaked, or the exposure was not long enough. Should the soluble image parts not be dissolved during this time, some incorrect procedure has been followed.

POST DEVELOPMENT BAKING OF THE RESIST

To remove any solvent remaining from the developing process, and to increase the durability of the resist coating, a postbaking operation of 10 minutes at 250° F (121° C) is recommended. Baking at this time also increases resist adhesion, important especially when strong etchants will be used. The result is a resist that forms a hard, tough, nonconductive stencil on the metal sheet, highly resistant to all common electroplating, electroforming, etching and electroetching solutions, while the metal's exposed areas will accept metallic buildup or allow controlled removal.

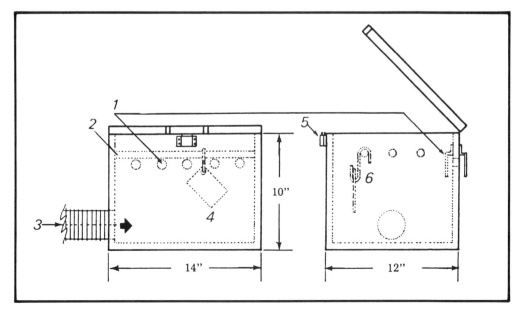

16–25 *DRYING BOX TO DRY EXPOSED AND PROCESSED PHOTORESIST*
1. *Vents with light baffle for vapor escape.*
2. *Dowel rod for hanging exposed and processed metal plate to dry.*
3. *Hot air blower, from a hair dryer or other source.*
4. *Plate with hole hanging by a hook to dry.*
5. *Magnetic catch to hold the box lid closed. A latch or hook catch could be used instead.*
6. *Wire hook over dowel to hold plate.*
A *lightproof black cloth,* not shown, could be used with both these boxes to cover them in case they are not completely lightproof when the lights are on.

ELECTROPLATING USING THE PHOTORESIST STENCIL

The mandrel must be chemically clean. To remove any possible remaining films in the open patterned areas, it is dipped into a weak etchant, and rinsed. It can then be electroplated with the same metal as the base sheet, or with a metal whose color contrasts with the base metal. The work is attached to a *copper wire* and is made cathodic by attaching it to the cathode bar while it is immersed in the electroplating solution. Plating procedures have already been described.

Resist manufacturers recommend that photoresists be used with plating baths having a neutral (pH 7) or acidic (below pH 7) content. Baths containing cyanide are dangerous, and besides are alkaline and should be avoided because of the violent formation of hydrogen gas bubbles that takes place on the exposed metal areas which results in a violent scrubbing action that can act to remove the resist. Compatible plating bath solutions include acid copper baths, neutral or near-acid gold plate baths, acid-type rhodium baths, nickel sulphamate and nickel fluoborate baths.

Because plated metals are very thin, plated mandrel results will have to be mounted in a jewel by methods that do not require heat which would destroy the image. They can be set in a bezel, or riveted in place.

PHOTOELECTROFORMING:
Stripped or adhesive electroforms

Either of two directions can be followed: the creation of *stripped electroforms* or *adhesion electroforms*. In the case of stripped electroforms, the aim is to build up an electroformed image on a mandrel, from which it is then stripped off. Adhesion electroforms are built up on the mandrel by establishing conditions that make them permanently a part of it.

STRIPPED ELECTROFORMS

Stripped electroforms require the use of an image whose parts are *connected* so that when subsequently stripped off the mandrel, they come off as a unit. The simplest way of assuring that the image can be stripped off after electroforming is to use a base metal mandrel that is *inherently passive*, such as stainless steel, nickel alloys with low thermal-expansion percentages such as Invar (Ni 36 - Fe 63 - others 1) or Kovar (Ni 28 - Fe 54 - Co 18), and chromium, or a metal plated with nickel or chromium. While all these allow a metal deposit to be built up on their surfaces, the buildup is not adherent. Such mandrels

are called permanent because they can be repeatedly reused as long as their resist stencils remain intact. Care must be taken when they are stripped not to damage the stencil.

To be sure a mandrel surface is *equally passive*, before metallic buildup takes place, stainless steel and chromium surfaces are passivated in a nitric acid bath, and nickel alloys are immersed for 30–60 seconds in a solution containing ½ oz sodium dichromate dissolved in 1 gal water, then rinsed.

Electroplating deposits should be free of tensile stress or the deposit may prematurely self-strip and curl off the mandrel. For copper deposits, copper sulphate or copper fluoborate baths are recommended for low-stress deposits. For nickel deposits, nickel sulphamate solutions are recommended.

Before metal buildup commences, if there is any reason to doubt the cleanliness of the areas to be plated, the surface can be tested for water break. If breaks occur, clean the mandrel with a mild alkaline cleaner, and repassivate the surface. The current distribution should be even, and the anodes (if more than one is used) should be distributed equidistantly, not more than 2 in (5.1 cm) from the mandrel. Plating continues to the desired thickness.

If the mandrel surface has been properly passivated, the electroform will strip off easily. Stripping is done by inserting a sharp edge such as a *razor blade* under the deposit, and lifting it slowly upward, gripped between the thumb and the blade. Another way is to flex the mandrel and allow it to return to its original shape, a method that works if the mandrel will flex without permanent deformation. Separation must be carried out carefully, especially when the intention is to reuse the mandrel stencil, as its edges can be damaged by rough stripping.

POSTELECTROFORMING TREATMENTS OF A STRIPPED ELECTROFORM An electroform can be allowed to start and develop to less than the final desired thickness, but developed sufficiently to allow it to be stripped. Once removed, electroforming can be allowed to continue on all the surfaces of the independent electroform to a total thickness that makes it rigid. Thin stripped electroforms can be somewhat shaped three dimensionally using fingers and tools, depending on the structure of the image. Because they tend to be brittle, shaping must be done carefully. Parts can be cut away to bring the rest to a curvature. An image can be pressed over a shaped metal base to take on its convex or concave form, and then be soldered or electroformed to this base which can be of the same or a contrasting metal.

A shaped image can be applied to a dimensional mandrel made of sticky wax to which it will adhere. Several images, or repeats of a single image can be combined into one larger image to form a unit by first cementing them together with epoxy, then painting the joins with an electroconductive lacquer, and continuing the electroforming process to unite them. An electroform can be all of one metal, or started in one and finished in a second metal, as for instance a copper electroform finished in silver or gold. The photoelectroformed result can be an independent object or incorporated as an element in a fabricated jewel that includes other structures and stones. These are only some of the directions that suggest themselves; others can be explored.

16-26 MONA R. BERMAN, U.S.A. "Waterform Ring II." Made of photoelectroformed matrix-stripped units shaped three dimensionally, with freshwater and baroque pearls. *Photo: Gerald Wenner*

Plate 21–1 BULGARI, Rome, Italy, fabricator. Brooch in gold with black enamel, rubies, diamonds, and sapphire. *Photo: Courtesy Bulgari, Rome*

Plate 21–2 GLENDA ARENTZEN, U.S.A. Cast and fabricated brooch in colored golds (14k, 18k, 24k), with naturally colored diamonds (yellow, brown, green, lavender, and white). *Photo Glenda Arentzen*

21–1

21–2

22–1

Plate 23–1 STANLEY LECHTZIN, U.S.A. "Photo Cameo Brooch No. 56D." Silver gilt, electroformed, with cast and carved acrylic, and photoetched images pigmented in red and green. *Photo: Stanley Lechtzin*

Plate 23–2 EDWARD DE LARGE, England. Pendant/necklace fabricated of silver and colored titanium. *Photo: Francis Warwick*

Plate 23–3 JAMES B. WARD, England. "Scottish Camel." Brooch fabricated in colored titanium. *Photo: James B. Ward*

Plate 22–1 CHARLOTTE DE SYLLAS, England. Earrings fabricated of mercury-gilded silver, with carved coral flowers. *Photo: Courtesy Crafts Council, London*

Plate 22–2 LEE BARNES PECK, U.S.A. "Bird Pendant." Cast and fabricated in sterling silver, plated in 24k gold and copper, with agate. *Photo: Lee Barnes Peck*

22–2

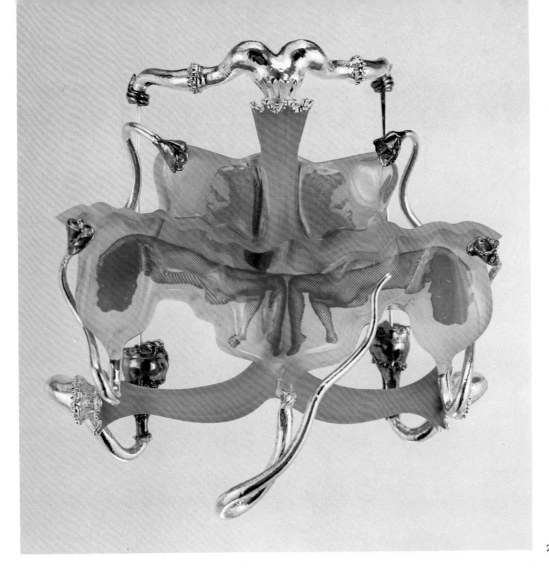

23-1

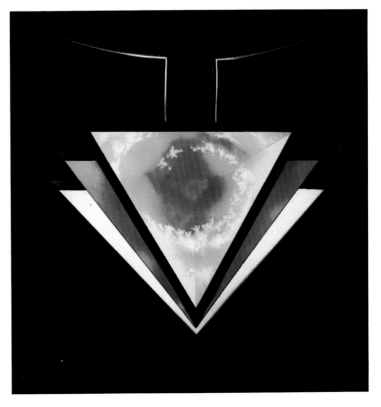

23-3

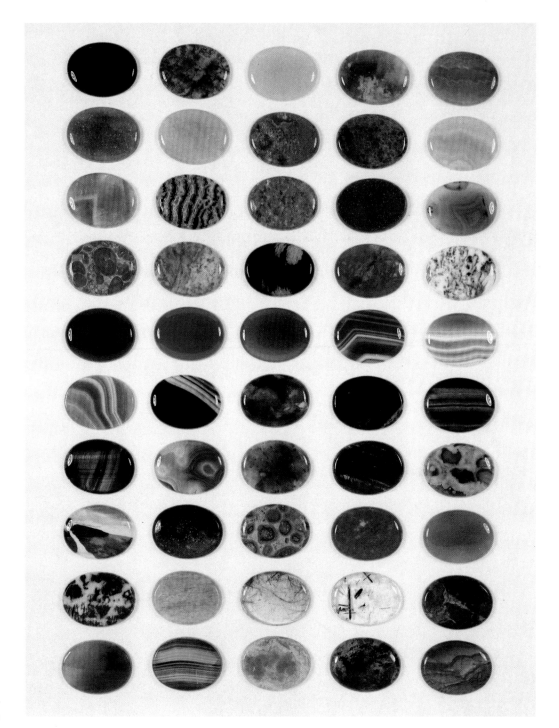

24–1

Plate 24–1 *Semiprecious stones, cabachon cut. Photo: Courtesy Johann Philipp Wild, Idar Oberstein, West Germany.* This family corporation of stone cutters, established in the 18th century, is outstanding today among the many stone-cutting establishments in Idar Oberstein, Europe's fabuous stone-cutting center.

1. Onyx: Brazil, Uruguay
2. Green moss agate: India
3. Rose quartz: Brazil, Namibia
4. Fancy jasper: India
5. Perelivt: U.S.S.R.
6. Aventurine: India
7. Light aventurine: Brazil
8. Mexican agate: Mexico
9. Rhodonite: Australia, Madagascar
10. Blue natural banded agate: South Africa
11. Striped amethyst quartz: Namibia
12. Zebra agate: India, Mexico

13. Epidote: U.S.A.
14. Goldstone: Italy
15. Banded carnelian: Brazil, Uruguay
16. Bird's eye agate: U.S.A.
17. Maquay agate: Mexico
18. Snowflake obsidian: U.S.A.
19. Vaquilla agate: Mexico
20. Tree agate: India
21. Carnelian: Brazil, Uruguay
22. Blue agate: Brazil, Uruguay
23. Green agate: Brazil, Uruguay
24. Red striped agate: Brazil, Madagascar, Uruguay
25. Green striped agate: Brazil, Madagascar, Uruguay
26. Blue striped agate: Brazil, Madagascar, Uruguay
27. Black striped agate: Brazil, Madagascar, Uruguay
28. Red moss agate: India
29. Sodalite: Canada, Namibia

30. Tiger's eye: South Africa
31. Variegated tiger's eye: South Africa
32. Botswana agate: Botswana
33. Coramite: South Africa
34. Tiger iron: Australia
35. Ryolite: Australia
36. Mookaite: Australia
37. Zoisite: Tanzania
38. Poppy jasper: Namibia
39. Plum chalcedony: South Africa
40. Orange aventurine: India
41. Russian lapis: Siberia
42. Amazonite: South Africa, U.S.A.
43. Rutilated quartz: Brazil
44. Tourmalinated quartz: Brazil
45. Chile lapis: Chile
46. Russian jade: Siberia
47. Malachite: Zaire
48. Rhodocrosite: Argentina
49. Eilat stone: Israel
50. Landscape jasper: U.S.A.

ADHESIVE ELECTROFORMS

PHOTOETCHING The photoresist can be etched in the usual way with any etchant suitable for use with the particular metal of which the mandrel is made. (See The Acid Etching of Metals, Chapter 8.) Tank etch or electroetch methods can be used. Be sure all surfaces of the mandrel are suitably protected with a resist where necessary. Take care not to overetch, particularly when real halftone metal plate images are used. The advantage of this etching process over ordinary etching is that the photosensitized resist allows the use of an *image on metal created through photography*, which considerably broadens the scope of design possibilities.

BI-METAL ELECTRODEPOSITED INLAY After the mandrel has been thoroughly rinsed to prevent the possibility of entrapping acid traces, the etching process can be used as a prelude to the electrodeposition of a second metal, different from that of the mandrel, into the depression made by the etching process. The result can be called a *bi-metal electrodeposited inlay*. This inlay can be permanently adherent provided the etching depth is sufficient to activate the surface and expose the true crystal structure of the etched areas. The atoms of the electrodeposited metal will then form a permanent bond with those of the mandrel metal. Deliberately deep etching accompanied by a laterally spreading, sidewall-etched groove automatically forms an undercut that acts to *lock in place* any metal electrodeposited into these etched grooves.

This system could be used, for example, to electrodeposit a silver inlay into an etched image on a copper mandrel base. The resulting image can be in a *flat plane* with that of the mandrel, smoothed level by drawfiling if necessary, then polished. Alternately, the electrodeposition can be extended to allow the second metal to build up *in relief* above the mandrel metal plane.

TRI-METAL ELECTROFORMING Three metals can be used in this system. The first is the mandrel base metal; the second, any other metal electrodeposited into an etched image; the third, a metal deposited after portions of the second metal have been stopped out. For example, in such a sequence, a copper base could be inlaid with silver, then parts of the inlay plated in gold.

REMOVING THE PHOTORESIST FROM THE MANDREL

In mandrels used for stripped-off electroforms, the resist can be retained to allow the mandrel to be reused. If the work employs the resist only once, it must be removed. To remove a resist, the mandrel is soaked in a fast-working resist-stripping chemical available from Kodak, acetone, or a lacquer thinner placed in a *glass* or *polypropylene tank*. Kodak manufactures resist strippers for use with specific resists. After a few minutes of immersion, the resist swells and lifts away from the mandrel, which is spray rinsed with cold water.

16–27 MONA R. BERMAN, U.S.A. "Sun Pin I." Made from a nonadhesive, matrix-stripped, arborescent photoelectroform, combined with a repoussé-worked unit, forged wire, and a crazy lace agate. Parts are in sterling, 14K, 18K, and 22K gold, and gold plated. *Photo: Gerald Wenner*

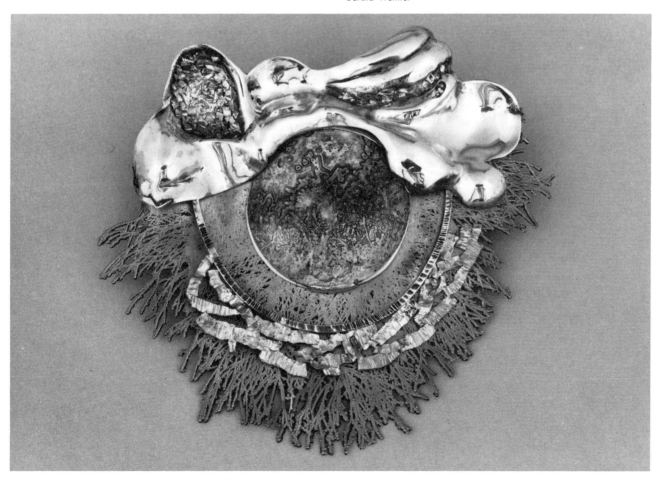

17

COLORING METALS
Achieving Patinas Through Heat, Chemicals, and Electrolysis

METAL COLORING

Broadening the basic color range of metals

Tarnishing is the term given to the *undesirable* dulling, discoloring, luster-destroying film that forms on a metal surface during its exposure to atmospheric conditions. Taking *silver tarnish* as an example, this consists mainly of silver sulphide (Ag_2S) and some silver oxide (Ag_2O), which develop when the object is in a humid atmosphere, and where even a low concentration of hydrogen sulphide (H_2S) exists, as well as acids and dust. The rate of tarnish on silver increases with the relative increase in humidity and rise in atmospheric temperature. Under such conditions, these substances interact, the atmospheric gas diffusing inward through the developing film which causes the thickness of the layer of tarnish to grow. In time, the film develops a series of interference oxide colors before finally turning black, its normal color on silver.

Tarnish also develops for other reasons. The relative purity of the metal has its effect: alloys with greater alloying metal content, such as copper, tarnish more rapidly in proportion to their alloy metal content. Rough surfaces tarnish more quickly than smooth ones, which makes electrodeposited silver relatively more resistant to tarnish because its crystalline orientation is surface smooth. If a silver object contacts sulphur contained in rubber, local tarnish occurs, as when a rubber band is placed around it, the sulphur even penetrating through paper. Silver objects tarnish when stored in cardboard boxes containing sulphur compounds, humidity causing the liberation of sulphur. The composition of fibrous jewel boxes therefore must be sulphur-free. To prevent the development of tarnish, metal jewelry is best kept enclosed in an airtight *plastic envelope*.

These are conditions and circumstances in which tarnishing occurs *naturally*. When it is induced *by choice* in a controlled manner on a metal surface to give it a color different from its normal basic state, or to create special, esthetic effects, tarnishing becomes *coloring*, or in the jeweler's vernacular, *"oxidizing."*

Coloring a metal object is done after all fabrication, machining, and heat treatments have been completed, and the metal-jewel is finished and in its final surface condition. The *color* or *patina* a jeweler may choose to give to a metal may be unusual, or may be designed to artificially duplicate a predictable patina or film that the object would normally acquire in time after a long, slow exposure to the

effects of atmosphere and moisture and during use. Once formed, such patinas tend to protect the metal from further change, and require only a little maintenance, such as occasional surface rubbing with a *soft cloth*.

Coloring is done on a metal object to age or "antique" the appearance of a surface; to deliberately change its

17–1 NETHERLANDS, 17th century. "Popinjay." Guild necklace, silver, with a series of repoussé-worked badges, each representing a Head of the Guild at different periods, the flat sheet back engraved with dated inscriptions. Time-caused natural coloring brings dimension to the relatively low relief surface decorations. The originally bright-cut engraved inscriptions are now black and more visible. *Photo: Victoria and Albert Museum, London, Crown Copyright*

17–2 HOPI PUEBLO, U.S.A. "Labyrinth." Silver pin with a flat, pierced work sheet soldered as an overlay to a flat, previously textured sheet. The depression was colored black with a locally applied coloring solution to emphasize the pattern and the upper sheet surface polished bright for contrast and dimensionality. This traditional design is called Sé-e-he Ki. Elder brother (sé-e-he) built his house (ki) in the form of a labyrinth to confuse his enemies. Ø 2⅜ in. *Photo: Courtesy the U. S. Department of the Interior, Indian Arts and Crafts Board*

17–3 PATRIZ HUBER, West Germany, 1901. Silver belt buckle with 24K green-dyed agates. Each half is made from one sheet by repoussage. The intaglio punch-matted ground is colored black, and the relief forms polished bright. Width 8.7 cm. *Photo: Günter Meyer, Schmuckmuseum, Pforzheim*

color; to reduce light reflection; to emphasize a part or unit by giving it a color different from another part or unit; to differentiate one metal from another; to heighten the effect of relief between uncolored and colored areas; or to emphasize a pattern or texture. The colors achieved generally possess a subdued luster that is peculiar to metals alone, and are harmonious with the character of metals as they develop from its natural, organic products.

COLORING PROCESSES

Coloring may be accomplished by different processes: *heat treatments; chemical dips;* or *electrochemical processes.* Examples of each of these are described below. Creating all metal colors should take place under conditions of *good ventilation.* Chemicals should be handled with care while wearing *rubber* or *plastic gloves.* A ready supply of running water should be nearby. *Antidotes* to the chemicals used should be known and available, made ready beforehand to immediately counteract possibly harmful effects.

HEAT TREATMENT COLORING

In *heat treatment coloring,* the color of a metal surface is changed by applying the heat from an oxidizing flame or from other sources directly to the object, to its immediate environment, to a substance on which it rests, or to a substance into which the object is immersed or buried. Starting at a different temperature for each metal, heat causes the formation of an oxide film on the surface which in most metals progresses through a series of interference colors, and can be arrested at a particular point to preserve a particular color or color range. When a metal surface is slowly oxidized, its surface atoms combine with oxygen, and normally, the result is an adherent oxide film that is a binary compound of the elemental metal plus oxygen. The *oxidizing agent* is *heat* in conjunction with

atmospheric *air,* and the character of the oxide is *basic,* that is, the opposite of acidic.

HEAT COLORING COPPER

When a clean copper object is heated in air to temperatures over 1112° F (600° C), its surface develops a scale of *red cuprous oxide* (CU_2O). If the heat is prolonged, even at a given temperature, the oxide layer thickens and toughens, and the outer layer becomes a *black cupric oxide* (CuO), while the inner layer remains red. If heating was rapid, the outer layer is in a state of stress and may of itself peel off in fragments, leaving the surface spotted red and black.

Copper oxide films can be preserved on the metal by creating them slowly, allowing partial cooling, then quenching the object in oil (which also acts to deepen the color). If wanted, the outer black layer can be partially removed down to the red layer or to the copper itself by *relieving* (see Postcoloring Treatments in this chapter) to create graded color effects ranging from black to red to pink.

HEAT COLORING GOLD ALLOYS

Pure gold (24K) does not oxidize when exposed to heat, and is also not acted upon by compounds containing sulphur. Gold alloys containing copper can be heat oxidized because the copper content in the surface passes through the same sequence as described above for pure copper. This oxide can be retained and partially relieved to expose the gold.

HEAT BLUING STEEL: Amozoc, Mexico

In Amozoc, a town near Puebla, Mexico, for over 400 years craftsmen have made a specialty of fabricating horsemen's personal decorative items (*adornos para charros*) such as buttons, buckles, hatband ornaments, and spurs, as well as horse and saddle furnishings such as stirrups, saddle, bridle, and harness decorations. These are made in mild steel because it is more easily shaped, inlaid, or damascened with silver, gold, or both—a usual form of decoration. The steel is then blued by heat treatment. In this process, the basic steel ornament is first formed by casting or forging, and its finished surface is given a *high bright polish.* Using *cold chisels,* linear and shaped grooves are carved into the surface. Into these silver and/or gold, in wire and/or sheet form are inlaid. Engraved linear patterns are then commonly made on the inlaid precious metal forms. The surface is again polished and cleaned, after which it is not touched. It is then ready for coloring the steel parts.

THE STEEL OXIDATION COLOR SPECTRUM All steels, whether mild or the high-carbon types used for tools will exhibit a color spectrum change if their polished surface is gradually heated. (See the oxidation color spectrum sequence a polished high-carbon steel surface takes when heated gradually, in Table, "Tempering Temperatures: Judgment by Heat-Produced Colors on Polished Steel," p. 240.) The sequence of colors follows the buildup of heat and is always the same so one knows what colors to expect and can be prepared to act rapidly. In the case of high-carbon tool steels, this color development is used as an indication of the degree of temper or hardness the metal has reached, but this does not apply to mild steels. A practical function of bluing mild steel is that the oxide that forms inhibits the development of surface rust.

The deep blue color aimed for in Amozoc is called *pavón* literally meaning "peacock." First the surface is coated with a thin layer of oil, then immersed into the heat medium which is a hot *molten niter bath* (potassium nitrate or saltpeter, KNO_3). For this reason this technique is also called *niter bluing.* The metal must be *clean* and *water-free* or a violent spitting will take place. Other heat mediums can be used, such as an *oven,* or *heated dry sand* in a metal box into which the object is immersed and buried. For a small object, a piece of heated steel can be brought into contact with it.

The niter bath temperature is over 600° F (315° C) which will bring the color of the polished steel surface to the peacock blue state when the object's temperature reaches about 540° F (282° C). When the blue color is approaching, the object is watched closely, and once it is reached, the object is immediately withdrawn from the bath and quenched in cold water to arrest the color. It is then dipped into boiling water, and finally into hot oil which acts to preserve the oxide. Under normal conditions, the steel will indefinitely retain its blue patina which makes a handsome contrast with the silver and/or gold inlay. The precious metals do not oxidize at that temperature, but if they become tarnished, they can be rubbed with a cloth and if necessary a mild abrasive such as charcoal powder or soot to remove the superficial tarnish.

Steel can also be blued by the use of steam, or by immersion in chemical dip solutions at room temperature. (See Chemical Dip Coloring Formulas for Particular Metals, p. 718.) Copper and its alloys when colored in molten sodium nitrate develop a red patina, and stainless steel a straw-colored to red gold patina.

CHEMICAL DIP COLORING

Chemical dip or *immersion coloring* is probably the most widely used of coloring methods because it can be done in a variety of ways, at relatively low temperatures, to the *total surface* of an object made entirely of one or more metals. The same coloring solutions can also be applied *locally* with a swab or brush applicator so that the whole work need not be uniformly colored. This is important when only a small area is to be colored; when the work includes stones or other substances that might be affected by the dip chemicals; or to reduce the work of *relieving,* the removal of color from unwanted areas.

Coloring solutions contain a combination of water and chemical constituents in specific proportions for use at particular temperatures and for prescribed time intervals. The result is a thin layer of a compound on the base metal surface, usually more or less even in thickness and color. A properly achieved, chemically created color normally is

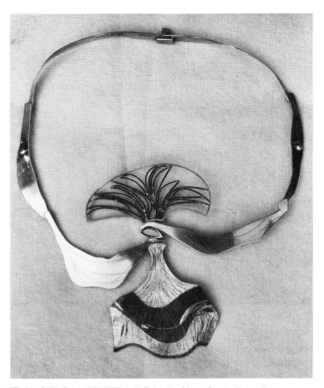

17–5 GLENDA ARENTZEN, U.S.A. Necklace in sterling silver, copper, and brass, with ivory. The etched lower pendant unit combines all three metals and is locally colored to emphasize the contrast between the different metal parts. The upper wire unit has a brass frame enclosing colored copper wires. The neckpiece parts are held together by ball and post rivets. *Photo: Bill Byers*

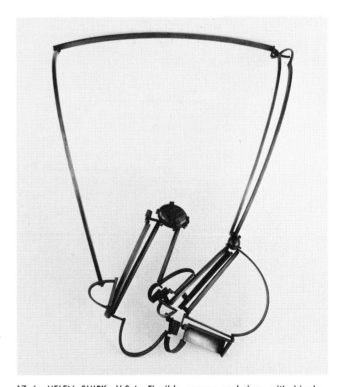

17–4 JOAQUÍN CAPDEVILA, Spain. Brooch in gold, silver, and plastic tubes. The upper surface of the silver ground is locally colored to surround the two surface-textured gold forms for contrast. Size 5 × 5 cm. *Photo: Ferrán Borrás*

17–6 HELEN SHIRK, U.S.A. Flexible copper neckpiece with binghamite, constructed of 8, 11, and 14 gauge B.&S. copper sheet. The surface was given a "low key" texture with a *cut 4* file before coloring. The piece was dipped repeatedly in a liver of sulphur solution to color it black. After each immersion, it was rinsed and rubbed lightly with *steel wool* to achieve an even color. After the last dip and drying, the surface was rubbed with *000 grade steel wool* to produce a soft sheen, and to emphasize some areas by relieving the color to create light to dark gradations. Size 10½ × 8 in. *Photo: Helen Shirk*

adherent and can only be removed by the use of high heat, an acid solution, an abrasive with a polishing wheel or wire scratch brush, or by electrochemical means.

OXIDIZING VS. SULPHIDING

Oxidizing is the term commonly used to describe what happens when a metal reacts to a chemical dip. When a solution is used in which sulphur is the activating chemical, this term is actually a misnomer as it is not an oxide that forms, as in heat-created coloring, but a *metallic sulphide compound* surface film that is a combination of the chemicals in the solution and the base metal. For instance, when the commonly used *liver of sulphur* (a crude mixture of potassium polysulphides and thiosulphate) is applied, a wide range of browns and blacks are achieved that are *metallic sulphides,* not oxides. The term "oxidation" used to mean coloring, is, however, entrenched in the jeweler's terminology, though the general term *coloring* is preferable. The term oxidation is also propagated by jewelry suppliers who manufacture special, concentrated proprietary mixtures of "oxidizing liquids" used to color metals. These usually contain sodium, potassium, barium, and ammonium sulphides or polysulphides.

FACTORS THAT INFLUENCE SUCCESSFUL CHEMICAL DIP COLORING

Because of the wide range of variables in the conditions and materials used in coloring techniques, the process of coloring by chemical dipping is not always under total control or completely predictable. Satisfactory results can be achieved without a knowledge of chemistry by simply following given formulas and practices, but knowing what is happening chemically is a decided help. Even so, a certain degree of empirical, trial and error experimentation is necessary since the same chemical compound may take on variations of color on metal by changes in any of the variable conditions.

First in importance is the *composition of the metal* to be colored. Different metals, pure or alloyed, accept coloring compounds in relation to their particular character. The *natural, basic color* of the metal has an influence on the appearance of the patina, which can be seen when using the same coloring solution for different metals. *Impurities present in the metal,* even in small traces, will have an effect on the resulting color, as Japanese metal craftsworkers, masters in the art of coloring metals, well know. The *method by which the metal was worked,* whether by casting, stamping, rolling, forging, or extrusion also will cause differences in the result. Cast metals, for instance, are colored with greater difficulty than forged metals.

Next in importance is the *condition of the metal surface.* To achieve a uniform result, all surfaces on the object, whether being colored or not, must be in condition to receive coloring. This means they must be free of all foreign matter such as oil, grease, fingerprints, polishing compounds, oxide films, or fused borax from soldering. If they are not *completely clean* the coloring film will not adhere to the surface. These substances are removed by cleaning methods already discussed. The resulting surface must be *chemically clean.* The *surface texture,* whether smooth or

Some Chemicals Used in Coloring Solutions

Chemical	Atomic Composition	Common Name
Acetic acid	CH_3COOH	Vinegar
Acid potassium tartrate	$KHC_4H_4O_6$	Cream of tartar
Alcohol	C_2H_5OH	Grain alcohol
Aluminum chloride	$AlCl_3$	
Ammonium chloride	NH_4Cl	Sal ammoniac
Ammonium hydroxide	NH_4OH	Ammonium base
Ammonium molybdate	NH_4HMoO_4	
Ammonium sulphide	$(NH_4)_2S$	
Aqua ammonia	NH_3+H_2O	Spirit of hartshorn
Barium sulphide	BaS	Bologna phosphorus
Calcium carbonate	$CaCO_2$	Precipitated chalk, whiting
Calcium chloride	$CaCl_2$	
Chromic acid	H_2CrO_4	
Copper acetate	$Cu(C_2H_3O_2)_2$	French verdigris
Copper carbonate	$CuCO_3$	Green verditer
Copper nitrate	$Cu(NO_3)_2$	
Copper sulphate	$(CuSO_4.5H_2O)$	Bluestone, blue vitriol, blue copperas
Lead acetate	$Pb(C_2H_3O_2)_2.3H_2O$	Sugar of lead
Mercuric chloride	$HgCl_2$	Corrosive sublimate
Nickel sulphate	$NeSO_4$	Blue salts
Nitric acid	HNO_3	Aqua fortis
Potassium aluminum sulphate	$KAl(SO_4)_2.12H_2O$	Alum
Potassium chlorate	$KClO_3$	
Potassium chloride	KCl	Sylvite
Potassium nitrate	KNO_3	Saltpeter
Potassium nitrite	KNO_2	
Potassium sulphide (impure)	K_2S	Liver of sulphur, hepar sulphuris
Selenious acid	H_2SeO_3	
Sodium chloride	$NaCl$	Common salt
Sodium hydroxide	$NaOH$	Caustic soda
Sodium hyposulphite	$Na_2S_2O_2$	Hydrosulphite
Sodium sulphide	Na_2S	
Sodium thiosulphate	$Na_2S_2O_3$	Hypo, hyposulphate of soda

rough, shiny or matte, will have an effect on the appearance of the color as these qualities are retained in the result, influencing the way in which light is reflected from its surface.

Other factors involve the *nature and use of the coloring solution.* The natural chemical content of the water used; the degree of purity of the chemicals used; the composition of the solution; the length of time of immersion; the temperature of the solution and/or metal object upon immersion; whether a still or agitated solution is used; and, not least important, the skill and judgment of the craftsperson in controlling and manipulating these variables. All these factors have their effect on the result, and the ability to reproduce it when desired.

EQUIPMENT USED FOR CHEMICAL DIP COLORING

Glass beaker or *Pyrex container* that will withstand thermal shock, and of a size that will hold the entire object, if necessary.
Dipping wire of the same metal as being colored; a nonmetal *plastic* or *wooden tongs;* or *plastic fishing line.*
Hair brush applicator for local coloring.
A heat source: electric hot plate; gas burner.
Relieving medium: whiting, pumice, or mild abrasive.

PREPARING A COLORING SOLUTION

When preparing a coloring solution, weigh out the dry chemical, and dilute it in water *before* adding it to the solution as it will take longer to dissolve in the solution if it is added to it dry. Ready-made commercial proprietary coloring solutions are also available from suppliers for use with all metals.

CHEMICAL DIP COLORING FORMULAS FOR PARTICULAR METALS

Hundreds of formulas have been developed for producing various colors on different metals and alloys. Some of the more successful ones whose ingredients are available from chemical supply houses are given here. In general, fairly dilute solutions are used to build up films slowly rather than highly concentrated solutions which tend to produce nonadhering films. Also generally speaking, coloring solutions work better on scratch-brushed surfaces rather than those that are highly polished. Scratch brushing can be done manually or mechanically. Color films can withstand some degree of polishing, depending on their adhesive quality and thickness.

LIVER OF SULPHUR: The classic coloring sulphide

This ancient and widely used coloring chemical which is an impure potassium sulphide, will produce a brown to black range of colors on low gold and copper alloys, sterling silver alloys, and on copper and copper alloys. It is available in a solid state which facilitates storage, and is dissolved to prepare a solution when needed because a standing solution has a short life.

To prepare a dip solution, dissolve less than 1 oz of the solid into 2 pt warm (not boiling) water by stirring. The result should be a deep yellow color, and if not, add more liver of sulphur, but not much in excess of 1 oz to ½ gal water or the solution will be too concentrated, which can cause the coloring compound to form a brittle film that may peel off.

To *totally color* an object, attach it to a silver or copper wire, or a plastic line that will withstand heat. Because a warm solution will color metal more quickly than a cold one, it can be *heated but not boiled.* Also warm the object and immerse it into the solution. Allow the color to develop, removing the object by the wire at intervals for inspection. When it has attained the desired depth of color, rinse it under cold running water, then hot water, then dry the object in air or in sawdust. If the color then appears uneven, scratch brush the surface and repeat the process.

To *locally color* a part, warm the object, and paint the area with a *brush* that has been dipped into this solution. The depth of the black color can be increased by adding ⅛ oz aqua ammonia to the above-mentioned solution.

Gold alloys (below 18K containing copper): Brown to black
Sterling silver: Brown
Copper: Warm brown
Bronze: Dark brown

Copper sulphate	5 oz
Copper acetate	5 oz
Water	1 gal

Immerse the object by a wire into a cold solution, then heat the solution to boiling and allow it to cool. Repeat this procedure several times until the desired depth of color is achieved. A larger amount of copper sulphate deepens the color. Increasing the copper acetate produces a bluish tinge on scratch-brushed surfaces.

Copper (85% or more): Black, dull

Sulphurated potash	2 oz
Ammonium hydroxide	¼ oz
Water	1 gal
Temperature	70° F (21° C)

Copper: Reddish bronze to dark brown

Sulphurated potash	2 oz
Sodium hydroxide	3 oz
Water	1 gal
Temperature	170° F (76° C)

Brass: Blue black

Copper carbonate	¼ lb
Ammonia	1 pt
Water	2½ pt
Temperature	175° F (79° C)

Mix the copper carbonate with the ammonia before adding water. After coloring, fix the color by a dip into a 2½% caustic soda solution.

Brass: Brown

Potassium chlorate	5½ oz
Nickel sulphate	2¾ oz
Copper sulphate	24 oz
Water	1 gal
Temperature	195–212° F (90–100° C)

Brass: Blue

Lead acetate	2–4 oz
Sodium thiosulphate	8 oz
Acetic acid	4 oz
Water	1 gal
Temperature	180° F (82° C)

Brass: Antique green

Nickel ammonium sulphate	8 oz
Sodium thiosulphate	8 oz
Water	1 gal
Temperature	160° F (71° C)

17-7 BJÖRN WECKSTRÖM, Finland, designer; manufacturer Lapponia Jewelry Ltd., Helsinki. "Maginot." A "flame bronze" bracelet, colored blue by first heating the work, then dipping it into the coloring solution. *Photo: Winfrid Zakorski, courtesy Lapponia Jewelry Ltd.*

Brass and copper: Antique yellowish green

Copper nitrate	4 oz
Ammonium chloride	4 oz
Calcium chloride	4 oz
Water	1 gal

If desired, a dark ground can be made first with a sulphide solution for black, upon which this solution can be used. Stipple the solution on with a brush and allow it to dry. Repeat the stippling, and when color appears, boil the object in water, dry it in air. To increase the color, repeat the application. Wax or lacquer the object.

Brass: Yellow to bright red

Copper carbonate	2 parts by volume
Caustic soda	1 part by volume
Water	10 parts by volume

Dip until the desired depth of color appears, then rinse in water.

Bronze: Gray

Copper sulphate	1 oz
Sodium chloride	⅕ oz
Water	¼ oz

Apply and allow to dry, then wash in warm water. Repeat until desired color is achieved.

Steel (highly polished):   Black

Nitric acid	¾ oz
Copper sulphate	1½ oz
Selenious acid	1 oz
Water	1 gal

Use below boiling point; dip repeatedly until desired color is achieved.

Steel (highly polished):   Caustic black

Caustic soda	40 oz
Potassium nitrite	15 oz
Potassium nitrate	10 oz
Water	½ gal

Use at boiling point; dip until desired color depth, then rinse.

Steel (highly polished):   Blue

Potassium chlorate	3 parts by volume
Mercuric chloride	4 parts by volume
Alcohol	8 parts by volume
Water	85 parts by volume

Use at room temperature.

Steel (highly polished):   Blue

Sodium thiosulphate	8 oz
Lead acetate	2 oz
Water	1 gal

Use at boiling temperature.

POSTCOLORING TREATMENTS

Several different postcoloring treatments are possible, depending on their purpose and the desired effect.

RELIEVING

Relieving is the process of using abrasives to vary the thickness and therefore the tone of the uniform color film created on the metal surface with chemicals. Abrasives can be used to completely remove the color in specific areas where it might anyway wear off in use, such as raised surfaces, to bring the metal there to a desired degree of brightness and create highlights on the object while leaving the color film in the depressions; to create the effect of depth and to heighten relief, even in the case of low-relief figures or textures; to give prominence to or to subordinate a particular area; to set off an area by contrast with the colored area; or simply to alter the monotony of a uniform color and introduce variety by contrast.

The method used for relieving may depend on the shape of an object, or the accessibility of parts to be reached. It is accomplished with greatest control manually by rubbing the high places with *fingers* that have been made wet and dipped into a mild abrasive such as *chalk powder* (whiting), *finely powdered pumice,* or *tripoli.* With care, relieving can also be done mechanically to remove excessive deposits by using a *bristle* or *scratch brush* with a slurry of *pumice;* or on a *buffing wheel* with a greaseless compound or rouge.

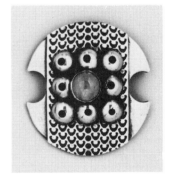

17-8 PENTTI SARPANEVA, Finland, designer; manufacturer Kalevala Koru, Helsinki. Bronze pendant utilizing a central stone, pierced bead forms, and a colored, stamp-textured surface relieved after coloring to remove unwanted color while allowing it to remain in the depressions. *Photo: Studio Wendt, courtesy Kalevala Koru*

WAXING OR OILING

Molten wax such as beeswax, carnauba wax, or paraffin can be applied by manual or mechanical methods to an already colored surface to provide it with a semiglossy film that protects metal patinas from deterioration, and also has the effect of deepening or enriching their appearance. A neutral sweet oil can be substituted for wax, but is not as enduring. Molten wax can be applied with a *brush* or a *clean cloth,* then rubbed with a *clean, soft cloth* to remove any surplus and to heighten the degree of surface reflection. Frictional heat also hardens the wax coating, making it last longer. Wax can also be polished mechanically with a *soft flannel wheel* at a very low speed of about 750 sfpm. In some cases, a color can be deepened by warming the object, and rubbing it with a cloth dipped into *soot* (a fine carbon powder) to leave the surface lustrous. Soot can be collected by holding a piece of glazed ceramic over a candle flame.

LACQUERING

Clear lacquers are rapidly drying compositions that can be applied to an uncolored finished metal surface after polishing to retard or prevent tarnishing or oxidation, or to provide colored metal surfaces with a waterproof, air-excluding surface that protects and extends the life of the coloring. The question of whether or not to use lacquers on jewelry is one of taste and principle. Some jewelers prefer to leave all metal surfaces open to air which will eventually cause natural oxidation and patination.

The metal lacquers commonly used today are made of *cellulose derivatives* such as cellulose nitrate, cellulose acetate, methyl, ethyl, and benzyl cellulose to which *synthetic resins* such as vinyls, alkyds, epoxy, or acrylics are added, dissolved in *organic solvents* plus *diluents* to reduce their viscosity. Lacquers dry by solvent evaporation and form a hard, smooth, tough film on the metal surface with their nonvolatile constituents, which are resistant to abrasives and chemical action. They can be highly glossy or matte, depending on the lacquer composition. The harder the surface of the result, the longer lasting it is.

Before applying any lacquer to an uncolored surface, it must be chemically clean and dry or the lacquer will not adhere properly and oxidation and corrosion may take place beneath the lacquer film. Lacquers can also be applied to colored metals which are grease-free. Lacquer can be applied by dipping the entire object into the container holding the lacquer, then allowing the surplus to drain off;

it can be painted on the object with a clean brush; or it can be sprayed on, in which case it must be thinned. Only one coat should be given as the solvent in a second film may soften and penetrate the first and cause raising and wrinkling.

After application, the resin is converted to a hard gel by solvent evaporation, oxidation, or polymerization. These actions can take place in air at room temperature. Thermosetting-based lacquers can be force dried and their setting action accelerated by hastening the solvent evaporation through curing in the heat of an oven. The use of artificial heat provides such lacquers with a lasting ability superior to air-dried lacquers. Normally, a heat of from 250–400° F (121–204° C) lasting 5–60 minutes depending on the lacquer, is sufficient to cause polymerization to take place.

Varnishes are sometimes used on metals to protect their surfaces. These are oleoresins, meaning they are made from a combination of an oil and a resin, and leave a thin transparent or translucent film on the object that dries in air. *Spirit varnishes* contain a resin in a solvent that dries in air by the evaporation of the solvent. *Oil varnishes* contain a combination of resins, vegetable oils, driers (catalytic substances that accelerate the drying or hardening time), and a solvent or thinner; they dry by evaporation and oxidation or polymerization, or both.

Thinners, also termed *reducers,* are combinations of organic solvents and diluents introduced to lacquers and varnishes to reduce their viscosity. They can also be used to dissolve and remove lacquer from an object.

ANODIZING METALS

Electrochemical conversion coating and dye coloring

Anodizing is the popular term given to the electrochemical process of forming an integral *conversion coating* on a metal surface consisting of a stable oxide compound created for decorative or functional purposes. Aluminum, titanium, and their alloys are the metals most commonly and successfully anodized, but tantalum, niobium (formerly called columbium), magnesium, zirconium, hafnium, tungsten, and other metals can also be anodized. The anodic film initially created on the surface of aluminum and titanium by this process is relatively hard, transparent to opaque, and in the case of aluminum, highly porous in nature. Once the pores of an aluminum anodic film are sealed, however, the film then acts to protect the base metal and minimizes its corrosion, streaking, or discoloration by shielding it from atmospheric contact.

Anodized coatings have other than decorative purposes. Metal surfaces are anodized to prepare them to accept paint: the anodic film provides an inert surface between the metal and the paint film applied to it, thereby preventing moisture from penetrating to the metal which would result in lack of adhesion. (The paint referred to is the type that consists of a pigment combined with a drying oil, and cures by the absorption of oxygen from the atmosphere.) In some cases, metal is anodized to create a porous film or roughened surface that acts to increase the adhesion of electroplated metal.

The purpose and method of anodizing discussed first here is to provide a surface on an *aluminum base metal* that can accept organic dye colors. Titanium anodizing is discussed separately in this chapter. Anodic films are not ductile, therefore objects to be dyed after anodization must be completely fabricated as they cannot be subjected to any other processing without injuring the film—except possibly polishing which can be done to aluminum as the anodized aluminum oxide layer is hard when sufficiently thick, and then has good abrasion resistance.

The usual aluminum *anodizing and dyeing sequence* consists of mechanically or chemically finishing the metal, cleaning, rinsing, anodizing, rinsing, dyeing, sealing, and rinsing.

PREANODIZING TREATMENT AND METAL SURFACE PREPARATION

The crystal formation and appearance of the anodized surface is governed by the condition of the metal substrate when subjected to anodizing, and by the composition of the electrolyte. For instance, for a high degree of luster in the result, the metal must be polished bright, or made bright by subjecting it to the chemical action of a bright dip solution.

Aluminum bright dip

Phosphoric acid	75% by weight
Hydrogen peroxide	3.5% by weight
Water	21.5% by weight
Temperature	195° F (90° C)

For duller, textured effects, the surface can be drawfiled, scratch brushed, sandpapered, steel wooled, sandblasted, etc., each process producing a different texture and degree of reflectivity through the always transparent dye. Anodizing emphasizes textural effects, but also brings out undesirable existing scratches. To achieve a matte surface on aluminum, the object is first etched in a 5% sodium hydroxide solution at 122° F (50° C), and rinsed.

Prior to anodizing, the surface must be *chemically clean* for the process to be successful, and in a neutral state. To accomplish this, normally the object is washed with a brush in a mild alkaline solution, but other cleaning processes can be used, depending on the kind of soil to be removed.

ANODIZING ALUMINUM:
Preparing the oxide coating

To anodize an aluminum object, it must be attached by an *aluminum wire* to the anode in an electric cell, or no anodized film will build up. It is then immersed in the *electrolyte* or acid anodizing bath. It is handled by this wire in all subsequent processes as the surface must not be touched. When the current is then turned on, because the object is anodic (positive) in the cell, oxygen is liberated from its surface on which oxidation occurs, forming an adherent oxide compound or film. In the case of pure aluminum, the resulting oxide film is a coating of hard, colorless aluminum oxide (Al_2O_3) that varies in thickness from 0.00005–0.001 in (0.00127–0.0254 mm). Its outer layer is highly porous, possessing billions of pores in a cellular structure and, depending on the formation voltage and the electrolyte used, its appearance ranges from transparent to opaque. Below this is a compact barrier layer.

When transparent anodized coatings on pure aluminum

are dyed, the transparent color appears bright, the metal reflecting through it. When alloying metals are present, they may cause the oxide to appear grayish, brownish, or other colors depending on the metal. Some of these colors are attractive in themselves. The degree of dullness increases with the increase in the percentage of the alloying constituents, and when the anodized film is dyed, these discolorations affect the intensity of the color results.

In industry, when numerous objects are to be anodized at the same time, they are normally suspended on *racks* made of commercially pure titanium which is completely passive in the temperature range used in anodizing baths, and they are therefore repeatedly usable. (Titanium racks are also used to hold objects being metal plated.)

THE ANODIZING ELECTROLYTIC SOLUTIONS

When anodizing pure aluminum, or an aluminum alloy that contains more than 5% copper, the recommended active agent is a *sulphuric acid bath;* if the alloy contains less than 5% copper, a *chromic acid bath* is used. The oxide film produced is a compound that forms on the surface of the object from its electrochemical corrosion into the solution once it is electrically activated. When such an anodic film is created in chromic acid baths, it is thinner, more flexible, and tends to appear opaque and dull when dyed, therefore it is dyed pastel or deep opaque colors. If a clear bright color result with metallic luster is wanted, it is preferable to use a sulphuric acid solution. During any anodizing operation, wear *rubber gloves* as an insulation against electrical shock, and work with the electrolyte solution under a *hood* equipped with an *exhaust fan.* In general, harder oxide films are created at lower temperatures and dilute solutions. Concentrated solutions (15–25%) are used if the oxide film will be dyed a deep color.

CHROMIC ACID ANODIZING
ELECTROLYTIC SOLUTION

Chromic acid, technical 5–10%	6.7–13.4 oz/gal
Chloride as NaCl	less than 0.2 g/liter
Sulphate as H_2SO_4	less than 0.5 g/liter
pH	0.5–1.0
Voltage	10–40 volts
Temperature	95°–120° F (35–48° C)
Time	30 minutes at 40 volts

The direct current for either acid solution is supplied by a *DC rectifier* with an attached *voltmeter* and *ammeter,* and must be capable of allowing controlled regulation of 10–40 volts. A *stainless steel tank* is used to hold chromic acid solutions which have good throwing power and will anodize even recessed parts. The *contact clamps* attached to the wire that brings the current to the object can be of any metal provided they do not come into contact with the solution. The tank containing the solution is made the cathode by attaching it to the cathode wire. If a glass tank is used, a stainless steel cathode sheet must be immersed in the solution. Large objects can be anodized in sections, if necessary. The solution is heated to the desired temperature by a *thermostatically controlled immersion heater,* and the object is agitated to maintain an even heat in the solution.

17–9 ERIC SPILLER, England. Aluminum brooches anodized in various colors. The patterns are created by the use of a milling machine. The metal is cut into radiating slots whose size and placement have been worked out mathematically. Steel pins (not visible) hold the brooches to clothing. Ø sizes *top:* 26 mm; *bottom:* 50 mm, 26 mm, and 48 mm. *Photo: Eric Spiller*

At first keep the current voltage low, then after 5–10 minutes, rapidly increase it to 40 volts. Avoid overloading the rectifier as this may result in its damage. Maintain this voltage about 30–40 minutes, then gradually reduce the current to zero, remove the object, and rinse it. When using a chromic acid electrolyte, the resulting anodized aluminum surface has a dull, greenish gray appearance.

SULPHURIC ACID ANODIZING ELECTROLYTIC SOLUTION

To prepare an aluminum object for the acceptance of dye, a solution such as the following containing sulphuric acid produces the most satisfactory anodized coating.

Sulphuric acid	15%: 12 fl oz/gal
	18%: 14.7 fl oz/gal
pH	0.5–1.0
Current density	10–25 amp/ft²
Voltage	14–18 volts
Temperature	60–80° F (15–26° C)
Time	15–30 minutes, the longer time for deep, dark colors

Place the prepared solution in a *glass, plastic, rubber-lined,* or *lead-lined tank.* A lead-lined tank may be used as the cathode, otherwise use a *lead sheet cathode* equal in surface area to that of the object. Establish the current density of an average of 10 amp/ft² at the start. As the aluminum content in the bath increases due to its dissolution, increase the voltage slightly to about 15 amp/ft². A solution temperature of 70° F (21° C) is ideal, and the solution must be agitated. Increasing the temperature makes the coating more porous and later able to absorb more dye, but sealing the resulting larger pores is more difficult, and the dye tends to leach out in the sealing bath. Also, the hardness of the anodized film and its luster are decreased. After the desired coating is produced, reduce the current to zero, and immediately withdraw the object from the solution and rinse it.

If an electrolyte of boric acid and ammonium borate is used for aluminum, and operated at 50–500 volts, the anodized coating will appear iridescent, and its thickness will be in proportion to the formation voltage.

An electrolyte will last for about one month, depending on the frequency of its usage. To avoid evaporation, when not in use, store it in a covered or closed container such as a *plastic bottle* (this will also keep dust out).

SEALING A COLORLESS ALUMINUM ANODIZED SURFACE

If a clear, colorless finish is wanted on aluminum, the surface must then be sealed from further absorption, but if dyeing follows, sealing is done *after* dyeing. In the former case, the aluminum anodized film now present is sealed by soaking the object in neutral (pH 7) boiling water for 10–20 minutes, and the object is then air dried.

RINSING   After anodizing in either a chromic or sulphuric acid bath, and before dyeing, the object must be thoroughly rinsed to remove any traces of acid to render neutral the object's anodized surface. The object must always be handled by its attached anode wire to avoid touching its surface. Inadequate rinsing will result in streaked and discolored effects as the dye color will react to any trapped traces of acid still present. If the work has deep recesses or inaccessible hollow parts, these may be difficult to rinse, and a neutralizing bath of sodium bicarbonate is recommended after rinsing, followed by a rinse in clear water.

To rinse an object, it is first placed under running cold water, then immersed into clean water heated to 150–185° F (65–85° C), and agitated. Upon removal, a hot object will air dry rapidly, therefore it is immediately immersed into the dyebath.

DYE COLORING ANODIZED ALUMINUM OBJECTS

Dyeing an aluminum object that has been anodized is a relatively simple process. Dyeing must be done *before sealing* because the pores of the anodic coating are then open to receive the dye. The anhydrous form of the aluminum oxide coating links with dyes more easily, which the monohydrate form that the oxide becomes after sealing will not do. Several hundred transparent, specially manufactured proprietary *organic dyes* are available from suppliers for use in dyeing aluminum. However, organic dyes tend to break down upon exposure to sunlight. For greater light fastness, *inorganic pigments* such as yellow cadmium sulphide, violet gold chloride, or orange sodium molybdate are used.

Upon immersing the object in the dye solution, the color penetrates and coats within the open pores of the anodized surface. The depth of the dye penetration is determined by the thickness and degree of porosity of the anodized coating. Because the dye color is transparent, light is reflected from the metal below the anodic film through the dye in a manner similar to that of transparent enamels on metal. Only a few of these colors are highly resistant to fading after exposure to direct sunlight. Fading resistance is increased in proportion to the strength of the color absorbed.

THE DYEBATH

Water	deionized, pH 7
Dye content	0.025–1.0%
Temperature	150° F (65° C)
Dye tank	glass, stainless steel, plastic, or fiber glass

During dyeing, as during anodizing, the object is handled by an attached wire of the same metal, and must not be touched. The dyebath variables that must be controlled are color concentration, temperature, and length of time of immersion. The color concentration depends on the desired depth of color, and manufacturer's suggestions should be followed for each dye. For full colors, however, a typical dye concentration contains two grams of dye per liter of water. Tints of colors require smaller concentrations, but these tend to be more likely to deteriorate. For most dyes, a pH value of 6–7 is best. To slightly lower the pH value of neutral water, add a small amount of acetic acid (vinegar) to the solution.

The dyebath must be made ready *before anodizing* the object because it is most important that the anodized object, once rinsed, be *immediately immersed* into the dye solution and not be allowed to dry. The temperature of the dyebath must be maintained at the recommended degree, usually done with a thermostatically controlled *immersion heater,* but other means can also be used. The solution must be agitated during the entire dyeing process which can be done manually by jiggling the attached wire, while wearing rubber gloves. Agitation can also be accomplished by the use of a *magnetic stirrer,* or by other means. After agitating the object in the dyebath for about 10 minutes, it is removed.

SEALING AFTER DYEING To eliminate film porosity and make the surface resistant to further dyeing, staining, or corrosion, the outer, porous oxide layer must be sealed. This is done by immersing and agitating the object in a sealing bath of slightly acidified (pH 4–6) water in a glass or stainless steel tank, or one of any other inert material, and heated to 200° F (93° C). To prevent the formation of surface smut, add 0.1% of a *wetting agent* to the water. During the sealing process, the existing amorphous aluminum oxide anodized coating (Al_2O_3) is converted to aluminum monohydrate ($Al_2O_3 \cdot H_2O$), known as Boehmite. Chromic acid anodized surfaces are sealed by a 5-minute immersion, and sulphuric acid anodized objects require an immersion of 10–15 minutes. During this time, the pore walls swell and close so the surface is no longer absorptive and the dye is locked in, but there is no change in the appearance of the dyed film. The object is then air dried at a temperature no higher than 225° F (107° C). Other sealants are also used, and these include hot dilute solutions of nickel or cobalt acetate, waxes, oils, or resins. Wax or grease films are also applied to water-sealed surfaces to provide additional protection.

POSTSEALING POLISHING After dyeing, sealing, and drying, because of the relative hardness of the aluminum oxide coating, an aluminum object can be color buffed using a *lime-containing polishing compound* that also contains wax. In this process, any existing surface smut is also removed. Irregularly shaped surfaces can be polished with a tampico brush wheel, or by sawdust tumbling.

It is conceivable that a jeweler may wish to remove *part* of a dyed anodic coating down to the basis metal to expose selected areas of the metal while the rest remains dye colored. This can be done manually or mechanically simply by using an abrasive whose action is enough to remove the coating.

ANODIZED METAL DYEING TECHNIQUES

Multicolor selective dyeing of an anodized surface is possible. The object is first completely, or partially ano-
dized. Selected areas are protected against the acceptance of dye by the use of any *masking resist* that is capable of remaining intact on the metal surface and withstanding the dyebath temperature. Masking materials include suitable *stop-off lacquers.* New types of waxes have been developed for this purpose and are used successfully provided the object is not placed in solutions heated to more than their melting point. *Pressure-sensitive tapes,* also called stop-off tapes, are available, made of vinyl or other plastic, and one has a lead backing. These tapes can be cut into any shape, and are applied to a surface by simple finger pressure. They are peeled off to be removed.

Adjoining area color dyeing is one possible procedure in which a resist is applied to selected areas of the anodized object, and the exposed areas are dyed. A second application of a resist can then be applied to protect the already dyed area, and parts formerly covered by the resist are then exposed to a second color dyeing. The same procedure can be repeated for any subsequent color areas. Finally, the resist is removed, and the work sealed.

Overdyeing of a color area with a second color, covering the first one either completely or partially, is also possible. In this case, the colored areas not to be overdyed are covered with a resist. After dyeing, the resist is removed and the entire surface is sealed.

Patterns can be painted or printed on an already anodized surface using a liquid resist, or a proprietary ink and resist combination available from suppliers. The exposed ground can then be dyed and sealed; or dyed, further resists applied, overdyed, and sealed. The resist-cum-ink can then be dissolved with its solvent, and the object's surface sealed.

Photosensitizing an anodized metal surface is also possible as it allows the application of emulsions, the porous nature of the anodic film providing a mechanical means of gripping the emulsion. An image can be created on the emulsion, then developed, leaving a part of the surface, such as the ground, emulsion-free. The exposed area can then be colored by the usual immersion in a dyebath, followed by sealing, and the removal of the remaining emulsion.

TITANIUM COLORING

Heat and anodic oxidizing methods

Coloring titanium for its purely decorative effect is one of those processes that ignores the conventional aims, thinking, and criteria of industrial practice and substitutes aims that are purely subjective and creative. Do not use any titanium containing even a small amount of tin which inhibits titanium coloring. Coloring titanium is possible because its surface, when properly prepared, is highly reactive upon exposure to certain conditions, and forms a series of colors due to the development of a tenacious oxide film. Decidedly decorative in appeal, this oxide film is highly resistant to a wide variety of corrosive substances that would affect other metals. Colors are permanent if unabraded, and if the oxide film is thick enough, will not fade or tarnish.

Two methods for coloring titanium are possible: coloring by the use of *heat,* which is more difficult to control; and coloring by *electrochemistry* which with proper controls allows exact, predictable color results. These methods are discussed separately on pp. 726 & 727. Heat coloring is not applicable to tantalum and niobium which develop gray to black surface oxides, but these metals can be colored electrochemically. (See Refractory Metals Used in Jewelry, Chapter 3, for working titanium, tantalum, and niobium.)

OPTICAL INTERFERENCE COLORS

The colors apparent on a light-reflecting refractory metal surface occur when the surface oxide that forms reaches a specific thickness range. Colors are not due to color present in the oxide, but are explained by the phenomenon called *optical interference*. In this phenomenon, two parallel reflecting surfaces exist: the upper surface which is variably transparent depending on oxide thickness, and within a small distance from it, the lower surface which is the true metal surface. White light rays striking the metal surface enter the oxide film and reach the reflective interface between the basis metal and the oxide film. Part of them are absorbed in the metal, but most are broken up and refracted from this surface as multiple reflections that pass back into and through the transparent oxide film to the eye of the observer. Differences in oxide thickness cause the film to appear as different colors. Color intensity depends on the degree of initial metal reflectivity.

The same optical effect of absorption, refraction, transmission, and multiple reflections within a film is observed, for the same reasons, in the colors that appear on a soap bubble or an oil film floating on water, but in metal they are permanent. Because of the structure of the substance, permanent interference colors also occur on nacreous shells, feathers, butterfly wings, and beetle elytrae.

TITANIUM OXIDATION COLOR SPECTRUM

The same color sequence that occurs when titanium is *heat colored* also develops when the metal is *anodize colored*. In the latter case, the colors do not develop in relation to a degree of heat, but to the *degree of voltage* allowed to pass through the electrolyte and the metal, and the process is called *anodic interference coloring*.

The specific temperature- or voltage-linked oxide colors that develop on a clean titanium surface are given in Table, "Titanium Heat Oxidation and Anodized Color Spectrum" in this chapter. (The sequence of colors is different for electrochemically colored niobium and tantalum.) As the chart indicates, these colors succeed each other in a characteristic, therefore completely predictable order. The whole color sequence for a particular metal can be termed its *oxidation color spectrum*. Utilizing this predictability, a titanium (niobium and tantalum) surface can be oxidation colored with a great degree of control, and the color arrested and preserved. Depending on the method used, the color can be uniform on the entire object or on parts of it, or seen as a blended spectrum of colors. Methods of achieving these effects are discussed ahead.

TITANIUM SURFACE PREPARATION BEFORE COLORING

Before coloring by either method can take place, the metal's surface condition must be prepared by manual or mechanical abrasion, or chemical means through etching solutions, and the surface must be clean. It is important to note that the character of the textural condition of the surface, its degree of brightness or dullness, has a distinct effect on the intensity of the color produced due to differences in the degree of reflection from these differently prepared surfaces. Such differences can be used as a means of deliberately achieving color variations.

TITANIUM ABRASION PREPARATION METHODS

Some of the methods mentioned here can be carried out manually or mechanically, and others only mechanically. The different textural surface results are visible through the color.

WARNING:
Titanium Dust and Combustion

In cases where surface preparation methods produce dusts of titanium particles, there is a danger of a fire hazard or an explosion occurring from the ignition of the titanium by sparks. To avoid such an occurrence in these processes, *always use a liquid lubricant,* and do not allow titanium dusts to accumulate in the air, on work, or on bench surfaces, but remove and dispose of them.

Polishing a titanium surface for all-over brightness is done with a *polishing lathe* in the same manner as polishing stainless steel. Use a *canvas wheel* coated with 80, 100, 120, or 150 grit *silicon carbide* containing abrasives blended with stearic acid, in successively finer particle stages. The wheel speed, however, should not exceed 2800 sfpm. Do not allow an extended dwell time on the metal at any one position or it will overheat at that point and burn. Use light pressure at the end for a high polish.

Sandblasting can be carried out for a nondirectional, all-over matte surface, at 5 psi, using a wet slurry of an *aluminum oxide abrasive*. Masking materials can be used on the object to protect previously created bright or textured areas, while exposed areas are made matte for surface texture contrast. Colored areas previously created can also be protected by masking while new areas are sandblasted clean and left that way, or to prepare them for coloring.

Directionally texturing an area masked out with tape is possible using a *glass fiber brush* or *paper- or cloth-backed abrasive*. Areas brushed or rubbed in different directions create shifting color intensities as reflected light picks up the color at different angles when the work moves. This technique can be used to create illusory effects of depth on a flat surface.

Surface scraping can be done manually with a *coarse file* or a *diamond file* to create directional texture. Curved *riffle files* can be used to texture local areas only rather than whole surfaces because of their curved forms. Make sure to rinse the filings away at intervals with water. Series of parallel or crossing lines can also be made on the metal with *gravers* or *scorers*, the bright lines reflecting light through the colored oxide film. Line scoring can be a postcoloring technique, the lines left unoxidized, or color oxidized.

Rotary bur texturing is possible using *high-speed steel* or *tungsten carbide abrasive burs* and a lubricant. By varying speeds and bur types, several surface textures are possible, each creating different effects.

Surface grinding can be done manually with an *abrasive stick*, or mechanically at one-third to one-half of conventional grinding speeds. Use *vitrified bond wheels* with 46–70 grit sizes, and a wheel hardness of J-1; or an A 60M wheel at 500 sfpm. Use light pressure cuts to avoid burning or cracking the metal, and as a lubricant-coolant use a continual flow of a water-soluble oil, or a chlorinated or sulphurizing oil. *Never dry grind titanium* or its alloys because the dry dust thrown into the air can be ignited by a spark and cause an explosion or fire.

DEGREASING A TITANIUM OBJECT BEFORE COLORING

To degrease the surface, wash it first in an ammonium, detergent, and water solution, then rinse it in deionized or distilled water. If water break still occurs, repeat the washing, or rub it with denatured alcohol on clean cotton wadding.

TITANIUM CHEMICAL CLEANING AND BRIGHTENING

To prepare a titanium surface for coloring by heat or electrochemical means, it can first be etched in an acid solution. Etching and pickling should be allowed to progress until a uniform gas evolution appears on the whole surface of the object, as otherwise the oxide color thickness will not be uniform. If etching is protracted, the surface will take on a semimatte appearance. Should etching continue longer on titanium that has been grain enlarged by heating, the surface appears spangled with facetlike markings called *etch figures,* characteristically produced when metal crystal surfaces are relatively deeply attacked chemically. The true crystal structure of sheet metal exists below its upper layer where, due to rolling or polishing, crystals are considerably distorted. Not until the etchant eliminates all traces of that upper distorted layer and eats down to its undistorted crystal structure is the etch figure revealed. Titanium crystals are hexagonal and close packed below 1620° F (882° C). Bright dipping such a grain-coarsened titanium surface produces a result attractive enough by itself for use in jewelry without coloring. When this surface is anodized, it provides a facet-patterned base that reflects light through the oxide colors with every change of direction, much as in basse taille enameling in which a pattern engraved on metal and covered with transparent enamel reflects light through the enamel.

During all methods involving the use of acids, wear *rubber gloves,* and a *face shield,* and work under conditions of *good ventilation.*

ACID SOLUTIONS USED IN PROCESSING TITANIUM

TITANIUM SCALE-LOOSENING SOLUTION

In cases where titanium has been subjected to heat treatment, and an undesirable, heavy oxide scale remains, its removal may require an initial scale-loosening treatment with an alkaline oxidizer before pickling or bright dipping can take place.

Potassium permanganate ($KMnO_4$)	3–12 oz/gal
Soda ash (Na_2CO_3)	3–12 oz/gal
Temperature	170–212° F (76–100° C)

TITANIUM OXIDE SCALE-REMOVAL SOLUTION

Nitric acid	10–40% by weight (20% recommended)
Hydrofluoric acid	1.0–4.0% by weight (4% recommended)
Distilled water	Remainder
Temperature	75–140° F (23–60° C)

Hydrofluoric acid attacks any film of oxide, and nitric acid corrodes the exposed metal unprotected by a resist.

WARNING:
Caution in the Use of Hydrofluoric Acid

Hydrofluoric acid (HF or H_2F_2) which attacks refractory metals is a *dangerous, highly corrosive acid* with a suffocating odor. *Solutions must be prepared, used, and stored with utmost care and caution, and used under highly controlled conditions.* It attacks all silicates such as glass, eyeglass lenses, porcelain, sand, and the silicate content of investment plaster-forming silicon tetrafluoride (SiF_4) which is passed off as a gas. Therefore *good ventilation* and working under a *fume hood* is essential, and if you do not have this facility, do not use this acid. Eye, face, and breathing protection, protective clothing, and rubber gloves are all *essential* to its use. It must be stored in a *lead-, rubber-, gutta percha-,* or *paraffin-lined container* (*never glass*), and kept in a cool, dry place.

When using a titanium oxide scale removal solution containing hydrofluoric acid, place it in a *stainless steel* or *inert plastic container* or tank. Carefully remove the object with *wooden* or *plastic tongs,* and avoid splashes.

Whenever using a hydrofluoric acid solution, *beforehand,* prepare a *bicarbonate of soda and water paste,* and keep it available for use should the acid make skin contact. In such a case, quickly but gently rub the affected area with this paste, and immediately rinse it off in large quantities of cold running water.

TITANIUM PICKLING SOLUTION

Hydrofluoric acid	4% by volume
(or sodium fluoride)	(4% by volume)
Hydrochloric acid	20% by volume
Distilled water	remainder
Temperature	68° F (20° C)

Rinse, and follow by:

TITANIUM BRIGHT DIP SOLUTION

Nitric acid	5% by weight
Hydrofluoric acid	1% by weight
Distilled water	remainder
Temperature	68° F (20° C)

TITANIUM ETCHING SOLUTION

Hydrofluoric acid	10% by volume
Nitric acid	9% by volume
Distilled water	remainder
Temperature	68° F (20° C)

Use a stainless steel or plastic tank.

When desired, a titanium oxide film already existing can be dissolved by immersing the object in a titanium pickling solution.

VACUUM-ETCHED AND ANODIZED COMMERCIAL TITANIUM PRODUCTS

Metal manufacturers and processors have not been idle in regard to the possibilities of surface texturing and coloring titanium. In recent years, Metaux Precieux S.A., Neuchatel, Switzerland, and the Imperial Metal Industries-Titanium (IMI-Titanium), Birmingham, England, have developed patented processes by which titanium sheet metal is given a ready-made, uniformly textured decorative surface, then oxide colored. This product is designed for use in the jewelry and watchmaking fields. The Swiss-registered, colored titanium product is called *Ticolor,* and its colored oxide layer is stated to have a wear resistance equal to 20 micron gold plating (7 microns are normal in a well-wearing gold plate).

In the preparation of these products, the surface texture is created before coloring by thermally etching the metal at 1652–2192° F (900–1200° C) in an inert, very high vacuum atmosphere. The metal, previously evenly worked by controlled mechanical means, develops a surface with an exposed, enlarged, more or less uniformly sized grain structure pattern, randomly oriented and facetlike, and visible to the naked eye. The effect is similar to results achieved when acid etching other metals for microanalysis. Coloring follows, and is achieved by electrochemical anodizing. The color distribution of the result relates to the orientation of the facetlike crystal surface pattern, one color predominating, and other colors intervening, creating an opallike appearance, depending on the manner of anodizing and the thickness of the oxide film.

The IMI-Titanium product is available with crystal surfaces on both sides, in the following grain sizes: very large, large, medium, small, and normal. The dominant colors available are: light brown, brown, purple, dark blue, mid-blue, light blue, light yellow, yellow, orange, salmon, pink, purple, blue, blue green, dark green, mid-green, or light green. These colors result from the different voltages used during anodization. The maximum sheet size available is 7½ in × 84 in (19.1 cm × 213.3 cm). No polishing of the surface is necessary as it remains scintillatingly bright. These colors penetrate into the depressions between the grains, making the surface more resistant to handling. When the surface becomes abraded, it shows bright grains outlined with color that remains in the depressions surrounding them, an effect that might be done deliberately.

Precolored titanium sheet can be heated to modify or modulate the existing colors. It cannot be shaped by plastic deformation methods, and generally is used flat, cut or stamped into any shape. It can be cut into long strips which permits it to be bent into a curve without plastic deformation and held in a mount of another metal. Because of these limitations on design concepts using titanium, such units must be fabricated by cold methods, and held to the object by mechanical means.

TITANIUM DIRECT HEAT TREATMENT COLORING

Titanium oxidizes at room temperature, but the oxide films that develop are not sufficiently thick to show color. Upon being heated in air or in an enclosed heat chamber to temperatures above 700° F (371° C), the passive oxide film develops sufficient thickness to exhibit optical interference colors. The oxide film thickness increases in direct relation to the increase in temperature, and the duration of the heat treatment which can last from less than a minute to an extended time of 30 minutes, developing within a range of from 0.04–0.2+ microns. The oxidation rates of titanium alloys vary considerably, depending on the particular alloy content. When pure titanium is heated in air to above 932° F (500° C) the initial visible interference color oxide appears, the color series developing as the temperature increases to 1634° F (890° C). Thereafter, colors appear dull and the oxide becomes soluble into the titanium base metal which as a result becomes severely embrittled.

Before any coloring can be carried out, it is extremely important that the surface of the metal be *chemically clean.* Once clean, *the surface must never be touched* until coloring is completed. The salt from a fingerprint, for example, may cause stress-corrosion cracking at temperatures of 600° F (315° C) and above.

The *heat source* used for oxidizing can be a *kiln* or *furnace* equipped with a *pyrometer,* an accurate heat measuring device consisting of a *thermocouple* in the heating chamber connected to an *ammeter* outside that is calibrated to indicate inside temperature in degrees Fahren-

17–10 GUNILLA TREEN, England. Brooch with silver birds mounted on a mosaiclike, divided titanium ground in one plane, torch heated to create cloudlike effects. The whole is surrounded by a plastic frame silver wire riveted to the ground. *Photo: Cyril Wilson*

17–11 NANNY STILL-McKINNEY, Finland, designer; manufacturer Kultakeskus Oy, Hämeenlinna. Silver pendants made of stamped units assembled by solder. *Left:* "Grapes," 5 cm high; *right:* "Pear," 5.5 cm high. Both use stamped units of precolored titanium sheets with a crystalline grain surface. In the first, the components are cemented in place, and in the second, they are mounted from below in a reverse bezel construction. *Photo: Courtesy Kultakeskus Oy*

heit or Centigrade or both. The heat chamber is preheated to the desired temperature for the wanted color. The object is placed on a *metal trivet,* the kiln door is opened, it is inserted into the heat chamber by the use of *tongs,* and the door is closed. After a suitable time lapse, the object is withdrawn by the same means. Due to uniform temperature within the kiln chamber, an *overall* color appears on the metal. A certain difficulty exists in observing the color development on the metal because it can be seen only after withdrawing the metal from the heating chamber.

When *heat coloring in air,* no problem of visibility exists. The object is placed on a clean *refractory surface* such as charcoal or firebrick. Heat is directed on the object with a *jeweler's torch* or a *microwelding torch* which has a small intense flame. Heat buildup in the object depends on the duration of heat application. Heat can be concentrated in a *local area* on the object in which case small-area variable color effects are possible. The radius of color variation from the point of heat application depends on flame size. When a large, gentle, oxidizing flame is applied to a relatively large area, the resulting blend of colors is more spaced out and gradual. Once the anticipated, desired color sequence is achieved, the color or colors are retained by immediately withdrawing the object from the heat source, or the heat source from the object. Quenching is not necessary, and the colors retain their brightness upon cooling.

Wherever color-blended effects are seen on a colored titanium object, this indicates the colors have been achieved by heating in air. It is not necessary, however, to confine the coloring method to one heating technique. For instance, an overall, even color can be created first by the use of an even heat source such as a kiln, then parts of the object can be color graded by local applications of heat from a torch.

Several variations in achieving in-air color effects are possible, based on the fact that heat diminishes in degree as it is conducted away from the hottest point on the metal. This is what accounts for the spectrum series of colors that appear from the hot point outward. By keeping the flame on the undersurface of the metal, these color changes are easier to observe. When the hot point is in an internal portion of the object, colors will radiate in a concentric sequence around that place, each color blending imperceptibly into another. When the hot point is at an object's edge, the colors radiate from there inward. By repeating the heating process and changing the position of the hot spot, overlapping or intersecting rainbow and cloudlike effects can be created.

To *prevent* the formation of an oxide color on a portion of a pure titanium surface, that area can be brushed or sprayed with an even layer of a *paint containing aluminum particles*. The object is then baked at 400° F (204° C) for a minimum of 4 hours. The resulting coating will provide protection up to about 1350° F (732° C), and is removed once coloring is finished. The paint could also be spattered irregularly on a surface to cause a spotted effect.

It is also possible to heat the metal while a portion of it is held by *clamps* between two insulating or *heat sink sheets,* such as mild steel, or *asbestos composition boards.* Heat applied to the exposed portion will develop up to the protected portion, and the color will then change because of the reduction in heat, creating a color demarcation on the metal. This can be repeated with color areas overlapping by changing the position of the heat shield material.

Lines can be scored through any resulting colored surface oxide film by using a *diamond-mounted scriber,* producing bright metal lines on a colored ground. In the same way, surfaces can be scratched to free them of oxide coloring and expose portions of the base metal.

Outlines of shapes and figures can be made first on the object's surface by etching, and the shapes within the lines then colored. Coloring can be carried out first, and the outlines then etched, with the already achieved colors protected by a resist that is afterward removed by its solvent. The etched, depressed lines can be left untouched, or filled with an inlay of a colored liquid plastic material such as a colored epoxy, or a two-part polyurethane resin. Such lines can act as borders around figures, or as lines integrated with an abstract composition.

The table, "Titanium Heat Oxidation and Anodized Color Spectrum," indicates the relationship between the formation of an oxide color on the surface of pure titanium by the application of various approximate *temperatures* or *voltages*.

TITANIUM OVERALL ANODIZING:
Coloring by electrochemical immersion

Total immersion coloring of a titanium component uses an *electrolyte* which is an acid solution made electroconductive by immersed electrodes. The electrolyte acts as a

Titanium Heat Oxidation and Anodized Color Spectrum

Color	Temperature		Voltage	Oxide Film Thickness
	°F	°C	DC	Approximate in Microns
Pale yellow	700	371	3-5	0.03
Pale gold-straw	725	385	10	0.035
Dark gold-brown	750	398	15	0.04
Purple	775	412	20	0.046
Blue-purple	800	426	25	0.0527
Deep blue	825	440	30	0.06
Medium blue	850	454	35	0.063
Pale blue	875	468	40	0.0658
Blue-green	900	482	45	0.07
Green-blue	925	496	50	0.0825
Pale green	950	510	55	0.095
Green-gold	975	523	60	0.1075
Green-gold, purple-marked	1000	537	65	0.12
Rose-gold	1025	551	70	0.13
Red-purple	1050	565	75	0.14
Purple-gold	1075	579	80	0.15
Dull purple, blue-marked	1100	593	85	0.16
Green, purple-marked	1125	607	90	0.17
Dull green with red	1150	621	95	0.18
Brown-gray, matt	1175	635	100	0.19
Mottled gray, opaque	1200	648	110	0.2+

Some data courtesy Imperial Metal Industries, Titanium, Birmingham, England.

medium for transmitting the current to the object immersed in it. Color is not achieved by dyeing a colorless anodized coating as with aluminum, because anodized titanium has no appreciable affinity for dye colors. When titanium immersed in an electrolyte is subjected to different voltages, its surface forms a compact anodic film of titanium dioxide (TaO_2), the most stable of all titanium oxides. This develops from the active combination of the metal and oxygen that forms at the anode to which the object is attached. The particular colors that develop, as already explained, depend on the amount of voltage used: the higher the voltage, the thicker the oxide film, which is also dense and adherent.

Electrochemically created color sequences are the same as those that are created by heat. These color sequences occur as *first-, second-,* or *third-order colors,* that is, at low voltages, one distinct series of colors develop, but when the voltages are increased, a similar series of colors occurs a second or third time. The film of the first series is much thinner than that of the second or third series or order. Since thicker oxide films are more durable than thin ones, higher voltage color series are preferable. High-voltage colors are less susceptible to abrasion and fading on exposure to the atmosphere and light than are low-voltage colors. Colors made on mechanically highly polished surfaces are relatively more subject to fading than those created on surfaces that have been chemically brightened.

To achieve an *even color,* surface cleanliness prior to the immersion of the whole object in the electrolyte is of critical importance. Fingerprints, for instance, will seriously interfere with an even buildup of the anodic oxide film.

ELECTROLYTES The electrolytes recommended for a particularly coherent film are either a 10% sulphuric acid, 80% phosphoric acid, 10% water solution; or one containing 5–10% ammonium sulphate. The latter is cheaper and safer, though the result is less resistant to galling or contact abrasion from rubbing. When not in use, the electrolyte can be stored in a well-closed *plastic* or *glass bottle*. These solutions are used at room temperature, and may require cooling after high currents have been used. When colors are no longer bright, the electrolyte is exhausted or contaminated, and must be discarded.

RECTIFIER *Rectifiers* used for titanium anodizing must have a variable voltage range output of 0–140 volts, necessary for the production of a full color range. For titanium, the normal voltage range is 3–90 volts; for niobium 12–140 volts; for tantalum 20–120 volts. *Single-phase* DC *rectifiers* are used, capable of delivering 10 amps/ft² of treated surface. (Some craftspersons report on successful titanium coloring with AC current but this is not common practice.) In the rectifier, the main power supply passes through a variable transformer whose output is isolated from the main supply. The rectifier should be equipped with a *digital voltmeter* controllable in units of 1 volt, necessary for accuracy in color control through voltage control. Current and output voltage are seen on *two-scaled meters* on the front panel of the rectifier.

RESISTS To confine a particular color to a specific, exposed workpiece area, the rest of the object must be masked by a *resist*. (Some resist materials have been mentioned under Anodized Metal Dyeing Techniques, p. 723.) When high voltages are used, the chosen resist must also be heat resistant. A layer of an *adhesive cellulose tape* can be used as a resist to create straight edges, or it can be cut into curves or shapes. Another material that will give sufficient protection is a *solution of cellulose in benzyl acetate,* such as the British product Canning's Lacomit, or the Swiss product Napon. These are applied in two even coats, and allowed to air dry between applications. They are removed after use *under good ventilation* by a *benzyl acetate solvent,* or *chloroform,* neither of which has any effect on the appearance or condition of the achieved oxide film.

WARNING:
Caution in the Use of High Voltages

Voltages produced by the necessary electrical equipment go high enough to be *lethal*. To be certain the electrical equipment and the setup are correct and usable without danger, selection, installation, and checking should be done with the advice or help of a qualified electrician. Proper safety precautions are of *prime importance* during work. Since wet mediums are electroconductive, to avoid electrical shock, it is essential to keep the work area *dry*. Work on a *nonmetallic, nonelectroconductive surface* such as plastic, rubber, or wood. Never allow any exposed body parts to contact electrical parts. *Never touch the workpiece* with bare hands at any time when current is on, and always wear *rubber gloves* (without holes). Handle the workpiece directly only when the current is off, and then only by its attached wire or jig.

PROCEDURE

The *anode* (positive) is the object, made anodic *while the electric power is off,* by attaching it to an *insulated wire lead*. The lead can terminate in *alligator clamps* at the end where it is attached to the anode contact on the rectifier. Clamps should not contact the electrolyte. Alternately, the workpiece can be placed in or held by a *titanium jig* which is connected to the anodic contact by an insulated wire lead. The *cathode* (negative) is a titanium strip, bar, or disc; platinized titanium mesh; or stainless steel. Its total surface area should be approximately equal to that of the average workpiece. The cathode is connected by an insulated wire lead to the cathode contact on the rectifier. Clips can be used at both lead ends, but again, must not contact the electrolyte. Anodic object and the cathode *must not touch* while the workpiece is suspended in the electrolyte or a short circuit and fuse blowout will occur. Keep the anodic object and the cathode as far apart as possible as this aids in color control and in the achievement of clearer colors.

With the *power turned off,* completely or partially immerse the prepared, power-connected workpiece into the electrolyte. As an electrolyte container use a *glass* or *inert plastic tank*. If a *stainless steel tank* is used, it can substitute for the cathode by attaching a lead clamp to it.

Turn on the current, and raise it gradually, 10 volts at a time, until the voltage necessary for achieving the desired color is reached. The highest voltage color must be produced *first,* followed by others in order of decreasing voltage. Between each voltage increase, the circuit ammeter should indicate a current decay by returning to zero between stages. This is also visible on the workpiece when oxygen bubbles cease to form on its surface. Current flow should not exceed 10 amps/ft². The potential increase in current voltage to 110 volts should take at least 10 minutes, and proportionately less for lower voltages, the lowest voltage colors requiring only a few seconds of immersion. Time factors are the workpiece surface area size, the distance between anode and cathode, the electrolyte used, and whether the latter is still or agitated (agitation reduces time).

As the current increases and the cathode visibly effervesces, color changes become visible on the object. Once the desired voltage and color are reached, hold the voltage steady at that point for 30 seconds while the current decays; during this time, the oxide layer thickness builds up to the maximum possible under those conditions. Once the film is formed, the electric current flow from the titanium being anodized ceases almost completely. The oxide then acts as an electrical insulator, causing the oxidizing action to stop at the given point when a uniform oxide film of specific thickness develops on the exposed area. Reduce the current gradually until it is back to 0 volts and the rectifier is off. *Then* remove the object from the electrolyte, rinse it in deionized or distilled water, and dry it.

The procedure is the same when producing the *next lower voltage color* on another part of the same object. Former color areas can be left exposed as they are not affected, but, depending on design requirements, they may be masked off with a resist leaving only the next color area exposed.

TITANIUM LOCALIZED ANODIZING:
Selective area coloring

This anodizing method has the advantage of making possible the controlled creation of a color in a small design area of a titanium component, without the use of a tank containing electrolyte. With the current turned *off,* make the work anodic by attaching an insulated lead wire, as al-

17-12 ANN MARIE SHILLITO, England. Buckle in etched and selective anodize-colored titanium. The buckle is produced in a limited series. Several identical units are created simultaneously on a single titanium sheet that has been previously etched to expose its crystalline structure as the colors appear more intense on such a reflecting surface. The photoresist-covered sheet is exposed to a projected outline image, then developed, and the lines are etched to a desired depth. While the resist is still present, the etched lines are filled with a two-part polyurethane pigment which is not affected by subsequent processes, and the resist is then removed. The colors are created within the outlines by the use of an *anodic stylus* with an electrolyte-applying tip, using the necessary voltages; highest voltage colors first, followed by others in order of decreasing voltages. The colors are fairly close to natural: brown cows, blue sky, brown ground, yellow and purple flowers, and green grass (a mixture of yellow and blue). *Photo: Ann Marie Shillito*

17-13 *THE BELT WITH BUCKLE.* Photo: Crafts Advisory Committee, London

17-14 EDWARD A. DE LARGE, England. Necklace in silver with titanium pendant unit whose surface has been textured in different directions to create the triangular planes that give the object an illusion of three dimensions. Parts of the titanium oxide pattern were created by masking out other parts using masking tape, petroleum-based glue, or etching stop-out varnish. The exposed areas were then anodize colored in an electrolyte at a range of 12–80 volts. Depending on the design requirements, masking may be carried out several times, always working from the highest voltage color downward. Those colors produced at higher voltages are unaffected by the lower voltages used to create the following colors. Masking materials are removed by their appropriate solvent. After cleaning the entire unit, parts of it were then heat treated directly with a gas torch to create additional graded color effects. Pendant width 7.5 cm. *Photo: Günter Meyer*

ready described. Place the cleaned workpiece flat on a *dry rubber mat* and immobilize it. Alternately, the workpiece can be held down by a sheathed titanium wire whose exposed point contacts it and delivers the current. Attach the cathode wire to an *electrolyte applicator* which can be a plastic- or wood-handled *brush* with natural or nylon hair and a *metal ferrule*. The cathode wire is fixed to the ferrule which conducts current to the electrolyte fluid into which the brush has been dipped. The ferrule should be insulated after wire attachment with sufficient electrical tape, and it should not be allowed to touch the workpiece or a short circuit and fuse blowout will occur.

Another improvised electrolyte applicator device that will serve the same purpose is a pen-length *glass capillary tube* through which a cathode-attached titanium wire passes just short of the tube end, where it reaches a *wad of cotton* stuffed into the working end of the tube. The opposite end is left open for the escape of evolved gases.

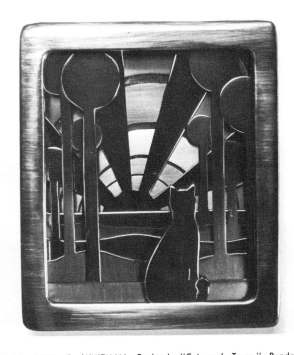

17-15 JULIA C. WHITMAN, England. "Cat and Trees." Pendant fabricated from several units of pierced titanium, and a silver frame. High-speed drills, 0.5–1.5 mm, mounted in a flex-shaft, were used to make holes for the entry of normal, high-quality piercing saw blades which were used to remove pierced areas. The negative shapes were finished with variously sectioned needle files. After coloring, the flat units were assembled one above the other, and placed within a flange behind the frame, and glued there with cyanoacrylate adhesive. The flange was then rubbed over the layers' edges, as with a bezel setting, to hold them in place. Alternately, the assembled layers can be drilled with holes, and silver rivet pins soldered to the back of the silver frame at positions corresponding to these holes. Once the pins are passed through the holes, their heads can be hammer formed at the reverse. Size 40 × 35 mm. *Photo: Pete Norman*

While holding the tube (or the brush) with a *rubber-gloved* hand, the cotton (or brush hairs) is dipped into the electrolyte and absorbs the solution. In the case of the tube, electrolyte also enters the tube, creating a surplus that thereafter acts as a reservoir to supply new solution to the cotton swab as needed.

Turn on the current, and gradually bring it up to the highest voltage that will produce the desired color. Brush or swab the electrolyte over the exact area where that color is wanted. At intervals, recharge the applicator with electrolyte, especially necessary when colors are created above 50 volts, or the solution will boil and evaporate. If the applicator is allowed to completely dry out, due to voltage-generated heat, brush hairs or wadding will burn, and the glue holding the hair will melt. Rinse the applicator occasionally in water to dissolve accumulated salts. Once the desired oxide color appears, continue to rub the area another 2–10 minutes, then gradually turn the current off. Finally, rinse the object in water to remove acid traces left from the electrolyte. After drying, the actual full color is visible, and is somewhat different when the surface is wet. The same procedure is followed for remaining lower voltage colors. When a design requires several colors, for area control, masking may follow the creation of each color. Unwanted color areas can be removed with abrasives or by an acid etch.

The different color creation methods described can be combined on the same workpiece. For example, the entire object may be immersion anodized. Parts of the color can be removed by abrasion or etching while the rest is covered with a resist. Etched parts without color can be colored with lower voltage colors. Parts can then be subjected to direct heat from a torch. By superimposition or juxtaposition, coloring effects achievable by all processes can be interrelated or modified.

MAINTENANCE AND PROTECTIVE COATINGS ON TITANIUM OXIDE FILMS

Although the oxide film on titanium is relatively tough —actually it is claimed to be harder than the metal itself —it can be scratched if it comes into contact with other hard metals, abrasives, or sharp points. Therefore, titanium jewelry components should be mounted in a way that offers them some protection and minimizes possible abrasion, and titanium jewelry should be stored in a cloth or plastic bag when not in use.

Small amounts of grease left by a fingerprint made on a *finished*, colored, smooth surface is more noticeable than such marks made on titanium colored over a coarse-grained or deeply-etched surface. Fingerprints can, however, be removed by washing the object with a detergent solution, in which case the original condition is restored.

Some experimenting has been done on coating the anodized film with a transparent substance to protect it. Various materials such as lacquers, and clear epoxy have been tried. These materials have been only relatively successful because they modify the manner by which the interference colors are produced. This area is, however, open for experimentation.

For protection of the surface, titanium units in a jewel could be covered with clear, flat or cabochon-curved, lenslike pieces of rock crystal through which the colors and patterns would be visible.

ABBREVIATIONS USED IN WEIGHTS, MEASURES, AND OTHER AREAS

ap	apothecary weight	lb	pound
av or avdp	avoirdupois	lb av	pound avoirdupois
B.&S.	Brown and Sharpe gauge	lb t	pound troy
°C	degree Celsius (centigrade)	m	meter
cg	centigrams	max.	maximum
cir.	circumference	min.	minimum, minute
c.p.	chemically pure	mg	milligram
cm	centimeter	ml	milliliter
ct	carat	mm	millimeter
cwt	hundredweight	OD	outside diameter
deg	degree	o.f.	oxidizing flame
dkg	decagram	oz	ounce
dia., Ø	diameter	oz ap	ounces apothecary weight
dm	decimeter	oz t	ounces troy
dr	dram	pt	pint
dwt	pennyweight (troy)	p.s.	pearl size
°F	degree Fahrenheit	psi	pounds per square inch
fl oz	fluid ounces	qt	quart
ft	foot	r.f.	reducing flame
g	gram	rpm	revolutions per minute
gal	gallon	rps	revolutions per second
gr	grains	sec.	second
hr	hour	sfpm	surface feet per minute
ID	inside diameter	sq	square
in	inch	s.s.	stone size
K, kt	karat	yd	yard
kg	kilogram	wt	weight
l	liter		

18

STANDARD WEIGHTS, MEASURES, AND TABLES

LINEAR MEASUREMENTS

LENGTH

Barter, in which exact weights and measures was not needed, preceded the development of standard weights and measures of length, weight, and capacity. Measures of length came about by the development of the building arts.

Standards of linear measurement for use as a permanent reference were first based on the proportions of human limbs. The *cubit,* among the earliest measurements of length, is the distance from the elbow to the end of the middle finger. This probably came into use because within a small range of variables, this was available to all. The main subdivision was the span of outstretched fingers from thumb to little finger, which was called half a cubit. Other parts of the body, the foot length, the palm, finger or digit width (four to a palm), and outstretched arms were all used as measures, the number of each smaller unit made to correspond with the larger unit.

These concepts of measurements were the basis of later European measurements that spread westward through trade and migrations from the great civilizations of the Middle East where they originated. Equivalents exist with all peoples, under different names. Below are some of their values in terms of today's units.

Ancient Measurements, Approximate Equivalents

1 hand	=	4 in	= 10.2 cm
1 span	=	9 in	= 22.9 cm
1 cubit	=	18 in	= 45.7 cm
1 pace	=	30 in	= 76.2 cm

BRITISH AND AMERICAN MEASURING SYSTEMS

Although there are still thousands of locally used units also currently in use in various countries, the two systems that are internationally most widely used and of which there is almost universal knowledge today are the *British System* and the *Metric System*. These were adopted for use by most countries in the mid-late 19th century. Either of these (and in some cases both) is the fundamental system of measurement used, with the majority of countries following the metric system or planning to do so in the near future. Areas originally a part of the British Empire generally use the British System to which the *American System* is almost exactly equivalent. However, different metric equivalents have been established for British units in the U.K. and the U.S.A. These differences are not very significant, and in almost all cases, appear after the fourth significant number. Countries formerly under the influence of other European countries use the Metric System. Independent countries in general use the Metric System, and all European countries except the U.K. do so.

There seems to be a growing tendency for the eventual universal adoption of the Metric System by all countries of the world. With its equivalent conversion units of capacity to units of weight clearly interrelated (and vice versa), and its divisions based on 100 parts, this system has great logic and usefulness.

THE DECIMAL SYSTEM

The decimal system used within both the Metric and the British Systems is almost universally standardized. In it, numbers smaller than one unit are shown to the *right* of the decimal point, and their place distant from the point indicates tenths, hundredths, thousandths, etc. Whole numbers are shown to the *left* of the decimal point, divided into groups of three by a comma.

Feet and Inches to Meters
(based on 1 inch = 25.4 millimeters)

ft	0 in m	1 in m	2 in m	3 in m	4 in m	5 in m
0		0.0254	0.0508	0.0762	0.1016	0.1270
1	0.3048	0.3302	0.3556	0.3810	0.4064	0.4318
2	0.6096	0.6350	0.6604	0.6858	0.7112	0.7366
3	0.9144	0.9398	0.9652	0.9906	1.0160	1.0414
4	1.2192	1.2446	1.2700	1.2954	1.3208	1.3462
5	1.5240	1.5494	1.5748	1.6002	1.6256	1.6510
6	1.8288	1.8542	1.8796	1.9050	1.9304	1.9558
7	2.1336	2.1590	2.1844	2.2098	2.2352	2.2606
8	2.4384	2.4638	2.4892	2.5146	2.5400	2.5654
9	2.7432	2.7686	2.7940	2.8194	2.8448	2.8702
10	3.0480	3.0734	3.0988	3.1242	3.1496	3.1750
11	3.3528	3.3782	3.4036	3.4290	3.4544	3.4798
12	3.6576	3.6830	3.7084	3.7338	3.7592	3.7846
13	3.9624	3.9878	4.0132	4.0386	4.0640	4.0894
14	4.2672	4.2926	4.3180	4.3434	4.3688	4.3942
15	4.5720	4.5974	4.6228	4.6482	4.6736	4.6990
16	4.8768	4.9022	4.9276	4.9530	4.9784	5.0038
17	5.1816	5.2070	5.2324	5.2578	5.2832	5.3086
18	5.4864	5.5118	5.5372	5.5626	5.5880	5.6134
19	5.7912	5.8166	5.8420	5.8674	5.8928	5.9182
20	6.0960	6.1214	6.1468	6.1722	6.1976	6.2230

ft	6 in m	7 in m	8 in m	9 in m	10 in m	11 in m
0	0.1524	0.1778	0.2032	0.2286	0.2540	0.2794
1	0.4572	0.4826	0.5080	0.5334	0.5588	0.5842
2	0.7620	0.7874	0.8128	0.8382	0.8636	0.8890
3	1.0668	1.0922	1.1176	1.1430	1.1684	1.1938
4	1.3716	1.3970	1.4224	1.4478	1.4732	1.4986
5	1.6764	1.7018	1.7272	1.7526	1.7780	1.8034
6	1.9812	2.0066	2.0320	2.0574	2.0828	2.1082
7	2.2860	2.3114	2.3368	2.3622	2.3876	2.4130
8	2.5908	2.6162	2.6416	2.6670	2.6924	2.7178
9	2.8956	2.9210	2.9464	2.9718	2.9972	3.0226
10	3.2004	3.2258	3.2512	3.2766	3.3020	3.3274
11	3.5052	3.5306	3.5560	3.5814	3.6068	3.6322
12	3.8100	3.8354	3.8608	3.8862	3.9116	3.9370
13	4.1148	4.1402	4.1656	4.1910	4.2164	4.2418
14	4.4196	4.4450	4.4704	4.4958	4.5212	4.5466
15	4.7244	4.7498	4.7752	4.8006	4.8260	4.8514
16	5.0292	5.0546	5.0800	5.1054	5.1308	5.1562
17	5.3340	5.3594	5.3848	5.4102	5.4356	5.4610
18	5.6388	5.6642	5.6896	5.7150	5.7404	5.7658
19	5.9436	5.9690	5.9944	6.0198	6.0452	6.0706
20	6.2484	6.2738	6.2992	6.3246	6.3500	6.3754

Length: British and American System

Unit	Inches	Feet	Yards	Centimeters
1 inch (in) =	1	0.083	0.027	2.540005
1 foot (ft) =	12	1	0.33	30.480
1 yard (yd) =	36	3	1	91.44018

The **inch** is a measure of length, being the twelfth part of a **foot**. The English inch is equal to 2.54 centimeters. It is commonly divided into halves, quarters, eighths, sixteenths, etc. or tenths, hundredths, etc. In the mechanical arts " stands for inches, and ' for feet.

Inch Fractions to Decimals and Millimeters

Fractions of an Inch	Decimals of an Inch	Millimeters	Fractions of an Inch	Decimals of an Inch	Millimeters
$\frac{1}{64}$	.0156	0.397	$\frac{33}{64}$	.5156	13.097
$\frac{1}{32}$	.0312	0.794	$\frac{17}{32}$	.5312	13.494
$\frac{3}{64}$	.0469	1.190	$\frac{35}{64}$	.5469	13.890
$\frac{1}{16}$	.0625	1.588	$\frac{9}{16}$	.5625	14.288
$\frac{5}{64}$	.0781	1.984	$\frac{37}{64}$	.5781	14.684
$\frac{3}{32}$	.0937	2.381	$\frac{19}{32}$	.5937	15.081
$\frac{7}{64}$	.1094	2.778	$\frac{39}{64}$	.6094	15.478
$\frac{1}{8}$	.1250	3.175	$\frac{5}{8}$	.6250	15.875
$\frac{9}{64}$	.1406	3.572	$\frac{41}{64}$	.6406	16.272
$\frac{5}{32}$	.1562	3.969	$\frac{21}{32}$	.6562	16.669
$\frac{11}{64}$	.1719	4.365	$\frac{43}{64}$	.6719	17.066
$\frac{3}{16}$	.1875	4.763	$\frac{11}{16}$	.6875	17.463
$\frac{13}{64}$	.2031	5.159	$\frac{45}{64}$	.7031	17.859
$\frac{7}{32}$	.2187	5.556	$\frac{23}{32}$	.7187	18.256
$\frac{15}{64}$	.2344	5.953	$\frac{47}{64}$	.7344	18.653
$\frac{1}{4}$	.2500	6.350	$\frac{3}{4}$	.7500	19.050
$\frac{17}{64}$	.2656	6.747	$\frac{49}{64}$	.7656	19.447
$\frac{9}{32}$	.2812	7.144	$\frac{25}{32}$	.7812	19.844
$\frac{19}{64}$	.2969	7.540	$\frac{51}{64}$	.7969	20.241
$\frac{5}{16}$	.3125	7.938	$\frac{13}{16}$	.8125	20.638
$\frac{21}{64}$	.3281	8.334	$\frac{53}{64}$	.8281	21.034
$\frac{11}{32}$	.3437	8.731	$\frac{27}{32}$	.8437	21.431
$\frac{23}{64}$	.3594	9.128	$\frac{55}{64}$	.8594	21.828
$\frac{3}{8}$	.3750	9.525	$\frac{7}{8}$	.8750	22.225
$\frac{25}{64}$	.3906	9.922	$\frac{57}{64}$	.8906	22.622
$\frac{13}{32}$	.4062	10.319	$\frac{29}{32}$	.9062	23.019
$\frac{27}{64}$	.4219	10.715	$\frac{59}{64}$	.9219	23.416
$\frac{7}{16}$	.4375	11.113	$\frac{15}{16}$	.9375	23.813
$\frac{29}{64}$	.4531	11.509	$\frac{61}{64}$	.9531	24.209
$\frac{15}{32}$	.4687	11.906	$\frac{31}{32}$	.9687	24.606
$\frac{31}{64}$	.4844	12.303	$\frac{63}{64}$	.9844	25.003
$\frac{1}{2}$	.5000	12.700	1	1.0000	25.400

Decimal Equivalents of Fractions
(in decimal inches)

8ths, 16ths, 32nds, 64ths			
8ths	**32nds**	**64ths**	**64ths**
$\frac{1}{8}$ = .125	$\frac{1}{32}$ = .03125	$\frac{1}{64}$ = .015625	$\frac{33}{64}$ = .515625
$\frac{1}{4}$ = .250	$\frac{3}{32}$ = .09375	$\frac{3}{64}$ = .046875	$\frac{35}{64}$ = .546875
$\frac{3}{8}$ = .375	$\frac{5}{32}$ = .15625	$\frac{5}{64}$ = .078125	$\frac{37}{64}$ = .578125
$\frac{1}{2}$ = .500	$\frac{7}{32}$ = .21875	$\frac{7}{64}$ = .109375	$\frac{39}{64}$ = .609375
$\frac{5}{8}$ = .625	$\frac{9}{32}$ = .28125	$\frac{9}{64}$ = .140625	$\frac{41}{64}$ = .640625
$\frac{3}{4}$ = .750	$\frac{11}{32}$ = .34375	$\frac{11}{64}$ = .171875	$\frac{43}{64}$ = .671875
$\frac{7}{8}$ = .875	$\frac{13}{32}$ = .40625	$\frac{13}{64}$ = .203125	$\frac{45}{64}$ = .703125
16ths	$\frac{15}{32}$ = .46875	$\frac{15}{64}$ = .234375	$\frac{47}{64}$ = .734375
$\frac{1}{16}$ = .0625	$\frac{17}{32}$ = .53125	$\frac{17}{64}$ = .265625	$\frac{49}{64}$ = .765625
$\frac{3}{16}$ = .1875	$\frac{19}{32}$ = .59375	$\frac{19}{64}$ = .296875	$\frac{51}{64}$ = .796875
$\frac{5}{16}$ = .3125	$\frac{21}{32}$ = .65625	$\frac{21}{64}$ = .328125	$\frac{53}{64}$ = .828125
$\frac{7}{16}$ = .4375	$\frac{23}{32}$ = .71875	$\frac{23}{64}$ = .359375	$\frac{55}{64}$ = .859375
$\frac{9}{16}$ = .5625	$\frac{25}{32}$ = .78125	$\frac{25}{64}$ = .390625	$\frac{57}{64}$ = .890625
$\frac{11}{16}$ = .6875	$\frac{27}{32}$ = .84375	$\frac{27}{64}$ = .421875	$\frac{59}{64}$ = .921875
$\frac{13}{16}$ = .8125	$\frac{29}{32}$ = .90625	$\frac{29}{64}$ = .453125	$\frac{61}{64}$ = .953125
$\frac{15}{16}$ = .9375	$\frac{31}{32}$ = .96875	$\frac{31}{64}$ = .484375	$\frac{63}{64}$ = .984375

7ths, 14ths, and 28ths								6ths, 12ths, and 24ths							
7th	14th	28th	Decimal	7th	14th	28th	Decimal	6th	12th	24th	Decimal	6th	12th	24th	Decimal
		1	.035714			15	.535714			1	.041667	3			.5
	1		.071429	4			.571429		1		.083333			13	.541666
		3	.107143			17	.607143			3	.125		7		.583333
1			.142857		9		.642867	1			.166666			15	.625
		5	.178571			19	.678571			5	.208333	4			.666666
	3		.214286	5			.714286		3		.25			17	.708333
		7	.25			21	.75			7	.291666		9		.75
2			.285714		11		.785714	2			.333333			19	.791666
		9	.321429			23	.821429			9	.375				.833333
	5		.357143	6			.857143		5		.416666	5		21	.875
		11	.392857			25	.892857			11	.458333				.916666
3			.428571		13		.928571						11		
		13	.464286			27	.964286							23	.958333
	7		.5												

Ring Sizes,
Approximate Comparison Table

American	British	European	Inside Diameter inch	mm
	A		.4750	12.065
		38	.4762	12.096
	A½		.4828	12.263
1			.486	12.344
		39	.4887	12.414
	B		.4905	12.459
	B½		.4983	12.657
		40	.5013	12.733
1½			.502	12.751
	C		.5060	12.852
	C½	41	.5138	13.051
2			.518	13.157
	D		.5215	13.246
		42	.5263	13.369
	D½		.5293	13.444
2½			.534	13.564
	E		.5370	13.640
		43	.5389	13.687
	E½		.5448	13.838
3			.550	13.970
		44	.5514	14.006
	F		.5525	14.034
	F½		.5603	14.232
		45	.5639	14.324
3½			.566	14.376
	G		.5680	14.427
	G½		.5758	14.625
		46	.5765	14.642
4			.582	14.783
	H		.5835	14.821
		47	.5890	14.961
	H½		.5913	15.019
4½			.598	15.189
	I		.5990	15.215
		48	.6015	15.279
	I½		.6068	15.413
5		49	.6141	15.597
	J		.6145	15.608
	J½		.6223	15.806
		50	.6266	15.916
5½	K		.6300	16.002
	K½		.6378	16.200
		51	.6391	16.234
6	L		.6455	16.396
		52	.6517	16.552
	L½		.6533	16.594
	M		.6610	16.789
6½			.662	16.815
		53	.6642	16.871
	M½		.6688	16.988
	N		.6765	17.183

American	British	European	Inside Diameter inch	mm
		54	.6767	17.189
7			.678	17.221
	N½		.6843	17.381
		55	.6893	17.507
	O		.6920	17.577
7½			.694	17.628
	O½		.6998	17.775
		56	.7018	17.826
	P		.7075	17.971
8			.710	18.034
		57	.7143	18.144
	P½		.7153	18.169
	Q		.7230	18.364
8½			.7265	18.453
		58	.7269	18.462
	Q½		.7308	18.562
	R		.7385	18.758
		59	.7394	18.780
9			.743	18.872
	R½		.7463	18.956
		60	.7519	19.098
	S		.7540	19.152
9½			.759	19.279
	S½		.7618	19.350
		61	.7644	19.416
	T		.7695	19.545
		62	.7770	19.736
	T½		.7772	19.741
10			.778	19.761
	U		.7850	19.939
		63	.7895	20.054
	U½		.7928	20.137
10½			.794	20.168
	V		.8005	20.333
		64	.8020	20.372
	V½		.8083	20.531
11			.811	20.599
		65	.8146	20.690
	W		.8160	20.726
	W½		.8238	20.925
11½		66	.8271	21.008
	X		.8315	21.120
	X½		.8393	21.318
		67	.8396	21.326
12			.843	21.412
	Y		.8470	21.514
		68	.8522	21.645
	Y½		.8548	21.712
12½			.859	21.819
	Z		.8625	21.908
		69	.8647	21.963
	Z½		.8703	22.106
13			.875	22.225

Courtesy Jewellery Advisory Centre, London.

Determining Ring Blank Lengths in B. & S. Gauge

Sizes (U.S.A.)	Length (mm)	Metal Thickness, B.&S. Gauge						
		12	14	16	18	20	22	24
1	39.0	45.5	44.2	43.0	42.1	41.5	40.9	40.5
1¼	39.6	46.2	44.6	43.6	42.7	42.1	41.5	41.1
1½	40.2	46.9	45.2	44.3	43.3	42.7	42.1	41.8
1¾	40.8	47.7	45.8	44.9	44.0	43.3	42.7	42.4
2	41.5	48.0	46.5	45.5	44.6	44.0	43.3	43.0
2¼	42.1	48.7	47.1	46.2	45.2	44.6	44.0	43.6
2½	42.7	49.3	47.7	46.8	45.8	45.2	44.6	44.3
2¾	43.4	49.9	48.4	47.4	46.5	45.8	45.2	44.9
3	44.0	50.6	49.0	48.0	47.1	46.5	45.8	45.6
3¼	44.6	51.2	49.6	48.7	47.7	47.1	46.5	46.2
3½	45.2	51.8	50.2	49.3	48.4	47.7	47.1	46.8
3¾	45.9	52.4	50.9	49.9	49.0	48.4	47.7	47.4
4	46.5	53.1	51.5	50.6	49.6	49.0	48.3	48.0
4¼	47.1	53.7	52.1	51.2	50.2	49.6	49.0	48.7
4½	47.8	54.3	52.8	51.8	50.9	50.2	49.6	49.3
4¾	48.4	55.0	53.4	52.4	51.5	50.9	50.2	49.9
5	49.0	55.6	54.0	53.1	52.1	51.5	50.9	50.6
5¼	49.6	56.2	54.6	53.7	52.8	52.1	51.5	51.2
5½	50.3	56.8	55.3	54.3	53.4	52.7	52.1	51.8
5¾	50.9	57.5	55.9	55.0	54.0	53.4	52.8	52.4
6	51.5	58.1	56.5	55.6	54.6	54.0	53.4	53.1
6¼	52.2	58.7	57.1	56.2	55.3	54.6	54.0	53.7
6½	52.8	59.3	57.8	56.8	55.9	55.3	54.6	54.3
6¾	53.4	60.0	58.4	57.5	56.5	55.9	55.3	55.0
7	54.0	60.6	59.0	58.1	57.1	56.5	55.9	55.6
7¼	54.7	61.2	59.7	58.7	57.8	57.1	56.5	56.2
7½	55.3	61.9	60.3	59.3	58.4	57.8	57.1	56.8
7¾	55.9	62.5	60.9	60.0	59.0	58.4	57.8	57.5
8	56.6	63.1	61.5	60.6	59.7	59.0	58.4	58.1
8¼	57.2	63.7	62.2	61.2	60.3	59.7	59.0	58.7
8½	57.8	64.4	62.8	61.9	60.9	60.3	59.7	59.3
8¾	58.4	65.0	63.4	62.5	61.5	60.9	60.3	60.0
9	59.1	65.6	64.1	63.1	62.2	61.5	60.9	60.6
9¼	59.7	66.3	64.7	63.7	62.8	62.2	61.5	61.2
9½	60.3	66.9	65.3	64.4	63.4	62.8	62.2	61.9
9¾	60.9	67.5	65.9	65.0	64.1	63.4	62.8	62.5
10	61.6	68.1	66.6	65.6	64.7	64.1	63.4	63.1
10¼	62.2	68.8	67.2	66.3	65.3	64.7	64.1	63.7
10½	62.8	69.4	67.8	66.9	65.9	65.3	64.7	64.4
10¾	63.5	70.0	68.5	67.5	66.6	65.9	65.3	65.0
11	64.1	70.7	69.1	68.1	67.2	66.6	65.9	65.6
11¼	64.7	71.3	69.7	68.8	67.8	67.2	66.6	66.3
11½	65.3	71.9	70.3	69.4	68.5	67.8	67.2	66.9
11¾	66.0	72.5	71.0	70.0	69.1	68.5	67.8	67.5
12	66.6	73.2	71.6	70.7	69.7	69.1	68.5	68.1
12¼	67.2	73.8	72.2	71.3	70.3	69.7	69.1	68.8
12½	67.9	74.4	72.8	71.9	71.0	70.3	69.7	69.4
12¾	68.5	75.0	73.5	72.5	71.6	71.0	70.3	70.0
13	69.1	75.7	74.1	73.2	72.2	71.6	71.0	70.7

Add 0.5mm to these lengths if the ring band is wider than 4mm.

Approximate Length per Troy Ounce of Sterling Silver Wire

Nearest Fractional Size	Rectangular		Square		Round		Half Round	
	B.&S. Gauge	Feet	B.&S. Gauge	Feet	B.&S. Gauge	Feet	B.&S. Gauge	Feet
5/16″							5/16″ base	5 inches
5/32″							6 ″	1½
1/8″			8	1	8	1¼	8 ″	2½
					10	2	10 ″	3¾
5/64″			12	2¼	12	3		
1/16″			14	3¾	14	4¾	14 ″	9½
	4 × 16	1½	16	6	16	7½		
	6 × 18	2¼	18	9¼	18	12		
1/32″					20	19		
	8 × 22	4¾			22	30		
1/64″	8 × 26				24			
	14 × 30							
	14 × 32							

THE METRIC SYSTEM

The Metric System as a standard of measurement originated in France about 1790. Its use is required by law in a majority of countries in the world, and is permitted in others such as the U.S.A. and the U.K. As mentioned, eventually its use will become universal.

The Metric System is a decimal system of measures and weights in which the *meter* and the *gram* are used as basic measures. All units are derived from the meter, the basic unit of length. It is intended to be, and nearly is, one ten-millionth part of the distance measured on a meridian from the equator to the pole.

Other primary measurement units are based on the meter, such as the *square meter,* the *cubic meter,* the *liter,* and the *gram.* Because it was found that it was possible to have greater accuracy when a standard of mass of a material substance was specifically defined, the *kilogram* was adopted as the standard of mass, rather than a standard used for volume. The *liter,* the unit of volume, was then redefined in terms of the standard of mass, as the volume of kilogram of pure water at the temperature of its maximum density. It is equal to 1.000027 cubic decimeters.

In the metric system the following measures used as a prefix before a unit have these meanings:

micro   means one millionth
milli   means one thousandth
centi   means one hundredth
deci   means one tenth
deca   means ten
hecto   means one hundred
kilo   means one thousand
myria   means ten thousand
mega   means one million

Metric System Measures of Length
(with decimal equivalents in inches)

Unit	Abbreviation	Equivalents	
1 millimeter	mm		0.039370 inch
1 centimeter	cm	= 10 millimeters	0.39370 inch
1 decimeter	dm	= 10 centimeters	3.9370 inches
1 meter	m	= 10 decimeters	39.37008 inches
			3.2808399 feet
			1.09361 yards
1 decameter	Dm	= 10 meters	32.808399 feet
1 hectometer	Hm	= 10 decameters	19.883878 rods
1 kilometer	Km	= 10 hectometers	1,093.61 yards
		= 1,000 meters	0.6213712 mile
1 myriameter	Mm	= 10 kilometers	6.213712 miles
1 megameter	Mg	= 1,000 kilometers	621.4 miles

Decimal Equivalents of Millimeters to Decimal Inches

mm	Inches	mm	Inches	mm	Inches	mm	Inches	mm	Inches
.01	.00039	.41	.01614	.81	.03189	21	.82677	61	2.40157
.02	.00079	.42	.01654	.82	.03228	22	.86614	62	2.44094
.03	.00118	.43	.01693	.83	.03268	23	.90551	63	2.48031
.04	.00157	.44	.01732	.84	.03307	24	.94488	64	2.51968
.05	.00197	.45	.01772	.85	.03346	25	.98425	65	2.55905
.06	.00236	.46	.01811	.86	.03386	26	1.02362	66	2.59842
.07	.00276	.47	.01850	.87	.03425	27	1.06299	67	2.63779
.08	.00315	.48	.01890	.88	.03465	28	1.10236	68	2.67716
.09	.00354	.49	.01929	.89	.03504	29	1.14173	69	2.71653
.10	.00394	.50	.01969	.90	.03543	30	1.18110	70	2.75590
.11	.00433	.51	.02008	.91	.03583	31	1.22047	71	2.79527
.12	.00472	.52	.02047	.92	.03622	32	1.25984	72	2.83464
.13	.00512	.53	.02087	.93	.03661	33	1.29921	73	2.87401
.14	.00551	.54	.02126	.94	.03701	34	1.33858	74	2.91338
.15	.00591	.55	.02165	.95	.03740	35	1.37795	75	2.95275
.16	.00630	.56	.02205	.96	.03780	36	1.41732	76	2.99212
.17	.00669	.57	.02244	.97	.03819	37	1.45669	77	3.03149
.18	.00709	.58	.02283	.98	.03858	38	1.49606	78	3.07086
.19	.00748	.59	.02323	.99	.03898	39	1.53543	79	3.11023
.20	.00787	.60	.02362	1.00	.03937	40	1.57480	80	3.14960
.21	.00827	.61	.02402	1	.03937	41	1.61417	81	3.18897
.22	.00866	.62	.02441	2	.07874	42	1.65354	82	3.22834
.23	.00906	.63	.02480	3	.11811	43	1.69291	83	3.26771
.24	.00945	.64	.02520	4	.15748	44	1.73228	84	3.30708
.25	.00984	.65	.02559	5	.19685	45	1.77165	85	3.34645
.26	.01024	.66	.02598	6	.23622	46	1.81102	86	2.38582
.27	.01063	.67	.02638	7	.27559	47	1.85039	87	3.42519
.28	.01102	.68	.02677	8	.31496	48	1.88976	88	3.46456
.29	.01142	.69	.02717	9	.35433	49	1.92913	89	3.50393
.30	.01181	.70	.02756	10	.39370	50	1.96850	90	3.54330
.31	.01220	.71	.02795	11	.43307	51	2.00787	91	3.58267
.32	.01260	.72	.02835	12	.47244	52	2.04724	92	3.62204
.33	.01299	.73	.02874	13	.51181	53	2.08661	93	3.66141
.34	.01339	.74	.02913	14	.55118	54	2.12598	94	3.70078
.35	.01378	.75	.02953	15	.59055	44	2.16535	95	3.74015
.36	.01417	.76	.02992	16	.62992	56	2.20472	96	3.77952
.37	.01457	.77	.03032	17	.66929	57	2.24409	97	3.81889
.38	.01496	.78	.03071	18	.70866	58	2.28346	98	3.85826
.39	.01535	.79	.03110	19	.74803	59	2.32283	99	3.89763
.40	.01575	.80	.03150	20	.78740	60	2.36220	100	3.93700

Metric System Conversion Table

Millimeters	× .03937	= Inches
Millimeters	= 25.400	× Inches
Meters	× 3.2809	= Feet
Meters	= .3048	× Feet
Square centimeters	× .15500	= Square inches
Square centimeters	= 6.4515	× Square inches
Square meters	× 10.76410	= Square feet
Square meters	= .09290	× Square feet
Cubic centimeters	× .061025	= Cubic inches
Cubic centimeters	= 16.3866	× Cubic inches
Cubic meters	× 35.3156	= Cubic feet
Cubic meters	= .02832	× Cubic feet
Cubic meters	× 1.308	= Cubic yards
Cubic meters	= .765	× Cubic yards
Liters	× 61.023	= Cubic inches
Liters	= .01639	× Cubic inches
Liters	× .26418	= U.S. gallons
Liters	= 3.7854	× U.S. gallons
Grams	× 15.4324	= Grains
Grams	= .0648	× Grains
Grams	× .03527	= Ounces, avoirdupois
Grams	= 28.3495	× Ounces, avoirdupois
Kilograms	× 2.2046	= Pounds
Kilograms	= .4536	× Pounds
Kilograms per square cm	× 14.2231	= Pounds per square inch
Kilograms per square cm	= .0703	× Pounds per square inch
Kilograms per cubic meter	× .06243	= Pounds per cubic foot
Kilograms per cubic meter	= 16.01890	× Pounds per cubic foot

THICKNESS

Wire Gauge Standards, U.S.A.
(in decimal inches)

Number of Wire Gauge	American or Brown & Sharpe	Birmingham or Stubs' Iron Wire	Washburn & Moen, Worcester, Mass.	Stubs Steel Wire	U.S Standard Gauge for Sheet and Plate Iron and Steel
00000000	–	–	–	–	–
0000000	–	–	–	–	–
000000	–	–	–	–	.46875
00000	–	–	–	–	.4375
0000	.460	.454	.3938	–	.40625
000	.40964	.425	.3625	–	.375
00	.3648	.380	.3310	–	.34375
0	.32486	.340	.3065	–	.3125
1	.2893	.300	.2830	.227	.28125
2	.25763	.284	.2625	.219	.265625
3	.22942	.259	.2437	.212	.250
4	.20431	.238	.2253	.207	.234375
5	.18194	.220	.2070	.204	.21875
6	.16202	.203	.1920	.201	.203125
7	.14428	.180	.1770	.199	.1875
8	.12849	.165	.1620	.197	.171875
9	.11443	.148	.1483	.194	.15625
10	.10189	.134	.1350	.191	.140625
11	.090742	.120	.1205	.188	.125
12	.080808	.109	.1055	.185	.109375
13	.071961	.095	.0915	.182	.09375
14	.064084	.083	.0800	.180	.078125
15	.057068	.072	.0720	.178	.0703125
16	.05082	.065	.0625	.175	.0625
17	.045257	.058	.0540	.172	.05625
18	.040303	.049	.0475	.168	.050
19	.03589	.042	.0410	.164	.04375
20	.031961	.035	.0348	.161	.0375
21	.028462	.032	.03175	.157	.034375
22	.025347	.028	.0286	.155	.03125
23	.022571	.025	.0258	.153	.028125
24	.0201	.022	.0230	.151	.025
25	.0179	.020	.0204	.148	.021875
26	.01594	.018	.0181	.146	.01875
27	.014195	.016	.0173	.143	.0171875
28	.012641	.014	.0162	.139	.015625
29	.011257	.013	.0150	.134	.0140625
30	.010025	.012	.0140	.127	.0125
31	.008928	.010	.0132	.120	.0109375
32	.00795	.009	.0128	.115	.01015625
33	.00708	.008	.0118	.112	.009375
34	.006304	.007	.0104	.110	.00859375
35	.005614	.005	.0095	.108	.0078125
36	.005	.004	.0090	.106	.00703125
37	.004453	–	–	.103	.006640625
38	.003965	–	–	.101	.00625
39	.003531	–	–	.099	–
40	.003144	–	–	.097	–

Courtesy L.S. Starrett Co.

British (Imperial) Standard Wire Gauge
(in decimal inches and millimeters)

SWG No	Diameter in	Diameter mm	SWG No	Diameter in	Diameter mm	SWG No	Diameter in	Diameter mm
7/0	0.500	12.70	13	0.092	2.34	32	0.0108	0.274
6/0	0.464	11.79	14	0.080	2.03	33	0.0100	0.254
5/0	0.432	10.97	15	0.072	1.83	34	0.0092	0.234
4/0	0.400	10.16	16	0.064	1.63	35	0.0084	0.213
3/0	0.372	9.45	17	0.056	1.42	36	0.0076	0.193
2/0	0.348	8.84	18	0.048	1.22	37	0.0068	0.173
1/0	0.324	8.23	19	0.040	1.016	38	0.0060	0.152
1	0.300	7.62	20	0.036	0.914	39	0.0052	0.132
2	0.276	7.01	21	0.032	0.813	40	0.0048	0.122
3	0.252	6.40	22	0.028	0.711	41	0.0044	0.112
4	0.232	5.89	23	0.024	0.610	42	0.0040	0.102
5	0.212	5.38	24	0.022	0.559	43	0.0036	0.0914
6	0.192	4.88	25	0.020	0.508	44	0.0032	0.0813
7	0.176	4.47	26	0.018	0.457	45	0.0028	0.0711
8	0.160	4.06	27	0.0164	0.417	46	0.0024	0.0610
9	0.144	3.66	28	0.0148	0.376	47	0.0020	0.0508
10	0.128	3.25	29	0.0136	0.345	48	0.0016	0.0406
11	0.116	2.95	30	0.0124	0.315	49	0.0012	0.0305
12	0.104	2.64	31	0.0116	0.295	50	0.0010	0.0254

Birmingham Metal Gauge (British)
(in decimal inches and millimeters)

Gauge Number	Dimensions in	Dimensions mm	Gauge Number	Dimensions in	Dimensions mm
8/0	0.7083	18.0	23	0.0278	0.707
7/0	0.6666	16.93	24	0.0248	0.629
6/0	0.625	15.875	25	0.0220	0.560
5/0	0.5883	14.94	26	0.0196	0.498
4/0	0.5416	13.76	27	0.0174	0.4432
3/0	0.500	12.7	28	0.0156	0.3969
2/0	0.4452	11.31	29	0.0139	0.3531
1/0	0.3964	10.07	30	0.0123	0.3124
1	0.3532	8.971	31	0.0110	0.2794
2	0.3147	7.993	32	0.0098	0.2489
3	0.2804	7.122	33	0.0087	0.2210
4	0.250	6.35	34	0.0077	0.1956
5	0.2225	5.651	35	0.0069	0.1753
6	0.1981	5.032	36	0.0061	0.1549
7	0.1764	4.48	37	0.0054	0.137
8	0.1570	3.988	38	0.0048	0.122
9	0.1398	3.55	39	0.0043	0.109
10	0.1250	3.175	40	0.00386	0.098
11	0.1113	2.827	41	0.00343	0.087
12	0.0991	2.517	42	0.00306	0.078
13	0.0882	2.24	43	0.00272	0.069
14	0.0785	1.994	44	0.00242	0.0615
15	0.0699	1.775	45	0.00215	0.0546
16	0.0625	1.587	46	0.00192	0.0488
17	0.0556	1.412	47	0.00170	0.0432
18	0.0495	1.257	48	0.00152	0.0386
19	0.0440	1.118	49	0.00135	0.0343
20	0.0392	0.996	50	0.00120	0.0305
21	0.0349	0.886	51	0.00107	0.0272
22	0.0312	0.794	52	0.00095	0.0241

High-Speed Steel Twist Drills

(equivalent measurements with B.&S. gauge and Stubs Steel Wire gauge)

Inch	mm	B.&S. Gauge	Stubs Steel Wire	Drill No.	Inch	mm	B.&S. Gauge	Stubs Steel Wire	Drill No.	Inch	mm	B.&S. Gauge	Stubs Steel Wire	Drill No.
.0030	0.076	–	–	–	.0403	1.024	18	–	–	.1200	3.048	–	31	31
.0040	0.102	–	–	–	.0410	1.041	–	58	59	.1270	3.226	–	30	–
.0050	0.127	–	–	–	.0420	1.067	–	57	58	.1285	3.264	8	–	30
.0059	0.150	–	–	97	.0430	1.092	–	–	57	.1340	3.404	–	29	–
.0060	0.152	–	–	–	.0450	1.143	–	56	–	.1360	3.454	–	–	29
.0063	0.160	–	–	96	.0453	1.151	17	–	–	.1390	3.531	–	28	–
.0067	0.170	–	–	95	.0465	1.181	–	–	56	.1405	3.573	–	–	28
.0070	0.178	–	–	–	.0500	1.270	–	55	–	.1430	3.636	–	27	–
.0071	0.180	–	–	94	.0508	1.290	16	–	–	.1440	3.662	–	–	27
.0075	0.190	–	–	93	.0520	1.321	–	–	55	.1443	3.670	7	–	–
.0079	0.200	–	–	92	.0550	1.397	–	54	54	.1460	3.712	–	26	–
.0080	0.203	–	–	–	.0571	1.450	15	–	–	.1470	3.758	–	–	26
.0083	0.210	–	–	91	.0580	1.473	–	53	–	.1480	3.763	–	25	–
.0087	0.220	–	–	90	.0595	1.512	–	–	53	.1495	3.802	–	–	25
.0090	0.229	–	–	–	.0630	1.600	–	52	–	.1510	3.835	–	24	–
.0091	0.230	–	–	89	.0635	1.613	–	–	52	.1520	3.861	–	–	24
.0095	0.241	–	–	88	.0641	1.629	14	–	–	.1530	3.886	–	23	–
.0100	0.254	–	–	87	.0660	1.676	–	51	–	.1540	3.912	–	–	23
.0105	0.267	–	–	86	.0670	1.702	–	–	51	.1550	3.937	–	22	–
.0110	0.279	–	–	85	.0690	1.753	–	50	–	.1570	3.988	–	21	22
.0115	0.292	–	–	84	.0700	1.778	–	–	50	.1590	4.039	–	–	21
.0120	0.305	–	–	83	.0720	1.829	13	49	–	.1610	4.085	–	20	20
.0125	0.320	–	–	82	.0730	1.854	–	–	49	.1620	4.111	6	–	–
.0130	0.330	–	80	81	.0750	1.905	–	48	–	.1640	4.162	–	19	–
.0135	0.343	–	–	80	.0760	1.930	–	–	48	.1660	4.212	–	–	19
.0140	0.356	–	79	–	.0770	1.956	–	47	–	.1680	4.263	–	18	–
.0142	0.361	27	–	–	.0785	1.994	–	–	47	.1695	4.302	–	–	18
.0145	0.369	–	–	79	.0790	2.007	–	46	–	.1720	4.371	–	17	–
.0150	0.381	–	78	–	.0808	2.052	12	–	–	.1730	4.396	–	–	17
.0159	0.404	26	–	–	.0810	2.057	–	45	46	.1750	4.447	–	16	–
.0160	0.406	–	77	78	.0820	2.083	–	–	45	.1770	4.498	–	–	16
.0179	0.455	25	–	–	.0850	2.159	–	44	–	.1780	4.523	–	15	–
.0180	0.457	–	76	77	.0860	2.184	–	–	44	.1800	4.570	–	14	15
.0200	0.508	–	75	76	.0880	2.235	–	43	–	.1819	4.618	5	–	–
.0201	0.511	24	–	–	.0890	2.261	–	–	43	.1820	4.621	–	13	14
.0210	0.533	–	–	75	.0907	2.304	11	–	–	.1850	4.697	–	12	13
.0220	0.559	–	74	–	.0920	2.337	–	42	–	.1880	4.773	–	11	–
.0225	0.572	–	–	74	.0935	2.378	–	–	42	.1890	4.799	–	–	12
.0226	0.574	23	–	–	.0950	2.413	–	41	–	.1910	4.855	–	10	11
.0230	0.584	–	73	–	.0960	2.438	–	–	41	.1935	4.919	–	–	10
.0240	0.610	–	72	73	.0970	2.464	–	40	–	.1940	4.932	–	9	–
.0250	0.635	–	–	72	.0980	2.489	–	–	40	.1960	4.982	–	–	9
.0253	0.643	22	–	–	.0990	2.515	–	39	–	.1970	5.008	–	8	–
.0260	0.660	–	71	71	.0995	2.528	–	–	39	.1990	5.059	–	7	8
.0270	0.685	–	70	–	.1010	2.565	–	38	–	.2010	5.105	–	6	7
.0280	0.712	–	–	70	.1015	2.578	–	–	38	.2040	5.182	–	5	6
.0285	0.724	21	–	–	.1019	2.588	10	–	–	.2043	5.189	4	–	–
.0290	0.737	–	69	–	.1030	2.616	–	37	–	.2055	5.220	–	–	5
.02925	0.743	–	–	69	.1040	2.642	–	–	37	.2070	5.258	–	4	–
.0300	0.762	–	68	–	.1060	2.692	–	36	–	.2090	5.309	–	–	4
.0310	0.787	–	67	68	.1065	2.705	–	–	36	.2120	5.381	–	3	–
.0320	0.813	20	66	67	.1080	2.743	–	35	–	.2130	5.406	–	–	3
.0330	0.838	–	65	66	.1100	2.794	–	34	35	.2190	5.559	–	2	–
.0350	0.889	–	64	65	.1110	2.819	–	–	34	.2210	5.615	–	–	2
.0359	0.912	19	–	–	.1120	2.845	–	33	–	.2270	5.768	–	1	–
.0360	0.914	–	63	64	.1130	2.870	–	–	33	.2280	5.793	–	–	1
.0370	0.940	–	62	63	.1144	2.906	9	–	–	.2294	5.829	3	–	–
.0380	0.965	–	61	62	.1150	2.921	–	32	–	.2576	6.543	2	–	–
.0390	0.990	–	60	61	.1160	2.946	–	–	32	.2893	7.346	1	–	–
.0400	1.016	–	59	60										

Comparison Table, Drill, Wire, Douzieme, Ligne
(in inches and millimeters)

Inch	mm	B.&S. Twist Drill No.	B.&S. and Amer. Wire No.	Douzieme	Ligne	Inch	mm	B.&S. Twist Drill No.	B.&S. and Amer. Wire No.	Douzieme	Ligne
.001						.051	1 3/10			16	
.002						.052		55		7	7/12
.003			40			.053					
.004	1/10		38			.054					
.005			36			.055	1 4/10	54			
.006			34			.056					
.007			33	1	1/12	.057			15		
.008	2/10		32			.058					
.009			31			.059	1 5/10	53		8	8/12
.010			30			.060					
.011			29			.061					
.012	3/10		28			.062					
.013		80				.063	1 6/10	52			
.014		79	27			.064			14		
.015				2	2/12	.065					
.016	4/10	78	26			.066					
.017						.067	1 7/10	51		9	9/12
.018		77	25			.068					
.019						.069					
.020	5/10	76	24			.070		50			
.021		75				.071	1 8/10				
.022		74	23	3	3/12	.072			13		
.023						.073		49			
.024	6/10	73				.074				10	10/12
.025		72	22			.075	1 9/10				
.026		71				.076		48			
.027						.077					
.028	7/10	70	21			.078		47			
.029		69				.079	2				
.030				4	4/12	.080					
.031	8/10	68				.081		48	12	11	11/12
.032		67	20			.082		45			
.033		66				.083	2 1/10				
.034						.084					
.035	9/10	65				.085					
.036		64	19			.086		44			
.037		63		5	5/12	.087	2 2/10				
.038		62				.088					
.039	1	61				.089		43		12	1
.040		60	18			.090					
.041		59				.091	2 3/10		11		
.042		58				.092					
.043	1 1/10	57				.093		42			
.044				6	6/12	.094	2 4/10				
.045			17			.095					
.046		56				.096		41		13	1 1/12
.047	1 2/10					.097					
.048						.098	2 5/10	40			
.049						.099		39			
.050						.100					

Courtesy Myron Toback, Inc.

The **douzieme gauge** used by watchmakers and sometimes by jewelers is also called a **spring gauge** and **degree gauge**. Douzieme in French means 1/12.
1 douzieme = 1/12 ligne = 0.0074″ = 0.188mm
1 ligne (or line) = 12 douzieme = 0.0888″ = 2.256mm
Note: Maximum error = one half of one one thousandth of an inch.

Decimal Equivalents of Letter-Sized Drills
(in inches)

Letter	Size of Drill	Letter	Size of Drill
A	.234	N	.302
B	.238	O	.316
C	.242	P	.323
D	.246	Q	.332
E	.250	R	.339
F	.257	S	.348
G	.261	T	.358
H	.266	U	.368
I	.272	V	.377
J	.277	W	.386
K	.281	X	.397
L	.288	Y	.404
M	.295	Z	.413

Wire, Tap, and Drill Sizes

B.&S. size wire used for making screws to fit the nearest tap and tap drill sizes that accommodate them. All dimensions are in inches.

Wire B.&S.	Decimal Equivalent	Tap Size	Root Diameter	Outer Diameter	Tap Drill Size	
					Number	Decimal Equivalent
3	.22942	12-24	0.1619	0.2160	16	0.1770
4	.20431	10-24	0.1359	0.1900	25	0.1495
5	.18194	8-32	0.1234	0.1640	29	0.1360
7	.14428	6-32	0.0974	0.1380	36	0.1065
8	.12849	5-40	0.0925	0.1250	38	0.1015
9	.11443	4-40	0.0795	0.1120	43	0.0890
10	.10189	3-48	0.0719	0.0990	47	0.0785
11	.09074	2-56	0.0628	0.0860	50	0.0700
12	.08080	1-64	0.0527	0.0730	53	0.0595

AREA OR SURFACE

Equivalents of Area, Metric, and British Systems

Square Millimeters	Square Centimeters	Square Inches
1	0.01	0.00155
100	1	0.155
645.2	6.45	1

Squares and Circles, Areas and Circumferences
(in inches)

Size in Inches	Area of □ in Square Inches	Area of ○ in Square Inches	Circumference of ○ in Inches	Size in Inches	Area of □ in Square Inches	Area of ○ in Square Inches	Circumference of ○ in Inches
¼	.0625	.0491	.7854	10¼	105.06	82.52	32.20
½	.2500	.1964	1.571	10½	110.25	86.59	32.99
¾	.5625	.4418	2.356	10¾	115.56	90.76	33.77
1	1.000	.7854	3.142	11	121.00	95.03	34.56
1¼	1.563	1.227	3.927	11¼	126.56	99.40	35.34
1½	2.250	1.767	4.712	11½	132.25	103.87	36.13
1¾	3.063	2.405	5.498	11¾	138.06	108.43	36.91
2	4.000	3.142	6.283	12	144.00	113.10	37.70
2¼	5.063	3.976	7.069	12¼	150.06	117.86	38.48
2½	6.250	4.909	7.854	12½	156.25	122.72	39.27
2¾	7.563	5.940	8.639	12¾	162.56	127.68	40.06
3	9.000	7.069	9.425	13	169.00	132.73	40.84
3¼	10.56	8.296	10.21	13¼	175.56	137.89	41.63
3½	12.25	9.621	11.00	13½	182.25	143.14	42.41
3¾	14.06	11.04	11.78	13¾	189.06	148.49	43.20
4	16.00	12.57	12.57	14	196.00	153.94	43.98
4¼	18.06	14.19	13.35	14¼	203.06	159.49	44.77
4½	20.25	15.90	14.14	14½	210.25	165.13	45.55
4¾	22.56	17.72	14.92	14¾	217.56	170.87	46.34
5	25.00	19.64	15.71	15	225.00	176.72	47.12
5¼	27.56	21.65	16.49	15¼	232.56	182.65	47.91
5½	30.25	23.76	17.28	15½	240.25	188.69	48.69
5¾	33.06	25.97	18.06	15¾	248.06	194.83	49.48
6	36.00	28.27	18.85	16	256.00	201.06	50.27
6¼	39.06	30.68	19.64	16¼	264.06	207.39	51.05
6½	42.25	33.18	20.42	16½	272.25	213.83	51.84
6¾	45.56	35.78	21.21	16¾	280.56	220.35	52.62
7	49.00	38.48	21.99	17	289.00	226.98	53.41
7¼	52.56	41.28	22.78	17¼	297.56	233.71	54.19
7½	56.25	44.18	23.56	17½	306.25	240.53	54.98
7¾	60.06	47.17	24.35	17¾	315.06	247.45	55.76
8	64.00	50.27	25.13	18	324.00	254.47	56.55
8¼	68.06	53.46	25.92	18¼	333.06	261.59	57.33
8½	72.25	56.75	26.70	18½	342.25	268.80	58.12
8¾	76.56	60.13	27.49	18¾	351.56	276.12	58.91
9	81.00	63.62	28.28	19	361.00	283.53	59.69
9¼	85.56	67.20	29.06	19¼	370.56	291.04	60.48
9½	90.25	70.88	29.85	19½	380.25	298.65	61.26
9¾	95.06	74.66	30.63	19¾	390.06	306.36	62.05
10	100.00	78.54	31.42	20	400.00	314.16	62.83

Rules relating to circles and ovals

The circumference of a circle is the diameter × 3.1416.

The diameter of a circle is the circumference multiplied by .31831.

The area of a circle is the diameter × itself × .7854.

A circle is .7854 times as heavy as a square of the same size, i.e. the loss in cutting a circle from a square is .2146 of the weight of the square.

MEASURES OF WEIGHT AND MASS

WEIGHT MEASUREMENTS

Archeological evidence indicates that *weights* and *balances* came into use in Egypt about 5000 B.C. for the measurement of gold dust and gold ingots, and for use by goldsmiths and jewelers. Contrary to what one might expect, they were not used for commercial purposes because the main form of commerce was barter. The earliest record of the use of weight and balances for commercial purposes seems to have occurred in the Indus Valley civilizations of India (present-day Pakistan) about 2500 B.C. The weighing of gold therefore has the longest history of any weight standard invented by man. The weights used for measuring small amounts of gold are believed to have been seeds which are still used for this purpose in some countries today. For heavier amounts, the weights were made of polished stone, geometric in form, or of bronze made in the shape of animals or birds.

Tests have shown that the beam balances in use from 5000–1500 B.C. have a sensitivity range of from 2–30 grains with 100–2000 grains (6.48–130 g) respectively in each pan. From 1500 B.C. to 400 A.D. this divergence was reduced as the balance sensitivity improved to 1–5 grains for the same amount.

WEIGHING SCALES

When the jeweler deals with precious metals and stones, makes alloys, or prepares recipes, a *balance* or *scale* must be used to determine weights and to measure amounts with accuracy. The basic concept of the scale works on the principle of the lever and counterweights. Today, several different forms and constructions of scales are available.

THE BEAM BALANCE The balance—the most ancient instrument for weighing, and still in use today—in its simplest form consists of a beam or lever that is supported exactly at its center so that both lever arms are of *equal lengths*. From each arm end hangs three cords, each supporting a *scale* or *pan,* one for containing the substance weighed, and the other to contain the counterweight. It is hand held and is accurate to one-tenth of a gram. The most accurate balance of this type, termed a *precision balance,* has a *mechanically* supported beam, is made of corrosion-resistant materials, and is enclosed in a glass case to protect it from drafts when in use and against the corrosive action of the atmosphere when stored. Different weights are used with this scale for weighing precious stones or metals. Accuracy is very important as slight differences of weight make great differences in value. For instance, scales used for weighing stones, because the *carat unit* used is small, must be capable of an accuracy of one-hundredth of a carat in gram equivalents. Such scales are sometimes equipped with a magnifying glass so the very finely divided weight graduations can be read.

THE COUNTERPOISE SCALE The counterpoise scale also uses the principle of the beam or lever, but its arms are of unequal lengths. In this case, the substance weighed is placed on the short arm side, ordinarily on a load platform, and a counterweight is placed at a position on the beam where a state of counterbalance or equilibrium is achieved, one force acting in opposition to the other in equal amounts. As the beam is marked at regular intervals, a reading is taken from the position of the sliding counterweight which gives the weight of the substance or object being weighed. Models exist with one, two, or three beams, each capable with the use of the correct counterweight of a certain range of weights. Extra weights can be placed on the beam to bring the scale capacity to its maximum.

The *steelyard* is a type of large counterpoise scale used for weighing heavy nonferrous and ferrous metals. Its beam is hung by a hook, and a sliding *poise* or movable weight moves on the beam bar which is notched, graduated, and marked, until it balances the weight of the material suspended from a hook which hangs below the short arm; a reading is then taken.

SPRING BALANCES In this group are all scales employing an elastic spring or springs which change shape under the force of weights, the change being shown by an indicator that passes before a marked chart. If such a scale is used on a table it is called a *counter scale,* or if on the floor a *floor scale.* These scales can be mounted with a beam and poise mechanism; if they have a fan-shaped chart over which the indicator sweeps in an arc, they are termed a *fan scale.*

DIGITAL-ELECTRONIC PRECISION SCALES In recent times, automatic precision scales with single-load receiving platforms have been developed having electronic weight-registering systems with the weight seen as numbers on lighted panels. They can be battery- or direct-electric-line-operated, and are available in ranges of 0–150 g, 0–1000 g, and 0–5000 g.

SCALE MAINTENANCE It is important to treat scales and balances with great care as their accuracy can be destroyed by careless handling. If a pan or pans are used, their good condition must be maintained. When corrosive materials are weighed in them, first place a piece of paper in the pan, counterbalanced by a similar paper in the second pan, if one exists. The *weights* used in counterbalancing should also be treated with care or their accuracy may be impaired. Small weights are handled with tweezers for this reason, and they should be stored in protective containers. When scales are not in use, they should be covered, and stored in clean, cool, dry places.

SPECIFIC GRAVITY

Specific gravity for solids and liquids is a numerical value representing the weight of a given substance as compared to the weight of an equal volume of water at 4° C (39.2° F) for which the specific gravity is taken as 1.0000.

Specific Gravities (Densities) of Metals

Metal	Value	Metal	Value
Aluminum	2.69	Lead	11.34
Antimony	6.62	Magnesium	1.73
Bismuth	9.80	Manganese	7.43
Cadmium	8.65	Mercury	13.54
Carbon	2.25	Nickel	8.90
Chromium	7.19	Niobium (Columbium)	8.57
Copper	8.94	Osmium	22.58
Gold (pure)	19.32	Palladium	12.02
18K green	15.90	Platinum	21.45
18K yellow	15.58	15% Iridio-Plat	21.57
18K white	15.18	10% Iridio-Plat	21.53
18K red	14.64	5% Iridio-Plat	21.49
14K green	14.20	Rhodium	12.44
14K yellow	13.07	Ruthenium	12.20
14K white	12.61	Silicon	2.33
14K red	13.26	Silver (pure)	10.49
10K green	11.03	Sterling	10.40
10K yellow	11.57	Coin	10.35
10K white	11.07	Tantalum	16.60
10K red	11.59	Tin	7.30
Iridium	22.50	Titanium	4.50
Iron	7.87	Zinc	7.13

(See chart *Making Gold and Silver Alloys,* p. 38, for colored gold alloy compositions.)

18-1 WEIGHTS AND SCALES

1. *Precision precious metal weights*, 1–20 mg, made of aluminum; 50–500 mg, made of white metal.
2. *Precision precious metal brass knob weights*, 1–200 g.
3. *Portable, pocket precious stone weight set* in hardwood box with sliding lid, and weight-handling tweezers, 1–500 mg.
4. *Set of brass knob weights* for weighing precious metals, 1–200 g, mounted in hardwood block, with place for smaller weights.
5. *Set of metric diamond weights* for weighing precious stones, $\frac{1}{100}$–$\frac{50}{100}$ct.
6. *Set of metric diamond weights*, square form, for weighing precious stones, 1–500ct.
7. *Set of metric diamond weights*, round knob form, for weighing precious stones, 1–100ct.
8. *Hand-held beam balance* with weighing scales or pans, the oldest scale in existence, for weighing small amounts of precious metals and precious stones.
9. *Pocket stone scale*, a beam balance for weighing diamonds and precious stones, with hardwood case 7 in long, 2½ in wide, 1½ in high, with weight-handling tweezers and metric weights from $\frac{1}{100}$–50ct, capacity 100ct. Also available with weights for weighing precious metals.
10. *Precision gold weight scale*, with glass-enclosed weighing pans for protection against dust and drafts; anti-magnetic; adjustable screw legs, and built-in water level for leveling; lower drawers with built-in weight compartments and weight-handling tweezers; two-sided weight dial; transporting clamp; agate bearings; removable pans; weight range available: 20–500 mg; 50 mg to 1 kg; 100 mg to 2 kg. (Karl Fischer)
11. *Precision speed scale* with single-load receiving platform, optical weight range: 0–2000 g; height 300 mm, width 250 mm, depth 330 mm.
12. *Typical scale reading dial* for the above scale, registering 1053.15 g.

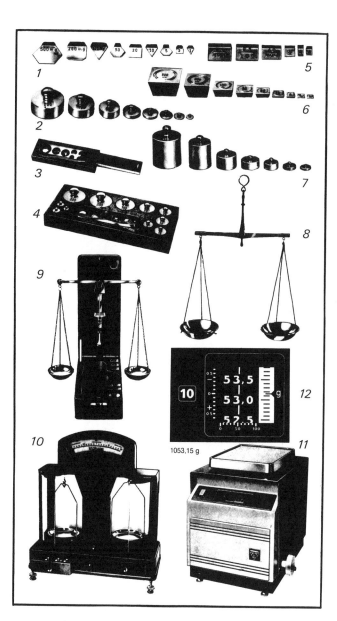

1053,15 g

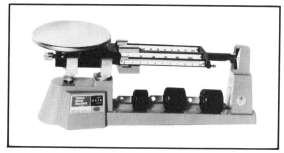

18-2 PRECISION SCALES, COUNTERPOISE TYPES

1. *Pennyweight scale*, a precision scale for weighing precious metals, capacity 35 dwt. Springs and movable weights are eliminated by the permanent counterweight fulcrum action. Leveling screw allows placement on uneven surfaces to achieve perfect balance.
2. *Precision double-beam balance* with two removable platform pans. Capacity 60 oz (1200 dwt), 105 dwt without adding weights. Upper beam: scale 0.10–5 dwt; lower beam: 5–100 dwt; capacity can be increased by the use of additional 4 oz weights placed on the beam. Pan Ø 5¾ in; scale: height 8 in, length 13 in, depth 6 in.
3. *Triple-beam balance scale*, available in *metric* or *avoirdupois* models, with set of *attachment weights* to bring the capacity to its maximum.

   Metric: Capacity 2610 g; weight set: two 1 kg weights, one 500 g weight; scales: 10 g × 0.1 g; 500 g × 100 g; 100 g × 10 g. Sensitivity: 0.1 g.

   Avoirdupois: Capacity 5 lb 2 oz; weight set: two 2 lb weights, one 1 lb weight; scales: 1 oz × $\frac{1}{64}$ oz; 1 oz × 0.01 oz; 16 oz × 1 oz. Sensitivity: $\frac{1}{64}$–$\frac{1}{100}$ oz.

Atomic Weights of Common Elements
(alphabetically arranged)

	Symbol	Atomic Number	Atomic Weight		Symbol	Atomic Number	Atomic Weight
Aluminum	Al	13	26.97	Molybdenum	Mo	42	95.95
Antimony	Sb	51	121.76	Neodymium	Nd	60	144.27
Argon	A	18	39.944	Neon	Ne	10	20.183
Arsenic	As	33	74.91	Nickel	Ni	28	58.69
Barium	Ba	56	137.36	Nitrogen	N	7	14.008
Beryllium	Be	4	9.02	Osmium	Os	76	190.2
Bismuth	Bi	83	209.00	Oxygen	O	8	16.0000
Boron	B	5	10.82	Palladium	Pd	46	106.7
Bromine	Br	35	79.916	Phosphorus	P	15	30.98
Cadmium	Cd	48	112.41	Platinum	Pt	78	195.23
Calcium	Ca	20	40.08	Potassium	K	19	39.096
Carbon	C	6	12.010	Praseodymium	Pr	59	140.92
Cerium	Ce	58	140.13	Protactinium	Pa	91	231
Cesium	Cs	55	132.91	Radium	Ra	88	226.05
Chlorine	Cl	17	35.457	Radon	Rn	86	222
Chromium	Cr	24	52.01	Rhenium	Re	75	186.31
Cobalt	Co	27	58.94	Rhodium	Rh	45	102.91
Columbium	Cb	41	92.91	Rubidium	Rb	37	85.48
Copper	Cu	29	63.57	Ruthenium	Ru	44	101.7
Dysprosium	Dy	66	162.46	Samarium	Sm	62	150.43
Erbium	Er	68	167.2	Scandium	Sc	21	45.10
Europium	Eu	63	152.0	Selenium	Se	34	78.96
Fluorine	F	9	19.00	Silicon	Si	14	28.06
Gadolinium	Gd	64	156.9	Silver	Ag	47	107.880
Gallium	Ga	31	69.72	Sodium	Na	11	22.997
Germanium	Ge	32	72.60	Strontium	Sr	38	87.63
Gold	Au	79	197.2	Sulphur	S	16	32.066
Hafnium	Hf	72	178.6	Tantalum	Ta	73	180.88
Helium	He	2	4.003	Tellurium	Te	52	127.61
Holmium	Ho	67	164.94	Terbium	Tb	65	159.2
Hydrogen	H	1	1.0080	Thallium	Tl	81	204.39
Indium	In	49	114.76	Thorium	Th	90	232.12
Iodine	I	53	126.92	Thulium	Tm	69	169.4
Iridium	Ir	77	193.1	Tin	Sn	50	118.70
Iron	Fe	26	55.85	Titanium	Ti	22	47.90
Krypton	Kr	36	83.7	Tungsten	W	74	183.92
Lanthanum	La	57	138.92	Uranium	U	92	238.07
Lead	Pb	82	207.21	Vanadium	V	23	50.95
Lithium	Li	3	6.940	Xenon	Xe	54	131.3
Lutecium	Lu	71	174.99	Ytterbium	Yb	70	173.04
Magnesium	Mg	12	24.32	Yttrium	Y	39	88.92
Manganese	Mn	25	54.93	Zinc	Zn	30	65.38
Mercury	Hg	80	200.61	Zirconium	Zr	40	91.22

SPECIFIC GRAVITIES OF VARIOUS

OTHER SOLIDS

Cork	0.24
Ebony	1.22
Fats	0.92–0.94
Glass, plate	2.40–2.72
Glass, crystal	2.90–3.00
Porcelain, china	2.30–2.50
Resins, rosin, amber	1.07
Rubber	0.93
Wax	0.95–0.98

LIQUIDS

Acids, nitric, 91%	1.50
Acids, sulphuric, 87%	1.80
Lye, soda, 66%	1.70
Oils, mineral	0.90–0.93
Gasoline	0.66–0.69
Water, 4° C	1.0
Water, 100° C	0.9584
Water, frozen	0.88–0.92
Water, sea	1.02–1.03

GASES

The specific gravity of gases is based on air at 0° C (32° F) and 760 mm pressure. (Air = 1)

Air, 0° C (32° F), 760 mm	1.0
Ammonia	0.5920
Carbon dioxide	1.5291
Gas, natural	0.47–0.48
Hydrogen	0.0693
Nitrogen	0.9714
Oxygen	1.1056

Conversion of Common Weights Used by Goldsmiths

Grams	Kilograms	Ounces Avoirdupois	Ounces Troy and Apothecary	Pounds Avoirdupois	Pounds Troy and Apothecary	Grains
1	0.001	0.03527	0.03215	0.002205	0.002679	15.432
1000	1	35.274	32.151	2.2046	2.679	15432.4
28.349	0.028349	1	0.91146	0.0625	0.07596	437.5
31.103	0.031103	1.0971	1	0.068571	0.08333	480
453.59	0.45359	16	14.583	1	1.2153	7000
373.24	0.37324	13.166	12	0.8229	1	5760
0.06480	0.00006480	0.002285	0.002083	0.0001428	0.0001736	1

GOLDSMITH'S WEIGHTS

APOTHECARIES' WEIGHT

20 grains (gr)	= 1 scruple (s ap)	= 20 grains
3 scruples	= 1 dram (or drachms) (dr ap)	= 60 grains
8 drams	= 1 ounce (oz ap)	= 24 scruples = 480 grains
12 ounces	= 1 pound (lb ap)	= 96 drams = 288 scruples = 5,760 grains

TROY WEIGHT
(Used to weigh precious metals and stones)

1 grain (gr)	= 0.0648 g
24 grains	= 1 pennyweight (dwt) ("d" = English penny; "wt" = weight)
20 pennyweights (dwt)	= 1 ounce (oz t) = 480 grains
12 ounces	= 1 pound (lb t) = 240 pennyweights = 5,760 grains

To convert troy ounces to avoirdupois ounces, multiply by 1.09714.
The troy ounce is about 10% heavier than the commonly used avoirdupois ounce.

AVOIRDUPOIS WEIGHT
(Used to weigh base metals and chemicals)

27 $\frac{11}{32}$ grains (gr)	= 1 dram
16 drams (or drachms)	= 1 ounce (oz) = 437½ grains = 28.35 g
16 ounces	= 1 pound (lb) = 256 drams = 0.4536 kg = 7,000 grains
100 pounds	= 1 hundredweight (cwt) = 1,600 ounces
20 hundredweight	= 1 ton (tn) = 2,000 pounds (in short measure)
112 pounds	= 1 long hundredweight (L. cwt)
20 long hundredweight	= 1 long ton (L. tn) = 2,240 pounds

To convert avoirdupois ounces to troy ounces, multiply by 0.91146.
The avoirdupois pound is about 21.5% heavier than the troy pound.

GRAM WEIGHT

A gram (g) is a unit of weight and mass used in the metric system. It was intended to be, and very nearly is equal to the weight in a vacuum of one cubic centimeter (1cc) of pure water at maximum density.

1 gram = 15.4324874 grains troy (gr t), or 0.03215 ounce troy (oz t), or 0.03527398 ounce avoirdupois (oz av)
10 grams = 1 decagram (dkg) = 0.3527398 oz av
10 decagrams = 1 hectogram (hg) = 3.527398 oz av
10 hectograms = 1 kilogram (kg) = 2.20462125 pounds
1000 kilograms = 1 metric ton (t) = 2204.62125 pounds
1 carat = ⅕ gram (g) = 200 milligrams (mg) = 4 pearl grains

CONVERSIONS OF WEIGHT AND MASS

Carat (ct) (metric)
  3.08647 grains; 0.2 gram
Grain (gr)
  0.00208 oz t; 0.0022857 oz av;
  0.0648 gram
Gram (g)
  0.03215 oz t; 0.035274 oz av;
  0.643 pennyweight
Kilogram (kg)
  2.2046 lb av; 1000 grams
Milligram (mg)
  0.001 gram
Ounce, fluid (fl oz)
  0.0078125 gallon; 0.03125 quart (liquid);
  1.80469 cubic inches;
  29.5737 cubic centimeters

Ounce, avoirdupois (oz av)
  0.0625 lb av; 0.911458 oz t; 18.2292 pennyweights;
  437.5 grains; 28.3495 grams
Ounce, troy (oz t)
  0.068571 lb av; 0.0833 lb t; 20 pennyweights;
  480 grains; 28.3495 grams
Pennyweight, troy (dwt)
  0.0034286 lb av; 0.004167 lb t; 1/20 oz t; 24 grains;
  1.1552 grams
Pound, avoirdupois (lb av)
  1.2153 lb t; 14.583 oz t; 16 oz av; 291.667 pennyweights;
  7000 grains; 453.592 grams
Pound, troy (lb t)
  0.82286 lb av; 12 oz t; 13.166 oz av; 240 pennyweights;
  5760 grains; 373.24 grams
Square centimeter (cm²)
  0.0010764 sq ft; 0.155 sq in
Square decimeter (dm²)
  15.50 sq in; 0.01 sq meter; 100 sq cm

Comparative Weights
of Different Precious Metals

Metal	Times Heavier	Than Other Metal
Sterling silver	.796	14k Gold
Sterling silver	.485	Platinum
14k yellow gold	1.257	Sterling silver
14k yellow gold	.609	Platinum
14k yellow gold	1.089	Palladium
Platinum	1.788	Palladium
Platinum	1.650	14k yellow gold
Platinum	2.063	Sterling silver

Precious Metal Sheet

(weight per square inch, B.&S. gauge)

B.&S. Gauge	Thickness in Inches	Platinum	Palladium	Fine Gold	18k Yel. Gold	14k Yel. Gold	10k Yel. Gold	Fine Silver	Sterling Silver	Coin Silver
		Ozs	Ozs	Dwts	Dwts	Dwts	Dwts	Ozs	Ozs	Ozs
1	.28930	3.27	1.83	58.9	47.5	39.8	35.3	1.60	1.58	1.58
2	.25763	2.91	1.63	52.5	42.3	35.5	31.4	1.42	1.41	1.40
3	.22942	2.59	1.45	46.7	37.7	31.6	28.0	1.26	1.25	1.25
4	.20431	2.31	1.29	41.6	33.6	28.1	24.9	1.12	1.12	1.11
5	.18194	2.06	1.15	37.0	29.9	25.1	22.2	1.00	.993	.988
6	.16202	1.83	1.02	33.0	26.6	22.3	19.8	.894	.884	.880
7	.14428	1.63	.912	29.4	23.7	19.9	17.6	.796	.787	.783
8	.12849	1.45	.812	26.2	21.1	17.7	15.7	.709	.701	.697
9	.11443	1.29	.723	23.3	18.8	15.8	14.0	.631	.624	.622
10	.10189	1.15	.644	20.8	16.7	14.0	12.4	.562	.556	.553
11	.09074	1.03	.574	18.5	14.9	12.5	11.1	.500	.495	.494
12	.08080	.913	.511	16.5	13.3	11.1	9.85	.446	.441	.439
13	.07196	.813	.455	14.7	11.8	9.91	8.77	.397	.392	.391
14	.06408	.724	.405	13.1	10.5	8.82	7.81	.354	.350	.348
15	.05706	.645	.361	11.6	9.37	7.86	6.96	.316	.311	.310
16	.05082	.574	.321	10.4	8.35	7.00	6.21	.281	.277	.276
17	.04525	.511	.286	9.21	7.43	6.23	5.52	.250	.247	.246
18	.04030	.455	.255	8.20	6.62	5.55	4.91	.223	.220	.219
19	.03589	.406	.227	7.32	5.89	4.94	4.38	.198	.196	.195
20	.03196	.361	.202	6.51	5.25	4.40	3.90	.176	.174	.173
21	.02846	.322	.180	5.80	4.67	3.92	3.47	.157	.155	.154
22	.02534	.286	.160	5.16	4.16	3.49	3.09	.140	.138	.138
23	.02257	.255	.143	4.59	3.71	3.11	2.75	.124	.123	.123
24	.02010	.227	.127	4.09	3.30	2.77	2.45	.111	.110	.110
25	.01790	.202	.113	3.64	2.94	2.46	2.18	.0988	.0976	.0973
26	.01594	.180	.101	3.24	2.62	2.19	1.94	.0879	.0870	.0866
27	.01419	.160	.0897	2.88	2.33	1.95	1.73	.0783	.0774	.0770
28	.01264	.143	.0799	2.58	2.08	1.74	1.54	.0697	.0690	.0686
29	.01125	.127	.0711	2.29	1.85	1.55	1.37	.0620	.0614	.0611
30	.01002	.113	.0633	2.04	1.65	1.38	1.22	.0553	.0547	.0544
31	.00892	.101	.0564	1.82	1.46	1.23	1.09	.0492	.0487	.0484
32	.00795	.0898	.0503	1.62	1.31	1.09	.969	.0438	.0434	.0432
33	.00708	.0800	.0448	1.44	1.16	.975	.863	.0391	.0386	.0385
34	.00630	.0712	.0398	1.29	1.03	.868	.768	.0348	.0344	.0342
35	.00561	.0634	.0355	1.14	.921	.772	.684	.0310	.0306	.0305
36	.00500	.0565	.0316	1.02	.821	.689	.610	.0276	.0273	.0272
37	.00445	.0503	.0281	.908	.731	.613	.543	.0246	.0243	.0242
38	.00396	.0448	.0250	.808	.650	.545	.483	.0219	.0216	.0215
39	.00353	.0399	.0223	.712	.580	.486	.430	.0195	.0193	.0191
40	.00314	.0355	.0199	.640	.516	.432	.383	.0173	.0172	.0171

Conversion of Ounces Troy to Grams

Oz Tr	0.00	0.01	0.02	0.03	0.04	0.05	0.06	0.07	0.08	0.09
0.0	–	0.3	0.6	0.9	1.2	1.6	1.9	2.2	2.5	2.8
0.1	3.1	3.4	3.7	4.0	4.4	4.7	5.0	5.3	5.6	5.9
0.2	6.2	6.5	6.8	7.2	7.5	7.8	8.1	8.4	8.7	9.0
0.3	9.3	9.6	10.0	10.3	10.6	10.9	11.2	11.5	11.8	12.1
0.4	12.4	12.8	13.1	13.4	13.7	14.0	14.3	14.6	14.9	15.2
0.5	15.6	15.9	16.2	16.5	16.8	17.1	17.4	17.7	18.0	18.4
0.6	18.7	19.0	19.3	19.6	19.9	20.2	20.5	20.8	21.2	21.5
0.7	21.8	22.1	22.4	22.7	23.0	23.3	23.6	23.9	24.3	24.6
0.8	24.9	25.2	25.5	25.8	26.1	26.4	26.7	27.1	27.4	27.7
0.9	28.0	28.3	28.6	28.9	29.2	29.5	29.9	30.2	30.5	30.8

Oz Tr	0	1	2	3	4	5	6	7	8	9
0	–	31.1	62.2	93.3	124.4	155.5	186.6	217.7	248.8	279.9
10	311.0	342.1	373.2	404.3	435.4	466.6	497.7	528.8	559.9	591.0
20	622.1	653.2	684.3	715.4	746.5	777.6	808.7	839.8	870.9	902.0
30	933.1	964.2	995.3	1026.4	1057.5	1088.6	1119.7	1150.8	1181.9	1213.0

Example: To convert 25.75oz tr to grams:
From the lower table read: 25.00 = 777.6
From the upper table read: 0.75 = 23.3

25.75oz tr = 800.9 grams

Sterling Silver Sheet

(weight in ounces per square foot; various widths, B.&S. gauge)

B.&S. Gauge	Thickness in Inches	1 Foot X									
		1"	2"	3"	4"	5"	6"	7"	8"	9"	10"
1	.28930	19.0	37.9	56.9	75.8	95.1	114	133	152	171	190
2	.25763	16.9	33.9	50.8	67.7	84.7	102	119	135	152	169
3	.22942	15.1	30.2	45.2	60.3	75.4	90.5	106	121	136	151
4	.20431	13.4	26.9	40.3	53.7	67.1	80.6	94.1	107	121	134
5	.18194	12.0	23.9	35.9	47.8	59.8	71.7	83.7	95.7	108	120
6	.16202	10.6	21.3	31.9	42.6	53.2	63.9	74.5	85.2	95.8	106
7	.14428	9.48	19.0	28.4	37.9	47.4	56.9	66.4	75.9	85.3	94.8
8	.12849	8.44	16.9	25.3	33.8	42.2	50.7	59.1	67.6	76.0	84.4
9	.11443	7.52	15.0	22.6	30.1	37.6	45.1	52.6	60.2	67.7	75.2
10	.10189	6.70	13.4	20.1	26.8	33.5	40.2	46.9	53.6	60.3	67.0
11	.09074	5.96	11.9	17.9	23.9	29.8	35.8	41.7	47.7	53.7	59.6
12	.08080	5.31	10.6	15.9	21.2	26.6	31.9	37.2	42.5	47.8	53.1
13	.07196	4.73	9.46	14.2	18.9	23.6	28.4	33.1	37.8	42.6	47.3
14	.06408	4.21	8.42	12.6	16.8	21.1	25.3	29.5	33.7	37.9	42.1
15	.05706	3.75	7.50	11.3	15.0	18.8	22.5	26.3	30.0	33.8	37.5
16	.05082	3.34	6.68	10.0	13.4	16.7	20.0	23.4	26.7	30.1	33.4
17	.04525	2.97	5.95	8.92	11.9	14.9	17.8	20.8	23.8	26.8	29.7
18	.04030	2.65	5.30	7.95	10.6	13.2	15.9	18.5	21.2	23.8	26.5
19	.03589	2.36	4.72	7.08	9.43	11.8	14.2	16.5	18.9	21.2	23.6
20	.03196	2.10	4.20	6.30	8.40	10.5	12.6	14.7	16.8	18.9	21.0
21	.02846	1.87	3.74	5.61	7.48	9.35	11.2	13.1	15.0	16.8	18.7
22	.02534	1.67	3.33	5.00	6.66	8.33	9.99	11.7	13.3	15.0	16.7
23	.02257	1.48	2.97	4.45	5.93	7.42	8.90	10.4	11.9	13.3	14.8
24	.02010	1.32	2.64	3.96	5.28	6.61	7.93	9.25	10.6	11.9	13.2
25	.01790	1.18	2.35	3.53	4.71	5.88	7.06	8.23	9.41	10.6	11.8
26	.01594	1.05	2.10	3.14	4.19	5.24	6.29	7.33	8.38	9.43	10.5
27	.01419	.933	1.87	2.80	3.73	4.66	5.60	6.53	7.46	8.39	9.33
28	.01264	.831	1.66	2.49	3.32	4.15	4.98	5.81	6.65	7.48	8.31
29	.01125	.739	1.48	2.22	2.96	3.70	4.44	5.18	5.92	6.65	7.39
30	.01002	.659	1.32	1.98	2.63	3.29	3.95	4.61	5.27	5.93	6.59
31	.00892	.586	1.17	1.76	2.34	2.93	3.52	4.10	4.69	5.28	5.86
32	.00795	.523	1.05	1.57	2.09	2.61	3.14	3.65	4.18	4.70	5.23
33	.00708	.465	.931	1.40	1.86	2.33	2.79	3.26	3.72	4.19	4.65
34	.00630	.414	.828	1.24	1.66	2.07	2.48	2.90	3.31	3.73	4.14
35	.00561	.369	.737	1.11	1.47	1.84	2.21	2.58	2.95	3.32	3.69
36	.00500	.329	.657	.986	1.31	1.64	1.97	2.30	2.63	2.96	3.29
37	.00445	.293	.585	.878	1.17	1.46	1.76	2.05	2.34	2.63	2.93
38	.00396	.260	.521	.781	1.04	1.30	1.56	1.82	2.08	2.34	2.60
39	.00353	.232	.464	.696	.928	1.16	1.39	1.62	1.86	2.09	2.32
40	.00314	.206	.413	.619	.826	1.03	1.24	1.44	1.65	1.86	2.06

Handy and Harman

Troy Weight

Subdivisions of the Ounce with Their Decimal Equivalents

Dwt	Decimals of an Ounce Troy	Grains	Nearest Decimals of an Ounce Troy	Avoirdupois Ounces	Decimals of an Ounce Troy
1	.050	1	.002	1	.91
2	.100	2	.004	2	1.82
3	.150	3	.006	3	2.73
4	.200	4	.008	4	3.64
5	.250	5	.010	5	4.55
6	.300	6	.012	6	5.47
7	.350	7	.014	7	6.38
8	.400	8	.016	8	7.29
9	.450	9	.019	9	8.20
10	.500	10	.021	10	9.11
11	.550	11	.023	11	10.02
12	.600	12	.025	12	10.93
13	.650	13	.027	13	11.85
14	.700	14	.029	14	12.76
15	.750	15	.031	15	13.67
16	.800	16	.033	16 (1lb)	14.58
17	.850	17	.035		
18	.900	18	.037		
19	.950	19	.040		
20	1.000	20	.042		

Precious Metal Round Wire
(weight in pennyweights or ounces per foot)

B.&S. Gauge	Thickness in Inches	Platinum Ozs	Palladium Ozs	Fine Gold Dwts	18k Yel. Gold Dwts	14k Yel. Gold Dwts	10k Yel. Gold Dwts	Fine Silver Ozs	Sterling Silver Ozs	Coin Silver Ozs
1	.28930	8.91	4.99	161.	130.	109.	96.2	4.36	4.30	4.28
2	.25763	7.07	3.94	128.	104.	86.1	76.3	3.45	3.41	3.40
3	.22942	5.61	3.49	101.	81.5	68.3	60.5	2.74	2.71	2.69
4	.20431	4.45	2.12	80.1	64.6	54.2	48.0	2.17	2.14	2.13
5	.18194	3.53	1.97	63.5	51.2	43.0	38.0	1.72	1.70	1.89
6	.16202	2.80	1.56	50.4	40.6	34.1	30.2	1.36	1.35	1.34
7	.14428	2.22	1.24	39.9	32.2	27.0	23.9	1.09	1.07	1.07
8	.12849	1.76	.984	31.6	25.6	21.4	19.0	.859	.848	.844
9	.11443	1.39	.780	25.2	20.3	17.0	15.1	.682	.673	.670
10	.10189	1.11	.619	20.0	16.1	13.5	11.9	.541	.534	.530
11	.09074	.877	.491	15.8	12.7	10.7	9.46	.429	.423	.421
12	.08080	.695	.389	12.6	10.1	8.47	7.50	.339	.335	.333
13	.07196	.552	.309	9.94	8.01	6.72	5.95	.270	.266	.265
14	.06408	.437	.245	7.87	6.36	5.33	4.72	.214	.211	.210
15	.05706	.347	.194	6.25	5.04	4.23	3.74	.169	.167	.166
16	.05082	.275	.154	4.96	4.00	3.35	2.97	.135	.132	.132
17	.04525	.218	.122	3.93	3.17	2.66	2.35	.107	.105	.105
18	.04030	.173	.0968	3.11	2.51	2.11	1.87	.0846	.0835	.0834
19	.03589	.137	.0767	2.48	1.99	1.67	1.48	.0671	.0662	.0659
20	.03196	.109	.0609	1.96	1.58	1.33	1.17	.0532	.0525	.0522
21	.02846	.0863	.0483	1.56	1.25	1.05	.931	.0422	.0416	.0414
22	.02534	.0684	.0383	1.23	.994	.833	.738	.0335	.0330	.0328
23	.02257	.0543	.0304	.977	.789	.661	.585	.0265	.0262	.0261
24	.02010	.0430	.0241	.775	.625	.524	.464	.0210	.0208	.0207
25	.01790	.0341	.0191	.615	.496	.416	.368	.0167	.0165	.0164
26	.01594	.0271	.0151	.488	.393	.330	.292	.0133	.0131	.01304
27	.01419	.0214	.0120	.386	.312	.261	.231	.0105	.0103	.0103
28	.01264	.0170	.00952	.306	.247	.207	.184	.00831	.00821	.00817
29	.01125	.0135	.00754	.243	.196	.164	.145	.00659	.00650	.00647
30	.01002	.0107	.00598	.193	.155	.130	.115	.00522	.00516	.00513
31	.00892	.00847	.00474	.153	.123	.103	.0914	.00414	.00410	.00407
32	.00795	.00673	.00377	.122	.0978	.0820	.0726	.00328	.00325	.00323
33	.00708	.00534	.00299	.0962	.0776	.0651	.0576	.00261	.00258	.00257
34	.00630	.00423	.00236	.0761	.0614	.0515	.0456	.00207	.00204	.00203
35	.00561	.00335	.00188	.0604	.0487	.0408	.0362	.00164	.00162	.00161
36	.00500	.00266	.00149	.0480	.0387	.0324	.0287	.00130	.00128	.00127
37	.00445	.00211	.00118	.0380	.0306	.0257	.0228	.00104	.00102	.00102
38	.00396	.00167	.000934	.0301	.0243	.0204	.0180	.000816	.000806	.000802
39	.00353	.00133	.000742	.0240	.0193	.0162	.0143	.000649	.000641	.000637
40	.00314	.00105	.000587	.0190	.0153	.0128	.0113	.000513	.000507	.000504

Sterling Silver Circles
(diameter in inches, weight in ounces)

Thickness B.&S. Gauge	11/32 ozs	½″ ozs	⅝″ ozs	¾″ ozs	⅞″ ozs	1″ ozs	1⅛″ ozs	1¼″ ozs	1½″ ozs	2″ ozs	3¼″ ozs	3½″ ozs	4″ ozs	5″ ozs	6″ ozs	7″ ozs	8″ ozs	9″ ozs	10″ ozs	11″ ozs
30	.001	.010	.016	.024	.035	.043	.051	.067	.097	.172	.460	.530	.690	1.08	1.60	2.11	2.80	3.50	4.31	5.20
28	.010	.014	.022	.030	.044	.054	.060	.085	.122	.217	.570	.670	.870	1.40	1.96	2.66	3.50	4.40	5.44	6.60
26	.013	.017	.028	.039	.056	.069	.076	.107	.154	.274	.724	.840	1.10	1.70	2.50	3.36	4.40	5.60	6.90	8.30
24	.016	.022	.037	.049	.070	.087	.095	.135	.195	.346	.913	1.06	1.40	2.20	3.11	4.24	5.50	7.00	8.70	10.50
22	.020	.027	.044	.061	.078	.110	.153	.170	.250	.440	1.20	1.34	1.70	2.70	3.90	5.34	6.98	8.80	10.90	13.20
20	.028	.034	.052	.077	.088	.137	.181	.215	.309	.550	1.45	1.68	2.20	3.44	4.95	6.74	8.80	11.10	13.70	16.67
18	.036	.043	.075	.098	.139	.173	.235	.271	.390	.693	1.83	2.12	2.77	4.33	6.24	8.49	11.1	14.0	17.3	21.0
16	.045	.055	.110	.123	.140	.219														

All weights are approximate, shown to help in the calculation of approximate weight and cost.

Courtesy Swest, Inc.

STERLING SILVER WIRE

SPECIAL SHAPES

HALF ROUND

WIDTH	APPROX. WT. (Troy oz./ft.)	NO. FT. 1 oz. Coil
5/16″	2.5	5/12
1/4″	1.6	3/4
6 ga.	0.7	1-1/2
8 ga.	0.4	2-1/3
10 ga.	0.3	3-1/2
12 ga.	0.2	6

SQUARE

B & S GAUGE	APPROX. WT. (Troy oz./ft.)	NO. FT. 1 oz. Coil
8	1.1	11/12
10	0.7	1-1/2
12	0.4	2-1/3
14	0.3	3-3/4
16	0.2	6
18	0.1	9-1/3

TRIANGULAR

BASE SIZE	APPROX. WT. (Troy oz./ft.)
6 ga.	1.2
8 ga.	1.1
12 ga.	0.2

FLAT

B & S Width	B & S Thickness	APPROX. WT. (Troy oz./ft.)	NO. FT. 1 oz. Coil
4	16	0.7	1-1/2
6	18	0.4	2-1/4
8	26	0.1	7-1/2
14	30	0.04	23-1/4

BEAD WIRE (Round)

B & S GAUGE
9
15

HALF BEAD WIRE (Half Round)

B & S GAUGE	STOCK NO.
9	5-16
12	5-17
14	5-18

TWIST WIRE (Double Strand)

B & S GAUGE
12
14

BEZEL WIRE

STOCK NO.
5-1
5-2
5-3
5-4

Courtesy Swest, Inc.

GOLD WIRE

SPECIAL SHAPES

APPROXIMATE WEIGHT PER FOOT

HALF ROUND

SIZE (Millimeters)	APPROX. WT. 14K (Dwts/foot)
6 x 2	21 − 23
5 x 2	18 − 20
4 x 2	14 − 17
6 x 1½	16 − 19
5 x 1½	14 − 16
4 x 1½	12 − 13
3 x 1½	11 − 12
2 x 1½	6 − 7
1½ x 1	3 − 4

FLAT

SIZE (Millimeters)	APPROX. WT. 14K (Dwts/foot)
6 x 2	27 − 31
5 x 2	23 − 25
4 x 2	19 − 21
6 x 1½	20 − 23
5 x 1½	18 − 19
4 x 1½	14 − 15
3 x 1½	11 − 12
2 x 1½	7 − 8
4 x 1	9 − 10
3 x 1	7 − 8
2 x 1	4½ − 5
1½ x 1	3½ − 4

SQUARE

SIZE (Millimeters)	APPROX. WT. 14K (Dwts/foot)
4 x 4	37 − 41
3 x 3	21 − 23
2½ x 2½	14 − 16
2 x 2	9 − 11
1½ x 1½	5½ − 7
1 x 1	2½ − 3

BEZEL WIRE

APPROX. WT. 10K (Dwts/foot)	APPROX. WT. 14K (Dwts/foot)
5.6	6.2
6.6	7.1
4.0	4.5
3.5	3.6

Courtesy Swest, Inc.

CAPACITY: LIQUIDS

CAPACITY MEASUREMENTS

Unlike measurements of weight, those of capacity have not been as widely recorded in the past. These evolved mainly in relation to the measurement of wine, oil, and water. There seems to be no evidence that ancient standards of mass weight derived from any standard of linear measurement. Such connections came about at a much later time.

When weighing liquids on counterbalances, weigh the vessel first, note this weight, then fill the vessel with liquid and weigh it again. Subtract the weight of the vessel from the total to get the actual weight of the liquid.

Formulas given in *parts* are usable in Metric or any other weight system, the *unit of measure* being substituted for the word *part*.

CONVERSIONS OF LIQUID MEASURES OF CAPACITY

Cubic centimeter (cm³ or cc)
  0.03381 fluid ounces; 0.001 liter;
  0.061023 cubic inch

Cubic foot (ft³ or cu ft)
  7.481 gallons; 1728 cubic inches; 28.317 liters;
  28,317 cubic centimeters

Cubic inch (in³ or cu in)
  0.004329 gallon; 0.5541 ounces; 16.3872 cubic centimeters

Gallon (gal)
  (of water) weighs 8.337 pounds at 62° F;
  0.13368 cubic foot; 128 fluid ounces; 231 cubic inches;
  3.7853 liters (American); 4.543 liters (British);
  3785.4 cubic centimeters

1 liter (1) = 1 cubic decimeter = 61.0270515 cu in,
  or 0.03531 cu ft, or 1.0567 liquid qts, or 0.908 dry qt,
  or 0.26417 gal U.S.

10 liters = 1 decaliter (dkl) = 2.26417 gal U.S.

10 decaliters = 1 hectoliter (hl)

10 hectoliters = 1 kiloliter (kl) = 61027.0515 cu in

1 quart = 0.03342 cu ft, 0.25 gal, 32 fl oz,
  57.749 cu in, 946.358 cc

Capacity to Liquid Measure Conversion

Minims	Fluid Ounces	Milliliters
1.0	0.002083	0.06161
480.0	1.0	29.5729
16.2311	0.033814	1.0

Fluid Ounce Conversion to Cubic Centimeters (cm³ and cc) or Milliliters

oz fl	U.S.	cm³, cc, ml British	oz fl	U.S.	cm³, cc, ml British	oz fl	U.S.	cm³, cc, ml British	oz fl	U.S.	cm³, cc, ml British
1/2	15	14	8 1/2	251	242	16 1/2	488	469	24 1/2	725	696
1	30	28	9	266	256	17	503	483	25	739	710
1 1/2	44	43	9 1/2	281	270	17 1/2	518	497	25 1/2	754	725
2	59	56	10	296	284	18	532	511	26	769	739
2 1/2	74	71	10 1/2	310	298	18 1/2	547	526	26 1/2	784	753
3	89	85	11	325	313	19	562	540	27	798	767
3 1/2	104	99	11 1/2	340	327	19 1/2	577	554	27 1/2	813	781
4	118	114	12	355	341	20	591	568	28	828	796
4 1/2	133	128	12 1/2	370	355	20 1/2	606	582	28 1/2	843	810
5	148	142	13	384	369	21	621	597	29	858	824
5 1/2	163	156	13 1/2	399	384	21 1/2	636	611	29 1/2	872	838
6	177	170	14	414	398	22	651	625	30	887	852
6 1/2	192	185	14 1/2	429	412	22 1/2	665	639	30 1/2	902	867
7	207	199	15	444	426	23	680	653	31	917	881
7 1/2	222	213	15 1/2	458	440	23 1/2	695	668	31 1/2	932	895
8	237	227	16	473	455	24	710	682	32	946	909

Conversion Formulas

To get cubic centimeters from U.S. fluid ounces, multiply by 29.57.
To get cubic centimeters from British fluid ounces, multiply by 28.41.
To get U.S. fluid ounces from cubic centimeters, multiply by 0.034.
To get British fluid ounces from cubic centimeters, multiply by 0.035.
One cubic centimeter almost exactly equals one milliliter (1cc = 0.99997ml)
One U.S. fluid ounce is equal to 29.57cm³, and a British fluid ounce is equal to 28.41cm³, therefore the conversions are slightly different, and a column is used for each in this table.

TEMPERATURE

There are two practical scales of temperature in use today, the *Celsius* or *centigrade* scale (° C), and the *Fahrenheit* scale (° F). Conversion from one to the other is simple and makes use of the following formulas:

(Degrees Fahrenheit — 32) × ⅝ = degrees Celsius
(Degrees Celsius × ⅑) + 32 = degrees Fahrenheit

Verbally expressed: To find the Celsius (centigrade) equivalent of a Fahrenheit figure, subtract 32 from that figure, divide it by 9, then multiply it by 5.

To find the Fahrenheit equivalent of a Celsius (centigrade) figure, divide by 5, then multiply by 9, then add 32 to the result.

The *Fahrenheit* scale was invented by Gabriel Daniel Fahrenheit who in 1709 devised a thermometer containing alcohol, and in 1714 one containing mercury. At sea level on the Fahrenheit thermometer, water boils at 212° F and freezes at 32° F above zero. This scale is commonly used in the United States and Great Britain.

The *Celsius* scale is named after the Swedish astronomer Anders Celsius who in 1742 proposed a similar scale which was adopted internationally in 1954. It is proper to read 20° C as "20 degrees Celsius," and not "20 degrees centigrade" as is customary in the United States. In this scale, water boils at 100° C and freezes at 0° C at 760 mm (or about 30 inches) barometric pressure. This scale is far more widely used in the world than the Fahrenheit scale, and it is probable that at some time its use might become universal.

Melting Points of Selected Metals

Metal	Sym-bol	Atomic Number	Atomic Weight	°C	°F
Aluminum	Al	13	26.9815	660.2	1220.4
Antimony	Sb	51	121.75	630.5	1166.9
Bismuth	Bi	83	208.980	271.3	520.3
Cadmium	Cd	48	112.40	320.0	608.0
Carbon	C	6	12.01115	3500	6332
Chromium	Cr	24	51.996	1765	3209
Cobalt	Co	27	58.9332	1480	2696
Copper	Cu	29	63.54	1083	1981.4
Gold	Au	79	196.967	1063	1945.4
18k green	—	—	—	988	1810
18k yellow	—	—	—	927	1700
18k white	—	—	—	943	1730
18k red	—	—	—	902	1655
14k green	—	—	—	963	1765
14k yellow	—	—	—	879	1615
14k white	—	—	—	996	1825
14k red	—	—	—	935	1715
10k green	—	—	—	860	1580
10k yellow	—	—	—	907	1665
10k white	—	—	—	1079	1975
10k red	—	—	—	960	1760
Iridium	Ir	77	192.2	2454	4449
Iron	Fe	26	55.847	1539	2802
Lead	Pb	82	207.19	327.35	621.2
Magnesium	Mg	12	24.312	651	1204
Manganese	Mn	25	54.9380	1260	2300
Mercury	Hg	80	200.59	−38.85	−37.67
Molybdenum	Mo	42	95.94	2620	4748
Nickel	Ni	28	58.71	1455	2651
Osmium	Os	76	190.2	2700	4892
Palladium	Pd	46	106.4	1554	2829
Phosphorus	P	15	30.9738	44.1	111.4
Platinum	Pt	78	195.09	1773.5	3224.3
15% Iridio-Plat.		—	—	1821	3310
10% Iridio-Plat.		—	—	1788	3250
5% Iridio-Plat.		—	—	1779	3235
Rhodium	Rh	45	109.905	1966	3571
Ruthenium	Ru	44	101.07	2500	4532
Silicon	Si	14	28.086	1420	2588
Silver	Ag	47	107.870	960.5	1760.9
Sterling				893	1640
Coin				879	1615
Tin	Sn	50	118.69	231.9	449.4
Tungsten	W	74	183.85	3400	6152
Vanadium	V	23	50.942	1710	3110
Zinc	Zn	30	65.37	419.4	787

High Temperatures Judged by Color

°F	°C	Color
752	400	Red heat, visible in dark
885	474	Red heat, visible in twilight
975	525	Red heat, visible in daylight
1077	581	Red heat, visible in sunlight
1292	700	Dark red
1472	800	Dull cherry red
1652	900	Cherry red
1832	1000	Bright cherry red
2012	1100	Orange-red
2192	1200	Orange-yellow
2372	1300	Yellow-white
2552	1400	White welding heat
2732	1500	Brilliant white
2912	1600	Dazzling white, blue-white

Melting Points of Metals from Low to High

Metal	°C	°F
Mercury	−38.85	−37.9
Phosphorus	44.1	47.3
Tin	231.9	448.3
Bismuth	271.3	520.3
Cadmium	320.0	608.0
Lead	327.35	621.2
Zinc	419.4	786.9
Antimony	630.5	1166.9
Magnesium	651.0	1203.8
Aluminum	660.2	1220.3
Silver	960.5	1760.9
Gold	1063.0	1945.4
Copper	1083.0	1981.4
Manganese	1260.0	2300.0
Silicon	1420.0	2588.0
Nickel	1455.0	2651.0
Cobalt	1480.0	2696.0
Iron	1539.0	2802.2
Palladium	1554.0	2829.2
Vanadium	1710.0	3110.0
Chromium	1765.0	3209.0
Platinum	1773.5	3224.3
Titanium	1820.0	3300.0
Rhodium	1966.0	3570.8
Iridium	2454.0	4449.2
Ruthenium	2500.0	4532.0
Molybdenum	2620.0	4748.0
Osmium	2700.0	4892.0
Tungsten	3400.0	6152.0
Carbon	3500.0	6332.0

Temperature Conversions

The general arrangement of this table was devised by Sauveur and Boylston. The middle column of figures (in bold-faced type) contains the reading (°F or °C) to be converted. If converting from degrees Fahrenheit to degrees Centigrade, read the Centigrade equivalent in the column headed "C." If converting from degrees Centigrade to degrees Fahrenheit, read the Fahrenheit equivalent in the column headed "F."

F		C	F		C	F		C	F		C	F		C
—	-458	-272.22	—	-308	-188.89	-252.4	-158	-105.56	+17.6	-8	-22.22	287.6	142	61.11
—	-456	-271.11	—	-306	-187.78	-248.8	-156	-104.44	+21.2	-6	-21.11	291.2	144	62.22
—	-454	-270.00	—	-304	-186.67	-245.2	-154	-103.33	+24.8	-4	-20.00	294.8	146	63.33
—	-452	-268.89	—	-302	-185.56	-241.6	-152	-102.22	+28.4	-2	-18.89	298.4	148	64.44
—	-450	-267.78	—	-300	-184.44	-238.0	-150	-101.11	+32.0	±0	-17.78	302.0	150	65.56
—	-448	-266.67	—	-298	-183.33	-234.4	-148	-100.00	+35.6	+2	-16.67	305.6	152	66.67
—	-446	-265.56	—	-296	-182.22	-230.8	-146	-98.89	+39.2	+4	-15.56	309.2	154	67.78
—	-444	-264.44	—	-294	-181.11	-227.2	-144	-97.78	+42.8	+6	-14.44	312.8	156	68.89
—	-442	-263.33	—	-292	-180.00	-223.6	-142	—96.67	+46.4	+8	-13.33	316.4	158	70.00
—	-440	-262.22	—	-290	-178.89	-220.0	-140	-95.56	+50.0	+10	-12.22	320.0	160	71.11
—	-438	-261.11	—	-288	-177.78	-216.4	-138	-94.44	+53.6	+12	-11.11	323.6	162	72.22
—	-436	-260.00	—	-286	-176.67	-212.8	-136	-93.33	+57.2	+14	-10.00	327.2	164	73.33
—	-434	-258.89	—	-284	-175.56	-209.2	-134	-92.22	+60.8	+16	-8.89	330.8	166	74.44
—	-432	-257.78	—	-282	-174.44	-205.6	-132	-91.11	+64.4	+18	-7.78	334.4	168	75.56
—	-430	-256.67	—	-280	-173.33	-202.0	-130	-90.00	+68.0	+20	-6.67	338.0	170	76.67
—	-428	-255.56	—	-278	-172.22	-198.4	-128	-88.89	+71.6	+22	-5.56	341.6	172	77.78
—	-426	-254.44	—	-276	-171.11	-194.8	-126	-87.78	+75.2	+24	-4.44	345.2	174	78.89
—	-424	-253.33	—	-274	-170.00	-191.2	-124	-86.67	+78.8	+26	-3.33	348.8	176	80.00
—	-422	-252.22	-457.6	-272	-168.89	-187.6	-122	-85.56	+82.4	+28	-2.22	352.4	178	81.11
—	-420	-251.11	-454.0	-270	-167.78	-184.0	-120	-84.44	+86.0	+30	-1.11	356.0	180	82.22
—	-418	-250.00	-450.4	-268	-166.67	-180.4	-118	-83.33	+89.6	+32	±0.00	359.6	182	83.33
—	-416	-248.89	-446.8	-266	-165.56	-176.8	-116	-82.22	+93.2	+34	+1.11	363.2	184	84.44
—	-414	-247.78	-443.2	-264	-164.44	-173.2	-114	-81.11	+96.8	+36	+2.22	366.8	186	85.56
—	-412	-246.67	-439.6	-262	-163.33	-169.6	-112	-80.00	+100.4	+38	+3.33	370.4	188	86.67
—	-410	-245.56	-436.0	-260	-162.22	-166.0	-110	-78.89	+104.0	+40	+4.44	374.0	190	87.78
—	-408	-244.44	-432.4	-258	-161.11	-162.4	-108	-77.78	107.6	42	5.56	377.6	192	88.89
—	-406	-243.33	-428.8	-256	-160.00	-158.8	-106	-76.67	111.2	44	6.67	381.2	194	90.00
—	-404	-242.22	-425.2	-254	-158.89	-155.2	-104	-75.56	114.8	46	7.78	384.8	196	91.11
—	-402	-241.11	-421.6	-252	-157.78	-151.6	-102	-74.44	118.4	48	8.89	388.4	198	92.22
—	-400	-240.00	-418.0	-250	-156.67	-148.0	-100	-73.33	122.0	50	10.00	392.0	200	93.33
—	-398	-238.89	-414.4	-248	-155.56	-144.4	-98	-72.22	125.6	52	11.11	395.6	202	94.44
—	-396	-237.78	-410.8	-246	-154.44	-140.8	-96	-71.11	129.2	54	12.22	399.2	204	95.56
—	-394	-236.67	-407.2	-244	-153.33	-137.2	-94	-70.00	132.8	56	13.33	402.8	206	96.67
—	-392	-235.56	-403.6	-242	-152.22	-133.6	-92	-68.89	136.4	58	14.44	406.4	208	97.78
—	-390	-234.44	-400.0	-240	-151.11	-130.0	-90	-67.78	140.0	60	15.56	410.0	210	98.89
—	-388	-233.33	-396.4	-238	-150.00	-126.4	-88	-66.67	143.6	62	16.67	413.6	212	100.00
—	-386	-232.22	-392.8	-236	-148.89	-122.8	-86	-65.56	147.2	64	17.78	417.2	214	101.11
—	-384	-231.11	-389.2	-234	-147.78	-119.2	-84	-64.44	150.8	66	18.89	420.8	216	102.22
—	-382	-230.00	-385.6	-232	-146.67	-115.6	-82	-63.33	154.4	68	20.00	424.4	218	103.33
—	-380	-228.89	-382.0	-230	-145.56	-112.0	-80	-62.22	158.0	70	21.11	428.0	220	104.44
—	-378	-227.78	-378.4	-228	-144.44	-108.4	-78	-61.11	161.6	72	22.22	431.6	222	105.56
—	-376	-226.67	-374.8	-226	-143.33	-104.8	-76	-60.00	165.2	74	23.33	435.2	224	106.67
—	-374	-225.56	-371.2	-224	-142.22	-101.2	-74	-58.89	168.8	76	24.44	438.8	226	107.78
—	-372	-224.44	-367.6	-222	-141.11	-97.6	-72	-57.78	172.4	78	25.56	442.4	228	108.89
—	-370	-223.33	-364.0	-220	-140.00	-94.0	-70	-56.67	176.0	80	26.67	446.0	230	110.00
—	-368	-222.22	-360.4	-218	-138.89	-90.4	-68	-55.56	179.6	82	27.78	449.6	232	111.11
—	-366	-221.11	-356.8	-216	-137.78	-86.8	-66	-54.44	183.2	84	28.89	453.2	234	112.22
—	-364	-220.00	-353.2	-214	-136.67	-83.2	-64	-53.33	186.8	86	30.00	456.8	236	113.33
—	-362	-218.89	-349.6	-212	-135.56	-79.6	-62	-52.22	190.4	88	31.11	460.4	238	114.44
—	-360	-217.78	-346.0	-210	-134.44	-76.0	-60	-51.11	194.0	90	32.22	464.0	240	115.56
—	-358	-216.67	-342.4	-208	-133.33	-72.4	-58	-50.00	197.6	92	33.33	467.6	242	116.67
—	-356	-215.56	-338.8	-206	-132.22	-68.8	-56	-48.89	201.2	94	34.44	471.2	244	117.78
—	-354	-214.44	-335.2	-204	-131.11	-65.2	-54	-47.78	204.8	96	35.56	474.8	246	118.89
—	-352	-213.33	-331.6	-202	-130.00	-61.6	-52	-46.67	208.4	98	36.67	478.4	248	120.00
—	-350	-212.22	-328.0	-200	-128.89	-58.0	-50	-45.56	212.0	100	37.78	482.0	250	121.11
—	-348	-211.11	-324.4	-198	-127.78	-54.4	-48	-44.44	215.6	102	38.89	485.6	252	122.22
—	-346	-210.00	-320.8	-196	-126.67	-50.8	-46	-43.33	219.2	104	40.00	489.2	254	123.33
—	-344	-208.89	-317.2	-194	-125.56	-47.2	-44	-42.22	222.8	106	41.11	492.8	256	124.44
—	-342	-207.78	-313.6	-192	-124.44	-43.6	-42	-41.11	226.4	108	42.22	496.4	258	125.56
—	-340	-206.67	-310.0	-190	-123.33	-40.0	-40	-40.00	230.0	110	43.33	500.0	260	126.67
—	-338	-205.56	-306.4	-188	-122.22	-36.4	-38	-38.89	233.6	112	44.44	503.6	262	127.78
—	-336	-204.44	-302.8	-186	-121.11	-32.8	-36	-37.78	237.2	114	45.56	507.2	264	128.89
—	-334	-203.33	-299.2	-184	-120.00	-29.2	-34	-36.67	240.8	116	46.67	510.8	266	130.00
—	-332	-202.22	-295.6	-182	-118.89	-25.6	-32	-35.56	244.4	118	47.78	514.4	268	131.11
—	-330	-201.11	-292.0	-180	-117.78	-22.0	-30	-34.44	248.0	120	48.89	518.0	270	132.22
—	-328	-200.00	-288.4	-178	-116.67	-18.4	-28	-33.33	251.6	122	50.00	521.6	272	133.33
—	-326	-198.89	-284.8	-176	-115.56	-14.8	-26	-32.22	255.2	124	51.11	525.2	274	134.44
—	-324	-197.78	-281.2	-174	-114.44	-11.2	-24	-31.11	258.8	126	52.22	528.8	276	135.56
—	-322	-196.67	-277.6	-172	-113.33	-7.6	-22	-30.00	262.4	128	53.33	532.4	278	136.67
—	-320	-195.56	-274.0	-170	-112.22	-4.0	-20	-28.89	266.0	130	54.44	536.0	280	137.78
—	-318	-194.44	-270.4	-168	-111.11	-0.4	-18	-27.78	269.6	132	55.56	539.6	282	138.89
—	-316	-193.33	-266.8	-166	-110.00	+3.2	-16	-26.67	273.2	134	56.67	543.2	284	140.00
—	-314	-192.22	-263.2	-164	-108.89	+6.8	-14	-25.56	276.8	136	57.78	546.8	286	141.11
—	-312	-191.11	-259.6	-162	-107.78	+10.4	-12	-24.44	280.4	138	58.89	550.4	288	142.22
—	-310	-190.00	-256.0	-160	-106.67	+14.0	-10	-23.33	284.0	140	60.00	554.0	290	143.33

(continued on the next page)

F		C	F		C	F		C	F		C	F		C
557.6	292	144.44	870.8	466	241.11	1832.0	1000	537.78	3398.0	1870	1021.1	4964.0	2740	1504.4
561.2	294	145.56	874.4	468	242.22	1850.0	1010	543.33	3416.0	1880	1026.7	4982.0	2750	1510.0
564.8	296	146.67	878.0	470	243.33	1868.0	1020	548.89	3434.0	1890	1032.2	5000.0	2760	1515.6
568.4	298	147.78	881.6	472	244.44	1886.0	1030	554.44	3452.0	1900	1037.8	5018.0	2770	1521.1
572.0	300	148.89	885.2	474	245.56	1904.0	1040	560.00	3470.0	1910	1043.3	5036.0	2780	1526.7
575.6	302	150.00	888.8	476	246.67	1922.0	1050	565.56	3488.0	1920	1048.9	5054.0	2790	1532.2
579.2	304	151.11	892.4	478	247.78	1940.0	1060	571.11	3506.0	1930	1054.4	5072.0	2800	1537.8
582.8	306	152.22	896.0	480	248.89	1958.0	1070	576.67	3524.0	1940	1060.0	5090.0	2810	1543.3
586.4	308	153.33	899.6	482	250.00	1976.0	1080	582.22	3542.0	1950	1065.6	5108.0	2820	1548.9
590.0	310	154.44	903.2	484	251.11	1994.0	1090	587.78	3560.0	1960	1071.1	5126.0	2830	1554.4
593.6	312	155.56	906.8	486	252.22	2012.0	1100	593.33	3578.0	1970	1076.7	5144.0	2840	1560.0
597.2	314	156.67	910.4	488	253.33	2030.0	1110	598.89	3596.0	1980	1082.2	5162.0	2850	1565.6
600.8	316	157.78	914.0	490	254.44	2048.0	1120	604.44	3614.0	1990	1087.8	5180.0	2860	1571.1
604.4	318	158.89	917.6	492	255.56	2066.0	1130	610.00	3632.0	2000	1093.3	5198.0	2870	1576.7
608.0	320	160.00	921.2	494	256.67	2084.0	1140	615.56	3650.0	2010	1098.9	5216.0	2880	1582.2
611.6	322	161.11	924.8	496	257.78	2102.0	1150	621.11	3668.0	2020	1104.4	5234.0	2890	1587.8
615.2	324	162.22	928.4	498	258.89	2120.0	1160	626.67	3686.0	2030	1110.0	5252.0	2900	1593.3
618.8	326	163.33	932.0	500	260.00	2138.0	1170	632.22	3704.0	2040	1115.6	5270.0	2910	1598.9
622.4	328	164.44	935.6	502	261.11	2156.0	1180	637.78	3722.0	2050	1121.1	5288.0	2920	1604.4
626.0	330	165.56	939.2	504	262.22	2174.0	1190	643.33	3740.0	2060	1126.7	5306.0	2930	1610.0
629.6	332	166.67	942.8	506	263.33	2192.0	1200	648.89	3758.0	2070	1132.2	5324.0	2940	1615.6
633.2	334	167.78	946.4	508	264.44	2210.0	1210	654.44	3776.0	2080	1137.8	5342.0	2950	1621.1
636.8	336	168.89	950.0	510	265.56	2228.0	1220	660.00	3794.0	2090	1143.3	5360.0	2960	1626.7
640.4	338	170.00	953.6	512	266.67	2246.0	1230	665.56	3812.0	2100	1148.9	5378.0	2970	1632.2
644.0	340	171.11	957.2	514	267.78	2264.0	1240	671.11	3830.0	2110	1154.4	5396.0	2980	1637.8
647.6	342	172.22	960.8	516	268.89	2282.0	1250	676.67	3848.0	2120	1160.0	5414.0	2990	1643.3
651.2	344	173.33	964.4	518	270.00	2300.0	1260	682.22	3866.0	2130	1165.6	5432.0	3000	1648.9
654.8	346	174.44	968.0	520	271.11	2318.0	1270	687.78	3884.0	2140	1171.1	5450.0	3010	1654.4
658.4	348	175.56	971.6	522	272.22	2336.0	1280	693.33	3902.0	2150	1176.7	5468.0	3020	1660.0
662.0	350	176.67	975.2	524	273.33	2354.0	1290	698.89	3920.0	2160	1182.2	5486.0	3030	1665.6
665.6	352	177.78	978.8	526	274.44	2372.0	1300	704.44	3938.0	2170	1187.8	5504.0	3040	1671.1
669.2	354	178.89	982.4	528	275.56	2390.0	1310	710.00	3956.0	2180	1193.3	5522.0	3050	1676.7
672.8	356	180.00	986.0	530	276.67	2408.0	1320	715.56	3974.0	2190	1198.9	5540.0	3060	1682.2
676.4	358	181.11	989.6	532	277.78	2426.0	1330	721.11	3992.0	2200	1204.4	5558.0	3070	1687.8
680.0	360	182.22	993.2	534	278.89	2444.0	1340	726.67	4010.0	2210	1210.0	5576.0	3080	1693.3
683.6	362	183.33	996.8	536	280.00	2462.0	1350	732.22	4028.0	2220	1215.6	5594.0	3090	1698.9
687.2	364	184.44	1000.4	538	281.11	2480.0	1360	737.78	4046.0	2230	1221.1	5612.0	3100	1704.4
690.8	366	185.56	1004.0	540	282.22	2498.0	1370	743.33	4064.0	2240	1226.7	5702.0	3150	1732.2
694.4	368	186.67	1007.6	542	283.33	2516.0	1380	748.89	4082.0	2250	1232.2	5792.0	3200	1760.0
698.0	370	187.78	1011.2	544	284.44	2534.0	1390	754.44	4100.0	2260	1237.8	5882.0	3250	1787.7
701.6	372	188.89	1014.8	546	285.56	2552.0	1400	760.00	4118.0	2270	1243.3	5972.0	3300	1815.5
705.2	374	190.00	1018.4	548	286.67	2570.0	1410	765.56	4136.0	2280	1248.9	6062.0	3350	1843.3
708.8	376	191.11	1022.0	550	287.78	2588.0	1420	771.11	4154.0	2290	1254.4	6152.0	3400	1871.1
712.4	378	192.22	1040.0	560	293.33	2606.0	1430	776.67	4172.0	2300	1260.0	6242.0	3450	1898.8
716.0	380	193.33	1058.0	570	298.89	2624.0	1440	782.22	4190.0	2310	1265.6	6332.0	3500	1926.6
719.6	382	194.44	1076.0	580	304.44	2642.0	1450	787.78	4208.0	2320	1271.1	6422.0	3550	1954.4
723.2	384	195.56	1094.0	590	310.00	2660.0	1460	793.33	4226.0	2330	1276.7	6512.0	3600	1982.2
726.8	386	196.67	1112.0	600	315.56	2678.0	1470	798.89	4244.0	2340	1282.2	6602.0	3650	2010.0
730.4	388	197.78	1130.0	610	321.11	2696.0	1480	804.44	4262.0	2350	1287.8	6692.0	3700	2037.7
734.0	390	198.89	1148.0	620	326.67	2714.0	1490	810.00	4280.0	2360	1293.3	6782.0	3750	2065.5
737.6	392	200.00	1166.0	630	332.22	2732.0	1500	815.56	4298.0	2370	1298.9	6872.0	3800	2093.3
741.2	394	201.11	1184.0	640	337.78	2750.0	1510	821.11	4316.0	2380	1304.4	6962.0	3850	2121.1
744.8	396	202.22	1202.0	650	343.33	2768.0	1520	826.67	4334.0	2390	1310.0	7052.0	3900	2148.8
748.4	398	203.33	1220.0	660	348.89	2786.0	1530	832.22	4352.0	2400	1315.6	7142.0	3950	2176.6
752.0	400	204.44	1238.0	670	354.44	2804.0	1540	837.78	4370.0	2410	1321.1	7232.0	4000	2204.4
755.6	402	205.56	1256.0	680	360.00	2822.0	1550	843.33	4388.0	2420	1326.7	7322.0	4050	2232.2
759.2	404	206.67	1274.0	690	365.56	2840.0	1560	848.89	4406.0	2430	1332.2	7412.0	4100	2260.0
762.8	406	207.78	1292.0	700	371.11	2858.0	1570	854.44	4424.0	2440	1337.8	7502.0	4150	2287.7
766.4	408	208.89	1310.0	710	376.67	2876.0	1580	860.00	4442.0	2450	1343.3	7592.0	4200	2315.5
770.0	410	210.00	1328.0	720	382.22	2894.0	1590	865.56	4460.0	2460	1348.9	7682.0	4250	2343.3
773.6	412	211.11	1346.0	730	387.78	2912.0	1600	871.11	4478.0	2470	1354.4	7772.0	4300	2371.1
777.2	414	212.22	1364.0	740	393.33	2930.0	1610	876.67	4496.0	2480	1360.0	7862.0	4350	2398.8
780.8	416	213.33	1382.0	750	398.89	2948.0	1620	882.22	4514.0	2490	1365.6	7952.0	4400	2426.6
784.4	418	214.44	1400.0	760	404.44	2966.0	1630	887.78	4532.0	2500	1371.1	8042.0	4450	2454.4
788.0	420	215.56	1418.0	770	410.00	2984.0	1640	893.33	4550.0	2510	1376.7	8132.0	4500	2482.2
791.6	422	216.67	1436.0	780	415.56	3002.0	1650	898.89	4568.0	2520	1382.2	8222.0	4550	2510.0
795.2	424	217.78	1454.0	790	421.11	3020.0	1660	904.44	4586.0	2530	1387.8	8312.0	4600	2537.7
798.8	426	218.89	1472.0	800	426.67	3038.0	1670	910.00	4604.0	2540	1393.3	8402.0	4650	2565.5
802.4	428	220.00	1490.0	810	432.22	3056.0	1680	915.56	4622.0	2550	1398.9	8492.0	4700	2593.3
806.0	430	221.11	1508.0	820	437.76	3074.0	1690	921.11	4640.0	2560	1404.4	8582.0	4750	2621.1
809.6	432	222.22	1526.0	830	443.33	3092.0	1700	926.67	4658.0	2570	1410.0	8672.0	4800	2648.8
813.2	434	223.33	1544.0	840	448.89	3110.0	1710	932.22	4676.0	2580	1415.6	8762.0	4850	2676.6
816.8	436	224.44	1562.0	850	454.44	3128.0	1720	937.78	4694.0	2590	1421.1	8852.0	4900	2704.4
820.4	438	225.56	1580.0	860	460.00	3146.0	1730	943.33	4712.0	2600	1426.7	8942.0	4950	2732.2
824.0	440	226.67	1598.0	870	465.56	3164.0	1740	948.89	4730.0	2610	1432.2	9032.0	5000	2760.0
827.6	442	227.78	1616.0	880	471.11	3182.0	1750	954.44	4748.0	2620	1437.8	9122.0	5050	2787.7
831.2	444	228.89	1634.0	890	476.67	3200.0	1760	960.00	4766.0	2630	1443.3	9212.0	5100	2815.5
834.8	446	230.00	1652.0	900	482.22	3218.0	1770	965.56	4784.0	2640	1448.9	9302.0	5150	2843.3
838.4	448	231.11	1670.0	910	487.78	3236.0	1780	971.11	4802.0	2650	1454.4	9392.0	5200	2871.1
842.0	450	232.22	1688.0	920	493.33	3254.0	1790	976.67	4820.0	2660	1460.0	9482.0	5250	2898.8
845.6	452	233.3	1706.0	930	498.89	3272.0	1800	982.22	4838.0	2670	1465.6	9572.0	5300	2926.6
849.2	454	234.44	1724.0	940	504.44	3290.0	1810	987.78	4856.0	2680	1471.1	9662.0	5350	2954.4
852.8	456	235.56	1742.0	950	510.00	3308.0	1820	993.33	4874.0	2690	1476.7	9752.0	5400	2982.2
856.4	458	236.67	1760.0	960	515.56	3326.0	1830	998.89	4892.0	2700	1482.2	9842.0	5450	3010.0
860.0	460	237.78	1778.0	970	521.11	3344.0	1840	1004.4	4910.0	2710	1487.8	9932.0	5500	3037.7
863.6	462	238.89	1796.0	980	526.67	3362.0	1850	1010.0	4928.0	2720	1493.3	10,022.0	5550	3065.5
867.2	464	240.00	1814.0	990	532.22	3380.0	1860	1015.6	4946.0	2730	1498.9	10,112.0	5600	3093.3

TIME AND SPEED

TIME MEASUREMENTS

Time measurements are uniform throughout the world as far as periods of one week or less are concerned. The basic unit is the mean solar day, divided into 24 hours of 60 minutes each, or 3,600 seconds.

SPEED MEASUREMENTS

Speed measurements are always stated in a frame of reference to have meaning. For example, *revolutions per minute* means the number of times in which an object will rotate one complete turn in one full minute. Therefore speed in general means the rate of motion or performance accomplished in a given time.

Drill feeds are governed by the size of the drill and the metal or other material to be drilled. For drills smaller than ⅛ in the recommended feed is 0.001–0.002 in per revolution; for drills ¼–½ in, 0.002–0.004 in; for drills ¼–½ in, 0.004–0.007 in, for drills ½–1 in, 0.007–0.015 in; and for drills larger than 1 in, 0.015–0.025 in per revolution. When drilling relatively hard materials such as alloy steels, the lower feeds should be used, and when drilling relatively soft materials such as the precious metals, brass, and aluminum, the higher feeds should be used. Recommended peripheral speeds for carbon steel drills are 60 fpm (feet per minute) for precious metals and brass, and 30 fpm for steel. For high-speed drills, recommended peripheral speeds are 200 fpm for precious metals and brass, and 80–100 fpm for steel and iron.

Peripheral or Surface Speed
(In feet per minute)

rpm	1″ Diameter	4″ Diameter	6″ Diameter	8″ Diameter
900	235	950	1400	1900
1150	300	1200	1800	2400
1200	315	1250	1900	2500
1500	400	1550	2350	3150
1750	450	1800	2750	3650
2000	525	2100	3100	4200
2400	625	2500	3800	5000
2800	730	2900	4400	5850
3000	785	3100	4700	6300
3200	840	3350	5000	6700
3450	900	3600	5400	7200
3750	980	3900	5900	7800
4000	1045	4200	6300	8400
4500	1180	4700	7200	9400
5000	1310	5200	7800	10500
5400	1410	5600	8500	11300
6000	1570	6300	9400	12500

Suggested Drill Cutting Speeds and Feeds
(drills mounted on drill presses)

Drill Diam., Inches	Feet per Minute										
	30	40	50	60	70	80	90	100	150	200	250
	Revolutions per Minute										
¹⁄₁₆	1833	2445	3056	3667	4278	4889	5500	6112	9167	12223	15279
⅛	917	1222	1528	1833	2139	2445	2750	3056	4584	6112	7639
³⁄₁₆	611	815	1019	1222	1426	1630	1833	2037	3056	4074	5093
¼	458	611	764	917	1070	1222	1375	1528	2292	3056	3820
⁵⁄₁₆	367	489	611	733	856	978	1100	1222	1833	2445	3056
⅜	306	407	509	611	713	815	917	1019	1528	2037	2546
⁷⁄₁₆	262	349	437	524	611	698	786	873	1310	1746	2183
½	229	306	382	458	535	611	688	764	1146	1528	1910
⅝	183	244	306	367	428	489	550	611	917	1222	1528
¾	153	204	255	306	357	407	458	509	764	1019	1273
⅞	131	175	218	262	306	349	393	473	655	873	1091
1	115	153	191	229	267	306	344	382	573	764	955
1⅛	102	136	170	204	238	272	306	340	509	679	849
1¼	92	122	153	183	214	244	275	306	458	611	764
1⅜	83	111	139	167	194	222	250	278	417	556	694
1½	76	102	127	153	178	204	229	255	382	509	637
1⅝	71	94	118	141	165	188	212	235	353	470	588
1¾	66	87	109	131	153	175	196	218	327	437	546
1⅞	61	82	102	122	143	163	183	204	306	407	509
2	57	76	96	115	134	153	172	191	287	382	477

Courtesy L. S. Starrett Co.

19
GLOSSARIES

VISUAL GLOSSARY

Geometric and morphic shapes, forms, and concepts

The arts incorporate the most important manifestations of principles and concepts inexhaustibly active in the phenomenal, biological, and physical world of *nature,* the main source of creative inspiration. Throughout history, humanity has interpreted nature and natural phenomena by representing them as abstract *shapes* and *forms* that express their essences, and has attributed to these abstractions conceptual, magical, and other significances. By their use, entire cultural environments have been created. It is therefore important that when we create an object that utilizes such shapes and forms, we understand these universal meanings. To think of them simply in terms of their decorative qualities and to ignore their greater meaning and its implications is to experience only a fraction of their potential for appreciation, enjoyment, and their ability to heighten the communication of an idea.

The *idea* or internal concept contained in a jewel is expressed essentially by what is external or physically visible. Ideas in the arts are substantially communicated by the use of *two-dimensional shapes,* and *three-dimensional forms,* qualified by material, color, and surface treatment. Because shapes and forms, and the images and constructions created by their use represent *thought,* every creative work embodies mental concepts capable of being either sensed intuitively, or intellectually understood and assimilated. In effect, concepts become a visual language of communication.

By giving a concept a name, and depicting it graphically, as is done here, the possibly complex idea that it represents—which may be difficult to describe verbally—becomes intuitively obvious when seen concretely in one of its visual manifestations in a flat plane. All of the concepts depicted can be found in the designs and constructions of ancient, historic, ethnic, and contemporary jewelry. Concepts representing shapes and forms may physically consist of a single unit, or include a number of components. Almost every figure embraces *several meanings* and can be interpreted or explained on *several levels.* Pertinent to this explanation, among others, are the areas of *geometry,* involving regular shapes and forms whose physical existence relate to a central point or axis; *morphology,* which covers the nature, type, and structure of irregular or biomorphic shapes and forms; *conceptuality,* dealing with the idea or abstract thought expressed; *symbolism,* which explains the spiritual, often universal, inner, general or specific meaning associated with the configuration; and *cosmology,* which reveals the relation of their various shapes and forms to aspects of systems exhibited in the universe. Wherever possible and appropriate, these areas have been mentioned in the descriptions and discussions of particular items that follow.

The most basic of all elements used to create the shapes and forms employed in jewelry, as well as in other arts, are the *point* and the *line.* This visual glossary therefore begins with these generic concepts. From there onward, an attempt has been made to represent and include the more important concepts

that enter into a jeweler's thinking, though the glossary is by no means complete. The organization first deals with concepts, shapes, and forms involving an increasing progression of *numbers* which are units that define and allow for the comprehension of shapes, forms, space, and directions. Thereafter, the visual concepts are presented in increasing complexity, and/or are grouped by principles they have in common.

In all cultures, jewelers seek an integration or conceptual synthesis of form relationships in their work through the use of materials and techniques, shaped by ideas. The general *primary aim* is to successfully compose components in an organization that first of all exhibits a satisfying *sense of unity* or *wholeness.* The work in addition, by dealing with the messages of shape and form as well as esthetic and intellectual concerns, can communicate its higher realization, which is the expression of its *significance.*

1 POINT: A *point* is an imaginary or real place having definite position in space, but no volume or parts. It is the smallest possible unit, graphically indicated by a dot. By representing the unit, it also indicates the number *one* (1), which is the origin of all numbers. Symbolically, numbers do not simply denote quantities, but are ideas, each with its own qualities. Even numbers express the principle of negativeness and passivity; odd numbers, positiveness and activity. A point can be thought of as fixed or moving through dimensional space. It also represents the tapering end of anything; a position by itself or in relation to other positions; and the meeting place of any two elements in infinite space. Symbolically, the point represents the concept of the Creator, spirit, the center, nucleus, and the force of resistance.

2 NODE: A *node* consists of the figure made by the indirect distance between two nonconsecutive points on a curve. The curve itself can be regarded as a series of points, or as a moving point.

3 STRAIGHT LINE: A *straight line* has length but no breadth, and is the graphically depicted unbroken linkage of the direct distance between two points. Two points can also be thought of as being connected by an arc on a line, in this case, the arc describing an angle of 180°. Connected with this concept is the *straight edge,* a tool used to test the straightness of surfaces; and the *ruler,* a metal, wood, or plastic tool also with a straight edge, but used to measure its length. The space between the two points therefore involves the concepts of *distance* and *measurement.* The number *two* (2) introduces the concept of *duality,* and the idea of *division* into halves. From the basic elements of *point* and *line,* many other elements can be created. For example, when one point is fixed, and the other to which it is connected by a line moves from it equidistantly, the line acts as the *radius* of a circle. Symbolically, when a line is horizontal it is passive; when vertical, active.

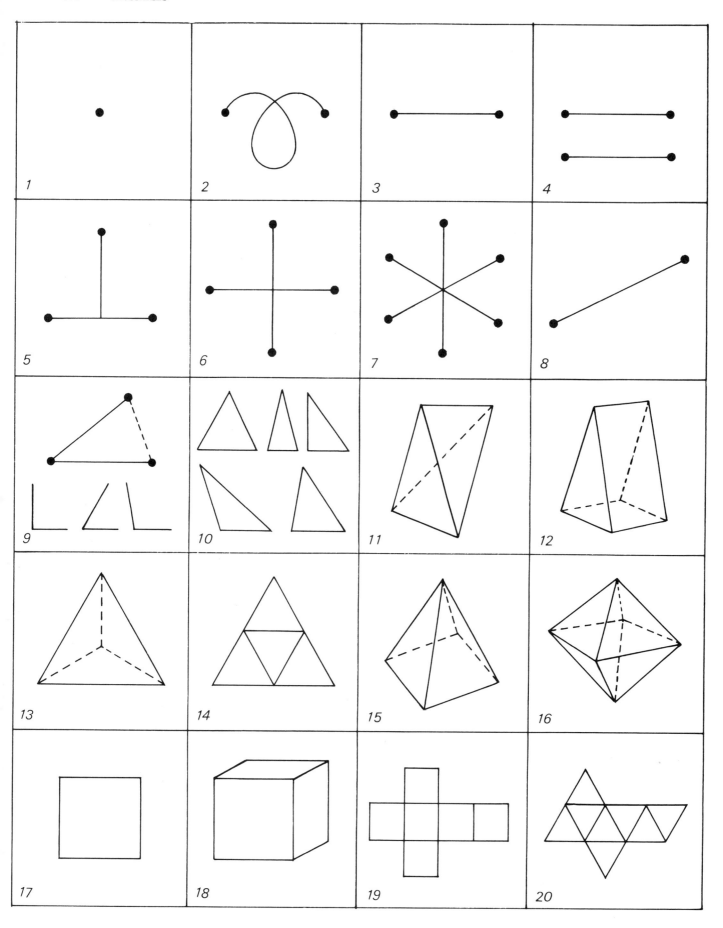

4 PARALLEL LINES: *Parallel lines* are two lines (or planes) everywhere lying equally distant from each other, and moving in the same direction, but never meeting, however far they are extended. Parallel curves are also possible. Conceptually, by their theoretical endlessness, they represent infinity. Symbolically, parallel lines represent constancy.

5 PERPENDICULAR LINES (AND PLANES): *Perpendicular lines* consist of one line (or plane) exactly upright or vertical and a second line (or plane) exactly horizontal, the two meeting at a point of incidence. The vertical line points toward the horizontal line in the direction of gravity toward the earth's center; the horizontal line is parallel with the horizon, and the angles they make with each other are 90° (a right angle). The action of the *plumb line,* a line with an attached *conoidal weight* or *plumb bob* containing lead that hangs freely in space for use in determining verticality, works by gravitational force to establish the vertical in a perpendicular relationship. Symbolically, perpendicular lines represent opposition, verticality, and uprightness.

6 TWO INTERSECTING LINES: TWO-DIMENSIONAL SPACE: *Two intersecting lines,* one horizontal the other vertical, when drawn from four points, cut across each other, form right angles and four equal compartments. This figure can be used to illustrate the concept of *two-dimensional space* which implies four directions (five, if the *center* or crossing point is included). The vertical line indicates *height* which has two directions: top and bottom, or up and down; and the horizontal represents *width* which also has two directions: left and right. In terms of the *terrestrial plane,* all these directions are horizontal and become the *cardinal points:* (north-south; east-west). The concept of *intersection* can also be applied to surfaces and volumes in which the place of intersection is not a point, but a *line.* Together, besides symbolizing directions, they also indicate conjunction, communication, inversion, the union of opposites, and change.

7 THREE INTERSECTING LINES: THREE-DIMENSIONAL SPACE: *Three lines intersecting* each other perpendicularly in three-dimensional space (here represented by a flat plane) depict the concept of the *six basic directions of motion:* up, down, left, right, front, back (*seven* if the center at the crossing point, "static motion," is added). With these directions established, a coordinated system becomes possible by which *magnitudes* can be measured. Symbolically, this directional concept embodies the idea of orientation in both the physical and psychic worlds.

8 OBLIQUE LINE (OR PLANE): An *oblique line* (or plane) slants, which makes it neither horizontal nor vertical because of its deviation from perpendicularity and parallelism. (In the case of an *oblique solid,* it is so called because its main axis is not perpendicular to the base.) Oblique lines are used in oblique or *linear perspective* in which when depicting the illusion of depth in a two-dimensional plane, all receding parallel lines are made to move obliquely (at an angle) toward a vanishing point on the horizon. Conceptually, an oblique line implies the idea of *ascent* and *descent.* Symbolically, the ideas of unbalance, movement, change, deviation, and action are involved.

9 ANGLE: An *angle* is the figure formed by the coming together or intersection of two lines to an end point, the space between such lines constituting the figure called an *angle.* The concept implies the *joining of three points,* and the forming of a *plane* which occurs when the first and the third points in this configuration are joined with a line, thus making a *triangle.* By one definition, a *plane* is defined as any surface determined by any three points which are not collinear. An angle's measure is expressed in *degrees* (°), the complete revolution of one leg rotating through 360°. Three *basic angle types* exist: *right* (90°), *acute* (more than 0° but less than 90°), and *obtuse* (more than 90° and less than 180°). When the two legs of the angle are equal and acute, the configuration symbolically represents the *compass* which implies the act of creation by measurement and delineation. Among other symbolic meanings given to the *ternary* or the concept of *three* is that the in-

troduction of a third element solves the problem of conflict posed by the idea of two or duality. A great many other symbolic meanings evolve from the idea of three, the first odd number larger than one. An important religious idea is the Trinity which exists not only in Christianity, but also in other religions.

10 TRIANGLES: A *triangle* is a plane figure (unless otherwise indicated) formed by *three points* that are not on the same line (noncollinear) and the *three line segments* that connect them, intersecting by twos in three places, forming three internal angles or *vertices.* The sum total of the interior angles of any triangle always equals 180°. The basic triangle types depend on the relation of the sides and angles to each other. These are: *equilateral triangle* in which all sides are of equal length and each interior angle is 60°; *isosceles triangle* in which two sides are equal; *right triangle* in which one of the interior angles is 90°; *obtuse triangle* in which one interior angle is obtuse; *scalene triangle* in which all the angles are acute and no two sides have an equal length. Equilateral and isosceles triangles also have all acute angles, but in the first, all sides are equal, and in the second, two sides are equal. The *area* of a plane triangle is figured by multiplying any side by one-half the perpendicular distance of that side from the opposite vertex. The triangle is used in art both decoratively and symbolically, representing a variety of concepts involving the ternary or three. It is connected with the concept of activity. In some primitive cultures, the triangle, apex down, symbolizes the female genitalia, and life, the soul, or the spirit. Curved-line and curved-plane triangles are also possible. Connected with the triangle is the *triskele,* any pattern consisting of three, usually curved branches that radiate from a center.

11 TETRAGONAL SPHENOID: A *tetragonal sphenoid* is a wedge-shaped form having *four similar isosceles triangular faces,* the base lines of two of them coinciding and forming an edge in one direction, and the base lines of the other two an edge in a different, usually opposite direction. (A *tetrad* is anything involving the concept of *four* by grouping, collecting, juxtaposing, combining, two variables in pairs, etc.) The tetragonal sphenoid is one of the basic forms used in forging. It results from the suppression of alternate faces of a double pyramid, and the extension of the remaining faces until they intersect. Symbolically, the form represents opposition in duality.

12 WEDGE: A *wedge* is a *five-faced* form with a four-sided base, two rectangular faces that meet in one edge whose position is parallel with the edges of the base, and two triangular ends. The pointed edge is considered the active end as it is the end that does the main work. In one method, the wedge is gradually driven into a substance to force an entrance or passage in order to effectuate its cleavage by causing a break. Chisels and engraving tools are based on the wedge shape and variations of this shape, and utilize this shape in another fashion, to remove material from the mass. Wedges are also used to create a state of fixation by pressure, as in a ring clamp. Symbolically, the form implies aggression.

13 TETRAHEDRON: A *tetrahedron* is a polyhedron or multifaced form with *four faces,* each of which is an equilateral triangle in shape. The form is a triangular-based pyramid, all sides meeting at a common vertex at a point on the vertical axis. This form is the simplest of primary solids. Symbolically, it involves the *quaternary* or principle of four, and is associated with the concept of site, and an intuitive sense of spacial order.

14 TETRAHEDRON SOLID: PLAN PATTERN: For purposes of understanding the following terms as used in the text ahead, they are defined here:
Plan: The graphic depiction of the top view of a form, represented in one plane.
Elevation: The graphic depiction of an object projected on a vertical plane perpendicular to the horizon.
Development: The flattening out of a developable form upon a plane without stretching it, to show the pattern from which it can be constructed three dimensionally. (See 63, Ring; and 72, Cone.)

In the plan of a solid tetrahedron, all sides are flattened to one plane. The form is created by cutting out this shape, then bending along the lines. To find the *volume* of this pyramid, multiply one-third of the area of the base by the altitude. To find the *surface area,* add to the base area one-half of the product of the perimeter of the base times the slant height of the pyramid.

15 PYRAMID: A *typical pyramid* is a *five-surfaced form* with a square base and four triangular faces meeting at a point at the top which is directly over and on the central vertical axis line. Pyramid bases may also have the shape of a triangle (as in the tetrahedron), rectangle, or other polygon, and in each case, these have as many triangular-shaped sides as the number of straight sides on the base figure. In regular pyramids, the sides always meet at a common vertex over a center point in the base. Pyramids are named after the shape of their bases: triangular pyramid, square pyramid, rectangular pyramid, etc. In terms of symbols, the pyramid signifies fire as the apex is the finishing point of all things. Square-based pyramids symbolize the maternal earth.

16 OCTAHEDRON: A *regular octahedron* is an *eight-sided* or eight-faced form, each face an equilateral triangle. It can be thought of as a double pyramid with a common base, and an apex at top and bottom occurring on the same vertical axis line at an equal distance from the base plane. Symbolically, it embodies the concept of opposites, such as fire and water.

17 SQUARE: A *square* is a parallelogram having *four equal sides,* and four internal *right angles.* It belongs to the family of *tetragons* or plane figures having four sides, which includes the rectangle, quadrangle, rhombus, and parallelogram—all *tetragonal figures.* Symbolically, the square is associated with the *quaternary* and the number *four*—the first *square number.* These concepts include the four seasons; the four elements: earth (solids), water (liquids), air (gases), and fire (temperature), the latter transforming all matter; and the cardinal points. It is also connected with the concepts of construction, artifice, stability, reality, earth, the material aspects of life, and the body.

18 CUBE: A *cube* is a regular solid having *six equal square sides,* making it a *hexahedron* or six-faced polyhedron, and corresponds to the solid of a square. In this solid, which belongs to the tetragonal system, all three axes are at right angles and are equal. The cube symbolizes the idea of stability because by itself, it cannot rotate. In hollow form, it symbolizes a box or container in which something is kept. *Box construction* is a term indicating the fabrication of a hollow object by the use of sheet metal.

19 CUBE: PLAN PATTERN: The six sides of the cube form, projected flat. Once cut out, the form is constructed by bending along lines.

20 OCTAHEDRON: PLAN PATTERN: The eight sides of the octahedron, each one an equilateral triangle, projected flat. Once cut out, the form is constructed by bending along the lines.

21 RECTANGLE: A *rectangle* is a right-angled parallelogram with *two pairs of sides,* one pair longer than the other. Its area is found by multiplying the dimensions of two adjacent sides. Symbolically it is considered to be the most rational, secure form, probably because it is used in relation to life's basic, physical needs in the shape of a door, window, table, etc.

22 RECTANGULAR SOLID: The corresponding solid of a rectangle is an elongated cube. Symbolically it is associated with the shape of a room or a house.

23 RECTANGULAR SOLID: PLAN PATTERN: Depicted here is the flat plan of a rectangular solid with its three pairs of matching sides. Once cut out, it is constructed by bending along lines.

24 QUADRANGLE: A *quadrangle* is a rectangular-plane tetragonal figure with four sides and four angles connected by two diagonal lines from corner to corner, totaling *six lines,* determined by *four points.* Like all tetragons, it is connected

with the idea of *four* in many areas, reinforced by the division of its interior into four triangles.

25 RHOMBUS: A *rhombus* is an equilateral parallelogram with *two pairs of parallel sides,* one pair *oblique.* Like all four-sided figures having acute and oblique angles, it produces a leaning effect, and therefore implies the idea of *motion* in the direction toward which the figure leans.

26 RHOMBOID: A *rhomboid* is a parallelogram in which opposite angles are obtuse or acute, the sides adjacent to each other are unequal, and opposite sides are parallel.

27 PARALLELEPIPEDON: A *parallelepipedon* is a *six-sided prism* whose three pairs of matching faces are parallelograms. It is the corresponding solid of a parallelogram.

28 TRAPEZIUM: A *trapezium* is a plane figure with *four sides* of which *no two are parallel,* therefore, it is any irregular four-sided figure. Symbolically it represents irregularity or abnormality.

29 PENTAGON: A *pentagon* is a regular polygon having *five sides* and *five equal interior angles.* To draw *any regular polygon,* the most accurate and fastest way is to use a *protractor* and lay out its central angles. In a pentagon, each central angle is 72°, and the interior angle between sides is 108° (half = 54°). The *quinary* or the concept of *five* involves any group of *five elements,* and represents an extremely important concept that commonly occurs in nature. This may account for its frequent use in amulets and talismans. The human body has five extremities: four limbs and a head that controls them; the hand has five fingers, and the toes are five in number; there are five senses: hearing, sight, taste, smell, and touch. Plants often grow with an inflorescence or general arrangement and disposition of flowers or leaves on an axis in groups of five.

30 PENTAGRAM, PENTACLE, OR PENTALPHA: A *pentagram* or five-pointed star is also called a *pentacle* or *pentalpha,* as well as a *cross polygon* because its lines intersect. Symbolically, this is a universally powerful figure, very commonly used for talismanic purposes. It has variously been interpreted to symbolize the forces of the spirit struggling against night or darkness; as a sign of the microcosmos or man who represents the world in miniature, and whose five extremities outstretched fit within this figure with the generative organs at the center; and a variety of other concepts.

31 PENTAGONAL PYRAMID: A *pentagonal pyramid* is a right pyramid or polyhedron with a pentagonal base, each of whose triangular sides is a projection of one line or side of that figure, all sides meeting at a common vertex or point directly above its center. Its pattern or plan is the pentagon.

32 PENTACRON: A *pentacron* is a solid having five angular, conical summits or points. The principle of five is applied to any figure having five similar elements.

33 HEXAGON: A *hexagon* is a regular *six-sided polygon* with six central angles of 60° each, and the interior angle between sides is 120° (half = 60°). It contains six equilateral triangles, each with three 60° interior angles. It can also contain three crossing rectangles (see next figure) whose sides are formed by sides of the hexagon, all together forming a *hexagram* contained within the hexagon. *Six* is the first complete number, divisible into three twos, or two threes. Symbolically it represents the cessation of movement; equilibrium; and also the six directions: up, down, front, back, left, right.

34 HEXAGRAM: A *hexagram* is a regular figure which encompasses a regular hexagon, created by extending each of the hexagon's sides until they form *six equal appexes.* This figure can also be contained within a hexagon. The hexagram is an important symbolic figure, commonly with the connotation of a star. When thought of as the union of two superimposed equilateral triangles, it represents the Seal of Solomon; and is also a symbol of the human soul. Because it is equally divisible, it is also a symbol of dualism or the union of opposites as when the triangle with its vertex up symbolizes fire, and one with its apex down symbolizes water.

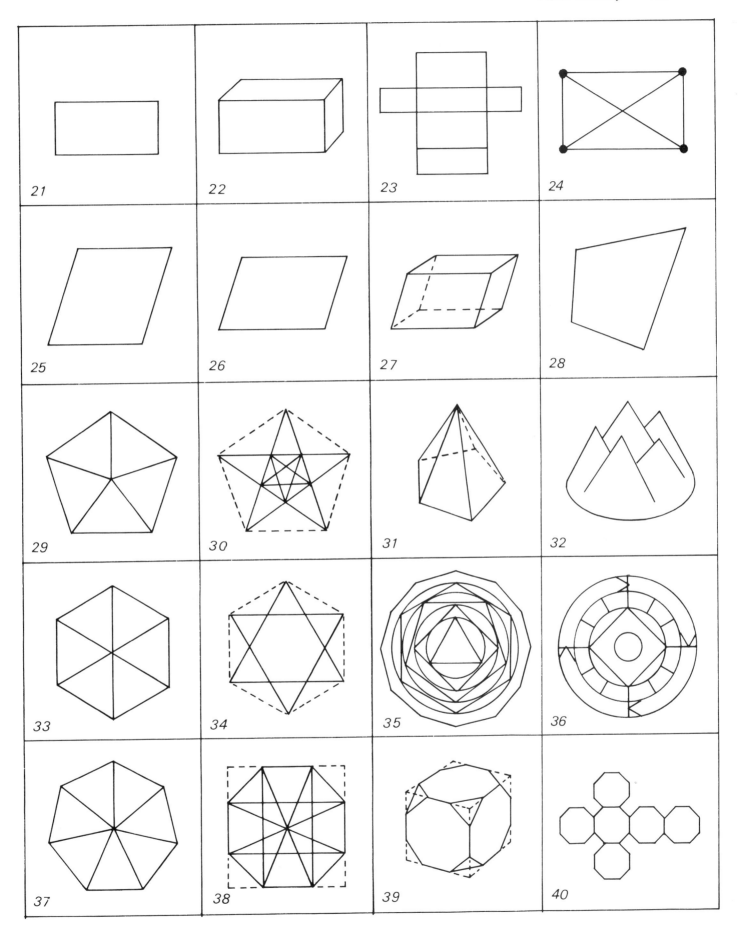

35 POLYGONS: *Polygons* are closed figures that have three or more straight sides, all lying in a *single plane*. A *spherical polygon* is a similar figure drawn on the surface of a sphere. A *skew polygon* is made up of segments lying in different planes. *Regular polygons* are equilateral and equiangular. *Irregular polygons* have different angles at their vertices, or line segments of different lengths. *Convex polygons* have all interior angles less than straight angles (180°). *Concave polygons* have at least one interior angle of more than 180°. *Cross polygons* have line segments that intersect. Regular polygons are given names according to the number of their sides: 3 sides, triangle; 4 sides, square or quadrangle; 5 sides, pentagon; 6 sides, hexagon; 7 sides, heptagon; 8 sides, octagon; 9 sides, nonagon; 10 sides, decagon; 12 sides, dodecagon.

THE FIVE PLATONIC POLYHEDRONS OR SOLIDS

The *five regular polygons* (triangle, square, pentagon, octagon, and dodecagon) can be enscribed within a circle, or can be encompassed by a circle, as shown here. Their solids, called the *five Platonic solids or bodies,* or regular solids, because they were mentioned by Plato, are convex polyhedra formed by four or more plane faces which are *all equal,* and have vertices which are all equal angles. These solids, given below, may be enscribed within or circumscribed about a sphere with which they all have homeomorphic surfaces. They can be described as follows, the first three having sets of equilateral triangles as faces:

Tetrahedron:	4 vertices,	6 edges,	4 faces
Octahedron:	6 vertices,	12 edges,	8 faces
Icosahedron:	12 vertices,	30 edges,	20 faces
Hexahedron:	8 vertices,	12 edges,	6 faces
Dodecahedron:	20 vertices,	30 edges,	12 faces

Symbolically, regular figures in general when enscribed within a circle represent unity in multiplicity, as embodied in the concept of the *mandala.* Because a mandala in essence is a cosmogram, the harmonic patterns it contains involve laws of proportion and the idea of the cosmos and transformation.

36 ZODIACAL CYCLE: Several important circular systems are based on the idea of a relationship of 12 *divisions.* The most important, involving a cyclic alternation of "12" is *time,* symbolized by the *clock.* This is usually thought of as a circular diagram divided into 12 divisions representing the hours. By the use of this device, the day is divided into day and night, and by extension, the months and the year can be calculated. Another important symbolic connection with such a division is the *wheel* which can be constructed with 12 spokes, its total concept involving ideas of motion, rotation, and cyclic repetition. In ancient symbolism, the sun is sometimes thought of as a wheel because of its cyclic passage through the heavens.

From the apparent rotational action of the sun (actually it is the earth that rotates), and the positions of the planets in the heavens comes the *zodiacal cycle* (Greek *zoe,* "life"; *diakos,* "wheel"), among symbols, probably the most widespread and continually used in the world. (See Astrological Stones, p. 583, for the symbols and the gemstones associated with them.) In systems based on twelve, the total can be subdivided into four groups of three, three groups of four, or two groups of six, and these ideas, also used in the zodiacal cycle, also give rise to other symbolic uses. The zodiacal cycle is based on a system of 12 divisions, its basic representation indicating a time-space relationship dependent on the motion of the planets in the heavens. Like all circular diagrams, this representation of the zodiacal cycle can be interpreted as a kind of mandala.

The use of the zodiacal diagram is far too complex to go into here, but its general structure can be briefly explained. The *blank form* called a *natal map,* is marked with the positions of the planets at the moment of the birth of a child in order to determine their influence on its personality and life. The outer circle is divided into four equal *quadrants* or *quar-*

ters, two above the earth in the heavens, and two below, by a horizontal line (the horizon) and a vertical line (the upper part pointing to the mid-heaven or *medium coeli,* indicating south; the lower part to the nadir or *imum coeli,* indicating north). The right end of the horizontal line points to the western horizon, the left to the eastern horizon. The 12 divisions or spokes of the wheel, each 30° apart, are called *cusps,* and the spaces between them are *houses.* The first house is the one below the eastern horizon, and the others follow counterclockwise around the circle. The cusps above the horizon are the six houses over earth, and those below the horizon are the six houses under earth. At the left-hand horizontal cusp is the *ascendant* where the sun rises; at the right-hand horizontal cusp is the *descendant* where the sun sets. At the center is the observer. When a zodiacal figure of the heavens is erected for an individual, the spaces are marked within with the zodiacal symbolic signs of the seven planets in regard to their position in the cusps at the moment of birth, and within the houses of the two luminaries—the sun and moon—as seen from the place of birth at a particular moment in time. Interpreting the relationships of these symbols is what constitutes "reading" the natal map.

37 HEPTAGON: A *heptagon* is a polygon with *seven sides,* seven central angles, each 51.4°, and seven interior angles each 128.6° (half = 64.3°). The number *seven* or the *septenary* is called the first complete odd number. Because of its exceptional character—it incorporates the ternary and the quaternary, graphically represented by the superimposition of a triangle on a square, or a triangle within a square—it has always been held in special reverence. Symbolically it represents a symbol of conflict. Many concepts are connected with the idea of seven. Probably most important are those concerning the serial arrangement of the universe. There are seven directions in space (when the center is included), seven traditional planets (the sun, moon, and the five nearest planets), seven days of the week (six of work and one of rest—to symbolize a return to the center). In addition we have the ideas of the existence of seven virtues and seven deadly sins; seven degrees of perfection; and the basic series of Western musical notes. Because seven is an odd number, it is believed to be active.

38 OCTAGON: An *octagon* is a polygon with *eight sides,* eight center angles of 45° each, and eight interior angles, each 135° (half = 67.5°). By drawing four diameters to its eight points, it can be divided into eight triangles. Divided by interior vertical and horizontal lines connecting the eight vertices, a cross shape is produced that is widely used in folk art to symbolize the sun. A perpendicular line from the center to one if its sides is called an *apothem,* the same term also used when the same is done with any regular polygon. The octagon involves the *octonary* or the concept of eight. One of the most important characteristics of this figure is its relationship with the square.

39 TRUNCATED CUBE: *Truncation* is the process of cutting off a figure by an intersecting plane. By truncating the corners of a cube in identical degrees, making each side an octagon, the resulting 14-sided figure approaches a circular shape.

40 TRUNCATED CUBE: PLAN PATTERN: The pattern of a six-sided, *truncated cube* projected on one plane is represented here. After being cut out and bent along the lines, the form at the left can be constructed.

41 CIRCLE: A *circle* is a closed-plane curve with all of its points equidistant from an inner point, termed its *center.* The length of the line describing its closed plane is called the *circumference.* The *area* of a circle is found by multiplying the square of the radius by π (pi) which equals 3.14159265. Symbolically the circle has a great many meanings, possibly more than any other geometric figure. It represents the universe; the sun or source of life; a halo or aureole; enlightenment; wholeness; self and the psyche. Divided into halves vertically, the right half is termed the arc of descent, and the left half the arc of ascent, the arrows indicating a clockwise direction of rotation. In this concept, the microcosm is at the top, and the macrocosm at the bottom. A *double circle* represents a loop or ring.

42 CONCENTRIC CIRCLES: A series of *concentric circles,* each drawn from the same central point, together imply two concepts: one of outward movement, as when rings form on a still water surface when a stone is thrown into it; and the other the idea of rotation around a fixed point. Symbolically, concentric circles represent the movement of the planets in the universe around the central point of the sun. Mechanically, the figure expresses the movement of a swivel, hinge, and the wheel.

43 QUADRANT: A *quadrant* is an arc of 90° forming a right angle at the center of the circle. The area within its sides, actually two radii, constitutes the quarter part of a circle.

44 FUNCTIONS OF A CIRCLE: AB = diameter; C = center; CD = radius; GH = secant; EF = chord; EPF = an arc on chord EF; IPJ = a tangent at point P.

45 SPACE LIMIT AND FOCAL POINT: The circumference of a circle symbolizes the concept of the *limit* of a shape in space, which embodies the ideas of *definition,* and an *integrated whole.* The *center point* symbolizes the concept of a *focal point* within a shape, sometimes a generating point as in this case. It also symbolizes the ideas of origin, unity, and the self, and identity with the Supreme Principle of the universe. The idea of center also includes the concepts of a passage from the outside to the inside; a movement toward the center or contemplation; from space to spacelessness; and time to timelessness.

46 SPHERE: The *sphere* is the corresponding solid of a circle. Symbolically it is a form that embodies the idea of *perfection.* It is associated with the planets, the sun, and the moon, and has many other symbolic associations.

47 CONVEX: The *hemisphere* (half sphere) or *dome* encompasses the concept of *convexity.* Symbolically convexity implies the idea of swelling, raising, or *relief.* Variations on the convex dome are the *pointed dome,* and the so-called *onion dome* which is pointed at the top and contracts at the base.

48 CONCAVE: By reversing the convex, its opposite, the *concave* is created. In the idea of concavity are included the concepts of hollowness, sinking, and *intaglio.* Concavity also implies the idea of a container.

49 DOUBLE CONVEX: The *double convex* or almond-shaped figure on *one plane* is called a *mandorla,* and is formed by the intersection of two circles. Symbolically, when used in the vertical position, it represents the conjunction of earth and heaven. In a solid or hollow three-dimensional form, the double convex can be two matching, superimposed convex forms, base to base, or a lens of this shape.

50 CONVEX-CONCAVE CONCEPTS: Variations on combinations of the concepts of concavity and convexity are several. In the upper figure is a single concave appearing as a part of a hollow or solid object. The center figure is a hollow or solid object that is doubly concave on opposite sides. The lower figure is a hollow or solid convex-concave form with opposite sides in the same direction.

51 RELATIONSHIPS: SCALE: The concept of *relationships* implies a correspondence or comparison between two bodies, involving size, sequence, series, linkage, and other considerations. *Scale,* another relationship concept, refers to a *relative comparison* of the dimensions of two similar objects related by juxtaposition. Such a comparison involves proportion, size, extent, or degree.

52 REST AND SUPPORT: In the upper figure, the relationship is one created by *gravitational force.* One object makes *contact* or physically touches and *rests* on the other which in turn *supports* the first. In the lower figure, the relationship concept of *equilibrium* or physical balance is represented. A heavier weight and a lighter weight are kept in physical balance on the same level by shifting the *fulcrum* or center of support toward the heavier object to a position where the force of gravity on both objects is equalized.

53 CONNECTION: In the relationship illustrated here as one possibility, a smaller form is physically joined to a larger form by means of a third or transitional form that while maintaining their separateness, also unites them. The concepts active in their relationship can be described as *introduction, transition,* and *culmination.*

54 CONJUNCTION OF OPPOSITES: This idea, represented by a diagram, involves a relationship of *duality.* Two bodies, after an initial point of contact, are impelled by a mutually attracting force or energy emanating from without that urges them toward unity at a hidden center. The *heart shape* takes its configuration from the limit shape of this figure which symbolizes the *conjunction* of opposites or unification, and the elimination of separation or dualism. The two elements, the lover and the beloved, are reconciled. Symbolically the heart configuration connotes the merging of the brain (thought) and the sexual urge, and represents a potential eternal center of happiness, peace, rest, and satisfaction.

55 OVERLAPPING: *Overlapping* is a form of relationship in which one shape or form is partially or totally superimposed on another or others. As an example, three circles of the same size are used here. When these overlap each other by the same amounts, they form a limit figure called the *trefoil* which symbolically represents the Trinity, and knowledge of the divine essence. When four circles are similarly, uniformly overlapped, the resulting limit figure is a *quatrefoil* or four-lobed clover leaf, which in some parts of the world signifies good luck.

56 MAGNITUDE: *Magnitude* is a relationship involving a *physical comparison of sizes* between two or more units, and the possibility of their being larger or smaller. Variations of this concept can be illustrated by the representation of the serial relationship existing in a string of beads. In the first, all forms have the same magnitude—they are of equal size. In the next, a regular *increase* in size occurs, and in the third, a gradual *increase and decrease.* The result is a rhythmic unity.

57 SURROUNDING: In a *surrounding* relationship, one shape or form is encompassed by another shape or form. Symbolically, the concept is one of *holding* in a passive manner. The central *hole* illustrates the concept of *negative space* which is surrounded and in a sense passively held by a solid or positive shape.

58 GRASPING: *Grasping* is a relationship that involves surrounding, but by implication, the force of *pressure* exists. This concept is used in stone setting.

59 DIVISION AND MULTIPLICATION: In *division,* an object is either physically severed into two or more separate units, or visually separated into parts by the use of a line or other form of demarcation to distinguish one unit from another. The concept stresses the resulting units, and their separation implies placing or keeping them physically or visually independent. Inherent in the concept of division is the act of *multiplication,* which can also take place by the process of *addition.* A violent form of division is *dismemberment,* in which an object is divided into parts with violence.

60 CONTRAST: DUALISM: *Contrast* as a concept implies a *dualistic relationship,* in principle based on a distinction between the two opposites, each element being irreducible, an extreme of its type, and incapable of synthesis. The existence of opposites implies the presence of a tension between them. This dualistic concept appears often in designs used by all cultures, in all ages, and includes contrast of color, shape, form, texture, etc.

The Chinese *yin-yang* symbol depicts the concept of dualism or the *duad*—the union of two—by the *yin-yang disc* which perfectly exemplifies the negative-positive dualistic state in all things. The figure employs the idea of correspondence in a pattern of opposites. In this integrated antithesis, *yang* represents the universal, active, positive, male principle (also heaven, light, penetration, and the odd numbers), and *yin* the passive, negative, female principle (also earth, darkness, absorption,

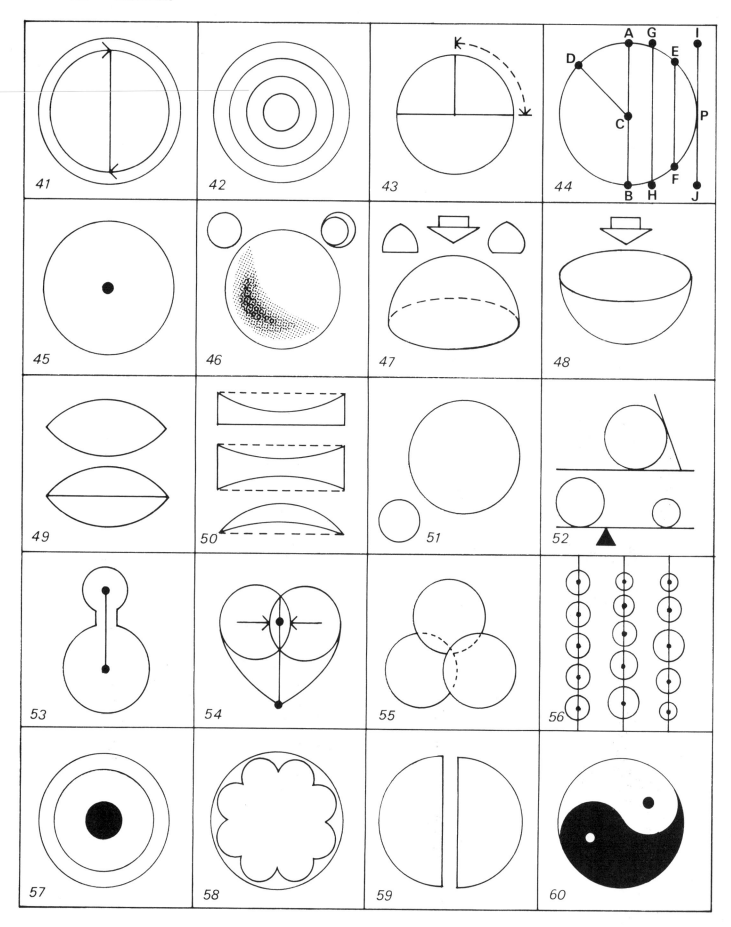

and even numbers). These ideas are graphically depicted by the use of a circle which is divided into two equal sections by a sigmoid curve created by cutting an arc from the opposite side, thus making the resulting figure far more dynamic than if it were simply a diameter bisection. The curve by its implication of movement or rotation also expresses intercommunication between the opposites. The dark half represents the yin; and the light half represents the yang. The white dot within the yin and the black dot within the yang indicate that no essence is ever totally one, and some of each is always present within the other. Although the circle that contains them is a symbol of stability, its use in no way causes the opposing elements to neutralize each other, but instead infinitely prolongs the condition of duality.

In Chinese symbolism, the circle is the symbol of the *T'ai Chi* or the "grand origin" which is the source of existence. The idea of the yin-yang evolved through a process of differentiation that took place within the *T'ai I* or cosmic matter before it congealed into concrete shapes. From this process came the *T'ai Chi* which is the primal monad or unit that reflects the universe, and which possesses a mingled potential of form, breadth, and substance whose revolutions constituted the yin-yang. In Tao, The Way, founded by Lao Tzu (the patron of blacksmiths), T'ai I is worshipped.

61 CYLINDER: The *cylinder* and the *cone* bear a relationship to each other by their common use of the circle. A *cylinder* is a surface or form achieved by rotating one side of a rectangle 360° around its other, parallel side which is the axis. The cylinder is the resulting volume so generated. Symbolically, an upright cylinder represents ascent and elevation, as in a tower, and the upward impulse in general, therefore the phallic implication of towers.

62 HALF CYLINDER: This is a vertical section of a cylinder through its center, making an arc of 180°. When horizontal, it becomes a *vault* which symbolizes the union of sky and earth, or a tunnel under earth.

63 RING: A *ring* or annular band can be described as a cross section of a cylinder, the idea of *sectioning* implying a cutting, slicing, or dismembering action. The ring, a closed circle, symbolizes wholeness and eternal continuity, which is the main reason that it is used as a marriage symbol. Shown here is the *perspective view* (right), the *elevation view* (top left), the *plan view* (left center), and the *development* of the form (bottom).

64 ELONGATED, AND CANTED CYLINDER: An *elongated cylinder* when longer than wide becomes a *tube*. Tubes also exist with oval, square, or other polygonal-shaped sections. The *canted cylinder* is one whose ends have been sectioned at an oblique angle to the longitudinal axis, making the end appear as an ellipse. When stood on one end, as shown, the tube axis leans or is canted to one side, the angle depending on the angle of severance.

65 TAPERED CYLINDER: In a *tapered cylinder,* the diameter of one end is larger than the diameter of the opposite end toward which the sides diminish. The form is used in a *funnel* whose function is to conduct liquids through a small opening in a container, the tapered cylinder acting to ease the transition. A *tapered and curved* cylindrical form occurs naturally in an *animal's horn,* a form that is widely used in the arts. Besides symbolizing power and strength, the horn is dualistic in that its outer form is penetrating, while the inner form can be a receptacle, as in a cornucopia or rhyton.

66 TRANSFORMATIONS OF CYLINDERS: By exerting pressure externally with tools on the sides of an existing, tapered, seamless cylinder or tube, it can be shaped into a concave curve, a form sometimes used in a spout. By exerting pressure *internally* on the form, its sides can be made to bulge outward into a convex curve, as in a barrel form.

67 HALF CYLINDER, TAPERED: Longitudinally bisecting a straight, tapered cylinder produces a straight, tapered half cylinder (center). Keeping the open side edge straight, and curving the lower part of the form produces a *spathe* form

(lower right) as found in some flowers. Reversing the form so it opens at the bottom, and curving the plane upward to a termination in a point results in a typical *claw* shape (top).

68 HALF CYLINDER, CURVED BASE: A half cylinder can be formed with its base making a rising or *anticlinal* curve (top), or with a falling or *synclinal plane* that inclines downward from opposite directions (bottom).

69 CURVED TUBE: Any tube shape, provided it is long enough, can be bent into a curve either manually or mechanically, with or without an internal supporting material, the curve depending on tube diameter dimensions, wall thickness, and degree of curvature.

70 FLARED TUBE: A *flared tube* is one whose end spreads in an outward curve—in the case of metal, accomplished by stretching—and resembles a trumpet.

71 TRACTRIX: A *tractrix* form appears as two tube shapes with matching diameter flared ends. The point at which the figure reaches its greatest swelling is called the *nodal space.* Here the ascending node meets the descending node forming a *tractrix curve* which is the involute of a *catenary curve* (see 81).

72 CONE: DEVELOPMENT PATTERN: A *right circular cone* is shown here along with the method of creating the development of its shape for the purpose of construction. To draw the development of a cone, first draw its *elevation* (lower solid-line figure). Draw the cone *plan* (left circle), and divide it into an equal number of parts. Using a compass, measure the distance from the vertex to the base point (the sloping line at the right), and with this as a radius, draw a curve with the vertex as the center. On this curve, step out or mark off the same division distances as on the plan. Draw a straight line from the vertex to the last marked division. The resulting fan shape is the *development* which when curved until the edges butt, will produce a cone that matches the elevation form, three dimensionally.

73 RIGHT CIRCULAR CONE: The *right circular cone* form is based on the association of a circle and a right triangle, and is generated by the rotation of such a triangle about its perpendicular leg used as an axis. The length of this vertical leg is termed the *altitude* of the cone, and the length of the slanting leg or hypotenuse of the right triangle is called the *slant height* of the cone. The point at the top is termed the *vertex,* the highest point on the perpendicular from the base of any figure having a base. The *apex* is a general term indicating the tip or point of a form which can occur in any direction, and this term is often loosely used interchangeably with vertex. *Vertex* can also mean a common point through which several lines pass. Variations of the cone shape include the *conoid,* which is any form made by the revolution of a *conic section* about its axis. Such forms are the *outward-swelling cone* (upper left) or bullet shape, and the *concave-surfaced cone* (upper right). Cone shapes occur as natural formations, as in a mountain peak, and in shells. The symbolic meanings of the cone are complex, in the main, derived from its association with the circle and the triangle.

74 DOUBLE CONE: THE COLOR SOLID: A *double cone* (two cones mounted base to base) is a three-dimensional figure utilized to illustrate facts about the relationships of colors. This figure is termed the *color solid.* In this system, at the vertex is white, and at the lower apex black. All colors become increasingly lighter *tints* as they approach white, and increasingly darker *shades* as they approach black. The diagram is divided by a vertical plane toward whose right are placed the *warm colors* (red, orange, yellow) and toward whose left are placed the *cool colors* (green, blue, purple). All colors are arranged in the horizontal circular plane according to their sequence in the spectrum. At the center is a median gray. The degree of brilliance of a color, called its *saturation,* decreases as it approaches the central neutral gray.

75 CONOIDS: Shown here are variations and combinations of cone sections or *conoids.*

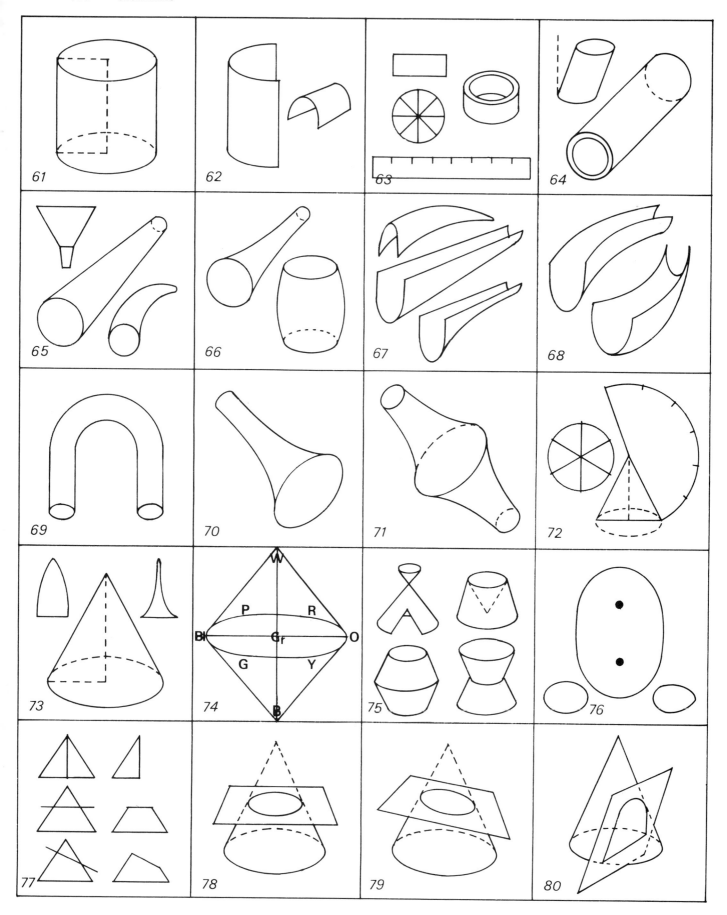

76 ELLIPSE: An *ellipse* is defined as a plane curve created by the path of a point the sum of whose distances from two fixed points, called *focii* (plural of "focus"), is constant. It can be created by taking an oblique slice on a cone, making it obliquely truncated (see 79). The solid of an ellipse is an *ellipsoid* which is a *compressed sphere* (lower left), and a variant is the *egg shape* (lower right). These shapes are said to be *homeomorphic* or equivalent to the original form as one can be changed into another by stretching or contracting.

77 CONE SECTIONS: To *section* a form or object is the physical act of cutting or separating a portion, or making a slice through it; or depicting on one plane how it appears when cut through that plane. *Longitudinal section* (top): a cut through the vertical center of an object. *Cross or transverse section* (not shown): a cut vertically through its width when the long axis is horizontal. *Horizontal section* (center): a cut horizontally through its width. *Oblique section* (bottom): a cut made at an angle through the perpendicular axis of a form.

78 FRUSTUM: HORIZONTAL CONE SECTION: A *frustum* is the part of a cone remaining next to the base after horizontally cutting off, or making a section through the upper portion, parallel to the base. Also, any *part* of a cone (or pyramid) intersected between *two planes,* either parallel with the base, or less frequently, at an angle to the base. This form is widely used in jewelry stone settings.

79 OBLIQUE CONE SECTION: An *oblique section* cut through a cone or a tube creates an *ellipse.* Symbolically, the ellipse is connected with the concept of cyclic phenomena.

80 PARABOLA: A *parabola* is created by the intersection of a right circular cone by a plane parallel to the angle of its side surface slant. Parabolic curves can be depicted in two or three dimensions.

81 CURVES: A *curve* is a line or plane that bends without angles. All curves are forms of energy. They can also be described as the undulating path of a moving point that does not move in a straight line, or the intersection of two surfaces similarly bent. Curves therefore exist in one plane, or in more than one. Because of the many curve types, only a few of the more regular ones can be shown and described here.

A *catenary curve* (upper, descending figure) is the shape assumed by a flexible but inextensible cord or chain whose ends are fixed at two level horizontal points, while the rest is allowed to fall freely. Because of gravitational force, the cord or chain makes a natural, *common catenary curve* proportionate to its length. An *arch* (lower rising figure) is any curve or structure that moves in an upward curve, then down to span a distance. Several kinds of architectural arches exist, each identified by the shape of its curve. These include the *round* arch, *horseshoe* arch, *flat* (a flattened curve), *pointed* (rising to a point), *ogee* (a pointed arch having a reverse curve near the apex), and *trefoil* arch (having three curved forms or lobes). Symbolically, the arch represents a vault, or the sky over earth.

82 OPEN AND CLOSED CURVES: A *loop* (top figure) is a curve that passes over on itself, therefore forming a *closed curve* when in one plane, but possibly open when it is three dimensional. Because it is a form used in making knots, symbolically it represents the idea of binding or snaring. *Periodic curves* (below) are *open curves* in which one basic curve is regularly repeated several times, creating an undifferentiated rhythmic pattern. One of the terms used to describe a curve is its degree of *slope* or its inclination from the horizontal or perpendicular, described as right or left, upward or downward, slight, moderate, or steep, slow or fast. In the first periodic curve shown, all slopes are equal, therefore the undulating motion is nondirectional, each part canceling out the other. In the second example, the upward, moderate slope is toward the right, creating a rightward movement, as in the motion of waves in water.

83 REVERSE CURVES: SIGMOID: *Reverse curves* turn back on their initial direction, and the classic example is the curves in the letter S whose upper part is hollow, termed

cyma recta, and whose lower part seen from the same side swells or projects, termed *cyma reversa* (from the Greek *kyma* or *cyma* = swollen). A *sigmoid curve* (from Greek = sigma, the 18th Greek letter, S), is a regular curve that flexes in reverse directions. It is an example of *rotational symmetry,* the axis projecting perpendicularly from the center of the curve. Two sigmoid curves placed horizontally, one above the other in reverse, form one figure, like an "8" on its side. This shape is the common symbol for *infinity* because its curves are in endless, constant motion.

84 RANDOM CURVES: *Random curves* are made freely or by chance, and do not follow any regular curve. They can be *open* or *closed curves,* the latter forming *closed free-form shapes,* and can have *slow* or *fast slopes,* on one plane, or in three dimensions. When in one plane, the existence of space is still implied at points of overlapping. *Arabesques,* in the usual meaning of this term, are any intricate pattern of curviform, flowing lines, but can also be geometric and angular in character.

85 SPIRAL CURVES: A *two-dimensional* or *flat spiral curve* is the path of a point or a plane that moves around an axis while continuously approaching, or receding from it. When on one plane, we have the kind of spiral in which the spaces between the curves diminish as the line approaches the center. The spiral in which the space between the curves remains constant is called the *spiral of Archimedes.* A spiral formed in a cone shape is also possible, as in some sea shells, or as a helix (see 86). A *lituus* (below) is a spiral that starts with a plane almost parallel to a polar line, then curves inward until it meets the line. Spirals are among the basic, universal ornamental motifs in the world of art. All spirals symbolically denote pure energy, which is physically true of a spiral spring, and also evolutive power or growth, since many plants grow spirally to provide maximum light access to all parts. Spirals are also physical forms in motion, as exemplified by whirlpools, whirlwinds, and nebulae. The pattern also symbolizes the relationship between the circle and the mystic center.

86 HELIX: A *helix* in general is a three-dimensional form of spiral that moves around a cylindrical or cone-shaped volume. A *solenoid helix* (above) is a tubular coil that moves in *uniform diameters* around a single straight or curved axis. A *cochleiform helix* (below) is one that moves in a tapering direction, as around a cone-shaped volume, a type found in the thread of a wood screw, and in some tapering shells.

87 SCROLL: LINE INTO FORM: A *scroll* in essence is a kind of spiral or convoluted form, typified by the curves found in a parchment scroll. Several variations of this concept are possible in linear form, such as the *single scroll* (top), the involuted or *double scroll* (center) which symbolically is related to a bull's horns, and a sigma-shaped or *reverse scroll* (bottom).

88 DIMENSIONAL SCROLLS: Any scroll form in line can be realized as a plane in three dimensions.

89 DEVELOPMENT FROM LINE TO PLANE: Any open, undulating curved line can be formed into a plane in space by simple extension.

90 DEVELOPMENT FROM PLANE TO SOLID: In this example, to create a solid, the curve is reversed and a matching plane created. Two additional planes perpendicular to both ends close the form and make it a solid. In the fabrication process, these forms would be of sheet metal, joined by soldering, leaving a small hole somewhere for the escape of gases.

91 SERIAL REPETITION: In this case (top line), equidistant, matching curved lines whose meeting places form repeating peaks, create a line symbolic of waves. By extending the line into a plane (center), the result is a series of parallel ribbed or fluted forms, the flutes concave on one side and convex on the other, each separated from the others by an *arris* or ridge. When the arrises converge (bottom), the result is tapering flutes. An arris is also formed by the meeting of any two surfaces, planar or curved, wherever a ridged, sharp edge, or raised angle occurs in the form or in a join.

92 CORRUGATIONS: STEPS: *Corrugation* is the forming of any plane into folds or alternating ridges and grooves by folding or bending the plane. The bends can be angular or curved, and follow each other in straight or curved parallel series. In metalwork, rolling mills with matched positive and negative rolls are used to create corrugated sheet. In Japan, hand machines of this type are available to make small-scale sheets, as when preparing copper sheets for temple roofing. In principle, the corrugated form is applied to the abstract concept of *steps*, or any steplike arrangement of forms. When the steps are horizontal, the concepts of ascent and descent, and communication between levels are in operation. The form can also be used in any other position. The *zigzag* line, or *chevrons* in series follow this same concept, and these basic decorative figures are used in all art forms.

93 REPETITION: LINEAR NETWORK: Equally spaced vertical and horizontal superimposed lines create a figural concept that has several applications. First, because these lines are *open ended* and extensible in any direction, the potential of their repetition and therefore the dimension of the pattern is limitless. In this figure, the *opposition* of two elements is illustrated, as in weaving during which one set of threads (the warp) is passive, and the other set (the weft) is active, passing alternately over and under the warp. The symbolism of the resulting pattern or structure is a resolution of opposing forces into stability and rationality. The *net* is another object employing the principle of the repetition of opposites. Physically and symbolically, a net expresses the idea of the power of trapping, binding, or encompassing, and also transparency. When the *spaces* of a pattern structured in this arrangement are thought of as being *solid* shapes or forms, the result is a series of abutting objects, as in a mosaic. By alternating the colors of each squa.e, as in a checkerboard, the figure adopts a positive-negative or dualistic relationship.

94 REPETITION: SHAPE AND FORM: *Shapes* (above) and *forms* (below) can create a regular rhythmic pattern by their repetition. Placement can be greatly varied: side by side; half drop; alternating reverse; all-over or diaper; running linear; and alternation, etc. (See Lap Joints, p. 396.) Further variation is introduced by an increase and decrease in size.

95 CONVERGENCE: In *convergence*, lines or forms are oriented toward one point, either within the field of vision, or beyond it. By implication, they incline or move closer toward each other, and in so doing, gradually decrease in size. The concept is used to create an illusion of distance, as in *perspective*. Theoretically, when converging lines meet in one plane and are continued *beyond* the meeting point, a *reverse pattern* develops. As shown in the illustration, the ends of lines in such a repeated pattern can be straight or form curves.

96 RADIATION: *Radiation* is the diffusion of lines or forms away from a visible or imaginary center within the field of vision. The concept ordinarily implies the action of a force or energy from the center outward. Symbolically, typical radiation figures include the sun which by its radiation of light is the source of all earthly energy; an aureole or halo which is a relic of solar cults; the spokes of a wheel such as the Buddhist Wheel of Life meant to bring to mind the nature of existence and cause and effect; or in representations such as the *six chakras* of Kundalini yoga. Radiation is used in the directional device of the *compass card* attached to the face of a mariner's compass. On it are marked the 32 points or *rhumbs*, and the graduated 360° of the circle. From the central point radiate lines that give the main directions: North, East, South, and West, and the intermediary directions NNE, ENE, ESE, SSE, SSW, WSW, WNW, and NNW. The concept of radiation need not be rigidly conceived, as exemplified by the irregularly radiating or *actiniform* tentacles of a sea anemone. Radiation can proceed three dimensionally as from the central point of a sphere, or in an explosion.

97 BILATERAL SYMMETRY OF SHAPE: *Basic symmetry* is described as the angle that any line (or image) that falls on a reflecting surface makes with a perpendicular to that surface at the point of incidence, the angle of incidence being equal to the angle of reflection. Numerous types of two- and three-dimensional symmetry exist, and only the simplest two-dimensional types are mentioned here. *Bilateral symmetry*, shown here, is most evident in the human body which is divisible in halves by a vertical axis line or plane; in reflections in water in which the axis is horizontal; and in a mirror image in which the plane of the glass is the axis. Symmetry implies the equipoise of opposite images in a physical, static balance. A *mirror*, because it formally reflects reality in the world of vision, symbolizes passivity.

98 DOUBLE SYMMETRY: In *double symmetry* the image itself is already symmetrical, therefore there is one horizontal plane of reflection, and one axis of twofold symmetry.

99 TETRAGONAL SYMMETRY: In *tetragonal symmetry* there is a horizontal and a vertical plane of reflection, and two axes of twofold symmetry. The resulting regular figure created on one plane is divisible by a horizontal and a vertical axis into four identical parts. When a square figure such as this contains an arrangement of five identical units, one at each corner and one in the center, the arrangement is called a *quincunx*.

100 ASYMMETRY: In *asymmetry*, there is a total lack of any formal symmetry in the sense of the possibility of dividing the figure with a line-axis into two parts. Instead, balance is achieved *visually*. Because such a balance involves unequal shapes or forms, their relationship is dynamic.

101 BASIC FORMS OF METAL: The *basic forms of metal* are sheet, wire, tube, and solid mass (not shown).

102 FREE SHAPE: ORGANIC FORM: The general term *free shape* is used to describe any shape that cannot be explained in geometric terms. A one-plane figure of this type made with a continuously curving line is commonly called *amoeboid* after the protozoan that is the simplest of known animals and which constantly changes its shape, taking any form of which curves are capable. Such shapes are therefore amorphous and irregular. Three-dimensional objects in this category could be termed *organic forms*.

103 SOLID: DENSITY: A *solid*, representing *density*, is any three-dimensional form whose interior has no cavities, being filled with matter, typically as when an object is cast solid when it has density. The term is also applied to an object that *appears* to be solid, therefore "solid-looking," though in fact it may contain an invisible void. A test of solidity is the *weight* of an object of a known material in reference to its *specific gravity*.

104 HOLLOW: SPACE: *Space*, in which all is possible, is chaotic until it is given shape or form. A *hollow form* is one whose interior is an empty cavity, usually containing air. The form of that space is related to the form of the surrounding objects. The space is inert and inactive when invisible, but when visible, becomes an active part of the total design of an object. The form-space relationship depends in part on the manner of fabrication of the object. Various methods of fabrication create their particular kinds of space. For example, in sheet metal fabrication, a form can be made by using a single piece of metal which is stretched and deformed until it attains a desired volume or state of hollowness. Other kinds of hollow space are made by a combination of two, three, or more separately made parts which are then assembled. Psychologically, the concept of the hollow represents the unconscious. Symbolically, a contained space implies the world of manifestation and reality.

105 ONE-ELEMENT RELATIONSHIPS: BIFURCATION: *Bifurcation* is the division of any single body into *two* branches while still maintaining a partial unity in the object. Philosophically, in the *bifurcation theory*, reality is divided into two distinctly separated compartments—the external world of reality, and the internal world of the mind.

106 BRANCHING: A *branch* is any subdivision, outgrowth, or offshoot from a main body, possible in any number, the

branch being either comparable in size with the main body, or smaller. By implication, there is a motion emanating away from the main body. *Dendritic* forms are finely branching units that resemble shrubs more than trees, and such forms are found in nature in the mineral and physiological world. Symbolically, a branch represents the concepts of relationship and subdivision.

107 KNOT: A *knot* consists of the self-bending of the two ends of a flexible body on itself to form loops in many planes, through which the ends pass in various configurations. When the ends are pulled tightly, a thickening or swelling lump or knob occurs at that point. Knots are also used to combine more than two ends by similar means. Many different knotting systems exist, each with its own name. The knot illustrated here is the simplest—the overhand knot. Symbolically, a knot represents binding, fettering, or a tightly closed linkage.

108 TWO-ELEMENT RELATIONSHIPS: DIVERGENCE-CONVERGENCE: *Divergence* is the gradual receding of one body from another, in a straight or curving direction, the distance increasing indefinitely. *Convergence,* the opposite, is the approach of one body toward another until they merge. Symbolically a repellence, or an attraction between the bodies is implied.

109 LINKAGE: *Linkage* is a system of uniting, binding, connecting, or looping two or more units or elements, causing them to manifest a rigid or flexible relationship. The simplest example of flexible linkage is found in the links of a chain. Linkage can be *planar* or *solid,* depending on whether the movement is a linkage on one plane, or in space; and *complete* as when the motion is defined, as in a sliding motion. Linkages are termed primary, secondary, infinite, etc., according to the number of degrees of freedom the system has, assuming these can be counted. Symbolically, linkage contains the concepts of integration, continuity, and unity in action.

110 TWISTING AND WRAPPING: *Twisting* or twining is the act of combining or uniting two or more *active* flexible elements that do not resist this action, but adapt themselves to it. The bending and turning torsion motion proceeds in a spiral direction, one part relative to another around an imaginary common axis. In the result, the elements are rigidly or flexibly bound together into a single unit. *Wrapping* resembles twisting, but in this case, one element remains physically unchanged while the other is twisted around it, the first acting as the axis of the wrapping action, and supporting the wrapping element without entering the twisting motion. *Self-twisting* (not shown) is the twisting of a form about or upon itself, the form being one capable of showing such twisting.

111 INTERLOCKING: *Interlocked* forms are connected, engaged, or united either in a way that creates a form association, as shown, in which the motion of one part is constrained by the position or presence of the other, preventing the parts from moving or working independently; or in ways that permit a degree of movement. Two or more forms can be so interlocked, the total creating a structure, simple or complex. Some interlocking systems involve the concept of *inversion* or a reversed arrangement where one form accommodates another, as shown here. Symbolically, inversion denotes the turning of an idea to its opposite, or a confrontation of opposites at a focal point or axial plane.

112 CONTAINING AND PIERCING: When one element penetrates another but does not pass through it, the first is said to be *contained* within the second, or held enclosed within those fixed limits. The concept can be applied to three-dimensional objects as in the sleeve and tube shank shown, or to two-dimensional relationships as in the inlay of one substance within another, both appearing in a two-dimensional plane. Should the first object *pass through* the second, the latter is *pierced* or *penetrated.* The piercing object can remain in place, or be removed, leaving a pierced opening caused by its penetration, as in pierced work done with chisels.

113 TRANSFORMATIONS   AND   DEFORMATIONS: BENDING: When an operation involves twisting, stretching, contracting, or cutting, a distortion or *deformation* of the original plane or form occurs. In simple *bending,* there is no distortion of the planes, but instead the object is transformed without distortion by a change in direction from its original state to another.

114 SELF-TWIST: DEFORMATION BY TORQUE: The *self-twist* is an example of deformation by *torque* in which stretch distortion occurs due to the application of torsional stress on the object. In such a case, the object is moved out of a single plane into a curving plane or planes which are permanent. Whatever the sectional shape of the object, the torsional stress force can be controlled and causes a movement of the object in a spiral course around its core. This can take place in *one* direction, or in *alternating* directions.

115 TAPERING: FLATTENING AND DRAWING OUT: *Tapering* as it occurs in forging, is a deformation process in which a gradual decrease in the dimensions of an object occurs in width, or thickness, or both. The decrease normally proceeds regularly to a wedge, pyramidal, pointed, or other attenuated shape. In *flattening,* the alternating faces of the object are worked to draw them out and taper them to a thin edge. This action usually is accompanied by a degree of lateral stretching unless this is prevented by working the sides of the taper as well as its faces. In the act of tapering toward a *conical section* or *point,* a rod or wire of any section is *drawn out* and slowly *rounded* by rotating the form as it receives hammer blows. Deformation and stretching occur in both cases, longitudinally and laterally, or only longitudinally.

116 TRANSITIONAL DEFORMATION BY COMPRESSION: Deformation can alter a form either by a sudden or gradual transition. When the cross section of the parts before and after deformation are different, or when a change in direction occurs, the transition may create an *easement curve* between the two forms or its directional change. In transitional changes, the result appears different from the original. For example, in the illustration, a square-sectioned rod is being transformed by transition into a cylindrical one. In forging, this is done by first applying lateral hammer blows to suppress the edges of the square form on opposing sides, causing them to merge in an easement curve into the cylindrical form. By this compressive force, the diameter of the cylinder is at the same time decreased and the form is *stretched* in length.

117 CONTRACTION: OPPOSITION, UPSETTING: *Contraction* is an oppositional deformation force applied against the inertia of the longitudinal direction of a metal rod, ultimately causing it to contract or decrease in length. (The process is called *upsetting* in forging.) In the result, the point of immediate contact with the force, or the place of greatest softness spreads laterally and becomes permanently deformed in a direction away from that of the applied force. An example is the formation of a rivet head. By applying the same force to opposite ends of the same object, as shown, a lateral deformation occurs at both ends.

118 THE DEVELOPED SURFACE: DIRECTIONAL WARPAGE: The deformation of a *flat metal surface* can occur in a variety of ways. When a deformation phenomenon results from one action, as above, it can be easily described, but when a combination of actions produces compound effects on the same object, describing it is more difficult. For example, in the illustration, two opposing forces have worked the originally square, flat plane to cause it to warp by stretching in two opposite directions at its maximum curvature, creating a convex-concave form. To properly describe such a form would require the terminology of *topology,* a branch of mathematics related to geometry that deals with the properties of a form independent of magnitudes and measurable qualities such as angles, distances, and areas. It is concerned instead with the position and relative position of elements without reference to size, using concepts that are basic in our comprehension of the physical world. Topological space first involves the concept of *limit,* within which *positional* descriptions then use the terms *borders, paths,* and *crossings;* a point represents an actual point

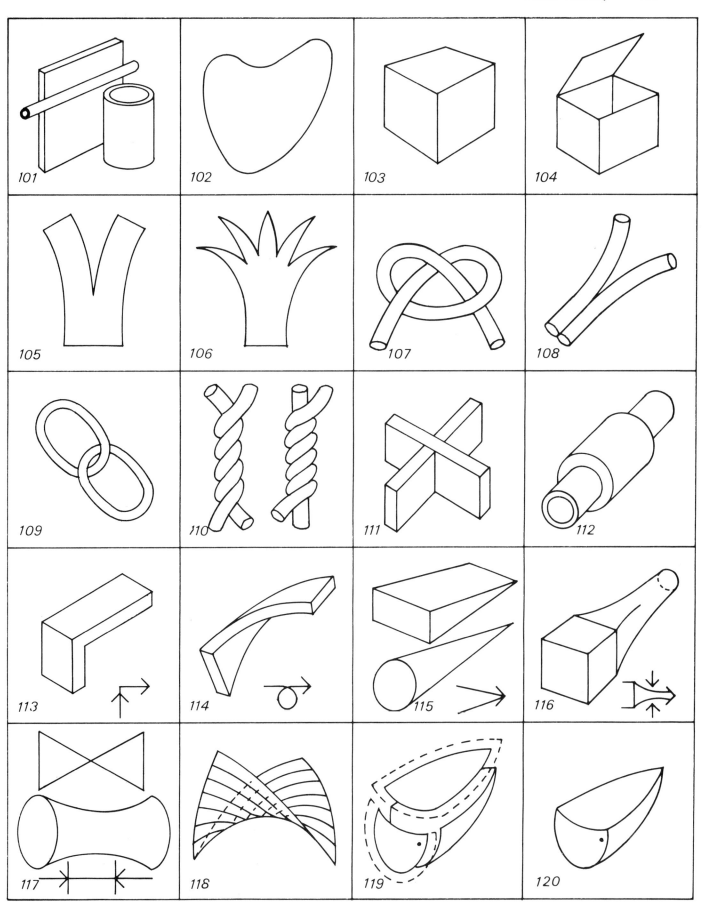

or a whole figure; and the ideas of connectedness, curvature, and slope are used to describe forms. The effect of directional warpage can be created as an *illusion* on one plane by graphic means.

119 FABRICATING A MULTICOMPONENT HOLLOW FORM: Hollow forms can be fabricated from two or more components, each shaped separately to conform with the edges or limits of the other. To facilitate joining, parts upon which others butt can have surplus material projecting beyond the join line. These parts are then bound together, and solder joined, leaving a small hole somewhere for the escape of expanding gases during soldering. This boat-shaped form is made of three components. Other forms might require two or more components, depending on their structure.

120 ASSEMBLING A MULTICOMPONENT HOLLOW FORM: After all components are solder joined, the surplus of each component is trimmed off, and the seams filed smooth. The form is then polished. Any nongeometric form that can be made of sheet metal shaped without or with deformation processes can be fabricated in this way.

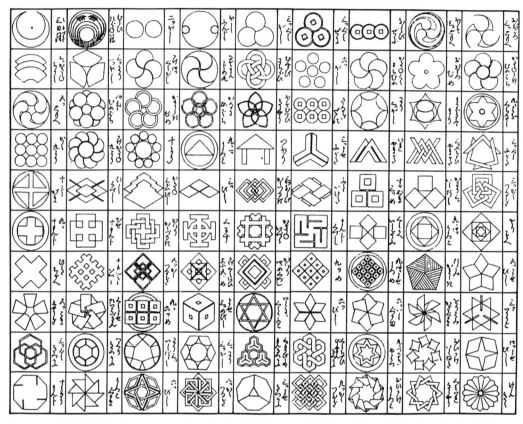

19-1A   Japan. *Mons* (family crests). These designs, taken from an old Japanese book, were embroidered on kimonos, especially by families of the ancient feudal nobility. Commonly they consisted of conventionalized natural forms, but symbolic geometric figures were also used, and some of these are shown here, arranged by shape and arithmetic progression. Many utilize concepts discussed above.

19–1   *Opposite Page:* Japanese jewelers' works that embody concepts discussed above. Reading from *left to right:*
1 AKINOBU KUMAGAYA. Brooch, silver, gold plated.
2 NORIKO HATANAKA. Brooch, silver, 24K gold.
3 TOSHIYA MASUOKA. Brooch, silver, 18K gold, copper.
4 MICHIKO HIDEHI. Brooch, silver.
5 AIKO NOMOTO. Brooch, silver.
6 SETSUKO KIMURA. Brooch, silver, mercury amalgam, gold finish (kinkesh 1).
7 FUMIAKI NISHIYAMA. Brooch, silver.
8 KYOKO KOJIMA. Brooch, silver.
9 KAZUYO MATSUMOTO. Brooch, silver.
10 REIKO KAGOTEDA. Brooch, silver, gold plated.
11 TEREZU INAGAKI. Brooch, silver, 18K gold, ebony, ivory.
12 OKINARI KUROKAWA. Brooch, 18K gold, stainless steel.
13 KEIKO MATSUSHITA. Brooch, silver.
14 MASARU NEO. Brooch, 18K gold.
15 JUNKO MURAKAWA. Brooch, silver.
16 JUNYOL JUNG. Brooch, silver, mirror.
17 MITSUKO YAMAGUCHI. Brooch, silver, plastic, mirror.
18 FUMIKO FUJIMOTO. Brooch, silver, 18K gold.
19 KAZUKO MITSUSHIMA. Ring, silver, glass.
20 IKUKO MATSUZAWA. Brooch, silver, copper, iron pyrites.
21 YOSHIKO NAKAMURA. Brooch, silver, gold plated.
22 MACHIO HIROUCHI. Brooch, silver, copper.
23 NAMIO TSUTSUMI. Brooch, copper, shakudo.
24 AYAKO TSUBO. Brooch, silver.
25 NORIKO AOYAGI. Brooch, silver, rhodium plated, gold plated, zircon, plastic.
26 MIYUKI IMOTO. Brooch, silver, rhodium plated.
27 JUNKO MAKITA. Brooch, copper, silver.
28 MASAFUMI SEKINE. Brooch, silver.
29 SHINO INOUE. Brooch, silver, rhodium plated, watermelon tourmaline.
30 CHIHARU KINOSHITA. Brooch, silver, gold plated.
31 HARUKO SUGAWARA. Brooch, silver, plastic.
32 KYOKO IKEDA. Brooch, silver.
33 TOSHIO NISHIKAWA. Brooch, silver, enamel.
34 YOKO SATO. Brooch, silver.
35 HIROKO MIYACHI. Bracelet, silver, rhodium plated.
Photos: Yasushi Sugimata, courtesy Japan Jewelry Designer's Association, Tokyo.

GLOSSARY: FORMS OF JEWELRY

M = worn by men
w = worn by women

AEGIS: (M, w) A breast ornament worn for protection or defense.

AGLET: (M, w) A small, broochlike ornament sewn to clothing.

AIGRETTE: (M, w) A head ornament worn on a turban, hat, or in the hair to hold aigrette bird feathers, or made entirely of metal and jewels often shaped in the form of feathers.

AIGUILLETTE: (w) A shoulder knot, often jeweled.

ALBERT: (M) A gold watch chain holding a watch at one end, and having a safety bar at the other.

AMULET: (M, w) An object attributed with magical value worn on a person.

AMULET HOLDER: (M, w) A container for an amulet. It can be worn around the neck, upper arm, wrist, waist, ankle, or other body part.

ANKLET: (w) A chain or other ornament worn around the ankle. Sometimes termed a *slave bracelet*.

ANKLET WITH ATTACHED TOE RINGS: (w) A composite ornament consisting of toe rings attached by chains or loops to an ankle bracelet.

ARCHER'S RING: (M) A ring worn on the thumb to aid in drawing the bow string, and to protect the thumb against its backlash.

ARCHER'S WRIST GUARD: (M) A wristband, often highly ornamented, worn to provide strength. Called a *ketoh* by American Indians.

BADGE: (M, w) A distinctive mark, token, or sign worn as an indication of social position or office.

BADGE AND CHAIN: (M, w) A long necklace worn by persons of high social or political rank, consisting of a central pendant usually ornamented with a symbol of office, held by a long, decorative chain.

BALUSTER: (w) A dress pin, straight and single, or earrings having vaselike or curved decoration done by turning, in forms reminiscent of stair rails.

BANDEAU: (M, w) A narrow band or fillet worn around the hair, across the brow.

BANDOLIER: (M, w) A broad belt that passes over one shoulder, across the chest, and under one arm. Formerly it was a means of suspending articles at the side, such as a wallet, but was adopted by soldiers, originally to support a musket, later to carry cases of powder charges, and now, cartridges.

BANGLE: (M, w) A seamless, usually rigid bracelet.

BARRETTE: (M, w) A device to hold the hair in place, worn at the sides or the back of the head, and held to the hair by a clip or other manner.

BARM: (M, w) A shoulder brooch or decorative ornament worn on festive dress in Europe, especially during the 12th century.

BEARD: (M, w) An articulated ornament worn around the chin or across the lower part of the face in some cultures.

BELT: (M, w) Anything encircling or engirdling the waist, used as pure ornament; to support dress, ornaments, weapons; to serve as a bandage for warmth or protection; or to indicate office or social position. Made rigid as a single unit, from a series of joined parts, or a combination of these. When wide enough, a belt becomes a *corset* or *corselet*. The belt is a symbol of the protection of the body, and also a symbol of virginity.

BELT FURNITURE: (M, w) The parts of a belt that are used to help its functioning. They can be simple or highly ornamented.

Belt buckle: A catch device for fastening the two loose ends of a belt or strap used on a belt or on any other object employing straps. It is attached to one end and usually has the form of a linklike frame having a movable tongue that goes through a hole in the other end of the belt. There are many variations and systems of buckle closings. The buckle symbolically represents protection and self-defense.

Belt hook: A system of closing a belt by means of a hook.

Belt clasp: A device for closing and holding a belt.

Belt catch: Any other holding system for a belt.

Belt guard: A loop through which a belt end passes to keep it from flapping.

Belt mordant: A metal plate or *chape* at the tip end of a belt opposite the buckle, sometimes ornamented and jeweled.

Belt tongue: An ornamental end of the part of the belt opposite from the buckle, meant to prevent its wearing out.

BETROTHAL RING: (M, w) A ring by which a person becomes affianced, given to indicate a pledge or engagement to marry.

BIB CLASP: (w) A series of hooks with ornament, used to close a bodice.

BIRTHSTONE RING: (M, w) A ring holding a birthstone.

BLAZON: (M, w) A heraldic shield or coat of arms repre-

19–2 PLOEM and C. COLSOEL, Amsterdam, ca. 1830. Parure of gold filigree including a necklace with pendant, earrings, brooch, cuff links, two hatpins, and a pair of matching bracelets, all in their original fitted box. *Photo: Rijksmuseum, Amsterdam*

19–3 MIRJAM SALMINEN, Finland, designer; manufacturer Kaunis Koru Oy, Helsinki. Contemporary parure, consisting of a necklace, bracelet, and ring in 18K gold, with diamonds set in tube settings. *Photo: Hannu Ritvanen, courtesy Kaunis Koru Oy*

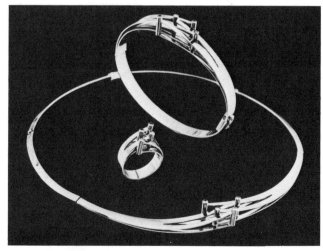

senting armorial bearings, often used to embellish ornaments, or as a brooch, badge, pendant, etc.

BODY ORNAMENT: (w) Usually a large ornament that does not fit conveniently into any one category, but may belong to a combination of several.

BODY STAMP: (M, W) A metal stamp bearing a symbolic device, usually religious, pressed into a paste and then stamped on exposed parts of the body as a sign of devotion. Used in India.

BOLO: (M) A man's neck ornament, usually strung on leather thongs, meant to take the place of a conventional tie. Invented in the Southwest United States by American Indian jewelers and extensively used there. Takes its name from the *bolo,* a leather-thong-weighted instrument used by South American cowboys in cattle control.

BRACELET: (M, W) A rigid or flexible ornament worn around the wrist or arm. It can be divided into several basic types:
Hook and eye: Flexible, made with a closing and opening device.
Penannular: A ring or almost ringed, rigid ornament.
Spiral: Formed in the shape of a spiral.

BRACELET WITH ATTACHED FINGER RINGS: (w) In some cultures, as in India, this is conceived of as a single compound ornament.

BRACER: (M, W) An ornament worn on the wrist serving to bind and strengthen it.

BRAID ORNAMENT: (w) Any ornament worn attached to a braid of hair, or suspended from it.

BRASSIÈRE: (w) Sometimes, an ornament worn over the breasts of a woman, aiding in their support.

BREAST ORNAMENT: (M, W) An ornament displayed on the breast.

BREASTPLATE: (M, W) A plate of metal or other material covering the breast, formerly used as protective armor. In ancient times (Hebrew), an ornament worn by the priesthood bearing the twelve gems representing the tribes of Israel.

BRIDAL CROWN: (w) An ornamental crown worn by brides (Scandinavia).

BROACH: (w) A pointed rod of metal or wood used for any ornament requiring a pin for its closing.

BROOCH OR BROACH: (M, W) Derived from the French *broche,* "a spit or skewer." An ornamental clasp of various forms, originally having a tongue, now a pin or loop by which it is attached to a garment.

BUCKLE: (M, W) See belt buckle.

BULLA: (w) A round pendant with a broad upper loop, worn on a chain. Originally Etruscan, adopted by Romans as an amulet.

BUN ORNAMENT: (w) An ornament helping to form a bun of hair or worn on or around it.

BURSA: (M, W) A purse, used for cosmetics, small objects, money, etc.

BUTTON: (M, W) A catch of various forms and materials, usually a knob or stud—round, oval, square, etc. in shape—used to hold together certain parts of a garment. It is attached to one part and then passes through a loop on the other, or through a buttonhole. Some are an indication of membership in an organization (Army, etc.) or a badge of honor.

BUTTON ORNAMENT: (M, W) A series of shirt studs or buttons, attached to each other by a chain or other decorative device to form one flexible connected unit. In this way, used as an ornament by both men and women in India.

CACHE-SEX: (M, W) An ornament worn to cover the pubic area of children, men, or women.

CAMEO: (w) A jewel set with a carved cameo, also the stone itself.

CARCANET: (w) A short, chokerlike collar necklace, which takes its name from the French *carcan,* the iron collar or chain of a prisoner. Now it is an ornamental necklace or collar usually of gold with jewels, or a gold ornamental headband.

CEREMONIAL JEWELRY: (M, W) Jewelry whose function is to decorate the wearer during a particular ceremony, or state occasion and therefore not worn otherwise.

CHAIN: (M, W) A series of plain or ornamental metal links, made of wire, connected or fitting through each other, ordinarily used for the purpose of supporting something (such as a pendant) but also alone or multiply for purely decorative uses. Made by hand or commercially by a chainer.

CHAIN OF OFFICE: (M, W) A necklace worn by an official to indicate his or her position or office, usually at times of ceremony. (Wine taster; burgomeister; ambassador; guild leader; etc.)

CHAIN TYPES: (M, W) Symbolically, the chain represents bonds and communication, matrimony, social or psychic integration. There are many chain types, some of which are:
Anchor: Has links of the form used in anchors.
Band: Series of interlocking links that form a wide, flexible, flat band.
Curb: The links are twisted so that they lie flat, a common pattern.
Fancy: Developments and combinations of different types.
Fetter: Originally a chain for the feet to hinder movement, now a chain in which long links are combined with an alternation of a series of short links.
Rope: A chain of interlocking links, flexible and ropelike.
Trace: Equal sized, oval, looped links which when stretched will not lie flat because of the alternating horizontal and vertical placement of the links.
Venetian: Interlocking squares.

CHAPLET: (M, W) A garland or wreath worn on the head, also a string of beads or a necklace.

CHARM: (M, W) An object originally worn because of its protective properties, its efficacy to the wearer in averting illness or to secure good luck. Now often just an amusing or commemorative object worn singly or in bunches on a chain.

CHARM BOX: (M, W) An ornamental box used to contain charms, worn as a pendant on a chain or on a beaded necklace (Tibet).

CHARM BRACELET: (w) A bracelet usually of chain from which charms hang by loops.

CHATELAINE: (w) An ornamental brooch, clasp, or hook worn at a woman's waist, having links or chains attached, from which hang various objects such as keys, a watch, a purse, or trinkets. Chatelaine in French literally means "woman owner of objects."

CHOKER: (w) A short necklace, about 15 in (38 cm) long, worn flat against the neck.

CLASP: (M, W) Several types of releasable catch meant to hold together two or more complementary parts of a necklace, bracelet, beads, etc. Can be completely simple and functional, or highly decorated.

CLASP HOOK: (M, W) A pair of hooks made so that each part forms a *mousing* (a clasp or fastening unit that joins the point and shank of a hook) to prevent its unhooking or straightening out.

CLIP: (M, W) An ornament that grips and tightly holds to the body (as on the ear or hair) or clothing by means of a pressure clip at its back, usually operating by a spring device that keeps it from shifting.

CLOAK PIN: (M, W) A pin meant to hold a heavy garment to the body, usually having a heavy pinstem or a pair of pinstems.

COCKTAIL RING: (w) A fancy ring worn for dressy occasions, usually set with stones, produced mainly by commercial jewelers since 1925.

COLLAR OR COLLIER: (M, W) An upstanding short necklace (Latin: *collum,* "neck") that rests on the base of the neck. Also a necklace of an order showing insignia (knighthood); also the collar used on an animal.

COMB: (M, W) Any toothed device used to straighten, clean, or confine the hair, or to ornament it when it is left placed in the hair.

COMMEMORATIVE JEWEL: (M, W) A ring or other ornament meant to celebrate a particular occasion or event.

CORDELIÈRE: (w) A long, beaded or braided girdle, knotted in front with the ends hanging down. Also called *cordonnière* because it was made to resemble a cord.

CORONET: (m, w) A small crown worn as a sign of high rank but lower than that of an emperor or king. In some countries, their basic form and subject matter is defined by protocol. The word is also used for any ornamental fillet or wreath worn around the temples as a decorative headdress.

CORSAGE: (w) An elaborate ornament, usually designed for flexibility in hinged or joined parts, worn on the bosom to cover the waist or bodice of a woman's dress.

COSTUME JEWELRY: (w) Jewelry made of non-precious materials and metals, usually of short fashion.

CROSS: (m, w) A religious symbol of divinity and Christianity worn as an amulet or ornament, at the neck, held in the hands, or at the end of a rosary.

CROWN: (m, w) A wreath, garland, or fillet worn around the head as a symbol of success, pre-eminence, sign of honor, as a reward for victory. A royal or imperial headdress denoting imperial power, worn by those entitled to it, as a symbol of having reached the highest goal. Certain forms or materials and colors used have specific symbolic meaning.

CUFF LINKS: (m, w) A pair of ornamental, easily removable buttons worn by men and women in the cuffs of a shirt, holding the cuffs together without overlapping their ends.

DEMI-PARURE: (w) A brooch with earrings (see *parure*).

DEVOTIONAL JEWELRY: (m, w) Jewelry meant to indicate one's attachment to a deceased person or for a religious purpose.

DIADEM: (w) A headband or fillet earlier worn as an emblem of power or royalty, now as any head decoration that crosses above the brow.

DINNER RING: (w) A fancy ring worn at important social occasions and not for everyday use.

DOG COLLAR: (w) An ornamented broad necklace worn tightly around the neck; also a close-fitting one worn by the clergy; also a collar worn by dogs.

EAR AND HAIR ORNAMENT: (w) A single ornament, usually consisting of a chainlike band that passes over the head, to which earrings are attached, and by which the earrings, usually heavy, are supported (India).

EAR PLUG: (w) An ornament worn by passing a part of it through a large hole preformed in the earlobe or other ear part. Sometimes this hole is very large due to progressive stretching.

EARRINGS: (m, w) Ornaments usually worn on the earlobe, and held to it by various devices such as studs, clips, loops, chains, sometimes with attachments to the hair to relieve the weight; with or without a pendant. Two basic types are those held by the insertion of a wire through the pierced lobe, and those held by a pressure device such as a screw or clip. Each of these presents its particular design problems depending on the manner in which they are supported on the ear.

EAR STUD: (m, w) An ear ornament worn by inserting a stud through a preformed hole in any part of the ear, then held there by a spring-operated closing device pressed over the stud shank from the reverse side.

ECCLESIASTICAL RING: (m) An oversized ring worn by some priests, bishops, archbishops, and the Pope.

EMBLEM: (m, w) A button, stud, or pin worn only by those entitled to it by membership; decorated, often with enamel, bearing the symbols or in the form of a design adopted by a fraternal or service organization.

ENGAGEMENT RING: (m, w) A ring given as a sign of betrothal.

ENSEIGNE: (m) A men's hat badge often worn as an emblem of rank and having a decoration with subject matter symbolic of lineage; worn during the Renaissance.

EPAULETTE: (m) A shoulder ornament or badge consisting of a strap ending in a fringe, worn on officers' dress uniforms. Originally meant to retain a shoulder belt.

EPISCOPAL RING: (m) A bishop's ring, one of his signs of office.

ETERNITY RING: (w) A circular ring set with a continual band of stones or a few stones, used as a wedding ring, symbolic of eternal love or fidelity.

FACE VEIL: (w) An ornament, often of suspended chains worn so as to fall in front of the face. An Eastern concept that may be in daily use or only for special occasions such as marriages.

FASTENINGS: (m, w) Any findings used on a jewel that are treated with a form of decoration beyond its functional framework.

FEDE RING: (m, w) A ring whose subject is clasped hands, a symbol of fidelity.

FERRONNIÈRE: (w) A chain that crosses the forehead and circles the head, with a pendant or fixed jewel, named after da Vinci's "La Belle Ferronnière."

FIBULA: (w) A pin brooch, clasp, or buckle whose form originated in the Bronze Age and has persisted in developed forms until present times.

FILLET: (m, w) A thin, narrow band worn across the forehead and around the head to encircle the hair.

FINGER AND TOE SHIELDS: (m, w) An ornamental casing worn over the finger or toes. The Chinese used such devices to protect extremely long fingernails, a symbol of wealth (fingernails could not be cultivated by anyone who had to do manual labor). The Egyptians covered the fingers and toes of mummies with protective shields. In Bali such shields are worn by fierce characters during dance-pantomimes to create the effect of claws.

FINIAL: (m, w) An ornamental decoration at the top or ends of a jewel, or on an object such as a hat.

FOB: (m, w) A small ornament, weight, or jewel hung on a watch chain.

FOREHEAD ORNAMENT: (w) Any ornament worn on the forehead, by suspension from a chain, band, or other device.

FRIENDSHIP RING: (m, w) Any ring given as a token of friendship.

GARTER: (m, w) Usually a restricting band worn around the thigh, calf, or upper arm to bind or secure clothing. It can also be ornamented. Members of the Order of the Garter in England, an order of knighthood begun in 1346 by Edward III, are entitled to wear a jeweled garter below the left knee, a badge or star bearing St. George's cross, and a collar used by this order bearing a badge depicting St. George and the Dragon.

GIMMAL RING: (m, w) A ring made of two or more interlocked parts, linked hoops that when worn fit together to make a total ornament. In general, a gimmal is any joined work whose parts move within each other, such as a *puzzle ring*.

GIRDLE: (m, w) An ornamental belt that encircles the waist, or rests on the hips, used to hold garments to the body, or for the suspension of objects.

GORGET: (w) Originally a piece of armor that protected the throat, now also a collar or ornament covering the neck and breast; or a neck ornament that is more or less rigid.

GUARD CHAIN: (m, w) A long chain from which a key, watch, or other object of use is hung.

GUARD RING: (w) A ring or a pair of rings worn to protect a more precious ring, or to hold in place one that may be too large for the wearer.

HAIR CLIP: (w) An ornament worn in the hair and held by a clip, used to hold hair in place.

HAIR JEWELRY: (w) Jewelry made of human or animal hair, the former popular during Victorian times.

HAIRNET: (w) A netlike jewel worn over the hair or around a bun.

HAIR ORNAMENT: (w) Any ornament meant to be worn in the hair.

HAIR PENDANT: (w) A pendant suspended from the hair.

HAIRPIN: (w) An ornamental pin used to hold hair in place, in a bun, as a decoration, etc.

HAT: (m, w) A head covering, made of metal in some form, sometimes jeweled.

HAT FINIAL: (M) Ornament worn at the crown of a hat; in some cultures, its form, color, and materials are an indication of rank.

HAT ORNAMENT: (M, W) Any ornament meant to be attached to a hat, as a hatband, brooch, egrette, etc.

HATPIN: (W) An ornamental large-headed pin used to pierce a hat, especially a large one, and by including some hair, hold it securely on the head.

HEAD AND EAR ORNAMENT: (W) A combination of a head ornament such as a tiara or fillet to which are attached ear ornaments, making a compound ornament.

HEADBAND: (M, W) A band or fillet worn around the head.

HEADDRESS: (M, W) A covering or ornament for the head, usually one of major importance.

HUNTING TROPHY (M) A trophy from a hunted animal mounted in a jewel. Bird beaks, animal claws, teeth, skulls, horns, legs, tails, feathers, etc., have all been used. Such a jewel may be worn on a hat, used as a pendant, attached to a coat, etc.

ICON: (M, W) A religious amulet worn on the body, usually bearing an image of a saint or a god.

INFULA: (M, W) A fillet worn on the head as a token of inviolability or religious consecration.

KEEPER RING: (W) Any ring or rings worn to prevent the loss of a more valuable ring worn with it.

KEY: (M, W) A real or ornamental key, worn as decoration; worn as an indication of membership in a society, or as an indication of an honor granted.

KEY CHAIN: (M, W) A chain used to hold a key, worn as an ornament.

KEY HOLDER ORNAMENT: (W) An ornament, often very elaborate, worn at the waist by the mistress of a large household, having attached rings from which many keys are suspended—the number, by implication, indicating the relative wealth of the household, since the ownership of more objects of value necessitates a greater number of keys for their security (India).

LABRET: (W) A jewel worn in a perforation made in the lip, or close to it (Central and South America).

LAPEL BUTTON: (M, W) A small ornament worn in the lapel of a jacket as an indication of membership in an organization; to indicate an honor given; in support of a person or cause; or as a sign of mourning.

LAVALIERE: (W) A pendant with singly mounted stones, also known as a *negligé.*

LOCKET: (W) A pendant or pin usually made in two parts hinged together so that it can be opened. Inside it may contain a miniature painting of a loved one, a photograph, or a good-luck charm.

MAGICAL JEWELRY: (M, W) Any jewelry worn for a magical purpose.

MANCHETTE: (W) A wide cufflike bracelet.

MAN'S SHIRT BROOCH: (M) A brooch worn by a man in place of a tie, at the base of the neck.

MASK: (M, W) A decorative mask worn to conceal one's identity.

MEDAL: (M, W) A metal ornament bearing a design on the front, and often on the back as well, usually disclike in shape, but also in other forms. Worn as a charm; ornament; conferred as a symbolic reward for services or achievement; or in remembrance of a notable event. It may also include an inscription. Some are worn as a pendant, others at the waist, on the breast, or suspended by a ribbon. Within this category are also orders of honor and merit issued by governments and societies.

MEDALLION: (M, W) A large medal, tablet, or panel often issued for a memorial purpose. The front and sometimes also the back are decorated, may contain a portrait, figures, or other subject molded in relief. The term is also generalized to mean any large, round, decorative shape used in a design, as in a jewel, a rug, etc.

MEMORIAL JEWELRY: (M, W) Jewelry meant to commemorate an occasion, event, or an individual.

MONEY: (M, W) Stamped metal coins issued by a recognized authority as a medium of exchange. Real coins and imitations are often used as ornament in jewelry by all cultures.

MORSE: (M) A kind of clasp or brooch used to fasten a clergyman's cope.

NECKBAND: (M, W) A cloth band worn around the neck, to which a metal or other ornament may be attached.

NECKLACE: (M, W) A general term for a variety of ornaments worn around the neck, often made of a material of some value.

NECKLACE CLASP: (M, W) A decorated clasp for a necklace, worn at the nape of the neck, and at times, more ornamental than the necklace.

NECKLET: (W) A short necklace, usually not more than 18 in (45.7 cm) long.

NECKPIECE: (M, W) A general term for any ornament worn around the neck. The contemporary implication is that it is made of materials of lesser intrinsic value, also one that is larger in size than a conventional necklace.

NOSE RING: (W) An ornamental ring worn through a hole pierced in the septum or *alae nasi,* in India symbolic of a woman's married state. It may also be clipped to the part concerned if no hole exists.

OUCHES: (W) Cameo brooch sewn onto clothing, 14th century.

PAPAL RING: (M) A large ceremonial ring worn by a Pope.

PARURE: (W) French: "ornamenting, adorning." A set of jewelry matching in materials used, meant to be worn together. Such sets often included a necklace, earrings, brooch, bracelet or bracelets, and ring, but could also include hair ornaments, pendants, hair combs, etc. A *demi-parure* is an abbreviated set, such as bracelet and earrings, etc.

PECTORAL: (M, W) A large ornamental plate worn on the chest, hung as a pendant, or held by a pin like a broach.

PENANNULAR BRACELET: (W) A broken circle bracelet, in classical form often having animal head terminals. Often rigid, but sometimes made with a removable section to allow its placement and removal on the wrist or ankle.

PENANNULAR BROOCH: (W) A circular brooch with a break, fitted with a long, movable pin pushed through the cloth at two points. The end of the ring is then passed under the other, exposed pin end, and turned, causing the cloth to hold the pin against the ring. Characteristically a Celtic type.

PENDANT: (M, W) A movable ornament that hangs suspended from another device such as another part of the same ornament, or from a chain.

PIN: (M, W) Any ornamental brooch worn by piercing the clothing with its attached pointed pinstem which is then locked in place by a closing device. It may have a functional purpose such as holding clothing together, or be purely decorative. Pins are also used to support other pendant ornaments, and to hold the hair, a hat, or tie in place (see *hatpin, hairpin, scarfpin, tiepin*). The term also refers specifically to the pin itself, termed the pinstem.

PILGRIM'S BADGE: (M, W) A brooch worn by a pilgrim to commemorate a journey, usually made as an act of devotion.

PLAQUE: (M, W) An ornament in the form of a decorated sheet of metal, worn singly as a pendant, or as one of several in series in a necklace.

POISON RING: (W) A ring whose ornamental upper part is hinged to the shank so that it can be opened, exposing a small inside chamber large enough for carrying small pills or "poisons." Also called a "Borgia ring" after the Italian Lucretia Borgia, Duchess of Ferrara (1480–1519) (sister of the equally famous Cesare Borgia), who is said to have used such a device to poison the drink of victims.

POMANDER: (W) A pendant scent case used from medieval times to the 18th century, worn hanging from the girdle or from a long neck chain, or hanging from a chatelaine.

PONYTAIL ORNAMENT: (W) A device used to clasp and hold hair worn tightly gathered with ends loose, at the nape of the neck, or higher on the head.

PUZZLE RING: (M, W) A ring made of movable parts that fit together in a knotlike pattern (see *gimmal ring*).

REGALIA: (M, W) Jewels and objects worn or held by reigning monarchs as a symbol of their sovereignty.

RING: (M, W) Originally a metal circlet worn on the finger, arm, or neck. Now an ornament worn on a finger or fingers, but in other forms also worn on the nose, ear, ankle, neck, etc. The word also refers to any band of metal used to connect, hold, or hang something, also called a hoop, band, or circle. There are an infinite number of kinds of rings, some of which are mentioned in this glossary. Very important and almost universal in the West is the use of a ring or rings on the ring finger (the third finger of the left hand) on which engagement and wedding rings are placed. A conventional ring may have a *hoop* or *shank*, a *shoulder* (ornamented), and a *bezel* or *claws* to hold a stone.

RIVIÈRE: (W) A long necklace made of a series of set stones, usually diamonds.

ROSARY: (M, W) A necklace worn around the neck or a string of beads etc. held in the hands, used for counting prayers. In Catholicism, a rosary is used in a form of devotion to the Virgin Mary. Rosaries are also used by Tibetan Buddhists to count the times that the prayer *Aum Mani Padme Hum* ("Praised be the Jewel in the Lotus," i.e., Buddha) is said, and by Moslems during the worship of Allah. They are sometimes referred to as "worry beads" because they are often harassed with the fingers during periods of great stress or worry. Rosaries can be a very simple string of beads or highly ornamented and jeweled beads and links.

ROSETTE: (W) A round ornament resembling the form of a stylized rose.

SAFETY PIN BROOCH: (W) A brooch having a pinstem given one or more turns to create a spring, and a closing that holds the point end. This may be an integral part of the brooch when made of wire, or added to it.

SAUTOIR: (W) A very long, narrow necklace of chains, beads, etc., sometimes with an end tassel.

SCARFPIN: (M, W) A pin or brooch meant to secure a scarf or tie.

SCARFSLIDE: (M, W) An ornament having a circular part through which the ends of a scarf are drawn, the ornament then being pulled to the chest or the base of the neck to hold the scarf in place.

SEAL: (M, W) Any stamping device bearing a design, figure, or inscription. The design on the stamp can be imparted to make an impression in relief on a soft substance capable of being impressed such as wax or clay. The word "seal" is also used for the impression so made. Originally seals were used in place of signatures to authenticate documents, and to confirm formal contracts, or simply as an ornamental stamp affixed to sealing wax used on letters and documents to identify the sender, ensure the authenticity of a document, or prevent pilferage of the contents of a package prior to delivery.

SEAL RING: (M, W) A ring on which a seal is mounted.

SEAL STAMP: (M, W) A stamp on which a seal is mounted, this being attached to a chain worn on a person, or by a loop to some other part of the body or clothing, for use when stamping wax to seal a document or letter.

SIGNET RING: (M, W) A ring that contains a signet or private seal, also called a seal ring.

SHOE BUCKLE OR ORNAMENT: (M, W) Any ornament worn on a shoe, such as a shoe buckle or stud.

SLEEPERS: (W) Small stud earrings, usually gold, inserted in a newly pierced ear to keep the hole open while it heals. Also called dormuses and abridores.

SPLIT-SHANK RING: (M, W) A ring having an open split shank which allows it to be adjusted for size by compression or spreading.

STOMACHER: (W) A usually triangular bodice ornament of the 18th century that covered much of the front of a dress, and often made in detachable sections so that a part could be worn separately as a corsage brooch.

STRAP UNION: (M, W) A metal joining part between two pieces of a leather strap, not a buckle, but permanently closed.

STUD: (M, W) An ornamental knob or boss, rod, pin, or nail with a decorative head. Also a *detachable,* buttonlike device inserted through one or more holes, buttonholes, loops, eyelets of any material, meant to serve as a decorative fastener. Also a short rod or pin with a decorative head whose plain shaft is inserted through a hole in two materials, holding them together by various methods such as split or whole rivets, while the ornamental head projects upward from the surface. Sometimes it holds a loose metal plaque in place at the same time.

TAG: (W) A decorative end ornament that acts as a terminal device on a chain.

TALISMAN: (M, W) A protective jewel to which magic properties are attributed.

TASSELS: (W) A terminal decorative device, originally a clasp for a cloak, but now a pendant ornament with parallel, bunched but free hanging elements, attached at one end to a cord, chain, or other article.

TEMPORAL: (W) An ornament worn on the temples at either side of the head.

THUMB RING: (M, W) A ring worn on the thumb.

TIARA: (W) A frontlet, coronet, or half crown ornament worn at the front of the head. Often made with an added wire below to raise it somewhat above the hair when in use, the latter becoming invisible when depressed into the hair. Also the Pope's *triple crown,* symbolic of the Papal dignity. A *tiarella* is a little tiara.

TIE CLASP OR CLIP: (M) A clasp worn to hold a tie with pressure clasp at its back which grips both the tie and the shirt beneath.

TIEPIN: (M) A straight pin with a decorative head which pierces the tie to hold it in place; in use, only the decorated head is seen.

TIE TACK: (M) A stud worn to pierce a tie and the shirt beneath it to secure the tie in place.

TOE RING: (W) A ring worn on a single toe, or in series for more than one toe, or on all five.

TOGGLE: (M, W) A kind of button or frog that can be easily engaged and disengaged for temporary purposes. Also a chain ending with a swivel and loop that easily turns so that what is attached to it lies flat and the chain does not bind in movement.

TOOTHPICK, EARPICK, TWEEZER, FINGERNAIL CLEANER: (M, W) All these in miniature are held as a set in a ring, a chatelaine, or other device, often attached to a chain and worn as an ornament at the front or at the waist.

TORQUE, TORC, TORCH: (W) A stiff, originally twisted necklace or collar (from Latin: *torquere,* "to twist") with a back opening, commonly worn by ancient peoples.

WATCH: (M, W) An instrument to keep time, ordinarily worn on the wrist with a plain or ornamental strap, but also as a pocket watch, as a pendant, in a ring, and sometimes in a jewel. The size of a conventionally mechanized watch is indicated by the diameter of the pillar plates, 0 size having a $1\frac{5}{30}$ in (2.96 cm) diameter, with each larger or smaller watch size showing a difference of $\frac{1}{30}$ of an inch (0.847 mm). A watch is contained in a *watchcase,* which covers the works and prevents foreign matter from entering and clogging it, and these can be highly ornamented. Some models are worn on a watch chain to prevent their loss. A *watch charm, seal,* or *fob* can dangle ornamentally from the *watch chain.*

WEDDING RING: (M, W) A plain or ornamented band ring worn in the West on the third finger of the left hand, by women and men. It is given during the wedding ceremony and worn as an indication of a marital state.

WREATH: (M, W) A decorative head ornament, when in metal, often made in imitation of real leaves, especially the laurel which is traditionally used as a sign of honor to the person to whom it is given.

GLOSSARY: JEWELRY FINDINGS

Findings are small metal parts that have functional uses in the construction of and wearing of jewelry. A wide range of items are available manufactured by suppliers to the jewelry trade in more or less standardized forms and sizes. The choice of whether to use a commercial finding or whether to make your own which duplicates the function of any of these items is a matter of personal feeling, and/or the demands made by the work. Some jewelers insist that a greater harmony exists between the rest of the work and the finding if it is handmade. Others do not hesitate to use one that is a machine-manufactured, ready-made object. Still others invent a finding required by a particular jewel, or one that serves a function not supplied by a finding having a conventional form. Every jeweler should make it a point to study the concepts of findings used in historic jewelry of all cultures, all of which, until the Industrial Revolution, were handmade. The variety of these concepts and the problem solving invested in these devices is simply staggering.

Among findings, a distinction exists between those whose functional concepts involve *closing, fastening,* or *joining.*

Closings are devices used to close parts of a jewel with or upon each other to hold the piece in place on a body part. Among findings that work in this way are hinges, removable pins, clasps, catches (box catches, foldover catches), hooks of various types (sister, swivel, belt), steel springs, spring rings, belt buckles, and lacings.

Fastenings are devices by which a jewel is held either to clothing or to a part of the body by passing through it or clutching it. Examples that are *attached to clothing* include pinstems with catch and joint, clips, tack and clutch buttons, tie bar clips, scarf, hat and tiepins, cuff link backs, and studs through clothing. Among those fastenings that *pass through* or *engage body parts* directly are pierced ear wires with friction nuts or screws, screw ear wires, ear clips, hair clips, nose rings, lip studs, and ear studs.

Joinings are devices for holding together parts of a jewel and do not directly serve either of the above functions. These include cord, chain, wire, jump rings, split spiral rings, head pins, eye pins, swivels, caps, bails, up eyes, flat eyes, pendant loops with or without posts, screws, bolts and nuts, rivets, permanent pins, stone settings, and bezels.

The list given below in alphabetical order includes findings in most common use. Most of them are available made of precious metals, and also of nickel silver, copper-plated and nickel-plated white metal, brass, and bronze. Manufacturers' finding supply catalogs must be consulted for details.

BEZELS: Commercial bezels are upstanding flanges that are soldered or otherwise joined to a jewel and folded over a stone to hold it in place. They are available ready-made in standard shapes in calibrated, graduated sizes to match stones of similarly calibrated sizes.

BROOCH OR PIN FINDINGS: Conventional brooch findings used to attach a brooch to clothing consist of three parts: the *catch,* the *pinstem,* and *joint.*

Catch: Basically a hook-shaped holding device that engages the pinstem after it passes through the cloth (see separate listing below).

Pinstem: The rigid wire or slender rod whose pointed end passes through the cloth or clothing accessory to which the brooch is attached, and which engages the catch while the other end is held by a joint attached to the brooch.

Joint: The device that holds the end of the pinstem op-

19–4 *JEWELRY FINDINGS*
Photo: Fern Hanaway, Inc., courtesy B. A. Ballou, Providence, Rhode Island

posite the point and allows it to rotate 45–180°, the joint acting as a fulcrum. Catches and joints are made with attached *round patches* to facilitate their being soft soldered in position. Those without patches are meant to be hard soldered in place.

CAP, CASING, FERRULE OR SLEEVE: Basically, a tube or cone-shaped cup closed at one end, often with attached loop at the closed end. Into the open end a cord, woven or loop-in-loop chain, or a stone may be placed. The shape may be plain or ornamental. In general, a ferrule serves to cover the end of whatever is inserted, and acts as a coupling. Some ferrules are movable.

CATCH: Catches are any of several devices that seize or engage, hold, and arrest another part.

Pin catch: This holds a pinstem. It can be made of a simple curved wire, flat metal, or be a cast hook that incorporates a safety device that can be turned to close the opening after the pinstem is engaged, to keep it secure.

Foldover snap catch: A hinged, two-part catch, generally of oblong or square shape, that folds over and snaps shut after enclosing a loop. Used on bracelets and necklaces or other ornaments requiring such a closing.

Ring catch with bar swivel: This is a simple, easily made device used to close necklaces or bracelets. It consists of a larger ring with an attached small link loop. Through the larger ring a bar with an attached small link ring is passed. The length of the bar is greater than the diameter of the large ring and therefore while there is a weight on it as when in use, it cannot become disengaged, unless this is done deliberately as when putting on or taking off the article. Disengagement is performed by turning the bar so that one end passes through the ring. In some, the bar ends have a melted ball.

Screw catch: A catch in which the two circular parts screw together. Each half has a small attached loop, to which the ends of a necklace or string of beads is at-

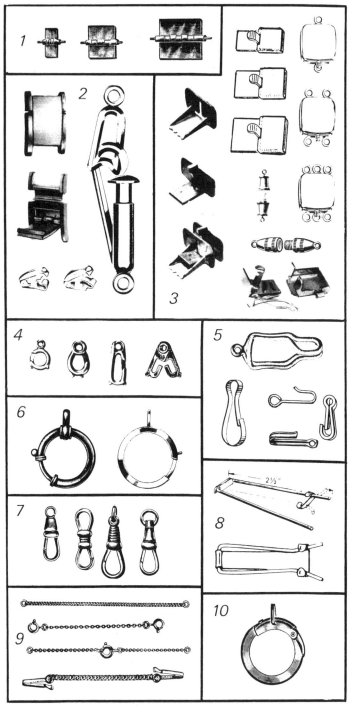

19–5 CLOSINGS

1. *Hinges, ready-made;* 2. *Foldover clasps;* 3. *Box clasps and screw clasps;* 4. *Sister hooks;* 5. *Belt hooks, strung bead hooks;* 6. *Spring rings;* 7. *Swivel hooks;* 8. *Barrette clips;* 9. *Guard chains;* 10. *Key ring.*

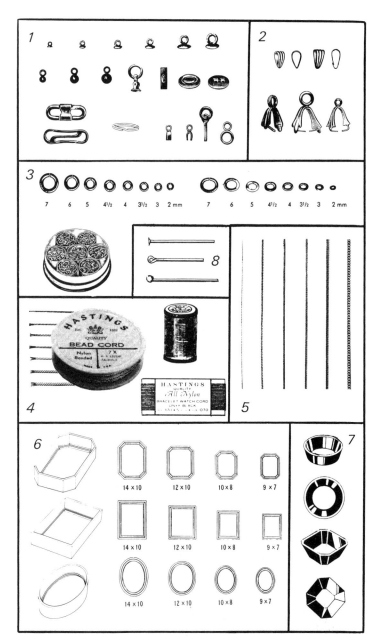

19–6 JOININGS

1. *Up eyes; flat eyes; pendant swivel loop; other forms of up eyes; oval loops; split rings; screw eye and eye joinings.*
2. *Pendant bails; stone-holding bails.*
3. *Round jump rings; oval jump rings; a box containing one gross (12 dozen or 144) of round and oval jump rings in assorted sizes.*
4. *Nylon cord on spools; heavy nylon watchband cord, available in black, gray, and rose, 5 yards on a card, 0.070–0.110 in diameter.*
5. *Pigtail chain in stainless steel (first three); remainder: foxtail chain in nickel- or gold-plated stainless steel, used for stringing and other purposes.*
6. & 7. *Bezels: plain octagon, cushion, and oval, all in 14 × 10 mm, 12 × 10 mm, 10 × 8 mm, and 9 × 7 mm; larger sizes available: 14 × 12 mm, 16 × 12 mm, 18 × 13 mm, 20 × 15 mm; round available in 7–12 mm; all in 14K white or yellow gold, and other metals.*
8. *Head pin, eye pin, ball pin, in sterling silver.*

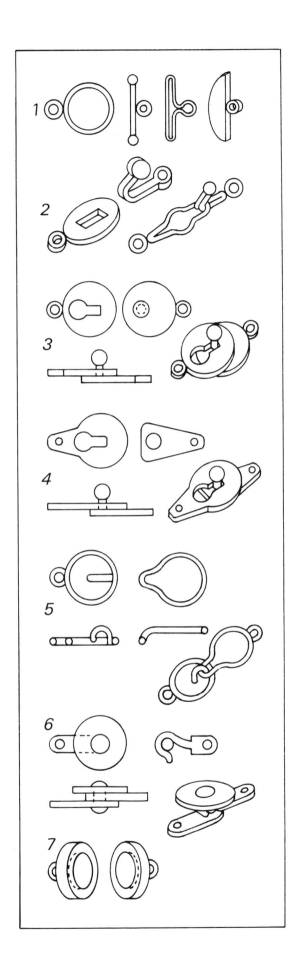

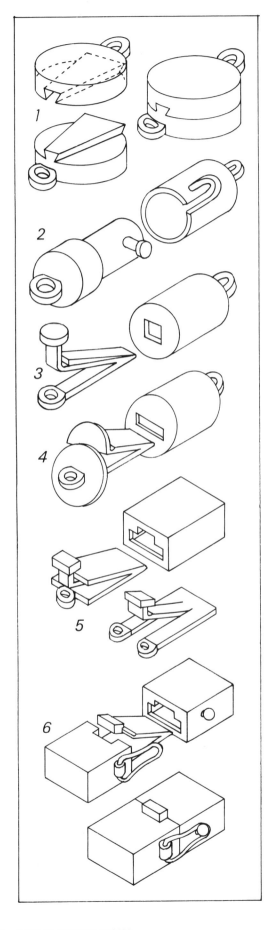

19-7 HAND FABRICATED CATCHES
1. Ring and T-bar catch; 2. Hook and slot catch, sheet and wire; 3. Keyhole catch with attached loops; 4. Keyhole catch variation, one-piece sheet; 5. Internal wire hook and loop catch; 6. Covered side hook catch; 7. Disc contact magnet, two parts.

19-8 HAND FABRICATED CLASPS
1. Tapered wedge-slot, positive-negative clasp, open and closed; 2. Spike and tube slot-lock clasp; 3. Tube clasp with spring catch; 4. Tube clasp with spring catch, variation; 5. Box clasp with two forms of spring catch; 6. Box clasp with safety side latch, open and closed.

tached. These are manufactured or can easily be made of tubing and wire, without even the necessity for threading. (See Making a Pseudoscrew, p. 427.)

CHAINS: Craftspersons can make their own chains. Machine-made chains are available in a great variety of systems and weights, many of which are of standardized construction, while others are so-called novelty chains. They may be had with soldered or unsoldered links. Craftspersons generally have a prejudice against their use with handmade jewelry, but this attitude is being overcome as new ways are found to use them creatively. They should be thought of as another resource available to the craftsperson like any other metal form. (See Chains, Chapter 6.)

CLASP: Clasps are devices meant to join and hold two parts of a necklace, bracelet, or the like. They may be of several shapes.

Box clasp: A clasp in two parts: the *box* containing a *socket* which is attached by a loop or loops to one side of the article, and the tonguelike *spring catch* (sometimes called the *click* for the sound it makes in engaging the socket) attached to the other side, also having an attached loop for attachment. The spring catch is pressed into and engages the socket in the box. Box clasps are available plain or ornamented, and can be made by hand by box construction.

Hook clasp: A box clasp that employs a hook instead of a spring catch to engage the box.

Tube clasp: The principle of this clasp with socket and spring catch is the same as that of the box clasp, but it is made from a tube. It is also used on necklaces and bracelets.

CLIP: A device used on brooches, earrings, and hair ornaments, it clutches a part of the body, hair, or cloth in a firm grip, and is held in place by spring pressure. For additional security, the clip may have teeth which penetrate and grip the cloth. A special type is a *ring size clip.*

CUFF LINK BACK: A device used to hold the ornamented portion in place in the shirt cuff. They are available in several styles. One is made with a separate joint that is first hard soldered to the ornamented part, then the rest is riveted in this; one with an attached round disc is used for soft soldering; one has a steel spring. Links and other systems can be used for this function.

EAR WIRES: Ear wires are devices for holding an earring to the ear. These can be divided into several basic types, and several variations are available in each category.

Screw: This contains a threaded post that winds through a matching threaded opening in the wire that curves under and around to the front of the earlobe. The post is screwed closed to bring pressure on an end-mounted pad against the earlobe to hold the earring tightly on the ear. The post is unscrewed to release the earring. Variations in form exist: some have a ring to hold attachments, others are flattened, have a pad, cup, cup with peg, cup with ring, half ball, or full ball.

Pierced ear: Several types of pierced ear finding exist. One employs a straight *pointed post* or stud that passes through the pierced ear hole. A *threaded stud* has a *matching nut* that is screwed on it, and this is very safe. A *butterfly clip* has a flat wire double scroll with a central hole through which a smooth stud passes, and holds by pressure. A groove surrounding the stud end before it tapers keeps the clip from falling off. Another is a *hook-shaped wire* that passes through the ear hole. Some of these then engage a hook or clasp to close them. Variations have attached loops or domes. Still another is a lever lock type.

Wing-back type: A wire bent to the conformity of the shape of the space just *within* the ear, fits there and comfortably distributes the weight of the earring without noticeable pressure.

Spring clip: A clip type, more comfortable than a screw because when closed, the pressure is distributed over a larger area.

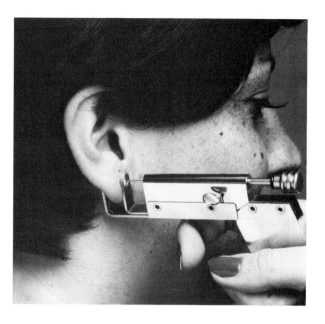

19-9   *EAR PIERCING INSTRUMENT, OHRFIX*
Manufactured by Ohrfix, Erich W. Wittman GmbH & Co. KG, Erlangen, West Germany.

To pierce an earlobe with this instrument, first clean the lobe on both sides with an antiseptic, and likewise disinfect the parts of the instrument that contact the lobe. Mark the position of the hole on the lobe with a sterile *metal point* or *needle*. This instrument uses special 24K gold-plated stainless steel *one-way studs* to make the hole. The stud consists of two parts: a pointed post with a decorative end ball, and a flat, round stud receptacle with a central hole into which the post end goes and which holds it firmly. Both stud and holder are sold in pairs for use with this instrument, mounted on a sterile Styrofoam backing, enclosed in a sterile container from which they must be removed without touching any parts. Basically, the instrument is a gun-shaped mechanism that uses spring energy to shoot the stud shaft through the earlobe. It has a U-shaped space at the front into which the lobe fits and by which it is held. Each flange of this holder has an upper, central groove—one designed to hold the stud back, and the other to hold the stud.

First cock the stud release trigger or plunger at the opposite end by pulling the knob back until it audibly click-stops in place, which also prepares the pressure spring for use. Hold the instrument at a 45° angle to the Styrofoam mount, and gently slide the *stud back* or *retainer* into the front groove and lift it out. Invert the Styrofoam mount and place the *stud with ball* into the second flange groove or stud holder at the tip of the barrel with its pointed end forward, then lift the Styrofoam mount straight up. Since these parts are sterile, they must not be touched. Engage the earlobe in the U-shaped holder with the stud point exactly over the marked hole position, with the retainer at the opposite point at the back of the earlobe. Aiming the stud point through the aiming sight, slowly squeeze the slide trigger to hold the earlobe steady, into the fully closed position. Press the firing lever straight down with the thumb. The stud will instantly spring forward, pierce the lobe, and simultaneously the stud clasp shaft is engaged in the hole of the stud holder on the other side of the lobe. Release the trigger, and bring the instrument *straight downward* to disengage the stud and stud back, without recocking the instrument. The stud ball remains visible at the front of the earlobe. Both parts stay in place until the hole has healed. The small wound is dressed with an antiseptic on a wad of sterile cotton. The healing period varies with each individual. Thereafter, a stud or earring should be left in the hole to prevent it from growing closed. *Photo: Courtesy Ohrfix*

GALLERY WIRE: Round wire or flat, narrow strips stamped by hand or machine with various patterns by means of one- or two-part molds. Some have balls or beads in series, or other shapes, sometimes inspired by designs from classical antiquity. Others have openwork suggestive of galleried arcades and balustrades, hence the name. They are often used around traditional stone settings, or as borders on holloware.

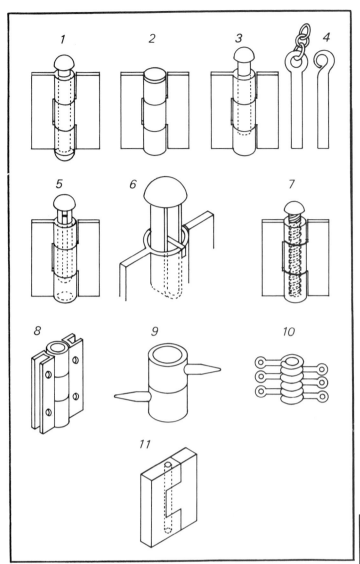

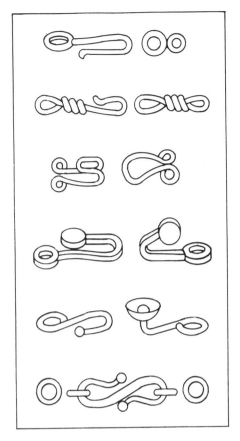

19-11 HAND-FABRICATED HOOKS MADE OF WIRE, USED FOR CLOSINGS.

19-10 HINGE TYPES

1. A *typical hinge* which consists of *flaps* (leaves or bearers); cheniers or *knuckles*; and a *pin*. This is a three-knuckle hinge, the top and bottom knuckles attached to the left flap, and the center one to the right flap. The pin head has been shown raised above the top knuckle only to illustrate its position. In fact, both top and bottom heads would be formed like rivet heads, close upon the knuckles, but with just enough space so as not to freeze the hinge action. If this occurs, inject some tripoli and work the flap back and forth slowly till it moves freely.

2. A *permanent pin hinge* with flattened heads.

3. A *removable pin hinge*, which allows disengagement of the lugs.

4. *Removable pin* with soldered-on ring eye and attached guard chain to prevent loss; a pin with a forged eye, one piece.

5. A *removable split pin hinge*.

6. A *permanent split pin hinge* with soldered-in retaining crossbar.

7. *Removable screw pin* in internally threaded knuckles.

8. *Soft material hinge* with U-flaps having holes to allow for rivets or screws.

9. *Hook and eye hinge* with tapered pins to allow them to be cemented in place in soft materials.

10. *Wire ring hinge*, each unit riveted or screwed in place.

11. *Dovetail hinge* with internal, invisible riveted pin.

19-12 FASTENINGS

1. *Tie tack clutch button backs* and *stud posts* of various types; assembled with safety guard chain and buttonhole bar.

2. *Screw-type button back* with screw post.

3. *Pipe stem stud back* with internal spring allowing retraction of the short stem.

4. *Scarf, hat, or tie pinstem*; straight, and with attached disc; *scarf pinstem safety clutches*.

5. *Cuff link back types*: hard solder, plain top; hard solder, ribbed top; hard solder, swivel back, also shown disassembled with separate joint and rivet; soft solder type with attached patch; fold-back hinged type. (V. M. Christensen A/S)

6. *Tie clasps*: spring type; alligator-jaw clip type.

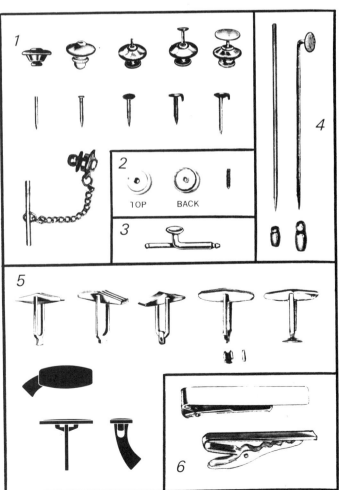

19–13 *UNIT LINKING SYSTEMS*
1. Ring and bent flat wire loops, invisible.
2. Ring with four half loops, invisible.
3. Flat wire loops with pierced openings, visible.
4. Rings in series with pierced openings, visible.
5. Flange with ball-ended wire, invisible.
6. Pierced lugs of various types.
7. Self-hooks engaging half loops.

Threading devices
8. Double strip through half loops, threaded with a fibrous material or metal wire or strip.
9. Tube top lug threaded with wire or nylon line.
10. Lug-threading units of round tube, square tube, or spiral wire, with various shapes.
11. Double-lug units, threaded top and bottom.
12. Double-lug units, threaded top and bottom, the lowest unit with ornamental lower portion.

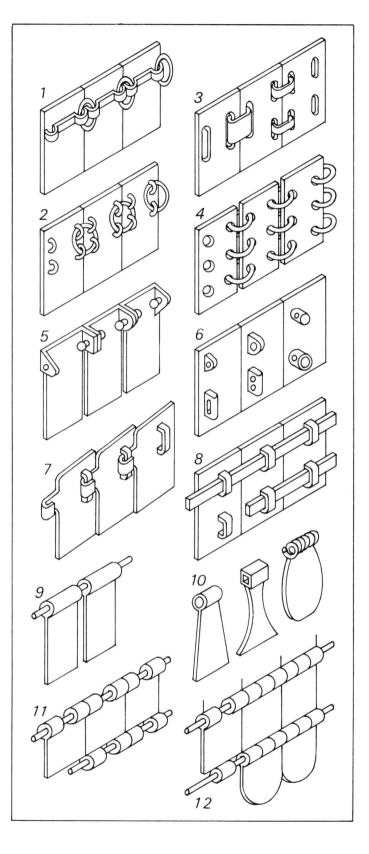

HINGES: An articulated joint usually made of two flat, rectangular parts, each bearing alternating tubular lugs that interlock, so that all the lugs form one continuous tube through which a rod or pin passes, thus holding the two parts together. The holding rod can be temporary (as in a bracelet) or permanent, in which case both ends are upset like a rivet, to form a mushroom that prevents it from slipping out. (See Functional Uses of Tubing, p. 260 and The Hinge in this chapter.)

HOOKS: Any curved or angular device, often ending in a point or taper, made of wire or sheet are hooks. They are meant to pass over and engage a projecting retaining stud, or to pass through a ring or loop, to fasten and sustain the closing.

Sister hook: Two hooks with facing pointed ends, both overlapping, held together at a swivel joint by an open tube rivet. They can be separated by sliding one over the other to form an opening between them to allow a loop to enter, and are then pressed closed to form a continuous loop, safe, holding device.

Belt hook: Generally a circular shape with wire hook.

Swivel hook: A hook whose normal position is closed by spring pressure. One of its legs can be moved inward by applying pressure against it to compress the inner spring. There is a loop at the top, rigid on some swivels, and freely rotating on others so that whatever it holds can stay in place without twisting.

LINK OR LOOP: A single ring unit of any size. A *jump ring* is used alone, other loops are soldered to another part, or to a single last part of a series of links or loops in a chain. In general, loops are used as a connecting element to hold parts together. They may be open or soldered closed, circular, oval, or other shape, made of wire or sheet.

RINGS: Any continuous circular or oval form made of wire, sheet, or tube cross section, used for holding, connecting, spacing, hanging, etc. Some examples:

Jump ring: A connecting ring of wire, made in many sizes, open or soldered closed.

Key ring: A circular ring or hoop with some system of opening and closing to admit the threading of keys. They usually have a spring- or latch-closing, safe locking device, and a loop attached to hold a chain and/or a decorated tab or ornament.

Spring ring: Also called a *bolt ring*, this consists of a circular metal tube containing a concealed steel spring, and provided with a latch with attached knob that when pressed against the spring pressure with a fingernail, makes an opening in the ring. While held thus, a jump ring on the opposite side can be passed through the opening. Upon release of the spring tension, the latch is automatically forced back in place, closing the ring, which remains closed because of the spring's pressure. This finding is in universal use. Though it is not especially pleasing esthetically, it nevertheless is an ingenious and reliable invention that performs its function well. It is available in gold, silver, white metal, steel, etc.

RING SIZE CLIP: A spring-hardened metal strip with paired end flanges, placed within a ring shank, the flanges then bent onto the shank to reduce ring size and make a tighter fit.

RIVETS: Rivets are a metallic rod or wire in relatively short lengths used to unite two or more metal parts. Its shank or tube is passed through a hole in each part, then its ends are pressed, beaten down or upset to form heads or flanges that hold the shank in place. There are several types, some permanent, others movable.

Head: Has a preformed head at one end of various shapes: round, cone, pointed, flattened, countersunk.

Split: A rivet whose shank is divided into two parts or legs that are bent apart beneath to hold it in place.

Sliding: A rivet that holds two parts but not immovably, and can be slid within a groove or slot. Also called an *almain* rivet.

Integral: A rivet made by passing a projecting part of one unit through a hole in the other, then upsetting the end so that the parts cannot be separated. This is not a true rivet but works like one.

SCREW EYE: A loop, soldered to or engaging a second loop that is attached to a threaded post. Meant for winding into a soft substance such as wood, ivory, plastic, tortoiseshell, or drilled stone.

TIE CLASP OR CLIP: A device with a spring-held alligator clip, or a work-hardened metal spring clip, used to hold a tie, or a scarf in place.

TIE TACK: A pinlike device soldered to the back of an ornamental tiepin. The pin passes through the tie and shirt from the front of these layers of cloth, emerges at the back where it engages a *clutch back* which grasps the pinstem. To release this, a *pad* on the clutch back is pulled back, putting pressure against the restraining spring to enlarge the opening, which allows the pin to exit.

TOGGLE: A pin or bolt tapering at both ends with a groove around its middle, fixed transversely in the eye of a chain.

UNIT-LINKING SYSTEMS: Various systems of joining units to each other by the means of findings of different sorts, visible or invisible, can be used. Units can be made in parallel series to pass around cylindrical body parts such as the wrist, waist, or ankle; or in tapering sections to form radial shapes suited to these same places or to necklaces. The illustration shows only parallel units, but any of these systems could also be used for linking radial units.

SOLDERING JEWELRY FINDINGS

Commercial, mass-produced jewelry findings such as *joints* and *safety catches* used on brooches, *ear wires* for earrings, *posts* for earrings and tie tacks, *cuff link backs,* and *jump rings* used as a loop or a part, are widely used in jewelry making. They are placed on parts of a jewel after they have reached a stage of completion. The metal used in these devices should match that used in the piece, if possible. Joints and catches are available with or without attached cups or flat discs. Generally speaking, those without cups are hard soldered to the work, and those with cups are soft soldered on, as the cups provide a larger surface to lend strength to the less strong soft solder. Cuff link backs may be the type that contain a spring, and if there is no way to disassemble them, they should be soft soldered as the spring may lose its elasticity if subjected to hard soldering heat. Some are therefore made with a separate joint attachment, similar to that used for a pin, which is hard soldered in place, and then the rest of the finding is riveted to the joint in the same manner as a pinstem is riveted to a pin joint.

SOLDERING PIN FINDINGS

When the pinstem is horizontal on a brooch, pin findings should be placed *above the center line* so that the weight of the pin does not cause it to fall forward and it lies flat. Place the *joint* on the *right* at the *back* of the piece, and place the *catch* on the *left*. This is the usual arrangement to allow right-handed people to conveniently pass the pinstem point through the clothing with ease from right to left. If the pinstem must be placed vertically, it should then be centered, and the joint should be at the top and the catch at the bottom. Only use catches with safety locks or self-locking catches to prevent loss. Using a catch without a safety device is a false economy.

Mark the positions for both joint and catch and scrape or file those places as well as the backs of both joint and catch to be sure that the contacting metals are clean. With a flux brush, put a minimum of flux at each position—one dab is enough as more might swell and cause solder displacement or let the solder flood the catch. We assume that by the nature of the situation the finding will stand upright by itself. Be sure that joint and catch are lined up properly so that the pinstem when attached later will fit into the catch groove made to receive it. Some jewelers place the joint slightly above the horizontal so that when the pinstem is in place, it exerts a springlike pressure against the catch as a safety measure. The catch groove opening should point *downward* so that the weight of the brooch acts as a security factor by pressing the pinstem upward into the catch should the safety lock by some chance open.

When soldering, place the safety lock on the catch in the *open* position, and some jewelers paint it with yellow ochre or a solder-inhibiting medium to avoid the possibility of solder flooding it and thus freezing the catch and rendering it inoperative. One way of avoiding such an occurrence is not to use more solder than is necessary. Two small snippets, one on either *side* of the joint and catch is enough. Also, avoid overheating the work so that the solder does not spread to where it is not wanted.

Use a small-tipped soldering torch and a small, pointed flame that can concentrate the heat locally where it is needed. At the start of soldering, do not play the flame directly on *any kind of finding,* but pass the flame tip in a circle around it to slowly bring up the temperature of the area of metal to which it is attached. When the solder-melting temperature is reached, the flame can touch the finding briefly to be sure its temperature and that of the base are the same and to ensure a good flow of solder to both parts, then quickly withdraw the flame. After soldering place the work in the pickle solution to clean it.

In cases where the finding will *not* stand upright by itself in the desired position, the help of a wire jig or tool is needed. Usually *slide-locking* or *self-locking soldering tweezers* are resorted to, and these are preferred to ordinary tweezers because they hold the finding without the necessity of thinking about the need to apply constant pressure, which leaves the mind and hands free to concentrate on soldering. Clean and flux the bottom of the catch and joint, hold one of them bottom up with tweezers, and place a medium-sized solder snippet there. While continuing to hold each in turn separately in air, melt the solder in place and allow it to cool. Clean the place where each of them is to be at the back of the brooch and flux it. While holding the finding in readiness with the tweezers, heat the position on the brooch until it reaches near soldering temperature. With the ball of the hand resting on the bench for stability, lower the finding to its position, keeping it in contact with the rest while continuing the heating until the solder flows. Remove the flame, but continue to hold the finding in place for a few seconds until the solder freezes, then unlock the tweezers, and pickle the work. *Soldering clamps* such as a *third-hand clamp* can also be used to hold findings in place while they are soldered.

RIVET JOINING A PINSTEM

To complete the finding for the brooch, the pinstem must be attached. Pinstems are available in medium or heavy weights, in graduated sizes ½–3 in (1.3–7.6 cm) in length. Joining the pinstem to the joint is a riveting process which does not em-

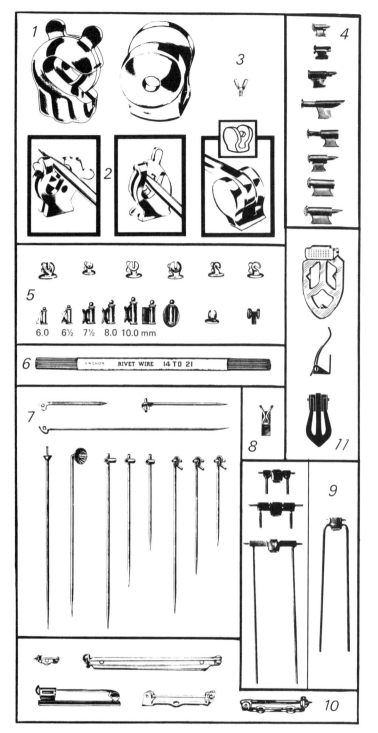

1. *Matching catch with safety lock, and joint, for hard soldering.*
2. *Self-locking catch whose latch closes when the pinstem is pressed* down into the notch, and *joint with internal posts, whose sides when pressed permanently engage the hole in an inserted pinstem and hold it in place.*
3. *Catch and joint with screw bases.*
4. *European-type catch in assorted sizes, consisting of a horizontal cylinder first pulled out by a head to allow the entry of the pinstem, then pressed to return it in place to hold the point locked within the cylinder.*
5. *Catches and joints with patches, designed for soft soldering, but when made of silver or gold, usable for hard soldering as well.*
6. *Rivet wire, assorted sizes, used to hold the pinstem to the joint.*
7. *Pinstems, various lengths, used with catch and joint of proportional size; with hole and pressure cam; attached pins; screw ends; and other systems used in Europe.*
8. *Safety lock, European style, soldered by a patch to a brooch back just below the pinstem, used to engage a pinstem when used with an ordinary, simple wire hook. After the pinstem is inserted and engaged with the hook, the hook is lifted upward, grasps and holds the pinstem under pressure against itself.*
9. *Double pinstem findings, French, with various joint systems.*
10. *One-piece assembled brooch finding with safety catches, used for soft soldering.*
11. *Brooch clips with spring device, demountable for hard soldering.*

in use points toward the brooch back. This flange acts as a stop when the pinstem is in a position just short of horizontal, so that it must be forced somewhat downward to engage the slot in the safety catch, the flange thus acting to provide spring to the pinstem.

If you are using a pinstem with attached rivets, spread the catch apart with *pliers* enough to allow the rivets to engage its holes. Then with *square-nosed pliers,* press the joint halves toward each other allowing the rivets to enter the holes. Before finally pressing the rivets to spread their ends which now project slightly beyond the sides of the joint, test the stop flange of the pinstem by moving it to engage the catch. If it is too high, as is often the case, return the pinstem so the flange is pointing upward, and file away some of its edge, then test it again. Assuming it now works well, now position the rivet ends well within the base of the jaws of a pair of square-nosed pliers, and exert maximum pressure to spread the ends of the rivets so that they no longer can come loose from the holes in the joint. Special *rivet-setting pliers* are available for this purpose.

Joints are available without holes and having two *internally* attached rivets that together make the distance of the parts when closed. In this case, a pinstem with a hole is placed within the joint and the joint halves are brought together with pliers.

When no attached rivets but only holes in both the joint and the pinstem exist, they must be held together with a length of rivet wire. Select a piece of nickel alloy pinstem rivet wire having a diameter that fits snugly in the joint and pinstem hole, and mark it, withdraw it, and cut off a section long enough so that a *small amount* passes through and projects beyond either side of the joint while the pinstem is in place. Be sure both ends are flat. Replace the rivet, grasp it as before and squeeze it with flat-nosed pliers. To be sure a rivet head has formed, place the rivet vertically in contact with any flat steel surface such as a small, flat *anvil.* With a small *riveting hammer* made for small work of this nature, lightly hammer the rivet ends, turning the work after every few blows so that both sides are hammered to upset the rivet ends and form heads. A fault to be avoided is cutting the length of the rivet too long so that when spreading the head, the rivet bends. In this case there is nothing to be done but to saw out the rivet, cut a new, shorter one, and repeat the process.

ploy heat, and the same procedure can be followed in the case of cuff link backs that use joints.

Pinstems are never in place before all soldering is finished in order to preserve their state of springiness which would be destroyed if they were allowed to reach soldering temperature. Some pinstems are made with *externally* attached rivets that project from each side, and others simply have a hole through which a separate rivet wire is passed. At one end the pinstem has a point. If for some reason the pinstem must be shortened, after cutting off the excess, the point must be restored by filing it to a taper and polishing it highly so that it passes through cloth easily. At the other end there is an attached flange which

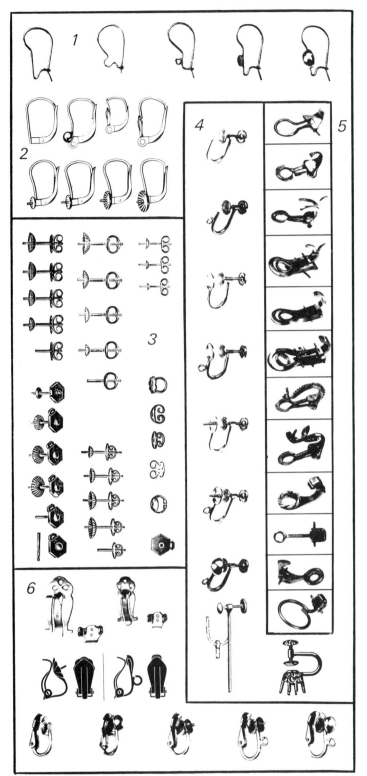

19–15 FASTENINGS: Earring findings

1. *Pierced ear wires, single wire; with cup; with dome.*
2. *Pierced ear rivet hinge clips: plain; with loop; with cup and post for mounting pearl or stone.*
3. *Pierced ear, plain-post friction type, and screw-threaded posts; ear nuts to accommodate both types.*
4. *Unpierced ear wires, screw-pressure type, with various accommodations: plain, soldering; with loop; with cup; with stone-mounting post; half-dome; straight; with claw stone setting.*
5. *French ear clips, various designs. (Comptoir Lyon-Alemand Louyot)*
6. *Ear clips, spring type, with separate joint mount for hard soldering to prevent loss of spring in clip: with various accommodations.*

SOLDERING ON EAR WIRES

There are several types of ear wires, but the most common ones are basically variants of those for unpierced or pierced ears. In terms of soldering them in place, we are concerned here only with the types that are soldered on, that area by which they are soldered to the rest of the earring, and the means of keeping it in contact with the rest while soldering takes place. Those having a flat area or domed cup are the easiest to solder in place because they usually can be made to stand upright without any support. Those which cannot so stand must be held in the position of contact by *clips,* or *self-locking tweezers.* A binding wire jig can be made of a length of wire by wrapping it at one end around the ear wire, extending it horizontally away from the work, then turning it to a right angle down into the soldering surface which it penetrates like a pin.

Ear wires can be hard soldered with easy-flow solder, though this can anneal them, making them too soft to use. In this case, it is necessary after soldering to restore the spring to the curved part of the wire. That part is placed on a *small anvil* and hammered with a small hammer. Other jewelers prefer to soft solder the ear wire in place, but in this case, no other soldering can be done on the work and it must be the last step that necessitates heat higher than that used in soft soldering.

Ear wires in the form of *posts* used for pierced ears can be soldered in the same way as described above, and so can *tie tack posts.*

BUTT JOINT SOLDERING CIRCULAR WIRE AND STRIP FORMS: links, jump rings, band rings

Oval or circular links and jump rings made of wire are used in chains and in construction systems where parts are attached by loops. To be sure that such parts do not separate and are strong, once in place they must be soldered closed. This often means that the rest of the work must be isolated or as much as possible brought out of the way of the soldering and only the individual ring is raised with the opening upward while the rest is below.

If it is necessary before soldering to open and close the ring to admit another part or pass it through another loop or part, when closing it, remember the correct way to open and close rings. (See Chain Mail, Chapter 6.) The two ends should come together as a well-fitting butt joint without any gap.

In soldering wire rings or links, use one or two *self-locking tweezers* or *slide-locking tweezers.* A *two-clamp soldering jig* is especially useful in cases where the link or ring joins two heavy parts whose weight must be supported. Clamp them to the lower portion of the ring leaving the opening at the top, or hold the ring with tweezers as far from the joint as possible while the parts it joins hang below. We assume the ring is clean. Flux the seam, pick up one small solder snippet with the *flux brush,* and place it on top of the joint so that it straddles both its sides. With a small torch tip that produces a small, pointed flame, pass the heat *around* the ring joint to drive off the flux moisture. The ring heats up very quickly as it is a small amount of metal. Touch the joint with the flame pointing away from you across the joint, withdraw it, then touch the joint again to melt the solder. Remove the flame just when the solder flows. A joint made with just enough solder will be almost invisible. If too much solder is used, it may form an unsightly lump at the joint which must be filed away.

Band rings and ring shanks made of heavier metal than the wire used for jump rings require the use of binding wire to bring the joint ends together and hold them that way during soldering, or the soldering heat may cause them to draw apart. First clean the joint and apply flux to it. Wrap the *outside circumference* of the band with a single strand of medium-weight iron binding wire, and twist the ends together with *pliers* until the two parts of the seam come into contact. By another system that avoids contact of the binding wire with the seam, pass the wire around the *diameter* of the ring and twist the ends together at one side until the pressure makes the ends meet. Position the ring upright, ordinarily with the seam *down* so gravity helps the solder flow, by propping it up against a charcoal block. Place a single narrow solder snippet as long as the joint, on top of the joint on the inside of the band, and in contact with both joint sides. First heat the band or ring with a circular motion of the flame tip to bring up the temperature of the metal. When solder flow temperature is near, briefly place the flame tip on the seam which will cause the solder to flow. Be sure it flows the joint length, then quickly remove the flame. Do not unnecessarily prolong the heating process. Snip off the binding wire and immerse the band in pickle to clean it, remove, and rinse.

THE HINGE

A *hinge* is an articulated construction used as a joining device. For purposes of discussion, we speak here of a hinge as a separate entity though in fact in jewelry it is also often an integral part of the piece. The diagram shows a typical hinge as a separate unit. It consists of two side *flaps* or *leaves* in their simplest form, as flat rectangles, but they may be curved or in any ornamental shape. Attached to the flaps are cylindrical forms variously called *lugs, cheniers,* or *knuckles,* that match in both external and internal diameter, and are lined up with each other. The lugs are called knuckles because they act in the same way as those finger joints of the hand. In jewelry, lugs are usually made of short sections of tubing, with exactly squared ends, but they can also be made of a tube shape made of a spiral of wire, or they can be an integral lug made of a cylindrically bent extension of the metal used for the flap. A hinge has a minimum of two, but usually is more stable with three or more lugs attached alternately to the two flaps. In the diagram, two are attached to the left flap and one to the right. They must be lined up with each other to allow the passage of a *retaining pin* that holds the hinge parts together. The flaps

rotate around the pin. The amount of movement may be minimal to an angle of 180° (depending on where the restraining flange or stop device is placed), or up to a full 360°, called a *turnover hinge* (in which the flaps come completely flat on each side). The hinge can be completely invisible and used to articulate a part of the design concept. If flaps are used, they can be soldered to the back of the piece so that only the lugs show, or they can be visible and highly decorated.

PERMANENT PIN HINGES   Hinges can be used to permanently hold parts together, in which case the pin is fixed in place like a flush-headed rivet by hammering down and upsetting its two ends. Such hinges are used to join units in a bracelet, pendant, or a necklace, and they can be almost invisible. The pin head can have any other shape such as round, as in the illustration.

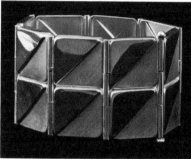

19–20   KAIJA AARIKKA, Finland, designer; manufacturer Aarikka Koru, Helsinki. Silver bracelet with three-lug hinges holding stamped parts that are half polished, half matte. The opening is a headed removable pin. Photo: Seppo Vikman, courtesy Aarikka Koru

19–21   JEREMY ROSS, England. Silver bracelet made of curved sheet parts joined by seven-lug hinges which are exposed and form decorative edges. Photo: Ross

19–16   HELY JUVONEN, Finland, designer; manufacturer Kultakeskus Oy, Hämeenlinna. Gold cuff links with hinged findings that fold back and flatten completely for ease in insertion. Photo: Kalevi Pekkonen, courtesy Kultakeskus Oy

19–17   PAULA HÄIVÄOJA, Finland, designer; manufacturer Kalevala Koru, Helsinki. Silver cuff link in the form of a dovetail hinge with hidden rivet. Photo: Studio Wendt, courtesy Kalevala Koru

19–22   CHRISTA LÜHTJE, West Germany. Bracelet in green jade and gold. The stone parts were cut for the maker from drawings supplied to the lapidary. To hold them together, a gold tube was inserted in the vertically drilled holes that pass through each section, which makes the stone parts act as dovetail hinges. The gold closing is also a hinge with decorative side flaps and a removable pin. Photo: Claus Hansmann

19–18   TAISTO PALONEN, Finland, designer: manufacturer Kultateollisuus Oy, Turku. The hinges are used at right angles which gives great flexibility to the bracelet. Photo: Oppi

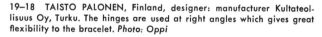

19–19   KARL GUSTAV HANSEN, Denmark, designer; manufacturer Hans Hansen Sølvsmedie, Kolding. Silver bracelet No. 2276. The concept of the entire design is a hinge with flaps in series. A headed removable screw-pin is used for opening and closing. Photo: Courtesy Hans Hansen Sølvsmedie

REMOVABLE PIN HINGES Hinges can also be used in a bracelet or belt to make a closing that can be opened. In this case, the pin is removable, and its head is usually large enough to allow it to be grasped. It may have an attached loop to simplify its removal, or allow the attachment of a *guard chain* to prevent its loss when removed.

THE SPLIT-PIN HINGE The pin in this case is made of a U-shaped half-round wire or flat wire with a space between. Into this space goes a crossbar that is soldered to the top of the top lug. A pin head is then soldered to the ends of the pin. This arrangement (see diagram) allows the pin to be removed as far as the top lug so the hinge can be opened. Because the pin cannot go further than the crossbar, it is attached to the piece and cannot be lost. Such a pin is commonly used on jewelry in the East.

THE REMOVABLE SCREW-PIN HINGE This headed pin has an external threaded screw that fits the internal thread of the lugs. It is safer than a plain, straight pin. It is also commonly used in jewelry in the East. The screw thread is often made from a wire coil. (See Making a Pseudoscrew, p. 427.) The screw-pin is completely removable.

HOOK AND EYE SOFT-MATERIAL HINGE A two-knuckle hinge with a tapered rod or spur soldered to each knuckle instead of a flap is used for hinging soft materials. The spur enters a hole drilled in soft materials such as wood or plastic, and is cemented there.

THE U-FLAP HINGE Another hinge type used on soft materials has U-shaped flaps that surround the soft material. They are pierced with holes that also penetrate the soft material, and pins are inserted and riveted into the hole to hold the ensemble together.

CONSTRUCTING A HINGE

Measure the total length for the lugs or knuckles. Divide this measurement into a minimum of three equal parts, the most common number used. Two-lug hinges are sometimes used when each of them is long enough, but they are not as strong or as stable as a three-lug hinge. Hinges with more than three lugs are common. An odd number of lugs keeps the pin in line as both ends are held by the same side or flap, and this prevents the pin from bending.

When cutting tubing, to assure squared ends, avoid waste, and unnecessary work, some device to hold the tube perpendicular to the cut is needed as this can rarely be done freehand with accuracy. A simple device is a *hardwood block* with squared ends and a V-shaped lengthwise groove perpendicular to its ends. This can be easily made, and is useful in guiding the saw to make accurate, true cuts and it also serves as a template when finishing a cut end. *Joint tools* are also used to hold tubing and wire while it is cut. (See Tubing, Chapter 7, Illustration 7–29.)

Mark and cut the lugs one at a time from seamed or seamless tubing, on each of them allowing a fraction more than is needed for trimming and truing. They are marked and cut *separately* because there is some loss of metal in the cutting groove and inaccuracies can occur. Place the tube in the V-groove of the wood block and while holding it down firmly with the fingers, cut through the tube, holding the saw blade close to the block end. When sawing tubing, make an initial groove, start slowly, and use little pressure before arriving at midway, then increase the pressure.

To assure a close-fitting hinge, the lug ends must be finished at a 90° angle to the tube axis. After the tube is sawed through, finish and square the end by placing it flush with the block end, and while holding it firmly, file or stone the end true. The tube can also be placed between two pieces of hardwood with a groove to hold the tube in place, then clamped together. Measure the tube from this finished end, and again allowing a fraction for trimming and truing, cut off the lug and finish its ends in the same way. Do the same for the others needed.

To check the accuracy of fit and total length, thread all lugs on a straight iron or steel wire *driftpin* having the same gauge thickness as the metal pin used later. Aligning two or more holes in an object by inserting a pin is termed *drifting*. This same wire driftpin is used during soldering, as described below. Assembled, the lugs appear as they will be after soldering. Defects such as space between lugs due to inaccurate end squaring can be seen and corrected. Lugs that do not fit closely together allow an undesirable looseness and eccentric, lengthwise movement of the hinge.

LUG PLACEMENT

There are various ways of placing the lugs depending on whether they are to be visible or not. If visible, they are butt ended with the flaps. If invisible, the flap or sheet metal edge must be either chamfered or cut off at the corners to an angle, or a rounded, concave depression must be made to accommodate the lugs as illustrated in the diagrams in this section.

SOLDERING THE LUGS

The lugs are soldered in alternating order to the opposite flaps. Place them in position, assembled on the iron driftpin wire mentioned. Iron or steel wire is used in the soldering operation because it has a higher melting temperature than the precious and nonferrous metals, therefore there is less chance of the solder fusing to it. For future reference, mark the position of each lug location on the flap with a *scriber*.

The biggest problem in hinge making is to prevent the flow

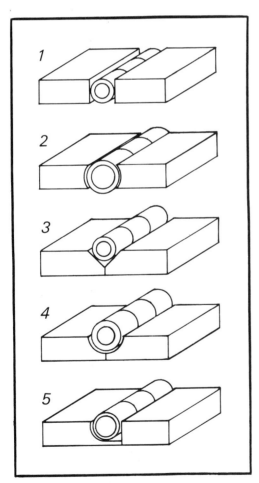

19–23 *THREE-KNUCKLE HINGES*
1. Flush hinge, squared-gap flaps, 360° hinge.
2. Flush hinge, curved profile gap flaps, 360° hinge.
3. Hidden hinge, angle-chamfer gap, 180° hinge.
4. Hidden hinge, book joint type, with curved profile gap, 180°.
5. Hidden hinge, with one gap side having curved profile horn, and the other a straight side, 180°.

of solder to unwanted places which can cause the hinge to freeze. Remove the iron driftpin, coat it with a solder inhibitor such as yellow ochre, and allow this to dry. Clean each lug and carefully coat each *end only* with yellow ochre and allow it to dry. Coat the flaps with flux and dry. The reason for drying in advance is to eliminate all mechanically combined liquid which can cause the yellow ochre to flow to unwanted places and thus make complications by preventing the flow of solder to where it *is* wanted.

Reassemble the lugs on the iron driftpin and place them according to the marked position in contact with the flaps which are now resting on a soldering surface. Leave the iron driftpin inside during soldering to assure the correct alignment of the lugs by holding them in place. If *seamed tubing* is used for lugs, place the seam in contact with the flap so it is soldered closed at the time of joining. To increase the contact area between the lug and the flap, before placing the lugs, while they are on the iron pin, run a *file* down their length to flatten one side. Put this flat side in contact with the flaps.

Dip a small minimal snippet of hard solder in flux, and dry it. Place one of these snippets in contact with *each* lug and flap, *on the side to which it is to be joined.* Avoid using too large a piece of solder which can flood the joint and freeze the hinge. With a small-size torch tip and a soft flame, slowly heat the metal to drive off any moisture in the assembly, and when all evidence of moisture disappears, add more air to point the flame. Concentrate the heat on the solder, and remove the flame as soon as the solder flows. Do not unnecessarily prolong the heat.

Allow the hinge to cool. While the pin is still in the lugs, test the movement of the hinge to see that it is operative and that the lugs have been joined. If a lug comes loose, reflux the joint and repeat the heating. If solder flows *inside* the lug, remove it with a *reamer* of appropriate size.

Before pickling, remove the iron driftpin with pliers, and scrub off the yellow ochre to avoid contaminating the pickle. Again check each lug to see if it is held securely. Small adjustments can be made with a file if needed. Should the hinge freeze with solder, it must be heated again to solder flow temperature, and the frozen parts removed. All solder is then filed away and the process repeated.

RIVETING A PERMANENT HINGE PIN

The pin used (also called a *joint pin*) should be of the same diameter as the inside of the lug. Its thickness should be not less than the thickness of the lug wall. Preferably the pin should be of the same metal as used for the work. However, high-karat gold and sterling silver are weaker for this purpose than a lower karat gold or coin or 830/1000 silver, or nickel silver pin wire. If a question of preserving the appearance of the work comes up, a head of the same metal as the work can be soldered to the pin if it is a different metal. It is also possible to use *tubing* as a pin, which then becomes a form of open rivet.

Cut the pin somewhat longer than the total length needed,

and anneal it. Hammer one end, holding the pin upright in the hinge while the other end is supported in the depression of a *dapping block* (for round-headed pins) or a *flat surface block* (for flat-headed pins). After a few blows to spread the pin end, reverse its position on the support and upset the other end in the same way. To flange out a tube rivet end, place the tube on a *round-ended dapping tool* fixed upright in a bench vise, then place another dapping tool on the opposite end and hammer straight down. This should flange both ends simultaneously. Avoid hammering the pin ends to the point where hinge movement is hindered. Test the hinge movement in stages during this process. In some circumstances, it may be convenient to first form a head on one end of the pin, or solder on a head at one end, then insert the pin and form the opposite end, as when making a rivet.

When the pin is fixed, it should not shake. If it seems loose, the pin gauge was probably too small for the inner lug diameter. There should be no play between pin and lug thickness.

THE INTEGRAL LUG

A hinge can be made by making the lug an integral extension of the flap. In this case, the metal for the lug part must be bent into a round cylindrical shape to accommodate the pin. This is done by first bending the lug ends on one flap with *round-nosed pliers* to form the initial curve. Then insert a steel rod the size of the pin to act as a mandrel, and *hammer* the lug over it to form a cylinder. Remove the rod. Repeat the process for the lug ends on the opposite flap. Assemble the hinge on the same rod and make adjustments to be sure they are lined up.

THE SPRING

The spring is a form of spiral. Spring forms exist everywhere in nature, so it is no surprise that at an early date, they were imitated and used by man. The spring is a means of storing energy. In the case of metal, this storage occurs when the metal of the spring has resilience that allows it to be stretched or compressed, and then, of its own will, to recover and return to its original shape by *elasticity.*

Springs are used in kinetic jewelry such as headdresses, combs, and brooches. When used to mount a part of an ornament, the part will move in air with the movement of the wearer. Brooches sometimes have faceted precious stones such as diamonds mounted on a spring *en tremblant,* so that with the slightest movement, they scintillate.

Springs are also used to put tension on a member in a way that is otherwise impossible, as when tensioning a wire.

19–24 JEREMY ROSS, England. Silver ring with hinged shank, and resin-filled lid with silver inserts. The ring opens to reveal two compartments, each with its own hinged lid. *Photo: Michael Goldwater*

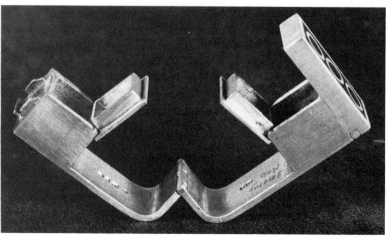

BIBLIOGRAPHIES

HISTORIC JEWELRY

ADAIR, JOHN. *The Navajo and Pueblo Silversmiths*. Norman, Oklahoma: University of Oklahoma Press, 1958.

AGRICOLA, GEORGIUS. *De Rē Metallica*. Basel, 1556. Translated by Herbert Clark Hoover and Lou Hoover, 1912. Reprint. New York: Dover Publications, 1950.

AITCHISON, LESLIE. *A History of Metals*. 2 vols. New York: Interscience Publishers, Inc., 1960; London: Macdonald and Evans, 1960.

ALEXANDER, C. *Jewelry: Art of the Goldsmith in Classical Times*. New York: The Metropolitan Museum of Art, 1928.

ALDRED, CYRIL. *Jewels of the Pharaohs: Egyptian Jewelry of the Dynastic Period*. New York: Praeger Publishers, 1971.

ANDERSON, LAWRENCE LESLIE. *The Art of the Silversmith in Mexico: 1519-1936*. New York: Hacker, 1975.

ARAI, HAKUSEKI. *The Armour Book in Honcho Gunki Ko*. Rutland, Vermont: Charles E. Tuttle Co., n.d.

ARMSTRONG, NANCY. *Jewellery: An Historical Survey of British Styles and Jewels*. Guildford and London: Lutterworth Press, 1973.

———. *Victorian Jewelry*. London: Studio Vista, 1976.

BAINBRIDGE, HENRY CHARLES. *Peter Carl Fabergé: Goldsmith and Jeweler to the Russian Imperial Court*. B. T. Batsford Ltd., 1949; London: Second Impression, Spring Books, 1967.

BAPST, G. *Histoire des joyaux de la couronne de la France*. Paris: 1889.

BARRADAS, JOSÉ PEREZ DE. *Orfebreria prehispánica de Columbia*. Bogota, Colombia: Banco de la República, 1958.

BARSALI, I. B. *Medieval Goldsmiths' Work*. London: Hamlyn, 1969; New York: Tudor, 1969.

BARTEN, SIGRID. *René Lalique: Schmuck und Objets d'Art 1890-1910*. Munich: Prestel-Verlag, 1977.

BECKER, VIVIENNE. *Antique and Twentieth Century Jewellery*. London: NAG Press Ltd., 1980.

BEDINGER, MARGERY. *Indian Silver: Navajo and Pueblo Jewelers*. Albuquerque: University of New Mexico Press, 1973.

BENITEX, JOSÉ R. *El traje y el adorno en México, 1500-1910*. Guadalajara, Mexico: Imprenta Universitaria, 1946.

BHUSHAN, JAMILA BRIJ. *Indian Jewellery, Ornaments and Decorative Designs*. Bombay: D. B. Taraporevala Sons & Co. Pvt. Ltd., 1964.

BIRINGUCCIO, NAVVOCCIO. *The Pirotechnica (De la Pirotechnica)*. Venice, 1540. English translation by Cyril Stanley Smith and Martha Teach Gnudi. The American Institute of Mining and Metallurgical Engineers, Inc., 1942.

BLACK, J. ANDERSON. *A History of Jewels*. London: Orbis Publishing, 1974.

BLAKEMORE, KENNETH. *Book of Gold*. New York: Stein and Day, 1971; London: November Books, 1971.

———. *Management for the Retail Jeweller*. London: Iliffe Books Ltd., 1973.

———. *The Retail Jeweller's Guide*. London: Iliffe Books Ltd., 1969.

BOARDMAN, JOHN and SCARISBRICK, DIANA. *The Ralph Harari Collection of Finger Rings*. London: Thames and Hudson Ltd., 1977.

BOTT, GERHARD. *Schmuck als künstlerische Aussage unserer Zeit*. Königsbach bei Pforzheim: Verlag Hans Schöner, 1971.

———. *Juwelenbuch*. Köln: Verlag Du Mont, 1972.

BOYER, MARTHA. *Mongol Jewellery*. Nationalsmuseets Skrifter, Etnografisk Raekke, Copenhagen: I Kommission Hos Gyldendalske Boghandel, Nordisk Forlag, 1952.

BRADFORD, ERNLE DUSGATE SELBY. *Contemporary Jewellery and Silver Design*. London: Heywood and Co. Ltd., 1950.

———. *Four Centuries of European Jewellery*. New York: Philosophical Library, 1953; London: Country Life, 1953.

———. *English Victorian Jewellery*. New York: Robert M. McBride Co., 1959.

BRUNEL, FRANCIS. *Jewellery of India, Five Thousand Years of Tradition*. New Delhi: National Book Trust, 1972.

BUDGE, SIR E. A. WALLIS. *Amulets and Superstitions*. London: Oxford University Press, 1930. Reprint. Dover Publications, Inc. New York, 1978.

BULGARI, C. G. *Argentieri, gemmari e orafi d'Italia*. Rome: 1958.

BURY, SHIRLEY. *Alessandro Castellani and the Revival of Granulation*. Burlington Magazine CXVII, 1975, pp. 664-68.

CARLI, ENZO. *Pre-Conquest Goldsmiths' Work of Colombia*. London: William Heinemann, Ltd., 1957.

CASTELLANI, A. *Antique Jewellery and its Revival*. London: 1862.

CELLINI, BENVENUTO. *Treatises on the Arts of Goldsmithing and Sculpture*. (Translated by C. R. Ashbee.) London: Edward Arnold, 1898; New York: Dover Publications Inc., 1967.

CELLINI, BENVENUTO. *Abhandlungen über die Goldschmiedekunst und die Bildhauerei*. (Übersetzt von Ruth und Max Fröhlich). Basel: Gewerbemuseum, n.d. (1979)

CLIFFORD, ANNE. *Cut-Steel and Berlin Iron Jewellery*. Cranbury, New Jersey: A. S. Barnes & Co., 1971.

COARELLI, FILIPPO. *Greek and Roman Jewellery*. London: Hamlyn, 1970; New York: Tudor, 1971.

COOPER, DIANA, and BATTERSHILL, NORMAN. *Victorian Sentimental Jewelry*. Cranbury, New Jersey: A. S. Barnes & Co., 1973; London: David & Charles Newton Abbot, 1972.

CURTIS, CHARLES DENSMORE. *Ancient Granulated Jewelry*. Rome: American Academy Memoirs, 1917.

Dali, Salvador: A Study in his Art-in-Jewels. (The Collection of the Owen Cheatham Foundation.) Greenwich, Connecticut: New York Graphic Society, 1965, 1970; London: Studio Books, 1959.

DAVIDSON, PATRICIA F., and HOFFMAN, HERBERT. *Greek Gold: Jewelry from the Age of Alexander*. Mainz: Philip von Zabern, 1966.

DE KERTESZ, M. WAGNER. *Historia universal de las joyas*. Buenos Aires: Ediciones Centurión, 1947.

DONGERKERY, KAMALA. *Jewelry and Personal Adornment in India*. New Delhi: Indian Council for Cultural Relations, Vikas Publications, 1971.

DUZHENKO, Y., and SMIRNOVA, E. *Treasures of the U.S.S.R. Diamond Fund.* Moscow: Iskusstvo, 1969.

EMMERICH, ANDRÉ. *Sweat of the Sun and Tears of the Moon: Gold and Silver in Pre-Columbian Art.* Seattle: University of Washington Press, 1965.

EVANS, JOAN. *A History of Jewellery: 1100–1870.* New York: Pitman Publishing Co., 1953; rev. ed. Boston: Boston Book and Art, Publisher, 1970.

———. *Magical Jewels of the Middle Ages and the Renaissance, Particularly in England.* London: Oxford University Press, 1922.

FFOULKES, CHARLES M. *The Armourer and His Craft.* New York: Benjamin Blom, 1967.

FINLAY, IAN. *Celtic Art, An Introduction.* London: Faber and Faber Ltd., 1973.

FLOWER, MARGARET. *Victorian Jewelry.* New York: Duell, Sloane & Pearce, 1951.

FOSCUE, EDWIN J. *Taxco: Mexico's Silver City.* Dallas: Southern Methodist University Press, 1947.

GALLO, M. M. *The Gold of Peru.* Recklinghausen, West Germany: Aurel Bongers, 1959.

GARSIDE, ANNE, ed. (six contributors). *Jewelry Ancient to Modern.* New York: The Viking Press, in cooperation with The Walters Art Gallery, Baltimore, 1980.

GERE, CHARLOTTE. *American & European Jewelry, 1830–1914.* New York: Crown Publishers, Inc., 1975.

GERLACH, MARTIN. *Primitive and Folk Jewelry.* 1901. Reprint. New York: Dover Publications, 1973.

GODDARD, ANDRÉ. *Le Trésor de Ziwiye.* Haarlem: 1950.

GREGORIETTI, GUIDO. *Jewelry Through the Ages.* New York: Crescent, 1969.

GREIFENHAGEN, ADOLF. *Schmuck der Alten Welt.* Berlin: Gebr. Mann Verlag, 1974.

GUNSAULUS, HELEN. *The Japanese Sword and Its Decoration.* Chicago: Field Museum of Natural History, 1924.

HACKENBROCH, YVONNE. *Renaissance Jewellery.* Munich: Verlag C. H. Beck, 1980.

HANSMANN, LISELOTTE, and KRISS-RETTENBECK, LENZ. *Amulett und Talisman: Erscheinungsform und Geschichte.* München: Verlag Georg D. W. Callwey, 1977.

HAUSEN, MARIKA (text); KIHLMAN, CHRISTER (preface). *Björn Weckström.* Helsinki: Otava, 1980.

HAWLEY, HENRY. *Fabergé and His Contemporaries.* The India Early Minshall Collection. Cleveland: The Cleveland Museum of Art, 1967.

HAYWARD, J. F. *Virtuoso Goldsmiths.* London: Sotheby Park Bernet, 1976.

HEINIGER, ERNST A., and HEINIGER, JEAN. *The Great Book of Jewels.* Lausanne: Edita S.A., 1974; Boston: New York Graphic Society, 1974.

HÉJJ-DETARI, ANGÉLA. *Hungarian Jewellery of the Past (Régi magyar ékszerek).* Budapest: Corvina Press, 1976; London: Collet's, 1965; New York: Heinemann, 1965.

HENDLEY, COLONEL THOMAS HOLBEIN. "Monograph on Indian Jewellery." In *The Journal of Indian Art,* vol. 12, nos. 95–107. London: W. Griggs & Sons, Ltd., 1909.

HIGGINS, REYNOLD ALLEYNE. *Greek and Roman Jewellery.* London: Methuen & Co., 1961; New York: Methuen/Barnes and Noble, 1962.

———. *Jewellery from Classical Lands.* London: The British Museum, 1965.

———. *Minoan and Mycenaean Art.* London: Thames and Hudson, 1967.

HINKS, PETER. *Nineteenth Century Jewellery.* London: Faber and Faber Ltd., 1975.

HOLLIS, JILL, ed. (fifteen contributors). *Princely Magnificence, Court Jewels of the Renaissance 1500–1630.* London: Debrett's Peerage Ltd. and Victoria and Albert Museum, 1980.

HOLZHAUSEN, WALTER *Goldschmiedekunst in Dresden.* Tübingen: 1966.

HORNUNG, CLARENCE. *A Source Book of Antiques and Jewelry Designs.* New York: Braziller, 1968.

HUGHES, GRAHAM. *Modern Jewelry: An International Survey, 1890–1963.* New York: Crown Publishers, 1963.

———. *Jewellery.* London: Studio Vista, 1966.

———. *The Art of Jewelry.* New York: Viking Press, 1972; London: Studio Vista, 1972.

———. *Gems and Jewellery: A Pictorial History.* Oxford: Phaidon, 1978.

JESSUP, RONALD. *Anglo-Saxon Jewellery.* New York: Frederick A. Praeger, Inc., 1953; Aylesbury, Buckinghamshire, U.K.: Shire Publications, Ltd., 1974.

KALTER, JOHANNES. *Schmuck aus Nordafrica.* Stuttgart: Linden Museum, Staatliches Museum für Völkerkunde, 1976.

KIHLMAN, CHRISTER, and HAUSEN, MARIKA. *Björn Weckström.* Helsinki: Otava, 1980.

KLEVER, KATRIN, and KLEVER, ULRICH. *Exotischer Schmuck.* Munich: Mosaik Verlag GmbH, 1977.

KUNZ, GEORGE F. *Rings for the Finger.* 1917. Reprint. New York: Dover Publications, Inc., 1973.

LAPKOVSKAYA, E. A. *Applied Art of the Middle Ages in the Collection of the State Hermitage: Metalwork.* Moscow: Iskusstvo, 1971.

LÁZLÓ, GYULA. *The Art of the Migration Period (A népvandoriáskor müvészete Magyarországon).* Budapest: Corvina Press, 1970; Miami: The University of Miami Press, 1974.

LAURVIK, J. N. *René Lalique.* New York: 1912.

LEHTINEN, ILDIKÓ. *Women's Jewelry in Central Russia and Western Siberia (Naisten Korut Keski-Venäjällä ja Länsi-Siperiassa).* Helsinki: Museovirasto, 1979. (In Finnish, with English photo captions and summary.)

LESLEY, PARKER (introduction and catalog). *Renaissance Jewels and Jeweled Objects from the Melvin Gutman Collection.* Baltimore: The Baltimore Museum of Art, 1968.

———. *Fabergé.* A Catalog of the Lillian Thomas Pratt Collection of Russian Imperial Jewels. Richmond, Virginia: Virginia Museum of Fine Arts, 1976.

LEUZINGER, E. *Wesen und Form des Schmuckes afrikanischer Völker.* Zürich: 1950.

LEWIS, M. D. S. *Antique Paste Jewellery.* London: Faber and Faber, Ltd., 1970.

LINS, P. A., and ODDY, W. A. "The Origins of Mercury Gilding," *Journal of Archeological Science II,* 1975.

MALCHENKO, M. *Art Objects in Steel by Tula Craftsmen.* Leningrad: Aurora Art Publishers, 1974.

MASON, ANITA. *An Illustrated Dictionary of Jewellery.* Reading, Berkshire, England: Osprey Publishing Ltd., 1973.

MAXWELL-HYSLOP, K. R. *Western Asiatic Jewellery, c. 3000–612 B.C.* New York: Barnes and Noble, 1971; London: Methuen, 1971.

MCCARTHY, JAMES REMINGTON. *Rings through the Ages.* New York: Harper & Brothers, 1945.

MCDONALD, DONALD. *A History of Platinum.* London: Johnson Matthey, 1960.

MEEN, V. B., and TUSHINGHAM, A. D. *Crown Jewels of Iran.* Toronto: University of Toronto Press, 1968.

MĚŘIČKA, VÁCLAV. *Orders and Decorations.* London: Paul Hamlyn, Ltd., 1967.

MOUREY, GABRIEL; VALLANCE, AYMER; FRED, W.; MORAWE, CHR. FERDINAND; KHNOPFF, F.; BROCHNER, GEORG. *Art Nouveau Jewellery and Fans.* 1903. Reprint. New York: Dover Publications Inc., 1973.

MULLER, PRISCILLA.. *Jewels in Spain, 1500–1800.* New York: Hispanic Society of America, 1972.

OMAN, CHARLES C. *British Rings, 800–1914.* Totowa, New Jersey: Rowman & Littlefield, 1974; London: B. T. Batsford, 1974.

OVED, SAH. *The Book of Necklaces.* London: Arthur Barker, 1953; Toronto: McClelland, 1953.

PACK, GRETA, AND DAVIS, MARY L. *Mexican Jewelry.* Austin: University of Texas Press, 1963.

PETRIE, SIR W. M. FLINDERS. *The Arts and Crafts of Ancient Egypt.* London: Foulis, 1909.

RACZ, ISTVAN. *Kivikirves ja Hopearisti (Stone Axe and Silver Cross).* Helsinki: Kustannusosakeyhtiö Otava, 1962. In Finnish.

RADOJKOVIĆ, BOJANA. *Jewellery with the Serbs (XII–XVIII Century).* Belgrade: Museum of Decorative Arts, 1969. Yugoslavian text, English summary.

REILING, REINHOLD. *Goldschmiedekunst-Arbeiten von 32 europäischen Goldschmieden.* Königsbach/Pforzheim: Verlag Hans Schöner, 1978.

RICKETTS, HOWARD. *Antique Gold and Enamelware in Color.* Garden City, New York: Doubleday & Co., Inc., 1971.

RITZ, GISLIND, and SCHMIDT-GLASSNER, HELGA. *Alter Bäuerlicher Schmuck.* Munich: Verlag Georg D. W. Callwey, 1979.

ROBINSON, B. W. *The Arts of the Japanese Sword.* Rutland, Vermont: Charles E. Tuttle Co., 1961.

ROGERS, FRANCES, and BEARD, ALICE. *5000 Years of Gems and Jewelry.* Philadelphia: J. B. Lippincott Co., 1947.

ROSS, HEATHER COLYER. *Bedouin Jewellery in Saudi Arabia.* London: Stacey International, 1978.

ROSS, MARVIN C. *The Art of Karl Fabergé and His Contemporaries.* Norman, Oklahoma: University of Oklahoma Press, 1965.

ROSSI, FILIPPO. *Italian Jeweled Arts.* New York: Harry N. Abrams, Inc., 1954.

RYBAKOV, B. A. *Russian Applied Art of the Tenth–Thirteenth Centuries.* Leningrad: Aurora Art Publishers, 1970.

SAVILLE, MARSHALL H. *The Goldsmith's Art in Ancient Mexico.* New York: Museum of the American Indian, Heye Foundation, 1920.

SCHOLLMAYER, KARL. *Neuer Schmuck: Ornamentum humanum.* Tübingen: Verlag Ernst Wasmuth, 1974.

SIJELMASSI, DR. MOHAMED. *Les Arts traditionnels au Maroc.* "Les Bijoux," pp. 89–125. Paris: Avenir Graphique, 1974.

SINGER, CHARLES; HOLMYARD, E. J.; and HALL, A. R. *A History of Technology.* 6 vols. London: Oxford University Press, 1954.

SITWELL, H. D. W. *The Crown Jewels and Other Royal Regalia, in the Tower of London.* London: Dropmore Press, 1953.

SIVIERO, RODOLFO. *Jewelry and Amber of the National Museum of Naples (Gli Ori e le ambre del Museo Nazionale di Napoli).* Sansoni: Sotto L'Alto Patronato della Accademia Nazionale dei Lincei, 1959; New York and London: McGraw-Hill, 1959.

SMITH, CYRIL STANLEY. *A History of Metallography: The Development of Ideas on the Structure of Metals before 1890.* Chicago: University of Chicago Press, 1960.

SNOWMAN, A. KENNETH. *The Art of Carl Fabergé.* Greenwich, Connecticut: New York Graphic Society, 1974.

———. *Carl Fabergé, Goldsmith to the Imperial Court of Russia.* London: Debrett's Peerage, Ltd., 1979.

SPRATLING, WILLIAM. "25 años de platería moderna," *Artes de México,* vol. 3, no. 10, 1955.

STEINGRÄBER, ERICH. *Antique Jewelry.* New York: Frederick A. Praeger, Inc., 1957; London: Thames and Hudson, 1957.

———. *Royal Treasures.* London: Weidenfeld and Nicolson, 1968.

SUTHERLAND, C. H. V. *Gold.* London: Thames and Hudson, 1959.

SVIRIN, A. N. *Early Russian Jewellery Work in the XI to the XVIII Centuries.* Moscow: Iskusstvo, 1972.

TURNER, RALPH. *Contemporary Jewelry, A Critical Assessment 1945–75.* London: Studio Vista, 1976.

TWINING, LORD E. F. *A History of the Crown Jewels of Europe.* London: B. T. Batsford Ltd., 1960.

———. *European Regalia.* London: Batsford, 1967.

UYLDERT, MELLIE. *Metal Magic.* Wellingborough, Northamptonshire: Turnstone Press Ltd., 1980.

VEVER, HENRI. *La Bijouterie Française au XIXe Siècle.* 63 vol. Paris: 1904–8.

VILIMKOVA, MILADA. *Egyptian Jewelry.* New York: Tudor Publishing Co., 1970; London: Paul Hamlyn, 1970.

VON HABSBURG-LOTHRINGEN, GEZA. *Fabergé, Court Jeweler to the Tsars.* London: Studio Vista/Christie's, 1979.

WARNER, O. *The Crown Jewels.* London: Penguin Books, 1951.

WHEELER, R. *The Cheapside Horde.* London: Lancaster House, 1928.

WILCOX, DONALD J. *New Design in Jewelry.* New York: Van Nostrand Reinhold Company, 1970.

———. *Body Jewellery.* London: Pitman Publishing, 1974.

WILKERSON, ALIX. *Ancient Egyptian Jewellery.* London: Methuen, 1971; New York: Methuen/Barnes & Noble, 1971.

WILLSBERGER, JOHANN. *Gold.* Garden City, New York: Doubleday & Co., Inc., 1976.

JEWELRY TECHNOLOGY

ABBEY, STATON. *The Goldsmith's and Silversmith's Handbook.* London: Technical Press Ltd., 1952; New York: W. S. Heinman, 1968.

ALLEN, B. M. *Soldering Handbook.* New York: Drake Publishers, 1970.

ASHLEY, CLIFFORD W. *The Ashley Book of Knots.* New York: Doubleday, Doran & Company, 1947; London: Faber and Faber Ltd., 1947; reprinted 1979.

BARBER, CLIFFORD L. *Solder: Its Fundamentals and Usage.* Chicago: Kester Solder Company, Third Division, 1965.

BEALER, ALEX W. *The Art of Blacksmithing.* New York: Funk & Wagnalls, 1969.

BLUM, WILLIAM, and HOGABOOM, GEORGE. *Principles of Electroplating and Electroforming.* New York: McGraw-Hill Book Co., 1949.

BOVIN, MURRAY. *Jewelry Making for Schools, Tradesmen, Craftsmen.* Forest Hills, New York: Murray Bovin, 1953.

———. *Silversmithing and Art Metal for Schools, Tradesmen, Craftsmen.* Forest Hills, New York: Murray Bovin, 1963; Revised 1979.

———. *Centrifugal or Lost-Wax Casting for Schools, Tradesmen, Craftsmen.* Forest Hills, New York: Murray Bovin, 1973.

BOWMAN, JOHN J., and HARDY, R. ALLEN. *The Jewelry Engraver's Manual.* Princeton, New Jersey: D. Van Nostrand Company, 1954.

BRANSON, OSCAR T. *Indian Jewelry Making.* Tucson, Arizona: Treasure Chest Publications Inc., 1977.

BRAUN-FELDWEG, WILHELM. *Metal Design and Technique.* New York: Van Nostrand Reinhold Co., 1975.

BREPOHL, ERHARD. *Theorie und Praxis des Goldschmieds.* Leipzig: VEB Fachbuchverlag, 1978.

BRITTAIN, A.; WOLPERT, S.; and MORTON, P. *Engraving on Precious Metals.* 1958. Reprint. London: N. A. G. Press Ltd., 1973.

BRYNNER, IRENA. *Modern Jewelry: Design and Technique.* New York: Van Nostrand Reinhold Co., 1968.

CHOATE, SHARR. *Creative Casting: Jewelry, Silverware, Sculpture.* New York: Crown Publishers, 1966.

———. *Creative Gold and Silversmithing: Jewelry, Decorative Metalcraft.* New York: Crown Publishers, 1970.

CLARK, CARL D. *Molding and Casting: Its Technique and Application.* Butler, Maryland: Standard Arts Press, 1972.

COYNE, JOHN, ed. *The Penland School of Crafts Book of Jewelry Making.* New York: Bobbs-Merrill, 1975.

CUZNER, BERNARD. *Goldsmith's Handbook.* London: Technical Press, 1936.

———. *A Silversmith's Manual.* London: N. A. G. Press Ltd., 1958.

DIPASQUALE, DOMINIC; DELIUS, JEAN; and ECKERSLEY, THOMAS. *Jewelry Making: An Illustrated Guide to Technique.* Englewood Cliffs, New Jersey: Prentice-Hall, Inc., 1975.

EDWARDS, KEITH. *Lost Wax Casting of Jewelry.* Chicago: Henry Regnery Co., 1975.

FEIRER, JOHN. *General Metals.* New York: McGraw-Hill Book Co., 1967.

———. *Machine Tool Metalworking: Principles and Practices.* New York: McGraw-Hill Book Co., 1973.

FIELD, SAMUEL, and BONNEY, SAMUEL R. *The Chemical Coloring of Metals.* London: Chapman & Hall, 1925.

Finishing Handbook and Directory. Published annually by Product Finishing, Sawell Publications, London.

FISCH, ARLINE M. *Textile Techniques in Metal.* New York: Van Nostrand Reinhold Company, 1975.

FISCHER, JOHANNES, and WEIMER, DENNIS. *Precious Metal Plating.* New York: International Publications Service, 1964.

FISHLOCK, DAVID. *Metal Coloring.* New York: International Publications Service, 1962.

FORBES, R. J. *Metallurgy in Antiquity.* Studies in Ancient Technology, vols. 8 and 9. New York: W. S. Heinman, 1971–72.

FRANKE, LOIS E. *Handwrought Jewelry.* Bloomington, Illinois: McKnight and McKnight Publishing Co., 1962.

FURNESS, R. W., and DRAPER, R. *The Practice of Plating on Plastics.* Teddington: Robert Draper Ltd., 1968.

GARRISON, WILLIAM E., and DOWDE, MERLE E. *Handcrafting Jewelry: Designs and Techniques.* Chicago: Henry Regnery, 1972.

GEHRING, OSCAR. *Josef Wilm, der Gold und Silberschmied.* Verlag Gold und Silber; New York: Stechert-Hafner, Inc.

GENTILLE, THOMAS. *Step-by-Step Jewelry: A Complete Introduction to the Craft of Jewelry.* New York: Golden Press, 1968.

GOODEN, ROBERT, and POPHAM, PHILIP. *Silversmithing.* London: Oxford University Press, 1971.

Guide to Dental Material and Devices. 6th ed. Chicago: American Dental Association, 1972–1973.

HACK, JOHN. *Metal: Designs, Material, Technique.* New York: Van Nostrand Reinhold Co., 1972.

HARDY, R. ALLEN, and BOWMAN, JOHN J. *The Jewelry Repair Manual.* New York: Van Nostrand Reinhold Company, 1956.

HIORNS, ARTHUR H. *Metal Coloring and Bronzing.* London: Macmillan and Co., 1920.

HOLLANDER, HARRY B. *Plastics for Jewelry.* New York: Watson-Guptill Publications, 1974.

HOLMSTROM, J. G. *Modern Blacksmithing.* New York: Drake Publishers, 1970.

HORTH, A. C. *Repoussé Metalwork.* London: Methuen and Co., 1905.

JARVIS, CHARLES A. *Jewellery Manufacture and Repair.* London: N. A. G. Press Ltd., 1978.

KRONQUIST, EMIL F. *Metalwork for Craftsmen.* New York: Dover Publications, Inc., 1972.

LIDDICOAT, RICHARD, JR., and COPELAND, L. L. *Jeweller's Manual.* Los Angeles: Gemmological Institute of America, 1967.

LINICK, LESLIE L. *Jeweller's Workshop Practices.* Chicago: Henry Paulson & Co., 1948.

MARYON, HERBERT, F.S.A. *Metalwork and Enameling.* 3rd ed. New York: Dover Publications, Inc., 1971.

MERIEL-BUSSY, YVES. *Embossing of Metal Repoussage.* New York: Sterling Publishing Co., 1970.

Metal Finishing Guidebook and Directory. Published annually by Metals and Plastics Publications, Inc. One University Plaza, Hackensack, New Jersey 07601, U.S.A.

MEYEROWITZ, PATRICIA. *Jewelry and Sculpture through Construction.* New York: Van Nostrand Reinhold Co., 1967; London: Studio Vista, 1967.

MORTON, PHILIP. *Contemporary Jewelry: A Studio Handbook.* Rev. ed. New York: Holt, Rinehart & Winston, 1976.

MURPHY, J. A., ed. *Surface Preparation and Finishes for Metals.* New York: McGraw-Hill, 1971.

NEWMAN, JAY HARTLEY, and NEWMAN, LEE SCOTT. *Plastics for the Craftsman: Basic Techniques for working with Plastics.* New York: Crown Publishers, 1973.

———. *Electroplating and Electroforming for Artists and Craftsmen.* New York: Crown Publishers Inc., 1980.

———. *Wire Art.* New York: Crown Publishers, Inc., 1975.

OLLARD, E. A. *Elementary Science for Electroplating Students and Foreman.* Teddington: Robert Draper Ltd., 1969.

PACK, GRETA. *Chains and Beads.* New York: Van Nostrand Reinhold Co., 1951.

———. *Jewelry and Enameling.* New York: Van Nostrand Reinhold Co., 1953.

———. *Jewelry Making for the Beginning Craftsman.* New York: Van Nostrand Reinhold Co., 1957.

———. *Jewelry Making by the Lost Wax Process.* Rev. ed. New York: Van Nostrand Reinhold Co., 1975.

RAPSON, W. S., and GROENEWALD, T. *Gold Usage.* London: Academic Press, 1978.

RICHARDSON, M. T. *Practical Blacksmithing.* 4 vols. 1889–1891. Reprint (4 vols. in 1). New York: Weathervane Books, 1978.

ROSE, AUGUSTUS F., and CIRINO, ANTONIO. *Jewelry Making and Design.* Worcester: Davis Press, 1949. New York: Dover Publications, Inc., 1967.

ROSE, T. K. *The Precious Metals.* London: Constable and Co., 1910.

SAX, N. IRVING. *Dangerous Properties of Industrial Materials.* 4th ed. New York: Van Nostrand Reinhold Co., 1975.

SEPPÄ, HEIKKI. *Form Emphasis for Metalsmiths.* Kent, Ohio: The Kent State University Press, 1978.

SJOBERG, JAN, and SJOBERG, OVE. *Working with Copper, Silver, Enamel.* New York: Van Nostrand Reinhold Co., 1974.

SMERDJIEV, S. *Metal-to-Metal Adhesive Bonding.* Boston: Cahners Publishing Co., 1970.

SMITH, ERNEST A. *Working in Precious Metals.* 1933. Reprint. London: N. A. G. Press Ltd., 1978.

SOLBERG, RAMONA. *Inventive Jewelry-Making.* New York: Van Nostrand Reinhold Co., 1972.

SPIRO, PETER. *Electroforming.* New York: International Publications Service, 1971.

STEAKLEY, DOUGLAS. *Holloware Techniques: Basic Methods for Making Three-Dimensional Objects in Metal.* New York: Watson-Guptill Publications, 1980.

STOREY, MICKEY. *Centrifugal Casting as a Jewelry Process.* Scranton, Pennsylvania: International Text Book Educational Publishers, 1963.

Symposium on Electroforming, Application, Uses and Properties of Electroformed Metals. Philadelphia: American Society for Testing and Materials, 1962.

The Marking of Precious Metals: A Guide to Markings and Descriptions Used in the Jewelry Trade. Jewelers Vigilance Committee, 45 West 45th Street, New York, New York, n.d.

THEOPHILUS PRESBYTER (Roger of Helmarshausen). *Schedula Diversarium Artium (On Diverse Arts).* A 12th-century treatise, translated by John C. Hawthorne and Cyril Stanley Smith. Chicago: The University of Chicago Press, 1963.

THOMAS, RICHARD. *Metalsmithing for the Artist-Craftsman.* New York: Chilton Company, Book Division, 1960.

TRESKOW, ELISABETH. *Geschichte, Kunst und Technik der Granulation.* (Diebeners Goldschmiede-Jahrbuch 1959), Stuttgart: Verlag Diebener, 1959.

TYLECOTE, R. F. *A History of Metallurgy.* London: Metals Society, 1976.

UNTRACHT, OPPI. *Enameling on Metal.* Radnor, Pennsylvania: Chilton Company, Book Division, 1957.

———. *Metal Techniques for Craftsmen.* Garden City, New York: Doubleday & Co., Inc., 1968; London: Robert Hale Ltd., 1968.

VON FRAUNHOFER, J. A. *Basic Metal Finishing.* New York: Chemical Publishing Co., Inc., 1976; London: Paul Elek (Scientific Books) Ltd., 1976.

VON NEUMAN, ROBERT. *The Design and Creation of Jewelry.* Rev. ed. Radnor, Pennsylvania: Chilton Company, Book Division, 1972.

WALKING, W. P. *Pantograph Engraving.* Kansas City: Privately published, 1975.

WEINER, LOUIS. *Hand Made Jewelry.* New York: Van Nostrand Co., 1948.

WESTBURY, E. T. *Metal Turning Lathes: Their Design, Applica-*

tion and Operation. New York: International Publications Service, 1968.

WEYGERS, ALEXANDER G. *The Making of Tools.* New York: Van Nostrand Co., 1973.

——. *The Modern Blacksmith.* New York: Van Nostrand Co., 1974.

WIGLEY, THOMAS B. *The Art of the Goldsmith and Jeweller.* London: Charles Griffin & Co., 1898.

WILSON, HARRY. *Silverwork and Jewellery: A Textbook for Students and Workers in Metal.* 1902. Reprint. London: Sir Isaac Pitman and Sons, 1951.

WINEBRENNER, D. KENNETH. *Jewelry-Making as an Art Expression.* Scranton, Pennsylvania: International Textbook Co., 1953.

WINSTON, BOB, and WINSTON, GINA. *Cast Away.* Scottsdale, Arizona: Shelfhouse Publications, 1975.

YEATES, R. L. *Electroplating: A Survey of Principles and Practice.* New York: International Publications, 1971.

LAPIDARY; MINERALOGY; AND GEMOLOGY

ANDERSON, B. W. *Gem Testing.* London: The Butterworth Group, Iliffe Books, 1971; Buchanan, New York: Emerson Books, 1948; New York: Van Nostrand Reinhold Co., 1971.

AREM, JOEL E. *Color Encyclopedia of Gemstones.* New York: Van Nostrand Reinhold Co., 1977.

BALEJ, RONALD J. *Tumbler's Guide.* Minneapolis: Minnesota Lapidary Supplies Inc., 1963.

——. *Gemcutter's Guide.* Minneapolis: Minnesota Lapidary Supplies Inc., 1963.

BALL, SYDNEY. *A Roman Book on Precious Stones.* Los Angeles: Gemological Institute of America, 1950.

BANK, H. *Precious Stones and Minerals.* London: Fredk. Warne and Co. Ltd., 1970.

BAXTER, WILLIAM T. *Jewelry, Gem Cutting and Metal-Craft.* New York: McGraw-Hill Book Co., 1950.

BAUER, MAX. *Precious Stones.* New York: Dover Publications Inc., 1968.

BLAKEY, GEORGE G. *The Diamond.* New York and London: Paddington Press Ltd., 1977.

BOARDMAN, JOHN. *Archaic Greek Gems.* Evanston, Illinois: Northwestern University Press, 1968.

BUCHESTER, K. J. *The Australian Gemhunter's Guide.* Sydney: Ure-Smith, 1967.

CAMPBELL, IAN, and COURT, ARTHUR. *Minerals: Nature's Fabulous Jewels.* New York: Harry N. Abrams, 1974.

CROW, W. B. *Precious Stones: Their Occult Powers and Hidden Significance.* London: Aquarian Publishing Co., 1968; New York: Weiser, 1968.

DANIEL, G. L. *Tumbling Techniques.* Gordon's, 1810 E. Anaheim Street, Long Beach, California 90801.

DE MICHELE, VINCENZO. *The World of Minerals.* New York: Crown Publishers, 1973.

DESAUTELS, PAUL E. *The Mineral Kingdom.* New York: Grosset and Dunlap, 1968.

——. *Gems in the Smithsonian Museum.* Washington, D.C.: Smithsonian Institution Press, 1972.

——. *Collector's Series: Rocks and Minerals.* New York: Grosset and Dunlap, 1974.

DICKINSON, JOAN YOUNGER. *The Book of Pearls.* New York: Crown Publishers Inc., 1968.

——. *Book of Diamonds, Their History and Romance.* New York: Bonanza Books, 1975.

EICHLER, F., and KRIS, E. *Die Kameen im Kunsthistorischen Museum.* Vienna: 1927.

EVANS, I. O. *Rocks, Minerals and Gemstones.* Feltham, England: Hamlyn, 1972.

EYLES, WILFRED CHARLES. *The Book of Opals.* Rutland, Vermont: Charles E. Tuttle Co., 1954.

FENTON, CARROLL LANE, and FENTON, MILDRED ADAMS. *The Fossil Book.* Garden City, New York: Doubleday & Co., 1958.

FIRSOFF, V. A. *Working with Gemstones.* Newton Abbot, England: David & Charles, 1974; New York: Arco Publishing Co., 1974.

FISHER, P. J. *Jewels.* London: Batsford, 1965.

Gemstones of the United States. Catalog I 19.3:1042-G. Washington, D.C.: U. S. Government Printing Office.

GOITIEN, G. D. *Letters from Indian Merchants.* Berkeley: University of California, 1974.

GROSZINSKI, PAUL. *Diamond Technology.* London: N. A. G. Press, 1953.

GÜBELIN, EDVARD J. *The Internal World of Gemstones.* Zürich: ABC Edition, 1974.

GUMP, RICHARD. *Jade: Stone of Heaven.* Garden City, New York: Doubleday & Co., Inc., 1962.

KAGAN, JU. *Western European Cameos in the Hermitage Collection.* Leningrad: Aurora Art Publishers, 1973.

KRAUS, E. M., and SLAWSON, C. B. *Gems and Gem Materials.* New York and London: McGraw-Hill, 1947.

KUNZ, GEORGE FREDERICK. *Gems and Precious Stones of North America.* New York: Dover Publications, Inc., 1968.

——. *The Curious Lore of Precious Stones.* New York: J. B. Lippincott Co., Reprinted New York: Dover Publications, Inc., 1971.

LENZEN, GODELHARD. *History of Diamond Production and the Diamond Trade.* London: Barrie and Jenkins, 1970.

LEWIS, M. D. S. *Antique Paste Jewellery.* London: Faber and Faber, 1970.

LIDDICOAT, RICHARD T, JR. *Handbook of Gem Identification.* Los Angeles: Gemological Institute of America, 11940 San Vicente Blvd., Los Angeles, California, 1969.

MARTYNOVA, M. V. *Precious Stone in Russian Jewelry Art in XIIth–XVIIIth Centuries.* Moscow: Iskusstvo, 1973.

NEVEROV, O. *Antique Intaglios in the Hermitage Collection.* Leningrad: Aurora Art Publishers, 1976.

NOTT, STANLEY CHARLES. *Chinese Jade Throughout the Ages.* Rutland, Vermont: Charles E. Tuttle Co., 1962.

ORCHARD, WILLIAM C. *Beads and Beadwork of the American Indians.* New York: Museum of the American Indian, Heye Foundation, 1929.

OSBORNE, DUFFIELD. *Engraved Gems: Signets, Talismans, and Ornamental Intaglios, Ancient and Modern.* New York: Henry Holt and Co., 1912.

QUICK, LELAND; LEIPER, HUGH. *Gemcraft: How to Cut and Polish Gemstones.* Radnor, Pennsylvania: Chilton Book Co., 1975.

——. *The Book of Agates and Other Quartz Gems.* Radnor, Pennsylvania: Chilton Book Co., 1963.

RAPP, GEORGE R., JR.; ROBERTS, WILLARD; and WEBER, JULIUS. *Encyclopedia of Minerals.* New York: Van Nostrand Reinhold Co., 1974.

RIBAKOVA, B. A. *Treasures of the USSR Diamond Fund.* Moscow: Iskusstvo, 1975.

REESE, NADINE. *Cultured Pearl.* Rutland, Vermont: Tuttle Press, 1959.

RICHTER, GISELA. *Engraved Gems of the Greeks, Etruscans and Romans.* London: Phaidon, 1968; New York: Phaidon/Praeger, 1968.

RITCHIE, CARSON I. A. *Modern Ivory Carving.* Cranbury, New Jersey: A. S. Barnes, 1972.

————. *Carving Shells and Cameos*. London: Arthur Barker, 1953.

SCARFE, HERBERT. *Cutting and Setting Stones*. New York: Watson-Guptill Publications, 1972; London: B. T. Batsford, 1972.

SCHEDEL, JOSEPH. *The Splendor of Jade: 4,000 Years of the Art of Chinese Jade Carving*. New York: E. P. Dutton & Co., 1974.

SCHUBNEL, HENRI-JEAN. *Pierres précieuses dans le monde*. Paris: Horizons de France, 1972.

SHIPLEY, ROBERT M. *Dictionary of Gems and Gemology*. Los Angeles: Gemological Institute of America, 1951.

————. *Famous Diamonds of the World*. Los Angeles: Gemological Institute of America, 1955.

SINKANKAS, JOHN. *Standard Catalog of Gems*. New York: D. Van Nostrand Co. Inc., 1968.

————. *Gem Cutting: A Lapidary's Manual*. New York: D. Van Nostrand Co. Inc., 1955, 1962.

————. *Gemstone and Mineral Data Book*. New York: Macmillan Publishing Co., 1974.

SMITH, G. F. HERBERT. *Gemstones*. London: Methuen, 1952; revised edition, London: Chapman and Hall, 1973; New York: Pitman Publishing Corp., 1973.

SPERISEN, FRANCIS J. *The Art of the Lapidary*. Milwaukee: The Bruce Publishing Company, 1950, 1961.

STURZAKER, JAMES. *Gemstones and their Occult Powers*. London: Metatron Publications, 1977.

SUTHERLAND, B. B. *The Romance of Seals and Engraved Gems*. New York and London: Macmillan, 1965.

THOMAS, WILLIAM, and PAVITT, KATE. *The Book of Talismans, Amulets and Zodiacal Gems*. 1914. Reprint. London: The Aquarian Press, 1970.

TOLANSKY, S. *The History and Use of Diamonds*. London: Methuen & Co. Ltd., 1962.

WAINWRIGHT, JOHN. *Discovering Lapidary Work*. London: Mills & Boon Limited, 1971.

WEBSTER, ROBERT. *Gemologists Compendium*. New York: Henry Paulson & Co., 1947; London: N. A. G. Press, 1970.

————. *Practical Gemology*. Los Angeles: Gemological Institute of America, 1952.

————. *Gems: Their Sources, Descriptions and Identification*. 2 vols. London: Butterworths, 1962; New York: Anchor Books, 1970.

————. *Gems in Jewellery*. London: N. A. G. Press, 1975.

WEINSTEIN, MICHAEL. *The World of Jewel Stones*. New York: Sheridan, 1958.

WERTZ, ED, and WERTZ, LEOLA. *Handbook of Gemstone Carving*. Mentone, California: Gembooks, n.d.

WILLEMS, J. DANIEL. *Gem Cutting*. Peoria, Illinois: Manual Arts Press, 1948.

WILSON, DEREK, and AYERST, P. *White Gold. The Story of African Ivory*. New York: Taplinger, 1976.

WOLLASTON, TULLY CORNTHWAITE. *Opal: The Gem of the Never Never*. London: Thomas Murby & Co., 1924.

ZUCKER, BENJAMIN. *How to Buy and Sell Gems*. New York: Times Books, 1979.

EXHIBITION CATALOGS AND HANDBOOKS ON JEWELRY

ARMSTRONG, E. C. R. *Catalogue of Irish Gold Ornaments in the Collection of the Royal Irish Academy*. 2d ed. Dublin: 1933.

BARSNESS, JOHN C. *Photographing Crafts*. New York: American Crafts Council, 1974.

BOTT, GERHARD, and CITROËN, K. *Jugendstil; Sammlung K. A. Citroën, Kunsthandwerk um 1900*. Darmstadt: Hessisches Landesmuseum, 1962.

BRAY, WARWICK. *The Gold of El Dorado*. (Catalog: The Royal Academy, Piccadilly.) London: Times Newspapers Ltd., 1978.

BRUCE-MITFORD, RUPERT. *The Sutton Hoo Ship-Burial, A Handbook*. 2d ed. London: The Trustees of the British Museum, 1972.

CASO, A. "Lapidary work, Goldwork and Copperwork from Oaxaca," in G. R. Willey (ed.), *Handbook of Middle American Indians*. Austin, Texas: 1965.

CHAMPAULT, D., and VERBRUGGE, A. R. *La Main*. Paris: Catalogues du Musée de l'Homme, 1965.

Christie, Manson & Woods, Ltd., London, New York, Beverly Hills, Montreal, etc. *Illustrated catalogs of jewelry auctions*.

Contemporary Southern Plains Indian Metalwork. Indian Arts and Crafts Board, U.S. Department of the Interior in cooperation with the Oklahoma Indian Arts and Crafts Cooperative, 1976.

DALTON, O. M. *Catalogue of the Finger Rings*. London: Franks Bequest, British Museum, 1912.

————. *Catalogue of the Engraved Gems of the Post-classical Periods in the British Museum*. London, 1915.

Diebener's Handbuch des Goldschmieds. Bands 1–5. Stuttgart: Rule-Diebener-Verlag K.G., 1963.

El Dorado: Goldschätze aus Kolumbien, Kunstwerke der Indios aus dem Goldmuseum, Bogotá. Basel: Schweizerischer Bankverein, 1975.

Fabergé, Goldsmith to the Russian Imperial Court. San Francisco: M. H. De Young Memorial Museum, 1964.

FIROUZ, I. A. *Silver Ornaments of the Turkoman*. Teheran, 1978.

From the Lands of the Scythians. Ancient treasures from the Museums of the U.S.S.R., 3000 B.C.–100 B.C. New York: The Metropolitan Museum of Art Bulletin, Volume XXXII, Number 5, 1975.

FUJIWARA, KAKUICHI. *Nihon no Musubi (Japanese Knotwork)*. Tokyo: Tsukigi Shokan, 1974. (In Japanese, illustrated with 629 sets of line drawings)

GABUS, JEAN. "Contributions a l'Étude des Touaregs." Neuchatel, 1972.

GEE, GEORGE E. *The Practical Gold Worker*. London: Crosby, Lockwood and Son, 1877.

————. *The Goldsmiths' Handbook*. London: Crosby, Lockwood and Son, 1903.

————. *Silversmiths' Handbook*. 5th ed. London: Crosby, Lockwood and Son, 1921.

GETTY, NILDA C. FERNÁNDEZ, and FORSYTH, ROBERT J. *Contemporary Crafts of the Americas: 1975*. Chicago: Henry Regnery Co., 1975.

Goldschätze der Thraker; Thrakische Kultur und Kunst auf bulgarischen Boden. Wein: Österreichisches Museum für angewandte Kunst, 1975.

HACKENS, TONY. *Catalogue of the Classical Collection, Classical Jewelry*. Providence, Rhode Island: Museum of Art, Rhode Island School of Design, 1976.

HARTMANN, GÜNTHER. *Silberschmuck der Araukaner, Chile*. Berlin: Staatliche Museen Preussischer Kulturbesitz, Museum für Völkerkunde, 1974.

HEIGL, CURT. *Gold + Silber, Schmuck + Gerät von Albrecht Dürer bis zur Gegenwart*. München: Verlag Karl M. Lipp, 1971.

HIGGINS, REYNOLD. *Jewellery from Classical Lands*. The Trustees of the British Museum, Oxford: The University Press, 1965.

HÖPFNER, GERD, and HAASE, GESINE. *Metallschmuck aus Indien*.

Berlin: Staatliche Museen Preussischer Kulturbesitz, Museum für Völkerkunde, 1978.
International Jewellery Arts Exhibition, Tokyo Triennial. Japan Jewellery Designer Association (Nihon Keizai Shimbun), Catalogs published for the years 1970, 1973, 1976, and *The 4th Tokyo Triennial, '79.*
Jeweller's Art of Peoples of Russia, USSR 1973. Catalog of the State Museum of Folk Art of the USSR. Leningrad, 1974.
JONES, J. "Gold and the New World" and "Pre-Columbian Gold," in *El Dorado, The Gold of Ancient Colombia.* Bogotá: 1974.
KALTER, J. *Orientalischer Volksschmuck.* (Ausstellungskatalog.) Stuttgart: Linden Museum, 1979.
Later Prehistoric Antiquities of the British Isles. London: The Trustees of the British Museum, 1953.
Le Bijou 1900. Hotel Solvay, Brussels: 1965.
Lists of Publications. National Bureau of Standards, U.S. Department of Commerce, Washington, D.C.
MENZEL, BRIGITTE. *Goldgewichte aus Ghana.* Berlin: Staatliche Museen Preussischer Kulturbesitz, Museum für Völkerkunde, 1968.
Metals Handbook. The American Society for Metals, Metals Park, Novelty, Ohio, 1960.
MAY, F. *Silberschmuck aus der Sammlung Fraschina.* Bern: 1961/2.
Merovingische Kunst. Brussels: Koninklijke Musea voor Kunst en Geschiedenis, 1954.
Modern Jewellery in Japan. Japan Jewellery Designer Association Exhibition at Wako, Ginza, Tokyo. Tokyo: Reine Publishing Co. Ltd., 1978.
MORAN, LOIS, et al. *Contemporary Crafts Market Place.* American Crafts Council, New York and London: R. R. Bowker Co., 1975.
O'CONNOR, HAROLD. *New Directions in Goldsmithing, A Workshop Guide.* Crested Butte, Colorado: Dunconor Books, 1975.
———. *The Jeweler's Bench Reference.* Crested Butte, Colorado: Dunconor Books, 1977.
OMAN, CHARLES L. *Catalogue of the Rings.* London: Victoria and Albert Museum, 1930.
ROSSI, A. *Oreficeria popolare italiana.* Catalogo Mostra al Museo dello Arte e Tradizioni Populari, Roma: 1964.
Schatzkammer der Residenz: *Führer durch die Schatzkammer der Residenz.*, München: 1931.
Schmuck aus Zentralasien: Sammlung Inge Prokot. Köln: Museum für Ostasiatische Kunst; Pforzheim: Schmuckmuseum; Hanau: Deutsches Goldschmiedehaus, 1980.
Schmuckmuseum, Pforzheim Reuchlinhaus, Catalogs:
Schmuck aus dem Schmuckmuseum Pforzheim. 1971.
Friedrich Becker. 1972.
Schmuck 73- Tendenzen. 1973.
Claus Bury: Schmuck Zeichnungen objecte. 1974.
Schmuck aus Stahl. 1974.

Schmuck 75- Tendenzen, 1975.
Schmuck 77- Tendenzen, 1977.
Bezalel Academy Jerusalem, 1978.
SNAG, 1979.
Therese Hilbert, 1979.
Otto Künzli, 1979.
Email, 1980.
Schmuckmuseum Pforzheim, Von der Antike bis zur Gegenwart, 1980.
Zeitgenössischer Schmuck aus Polen, 1980.
SCHULER-SCHÖMIG, IMMINA. *Werke Indianischer Goldschmiedekunst.* Berlin: Staatliche Museen Preussischer Kulturbesitz, Museum für Völkerkunde, 1972.
SELLING, GÖSTA, et al. *Golden Age and Viking Art in Sweden.* Historiska Museet, Stockholm: 1964.
SELWYN, A. *Retail Jeweler's Handbook.* New York: Chemical Publishing Co., 1955.
SHIPLEY, ROBERT M. *Jeweler's Pocket Reference Book.* Los Angeles: Gemological Institute of America, 1950.
SKUBIC, PETER, et al. *Schmuck International 1900–1980.* Wien. Künstlerhaus, 1980.
Sotheby & Co., London; Sotheby Parke Bernet Inc., New York, Los Angeles, etc. Illustrated catalogs of jewelry auctions.
TAIT, HUGH. *Jewellery through 7000 Years.* Catalogue published for The Trustees of the British Museum. London: British Museum Publications Ltd., 1976.
TAIT, HUGH, and GERE, CHARLOTTE. *The Jeweller's Art, An Introduction to the Hull Grundy Gift to the British Museum.* London: British Museum Publications Ltd., 1978.
TAYLOR, GERALD, and SCARISBRICK, DIANA. *Finger Rings from Ancient Egypt to the Present Day.* London: Lund Humphries, for the Ashmolean Museum, Oxford, and The Worshipful Company of Goldsmiths, London, 1978.
The Art of Peter Carl Fabergé. New York: A La Vielle Russie, Inc., 1961.
The Diamond Dictionary. Los Angeles: Gemological Institute of America, 1977.
The Jewelry of Margaret de Patta: A Retrospective Exhibition. Oakland, California: The Oakland Museum: Oakes Gallery, 1976.
The Worshipful Company of Goldsmiths, London. Catalogues:
International Exhibition of Modern Jewellery 1890–1961. 1961.
Omar Ramsden, 1873–1939. 1973.
Seven Golden Years. 1974.
Explosion (650th Anniversary of the Goldsmiths' Company). 1977.
Loot and Superloot. 1979.
Others.
U.S. Bureau of Standards, Washington, D.C. Publications.
U.S. Bureau of Mines, Washington, D.C. Publications.
VOLBACH, W. F. *Monili dell' Asia dal Caspio all' Himalaya.* Catalogo mostra a Palazzo Brancaccio, Roma: 1963.

PERIODICALS

Jewelry

American Craft (Formerly *Craft Horizons*). American Craft Council, 22 West 55th Street, New York, New York 10019. (Bi-Monthly)
American Horologist and Jeweler. Robert Publishing Co., P.O. Box 7127, Capitol Hill Station, Denver, Colorado. (Monthly)
American Jewelry Manufacturer. The Manufacturing Jewelers

and Silversmiths of America Inc., 1271 Avenue of the Americas, New York, New York 10020.
Apollo. 22 Davies Street, London W1Y ILH. (Occasional articles on jewelry)
Arte y Joya. Revista Professional Española de Joyeria, Relojeria, Orfebreria, Artes Suntuarias, Artesania y Bisuteria. Printed by Instituto Grafico Para Publicidad, Trabajo 125,

Barcelona, Spain; Administration y Publicidad: Rosellón, 362, Barcelona 13, Spain. (Bi-Monthly)

Aurum, The International Technical Revue for Jewellery Manufacturers and Goldsmiths. The Technical Advisory Service of the International Gold Corporation Ltd., P.O. Box 445, CH-1211, Geneva 1, Switzerland. (Quarterly)

Bijou. Suite 205, 2950 Masson Street, East; Montreal, Quebec, Canada H1Y1X4. (Monthly)

British Jeweller and Watchbuyer. St. Dunstan's House, Carey Lane, London EC2V 8AA. (Monthly)

Buyer's Guide. Published by the British Jeweler and Watchbuyer for the British Jeweller's Association and the British Wholesale Jeweller's Association, St. Dunstan's House, Carey Lane, London EC2V 8AA.

Canadian Jeweler. 481 University Avenue, Toronto, Ontario, Canada M5W1A7. (Monthly)

Casting and Jewelry Craft. Allan Publications Inc., 507 Fifth Avenue, New York, New York 10017. (Bi-Monthly)

Commonwealth Jeweller and Watchmaker. Sydney, Australia.

Crafts. Crafts Council, 8 Waterloo Place, London SW1Y 4AU. (Six times a year: January, March, May, July, September, and November)

Craft Australia. Crafts Council of Australia,. 27 King Street, Sydney 2000, Australia.

Deutche Goldschmiede-Zeitung. Rühle-Diebener Verlag, Stuttgart, Olgastrasse 110, West Germany.

18 Karati. Rivista Italiana di Arte Orafa e Moda. Viale Stefini 3, 20125 Milano, Italia. (Bi-Monthly)

Europe Star. P.O. Box 4021211, Geneva 11, Switzerland. (Bi-Monthly)

Four Seasons of Jewelry (Hoseki No Shiki). Jewelry Journal Co., Ltd. 44-7, Hongo 3 Chome, Bunkyo-Ku, Tokyo, Japan. (Bi-Monthly)

Gold und Silber, Uhren und Schmuck. Konradin-Verlag Robert Kohlhammer GmbH, Postfach 625, 7 Stuttgart 1, West Germany. (Monthly)

Goldschmiede-Zeitung, European Jeweler. Ruehle-Diebener-Verlag GmbH & Co. K. G., Wolfschlugenstrasse 5A, Stuttgart 70, West Germany. (Monthly)

Guldsmedebladet. Guldsmedefagets Faellesraad, Box 362, DK-6000 Kolding, Denmark.

Gullsmed Kunst. Storgate 14, Oslo 1, Norway.

Jewel. Reine Publishing Co. Ltd., Hamada Building, 2-38 Ichigaya Tamachi, Shinjuku ku, Tokyo 162, Japan. (Bi-Monthly)

Jewelers Circular Keystone. Chilton Company, Chilton Way, Radnor, Pennsylvania 19089. New York Office: 212-697-3400. (Monthly)

———. *Annual Directory.* (Listing wholesalers of jewelry suppliers)

Jeweller. Allens (Clerkenwell) Ltd., Wheathampstead, Herts., England.

Jewelry World. 33 Marmot Street, Toronto, Ontario, Canada M4S2T4. (Bi-Monthly)

Metalsmith. (Formerly *Goldsmiths Journal*) The Society of North American Goldsmiths (SNAG). Art Department, Longwood College, Farmville, Virginia, 23901. (Quarterly)

Montres et Bijoux. Amsermet 18, Geneva, Switzerland.

National Jeweler. Gralla Publications, 1515 Broadway, New York 10036, New York. (Bi-Monthly)

Ontario Craft and *Craft News.* Ontario Crafts Council, 346 Dundas Street West, Toronto, Ontario M5T 1G5 Canada.

Ornament (Formerly *The Bead Journal*). P.O. Box 24-C-47, Los Angeles, California, 90024. (Quarterly)

Réalités. 13 rue St. Source, Paris 9, France. (Occasional articles on jewelry)

Revue Francaise des Bijoutiers Horlogers. Pierre Johanet et ses Fils, Editeurs S.A., 7 Avenue F. D. Roosevelt, Paris 8, France. (Monthly)

Small Business Bulletins. Small Business Administration, Washington, D.C., and Field Offices. *Jewelry Retailing.*

Swiss Watch and Jewelry Journal. International Edition: available in English, French, German, and Spanish. Scriptar S.A., Lausanne, Switzerland. (Bi-Monthly)

LAPIDARY PERIODICALS/SAFETY AND HEALTH PUBLICATIONS

Australian Lapidary Magazine. The Jay Kay Publications, 11 Robinson Street, Sydney, New South Wales. (Bi-Monthly)

Canadian Rockhound. P.O. Box 194, Station A, Vancouver, British Columbia, Canada. (Bi-Monthly)

Gems & Gemology. Gemological Institute of America, 11940 San Vicente Blvd., Los Angeles, California 90049. (Quarterly)

Gems. Lapidary Publications, 29 Ludgate Hill, London EC4. (Monthly)

Gems and Minerals. P.O. Box 687, Mentone, California 92359. (Monthly)

Journal of Gemmology. The Gemmological Association of Great Britain, St. Dunstan's House, Carey Lane, London EC2V 8AA. (Quarterly)

Lapidary Journal. Box 80937, San Diego, California 92138. (Monthly)

A Guide to Industrial Respiratory Protection. NIOSH Technical Information Bulletin, HEW Publication No. 76-189, Stock No. 017-033-00153-7, Superintendent of Documents, U.S. Government Printing Office, Washington, D.C. 20402.

Accident Prevention Manual for Industrial Operators. Vol. 1: *Engineering and Technology,* edited by Frank McElroe. 8th ed., Chicago: National Safety Council, 1980.

BARAZANI, GAIL. *Safe Practices in the Arts and Crafts: A Studio Guide.* College Art Association, 16 East 52nd St., New York, N.Y. 10022.

CARNOW, BERTRAM, M.D. *Health Hazards in the Arts and Crafts.* Art Hazards Supply Co., Route 1, Box 87-A, Blue Mounds, Wisc. 53517.

EPSTEIN, SAMUEL S., M.D. *The Politics of Cancer.* Sierra Club Books, 580 Bush St., San Francisco, Calif. 94108.

Fire Prevention Handbook. National Fire Protection Association, 470 Atlantic Avenue, Boston, Mass. 02110.

GOSSELIN, HODGE, SMITH, and GLEASON. *Clinical Toxicology of Commercial Products.* 4th ed., Baltimore: Williams and Wilkins, 1976.

Handbook of Organic Industrial Solvents. American Mutual Insurance Alliance, 20 North Wacker Drive, Chicago, Ill. 60606.

Hazards in the Arts. Newsletter, edited and published by Gail Barazani, Chicago.

HUNTER, DONALD. *The Diseases of Occupations.* Boston: Little, Brown, 1969.

MCCANN, MICHAEL. *Artists Beware.* Cincinnati: Watson Guptill Publications, 1982.

SAX, N. IRVING. *Dangerous Properties of Industrial Materials.* New York: Van Nostrand-Reinhold, 1975.

Superintendent of Documents, U.S. Government Printing Office, Washington, D.C. 20402. (Safety and hazards publications).

The Household Pollutants Guide. Center for Science in the Public Interest, Doubleday/Anchor, Garden City, N.Y.

WEISS, LINDA. *Health Hazards in the Field of Metalsmithing.* Society of North American Goldsmiths, c/o Mark Baldridge, Art Department, Longwood College, Farmville, Va. 23901.

SOURCES OF TOOLS, SUPPLIES, AND SERVICES

U.S.A.

In addition to all the sources given below, it is suggested that the reader investigate the Classified Telephone Directory of his/her own town or that of the nearest large city. They often contain surprises that may solve your supply or service problem.

PRECIOUS METALS

The companies listed here are primarily precious metal refiners and suppliers. They will sell precious metals in certain minimum amounts. Besides the usual stock items, some will make up special alloys in desired forms of sheet, wire, or tubing upon request. Many of these companies also accept scrap, lemel, and sweeps in certain minimum amounts for refining. They will then either give you a credit against the resulting amount of reclaimed precious metal or make an equivalent exchange in finished metal.

Englehard Industries, Inc.
768 Market Street
San Francisco, California 94104

429 Delancy
Newark, New Jersey 07105

General Refineries
292 Walnut Street
St. Paul, Minnesota 55102

Goldsmith Bros.
Division National Lead Co.
111 N. Wabash Avenue
Chicago, Illinois 60603

Handy and Harman
850 Third Avenue
New York, New York 10022

Branches:
Bridgeport, Connecticut 06607
845 Waterman Avenue
East Providence, Rhode Island 02914

1900 Eastes Avenue
Elkgrove Village, Illinois 60007

4140 Gibson Road
El Monte, California 91731

Frank Mossberg Drive
Attleboro, Massachusetts 02703

4402 West 215th Street
Cleveland, Ohio 44126

1700 West & Mile Road
Southfield, Michigan 48075

1234 Exchange Bank Bldg.
Dallas, Texas 75235

141 John Street
Toronto, Canada

L-S Plate and Wire
70-17 51st Avenue
Woodside, New York 11375
(gold and gold filled)

Martin Hanum Inc.
810 South Mateo Street
Los Angeles, California 90021

Hauser and Miller Co.
4011 Forest Park Boulevard
St. Louis, Missouri 63108

Hoover and Strong
119 W. Tupper Street
Buffalo, New York 14201

Leach and Garner Co.
608 Fifth Avenue
New York, New York 10020

Western Division
7327 Lankershim Boulevard
N. Hollywood, California 90068

The J. M. Ney Co.
Bloomfield, Connecticut 06002

Simmons Refining Co.
Dept. MF
1704 S. Normal Avenue
Chicago, Illinois 60616
(Refiners of scrap, etc.)

Spreyers Smelting and Refining Co.
Medical-Dental Building
Seattle, Washington 98101

Vennerbeck & Clase Co.
150 Chestnut Street
Providence, Rhode Island 02903
(gold and gold filled)

Western Gold and Platinum Co.
525 Harbor Boulevard
Belmont, California 94002

PRECIOUS METAL LEAF

Gold Leaf and Metallic Powders, Inc.
145 Nassau Street
New York, New York 10038

Ralph W. Grauert, Inc.
100 Gold Street
New York, New York 10038

Hastings and Co. Inc.
2314 Market Street
Philadelphia, Pennsylvania 19103

43 West 16th Street
New York, New York 10011

330 South Wells Street
Chicago, Illinois 60606

Peerless Roll Leaf Co.
Division of Howe Sound Co.
4511 New York Avenue
Union City, New Jersey 07087

TITANIUM, TANTALUM, AND NIOBIUM (COLUMBIUM): U.S.A.

Astro Metallurgical
3225 Lincoln Way West
Wooster, Ohio 44691

Du Pont de Nemours
1007 Market Street
Wilmington, Delaware 19898

Union Carbide Corp.
(Electro Metallurgical Co.)
270 Park Avenue
New York, New York 10017

Fansteel Metals Inc.
1 Tantalum Place
North Chicago, Illinois 60064

Futura Titanium
P.O. Box 5004
West Lake Village, California 91359

Kawecki Berylco Industries Inc.
220 East 42nd Street
New York, New York 10017

Leico Industries
250 West 57th Street
New York, New York 10019

Timet
400 Rouser Road
Pittsburgh, Pennsylvania

Titanium Sales Corp.
17 Industrial Road
Fairfield, New Jersey 07006

*Wah Chang Smelting and Refining
of America Inc.*
65 Herbhill Road
Glen Cove, New York 11542
P.O. Box 460
Albany, Oregon 97321

NONFERROUS METALS

Advanced Laboratory Associates, Inc.
517 Milltown Road
N. Brunswick, New Jersey 08902
(dental mercury)

Belden Corp.
2000 S. Batavia Avenue
Chicago, Illinois
(copper wire)

Ernest W. Beissinger
3 Charter Oak Drive
Carnegie, Pennsylvania 15103

Chase Brass and Copper Co. Inc.
150–156 Lafayette Street
New York, New York 10013

T. E. Conklin Brass and Copper Co.
322–324 West 23rd Street
New York, New York 10011

Ducommun Metals & Supply Co.
4890 S. Alameda Street
Los Angeles, California 90058

Revere Copper and Brass, Inc.
230 Park Avenue
New York, New York 10010

Totten Tubes, Inc.
1555 Los Palos Street
Los Angeles, California 90023

Investigate local metal suppliers.

GENERAL JEWELER'S EQUIPMENT AND MATERIALS

The following are mainly comprehensive supply houses for jewelers and metalworkers, and most of them offer mail order service. Normally they carry a wide range of *tools, materials,* and *equipment* used by jewelers. Often they also accept small-quantity orders of the precious metals in all forms, and stock semiprecious stones. For exact information on what they offer, it is suggested that readers write for their catalog, which almost all offer free, or at a minimal cost, this amount often deducted from the next purchase order. This list is alphabetically arranged.

Abbey Materials Corp.
116 West 29th Street
New York, New York 10001

Allcraft Tool & Supply Co. Inc.
215 Park Avenue
Hicksville, New York 11801

22 West 48th Street
New York, New York 10036

204 North Harbor Boulevard
Fullerton, California 92632

American Edelstaal, Inc.
One Atwood Avenue
Tenafly, New Jersey 07670
(Unimat Lathes)

American Handicrafts Co., Inc.
1011 Foch Street
Forth Worth, Texas 76107

American Metalcraft Inc.
4100 Belmont Avenue
Chicago, Illinois 60641

Anchor Tool & Supply Co., Inc.
231 Main Street (*or* P.O. Box 265)
Chatham, New Jersey 07928

Are Creations Inc.
Box 155
N. Montpelier Road
Plainfield, Vermont 05667

Bartlett & Co., Inc.
5 S. Wabash
Chicago, Illinois 60603

Bergen Arts & Crafts Inc.
Box 381 H-6
Marblehead, Massachusetts 01945

Dick Blick
Box 1268
Galesbury, Illinois 61401

Boin Arts & Crafts Co.
87 Morris Street
Morristown, New Jersey 07960

Jules Borel & Co.
1110 Grand Avenue
Kansas City, Missouri 64106

Bourget Bros.
1626 11th Street
Santa Monica, California 90404

Brodhead Garrett & Co.
4560 East 71st Street
Cleveland, Ohio 44105

Buehler Limited
2120 Greenwood Street
Box 1459
Evanston, Illinois 60204

California Crafts Supply
1096 N. Main Street
Orange, California 92667

Craft Service
337 University Avenue
Rochester, New York 14607

The Craftool Co.
1421 West 240 Street
Harbor City, California 90710
Industrial Road
Woodbridge, New Jersey 07075

William Dixon Co.
750 Washington Avenue
Carlstadt, New Jersey 07072

Donegan Optical Co.
1405 Kansas Avenue
Kansas City, Missouri 64127
(Optical supplies)

Ekbergs
1404 South Glendale
Sioux Falls, South Dakota 57105

Dick Ells Co.
908 Venice Boulevard
Los Angeles, California 90015

The Foredom Electric Co.
A Division of Blackstone Industries, Inc.
Bethel, Connecticut 06801
(Flexible shafts)

Friedheim Tool Supply Co.
412 West 6th Street
Los Angeles, California 90014

Gamzon Bros. Inc.
21 West 46th Street
New York, New York 10036

Paul H. Gesswein & Co., Inc.
255 Hancock Avenue
Bridgeport, Connecticut 06605

Grieger's Inc.
900 S. Arroyo Parkway
Pasadena, California 91109

Gwinn Craft Supply Co.
142 N. Market Street
Wichita, Kansas 67202

T. B. Hagstoz & Son
709 Sansom Street
Philadelphia, Pennsylvania 19106

C. R. Hill Co.
2734 W. 11 Mile Road
Berkley, Michigan 48072

Immerman Crafts Inc.
21668 Libby Road
Cleveland, Ohio 44137

B. Jadow and Sons, Inc.
53 West 23rd Street
New York, New York 10010

J. J. Jewelcraft
4959 York Boulevard
Los Angeles, California 90042

Jeweler Aids Co.
130–40 277 Street
Laurelton, New York 11413

Marshall-Swartchild Co.
2040 N. Milwaukee Avenue
Chicago, Illinois 60647

Metal Crafts and Supply Co.
10 Thomas Street
Providence, Rhode Island 02903

Microflame Inc.
3724 Oregon Avenue
Minneapolis, Minnesota 55426

I. Miller Inc.
304 Colonial Arcade
Cleveland, Ohio 44115

New Orleans Jeweler's Supply Co.
206 Charters Street
New Orleans, Louisiana 70130

Nicholson File Co.
667 Waterman Avenue
Providence, Rhode Island 02914

Norvell Marcum Co.
1609 S. Boston
P.O. Box 2887
Tulsa, Oklahoma 74119

Ohio Jewelers Supply
1030 Euclid Avenue
Cleveland, Ohio 44115

Wm. J. Orkin, Inc.
373 Washington Street
Boston, Massachusetts 02108

Rosenthal Jewelers Supply Corp.
117 NE First Avenue
Miami, Florida 33132

Sax Arts and Crafts
207 N. Milwaukee Street
Milwaukee, Wisconsin 53202

I. Schor Co.
71 Fifth Avenue
New York, New York 10003

H. Serabian
74 West 45th Street
New York, New York 10036

Skil-Crafts
305 Virginia Avenue
Joplin, Missouri 64801

Snapvent Co.
1107 West Cumberland Avenue
Knoxville, Tennessee 37916

C. W. Somers & Co. Inc.
387 Washington Street
Boston, Massachusetts 02108

Standard Diamond Tool Co. Inc.
71 West 47th Street
New York, New York 10036

The L. S. Starrett Co.
121 Crescent Street
Athol, Massachusetts 01331
4949 West Harrison Street
Chicago, Illinois 60644
5946 East Washington Boulevard
Los Angeles, California 90040
(Hand measuring tools, precision instruments, etc.)

Swest Inc.
(Formerly Southwest Smelting and Refining Co.)
10803 Composite Drive
Dallas, Texas 75220
431 Isom Road
San Antonio, Texas 78206
1725 Victory Boulevard
Glendale, California 91201

Tepping Studio Supply Co.
3003 Salem Avenue
Dayton, Ohio 45406

Myron Toback
23 West 47th Street
New York, New York 10036

TSI Inc.
(Technical Specialties International)
Nickerson Street Business Park
101 Nickerson Street
Seattle, Washington 98119

CASTING EQUIPMENT AND MATERIALS

Alexander Saunders & Co. Inc.
28 Chestnut Street (Route 9D)
Cold Spring, New York 10516

Casting Supply House Inc.
62 W. 47th Street
New York, New York 10036

Cleveland Dental Laboratories Co.
Caxton Building
812 Huron Road East
Cleveland, Ohio 44115

General Refineries Inc.
292 Walnut Street
St. Paul, Minnesota 55102

The Jelrus Co. Inc.
136 W. 52nd Street
New York, New York 10019

Kerr Dental Mfg. Co.
6081–6095 Twelfth Street
Detroit, Michigan 48208
28200 Wick Road
Romulus, Michigan 48174

Marketeers, Inc.
19101 Villaview Road
Cleveland, Ohio 44119

The Newall Mfg. Co.
139 N. Wabash Avenue
Chicago, Illinois 60602
(Casting wax)

Romanoff Rubber Co. Inc.
153 W. 27th Street
New York, New York 10001

Frank B. Ross Co. Inc.
6 Ash Street
Jersey City, New Jersey 07304
(Industrial waxes)

F. W. Steadman Co. Inc.
59 Pearl Street
New York, New York 10004
(Steadco Waxes)

Torit Division
Donaldson Co. Inc.
1133 Rankin Street
St. Paul, Minnesota 55116

S. S. White Dental Mfg. Co.
55 E. Washington Street
Chicago, Illinois 60602

Pennwalt Building, Three Parkway
Philadelphia, Pennsylvania 19103

WIN-OX Products
2105 S. Hardy Road
Scottsdale, Arizona 85251

JEWELRY CASTING SPECIALISTS

Abud Casting, Inc.
17 West 45th Street
New York, New York 10036
(Casters and mold makers)

Adwar Casting Co.
243 West 30th Street
New York, New York 10001
(Platinum casters)

Ampex Casting Corp.
64 West 48th Street
New York, New York 10036

Avante Products Corp.
7700 River Road
North Bergen, New Jersey 07047
(White metal casters)

Billanti Casting Co.
64 West 48th Street
New York, New York 10036

Conrado Casting Inc.
49 West 47th Street
New York, New York 10036

Karbra
62 West 47th Street
New York, New York 10036
(Platinum casters)

Precious Metal Casting and Design
P.O. Box 2627
Key West, Florida 33040

FINDINGS AND CHAINS

Most of these are manufacturers to the trade and require minimum orders.

American Jewelry Chain Co.
560 Atwells Avenue
Providence, Rhode Island 02909

303 Fifth Avenue
New York, New York 10016

Atlas Chain Co.
47 West 43rd Street
New York, New York 10001

B. A. Ballou & Co. Inc.
800 Waterman Avenue
East Providence, Rhode Island 02914

Joseph M. Dattoli
62 West 47th Street
Room 312
New York, New York 10036

Eastern Findings Corp.
152 West 22nd Street
New York, New York 10011

Karlan & Bleicher, Inc.
195 Danbury Road
Wilton, Connecticut 06897

Marshall-Swartchild Co.
2040 N. Milwaukee Avenue
Chicago, Illinois 60647

C. E. Marshall Co.
1113 W. Belmont
P.O. Box 7737
Chicago, Illinois 60657

Metal Crafts and Supply Co.
10 Thomas Street
Providence, Rhode Island 02903

Metal Findings Corp.
152 West 22nd Street
New York, New York 10011

Swest Inc.
10803 Composite Drive
Dallas, Texas 75220

Universal Chain Co., Inc.
110 West 34th Street
New York, New York 10001
(Fancy link chains)

FINISHING, POLISHING, AND BUFFING EQUIPMENT AND MATERIALS

A. E. Aubin Co.
85M Charter Oak Avenue
Hartford, Connecticut 06106
(Bench model abrasive blaster)

Bacon Felt Co.
11 Fifth Street
Taunton, Massachusetts 02780
(Felt wheels)

Behr-Manning Co.
10th Avenue and 27th Street
Watervliet, New York 12189
(Sharpening and grinding stones)

Brightboy Industrial
351 Sixth Avenue
Newark, New Jersey 07107
(Bonded abrasives)

The Buckeye Products Co.
7031 Vine Street
Cincinnati, Ohio 45216
(Abrasives)

The Carborundum Co.
Abrasives Marketing Division
P.O. Box 337-T
Niagara Falls, New York 14302

Diamond Pacific Tool Corp.
24063 W. Main Street
Barstow, California 92311
(Diamond abrasives and drills)

The Enequist Chemical Co., Inc.
100 Varick Street
Brooklyn, New York 11237
(Coloring chemical solutions)

Felker Operations
Dresser Industries, Inc.
1900 E. South Crenshaw Boulevard
Torrance, California 90509
(Diamond abrasives)

Formax Manufacturing Corp.
3171 Bellevue
Detroit, Michigan 48207
(Polishing and buffing compounds)

Hammel, Riglander and Co. Inc.
P.O. Box 222
New York, New York 10014
(Polishers and dust collectors)

The Lea Manufacturing Co.
237 East Aurora Street
Waterbury, Connecticut 06720
(Polishing and buffing compounds)

Merit Abrasive Products, Inc.
201 West Manville Street
Compton, California 90224

Norton Co.
50 New Bond Street
Worcester, Massachusetts 01606

Schaffner Manufacturing Co.
1 Schaffner Center
Pittsburgh, Pennsylvania 15202
(Compounds, buffs, and coated abrasives)

United Abrasives, Inc.
910 Brown Street
Norway, Michigan 49870

LAPIDARY EQUIPMENT

Allen Lapidary Equipment Mfg. Co.
P.O. Box 75411
Oklahoma City, Oklahoma 73107

B. & I. Manufacturing
Dept. L, Box 146
Adrian, Michigan, 49221

Covington Lapidary Eng. Co.
Box 35
Redlands L., California 92373

The Exolon Co.
1033 East Niagara Street
Tonawanda, New York 14150
(Gem polishing abrasives)

Geo-Sonics
102 Lincoln Street
New London, Iowa 52645
(Vibrasonic tumblers, ultrasonic
drilling machines)

*Great Western Lapidary Equipment
Co.*
3444 Main Street
Chula Vista, California 92011

Grieger's, Inc.
900 S. Arroyo Parkway
Pasadena, California 91109

Henry B. Graves Co.
1190 South Old Dixie Highway
Delray Beach, Florida 33444

Lorton's Inc.
2854 N. W. Market Street
Seattle, Washington 98107
(Slab and trim saws)

M. D. R. Manufacturing Co.
2686 S. La Cienega Boulevard
Los Angeles, California 90034

*MK Diamond Products
Highland Park Manufacturing*
12600 Chadron Avenue
Hawthorne, California 90250

Murray American Corp.
15 Commerce Street
Chatham, New Jersey 07928
(Tumbling materials)

Scott-Murray Mfg. Co.
Box 25077 Northgate Station
Seattle, Washington 98125
(Tumblers)

Star Diamond Industries Inc.
1421 W. 240 Street
Harbor City, California 90710

Technicraft Lapidaries Corp.
3560 Broadway
New York, New York 10031

3M Company
Building 224–55
3M Center
St. Paul, Minnesota 55101

United Abrasives Inc.
910 Brown Street
Norway, Michigan 49870

Vreeland Manufacturing Co.
4105 N. E. 68th Avenue
Portland, Oregon 97213

MINERAL GEMSTONES

Jerry Barkas
29 West 47th Street
Arcade Store No. 5
New York, New York 10036

John Barry & Co.
P.O. Box 15, Dept. C
Detroit, Michigan 48218

Ernest W. Bessinger
P.O. Box 454
Carnegie, Pennsylvania 15106

Eugene Chaput
210 Post Street
San Francisco, California 94108

Coffey's Lapidary
9120 Jamacha Road
Spring Valley, California 92077

Elvin
P.O. Box 787
Westfield, New Jersey 07090
(Lindé star boules)

Raymond Gabriel
Dept. CR
1469 Rosena Avenue
Madison, Ohio 44057

Grieger's, Inc.
900 S. Arroyo Parkway
Pasadena, California 91109

Russ Hind
1273 South Coast Highway
Laguna Beach, California 92651

Francis Hoover
12445 Chandler Boulevard
North Hollywood, California 91607

International Gem Corp.
15 Maiden Lane
New York, New York 10038

Carol Kramer
20 Bethune Street
New York, New York 10014

The Lapidary Journal
Box 80937
San Diego, California 92138
(Contains many advertisements for
others)

Lochs
R.D. 1
Center Valley, Pennsylvania 18034

William Mercer
665 Fifth Avenue
New York, New York 10031

O'Brien Lapidary
1116 N. Wilcox Avenue
Hollywood, California 90038

Oceanside Gem Imports, Inc.
P.O. Box 222
Oceanside, New York 11572

Precious Stones Company
580 Fifth Avenue
New York, New York 10036

Kenneth F. Rose
P.O. Box 84
Southfield, Michigan 48037

William V. Schmidt Co., Inc.
30 Rockefeller Plaza
New York, New York 10020

Francis Sperisen
166 Geary Street
San Francisco, California 94108

Universal Gems & Minerals Inc.
5951 Griems Court
El Paso, Texas 79905

Vermont Gems and Minerals
P.O. Box 101
Ctr. Rutland, Vermont 05736

Charles Weidinger
631 W. 54th Place
Chicago, Illinois 60609

World Wide Gems
146 Rose Street
Kalamazoo, Michigan 49006

ORGANIC SUBSTANCES

Benjane Arts
320 Hempstead Avenue
West Hempstead, New York 11552
(Shells, organic products)

Benson Co.
220 E. Pacific Coast Highway
Long Beach, California 90806
(Coral, shells)

Crown Cultured Pearl Corp.
580 8th Avenue
New York, New York 10018
(Pearls, jade, coral, ivory)

Judie Joseph
4253 Trout River Boulevard
Jacksonville, Florida 32208
(Ivory)

PLASTICS, RESINS, RESIN DYES, AND ADHESIVES

Cadillac Plastic and Chemical Co.
1245 W. Fulton
Chicago, Illinois 60607

Castolite Co.
P.O. Box 391
Woodstock, Illinois 60098

Cosmos Dental Products, Inc.
180 Varick Street
New York, New York 10014
(Denture base polymer and cold
curing repair resins)

Du Pont de Nemours, E. I. & Co.
350 Fifth Avenue
New York, New York 10017

Federal Prosthetics, Inc.
15 Parkville Avenue
Brooklyn, New York 11230
(Dental chromium-cobalt casting
alloy)

Mail Order Plastics
56 Lispenard Street
New York, New York 10013

Nasco
901 Janesville Avenue
Ft. Atkinson, Wisconsin 53538

Plastic Center, Inc.
1215–1221 Wood Street
Philadelphia, Pennsylvania 19107

The Plastics Factory
119 Avenue D
New York, New York 10009

Polyproducts Corp.
13810 Nelson Avenue
Detroit, Michigan 48227

Resin Coatings Corp.
14940 N.W. 25 Court
Opa Locka, Florida 33054

Tap Plastics, Inc.
3011 Alvarado
San Leandro, California 94577

ELECTROPLATING AND ELECTROFORMING EQUIPMENT AND MATERIALS

Acheson Colloids
P.O. Box 288
Port Huron, Michigan 48060
(Silver conductive coatings)

*American Chemicals and Refining Co.
Inc.*
Sheffield Street
Waterbury, Connecticut 06714
(Precious metal plating solutions)

Auromet Corp.
199 Canal Street
New York, New York 10013
(Precious metal solutions and salts)

B. & D. Polishing and Plating Corp.
1575 York Avenue
New York, New York 10028
(Gold and silver plating)

Cole-Parmer Instruments Co.
7425 N. Oak Park Avenue
Chicago, Illinois 60648
(Stainless steel and plastic beakers)

Englehard Industries Division
430 Mountain Avenue
Murray Hill, New Jersey 07974
(Gold plating solutions, silver anodes)

Paul Frank
153 East 26th Street
New York, New York 10010
(pH papers)

*Franklin Plating and Polishing Co.,
Inc.*
630 South Sixth Street
Columbus, Ohio 43206

The Harshaw Chemical Co.
1945 East 97th Street
Cleveland, Ohio 44106

Hill Cross Co., Inc.
393 Pearl Street
New York, New York 10038

J. Holland & Sons, Inc.
475 Keap Street
Brooklyn, New York 11211

Hoover and Strong, Inc.
119 W. Tupper Street
Buffalo, New York 14201

Lea-Ronal, Inc.
272 Buffalo Avenue
Freeport, New York 11520
(Cyanide free plating materials)

Ramyr Manufacturing Co.
6750 Caballero Boulevard
Bueno Park, California 90620
(Periodic reverse plater)

E. H. Sargent & Co.
4647 West Forster Avenue
Chicago, Illinois 60630
(Chemicals for plating)

Swest Inc.
10803 Composite Drive
Dallas, Texas 75220

Technic Inc.
P.O. Box 965
Providence, Rhode Island 02901
(Gold plating solutions, silver anodes)

CHEMICALS AND CHEMICAL EQUIPMENT

Allied Chemical Corp.
40 Rector Street
New York, New York 10006

Berg Chemical Corp.
331 West 37th Street
New York, New York 10018

Braun-Knecht-Heimann Co.
2301 Blake Street
Denver, Colorado 80205

Burrell Corp.
2223 Fifth Avenue
Pittsburgh, Pennsylvania 15219

Canadian Laboratory Supplies Co.
403 St. Paul Street West
Montreal 1, Quebec, Canada

*Copper Pigment & Chemical Works,
Inc.*
7 Arbor Street
Sewaren, New Jersey 07077

W. H. Curtain & Co.
P.O. Box 606
Jacksonville, Florida 33033
P.O. Box 1491
New Orleans, Louisiana 70113
1812 Griffin Street
Dallas, Texas 75202

Harshaw Scientific Co.
1945 E. 97th Street
Cleveland, Ohio 44106

Howe and French, Inc.
99 Broad Street
Boston, Massachusetts 02110

Kansas City Laboratory Supply Co.
307 Westport Road
Kansas City, Kansas 66111

New York Laboratory Supply Co.
78 Varick Street
New York, New York 10013

Roemer-Karrer Co.
810 N. Plankinton Avenue
Milwaukee, Wisconsin 53203

E. H. Sargent & Co.
4647 W. Foster Avenue
Chicago, Illinois 60630

Scientific Supplies Co.
600 Spokane Street
Seattle, Washington 98104

Seidler Chemical & Supply Co.
12–16 Orange Street
Newark, New Jersey 07102

Will Corporation of Georgia
P.O. Box 966
Atlanta, Georgia 30301

MISCELLANEOUS

American Balance Co.
527 Fifth Avenue
New Rochelle, New York 10801
(Diamond, gold scales)

Art Hazards Information Center
Center for Occupational Hazards
5 Beekman Street
New York, New York 10038

Bead Game
505 N. Fairfax Avenue
Los Angeles, California 90036
(Beads, organic materials, findings)

Carpenter and Wood Co., Inc.
15 Cedar Street
Providence, Rhode Island 02903
(Enamels)

Home Safety Equipment Co., Inc.
P.O. Box 691
New Albany, Indiana 47150
(Sluice boxes)

H. A. Evers Co. Inc.
72C Oxford Street
Providence, Rhode Island 02905
(Quality and trademark stamps)

*M. McNamara Stamp & Stencil
   Works, Inc.*
40 East 20th Street
New York, New York 10003
(Quality and trademark stamps)

Mine Safety Appliances Co.
400 Penn Center Bldg.
Pittsburgh, Pennsylvania 15235
(Respirators)

Paasche Airbrush Co.
1909 West Diversey Parkway
Chicago, Illinois 60614
(Airbrushes)

Thomas C. Thompson Co.
1539 Deerfield Road
Highland Park, Illinois 60035
(Enamels)

SAFETY EQUIPMENT (Write for catalogs)

A. M. Best Co.
Oldwick, New Jersey 08858
(General safety equipment)

Art Hazards Supply Co.
Route 1, Box 87A
Blue Mounds, Wisconsin 53517

Bilsom International, Inc.
11800 Sunrise Valley Drive
Reston, Virginia 22091
(Ear protection)

Direct Safety Equipment
1607 West 17th Street
Tempe, Arizona 85281

E.A.R. Division Cabot Corporation
7911 Zionsville Road
Indianapolis, Indiana 46268
(Hearing protection)

Eastco Industrial Safety Corp.
26–15 123rd Street
Flushing, N.Y. 11345

International Glove Division
International Playtex Co.
45 Church Street
Stamford, Connecticut 06906
(Gloves)

Lab Safety Supply Co.
P.O. Box 1368
Janesville, Wisconsin 53547

M. Setlow & Son, Inc.
Indian River Road
Orange, Connecticut 06477
(Apparel, flame-retarding)

Mine Safety Appliances Co.
600 Penn Center Building
Pittsburgh, Pennsylvania 15235
(Respirators)

Norton Company
Safety Products Division
Cranston, Rhode Island 02920

*Occupational Health & Safety
Products Division/3M*
Dept. OCH-102
P.O. Box 3708
St. Paul, Minnesota 55101

Raybestos Industrial Products
Raybestos Manhattan, Inc.
P.O. Box 5205
N. Charleston, South Carolina 29406
(Asbestos substitute products)

Safety Supply Canada
214 King Street East
Toronto, Ontario M5A 1J8
Canada

United States Safety Service Co.
1535 Walnut Street
Kansas City, Missouri 64108
(Respiratory devices; goggles)

Universal Safety Equipment Co.
5001 West Belmont
Chicago, Illinois 60641

United Kingdom

PRECIOUS METALS

Abelson (Hatton Garden) Ltd.
Abelson House
16 Greville Street
London EC1

J. Betts and Sons Ltd.
84 Hatton Garden
London EC1
64 Charlotte Street
Birmingham 3

J. Blundell & Sons, Ltd.
199 Wardour Street
London W1

Commercial Smelting and Refining Co.
15 Farringdon Road
London EC1

Englehard Sales Ltd.
Primate House
Hatton Garden
London EC1 and 49–63 Spencer Street
Birmingham 18

Johnson Matthey Metals Ltd.
43 Hatton Garden
London EC1N 8EE
Victoria Street, Birmingham
175 Arundel Gate, Sheffield S1 1JY
(Also tools, supplies and findings)

Johnson & Sons Smelting Works Ltd.
104 Spencer Street
Birmingham 18

Sheffield Smelting Co. Ltd.
132 St. John Street
London EC1V 4JU
Royds, Mill Street, Sheffield
St. Paul's Square
Charlotte Street
Birmingham 13

Gold and Silver Leaf and Foil
G. M. Whiley Ltd.
Victoria Road
South Ruislip
Middlesex

E. Winter and Co. Ltd.
12 Charterhouse Buildings
London EC1

Titanium

IMI-Titanium
Witton Birmingham B6 7BA

Titanium International Ltd.
Thornhill Road
Solihull

Titanium Metals and Alloys, Ltd.
85 London Wall
London EC2

Niobium (Columbium), and Tantalum

Elvanth Ltd.
Sinclair House
The Avenue
London W13

Murex Ltd.
Murex Works
Ferry Lane
Rainham, Essex

NONFERROUS METALS

Brown Bros. Ltd.
Downs Road
London E5

Clay Bros. & Co.
6B Spring Bridge Road
London W5

Deutch & Brenner Ltd.
Alliance Works
Barford Street
Birmingham 18

H. J. Edwards & Sons Ltd.
93–95 Barr Street
Birmingham 19

Godwin Warren & Co., Ltd.
117 Radcliffe Street
Bristol 1

B. Grundy & Co. Ltd.
Shelford Place
London N16

Henry Righton & Co. Ltd.
70 Pentonville Road
London N1
(Copper, brass, etc.)

Johnson Clapham & Morris, Ltd.
Jacem House, Trafford Park
Manchester

A. D. Keeling & Co., Ltd.
Warstone Metal Works
Hall Street
Birmingham 18

Randalls Ltd.
20–22 St. Mary Street
Bedford

J. F. Ratcliff (Metals) Ltd.
New Summer Street
Birmingham B19 3QN

H. Rollet & Co. Ltd.
Howie Street
London SW11 4AR

Rowe Bros., Ltd.
7 Unity Street, College Green
Bristol 1

J. Smith & Sons Ltd.
50 St. John's Square
Clerkenwell
London EC1
(Copper, brass, etc.)

JEWELER'S TOOLS AND SUPPLIES

Allcraft/Enamelaire Ltd.
Holywell Industrial Estate
Mail Order: Dept. C.5
Watford WD1 8SE, Herts.
Retail showroom: 11 Market Street
Watford, Herts.
(Tools, enamels, wax, lapidary)

Arts and Crafts Unlimited
49 Shelton Street
London WC2

Bede-Brown (Metalcraft)
1 Hereford Way
Fellgate, Jarrow
Co. Durham

Buck and Ryan
101 Tottenham Court Road
London W1
(Precision tools)

Charles Cooper (Hatton Garden) Ltd.
Knights House
23–27 Hatton Wall
Hatton Garden
London EC1N 8JJ
(Also polishing materials and findings)

Coronet Trading Co.
44 Station Lane
Hornchurch
Essex RM12 6NB
(Jewelry and enameling tools and
supplies)

Craftorama (Wholesale) Co.
14 Endell Street
London WC2H 9HE

Crafts Unlimited
21 Macklin Street
London WC2

202 Bath Street
Glasgow

Dryad
Northgates
Leicester

Fred Aldons Ltd.
Lever Street
Manchester M60 1UX

George Panton & Sons
Buchanan Street
Glasgow

E. Gray & Son
Grayson House
12–16 Clerkenwell Road
London EC1

Herring, Morgan & Southon, Ltd.
9 Berwick Street
London W1
(Also findings)

R. Holt & Co. Ltd.
92 Hatton Garden
London EC1

Hydebourne Ltd.
376 Finchley Road
London NW3 7AJ
(Jewelry, enameling, casting supplies)

Lionel Pepper
4A Abbeville Road
London SW4

Macready's Metal Co., Ltd.
Pentonville Road
London N1
(Tool steel)

Microflame (U.K.) Ltd.
Rickinghall, Diss,
Norfolk, 1P22 1BR
(Miniature torches)

Microweld
110 Churchill Road
Launton Industrial Estate
Bicester, Oxon.
(Miniature torches)

B. R. Perris Machine Tools
10 Sprowston Road
Norwich
Norfolk NOR 67P

F. Pike
58g Hatton Garden
London EC1

Record Ridgway Tools Ltd.
Parkway Works
Sheffield S9 3BL

Rhodes Flamefast Ltd.
Pendleburry Industrial Estate
Bridge Street
Swinton, Manchester M27 IFJ
(Torches, furnaces, kilns)

Ronson Ltd.
352 Strand
London WC2 and
66 Jermyn Street
London WC1
(Soldering equipment)

C. V. Salvo Ltd.
88 Hatton Garden
London EC1

Wm. A. Meyer Sievert Ltd.
P.O. Box 562
9–11 Gleneldon Road
London SW 162A

Stanley Tools Ltd.
Woodside
Sheffield S3 9PD

Henri Picard & Supa Nove II Freres
Ltd.
34–35 Furnival Street
London EC4
(Soldering equipment)

Thomas Sutton
166 Warstone Lane
Birmingham 18

William Allday & Co. Ltd.
Alcosa Works
Stourport-on-Severn
Worcestershire DY13 9AP
(Gas-fired torches, forges, and
furnaces)

CASTING MATERIALS AND EQUIPMENT

Amalgamated Dental Co. Ltd.
26 Broadwick Street
London W1
(Dental wax, investment plaster, etc.)

Ferro (Great Britain) Ltd.
Wombourne
Wolverhampton WV5 8DA
(Kilns)

Fuel Furnaces Ltd.
Shady Lane
Birmingham B44 9EX

Hoben Davis Ltd.
Holditch Industrial Estate
Spencroft Road
Newcastle-under-Lyme
Staffordshire ST5 9JD
(Lost wax casting supplies)

W. J. Hooker Ltd.
Waterside
Brightlingsea
Colchester
Essex

Midlands Silicones Ltd.
68 Knightbridge
London SW1
(Silicone rubber for flexible molds)

Nesor Products Ltd.
Claremont Hall
Pentonville Road
London N1
(Investment plaster, wax, etc.)

Podmore and Sons Ltd.
Shelton Stoke-on-Trent
Staffordshire
(Kilns)

Vinatex Ltd.
Devonshire House
Carshalton
Surrey
(Vinyl for molds)

PLASTICS, RESINS, DYES, ADHESIVES

Alec Tiranti Ltd.
21 Goodge Place
London W1

70 High Street
Theale Berks

Bartoline (Hull) Ltd.
Swinemoor Industries Estate
Beverley, Yorks

B.I.P. Chemicals Ltd.
Popes Lane
Oldbury, P.O. Box 6
Warley, Worcs.
(Polyester resins, large amounts)

CIBA (A.R.L.) Ltd.
Duxford
Cambridge
(Epoxy resins, catalysts, and
accelerators)

Cornelius Chemical Co. Ltd.
Ibex House
Minories
London EC3
(Acrylic)

Emerson & Cuming (U.K.) Ltd.
Colville Road, Acton
London W3
(Epoxy resins)

ICI Plastics Division
Welwyn Garden City
Herts
(Other locations: Bristol, Birmingham,
Manchester, Glasgow, and Belfast)

James Coates Bros. Ltd.
1 Townley Street
Middleton, Manchester

Kingsmead Glass & Resin Suppliers
Shire Hill Industrial Estate
Saffron Walden
Essex CB11 3AQ

Scott Bader Ltd.
Wollaston
Willingborough
Northhamptonshire
(Resins, large amounts)

Trylon Ltd.
Thrift Street
Wollaston
Northants NN9 7QJ
(Polyester resins and associated
materials)

LAPIDARY AND GEMSTONES

P. W. Allen & Co.
253 Liverpool Road
London N1
(Illuminated magnifiers)

Ammonite Ltd.
Llandow Industrial Estate
Cowbridge
Glamorgan

M. L. Beach Ltd.
41 Church Street
Twickenham, Middlesex
7 King's Parade
Brighton
(Tumblers, roughs, abrasives, findings)

Bezalel Gems Co.
67/68 Hatton Garden
London EC1

Gemrocks Ltd.
Halton House
7/8 Holborn
London EC1

Gemset of Broadstairs Ltd.
31 Albion Street
Broadstairs, Kent

Gemstones
44 Walmsley Street
Spring Bank
Hull, E. Yorks
(Lapidary machines, supplies)

Glenjoy Lapidary Supplies
89 Westgate
Wakefield, Yorkshire

*Hirsh Jacobson Merchandising Co.,
Ltd.*
91 Marylebone High Street
London W1m 4AY
(Lapidary equipment, roughs,
gemstones, materials)

A. and D. Hughes Ltd.
Pope's Lane
Oldbury, Warley, Worcestershire

Lapidary Abrasives
14 Market Street
Altrincham, Cheshire

Opie Gems
13 Gilbert Close
Hempstead
Gillingham, Kent

Mr. K. Parkinson, F.G.A.
11 Fitzroy Street
Hull

R. F. D. Parkinson & Co. Ltd.
Doulton, Shepton Mallet, Somerset

P. & M. Roberts
Atholl Road
Pitlochry, Perthshire
Scotland
(P.M.R. lapidary machines and
supplies)

Shipton and Co. Ltd.
27–33 Spencer Street
Birmingham 18

Withear Lapidary Co.
35 Ballards Lane
London N3

INDEX

(Page references in bold face refer to illustrations)

Color Plates   (*Jeweler's names alphabetically arranged*)

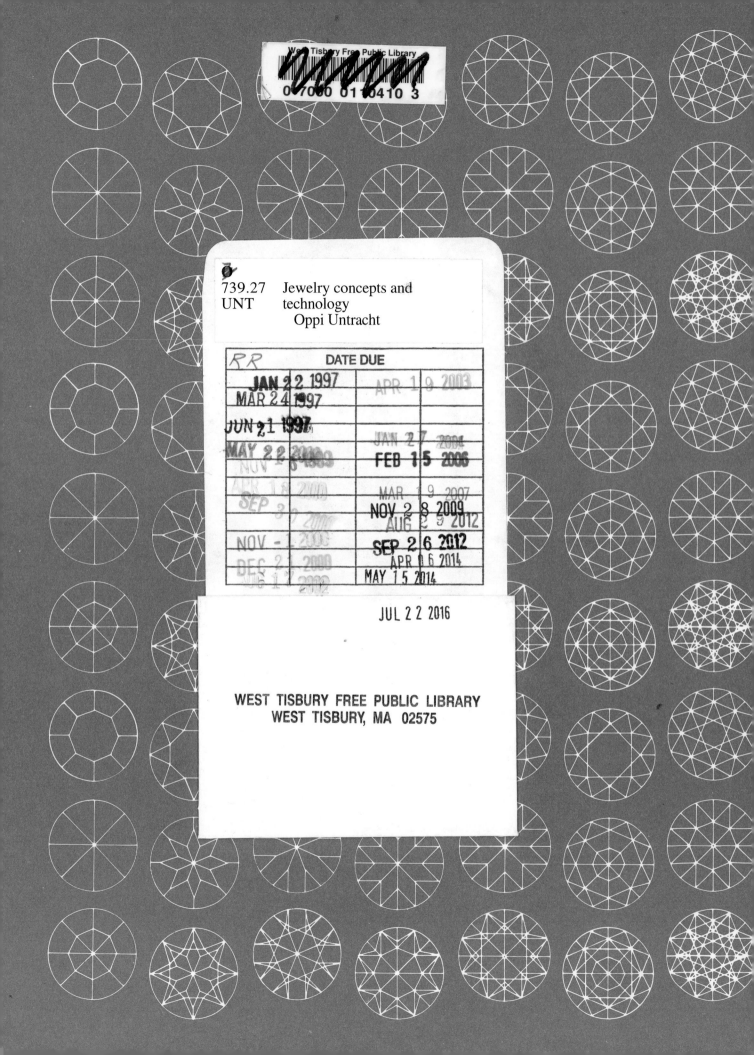